Praise for *International Law: a European Perspective*

This new textbook provides a remarkable tool for the teaching of international law at the graduate and postgraduate levels. By emphasizing legal practices which are too often ignored or overlooked in the teaching of international law, it comes to offer an account of the subject that is not only refreshing but that is also most nuanced and balanced. In doing so, it recognizes that there are multiple ways to approach and teach international law, thereby doing justice to the pluralism of the field in both theory and practice. This textbook surely makes the study of international law even more fascinating.

Jean d'Aspremont,
Sciences Po Law School, and University of Manchester

A much needed international law textbook in English that offers a systematic coverage of the practice of the EU, European governments and courts in international law, and highlights the important contributions by continental and civil law countries to the evolution of the law.

Eyal Benvenisti,
the Whewell Professor of International Law, University of Cambridge, and the Director of the Lauterpacht Centre for International Law

This is a book on the momentous contribution of the European institutions to the development of international law: the missing book in international law studies.

Enzo Cannizzaro,
Full Professor of International and EU Law, University of Rome La Sapienza

The book is a splendid gift to all those seeking a global approach to the impact and application of international law. It gives a comprehensive account of how European courts – in particular the Court of Justice of the EU and the European Court of Human Rights – have integrated international law into their own legal orders and in turn contributed to its development.

Eileen Denza,
Formerly Legal Counsellor, UK Foreign and Commonwealth Office; Counsel to EC Committee, House of Lords; Visiting Professor, University College London

This textbook very efficiently fills a gap in the English literature when dealing with the main fields of International law while privileging a European perspective informed by the comprehensive treatment of the practice provided by European countries, European interstate organizations and European courts. Indeed, a most useful instrument for assessing the European contribution to the modern development of international law.

Pierre-Marie Dupuy,
Honorary Professor of International Law, Graduate Institute of International and Development Studies, Geneva

The present publication is highly recommended as an outstanding new textbook on public international law. This textbook is distinguished from the other existing textbooks in that it offers the 'European' perspective on public international law and is based on the analysis of the EU and broader 'European' law practice in this field. It examines practice of the EU, the Council of Europe, and national practice both in common and civil law jurisdictions, as well as European practice in various international organisations. This textbook adopts, however, a holistic approach to international law and takes into consideration other than European practice and contributions to the development of public international law. It has a classical format of a public international law textbook. It includes, however, the analysis of several special branches of international law, such as international environmental law. This textbook is characterised by an in-depth analysis of the case law of various international courts and tribunals, including the International Court of Justice and a very wide use of primary and secondary sources. This is an excellent and innovative textbook, which is in my view, is a necessary and essential reading for scholars, practitioners and students of international law.

Malgosia Fitzmaurice,
Chair of Public International Law at the Department of Law,
Queen Mary University of London

This is a very authoritative textbook on the theory and practice of international law. It excels in up-to date comprehensiveness and academic rigour. It uses highly innovative methods integrating European legal history, the practice of civil law and common law legal systems and the experiences of the European Union and the Council of Europe. An indispensable companion for academics, practitioners and students of international law and in particular for everyone who cares about opening pathways to new ideas.

Ricardo Gosalbo Bono,
Professor of Law, VUB, Former Director in the Legal Service,
Council of the European Union

A truly European book, with many references to different European legal systems and their courts, including the European Union and its courts. Without doubt it is a book that will prove itself very serviceable in Master's courses in European universities and that can be very useful to practitioners and judges in national courts, who want to give themselves a first impression of the different sectors of international law and how they have been approached in different jurisdictions of European countries and the EU.

Pieter Jan Kuijper, Professor Emeritus
of the Law of International Organizations,
University of Amsterdam

This is the first, complete account of the EU positioning in the realm of international law. Thoroughly researched, and elegantly written, this volume is a most valuable source of information and inspiration to academics, and practitioners alike.

Petros C Mavroidis, Edwin B. Parker
Professor of Foreign and Comparative Law, Columbia University

Contemporary international law treatises in English are dominated by writers hailing from common law countries. This rigorous and comprehensive volume provides much-needed insights about international law through the lens of the civil law tradition, while drawing salient connections with the law of the European Union and the Council of Europe system.

Sean D Murphy, Manatt/Ahn
Professor of International Law, George Washington University;
President, American Society of International Law

Public international law professes universality but is, in reality, partly dependent on geographical and political context. International law as applied by the United States of America is not quite the same as the international law applied by the EU and European nations. While much has been written about the status of public international law in EU law, there is scant literature on public international law as such, but seem from a European perspective. The present *magnum opus* fills this void and will constitute an indispensable source for academics and practitioners alike.

Allan Rosas,
Judge in the Court of Justice of the European Union

This comprehensive, balanced and altogether excellent textbook on international law is unique in presenting, in English, continental European and civil law viewpoints and materials bearing on the structure, function, and dynamics of international law. Because our ability to manage international relations depends on understanding the frameworks through which our counterparts understand the world, this volume is essential reading for those from outside the European and civil law traditions.

Joel P Trachtman,
Professor of International Law, The Fletcher School of Law and Diplomacy,
Tufts University

International Law – A European Perspective is *the* textbook to use if teaching international law in Europe in English. It is a comprehensive and excellent textbook taking into account European institutional specialities such as the EU as “a new legal order” and the Council of Europe as well as civil and common law traditions. It thus paints a comprehensive picture of International Law against the European background, including international legal theory and legal history. It is very well structured and easily accessible for readers.

Anne van Aaken, Alexander von Humboldt Professor,
University of Hamburg

INTERNATIONAL LAW: A EUROPEAN PERSPECTIVE

International Law

A European Perspective

Jan Wouters
Cedric Ryngaert
Tom Ruys
Geert De Baere

With the editorial assistance of
Thomas Van Poecke and Evelien Wauters

•HART•
OXFORD • LONDON • NEW YORK • NEW DELHI • SYDNEY

HART PUBLISHING

Bloomsbury Publishing Plc

Kemp House, Chawley Park, Cumnor Hill, Oxford, OX2 9PH, UK

1385 Broadway, New York, NY 10018, USA

29 Earlsfort Terrace, Dublin 2, Ireland

HART PUBLISHING, the Hart/Stag logo, BLOOMSBURY and the Diana logo are trademarks of Bloomsbury Publishing Plc

First published in Great Britain 2019

Reprinted 2021, 2023

A catalogue record for this book is available from the British Library.

Library of Congress Cataloging-in-Publication data

Names: Wouters, Jan, 1964- author. | Ryngaert, Cedric., author. | Baere, Geert de, 1979- author. | Ruys, Tom, author. | Van Poecke, Thomas. | Wauters, Evelien.

Title: International law : a European perspective / Jan Wouters, Cedric Ryngaert, Tom Ruys, Geert De Baere ; with the editorial assistance of Thomas Van Poecke and Evelien Wauters.

Description: Oxford, UK ; Portland, Oregon : Hart Publishing, an imprint of Bloomsbury, 2019.

Identifiers: LCCN 2018037231 (print) | LCCN 2018038058 (ebook) | ISBN 9781509909049 (Epub) | ISBN 9781849464161 (pbk. : alk. paper)

Subjects: LCSH: International law. | International law—Europe.

Classification: LCC KZ3410 (ebook) | LCC KZ3410 .W68 2018 (print) | DDC 341—dc23

LC record available at https://lccn.loc.gov/2018037231

ISBN: PB: 978-1-84946-416-1
ePDF: 978-1-50990-903-2
ePub: 978-1-50990-904-9

Typeset by Compuscript Ltd, Shannon
Printed and bound in Great Britain by CPI Group (UK) Ltd, Croydon CR0 4YY

MIX
Paper | Supporting responsible forestry
FSC® C013604

Acknowledgements

This book has gone through a long gestation period. The idea goes back 20 years in time, to 1998 to be precise, when the first author was appointed chair in public international law at KU Leuven. Looking for English language teaching materials, it turned out that nearly all textbooks were written for common law jurisdictions. Very few, if any, paid attention to the international law practice of continental European States, the European Union (EU) and the Council of Europe. In Leuven, where we are just a stone's throw away from Brussels, the heart of the EU, and have a long tradition of comparative law, we felt the need to study international law through the multiple layers of transnational legal engagement that European countries have developed in the past 70 years: that is, with sufficient attention for the international law practice of a wide number of European countries – both civil and common law – and the EU institutions and the Council of Europe, in particular the 'supreme courts' of both organisations, ie the European Court of Justice and the European Court of Human Rights. Earlier attempts to do this include the textbook in Dutch which the first author published in 2005 with Marc Bossuyt, *Grondlijnen van Internationaal Recht* (Intersentia Publishers) and the edited volume *The Europeanisation of International Law* published with Jan Wouters, Erika De Wet and André Nollkaemper as co-editors in 2008 (TMC Asser Press).

Some ten years ago, three bright young scholars teamed up with the first author in Leuven to make the dream of an English textbook on international law from a European perspective come true: Cedric Ryngaert (who had defended his PhD in Leuven in 2007 and was subsequently appointed in Leuven and Utrecht), Tom Ruys (who obtained his PhD in Leuven in 2009 and was appointed in Ghent soon after) and Geert De Baere (who was appointed in Leuven in 2009 and became a judge of the EU's General Court in 2017). It has been a privilege to work together throughout all these years. Each of us wrote different chapters, but we take common responsibility for the whole book, which has gone through various phases of editing.

That brings us to the precious help of a great number of researchers affiliated to the Leuven Centre for Global Governance Studies and Institute for International Law at KU Leuven. They generously contributed their time and expertise in the various subfields of international law to make the manuscript as accurate and well-referenced as possible. They include, in alphabetical order: Hanna Bourgeois, Samuel Cogolati, Hanne Cuyckens, Philip De Man, Sanderijn Duquet, Linda Hamid, Elke Hellinx, Marieke Koekkoek, Ward Munters, Olivia Herman, Nina Pineau, Hendrik Vandekerckhove, Thomas Van Poecke, Nils Vanstappen, Evelien Wauters and Ines Willemyns. Student assistants or research interns who provided valuable assistance included Julia Bowley, Elizabeth Tomassetti, Lies Van Welde and Louise Willocx. In Utrecht, precious assistance was provided by Noémie Gagnon-Bergeron, Johanna Ohlman, Raluca Racasan, and Benjamin Thompson; in Ghent, by Mats Cuvelier and Luca Ferro.

A special word of gratitude goes to those colleagues in Leuven who were involved in the editorial process: initially Jed Odermatt and, when the book manuscript reached its full scope and an enormous amount of editorial fine-tuning needed to be done, Thomas Van Poecke and Evelien Wauters. Cedric Ryngaert thanks the European Research Council (Starting Grant Scheme, Proposal 336230—UNIJURIS), the Dutch Organization for Scientific Research (VIDI Scheme, No 016.135.322), and the UU Department of Law's research programme on Regulation and Enforcement in Europe (RENFORCE) for funding the author's research time that went into contributing to this book.

Various chapters in this book benefited from the helpful remarks of a number of colleagues: Professor Alex Mills, Dr Leonie Reins and Professor Geert Van Calster.

Last but not least our thanks go to the team of Hart Publishing, in particular Sinead O'Moloney, Tom Adams and Maria Skrzypiec, for their very professional service and enthusiastic support for our book project.

We dedicate this book to our families and to our students of the present and future generations, hoping that it may encourage them to contribute to a more just and sustainable international legal order.

We have strived to adequately describe the law as it stands mid-July 2018, with some last additions afterwards. This implies *inter alia* that the United Kingdom is counted as an EU Member State.

Leuven
14 July 2018

Contents

Table of Cases

International and European

National

Albania

Australia

Austria

Norway

Poland

United States

Table of International Instruments

International, Multilateral and Bilateral Instruments

Netherlands

Peru

Romania

Serbia

Spain

Switzerland

United Kingdom

United States

Vatican

List of Abbreviated Legal Instruments

International Treaties

Convention (II) with Respect to the Laws and Customs of War on Land and its annex: Regulations concerning the Laws and Customs of War on Land (adopted 29 July 1899, entered into force 4 September 1900) 187 CTS 429 ('**Hague Convention 1899**').

Convention (IV) respecting the Laws and Customs of War on Land and its annex: Regulations concerning the Laws and Customs of War on Land (adopted 18 October 1907, entered into force 26 January 1910) 187 CTS 227 ('**Hague Convention 1907**').

Treaty of Peace with Germany (adopted 28 June 1919, entered into force 10 January 1920) 225 CTS 188 ('**Treaty of Versailles**').

Montevideo Convention on the Rights and Duties of States (adopted 26 December 1933, entered into force 26 December 1934) 165 LNTS 19.

Chicago Convention on International Civil Aviation (adopted 7 December 1944, entered into force 4 April 1947) 15 UNTS 295.

Charter of the United Nations (adopted 26 June 1945, entered into force 24 October 1945) 1 UNTS 16 ('**UN Charter**').

Statute of the International Court of Justice (adopted 26 June 1945, entered into force 24 October 1945) 33 UNTS 933 ('**ICJ Statute**').

General Agreement on Tariffs and Trade (adopted 30 October 1947, entered into force 1 January 1948) ('**GATT 1947**').

Convention on the Prevention and Punishment of the Crime of Genocide (adopted 9 December 1948, entered into force 2 January 1951) 78 UNTS 277 ('**Genocide Convention**').

North Atlantic Treaty (adopted 4 April 1949, entered into force 24 August 1949) 34 UNTS 243 ('**NATO Treaty**').

Geneva Convention for the Amelioration of the Condition of the Wounded and Sick in Armed Forces in the Field (adopted 12 August 1949, entered into force 21 October 1950) 75 UNTS 31 ('**Geneva Convention I**'; '**GC I**').

Geneva Convention for the Amelioration of the Condition of Wounded, Sick and Shipwrecked Members of Armed Forces at Sea (adopted 12 August 1949, entered into force 21 October 1950) 75 UNTS 85 ('**Geneva Convention II**'; '**GC II**').

Geneva Convention relative to the Treatment of Prisoners of War (adopted 12 August 1949, entered into force 21 October 1950) 75 UNTS 135 ('**Geneva Convention III**'; '**GC III**').

Geneva Convention relative to the Protection of Civilian Persons in Time of War (adopted 12 August 1949, entered into force 21 October 1950) 75 UNTS 287 ('**Geneva Convention IV**'; '**GC IV**').

Convention relating to the Status of Refugees (adopted 28 July 1951, entered into force on 22 April 1954) 189 UNTS 150 ('**Refugee Convention**').

Convention on the Organization for Economic Co-operation and Development (adopted 14 December 1960, entered into force 30 September 1961) 888 UNTS 179 ('**OECD Convention**').

International Convention on the Elimination of All Forms of Racial Discrimination (adopted 21 December 1965, entered into force 4 January 1969) 660 UNTS 195 ('**ICERD**').

Vienna Convention on Diplomatic Relations (adopted 18 April 1961, entered into force 24 April 1964) 500 UNTS 95 ('**VCDR**').

Convention on the Reduction of Statelessness (adopted 30 August 1961, entered into force 13 December 1975) 989 UNTS 175.

Vienna Convention on Consular Relations (adopted 24 April 1963, entered into force 19 March 1967) 596 UNTS 261 ('**VCCR**').

International Covenant on Civil and Political Rights (adopted 16 December 1966, entered into force 23 March 1976) 999 UNTS 171 ('**ICCPR**').

International Covenant on Economic, Social and Cultural Rights (adopted 16 December 1966, entered into force 3 January 1976) 993 UNTS 3 ('**ICESCR**').

Treaty on the Non-Proliferation of Nuclear Weapons (adopted 1 July 1968, entered into force 5 March 1970) 729 UNTS 161 ('**Non-Proliferation Treaty**'; '**NPT**').

Vienna Convention on the Law of Treaties (adopted 23 May 1969, entered into force 27 January 1980) 1155 UNTS 331 ('**VCLT**').

Protocol Additional to the Geneva Conventions of 12 August 1949, and relating to the Protection of Victims of International Armed Conflicts (adopted 8 June 1977, entered into force 7 December 1978) ('**Additional Protocol I**'; '**AP I**').

Protocol Additional to the Geneva Conventions of 12 August 1949, and relating to the Protection of Victims of Non-International Armed Conflicts (adopted 8 June 1977, entered into force 7 December 1978) 1125 UNTS 609 ('**Additional Protocol II**'; '**AP II**').

Convention on the Elimination of All Forms of Discrimination against Women (adopted 18 December 1979, entered into force 3 September 1981) 1249 UNTS 13 ('**CEDAW**').

United Nations Convention on the Law of the Sea (adopted 10 December 1982, entered into force on 16 November 1994) 1833 UNTS 397 ('**UNCLOS**').

Convention against Torture and Other Cruel, Inhuman or Degrading Treatment or Punishment (adopted 10 December 1984, entered into force 26 June 1987) 1465 UNTS 85 ('**Convention against Torture**').

Convention on the Rights of the Child (adopted 20 November 1989, entered into force on 2 September 1990) 1577 UNTS 3 ('**CRC**').

United Nations Framework Convention on Climate Change (adopted 9 May 1992, entered into force 21 March 1994) 1771 UNTS 107 ('**UNFCCC**').

Convention on Conciliation and Arbitration within the OSCE (adopted on 15 December 1992, entered into force 5 December 1994) 1842 UNTS 121 ('**OSCE Convention**').

North American Free Trade Agreement (adopted 17 December 1992, entered into force 1 January 1994) (1993) 32 ILM 296 ('**NAFTA**').

Declaration of Principles on Interim Self-Government Arrangements (13 September 1993) ('**Oslo I Accords**').

Agreement Establishing the World Trade Organization (adopted 15 April 1994, entered into force 1 January 1995) 1867 UNTS 154 (‘**WTO Agreement**’).

Kyoto Protocol to the United Nations Framework Convention on Climate Change (adopted 11 December 1997, entered into force 16 February 2005) 2303 UNTS 162 (‘**Kyoto Protocol**’).

Rome Statute of the International Criminal Court (adopted 17 July 1998, entered into force on 1 July 2002) 2187 UNTS 90; as amended (‘**ICC Statute**’).

International Convention for the Protection of All Persons from Enforced Disappearance (adopted 20 December 2006, entered into force 23 December 2010) 2716 UNTS 3 (‘**Enforced Disappearance Convention**’).

Comprehensive Economic and Trade Agreement between Canada, of the one part, and the European Union and its Member States, of the other part (adopted 26 September 2014, entered into force provisionally 21 September 2017) [2017] OJ L 11/23 (‘**CETA**’).

European Treaties

Convention for the Protection of Human Rights and Fundamental Freedoms (adopted 4 November 1950, entered into force 3 September 1953) 213 UNTS 221; CETS No 5 (‘**ECHR**’).

European Social Charter (revised) (adopted on 3 May 1996, entered into force 1 July 1999) CETS No 163 (‘**ESC**’).

Consolidated version of the Treaty on European Union [2016] OJ C 202/13 (‘**TEU**’).

Consolidated version of the Treaty on the Functioning of the European Union [2016] OJ C 202/47 (‘**TFEU**’).

Charter of Fundamental Rights of the European Union [2016] OJ C 202/389.

Resolutions, Declarations and Policy Instruments

United Nations General Assembly Resolution 217 A (III), ‘Universal Declaration of Human Rights’, 10 December 1948, UN Doc A/RES/3/217 (‘**UDHR**’).

United Nations General Assembly Resolution 2625 (XXV), ‘Declaration on Principles of International Law concerning Friendly Relations and Co-operation among States in accordance with the Charter of the United Nations’, 24 October 1970, UN Doc A/RES/25/2625 (‘**Friendly Relations Declaration**’).

United Nations General Assembly Resolution 37/10, ‘Manila Declaration on the Peaceful Settlement of International Disputes’, 15 November 1982, UN Doc A/RES/37/10 (‘**Manila Declaration**’).

Rio Declaration on Environment and Development (16 June 1992) (1992) 31 ILM 874 (‘**Rio Declaration**’).

United Nations Security Council Resolution 827, ‘Statute of the International Tribunal for the Prosecution of Persons Responsible for Serious Violations of International Humanitarian Law Committed in the Territory of the Former Yugoslavia since 1991’, 25 May 1993, UN Doc S/RES/827; as amended (‘**ICTY Statute**’).

United Nations Security Council Resolution 955, ‘Statute of the International Criminal Tribunal for the Prosecution of Persons Responsible for Genocide and Other Serious

Violations of International Humanitarian Law Committed in the Territory of Rwanda and Rwandan Citizens Responsible for Genocide and Other Such Violations Committed in the Territory of Neighbouring States, between 1 January 1994 and 31 December 1994', 8 November 1994, UN Doc S/RES/955; as amended ('**ICTR Statute**').

International Law Commission, 'Articles on Nationality of Natural Persons in relation to the Succession of States with commentaries' (1999) *YILC*, Vol II, Part Two, 23-47 ('**ILC Articles on Nationality**').

International Law Commission, 'Draft Articles on Responsibility for Internationally Wrongful Acts with commentaries' (2001) *YILC*, Vol II, Part Two, 31-143 ('**ASR**').

International Law Commission, 'Articles on Diplomatic Protection with commentaries' (2006) *YILC*, Vol II, Part Two, 26-55 ('**ADP**').

International Law Commission, 'Articles on the Responsibility of International Organizations' (2011) *YILC*, Vol II, Part Two, 46-105 ('**ARIO**').

Human Rights Council, Report of the Special Representative of the Secretary-General on the issue of human rights and transnational corporations and other business enterprises, John Ruggie: 'Guiding Principles on Business and Human Rights: Implementing the United Nations "Protect, Respect and Remedy" Framework', 21 March 2011, UN Doc A/HRC/17/31, Annex ('**UNGPs**').

List of Abbreviations

ACS	Association of Caribbean States
ACP	African, Caribbean and Pacific countries
ADB	Asian Development Bank
ACD	Asia Cooperation Dialogue
ADP	(International Law Commission) Articles on Diplomatic Protection (with Commentaries)
AEC	African Economic Community
AfCFTA	African Continental Free Trade Agreement
AfDB	African Development Bank
AFDI	Annuaire français de droit international
AG	Advocate General
AIS	Andean Integration System
AJIL	American Journal of International Law
AL	Albania
ALADI	Latin American Integration Association
ALBA	Bolivarian Alliance for the Peoples of our America
All ER	All England Law Reports
AMU	Arab Maghreb Union
AOSIS	Alliance of Small Island States
APEC	Asian-Pacific Economic Cooperation
AP I	Protocol Additional to the Geneva Conventions of 12 August 1949, and relating to the Protection of Victims of International Armed Conflicts (Protocol I)
AP II	Protocol Additional to the Geneva Conventions of 12 August 1949, and relating to the Protection of Victims of Non-International Armed Conflicts (Protocol II)
APRM	African Peer Review Mechanism
ARF	ASEAN Regional Forum
ARIO	Articles on the Responsibility of International Organizations
ASEAN	Association of South East Asian Nations
ASEM	Asia-Europe Meeting
ASR	International Law Commission Articles on the Responsibility of States for Internationally Wrongful Acts

AT	Austria
ATCM	Antarctic Treaty Consultative Meeting
ATCP	Antarctic Treaty Consultative Party
ATS	Antarctic Treaty System
AWACS	Airborne Warning and Control System
AU	African Union
BCEAO	Central Bank of West African States
BE	Belgium
BEAC	Bank of Central African States
BIMSTEC	Bay of Bengal Initiative for Multi-Sectoral Technical and Economic Cooperation
BIT(s)	Bilateral Investment Treaty(-ies)
BLEU	Belgium-Luxembourg Economic Union
BOAD	West African Development Bank
BOIP	Benelux Office for Intellectual Property
BRD	Bundesrepublik Deutschland
BSEC	Organization of the Black Sea Economic Cooperation
BSIC	Sahel-Saharan Bank for Investment and Trade
BYIL	British Yearbook of International Law
CAFTA-DR	Dominican Republic – Central America Free Trade Agreement
CARICOM	Caribbean Community and Common Market
CARIFTA	Caribbean Free Trade Association
CAT	Committee against Torture
CBSS	Council of Baltic Sea States
CCNR	Central Commission for Navigation on the Rhine
CEDAW	Convention on the Elimination of All Forms of Discrimination against Women
CEEAC	Communauté économique des Etats de l'Afrique Centrale (see also ECCAS)
CEFTA	Central European Free Trade Agreement
CEI	Central European Initiative
CELAC	Community of Latin American and Caribbean States
CEMAC	Economic and Monetary Community of Central Africa
CEN-SAD	Community of Sahel-Saharan States
CERD	Committee on the Elimination of Racial Discrimination
CERI	Centre for Educational Research and Innovation
CERN	European Organization for Nuclear Research
CETS	Council of Europe Treaty Series
CFE	Treaty on Conventional Armed Forces in Europe

CFP	Common Fisheries Policy
CFSP	Common Foreign and Security Policy
CH	Switzerland
CICAD	Inter-American Drug Abuse Control Commission
CICTE	Inter-American Committee against Terrorism
CIS	Commonwealth of Independent States
CFSP	Common Foreign and Security Policy
CJEU	Court of Justice of the European Union
CJICL	Cambridge Journal of International and Comparative Law
CJLJ	Canadian Journal of Law and Jurisprudence
CJIL	Chinese Journal of International Law
CLCS	Commission on the Limits of the Continental Shelf
CLR	Columbia Law Review
CLS	Critical Legal Studies
CMLR	Common Market Law Review
COBAC	Central African Banking Commission
COMESA	Common Market for Eastern and Southern Africa
CONFEJES	Conference of Francophone Ministers of Youth and Sports
CONFEMEN	Conference of Francophone Ministers of Education
COPAX	Council for Peace and Security in Central Africa
Coreper	Committee of Permanent Representatives (EU)
CPC	Conflict Prevention Centre (OSCE)
CPF	Permanent Council of the Francophonie
CPVO	Community Plant Variety Office
CRC	Convention on the Rights of the Child
CSBMs	Confidence and Security Building Measures
CSDP	Common Security and Defence Policy
CSME	CARICOM Single Market and Economy
CTBTO Prepcom	Preparatory Commission for the Comprehensive Nuclear-Test Ban Treaty Organization
CTC	Counter-Terrorism Committee
CTED	Counter-terrorism Committee Executive Directorate
CTS	Consolidated Treaty Series
CUP	Cambridge University Press
CZ	Czech Republic
DAC	Development Assistance Committee (OECD)
DDR	Deutsche Demokratische Republik
DE	Germany

DPPC	Defence Policy and Planning Committee (of the North Atlantic Treaty Organization)
DRC	Democratic Republic of the Congo
DSB	Dispute Settlement Body (of the World Trade Organization)
EAC	East African Community
EACJ	East African Court of Justice
EAEC	European Atomic Energy Community (also 'Euratom')
EAEU	Eurasian Economic Union
EAPC	Euro-Atlantic Partnership Council
EAS	East Asia Summit
EBID	ECOWAS Bank for Investment and Development
EBRD	European Bank for Reconstruction and Development
EC	European Community
ECA	Economic Commission for Africa
ECB	European Central Bank
ECC	Energy Charter Conference
ECCAS	Economic Community of Central African States (see also CEEAC)
ECE	Economic Commission for Europe
ECHR	European Convention for the Protection of Human Rights and Fundamental Freedoms
ECJ	European Court of Justice
ECLAC	Economic Commission for Latin America and the Caribbean
ECMT	European Conference of Ministers of Transport
ECMWF	European Centre for Medium-Range Weather Forecasts
ECSWA	Economic and Social Commission for Western Asia
ECtHR	European Court of Human Rights
ECOMOG	ECOWAS Cease-fire Monitoring Group
ECOSOC	United Nations Economic and Social Council
ECOWAS	Economic Community of West African States
ECSC	European Coal and Steel Community
ECST	European Civil Service Tribunal
EDRC	Economic and Development Review Committee (OECD)
EEA	European Economic Area
EEAS	European External Action Service
EEC	European Economic Community
EEZ	Exclusive Economic Zone
EFP	Enhanced Forward Presence (NATO)
EFTA	European Free Trade Association
EGC	European General Court

EJIL	European Journal of International Law
ELR	European Law Review
EMBL	European Molecular Biology Laboratory
EMU	Economic and Monetary Union
EP	European Parliament
EPA	European Partnership Agreement
EPC	Economic Policy Committee (OECD)
EPO	European Patent Office
EPPO	European and Mediterranean Plant Protection Organization
ES	Spain
ESA	European Space Agency
ESC	European Social Charter
ESCAP	Economic and Social Commission for Asia and the Pacific
ESDP	European Security and Defence Policy
ESO	European Organization for Astronomical Research in the Southern Hemisphere
ETS	European Treaty Series
EU	European Union
EuFMD	FAO Commission for the control of Foot-and-Mouth disease
EUIPO	European Union Intellectual Property Office
EUMETSAT	European Organization for the Exploitation of Meteorological Satellites
Euratom	European Atomic Energy Community (also 'EAEC')
Eurocontrol	European Organization for the Safety of Air Navigation
EUROFIMA	European Company for the Financing of Railroad Equipment
EWCA	Court of Appeal of England and Wales
EWHC	High Court of Justice of England and Wales
FAO	Food and Agriculture Organization
FATF	Financial Action Task Force
FCN (treaties)	Friendship, Commerce, and Navigation (treaties)
FOMAC	Central African Multinational Force
FR	France
FRY	Federal Republic of Yugoslavia
FTAA	Free Trade Area of the Americas
FYIL	Finnish Yearbook of International Law
G7	Group of Seven
G77	Group of 77
GATT	General Agreement on Tariffs and Trade

GC I	Geneva Convention for the Amelioration of the Condition of the Wounded and Sick in Armed Forces in the Field (Geneva Convention I)
GC II	Geneva Convention for the Amelioration of the Condition of Wounded, Sick and Shipwrecked Members of Armed Forces at Sea (Geneva Convention II)
GC III	Geneva Convention relative to the Treatment of Prisoners of War (Geneva Convention III)
GC IV	Geneva Convention relative to the Protection of Civilian Persons in Time of War (Geneva Convention IV)
GCC	Cooperation Council for the Arab Gulf States (Gulf Cooperation Council)
GDP	Gross Domestic Product
GJIL	Georgetown Journal of International Law
GNP	Gross National Product
GPGs	Global Public Goods
GRULAC	Latin American and Caribbean Group
GYIL	German Yearbook of International law
HC IV	Fourth Hague Convention Respecting the Laws and Customs of War on Land
HR	Croatia
HRC	(United Nations) Human Rights Council
HRCttee	(United Nations) Human Rights Committee
HR/VP	High Representative of the Union for Foreign Affairs and Security Policy/Vice-President of the European Commission
HU	Hungary
IACHR	Inter-American Commission on Human Rights
IACtHR	Inter-American Court on Human Rights
IADB	Inter-American Development Bank
IAEA	International Atomic Energy Agency
IBRD	International Bank for Reconstruction and Development
ICAO	International Civil Aviation Organization
ICC	International Criminal Court
ICCS	International Commission of Civil Status
ICCPR	International Covenant on Civil and Political Rights
ICERD	International Convention on the Elimination of All Forms of Racial Discrimination
ICESCR	International Covenant on Economic, Social and Cultural Rights
ICJ	International Court of Justice
ICLQ	International and Comparative Law Quarterly

ICSID	International Centre for Settlement of Investment Disputes
ICTR	International Criminal Tribunal for Rwanda
ICTY	International Criminal Tribunal for the former Yugoslavia
ICUMSA	International Commission for Uniform Methods of Sugar Analysis
IDA	International Development Association
IDB	Islamic Development Bank
IE	Ireland
IEA	International Energy Agency
IFAD	International Fund for Agricultural Development
IFC	International Finance Corporation
IIC	Inter-American Investment Corporation
ILA	International Law Association
ILC	International Law Commission
ILO	International Labour Organization
IMF	International Monetary Fund
IMO	International Maritime Organization
Interpol	International Criminal Police Organization
IOM	International Organization for Migration
ISA	International Seabed Authority
ISFP	Initiative on Soaring Food Prices
ISO	International Standardization Organization
IT	Italy
ITC	International Trade Centre
ITLOS	International Tribunal for the Law of the Sea
ITO	International Trade Organization
ITU	International Telecommunications Union
IUU (fishing)	Illegal, Unreported and Unregulated (fishing)
JEL	Journal of Environmental Law
JHA	Justice and Home Affairs
JICJ	Journal for International Criminal Justice
JIDS	Journal of International Dispute Settlement
JIEL	Journal of International Economic Law
LGDJ	Librairie générale de droit et de jurisprudence
LJIL	Leiden Journal of International Law
LV	Latvia
MARAC	Central African early warning system
MARPOL	International Convention for the Prevention of Pollution from Ships
MC	Military Committee (NATO)

Mercosur	Southern Common Market (Mercado Común del Sur)
MIF	Multilateral Investment Fund
MIGA	Multilateral Investment Guarantee Agency
MJIL	Michigan Journal of International Law
MLR	Modern Law Review
MoU	Memorandum of Understanding
MPEPIL	*Max Planck Encyclopedia of Public International Law* (R Wolfrum (ed), OUP))
MUP	Manchester University Press
NAC	North Atlantic Council
NACC	North Atlantic Cooperation Council
NAFO	Northwest Atlantic Fisheries Organization
NAFTA	North American Free Trade Agreement
NAM	Non-Aligned Movement
NAMCO	North Atlantic Marine Mammal Commission
NASCO	North Atlantic Salmon Conservation Organization
NATO	North Atlantic Treaty Organization
NEA	Nuclear Energy Agency
NEAFC	North-East Atlantic Fisheries Commission
NEPAD	New Partnership for Africa's Development
NILR	Netherlands International Law Review
NL	Netherlands
NPG	Nuclear Planning Group (NATO)
NPT	Non-Proliferation Treaty
NYIL	Netherlands Yearbook of International Law
OAPEC	Organization of Arab Petroleum Exporting Countries
OAS	Organization of American States
OCCAR	Organization for Joint Armament Cooperation
OCHA	See UNOCHA
OCTs	Overseas Countries and Territories
ODIHR	Office for Democratic Institutions and Human Rights (OSCE)
OECD	Organisation for Economic Co-operation and Development
OECS	Organization of Eastern Caribbean States
OEEC	Organisation for European Economic Cooperation
OEEPE	European Organization of Experimental Photogrammetric Studies
OHCHR	Office of the United Nations High Commissioner for Human Rights
OIC	Organization of the Islamic Cooperation
OJ	Official Journal of the European Union

OJLS	Oxford Journal of Legal Studies
OMRs	Outermost Regions
OPCW	Organization for the Prohibition of Chemical Weapons
OPEC	Organization of the Petroleum Exporting Countries
OSCE	Organization for Security and Co-operation in Europe
OTP	Office of the Prosecutor of the International Criminal Court
OUP	Oxford University Press
PACE	Parliamentary Assembly of the Council of Europe
PADF	Pan American Development Foundation
PAHO	Pan American Health Organization
PCA	Permanent Court of Arbitration
PCIJ	Permanent Court of International Justice
PfP	Partnership for Peace
PLO	Palestine Liberation Organization
PRGF	Poverty Reduction and Growth Facility
PRSP	Poverty Reduction Strategy Paper
PUF	Presses universitaires de France
QB	Queen's Bench Division
R2P	Responsibility to Protect
RAP	Readiness Action Plan (NATO)
RCC	Regional Cooperation Council
RdC	Recueil des cours de l'Académie de droit international de La Haye
REC(s)	Regional Economic Community(-ies)
REPAC	Network of Parliaments of the Economic Community of Central African States
RFB	Regional Fishing Body
RFMO	Regional Fisheries Management Organization
RIAA	Reports of International Arbitral Awards
Riv Dir Int	Rivista di Diritto Internazionale
RS	Serbia
RU	Romania
SAARC	South Asian Association for Regional Cooperation
SACEUR	Supreme Allied Commander Europe (NATO)
SACT	Supreme Allied Commander Transformation (NATO)
SADC	Southern African Development Community
SAFTA	South Asian Free Trade Area
SAPTA	South Asian Preferential Trading Arrangement
SARS	Severe Acute Respiratory Syndrome

SCO	Shanghai Cooperation Organization
SDRs	Special Drawing Rights
SECI	Southeast European Cooperative Initiative
SELA	Latin American and Caribbean Economic System
SFRY	Socialist Federal Republic of Yugoslavia
SHAPE	Supreme Headquarters Allied Commander for Europe
SI	Slovenia
SICA	Central American Integration System
SIECA	Secretariat for Central American Integration
SOFA	Status of Forces Agreements
SPC	Secretariat of the Pacific Community
STDs	Sexually Transmitted Diseases
STL	Special Tribunal for Lebanon
SYBIL	Singapore Yearbook of International Law
TAC	Total Allowable Catch
TCS	Trilateral Cooperation Secretariat
TEU	Treaty on European Union
TFEU	Treaty on the Functioning of the European Union
TNCs	transnational corporations
TRIPS	Agreement on Trade-Related Aspects of Intellectual Property Rights
TRNC	Turkish Republic of Northern Cyprus
TTIP EU-US	Transatlantic Trade and Investment Partnership
UDEAC	Central African Customs and Economic Union
UDHR	Universal Declaration of Human Rights
UEAC	Union Economique de l'Afrique Centrale
UEMOA	West African Economic and Monetary Union
UK	United Kingdom of Great Britain and Northern Ireland
UKHL	House of Lords of the United Kingdom
UKSC	Supreme Court of the United Kingdom
UMA	Arab Maghreb Union
UN	United Nations
UN-AIDS	Joint United Nations Programme on HIV/AIDS
UNASUR	Union of South American States (Unión de Naciones Suramericanas)
UNCDF	United Nations Capital Development Fund
UN Charter	Charter of the United Nations
UNCIO	United Nations Conference on International Organization
UNCITRAL	United Nations Commission on International Trade Law

UNCLOS	United Nations Convention on the Law of the Sea
UNCTAD	United Nations Conference on Trade and Development
UNDP	United Nations Development Programme
UNDCP	United Nations International Drug Control Programme
UNEP	United Nations Environment Programme
UNESCO	United Nations Educational, Scientific and Cultural Organization
UNFCCC	United Nations Framework Convention on Climate Change
UNFPA	United Nations Population Fund
UNGA	United Nations General Assembly
UNGPs	United Nations Guiding Principles on Business and Human Rights
UN-HABITAT	United Nations Human Settlements Programme
UNHCR	Office of the United Nations High Commissioner for Refugees
UNICEF	United Nations Children's Fund
UNICRI	United Nations Interregional Crime and Justice Research Institute
UNIDIR	United Nations Institute for Disarmament Research
UNIDO	United Nations Industrial Development Organization
UNISDR	United Nations Office for Disaster Risk Reduction
UNITAR	United Nations Institute for Training and Research
UNOCHA	United Nations Office for the Coordination of Humanitarian Affairs
UNODC	United Nations Office on Drugs and Crime
UNOPS	United Nations Office for Project Services
UNRISD	United Nations Research Institute for Social Development
UNRWA	United Nations Relief and Works Agency for Palestine Refugees in the Near East
UNSC	United Nations Security Council
UNSCOM	United Nations Observation, Verification and Inspection Commission
UNSG	United Nations Secretary General
UNTS	United Nations Treaty Series
UNU	United Nations University
UNV	United Nations Volunteers
UN Women	United Nations Entity for Gender Equality and the Empowerment of Women
UNWTO	United Nations World Tourism Organization
UPU	Universal Postal Union
US	United States of America
VCCR	Vienna Convention on Consular Relations
VCDR	Vienna Convention on Diplomatic Relations

VCLT	Vienna Convention on the Law of Treaties
VJTF	Very High Readiness Joint Task Force (of the North Atlantic Treaty Organization)
WEOG	Western Europe and Others Group
WEU	Western European Union
WFP	World Food Programme
WHO	World Health Organization
WIPO	World Intellectual Property Organization
WMO	World Meteorological Organization
WTO	World Trade Organization
XK	Kosovo
YILC	Yearbook of the International Law Commission
ZaöRV	Zeitschrift für ausländisches öffentliches Recht und Völkerrecht

List of Tables

Introduction

International Law, A European Perspective

Students of international law have a plethora of excellent English language textbooks and treatises at their disposal. What then could possibly justify the addition of yet another textbook to the catalogue? The idea for the present textbook started from the simple observation that many law faculties in Europe teach courses in international law in English, both at bachelor and master levels. However, the majority of the international law textbooks currently used were written or edited by academics and practitioners from the English-speaking world, often with a common law background. Inevitably and understandably, these textbooks focus principally on practice from common law countries, particularly from the United States of America and the United Kingdom, and less on practice from continental and civil law countries, and on the increasingly important interactions between international law on the one hand and the law of the European Union (EU)[1] or the European Convention for the Protection of Human Rights and Fundamental Freedoms (ECHR) on the other hand.

The present textbook aims to fill that void, by taking a comprehensive European perspective when discussing the classic doctrines and the main sub-branches of international law. That perspective notably includes the EU, the Council of Europe, and their respective Member States. Throughout the book, special attention is devoted to the reception of international law in the EU legal order and the EU's international legal action (see especially Chapter 4),[2] and to the dialectical relationship between general international law and the ECHR, as applied by the European Court of Human Rights (ECtHR).[3]

[1] That is to say, the law emanating from the EU, which is founded on the Treaty on European Union (TEU) and the Treaty on the Functioning of the European Union (TFEU).

[2] Examples of the Court of Justice of the EU's case law on the relationship between EU law and public international law more generally include the judgments of 3 September 2008, *Kadi and Al Barakaat International Foundation v Council and Commission*, C-402/05 P and C-415/05 P, EU:C:2008:461; of 21 December 2011, *Air Transport Association of America and others*, C-366/10, EU:C:2011:864; of 18 July 2013, *Commission and others v Kadi*, C-584/10 P, C-593/10 P and C-595/10 P, EU:C:2013:518; of 21 December 2016, *Council v Front Polisario*, C-104/16 P, EU:C:2016:973; of 27 February 2018, *Western Sahara Campaign UK*, C-266/16, EU:C:2018:118; and of 6 March 2018, *Achmea*, C-284/16, EU:C:2018:158.

[3] Interactions between the ECHR and general international law were notably at issue in the ECtHR decisions in *Behrami and Behrami v France*; *Saramati v France, Germany and Norway* App nos 71412/01 and 78166/ 01 (ECtHR, 2 May 2007); *Al-Skeini and others v UK* App no 55721/07 (ECtHR, 7 July 2011); *Al-Jedda v UK* App no 27021/08 (ECtHR, 7 July 2011); *Nada v Switzerland* App no 10593/08 (ECtHR, 12 September 2012); and *Al-Dulimi and Montana Management Inc v Switzerland* App no 5809/08 (ECtHR, 21 June 2016).

The European perspective espoused by our book is informed by a substantial amount of European practice at the level of States and international organisations. In particular, the book makes wide use of decisions of the Court of Justice of the European Union (CJEU),[4] the ECtHR, and national courts in Europe. The book also refers to practice at the diplomatic and executive level, which includes EU coordinated positions and statements on issues of international law. In so doing, the book subscribes to the idea that the further constitutionalisation of the EU is a feature of what can be termed the constitutionalisation of international law, in the sense that the EU remains an instance of particularly effective international law, or at least a 'laboratory' of international law.[5]

However, our book is not intended as a textbook on EU practice, nor more broadly on 'European' practice, in international law. It is an international law textbook. The book therefore follows a typical textbook structure, tackling the main tenets of international law. Crucially, what differentiates the present book from the existing literature is that, as an international law textbook, it devotes considerable attention to both EU and broader 'European' practice in public international law. In particular, the book explores, on the one hand, the dynamics of international law in Europe on the basis of the practice of European States (including non-EU Member States), the EU, and the Council of Europe, as well as of other organisations, such as the United Nations Economic Commission for Europe (UNECE) (see Chapter 19, Section II, and Chapter 20), and the European Space Agency (ESA) (see Chapter 18, Section XII(D)). On the other hand, the book examines European practice in a broad range of international organisations, including within the United Nations (UN) and the UN system (see notably Chapter 6, Section VIII),[6] the World

[4] Under Art 19(1), first subparagraph TEU, the institution of the Court of Justice of the EU encompasses the Court of Justice (ECJ), the General Court (EGC) and specialised courts. The only court falling in the final category, the Civil Service Tribunal (EU Civil Service Tribunal or ECST), established in 2004, ceased to operate on 1 September 2016 after its jurisdiction was transferred to the EGC in the context of the reform of the EU's judicial structure.

[5] KS Ziegler, 'International Law and EU Law: Between Asymmetric Constitutionalisation and Fragmentation' in A Orakhelashvili (ed), *Research Handbook on the Theory and History of International Law* (Cheltenham, Edward Elgar, 2011) 268–73.

[6] For earlier work see inter alia J Wouters, 'The European Union as an Actor within the United Nations General Assembly' in V Kronenberger (ed), *The EU and the International Legal Order: Discord or Harmony*? (The Hague, TMC Asser Press, 2001) 375–404; J Wouters, 'The United Nations, the EU and Conflict Prevention: Interconnecting the Global and Regional Levels' in V Kronenberger and J Wouters (eds), *The European Union and Conflict Prevention: Policy and Legal Aspects* (The Hague, TMC Asser Press, 2004) 369–92; J Wouters, F Hoffmeister and T Ruys (eds), *The United Nations and the European Union: An Ever Stronger Partnership* (The Hague, TMC Asser Press, 2006); M Emerson et al, *Upgrading the EU's Role as Global Actor: Institutions, Law and the Restructuring of European Diplomacy* (Brussels, Centre for European Policy Studies, 2011); J Wouters et al (eds), *The European Union and Multilateral Governance: Assessing EU Participation in United Nations Human Rights and Environmental Fora* (Basingstoke, Palgrave Macmillan, 2012); B Van Vooren, S Blockmans and J Wouters (eds), *The EU's Role in Global Governance: The Legal Dimension* (Oxford, OUP, 2013); J Wouters, J Odermatt and T Ramopoulos, 'The Status of the European Union at the United Nations General Assembly' in I Govaere et al (eds), *Liber Amicorum Marc Maresceau* (Leiden, Brill, 2013) 211–23; G De Baere and E Paasivirta, 'Identity and Difference: The EU and the UN as Part of Each Other' in HCFJA de Waele and J-J Kuipers (eds), *The Emergence of the European Union's International Identity* (Leiden, Nijhoff, 2013) 21–42; J Wouters and S Duquet, 'The United Nations, the European Union and Multilateral Action against Terrorism' in I Govaere and S Poli (eds), *EU Management of Global Emergencies: Legal Framework for Combating Threats and Crises* (Leiden, Brill, 2014) 351–87; J Wouters and AL Chané, 'Brussels Meets Westphalia: The European Union and the United Nations' in P Eeckhout and M Lopez-Escudero (eds), *The European Union's External Action in Times of Crisis* (Oxford, Hart, 2016) 299–323; AL Chané and J Wouters, 'The European Union in United Nations Economic Governance Fora' (2017) 8 *European Yearbook of International Economic Law* 541.

Trade Organization (WTO) (see Chapter 19, Section III),[7] and the International Criminal Court (ICC) (see Chapter 17, Section V(A)).[8]

More in particular, the textbook refers to practice of continental European 'civil law' jurisdictions, European common law practice, as well as practice of EU institutions and the Council of Europe. However, it also discusses relevant non-European practice regarding international law (for example with a view to comparing it to parallel European practice), as well as the main cases brought before international dispute-settlement mechanisms, in particular the International Court of Justice (ICJ) (see notably Chapter 13, Section III(B)).

The book aims to give a comprehensive overview of international law, with attention to all the 'classics' that form the core of any international law textbook: the sources (Chapters 2 and 3), the relationship and interactions between international and domestic law (including the EU, Chapter 4), the subjects (Chapters 5, 6, 7 and 8), jurisdiction (Chapter 9), diplomatic relations (Chapter 10), immunities (Chapter 11), State responsibility (Chapter 12), and the settlement of disputes (Chapter 13). But it goes beyond that core by entering into various sub-fields of international law, notably the law on the use of force (Chapter 14), the law of armed conflict (Chapter 15), human rights law (Chapter 16), international criminal law (Chapter 17), the law of the sea and global commons (Chapter 18), international economic law (Chapter 19), and international environmental law (Chapter 20). We have endeavoured to cover, at least with broad brushstrokes, the law of international organisations, paying attention to both global (Chapter 6) and regional organisations (Chapter 7), in Europe and in other continents.

In all these areas we have tried to pay attention to European contributions to, and engagement with, these fields and/or organisations. This includes inter alia EU treaty practice (see notably Chapter 2); European (EU and national) case law on the effects of international law in the domestic legal order; European practice on the recognition of States (see Chapter 5, Section IV(A)); EU practice with regard to the UN and its most important bodies, including the UN Human Rights Council (see Chapter 16, Section VII(A)); EU cooperation with non-European regional organisations (see Chapter 7); European conventions and case law (including both from national courts and the ECtHR) on immunities (see Chapter 11); the EU and the International Law Commission (ILC)'s work on the responsibility of international organisations and ECtHR case law on attribution of State responsibility (see Chapter 12); European practice on the peaceful settlement of disputes (including with regard to the acceptance of the jurisdiction of the ICJ) (see Chapter 13); practice in Europe regarding (collective) self-defence (see Chapter 14, Section III(D)); European dimensions (both under the ECHR and the Charter of Fundamental Rights of the EU) of human rights protection (including on social rights, minorities and torture prevention) (see Chapter 16); European practice on the law of the sea (from port State

[7] See eg G De Baere and I Van Damme, 'Co-Adaptation in the International Legal Order: The EU and the WTO' in J Crawford and S Nouwen (eds), *Select Proceedings of the European Society of International Law*, Vol 3, 2010 (Oxford, Hart, 2012) 311–25; J Wouters, 'The European Union and the World Trade Organization: Partners or Competitors?' in I Govaere and D Hanf (eds), *Liber Amicorum Paul Demaret* (Bern, Peter Lang, 2013) 373–83.

[8] See eg J Wouters and S Basu, 'The Creation of a Global Criminal Justice System: the European Union and the International Criminal Court' in C Ryngaert (ed), *The Effectiveness of International Criminal Justice* (Antwerp, Intersentia, 2009) 117–42. For relevant legal instruments on the interrelationship between the EU and the ICC, see in particular the Agreement between the International Criminal Court and the European Union on Cooperation and Assistance (adopted 10 April 2006, entered into force 1 May 2006) [2006] OJ L 115/50; Council Decision 2011/168/CFSP of 21 March 2011 on the International Criminal Court and repealing Common Position 2003/444/CFSP [2011] OJ L 76/56; and Council of the EU, 'Action Plan to follow-up on the Decision on the International Criminal Court', 12 July 2011, 12080/11, Annex.

control to naval operations and the EU common fisheries policy) and global commons (eg under the United Nations Convention on the Law of the Sea (UNCLOS), on the Arctic and outer space, be it through the EU or ESA) (see Chapter 18); the EU in the WTO, the EU's rich record of international trade agreements, the relationship between WTO law and the EU legal order, and European practice on international investment protection up to the Commission's proposals for a World Investment Court (see Chapter 19); European dynamics of international environmental law, including the EU's participation in many EU environmental treaties, such as the Convention on International Trade in Endangered Species of Wild Fauna and Flora (CITES)[9] and the Convention on Access to Information, Public Participation in Decision-Making and Access to Justice in Environmental Matters (the Aarhus Convention),[10] and the most prominent EU instruments for environmental and wildlife protection (see Chapter 20).

Finally, it bears emphasising what our book does *not* do. It does not put forward a 'provincial' European perspective on international law. It does not suggest a conception of the EU or of Europe more generally as the world centre of political virtue. It is not built on a conception of European identity based on the negation of the 'non-European otherness'[11] of the wider world, which arguably constituted part of Europe's identity during its past of colonialism and imperialism.[12] Narratives of international law depicting progress in terms of a unified international community have also been described as speaking 'a thoroughly Eurocentric language',[13] with Europe imagining its values as universal.[14] This book does not put forward such a narrative. Rather, it critically engages with the role of Europe in international law, including from a historical perspective (see Chapter 1).[15]

[9] Convention on International Trade in Endangered Species of Wild Fauna and Flora (adopted 3 March 1973, entered into force 1 January 1975) 993 UNTS 243 (CITES).

[10] Convention on Access to Information, Public Participation in Decision-Making and Access to Justice in Environmental Matters (adopted 28 June 1998, entered into force 30 October 2001) 2161 UNTS 447 (Aarhus Convention).

[11] M Koskenniemi, *The Gentle Civilizer of Nations: The Rise and Fall of International Law 1870–1960* (Cambridge, CUP, 2002) 112.

[12] cp S Marks, 'Empire's Law' (2003) 10 *Indiana Journal of Global Legal Studies* 460. On the intertwining of the development of international law and Europe's imperialism, see A Anghie, *Imperialism, Sovereignty and the Making of International Law* (Cambridge, CUP, 2004). See further M Craven, 'Colonialism and Domination' in B Fassbender and A Peters (eds), *The Oxford Handbook of the History of International Law* (Oxford, OUP, 2012) 862–89.

[13] Several strategies have been put forward to address the challenge of Eurocentrism in international law. Koskenniemi suggests four ways: first, a careful demonstration of the 'colonial origins' of a particular international legal rule or institution; second, focusing on encounters between the European and non-European world as a crucial moment in the history of international law; third, examining the hybridisation of international legal concepts as they are transferred between the coloniser and the colonies; and fourth, what Koskenniemi calls 'exotising' or 'provincialising' Europe and European laws: M Koskenniemi, 'Histories of International Law: Dealing with Eurocentrism' (2011) 19 *Rechtsgeschichte* 152, 170–175. Becker Lorca, in turn, suggests three trends followed by historians of international law aware of potential Eurocentric distortions: first, histories have been written in which international law both reflects the interests of powerful Western sovereigns and enables weaker actors to resist by using the universal language of rights; second, Koskenniemi's *Gentle Civilizer of Nations* represents a turning point in the historiography of international law in recounting the history of international law as an intellectual history, thereby showing a way beyond realist and post-colonial structuralism, as well as beyond histories of ideas committed to a narrative of progress; third, a number of legal scholars have explored the dynamics between centre and periphery as a heuristic to retrieve the history of international law in its global rather than solely Western dimensions: A Becker Lorca, 'Eurocentrism in the History of International Law' in B Fassbender and A Peters (eds), *The Oxford Handbook of the History of International Law* (Oxford, OUP, 2012) 1055–56.

[14] Koskenniemi (n 13) 160.

[15] Our book also does not advocate for or against the emergence of a customary international law norm favouring European integration, the existence of which has been suggested notably within the context of the World Trade Organization: see M Lickova, 'European Exceptionalism in International Law' (2008) 19 *EJIL* 490.

Furthermore, our book acknowledges that history demonstrates that international law 'has been as Asian or African as it has been European',[16] and that the first instruments and institutions of international law identified to date probably originate outside Europe.[17] At the same time, to the extent that some of the central precepts of current international law have their origins in early modern European political thought and practice, the book acknowledges that this fact may create tensions for any claims with respect to the universality of international law.[18]

The book's prime value, however, lies in presenting European contemporary practice and doctrine of international law. Surprisingly perhaps, due to the dominance of English-language scholarship, which tends to focus on common law practice, European (including EU) practice has received comparatively less attention. This book enables the reader better to grasp the contemporary 'European' approach to international law, which will in turn enrich the debate on the truly universal character of international law. Indeed, knowledge of the various approaches to international law is key to apprehend how international law events and arguments are globally understood, whether or not the reader or practitioner ultimately accepts all these approaches as valid.[19] Accordingly, this book is a starting point for, rather than the conclusion of, an international conversation on the content and meaning of international law, taking place in a diverse world with different power and knowledge centres – one of them being Europe.

In sum, the present textbook aims to complement the existing literature by providing a comprehensive European perspective that takes into account, next to relevant practice from across the international legal order, European practice, including from the EU, the Council of Europe, and a great number of European States, without taking this practice as 'standard' or paradigmatic.

[16] On which see eg TO Elias, *Africa and the Development of International Law*, 2nd edn (Dordrecht, Nijhoff, 1988).

[17] See A Orakhelashvili, 'The Idea of European International Law' (2006) 17 *EJIL* 315, 329 and 339, citing as an example the system of treaty law and diplomatic immunities in Sumerian cities in the third and second millennia BC.

[18] J Crawford, *Chance, Order, Change: The Course of International Law, General Course on Public International Law* (The Hague, Hague Academy of International Law, 2014) 311–14. See also M Koskenniemi, 'International Law in Europe: Between Tradition and Renewal' (2005) 16 *EJIL* 113.

[19] See further A Roberts, *Is International Law International?* (Oxford, OUP, 2017).

1

Foundations, History and Theory of International Law

I. Definitions of International Law

Defining 'international law' is less straightforward than it might seem. Up until the first half of the twentieth century, the majority scholarly opinion was that only States could be subjects of international law in the sense of possessing international legal personality and being bearers of international legal rights and obligations (among which the right to bring claims under international law). International law, in the past often referred to as 'the law of nations', could therefore have been defined as 'the totality of norms that regulates relations between States'.

That classic conception of international law gradually became less plausible during the course of the last century. After the First World War, international legal norms came into existence on an ever greater number of subject matters formerly well outside the scope of international law, and new actors emerged. These included in particular international organisations established by States (such as the League of Nations and the International Labour Organization, established in 1919 by the Treaty of Versailles), non-governmental organisations, transnational enterprises, and finally the individual itself.[1] Indeed, Hersch Lauterpacht went so far as to argue that 'the individual human being is the ultimate unit and end of all law, national and international'.[2]

In other words, international law evolved into a system recognising subjects other than States. A prima facie plausible adjusted definition of international law could therefore be: 'the law regulating the relationships between subjects of international law'. However, that definition suffers the defect of using a concept – 'subjects of international law' – that itself contains the concept 'international law' that is being defined. The present book therefore prefers a definition that is perhaps less clear-cut, but is logically coherent and flexible

[1] On individuals in international law in general, see eg K Parlett, *The Individual in the International Legal System: Continuity and Change in International Law* (Cambridge, CUP, 2011); A Peters, *Beyond Human Rights: The Legal Status of the Individual in International Law* (Cambridge, CUP, 2016).

[2] E Lauterpacht (ed), *International Law: Being the Collected Papers of Hersch Lauterpacht*, Vol I: The General Works (Cambridge, CUP, 1970) 149.

enough to adapt to the evolutive character of international law: 'international law is the law that regulates international relations'.

A further distinction needs to be drawn between public international law or international public law on the one hand, and private international law or conflict of laws on the other hand.[3] The latter traditionally consists of norms of national law that contain rules to determine the courts of what State have jurisdiction and the national law of what State applies to a certain private law dispute that has connections with more than one national legal order (such as a car accident between a French and a German car on Swiss territory or a marriage between an Argentine woman and a Belgian man). Nevertheless, States have since the nineteenth century been coordinating their systems of conflict of laws through treaties, in other words through an instrument of public international law. That has, in particular, been the case within the framework of the Hague Conference on Private International Law.[4] In other words, while it is useful to make a conceptual distinction between public international law and private international law, this should not be taken as implying that they belong to wholly different worlds. Rather, norms of public international law shape and are given effect through private international law, which in turn can be said to effect an international ordering of regulatory authority in private law, structured by international principles of justice, pluralism and subsidiarity.[5]

II. Functions of International Law

A first function of international law exists in delimiting the jurisdiction of the subjects of international law. In particular, international law delimits jurisdiction:

— *Ratione territoriae*: the jurisdiction of one State ends where that of another State begins, ie, at the internationally recognised border or where the international domain starts (eg, the high seas or space). In principle, territorial jurisdiction applies, which means that a State can only exercise its competences within its territory. However, a number of exceptions apply, which will be discussed in Chapter 9 on jurisdiction;

— *Ratione temporis*: international law governs issues that may arise regarding the emergence of new States, State succession (eg, the dissolution of the Soviet Union, Yugoslavia or Czechoslovakia or the absorption by the German Federal Republic of the German Democratic Republic), or the extinction of States;

— *Ratione materiae*: this is especially relevant for international organisations, which have only been attributed certain specific competences by the founding States.

Specifically with respect to States, the regulation of their jurisdiction is important because it is at the heart of an international legal order that seeks to provide for the lawful coexistence

[3] For an excellent introduction to private international law, see generally P Torremans, U Grušić, C Heinze, L Merrett, A Mills, C Otero García-Castrillón, ZS Tang, K Trimmings and L Walker (eds), *Cheshire, North & Fawcett: Private International Law*, 15th edn (Oxford, OUP, 2017); and, from a European perspective, G Van Calster, *European Private International Law*, 2nd edn (Oxford, Hart, 2016).

[4] Statute of the Hague Conference on Private International Law (adopted 31 October 1951, entered into force 15 July 1955) 220 UNTS 121.

[5] A Mills, *The Confluence of Public and Private International Law: Justice, Pluralism and Subsidiarity in the International Constitutional Ordering of Private Law* (Cambridge, CUP, 2009). See also A Mills, 'The Private History of International Law' (2006) 55 ICLQ 1.

of sovereigns. Rules of jurisdiction reflect fundamental requirements in the international system that flow from the acceptance by States that there are limits on their own regulatory authority, and that exercises of regulatory authority by foreign sovereigns are themselves legitimate.[6]

A second function of international law is therefore the regulation of the coexistence of subjects of international law. In particular, international law determines means of dispute settlement or conflict prevention, the use of force, the usage of territory, diplomatic and consular relations, and international responsibility.

A third function of international law is to regulate international cooperation between subjects of international law. This concerns, in particular, the law of international organisations, which has seen striking developments since the Second World War, but equally treaty regimes establishing specific duties of cooperation without giving rise to the establishment of an international organisation.[7]

The following table compares a number of basic characteristics of what can be termed the international law of coexistence and the international law of cooperation.[8] It must be kept in mind that international law is today still to an important extent a law of coexistence, ie, a framework of legal norms that delimit the jurisdictions of independent States. Nevertheless, the number of international legal rules that govern the cooperation between those States, which in practice have become ever more interdependent, is steadily growing.

Table 1 Comparison Law of Coexistence – Cooperation

THE LAW OF COEXISTENCE	THE LAW OF COOPERATION
1. Premises	
Sovereign equality of States	Awareness of the relativity of sovereignty and the need to pool it
States as hermetic entities ('billiard balls')	States as interdependent actors
No common interests between States, except for the need for rules of delimitation of jurisdiction	Common interests and values that cannot be protected or furthered unilaterally
2. Functions of international law	
How to maintain peaceful coexistence between States	How to enable efficient cooperation between States
Mostly questions of interstate relations ('international traffic rules')	A significant number of policy questions that until now were mostly discussed and settled within States
Mostly prohibitions	Mostly obligations
3. Norm-creating processes	
Essentially non-institutional	Essentially institutional
Identity of norm-givers and addressees of norms	Organs with normative competence as norm-givers and States and other subjects of international law as addressees of norms

(*continued*)

[6] A Mills, 'Rethinking Jurisdiction in International Law' (2014) 84 *BYIL* 188.

[7] See eg the duties of cooperation contained throughout the International Covenant on Economic, Social and Cultural Rights.

[8] See W Friedmann, *The Changing Structure of International Law* (London, Stevens & Sons, 1964). And see P-M Dupuy, 'International Law: Torn between Coexistence, Cooperation and Globalization. General Conclusion' (1998) *EJIL* 278.

Table 1 *(continued)*

THE LAW OF COEXISTENCE	THE LAW OF COOPERATION
4. Punishment of infringements	
Self-help through countermeasures, retorsions, reprisals or war	Institutionalised sanctions: penalties, suspension, expulsion, etc.

Lastly, international law plays an important role in the legal framework and development of 'global governance'. Global governance is not a legal notion; it concerns the entirety of formal and informal processes between States, organisations (including intergovernmental and non-governmental organisations as well as business enterprises) and/or people, which aim to address global challenges through the formulation and enforcement of rules and standards, by giving incentives and guidance, generating information and knowledge and/or settling disputes.[9] For instance, one can think of the international regulation of 'global commons', which in principle fall beyond the jurisdiction of States,[10] or the provision of global public goods, such as a sustainable environment or international security.[11] Moreover, in international relations, processes of informal law-making and soft law often take place,[12] while non-State actors are becoming ever more important.[13]

III. Features of International Law

International law has certain characteristics that flow from the fact that it is a legal order governing coexistence and cooperation between sovereign and equal States. Crucially, the international legal order in general and the United Nations in particular are based on the principle of sovereign equality.[14] As a consequence, international law is an essentially decentralised and horizontal legal order, especially when compared to the often heavily-centralised and institutionalised character of national legal orders. These features have also given rise to doubts as to the legal character of international law.[15] For example, HLA Hart argued that while the term 'law' is habitually used in relation to international law, 'the absence of an international legislature, courts with compulsory jurisdiction, and centrally organized sanctions have inspired misgivings, at any rate in the breasts of legal theorists'.[16] According to Hart, the absence of these institutions implies that the rules for States resemble

[9] R Thakur and L Van Langenhove, 'Enhancing Global Governance through Regional Integration' in AF Cooper, CW Hughes and P De Lombaerde (eds), *Regionalisation and Global Governance: The Taming of Globalisation?* (Abingdon, Routledge, 2008) 20. For a collection of some of the most salient scholarship on global governance, see A Marx and J Wouters (eds), *Global Governance*, Vol. 1: Different Manifestations of and Perspectives on Global Governance (Cheltenham, Edward Elgar, 2018).

[10] See Chapter 18 on Law of the Sea and Global Commons. See also S Cogolati and J Wouters (eds), *The Commons and a New Global Governance* (Cheltenham, Edward Elgar, 2018).

[11] See below, Section V(A).

[12] See Chapter 3, Section VII on Soft Law and Informal Law. This includes international standard-setting through experts and networks: see H Cullen, J Harrington, and C Renshaw (eds), *Experts, Networks and International Law* (Cambridge, CUP, 2017).

[13] See Chapter 8 on Non-State Actors.

[14] Art 2(1) UN Charter.

[15] See below, Section V.

[16] HLA Hart, *The Concept of Law*, 2nd edn (Oxford, OUP, 1994) 214.

'that simple form of social structure, consisting only of primary rules of obligation, which, when we find it among societies of individuals, we are accustomed to contrast with a developed legal system'.[17]

Conversely, scholars such as Finnis have warned that too often one particular characteristic of 'the central case of law' is emphasised, and any system not displaying that characteristic (eg, a system without sanctions) is then brand-marked as not really being law, thus banishing it to another discipline.[18] The character of international law as law will be further explored in Section V below on the theory of international law.

A. No Central Legislator

International law knows no central legislator, a consequence of what Dworkin described as the 'unmitigated Westphalian system'.[19] The UN General Assembly (UNGA) is certainly no 'World Legislator'. Indeed, its resolutions lack binding force except with respect to internal affairs of the UN. In international law, States are norm-givers and addressees of those norms at the same time. Given that international law is traditionally assumed to be based on the free will of sovereign States, international legal rules generally only bind States if they have accepted to be so bound. Exceptions to the rule that States only enter into international legal obligations to which they have voluntarily agreed are general or customary international law (to the extent that a State does not persistently object to the emergence of a new customary rule[20] or has acquired Statehood after the rule has come into existence) and *jus cogens* (to the extent that it suffices for the rule of *jus cogens* to be accepted by the 'international community as a whole').

The latter does not detract from the fact that the UN, and the UN General Assembly in particular, enjoys a unique legitimacy and 'convening power' because of the universal character of the organisation, which currently has 193 Member States. During its more than 70 years of history, the UN has made a fundamental contribution to the further development of international law and the international legal order.[21] It has done so in particular through the work of the UNGA, the UN Security Council (UNSC), the UN Economic and Social Council (ECOSOC), the International Court of Justice (ICJ) and other UN-related international judicial bodies,[22] as well as through the work of several subsidiary organs, such as the International Law Commission (ILC), the UN Commission on International Trade Law and the UN Committee on the Peaceful Uses of Outer Space. Nevertheless, the UN's unique and central position within the normative processes of international law should not be overstated, for three reasons. First, the UN has always struggled with the

[17] ibid. For a critique of Hart's analysis in this regard, see eg J Waldron, 'International Law: "A Relatively Small and Unimportant" Part of Jurisprudence?' in L Duarte d'Almeida, J Edwards and A Dolcetti (eds), *Reading HLA Hart's The Concept of Law* (Oxford, Hart, 2013) 209–23.

[18] J Finnis, *Natural Law and Natural Rights*, 2nd edn (Oxford, OUP, 2011) 277–78.

[19] R Dworkin, 'A New Philosophy for International Law' (2013) 41 *Philosophy & Public Affairs* 27. On the Peace of Westphalia and its impact on the history of international law, see below, Section IV(D).

[20] See also Chapter 3, Section II(E), on the role of the 'persistent objector' in the emergence of a norm of general international law.

[21] See eg C Joyner (ed), *The United Nations and International Law* (Cambridge, CUP, 1997); *Making Better International Law: The International Law Commission at 50* (New York, United Nations, 1998); M Forteau, 'Le droit international dans la Charte des Nations Unies' in JP Cot, A Pellet and M Forteau (eds), *La Charte des Nations Unies : commentaire article par article*, 3rd edn (Paris, Economica, 2005) 111–40.

[22] See further in general G De Baere and J Wouters (eds), *The Contribution of International and Supranational Courts to the Rule of Law* (Cheltenham, Edward Elgar, 2015).

political tensions intrinsically connected to a divided world, notably within the framework of its main political bodies: the General Assembly, the Security Council and ECOSOC.[23] During the first 45 years of its existence, this concerned first and foremost the East-West divide in the context of the Cold War. Following the process of decolonisation, an additional North-South tension emerged from the 1960s onwards. Further, one can add the more recent 'multipolarity' between the West and (re)emerging powers such as Brazil, Russia, India, China and South Africa.[24] Up until today, these tensions polarise debates and leave their mark on the development of international law. Second, the UN has numerous organs, subsidiary organs, programmes and funds (besides the specialised organisations of the UN system, the many conferences organised under its auspices and dozens of multilateral UN treaties with their own dynamics) that at times internally compete with each other and entail a strong need for system-wide coherence.[25] Third, while the UN and the UN system may well be particularly important and universal multilateral institutions, by no means do they have a monopoly on international lawmaking. Some global organisations, such as the World Trade Organization (WTO), operate outside of the UN system, and certain (sub) branches of international law, such as the law of armed conflict,[26] international economic law[27] and the law of Antarctica[28] have, for diverse reasons, largely developed through multilateral and bilateral channels outside the UN system.

Besides its contribution to the development of international law, the UN has used the abovementioned legitimacy and convening power also to give more general impulses to global governance. Of particular importance in this regard are the Millenium Development Goals (MDGs), which the UN drew up in 2000 for the period 2000–2015. After an intensive consultation round and two years of intergovernmental negotiations, the heads of State and government adopted the *Sustainable Development Goals* (SDGs) at the 2015 UN Sustainable Development Summit. The SDGs must be achieved by 2030, and are therefore also known as the '2030 Agenda for Sustainable Development'. This Agenda is a 'plan of action for people, planet and prosperity' that intends to eradicate poverty and hunger and safeguard the sustainability of the earth.[29] More concretely, the SDGs consist of 17 general goals and 169 more specific targets that are 'integrated and indivisible and balance the three dimensions of sustainable development: the economic, social and environmental'.[30]

[23] See eg A Roberts and B Kingsbury (eds), *United Nations, Divided World: The UN's Role in International Relations*, 2nd edn (Oxford, Clarendon Press, 1993).

[24] See eg M Donette and D Brown, *Multipolarity in the 21st Century: A New World Order* (London, Routledge, 2012); M Happold (ed), *International Law in a Multipolar World* (London, Routledge, 2012).

[25] More recently, this striving for coherence has strenghthened. See notably the 'One UN' initiative: Report of the High-level Panel on System-wide Coherence, 'Delivering as One', 20 November 2006, UN Doc A/61/583, 9–67.

[26] See Chapter 15.

[27] See Chapter 19.

[28] See Chapter 18, Section XI.

[29] UNGA Res 70/1, 'Transforming Our World: The 2030 Agenda for Sustainable Development', 25 September 2015, UN Doc A/RES/70/1, preamble, paras 1–2.

[30] ibid, para 3. On (the MDGs and) the SDGs, see further eg VP Nanda, 'The Journey from the Millennium Development Goals to the Sustainable Development Goals' (2016) 44 *Denver Journal of International Law and Policy* 389; RE Kim, 'The Nexus between International Law and the Sustainable Development Goals' (2016) 25 *Review of European, Comparative and International Environmental Law* 15; P Hugon, 'Du bilan mitigé des Objectifs du Millénaire pour le développement aux difficultés de mise en œuvre des Objectifs de développement durable' (2016) 174 *Mondes en développement* 15; P Orliange, 'Le financement des Objectifs de développement durable (ODD)' (2017) 88 *Annales des Mines – Responsabilité et environnement* 45; J Wouters and S Cogolati, 'Taking Sustainable Development Goal 17 Seriously: The World Bank's Legal Framework to Provide Global Public Goods' (2016) 7 *World Bank Legal Review* 35–51. On sustainable development and international law more generally, see also N Schrijver, *The Evolution of Sustainable Development in International Law: Inception, Meaning and Status* (Leiden, Nijhoff, 2008).

Table 2 The UN Sustainable Development Goals (SDGs)[31]

Goal 1. End poverty in all its forms everywhere
Goal 2. End hunger, achieve food security and improved nutrition and promote sustainable agriculture
Goal 3. Ensure healthy lives and promote well-being for all at all ages
Goal 4. Ensure inclusive and equitable quality education and promote lifelong learning opportunities for all
Goal 5. Achieve gender equality and empower all women and girls
Goal 6. Ensure availability and sustainable management of water and sanitation for all
Goal 7 Ensure access to affordable, reliable, sustainable and modern energy for all
Goal 8. Promote sustained, inclusive and sustainable economic growth, full and productive employment and decent work for all
Goal 9. Build resilient infrastructure, promote inclusive and sustainable industrialisation and foster innovation
Goal 10. Reduce inequality within and among countries
Goal 11. Make cities and human settlements inclusive, safe, resilient and sustainable
Goal 12. Ensure sustainable consumption and production patterns
Goal 13. Take urgent action to combat climate change and its impacts
Goal 14. Conserve and sustainably use the oceans, seas and marine resources for sustainable development
Goal 15. Protect, restore and promote sustainable use of terrestrial ecosystems, sustainably manage forests, combat desertification, and halt and reverse land degradation and halt biodiversity loss
Goal 16. Promote peaceful and inclusive societies for sustainable development, provide access to justice for all and build effective, accountable and inclusive institutions at all levels
Goal 17. Strengthen the means of implementation and revitalize the Global Partnership for Sustainable Development

As the example of the SDGs illustrates, there is an emerging tendency to engage in alternative processes of rule-making and standard-setting by States, sub-State entities and private actors alongside the more traditional ways to generate international law. The norms thus developed challenge dominant theories on sources of international law, and disagreement exists on the legal value of such non-traditional norms, which are sometimes referred to as 'soft law', 'global governance activities', 'international public administration' or 'informal lawmaking'.[32]

Finally, the absence of an international legislator also has an impact on international adjudication, as international judges must habitually find the law before being able to apply it.[33]

[31] UNGA Res 70/1 (n 29) 14.

[32] See S Duquet and J Wouters, 'Non-Traditional Norms in International Law: Approaches in Legal Scholarship' (2014) 5 *Czech Yearbook of International Law*.

[33] See D Regan, 'International Adjudication: A Response to Paulus – Courts, Custom, Treaties, Regimes, and the WTO' in S Besson and J Tasioulas (eds), *The Philosophy of International Law* (Oxford, OUP, 2010) 227–29; G De Baere, A-L Chané and J Wouters, 'International Courts as Keepers of the Rule of Law: Achievements, Challenges, and Opportunities' (2016) 48 *New York University Journal of International Law and Politics* 755.

B. No Central Judiciary

International law does not know a central judicial body with compulsory jurisdiction. The ICJ in The Hague can only take cases if the States Parties to the dispute have recognised its jurisdiction.[34] By contrast, national legal systems are built on courts with compulsory jurisdiction. International arbitration too is subject to acceptance of jurisdiction by the States involved in the dispute. Nevertheless, systems of compulsory jurisdiction have been introduced in certain areas of international law, usually in combination with an international judicial or quasi-judicial organ. Notable examples include the EU with the Court of Justice of the EU (CJEU),[35] and the Appellate Body of the WTO. Given the lack of one central judicial organ, international law knows a panoply of alternative dispute settlement mechanisms, ranging from diplomatic and judicial methods to the involvement of international organisations.[36]

For theorists such as Hans Kelsen,[37] the judicial process is the foundation of each legal organisation and every community of law, and the introduction of a judicial organ with compulsory jurisdiction is the turning point in the transition from a decentralised legal order to a more centralised and more effective legal order.[38] In the international legal order, that process is still in its infancy, as judicial dispute settlement remains an exception to the rule of autonomous interpretation by States of their international obligations and free choice of means of peaceful dispute settlement. Nevertheless, international courts play an ever-increasing central role in the debate about the meaning of international law and about what respect for the rule of law by governments entails.[39]

C. No Central Enforcement

There is no 'world police force'. Of course, the UN Security Council has important powers with respect to 'threats to the peace, breaches of the peace, and acts of aggression' under Chapter VII of the UN Charter. However, while collective enforcement does take place more often than in earlier times on the basis of UNSC action under Chapter VII, the actual exercise of these powers remains subject to important legal and political limitations.

Quite apart from the powers of the UN Security Council, international law knows several enforcement mechanisms, most of which are unilateral in character, ranging from peaceful means of enforcement such as retorsions or reprisals to the use of force. But in

[34] See Art 36 ICJ Statute. See also Chapter 13 on Peaceful Settlement of Disputes, Section III(B)(ii).

[35] Under Art 19(1) TEU, the institution of the CJEU encompasses the Court of Justice (ECJ), the General Court (EGC) and specialised courts. The only court falling in the final category, the Civil Service Tribunal, established in 2004, ceased to operate on 1 September 2016 after its jurisdiction was transferred to the EGC in the context of the reform of the EU's judicial structure.

[36] See Chapter 13, Section II on diplomatic and non-judicial methods of dispute settlement.

[37] See below, Section V(B).

[38] H Kelsen, *Peace through Law* (Chapel Hill, The University of North Carolina Press, 1944) 73. See C Leben, 'Hans Kelsen and the Advancement of International Law' (1998) 9 *EJIL* 287, 291–92; J von Bernstorff, *The Public International Law Theory of Hans Kelsen: Believing in Universal Law* (Cambridge, CUP, 2010) 191–224.

[39] De Baere, Chané and Wouters (n 33) 753–54. See also A Paulus, 'International Adjudication' in Besson and Tasioulas (n 33) 207–24; B Kingsbury, 'International Courts: Uneven Judicialisation in Global Order' in J Crawford and M Koskenniemi (eds), *The Cambridge Companion to International Law* (Cambridge, CUP, 2012) 203–27; KJ Alter, *The New Terrain of International Law: Courts, Politics, Rights* (Princeton, Princeton UP, 2014); E Benvenisti and GW Downs, *Between Fragmentation and Democracy: The Role of National and International Courts* (Cambridge, CUP, 2017).

fact, States are often brought to comply with their international law obligations through other incentives,[40] notably through self-interest.[41] That is, for example, why most States comply with the rules on privileges and immunities of diplomatic and consular staff most of the time: they are always simultaneously in the position of receiving State on their own territory and sending State in other States' territories.

Given the short supply of collective enforcement mechanisms, States in international law often have no other option but to turn to 'self-help'.[42] Contrary to most systems of national law, and with the exception of international systems with compulsory jurisdiction such as the EU and the WTO, international law does not in principle prohibit such self-help. International law does impose certain limitations on State action as a response to a violation of international law by another State. In particular, the UN Charter obliges all Members to 'settle their international disputes by peaceful means in such a manner that international peace and security, and justice, are not endangered',[43] and to 'refrain in their international relations from the threat or use of force against the territorial integrity or political independence of any state, or in any other manner inconsistent with the Purposes of the United Nations'.[44]

D. Dependence on Municipal Legal Orders

Given its horizontal and decentralised character, international law is heavily dependent for its implementation and enforcement on States and, by implication, on their national legal orders. That is why it is of fundamental importance to take the relationship between international law and national law into consideration. However, different national legal systems take different positions vis-à-vis the status of international law in the national legal order. In particular, so-called 'monist' and 'dualist' legal systems are traditionally seen as taking contrasting positions in that respect, it being understood that both types of systems are required to give effect to their international law obligations.[45]

E. Differentiation and Fragmentation

International law is a greatly differentiated system of law, both as regards its scope *ratione materiae* and *ratione territorii*. With respect to its scope *ratione materiae*, international law comprises every possible area of law: from human rights law[46] (eg, the International Covenant on Civil and Political Rights, the International Covenant on Economic, Social and Cultural Rights, and the Convention on the Rights of the Child) to international

[40] On compliance with international law, see generally L Henkin, *How Nations Behave: Law and Foreign Policy*, 2nd edn (New York, Columbia UP, 1979) 47, famously asserting that it is probably the case that '[a]lmost all nations observe almost all principles of international law and almost all of their obligations almost all of the time'.

[41] See also AT Guzman, *How International Law Works: A Rational Choice Theory* (Oxford, OUP, 2008) 9, referring to the three 'Rs' of compliance: reciprocity, retaliation, and reputation.

[42] See the regime covering the implementation of responsibility by extrajudicial process through retorsion, the exception of non-performance (*exceptio non adimpleti contractus*) or countermeasures under the ILC's Articles on State Responsibility, on which see J Crawford, *State Responsibility: The General Part* (Cambridge, CUP, 2013) 675–711. See further Chapter 12.

[43] Art 2(3) UN Charter.

[44] ibid Art 2(4).

[45] See also Chapter 4, Section III, on the position of international law in national legal orders.

[46] See Chapter 16 on Human Rights Law.

economic law[47] (eg, the Agreement establishing the WTO (WTO Agreement)), international criminal law[48] (eg, the Rome Statute of the International Criminal Court (ICC Statute)) or international environmental law[49] (eg, the United Nations Framework Convention on Climate Change (UNFCCC)[50]), and many other specialised fields.

With respect to the scope *ratione territorii* of international law, a distinction can be drawn between the following categories:

- general or universal international law, which applies to the community of States as a whole or at least a large part thereof on the basis of customary international law, multilateral treaties, or indeed *jus cogens*;
- regional international law, which only applies to a geographically limited group of States, such as for example the law of the EU or a right of passage by one State over the territory of another State. Such regional international law can flow both from a treaty and from regional customary law;
- special international law, ie, international norms that count only between two or an otherwise limited number of States that are not necessary geographically determined, such as for example double taxation treaties.

The above implies that international law is essentially heterogeneous. Moreover, diverging views or interpretations of norms of international law are naturally common in a world of nearly 200 independent States with their own political, economic, social, cultural, ideological and military characteristics. The individual characteristics of these States also contribute to significant differences in the effectiveness of international law in terms of compliance and possibilities for actual enforcement. Nevertheless, at the time of writing, no fewer than 193 States are Members of the United Nations, and have subscribed to its fundamental purposes, principles and rules.

Yet the absence of any vertical hierarchical structure in international law, combined with its rapid expansion and dispersal into a swathe of specialised fields, has led to concerns of fragmentation. As Koskenniemi wrote in his report for the ILC:

> What once appeared to be governed by 'general international law' has become the field of operation for such specialist systems as 'trade law', 'human rights law', 'environmental law', 'law of the sea', 'European law' and even such exotic and highly specialized knowledges as 'investment law' or 'international refugee law' etc – each possessing their own principles and institutions. The problem, as lawyers have seen it, is that such specialized law-making and institution-building tends to take place with relative ignorance of legislative and institutional activities in the adjoining fields and of the general principles and practices of international law. The result is conflicts between rules or rule-systems, deviating institutional practices and, possibly, the loss of an overall perspective on the law.[51]

Such fragmentation may be substantive, ie, the result of conflicting but equally authoritative pronouncements on international law by courts and tribunals, or institutional, ie, the expansion of international courts and tribunals with competing jurisdiction, also termed

[47] See Chapter 19 on International Economic Law.

[48] See Chapter 17 on International Criminal Law.

[49] See Chapter 20 on International Environmental Law.

[50] UN Framework Convention on Climate Change (adopted 9 May 1992, entered into force 21 March 1994) 1771 UNTS 107.

[51] ILC, Report of the Study Group of the International Law Commission Fragmentation of International Law: 'Difficulties Arising from the Diversification and Expansion of International Law', finalised by Martti Koskenniemi, 13 April 2006, UN Doc A/CN.4/L.682, para 8. On the ILC, see Chapter 3, Section II(F).

'proliferation'. However, it has been argued that open contradictions in the case law of different international courts are in fact few and far between, and that there is an increasing commonality in the practice of international courts.[52]

A particular substantive or institutional field of international law may also develop to such an extent that it effectively displaces general international law, thus becoming a so-called 'self-contained regime'.[53] Fragmentation may give rise to conflicts between such different regimes and between different fields of international law more generally, such as for example between trade and environmental law,[54] or indeed between EU law and general international law, as evidenced by the *Kadi* saga.[55] Nevertheless, international law has its own techniques and mechanisms to solve or at least to mitigate such conflicts.[56] In that sense, perhaps international law has not become more fragmented than it was, just more diverse.[57]

IV. History of International Law

A. Antiquity

The origins of diplomacy, or the sending of emissaries with a view to negotiations, goes back to the Near East at least to the second and possibly to the fourth millennium BC, while the oldest known diplomatic document is a letter inscribed on a cuneiform tablet sent around 2500 BC, discovered in what is currently Syria.[58] In turn, the oldest surviving complete treaty is an agreement between Ancient Egypt and the Hittite Empire on the division of spheres of influence and the extradition of fugitives, dating from the thirteenth century BC.[59]

Ancient Greek city States also concluded trade, peace and alliance agreements. Furthermore, a polis would select prominent citizens in other States as *προξενοι* (proksenoi, ie, 'State-guest-friends'), who were expected to host its ambassadors, give hospitality to its citizens, represent them in court, and in general to protect its interests.[60] Moreover, Roman usage of peace treaty-making was informed by Greek practice, which in turn drew on the practice of pre-classical civilisations of the Middle East, demonstrating the remarkable continuity in ancient peace treaty practice.[61]

[52] De Baere, Chané and Wouters (n 33) 787–88.

[53] J Crawford, *Chance, Order, Change: The Course of International Law, General Course on Public International Law* (The Hague, Hague Academy of International Law, 2014) 284–85. See also M Young (ed), *Regime Interaction in International Law: Facing Fragmentation* (Cambridge, CUP, 2015).

[54] See eg M Young, *Trading Fish, Saving Fish: The Interaction between Regimes in International Law* (Cambridge, CUP, 2013). See further D Pulkowski, *The Law and Politics of International Regime Conflict* (Oxford, OUP, 2014); K Blome, A Fischer-Lescano, H Franzki, N Markard and S Oeter (eds), *Contested Regime Collisions: Norm Fragmentation in World Society* (Cambridge, CUP, 2016).

[55] See Chapter 4, Section V(B)(iii)(b).

[56] See eg the mechanisms in the VCLT, on which see Chapter 2 on Sources: Treaty Law.

[57] Crawford (n 53) 308.

[58] I Rogers, *Satow's Diplomatic Practice*, 7th edn (Oxford, OUP, 2017) 6.

[59] DJ Bederman, *International Law in Antiquity* (Cambridge, CUP, 2001) 147–50.

[60] B Steinbock, *Social Memory in Athenian Public Discourse: Uses and Meanings of the Past* (Michigan, University of Michigan Press, 2013) 82.

[61] R Lesaffer, 'Peace Treaties and the Formation of International Law' in B Fassbender and A Peters (eds), *The Oxford Handbook of the History of International Law* (Oxford, OUP, 2012) 71–94.

The oldest form of Roman 'public international law'[62] is to be situated in the context of the *jus fetiale*, ie, rites by *fetiales* (fetial priests) comprising a body of procedures and norms that inter alia dealt with foreign relations, including binding Rome to treaties with a foreign people or declaring war, which were of Roman and not of international origin. The Romans also knew quite an elaborate law and practice of treaties, which was similar to that of the Ancient Near East or the Ancient Greeks, and provided for treaties to be essentially oral agreements rendered binding by oath and the invocation of gods, which were nevertheless commonly written down and published. The term *jus gentium*, Roman law's major contribution to the intellectual history of international law, originally denoted the law applicable to foreigners, and only by the time of the Digest of Justinian had evolved into both a universal private law and a law applicable to foreign relations. That double concept of *jus gentium* as universal law and as the law of foreign relations was subsequently carried over into the Middle Ages.[63] Roman peacemaking practice likewise did not disappear with the demise of the Roman Empire in the West in 476 AD. It continued to live on through the early Middle Ages, in particular in the practices of the Byzantine Empire, the Germanic successor Kingdoms, and the Islamic world.[64]

B. Middle Ages

From the seventh century onwards, the Islamic world developed the Siyar, a form of law of nations based on the Sharia. It was structured around a fundamental distinction between the territories in which Islamic law reigned supreme, called *dar-al-Islam* (the abode of Islam) on the one hand, and territories in which it did not, referred to as *dar-al-hard* (the abode of war), on the other hand. The Islamic law of nations contained rules inter alia on the inviolability of envoys, safe-conducts, the obligation to perform binding agreements (*pacta sunt servanda*) and the conduct of hostilities.[65]

Seeing international society as an extension of Chinese society that was hierarchical, imperial China adopted the tribute system in its relations with neighbouring States (and Western States), and the frequency of a State's ability to pay tribute to China, as China would permit, represented the degree of the tribute State's assimilation to Chinese culture and reflected the position of the tribute State in the Chinese world order. Western powers abhorred the tribute system for violating their Westphalian conception of world order based on the principles of State sovereignty and sovereign equality of States, and 'regarded it as a hierarchical regional order and an abnormal case of historical states systems'.[66]

In medieval Europe, Italian cities, Hanseatic cities, the Low Countries, France and England played an important role in the development of international law. For example, the so-called '*rôles d'Oléron*', a codification of decisions made in the maritime courts on the small island of Oléron off the western coast of France near La Rochelle, contained the international customary rules governing overseas trade.[67]

[62] R Lesaffer, 'Roman Law and the Intellectual History of International Law' in A Orford and F Hoffmann (eds), *The Oxford Handbook of the Theory of International Law* (Oxford, OUP, 2016) 38–58.

[63] Lesaffer (n 62) 41–45.

[64] Lesaffer (n 61) 72.

[65] J Allain, 'Acculturation through the Middle Ages: The Islamic Law of Nations and Its Place in the History of International Law' in A Orakhelashvili (ed), *Research Handbook on the Theory and History of International Law* (Cheltenham, Edward Elgar, 2011) 394–407.

[66] P Chan, *China, State Sovereignty and International Legal Order* (The Hague, Nijhoff, 2015) 69–71.

[67] See eg TJ Runyan, 'The Rolls of Oleron and the Admiralty Court in Fourteenth Century England' (1975) 19 *American Journal of Legal History* 95; E Frankot, 'Medieval Maritime Law from Oléron to Wisby: Jurisdictions

Furthermore, medieval scholars contributed to the development of the law of peacemaking through the application of concepts from Roman private law to peace treaties. In turn, medieval canon law made a major contribution to the development of treaty law through the articulation of such principles as *pacta sunt servanda* and the doctrine of *clausula rebus sic stantibus*.[68]

C. The Early Modern Era

Three significant developments between 1450 and 1550 heralded the end of the medieval legal order:[69] (i) the rise of major dynastic powers such as Valois France and Habsburg Spain; (ii) the reformation, which ended the unity of the Latin Church; and (iii) the expeditions and ensuing conquests by Spain and Portugal in the East Indies and the Americas, sounding in an era of European colonialism lasting well into the twentieth century.[70] The upshot was that by the second half of the sixteenth century, the medieval legal order of what has been referred to as the *respublica Christiana* had collapsed. For example, almost all references to the jurisdiction and ecclesiastical institutions and sanctions had disappeared from treaty practice by the end of the sixteenth century.[71] A profound political and legal crisis ensued, and the new order of *jus publicum Europaeum* (*droit public de l'Europe*) would only emerge after Westphalia.[72]

The early modern era[73] brought with it the collapse of religious unity in Europe, the emergence of the sovereign State, and the monopolisation of the practice of external relations by central governments, all of which had a crucial impact on the emergence of international law as a discipline. The loss of religious unity entailed the demise of the basis on which the authority of the doctrine and practice of *jus gentium* had rested, which on the one hand implied that doctrine lost much of its impact on the practice of international relations after 1500. On the other hand, it allowed international law to emerge as an autonomous scholarly discipline during the sixteenth and seventeenth centuries.[74]

The dawn of the sovereign State after 1500 also significantly impacted on treaties in general and peace treaties in particular, which gradually transformed from compacts between sovereign rulers to public treaties between States. Before that date, peace treaties were personal contracts made by sovereign rulers in their own name, binding themselves and not directly their realms or subjects. However, as they claimed the monopoly of war and peace and of representing their realm on the international scene, sovereign rulers were regarded more and more as representatives with the capacity to bind their realms

in the Law of the Sea' in J Pan Montojo and F Pedersen (eds), *Communities in European History: Representations, Jurisdictions, Conflicts* (Pisa, Edizioni Plus – Pisa UP, 2007) 151–72.

[68] Lesaffer (n 61) 74–75.

[69] R Lesaffer, 'The Classical Law of Nations (1500–1800)' in Orakhelashvili (n 65) 411–12.

[70] See further M Craven, 'Colonialism and Domination' in Fassbender and Peters (n 61) 862–89. Note that the Crowns of Castile and Portugal had been sponsoring expeditions down the West Coast of Africa and to islands in the Atlantic for nearly a century prior to Columbus's voyage to the Americas: ibid, 865.

[71] R Lesaffer, 'Peace Treaties from Lodi to Westphalia' in R Lesaffer (ed), *Peace Treaties and International Law in European History: From the Late Middle Ages to World War One* (Cambridge, CUP, 2004) 33–34.

[72] Lesaffer (n 69) 412–13.

[73] For a comprehensive overview of international law scholarship from the early modern era, see A Wijffels, 'Early-Modern Scholarship on International Law' in Orakhelashvili (n 65) 23–60.

[74] Lesaffer (n 69) 418–19.

and subjects directly.[75] Put differently, the concept of the State gradually emerged as an abstraction of the sovereignty of kings. Thus, treaties changed from being personal agreements between sovereigns as individuals, to binding the State in its international relations.

D. Westphalia and Beyond

A pivotal year in the emergence of the modern nation State after the Renaissance was 1648, the year of the Peace of Westphalia,[76] which was founded on three treaties:

(1) the Peace of Münster between the Dutch Republic and the Kingdom of Spain, signed on 30 January 1648;
(2) the Treaty of Münster (*Instrumentum Pacis Monasteriensis*, IPM), between the Holy Roman Empire and France and their respective allies, signed on 24 October 1648;
(3) the Treaty of Osnabrück (*Instrumentum Pacis Osnabrugensis*, IPO), between the Holy Roman Empire, the Kingdom of Sweden and their respective allies, signed on 24 October 1648.

The result was not only the recognition of the Republic of the Seven United Netherlands as a sovereign State, but also of the German Imperial States as nearly unlimited bearers of sovereignty, as well as the recognition of the principle that each prince had the right to determine the religion of his own State (*cujus regio, ejus religio*). The Peace of Westphalia is traditionally considered to have given rise to an international system based on independent sovereign States not under any superior authority. The three treaties also provided for a system of collective security and a mechanism of peaceful settlement of disputes, which was never applied.[77]

Nevertheless, important though it no doubt was in the development of international law, the sovereign State in Europe did not suddenly spring into existence at Westphalia. Rather, its emergence was a gradual process starting during the Late Middle Ages and only fully reaching its completion after the French Revolution, which started in 1789.[78] Indeed, following the demise of the *respublica Christiana*, the main princes and city States now possessed external sovereignty, in the sense of the complete or partial absence of any higher authority in the important elements of international relations, and Europe did consist of a collection of sovereign States by about 1550. However, the establishment of internal sovereignty properly speaking, ie, the sovereign power being the sole source of public authority

[75] Lesaffer (n 61) 81–83.

[76] On the era leading up to the Peace of Westphalia, see M Kintzinger, 'From the Late Middle Ages to the Peace of Westphalia' in Fassbender and Peters (n 61) 607–27.

[77] Further on the Peace of Westphalia and its impact, see eg C Harding and CL Lin, 'The Significance of Westphalia: An Archaeology of the International Legal Order' in C Harding and CL Lim (eds), *Renegotiating Westphalia: Essays and Commentary of the European and Conceptual Foundations of Modern International Law* (The Hague, Nijhoff, 1999) 1–23; D Croxton, 'The Peace of Westphalia of 1648 and the Origins of Sovereignty' (1999) 21 *The International History Review* 569; H Duchhardt, 'From the Peace of Westphalia to the Congress of Vienna' in Fassbender and Peters (n 61) 628–53. The emergence of the modern State post Westphalia also created a new intellectual environment for reviewing and evaluating the rights of indigenous peoples, which did not fit easily into a model of an international legal order based on sovereign States. For example, North American indigenous peoples lacked the agricultural, urban, and industrial capabilities of even the Central American indigenous peoples, rendering it impossible for most thinkers to categorise them as States in the legal sense of the word. K Coates, 'North American Indigenous Peoples' Encounters' in Fassbender and Peters (n 61) 794.

[78] See also J Branch, *The Cartographic State: Maps, Territory, and the Origins of Sovereignty* (Cambridge, CUP, 2014); and EJ Kolla, *Sovereignty, International Law, and the French Revolution* (Cambridge, CUP, 2017).

within the State, would take until the French Revolution or indeed the nineteenth century to take hold fully.[79] The crucial importance of the Peace of Westphalia rather lies in the fact that it marked the end of devastating religious wars, and created the stability for a new international legal order to emerge.[80]

The period between the 1648 Peace of Westphalia and the 1713 Peace of Utrecht, which ended the War of the Spanish Succession, saw the development of what could be termed the 'classical' law of nations or the *jus publicum Europaeum*, premised on State sovereignty.[81] A number of characteristics can be identified as typical for 'classical' international law.[82] First, sovereign rulers considered themselves to be part of a wider community. While until the end of the seventeenth century, that community was not referred to as 'Europe' but as '*Christianitas*' or as '*respublica Christiana*', these direct references to Christianity were gradually replaced by 'Europe' during the eighteenth century. Second, one of the principal elements of the international legal order became the principle of the balance of power, not through equality of States or equilibrated coalitions, yet nevertheless able to limit the freedom of States, such as in the 1713 Peace of Utrecht. The latter entailed the acceptance by the French and Spanish Bourbon princes of limits on their dynastic rights in favour of the balance of power and European peace. Third, the sanctity of treaties kept its status as a primordial principle of international law, de Vattel,[83] for example, considering it a 'sacred duty' to uphold treaties. Fourth, third-power guarantees became a fixture of late seventeenth and eighteenth century peace and alliance treaties. Fifth, the great powers had a specific role in upholding peace in Europe through the balance of power and the guarantee system, prefiguring to some extent the so-called 'Concert of Europe' that emerged after the 1814–1815 Congress of Vienna,[84] and indeed arguably also foreshadowing the role of the permanent members of the Council of the League of Nations or the UN Security Council.[85]

E. The Nineteenth Century

The nineteenth century has been described as both a 'long century, running from 1789 until 1914', and 'largely a European story: the Concert of Europe, the balance of power, nationalism in Europe and Latin America, the Age of Empire, the opening of Japan'.[86] Nevertheless, the nineteenth century was also a century of routine incorporation of multilateralism and a collective approach to common threats and problems.[87]

The rise of the doctrine of the 'sovereign State' described in the previous section can be regarded as an extrapolation to international relations of a political theory on the organisations of a State internally: the prince (later the nation) is the ultimate source of sovereignty and hence the highest authority (*suprema potestas*) within the national territory.

[79] ibid, 415.
[80] Lesaffer (n 69) 410 and 414. See further, Lesaffer (n 61) 85.
[81] Lesaffer (n 69) 414–15.
[82] ibid, 416–18.
[83] On which see also Section V(B) below.
[84] See eg G Simpson, *Great Powers and Outlaw States: Unequal Sovereigns in the International Legal Order* (Cambridge, CUP, 2004).
[85] Lesaffer (n 61) 87.
[86] D Kennedy, 'International Law and the Nineteenth Century: History of an Illusion' (1996) 65 *Nord J Intl* 390.
[87] A Orakhelashvili, 'The 19th-century Life of International Law' in Orakhelashvili (n 65) 442.

In a certain sense, that is a paradoxical evolution. Indeed, during the nineteenth century – at least in the western hemisphere – internal sovereignty was in most States organised on the basis of the doctrine of the separation of powers, and the authority of the sovereign or the government was limited through a constitution containing a division of powers and the recognition of fundamental rights and freedoms of citizens. By contrast, sovereignty on the international plane remained supreme and undivided for a long time.

International law developed into a law of coexistence during that period, ie, a framework of rules that formally demarcate the spheres of jurisdiction of entirely independent and sovereign States. Nevertheless, the Congress of Vienna in 1815 heralded a gradual evolution to a form of cooperation between the European great powers.[88] From the 1820s onwards, a form of cooperation existed termed the 'Concert of Europe', in essence a collection of ad hoc conferences between the great powers after a conflict or another event threatening to disturb the balance of power in Europe. Furthermore, from the mid-nineteenth century onwards, an increasing number of rules of general international law were codified in conventions. The peace treaties that ended the Napoleonic Wars, and in particular those emerging from the Congress of Vienna, were trailblazers in that regard.[89]

The nineteenth century was also characterised by two important phenomena that had a crucial impact on the development of international law. The first momentous development was the increased colonisation by European States of the rest of the world. International law served as an instrument to legitimise the European colonisation process,[90] much as it had in earlier days served to legitimise the freedom of the high seas.[91] Multilateral treaties were on occasion used to put in place colonial policies, such as the 1885 Berlin Act, through which European powers decided to carve up the African continent between them.[92] In other words, the multilateralism based on common values and interests and the need for collective action also provided a catalyst for colonialism.[93]

That process gave rise to a persistent tension between 'northern' and 'southern' States in shaping and interpreting international law. In particular, international law has often been regarded by States in the southern hemisphere as merely representing the law of the white man or of the northern States.

A second fundamental phenomenon was the industrial revolution during the late eighteenth and the nineteenth centuries. It gave rise to a tremendous increase in production and trade, which became ever more international with the emergence of steam trains and ships. The colonisation process and the industrial revolution together gave rise to a complex worldwide economic network. That in turn had a fourfold impact on the emergence of international organisations.

First, the increased intensity and frequency of international transactions and the concomitant interests of States increased the risk of international conflicts. That helps to explain the tendency of States during the nineteenth century to accept international

[88] See eg M Vec, 'From the Congress of Vienna to the Paris Peace Treaties of 1919' in Fassbender and Peters (n 61) 654–78.

[89] Lesaffer (n 61) 78.

[90] See eg M Koskenniemi, *The Gentle Civilizer of Nations: The Rise and Fall of International Law 1870–1960* (Cambridge, CUP, 2002) 98–178.

[91] See especially H Grotius, *Mare Liberum, sive de jure quod Batavis competit ad indicana commercia dissertatio* (Leiden, Elzevier, 1609).

[92] Orakhelashvili (n 87) 452.

[93] ibid, 454.

arbitration as an alternative form of settlement of disputes instead of war, at least where no vital interests were at stake.

Second, there was a growing need for common norms and standards on patenting inventions, classifying goods for the purposes of levying customs duties, and fixing exchange rates between currencies. This explains the emergence of the first international institutions, the so-called 'international unions' such as the International Telegraph Union in 1865,[94] the International Meteorological Organization in 1873,[95] and the General Postal Union in 1874,[96] which became the Universal Postal Union in 1878.[97] At the end of the nineteenth century, the trend towards international standardisation spread to politically more sensitive areas, such as the protection of workers and children.

Third, the rigid conception of what sovereignty entailed became a serious barrier for international trade. For example, before the establishment of the General Postal Union in 1875, international mail traffic was governed by a complex network of bilateral treaties, as States wanted to maximise their financial gains. That gave rise to increasingly prohibitive postal tariffs for international mail and to levies at every border crossing.

Fourth, the growing interdependence of the economies of the major powers engendered the emergence of certain common interests, which in turn led to the first initiatives to establish a permanent institutional framework in the form of so-called 'international commissions'. The early nineteenth century already saw the establishment of the Central Commission for Navigation on the Rhine[98] and the Commissions of the Danube River,[99] which aimed to promote free navigation on both rivers. Similar commissions were established for international trade in certain goods, such as the International Commission for Uniform Methods of Sugar Analysis, founded in 1897.[100] The growing interdependence also turned certain national problems into international issues. For example, the end of the nineteenth century saw the establishment of several international unions to prevent illnesses such as cholera.

Nevertheless, the inability of nineteenth century balance of power mechanisms to prevent the First World War demonstrated its limitations to secure peace and stability. As a consequence, the twentieth century focused on the need to build institutional safeguards for the proper operation of the international legal system, and on the rights of non-State entities,[101] notably through the development of human rights law.

[94] International Telegraph Convention (adopted 17 May 1865, entered into force 1 January 1866) 130 CTS 198. The International Telegraph Union was succeeded by the International Telecommunications Union, a UN specialided agency: see the Constitution of the International Telecommunication Union (adopted 22 December 1992, entered into force 1 July 1994) (1994) ATS 28.

[95] A nongovernmental organisation established in Vienna in 1873. It was succeeded by the World Meteorological Organization, a UN specialised agency: see the Convention of the World Meteorological Organization (adopted 11 October 1947, entered into force 23 March 1950) 77 UNTS 143.

[96] Treaty Concerning the Formation of a General Postal Union (adopted 9 October 1874, entered into force 1 July 1875).

[97] Universal Postal Union (UPU) Convention and Final Protocol (adopted 1 June 1878, entered into force on 1 April 1879) 49 Stat 2741. See now the Constitution of the Universal Postal Union (adopted 10 July 1964, entered into force on 1 January 1966) 611 UNTS 7. The UPU is a UN specialised agency.

[98] Convention for Rhine Navigation (adopted 17 October 1868, entered into force 14 April 1967), available at ccr-zkr.org/files/conventions/convrev_e.pdf.

[99] Established pursuant to the Treaty of Paris (adopted 30 March 1856, entered into force 23 July 1952), which also ended the Crimean War between the Russian Empire on the one hand, and the Ottoman Empire, the British Empire, the Second French Empire, and the Kingdom of Sardinia on the other hand.

[100] See icumsa.org.

[101] Orakhelashvili (n 87) 455.

F. The Twentieth Century

i. The Hague Peace Conferences

Great rivalry between nation States continued to exist during the period between the end of the nineteenth century and the beginning of the First World War, which complicated and hindered international cooperation. The most significant development in international law pertained to the conclusion of a number of important multilateral treaties on the laws of war during the 1899 and 1907 Hague Peace Conferences.[102] They were convened on the initiative of the Russian Tsar, Nicholas II, to promote disarmament, the agreement of basic rules on 'humane' warfare and the development of methods of peaceful settlement of disputes between nations. While neither conference established any form of compulsory arbitration, one of the great successes of the 1899 conference was the adoption of a Convention for the Pacific Settlement of International Disputes,[103] which established the still-functioning Permanent Court of Arbitration.[104]

The second Hague Peace Conference, held in 1907, was attended by nearly every existing European and non-European State, and could perhaps be considered as the first attempt at creating 'universal' international law.[105] It focused predominantly on regulating the conduct of warfare, and led to a series of conventions on that issue, the so-called 'Law of The Hague'.[106] One of the most notable developments emanating from the Hague Conventions was the Martens Clause, named after the Russian scholar Fyodor Fyodorovich Martens (1845–1909). It was first inserted in the Preamble of the 1899 Convention (II) with Respect to the Laws and Customs of War on Land,[107] and restated in the 1907 Convention (IV) respecting the Laws and Customs of War on Land,[108] and holds as follows:[109]

> Until a more complete code of the laws of war has been issued, the High Contracting Parties deem it expedient to declare that, in cases not included in the Regulations adopted by them, the inhabitants and the belligerents remain under the protection and the rule of the principles of the law of nations, as they result from the usages established among civilized peoples, from the laws of humanity, and the dictates of the public conscience.
>
> They declare that it is in this sense especially that Articles I [on belligerents] and 2 [on citizens, who, on the approach of the enemy, spontaneously take up arms to resist the invading troops, the so-called 'levée en masse'] of the Regulations adopted must be understood.

[102] C Focarelli, 'International Law in the 20th Century' in Orakhelashvili (n 65) 479. See GH Aldrich and CM Chinkin (eds), 'Symposium: the Hague peace conferences' (2000) 94 *AJIL* 1. On the crucial role played by Dutch academic lawyer and statesman TMC Asser in both conferences, see G De Baere and A Mills, 'T.M.C. Asser and Public and Private International Law: The Life and Legacy of "a Practical Legal Statesman"' (2012) 42 *NYIL* 25–26 and 28–29.

[103] The Hague Convention for the Pacific Settlement of International Disputes of 1899 (adopted 29 July 1899, entered into force 4 September 1900) (1907) 1 *AJIL* 103, replaced by the The Hague Convention for the Pacific Settlement of International Disputes of 1907 (adopted 18 October 1907, entered into force 26 January 1910) (1908) 2 *AJIL* Supp 43.

[104] See pca-cpa.org and Chapter 13, Section III(A) on arbitration.

[105] Focarelli (n 102) 480.

[106] On which see Chapter 15 on the Law of Armed Conflict.

[107] Convention (II) with Respect to the Laws and Customs of War on Land and its annex: Regulations concerning the Laws and Customs of War on Land (adopted 29 July 1899, entered into force 4 September 1900) 32 Stat 1803; TS 403.

[108] Convention (IV) respecting the Laws and Customs of War on Land and its annex: Regulations concerning the Laws and Customs of War on Land (adopted 18 October 1907, entered into force 26 January 1910) 36 Stat 2277; TS 539.

[109] On its interpretation, see eg A Cassese, 'The Martens Clause: Half a Loaf or Simply Pie in the Sky' (2000) 11 *EJIL* 187.

However, no concrete progress on disarmament was made. A third Hague Peace Conference was scheduled for 1915,[110] but was never held due to the outbreak of the First World War.

ii. World War I and the League of Nations

The First World War signalled the demise of what is sometimes referred to as the 'European Age', including the end of the permissibility of colonial expansion, and the rise of the two prime powers of the twentieth century, both of which non-European: the United States of America (USA) and the Union of Soviet Socialist Republics (USSR). The USSR in particular challenged the very foundations of international law in a number of ways: (i) by advocating the application of the principle of self-determination to national groups in Europe and to colonies; (ii) by claiming substantive and not just formal equality between all States; (iii) by pledging to intervene in the internal affairs of other States in order to assist the working class; and (iv) by repudiating existing rules of international law considered as 'bourgeois', and denouncing certain treaties binding on Russia, especially in the field of investor protection.[111]

After the First World War, the League of Nations was established on the initiative of US President Thomas Woodrow Wilson.[112] In his address to a joint session of the US Congress on 8 January 1918, President Wilson presented a programme of 14 points with a view to a comprehensive peace settlement. The 14th point proposed: 'A general association of nations must be formed under specific covenants for the purpose of affording mutual guarantees of political independence and territorial integrity to great and small states alike'. On 28 June 1919, the Paris Peace Conference adopted the 26 Article Covenant of the League of Nations,[113] which entered into force together with the Treaty of Versailles[114] on 10 January 1920. Other international organisations emerged within the framework of the League of Nations, such as the International Labour Organization, which was likewise established by the Treaty of Versailles.[115] Furthermore, the Assembly of the League of Nations on 13 December 1920 unanimously adopted the Statute of the Permanent Court of International Justice (PCIJ).[116] The League of Nations aimed at the enhancement of international cooperation and the assurance of international peace and security through a system of collective security, and the entry into force of its Covenant was an epochal event in the history of international law.[117]

[110] See JB Scott, 'Recommendation for a Third Peace Conference at the Hague' (1908) 2 *AJIL* 815.

[111] Focarelli (n 102) 482–83.

[112] For a recent biography, see eg A Scott Berg, *Wilson* (New York, GP Putnam's Sons, 2013). See also the (rather unflattering) biography of President Wilson co-authored by Sigmund Freud: S Freud and WC Bullitt, *Thomas Woodrow Wilson: A Psychological Study* (Boston and Cambridge, Houghton Mifflin Company and The Riverside Press, 1967).

[113] Covenant of the League of Nations (adopted 28 April 1919, entered into force 10 January 1920) 225 CTS 195.

[114] Treaty of Peace with Germany (adopted 28 June 1919, entered into force 10 January 1920) 225 CTS 188 (Treaty of Versailles).

[115] Constitution of the International Labour Organization (ILO) (adopted 28 June 1919, entered into force 20 April 1948) 15 UNTS 40. The ILO became a UN specialised agency in 1946.

[116] Statute of the PCIJ (adopted 16 December 1920, entered into force 20 August 1921) 6 LNTS 379.

[117] See further H Lauterpacht, 'The Covenant as the "Higher Law"' (1936) 17 *BYIL* 54, who argued that it followed from its Art 20 that the Covenant took precedence over other conflicting treaties. See also M Fosse, J Fox, *The League of Nations: From Collective Security to Global Rearmament* (Geneva, UN, 2012); BJC McKercher, 'The League of Nations and the Problem of Collective Security 1919–1939' in *The League of Nations 1920–1946: Organization and Accomplishments: A Retrospective of the First International Organization for the Establishment of World Peace* (New York, UN, 1996).

The League of Nations originally counted 45 Member States, ie, the allied victors and 13 neutral States. Other States would join later, such as Germany in 1926 and the Soviet Union in 1934. The maximum number of member States would be 60 in 1934, which had diminished to 54 by 1939. In total, 62 States were members of the League of Nations. Notoriously and despite the best efforts of President Woodrow Wilson, the US never became a member of the League of Nations, the Senate having refused to agree to the Treaty of Versailles.[118]

The three main organs of the League of Nations were the Assembly, the Council and the permanent Secretariat:[119]

(1) the Assembly[120] was the plenary meeting of the League of Nations, and consisted of Representatives of the Members of the League. The Assembly could deal at its meetings with any matter within the sphere of action of the League 'or affecting the peace of the world'. At meetings of the Assembly each Member of the League had one vote, and could not have more than three Representatives;[121]

(2) the Council[122] consisted of Representatives of the Principal Allied and Associated Powers, together with Representatives of four other Members of the League. The former was in fact the category of permanent members, consisting of the US, the British Empire, France, Italy and Japan. The fifth seat was initially unoccupied through the non-ratification by the US. After the Locarno Pact of 1925,[123] the seat was allocated to Germany. When Nazi Germany left the League of Nations in 1933, the seat was allocated to the Soviet Union. The first elected members of the Council were Representatives of Belgium, Brazil, Spain and Greece. The number of elected members was gradually increased to 6 in 1922, 9 in 1926 and 11 in 1936. At meetings of the Council, each Member of the League represented on the Council had one vote, and could have not more than one Representative. Like the Assembly, the Council could deal at its meetings with any matter within the sphere of action of the League or affecting the peace of the world;[124]

(3) the permanent Secretariat[125] was established at the Seat of the League in Geneva, and comprised of a Secretary General and such secretaries and staff as were required. The office of Secretary General was administrative rather than political, and was performed consecutively by the British politician and diplomat Sir Eric Drummond until 1932 and the French diplomat Joseph Avenol until 1940.[126]

[118] TD Grant, 'Universality versus Coherence: Membership, Participation and the Crisis of the League of Nations' (2015) 17 *International Community Law Review* 138.

[119] Art 2 Covenant of the League of Nations.

[120] See Art 3 Covenant of the League of Nations.

[121] See further ME Burton, *The Assembly of the League of Nations* (Chicago, University of Chicago Press, 1941); F Grob, *Die Kompetenzen des Völkerbundsrates und der Völkerbundsversammlung zur Streitschlichtung und Kriegsverhütung* (Berlin, Vahlen, 1933).

[122] See Art 4 Covenant of the League of Nations.

[123] Treaty of Mutual Guarantee between Germany, Belgium, France, Great Britain and Italy (adopted 16 October 1925, entered into force 14 September 1926) 54 LNTS 289.

[124] See further R Lange, *La composition du Conseil de la Société des Nations* (Paris, Au commerce des idées, 1928); AH Philipse, *Le rôle du Conseil de la Société des Nations dans le règlement pacifique des différends internationaux* (Leiden, Nijhoff, 1928); Grob (n 121).

[125] Art 6 Covenant of the League of Nations.

[126] See further A Cagne, *Le secrétariat général de la Société des nations* (Paris, Jel, 1936); TL Deibel, *Le secrétariat de la Société des Nations et l'Internationalisme Américain, 1919–1924* (Genève, Carnegie, 1972).

Except where otherwise expressly provided in the Covenant, decisions at any meeting of the Assembly or of the Council required the agreement of all the Members of the League represented at the meeting. However, all matters of procedure at meetings of the Assembly or of the Council, including the appointment of Committees to investigate particular matters, could be decided by a majority of the Members of the League represented at the meeting.[127]

The effectiveness of the collective security mechanism of the League of Nations was compromised from the start by the lack of participation by the US, the Soviet Union (which was admitted in 1934, only to be expulsed in 1939 after its invasion of Finland) and Germany (which was only admitted in 1926). The mechanism was similarly weakened by a number of countries leaving the League: Brazil in 1928, Germany and Japan in 1933 (the latter in reaction to a condemnation by the League of its invasion of Manchuria), Italy in 1937, and Hungary and Spain in 1939. Politically, the League of Nations was characterised by a growing powerlessness, as exemplified by the Japanese invasion of Manchuria in 1931, the Italian invasion of Ethiopia in 1934–1935, the Spanish Civil War in 1936, the German invasions of Austria in 1938 and of Czechoslovakia in 1939, and the Soviet invasion in Finland in 1939, leading to the so-called 'Winter War'.[128]

Nevertheless, the League of Nations has contributed to the development of international law in at least four ways:

— first, Article 14 of the Covenant of the League of Nations provided for the Council to formulate and submit to the Members of the League for adoption plans for the establishment of a PCIJ. The Court was to be competent 'to hear and determine any dispute of an international character which the parties thereto submit to it'. The Court could also give an advisory opinion upon any dispute or question referred to it by the Council or by the Assembly. The PCIJ, the predecessor of the ICJ, was also based in the Peace Palace in The Hague, and handled 66 cases between 1922 and 1939. These resulted in 32 judgments and 27 advisory opinions, which were all requested by the Council of the League (even though the Assembly also had the competence to request an advisory opinion). Like the ICJ now, the PCIJ did not have compulsory jurisdiction. The importance of the PCIJ lay mostly in (i) proving that a permanent international court had a role to play in the proper conduct of international relations; (ii) being a turning point in the acceptance by States that legal rules have a place in international politics; and (iii) contributing significantly through its case law to the clarification and further development of international law;[129]

— second, while the League of Nations was by no means an international legislator, around 120 treaties were negotiated and concluded under its aegis. The League of Nations was the first international organisation providing a permanent forum for negotiations between States with a view to the development of international (treaty) law;

— third, the League of Nations managed the Saarland, monitored the government of the Free City of Danzig and supervised the mandate system, which provided for the

[127] Art 5 Covenant of the League of Nations.

[128] For an early appraisal, see JE Harley, *The League of Nations and the New International Law* (Oxford, OUP, 1921). See, more recently, S Wertheim, 'The League of Nations: A Retreat from International Law?' (2012) *Journal of Global History* 210.

[129] See also O Spiermann, *International Legal Argument in the Permanent Court of International Justice* (Cambridge, CUP, 2005); and C Tams and M Fitzmaurice (eds), *Legacies of the Permanent Court of International Justice* (Leiden, Brill, 2013).

administration, by the Mandatory Power, of territories previously controlled by States defeated in World War I, principally Imperial Germany and the Ottoman Empire.[130]

— fourth and finally, the League of Nations introduced a remarkable system of protection of the rights of minorities.[131]

Furthermore, a number of principles were established by the League Covenant that survived the demise of the League:[132] (i) Article 10 of the Covenant provided a (somewhat qualified) ban on aggression; (ii) Article 18 of the Covenant contained an obligation to register treaties, thereby sanctioning Wilson's first point on the prevention of secret diplomacy; and (iii) the League gave an impetus to the codification of customary international law, notably by convening the 1930 League of Nations Codification Conference at the Hague.[133]

Outside the framework of the League of Nations, an initiative of Frank B Kellogg and Aristide Briand, respectively the US Secretary of State and the French Minister of Foreign Affairs, led to the conclusion of the Kellogg-Briand Pact in 1928,[134] which prohibited the use of force as a means to settle international disputes.[135] Despite the fact that 62 States, ie, nearly the entire community of States then in existence, became parties to the Pact, it was unable to call to halt the aggressive foreign policies of Germany, Japan and Italy in the 1930s, which would culminate in the Second World War. Nevertheless, the Pact lies at the origin of the prohibition of the use or threat of force in international relations, now laid down in Article 2(4) of the UN Charter and recognised as a rule of customary international law. It has been argued that the renunciation of war as a means of advancing national policy was more than just a cynical gesture of the statesmen of the time.[136] Indeed, it represented a fundamental shift in human history in that, up to that point, war had been accepted as a 'predominantly legitimate and often glorious way of defending or advancing national interests and of enforcing international obligations'. In sum, the prohibition of the use of force by States is arguably 'the greatest achievement of twentieth century civilization'.[137]

iii. World War II and the United Nations

The League of Nations was unable to prevent the outbreak of World War II. In fact, the German attack on Poland in September 1939 was not even formally put on the agenda of

[130] N Matz, 'Civilization and the Mandate System under the League of Nations as Origin of Trusteeship' (2005) 9 *Max Planck Yearbook of United Nations Law* 47.

[131] See P Kovács, 'The Protection of Minorities under the Auspices of the League of Nations' in D Shelton (ed), *The Oxford Handbook of International Human Rights Law* (Oxford, OUP, 2012) 325–41.

[132] Focarelli (n 102) 484–85.

[133] See MO Hudson, 'The First Conference for the Codification of International Law' (1930) 24 *AJIL* 447.

[134] General Treaty for the Renunciation of War as an Instrument of National Policy (adopted 27 August 1928, entered into force 24 July 1929) 94 LNTS 57. See generally RH Ferrell, *Peace in Their Time: The Origins of the Kellogg-Briand Pact* (New Haven, Yale UP, 1952); and OA Hathaway and SJ Shapiro, *The Internationalists And Their Plan to Outlaw War* (London, Allen Lane, 2017), arguing that the Pact was the beginning of a new attitude to war and that it shaped the thinking of those who framed a new world order.

[135] See further D Bolech Cecchi, 'The Outlawry of War and the Kellogg-Briand Pact' in M Petricioli (ed), *Pour la paix en Europe : institutions et société civile dans l'entre-deux-guerres* (Brussels, Lang, 2007); B Roscher, *Der Briand-Kellogg-Pakt von 1928: der 'Verzicht auf den Krieg als Mittel nationaler Politik' im völkerrechtlichen Denken der Zwischenkriegszeit* (Baden-Baden, Nomos, 2004); R Bermejo Garcia, 'El uso de la fuerza, la Sociedad de Naciones y el Pacto Briand-Kellogg' in Y Gamarra Chopo and CR Fernandez Liesa (eds), *Los origenes del Derecho internacional contemporaneo : estudios conmemorativos del Centenario de la Primera Guerra Mundial* (Zaragoza, Institucion Fernando el Catolico, 2015) 217–46.

[136] M Weller, *Iraq and the Use of Force in International Law* (Cambridge, CUP, 2010) 1.

[137] ibid.

the Council of the League of Nations. Nevertheless, during the Second World War, the idea that a new international organisation would be needed after the war to maintain international peace and security gained ground among the allied nations.

On 14 August 1941, the United States and the United Kingdom signed the Atlantic Charter, which contained the common views of both nations, which the Soviet Union, the British dominions and the Western governments in exile joined in September 1941.[138]

On 1 January 1942, 26 countries, including the Atlantic Charter countries, China, Poland, Czechoslovakia, Yugoslavia and a number of Latin-American countries,[139] signed the Declaration by United Nations, which in essence committed them to the maximum war effort while prohibiting them from making a separate peace. More detailed plans for the structure of a new international organisation were drawn up in 1943, a process culminating in the Declaration of the Four Nations or the Four Power Declaration, signed on 30 October 1943 at the Moscow Conference by the United States, the United Kingdom, the Soviet Union, and the Republic of China. The declaration recognised the need to establish as soon as possible a general international organisation, based on the sovereign equality of all peace-loving States with a view to maintaining international peace and security. Subsequently, lawyers of these four powers drafted the most important principles of what would become the UN Charter at the Dumbarton Oaks Conference, held from August to October 1944.[140]

President Franklin D Roosevelt, Prime Minister Winston Churchill and General Secretary Joseph Stalin, the heads of government of the United States, the United Kingdom and the Soviet Union, respectively, met at the Yalta Conference in February 1945 to discuss the fate of post-war Europe. At the same time, they agreed on a number of crucial points with respect to the organisation of decision-making in what would become the UN, in particular with respect to what would become the Security Council. Furthermore, they decided to call the United Nations Conference on International Organization (UNCIO) in San Francisco from 25 April–26 June 1945. On the final day of the conference, the Charter of the United Nations was signed by the representatives of the 50 participating countries. The UN Charter entered into force on 24 October 1945, and the first General Assembly met in London on 10 January 1946. It is worth quoting part of the preamble to the UN Charter:

> WE THE PEOPLES OF THE UNITED NATIONS,
>
> DETERMINED
>
> to save succeeding generations from the scourge of war, which twice in our lifetime has brought untold sorrow to mankind, and
>
> to reaffirm faith in fundamental human rights, in the dignity and worth of the human person, in the equal rights of men and women and of nations large and small, and
>
> to establish conditions under which justice and respect for the obligations arising from treaties and other sources of international law can be maintained, and
>
> to promote social progress and better standards of life in larger freedom

[138] See EA Laing, 'Relevance of the Atlantic Charter for a new world order' (1989) *Indiana Journal of International Law* 298.

[139] The original 26 signatories were: the US, the UK, the Union of Soviet Socialist Republics, China, Australia, Belgium, Canada, Costa Rica, Cuba, Czechoslovakia, Dominican Republic, El Salvador, Greece, Guatemala, Haiti, Honduras, India, Luxembourg, Netherlands, New Zealand, Nicaragua, Norway, Panama, Poland, Union of South Africa, Yugoslavia.

[140] See RC Hildebrand, *Dumbarton Oaks: The Origins of the United Nations and the Search for Postwar Security* (Chapel Hill, University of North Carolina Press, 1990).

The UN's organs are modelled on the organs of the League of Nations, with notably less concurring powers between the Council and the Assembly, and noticeably more power conferred on the Assembly.[141] As with respect to the Covenant of the League of Nations, the UN Charter has sometimes been considered as the 'constitution of the international community'.[142]

Nevertheless, it has been argued that the 'bifurcated regime' for dealing with aggression consisting of the authority of the Security Council on the one hand and the right of self-defence on the other hand, failed to address adequately 'four seismic developments that, even as the Charter was being signed, were beginning to transform the world':[143] (i) the advent of the Cold War, which froze the UN Security Council's ability to guarantee collective security because of the veto; (ii) the use of indirect aggression through the export of insurgency and covert meddling in civil wars, instead of the type of military aggression Article 2(4) of the Charter was designed to prohibit; (iii) the technological transformation of weaponry (nuclear, chemical, and biological) and of delivery systems (rocketry); and (iv) a rising global public consciousness of the importance of human freedom and the link between the repression of human rights and threats to the peace. As a consequence, like other treaties written for the long term, the UN Charter has had to 'meet the threat of obsolescence with adaption'.[144]

The establishment of the UN also created a legal order in which the principles of self-determination, sovereign equality, and the prohibition of the use of force were central for the determination of certain claims to authority over a territory as lawful or not. Indeed, these principles would go on to inspire the process of decolonisation. Furthermore, the reaffirmation of 'faith in fundamental human rights' and in 'the dignity and worth of the human person' in the preamble to the UN Charter would shape the development during the twentieth century of human rights law and humanitarian law as constraints on State action.[145] The UN therefore set the stage for a reassessment of the relationship between States and international law: on the one hand, principles such as self-determination and non-intervention[146] render intervention in the internal affairs of a State prima facie illegitimate; on the other hand, the developing human rights and humanitarian law principles imply that such intervention must under certain circumstances also be legitimate. It has been the fundamental task and perennial challenge of the UN to establish a delicate balance between those two tendencies.[147]

iv. The Cold War Period

A paradoxical situation developed after World War II. On the one hand, the world became increasingly interconnected due to technological and economic developments. That globalisation of problems went hand in hand with a substantial increase in multilateral treaties and international organisations. International law became to an important extent a 'law of

[141] Focarelli (n 102) 493.

[142] See eg B Fassbender, *The United Nations Charter as the Constitution of the International Community* (The Hague, Nijhoff, 2009).

[143] TM Franck, *Recourse to Force: State Action against Threats and Armed Attacks* (Cambridge, CUP, 2002) 3–4.

[144] ibid, 4.

[145] A Orford, 'Constituting order' in Crawford and Koskenniemi (n 39) 280–81.

[146] On which see eg Crawford (n 53) 384–89. See also Chapter 14, Section II(B), on the scope of Art 2(4) UN Charter and Section IV(A), on wars of national liberation.

[147] Orford (n 145) 281.

cooperation'. This evolution coincided with the rise of multilateral human rights treaties, which were in part an answer to the excesses of World War II.[148] A significant number of human rights treaties and other instruments were adopted at global and regional levels, in particular in Europe, the Americas, and Africa. Significant steps towards the development of a 'law of cooperation' were also taken outside the context of human rights, for example through the adoption of the 1982 UN Convention on the Law of the Sea (the 'Montego Bay Convention'),[149] sometimes referred to as the 'constitution of the oceans'.

On the other hand, the operation of the UN, and in particular the Security Council, was for a long time severely affected by the Cold War. The wave of decolonisation brought into being a significant number of States, which were mostly very keen to hang on to their newly acquired independence and sovereignty. Due to these developments, international law to an important extent retained its function as a law of coexistence.

Together with the establishment of a universal international organisation, the end of the Second World War brought about a significant rise in regional frameworks for cooperation. This is in particular the case in Europe with the EU, which provides for far-reaching limitations in and a 'pooling' of national sovereignty, it being understood that such pooling is in itself as much an attribute of sovereignty, as entering into treaties or organisations with other States.[150]

v. The Post-Cold War Period

The fall of the Berlin Wall in November 1989 symbolised the sudden end to the era of bipolarity between East and West, and the start of a new multipolar reality. International law and international governance structures have needed time to adjust. The constellation of events in the 1980s and 1990s gave rise to epochal changes in international law, notably in the area of regional integration and trade. The EU and the WTO have occupied an important place in the centre of this new hope for international law.[151]

However, the post-Cold War period has not just been determined by international organisations, but also by the rise of transnational structures such as multinational corporations and non-governmental organisations.[152] The latter, for example, played a crucial role in the negotiation of the 1997 Antipersonnel Mine Ban Convention[153] and the 1998 ICC Statute, both of which in turn symbolise the important developments the post-Cold War period has seen in the area of humanitarian law and international criminal law, and the latter of which

[148] Notably, on 9 December 1948 the UN General Assembly, meeting in Paris, adopted the Convention on the Prevention and Punishment of the Crime of Genocide (entered into force on 12 January 1951) 78 UNTS 277, which was followed on 10 December by the adoption of the Universal Declaration of Human Rights, GA res. 217A (III), UN Doc A/810 at 71 (1948). See e.g. D Mayers, 'Humanity in 1948: The Genocide Convention and the Universal Declaration of Human Rights' (2015) 26 *Diplomacy & Statecraft* 446–72. For a history of the concepts of genocide and crimes against humanity, see P Sands, *East West Street: On the Origins of Genocide and Crimes Against Humanity* (London, Weidenfeld & Nicolson, 2016). Other international human rights treaties were to follow. See further Chapter 16. See also T Meron, 'International Law in the Age of Human Rights: General Course on Public International Law' (2003) 301 *RdC* 9.

[149] See further Chapter 18 on Law of the Sea.

[150] Crawford (n 53) 111. See also Chapter 7 on Regional Organisations.

[151] G De Baere and I Van Damme, 'Co-Adaptation in the International Legal Order: The EU and the WTO' in J Crawford and S Nouwen (eds), *Select Proceedings of the European Society of International Law*, Vol 3, 2010 (Oxford, Hart, 2012) 311.

[152] Focarelli (n 102) 511–12.

[153] Convention on the Prohibition of the Use, Stockpiling, Production and Transfer of Anti-Personnel Mines and on their Destruction (adopted 18 September 1997, entered into force 1 March 1999) 2056 UNTS 241.

is a symptom of the significant increase in the number of international courts and tribunals witnessed in the last decades.[154]

In addition, two developments that had started in the 1970s took on particular urgency in the post-Cold War period. First, international terrorism has had a significant impact on many areas of international law, including the law on the use of force, as well as on international criminal law, humanitarian law, human rights, and the law of international responsibility.[155] Second, the environment has been at the forefront of international law-making during the past decades, notably but not exclusively in the area of climate change, through the conclusion of the UNFCCC,[156] which forms the cornerstone of the international law regime to combat climate change.[157]

In general, international law in the post-Cold War era is characterised by the tension between a reaffirmation of the importance of sovereign States as the most important actors on the international legal stage on the one hand, and the ever-greater importance of sub-State or non-State actors on that same stage. At the same time, the foundations of international law are arguably fundamentally shifting from a focus on State sovereignty to a greater concern with 'humanity' more generally, and hence from sovereignty as a 'right' to 'sovereignty as responsibility'.[158] Those tensions and developments, combined with the increasing awareness of transnational problems such as terrorism and climate change, that can only be tackled on an international or even on a global level, are likely to present crucial challenges for international law for the foreseeable future.

V. Theory of International Law

A theory of international law is to a significant extent a theory of its binding force or lack thereof, and more generally of the 'legal' character of international law.[159] What theory can explain the binding force of international law vis-à-vis independent sovereign States, in particular if sovereignty implies that no authority exists above the sovereign entity?[160] Scholars have variously attempted to find a theoretical underpinning for the binding force of international law or, conversely, have denied the possibility of any such

[154] On which see De Baere, Chané and Wouters (n 33).
[155] See eg KN Trapp, 'Back to Basics: Necessity, Proportionality, and the Right of Self-Defence against Non-State Terrorist Actors' (2007) 56 *ICLQ* 141; and KN Trapp, *State Responsibility for International Terrorism* (Oxford, OUP, 2011).
[156] n 50.
[157] See further Chapter 20 on International Environmental Law.
[158] Mills (n 6) 188–89. The idea of 'sovereignty as responsibility' is often associated with the 'responsibility to protect', on which see Chapter 14, Section IV(C) and eg A Peters, 'The Responsibility to Protect: Spelling Out the Hard Legal Consequences for the UN Security Council and its Members' in U Fastenrath, R Geiger, D-E Khan, A Paulus, S von Schorlemer and C Vedder (eds), *From Bilateralism to Community Interest: Essays in Honour of Bruno Simma* (Oxford, OUP, 2011) 297–326; regarding the role of the EU: G De Baere, 'The EU and the Responsibility to Protect' in B Van Vooren, S Blockmans and J Wouters (eds), *The EU's Role in Global Governance: The Legal Dimension* (Oxford, OUP, 2013) 95–109. On sovereignty and humanity, see further: A Peters, 'Humanity as the A and Ω of Sovereignty' (2009) 20 *EJIL* 513. But see JE Alvarez, 'State Sovereignty is not Withering Away: A Few Lessons for the Future' in A Cassese (ed), *Realizing Utopia: The Future of International Law* (Oxford, OUP, 2012) 26–37; and J Crawford, 'Sovereignty as a Legal Value' in Crawford and Koskenniemi (n 39) 117–33.
[159] See eg F Mégret, 'International Law as Law' in Crawford and Koskenniemi (n 39) 64–92.
[160] See generally P Eleftheriadis, 'Law and Sovereignty' (2010) 29 *Law and Philosophy* 535.

binding force. Some have rejected the legal character of international law,[161] or downplayed its significance.[162] By contrast, others have pointed out that the problem of the foundation for the binding force of norms is not at all unique to international law[163] or that international law is perhaps structurally different, but is not in any way less 'law-like' than municipal law.[164] Indeed, theories of law founded on a clear distinction between international law and municipal law may be in danger of becoming obsolete. Developments in the material and personal scope of international law increasingly make it an integral part of the law applying to individual subjects in domestic legal orders, thus integrating international law within municipal legal systems to a significantly greater extent than it was in the past. As Besson and Tasioulas put it: 'Law itself has changed as a result of globalization and so should legal theory'.[165]

However, it would be mistaken to believe that the theory of international law serves only to confirm or deny its existence or its legal character. It has been argued that international law has entered a 'post-ontological era', enabling international lawyers to 'undertake critical assessment' of their subject, instead of continuously having to defend its existence.[166] The following does not purport to put forward its own theory of international law, but provides an overview of some of the prevalent theories, without in any way aspiring to completeness. It hardly needs pointing out that the categories used in what follows are primarily useful for expository and didactic purposes. They are not set in stone, and the borders between them are often very fluid indeed.

A. Natural Law Theories

Natural law thinkers view law as a natural given of the human condition. For contemporary natural law thinkers, all norms must be practically reasonable to be valid or binding, and they can only be practically reasonable if they are consistent with a set of moral constraints. Natural lawyers therefore believe there to be a necessary connection between law and morality, a position denied by legal positivists,[167] who identify law on the basis of socio-legal facts.[168]

The Roman legal scholar Ulpian had posited the existence of a natural law common to all living creatures,[169] and applicable to all human beings as a *jus gentium*, to be distinguished from the particular laws of the different nations, the *jus civile*. Non-Roman inhabitants of

[161] Famously J Austin, *The Province of Jurisprudence Determined* (1832), WE Rumble (ed) (Cambridge, CUP, 1995) 20, also classifying constitutional law as' positive morality merely': ibid, 216.

[162] See eg Hart (n 16) 198, remarking that law in the international system has been confined to matters that do not 'affect "vital" issues'; cp A Orakhelashvili, 'The Relevance of Theory and History – The Essence and Origins of International Law' in Orakhelashvili (n 65) 3–22.

[163] See eg G Fitzmaurice, 'The Foundation of the Authority of International Law and the Problem of Enforcement' (1956) 19 *MLR* 1, 9–10.

[164] See eg H Lauterpacht, *The Function of Law in the International Community* (Oxford, OUP, 1933) 433, and 183–201 on the difficulty of distinguishing 'political' from 'legal' disputes in international tribunals, referring to a maxim of '*de maximis non curat praetor*'.

[165] S Besson and J Tasioulas, 'Introduction' in Besson and Tasioulas (n 33) 13.

[166] T Franck, *Fairness in International Law and Institutions* (Oxford, Clarendon Press, 1995) 6.

[167] See eg M Kramer, 'On the Separability of Law and Morality' (2004) 17 *CJLJ* 315; M Kramer, 'The Big Bad Wolf: Legal Positivism and Its Detractors' (2004) 49 *American Journal of Jurisprudence* 1, 1–10.

[168] On contemporary natural law theory, see further G Duke and RP George (eds), *The Cambridge Companion to Natural Law Jurisprudence* (Cambridge, CUP, 2017).

[169] P Krüger (ed), *Ulpiani liber singularis regularum* (Berlin, Weidmann, 1878).

the Roman empire, so-called *peregrine*, could rely on *jus gentium* for their relations with other inhabitants.

The Roman conception of natural law was adopted by Medieval Christian theology. Thomas Aquinas (1225–1274) defined *jus gentium* as part of natural law, which in addition consisted of certain institutions created by human custom.[170] Of particular importance was his *Summa Theologiae*, in which Aquinas further developed the 'just war' (*bellum justum*) theory of the Church, in particular putting forward three requirements for war to be just: (i) a legitimate authority declaring war (*auctoritas principis*); (ii) a just reason, namely the quest for legal reparation (*justa causa*); and (iii) the intention of achieving what is good (*intentio recta*).[171] The glossators in the twelfth and thirteenth centuries, especially in Bologna, and to an even larger extent post-glossators such as Bartolus (1314–1357) and Baldus (1327–1410) further developed numerous areas of international law on the basis of Roman legal concepts.

The authors of the Spanish school in the fifteenth and sixteenth centuries were still heavily influenced by medieval theological views, and in particular by Aquinas' work in the Aristotelian tradition. That was in part a consequence of the fact that political affairs, especially those of the Western Christian community, were considered as a natural subject of theological inquiry, and in part a consequence of the Catholic counter-reformation. Francisco de Vitoria (1483–1546), a Dominican who taught at the University of Salamanca, was particularly influential. Writing in the Thomistic tradition, he examined the question of the legitimacy of the Spanish conquests in the Americas in his *De Indis*[172] and *De jure belli*,[173] and emphasised the legitimacy of non-Western polities, as well as the necessary restrictions on the use of force, conquest, and enslavement of their populations flowing from that position. Vitoria's work was based on the view that all mankind formed a natural community preordained by divine will, premised on the common good of all mankind, and governed by the principles of natural law (*jus naturale*).[174]

Francisco de Vitoria postulated the existence of a *jus inter gentes*, which while derived from natural law, was itself positive law.[175] This law derives its binding force not just from treaties between States, but also from laws that are binding for all States. Francisco Suárez (1548–1617), a Jesuit who taught at the University of Coímbra, updated and systematised the medieval scholastic tradition, notably in his *De Legibus ac Deo Legislatore*.[176] He is also credited with using the notion of *jus gentium* to denote the law governing interstate relations rather than in the traditional sense stemming from Roman law.[177] Francisco Suárez took the view that while humanity was divided in different kingdoms, it still constituted one species with one political and moral unity, which ought to possess its proper customary law.[178] Nevertheless, he introduced the idea of a veritably positive international law in that the law of nations was founded on the consent of States. However, natural law did underpin the law of nations, in the sense that, according to Suárez, natural law stipulated the binding

[170] See eg JJ Baumann, *Die Staatslehre des h. Thomas von Aquino* (Leipzig, Hirzel, 1873).
[171] See eg J-P Rentto, 'Ius Gentium: A Lesson from Aquinas' (1992) *FYIL* 103.
[172] See A Pagden and J Lawrance (eds), *Vitoria: Political Writings* (Cambridge, CUP, 1992) 231.
[173] ibid, 293.
[174] See Lesaffer (n 69) 421.
[175] See eg A Truyol Serra, *The Principles of Political and International Law in the Work of Francisco de Vitoria* (Madrid, Cultura Hispanica, 1946); A Truyol Serra, H Mechoulan and P Haggenmacher, *Actualité de la pensée juridique de Francisco de Vitoria* (Brussel, Bruylant, 1988).
[176] F Suarez, *Tractatus de Legibus ac Deo Legislatore* (Coimbra, 1612).
[177] See Wijffels (n 73) 41–42.
[178] See eg C Barcia Trelles, 'Francisco Suárez (1548–1617)' (1933) 43 I *RdC* 385.

character of promises and hence of rules based on consent, thus providing the basis for the binding character of international law.[179]

Arguably because of the declining authority of the Holy Roman Empire and the emergence of the modern State system,[180] natural law-based theories were the preeminent theoretical position in international legal scholarship from the sixteenth century onwards.[181] For sixteenth century scholastics, this meant that the Divine law was inherently part of human nature, while seventeenth and eighteenth century rationalists saw law as the expression of a global reason operating in all human beings.

These predecessors of the natural law school were followed by Alberico Gentili (1552–1608), Regius Professor of Civil Law at the University of Oxford, who in his 1598 treatise *De jure belli libri tres*[182] argued that the law of nations should build on universal natural reason, and that natural law comprises normative constraints on actions of States both internally and externally.[183] It was the main exposition of the law of war and peace before Grotius' seminal work, and his division between *jus ad bellum*, *jus in bello*, and *jus post bellum* became standard.[184]

The true founder of the natural law school was Hugo De Groot or Grotius (1583–1645),[185] whose most important works are *De jure praedae*,[186] which includes the tract *Mare Liberum*[187] and *De jure belli ac pacis libri tres*. Grotius took the view that international law has to be founded on natural law, which in itself is the expression of rationality:

> The law of nature is a dictate of right reason, which points out that an act, according as it is or is not in conformity with rational nature, has in it a quality of moral baseness or moral necessity; and that, in consequence, such an act is either forbidden or enjoined by the author of nature, God.[188]

Grotius identified a set of basic natural rights needed for a basic sociability, which in turn is needed for being fully human. For Grotius, all people have such natural rights merely by virtue of being human, and these rights could therefore be regarded as basic human rights. However, these natural rights are alienated to the State, and in particular to the sovereign.[189] In that sense, Grotius' views may not be that far removed from Thomas Hobbes' (1588–1679) ideas,[190] and Grotius could therefore both be a natural lawyer and

[179] See Lesaffer (n 69) 421–22. See also JB Schneewind, *The Invention of Autonomy* (Cambridge, CUP, 1998) 59–66.

[180] R Lesaffer, 'The Grotian Tradition Revisited: Change and Continuity in the History of International Law' (2002) 73 *BYIL* 103, 105.

[181] See P Capps, 'Natural Law and the Law of Nations' in Orakhelashvili (n 65) 61.

[182] A Gentili, *De jure belli libri tres* (Oxford, Clarendon, 1933).

[183] See Capps (n 181) 64–71.

[184] See Lesaffer (n 69) 420 and 428.

[185] On Grotius as part of the natural law tradition in international law, see Capps (n 181) 71–80; Schneewind (n 179) 66–81. See further B Kingsbury and B Straumann, 'State of Nature versus Commercial Sociability as the Basis of International Law: Reflections on the Roman Foundations and Current Interpretations of the International Political and Legal Thought of Grotius, Hobbes, and Pufendorf' in Besson and Tasioulas (n 33) 33–51.

[186] HG Hamaker (ed), *De jure praedae commentarius* (The Hague, 1868). Grotius' work on prize law was commissioned by the Dutch East India Company (*Vereenigde Oost-Indische Compagnie* or VOC), and was intended to establish that the VOC's military clashes with the Portuguese could be classified as a just war. See Wijffels (n 73) 49.

[187] See Grotius (n 91); see R Feenstra (ed), *Hugo Grotius Mare Liberum 1609–2009* (Boston, Brill, 2009).

[188] H Grotius, *On the Law of War and Peace* (1625), SC Neff (ed and annot) (Cambridge, CUP, 2012) 28–29.

[189] R Harrison, *Hobbes, Locke and Confusion's Masterpiece* (Cambridge, CUP, 2003) 143 and 149.

[190] In reaction to the English Civil War (1642–1651), Thomas Hobbes argued that we cannot live in a community governed by rules of morality unless the system is set up so as to make it in each person's interest to abide by those rules. According to Hobbes, that can only be achieved through a powerful sovereign holding the monopoly on the

a 'proto-positivist'.[191] Grotius was above all a brilliant system-builder, who constructed a more or less consistent and logical system of the law of nations on the basis of the legal traditions of antiquity, medieval theology, canon law, Roman law, and the writings of humanists and scholastics.[192]

Both Gentili's *De jure belli libri tres* and Grotius' *De jure belli ac pacis libri tres* could perhaps be considered as general textbooks on international law in the modern sense.[193] However, in contrast to Gentili, Grotius understands the law of nations to be conventional and distinguishable from natural law as such.[194]

Grotius confirmed the unity of human society despite the diverging political and legal orders of modern States. The confrontation with the wars of religion during the sixteenth and seventeenth centuries forced him to abandon the universal religious inspiration of natural law. He attempted to restore unity by making the law of peoples dependent on a higher natural law that would in principle be knowable by the rational human mind.

The natural law school also included Samuel Pufendorf (1632–1694), whose principal work *De jure naturae et gentium*[195] appeared in 1672, and Christian von Wolff (1679–1754), whose most important work on international law, *Jus gentium methodo scientifica pertractatum*,[196] was published in 1749. Wolff used the device of a theoretical 'society of nations' (*civitas gentium maxima*) in order to provide a supreme source from which the law applying to relations between sovereign States could be derived.[197]

Another towering figure was the Swiss scholar Emmerich de Vattel (1714–1767), whose *Le droit des gens*[198] appeared in 1758. According to de Vattel, the State has the sovereign power to interpret natural law. Vattel emphasised that *jus gentium* was a law between States that did not as such apply to citizens.[199] In doing so, he laid the foundations for the classic theory of international law, which regards only States as subjects of international law. Furthermore, his impact on the emerging discipline of international law in particular in the US was substantial, and his work remained influential until well into the nineteenth century.[200]

While Vattel, Wolff, and Pufendorf lay the groundwork for positivism – a theory of law holding that the answer to the question whether a given norm is legally valid and hence belongs to a given legal system depends on its sources and not on its merits[201] – in international law, they were writing during a period of dominance of natural law

use of force. See in particular T Hobbes, *Leviathan* (1651), JCA Gaskin (ed) (Oxford, OUP, 2008). Hobbes' theory can be described as a 'social contract' theory, though markedly different than those put forward by J-J Rousseau and J Locke. See further J Wolff, *An Introduction to Political Philosophy*, 3rd edn (Oxford, OUP, 2015) Chapter 2. See also Schneewind (n 179) 82–100, referring to Hobbes as 'Grotianism at the limits'.

[191] Capps (n 181) 76–77.

[192] See Lesaffer (n 69) 423.

[193] Wijffels (n 73) 43–45.

[194] H Lauterpacht, 'The Grotian Tradition in International Law' (1946) 23 *BYIL* 1, 21–22.

[195] S Pufendorf, *De jure naturae et gentium libri octo* (Oxford, Clarendon, 1934).

[196] C von Wolff, *Jus gentium methodo scientifica pertractatum in quo jus gentium naturale ab eo, quod voluntarii, pactitii et consuetudinarii est, accurate distinguitur* (Prostat in officina libraria Rengeriana, 1749); and C von Wolff, *The Law of Nations Treated According to a Scientific Method* (Oxford, Clarendon Press, 1934). Wolff subsequently published an abridged version of his main argument: C von Wolff, *Institutiones juris naturae et gentium in quibus ex ipsa hominis natura continuo nexu omnes obligationes et jura omnia deducuntur* (Apud F ex N Pezzana, 1769).

[197] See Wijffels (n 73) 53.

[198] E de Vattel, *Le droit des gens, ou principes de la loi naturelle, appliqués à la conduite et aux affaires des nations et des souverains* (Leiden, Compagnie, 1758); and E de Vattel, *The Law of Nations, or the Principles of Natural Law, Applied to the Conduct and to the Affairs of Nations and Sovereigns* (1758), CG Fenwich (trans) (Washington DC, Carnegie Institute, 1916).

[199] ibid.

[200] See Lesaffer (n 69) 425.

[201] J Gardner, 'Legal Positivism: 5½ Myths' (2001) 46 *American Journal of Jurisprudence* 199.

theory, and their approach was therefore dependent on the foundations and principles of natural law.[202]

Immanuel Kant's approach to international law is rather different, for two reasons in particular: (i) Kant questions the status of the law of nations as a legal system as 'nations do not stand under any common external constraint'; and (ii) Kant regards Grotius, as well as Pufendorf and Vattel, as 'sorry comforters', whose writings are 'still dutifully quoted in justification of military aggression'.[203] For Kant, all people enjoy a 'right to communal possession of the earth's surface. Since the earth is a globe, they cannot disperse over an infinite area, but must necessarily tolerate one another's company'.[204] However, a single power under a 'universal monarchy' is undesirable, as 'laws progressively lose their impact as the government increases its range'.[205] However, Kant argues that 'distress must force men to form a state which is not a cosmopolitan commonwealth under a single ruler, but a lawful *federation* under a commonly accepted *international right*'.[206]

Put differently, reason requires States to enter into a non-coercive federative structure of republican States.[207] In *Toward Perpetual Peace*, structured as if itself a peace treaty, Kant aims to show how the closer a State approaches perpetual peace with its potential enemies, the more secure citizens' juridical freedom will be. Kant's account of the law of nations is a recognition of the need for non-coercive containment of coercive powers. Yet at the same time, his point is that our ultimate allegiance does not belong to a temporal power, but to the 'moral laws elaborated autonomously within an ever-expanding ethical community'.[208]

[202] See A Orakhelashvili, 'The Origins of Consensual Positivism – Pufendorf, Wolff and Vattel' in Orakhelashvili (n 65) 94–95. It should of course be kept in mind that Vattel, Wolff, and Pufendorf differed quite substantially in their approaches. With respect to Wolff and Vattel, compare, for example, the following two quotes: Wolff, *The Law of Nations Treated According to a Scientific Method* (n 196), Prolegomena, 11: 'Nature herself has established society among all nations and binds them to preserve society. For nature herself has established society among men and binds them to preserve it. Therefore, since this obligation, as coming from the law of nature, is necessary and immutable, it cannot be changed for the reason that nations have united into a state. Therefore society, which nature has established among individuals, still exists among nations and consequently, after states have been established in accordance with the law of nature and nations have arisen thereby, nature herself also must be said to have established society among all nations and bound them to preserve society'; and Vattel, *The Law of Nations* (n 198), Preface, 9: 'In the very outset of my work, it will be found that I differ entirely from Monsieur Wolf in the manner of establishing the foundations of that species of law of nations which we call voluntary. Monsieur Wolf deduces it from the idea of a great republic (*civitatis maximæ*) instituted by nature herself, and of which all nations of the world are members. According to him, the voluntary law of nations is, as it were, the civil law of that great republic. This idea does not satisfy me; nor do I think the fiction of such a republic either admissible in itself, or capable of affording sufficiently solid grounds on which to build the rules of the universal law of nations, which shall necessarily claim the obedient acquiescence of sovereign states. I acknowledge no other natural society between nations than that which nature has established between mankind in general. It is essential to every civil society (*civitati*) that each member have resigned a part of his right to the body of the society, and that there exist in it an authority capable of commanding all the members, of giving them laws, and of compelling those who should refuse to obey. Nothing of this kind can be conceived or supposed to subsist between nations. Each sovereign state claims, and actually possesses an absolute independence on all the others'. Many thanks to Alex Mills and Kimberley Trapp for drawing attention to these two passages. See also P Allott, *The Health of Nations: Society and Law beyond the State* (Cambridge, CUP, 2002) 412–16, paras 14.40–14.45.

[203] I Kant, *Perpetual Peace: A Philosophical Sketch* (1795), HS Reiss (ed) (Cambridge, CUP, 2003) 103 (ZeF 8:355). See also A Perreau-Saussine, 'Immanuel Kant on International Law' in Besson and Tasioulas (n 33) 53–76.

[204] Kant (n 203) 106.

[205] ibid, 113.

[206] I Kant, *On the Common Saying 'This May be True in Theory but it does not Apply in Practice'* (1793), HS Reiss (ed) (Cambridge, CUP, 2003) 90.

[207] Capps (n 181) 80–91.

[208] Perreau-Saussine (n 203) 55, 58, 60 and 69.

In the eighteenth century, a normative approach to international relations was developed, often referred to as the '*droit public de l'Europe*', which was characterised by understanding the international community as a 'system' governed by principles similar to natural laws.[209] In that sense, the '*droit public de l'Europe*' bridged the dichotomy between a natural law approach and the positive law oriented '*usus modernus*' approach, and strove to reduce the tension between a normative approach to international relations and Realpolitik. '*Droit public de l'Europe*' became a set phrase referring to a set of principles and rules governing international relations and international law, based on meta-legal principles, domestic constitutional law, and international custom and diplomacy.[210]

During the nineteenth and twentieth centuries, while natural law was sometimes used,[211] to underscore the universality of international law, that is to say the fact that it applied both to European and non-European States,[212] it was put on the back foot by the rise of positivism. However, gravely affected by the First and Second World Wars and by the instrumentalisation of law by totalitarian regimes, international law thinking incorporates important natural law tendencies, which nonetheless rarely – if ever – question the contribution of positivism. Alfred Verdross[213] and Hersch Lauterpacht,[214] for example, while both students of Hans Kelsen, set out to go beyond a critique of positive law from within a positivist theoretical framework. Both connected an appreciation of positivism to a grounding in natural law, thereby arguably attempting to bridge a gap between natural and positive law that had widened with Pufendorf and Vattel.[215]

Starting from what natural law thinkers see as the inadequacy of positivism to provide a solid basis for the binding nature of international law (such as the hypothetical *Grundnorm*), contemporary natural law theory posits the pre-existence of a transcendent law in relation to which formal rules would be subordinate. Positive law would only be valid to the extent that it complies with the eternal and universal rules derived from the rational and social nature of humans. Modern natural law thinking regards international natural law as the application of justice in international affairs.[216]

This justice would be free from any subjectivity, because it forms part of an objective universe of ethical values that everyone can determine on the basis of experience. International law counts as positive law, because it protects fundamental human interests and values. An example of that mechanism is the rise of *jus cogens* as positive law.[217] That body of law, which is predominantly inspired by the protection of the dignity of every human being, is binding for States independently of their consent, as no State can validly claim that a treaty could justify genocide or slavery.

[209] See eg G Bonnot de Mably, *Le droit public de l'Europe, fondé sur les traitez conclus jusqu'en l'année 1740* (The Hague, J Van Duren, 1746).
[210] See Wijffels (n 73) 26–27 and 55–56.
[211] eg R Phillimore, *Commentaries upon International Law*, 3rd edn, Vol I (London, Butterworths, 1871) 15.
[212] See also Orakhelashvili (n 162) 15–19.
[213] See eg A Verdross, *Universelles Völkerrecht*, 3rd edn (Berlin, Duncker and Humblot, 1984). See also B Simma, 'The Contribution of Alfred Verdross to the Theory of International Law' (1995) *EJIL* 33.
[214] See eg Lauterpacht (n 164); Lauterpacht (n 194). See also IGM Scobbie, 'The Theorist as Judge: Hersch Lauterpacht's Concept of the International Judicial Function' (1997) *EJIL* 264.
[215] G Gordon, 'Natural Law in International Legal Theory: Linear and Dialectical Presentations' in Orford and Hoffmann (n 62) 291.
[216] See eg JLA Garcia, 'Topics in the New Natural Law Theory' (2001) *American Journal of Jurisprudence* 51; RP George, *In Defense of Natural Law* (Oxford, OUP, 1999); RP George (ed), *Natural Law* (Aldershot, Ashgate, 2003); K Greenawalt, 'How Persuasive Is Natural Law Theory?' (2000) *Notre Dame Law Review* 1647.
[217] On which see eg R Kolb, *Théorie du jus cogens international: Essai de relecture du concept* (Paris, PUF, 2001); A Orakhelashvili, *Peremptory Norms in International Law* (Oxford, OUP, 2006).

At the same time, some natural law scholars argue that international natural law theory has the vocation of limiting the excesses of globalisation, by protecting global public goods that are not adequately protected by current positive law.[218] The legacy of natural law could therefore be discerned in theories proffering an appreciation of emergent global or transnational public goods that suggest new ways of conceptualising political organisation under changing historical circumstances, establishing new and naturally-occurring grounds for political organisation, tied to a certain appreciation of human nature.[219]

More generally, principles of natural law find expression in the contestation of international rules and institutions that are considered illegitimate or undemocratic.[220]

B. Positivism

As mentioned above, Pufendorf, Wolff, and Vattel had already emphasised the importance of consent and agreement in creating international law and in granting it binding force, and by and large allocated natural law a role that could in due course be taken over by positive international law.[221]

The English scholars John Selden (1548–1654) and Richard Zouche (1590–1660) are regarded as the first positivists, for whom only treaties and customary law counted as sources of international law. The star of positivism would rise in the eighteenth century, with important contributions by the Dutch scholar Cornelis van Bynkershoek (1673–1743),[222] and the German scholars Johann Jakob Moser (1701–1785) and Georg Friedrich von Martens (1756–1821), whose most important work bears the revealing title *Précis du droit des gens moderne de l'Europe, fondé sur les traités et l'usage*.[223] Nevertheless, it is important to bear in mind that while their focus lay on the positive law of nations, most of the authors of treatises on the subject writing in the seventeenth and eighteenth centuries acknowledged the existence and relevance of natural law and justice and even gave them a place in their system.[224]

Theoretical conceptions founded on legal positivism were put forward in the nineteenth century as a reaction against seventeenth century natural law thinking, which sought the quintessence of law outside law. Positivism maintains that law is what the State, as the representation of the moral ideal, mandates and imposes. Positivism considers only positive law as actual law, which implies a clear limitation of what law is in comparison to

[218] On global public goods, see eg I Kaul et al (eds), *Providing Global Public Goods: Managing Globalization* (New York, OUP, 2003); I Kaul, I Grunberg and MA Stern (eds), *Global Public Goods: International Cooperation in the 21st Century* (New York, OUP, 1999). See also S Cogolati, L Hamid, and N Vanstappen, 'Global Public Goods and Democracy in International Legal Scholarship' (2016) 5 *Cambridge Journal of International and Comparative Law* 4–30.

[219] Gordon (n 215) 300–301. That does not mean that proponents of the global public goods approach generally consider their views to be based on theories of natural law. See also Section V(I).

[220] See eg JM Coicaud and D Warner (eds), *Ethics and International Affairs: Extent and Limits* (Tokyo, UN UP, 2001); P De Greiff and C Cronin (eds), *Global Justice and Transnational Politics: Essays on the Moral and Political Challenges of Globalization* (Cambridge, MIT Press, 2002); JH Dunning (ed), *Making Globalization Good: The Moral Challenges of Global Capitalism* (Oxford, OUP, 2003).

[221] See Orakhelashvili (n 202) 93–110.

[222] C Van Bynkershoek, *De dominio maris dissertatio* (Lugduni Batavorum, Apud Joannem van Kerckhem, 1744). Bynkershoek argued in favour of effective *occupatio* as title to territory as part of an argument aiming at establishing the freedom of the high seas.

[223] GF von Martens, *Précis du droit des gens moderne de l'Europe, fondé sur les traités et l'usage: pour server d'introduction à un cours politique et diplomatique* (JC Dieterich, 1789).

[224] See Lesaffer (n 69) 426.

natural law theories. A rule has legal value when it can trace its coming into existence to an act of creation by a competent public authority.

In that respect, the most important function for legal scholarship is distinguishing the *lex lata* from the *lex ferenda*; a distinction that had become blurred in natural law theories. While codifications during the nineteenth century allowed a much clearer identification of positive law, international law seemed especially prone to failing to distinguish the law as actually applicable from the law that one desired to be applicable. Positivist scholars take the view that natural law principles can no longer form part of what the law is. All law-generating processes that cannot be traced back to the expression of the will of a State cannot be considered as a formal source of law.

However, determining the *lex lata* does not necessarily imply the rejection of moral values. It is possible to believe in the necessity of moral rules without admitting that whatever they prescribe should immediately become legally binding rules. In other words, the positivist method does not ipso facto approve of the law as it is. In fact, a correct identification of the *lex lata* makes a more acute and direct criticism of the applicable rules possible.

A legal theory that derives the binding force of the law from its source within a State de facto also questions the binding nature of constitutional law, the basic rules of which cannot be traced back to the State itself. Rather, they are a precondition for a State to exist that can promulgate laws. Likewise, will-based theories often lead to the questioning of the legal character of international law. A focus on formal hierarchy makes it theoretically impossible to create rights between sovereign and equal States that create law and are at the same time subject to it.

Along the same lines, traditional legal positivism in the nineteenth and twentieth centuries as a rule took the method of law-making within States as the model on the basis of which all other law-making had to be assessed. An eminent example was the nineteenth century British legal philosopher John Austin, who argued that law within a State amounts to a command issued by the sovereign with which the subjects have to comply, the so-called 'command theory' of law. Internally, Austin viewed sovereignty as a question of fact in that the power of the sovereign was above and beyond the law, as the source of all legal authority lay in sovereign commands.[225] If the command is disobeyed, a judge can intervene to impose compliance, and if the judgment is disobeyed, the executive can ensure enforcement. Such mechanisms are absent in interstate relationships. Furthermore, such mechanisms would be contrary to the idea of sovereignty, which per se excludes the existence of any higher authority. Externally, Austin viewed sovereignty as a question of fact in that 'obligations' on the international plane could only derive from the voluntary acts of sovereigns: thus Austin rejected the idea that international law, properly considered, was law.[226] International law therefore merely amounts to 'positive morality'.[227] For lack of a sovereign, relationships in the international order are based on power rather than law. Treaties merely represent a temporary point of balance in the power relationships between States, and can be renounced when their provisions are contrary to the national interest. Echoes of that approach, leaving aside evolutions as regards its theoretical underpinnings, are still part of the current debate, for example within the context of realist approaches to international law, which will be explored further below.[228] Nevertheless, a number of legal

[225] Mills (n 6) 191.
[226] ibid.
[227] Austin (n 161) 20, also classifying constitutional law as 'positive morality merely': ibid, 216.
[228] See Section V(E).

positivists have taken it upon themselves to find a theoretical basis for the binding force of international law.

A strand of positivism, represented by thinkers such as Georg Jellinek,[229] attempts to broaden the classic concept of law by granting treaties the status of an order. They succeed in leaving out a higher supranational authority that would promulgate international law by regarding the latter as a form of externalised national law.[230] This external public law is merely an aspect of constitutional law that delimits the powers to represent the State vis-à-vis other States. Indeed, apart from laying out the procedure to consent to and ratify treaties, the law of treaties in practice determines the organs of the State that are empowered to conclude treaties with other States.

While the State binds itself internationally, its exclusive autonomous will is preserved. The will of the State is sovereign and only it can bring into existence international law. In exercising its sovereignty, a State can determine its own fate and can if need be limit itself by creating international law. The latter's legal character is determined entirely by its incorporation in national law, which implies the denial of the existence of international law as a separate branch of the law. In fact, pooling sovereignty by entering into mutual obligations is a priori impossible, as the law that regulates the external relations of a State is purely dependent on the will of that State.

Jellinek suggested the theory of self-obligation to explain international law's binding force: as the State can bind itself in its own legal system to private entities and persons, it can also bind itself internationally.[231] While Jellinek sought to justify the binding force of international law (albeit as external public law), he admits that in case of conflict, the internal law of the State should prevail when the existence of the State is at stake. Jellinek's approach to international law determines that States are only bound by treaties to the extent that it is in their interest.[232] Jellinek therefore seeks to integrate the internal and external dimensions of State action while maintaining both the primacy and unitary nature of the State and its capacity to be bound by obligations contracted with other States.[233]

In his quest for grounding the binding force of international law, Triepel draws a distinction between the common will and the individual will of the States. In contrast to Jellinek's statist view, Triepel argued that the will of one individual State cannot as such create international law: it can only contribute to the formation of a common will that arises out of the unification of particular wills, a process he called '*Vereinbarung*'.[234] The latter can also take place silently, thereby granting binding legal force to customary international law. Faced with the problem of how the subjective will of the State can contribute to an objective international legal order, Triepel put forward an abstract form of '*Vereinbarung*' as a hypothetical 'agreement' ex ante between States that is hierarchically superior to the rules of international law created through it. While the common will is not created by a higher organ, Triepel uses the presence of a superior will that States cannot escape and that in other words leads a continued existence independent of their continued support.

While the common will is only presupposed among those participating in the '*Vereinbarung*', Lassa Oppenheim's common consent theory also incorporates the

[229] G Jellinek, *Die rechtliche Natur der Staatenverträge: ein Beitrag zur juristischen Konstruktion des Völkerrechts* (Vienna, Hölder, 1880).
[230] See eg PKL Zorn, *Die Zukunft des Völkerrechts* (Berlin, Voss, 1918).
[231] Jellinek (n 229) 5–7.
[232] ibid, 40.
[233] A Lev, 'The Transformation of International Law in the 19th Century' in Orakhelashvili (n 65) 135.
[234] H Triepel, 'Les rapports entre le droit interne et le droit international' (1923) 1 *RdC* 77.

minority of non-consenting States. The validity of international law is to be found in the explicit or implicit common consent of the great majority of States. Oppenheim's defence of the existence of international law starts from international practice, which shows that States do acknowledge the existence of some rules. There is no need for an international legislator, as a rule of law can exist on the basis of common consent that it will be enforced. International law exists, but only through the common will of civilised States. Indeed, for Oppenheim, the common European tradition guarantees similar notions of justice within a 'Family of Nations' that share the same concept of civilisation.[235] As the existence of international law is predicated on the common consent of States, sovereignty plays a crucial role in Oppenheim's theory.[236]

Around 1920, the Viennese school of public law revisited the classic positivist conceptions. This current, of which Hans Kelsen would be the preeminent representative,[237] could be described as 'neo-positivist' or 'normativist'. Normativism maintains that all law ought to be 'positive', ie wilfully created by human intervention. However, the existence of a rule cannot be derived from a certain historical material source, such as State consent. The Kelsenian 'Pure Theory of Law' grounds the validity of international law within the international legal norms themselves: legal norms have a formal, ahistorical and apolitical source within the system.[238] This formal source is turned into a source of law, because a higher systemic norm grants it that status. That higher norm in turn derives its validity from the legal character of its source of law. That regression finally leads back to the so-called 'Basic Norm' (*Grundnorm*), the validity of which cannot be derived from a higher systemic norm. Kelsen views international law as a monistic,[239] closed system of norms free from any natural law or moral presupposition. For Kelsen, law is not subject to but coincident with the State, which he regards as a legal pyramidal structure. The constitution as the basic norm of the State forms the top of the internal legal order, while the binding force of treaty law is grounded in the principle of *pacta sunt servanda*. Equating the international Basic Norm with *pacta sunt servanda* appears to imply an implicit admission that treaty law is hierarchically inferior to customary international law. However, for Kelsen, the Basic Norm as highest rule of law was not produced by another formal source of law. Hence, not having been promulgated by a law-creating organ in accordance with a legal procedure, the Basic Norm cannot be a norm of positive law. Its existence cannot therefore be proven: the norm at the top of the legal pyramid is a hypothesis or an axiom.

In turn, HLA Hart built his conception of the concept of law on the notion of a rule of recognition, ie, a social rule practised by judges and other officials that specifies the conditions for all legal norms to belong to the legal system, and is therefore constitutive of the system. However, in contrast with Kelsen, Hart never adopted Kelsen's view that all laws in

[235] L Oppenheim, *International Law*, 1st edn (Longmans, Green & Co, 1905) Vol I, 7–12.

[236] See also M Schmoeckel, 'Consent and Caution: Lassa Oppenheim and His Reaction to World War I' in R Lesaffer (ed), *Peace Treaties and International Law in European History: From the Late Middle Ages to World War One* (Cambridge, CUP, 2004) 270–88.

[237] Further on Kelsen's contribution to international law, see eg Leben (n 38); D Zolo, 'Hans Kelsen: International Peace through International Law' (1998) 9 *EJIL* 306; F Rigaux, 'Hans Kelsen on International Law' (1998) 9 *EJIL* 325; A Carty, 'The Continuing Influence of Kelsen on the General Perception of the Discipline of International Law' (1998) 9 *EJIL* 344; C Jabloner, 'Kelsen and his Circle: The Viennese Years' (1998) 9 *EJIL* 368; Von Bernstorff (n 38); J Kammerhofer, 'Hans Kelsen's Place in International Legal Theory' in Orakhelashvili (n 65) 143–67.

[238] H Kelsen, *Das Problem der Souveränität und die Theorie des Völkerrechts: Beitrag zu einer reinen Rechtslehre*, 2nd edn (Tübingen, Mohr, 1928). See further Kelsen (n 38); H Kelsen, *The Law of the United Nations* (Praeger, 1951).

[239] On monism and dualism, see Chapter 4, Section III.

the world must form one unity in a single legal system. Hart took the view that there exist international legal obligations, but no international legal system. In particular, international law lacks the secondary rules necessary for a legal system and therefore remains a primitive legal order composed of primary rules of obligation.[240] Put differently, as international law does not have courts and legislatures like those of States, international law resembles a primitive legal system.[241] Furthermore, according to Hart, international law arguably also lacks a unifying rule of recognition specifying sources of law.[242] Yet at the same time, Hart dismissed the notion of sovereignty as something external or prior to international law. Indeed, according to Hart, there is 'no way of knowing what sovereignty states have, till we know what the forms of international law are and whether or not they are mere empty forms'.[243] More broadly, Hart's variation on 'positivism', which is founded on collective belief and the internal perspective while rejecting Austin's idea of law as based on the threat of coercion, may arguably be applied to international law. In that way, even if such a theory was not developed by Hart himself, his positivism leaves scope for a conception of international law as law because States and other actors in the international legal order believe it to be law and mostly act accordingly.

While positivist approaches to international law have increasingly been subject to critiques founded in other theoretical approaches, a pragmatic espousal of positivism or at least of the importance of positive law remains prevalent in the practice of international law.[244] Indeed, a common approach to international law consists in adopting a positivist, ie, inductive and empirical, methodology, without necessarily adhering to a positivist theoretical framework, in the sense of a commitment to the idea that States are the key actors in international law and are independent, free, equal, and sovereign (seen as an a priori value above international law).[245]

C. Objectivism

The emergence of objectivist thinking at the start of the twentieth century is connected with the rise of sociology as a scientific discipline. To objectivist thinkers, such as Georges Scelle and Léon Duguit, the validity of international law can be empirically found in the social environment of which it is a part. This social environment contains 'objective norms' the formation of which does not depend on the subjective will of States. In contrast to voluntarism and normativism, objectivism does not focus solely or even predominantly on formal sources of law, but demands attention to the social context as a material source of international law.

240 Hart (n 16) 214.

241 For a critique of Hart's account, see eg Mills (n 6) 100–101 and Waldron (n 17) 213–18, both pointing out that rules on the creation of treaties are clear examples of secondary norms. Compare M Payandeh, 'The Concept of International Law in the Jurisprudence of H.L.A. Hart' (2010) 21 *EJIL* 981, arguing that rather than asking whether international law encompasses legislative, judicative, and executive structures comparable to the municipal system in form, we should ask whether the international order has structures which effectively fulfil the same fundamental functions attributed to law. If international law fulfils this requirement there are no grounds to deny it the status of a legal system. According to Payandeh, 'Hart offers no compelling reason why a legal system necessarily would have closely to resemble the archetype of the municipal legal order of a modern constitutional state'.

242 Hart (n 16) 214. See further M Giudice, 'Hart and Kelsen on International Law' in L Green and B Leiter (eds), *Oxford Studies in Philosophy of Law* (Oxford, OUP, 2013) Vol II, 148–49.

243 Hart (n 16) 224.

244 See J Kammerhofer, 'International Legal Positivism' in Orford and Hoffmann (n 62) 407–408.

245 Mills (n 6) 191–92.

Scelle argued that the content of objective law is determined by the need of coexistence.[246] The universal society carries within its structure the objective norms necessary for its survival. Scelle emphasises the social need for regulation as a material source of law, which through the intervention of formal sources of law is transformed into positive law. Nevertheless, the binding character of this positive law is not founded in the fact that it originates from a formal source of law, but on its compatibility with 'objective law', ie its material source or 'social necessity' (*nécessité sociale*). The compatibility of positive law with objective law is presupposed, but if the positive norm is nevertheless found to contradict the objective norm, Scelle's theory contemplates the possibility of a legitimate revolution. Rather like natural law norms, objective norms are part of a pre-existing system of which positive law is only a reflection. Objective law imposes itself on its subjects independently of their will or even of any consciousness of their existence.[247]

Duguit put forward a theory according to which objective law is brought into existence by social group consciousness.[248] He replaced the transcendent principles of natural law by the observation of social phenomena. In contrast to positivist thinkers, Duguit argued that it is not the State (being as it is an imaginary construction) that creates legal rules, but society, much like every social group promulgates its own rules of behaviour. Within a society, social feelings and sentiments of justice are always present that prescribe a certain behaviour. At a certain point in time, a consciousness takes shape within society that certain behavioural norms are in fact legal norms that need to be enforced. These norms are objective, in the sense that they are based on social necessity and are therefore independent of any State will. International law too contains objective norms, as the same social feelings and sentiments of justice present within States can also be found within the international community. Nevertheless, within the international community, 'intersocial feelings' are present rather than sentiments of close interdependence between members of the same group. Duguit attempted to do away with the dominant role of States in international law, and granted individuals an exclusive role in its formation.

D. Marxism

Marxist theory of international law cannot be understood separately from Marxist political and economic theory more generally and in particular from historical materialism.[249] In essence, that implies that any Marxist theory of international law is grounded in the conviction that idealist theories of international law, ie, those that rely on the power of ideas to explain the current state of international law, are inadequate. Instead, Marxism

[246] G Scelle, *Précis de droit des gens, principes et systématique* (Paris, Sirey, 1934). See also H Thierry, 'The Thought of Georges Scelle' (1990) *EJIL* 193; A Cassese, 'Remarks on Scelle's Theory of "Role Splitting" (*dédoublement fonctionnel*) in international law' (1990) *EJIL* 210; Koskenniemi (n 90) 327–38.

[247] cp also the work of Charles De Visscher, on which see eg P-M Dupuy, 'The European Tradition in International Law: Charles de Visscher. By Way of Introduction' (2000) *EJIL* 871; F Rigaux, 'An Exemplary Lawyer's Life (1884–1973)' (2000) *EJIL* 877; J Verhoeven, 'Charles de Visscher: Living and Thinking International Law' (2000) *EJIL* 887; P Couvreur, 'Charles de Visscher and International Justice' (2000) *EJIL* 905.

[248] L Duguit, *Traité de droit constitutionnel*, 3rd edn (Paris, Fontemoing, 1927). See further Koskenniemi (n 90) 297–302.

[249] S Marks, 'Introduction' in S Marks (ed), *International Law on the Left: Re-Examining Marxist Legacies* (Cambridge, CUP, 2008) 2; R Knox, 'Marxist Approaches to International Law' in Orford and Hoffmann (n 62) 306–307.

urges students of international law not to take international ideas and interpretations at face value, but to delve into the material conditions for their emergence and deployment.[250]

Arguably the most important Marxist theorist of international law is Evgeny Pashukanis, a Bolshevik lawyer who rose to prominence after the 1917 Russian Revolution. He was the main Soviet legal theorist in the 1920s and 1930s.[251] Pashukanis' theory of law is most fully set out in his seminal book, *The General Theory of Law and Marxism*, published originally in 1924,[252] where he sought to develop a theory of law based on the economic and social theory of historical materialism as developed by Karl Marx and Friedrich Engels.[253] In particular, in answer to the question 'in what sense can it be said that law regulates social relations?', Pashukanis replies that 'law represents the mystified form of a specific social relation' and that 'under certain conditions the *regulation* of social relations assumes a *legal character*'.[254] In Pashukanis' view, international law was the oldest form of law, because the exchange of commodities originally took place not between individuals, but between communities. Nevertheless, international law only came to full bloom through capitalism.[255] Pashukanis' theory of international law has in recent years been revived and further developed by China Miéville, who placed particular emphasis on the importance of coercion and violence as inherent in the legal character of international law.[256]

Important contemporary strands of Marxist theory of international law have focused on critique of ideology, defined by Susan Marks as 'ways in which meaning serves to establish and sustain relations of domination',[257] and on the role of international law in exploitation and domination of the developing world.[258]

E. Realism

Realist theories hold that law, and especially international law, is essentially epiphenomenal, in the sense that States, and in particular powerful States, will only obey international law when it is in their real or perceived interest to do so.[259] In that sense, traditional 'non-realist' theories of international law not only obfuscate power and interests, but are also destabilising and counterproductive. Well-intentioned efforts to institutionalise structures such as the ICC[260] can increase disorder and violence.[261]

[250] Marks (n 249) 3.
[251] Knox (n 249) 315.
[252] EB Pashukanis, *The General Theory of Law and Marxism* (New Brunswick, Transaction Publishers, 2002 (1924)).
[253] Marxist theory does not, of course, hold the monopoly of the application of insights from economic theory to international legal issues. See notably on the work of law and economics scholars on international law D Danielsen, 'International Law and Economics: Letting Go of the "Normal" in Pursuit of an Ever-Elusive Real' in Orford and Hoffmann (n 62) 452–70. See further: E Kontorovich and F Parisi (eds), *Economic Analysis of International Law* (Cheltenham, Edward Elgar, 2016).
[254] Pashukanis (n 252) 78–79.
[255] Pashukanis (n 252) 175; Knox (n 249) 316.
[256] C Miéville, *Between Equal Rights: A Marxist Theory of International Law* (Leiden, Brill, 2005).
[257] S Marks, *The Riddle of All Constitutions: International Law, Democracy and the Critique of Ideology* (Oxford, OUP, 2000) 10.
[258] See eg BS Chimni, *International Law and World Order: A Critique of Contemporary Approaches*, 2nd edn (Cambridge, CUP, 2017).
[259] Crawford (n 53) 29. See generally O Jütersonke, 'Realist Approaches to International Law' in Orford and Hoffmann (n 62) 327–43.
[260] On which see also Chapter 17 on International Criminal Law.
[261] S Krasner, 'Realist Views of International Law' (2002) 96 *American Society of International Law Proceedings* 268.

One consequence of the realist view, as notably put forward by Hans Morgenthau, is that the common distinction between legal disputes and disputes over conflicts of interests is of little use for any analysis that aims to have a practical impact, as all disputes are essentially related to the interests of the parties involved.[262] Morgenthau took the view that mainstream international lawyers had defined law in a manner excluding elements vital to it, in particular sociological, ethical, and other factors that constantly enter into, change and introduce rules. Law can therefore not be ascertained independently from political analyses. Furthermore, international law is only marginally binding, as it often lacks sanctions and therefore only amounts to mere subjective wishes.[263]

Along the same lines, the so-called 'new realists' essentially argue that since States are primarily motivated by self-interest, compliance with international law is optional and therefore nothing more than high-minded talk. It follows that international law is mostly irrelevant to determining how States, and in particular the US, deal with international threats, specifically those posed by terrorists, and that the US should obstruct any efforts to establish jurisdiction by international courts and tribunals, such as notably the ICC, over US citizens. That theory also has consequences for US constitutional law, in that it presumes that the President should be left to pursue the necessary international policies without interference by the US Congress or by courts.[264]

F. New Haven School of International Law

Developed by Myres McDougal and Harold Laswell, the New Haven School of international law (named after the city of New Haven, Connecticut, where Yale Law School is located) put forward a policy-oriented approach to international law, which aimed to substitute pragmatic interdisciplinary and social scientific reasoning for the traditional 'legalism'.[265] According to the approach proposed by them, decision-makers and lawyers have to treat each case in its individual context with a specific problem-solving aim.

Rules were regarded as merely trends of previous decisions, and lawyers were explicitly given a policy-making role.[266] At the same time, the New Haven School can be seen as a variant of liberal internationalism, an approach to international law geared towards the application of broadly-framed liberal values to international governance, often traced back to Kant's *Toward Perpetual Peace*,[267] and given renewed impetus by Woodrow Wilson's 14 points.[268] However, the New Haven School's belief that international law should serve

[262] H Morgenthau, *Die internationale Rechtspflege, ihr Wesen und ihre Grenzen* (Leipzig, Noske, 1929). See also H Morgenthau, *Politics among Nations: The Struggle for Power and Peace* (New York, Knopf, 1948).

[263] H Morgenthau, 'Positivism, Functionalism, and International Law' (1940) 34 *AJIL* 267. See also M Koskenniemi, *From Apology to Utopia: The Structure of International Legal Argument* (Cambridge, CUP, 2005) 197–201.

[264] See eg RJ Delahunty and J Yoo, 'Executive Power v. International Law' (2007) 30 *Harvard Journal of Law and Public Policy* 73; J Goldsmith and E Posner, *The Limits of International Law* (Oxford, OUP, 2007). For a powerful critique of this theory, see JD Ohlin, *The Assault on International Law* (Oxford, OUP, 2015).

[265] See HD Lasswell and M McDougal, *Jurisprudence for a Free Society: Studies in Law, Science and Policy* (New Haven, New Haven Press, 1992). See also WM Reisman, S Wiessner and AR Willard, 'The New Haven School: A Brief Introduction' (2007) 32 *Yale Journal of International Law* 575.

[266] See Koskenniemi (n 263) 474–80; H Saberi, 'Yale's Policy Science and International Law: Between Legal Formalism and Policy Conceptualism' in Orford and Hoffmann (n 62) 427–51.

[267] See above, Section V(A).

[268] See above, Section IV(F)(ii).

(liberal) foreign policy interests was often criticised for equating to a US-centric and hence limited approach to the international legal order.[269]

G. Global Administrative Law

Global administrative law,[270] which starts from the observation that much of global governance can be understood as regulation and administration, and that we are witnessing the emergence of a 'global administrative space', can be described as

> a space in which the strict dichotomy between domestic and international has largely broken down, in which administrative functions are performed in often complex interplays between officials and institutions on different levels, and in which regulation may be highly effective despite its predominantly non-binding forms.[271]

In the protagonists' own words, this relatively new field of international law is essentially preoccupied with

> the mechanisms, principles, practices, and supporting social understandings that promote or otherwise affect the accountability of global administrative bodies, in particular by ensuring [that] they meet adequate standards of transparency, participation, reasoned decision, and legality, and by providing effective review of the rules and decisions they make.[272]

Global administrative law essentially focuses on treaty-based intergovernmental regulatory bodies (such as the Food and Agriculture Organization, the World Bank, and WHO), but also on public-private partnerships (such as the Codex Alimentarius Commission), or nongovernmental organizations (such as the International Standardization Organization). It examines the design of global governance institutions and interactions with other extranational and national regulatory bodies, as well as their corresponding rules and decisions, procedural standards and mechanisms governing their processes.[273]

H. Cosmopolitanism

Cosmopolitan theories of international law and international relations build on core ideas from Kantian philosophy.[274] Notably, individual or liberal cosmopolitans regard the individual as the only unit of normative value with respect to the international legal system. Contemporary liberal cosmopolitans often build on John Rawls' seminal *A Theory of Justice*,[275] while at the same time globalising Rawls' update of the position of the individual

[269] See D Joyce, 'Liberal Internationalism' in Orford and Hoffmann (n 62) 474–80.
[270] Which is sometimes considered as a part of realism in the broader sense; see eg Jütersonke (n 259) 342.
[271] N Krisch and B Kingsbury, 'Introduction: Global Governance and Global Administrative Law in the International Legal Order' (2006) 17 *EJIL* 1.
[272] B Kingsbury, N Krisch and RB Stewart, 'The Emergence of Global Administrative Law' (2005) 68 *Law and Contemporary Problems* 15, 17.
[273] B Kingsbury, M Donaldson and R Vallejo, 'Global Administrative Law and Deliberative Democracy' in Orford and Hoffmann (n 62) 527. See further E Benvenisti, *The Law of Global Governance* (The Hague, Hague Academy of International Law, 2014).
[274] See W Werner and G Gordon, 'Kant, Cosmopolitanism, and International Law' in Orford and Hoffmann (n 62) 505–25. For reflections on international law from the perspective of moral philosophy more broadly, see eg S Besson, 'Moral Philosophy and International Law' in Orford and Hoffmann (n 62) 385–406.
[275] J Rawls, *A Theory of Justice*, revised edn (Cambridge, Belknap, 1999 (1971)).

in Kantian ethics instead of coming up with a different and altogether more limited set of normative requirements to be applied to international relations, as Rawls himself had done in *The Law of Peoples*.[276] For example, Thomas Pogge has argued that individuals are the ultimate units of concern for everyone and generate obligations that are binding on all, while 'the status of ultimate unit of concern attaches to every living human being equally'.[277]

By contrast, State-oriented or contractual cosmopolitans treat States as individuals and as the primary units of normative value, and hold that States have created cosmopolitan conditions and institutions on the basis of their free will as expressed in international law. Notably, Jürgen Habermas has argued in favour of preserving the State as the primary source and expression of democratic legitimacy, while subordinating its authority to an institution akin to a reformed UN,[278] with supranational capacity vested in a reformed UN Security Council and the UN General Assembly transformed into a World Parliament.[279] Other theorists, such as Ernst-Ulrich Petersmann, have steered a course closer to the currently existing international law, and have described certain developments through a constitutionalist lens.[280] The global constitutionalist school of thought offers an analytical framework that attempts to (empirically) describe the foundations of global governance, and (normatively) tackle the challenges posed by this 'new world order'.[281] While there is arguably no document that could currently serve as 'a global constitution',[282] global constitutionalists argue that the extension of constitutional principles and more centralised decision-making mechanisms at the global level would improve the democratic underpinnings of the international legal order.

A third form, sometimes termed innate cosmopolitanism, offers a collectivist perspective behind international law, based on the idea that proper legal rules will correspond with norms that characterise the reality of the world collective.[283] Notably, the 1951 Refugee Convention could be said to contain basic provisions that echo Kant's conception of cosmopolitan right, a basic norm of hospitality towards strangers.[284] Kant's cosmopolitan right of hospitality has also been the starting point for scholarship on the expansion of the concept of citizenship to alleviate the tension between universal human rights and State sovereignty.[285]

[276] J Rawls, *The Law of Peoples* (Harvard, Harvard UP, 1999). See AK Sen, *The Idea of Justice* (London, Penguin, 2009) 26, arguing that *The Law of Peoples* does not contain principles of justice, but rather principles of humanitarian behaviour.

[277] T Pogge, 'Cosmopolitanism and Sovereignty' (1992) 103 *Ethics* 49 and 103. Other examples of authors writing in that tradition are A Buchanan, *Justice, Legitimacy and Self-Determination: Moral Foundations for International Law* (Oxford, OUP, 2004) and K-C Tan, *Justice Without Borders: Cosmopolitanism, Nationalism and Patriotism* (Cambridge, CUP, 2004).

[278] J Habermas, *The Divided West* (Cambridge, Polity, 2006) 139–43.

[279] J Habermas, 'The Constitutionalization of International Law and the Legitimation Problems of a Constitution for World Society' (2008) 15 *Constellations* 449.

[280] E-U Petersmann, 'How to Constitutionalize International Law and Foreign Policy for the Benefit of Civil Society' (1999) 20 *MJIL* 1.

[281] On what this new order entails, see generally A-M Slaughter, *A New World Order* (Princeton, Princeton UP, 2005).

[282] But see B Fassbender, 'The United Nations Charter as Constitution of the International Community' (1998) 36 *Columbia Journal Transnational Law* 529.

[283] See eg G Teubner, *Constitutional Fragments: Societal Constitutionalism and Globalization* (Oxford, OUP, 2012); J Brunnée and SJ Toope, *Legitimacy and Legality in International Law: An Interactional Account* (Cambridge, CUP, 2010).

[284] Werner and Gordon (n 274) 521–23.

[285] See especially S Benhabib, *The Rights of Others: Aliens, Residents, and Citizens* (Cambridge, CUP, 2004).

I. Global Public Goods

Over the last decade, global public goods (GPGs) have been at the centre of the policy discourse of prominent international organisations, States, and non-governmental organisations alike. The concept emerged in 1999, in a seminal book sponsored by the United Nations Development Programme (UNDP), and finds its origins in economic theory.[286] The economic literature defines public goods as *non-rival*, since anyone can benefit from them without diminishing the quantity available to other consumers, and *non-excludable*, as no one can realistically be excluded from their consumption. Nowadays, an increasing number of public goods transcend national boundaries. For instance, climate change mitigation, the eradication of infectious diseases, the fight against corruption, or the protection of the ozone layer are all seen as GPGs. According to Inge Kaul and her co-authors, in addition to sharing the properties of non-rivalry and non-excludability indicated above, GPGs should produce benefits that are available worldwide and across social strata. In this regard, they define GPGs as 'outcomes (or intermediate products) that tend towards universality, in the sense that they benefit all countries, population groups, and generations'.[287]

The under-provision of such GPGs can be explained by drawing a parallel between the international and national levels. States, who – like individuals at the national level – are considered to act as rational, self-interested actors, will not be prepared to contribute or take upon themselves the task of providing GPGs without being somehow coerced to do so. Consider, for instance, major polluter countries that have never ratified the Kyoto Protocol.[288] States and other global actors have an incentive to free-ride on the efforts of others, and in the absence of agreed upon collective action, this will inevitably lead to global underinvestment and undersupply.

Surprisingly, the concept of GPGs has attracted little attention from international legal scholars, with the majority of authors writing on the topic coming from fields such as economics, political sciences, or international relations. International law has been relatively late in taking notice of the GPGs debate, since it took some years after the publication of the three UNDP volumes on GPGs before a limited, but slowly increasing number of legal scholars have started joining the debate. These legal scholars today claim that international law can serve as an instrument to contribute to the effective provision of GPGs. For instance, Bodansky argues that, '[s]ince GPGs cannot be adequately produced by the market, we need international institutions and international law to provide them'.[289] Likewise, Trachtman contends that international law 'comprises a kind of rudimentary government' to provide GPGs,[290] whereas Shaffer affirms that international law 'is required to produce global goods'.[291]

However, the vast majority of legal scholars writing on the topic argue that international law as it currently stands, with its cardinal principles of State sovereignty and State consent, constitutes a hindrance to the effective provision of GPGs. Shaffer, for example, warns

[286] See Kaul, Grunberg and Stern (n 218).
[287] ibid, 16.
[288] Kyoto Protocol to the United Nations Framework Convention (adopted 11 December 1997, entered into force 16 February 2005) 2303 UNTS 162.
[289] D Bodansky, 'What's in a Concept? Global Public Goods, International Law and Legitimacy' (2012) 23 *EJIL* 651, 652.
[290] JP Trachtman, *The Future of International Law: Global Government* (Cambridge, CUP, 2013) 7–9 and 68.
[291] G Shaffer, 'International Law and Global Public Goods in a Legal Pluralist World' (2012) 23 *EJIL* 669, 670–71.

that international law could 'potentially impede [the] dynamic processes that are needed to address GPGs challenges',[292] while Nico Krisch asserts that 'classical international law' is inadequate in providing proper solutions to the challenges posed by the provision of GPGs.[293] Similarly, Trachtman argues that, '[i]n the international system, based as it is on individual state consent, it may be tougher to make rules that would bind free riders'.[294] In this sense, Petersmann too concludes that, to limit the participation problem, one would need 'rights-based rules, institutions and governance mechanisms that go beyond those of "Westphalian intergovernmentalism"'.[295] In other words, these legal scholars argue that international law *de lege lata*, ie, organised along Westphalian lines, is ill-suited to the provision of GPGs as it lacks coercive mechanisms, but equally contend that international legal rules and institutions are essential to establish exactly those coercive mechanisms which are currently lacking. In order adequately to provide GPGs, a major overhaul of the international legal system would thus be required.[296]

J. Critical Approaches to International Law

The late twentieth century Critical Legal Studies (CLS) and deconstructivist movements focus on exposing the ideological conditioning of the formation of international law, and reject the claims of universality.[297] Lawyers are the product of their cultural environment, from which they derive certain values that colour their view of the world and hence of international law. Theories of international law can, therefore, never be value-neutral and free of subjective elements.

The CLS movement takes particular issue with consensus as the source and basis of the binding force of international law, as well as with the conflation of law and morality. It rejects as an unattainable ideal the existence of a basic consensus about the justice of the international order. Will-based theories are especially the object of critical commentary, in particular their aim of wedding the dynamic and ever-changing will of the State with the static positivist norm of international law by having recourse to constructions such as common will or common sense, which do not correspond to the actual will of the State.

The critical school also regards the foundations of international law as catch-all principles. One and the same principle of international law could justify contradictory results, and would therefore be useless in order to justify or criticise international behaviour. The fact that States rely on international law is to be explained through ideological mystification of international law propagating its own value.

[292] ibid, 671.
[293] N Krisch, 'The Decay of Consent: International Law in an Age of Global Public Goods' (2014) 108 *AJIL* 1.
[294] Trachtman (n 290) 154.
[295] E-U Petersmann, 'Introduction and Overview: Lack of Adequate Theories, Rules and Institutions for the Central Policy Challenge in the 21st Century?' in E-U Petersmann (ed), *Multilevel Governance of Interdependent Public Goods Theories, Rules and Institutions for the Central Policy Challenge in the 21st Century*, EUI Working Paper RSCAS 2012/23, 46, cadmus.eui.eu/bitstream/handle/1814/22275/RSCAS_2012_23final.pdf.
[296] For a more extensive account of the legal literature on GPGs, see Cogolati, Hamid, and Vanstappen (n 218).
[297] See eg R Unger, 'The Critical Legal Studies Movement' (1983) 96 *HLR* 561; A Carty, 'Critical International Law: Recent Trends in the Theory of International Law' (1991) *EJIL* 66; DZ Cass, 'Navigating the New Stream: Recent Critical Legal Scholarship in International Law' (1996) *Nord J Intl* 341; D Kennedy, 'A New Stream of International Law Scholarship' (1988) *Wisconsin International Law Journal* 1; A Anghie, *Imperialism, Sovereignty and the Making of International Law* (Cambridge, CUP, 2004); D Kennedy, *The Dark Side of Virtue* (Princeton, Princeton UP, 2005); Koskenniemi (n 263); S Marks, 'Big Brother is Bleeping Us – With the Message that Ideology Doesn't Matter' (2001) 12 *EJIL* 109.

A preeminent representative of that approach is Martti Koskenniemi, whose seminal *From Apology to Utopia* first appeared in 1989.[298] On Koskenniemi's account, international law is predicated on two opposing and irreconcilable concepts: 'apology', according to which State behaviour determines the content and binding force of international law, on the one hand, and 'utopia', according to which international law has a normative force beyond that described by State will or behaviour.[299] As a consequence, 'international law is singularly useless as a means for justifying or criticising international behaviour', because it is based on contradictory premises. It therefore remains both 'overlegitimising' in the sense that it can be invoked to justify just about any behaviour ('apologism'), and 'underlegitimising', as it is incapable of providing any convincing argument for the legitimacy of specific practices ('utopianism').[300] On Koskenniemi's own account, *From Apology to Utopia* is above all an 'an intervention in the practical world of international law that seeks to understand how to separate good and bad arguments in that field and how that competence might be used to deal with a profoundly unjust world'. Contradicting arguments to the effect that the structuralism in *From Apology to Utopia* leads to an 'anything goes' attitude, Koskenniemi insists that the very point of the book's analysis

> is to lay out the conditions within which important rules and policies emerge from the mass of legal materials available and within which they come to be interpreted and applied in certain ways instead of other prima facie plausible ways.[301]

More specific currents of critical theories of international law are the various feminist approaches to international law, which challenge the underlying normative assumptions of international law, and aim to introduce gender as a category of analysis in international law by challenging the 'masculinist' certainties of international law,[302] and Third World approaches to international law, which inter alia challenge the legitimacy of the limits on sovereignty and democratic control in developing countries imposed by development aid and lending.[303]

However, deconstructive theories of international law have also been challenged by scholars who, while taking on board the challenges to the normativity and universality of international law, have attempted to reconstruct a theory of international law on other grounds.[304]

One contemporary example is the theory of social idealism put forward by Philip Allott, which sets out a general social philosophy in which law plays a central role, and which cannot be fitted within existing schools of legal philosophy,[305] neither forming part of the

[298] It was reissued in 2005: see Koskenniemi (n 263).

[299] Koskenniemi (n 263) 58–60; on which see Crawford (n 53) 161–71.

[300] Koskenniemi (n 263) 67. For a sustained criticism of this approach, see I Scobbie, 'Towards the Elimination of International Law: Some Radical Scepticism about Sceptical Radicalism' (1990) 61 *BYIL* 339; Crawford (n 53) 171–78. See further J d'Aspremont, 'Martti Koskenniemi, the Mainstream, and Self-Reflectivity' (2016) 29 *LJIL* 625, arguing that while contemporary international lawyers have affected a critical attitude, few have really confronted and integrated the critical stance at the core of *From Apology to Utopia*.

[301] M Koskenniemi, 'What is Critical Research in International Law? Celebrating Structuralism' (2016) 29 *LJIL* 727 and 732.

[302] H Charlesworth, C Chinkin, and S Wright, 'Feminist Approaches to International Law' (1991) 85 *AJIL* 613. See further D Otto, 'Feminist Approaches to International Law' in Orford and Hoffmann (n 62) 488–504.

[303] See eg M Bennouna, *Droit international du développement : tiers-monde et interpellation du droit international* (Boulogne-Billancourt, Berger-Levrault, 1983); BS Chimni, 'International Institutions Today: An Imperial Global State in the Making' (2004) 15 *EJIL* 1; Anghie (n 297).

[304] See eg N MacCormick, 'Reconstruction after Deconstruction: A Response to CLS' (1990) 10 *OJLS* 539; Scobbie (n 300) 339–62.

[305] See M Koskenniemi, 'International Law as Therapy: Reading The Health of Nations' (2005) 16 *EJIL* 329.

analytical philosophical school, nor, despite being a 'critical' theory, of CLS.[306] Allott's work deliberately distances itself from Anglo-American philosophy of the last 100 years.[307] His vision as set out in *Eunomia* intends to 're-imagine the human world by proposing a new ideal of international society, the society of all-humanity, the society of all societies',[308] and is therefore essentially characterised by an ultimate conviction in the power of ideas to restructure the world.[309] Allott argues that Vattel's work on international law, in particular in using State sovereignty to reject a natural society of all human beings, provided the theoretical grounding for a world governed by the interests of States.[310] That, in turn, has led to the perception of domestic and international affairs as 'intrinsically and radically separate'.[311] Philip Allott's work sets out a vision of how the world could be or could have been if the 'Vatellian conception of international law' had not become dominant, but does not provide – nor aim to provide – in any detail the steps to be taken to achieve that aspiration, and simply points to a possible way to renewal.[312]

In sum, each of the theoretical approaches outlined in this section could be said to represent both disenchantment with contemporary representations of international law and a willingness to draw on ideas from outside the field of international law.[313]

VI. 'European' International Law

International law has often been described as originating in Europe sometime during the sixteenth and seventeenth centuries and then spreading progressively to other continents and eventually the entire world. In other words, the process of international law's globalisation has often been conceived of as the gradual expansion of the scope of application of 'European international law'. That expansion happened as and when non-European States were admitted as new members of the international community or, alternatively, when international legal rules, doctrines or ideas were imposed outside Europe to justify colonialism.[314]

It has now long been acknowledged that this Eurocentric conception of the history of international law is at least partly incomplete and partly incorrect.[315] Moreover, it ignores the violence and destruction that was part and parcel of the spread of 'European' international law, often in the form of subjugation and colonisation, disregards the relevance

[306] I Scobbie, '"The Holiness of Heart's Affection": Philip Allot's Theory of Social Idealism' in Orakhelashvili (n 65) 169–70.

[307] Besson and Tasioulas (n 165) 4.

[308] P Allott, *Eunomia: New Order For a New World* (Oxford, OUP, 2001) 192, para 13.37; and Allott (n 202) 152–53, paras 5.60–5.61.

[309] Scobbie (n 306) 176.

[310] Allott (n 202) 415–16, para 14.44.

[311] Allott (n 308) 243, para 13.105.

[312] Scobbie (n 306) 189–95. His most recent work, P Allott, *Eutopia: New Philosophy and New Law for a Troubled World* (Cheltenham, Edward Elgar, 2016), aims to resume the debate about the role of philosophy and society and law in making a better human future to which Thomas More contributed in his book *Utopia* (1516), 'responding to a human world that More could not have imagined'.

[313] A Orford and F Hoffmann, 'Introduction: Theorizing International Law' in Orford and Hoffmann (n 62) 6–7.

[314] A Becker Lorca, 'Universal International Law: Nineteenth-Century Histories of Imposition and Appropriation' (2010) 51 *Harvard International Law Journal* 475, 475–76.

[315] See ibid, 477; M Koskenniemi, 'Histories of International Law: Dealing with Eurocentrism' (2011) 19 *Rechtsgeschichte* 154–55; A Becker Lorca, 'Eurocentrism in the History of International Law' in B Fassbender and A Peters (eds), *The Oxford Handbook of the History of International Law* (Oxford, OUP, 2012).

of non-European forms of legal relations,[316] and tends to portray the non-European world as an object of European policy or thought about that policy.[317] The traditional narrative of the origins of international law as a European invention that subsequently globalised became contested when international lawyers from newly-independent nations started taking part actively in the scholarly debate on international law.[318] A careful study of the history of international law in fact shows that its origins are in no way inherently European,[319] and that the cultural and intellectual heritage of non-European nations had long developed fundamental ideas of international law, such as concepts of the sanctity of treaties, the inviolability of ambassadors, principles of humanity in conducting wars, including the distinction between combatants and non-combatants, and fundamental principles of the law of the sea.[320]

Furthermore, the universality of international law based on (natural law) principles applicable to all nations has been a fixture of European international lawyers for a long time. For example, as noted above, Vitoria argued that non-Christian Native American nations were not merely objects of conquest, and wars against them consequently could only be waged for a just cause. Later generations of legal scholars would in fact resurrect the writings of Vitoria and other writers to demonstrate that intellectual support for the rights of indigenous peoples lay deep in Europe's past.[321] Kant likewise condemned the brutality of European behaviour towards non-European peoples in *Towards Perpetual Peace*,[322] and the foundation of colonies in *The Metaphysics of Morals*.[323]

The works by classical writers such as Grotius, Wolff, and Vattel likewise do not appear to suggest in any way that the law of nations applied differently to different nations or peoples.[324] Moreover, while the term 'droit public de l'Europe' or '*jus publicum Europaeum*' discussed above might suggest otherwise, it was in fact not of necessity a doctrine of European exclusivity in international law, but a descriptive assessment of European treaty practice.

At any rate, membership of the 'public law of Europe' was never based on a coherent set of principles.[325] Specifically as regards treaty practice, for a long time two different patterns of behaviour could be discerned. On the one hand, when Europeans were faced with powerful contenders, such as Arab rulers in the Middle Ages, the Ottoman Empire, and empires and princes of East Asia and South-East Asia, peace treaties often built on the practices and laws of both civilisations. On the other hand, when European powers were in a dominant position, such as with respect to the indigenous peoples of the Americas, they imposed a different type of peace treaty, often including the attribution of guilt on the part of the indigenous peoples, as well as total subjection or the imposition of harsh conditions.[326]

316 B Fassbender and A Peters, 'Introduction: Towards A Global History Of International Law' in Fassbender and Peters (n 61) 1–3.
317 Koskenniemi (n 315) 161.
318 Becker Lorca (n 315) 1037.
319 Orakhelashvili (n 162) 19–20.
320 See A Orakhelashvili, 'The Idea of European International Law' (2006) 17 *EJIL* 328.
321 Coates (n 77) 793.
322 Kant (n 203) 106–107 (ZeF 8:358–9).
323 I Kant, *The Metaphysics of Morals* (1797), L Denis (ed), M Gregor (trans) (Cambridge, CUP, 2017) 58–59 (MdS 6:266). See also K Flikschuh and L Ypi (eds), *Kant and Colonialism: Historical and Critical Perspectives* (Oxford, OUP, 2014).
324 Orakhelashvili (n 320) 316.
325 ibid, 317 and 336–38.
326 Lesaffer (n 61) 90.

At the same time, certain canon law prohibitions on treaties with non-Christian States were gradually outweighed by the recognition of the necessity for European powers to interact with non-European powers.[327] That much is clear, for example, from the ICJ's judgment in the *Right of Passage* case, in which Portugal claimed a right of passage over Indian territory. In support of its claim, Portugal relied on the Treaty of Poona of 1779 between Portugal and the Maratha Empire. Significantly, the Court regarded the treaty as validly concluded under international law, holding:

> The Marathas themselves regarded the Treaty of 1779 as valid and binding upon them, and gave effect to its provisions. The Treaty is frequently referred to as such in subsequent formal Maratha documents, including the two sanads of 1783 and 1785, which purport to have been issued in pursuance of the Treaty. The Marathas did not at any time cast any doubt upon the validity or binding character of the Treaty.[328]

By referring to the practice and legal conviction of the Marathas, the ICJ implicitly confirmed their legal personality and participation in the international legal order on the basis of reciprocity.[329] Nevertheless, in their administration of colonies, colonial powers sometimes developed a form of 'imperial international law': a subcategory of international law regulating relations with the colonised peoples, with less extensive rights for the latter.[330]

However, the nineteenth century saw the rise of the idea of 'European international law', which was based on the assumption that international law developed through European treaty practice and custom, without the participation of non-European nations.[331] Western international lawyers and diplomats, often in an effort to advance mercantile or expansionist policies, advanced the idea of an exclusively European international law in order to justify the exclusion of non-European entities from the privileges of an international legal order based on sovereign equality. They thereby gave a legal basis inter alia for colonialism, notably by defining territory as *terra nullius* (ie, not subject to any sovereign authority and thus subject to acquisition through *occupation*), despite the fact that it was inhabited by indigenous peoples.[332] The twin doctrines of 'right of discovery' and '*terra nullius*' paved the way for a rapid occupation of indigenous lands.[333]

Non-Europeans were considered uncivilised and unable to understand international law, which implied that reciprocal observance of international law was inconceivable. The only relationship between Europeans and non-Europeans that was considered acceptable within the idea of European international law was the domination of the former over the latter through the imposition of unequal treaties or subjection by annexation, colonisation or transformation into a protectorate.[334] In other words, during the period beginning in the nineteenth century and extending at least until The Hague Peace Conferences, the international legal order was divided into 'a European-centred Family of Nations and a non-European zone of semi-sovereign, unequal or uncivilized states'.[335] That division had

[327] Orakhelashvili (n 320) 333.
[328] *Right of Passage over Indian Territory* [1960] ICJ Rep 6, 37.
[329] Orakhelashvili (n 320) 333.
[330] U Baxi, 'India-Europe' in Fassbender and Peters (n 61) 755–57. See also L Benton and L Ford, *Rage for Order: The British Empire and the Origins of International Law, 1800–1850* (Cambridge, MA, Harvard UP, 2016). See also Anghie (n 297).
[331] Orakhelashvili (n 320) 317. Becker Lorca (n 315) 1038.
[332] Becker Lorca (n 314) 479–80.
[333] Coates (n 77) 793–94.
[334] See Orakhelashvili (n 320) 327.
[335] Simpson (n 84) 234.

both theoretical and practical implications, in that, on the one hand, States were classified according to their capacity to meet certain culturally determined standards and, on the other hand, a number of doctrines arose that seemed hard to reconcile with sovereign equality, such as unequal treaties, certain forms of extraterritorial jurisdiction for European powers, and the exclusion of so-called peripheral States from international institutions.[336]

For example, when European powers in the nineteenth century attempted to understand the demise of the indigenous peoples in most parts of North America, their analysis followed a fairly simple pattern: European law was considered to be inherently superior to any constructs shaping indigenous societies. The incorporation of the indigenous peoples of North America in the European legal and political system was therefore viewed as both an inevitable and a positive outcome, and in fact a crucial step in their gradual civilisation. By the late nineteenth century, consideration of the rights of indigenous peoples had dropped out of most of the debates on international law, which addressed questions of relationships between nation States. Since indigenous peoples as such lacked the status of nation States, any legal issues pertaining to them were properly the responsibility of national and imperial legal systems.[337] Nevertheless, the emerging new legal regime after World War I prompted some leaders of indigenous peoples, such as the Council of the Iroquois Confederacy,[338] to seek support for their cause in the newly-established League of Nations. Yet these efforts came to nothing.[339]

More broadly, early postcolonial authors such as Alexandrowicz have argued that relations between European States and Islamic and East Indian communities were until the nineteenth century based on reciprocal treaty relations, and only following the rise of positivism did the Europeans begin to impose their standards on others.[340] In fact, the first generation of non-Western international lawyers did not put forward divergent narratives exposing a Eurocentric distortion or challenge the conventional narrative about the Western origins of international law. Rather, authors such as the Argentinian Carlos Calvo or Estonian-Russian Fedor Martens included their nations as part of the familiar European history of international law, as part of an effort to show that these States belonged to the family of civilised nations.[341]

By contrast, later postcolonial authors have argued that authors such as Alexandrowicz, in trying to prove that international law did exist between Europe and the non-European world, were in reality proceeding on the basis of an embedded conceptual Eurocentrism.[342] A new generation of international lawyers from non-European States rejected their predecessors' strategy of internalising classical international law, and instead advocated the dissolution of the standard of civilisation in favour of the coexistence of regional orders within international law.[343]

Notably, Anghie has argued that what he terms the self-sustaining and endless 'dynamic of difference', ie, 'the endless process of creating a gap between two cultures,

[336] ibid, 234.
[337] Coates (n 77) 788 and 797.
[338] See SJ Anaya, *Indigenous Peoples in International Law*, 2nd edn (Oxford, OUP, 2004) 57.
[339] Coates (n 77) 799. See further KT Kessler-Mata, *American Indians and the Trouble with Sovereignty: A Turn Toward Structural Self-Determination* (Cambridge, CUP, 2017).
[340] CH Alexandrowicz, *An Introduction to the Law of Nations in the East Indies (16th, 17th and 18th centuries)* (Oxford, Clarendon Press, 1967). See Koskenniemi (n 315) 163–64.
[341] Becker Lorca (n 315) 1038.
[342] Koskenniemi (n 315) 168.
[343] Becker Lorca (n 315) 1038.

demarcating one as "universal" and civilised and the other as "particular" and uncivilised, and seeking to bridge the gap by developing techniques to normalize the aberrant society' animated the development of many of the central doctrines of international law, in particular, the doctrine of sovereignty.[344] On Anghie's account, the rise of positivism coincided with the repudiation of the natural law idea, for example put forward by Wolff, that a universally applicable law governed a naturally constituted society of nations.[345] Instead, nineteenth century positivism limited international law to 'civilised nations'.[346]

Anghie has also argued that while scholars such as Vitoria and Wheaton recognised the existence of important cultural differences between, for example, Native Americans and Spanish colonists, Vitoria and his contemporaries sought to bridge the gap between the European and the non-European world through a universally applicable law, and Wheaton and other nineteenth century positivists argued that European international law ought to be applied to non-European 'uncivilised' nations. Only the practice of European States could therefore create international law, and non-European nations were as such excluded from the realm of international law. However, once that distinction was made, it served as a ground for applying different standards to European and non-European nations, in essence resulting in the precedence of European international law over any claims non-Europeans might have.[347] The idea is prevalent in international law textbooks from the second half of the nineteenth century that the system of international law embodies the usages of the civilised – ie, European – nations, which are united in a natural community, keeping in place the primacy of Europe in international law.[348] Of course, if international law were indeed inherently and irredeemably an instrument of European domination and imperialism, even a critical use of categories of international law would ipso facto be Eurocentric.[349]

Nevertheless, it has been argued that while the emphasis on the European character of international law is connected with the rise of positivism, this is true only in a chronological and not in a conceptual sense.[350] For example, next to positivists such as Wheaton, the idea of international law as put forward by scholars such as Lorimer was based on a natural law conception, and posited that positive law was declaratory of the law of nature. The law of nations, in turn, was to be discovered through inferences from the basic facts of nature, which according to Lorimer were essentially power relations. On that basis, Lorimer ruled out the possibility of formal legal equality among States that are unequal in fact, a difference that conferred on European States unilateral rights to expansion and conquest.[351] European international law as an idea of exclusivity and superiority therefore did not necessarily owe its existence to the dominance of positivism, but was simply based on the assumptions and prejudices of racial, cultural, and religious superiority of Europeans over non-Europeans, presenting the latter as naturally unfit to be part of the Family of Nations due to their lack of civilisation. As such, it was part of the ideology of colonialism, which found little or no support in classical international law.[352]

[344] Anghie (n 297) 4.
[345] eg H Wheaton, *Elements of International Law* (Carey, Lea and Blanchard, 1836) 10.
[346] Anghie (n 297) 52–53.
[347] ibid, 54–55.
[348] Lev (n 233) 132–33.
[349] Koskenniemi (n 315) 169. See also M Koskenniemi, W Rech and M Jiménez Fonseca (eds), *International Law and Empire: Historical Explorations* (Oxford, OUP, 2017).
[350] Orakhelashvili (n 320) 317.
[351] J Lorimer, *The Institutes of the Law of Nations* (Edinburgh, W Blackwood and Sons, 1880) 104 and 260–61. See Becker Lorca (n 314) 489; Orakhelashvili (n 320) 318.
[352] Orakhelashvili (n 320) 325–26.

In fact, non-European international lawyers welcomed positivist theories to the extent that they displaced natural law-based theories detrimental to the interests of non-European States.[353] Furthermore, it has persuasively been argued by Becker Lorca that the expansion of international law to reaching a global scope during the nineteenth century was achieved when the doctrines of recognition and the standard of civilisation, which erected boundaries between the regimes governing the relations between Western sovereigns under formal equality on the one hand and between the latter and non-Western polities on the other hand, were reinterpreted in such a way that non-Western sovereigns were admitted into the international community, thereby becoming governed by the regime recognising formal equality. That transformation was not done by way of a 'concession' by the West, but through the reinterpretation of the applicable rules by non-Western States, made possible by the fact that a generation of non-European international lawyers had appropriated Western international legal thinking. These lawyers internalised European legal thought in order to change it, and in doing so also transformed international law itself.[354]

In other words, instead of being a process of European expansion, international law universalised during the nineteenth century when jurists from non-European polities such as Japan, the Ottoman Empire, and Latin American States appropriated European international legal thought.[355] Faced with pressures to sign unequal treaties, non-European elites understood the importance of learning the prevailing international legal discourse. Consequently, after studying international law in Europe, many of them internalised the categories of classical international law, and ultimately used them in order to change, in the direction of equality, the rules of international law applicable to their polities.[356] Even when international law purely reflected power imbalances, the expression thereof in the language of law gave non-European international lawyers a starting point for resistance, as rules or principles set out in treaties set a baseline that could be invoked to fend off further encroachment by Western powers.[357] Their reinterpretation of the central elements of classical international law, such as positivism, absolute sovereignty and the standard of civilisation, progressively achieved the inclusion of non-Western States within the regime of autonomy and equality. That process took place despite the fact that it was neither in the interest of European States, nor of the US to expand the scope of European international law as a law sanctioning sovereign equality beyond the Western world.[358] Such analyses undermine the view that the adoption of a 'European' legal vocabulary or legal concepts would of necessity give rise to European dominance or at any rate would work in favour of European interests, and hence confound the idea of Europeanisation.[359]

Furthermore, recently, 'European' international law has sometimes been understood, first, as synonymous with the development of the extensive rights granted to individuals and the accompanying advanced enforcement machineries of the European Convention for the Protection of Human Rights and Fundamental Freedoms (ECHR) and the constitutive treaties of the EU,[360] or, second, as representing a contrasting attitude to the US allegedly

[353] Becker Lorca (n 314) 489–92.
[354] ibid, 477–78. See also A Becker Lorca, *Mestizo International Law: A Global Intellectual History 1842–1933* (Cambridge, CUP, 2015).
[355] Becker Lorca (n 314) 475–552.
[356] ibid, 481.
[357] ibid, 520.
[358] ibid, 481.
[359] Koskenniemi (n 315) 173.
[360] Orakhelashvili (n 320) 340–47.

rather more sceptical approach to international law.[361] With respect to the first aspect, it is arguably the specific and universal character of the obligations contained in the ECHR rather than its European scope of application that endows it with its public order character. Furthermore, unique though the EU no doubt is, in relation to international law the EU in effect constitutes a complex system of *lex specialis*, a phenomenon that can be fitted with and explained by traditional principles and categories of international law.[362] As regards the second aspect, the US attitude to international law has been described as a form of pervasive rule-scepticism: the contrast between legal norms and their compliance is in the US often treated as a form of 'cognitive dissonance', the solution to which is the redefinition or the abandonment of the normative.[363] At the same time, it has also been remarked that Europe's use of international law was for a long time determined from its position of overwhelming power, and that while Europe today does not speak from that position anymore, it still speaks the language of universal international law 'perhaps uncertain about who will listen'.[364] In particular, Europe is said to start from the premise that the international world will be how Europe itself is, and international law is understood in the light of its domestic legalism, with treaties as legislation, international courts as the judiciary, and the UN Security Council as the police. By contrast, the US is said to consider legalisation as just another policy choice and a matter of costs and benefits.[365] As demonstrated by the brief and rather schematic overview in the present section, the concept of 'European international law' has taken on divergent meanings with sometimes dramatically different implications over the course of the history of international law, and continues to evolve and to provoke debate.

VII. Conclusion

Any study of international law presupposes a thorough insight into its foundations, but equally at least a basic grasp of its history and its theory. The present chapter has found that international law evolved from a law regulating the coexistence of States or even, from some perspectives, of European States, to a law shaping the cooperation between all States and other subjects of international law, including international organisations and, at least partly, non-governmental organisations, transnational enterprises, and finally the individual itself. It has explored various theoretical underpinnings for the binding force of international law or lack thereof, but equally a number of critical approaches to international law. The present chapter has provided an expository overview of all these aspects, while at the same time addressing the possible meanings of 'European' international law. The foundations of

361 KS Ziegler, 'International Law and EU law: Between Asymmetric Constitutionalisation and Fragmentation' in Orakhelashvili (n 65) 273; cp also Ohlin (n 264), discussing the hostile attitude towards international law displayed by recent US governments.

362 Orakhelashvili (n 320) 341 and 347. See in the same sense with respect to the EU principle of loyalty and the principle of good faith in international law (and constitutional law): G De Baere and T Roes, 'EU Loyalty as Good Faith' (2015) 64 *ICLQ* 845.

363 G Verdirame, '"The Divided West": International Lawyers in Europe and America' (2007) 18 *EJIL* 572. For a nuanced and highly informative analysis of the attitude of the Supreme Court of the US towards international law, see S Breyer, *The Court and the World: American Law and the New Global Realities* (New York, Vintage Books, 2016).

364 M Koskenniemi, 'International Law in Europe: Between Tradition and Renewal' (2005) 16 *EJIL* 117.

365 ibid.

international law will be further examined in the following chapters on sources, the relationship and interactions between international law, EU law, and national law, on the subjects of international law, and on jurisdiction.

Bibliography

Besson, S, and Tasioulas, J (eds), *The Philosophy of International Law* (Oxford, OUP, 2010).

Crawford, J, *Chance, Order, Change: The Course of International Law, General Course on Public International Law* (The Hague, Hague Academy of International Law, 2014).

Crawford, J and Koskenniemi, M (eds), *The Cambridge Companion to International Law* (Cambridge, CUP, 2012).

Fassbender, B and Peters, A (eds), *The Oxford Handbook of the History of International Law* (Oxford, OUP, 2012).

Orakhelashvili, A (ed), *Research Handbook on the Theory and History of International Law* (Edward Elgar, 2011).

Orford, A and Hoffmann, F (eds), *The Oxford Handbook of the Theory of International Law* (Oxford, OUP, 2016).

Further Reading

Allott, P, *Eunomia: New Order for a New World* (Oxford, OUP, 2001).

Allott, P, *The Health of Nations: Society and Law beyond the State* (Cambridge, CUP, 2002).

Alter, KJ, *The New Terrain of International Law: Courts, Politics, Rights* (Princeton, Princeton UP, 2014).

Anghie, A, *Imperialism, Sovereignty and the Making of International Law* (Cambridge, CUP, 2004).

Becker Lorca, A, Mestizo *International Law: A Global Intellectual History 1842–1933* (Cambridge, CUP, 2015).

Bederman, DJ, *International Law in Antiquity* (Cambridge, CUP, 2001).

Benvenisti, E and Downs, GW, *Between Fragmentation and Democracy: The Role of National and International Courts* (Cambridge, CUP, 2017).

De Baere, G and Wouters, J (eds), *The Contribution of International and Supranational Courts to the Rule of Law* (Cheltenham, Edward Elgar, 2015).

Lauterpacht, H, *The Function of Law in the International Community* (Oxford, OUP, 1933).

Mills, A, *The Confluence of Public and Private International Law: Justice, Pluralism and Subsidiarity in the International Constitutional Ordering of Private Law* (Cambridge, CUP, 2009).

Guzman, AT, *How International Law Works: A Rational Choice* (Oxford, OUP, 2008).

Henkin, L, *How Nations Behave: Law and Foreign Policy*, 2nd edn (Council on Foreign Relations, 1979).

Jouannet, E, *Le droit international libéral-providence – Une histoire du droit international* (Brussels, Bruylant, 2011).

Kessler-Mata, KT, *American Indians and the Trouble with Sovereignty: A Turn Toward Structural Self-Determination* (Cambridge, CUP, 2017).
Kolb, R, *Théorie du droit international*, 2nd edn (Brussels, Bruylant, 2013).
Koskenniemi, M, *From Apology to Utopia*, 2nd edn (Cambridge, CUP, 2005).
Koskenniemi, M, Rech, W and Jiménez Fonseca, M (eds), *International Law and Empire: Historical Explorations* (Oxford, OUP, 2017).
Lesaffer, R (ed), *Peace Treaties and International Law in European History: From the Late Middle Ages to World War One* (Cambridge, CUP, 2004).
Marks, S (ed), *International Law on the Left: Re-Examining Marxist Legacies* (Cambridge, CUP, 2008).
Ohlin, JD, *The Assault on International Law* (Oxford, OUP, 2015).
Pulkowski, D, *The Law and Politics of International Regime Conflict* (Oxford, OUP, 2014).
Simpson, G, *Great Powers and Outlaw States: Unequal Sovereigns in the International Legal Order* (Cambridge, CUP, 2004).
Spiermann, O, *International Legal Argument in the Permanent Court of International Justice* (Cambridge, CUP, 2005).
von Bernstorff, J, *The Public International Law Theory of Hans Kelsen: Believing in Universal Law* (Cambridge, CUP, 2010).
Young, M (ed), *Regime Interaction in International Law: Facing Fragmentation* (Cambridge, CUP, 2015).

2

Sources: Treaty Law

I. Introduction

In this and the next chapter, the term 'sources' refers to the formal sources of international law, meaning the methods for establishing legal norms in the international legal system. It does not refer to the substantive or material sources of law, such as the content of certain treaty provisions or rules of customary international law: we focus on the *processes of lawmaking* in the international legal system.

The most authoritative statement regarding the formal sources of international law can still be found in Article 38 of the International Court of Justice (ICJ) Statute:

> 1. The Court, whose function is to decide in accordance with international law such disputes as are submitted to it, shall apply:
>
> (a) international conventions, whether general or particular, establishing rules expressly recognized by the contesting States;
> (b) international custom, as evidence of a general practice accepted as law;
> (c) the general principles of law recognized by civilized nations;
> (d) subject to the provisions of Article 59, judicial decisions and the teachings of the most highly qualified publicists of the various nations, as subsidiary means for the determination of rules of law.
>
> 2. This provision shall not prejudice the power of the Court to decide a case ex aequo et bono, if the parties agree thereto.

This provision dates from the early 1920s, as it also appeared in the Statute of the ICJ's predecessor, the Permanent Court of International Justice (PCIJ).[1] Its text was drafted by an Advisory Committee of Jurists appointed by the League of Nations. Even if the drafters only intended to draft a provision relating to the functioning of the PCIJ – or, in 1945, the ICJ – it is 'generally accepted as a correct statement of the sources of international law'.[2] Note that the Advisory Committee considered to introduce a formal order among the

[1] Statute for the Permanent Court of International Justice (adopted 16 December 1920, entered into force 20 August 1921) 6 LNTS 389. The words 'whose function is to decide in accordance with international law such disputes as are submitted to it' did not appear in Art 38 of the Statute of the PCIJ.

[2] D Harris and S Sivakumaran, *Cases and Materials on International Law*, 8th edn (London, Sweet & Maxwell, 2015) 16.

different sources, by inserting the words 'in the undermentioned order' in the first paragraph of the provision. Eventually, the members of the Committee were convinced that such a specification was unnecessary given the 'natural classification' of sources,[3] and thought it would be undesirable, as it would 'fail to recognise that these various sources may be applied simultaneously, and also that the nature of each source differs'.[4]

Article 38 of the ICJ Statute still offers a useful starting point, even if it should be emphasised that it is incomplete. It does not include equity as a source of international law (apart from a limited reference in paragraph 2), nor does it make reference to unilateral legal acts, decisions of international organisations, norms of *jus cogens*, soft law or informal law. These other sources of international law are discussed in Chapter 3. The present chapter discusses what is still considered to be the main source of international law: treaties.

II. The Vienna Convention on the Law of Treaties

Treaties currently represent the main source of international law, and treaty law remains a key pillar of public international law.[5] More than 158,000 treaties have been registered at the UN.[6] In many fields, treaties have replaced rules of customary international law,[7] particularly through the codification thereof. The advantages of this process are quite evident. The inclusion of rules in a treaty brings with it greater legal certainty, both regarding the substance of the legal rule as well as the parties bound by those rules. Treaties are the voluntary or consensual legal instrument *par excellence*. States are only bound by them insofar as they have expressed their consent to be so.[8]

Treaty law was traditionally governed by customary international law. However, in 1969, it was for the most part codified in the Vienna Convention on the Law of Treaties (VCLT).[9] This codification was one of the first projects of the International Law Commission (ILC). Following proposals by its consecutive British members and rapporteurs (James L Brierly, Hersch Lauterpacht, Gerald Fitzmaurice and Humphrey Waldock), in 1966, the ILC

[3] PCIJ Advisory Committee of Jurists, 'Procés Verbaux of the Proceedings of the Committee', 16 June–24 July 1920, 337.

[4] ibid. See also Harris and Sivakumaran (n 2) 16–17. On the genesis of Art 38 ICJ Statute, see further O Spiermann, 'The History of Article 38 of the Statute of the International Court of Justice: "A Purely Platonic Discussion"?' and M Fitzmaurice, 'The History of Article 38 of the Statute of the International Court of Justice: The Journey from Past to Present' in J d'Aspremont, S Besson and S Knuchel (eds), *The Oxford Handbook of the Sources of International Law* (Oxford, OUP, 2017), respectively at 165–78 and 179–201.

[5] See eg O Dörr and K Schmalenbach (eds), *Vienna Convention on the Law of Treaties: A Commentary*, 2nd edn (Heidelberg, Springer, 2018), v: 'The law of treaties forms the backbone of the international legal order'.

[6] These treaties are published in the United Nations Treaty Series (UNTS), which can be consulted as an online database via treaties.un.org.

[7] With the reservation that customary international law continues to exist alongside treaty law, and continues to apply to States that are not bound by the relevant treaty. On the interrelationship between treaties and customary international law, see further R Kolb, *The Law of Treaties: An Introduction* (Chelthenham, Edward Elgar, 2016) 260–69.

[8] Regarding the problem of consensualism in international law more generally, see eg O Elias and C Lim, *The Paradox of Consensualism in International Law* (The Hague, Kluwer, 1998); E Suy, 'Rôle et signification du consensus dans l'élaboration du droit international'; 'The Role and Significance of Consensus in the Forming of International Law: Provisional Report 1996' – 'Final Report 1996' (1997) 67 *Annuaire de l'Institut de Droit International*, respectively 16–35, 79–89 and 111–18.

[9] Vienna Convention on the Law of Treaties (adopted 23 May 1969, entered into force 27 January 1980) 1155 UNTS 331.

adopted 'Draft Articles on the Law of Treaties' that served as the basis for the diplomatic conference on treaty law held in Vienna in 1968–1969.[10] The text of the treaty was accepted by 79 votes to 1, with 19 abstentions. On 27 January 1980, the VCLT entered into force.[11] Currently, 116 States are parties to the VCLT, including 26 EU Member States.[12] Strictly speaking, the VCLT applies only to treaties that are concluded by States after the entry into force of the Convention with regard to such States.[13]

However, most, though not all, of the provisions of the VCLT are considered to represent customary international law, and are as such applicable to other treaties as well. Notably, numerous judgments and advisory opinions of the ICJ refer to the VCLT as an expression of customary international law.[14] The Court of Justice of the European Union (CJEU) has also held that, insofar as they represent rules of customary international law, provisions of the VCLT are applicable to treaties entered into by the EU.[15]

The VCLT is also applicable to treaties that are the constituent instrument of an international organisation and to treaties that have been adopted within an international organisation.[16] However, in this (as well as other) respect(s), the VCLT is of a dispositive nature. The rules that apply in the first place are the rules of the international organisation itself as established under its constituent instrument and internal law. Thus, when a constituent treaty of an international organsation does not contain any provisions concerning the termination of membership, the rules of the VCLT become relevant.[17]

In the context of the EU, the VCLT and rules of treaty law are not applied to the EU's founding treaties. This is because the EU represents a special type of international organisation, which has developed its own rules regarding the interpretation and application of primary law. The General Court has held that:

> The reference to international law, and in particular to Articles 54 and 70 of the Vienna Convention [on the Law of Treaties], fails to have regard to the sui generis nature of the Community legal order [...]. The indivisibility of the Community legal order and the *lex specialis* to *lex generalis* relationship between the ECSC and EC Treaties mean that the consequences of the expiry of the ECSC Treaty are not governed by the rules of international law but must be assessed in the light of the provisions existing within the Community legal order.[18]

[10] See ILC, 'Draft Articles on the Law of Treaties with commentaries' (1966) *YILC*, Vol II, 187–274 (ILC Draft Articles). Regarding the role of the ILC in this respect, see F Vallat, 'The Work of the International Law Commission – The Law of Treaties' (1975) 22 *NILR* 327.

[11] That is on the 30th day after the deposit of the 35th ratification or confirmation instrument; see Art 84(1) VCLT.

[12] France and Romania are neither signatories nor contracting parties.

[13] Art 4 VCLT.

[14] See eg *Legal Consequences for States of the Continued Presence of South Africa in Namibia (South West Africa) notwithstanding Security Council Resolution 276* (Advisory Opinion) [1971] ICJ Rep 16 (on the notion of 'material breach'); *Fisheries Jurisdiction* (United Kingdom of Great Britain and Northern Ireland v Iceland) [1974] ICJ Rep 3 (*rebus sic stantibus*); *Gabčíkovo-Nagymaros Project* (Hungary v Slovakia) [1997] ICJ Rep 7 (grounds for terminating a treaty, impossibility of performance, *rebus sic stantibus*).

[15] See eg judgments of 16 June 1998, *Racke*, C-162/96, EU:C:1998:293 (*rebus sic stantibus*); and of 25 February 2010, *Brita*, C-386/08, EU:C:2010:91 (interpretation, *pacta tertiis*); judgment of 21 December 2016, *Council v Front Polisario*, C-104/16 P, EU:C:2016:973, paras 86–87, 100 (good faith interpretation, interpretation taking account of any relevant rules of international law applicable in the relations between the parties, principle of self-determination, *pacta tertiis*); and of 27 February 2018, *Western Sahara Campaign UK*, C-266/16, EU:C:2018:118, paras 58–60 (interpretation in the light of a subsequent agreement between the parties).

[16] Art 5 VCLT.

[17] Art 56 VCLT. See eg *Interpretation of the Agreement of 25 March 1951 between the WHO and Egypt* (Advisory Opinion) [1980] ICJ Rep 73.

[18] See judgment of 25 October 2007, *SP v Commission*, T-27/03, T-46/03, T-58/03, T-79/03, T-80/03, T-97/03 and T-98/03, EU:T:2007:317, para 58.

Alongside the VCLT, which only applies to treaties between States,[19] there is also the 1986 Vienna Convention on the Law of Treaties between States and International Organizations or between International Organizations (VCLT-IO).[20] The VCLT-IO, which has not yet entered into force, applies to treaties between States and international organisations or between international organisations. To date, the VCLT-IO has only been ratified by 31 States, including 18 EU Member States (the EU itself is not a party). Only 12 international organisations, most of which belong to the UN family, have formally adopted the VCLT-IO. Pursuant to Article 85(1) of the VCLT-IO, 35 ratifications by States are needed for it to enter into force. Formal confirmations by international organisations are not taken into account for the purpose of determining the date on which the Convention enters into force. Pursuant to Article 73 of the VCLT-IO, as between States Parties to the VCLT, 'the relations of those States under a treaty between two or more States and one or more international organizations shall be governed by that convention'.

For the sake of completeness, it should also be noted here that there is a third convention that is related to the topic of treaties, namely the 1978 Vienna Convention on Succession of States in respect of Treaties.[21] This Convention, to which only few EU Member States are a party,[22] entered into force on 6 November 1996 and currently has 22 States Parties. It is discussed further in Chapter 5, Section VI(C), dealing with state succession in respect of treaty relations.[23]

III. Definition of a 'Treaty'

One of the questions the ILC had to face when preparing the Draft Articles, was how to define a treaty for the purposes thereof, as States enter into a variety of different types of agreements at the international level with different titles. The Draft Articles and Article 2(1)(a) VCLT define a treaty, for their respective purposes, as 'an international agreement concluded between States in written form and governed by international law, whether embodied in a single instrument or in two or more related instruments and whatever its particular designation'. The VCLT-IO employs a similar definition, adding that it must concern an agreement between one or more States and one or more international organisations, or between international organisations.[24]

[19] Art 1 VCLT.

[20] Vienna Convention on the Law of Treaties between States and International Organizations or between International Organizations (adopted 20 March 1986, not yet entered into force) 25 ILM 543, UN Doc A/CONF 129/15.

[21] Vienna Convention on Succession of States in Respect of Treaties (adopted 23 August 1978, entered into force 6 November 1996) 1946 UNTS 3.

[22] Only Croatia, Cyprus, the Czech Republic, Estonia, Poland, Slovakia and Slovenia are a party. These are all EU Member States for which problems of State succession have a particular relevance. The same applies for other European States that are a party, such as Bosnia and Herzegovina, Former Yugoslav Republic of Macedonia (whose name will in the future change to Northern Macedonia), Moldova, Montenegro, Serbia and Ukraine.

[23] See also G Distefano, G Gaggioli and A Hêche (eds), *La convention de Vienne de 1978 sur la succession d'états en matière de traités: commentaire article par article et études thématiques* (Brussels, Bruylant, 2016). For a short critique, see ST Korman, 'The 1978 Vienna Convention on Succession of States in Respect of Treaties: An Inadequate Response to the Issue of State Succession' (1992) 16 *Suffolk Transnational Law Review* 174.

[24] Art 2(1)(a)(i) VCLT-IO.

This definition reflects the main elements a treaty is required to have under customary international law: there must be (a) an agreement (b) concluded between two or more subjects of international law (c) with the intent to create legal effects and (d) governed by international law.[25] Nevertheless, the definitions under customary international law and the VCLT are not identical. The definition of the VCLT is only applicable for the purposes of the VCLT,[26] and is more limited than the customary international law definition of a treaty in two ways: it only covers (i) treaties concluded between States, and (ii) in written form. In any case, customary international law continues to apply to treaties that do not fall within the scope of the definition of the VCLT.[27] What follows discusses the elements required to have a treaty under customary international law and the specifics required by the VCLT.

A. An 'Agreement'

First, there must be an 'agreement' or, in the words of Robert Kolb, a 'consensual bond'.[28] This means that there must be a 'meeting of the minds' in the context of an interchange among participants that generates a normative commitment.[29] The agreement may be express or tacit. An express agreement is either embodied in a written instrument or concluded orally. A tacit agreement can follow from acquiescence; in this case acts or deeds that necessarily mean the acceptance of a certain proposal.[30] The requirement of an agreement could be understood as referring to the instrument(s) recording the parties' commitments rather than the underlying meeting of the minds; in particular, Article 2(1)(a) of the VCLT leaves this issue open.[31] However, as for the mere requirement of agreement, there is no need for a specific instrument,[32] at least under customary international law: it refers to the conceptual meeting of the minds rather than any such instrument.[33]

B. In Written Form

An additional requirement contained in the VCLT is that the agreement be 'in written form'. The preference given to the written form can be explained by its evidentiary value and the fact that international agreements are usually concluded in writing.[34] However, Article 2(1)(a) VCLT does not specify the formal requirements that have to be fulfilled by the (written) instrument.[35] Accordingly, this element is not applied restrictively, and the precise way in

[25] See also Kolb (n 7) 16, who does not speak of the requirement of an agreement, but of a 'consensual bond' (express or tacit). According to him, 'the word "treaty" is reserved for written instruments; the word "agreement" is broader, encompassing non-written bonds'.
[26] Art 1 VCLT.
[27] See eg Art 3(b) VCLT.
[28] See above (n 25).
[29] D Hollis 'Defining Treaties' in D Hollis (ed), *The Oxford Guide to Treaties* (Oxford, OUP, 2012) 20; Kolb (n 7) 16. See further K Widdows, 'What is an Agreement in International Law?' in S Davidson (ed), *The Law of Treaties* (Aldershot, Ashgate, 2004) 73.
[30] Kolb (n 7) 16–17.
[31] Hollis (n 29) 20–21.
[32] But see ibid, 21.
[33] Kolb (n 7) 16–17.
[34] P Gautier, 'Article 2: Use of Terms – 1969 Vienna Convention' in O Corten and P Klein (eds), *The Vienna Conventions on the Law of Treaties: A Commentary* (Oxford, OUP, 2011) Vol I, 38.
[35] ibid.

which a treaty is written is not relevant. It is simply required that some sort of permanent and readable record of the agreement exists.[36] As alluded to above, stressed by the ILC[37] and eventually evidenced by Article 3 VCLT, this element is not an intrinsic requirement for there to be a treaty under customary international law: the VCLT has excluded oral agreements simply for practical reasons and without prejudice to their legal force. In any case, due to the complexity of international relations and the difficulty of providing evidence, non-written treaties are currently rare.

C. Concluded between Two or More Subjects of International Law

A second requirement for there to be a treaty under customary international law, is that it is concluded by entities posessing treaty-making power under international law.[38] Chiefly, these are the subjects of international law, with the general understanding that treaty-making power is not granted to all subjects of international law to the same extent. According to Article 6 of the VCLT, '[e]very State has the capacity to conclude treaties'. The capacity to enter into treaties is an inherent right of every State and does not depend on the recognition by other States or subjects of international law.[39] At the same time, the State is the sole subject 'posessing a general and unlimited treaty-making capacity'.[40] In this line, and as discussed above, the VCLT limits itself to treaties concluded between States.[41] Nevertheless, there are plenty of examples of subjects of international law other than States that have concluded treaties, including international organisations, units of federal States, the Holy See, indigenous peoples, liberation movements and other non-State territorial entities.[42]

Special mention should be made of the *treaty practice of the European Union*. While the EU is surely not the only international organisation that has been endowed with treaty-making capacity, the impressive number and depth of the treaties it has concluded in a time-span of over five decades make it a very prolific treaty actor: the EU Treaty Office Database lists 959 bilateral and 281 multilateral agreements.[43] In the EU context, treaties to which the EU and the Member States are a party are commonly referred to as 'agreements'. They should not be confused with the EU Treaties, ie the constituent instruments establishing the EU (the TEU and TFEU).[44]

[36] ibid, 38–39; Hollis (n 29) 23.

[37] ILC, 'Report of the International Law Commission on the work of the first part of its seventeenth session, 3 May–9 July' (1965) *YILC*, Vol II, 158, para 21.

[38] Indeed, the very definition of a subject of international law is that it can have rights and obligations under international law, while concluding a treaty is the main way to acquire these rights and obligations.

[39] K Schmalenbach, 'Article 6. Capacity of States to Conclude Treaties' in Dörr and Schmalenbach (n 5) 118: 'The very moment a State comes into existence in accordance with international law, its treaty making capacity cannot be contested without denying the entity's legal status as a State'.

[40] Kolb (n 7) 18.

[41] Art 2(1)(a) VCLT.

[42] eg the Oslo Accords between the Government of the State of Israel and the Palestine Liberation Organization, namely the Declaration of Principles on Interim Self-Government Arrangements (Oslo I Accord) (13 September 1993) and the Israeli-Palestinian Interim Agreement on the West Bank and the Gaza Strip (Oslo II Accord) (28 September 1995). See further A Aust, *Modern Treaty Law and Practice*, 3rd edn (Cambridge, CUP, 2013) 56–70; O Elias, 'Who Can Make Treaties? International Organizations' and T Grant, 'Who Can Make Treaties? Other Subjects of International Law' in Hollis (n 29), respectively at 73–92 and 125–49.

[43] ec.europa.eu/world/agreements/default.home.do. This database includes an inventory of all agreements to which the EU, the European Community (EC), the European Economic Community (EEC), or the European Atomic Energy Community (EURATOM) are a party.

[44] See further M Cremona, 'Who Can Make Treaties? The European Union' in Hollis (n 29) 93.

Of particular relevance for several European States is that *units of federal States* can in certain circumstances conclude treaties.[45] This is, for instance, the case in a very systematic manner for the Communities and Regions of Belgium: they have treaty-making capacity for all matters for which they have an internal competence (*in foro interno, in foro externo*).[46] While the ILC Draft Articles took into account the possibility for units of federal States to conclude treaties, the relevant provision did not make it to the final text of the VCLT.[47] It is nevertheless apparent from the *travaux préparatoires* of the VCLT that international law does not exclude the competence of units of federal States to conclude treaties.[48]

The competence of units of federal States to conclude treaties must first and foremost exist under national law. Thus, this treaty-making capacity is often laid down in the concerned State's constitution. Article 167(3) of the Belgian Constitution, for example, explicitly provides for the possibility of the Belgian Communities and Regions to conclude treaties with regard to matters that fall within their competence under national law.[49] In other federal States, the competence of units to conclude treaties is generally less developed. While for example also the German *Länder* and Swiss cantons conclude international agreements, it is not clear wether these are treaties.[50] Second, this competence must also be recognised by other States and international organisations. Thus, at least in practice, the treaty-making capacity of units of federal States also depends on the attitude of other subjects of international law.

There is no consensus whether units of federal States can conclude treaties based on their own international legal personality, or merely as organs of the federal State. Therefore, depending on whether one or the other position is taken, treaties concluded exclusively by units of federal States are governed respectively by customary international law or by the provisions of the VCLT. Article 7 VCLT does not prevent the government of a federal entity from representing the State, while Article 29 VCLT acknowledges the possibility of treaties that are concluded only for a limited territory of a State, eg a specific unit of a federal State.

In addition to the possibility of treaties concluded by units of a federal State, a large number of agreements have been concluded between *sub-State actors*, specifically including municipalities, provinces, departments and regions. Such 'cross-border cooperation between local administrations' is usually enabled by a framework instrument between the States in which is are situated.[51] Agreements between sub-State actors are usually not governed by

[45] See Aust (n 42) 60–64.

[46] See J Wouters and L De Smet, 'The Legal Position of Federal States and their Federated Entities in International Relations: The Case of Belgium' in TAJA Vandamme and JH Reestman (eds), *Ambiguity in the Rule of Law: The Interface between National and International Legal Systems* (Groningen, Europa Law Publishing, 2001) 121–62.

[47] ILC Draft Articles (n 10), Art 5(2): 'States members of a federal union may possess a capacity to conclude treaties if such a capacity is admitted by the federal constitution and within the limits there laid down'. See also GI Hernández, 'Federated Entities in International Law: Disaggregating the Federal State?' in D French (ed), *Statehood and Self-Determination: Reconciling Tradition and Modernity in International Law* (Cambridge, CUP, 2013) 491–512.

[48] See O Lissitzyn, 'Territorial Entities Other than Independent States in the Law of Treaties' (1968) III 125 *RdC* 1; H Steinberger, 'Constitutional Subdivisions of States or Unions and their Capacity to Conclude Treaties: Comments on Art. 5 Para. 2 of the ILC's 1966 Draft Articles on the Law of Treaties' (1967) 27 *ZaöRV* 411; Wouters and De Smet (n 46).

[49] Belgian Constitution (7 February 1831), as amended, www.dekamer.be/kvvcr/pdf_sections/publications/constitution/GrondwetUK.pdf.

[50] Aust (n 42) 61.

[51] For instance within the EU, by means of Regulation (EC) 1082/2006 of 5 July 2006 on a European grouping of territorial cooperation (EGTC) [2006] OJ L210/19, as amended by Regulation (EU) No 1302/2013 of 17 December 2013 amending Regulation (EC) 1082/2006 on a European grouping of territorial cooperation (EGTC) as regards

international law, but by the national law of one of the States concerned. However, a strict application of national law, which is often difficult due to administrative differences, may then be tempered by the framework instrument. The interaction between national (administrative) law and such framework instruments is sometimes referred to as the 'law of cross-border relations' or 'neighbourhood law'.[52]

D. Intent to Create Legal Effects

i. General

A third requirement is that the agreement must purport to have legal effects. If States commit themselves, but do not want to assume legally binding obligations, the agreement is of a mere political, but not legal nature.[53] The UN Treaty Handbook sets out that '[a] treaty or international agreement must impose on the parties legal obligations binding under international law, as opposed to mere political commitments'.[54] As for the VCLT, the ILC did not see the need to make this requirement explicit, as it considered that the phrase 'governed by international law' embraces the element of an intention to create *legal* obligations.[55]

Many acts that were formulated within the framework of the Conference for Security and Co-operation in Europe, later renamed the Organization for Security and Co-operation in Europe (OSCE), are not treaties, because they were made exclusively as politically binding agreements. These agreements are therefore not registered as treaties with the UN.[56] One of the consequences of the non-legal nature of the founding instruments of the OSCE is that it has no international legal personality, and that there is uncertainty about its legal status. The attempt to adopt a Convention on International Legal Personality, Legal Capacity and Privileges and Immunities of the OSCE was made conditional upon the adoption of an OSCE Constituent Document, and has – in absence of consensus on the latter – failed.[57]

ii. Memorandums of Understanding

A memorandum of understanding (MOU) is an instrument concluded between States that is *not* legally binding (and thus by implication also not 'governed by international law',

the clarification, simplification and improvement of the establishment and functioning of such groupings [2013] OJ L347/303; within the Council of Europe, by means of the European Outline Convention on Transfrontier Co-operation between Territorial Communities or Authorities (adopted 21 May 1980, entered into force 22 December 1981) CETS No 106.

[52] See in particular Y Lejeune, *Le droit des relations transfrontalières entre autorités régionales ou locales relevant d'Etats distincts: les expériences franco-belge et franco-espagnole* (Brussels, Bruylant, 2005); M Niedobitek, *Das Recht der grenzüberschreitenden Verträge: Bund, Länder und Gemeinden als Träger* (Tübingen, Mohr Siebeck, 2001); R Seerden, 'The Public International Law Character of Transfrontier Agreements between Decentralized Authorities' (1992) 5 *LJIL* 187; J Wouters and D Van Eeckhoutte, 'Het nabuurschapsrecht: analyse van het snel evoluerende juridisch kader voor publiekrechtelijke grensoverschrijdende samenwerking tussen territoriaal gedecentraliseerde besturen' (2003) 7 *Chroniques de Droit Public* 443 and 633.

[53] Kolb (n 7) 19.

[54] UN Office of Legal Affairs (Treaty Section), *Treaty Handbook*, 2nd edn (New York, UN, 2012) 31.

[55] ILC Draft Articles (n 10) 189, para 6. See also (1959) *YILC* Vol II, 96: 'instruments which, although they might look like treaties, merely contain[ing] declarations of principle or statements of policy, or expressions or opinion, or voeux, would not be treaties'.

[56] See eg the Helsinki Final Act: Final Act of the Conference for Security and Co-operation in Europe (1 August 1975) 14 ILM 1292.

[57] OSCE, 'Report to the Ministerial Council on Strengthening the Legal Framework of the OSCE in 2016', 9 December 2016, MC GAL/7/16, para 6.

on which see below, Section III(E)).[58] MOUs have become a popular instrument for governments and international organisations, and the use thereof is now widespread in most areas of international relations.[59] It is generally accepted that it is negotiating States themselves that determine whether they want to conclude a treaty or a MOU.[60] If there is no express provision as to the (non-)legally binding status of the agreement, the States' intention is to be deduced primarily from the terms used in the instrument itself (eg 'shall' for treaties; 'will' for MOUs) and the circumstances of its conclusion (eg an agreement arrived at only following a failure to conclude a treaty).[61] However, what negotiating States say afterwards about their intention is not relevant.[62]

MOUs are concluded for several reasons, the main ones being confidentiality and convenience. Unlike treaties (see below, Section V(F)), MOUs are typically not under a national or international requirement of publication, let alone registration with the UN. This may for example be interesting for agreements on sensitive defence or commercial matters. Second, unlike treaties (see below, Section V(B)), a MOU will usually become effective upon signature. Thus, its conclusion is not subject to constitutional procedures, while also its amendment and termination are subject to few formalities.[63] While MOUs entail many advantages, they also come with certain dangers. Parties may disagree on their status, consider compliance less important and be less careful in drafting them. In addition, it may be more difficult to provide for implementing legislation for MOUs, which in any case do not have direct effect in the national legal order, as can be the case for treaties in monist States (see Chapter 4, Section III(B)). Lastly, as they are usually not public, MOUs are more difficult to find – not only for the public at large, but also for government officials.[64]

E. Governed by International Law

A fourth requirement is that the treaty be 'governed by international law'. Apart from being meant by the ILC to cover the requirement of 'intent to create legal effects' (see above, Section III(D)(i)), this expression mainly serves to distinguish treaties from agreements governed by national law.[65] The legal effects that ensue from the agreement must ensue under *international* law; if legal effects ensue under another legal order, the agreement is not a treaty and international law does not apply to it.[66] For example, States or international organisations may enter into legally binding agreements with each other that are governed by the national law of one or several of the parties. They will do so mainly for agreements that

[58] Aust (n 42) 28 and 29–30.
[59] ibid, 28–29 and 40.
[60] For an opposing view, see J Klabbers, *The Concept of Treaty in International Law* (The Hague, Kluwer, 1996) and J Klabbers, 'Not Revisiting the Concept of Treaty' in A Orakhelashvili and S Williams (eds), *40 Years of the Vienna Convention on the Law of Treaties* (London, British Institute of International and Comparative Law, 2010) 29–39.
[61] Aust (n 42) 23–34.
[62] ibid, 30; *Maritime Delimitation and Territorial Questions between Qatar and Bahrain* (Qatar v Bahrain) [1994] ICJ Rep 112, para 27.
[63] Aust (n 42) 40–44.
[64] ibid, 44–46. See further RM Rodriguez et al, *Binding and Non-binding Instruments in Intergovernmental Relations: A Diplomat's Guide to Understand the Concepts of Treaty and Memorandum of Understanding in Theory and Practice* (Washington DC, EUCLID UP, 2015).
[65] Aust (n 42) 29–30.
[66] Kolb (n 7) 21.

serve a commercial rather than political purpose,[67] and/or because it allows them to bypass the many formalities that come with the conclusion of a treaty (see below, Section V).[68]

F. Form

Some non-constitutive elements of treaties deserve attention. First of all, no particular form is required: as indicated above, treaties can be concluded 'in whatever form, solemn, express or tacit'.[69] Thus, any mutual intention on the part of States (or, where appropriate, other subjects of international law) to engage in a legally binding commitment, regardless of how it is expressed, qualifies as a treaty. Although the VCLT requires that a treaty be written, it adds to its definition that it covers treaties 'whether embodied in a single instrument or in two or more related instruments'.[70] Thus, a treaty may come into being through the exchange of letters or notes between parties; substantively, it will constitute one treaty, even if it has taken shape in more than one instrument.[71] In the same line, in the *Aegean Sea Continental Shelf* case of 1978, the ICJ held that a joint press communiqué signed by two States can have the same legal effects as a treaty.[72] In 1994, the ICJ considered that the minutes of a meeting between the Ministers of Foreign Affairs of Qatar and Bahrain were 'not a simple record of a meeting', but 'enumerate[d] the commitments to which the Parties ha[d] consented', created rights and obligations in international law for them and constituted an international agreement.[73] In addition, a number of treaties may form an integrated whole, thus connecting with one another. This often is the case in the context of international organisations. For instance, every EU Member State needs to be a party to both the TEU and the TFEU, all Member States of the Council of Europe need to be a party to the ECHR, and all Members of the WTO must be a party to all multilateral WTO agreements.

There have been a number of occasions on which the CJEU has been called upon to decide what constitutes an 'agreement' for the purposes of EU law. While the Court largely follows the definition of a treaty under international law, it has employed a slightly wider definition than that contained in the VCLT.[74] For example, in *France v Commission*,[75] the CJEU had to decide whether a cooperation agreement concluded between the European Commission and the United States in the field of competition law would constitute an international agreement for the purposes of EU law.[76] The issue was whether the Commission had the competence to conclude such an agreement. The CJEU found that the agreement fell within the definition of an 'international agreement' concluded between an international organisation and a State within the meaning of Article 2(1)(a)(i) VCLT-IO, and that in the

[67] eg, the acquisition or lease of land or buildings by an international organisation; the lease of land or buildings by the receiving State to the sending State for the embassy or a consulate of the latter.

[68] Kolb (n 7) 21.

[69] ibid, 25.

[70] Art 2(1)(a) VCLT.

[71] Hollis (n 29) 29–30.

[72] *Aegean Sea Continental Shelf* (Greece v Turkey) [1978] ICJ Rep 3, para 96.

[73] *Qatar v Bahrain* (n 62) para 25.

[74] See J Odermatt, 'The Use of International Treaty Law by the Court of Justice of the European Union' (2015) 17 *Cambridge Yearbook of European Legal Studies* 121 and D Verwey, *The European Community, the European Union and the International Law of Treaties* (The Hague, TMC Asser Press, 2004) 96.

[75] Judgment of 9 August 1994, *France v Commission*, C-327/91, EU:C:1994:305.

[76] Agreement between the Government of the USA and the Commission of the European Communities Regarding the Application of their Competition Laws (as modified) [1995] OJ L95/47.

event of non-performance of the Agreement by the Commission, the Community could incur liability at the international level.[77] In *Opinion 1/75*, the CJEU discussed the meaning of 'agreement' to determine whether the 'Understanding on a Local Cost Standard' drawn up under the auspices of the OECD was a treaty concluded by the EU (then still the European Economic Community (EEC)), for the purpose of determining the admissibility of the request for an opinion from the Court under Article 218(11) TFEU.[78] It defined an international agreement as 'any undertaking entered into by entities subject to international law which has binding force, whatever its formal designation'.[79] In the *Venezuelan Fishing Rights* case, the CJEU found that a Declaration on the granting of fishing opportunities in EU waters to Venezualan fishing vessels made by the EU and the subsequent action on the part of Venezuala constituted an 'offer' and 'acceptance' leading to the creation of an international agreement. According to the Court, the offer and acceptance need not take place simultaneously.[80]

G. Name

The precise name of the instrument is legally irrelevant. Article 2(1)(a) of the VCLT specifies that it applies to a treaty 'whatever its particular designation'. States enter into treaties with a wide variety of names, including 'treaty', 'convention', 'pact', 'covenant', 'agreement', 'instrument', 'arrangement', 'statute', 'understanding' and 'memorandum of understanding'. Before the VCLT came into force, the term 'agreement in simplified form' was used for agreements that were concluded through a simplified procedure (ie by an exchange of letters or notes, by joint statements between ministers or senior civil servants, or by signing without ratification). From an international law perspective, these are treaties nevertheless.[81] The term 'protocol' is often used to supplement or modify a treaty that has already entered into force.[82] A relatively popular recent phenomenon are so-called 'framework conventions' (*conventions-cadres*). Examples include the 1992 UNFCCC, the 1992 UNECE Water

[77] *France v Commission* (n 75) para 25.

[78] Providing that: 'A Member State, the European Parliament, the Council or the Commission may obtain the opinion of the Court of Justice as to whether an agreement envisaged is compatible with the Treaties. Where the opinion of the Court is adverse, the agreement envisaged may not enter into force unless it is amended or the Treaties are revised'.

[79] Opinion 1/75 (OECD Understanding on a Local Cost Standard) of 11 November 1975, EU:C:1975:145, 1355, 1360.

[80] Judgment of 26 November 2014, *Parliament v Council and Commission v Council ('Venezuelan Fishing Rights')*, C-103/12 and C-165/12, EU:C:2014:2400, paras 68–73. In so deciding, the Court disagreed with the Opinion of AG Sharpston in *Venezuelan Fishing Rights*, C-103/12 and C-165/12, EU:C:2014:334, who argued that there was no agreement under international law (at points 79–81), concluding (at point 81): 'I have found no evidence of Venezuela's intention to be bound by the terms of the Declaration. When Venezuela applied for fishing authorisations, it seems to me that it did not "accept" the EU's offer with an intention to be bound by it as an agreement. Rather, in so doing it relied in good faith on the EU's undertaking in the Declaration and subsequently confirmed in the 2012 TAC Regulation (which had by that stage already been adopted). The fact that the Declaration produced its intended effects, and thus benefited Venezuela, is an insufficient basis for finding that Venezuela accepted to be bound by the Declaration as an agreement concluded between it and the EU. Nor can mere receipt of the notification of the Declaration or Venezuela's subsequent inquiry into the effect of proceedings before the Court constitute such a basis'. See also below, p 164.

[81] P Gautier, *Essai sur la définition des traités entre Etats. La pratique de la Belgique aux confins du droit des traités* (Brussels, Bruylant, 1993) 149.

[82] See eg the Kyoto Protocol (adopted 11 December 1998, entered into force 16 February 2005) 2303 UNTS 162, which is a protocol to the UNFCCC or the 16 protocols to the ECHR.

Convention, the 2003 Framework Convention on Tobacco Control adopted by the WHO, and the 1995 Framework Convention for the Protection of National Minorities adopted within the Council of Europe. Characteristic for a framework convention is that it constitutes an agreement that formulates certain objectives and principles and sometimes also an institutional framework on the basis of which later more detailed treaties (possibly in the form of 'protocols') are meant to come about. A framework convention is a legally binding treaty under international law. However, its 'framework nature' implies that it outlines objectives and principles rather than laying down specific obligations, even though typically it contains a number of minimum obligations.[83]

IV. Types of Treaties

Treaties can be divided into various categories, based either on their substance, or on formal criteria (such as the manner in which they were concluded or the number of parties involved). Apart from the distinction between bilateral and multilateral treaties, there is limited legal – but still pedagogical – value in making these classifications.

A. Contractual, Law-making and Consitutional Treaties

Article 38(1)(a) of the ICJ Statute determines that the ICJ is to settle disputes by applying, amongst others, 'international conventions, whether *general or particular*' (emphasis added). This touches upon the distinction between so-called law-making treaties (*traités-lois*) and contractual treaties (*traités-contrats*). Law-making treaties develop (or codify) generally applicable rules in a particular area of international law, whereby the application of the rules does not, in general, depend on reciprocity. The VCLT and VCLT-IO themselves are examples of law-making treaties. Other examples include the Antarctic Treaty, the UN Convention on the Law of the Sea (UNCLOS) and treaties in the field of the protection of the environment and human rights. For example, the European Court of Human Rights (ECtHR) has held that the ECHR is a law-making treaty.[84] Contractual treaties, by contrast, provide for mutual rights and obligations based on reciprocity. They may touch upon a wide array of issues; from agreements on the delivery of grain or weapons to the transfer of territory. They are subject to international law, and not to be confused with inter-State contracts subject to the internal rules of law of one particular State (see above, Section III(E)). Admittedly, any sharp distinction between both types of treaties is somewhat artificial, and certain treaties may not easily fit within one category or another. Nevertheless, the distinction helps us to understand why treaty law (notably including the VCLT), which usually follows a contractual logic, at times fits uneasily for law-making treaties.[85]

[83] See inter alia AC Kiss, 'Les traités-cadres: une technique juridique caractéristique du droit international de l'environnement' (1993) 39 *Annuaire français de droit international* 792; N Matz-Lück, 'Framework Conventions as a Regulatory Tool' (2009) 1 *Goettingen Journal of International Law* 439; N Matz-Lück, 'Framework Agreements' in MPEPIL.

[84] *Loizidou v Turkey* App no 15318/89 (ECtHR, 23 March 1995) para 84. See further C Brölmann, 'Law-Making Treaties: Form and Function in International Law' (2005) 74 *Nord J Intl* 383.

[85] See further E Raftopoulos, *The Inadequacy of the Contractual Analogy in the Law of Treaties* (Athens, Hellenic Institute of International and Foreign Law, 1990); A Rasulov, 'Theorizing Treaties: The Consequences of the

A third category of treaties are constituent instruments of international organisations or 'constitutional treaties' (*traités-constitutions*). Indeed, international organisations are generally established through a constituent instrument that is an international treaty. Usually, these treaties not only establish an international organisation, but also set out the basic rules for its governance, membership and functions. The UN Charter and the EU Treaties are examples of such treaties. As mentioned above (Section II), the provisions of the VCLT apply to the founding treaties of international organisations 'without prejudice to any relevant rules of the organization'.[86]

B. Bilateral and Multilateral Treaties

Treaties can also be categorised based upon the number and nature of the parties involved. The main distinction is that between bilateral and multilateral treaties. In principle, bilateral treaties are treaties between two States, between a State and an international organisation or between two international organisations. Multilateral treaties are treaties to which three or more States (and/or international organisations) are a party. In the context of EU treaty practice, an agreement is still considered to be bilateral in nature when it includes the EU and its Member States on the one hand and a group of States on the other.[87] What is decisive in differentiating bilateral and multilateral treaties is not so much the number of States or organisations involved, but the way in which the relevant rights and obligations are structured. In a bilateral treaty, obligations are organised between two contracting parties; a multilateral treaty contains a set of mutual obligations among all contracting parties.

The distinction between multilateral and bilateral treaties has a number of consequences regarding the applicable law of treaties. For example, one provision in the VCLT – Article 60(1), concerning the material breach of a bilateral treaty (on which see below, Section XI(E)) – is limited to bilateral treaties. While a number of provisions expressly concern multilateral treaties,[88] also the provisions regarding reservations and depositaries are by nature only relevant for multilateral treaties.[89] In addition, whether a treaty is a bilateral or multilateral treaty affects several of the issues discussed below, notably including its conclusion, modification and the issue of withdrawal.

A third category of treaties that can be differentiated based on the number of parties is that of 'plurilateral' treaties. The term is used almost exclusively within the framework of the WTO (on which see Chapter 19, Section III(A)(vi)(d)), where, in addition to a long list of multilateral agreements (to which all WTO Members must be a party), there are

Contractual Analogy' in CJ Tams, A Tzanakopoulos and A Zimmermann (eds), *Research Handbook on the Law of Treaties* (Chelthenham, Edward Elgar, 2014) 74–122.

[86] Art 5 VCLT. On constituent treaties, see further E Suy, 'The Constitutional Character of Constituent Treaties of International Organizations and the Hierarchy of Norms' in U Beyerlin and R Bernhardt (eds), *Recht zwischen Umbruch und Bewahrung: Völkerrecht, Europarecht, Staatsrecht: Festschrift für Rudolf Bernhardt* (Berlin, Springer, 1995) 267–78; P Quayle, 'Treaties of a Particular Type: The ICJ's Interpretative Approach to the Constituent Instruments of International Organizations' (2016) 29 *LJIL* 853.

[87] See eg the Cotonou Partnership Agreement Between the Members of the African, Caribbean and Pacific Group of States, of the One Part, and the European Community and its Member States, on the Other Part [2000] OJ L317/3.

[88] ie Arts 40 (amendment of multilateral treaties), 41 (agreements to modify multilateral treaties between certain of the parties only), 58 (suspension of the operation of a multilateral treaty by agreement between certain of the parties only) and 60(2) (material breach of a multilateral treaty) VCLT.

[89] Aust (n 42) 9.

a number of plurilateral agreements, ie agreements to which Members of the WTO can, but do not have to, accede.[90]

C. 'Open' and 'Closed' Treaties

Another distinction is the one between 'open' and 'closed' treaties. 'Open' treaties are multilateral treaties to which States other than the original States Parties can accede. Through numerous ratifications and accessions, an open treaty can evolve into a universal or quasi-universal treaty. For instance, the Convention on the Rights of the Child is nearly universally ratified, and now has 196 parties. That openness may of course be limited. Closed treaties are bilateral or multilateral treaties that are not open to other States. These include, for example, treaties between two countries in the field of double taxation.

D. Treaties Established in the Framework of an International Organisation

As the number of international organisations increased substantially in the second half of the twentieth century, so did the number of treaties established within the framework of international organisations. Some of these treaties are created merely 'under the auspices' of an organisation: the organisation then is a driving force behind the treaty, but the negotiation and ratification of the treaty remains in the hands of States. UNCLOS, for example, came about under the auspices of the UN. In other circumstances, the organisation can be much more directly involved in the development of a particular treaty. Falling within the latter category are the International Labour Organization (ILO) conventions, which have been adopted by the ILO Conference by a two-thirds majority.[91] Within the World Health Organization (WHO), the World Health Assembly can adopt treaties or agreements[92] by a two-thirds majority.[93] Agreements that were developed between EU Member States on the basis of the EU Treaties, such as the Europol Convention,[94] also fall within this category.

A number of international organisations have been instrumental in developing key multilateral treaties. The UN, and especially the UN General Assembly (UNGA), has a particular role in this regard. Under the UN Charter, the UNGA is tasked with 'encouraging the progressive development of international law and its codification'.[95] It is for this purpose that the UNGA has established a particular subsidiary body, namely the International Law Commission (ILC), which has precisely the mandate to progressively develop

[90] See eg B Hoekman, 'Plurilateral Agreements, Variable Geometry and the WTO' in A Dür and M Elsig (eds), *Trade Cooperation: The Purpose, Design and Effects of Preferential Trade Agreements* (Cambridge, CUP, 2015) 533–54.

[91] Art 19(2) Constitution of the International Labour Organization (adopted 28 June 1919, entered into force 10 January 1920) 15 UNTS 40 (ILO Constitution).

[92] To date, only one treaty has been adopted in this way, namely the Framework Convention on Tobacco Control (adopted 21 May 2003, entered into force 27 February 2005) 2302 UNTS 166.

[93] Art 19 Constitution of the World Health Organization (adopted 22 July 1946, entered into force 7 April 1948) 14 UNTS 185 (WHO Constitution).

[94] Convention based on Article K.3 of the Treaty on European Union, on the Establishment of a European Police Office [1995] OJ C316/2 (Europol Convention); replaced by Council Decision 2009/371/JHA of 6 April 2009 establishing the European Police Office (Europol) [2009] OJ L121/37, as amended; replaced by Regulation (EU) 2016/794 of the European Parliament and of the Council of 11 May 2016 on the European Union Agency for Law Enforcement Cooperation (Europol) [2016] OJ L135/53.

[95] Art 13(1)(a) UN Charter.

and codify international law (see Chapter 3, Section II(F)).[96] At the regional level, the Council of Europe has sought to achieve its goal to foster greater unity between its Member States in part by developing key agreements in a number of fields.[97] Since it was founded in 1949, no fewer than 229 treaties and protocols have been adopted within the framework of the Council of Europe.[98] For the ILO, the number has reached 189 conventions;[99] in the context of the International Maritime Organization (IMO), 58 treaties and protocols have been adopted to date.[100]

Although upon their adoption, each of these treaties still has to be ratified by the Members or Member States, the constitutional documents of a number of international organisations provide for a follow-up procedure to facilitate expedient ratification. For instance, each Member of the WHO undertakes that it will, within 18 months after the adoption of a convention or agreement by the World Health Assembly, take action related to the acceptance of such convention or agreement. If a Member does not approve this treaty or agreement within the prescribed time limit, it must send a statement to the Director-General of the WHO in which it states its reasons for non-acceptance.[101]

V. Conclusion of Treaties

In the broad sense, the conclusion of a treaty refers to the entire procedure by which international treaties come about. In the strict sense, a treaty can only be considered 'concluded' when States (or other subjects of international law with treaty-making capacity) have expressed their consent to be bound. This section discusses the subsequent stages that come with the conclusion of a treaty in the broad sense.

A. Drafting of the Treaty Text

First, there are several stages to the drafting of a treaty text. These can broadly be categorised as the stages of negotiation, the adoption of the treaty text, and its authentication.

i. Negotiation

As a general rule, treaties are the result of a negotiation process. The negotiations will, depending on the number of parties, either be bilateral or multilateral in nature. Multilateral negotiations can take place within the framework of a diplomatic conference or of an international organisation (see above, Section IV(D)). Internally, each State has different

[96] UNGA Res 174 (II), 21 November 1947, UN Doc A/RES/147 (II).

[97] Art 1(a) and (b) Statute of the Council of Europe (adopted 5 May 1949, entered into force 3 August 1949) CETS No 1. An example of such an agreement is the Framework Convention for the Protection of National Minorities (adopted 1 February 1995, entered into force 1 February 1998) CETS No 157.

[98] For an overview, see the website of the Council of Europe Treaty Office: www.coe.int/en/web/conventions.

[99] For an overview, see the ILO Information System on International Labour Standards: ilo.org/dyn/normlex/en/f?p=NORMLEXPUB:1:0::NO:::.

[100] For an overview, see the List of IMO Conventions: imo.org/About/Conventions/ListOfConventions.

[101] Art 20 WHO Constitution (n 93). A similar follow-up mechanism is used in the ILO; see Art 19(5) ILO Constitution (n 91).

rules and procedures regarding the negotiation of treaties. On the international level, treaty negotiations have not truly been made the object of substantive regulation.[102] For example, the idea of a separate article on negotiations in the ILC Draft Articles was abandoned.[103] In 1999, the UNGA adopted the 'Principles and Guidelines for International Negotiations'.[104]

A first and most important procedural concern is who is entitled to negotiate a treaty on behalf of a State.[105] Remarkably, the VCLT addresses the authority to negotiate a treaty in Article 2(1)(c) when defining 'full powers', but not in the substantive rule of Article 7 concerning full powers (on the latter, see below, this subsection).[106] Article 2(1)(c) VCLT defines 'full powers' as

> a document emanating from the competent authority of a State designating a person or persons to represent the State for negotiating, adopting or authenticating the text of a treaty, for expressing the consent of the State to be bound by a treaty, or for accomplishing any other act with respect to a treaty.

Still, 'the opening of exploratory talks or even *in merito* negotiations are possible without "powers" understood in their original meaning, ie a formal document'.[107] In practice, a delegate attending an international conference at which a multilateral treaty is negotiated will usually participate on behalf of a State based on 'credentials' issued by that State. Credentials may allow negotiating and concluding the negotiations by adopting the final text of a treaty, but not to authenticate that text by signing it (even if the treaty is subject to ratification)[108] or to bind the State in any way. For the latter purposes, full powers – which can be combined in one document with credentials – are required.[109]

With the exception of the possibility of credentials, a person who represents a State in the negotiation, adoption or authentication of the text of a treaty or for the purpose of expressing the consent of the State to be bound, needs to show proof of appropriate 'full powers' for that purpose. As it is left for each State to decide on the scope of the full powers, they can allow representing the State for one particular treaty, or generally, for all sorts of treaties ('general full powers').[110] Article 7(2) VCLT considers the following persons, based on their duties and without having to show proof of full powers, as representing their State: (i) Heads of State, Heads of Government and Ministers of Foreign Affairs, for the purpose of performing all acts relating to the conclusion of a treaty; (ii) heads of diplomatic missions, only for the purpose of adopting the text of a treaty between the accrediting State and the State to which they are accredited; and (iii) representatives accredited by States to an international conference or to an international organisation or one of its organs, only for the purpose of adopting the text of a treaty in that conference, organisation or organ.

[102] G Korontzis, 'Making the Treaty' in Hollis (n 29) 179. See also J Wouters, 'Government by Negotiation' in S Cassese (ed), *Research Handbook on Global Administrative Law* (Cheltenham, Edward Elgar, 2016) 196–211.

[103] K Schmalenbach, 'Lawmaking by Treaty: Negotiation of Agreements and Adoption of Treaty Texts' in C Brölmann and Y Radi (eds), *Research Handbook on the Theory and Practice of International Lawmaking* (Cheltenham, Edward Elgar, 2016) 90.

[104] UNGA Res 53/101, 20 January 1999, UN Doc A/RES/53/101.

[105] Kolb (n 7) 38.

[106] P Kovacs, 'Article 7: Full Powers – 1969 Vienna Convention' in Corten and Klein (n 34) Vol I, 132; Schmalenbach (n 103) 90.

[107] Kovacs (n 106) 132.

[108] In which case signature refers to 'simple signature', as opposed to 'definitive signature', which also expresses the consent (of the State) to be bound; Aust (n 42) 89. See also below, Section V(B)(i).

[109] ibid, 72.

[110] F Hoffmeister, 'Article 7. Full Powers' in Dörr and Schmalenbach (n 5) 134. See further Aust (n 42) 71–78.

In addition, the ICJ appears to have recognised that other State ministers have the power to negotiate and conclude treaties in their sphere of competence.[111]

Apart from the procedural issue of the authority to negotiate, the aforementioned UNGA Negotiation Principles address issues such as the agreed framework of procedure for the negotiations, the principle of sovereign equality of the negotiating parties and the right to initiate and participate in negotiations and the duty to cooperate. More substantive rules governing the negotiation of treaties concern unlawful objects and purposes of negotiations, the threat or use of unlawful negotiation means and the duty to negotiate in good faith.[112]

The VCLT-IO determines that '[t]he capacity of an international organization to conclude treaties is governed by the rules of that organization'.[113] Article 7 VCLT-IO deals with the question of who is capable of representing an international organisation for the purposes of adopting or authenticating a text of a treaty or expressing its consent to be bound. As with States, the Article recognises as having such capacity those who produce appropriate full powers, or, where it appears from practice or other circumstances that this was the intention of the States and international organisations concerned, those who are considered 'as representing the organization for such purposes, in accordance with the rules of the organization'.[114]

The procedure for the negotiation of an international agreement by the EU is set out in Article 218 TFEU. The first step is for the Council to authorise the opening of negotiations, and to adopt 'negotiating directives' addressed to the party or parties undertaking the negotiations.[115] In most cases the European Commission will first have made a recommendation to the Council for the opening of negotiations.[116] It is well established that the European Commission has the power to represent the EU internationally and to negotiate international agreements on its behalf, though in some cases the Council may appoint a 'negotiating team'. The High Representative of the Union for Foreign Affairs and Security Policy may make such a recommendation to the Council where the envisaged agreement relates solely or predominantly to the Common Foreign and Security Policy (CFSP).[117] Once the Council has adopted the negotiation directives, the negotiator negotiates on behalf of the Union with the third State in question. Once authorised, the negotiator must conduct the negotiations in consultation with special committees appointed by the Council to assist him in this task and within the framework of such directives as the Council may issue.[118] In all cases, the European Parliament is to be immediately and fully informed at all stages of the procedure.[119] The CJEU has held in this repect that

> participation by the Parliament in the legislative process is the reflection, at Union level, of a fundamental democratic principle that the people should participate in the exercise of power through the intermediary of a representative assembly […]. As regards the procedure for negotiating and

[111] *Armed Activities on the Territory of the Congo (New Application: 2002)* (Democratic Republic of the Congo v Rwanda) [2006] ICJ Rep 6, para 47; Kolb (n 7) 37–41.
[112] In general, see further Schmalenbach (n 102) 90–96; on good faith, see further M-L Gächter-Alge, 'The Principle of Good Faith in Treaty Negotiations – Obligation to Choose Words in a Trustworthy Manner' in S Besson and N Levrat (eds), *Les principes en droit européen* (Genève, Schulthess, 2011) 139–60.
[113] Art 6 VCLT-IO.
[114] See further Kovacs (n 106) 145–54.
[115] Art 218(2) TFEU.
[116] eg Art 207(3) TFEU.
[117] Art 218(3) TFEU.
[118] Art 218(4) TFEU.
[119] Art 218(10) TFEU.

concluding international agreements, the information requirement laid down in Article 218(10) TFEU is the expression of that democratic principle, on which the European Union is founded [...]. The aim of that information requirement is, inter alia, to ensure that the Parliament is in a position to exercise democratic control over the European Union's external action and, more specifically, to verify that the choice made of the legal basis for a decision on the conclusion of an agreement was made with due regard to the powers of the Parliament [...].[120]

ii. Adoption

Adoption is the act by which the negotiating parties express their agreement with the final text of the treaty.[121] The adoption of the text of a treaty takes place, in principle, once the consent of all the States participating in its drafting is given.[122] For the adoption of the text of a treaty at an international conference, a majority of two-thirds of the States present and voting suffices, unless those States, by the same majority, decide to apply a different rule.[123] In case of bilateral treaties, a specific or distinct process of adoption is rare: the parties' very signature of the final text constitutes the act of adopting the text.[124]

The adoption of the text of a treaty marks the end of the negotiation process. However, this stage does not amount to the State expressing its consent to be bound by the treaty. In fact, it is simply 'the formal act by which the form and content of the treaty are settled'.[125] Even so, pursuant to Article 24(4) VCLT, the adoption of a treaty does have legal consequences:

> The provisions of a treaty regulating the authentication of its text, the establishment of the consent of States to be bound by the treaty, the manner or date of its entry into force, reservations, the functions of the depositary and other matters arising before the entry into force of the treaty apply from the time of the adoption of its text.[126]

iii. Authentication

Authentication is the 'process of establishing the final text'.[127] It signals that the text corresponds to the one agreed upon and constitutes the definitive text of the treaty.[128] Authentication usually takes place through initialling and/or signing the treaty.[129] It can also take place through a procedure that is provided for in the treaty text or agreed upon by the States participating in the treaty. For bilateral treaties, initialling/signing is normally

[120] Judgment of 14 June 2016, *Parliament v Council (Tanzania Pirates Agreement)*, C-263/14, EU:C:2016:435, paras 70–71. For an analysis of the impact of this judgment on the choice of legal basis and on the role of the European Parliament, see G De Baere and T Van den Sanden, 'Interinstitutional Gravity and Pirates of the Parliament on Stranger Tides: The Continued Constitutional Significance of the Choice of Legal Basis in Post-Lisbon External Action' (2016) 12 *European Constitutional Law Review* 85.

[121] Korontzis (n 102) 184.

[122] Art 9(1) VCLT.

[123] Art 9(2) VCLT. For example, the United Nations Diplomatic Conference of Plenipotentiaries on the Establishment of an International Criminal Court in Rome adopted the Rome Statute of the International Criminal Court on 17 July 1998 with a vote of 120 of the 160 participating States (7 votes against and 21 abstentions). See further F Hoffmeister, 'Article 9. Adoption of the Text' in Dörr and Schmalenbach (n 5) 151.

[124] Korontzis (n 102) 186–87. See also Aust (n 42) 79–80.

[125] Aust (n 42) 79.

[126] Art 24(4) VCLT; see also Korontzis (n 102) 188.

[127] Aust (n 42) 83.

[128] Korontzis (n 102) 188.

[129] Art 10 VCLT.

regarded as amounting both to adoption *and* authentication. Also for multilateral treaties, authentication can proceed in such a way. However, given the number of parties involved, the fact that the negotiation process may have been lengthy and hectic, and the possibility of multiple authentic texts in different languages, a formal procedure of adoption followed by a separate authentication is important and often preferred.[130]

B. Expression of Consent to be Bound

A State's consent to be bound by a treaty may be expressed by signature, exchange of instruments constituting a treaty,[131] ratification, acceptance, approval, accession, or 'by any other means if so agreed'.[132] This demonstrates the great flexibility of treaty law, as already discussed above (in Section III). In practice, this makes it possible for consent to be shown through particular behaviour or additional correspondence. Means worth mentioning include, in a bilateral context: proclamation, publication, mutual notification that domestic requirements have been fulfilled, joint public declaration[133] and oral expressions of consent to be bound; in a multilateral context: initialling a text (if explicitly so agreed; see Article 12(2)(a) VCLT),[134] decisions in an intergovernmental context, treaty-making under an institutionalised treaty regime and rule-making under the auspices of an international organisation (which are often situated at the borderline between treaty-making and law-making by the international organisation). Compliance with certain requirements of a treaty to which a State is not a party, lastly, is not a means of expressing consent to be bound.[135]

Because the expression of the consent of a State to be bound by a treaty and the establishment of this consent do not always coincide in time and constitute two distinct acts, Article 16 VCLT serves to determine precisely when the consent of a State to be bound can be established and take effect regarding other contracting States.[136] Thus, it determines that:

> Unless the treaty provides otherwise, instruments of ratification, acceptance, approval or accession establish the consent of a State to be bound by a treaty upon:
> a) their exchange between the contracting States;
> b) their deposit with the depositary; or
> c) their notification to the contracting States or to the depositary, if so agreed.[137]

[130] Aust (n 42) 83–84; Kolb (n 7) 41–42.
[131] A practice that, due to its very nature, is normally limited to treaties of a bilateral nature; Aust (n 42) 94.
[132] Art 11 VCLT.
[133] See eg the *Aegean Sea Continental Shelf* (n 72) as discussed above (Section III(F)).
[134] The use of initialling for the purpose of expressing consent to be bound is to be discouraged, as it is more commonly used as the means by which a text is adopted or authenticated (see above, Section V(A)(iii)); Aust (n 42) 93. Nevertheless, an example is the General Framework Agreement for Peace in Bosnia and Herzegovina (adopted 21 November 1995, entered into force 14 December 1995) 35 ILM 75 (Dayton Peace Agreement), which entered into force through the *initialling* of the Dayton Agreement, after the *signing* of an Agreement on Initialling, which provided that the initialling of the Dayton Agreement would express the respective States' consent to be bound; ibid, 93.
[135] F Hoffmeister, 'Article 11. Means of Expressing Consent to be Bound by a Treaty' in Dörr and Schmalenbach (n 5) 169.
[136] F Horchani and Y Ben Hammadi, 'Article 16: Exchange or Deposit of Instruments of Ratification, Acceptance, Approval or Accession – 1969 Vienna Convention' in Corten and Klein (n 34) Vol I, 335.
[137] Art 16 VCLT.

For treaties established in the framework of the UN and many other multilateral treaties, the Secretary General of the UN (UNSG) is designated as the depositary.[138] Today, the UNSG is the depository of more than 560 multilateral treaties, covering a broad range of subject matters.[139]

i. Signature

Article 12(1) of the VCLT provides that:

> The consent of a State to be bound by a treaty is expressed by the signature of its representative when:
>
> (a) The treaty provides that signature will have that effect;
> (b) It is otherwise established that the negotiating States were agreed that signature should have that effect; or
> (c) The intention of the State to give that effect to the signature appears from the full powers of its representative or was expressed during the negotiation.[140]

As mentioned above (Section V(A)(iii)), signature can serve for the cumulative purposes of authentication *and* expression of consent to be bound. In such cases, the signature is 'definitive' rather than 'simple', as in the latter case, the treaty is still subject to ratification.[141] Treaties concluded pursuant to Article 12 VCLT are traditionally known as 'treaties in simplified form' (*accords en forme simplifiée*). As they do not require ratification, their conclusion, and often also entry into force, is 'immediate'.[142] Today, the use of simplified treaties is widespread and represents a large proportion of the overall treaty practice.[143] In the US, for example, this procedure is often preferred in order not to be subjected to the constitutional obligation to obtain approval ('advice and consent') of treaties by a two-thirds majority in the Senate.[144] On the international level, agreements in simplified form have the same binding status as treaties.

For other treaties, it may not be the intention of the contracting States to be bound by the treaty simply upon signing it. Often, that is so because States are required by their constitutional system to go through internal procedures of consent (see below, Section V(B)(iv)). Thus, when a treaty provides that it is subject to ratification, that ratification is essential in order for States to be bound by that treaty and a mere signature will not suffice to express their consent. If a treaty does not provide for ratification and remains silent about the way in which consent to be bound can be expressed, it is assumed that

[138] See further A Hinojal-Oyarbide and A Rosenboom, 'Managing the Process of Treaty Formation' in Hollis (n 29) 248–76; UN Office of Legal Affairs (Treaty Section), 'Summary of Practice of the Secretary General as Depositary of Multilateral Treaties', 1994, UN Doc ST/LEG/7/Rev.1.
[139] See treaties.un.org.
[140] Art 12(1) VCLT.
[141] See already above (n 108).
[142] C van Assche, 'Article 12: Consent to be Bound by a Treaty Expressed by Signature – 1969 Vienna Convention' in Corten and Klein (n 34) Vol I, 211–13. See also Kolb (n 7) 42, and further C Chayet, 'Les accords en forme simplifiée' (1957) 3 *Annuaire français de droit international* 3 and FS Hamzeh, 'Agreements in Simplified Form – Modern Perspective' (1968–69) *BYIL* 179; PF Smets, *La conclusion des accords en forme simplifiée: étude de droit international et de droit constitutionnel belge et comparé* (Brussels, Bruylant, 1969).
[143] Korontzis (n 102) 196.
[144] Art II(2)(2) US Constitution. See further D Bodansky and P Spiro, 'Executive Agreements+' (2016) 49 *Vanderbilt Journal of Transnational Law* 885; FL Morrison, 'Executive Agreements' in MPEPIL.

signature suffices as an expression of consent to be bound.[145] Moreover, given their inherent capacity to represent their State on the international level, there is a presumption that the signature of a treaty by a Head of State, Head of Government or Minister of Foreign Affairs engages the State they represent. In this respect, in the *Land and Maritime Boundary* (Cameroon v Nigeria) case, when addressing Nigeria's argument that its constitutional rules regarding the conclusion of treaties were not complied with, the ICJ ruled that

> a limitation of a Head of State's capacity in this respect is not manifest in the sense of Article 46, paragraph 2, unless at least properly publicized. This is particularly so because Heads of State belong to the group of persons who, in accordance with Article 7, paragraph 2, of the Convention '[i]n virtue of their functions and without having to produce full powers' are considered as representing their State.[146]

When a State signs a treaty, exchanges instruments constituting a treaty or expresses its consent to be bound by a treaty still subject to ratification, pursuant to Article 18 VCLT, this triggers an interim obligation pending the treaty's entry into force. The State is then obliged to refrain from acts which would defeat the object and purpose of the treaty.[147] This is a manifestation of the broader principle of good faith in international treaty law and international law in general.[148] This principle does not mean that the obligations under the treaty apply before its entry into force (though this can be the case through the provisional application of the treaty, on which see below, Section V(E)). Rather, Article 18 is designed to protect the legitimate expectations of the contracting States, and to prevent acts that would render the performance of obligations under the treaty extremely difficult, impossible or meaningless.[149]

The General Court of the EU examined the interim obligation under Article 18 VCLT incidentally in *Opel Austria*. Rather than to base its reasoning on Article 18 VCLT, however, the Court found that there was a legitimate expectation on the part of a company that the

[145] In support of this view UNSC Res 687, 8 April 1991, UN Doc S/RES/687 is sometimes cited, in which the UNSC considered a border treaty between Kuwait and Iraq, drawn up in the form of agreed minutes that had been signed by both parties, to be binding (6th recital of the preamble and operative clause 2); Aust (n 42) 89.

[146] *Land and Maritime Boundary* (Cameroon v Nigeria; Equatorial Guinea intervening) [2002] ICJ Rep 303, para 265.

[147] For this reason, on 6 May 2002, the US Government sent the following Communication to the UNSG with respect to the ICC Statute, which it had signed on 31 December 2000: 'This is to inform you, in connection with the Rome Statute of the International Criminal Court adopted on July 17, 1998, that the United States does not intend to become a party to the treaty. Accordingly, the United States has no legal obligations arising from its signature on December 31, 2000. The United States requests that its intention not to become a party, as expressed in this letter, be reflected in the depositary's status lists relating to this treaty'; Under Secretary of State for Arms Control and International Security John R Bolton, 'International Criminal Court: Letter to UN Secretary General Kofi Annan', 6 May 2002, 2001–2009.state.gov/r/pa/prs/ps/2002/9968.htm. For an application before national courts, see eg Constitutional Court (DE), *G ('Extradition to India Case')*, 24 June 2003, Case No 2 BvR 685/03, BVerfGE 108, 129 (emphasising that according to Art 18 VCLT Germany and India were under the obligation not to defeat the purpose of their extradition treaty, even though they had not ratified it yet); Council of State (NL), *Dutch Seamen's Welfare Foundation v Minister of Transport, Public Works, and Water Management*, 27 July 2005, Case No ECLI:NL:RVS:2005:AU0095 (considering that the adoption of an ILO Convention merely constituted a collective legal act of the ILO Members, did not qualify as a signature and did not create any obligations for the Netherlands to comply with Art 18 VCLT); and Supreme Court (PL), *Stanisław v Zakład Techniczno-Budowlany P Spółka zoo*, 29 July 2005, Case No II PK 100/05 as well as Court of Cassation (IT), *Public Prosecutor at the Tribunal of Brescia v Elvis and el Mahdi*, 9 October 2015, Case No 40699 (both interpreting domestic law in conformity with the relevant treaty, even if it had not yet been ratified).

[148] O Dörr, 'Article 18. Obligation not to Defeat the Object and Purpose of a Treaty Prior to its Entry into Force' in Dörr and Schmalenbach (n 5) 244. See also Aust (n 42) 107–109; Kolb (n 7) 43–46.

[149] ibid. See further MA Rogoff, 'The International Legal Obligations of Signatories to an Unratified Treaty' in S Davidson (ed), *The Law of Treaties* (Aldershot, Ashton, 2004) 191–230.

Council and other parties to the EEA Agreement would not act so as to defeat the object and purpose of that agreement.[150] There have been a number of (other) cases in which the same interim obligation has been invoked before the EU courts.[151] In their judgments, the courts apply a good faith test rather than the actual Article 18 VCLT.[152]

Finally, it sometimes occurs that representatives sign a treaty *ad referendum*, because they are unsure whether signing exceeds the scope of their competence. This means that the signature must later be confirmed by the State in order for it to be considered an expression of consent to be bound by the treaty.[153]

With respect to the EU, under Article 218(5) TFEU, the Council, upon the proposal of the negotiator, is to adopt a decision authorising the signing of the agreement. However, the EU Treaties do not specify which party is actually responsible for signature at the conclusion of negotiations. Thus, the Council arguably has a wide discretion in deciding the party that is to sign the agreement. Depending on whether or not the agreement concerns matters of CFSP, the appropriate party would be the High Representative or the European Commission respectively. For international agreements concluded by both the EU and its Member States ('mixed agreements'), the EU Member State holding the rotating presidency will also be involved in the signing thereof.

ii. *Ratification*

According to Article 2(1)(b) VCLT, '"[r]atification", "acceptance", "approval" and "accession" mean in each case the international act so named whereby a State establishes on the international plane its consent to be bound by a treaty'. Pursuant to Article 14(1) VCLT, the consent of a State to be bound by a treaty must be expressed by ratification in scenarios similar to those required for signature, namely when:

(a) The treaty provides for such consent to be expressed by means of ratification;
(b) It is otherwise established that the negotiating States were agreed that ratification should be required;
(c) The representative of the State has signed the treaty subject to ratification; or
(d) The intention of the State to sign the treaty subject to ratification appears from the full powers of its representative or was expressed during the negotiation.

One notes from requirements (c) and (d) that prior to moving to ratification, a State must have signed the treaty, and made its consent to be bound 'subject to ratification'. As opposed to the rules on signature, if a treaty is silent on ratification, it is presumed not to be required.[154] Thus, ratification is the legal act following signature, through which the Head of State, Head of Government or the Minister of Foreign Affairs (or any other organ having received full powers) confirms that the treaty that has been developed by its authorised representatives, will be definitively binding and formally undertakes to uphold the treaty on behalf of the State. Usually, this is done by the exchange

[150] Judgment of 22 January 1997, *Opel Austria v Council*, T-115/94, EU:T:1997:3, paras 93–94 (in those days, the General Court was still called the 'Court of First Instance').
[151] See judgment of 27 November 1997, *Danisco Sugar*, C-27/96, EU:C:1997:563; judgment of 17 January 2007, *Greece v Commission*, T-231/04, EU:T:2007:9.
[152] Or even a 'manifest intent' test: J Klabbers, 'How to Defeat a Treaty's Object and Purpose Pending Entry into Force: Toward Manifest Intent' (2001) 34 *Vanderbilt Journal of Transnational Law* 283, 318.
[153] Art 12(2)(b) VCLT. See Aust (n 42) 90–91; van Assche (n 142) 235–38.
[154] Korontzis (n 102) 188.

(in case of bilateral treaties) or deposit (in case of multilateral treaties) of the instrument of ratification.[155]

The reason for a ratification procedure separate from signature lies in the democratic structure of most States. As the treaty is both negotiated and ratified by the executive, it may require some time in between both formalities to internally reflect on the treaty and consult the State's people or their elected representatives before expressing definitive consent to be bound.[156] Thus, even if the process of ratification and its effect within the legal order of a State differ from jurisdiction to jurisdiction, it normally involves legislative or parliamentary bodies.[157] Nevertheless, at least for the purpose of international law, the act of ratification – an act of the executive – needs to be clearly distinguished from what is normally called 'consent', 'assent' or 'approval', ie the internal act of parliament that authorises the executive to ratify.[158] From an international law perspective, it makes no difference which internal procedure precedes actual ratification and whether it is appropriately followed.[159]

In the VCLT-IO, the term 'act of formal confirmation' is used instead of 'ratification' for international organisations. According to the terminology in the EU context, the EU 'concludes' an international agreement. The EU generally expresses its consent to be bound by a treaty through a Council Decision on the conclusion (the EU law equivalent of ratification) of the agreement, in which it is stated that the treaty 'is hereby approved on behalf of the Union'.[160]

iii. Acceptance, Approval or Accession

Acceptance, approval or accession have the same legal consequences as ratification.[161] Acceptance and approval, which do not have any special technical significance, are just formal expressions of consent that may consist of the simple announcement that the domestic requirements have been fulfilled. They allow the government the opportunity to examine the treaty after its signature before expressing the final consent to be bound. Since using the term ratification may trigger domestic legislative procedures, and '[i]n order to preserve the possibility of a two-step procedure without parliamentary ratification',[162] 'acceptance' or 'approval' are used instead. According to one author, there would be a difference between both terms in that 'approval' is a simpler and more direct way to express consent to be bound. However, at the domestic level, and as opposed to 'acceptance', it would run the risk of being considered equal to ratification, making the treaty subject to parliamentary approval.[163] Most authors and the ILC consider that at least at the international level,

[155] Aust (n 42) 95–97; Kolb (n 7) 46–47; Korontzis (n 102) 197–98.
[156] Kolb (n 7) 47.
[157] Korontzis (n 102) 197.
[158] Kolb (n 7) 47.
[159] F Hoffmeister, 'Article 14. Consent to be Bound by a Treaty Expressed by Ratification, Acceptance or Approval' in Dörr and Schmalenbach (n 5) 205.
[160] See eg Art 1 of the Council Decision 2014/835/EU of 27 November 2014 on the conclusion of the Agreement between the European Union and the Republic of Iceland and the Kingdom of Norway on the surrender procedure between the Member States of the European Union and Iceland and Norway [2014] OJ L343/1.
[161] See Arts 14(2) and 15 VCLT.
[162] Hoffmeister (n 159) 205.
[163] ibid, 207.

the term 'acceptance' is an innovation of terminology rather than method, and that the choice between both terms is not a matter of substance.[164]

The term 'accession', on the other hand, is reserved for the act through which a State becomes a party to a treaty that has already been negotiated and signed by other States.[165] It is usual for multilateral treaties to be opened for signature for a limited period of time; afterwards they are open only to accession.[166] Moreover, in the majority of cases, the treaty in question will have already entered into force for the negotiating States. There is no guaranteed right for States to become parties to a treaty by accession since this form of consent is only available when the treaty in question so provides or the parties agree to it (see also above, Section IV(C), on the conceptual distinction between 'open' and 'closed' treaties).[167] Usually, treaties determine whether they are open to accession and the manner in which it has to take place. International organisations often set preconditions for the accession of States.[168] These preconditions may be geographical, such as the requirement of being 'European' in the case of the EU[169] and the North Atlantic Treaty Organization (NATO).[170] They may include substantive conditions, such as democracy[171] and respect for fundamental freedoms, as is the case for the Council of Europe[172] and the EU.[173] Accession of new Member States often leads to extensive negotiations and the conclusion of a separate Treaty of Accession. For example, a Treaty of Accession of the ten new Member States to the EU was signed on 16 April 2003 in Athens.[174]

iv. Parliamentary Consent

As already discussed above (Section V(B)(ii)), in many countries, treaties only have effect in the internal legal system when parliamentary consent has been granted. This is not a requirement of international law, but a constitutional requirement under the State's internal law.

For EU agreements on CFSP, the European Parliament has no role to play (other than being 'immediately and fully informed';[175] see also above, Section V(A)(i)). For other agreements, the Parliament needs to be consulted.[176] Moreover, for association agreements, an agreement on the accession of the EU to the ECHR, agreements establishing a specific institutional framework, agreements with important budgetary implications, agreements in

[164] Aust (n 42) 100–101; R Ben Achour, I Frikha and M Snoussi, 'Article 14: Consent to be Bound by a Treaty Expressed by Ratification, Acceptance or Approval – 1969 Vienna Convention' in Corten and Klein (n 34) Vol I, 295; ILC Draft Articles (n 10) 198, para 10; Korontzis (n 102) 199–200.

[165] Art 15 VCLT.

[166] Korontzis (n 102) 200.

[167] ibid, 201.

[168] Aust (n 42) 102–103.

[169] Art 49 TEU.

[170] Art 10 NATO Treaty.

[171] See in this regard inter alia J Wouters, B De Meester and C Ryngaert, 'Democracy and International Law' (2003) 34 *NYIL* 137, in particular at 159–62.

[172] See the Preamble and Art 3 of the Statute of the Council of Europe (n 96).

[173] Art 49 TEU.

[174] Treaty concerning the accession of the Czech Republic, the Republic of Estonia, the Republic of Cyprus, the Republic of Latvia, the Republic of Lithuania, the Republic of Hungary, the Republic of Malta, the Republic of Poland, the Republic of Slovenia and the Slovak Republic to the European Union (adopted 16 April 2003, entered into force 1 May 2004) [2003] OJ L 236/17.

[175] Art 218(10) TFEU.

[176] Art 218(6)(b) TFEU.

areas where the 'ordinary legislative procedure' applies,[177] and for the withdrawal agreement in case a Member State departs from the EU,[178] the consent of the Parliament needs to be obtained.

C. Reservations

A treaty is the result of negotiations between two or more States. This means that once the treaty text is adopted, it is no longer possible for any of the parties to amend it; it can either be accepted or rejected. In some cases, the practice of making reservations offers an exception to this rule.[179] It is not possible to make reservations to a bilateral treaty. In such a case, a counter-offer will immediately be made to reopen negotiations.[180] However, for multilateral treaties, it is, with particular exceptions (see below, this section), generally possible to make reservations.[181] Article 2(1)(d) VCLT describes a reservation as

> a unilateral statement, however phrased or named, made by a State, when signing, ratifying, accepting, approving or acceding to a treaty, whereby it purports to exclude or to modify the legal effect of certain provisions of the treaty in their application to that State.

Before World War II, when the text of a treaty needed to be adopted unanimously, reservations needed to be accepted unanimously as well: if a reservation was not accepted by all the other contracting States, the reserving State had to drop its reservation to be able to become a party (ie the 'unanimity approach').[182] Today, the treaty law on reservations (as embodied in the VCLT) has become more flexible.

The dilemma to be confronted is whether reservations are allowed when the treaty itself does not say anything on the topic. This often occurs, including for the VCLT itself. The provisions of the VCLT addressing this issue were to a large extent inspired by the ICJ's 1951 *Reservations regarding the Convention on the Prevention and Punishment of the Crime of Genocide* Advisory Opinion (*Genocide* Advisory Opinion).[183] The impetus for the case was provided by the fact that the socialist countries wanted to become a party to the Genocide Convention, but at the same time wanted to make a reservation with regard to the jurisdiction of the ICJ over disputes related to the Convention that is contained therein.[184] The UNGA decided to request an advisory opinion from the ICJ. The ICJ ruled that in the specific context of the Genocide Convention, a more flexible approach was required and that the classic rule of unanimity could not be maintained.[185] Instead, when a treaty is silent on the admissibility of reservations, it is permitted to make such reservations unless they are irreconcilable with the object and purpose of the treaty.[186] The VCLT made the possibility of reservations the default rule for all treaties,[187] except for some particular cases.

[177] Art 218(6)(a) TFEU.
[178] Art 50 TEU.
[179] Arts 19–23 VCLT.
[180] Kolb (n 7) 67; ET Swaine, 'Treaty Reservations' in Hollis (n 29) 278.
[181] Kolb (n 7) 71.
[182] ibid, 64–65. See also Swaine (n 180) 281–82.
[183] *Reservations to the Convention on the Prevention and Punishment of the Crime of Genocide* [1951] ICJ Rep 15.
[184] Art IX Genocide Convention.
[185] *Genocide* Advisory Opinion (n 183) 21–22.
[186] ibid, 24. See also M Fitzmaurice, 'The Practical Working of the Law of Treaties' in MD Evans (ed), *International Law*, 4th edn (Oxford, OUP, 2014) 184–86; Swaine (n 180) 282.
[187] Swaine (n 180) 283.

Article 19 VCLT sets out that a State may, when signing, ratifying, accepting, approving or acceding to a treaty, formulate a reservation, except for three cases. First, when the reservation is prohibited by the treaty.[188] Second, when the treaty provides that only specified reservations may be made, which do not include the reservation in question.[189] Such cases give rise to a question of treaty interpration regarding whether the reservation falls within the category of prohited reservations. Third, a State may not formulate a reservation that is incompatible with the object and purpose of the treaty,[190] as discussed above in relation to the *Genocide* Advisory Opinion. This again gives rise to questions of what constitutes the object and purpose of a treaty, and to particular problems with regard to human rights treaties.[191]

In addition, and even if the unanimity rule no longer applies, the reservation must in principle still be accepted explicitly or tacitly by at least one other contracting State.[192] Artice 20 VCLT sets out a number of rules regarding the acceptance of and objection to reservations by the other parties. Article 20(1) VCLT contains the general rule that '[a] reservation expressly authorised by a treaty does not require any subsequent acceptance by the other contracting parties unless the treaty so provides'.[193] However, the other parties to the treaty still need to accept the reservation

> [w]hen it appears from the limited number of the negotiating States and the object and purpose of a treaty that the application of the treaty in its entirety between all the parties is an essential condition of the consent of each one to be bound by the treaty.[194]

An example of such a case would be the EU Treaties. In the case of treaties that are the constituent instrument of an international organisation, acceptance by the 'competent organ of that organization' is required.[195] Such constituent treaties are a special type of instrument and need to be shielded from the rules on reservations that might otherwise jeopardise the functioning of an international organisation.

[188] Art 19(a) VCLT. A number of treaties stipulate that no reservation thereto is permitted. This is, for example, the case with many recent environmental conventions; see eg Art 24 UNFCCC (n 82); Art 37 Convention on Biological Diversity (adopted 5 June 1992, entered into force 29 December 1993) 1760 UNTS 79; Art 26 Kyoto Protocol to the UNFCCC (adopted 11 December 1997, entered into force 16 February 2005) 2303 UNTS 162; Art 27 Paris Agreement (adopted 12 December 2015, entered into force 24 November 2016) UNTS No 54113. The same is the case for Art 120 of the ICC Statute, which provides that '[n]o reservations may be made to this Statute'.

[189] Art 19(b) VCLT. As an example, reference can be made to Art 57(1) ECHR. While this article allows a State to make a reservation 'in respect of any particular provision of the Convention to the extent that any law then in force in its territory is not in conformity with the provision' it adds that '[r]eservations of a general character shall not be permitted under this Article'. The ECtHR has stated that '[b]y "reservation of a general character" […] is meant in particular a reservation couched in terms that are too vague or broad for it to be possible to determine their exact meaning and scope'; *Belilos v Switzerland* App no 10328/83 (ECtHR, 29 April 1988) para 55.

[190] Art 19(c) VCLT.

[191] For example, when in 1992, the US made a reservation to Art 6(5) ICCPR, reserving itself the right to execute minors '(other than a pregnant woman) duly convicted under existing or future laws permitting the imposition of capital punishment', 11 European States objected and held (inter alia) that it was incompatible with the object and purpose of the ICCPR; see Aust (n 42) 123–25 and further K Ash, 'U.S. Reservations to the International Covenant on Civil and Political Rights: Credibility Maximization and Global Influence' (2005) 3 *Northwestern Journal of International Human Rights*. See further also U Linderfalk, 'On the Meaning of the "Object and Purpose" Criterion, in the Context of the Vienna Convention on the Law of treaties, Article 19' (2003) 72 *Nord J Intl* 429.

[192] Art 20(4) VCLT; Kolb (n 7) 71.

[193] Art 20(1) VCLT.

[194] ibid, Art 20(2).

[195] ibid, Art 20(3).

If the treaty does not (i) expressly authorise a reservation,[196] (ii) require application in its entirety due to its nature,[197] or (iii) constitute the constituent instrument of an international organisation,[198] Article 20(4) VCLT provides for the rules that apply residually:

> (a) [a]cceptance by another contracting State of a reservation constitutes the reserving State a party to the treaty in relation to that other State if or when the treaty is in force for those States;
>
> (b) [a]n objection by another contracting State to a reservation does not preclude the entry into force of the treaty as between the objecting and reserving States unless a contrary intention is definitely expressed by the objecting State;
>
> (c) [a]n act expressing a State's consent to be bound by the treaty and containing a reservation is effective as soon as at least one other contracting State has accepted the reservation.[199]

Article 20(5) adds that if a State does not object to the reservation within a period of 12 months after the date it was notified of the reservation or after the date it expressed its consent to be bound by the treaty (whichever is later), the reservation is considered to be accepted. Accordingly, 'acceptance' does not require a formal instrument and may be expressed tacitly, even by the absence of an objection. Thus, the combined effect of that provision and Article 20(4) VCLT 'is that the reserving state will become a contracting state unless *all* the other contracting states (1) object to the reservation *and* (2) explicitly object to the reserving state becoming a contracting state. Yet this will never happen'.[200]

In terms of legal consequences, a reservation '*modifies* for the reserving State in its relations with the other parties the provisions of the treaty to which the reservation relates, to the extent of the reservation (emphasis added)'.[201] Article 21(3) complements Article 20(4)(b) VCLT and provides that in the relations between the reserving State and the State that objected to the reservation, but has not opposed the entry into force of the treaty between itself and the reserving State, 'the provisions to which the reservation relates do *not apply* [...] to the extent of the reservation' (emphasis added). However, the reservation 'does not modify the provisions of the treaty for the other parties to the treaty *inter se*'.[202] As a result

> three forms of future relations are possible: (i) no relations under that treaty at all, with respect to any State that has objected and made clear that it wishes to deny treaty relations; (ii) treaty relations but for the reserved-to provision(s), with respect to any State that has objected but not declined treaty relations; and (iii) treaty relations as amended by the reservation, with respect to any State that has explicitly (or tacitly) accepted the reservation.[203]

The issue of the legal consequences of a reservation becomes more complicated when the reservation is considered to be *invalid*. In its *Genocide* Advisory Opinion, the ICJ found that a State which adopts a reservation that is incompatible with the object and purpose of a convention – and therefore invalid – cannot be considered to be a party to that convention.[204] In *Belilos v Switzerland*, the ECtHR approached the issue differently. After the Court had

[196] ibid, Art 20(1).
[197] ibid, Art 20(2).
[198] ibid, Art 20(3).
[199] Aust (n 42) 127.
[200] ibid, 128.
[201] Art 21(1)(a) VCLT.
[202] ibid, Art 21(2).
[203] Swaine (n 180) 278.
[204] *Genocide* Advisory Opinion (n 183) 24 and 29.

established its jurisdiction to rule on the validity of a reservation made by Switzerland to the ECHR,[205] it found that the reservation's wording 'f[e]ll foul of the rule that reservations must not be of a general character',[206] following which it found the reservation to be invalid.[207] Nevertheless, the Court held that 'it is beyond doubt that Switzerland is, and regards itself as, bound by the Convention irrespective of the validity of the declaration containing the reservation'.[208] Accordingly, the Court considered the invalid reservation to be *severable* from Switzerland's instrument of ratification, to which the reservation was appended, and thus from its consent to be bound by the ECHR.[209] The Human Rights Committee (HRCttee) adopted a similar approach in its General Comment No 24, stating:

> The normal consequence of an unacceptable reservation is not that the [ICCPR] will not be in effect at all for a reserving party. Rather, such a reservation will generally be severable, in the sense that the [ICCPR] will be operative for the reserving party without benefit of the reservation.[210]

This 'severability doctrine' has been rejected by many States, notably including France, the UK and the US, as being a violation of the principle that a State cannot be bound by a treaty to which it has not consented.[211] Nevertheless, according to the ILC's Guide to Practice on Reservations to Treaties of 2011, a State which has adopted an invalid reservation remains bound by the treaty concerned without the benefit of the reservation, unless it expresses an intention to the contrary;[212] ie, the ILC considers that there is a rebuttable presumption in favour of the severability doctrine.[213] Some consider that severing reservations is a *lex specialis* only pertaining to human rights treaties, being non-reciprocal law-making treaties (see above, Section IV(A)) that aspire to universal ratification.[214] Nevertheless, contemporary general practice concerning objections to reservations and the stance taken by the ILC show that support for the severability doctrine is at least growing, also as regards other treaties.[215]

A reservation or objection to a reservation may be withdrawn at any time, unless the treaty otherwise provides.[216] This withdrawal does not need to be accepted by the other contracting parties; also not by those that accepted the reservation.[217] A reservation, an express acceptance of a reservation, an objection to a reservation and the withdrawal of a reservation or of an objection to a reservation must be formulated in writing.[218]

205 *Belilos v Switzerland* (n 189) para 50.
206 ibid, para 55; as required by then Art 64(1), now Art 57(1) ECHR (see above (n 189)). Similarly, at para 59, the Court found that Switzerland failed to comply with the requirement of Art 64(2), now Art 57(2) ECHR to provide 'a brief statement of the law concerned'.
207 ibid, para 60.
208 ibid.
209 This approach was confirmed in *Weber v Switzerland* App no 11034/84 (ECtHR, 22 May 1990) and *Loizidou v Turkey* (Preliminary Objections) App no 15318/89 (ECtHR, 23 March 1995).
210 HRCttee, General Comment No 24: 'Issues Relating to Reservations Made upon Ratification or Accession to the Covenant or the Optional Protocols thereto, or in Relation to Declarations under Article 41 of the Covenant', 4 November 1994, UN Doc CCPR/C/21/Rev.1/Add.6, para 18.
211 See notably: Report of the Human Rights Committee, 3 October 1995, UN Doc A/50/40, Annex VI: 'Observations of States Parties under article 40, paragraph 5, of the Covenant', 134–35 (for the US) and 138–39 (for the UK); KL McCall-Smith, 'Severing Reservations' (2014) 63 *ICLQ* 599, 615–16.
212 ILC, 'Guide to Practice on Reservations to Treaties' (2011) *YILC*, Vol II, Part 2, 35, 4.5.3.
213 McCall Smith (n 211) 623.
214 ibid, 600 and 610–11; cp M Craven, 'Legal Differentiation and the Concept of the Human Rights Treaty in International Law' (2000) 11 *EJIL* 489, 507–509.
215 McCall Smith (n 211) 633–34.
216 Art 22(1)–(2) VCLT.
217 Aust (n 42) 139.
218 Art 23(1) and (4) VCLT.

If formulated when signing the treaty subject to ratification, acceptance or approval, a reservation must be formally confirmed by the reserving State.[219] This is not required for the express acceptance of, or an objection to, a reservation.[220]

In cases where a treaty excludes reservations, States may still use the option of making an 'interpretative' declaration or statement. An interpretative declaration is 'a unilateral declaration, however phrased or named, made by a state whereby it purports to clarify the meaning or scope attributed to the treaty or certain of its provisions'.[221] Even if this option is not addressed by the VCLT, such declarations are often used by States. Whether the declaration does or does not constitute a 'disguised reservation' depends on the scope the State that has formulated the declaration intended to give to it.[222]

In *Belilos v Switzerland*, the ECtHR found that an interpretative declaration made by Switzerland was in fact a reservation. More precisely, the Court held that '[i]n order to establish the legal character of such declarations, one must look behind the title given to it and seek to determine the substantive content'.[223] Thereby, in line with the provisions of the VCLT, the Court recognised that it is necessary to ascertain the original intention of the drafters of the declaration. The ECtHR concluded that, although Switzerland described its declaration as 'interpretative', it in fact 'meant to remove certain categories of proceedings from the ambit of Article 6 § 1 (art 6-1) and to secure itself against an interpretation of that Article (art 6-1) which it considered to be too broad'.[224] Therefore, the declaration was found to be invalid (see above, this section).

Reservations can lead to an undesired fragmentation of multilateral treaties. For that reason, in 1952, the UN General Assembly recommended to provide conditions concerning the admissibility of reservations in the treaty itself as much as possible.[225] Additionally, in 2011, the ILC adopted the abovementioned Guide to Practice on Reservations to Treaties in order to provide assistance with problems concerning the permissibility and effects of reservations to treaties and interpretative declarations, explaining the relevant provisions of the VCLT and supplementing them.[226]

International organisations are also legally capable of making reservations, although this is quite rare. Nearly all practice of international organisations making reservations refers to the European Community (EC) or EU.[227] For example, the EU made a reservation when becoming a party to the UN Convention on the Rights of Persons with Disabilities.[228]

[219] ibid, Art 23(2).
[220] ibid, Art 23(3).
[221] Aust (n 42) 115.
[222] According to M Fitzmaurice (n 186) 191, 'such declarations must be subject to close scrutiny. If they change the scope of the obligation, they cease to be declarations and become reservations'. See also Aust (n 42) 117–18.
[223] *Belilos v Switzerland* (n 189) para 49.
[224] ibid.
[225] UNGA Res 598 (VI), 12 January 1952, UN Doc A/RES/598 (VI).
[226] ILC, 'Guide to Practice on Reservations to Treaties' (2011) *YILC*, Vol II, Part 2, 26–38 (see above (n 212)).
[227] Verwey (n 74) 129.
[228] Council Decision 2014/835/EU of 26 November 2009 concerning the conclusion, by the European Community, of the United Nations Convention on the Rights of Persons with Disabilities [2010] OJ L23/35; Annex III, Reservation by the European Community to Article 27(1) of the UN Convention of the Rights of Persons with Disabilities: 'The European Community states that pursuant to Community law (notably Council Directive 2000/78/EC of 27 November 2000 establishing a general framework for equal treatment in employment and occupation), the Member States may, if appropriate, enter their own reservations to Article 27(1) of the Disabilities Convention to the extent that Article 3(4) of the said Council Directive provides them with the right to exclude non-discrimination on the grounds of disability with respect to employment in the armed forces from the scope of the Directive. Therefore, the Community states that it concludes the Convention without prejudice to the above right, conferred on its Member States by virtue of Community law'.

Most EU practice regarding reservations has taken place within the context of 'European' treaties, such as those adopted within the framework of the Council of Europe.

D. Entry into Force

The moment a treaty enters into force, the rights and obligations enshrined in it become effective in international law and the instrument becomes fully binding upon the parties.[229] Pursuant to Article 24(1) VCLT, a treaty enters into force in such manner and upon such date as it may provide or as the negotiating States may agree. While some multilateral treaties only enter into force upon ratification by all signatory States, most simply require a minimum number of States to ratify the treaty.[230] It can be the case that certain States specified by name or category must be amongst them.[231] Multilateral treaties usually also stipulate that 'the *date* of entry into force will be a specified number of days, weeks or months following the deposit of the last instrument of ratification which is needed to bring the treaty into force'.[232] Only a few treaties establish a set date for entry into force, as this may run the risk of entry into force without a desirable number of ratifications.[233] For treaties that do not specify the manner in which they enter into force, Article 24(2) VCLT establishes that they shall enter 'into force as soon as consent to be bound by the treaty has been established for all the negotiating States'.

Noteworthy in this regard is that the VCLT makes an important terminological distinction between a 'Contracting State' and a 'State Party'. A Contracting State is a State that has consented to be bound by the treaty, irrespective of whether the treaty has entered into force.[234] A State Party is a State that has consented to be bound by the treaty *and* for which the treaty has entered into force.[235]

E. Provisional Application

Even before its entry into force, a treaty may generate several legal consequences. As discussed above (Section V(B)(i)), a State is obliged to refrain from acts which would defeat the object and purpose of a treaty during the period before it enters into force.[236] The provisions of a treaty regulating the authentication of its text and all matters arising necessarily before the entry into force of the treaty apply from the time of the adoption of its text.[237] Moreover, a treaty or a part thereof can be applied provisionally.

[229] Aust (n 42) 145.
[230] ibid, 145–47.
[231] ibid, 147–48. See eg Art XIV(1) Comprehensive Nuclear Test Ban Treaty (adopted 10 September 1996, not yet entered into force) 35 ILM 1439. This treaty has not yet entered into force as not all States listed in Annex 2 have ratified the treaty. For a deeper analysis of Art 24 VCLT and a review of a variety of different clauses regulating the entry into force of treaties, see Aust (n 42) 145–50; H Krieger, 'Article 24. Entry into Force' in Dörr and Schmalenbach (n 5) 423.
[232] Aust (n 42) 150–51.
[233] Thus, clauses specifying a specific date of entry into force are usually 'subject to a proviso'; ibid, 148–49.
[234] Art 2(1)(f) VCLT.
[235] ibid, Art 2(1)(g).
[236] ibid, Art 18.
[237] ibid, Art 24(4).

Often, a considerable amount of time passes between the adoption and entry into force of a (multilateral) treaty, especially when it requires a substantial number of ratifications.[238] Provisional application allows States to bridge this period by already applying the treaty or part of its substantive provisions prior to its entry into force.[239] Thus, the provisional application of a treaty can serve several purposes. It may (i) fill an urgent need to apply an adopted, but unratified treaty; (ii) allow States, if their domestic ratification requirements do not bar this, to apply a treaty that they favour in advance; (iii) provide a timeline for taking measures that pave the way for definitive application; (iv) give States the time required to prepare rules and regulations for an international organisation the treaty is to bring into force; and (v) 'serve as a second-best alternative to applying all or parts of a treaty' where circumstances temporarily (or permanently) preclude the treaty's entry into force.[240]

Today, provisional application is provided for in the context of a wide range of treaties.[241] Negotiating States can agree on the provisional application in the treaty itself,[242] or 'in some other manner',[243] eg through an exchange of notes[244] or a collateral agreement.[245] In any case, conceptually, provisional application is the product of a separate, ancillary agreement that is binding.[246] Usually, treaty clauses on provisional application provide that the latter starts for a State upon adoption or (simple) signature of the treaty by that State.[247] However, it is also possible that such a clause requires specific consent of a party to be bound before the treaty's entry into force.[248] If the treaty contains no clause on provisional application, the latter can only arise if the State somehow expresses support for provisional application (eg by voting for a resolution to that effect).[249] The provisional application of a treaty ends for a State when that State informs the other States between which the treaty is being applied provisionally that it does not want to be a party,[250] or when, for that State, the treaty enters into force.[251] The latter implies that even after the treaty has 'objectively' entered into force, the provisional application thereof may continue for States for which it is not (yet) in force.[252] The provisional application of a treaty can last a long time, as evidenced by the General Agreement on Tariffs and Trade (GATT), which applied provisionally from 1947 until 1994.[253]

[238] Aust (n 42) 154.
[239] RE Dalton, 'Provisional Application of Treaties' in Hollis (n 29) 220–21.
[240] ibid, 234.
[241] ibid.
[242] See eg Art 45 of the Energy Charter Treaty (adopted 17 December 1994, entered into force 16 April 1998) 2080 UNTS 95, a 'particularly robust and highly complex article on provisional application', which for example provides that 'parties terminating provisional application cannot escape jurisdiction over disputes arising during the period of provisional application for twenty years'; Dalton (n 239) 241–42.
[243] Art 25(1) VCLT.
[244] Dalton (n 239) 221.
[245] Kolb (n 7) 55.
[246] Dalton (n 239) 230 and 238.
[247] Aust (n 42) 154.
[248] See eg Art 18 of the Convention on the Prohibition of the Use, Stockpiling, Production and Transfer of Anti-Personnel Mines and on their Destruction (adopted 18 September 1997, entered into force 1 March 1999) 2056 UNTS 211, providing that '[a]ny State may at the time of its ratification, acceptance, approval or accession, declare that it will apply provisionally paragraph 1 of Article 1 of this Convention pending its entry into force'; Dalton (n 239) 240.
[249] Aust (n 42) 154.
[250] Art 25(2) VCLT.
[251] Dalton (n 239) 240.
[252] Aust (n 42) 154; Kolb (n 7) 56.
[253] By means of its Protocol on Provisional Application (adopted 30 October 1947, entered into force 1 January 1948) 55 UNTS 308.

Also in the context of the EU, there is often a significant delay between the moment of signing the agreement on behalf of the EU and the decision of the Council to conclude – ie to ratify – the agreement. That is the case not so much for 'EU only' or 'non-mixed' agreements, for which the internal approval can be a matter of months, but rather for 'mixed agreements' (see already above, Section V(B)(i)).[254] As EU Member States also have to become parties to such agreements, the process of conclusion can be a matter of years, because ratification by all of them is required.[255] Thus, in accordance with Article 25 VCLT, Article 218(5) TFEU allows the Council to declare the provisional application of agreements before their entry into force; something which, at least for mixed agreements, is consistently done. Recently, for example, the Council decided to apply provisionally most of the Comprehensive Economic and Trade Agreement (CETA) between Canada and the EU.[256]

Article 218(5) TFEU does not require the Council to wait for the European Parliament's consent before it decides to apply the agreement provisionally. Nevertheless, in cases where the consent of the Parliament is required for the conclusion of an agreement by the EU,[257] the Parliament often requests that agreements not be provisionally applied before it gives its consent.[258] The Council then normally agrees to forward the agreement to the European Parliament for its consent.[259] Neither does Article 218(5) TFEU deal with the scope of provisional application. However, in the case of mixed agreements, the Council cannot provisionally apply parts of the agreement within the exclusive competence of the EU Member States, while it is disputed whether the Council can provisionally apply parts of the agreement that relate to shared competences.[260] In any case, it is the Council's practice to exclude parts considered not to fall within the exclusive competence of the EU from provisional application.[261] A last unresolved issue not dealt with by Article 218(5) TFEU is whether a Member State's failure (or refusal) to ratify the agreement would preclude the provisional application of that agreement by the EU.[262] On the one hand, if a Member

[254] Dalton (n 239) 234.

[255] See eg the Agreement on Cooperation and Customs Union between the European Economic Community and the Republic of San Marino [2002] OJ L84/43, wich was signed on 16 December 1991, but only entered into force on 1 April 2002; cp A Rosas, 'The European Union and Mixed Agreements' in AA Dashwood and C Hillion (eds), *The General Law of EC External Relations* (London, Sweet and Maxwell, 2000) 208. See also the Free Trade Agreement between the European Union and its Member States, of the one part, and the Republic of Korea, of the other part [2011] OJ L127/6, which was signed on 6 October 2010, but only entered into force on 13 December 2015.

[256] Council Decision (EU) 2017/38 of 28 October 2016 on the provisional application of the Comprehensive Economic and Trade Agreement (CETA) between Canada, of the one part, and the European Union and its Member States, of the other part [2017] OJ L11/1080.

[257] See Art 218(6)(a) TFEU.

[258] eg, by way of its 'Resolution of 11 May 2011 on the state of play in the EU-India Free Trade Agreement negotiations', europarl.europa.eu/sides/getDoc.do?pubRef=-//EP//TEXT+TA+P7-TA-2011-0224+0+DOC+XML+V0//EN, at para 36, the Parliament 'call[ed] on the Commission and the Council not to propose any provisional application of the agreement before the EP has given its consent'.

[259] See eg the Council Conclusions on CETA, as adopted by the Council (Written Procedure) on 28 October 2016, 13887/16, data.consilium.europa.eu/doc/document/ST-13887-2016-INIT/en/pdf.

[260] D Kleimann and G Kübek, 'The Signing, Provisional Application, and Conclusion of Trade and Investment Agreements in the EU: The Case of CETA and Opinion 2/15', *European University Institute*, November 2016, Working Paper RSCAS 2016/58, 17.

[261] See eg Art 1 Council Decision 2017/38 (n 256).

[262] eg, the Belgian Region of Wallonia endangered the signing of CETA, and even thereafter renewed threats that it may not approve the agreement unless all of its conditions are met; C Stupp, 'After Parliament Approval, Final Ratification Could Still Put CETA in Legal Limbo', *Euractiv*, 15 February 2017, euractiv.com/section/trade-society/news/after-parliament-approval-final-ratification-could-still-put-ceta-in-legal-limbo.

State were to deposit a notification that it will not ratify a mixed agreement that requires the ratification of all the contracting parties to enter into force, this would imply that the agreement cannot be concluded. As the agreements or Council decisions (authorising the provisional application) often state that the agreement only provisionally applies pending its entry into force or conclusion, it can be argued that a Member State's failure to ratify the agreement requires the termination of provisional application if such failure is permanent and definitive.[263] On the other hand, it is submitted that as only matters within the scope of EU competences are subject to provisional application, also the termination of the provisional application of an international agreement is to be governed by Article 218(5) TFEU and can thus only be decided upon by the Council, and not a single Member State.[264]

F. Publication

Pursuant to Article 102(1) of the UN Charter, every treaty entered into by any Member of the United Nations must be registered as soon as possible with the Secretariat and published by it.[265] These treaties are published in the *United Nations Treaty Series* (UNTS).[266] Article 102(2) of the UN Charter states that no party to any treaty which has not been registered may invoke it before any organ of the UN, which includes the ICJ. This provision was introduced in order to prevent secret treaties, especially secret alliances.[267] It has been submitted that non-registered treaties may still be invoked if other appropriate forms of publication have taken place.[268]

Treaties to which the EU is a party are published in the *Official Journal of the European Union* (OJ). The EU Treaty Office Database[269] also contains a list of the bilateral and multilateral international treaties or agreements concluded by the EU, the European Atomic Energy Community and the former European Communities. In the same vein, conventions that are prepared and negotiated within the institutional framework of the Council of Europe are published in the *Council of Europe Treaty Series* (CETS), which groups together all the conventions concluded within the Council of Europe since 1949, including their explanatory reports, status of signatures and ratifications, as well as declarations and reservations made by States.[270] Within European countries, the rules regarding the publication of treaties differ from State to State.

[263] eg, regarding CETA, the Council held that '[i]f the ratification of CETA fails permanently and definitively because of a ruling of a constitutional court, or following the completion of other constitutional processes and formal notification by the government of the concerned state, provisional application must be and will be terminated. The necessary steps will be taken in accordance with EU procedures' (Statements to be entered in the Council minutes [2017] OJ L11/9, para 20).

[264] G Van der Loo and RA Wessel, 'The Non-Ratification of Mixed Agreements: Legal Consequences and Solutions' (2017) 54 *Common Market Law Review* 735, 743 and 746; A Suse and J Wouters, 'The Provisional Application of the EU's Mixed Trade and Investment Agreements', *Leuven Centre for Global Governance Studies*, May 2018, Working Paper No. 201, 19–20.

[265] See further WK Geck 'Die Registrierung und Veröffentlichung völkerrechtlicher Verträge' (1962) 22 *ZaöRV* 113.

[266] See further C-A Fleischhauer, 'The United Nations Treaty Series' in Y Dinstein and M Tabory (eds), *International Law at a Time of Perplexity: Essays in Honour of Shabtai Rosenne* (Dordrecht, Nijhoff, 1989) 131–48.

[267] See further M Brandon, 'The Validity of Non-Registered Treaties' (1952) 29 *BYIL* 186; R Caddell, 'Treaties, Secret' in MPEPIL; J Quigley, 'Leon Trotsky and the Prohibition against Secret Treaties' (2017) 19 *Journal of the History of International Law* 246.

[268] *South West Africa Cases* (Ethiopia v South Africa; Liberia v South Africa) [1962] ICJ Rep 319, Separate Opinion of Judge Jessup and Judge Bustamante.

[269] See above (n 43).

[270] See above (n 98).

VI. Application and Non-application of Treaties

Part III of the VCLT is titled 'Observance, Application and Interpretation of Treaties'. Under Section I, 'Observance of Treaties', the fundamental principle is *pacta sunt servanda*. Article 26 VCLT codifies a long-standing fundamental rule of customary international law, stating that '[e]very treaty in force is binding upon the parties to it and must be performed by them in good faith'.[271] Article 26 VCLT contains two components: the binding commitment regarding treaties that have entered into force and the principle of good faith in their implementation. The latter has an important significance for the interpretation and application of a treaty.[272] In the *Gabčíkovo-Nagymaros* case, the ICJ held that:

> Article 26 combines two elements, which are of equal importance. It provides that 'Every treaty in force is binding upon the parties to it and must be performed by them in good faith'. This latter element, in the Court's view, implies that, in this case, it is the purpose of the Treaty, and the intentions of the parties in concluding it, which should prevail over its literal application. The principle of good faith obliges the Parties to apply it in a reasonable way and in such a manner that its purpose can be realized.[273]

As a consequence of this rule, 'State Parties have the legal right to demand compliance and the legal duty to comply with the obligations imposed by the treaty'.[274] Article 27 VCLT, the second provision of Section I, adds that a party may not invoke the provisions of its internal law as justification for its failure to perform a treaty.[275] This rule is without prejudice to Article 46 VCLT, which deals with the violation of provisions of national law regarding competence (see below, Section X(A)(i)). The principle of primacy of a treaty over internal law has repeatedly been confirmed in international case law:

> From the standpoint of international law and of the Court which is its organ, municipal laws are merely facts which express the will and constitute the activities of States, in the same manner as do legal decisions or administrative measures.[276]
>
> It is a generally accepted principle of international law that in the relations between Powers who are contracting Parties to a treaty, the provisions of municipal law cannot prevail over those of the treaty.[277]

[271] cp G De Baere and T Roes, 'EU Loyalty as Good Faith' (2015) 64 *ICLQ* 829, arguing that the notions of loyalty and sincere cooperation in EU law are conceptually the same as the notions of good faith and *pacta sunt servanda* in international law.

[272] S Rosenne, *Developments in the Law of Treaties 1945–1986* (Cambridge, CUP, 1989) 135–79. See further R Kolb, *La bonne foi en droit international public: contribution à l'étude des principes généraux du droit* (Paris, Université de France, 2000); AD Mitchell, M Sornarajah and T Voon, *Good Faith and International Economic Law* (Oxford, OUP, 2015); G White, 'The Principle of Good Faith' in L Vaughan (ed), *The United Nations and the Principles of International Law: Essays in Memory of Michael Akehurst* (London, Routledge, 1994) 230–55.

[273] *Gabčíkovo-Nagymaros* (n 14) para 142. See further Fitzmaurice (n 186) 176–77.

[274] K Schmalenbach, 'Article 26. *Pacta sunt servanda*' in Dörr and Schmalenbach (n 5) 479. But see eg Court of Appeal The Hague (NL), *Organization of Asylum Lawyers in the Netherlands and The Netherlands Lawyers Committee for Human Rights v the Netherlands (Ministry of Justice)*, 31 October 2002, Case No ECLI:NL:GHSGR:2002:AE9573, at para 5.7, holding that the obligation to perform a treaty (the Refugee Convention) in good faith does not oblige the Netherlands to follow recommendations (of the Executive Committee of the UN High Commissioner for Refugees) it is not bound by.

[275] See generally Aust (n 42) 159–77; A Aust, *Handbook of International Law*, 2nd edn (New York, CUP, 2010) 74–80.

[276] *Certain German Interests in Polish Upper Silesia* (Germany v Poland) [1926] PCIJ Series A, No 7, 19.

[277] *Interpretation of the Convention Between Greece and Bulgaria Respecting Reciprocal Emigration, Signed at Neuilly-Sur-Seine on November 27th, 1919* (Question of the 'Communities') [1930] PCIJ Series B, No 17, 32.

> A State cannot adduce as against another State its own Constitution with a view to evading obligations incumbent upon it under international law or treaties in force.[278]

The CJEU has consistently applied this principle of international law in its legal reasoning. The Court has repeatedly held that a Member State cannot plead provisions, practices or situations prevailing in its domestic legal order to justify failure to observe obligations arising under EU law.[279] Moreover, the EU, like a State, cannot invoke its own legal order as a reason for failure to fulfill its obligations under a treaty.

Under Section II of Part III of the VCLT, titled 'Application of Treaties', the VCLT contains provisions concerning (i) the non-retroactivity[280] and (ii) the territorial scope of treaties,[281] as well as (iii) the application of successive treaties relating to the same subject matter.[282] Article 28 VCLT contains the principle of non-retroactivity. This entails that the provisions of a treaty will not bind a party in relation to any activity or situation that took place before the date of the entry into force of the treaty (with respect to that party). This general rule applies unless a different intention appears from the treaty.[283]

Regarding the territorial scope of a treaty, Article 29 VCLT provides that the treaty will be binding upon the entire territory of the party, unless another intention appears from the treaty.[284] In principle, the 'entire territory of a party' includes the metropolitan territory of the State as well as any overseas territories. Territory also includes the territorial sea, but does not extend to the continental shelf (on these concepts, see Chapter 18 on Law of the Sea).[285] In case of a change in territory (eg the transfer of a part of a territory), the treaty follows the change in borders in accordance with the principle of moving treaty boundaries. This is the case unless the treaty is specifically connected to a certain territory, such as a treaty that determines national borders (see also Chapter V, Section VI(C)).[286]

Strictly speaking, the EU does not possess its own 'territory'. Thus, Article 52 TEU sets out that the EU Treaties apply to the EU Member States whereas Article 355 TFEU defines in more detail the specific territorial scope of the EU Treaties, including the status of various overseas departments and territories. When the EU joins an international agreement, that treaty will often include a specific clause setting out its precise territorial application. This clause normally provides that the agreements will apply in the territory to which EU law is applied, thus linking the application of the agreement to the territorial application of EU law. This means that the territorial application of the EU Treaties or of international agreements to which the EU is a party can change depending on whether there is a new EU Member State, a withdrawal of a Member State, or a change in the territory or the

[278] *Treatment of Polish Nationals and Other Persons of Polish Origin or Speech in the Danzig Territory* [1932] PCIJ Series A/B, No 44, 24.

[279] See inter alia judgment of 8 February 1973, *Commission v Italy*, 30/72, EU:1973:16, para 11; judgment of 18 July 2007, *Commission v Germany,* C-503/04, EU:C:2007:432, para 38; judgment of 4 June 2009, *Commission v Greece*, C-568/07, EU:C:2009:342, para 50; judgment of 24 January 2018, *Commission v Italy*, C-433/15, EU:C:2018:31, para 56. A Schaus, 'Article 27: Internal Law and Observance of Treaties – 1969 Vienna Convention' in Corten and Klein (n 34) Vol I, 691.

[280] Art 28 VCLT.

[281] ibid, Art 29.

[282] ibid, Art 30.

[283] ibid, Art 28. See further F Dopagne, 'Article 28: Non-retroactivity of Treaties – 1969 Vienna Convention' in Corten and Klein (n 34) Vol I, 718.

[284] Art 29 VCLT. For an application by the CJEU, see *Council v Front Polisario* (n 15) paras 94–98.

[285] S Karagiannis, 'Article 29: Territorial Scope of Treaties – 1969 Vienna Convention' in Corten and Klein (n 34) Vol I, 751–54.

[286] See eg P Malanczuk, *Akehurst's Modern Introduction to International Law*, 7th edn (New York, Routledge, 1997) 163–64.

application of EU law within a Member State. For a number of reasons, the EU may seek to limit the territorial application of an agreement to a certain part of EU territory. Agreements relating to the Area of Freedom, Security and Justice contain special provisions regarding the UK, Ireland or Denmark due to their opt outs in this field (although often those States will conclude a bilateral agreement mirroring the one concluded by the EU).

In some cases, a so-called 'federal clause' may be included in a treaty, usually one that is multilateral in nature. The purpose of a federal clause is to ensure the autonomy of the units of a federal State by limiting the participation of the latter to those matters that fall within the scope of its competence.[287] Federal clauses have a number of drawbacks. In particular, the degree to which a multilateral treaty will enter into force thus depends on the constitutional system of the federal State. This may lead to a lack of transparency and legal uncertainty for the other contracting States. For that reason, States are reluctant to include federal clauses in treaties. Certain human rights treaties went so far as to include a 'reversed' or 'anti-federal' clause, stating that the treaty will apply to all parts of any federal State.[288]

Article 30 of the VCLT deals with the application of successive treaties relating to the same subject-matter. In some situations a treaty may contain an explicit rule applicable in case of conflict with other treaties. Article 30(2) VCLT establishes that '[w]hen a treaty specifies that it is subject to, or that it is not to be considered as incompatible with, an earlier or later treaty, the provisions of that other treaty prevail'.[289] For example, Article 7 of the NATO Treaty states that the treaty 'does not affect, and should not be interpreted as affecting in any way, the rights and obligations under the Charter of the Parties which are members of the United Nations, or the primary responsibility of the Security Council for the maintenance of international peace and security'.[290]

Conversely, Article 103 of the UN Charter provides that in the event of a conflict between the obligations under the UN Charter and obligations under any other international agreement, the obligations under the Charter prevail. Article 103 is comprehensive, and can only exist due to the fact that no international organisation is comparable to the UN in terms of universality, purposes and powers. Accordingly, its importance is recognised by Article 30(1) VCLT, which provides that its provisions are 'subject to' Article 103 of the UN Charter.[291] How the EU legal order deals with obligations on the basis of the UN Charter is discussed in Chapter 4, Section V(B)(iii)(b).

The EU Treaties also contain provisions concerning their relationship with pre-existing treaties concluded by Member States prior to their EU membership. Article 351 TFEU provides that obligations of EU Member States that existed before their EU membership

[287] For examples of federal clauses, see Art 37 of the Convention relating to the Status of Stateless Persons (adopted 28 September 1954, entered into force 6 June 1960) 360 UNTS 130 and Art 41 of the Refugee Convention. Also Art 19(7) of the ILO Constitution (n 91) contains a federal clause that extends to all Conventions and Recommendations adopted by the ILO.

[288] For example, Art 50 of the ICCPR stipulates that 'the provisions of the present Covenant shall extend to all parts of federal States without any limitations or exceptions'. Identical provisions can be found in Art 10 of the First Optional Protocol to the International Covenant on Civil and Political Rights (adopted 16 December 1966, entered into force 23 March 1976) 999 UNTS 302 and in Art 9 of the Second Optional Protocol to the International Covenant on Civil and Political Rights, aiming at the Abolition of the Death Penalty (adopted 15 December 1989, entered into force on 11 July 1991). The same provision is found in Art 28 of the ICESCR. See Karragiannis (n 285) 745–51.

[289] For an application by the CJEU, see *Council v Front Polisario* (n 15) paras 110–14.

[290] According to Art 8 of the NATO Treaty, in turn, each party 'undertakes not to enter into any international engagement in conflict with this Treaty'. See Aust (n 42) 196–97.

[291] Aust (n 42) 195–96.

are not affected by the EU Treaties. At the same time, the article contains an obligation for Member States to take appropriate steps to eliminate incompatibilities where they exist.[292] This provision seeks to strike a careful balance between two principles: the respect for prior agreements concluded by the Member States (and the principle of *pacta sunt servanda*) and the integrity and uniformity of EU law. This being said, the CJEU has applied Article 351 in a way that tends to protect the 'autonomy' of the EU legal order, rather than to safeguard the pre-existing obligations of EU Member States.[293] Moreover, the latter are obliged to eliminate incompatibilites with EU law even if these remain hypothetical and have failed to materialise.[294]

In case a treaty does not specify how it relates to another treaty, the following two scenarios are to be distinguished. In a first scenario, all the parties to the earlier treaty are also parties to the later treaty, while the earlier treaty is not terminated or suspended. In this case the earlier treaty applies only to the extent that its provisions are compatible with those of the later treaty.[295] This is an application of the *lex posterior derogat lege priori* (the later law prevails over the prior law) principle. In a second scenario, parties to the earlier treaty do not include all the parties to the later treaty. Then, the mutual rights and obligations between a State that is party to both treaties and a State that is party to only one of the treaties are governed by the treaty to which both States are parties. In the relations between States that are a party to both treaties, the *lex posterior* (later law) applies.[296]

VII. Treaty Interpretation

The process by which treaties are drafted entails that they often contain language that is broad and/or ambiguous. States may agree to (partly) disagree through what is euphemistically called 'constructive ambiguity'. Therefore, treaty law contains some rules on how treaties are to be interpreted. These rules are laid down in Articles 31–33 VCLT, which are considered to reflect customary international law.[297] However, at a preliminary level, it is to be noted that it is always human beings who interpret treaties, and that interpretation is part of the 'art of law' rather than a mechanical process.

The interpretation of treaties takes place at both the international and domestic level. At the international level, the authors of the text of the treaty in question are the primary actors

[292] See also J Crawford, *Brownlie's Principles of Public International Law*, 8th edn (Oxford, OUP, 2012) 378.

[293] See judgment 3 September 2008, *Kadi and Al Barakaat International Foundation v Council*, C-402/05 and C-415/05, EU:C:2008:461, para 304: 'Article 307 EC [now Art 351 TFEU] may in no circumstances permit any challenge to the principles that form part of the very foundations of the Community legal order'; judgment of 22 October 2009, *Bogiatzi*, C-301/08, EU:C:2009:649, paras 17–19: 'it is equally settled case-law that the provisions of an agreement concluded prior to the entry into force of the Treaty cannot be relied on in intra-Community relations'.

[294] See judgments of 3 March 2009, *Commission v Austria*, C-205/06, EU:C:2009:118 and *Commission v Sweden*, C-249/06, EU:C:2009:119; 19 November 2009, *Commission v Finland*, C-118/07, EU:C:2009:715. See further J Klabbers, *Treaty Conflict and the European Union* (Cambridge, CUP, 2009).

[295] Art 30(3) VCLT.

[296] ibid, Art 30(4). On 'successive treaties', see further Aust (n 42) 192–204; on 'conflict', Kolb (n 7) 182–92. See also CJ Borgen, 'Treaty Conflicts and Normative Fragmentation' in Hollis (n 29) 448–71.

[297] See inter alia Arbitral Award of 31 July 1989 ICJ Rep [1991] 69–70 para 48 (on Arts 31 and 32 VCLT); *Kasikili/Sedudu Island* (Botswana v Namibia) [1999] II 1074, para 18; *Certain Questions of Mutual Assistance in Criminal Matters* (Djibouti v France) ICJ Rep [2008] 219, para 112 (on Art 31(3)(c) VCLT). See R Gardiner, 'The Vienna Convention Rules on Treaty Interpretation' in Hollis (n 29) 476.

competent to interpret the treaty. Their interpretation is considered to be an 'authoritative' interpretation.[298] Second, international organisations, and especially the international judicial institutions part thereof, are often asked to interpret international treaties.[299] At the domestic level, it is mainly the legislator, the government and the national courts that are called upon to interpret treaties.[300] However, such unilateral interpretations do not bind other treaty parties.

At the European level, both the CJEU[301] and the ECtHR regularly apply the VCLT rules of interpretation 'respecting their structure and content in their natural sequence'.[302] In the landmark 1975 case of *Golder v UK*, the ECtHR held that:

> [it] is prepared to consider [...] that it should be guided by Articles 31 to 33 of the Vienna Convention of 23 May 1969 on the Law of Treaties. That Convention has not yet entered into force and it specifies, at Article 4, that it will not be retroactive, but its Articles 31 to 33 enunciate in essence generally accepted principles of international law to which the Court has already referred on occasion. In this respect, for the interpretation of the European Convention, account is to be taken of those Articles subject, where appropriate, to 'any relevant rules of the organization' – the Council of Europe – within which it has been adopted (Article 5 of the Vienna Convention).[303]

Nevertheless, it should be stressed that parallel to its application of the VCLT, the ECtHR has developed its own interpretative techniques and principles (see below, Subsection (A)(i)).

A. Interpretation Methods, Principles and Techniques

i. Interpretation Methods

Broadly speaking, there are three schools of interpretation. The three schools of or approaches to interpretation constitute three different methods that put emphasis on different means by which the meaning of a treaty provision can be established.[304]

A first approach is that of the *objective* or *textual* interpretation, and seeks to ascertain the 'ordinary' or 'plain' meaning of the treaty text. As the text is the 'vehicle for the necessary legal certainty and the exteriorization of the parties' intent', it is reasonable that the interpreter should start by analysing the text.[305] On the other hand, it has been submitted

[298] *Delimitation of the Polish-Czechoslovakian Frontier (Question of Jaworzina)* PCIJ [1923] Series B, No 8, 37, para 80: 'it is an established principle that the right of giving an authoritative interpretation of a legal rule belongs solely to the person or body who has power to modify or suppress it'. However, this does not mean that agreement between the parties is the *only* means of achieving an authoritative interpretation: R Gardiner, *Treaty Interpretation*, 2nd edn (Oxford, OUP, 2015) 123.

[299] See further Gardiner (n 298) 125–41.

[300] ibid, 142. Further, see eg the several relevant chapters in HP Aust and G Nolte (eds), *The Interpretation of International Law by Domestic Courts: Uniformity, Diversity, Convergence* (Oxford, OUP, 2016) and HP Aust, A Rodiles and P Staubach, 'Unity or Uniformity? Domestic Courts and Treaty Interpretation' (2014) 27 *LJIL* 75.

[301] For an illustration of an application of the VCLT rules on interpretation by the CJEU, see *Council v Front Polisario* (n 15) paras 86–127. However, note that, as mentioned above (Section II), the rules of treaty law (as embodied in the VCLT) are not considered to apply to the EU's founding treaties.

[302] Gardiner (n 298) 135; J-M Sorel and V Boré Eveno, 'General Rule of Interpretation – 1969 Vienna Convention' in Corten and Klein (n 34) Vol I, 821–22.

[303] *Golder v UK* App no 4451/70 (ECtHR, 21 February 1975) para 29.

[304] ibid.

[305] Kolb (n 7) 136.

that 'language as such conveys no clear and objective meaning, and that only by resorting to context and/or other extra-linguistic elements', 'meaning' may be considered clear.[306]

A second approach is that of the *subjective* interpretation, and seeks to determine what the intention of the parties to the agreement was, considering that it is they who negotiated the treaty.[307] The problem of this approach is that there may not have been a common intention regarding the contested issue. For instance, a certain text may have been adopted due to the fact that its very ambiguity reconciled the opposing points of view held by the parties (see above (this Section), on 'constructive ambiguity'). Moreover, the intention of the parties, and the meaning to be given to the treaty, may change over time.

Third, a *teleological* interpretation seeks to interpret the text in light of the object (subject matter) and purpose (aim) of the treaty. Thus, any ambiguity should be resolved by giving preference to the interpretation that gives effect to that object and purpose.[308] The danger of specifically paying attention to the general objectives of a treaty is that of 'trespassing over the intention of the parties' and lapsing into 'judicial legislation'.[309]

Sometimes, a fourth approach of *contextual* or *systematic* interpretation is distinguished. This approach seeks to interpret the words, sentences, paragraphs, provisions and sections of a treaty and the treaty as a whole in light of each other (context in the narrow sense), and/or in light of contemporary related agreements, or later elements such as subsequent conduct, agreements and other rules of international law (context in the broad sense).[310]

A potential fifth approach is that of *evolutive* interpretation, following which the treaty is interpreted in light of the contemporary legal order rather than in light of the law as it stood at the time of its adoption. This approach allows treaties to inform social life as it evolves.[311] While the ECtHR generally follows the VCLT rules on treaty interpretation, the Court has also developed an interpretative method of its own based on an approach of evolutive interpretation. The ECtHR first mentioned this approach in the *Tyrer v UK* case, where the Court had to decide whether judicial corporal punishment of juveniles amounted to degrading punishment within the meaning of Article 3 ECHR. The Court held that it

[306] A Bianchi, 'Textual Interpretation and (International) Law Reading: The Myth of (In)determinacy and the Genealogy of Meaning' in PHF Bekker, R Dolzer and M Waibel (eds), *Making Transnational Law Work In The Global Economy – Essays In Honour Of Detlev Vagts* (Cambridge, CUP, 2010) 36. For an application on the national level, see eg Court of Appeal Ghent (BE), *Sabanci v Erdal (Fehriye)*, 31 October 2005 (unreported), where the Court held that the term 'automatic firearm' as contained in Art 1(e) European Convention on the Suppression of Terrorism (adopted 27 January 1977, entered into force 4 August 1978) CETS No 90 does not include semi-automatic weapons. This judgment was overruled by the Belgian Court of Cassation, which applied Art 31(1) VCLT and argued that the offences referred to in Art 1(e) include the use of firearms that can at least be reloaded automatically so that they can fire quickly and arbitrarily and that a large number of victims can be made. According to the Court, such weapons, albeit semi-automatic, are, in contrast to non-automatic weapons, the firearms referred to in Art 1(e). Therefore, the wording 'automatic firearms' in Art 1(e) has a general scope and does not distinguish between fully automatic and semi-automatic firearms; Court of Cassation (BE), *Sabanci v Erdal (Fehriye)*, 27 June 2006, Case No P.05.1491.N, para 4.

[307] Kolb (n 7) 150.

[308] Crawford (n 292) 379.

[309] Kolb (n 7) 146. See eg Supreme Court (NO), *Dar and Norwegian Organization for Asylum Seekers (intervening) v Norwegian Immigration Appeals Board*, 16 April 2008, Case No HR-2008-681-A, (2008) *Norwegian Supreme Court Gazette* 513, where the Court refused to recognise that the object and purpose of the Convention against Torture imply that any interim measures ordered by the Committee against Torture would be binding upon States.

[310] ibid, 139.

[311] ibid, 158. See further G Distefano, 'L'interprétation évolutive de la norme internationale' (2011) 2 *Revue générale de droit international public* 373; C Djeffal, *Static and Evolutive Treaty Interpretation: A Functional Reconstruction* (Cambridge, CUP, 2015); ST Helmersen, 'Evolutive Treaty Interpretation: Legality, Semantics and Distinctions' (2013) 6 *European Journal of Legal Studies* 127.

did. For this purpose, it held that 'the Convention is a living instrument which [...] must be interpreted in the light of present day conditions', and that, '[i]n the case now before it the Court cannot but be influenced by the developments and commonly accepted standards in the penal policy of the Member States of the Council of Europe in this field'.[312] This passage inaugurated the Court's pervasive use of evolutive interpretation in later years.[313]

ii. Interpretation Principles and Techniques

Apart from the broader schools of interpretation, there are a number of more specific principles that play an important role in the interpretation of treaties.[314] First, there is the fundamental principle that treaties must be interpreted in *good faith*, which relates directly to the principle of *pacta sunt servanda*.[315] This principle requires fidelity to the intention of the parties without failing to acknowledge the object and purpose of a treaty by an interpretation that is too literal.[316]

A second principle is that it is *unnecessary to apply the principles of interpretation when the text is clear*. In that sense, the PCIJ stated that '[h]aving before it a clause which leaves little to be desired in the nature of clearness, [the Court] is bound to apply this clause as it stands'.[317] In the words of Vattel, the first general maxim concerning interpretation is that it is not permitted to interpret what does not require interpretation.[318] This principle is limited by a third, related principle called *argument ad absurdum*: 'an interpretation which yields an absurd or highly unreasonable result is legally wrong, since it cannot be thought that the parties could have intended it'.[319] Thus, the natural and ordinary meaning of words must be preferred, *unless* it leads to manifestly absurd or unreasonable results.[320]

Further, the principle of *effectiveness*, *principe de l'effet utile* or *ut res magis valeat quam pereat* (it may rather have effect than be destroyed) entail that where there are two possible interpretations of a treaty, the interpretation that facilitates the most effective application is to be preferred.[321] When it *reasons by analogy*, the interpeting body seeks to address a legal

[312] *Tyrer v UK* App no 5856/72 (ECtHR, 25 April 1978) para 31.

[313] See eg *Marckx v Belgium* App no 6833/74 (ECtHR, 13 June 1979). See further JE Helgesen, 'What are the Limits to the Evolutive Interpretation of the European Convention on Human Rights?' (2011) 31 *Human Rights Law Journal* 275; T Thienel, 'The "Living Instrument" Approach in the ECHR and Elsewhere: Some Remarks on the Evolutive Interpretation of International Treaties' in J Delbrück, UE Heinz, K Odendahl, N Matz-Lück and A von Arnauld (eds), *Aus Kiel in die Welt: Kiel's Contribution to International Law: Festschrift zum 100-jährigen Bestehen des Walther-Schücking-Instituts für Internationales Recht* (Berlin, Duncker & Humblot, 2014) 165–200. See also Chapter 16, Section IX(A)(ii) on the interpretation of the ECHR.

[314] For a summary of the principles of interpretation, see Fitzmaurice (n 186) 178–79.

[315] ILC Draft Articles (n 10) 221, para 12. See also *Council v Front Polisario* (n 15) para 124 (on the principle of good faith), referring to *Racke* (n 15) para 49 (on the principle of *pacta sunt servanda*).

[316] See also Kolb (n 7) 148–49.

[317] *Question Concerning the Acquisition of Polish Nationality* [1923] PCIJ Series B, No 7, 20.

[318] Cited by C Rousseau, *Droit international public* (Paris, Sirey, 1970) 269, own translation from French: '[l]a première maxime générale sur l'interprétation est qu'il n'est pas permis d'interpréter ce qui n'a pas besoin d'interprétation'.

[319] Kolb (n 7) 154.

[320] ILC Draft Articles (n 10) 223, para 19. For confirmations by the PCIJ and ICJ, see *Polish Postal Service in Danzig* [1925] PCIJ Series B, No 11, 39, para 113; *Temple of Preah Vihear* (Cambodia v Thailand) [1961] ICJ Rep 17, 32–33; *Competence of the General Assembly for the Admission of a State to the United Nations* [1950] ICJ Rep 4, 8. For a recent confirmation by the CJEU, see *Council v Front Polisario* (n 15) para 124.

[321] ILC Draft Articles (n 10) 219, para 6. See further H Gutièrrez Posse, 'La maxime ut res magis valeat quam pereat (interprétation en fonction de l'"effet utile"): les interprétations "extensives" et "restrictives"' (1972) 23 *Österreichische Zeitschrift für öffentliches Recht* 229.

void or an obscure text by referring to what is assumed in similar circumstances.[322] Another technique is to *reason a contrario* (see the Latin maxim *inclusio unius est exclusio alterius* (to include one thing, is to exclude the others)). This way of reasoning concludes that based on a contradiction in assumptions there is also a contradiction in the consequences.[323] Lastly, an interpretation *contra proferentem* interprets an ambiguous text to the benefit of whomever is obligated by the treaty and to the detriment of the beneficiary of the treaty, and especially to the detriment of the one who has drawn up the text and should have been more precise.[324]

In any case, '[t]he many maxims and phrases [...] are merely prima facie guides to the intention of the parties and must always give way to contrary evidence of the intention of the parties in a particular case'.[325]

B. Rules of Interpretation of the Vienna Convention on the Law of Treaties

i. Basic Rule

As discussed above, there are a number of schools, principles and techniques of interpretation. Several of them are united in Article 31 VCLT, containing the 'general rule of interpretation', which is a true example of compromise.[326] Article 31(1) contains the 'basic rule',[327] providing that '[a] treaty shall be interpreted in *good faith* in accordance with the *ordinary meaning* to be given to the terms of the treaty in their *context* and in the light of its *object and purpose*' (emphasis added).

ii. Context

Subsequently, Article 31(2) VCLT clarifies what constitutes 'context'. In addition to the text of the treaty itself, its preamble[328] and annexes, the following may comprise context: (i) any agreement relating to the treaty which was made between all the parties in connection with the conclusion of the treaty (eg a statement from all parties attached to the Final Act); and (ii) any instrument which was made by one or more parties in connection with the conclusion of the treaty and accepted by the other parties as an instrument related to the treaty (eg a statement from one party attached to the Final Act). These instruments do not form part of the treaty, but may be used to determine the treaty's 'ordinary meaning'. They are not unilateral instruments, but have been accepted in some way by the other parties to the treaty.[329]

iii. Issues Additional to Context

In addition to agreements and instruments that are made 'in connection with' the conclusion of a treaty (and that constitute context), Article 31(3) VCLT refers to interpretative

[322] See A Bleckmann, 'Analogie im Völkerrecht' (1977) 17 *Archiv des Völkerrechts* 161.
[323] On both, see Kolb (n 7) 151–53.
[324] See H Barati, 'La règle d'interprétation contra proferentem en droit international' (1999) 103 *Revue générale de droit international public* 891.
[325] AD McNair, *The Law of Treaties* (Oxford, Clarendon, 1986) 364–66.
[326] Sorel and Boré Eveno (n 302) 808.
[327] Aust (n 42) 208.
[328] On this specific issue, see further MH Hulme, 'Preambles in Treaty Interpretation' (2016) 164 *University of Pennsylvania Law Review* 1281.
[329] See Gardiner (n 298) 232–42.

agreements made *after* the conclusion of a treaty, which 'shall be taken into account, together with the context':

(a) Any subsequent agreement between the parties regarding the interpretation of the treaty or the application of its provisions;
(b) Any subsequent practice in the application of the treaty which establishes the agreement of the parties regarding its interpretation;
(c) Any relevant rules of international law applicable in the relations between the parties.

The first two of these elements deal with agreements between and practice of the parties themselves, whereas the final provision opens up the range of rules available to assist the interpreter to rules that are independent of the treaty. Article 31(3)(a) recognises that subsequent agreements by the parties can be taken into account. Such agreements represent 'an authentic interpretation by the parties which must be read into the treaty for purposes of its interpretation'.[330] This does not only apply to formal treaties, but can equally apply to other forms of agreement. However, there must be 'a relationship between the putative subsequent agreement and the treaty which is being interpreted sufficient to warrant the subsequent agreement being seen as providing evidence of meaning by way of interpretation or application'.[331] For example, in *Western Sahara Campaign UK*,[332] the CJEU took into account a 2013 Protocol[333] to interpret the Fisheries Partnership Agreement between the EU and Morocco.[334]

Article 31(3)(b) allows for the subsequent practice of the parties to be taken into account. The subsequent practice of the parties is important for interpretational purposes, because it 'constitutes objective evidence of the understanding of the parties as to the meaning of the treaty'.[335] Thus, subsequent practice 'can result in a departure from the original intent' of the parties.[336] In extraordinary cases, subsequent practice may even amount to an amendment of the treaty.[337] As regards the issue of *which* practice is relevant, both action and

[330] *Kasikili/Sedudu Island* (Botswana v Namibia) [1999] ICJ Rep 1045, para 49, quoting the commentary to the ILC Draft Articles (n 10) 221, para 14.

[331] Gardiner (n 298) 243. See eg *Maritime Delimitation in the Area between Greenland and Jan Mayen* (Denmark v Norway) [1993] ICJ Rep 38, para 28, where the Court rejected that there was 'any subsequent agreement between the parties', as '[n]o reference whatever was made in the 1979 Agreement to the existence or contents of the 1965 Agreement'.

[332] *Western Sahara Campaign UK* (n 15) paras 60 and 74–85.

[333] Protocol between the European Union and the Kingdom of Morocco setting out the fishing opportunities and financial contribution provided for in the Fisheries Partnership Agreement between the European Union and the Kingdom of Morocco [2013] OJ L328/2.

[334] Fisheries Partnership Agreement between the European Community and the Kingdom of Morocco [2006] OJ L141/4, as approved and implemented by Council Regulation (EC) No 764/2006 of 22 May 2006 on the conclusion of the Fisheries Partnership Agreement between the European Community and the Kingdom of Morocco [2006] OJ L141/1, by Council Decision 2013/785/EU of 16 December 2013 on the conclusion, on behalf of the European Union, of the Protocol between the European Union and the Kingdom of Morocco setting out the fishing opportunities and financial contribution provided for in the Fisheries Partnership Agreement between the European Union and the Kingdom of Morocco [2013] OJ L349/1, and by Council Regulation (EU) No 1270/2013 of 15 November 2013 on the allocation of fishing opportunities under the Protocol between the European Union and the Kingdom of Morocco setting out the fishing opportunities and financial contribution provided for in the Fisheries Partnership Agreement between the European Union and the Kingdom of Morocco [2013] OJ L328/40.

[335] *Kasikili/Sedudu Island* (n 330) para 49, quoting the commentary to the ILC Draft Articles (n 10) 221, para 15.

[336] *Dispute regarding Navigational and Related Rights* (Costa Rica v Nicaragua) [2009] ICJ Rep 213, para 64.

[337] See eg the subsequent practice of the UNSC to accept abstentions rather than 'concurring' votes of its permanent members as required by Art 27(3) of the UN Charter for it to adopt resolutions, as endorsed by the ICJ in *Legal Consequences for States of the Continued Presence of South Africa in Namibia* (n 14) para 22. On the possibility of amendment by subsequent practice, see further below on Art 39 VCLT.

inaction can be considered.[338] Practice can include votes within an international organisation, diplomatic correspondence, official statements and documents, legislative acts and judicial decisions.[339] In the context of multilateral treaties, not all parties must participate in the practice, but their 'manifested or imputed agreement' is required.[340] Thus, it is sufficient that there is practice of one or more parties, endorsed by the other parties.[341] This matter is of particular importance for subsequent practice in international organisations in general, and in relation to the constituent treaties of international organisations in particular.[342] Even if in principle, the practice of, or within, an international organisation is attributable to the organisation itself rather than the individual parties setting it up, such practice is taken into account.[343] The ICJ, for example, has made use of the practice of UN organs when interpreting the UN Charter.[344]

The CJEU does not take into account 'subsequent practice' of the EU Member States when interpreting EU primary law, arguing that 'mere practice cannot override the provisions of the Treaty'.[345] The CJEU has been equally reluctant to consider subsequent practice when interpeting agreements to which the EU is a party.[346] In *Anastasiou* the Court noted that, in accordance with Article 31 VCLT, 'substantial importance properly attaches to the object and purpose of a treaty and *any subsequent practice in its application*'.[347] Yet in that case the Court did not find the practice of the EU Member States to be sufficiently uniform. It has been argued that the Court's reluctance to take into account subsequent practice in these instances stems from the more general suspicion towards employing practices as a means of interpretation of EU law.[348]

The ECtHR, on the other hand, does refer and take into account the practice of parties to the Convention.[349] Moreover, 'in respect of the criterion set out in Article 31 § 3(b) of the Vienna Convention [...], the Court has [...] stated that a consistent practice on the part of

338 Gardiner (n 298) 262.

339 ibid, 257–59. See also Federal Administrative Court (DE), *Students' Union of the University of Paderborn v University of Paderborn*, 29 April 2009, Case No 6 C 16/08, BVerwGE 134, 127, para 48, where the Court held that the concluding observations and general comments of the Committee on Economic, Social and Cultural Rights reflect the practice of contracting parties under the ICESCR.

340 Gardiner (n 298) 266–67.

341 ibid, 270.

342 See further C Brölmann, 'Specialized Rules of Treaty Interpretation: International Organizations' in Hollis (n 29) 507–24.

343 Gardiner (n 298) 280. See eg Constitutional Court (DE), *Parliamentary Group of the Social Democratic Party (SPD) in the German Federal Parliament v Federal Government (Germany)*, 12 July 1994, Case Nos 2 BvE 3/92, 2 BvE 5/93, 2 BvE 7/93, 2 BvE 8/93, BVerfGE 90, 286, paras 272–79, where the Court considered that the sending of troops to Yugoslavia by NATO Member States to enforce relevant UNSC resolutions constituted subsequent practice allowing for a dynamic interpretation of the NATO Treaty rather than a modification thereof. Accordingly, the approval of the German parliament for the sending of German troops was not required.

344 See eg *Certain Expenses of the United Nations* [1962] ICJ Rep 151; *Legal Consequences for States of the Continued Presence of South Africa in Namibia* (n 14), para 22; *Legal Consequences of the Construction of a Wall in the Occupied Palestinian Territory* [2004] ICJ Rep 136, paras 27–28.

345 *France v Commission* (n 75) para 36. See G Slynn, 'The Use of Subsequent Practice as an Aid to Interpretation by the Court of Justice of the European Communities' in R Bieber and G Ress (eds), *Die Dynamik des Europäischen Gemeinschaftsrechts* (Baden-Baden, Nomos, 1987) 138–45.

346 eg *Council v Front Polisario* (n 15) paras 120–25.

347 Judgment of 5 July 1994, *Anastasiou*, C-432/92, EU:C:1994:277, para 43.

348 See J Odermatt, 'The Use of International Treaty Law by the Court of Justice of the European Union' (2015) 17 *Cambridge Yearbook of European Legal Studies* 121; G Nolte, 'Report 2. Jurisprudence Under Special Regimes Relating to Subsequent Agreements and Subsequent Practice' in G Nolte (ed), *Treaties and Subsequent Practice* (Oxford, OUP, 2013) 301.

349 See eg *Banković and others v Belgium and others* App no 52207/99 (ECtHR, 12 December 2001) para 62: 'The Court finds State practice in the application of the Convention since its ratification to be indicative of a lack of any apprehension on the part of the Contracting States of their extra-territorial responsibility in contexts similar to the present case'.

the High Contracting Parties, subsequent to their ratification of the Convention, could be taken as establishing their agreement not only as regards interpretation but even to modify the text of the Convention'.[350] Thus, in *Al-Saadoon and Mufdhi v UK*, the ECtHR ruled that the ratification rate of the Thirteenth Protocol to the ECHR[351] and 'consistent State practice in observing the moratorium on capital punishment, are strongly indicative that Article 2 has been amended so as to prohibit the death penalty in all circumstances'.[352] In *Hassan v UK*, which concerned the administrative detention of a civilian in a situation of an international armed conflict, the ECtHR was prepared to 'accommodate' the grounds of permitted deprivation of liberty set out in Article 5 ECHR without the UK having lodged a formal derogation from its obligations under that provision, as is normally required by Article 15 ECHR.[353] While Hassan was not detained based on one of the (exhaustive) grounds of permitted deprivation of liberty recognised by Article 5 ECHR, the Court accepted that the UK could administratively detain him in accordance with international humanitarian law despite the lack of a formal derogation, as '[t]he practice of the High Contracting Parties is not to derogate from their obligations under Article 5 in order to detain persons on the basis of the Third and Fourth Geneva Conventions during international armed conflicts'.[354] Also, the ECtHR often refers to 'subsequent social developments'[355] to adopt evolutionary interpretations, which are in fact linked with general practice.[356]

Article 31(3)(c) VCLT allows other rules of international law that are applicable to the parties to be taken into account. This rule recognises international law as a legal system, in which a treaty does not exist in isolation, but among a great number of other rules and obligations. Thus, the 'systemic approach' to treaty interpretation considers these other rules as relevant in determining the context. In an oft-quoted expression of this principle, the ICJ has stated that '[a]n international instrument has to be interpreted and applied within the framework of the entire legal system prevailing at the time of the interpretation'.[357]

The CJEU has used this provison to take into account a wider set of rules when interpreting an agreement. For example, in *Brita*,[358] the Court relied on Article 31(3)(c) in order to make use of the *pacta tertiis* principle (see below, Section VIII), according to which treaties do not impose obligations or confer rights upon third States (and which also finds expression in Article 34 VCLT).[359] Also the ECtHR has stated that

> the Convention must be interpreted in the light of the rules set out in the Vienna Convention of 23 May 1969 on the Law of Treaties, Article 31 § 3 (c) of which states that account must be taken of 'any relevant rules of international law applicable in the relations between the parties'.[360]

[350] *Hassan v UK* App no 29750/09 (ECtHR, 16 September 2014) para 101.

[351] Protocol No 13 to the Convention for the Protection of Human Rights and Fundamental Freedoms, concerning the abolition of the death penalty in all circumstances (adopted 3 May 2002, entered into force 1 July 2003) CETS No 187.

[352] *Al-Saadoon and Mufdhi v UK* App no 61498/08 (ECtHR, 2 March 2010) para 120. See also Chapter 16, Section IX(A)(i) on the right to life under the ECHR.

[353] On the possibility to derogate from the ECHR, see again Chapter 16, Section IX(A)(i).

[354] *Hassan v UK* (n 350) paras 101–104 (quote at para 101).

[355] See eg *Christine Goodwin v UK* App no 28957/95 (ECtHR, 11 July 2002) about 'the clear and uncontested evidence of a continuing international trend in favour not only of increased social acceptance of transsexuals but of legal recognition of the new sexual identity of post-operative transsexuals' (para 85) and 'major social changes in the institution of marriage since the adoption of the Convention as well as dramatic changes brought about by developments in medicine and science in the field of transsexuality' (para 100).

[356] Nolte (n 348) 246–48.

[357] *Legal Consequences for States of the Continued Presence of South Africa in Namibia* (n 14) para 53.

[358] See also *Council v Front Polisario* (n 15) paras 86, 88 and 123–24.

[359] *Brita* (n 15) paras 43–44.

[360] *Mamatkulov and Askarov v Turkey* App nos 46827/99 and 46951/99 (ECtHR, 4 February 2005) para 111.

Thus, the ECtHR often takes into account other human rights instruments and the way in which they have been interpreted by other international and regional bodies.[361]

Moreover, Article 31(3)(c) has more recently gained renewed attention and shown to have a capacity to become applicable in a greater variety of circumstances than was originally envisaged.[362] In particular, the provision has been central to an extensive study by the ILC on the fragmentation of international law, arguing that it 'may be taken to express what may be called the principle of "systemic integration", the process [...] whereby international obligations are interpreted by reference to their normative environment ("system")'.[363]

Lastly, Article 31(4) VCLT provides that '[a] special meaning shall be given to a term if it is established that the parties so intended'. Thus, while Article 31 places priority on textual interpretation, this provision makes space for the intention of the parties in a somewhat subsidiary manner. Nevertheless, it is often used to affirm the existence of a 'special meaning' to privilege the intention of the parties, thus providing a gateway for the subjective approach.[364] In principle, the burden of proof of a special meaning rests on the party that invokes it.[365]

iv. Supplementary Means of Interpretation

Pursuant to Article 32 VCLT, recourse may be had to 'supplementary means of interpretation'. These may be used only in order to *confirm* the meaning resulting from the application of Article 31, *or* to determine the meaning when the interpretation of these rules (i) leaves the meaning ambiguous or obscure; or (ii) leads to a result which is manifestly absurd or unreasonable. The supplementary means of interpretation include in particular the preparatory work of the treaty (also known as a treaty's *travaux préparatoires*) and the circumstances of its conclusion.[366]

Thus, the VCLT gives only a subordinate role to the subjective-historical approach, which stresses the importance of the preparatory work of a treaty (expressing the intention of the parties). This is in accordance with long-standing international case law that 'there is

[361] See eg *Al-Adsani v UK* App no 35763/97 (ECtHR, 21 November 2011) para 60; *Pini et al v Romania* App no 78028/01 (ECtHR, 22 June 2004) para 139; *Siliadin v France* App no 73316/01 (ECtHR, 26 October 2005) paras 85–87; *Sørensen and Rasmussen v Denmark* App nos 52562/99 and 52620/99 (ECtHR, 11 January 2006) para 72; *Emonet et autres*, App no 39051/03 (ECtHR, 13 December 2007) para 65; *Demir and Baykara* App no 34503/97 (ECtHR, 12 November 2008) paras 69–73.

[362] Gardiner (n 298) 290.

[363] ILC, 'Report of the Study Group on Fragmentation Of International Law: Difficulties Arising From The Diversification And Expansion of International Law', finalized by Martti Koskenniemi, 13 April 2006, UN Doc A/CN.4/L.682, para 413.

[364] Sorel and Boré Eveno (n 302) 829.

[365] Aust (n 42) 217.

[366] Art 32 VCLT. On the use of preparatory work in the interpretation of treaties, see eg E Canal-Forgues, 'Remarques sur le recours aux travaux préparatoires dans le contentieux international' (1993) 97 *Revue générale de droit international public* 901; J Klabbers, 'International Legal Histories: The Declining Importance of Travaux Préparatoires in Treaty Interpretation?' (2003) 50 *NILR* 267; R Lawson, 'Adieu les travaux! Het afgenomen belang van de travaux préparatoires voor de uitleg van het EVRM' (1996) 21 *Nederlands tijdschrift voor de mensenrechten* 61; M Raisch, 'Travaux préparatoires and United Nations Treaties or Conventions: Using the Web Wisely: Research Tips and Observations' (2002) 30 *International Journal of Legal Information* 324; M Ris, 'Treaty Interpretation and ICJ Recourse to Travaux Préparatoires: Toward a Proposed Amendment of Articles 31 and 32 of the Vienna Convention on the Law of Treaties' (1991) 14 *Boston College International and Comparative Law Review* 111; M Sassoli, 'Bedeutung von 'travaux préparatoires' zu Kodificationsvertragen für das allgemeine Völkerrecht' (1990) 41 *Österreichische Zeitschrift für öffentliches Recht und Völkerrecht* 109; WA Schabas, '"Travaux préparatoires" of Human Rights Instruments' in A Alen et al (eds), *Liberae Cogitationes: Liber Amicorum Marc Bossuyt* (Cambridge, Intersentia, 2013) 579–90.

no occasion to resort to preparatory work if the text of a convention is sufficiently clear in itself'.[367] The reasons for this reluctance were expressed during the Conference on the Law of Treaties by the British representative, among others:

> [...] preparatory work was almost invariably confusing, unequal and partial: confusing because it commonly consisted of the summary records of statements made during the process of negotiations, and early statements on the positions of the delegations might express the intention of the delegation at that stage, but bear no relation to the ultimate text of the treaty; unequal, because not all delegations spoke on any particular issue; and partial because it excluded the informal meetings between heads of delegations at which final compromises were reached and which were often the most significant feature of any negotiation.[368]

Nonetheless, in most disputes over the correct interpretation of a treaty provision, reference will be made to the preparatory work if it is available. Extreme care is warranted in these circumstances. Some of the questions that arise are *which* preparatory texts should be taken into account, and what *weight* should be given to them in the process of interpretation.[369]

As to the CJEU, it has proven to be rather reluctant to refer to preparatory works when interpreting either the EU Treaties or agreements to which the EU is a party. The Court has held that

> every provision of Community law must be placed in its context and interpreted in the light of the provisions of Community law as a whole, regard being had to the objectives thereof and to its state of evolution at the date on which the provision in question is to be applied.[370]

Thus, the CJEU favours the textual, systematic and teleological methods of interpretation, and has only rarely looked at the intent of the drafters when interpreting the law. As in recent years the 'preparatory documents issued by the different actors in the Community legislative process are gradually becoming more voluminous, detailed and carefully drafted', it has been submitted that they will become more relevant as aids to interpretation.[371] Furthermore, the *travaux préparatoires* reflecting the work of the 'Convention for the Future of Europe' in relation to the 'Treaty establishing a Constitution for Europe', a large proportion of the content of which was carried over into the Treaty of Lisbon, are now more readily accessible than any preparatory works of previous amendments to the Treaties. The CJEU has notably relied on these *travaux préparatoires* in its judgment in *Inuit Tapiriit Kanatami*, to interpret the locus standi requirements in the fourth paragraph of Article 263 TFEU.[372]

v. *Treaties Authenticated in Two or More Languages*

The terms used in treaties that have been authenticated in two or more languages are considered to have the same meaning in each authentic text.[373] When a comparison of the

[367] *Conditions of Admission of a State to Membership in the United Nations* (Advisory Opinion) [1948] ICJ Rep 57, 63; *Ambatielos* (Greece v United Kingdom) (Preliminary Objection) [1952] ICJ Rep 28, 45.

[368] Official Records of the United Nations Conference on the Law of Treaties, First Session (Summary Records of the Plenary Meetings and of the Meetings of the Committee of the Whole), 33rd meeting of the Committee of the Whole, 22 April 1968, UN Doc A/CONF.39/C.1/SR.33, 178, para 8.

[369] Aust (n 42) 218–19.

[370] Judgment of 6 October 1982, *CILFIT v Ministero della Sanità*, 283/81, EU:C:1982:335, para 20.

[371] K Frick and S Schonberg, 'Finishing, Refining, Polishing: On the Use of Travaux Preparatoires as an Aid to the Interpretation of Community Legislation' (2003) 28 *ELR* 149, 170–71. See also L Navel, 'Les travaux préparatoires dans la jurisprudence de la Cour de justice de l'Union européenne' (2016) *Revue du droit public et de la science politique en France et à l'étranger* 1547.

[372] Judgment of 3 October 2013, *Inuit Tapiriit Kanatami and Others v Parliament and Council*, C-583/11 P, EU:C:2013:625, paras 59 and 70.

[373] Art 33(3) VCLT.

authentic texts discloses a difference of meaning that is not eliminated by the application of Articles 31 and 32 VCLT, the meaning that best reconciles the texts, having regard to the object and purpose of the treaty, needs to be adopted.[374]

vi. Combination of Different Interpretative Methods

An interesting case to compare the different methods of interpreting treaties is the 1932 advisory opinion of the PCIJ on *Interpretation of the Convention of 1919 concerning Employment of Women during the Night*.[375] This advisory opinion concerned the question whether the prohibition laid down in the ILO Convention concerning Employment of Women during the Night[376] was also applicable to women in managerial positions. In its analysis, the PCIJ applied the method of textual interpretation,[377] systematic or contextual interpretation[378] and subjective-historical interpretation (referencing relevant preparatory works).[379] The dissenting opinion of Judge Anzilotti, on the other hand, principally emphasised the method of teleological interpretation,[380] combining it with a different implementation of the contextual[381] and the subjective-historical approach.[382]

VIII. Consequences of Treaties for Third Parties

According to the Latin maxim *pacta tertiis nocent nec prosunt* (literally 'agreements harm nor benefit third parties'), '[a] treaty does not create either obligations or rights for a third State without its consent'.[383] Treaties only have relative effect and remain *res inter alios acta* for third States.[384] Nonetheless, the VCLT provides that in exceptional cases, a treaty can create benefits or even obligations for third parties.[385] If the parties to the treaty intend this through a provision in the treaty, an *obligation* can arise for a third State if the third State expressly accepts that obligation in writing.[386] A *right* for a third State can arise from a treaty provision if the third State assents thereto. Assent is presumed so long as the contrary is not indicated, unless the treaty provides otherwise.[387]

374 Art 33(4) VCLT. See further Gardiner (n 298) 413–47, on 'Languages' and A Papaux and R Samson, 'Article 33: Interpretation of Treaties Authenticated in Two or More Languages' in Corten and Klein (n 34) Vol I, 866–84.
375 *Interpretation of the Convention of 1919 concerning Employment of Women during the Night* [1932] PCIJ Rep Series A/B, No 50.
376 Convention (No 4) concerning Employment of Women during the Night (adopted 28 November 1919, entered into force 13 June 1921) 38 UNTS 67.
377 *Interpretation of the Convention of 1919 concerning Employment of Women during the Night* (n 375) paras 31 and 49.
378 ibid, paras 32–48 and 63–66.
379 ibid, paras 51–61.
380 ibid, paras 74–77.
381 ibid, paras 77–88.
382 ibid, paras 90–91.
383 Art 34 VCLT. See also J Law and EA Martin, *A Dictionary of* Law, 8th edn (Oxford, OUP, 2015) 440.
384 See eg Higher Regional Court Stuttgart (DE), *Former Consular Employee at the Consulate General of Croatia in Stuttgart v Croatia*, 23 October 2014, Case No 5 U 52/14, para 39, where the Court held that Croatia could not invoke the European Convention on State Immunity (adopted 16 May 1972, entered into force 11 June 1976) CETS No 74 to its benefit, simply because it was not a party to the Convention.
385 Aust (n 42) 228.
386 Art 35 VCLT.
387 ibid, Art 36(1).

The CJEU applied the *pacta tertiis* principle in *Brita* (see above, Section VII(B)(iii)).[388] The Court employed the *pacta tertiis* principle in interpreting Article 83 of the EC-Israel Association Agreement,[389] which defines the territorial scope of that agreement. It considered that if it were to interpret this provision in a way that the Israeli customs authorities enjoy competence in respect of products originating in the West Bank, this would be tantamount to imposing on the Palestinian customs authorities an obligation to refrain from exercising the competence conferred upon them by virtue of the EC-PLO Protocol.[390] Such an interpretation, according to the Court, would create an obligation for a third party without its consent, and thus violate the *pacta tertiis* principle.[391]

Article 37 VCLT concerns the revocation or modification of obligations or rights of third States. Article 37(1) determines that once a third party has agreed to be bound by an *obligation* in conformity with Article 35 VCLT, it may only be revoked with the consent of the other parties, unless it is established that they agreed otherwise. This provision does not set out any formal requirement for how consent is to be expressed.[392] Regarding *rights* arising for third States (in accordance with Article 36 VCLT), Article 37(2) is worded negatively. The rights of a third State *may not* be revoked or modified 'if it is established that the right was intended not to be revocable or subject to modification without the consent of the third State'.[393] It is doubtful whether Article 37 VCLT constitutes an expression of customary international law, mainly due to the lack of international practice.[394]

Article 38 VCLT provides that nothing in Articles 34–37 precludes a rule set forth in a treaty from becoming binding on a third State as a rule of customary international law. In these situations, it is the rule of customary international law, not the treaty itself, that binds the third State. This exemplifies that a treaty that is not binding upon a State may nevertheless have an impact on that State by contributing to the development of customary international law.[395]

IX. Amendment and Modification of Treaties

A. Amendment

A treaty may be amended by agreement between the contracting parties.[396] Such amendments can pertain to certain provisions of the treaty or to the entire treaty. A distinction is

[388] For a more recent application of the principle of the relative effect of trearies, see *Council v Front Polisario* (n 15) paras 100–107.

[389] Euro-Mediterranean Agreement establishing an association between the European Communities and their Member States, of the one part, and the State of Israel, of the other part [2000] OJ L147/3.

[390] Protocol 3 concerning the definition of the concept of "originating products" and methods of administrative cooperation' as annexed to the Euro-Mediterranean Interim Association Agreement on trade and cooperation between the European Community, of the one part, and the Palestine Liberation Organisation (PLO) for the benefit of the Palestinian Authority of the West Bank and the Gaza Strip, of the other part [1997] OJ L187/3.

[391] *Brita* (n 15) paras 44–52.

[392] D Bederman 'Third Party Rights and Obligations in Treaties' in Hollis (n 29) 337.

[393] Art 37(2) VCLT. See also Aust (n 42) 230.

[394] A Proelss, 'Article 37. Revocation or Modification of Obligations or Rights of Third States' in Dörr and Schmalenbach (n 5) 740.

[395] Crawford (n 292) 385. See further Y Dinstein, 'The Interaction between Customary International Law and Treaties' (2006) 322 *RdC* 243.

[396] Art 39 VCLT.

sometimes made between the two procedures insofar that the first case involves an *amendment*, while the second case involves a *revision* of the treaty.[397] The VCLT speaks of the 'amendment' of treaties. As a general rule, if the treaty concerned does not provide otherwise, the rules of the VCLT concerning the conclusion and entry into force of treaties are applicable to amendments.[398]

For a bilateral treaty, an amendment can take place simply when both parties agree to it. Such amendments can be made even simpler by including a provision that specifies the form in which any amendment is to be expressed.[399] For multilateral treaties, reaching a unanimous decision to amend the treaty is in most cases practically impossible. Thus, these treaties often include provisions setting out a more facilitating procedure for amendment.[400] A first possibility is that the amendment needs to be adopted by the plenary body (usually by majority decision) and then binds all parties, who are presumed to have consented therewith tacitly, unless they opt out.[401] Second, to avoid differentiation of treaty commitments, the adopted amendment may require ratification by a certain majority, upon which non-ratifying States either cease to be treaty parties, or become bound by the amendment as well.[402] Third, in a procedure usually reserved for narrowly defined and relatively uncontroversial matters, the amendment process may simply collapse the adoption and consent steps into one (majority) vote by the treaty's plenary body.[403]

If the treaty contains no provisions on the amendment procedure, Article 40 VCLT applies. The dual purpose of this provision is, on the one hand, to protect State sovereignty by 'keeping with the formal model of strictly-consent-based treaty making' and, on the other hand, to preserve as much of the membership structure as possible and, if this proves impossible, to manage the legal relationships between the parties to the original treaty and the parties to the amended treaty as clearly as possible.[404] First, any proposal to amend a multilateral treaty (usually made by one or more of the parties, sometimes by a treaty body) must be notified to all the contracting States, each of which has the right to take part in the negotiation and conclusion of any agreement for the amendment of the treaty.[405] Second, the amendment must be adopted, after which it enters into force only upon acceptance by a specified majority, and only for those States that have ratified it.[406] Again, every State entitled to become a party to the treaty will also be entitled to become a party to the treaty as amended.[407] Any State that becomes a party to the treaty after the entry into force of the amendment will, failing an expression of a different intention by that State, be considered as a party to the treaty as amended, and be considered as a party to the unamended treaty in relation to any party to the treaty not bound by the amendment.[408]

[397] See eg Arts 108 and 109 UN Charter.
[398] Art 39 VCLT.
[399] Aust (n 42) 234–35; Kolb (n 7) 198.
[400] See eg Art 109 UN Charter and Art 48 TEU.
[401] J Brunnée, 'Treaty Amendments' in Hollis (n 29) 356–60; Kolb (n 7) 199.
[402] Brunnée (n 401) 360–62.
[403] ibid, 362–63. On methods of amending multilateral treaties, see also Aust (n 42) 235–40.
[404] Brunnée (n 401) 352–53.
[405] Art 40(2) VCLT.
[406] Brunnée (n 401) 352. Art 40(4) VCLT provides that in relation to States Parties to the original treaty that have not ratified the amending agreement, Art 30(4)(b), as discussed above (Section VI), applies.
[407] Art 40(3) VCLT.
[408] ibid, Art 30(5). See also Kolb (n 7) 199–200 and further MJ Bowman, 'The Multilateral Treaty Amendment Process: A Case Study' (1995) 44 *ICLQ* 540.

B. Modification

In addition to the practice of amendments, that of modifications *inter se* has developed, entailing that certain parties agree amongst each other to modify the treaty on certain points in their mutual relations.[409] Thus, for multilateral treaties, the VCLT distinguishes between the *amendment* of a treaty (changes to the treaty between all parties)[410] and the *modification* of a treaty (changes to the treaty that apply only between certain parties).[411] In practice, it will not always be possible to make a strict distinction between these two processes. All parties may choose to amend a treaty, but the ratification process may not take place simultaneously, with some States delaying the process or eventualy choosing not to ratify. Article 41 VCLT sets out the conditions for modification. First, this particular kind of *inter se* agreement is allowed only if there is an express provision allowing for such a possiblity in the treaty. Some treaties may, for example, allow parties to enhance or extend the duties already set out in the treaty. Second, where modification is not prohibited by the treaty, an *inter se* agreeement is allowed if two conditions are met: the modification (i) 'does not affect the enjoyment by the other parties of their rights under the treaty or the performance of their obligations' *and* (ii) 'does not relate to a provision, derogation from which is incompatible with the effective execution of the object and purpose of the treaty as a whole'.[412] Unless the treaty provides otherwise, the parties in question must notify the other parties of their intention to conclude the agreement and of the modification to the treaty for which it provides.[413] If an *inter se* agreement goes against the rules discussed above, it will still be legally valid *inter partes*,[414] unless its validity is affected by another issue (see below, Section X).

In the context of the EU, there are instances where a conflict may arise between a Member State's obligations under EU law, and its obligations under a particular international agreement. In order to deal with this scenario, some agreements have a so-called 'disconnection clause'. This clause states that for EU Member States, EU law will apply in their mutual relations, rather than the relevant provisions of the international agreement.[415] Such clauses operate automatically; they do not *allow* the EU Member States to apply EU law in their mutual obligations, but *require* them to do so.[416] What makes the disconnection clause different from an *inter se* agreement, is that the disconnection clause functions as a part of the treaty itself, rather than as a separate agreement.[417]

[409] Brunnée (n 401) 363–64.

[410] Art 40 VCLT.

[411] ibid, Art 41. Kolb makes the distinction between respectively 'objective' and 'subjective' amendments; see Kolb (n 7) 200.

[412] Art 41(1)(b) VCLT.

[413] On 'agreement to modify a multilateral treaty between certain parties only', see also Aust (n 42) 242.

[414] Kolb (n 7) 201.

[415] One of the earliest examples of such a clause can be found in Art 7 of the Joint Council of Europe/OECD Convention on Mutual Administrative Assistance in Tax Matters (adopted 25 January 1988, entered into force 1 April 1995) CETS No 127: 'Notwithstanding the rules of the present Convention, those Parties which are members of the European Economic Community shall apply in their mutual relations the common rules in force in that Community'.

[416] Cremona (n 44) 109.

[417] See further M Smrkolj, 'The Use of the "Disconnection Clause" in International Treaties: What Does it Tell us about the EC/EU as an Actor in the Sphere of Public International Law?', 14 May 2008, ssrn.com/abstract=1133002.

C. Non-written Amendments

Lastly, in connection with Article 39 VCLT, providing that '[a] treaty may be amended by agreement between the parties', the question has arisen whether, given the fact that the VCLT is only applicable to treaties in written form,[418] an amendment to a treaty based on a verbal agreement or by subsequent practice (see also above, Section VII(B)(iii)) is admissible. The ILC Draft Articles determined that a treaty can be modified by subsequent practice that shows the agreement of parties to modify the treaty.[419] However, this provision was struck out mainly due to the said limitation on the scope of application of the VCLT.[420] Since Article 3 VCLT explicitly determines that the VCLT does not encroach on the legal effect of international agreements that were established in non-written form, it is assumed that the amendment of a treaty can also take place verbally, by conclusive behaviour or by subsequent practice.[421]

X. Invalidity of Treaties

The (alleged) invalidity of treaties is a rarity and an issue of limited practical importance. There is a presumption that a treaty is valid, and its continuance in force is the normal state of affairs.[422] Nevertheless, the VCLT lists a number of defects that can result in the invalidity of a treaty. If a treaty becomes invalid, the treaty is considered void 'as from the moment of its conclusion' (ie with effect *ex tunc*).[423] The defects that can result in invalidity normally originate from one (or more) of three sources: (i) improper procedure or authorisation; (ii) misleading behaviour; or (iii) coercion. In all of these cases the consent to be bound has been affected in some way.[424] What follows succinctly discusses the defects that can result in the invalidity of a treaty, making the fundamental distinction between 'relative' and 'absolute' invalidity.[425]

A. Relative Invalidity

Relative invalidity is attached to grounds that affect the particular interests only of the State(s) concerned, and that are thus to be invoked by the affected State(s).[426] At the same time, Article 45 VCLT prohibits a State from invoking a ground for invalidity when the State has expressly, or implicity through its conduct, agreed to the validity or continuation

[418] Art 2(1)(a) VCLT (see above Section III(B)).
[419] ILC Draft Articles (n 10) 236, Art 38.
[420] Kolb (n 7) 194.
[421] For an example, see above (n 337) on the voting practice of the UNSC. See also the decision of the German Consitutional Court discussed above (n 343), illustrating that the difference with (dynamic) interpretation can be subtle. For a detailed discussion of the various forms of agreement that are available to amend a treaty, see P Sands, 'Article 39: General Rules regarding the Amendment of Treaties – 1969 Vienna Convention' in Corten and Klein (n 34) Vol II, 971–76.
[422] Aust (n 42) 273.
[423] Kolb (n 7) 108.
[424] J Klabbers, 'The Validity and Invalidity of Treaties' in Hollis (n 29) 557.
[425] See Kolb (n 7) 108–109.
[426] ibid, 108.

of the treaty after it became aware of the facts that could have constituted a ground of invalidity.[427] In relation to relative invalidity, it is – under certain circumstances (see below, Section X(C)) – possible to limit the invalidity to the vitiated clause, without extending it to the entire treaty. The grounds that according to the VCLT result in relative invalidity are the violation of provisions of national law regarding competence to conclude treaties,[428] error,[429] fraud[430] and corruption.[431]

i. Violation of Provisions of National Law Regarding Competence

According to Aust, 'Article 46 is probably the only provision on invalidity that may have some practical importance'.[432] To emphasise the exceptional character of the cases in which it can be invoked, Article 46(1) VCLT is worded negatively,[433] setting out that a State may *not* invoke the non-observance of its internal law regarding competence to conclude treaties as a ground for invalidating consent, except under two conditions. First, the violation must be manifest, meaning that it would be 'objectively evident to any State conducting itself in the matter in accordance with normal practice and in good faith'.[434] Second, it must concern a rule of the national law of that State which is of fundamental importance. This provision is a compromise between several schools of thought. At the one extreme is the 'internationalist' approach, which allows no possibility of unenforceability on the grounds of non-compliance with constitutional requirements. At the other extreme is the 'constitutionalist' view, which holds that it is always possible for provisions to be unenforceable due to lack of compliance with domestic legal requirements.[435]

The ICJ does not easily accept the invalidity of treaties under Article 46 VCLT. Thus, in the *Land and Maritime Boundary* (Cameroon v Nigeria) case, the Court rejected the argument of Nigeria that Cameroon knew or 'should have known that the Head of State of Nigeria did not have the authority to make legally binding commitments without referring back to the Nigerian government'.[436] The Court argued that 'a limitation of a Head of State's capacity in this respect is not manifest in the sense of Article 46, paragraph 2, unless at least properly publicized' (see also above, Section V(B)(i)).[437] Similarly, in the

[427] See ibid, 112–14.
[428] Art 46 VCLT, and the similar Art 47 VCLT, which concerns a violation of the specific restrictions on the authority to express the consent of a State (see below, this Subsection).
[429] Art 48 VCLT.
[430] ibid, Art 49.
[431] ibid, Art 50.
[432] Aust (n 42) 273.
[433] ibid.
[434] Art 46(2) VCLT.
[435] See the story of the preparatory work in IM Sinclair, *The Vienna Convention on the Law of Treaties*, 2nd edn (Manchester, MUP, 1984) 169–71. See also the ILC's comments on its final draft of Art 43 in RG Wetzel and D Rauschning (eds), *The Vienna Convention on the Law of Treaties: Travaux Préparatoires* (Frankfurt am Main, Metzner, 1978) 336–39. In the same line as Art 46, Art 47 VCLT provides that '[i]f the authority of a representative to express the consent of a State to be bound by a particular treaty has been made subject to a specific restriction, his omission to observe that restriction may not be invoked as invalidating the consent expressed by him unless the restriction was notified to the other negotiating States prior to his expressing such consent'; see also Aust (n 42) 275; Klabbers (n 424) 561–64; Kolb (n 7) 91–97. See further M Bothe, 'Article 46: Provisions of Internal Law regarding Competence to Conclude Treaties – 1969 Vienna Convention' and F Hofmann, 'Article 47: Specific Restrictions on Authority to Express the Consent of a State' in Corten and Klein (n 34) Vol II, respectively at 1090–99 and 1102–14. See also below p 175, in particular n 13.
[436] *Land and Maritime Boundary* (n 146) para 258.
[437] ibid, para 265.

Maritime Delimitation in the Indian Ocean (Somalia v Kenya) case, the Court dispensed with the argument of Somalia that it was not bound by a MOU – which the Court considered to constitute a treaty[438] – following the signature thereof by its Minister for National Planning and Cooperation because 'Somali law required ratification of the MOU'.[439] Considering that 'the Prime Minister of the Transitional Federal Government of Somalia had, by full powers "authorized and empowered" the Minister, under international law, to sign the MOU' and that '[n]o caveat relating to a need for ratification was mentioned in those full powers, nor in the MOU itself, which on the contrary provided for its entry into force upon signature', the Court found that there was 'no reason to suppose that Kenya was aware that the signature of the Minister may not have been sufficient under Somali law to express, on behalf of Somalia, consent to a binding international agreement'.[440]

Also in the context of the EU there may be situations where a representative of the EU expresses its consent to be bound by an international legal instrument when it has no authority to do so under EU law, or where a Member State enters into an agreement in violation of EU law. Due to the complex nature of EU law, however, it is very unlikely that a breach of internal EU rules could be described as 'manifest' under international law.[441]

ii. Error

Following Article 48 VCLT, error provides a second ground that can invalidate consent. The error must (i) pertain to a fact or a situation which was assumed by that State to exist at the time when the treaty was concluded and (ii) form an 'essential basis' of its consent to be bound by the treaty.[442] The error must not be inexcusable, meaning that the State in question must not have contributed to the error by its own conduct, or the circumstances must not have been such as to put that State on notice of a possible error.[443]

As such, the VCLT affirms the ruling of the ICJ in its 1962 judgment in *Temple of Preah Vihear* (Cambodia v Thailand):

> The plea of error cannot be allowed as an element vitiating consent if the party advancing it contributed by its own conduct to the error, or could have avoided it, or if the circumstances were such as to put that party on notice of a possible error.[444]

In this case, nearly all the errors were 'geographical errors, mostly on maps'.[445] The error must relate to a 'fact or situation' that reflects on the treaty, but cannot concern an error relating only to the wording of the treaty.[446]

[438] *Maritime Delimitation in the Indian Ocean* (Somalia v Kenya) (Preliminary Objections) [2017] ICJ Rep 3, paras 42 and 50. On MOUs, see above, Section III(D)(ii).
[439] ibid, para 48.
[440] ibid, para 49.
[441] Thus, even if in its judgment of 9 August 1994, *France v Commission*, C-327/91, EU:C:1994:305, the CJEU found that the Commission did not have the power to conclude a treaty with the US (paras 33–43), it did not decide that the treaty did not bind the then European Community; Aust (n 42) 274–75.
[442] Art 48(1) VCLT.
[443] ibid, Art 48(2).
[444] *Temple of Preah Vihear* (n 320) 26.
[445] ILC Draft Articles (n 10) 243.
[446] Art 48(3) VCLT. See also Aust (n 42) at 275–76; Klabbers (n 424) 564–66; Kolb (n 7) 97–99. See further H Schulte-Beerbühl, *Irrtum bei völkerrechtlichen Verträgen nach der Wiener Vertragsrechtskonvention* (Gelsenkirchen, Mannhold, 1982); E Wyler and R Samson, 'Article 48: Error – 1969 Vienna Convention' in Corten and Klein (n 34) Vol II, 1117–39.

iii. Fraud

Article 49 VCLT provides that a State may invoke fraud as invalidating its consent to be bound by the treaty if that State has been induced to conclude a treaty by the fraudulent conduct of another negotiating State. The expression 'fraudulent conduct' includes any deliberately false statements, misrepresentations or other deceitful proceedings by which a State is induced to give consent that it would not otherwise give.[447] While fraud is accepted as a way of vitiating consent in domestic legal systems, and *fraus omnia corrumpit* can be considered a general principle of law, there is barely any practice of it being invoked to invalidate a treaty. The ILC decided to allow the proper scope of this provision to be developed in practice and in the rulings of international courts.[448]

iv. Corruption

At least as rare are the precedents concerning corruption of a representative of a State, also noted as a reason for invalidating consent in the VCLT. Pursuant to Article 50 VCLT, a State may invoke corruption as invalidating its consent to be bound by the treaty if the expression of its consent to be bound has been procured through the corruption of its representative directly or indirectly by another negotiating State. The ILC clarified that only acts that have a substantial influence on the will of the representative are applicable, with the exclusion of small favours or gestures of comity.[449]

B. Absolute Invalidity

Absolute invalidity is connected to grounds that affect the collective interests of the international legal order.[450] Thus, in cases of absolute invalidity the treaty is rendered void and without legal effect *ab initio*, meaning that the affected State does not need to invoke the relevant ground for the treaty to become invalid.[451] Absolute invalidity normally affects the entire treaty (see below, Section X(C) on limited invalidity).

i. Coercion of a Representative of a State

If a State's consent has been procured by coercion of its representative through acts or threats directed against him or her, the consent is without legal effect and the entire treaty is void.[452] The coercion mentioned in Article 51 VCLT concerns the representative of the State as an individual and not as an organ of the State. It seems that what the ILC had in mind when drafting this provision were situations of physical violence and/or blackmail.[453]

447 Aust (n 42) 276.

448 ILC Draft Articles (n 10) 244. See also Klabbers (n 424) 566; Kolb (n 7) 99. See further G Niyungeko, 'Article 49: Fraud – 1969 Vienna Convention' in Corten and Klein (n 34) Vol II, 1142–66.

449 ILC Draft Articles (n 10) 245. See also Aust (n 42) 277; Klabbers (n 424) 566; Kolb (n 7) 100. See further JP Cot, 'Article 50: Corruption of a Representative of a State – 1969 Vienna Convention' in Corten and Klein (n 34) Vol II, 1169–76.

450 Kolb (n 7) 108.

451 ibid.

452 Art 51 VCLT; Aust (n 42) 277.

453 Aust (n 42) 277; Klabbers (n 424) 567; Kolb (n 7) 100.

However, most of the historic examples (François I as a prisoner of the Holy Roman Emperor Charles V in 1526; Korean negotiators coerced by Japan in 1905; German coercion of Czechoslovak President Hach in 1939) show that the individuals that were coerced were those that were at the top of the State's hierarchy, making it difficult to separate it from coercion of the State itself.[454]

ii. Coercion of a State

Article 52 VCLT provides for the absolute invalidity of a treaty 'if its conclusion has been procured by the threat or use of force in violation of the principles of international law embodied in the Charter of the United Nations'. Under classical international law, the threat or use of force was not forbidden; therefore, the validity of treaties concluded by such means was not affected.[455] Especially since the 1928 Kellogg–Briand Pact[456] and Article 2(4) of the UN Charter, the threat or use of force is no longer permitted.[457] Thus, the ILC concluded that 'the invalidity of a treaty procured by the illegal threat or use of force is a principle which is *lex lata* in the international law of today'.[458] The expression 'principles of international law, as laid down in the Charter of the United Nations', was chosen over 'the Charter' in general, to avoid giving the impression that the article limited its application to UN Member States.[459] Article 52 VCLT does not apply to the threat or use of *lawful* force.[460] During the drafting of the VCLT, it was discussed whether the notion of coercion should not only address military force but also political and economic pressure. Since many States found that this would seriously undermine the viability of treaty negotiations, this proposal never made it into Article 52. However, the Final Act of the Vienna Conference includes a declaration also condemning coercion by non-forceful means.[461] In the *Fisheries Jurisdiction* case, the ICJ rejected what could be a 'veiled charge of duress' under Article 52 VCLT, holding that 'a court cannot consider an accusation of this serious nature on the basis of a vague general charge unfortified by evidence in its support', while the instruments at hand 'were freely negotiated by the interested parties on the basis of perfect equality and freedom of decision on both sides'.[462]

[454] See further G Distefano, 'Article 51: Coercion of a Representative of a State – 1969 Vienna Convention' in Corten and Klein (n 34) Vol II, 1179–98.

[455] Kolb (n 7) 101.

[456] General Treaty for Renunciation of War as an Instrument of National Policy (adopted 27 August 1928, entered into force 24 July 1929) 94 LNTS 57 ('Kellogg-Briand Pact').

[457] On the prohibition of the use of force, see Chapter 14, Section II.

[458] ILC Draft Articles (n 10) 246.

[459] ibid, 247.

[460] Aust (n 42) 278.

[461] Official Records of the United Nations Conference on the Law of Treaties, First and Second Sessions, 26 March–24 May 1968 and 9 April–22 May 1969, UN Doc A/CONF.39/11/Add.2, containing the Final Act of the United Nations Conference on the Law of Treaties, UN Doc A/CONF.39/26, 281, with Annex: Declaration on the Prohibition of Military, Political or Economic Coercion in the Conclusion of Treaties, 285: 'The United Nations Conference on the Law of Treaties [...] [s]olemnly condemns the threat or use of pressure in any form, whether military, political, or economic, by any State in order to coerce another State to perform any act relating to the conclusion of a treaty in violation of the principles of the sovereign equality of States and freedom of consent'.

[462] *Fisheries Jurisdiction* (n 14) 14, para 24. See Aust (n 42) 277–78; Klabbers (n 424) 568–70; Kolb (n 7) 101–104. See further O Corten, 'Article 52: Coercion of a State by the Threat or Use of Force – 1969 Vienna Convention' in Corten and Klein (n 34) Vol II, 1201–20; HG de Jong, 'Coercion in the Conclusion of Treaties: A Consideration of Articles 51 and 52 of the Convention of the Law of Treaties' (1984) 15 *NYIL* 209.

iii. Violation of Jus Cogens

Traditionally, it was assumed that States could conclude treaties on any matter. However, during the preparation of the VCLT, the ILC considered that this situation had changed, and that there are rules of international law from which States cannot deviate in their mutual agreements:

> The view that in the last analysis there is no rule of international law from which States cannot at their own free will contract out, has become increasingly difficult to sustain [...]. [...] [T]he Commission concluded [...] that to-day there are certain rules from which States are not competent to derogate at all by a treaty arrangement, and which may be changed only by another rule of the same character [...]. The emergence of rules having the character of jus cogens is comparatively recent [...]. The Commission considered the right course to be [...] to leave the full content of this rule to be worked out in State practice and in the jurisprudence of international tribunals. [...] Examples suggested included (a) a treaty contemplating an unlawful use of force contrary to the principles of the Charter, (b) a treaty contemplating the performance of any other act criminal under international law, and (c) a treaty contemplating or conniving at the commission of acts, such as trade in slaves, piracy or genocide, in the suppression of which every State is called upon to co-operate. [...] [T]reaties violating human rights, the equality of States or the principle of self-determination were mentioned as other possible examples.[463]

The ILC decided not to add any more examples of *jus cogens* rules, inter alia because 'the mention of some cases [...] might, even with the most careful drafting, lead to misunderstanding as to the position concerning other cases'.[464] Up until today, there is a lack of general agreement regarding the question of which rules of international law constitute norms of *jus cogens*. There is, however, a broad consensus that it includes the following: the ban on aggression and the illegitimate use of force more generally; genocide; racial discrimination; slavery and torture.[465]

Without denying the *jus cogens* status of rules in international law, representatives of Western States raised certain objections during the Vienna Conference on introducing a violation of *jus cogens* as a ground for the invalidation of treaties. They opposed such a rule as long as the concept of *jus cogens* had not been further defined and as long as it was not accompanied by a satisfactory mechanism for an independent judicial settlement.[466] To a certain extent, these objections were addressed by qualifying the draft text of the ILC, acccording to which 'a peremptory norm of general international law is a norm from which no derogation is permitted and which can be modified only by a subsequent norm of general international law having the same character', namely by specifying that it must concern a norm 'accepted and recognized by the international community of States as a whole'.[467] The expression 'as a whole' was inserted to indicate that no individual State has the right of veto, that it is not necessary for the norm in question to be accepted and recognised by all States, that it is sufficient if a large majority does so, and that it is not States individually, but rather States as a collective that must accept and recognise the non-derogability of the norm.[468] However, the deciding factor is not just the quantitative aspect,

[463] ILC Draft Articles (n 10) 247–48.
[464] ibid, 248.
[465] See generally S Verhoeven, *Norms of Jus Cogens in International Law: A Positivist and Constitutionalist Approach* (DPhil thesis, KU Leuven, 2011) 342–407.
[466] IM Sinclair, 'Vienna Conference on the Law of Treaties' (1970) 19 *ICLQ* 47, 66.
[467] Art 53 VCLT.
[468] ILC, Second Report on *Jus Cogens* by Dire Tladi, Special Rapporteur, 16 March 2017, UN Doc A/CN.4/706, 34, para 67.

but also the fundamental interest of the international community at hand, which implies a value judgement.[469]

Article 53 VCLT deals with the invalidity of a treaty that 'at the time of its conclusion' is in violation of a peremptory norm of general international law. Article 64 VCLT, which concerns treaties that become invalid when a new peremptory norm of general international law appears, constitutes its counterpart. Both provisions stipulate that the main consequence for a treaty that conflicts with a norm of *jus cogens* is that it becomes invalid.[470] The consequences of this invalidity are, in turn, regulated by Article 71 VCLT. In the case where a newly-concluded treaty is void pursuant to Article 53 VCLT, parties are under an obligation to (i) eliminate wherever possible the consequences of any provision that is in violation with the rule of *jus cogens*; and (ii) align their mutual relations with the rule of *jus cogens*.[471] In the case of a treaty that becomes void in accordance with Article 64 VCLT: (i) the termination of the treaty releases the parties from any further obligation to perform the treaty; and (ii) the termination of the treaty does not affect any right, obligation or legal situation of the parties created through the execution of the treaty prior to its termination. These rights, obligations or legal situations can afterwards be maintained only to the extent that their maintenance is not in itself in conflict with the new peremptory norm of *jus cogens*.[472]

C. Severability of Invalid Clauses

The question arises whether the invalidity can be limited to the vitiated clause, or whether it necessarily affects the entire treaty. Article 44(2) VCLT contains the general rule that '[a] ground for invalidating […] the operation of a treaty recognized in the present Convention may be invoked only with respect to the whole treaty'. This general principle is justified by the usual interconnectedness of the different treaty provisions. Thus, the invalidity normally affects the entire treaty, and if States want to continue their treaty relations – apart from the vitiated clause – they need to conclude a new agreement.[473] However, Article 44(3) provides an exception to this rule, stating that

> If the ground relates solely to particular clauses, it may be invoked only with respect to those clauses where:
>
> (a) The said clauses are separable from the remainder of the treaty with regard to their application;
> (b) It appears from the treaty or is otherwise established that acceptance of those clauses was not an essential basis of the consent of the other party or parties to be bound by the treaty as a whole; and
> (c) Continued performance of the remainder of the treaty would not be unjust.

[469] ibid, 11–12, para 22.
[470] Arts 53 and 64 VCLT.
[471] Art 71(1) VCLT.
[472] ibid, Art 71(2). See also Aust (n 42) 278–79; Klabbers (n 424) 570–74; Kolb (n 7) 104–108. See further E Suy, 'Article 53: Treaties Conflicting with a Peremptory Norm of General International Law ("Jus Cogens") – 1969 Vienna Convention' in Corten and Klein (n 34) 1224–33 and A Lagerwall, 'Article 64: Emergence of a New Peremptory Norm of General International Law ("Jus Cogens") – 1969 Vienna Convention' in ibid, 1455–80. On *jus cogens* more generally, see Verhoeven (n 465); R Kolb, *Peremptory International Law – Jus Cogens: A General Inventory* (Oxford, Hart, 2015).
[473] Kolb (n 7) 110.

Article 44(5) VCLT excludes this possibility for 'cases falling under Articles 51, 52 and 53', covering all cases of absolute invalidity, with the exception of Article 64 VCLT: in cases of a new norm of *jus cogens* with which the treaty comes to conflict, severability of the affected clause(s) remains possible.[474]

XI. Termination of Treaties

Articles 54–64 VCLT deal with the – definitive – termination of or withdrawal from a treaty and with the – provisional – suspension of a treaty. These three situations have in common that 'the rights and obligations enshrined in the treaty are no longer applicable, either in whole and definitively, or for a certain defined or undefined time-span, or for some parties and not for others'.[475] As opposed to what is the case for invalidity (see above, Section X), the consequences of termination, withdrawal and suspension only take effect from the moment it is determined that the conditions for one of these three situations to materialise have been met (*ex nunc*).[476] According to Articles 54 (on termination and withdrawal) and 57 VCLT (on suspension), these situations may be governed by the provisions of the treaty itself, or can take place at any time with the consent of all the parties after consultation with the other contracting States. Articles 65–68 VCLT lay down the procedure to be followed in case of termination, withdrawal or suspension (see below, Section XII).

A. Termination

'Termination' concerns the extinction of the treaty: the treaty ceases to exist as a whole.[477] Most treaties include explicit provisions concerning their (duration and) termination.[478] Such provisions can take many forms. For example, a treaty may set out that it only applies within a certain period of time[479] or ends on a certain date.[480] A treaty may stipulate that its duration, unless terminated, is automatically extended for a certain period of time.[481] The decision to extend a treaty, be it for a definite or indefinite period of time, may also be left in the hands of a conference.[482] Treaties of a contractual nature may have a clause providing that the treaty can be terminated by one of the parties when

[474] See ibid, 109–12. See further M Falkowska, M Bedjaoui and T Leidgens, 'Article 44: Separability of Treaty Provisions – Vienna Convention 1969' in Corten and Klein (n 34) Vol II, 1046–61.
[475] Kolb (n 7) 206.
[476] Art 70(1)(b) VCLT; ibid, 108 and 250.
[477] Kolb (n 7) 206.
[478] LR Helfer, 'Terminating Treaties' in Hollis (n 29) 634.
[479] eg Art 97 Treaty establishing the European Coal and Steel Community (adopted 18 April 1951, entered into force 23 July 1952) 261 UNTS 140: 'The present Treaty is concluded for a period of fifty years from the date of its entry into force'.
[480] eg Art II(2) Panama Canal Treaty (adopted 7 September 1977, entered into force 1 October 1979) 1280 UNTS 4: 'This Treaty shall terminate at noon, Panama time, December 31, 1999'.
[481] eg Art XIV Genocide Convention: 'The present Convention shall remain in effect for a period of ten years as from the date of its coming into force. It shall thereafter remain in force for successive periods of five years for such Contracting Parties as have not denounced it at least six months before the expiration of the current period'.
[482] See eg Art X(2) Non-Proliferation Treaty: 'Twenty-five years after the entry into force of the Treaty, a conference shall be convened to decide whether the Treaty shall continue in force indefinitely, or shall be extended for an additional fixed period or periods. This decision shall be taken by a majority of the Parties to the Treaty'.

the obligation(s) concerned (eg the delivery of material) have not taken place as agreed (eg before a certain date).[483]

If a treaty does not contain provisions on its termination, there are certain grounds that can lead to its termination. For example, treaties can be terminated by falling into disuse (*desuetudo*).[484] On the other hand, the fact that the number of parties to a multilateral treaty decreases below the number necessary for its entry into force has no legal effects for its application with regard to those that are still a party thereto, unless the treaty states otherwise.[485] The (possible) grounds for termination as dealt with by the VCLT are discussed below under specific headings.

Following Article 70(1) VCLT, the consequences of the termination of a treaty are that (a) it '[r]eleases the parties from any obligation further to perform the treaty', which, however, (b) '[d]oes not affect any right, obligation or legal situation of the parties created through the execution of the treaty prior to its termination'.

B. Withdrawal

Withdrawal differs from termination in that it concerns a unilateral act of one State Party that wishes to free itself from its treaty obligations (and that is in a capacity to do so). Even if treaties themselves do not always do so, it is preferable to make a terminological difference between 'denunciation' (*dénonciation*), which concerns bilateral treaties, and 'withdrawal' (*retrait*), which concerns multilateral treaties. In the case of bilateral treaties, the denunciation terminates the treaty (and is thus, even if in nature a case of unilateral 'withdrawal', in effect also a case of termination). In the case of withdrawal from a multilateral treaty, the treaty continues to apply to the other treaty parties.[486] Thus, Art 70(2) VCLT provides that '[i]f a State denounces or withdraws from a multilateral treaty, [Art 70(1) VCLT] applies in the relations between that State and each of the other parties to the treaty from the date when such denunciation or withdrawal takes effect'.

Treaties often explicitly provide for the possibility of withdrawal. If they do, they usually also arrange its modalities (notably the term following which the withdrawal can take effect)[487] and consequences (eg whether or not the withdrawal has retroactive effect).[488] Also the founding treaties of international organisations normally contain provisions for

The parties agreed to extend the treaty indefinitely at the fifth conference in 1995. For a more detailed account on the types of termination clauses, see Aust (n 42) 246–54.

483 Even if they do not provide for such a clause, such a failure to perform the obligation would most probably constitute a 'material breach' under Art 60 VCLT, allowing the other party to terminate the treaty (see below, Section XI(E)) or such a termination clause could be considered to be present implicitly.

484 Aust (n 42) 270.

485 Art 55 VCLT. For an example of the latter, see Art XV Genocide Convention: 'If, as a result of denunciations, the number of Parties to the present Convention should become less than sixteen, the Convention shall cease to be in force as from the date on which the last of these denunciations shall become effective'.

486 Aust (n 42) 245.

487 See eg Art 58(1) ECHR (6 months); Art 52 Convention on the Rights of the Child (1 year); Art 317(1) UNCLOS (1 year); Art 10(1) Non-Proliferation Treaty (3 months).

488 See eg Art 58(2) ECHR, stating that withdrawal will not have any retroactive effect. See also Art 63(3) GC I, Art 62(3) GC II, Art 142(3) GC III and Art 158(3) GC IV, stipulating that a withdrawal of which notice is given while the withdrawing State is involved in a conflict will not in any way take effect as long as peace is not concluded and in any case not until after operations connected with the release and repatriation of the persons protected by the relevant Convention have been terminated.

withdrawal.[489] For instance, Article 50(1) TEU provides that '[a]ny Member State may decide to withdraw from the Union in accordance with its own constitutional requirements'. Overall, the procedure laid down in Article 50 TEU, which includes the requirement that the EU and the State concerned negotiate and conclude an agreement setting out the arrangements for the withdrawal,[490] draws on the rules laid down in the VCLT,[491] and must be presumed to be compatible therewith.[492] Thus, while the question arose as to whether the rules laid down in Article 70 VCLT apply to 'Brexit' as a matter of customary international law, or whether Article 50 TEU should be considered to be a *lex specialis* governing the matter, the most elegant solution appears to apply both provisions concurrently by interpreting them in a manner in which they do not conflict.

If a treaty contains no provision regarding these matters, denunciation or withdrawal is only possible if (i) it is established that the parties intended to admit that possibility; or (ii) a right of denunciation or withdrawal may be implied by the nature of the treaty.[493] In these cases, a notification of not less than 12 months in advance is required.[494] Whether the parties intended to allow the possibility of denunciation or withdrawal may appear from the preparatory works, if available. Thus, it was confirmed at the San Francisco Conference, which preceded the adoption of the UN Charter, that in principle, States can withdraw from the UN (Charter).[495] Second, whether denunciation or withdrawal is possible can be implied from the nature of a treaty. It is assumed that – if they are silent on the matter – this is impossible for border treaties or treaties that concern the transfer of territory or the establishment of a boundary,[496] for peace and demilitarisation treaties and treaties that establish permanent regimes.[497] On the other hand, it is assumed that denunciation or withdrawal is possible for cooperative treaties, including those based on friendship, treaties concerning commerce and cultural grounds, as well as treaties that establish an international organisation or a military alliance.[498]

A notorious example of a withdrawal is that of the Democratic People's Republic of Korea (DPRK) from the ICCPR in 1977. The HRCttee responded to this withdrawal with a general comment, stating that a State Party cannot withdraw from the ICCPR as the rights contained therein 'belong to the people living in the territory of the State Party', 'notwithstanding change in government of the State Party […] or State succession or any subsequent action of the State Party designed to divest them of the rights guaranteed by the Covenant'.[499] The UN Secretary General also rejected North Korea's withdrawal,

[489] See eg Art 7 Statute of the Council of Europe (n 96); Art XV(1) WTO Agreement.

[490] Art 50(2) TEU.

[491] Praesidium, 'Title X: Union Membership', 2 April 2003, CONV 648/03 – Annex II, 9.

[492] A Sari, 'Reversing a Withdrawal Notification under Article 50 TEU: Can a Member State Change Its Mind?' (2017) 42 *ELR* 451, 470–71.

[493] Art 56(1) VCLT.

[494] ibid, Art 56(2).

[495] (1946–1947) *Yearbook of the United Nations*, Part One – Chapter 1. Origin and Evolution, 21. However, the only example of a (de facto) withdrawal from the UN, ie that of Indonesia in 1965, was upon its return in 1966 formally treated as a 'cessation of cooperation' rather than a withdrawal; UNGA Official Records 21st Session, 1420th Plenary Meeting, 28 September 1966, UN Doc A/PV.1420, 2, para 7.

[496] Consider Art 62(2)(a) VCLT.

[497] ILC, Second Report on the Law of Treaties by Sir Humphrey Waldock, Special Rapporteur (1963) *YILC*, Vol II, 64 (draft Art 17(4)). See also Aust (n 42) 256; Helfer (n 478) 638.

[498] Second Report by Sir Humphrey Waldock (n 497) 64 (draft Art 17(3)). See also Aust (n 42) 257; Helfer (n 478) 638.

[499] HRCttee, General Comment No 26: 'Continuity of Obligations', 8 December 1997, UN Doc CCPR/C/21/Rev.1/Add.8/Rev.1, para 4.

but argued that it was precluded by Article 54 VCLT (see above, introduction to Section XI), which he considered to allow withdrawal only in case all other State Parties consented therewith.[500] The DPRK appears to have accepted this.[501]

C. Suspension

Suspension concerns a temporary release from treaty obligations. Article 58 VCLT sets out the conditions under which a multilateral treaty can be suspended between certain parties. Such is possible only if: (a) the treaty provides for such a possibility; or (b) does not prohibit it *and* (i) the suspension does not affect the enjoyment by the other parties of their rights under the treaty or the performance of their obligations, and (ii) is not incompatible with the object and purpose of the treaty.[502] The suspension of a treaty: (a) releases the parties between which the operation of the treaty is suspended from the obligation to perform it in their mutual relations during the period of the suspension; and (b) does not otherwise affect the legal relations between the parties established by the treaty.[503] However, during the suspension, the parties must refrain from acts 'tending to obstruct the resumption of the operation of the treaty'.[504]

Article 218(9) TFEU provides that 'on a proposal from the Commission or the High Representative of the Union for Foreign Affairs and Security Policy', the Council can 'adopt a decision suspending application of an agreement'. For example, following the outbreak of the war in Yugoslavia, the then EEC unilaterally suspended its cooperation agreement with the Socialist Federal Republic of Yugoslavia.[505] A more recent example is the partial suspension of the application of the Cooperation Agreement with the Syrian Arab Republic.[506]

D. Concluding a Later Treaty

Article 59 VCLT sets out the first specific mode of termination or suspension: the abrogation or supension of a treaty implied by the conclusion of a later treaty. This article is based on the legal principle *lex posterior derogat priori* (the later law prevails over the earlier law). Thus, a treaty is considered to have been terminated if all the parties to it conclude a later treaty relating to the same subject matter and: (i) it appears from the later treaty

[500] UNSG, Notification by the Democratic People's Republic of Korea, 12 November 1997, UN Doc C.N.467.1997. TREATIES-10.

[501] See Aust (n 42) 257; Helfer (n 478) 639–40. See further E Evatt, 'Democratic People's Republic of Korea and the ICCPR: Denunciation as an Exercise of the Right of Self-defence?' (1998) 5 *Australian Journal of Human Rights* 215 and more generally Y Tyagi, 'The Denunciation of Human Rights Treaties' (2008) 79 *BYIL* 86.

[502] Art 58(1) VCLT. Art 58(2) VCLT adds the (default) obligation to notify the other parties to the treaty.

[503] Art 72(1) VCLT.

[504] ibid, Art 72(2). On the matter of termination, withdrawal and suspension in general, see eg C Feist, *Kündigung, Rücktritt und Suspendierung von multilateralen Verträgen* (Berlin, Duncker & Humblot, 2001).

[505] Council Regulation (EEC) No 3300/91 of 11 November 1991 suspending the trade concessions provided for by the Cooperation Agreement between the European Economic Community and the Socialist Federal Republic of Yugoslavia [1991] OJ L315/1. On this suspension, see *Racke* (n 15) and DR Verwey, *The European Community, the European Union and the International Law of Treaties* (The Hague, TMC Asser Press, 2004) 148–49.

[506] Council Decision 2011/523/EU of 2 September 2011 partially suspending the application of the Cooperation Agreement between the European Economic Community and the Syrian Arab Republic [2011] OJ L228/19.

or is otherwise established that the parties intended that the matter should be governed by that treaty; and (ii) the provisions of the later treaty are so incompatible with those of the earlier one that the two treaties cannot be applied at the same time.[507] The rule established by Article 59 applies where two treaties that are in force, while neither of them is expressly terminated, and seeks to regulate a specific matter giving rise to a conflict between the successive treaties.[508] Whether two treaties relate to the same subject matter is to be determined as a matter of treaty interpretation, according to the relevant provisions of the VCLT (see above, Section VII).[509]

E. Violation of the Treaty (Material Breach)

Article 60 VCLT deals with the consequences that flow from the violation of the treaty by one of its parties. This article had to carefully balance the consideration of an effective response agains treaty breaches, to avoid abuse by the law-breaking State that could otherwise benefit from its own wrong, and that of preserving treaty commitments, to avoid abuse by a State Party that no longer wants to be bound by the treaty and thus invokes an invented or innocent breach by another party to unilaterally denounce or suspend the operation of the treaty.[510] Thus, the breach of a treaty is considered to be a valid ground for its termination or suspension, but only if it is material (*violation substantielle*).[511] The principle underlying Article 60 VCLT is similar to that of the *exceptio non adimpleti contractus* (exception of a non-performed contract), a remedy that allows a party to a reciprocal contract to withhold its own performance, and that is known in various national legal systems (see also Chapter 12, Section VI(A)). In its *Namibia* advisory opinion, the ICJ acknowledged the existence of

> the general principle of law that a right of termination on account of breach must be presumed to exist in respect of all treaties, except as regards provisions relating to the protection of the human person contained in treaties of a humanitarian character.[512]

Pursuant to Article 60(3)(b) VCLT, a 'material breach' consists of: (i) a repudiation of the treaty not sanctioned by the VCLT; or (ii) the violation of a provision essential to the accomplishment of the object or purpose of the treaty.[513] It is therefore not so much about

[507] Art 59(1) VCLT. Art 59(2) VCLT provides that '[t]he earlier treaty shall be considered as only suspended in operation if it appears from the later treaty or is otherwise established that such was the intention of the parties'. For an application on the national level, see eg Supreme Court (PL), *Question of law regarding the interpretation of Article 17(2) of Treaty on Extradition between the Republic of Poland and Australia*, 19 February 2003, Case No I KZP 47/02, where the Court considered that an earlier extradition treaty (1932) no longer applied to an extradition request, as a later extradition treaty (1998) provided that the earlier treaty ceased to be in force and that extradition requests submitted after the entry into force of the later treaty are governed by that treaty, despite the fact that the request was pending upon, but submitted before the later treaty's entry into force.

[508] F Dubuisson, 'Article 59: Termination or Suspension of the Operation of a Treaty Implied by Conclusion of a Later Treaty – 1969 Vienna Convention' in Corten and Klein (n 34) Vol II, 1325–47.

[509] See also Aust (n 42) 257–58; Kolb (n 7) 211–12; Sinclair (n 435) 93–98. See further Dubuisson (n 508).

[510] B Simma and CJ Tams, 'Reacting against Treaty Breaches' in Hollis (n 29) 582; Kolb (n 7) 220–21.

[511] This means that an 'ordinary' violation does not suffice in respect of this article. However, such an ordinary violation does in effect make it possible to appeal to the rules concerning State responsibility, and thus to take appropriate countermeasures and claim reparations; see Kolb (n 7) 221. On the relation between material breach and state responsibility, see M Fitzmaurice, 'Material Breach of Treaty: Some Legal Issues' (2001) 6 *Austrian Review of International and European Law* 3, 11–29. See also Chapter 12 on International Responsibility.

[512] *Legal Consequences for States of the Continued Presence of South Africa in Namibia* (n 14) para 96.

[513] This rule appears to have been sanctioned as being part of customary international law in ibid, para 94.

the seriousness of the violation, but rather about the importance of the rule that has been violated.[514] At least in theory, this means that serious violations of provisions that, no matter how important, do not essentially affect the realisation of the object or purpose of the treaty, are not sufficient to invoke Article 60 VCLT. However, in practice, this rule has proved unworkable: typically, when tribunals discuss Article 60 VCLT, 'they conceptualize it as referring to grave breaches'.[515]

Pursuant to Article 60(1) VCLT, a material breach of a *bilateral* treaty by one of its parties gives the other party the right to invoke the breach 'as a ground for terminating the treaty or suspending its operation in whole or in part'. Thus, consequences do not follow automatically: the aggrieved party simply has the option to pursue the treaty's termination or suspension.[516] In the *Gabčíkovo-Nagymaros* case, the ICJ stressed that a party cannot invoke a material breach if it committed a wrongful act itself and thus prevented the other party from complying with the treaty.[517]

The EU has included an 'essential elements' or human rights clause in a large number of bilateral cooperation and trade agreements with third countries that concern respect for a number of values which the EU has committed to promote in its external relations, such as human rights, democracy and the rule of law.[518] In 1991, the Council first gave the Commission a specific mandate to include human rights clauses in agreements with third countries, emphasising the need to favour a positive, dialogue-centred approach to human rights and that suspensions or other punitive measures under the clause should only be invoked as a last resort.[519] In 1995, responding to a communication of the Commission, the Council adopted the policy to systematically include operative human rights clauses in all future EU cooperation and trade agreements.[520] Even then, all EU trade agreements since 1992 had already included one. As a result, roughly over 120 EU trade agreements with countries all over the world now contain such clauses.[521] While the specific clauses vary somewhat, they are normally included at the beginning of the agreement. They reference the democratic principles and fundamental human rights underpinning the agreement at hand and (together with a non-execution clause, to be discussed right below) condition the agreement upon the parties' compliance therewith. Article 1 of the EU-Central America Association Agreement can serve as an example:

> Respect for democratic principles and fundamental human rights, as laid down in the Universal Declaration of Human Rights, and for the principle of the rule of law, underpins the internal and international policies of both Parties and constitutes an essential element of this Agreement.[522]

[514] J Klabbers, *International Law* (Cambridge, CUP, 2013) 63.

[515] ibid. On this, see B Simma, 'Reflections on Article 60 of the Vienna Convention on the Law of Treaties and its Background in General International Law' (1970) 20 *Austrian Journal of Public and International Law* 5. See also Aust (n 42) 260–61 and Fitzmaurice (n 511) 4–11.

[516] Kolb (n 7) 222.

[517] *Gabčíkovo-Nagymaros* (n 14) para 110; see also Aust (n 42) 259.

[518] Arts 3(5) and 21(1) TEU.

[519] Resolution of the Council and of the Member States meeting in the Council on human rights, democracy and development, 28 November 1991, reported in 11-1991 *Bulletin of the European Communities* 122–23.

[520] Commission of the European Communities, 'Communication on the Inclusion of Respect for Democratic Principles and Human Rights in Agreements between the Community and Third Countries', 23 May 1995, COM(95) 216 final; and Council Conclusions of 29 May 1995, both reported in 5-1995 *Bulletin of the European Union* at 9, and as interpreted by L Bartels, 'The European Parliament's Role in relation to Human Rights in Trade and Investment Agreements', Study for the DROI and INTA Committees of the European Parliament, europarl.europa.eu/RegData/etudes/etudes/join/2014/433751/EXPO-JOIN_ET%282014%29433751_EN.pdf, 6.

[521] Bartels (n 520) 6–8.

[522] Agreement establishing an Association between the European Union and its Member States, on the one hand, and Central America on the other (29 June 2012) [2012] OJ L346/3.

As alluded to, a non-execution clause is inherently attached to an essential elements clause. Such a clause is usually added in the final dispositions of the agreement. It allows for either contracting party to take 'appropriate measures' in the case of a violation of an essential element, including the suspension of the agreement at large under the rules of the VCLT, if necessary 'as reflecting customary international law'. Thus, the violation of an essential elements clause in essence results in a material breach in the sense of Article 60 VCLT. Here, Article 355 of the EU-Central America Association Agreement can serve as an example:

> 2. If a Party considers that another Party has failed to fulfil an obligation under this Agreement, it may have recourse to appropriate measures. Before doing so, except in cases of special urgency, it shall submit to the Association Council within thirty days all relevant information required for a thorough examination of the situation with a view to seeking a solution acceptable to the Parties. In selecting which measures to adopt, priority shall be given to those which are least disruptive to the implementation of this Agreement. Such measures shall be notified immediately to the Association Committee and shall be the subject of consultations in the Committee if a Party so requests.
>
> 3. The Parties agree that the term 'cases of special urgency' in paragraph 2 means a case of material breach of this Agreement by one of the Parties. The Parties further agree that the term 'appropriate measures' referred to in paragraph 2 means measures taken in accordance with international law. It is understood that suspension would be a measure of last resort.
>
> 4. A material breach of this Agreement consists in:
>
> (a) repudiation of this Agreement not sanctioned by general rules of international law;
>
> (b) violation of the essential elements of this Agreement.[523]

The EU has only unsystematically applied human rights clauses, leading to twofold criticism. First, is has been held that the EU does not enforce human rights conditionality often enough, regularly letting human rights violations by trade partners go unpunished. Second, it has been held that the EU applies the human rights clauses in a seemingly selective way, using double standards: only developing countries in a highly dependent relation with the EU have so far been subjected to an activation of the clauses, while other, stronger trading partners have remained out of reach. In combination with a lack of monitoring and enforcement capacity, this has largely caused human rights clauses to lack the necessary credibility to present a viable tool for human rights promotion.[524]

Pursuant to Article 60(2) VCLT,

> A material breach of a *multilateral* treaty by one of its parties entitles (emphasis added):
>
> (a) The other parties by unanimous agreement to suspend the operation of the treaty in whole or in part or to terminate the treaty either
>
> (i) In the relations between themselves and the defaulting State, or
>
> (ii) As between all the parties;
>
> (b) A party specially affected by the breach to invoke it as grounds for suspending the operation of the treaty in whole or in part in the relations between itself and the defaulting State;
>
> (c) Any party other than the defaulting State to invoke the breach as grounds for suspending the operation of the treaty in whole or in part with respect to itself if the treaty is of such a

[523] ibid.

[524] See further N Hachez, '"Essential Elements" Clauses in EU Trade Agreements – Making Trade Work in a Way that Helps Human Rights?' (2015) 53 *Cuadernos Europeos de Deusto* 81 and *Leuven Centre for Global Governance Studies*, Working Paper No 158.

> character that a material breach of its provisions by one party radically changes the position of every party with respect to the further performance of its obligations under the treaty.

Article 60(2)(a) VCLT recognises that some treaties may have a public law character, and cannot be reduced to mere bilateral sets of rights and obligations.[525] Moreover, the options granted to all States Parties in unanimous agreement are broader than those granted to any individual State Party: the former can suspend *or* terminate, the latter can only suspend the treaty. This difference is made to prevent abusive claims by a single State.[526] Provision (c) is specifically meant for 'integral treaties' like disarmament treaties, where a breach by one party could undermine the entire treaty regime, and (a) and (b) would thus not adequately protect the interests of an individual party.[527]

With regard to a material breach of a multilateral treaty on which an international organisation is founded, in some cases provisions are made for revocation or suspension of membership or membership rights. Thus, under Article 6 of the UN Charter, a Member that has persistently violated the principles contained in the Charter may be expelled by the General Assembly upon recommendation by the Security Council. This provision, due partly to deadlocks within the UNSC, and partly to the efforts of the UN to be a truly universal organisation, has never been applied.[528]

Within the EU, Article 7(3) TEU sets out the process by which certain rights of Member States may be suspended in cases where the existence of a serious and persistent breach of certain fundamental principles of EU law has been established. More recently, the European Parliament has called for triggering of Article 7 with regard to Hungary[529] and Poland.[530] On 20 December 2017, the Commission for the first time issued a reasoned proposal for a Council decision on the determination of a clear risk of a serious breach by Poland of the rule of law.[531] The proposal was welcomed by the European Parliament in a resolution on 1 March 2018, which also called on the Council 'to take swift action in accordance with the provisions set out in Article 7(1) TEU'.[532]

[525] Klabbers (n 514) 63. See further DHN Hutchinson, 'Solidarity and Breaches of Multilaterial Treaites' (1988) 59 *BYIL* 5.

[526] Kolb (n 7) 223.

[527] Aust (n 42) at 260; Kolb (n 7) at 224.

[528] See further JM Lavieille, 'La procédure de suspension des droits d'un état membre des Nations Unies' (1977) 81 *Revue générale de droit international public* 431 and KD Magliveras, *Exclusion from Participation in International Organisations: The Law and Practice Behind Member States' Expulsion and Suspension of Membership* (The Hague, Kluwer, 1999) 31–64, on 'Expulsion from the United Nations'.

[529] European Parliament Resolution of 17 May 2017 on the situation in Hungary (2017/2656(RSP)); Resolution of 12 September 2018 (2017/2131 (INL)).

[530] European Parliament Resolution of 15 November 2017 on the situation of the rule of law and democracy in Poland (2017/2931(RSP)). See further L Besselink, 'The Bite, the Bark, and the Howl: Article 7 TEU and the Rule of Law Initiatives' in A Jakab and D Kochenov (eds), *The Enforcement of EU Law and Values: Ensuring Member States' Compliance* (Oxford, OUP, 2017) 128–44; B Bugarič, 'Protecting Democracy inside the EU: On Article 7 TEU and the Hungarian Turn to Authoritarianism' in C Closa and D Kochenov (eds), *Reinforcing Rule of Law Oversight in the European Union* (Cambridge, CUP, 2016) 82–101.

[531] European Commission, Reasoned Proposal in accordance with Article 7(1) of the Treaty on European Union regarding the Rule of Law in Poland: 'Proposal for a Council Decision on the determination of a clear risk of a serious breach by the Republic of Poland of the rule of law', 20 December 2017, COM(2017) 835 final. See also below, p 265.

[532] European Parliament Resolution of 1 March 2018 on the Commission's decision to activate Article 7(1) TEU as regards the situation in Poland (2018/2541(RSP)). See further A von Bogdandy, P Bogdanowicz, I Canor, M Taborowski and M Schmidt, 'Guest Editorial: A Potential Constitutional Moment for the European Rule of Law – The Importance of Red Lines' (2018) 55 *CMLR* 983.

The provisions concerning the termination or suspension of a treaty due to a violation of the treaty are not applicable 'to provisions relating to the protection of the human person contained in treaties of a humanitarian character, in particular to provisions prohibiting any form of reprisals against persons protected by such treaties'.[533] Though this rule is in particular applicable to the Geneva Conventions, it is also assumed to apply to human rights treaties.[534] In its *Namibia* advisory opinion, as quoted above, the ICJ recognised this rule as a general principle of law.[535]

F. Supervening Impossibility of Performance

Article 61(1) VCLT sets out the circumstances under which a party may invoke a supervening impossibility of performance of a treaty as a ground for terminating or withdrawing (from) it. This impossibility must result from the permanent disappearance or destruction of an object indispensable for the execution of the treaty.[536] The effect of the impossibility is not automatic, and a party must invoke the ground for termination.[537] Among the rare examples of general practice regarding this matter, the ILC gave examples of 'the submergence of an island, the drying up of a river or the destruction of a dam or hydro-electric installation indispensable for the execution of a treaty'.[538] As is apparent from the preparatory works of the VCLT,[539] and confirmed by the ICJ, serious financial difficulties cannot constitute impossibility of performance.[540] When the impossibility is temporary (eg a failed harvest), this can, according to Article 61(1) VCLT, be invoked as a ground for suspension of the operation of the treaty. A party may not invoke impossibility of performance 'if the impossibility is the result of a breach by that party either of an obligation under the treaty or of any other international obligation owed to any other party to the treaty'.[541] Although there might be borderline cases in which the two tend to overlap, 'impossibility of performance' should be distinguished from the concept of 'fundamental change of circumstances', as the criteria to be employed in applying both grounds are not the same.[542]

[533] Art 60(5) VCLT.
[534] Aust (n 42) 260; Simma and Tams (n 510) 587–88.
[535] *Legal Consequences for States of the Continued Presence of South Africa in Namibia* (n 14) para 96. On Art 60, see further MM Gomaa, *Suspension or Termination of Treaties on Grounds of Breach* (The Hague, Nijhoff, 1996); B Simma and CJ Tams, 'Article 60: Termination or Suspension of the Operation of a Treaty as a Consequence of its Breach – 1969 Vienna Convention' in Corten and Klein (n 34) Vol II, 1351–78.
[536] Art 61(1) VCLT.
[537] Crawford (n 292) 392.
[538] ILC Draft Articles (n 10) 256, para 2.
[539] Official Records of the United Nations Conference on the Law of Treaties, First Session (Summary Records of the Plenary Meetings and of the Meetings of the Committee of the Whole), 62nd Meeting of the Committee of the Whole, 9 May 1968, UN Doc A/CONF.39/C.1/SR.62, 361–65.
[540] *Gabčíkovo-Nagymaros* (n 14) para 102.
[541] Art 61(2) VCLT. Thus, in *Gabčíkovo-Nagymaros* (n 14) para 103, the ICJ rejected the argument of Hungary that the object of the disputed treaty (a dam on the Danube to be built and operated jointly by Hungary and Czechoslovakia) had permanently disappeared because Hungary had not carried out most of the works for which it was reponsible under the Treaty.
[542] ILC Draft Articles (n 10) 256, para 1. See also Aust (n 42) 261–62; Kolb (n 7) 235–37. See further P Bodeau-Livinec and J Morgan-Foster, 'Article 61: Supervening Impossibility of Performance – 1969 Vienna Convention' in Corten and Klein (n 34) Vol II, 1382–408.

G. Fundamental Change of Circumstances (*Rebus Sic Stantibus*)

It has long been acknowledged that a fundamental change of circumstances (*clausula rebus sic stantibus*) is a ground for termination of a treaty or the withdrawal from it. Such a change must be one that was unforeseen by the parties at the time of the conclusion of the treaty. As it is an important exception to the principle of *pacta sunt servanda*, and the principle has been abused for political ends in the past, the VCLT has imposed strict conditions on the possibility to invoke it.[543] The ICJ has acknowledged that Article 62 VCLT can in many ways be considered a codification of customary international law.[544] As noted by the Court in the *Gabčíkovo-Nagymaros* case, its negative and conditional wording clearly indicates that the stability of treaty relations demands that *rebus sic stantibus* can only be applied in exceptional circumstances.[545]

Thus, Article 62(1) VCLT states that a party *cannot* invoke *rebus sic stantibus* as a ground for termination of a bilateral treaty or withdrawal from a multilateral treaty, unless the following five conditions are cumulatively met:

(1) there needs to be a change in the circumstances which existed at the time of the conclusion of the treaty;
(2) the change needs to be fundamental;
(3) the change may not have been foreseen by the parties;[546]
(4) the existence of those circumstances must have constituted an essential basis for the consent of the parties to be bound by the treaty; and
(5) the effect of the change needs to be such that the extent of the obligations still to be performed under the treaty is 'radically' altered.[547]

Moreover, Article 62(2) VCLT states that a fundamental change of circumstances may not be invoked (i) if the treaty establishes a boundary; or (ii) if the fundamental change is the result of a breach by the party invoking it either of an obligation under the treaty or of any other international obligation owed to any other party to the treaty. The latter is an application of the general principle of *nemo auditur propriam turpitudinem allegans* (no one can take advantage of his or her own wrongdoing).[548]

[543] Aust (n 41) 262.

[544] *Fisheries Jurisdiction* (n 14) para 36.

[545] *Gabčíkovo-Nagymaros* (n 14) para 104.

[546] The ICJ ruled that new developments in knowledge of the environment and environmental law can not be considered completely unforeseen; *Gabčíkovo-Nagymaros* (n 14) para 104.

[547] Art 62(1) VCLT, as rephrased. For a much contested application of *rebus sic stantibus* on the national level, see Supreme Commercial Court (RU), *Sentyabr v MIA Trans and LSV-Trans (joining)*, 23 April 2013, Case No 15497/12, where the Court held that the Geneva Convention on the Contract for the International Carriage of Goods by Road (adopted 19 May 1956, entered into force 2 July 1961) 399 UNTS 189, applied to the transport of goods from Kaliningrad to Moscow through Lituania and Belarus. Art 1(1) of the Convention explicitly states that the Convention 'appl[ies] to every contract for the carriage of goods [...] when the place of taking over of the goods and the place designated for delivery [...] are situated in two different countries'. While Kaliningrand and Moscow are both part of Russia, the Court considered that the Convention was ratified by the USSR at a time that these places were part of the unified territory of the USSR, and that the changed geographical circumstances constituted a fundamental change of circumstances that allowed it to apply the Convention.

[548] Aust (n 42) 264. See further P Cahier, 'Le changement fondamental de circonstances et la convention de Vienne de 1969 sur le droit des traités' in *Le droit international à l'heure de sa codification: Etudes en l'honneur de Roberto Ago* (Milan, Giuffrè, 1987) Vol I, 163–86; Kolb (n 7) 226–35; MN Shaw and C Fournet, 'Article 62: Fundamental Change of Circumstances – 1969 Vienna Convention' in Corten and Klein (n 34) Vol II, 1411–33; DF Vagts, 'Rebus Revisited: Changed Circumstances in Treaty Law' (2005) 43 *Columbia Journal of Transnational Law* 459.

The CJEU applied the *rebus sic stantibus* rule, which it found to be part of customary international law (as reflected in Article 62(1) VCLT)[549] in its 1998 *Racke* judgment. The Court found that the outbreak of armed conflict in Yugoslavia constituted a fundamental change in circumstances, and that

> 'the maintenance of a situation of peace in Yugoslavia, indispensable for neighbourly relations, and the existence of institutions capable of ensuring implementation of the cooperation envisaged by the Agreement throughout the territory of Yugoslavia constituted an essential condition for initiating and pursuing that cooperation'.[550]

Thus, by unilaterally suspending the Agreement, the Council of the EU had not violated the *rebus sic stantibus* rule.[551] As noted by Klabbers, this decision is vulnerable to criticism, as it 'casts its net far too wide', mainly for two reasons: first, almost all treaties presuppose peace and stable institutions (with the obvious exception of treaties concerning the law of armed conflict); second, as the VCLT explicitly excludes armed conflict from its scope (see below, Section XI(I)), it is somewhat incongruous to introduce it through an application of the *rebus sic stantibus* rule.[552] Aust considers that as the Court merely concluded that the Council did not make 'a manifest error of assessment',[553] it did not consider the international law point in depth, but rather approached the case as one of judicial review of action taken under EC law (as it was then).[554]

H. Severance of Diplomatic or Consular Relations

Following Article 63 VCLT, the severance of diplomatic or consular relations between treaty parties does not affect the legal relations established between them by a treaty, except insofar as the existence of diplomatic or consular relations are indispensable for the application of the treaty. The exception could concern extradition treaties, as it would be difficult to apply these in practice without diplomatic relations. However, even if diplomatic relations between Iraq and the United Kingdom broke off in 1990, between then and 2002, Iraq applied at least three times for the extradition of Iraqi nationals under the Iraq-UK Extradition Treaty,[555] be it through third States. While the applications were refused, they were not so based on the fact that the treaty had been suspended.[556]

[549] *Racke* (n 15) para 53.
[550] ibid, paras 54–56.
[551] ibid, paras 53 and 60.
[552] Klabbers (n 514) 65. Regarding the latter argument, one could argue that the Court was not applying the VCLT but customary international law (as it stressed in *Racke* (n 15) para 40). This would imply that the Court does not think Art 73 VCLT (excluding armed conflict from the scope of the VCLT) should be factored in the *rebus sic stantibus* rule as part of customary international law. Thus, at least with respect to States involved in an armed conflict, Kolb argues that they can still found themselves on the (general) *rebus sic stantibus* rule, as 'the *lex specialis* is here complementary and not derogatory'; Kolb (n 7) 243 and 245.
[553] *Racke* (n 15) para 56 (see also para 52).
[554] Aust (n 42) 263. For a detailed discussion of the Racke decision, see J Wouters and D Van Eeckhoutte, 'Enforcement of Customary International Law through European Community Law' in JM Prinssen and A Schrauwen (eds), *Direct Effect: Rethinking a Classic of EC Legal Doctrine* (Groningen, European Law Publishing, 2002) 181–234.
[555] Extradition Treaty between the United Kingdom and Iraq (adopted 2 May 1932, entered into force 5 May 1933) 141 LNTS 277.
[556] Aust (n 42) 270–71. See also Kolb (n 7) 238–39. In the same vein, Art 74 provides that: 'The severance or absence of diplomatic or consular relations between two or more States does not prevent the conclusion of treaties between those States. The conclusion of a treaty does not in itself affect the situation in regard to diplomatic or consular relations'.

I. Outbreak of Armed Conflict

The VCLT does not spell out the consequences for a treaty in case war or armed conflict breaks out between parties to a treaty. Article 73 VCLT merely stipulates that its provisions 'shall not prejudge any question that may arise in regard to a treaty […] from the outbreak of hostilities between States'. Indeed, the ILC has carried out separate work on the effect of armed conflict on treaties.[557] However, for now, the issue is still governed by customary international law, except in so far as a treaty, either implicity or explicitly, addresses the effect of armed conflict.[558]

If a treaty does not address the issue, the matter is uncertain. In the past, treaties were often terminated upon the outbreak of armed conflict between treaty parties. Today, however, no presumption for termination or suspension exists.[559] While armed conflict does not by definition terminate a treaty between warring parties, it is unclear exactly which treaties would be affected and how.[560] The general rule is that treaties continue to apply, unless their application is made reasonably impossible by the outbreak of hostilities.[561] In this light, Kolb distinguishes several categories of treaties.[562] *Bilateral* treaties between belligerents supposing a state of peace (eg commercial treaties) and those with a political nature (eg friendship treaties) are to be considered 'extinguished', while their final fate should be determined at the end of the armed conflict by agreements between the belligerents.[563] With the exception of: (i) treaties concluded in order to apply in situations of armed conflict; and (ii) treaties that concern the transfer of territory or the establishment of a boundary, all other treaties either continue to apply, or *may* be suspended by any of the belligerents.[564] As for *multilateral* treaties, law-making and codification treaties are in principle not affected; international humanitarian and human rights law treaties (for the latter, with the possible exception of derogations) continue to apply; any other multilateral treaties may be suspended between the belligerents, but continue to apply between belligerents and non-belligerents (and between non-belligerents).[565]

XII. Procedure and Settlement of Disputes

Articles 65–68 VCLT set out the procedure to be followed by treaty parties in case of invalidity, termination, withdrawal or suspension of a treaty. These rules aim to protect the

[557] See ILC, 'Draft Articles on the Effects of Armed Conflicts on Treaties, with commentaries' (2011) *YILC*, Vol II, Part 2, 107–21. Further, see eg B Tan Zhi Peng, 'The International Law Commission's Draft Articles on the Effects of Armed Conflicts on Treaties: Evaluating the Applicability of Impossibility of Performance and Fundamental Change' (2013) 3 *The Asian Journal of International Law* 51.

[558] Aust (n 42) 271; Kolb (n 7) 243–44.

[559] Kolb (n 7) 242–43.

[560] Aust (n 42) 271.

[561] ibid, 272; Kolb (n 7) 243.

[562] Kolb (n 7) 243.

[563] ibid, 244.

[564] ibid.

[565] ibid, 244–45. See further R Provost, 'Article 73: Cases of State Succession, State Responsibility and Outbreak of Hostilities – 1969 Vienna Convention' in Corten and Klein (n 34) Vol II, 1645–59; Crawford (n 292) 390–91; Aust (n 42) 271–72.

stability of treaties and the continuity of treaty relations by preventing States from taking arbitrary action and invoking grounds of invalidity or termination to avoid their treaty obligations.[566] In the *Gabčíkovo-Nagymaros* case, the ICJ held that:

> Both Parties agree that Articles 65 to 67 of the Vienna Convention on the Law of Treaties, if not codifying customary law, at least generally reflect customary international law and contain certain procedural principles which are based on an obligation to act in good faith.[567]

First of all, a State Party has the duty to notify the other State Parties of its claim, 'the measure proposed to be taken with respect to the treaty and the reasons therefor'.[568] Except when another treaty party, within a period which must not be less than three months after the receipt of the notification (except in cases of special urgency), has raised any objection, the party making the notification may carry out the measure in the manner it has proposed.[569] If an objection has been raised, the parties must seek a solution through the means indicated in Article 33 of the UN Charter, providing that

> The parties to any dispute, the continuance of which is likely to endanger the maintenance of international peace and security, shall, first of all, seek a solution by negotiation, enquiry, mediation, conciliation, arbitration, judicial settlement, resort to regional agencies or arrangements, or other peaceful means of their own choice.

That article leaves the choice of means entirely up to the parties themselves. Thus, while the ILC Draft Articles limited themselves to referring to Article 33(1) UN Charter,[570] at the urgent request of a number of – mostly Western – States for procedural guarantees, the procedural framework was eventually expanded, now including also an additional Article 66 VCLT.[571] Article 66 provides a supplementary procedure in case it proves not to be possible to reach a solution within a period of 12 months following the date on which the objection was raised. A distinction is made based on whether the dispute concerns the application or the interpretation of a norm of *jus cogens* as set out in Articles 53 or 64 VCLT or any of the other articles of Part V of the VCLT. For the former, one of the parties may submit the dispute to the ICJ, unless the parties by common consent agree to submit the dispute to arbitration.[572] Regarding the latter, a request may be submitted to the Secretary General of the United Nations.[573] This, in turn, sets in motion a conciliation procedure set out by the Annex to the VCLT, the outcome of which is a non-binding recommendation.[574]

Many developing and socialist States issued reservations to Article 66 VCLT, essentially stating that any dispute settlement procedure requires the consent of both parties to the dispute.[575] Many developed and European States, in turn, objected to these reservations.[576]

[566] Kolb (n 7) 253; H Krieger, 'Article 65. Procedure to Be Followed with respect to Invalidity, Termination, Withdrawal from or Suspension of the Opreation of a Treaty' in Dörr and Schmalenbach (n 5) 1212.
[567] *Gabčíkovo-Nagymaros* (n 14) para 109.
[568] Art 65(1) VCLT.
[569] Art 65(2) VCLT.
[570] ILC Draft Articles (n 10) 261–64.
[571] H Krieger, 'Article 66. Procedures for Judicial Settlement, Arbitration and Conciliation' in Dörr and Schmalenbach (n 5) 1233–34.
[572] Art 66(a) VCLT.
[573] Art 66(b) VCLT.
[574] Point 6 Annex to the VCLT.
[575] See the reservations of Algeria, Armenia, Brazil, China, Cuba, Guatemala, Saudi Arabia, Syria, Tunisia, the USSR and its client States and Vietnam.
[576] See the objections of Austria, Canada, Denmark, Egypt, Finland, Germany, Japan, the Netherlands, New Zealand, Sweden, Tanzania, the UK and the US.

Similarly, a number of developed and European States reacted by adopting their own reservations to make clear that they only considered Article 66 to apply in cases where the other party to the dispute accepts compulsory jurisdiction under Article 66,[577] or issued interpretive declarations stating that nothing in the article can be considered to oust the jurisdiction of the ICJ where it has jurisdiction on another basis.[578] In any case, the practical relevance of Article 66 VCLT is limited.[579] As considered by the ICJ in the *Armed Activities* case, the rules contained therein are not declaratory of customary international law.[580]

XIII. Concluding Remarks

Up until today, treaties are the main source of international law and thereby essential to the study of public international law. The rules on treaty law are codified in the VCLT, of which most provisions constitute customary international law. Treaties come in various types and forms: they can be contractual or law-making, bilateral or multilateral and open or closed. In any case, such distinctions have a limited legal value, as all treaties are principally governed by the same rules, considering that in essence, a treaty is an agreement concluded between two or more subjects of international law with the intent to create legal effects that is governed by international law.

The conclusion of a treaty starts with its drafting process, which includes the phases of negotiation, adoption and authentication. After the drafting process, the States – or other subjects of international law – involved in the process have to express their consent to be bound, either through signature, ratification, acceptance, approval or accession. Parliamentary consent, if applicable, is a requirement under domestic law and not under international law. States can make their consent subject to reservations to the treaty. Only after these two general stages, and with the particular exception of the possibility of provisional application, can the treaty enter into force and become legally binding on the parties.

The two intrinsically related and cardinal principles of *pacta sunt servanda* and good faith make clear that a State Party to a treaty has a binding commitment and that it must implement the treaty in a way that realises its purpose. As the meaning of treaty provisions is hardly ever crystal clear, the rules on treaty interpretation pragmatically provide for a wide array of methods, principles and techniques that can be employed by the interpreter, who should also consider the treaty at hand as part of the broader, interconnected whole of international law that pursues systemic integration.

Treaties can be affected by relative or absolute invalidity for reasons linked to an improper procedure or authorisation, misleading behaviour or coercion. They can also be terminated, withdrawn from or denounced or, alternatively, suspended by the conclusion of

[577] See the reservations of Belgium, Denmark, Finland, Portugal and Tanzania.
[578] See the declarations of Canada, Germany the Netherlands, New Zealand and the UK.
[579] Krieger (n 571) 1233–35.
[580] *Armed Activities (New Application: 2002)* (n 111) para 125. See further M Prost, 'Article 65: Procedure to Be Followed with respect to Invalidity, Termination, Withdrawal from or Suspension of the Opreation of a Treaty – 1969 Vienna Convention' and H Ruiz Fabri, 'Article 66: Procedures for Judicial Settlement, Arbitration and Conciliation' in Corten and Klein (n 34) Vol II, respectively at 1483–1508 and 1513–36.

a later treaty, a material breach of the treaty, an impossibility of performance, or a fundamental change of circumstances. The severance of diplomatic or consular relations or the outbreak of hostilities between treaty partners, on the other hand, are generally presumed not to affect their treaty relations. Both in case of invalidity and termination, States Parties to the VCLT should – at least in theory – follow the procedure laid down in Articles 65–68 thereof.

While treaties are the main source of international law, they are part of a more comprehensive system, and international law is not and can in no way be limited to this specific type of source. As will be seen in the next chapter, other sources of international law, notably customary international law, unilateral acts, general principles, case law, doctrinal writings, soft law and informal lawmaking, are important, and may well challenge treaties' traditional centrality to international law.

Bibliography

Aust, A, *Modern Treaty Law and Practice*, 3rd edn (Cambridge, CUP, 2013).
Corten, O, and Klein, P (eds), *Les Conventions de Vienne sur le droit des traités: commentaire article par article* (Brussels, Bruylant, 2006).
Corten, O and Klein, P (eds), *The Vienna Conventions on the Law of Treaties: A Commentary* (Oxford, OUP, 2011).
Davidson, S, *The Law of Treaties* (Aldershot, Ashgate, 2004).
Dörr, O and Schmalenbach, K (eds), *Vienna Convention on the Law of Treaties: A Commentary*, 2nd edn (Heidelberg, Springer, 2018).
Heintschel von Heinegg, W, 'Die völkerrechtlichen Verträge als Hauptrechtsquelle des Völkerrechts' in Ipsen, K (ed), *Völkerrecht*, 6th edn (München, Beck, 2014) 390–470.
Hollis, DB (ed), *The Oxford Guide to Treaties* (Oxford, OUP, 2012).
International Law Commission, 'Draft Articles on the Law of Treaties with commentaries' (1966) *YILC*, Vol II, 187.
Kearney, RD, and Dalton, RE, 'The Treaty on Treaties' (1970) 64 *AJIL* 495.
Klabbers, J, *The Concept of Treaty in International Law* (The Hague, Kluwer, 1996).
Kolb, R, *The Law of Treaties: An Introduction* (Cheltenham, Edward Elgar, 2016).
Reuter, P, *La Convention de Vienne du 29 mai 1969 sur le droit des traités* (Paris, Colin, 1970).
Rosenne, S, *The Law of Treaties: A Guide to the Legislative History of the Vienna Convention* (New York, Oceana Dobbs Ferry, 1970).
Sinclair, I, *The Vienna Convention on the Law of Treaties*, 2nd edn (Manchester, MUP, 1984).
Tams, CJ, Tzanakopoulos, A and Zimmermann, A (eds), *Research Handbook on the Law of Treaties* (Chelthenham, Edward Elgar, 2014).
Verwey, D, *The European Community, the European Union and the International Law of Treaties* (The Hague, TMC Asser Press, 2004).
Villiger, ME, *Commentary on the 1969 Vienna Convention on the Law of Treaties* (Leiden, Nijhoff, 2009).
Wetzel, RG, and Rauschning, D, *The Vienna Convention on the Law of Treaties: Travaux Préparatoires* (Frankfurt am Main, Metzner, 1978).

Further Reading

Buffard, I, and Zemanek, K, 'The "Object and Purpose" of a Treaty: An Enigma?' (1998) 3 *Austrian Review of International and European Law* 311.

Cahier, P, 'Le changement fondamental de circonstances et la convention de Vienne de 1969 sur le droit des traités' in *Le droit international à l'heure de sa codification: etudes en l'honneur de Roberto Ago* (Milano, Giuffrè, 1987) 163–186.

de Jong, HG, 'Coercion in the Conclusion of Treaties: A Consideration of Articles 51 and 52 of the Convention of the Law of Treaties' (1984) 15 *NYIL* 209.

Distefano, G, Gaggioli, G, and Hêche, A (eds), *La Convention de Vienne de 1978 sur la succession d'Etats en matière de traités: commentaire article par article et études thématiques* (Brussels, Bruylant, 2016).

Feist, C, *Kündigung, Rücktritt und Suspendierung von multilateralen Verträgen* (Berlin, Duncker & Humblot, 2001).

Fitzmaurice, M, 'Third Parties and the Law of Treaties' (2002) 6 *Max Planck Yearbook of United Nations Law* 37.

Fleischhauer, C-A, 'The United Nations Treaty Series' in Dinstein, Y, and Tabory, M (eds), *International Law at a Time of Perplexity: Essays in Honour of Shabtai Rosenne* (Dordrecht, Nijhoff, 1989) 131–148.

Gardiner, RK, 'Treaties and Treaty Materials: Role, Relevance and Accessibility' (1997) 46 *ICLQ* 643.

Gardiner, RK, *Treaty Interpretation*, 2nd edn (Oxford, OUP, 2015).

Geck, WK, 'Die Registrierung und Veröffentlichung völkerrechtlicher Verträge' (1962) 22 *ZaöRV* 113.

Gomaa, MM, *Suspension or Termination of Treaties on Grounds of Breach* (The Hague, Nijhoff, 1996).

Guzman, A, 'The Design of International Agreements' (2005) 16 *EJIL* 579.

Hutchinson, DN, 'The Significance of the Registration or Non-Registration of an International Agreement in Determining Whether or Not It Is a Treaty' (1993) 46 *Current Legal Problems* 257.

Klabbers, J, *Treaty Conflict and the European Union* (Cambridge, CUP, 2009).

Linderfalk, U, 'On the Meaning of the "Object and Purpose" Criterion, in the Context of the Vienna Convention on the Law of Treaties, Article 19' (2003) 72 *Nord J Intl* 429.

Luhashuk, II, 'The Principle *Pacta Sunt Servanda* and the Nature of Obligation under International Law' (1989) 83 *AJIL* 513.

Matz-Lück, N, 'Framework Conventions as a Regulatory Tool' (2009) 1 *Goettingen Journal of International Law* 439.

Nolte, G (ed), *Treaties and Subsequent Practice* (Oxford, OUP, 2013).

Raustiala, K, 'Form and Substance in International Agreements' (2005) 99 *AJIL* 581.

Rodriguez, RM, Scully, M, and Tollefsen, J, *Binding and Non-binding Instruments in Intergovernmental Relations: A Diplomat's Guide to Understand the Concepts of Treaty and Memorandum of Understanding in Theory and Practice* (Washington DC, EUCLID UP, 2015).

Ruda, JM, 'Nulidad de los tratados' in Dinstein, Y (ed), *International Law at a Time of Perplexity: Essays in Honour of Shabtai Rosenne* (Dordrecht, Nijhoff, 1989) 661–678.

Schulte-Beerbühl, H, *Irrtum bei völkerrechtlichen Verträgen nach der Wiener Vertragsrechtskonvention* (Gelsenkirchen, Mannhold, 1982).
Vagts, DF, 'Rebus Revisited: Changed Circumstances in Treaty Law' (2005) 43 *Columbia Journal of Transnational Law* 459.
White, G, 'The Principle of Good Faith' in Vaughan, L (ed), *The United Nations and the Principles of International Law: Essays in Memory of Michael Akehurst* (London, Routledge, 1994) 230–255.
Wolfrum, R and Röben, V (eds), *Developments of International Law in Treaty Making* (Berlin, Springer, 2005).

3

Other Sources – Hierarchy

I. Introduction

The previous chapter examined the primary instrument of lawmaking in international law: treaties. Yet alongside international conventions, Article 38 of the ICJ Statute lists three other sources of international law: international custom; general principles of law; and 'judicial decisions and the teachings of the most highly qualified publicists of the various nations'. This chapter discusses these other sources of international law as well as the issue of hierarchy of sources and the relationship between sources. It should also be pointed out that while Article 38 of the ICJ Statute is recognised as reflecting the sources of international law, new sources of international law that are not listed in Article 38 have become relevant. For example, unilateral acts of States and decisions of international organisations are not listed as a source, yet one cannot deny their importance for international law. Moreover, so-called 'informal' and 'soft law' instruments are having an ever larger impact on the international legal order. The diversity of sources begs the question about the mutual relationship between, or hiearchy of, the sources.

II. Customary International Law

Custom[1] is the oldest and original formal source of international law (and of law more generally). Numerous rules that are now found in international conventions – for instance,

[1] See eg M Akehurst, 'Custom as a Source of International Law' (1977) 47 *BYIL* 1; DJ Bederman, *Custom as a Source of Law* (Cambridge, CUP, 2010); M Bos, 'The Identification of Custom in International Law' (1982) 25 *GYBIL* 9; H Bourgeois and J Wouters, 'Methods of Identification of International Custom: A New Role for *Opinio Juris*' in R Pisillo Mazzeschi and P De Sena (eds), *Global Justice, Human Rights and the Modernization of International Law* (Cham, Springer, 2018), 69–111; CA Bradley (ed), *Custom's Future: International Law in a Changing World* (Cambridge, CUP, 2016); M Byers, *Custom, Power and the Power of Rules: International Relations and Customary International Law* (Cambridge, CUP, 1999); GM Danilenko, 'The Theory of International Customary Law' (1988) 31 *GYBIL* 9; L Ferrari Bravo, 'Méthodes de recherche de la coutume internationale dans la pratique des Etats' (1985-III) 192 *RdC* 233; P Haggenmacher, 'La doctrine des deux éléments du droit coutumier dans la pratique de la Cour internationale' (1986) 90 *Revue générale de droit international public* 5; BD Lepard, *Customary International Law – A New Theory with Practical Applications* (Cambridge, CUP, 2010);

those relating to diplomatic relations or treaty law – formed part of customary international law long before they were put on paper. And while the number of bilateral, regional and multilateral treaties has increased exponentially over the past decades, custom continues to play an important role as a source of international law in addition to, and alongside, existing treaty law.

A definition of 'custom' can be found in Article 38(1) of the ICJ Statute, which refers to 'international custom as evidence of a general practice accepted as law'. A useful 'working definition' can moreover be found in the 2000 Final Report of the International Law Association (ILA) Committee on the formation of customary (general) international law (ILA Final Report):

> [A] rule of customary international law is one which is created and sustained by the constant and uniform practice of States and other subjects of international law in or impinging upon their international legal relations, in circumstances which give rise to a legitimate expectation of similar conduct in the future.[2]

Both definitions illustrate that custom is comprised of two elements. First, there is the objective element, namely general practice. The subjective element entails the recognition that such practice is required, prohibited or allowed as a matter of law, and is generally described as *opinio juris*.[3] If general practice provides the raw material for the customary process, it is clear that there must be something supplementary to accomplish its transformation into a rule of customary international law. This is where the subjective or psychological element comes in. As the ICJ emphasised in the *North Sea Continental Shelf* cases:

> Not only must the acts concerned amount to a settled practice, but they must also be such, or be carried out in such a way, as to be evidence of a belief that this practice is rendered obligatory by the existence of a rule of law requiring it. The need for such a belief, i.e., the existence of a subjective element, is implicit in the very notion of the opinio juris sive necessitatis. The States concerned must therefore feel that they are conforming to what amounts to a legal obligation. The frequency or even habitual character of the acts is not in itself enough.[4]

In other words, *opinio juris* serves to make customary international law. It distinguishes custom from a wide range of 'international acts, eg, in the field of ceremonial and protocol, which are performed almost invariably, but which are motivated only by considerations of courtesy, convenience or tradition, and not by a sense of legal duty'.[5] Examples of the latter type include, for instance, the lowering of the flag to half-mast for the funeral

BD Lepard (ed), *Reexamining Customary International Law* (New York, CUP, 2017); MH Mendelson, 'The Formation of Customary International Law' (1998) 272 *RdC* 155; K Skubiszewski, 'Elements of Custom and the Hague Court' (1971) 31 *ZaöRV* 810; A Roberts, 'Traditional and Modern Approaches to Customary International Law: A Reconciliation' (2001) 95 *AJIL* 757–791; HWA Thirlway, *International Customary Law and Codification: An Examination of the Continuing Role of Custom in the Present Period of Codification of International Law* (Leiden, Sijthoff, 1972); ME Villiger, *Customary International Law and Treaties: A Manual on the Theory and Practice of the Interrelation of Sources*, 2nd edn (The Hague, Kluwer, 1997); K Wolfke, *Custom in Present International Law*, 2nd edn (Dordrecht, Nijhoff, 1993).

[2] ILA, Committee on Formation of Customary (General) International Law, 'Final Report of the Committee: Statement of Principles applicable to the formation of General Customary International Law', Report of the Sixty-Ninth Conference, 2000, 712–77, law.umich.edu/facultyhome/drwcasebook/Documents/Documents/ILA%20Report%20on%20Formation%20of%20Customary%20International%20Law.pdf.

[3] eg *Continental Shelf* (Libyan Arab Jamahiriya v Malta) [1985] ICJ Rep 13, para 27: 'It is of course axiomatic that the material of customary international law is to be looked for primarily in the actual practice and *opinio juris* of States.'

[4] *North Sea Continental Shelf* (Federal Republic of Germany v Denmark and the Netherlands) [1969] ICJ Rep 3, para 77.

[5] ibid.

of third-country Heads of State, the alphabetical seating order of States at international conferences, or the use of white paper for diplomatic correspondence. Still, the line between custom and comity may at times be rather thin. Certain conduct that is initially applied as a matter of courtesy (eg, fiscal privileges for foreign diplomats) may also gradually evolve into actual custom.

An example of the creation of a norm of customary international law concerns the principle that coastal States have certain entitlements to the natural resources within the continental shelf extending beyond their coastline. In 1945, US President Harry Truman first issued a declaration asserting such claim.[6] The 'Truman Proclamation' was quickly followed by similar claims by other countries in Latin America, the Persian Gulf and elsewhere. This gradually led to the emergence of a customary norm, which was subsequently affirmed and clarified in the 1958 Geneva Convention on the Continental Shelf, and later in the 1982 UN Convention on the Law of the Sea (see Chapter 18 on the Law of the Sea and Global Commons, Section III).

A. Treaty and Custom

Custom is a primary source of international law and holds the same normative power as treaty law. The implication is that the relationship between custom and treaty law is subject to the principles of *lex posterior derogat priori* (later rules prevail over earlier rules) and *lex specialis derogat generali* (more 'specific' rules prevail over more 'general' rules).[7] This means that rules of customary international law may be modified by later and more specific treaties, including those that seek to codify principles of customary international law. This does not mean that an existing treaty cannot be modified by a later customary norm. However, this remains a rather exceptional situation.

The main 'weakness' of custom in comparison to treaty law is that it may at times be difficult to ascertain whether and when a customary rule has come into being, and what its precise content is. This is particularly true when there exist few or no explicit written restatements of an alleged customary rule, such as in the form of non-binding resolutions. By its very nature, customary international law is indeed the result of an informal process of rule-creation,[8] and is therefore inherently subject to a greater degree of uncertainty than treaty law.[9] However, as discussed in the previous chapter, treaty provisions are not always

[6] The text of the Proclamation is reproduced in M Whiteman (1965) 4 *Digest of International Law*, Washington, US Government Printing Office, 756. See further, J Crawford and T Viles, 'International Law on a Given Day' in K Ginther, G Hafner, W Lang, H Neuhold and L Sucharipa-Behrmann (eds), *Völkerrecht zwischen normativen Anspruch und politischer Realität. Festschrift für Karl Zemanek zum 65. Geburtstag* (Duncker & Humblot, Berlin, 1994) 45–68.

[7] Note, a later general rule does not, however, prevail over a prior and more specific rule (*lex posterior generalis non derogat legi priori speciali*).

[8] This also explains why, even in dualist countries, customary rules need not be transformed into national law, but can be invoked before the national courts as the 'law of the land'.

[9] See among others, Court of Cassation (FR), *Movement Against Racism and for Peoples' Friendship v Aussaresses*, 17 June 2003, Appeal no 02-80719, Decision no 122 (no criminalisation of crimes against humanity under customary international law if crimes predate inclusion in the French Criminal Code); House of Lords (UK), *R v Jones (Margaret) and others*, 30 March 2006 [2006] UKHL 16 (customary international law not enough to prosecute a crime that is not enshrined in English law); High Court (IE), *Horgan v Ireland and others*, 28 April 2003, Case No 3739P, [2003] IEHC 64 (customary international law acts as a (mere) 'rule for conduct'); Court of Appeal (SE), *Public Prosecutor (on behalf of Behram (Hussein) and others) v Arklöf (Jackie)*, 18 December 2006,

drafted with a great deal of precision, and often give rise to interpretative difficulties of their own (see Chapter 2 on Sources: Treaty Law, Section VII).

The uncertainty inherent to custom explains why, as a matter of practical expediency, national and international judges will generally first assert the existence of relevant treaty law, before turning their eye to customary international law. When it comes to the identification of customary international law, the CJEU will tend to look at whether the ICJ has itself pronounced on the customary status of a rule,[10] or whether it has been codified in an international legal instrument (treaty or draft articles). It also explains why national judges will rarely set aside an explicit norm of national law by reason of its alleged incompatibility with customary international law (see further, Chapter 4 on the Interaction between International Law, EU Law and National Law, Section IV(B)).[11]

Furthermore, the aforementioned uncertainty also explains why the international community has often sought to codify various branches of (unwritten) customary international law into treaty law. The process of codification of customary international law is discussed in more detail below. Despite these codification efforts in numerous branches of international law, and, more generally, the exponential growth of treaty law, custom remains a key primary source of international law.

First, various sub-domains of international law, such as the law of neutrality, the rules governing naval warfare or the rules governing the immunities of foreign officials, have not, or only partially, been codified in written treaty law, and continue to consist to a large extent of unwritten customary rules. Second, it must be recalled that treaty law only applies to the parties who have given their consent to be bound, and that only very few treaties have reached universal, or near universal, ratification. Customary international law, however, in principle applies to all States alike.[12] Accordingly, in order to ascertain whether certain rules enshrined in treaty law also apply vis-à-vis non-State Parties, it remains crucial to verify whether those rules are also reflective of customary international law.

By way of illustration, in the 1969 *North Sea Continental Shelf* cases, Denmark and the Netherlands claimed that Article 6 of the 1958 Geneva Convention on the Continental Shelf was binding on Germany even if Germany had never ratified the instrument.[13] The provision proclaimed that the boundaries of the continental shelves of neighbouring States should in principle be drawn by applying the equidistance method. In light of the concave trajectory of Germany's coastline, application of this method would have meant that only a small portion of the North Sea continental shelf would be apportioned to Germany, in contrast to more sizeable portions on the part of Denmark and the Netherlands.

Case No B 4084-04 (customary international law sufficiently specific, foreseeable, and clear legal basis for prosecution); National Court (ES), *Public Prosecutor's Office, de Lois (Graciela) (intervening) and others (intervening) v Manzorro (Adolfo)*, 19 April 2005, ES:AN:2005:2016 (crimes against humanity punishable in the Spanish legal order, because they are customary international law – even though originally not penalised under Spanish law).

[10] In its judgment of 24 November 1992, *Anklagemindigheden v Poulsen and Diva Navigation*, C-286/90, EU:C:1992:453, the CJEU referred to the following cases in support of the proposition that the provisions of certain treaties represented the state of customary international law: *Delimitation of the Maritime Boundary in the Gulf of Maine Region* (Canada v United States of America) [1984] ICJ Rep 246; *Continental Shelf* (n 3) 13; and *Military and Paramilitary Activities in and against Nicaragua* (Nicaragua v United States of America) [1984] ICJ Rep 392, 14

[11] See eg Council of State (FR), *Stanislas Aquarone v France*, 6 June 1997, FR:CEASS:1997:148683.19970606 (no priority for customary international law); Court of Cassation (BE), *Sharon*, 12 February 2003, Case No P.02.1139.F/2 (duty to interpret national law consistently with customary international law).

[12] But see below, p 152, on the concept of the persistent objector and on the notion of regional or local custom.

[13] *North Sea Continental Shelf* (n 4).

The ICJ, however, ultimately found that there was insufficient evidence of general practice and *opinio juris* to conclude (i) that Article 6 was declaratory of pre-existing custom, (ii) that its inclusion had led to the 'crystallisation' of a new customary norm, or (iii) that it had developed into a customary norm in the years following the adoption of the Convention.

Third, evolving practice and *opinio juris* may result in the emergence of new customary rules, possibly even replacing pre-existing conflicting treaty norms. Finally, the parallel existence of customary rules and treaty rules may have practical repercussions, for example with regard to the jurisdiction of international courts and tribunals,[14] or in relation to the possibility to 'escape' from certain binding rules by withdrawing from a treaty, or by lodging reservations to a treaty.

B. The Formation and Identification of Custom

The methods for establishing the existence of a customary rule and for ascertaining its content are essentially identical. Both require a careful analysis of relevant practice and *opinio juris*. Guidance on how to identify and assess relevant evidence is found first and foremost in the case law of the ICJ. The Court, however, has at times been criticised for failing to properly substantiate findings that a certain norm reflects customary international law. In 2016, the ILC has adopted on first reading a set of guiding principles on the 'Identification of Customary International Law' (2016 ILC Draft Conclusions).[15] These draft conclusions are largely based on the case law of the ICJ, and endorse the 'two element' approach that is now widely accepted by States, international courts and in the literature.[16] In certain cases, ascertaining the existence and content of a customary norm may be relatively straightforward. For numerous customary rules, there is little or no controversy as to their core content. In other situations, however, especially where relevant practice is thought to have evolved over time, the content of customary rules gives rise to considerable disagreement. By way of illustration, scholars hold differing interpretations as to whether Article 51 of the UN Charter allows for self-defence against 'imminent' attacks. The different conclusions arrived at can often be traced back to different methods in terms of identifying relevant practice and *opinio juris* and in terms of assessing the relative weight of the assembled evidence.[17] It is important to keep in mind in such contexts that, while identifying custom is not an exact science, a balanced assessment of all available evidence goes a long way in clarifying the norms concerned.

[14] Thus, in the *Nicaragua* case, a reservation included in the United States' declaration accepting compulsory jurisdiction barred the ICJ from testing the compatibility of US conduct against multilateral treaties, such as the UN Charter. The Court nonetheless (controversially) circumvented this reservation (the 'Vandenberg reservation') by holding that it did not prevent the Court from testing US conduct against the customary equivalent of these treaty rules (in particular, the customary equivalent of the Charter rules on the use of force). See *Nicaragua* (n 10).

[15] ILC, Text of the Draft Conclusions Provisionally Adopted by the Drafting Committee on Identification of Customary International Law, Sixty-Eight Session, 2 May–10 June and 4 July–12 August 2016, 30 May 2016, UN Doc A/CN.4/L.872. While the 2016 ILC Draft Conclusions were adopted on first reading only in 2016, it is interesting to see that they have already been relied upon by domestic judges. See eg High Court of Justice, *The Freedom and Justice Party and others v Secretary of State for Foreign and Commonwealth Affairs* [2016] EWHC 2010, para 77.

[16] In 2016 ILC Draft Conclusion 2 (n 15) it is established that '[t]o determine the existence and content of a rule of customary international law, it is necessary to ascertain whether there is a general practice that is accepted as law (*opinio juris*)'.

[17] See eg O Corten, 'The Controversies over the Customary Prohibition on the Use of Force: A Methodological Approach' (2005) 16 *EJIL* 803.

An interesting exercise in this regard concerns the Customary Law Study of the International Committee of the Red Cross (ICRC).[18] This study, published in 2005, identifies a set of 161 rules that are deemed to reflect customary international humanitarian law. The identification of the rules is based on an in-depth study of relevant materials, including international and national case law, military manuals, national legislation, decisions of international organisations, etc, all published in a separate volume.[19] Even if the study itself is not free from controversy, it illustrates the importance of a rigorous methodology for the purposes of identifying custom.

The CJEU has on numerous occasions been called upon to deal with issues regarding customary international law. Like many domestic courts (see Chapter 4 on between Relationship and Interactions between International Law, EU Law and National Law, Section (IV)(B)), the CJEU is reluctant to allow the invocation of customary international law to *contest* the legal validity of EU acts.[20] This being said, the CJEU has referred to the codification process of the ILC in a number of its judgments. In *Walz*[21] the Court referred to the ASR in determining the meaning of 'damage'. The Court also refers, from time to time, to the provisions of the 1986 and 1969 Vienna Convention on the Law of Treaties (VCLT) insofar as they reflect customary international law (see Chapter 2 on Sources: Treaty Law).

C. General Practice

Practice consists of any behaviour of subjects of international law (primarily States but on some occasions also international organisations) that discloses their conscious attitude with respect to an international legal situation.[22] Only conscious conduct may qualify, implying,

[18] ICRC, *Customary International Humanitarian Law – Volume I: Rules* (Cambridge, CUP, 2005).

[19] ICRC, *Customary International Humanitarian Law – Volume II: Practice* (Cambridge, CUP, 2005). A regularly updated version of the ICRC's Customary IHL database (with relevant materials) is available at www.icrc.org/customary-ihl/eng/docs/home.

[20] See eg judgment of 21 December 2011, *Air Transport Association of America and others*, C-366/10, EU:C:2011:864, paras 107–10: 'The principles of customary international law [...] may be relied upon by an individual for the purpose of the Court's examination of the validity of an act of the European Union in so far as, first, those principles are capable of calling into question the competence of the European Union to adopt that act [...] and, second, the act in question is liable to affect rights which the individual derives from European Union law or to create obligations under European Union law in his regard. [...] However, since a principle of customary international law does not have the same degree of precision as a provision of an international agreement, judicial review must necessarily be limited to the question whether, in adopting the act in question, the institutions of the European Union made manifest errors of assessment concerning the conditions for applying those principles [...]'. See earlier also judgment of 16 June 1998, *Racke*, C-162/96, EU:C:1998:293, judgment of 22 January 1997, *Opel Austria v Council*, T-115/94, EU:T:1997:3. See *inter alia* PJ Kuijper, 'Customary International Law, Decisions of International Organizations and Other Techniques for Ensuring Respect for International Rules in European Community Law' in J Wouters, A Nollkaemper and E De Wet (eds), *The Europeanisation of International Law. The Status of International Law in the EU and its Member States* (The Hague, TMC Asser Press, 2008), 87–106; Id, 'From Dyestuffs to Kosovo Wine: From Avoidance to Acceptance by the European Community Courts of Customary International Law as Limit to Community Action' in IF Dekker and HHG Post (eds), *On the Foundations and Sources of International Law* (The Hague, TMC Asser Press, 2003) 149–76; J Wouters and D Van Eeckhoutte, 'Enforcement of Customary International Law through European Community Law' in JM Prinssen and A Schrauwen (eds), *Direct effect. Rethinking a Classic of EC Legal Doctrine* (Groningen, European Law Publishing, 2002), 183–234.

[21] Judgment of 6 May 2010, *Walz v Clickair SA*, C-63/09, EU:C:2010:25.

[22] See Ferrari Bravo as referred to in Akehurst (n 1) 261. See also 2016 ILC Draft Conclusion 4 (n 15) para 1, in which the ILC established that '[t]he requirement, as a constituent element of customary international law, of a general practice means that it is primarily the practice of States that contributes to the formation, or expression,

for instance, that the unintentional trespassing of another State's territory has no bearing on customary international law. Furthermore, for acts to qualify as practice, it is imperative that they are public or communicated to some extent. Acts that are never disclosed cannot influence the evolution of custom, since other States must in principle be given the opportunity to react to the behaviour within a reasonable period of time. Hence, clandestine operations and acts for which a State denies responsibility do not count as 'general practice'.

To give rise to general custom, a certain 'density' of practice is also required. First, practice must be virtually uniform.[23] This means that the acts must indicate a certain similarity or consistency, both at the internal level (regarding different acts of the same State)[24] and the collective level (regarding acts of different States).[25] Absolute consistency is not required. The ICJ has affirmed that 'too much importance need not be attached to [a] few uncertainties or contradictions, real or apparent'.[26] In this context, it is important to recall the famous dictum of the Court in the *Nicaragua* case, according to which inconsistent conduct must ultimately be assessed by reference to the State's justification of its conduct and the reactions of other States:

> The Court does not consider that, for a rule to be established as customary, the corresponding practice must be in absolute rigorous conformity with the rule. In order to deduce the existence of customary rules, the Court deems it sufficient that the conduct of States should, in general, be consistent with such rules, and that instances of State conduct inconsistent with a given rule should generally have been treated as breaches of that rule, not as indications of the recognition of a new rule. If a State acts in a way prima facie incompatible with a recognized rule, but defends its conduct by appealing to exceptions or justifications contained within the rule itself, then whether or not the State's conduct is in fact justifiable on that basis, the significance of that attitude is to confirm rather than to weaken the rule.[27]

This reasoning explains why certain rules, such as the prohibition of torture, undoubtedly form part of customary international law (and even constitute *jus cogens* norms: see above, Chapter 2 on Sources: Treaty Law, Section X(B)(iii)), even though violations regrettably do take place all too often.

A second requirement is that practice must also be 'extensive'.[28] Practice does not need to be universal for all States to be bound by it – 'general' practice suffices.[29] A few dissenting States will not normally prevent the formation of a rule of customary international law. On the other hand, it is impossible to fix a precise number or percentage of States whose active

of rules of customary international law'. In para 2, the ILC, however added that, '[i]n certain cases, the practice of international organizations also contributes to the formation, or expression, of rules of customary international law'. See further below, Section II(C)(iv), on the role of international organisations in the development of customary international law.

[23] eg *North Sea Continental Shelf* (n 4) para 75.

[24] eg *Fisheries* (United Kingdom v Norway) [1951] ICJ Rep 116–44, para 138. See also 2016 ILC Draft Conclusion 7 (n 15) on assessing a State's practice: '1. Account is to be taken of all available practice of a particular State, which is to be assessed as a whole. 2. Where the practice of a particular State varies, the weight to be given to that practice may be reduced'.

[25] ibid, 131; *Asylum* (Colombia v Peru) [1950] ICJ Rep 266–89, para 277.

[26] *Fisheries* (n 24) para 138.

[27] *Nicaragua* (n 10) para 186.

[28] *North Sea Continental Shelf* (n 4) para 74.

[29] See also 2016 ILC Draft Conclusion 8 (n 15) para 1, which establishes that '[th]e relevant practice must be general, meaning that it must be sufficiently widespread and representative, as well as consistent'.

or passive support is required. Indeed, the criterion of 'generality' is a highly relative one, the fulfilment of which is closely linked to its representativeness in relation to the nature of the practice. What matters are the actions of those States which are in a position to participate in the practice and/or which have an interest in the subject matter (so-called 'specially affected States'). By way of illustration, the consistent practice of land-locked States is unlikely to create new rules pertaining to the law of the sea. To this end, one should rather first look at the practice of coastal States. By analogy, the practice of States that possess the technology and equipment to launch objects into space will logically have a greater impact on the formation of customary rules of space law than the practice of other States.

Passive behaviour may under certain conditions also qualify as relevant practice. In other words, 'extensive' practice does not presuppose that a majority of the international community has *actively* engaged in a certain practice. When there exists a uniform practice by certain States which is repeated on several occasions without significant objections by other States, this may provide the required material element for the formation of a rule of customary international law.

The third and last aspect of the density of practice concerns the temporal element, that is the time lapse during which a practice must substantiate to give rise to custom.[30] In the *Fisheries Jurisdiction* case, for instance, the ICJ accepted a period of about 12 years for a customary rule to emerge.[31] However, it is commonly accepted today that custom can emerge in a relatively short time. This accelerated pace of customary lawmaking is explained by the development of modern means of communication and the proliferation of international fora and exchanges, which enable States to express their views on various international legal problems and to learn the views of other States without a substantial passing of time. As with the two previous criteria, it is impossible to set a fixed time limit. Again, the criterion is a relative one, depending on the circumstances of each particular case.

Furthermore, the three different aspects of the 'density' of customary international law are closely interrelated, in the sense that the limited duration may to some extent be compensated for by a greater uniformity and generality, and so on.[32] Thus, the ICJ has acknowledged that:

> [T]he passage of only a short period of time is not necessarily, of itself, a bar to the formation of a new rule of customary international law (…) [provided that] within the period in question, short though it might be, State practice, including that of States whose interests are specially affected, should have been both extensive and virtually uniform (…).[33]

Does this mean that a single act of practice could inspire a new (or modified) rule of customary international law, provided it would be supported (actively or passively) by a broad majority of the international community? Some have suggested the emergence of so-called 'instant custom', for example, in the realm of space law as well as in relation to the rules governing the use of force in international law.[34] When relevant practice is rare,

[30] *Asylum* (n 25) paras 275–76.

[31] *Fisheries Jurisdiction* (United Kingdom v Iceland) [1974] ICJ Rep 3.

[32] 2016 ILC Draft Conclusion 8 (n 15) para 2, reads as follows: '[p]rovided that the practice is general, no particular duration is required'.

[33] *North Sea Continental Shelf* (n 4) para 74.

[34] For example, following the 9/11 terrorist atttacks in the United States. cp B Langille, 'It's "Instant Custom": How the Bush Doctrine Became Law after the Terrorist Attacks of September 11, 2001' (2003) 26 *Boston College International and Comparative Law Review* 145.

single instances of practice may carry considerable weight. On the other hand, some time will normally need to elapse before a practice matures into a rule:

> [E]ven in the present era of easy and instantaneous communications, if a State or group of States adopts a practice, others will need to consider how (if at all) they wish to respond. These responses may give rise to further responses, and so on. All of this will usually involve some delay.[35]

A certain time lapse may also serve to clarify whether the practice under consideration and the concomitant reaction of third States was inspired by a sense of legal conviction, or whether States' positions were, for instance, motivated by factual or circumstantial particularities. In practice it would seem highly unlikely that a single instance of active practice would, without any repetition or significant time lapse, give rise to the formation or modification of a rule of customary international law.

i. *Physical and Verbal Acts*

There is an inclination to automatically tend to equate practice with the 'physical acts' or 'material deeds' of States. The use of a certain weapon might make up relevant practice for customary international humanitarian law, as might the imposition of discriminatory import tariffs vis-à-vis international economic law. Such physical acts have for centuries constituted the engine driving the formation of customary international law, and continue to do so.[36]

Are these acts the *only* material constitutive of practice? Some authors answer in the positive, narrowing the definition of practice to physical acts to the exclusion of 'verbal acts' or claims. Prominent among this group of scholars is D'Amato, who stresses that: 'a claim is not an act (…). Claims (…), although they may articulate a legal norm, cannot constitute the material component of custom'.[37] The danger of this approach is that the verbal reactions to certain physical acts – such as objections to aerial incursions by military aircraft – will only be considered as supplementary evidence or as a reflection of *opinio juris*, and will not be integrated in the analysis of actual practice. This results in a slippery slope whereby certain actions might be interpreted as giving rise to the emergence of new custom, despite the verbal opposition of a large share, possibly even the majority, of the international community. Thirlway adopts a more nuanced approach and distinguishes between 'mere assertions *in abstracto*' of a legal rule, on the one hand, and claims made in relation to some specific dispute.[38] While the latter are considered to qualify as practice, the former merely offer 'supplementary evidence', without contributing to the required generality of the objective element.[39] However, as Akehurst correctly observes, the distinction between concrete and abstract assertions is not very realistic, as the two classes generally merge into one another:

> For instance, at a conference on the law of the sea the Arab States and Israel may appear to be making abstract assertions about the right of passage through straits, but it is probable that what they really have in mind is the right of passage through the Straits of Tiran.[40]

[35] ILA Final Report (n 2) 731–32.

[36] See eg Y Dinstein, 'The Interaction between Customary International Law and Treaties' (2006) 322 *RdC* 243, 275.

[37] A D'Amato, *The Concept of Custom in International Law* (Ithaca, Cornell University Press, 1971) 88.

[38] HWA Thirlway (n 1) 58.

[39] ibid.

[40] M Akehurst (n 1) 4. In similar vein, when a dictatorial regime renowned for its disrespect for human rights at home takes the floor in a general debate at the UN General Assembly to denounce the lawfulness of humanitarian intervention, it may well be aware that such right could at some future time be invoked against it.

It is well-established in international case law that the concept of practice is not confined to physical practice but equally covers verbal practice, whether of an abstract or a concrete nature. For instance, State positions throughout successive UN conferences on the Law of the Sea were taken into account in the *Fisheries Jurisdiction* case[41] and in the *Continental Shelf* case.[42] Also, when dealing with the law on the use of force in the *Nicaragua* case, the ICJ argued that 'further confirmation of the validity as customary international law' of the principle expressed in Article 2(4) of the UN Charter could be found in the fact that it was frequently recognised as such 'in statements by State representatives'.[43] And in the *Tadić* case, the International Criminal Tribunal for the Former Yugoslavia (ICTY) emphasised that 'in appraising the formation of customary rules (…) reliance must primarily be placed on such elements as official pronouncements of States, military manuals and judicial decisions'.[44] Both the ILC[45] and the ILA Final Report support the view that verbal acts count as practice.[46]

ii. *Omissions*

Practice not only covers 'active' physical and verbal practice; it equally includes negative actions or omissions.[47] Assuming that a customary norm may take three different forms – it can be an obligation, a permission, or a prohibition – this is of particular importance when dealing with the latter category. Indeed, if 'omissions' were excluded from the scope of practice, it would be virtually impossible for a prohibitive norm to acquire and/or maintain customary status. Actions going against a customary prohibition – and hence violating the rule – would be given disproportionate weight. In light of this, it comes as no surprise that

[41] *Fisheries Jurisdiction* (n 31) paras 55–58.

[42] *Continental Shelf* (n 3) para 45. See also *Asylum* (n 25) para 277 (where the Court considered both the actual exercise of diplomatic asylum as well as the 'official views expressed on various occasions'); *Rights of Nationals of the United States of America in Morocco* (France v United States of America) [1952] ICJ Rep 176, 200 and 209 (where the Court looked for evidence of custom inter alia in diplomatic correspondence between France and the United States, and in the records of the Conference of Algericas of 1906).

[43] *Nicaragua* (n 10) para 190.

[44] ICTY, Appeals Chamber, *Prosecutor v Tadić, Decision on the Defence Motion for Interlocutory Appeal on Jurisdiction*, 2 October 1995, Case No IT-94-1, para 99.

[45] eg ILC, 'Addendum to the eighth report on State responsibility, by Mr Roberto Ago' (1980) *YILC*, Vol II, 34; ILC, 'Report of the International Law Commission to the General Assembly' (1950) *YILC*, Vol II, 368; ILC, Second Report on Identification of Customary International Law by Michael Wood, Special Rapporteur, 22 May 2014, UN Doc A/CN.4/672 para 37; ILC, Third Report on the Identification of Customary International Law by Michael Wood, Special Rapporteur, Sixty-Sixth Session, 5 May–6 June and 7 July–8 August 2014, UN Doc A/CN.4/672 (ILC Third Report) para 16 (in his Second and Third Report, the ILC Special Rapporteur Michael Woods confirmed that practice may comprise both physical and verbal (written and oral) conduct). In its 2016 ILC Draft Conclusion 6 (n 15) para 1, the ILC eventually stipulated that '[p]ractice may take a wide range of forms. It includes both physical and verbal acts'. In para 2, the ILC gave a non-exhaustive list of different forms of State practice, including verbal practice: 'diplomatic acts and correspondence; conduct in connection with resolutions adopted by an international organization or at an intergovernmental conference; conduct in connection with treaties; executive conduct, including operational conduct "on the ground"; legislative and administrative acts; and decisions of national courts'.

[46] ILA Final Report (n 2) 725.

[47] In its 2016 ILC Draft Conclusion 6 (n 15) para 1, the ILC also determined that 'under certain circumstances', inaction may also serve as practice. In its commentaries to the 2016 ILC Draft Conclusions, the ILC's drafting committee on the identification of customary international law noted that the words 'under certain circumstances' imply that only 'deliberate abstention from acting' may be taken into account, see ILC, Report of the International Law Commission on the Work of Its Fifty-Eighth Session, Sixty-Fifth Session, 1 May–9 June and 3 July–11 August 2016, Supplement No 10, UN Doc A/61/10 (2016 ILC Commentaries) 91.

the ICJ has on occasion held that abstentions can contribute to the creation of customary rules.[48] Omissions are included in the scope of practice, but will not, on their own, suffice to give rise to customary norms. As with physical acts, the element of *opinio juris* is also required. Furthermore, abstentions as such are often of limited use in ascertaining the concrete content of the customary rule, given their inherent ambiguity and the resulting difficulty in identifying and qualifying them.

iii. States

When it comes to the formation of customary international law, it is primarily the practice of States that matters. This raises the question of *whose* practice amounts to 'general practice' for the purpose of customary lawmaking. Two different aspects must be distinguished. First, it must be determined what agents of the State contribute to this process. Second, the question arises whether other actors, such as private individuals or international organisations, may be involved.

As to the first question, some authors traditionally argued that the only relevant State practice was the practice of those organs capable of entering into binding agreements on behalf of the State. In other words, State practice would essentially be confined to heads of State, heads of government and foreign ministers.[49] Today, however, this approach is widely rejected as overly restrictive.[50] Just as any State organ can engage that State's international legal responsibility, so it can contribute to the formation and evolution of customary international law, regardless of whether it belongs to the executive, legislative or judicial branch.[51] All *official* practice may be taken into account, as long as it fulfils the general conditions discussed above. It must be public or communicated in some way, and it must bear on the State's international legal relations. Evidently, the capability of each State organ to contribute to the customary process is largely determined by its competences in the broader international domain.

In accordance with these general principles, the actions of the whole of the executive should count, not only those of the foreign ministry. For example, the ministry for home affairs and the ministry of transport (or their equivalents) clearly produce relevant State practice with regard to the expulsion of aliens and the regulation of civil aviation. As discussed above (see above, Section II(C)(i)), one should not only examine *physical* practice, but also *verbal* practice. The latter category covers a wide range of oral and written statements, which can take numerous forms, including inter alia, official statements and (non-confidential) doctrines (eg, the aforementioned 'Truman Proclamation' or various national security strategies); ministerial declarations and press communiqués; inter-State diplomatic correspondence; statements made in international fora such as the UN Security Council or the UN General Assembly, or positions submitted to the ILC; oral and written observations in the course of proceedings before the ICJ; opinions of national legal advisors expressed in their position as representative of the government (insofar as they are not strictly confidential), etc.

[48] eg *Nottebohm* (Liechtenstein v Guatemala) [1955] ICJ Rep 4 22 (the Court partly relied on 'the practice of certain States which refrain from exercising protection in favour of a naturalized person'). See also ILA Final Report (n 2) 726–27.

[49] eg K Strupp, 'Les règles générales du droit de la paix' (1934-I) 47 *RdC* 259, 313–14.

[50] eg ILA Final Report (n 2) 728–29.

[51] According to 2016 ILC Draft Conclusion 5 (n 15): 'State practice consists of conduct of the State, whether in the exercise of its executive, legislative, judicial or other functions'.

Furthermore, State practice is not limited to acts of the executive. As the *Nottebohm*[52] and *Arrest Warrant* cases[53] illustrate, national legislation may also contribute insofar as it touches upon the international legal sphere.[54] In a similar vein, the PCIJ and the ICJ have on several occasions referred to decisions of national courts when examining the existence and/or content of a customary rule.[55] There is indeed no reason to exclude a priori acts of the legislative and judicial organs of the State from the customary process. On the other hand, as the ILA Final Report observes: 'since it is the executive which has primary responsibility for the conduct of foreign relations, that organ's formal position ought usually to be accorded more weight than conflicting positions of the legislature or the national courts'.[56]

Useful (non-exhaustive) compilations of relevant practice of different States can be found in a variety of 'national' international law journals.[57] A country such as the United States moreover publishes an annual 'Digest of United States Practice in International Law' on its own initiative.[58]

iv. Actors Other Than States

While States remain the main drivers of customary international law, other entities may nevertheless play a role in its development. What importance should be given to, for example, acts performed by private individuals, international courts and tribunals, or international organisations?

Regarding *private individuals*, some authors have argued in the past that customary rules may be created by the constant and uninterrupted practice of private persons.[59] Judge Van den Wyngaert raised the following in her dissenting opinion attached to ICJ judgment in the *Arrest Warrant* case:

> Major scholarly organizations, including the International Law Association and the Institut de droit international have adopted resolutions and newly established think tanks, such as the drafters of the 'Princeton principles' and of the 'Cairo principles' have made statements on the issue. Advocacy organizations, such as Amnesty International, Avocats Sans Frontières, Human Rights

[52] *In casu*, the ICJ partially relied on the fact that national laws make naturalisation dependent on conditions indicating the existence of a certain link with the State (*Nottebohm* (n 48) para 22).

[53] *In casu*, the Court carefully examined practice, 'including national legislation', to determine whether there existed under customary international law any form of exception to the rule according immunity from criminal jurisdiction and inviolability to incumbent Ministers for Foreign Affairs, where they are suspected of having committed war crimes or crimes against humanity (*Arrest Warrant of 11 April 2000* (DRC v Belgium) [2002] ICJ Rep 3, para 58).

[54] eg ILA Final Report (n 2) 729; ILC, 'Report of the International Law Commission to the General Assembly' (1950), *YILC*, Vol II, 370.

[55] eg *SS Lotus* (France v Turkey) [1927] PCIJ Series A no 10, ICGJ 248; *Nottebohm* (n 48) 22–23; *Arrest Warrant* (n 53) para 58 (referring to 'decisions of national higher courts, such as the House of Lords or the French Court of Cassation').

[56] ibid.

[57] Overviews of State practice can be found inter alia in the *American Journal of International Law*, the *Annuaire français de droit international*, the *British Yearbook of International Law*, the *Chinese Journal of International Law*, the *German Yearbook of International Law*, the *Italian Yearbook of International Law*, the *Netherlands Yearbook of International Law*, the *Polish Yearbook of International Law*, the *Revista española de derecho internacional*, the *Revue belge de droit international*, or the *Revue générale de droit international public*.

[58] See eg Office of the Legal Adviser, US Department of State, 'Digest of United States Practice in International Law 2013', state.gov/documents/organization/226409.pdf.

[59] See eg L Kopelmanas, 'Custom as a Means of the Creation of International Law' (1937) 18 *BYIL* 127, 149–50; K Wolfke, 'Some Persistent Controversies Regarding Customary International Law' (1993) 24 *NYIL* 1, 4.

> Watch, The International Federation of Human Rights Leagues (FJDH) and the International Commission of Jurists, have taken clear positions on the subject of international accountability. This may be seen as the opinion of civil society, an opinion that cannot be completely discounted in the formation of customary international law today.[60]

However, precedents in support of this view seem to be virtually non-existent. A broad majority of legal scholars agree that even if individuals are to a certain extent capable of holding rights and duties under international law, they cannot, by themselves, contribute to the formation of customary international law, unless their conduct can be attributed to a State.[61] The acts of private individuals, including corporations, or lobby groups, may nonetheless cause a certain reaction of the State, thereby *indirectly* provoking developments in the customary lawmaking process. However, it is the reaction by the State, not the individual, that is developing customary international law.

Regarding the decisions of *international courts and tribunals*, these should not be seen as reflecting States' official positions. Hence, contrary to domestic judgments, they do not qualify as practice.[62] Decisions of international courts and tribunals are only binding upon the parties to the particular case. However, the persuasive force of these decisions can be considerable. While the doctrine of *stare decisis* is not used in international law, the judicial decisions of international courts and tribunals regarding the development and content of customary international law can carry an important precedential value and may in turn influence the subsequent practice of States and international organisations. As ILC Special Rapporteur Sir Michael Wood has observed, 'their weight varies depending on the quality of the reasoning, the composition of the court or tribunal, and the size of the majority by which they were adopted'.[63] International courts and tribunals remain ultimately a subsidiary means for the determination of the law (see below, Section IV(A)),[64] rather than an independent actor contributing to general practice.

What role do *international organisations* play in the process of forming and identifying customary international law?[65] Several indications suggest that their activities may count as practice.[66] The ILC recognised this as far back as 1950.[67] Also in its 2016 Draft Conclusions, the ILC stipulated that '[i]n certain cases, the practice of international organizations also contributes to the formation, or expression, of rules of customary international law'.[68] In its commentaries to the 2016 ILC Draft Conclusions (2016 ILC Commentaries), the

[60] *Arrest Warrant* (n 53) 154–55, Dissenting Opinion by Judge Van Den Wyngaert, as referred to by Bourgeois and Wouters (n 1) 96.

[61] See, among others, ILA Report (n 2) 727; M Akehurst (n 1) 11; see also, 2016 ILC Draft Conclusion 4 (n 15) para 3: '[c]onduct of other actors [than States and international organisations] is not practice that contributes to the formation, or expression, of rules of customary international law, but may be relevant when assessing the practice referred to in paragraphs 1 and 2'.

[62] ILA Final Report (n 2) 729–30; Mendelson (n 1) 202.

[63] ILC Third Report (n 45) para 60.

[64] 2016 ILC Draft Conclusion 13 (n 15) para 1.

[65] On this, see eg N Blokker, 'International Organizations and Customary International Law' (2017) 14 *International Organizations Law Review* 1; J Klabbers, 'International Organizations in the Formation of Customary International Law' in E Cannizzaro and P Palchetti (eds), *Customary International Law on the Use of Force* (Leiden, Nijhoff, 2005) 179–95; G Cahin, *La coutume internationale et les organisations internationales: l'incidence de la dimension institutionelle sur le processus coutumier* (Paris, Pedone, 2001); J Odermatt, 'The Development of Customary International Law by International Organizations' (2017) 66 *ICLQ* 491.

[66] Mendelson suggests that 'State practice' would more precisely be called the 'practice of subjects of international law'; Mendelson (n 1) 201.

[67] ILC, 'Report of the International Law Commission to the General Assembly' (1950) *YILC*, Vol II, 372.

[68] 2016 ILC Draft Conclusion 4 (n 15) para 2.

ILC's drafting committee on the identification of customary international law stressed that '[r]eferences in the draft conclusions and commentaries to the practice of States should (…) be read as including, in those cases where it is relevant, the practice of international organizations'.[69] With respect to resolutions adopted by an international organisation or at an intergovernmental conference, the ILC, however, specifically noted that these instruments, of themselves, can neither 'create a rule of customary international law' nor 'provide evidence for establishing the existence and content of a rule of customary international law, or contribute to its development'.[70] A provision in a resolution may, however, 'reflect a rule of customary international law if it is established that the provision corresponds to a general practice that is accepted as law (*opinio juris*)'.[71]

The ICJ seems to have followed a similar view in the *Reservations to the Genocide Convention* case[72] and in the *Fisheries Jurisdiction* case by taking into account the practice of international organisations to identify rules of customary international law.[73]

The conduct of/within an international organisation can first and foremost have an impact on its internal functioning. Conduct related to the organisation's internal legal order, such as issues related to its competences and functioning, can indeed establish a binding 'institutional practice' or '*coutume institutionnelle*'.[74] An example concerns the institutional practice of the UN Security Council whereby it is accepted that the abstention of a permanent member does not as such prevent the adoption of a resolution. This is the case even though Article 27(3) of the UN Charter in principle requires that all permanent members concur.

The question whether the conduct of international organisations can contribute to the creation of customary international rules of a general normative nature is, however, a different matter altogether. In this context, a further distinction is necessary between: (i) the practice of international organisations endowed with international legal personality acting in their own capacity, independently of their Member States; and (ii) situations where the international organisation merely acts as a conglomerate of State representatives. In the former situation, the practice of the international organisation can indeed contribute, of itself, to the formation and development of customary international law. For instance, in matters where the EU has been endowed with exclusive competence and acts in a supranational capacity (eg, trade policy), it clearly contributes (directly) to the customary lawmaking process.[75]

[69] 2016 ILC Commentaries (n 47) 88.

[70] 2016 ILC Draft Conclusion 12 (n 15) paras 1 and 2.

[71] 2016 ILC Draft Conclusion 12 (n 15) para 3.

[72] *Reservations to the Convention on the Prevention and Punishment of the Crime of Genocide* [1951] ICJ Rep 15, 25.

[73] *Fisheries Jurisdiction* (n 31) 58 (the Court inter alia took account of the practice of international fisheries commissions to examine customary fishing rights).

[74] See eg O Corten, 'La participation du Conseil de Sécurité à l'élaboration, à la cristallisation ou à la consolidation de règles coutumières' (2004) 37 *Revue belge de droit international* 552 (distinguishing between '*coutume institutionelle*' on the one hand, and '*coutume de droit international*' on the other, and giving examples of both in relation to the practice of the UN Security Council). See also JA Barberis, 'Réflexions sur la coutume internationale' (1990) 36 *AFDI* 9, 33–34; P-M Dupuy, 'Le droit des Nations Unies et sa pratique dans la jurisprudence de la Court internationale de Justice' in Société Française pour le Droit International (ed), *La pratique et le droit international: colloque de Genève* (Paris, Pedone, 2004) 139–57.

[75] The same may exceptionally be true for other non-State actors. Thus, the ICTY has recognized that the acts of the ICRC may influence customary international law. *Tadic* (n 44) para 109: 'the ICRC has promoted and facilitated the extension of general principles of humanitarian law to internal armed conflict. The practical results the ICRC has thus achieved in inducing compliance with international humanitarian law ought therefore to be regarded as an element of actual international practice; this is an element that has been conspicuously instrumental in the emergence or crystallization of customary rules'.

In his Third Report on 'Identification of Customary International Law' (2015), ILC Special Rapporteur Sir Michael Wood discussed, among other things, whether it would be possible for international organisations to contribute to the development of customary international law 'as such', that is, as autonomous actors in international law, rather than as a forum for the Member States to contribute such practice.[76] The Report speaks of one 'clear cut' case where an organisation's external practice (its relations with other States and organisations, rather than its internal practice) can contribute to the formation and identification of rules of customary international law.[77] This is where States have assigned competences to an organisation in a particular field, the best example of which is the EU.[78] In many cases it is the EU, and not the EU Member States, that conducts external relations with third parties, negotiating and concluding international agreements and participating in international organisations. Here such 'organisation practice' can be equated with that of States since, if it were not, 'Member States would themselves be deprived of or reduced in their ability to contribute to State practice'.[79] This approach recognises that regional organisations which exercise considerable external competences can contribute to customary international law as such, although practice is limited.

By contrast, in the second scenario, the international organisation is a forum in which the individual States participate. It is still States, rather than the organisation as such, that contribute relevant practice. Thus, when the Council of the EU acts within the context of the Common Security and Defence Policy (CSDP), or when the UN Security Council or the UN General Assembly adopt a resolution, the relevant practice of these entities can be regarded as collective practice expressed via an international forum. In such situations, even if the decision is formally recorded as a resolution of (the organ of the) organisation, it is best regarded (in the context of the formation and development of customary international law) as a series of verbal acts by the individual Member States participating in the organ. Apart from the decision itself, these verbal acts consist in positive or negative votes, abstentions, explanations of vote, statements made during the debates preceding the adoption of the act, etc.[80] As the ILA Committee concludes,

> it would add little or nothing to the weight of such practice by the Member States themselves to treat the resolution itself (as distinct from voting for it) as a further piece of practice, this time on the part of the organization.[81]

Particular attention has been paid to whether and, if so, how resolutions of the UN General Assembly impact the formation of customary international law.[82] Moreover, from the case

[76] ILC Third Report (n 45) 76.
[77] ibid, 77.
[78] ibid. This approach has also been reflected in the 2016 ILC Commentaries (n 47) 89–99.
[79] ILC Third Report (n 45) 77.
[80] As mentioned above (see Section II(C)(i)), in 2016 ILC Draft Conclusion 6 (n 15) para 2, the ILC identified the conduct in connection with resolutions adopted by an international organisation or at an intergovernmental conference as a form of State practice.
[81] ILA Final Report (n 2) 730.
[82] See eg OY Asamoah, *The Legal Significance of the Declarations of the General Assembly of the United Nations* (The Hague, Nijhoff, 1966); J Castenada, *Legal Effects of United Nations Resolutions* (New York, Columbia UP, 1969); G Arangio-Ruiz, 'The Normative Role of the General Assembly of the United Nations and the Development of Principles of Friendly Relations' (1972) III *RdC* 419; P Weil, 'Towards Relative Normativity in International Law?' (1983) 77 *AJIL* 413; C Tomuschat, 'The Concluding Documents of World Order Conferences' in J Makarczyk (ed), *Theory of International Law at the Threshold of the 21st Century: Essays in Honour of Krzysztof Skubiszewski* (Alphen aan den Rijn, Kluwer, 1996) 563–85.

law of the ICJ it clearly follows that resolutions of the UN General Assembly, such as the 1948 'Universal Declaration on Human Rights' (UDHR) or the 1974 'Definition of Aggression', can indeed contribute to the formation of customary international law.[83] At the same time, a cautious approach is needed. A careful analysis of the text, for example its language and title, is indispensable to verify whether its provisions were inspired by legal considerations, or by political or other non-legal ones. Furthermore, one must also take account of the mode of adoption of the resolution (majority, consensus or unanimity) as well as surrounding verbal practice, such as reservations or vote explanations. In principle, some degree of additional physical practice will be needed – UN General Assembly resolutions do not create 'instant custom' out of thin air.

In the *North Sea Continental Shelf* cases, the ICJ confirmed that *multilateral treaties* can also contribute to the formation of customary international law. In essence, three possibilities arise: (i) a treaty can codify pre-existing customary rules; (ii) it can 'crystallise' an emerging customary norm; or (iii) it can contribute to the formation of a new customary norm.[84] Treaties thus effectively qualify as relevant practice. At the same time, it follows from the *North Sea Continental Shelf* cases that treaty norms can only give rise to the formation of new custom insofar as they also find confirmation in the practice of other States which are not parties to the treaty or treaties concerned.[85] There must be some practice outside the treaty context.[86]

In other words, for treaty norms to give rise to customary international law, further evidence is needed to establish that it was the clear intention of the parties to accept more than a merely conventional norm.[87] Especially in relation to *bilateral* treaties, caution is needed. Indeed, in many cases, States conclude bilateral treaties in order to go beyond what general international law would otherwise permit them to do (eg, when States conclude bilateral 'hot pursuit' agreements allowing the pursuit of criminals across a mutual border). It would be erroneous in such situations to construe the existence of a series of similar bilateral treaties as proof of the existence of a customary norm of a more general nature.

D. *Opinio Juris*

General practice provides the raw material of the customary process. Yet it is clear that there must be something supplementary to accomplish its transformation into a rule of customary international law. This leads to the second constitutive element, that is, the psychological or subjective element: *opinio juris*. This element primarily refers to the

[83] *Legality of the Threat or Use of Nuclear Weapons* [1996] ICJ Rep 226, para 70. See also *Nicaragua* (n 10) para 188.

[84] *North Sea Continental Shelf* (n 4). Although the record is not unambiguous, the ICJ has on several occasions made reference to treaties to ascertain the existence of a customary rule (eg *Nottebohm* (n 48) para 183). See also 2016 ILC Draft Conclusion 11 (n 15) para 1, in which the ILC listed the same three occassions in which a treaty rule *as such* can be found to echo a rule of customary international law.

[85] *North Sea Continental Shelf* (n 4) para 76. In relation to multilateral treaties enjoying (near-)universal participation, the problem arises that there may be very little room left for possible 'non-State Party State practice'. This is the so-called 'Baxter paradox'.

[86] ibid. See also *Van Anraat v The Netherlands* (Decision on Admissibility) App no 65389/09 (ECtHR, 6 July 2010) paras 35–36, 88.

[87] ILA Final Report (n 2) 763. According to 2016 ILC Draft Conclusion 11 (n 15) para 2: '[t]he fact that a rule is set forth in a number of treaties may, but does not necessarily, indicate that the treaty rule reflects a rule of customary international law'.

recognition or acceptance by States that a certain (uniform, durable and extensive) practice reflects not simply a usage or tradition, but instead reflects a legal norm permitting, ordering or prohibiting certain conduct.[88] In other words, it relates to the need for the practice to be carried out 'as of right'.[89]

By way of illustration, the fact that States abstain from exercising jurisdiction in criminal matters in certain situations or vis-à-vis certain persons, may flow both from practical and legal considerations.[90] Only in the latter case will such practice give rise to customary international law: 'abstention from exercising criminal jurisdiction over aliens for certain crimes committed on the high seas could only result in a customary rule if such abstention were based on their being conscious of having a duty to abstain'.[91]

Whereas *physical* practice generally constitutes the engine driving the formation of customary international law, evidence of *opinio juris* can first and foremost be found in (oral or written) declarations in which States themselves pronounce on the legal character of a certain practice.[92] Express or implicit declarations recognising the content or the binding character of a customary rule indeed provide useful proof of the subjective element. For instance, in the *Nuclear Weapons* advisory opinion, the ICJ recognised that UN General Assembly resolutions 'can, in certain circumstances, provide evidence important for establishing the existence of a rule or the emergence of an *opinio juris*', and proceeded to an analysis of resolutions dealing with the use of nuclear weapons.[93] Likewise, in the *Nicaragua* case, it acknowledged that *opinio juris* could 'with all due caution, be deduced from, inter

[88] See also 2016 ILC Draft Conclusion 9 (n 15) on the requirement of acceptance as law (*opinio juris*).

[89] There is a long-standing debate as to the exact nature of the subjective element. One approach equates the element with the explicit or implicit will of the State that the practice would become a rule of law – in other words, with the State's *consent* to the (would-be) rule. A second group prefers to regard the subjective element as the belief (or conviction) of States that a certain practice is legally permissible, obligatory or prohibited. The ICJ has so far failed to resolve the controversy and both theories can cite judgments which to a greater or lesser degree support their contentions. Both views suffer from theoretical flaws (see eg M Byers, *Custom, Power and the Power of Rules: International Relations and Customary International Law* (Cambridge, CUP, 1999) 130 ff; O Elias, 'The Nature of the Subjective Element in Customary International Law' (1995) 44 *ICLQ* 501; R Kolb, 'Selected Problems in the Theory of Customary International Law' (2003) 50 *NILR* 119; IM Lobo de Souza, 'The Role of State Consent in the Customary Process' (1995) 44 *ICLQ* 521; S Yee, 'The News that *Opinio Juris* "Is Not a Necessary Element of Customary [International] Law" Is Greaty Exaggerated' (2001) 43 *GYIL* 227, 231–32). A more neutral formula, combining both approaches and building on the text of Art 38(1)(b) ICJ Statute, defines the subjective element as the 'acceptance or recognition of a practice as law'. This has also been reflected in 2016 ILC Draft Conclusion 9 (n 15) para 1, in which the ILC established that 'the general practice be accepted as law (*opinio juris*)' implies that the practice in question must be undertaken with a sense of legal right or obligation'. For an example of national practice, see Administrative Court of Appeal (FR), *Association France-Palestine Solidarité (AFPS) and Palestine Liberation Organization (PLO) v Société Alstom transport SA and others*, 22 March 2013, Case No 11/05331.

[90] Federal Supreme Court (CH), *Swiss Compensation Office v M*, 19 June 2013, Case No 9C_662/2012.

[91] *SS Lotus* (n 55), 28.

[92] As mentioned above (see above, Section II(C)(i)), oral and written declarations can also qualify as (verbal) practice. For example, in 2016 ILC Draft Conclusion 10 (n 15) para 2, the ILC included a non-exhaustive list of forms of evidence of *opinio juris*, including: 'public statements made on behalf of States; official publications; government legal opinions; diplomatic correspondence; decisions of national courts; treaty provisions; and conduct in connection with resolutions adopted by an international organization or at an intergovernmental conference'. However, since oral and written declarations can also qualify as both practice and *opinio juris*, one and the same act can count as an instance of both the subjective and the objective element. Mendelson warns of the risk of 'double-counting' in this context (Mendelson (n 1) 207). But see eg ME O'Connell, 'Taking *Opinio Juris* Seriously, a Classical Approach to International Law on the Use of Force' in E Cannizzaro and P Palchetti (n 65) 16 (arguing that 'double-counting' only takes place if the same act is counted twice for the purpose of establishing the required density of the practice). See also, N Arajärvi, 'The Requisite Rigour in the Identification of Customary International Law: A Look at the Reports of the Special Rapporteur of the International Law Commission' (2017) 19 *International Law Community Review* 9, 35, as cited by Bourgeois and Wouters (n 1) 94-95. On the 'epistemological circle', see M Byers (n 89) 136 ff.

[93] *Nuclear Weapons* (n 83) para 70 ff.

alia, the attitude (…) of States towards certain UN General Assembly resolutions'.[94] Verbal practice may also provide counter-evidence, in the sense that protests against a certain conduct will not only hamper the required density of practice, but also supply indications of a negative *opinio*.

At the same time, absent oral or written declarations, *opinio juris* is sometimes implicitly deduced from the physical conduct of States. In the *Right of Passage* case, for example, the ICJ found that 'there existed during the British and post-British periods a constant and uniform practice allowing free passage between Daman and the enclaves'.[95] Having observed that this practice had continued over a period extending beyond a century and a quarter unaffected by regime change, the Court was satisfied that it was 'accepted as law'.[96] In other cases, however, the ICJ refrained from deducing the *opinio juris* from the conduct of States. In the *Lotus* case, the PCIJ argued that States' abstention from exercising criminal jurisdiction over aliens for certain crimes committed on the high seas could only result in a customary rule if such abstention were based on States being conscious of having a duty to abstain.[97] In the *North Sea Continental Shelf* cases, the ICJ concluded that the drawing of the continental shelf boundaries according to the principle of equidistance did not constitute evidence of States' *opinio juris* since it might have been motivated by other obvious factors.[98]

The problem, indeed, is that omissions are often ambiguous as to their legal relevance. An abstention may be motivated by a sense of legal conviction, but there may also be other reasons, unconnected with international law.[99] A State's abstention from torturing its citizens could potentially be inspired by its belief that this would be counterproductive, and its non-recourse to the use of force could originate from mere military weakness. Consequently, as was recognised in the *Lotus* case[100] and the *Nicaragua* case,[101] when dealing with omissions, it is imperative that evidence of *opinio juris* can be provided (see also below).

The ICJ has often focused its analysis on general practice, while using *opinio juris* as a *negative* element of proof, which can rebut the idea that a continuous practice of States has transformed into a rule of customary international law. A good illustration is the Advisory Opinion on the *Legality of Nuclear Weapons*. In this case the ICJ rejected the existence of a customary prohibition on the recourse to nuclear weapons on the grounds that members of the international community are profoundly divided on the matter, even though no nuclear weapons have been used in warfare since 1945.[102] Conversely, the absence of protests against

[94] *Nicaragua* (n 10) para 188. The Court moreover found evidence of the *opinio juris* of the United States in its ratification of the Montevideo Convention and its acceptance of the Final Act of the Conference for Security and Co-operation in Europe (1 August 1975) 14 ILM 1292 (Helsinki Final Act), as well as of a resolution of the Sixth International Conference of American States condemning aggression (para 189).

[95] *Right of Passage over Indian Territory* (Portugal v India) [1960] ICJ Rep 6, para 40.

[96] See also *Nottebohm* (n 48) para 22.

[97] *SS Lotus* (n 55) para 28.

[98] *North Sea Continental Shelf* (n 4) para 78.

[99] See GP Buzzini, 'Les comportements passifs des Etats et leur incidence sur la réglementation de l'emploi de la force en droit international général' in E Cannizzaro and P Palchetti (n 65) 81–84. See also ILA Final Report (n 2) 726.

[100] In the *Lotus* case, for example, the PCIJ held that the absence of prosecutions did not prove the existence of a rule of customary law, because the omission had not been accompanied by *opinio juris* (*SS Lotus* (n 55) para 28).

[101] *Nicaragua* (n 10) para 188 (the ICJ stressed that absentions from the threat or use force needed to be supported by *opinio juris* as to their binding character).

[102] *Nuclear* Weapons (n 83) paras 66–67. Note: as Rijpkema observes, the Court's *modus operandi* differs depending on whether the parties concord as to the existence of a particular rule of customary international law. PP Rijpkema, 'Customary International Law in the *Nicaragua* case' (1989) 20 *NYIL* 91, 97.

certain conduct or the 'general toleration' by governments in general,[103] as well as the acquiescence by certain directly affected States who could have been expected to protest 'if they had really thought that [the conduct] was in violation of international law',[104] has occasionally been considered as implicit proof of States' *opinio juris*.[105]

While negative and positive acts of States may provide an *implicit* indication of a State's *opinio juris*, it is imperative to proceed cautiously. First, when verbal practice is readily available, the *opinio juris* expressed therein should not be disregarded. Furthermore, apart from its density, the nature of the physical conduct and the context in which it takes place must be taken into account. To distinguish between customary international law and international comity, the practice would moreover have to be carried out 'in areas of inter-state relations, which (…) objectively require legal regulation'.[106] Finally, there are certain situations where the conduct will only 'count' if there is positive evidence that the State(s) concerned intended, understood or accepted that a customary rule could result from, or lay behind, the conduct in question. This is firstly the case when dealing with omissions, which, as seen above, are often ambiguous as to their legal relevance.[107] The same is true for other forms of ambiguous conduct, 'the basis of which remains speculative'.[108] The conduct under consideration will therefore only count towards the formation or development of a customary rule if accompanied by other (verbal) indications of *opinio juris*.

E. Binding Scope of Customary International Law

It is well-known that international law in essence derives its binding character from State consent.[109] Treaties, for instance, do not create obligations for third parties (see Chapter 2 on Sources: Treaty Law, Section VIII). In the context of the formation of customary international law, a clarification is nonetheless in order. Indeed, customary rules are in principle also binding on States that have not *actively* participated (through their practice) to the creation of the norm, but which have instead acquiesced.

States will only be able to 'escape' from the binding nature of a norm of customary international law insofar as they have 'persistently objected' to the norm *as from its emergence*.[110] A mere absence of acquiescence is insufficient.[111] A State that speaks out

[103] eg *Fisheries* (n 24) paras 139–40; *SS Lotus* (n 55) para 23. A good example of national practice can be found in Constitutional Court (LV), *Agešins and others v Parliament of Latvia (Saeima)*, 23 November 2006, Case No 2006-03-0106.

[104] eg *SS Lotus* (n 55) para 29.

[105] See also 2016 ILC Draft Conclusion 10 (n 15) para 3, in which the ILC provided that '[f]ailure to react over time to a practice may serve as evidence of acceptance as law (*opinio juris*), provided that States were in a position to react and the circumstances called for some reaction'.

[106] Danilenko (n 1) 36. In a similar vein, Mendelson (n 1) 208; ILA Report (n 2) 747.

[107] eg ILA Report (n 2) 726; Mendelson (n 1) 207–209; Buzzini (n 99) 82.

[108] ILA Final Report (n 2) 748–49; eg *North Sea Continental Shelf* (n 4) paras 76–77.

[109] DK Anton, P Mathew and W Morgan, *International Law: Cases and Materials* (Oxford, OUP, 2005) 414–18.

[110] See also 2016 ILC Draft Conclusion 15 (n 15) on persistent objectors, in which the ILC determined that a rule of customary international law cannot be opposed to a State if that State has objected to the rule during the process of formation, for so long as it maintains its objection. In order to avoid the binding nature of the rule, the following three conditions have to be met: (1) the objection must be clearly expressed; (2) the objection must be made known to other States; and (3) the objection must be maintained persistently. See further, JI Charney, 'The Persistent Objector Rule and the Development of Customary International Law' (1985) 56 *BYIL* 1; Lepard (n 1) 229–42; D Kritsiotis, 'On the Possibilities of and for Persistent Objection' (2010) 21 *Duke Journal of Comparative and International Law* 121; JA Green, *The Persistent Objector Rule in International Law* (Oxford, OUP, 2016).

[111] According to 2016 ILC Draft Resolution 15 (n 15) para. 2: '[t]he objection must be clearly expressed, made known to other States, and maintained persistently'. See further, Green (n 110).

against a norm of customary international law *after* its emergence moreover no longer qualifies as a 'persistent objector' and remains bound. Even if a State can be considered to be a persistent objector and therefore might not be bound by a customary norm at first, the question can be posed whether that State can *remain* a persistent objector with regard to that norm for a very long time. Such States may be under pressure by other States to comply, and there are disadvantages to being outside the legal orthodoxy. For instance, the United Kingdom soon agreed to the extension of the territorial sea from 3 to 12 miles because of the wide acceptance, even though it first objected to such an extension.[112] Of course, if a large number of States oppose the coming into being of a new customary norm, the question arises whether the practice is sufficiently extensive for this norm to materialise in the first place.

Finally, it must be observed that the term 'customary international law' is generally understood to refer to 'general' customary international law, that is, customary rules binding on all States (except for possible 'persistent objectors'). It nonetheless follows from the case law of the ICJ that custom can also be 'regional' or even 'local' in nature. In the *Asylum* case, for instance, the ICJ examined whether there existed within Latin America a regional custom concerning the granting of asylum to political refugees.[113] In the *Right of Passage* case, it recognised the possibility of 'local custom', assuming consent of the parties concerned:

> The Court sees no reason why long continued practice between two States accepted by them as regulating their relations should not form the basis of mutual rights and obligations between the two States.[114]

Also in its 2016 ILC Draft Conclusions, the ILC confirmed that certain rules of particular customary international law only apply among a limited number of States due to their regional, local, or other nature.[115] Regional and local custom nonetheless remain the exception; *general* custom remains the rule. In spite of occasional suggestions of possible norms of European regional customary law,[116] little research has been conducted on the issue. The prohibition of the death penalty could possibly qualify as such. The issue of European regional customary human rights law could arise if a State were to withdraw from the ECHR.

F. Codification of Customary International Law

Given the uncertainties that accompany the adoption of customary international law – issues with evidence, ambiguities or controversy regarding the exact scope of an unwritten rule of law – the pursuit towards a gradual codification of customary international law by

[112] M Dixon, *Textbook on International Law*, 7th edn (Oxford, OUP, 2013) 34; MN Shaw, *International Law*, 8th edn (Cambridge, CUP, 2017) 66–68.

[113] *Asylum* (n 25) 277 (the Court ultimately found that there was insufficient proof to establish any regional custom).

[114] *Right of Passage* (n 95) 39.

[115] 2016 ILC Draft Conclusion 16 (n 15) on particular customary international law. Interestingly, the ILC provided that 'to determine the existence and content of a rule of particular customary international law, it is necessary to ascertain whether there is a *general practice among the States concerned* that is accepted by them as law (*opinio juris*)' (emphasis added).

[116] eg Q Qerimi, *Development in International Law: A Policy-oriented Inquiry* (Leiden, Nijhoff, 2012) 149 (suggesting that the polluter-pays principle represents 'at least European custom').

means of treaties has been going on for a considerable time. This process dates back to the end of the nineteenth century, illustrated by the codification of the laws of war, which was set into motion by the Peace Conferences at The Hague in 1899 and 1907. The League of Nations, the predecessor of the UN, also tried to promote the codification of customary international law. The most tangible result of those efforts was the 1930 Convention on Certain Questions Relating to the Conflict of Nationality Laws.[117]

The UN has pursued this undertaking with far greater success.[118] With the advent of the UN Charter era, the effort to codify customary international law has become more systematic and has increased its pace. In accordance with Article 13 of the UN Charter, one of the tasks of the UN General Assembly consists of '[initiating] studies and [making] recommendations for the purpose of (…) encouraging the progressive development of international law and its codification'. To this end, the UN General Assembly in 1947 established the ILC,[119] a body composed of 34 independent international law experts, which meet for a period of 10–12 weeks per year in Geneva.[120] According to the Statute of the ILC, its aim is to promote the progressive development and codification of international law.[121] The meaning of these terms is detailed further in Article 15 of the ILC Statute.[122]

The efforts of the ILC to codify and 'progressively develop' international law have resulted in a wide range of instruments, with some being regarded as highly authoritative (eg, in the realm of diplomatic and consular relations) and others perhaps less successful (eg, the effort to codify the rules pertaining to various aspects of State succession).

[117] Convention on Certain Questions relating to the Conflict of Nationality Laws (12 April 1930) 179 LNTS 89; VD Mahajan, *Public International Law* (Delhi, Eastern Book Company, 1974) 60–71.

[118] See inter alia G Abi-Saab, 'De la codification: quelques réflexions sur la signification et son rôle en droit international' in *Le développement du droit international: réflexions d'un demi-siècle* (Paris, Presses universitaires de France, 2013) 107–20; Y Daudet, 'Actualités de la codification du droit international' (2003) 303 *RdC* 9; Y Daudet, *Les conferences des Nations Unies pour la codification du droit international* (Paris, LGDJ, 1968); M de Serpa Soares, 'UN70: Contributions of the United Nations to the Development of International Law' (2016) 40 *Fletcher Forum of World Affairs* 99; R Higgins, 'The United Nations at 70 Years: the Impact upon International Law' (2016) 40/1 *L'Observateur des Nations Unies* 15; *International Law at the Time of its Codification: Essays in Honour of Roberto Ago* (Milan, Giuffrè, 1987); *La codification du droit international* (Paris, Pedone, 1999); R Pisillo-Mazzeschi, 'Treaty and Custom: Reflections on the Codification of International Law' (1997) 23 *Commonwealth Law Bulletin* 549; P Tomka, 'Customary International Law in the Jurisprudence of the World Court: the Increasing Relevance of Codification' in L Lijnzaad (ed), *The Judge and International Custom* (Leiden – Boston, Brill Nijhoff, 2016) 1–24; HWA Thirlway, *International Customary Law and Codification: an Examination of the Continuing Role of Custom in the Present Period of Codification of International Law* (Leiden, Sijthoff, 1972); H Torrione, *L'influence des conventions de codification sur la coutume en droit international public* (Fribourg, Editions universitaires Fribourg, 1989).

[119] UNGA Res 174 (II), 21 November 1947, UN Doc A/RES/174 (II). See on the ILC inter alia FL Bordin, 'Reflections of Customary International Law: the Authority of Codification Conventions and ILC Draft Articles in International Law' (2014) 63 *ICLQ* 535; G Nolte (ed), *Peace through International Law: the Role of the International Law Commission* (Dordrecht, Springer, 2009); *Making Better International Law: the International Law Commission at 50* (New York, United Nations, 1998); A Pellet, 'La Commission du droit international, pour quoi faire?' in *Boutros Boutros-Ghali Amicorum Discipulorumque Liber: Peace, Development, Democracy* (Brussels, Bruylant, 1998) 583–612; I Sinclair, *The International Law Commission* (Cambridge, Grotius, 1987); A Watts (ed), *The International Law Commission 1949–1998* (Oxford, OUP, 1999).

[120] See un.org/law/ilc.

[121] Art 1(1) Statute of the International Law Commission, Annex to UNGA Res 174 (II), 21 November 1947, A/RES/174 (II) (ILC Statute).

[122] Article 15 ILC Statute reads: 'In the following articles the expression "progressive development of international law" is used for convenience as meaning the preparation of draft conventions on subjects which have not yet been regulated by international law or in regard to which the law has not yet been sufficiently developed in the practice of States. Similarly, the expression "codification of international law" is used for convenience as meaning the more precise formulation and systematisation of rules of international law in fields where there already has been extensive State practice, precedent and doctrine.'

Some efforts have been converted into multilateral conventions under the auspices of the UN General Assembly (eg, the 1969 Vienna Convention on the Law of Treaties). Others have retained the status of 'Draft Articles' (eg, the ASR and the 2011 Articles on the Responsibility of International Organizations). While the latter instruments do not qualify as actual treaty law, they often command considerable authority, and have at times been taken to (partially) reflect customary international law in relevant case law. The ILC has also adopted various sets of guiding principles, such as the 2006 Guiding Principles applicable to unilateral declarations of States capable of creating legal obligations, or the 2011 Guide to Practice on Reservations to Treaties.[123]

Some of the current work of the ILC focuses on the immunity of State officials from foreign criminal jurisdiction; subsequent agreements and subsequent practice in relation to the interpretation of treaties; provisional application of treaties; identification of customary international law; protection of the environment in relation to armed conflicts; protection of the atmosphere; succession of States in respect of State responsibility; crimes against humanity; and peremptory norms of general international law (*jus cogens*). In addition to codification, the ILC has also undertaken studies on a number of topics, such as the 'fragmentation of international law' (2002–2006), 'the most-favoured-nation clause' (2009–2011) and 'Treaties over time' (2009–2011).

The EU seeks to contribute to the development and codification of international law by the ILC. One example of this is the ILC's work on the responsibility of international organisations. The EU paid particularly close attention to the work of the ILC and the Special Rapporteur, submitting comments at each stage of the process. The EU was critical of the ILC's 2011 Draft Articles on the Responsibility of International Organizations, arguing that they failed to take into account the specific nature of the EU legal order.[124] More recently, the EU is paying close attention to the ILC's work on the identification of customary international law.[125] The EU, via its statements at the UNGA Sixth Committee, has argued that international organisations such as the EU are capable of contributing to the development of customary international law in their own right.[126] The ILC is sometimes criticised for failing to sufficiently take into account international organisations, especially regional organisations such as the EU.[127] The EU, however, continues to cooperate with the ILC in a range of areas. This includes the provisional application of treaties,[128] the protection of persons in disasters,[129] and the expulsion of aliens.[130] The positions to be

[123] For a full list of the texts, instruments and final reports of the ILC, see un.org/law/ilc.

[124] See J Wouters and J Odermatt, 'Are All International Organizations Created Equal?' (2012) 9 *International Organizations Law Review* 7.

[125] ILC Third Report (n 45).

[126] E Cujo, Legal Adviser, Delegation of the European Union to the United Nations, Statement on behalf of the European Union at the UNGA Sixth Committee on Agenda item 78 on Identification of customary international law, 3 November 2015, eu-un.europa.eu/eu-statement-united-nation-6th-commission-identification-of-customary-international-law.

[127] See J-M Cortés Martín, 'European Exceptionalism in International Law? The European Union and the System of International Responsibility' in M Ragazzi (ed), *The Responsibility of International Organizations: Essays in Memory of Sir Ian Brownlie* (Leiden, Nijhoff, 2013) 192.

[128] Cujo (n 126).

[129] L Gussetti, Director, European Commission Legal Service, Statement on behalf of the European Union at the 69th UNGA Sixth Committee on Agenda item 78 on Protection of persons in the event of disasters, 27 October 2014, eu-un.europa.eu/eu-statement-united-nations-6th-committee-protection-of-persons-in-disasters.

[130] ibid.

taken by the EU at the UN Sixth Committee are often developed by the Comité Juridique (COJUR), who will prepare statements for the meetings of the UN General Assembly and ILC Sessions.[131] The EU and its Member States have also delivered statements at the Sixth Committee on topics such as the Rule of Law,[132] the Protection of Diplomats,[133] and Protocols Additional to the Geneva Conventions of 1949.[134]

Codification has some indisputable advantages. It contributes to the development of international law by clarifying and consolidating such law. It also acts as an instrument of broader dissemination of international law, an incentive for scientific research on international law, and a factor in increased certainty in positive law and therefore an enhancement of opportunities to settle disputes on legal grounds. However, codification is sometimes accused of being a contributing factor in conservatism and legal paralysis. The principal danger may lie in excessively ambitious attempts at codification that are thus doomed to fail, leaving customary international law in a worse state than before. For example, the treaties on succession of States (see Chapter 5 on States) have not proven very successful.[135]

III. General Principles of Law

General principles of law are principles that are common to the legal systems of 'civilised nations'. The qualification of 'civilised' dates from the original Article 38(1)(c) in the Statute of the PCIJ from 1920. Now that practically all States have joined the UN this has clearly become irrelevant and anachronistic.[136]

According to the prevailing opinion, this paragraph was included in order to resolve the issue of possible lacunae in international law and to eliminate the risk that a judge would

[131] See J Wouters and M Hermez, 'The EU's Contribution to "the Strict Observance and the Development of International Law" at the UNGA Sixth Committee' in S Blavoukos and D Bourantonis (eds), *The EU in UN Politics. Actors, Processes and Performance* (Basingstoke, Palgrave, 2017) 147–63.

[132] G Marhic, Minister Counsellor, Delegation of the European Union to the United Nations, Statement on behalf of the European Union and its Member States at the UNGA Sixth Committee on Agenda item 82: 'The Rule of Law at the National and International Levels', 13 October 2014, eu-un.europa.eu/eu-statement-united-nations-6th-committee-rule-of-law.

[133] E Cujo, Legal Adviser, Delegation of the European Union to the United Nations, Statement on behalf of the European Union and its Member States by at the UNGA Sixth Committee on Agenda item 80: 'Consideration of Effective Measures to Enhance the Protection, Security and Safety of Diplomatic and Consular Missions and Representatives', 20 October 2014, eu-un.europa.eu/eu-statement-united-nations-6th-committee-protection-of-diplomats.

[134] G Marhic, Minister Counsellor, Delegation of the European Union to the United Nations, Statement on behalf of the European Union and its Member States by at the UNGA Sixth Committee on Agenda item 79: 'Status of Protocols Additional to Geneva Conventions of 1949 and Relating to the Protection of Victims of Armed Conflicts', 20 October 2014, eu-un.europa.eu/eu-statement-united-nations-6th-committee-protocols-additional-to-geneva-conventions.

[135] See inter alia PM Eisemann and M Koskenniemi (eds), *La succession d'Etats: la codification à l'épreuve des faits* (The Hague, Nijhoff, 2000); A Zimmermann, 'La Convention de Vienne sur la succession d'Etats en matière de traités: codification réussie ou échouée?' in G Distefano, G Gaggioli and A Hêche (eds), *La Convention de Vienne de 1978 sur la succession d'Etats en matière de traités: commentaire article par article et études thématiques* (Brussels, Bruylant, 2016) 1547–78.

[136] Dixon (n 112) 42. An interesting variation to this expression is the one used in Art 15(2) ICCPR: 'Nothing in this article shall prejudice the trial and punishment of any person for any act or omission which, at the time when it was committed, was criminal according to the *general principles of law recognized by the community of nations*' (emphasis added).

refuse to decide on an issue due to the lack of an existing rule of law (what is known as '*non liquet*').[137] Therefore, general principles of law constitute a *subsidiary* – but not secondary – source of law to which recourse can be had when no applicable treaty rule or rule of customary international law is at hand.[138] They are also generally considered to be an *autonomous* source of law that are distinguished from treaty and custom, as reflected in the fact that Article 38(1) of the ICJ Statute dedicates a separate paragraph to general principles of law.[139] Last but not least, they constitute principles of positive law, since they are 'the general principles of law *recognized* by civilized nations'.[140]

The preparatory works show that Article 38(1)(c) of the ICJ Statute refers to principles of national law. They are principles that have been developed in a specific context and, if sufficiently abstracted, can be applied by analogy in certain cases in order to prevent gaps in obtaining a legal solution. However, not every general principle of national law qualifies.[141] To qualify, two conditions must be met. First, the principles must be common to the various national legal systems.[142] The principle must exist in most, if not all, legal systems. The principles must also be transposable to the international level. In other words, it must be examined whether they can be adopted in international law, taking into account the fundamental features of the latter (see Chapter 1 on Foundations, History and Theory of International Law) and the differences in structure between the international and national legal orders.

[137] *Nicaragua* (n 10) 135; *North Sea Continental Shelf* (n 4) 46; Shaw (n 112) 66–68. More recently, it has been found that general principles also contribute to the coherence of international law, see M Andenas, M Fitzmaurice, A Tanzi and J Wouters (eds), *General Principles and the Coherence of International Law* (Leiden, Brill, 2018).

[138] A Pellet, 'Article 38' in A Zimmerman, C Tomuschat and K Oellers-Frahm (eds), *The Statute of the International Court of Justice: A Commentary* (Oxford, OUP, 2012) 852.

[139] B Schlütter, *Developments in Customary International Law* (Leiden, Nijhoff, 2010) 71–86.

[140] R Jennings and A Watts, *Oppenheim's International Law*, 9th edn (London, Longman, 1992) 36–37.

[141] The following principles were not recognised as general principles of international law by domestic courts: the stand-still principle (Court of Cassation (BE), *AAZ and others v FT and others*, 14 January 2004, Case No P.03.1310.F); the principle of *ne bis in idem* (Court of Cassation (BE), *BVD and others, Re, DBCV and others v NV Deutsche Bank*, 26 July 2005, Case No P.05.0767.N); the principle of necessity as a defense against private parties (Constitutional Court (DE), *K and others v Argentina (represented by President Néstor Kirchner)*, 8 May 2007, DE:BVerfG:2007:ms20070508.2bvm000103); the principle of immunity of international organizations (Court of Cassation (BE), *League of Arab States v TM*, 12 March 2001, Case No S.99.0103.F); the prohibition to cause statelessness (Constitutional Court (DE), *O*, 24 May 2006, DE:BVerfG:2006:rs20060524.2bvr066904).

[142] The following principles have, for instance, been recognised as general principles of international law by national courts: the principle of legality in criminal law (Constitutional Court (HU), *President of Hungary*, 12 October 1993, Case no 53/1993 (X 13), (1993) *Official Gazette of Constitutional Court* 323); the principle of non-retroactivity in criminal law (Court of First Instance of Piedmont (IT), *De Guglielmi and De Guglielmi v Germany*, 19 May 2010, (2010) 46 *Rivista di Diritto Internazionale Privato e Processuale* 1006; Court of Cassation (FR), *Movement Against Racism and for Peoples' Friendship v Aussaresses*, 17 June 2003, Appeal No 02-80719, Decision No 122); the principle of condemnation of fascist regimes (Constitutional Court (SI), *Dolenc and Petan*, 9 November 2006, SI:USRS:2006:U.I.266.04); the principle of comity (Queen's Bench Division of the High Court (UK), *R v Secretary of State for the Home Department, ex parte Belgium*, 15 February 2000, Case Nos CO/236/2000, CO/238/2000); the principle *uti possidetis* (Constitutional Court (SI), *Re Agreement between the Republic of Slovenia and the Republic of Croatia on Border Traffic and Cooperation*, 19 April 2001, SI:USRS:2001:Rm.1.00; Constitutional Court (SI), *Re Arbitration Agreement between the Government of the Republic of Slovenia and the Government of the Republic of Croatia*, 18 March 2010, SI:USRS:2010:Rm.1.09); the prohibition of the use of force (High Court (IE), *Horgan v Ireland and others*, 28 April 2003, Case No 3739P; Council of State (IT), *Italia Nostra v Ministry of Cultural Heritage and Libyan Arab Jamahiriya (intervening)*, 23 June 2008, Case No 3154/2008); the principle of self-determination (Council of State (IT), *Italia Nostra v Ministry of Cultural Heritage and Libyan Arab Jamahiriya (intervening)*, 23 June 2008, Case No 3154/2008); the principle of separation of powers (Federal Constitutional Court (RS), *Supreme Court of the Republic of Serbia and others v People's Assembly of the Republic of Serbia*, 13 February 2003, Case No 17/2003); the principle of primacy of international law (Constitutional Court (TRNC), *National Unity Party v TRNC Assembly of the Republic*, 21 June 2006, Case No D 3/2006).

A number of general principles of law that are common to national legal systems can be found in the field of contract and tort law.[143] In addition, some procedural norms also constitute general principles, such as the *res judicata* principle,[144] the principle that no one can be both judge and party to its own case (*nemo judex in sua causa*),[145] and denial of justice (*déni de justice*).[146] Two other important general principles are acquiescence and estoppel.[147] In the *Gulf of Maine* case, the ICJ held that:

> [T]he concepts of acquiescence and estoppel, irrespective of the status accorded to them by international law, both follow from the fundamental principles of good faith and equity. They are, however, based on different legal reasoning, since acquiescence is equivalent to tacit recognition manifested by unilateral conduct which the other party may interpret as consent, while estoppel is linked to the idea of preclusion.[148]

One of the most important general principles of law that underlies numerous international rules of law is the principle of good faith. This principle is contained in Article 2(2) of the UN Charter, which provides that all UN Member States shall fulfil their obligations under the Charter in good faith. This was also confirmed in the 1970 *Friendly Relations Declaration* and in the 1976 Helsinki Final Act.[149] The EU law incarnation of good faith is the principle of sincere cooperation,[150] which in turn is the foundation for the primacy of EU law.[151] The principle is also at the core of another essential treaty law principle, namely the principle of *pacta sunt servanda* (as set out in Article 26 VCLT).[152] The ICJ emphasised the importance of this principle in the *Nuclear Tests Case*[153] and has repeatedly confirmed it ever since. Nevertheless, the ICJ has also found that good faith as a concept is not in itself a source of obligations when no other obligation exists.[154] Good faith is therefore a principle that complements and specifies the operation of existing international rules of law.[155]

[143] *Factory at Chorzów* [1927] PCIJ Series A, No 9.

[144] *Application of the Convention on the Prevention and Punishment of the Crime of Genocide* (Bosnia and Herzegovina v Serbia and Montenegro) [2007] ICJ Rep 43, para 113; *Effect of Awards of Compensation Made by the United Nations Administrative Tribunal* [1954] ICJ Rep 47, 53 and *Corfu Channel* (United Kingdom of Great Britain and Northern Ireland v Albania) [1949] ICJ Rep 4, 18.

[145] *Interpretation of Article 3, Paragraph 2, of the Treaty of Lausanne* [1925] PCIJ Series B, No 12, 32.

[146] *Barcelona Traction, Light and Power Company, Limited* (Belgium v Spain) [1970] ICJ Rep 36. For examples of national practice, see Stockholm Chamber of Commerce (SSC) Arbitration Institute (UA), *AMTO LLC v Ukraine*, 26 March 2008, SCC Case No 080/2005; Court of Cassation (FR), *Israel v National Iranian Oil Company*, 1 February 2005, Civil Appeal Nos 01-13742 and 02-15237: Court of Cassation (FR), *African Development Bank v X*, 25 January 2005, Case No 04-41012.

[147] On estoppel, see in particular, *Land and Maritime Boundary between Cameroon and Nigeria* (Cameroon v Nigeria: Equatorial Guinea intervening) [1998] ICJ Rep 275, 303; *Elettronica Sicula S.p.A. (ELSI)* (United States of America v Italy) [1989] ICJ Rep 15, 44; *Temple of Preah Vihear* (Cambodia v Thailand) [1962] ICJ Rep 6, 23, 31–32 and *Serbian Loans* [1929] PCIJ Series A, No 20.

[148] *Delimitation of the Maritime Boundary in the Gulf of Maine Area* [1984] ICJ Rep 246, para 130.

[149] See above (n 94).

[150] Art 4(3) TEU.

[151] See G De Baere and T Roes, 'EU Loyalty as Good Faith' (2015) 64 *ICLQ* 829.

[152] See eg Constitutional Court (SI), *Constitutional Review*, 5 June 1997, SI:USRS:1997:RS.40.97; Constitutional Court (CZ), *Novotný (Emil) v Ministry of Justice*, 21 February 2007, CZ:US:601.04.1; Supreme Administrative Court (CZ), *Explosive Service, as v Customs Directorate Prague*, 27 March 2008, Case No 9 Afs 130/2007-44.

[153] *Nuclear Tests* (Australia v France) [1974] ICJ Rep 253.

[154] *Borders and Transborder Armed Actions* (Nicaragua v Honduras) [1988] ICJ Rep 105.

[155] *Nuclear Weapons* (n 83) 264; *Fisheries Jurisdiction* (n 31) 33; and *North Sea Continental Shelf* (n 4) 46–47. See also the confirmation of the principle of good faith within the scope of international environmental law in principles 19 and 27 of the Rio Declaration.

IV. Case Law and Legal Writings

Article 38(1)(d) of the ICJ Statute states that the Court shall apply, 'subject to the provisions of Article 59, judicial decisions and the teachings of the most highly qualified publicists of the various nations, as subsidiary means for the determination of rules of law'. As is evident from this provision, both case law and scholarly writings are only 'subsidiary means for the determination of rules of law'.

A. Case Law

The case law of the PCIJ and its successor, the ICJ, has a privileged place in international law since the latter is the 'principal judicial organ of the United Nations'.[156] Pursuant to Article 59 of the ICJ Statute, however, the decisions of the Court have 'no binding force except between the parties and in respect of that particular case'.[157] The Court is not bound by its previous judgments, that is, there is no rule of *stare decisis.* Yet it is beyond doubt that its case law has great legal value.[158] The rulings of the ICJ have a major influence on the decisions of other international courts and tribunals. This is largely due to the high qualifications and wide diversity in legal establishment and the experience of its members, as well as the fact that the Court as a body should represent 'the main forms of civilization and the principal legal systems of the world'.[159] However, this influence rests most strongly on the force of conviction of the reasoning that was developed in these rulings, rather than any principle of precedent in international law.

Although the ICJ is the 'principal judicial organ' of the UN that settles disputes between States, it is no longer the only one.[160] As discussed further (see Chapter 13 on Peaceful Dispute Settlement, Section III), there are a multitude of other international and regional courts and tribunals. These include courts established under a treaty to settle disputes between States, as well as judicial organs that rule on individual criminal responsibility, such as the ICTY, ICTR and the ICC. In addition, there are several international arbitral tribunals, such as the Iran-US Claims Tribunal, or the ad hoc arbitral panels formed within the scope of the Permanent Court of Arbitration and the International Centre for Settlement of Investment Disputes (ICSID). There are also a number of semi-judicial organs, such as the UN Human Rights Committees and, within the framework of the WTO, the different panels and the Appellate Body. Again, pronouncements by these bodies will possess various degrees of authoritativeness. Judicial pronouncements by the International Tribunal for the Law of the Sea, for example, are highly authoritative in the field of the law of the sea.

[156] Art 92 UN Charter; see also Art 1 ICJ Statute.
[157] Constitutional Court (HU), *Member of Parliament*, 7 October 2003, *Decisions of the Constitutional Court*, Vol XII, No 10, 31 October 2003, 1281; Court of First Instance (IT), *Alessi and others v Germany and Presidency of the Council of Ministers of the Italian Republic (intervening)*, 21 January 2014, Order No 85/2014; Constitutional Court (IT), *Simoncioni and others v Germany and President of the Council of Ministers of the Italian Republic (intervening)*, 22 October 2014, Case No 238/2014; Court of Cassation (IT), *Opačić*, 29 October 2015, Case No 43696/2015.
[158] C Brown, 'Article 59' in Zimmerman (n 138) 1416.
[159] Art 9 ICJ Statute.
[160] Dixon (n 112) 112.

B. Legal Doctrine

Like case law, legal doctrine is not an actual source of law. Still, such writings help to determine the law's content, comment on it, explain it and, where necessary, criticise it.[161] In such instances, a clear division must be made between the attempts at objective explanation of the international practice of law (*de lege lata*) and the expression of personal views about what the law should be (*de lege ferenda*). Especially in the period when international law was still being formed, 'the opinions of the most qualified publicists' such as Pufendorf, Van Bynkershoek, Grotius and de Vattel were exceptionally influential. Writings on international law are rather less influential today, however, and the ICJ and other courts rarely invoke scholarly writings in their judgments and opinions.[162] One reason may be that it is difficult to identify who counts as 'the most highly qualified publicists' in international law.[163] At the European level, legal doctrine is also rarely invoked by the ECtHR[164] and never by the CJEU.[165] The lack of explicit citations does not mean, however, that legal writings or legal theory do not carry weight in the judicial reasoning of these courts.

V. Equity

Equity is the application of the principles of fairness and reasonableness to a certain case, taking into account all the elements of the matter at hand and abstracting solely the technical requirements of positive law.[166] In international law, equity can play a threefold role: (i) *infra legem*, as a means to mitigate or relieve the application of the law; (ii) *praeter legem*, as a means to supplement the application of the law; and (iii) *contra legem*, as a means to overrule the application of a rule of law.[167]

When considerations of fairness demand it, a judge may appeal, even without the consent of the parties, to principles of equity in order to mitigate the severity or inflexibility of positive law. This equity *infra legem* is included in positive law itself: it allows the judge to choose from several possible options, selecting the one which is best suited to the details of the matter and the situation of the parties.[168]

The complementary function of equity, ie, *praeter legem*, makes it possible for the judge to fill in the gaps in international law. It is a matter of dispute whether the international judge is allowed to apply this on his or her own initiative, or if, pursuant to Article 38(2)

[161] Shaw (n 112) 66–68.
[162] Dixon (n 112) 49; Shaw (n 112) 66–68.
[163] Dixon (n 112) 49.
[164] The ECtHR referred to scholarly writings to support its conclusions on jurisdiction in *Banković v Belgium* App no 52207/99 (ECtHR, 12 December 2001).
[165] At least in the decisions of the Court of Justice and the General Court. By contrast, Attorneys General do regularly cite academic scholarship; eg Opinion of AG Poiares Maduro of 16 January 2008 in *Kadi v Council and Commission*, C-402/05 P, EU:C:2008:11; Opinion of AG Bot of 19 March 2013 in *Commission and others v Kadi*, C-584/10 P, C-593/10 P and C-595/10 P, EU:C:2013:176; Opinion of AG Wahl of 8 September 2016 in Opinion 3/15 (Marrakesh Treaty on access to published works), EU:C:2016:657; Opinion of AG Wathelet of 10 January 2018 in *Western Sahara Campaign*, C-266/16, EU:C:2018:1.
[166] *Kutch Arbitration* (India v Pakistan), Award of 19 February 1968, 50 ILR 2.
[167] *Maritime Delimitation in the Area between Greenland and Jan Mayen* (Denmark v Norway) [1993] ICJ Rep 226, Separate Opinion of Judge Weeramantry. See also V Lowe, 'The Role of Equity in International Law' in M Koskenniemi (ed), *The Sources of International Law* (Aldershot, Dartmouth, 2000) 403–32.
[168] ibid, paras 69–72.

of the ICJ Statute, he or she needs explicit consent from the parties.[169] In the *North Sea Continental Shelf* cases, the ICJ put forward equity as one of the guiding principles when negotiating boundaries for the continental shelf between Germany and the Netherlands, and between Germany and Denmark, because it had found that there was no rule of treaty law or customary international law that bound these parties to such a boundary.[170]

To apply equity *contra legem,* in other words to overrule positive law, the consent of both parties is required.[171] Article 38(2) of the ICJ Statute states explicitly that the ICJ can only decide '*ex aequo et bono* (…) if the parties agree thereto'. Article 293(2) of the Convention on the Law of the Sea also provides that a court or tribunal has jurisdiction in the matter of a dispute on the interpretation or application of this Convention to decide the case *ex aequo et bono*, if the parties so agree. A similar provision holds true for arbitral tribunals within the framework of the ICSID.[172]

VI. Unilateral Acts

Article 38 of the ICJ Statute does not mention unilateral acts as a source of international law. Nonetheless, they may be defined as the will expressed by one single legal subject with the intent of bringing about legal consequences;[173] they are acts or statements by which subjects of law unilaterally indicate where they stand with regard to a certain matter in international law. 'Unilaterally' here means that there is no connection to the acts or statements of another subject of international law. A distinction is made in international law between the unilateral acts made by States and those made by international organisations.

A. Unilateral Acts of States

The ICJ has recognised in the *Nuclear Tests Case*[174] that States can impose unilateral obligations upon themselves.[175] According to the Court, unilateral acts of States are characterised by the following: (i) the intent of States to bind themselves must be clear from the circumstances of the statement or act; (ii) the unilateral legal act must be publicly known or at least generally known; (iii) the form of the unilateral legal act is irrelevant, but it must be explicit, in other words not ambiguous; and (iv) acceptance or any other response by any subject of international law is not necessary.

Both legislative and executive powers can bind a State internationally by unilateral legal acts. In the latter case, it may involve acts by the Head of State, the Minister of Foreign

[169] ibid, paras 65–68.
[170] *North Sea Continental Shelf* (n 4) 4.
[171] *Jan Mayen* (n 167) para 73. For an example of national practice, see Constitutional Court (AL), *Socialist Party of Albania v President of Albania and others*, 15 April 2010, Case No V-15/10.
[172] Art 42(3) Convention on the Settlement of Investment Disputes between States and Nationals of Other States (adopted 18 March 1965, entered into force 14 October 1966) 575 UNTS 159: 'The provisions of paragraphs (1) and (2) shall not prejudice the power of the Tribunal to decide a dispute *ex aequo et bono* if the parties so agree'.
[173] ILC, Report of the International Law Commission on the Work of its Fifty-Eighth Session, Sixty-First Session, 1 May–9 June and 3 July–11 August 2006, Supplement 10, 369–70.
[174] *Nuclear Tests* (n 153) 253.
[175] P-M Dupuy, *Droit international public* (Paris, Dalloz, 2016).

Affairs or even an embassy.[176] In terms of validity, unilateral legal acts in international law are largely subject to the same conditions as treaties. These legal acts must respect, for example, norms of *jus cogens*.[177] Opinions vary widely on the foundation of the binding nature of unilateral legal acts. In the *Nuclear Tests Case*, the ICJ mentions good faith as its foundation.[178] References are also often made to equity and to the principle of estoppel in the sense that it would be unreasonable to hold other States responsible for damage suffered if the State reconsiders its previous statements or acts.

A distinction can be made between several kinds of unilateral legal acts. First, unilateral legal acts are *autonomous* when they are not connected to a treaty or customary international law and their validity does not depend on another legal act (whether unilateral, bilateral or multilateral). In this category, a distinction can be made between the following types. The first is *notification*. This is an act by which a State officially notifies a third party of a fact or a situation, which from that moment on will be considered as legally known to the recipient. The second is *recognition*, an act by which a State establishes the existence of certain facts. For example, it may recognise a new State or a new government of another State (see below, p 266), or recognise certain acts, such as the conferral of a State's nationality on an individual (see below, p 432). Recognition is the most important and most common form of unilateral legal acts. A third type of unilateral act is *protest*, ie, an act by which a State announces that it does not recognise a certain situation, claim or behaviour as legal. This includes, for example, the sustained protest against an emerging rule of customary international law by a State acting as a 'persistent objector' (see above, Section II(E)). The fourth form is that of the *waiver*. This is an act by which a State announces its intention to waive or renounce a right, power, claim or complaint. Such a waiver must be explicit and cannot be merely assumed. This may include, for example, the waiver of immunity within the framework of a specific judicial procedure against a State, or the waiver of the diplomatic immunity of a diplomatic agent. The final type of unilateral act is the *promise*. This is an act by which a State binds itself to behave in a specific way towards another subject of international law.[179]

In addition to the unilateral acts discussed above, there are unilateral legal acts that are *connected to of treaty law or customary international law*. An example of the former is the accession, denunciation or withdrawal from a treaty, including a founding treaty of an international organisation. This also includes the making of a statement that accepts the compulsory jurisdiction of the ICJ within the meaning of Article 36(2) of the ICJ Statute. A unilateral legal act may also be exercised based on a rule of customary international law that grants specific rights to States.[180]

B. Unilateral Acts of International Organisations

International organisations, as subjects of international law, can make various contributions to international lawmaking: through the conclusion of treaties (see Chapter 2 on Sources: Treaty Law), in the context of the formation of customary international law (see above,

[176] ILC Report (n 173) Supplement 10, 372–74.
[177] ibid, 378–79.
[178] *Nuclear Tests* (n 153) 267–68, paras 43 and 46; and 472–73, paras 46 and 49.
[179] K Skubiszewski, 'Unilateral Acts of States' in M Bedjaoui, *International Law: Achievments and Prospects* (Leiden, Nijhoff, 1991) 223–29.
[180] ibid, 226.

Section II(C)(iv)), through participation in the work of other international organisations, but also through unilateral legal acts adopted within the scope of their conferred powers. Even though these acts do not appear in Article 38(1) of the ICJ Statute, they are becoming increasingly important as a formal source of international law.[181]

Unilateral acts of international organisations usually take the form of resolutions. Their legal status is highly diverse. The founding treaties of international organisations sometimes grant them the power to propose legally binding acts ('decisions'). As States are loath to relinquish sovereignty, these cases generally remain limited. In most cases, the power of international organisations remains limited to the adoption of legally non-binding acts ('recommendations').

Acts of international organisations often include both a consensual and a unilateral element. The consensual element lies in the fact that the acts are based on a convergence of the will expressed by members of the decision-making organ. Indeed, decision-making takes place by consensus in most cases.[182] The Council of the EU represents a notable exception, as the EU Treaties provide in numerous cases that it decides by qualified majority voting[183], even though decision-making practice in those cases is usually consensual as well.[184] However, such acts also contain a unilateral element when an organ in which not all members are represented makes a decision that is binding on all members of the organisation. For instance, pursuant to Article 25 UN Charter, the decisions of the UN Security Council, composed of only 15 Members, are binding on all UN Member States.

The EU institutions have been granted the most comprehensive competences to make legally binding decisions. Article 288 TFEU stipulates that, under the conditions specified in the Treaty, the European Parliament and the Council jointly, the Council and the European Commission can adopt regulations and directives and make decisions. The following instruments are defined in Article 288 TFEU itself. *Regulations* have general application and are binding in their entirety and directly applicable in all EU Member States. *Directives* are binding, as to the result to be achieved, upon each Member State to which they are addressed, but leave to the national authorities the choice of form and methods. *Decisions* are binding in their entirety; if they specify those to whom they are addressed, they are binding only on them.[185]

Another example is decisions of the UN Security Council within the meaning of Article 25 of the UN Charter. According to this provision, UN Member States have

[181] M Sørensen (ed), *Manual of Public International Law* London, (London, Macmillan, 1968) 157–65.

[182] On decision-making by international organisations, see Chapter 6, Section (V)(B).

[183] See Arts 16(3) and (4) TEU, and 238(2) TFEU.

[184] See JP Jacqué, 'Le vote majoritaire au Conseil de l'Union européenne: une vision pragmatique' in F Picod (ed), *Le principe majoritaire en droit de l'Union européenne* (Brussels, Larcier, 2016) 105–14.

[185] Apart from these three instruments, Article 188 TFEU also lists recommendations and opinions, 'which shall have no binding force'. See generally R Schütze, 'The Morphology of Legislative Power in the European Community: Legal Instruments and the Federal Division of Powers' (2006) 25 *YEL* 91–151. On regulations, see JV Louis, Les règlements de la Communauté économique européenne (Brussels, Presses universitaires de Bruxelles, 1969). On directives, see A Pinto Pereira, A diretiva comunitária (Coimbra, Coimbra Editora, 2014) ; S Prechal, Directives in EC Law (Oxford, OUP, 2005, 2nd edn) ; D Simon, La directive européenne (Paris, Dalloz, 1997). On decisions within the meaning of Art 288 TFEU (not to be confounded with decisions adopted under the EU's CFSP), see M Nettesheim, 'Art 288', in E Grabitz, M Hilf and M Nettesheim (eds), Das Recht der europaïschen Union (Munich, Beck, 2017), paras 172–99. On various other acts of the Council see U Everling, 'Zur rechtlichen Wirkung von Beschlüssen, Entschließungen, Erklärungen und Vereinbarungen des Rates oder der Mitgliedstaaten der Europäischen Gemeinschaft' in G Lüke, G Ress and MR Will (eds), Rechtsvergleichung, Europarecht und Staatenintegration: Gedächtnisschrift für Léontin-Jean Constantinesco (Cologne, Heymanns, 1983) 133–56.

agreed 'to accept and carry out the decisions of the UN Security Council in accordance with the present Charter'. A legal debate took place for an extended period with regard to the proper meaning of the term 'decisions'. Often the view was defended, specifically within the UN Security Council and in the UN General Assembly, that this term only refers to decisions within the framework of Chapter VII of the UN Charter,[186] in other words, enforcement measures to re-establish peace and security. During the San Francisco Conference, the Belgian delegation had proposed to limit the scope of Article 25 to decisions made within the framework of Chapters VI, VII and VIII of the UN Charter, but that proposal was rejected. In its *Namibia* advisory opinion,[187] the ICJ rejected this restrictive interpretation. The Court ruled that, in order to assess whether it is a 'decision' of the UN Security Council within the meaning of Article 25, an analysis must be made of the language of the resolution, taking into account the discussions that have led to the resolution, the provisions of the UN Charter that were put forward and, in general, all of the circumstances that serve to determine the legal consequences of a resolution of the UN Security Council.

Both international practice and legal literature show that the 'recommendations' of international organisations do not in principle have legally binding value. A State is free to determine the consequences that will flow from such a recommendation. However, simply because recommendations are not legally binding does not mean that they have no legal or other importance.[188] For example, in light of the principle of good faith, UN Member States should not simply disregard UN resolutions. Non-binding recommendations may also be given effect in the domestic legal orders of States or international organisations. For instance, a court may decide to interpret the meaning of a term in light of such recommendations.[189]

There is little practice of international organisations making *binding* unilateral declarations in the same manner as States. Such practice may be beginning to emerge in the context of the EU. In *Venezuelan Fishing Rights*,[190] a case before the CJEU, there was disagreement over whether the instrument in question constituted an 'agreement' for the purposes of Article 218 TFEU, or whether it was a 'unilateral binding instrument'. The Advocate General categorised a Council Decision unilaterally granting fishing opportunities to Venezuelan fishing vessels off the coast of French Guyana[191] as a 'binding unilateral declaration' under international law,[192] yet the Court ultimately found that it should be regarded as an international agreement between the EU and Venezuela.

As discussed to some extent above (see Section II(C)(iv)), resolutions of the UN General Assembly can also make a particular contribution to the development of international law.

[186] See Security Council Report, 'Special Research Report No. 1: Security Council Action under Chapter VII: Myths and Realities', 23 June 2008, 8.

[187] *Legal Consequences for States of the Continued Presence of South Africa in Namibia (South West Africa) notwithstanding Security Council Resolution 276 (1970)* (Advisory Opinion) [1971] ICJ Rep 16.

[188] M Virally, 'Unilateral Acts of International Organisations' in Bedjaoui (n 179) 256.

[189] Supreme Court (CY), *Re Constantinou v Cyprus*, 24 March 1984, Case No 302/80. In the EU context, see J Wouters and J Odermatt, 'Norms Emanating from International Bodies and Their Role in the Legal Order of the European Union' in R Wessel and S Blockmans (eds), *Between Autonomy and Dependence: The EU Legal Order under the Influence of International Organisations* (The Hague, TMC Asser Press, 2012) 47–68.

[190] Judgment 26 November 2014, *Parliament v Council and Commission v Council* ('*Venezuelan Fishing Rights*'), C-103/12 and C-165/12, EU:C:2014:2400. See also above, p 70.

[191] Council Decision 2012/19/EU of 16 December 2011 on the approval, on behalf of the European Union, of the Declaration on the granting of fishing opportunities in EU waters to fishing vessels flying the flag of the Bolivarian Republic of Venezuela in the exclusive economic zone off the coast of French Guiana [2012] OJ L6, 8.

[192] Opinion of AG Sharpston of 15 May 2014 in Joined Cases *Parliament and Commission v Council* ('*Venezuelan Fishing Rights*'), C-103/12 and C-165/12, EU:C:2014:334, points 69–124.

They can, for example, provide an interpretation of existing international law and thereby contribute to the establishment of rules of customary international law. When the legal view expressed in a resolution is in fact supported by general practice aligned with that view, rules of customary international law can be established in an accelerated manner. The resolution should represent a general expression of will, formulating general rules of behaviour, directed to the UN Member States as a whole and intended to govern an indefinite number of cases.[193]

A good example of such a UN General Assembly resolution is the 1960 Declaration on the Granting of Independence to Colonial Countries and People,[194] which contributed to the formation of customary international law with regard to the principle of self-determination. This resolution was adopted with 89 votes in favour, none against and nine abstentions. Not all resolutions can count on such broad support. A highly controversial matter at that time was the adoption of the 1974 Charter of Economic Rights and Duties of States,[195] which was adopted with 120 in favour, six against and ten abstentions. The States that were against it or abstained included the key industrialised countries (15 OECD countries), representing two-thirds of world trade.

An entirely different matter relates to the international law status of the UDHR, adopted by the UN General Assembly on 10 December 1948. The Declaration was adopted without any negative votes, but with eight abstentions (by socialist countries, South Africa and Saudi Arabia). Even though it is not intended to be a legally binding document but rather, as its preamble states, as a 'common standard of achievement' to strive for by all peoples and nations, many of its provisions have achieved the status of customary international law, and some even of *jus cogens* (see below, p 670). The UDHR without a doubt influenced many national constitutions as well as numerous global and regional human rights treaties. At the very least, the UDHR can be considered as an especially authoritative interpretation of the obligations with regard to human rights and fundamental freedoms that UN Member States have taken upon themselves by becoming parties to the UN Charter.[196]

VII. Soft Law and Informal Law

In international relations, States and international organisations often develop instruments or documents that are not treaties or unilateral legal acts, but nevertheless deal with their mutual relations or at least are intended to determine their general conduct. For lack of a better term, 'soft law' is often used to indicate that the instruments or documents concerned are not legally binding acts. Nevertheless, apart from their important political meaning, these acts play a role in the formation and development of international law that is by no

[193] *Nuclear Tests* (n 153) 226 and *Nicaragua* (n 10) 100.

[194] UNGA Res 1514 (XV), 'Declaration on the Granting of Independence to Colonial Countries and Peoples', 14 December 1960, UN Doc A/RES/1514. See in this context *Western Sahara* (Advisory Opinion) [1975] ICJ Rep 12. On the right to self-determination, see below, pp 218 ff.

[195] UNGA Res 3281 (XXIX), 'Charter of Economic Rights and Duties of States', 12 December 1974, UN Doc A/RES/3281. See also below, p 874.

[196] See J von Bernstorff, 'The Changing Fortunes of the Universal Declaration of Human Rights: Genesis and Symbolic Dimensions of the Turn to Rights in International Law' (2008) 19 *EJIL* 903, 913–14.

means insignificant.[197] A typical example of such a document is the Helsinki Final Act, signed on 1 August 1975.[198] This document is not a legally binding treaty, but its significance in the relations between East and West can hardly be overestimated.

In many newer domains of international law, such as international economic, environmental, human rights and space law, soft law has been created in the form of codes of conduct, principles, best practices, statements, guidelines, etc. These instruments are an important non-legally binding way to build consensus between States on certain principles. In terms of international environmental law, examples include the 1972 Stockholm Declaration[199] and the 1992 Rio Declaration, as well as the 'Forest Declaration' adopted at the UN Conference in Rio de Janeiro on environment and development on 13 June 1992.[200]

In addition to these soft law processes, one can add what has been described as 'informal international lawmaking' or 'IN-LAW'.[201] This includes lawmaking via international cooperation outside the traditional frameworks of international law. IN-LAW norms all share one characteristic: they do not fall neatly within the traditional sources of custom, treaty and general principles of law. This process has been defined as

> Cross-border cooperation between public authorities, with or without the participation of private actors and/or international organizations, in a forum other than a traditional international organization (process informality), and/or as between actors other than traditional diplomatic actors (such as regulators or agencies) (actor informality), and/or which does not result in a formal treaty or traditional source of international law (output informality).[202]

[197] See generally eg K Abbott and D Snidal, 'Hard and Soft Law in International Governance' in C Ku and PF Diehl (eds) *International Law: Classic and Contemporary Readings* (Boulder, Rienner, 2009) 21–48; GM Abi-Saab, 'Eloge du « droit assourdi »: quelques réflexions sur le rôle de la « soft law » en droit international contemporain' in GM Abi-Saab, MG Kohen and MJ Langer (eds), *Le développement du droit international : réflexions d'un demi-siècle* (Paris, PUF, 2013), 137–44; A Boyle, 'Soft-law in International Law-making', in M Evans (ed) *International Law* (Oxford, OUP, 4th edn, 2014), 118–36; CM Chinkin, 'The Challenge of Soft Law: Development and Change in International Law' in J Weiler and AT Nissel (eds) *International Law* (London, Routledge, 2011), 210–25; C Giersch, *Das internationale Soft Law: eine völkerrechtsdogmatische und völkerrechtssoziologische Bestandsaufnahme* (Berlin, LIT, 2015); AT Guzman and T Meyer, 'Soft Law' in *Economic Analysis of International Law* (Cheltenham, Edward Elgar, 2016) 123–54; G Shaffer, 'Hard and Soft Law' in JL Dunoff and MA Pollack (eds) *Interdisciplinary Perspectives on International Law and International Relations* (New York, CUP, 2013), 197–222; D Shelton, *Commitment and Compliance: The Role of Non-Binding Norms in the International Legal System* (Oxford, OUP, 2010). In the sphere of human rights law, see eg S Lagoutte, T Gammeltoft-Hansen and J Cerone (eds), *Tracing the Roles of Soft Law in Human Rights* (Oxford, OUP, 2016). In international environmental law, see eg J Friedrich, *International Environmental « Soft Law »: the Functions and Limits of Nonbinding Instruments in International Environmental Governance and Law* (Heidelberg, Springer, 2013); CC Joyner, 'Recommended Measures under the Antarctic Treaty: Hardening Compliance with Soft International Law' in JN Moore (ed), *Common Resources. Law of the Sea, Outer Space, and Antarctica* (Leiden, Brill, 2018), 710–53. In the area of financial law, see eg C Brummer, *Soft Law and the Global Financial System: Rule Making in the 21st Century* (New York, CUP, 2015, 2nd edn); F Weiss and AJ Kammel (eds), *The Changing Landscape of Global Financial Governance and the Role of Soft Law* (Leiden, Brill, 2015). In space law, see eg I Marboe (ed), *Soft Law in Outer Space: the Function of Non-Binding Norms in International Space Law* (Vienna, Böhlau, 2012).

[198] Helsinki Final Act (n 94).

[199] Declaration of the United Nations Conference on the Human Environment (adopted 16 June 1972) 11 ILM 1416.

[200] Non-legally binding authoritative statement of principles for a global consensus on the management, conservation and sustainable development of all types of forests, adopted by the Conference of the United Nations on Environment and Development, 13 June 1992, 31 ILM 881.

[201] See J Pauwelyn, R Wessel and J Wouters (eds), *Informal International Lawmaking* (Oxford, OUP, 2012). For case-studies, see J Pauwelyn, RA Wessel, J Wouters, A Berman and S Duquet (eds), *Informal International Lawmaking: Case Studies* (Oslo, Torkel Opsahl Academic EPublisher, 2013).

[202] For a comprehensive overview of the concept, see J Pauwelyn, 'Informal International Lawmaking: Framing the Concept and Research Questions' in Pauwelyn, Wessel and Wouters (n 201) 13.

Contrasted with so-called 'traditional' international lawmaking, it is characterised by the absence of the formalities associated with international law in terms of output, process, and actors involved. In this way, IN-LAW is not the same as soft law, which is characterised mainly by its non-binding legal nature, although the two concepts may at times overlap.

The EU has been drawn into the developments of 'soft law' and 'informal international lawmaking'. First, the EU seeks to influence the developments of soft law in a number of international fora. For instance, in the wake of the global economic crisis, the EU along with its international partners and Member States have sought to address a range of issues through the Group of Twenty (G20)[203] or the Financial Stability Board.[204] These bodies tend to produce non-binding recommendations and commitments, which are not legally binding but nevertheless highly influential. Second, the EU and the EU legal order are also increasingly affected by the developments in soft law and informal international lawmaking. The CJEU, for instance, has been faced with questions regarding how to deal with 'soft law' instruments that, although not strictly legally binding in the EU legal order, may still be given effect in other ways, such as through methods of interpretation.[205] Moreover, much of the EU's recent legislative action involves the implementation of soft or informal law, such as G20 commitments, or makes reference to non-binding instruments, such as resolutions of the UN General Assembly, in the preamble or text.

VIII. Hierarchy of Sources

The discussion about the sources of international law says precious little about the issue of hierarchy. The issue of the hierarchical relations between the sources of international law arises when there is a conflict between norms, regardless of whether or not they belong to the same source. Due to its horizontal nature, international law does not have any hierarchy of standards as is the case with national legal orders.[206] Nevertheless, there is the important exception of *jus cogens*. If there is a conflict between a treaty rule or a rule of customary international law and such a *jus cogens* norm, the *jus cogens* norm takes precedence and the treaty rule or rule of customary international law becomes invalid.[207]

[203] See J Wouters, S Van Kerckhoven and J Odermatt, 'The EU at the G20 and the G20's Impact on the EU' in B Van Vooren, S Blockmans and J Wouters (eds), *The EU's Role in Global Governance: The Legal Dimension* (Oxford, OUP, 2012) 259–71.

[204] See eg in the field of international banking J Wouters and J Odermatt, 'International Banking Standards, Private Law and the European Union' in M Cremona and H Micklitz (eds), *The External Dimension of European Private Law* (Oxford, OUP, 2015), 171–91.

[205] For a discussion on how the CJEU has dealt with non-binding norms, see J Wouters and J Odermatt, 'Norms Emanating from International Bodies and Their Role in the Legal Order of the European Union' in Wessel and Blockmans (n 189) 47–68. See eg judgment of 28 July 2016, *Council v Commission*, C-660/13, EU:C:2016:616, in which the Court was faced with the question of the status under EU constitutional law of a Memorandum of Understanding (MoU) on a financial contribution by Switzerland to the Member States that acceded to the Union as a result of the 2004 enlargement. See more generally on the position of soft law in EU law, J Iliopoulos-Strangas and JF Flauss (eds) *Das Soft Law der europäischen Organisationen* (Baden-Baden, Nomos, 2012); J Schwarze, 'Soft Law im Recht der Europäischen Union' (2011) 46 *Europarecht* 3–18; L Senden, *Soft Law in European Community Law* (Oxford, Hart, 2004); F Terpan, 'Soft Law in the European Union: the Changing Nature of EU Law' (2015) 21 *European Law Journal* 68–96.

[206] *Nicaragua* (n 10) 14.

[207] Arts 53 and 64 VCLT; see Chapter 2 on Sources: Treaty Law, Section X(B)(iii).

A controversial question is whether it is possible to discern a hierarchy in Article 38 of the ICJ Statute. During the preparatory works of the Advisory Committee of Jurists, the proposal to include in Article 38 the stipulation that the ICJ needed to apply the sources 'in the undermentioned order' was rejected.[208] The chairman of the Committee, Édouard Descamps, defended the view that there is a certain natural order of sources. When two States conclude a treaty in which the solution to a dispute can be found, the Court may not apply a rule of customary international law and disregard the treaty. Similarly, when there is a well-known rule of customary international law, there is no reason to appeal to the general principles of law.[209] However, this opinion was rejected by the other members, in particular because – as the ICJ ruled in the *Nicaragua* case (1986) – different sources can be applied at the same time, and because the nature of each source is different.[210]

What if a conflict arises between a rule of treaty law and a rule of customary international law? It happens frequently that a provision in a treaty deviates from a previously established rule of customary international law, but a treaty may also fall into disuse (*desuetudo*) when a new rule of customary international law is established. It is assumed that this entails the termination of a treaty with the tacit consent of the parties. Nonetheless, there is no fundamental hierarchical relationship between the two sources, and both are equal in status. Since customary international law – with the exception of *jus cogens* – is dispositive in nature, the subjects of international law are free to change, replace or exclude these rules by treaties. In case of a conflict between a treaty norm and an earlier rule of customary international law, the former therefore in principle applies between the parties.[211] When, however, a new rule of customary international law is established after the conclusion of a treaty, the former will prevail.[212]

The conflicts referred to here must therefore be resolved by means of the principle of *lex posterior derogat priori*, by which more recent law prevails over inconsistent earlier law.[213] However, it should be clarified that a later general rule does not prevail over a specific earlier rule: *lex posterior generalis non derogat legi priori speciali*. For example, a specific bilateral treaty will not be changed by later general custom.

It should be emphasised that a treaty rule and a rule of customary international law that deal with the same substance do not cancel each other out. Rather, they exist separately alongside one another and can as such be applicable simultaneously.[214] In the *Nicaragua* case the ICJ held in this respect:

> [E]ven if the customary norm and the treaty norm were to have exactly the same content, this would not be a reason for the Court to hold that the incorporation of the customary norm into treaty law must deprive the customary norm of its applicability as distinct from that of the treaty norm. (…) More generally, there are no grounds for holding that when customary international law is comprised of rules identical to those of treaty law, the latter 'supervenes' the former, so that the customary international law has no further existence of its own.[215]

[208] PCIJ Advisory Committee of Jurists, 'Procés Verbaux of the Proceedings of the Committee', 16 June–24 July 1920.
[209] ibid.
[210] *Nicaragua* (n 10) 14.
[211] See *SS 'Wimbledon'* (United Kingdom, France, Italy and Japan v Germany) [1923] PCIJ Series A, No 1.
[212] *Continental Shelf* (n 3).
[213] See also Art 30 VCLT as elaborated on in Section VI of Chapter 2 on Sources: Treaty Law.
[214] By relying on the customary rules on the use of force, rather than the parallel UN Charter rules, the ICJ managed to circumvent the US reservation to the ICJ's jurisdiction.
[215] *Nicaragua* (n 10) para 177.

Both standards continue to exist separately, for a number of reasons.[216] First, from the perspective of their applicability, if a treaty party exercises its right to terminate or suspend a treaty (eg, because of a material breach by the other party), it is no longer bound by the treaty, but it is still bound by the identical rule of customary international law. It is also possible that a party has made a reservation to the treaty provision concerned; but this does not affect the applicability of the similar rule of customary international law with regard to this party. Second, States that are not party to the treaty will – unless they are 'persistent objectors' (see above, Section II(E)) – be bound by the rules of customary international law. Third, a State may have accepted a treaty rule because the treaty provides appropriate implementing mechanisms or institutions.

Conflicts between norms enshrined in separate treaties must be tackled by reference to conflict or priority rules, which may be included in those treaties, or by reference to the general rules of treaty law, in particular those set out in Article 30 VCLT, apply (see Chapter 2 on Sources: Treaty Law, Section VI).

As far as the hierarchy between treaties is concerned, one must point again to the relevance of Article 103 of the UN Charter. As stated above, this provision determines that in the event of a conflict between the obligations of the Members under the UN Charter and their obligations under any other international agreement, their obligations under the UN Charter shall prevail. This is a special priority rule, also referred to in Article 30(1) VCLT.

Combined with Article 25 of the UN Charter, which obliges UN Member States to accept and carry out the decisions of the UN Security Council in accordance with the UN Charter, Article 103 of the UN Charter bestows great power on the UN Security Council. For example, when the UN Security Council imposes economic sanctions on a UN Member State pursuant to Article 41 of the UN Charter, its decision will prevail over conflicting obligations of UN Member States pursuant to bilateral or multilateral trade and investment agreements with the UN Member State concerned.[217]

In the EU legal order, Article 351 TFEU also provides for a specific conflict clause. On the one hand, Article 351, first paragraph, sets out that

> the rights and obligations arising from agreements concluded before 1 January 1958 or, for acceding States before the date of their accession, between one or more EU Member States on the one hand, and one or more third countries on the other, shall not be affected by the provisions of the Treaties.

On the other hand, '[t]o the extent that such agreements are not compatible with the Treaties', Article 351, second paragraph, obliges the EU Member State(s) concerned to 'take all appropriate steps to eliminate the incompatibilities established. EU Member States shall, where necessary, assist each other to this end and shall, where appropriate, adopt a common attitude'. As indicated above (p 95), the CJEU has developed case law regarding the application of this provision and the legal questions that arise from agreements entered into by EU Member States prior to their EU membership.[218]

[216] See ibid, para 178.

[217] On the UN Security Council's lawmaking role, see inter alia J Wouters and J Odermatt, '*Quis Custodiet Consilium Securitatis?* Reflections on the Lawmaking Powers of the Security Council' in V Popovski and T Fraser (eds), *The Security Council as Global Legislator* (London, Routledge, 2014) 71–96.

[218] See the references made in note 295 at p 95, as well as P Manzini, 'The Priority of Pre-Existing Treaties in EC Member States within the Framework of International Law' (2001) 12 *EJIL* 781–792. See also judgment of 6 March 2018, *Achmea*, C-284/16, EU:C:2018:158.

Given the informal character of the process of formation of customary international law, conflicts between different rules of general custom are essentially excluded. When a new rule of customary international law is established, the older rule disappears and only the new norm will apply. It is theoretically conceivable, however, that a conflict might arise between a norm of general customary international law and a norm of regional or local customary law. In that case, the regional or local customary norm applies between the subjects of international law to which that norm is applicable. In their relations with other subjects, the norm of general custom will apply.

IX. Concluding Remarks

Besides treaties, international law has various types of sources that need to be taken into account. Some of them can be found in Article 38 of the ICJ Statute. Customary international law has the same normative power as treaty law. It is composed of two elements: an objective one, namely the consistent, extensive, and relatively long practice of subjects of law (primarily States but on some occasions also international organisations); and a subjective one, the *opinio juris*, or the belief that this practice depends on a legal obligation. The general principles of law are a subsidiary and autonomous source of law. In order to be considered, a principle has to be common to the various legal systems of the world, and must be transposable to the international level. Finally, Article 38 of the ICJ Statute mentions case law and legal writings. These sources are subsidiary means for the determination of rules of law.

However, in order to be fully comprehensive, one must not forget about sources that are not mentioned in the ICJ Statute. This is the case of equity, unilateral acts of States and international organisations, and soft and informal law. The latter especially have become ever more widespread in international relations.

With such a wide number of international law sources, conflicts can emerge between norms, and the question of hierarchy arises. Due to the horizontal nature of international law, no rule can be considered above another – treaty and custom, among others, exist side by side. However, a number of principles can help solving some issues. First of all, *jus cogens* norms take precedence over any other norm of international law. Moreover, a later rule takes precedence over an earlier one (*lex posterior derogat priori*), except if that earlier one is a *lex specialis* and the later one a general one (*lex posterior generalis non derogat legi priori speciali*).

Beyond the problem of hierarchy between norms within the international legal system, the question of the relationship and interactions between international, EU and national law arises. The next chapter will tackle this issue.

Bibliography

Andenas, M, Fitzmaurice, M, Tanzi, A and Wouters, J (eds), *General Principles and the Coherence of International Law* (Leiden, Brill, 2018).

Besson, S, 'Theorizing the Sources of International Law' in Besson, S and Tasioulas, J (eds), *The Philosophy of International Law* (Oxford, OUP, 2010) 163–85.

Cahin, G, *La coutume internationale et les organisations internationales: l'incidence de la dimension institutionnelle sur le processus coutumier* (Paris, Pedone, 2001).
d'Aspremont, J, Besson, S and Knuchel, S (eds), *The Oxford Handbook of the Sources of International Law* (Oxford, OUP, 2017).
Green, JA, *The Persistent Objector Rule in International Law* (Oxford, OUP, 2016).
Kolb, R, 'Principles as Sources of International Law (With Special Reference to Good Faith)' (2006) 53 *NILR* 1.
Koskenniemi, M (ed), *Sources of International Law* (Aldershot, Dartmouth, 2000).
Oraison, A, 'La Cour Internationale de Justice, l'Article 38 de son Statut et les Principes Généraux' (2002) 80 *Revue de Droit International* 103.
Pellet, A, 'Article 38' in Zimmermann, A, Tomuschat, C and Oellers-Frahm, K (eds), *The Statute of the International Court of Justice, A Commentary* (Oxford, OUP, 2006) 731–870.
Thirlway, H, *The Sources of International Law* (Oxford, OUP, 2014).
van Hoof, GJH, *Rethinking the Sources of International Law* (The Hague, Kluwer, 1983).
Villiger, ME, *Customary International Law and Treaties: A Manual on the Theory and Practice of the Interrelation of Sources*, 2nd edn (The Hague, Kluwer, 1997).

Further Reading

Blum, YZ, 'The Role of Equity in International Law' in *Will 'Justice' Bring Peace?: International Law – Selected Articles and Legal Opinions* (Leiden, Nijhoff, 2016) 392–99.
Buzzini, GP, 'La théorie des sources face au droit international général: Réflections sur l'émergence du droit objectif dans l'ordre juridique international' (2002) 106 *Revue Générale de Droit International Public* 581.
Byers, M, *Custom, Power and the Power of Rules: International Relations and Customary International Law* (Cambridge, CUP, 1999).
Carrillo Salcedo, JA, 'Reflections in the Existence of a Hierarchy of Norms in International Law' (1997) 8 *EJIL* 583.
d'Aspremont, J, *Formalism and the Sources of International Law: A Theory of the Ascertainment of Legal Rules* (Oxford, OUP, 2011).
Druzin, BH, 'Why Does Soft Law Have any Power Anyway?' (2017) 7 *The Asian Journal of International Law* 361.
Giersch, C, *Das internationale Soft Law: eine völkerrechtsdogmatische und völkerrechtssoziologische Bestandsaufnahme* (Berlin, LIT, 2015).
Jennings, R, 'Reflections on the Subsidiary Means for the Determination of Rules of Law' in Jennings, R (ed), *Studi di diritto internazionale in onore di Gaetano Arangio-Ruiz* (Napoli, Editoriale Scientifica, 2004) 319–38.
Kassoti, E, *The Juridical Nature of Unilateral Acts of States in International Law* (Leiden, Nijhoff, 2015).
Mosler, H, 'To What Extent Does the Variety of Legal Systems of the World Influence the Application of the General Principles of Law within the Meaning of Art 38(1)(c) of the Statute of the International Court of Justice' in *International Law and the Grotian Heritage* (The Hague, TMC Asser Instituut, 1985) 173–85.
Mrljic, R, 'Some remarks on Soft Law and Some Specific Forms of Treaty Making' in Wolfrum, R, Sersic, M and Sosic, TM (eds), *Contemporary Developments in International Law: Essays in Honour of Budislav Vukas* (Leiden, Nijhoff, 2016) 840–50.

Nasser, SH, *Sources and Norm of International Law: A Study on Soft Law* (Berlin, Galada and Wilch, 2008).
Pauwelyn, J, Wessel, RA and Wouters, J (eds), *Informal International Lawmaking* (Oxford, OUP, 2012).
Prost, M, 'Hierarchy and the Sources of International Law: A Critique' (2017) 39 *Houston Journal of International Law* 285.
Raimondo, FO, *General Principles of Law in the Decisions of International Criminal Courts and Tribunals* (Leiden, Nijhoff, 2008).
Saganek, P, *Unilateral Acts of States in Public International Law* (Leiden, Nijhoff, 2016).
Shelton, D (ed), *Commitment and Compliance: The Role of Non-Binding Norms in the International Legal System* (Oxford, OUP, 2000).
Sivakumaran, S, 'The Influence of Teachings of Publicists on the Development of International Law' (2017) 66 *ICLQ* 1.
Tahvanainen, A, 'Hierarchy of Norms in International and Human Rights Law' (2006) 24 *Nordisk tidsskrift for menneskerettigheter* 191.
Torres Cazorla, MI, *Los actos unilaterales de los Estados: Un análisis a la luz de la práctica estatal y de la labor de la Comisión de Derecho Internacional* (Madrid, Tecnos, 2010).
Vismara, F, 'La prova di una pratica generale accettata come diritto nella prassi della Corte internazionale di giustizia' (2000) *La Comunità Internazionale* 439.
Weil, P, 'L'équité dans la jurisprudence de la Cour internationale de justice: un mystère en voie de dissipation?' in Lowe, V and Fitzmaurice, M (eds), *Fifty Years of the International Court of Justice: Essays in Honour of Sir Robert Jennings* (Cambridge, CUP, 1996) 121–44.
Weiler, JHH and Paulus, AL, 'The Structure of Change in International Law or Is There a Hierarchy of Norms in International Law?' (1997) 8 *EJIL* 545.
White, M, 'Equity – A General Principle of Law Recognised by Civilised Nations?' (2004) 4 *Queensland University of Technology Law and Justice Journal* 103.

4

The Relationship and Interactions between International Law, EU Law and National Law

I. Introduction

International law is crucially dependent on States for its effectiveness, and accordingly also on the domestic legal orders of States. International law is, in principle, neutral towards the effect given to it in the domestic legal order. It is only interested in compliance with its norms, irrespective of the means employed to realise compliance. This means that a State is free to decide on the domestic effect that is to be given to international law. Nevertheless, this freedom does not imply that a State can 'rely on her own legislation to limit the scope of her international obligations'.[1] Indeed, it is now well established that, under international law, international law takes precedence over municipal law.[2] Whether international law also prevails over municipal law in *domestic courts*, however, depends on the applicable norms of national constitutional law.

[1] *Free Zones of Upper Savoy and the District of Gex* (France v Switzerland) (Order) [1930] PCIJ Series A, No 24, 12; and (Judgment) [1932] PCIJ Series A/B, No 46, 167. See *SS 'Wimbledon'* (United Kingdom, France, Italy and Japan v Germany) [1923] PCIJ Series A, No 1, 29–30; *Greco-Bulgarian 'Communities'* (Advisory Opinion) [1930] PCIJ Series B, No 17, 32; *Treatment of Polish Nationals and Other Persons of Polish Origin or Speech in the Danzig Territory* (Advisory Opinion) [1932] PCIJ Series A/B, No 44, 24; *Exchange of Greek and Turkish Populations* (Advisory Opinion) [1925] PCIJ Series B, No 10, 20; *Jurisdiction of the Courts of Danzig* (Advisory Opinion) [1925] PCIJ Series B, No 15, 26–27; *Fisheries* (United Kingdom v Norway) [1951] ICJ Rep 116, 132; *Nottebohm* (Liechtenstein v Guatemala) [1953] ICJ Rep 111, 123; *Application of the Convention of 1902 Governing the Guardianship of Infants* (Netherlands v Sweden) [1958] ICJ Rep 55, 67; *Applicability of the Obligation to Arbitrate under Section 21 of the United Nations Headquarters Agreement of 26 June 1947* (Advisory Opinion) [1988] ICJ Rep 12, 34–35. The principle is codified in Art 27 VCLT and Arts 3 and 32 ASR. See further Chapters 2 and 12.

[2] See also *Elettronica Sicula SPA (ELSI)* (United States of America v Italy) [1989] ICJ Rep 15, paras 71–73, where the Court responded to an argument by Italy that there was no breach of the relevant treaty because the decision at issue 'was issued by the competent authority on a regular legal basis' by explaining that even if the State authority in question had 'held the requisition to be entirely justified in Italian law, this would not exclude the possibility that it was a violation of the […] Treaty'.

This chapter looks at the interaction between international law and internal legal systems, and is structured as follows. First, the role of national law in international law is briefly considered. The remainder of the chapter is then devoted to exploring the position of international law in internal legal systems. The final section of the chapter explores the extent to which the legal order of the EU fits within the traditional conception of the relationship between international law and internal legal systems.

II. The Role of National Law in International Law

While every State remains free to decide how international obligations are to be implemented in its internal law, it must give effect to these obligations in good faith.[3] This principle, known as *pacta sunt servanda*, finds expression in the text of Article 26 VCLT: 'Every treaty in force is binding upon the parties to it and must be performed by them in good faith'.[4] It is worth recalling that, in *Gabčíkovo-Nagymaros Project*, the ICJ clarified that Article 26 VCLT combines two elements of equal importance:

> It provides that 'Every treaty in force is binding upon the parties to it and must be performed by them in good faith.' This latter element, in the Court's view, implies that, in this case, it is the purpose of the Treaty, and the intentions of the parties in concluding it, which should prevail over its literal application. The principle of good faith obliges the Parties to apply it in a reasonable way and in such a manner that its purpose can be realized.[5]

The corollary of the *pacta sunt servanda* principle is the prohibition for a State 'to invoke the provisions of its internal law as justification for its failure to perform a treaty', as laid down in Article 27 VCLT. Article 13 of the 1949 Draft Declaration on Rights and Duties of States makes explicit the basic idea underpinning this prohibition, namely that States must fulfil their obligations in good faith.[6] Allowing States to invoke their internal law as an excuse for a failure to fulfil their treaty obligations would amount to allowing them unilaterally to determine the extent of their own obligations. As the PCIJ held in *Interpretation of the Convention between Greece and Bulgaria respecting reciprocal emigration*, it is 'a generally accepted principle of international law that in relations between Powers who are contracting parties to a treaty, the provisions of municipal law cannot prevail over those of the treaty'.[7] The ICJ too has confirmed that principle on many occasions. It did so, for example, in *Obligation to Arbitrate*, where in response to an argument submitted by the US that it had taken certain measures irrespective of any obligations under the agreement at issue, the ICJ held that:

> It would be sufficient to recall the fundamental principle of international law that international law prevails over domestic law. This principle was endorsed by judicial decision as long ago as the

[3] G De Baere and T Roes, 'EU Loyalty as Good Faith' (2015) 64 *ICLQ* 829, 839–45.

[4] See also the Separate Opinion of Judge Ajibola in *Territorial Dispute* (Libyan Arab Jamahiriya v Chad) [1994] ICJ Rep 6, para 79. The ILC has on several occasions stressed that 'the rule *pacta sunt servanda* is itself founded upon good faith'; see eg (1964) *YILC*, Vol II, 8. For a summary of the ILC's work on the issue, see P Gormley, 'The Codification of Pacta Sunt Servanda by the International Law Commission: The Preservation of Classical Norms of Moral Force and Good Faith' (1969) 14 *Saint Louis University Law Journal* 367.

[5] *Gabčíkovo–Nagymaros Project* (Hungary v Slovakia) [1997] ICJ Rep 7, para 142. See also Chapter 2.

[6] ILC, 'Draft Declaration on Rights and Duties of States' (1949) *YILC*, Vol I, 178.

[7] *Interpretation of the Convention between Greece and Bulgaria respecting reciprocal emigration, signed at Neulilly-sur-Seine on November 27th, 1919* (Advisory Opinion) [1930] PCIJ Series B, No 17.

> arbitral award of 14 September 1872 in the Alabama case between Great Britain and the United States, and has frequently been recalled since [...].[8]

The nature of the legal provisions of domestic law does not matter. In *Treatment of Polish nationals and other persons of Polish origin or speech in the Danzig territory*, the PCIJ held that the same principle applies to a State's constitutional law.[9] In turn, some domestic courts have recognised the supremacy of international treaties over their respective State's constitution.[10]

The principle is also reflected in Articles 3 and 32 of the ILC Articles on State Responsibility. The former makes clear that the characterisation of an act of a State as internationally wrongful is governed by international law and is not affected by the characterisation of the same act as lawful by internal law. The latter provides that the responsible State 'may not rely on the provisions of its internal law as justification for failure to comply with its obligations'. As the ICJ held in *LaGrand*: 'the international responsibility of a State is engaged by the action of the competent organs and authorities acting in that State, whatever they may be'.[11] As a corollary, the principle of supremacy ordinarily implies that all public authorities are competent to set aside domestic law provisions that conflict with international law without the need for them to obtain a court order to this effect.[12]

Nevertheless, as explained earlier (in Chapter 2), the principle in Article 27 VCLT, according to which a party 'may not invoke the provisions of its internal law as justification for its failure to perform a treaty', is without prejudice to Article 46 VCLT, which provides that a State

> may not invoke the fact that its consent to be bound by a treaty has been expressed in violation of a provision of its internal law regarding competence to conclude treaties as invalidating its consent unless that violation was manifest and concerned a rule of its internal law of fundamental importance.[13]

It is understood that a violation is manifest if it would be objectively evident to any State conducting itself in the matter in accordance with normal practice and in good faith.[14]

However, it would be misguided to hold that national law is irrelevant for international law. Indeed, national law-making is of crucial importance for the formation of customary international law, as it indicates state practice and *opinio juris*. In *Certain German Interests in Polish Upper Silesia*, the PCIJ clarified that while from the standpoint of international law – and that of the Court, which only applies international law – 'municipal laws are

[8] *Applicability of the Obligation to Arbitrate under Section 21 of the United Nations Headquarters Agreement of 26 June 1947* (Advisory Opinion) [1988] ICJ Rep 12, para 57.

[9] *Treatment of Polish Nationals* (n 1) 24; cp *Greco-Bulgarian 'Communities'* (n 1) 32.

[10] cp eg Court of Cassation (BE), *BM v Belgium*, 16 November 2004, Case No P.04.0644.N, para 16 (holding that a treaty provision with direct effect has priority over the Belgian Constitution).

[11] *LaGrand* (Germany v United States of America) (Order on Provisional Measures) [1999] ICJ Rep 9, para 28.

[12] Court of Appeal Brussels (BE), *Gruyez and Rolland v Municipality of Sint-Genesius-Rode*, 28 January 2003, Case No 2002/KR/412, para 2.

[13] Art 46(1) VCLT. As noted above (see Chapter 2.X.A.i.), this provision, or its customary law version, is rarely successfully applied. For instance, the PCIJ, in the *Eastern Greenland Case* (Norway v Denmark) [1933] PCIJ Series A/B, No 53, rejected Norway's claim that its minister of foreign affairs could not enter into a binding international agreement on 'matters of importance' without approval of the 'King in Council', and satisfied itself with the observation that the foreign minister acted 'within his province'. For a discussion of Art 46 VCLT and relevant case law, see T Meron, 'Article 46 of the Vienna Convention on the Law of Treaties (Ultra Vires Treaties)' (1978) 49 *BYIL* 175.

[14] Art 46(2) VCLT. See further Chapter 2.

merely facts', they are not ordinary facts, as they 'express the will and constitute the activities of States, in the same manner as do legal decisions or administrative measures'.[15] For instance, in the *Tadić* case, the ICTY Appeals Chamber relied on examples of national laws, inter alia from the German and Belgian legal systems, providing evidence of international practice showing 'that States intend to criminalise serious breaches of customary rules and principles on internal conflicts'.[16]

Furthermore, the potential usefulness of internal law principles as sources of international law is ingrained in Article 38(1)(c) of the Statute of the ICJ, which provides for the Court to apply 'the general principles of law recognized by civilized nations'.[17] Lord Phillimore, a member of the Advisory Committee of Jurists that drafted the identical provision of the original PCIJ Statute, clarified that the general principles referred to 'were accepted by all nations *in foro domestico*, such as certain principles of procedure, the principle of good faith, and the principle of *res judicata*, etc'.[18] For example, in *Barcelona Traction*, the ICJ relied on national law in order to recognise the concept of the corporate entity. The Court held that international law was

> called upon to recognize institutions of municipal law that have an important and extensive role in the international field. This does not necessarily imply drawing any analogy between its own institutions and those of municipal law, nor does it amount to making rules of international law dependent upon categories of municipal law. All it means is that international law has had to recognize the corporate entity as an institution created by States in a domain essentially within their domestic jurisdiction. This in turn requires that, whenever legal issues arise concerning the rights of States with regard to the treatment of companies and shareholders, as to which rights international law has not established its own rules, it has to refer to the relevant rules of municipal law. Consequently, in view of the relevance to the present case of the rights of the corporate entity and its shareholders under municipal law, the Court must devote attention to the nature and interrelation of those rights.[19]

Similarly, when international law places certain limits on the extent to which a State can rely on the nationality of one of its citizens in order to exercise diplomatic protection, it does so in the understanding that nationality is conferred by national law.[20] The ICJ explained the different roles of national law and international law in that respect in the *Nottebohm* case:

> It is for Liechtenstein, as it is for every sovereign State, to settle by its own legislation the rules relating to the acquisition of its nationality, and to confer that nationality by naturalization granted by its own organs in accordance with that legislation. […] Nationality serves above all to determine that the person upon whom it is conferred enjoys the rights and is bound by the obligations which the law of the State in question grants to or imposes on its nationals. This is implied in the wider concept that nationality is within the domestic jurisdiction of the State. But the issue

[15] *Certain German Interests in Polish Upper Silesia* (Germany v Poland) [1926] PCIJ Series A, No 7, 19; cp, in that sense, *Free Zones of Upper Savoy and the District of Gex* (n 1) 12.

[16] ICTY, Appeals Chamber, *Prosecutor v Tadić*, Decision on the Defence Motion for Interlocutory Appeal on Jurisdiction, 2 October 1995, Case No IT-94-1, paras 130–32.

[17] see further Chapter 3.III.

[18] PCIJ Advisory Committee of Jurists, 'Procés Verbaux of the Proceedings of the Committee', 16 June–24 July 1920, 335. See De Baere and Roes (n 3) 867. See also G Ripert, 'Les règles du droit civil applicables aux rapports internationaux' (1933) 44 *RdC* 565, 637. R Dworkin, 'A New Philosophy for International Law' (2013) 41 *Philosophy and Public Affairs* 2, 20, considered the principles mentioned in Art 38(1)(c) of the Statute of the ICJ to be a 'fossilisation' of a *jus gentium* of legal principles common to nations as inherited from imperial Rome.

[19] *Barcelona Traction, Light and Power Company, Limited* (Belgium v Spain) [1970] ICJ Rep 3, para 38.

[20] *Nottebohm* (Liechtenstein v Guatemala) [1955] ICJ Rep 4, 20–21.

> which the Court must decide is not one which pertains to the legal system of Liechtenstein. It does not depend on the law or on the decision of Liechtenstein whether that State is entitled to exercise its protection, in the case under consideration. To exercise protection, to apply to the Court, is to place oneself on the plane of international law. It is international law which determines whether a State is entitled to exercise protection and to seise the Court. The naturalization of Nottebohm was an act performed by Liechtenstein in the exercise of its domestic jurisdiction. The question to be decided is whether that act has the international effect here under consideration.[21]

The concept of 'domestic jurisdiction', intended to delineate the scope of application of national law as independent of international law, remains one of the cornerstones of the international legal order and is as such enshrined in Article 2(7) UN Charter. However, the scope of that domestic jurisdiction has been significantly diminished over the past century, notably as a consequence of human rights law. Nevertheless, national law remains of particular relevance for human rights law, notably in the 'domestic remedies rule',[22] and the habitual possibility to vary the application of certain rights through exceptions or restrictions 'prescribed by law'.[23]

III. The Position of International Law in National Legal Orders: Beyond Monism and Dualism

International law essentially leaves States free to choose how to give effect to international law in their domestic legal order,[24] as long as States meet their international law obligations.[25] Thus, the position of international law in the national legal order is a matter of domestic law. Since the late nineteenth century, two broad approaches of giving effect to international law in the domestic legal order can be discerned: monism and dualism. These approaches should be seen as ideal-typical descriptions of a state of affairs rather than a true reflection of the position of the domestic legal order vis-à-vis international norms. No national system perfectly fits the mould of either monism or dualism.

In essence, pursuant to the monist approach, international law is automatically incorporated into the domestic legal order, whereas pursuant to the dualist approach, international law first needs to be transformed into national law before it can be invoked before a national court. Both approaches stem from domestic law (since, as indicated, international law does not prescribe any specific mode of giving effect to international law), and, as such, reflect a

[21] ibid.

[22] See eg Art 35(1) ECHR and Art 44(b) ASR. See further AA Cançado Trindade, *The Application of the Rule of Exhaustion of Local Remedies in International Law: Its Rationale in the International Protection of Individual Rights* (Cambridge, CUP, 1983); CF Amerasinghe, *Local Remedies in International Law* (Cambridge, Grotius, 1990).

[23] See eg Arts 5(1), 9(2), 10(2) and 11(2) ECHR.

[24] See eg *LaGrand* (Germany v United States of America) (Judgment on Merits) [2001] ICJ Rep 466, para 128 (after having found that the US had violated Art 36 of the Vienna Convention on Consular Relations (VCCR) by failing to inform German nationals of their right to consular assistance in a case leading to the imposition of a death penalty, stating that 'the United States of America, by means of its own choosing, shall allow the review and reconsideration of the conviction and sentence').

[25] *Case Concerning Avena and other Mexican Nationals* (Mexico v United States of America) [2004] ICJ Rep 12, para 141 (concerning a similar violation as in *LaGrand*, holding that 'what is crucial in the review and reconsideration process is the existence of a procedure which guarantees that full weight is given to the violation of the rights set forth in the Vienna Convention, whatever may be the actual outcome of such review and reconsideration').

particular political philosophy.[26] In particular, monism can broadly be understood against the background of the centrality of the individual, while dualism is based on the traditional central position of State sovereignty.[27]

A. Dualism

One of the most influential proponents of dualism was the German-English legal scholar Lassa Oppenheim.[28] Oppenheim argued that because international and domestic law differ fundamentally from each other, it is impossible for international law to be part of domestic law. Both legal spheres would differ in terms of formal sources. National law is promulgated by the legislature of one State and applicable within that State, whereas international law is agreed upon, and applied, by different States. In terms of the relations they govern, national law governs the relations between individuals and between the State and individuals, whereas international law governs the relations between States. Because of these differences, international law could only have effect in the domestic legal order if it is transformed into national law.[29] National judges, then, have to apply *only* domestic law, that is, law resulting from the will of one single State. According to this theory, international law is relegated to a purely contractual level that governs inter-State relations, and individuals can only derive rights from an international norm to the extent that the norm has been transformed into the law of the domestic system.

In a dualist system, a conflict between an international norm and a domestic norm is conceptually impossible. At most, a conflict may arise between a domestic norm of international origin and another norm. Ordinarily, pursuant to the maxim *lex posterior derogat legi priori*, the later norm will prevail over the earlier, whatever its origin. But because a rigid application of this maxim might engage the international responsibility of the State (as the earlier norm may well be of international origin, and may as such bind the State at the international level), many dualist systems (and monist systems, for that matter) apply a principle of consistent or harmonious interpretation, by virtue of which the national judge ought to choose the interpretation of a norm that is most in line with international law.[30]

[26] It has been pointed out, however, that the influence of particular political philosophies on the legal practice of giving effect to international law in national law should not be exaggerated, as the theoretical differences between the various philosophies are often subtle. cp L Ferrari-Bravo, 'International and Municipal Law: The Complementarity of Legal Systems' in R St John Macdonald and DM Johnston (eds), *The Structure and Process of International Law: Essays in Legal Philosophy, Doctrine, and Theory* (The Hague, Nijhoff, 1986) 716.

[27] J Crawford, *Chance, Order, Change: The Course of International Law* (The Hague, Hague Academy of International Law, 2014) 219–20.

[28] L Oppenheim (H Lauterpacht ed), *International law: A Treatise*, 7th edn, Vol I: Peace (London, Longmans, 1948) 37.

[29] ibid.

[30] The doctrine of consistent interpretation is known in US constitutional law as 'The Charming Betsy' doctrine, which has its origins in Supreme Court (US), *Murray v The Charming Betsy*, 6 US 64 (1804) 118, where Marshall CJ held that 'an act of Congress ought never to be construed to violate the law of nations if any other construction remains'. As the phrasing indicates, the canon only applies if the national law in question is ambiguous: see Crawford (n 27) 233, noting that the same applies in the UK. See further eg CA Bradley, 'The Charming Betsy Canon and Separation of Powers: Rethinking the Interpretive Role of International Law' (1998) 86 *Georgetown Law Journal* 479; AJ Bellia Jr and BR Clark, *The Law of Nations and the United States Constitution* (Oxford, OUP, 2017) 83–85; and more generally G Betlem and A Nollkaemper, 'Giving Effect to Public International Law and European Community Law before Domestic Courts: A Comparative Analysis of the Practice of Consistent Interpretation' (2003) 14 *EJIL* 569.

The principle of 'consistent interpretation' is also well known in EU law, and enables Member State courts to interpret domestic law consistently with an EU norm that may possibly not have direct effect.[31] Consistent interpretation also allows domestic and EU law to be interpreted in light of international law.[32] Both aspects will be studied in more detail with respect to the EU legal order below, in Section V.

Dualist systems have a number of apparent advantages over monist systems. First, they provide clarity and legal certainty, as the citizen and the judge need only to take into account one legal order, that is, the domestic one. Second, a dualist system is supposedly more democratic and protective of national sovereignty, since it requires rigorous parliamentary intervention before international law is given effect. However, parliamentary intervention exists in monist systems as well. In many monist systems parliament needs to approve international treaties before the executive branch can deposit its instrument of ratification, which expresses the State's consent to be bound. However, when approving the treaty, parliament cannot change the terms of the treaty (it can only approve or disapprove). Once approved, the treaty automatically becomes part of the domestic legal order.

A major drawback of dualism is that individuals are entirely dependent on national legislatures for the effectuation of their rights under international law. In particular, individuals must rely on the skill of national legislators to transform faithfully the international obligations in question into national law. Not infrequently, the drafting may leave something to be desired. Keith cites the examples of the UK and New Zealand implementing legislation of the Hague Convention on International Child Abduction, which had respectively omitted certain provisions and used terms different from those in the Convention.[33] When confronted with a partial or incorrect incorporation of international law into the internal legal system, individuals cannot directly invoke international law. This may affect them in a particularly adverse manner in cases where international norms provide checks on discretionary government action; for example, in the context of the 'war on terror'.[34]

B. Monism

Most domestic legal systems now have monist features in that they display a certain openness towards the invocation of international law before domestic courts.[35] Monism basically posits that international law and domestic law are just two manifestations of the concept of law, and that international law is superior to domestic law. From the latter characteristic it flows that international law, in order for it to have effect in the domestic legal order,

[31] See eg judgments of 19 April 2016, *DI*, C-441/14, EU:C:2016:278, paras 31–33 and the case law cited there, and of 17 May 2018, *Karel de Grote – Hogeschool Katholieke Hogeschool Antwerpen*, C-147/16, EU:C:2018:320, para 41. The principle is also known as 'indirect effect' or 'harmonious interpretation'. See further eg P Craig and G de Búrca, *EU Law: Text, Cases, and Materials*, 6th edn (Oxford, OUP, 2015) 209–16; and M Bobek, 'The Effects of EU Law in the National Legal Systems' in C Barnard and S Peers (eds), *European Union Law*, 2nd edn (Oxford, OUP, 2017) 156–61.

[32] See eg judgment of 8 September 2015, *Philips Lighting Poland and Philips Lighting v Council*, C-511/13 P, EU:C:2015:553, para 60 and the case law cited there.

[33] KJ Keith, '"International Law is Part of the Law of the Land": True or False?' (2013) 26 *LJIL* 351, referring in particular to *Re H* (Abduction: *Custody Rights*) [1991] 2 AC 476 and *Gross v Boda* [1995] 1 NZLR 569.

[34] On the role of domestic courts in the maintenance of the rule of international law by providing judicial control over the exercises of public powers that may conflict with international law, see A Nollkaemper, *National Courts and the International Rule of Law* (Oxford, OUP, 2010) 250.

[35] P Daillier, 'Monisme et dualisme: un débat dépassé?' in R Ben Achour and S Laghmani (eds), *Droit international et droits internes; développements récents* (Paris, Pedone, 1999) 12.

need not be transformed into domestic law, and that, in case of conflict between norms of international and domestic law, the international norm prevails and the domestic norm is set aside. Arguably the leading proponent of monism was the famous Austrian legal scholar Hans Kelsen, for whom the unity of national and international law, and the supremacy of international law over domestic law, were epistemological postulates.[36] In fact, Kelsen considered international law to be an objective *Grundnorm* (basic norm) from which national legal orders borrow their validity, and which also encompasses all national legal orders. His former student, Hersch Lauterpacht, likewise espoused a monistic theory of the relationship between international law and national law, but his approach was rooted in a more natural law oriented conception of the wellbeing of individual humans as the ultimate purpose of international law. Lauterpacht argued that this purpose could more readily be achieved by granting international law full effect in and primacy over national law.[37]

The advantages provided by a monist approach mirror the disadvantages of the dualist approach. Monism reduces the risk of invoking State responsibility, as, unlike in a dualist approach, the judge has to give priority to the international norm in case of conflict with a domestic norm. Moreover, individuals can invoke international law directly in case the national legislature has failed to transform international law into domestic law. The plurality of sources applicable to cases heard by domestic judges and the democratic deficit of international law can be cited as the major drawbacks of monism.

C. Beyond Monism and Dualism

Throughout the twentieth century, various leading European international lawyers have taken issue with the usefulness of the distinction between monism and dualism. Gerald Fitzmaurice, for instance, considered the controversy over the effect of international law in the domestic legal order as artificial and misguided.[38] He did not just regard domestic and international law as different spheres, as dualism would do, but as two entirely separate systems operating in different fields and having no common subject-matter, just like the legal systems of two States are ships passing in the night.[39] Since, in principle, they have nothing in common, they can also not come into conflict with each other. Each system is superior in its own domain. However, it is not excluded that domestic obligations can clash with international obligations. In order to solve this conflict, Fitzmaurice did not advocate the supremacy of international law, but proposed applying conflict rules borrowed from 'natural law'.[40]

[36] H Kelsen, *Principles of International Law*, 2nd edn (New York, Holt, Rinehart and Winston, 1967) 569. See further Chapter 1.V.B.

[37] See eg H Lauterpacht, 'General Rules of the Law of Peace' in E Lauterpacht (ed), *International Law: Being the Collected Papers of Hersch Lauterpacht*, Vol I: The General Works (Cambridge, CUP, 1970) 214. See further M Koskenniemi, 'Lauterpacht: The Victorian Tradition in International Law' (1997) 8 *EJIL* 215. See also Chapter 1.I.

[38] G Fitzmaurice, 'The General Principles of International Law Considered from the Standpoint of the Rule of Law' (1957) II 68 *RdC* 71.

[39] ibid, 71–72. cp the Opinion of AG Poiares Maduro in *Kadi v Council and Commission (Kadi 2008)*, C-402/05 P, EU:C:2008:11, point 22, arguing that the fact that the EU is an autonomous legal order 'does not mean, however, that the Community's municipal legal order and the international legal order pass by each other like ships in the night'.

[40] ibid, 82. cp along similar lines, C Rousseau, *Droit international public: introduction et sources* (Paris, Sirey, 1970) 46–47; C Rousseau 'Principes de droit international public' (1958) 93 *RdC* 370, 473–74, proposing the application of 'le droit des gens'.

However, the distinction made between clashing legal orders and clashing legal obligations seems artificial, and the solution propounded to solve conflicts between obligations – 'natural law' – somewhat esoteric. More importantly, practice has caught up with this view. One can no longer realistically negate any interaction between international and domestic law,[41] as an increasing number of international norms purport to regulate domestic situations, for example, in the fields of environmental law, human rights law and criminal law. These are fields that are also regulated by domestic law. In fact, at a time when dualism was still very much in vogue, the PCIJ already referred to the direct enforceability of international law by individuals before domestic courts, in the *Jurisdiction of the Courts of Danzig* case (1928):

> It may be readily admitted that, according to a well established principle of international law, the [treaty], being an international agreement, cannot, as such, create direct rights and obligations for private individuals. But it cannot be disputed that the very object of an international agreement, according to the intention of the contracting Parties, may be the adoption by the Parties of some definite rules creating individual rights and obligations and enforceable by the national courts.[42]

Because monism and dualism may fail to describe adequately how international and domestic law truly relate to each other, new approaches have put more emphasis on the multifaceted process of interaction between international and national law. For example, von Bogdandy, who hails from a German constitutional tradition, has polemically stated:

> Monism and dualism should cease to exist as doctrinal and theoretical notions for discussing the relationship between international law and internal law. Perhaps they can continue to be useful in depicting a more open or more hesitant political disposition toward international law. But from a scholarly perspective, they are intellectual zombies of another time and should be laid to rest, or "deconstructed".[43]

Instead, von Bogdandy proposes to reconstruct the system on the basis of a theory of 'legal pluralism'. Unlike monism and dualism, legal pluralism would not turn a blind eye to the reality of diversity in international law-national law interaction. Legal pluralism 'does not imply a strict separation between legal regimes' but 'promotes the insight that there is an interaction among the different legal orders',[44] which are 'coupled'.[45] Legal pluralism has also been relied on to explain the apparent clash between EU law on the one hand and national law[46] or obligations under the UN Charter on the other,[47] but it remains to be seen whether it is able to solve the practical consequences of the conflict.[48]

[41] R Müllerson, *Ordering Anarchy: International Law in International Society* (The Hague, Nijhoff, 2000) 178.

[42] *Jurisdiction of the Courts of Danzig* (n 1) 17–18. Crawford has observed that this example shows that, 'even in reliance on decisions from the period of classical dualism, the boundaries between the international and the national, the public and the private, turn out to be more permeable than it might have been thought': J Crawford, 'Continuity and Discontinuity in International Dispute Settlement: An Inaugural Lecture' (2010) 1 *Journal of International Dispute Settlement* 1, 9.

[43] A von Bogdandy 'Pluralism, Direct Effect, and the Ultimate Say: On the Relationship Between International and Domestic Constitutional Law' (2008) 6 *International Journal of Constitutional Law* 397.

[44] ibid, 401.

[45] cp also Crawford (n 27) 222.

[46] E Cloots, 'Germs of Pluralist Judicial Adjudication: *Advocaten voor de Wereld* and Other References from the Belgian Constitutional Court' (2010) 47 *CMLR* 645.

[47] See eg S Besson, 'European Legal Pluralism after Kadi' (2009) 5 *European Constitutional Law Review* 237; G de Búrca, 'The European Court of Justice and the International Legal Order after Kadi' (2010) 51 *Harvard International Law Journal* 1.

[48] See in general eg P Eleftheriadis, 'Pluralism and Integrity' (2010) 23 *Ratio Juris* 365.

At any rate, the usefulness of the monism-dualism distinction has come under particular pressure owing to the interaction between the law of the EU and domestic law, as well as the interaction between the international legal order and the EU 'constitutional order',[49] which the present chapter examines more closely below in Section V. Yet national legal orders too mostly belie any rigid distinction between monism and dualism. For example, the US, Germany, the Netherlands and Poland have been described as 'hybrid monist' States.[50] In *Malgorzata v Poland*, the Polish Supreme Administrative Court confirmed that international treaties ratified on the basis of a prior statutory consent for ratification are directly applicable in the domestic legal order and take precedence over a statute if the two cannot be reconciled.[51] In short, classifying national legal systems as monist or dualist is rather an exercise in degree than in absolutes, and monism and dualism are therefore more appropriately looked at as ends of a continuum or spectrum with much diversity between the various systems situated on it.[52]

More pragmatically, the difference between monist and dualist systems may disappear where rules of international law are permissive or use broad, open, or programmatic terms; or indeed depending on the knowledge of or attitude towards international law by judges and lawyers in general in specific legal systems.[53]

IV. Domestic Effect of Specific Sources of International Law

This section examines the effect that European courts, both of the EU and of European States, give to various sources of international law in their domestic legal order. The effect of international treaties, customary international law, decisions of international judicial bodies and decisions of international organisations will be discussed successively.

A. Treaties

When a legal system is described as dualist, this means in the first place that it opposes *international treaties* automatically becoming part of the domestic legal order upon ratification.

[49] In this respect, Tietje discarded monism and dualism as useful theories, and suggested 'communitarisation' of international law as a rival theory. C Tietje, 'The Status of International Law in the European Legal Order: The Case of International Treaties and Non-binding International Instruments' in J Wouters, A Nollkaemper and E de Wet (eds), *The Europeanisation of International Law: The Status of International Law and its Member States* (The Hague, TMC Asser Press, 2008) 59. Given that the Union has replaced the European Community with the Treaty of Lisbon, one may possibly want to refer to 'unionisation'. Rosas, however, has characterised the approach of the CJEU towards international law as monist, at least with respect to treaties. cp A Rosas, 'The European Court of Justice and Public International Law' in Wouters, Nollkaemper and de Wet (n 49) 75. See *in extenso* on the interaction between international, European and domestic law, N Lavranos, 'UN Sanctions and Judicial Review' in Wouters, Nollkaemper and de Wet (n 49) 185–204. See K Lenaerts, 'Direct Applicability and Direct Effect of International Law in the EU Legal Order' in I Govaere, E Lannon, P van Elsuwege and S Adam (eds), *The European Union in the World: Essays in Honour of Marc Maresceau* (Leiden, Nijhoff, 2014) 45: 'The incorporation of public international law into EU law follows, to some extent, a "monist approach"'.

[50] D Sloss, 'Treaty Enforcement in Domestic Courts' in D Sloss (ed), *The Role of Domestic Courts in Treaty Enforcement: A Comparative Study* (Cambridge, CUP, 2009) 7.

[51] Supreme Administrative Court (PL), *Malgorzata v Poland*, 29 May 2002, Case No I SA/Lu 883/01, para 49.

[52] Crawford (n 27) 218–19.

[53] Keith (n 33) 357.

In a dualist system, the substantive content of a treaty can only be invoked to the extent that the treaty has been transformed into domestic law. For example, while since 3 May 1953, the UK has been a party to the ECHR and bound by its provisions, the rights contained in the Convention have only been part of its national legal order since the adoption of the Human Rights Act (1998).[54] This also implies that the rights enshrined in the Convention are only enforceable at the national level in respect of acts occurring after the entry into force of the implementing legislation.[55]

Still, monist systems likewise do not allow provisions of international treaties to be invoked in all circumstances. Most monist systems only recognise that treaty provisions have direct effect – which allows individuals directly to invoke them before domestic courts – if the provisions are self-executing. Treaty provisions are considered to be self-executing when they are sufficiently clear to be directly applied to a case, and are not in need of further implementing measures. The judgment of the Swiss Federal Supreme Court in *A and B v Government of the Canton of Zürich* offers an illustration of the approach commonly taken to the notion of 'self-executing':

> [P]rovisions of an international treaty could only be invoked by individuals before the national courts if they were self-executing, that is: if they had a sufficiently clear and tangible content to form the basis of a decision. Treaty provisions of a programmatic character could not be considered as self-executing: they did not establish individual rights that could be invoked before national courts, but needed to be elaborated and given appropriate form by the legislator.[56]

Sometimes, a 'subjective' yardstick is added to this 'objective' criterion: the treaty drafters' intention to grant subjective rights to and/or to impose duties on persons[57] or more generally to convey direct effect to a treaty provision. Because it is often difficult to trace this intention, the objective yardstick will frequently be decisive, as illustrated by the judgment of the Dutch Council of State (Raad van State) in *Reinier van Arkel Foundation and others v Minister for Transport, Public Works and Water Management*:

> Since neither the wording nor the legal history of the European Agreement on Main International Traffic Arteries [AGR] contained any evidence as to the question whether or not the contracting parties intended to give direct effect to the Agreement's provisions, the answer to the question whether the provisions had direct effect depended only upon their content. In order to provide an affirmative answer, the provisions of the AGR should be concrete and sufficiently manageable for the courts to apply. In this respect, the wording, object, and purpose of the provisions and their interrelationship with other provisions of the AGR may be taken into account.[58]

[54] See eg D McGoldrick, 'The United Kingdom's Human Rights Act 1998 in Theory and Practice' (2001) 50 *ICLQ* 901. Note that the Human Rights Act has recently come under attack in the UK. See eg 'The Conservatives' Proposals to Change Britain's Human Rights Laws: Protecting Human Rights in the UK', *The Guardian*, 3 October 2014, theguardian.com/politics/interactive/2014/oct/03/conservatives-human-rights-act-full-document; and 'Theresa May bows to EU by keeping UK in human rights convention after Brexit, enraging Tory right', *The Independent*, 12 July 2018, https://www.independent.co.uk/news/uk/politics/theresa-may-brexit-white-paper-eu-european-convention-on-human-rights-tory-mps-a8444386.html.

[55] cp *In re McKerr* [2004] UKHL 12 (holding that the right to an adequate investigation into a next-of-kin's killing by State forces was not enforceable in respect of a death occurring before the Human Rights Act's entry into force).

[56] Federal Supreme Court (CH), *A and B v Government of the Canton of Zürich, Appeal against a Regulation of 15 September 1999 adopted by the Canton of Zürich on the Tuition at Schools of Higher Education*, 22 September 2000, Case No 2P.273/1999, BGE 126 I 242.

[57] See in that sense Court of Cassation (BE), *Thonon*, 21 April 1983, (1983–1984) *Rechtskundig Weekblad* 2315.

[58] Council of State (NL), *Reinier van Arkel Foundation (Stichting Reinier van Arkel) and others v Minister for Transport, Public Works and Water Management (Minister van Verkeer en Waterstaat)*, 15 September 2004, Case No 200401178/1, LJN: AR2181, AB 2005/12, para 2.2.6.

At the domestic level, courts are often called upon to determine whether provisions of human rights treaties are self-executing. European courts have accepted that most treaty provisions concerning civil and political rights are self-executing,[59] but have been more reluctant to find human rights treaties such as the provisions of the International Covenant on Economic, Social and Cultural Rights (ICESCR) and the Convention on the Rights of the Child (CRC), to be self-executing. The Swiss Federal Supreme Court has adopted the European approach when ruling that the provisions of the ICESCR are not self-executing except in rare cases.[60] By contrast, the Belgian Council of State has deduced a standstill duty from Article 13(2)(a) ICESCR, which provides for primary education to be compulsory and available free to all.[61] As far as CRC provisions are concerned, it is notable that European courts have rendered contradictory judgments. For example, while one court recognised the self-executing character of Article 3(1) CRC, another court rejected the same position.[62]

Determinations of whether treaty provisions are self-executing are largely limited to treaties that confer rights on individuals, who invoke them before domestic courts. Where treaties codify basic principles of inter-State conduct, and a fortiori when foreign States themselves rely on treaty provisions protecting their rights, domestic courts will accept the direct effect of such provisions at face value. Thus, at least in monist States, courts have directly applied the provisions of the Vienna Convention on Diplomatic Relations, which grants privileges and immunities to diplomatic representatives, given the importance of smooth diplomatic relations and the avoidance of international discord.

Finally, while international law generally leaves it to States to decide how to give effect to their international legal obligations, this is not always the case. One obvious example concerns the 1949 Geneva Conventions, which oblige the High contracting parties to 'undertake to enact any legislation necessary to provide effective penal sanctions for persons committing, or ordering to be committed, any of the grave breaches' of the Conventions.[63] Similar obligations can be found in the Convention against Torture, which obliges the contracting

[59] Some courts have also accepted this for provisions of the Convention on the Elimination of All Forms of Discrimination against Women (CEDAW). cp District Court The Hague (NL), *Test Trial Fund Clara Wichmann and others v Netherlands*, 7 September 2005, Case No HA ZA 03/3395, LJN: AU2088, NJ 2005/473, AB 2005/398, NJCM 2005/30(8), in relation to Art 7 CEDAW. Also, and rather interestingly, the German Constitutional Court ruled that Art 36(1) of the Vienna Convention on Consular Relations (VCCR) was self-executing (*German Consular Notification Case*, 19 September 2006, Case No 2 BvR 2115/01, paras 51–53), after the ICJ had held that 'Article 36, paragraph 1, creates individual rights' (*LaGrand* (n 24) para 77), while later refusing to decide on Mexico's contention that the right to consular notification and consular communication under the VCCR is a human right, nevertheless observing 'that neither the text nor the object and purpose of the Convention, nor any indication in the *travaux préparatoires*, support the conclusion that Mexico draws from its contention in that regard' (*Avena* (n 25) paras 60–61).

[60] *A and B v Government of the Canton of Zürich* (n 56).

[61] Council of State (BE), *M'feddal*, 6 September 1989, Case No 32.989, in which it held that it follows from Art 13(2)(a) ICESCR that Belgium, which has known free primary school education since 1914, could not derogate from that principle after having become a party to the ICESCR. The later introduction of school fees for non-Belgians was therefore incompatible with Art 13(2)(a) ICESCR.

[62] Compare Court of Cassation (FR), *X v Y*, 1 October 2005, Case No 1810, Information Bulletin Court of Cassation 626 (holding that Art 3(1) CRC was self-executing and could be invoked before French courts) with District Court The Hague (NL), *Minister for Immigration Affairs and Integration v A and B*, Appeal Decision, 22 February 2006, Case No 200507814/1 (JV 2006/132) (holding that the same provision was not self-executing). However, another Dutch court considered Art 2(1) CRC to be self-executing (Central Appeals Tribunal (NL), *Appellant 1 and Appellant 2 (joining) v Council of the Mayor and Aldermen of the City of Zaanstad*, Final Appeal Judgment, 24 January 2006, Case No 05/3621 WWB, 05/3622 WWB, Decision No LJN: AV0197, USZ 2006/85, RSV 2006/84.

[63] Art 49 GC I; Art 50 GC II; Art 129 GC III; Art 146 GC IV. cp Keith (n 33) 352.

States to make conduct within the scope of the Convention 'punishable by appropriate penalties which take into account their grave nature',[64] or the Genocide Convention, which requires 'effective penalties'.[65] Such treaty provisions also nuance the distinction between monism and dualism, in that in both types of systems the legislature will have to intervene to determine inter alia the prosecuting authority, the courts having jurisdiction, and the specific penalties to be imposed.[66] Exceptionally, some treaties even explicitly assert that their provisions are self-executing.[67]

B. Customary International Law

Even in 'dualist' States, courts are often willing to give effect to customary international law in the domestic legal order. In the dualist UK system, notably, customary international law is part of the 'law of the land'.[68] In most States, customary norms regarding jurisdiction and immunity, which are so closely tied to the principle of sovereignty and the smooth conduct of inter-State relations, also apply directly in the domestic legal order,[69] except possibly when they conflict with domestic legislation.

That said, domestic courts often consider that they are not in an appropriate position to identify norms of customary international law, and may sometimes flatly deny the customary law character of a norm without much examination of State practice or *opinio juris*. Instead, they may limit themselves to giving effect to uncontroversial customary law principles such as the law of treaties, for instance the rules on treaty interpretation.[70] At any rate, domestic courts that are willing to give effect to customary international law are typically reluctant to recognise customary international law as a ground for invalidity of domestic legislation (or, put differently, to recognise the supremacy of customary international law). The CJEU, as will be seen below, has not ruled out reviewing secondary EU law in light of customary international law, although this is unlikely to lead to the invalidity or annulment of the EU act in question.[71] Courts' reluctance to apply customary international law may

[64] Art 4(2) Convention against Torture.
[65] Art 5 Genocide Convention.
[66] Keith (n 33) 358.
[67] eg Art 4(7) Benelux Convention on Intellectual Property (adopted 25 February 2005, entered into force 1 September 2006) 2386 UNTS 29.
[68] Keith (n 33) 360. See further R O'Keefe, 'The Doctrine of Incorporation Revisited' (2009) 79 *BYIL* 7, 12–17.
[69] C Ryngaert, *Jurisdiction in International Law*, 2nd edn (Oxford, OUP, 2015) 46–48.
[70] The same appears by and large to apply to the CJEU: See eg judgments of 3 June 2008, *International Association of Independent Tanker Owners and others (Intertanko)*, C-308/06, EU:C:2008:312, para 51 (holding, without justifying why, that 'it does not appear that [a number of regulations of two annexes to the International Convention for the Prevention of Pollution from Ships, signed in London on 2 November 1973, as supplemented by the Protocol of 17 February 1978 (MARPOL 73/78)] are the expression of customary rules of general international law'; 17 February 2016, *Air Baltic Corporation*, C-429/14, EU:C:2016:88, para 24 (recalling settled case law according to which 'an international treaty must be interpreted by reference to the terms in which it is worded and in the light of its objectives. [Art 31 VCLT], which codifies general international law and is binding on the European Union, states that a treaty is to be interpreted in good faith in accordance with the ordinary meaning to be given to its terms in their context and in the light of its object and purpose'); 27 February 2018, *Western Sahara Campaign* UK, C-266/16, EU:C:2018:118, para 58 (holding that in order to interpret the relevant provisions of the agreement at issue, 'it is necessary to refer to the rules of customary international law reflected by [Art 31 VCLT], which are binding on the EU institutions and are part of the EU legal order'); 11 July 2018, *Bosphorus Queen Shipping*, C-15/17, EU:C:2018:557, para 67 (referring to Art 31 VCLT, adding that it is clear from that provision 'that a treaty must be interpreted in good faith, in accordance with the ordinary meaning to be given to the terms of the treaty in their context and in the light of its object and purpose').
[71] Judgments of 24 November 1992, *Poulsen and Diva Navigation*, C-286/90, EU:C:1992:453, paras 9–10; of 16 June 1998, *Racke*, C-162/96, EU:C:1998:293, para 45; and *Intertanko* (n 70) para 51. Primary EU law consists

also be caused by concerns with respect to the democratic legitimacy of the formation of customary international law (which, unlike treaty law, is not put before a parliament for approval).[72]

Just as it is common for national courts to construe domestic norms in light of (ratified) treaties, the same applies to customary international law.[73] This 'light touch' approach enables domestic courts to apply international law without giving direct effect to it, while the latter technique controversially implies that courts may have to set aside domestic law in favour of international law. That said, courts may at times nominally apply the principle of consistent interpretation, while actually invalidating a domestic norm that could only be fairly construed in violation of a norm of international law (thereby giving direct effect to the international norm). The judgment of the Belgian Court of Cassation in the *Sharon and Others* case provides a striking illustration of that practice. There, the Court of Cassation took the view that customary international law does not permit heads of State and government to be prosecuted before the criminal courts of a foreign State. The Court of Cassation then went on to interpret the relevant provision of the Belgian law on the punishment of grave breaches of international humanitarian law, pursuant to which immunities provided no obstacle to the application of the law, in the light of customary international law:

> Nevertheless, that rule of internal law would infringe the aforementioned principle of customary international criminal law if it were to be interpreted as intending to put aside the immunity sanctioned by that principle[.] That rule can therefore not have that object, but has to be understood as solely excluding that the official capacity of a person could entail his lack of criminal liability for the international crimes enumerated by the law.[74]

Given that the language of the relevant internal law was clear and fairly unambiguous, this can only be described as an interpretation *contra legem*.[75]

of the constitutional Treaties of the EU (TEU, TFEU, and the Treaty establishing the European Atomic Energy Community) and the protocols and annexes attached to those Treaties, the Charter of Fundamental Rights of the EU, and any amending Treaties and accession agreements. Secondary law consists of legal instruments based on primary EU law, such as regulations, directives, and decisions.

[72] PJ Kuijper, 'Customary International Law, Decisions of International Organisations and Other Techniques for Ensuring Respect for International Legal Rules in European Community Law' in Wouters, Nollkaemper and de Wet (n 49) 96. Further on the legitimacy of customary international law, see eg M Byers, *Custom, Power and the Power of Rules: International Relations and Customary International Law* (Cambridge, CUP, 1999); J Tasioulas, 'Customary international law and the quest for global justice' in A Perreau-Saussine and JB Murphy (eds), *The Nature of Customary Law: Legal, Historical and Philosophical Perspectives* (Cambridge, CUP, 2007) 307–35; WS Dodge, 'Customary International Law and the Question of Legitimacy' (2007) 120 *Harvard Law Review* 19–27; Crawford (n 27) 70–75.

[73] eg Supreme Court (IS), *State Social Security Institute v Organization of the Disabled in Iceland*, 19 December 2000, Case No 125/2000, H 2000 4480, para 18 (noting that it was a recognised rule in Nordic legislation that legislation should be construed, as far as possible, in accordance with the international conventions that the State had ratified).

[74] Court of Cassation (BE), *HAS v Ariel Sharon*, 12 February 2003, (2003) 42 ILM 596. See further A Cassese, 'The Belgian Court of Cassation v. the International Court of Justice: The *Sharon and others* Case' (2003) 1 *JICJ* 437.

[75] The Court of Cassation appears to have found inspiration in the ICJ's judgment in the *Arrest Warrant* case, which pertained to the same Belgian law, this time as applied to the Congolese Minister of Foreign Affairs, Abdoulaye Yerodia Ndombasi. The ICJ had rejected Belgium's argument that under customary international law, there exists an 'exception to the rule according immunity from criminal jurisdiction and inviolability to incumbent Ministers for Foreign Affairs, where they are suspected of having committed war crimes or crimes against humanity'; *Arrest Warrant of 11 April 2000* (Democratic Republic of the Congo v Belgium) [2002] ICJ Rep 3, para 58. However, at para 60, the Court emphasised that 'the *immunity* from jurisdiction enjoyed by incumbent Ministers for Foreign Affairs does not mean that they enjoy *impunity* in respect of any crimes they might have

C. Decisions of International Courts

Domestic courts may rely on decisions of international courts or courts from other national jurisdictions when they apply international law even if, strictly speaking, they are not bound by the decision to which they refer.[76] Such reliance is not necessarily easily traceable, as national courts may at times fail to refer to such decisions directly, even if it is clear that their decision is influenced by a decision of a foreign or international court. A clear example is the judgment of the Belgian Court of Cassation in *Sharon and Others* discussed above.[77] There, the Court of Cassation drew on a decision of the French Court of Cassation without citing it,[78] while also failing to cite the ICJ judgment in the *Arrest Warrant* case, which was of particular relevance.

In some instances, reliance on or compliance with decisions of international courts may even be mandated by the national legal system. For example, Section 10(2) of the Spanish Constitution provides that:

> Provisions relating to the fundamental rights and liberties recognised by the Constitution shall be construed in conformity with the Universal Declaration of Human Rights and international treaties and agreements thereon ratified by Spain.

That provision is understood as implying that Spanish courts should interpret the treaties and agreements referred to in line with how they are interpreted by the competent international courts.[79] The German Constitutional Court ruled that German courts are under a constitutional *obligation* to consider decisions of the ICJ, even if rendered in proceedings to which Germany was not a party. However, the Court limited the 'normative directing function' of the ICJ's case law to situations in which the ICJ had accepted its jurisdiction to interpret the treaty in question, and added that even then, German authorities could still deviate from the ICJ's case law.[80] The courts of other countries are much less open to giving effect to decisions of the ICJ in their domestic legal order. The Hungarian Constitutional Court, for instance, ruled that the ICJ's judgment in the *Gabčíkovo-Nagymaros* case did not create international obligations that are enforceable in Hungarian courts.[81] In the *Medellin* case,[82] the US Supreme Court refused to endorse the binding effect in US state courts of the ICJ's judgment in the *Avena* case,[83] even though the US executive branch had called

committed, irrespective of their gravity' (emphasis added). Given that Belgium was a party in the *Arrest Warrant* case, and that pursuant to Art 59 of the ICJ Statute, decisions of the Court have binding force 'between the parties and in respect of that particular case', the similarity in result and indeed in part of the phrasing is not surprising.

[76] cp Nollkaemper (n 34) 235.

[77] *HAS v Ariel Sharon* (n 74).

[78] Court of Cassation (FR), *Gaddafi*, 13 March 2001, (2001) 125 ILR 490.

[79] Nollkaemper (n 34) 236. For a recent application, see eg Constitutional Court (ES), 22 September 2014, Case No 145/2014, *Official State Gazette* No 261 of 28 October 2014, 34. Note, however, that a tension may exist between the obligation under Section 10(2) and the possibility under Section 93 for the constitutional powers to be transferred by international treaty, notably to the EU. See judgment of 26 February 2013, *Melloni*, C-399/11, EU:C:2013:107 and Constitutional Court (ES), 13 February 2014, Case No 26/2014, *Official State Gazette* No 60 of 11 March 2014, 85.

[80] cp Federal Constitutional Court (DE), *German Consular Notification Case*, 19 September 2006, 2 BvR 2115/01, paras 57–62.

[81] Constitutional Court (HU), *Re Member of Parliament*, 31 October 2003, *Decisions of the Constitutional Court* Vol XII, No 10 of 31 October 2003, 1281–91, relating to the *Gabčíkovo-Nagymaros* case (n 5), para 3.3.

[82] Supreme Court (US), *Medellín v Texas*, 25 March 2008, 552 US 491 (2008) (No 06-984).

[83] In *Avena* (n 25), the ICJ had required the relevant US authorities to grant review and reconsideration of decisions convicting a number of Mexican nationals to the death penalty in violation of the duty of consular notification provided in the VCCR (see further Chapter 10.II(B) on consular functions).

upon US domestic courts to allow review.[84] In the *Ara Libertad* case, the Supreme Court of Ghana refused to give direct effect to an order of the International Tribunal for the Law of the Sea (ITLOS).[85] The Italian Constitutional Court annulled Italian legislation implementing the 2012 ICJ judgment in *Jurisdictional Immunities of the State* (which found that Italy had violated international law by not recognising the immunity of Germany, even in the face of violations of *jus cogens*),[86] on the ground that the implementation of the ICJ decision violated Italian constitutional law.[87]

D. Decisions of International Organisations

Apart from resolutions of the UN Security Council (UNSC), in particular those adopted under Chapter VII of the UN Charter (see Chapter 14) and of course EU legal acts, very few decisions of international organisations are endowed with binding effect.[88] However, such binding effect may in itself entail problems for domestic legal orders, especially if a conflict arises with domestic legal standards. In particular, an issue that has arisen in relation to UNSC resolutions before domestic courts is whether they can be declared invalid on the ground that they violate a superior norm of *jus cogens*, or a domestic constitutional norm. This was one of the questions faced by the Swiss Federal Supreme Court in *Nada*.[89] That court found that the fundamental rights and procedural guarantees invoked by Nada were in principle not recognised internationally as *jus cogens*. Still, it admitted that the Security Council's delisting procedure for individuals appearing on the sanctions list was not in conformity with the standards of judicial control granted by domestic and international human rights law, yet found that it could not correct this situation.[90] The ECtHR later held that Switzerland had violated the ECHR, on the grounds that it had failed to exercise the *discretion* it had in implementing the resolution.[91] That reasoning was based on the presumption the Court had established in *Al-Jedda*. There, the ECtHR had held that

> in interpreting its resolutions, there must be a presumption that the Security Council does not intend to impose any obligation on Member States to breach fundamental principles of human

[84] See the Presidential determination by President George W Bush on 28 February 2005, published in SJ Cummins (ed), *Digest of United States Practice in International Law 2005* (Office of the Legal Adviser, United States Department of State, Oxford University Press, and International Law Institute, 2007) 30: 'I have determined, pursuant to the authority vested in me as President by the Constitution and the laws of the United States of America, that the United States will discharge its international obligations under the decision of the International Court of Justice in the Case Concerning Avena and Other Mexican Nationals (Mexico v. United States of America) (Avena), 2004 ICJ 128 (Mar. 31), by having State courts give effect to the decision in accordance with general principles of comity in cases filed by the 51 Mexican nationals addressed in that decision'.

[85] Supreme Court (GH), *Republic v High Court (Commercial Division) Accra, Ex Parte; Attorney General*, 20 June 2013, Case No J5/10/2013; *Ara Libertad Case* (Argentina v Ghana), Order of 15 December 2012, ITLOS Case No 20.

[86] *Jurisdictional Immunities of the State* (Germany v Italy: Greece intervening) [2012] ICJ Rep 99.

[87] Constitutional Court (IT), Case No 238, 22 October 2014.

[88] Domestic courts may sometimes invoke non-binding decisions of international organisations so as to clarify the law. Thus, such decisions play a limited normative role in the domestic legal order. See also Chapter 3.

[89] Federal Supreme Court (CH), *Youssef Nada v State Secretariat for Economic Affairs and Federal Department of Economic Affairs*, 14 November 2007, Case No 1A 45/2007, BGE 133 II 450.

[90] Constitutional review of UNSC resolutions was also rejected by a Croatian court: Constitutional Court (HR), *Bobetko Report, Review of constitutionality and legality*, 12 November 2002, Case No U-X-2271/2002.

[91] *Nada v Switzerland* App no 10593/08 (ECtHR, 12 September 2012).

> rights. In the event of any ambiguity in the terms of a United Nations Security Council resolution, the Court must therefore choose the interpretation which is most in harmony with the requirements of the Convention and which avoids any conflict of obligations. In the light of the United Nations' important role in promoting and encouraging respect for human rights, it is to be expected that clear and explicit language would be used were the Security Council to intend States to take particular measures which would conflict with their obligations under international human rights law.[92]

The Court applied the same reasoning in *Al-Dulimi*, another UNSC sanctions case involving Switzerland. However, the discretion available to UN Member States was very narrow indeed,[93] and in finding that Switzerland had violated the ECHR, the Court arguably stretched the presumption it had established in *Al-Jedda* nearly to breaking point. Nevertheless, such an interpretative presumption could be an important tool for securing human rights compliance with respect to UNSC decisions: if the Security Council wishes to release States from their human rights obligations, it will have to do so through clear and unambiguous language – a rare occurrence in UNSC resolutions.[94]

At the same time, these judgments could be considered as indirectly reviewing the relevant resolutions of the UN Security Council. Furthermore, the CJEU's ruling in *Kadi*, discussed below (Section V(B)), may embolden Member States to conduct a constitutional review of UNSC resolutions that do not conform with rule of law tenets.[95]

V. The EU as a New Legal Order of International Law

In *van Gend & Loos*,[96] the CJEU held that the EEC Treaty was 'more than an agreement which merely creates mutual obligations between the contracting states'. Indeed:

> the states have acknowledged that Community law has an authority which can be invoked by their nationals before [national] courts and tribunals. The conclusion to be drawn from this is that the Community constitutes a new legal order of international law for the benefit of which the states have limited their sovereign rights, albeit within limited fields, and the subjects of which comprise not only Member States but also their nationals. Independently of the legislation of Member States, Community law therefore not only imposes obligations on individuals but is also intended to confer upon them rights that become part of their legal heritage.

Subsequently, the Court elaborated on what the new legal order entailed in *Costa v ENEL*:[97]

> By contrast with ordinary international treaties, the EEC Treaty has created its own legal system which, on the entry into force of the Treaty, became an integral part of the legal systems of the Member States and which their courts are bound to apply.
>
> By creating a Community of unlimited duration, having its own institutions, its own personality, its own legal capacity and capacity of representation on the international plane and, more particularly, real powers stemming from a limitation of sovereignty or a transfer of powers from

[92] *Al-Jedda v the United Kingdom* App no 27021/08 (ECtHR, 7 July 2001), para 102.
[93] *Al-Dulimi and Montana Management Inc v Switzerland* App no 5809/08 (ECtHR, 21 June 2016).
[94] M Milanovic, '*Al-Skeini* and *Al-Jedda* in Strasbourg' (2012) 23 *EJIL* 138.
[95] On review of UN sanctions decisions, see further A Tzanakopoulos, *Disobeying the Security Council: Countermeasures against Wrongful Sanctions* (Oxford, OUP, 2011).
[96] Judgment of 5 February 1963, *van Gend & Loos*, 26/62, EU:C:1963:1, 12.
[97] Judgment of 15 July 1964, *Costa*, 6/64, EU:C:1964:66, 593.

> the States to the Community, the Member States have limited their sovereign rights, albeit within limited fields, and have thus created a body of law which binds both their nationals and themselves.

Those canonical statements have become part of the settled case law of the CJEU, with some modifications. Notably, 'of international law' has been omitted after 'new legal order'. For example, in Opinion 2/13 (Accession of the European Union to the ECHR), the CJEU held that

> the founding treaties of the EU, unlike ordinary international treaties, established a new legal order, possessing its own institutions, for the benefit of which the Member States thereof have limited their sovereign rights, in ever wider fields, and the subjects of which comprise not only those States but also their nationals.[98]

The Court has also clarified, most recently in Opinion 1/09 (Agreement creating a Unified Patent Litigation System), that the essential characteristics of the EU legal order 'are in particular its primacy over the laws of the Member States and the direct effect of a whole series of provisions which are applicable to their nationals and to the Member States themselves'.[99]

All this taken together amounts to what the CJEU conceives of as 'the autonomy of EU Law'. In *Achmea*, the Court held in that regard that

> the autonomy of EU law with respect both to the law of the Member States and to international law is justified by the essential characteristics of the EU and its law, relating in particular to the constitutional structure of the EU and the very nature of that law. EU law is characterised by the fact that it stems from an independent source of law, the Treaties, by its primacy over the laws of the Member States, and by the direct effect of a whole series of provisions which are applicable to their nationals and to the Member States themselves. Those characteristics have given rise to a structured network of principles, rules and mutually interdependent legal relations binding the EU and its Member States reciprocally and binding its Member States to each other.[100]

This section examines the place of the EU within the international legal order. In what way can it be said that the Union is a *new* legal order, and in what way is it a new legal order of *international law*? The following section first examines what the essential characteristics of the EU legal order imply for its status as an international organisation. That examination is followed by an analysis of the attitude of the Union towards international law and the position of the latter in the EU legal order.

A. Direct Effect, Primacy, and the New Legal Order

It is clear from the passage quoted above that the Court's conception of international law as expressed in *van Gend & Loos* was rooted in the classical conception of international law as purely inter-State law, with only States as its subjects.[101] The Community, by contrast, had individual citizens as its subjects, who could invoke Community law through the doctrine of direct effect, which the Court also saw as being foreign to international law. The Commu-

[98] Opinion 2/13 (Accession of the European Union to the ECHR) of 18 December 2014, EU:C:2014:2454, para 157, referring to *van Gend & Loos* (n 96), and *Costa* (n 97), and to Opinion 1/09 (Agreement creating a Unified Patent Litigation System) of 8 March 2011, EU:C:2011:123, para 65. See also judgment of 28 April 2015, *Commission v Council*, C-28/12, EU:C:2015:282, para 34.

[99] Opinion 1/09 (n 98) para 65.

[100] Judgment of 6 March 2018, *Achmea*, C-284/16, EU:C:2018:158, para 33.

[101] G De Baere, *Constitutional Principles of EU External Relations* (Oxford, OUP, 2008) 34.

nity, therefore, constituted a 'new legal order'.[102] It is now acknowledged by many that the new legal order was not entirely as new as the Court appeared to think it was.[103]

Indeed, the example of the PCIJ's judgment in *Jurisdiction of the Courts of Danzig*,[104] shows that in *van Gend & Loos*, the CJEU remained within the bounds of traditional international law in introducing the doctrine of direct effect into Community law.[105] The Court made direct effect conditional upon the fulfilment of criteria directly drawn from international law:[106] (i) direct effect must be consistent with 'the spirit, the general scheme and the wording of those provisions';[107] and (ii) the provision in question must be 'clear and unconditional and not contingent on any discretionary implementing measure'.[108] These conditions, especially the second, can be explained by the original *ratio legis* of direct effect: the doctrine of the separation of powers. Courts are traditionally kept out of the area of foreign relations, for reasons of political sensitivity, diplomacy, national security, and because much scope for negotiation and manoeuvre is deemed necessary. The formulation of the commitments agreed is frequently vague or ambiguous, and 'programmatic' terms have often resulted in little involvement of courts. Only where unequivocal rights and duties are at stake, would judicial intervention be conceivable.[109]

The Court further elaborated its conception of the core of the EU legal order in *Costa v ENEL*,[110] in which it affirmed the primacy of EU law over national law, and *Simmenthal*,[111] in which the Court ruled that national courts have a duty to disapply national provisions that conflict with EU law, and must not wait for the national constitutional court to set the national provisions aside.[112]

Arguably, 'supremacy', 'primacy' or 'precedence' in EU law, founded on the duty of loyalty,[113] are essentially used interchangeably as 'appropriate synonyms'[114] of *pacta sunt servanda*. In *Costa v ENEL*, the CJEU held that:

> The integration into the laws of each Member State of provisions which derive from the Community, and more generally the terms and the spirit of the Treaty, make it impossible for

[102] O Spiermann, 'The Other Side of the Story: An Unpopular Essay on the Making of the European Community Legal Order' (1999) 10 *EJIL* 763, 766; note, eg, that the ICJ in the *LaGrand* case (n 24) para 77 ruled that Art 36(1) VCCR creates individual rights.

[103] For a general discussion, see eg D Wyatt, 'New Legal Order, or Old?' (1982) 7 *ELR* 147; B de Witte, 'Retour à "Costa": La primauté du droit communautaire à la lumière du droit international' (1984) *Revue trimestrielle de droit européen* 425; P Eleftheriadis, 'Aspects of European Constitutionalism' (1996) 21 *ELR* 32; A Verhoeven, *The European Union in Search of a Democratic and Constitutional Theory* (The Hague, Kluwer, 2002) 98–100; R Barents, *The Autonomy of Community Law* (The Hague, Kluwer, 2004).

[104] See above (n 1) 17–18.

[105] De Baere (n 101) 35; on the distinction between direct effect and direct applicability (which is not always made by the CJEU), see eg A Arnull, *The European Union and its Court of Justice* (Oxford, OUP, 2006) 185–87.

[106] See also Verhoeven (n 103) 311–12.

[107] *van Gend & Loos* (n 96).

[108] See eg judgment of 15 January 1986, *Hurd*, 44/84, EU:C:1986:2, para 47; and, specifically with respect to the direct effect of directives, judgment of 4 October 2018, *Kantarev*, C-571/16, EU:C:2018:807, para 98.

[109] S Prechal, 'Does Direct Effect Still Matter?' (2000) 37 *CMLR* 1047, 1065. See further below, Section V(B)(iii)(a).

[110] See above (n 97).

[111] Judgment of 9 March 1978, *Simmenthal*, 106/77, EU:C:1978:49. See also judgment of 22 October 1998, *IN. CO. GE.'90 and others*, C-10/97 to C-22/97, EU:C:1998:498, para 21 (holding that it could not 'be inferred from the judgment in *Simmenthal* that the incompatibility with Community law of a subsequently adopted rule of national law has the effect of rendering that rule of national law non-existent. Faced with such a situation, the national court is, however, obliged to disapply that rule, provided always that this obligation does not restrict the power of the competent national courts to apply, from among the various procedures available under national law, those which are appropriate for protecting the individual rights conferred by Community law').

[112] De Baere (n 101) 36.

[113] De Baere and Roes (n 3) 840.

[114] cp Spiermann (n 102) 785 (with respect to precedence).

> the States, as a corollary, to accord precedence to a unilateral and subsequent measure over a legal system accepted by them on a basis of reciprocity. The executive force of Community law cannot vary from one State to another in deference to subsequent domestic laws, without jeopardizing the attainment of the objectives of the Treaty [intended by[115]] Article 5(2) [now Article 4(3) TEU] and giving rise to the discrimination prohibited by Article 7 [now Article 18 TFEU].[116]

It has often been argued that the primacy of EU law differs from the supremacy of international law.[117] In several paragraphs of the *Costa* judgment, the CJEU seemingly contrasted the EU legal order with those established by 'ordinary international treaties'. While the latter leave contracting parties the choice as to form and methods, including the choice between a 'monist' and a 'dualist' attitude towards international law, the EU Treaties are 'an integral part of the legal systems of the Member States' which their courts 'are bound to apply'.[118] In assessing compliance with obligations, international law only looks at the result but leaves the contracting parties free as to the means to attain that result ('external primacy'). EU law primacy is said to be different, because it is also concerned with how the Member States implement their EU law obligations ('internal primacy'). The Court established internal primacy by presenting EU law as different from international law and as in some way part of national law. This was intended to convince national courts in dualist Member States not to treat EU law as they would allegedly treat international law, that is, by transposing it, and applying the maxim *lex posterior derogat priori* in case of conflict with national law.[119]

However, as to actual content, there is arguably no such contrast between EU law and international law.[120] 'Internal primacy' is not specific to EU law but is inherent in the *pacta sunt servanda* principle applied in international law.[121] International law as a rule simply does not have the same judicial tools (most importantly the preliminary ruling procedure)[122] at its disposal to fully develop this consequence of *pacta sunt servanda*.[123] In other words, States are obliged to ensure the internal primacy of international law, but they do so in accordance with their own national constitutions. As a consequence, the existing potential in international law is only rarely realised, as its effectiveness is at the mercy of municipal courts.[124] In the EU legal order, by contrast, the preliminary ruling procedure occupies a central and unique place.[125] This procedure allows for ex ante control over compatibility of

[115] De Baere and Roes (n 3) 840, fn 55.
[116] *Costa* (n 97) 593–94. cp K Lenaerts and JA Gutiérrez-Fons, 'To Say What the Law of the EU Is: Methods of Interpretation and the European Court of Justice' (2014) 20 *Columbia Journal of European Law* 3, 25 citing this passage as an example of 'consequentialist interpretation'.
[117] See further De Baere and Roes (n 3) 840–41.
[118] *Costa* (n 97) 593.
[119] See Spiermann (n 102) 763.
[120] De Witte (n 103) 425.
[121] See De Baere and Roes (n 3) 841–42.
[122] Art 267 TFEU, on which see K Lenaerts, I Maselis and K Gutman (JT Nowak ed), *EU Procedural Law* (Oxford, OUP, 2014) chapters 6, 10, and 24.
[123] cp C Leben, 'Hans Kelsen and the Advancement of International Law' (1998) 9 *EJIL* 287, 291–92, noting that, for Kelsen, the introduction of a judicial organ with compulsory jurisdiction is the turning point in the transition from a decentralised legal order to a more centralised and more effective legal order, and citing the CJEU as an example. See H Kelsen, *Peace Through Law* (Chapel Hill, University of North Carolina Press, 1944) 73. See also Chapter 1.III.B.
[124] Leben (n 123) 297.
[125] JHH Weiler, 'The Transformation of Europe' (1991) 100 *Yale Law Journal* 2403.

national law with Union law,[126] in contrast with general international law, which normally only acts ex post, by way of international responsibility. The purpose of the preliminary ruling procedure, the CJEU has held from early on, is that of harmonising the interpretation of EU law.[127] This emphasis on uniformity, De Witte argues, was an additional reason for the Court to speak out on internal primacy as well.[128] However, it is important to note that the CJEU framed the issue not as a conflict between municipal law and international law, but between two types of municipal law, one of which (EEC law) took precedence over the other. As Spiermann has pointed out, that does constitute a departure from international law, but only in the sense that the CJEU appears to have been more deferential to state sovereignty than general international law would be.[129]

While general international law may often lack the judicial machinery the EU has at its disposal, the binding nature of international law and the obligations flowing from it appear to be conceptually the same and based on the same premise of good faith or loyalty as those flowing from primacy in EU law.[130] Equipped as it is with a formidable enforcement machinery largely lacking in other treaty-based systems or indeed in general international law, EU law could perhaps accurately be described as 'successful international law'[131] or at least 'uncommonly successful'[132] or 'particularly effective'[133] international law. Nevertheless, a glance at the long list of cases[134] brought by the European Commission before the CJEU against Member States for failure to fulfil their obligations under EU law[135] leaves no doubt that EU law too is not invariably as diligently implemented as it ought to be. The difference with general international law is therefore one of degree, not of kind. The EU may constitute an exceptional international legal order, but its very existence – which could possibly be emulated by other such orders – signals that the monism-dualism distinction is not satisfactory. Since *van Gend & Loos*, 'dualist' Member States could no longer prevent individuals from directly invoking EU law before domestic courts, a process which inevitably implies a degree of monism, especially in combination with primacy, as has been clear since *Costa v ENEL*.

126 Though only indirectly. See eg judgments of 26 January 2010, *Transportes Urbanos y Servicios Generales*, C-118/08, EU:C:2010:39, para 23; and of 26 July 2017, *Europa Way and Persidera*, C-560/15, EU:C:2017:593, para 35 (recalling that although it is not the task of the Court, in preliminary ruling proceedings, to rule upon the compatibility of provisions of national law with EU law, it has jurisdiction to give the national court full guidance on the interpretation of EU law in order to enable it to determine the issue of compatibility for the purposes of the case before it).

127 Judgment of 6 April 1962, *de Geus*, 13/61, EU:C:1962:11, 51. See more recently *Achmea* (n 100) para 37 (holding that the judicial system of the EU 'has as its keystone the preliminary ruling procedure provided for in Article 267 TFEU, which, by setting up a dialogue between one court and another, specifically between the Court of Justice and the courts and tribunals of the Member States, has the object of securing uniform interpretation of EU law, thereby serving to ensure its consistency, its full effect and its autonomy as well as, ultimately, the particular nature of the law established by the Treaties').

128 De Witte (n 103) 434–35 and 440–42.

129 Spiermann (n 102) 773–75.

130 De Baere and Roes (n 3) 845.

131 Leben (n 123) 298.

132 De Baere and Roes (n 3) 845.

133 A Pellet, 'Les fondements juridiques internationaux du droit communautaire' (1994) *Collected Courses of the Academy of European Law* 221; and KS Ziegler, 'International Law and EU law: Between Asymmetric Constitutionalisation and Fragmentation' in A Orakhelashvili (ed), *Research Handbook on the Theory and History of International Law* (Cheltenham, Edward Elgar, 2011) 272, also arguing that the 'constitutionalisation' of the EU is at the same time a feature of the 'constitutionalisation' of international law (268–69).

134 See www.curia.europa.eu.

135 Pursuant to Arts 258–260 TFEU, on which see Lenaerts, Maselis and Gutman (Nowak ed) (n 122) chapter 5; L Prete, *Infringement Proceedings in EU Law* (Alphen aan den Rijn, Kluwer, 2017).

B. International Law in the EU Legal Order

Having established that the EU constitutes an international legal order that cuts across the classic dichotomy between monism and dualism, the question arises whether a similar qualification applies to the position of general international law in the EU legal order. The following examines that issue with respect to a number of sources of international law, notably treaties, customary international law, and acts of other international organisations.[136]

i. Treaties

Article 216(2) of the Treaty on the functioning of the EU (TFEU) provides for agreements concluded by the Union to be 'binding upon the institutions of the Union and on its Member States'. Such agreements prevail over EU acts,[137] and their provisions form an integral part of the EU legal order as from their entry into force.[138] A number of consequences follow from that position. First, the CJEU has jurisdiction to review the validity of an agreement concluded by the Union in the light of EU constitutional law and international law binding on the Union. Second, the validity of an EU act may be affected by the fact that it is incompatible with rules of international law. Third, Member States are under a duty under Article 216(2) TFEU to implement those parts of an international convention for which the Union has declared competence and to refrain from bringing international disputes against each other relating to those parts. In what follows, these consequences will be briefly addressed in turn.

First, in *Western Sahara Campaign UK*, the CJEU held that the provisions of international agreements concluded by the Union must be entirely compatible with the Treaties and with EU constitutional principles.[139] More specifically, the Court held that first, the substantive content of such agreements must be compatible with the rules governing the powers of the EU institutions and with the relevant rules of substantive law, and second, the procedure adopted for their conclusion must comply with the formal and procedural rules applicable under EU law. The Court also recalled that the EU is bound, when exercising its powers, 'to observe international law in its entirety, including not only the rules and principles of general and customary international law, but also the provisions of international conventions that are binding on it'. On that basis, the Court concluded that it had jurisdiction to assess whether an international agreement concluded by the EU is compatible with the Treaties and with the rules of international law which, in accordance with the Treaties, are binding on the Union.[140] Finally, the Court clarified that in a situation where the Court has received a request for a preliminary ruling concerning the validity of an

[136] See PJ Kuijper, J Wouters, F Hoffmeister, G De Baere and T Ramopoulos, *The Law of EU External Relations: Cases, Materials, and Commentary on the EU as an International Legal Actor*, 2nd edn (Oxford, OUP, 2015) 695–796.

[137] Judgments of 21 December 2011, *Air Transport Association of America and others (ATAA)*, C-366/10, EU:C:2011:864, para 50; and of 18 March 2014, *Z.*, C-363/12, EU:C:2014:159, para 71. On the latter judgment, see G De Baere, 'Shall I Be Mother? The Prohibition on Sex Discrimination, the UN Disability Convention, and the Right to Surrogacy Leave under EU Law' (2015) 74 *Cambridge Law Journal* 44–48.

[138] Judgment of 30 April 1974, *Haegeman*, 181/73, EU:C:1974:41, para 5; *ATAA* (n 137) para 73; *Western Sahara Campaign UK* (n 70) para 46.

[139] *Western Sahara Campaign UK* (n 70) para 46, effectively confirming what it had held in the judgment of 3 September 2008, *Kadi and Al Barakaat International Foundation v Council and Commission (Kadi 2008)*, C-402/05 P and C-415/05 P, EU:C:2008:461, para 285.

[140] *Western Sahara Campaign UK* (n 70) paras 46–48.

international agreement concluded by the Union, that request must be understood as relating to the EU act approving the conclusion of that international agreement. However, the review of validity that the Court may be required to carry out in that context can nonetheless encompass the legality of that act in the light of the actual content of the international agreement at issue.[141]

Second, the validity of an EU act may be affected by the fact that it is incompatible with rules of international law when a number of conditions are fulfilled as outlined notably by the CJEU in *Intertanko*[142] and *Air Transport Association of America.*[143] First, the EU must be bound by those rules.[144] Second, the nature and the broad logic of the international treaty in question must not preclude the CJEU from examining the validity of an EU act in the light of its provisions.[145] Third, the treaty provisions relied upon for the purpose of examining the validity of the EU act in question appear, as regards their content, to be unconditional and sufficiently precise;[146] that is, they contain a clear and precise obligation that is not subject, in its implementation or effects, to the adoption of any subsequent measure.[147] On that basis, direct effect of treaties in the EU legal order has been recognised with respect to the Lomé and Montreal Conventions,[148] but not with respect to the ECHR, the United Nations Convention on the Law of the Sea (UNCLOS),[149] the WTO Agreements,[150] and the United Nations Convention on the Rights of Persons with Disabilities.[151]

It is worth pausing for a moment at the first of the three conditions with respect to international agreements outlined above, ie that the EU must be bound by the provision of the international agreement relied upon. That is obviously the case when the Union is a party to the agreement at issue.[152] The EU is also internally bound by an international agreement if the EU Treaties provide for the Union to exercise its competences in accordance with that agreement,[153] or if the agreement reflects customary international law, such as many provisions of the VCLT.[154] Nevertheless, the Union can also be bound by an international agreement if and in so far as, pursuant to the EU Treaties, the EU has assumed the powers previously exercised by its Member States in the field to which that international agreement

[141] ibid, paras 50–51, referring to *Kadi 2008* (n 139) paras 286–89.
[142] *Intertanko* (n 70).
[143] *ATAA* (n 137) paras 52–55. See further Chapter 6.
[144] See judgment of 12 December 1972, *International Fruit Company and others*, 21/72 to 24/72, EU:C:1972:115, para 7.
[145] See judgment of 9 September 2008, *FIAMM and others v Council and Commission*, C-120/06 P and C-121/06 P, EU:C:2008:476, para 110.
[146] Judgment of 10 January 2006, *IATA and ELFAA*, C-344/04, EU:C:2006:10, para 39.
[147] See judgment of 30 September 1987, *Demirel*, 12/86, EU:C:1987:400, para 14.
[148] See the list of relevant cases and the conventions concerned in Rosas (n 49) 77, fn 32.
[149] See *Intertanko* (n 70) para 64. See nevertheless *Bosphorus Queen Shipping* (n 70) para 44.
[150] cp eg Judgment of 23 November 1999, *Portugal v Council*, C-149/96, EU:C:1999:574, paras 41–47.
[151] See *Z* (n 137) paras 84–90.
[152] Art 216(2) TFEU.
[153] eg Art 78(1) TFEU, which provides for the Union to develop a 'common policy on asylum, subsidiary protection and temporary protection with a view to offering appropriate status to any third-country national requiring international protection and ensuring compliance with the principle of *non-refoulement*. This policy must be in accordance with the Geneva Convention of 28 July 1951 and the Protocol of 31 January 1967 relating to the status of refugees, and other relevant treaties'; as well as Art 18 of the Charter of Fundamental Rights of the EU, which provides that the right to asylum is to be 'guaranteed with due respect for the rules of the Geneva Convention of 28 July 1951 and the Protocol of 31 January 1967 relating to the status of refugees'. See below (n 163).
[154] *Western Sahara Campaign UK* (n 70), para 21.

applies: so-called 'functional succession'. As the Court made clear in *Intertanko*, the standard for a 'functional succession' to take place is rather high: the EU must have assumed, and thus the Member States must have transferred to it, all the powers which they previously exercised and which fall within the scope of the convention. The fact that one or more EU law acts may have the object or effect of incorporating into EU law certain provisions that are set out in an international agreement to which the EU is not itself a party is not sufficient for it to be 'bound' in the sense above, and hence for it potentially to trigger a review by the Court of the legality of the act or acts of EU law in the light of that agreement.[155] In *Air Transport Association of America*, the CJEU confirmed that what is needed is not just for the EU to have effectively taken over the place of the Member States in the international agreement in question, but also for that to have happened on the basis of *exclusive* competence. Functional succession at the international level is therefore crucially linked to exclusive competence at the EU level. The CJEU thereby follows the model of the only undisputable example of functional succession, namely the EU's position in the General Agreement on Tariffs and Trade (GATT).[156]

Nevertheless, the fact that the Member States are parties to a treaty is liable to have consequences for its interpretation. In light of the customary principle of good faith, which forms part of general international law, and of Article 4(3) of the Treaty on European Union (TEU) its specific expression in the EU legal order, the CJEU must interpret the EU act based on the treaty taking account of the text of that treaty.[157] This point was made by Advocate General Kokott in her Opinion in *Air Transport Association of America*,[158] but not included in the judgment. That said, in previous case law, neither the Advocates General nor the CJEU have provided clear guidance on what such an interpretation in conformity with international law would entail. However, the principle of consistent interpretation has allowed the CJEU to give 'indirect effect' to treaties to which the EU is not a party and to which it is thus technically not bound, such as the ECHR.[159]

Furthermore, EU Member State courts arguably respond differently to rules of international law, and in particular treaties, when at the same time EU law obligations are involved.[160] A core element in this appears to be the judicial architecture of the EU, with the CJEU playing the role of a catalyst through the preliminary ruling procedure. By attaching its authority and the EU principle of primacy to treaties, the CJEU can oblige national courts of EU Member States to leave aside rules of national law and to give full effect to EU law and hence to international law. The effect of the intervention by the CJEU should not be underestimated: strong supranational courts of regional integration organisations

[155] *Intertanko* (n 70) paras 49–50. See nevertheless *Bosphorus Queen Shipping* (n 70) para 44.

[156] *International Fruit Company* (n 144) paras 14–18. That corresponds to its exclusive competence regarding the common commercial policy as per Art 3(1)(e) TFEU. The question that remains is whether the CJEU would limit the possibility for functional succession strictly to EU adherence to international agreements on the basis of the a priori exclusive competences listed in Art 3(1) TFEU, or whether shared competences that have become exclusive through the operation of Arts 2(2) and 3(2) TFEU would also qualify.

[157] *Intertanko* (n 70) para 52.

[158] Opinion of AG Kokott in *Air Transport Association of America and others*, C-366/10, EU:C:2011:637, point 66.

[159] See Tietje (n 49) 68, submitting that 'the Court usually tries to interpret and apply Community law in full conformity with international standards, even though the EC might not be bound in strict legal terms to the international agreements in question'. See also *Intertanko* (n 70) para 52 and *Bosphorus Queen Shipping* (n 70) para 45 (with respect to MARPOL 73/78 (n 70)).

[160] See G De Baere and JT Nowak, 'The Right to "Not Prohibitively Expensive" Judicial Proceedings under the Aarhus Convention and the ECJ as an International (Environmental) Law Court: *Edwards and Pallikaropoulos*' (2016) 53 *CMLR* 1748.

like the EU can play an important role in the development and enforcement of international law.[161] The Union legal order in general and the CJEU in particular has functioned as a powerful catalyst for the effect of international treaties in the national legal orders of the Member States.[162] For the Court to play that role, it is not even strictly necessary that the Union should be a party to the international agreement in question:[163] as soon as EU law contains certain norms originating from international treaties, the Court acts as the guarantor of uniform interpretation and enforcement within the EU legal order.[164]

Third, and conversely, Member States must not violate the monopoly of the CJEU to interpret and apply Union law under Article 344 TFEU.[165] This point was at the heart of the so-called *Mox Plant* case, where the Commission brought a case against Ireland for having instituted dispute-settlement proceedings against the UK under UNCLOS concerning the MOX plant located at Sellafield (UK), even though the subject matter had been covered by the Community declaration of competence upon accession to UNCLOS.[166] Article 282 UNCLOS specifically regulates the relationship between obligations under that treaty and obligations under general, regional, or bilateral agreements:

> If the States Parties which are parties to a dispute concerning the interpretation or application of this Convention have agreed, through a general, regional or bilateral agreement or otherwise, that such dispute shall, at the request of any party to the dispute, be submitted to a procedure that entails a binding decision, that procedure shall apply in lieu of the procedures provided for in this Part, unless the parties to the dispute otherwise agree.

In its judgment, the CJEU emphasised that the Member States and the EU institutions have an obligation of close cooperation in fulfilling the commitments undertaken by them under joint competence when they conclude a mixed agreement (ie an agreement to which both the EU and the Member States are parties).[167] The Court held that this is so particu-

[161] See also A Nollkaemper, 'The Role of National Courts in Inducing Compliance with International and European Law – A Comparison' in M Cremona (ed), *Compliance and the Enforcement of EU Law* (Oxford, OUP, 2012) 188–93.

[162] See in that sense also Ziegler (n 133) 280–81, arguing that through its special enforcement instruments, EU law reinforces international law substantively and procedurally.

[163] That is well illustrated by the Court's case law with respect to the Refugee Convention. By generally aligning its case law with the Refugee Convention, the Court has enabled the Member States to align their judicial and administrative practices both with their international obligations under the Refugee Convention and their obligations under EU law. In that way, the CJEU, in particular through the preliminary ruling procedure, plays a critical role in providing within the EU the consistency and unity in application and implementation that the Refugee Convention lacked in its original set-up. That alignment of EU law with the Refugee Convention has now become part of settled case law: see judgments of 2 March 2010, *Salahadin Abdulla and others*, C-175/08, C-176/08, C-178/08 and C-179/08, EU:C:2010:105, paras 52–53, and most recently, of 13 September 2018, *Ahmed*, C-369/17, EU:C:2018:713, paras 40–41 and the case law cited there. See further G De Baere, 'The Court of Luxembourg Acting as an Asylum Court' in A Alen, V Joosten, R Leysen and W Verrijdt (eds), *Liberae Cogitationes: Liber Amicorum Marc Bossuyt* (Antwerp, Intersentia, 2013) 107–24.

[164] De Baere and Nowak (n 160) 1748–49.

[165] See G De Baere, 'EU Status in Other International Organizations' in R Schütze and T Tridimas (eds), *Oxford Principles of European Union Law*, Vol 1: The European Union Legal Order (Oxford, OUP, 2018) 1246–52.

[166] 'When Community rules exist but are not affected, in particular in cases of Community provisions establishing only minimum standards, the Member States have competence, without prejudice to the competence of the Community to act in this field. Otherwise competence rests with the Member States': judgment of 30 May 2006, *Commission v Ireland ('Mox Plant')*, C-459/03, EU:C:2006:345, paras 8 and 104. On this declaration see Opinion of AG Poiares Maduro in *Commission v Ireland ('Mox Plant')*, C-459/03, EU:C:2006:42, point 36. cp R Churchill and J Scott, 'The Mox Plant Litigation: The First Half-Life' (2004) 53 *ICLQ* 643–76.

[167] *Mox Plant* (n 166) para 175; see judgment of 4 November 1997, *Parfums Christian Dior*, C-337/95, EU:C:1997:517, para 36. On mixed agreements, see J Heliskoski, *Mixed Agreements as a Technique for Organizing*

larly when a Member State submits to an arbitral tribunal outside the Union framework a dispute essentially on undertakings resulting from a mixed agreement that relates to an area, in which the respective areas of competence of the Union and the Member States are liable to be closely interrelated.[168] In those circumstances, the obligation of close cooperation within the framework of a mixed agreement involved a duty to inform and consult the competent Union institutions prior to instituting dispute-settlement proceedings concerning the MOX plant within the framework of UNCLOS.[169] By bringing proceedings under the UNCLOS dispute-settlement system, without having first informed and consulted the competent Union institutions, Ireland had therefore failed to comply with its duty of cooperation under Articles 4(3) TEU and 192 EURATOM.[170]

However, what would happen if the international agreement in question does not contain a provision such as Article 282 UNCLOS, containing a 'friendly' conflict rule with respect to other dispute settlement mechanisms? The absence of such a rule in the ECHR was one of the elements that led the CJEU in Opinion 2/13 to the conclusion that the Draft agreement on the accession of the EU to the ECHR was liable to affect Article 344 TFEU. Opinion 2/13 inevitably appears to imply that provisions in an international agreement much like Article 344 TFEU, which prevent parties from bringing disputes pertaining to the agreement in question before other dispute settlement mechanisms, are inherently problematic.[171]

Further building on that case law, the CJEU in *Achmea* contrasted commercial arbitration with the arbitration procedure set up by the Agreement on encouragement and reciprocal protection of investments between the Kingdom of the Netherlands and the Czech and Slovak Federative Republic (the BIT).[172] With respect to commercial arbitration, the Court held that the requirements of efficient arbitration proceedings justify the review of arbitral awards by the courts of the Member States being limited in scope, provided that the fundamental provisions of EU law can be examined in the course of that review and, if necessary, be the subject of a reference to the CJEU for a preliminary ruling. By contrast, the Court considered arbitration proceedings such as those referred to in Article 8 of the BIT to be different from commercial arbitration proceedings. The fundamental difference, according to the Court, lay in the fact that while the latter originate in the freely expressed wishes of the parties, the former derive from a treaty by which Member States agree to remove from the jurisdiction of their own courts, and hence from the system of judicial remedies which the second subparagraph of Article 19(1) TEU requires them to establish in the fields covered by EU law, disputes which may concern the application or interpretation of EU law. Consequently, the Court considered that, by concluding the BIT,

the International Relations of the European Community and Its Member States (The Hague, Kluwer, 2001); C Hillion and P Koutrakos (eds), *Mixed Agreements Revisited: The EU and Its Member States in the World* (Oxford, Hart, 2010); G De Baere, 'EU External Action' in Barnard and Peers (n 31) 746–48. In Opinion 2/15 (EU-Singapore Free Trade Agreement) of 16 May 2017, EU:C:2017:376, para 29, the CJEU defined a mixed agreement simply as an agreement that has to be 'signed and concluded both by the European Union and by each of its Member States'.

[168] *Mox Plant* (n 166) para 176.

[169] ibid, para 179.

[170] ibid, para 182 and see also Opinion of AG Poiares Maduro in *Mox Plant* (n 166), points 57–58.

[171] See eg Art 23(1) of the WTO Understanding on Rules and Procedures Governing the Settlement of Disputes (adopted 15 April 1994, entered into force 1 January 1995) 1869 UNTS 401: 'When Members seek the redress of a violation of obligations or other nullification or impairment of benefits under the covered agreements or an impediment to the attainment of any objective of the covered agreements, they shall have recourse to, and abide by, the rules and procedures of this Understanding'.

[172] *Achmea* (n 100) paras 54–55.

the Member States parties to it established a mechanism for settling disputes between an investor and a Member State which could prevent those disputes from being resolved in a manner that ensures the full effectiveness of EU law, even though they might concern the interpretation or application of that law. While the CJEU recalled that an international agreement providing for the establishment of a court responsible for the interpretation of its provisions and whose decisions are binding on the institutions, including the CJEU, is not in principle incompatible with EU law, provided that the autonomy of the EU and its legal order is respected, it held that, apart from the fact that the disputes falling within the jurisdiction of the arbitral tribunal referred to in Article 8 of the BIT may relate to the interpretation both of that agreement and of EU law, the possibility of submitting those disputes to a body which is not part of the judicial system of the EU is provided for by an agreement which was concluded not by the EU but by Member States. According to the Court, that calls into question not only the principle of mutual trust between the Member States but also the preservation of the particular nature of the law established by the Treaties, ensured by the preliminary ruling procedure provided for in Article 267 TFEU, and is therefore incompatible with the principle of sincere cooperation in Article 4(3) TEU. Article 8 of the BIT therefore has an adverse effect on the autonomy of EU law. Consequently, the Court concluded that Articles 267 and 344 TFEU preclude a provision in an international agreement concluded between Member States under which an investor from one of those Member States may, in the event of a dispute concerning investments in the other Member State, bring proceedings against the latter Member State before an arbitral tribunal whose jurisdiction that Member State has undertaken to accept.[173] It remains to be seen how that conclusion will impact on the Court's assessment of the compatibility of investor-State dispute resolution mechanisms contained in trade agreements to which the EU is or wishes to become a party.[174]

ii. Customary International Law

Since the entry into force of the Lisbon Treaty, the CJEU appears to start its analysis of the effect of general or customary international law with a reference to Article 3(5) TEU, pursuant to which the Union is to contribute to the strict observance and the development

[173] *Achmea* (n 100) paras 56–60.

[174] See request for an Opinion 1/17, currently pending before the CJEU, on the compatibility with the Treaties of the mechanism for the resolution of investment disputes between investors and States as contained in the Comprehensive Economic and Trade Agreement between Canada, of the one part, and the European Union and its Member States, of the other part, signed in Brussels on 30 October 2016. See further also, on the one hand, *Micula* v *Commission*, T-694/15 and *Micula and others* v *Commission*, T-704/15, both pending before the General Court of the EU, and on the other hand, High Court of Justice of England and Wales, Queen's Bench Division (Commercial Court), *Micula & others v Romania & another* [2017] Bus LR 1147, [2017] EWHC 31 (Comm), [2017] WLR(D) 35 (20 January 2017), in which the High Court stayed the enforcement of the International Centre for Settlement of Investment Disputes (ICSID) award in *Micula v Romania* (ICSID Case No ARB/05/20), 'pending the resolution of the claimants' proceedings in the European court seeking the annulment of the Commission's Final Decision of 30 March 2015' (ie Commission Decision (EU) 2015/1470 of 30 March 2015 on State aid SA.38517 (2014/C) (ex 2014/NN) implemented by Romania [Arbitral award *Micula v Romania* of 11 December 2013 (notified under document C(2015) 2112)], [2015] OJ L232/43), 'because the Commission's Final Decision prohibits Romania from paying the Award, and the "principle of sincere cooperation" in Art 4(3) TEU as interpreted both in European and in English case law precludes national courts from taking decisions which conflict with a decision of the Commission'. The Arbitral Tribunal that rendered the Award was established pursuant to the bilateral investment treaty entered into between the Government of the Kingdom of Sweden and the Government of Romania on the Promotion and Reciprocal Protection of Investments on 1 April 2003 (ie the Sweden/Romania BIT).

of international law. The Court has derived from that provision the obligation for the EU to observe international law in its entirety when it adopts an act, including customary international law, which is binding upon the EU institutions.[175]

The CJEU has relied on the case law of the ICJ and the PCIJ, as well as on a number of international agreements, as a basis for determining the status in international law of the principles at issue. Such reliance has become habitual, and is a notable example of deference towards the ICJ and towards international law more broadly,[176] as well as arguably a technique to mitigate the risk of conflicting interpretations threatening the consistency of international law.[177]

For example, in *Air Transport Association of America*, the CJEU regarded the principles that each State has complete and exclusive sovereignty over its airspace, that no State may validly purport to subject any part of the high seas to its sovereignty, and the principle of freedom to fly over the high seas, as 'embodying the current state of customary international maritime and air law'. Moreover, it noted that they had been respectively codified in Article 1 of the Chicago Convention,[178] Article 2 of the 1958 Geneva Convention on the High Seas,[179] and the third sentence of Article 87(1) UNCLOS. By contrast, as regards the principle that aircrafts overflying the high seas are subject to the exclusive jurisdiction of the State in which they are registered, the CJEU held that there existed insufficient evidence to establish that the principle of customary international law pursuant to which a vessel on the high seas is in principle governed only by the law of its flag State, and to which the Court had referred in *Poulsen and Diva Navigation*,[180] would apply by analogy to aircraft overflying the high seas.[181]

Furthermore, in *Front Polisario*, the Court referred to 'the customary principle of self-determination referred to in particular in Article 1 of the Charter of the United Nations' as a principle of international law applicable to all non-self-governing territories and to all peoples who have not yet achieved independence, a legally enforceable right *erga omnes*, and one of the essential principles of international law.[182]

In *ATAA*, the CJEU also examined the conditions under which customary international law could be relied upon by individuals for the purpose of examining the validity of an EU act. The Court found that this is subject to two conditions. First, those principles should be

[175] *ATAA* (n 137) para 101. On the status of customary international law in EU law, see also the Opinion of AG Jacobs in *Racke*, C-162/96, EU:C:1997:582.

[176] See also Kuijper (n 72) 95.

[177] J Pauwelyn, 'Europe, America and the "Unity" of International Law' in Wouters, Nollkaemper and de Wet (n 49) 212. See also ILC, 'Fragmentation of International Law: Difficulties Arising from the Diversification and Expansion of International Law', Report of the Study Group of the International Law Commission, Finalised by Martti Koskenniemi, UN Doc A/CN.4/L.682. See further Chapter 1, Section III(E).

[178] Referring to the *Military and Paramilitary Activities in and against Nicaragua* (Nicaragua v United States of America) [1986] ICJ Rep 392, para 212.

[179] Convention on the High Seas (adopted 29 April 1958, entered into force 30 September 1962) 450 UNTS 11. The CJEU also referred to the *SS Lotus* [1927] PCIJ Series A, No 10, 25.

[180] *Poulsen and Diva Navigation* (n 71) para 22.

[181] *ATAA* (n 137) paras 103–106.

[182] Judgment of 21 December 2016, *Council v Front Polisario*, C-104/16 P, EU:C:2016:973, para 88, referring to *Western Sahara* (Advisory Opinion) [1975] ICJ Rep 12, paras 54–56, and *East Timor* (Portugal v Australia) [1995] ICJ Rep 90, para 29 and the case law cited. It also relied on the customary rule codified in Art 29 VCLT, which provides that, unless a different intention appears from the treaty or is otherwise established, that treaty is binding upon each party in respect of its entire territory (paras 94–98), but without citing any sources. For a commentary, see eg J Odermatt, 'Council of the European Union v Front populaire pour la libération de la saguia-el-hamra et du rio de oro (Front Polisario) – Case C-104/16 P' (2017) 111 *AJIL* 731.

capable of calling into question the competence of the EU to adopt that act;[183] and second, the act in question must be liable to affect rights which the individual derives from EU law or to create obligations under EU law in his regard.[184] It is important to note that these conditions differ from those applicable to international agreements as outlined above.[185]

In her Opinion in *ATAA*, Advocate General Kokott proposed that principles of customary international law ought to be subject to the same conditions as provisions of international agreements in order to form the basis of a review of legality, and ruled out that possibility in the case at hand.[186] By contrast, the CJEU held that even though the principles at issue appeared only to have the effect of creating obligations between States, it was nevertheless possible for the claimants in the main proceedings to rely on them and for the Court to examine the validity of an EU measure in their light. In other words, contrary to what was feared after the judgment in *Intertanko*,[187] the CJEU did not impose the same strict conditions on principles of customary international law as it did on provisions of international agreements in order for them to be capable of being relied upon. However, the Court immediately toned down the impact of its principled stance by adding that since a principle of customary international law does not have the same degree of precision as a provision of an international agreement, judicial review must necessarily be limited to the question whether, in adopting the act in question, the EU institutions made manifest errors of assessment concerning the conditions for applying those principles,[188] citing its judgment in *Racke* to that effect.[189]

In other words, the reason why the CJEU did not apply the same conditions to principles of customary international law and to international agreements appears to be that it believes that those conditions can *never* be met by customary international law. One wonders why an intermediate position between that of the CJEU and the Advocate General would not be preferable: if principles of customary international law appear, as regards their content, to be unconditional and sufficiently precise, individuals should be able to rely on them in the same way as with respect to international agreements. If such principles miss the necessary degree of precision, they could be relied on for the marginal review suggested by the CJEU.[190] So far, the CJEU has not yet declared an act of secondary EU law invalid on the ground of incompatibility with a customary norm.

Nevertheless, the CJEU has relied on customary international law in order to interpret international agreements concluded by the EU. For example, in *Brita*,[191] the Court invoked Article 34 VCLT and the principle of general international law that it codifies – the relative effect of treaties and their legal neutrality towards third parties (*pacta tertiis nec nocent nec prosunt*) – for the purposes of delineating the scope of application of the EC-Israel Association Agreement. The CJEU held that the EU's agreement with Israel could not as such

[183] Judgments of 27 September 1988, *Ahlström Osakeyhtiö and others v Commission ('Wood Pulp')*, 89/85, 104/85, 114/85, 116/85, 117/85 and 125/85 to 129/85, EU:C:1988:447, paras 14–18; and of 24 November 1993, *Mondiet*, C-405/92, EU:C:1993:906, paras 11–16.

[184] *ATAA* (n 137) para 107.

[185] G De Baere and C Ryngaert, 'The ECJ's Judgment in Air Transport Association of America and the International Legal Context of the EU's Climate Change Policy' (2013) 18 *European Foreign Affairs Review* 394.

[186] AG Kokott (n 158) points 134–38.

[187] Eg J Wouters and P De Man, 'Case-Note to European Court of Justice, International Association of Independent Tanker Owners (Intertanko) Case C-308/06' (2009) 103 *AJIL* 555, 558.

[188] *ATAA* (n 137) paras 109–10.

[189] *Racke* (n 71) para 52.

[190] De Baere and Ryngaert (n 185) 397–98.

[191] Judgment of 25 February 2010, *Brita*, C-386/08, EU:C:2010:91.

create an obligation on a third party (Palestinian customs authorities) to refrain from exercising their competence under the EC-PLO Protocol.[192] The same principle of international law formed the basis of the Court's appraisal in *Front Polisario* of the position of Western Sahara in the EU-Morocco Association Agreement and led to a similar conclusion.[193]

iii. Acts of International Organisations

International agreements to which the Union is a party quite often provide for certain bodies to be established. The Court of Justice has held that legally binding decisions taken by such bodies have in principle the same status as the international agreement itself. The Court did so first as regards decisions taken by the EEC–Turkey Association Council.[194] In Opinion 1/91, the Court confirmed that decisions of an Association Council, but equally in principle, any decision taken by an institution set up through an international agreement concluded by the Union, including decisions taken by a court set up by such an international agreement, become an integral part of the EU legal order.[195] The following section will take a closer look at the position of respectively WTO law and obligations on the basis of the UN Charter in the EU legal order.

a. WTO Law

A particular issue has arisen with respect to the status of WTO law in the EU legal order. In the preamble to the decision concluding the WTO Agreement, the Council of Ministers gave an indication of what it intended the status of WTO to be within the EU legal order: Recital 11 provides that 'by its nature, the Agreement establishing the World Trade Organization, including the Annexes thereto, is not susceptible to being directly invoked in Community or Member State courts'.[196]

However, this does not per se settle the debate as to the effect of WTO law within the Union legal order. The content of recital 11 is nowhere reflected in the decision as enacted, and the preamble to a Union act has no binding legal force.[197] Therefore, in the absence of an explicit determination by the parties, the effect of treaties within the EU legal order is for the CJEU to determine, and not for an institution that forms part of one of the parties to the agreement, and even less in a non-binding recital to the internal act concluding the agreement. Recital 11 is merely an indication as to the intention of one of the parties to the WTO Agreements and as such at most a supplementary means of interpretation in the sense of Article 32 VCLT. In his Opinion in *Hermès*, Advocate General Tesauro argued that, since there is no provision agreed to by all the contracting parties that excludes direct effect, the recital in question cannot prevent the Court from coming to a different conclusion.[198]

[192] ibid, para 52.

[193] *Front Polisario* (n 182) para 107.

[194] Judgment of 14 November 1989, *Greece v Commission*, 30/88, EU:C:1989:422, paras 12–13.

[195] Opinion 1/91 (First Opinion on the EEA Agreement) of 14 December 1991, EU:C:1991:490.

[196] Council Decision 94/800/EC of 22 December 1994 concerning the conclusion on behalf of the European Community, as regards matters within its competence, of the agreements reached in the Uruguay Round multilateral negotiations (1986–1994) [1994] OJ L336/1, final recital of the preamble.

[197] See judgments of 19 June 2014, *Karen Millen Fashions*, C-345/13, EU:C:2014:2013, para 31 and the case law cited therein, and of 13 September 2018, *Česká pojišťovna*, C-287/17, EU:C:2018:707, para 33.

[198] Opinion of AG Tesauro in *Hermès*, C-53/96, EU:C:1997:539, point 24. Bourgeois has argued that recital 11 reflects the view traditionally held by most governments of EU Member States that trade policy, as part of foreign policy, is the domain of governments and that interference by courts is to be avoided in order to pursue fully the

The *International Fruit* case concerned the compatibility of certain regulations of the Commission with Article XI GATT. There, the Court confirmed that the task to determine the effect of GATT/WTO law within the EU legal order fell squarely within its jurisdiction, and determined that the obligations under the GATT did not meet the conditions for direct effect.[199] After the Marrakech Agreement had established the WTO and introduced an elaborate system of dispute settlement, many predicted that the CJEU would accept the direct effect of WTO law within the EU legal order. However, in an action brought by Portugal for the annulment of a Council Decision on agreements between the Community and Pakistan and India,[200] the Court maintained its pre-Marrakech stance. It referred inter alia to the need not to deprive the legislative or executive organs of the contracting parties from reaching negotiated solutions to disagreements and, controversially, to the fact that other contracting parties did not grant WTO law any direct effect, thereby introducing a political reciprocity argument.[201] The upshot is that, according to the CJEU's settled case law, 'given their nature and purpose, the WTO agreements are not in principle among the rules in the light of which the Court is to review the legality of measures adopted by the European Union institutions'.[202]

Nevertheless, in principle, the Court accepts two exceptions to the impossibility of reviewing EU acts on the basis of GATT/WTO law, the so-called *Fediol* and *Nakajima* exceptions, named after the judgments in which they were first recognised. In *Fediol*, the Court held that it would review an EU act on the basis of GATT/WTO law if the act in question explicitly refers to the relevant GATT/WTO rules.[203] The *Nakajima* exception

possibilities of resolving disputes by negotiation. If EU courts enforce WTO law, the political institutions would have their hands tied behind their backs. However, Bourgeois argues that this argument has become less persuasive as the flexibility of the GATT gave way to a determination by the WTO Dispute Settlement Body of who is legally right or wrong, with the only flexibility left being that with regard to remedies: JHJ Bourgeois, 'The European Court of Justice and the WTO: Problems and Challenges' in JHH Weiler (ed), *The EU, the WTO and the NAFTA: Towards a Common Law of International Trade* (Oxford, OUP, 2000) 114–15.

[199] *International Fruit Company* (n 144).

[200] Council Decision 96/386/EC of 26 February 1996 concerning the conclusion of Memoranda of Understanding between the European Community and the Islamic Republic of Pakistan and between the European Community and the Republic of India on arrangements in the area of market access for textile products [1996] OJ L153/47.

[201] *Portugal v Council* (n 150) paras 40 and 43–46 (holding that 'to require the judicial organs to refrain from applying the rules of domestic law which are inconsistent with the WTO agreements would have the consequence of depriving the legislative or executive organs of the contracting parties of the possibility [...] of entering into negotiated arrangements even on a temporary basis. [...] It is common ground, moreover, that some of the contracting parties, which are among the most important commercial partners of the Community, have concluded from the subject-matter and purpose of the WTO agreements that they are not among the rules applicable by their judicial organs when reviewing the legality of their rules of domestic law. Admittedly, the fact that the courts of one of the parties consider that some of the provisions of the agreement concluded by the Community are of direct application whereas the courts of the other party do not recognise such direct application is not in itself such as to constitute a lack of reciprocity in the implementation of the agreement [...]. However, the lack of reciprocity in that regard on the part of the Community's trading partners, in relation to the WTO agreements which are based on "reciprocal and mutually advantageous arrangements" and which must *ipso facto* be distinguished from agreements concluded by the Community, [...] may lead to disuniform application of the WTO rules. To accept that the role of ensuring that Community law complies with those rules devolves directly on the Community judicature would deprive the legislative or executive organs of the Community of the scope for manoeuvre enjoyed by their counterparts in the Community's trading partners.' See, however, Opinion of AG Ruiz-Jarabo Colomer in *Merck Genéricos – Produtos Farmacêuticos*, C-431/05, EU:C:2007:48, point 81, pointing out that if that is the real reason for which the Court refuses to acknowledge the direct effect of the WTO agreements, 'that applies only to fields in which compromise is genuinely possible'.

[202] See eg the judgment of 4 February 2016, *C & J Clark International*, C-659/13 and C-34/14, EU:C:2016:74, para 85 and the case law cited there.

[203] Judgment of 22 June 1989, *Fediol v Commission*, 70/87, EU:C:1989:254, paras 18–22.

pertains to the situation in which an EU act was adopted in order to comply with the international obligations of the Union under WTO law.[204] The Court tends to interpret the existing exceptions rather strictly. In particular, the fact that the Union adopts a measure specifically to comply with a decision of the Dispute Settlement Body (DSB) of the WTO is not sufficient to qualify for the *Nakajima* exception, as the Court made clear in *Van Parys*.[205] Indeed, even the failure to implement a DSB finding as to the breach of WTO law by the Union does not entail the non-contractual liability of the Union.[206] Finally, the Court has made it quite clear that the *Fediol* and *Nakajima* exceptions do not apply outside the area of WTO law.[207] The CJEU's approach to WTO law has evidently also had an effect on the approach taken by EU Member States' national courts, as is for example clear from the Belgian Court of Cassation's judgment in *Art Research & Contact*, in which it refused to grant direct effect to the WTO Agreement on Trade-Related Aspects of Intellectual Property Rights (TRIPS).[208]

Despite the principled view of the CJEU denying direct effect to WTO law, the Court does seem to attempt to achieve results that diverge as little as possible from WTO law obligations through 'WTO conform' interpretations, such as those adopted in *FTS International* and in *Ikea Wholesale*.[209]

b. Obligations on the Basis of the UN Charter

The relationship between EU law and obligations on the basis of the UN Charter also merits closer examination. As is well known, pursuant to Article 103 of the UN Charter, in the event of conflict with obligations arising out of any other international agreement, the obligations arising from the Charter prevail. The UN Charter also features prominently in the constituent Treaties of the EU. In particular, even though the EU is not a member of the UN and is not 'bound' by the UN Charter in the same way as it is by the WTO Agreements, the Treaties contain an obligation for the Union to respect the principles of the UN Charter.[210]

It is generally agreed that resolutions of the UN Security Council do not have direct effect in the domestic legal order of the EU or its Member States, unless they have been incorporated in that order;[211] nor does the UN Charter itself.[212] That being said, quite a

[204] Judgment of 7 May 1991, *Nakajima v Council*, C-69/89, EU:C:1991:186, paras 26–32.

[205] Judgment of 1 March 2005, *Van Parys*, C-377/02, EU:C:2005:121, paras 37–54.

[206] *FIAMM and others* (n 145) paras 106–33.

[207] It did so in the judgments of 13 January 2015, *Council and others v Vereniging Milieudefensie and Stichting Stop Luchtverontreiniging Utrecht*, C-401/12 P to C-403/12 P, EU:C:2015:4; and of 13 January 2015, *Council and Commission v Stichting Natuur en Milieu and Pesticide Action Network Europe*, C-404/12 P and C-405/12 P, EU:C:2015:5, which concerned the Aarhus Convention (on which see Chapter 20.II(A)(iv)).

[208] Belgian Court of Cassation (BE), *Art Research & Contact Naamloze Vennootschap v BS*, 11 May 2001, Case No C.00.0391.N.

[209] Judgments of 18 July 2007, *FTS International*, C-310/06, EU:C:2007:456, paras 15 and 19–25; and of 27 September 2007, *Ikea Wholesale*, C-351/04, EU:C:2007:547, paras 29–69.

[210] Arts 3(5), 21(1) and (2)(c) TEU. See further in general on the relationship between the EU and the UN the works cited in n 6 of the Introduction.

[211] eg Court of Cassation (FR), *Iraqi State v Corporation Dumez GTM (SA)*, 25 April 2006, para 2. cp Kuijper (n 72) 101, who argues that there exists a legitimacy problem with granting direct effect to UNSC resolutions in the EU legal order, since the Union is not a party to the UN Charter and the European Parliament 'has never had the chance to express itself on it'.

[212] eg Supreme Court (NL), *Association of Lawyers for Peace and others v Netherlands*, 6 February 2004, Case No C02/217HR, LJN: AN8071, para 3.4 (ruling that the prohibition of the use of force enshrined in Art 2(4) of

number of UNSC resolutions imposing sanctions on States or non-State entities have been incorporated into EU law by means of regulations whose substantive provisions thereby produce effect in the EU legal order.[213]

The relationship between obligations under the UN Charter and the constituent Treaties of the EU was the subject of the *Kadi* litigation, which concerned the implementation by the EU of sanctions taken by the UNSC against an individual suspected of terrorist acts. The then Court of First Instance held that EU acts implementing binding obligations under Chapter VII of the UN Charter could not be reviewed by it, except for their compliance with *jus cogens*.[214] On appeal, the Court of Justice overturned the Court of First Instance's judgment, taking the view that the respect for the UN Charter could not reach so far as to affect the protection of fundamental rights within the EU legal order. Thus, the primacy of international agreements has one clear limitation: it does not extend to primary Union law, including general principles of EU law, of which fundamental rights form an integral part.[215] The judgment of the Court of Justice in *Kadi* had a direct impact on the functioning of the UN, and led to the establishment[216] of the Office of the Ombudsperson,[217] to whom individuals, groups, undertakings or entities seeking to be removed from the UN Security Council's ISIL (Da'esh) and Al-Qaida Sanctions Committee List can submit their request for delisting.[218]

In the second *Kadi* case, the General Court followed the Court of Justice's approach, holding that its task was to ensure 'in principle the full review' of the lawfulness of the contested EU act in the light of fundamental rights, without affording it any immunity from jurisdiction on the ground that it gives effect to resolutions adopted by the UNSC under Chapter VII of the UN Charter. It did, however, precede that holding by a thinly-veiled criticism of the Court of Justice's judgment in the first *Kadi* case.[219] The General Court also held that, 'even if account is taken of the "Office of the Ombudsperson"', the UNSC had 'still not deemed it appropriate to establish an independent and impartial body responsible

the UN Charter, and the closely related provisions of Arts 42 and 51 were intended to protect States and could therefore not be invoked by a citizen before a national court).

[213] eg Council Regulation (EEC) No 990/93 of 26 April 1993 concerning trade between the European Economic Community and the Federal Republic of Yugoslavia (Serbia and Montenegro) [1993] OJ L102/14; Council Regulation (EC) No 881/2002 of 27 May 2002 imposing certain specific restrictive measures directed against certain persons and entities associated with Usama bin Laden, the Al-Qaida network and the Taliban [2002] OJ L139/9.

[214] Judgment of 21 September 2005, *Kadi v Council and Commission (Kadi 2005)*, T-315/01, EU:T:2005:332 paras 181–231. On *jus cogens* as a constraint on the UN Security Council, see Crawford (n 27) 420–24.

[215] *Kadi 2008* (n 139) paras 280–327.

[216] By UNSC Res 1904, 17 December 2009, UN Doc S/RES/1904.

[217] See the Opinion of AG Bot in *Commission and others v Kadi (Kadi 2013)*, C-584/10 P, C-593/10 P and C-595/10 P, EU:C:2013:176, point 83.

[218] The mandate of the Ombudsperson was most recently extended by UNSC Res 2368, 20 July 2017, UN Doc S/RES/2368.

[219] Judgment of 30 September 2010, *Kadi v Commission (Kadi 2010)*, T-85/09, EU:T:2010:418, paras 112–21: 'More fundamentally, certain doubts may have been voiced in legal circles as to whether the judgment of the Court of Justice in *Kadi* is wholly consistent with, on the one hand, international law and, more particularly, Articles 25 and 103 of the Charter of the United Nations and, on the other hand, the EC and EU Treaties, and more particularly Article 177(3) EC, Articles 297 EC and 307 EC, Article 11(1) EU and Article 19(2) EU (see, also Article 3(5) TEU and Article 21(1) and (2) TEU, as well as declaration No 13 of the Conference of the Representatives of the Governments of the Member States concerning the common foreign and security policy annexed to the Treaty of Lisbon, which stresses that "the [EU] and its Member States will remain bound by the provisions of the Charter of the United Nations and, in particular, by the primary responsibility of the Security council and of its members for the maintenance of international peace and security"[)]. […] The General Court acknowledges that those criticisms are not entirely without foundation'.

for hearing and determining, as regards matters of law and fact, actions against individual decisions taken by the Sanctions Committee'.[220] On appeal, the CJEU essentially confirmed its earlier approach and the General Court's analysis, relying both on judgments of the ECtHR and the Supreme Court of Switzerland, holding that

> despite the improvements added, in particular after the adoption of the contested regulation, the procedure for delisting and ex officio re-examination at UN level they do not provide to the person whose name is listed on the Sanctions Committee Consolidated List and, subsequently, in Annex I to Regulation No 881/2002, the guarantee of effective judicial protection, as the European Court of Human Rights, endorsing the assessment of the Federal Supreme Court of Switzerland, has recently stated in paragraph 211 of its judgment of 12 September 2012, Nada v. Switzerland (No 10593/08 […]).[221]

The hierarchical, pyramidal approach to the relationship between (what was then) Community Law and national law, empowering individuals, that was taken in the early days of the Community is arguably typical of Kelsenian monism. However, in the *Kadi* judgments, the CJEU has patently refused to endorse the subordinate place of the Union itself within the larger international legal system, essentially citing rule of law deficiencies at the international law level that the constitutional system underpinning the Union could not gloss over. In so doing, the CJEU has effectively installed a form of regional review of UN Security Council Resolutions.[222] More broadly, *Kadi* stands for the notion that international law will only be given effect in the domestic legal order to the extent that it comports with basic rule of law and due process guarantees. This approach is neither monist nor dualist, as it does not favour automatic incorporation of international law in the domestic legal order, nor does it require transformation, but instead makes the effect of international norms dependent on their substantive rule of law quality. This provides an illustration of the connection between the rule of law at the international and EU levels. The defects in how the rule of law operates at the international level bring the Union to a partial rejection of the existing international rules to the extent that they do not comply with internal rule of law standards. The *Kadi* judgments expose a systemic rule of law problem in the relationship between EU law and international law in general and between EU law and UN law in particular.[223]

This is arguably somewhat akin to the approach taken in the *Solange* cases, in which the German Constitutional Court emphasised the priority of German constitutional law over EU law to the extent that the fundamental rights protections provided by EU law would not rise to the level of protection provided by German constitutional law.[224] It could be argued

[220] ibid, para 128.

[221] Judgment of 18 July 2013, *Commission and others v Kadi (Kadi 2013)*, C-584/10 P, C-593/10 P and C-595/10 P, EU:C:2013:518, para 133.

[222] Crawford (n 27) 437–38.

[223] For a commentary on the *Kadi* cases and on the relationship between international law and EU law through the prism of the rule of law, see eg G De Baere, 'European Integration and the Rule of Law in Foreign Policy' in J Dickson and P Eleftheriadis (eds), *Philosophical Foundations of European Union Law* (Oxford, OUP, 2012) 374–80. See further eg D Halberstam and E Stein, 'The United Nations, the European Union, and the King of Sweden: Economic Sanctions and Individual Rights in a Plural World Order' (2009) 46 *Common Market Law Review* 13–72; G de Búrca, 'The European Court of Justice and the International Legal Order After Kadi' (2010) 51 *Harvard International Law Journal* 1–49; J Wouters, 'The tormented relationship between international law and EU law' in P Bekker, R Dolzer, and M Waibel (eds), *Making Transnational Law Work in the Global Economy: Essays in Honour of Detlev Vagts* (Cambridge, CUP, 2010) 198–221; A Cuyvers, '"Give me one good reason": The unified standard of review for sanctions after Kadi II" (2014) 51 *Common Market Law Review* 1759–1788.

[224] Federal Constitutional Court (DE), *Internationale Handelsgesellschaft v Einfuhr und Vorratsstelle für Getreide und Futtermittel ('Solange I')*, 29 May 1974, 37 BVerfGE 271; (1974) 2 CMLR 540; Federal Constitutional Court (DE), *Wünsche Handelsgesellschaft ('Solange II')*, 22 October 1986, 2 BvR 197/83; (1987) 3 CMLR 225.

that part of the reason the Court of Justice in *Kadi* came out so strongly in favour of fundamental rights was that it was well aware that national constitutional courts might be tempted to review EU measures considered unreviewable by the Court of Justice. The General Court appears to have hinted to the parallel with the *Solange* cases in its judgment, by noting that it was its task to ensure the full review of the lawfulness of the contested regulation in the light of fundamental rights '*so long as* the re-examination procedure operated by the Sanctions Committee clearly fails to offer guarantees of effective judicial protection' (emphasis added).[225] With the Court of Justice confirming with ever more vigour and emphasis the existential importance of the rule of law for the EU legal order,[226] and the UN Security Council sanctions regime not moving significantly closer to a possibility for independent judicial review,[227] that position is unlikely to change substantially in the foreseeable future.

VI. Concluding Remarks

Given the critical importance of national legal systems for the effective implementation of international law, the question of the relationship between international law and national law is of great practical relevance. That issue is also directly linked with the possibility for individuals to rely within their national constitutional systems on norms originating in international obligations. The present chapter examined both issues, and found that the classical position of international law in national legal systems and the corresponding possibility for individuals to rely on international law before national courts have gone through significant changes. Those evolutions are particularly marked within the legal order of the EU, which cuts across the standard dichotomy between monist and dualist

[225] *Kadi 2010* (n 219) paras 126–27, referring to *Kadi 2008* (n 139) para 322 and the Opinion of AG Poiares Maduro in *Kadi 2008* (n 39) point 54.

[226] See eg judgments of 28 March 2017, *Rosneft*, C-72/15, EU:C:2017:236, paras 72–73 ('As is apparent from both Article 2 TEU, which is included in the common provisions of the EU Treaty, and Article 21 TEU, concerning the European Union's external action, to which Article 23 TEU, relating to the CFSP, refers, one of the European Union's founding values is the rule of law [...] It may be added that Article 47 of the Charter, which constitutes a reaffirmation of the principle of effective judicial protection, requires, in its first paragraph, that any person whose rights and freedoms guaranteed by EU law are violated should have the right to an effective remedy before a tribunal in compliance with the conditions laid down in that article. It must be recalled that the very existence of effective judicial review designed to ensure compliance with provisions of EU law is of the essence of the rule of law'); 27 February 2018, *Associação Sindical dos Juízes Portugueses*, C-64/16, EU:C:2018:117, paras 30–45 (in order for effective judicial protection by courts or tribunals to be ensured 'maintaining such a court or tribunal's independence is essential, as confirmed by the second subparagraph of Article 47 of the Charter, which refers to the access to an "independent" tribunal as one of the requirements linked to the fundamental right to an effective remedy'); 25 July 2018, *Minister for Justice and Equality*, C-216/18 PPU, EU:C:2018:586, paras 63-67.

[227] See eg the dissenting opinion of President Schwebel in *Questions of Interpretation and Application of the 1971 Montreal Convention arising from the Aerial Incident at Lockerbie* (Libyan Arab Jamahiriya v United States of America) [1998] ICJ Rep 9, 64, concluding from the *travaux préparatoires*, and especially the episode of the failed Belgian proposal to introduce a limited possibility of review, that the ICJ was not and was not meant to be invested with a power of judicial review of decisions of the Security Council, and summing up: 'Judicial review, in varying forms, is found in a number of democratic polities, most famously that of the United States, where it was developed by the Supreme Court itself. But it is by no means a universal or even general principle of government or law. It is hardly found outside the democratic world and is not uniformly found in it. Where it exists internationally, as in the European Union, it is expressly provided for by treaty in specific terms. The United Nations is far from being a government, or an international organisation comparable in its integration to the European Union, and it is not democratic' (77–80).

constitutional systems. Furthermore, while remaining a legal order based on international law, the EU is equipped with uncommonly strong enforcement machinery, in particular through the preliminary ruling system, which it can also deploy to enforce international treaties to which the EU or its Member States are parties. At the same time, what the CJEU conceives of as the autonomy of EU law vis-à-vis national law and international law has also engendered tensions and even a certain antagonism with respect to other international systems, such as notably the structural problems in the relationship between the EU and UN legal systems as evident from the *Kadi* cases.

The more general lessons to be learned from the interactions between EU law and national constitutional law, and between international law and EU (constitutional) law, for the effect of international law in domestic courts and the empowerment of the individual in particular, is that advanced legal systems that provide a high level of legal protection to the individual do not necessarily give up their *acquis* in the face of international norms that have an arguably lower rule of law quality. After all, unlike what monism may appear to imply, the direct application of international law in domestic courts does not as a matter of course benefit the individual. It does if it is used as a shield against unwarranted government action, but it does not if the international norm itself unjustifiably targets the individual. In the latter case, a domestic constitutional norm or another international norm that is more protective of the individual may have to be relied on as a countervailing force. Nevertheless, as Crawford remarked with respect to the *Kadi* case law, 'it would be better if what can be achieved indirectly in Europe were available directly and universally'.[228]

Bibliography

Bleckmann, A, *Grundgesetz und Völkerrecht* (Berlin, Duncker & Humblot, 1975).

Crawford, J, *Chance, Order, Change: The Course of International Law* (The Hague, Hague Academy of International Law, 2014).

Daillier, P, 'Monisme et dualisme: un débat dépassé?' in Ben Achour, R and Laghmani, S (eds), *Droit international et droits interne, développements récents* (Paris, Pedone, 1999) 9–21.

De Witte, B, 'Retour à "Costa": La primauté du droit communautaire à la lumière du droit international' (1984) *Revue trimestrielle de droit européen* 425.

Follesdal, A, Wessel, RA and Wouters, J (eds), *Multilevel Regulation and the EU. The Interplay between Global, European and National Normative Processes* (Leiden – Boston, Martinus Nijhoff Publishers, 2008).

Hölscheidt, S, Ridinger, M and Zitterbart, A, Grundzüge des Völkerrechts und seine Bezüge zum Europa- und Verfassungsrecht (Jura, 2005).

Kaufmann, E, 'Traité international et loi interne' (1958) 41 *Rivista di diritto internazionale* 369.

[228] Crawford (n 27) 438, referring to J Crawford and S Marks, 'The Global Democracy Deficit: An Essay in International Law and Its Limits' in D Archibugi, D Held, and M Köhler (eds), *Re-imagining Political Community* (Cambridge, Polity Press, 1998) 84 (arguing in favour of the conferral of standing on international organisations before the ICJ and concluding that only if the ICJ were to have clear jurisdiction judicially to review action of all UN political agencies, including the UNSC, could the rule of law be said to extend to international political life).

Keith, KJ, '"International Law is Part of the Law of the Land": True or False?' (2013) 26 *LJIL* 351.
Kelsen, H, 'Les rapports de système entre le droit interne et le droit international public' (1926) 14 *RdC* 227.
Lenaerts, K, 'Direct Applicability and Direct Effect of International Law in the EU Legal Order' in Govaere, I, Lannon, E, van Elsuwege, P and Adam, S (eds), *The European Union in the World: Essays in Honour of Marc Maresceau* (Leiden, Nijhoff, 2014) 45–64.
Nollkaemper, A, *National Courts and the International Rule of Law* (Oxford, OUP, 2011).
O'Keeffe, R, 'The Doctrine of Incorporation Revisited' (2009) 79 *BYIL* 7.
Partsch, KJ, *Die Anwendung des Völkerrechts im innerstaatlichen Recht* (Karlsruhe, Müller, 1964).
Ripert, G, 'Les règles du droit civil applicables aux rapports internationaux' (1933) 44 *RdC* 637.
Rougeaux, JP, 'Les renvois du droit international au droit interne' (1977) 81 *Revue Générale de Droit International Public* 361.
Santulli, C, *Le statut international de l'ordre juridique étatique* (Paris, Pedone, 2001).
Spiermann, O, 'The Other Side of the Story: An Unpopular Essay on the Making of the European Community Legal Order' (1999) 10 *EJIL* 763.
von Bogdandy, A, 'Pluralism, Direct Effect, and the Ultimate Say: On the Relationship Between International and Domestic Constitutional Law' (2008) 6 *International Journal of Constitutional Law* 397.
Wouters, J, Nollkaemper, A and de Wet, E (eds), *The Europeanisation of International Law: The Status of International Law and its Member States* (The Hague, TMC Asser Press, 2008).
Ziegler, KS, 'International Law and EU Law: Between Asymmetric Constitutionalisation and Fragmentation' in Orakhelashvili, A (ed), *Research Handbook on the Theory and History of International Law* (Cheltenham, Edward Elgar, 2011) 268–327.

Further Reading

Betlem, G and Nollkaemper, A, 'Giving Effect to Public International Law and European Community Law before Domestic Courts: A Comparative Analysis of the Practice of Consistent Interpretation' (2003) 14 *EJIL* 569.
Bourgeois, JHJ, 'The European Court of Justice and the WTO: Problems and Challenges' in Weiler, JHH (ed), *The EU, the WTO and the NAFTA: Towards a Common Law of International Trade* (Oxford, OUP, 2000) 71–124.
De Baere, G, 'European Integration and the Rule of Law in Foreign Policy' in Dickson, J and Eleftheriadis, P (eds), *Philosophical Foundations of European Union Law* (Oxford, OUP, 2012) 354–83.
De Baere, G and Paasivirta, E, 'Identity and Difference: The EU and the UN as Part of Each Other' in de Waele, HCFJA and Kuipers, J-J (eds), *The Emergence of the European Union's International Identity* (Leiden, Nijhoff, 2013) 21–42.
De Baere, G and Roes, T, 'EU Loyalty as Good Faith' (2015) 64 *ICLQ* 829.
De Baere, G and Ryngaert, C, 'The ECJ's Judgment in *Air Transport Association of America* and the International Legal Context of the EU's Climate Change Policy' (2013) 18 *European Foreign Affairs Review* 394.

Dhommeaux, J, 'Monismes et dualismes en droit international des droits de l'homme' (1995) 41 *Annuaire Français de Droit International* 447.

Dworkin, R, 'A New Philosophy for International Law' (2013) 41 *Philosophy & Public Affairs* 2.

Escobar Hernández, C, 'La aplicación de los Tratados internacionales en España' in Mangas Martín, A, *Cuestiones prácticas de Derecho Internacional Público y cooperación jurídica internacional* (Madrid, Cuadernos de Derecho Judicial, 1994) 39–90.

Kuijper, PJ, Wouters, J, Hoffmeister, F, De Baere, G and Ramopoulos, T, *The Law of EU External Relations: Cases, Materials, and Commentary on the EU as an International Legal Actor*, 2nd edn (Oxford, OUP, 2015).

Lenaerts, K and José, G-FA, 'To Say What the Law of the EU Is: Methods of Interpretation and the European Court of Justice' (2014) 20 *Columbia Journal of European Law* 3.

McGoldrick, D, 'The United Kingdom's Human Rights Act 1998 in Theory and Practice' (2001) 50 *ICLQ* 4.

Perrin, G, 'Les rapports entre le droit international et le droit interne en particulier dans l'arrêt Barcelona Traction' in Baer-Kaupert, F-W (ed), *Liber Amicorum BCH Aubin* (Kehl am Rhein, Engel, 1979) 107–28.

Tzanakopoulos, A, *Disobeying the Security Council Countermeasures against Wrongful Sanctions* (Oxford, OUP, 2011).

Wouters, J, 'The Tormented Relationship between International Law and EU Law', in Bekker, PHF, Dolzer, R and Waibel, M (eds), *Making Transnational Law Work in the Global Economy. Essays in Honour of Detlev Vagts* (Cambridge, CUP, 2010) 198–221.

Wouters, J and De Man, Ph, 'Case-Note to European Court of Justice *International Association of Independent Tanker Owners (Intertanko)* Case C-308/06' (2009) 103 *AJIL* 555.

Wouters, J and Wessel, RA, 'The Phenomenon of Multilevel Regulation: Interactions between Global, EU and National Regulatory Spheres' (2007) 4 *International Organizations Law Review* 169.

5

States

I. Introduction

A. International Legal Personality

The next chapters take a closer look at the different subjects of international law and the extent to which they possess a greater or lesser degree of international legal personality.[1] Subjects of international law are those entities or persons that are recognised by customary law as being capable of possessing certain rights and duties under international law. They can invoke said rights and, conversely, be held accountable for breaches of these obligations. The substantive core of this concept (the capacity to possess certain rights and obligations under international law) is accompanied by a set of more formal corollaries, mainly: (i) the capacity to contribute to the formation of international law (in particular through the conclusion of treaties or by contributing to evolutions in customary international law); (ii) the enjoyment of certain privileges and immunities; and (iii) access to international dispute settlement mechanisms.

States were long regarded as being the only subjects of international law.[2] Other entities were mere 'objects' of international law. Objects could be the ultimate beneficiaries of certain arrangements between States, but they did not enjoy rights in their own capacity or otherwise play a meaningful role in international law. However, in light of developments in the international arena, including the impact of globalisation, as well as the advance of numerous sub-domains of international law, such as human rights law, international economic law or international criminal law,[3] it is clear that this exclusivist approach has become outdated.

[1] On this concept, see further R Portmann, *Legal Personality in International Law* (Cambridge, CUP, 2010); E Nijman, *The Concept of International Legal Personality: An Inquiry Into the History and Theory of International Law* (The Hague, TMC Asser Press, 2004); F Johns (ed), *International Legal Personality* (Farnham, Ashgate, 2010).

[2] Eg L Oppenheim, *International Law, A Treatise – Vol 1: Peace*, 2nd edn (New York, Longmans, 1912) para 289 ('Since the Law of Nations is a law between States only and exclusively, States only and exclusively are subjects of the Law of Nations').

[3] Consider eg A-L Vaurs-Chaumette, *Les sujets du droit international pénal: vers une nouvelle définition de la personnalité juridique internationale?* (Paris, Pedone, 2009).

As early as 1949, in its *Reparation for Injuries* Advisory Opinion, the ICJ recognised that international legal personality can take different forms, depending on the underlying functional needs: 'the subjects of law in any legal system are not necessarily identical in their nature or in the extent of their rights, and their nature depends upon the needs of the community'.[4]

It is now commonplace that international organisations (see Chapters 6 and 7) and various non-State actors (see Chapter 8) enjoy some form of international legal personality. By way of illustration, a glance at the EU Treaties Office Database reveals that the EU is now party to hundreds of bilateral and multilateral treaties.[5] At the level of the Council of Europe, individuals can, after having exhausted local remedies, bring a claim for alleged breaches of their rights under the ECHR. In addition, numerous bilateral investment treaties make it possible for multinational enterprises to initiate arbitral proceedings, for example, in the case of unlawful expropriation, against the State in which they operate (often without first having to exhaust local remedies).

It is important to stress the continuing primary role of States as the only subjects with full and 'original' international legal personality. This is reflected in the fact that only States can become a member of the UN (whereas international organisations can only be granted observer status),[6] and only States can initiate a contentious procedure before the ICJ.[7] Moreover, the powers of international organisations, including their treaty-making prerogatives, are ultimately determined by their founding States. Individuals and companies will only have access to international dispute settlement mechanisms insofar as States have so decreed. It follows that entities other than States, which remain the primary subjects, only have a limited and 'derived' international legal personality.

B. The Fundamental Rights and Obligations of States

States can create the most diverse rights and obligations under international law, especially by entering into treaties. They also possess certain rights and duties that are inextricably linked to statehood. The idea that there are certain fundamental rights and duties which States need not accept, but which they are 'born with', finds its origins in natural law,[8] and constitutes a deviation from the essentially 'consensualist' nature of international law.[9] An interesting document in this context is the 'Draft Declaration on Rights and Duties of States', drafted by the International Law Commission in 1949.[10] In a set of 14 articles, this document restates the basic customary rules of the so-called 'law of co-existence', which form the foundations upon which the international legal order is built.[11]

[4] *Reparation for Injuries Suffered in the Service of the United Nations* (Advisory Opinion) [1949] ICJ Rep 174, 178.

[5] Treaties Office Database of the European External Action Service, ec.europa.eu/world/agreements/.

[6] Art 4(1) UN Charter.

[7] Art 34 ICJ Statute.

[8] See eg HP Aust, 'Fundamental Rights of States: Constitutional Law in Disguise?' (2015) 4 *CJICL* 521.

[9] The same is true for the fact that new States are considered to be bound by pre-existing rules of (general) customary international law (see Chapter 3, Section II).

[10] ILC, 'Draft Declaration on Rights and Duties of States' (1949) *YILC*, Vol I, 178.

[11] These rules are mostly part of general customary international law, and are also reflected in various other instruments, such as the UN Charter, the Montevideo Convention on the Rights and Duties of States and the UNGA Friendly Relations Declaration.

Among these rules is the principle of 'sovereign equality',[12] which holds that, in spite of immense differences in terms of economic and military clout, States are regarded as equal in the eyes of international law. This principle finds expression, for example, in the one member-one vote system of the UN General Assembly and of many other international organisations. Other rules relate to States' right to respect for their territorial integrity and political independence, as reflected in the prohibition on the use of force, the principle of non-intervention and the right of individual or collective self-defence against armed attack (see Chapter 14). The Declaration also refers to the right of States 'to exercise jurisdiction over [their] territory and over all persons and things therein' (see Chapter 11).[13] The Declaration moreover affirms that every State 'has the duty to carry out in good faith its obligations' under international law and may not invoke national law as an excuse for failure to perform this duty.[14] Failure to abide by this duty will give rise to State responsibility (see Chapter 12). The list of rights and obligations in the Draft Declaration is not exhaustive and several others have been suggested in legal literature, including, for instance, the presumption that States enjoy an unlimited freedom subject only to those constraints determined by law (the so-called 'Lotus principle').[15]

II. Elements of Statehood

A. General

Since the 1648 Peace of Westphalia and the 1815 Congress of Vienna, the Westphalian State has come to be regarded as the primary actor of the international legal order, endowed with full and original international legal personality. However, defining what entities qualify as States is by no means a straightforward exercise. The list of Member States of the United Nations – which grew from 51 in 1945 to its present 193 in 2011 – forms a useful starting point, since membership is in principle open only to States.[16] But UN membership is not a decisive factor for determining statehood. By way of illustration, Switzerland only joined the UN in 2002, yet it is clear that it became a sovereign State long before that date. In a similar vein, the list of parties to the Convention on the Rights of the Child – the most widely ratified international treaty, which is open only to States – features a number of entities, such as Niue and the Cook Islands, which do not occupy a seat in the UN General Assembly. Furthermore, there are numerous territorial entities with de facto self-government, but

[12] Art 5 ILC Declaration (n 10). On the implications of the principle of sovereign equality, see eg Oppenheim (n 2) para 115. But see A Clapham, *Brierly's Law of Nations*, 7th edn (Oxford, OUP, 2012) 146–47 (finding it difficult to draw any consequence from the principle, which is not better explained than by the mere fact that States are independent). See further PH Kooijmans, *The Doctrine of the Legal Equality of States: An Inquiry into the Foundations of International Law* (Leiden, Sijthoff, 1964).

[13] Art 2 ILC Declaration (n 10). The State's right to exercise (legislative, adjudicative and enforcement) jurisdiction over its own territory is in principle comprehensive and exclusive. As further explained in Chapter 11, however, this right is nonetheless subject to various restrictions flowing from treaty and customary law, including immunities recognised by international law.

[14] Art 13 ILC Declaration (n 10).

[15] Eg J Crawford, *The Creation of States in International Law*, 2nd edn (Oxford, OUP, 2007) 40–41.

[16] But see UN Secretary General Trygve Lie, 'Letter dated 8 March 1950 from the Secretary General to the President of the Security Council transmitting a Memorandum on the Legal Aspects of the Problem of Representation in the United Nations', 9 March 1950, UN Doc S/1466.

which are not as such recognised as States and which are not members of international organisations (eg Somaliland), or which survive in 'an apparent twilight zone of partial recognition' (see also below, Section VII on 'contested States').[17]

Questions over entitlement to statehood may arise in various contexts. For example, the question may arise when the depositary of a multilateral treaty receives a request for accession, when an international judicial body receives an application to open proceedings, when a national judge is confronted with a person claiming immunities under international law, or when a State wishes to conclude a treaty and/or establish diplomatic relations with another entity. The legal and political stakes are not to be underestimated. In recent years, Israel and the United States vehemently opposed a UN General Assembly resolution recognising Palestine as a 'Non-Member Observer State'. While it was argued that such move would hinder the peace negotiations between Israelis and Palestinians, opposition was to no small extent inspired by fears that Palestine would seek to initiate an investigation by the International Criminal Court (ICC) into alleged war crimes committed by Israeli armed forces in Gaza.[18] Another case that caused deep rifts in the international community, including divergent views within Europe, is the status of Kosovo, which declared its independence in 2008 (see also below, Section III(D) on 'remedial secession' and Section IV(A) on recognition of States).[19]

In spite of the underlying political sensitivities, it is generally accepted that entitlement to statehood is a matter governed by law. In particular, it is considered to be governed by a set of (mostly) objective criteria that form part of customary international law. This is so even if State practice is not always consistent in this context and even if the criteria display a certain degree of circularity. In essence, there is an intrinsic contradiction in the legal concept of statehood in that it is both an antecedent to, and a product of international law.[20]

The classical starting point is the Montevideo Convention on the Rights and Duties of States.[21] According to Article 1 of the Convention, a State 'as a person of international law should possess the following qualifications: a) a permanent population; b) a defined territory; c) government; and d) capacity to enter into relations with the other States'. The first three criteria are discussed succinctly below. The fourth requirement can be framed somewhat differently as a requirement of 'independence', which is ultimately the decisive criterion of statehood, and is discussed at some length below.

[17] M Craven, 'Statehood, Self-Determination, and Recognition' in MD Evans (ed), *International Law*, 4th edn (Oxford, OUP, 2014) 202.

[18] These fears have not proven unsubstantiated. In April 2012, the Office of the Prosecutor of the ICC decided that a Palestinian declaration accepting the exercise of jurisdiction of the ICC for 'acts committed on the territory of Palestine since 1 July 2002' could not be accepted because the legal status of Palestine had not been settled, holding that '[i]n instances where it is controversial or unclear whether an applicant constitutes a "State", it is the practice of the Secretary General to follow or seek the General Assembly's directives on the matter'; ICC, Office of the Prosecutor, 'Situation in Palestine', 3 April 2012, icc-cpi.int/NR/rdonlyres/C6162BBF-FEB9-4FAF-AFA9-836106D2694A/284387/SituationinPalestine030412ENG.pdf. After it was recognised as a UN 'Non-Member Observer State' by the UN General Assembly (UNGA Res 67/19, 29 November 2012, UN Doc A/RES/67/19), in early January 2015, Palestine declared its acceptance of ICC jurisdiction as of 13 June 2014 and subsequently acceded to the Rome Statute. Shortly hereafter, the ICC Prosecutor effectively opened a preliminary examination into the situation in Palestine (ICC, Press Release, 16 January 2015, ICC-OTP-20150116-PR1083, icc-cpi.int/Pages/item.aspx?name=pr1083). See further J Salmon, 'La Qualité d'Etat de la Palestine' (2012) 45 *Revue belge de droit international* 13; T Van Poecke, 'Possibility of Opening a Preliminary Investigation into Crimes Allegedly Committed on the Territory of Palestine' (2016) 52 *Jura Falconis* 301.

[19] See further eg M Weller, *Contested Statehood: Kosovo's Struggle for Independence* (Oxford, OUP, 2009).

[20] Craven (n 17) 201.

[21] Convention on Rights and Duties of States (adopted 26 December 1933, entered into force 26 December 1934) 165 LNTS 19. The Convention was concluded in 1933 during the seventh International Conference of American States.

B. A Permanent Population

A first requirement holds that a State must have a 'permanent population'. This physical basis provides the State with its *raison d'être*, as the State exists first and foremost to promote the well-being of its population and, at least in Western liberal thinking, State authority finds its legitimacy in an unwritten social contract between the government and the governed.

The population requirement is not subject to any quantitative threshold and must be interpreted in a flexible manner. In the past, there existed doubt as to whether smaller entities could be regarded as actual States. This explains in part the reluctance to grant Liechtenstein membership in the League of Nations.[22] More recently, however, numerous micro-States (including island States such as Nauru and Tuvalu with populations of around 10,000 inhabitants) have joined the United Nations, illustrating that the preference for universality of UN membership has prevailed over a restrictive interpretation of the population requirement.

The population is linked to the State through the bond of nationality. The conferral and withholding of nationality is a matter which largely falls within the discretion of the State concerned and belongs to its *domaine réservé*. It is a matter in which international law intervenes only marginally; for example, by providing that all individuals have a right to nationality under human rights law,[23] by excluding the conferral of nationality in violation of the non-discrimination principle or *jus cogens* norms,[24] or by determining the opposability of nationality in the context of the exercise of diplomatic protection.[25] Otherwise, a population need not be characterised by a certain homogeneity in terms of ethnicity, language, culture or religion. Such homogeneity is nonetheless relevant in the context of the right of *peoples* to self-determination (see below, Section III(B)). A 'State' is not the same as a 'nation' or a 'people'.[26]

C. Defined Territory

The existence of a State also presupposes a territorial basis, that is, a defined territory. This territory encompasses the landmass, separated from neighbouring States by the external borders of the State, and includes the subsoil, the territorial sea (for coastal States), the internal waters and the national airspace. The territory is the locus where the State can exercise is territorial jurisdiction, in principle to the exclusion of other States.[27] This prerogative

[22] JC Duursma, *Fragmentation and the International Relations of Micro-States: Self-Determination and Statehood* (Cambridge, CUP, 1996) 173–74.

[23] See eg Art 15 UDHR; Art 24(3) ICCPR. See also the Convention on the Reduction of Statelessness (adopted 30 August 1961, entered into force 13 December 1975) 989 UNTS 175.

[24] Consider eg the section on 'conditions for the international legality of naturalisation' in the Report of the Independent International Fact-Finding Mission on the Conflict in Georgia, September 2009, Vol II, mpil.de//files/pdf4/IIFFMCG_Volume_II1.pdf, 155. See further A Peters, 'Extraterritorial Naturalizations: Between the Human Right to Nationality, State Sovereignty and Fair Principles of Jurisdiction' (2010) 53 *GYIL* 623.

[25] See further Chapter 12, Section V on 'invocation of State responsibility'.

[26] The notion of a 'people' may refer both to *all* the peoples of a given territory as well as to distinct self-determination units *within* a State; see R Higgins, *Problems and Process: International Law and How We Use It* (Oxford, Clarendon, 1994) 124; Crawford (n 15) 126.

[27] In Court of Cassation (BE), *MB and DV v Belgium*, 11 March 2011, Case No F.10.0011.N, the Belgian Court of Cassation struck down the argument that foreign States' embassy premises are part of the territory of the sending State.

also comes at a certain price. States must, within their territory, comply among other things, with the customary rules governing the treatment of aliens and act diligently to make sure their territory is not used in a way that causes harm to other States.[28]

As with the population requirement, there is no established minimum surface threshold. Numerous European and other micro-States are now UN Member States. Nauru, for instance, spans a territory of no more than 21 km², whereas Monaco has a territory of less than 2 km². There is no requirement that the territory consist of a single piece of land.

It has been argued that it is not so much the size or the factual possession or control over territory that matters, but rather the ability to rightfully claim the territory as a domain of exclusive authority.[29] It follows that this requirement, which is at first sight straightforward and objective, is closely interrelated to questions concerning the achievement of independence (see Section (II)(E)) and the acquisition of title over territory (see Section V, on 'acquisition of territory').

State practice illustrates that the existence of clearly and conclusively defined territorial boundaries is no precondition for statehood. Thus, Albania and Israel were respectively admitted to the League of Nations and the United Nations (in 1920 and 1949) in spite of a lack of settled borders. In the *North Sea Continental Shelf* cases, the ICJ similarly accepted that there is 'no rule that the land frontiers of a State must be fully delimited and defined, and often in various places and for long periods they are not'.[30] Numerous neighbouring States are indeed involved in – often long-standing – border disputes. What matters in the end is that a State controls a sufficiently identifiable territorial core.

D. (Effective) Government

The requirement of an effective government refers to the existence of public authorities capable of expressing the will of the State, exercising a certain degree of effective control over the territory concerned and providing for internal order and stability. It is best illustrated by the existence of centralised administrative and legislative organs and an enforcement branch that enjoys the monopoly over the exercise of legitimate violence within the State's territory.[31]

The importance of this criterion is illustrated by the report of the International Committee of Jurists established by the League of Nations in 1920 to examine the dispute between Finland and Sweden over the Aaland Islands. In the context of its analysis, the Committee itself needed to pronounce on the question whether and when Finland became a sovereign State in the aftermath of the Russian revolution. According to the Committee, '[t]his certainly did not take place until a stable political organisation had been created, and until the public authorities had become strong enough to assert themselves throughout the territories of the State without the assistance of foreign troops'.[32] The requirement explains the debate in legal doctrine as to whether the 'State of Palestine', as

[28] cp *Island of Palmas* (Netherlands v United States of America), Award of 4 April 1928, II RIAA 829, 839; *Trail Smelter Case* (United States v Canada), Award of 16 April 1938 and 11 March 1941, III RIAA 1905, 1963 ff.

[29] Craven (n 17) 219.

[30] *North Sea Continental Shelf* (Federal Republic of Germany v Denmark and Federal Republic of Germany v Netherlands) (Merits) [1969] ICJ Rep 4, para 46.

[31] Consider eg Crawford (n 15) 129: 'The existence of effective government, with centralized administrative and legislative organs, is the best evidence of a stable political community'.

[32] Report of the International Committee of Jurists entrusted by the Council of the League of Nations with the task of giving an advisory opinion upon the legal aspects of the Aaland Islands question, *Official Journal of the League of Nations*, Special Supplement No 3, October 1920.

declared in 1988, effectively qualified for statehood, having regard to its lack of control over the territory claimed.[33] It was also invoked by the District Court of The Hague to hold that Timor-Leste could not be regarded as a State at a time when it remained largely under Indonesian control.[34]

At the same time, State practice is not fully consistent in this regard.[35] Croatia and Bosnia-Herzegovina, for instance, were recognised as independent States by their European neighbours at a time when considerable parts of their territory were still controlled by non-State armed groups.[36] It appears in particular that when a certain entity has a strong entitlement to independence pursuant to the right of self-determination (especially in the context of newly-independent colonial States), the 'effective government' requirement is interpreted in a more flexible manner.[37] Thus, in relation to the Democratic Republic of the Congo's independence in 1960, Crawford notes how '[a]nything less like an effective government would be hard to imagine. Yet despite this there can be little doubt that in 1960 Congo was a State in the full sense of the term'.[38] Conversely, when an entity's claim to independence is vitiated by its being achieved in violation of the prohibition on the use of force or other peremptory norms, the presence of an 'effective government' will not suffice to establish statehood.

Once a State has come into existence, there is a strong presumption that it continues to exist, even if there is a disruption in the exercise of governmental functions. In this context, the international legal order clearly opts for stability and continuity. Thus, the fact that a State undergoes a period of political turmoil or is the theatre of a *coup d'état*, does not affect its qualification as a State. The same holds true for countries undergoing a civil war (eg Syria after 2011) and for so-called 'failed' or 'failing' States (eg Somalia). In such scenarios, delicate questions may arise as to which persons must be considered to represent the State (see below, Section IV(B) on 'recognition of governments'). Yet, these questions are ultimately distinct from the existence of the State as such.[39]

E. Independence

Apart from the foregoing more objective criteria, a fourth precondition must be added, namely the requirement of 'independence'. The Montevideo Convention frames this as the

[33] See eg FA Boyle, 'The Algiers Declaration on Palestine' (1990) 1 *EJIL* 301; J Crawford, 'The Creation of the State of Palestine: Too Much Too Soon?' (1990) 2 *EJIL* 307; J Salmon, 'Declaration of the State of Palestine' (1989) 5 *Palestine Yearbook of International Law* 48.

[34] District Court The Hague (NL), *East Timor and others v Netherlands*, Decision on admissibility, 21 February 1980, (1992) 87 ILR 73, para 6.

[35] According to Koskenniemi, '[c]ommunities which have lacked the actual legal effectiveness normally connected with statehood have been regarded as States (Monaco, Tuvalu, the Holy See, etc.) while communities with much greater effectiveness have been denied it (Rhodesia, Transkei, Taiwan)'; M Koskenniemi, *From Apology to Utopia: The Structure of International Legal Argument* (Cambridge, CUP, 2005) 276.

[36] Eg E Denza, 'European Practice on the Recognition of States' (2011) 36 *ELR* 321, 327. See further A Pellet, 'The Opinions of the Badinter Arbitration Committee: A Second Breath for the Self-Determination of Peoples' (1992) 3 *EJIL* 178; M Weller, 'The International Response to the Dissolution of the Socialist Federal Republic of Yugoslavia' (1992) 86 *AJIL* 569.

[37] Raič speaks of the 'compensatory force principle', that is, the compensating effect of the right to external self-determination in situations of a lack of effective government; D Raič, *Statehood and the Law of Self-Determination* (The Hague, Kluwer, 2002) 408. According to Raič, this principle also applies beyond the colonial context (ibid, 411).

[38] Crawford (n 15) 57.

[39] Even a failed State continues to enjoy the fundamental rights of States under international law. It also remains bound by its obligations under international law.

'capacity to enter into international relations with other States',[40] which manifests itself through the initiation of diplomatic relations and the exchange of ambassadors with other States, the conclusion of bilateral and multilateral treaties, membership of international organisations, submitting claims at the international level, and so on.

'Independence' presupposes that a State is capable of taking part in international relations in its own right, without being subordinate to another State. 'Independence' does not mean freedom from law – any State is in principle bound by pre-existing customary international law upon its coming into existence – but rather freedom from control by other States.[41] The distinction is well captured in the Individual Opinion of Judge Anzilotti to the PCIJ's 1933 Advisory Opinion on the *Customs Regime between Germany and Austria*. In this case, the PCIJ was asked to pronounce on whether a proposed customs union between the two countries was contrary to Austria's obligations pursuant to a post-war Protocol 'not to alienate its independence' and to 'abstain from any negotiations or from any economic and financial engagement calculated [...] to compromise its independence'.[42] While a majority of the Court found that the customs union contravened the aforementioned commitment, Judge Anzilotti stressed that:

> restrictions upon a State's liberty, whether arising out of ordinary international law or contractual engagements, do not as such in the least affect its independence. As long as these restrictions do not place the State under the legal authority of another State, the former remains an independent State however extensive and burdensome those obligations may be.[43]

It follows that independence is not affected by participation in a confederation,[44] whereby States agree to exercise certain governmental functions (eg foreign affairs or military matters) jointly, or when a State voluntarily (and temporarily) delegates certain sovereign prerogatives to a State or international organisation. Nor is it affected by the existence of a 'personal union', where several States share the same monarch.[45] In a similar vein, even though EU Member States have conferred considerable powers upon the EU, which has exclusive competence in fields such as trade, they still remain independent States. This is confirmed by Article 50(1) TEU, which recognises that '[a]ny Member State may decide to withdraw from the Union in accordance with its own constitutional requirements'.[46] Nor does an entity's de facto dependence on another State (eg in the form of dependence of foreign aid and loans, or from economic trade with a powerful neighbour) undermine its qualification as a State.[47]

[40] Art 1 Montevideo Convention.

[41] Clapham (n 12) 145.

[42] *Customs Regime between Germany and Austria* (Advisory Opinion) [1931] PCIJ Series A/B No 41, 37.

[43] *Customs Regime between Germany and Austria*, Separate Opinion of Judge Anzilotti, Series A/B No 41, 58.

[44] There would seem to be no true contemporary examples of confederations. Even if Switzerland officially goes by the name of the 'Swiss Confederation', it undoubtedly constitutes a single sovereign State (cp the Swiss constitution goes by the name of the 'Federal Constitution of the Swiss Confederation').

[45] Queen Elizabeth II, for instance, acts as the Head of State of the UK as well as of 15 Commonwealth realms, including Australia, New Zealand, Canada and Jamaica.

[46] Following a referendum in June 2016, on 29 March 2017, the UK formally invoked Art 50 TEU, triggering the process of withdrawal from the EU. See the letter of the Prime Minister of the UK, Theresa May, to the President of the European Council, Donald Tusk: gov.uk/government/uploads/system/uploads/attachment_data/file/604079/Prime_Ministers_letter_to_European_Council_President_Donald_Tusk.pdf.

[47] In Regional Social Court (DE), *Slovak Citizen v Claims Conference Frankfurt (CEEF)*, 23 January 2007, L 14 R 612/06, it was held that Slovakia's situation of vassalage towards Germany after 1939 did not affect its status as a State under international law.

By contrast, territorial entities within a federal State do not enjoy independence. This is so even if several such entities (eg the Flemish, Walloon and Brussels-Capital Regions in Belgium) have a treaty-making competence pursuant to the federal State's constitutional order. Article 2 of the Montevideo Convention confirms that '[t]he federal state shall constitute a sole person in the eyes of international law'. This explains why, when decentralised authorities within a federal State commit a breach of international law, it will be the federal State itself which will be internationally responsible. The same is true *mutatis mutandis* at the EU level. Thus, when the Flemish Region grants unlawful State aid in the sense of Article 107(1) TFEU or issues decrees contravening the free movement of persons, the resulting infringement procedures will be addressed to the Kingdom of Belgium.

On occasion, debate may arise as to whether an entity is effectively independent or whether it is legally (and not just factually) dependent on another State.[48] In the past, this question arose in the context of so-called 'protectorates'.[49] Thus, in the *US Nationals in Morocco* case, the ICJ looked at the impact of the creation of a French protectorate and in particular to the 1912 Treaty of Fez, whereby France undertook inter alia to exercise 'all of the international relations of Morocco'. The Court nonetheless noted that this was an arrangement 'of a contractual character' whereby Morocco 'remained a sovereign State'.[50] More recently, it may be observed that Andorra was admitted to UN membership only after significant reforms which removed doubts as to its independence from France and Spain.[51]

While the 'protectorate' has become a thing of the past, there remain numerous '*territoires d'outre-mer*', 'crown dependencies' and other 'non-self-governing' territories. Such dependent territories, including, for instance, Anguilla, the Netherlands Antilles, Greenland, or the Falkland Islands, have not (yet) become independent and/or have chosen a limited form of self-government, but remain associated with the former colonial power or 'metropolitan State'.[52] While these entities generally do not qualify as 'independent' States, their specific status and degree of autonomy varies strongly.

From an EU perspective, reference can be made in this context to so-called 'overseas countries and territories' (OCTs) in the sense of Articles 198–204 TFEU, on the one hand, and so-called 'outermost regions' (OMRs) in the sense of Article 349 TFEU, on the other.[53] The former category refers to a series of 'non-European countries and territories which have special relations with Denmark, France, the Netherlands and the United Kingdom', and which the EU Member States 'agree to associate with the Union'.[54] The stated purpose of this association is 'to promote the economic and social development of the countries and territories and to establish close economic relations between them and the Union as a

[48] According to Crawford, '[i]t would be possible for a tribunal to hold that a state which had granted away piecemeal a high proportion of its legal powers had ceased to have a separate existence as a consequence. But it may be difficult to distinguish granting away of capacities and the existence of agency or representation, and there is a strong presumption against loss of status'; Crawford (n 15) 135.

[49] See inter alia Crawford (n 15) 282–320; R Jennings and A Watts, *Oppenheim's International Law*, 9th edn (London, Longman, 1992) 266–274; M Trilsch, 'Protectorates and Protected States' (2011) *MPEPIL*.

[50] *Rights of Nationals of the United States of America in Morocco* (France v United States of America) [1952] ICJ Rep 176, 188.

[51] Crawford (n 15) 129; Duursma (n 22) 316–73.

[52] For the US State Department's list of 'dependencies and areas of special sovereignty', see: state.gov/s/inr/rls/10543.htm. For the United Nations list of 'non-self-governing territories', see: un.org/en/decolonization/nonselfgovterritories.shtml.

[53] For a discussion of how EU law principles apply to overseas territories, see D Kochenov (ed), *EU Law of the Overseas: Outermost Regions, Associated Overseas Countries and Territories, Territories Sui Generis* (Alphen aan den Rijn, Kluwer, 2011).

[54] Art 198 TFEU.

whole'.[55] The list of OCTs concerned can be found in Annex II to the TFEU.[56] The OMRs refer to a number of areas, such as Guadeloupe or the Canary Islands, which are geographically very distant from the European continent, but which are part of an EU Member State and which are in principle fully part of the EU (save for specific measures of derogation).[57] According to Article 355(6) TFEU, the status of the OCTs and OMRs can be amended by the Council, acting on the initiative of the Member State concerned.[58]

The key question in this context is how an entity, which, at a certain point in time, does not enjoy independence, can acquire such independence and consequently claim statehood. Ultimately, this question is closely related to the different ways in which new States can come into existence (see below, Section III). It is also linked to the issue of recognition of States, and to the debate whether recognition by existing States is constitutive of statehood, or whether it has a mere 'declaratory' effect (see below, Section IV).

F. Other Criteria?

In past centuries, international law was regarded as the law governing the relations between European Christian States.[59] As the European version of a family of nations gradually expanded to include non-European States, such as the United States, the Ottoman Empire or Japan, the focus shifted to the newcomer's alleged 'civilised' credentials, which in fact meant that States were expected to have a central administration modelled after that found in Western Europe.[60] In the twentieth century, the emphasis on a State's alleged 'civilised' character was abandoned for a more neutral and inclusive approach.

This evolution did not happen overnight. Article 22 of the Covenant of the League of Nations, which deals with the League's mandate system, contrasts the 'advanced nations' of the world with those more '[remote] from the centres of civilization'. Still today, a relic of this approach can be found in Article 38 of the ICJ Statute, which lists as one of the sources of international law 'the general principles of law recognized by civilized nations' (see Chapter 3, Section III).

Finally, statehood is not limited to liberal democracies, nor is it contingent on a State's willingness to observe international human rights law or international law more generally. It would indeed appear 'indefensible to express as a criterion of statehood a condition which the entity can only accept *because* it is a state'.[61] Still, factors such as these may well have

[55] Art 198(2) TFEU.

[56] As of October 2017, the list contained 21 entries. For further information, see the website of the Association of the Overseas Countries and Territories of the EU (OCTA), at octassociation.org/.

[57] See European Commission, 'Regional policy & outermost regions' ec.europa.eu/regional_policy/en/policy/themes/outermost-regions/.

[58] Thus, on 1 January 2014 Mayotte became an 'outermost region' of the EU within the meaning of Art 349 TFEU; European Council Decision of 11 July 2012 amending the status of Mayotte with regard to the European Union, [2012] OJ L204/131, taking into account the opinion of the European Commission (Commission Opinion under Article 355(6) of the Treaty on the Functioning of the European Union on a French Government initiative to amend the status of Mayotte with regard to the European Union, 8 June 2012, C(2012) 3506 final). Upon the entry into force of the Council Decision, EU law began to apply to the territory (subject to certain transitional arrangements).

[59] See above pp 51–54. See also below on the concept of '*terra nullius*' pp 240–241.

[60] See Craven (n 17) 210.

[61] See Crawford (n 15) 134. On the impact of democracy and democratic processes on the creation of States (eg, in the context of independence referenda), see J Vidmar, *Democratic Statehood in International Law* (Oxford, Hart, 2013).

an increasing impact on the extent to which existing States are willing to formally recognise new States,[62] and therefore indirectly influence the coming into existence of the State (see below, Section III).

An important example relates to the EC Declaration on the 'Guidelines on the Recognition of New States in Eastern Europe and in the Soviet Union' of 16 December 1991.[63] In the wake of the dissolution of the Soviet Union and of the Socialist Federal Republic of Yugoslavia, the EC and its Member States adopted a set of guidelines aiming at harmonising their policies with regard to the recognition of these new States. Interestingly, these guidelines made no reference to the abovementioned criteria for statehood, but instead spelled out a series of conditions upon which the formal recognition of these new States was made contingent, including respect for the UN Charter, respect for minority rights, respect for prior disarmament commitments, and commitment to peaceful dispute settlement. With regard to Yugoslavia, a separate EC 'Declaration on Yugoslavia'[64] was adopted, imposing further conditions, and providing that applications for recognition of the (former) Yugoslav Republics would be submitted for advice to the EC-established Arbitration Commission on the Former Yugoslavia (also known after its President as the 'Badinter Commission'), consisting of legal experts. It follows that the EC Member States saw the process of formal recognition as a tool to induce compliance with the rules of the international community, which in the case of the former Yugoslav Republics even took the form of a formal vetting process.[65] The result was a concerted recognition policy on the part of EC Member States.[66] At the same time, it has been observed that little to no efforts were made to substantively verify compliance with the various conditions spelled out in the Guidelines and that the effect was 'largely limited to requiring from the aspiring new states formal assurances of good conduct'.[67] In the end, the political conditions for recognition listed in the Guidelines should not be mistaken for constitutive criteria for statehood.

III. How States Come into Existence

A. General

For a State to come into existence, it should in principle meet each of the four requirements discussed above. In the past, this sometimes happened when groups of people moved from one area to another and settled on hitherto unexplored land, gradually building a self-governing society with a defined territorial basis. In the modern era, however, there is no more *terra nullius* on earth (see also below, Section V(B)) that lends itself to the creation of a

[62] See the discussion below (n 170).

[63] European Communities, 'Declaration on the "Guidelines on the Recognition of New States in Eastern Europe and in the Soviet Union"', 16 December 1991, (1992) 31 ILM 1486.

[64] European Communities, 'Declaration on Yugoslavia', 16 December 1991, (1992) 31 ILM 1485.

[65] See Denza (n 36) 325, 337.

[66] As Denza notes, when Germany broke ranks with the EC and other Member States by recognising Slovenia and Croatia in December 1991, it was 'extensively pilloried' by the other Member States (ibid, 326).

[67] ibid, 330. According to Denza, the implementation of the Guidelines was 'erratic and unsatisfactory (ibid, 321). Denza also suggests that the recognition policy 'showed a blithe disregard for the previously accepted criteria of sovereign statehood' (ibid, 325). Consider also A Aust, *Handbook of International Law*, 2nd edn (Cambridge, CUP, 2010) 17 (speaking of 'a political fig leaf to cover overhasty recognition').

new State. Still, the enormous increase of UN membership since 1945 reveals that numerous States have come into existence in recent decades. It follows that the creation of new States has generally taken place pursuant to the division of a pre-existing State into more than one State. Whether and when an entity acquires independence in such context is a delicate matter. At times, the outcome may be clear; for instance, where two or more territorial units formerly belonging to a single State agree to part ways. Where no such agreement exists, however, international law does not provide easy and clear-cut answers, and uncertainty often exists (sometimes for prolonged periods of time) as to whether a new State has come into existence and whether it is permitted for others to recognise it as such.

B. The Right of Self-Determination

The main explanation for the increase in States throughout the twentieth century relates to the application of the right of (external) self-determination in the colonial context, resulting in the separation of former colonies from their colonial powers. Pursuant to the right of self-determination, all peoples indeed have the right to 'freely determine their political status and freely pursue their economic, social and cultural development'.[68] The concept of a 'people' is not authoritatively defined, but is generally considered to refer to a group of persons characterised by a degree of homogeneity in terms of their language, culture, religion, ethnicity, history, etc. The right to self-determination was initially a political concept and gained in prominence after US President Wilson issued his famous 'Fourteen Points'. It was picked up by the International Committee of Jurists tasked with examining the Aaland Islands dispute.[69] At present, it is firmly grounded in the UN Charter,[70] and in various human rights treaties.[71] It has been recognised by the ICJ as 'one of the essential principles of contemporary international law' and as having an *erga omnes* character.[72]

Several resolutions of the UN General Assembly have further shaped the implications of the right of self-determination in the colonial context. Key instruments include the UNGA 'Friendly Relations Declaration'[73] and the UNGA 'Declaration on the Granting of Independence to Colonial Countries and Peoples'.[74] These and other instruments have led to the creation of a customary 'right to independence for the peoples of non-self-governing territories and peoples subject to alien subjugation, domination and exploitation', repeatedly affirmed by the ICJ.[75] Thus, the aforementioned peoples have a right to freely determine

[68] Art 1 ICCPR. Further, see eg D French (ed), *Statehood and Self-Determination* (Cambridge, CUP, 2015).

[69] International Committee of Jurists (n 32).

[70] Arts 1(2) and 55 UN Charter.

[71] See eg Art 1 ICCPR and Art 1 ICESCR.

[72] *East Timor* (Portugal v Australia) [1995] ICJ Rep 90, para 29. See also *Legal Consequences for States of the Continued Presence of South Africa in Namibia (South West Africa) notwithstanding Security Council Resolution 276 (1970)* (Advisory Opinion) [1971] ICJ Rep 16, paras 52–53; *Western Sahara* (Advisory Opinion) [1975] ICJ Rep 12, paras 54–59; CJEU case C-104/16P *Council of the EU v Polisario Front*, para 88.

[73] UNGA, 'Declaration on Principles of International Law concerning Friendly Relations and Co-operation among States in Accordance with the Charter of the United Nations', 24 October 1970, UN Doc A/RES/25/2625 (XXV).

[74] UNGA, 'Declaration on the Granting of Independence to Colonial Countries and Peoples', 14 December 1960, UN Doc A/RES/1514 (XV).

[75] *East Timor* (n 72) para 29; *South West Africa* (n 72) paras 52–53; *Legal Consequences of the Construction of a Wall in the Occupied Palestinian Territories (Advisory Opinion)* [2004] ICJ Rep 136, para 88; *Accordance with International Law of the Unilateral Declaration of Independence in Respect of Kosovo (Advisory Opinion)* [2010] ICJ Rep 403, para 79.

their political status, without external interference, including by pursuing so-called 'external' self-determination through the establishment of a sovereign and independent State. At the same time, political 'independence' is not the only option. Other modes of implementing the right of self-determination include 'the free association or integration within an independent State or the emergence into any other political status freely determined' by the people concerned.[76]

The principle of *uti possidetis* (in full: *uti possidetis juris ita possideatis*, which translates into: 'as you possessed by right, you will possess') imposes an important restriction on the exercise of the right of 'external' self-determination (and, more generally, in situations of secession or of dismemberment of a State) by commanding respect for existing external boundaries. It does so even if, from a historical perspective, these boundaries may have been drawn on an artificial basis by colonial powers with little regard for cultural and ethnic differences.[77] In other words, international law opts for continuity and stability in this context. Thus, the ICJ has repeatedly confirmed that boundary treaties have 'a legal life of their own' and that '[o]nce agreed the boundary stands, for any other approach would vitiate the fundamental principle of the stability of boundaries'.[78]

Dozens of former colonies, mostly in Africa, Latin America and Asia, have become independent over time, mostly in the second half of the twentieth century. A number of other entities have opted for an alternative formula such as a limited degree of autonomy while still retaining legal links with the colonial power. What is then the contemporary relevance of the right to independence of peoples subject to alien subjugation, domination and exploitation? In 1945, an 'international trusteeship system' was introduced in the context of the UN, which replaced the prior 'mandate' system of the League of Nations.[79] The underlying idea was that the trust territories concerned were to temporarily remain under the supervision of an administering authority (such as France or the UK), which was tasked with preparing the territory for full independence and which was answerable in this context to the Trusteeship Council.[80] Since then, all of the 11 territories placed under the

[76] 'Friendly Relations Declaration' (n 73).

[77] *Frontier Dispute* (Burkina Faso v Republic of Mali) [1986] ICJ Rep 554, 566 ('The essence of the principle lies in its primary aim of securing respect for territorial boundaries at the moment when independence is achieved. Such territorial boundaries might be no more than delimitations between different administrative divisions or colonies all subject to the same sovereign. In that case, the application of the principle of *uti possidetis* resulted in administrative boundaries being transformed into international frontiers in the full sense of the term.'); Opinion No 2 of the Arbitration Commission of the Peace Conference on Yugoslavia, 11 January 1992, (1992) 31 ILM 1497, 1498 (affirming that the right to self-determination must not involve changes to existing frontiers at the time of independence 'except where the States concerned agree otherwise'). For a critique, see eg Crawford (n 15) 239. See further O Corten et al (eds), *Démembrements d'Etats et delimitations territoriales: l'uti possidetis en question(s)* (Brussels, Bruylant, 1999); A Peters, 'The Principle of 'Uti Possidetis Juris': How Relevant Is It for Issues of Secession?' in C Walter, A von Ungern-Sternberg and K Abushov (eds), *Self-Determination and Secession in International Law* (Oxford, OUP, 2014) 95–137.

[78] See eg *Territorial Dispute* (Libyan Arab Jamahiriya v Chad) [1994] ICJ Rep 6, para 72; *Temple of Preah Vihear* (Cambodia v Thailand) (Merits) [1962] ICJ Rep 6, 34.

[79] The League's mandate system (Art 22 Covenant of the League of Nations) essentially applied to the former colonies of Germany and the Ottoman Empire. These entities were divided into three categories (Class 'A', 'B' and 'C' mandates), depending on their alleged 'stage of development', or, put differently, the degree to which they were considered 'ready' to become fully independent in the near future or not. See further N Matz, 'Civilization and the Mandate System under the League of Nations as Origin of Trusteeship' (2005) 9 *Max Planck Yearbook of United Nations Law* 47.

[80] See Arts 75–85 UN Charter. The Trusteeship system extended to (a) the territories held under 'mandate' under the League of Nations system, (b) colonies of the Axis powers, and (c) territories voluntarily placed under the system by States responsible for their administration (in reality, this third category remained dead letter). See also Arts 82–83 UN Charter on the role of the Security Council vis-à-vis 'strategic areas'.

trusteeship system have either become independent or have voluntarily associated themselves with a State. The last trust territory was Palau, which became independent in 1994. Since then, the Trusteeship Council has led a dormant existence. In the 2005 World Summit Outcome, States agreed that it would be appropriate to amend the UN Charter to delete the provisions related thereto.[81] No such amendment has taken place so far.

In a similar vein, most other 'non-self-governing territories' have in the meantime 'exhausted' their right of self-determination. The former concept refers to other entities whose peoples 'have not yet attained a full measure of self-government', but which were (mostly for political reasons) never placed under the aforementioned trusteeship system. Pursuant to Article 73 of the UN Charter, the States acting as administering authorities of these territories are required to assist them in the progressive development of their free political institutions and to report to the UN Secretary General on a regular basis.[82] In 1946, eight UN Member States[83] enumerated 72 territories under their control which they identified as 'non-self-governing'.[84] Since the early 1960s, the list of non-self-governing territories has been defined and adjusted on a regular basis by the UN General Assembly. It has also set up a Special Committee on Decolonization (the 'Committee of 24') to review the situation of the non-self-governing territories and report to the General Assembly.[85] Most of the territories concerned have now become independent States (eg East Timor) or have otherwise freely chosen their political status (eg Hong Kong). As a result, only 17 'non-self-governing' territories remain on the list (as of 2018), including, for instance, Western Sahara and Gibraltar.[86] It must be stressed, however, that the UN General Assembly

[81] UNGA, '2005 World Summit Outcome', 16 September 2005, UN Doc A/RES/60/1, para 176. On the other hand, some have construed the UN's involvement in post-conflict international territorial administration as a return of the trusteeship model. See in particular R Wilde, *International Territorial Administration: How Trusteeship and the Civilizing Mission Never Went Away* (Oxford, OUP, 2008). There have also been occasional suggestions to place 'failed' or 'failing' States under some form of UN conservatorship (see in particular G Helpman and S Ratner, 'Saving Failed States' (1992) 89 *Foreign Policy* 3).

[82] On 12 February 2002, then UN Under-Secretary General for Legal Affairs Hans Correll submitted a legal opinion at the request of the UN Security Council concerning contracts between the Moroccan authorities and foreign companies pertaining to the exploration of mineral resources in the Western Sahara (UN Doc S/2002/161). The Opinion observes that 'the General Assembly has consistently condemned the exploitation and plundering of natural resources and any economic activities which are detrimental to the interests of the peoples of these territories and deprive them of their legitimate rights over their natural resource' (para 22). By contrast, 'where resource exploitation activities are concluded in Non-Self-Governing Territories for the benefit of the peoples of these territories, on their behalf, or in consultation with their representatives, they are considered compatible with the Charter obligations of the administering Power'. Relying on the aforementioned opinion, on 10 December 2015, the General Court of the EU partially annulled a Council decision approving a fisheries agreement between Morocco and the EU inasmuch as it extended to the Western Sahara (judgment of 10 December 2015, *Front Polisario v Council*, T-512/12, EU:T:2015:953). In particular, the Court held that the Council had failed to satisfy itself 'that there was no evidence of an exploitation of the natural resources of the Western Sahara under Moroccan control likely to be to the detriment of its inhabitants and to infringe their fundamental rights' (para 241). Upon appeal, the Court of Justice nonetheless found that the General Court had erred in interpreting the agreement as being legally applicable to Western Sahara in the first place; judgment of 21 December 2016, *Council v Front Polisario*, C-104/16 P, EU:C:2016:973.

[83] Australia, Belgium, Denmark, France, the Netherlands, New Zealand, the UK and the US.

[84] UNGA, 'Transmission of Information under Article 73e of the Charter', 14 December 1946, UN Doc A/RES/66 (I).

[85] UNGA, 'The Situation with Regard to the Implementation of the Declaration on the Granting of Independence to Colonial Countries and Peoples', 27 November 1961, UN Doc A/RES/1654 (XVI).

[86] The UK acts as the 'administering power' for 10 territories, France for two; see un.org/en/decolonization/nonselfgovterritories.shtml. The Western Sahara, which, since the withdrawal of Spain is mostly under the *de facto* control of Morocco, is the sole self-governing territory without an official administering power.

occasionally adds entities to the list. In May 2013, for instance, at the request of a number of neighbouring island States, it decided to re-inscribe French Polynesia on the list.[87] While France was quick to denounce the move as an '*ingérence flagrante*' or a blatant interference with the internal affairs of the Polynesians,[88] this illustrates that, in essence, the UN General Assembly (still) deems itself competent to identify those entities that are entitled to 'external' self-determination. It also illustrates the intrinsic nexus between law and politics in questions of statehood.

While there is an established right to independence on the part of 'peoples subject to alien subjugation, domination and exploitation', the exact interpretation of both the terms 'people' and 'alien subjugation, domination and exploitation' remains controversial.[89] With regard to the former term, it has been observed that (at least in the present context) it does not simply refer to any 'minority' or 'ethnic group', but is strictly confined to pre-determined political entities with a clear, historically defined, territorial basis.[90] The latter concept was sometimes extended to the apartheid regimes in South Africa and Southern Rhodesia, or to situations of foreign military occupation (eg in the Occupied Palestinian Territories). Yet, it has always been closely linked to the colonial context and the process of decolonisation.

C. Mergers or State Dissolution

New States may also come into existence pursuant to mutual agreement. Two or more pre-existing States may decide to merge into a single entity. Conversely, territorial entities within a State may part ways; a process known as the dissolution of the State. Two situations of dissolution can be discerned: first, it is possible that newly-formed States secede from another State whose existence is considered to continue (secession). Second, the dissolution can be complete and lead just to the creation of new States without having a 'continuator State' (dismemberment or '*dismembratio*'). Ultimately, the extent to which such processes give rise to the creation of new States differs from one case to another.

As far as mergers are concerned, for instance, it is generally accepted that the unification of Germany in 1990 pursuant to the German Unification Treaty (*Einigungsvertrag*) did not result in the creation of a new State. Rather, the German Democratic Republic (DDR) 'extinguished' and became part of the Federal Republic of Germany (BRD) under the latter's constitution, while the BRD's governmental authorities remained in place; the BRD 'absorbed' the DDR.[91] Another question that arose was whether after reunification the former DDR would automatically enter the EU or whether it would have to reapply as a new Member State. Since reunification did not create a new State, this was seen as a territorial change of a Member State and Germany did not have to reapply for admission.[92] By contrast, views differ on whether the 1707 Treaty of Union between England and Scotland

[87] UNGA, 'Self-Determination of French Polynesia', 17 May 2013, UN Doc A/RES/67/265.
[88] Ministry of Foreign Affairs (FR), 'Résolution adoptée par l'Assemblée générale des Nations Unies sur la Polynésie française', 17 May 2013.
[89] S Joseph and M Castan, *The International Covenant on Civil and Political Rights: Cases, Materials and Commentary*, 3rd edn (Oxford, OUP, 2013) para 7.05.
[90] S Oeter, 'Self-Determination' in B Simma (ed), *The Charter of the United Nations: A Commentary*, 3rd edn (Oxford, OUP, 2012) paras 23–27.
[91] See further D Papenfuss, 'The Fate of the International Treaties of the GDR Within the Framework of German Unification' (1998) 92 *AJIL* 469.
[92] J-P Jacqué, 'German Unification and the European Community' (1991) 2 *EJIL* 1.

resulted in the creation of a new State, Great Britain, or whether, as a matter of international law, England continued, albeit under a new name and with an enlarged territory.[93]

Similarly, in situations of dissolution of a State, questions may arise as to whether any of the resulting territorial entities continue the legal personality of the predecessor State – put differently, whether there is a so-called 'continuator State' – or whether all are to be regarded as new 'successor' States entirely. The former scenario is sometimes described as one of 'partial' State succession, the latter as 'universal' State succession. The consequences of the discussion may be considerable, for example with regard to the resulting entities' membership of international organisations (see below, Section VI(C)).

If the entities concerned reach an agreement, this normally closes the discussion. Thus, when Czechoslovakia disintegrated into two separate States, the extinction of Czechoslovakia was ostensibly effected by the consent of both new States (the Czech Republic and Slovakia): neither claimed to continue its legal personality, and both applied for membership of the UN and other international organisations.[94] In a similar vein, the dissolution of Serbia and Montenegro in 2006 was governed by a Constitutional Charter which foresaw that, in case of a breakaway of Montenegro pursuant to a referendum, Serbia would be the continuator State.[95]

However, difficulties may arise where one or more entity claims to be the continuator State, but there is no agreement on the matter between the entities involved, or when there is no agreement to dissolve the predecessor State in the first place. Following the dissolution of the Soviet Union in 1990–91, formalised by the Minsk Agreement[96] and the Alma-Ata Declaration,[97] the Russian Federation made it clear that it regarded itself as the rightful heir of the Soviet Union's position under international law, including its permanent seat on the UN Security Council. The other former Soviet Republics all accepted this position, and no other State objected to it.[98] Immediately after the Alma-Ata Declaration, the European Communities explicitly accepted that 'the international rights and obligations of the former USSR [...] will continue to be exercised by Russia'.[99]

This situation stands in marked contrast to the break-up of the Socialist Federal Republic of Yugoslavia (SFRY), which combines features of State dissolution and of a series of unilateral secessions. Importantly, in April 1992, the Federal Republic of Yugoslavia (FRY) claimed to continue the international legal personality of the SFRY.[100] However, this position was not accepted by the other former Yugoslav Republics, nor by the ICJ.[101]

[93] See J Crawford and A Boyle, 'Annex A Opinion: Referendum on the Independence of Scotland – International Law Aspects', 10 December 2012, gov.uk/government/uploads/system/uploads/attachment_data/file/79408/Annex_A.pdf, paras 33–37.

[94] ibid, paras 74–78. See further J Malenovsky 'Problèmes juridiques liés à la partition de la Tchécoslovaquie' (1993) 39 *Annuaire français de droit international* 305, 317–18.

[95] *Constitutional Charter of the State Union of Serbia and Montenegro*, worldstatesmen.org/SerbMont_Const_2003.pdf. Consider also Agreement Relating to the Separation of Singapore from Malaysia as an Independent and Sovereign State (adopted 7 August 1965, entered into force 9 August 1965) 563 UNTS 89.

[96] Agreement establishing the Commonwealth of Independent States, 8 December 1991, (1991) 31 ILM 138. There were three parties to this agreement: Belarus, the Russian Federation and Ukraine.

[97] Alma Ata Declaration, 21 December 1991, (1991) 31 ILM 148 (subscribed to by all of the former Soviet Republics except for Georgia and the Baltic States).

[98] See Crawford and Boyle (n 93) para 57.3. See further YZ Blum, 'Russia Takes over the Soviet Union's Seat at the United Nations' (1992) 3 *EJIL* 354.

[99] Declaration of the European Communities, 23 December 1991, (1991) *EC Bulletin* 12, 121.

[100] Declaration of the Assemblies of Serbia, Montenegro and the FRY, 27 April 1992, UN Doc S/23877, Annex, 2.

[101] *Legality of Use of Force* (Serbia and Montenegro v United Kingdom) (Preliminary Objections) [2004] ICJ Rep 1307, para 89. On the different approach in the *Bosnian Genocide* case, see below, p 581.

Both the UN Security Council[102] and the Badinter Commission[103] took the view that the SFRY had ceased to exist. Uncertainty over the FRY's position continued until 2000–01, when it was admitted as a new UN Member State and abandoned its claim to continuity.[104]

In a legal opinion commissioned by the British government in the run-up to the Scottish independence referendum of September 2014, Crawford and Boyle identify several variables that may determine whether the legal personality of the State continues, and which entity acts as the 'continuator State'.[105] Relevant issues include the following: whether there is an agreement between the entities concerned; which unit retains the majority of the predecessor State's population and territory; which unit retains the governmental institutions of the predecessor State; and how third States and international organisations respond.[106]

The same factors may also be relevant in situations of (unilateral) 'secession' (see below, Section III(D)), albeit in the latter scenario the starting point is that there exists a presumption that the remaining territory continues the legal personality of the State. Even if a substantial part of the original territory is lost, the breakaway province will normally constitute a new State.

D. (Remedial) Secession beyond the Colonial Context

Above (Section III(B)), it was explained that international law recognises a right to independence on the part of colonial territories. The idea of extending this right to situations of unilateral 'secession' beyond the colonial context remains extremely controversial (as demonstrated by the reactions to the referenda on independence in Catalonia (Spain) and (Iraqi) Kurdistan in 2017). In general, States have been reluctant to extend the scope of the right of (external) self-determination for fear of creating undesired precedents. In particular, there is often a fear of opening the floodgates to the secessionist ambitions of various religious, ethnic or other polities within their own territory. This reluctance is reflected in the Friendly Relations Declaration's assertion that the right of self-determination should not be interpreted 'as authorizing or encouraging any action which would dismember or impair, totally or in part, the territorial integrity or political unity of sovereign and independent States'.[107]

In a 1998 landmark case concerning the position of Quebec, the Canadian Supreme Court stressed that peoples are expected first and foremost 'to achieve self-determination

[102] UNSC Res 757, 30 May 1992, UN Doc S/RES/757. See UNGA, 'Recommendation of the Security Council of 19 September 1992', 22 September 1992, UN Doc A/RES/47/1.

[103] Opinion No 8 of the Arbitration Commission of the Peace Conference on Yugoslavia, 4 July 1992, (1992) 31 ILM 1521–23. See further Pellet (n 36).

[104] See Crawford and Boyle (n 93) paras 79–92. Note: in the Dayton Agreement of 14 December 1995 ((1996) 35 ILM 68), the Federal Republic of Yugoslavia and Bosnia Herzegovina recognised each other as 'sovereign independent States within their international borders' (Art X).

[105] See Crawford and Boyle (n 93) paras 50–115.

[106] According to Crawford and Boyle, all of the factors would count in favour of the remaining territory of the UK to be the continuator State of the UK in case of a hypothetical Scottish independence; ibid, para 69.

[107] 'Friendly Relations Declaration' (n 73). Tomuschat frames the problem as follows: 'After all, international law [...] is a creation by those same States which, through its rules, seek to guarantee stability in their mutual relations. If, on the contrary international law should aspire critically to assess the *raison d'être* of States, including judgments to the effect that a State must disintegrate, it would become an instrument of revolutionary change, almost the opposite of a legal rule'; C Tomuschat, 'Self-Determination in a Post-Colonial World' in C Tomuschat (ed), *Modern Law of Self-Determination* (Dordrecht, Nijhoff, 1993) 5.

within the framework of their existing state'.[108] The Court left open whether this meant that peoples had a 'remedial' right to secession when they were denied any meaningful exercise of this right to 'internal' self-determination, for example, in situations where they are denied access to existing political institutions. The Court noted such scenario was 'possible', but did not deem it necessary to take a firm position since the Quebecers could in any event properly exercise their right of internal self-determination.[109]

The matter also surfaced in the ICJ's 2010 Advisory Opinion on the legality of the declaration of independence of Kosovo of 17 February 2008.[110] In this case, the Court noted that 'radically different views' existed as to whether there was a right to 'remedial secession' and, if so, in what circumstances.[111] At the same time, the Court decided that it was not called upon to resolve the conundrum, since the UN General Assembly had only requested it to rule whether the Kosovar declaration of independence – following a lengthy deadlock in the negotiations over the final status of Kosovo between the main protagonists – was 'in accordance with international law', and not to rule on the existence of any 'right to separate from a State'.[112] The Court held that there is no rule in international law *prohibiting* a unilateral declaration of independence. It admitted that there had been various instances where particular declarations of independence had been condemned by the UN Security Council. Yet,

> in all of those instances the Security Council was making a determination as regards the concrete situation existing at the time that those declarations of independence were made; the illegality attached to the declarations of independence thus stemmed not from the unilateral character of these declarations as such, but from the fact that they were, or would have been, connected with the unlawful use of force or other egregious violations of norms of general international law, in particular those of a peremptory character (*jus cogens*).[113]

In the context of Kosovo, no such objections were found to exist.[114] Consequently, the ICJ concluded that the declaration was not contrary to international law.

It follows that, beyond the scenarios discussed above, international law as it currently stands does not provide for a *right* to unilateral (remedial or other) secession.[115] Of course, international law must accept that, as a matter of fact, an unconstitutional declaration of independence may result in a de facto secession.

This was also acknowledged by the Canadian Supreme Court in its 1998 judgment, where it held that

> [t]he ultimate success of such a secession would be dependent on recognition by the international community, which is likely to consider the legality and legitimacy of secession having regard to,

[108] *Secession of Quebec, Re, Reference to Supreme Court*, 20 August 1998, (1998) 37 ILM 1342, para 154 ('A state whose government represents the whole of the people or peoples resident within its territory, on a basis of equality and without discrimination, and respects the principles of self-determination in its internal arrangements, is entitled to maintain its territorial integrity under international law and to have that territorial integrity recognized by other states').

[109] ibid. Note: the Court also left undecided whether the Quebecers qualified as a 'people' for present purposes.

[110] *Accordance with International Law of the Unilateral Declaration of Independence in Respect of Kosovo* (Advisory Opinion) [2010] ICJ Rep 403.

[111] ibid, para 82.

[112] ibid, para 83.

[113] ibid, para 81.

[114] Note that most of the Opinion focused on the compatibility of the declaration of independence with UNSC Resolution 1244 (1999), which installed a temporary UN administration in Kosovo (UNMIK) in the aftermath of NATO's military intervention, and with the subsequent UNMIK regulations.

[115] See eg the Report of the International-Fact-Finding Mission on the Conflict in Georgia (n 24) at 141.

amongst other facts, the conduct of Quebec and Canada, in determining whether to grant or withhold recognition.[116]

As the above quote indicates, international law does provide some indications to assess the legal implications if such de facto secession materialises, in particular as to whether it results in the creation of a new State and whether it is permissible to recognise the secessionist entity as such. The situation will be most straightforward if the predecessor State itself gradually accepts the de facto secession and (explicitly or implicitly) relinquishes its claims over the territory concerned. This is the case even if the independence thus achieved was not a 'negotiated' one at the outset.[117] In the absence of such acceptance, international law traditionally dictates that third States must abstain from 'premature recognition' of the new entity.[118] This means, for instance, that a new State should not be recognised while fighting is still ongoing and the secessionist entity has not (yet) been able to establish a stable government exercising effective control over a defined territory.[119] Otherwise, peoples that are manifestly prevented from exercising their (internal) right of self-determination within the existing State structure or that have been the victim of grave human rights violations will have a stronger entitlement to statehood or recognition.[120] Thus, the fact that Kosovo has been recognised as an independent State by over 110 UN Member States since the unilateral declaration of independence in 2008 may be explained in part as a reaction to the withdrawal of Kosovo's regional autonomy under the regime of Slobodan Milošević and the brutal repression by the Serbian authorities preceding the 1999 NATO intervention. By contrast, as indicated in the *Kosovo* Opinion, a claim to statehood will in principle be undermined if the de facto secession came about as a result of an unlawful military intervention or another breach of *jus cogens* (see also below, Section IV(A)).[121] Furthermore, as explained below, the degree of recognition by third States and international or regional organisations is not altogether without legal significance.

IV. The Role of Recognition

A. Recognition of States

The adoption and impact of 'recognition' finds itself at the intersection of law and politics. Recognition is an act which, at least partially, is inspired by political considerations, but

[116] *Secession of Quebec* (n 108) para 155: 'Such recognition, even if granted, would not, however, provide any retroactive justification for the act of secession, either under the Constitution of Canada or at international law'.

[117] The creation of the State of Eritrea strikes as an example of a unilateral secession that was later accepted by the predecessor State (Ethiopia). See Crawford (n 15) 402–403.

[118] See below (n 172).

[119] Note: on the application of the law on the use of force to so-called contested States, see C Henderson, 'Contested States and the Rights and Obligations of the Jus Ad Bellum' (2013) 21 *Cardozo Journal of International and Comparative Law* 367.

[120] Crawford seems to suggest in this context that the term 'people' is defined circularly. In particular, where a certain group or 'concentrated [minority] forming a distinctive unit in a particular area of the state and constituting a substantial majority of the population in that area' can be distinguished from 'the people of the state as a whole' and is struck, as a group, by an injustice recognised as triggering a right to self-determination, this group qualifies as a people in that circumstance; J Crawford, 'The Right of Self-Determination in International Law: Its Development and Future' in P Alston (ed), *People's Rights* (Oxford, OUP, 2001) 64.

[121] But see below (n 188).

which nonetheless generates legal consequences. A distinction must be made between the recognition of States and the recognition of governments.

The recognition of States concerns the unilateral act whereby a State recognises a new State as a member of the international community, accepting that the entity meets the constitutive requirements of a State and indicating its readiness to treat it as such. Such recognition can take various, explicit or implicit, forms. An obvious example consists in an explicit declaration to this end by the head of State or foreign minister of a third country. Other examples include: the opening of diplomatic relations between the respective States and the exchanging of ambassadors; the conclusion of bilateral treaties which explicitly or implicitly reveal that the contracting parties regard one another as States properly so termed, or the active support for another entity's application of membership to an international organisation open only to States. By contrast, the opening of consular relations or the mere shared membership of an international organisation is not of itself equivalent to mutual recognition as States on the part of the entities concerned.[122]

The recognition of a State – by whichever measure – is in principle a discretionary unilateral act. Thus, States are not obliged to engage in any of the acts of recognition identified above.[123] They are free to make recognition contingent upon the fulfilment of certain political preconditions, as the EC Member States did through the adoption of the aforementioned 'Guidelines on the Recognition of New States in Eastern Europe and in the Soviet Union' (see above, p 217). By contrast, customary international law does impose a number of restrictions on the freedom to recognise another entity as a State. In particular, a 'premature' recognition of a secessionist entity at a time when it has not yet established a stable government and fighting with the (predecessor) State is still ongoing, is traditionally deemed unlawful and contrary to the non-intervention principle.[124] In addition, the general duty of non-recognition of acts offending against peremptory norms enshrined in Article 41(2) of the ILC's Articles on State Responsibility (see also Chapter 12, Section IV(B)),[125] also applies to the recognition of States. This principle can be said to explain why in 1965, the UN Security Council called upon all States not to recognise the declaration of independence by an 'illegal racist minority régime' in Southern Rhodesia.[126] The archetypical example of the general duty of non-recognition is the non-recognition of territorial acquisition through conquest.[127] This principle has been affirmed in the UNGA's Friendly Relations Declaration,[128] and in its Definition of Aggression.[129] It has likewise been applied on several occasions by the UN Security Council; for instance, in relation to the Iraqi invasion of Kuwait in 1990,[130] pursuant to the Turkish invasion of northern Cyprus

[122] See R Jennings and A Watts (n 49) 169–74. Consider also Federal Supreme Court (CH), *Wang (Chuan Pu Andrew) and others v Office of the Federal Prosecutor*, 3 May 2004, Case No 1A.3/2004, where the Court held that a court decision to grant legal assistance in criminal matters to Taiwan could never amount to an official or implicit recognition of statehood by Switzerland.

[123] See Crawford (n 15) 148.

[124] See below (n 172). See also M Jamnejad and M Wood, 'The Principle of Non-intervention' (2009) 12 *LJIL* 345, 373.

[125] A Orakelashvili, *Peremptory Norms in International Law* (Oxford, OUP, 2006) 282.

[126] UNSC Res 216, 12 November 1965, UN Doc S/RES/216; UNSC Res 217, 20 November 1965, UN Doc S/RES/217. See also *Kosovo* Opinion (n 110) para 81.

[127] However, on the possibility of 'consolidation' of original illegality over time, see below (n 188).

[128] 'Friendly Relations Declaration' (n 73): 'No territorial acquisition resulting from the threat or use of force shall be recognized as legal'.

[129] UNGA, 'Definition of Aggression', Annex to UNGA Res 3314 (XXIX), 14 December 1974, UN Doc A/RES/3314 (XXIX), Art 5(3).

[130] UNSC Res 662, 9 August 1990, UN Doc S/RES/662 (deciding that the annexation had 'no legal validity, and is considered null and void').

and the subsequent creation of a so-called 'Turkish Republic of Northern Cyprus',[131] or in relation to Republika Srpska in 1992.[132] The EC Guidelines also stress that '[t]he Community and its Member States will not recognise entities which are the result of aggression'.[133]

A recent precedent concerns the Crimean peninsula, which, following a controversial referendum on 16 March 2014, declared its independence on 17 March and immediately thereafter concluded a 'treaty' with Russia, making it part of the Russian Federation.[134] As the referendum was organised against the background of a Russian military intervention – widely viewed as unlawful – the EU regarded the referendum as illegal and refused to recognise its outcome.[135] The Council of Europe's Venice Commission for its part opined that Russian legislation providing for the incorporation of Crimea into the Russian Federation was 'not compatible with international law', since it violated 'the principles of territorial integrity, national sovereignty, non-intervention in the internal affairs of another state and *pacta sunt servanda*'.[136] On 27 March 2014, the UNGA adopted a resolution calling upon all States 'not to recognise any alteration of the status of [Crimea] on the basis of the above-mentioned referendum and to refrain from any action or dealing that might be interpreted as recognizing any such altered status'.[137]

Recognition or non-recognition of States often generates repercussions at the domestic legal level.[138] Questions arise regarding whether certain persons or entities will be able to invoke immunities before the national courts of third States, whether they have legal standing to bring claims before these courts, and whether or not the acts adopted by the entity claiming statehood will be recognised. In many States, the answers to these questions depend on whether or not the executive has recognised the entity concerned. In the UK, for instance, this approach is grounded in the view that only the executive (and not the judiciary) is competent to determine foreign policy, and on the premise that the State cannot speak with two voices, 'the judiciary saying one thing, the executive another'.[139]

[131] See eg UNSC Res 541, 18 November 1983, UN Doc S/RES/541.

[132] UNSC Res 787, 16 November 1992, UN Doc S/RES/787. See also eg the preamble of UNSC Res 822, 30 April 1993, UN Doc S/RES/822 (concerning Nagorno-Karabakh). See further, on the non-recognition of the Republika Srpska: Opinion No 2 of the Arbitration Commission of the Peace Conference on Yugoslavia (n 77), where the Badinter Commission inter alia referred to the 'now peremptory norms of international law requir[ing] States to ensure respect for the (sic) rights of minorities'; Crawford (n 15) 406–407.

[133] 'Declaration on Yugoslavia' (n 64) 1487.

[134] See TD Grant, 'Annexation of Crimea' (2015) 109 *AJIL* 68.

[135] Joint statement by President of the European Council Herman Van Rompuy and President of the European Commission José Manuel Barroso on Crimea, 16 March 2014, EUCO 63/14; Council of the EU, Foreign Affairs Council meeting, 'Council Conclusions on Ukraine', 17 March 2014.

[136] Council of Europe, European Commission for Democracy through Law (Venice Commission), Opinion on 'whether draft Federal Constitutional Law No 462741-6 on amending the Federal Constitutional Law of the Russian Federation on the procedure of admission to the Russian Federation and creation of a new subject within the Russian Federation is compatible with international law', endorsed by the Venice Commission at its 98th plenary session, 21–22 March 2014, Opinion No 763/2014, CDL-AD(2014)004, at para 46. See also Council of Europe, European Commission for Democracy through Law (Venice Commission), Opinion on 'whether the decision taken by the Supreme Council of the Autonomous Republic of Crimea in Ukraine to organise a referendum on becoming a constituent territory of the Russian Federation or restoring Crimea's 1992 Constitution is compatible with constitutional principles', adopted by the Venice Commission at its 98th plenary session, 21–22 March 2014, Opinion No 762/2014, CDL-AD(2014)002.

[137] UNGA, 'Territorial integrity of Ukraine', 27 March 2014, UN Doc A/RES/68/262.

[138] These repercussions overlap in part with the domestic consequences attached to the recognition of governments, which is discussed below, Section IV(B).

[139] Eg *British Arab Commercial Bank plc v National Transitional Council of the State of Libya, ex parte Foreign and Commonwealth Office* [2011] EWHC 2274 (Comm), para 25. More generally, see ILA Committee on Recognition/Non-Recognition in International Law, 'Second (Interim) Report', March 2014, ila-hq.org/index.php/committees,

Thus, Crawford observes that as a general rule, 'non-recognized States have no right of appearance, and their acts will not be given effect by European courts'.[140]

The foregoing must nonetheless be nuanced to some extent. First, in the past, national courts went very far in refusing to give effect to the acts of unrecognised entities (eg by refusing to acknowledge marriages concluded under the laws of such entities).[141] This position has been softened, in particular to improve legal certainty on the part of individuals and corporations.[142] Thus, domestic courts often give effect to laws and acts of public authorities of unrecognised States when they concern day-to-day aspects of life, such as birth, marriages, divorces, deaths, and certain commercial matters.[143] For instance, in a 1975 judgment, the Italian Supreme Court asserted that recognition is irrelevant for establishing the effects in Italy 'of an act of private law executed abroad'.[144] On a related note, pursuant to the '*Namibia* principle', it is accepted that the duty of non-recognition of acts offending *jus cogens* norms does not extend to the effect of everyday transactions that are unavoidable in the daily relations of individuals.[145] Second, in a number of countries, such as Belgium and the Netherlands, national courts will independently assess the question of statehood 'on the basis of the factual criteria [...] laid down by international law', rather than by simply deferring to the recognition or non-recognition by the executive.[146] In a 2004 judgment, the Italian Supreme court similarly held that 'whether Italy (like other States) has recognized Montenegro as a sovereign State [was] totally irrelevant for the purposes of granting immunity from criminal jurisdiction to its top-ranking officials'.[147]

If recognition (explicit or implicit) by the executive often generates legal consequences at the national level, the question remains what the legal significance is at the *international* level. In the past, it was often argued that 'recognition' constituted one of the constituent elements of statehood, and that it was a *sine qua non* to qualify as a State under international law.[148] There are, however, intrinsic difficulties in this approach, in that it does not

26–27: 'There is a strong tradition of deference to the executive regarding whether or not an entity is recognized as a state, especially in the common law countries among the States surveyed'.

[140] Crawford (n 15) 162.

[141] See eg Royal Court of Appeal (HU), *Soviet Marriages* case (1925) ILR 31.

[142] Crawford (n 15) 162–63.

[143] Aust (n 67) 21.

[144] Court of Cassation (IT), *Warenzeichenverband Regelungstechnik EV v Ministry of Trade and Industry* (1975) 77 ILR 571, 571: 'The only prerequisite for the enforcement of a foreign legal rule is its effectiveness, provided that the particular legal provision does not also require reciprocity of treatment and so long as the principles of the foreign law to be enforced do not appear incompatible with the fundamental rule of the lex fori, in which case the foreign law is unenforceable for reasons of public policy'. In a similar vein, the (unofficial) Restatement of the Foreign Relations Law of the United States (Third) finds that 'courts in the United States ordinarily give effect to acts of a regime representing an entity not recognized as a state, or of a regime not recognized as a government of a state, if those acts apply to territory under the control of that regime and relate to domestic matters only'. American Law Institute, *Restatement of the Law – Third: The Foreign Relations Law of the United States* (St Paul, American Law Institute Publishers, 1990), Section 205.

[145] *Legal Consequences for States of the Continued Presence of South Africa in Namibia* (n 72) para 118.

[146] *East Timor v Netherlands* (n 34).

[147] Court of Cassation (IT), *Italy v DM*, 28 December 2004, Case No 49666, Diritto e Giustizia 30 (11/2005), (2006) 2 Riv Dir Int 568, para 14. The Court did acknowledge that the 'opinion of the Italian Ministry of Foreign affairs' was one of several 'significant factors' to be considered, yet not a binding or decisive one (ibid, para 17). See also Federal Supreme Court (CH), *Wang (Chuan Pu Andrew) and others v Office of the Federal Prosecutor*, 3 May 2004, Case No 1A.3/2004, where the Court held that the fact that the Swiss government did not recognise Taiwan was not the final word on Taiwan's statehood and, more specifically, did not preclude Switzerland from giving legal aid to Taiwanese authorities.

[148] Oppenheim (n 2) para 71. This approach seems to have been followed more recently in Higher Regional Court of Munich (DE), *Republic of Cyprus and others v Dikmen*, 18 March 2013, 19 U 4878/10 (pertaining to the so-called Turkish Republic of Northern Cyprus).

resolve the conundrum where an entity is recognised as a State by some, but not by others (as is often the case) and raises the question whether there ought to be a threshold of a minimum number of recognitions. The *'constitutive' approach* also raises fundamental questions pertaining to the foundations of the international legal order and the role of consent, as it essentially enables existing States to prevent new entrants from joining that order as 'full' subjects of international law.[149]

Pursuant to the *'declaratory' approach*, recognition does not bring into legal existence a State which did not exist before. Recognition merely acknowledges as a fact something which was previously uncertain, ie that an entity meets the criteria of statehood. At the same time, it signals the recognising State's willingness to treat the other entity as a fully-fledged State and normalise international relations with it. This 'declaratory' approach to the role of recognition finds support, for example, in the Montevideo Convention[150] and the work of the Badinter Commission.[151]

Whereas the declaratory approach has come to hold the upper hand in legal doctrine and State practice in recent times,[152] this is not to say that recognition bears no relevance. *First*, it is clear that States are not under any obligation to engage in international relations with one another to the fullest extent. Thus, it may be noted that while over 114 States have recognised Kosovo as a State,[153] numerous others have refrained from doing so. States are free not to engage in diplomatic relations with another entity, not to conclude bilateral treaties with it, and so on. If they choose not to establish diplomatic relations with another entity (such as Kosovo), 'statehood remains a question which for them can remain unanswered' – at least to a large extent.[154]

States can, if so desired, establish alternative relations with other unrecognised entities in light of functional needs. By way of illustration, in line with its 'One China' policy, the EU 'recognises the Government of the People's Republic of China as the sole legal government of China', and therefore 'is not engaged in relations of a diplomatic nature' with Taiwan.[155] At the same time, however, the EU does support Taiwan's meaningful participation in international organisations where this does not require statehood. The EU has bilateral consultations with Taiwan every year on a variety of issues, including education, environment, fisheries, etc.

The mere fact of withholding recognition does not make it permissible to ignore the customary rights and *erga omnes* entitlements of an entity that effectively meets the criteria of statehood. This applies, for example, to the prohibition on the use of force, the personal immunity for heads of State or the customary right to exclusive control over fishing within the Exclusive Economic Zone, and so on.

[149] For an illustration of this approach, see Oppenheim (n 2) para 27: 'those States which have hitherto formed the Family of Nations must expressly or tacitly consent to the reception of the new member'.

[150] Art 3 Montevideo Convention: 'The political existence of the state is independent of recognition by the other states. Even before recognition the state has the right to defend its integrity and independence, to provide for its conservation and prosperity, and consequently to organize itself as it sees fit, to legislate upon its interests, administer its services, and to define the jurisdiction and competence of its courts'.

[151] Opinion No 1 of the Arbitration Commission of the Peace Conference on Yugoslavia, 29 November 1991, (1992) 31 ILM 1494, 1495.

[152] In this sense eg Federal Supreme Court (CH), *Wang (Chuan Pu Andrew) and others v Office of the Federal Prosecutor*, 3 May 2004, Case No 1A.3/2004, para 5.3 (with references).

[153] See Republic of Kosovo, Ministry of Foreign Affairs, 'International Recognitions of the Republic of Kosovo', mfa-ks.net/?page=2,224.

[154] Clapham (n 12) 153.

[155] See EEAS, 'Taiwan and the EU', eeas.europa.eu/delegations/taiwan_en/2000/Taiwan%20and%20the%20EU.

Second, paraphrasing the Montevideo Convention, it is clear that the degree of recognition has repercussions for the 'capacity [of the entity concerned] to enter into international relations with other States', which is interwoven with the independence requirement of statehood (see above, Section II(E)). Recognition also carries a certain probative value in that the executive authorities will normally only proceed to recognition after having conducted an internal analysis to verify whether the entity concerned meets the criteria of statehood and is deemed to have an established expertise in this context. This is also the way in which recognition is oftentimes considered by national courts. Thus, in the abovementioned judgment of 2004, the Italian Court of Cassation held that

> although they do not create legal personality, significant factors to be considered in resolving [whether Montenegro has statehood] are […] the behaviour of other States towards Montenegro and vice versa, and in particular its participation in international treaties or conventions or intergovernmental organisations and the opinion of the Italian Ministry of Foreign affairs, which is the authority our law designates for international relationships and the observing and collection of data and relevant matters under international law.[156]

In a 1980 judgment concerning the situation in Timor-Leste, the District Court of Amsterdam noted that the absence of recognition of Timor-Leste by the large majority of the international community at that stage established a presumption that the factual criteria for statehood were deemed not to be fulfilled.[157] The probative value would seem particularly strong in respect of collective recognitions, as in the case of the recognition of Palestine as a 'Non-Member Observer State' by the UN General Assembly in 2012.[158]

Attempts to arrive at a more coherent and concerted recognition policy at the level of the EU have seen mixed results.[159] While the EC adopted a set of guidelines on the recognition of new States in the wake of the break-up of the Soviet Union and of the Socialist Federal Republic of Yugoslavia (see above, Section II(F) and IV(A)), the implementation of these guidelines has been deemed inconsistent and unsatisfactory.[160] The EU was more cohesive regarding the recognition by its Member States of Timor-Leste (2002), Montenegro (2006) and South Sudan (2011). However, the EU has failed to arrive at a common approach vis-à-vis the recognition of Kosovo. On 18 February 2008, the Council of the EU adopted a declaration stressing that Kosovo constituted a '*sui generis* case' and left it to the Member States to 'decide, in accordance with national practice and international law, on their relations with Kosovo'.[161] While the large majority of EU Member States has recognised Kosovo's independence, Spain, Slovakia, Cyprus, Romania and Greece have not. In a similar vein, there is no joint recognition policy with regard to Palestine, and EU Member States have voted differently with regard to the aforementioned UNGA resolution granting Palestine 'Non-Member Observer State' status.

In the end, as Koskenniemi points out, neither the declaratory nor the constitutive approach 'seems defensible alone and neither provides a satisfactory interpretation of State

[156] *Italy v DM* (n 147) paras 14 and 17. See also *Slovak Citizen* (n 47), where reference was made to the number of States that recognised Slovakia and the position of those States. In particular, the Court deemed it significant that enemy States recognised its status as a State under international law.

[157] *East Timor v Netherlands* (n 34) para 4.

[158] See above (n 18).

[159] For a call for a more coherent and concerted approach to recognition at the EU level, see Denza (n 36).

[160] See above (n 67).

[161] Council of the European Union, General Affairs and External Relations, External Relations, 18 February 2008, Doc 6596/08, 8.

practice'.[162] It is possible that a de facto secession comes about without recognition. If, in such a setting, a stable (de facto) government is established and a number of States choose to recognise the secessionist entity as a State whereas others do not, it is difficult to sustain that one group is necessarily (legally) correct and the other is wrong.[163] Rather, as acknowledged by the Canadian Supreme Court in 1998,[164] in case of a *fait accompli* secession, recognition by the international community may actually have a determining influence, in that it may tilt the balance in favour of statehood (or not). Thus, the fact that Abkhazia, South Ossetia and Taiwan are recognised only by a handful of States, whereas Kosovo is recognised by 114 States may actually have a direct impact on their claim to statehood. When an entity is admitted to UN membership pursuant to a recommendation by the UN Security Council and a two thirds majority vote in the UN General Assembly, such recognition could be argued to conclusively settle its claim to statehood, also vis-à-vis those UN Member States that opposed its application.

B. Recognition of Governments

States are abstract legal entities that act through their government and subsidiary State organs. Identifying this government and these State organs may be legally relevant for various reasons. For example, it may be relevant to identify who is competent to conclude treaties on the part of the State concerned and to represent it at the diplomatic level, including in international organisations; who can benefit from immunities under international law; whose conduct triggers the responsibility of the State; who has access to funds and assets of the State abroad; who can invite outside military 'intervention by invitation', etc. In many cases, the answers are self-evident: for most States, a stable and uncontested government can easily be identified. Problems may arise, however, where a new regime comes to power through unconstitutional or violent means, in particular where competing groups both claim to be the State's government. This was the case, for instance, in Libya after the fall of Gadhafi in 2011.[165]

It is in such situations that the concept of 'recognition of governments' comes into play. A recognition of a government is the act whereby the executive of a third State takes a public position – eg following a coup d'état or civil war – as to which body or group it regards as having the sole competence to represent the State concerned to the exclusion of all other groups. The term is usually taken to refer to acts of explicit recognition, although a State may also implicitly, through its conduct, reveal its position on the matter. De jure recognition signals that the entity concerned is regarded as fully satisfying the applicable legal criteria to represent the State. De facto recognition is a more cautious and provisional acknowledgment that a regime exercises de facto control over the State, but whereby the recognising State reserves its final position as to this regime's legal status.[166]

Recognition may have an impact at the judicial level inasmuch as national courts that are confronted with questions over who acts as the government of a third State may look at the position adopted by the executive (in particular the foreign ministry) for guidance

[162] Koskenniemi (n 35) 280.
[163] In this sense, see Clapham (n 12) 151–52.
[164] *Secession of Quebec* (n 108) para 155.
[165] See eg 'Libya's Rival Governments', *The Economist*, 27 September 2014.
[166] See Crawford (n 15) 152–53.

and may regard a recognition by the executive as binding or as conclusive evidence to this end. By way of illustration, in a judgment of 2011, a UK Court decided that the 'National Transitional Council of the State of Libya' (NTC) should be given access to English bank accounts in Libya's name formerly under the control of the Gadhafi regime.[167] The fact that the NTC had previously been recognised as the government of Libya by a certificate signed by the British Foreign Secretary was deemed to settle the matter.[168]

Does recognition of a government also entail consequences at the *international* level? As with the recognition of States, it would seem that its impact is mostly declaratory. Indeed, just as is the case for the recognition of States, there is no duty for States to explicitly and formally recognise new governments – and in fact the large majority of States do not practise such policy. Non-recognition of an entity does not automatically entail that it does not qualify as the government of a State, nor that third States can or will ignore this legal status and the ramifications thereof. Thus, in the *Tinoco Concessions* case, the arbitrator observed that, even if Tinoco's government was unconstitutional under the law of Costa Rica and even if it had not been recognised by third countries, Tinoco was nonetheless 'in actual and peaceable control without resistance or conflict or contest by any one'.[169] In light of this, the arbitrator held that it had been the actual government of Costa Rica, whose actions, including the granting of concessions, were binding upon Costa Rica.

This precedent suggests that the identification of the government of a State is a matter that is governed not by the subjective preferences of recognising States but by objective legal parameters. In particular, while a State may, for instance, express its support for the democratic 'legitimacy'[170] of a certain regime through an act of formal recognition, the 'standard set by international law' is the standard of secure de facto control of all or most of the State's territory.[171] Premature recognition of a new government absent such territorial control will in principle amount to a tortious act against the lawful government in breach of international law.[172] Furthermore, according to the traditional position in international law, in cases of civil war, 'the presumption in favour of the lawful government is

[167] *British Arab Commercial Bank* (n 139) para 21.

[168] A similar approach can be found in the US. Thus, Section 205 of the *Restatement of Foreign Relations Law* (n 144) stresses inter alia that a regime not recognised as the government of a State is ordinarily denied access to courts in the US and is not entitled to property belonging to that state located in the US. In the absence of explicit recognition by the executive, the UK courts have developed a set of factors to determine the existence of a government (see below, n175 and accompanying text).

[169] Arbitration between Great Britain and Costa Rica, Opinion and Award of William H Taft, 18 October 1923, reprinted in (1924) 18 *AJIL* 147, 152.

[170] On the increased focus on 'democratic governance' and 'democratic legitimacy' as emerging criteria for recognition, see eg T Franck, 'The Emerging Right to Democratic Governance' (1992) 86 *AJIL* 46; S Marks, 'What has Become of the Emerging Right to Democratic Governance?' (2011) 22 *EJIL* 507; SD Murphy, 'Democratic Legitimacy and the Recognition of States and Governments' (1999) 48 *ICLQ* 54; J Wouters, B De Meester and C Ryngaert, 'Democracy and International Law' (2003) 34 *NYIL* 139.

[171] Crawford (n 15) 152. For a recent affirmation, see eg US Senate, Committee on Foreign Relations, Libya and War Powers, Hearing, S Hrg 112189, 28 June 2011, 39 (US Legal Advisor: 'international law focuses on the question of recognition, and recognition tends to follow facts on the ground, particularly control over territory. As a general rule, we are reluctant to recognize entities that do not control entire countries because then they are responsible for parts of the country that they don't control, and we're reluctant to derecognize leaders who still control parts of the country because then you're absolving them of responsibility in the areas that they do control').

[172] H Lauterpacht, *Recognition in International Law* (Cambridge, CUP, 1947) 95 (warning that, if States could freely choose to recognise either side in a civil war as the lawful government, they could unilaterally 'reduce the established government to the status of a rebellious group and […] raise the newly recognized authority to the position of the legitimate government to which support and encouragement may lawfully be given'). See also Institut de Droit International, 'The Principle of Non-intervention in Civil Wars', Session of Wiesbaden, 1975, Art 2(f), idi-iil.org/app/uploads/2017/06/1975_wies_03_en.pdf.

above controversy: the latter is entitled to continued recognition de jure so long as the civil war, whatever its prospects, is in progress'.[173]

At the same time, it is a bridge too far to conclude that (explicit or implicit) recognition of a government by third States or organisations has no impact whatsoever on its legal position under international law. This is especially the case for 'collective' recognition, for instance, by the UN Security Council.[174] The degree of recognition has indeed been considered by national courts. Thus, British Courts have, for instance, identified a number of 'factors to be taken into account in deciding whether a government exists as the government of a state':

> (a) whether it is the constitutional government of the state; (b) the degree, nature and stability of administrative control, if any, that it of itself exercises over the territory of the state; (c) whether Her Majesty's Government has any dealings with it and if so what is the nature of those dealings; and (d) in marginal cases, the extent of international recognition that it has as the government of the state.[175]

Similarly, where two rival governments both claim to represent the State concerned, the degree of international recognition, in particular by the main political bodies of the UN, has an impact; for instance, on the assessment whether an entity is competent to invite outside military intervention.[176] Whether in such cases the degree of recognition merely plays a 'probative' or 'evidentiary' role or has a more 'constitutive' impact remains open to debate.

In recent decades, many States have by and large abandoned the practice of formally and explicitly recognising foreign governments.[177] The reason for this was that this practice was often politically embarrassing, as recognition was sometimes perceived as approval of a regime that came to power through unconstitutional means. Thus, in 1980, the British government stated that it would halt its past policy of making and announcing a decision formally 'recognising' new governments.[178] In spite hereof, after 2011, there was a flurry

[173] Lauterpacht (n 172) para 38 ('So long as the lawful government offers resistance which is not ostensibly hopeless or purely nominal, the de jure recognition of the revolutionary party as a government constitutes premature recognition which the lawful government is entitled to regard as an act of intervention contrary to international law'). Note: The de jure authorities of a State will not normally be internationally responsible for the conduct of an insurrectional movement fighting against it. The situation is different if the insurrectional movement is successful and becomes the new government of the State. In such case, its acts will *ab initio* be regarded as acts of the State. See Chapter 12, Section III(B).

[174] Consider eg UNSC Res 2174, 27 August 2014, UN Doc S/RES/2174 (concerning Libya), UNSC Res 2216, 14 April 2015, UN Doc S/RES/2216 (adopted in the midst of an ongoing civil war in Yemen and 'reaffirming its support for the legitimacy of the President of Yemen, Abdo Rabbo Masnsour Hadi') or UNSC Res 2337, 19 January 2017, UN Doc S/RES/2337 (endorsing the decisions of ECOWAS and the AU to recognise Mr Adama Barrow as President of the Gambia).

[175] *Republic of Somalia v Woodhouse Drake & Carey (Suisse) SA* [1993] QB 54 (the case dealt with access to property belonging to the State of Somalia at a time when no single group had control over the country); *Sierra Leone Telecommunications Co Ltd v Barclays Bank plc* [1998] 2 All ER 821. *British Arab Commercial Bank* (n 139) para 24 ('I should however note that [...] a growing number of states have recognised [the TNC] as the legitimate government of Libya').

[176] See further eg D Wippman, 'Pro-Democratic Intervention by Invitation' in G Fox and B Roth (eds), *Democratic Governance and International Law* (Cambridge, CUP, 2000) 293–327; T Ruys and L Ferro, 'Weathering the Storm: Legality and Legal Implications of the Saudi-led Military Intervention in Yemen' (2016) 65 *ICLQ* 61; MS Helal, 'The ECOWAS Intervention in The Gambia – 2016' in T Ruys, O Corten and A Hofer (eds), *The Use of Force in International Law: A Case-Based Approach* (Oxford, OUP, 2018) (912–932).

[177] I Roberts, *Satow's Diplomatic Practice* (Oxford, OUP, 2009) para 6.13 ('Modern practice is for other States to make no express statement recognizing a new government and for the continuation of relations – whether through the same ambassador or through a replacement appointment – to take place as inconspicuously as possible').

[178] Reprinted in (1980) 51 *BYIL* 255, 367–68 ('We have [...] concluded that there are practical advantages in following the policy of many other countries in not according recognition to Governments. Like them, we shall

of declarations by numerous States recognising the Libyan National Transitional Council (in the context of the civil war in Libya in 2011) and the Syrian Opposition Council (in the context of the Syrian civil war).[179] Importantly, these declarations were initially phrased as recognising these opposition movements as the 'legitimate representative of (the interests of) the people' of Libya/Syria. Such declarations are of a political nature and must not be confused with actual recognition of governments. They aim to signal political approval and grant legitimacy to the entities concerned and may entail practical consequences, such as periodic consultation or provision of funding.[180] They do not generate international legal implications. In particular, they do not normally detract from the fact that the State making the declaration still regards the 'old' regime as the de jure government.

Recognition of States and governments should not be confused with *recognition of belligerency*.[181] The latter concept refers to declarations made in the context of large-scale non-international armed conflicts whereby a non-State armed group has obtained effective control over part of the State's territory. In such setting, rebel groups can be recognised as 'belligerent parties' by the de jure government of the State and by third parties. Such recognition bears consequences for the application of the law of armed conflict, in that it triggers the application by analogy of the law governing international armed conflicts (including neutrality law). Recognition of belligerency is mostly a historical phenomenon and there have been no clear-cut applications in the Charter era.[182]

V. Acquisition of Territory

A. General

As noted above, a 'defined territory' forms one of the constitutive requirements of statehood, albeit that contestations about the specific demarcation of the boundaries do not prevent this condition from being fulfilled. Numerous countries have – often long-standing – land and/or maritime boundary disputes. The dispute between Japan and China, for instance, over the Senkaku/Diaoyu islands in the East China Sea,[183] or the dispute

continue to decide the nature of our dealings with regimes which come to power unconstitutionally in the light of our assessment of whether they are able of themselves to exercise effective control of the territory of the State concerned, and seem likely to continue to do so').

[179] See S Talmon, 'Recognition of Opposition Groups as the Legitimate Representative of a People' (2013) 12 *Chinese Journal of International Law* 219.

[180] Exceptionally, these recognitions have also been seen as a factor justifying the supply of weapons to rebel groups. See eg Letter by the Dutch Foreign Minister to the House of Representatives, 'Volkenrechtelijke aspecten van het sanctieregime tegen Syrië', 4 June 2013, rijksoverheid.nl/documenten/brieven/2013/06/04/brief-volkenrechtelijke-aspecten-van-het-sanctieregime-tegen-syrie) ('The lack of legitimacy of the Assad regime and the broad recognition of the [Syrian Opposition Council] as the legitimate representative of the Syrian people have led the government to conclude that the supply of military equipment to the SOC, in exceptional cases and under specific conditions, need not be contrary to international law' (our translation)). Whether this position is legally valid is most questionable. See further T Ruys, 'Of Arms, Funding and "Non-Lethal Assistance" – Issues Surrounding Third-State Intervention in the Syrian Civil War' (2014) 13 *Chinese Journal of International Law* 13.

[181] See further S Sivakumaran, *The Law of Non-International Armed Conflict* (Oxford, OUP, 2012) 9–20.

[182] See also Chapter 15, Section II(A), on the scope of application of the law of armed conflict.

[183] See eg G Poissonnier and P Osseland, 'A qui appartiennent les îles Senkaku/Diaoyu ?' (2008) 135 *Journal du droit international* 467.

between Mauritius and the United Kingdom over the British Indian Ocean Territory,[184] are but two of numerous examples. A large proportion of the cases brought before the ICJ or before inter-State arbitration indeed concern such conflicting claims.

Often, these disputes relate to the precise delimitation of land or maritime boundaries between neighbouring States. The issue of maritime delimitation is briefly addressed in Chapter 18 (Law of the Sea), Section VII. Equally, the delimitation of land is governed by a special body of rules. Thus, according to the *thalweg* principle, it is accepted that where a boundary is formed by a navigable river, it should be drawn in the middle of the principal channel of navigation (see also below, p 420).[185] If the watercourse separating the two countries is non-navigable, the boundary is constituted by the median line between the two river banks. International case law features numerous cases concerning the validity and interpretation of the decisions of joint boundary commissions and of boundary treaties.[186]

On other occasions, it will be the very *title* to territory, that is, the validity of a claim to a defined piece of territory, that is in dispute. This is where the so-called 'law of territory' or the 'law of acquisition of territorial sovereignty' comes into play. Historically, the law of territory developed alongside European colonisation. Until the fifteenth century, the territorial order among European States was settled through legal systems similar to those used to transfer property. Thus, title to territory could be obtained through mechanisms such as inheritance, marriage, cession or a peace treaty.[187] With the colonial expansion of Europe, European States developed a new legal framework to regulate and validate their colonial endeavours.

A key point of departure in the law of territory is that the acquisition of territory must be assessed in light of the rules of international law as they existed at the time of acquisition, and not as they exist today. This is the so-called principle of 'intertemporal law'. Thus, while today, acquisition of territory by conquest is clearly unlawful and must not be recognised by third States, this has not always been the case (see above, Section IV(A)).[188] Further, since

[184] See further *In the matter of the Chagos Marine Protected Area Arbitration* (Mauritius v UK), before an Arbitral Tribunal constituted under Annex VII of the United Nations Convention on the Law of the Sea, 18 March 2015, pcacases.com/pcadocs/MU-UK%2020150318%20Award.pdf; UNGA, 'Request for an advisory opinion of the International Court of Justice on the legal consequences of the separation of the Chagos Archipelago from Mauritius in 1965', 22 June 2017, UN Doc A/RES/71/292.

[185] See further M Forteau, 'Délimitation la rive au Thalweg, au milieu du chénal' in B Aurescu and A Pellet (eds), *Actualité du droit des fleuves internationaux* (Paris, Pedone, 2010) 29–39.

[186] See eg *Sovereignty over Certain Frontier Land* (Belgium v Netherlands) [1959] ICJ Rep 209; *Preah Vihear* (n 78) 26 (in both cases, the ICJ rejected the invocation of an error on the part of the State to vitiate its consent to the contested boundary).

[187] S Huh, 'Title to Territory in the Post-Colonial Era: Original Title and Terra Nullius in the ICJ Judgments on Cases Concerning Ligitan/Sipadan (2002) and Pedra Branca (2008)' (2015) 26 *EJIL* 709, 710.

[188] By way of illustration, when the three Baltic States became independent following the dissolution of the Soviet Union, the EC 'warmly welcome[d] the restoration of the sovereignty and independence of the Baltic States which they lost in 1940' (Declaration on Yugoslavia adopted at the [European Political Cooperation] Extraordinary Ministerial Meeting, 27 August 1991, reprinted in (1991) 62 *BYIL* 558). Statements such as these are ostensibly premised on the idea that States preserve their identity throughout a period (even if prolonged) of illegal annexation. Supreme Court of Justice (AT), *J v Social Insurance Institution for Farmers*, 9 November 2004, Case No 10 Ob S119/04d; Supreme Court (CY), *Re, Tomko (Tetyana) v Cyprus and Department of Population Register and Immigration of the Ministry of Interior*, 20 June 2007, Case No 709/2006; Constitutional Court (LV), *Re, Kariņš and others v Parliament of Latvia and Cabinet of Ministers of Latvia*, 29 November 2007, Case No 2007-10-0102. Dinstein nonetheless suggests that if the de facto control of territory annexed by an aggressor State continues uninterrupted for generations, international law may ultimately have no choice but to 'capitulate to the facts'. Y Dinstein, *War, Aggression and Self-defence*, 5th edn (Cambridge, CUP, 2011) 183–84. In a similar vein, others have suggested that 'original illegality may be corrected in a process of consolidation, that is, the passing of time during which it becomes generally accepted to be best to let the sleeping dogs lie'; Koskenniemi (n 35) 284.

there is no system of formal registration of title to territory under international law similar to such systems under domestic law, the main guiding principle is – as stated by Judge Huber in the *Island of Palmas* case – that 'the actual continuous and peaceful display of state functions is […] the sound and natural criterion of territorial sovereignty'.[189]

Traditionally, a distinction is made between five so-called 'modes of acquisition': occupation, accretion, cession, conquest and prescription.[190] Alternative distinctions are those between 'original' acquisition and 'derivative' acquisition (depending on whether there was a prior State holding title over the territory concerned or not), or between acquisition on the part of newly independent States and additional acquisitions by existing States. However, the validity of these categories is often challenged, and in reality, it is often difficult to separate them neatly.

B. Acquisition of Original Title

The classic example of 'original' acquisition is the 'occupation' of '*terra nullius*', that is, territory belonging to no one. It has indeed long been accepted that States can acquire valid title over uninhabited and unexplored land on a 'first come, first served' basis through effective occupation. Effective occupation requires both an objective element (the '*corpus occupendi*') and a subjective element (the '*animus occupendi*'). The objective element presupposes that the State has effective control over the land concerned and that it exercises this control through various forms of State activity with a certain degree of continuity and effectiveness. Displays of sovereignty may include formal declarations, the physical presence of State organs (eg military personnel), the collection of taxes, etc. The subjective element implies that there is an '*intentional* display of power and authority over the territory'[191] by the State itself (rather than by unauthorised persons) and acting on an autonomous basis (rather than eg pursuant to a delegation of powers by another State).[192]

The degree of recognition, or, conversely, the absence of competing claims, as well as considerations of contiguity, play a considerable role in assessing title to territory.[193] On the other hand, as indicated in the *Island of Palmas* case, State authority should not necessarily be displayed 'in fact at every moment on every point of territory'.[194] The relevant threshold depends on the specific circumstances of each case.[195] Thus, the PCIJ's 1933 *Eastern Greenland* judgment illustrates that the inaccessible or uninhabitable character of certain territory can compensate for a lesser degree of physical State activity (and exceptionally even a complete absence thereof).[196] In this case, the Court placed considerable emphasis on 'the absence of any claim to sovereignty by another Power' to hold that 'the King of

[189] *Island of Palmas* (n 28) 870–71.
[190] Oppenheim (n 2) para 211.
[191] *Eritrea v Yemen*, Award on Territorial Sovereignty and Scope of the Dispute, 9 October 1998, XXII RIAA 211, para 239.
[192] Crawford (n 15) 226.
[193] According to Koskenniemi (n 35) (at 286), the law of territorial acquisition 'oscillates between basing title on effective possession (and its derivatives) and on external recognition (acquiescence)', but neither is ultimately sufficient of its own.
[194] *Island of Palmas* (n 28) 840.
[195] *Sovereignty over Pedra Branca/Pulau Batu Puteh, Middle Rocks and South Ledge* (Malaysia v Singapore) [2008] ICJ Rep 12, para 67.
[196] *Legal Status of Eastern Greenland* [1933] PCIJ Rep Series A/B No 53. See also *Pedra Branca* (n 195) para 66: 'If this conclusion was valid with reference to the thinly populated and unsettled territory of Eastern Greenland,

Denmark and Norway displayed [...] in 1721 to 1814 his authority to an extent sufficient to give his country a valid claim to sovereignty, and that his rights over Greenland were not limited to the colonised area' of Greenland.[197]

In the contemporary world, the occupation of *terra nullius* has lost its significance as a means for acquiring territory, simply due to the fact that – save for some very small rocks and a small sector of Antarctica (over which no sovereignty may in any case be claimed pursuant to Article IV(2) of the Antarctic Treaty) – there is no more *terra nullius*.[198] Exceptionally, States can acquire 'new' territory in the form of new geological formations, such as when deposits result in an extension of the coastline, or when an underwater volcanic eruption results in the emergence of a new island in their vicinity.[199] Such acquisition of territory pursuant to 'accretion' nonetheless remains a relatively marginal phenomenon. The process of acquisition through 'occupation' is mostly important to assess historical claims to territory.

In the past, the concept of '*terra nullius*' was understood to cover not only uninhabited land, but also non-European land that was regarded as 'uncivilised', and accordingly open to occupation by the European powers.[200] The law of territory was thus developed and used to validate the European powers' colonial ambitions. This approach is also implicit in the aforementioned *Island of Palmas* case (1928), where Judge Huber noted that the 'native princes or chiefs of peoples' were 'not recognized as members of the community of nations' in the sixteenth century and beyond,[201] implying that European States could acquire title to the island of Palmas as *terra nullius*. Contracts between the Netherlands (and the Dutch East Indies Company), on the one hand, and the King of Tabukan (the local ruler of the area that included Palmas), were not regarded as treaties, but rather as 'a form of internal organisation of a colonial territory', and a display of Dutch sovereignty.[202] Because of its imperialist connotations, the concept of *terra nullius* has become controversial, and to some extent outmoded, in the post-colonial era. Thus, in its *Western Sahara* Opinion of 1975, the ICJ stressed that 'territories inhabited by tribes or peoples having a social and political organization' (such as Western Sahara in the nineteenth century), did not qualify as 'terrae nullius'.[203] It regarded the acquisition of such land pursuant to agreements with local rulers not as 'occupation' of 'terra nullius' by original title, but rather as a form of derivative acquisition.

More recent ICJ judgments confirm that, leaving aside the process of accretion, there exist essentially two ways of acquiring 'original title' to territory: (i) the acquisition of *terra nullius* by a pre-existing State; and (ii) the acquisition of title that coincides with the very birth of the State as a political entity within a given territorial domain.[204] Thus, in the *Pedra*

it should also apply to the present case involving a tiny uninhabited and uninhabitable island, to which no claim of sovereignty had been made by any other Power throughout the years from the early sixteenth century until the middle of the nineteenth century'.

[197] *Eastern Greenland* (n 196) 50–51.

[198] On the legal position of Antarctica, the Moon and other celestial bodies, see Chapter 18, Sections XI (on 'Antarctica') and XII (on 'Outer Space').

[199] Eg R Hughes, 'Hunga Tonga volcano eruption forms new S Pacific island', *BBC News*, 12 March 2015.

[200] According to Bedjaoui: '*[d]ans l'Antiquité romaine, est nullius tout territoire qui n'est pas romain. A l'époque des grandes découvertes des XVe et XVe siècles, est nullius tout territoire qui n'appartient pas à un souverain chrétien. Au XIXe siècle, est nullius tout territoire qui n'appartient pas à un Etat civilisé*'; ICJ, *Western Sahara*, ICJ Pleadings (1975), Vol IV, 445, 448.

[201] *Island of Palmas* (n 28) 858.

[202] ibid. See also Huh (n 187) 724.

[203] *Western Sahara* (n 72) para 80.

[204] See *Sovereignty over Pulau Ligitan and Pulau Sipadan* (Indonesia v Malaysia) [2002] ICJ Rep 625; *Pedra Branca* (n 195).

Branca case, the ICJ started from the observation that the Sultanate of Johor undoubtedly established itself as a sovereign State since it came into existence in 1512.[205] It subsequently went on to examine whether the contested Pedra Branca/Pulau Batu Puteh island fell within 'the general geographical scope of' the Sultanate – a question that was answered in the affirmative.[206]

C. Derivative Acquisition

A first form of derivative acquisition is prescription (or '*usucapio*'). Prescription refers to the situation whereby a State gradually acquires title to territory pursuant to the usurpation of another State's sovereignty, combined with the acquiescence of the former sovereign. It presupposes first and foremost that a State, acting in its sovereign capacity, exercises possession of territory (previously) belonging to another State, and that it does so for a certain period of time, and does so openly and peacefully.[207] In such a setting, it is possible that the other State relinquishes its claim over the territory concerned; eg through a formal declaration.[208] Alternatively, the usurper State may gradually acquire title over the territory if the other State fails to respond to its possession and acquiesces to the usurper's conduct. Case law nonetheless illustrates that such acquiescence is not to be presumed lightly. Assertion of the State of its sovereignty over the territory concerned or occasional acts of administration will normally prevent prescription from taking place. It would indeed seem that 'nothing short of the total (or near-total) absence of conduct *à titre de souverain* in an area by the title-holder will be sufficient to signal movement away from the status quo'.[209]

In reality, the difference between 'occupation' and 'prescription' may be hard to make and international judges will often balance the relative strengths and weaknesses of the claims put forward by the contending States, without explicitly using either label. The focus will generally lie on the degree of effective control, evidence of acquiescence, recognition or admission, as well as subsidiary factors such as the locus and character of the territory concerned.[210]

Another form of derivative acquisition relates to the transfer of title to territory from one State to another pursuant to a treaty between them. There exist many such historical cases of 'cession' of territory.[211] A well-known example is the 'Louisiana purchase' of 1803,[212] whereby the United States 'bought' an area covering more than two million km^2 from France. A key limitation is the principle that a State cannot transfer more rights than it possesses (*nemo dat quod non habet*). Thus, in the *Island of Palmas* case, the arbitrator found that Spain could not cede Palmas to the US pursuant to the Treaty of Paris, since it

[205] *Pedra Branca* (n 195) para 52.

[206] ibid, para 61 (the Court relied on the fact that the island was no *terra incognita* since it had always been known as a navigational hazard, as well as on the absence of any competing claim over the islands in the area of the Strait of Singapore at the time).

[207] Crawford (n 15) 231.

[208] See eg *Pedra Branca* (n 195) para 230.

[209] Crawford (n 15) 233.

[210] Procedures concerning territorial disputes tend to be highly technical and fact-specific. Much will depend on the arguments and the 'critical dates' brought forward by the respective parties. On the concept of the 'critical date', see eg Jennings and Watts (n 49) 710, nr 273.

[211] Some historical cases are more akin to renunciation of title to territory than to actual cession.

[212] Treaty for the Cession of Louisiana and Payments Conventions between France and the United States (adopted 30 April 1803, entered into force 21 October 1803) 57 CTS 27.

no longer had title to the territory concerned.[213] Examples of fully-fledged 'cession' of territory pursuant to treaty have become highly exceptional today. Treaties are occasionally used to implement (minor) border corrections or land swaps.[214] Finally, cession should not be confused with various arrangements whereby States grant certain (limited and temporary) rights to other States vis-à-vis part of their sovereign territory. There exist, for instance, numerous lease agreements (such as the controversial Guantanamo lease),[215] the duration and content of which may vary considerably.[216]

VI. State Succession

The doctrine of State succession involves the domestic and international legal effects of territorial changes of a State. The Vienna Convention of 23 August 1978 on the Succession of States in Respect of Treaties defines 'succession of States' as 'the replacement of one State (the "successor State") by another (the "predecessor State") in the responsibility for the international relations of territory'.[217] The replacement of a State by another State means that the principle of State sovereignty regulates the succession. This brings about an element of discontinuity: the successor State is not the 'continuation' of the predecessor State since both have a distinct international legal personality. Because the successor State exercises full authority as a sovereign and independent State within its territory, it is not automatically bound by all of the earlier actions of its predecessor State when exercising its competences.[218] However, this does not entail that every element of continuity would be excluded and that the *tabula rasa* principle may be applied across the board.[219]

There are several modes of State succession. Obviously, when a State disappears as an international person and ceases to exist, this leads to a situation of State succession (so-called 'universal succession of States'). In practice this can occur through a merger, dissolution and annexation. State succession can also occur in case of secession, a partial transfer of territory[220] and decolonisation, in which the predecessor State continues to exist (so-called 'partial succession of States').

International law relating to State succession is a disparate tangle, known for its plurality of sources. Many solutions are ad hoc and regulated by treaty, in many cases by

[213] *Island of Palmas* (n 28) 842.

[214] See eg 'India, Bangladesh swap border enclaves, settle old dispute', *The Hindu*, 1 August 2015; Traité entre le Royaume des Pays-Bas et le Royaume de Belgique visant à adapter la frontière entre les communes néerlandaises d'Eijsden-Margraten et de Maastricht et la ville belge de Visé (adopted 28 November 2016, entered into force 1 January 2018), *Tractatenblad* 29 (2016), Nr 1.

[215] Convention between Cuba and the United States for the Establishment of Naval and Coaling Stations at Guantanamo and Bahia Honda (adopted 2 July 1903, entered into force 6 October 1903) 193 CTS 314.

[216] See further MJ Strauss, *Territorial Leasing in Diplomacy and International Law* (Brill, Dordrecht, 2015).

[217] Art 2(1)(b) Vienna Convention on the Succession of States in Respect of Treaties (adopted 23 August 1978, entered into force 6 November 1996) 1946 UNTS 3; see also *Arbitral Award of 31 July 1989* (Guinea-Bissau v Senegal) [1991] ICJ Rep 53; *Land, Island and Maritime Frontier Dispute* (El Salvador v Honduras: Nicaragua Intervening) [1992] ICJ Rep 351, 598 and Opinion No 1 of Arbitration Commission (n 151).

[218] P Daillier, M Forteau, N Quoc Dinh and A Pellet, *Droit international public*, 8th edn (Paris, LGDJ, 2009) 540–41.

[219] DP O'Connell, *State Succession in Municipal Law and International Law*, Vol I (Cambridge, CUP, 1967).

[220] Examples thereof are the transfer of Eupen and Malmédy to Belgium and the transfer or Alsace-Lorraine to France (Treaty of Peace with Germany (adopted 28 June 1919, entered into force 10 January 1920) 225 CTS 188 (Treaty of Versailles), note 39).

peace treaties.[221] Sometimes predecessor and successor States conclude treaties, so-called devolution agreements, which regulate the matter in detail.[222] For example, the succession issues with regard to the German re-unification were settled in detail in the German Unification Treaty (*Einigungsvertrag*; see also above, Section III(C)).[223] Finally, within the framework of decolonisation, agreements were reached more than once between the (former) colonial power and the decolonised State, either before or after independence.[224] However, these treaties cannot exhaustively regulate the legal issues of State succession concerning the rights of third States; being a *res inter alios acta*, they cannot bind the latter.[225] In the absence of treaties, customary international law governs the matter.[226] Due to an inconsistent State practice that displays many ad hoc solutions and the limited number of relevant judicial decisions, this is not evident.[227] In addition, a number of formerly established rules have become contested by newly-independent States for being one-sided and in favour of the former colonial powers.[228]

Considering the rather chaotic state of the law on this matter and the decolonisation process, in the 1970s, the ILC prioritised State succession as a topic in its programme of work. It laid the basis for two treaties: the Vienna Convention on the Succession of States in Respect of Treaties (1978)[229] and the Vienna Convention on the Succession of States in Respect of State Property, Archives and Debt (1983).[230] Given their limited number of ratifications, these treaties can hardly be called a success. Neither are they regarded as a successful codification of customary international law, as many consider that they focus too much on the specific problems and interests of newly-independent States in the context of decolonisation.[231] Nevertheless, they provide useful inspiration to the international community in a number of cases and thus contributed to the development of customary international law.[232] Lastly, it is noteworthy that the ILC also adopted the 'Draft Articles on Nationality of Natural Persons in relation to Succession of States' (1999)[233] and started a codification effort as regards the succession of States in respect of State responsibility (2017).[234]

[221] MN Shaw, *International Law*, 8th edn (Oxford, OUP, 2017) 726; MN Shaw, 'State Succession Revisited' (1994) 5 *FYIL* 34. Examples are the Peace Treaty between the Allied Powers and Austria, its Protocol and Special Declaration (adopted 10 September 1919, entered into force 19 July 1920) 226 CTS 8; and the Peace Treaty between the Allied Powers and Hungary, its Protocol and Declaration (adopted 4 June 1920, entered into force 26 July 1921) 6 LNTS 187. See also the Treaty of Peace with Italy (adopted 10 February 1947, entered into force 15 September 1947) 49 UNTS 3.

[222] Shaw (n 221) 726; IRC Kawaley, 'How Useful are Devolution Agreements? The Seychelles Experience' (1986) 35 *ICLQ* 717; N Mugerwa, 'Subjects of International Law' in M Sorensen (ed), *Manual of Public International Law* (London, Macmillan, 1968) 300–301 and O'Connell (n 219) 352–73.

[223] Treaty on the Final Settlement with Respect to Germany (adopted 12 September 1990, entered into force 15 March 1991) 1696 UNTS 124. Another example is the Treaty relative to the Separation of Belgium from the Netherlands (adopted 19 April 1839, entered into force 8 June 1839, so-called 'Treaty of the XXIV Articles') 27 British and Foreign State Papers 990.

[224] Shaw (n 221) 726; Mugerwa (n 222) 300–301. See also O'Connell (n 219) 352–73.

[225] See Chapter 2, Section VIII, on the consequences of treaties for third parties.

[226] Shaw (n 221) 727.

[227] Shaw (2014) (n 221) 726–27; Shaw (1994) (n 221) 34.

[228] Jennings and Watts (n 49) 236, nr 68.

[229] See above (n 217).

[230] Vienna Convention on the Succession of States in Respect of State Property, Archives and Debt (adopted 8 April 1983, not yet in force) (1983) 22 ILM 306.

[231] P Malanczuk, *Akehurst's Modern Introduction to International Law*, 7th edn (London, Routledge, 1997) 161.

[232] See Opinion No 1 of Arbitration Commission (n 151) and Opinion No 3 of the Arbitration Commission of the Peace Conference on Yugoslavia, 11 January 1992, (1992) 31 ILM 1499.

[233] ILC, 'Draft Articles on Nationality of Natural Persons in relation to Succession of States' (1999) *YILC*, Vol I, Part Two, 23.

[234] See notably ILC, 'First Report on Succession of States in respect of State Responsibility' by Pavel Šturma, Special Rapporteur, 31 May 2017, UN Doc A/CN.4/708.

A. Relations between Successor State and Individuals

A first set of legal issues of State succession can be situated in the relations between the successor State and individuals. The award (or refusal) of nationality is one of the sovereign competences of a State (see also below, p 431).[235] Nevertheless, the successor State cannot determine who will be awarded its nationality with unhampered discretion. It needs to take into account every person's right to a nationality and the prohibition to deprive someone arbitrarily from his or her nationality, as recognised in Article 15 of the Universal Declaration of Human Rights.[236] Article 1 of the ILC Draft Articles on Nationality stipulates that '[e]very individual who, on the date of the succession of States, had the nationality of the predecessor State [...] has the right to the nationality of at least one of the States concerned'. Article 5 establishes a presumption of nationality, determining that those 'having their habitual residence in the territory affected by the succession of States are presumed to acquire the nationality of the successor State on the date of such succession'.[237] Conversely, a successor State is not obliged to award its nationality to persons whose habitual residence is located in another State and who have the nationality of that State or of a third State.[238]

Property rights acquired by individuals in accordance with the law of the predecessor State or based on contracts concluded before the change in territory, were traditionally upheld according to the 'doctrine of acquired rights'.[239] However, this doctrine was criticised by socialist countries and countries which emerged from decolonisation. The criticism related to the equality of successor States. First, it was argued that the fact that they would be bound by decisions of predecessor States runs counter to the principle of consensualism. Second, it was argued that this placed a heavy burden on the economic choices the – usually vulnerable and poor – newly-independent States could make.[240] International law has indeed traditionally allowed a successor State to freely determine the economic policy of its choice, including the freedom to expropriate alien property for public policy purposes.[241] The 1978 Convention seems to confirm this, by recognising that nothing in the Convention affects the principles of international law which affirm the permanent sovereignty of every people and every State over its natural wealth and resources.[242] Thus, the successor State remains

[235] Art 1 of the Hague Convention on Certain Questions relating to the Conflict of Nationality Laws (adopted 13 April 1930, entered into force 1 July 1937) 179 LNTS 89; *Nottebohm* (Liechtenstein v Guatemala) [1955] ICJ Rep 4, 23; *Acquisition of Polish Nationality* (Advisory Opinion) [1923] PCIJ Series B No 7, 16 and *Nationality Decrees in Tunis and Morocco* (Advisory Opinion) [1923] PCIJ Series B No 4, 24; Federal Supreme Court (CH), *Swiss Compensation Office v M*, 19 June 2013, Case No 9C_662/2012.

[236] Higher Administrative Court of Baden-Württemberg (DE), *Anonymous v German Office for the Recognition of Foreign Refugees*, 24 September 2008, Case No 13 S 1812/07, paras 33, 35 and 39.

[237] In *Swiss Compensation Office* (n 235), the Swiss Federal Supreme Court made clear that this acquisition of nationality is not automatic.

[238] Art 8(1) 'Draft Articles on Nationality' (n 233).

[239] *Land, Island and Maritime Frontier Dispute* (n 217) 400; *German Settlers in Poland* (Advisory Opinion) [1923] PCIJ Series B No 6, para 86; O'Connell (n 219) 239–40; Jennings and Watts (n 49) 215; Shaw (n 221) 757–58. See also TH Cheng, *State Succession and Commercial Obligations* (New York, Brill, 2006). For an example of a decision that upheld the doctrine of acquired rights, see Constitutional Court (SI), *AA*, 15 March 2007, Case No Up-1299/06-16, paras 2–3. The doctrine has been applied broadly; for example, in Supreme Court (CY), *Yemen v Compagnie d'Enterprises CFE SA*, 28 June 2002, Case No 10717, the Cypriot Supreme Court endorsed it in respect of a company claiming the right to resort to arbitration.

[240] Daillier, Forteau, Quoc Dinh and Pellet (n 218) 545–46.

[241] *Certain German Interests in Polish Upper Silesia* (Merits) [1926] PCIJ Series A No 7 and ICSID, *Amco Asia Corporation and others v Republic of Indonesia*, 20 November 1984, Case No ARB/81/1.

[242] Art 13 1978 Vienna Convention (n 230).

free to enact legislation affecting acquired rights, within the confines of international law; for example, in case it expropriates foreigners, it is limited by the duty to provide appropriate compensation.[243] Accordingly, the doctrine of acquired rights 'appears less a rigid and strict rule and more a flexible and limited principle':[244] while, together with other rules of international law, it serves to protect the individual against a total deprivation of acquired rights by the successor State, it does not prohibit that State from negatively affecting them.

B. Relations between Successor and Predecessor State

State succession also has legal effects in the relationship between the successor and predecessor State. Within the territory of the successor State, the legal system of the predecessor State disappears and is replaced by the legal system of the successor State. However, in the interest of legal certainty, the latter can freely decide to retain a part of the formerly applicable legislation. Concerning the transfer of assets of the predecessor State to the successor State, it is an established principle of customary international law that this occurs by right, both for movable and for immovable property.[245] As far as foreign public debt is concerned, the 1983 Convention differentiates between: (i) the creation of new States in the framework of decolonisation, in which case debts are not transferred to the newly-independent State, unless they were specifically incurred on behalf of the former colony; and (ii) the separation or dissolution of a State, in which case the debts of the predecessor State are transferred to the successor State 'in equitable proportions'.[246]

C. Treaty Relations of Successor State

State succession also generates legal affects in the relationship between the successor State and the international legal order. This concerns the fate of existing treaties, the membership of international organisations and international responsibility.

As far as existing treaties are concerned, the law is clear on treaties establishing a boundary and so-called 'political treaties'. For other treaties, their enduring effect depends on the mode of succession. With regard to treaties establishing a boundary, it should first of all be observed that the principle of the inviolability of national boundaries established by international law (ie by way of a treaty or based on customary rules on the acquisition of sovereign claims) dominates in case of State succession.[247] The *uti possedetis* principle was

[243] See eg the 'World Bank Guidelines on the Treatment of Foreign Direct Investment' (1992) 31 ILM 1363, Section IV.

[244] PA Lalive, 'The Doctrine of Acquired Rights' in *Rights and Duties of Private Investors Abroad* (New York, Matthew Bender, 1965) 167.

[245] *Appeal from a Judgment of the Hungaro/Czecoslovak Mixed Arbitral Tribunal (The Peter Pázmány University)* (Czechoslovakia v Hungary) [1933] PCIJ Series A/B No 61, 237; Crawford (n 15) 624–25.

[246] Arts 37–41 of the 1983 Vienna Convention (n 230). See eg Art 1 of Annex F to the 'Agreement on Succession Issues between the Five Successor States of the Former State of Yugoslavia (adopted 29 June 2001, entered into force 2 June 2004), (2002) 41 ILM 3, at 34, which provides that 'All rights and interests which belonged to the SFRY and which are not otherwise covered by this Agreement (including, but not limited to, patents, trademarks, copyrights, royalties, and claims of and debts due to the SFRY) shall be shared among the successor States, taking into account the proportion for division of SFRY financial assets in Annex C of this Agreement'.

[247] ILC, 'First report on succession of States and Governments in respect of treaties, by Sir Humphrey Waldock, Special Rapporteur' (1968) *YILC*, Vol II, 92–93.

discussed above (Section III(B)) in relation to the right of self-determination. The principle was applied on a large scale for the first time during the decolonisation period in Latin America in the nineteenth century, was relied upon by most African countries in the 1960s, and was considered to apply also to the dissolution of the socialist federations in the 1990s. The boundaries of the constituent republics became international boundaries.[248] Boundary treaties therefore cannot be affected by successor States, applying the principle *res transit cum suo onere* ('the thing passes with its burden'). On the date of the succession of States, the successor State receives a territory of which the boundaries are the existing boundaries of the predecessor State (in case of universal succession of States) or are determined by way of an act of cession (in case of partial succession of States). As mentioned above, the inviolability of national boundaries also resonates in the VCLT. Pursuant to Article 62(2)(a) VLCT, a fundamental change of circumstances (*rebus sic stantibus*) cannot be invoked as a ground for terminating or withdrawing from a treaty 'if the treaty established a boundary'.[249] Even if the treaty at issue is no longer in force, the established boundary still has to be accepted. The 1978 Convention contains a parallel rule for all territorial regimes established by treaty, such as demilitarised zones, rights of transit, port facilities or other servitudes, like the ones concerning the use of waterways.[250] In the *Gabčikovo-Nagymaros* case, the ICJ held that the Convention reflects a rule of customary international law in this regard.[251]

Second, political treaties establish rights or obligations deemed to be firmly linked to the regime in power in a certain territory and to its political orientation. Examples are treaties of alliance, friendship or neutrality. Such treaties do not bind a successor State, since they are viewed as intimately linked to the nature of the predecessor State.[252] An example is the Warsaw Pact,[253] to which the German Democratic Republic (DDR) was a State Party and to which the Federal Republic of Germany (BRD), as a successor State, did not accede. While trade and extradition treaties often have a distinctly political character, it is less clear what their fate is in case of State succession.[254] At least when the succession involves a State becoming part of another State by way of a merger, the dominant position is that such treaties do not bind the successor State.[255]

Third, as far as other treaties are concerned, the legal effects depend on the mode of State succession. In cases of decolonisation or, more broadly, cases of 'newly-independent States', the general rule is the 'clean slate' or *tabula rasa* principle. The successor State is considered to be a third party in respect of all treaties concluded by the predecessor State. This is an

[248] *Frontier Dispute* (n 77) 565; Opinion No 3 of Arbitration Commission (n 232) 171; *Beagle Channel* (Argentina v Chile), Arbitral Award of 18 February 1977, XXI RIAA 53 and *Affaire des frontières Colombo-vénézuéliennes* (Colombia v Venezuela), Arbitral Award of 1922, I RIAA 223, 228.

[249] See also Chapter 2, Section XI(G) on a 'fundamental change of circumstances (*rebus sic stantibus)*' as a ground for the termination of treaties.

[250] Article 12 1978 Vienna Convention (n 217) and *Case of the Free Zones of Upper Savoy and the District of Gex* (France v Switzerland) [1932] PCIJ Series A/B No 46, 145.

[251] *Gabčikovo–Nagymaros Project* (Hungary v Slovakia) [1997] ICJ Rep 7, 72.

[252] Shaw (n 221) 735.

[253] Treaty on Friendship, Cooperation and Mutual Assistance between Albania, Bulgaria, Hungary, German Democratic Republic, Poland, Romania, Union of Soviet Socialist Republics and Czechoslovakia (adopted 14 May 1955, entered into force 6 June 1955) 219 UNTS 3.

[254] Shaw (n 221) 703. Nevertheless, in Supreme Court (XK), *BA*, 7 September 2010, Case No PN KR 386/2010, the Court ignored the specificity of an extradition treaty and applied the general rules as stipulated in the 1978 Vienna Convention (n 217). Similarly, in Supreme Court (RU), *CJSC 'LUCH' v Ministry of Transportation and others*, 18 September 2009, Case No ГКПИ09-1184, the Court ignored the specificity of a trade agreement and applied the general rules.

[255] Jennings and Watts (n 49) 211 and Shaw (n 221) 736–37.

application of the *res inter alios acta* principle.[256] Of course, the State remains bound by the content of treaty provisions that reflect customary international law.[257] Bilateral treaties only remain in force in case of decolonisation if the newly-independent State and the other contracting party explicitly or implicitly agree to this. In the latter case, agreement can be deduced from the conduct of the States concerned.[258] With regard to multilateral treaties, a newly-independent State can, by a notification of succession, determine its status as a State Party, except when its participation would be incompatible with the object and purpose of the treaty or would radically change the circumstances of its operation. A formal accession is therefore not required. When, under the terms of the treaty or by reason of the limited number of the negotiating States and the object and purpose of the treaty, the consent of all the parties is required for the participation of another State, the newly-independent State may establish its status as a party to the treaty only with such consent.[259] In practice, newly-independent States have accepted – be it explicitly or implicitly – a significant number of treaties which were concluded by their respective colonial powers, usually after an individual examination. This is often to the advantage of the State concerned and of legal certainty and stability.[260]

In the case of *dismembratio* or secession, the 1978 Convention provides for the general rule of automatic succession. Treaties concluded by the predecessor State remain in force for every successor State, unless the States concerned agree otherwise, this goes against the object and purpose of the treaty, or it would radically change the conditions of its operation.[261] This general rule does not seem to be in line with State practice and cannot be considered to be a codification of customary international law.[262] This is so because in practice, seceding States regularly invoke the *tabula rasa* principle, which is nevertheless controversial, especially with regard to demilitarisation treaties.[263] As far as mergers are concerned, the rule is that each of the treaties concluded by one of the States concerned remains in force for the successor State, unless the successor State and the other State Party or Parties agree otherwise or if it would appear that the application of the treaty to the successor State would be incompatible with the object and purpose of the treaty or would

[256] See above, introduction to this Section. See also Art 16 1978 Vienna Convention (n 217) and, for an illustration, Oporto Civil Court of Appeal (PT), *State (Public Ministry) v B*, 24 October 2007, Case No 07443294, paras 9–10.

[257] *Military and Paramilitary Activity in and against Nicaragua* (Nicaragua v United States of America) (Merits) [1986] ICJ Rep 14.

[258] Art 24 1978 Vienna Convention (n 217); ILC, 'Succession of States in Respect of Treaties' (1974) *YILC*, Vol II, Part One, 237–39. For an example of the application of this rule, see Supreme Court (XK), *BA* (n 254) para 30. Interestingly, the Supreme Court of Kosovo relies on the part of the 1978 Vienna Convention on newly-independent States rather than on the part on separated States.

[259] Art 17 1978 Vienna Convention (n 217).

[260] ILC (n 258) 182–93; O'Connell (n 219) 352; Shaw (n 221) 739 and 741–42.

[261] Art 34 1978 Vienna Convention (n 217). For applications thereof, see: Supreme Administrative Court (CZ), *VJ v Czech Social Security Administration*, 28 November 2008, Case No 6 Ads 42/2007, paras 14–18, where the general rule of Article 34 was affirmed, but where it was decided that a treaty that applied between the Czech Republic and the Soviet Union no longer applied in the relations between the Czech Republic and one of the Soviet Union's successor States (Armenia), because the Czech Republic unilaterally declared so.

[262] Shaw (n 221) 739. See also Federal Supreme Court (CH), *Swiss Compensation Office v M*, 19 June 2013, Case No 9C_662/2012, at para 4.2.3–4.24, where the Court generally held that the 1978 Vienna Convention partially codified rules that deviate from customary international law and specified that there is no rule of customary international law postulating automatic succession to treaties concluded by the predecessor State.

[263] ILC (n 258) 263, 265–66. See also *VJ v Czech Social Security Administration* (n 261) para 18, recognising that many successor States of the Soviet Union rejected succession to the treaties concluded by the latter, and *Swiss Compensation Office v M* (n 262) para 4.4, generally affirming Switzerland's practice of discontinuity in treaty relations in case of succession.

radically change the circumstances of its operation.[264] When State succession occurs in a partial manner, eg following a cession of territory, the 'principle of moving treaty boundaries' comes into play (see above, p 94).[265] The territorial scope of the treaty follows the change in boundaries.[266] An exception to this occurs when the treaty is connected specifically to a certain territory, such as a border treaty. In that case, the rights and obligations of the predecessor State are transferred.[267] Nothing prevents the successor State from accepting that also other treaties concluded by the predecessor State remain valid in relation to the territory at hand. For instance, human rights treaties at the time of regaining sovereignty over Hong Kong, China declared that human rights treaties applicable to the former would continue to apply, even if China was not a party to it.[268]

The fate of multilateral human rights treaties in cases of State succession deserves special attention. The international community tends to assume succession to these treaties because of their special nature. The ICJ has emphasised this special nature with regard to the Genocide Convention in its 1951 Advisory Opinion on *Reservations to the Genocide Convention*.[269] The ECtHR did so too in the 2009 *Bijelić* case by recognising 'the principle that fundamental rights protected by international human rights treaties should indeed belong to individuals living in the territory of the State Party concerned, notwithstanding its subsequent dissolution or succession'.[270] The ethnic cleansing that took place after the break-up of the former Yugoslavia shows the importance of the issue. In 1994, the presidents of the different UN human rights committees considered that successor States were automatically bound by international human rights treaties from their respective date of independence onwards, and that respect for these treaties cannot depend on the confirming declaration by the government of the successor State.[271]

D. Membership of International Organisations

As to the membership of international organisations, in principle, the following rules apply. In case of partial State succession, the continuator State retains its membership of

[264] Art 31(1) 1978 Vienna Convention (n 217). In Federal Supreme Court (CH), *Limited Partnership v High Court of the Canton of Thurgau*, 15 June 2005, Case No 7B.31/2005, the Swiss Court seemed to suggest otherwise, stating that the territory of the agreement was limited to that of the original party as the scope of the agreement had not been explicitly extended.

[265] ILC (n 258) 208.

[266] Art 15 1978 Vienna Convention (n 217).

[267] See above (nn 248–251).

[268] See inter alia R Mushkat, 'Hong Kong and Succession of Treaties' (1997) 46 *ICLQ* 181; P Slinn, 'Aspects juridiques du retour à la Chine de Hong-Kong' (1996) *Annuaire français de droit international* 273 and J Chan, 'State Succession to Human Rights Treaties: Hong Kong and the International Covenant on Civil and Political Rights' (1996) 45 *ICLQ* 928.

[269] *Reservations to the Convention on the Prevention and Punishment of the Crime of Genocide* (Advisory Opinion) [1951] ICJ Rep 15, 23.

[270] *Bijelić v Montenegro and Serbia* App no 11890/05 (ECtHR, 6 November 2009) para 69.

[271] UNSG, 'Succession of States in respect of International Human Rights Treaties', 8 November 1994, UN Doc E/CN.4/1995/80, 3–4. However, in the *Croatia v Serbia* case, the ICJ implicitly required a notification for a successor State to be bound by a human rights treaty, as it only accepted jurisdiction based on Article IX of the Genocide Convention because the FRY had, by means of a declaration and note to the UNSG, committed itself to continue to fulfil all obligations assumed by the SFRY (which was a party to the Genocide Convention); *Application of the Convention on the Prevention and Punishment of the Crime of Genocide* (Preliminary Objections) (Croatia v Serbia) [2008] ICJ Rep 412, paras 93–117.

international organisations.[272] For instance, the Russian Federation preserved the UN membership of the Soviet Union, including the latter's permanent seat in the Security Council.[273] In case of a merger, the membership of an international organisation will be continued automatically if all predecessor States were a member of the organisation concerned. If the predecessor State ceases to exist, the membership is lost. In case of decolonisation, *dismembratio* and secession, the new States have to request their admission to the international organisation concerned.[274]

E. International Responsibility

As far as responsibility for internationally wrongful acts is concerned, international claims for compensation following actions in violation of public international law are considered 'personal' (see Chapter 12, Section III on 'State imputability'). This means that State succession takes place neither for the rights of the claimant State nor for the obligations of the defendant State: (i) only the predecessor State remains responsible for internationally wrongful acts which it would have committed with regard to a third State; and (ii) the successor State cannot exercise the right of diplomatic protection on behalf of a person who at the moment of the damage was not (yet) its national.[275] However, when the predecessor State ceases to exist and a new State is or new States are created, according to the Institut de Droit International, the general principle is that the successor State(s) can be held liable for the acts of the predecessor State.[276]

The Special Rapporteur of the ILC has stressed that '[t]raditionally, neither State practice nor doctrine gave a uniform answer to the question of whether and in what circumstances a successor State may be responsible for an internationally wrongful act of its predecessor' and that 'most authors assert that there is no transfer of obligations arising from international responsibility to a successor State – the theory of non-succession'.[277] Nevertheless, he considers that 'in the past twenty years, the view has evolved and has become more nuanced in this regard and critical of the theory of non-succession, to the extent that succession is admitted in certain cases'.[278] Many ILC members have criticised this argument, notably because they consider that the State practice the Special Rapporteur relied on consists of agreements between or unilateral declarations by States that do not depend on a sense of obligation (*opinio juris*) and accordingly do not warrant a departure from the traditional rule of non-succession.[279]

[272] Shaw (n 221) 746.
[273] See R Müllerson, *International Law, Rights and Politics* (London, Routledge, 1994) 141–47 and Blum (n 98).
[274] Shaw (n 221) 746.
[275] See generally O'Connell (n 219) chapter 19; P Dumberry, *State Succession to International Responsibility* (The Hague, Brill, 2007); MJ Volkovitsch, 'Righting Wrongs: Towards a New Theory of State Succession to Responsibility for International Delicts' (1992) 92 *Columbia Law Review* 2162 and W Czaplinski, 'State Succession and State Responsibility' (1990) 28 *Canadian Yearbook of International Law* 339.
[276] Institut de Droit International, 'State Succession in Matters of State Responsibility', 9 August 2013, idi-iil.org/app/uploads/2017/06/IDI_14_Kohen.pdf, para 43. See also *Gabčíkovo-Nagymaros Project* (n 251) 7; Court of Cassation (IT), *Podrute Massacre case*, 29 October 2015, Case No 43696/2015, para 3.2; Shaw (n 221) 762.
[277] First report of the Special Rapporteur (n 234) paras 30 and 32.
[278] ibid, para 33.
[279] Report of the International Law Commission, Sixty-ninth Session (1 May–2 June and 3 July–4 August 2017), UN Doc A/72/10, paras 228–234.

VII. Contested States

The international system is traditionally seen as consisting of a community of sovereign States and little else. However, the reality is much more complex, and a number of territories exist that do not fit into this idealised model. Various claims to statehood that are contested by the vast majority of existing States have led to the creation of a number of territorial entities that are often referred to as 'contested States',[280] 'unrecognised States',[281] 'de facto States',[282] 'de facto regimes',[283] or even 'self-proclaimed authorities'.[284] The internationally disputed nature of their claim to statehood is manifested either in a complete lack of formal recognition or in recognition by only a limited number of States.

For instance, in 1974, a military coup in Cyprus led to the invasion of the island by Turkish forces and, almost a decade later, to a proclamation of independence by the Turkish Republic of Northern Cyprus (TRNC).[285] The TRNC is a 'purported' State[286] that, with the support of Turkey, has been able to maintain its self-proclaimed independence over the years, albeit being recognised by no other State than its sponsor.[287] Another relevant example is Somaliland, a territory that asserted its independence from Somalia as early as 1991, but remains unrecognised by any State or international organisation,[288] despite the ability of its governing authority to exert control over the territory it claims as its own.[289] Following the collapse of the Soviet Union, a number of similar territorial entities emerged when the areas of Abkhazia and South Ossetia (Georgia), Nagorno-Karabakh (Azerbaijan), and Transnistria (Moldova) declared their independence.[290] Although their claims to sovereignty largely remain unheeded, these entities have successfully maintained their self-proclaimed independent status, frequently through pervasive and violent armed confrontation.[291] The UN Security Council has constantly reaffirmed the sovereignty and territorial integrity of their respective territorial States,[292] often calling on the international community to refrain from

[280] See eg D Geldenhuys, *Contested States in World Politics* (Basingstoke, Palgrave Macmillan, 2009).

[281] N Caspersen, *Unrecognized States: The Struggle for Sovereignty in the Modern International System* (Cambridge, Polity Press, 2012).

[282] J Frowein, *Das de facto-Regime im Volkerrecht* (Köln, Carl Heymanns Verlag, 1968); S Pegg, *International Society and the De Facto State* (Aldershot, Ashgate, 1998).

[283] M Schoiswohl, *Status and Human Rights Obligations of Non-Recognized De Facto Regimes in International Law: The Case of 'Somaliland'* (Leiden, Nijhoff, 2004).

[284] The term was first used by the ECtHR in a case against Moldova and Russia in relation to Transnistria. See *Ilaşcu and others v Moldova and Russia* App no 48787/99 (ECtHR, 8 July 2004) para 318. See also *Solomou and others v Turkey* App no 36832/97 (ECtHR, 24 June 2008) para 46.

[285] Shaw (n 221) 184–85.

[286] See UNSC Res 550, 11 May 1984, UN Doc S/RES/550.

[287] Shaw (n 221) 184–85. See also Chapter 9, Section IV(B), on the extent to which 'sponsors' such as Turkey and Russia are considered to exercise jurisdiction over territories such as respectively the TRNC and Transnistria.

[288] For a more detailed description of Somaliland, see Crawford (n 15) 412–15.

[289] A Arieff, 'De Facto Statehood? The Strange Case of Somaliland' (2008) 3 *Yale Journal of International Affairs* 60, 60.

[290] See eg 'Act of State Independence of the Republic of Abkhazia', 12 October 1999, unpo.org/article/705.

[291] Consider eg the five-day war that Georgia and Russia fought over South Ossetia in 2008. The conflict now forms the object of a preliminary investigation at the ICC. In this regard, see Office of the Prosecutor, Corrected Version of 'Request for Authorisation of an Investigation Pursuant to Article 15', 16 October 2015, ICC-01/15-4-Corr; ICC, Pre-Trial Chamber I, Decision on the Prosecutor's Request for Authorization of an Investigation, 27 January 2016, Case No ICC-01/15-12.

[292] See eg UNSC Res 1393, 31 January 2002, UN Doc S/RES/1393, where Abkhazia is described as an area 'within the State of Georgia'; UNSC Res 853, 29 July 1993, UN Doc S/RES/853, with respect to Nagorno-Karabakh,

recognising or assisting them in any way.[293] Nevertheless, a limited number of UN Member States have recognised contested States.[294] What ultimately defines these entities is that they are de facto self-governing and autonomous, but they have yet to be fully endorsed as States by the international community.[295]

Regardless of their level of recognition, these territorial entities share some State-like characteristics.[296] The EU's Independent International Fact-Finding Mission on the Conflict in Georgia described South Ossetia as an entity that has 'a territory, a population and a government acting on a newly established constitutional basis', but, since it was not sufficiently independent from Russia, 'South Ossetia came close to statehood without quite reaching the threshold of effectiveness'.[297] In this sense, the authors of the report argued that, from the perspective of international law, South Ossetia is 'an entity short of statehood'.[298] Abkhazia, on the other hand, was seen as more independent from Russia and 'more advanced than South Ossetia in the process of state-building'. For these reasons, it was contended that Abkhazia may 'be qualified as a state-like entity'.[299] However, it should be noted that the Fact-Finding Mission found that, 'although it shows the characteristics of statehood', the process of state-building in South Ossetia and Abkhazia is not legitimate.[300]

The contested States mentioned here satisfy, or at least come close to satisfying the Montevideo criteria for statehood discussed above. They all have a population, a territory, some form of governmental institutions, and even the potential to enter into relations with other States.[301] These territorial entities seek to present themselves and function as States. They have constitutions, working State institutions, armies, flags and individual currencies, and are often capable of providing basic public services, such as healthcare or education.[302] However, since their claims to statehood are contested, they remain in what some have called 'international legal limbo' with respect to many of the international rights and obligations that normally apply to States.[303]

where the UNSC stresses that the 'sovereignty and territorial integrity of the Azerbaijani Republic' must be guaranteed; UNSC Res 896, 31 January 1994, UN Doc S/RES/896, whereby, with respect to South Ossetia, the UNSC stressed the importance of 'respecting fully the sovereignty and territorial integrity of the Republic of Georgia'.

[293] See UNSC Res 550, 11 May 1984, UN Doc S/RES/550. See also *Cyprus v Turkey* App no 25781/94 (ECtHR, 10 May 2001) para 61, where the ECtHR held that 'it is evident from international practice and the condemnatory tone of the resolutions adopted by the United Nations Security Council and the Council of Europe's Committee of Ministers that the international community does not recognize the "TRNC" as a State under international law'.

[294] To give just two examples, Abkhazia is recognised by six UN Member States (Russia, Nicaragua, Venezuela, Nauru, Tuvalu and Vanuatu), whereas Transnistria is recognised by none. On the issue of recognition, see more extensively C Ryngaert and S Sobrie, 'Recognition of States: International Law or Real Politik? The Practice of Recognition in the Wake of Kosovo, South Ossetia and Abkhazia' (2009) 24 *LJIL* 467.

[295] Caspersen (n 281) 6–7. See also N Caspersen and G Stansfield, 'Introduction' in N Caspersen and G Stansfield (eds), *Unrecognized States in the International System* (Abingdon, Routledge, 2011) 1–2.

[296] See C Henderson (n 119) 370; L Hamid and J Wouters, 'We the People: Self-Determination v. Sovereignty in the Case of De Facto States' (2016) 1 *Inter Gentes – The McGill Journal of International Law and Legal Pluralism* 53.

[297] Georgia International Fact-Finding Mission (n 24) 134.

[298] ibid.

[299] ibid.

[300] ibid, 135.

[301] Montevideo Convention (n 21).

[302] N Caspersen, 'States Without Sovereignty: Imitating Democratic Statehood' in Caspersen and Stansfield (n 295) 73–89.

[303] Henderson (n 119) 371. For these obligations, see the Draft Declaration on Rights and Duties of States (n 10).

The territorial entities described are often seen as posing a challenge to the international legal system. For instance, Shaw notes that '[n]on-recognition, with its consequent absence of diplomatic relations, may affect the unrecognised state in asserting its rights or other states in asserting its duties under international law, but will not affect the existence of such rights and duties'.[304] Similarly, Crawford mentions that 'if international law withholds legal status from effective illegal entities, the result is a legal vacuum undesirable both in practice and principle'.[305] Indeed, since these contested States are often perceived as lacking in international legal personality,[306] various questions arise, including, inter alia, whether they are subjected to the rules of *jus ad bellum*,[307] or whether they owe any type of human rights obligations to the individuals living in their territories.[308] More generally, their existence challenges some of the deeply ingrained views that we hold on matters of statehood and State recognition.[309]

VIII. Conclusion

Traditionally, only States had the capacity to possess rights and obligations under international law. Up until today, they are the only entities enjoying full international legal personality. International law remains a legal system built upon the bedrocks of State consent and sovereign equality in which the Westphalian State is the primary actor. The proper functioning of that legal system presupposes that a State has certain characteristics: it must have a permanent population, a defined territory, an effective government and it must be independent. At least pursuant to the declarative approach, according to which recognition is not a requirement for statehood, any entity that acquires these four characteristics is a State.

As there is no more *terra nullius*, States can no longer acquire original title to territory by occupation. Annexation being prohibited, a contractual cession of territory is the primary legal way in which existing States can still acquire title to territory. New States can only come into existence following a change in the identity of a pre-existing State. Notably, decolonisation has led to the creation of a large number of newly-independent States that were considered to have an external right to self-determination. While the existence of a more general right of remedial secession beyond the colonial context is uncertain, new States can still be created through a merger or dissolution.

When a successor State with a new legal personality replaces a predecessor State, the law of State succession comes into play. Even if there are treaties governing State succession in respect of treaties and State property, archives and debt, the matter is largely governed by ad

[304] Shaw (n 221) 349.

[305] J Crawford, 'The Criteria for Statehood in International Law' (1976) 48 *BYIL* 93, 145.

[306] See M Schoiswohl, 'De Facto Regimes and Human Rights Obligations: The Twilight Zone of Public International Law?' (2001) 6 *Austrian Review of International and European Law* 45, 47–54.

[307] See Henderson (n 119).

[308] See A Cullen and S Wheatley, 'The Human Rights of Individuals in *De Facto* Regimes under the European Convention of Human Rights' (2013) 13 *Human Rights Law Review* 691; Y Ronen, 'Human Rights Obligations of Territorial Non-State Actors' (2013) 46 *Cornell International Law Journal* 21; D Murray, *Human Rights Obligations of Non-State Armed Groups* (Oxford, Hart, 2016).

[309] See generally A Peters, 'Statehood after 1989: "Effectivités" between Legality and Virtuality' (2010) 3 *Select Proceedings of the European Society of International Law* 171.

hoc devolution agreements and customary international law. But while there is agreement that newly-independent States start with a clean slate and do not inherit the obligations of their former coloniser (the *tabula rasa* principle), many other rules regarding State succession are contested.

Statehood is governed by international law. Nevertheless, law must give way to politics when it comes to recognition. Through the unilateral act of recognition, a State can recognise another State as a member of the international community and accept that it meets the requirements for statehood. While recognition itself does not constitute one of these requirements (except according to the largely surpassed constitutive approach), it has a severe impact on a State's capacity to conduct international relations. Thus, claims of statehood that are not met by (extensive) recognition, be it due to an alleged failure to meet the requirements of Statehood and/or for mere political reasons, result in contested States. These State-like entities do not fit the idealised model of the Westphalian State, but may nevertheless claim their position in the international legal order. Much like international and regional organisations (Chapters 6 and 7) and other non-state actors (Chapter 8), contested States challenge the traditional monopoly of the State on international legal personality, expose the tension between their status before international law and their role as a matter of fact, and demand that international law reflects the reality of international relations.

Bibliography

Corten, O, Delcourt, B, Klein, P and Levrat, N, *Démembrements d'Etats et délimitations territoriales: L'uti possidetis en question(s)* (Bruxelles, Bruylant, 1999).

Craven, M, 'Statehood, Self-Determination, and Recognition' in MD Evans (ed), *International Law*, 4th edn (Oxford, OUP, 2014) 202–47.

Crawford, J, 'The Criteria for Statehood in International Law' (1976) 48 *BYIL* 93.

Crawford, J, *The Creation of States in International Law*, 2nd edn (Oxford, OUP, 2007).

Denza, E, 'European Practice on the Recognition of States' (2011) 36 *European Law Review* 321.

Franck, T, 'The Emerging Right to Democratic Governance' (1992) 86 *AJIL* 46.

Frowein, J, *Das de facto-Regime im Völkerrecht* (Köln, Carl Heymanns Verlag, 1968).

Lauterpacht, H, *Recognition in International Law* (Cambridge, CUP, 1947).

O'Connell, DP, *State Succession in Municipal Law and International Law* (Cambridge, CUP, 1967).

Stern, B, 'La Succession d'Etats' (1996) 262 *Recueil des Cours* 9.

Further Reading

Cassese, A, *Self-Determination of Peoples: A Legal Reappraisal* (Cambridge, CUP, 1995).

Caspersen, N, *Unrecognized States: The Struggle for Sovereignty in the Modern International System* (Cambridge, Polity Press, 2012).

Dumberry, P, *State Succession to International Responsibility* (The Hague, Brill, 2007).

French, D (ed), *Statehood and Self-Determination* (Cambridge, CUP, 2015).
Kohen, MG (ed), *Secession: International Law Perspectives* (Cambridge, CUP, 2006).
Kohen, MG (ed), *Research Handbook on Territorial Disputes in International Law* (Cheltenham, Edward Elgar, 2018).
L Hamid and J Wouters, 'We the People: Self-Determination v. Sovereignty in the Case of De Facto States' (2016) 1 *Inter Gentes – The McGill Journal of International Law and Legal Pluralism* 53.
Marks, S, 'What has Become of the Emerging Right to Democratic Governance?' (2011) 22 *EJIL* 507.
Menon, PK, *The Succession of States in Respect to Treaties, State Property, Archives and Debts* (Lewiston, Edwin Mellen, 1991).
Murphy, SD, 'Democratic Legitimacy and the Recognition of States and Governments' (1999) 48 *ICLQ* 54.
Portmann, R, *Legal Personality in International Law* (Cambridge, CUP, 2010).
Raič, D, *Statehood and the Law of Self-Determination* (Leiden, Nijhoff, 2002).
Ronen, Y, 'Human Rights Obligations of Territorial Non-State Actors' (2013) 46 *Cornell International Law Journal* 21.
Shaw, MN, 'State Succession Revisited' (1994) 5 *FYIL* 34.
Talmon, S, *Recognition in International Law: A Bibliography* (The Hague, Nijhoff, 2000).
Vidmar, J, *Democratic Statehood in International Law* (Oxford, Hart, 2013).

6

International Organisations

I. Introduction – Definition

Chapter 1 already mentioned the gradual rise of international organisations since the nineteenth century: from the first international institutions, the so-called 'international unions' and 'international commissions' to the League of Nations ('LoN') and the International Labour Organization ('ILO'), both established in 1919 by the Treaty of Versailles. Especially since the end of the Second World War the number of international organisations has increased significantly. Although international organisations come in many shapes and sizes, they share a number of fundamental characteristics. This being said, there is no universally accepted legal definition of an "international organisation". In its 2011 *Articles on the Responsibility of International organisations* (ARIO, on which see below, Chapter 12, Section VII) the ILC defines the term as follows:

> "international organization" means an organization established by a treaty or other instrument governed by international law and possessing its own international legal personality. International organizations may include as members, in addition to States, other entities"[1]

The definition has been criticised as it suffers from certain shortcomings, particularly with regard to the requirement of legal personality. The following features can be listed to distinguish an international organisation from other subjects of international law, in particular non-governmental organisations (on which see below, Chapter 8, Section V):

a. An association of subjects of international law, most often States, but sometimes also (or even exclusively) other international organisations. For instance, the EU is a co-founder of the World Trade Organization (WTO);
b. Established by a treaty or other instrument governed by international law. There are indeed examples of international organisations, such as the Organization for Security

[1] Article 2(a) ARIO (2011) *YILC*, Vol II, Part 2. See S Bouwhuis, 'The International Law Commission's Definition of International Organizations' (2012) 9 *International Organizations Law Review* 451–65; M Mendelson, 'The Definition of 'International Organization' in the International Law Commission's Current Project on the Responsibility of International Organizations' in M Ragazzi (ed) *International Responsibility Today: Essays in Memory of Oscar Schachter* (Leiden, Brill, 2005), 371–89.

and Co-operation in Europe (OSCE) and the Organization of Petroleum Exporting Countries (OPEC), which have not been founded on the basis of a treaty;

c. The pursuit of common objectives;
d. The existence of one or more organs which are able to generate an "autonomous will" distinct from the organisation's members (*"volonté distincte"*).[2]

The first part of this Chapter addresses the general aspects of international institutional law: the types, powers, membership, organs, legal personality, decision-making, and finances of international organisations. Immunities of international organisations are discussed in Chapter 11, Section IV. The second part of this Chapter focuses on some of the key international organisations with a global membership, with particular emphasis on the United Nations (UN). Regional organisations are the subject of next Chapter, and the WTO is discussed in Chapter 19, Section VIII(A).

II. Types of International Organisations

International organisations can be divided into a number of different categories. While such categorisation is certainly useful (if only to clarify to some extent the broad spectrum of international organisations), realities are far more complex and nuanced than these categorisations may suggest. Also the legal relevance of any categorisation is limited.

A first distinction is that between universal (or global) and regional organisations. Universal international organisations comprise (almost) the entire international community of States, whereas regional organisations only include a limited number of States, typically tied to a certain geographical location.[3] As this book also makes this principal distinction, regional organisations are addressed in Chapter 7.

A second distinction that can be made is that between 'open' and 'closed' international organisations.[4] An open organisation is one that, in principle, all States can become a member of. The quintessential example of an open international organisation is the UN, whose membership is open to 'all peace-loving States which accept the obligations contained in the present Charter and, in the judgment of the Organization, are able and willing to carry out these obligations' (Article 4(1) UN Charter). In a closed (or non-universal) organisation, membership is only open to States that belong to a specified group. This group may be defined by means of geographic boundaries. This is, for instance, the case for the EU and the Council of Europe, which require that its members are 'European States',[5] as well as the Association of Southeast Asian Nations (ASEAN), which requires its members

[2] See inter alia J Klabbers, *An Introduction to International Organizations Law*, 3rd edn (Cambridge, CUP, 2015) 6–12; HG Schermers and NM Blokker, *International Institutional Law*, 5th edn (Leiden, Nijhoff, 2011), 37–47; K Schmalenbach, 'International Organizations or Institutions, General Aspects' (2014) *MPEPIL*.

[3] About the relationship between universal and regional organisations, see eg L Boisson de Chazournes, *Interactions between Regional and Universal Organizations: A Legal Perspective* (Leiden, Brill, 2017); C Dominicé, 'Co-ordination between Universal and Regional Organizations' in NM Blokker and HG Schemers (eds), *Proliferation of International Organizations: Legal Issues* (The Hague, Kluwer, 2001) 65–84.

[4] Klabbers (n 2) 24–25; Schermers and Blokker (n 2) 51–55; JA Pastor Ridruejo, *Curso de derecho internacional público y organizaciones internacionales* (Madrid, Tecnos, 2017) 712–13.

[5] See Art 49 TEU: 'Any European State'; Art 4 of the Statute of the Council of Europe (adopted 5 May 1949, entered into force 3 August 1949) CETS No 1 (Statute Council of Europe): 'Any European State'. cp Art 10 NATO Treaty: 'any other European State'.

to be located 'in the recognized geographical region of Southeast Asia'.[6] Membership in an international organisation may also be limited by other criteria than geographical ones. Membership in OPEC, for example, requires substantial net exports of crude oil.[7]

Another distinction can be made between general and functional organisations.[8] General (or political) organisations are active in a wide range of domains. An example of such a general organisation is the UN. At the regional level, also the EU may be regarded as a general organisation, as it has gradually expanded its work (which started off with one (the European Coal and Steel Community (ECSC)) and then three (in addition to the ECSC, the European Economic Community (EEC) and the European Atomic Energy Community (EAEC or Euratom) 'functional' Communities in the economic sphere; see Chapter 7, Section II(B)(i)) into a broad range of policy fields. At the opposite end of the spectrum one finds functional organisations, which typically focus on more specific and technical tasks, such as the specialised agencies of the UN (see below, Section VIII(E)) and the Organisation for the Prohibition of Chemical Weapons (OPCW).

Finally, a distinction is sometimes made between purely intergovernmental organisations and organisations with supranational features.[9] In intergovernmental organisations, Member States cooperate while retaining their sovereignty, and decisions are usually adopted by consensus or by unanimity (on the distinction, see below, Section V(B)(i)). In supranational organisations, on the other hand, certain powers are transferred to an organisation that can exercise these powers independently.[10] A supranational organisation is, inter alia, characterised by the fact that it has the power to adopt decisions that are binding upon its Member States, that the organs taking these decisions are not entirely dependent on the cooperation of all Member States (for example, because they are composed of independent individuals, or because decision-making takes place by majority vote), and that the organisation has the power to enforce its decisions (even if only through the help of an organ or the Member States).[11] The EU is the quintessential example of a supranational organisation. In so far as the UN Security Council adopts binding decisions under Chapter VII of the UN Charter in the case of a 'threat to the peace, breach of the peace, or act of aggression' by a special majority of its 15 members (see below, Section VIII(C)(ii)(b)), it can also be seen as supranational. However, even in intergovernmental organisations, the sovereignty of the members is often substantially eroded in practice. More generally, various scholars have

[6] Art 6(2) Charter of the Association of Southeast Asian Nations (adopted 20 November 2007, entered into force 15 December 2008) 2624 UNTS 46745.

[7] Art 7 Statute of the Organization of the Petroleum Exporting Countries (adopted 10 April 1965, entered into force 1 May 1965) 4 ILM 1175. See also SA Broome, 'Conflicting Obligations for Oil Exporting Nations? Satisfying Membership Requirements of Both OPEC and the WTO' (2006) 38 *The George Washington International Law Review* 409.

[8] P Sands and P Klein, *Bowett's Law of International Institutions*, 6th edn (London, Sweet & Maxwell, 2009) 17; Pastor Ridruejo (n 4) 713; M Diez de Velasco Vallejo *Les organisations internationales* (Paris, Economica, 2002) 15–16; Klabbers (n 2) 25–26; Schermers and Blokker (n 2) 58–59.

[9] Sands and Klein (n 8) 18; Pastor Ridruejo (n 4) 713–15; Diez de Velasco Vallejo (n 8) 19–21; Klabbers (n 2) 26–27; Schermers and Blokker (n 2) 55–57.

[10] PL Lindseth, 'Supranational Organizations' in J Katz Cogan, I Hurd and I Johnstone (eds), *The Oxford Handbook of International Organizations* (Oxford, OUP, 2016) 152–70; M Böckenförde and DA Sabsay, 'Supranational Organizations and their Impact on National Constitutions' in MV Tushnet (ed), *Routledge Handbook of Constitutional Law* (London, Routledge, 2013) 469–83.

[11] Schermers and Blokker (n 2) 56, who add that the organisation enjoys some financial autonomy, that no unilateral withdrawal from the organization is possible and that the organisation cannot be dissolved without the collaboration of its own organs. See also JE Alvarez, *International Organizations as Law-Makers* (Oxford, OUP, 2005) 16; Klabbers (n 2) 27.

identified different characteristics that they associate with supranational organisations.[12] Some have doubted the usefulness of the concept of supranationalism; others have rejected it altogether.[13] While the concept is probably ill-suited to characterise an international organisation in its entirety, it arguably has some value in highlighting particular characteristics in a certain body that indicate the extent to which it can validly be considered to be above, or 'supra', its Member States.[14]

III. Competences

International organisations do not have '*Kompetenz-Kompetenz*', ie the power to determine the scope of their own competences. They are subject to the principle of conferral of powers, also referred to as the 'principle of speciality'.[15] International organisations only have competences insofar as those have been conferred upon them by their Member States. Although this principle of conferral of powers or of speciality is not always mentioned in the constituent instrument of the organisation (typically the latter's founding treaty, like the UN Charter or the EU Treaties), it is generally accepted that all international organisations are governed by it.[16]

Probably the most explicit example is offered by the EU Treaties. Article 5 TEU provides that '[t]he limits of Union competence are governed by the principle of conferral', that the EU must act 'only within the limits of the competences conferred upon it by the Member States in the Treaties to attain the objectives set out therein', and that '[c]ompetences not conferred upon the Union in the Treaties remain with the Member States' (for the latter, see also Article 4(1) TEU).[17] The principle of conferral applies both to the internal and to the external action of the EU.[18] In addition to the question whether the EU possesses competence, the nature of that competence must be established. In that regard, the TFEU provides for various categories of EU competence: exclusive competence;[19] shared competence;[20] competence to provide arrangements for the Member States to coordinate their economic and employment policies;[21] competence to define and implement a common foreign and

[12] See eg Schermers and Blokker (n 2) 56–57; see also Alvarez (n 11) 16.

[13] See Schermers and Blokker (n 2) 57, fn 236 (referencing critical authors).

[14] G De Baere, A-L Chané and J Wouters, 'International Courts as Keepers of the Rule of Law: Achievements, Challenges, and Opportunities' (2016) 48 *New York University Journal of International Law and Politics* 736 (arguing that the internationalism-supranationalism spectrum can usefully be applied to bring out the marked differences that exist between different international judicial bodies in that regard).

[15] See P Klein, 'Quelques réflexions sur le principe de spécialité et la 'politisation' des institutions spécialisées' in L Boisson De Chazournes and P Sands (eds), *International Law, the International Court of Justice and Nuclear Weapons* (Cambridge, CUP, 1999) 78–91; C Chaumont, 'La signification du principe de spécialité dans les organisations internationales' in *Mélanges offerts à Henri Rolin* (Paris, Pedone, 1964) 55–66.

[16] MN Shaw, *International Law*, 8th edn (Cambridge, CUP, 2017) 998–1000; Klabbers (n 2) 50–69; Pastor Ridruejo (n 3) 716–717; D Sarooshi, *International Organizations and Their Exercise of Sovereign Powers* (Oxford, OUP, 2005); Schermers and Blokker (n 2) 155–89.

[17] See also Art 7 TFEU: 'The Union shall ensure consistency between its policies and activities, taking all of its objectives into account and in accordance with the principle of conferral of powers'.

[18] See Opinion 2/94 (Accession of the Community to the ECHR) of 28 March 1996, EU:C:1996:140, para 24; and judgment of 5 December 2017, *Germany v Council*, C-600/14, EU:C:2017:935, para 44.

[19] Arts 2(1) and 3 TFEU.

[20] ibid, Arts 2(2) and 4.

[21] ibid, Arts 2(3) and 5.

security policy (CFSP);[22] and competence to carry out actions to support, coordinate or supplement the actions of the Member States[23] – on the basis of which the EU institutions may exercise a varying degree of power.[24]

The competences that have been conferred on an international organisation first and foremost include those that have been conferred expressly in the organisation's constituent instrument. In addition, the question has been raised whether an organisation can also have powers that have not been explicitly conferred, but may be logically derived from the object and purpose of the constituent instrument, ie so-called 'implied powers'. In its 1949 advisory opinion *Reparation for Injuries Suffered in the Service of the United Nations*,[25] the International Court of Justice (ICJ) accepted the theory of implied powers. The case concerned the question whether (following the assassination of the UN mediator Count Bernadotte of Sweden by terrorists in the new town of Jerusalem, which was under the control of Israel, which was not a UN Member at the time) the UN had the competence to file an international legal claim for damages with respect to injuries suffered by it and the victim and its relatives. The ICJ concluded that '[u]nder international law, the Organization must be deemed to have those powers which, though not expressly provided in the Charter, are conferred upon it by necessary implication as being essential to the performance of its duties'.[26]

This doctrine of implied powers is currently widely recognised, and also extends to other international organisations.[27] The CJEU, for instance, in its 1956 *Fédéchar* judgment, referred to

> a rule of interpretation generally accepted in both international and national law according to which the rules laid down by an international treaty or a law presuppose the rules without which that treaty or law would have no meaning or could not be reasonably and usefully applied.[28]

Within the EU, implied competences have been relied on mostly with regard to external action, as first recognised by the CJEU in its 1971 *ERTA* judgment.[29] Of course, implied

[22] ibid, Art 2(4).
[23] ibid, Art 2(5).
[24] See further Chapter 7, Section II(B)(iii).
[25] *Reparation for Injuries Suffered in the Service of the United Nations* (Advisory Opinion) [1949] ICJ Rep 174.
[26] ibid, 12. See RA Wessel's annotation to this case in C Ryngaert, IF Dekker, RA Wessel and J Wouters (eds), *Judicial Decisions on the Law of International Organizations* (Oxford, OUP, 2016) 11–18. See also D Akande, 'The Competence of International Organizations and the Advisory Jurisdiction of the ICJ' (1998) 9 *EJIL* 437.
[27] V Engström, 'Implied Powers of International Organizations: On the Character of a Legal Doctrine' (2003) 14 *FYIL* 129; M Rama-Montaldo, 'International Legal Personality and Implied Powers of International Organizations' (1970) 44 *BYIL* 111; B Rouyer-Hameray, *Les compétences implicites des organisations internationales* (Paris, LGDJ, 1962); R Khan, *Implied Powers of the United Nations* (Delhi, Vikas Publications, 1970); K Skubiszewski, 'Implied Powers of International Organizations' in S Rosenne, Y Dinstein and M Tabory (eds), *International Law at a Time of Perplexity: Essays in Honour of Shabtai Rosenne* (Leiden, Nijhoff, 1989) 855–68.
[28] Judgment of 29 November 1956, *Fédération charbonnière de Belgique v High Authority*, 8/55, EU:C:1956:11, 292 and 299.
[29] Judgment of 31 March 1971, *Commission v Council ('ERTA')*, 22/70, EU:C:1971:32. See J Klabbers' annotation to this case in Ryngaert, Dekker, Wessel and Wouters (n 26) 19–27. The *ERTA* judgment is authority for the acquisition of implied external competences through the exercise of Union rules, and for their exclusive nature on the same basis. The former aspect is now codified in Art 216(1) TFEU, which provides that the Union may conclude an agreement with one or more third countries or international organisations inter alia where the conclusion of an agreement 'is likely to affect common rules or alter their scope'. The latter aspect is codified in Art 3(2) TFEU, which provides for the Union to have exclusive competence for the conclusion of an international agreement 'in so far as its conclusion may affect common rules or alter their scope': see judgments of 4 September 2014, *Commission v Council* ('Broadcasting Rights Convention'), C-114/12, EU:C:2014:2151, paras 65–67, and of 26 November 2014, *Green Network*, C-66/13, EU:C:2014:2399, paras 28–29; *Opinion 1/13* (Accession of third

powers cannot be stretched to such an extent that they would exceed the constitutional limitations set forth in the constituent instrument of the organisation in question.[30]

Some clauses in the constituent instrument of international organisations aim at ensuring a form of 'reserved powers' or *domaine réservé* of the Member States. A well-known example is Article 2(7) UN Charter, according to which '[n]othing contained in the present Charter shall authorize the United Nations to intervene in matters which are essentially within the domestic jurisdiction of any State', although this does not prejudice the application of enforcement measures adopted by the UN Security Council under Chapter VII of the Charter. A similar provision is found in the United Nations Educational, Scientific and Cultural Organization (UNESCO) Statute to preserve the cultural integrity and diversity of the Member States of the Organization.[31]

In the context of the EU, one can point to Article 4(2) TEU, pursuant to which the Union must 'respect [the] national identities [of Member States], inherent in their fundamental structures, political and constitutional, inclusive of regional and local self-government' as well as their 'essential State functions, including ensuring the territorial integrity of the State, maintaining law and order and safeguarding national security. In particular, national security remains the sole responsibility of each Member State'.[32] However, such clauses must be read from a dynamic and evolutionary perspective. For example, there is now a general consensus that UN Member States cannot invoke Article 2(7) UN Charter to defend serious and systematic violations of human rights within their territory.[33]

States to the Hague Convention) of 14 October 2014, EU:C:2014:2303, para 71; and *Opinion 2/15* (EU-Singapore Free Trade Agreement) of 16 May 2017, EU:C:2017:376, paras 170–72. Further, see eg G De Baere, 'EU External Action' in C Barnard and S Peers (eds), *European Union Law*, 2nd edn (Oxford, OUP, 2017) 717–18 and 720–22.

[30] For an illustration thereof, see *Opinion 2/94* (n 18), where the CJEU held that no Treaty provision conferred on the Community institutions any general power to enact rules on human rights or to conclude international conventions in this field (para 27). 'In the absence of express or implied powers for this purpose', the Court examined whether Art 235 of the EC Treaty (currently, after amendment, Art 352 TFEU, ie the so-called 'flexibility clause') could constitute a legal basis for accession to the ECHR. The Court held that provision to be 'designed to fill the gap where no specific provisions of the Treaty confer on the Community institutions express or implied powers to act, if such powers appear none the less to be necessary to enable the Community to carry out its functions with a view to attaining one of the objectives laid down by the Treaty' (para 29). However, after taking the position that accession to the ECHR would 'entail a substantial change in the present Community system for the protection of human rights in that it would entail the entry of the Community into a distinct international institutional system as well as integration of all the provisions of the Convention into the Community legal order', the Court concluded that such 'a modification of the system for the protection of human rights in the Community, with equally fundamental institutional implications for the Community and for the Member States, would be of constitutional significance and would therefore be such as to go beyond the scope of article 235. It could be brought about only by way of Treaty amendment' (paras 34–35). That Opinion provided the necessary impetus for the drafters of the Lisbon Treaty to insert a new Art 6(2) in the EU Treaty stating that the Union is to accede to the ECHR. An agreement on the EU's accession to the ECHR was reached in April 2013. However, the CJEU held that agreement to be 'not compatible with article 6(2) TEU or with Protocol (No 8)' relating to Art 6(2) TEU on the accession of the Union to the ECHR: *Opinion 2/13* (Accession of the European Union to the ECHR) of 18 December 2014, EU:C:2014:2454. See eg P Eeckhout, 'Opinion 2/13 on EU Accession to the ECHR and Judicial Dialogue: Autonomy or Autarky' (2015) 38 *Fordham International Law Journal* 955–92; J Odermatt, 'A Giant Step Backwards? Opinion 2/13 on the EU's Accession to the European Convention on Human Rights' (2015) 47 *New York University Journal of International Law and Politics* 783–97. On the accession of the EU to the ECHR, see Chapter 16, Section X(D)(ii).

[31] Art I(3) Constitution of the United Nations Educational, Scientific and Cultural Organization (adopted 16 November 1945, entered into force 4 November 1946) 4 UNTS 275 (UNESCO Constitution).

[32] See further E Cloots, *National Identity in EU Law* (Oxford, OUP, 2015).

[33] R Kolb, 'Du domaine réservé: réflexions sur la théorie de la compétence nationale' (2006) 110 *Revue générale de droit international public* 597; G Arangio-Ruiz, 'Le domaine réservé: l'organisation internationale et le rapport entre droit international et droit interne: cours général de droit international public' (1990) 225 *RdC* 9.

Another issue that arises in the context of the competences of international organisations relates to the powers of the respective organs of such organisations. The competences of those organs are usually specified in the organisation's constituent instrument. However, the scope of such competence is not always clearly delineated, and conflicts of competence may arise between organs of the same organisation. One such conflict arose within the UN when the General Assembly adopted its 'Uniting for Peace' resolution on 3 November 1950 (on which see also below, Section VIII(C)(i)(c)), holding that

> if the Security Council, because of lack of unanimity of the permanent members, fails to exercise its primary responsibility for the maintenance of international peace and security […], the General Assembly shall consider the matter immediately with a view to making appropriate recommendations to Members for collective measures.[34]

Permanent Security Council members France and the Soviet Union – who perceived this as undermining their veto rights – stated that this was not a competence of the General Assembly, but of the Security Council. In its 1962 advisory opinion *Certain Expenses of the United Nations*,[35] the ICJ ruled that the UN General Assembly did not overstep the boundaries of its competence in adopting the Uniting for Peace resolution.

Within the framework of the EU, Article 13(2) TEU provides for each EU institution to 'act within the limits of the powers conferred on it in the Treaties, and in conformity with the procedures, conditions and objectives set out in them'. That provision codifies the principle of institutional balance, which the CJEU had developed in extensive case law.[36] The institutional balance is crucially affected by the choice of the appropriate legal basis of a Union act.[37] That choice has constitutional significance, since, having only conferred powers, the EU must link the acts which it adopts to provisions of the Treaties which actually empower it to adopt such acts.[38] Further, the indication of the legal basis is of particular significance in order to preserve the prerogatives of the EU institutions concerned by the procedure for the adoption of a measure.[39]

[34] UNGA Res 377 (V), 'Uniting for Peace', 3 November 1950, UN Doc A/RES/337(V), 10. See inter alia AJ Carswell, 'Unblocking the UN Security Council: The Uniting for Peace Resolution' (2013) 18 *Journal of Conflict and Security Law* 453–80; C Tomuschat, 'Uniting for Peace: Ein Rückblick nach 50 Jahren' (2001) 76 *Die Friedens-Warte: Blätter für internationale Verständigung und zwischenstaatliche Organisation* 289; A Kosonen, *The United Nations General Assembly and the Authority to Establish UN Forces: An Interpretative Analysis of the Charter, the Theories of Implied and Inherent Powers, and the Uniting for Peace Resolution* (Helsinki, Institute of Public Law at the University of Helsinki, 1986); K Prössdorf, *Die 'Uniting for Peace' Resolution: eine Untersuchung der Satzungsmässigkeit der am 3. November 1950 von der Generalversammlung der Vereinten Nationen gefassten Resolution 377 (V)* (Uetersen bei Hamburg, Johannes Röbcke, 1960).

[35] *Certain Expenses of the United Nations* (Article 17, Paragraph 2, of the Charter) (Advisory Opinion) [1962] ICJ Rep 151; see the annotation of the case by J Wouters and J Odermatt, in Ryngaert, Dekker, Wessel and Wouters (n 26) 91–101.

[36] See eg judgments of 29 October 1980, *Roquette Frères v Council*, 138/79, EU:C:1980:249; and of 4 October 1991, *Parliament v Council ('Chernobyl')*, C-70/88, EU:C:1991:373. See inter alia S Gabbi, 'The Principle of Institutional (Un)Balance after Lisbon' (2014) 5 *European Journal of Risk Regulation* 259; JP Jacqué, 'The Principle of Institutional Balance' (2004) *CMLR* 383; K Lenaerts and JA Gutiérrez-Fons, 'A Constitutional Perspective' in R Schütze and T Tridimas (eds), *Oxford Principles of European Union Law – Vol 1: The European Union Legal Order* (Oxford, OUP, 2018) 124–32.

[37] Opinion of AG Poiares Maduro in *Parliament v Council*, C-133/06, EU:C:2007:551, point 32. See further E Sharpston and G De Baere, 'The Court of Justice as a Constitutional Adjudicator' in A Arnull et al (eds), *A Constitutional Order of States? Essays in EU Law in Honour of Alan Dashwood* (Oxford, Hart, 2011) 123–50.

[38] Opinion 1/15 (EU-Canada PNR Agreement) of 26 July 2017, EU:C:2017:592, para 71; and judgment of 25 October 2017, *Commission v Council ('WRC-15')*, C-687/15, EU:C:2017:803, para 49.

[39] *WRC-15* (n 38) para 50. The Court's settled case law on the choice of the appropriate legal basis states that the choice of legal basis must rest on objective factors amenable to judicial review, including the aim and content of the measure: see eg judgment of 12 September 2017, *Anagnostakis v Commission*, C-589/15 P, EU:C:2017:663,

IV. Membership

Initially, international organisations could only be created by States, and only States could become members of such organisations. In recent times, international organisations are increasingly involved in the setting up of new international organisations, although usually together with States. For example, the EU is a co-founding Member of the WTO and of the European Bank for Reconstruction and Development (EBRD).[40] Besides membership, which can be acquired through various procedures, the status of associate member or observer can be granted in various international organisations. Membership may also be suspended or revoked.[41]

A. Ways of Acquiring Membership

Usually, the constituent instrument of the international organisation in question contains provisions regarding the procedure through which States, or even international organisations, can become members.[42] For some organisations, all Member States must agree unanimously on the admission of a new Member State. This is the case, for example, for accession to the EU[43] and the North Atlantic Treaty Organization (NATO).[44] In other organisations, admission is possible if one or more organs agree by a certain majority. For example, a decision of the Ministerial Conference by a two-thirds majority is required for admission to the WTO.[45] Admission to the UN requires a decision of the General Assembly[46] (by a two-thirds majority of the Member States present) upon recommendation of the Security Council.[47] This implies that Permanent Members of the latter can veto any membership requests.

para 41. See further G De Baere and T Van den Sanden, 'Interinstitutional Gravity and Pirates of the Parliament on Stranger Tides: The Continued Constitutional Significance of the Choice of Legal Basis in Post-Lisbon External Action' (2016) 12 *European Constitutional Law Review* 85.

[40] See further G De Baere, 'EU Status in Other International Organizations' in Schütze and Tridimas (eds) (n 36) 1234–81.

[41] For a general overview, see eg A Duxbury, *The Participation of States in International Organisations* (Cambridge, CUP, 2011); S Mathias and S Tengrove, 'Membership and Representation' in Katz Cogan, Hurd and Johnstone (n 10) 962–84; KD Magliveras, 'Membership in International Organizations' in J Klabbers and Å Wallendahl (eds), *Research Handbook on the Law of International Organizations* (Cheltenham, Edward Elgar, 2011) 84–107.

[42] For a general overview on admission, see eg Sands and Klein (n 8) 538–45; Klabbers (n 2) 91–96; Diez de Velasco Vallejo (n 8) 60–65; Schermers and Blokker (n 2) 76–98.

[43] Art 49 TEU. Consent of the European Parliament is also required. See also JE Scalera, *Negotiating Membership in the WTO and the EU: The Politics of Accession* (London, Routledge, 2017).

[44] Art 10 NATO Treaty. See also AA Bebler, 'A Research Note on Eligibility for NATO Membership' in AA Bebler (ed), *The Challenge of NATO Enlargement* (Westport, Praeger, 1999) 49–57.

[45] Art XII(2) WTO Agreement. However, in practice decision-making takes place by consensus: see below, p 851.

[46] Art 18(2) UN Charter. See also *Competence of Assembly regarding admission to the United Nations* (Advisory Opinion) [1950] ICJ Rep 4.

[47] Art 4(2) UN Charter.

B. Associated Members and Observers

Besides ordinary membership, there are also other modalities for States or non-State actors to be involved in the functioning of an international organisation without becoming a full member. A considerable variation in possible statuses exists.

States with *associated membership* typically possess some form of participation rights in the organisation and have representation in (certain) organs of the organisation, but do not have voting rights.[48] Examples of associated membership can be found in certain specialised agencies of the UN, such as the World Health Organization (WHO), UNESCO, the Food and Agriculture Organization (FAO) as well as in the World Tourism Organization (UNWTO).

Non-Member States, liberation movements or non-governmental organisations may be granted *observer status* in certain international organisations.[49] This means that they have access to, and limited participation rights in, formal meetings of the organ of the international organisation where they have such status, without having voting rights. In general, observers receive the documents that are being discussed and may be given a limited opportunity to speak during the meetings. The practical significance of observer status varies from organisation to organisation. The UN offers an example where, in addition to the capacity of Non-Member Observer State of the Holy See[50] and Palestine,[51] a number of widely diverse entities have acquired observer status at the General Assembly, such as eg: the African Union, the League of Arab States, the International Tribunal of the Law of the Sea, the International Committee of the Red Cross (ICRC)[52] and even the Sovereign Military Order of Malta. Within the framework of the Economic and Social Council of the UN (ECOSOC), a longstanding institutionalised dialogue exists with a large number of NGOs, which have a consultative status (see also below, p 284). The EU has been granted 'enhanced participation rights' at the UN General Assembly,[53] allowing the EU inter alia to speak among the representatives of major groups. Also in a number of other international organisations or conferences the EU has been granted an 'enhanced observer' status or 'full participant' status, which gives it stronger participation rights while falling short of membership. This applies inter alia to the OECD and many of the UN's world conferences.

[48] Klabbers (n 2) 96–99; Diez de Velasco Vallejo (n 8) 69–70; Schermers and Blokker (n 2) 125–28.

[49] eg FB Vabulas, 'Consultative and Observer Status of NGOs in Intergovernmental Organizations' in B Reinalda (ed), *Routledge Handbook of International Organizations* (London, Routledge, 2012) 189–202; RA Jay, *United Nations Observer Status: An Accumulation of Contemporary Developments* (Washington, World Association of Lawyers, 1976); Schermers and Blokker (n 2) 131–49; Diez de Velasco Vallejo (n 8) 70–71; E Suy, 'The Status of Observers in International Organisations' (1978) 160 *Rec Cours* II 75–179.

[50] See UNGA Res 58/314 'Participation of the Holy See in the work of the United Nations', 1 July 2003, UN Doc A/RES/58/314.

[51] In 2012 the General Assembly voted to accord the State of Palestine the status of 'Non-Member Observer State'; UNGA Res A/RES/67/19, 'Status of Palestine in the United Nations', 29 November 2012, UN Doc A/RES/67/19. See also JP Cerone, 'Legal Implications of the UN General Assembly Vote to Accord Palestine the Status of Observer State' (2012) 37 *ASIL Insights* 16; S Burra, 'Palestine and the Belated UN Non-Member Observer State Status' (2012) 52 *Indian Journal of International Law* 591.

[52] W Remans, 'The Granting of Observer Status by the General Assembly of the United Nations to the International Federation of Red Cross and Red Crescent Societies' in KC Wellens (ed), *International Law: Theory and Practice: Essays in Honour of Eric Suy* (The Hague, Nijhoff, 1998) 347–62; C Koenig, 'Observer Status for the International Committee of the Red Cross at the United Nations: A Legal Viewpoint' (1991) 280 *IRRC* 37.

[53] UNGA Res 65/276, 'Participation of the European Union in the Work of the United Nations', 3 May 2011, UN Doc A/RES/65/276. See J Wouters, J Odermatt and T Ramopoulos, 'The Status of the European Union at the United Nations General Assembly' in I Govaere et al (eds), *The European Union in the World: Essays in Honour of Marc Maresceau* (Leiden, Nijhoff, 2014) 211–23.

In some cases this status was recognised only selectively or thematically, eg for the negotiation of a multilateral treaty within the framework of the organisation in question.[54]

C. Suspension and Termination of Membership

Membership of international organisations can be suspended temporarily or terminated permanently.

i. Suspension of Membership

Some international organisations explicitly provide for the option of suspending the membership of a Member State, or of suspending certain membership rights.[55]

Within the framework of the UN, Article 5 UN Charter provides the General Assembly with the possibility, acting on a recommendation of the Security Council, to suspend a UN Member State against whom preventive or enforcement action has been taken by the Security Council. Article 19 of the UN Charter strips a Member State of its voting rights in the General Assembly when such Member State is in arrears in the payment of its financial contributions equal to or exceeding the amount of the contributions due from it for the preceding two full years. In certain specialised agencies of the UN, suspension of voting rights may also be a sanction when membership contributions have not been paid.[56]

Membership rights can also be suspended for EU Member States within the EU in relation to a serious breach of the fundamental values upon which the EU is founded (as laid down in Article 2 TEU), under the procedures laid down in Article 7 TEU. This possibility, sometimes referred to as the 'nuclear option', has not yet been applied in practice, although the European Commission has recently recommended action under Article 7(1) TEU against Poland, and the European Parliament has invited the Council to do the same vis-à-vis Hungary.[57]

[54] See eg F Hoffmeister and PJ Kuijper, 'The Status of the European Union at the United Nations: Institutional Ambiguities and Political Realities' in J Wouters, F Hoffmeister and T Ruys (eds), *The United Nations and the European Union: An Ever Stronger Partnership* (The Hague, TMC Asser Press, 2006) 9–34; G De Baere and E Paasivirta, 'Identity and Difference: The EU and the UN as Part of Each Other' in H de Waele and J Kuipers (eds), *The European Union's Emerging International Identity: Views from the Global Arena* (Leiden, Nijhoff, 2013) 21–42; J Wouters, AL Chané, J Odermatt and T Ramopoulos, 'Improving the EU's Status in the UN and the UN System: An Objective Without a Strategy?' in C Kaddous (ed), *The European Union in International Organisations and Global Governance: Recent Developments* (Oxford, Hart, 2015) 45–74.

[55] H Hardt and BE Sasley, 'When States Break the Rules: Membership Suspension in International Organizations' (Annual Convention of the American Political Science Association, Washington, DC, 2014); KD Magliveras, *Exclusion from Participation in International Organizations: The Law and Practice Behind Member States' Expulsion and Suspension from Membership* (The Hague, Kluwer, 1999); Sands and Klein (n 8) 545–50.

[56] eg, Art IV UNESCO Constitution (n 31) sets out that 'A Member State shall have no vote in the General Conference if the total amount of contributions due from it exceeds the total amount of contributions payable by it for the current year and the immediately preceding calendar year'. Similarly, Art 56 of the Convention on the International Maritime Organization (adopted 6 March 1948, entered into force 17 March 1958) 289 UNTS 3 suspends voting rights for members that fail to discharge their financial obligations after one year. See also Art 7 of the Constitution of the World Health Organization (adopted 22 July 1946, entered into force 7 April 1948) 14 UNTS 185 (WHO Constitution), or Art 62 of the Chicago Convention on International Civil Aviation. See also JH Lavieille, 'La procedure de suspension des droits d'un Etat membre des Nations Unies' (1977) 1 *Revue Générale de Droit International Public* 431; BN Krylov, 'On the Suspension of Membership in International Organisations of the UN system' (1983) *Soviet Yearbook of International Law* 109.

[57] See respectively, European Commission, Reasoned Proposal in accordance with Article 7(1) of the Treaty on European Union regarding the Rule of Law in Poland, 20 December 2017, COM(2017) 835 final; European

ii. Termination of Membership

Membership in an international organisation can be terminated in four ways:[58]

a) the Member State can withdraw from the organisation (eg Greece from the Council of Europe in 1969, the United States from UNESCO in 1984[59] and again in 2018);
b) the organisation can expel the Member State (eg South Africa's expulsion from the UPU and the ITU because of the apartheid regime);[60]
c) the Member State ceases to exist (eg the German Democratic Republic in 1990);
d) the organisation ceases to exist (eg the League of Nations in 1946 or the Warsaw Pact in 1991).

The constituent instrument of international organisations often contains a provision which gives Member States the possibility to withdraw from the organisation.[61] Usually, for a Member State to withdraw from an international organisation, it is required to give prior notice and to observe a specified notice period. Such notice period may vary from six months (WTO)[62] to two years (ILO).[63] Interesting in this respect is the procedure for withdrawal from the International Criminal Court under Article 127 of the ICC Statute. This does not come into effect until one year after notification to the UN Secretary General and does not prejudice the consideration of matters that were brought before the Court before the withdrawal became effective.[64] With the International Monetary Fund (IMF) and the World Bank, on the other hand, withdrawal of membership has immediate effect. This was deemed necessary to guarantee the economic independence of their Members.

Article 50 TEU provides that an EU Member State may decide 'to withdraw from the Union in accordance with its own constitutional requirements'. On 23 June 2016 the United Kingdom voted in a referendum to leave the EU. It notified the latter of its intention to leave on 29 March 2017, triggering a period of negotiation with the Union in order to reach an agreement setting out the arrangements for withdrawal and the future relationship with the Union (see also below, p 316). The EU Treaties cease to apply in respect of the withdrawing

Parliament Resolution of 12 September 2018 (2017/2131 (INL)), See inter alia D Kochenov and L Pech, 'Monitoring and Enforcement of the Rule of Law in the EU: Rhetoric and Reality' (2015) 11 *European Constitutional Law Review* 512; H Schmitt von Sydow, 'Liberté, démocratie, droits fondamentaux et Etat de droit: analyse de l'article 7 du traité UE' (2001) 2 *Revue du droit de l'Union européenne* 285. See also above, p 124.

[58] N Singh, *Termination of Membership of International Organizations* (London, Stevens, 1957); Sands and Klein (n 8) 550–56; Klabbers (n 2) 106–11; Schermers and Blokker (n 2) 98–121; Diez de Velasco Vallejo (n 8) 65–68.

[59] JH Rosenthal, *The Withdrawal from UNESCO: International Organizations and the U.S. Role* (Washington, Institute for the Study of Diplomacy, 1990).

[60] See Magliveras (n 55) in general, and 69–75 on the case of South Africa in particular; LB Sohn, 'Expulsion or Forced Withdrawal from an International Organization' (1964) 77 *Harvard Law Review* 1381; B Blagoev, 'Expulsion of a Member State from the EU after Lisbon: Political Threat or Legal Reality?' (2011) 16 *Tilburg Law Review* 191.

[61] eg the WTO, Art XV WTO Agreement; the ILO, Art 1(5) Constitution of the International Labour Organization (adopted 28 June 1919, entered into force 10 January 1920, as amended 20 April 1948) (ILO Constitution) 15 UNTS 40; NATO, Art 13 NATO Treaty; the Council of Europe, Art 7 Statute Council of Europe (n 5); the OECD, Art 17 Convention on the Organization for Economic Co-operation and Development (adopted 14 December 1960, entered into force 30 September 1961) 888 UNTS 179. See also F Dehousse, 'Le droit de retrait des Nations Unies' (1965) 1 *Revue Belge de Droit International* 30; E Schwelb, 'Withdrawal from the United Nations: The Indonesian Intermezzo' (1967) 61 *AJIL* 661; E Stein and D Carreau, 'Law and Peaceful Change in a Subsystem: 'Withdrawal' of France from the North Atlantic Treaty Organization' (1968) 62 *AJIL* 577; MC Dock, 'Le retrait des Etats membres des organisations internationales de la famille des Nations Unies' (1994) 40 *Annuaire Français de Droit International* 106.

[62] Art XV WTO Agreement.

[63] Art 1(5) ILO Constitution.

[64] Art 127(2) ICC Statute.

State either when the agreement enters into force or two years after the notification of withdrawal was made (although this period can be extended by the European Council). Once an EU Member State has left the Union, it may re-join, but must follow the same procedure as a new Member State applying to join.

Constituent instruments of international organisations which provide the possibility to expel a member are relatively rare. Examples of organisations that have incorporated the express possibility for expulsion include the UN,[65] the IMF,[66] and the Council of Europe.[67] The grounds and procedures for expulsion vary. A UN Member State which has persistently violated the principles set out in the UN Charter may be expelled from the organisation by the General Assembly upon the recommendation of the Security Council, on the basis of a two-thirds majority decision.[68] Thus far, this has never happened. At the end of 1955, a draft resolution was submitted to the Security Council which called for the expulsion of Israel from the UN. In the 1960s and 1970s, the same was repeatedly done with respect to South Africa, but the Security Council was never able to reach a decision. It should be noted that it is rather difficult to reconcile the concept of expulsion with the universality propagated by the UN.

V. Organs and Decision-Making

Most international organisations have organs such as a General Assembly, a Council, a Secretariat and sometimes even a judicial and a parliamentary organ. These bodies can, often unanimously or by consensus, adopt decisions, which are usually non-binding.

A. Organs

International organisations normally have a number of bodies with more or less delineated competences.[69] The supreme organ is usually the one in which all Member States are represented. Such body may be called the General Assembly, (General) Conference, or (often in regional organisations) Council. The delegates in these organs are the representatives of national governments.[70]

The ILO is an interesting exception to this rule. In the International Labour Conference, every Member Country is represented by a tripartite delegation composed of two government representatives and one representative of national employer organisations and one

[65] Art 6 UN Charter. See also F Zeidler, *Der Austritt und Ausschluss von Mitgliedern aus den Sonderorganisationen der Vereinten Nationen* (Bern, Peter Lang, 1990).

[66] Articles of Agreement of the International Monetary Fund (adopted 22 July 1944, entered into force 27 December 1945) 2 UNTS 39 (IMF Articles of Agreement).

[67] Art 8 Statute Council of Europe (n 5).

[68] Art 6 juncto Art 18(2) UN Charter.

[69] ZM Klepacki, *The Organs of International Organizations* (The Hague, Nijhoff, 1978); Klabbers (n 2) 207–41; I Österdahl, 'International Organizations: Institutions and Organs' in Klabbers and Wallendahl (n 41) 156–89; P Reuter, 'Les organes subsidiaires des organisations internationales' in *Hommage d'une génération de juristes au Président Basdevant* (Paris, Pedone, 1960) 415–40; Schermers and Blokker (n 2) 189–290; Diez de Velasco Vallejo (n 8) 75–83; Pastor Ridruejo (n 3) 718–22.

[70] MP Karns, 'General Assemblies and Assemblies of States Parties' in Katz Cogan, Hurd and Johnstone (n 10) 757–81; Schermers and Blokker (n 2) 297–307.

representative of national employee organisations. Both of the latter representatives act independently of their government – at least in theory. Within the framework of the UN, the General Assembly is not the supreme organ, but a 'main organ' alongside the Security Council, ECOSOC, the Trusteeship Council, the ICJ and the Secretariat.[71] As a rule, the plenary bodies of international organisations convene only periodically, typically once a year (eg the UN General Assembly, the International Labour Conference of the ILO, the World Health Assembly of the WHO) or once every two years (eg UNESCO General Conference, WTO Ministerial Conference). Such body usually determines the general policy of the organisation and decides on issues such as the admission of new members and budgetary matters.

In many international organisations, operational management is entrusted to a body of more limited size, often called a Council, Governing Council, Administrative Council or Executive Council or Board.[72] The members of such organ are usually elected taking into account a certain geographical distribution, although the most important Member States often have permanent representation. The size of such a Council is usually limited to one-fifth or one-third of the total membership of the organisation in question. The ILO, for instance, has a Governing Body composed of 56 members.[73] The WHO has a 32-member Executive Board.[74]

The work of the organisation is usually supported by a Secretariat, which is managed by a Secretary General.[75] The Secretary General sometimes has a purely administrative function, but in some organisations he or she also fulfils an important political role. This is especially the case in the UN, since the Secretary General can bring any matter, which in his or her opinion may threaten the maintenance of international peace and security, to the attention of the Security Council (see below, Section VIII(C)(v)(b)).[76] Even where the constituent instrument of an organisation only provides for an administrative role, the Secretariat will frequently play an important role in reality. The WTO Secretariat, for instance, although lacking any formal decision-making competence, has a significant influence on the panels in the framework of the dispute settlement mechanism. It also provides technical support to several councils and committees, conducts studies and informs the public and the media.[77]

Although it remains a rare occurrence, international organisations can establish a judicial (or quasi-judicial) body.[78] These bodies adjudicate disputes between Member States and interpret the constitutive treaty of the organisation. Some of the main dispute settlement bodies are discussed in Chapter 13 on Peaceful Dispute Settlement.

[71] Art 7(1) UN Charter.

[72] RA Wessel, 'Executive Boards and Councils' in Katz Cogan, Hurd and Johnstone (n 10) 802–21.

[73] This organ is also constituted in a tripartite manner, ie by 28 government representatives, 14 employer representatives and 14 employee representatives: see Art 7(1) ILO Constitution (n 61).

[74] Art 24(1) WHO Constitution (n 56).

[75] T Piiparinen, 'Secretariats' in Katz Cogan, Hurd and Johnstone (n 10) 839–58; Schermers and Blokker (n 2) 320–51.

[76] Art 99 UN Charter.

[77] CP Bown and R Malacrida, 'The WTO Secretariat and the Role of Economics in Panels and Arbitrations' in CP Bown, *The Law, Economics and Politics of Retaliation in WTO Dispute Settlement* (New York, CUP, 2010) 391–433. See also below, pp 858–859.

[78] C Giorgetti, 'International Adjudicative Bodies' in Katz Cogan, Hurd and Johnstone (n 10) 881–902; Schermers and Blokker (n 2) 435–95. See further G De Baere and J Wouters (eds), *The Contribution of International and Supranational Courts to the Rule of Law* (Cheltenham, Edward Elgar, 2015).

Even rarer are international organisations that have established their own parliamentary body.[79] A number of – primarily European – organisations have a parliamentary assembly, whose powers are typically very limited. Such assemblies often have little more than a consultative vote and mostly provide a forum for mutual consultation and cooperation between national members of parliament of Member States. Unlike national parliaments, parliamentary bodies in international organisations have no genuine supervisory powers vis-à-vis the executive body of the organisation. A well-known example of a parliamentary body is the Parliamentary Assembly of the Council of Europe. The parliamentary assemblies of NATO and the OSCE have no formal treaty status.[80] In the context of the WTO, plans were made to establish a WTO parliamentary assembly, also without any treaty status. A very important exception, especially in terms of direct representation and powers, to the abovementioned parliamentary bodies is the European Parliament. The European Parliament is directly elected and has far-reaching powers in the EU's internal legislative procedures (especially under the 'ordinary legislative procedure')[81] and in the EU's treaty-making procedure (see Chapter 7, Section II(B)(ii)).

B. Decision-Making

The effectiveness of an international organisation is often measured by its decision-making procedures. International organisations display a great level of diversity in this respect.[82] In each case, the constituent instrument must be examined together with the institutional processes that have developed in practice. In addition to these procedures, it should also be examined which types of decisions the international organisations can adopt.[83]

i. Procedures

Before the Second World War, the constituent instruments of international organisations almost always required decisions to be adopted unanimously.[84] An exception was often made for procedural decisions. After the Second World War, in order to guarantee a minimum of effectiveness for decision-making procedures, the rule of unanimity was gradually abandoned in favour of different forms of majority voting.[85]

It is difficult to speak in general terms, because the modalities of decision-making differ substantially between organisations. In most cases, each Member State has one vote,

[79] See B Høyland, 'Parliaments' in Katz Cogan, Hurd and Johnstone (n 10) 782–801; Schermers and Blokker (n 2) 408–35.

[80] eg M Fuchs and A Pendzich-von Winter, 'The OSCE Parliamentary Assembly: Origins, Functions, Method of Work and Constituent Bodies' (1995–1996) 1–2 *OSCE Yearbook* 355.

[81] Arts 289(1) and 294 TFEU.

[82] See inter alia CW Jenks, 'Unanimity, the Veto, Weighted Voting, Special and Simple Majorities and Consensus as Modes of Decision in International Organizations' in *Cambridge Essays in International Law* (London, Stevens and Sons, 1965) 48–63; ND White, 'Decision-making' in Klabbers and Wallendahl (n 41) 225–50; Diez de Velasco Vallejo (n 8) 83–86; Pastor Ridruejo (n 3) 722–27.

[83] For a general overview on the legality of decisions, see eg J Wouters and J Odermatt, 'Assessing the Legality of Decisions' in Katz Cogan, Hurd and Johnstone (n 10) 1006–25.

[84] The ILO was the major exception to that rule, since it could adopt conventions by a two-thirds majority.

[85] CA Riches, *Majority Rule in International Organization: A Study of the Trend from Unanimity to Majority Decision* (Baltimore, The Johns Hopkins Press, 1940).

regardless of its size, power or economic status ('one country, one vote').[86] This is linked to the underlying principle of the sovereign equality of States. However, a few notable exceptions to this rule exist. In organisations such as the IMF and the World Bank,[87] votes are weighted on the basis of a system of quota allocated according to financial contributions. In the context of the EU, before the changes brought about by the Treaty of Lisbon in 2007, weighted voting also took place in the Council under the system of qualified majority voting (QMV).[88]

Even when the constituent instrument of an organisation requires decisions to be made by majority vote, many instances exist where institutional practice has developed into decision-making by *consensus*.[89] This means that decisions are taken without a formal vote. In global organisations, this practice can be explained in part by the number of developing countries that have become member following the different waves of decolonisation. Industrialised countries in particular (which often contribute the bulk of the organisation's budget) insisted on decision-making by consensus, so that majority decisions would not be 'imposed' on them. By taking decisions by consensus, it is more likely that negotiations will continue until a formula is worked out that is acceptable to all Member States. Also in the EU decision-making takes place by consensus in the European Council[90] and, in most cases in practice (even though the Treaties require qualified majority voting), in the Council.[91]

[86] R Monaco, 'Le système de vote dans les organisations internationales' in *Mélanges en l'honneur de Gilbert Gidel* (Paris, Sirey, 1961) 469–82; W Koo, *Voting Procedures in International Political Organizations* (New York, Columbia UP, 1947); P Jessup, 'Parliamentary Diplomacy: An Examination of the Legal Quality of the Rules of Procedures of Organs in the UN' (1956) 89 *RdC* 185; R Ben Achour, *Evolution des modes de décision dans les organisations internationales* (Tunis, CNUDST, 1986); Schermers and Blokker (n 2) 547–92.

[87] See for the IMF Art XII(5) IMF Articles of Agreement; for the World Bank, see Art V(3)(a): Articles of Agreement of the International Bank for Reconstruction and Development (adopted and entered into force 27 December 1945) 2 UNTS 134 (IBRD Articles of Agreement), 'The voting power of each member shall be equal to the sum of its basic votes and share votes'.

[88] See nowadays Art 16 TEU and Art 238 TFEU. The basic rules with respect to QMV in the Council that are currently in force are as follows. First, pursuant to Art 16(4) TEU, as from 1 November 2014, a qualified majority is to be defined as 'at least 55% of the members of the Council, comprising at least fifteen of them and representing Member States comprising at least 65% of the population of the Union'. Second, Art 238(2) TFEU provides that, by way of derogation from Art 16(4) TEU, 'as from 1 November 2014 and subject to the provisions laid down in the Protocol on transitional provisions, where the Council does not act on a proposal from the Commission or from the High Representative of the Union for Foreign Affairs and Security Policy, the qualified majority shall be defined as at least 72% of the members of the Council, representing Member States comprising at least 65% of the population of the Union'. Third, in both cases, a 'blocking minority must include at least four Council members, failing which the qualified majority shall be deemed attained' (Art 16(4) TEU). About weighted voting in other international organisations, see inter alia C Barrett and H Newcombe, *Weighted Voting in International Organizations* (Oakville, Canadian Peace Research Institute, 1968); J Kranz, 'Le vote pondéré dans les organisations internationales' (1981) 85 *Revue Générale de Droit International Public* 313; HA Schwarz-Liebermann von Wahlendorf, *Mehrheitsentscheidung und Stimmenwägung* (Tübingen, Mohr, 1953); E McIntyre, 'Weighted Voting in International Organizations' (1954) 8 *International Organizations* 484; H Newcombe, C Young and E Sinaiko, 'Alternative Pasts: A Study of Weighted Voting at the United Nations' (1977) 31 *International Organizations* 579; R Drago, 'La pondération dans les organisations internationales' (1956) 2 *Annuaire français de droit international* 529.

[89] C Guillerment Fernandez, 'The Search for Consensus and Unanimity within the International Organizations' (2016) 13 *US-China Law Review* 53; E Suy, 'Rôle et signification du consensus dans l'élaboration du droit international' (1997) 67 *Annuaire de l'Institut de Droit International* 16; P Jessup, 'Procedure by Consensus: Silence Gives Consent' (1975) 14 *Communicazione e studi* 173; H Cassan, 'Le consensus dans la pratique des Nations Unies' (1974) 20 *Annuaire français de droit international* 456; Schermers and Blokker (n 2) 533–47.

[90] Except where the Treaties provide otherwise: Art 15(4) TEU. For example, the European Council is to elect its President by a qualified majority: Art 15(5) TEU.

[91] For the European Council, see Art 15(4) TEU. See more generally F Picod (ed), *Le principe majoritaire en droit de l'Union européenne* (Brussels, Bruylant, 2016) 135–54.

It is important to distinguish decision-making by consensus from decision-making by *unanimity*.[92] In consensus-based decision-making, no formal vote is held. The chairman will instead establish that no-one has called for a formal vote and that the proposal is therefore adopted. Decision-making by unanimity, on the other hand, implies that there will be a vote and that all Member States must vote in favour. The abstention by a Member State does not prevent the adoption of the decision, unless the constituent instrument provides otherwise; this may also be accepted based on institutional practice.[93] An example of institutionalised decision-making by consensus can be found in the WTO. Pursuant to Article IX(1) of the WTO Agreement, 'the WTO shall continue the practice of decision-making by consensus followed under GATT 1947'. A footnote to this provision specifies that 'the body concerned shall be deemed to have decided by consensus on a matter submitted for its consideration, if no Member, present at the meeting when the decision is taken, formally objects to the proposed decision'. The same provision also stipulates that where a decision cannot be arrived at by consensus, the matter at issue shall be decided by voting, except as otherwise provided by the WTO Agreement. This has not happened in the WTO thus far.[94]

ii. Types of Decisions

Most international organisations can only adopt non-binding decisions, usually termed *resolutions*. They can also adopt *conventions*, to which States are only bound if they ratify the convention at hand. This is the case for a large number of conventions that have been adopted in the framework of the ILO and the Council of Europe. With regard to the ILO and the WHO, specific mechanisms are in place that oblige States, or at least pressure them, to ratify the conventions adopted within the framework of the organisation within a certain period of time.

It is rare for an organ of an international organisation to be able to adopt decisions that are directly binding on the Member States. The best-known examples are resolutions taken by the Security Council under Chapter VII of the UN Charter, and regulations, directives or decisions adopted by the Council of the EU (together with the European Parliament in case of a legislative procedure: see above, p 161).

In spite of the aforementioned limitations, the normative activities of international organisations have greatly expanded over the past three decades, making them important regulatory actors in an increasing number of areas of global governance.[95]

[92] Schermers and Blokker (n 2) 547–49.

[93] An example of such practice is found under Art 27(3) UN Charter with regard to the vote of permanent members of the Security Council, on which see Chapter 2, Section VII(B)(iii), n 337. See also M Fromont, 'L'abstention de vote dans les organisations internationales' (1961) 7 *Annuaire français de droit international* 492.

[94] J Tijmes-Lhl, 'Consensus and Majority Voting in the WTO' (2009) 8 *World Trade Review* 417; ME Footer, 'The Role of Consensus in GATT/WTO Decision-Making' (1997) 17 *Northwestern Journal of International Law and Business* 653.

[95] See inter alia Alvarez (n 11); S Block-Lieb and TC Halliday, *Global Lawmakers. International Organizations in the Crafting of World Markets* (Cambridge, CUP, 2017); I Johnstone, 'Law-Making by International Organizations' in JL Dunoff and MA Pollack (eds), *Interdisciplinary Perspectives on International Law and International Relations* (Cambridge, CUP, 2012) 266; J Wouters and P De Man, 'International Organizations as Law-Makers' in Klabbers and Wallendahl (n 41), 190. Specifically on the UNSC, see J Wouters and J Odermatt, '*Quis Custodiet Consilium Securitatis?* Reflections on the Lawmaking Powers of the Security Council' in V Popovski and T Fraser (eds), *The Security Council as Global Legislator* (London, Routledge, 2014) 71.

VI. Legal Personality

With respect to the legal personality enjoyed by international organisations, a distinction should be made between legal personality under national law and international law.[96] Legal personality under *national* law implies that the international organisation is capable of acquiring or disposing of movable and immovable property, entering into contracts, etc. It entails the capacity of the international organisation to engage in legal transactions under domestic law. The constituent instrument of most international organisations explicitly specifies that the organisation has legal personality under the national law of its Member States.[97]

On the other hand, the constituent instruments of international organisations usually fail to include a similar provision to endow the organisation with *international* legal personality, ie the capacity to enjoy rights and incur obligations under international law.[98] Exceptions include the former European Coal and Steel Community,[99] the former European Community[100] and the Eurasian Economic Union.[101] With the entry into force of the Treaty of Lisbon, the EU was explicitly granted international legal personality,[102] although arguably the Union already met the conditions of international legal personality prior to this.[103] Even when the constituent instrument does not explicitly confer international legal personality on the organisation, the existence of such international legal personality may, in some cases, be implied. Following the ICJ's 1949 landmark advisory opinion in *Reparation for Injuries*,[104] most international organisations have met the conditions for implied international legal personality.[105] In this case, the ICJ made it clear that

[96] Sands and Klein (n 8) 473–536; T Gazzini, 'Personality of International Organizations' in Klabbers and Wallendahl (n 41) 33–55.

[97] See eg Art 104 UN Charter; Art 39 ILO Constitution (Part XIII Treaty of Versailles); Art VIII(1) WTO Agreement; Art 335 TFEU. See also Klabbers (n 2) 43–46; Schermers and Blokker (n 2) 1021–40.

[98] Klabbers (n 2) 46–50; Diez de Velasco Vallejo (n 8) 41–58; E Lagrange, *La représentation institutionnelle dans l'ordre international: une contribution à la théorie de la personnalité morale des organisations internationales* (The Hague, Kluwer, 2002); Schermers and Blokker (n 2) 986–1021.

[99] Art 6 Treaty Establishing the European Coal and Steel Community (adopted 18 April 1951, entered into force 23 July 1952) 261 UNTS 140.

[100] Art 281 Consolidated Version of the Treaty Establishing the European Community (adopted 16 April 2003, entered into force 1 May 2004) [2006] OJ 321E/37: 'The Community shall have legal personality'.

[101] Art 1(2) Treaty on the Eurasian Economic Union (adopted 29 May 2014, entered into force 1 January 2015) un.org/en/ga/sixth/70/docs/treaty_on_eeu.pdf ('courtesy translation').

[102] Art 47 TEU: 'The Union shall have legal personality'.

[103] eg A Dashwood, 'External Relations Provisions of the Amsterdam Treaty' in D O'Keeffe and P Twomey (eds), *Legal Issues of the Amsterdam Treaty* (Oxford, Hart, 1999) 220: 'In the view of the writer, applying the criteria enunciated by the International Court of Justice in the Reparation for Injuries case, there are solid grounds for regarding the European Union as being already possessed of international legal personality'. See similarly W Devroe and J Wouters, *De Europese Unie: Het Verdrag van Maastricht en zijn uitvoering: analyse en perspectieven* (Leuven, Peeters, 1996) 65–66.

[104] *Reparation for Injuries Suffered in the Service of the United Nations* (Advisory Opinion) (n 25).

[105] See, however, the example of the OSCE, which does not have international legal personality, mainly because it is founded upon non-binding political instruments rather than a treaty. At least for now, the attempt to adopt a Convention on International Legal Personality, Legal Capacity and Privileges and Immunities of the OSCE has failed; see OSCE, 'Report to the Ministerial Council on strengthening the legal framework of the OSCE in 2016', 9 December 2016, MC GAL/7/16, para 6. See inter alia O Herman and J Wouters, 'The OSCE as a Case of Informal International Lawmaking?' in A Peters, M Steinbrück Platise and C Moser (eds), *Revisiting the Legal Status of the OSCE* (Cambridge, CUP, 2018). See also Chapter 2, Section III(D)(i).

the conferral of international legal personality upon international organisations does not in any way mean that this is the same legal personality as that of a State:

> Whereas a State possesses the totality of international rights and duties recognized by international law, the rights and duties of an entity such as the Organization must depend upon its purposes and functions as specified or implied in its constituent instrument and developed in practice.[106]

Moreover, while international legal personality means that the organisation may exercise rights and incur obligations at the international level, it does not tell us what the organisation may actually do on the international plane: this will depend on the competences conferred upon it and institutional practice.[107]

VII. Financing

Most international organisations depend on their Member States for financing.[108] The latter typically have to pay contributions once a year or once every two years. Usually, the size of that contribution is determined by the financial capacity of the Member State in question. The organisation's plenary body adopts the budget.[109] This body decides on the share every Member State must contribute to the overall budget.[110] Such budgetary decisions are binding for the membership, since no international organisation could reasonably function otherwise.

In addition to membership contributions (sometimes called 'assessed contributions'), many international organisations have various other sources of income. Voluntary contributions and donations play an important role here. For example, UNICEF (the UN Children's Fund) receives a large number of voluntary contributions. Some organisations have their own sources of income: the World Intellectual Property Organization (WIPO) and the European Patent Organisation (EPO), for instance, are partly funded by revenues from patent registrations.

The EU – which itself has a complicated system of 'own resources'[111] – is a member of a number of international organisations, but in most cases it does not pay contributions in the same manner as members that are States. Instead, the EU makes a contribution to cover

[106] *Reparation for Injuries* (n 25) 180.

[107] G Hafner, 'The Legal Personality of International Organizations: The Political Context of International Law' in A Reinisch and U Kriebaum (eds), *The Law of International Relations: Liber Amicorum Hanspeter Neuhold* (Utrecht, Eleven International Publishing, 2007) 81; JW de Zwaan, 'The Legal Personality of the European Communities and the European Union' (1999) 30 *NYIL* 75; Lagrange (n 98); Sarooshi (n 16). cp E Lauterpacht, 'The Development of the Law of International Organizations by the Decisions of International Tribunals' (1976) 152 *RdC* 403–13, who starts his explanation of the concept of international legal personality as follows: 'It is important to bear in mind that in itself the attribution of personality to an entity means nothing'.

[108] For a general overview on financing, see eg Klabbers (n 2) 113–29; T Ingadottir, 'Financing International Institutions' in Klabbers and Wallendahl (n 41); J Katz Cogan, 'Financing and Budgets' in Katz Cogan, Hurd and Johnstone (n 10) 903–19; Sands and Klein (n 8) 569–86; Schermers and Blokker (n 2) 609–722; Diez de Velasco Vallejo (n 8) 96–98.

[109] eg the General Assembly of the UN; see Art 17(1) UN Charter.

[110] See Art 17(2) UN Charter.

[111] See inter alia R Crowe, 'The European Budgetary Galaxy' (2017) 13 *European Constitutional Law Review* 428; A Potteau, 'Les finances de l'Union européenne' in R Dehousse (ed), *L'Union européenne*, 4th edn (Paris, La Documentation Française, 2014); S Storr, 'Die Finanzverfassung der Union' in M Niedobitek (ed) *Europarecht: Grundlagen der Union* (Berlin, De Gruyter, 2014), 783.

the administrative expenses relating to its membership. This is the case, for example, with the EU in the FAO and the Hague Conference on Private International Law.[112]

VIII. The United Nations[113]

A. Objectives

The UN's main objective is to maintain international peace and security. The founders of the UN were nevertheless aware that attaining such goal would depend not only on the absence of violence, but also on several other factors. That is why the objectives of the UN, as set out in Article 1 of the UN Charter, were formulated more broadly. In addition to (i) the maintenance of international peace and security, they include: (ii) the development of 'friendly relations among nations based on respect for the principle of equal rights and self-determination of peoples'; (iii) achieving 'international co-operation in solving international problems of an economic, social, cultural, or humanitarian character, and in promoting and encouraging respect for human rights and for fundamental freedoms for all without distinction as to race, sex, language, or religion'; and (iv) '[t]o be a center for harmonizing the actions of nations in the attainment of these common ends'.[114]

B. Membership

The UN is intended to be a universal organisation. In stark contrast to the League of Nations, it has achieved this purpose to a significant extent. In 2018, its membership includes 193 States. The UN Charter distinguishes the 51 'original Members', i.e. 'the states which, having participated in the United Nations Conference on International Organization in San Francisco, or having previously signed the Declaration by United Nations of 1 January 1942, sign the present Charter and ratify it in accordance with Article 110',[115] from the other members, which, in order to be admitted, have to be 'peace-loving states which accept the obligations contained in the present Charter and, in the judgment of the Organization, are able and willing to carry out these obligations'.[116] Admission is granted by a decision of the General Assembly (by a two-thirds majority of the Member States

[112] For the FAO, see Art XVIII(6): 'A Member Organization shall not be required to contribute to the budget as specified in paragraph 2 of this Article, but shall pay to the Organization a sum to be determined by the Conference to cover administrative and other expenses arising out of its membership in the Organization'. For the Hague Conference on Private International Law, see Art 9(2) of the Statute of the Hague Conference on Private International Law (adopted 32 October 1951, entered into force 15 July 1955; amendments adopted 30 June 2005, entered into force 1 January 2007) hcch.net/en/instruments/conventions/full-text. For a general overview, see eg HG Schermers, 'The Financing of International Organizations' (1995) 16 *Liechtensteinische Juristen-Zeitung* 74.

[113] For the antecedents, genesis and history of the UN, see Chapter 1, Section IV(F).

[114] For an overview, see inter alia JP Cot, A Pellet and M Forteau (eds), *La Charte des Nations Unies: commentaire article par article*, 3rd edn (Paris, Economica, 2005); Diez de Velasco Vallejo (n 8) 139–78; SB Gareis, *The United Nations: An Introduction*, 2nd edn (New York, Palgrave Macmillan, 2012) 16–22; B Simma (ed), *The Charter of the United Nations: A Commentary*, 3rd edn (Oxford, OUP, 2012); S von Schorlemer, 'The United Nations' in Klabbers and Wallendahl (n 41) 466–506.

[115] Art 3 UN Charter.

[116] Art 4(1) UN Charter.

present) upon the recommendation of the Security Council,[117] where the right of veto of the permanent members applies. Without such recommendation of the Security Council, a State cannot be admitted as a Member State of the UN.

The number of UN Member States has evolved from 51 at the outset, to 100 in 1960, and to 193 in 2011. In 1946, four new were members were admitted to the UN (Afghanistan, Iceland, Sweden and Thailand); there were only five admissions between 1947 and 1951 (North Yemen, Pakistan, Burma, Israel and Indonesia). The antagonism between the United States and the Soviet Union prevented other admissions. In 1956, a 'package deal' was agreed which arranged for the admission of 16 new Member States (Albania, Austria, Bulgaria, Cambodia, Finland, Hungary, Ireland, Italy, Jordan, Laos, Libya, Nepal, Portugal, Romania, Spain and Sri Lanka). From that moment on, with the exception of the admission of Vietnam, which was delayed in 1976 by the United States, admission to the UN was virtually automatic. In 1960, 16 African countries and Cyprus joined. On 18 December 1973, both the Federal Republic of Germany and the German Democratic Republic became Member States. Another issue was the recognition in 1971 of the government of the People's Republic of China (mainland China) rather than that of the Republic of China (Taiwan) as the legal representative of China.

At the beginning of the 1990s, there was a new and considerable expansion in the number of Member States. This included the admission in 1990 of Namibia and Liechtenstein, in 1991 of Lithuania, Latvia, Estonia, North and South Korea, Micronesia and the Marshall Islands, in 1992 of Moldova, Kazakhstan, Kyrgyzstan, Azerbaijan, Uzbekistan, Tajikistan, Turkmenistan, Armenia, San Marino, Croatia, Slovenia, Bosnia-Herzegovina and Georgia, and in 1993 of Eritrea, Monaco, Macedonia and Andorra, while Czechoslovakia dissolved into the Czech Republic and Slovakia. In contrast, on 19 September 1992, the Security Council decided that Serbia and Montenegro could not be considered to be the automatic successor to the Socialist Federal Republic of Yugoslavia and that, pending its admission as a new Member (which happened on 1 November 2000), the Federal Republic of Yugoslavia could not participate in the workings of the General Assembly (see also above, pp 226–227). Since then, new Member States have included Timor-Leste and Switzerland (2002), Montenegro (2006) and South Sudan (2011).

As indicated above, the General Assembly may suspend a Member State on the recommendation of the Security Council[118] or expel it altogether.[119] Suspension is possible for Member States 'against which preventive or enforcement action has been taken'; expulsion is possible where it involves a Member State 'which has persistently violated the Principles contained in the [UN] Charter'. Until today, matters have never progressed that far. In 1965, Indonesia voluntarily withdrew, resuming its position again in 1966.[120]

[117] Art 4(2) UN Charter. See also *Competence of the General Assembly for the admission of a state to the United Nations* (Advisory Opinion) [1958] ICJ Rep 4; *Conditions of admission of a State to the United Nations* (Charter, Art 4) (Advisory Opinion) [1948] ICJ Rep 57. See the annotation of these advisory opinions by JD Fry and A Chong in Ryngaert, Dekker, Wessel, and Wouters (n 26) 138–55.

[118] Art 5 UN Charter.

[119] ibid, Art 6.

[120] This is the only example of a (de facto) withdrawal from the UN. Upon Indonesia's return in 1966, the withdrawal was formally treated as a 'cessation of cooperation'; UNGA Official Records 21st Session, 1420th Plenary Meeting, 28 September 1966, UN Doc A/PV.1420, 2, para 7; see Chapter 2, Section XI(B), n 495. See further N Feinberg, 'Unilateral Withdrawal from the UN, The Indonesian Intermezzo' (1967) 61 *AJIL* 182.

Table 3 Organisational Chart of the UN and the UN Family

The United Nations System

UN PRINCIPAL ORGANS

- GENERAL ASSEMBLY
- SECURITY COUNCIL
- ECONOMIC AND SOCIAL COUNCIL
- SECRETARIAT
- INTERNATIONAL COURT OF JUSTICE
- TRUSTEESHIP COUNCIL[6]

Subsidiary Organs

- Main Committees
- Disarmament Commission
- Human Rights Council
- International Law Commission
- Joint Inspection Unit (JIU)
- Standing committees and ad hoc bodies

Funds and Programmes[1]

UNDP United Nations Development Programme

- **UNCDF** United Nations Capital Development Fund
- **UNV** United Nations Volunteers

UNEP[8] United Nations Environment Programme

UNFPA United Nations Population Fund

UN-Habitat[8] United Nations Human Settlements Programme

UNICEF United Nations Children's Fund

WFP World Food Programme (UN/FAO)

Research and Training

UNIDIR United Nations Institute for Disarmament Research

UNITAR United Nations Institute for Training and Research

UNSSC United Nations System Staff College

UNU United Nations University

Other Entities

ITC International Trade Centre (UN/WTO)

UNCTAD[1,8] United Nations Conference on Trade and Development

UNHCR[1] Office of the United Nations High Commissioner for Refugees

UNOPS[1] United Nations Office for Project Services

UNRWA[1] United Nations Relief and Works Agency for Palestine Refugees in the Near East

UN-Women[1] United Nations Entity for Gender Equality and the Empowerment of Women

Related Organizations

CTBTO Preparatory Commission Preparatory Commission for the Comprehensive Nuclear-Test-Ban Treaty Organization

IAEA[1,3] International Atomic Energy Agency

ICC International Criminal Court

IOM[1] International Organization for Migration

ISA International Seabed Authority

ITLOS International Tribunal for the Law of the Sea

OPCW[3] Organization for the Prohibition of Chemical Weapons

WTO[1,4] World Trade Organization

Subsidiary Organs

- Counter-Terrorism Committee
- International Tribunal for the former Yugoslavia (ICTY)
- International Residual Mechanism for Criminal Tribunals
- Military Staff Committee
- Peacekeeping operations and political missions
- Sanctions committees (ad hoc)
- Standing committees and ad hoc bodies

Peacebuilding Commission

HLPF High-level political forum on sustainable development

Functional Commissions

- Crime Prevention and Criminal Justice
- Narcotic Drugs
- Population and Development
- Science and Technology for Development
- Social Development
- Statistics
- Status of Women
- United Nations Forum on Forests

Regional Commissions[8]

ECA Economic Commission for Africa

ECE Economic Commission for Europe

ECLAC Economic Commission for Latin America and the Caribbean

ESCAP Economic and Social Commission for Asia and the Pacific

ESCWA Economic and Social Commission for Western Asia

Other Bodies

- Committee for Development Policy
- Committee of Experts on Public Administration
- Committee on Non-Governmental Organizations
- Permanent Forum on Indigenous Issues

UNAIDS Joint United Nations Programme on HIV/AIDS

UNGEGN United Nations Group of Experts on Geographical Names

Research and Training

UNICRI United Nations Interregional Crime and Justice Research Institute

UNRISD United Nations Research Institute for Social Development

Specialized Agencies[1,5]

FAO Food and Agriculture Organization of the United Nations

ICAO International Civil Aviation Organization

IFAD International Fund for Agricultural Development

ILO International Labour Organization

IMF International Monetary Fund

IMO International Maritime Organization

ITU International Telecommunication Union

UNESCO United Nations Educational, Scientific and Cultural Organization

UNIDO United Nations Industrial Development Organization

UNWTO World Tourism Organization

UPU Universal Postal Union

WHO World Health Organization

WIPO World Intellectual Property Organization

WMO World Meteorological Organization

WORLD BANK GROUP[7]

- **IBRD** International Bank for Reconstruction and Development
- **IDA** International Development Association
- **IFC** International Finance Corporation

Departments and Offices[9]

EOSG Executive Office of the Secretary-General

DESA Department of Economic and Social Affairs

DFS Department of Field Support

DGACM Department for General Assembly and Conference Management

DM Department of Management

DPA Department of Political Affairs

DPI Department of Public Information

DPKO Department of Peacekeeping Operations

DSS Department of Safety and Security

OCHA Office for the Coordination of Humanitarian Affairs

ODA Office for Disarmament Affairs

OHCHR Office of the United Nations High Commissioner for Human Rights

OIOS Office of Internal Oversight Services

OLA Office of Legal Affairs

OSAA Office of the Special Adviser on Africa

PBSO Peacebuilding Support Office

SRSG/CAAC Office of the Special Representative of the Secretary-General for Children and Armed Conflict

SRSG/SVC Office of the Special Representative of the Secretary-General on Sexual Violence in Conflict

SRSG/VAC Office of the Special Representative of the Secretary-General on Violence Against Children

UNISDR United Nations Office for Disaster Risk Reduction

UNODC[1] United Nations Office on Drugs and Crime

UNOG United Nations Office at Geneva

UN-OHRLLS Office of the High Representative for the Least Developed Countries, Landlocked Developing Countries and Small Island Developing States

UNON United Nations Office at Nairobi

UNOP[2] United Nations Office for Partnerships

UNOV United Nations Office at Vienna

Notes:

1 Members of the United Nations System Chief Executives Board for Coordination (CEB).

2 UN Office for Partnerships (UNOP) is the UN's focal point vis-a-vis the United Nations Foundation, Inc.

3 IAEA and OPCW report to the Security Council and the General Assembly (GA).

4 WTO has no reporting obligation to the GA, but contributes on an ad hoc basis to GA and Economic and Social Council (ECOSOC) work on, inter alia, finance and development issues.

5 Specialized agencies are autonomous organizations whose work is coordinated through ECOSOC (intergovernmental level) and CEB (inter-secretariat level).

6 The Trusteeship Council suspended operation on 1 November 1994, as on 1 October 1994 Palau, the last United Nations Trust Territory, became independent.

7 International Centre for Settlement of Investment Disputes (ICSID) and Multilateral Investment Guarantee Agency (MIGA) are not specialized agencies in accordance with Articles 57 and 63 of the Charter, but are part of the World Bank Group.

8 The secretariats of these organs are part of the UN Secretariat.

9 The Secretariat also includes the following offices: The Ethics Office, United Nations Ombudsman and Mediation Services, Office of Administration of Justice and the Office on Sport for Development and Peace.

This Chart is a reflection of the functional organization of the United Nations System and for informational purposes only. It does not include all offices or entities of the United Nations System.

Published by the United Nations Department of Public Information DPI/2470 rev.5—17-00023—March 2017

C. Principal Organs

The principal organs of the UN specified in Article 7(1) of the UN Charter are the General Assembly, the Security Council, ECOSOC, the Trusteeship Council, the ICJ and the Secretariat.[121] They will be discussed in turn, with the exception of the ICJ, which is dealt with in Chapter 13 on Peaceful Settlement of Disputes, Section III(B).

i. The General Assembly[122]

a. Composition

The General Assembly comprises all UN Member States.[123] Each Member State has no more than five representatives in the General Assembly.[124] The General Assembly meets in regular annual sessions, beginning on the third Tuesday of September and usually ending at Christmas. If circumstances so demand, at the request of the Security Council or of a majority of UN Member States, the Secretary General can call special sessions.[125]

The General Assembly adopts its own rules of procedure. For each session, it elects its President on a rotating basis from the delegates of five geopolitical groups (the African Group, the Western Europe and Others Group (WEOG), the Eastern European Group, the Asia-Pacific Group and the Latin American and Caribbean Group (GRULAC)).[126] The Bureau consists of 21 vice-presidents and the chairmen of the six Main Committees, respectively the Disarmament and International Security Committee (First Committee), Economic and Financial Committee (Second Committee), Social, Humanitarian and Cultural Committee (Third Committee), Special Political and Decolonization Committee (Fourth Committee), Administrative and Budgetary Committee (Fifth Committee) and Legal Committee (Sixth Committee).[127]

As mentioned above (p 264), the European Economic Community had been granted the status of permanent observer in the General Assembly since 1974. With the General Assembly Resolution of 3 May 2011 on participation of the EU in the work of the UN, the EU was granted enhanced participation rights.[128] Pursuant to that resolution, the EU, in its capacity as observer in the General Assembly, has the right, inter alia, to: (i) be inscribed on the list of speakers among representatives of major groups, in order to make interventions; (ii) participate in the general debate of the General Assembly; (iii) present proposals and amendments orally as agreed by the EU Member States; and (iv) exercise the right of reply regarding positions of the EU.[129] The representatives of the EU have no voting rights in the

[121] See also P Taylor and AJR Groom (eds), *The United Nations at the Millennium: The Principal Organs* (London, Continuum, 2000); Gareis (n 114) 23–36; Diez de Velasco Vallejo (n 8) 193–211; I Hurd, *International Organizations: Politics, Law, Practice*, 3rd edn (Cambridge, CUP, 2018) 42–79.

[122] For a general overview, see eg MJ Peterson, *The UN General Assembly* (London, Routledge, 2006); Sands and Klein (n 8) 25–36.

[123] Art 9(1) UN Charter.

[124] ibid, Art 9(2).

[125] ibid, Art 20.

[126] ibid, Art 21.

[127] B Finley, *The Structure of the United Nations General Assembly, Its Committees, Commissions and Other Organisms, 1946–1973* (Dobbs Ferry, Oceana Publications, 1977).

[128] UNGA Res 65/276, 'Participation of the European Union in the Work of the United Nations', 3 May 2011, UN Doc A/RES/65/276.

[129] ibid.

General Assembly, and do not have the right to co-sponsor draft resolutions or decisions, or to put forward candidates.[130]

b. Voting Procedures

Each member of the General Assembly has one vote.[131] Decisions of the General Assembly on important questions are made by a two-thirds majority of the members present and voting.[132] Important questions include: (i) recommendations with respect to the maintenance of international peace and security; (ii) the election of the non-permanent members of the Security Council, the members of ECOSOC, and the members of the Trusteeship Council; (iii) questions relating to membership (admission, suspension and expulsion); (iv) questions relating to the operation of the trusteeship system; and (v) budgetary questions. Decisions on other questions, including the determination of additional categories of questions to be decided by a two-thirds majority, are made by a majority of the members present and voting.[133] In practice, many resolutions are adopted by consensus; that is, without a Member State requesting a vote (see above, Section V(B)(i)).[134]

c. Functions

The General Assembly has very broad powers, primarily of a political nature. Pursuant to Article 10 of the UN Charter, 'the General Assembly may discuss any questions or any matters within the scope of the present Charter or relating to the powers and functions of any organs provided for in the present Charter'. The only limitations on these general functions are those set out in the Charter. As indicated above (p 261), Article 2(7) of the UN Charter provides that the UN may not intervene in matters that are essentially within the domestic jurisdiction of any State. Article 11(2), final sentence, stipulates that any question relating to the maintenance of international peace and security on which action is necessary, shall either before or after discussion be referred to the Security Council by the General Assembly.[135] Article 12(1) moreover ensures that:

> While the Security Council is exercising in respect of any dispute or situation the functions assigned to it in the present Charter, the General Assembly shall not make any recommendation with regard to that dispute or situation unless the Security Council so requests.

However, as discussed above (p 262), in 1950 the General Assembly adopted Resolution 377 A (V) ('Uniting for Peace'), which provides that a dispute can be submitted to the General Assembly when the Security Council cannot act because of a veto by a Permanent Member. Even though the legality of this resolution was disputed, especially by socialist countries, it has been applied a number of times. Ten emergency sessions have been held since its first use in the Korean crisis in 1950, inter alia on the Suez crisis (1956), Lebanon (1958),

[130] ibid.

[131] Art 18(1) UN Charter.

[132] ibid, Art 18(2).

[133] Art 18(3) UN Charter. See also M Marin-Bosch, *Votes in the UN General Assembly* (The Hague, Kluwer, 1997).

[134] UNGA Res A/520/Rev.18, 'Rules of Procedure of the General Assembly (embodying amendments and additions adopted by the General Assembly up to September 2016)', UN Doc A/520/Rev.18.

[135] JM Ruda, 'Drafting History of Articles 10 and 11 of the Charter of the United Nations on the Functions and Powers of the General Assembly' in J Tittel (ed), *Multitudo legum ius unum: Festschrift für Wilhelm Wengler zu seinem 65. Geburtstag* (Berlin, Interrecht, 1973) 375–449.

the DRC (1960), Afghanistan (1980), Namibia (1981), Palestine (1982), the territories occupied by Israel (1997–2009) and, most recently, the status of Jerusalem (2017).[136]

A number of competences are exercised by the General Assembly in conjunction with the Security Council:

- matters of membership, such as admission[137] and expulsion:[138] the General Assembly decides based on a recommendation of the Security Council;
- the election of the judges of the ICJ:[139] the General Assembly and Security Council (where the Permanent Members do not have a veto right for this matter) vote independently from each other; the candidate that is elected in both organs with a complete majority of votes is considered to have been chosen;
- the appointment of the Secretary General:[140] the General Assembly decides based on a recommendation of the Security Council.

For other matters, the General Assembly has an exclusive competence:

- the election of the members of the other principal organs (non-permanent Members of the Security Council, ECOSOC and the Trusteeship Council) and of the subsidiary organs;
- the approval of the budget of the Organization;[141]
- the authority over ECOSOC[142] and the Trusteeship Council;[143]
- the authorisation of organs of the UN other than the Security Council and other specialised agencies to request advisory opinions from the ICJ.[144]

The resolutions of the General Assembly are not legally binding, unless they concern resolutions that are related to the internal organisation of the UN, such as adoption of the budget and staff regulations, matters of membership, the adoption of the internal rules of procedure or the establishment of subsidiary organs. Nonetheless, resolutions of the General Assembly can contribute to customary international law (on which see Chapter 3, Section II).

ii. The Security Council

a. Composition

The Security Council consists of 15 UN Member States.[145] There are five permanent Members: China, France, the Russian Federation (since 1992 as successor to the Soviet Union), the United Kingdom and the United States. Ten other UN Member States are

[136] Regarding the Uniting for Peace Resolution, see also Chapter 14, Section VI(A), on peacekeeping.
[137] Art 4(2) UN Charter; ibid, Art 5 (suspension).
[138] ibid, Art 6 UN Charter.
[139] Arts 8 and 10–12 ICJ Statute.
[140] Art 97 UN Charter.
[141] ibid, Art 17(1).
[142] ibid, Art 60.
[143] ibid, Art 85(2).
[144] ibid, Art 96(2). On General Assembly resolutions, see also B Sloan, *United Nations General Assembly Resolutions in our Changing World* (New York, Brill, 1991).
[145] Art 23 UN Charter. For a general overview, see eg Sands and Klein (n 8) 36–52; MN Shaw, *International Law*, 8th edn (Cambridge, CUP, 2017) 925–28; Alvarez (n 11) 184–217; Diez de Velasco Vallejo (n 8) 198–201.

chosen as non-permanent Members for two-year terms. This is done through a rotation system in which the General Assembly annually elects five non-permanent Security Council Members for a two-year term. Amongst the chosen Members, there are five Members from the African and Asia-Pacific Groups, one from the Eastern European Group, two from the GRULAC and two from the WEOG.[146]

The organisation of the Security Council is aimed at ensuring a continuous performance of its functions. To this end, every member of the Security Council must at all times be represented at the seat of the Organization.[147] This has led to the institution of 'permanent representations', which is what nearly all UN Member States currently have in New York.[148]

The Security Council adopts its own rules of procedure, including the method of selecting its President.[149] The presidency of the Security Council is exercised on a rotating monthly basis according to the alphabetical order of the English name of its members. Any UN Member State that is not a member of the Security Council may participate, without voting rights, in the discussion of any question brought before the Security Council whenever the latter considers that the interests of that Member State are particularly affected.[150] If any UN Member State that is not a member of the Security Council or any State that is not a member of the UN is a party to a dispute under consideration by the Security Council, it must be invited to participate in the discussion relating to the dispute, also without voting rights.[151]

The EU has no formal status at the UN Security Council. Yet, the EU Treaties set out some obligations regarding EU Member States that are a member of the Council. These Member States must keep the High Representative and other Member States 'fully informed', concert their position among themselves, and, where the EU has a defined position on a subject on the Council's agenda, ask that the High Representative be invited to present that position.[152]

b. Voting Procedures

In contrast to the rule of unanimity that existed in the League of Nations, the Security Council adopts decisions on the basis of a special majority. With respect to procedural matters, nine affirmative votes out of the fifteen are required.[153] For all other matters,

[146] A Rodiles, 'Non-Permanent Members of the United Nations Security Council and the Promotion of the International Rule of Law' (2013) 5 *Goettingen Journal of International Law* 333.

[147] Art 28(1) UN Charter.

[148] There are permanent representatives with the UN not only in New York, but also in Geneva (especially regarding disarmament and human rights), in Vienna (regarding the fight against narcotics, the prevention of crime and the peaceful use of outer space) and in Nairobi (regarding the environment and human settlement). See ER Appathurai, *Les missions permanentes auprès de l'Organisation des Nations Unies* (Bruxelles, Bruylant, 1975); E Hambro, 'Permanent Representatives to International Organizations' (1976) 30 *Yearbook of World Affairs* 30; D Ciobanu, 'Credentials of Delegations and Representation of Member States at the UN' (1976) 25 *ICLQ* 351.

[149] Art 30 UN Charter. See also I Pogany, 'The Role of the President of the U.N. Security Council' (1982) 31 *ICLQ* 231. For more detail on the President's declarations, see P Tavernier, 'Les déclarations du Président du Conseil de Sécurité' (1993) 39 *Annuaire français de droit international* 86; S Talmon, 'The Statements by the President of the Security Council' (2003) 2 *CJIL* 419.

[150] Art 31 UN Charter.

[151] ibid, Art 32.

[152] Art 34(2) TEU: 'Member States which are also members of the United Nations Security Council will concert and keep the other Member States and the High Representative fully informed. Member States which are members of the Security Council will [...] defend the positions and the interests of the Union, without prejudice to their responsibilities under the provisions of the United Nations Charter'. See eg De Baere (n 40) 1267–68.

[153] Art 27(2) UN Charter.

nine affirmative votes, 'including those of the permanent members', out of the fifteen are required.[154] Accordingly, the Permanent Members of the Security Council have a right of veto for all matters other than procedural ones. In the 'San Francisco Declaration', the four inviting powers clarified that a number of affairs, such as the adoption of the internal rules of procedure, the establishment of subsidiary bodies, the invitation of a non-member to participate in the discussion and the listing of an item on the agenda, are considered to be procedural matters. In case of doubt on the procedural nature of other resolutions, the matter must be dealt with by holding a vote that is subject to the right of veto ('double veto'). In practice the requirement of the 'affirmative vote' of the Permanent Members has been softened by the institutional practice that the abstention – or absence – of a Permanent Member does not prevent the adoption of a Security Council resolution.[155] See also below, Section VIII(C)(ii)(d), on the Code of Conduct regarding the use of the right of veto.

c. Functions

Pursuant to Article 24(1) of the UN Charter, the Security Council has the 'primary responsibility' for the maintenance of international peace and security.[156] In carrying out its duties, the Security Council must act in accordance with the aims and principles of the UN.[157] A distinction should be made depending on whether the Security Council exercises its functions on the basis of Chapter VI (pacific settlement of disputes) or on the basis of Chapter VII (action with respect to threats to the peace, breaches of the peace, and acts of aggression) of the Charter. Pursuant to Chapter VI,

> The Security Council may investigate any dispute, or any situation which might lead to international friction or give rise to a dispute, in order to determine whether the continuance of the dispute or situation is likely to endanger the maintenance of international peace and security.[158]

The Security Council may, at any stage of a dispute, recommend appropriate procedures or methods of adjustment.[159]

Chapter VII of the UN Charter becomes applicable when the Security Council determines that there is a 'threat to the peace, breach of the peace, or act of aggression' and can make recommendations, or decide what measures shall be taken in accordance with

[154] ibid, Art 27(3). See also H Köchler, *The Voting Procedure in the United Nations Security Council: Examining a Normative Contradiction in the UN Charter and its Consequences on International Relations* (Vienna, International Progress Organization, 1991); L Gross, 'Voting in the Security Council: Abstention from Voting and Absence from Meetings' in L Gross, *Selected Essays on International Law and Organization* (Irvington-on-Hudson, Transnational Publishers, 1993) 201–43; B Broms, 'Voting in the Security Council' in LAE Hjerner and J Ramberg (eds), *Festskrift till Lars Hjerner: Studies in International Law* (Stockholm, Norstedts, 1990) 93–101.

[155] See above (n 93).

[156] V Gowlland-Debbas, 'The Functions of the United Nations Security Council in the International Legal System' in M Byers (ed), *The Role of Law in International Politics: Essays in International Relations and International Law* (Oxford, OUP, 2000) 277–313; M Leilach, *Die Wahrung des Weltfriedens und der internationalen Sicherheit als Aufgabe des Sicherhaitsrates der Vereinten Nationen* (Berlin, Duncker & Humblot, 1998); K Herndl, 'Reflections on the Role, Functions and Procedures of the Security Council of the United Nations' (1987) 206 *RdC* 289.

[157] Art 24(2) UN Charter. See also AF Lang Jr, 'Constitutionalism and the Law: Evaluating the Security Council' in Popovski and Fraser (n 95), 12–33; A Tzanakopoulos, 'Transparency in the Security Council' in A Bianchi and A Peters (eds), *Transparency in International Law* (Cambridge, CUP, 2013) 367–91; T Bruha and M Krajewski, 'Funktionswandel des Sicherheitsrates als Verfassungsproblem – Zur rechtlichen Sicht der neueren Praxis' (1998) 46 *Vereinte Nationen* 13.

[158] Art 34 UN Charter.

[159] ibid, Art 36(1).

Articles 41 and 42 of the UN Charter to enforce or restore international peace and security.[160] The Security Council can then also call upon the parties concerned to comply with such provisional measures as it deems necessary or desirable.[161] The Security Council may decide which measures, that do not involve the use of armed force, are to be employed.[162] Should the Security Council consider that measures provided for in Article 41 would be inadequate or have proved to be inadequate, it may take such action by air, sea, or land forces as may be necessary to maintain or restore international peace and security.[163] While Chapter VI deals with non-binding resolutions, Chapter VII concerns binding resolutions that may even entail the use of armed force (see Chapter 14, Section V on 'Chapter VII Action by the UN Security Council'). Action taken by the Security Council under Chapter VII should not be confused with what is known as the 'peacekeeping operations' that are undertaken with the consent of the State involved (see Chapter 14, Section VI on 'Peacekeeping Operations').

d. Reform

The issue of reform of the Security Council has been on the table for more than 25 years. However, it is proving to be very difficult for the international community – and also for the EU – to find consensus on expanding the list of Permanent Members.[164]

Whereas States generally support the importance of the UN Security Council as the principal actor with regard to peace and security, many object to the lack of representativeness in its composition, the lack of accountability to the UN General Assembly, the secrecy of its working methods and the inherently undemocratic character of the veto power. If reform proves successful, the UNSC may be endowed with a renewed legitimacy, lifting its authority beyond contestation. If no reform is achieved, it cannot be excluded that the post-Cold War revitalisation of the UNSC will grind to a halt and that States will increasingly challenge the validity and binding character of its resolutions. However, as intensive negotiations to expand the membership of the UNSC failed to produce a breakthrough in the context of the 2005 UN World Summit, the reform momentum seems to have faded. In the meantime, the so-called 'Accountability, Coherence, Transparency (ACT) Group' has drafted a Code of Conduct under which States pledge inter alia 'not to vote against a credible draft resolution before the Security Council on timely and decisive action to end the commission of genocide, crimes against humanity or war crimes, or to prevent such crimes' when they serve as a member of the UNSC.[165] At the time of writing, the Code of Conduct

[160] ibid, Art 39. See also E De Wet, *The Chapter VII Powers of the United Nations Security Council* (Oxford, Hart, 2004); B Lorinser, *Bindende Resolutionen des Sicherheitsrates* (Baden-Baden, Nomos, 1996).

[161] Art 40 UN Charter.

[162] ibid, Art 41.

[163] ibid, Art 42.

[164] See inter alia S Chesterman, 'Reforming the United Nations: Legitimacy, Effectiveness and Power after Iraq' (2006) 10 *Singapore Yearbook of International Law* 59; H Corell, 'Who Needs Reforming the Most – The UN or Its Members?' (2007) 76 *Nord J Intl* 265; N Schrijver, 'Reforming the UN Security Council in Pursuance of Collective Security' (2007) 12 *Journal of Conflict and Security Law* 127; K van Kesteren, 'Reforming the Security Council: Views from Practice' and J-P Cot, 'Reforming the Security Council: Is There a Hidden Agenda?' in N Blokker and N Schrijver (eds), *The Security Council and the Use of Force: Theory and Reality – A Need for Change?* (Dordrecht, Nijhoff, 2005) at respectively 261–68 and 269–80; J Wouters and T Ruys, 'Security Council Reform: A New Veto for a New Century?' 44 (2006) *Revue de droit militaire et de droit de la guerre* 139–74.

[165] 'Code of conduct regarding Security Council action against genocide, crimes against humanity or war crimes', 14 December 2015, UN Doc A/70/621–S/2015/978, Annex I, operative clause 2.

had been signed by 115 States, including the two European Permanent Members of the UNSC, but not the other Permanent Members.[166]

iii. The Economic and Social Council

ECOSOC is the coordinating organ for the economic and social activities of the UN, its specialised agencies and other institutions that are a part of the 'UN family'. Initially it consisted of 18 members. This number later rose to 27, and currently stands at 54 members, a third of which are annually elected by the General Assembly for a three-year term.[167] Each member has a representative in the Council and one vote. The Council decides by majority of the members present and voting.[168]

Pursuant to UN General Assembly Resolution 2847 (XXVI) of 23 December 1971, the geographical division of the seats within ECOSOC is as follows: 14 for the African Group, 13 for the WEOG, 11 for the Asia-Pacific Group, 10 for the GRULAC, and 6 for the Eastern European Group. Since 1992, ECOSOC holds annual five-week working sessions, which are alternately held in New York and Geneva. In addition, at least two organisational meetings are held in New York. The main session consists of a special meeting with ministers and senior officials on important economic and social matters. The operational work of the Council is carried out by its subsidiary organs (commissions and committees), all of which report to the Council.

ECOSOC acts as a central forum for the discussion of international economic and social matters of general or interdisciplinary nature, and formulates policy recommendations on those matters that are addressed to the UN Member States and to the UN system as a whole. ECOSOC plays a pivotal role in fostering international cooperation on the economic, social and humanitarian front, especially with respect to development issues.[169] Its main tasks and powers are: (i) to conduct studies and reports (or take the initiative thereto), and make recommendations with respect to international economic, social, cultural, educational, health, and related matters;[170] (ii) to make recommendations with a view to promoting respect for, and observance of, human rights and fundamental freedoms for all;[171] (iii) to organise international conferences and to compile draft conventions for submission to the General Assembly on matters falling within its competence;[172] (iv) to enter into agreements with specialised agencies, defining their relationship with the UN and coordinating the activities of those agencies through consultation with and recommendations to such agencies and through recommendations to the General Assembly and to UN Member States.[173]

[166] Global Centre for the Responsibility to Protect, 'List of Signatories to the ACT Code of Conduct', last updated 1 June 2018, globalr2p.org/resources/893.

[167] Art 61 UN Charter.

[168] ibid, Art 67(2).

[169] For a general overview of the role of ECOSOC, see eg Sands and Klein (n 8) 52–60; G Fedele, 'L'ECOSOC: l'attivitá dell'ONU nel campo economico e sociale' in S Baldi (ed), *Le Nazioni Unite viste da vicino: aspetti e problemi dell'attivitá dell'ONU e dell'azione dell'Italia* (Padova, CEDAM, 2006) 63–80. On calls to reform ECOSOC, see eg M Garrich and J Xercavins, 'Reforming the Economic and Social Council (ECOSOC)' in UBUNTU Forum Secretariat, *Reforming International Institutions: Another World is Possible* (London, Earthscan, 2009) 253–60; C Breen, 'The Necessity of a Role for the ECOSOC in the Maintenance of International Peace and Security' (2007) 12 *Journal of Conflict and Security Law* 261; I Gonzalez Garcia, 'El ECOSOC: la necesaria reforma de un ineficuente modelo de coordinacion para el desarollo' in JM Beneyto Perez and B Becerril (eds), *Una nueva Organizacion de Naciones Unidas para el siglo XXI* (Madrid, Biblioteca Nueva, 2007) 211–38.

[170] Art 62(1) UN Charter.

[171] ibid, Art 62(2).

[172] ibid, Art 62(3) and (4).

[173] ibid, Art 63.

ECOSOC may take appropriate measures to obtain regular reports from the specialised agencies.[174]

ECOSOC has established a multitude of commissions and committees. Pursuant to Article 68 of the UN Charter, it has established eight 'functional commissions' and five 'regional commissions'. The eight functional commissions are: the Statistical Commission, the Commission on Population and Development, the Commission on Science and Technology for Development, the Commission for Social Development, the Commission on Crime Prevention and Criminal Justice, the Commission on the Status of Women, the Commission on Narcotic Drugs, and the UN Forum on Forests. The UN Commission on Human Rights, which was a functional commission, was dissolved by the General Assembly in 2006 and replaced by the UN Human Rights Council (on which see Chapter 16, Section VII).[175]

The five regional economic commissions are: the Economic Commission for Africa (ECA) in Addis Ababa, Ethiopia (1958), the Economic and Social Commission for Asia and the Pacific (ESCAP) in Bangkok, Thailand (1947), the Economic Commission for Europe (ECE/CEE) in Geneva (1947), the Economic Commission for Latin America and the Caribbean (ECLAC) in Santiago, Chile (1948) and the Economic and Social Commission for Western Asia (ECSWA) in Beirut, Lebanon (1973).

In addition, ECOSOC has established a number of permanent committees and expert bodies (Committee for Programme and Coordination, Commission on Human Settlements, Committee on Non-Governmental Organizations, Committee on Negotiations with Intergovernmental Agencies, Committee on Energy and Natural Resources), as well as a number of non-permanent expert bodies with regard to matters such as development policy, natural resources and economic, social and cultural rights.

The relationship between ECOSOC and non-governmental organisations (NGOs) deserves special mention. Pursuant to Article 71 of the UN Charter, ECOSOC may make suitable arrangements for consultation with NGOs that are involved in matters that fall within the scope of its competence. The number of NGOs that have consultative status with ECOSOC has risen enormously, from 41 in 1946 to more than 4,800 today. In its Resolution 1996/31, ECOSOC has set criteria for granting consultative status to NGOs, thereby distinguishing between Category I (general consultative status, ie for NGOs which are involved in most of ECOSOC's activities), Category II (special consultative status, ie NGOs with an internationally recognised special competence in specific fields – most new accreditations are in this category), and Category III (roster consultative status, for ad hoc consultations). Consultative status provides NGOs with access not only to ECOSOC, but also to its many subsidiary bodies, the various human rights mechanisms of the UN and special events organised by the President of the General Assembly. General and special status NGOs are required to submit a 'quadrennial report' every four years. The Committee on NGOs reviews new applications twice a year (see also Chapter 8, Section V(A) on 'NGO Participation in International Organisations').

iv. Trusteeship Council

The international trusteeship system was established by the UN Charter in 1945 to oversee the 'trust territories', ie the territories that had been placed under this regime by special

[174] ibid, Art 64.
[175] UNGA Res 60/251, 3 April 2006, UN Doc A/RES/60/251.

agreement with the administrative authority concerned.[176] The Trusteeship Council, which is the subject of Chapter XIII of the UN Charter, was entrusted with the supervision of the 11 trust territories that were placed under the administration of seven UN Member States. Pursuant to Article 77 of the UN Charter, the system of trusteeship was applicable to: (i) territories that, in 1945, were under a mandate by the League of Nations (it was applied to the former B and C mandates of the League of Nations, with the exception of Southwest Africa); (ii) territories that were detached from 'enemy states' as a result of the Second World War (only Somalia, a colony of Italy, became a trust territory administered by Italy); and (iii) territories that were voluntarily placed under this system by the States responsible for their administration (this provision was never applied). The Trusteeship Council was evenly composed of governing and non-governing Members, it being understood that the Permanent Members of the Security Council were members of the Council in any case.[177] In the meantime, the objectives of the international trusteeship system have been fulfilled. All original trust territories have attained self-government or independence, be it as separate States, or by joining neighbouring independent States. The last trust territory was the Pacific Islands, which became independent as Palau, and joined the UN as its 185th Member State in 1994. The same year, the Trusteeship Council suspended its operations after having changed its rules of procedure, which no longer require that the Council meets annually, but provide that it shall meet when and where the situation so demands.[178] While the 2005 World Summit Outcome adopted by the General Assembly provides that Chapter XIII of the UN Charter and references to the Trusteeship Council in Chapter XII should be deleted as the Council no longer meets and has no remaining functions,[179] no such amendment of the Charter has materialised as yet (see also Chapter 5, Section III(B) on 'The Right of Self-Determination').

v. The Secretariat

The UN Secretariat comprises the UN staff as well their chief administrative officer, the Secretary General. These are discussed below.

a. The UN Staff

The Secretariat, the workings of which are outlined in Chapter XV UN Charter, comprises an international staff of employees who are responsible for the day-to-day workings of the UN in its headquarters in New York and elsewhere in the world.[180] The Secretariat performs a supportive function for the other UN organs and handles the administration of the programmes and policies of those other UN bodies. It is headed by a Secretary

[176] For a general overview, see eg Sands and Klein (n 8) 60–65; T Sellström, 'The Trusteeship Council: Decolonisation and Liberation' in A Adebajo (ed), *From Global Apartheid to Global Village: Africa and the United Nations* (Scottsville, University of KwaZulu-Natal Press, 2009) 107–37.
[177] Art 86(1) UN Charter.
[178] Draft Resolution T/L.1292, as adopted on 25 May 1994; see UN Trusteeship Council, 1705th meeting, 25 May 1994, UN Doc T/PV.1705, 4–5. About calls to reform the Trusteeship Council, see eg T Parker, *The Ultimate Intervention: Revitalising the UN Trusteeship Council for the 21st Century* (Sandvika, Norwegian School of Management, Centre for European and Asian Studies, 2003); C Redgwell, 'Reforming the United Nations Trusteeship Council' in WB Chambers and JF Green (eds), *Reforming International Environmental Governance: From Institutional Limits to Innovative Reforms* (Tokyo, United Nations University Press, 2005) 178–203.
[179] UNGA, '2005 World Summit Outcome', 16 September 2005, UN Doc A/RES/60/1, para 176.
[180] Schermers and Blokker (n 2) 351–97.

General. The tasks of the Secretariat are almost as diverse as those of the UN itself: coordinating peace operations,[181] mediating international disputes, investigating socio-economic problems, conducting and compiling studies on human rights and sustainable development, organising international conferences on problems with a global dimension, overseeing the execution of decisions of UN organs, providing translation services in the official languages of the UN (Arabic, Chinese, English, French, Russian and Spanish), and informing the global press and media. Today, the UN Secretariat has a staff of about 40,000 people. In the performance of their duties, the Secretary General and the staff are not permitted to seek or receive instructions from any government or from any other external authority, and must recuse themselves from any activity that might detract from their position as international civil servants who are exclusively responsible to the UN.[182] The UN Member States have undertaken to respect the exclusively international character of the responsibilities of the Secretary General and the staff, and not to seek to influence them in the discharge of their responsibilities.[183]

b. The Secretary General

The Secretary General is the chief administrative officer of the UN.[184] He is appointed by the General Assembly, upon the recommendation of the Security Council.[185] His or her mandate is fixed for five years and is renewable. The office of Secretary General has been successively held by Trygve Lie (Norway, 1946–1952), Dag Hammarskjöld (Sweden, 1953–1961), U Thant (Burma, 1961–1971), Kurt Waldheim (Austria, 1972–1981), Javier Perez de Cuellar (Peru, 1982–1991), Boutros Boutros-Ghali (Egypt, 1992–1996), Kofi Annan (Ghana, 1997–2006), Ban Ki-Moon (2007–2016) and António Guterres (Portugal, 2017–present).

The Secretary General has a number of administrative functions and powers. As the highest civil servant of the UN, the Secretary General acts in all meetings of the General Assembly, the Security Council, ECOSOC and the Trusteeship Council,[186] as well as in all meetings of their commissions, committees and subcommittees. The Secretary General draws up special reports in many fields and reports to the General Assembly on the work of the Organization on an annual basis.[187]

The Secretary General also prepares the provisional agenda of the meetings of the UN organs, helps prepare the practical aspects of meetings and conferences (eg by checking credentials and by providing staff, infrastructure and services), and functions as a central channel to transfer notifications from and to the UN. The Secretary General also is a depositary for a large number of multilateral treaties. He or she coordinates the activities of the

[181] See inter alia S Weinlich, *The UN Secretariat's Influence on the Evolution of Peacekeeping* (New York, Palgrave Macmillan, 2014); H Shimura, 'The Role of the UN Secretariat in Organizing Peacekeeping' in R C Thakur (ed), *United Nations Peacekeeping Operations: Ad Hoc Missions, Permanent Engagement* (Tokyo, United Nations University Press, 2001) 46–56.

[182] Art 100(1) UN Charter. See also P Novosad and E Werker, 'Who Runs the International System? Power and the Staffing of the United Nations Secretariat', Center for Global Development, Working Paper 376, September 2014, cgdev.org/sites/default/files/un_paper_0.pdf.

[183] Art 100(2) UN Charter.

[184] Art 97 UN Charter. See also L Gordenker, *The UN Secretary-General and Secretariat*, 2nd edn (London, Routledge, 2010); S Chesterman (ed), *Secretary or General? The UN Secretary-General in World Politics* (Cambridge, CUP, 2007).

[185] Art 97 UN Charter.

[186] ibid, Art 98.

[187] ibid.

UN on an internal level (amongst other things, by drawing up a calendar of conferences and meetings) and to some extent also on an external level, that is, between the UN and its specialised agencies and other intergovernmental organs. The Secretary General has a very important representative function. He or she represents the UN (i) vis-à-vis the public, (ii) at the negotiation and conclusion of agreements with governments and other intergovernmental organisations, and (iii) in any legal action for or against the Organization before courts and arbitral tribunals.

The Secretary General also appoints the staff in accordance with rules established by the General Assembly.[188] The primary criterion for the appointment of the staff and the determination of the conditions of service is the necessity of securing the highest standards of efficiency, competence, and integrity; due regard is paid to the importance of recruiting the staff on the broadest possible geographical basis.[189] The Secretary General has the power to waive the immunity of UN officials.[190]

The Secretary General also has a number of political functions and powers. Thus, '[t]he Secretary General may bring any matter which, in his opinion, may threaten the maintenance of international peace and security, to the attention of the Security Council',[191] as well as include any item he or she deems necessary to put before the General Assembly on the latter's provisional agenda.[192] The Secretary General shall also perform any other functions entrusted to him by the General Assembly, the Security Council or ECOSOC.[193]

The Secretary General often – either publicly or behind the scenes – offers his or her good offices; for example, in the context of preventive diplomacy, to prevent the outbreak, escalation or expansion of international conflicts, or in order to help defuse existing international problems. The political and diplomatic role of the Secretary General has increased over the years.

c. Operational Resources

The budget of the UN is approved by the General Assembly.[194] Since 1973, the budget has been set every two years. The expenses of the Organization are borne by the Member States as apportioned by the allocation key determined by the General Assembly.[195] For 2016–2017, the overall budget for the UN was US$5.4 billion,[196] with as main contributors

[188] ibid, Art 101(1).
[189] ibid, Art 101(3).
[190] Art 20 of the Convention on the Privileges and Immunities of the United Nations (adopted 13 February 1946, entered into force 17 September 1946) 1 UNTS 15.
[191] Art 99 UN Charter.
[192] Art 13(g) Rules of Procedure of the General Assembly (embodying amendments and additions adopted by the General Assembly up to September 2016), UN Doc A/520/Rev.18.
[193] Art 98 UN Charter. For a general overview of the Secretary General's role, see eg J Perez de Cuellar, 'The Role of the UN Secretary-General' in PF Diehl (ed), *The Politics of Global Governance: International Organizations in an Interdependent World* (Boulder, Rienner, 1997) 91–101; K Skjelsbaek and G Fermann, 'The UN Secretary-General and the Mediation of International Disputes' in J Bercovitch (ed), *Resolving International Conflicts: The Theory and Practice of Mediation* (Boulder, Rienner, 1996) 75–105; CSR Murthy, 'The Role of the UN Secretary-General Since the End of the Cold War' in MS Rajan (ed), *United Nations at Fifty Beyond* (New Delhi, Lancer Books, 1996) 297–321; B Rivlin and L Gordenker (eds), *The Challenging Role of the UN Secretary-General: Making 'the Most Impossible Job in the World' Possible* (Westport, Praeger, 1993).
[194] Art 17(1) UN Charter.
[195] ibid, Art 17(2). For a general overview, see eg Gareis (n 114) 38–42.
[196] UNGA A/Res/70/249, 'Programme budget for the biennium 2016–2017', 23 December 2015, UN Doc A/Res/70/249.

the US (22%), Japan (9.68%), China (7.921%), Germany (6.389%), France (4.859%), the UK (4.463%), Brazil (3.823%), Italy (3.748%), Russia (3.088%), Canada (2.921%), Spain (2.443%) and Australia (2.337%). The EU Member States taken together contribute more than 30% of the UN budget.[197]

The 'assessed contributions' of the Member States are the primary source of income for the regular budget. They are calculated on the basis of States' ability to pay (based on the total gross national product (GNP), modified by several factors, including the income per capita). The General Assembly uses 22% of the UN budget as a maximum contribution for a State (since 2000) and 0.001% as a minimum. The financial situation of the UN has been worrying for years, due to the fact that many Member States have made late or incomplete payments of their contributions to the regular budget (the biggest defaulter being the US).[198] Based on a modified allocation key, Member States also pay individually for UN peacekeeping operations. UN funds and programmes – such as the Development Programme of the UN (UNDP), the World Food Programme (WFP), the Office of the High Commissioner for Refugees (UNHCR), the UN Children Fund (UNICEF) and the UN Population Fund (UNFPA) – all have separate budgets. These are mainly financed by voluntary contributions from governments and individuals (the latter especially in the case of UNICEF). UN specialised agencies also have a separate budget.

D. Subsidiary Organs

Pursuant to Article 7(2) of the UN Charter, subsidiary organs may be established as deemed necessary in accordance with the Charter. The power to establish subsidiary organs is specifically given to the General Assembly,[199] the Security Council[200] and ECOSOC.[201] However, the UN Charter contains no uniform procedure for the structure, composition, functions, competences and financing of the subsidiary organs. Actual practice is so diverse that the current UN organisational chart no longer mentions 'subsidiary organs' but uses terminology such as 'programmes and funds', 'other UN entities' and 'research and training institutes'. It is nevertheless clear that these entities are 'subsidiary organs' established according to Article 7(2) UN Charter.

There is an important difference between the subsidiary organs and the specialised agencies of the UN. The latter were established pursuant to a multilateral treaty, while the former are based on a decision of a UN body. In addition, the existence of a subsidiary organ, however autonomous that organ may be in performing its tasks (eg the Administrative Tribunal of the UN), remains dependent on the principal by which it was established. Even though every subsidiary organ is in a subordinate position vis-à-vis the principal organ in question, this does not mean that the subsidiary organ cannot have a large

[197] UNGA A/Res/70/245, 'Scale of assessments for the apportionment of the expenses of the United Nations', 23 December 2015, UN Doc A/Res/70/245.

[198] F Francioni, 'Multilateralism à la Carte: The Limits to Unilateral Withholdings of Assessed Contributions to the UN budget' (2000) 11 *EJIL* 43.

[199] Art 22 UN Charter.

[200] ibid, Art 29.

[201] ibid, Art 68, which mentions 'commissions' and is formulated with more limitations.

measure of autonomy towards the latter, and, if it has been given the competence, can even make decisions that are binding on the principal organ.

In this context, the question has arisen whether the UN General Assembly had the right to refuse to follow up on a judgment by the UN Administrative Tribunal which granted indemnities to a member of the UN staff due to the termination of his employment without his consent. In its 1954 advisory opinion, *Effect of Awards of Compensation Made by the UN Administrative Tribunal*,[202] the ICJ answered this question in the negative. Basing its reasoning on the principle of implied powers, the Court ruled that

> the power to establish a tribunal, to do justice as between the Organization and the staff members, was essential to ensure the efficient working of the Secretariat, and to give effect to the paramount consideration of securing the highest standards of efficiency, competence and integrity. Capacity to do this arises by necessary intendment out of the Charter.[203]

Regarding the argument that the principle of implied powers would not give the General Assembly the power to establish a tribunal whose judgments would be binding to itself, the Court answered that '[t]he precise nature and scope of the measures by which the power of creating a tribunal was to be exercised, was a matter for determination by the General Assembly alone'.[204]

The most important group of subsidiary organs are the ones that are established by a decision of the General Assembly to fulfil specific functional tasks. But other UN principal organs have also established subsidiary organs. For example, in the wake of 9/11, the Security Council established the Counter-Terrorism Committee (CTC) to help improve the ability of UN Member States to prevent terrorist attacks.[205] In 2004, the Security Council established the Counter-Terrorism Committee Executive Directorate (CTED) to assist the work of the CTC and coordinate the process of monitoring the implementation of UNSC Res 1373. Relatedly, the Security Council has established so-called 'sanctions committees', which oversee the implementation of the sanctions measures imposed by the UN Security Council under Article 41 of the UN Charter (on which see above, Section VIII(D).[206] Peacekeeping operations established by the Security Council (on which see Chapter 14, Section VI) are also subsidiary bodies of the Council. Further, the Security Council has established two ad hoc criminal tribunals, namely that for the former Yugoslavia (ICTY) and Rwanda (ICTR) (on which see Chapter 17 on International Criminal Law, Section V), as well as the UN Observation, Verification and Inspection Commission (UNSCOM), which was active within the scope of weapon inspections after the Gulf War. For its part, ECOSOC has established many subsidiary organs.[207]

[202] *Effect of awards of compensation made by the UN Administrative Tribunal* (Advisory Opinion) [1954] ICJ Rep 47. See the annotation by K Keith in Ryngaert, Dekker, Wessel, and Wouters (n 26) 80–90.

[203] *Effect of awards of compensation made by the UN Administrative Tribunal* (n 202) 14.

[204] ibid, 15.

[205] UNSC Res 1373, 28 September 2001, UN Doc S/RES/1373, operative clause 6.

[206] See notably the 'Security Council Committee pursuant to resolutions 1267 (1999), 1989 (2011) and 2253 (2015) concerning ISIL (Da'esh) Al-Qaida and associated individuals groups undertakings and entities', more information regarding which can be found here: un.org/sc/suborg/en/sanctions/1267.

[207] For a general overview of UN subsidiary organs, see eg Sands and Klein (n 8) 65–74; S Torres Bernardez, 'Subsidiary Organs' in RJ Dupuy (ed), *Manuel sur les organisations internationales*, 2nd edn (Dordrecht, Nijhoff, 1998) 109–53; D Sarushi, 'The Legal Framework Governing United Nations Subsidiary Organs' (1996) 67 *BYIL* 413.

Table 4 Overview of UN Subsidiary Bodies, Funds and Programmes (in Chronological Order)

1	UNICEF: United Nations Children's Fund (1946)
2	UNRWA: United Nations Relief and Works Agency for Palestine Refugees in the Near East (1949)
3	UNHCR: Office of the United Nations High Commissioner for Refugees (1950)
4	WFP: World Food Programme (1961)
5	UNITAR: United Nations Institute for Training and Research (1963)
6	UNRISD: United Nations Research Institute for Social Development (1963)
7	UNCTAD: United Nations Conference on Trade and Development (1964), of which the ITC, the International Trade Centre, is a subsidiary organ
8	UNDP: United Nations Development Programme (1965)
9	UNFPA: United Nations Population Fund (1966)
10	UNCDF: United Nations Capital Development Fund (1966)
11	UNICRI: United Nations Interregional Crime and Justice Research Institute (1968)
12	UNV: United Nations Volunteers (1970)
13	UNOCHA: United Nations Office for the Coordination of Humanitarian Affairs (1971)
14	UNEP: United Nations Environment Programme (1972)
15	UNU: United Nations University (1973)
16	UNIDIR: United Nations Institute for Disarmament Research (1980)
17	OHCHR: Office of the UN High Commissioner for Human Rights (1993)
18	UNOPS: United Nations Office for Project Services (1995)
19	UN-AIDS: Joint United Nations Programme on HIV/AIDS (1996)
20	UNODC: United Nations Office on Drugs and Crime (named before 2002 ODCCP: Office for Drug Control and Crime Prevention)
21	UNISDR: United Nations Office for Disaster Risk Reduction (1999)
22	UN-HABITAT: United Nations Human Settlements Programme (2002), replacing the former UNCHS, the United Nations Centre for Human Settlements (1978)
23	UN Women: United Nations Entity for Gender Equality and the Empowerment of Women (2010), uniting the former UNIFEM, the United Nations Development Fund for Women, INSTRAW, the United Nations International Research and Training Institute for the Advancement of Women, DAW, the Division for the Advancement of Women, and OSAGI, the Office of the Special Adviser to the Secretary General on Gender Issues and Advancement of Women

E. Specialised Agencies and Related Organisations of the UN

The *specialised agencies* of the UN[208] are autonomous international organisations 'established by intergovernmental agreement and having wide international responsibilities, as defined in their basic instruments, in economic, social, cultural, educational, health,

[208] For a general overview, see eg Sands and Klein (n 8) 75–113; Gareis (n 114) 36–38; Diez de Velasco Vallejo (n 8) 348–472.

and related fields'[209] that are brought into relationship with the UN through agreements concluded with ECOSOC and approved by the General Assembly.[210] There are around 19 functional organisations whose policy is coordinated within the framework of ECOSOC (see above, Section VIII(C)(iii)). These can be divided into the following categories: the large – politically important – specialised agencies; the financial specialised agencies; and the more technical specialised agencies.

Apart from this, a number of international organisations have concluded a cooperation agreement with the UN and are recognised as *related organisations*. They cooperate with the UN but do not constitute specialised agencies within the meaning of Article 57 UN Charter.

Table 5 Overview of Specialised Agencies and Related Organisations of the UN

A	'Large' – politically important – specialised agencies	
	1	ILO: International Labour Organization
	2	WHO: World Health Organization
	3	UNESCO: United Nations Educational, Scientific and Cultural Organization
	4	FAO: Food and Agriculture Organization
	5	IFAD: International Fund for Agricultural Development
B	'Financial' specialised agencies	
	1	IMF: International Monetary Fund
	The World Bank Group:	
	2	IBRD: International Bank for Reconstruction and Development
	3	IDA: International Development Association
	4	IFC: International Finance Corporation
	5	MIGA: Multilateral Investment Guarantee Agency
	6	ICSID: International Centre for Settlement of Investment Disputes
C	'Technical' specialised agencies	
	1	ITU: International Telecommunication Union
	2	WMO: World Meteorological Organization
	3	WIPO: World Intellectual Property Organization
	4	UPU: Universal Postal Union
	5	ICAO: International Civil Aviation Organization
	6	IMO: International Maritime Organization
	7	UNIDO: United Nations Industrial Development Organization
	8	UNWTO: United Nations World Tourism Organization
D	'Related' organisations	
	1	IAEA: International Atomic Energy Agency
	2	CTBTO Prepcom: Preparatory Commission for the Comprehensive Nuclear-Test-Ban Treaty Organization
	3	ICC: International Criminal Court
	4	IOM: International Organization for Migration
	5	ISA: International Seabed Authority
	6	ITLOS: International Tribunal for the Law of the Sea
	7	OPCW: Organization for the Prohibition of Chemical Weapons
	8	WTO: World Trade Organization

[209] Art 57(1) UN Charter.
[210] ibid, Art 63.

IX. Other Global Organisations

This section focuses only on a selected number of universal international organisations, primarily from the UN system: the ILO, WHO, UNESCO, FAO, IMF, World Bank and IAEA.

A. International Labour Organization

The ILO was established in 1919 by the Treaty of Versailles as an autonomous institution connected to the League of Nations. In 1946, an agreement was approved through which the ILO became the first specialised agency of the UN. Today, 187 States are members of the ILO. The Organization is built upon several basic principles, the foundation of which can be traced back to the nineteenth century industrialists Robert Owen (1771–1853) from Wales and Daniel Legrand (1783–1859) from France. The aspirations of the ILO Constitution, as expressed in its preamble, are: (i) idealistic: a sustainable world peace can only be achieved if it is based upon social justice; (ii) humanitarian: to ameliorate the labour conditions of workers; (iii) political: labour conditions resulting in injustice, hardship and privation risk fomenting unrest among workers ('unrest so great that the peace and harmony of the world are imperilled'); and (iv) economic: if all countries improve the situation of workers, none of them can benefit from a competitive advantage due to poor labour conditions.[211] During the General Conference in Philadelphia, on 19 May 1944, the fundamental principles and aims of the ILO were clarified in a 'Declaration concerning the aims and purposes of the International Labour Organization', the so-called 'Philadelphia Declaration', which was annexed to the ILO Constitution.[212] By virtue of the Philadelphia Declaration, the basic principles upon which the ILO is based are:

(i) labour is not a commodity;
(ii) freedom of expression and of association are essential to sustained progress;
(iii) poverty anywhere constitutes a danger to prosperity everywhere;
(iv) the war against want must be carried on with unrelenting vigour within each nation, and by continuous and concerted international effort in which the representatives of workers and employers, enjoying equal status with those of Governments, join with them in free discussion and democratic decision with a view to the promotion of the common welfare.[213]

The ILO is composed of the following bodies: (i) the International Labour Conference, sometimes called the 'international parliament of labour', composed of representatives of all ILO Members; (ii) a Governing Body, the ILO's executive body, composed of representatives of a more limited number of ILO Members; and (iii) an International Labour Office, the ILO's permanent secretariat, which is supervised by the Governing Body.[214] The ILO is

[211] Preamble ILO Constitution (n 61).
[212] ibid, Annex: Declaration concerning the aims and purposes of the International Labour Organisation (Declaration of Philadelphia).
[213] ibid, Section I.
[214] Art 2 ILO Constitution (n 61).

unique because of its tripartite nature.[215] At the International Labour Conference and in the Governing Body, votes of delegates of employee organisations and delegates of employer organisations carry the same weight as the votes of the two delegates of the governments of the Members.

The International Labour Conference is organised annually in June in Geneva to address issues related to international labour standards and to approve the Organization's budget. Every national delegation at the Conference consists of two government representatives, one employee representative and one employer representative. The latter two delegates are nominated by the government in agreement with the industrial organisations.[216] One of the most pertinent functions of the Conference is the drafting of international conventions and recommendations concerning international labour standards on matters such as freedom of association, wages, working hours, labour conditions, labour compensations, social security, paid leave, industrial safety, employment offices and employment inspection. The importance of the conventions and recommendations of the ILO cannot be underestimated. While, for the members that ratified them, the conventions create binding obligations the implementation of which is supervised by the ILO, the recommendations serve as guidelines for domestic policy, legislation and practice. Since its establishment, the ILO has adopted 189 conventions and 205 recommendations.

The Governing Body meets three times per year in Geneva. It consists of 56 members: 28 government representatives and 14 representatives of each of the industrial partners.[217] This Body has the right of initiative with regard to drafting labour standards. It is this Body that tasks the Office with drafting a report to be discussed by the Conference. Furthermore, the Governing Body takes policy decisions, adopts ILO programmes, prepares the programmes and the budget and studies cases of non-compliance with ILO standards.

The International Labour Office is responsible for the collection and distribution of information on all subjects relating to the international adjustment of conditions of industrial life and labour, and, in particular, for the examination of subjects it proposes to bring before the Conference, aiming at the conclusion of an international convention.[218] The Office is headed by the ILO's Director-General, who is appointed by the Governing Body for five years (and can be re-elected), and who, subject to the instructions of the Governing Body, is responsible for the efficient operation of the Office and for such other duties as may be assigned to him or her.[219]

The follow-up mechanisms provided for in the ILO Constitution, which serve to evaluate whether Members comply with their obligations, are of particular interest. In this regard, the ILO has a regular supervisory mechanism and special procedures at its disposal. The regular supervisory mechanism consists of the obligation for Member States to report to the International Labour Office on measures they have taken to implement the conventions

[215] GA Johnston, *The International Labour Organization* (London, Europa Publications, 1970); F Blanchard, *L'OIT* (Paris, Seuil, 2004); Hurd (n 121) 168–91; Diez de Velasco Vallejo (n 8) 349–54; B Beguin, *Le tripartisme dans l'OIT* (Genève, Droz, 1959); E Vogel-Polsky, *Du tripartisme à l'OIT* (Bruxelles, ULB, 1966). About the role of the EU in the ILO, see eg R Delarue, 'ILO-EU Cooperation on Employment and Social Affairs' in Wouters, Hoffmeister and Ruys (n 54) 93–114: R Kissack, 'The Performance of the European Union in the International Labour Organization' in S Oberthür, KE Jørgensen and J Shahin (eds), *The Performance of the EU in International Institutions* (London, Routledge, 2013) 53–67.

[216] See Arts 3–6 ILO Constitution (n 61).

[217] ibid, Art 7.

[218] ibid, Art 10. See also F Maupain, 'The Settlement of Disputes within the International Labour Office' in BJ Fick (ed), *International Labour Law* (Cheltenham, Edward Elgar, 2015) 97–117.

[219] Art 8 ILO Constitution (n 61).

they have ratified,[220] and the steps they have taken to give effect to the conventions they have not ratified[221] and the recommendations.[222] These reporting obligations are the predecessor to and have been the source of inspiration for reporting obligations in human rights treaties. The special procedures consist of: (i) a representation procedure, in the framework of which an industrial organisation can bring a complaint before the Governing Body if it considers that a Member Country does not comply with a convention it ratified;[223] (ii) a complaint procedure, in the framework of which a Member Country that ratified the relevant convention, a member of the International Labour Conference, or the Governing Body may bring a complaint against a State alleged not to comply with a convention it ratified before a commission of inquiry to be established by the Governing Body;[224] and (iii) the possibility for representatives of industrial organisations to bring complaints against any Member Country regarding that matter before the Committee of Freedom of Association, a committee set up by the Governing Body.

In recent years, the ILO has sought to present itself as the forum *par excellence* for guaranteeing minimal labour standards in the globalising economy.[225] It has also been recognised as such: both the 1995 UN World Summit for Development in Copenhagen and the 1996 WTO Ministerial Declaration in Singapore expressed support for an internationally recognised core of labour standards and viewed the ILO as the appropriate organisation for developing and defining these standards.[226] The ILO's response was formed at the 86th International Labour Conference of June 1998, where a Declaration on Fundamental Principles and Rights at Work was adopted.[227] This Declaration was innovative by reiterating the fact that all ILO Member Countries are, by virtue of their membership, obliged to respect, improve and accomplish the fundamental principles included in eight fundamental (or 'core') conventions of the ILO, even if they did not ratify them. These 'principles concerning the fundamental rights which are the subject of those Conventions' are:

(a) freedom of association and the effective recognition of the right to collective bargaining;
(b) the elimination of all forms of forced or compulsory labour;
(c) the effective abolition of child labour; and
(d) the elimination of discrimination in respect of employment and occupation.[228]

The (revised) Annex to the Declaration provides for a follow-up to the Declaration, which consists of: (i) an 'annual follow-up concerning non-ratified fundamental conventions'; and

[220] ibid, Art 22.
[221] ibid, Art 19(5)(e).
[222] ibid, Art 19(6)(d).
[223] ibid, Art 24.
[224] ibid, Art 26.
[225] See eg L Picard, 'The Role of the International Labour Organization in Implementing Social Rights' in N Aliprantis and I Papageorgiou (eds), *Social Rights: Challenges at European, Regional and International Level* (Brussels, Bruylant, 2010) 147–60; A Yupsanis, 'The International Labour Organization and its Contribution to the Protection of the Rights of Indigenous Peoples' (2011) 49 *Canadian Yearbook of International Law* 117; F Maupain, *The Future of the International Labour Organization in the Global Economy* (Oxford, Hart, 2013).
[226] See respectively UN, Report of the World Summit for Social Development, 6–12 March 1995, UN Doc A/CONF.166.9, Commitment 3(i) and paras 47, 54(b) and 98(c); and WTO, Singapore Ministerial Declaration, 13 December 1996, WTO Doc WT/MIN(96)/DEC, para 4.
[227] International Labour Conference, ILO Declaration on Fundamental Principles and Rights at Work, 18 June 1998, ilo.org/declaration/thedeclaration/textdeclaration/lang--en/index.htm.
[228] ibid, para 2. The eight fundamental ILO conventions include: (i) the Freedom of Association and Protection of the Right to Organise Convention, 1948 (No 87); (ii) the Right to Organise and Collective Bargaining Convention, 1949 (No 87); (iii) the Forced Labour Convention, 1930 (No 29); (iv) the Abolition of Forced Labour Convention, 1957 (No 105); (v) the Minimum Age Convention, 1973 (No 138); (vi) the Worst Forms of Child Labour Convention, 1999 (No 182); (vii) the Equal Remuneration Convention, 1951 (No 100); and (viii) the Discrimination (Employment and Occupation) Convention, 1958 (No 111).

(ii) an annual 'global report' on one of the four categories of fundamental rights and principles.[229] In its 'Special Incentive Arrangement for Sustainable Development and Good Governance' (GSP+ programme), the EU lists the aforementioned eight fundamental ILO conventions among the 27 core international conventions on human and labour rights, environmental protection and good governance that beneficiaries of the programme (who are granted full removal of tariffs on over 66 per cent of product categories) have to comply with.[230]

In addition, in March 2002, the ILO composed a World Commission on the Social Dimension of Globalization and in February 2004 the report 'A Fair Globalization: Creating Opportunities for All' was issued.[231] In 2008, the 'Declaration on Social Justice for Fair Globalization' focused specifically on gender equality.[232] In response to the financial crisis, and the consequences thereof for the labour market, the 2009 Global Jobs Pact was adopted.[233] The Pact proposes several measures governments could take to enhance the recovery of the labour market, taking into account social protection of workers.

B. World Health Organization

With 194 Member States, the World Health Organization (WHO) is a global organisation aimed at improving international cooperation so as to achieve a maximal health level for all throughout the world.[234] International initiatives to improve public health began in the nineteenth century, in particular because the risk of epidemics significantly increased due to trade and migration. In 1945, the United Nations Conference on International Organization authorised the creation of a new, autonomous and international health organisation. The Constitution of the WHO dates from 1946 and entered into force on 7 April 1948

[229] ibid, Annex, as revised 15 June 2010.

[230] See Regulation (EU) No 978/2012 of the European Parliament and of the Council of 25 October 2012 applying a scheme of generalized tariff preferences and repealing Council Regulation (EC) No 732/2008 [2012] OJ L303/1. See inter alia L Beke and N Hachez, 'The EU GSP: a Preference for Human Rights and Good Governance?' in J Wouters, A Marx, D Geraets and B Natens (eds), *Global Governance Through Trade. EU Policies and Approaches* (Cheltenham, Edward Elgar, 2015) 185–213; J Orbie and F De Ville, 'Core Labour Standards in the GSP Regime of the European Union: Overshadowed by other Considerations' in C Fenwick and T Novitz (eds), *Human Rights at Work: Perspectives on Law and Regulation* (Oxford, Hart, 2010) 487–508; S Velluti, 'The EU's Social Dimension and its External Trade Relations' in A Marx, J Wouters, G Rayp and L Beke (eds), *Global Governance of Labour Rights. Assessing the Effectiveness of Transnational Public and Private Policy Initiatives* (Cheltenham, Edward Elgar, 2015) 42–62.

[231] World Commission on the Social Dimension of Globalization, 'A Fair Globalization: Creating Opportunities for All', February 2004, ilo.org/public/english/wcsdg/docs/report.pdf.

[232] International Labour Conference, ILO Declaration on Social Justice for a Fair Globalization', 10 June 2008, ilo.org/wcmsp5/groups/public/---dgreports/---cabinet/documents/genericdocument/wcms_371208.pdf.

[233] International Labour Conference, 'Recovering from the Crisis: A Global Jobs Pact', 19 June 2009, ilo.org/wcmsp5/groups/public/---ed_norm/---relconf/documents/meetingdocument/wcms_115076.pdf.

[234] For a general overview, see eg A Kamradt-Scott, 'The World Health Organization, Global Health Security and International Law' in H Nasu and K Rubenstein (eds), *Legal Perspectives on Security Institutions* (Cambridge, CUP, 2015) 225–47; DP Fidler, 'The Future of the World Health Organization: What Role for International Law?' in GL Burci (ed), *Global Health Law*, Vol I (Cheltenham, Edward Elgar, 2016) 203–50; AL Taylor, 'Making the World Health Organization Work: A Legal Framework for Universal Access to the Conditions for Health' in ibid, 251–96; PM Weller and X Yi-chong, 'The World Health Organization: Some Views from Inside' in PM Weller and X Yi-chong, *The Politics of International Organizations: Views from Insiders* (London, Routledge, 2015) 218–39; Diez de Velasco Vallejo (n 8) 354–58. Concerning the relationship between the EU and the WHO, see inter alia GL Burci, 'The European Union and the World Health Organization: Interactions and Collaboration from a Governance and Policy Perspective' in C Kaddous (ed), *The European Union in International Organisations and Global Governance: Recent Developments* (Oxford, Hart, 2015) 155–73; B Eggers and F Hoffmeister, 'UN-EU Cooperation on Public Health: the Evolving Participation of the European Community in the World Health Organization' in Wouters, Hoffmeister and Ruys (n 54) 155–68.

(this day is annually celebrated as World Health Day).[235] The objective of the WHO is the attainment of the highest possible level of health for all peoples.[236] The Preamble defines 'health' very broadly as 'a state of complete physical, mental and social well-being and not merely the absence of disease or infirmity'. Indeed, the Preamble of the WHO Constitution stipulates that the 'enjoyment of the highest attainable standard of health is one of the fundamental rights of every human being without distinction of race, religion, political belief, economic or social condition'.

The organs of the WHO are the World Health Assembly, the Executive Board and the Secretariat,[237] headed by a Director-General.[238] The highest organ is the World Health Assembly, in which all Member States are represented.[239] The Assembly meets annually,[240] mostly in May, in Geneva. During such meetings, the budget is approved and decisions are made concerning important policy affairs. The Executive Board is composed of 34 members who have technical expertise in the field of health.[241] These members are designated by 34 States elected by the World Health Assembly, taking into account an equitable geographical distribution,[242] and meet twice a year, in January and once again in May, following a meeting of the World Health Assembly. The Secretariat employs around 8,000 people and is located in six regional offices spread across the world.

The two pivotal tasks of the WHO involve managing technical cooperation with countries in the field of health, and directing and coordinating international health work. These tasks are complementary. They involve pioneering work in the field of health care, encouraging specific health projects and awareness, and developing norms and standards, namely through drafting International Health Regulations, which have been revised several times.[243] Additionally, the WHO centralises a great deal of information and many documents, in particular concerning the use of medicine, and ensures worldwide awareness with regard to health.

In terms of directing and coordinating international health work, the WHO inter alia undertook several global campaigns with a view to eradicate diseases such as malaria and smallpox, the latter of which has been eradicated. Polio (poliomyelitis) disappeared entirely in the Americas due to the WHO's assistance. Together with UNICEF, the WHO continues to seek worldwide eradication of this disease by way of encouraging the 30 countries in which the disease still occurs to organise largescale vaccination campaigns. In 2018, polio is only endemic in three countries: Afghanistan, Nigeria and Pakistan. In the past decades, the immunization coverage against polio, tetanus, measles, whooping cough, diphtheria and tuberculosis was raised to 80 per cent. Furthermore, the WHO can fight new and nascent diseases with teams that can be present anywhere in the world within 24 hours. These teams are capable of controlling a possible epidemic in case of an outbreak of a highly infectious disease.

Nowadays, sexually transmitted diseases (STDs), tuberculosis and diseases such as Ebola are the new focus of the WHO. For example, on 8 August 2014 the WHO declared the outbreak of the Ebola virus in West Africa to be an international emergency in the field

[235] See above (n 56).
[236] Art 1 WHO Constitution (n 56).
[237] ibid, Art 9.
[238] ibid, Art 30.
[239] ibid, Arts 10–11.
[240] ibid, Art 13.
[241] ibid, Art 24.
[242] ibid.
[243] See most recently WHO, 'International Health Regulations (2005)', 3rd edn, apps.who.int/iris/bitstream/handle/10665/246107/9789241580496-eng.pdf.

of health.[244] In February 2016, the WHO declared the Zika virus to be a worldwide health crisis.[245] In addition, especially since 9/11, the WHO has concentrated on the consequences of a possible attack with biological or chemical weapons. It played a prominent role in the fight against the Severe Acute Respiratory Syndrome (SARS) and more recently in the fight against the H1N1 flu (also known as swine flu) pandemic.

Lastly, on 21 May 2003, Members unanimously adopted the Framework Convention on Tobacco Control, the first treaty ever to be concluded under the auspices of the WHO, which strictly regulates the advertising of tobacco products.[246] The EU and all its Member States are parties to this Convention.

C. United Nations Educational, Scientific and Cultural Organization

UNESCO was established in November 1946, following an international conference held in 1945 in London, initiated by the British and the French.[247] The primary goal of UNESCO is to contribute to peace and safety in the world by improving collaboration among nations in the fields of education, science, culture and communication.[248] In order to achieve this aim, UNESCO is mainly committed to providing education for everyone. This involves improving literacy, providing development aid for training teachers and for educating education planners and policymakers, adjusting learning programmes, building local schools, etc, all in cooperation with the UN's development agencies. UNESCO encourages the preservation of national cultural values and of cultural heritage, so as to ensure that peoples can benefit from the advantages of modernisation without having to renounce their cultural identity and diversity. UNESCO is committed to: (i) free access to information, freedom of press and development of pluralistic media; (ii) the further strengthening of communication possibilities of developing countries and the improvement of social sciences; (iii) the dissemination and improvement of human rights and democracy, the abolition of all forms of discrimination, the amelioration of the position of women and the search for solutions to problems of the youth.

Institutionally, UNESCO is organised as follows. The General Conference, which consists of representatives of the 195 Member States (additionally, UNESCO counts 10 associate members), meets every two years in order to determine the policy, programme and budget of the organisation.[249] Of note is Palestine's accession on 23 November 2011 after the General Conference voted with 107 votes in favour, 52 abstentions and 14 votes against. The Executive Board meets twice a year, consists of 58 members elected by the General Conference and is tasked with the supervision of the programme adopted by the

[244] See WHO, 'Statement on the 1st meeting of the IHR Emergency Committee on the 2014 Ebola outbreak in West Africa', 8 August 2014, who.int/mediacentre/news/statements/2014/ebola-20140808/en.

[245] See WHO, 'WHO Director-General summarizes the outcome of the Emergency Committee regarding clusters of microcephaly and Guillain-Barré syndrome', 1 February 2016, who.int/en/news-room/detail/01-02-2016-who-director-general-summarizes-the-outcome-of-the-emergency-committee-regarding-clusters-of-microcephaly-and-guillain-barr%c3%a9-syndrome.

[246] Framework Convention on Tobacco Control (adopted 21 May 2003, entered into force 27 February 2005) 2302 UNTS 166. See also above, p 71.

[247] For a general overview, see eg Diez de Velasco Vallejo (n 8) 358–61; Sands and Klein (n 8) 86–87; H Arsheim, 'Religion' in Katz Cogan, Hurd and Johnstone (n 10) 501–502.

[248] Art I UNESCO Constitution (n 31); K Singh, 'Le rôle de l'UNESCO' (1999) 12 *Revue québécoise de droit international* 41.

[249] See Art IV UNESCO Constitution (n 31).

General Conference.[250] A Director-General, who is nominated by the Executive Board and appointed by the General Conference for a renewable term of six years, heads the secretariat, which is located in Paris.[251]

Like in the ILO, UNESCO Member States have the obligation to transfer the conventions – which are adopted by the General Conference with a two-thirds majority – within one year to the competent national governments and to report to the General Conference on their implementation.[252] On 20 October 2005, UNESCO adopted the Convention on the Protection of the Diversity of Cultural Expressions.[253] This Convention is based on several important principles, such as the respect for human rights and fundamental freedoms, sovereignty, equal dignity of and respect for all cultures, and international solidarity and cooperation. The most important aim is to protect and promote the diversity of cultural expressions. The EU itself is a party to the Convention, in addition to all EU Member States.[254]

D. Food and Agriculture Organization

The core purpose of the Food and Agriculture Organization (FAO), which was established in 1945, is to achieve food security for the entire world population by ensuring a rise in the levels of nutrition, an increase in agricultural productivity, an amelioration of living conditions of inhabitants of rural areas and a contribution to the expansion of the world economy in general.[255] In order to achieve these goals, the FAO centralises information on food security, offers expertise to its Members and provides an international forum where Members can consider the problems and challenges related to food security. In addition, the FAO works out projects on technical assistance at the request of interested countries, which are financed by international donors (eg industrialised countries or development banks). Doing so, the FAO mainly offers its technical knowhow as it can only provide funding to a limited extent. In crisis situations, the FAO acts together with the World Food Programme (WFP), a UN programme which was created in 1961. Furthermore, the FAO, in cooperation with the WHO, has established the Codex Alimentarius Commission in 1962, an international organisation which develops standards for food products.[256]

[250] See ibid, Art V.

[251] See ibid, Art VI.

[252] ibid, Arts IV(B)(4) and VIII.

[253] Convention on the Protection and Promotion of the Diversity of Cultural Expressions (adopted 20 October 2005, entered into force 18 March 2007) 2440 UNTS 311. See inter alia T Kono and S Van Uytsel (eds), *The UNESCO Convention on the Diversity of Cultural Expressions: A Tale of Fragmentation in International Law* (Antwerp, Intersentia, 2012); H Schneider and P Van den Bossche (eds), *Protection of Cultural Diversity from a European and International Perspective* (Antwerp, Intersentia, 2007); J Wouters and B De Meester, 'The UNESCO Convention on Cultural Diversity and WTO Law: A Case-Study in Fragmentation of International Law' (2008) 42 *Journal of World Trade* 205–40; J Wouters and M Vidal, 'UNESCO and the Promotion of Cultural Exchange and Cultural Diversity' in AA Yusuf (ed), *Standard-Setting in UNESCO. Normative Action in Education, Science and Culture* (Paris, Unesco/Nijhoff Publishers, 2007) 147–68.

[254] See inter alia L Cavicchioli, 'The European Community at UNESCO: An Exceptionally Active Observer?' in Wouters, Hoffmeister and Ruys (n 54) 135–54.

[255] I Rae, J Thomas and M Vidar, 'The Right to Food as a Fundamental Human Right: FAO's Experience' in B Guha-Khasnobis (ed), *Food Insecurity, Vulnerability and Human Rights Failure* (Basingstoke, Palgrave Macmillan, 2007) 266–85; X Pons Rafols, 'La seguridad alimentaria mundial: la acción política e institucional de la FAO' in X Pons Rafols and D Bondia Garcia (eds), *Alimentación y derecho internacional: normas, instituciones y procesos* (Madrid, Marcial Pons, 2013) 27–81; Diez de Velasco Vallejo (n 8) 396–99.

[256] See inter alia T Büthe and N Harris, 'Codex Alimentarius Commission' in T Hale and D Held (eds), *Handbook of Transnational Governance: Institutions and Innovations* (Cambridge, Polity, 2011) 219; ND Fortin, 'Codex

The FAO Conference consists of 197 Members, ie 194 States, two associated members and one international organisation, namely the EU (which is a member organisation, along with the full membership of individual EU Member States),[257] and meets every two years.[258] It determines the policy and approves the budget and programme of the organisation.[259] The Council consists of 49 members, elected by the Conference, and functions as governing organ of the FAO.[260] The FAO has a Director-General who is appointed by the Conference for a renewable term of four years.[261]

In response to the food crisis, the FAO Initiative on Soaring Food Prices (ISFP) was launched in December 2007. The ISFP encompasses several projects of the FAO which are aimed at allowing small farmers to produce more and to increase their revenues. Within the framework of the ISFP, the FAO collaborates with several other relevant actors like the UN High-Level Task Force on the Global Food Crisis, the EU (the EU Food Facility provides €228 million for FAO projects), national governments and local farmers. In 2008, special attention was paid to the impact of climate change on food security.[262] In 2014, the Second International Conference on Nutrition adopted the Rome Declaration on Nutrition and the Framework for Action.[263]

E. International Monetary Fund

The IMF has 189 Member Countries and is the international monetary watchdog.[264] Its establishment has to be viewed in light of the economic recession between the two World Wars. In order to overcome economic problems, countries sought refuge in competitive depreciations (currency devaluations aimed at obtaining a competitive advantage), which contributed to a global recession which, in its turn, contributed to the outbreak of World War II. During the Second World War, it became clear that international economic cooperation was necessary in order to ensure stability of exchange rates. In June 1944, this concern prompted the establishment of the IMF at the Conference of Bretton Woods (New Hampshire, US). At the same time, the International Bank for Reconstruction and Development (IBRD) was created. At first, stability of exchange rates was achieved

Alimentarius Commission' in C Tietje and A Brouder (eds), *Handbook of Transnational Economic Governance Regimes* (Leiden, Nijhoff, 2009) 645; MD Masson-Matthee, *The Codex Alimentarius Commission and Its Standards* (The Hague, TMC Asser Press 2007). All EU Member States are Members of the Codex Alimentarius Commission, and in 2003 the EU itself became a Member: see Council Decision 2003/822/EC of 17 November 2003 [2003] OJ L309/26.

[257] On the relationship between the EU and the FAO, see inter alia AL Chané and J Wouters, 'The European Union in United Nations Economic Governance Fora' (2017) 8 *European Yearbook of International Economic Law* 549–52; JM Pedersen, 'FAO-EU Cooperation: An Ever Stronger Partnership' in Wouters, Hoffmeister and Ruys (n 54) 63–91.

[258] Art III Constitution of the Food and Agriculture Organization of the United Nations (adopted and entered into force 16 October 1945; as amended) 12 UST 980 (FAO Constitution).

[259] ibid, Art IV(1).

[260] ibid, Art V.

[261] ibid, Art VII(1).

[262] See notably FAO, 'Climate Change and Food Security: A Framework Document', 2008, fao.org/forestry/15538-079b31d45081fe9c3dbc6ff34de4807e4.pdf.

[263] FAO Conference, Second International Conference on Nutrition, Conference Outcome Document: 'Rome Declaration on Nutrition', 19–21 November 2014, FAO Doc ICN2 2014/2.

[264] For a general overview, see eg Hurd (n 121) 138–67; Diez de Velasco Vallejo (n 8) 394–96; RM Lastra, 'The Role of the International Monetary Fund' in RM Lastra and L Buchheit (eds), *Sovereign Debt Management* (Oxford, OUP, 2014) 49–68; E Denters and A Viterbo, *International Monetary Fund (IMF)* (Alphen aan den Rijn, Kluwer, 2013).

through the implementation of a fixed exchange rate system (in accordance with this system, the exchange rates of other currencies were pegged to the US Dollar, and the US Dollar was in turn linked to a fixed amount of gold). At the beginning of the 1970s this system, sometimes referred to as the 'gold exchange standard', collapsed. Since 1978, IMF Member Countries can once again freely determine their exchange rate system.

The goals of the IMF are set forth in Article I of the Articles of Agreement of the IMF:[265] (i) the promotion of international monetary cooperation through a permanent institution that provides the machinery for consultation and collaboration on international monetary problems; (ii) the facilitation of the expansion and balanced growth of international trade, contributing thereby to the promotion and maintenance of high levels of employment and real income, and to the development of productive resources; (iii) the promotion of exchange stability, the maintenance of orderly exchange arrangements among Member Countries, and the avoidance of competitive exchange depreciation; (iv) the establishment of a multilateral system of payments in respect of current transactions between members and the elimination of foreign exchange restrictions hampering the growth of world trade; (v) the building of confidence among Member Countries by making the general resources of the Fund temporarily available to them under adequate safeguards, thus providing them with opportunity to correct maladjustments in their balance of payments; and (vi) the shortening of the duration and the lessening of the degree of disequilibrium in the international balances of payments of Member Countries.

An important task of the IMF is supervising the monetary policy of its Member Countries.[266] While IMF Member Countries may choose their own exchange rate system, the IMF still supervises their decisions. IMF staff consult with any relevant Member Country on a yearly basis,[267] which results in a report discussed by the Executive Board and based on which non-binding recommendations are made to the Member Country involved. Through several facilities, the IMF offers credit to countries that have temporary balance of payment problems. The extension of credit is attached to conditions intended to ensure that the country receiving the credit will in fact be able to implement a recovery policy in order to solve its balance of payment problems and, in addition, to relieve its debts. Since 1999, countries with a low GDP can access the Poverty Reduction and Growth Facility (PRGF), which, in comparison to other credit facilities, provides for a lower interest rate (0.5 per cent) with more favourable terms. The main condition of this facility is that the involved country drafts a Poverty Reduction Strategy Paper (PRSP). The PRSP has to be the end result of a participatory process in which the different parts of society are involved and has to formulate a policy that can solve structural macro-economic problems and reduce poverty.

The IMF consists of the following organs: a Board of Governors, an Executive Board and a Managing Director.[268] In the Board of Governors, the highest organ of the IMF, every Member Country is represented.[269] The Board meets annually, often in September.

[265] See above (n 66).

[266] RM Lastra, 'The Role of the IMF as a Global Financial Authority' (2011) 2 *European Yearbook of International Economic Law* 121; G Parigi and F Paterno, 'The Evolution of the International Monetary Fund in Response to the Global Financial Crisis' in E Sciso (ed), *Accountability, Transparency and Democracy in the Functioning of Bretton Woods Institutions* (Cham, Springer, 2017) 17–27.

[267] Art IV(3) IMF Articles of Agreement (n 66).

[268] ibid, Art XII(1).

[269] ibid, Art XII(2)(a). See further eg D Leech, 'Transparency and Democracy in the Governance of the International Monetary Fund and Reforms in Progress: A Voting Power Analysis' in E Sciso (ed), *Accountability, Transparency and Democracy in the Functioning of Bretton Woods Institutions* (Cham, Springer, 2017) 3–15.

The governors are generally the ministers of finance or the presidents of central banks, who speak on behalf of their government. The Board of Governors decides on important issues such as broadening the extent of the IMF, the accession of new Member Countries or the granting of special drawing rights (SDRs).[270] The Board is advised by two ministerial committees, the International Monetary and Financial Committee and the Development Committee. The daily course of events is monitored by the Executive Board, consisting of 24 executive directors and one managing Director.[271] The Executive Board meets at least three times per week and supervises the implementation of their policy by the Member Countries. The five countries with the biggest quota – the US, the UK, France, Germany and Japan – were until recently entitled to one permanent executive director. Most of the other countries bundle their votes in regional groups: their director represents several countries. These directors are obliged to cast the votes of the countries they represent as one whole. The Managing Director, who is appointed by the Executive Board, is the head of the staff of the Fund and chairs its Executive Board.[272]

In 2006, a two-year plan was adopted with a view to adjust the quota of IMF Member Countries. The goal was to increase the representation of the emerging market economies and developing countries. During a first round of negotiations the quota of the four most under-represented countries (China, Korea, Mexico and Turkey) were increased. A general agreement to change the voting weight was only adopted in 2008. In October 2010, during a meeting of the ministers of finance of the G-20 countries in Gyeongju, South Korea, it was decided to adjust the quota. Because of this adjustment, which relates to almost 6 per cent of the total amount of votes, dynamic and emerging economies, such as Brazil, Russia, India, China and South Africa (the BRICS), now receive relatively more influence. The changes in the Executive Board equally reflect the changing power relations at the international level; two European countries had to relinquish their seats. A package of measures was adopted by the Executive Board in November 2010 and approved by the Board of Governors in December 2010. The reforms became effective on 26 January 2016.

In spite of having the world's second-largest currency, the EU is not systematically represented in the IMF. Article 138 TFEU provides a legal basis for establishing 'unified representation' of the Eurozone countries in international financial institutions, but in spite of a 2015 Commission proposal to that effect, no such measures have been agreed upon as yet.[273]

[270] The 'SDR' is an international reserve asset that can be allocated to Member Countries by the IMF in proportion to their IMF quotas and relative economic standing in the world economy. The value of the SDR is determined by a basket of five major currencies (the US dollar (USD), British pound sterling (GBP), the euro (EUR), the Chinese yuan (CNY) and the Japanese yen (JPY)). It can be exchanged against the freely usable currencies of IMF Member Countries. See IMF, 'Special Drawing Right (SDR)', 19 April 2018, imf.org/en/About/Factsheets/Sheets/2016/08/01/14/51/Special-Drawing-Right-SDR.

[271] Art XII(3) IMF Articles of Agreement (n 66).

[272] ibid, Art XII(4).

[273] See inter alia J Wouters and T Ramopoulos, 'Time to Reconsider Status: The IMF, the EU, the Euro Area and Its Sovereign Debt Crisis' in M Guderzo and A Bosco (eds), *A Monetary Hope for Europe: The Euro and the Struggle for the Creation of a New Global Currency* (Florence, Firenze UP, 2016) 21–37; J Wouters, S Van Kerckhoven and T Ramopoulos, 'The EU and the Euro Area in International Economic Governance: The Case of the IMF' in F Amtenbrink and D Kochenov (eds), *The European Union's Shaping of the International Legal Order* (Cambridge, CUP, 2013) 306–27; J Wouters and S Van Kerckhoven, 'The International Monetary Fund' in KE Jørgensen and KV Laatikainen (eds), *Routledge Handbook on the European Union and International Institutions: Performance, Policy, Power* (Oxford, Routledge, 2012) 221–33; De Baere (n 40) 1268–69.

F. World Bank

The International Bank for Reconstruction and Development (IBRD)[274] is the first of five institutions that together form the World Bank Group. The Group also consists of the International Development Agency (IDA), the International Finance Corporation (IFC), the Multilateral Investment Guarantee Agency (MIGA) and the International Centre for Settlement of Investment Disputes (ICSID).[275]

Together, the IBRD and IDA form the World Bank. The two common goals of these institutions are to end extreme poverty and to improve shared welfare. The IBRD was established as the first institution of the World Bank Group at the Bretton Woods Conference in June 1944. While the IBRD initially had to provide funds to countries which had been struck by the war,[276] this function was taken over by the Marshall Plan not long afterwards. Quickly, the focus shifted to developing countries. In the beginning, the IBRD adopted a 'project approach', whereby it only looked at the project on its own terms. However, since the 1970s, the IBRD approaches projects in a more programmatic manner, whereby the focus is broadened to structural adjustments of government policies (Development Policy Loans). Because of changing trends in the field of development aid, the World Bank today pays more attention to good governance, the fighting of corruption and climate change.[277] In fact, the IBRD functions as a buffer between the private capital market and developing countries. The IBRD borrows money from the private capital market, at a low interest rate due to its credit rating, and lends this money, at a slightly higher interest rate, to some of the developing countries. Like the IMF, the IBRD imposes conditions that can only be of an economic nature.[278] In addition to providing loans, the IBRD also offers technical assistance. The decision-making process resembles the one at the IMF. Acceding to the IBRD, which counts 189 members, is only a possibility for countries that are members of the IMF. The president of the Bank is elected by the Executive Board, of which he or she is officially the president as well.[279]

Despite being a major donor of official development assistance in general and ranking third among the contributors to World Bank trust funds, the EU has no formal status in the World Bank.[280]

G. International Atomic Energy Agency

In 1957 the International Atomic Energy Agency (IAEA) was established as an autonomous organisation that maintains relations with the UN through a special agreement.[281]

[274] C von Monbart, 'IBRD' in R Wolfrum (ed), *UN: Law, Policies and Practice* (Boston, Nijhoff, 1995) 656–64; Hurd (n 121) 138–67; Diez de Velasco Vallejo (n 8) 389–91.
[275] On the ICSID, see Chapter 19, Section IV on International Investment Law.
[276] See Art I(i) IBRD Articles of Agreement (n 87).
[277] See eg B Graham and K Zvobgo, *The World Bank as an Enforcer of Human Rights* (Berlin, ResearchGate, 2018); Y Chen, 'International Organizations and Strategies of Self-Legitimization: The Example of the World Bank Anti-Corruption Sanctions Regime' (2016) 13 *Manchester Journal of International Economic Law* 314; D Van Der Meersche, 'Accountability in International Organisations: Reviewing the World Bank's Environmental and Social Framework' in E Sciso (ed), *Accountability, Transparency and Democracy in the Functioning of Bretton Woods Institutions* (Cham, Springer, 2017) 157–87.
[278] Art IV(10) IBRD Articles of Agreement (n 87).
[279] ibid, Art V(5)(a).
[280] Chané and Wouters (n 257) 557–59.
[281] UNGA Res 1145 (XII), 'Agreement governing the relationship between the United Nations and the International Atomic Energy Agency', 14 November 1957, Annex.

The IAEA counts 168 Member States and is the central intergovernmental forum for scientific and technical collaboration with regard to the peaceful use of atomic energy. The IAEA has two main objectives, namely 'to accelerate and enlarge the contribution of atomic energy to peace, health and prosperity throughout the world', and to ensure that 'assistance provided by it or at its request or under its supervision or control is not used in such a way as to further any military purpose'.[282] The IAEA sets standards on nuclear safety (such as standards on the protection against radiation and on safe transport of nuclear material) and on the protection of the environment, assists Member States through technical cooperation, and encourages the exchange of scientific and technical information on nuclear energy. It offers emergency aid to Member States in case of a nuclear accident, most recently following the nuclear disaster in Fukushima, Japan. One of the most important functions of the IAEA is the taking of precautionary measures to guarantee that nuclear installations and materials, which are to be used for peaceful purposes, are not employed for military use.[283] The IAEA therefore assists States in verifying that this is not the case: it sends inspectors all over the world to inspect nuclear installations and other locations falling within the scope of the IAEA Safeguards Programme.[284] The IAEA operates through several 'precautionary agreements', including precautionary agreements concluded within the context of the Non-Proliferation Treaty (NPT), the Tlatelolco Treaty for the Prohibition of Nuclear Weapons in Latin-America[285] and the Rarotonga South Pacific Nuclear Free Zone Treaty.[286]

The policy and programmes of the IAEA are drafted by both the General Conference, which meets annually and includes all Member States of the IAEA, and the Board of Governors (35 members of which 13 are appointed by the Board itself and 22 are appointed by the Conference), which meets five times each year.[287]

The IAEA sometimes carries out sensitive supervisory tasks. Currently, the most delicate files are the ones concerning North Korea and Iran. In 2007, North Korea, which withdrew from the NPT, decided to no longer allow inspections as stipulated by the Safeguards Programme. Therefore, inspections were carried out in line with an ad hoc programme to which North Korea, under pressure of the international community, agreed. In April 2009, North Korea announced that it would end every form of cooperation with the IAEA, following which the IAEA inspectors were expelled from the country. One month later, North Korea made public that it had been performing nuclear tests. UN Security Council Resolution 1874 condemned such nuclear tests, tightened the weapons embargo and called upon North Korea to implement its obligations under the NPT and to adopt a more transparent attitude towards the IAEA.[288] In 2013, North Korea performed a third nuclear test.

[282] Art II Statute of the International Atomic Energy Agency (adopted 23 October 1956, entered into force 29 July 1957; as amended up to 28 December 1989) iaea.org/sites/default/files/statute.pdf (IAEA Statute); A Behar, 'Preventing Nuclear Proliferation: The Role of the IAEA' in G Devin (ed), *Making Peace: The Contribution of International Institutions* (New York, Palgrave Macmillan, 2011) 49–66; TR Salomon and J Udich, 'Die Rolle der Internationalen Atomenergie-Organisation (IAEA) bei der Bewältigung nuklearer Unfälle' (2011) 59 *Vereinte Nationen* 120; Diez de Velasco Vallejo (n 8) 418–21.

[283] CB Wing and F Simpson, *Detect, Dismantle, and Disarm: IAEA Verification, 1992–2005* (Washington, United States Institute of Peace Press, 2013).

[284] T Rauf, 'The General Framework of IAEA Safeguards' in JL Black-Branch and DH Fleck (eds), *Nuclear Non-Proliferation in International Law*, Vol II (The Hague, Asser Press, 2016) 11–21.

[285] Treaty for the Prohibition of Nuclear Weapons in Latin America (adopted 14 February 1967, entered into force 22 April 1968) 634 UNTS 281 (Tlatelolco Treaty).

[286] South Pacific Nuclear Free Zone Treaty (adopted 6 August 1985, entered into force 11 December 1986) 1445 UNTS 177 (Rarotonga Treaty).

[287] See Art V IAEA Statute (n 282).

[288] UNSC Res 1874, 12 June 2009, UN Doc S/RES/1874.

In August 2015, the IAEA published a report concerning the application of safety measures with respect to North Korea,[289] and in September of the same year, the General Conference adopted a resolution with respect to the implementation of the safeguards agreement between the IAEA and North Korea.[290] However, North Korea performed further nuclear tests in January and September 2016, as well as in September 2017. As a reaction to said last test, the Security Council unanimously adopted a resolution, which paved the way for far-reaching sanctions against North Korea.[291]

It is also feared that Iran's nuclear technology might be used for military purposes. Several reports of the Board of Governors of the IAEA and Resolutions of the Security Council have called upon Iran to cooperate with the IAEA. In June 2010, Security Council Resolution 1929 imposed economic sanctions upon Iran (including prohibitions of arms trade and of every cooperation which can relate to the development of nuclear technology).[292] In July 2015, a Joint Comprehensive Plan of Action was approved between China, France, Germany, Russia, the UK, the US, the EU and Iran.[293] The Security Council, considering the Plan of Action to present a fundamental shift in the Iranian nuclear issue, ratified the Joint Comprehensive Plan of Action in a resolution in July 2015, and terminated the implementation of prior resolutions (including Resolution 1929), on the condition the Plan of Action would be respected.[294] Since 16 January 2016, the IAEA has verified and monitored Iran's implementation of its nuclear-related commitments in accordance with the modalities set out in the Plan of Action, and has issued quarterly reports on this subject. However, on 8 May 2018, the President of the United States, Donald Trump, announced the United States' withdrawal from the Plan.[295]

While all EU Member States are IAEA Members, based on a 1975 agreement with the IAEA,[296] EURATOM is an observer and participates in all formal and informal meetings within its responsibility.[297] The European Commission has extensive scientific and technological co-operation with the IAEA and is also represented in the main technical bodies developing nuclear safety standards and nuclear security guidance.

X. Concluding Remarks

International organisations constitute a very heterogeneous group of international law subjects. They vary in terms of types and categories, fields of expertise, membership rules,

[289] IAEA, Report by the Director General: 'Application of Safeguards in the Democratic People's Republic of Korea', 26 August 2015, IAEA Doc GOV/2015/49-GC(59)/22.

[290] IAEA General Conference, 'Implementation of NPT safeguards agreement between the Agency and the Democratic People's Republic of Korea', 18 September 2015, IAEA Doc GC(59)/RES/14.

[291] UNSC Res 2375, 11 September 2017, UN Doc S/RES/2375.

[292] UNSC Res 1929, 9 June 2010, UN Doc S/RES/1929.

[293] Joint Comprehensive Plan of Action (adopted 14 July 2015, entered into force 18 October 2015) state.gov/documents/organization/245317.pdf.

[294] UNSC Res 2231, 20 July 2015, UN Doc S/RES/2231.

[295] White House, 'Remarks by President Trump on the Joint Comprehensive Plan of Action', 8 May 2018, whitehouse.gov/briefings-statements/remarks-president-trump-joint-comprehensive-plan-action.

[296] Cooperation Agreement between the European Atomic Energy Community and the International Atomic Energy Agency (75/780/EURATOM) (adopted 1 December 1975, entered into force 1 January 1976) [1975] OJ L329/28.

[297] ibid, Art II(1).

financing, decision-making processes, etc. International organisations are all limited in their competences by the principle of speciality, even if they can have implied powers. In spite thereof, their normative activities have greatly expanded over the past three decades. Within organisations, typically various organs exist which have to work with, and respect, each other. Another point of attention is the organisations' relationship to their Member States. On the one hand, an international organisation is dependent on its Member States, at least financially. On the other hand, it typically has international legal personality, which allows it to exercise rights and enter into obligations at the international level independently from its Member States.

The UN and its programmes, funds and specialised agencies constitute the most important global group of organisations. Another international organisation which is on its way to quasi-universal membership is the WTO, which is dealt with in Chapter 19. Regional organisations such as the EU constitute a specific type of international organisations and are discussed in the next chapter.

Bibliography

Archer, C, *International Organizations*, 4th edn (London, Routledge, 2015).

Cede, F and Sucharipa-Behrmann, L (eds), *The United Nations: Law and Practice* (The Hague, Kluwer, 2001).

Charpentier, J and Sierpinski, B, *Institutions Internationales*, 18th edn (Paris, Dalloz, 2012).

Conforti, B and Focarelli, C, *The Law and Practice of the United Nations*, 5th edn (Leiden, Nijhoff, 2016).

Conforti, B and Focarelli, C, *Le Nazioni Unite*, 12th edn (Milano, Kluwer, 2015).

Cot, JP, Pellet, A and Forteau, M (eds), *La Charte des Nations Unies: commentaire article par article*, 3rd edn (Paris, Economica, 2005).

David, E, *Droit des organisations internationales* (Brussels, Bruylant, 2016).

Diez de Velasco, M, *Las Organisaciones Internacionales*, 16th edn (Madrid, Tecnos, 2010).

Dupuy, R (ed), *Manuel sur les organisations internationales/A Handbook on International Organizations*, 2nd edn (Dordrecht, Nijhoff, 1998).

Gareis, SB and Fraser, T (eds), *United Nations: An Introduction*, 2nd edn (Basingstoke, Palgrave Macmillan, 2012).

Karns, MP, Mingst, KA and Stiles, KW, *International Organizations: The Politics and Processes of Global Governance*, 3rd edn (Boulder, Lynne Rienner, 2015).

Klabbers, J, *Advanced Introduction to the Law of International Organizations* (Cheltenham, Edward Elgar, 2015).

Klabbers, J, *An Introduction to International Organizations Law*, 3rd edn (Cambridge, CUP, 2015).

Klabbers, J (ed), *International Organizations* (Aldershot, Ashgate, 2005).

LeRoy Bennett, A, *International Organizations: Principles and Issues*, 7th edn (New York, Pearson, 2001).

Ozmanczyk, EJ and Mango, A (eds), *Encyclopedia of the United Nations and International Agreements*, 3rd edn (New York, Routledge, 2003).

Ruffert, M and Walter, C, *Institutionalisiertes Völkerrecht*, 2nd edn (München, Beck, 2015).

Sands, P and Klein, P, *Bowett's Law of International Institutions*, 6th edn (London, Sweet & Maxwell, 2009).

Schermers, H and Blokker, NM, *International Institutional Law: Unity within Diversity*, 5th edn (Leiden, Nijhoff, 2011).
Schiavone, G, *International Organizations: A Dictionary and Directory*, 7th edn (New York, Palgrave, 2008).
Seidl-Hohenveldern, I and Loibl, G, *Das Recht der Internationalen Organisationen einschließlich der Supranationalen Gemeinschaften*, 7th edn (Keulen, Heymann, 2000).
Simma, B, Khan, DE, Nolte, G, Paulus, A, (eds) and Wessendorf, N (assistant ed), *The Charter of the United Nations: A Commentary*, 3rd edn (Oxford, OUP, 2012).
Singh, MK and Kumar, A, *United Nations Organisation* (New Delhi, KK Publications, 2001).
Volger, H (ed), *A Concise Encyclopedia of the United Nations*, 2nd edn (Den Haag, Nijhoff, 2009).
Weiss, TG and Daws, S (eds), *The Oxford Handbook on the United Nations* (Oxford, OUP, 2008).
White, ND, *The Law of International Organisations*, 2nd edn (Manchester, Manchester UP, 2005).

Further Reading

Alvarez, JA, *International Organizations as Law-Makers* (Oxford, OUP, 2006).
Amerasinghe, CF, *Principles of the Institutional Law of International Organizations*, 2nd edn (Cambridge, CUP, 2005).
Boisson de Chazournes, C, Romano, CPR and Mackenzie, R (eds), *International Organizations and International Dispute Settlement: Trends and Prospects* (Ardsley, Transnational, 2002).
Chemain, R and Pellet, A (eds), *La Charte des Nations Unies, constitution mondiale ?* (Paris, Pedone, 2006).
Cogan, JK, Hurd, I and Johnstone, I (eds), *The Oxford Handbook of International Organizations* (Oxford, OUP, 2017).
Coicauld, JM and Heiskanen, V (eds), *The Legitimacy of International Organizations* (Tokyo, United Nations University Press, 2001).
da Conceição-Heldt, E et al (eds), *Internationale Organisationen: Autonomie, Politisierung, interorganisationale Beziehungen und Wandel* (Baden-Baden, Nomos, 2015).
Denis, C, *Le pouvoir normatif du Conseil de securité des Nations Unies: portées et limites* (Brussels, Bruylant, 2004).
Diallo, A, *Les Nations Unies face aux nouveaux enjeux de la paix et de la sécurité internationales* (Paris, L'Harmattan, 2005).
Kirgis, FL, *International Organizations in Their Legal Setting*, 2nd edn (St Paul, West, 1993).
Klabbers, J and Wallendahl, Å (eds), *Research Handbook on International Organizations Law: Between Functionalism and Constitutionalism* (Cheltenham, Edward Elgar, 2011).
Knipping, F, von Mangoldt, H and Rittberger, V (eds), *The United Nations System and Its Predecessors* (Oxford, OUP, 1997).
Lagrange, E, *La représentation institutionnelle dans l'ordre international: une contribution à la théorie de la personnalité morale des organisations internationales* (The Hague, Kluwer, 2002).

Reinalda, B, *Decision Making within International Organisations* (London, Routledge, 2004).

Schlesinger, SC, *Act of Creation: The Founding of the United Nations* (Cambridge, Westview Press, 2004).

Thakur, R, *The United Nations, Peace and Security: From Collective Security to the Responsibility to Protect* (Cambridge, CUP, 2006).

Thomé, N, *Les pouvoirs du Conseil de sécurité au regard de la pratique récente du chapitre VII de la Charte des Nations Unies* (Aix-Marseille, Presses Universitaires d'Aix-Marseilles, 2006).

Wouters, J, Bruyninckx, H, Basu, S and Schunz, S (eds), *The European Union and Multilateral Governance: Assessing EU Participation in United Nations Human Rights and Environmental Fora* (Basingstoke, Palgrave Macmillan, 2012).

Wouters, J, Hoffmeister, F and Ruys, T (eds), *The United Nations and the European Union: An Ever Stronger Partnership* (The Hague, TMC Asser Press, 2006).

7

Regional Organisations

I. Introduction: The Rise of Regional Integration

International organisations at the level of particular (macro-) regions or continents are a relatively recent phenomenon in international law. Whereas the Organization of American States (OAS) finds its roots in the regional dynamics in the Americas at the end of the nineteenth century and the League of Arab States was created in 1944 (WWII), most regional and sub-regional organisations were set up after the Second World War, and sometimes much more recently.[1] Especially in Europe, a flurry of regional dynamics has been witnessed since the end of the 1940s, strongly driven by a European movement of citizens and prominent politicians looking for ways of pacifying a continent which, in the twentieth century alone, had been at the heart of two devastating wars which set the entire world ablaze. We begin this chapter with an overview of the most important regional organisations in Europe (Section II). Partly inspired by the European examples, regional organisations have also mushroomed in Latin-America, Africa and Asia. The most important ones will be discussed as well (Sections III–V). Some regional organisations span more than one continent and are dealt with in the section on so-called 'transcontinental' organisations (Section VI). Last but not least, this chapter will take a brief look at more informal cooperative groupings between States, whether based on regional togetherness or other criteria, such as politico-economic like-mindedness or systemic economic importance (Section VII).

II. Regional Organisations in Europe

The oldest regional organisation that was created in Europe after the Second World War has by now been firmly relegated to the history books: the Western European Union (WEU). The seeds of the WEU were sown with the Treaty of Brussels, which was

[1] On the institutional and legal dynamics of regional integration see inter alia C Closa and L Casini, *Comparative Regional Integration: Governance and Legal Models* (Cambridge, CUP, 2016); M Forteau, 'Regional Co-operation' (2007) *MPEPIL*. See also S Doumbé-Billé (ed), *La régionalisation du droit international* (Brussels, Bruylant, 2012).

signed on 17 March 1948 by Belgium, France, Luxembourg, the Netherlands and the United Kingdom.[2] The Treaty of Brussels provided for mutual self-defence – a first initiative in the face of the Soviet threat in the unfolding Cold War, and predating the North Atlantic Treaty Organization (NATO) – but also for intergovernmental mechanisms for economic, cultural and social cooperation. The actual WEU was only established with the modified Treaty of Brussels in 1954, with Italy and West Germany joining after the failure of the European Defence Community (on which see below, p 313). In the meantime, other European initiatives had also found their footing. The Council of Europe had been set up in 1949 and, in 1951, the European Coal and Steel Community had also seen the light of day. In 1949 another collective defence pact was concluded, involving the aforementioned European States, together with Canada and the United States: the Treaty of Washington (or NATO Treaty), which would become the bedrock of NATO. Having become redundant in light of the European Union's gradually evolving common security and defence policy, the WEU was officially declared defunct on 30 June 2011.[3]

Another early European post-WWII organisation, set up in 1948 and long since vanished, is the Organisation for European Economic Cooperation (OEEC). It was founded to distribute American recovery aid, in particular under the Marshall Plan. It was meant to be a permanent organisation for economic cooperation with a view to the post-war reconstruction of 18 European countries,[4] and was headquartered in Paris. Under American pressure, the OEEC liberalised intra-European trade, created a European Payments Union (dissolved at the end of 1958 after currencies were made convertible) and set up a European Nuclear Energy Agency in 1957.[5] It fell into decline in the course of the 1950s and was superseded in September 1961 by the Organisation for Economic Co-operation and Development (OECD), which counted the same members, expanded with the US and Canada. Although the current membership of the OECD spans five continents, it is included in this section because of its historical roots.

A. Council of Europe

After the Second World War, the international political debate largely revolved around finding a way to respond to the need felt by European States for further integration in order to preserve the situation of peace. From 7–10 May 1948, a non-governmental conference in The Hague with several prominent intellectuals and (former) politicians in attendance considered this very question. Following the proposals flowing from the conference and a speech by Winston Churchill in Zurich on 7 May 1948, the French government put forward

[2] Treaty between Belgium, France, Luxembourg, Netherlands and the United Kingdom of Great Britain and Northern Ireland for Collaboration in Economic, Social and Cultural Matters and for Collective Self-Defense (adopted 17 March 1948, entered into force 25 August 1948) 19 UNTS 52.

[3] S Rohan, *The Western European Union: International Politics between Alliance and Integration* (London, Routledge, 2014); J Litten, *Beitrag der Westeuropäischen Union (WEU) zur Europäischen Sicherheits- und Verteidigungspolitik (ESVP): eine rechtspolitische Untersuchung* (Aachen, Shaker, 2005); R Wegener, 'WEU: The European Pillar of the Atlantic Alliance' in S Baier-Allen (ed), *The Future of Euro-Atlantic Relations* (Baden-Baden, Nomos, 2000) 53–58.

[4] Austria, Belgium, Denmark, France, Greece, Iceland, Ireland, Italy, Luxembourg, the Netherlands, Norway, Portugal, Sweden, Switzerland, Turkey, the UK and West Germany (*Bundesrepublik Deutschland*).

[5] See eg Royal Institute of International Affairs, *The Organisation for European Economic Co-operation (O.E.E.C.)* (Oxford, OUP, 1958); E Veil, *Die Wohlstandswirkungen der handelspolitischen Integration Westeuropas: unter besonderer Berücksichtigung der Integrationsmassnahmen im Rahmen der Organisation für europäische wirtschaftliche Zusammenarbeit (OEEC)* (Munich, Universität München, 1965).

a proposal for a preparatory intergovernmental conference to set up a European organisation. However, fierce British opposition would not allow plans to develop beyond a strictly intergovernmental organisation, with limited powers and a non-threatening institutional structure: the Council of Europe was born. The Statute of the organisation was signed in London on 5 May 1949 by 10 European States.[6]

The Council of Europe's stated aim is 'to achieve a greater unity between its members for the purpose of safeguarding and realising the ideals and principles which are their common heritage and facilitating their economic and social progress'.[7] Every Member State 'must accept the principles of the rule of law and of the enjoyment by all persons within its jurisdiction of human rights and fundamental freedoms, and collaborate sincerely and effectively in the realisation of the [aforementioned] aim'.[8]

The seat of the organisation was established, for symbolic reasons, in the Franco-German war-stricken city of Strasbourg. It was only after the end of the Cold War that the Council of Europe became a truly pan-European organisation, thanks to the accession of Central and Eastern European countries and a number of the former Soviet Republics (including the Russian Federation). The accession process gave the organisation considerable leverage over prospective members, with regard to their commitment to democracy, human rights and the rule of law.[9] The membership of the Council of Europe stands at 47 States, together representing over 800 million citizens. Belarus is currently the only European State that remains outside the organisation. Canada, the Holy See, Japan, Mexico and the US have observer status in the Committee of Ministers.[10]

The Council of Europe has three main organs: the Committee of Ministers, the Parliamentary Assembly and the Secretariat, headed by a Secretary General.[11] The Committee of Ministers[12] is the main decision-making body of the organisation: it draws up the budget, decides on the activities and policies, and monitors the implementation of the decisions of the European Court of Human Rights (ECtHR) and the follow-up of the recommendations of the Parliamentary Assembly.[13] Resolutions are passed by a two-thirds majority and procedural decisions by a simple majority, but the former only bind Member States after their approval and ratification. The Parliamentary Assembly, which consists

[6] Statute of the Council of Europe (adopted 5 May 1949, entered into force 3 August 1949, last amended 4 May 1953) 87 UNTS 103, CETS No 11 (Statute Council of Europe). The States concerned were: Belgium, Denmark, France, Ireland, Italy, Luxembourg, the Netherlands, Norway, Sweden and the UK.

[7] Art 1, first para, Statute Council of Europe (n 6).

[8] ibid, Art 3.

[9] PA Jordan, 'Does Membership Have its Privileges? Entrance into the Council of Europe and Compliance with Human Rights Norms' (2003) 25 *Human Rights Quarterly* 660; V Djeric, 'Admission to Membership of the Council of Europe and Legal Significance of Commitments Entered into by New Member States' (2000) 60 *Zeitschrift für ausländisches öffentliches Recht und Völkerrecht* 605; and W Sadurksi, 'Partnering with Strasbourg: Constitutionalisation of the European Court of Human Rights, the Accession of Central and East European States to the Council of Europe, and the Idea of Pilot Judgments' (2009) 9 *Human Rights Law Review* 397, 411.

[10] Moreover, Canada, Israel and Mexico enjoy observer status, and Belarus the status of 'special guest' at the Parliamentary Assembly.

[11] For a general overview, see eg M Bond, *The Council of Europe: Structure, History and Issues in European Politics* (London, Routledge, 2012); T Kleinsorge, 'Council of Europe' in J Wouters (ed), *International Encyclopedia for Intergovernmental Organisations* (Alphen aan den Rijn, Kluwer, 2015); and *The Council of Europe: Achievements and Activities* (Strasbourg, Council of Europe, 1996).

[12] See Arts 13–21 Statute Council of Europe (n 5). It is composed of the Ministers of Foreign Affairs of the Member States. Twice a year the Committee meets at the ministerial level. The rest of the year it is composed of diplomatic representatives.

[13] LF Zwaak, 'The Role of the Council of Europe and its Committee of Ministers: Analysing the Efficiency of Measures taken under Article 46(2) of the ECHR' in C Boerefijn, JE Goldschmidt and C Flinterman (eds), *Changing Perceptions of Sovereignty and Human Rights: Essays in Honour of Cees Flinterman* (Antwerp, Intersentia, 2008) 355–80.

of 630 members,[14] focuses on strengthening Member States democratic structures and principles. To this end, it adopts a range of recommendations regarding the objectives and working areas of the organisation, addressed to the Committee of Ministers. In order to ensure the coordination between the two bodies, there is a 'Joint Committee', which meets *in camera* and consists of one representative of each government and an equal number of members of the Parliamentary Assembly.[15] The Secretariat is under the direction of a Secretary General and is in charge of the day-to-day tasks of the organisation. It has gradually expanded its activities and has played a more important role in recent years through country visits, fact-finding missions and related reports. In 1999, the Council established the office of the Commissioner for Human Rights within the General Secretariat in the furtherance of education and awareness in the field of human rights. The Commissioner has an important monitoring and advocacy function, as he or she may issue opinions,[16] make recommendations,[17] and undertake visits.[18]

The greatest contribution of the Council of Europe undoubtedly lies in the field of human rights. This began with the adoption of the European Convention for the Protection of Human Rights and Fundamental Freedoms (ECHR) on 4 November 1950. The ECHR, which has been amended and complemented by various protocols,[19] has laid the

[14] See Arts 22–35 Statute Council of Europe (n 6). Before 1974, and in the Statute of the Council of Europe, it is named the 'Consultative Assembly'. The 630 members comprise 315 representatives of the national parliaments and 315 deputies; to this, one should add 18 observers from non-Member States. In relation to the number of its population, each Member State has a national delegation from 2 to 18 delegates which reflects the proportions of the political parties in its national parliament.

[15] E Lambert-Adbelgawad, 'The Court as a Part of the Council of Europe: The Parliamentary Assembly and the Committee of Ministers' in A Føllesdal (ed), *Constituting Europe: The European Court of Human Rights in a National, European and Global Context* (Cambridge, CUP, 2013) 263–300.

[16] See eg Opinion of the Commissioner for Human Rights, 'Hungary's media legislation in light of Council of Europe standards on freedom of the media', 25 February 2011, CommDH(2011)10.

[17] See eg Recommendation of the Commissioner for Human Rights on the implementation of the right to housing, 30 June 2009, CommDH(2009)5.

[18] See eg the two visits to Turkey in April and September 2016; Commissioner for Human Rights, 'Memorandum on the freedom of expression and media freedom in Turkey', 15 February 2017, CommDH(2017)5.

[19] For the original text, see Convention for the Protection of Human Rights and Fundamental Freedoms (adopted 4 November 1950, entered into force 3 September 1953) 213 UNTS 222, ETS No 5. The amending protocols are Protocol No 11 to the Convention for the Protection of Human Rights and Fundamental Freedoms, restructuring the control machinery established thereby (adopted 11 May 1994, entered into force 1 November 1998) 2061 UNTS 12, CETS No 155 (Protocol No 11 replaced Protocols No 2, 3, 5, 8, 9 and 10); Protocol No 14 to the Convention for the Protection of Human Rights and Fundamental Freedoms, amending the control system of the Convention (adopted 13 May 2004, entered into force 1 June 2010) CETS No 194; Protocol No 15 to the Convention for the Protection of Human Rights and Fundamental Freedoms (adopted 24 June 2013, not yet entered into force) CETS No 213; Protocol No 16 to the Convention for the Protection of Human Rights and Fundamental Freedoms (adopted 2 October 2013, entered into force 1 August 2018) CETS No 214. The complementary protocols are: Protocol to the Convention for the Protection of Human Rights and Fundamental Freedoms (adopted 20 March 1952, entered into force 18 May 1954) 213 UNTS 262, CETS No 9; Protocol No 4 to the Convention of 4 November 1950 for the Protection of Human Rights and Fundamental Freedoms, securing certain rights and freedoms other than those already included in the Convention and in the first Protocol thereto (adopted 16 September 1963, entered into force 2 May 1968) 1496 UNTS 232, CETS No 46; Protocol No 6 to the Convention of 4 November 1950 for the Protection of Human Rights and Fundamental Freedoms, concerning the abolition of the death penalty (adopted 28 April 1983, entered into force 1 March 1985) 1496 UNTS 232, CETS No 114; Protocol No 7 to the Convention for the Protection of Human Rights and Fundamental Freedoms of 4 November 1950 (adopted 22 November 1984, entered into force 1 November 1988) 1525 UNTS 195, CETS No 117; Protocol No 12 to the Convention for the Protection of Human Rights and Fundamental Freedoms (adopted 4 November 2000, entered into force 1 April 2005) 2465 UNTS, CETS No 177; Protocol No 13 to the Convention for the Protection of Human Rights and Fundamental Freedoms, concerning the abolition of the death penalty in all circumstances (adopted 3 May 2002, entered into force 1 July 2003) 2246 UNTS, CETS No 187.

foundation for the most advanced international system of human rights protection in the world (which is discussed in more detail in Chapter 16, Section IX(A)). At first, the ECtHR and the Committee of Ministers were jointly tasked with monitoring compliance with the Convention. Since the entry into force of the Eleventh Protocol on 1 November 1998,[20] the Court consists of full-time judges (one per Member State) and bears full responsibility for the supervision of the Convention, while the Committee of Ministers supervises the execution of the Court's judgments. The ECtHR receives tens of thousands of individual complaints per year. Its case law has been of considerable importance and quality and has in some instances triggered major reforms of national legal systems.[21]

The Council of Europe has also shown itself to be a major driver of effective human rights protection through the European Social Charter, the Convention on the Prevention against Torture,[22] and the Framework Convention for the Protection of National Minorities[23] (the contents and oversight of which are discussed in Chapter 16, respectively Section IX(B), (C) and (D)). Moreover, in May 2011, the Council of Europe adopted the Convention on preventing and combating violence against women and domestic abuse (the Istanbul Convention).[24] It is one of only two treaties that focus exclusively on eliminating all forms of violence against women.[25]

The Council of Europe has overseen the genesis of more than 200 multilateral treaties in the field of legal cooperation (law of persons and family law, international criminal law, etc), cultural cooperation, youth and media. Until 2003, these treaties were published in the European Treaties Series (ETS); as of 2004 in the Council of Europe Treaties Series (CETS).

The Council of Europe has put in place various programmes with a view to protecting, promoting and respecting human rights.[26] The Secretary General and the Commissioner for Human Rights play a crucial role in this respect, by conducting missions in Member States and issuing reports.[27] These programmes focus on children's rights, the rights of persons with disabilities, the rights of migrants, the rights of regional and national minorities, the rights of Roma and travellers, the fight against discrimination, intolerance, xenophobia, gender inequality, violence against women and domestic violence, social and economic rights, the relationship between biotechnology, ethics and protection of human rights.[28]

[20] See above (n 19).

[21] A few examples are *Thlimmenos v Greece* App no 34369/97 (ECtHR, 6 April 2000) and *Tsirlis and Kouloumpas v Greece* App no 19234/91 (ECtHR, 29 May 1997), which triggered a major overhaul of Greece's Constitution with respect to the right to conscientious objection. For more examples, see D Anagnostou, 'Does European Human Rights Law Matter? Implementation and Domestic Impact of Strasbourg Court Judgments on Minority-Related Policies' (2010) 14 *The International Journal of Human Rights* 721.

[22] European Convention for the Prevention of Torture and Inhuman or Degrading Treatment or Punishment (adopted 26 November 1987, entered into force 1 February 1989) 1561 UNTS 363, CETS No 126.

[23] Framework Convention for the Protection of National Minorities (adopted 1 February 1995, entered into force 1 February 1998) 2151 UNTS 243, CETS No 157.

[24] Convention on Preventing and Combating Violence against Women and Domestic Violence (adopted 11 May 2011, entered into force 1 August 2014) CETS No 210.

[25] See below (n 215) for the other instrument, the Convention of Belém do Para.

[26] For a general overview, see eg S Schmahl and M Breuer (eds), *The Council of Europe: Its Laws and Policies* (Oxford, OUP, 2017).

[27] Country reports by the Commissioner of Human Rights can be accessed on coe.int/en/web/commissioner/country-monitoring.

[28] See eg N Muiznieks, Commissioner for Human Rights, 1st Quaterly Activity Report 2017: 1 January to 31 March 2017, 31 May 2017, CommDH (2017)19.

The Council of Europe maintains a close working relationship with the EU, which is governed by a multitude of specific legal texts.[29] In general, both organisations share the same fundamental values and they cooperate in many fields.[30] The adoption of the Lisbon Treaty ensured the further strengthening of the partnership between the two European organisations, notably providing the legal basis for the EU to accede to the ECHR (see Chapter 16, Section X(D)(ii)).

B. European Union

i. Genesis and Development

One of the key conundrums following the Second World War was the so-called 'German question', ie how to allow for a re-emergence of German economic power without putting European peace and security at risk. For the US, an economically strong Germany constituted a key element to ensure the security of Western Europe against Soviet influence. As France was struggling economically, its Foreign Minister, Robert Schuman, proposed a solution to both problems on 9 May 1950. In his famous 'Schuman Declaration', he put forward the idea of a common coal and steel market governed by a supranational High Authority, the European Coal and Steel Community (ECSC). He asserted that, by binding together, in particular, French and German markets, such an institution would make war 'materially impossible'.[31] In 1951, six European States signed the Treaty of Paris setting up the ECSC, with four institutions that would provide the basis for the EU institutions as they exist today.[32]

After the failure of the European Defence Community and the European Political Community in 1954, European economic integration regained momentum at a meeting of foreign ministers in Messina in 1955.[33] On 25 March 1957, the European Economic Community (EEC) and European Atomic Energy (Euratom) Treaties[34] were signed by the six Member States of the ECSC in Rome, with the former notably establishing a customs union and a common market. The EEC was to share the Parliamentary Assembly and Court of Justice with the ECSC, but was to have its own separate Commission and Council of Ministers.

Among the most important Treaty changes since the 1950s were the 1965 Merger Treaty (merging the Communities' institutions),[35] the 1970 and 1975 budgetary/financial Treaties,[36]

[29] For a general overview, see eg Council of Europe, *Compendium of Texts Governing the Relations between the Council of Europe and the European Union* (Strasbourg, Council of Europe, 2001).

[30] Memorandum of Understanding between the Council of Europe and the European Union (signed 11 May 2007) eeas.europa.eu/sites/eeas/files/mou_2007_en.pdf.

[31] Robert Schuman, 'Declaration of 9 May 1950', robert-schuman.eu/en/doc/questions-d-europe/qe-204-en.pdf.

[32] See further eg P Craig, 'Development of the EU' in C Barnard and S Peers (eds), *European Union Law*, 2nd edn (Oxford, OUP, 2017) 9–36.

[33] D Dinan, *Europe Recast: A History of European Union*, 2nd edn (Basingstoke, Palgrave Macmillan, 2014) 72. On the history of the Treaty establishing the European Defence Community, which failed to obtain approval in the French Parliament in 1954 and never entered into force, see E Fursdon, *The European Defence Community: A History* (London, MacMillan, 1980).

[34] Treaty establishing the European Economic Community (adopted 25 March 1957, entered into force 1 January 1958) 298 UNTS 11; Treaty establishing the European Atomic Energy Community (EURATOM) (adopted 25 March 1957, entered into force 1 January 1958) 298 UNTS 169 (Treaties of Rome).

[35] Treaty establishing a Single Council and a Single Commission of the European Communities (adopted 8 April 1965, entered into force 1 July 1967) 1348 UNTS 81 (Brussels Treaty).

[36] Treaty amending Certain Budgetary Provisions of the Treaties establishing the European Communities and of the Treaty establishing a Single Council and a Single Commission of the European Communities (adopted 22 April 1970, entered into force 1 January 1971) [1971] OJ L 2/1 (1970 Budgetary Treaty); Treaty amending

and especially the 1986 Single European Act,[37] the 1992 Maastricht Treaty,[38] the 1997 Amsterdam Treaty,[39] the 2001 Nice Treaty[40] and the 2008 Lisbon Treaty.[41] The EU's founding Treaties were also adapted, especially as far as the composition of the institutions was concerned, by the various Accession Treaties of 1972 (UK, Ireland, Denmark),[42] 1979 (Greece),[43] 1985 (Spain, Portugal),[44] 1994 (Austria, Finland, Sweden),[45] 2004 (Czech Republic, Estonia, Cyprus, Latvia, Lithuania, Hungary, Malta, Poland, Slovenia, Slovakia),[46] 2005 (Bulgaria, Romania)[47] and 2012 (Croatia).[48]

The 1986 Single European Act, which entered into force on 1 July 1987, aimed to complete, by the end of 1992, an essential aspect of the integration process, namely the single market: 'an area without internal frontiers in which the free movement of goods, persons, services, and capital is ensured'.[49] To this end, it provided for the extension of qualified majority voting in the Council and introduced the legislative 'cooperation' procedure, allowing for a stronger participation of the European Parliament in the adoption of Community legislation. Progress was made towards the abolition of restrictions on free movement of persons with the 1985 Schengen Agreement[50] and its 1990 Implementing Agreement.[51] While the

Certain Financial Provisions of the Treaty establishing the European Communities and of the Treaty establishing a Single Council and a Single Commission of the European Communities (adopted 22 July 1975, entered into force 1 June 1977) [1977] OJ L 359/1 (1975 Budgetary Treaty).

[37] Single European Act (adopted 17 February 1986 (Luxembourg) and 28 February 1986 (The Hague), entered into force 1 July 1987) [1987] OJ L 169/20.

[38] Treaty on European Union (adopted 7 February 1992, entered into force 1 November 1993) [1992] OJ C 191/1 (Maastricht Treaty).

[39] Treaty of Amsterdam amending the Treaty on European Union, the Treaties establishing the European Communities and certain related acts (adopted 2 October 1997, entered into force 1 May 1999) [1997] OJ C 340/115 (Amsterdam Treaty).

[40] Treaty of Nice amending the Treaty on European Union, the Treaties establishing the European Communities and certain related acts (adopted 26 February 2001, entered into force 1 February 2003) [2001] OJ C 80/1 (Nice Treaty).

[41] Treaty of Lisbon amending the Treaty on European Union and the Treaty establishing the European Community (adopted 13 December 2007, entered into force 1 December 2009) [2007] OJ C 306/1 (Lisbon Treaty).

[42] Treaty concerning the accession of the Kingdom of Denmark, Ireland, the Kingdom of Norway and the United Kingdom of Great Britain and Northern Ireland to the European Economic Community and to the European Atomic Energy Community (adopted 22 January 1972, entered into force 1 January 1973) [1972] OJ L 73/5.

[43] Treaty concerning the accession of the Hellenic Republic to the European Economic Community and to the European Atomic Energy Community (adopted 28 May 1979, entered into force 1 January 1981) [1979] OJ L 291/9.

[44] Treaty concerning the accession of the Kingdom of Spain and the Portuguese Republic to the European Economic Community and to the European Atomic Energy Community (adopted 12 June 1985, entered into force 1 January 1986) [1985] OJ L 302/9.

[45] Treaty concerning the accession of the Republic of Austria, the Kingdom of Sweden, the Republic of Finland and the Kingdom of Norway to the European Union (adopted 26 July 1994, entered into force 1 January 1995) [1994] OJ C 241/9.

[46] Treaty concerning the accession of the Czech Republic, the Republic of Estonia, the Republic of Cyprus, the Republic of Latvia, the Republic of Lithuania, the Republic of Hungary, the Republic of Malta, the Republic of Poland, the Republic of Slovenia and the Slovak Republic to the European Union (adopted 16 April 2003, entered into force 1 May 2004) [2003] OJ L 236/17.

[47] Treaty concerning the accession of the Republic of Bulgaria and Romania to the European Union (adopted 25 April 2005, entered into force 1 January 2007) [2005] OJ L 157/11.

[48] Treaty concerning the accession of the Republic of Croatia to the European Union (adopted 9 December 2011, entered into force 1 July 2013) [2012] OJ L 112/10.

[49] Single European Act (n 37), Art 13, nowadays laid down in Art 26(2) TFEU.

[50] Agreement between the Governments of the States of the Benelux Economic Union, the Federal Republic of Germany and the French Republic on the gradual abolition of checks at their common borders (adopted 14 June 1985, entered into force 2 March 1986) UNTS Registration No 52750 (Schengen Agreement).

[51] Convention implementing the Schengen Agreement of 14 June 1985 between the Governments of the States of the Benelux Economic Union, the Federal Republic of Germany and the French Republic on the gradual

Schengen 'acquis' (ie these agreements and all rules adopted thereunder) initially lay outside the EU framework, it was integrated in EU law with the Treaty of Amsterdam.[52]

The 1992 Maastricht Treaty, which entered into force on 1 November 1993, integrated the three European Communities within the framework of a European Union, extending them beyond economic integration towards 'a union of a political nature'.[53] The Treaty established a Union of three pillars, governed by a single institutional framework, with the first (supranational) Community pillar comprising the EEC, ECSC and Euratom Treaties, the second pillar introducing an intergovernmental Common Foreign and Security Policy (CFSP) and the third pillar fostering co-operation in Justice and Home Affairs (JHA). The Maastricht Treaty inserted a detailed legal and institutional framework for Economic and Monetary Union (EMU) in the EC Treaty, reinforced the legislative role of the European Parliament by introducing the 'co-decision procedure' (in which the Council and the Parliament need to agree jointly on new legislation; since the Treaty of Lisbon this is called the 'ordinary legislative procedure'), elevated the Court of Auditors to an institution, and created – as an advisory body – the Committee of the Regions. With the move towards a political union, the Maastricht Treaty marked another momentous development by introducing citizenship of the Union for all nationals of EU Member States, conferring substantive rights on Union citizens, such as the right to vote or stand for elections in municipal and European elections.

The Treaty of Amsterdam entered into force on 1 May 1999. It transferred matters of asylum, migration and judicial cooperation in civil matters from the JHA pillar to the Community pillar. It also recognised that the EU is 'founded on the principles of liberty, democracy, respect for human rights and fundamental freedoms, and the rule of law, principles which are common to the Member States'[54] and provided for a sanction mechanism in case of a 'serious and persistent breach' by a Member State of these principles.[55] Whereas the Maastricht Treaty allowed the EU to call upon the WEU (see above, introduction to Section II) for carrying out peace and crisis-related operations (the so-called 'Petersberg tasks'), the Amsterdam Treaty integrated these tasks within the EU framework and created the post of 'High Representative for Common Foreign and Security Policy' in order to speak with one voice on foreign policy matters.

The Treaty of Nice entered into force on 1 February 2003 and focused on adapting the EU institutions to the upcoming enlargement wave, but was generally seen as only an interim step.

The Treaty of Lisbon is the most recent treaty amendment and entered into force on 1 December 2009.[56] It followed the failure of the 2004 'Treaty establishing a Constitution for Europe',[57] which was rejected in French and Dutch referenda in the Spring of 2005, yet saw a large portion of its substance carried over into the Treaty of Lisbon. The latter

abolition of checks at their common borders (adopted 19 June 1990, entered into force 1 September 1993) [2000] OJ L 239/19.

[52] See the 'Protocol integrating the Schengen *acquis* into the framework of the European Union', as annexed to the Amsterdam Treaty (n 39). Further, see eg PJ Kuijper, 'Some Legal Problems Associated with the Communitarization of Policy on Visas, Asylum and Immigration under the Amsterdam Treaty and Incorporation of the Schengen Acquis' (2000) 37 *CMLR* 345.

[53] Bulletin EC 6-1990.

[54] Art 1(8)(a) Amsterdam Treaty.

[55] ibid, Art 1(9); Art 7(2) TEU.

[56] See above (n 41).

[57] Treaty establishing a Constitution for Europe (adopted 29 October 2004, not entered into force) [2004] OJ C 310/1.

amended the Treaty on European Union (TEU) and the EC Treaty, which in a revamped version became the Treaty on the Functioning of the European Union (TFEU). The Treaty of Lisbon provided for the foundation of the EU on the basis of the TEU and the TFEU as the EU's two equal constituent Treaties and gave the EU Charter of Fundamental Rights 'the same legal value as the Treaties', as confirmed in Article 1 TEU.[58] It discarded the previous pillar structure of Maastricht, replacing the EC with the EU, which it endowed with international legal personality.[59] However, CFSP, because of its strongly intergovernmental nature, remains de facto a second pillar next to the 'integrated' policies, ie the supranational policies which follow the ordinary Union – formerly Community – method of cooperation, with a strong role for the Commission, European Parliament and CJEU, and in most cases qualified majority voting in the Council. The Lisbon Treaty introduced a mutual assistance[60] and solidarity clause[61] and paid special attention to the EU's role as a global actor, inter alia by allowing for the creation of the European External Action Service (EEAS)[62] and creating the function of High Representative of the Union for Foreign Affairs and Security Policy, who is at the same time one of the Vice-Presidents of the European Commission (HR/VP), as Europe's foreign policy voice in the world.

As mentioned above, throughout the history of the EU the number of Member States continued to expand. Currently, the EU consists of 28 Member States, and five States (Albania, the Former Yugoslav Republic of Macedonia, Montenegro, Serbia and Turkey) have applied for EU membership. However, on 29 March 2017 the United Kingdom notified its intention to leave the EU on the basis of Article 50 TEU (referred to as 'Brexit').[63]

ii. Institutions

The EU today has seven institutions: the European Parliament; the European Council; the Council of the European Union (Council); the Commission; the Court of Justice of the European Union (CJEU); the European Central Bank (ECB); and the European Court of Auditors.[64] The European Parliament and the Council share the EU's legislative power, while the Commission holds the exclusive right of initiative to make legislative proposals (except in the area of CFSP). These three institutions are assisted by two advisory bodies, ie the Economic and Social Committee and the Committee of the Regions. Executive power is predominantly held by the Commission, which is responsible for both the implementation of legislation and the monitoring and enforcement of EU law. The CJEU upholds the respect for the rule of law through a variety of judicial procedures (see below, this subsection).

[58] Art 6(1) TEU.

[59] ibid, Art 47.

[60] See ibid, Art 42(7): 'If a Member State is victim of an armed aggression on its territory, the other Member States have towards it an obligation of aid and assistance by all the means in their power, in accordance with Article 51 of the United Nations Charter'. On the right of self-defence, see Chapter 14, Section III.

[61] See Art 222 TFEU: 'The Union and its Member States shall act jointly in a spirit of solidarity if a Member State is the object of a terrorist attack or the victim of a natural or man-made disaster'.

[62] The EEAS, a truly European diplomatic service, was established by Council Decision 2010/427/EU of 26 July 2010 [2010] OJ L201/30.

[63] Government of the UK, 'Prime Minister's Letter to Donald Tusk triggering Article 50', 29 March 2017, assets.publishing.service.gov.uk/government/uploads/system/uploads/attachment_data/file/604079/Prime_Ministers_letter_to_European_Council_President_Donald_Tusk.pdf. Further, see eg S Peers and D Harvey, 'Brexit: The Legal Dimension' in Barnard and Peers (n 32) 815–36.

[64] Art 13(1) TEU.

As the intergovernmental body with the essential decision-making role in EU law – and policymaking, the Council is composed of national ministers representing their respective Member States. Depending on the policy area, the Council meets in one of ten configurations. The Presidency of the Council rotates between the Member States and is held for a period of six months,[65] with the exception of one format, namely the Foreign Affairs Council, which is presided by the HR/VP. While the Council was initially the EU's sole legislator, it now shares this function, as well as budgetary powers, with the European Parliament. Decisions of the Council are prepared by a great number (more than 150) of working parties and committees, and in the end, by the Committee of Permanent Representatives (Coreper), ie the Ambassadors of the Member States.

The European Parliament has undergone a large transformation since its birth as an assembly under the ECSC and Rome Treaties. Following its first direct elections held in 1979 and the Maastricht Treaty's introduction of the co-decision procedure (the 'ordinary legislative procedure' since the Treaty of Lisbon),[66] the European Parliament has become one of the most important EU institutions. It is 'composed of representatives of the Union's citizens' who are elected in accordance with national rules.[67] Although elected by the nationals of their country, most members of the European Parliament form part of parliamentary groups.[68]

At the heart of the EU's executive is the Commission, whose function is to 'promote the general interest of the Union'.[69] It is predominantly responsible for initiating legislation, ensuring compliance with EU law (it can bring Member States before the CJEU in the context of infringement proceedings), executing the budget and representing the EU internationally. The Commission sits as a 'college', meaning that its decisions are taken collectively by its Commissioners. Although each Member State sends one national to the Commission, Commissioners are required to act independently of their Member States and to represent the interests of the Union.

The European Council, the EU's decision-maker of last instance, determines the political direction of the EU and is made up of the heads of State or government of all Member States. The President of the European Council and the President of the Commission are also members of the European Council but hold no voting right.[70] The HR/VP also 'take[s] part in its work'.[71]

The CJEU consists of two courts based in Luxembourg, ie the Court of Justice and the General Court. Its role is to 'ensure that in the interpretation and application of the Treaties the law is observed'.[72] The Court of Justice is composed of 28 judges, equating to one judge per Member State, and 11 Advocates General. By 2019 the General Court

[65] For the current revised order in which the Member States will hold the presidency of the Council until 2030, see Council Decision (EU) 2016/1316 of 26 July 2016 amending Decision 2009/908/EU, laying down measures for the implementation of the European Council Decision on the exercise of the Presidency of the Council, and on the chairmanship of preparatory bodies of the Council [2016] OJ L208/42.

[66] Arts 289(1) and 294 TFEU. See above, Section II(B)(i).

[67] Art 14 TEU.

[68] These are: the European People's Party (EPP), the Progressive Alliance of Socialists and Democrats (S&D), the European Conservatives and Reformists, the Alliance of Liberals and Democrats for Europe (ALDE), the Greens/European Free Alliance, the European United Left/Nordic Green Left (GUE/NGL) and the Europe of Freedom and Direct Democracy Group (EFDD).

[69] Art 17 TEU.

[70] Art 235 TFEU.

[71] Art 15(2) TEU.

[72] ibid, Art 19.

will be composed of 56 judges,[73] amounting to two judges per Member State. Both judges and Advocates General are appointed for a renewable six-year term. The Court of Justice has jurisdiction with respect to infringement actions,[74] references for a preliminary ruling,[75] actions for annulment,[76] actions for failure to act,[77] appeals against rulings of the General Court,[78] and a number of specific actions.[79] In turn, the General Court has jurisdiction regarding actions for annulment,[80] actions for failure to act,[81] actions relating to compensation for non-contractual damage brought against the Union,[82] actions pursuant to an arbitration clause contained in a contract concluded by or on behalf of the Union,[83] cases brought against the European Union Intellectual Property Office (EUIPO),[84] cases brought against the Community Plant Variety Office (CPVO),[85] and appeals against decisions of specialised courts.[86]

The European Central Bank was made a formal institution only since the 2007 Treaty of Lisbon, but has been in operation since the introduction of the Euro in 1999. It is responsible for the EU's monetary policy[87] and comprises an Executive Board and a Governing Council. The Executive Board is constituted by its President, Vice-President and four other 'persons of recognised standing and professional experience in monetary or banking matters'.[88] These six members of the Executive Board also sit in the Governing Council alongside the Governors of Central Banks of Eurozone countries. All members of both organs must act independently of their Member States and in the interest of the EU.

Finally, the Court of Auditors was established with the 1975 Budgetary Treaty.[89] It is responsible for examining 'the accounts of all revenue and expenditure of the Union' and the bodies, offices and agencies the EU has set up.[90]

[73] 54 judges after Brexit.

[74] Arts 258–260 TFEU.

[75] ibid, Art 267.

[76] ibid, Art 263.

[77] ibid, Art 265.

[78] ibid, Art 256(1), second para.

[79] Actions concerning disputes regarding the fulfilment by Member States of obligations under the Statute of the European Investment Bank (EIB), measures adopted by the Board of Governors and of the Board of Directors of the EIB, and the fulfilment by national central banks of obligations within the framework of the monetary Union (Art 271(a)–(d) TFEU), actions concerning any dispute between Member States that relates to the subject-matter of the Treaties, submitted to the Court under a special agreement between the parties (ibid, Art 273), actions relating to the legality of acts adopted by the European Council or by the Council pursuant to Art 7 TEU (ibid, Art 269), review of decisions which the General Court took on appeal against decisions of specialised courts (ibid, Art 256(2), second para).

[80] Art 263 TFEU.

[81] ibid, Art 265.

[82] ibid, Arts 268 and 340, second and third paras.

[83] ibid, Art 272.

[84] See Regulation (EU) 2017/1001 of the European Parliament and of the Council of 14 June 2017 on the European Union trade mark (Text with EEA relevance) [2017] OJ L154/1; and Council Regulation (EC) No 6/2002 of 12 December 2001 on Community designs [2002] OJ L3/1, amended by Council Regulation No 1891/2006 of 18 December 2006 amending Regulations (EC) No 6/2002 and (EC) No 40/94 to give effect to the accession of the European Community to the Geneva Act of the Hague Agreement concerning the international registration of industrial designs [2006] OJ L386/14.

[85] Council Regulation (EC) No 2100/94 of 27 July 1994 on Community plant variety rights [1994] OJ L227/1.

[86] Art 256(2), first para, TFEU. The only court falling in the category of 'specialised courts', the Civil Service Tribunal, established in 2004, ceased to operate on 1 September 2016 after its jurisdiction was transferred to the General Court in the context of the reform of the EU's judicial structure.

[87] See eg A Hinarejos, 'Economic and Monetary Union' in Barnard and Peers (n 32) 573–97.

[88] Art 283 TFEU.

[89] Art 1 of the 1975 Budgetary Treaty (n 36).

[90] Art 287 TFEU.

iii. Powers

As the EU constitutes a regional organisation and not a State, the powers possessed by the EU are not unlimited and often shared with the Member States. As set out in Article 5 TEU, in accordance with the principle of conferral (see Chapter 6, Section III), the Union can only act to the extent that powers have been conferred upon it by the Member States in the Treaties. The TFEU provides for various categories of EU competence – exclusive competence,[91] shared competence,[92] competence to provide arrangements for the Member States to coordinate their economic and employment policies,[93] competence to define and implement a CFSP,[94] and competence to carry out actions to support, coordinate or supplement the actions of the Member States[95] – on the basis of which the EU institutions may exercise a varying degree of power. Decision-making concerning CFSP is predominantly intergovernmental and largely escapes this categorisation of competences.[96]

All competences conferred upon the EU must be exercised in accordance with the principle of proportionality and all non-exclusive competences must be exercised in accordance with the principle of subsidiarity. According to the principle of proportionality, 'the content and form of Union action shall not exceed what is necessary to achieve the objectives of the Treaties'.[97] The principle of subsidiarity requires that the EU only acts where Member States cannot sufficiently achieve the objective set out in the Treaties, or where the objective can 'be better achieved at Union level'.[98] It is important to note that the principle of subsidiarity is intended to determine whether the EU ought to exercise a certain competence that has been conferred on it, and not whether certain competences ought to be conferred on it or should be reattributed to the Member States. Article 5(1) TEU is clear on that issue: 'The limits of Union competences are governed by the principle of conferral. The use of Union competences is governed by the principles of subsidiarity and proportionality'.

[91] ibid, Arts 2(1) and 3.
[92] ibid, Arts 2(2) and 4.
[93] ibid, Arts 2(3) and 5.
[94] ibid, Art 2(4).
[95] ibid, Arts 2(5) and 6.
[96] Arts 23–46 TEU. On EU external action, including the CFSP, see further P Eeckhout, *External Relations of the European Union, Legal and Constitutional Foundations*, 2nd edn (Oxford, OUP, 2011); B Van Vooren and R Wessel, *EU External Relations Law: Text, Cases and Materials* (Cambridge, CUP, 2014); P Koutrakos, *EU International Relations Law*, 2nd edn (Oxford, Hart, 2015); PJ Kuijper, J Wouters, F Hoffmeister, G De Baere and T Ramopoulos, *The Law of EU External Relations. Cases, Materials, and Commentary on the EU as an International Legal Actor*, 2nd edn (Oxford, OUP, 2015); G De Baere, 'EU External Action' in Barnard and Peers (n 32) 710–60; J Wouters and T Ramopoulos, 'The External Relations of the Union: The Institutional Structure' in R Schütze and T Tridimas (eds), *Oxford Principles of European Union Law*, Volume 1: The European Union Legal Order (Oxford, OUP, 2018) 1067–1109.
[97] Art 5(4) TEU.
[98] ibid, Art 5(3). The CJEU's possibilities to monitor compliance with subsidiarity have been enhanced by the fact that it now has jurisdiction in actions on grounds of its infringement by a legislative act, brought in accordance with Art 263 TFEU by Member States, or 'notified by them in accordance with their legal order on behalf of their national Parliament or a chamber thereof': see Art 8 Protocol (No 2) on the application of the principles of subsidiarity and proportionality [2016] OJ C202/206. See P Craig, *The Lisbon Treaty: Law, Politics, and Treaty Reform* (Oxford, OUP, 2010) 186–87. Pursuant to the same provision in Protocol No 2, the Committee of the Regions may also bring such actions against legislative acts for the adoption of which the TFEU provides that it be consulted. See further in general eg R Von Borries, 'Das Subsidiaritätsprinzip im Recht der Europäischen Union' (1994) *Europarecht* 263; P Craig, 'Subsidiarity: A Political and Legal Analysis' (2012) *Journal of Common Market Studies* 72; X Groussot and S Bogojevic, 'Subsidiarity as a Procedural Safeguard of Federalism' in L Azoulai (ed), *The Question of Competence in the European Union* (Oxford, OUP, 2014) 234–52; G De Baere, '"Единство в многообразието": Balancing Unity and Diversity in EU Competences through Subsidiarity, Proportionality and Flexibility' (2015) XII *Evropeiski praven pregled* 8.

However, while being an international organisation, the Union is also a legal order organised along federal lines. Article 4 TEU provides the 'programme' for the Union's conception of federalism.[99] It provides that competences that are not conferred upon the Union remain with the Member States,[100] that the Union is under an obligation to respect the equality of Member States before the Treaties 'as well as their national identities',[101] and entrenches the mechanism to keep the federal construction together, in the form of the principle of sincere cooperation.[102]

A unique feature of the EU is that the CJEU has played a preeminent role in the development of the EU's legal order, in particular through the preliminary ruling procedure provided for by Article 267 TFEU, under which national courts of all levels can (and in some circumstances must) refer questions on the interpretation or validity of EU law to the CJEU, and thereby engage in a judicial dialogue with the latter. In particular, as indicated above (pp 189–90) in its 1963 judgment in *van Gend & Loos*, the Court confirmed the doctrine of direct effect,[103] thereby granting individuals certain rights that can be directly invoked before national courts, and declared the then European Communities to be 'a new legal order of international law'.[104] The CJEU has progressively granted direct effect to a great number of provisions of the EU law, including the TEU and TFEU, directives, and international agreements concluded by the EU, thereby empowering individuals.[105] Furthermore, in its 1964 *Costa v ENEL* judgment the CJEU declared the primacy of EU law, ensuring that EU law would prevail in national courts when in conflict with national law.[106]

In the course of their existence, the EC and EU have also deepened their commitment to the respect of human rights, the rule of law and democracy. In particular, the EU adopted in 2000 the Charter of Fundamental Rights of the European Union, which, in a slightly adapted version of 2007, has been given the status of primary law by the Treaty of Lisbon (see Chapter 16, Section X(B)).[107] The CJEU's 1986 judgment in *Parti Ecologiste 'Les Verts' v Parliament* made it clear – long before Article 2 TEU, as inserted by the Treaty of Lisbon, recognised the rule of law as a foundational value of the Union, next to human rights and democracy – that adherence to the rule of law in the EU is fundamental and that no Member State or EU institution can escape judicial review of its actions.[108] More recently, the Court confirmed in its 2018 judgment in *Associação Sindical dos Juízes Portugueses* that mutual trust between the Member States and, in particular, their courts and tribunals is based on the fundamental premise that Member States share a set of common values, such as the rule of law, on which the Union is founded, as stated in Article 2 TEU, and that Article 19 TEU, which gives concrete expression to the value of the rule of law, entrusts the

[99] E Sharpston, 'Preface' in E Cloots, G De Baere and S Sottiaux (eds), *Federalism in the European Union* (Oxford, Hart, 2012) viii.
[100] Art 4(1) TEU.
[101] ibid, Art 4(2); cp E Cloots, *National Identity in EU Law* (Oxford, OUP, 2015).
[102] ibid, Art 4(3); cp G De Baere and T Roes, 'EU Loyalty as Good Faith' (2015) 64 *ICLQ* 829.
[103] Judgment of 5 February 1963, *van Gend & Loos*, 26/62, EU:C:1963:1. See further eg B de Witte, 'The Continuous Significance of *Van Gend en Loos*' in M Poiares Maduro and L Azoulai (eds), *The Past and Future of EU Law: The Classics of EU Law Revisited on the 50th Anniversary of the Rome Treaty* (Oxford, Hart, 2010) 9–15; JHH Weiler, '*Van Gend en Loos*: The Individual as Subject and Object and the Dilemma of European Legitimacy' (2014) 12 *International Journal of Constitutional Law* 94.
[104] *Van Gend & Loos* (n 103) 12. See further Chapter 4, Section V.
[105] See eg S Prechal, 'Does Direct Effect Still Matter?' (2000) 37 *CMLR* 1047.
[106] Judgment of 15 July 1964, *Costa*, 6/64, EU:C:1964:66.
[107] Art 6(1) TEU.
[108] Judgment of 23 April 1986, *Les Verts* v *Parliament*, 294/83, EU:C:1986:166.

responsibility for ensuring judicial review in the EU legal order not only to the CJEU but also to national courts and tribunals.[109]

C. North Atlantic Treaty Organization

NATO was established by virtue of the 1949 North Atlantic Treaty, also known as the Treaty of Washington or NATO Treaty. NATO is a political-military intergovernmental alliance and constitutes a forum for both political consultation and operational cooperation. The organisation is structured as a system of collective defence, as envisaged in Article 51 UN Charter, with at its core a mutual assistance obligation. The alliance was mainly formed as a bastion against Soviet expansion.[110] After the fall of the Berlin Wall and the dissolution of the Soviet Union, NATO was forced to reinvent itself.[111] In recent years, it has redirected its focus towards crisis management, counter-terrorism and cyber defence.[112] Nonetheless, over time, the NATO Treaty has never been amended; NATO has rather shifted its tasks mainly through the adoption of so-called 'Strategic Concepts'.[113] This reinterpretation means that collective defence, crisis management and cooperative security are now considered as NATO's three core tasks.

Over time, NATO's membership has gradually expanded. After the 12 founding countries[114] were joined by Greece and Turkey (1952), West Germany (1955) and Spain (1982), there were 16 Member States for quite some time. In 1999, the Czech Republic, Hungary and Poland became Member States. Bulgaria, Estonia, Latvia, Lithuania, Romania, Slovakia and Slovenia joined in 2004. Albania and Croatia joined in 2009 and most recently, Montenegro became a Member State in 2017. NATO today counts 29 Member States. At this moment, it officially recognises Bosnia and Herzegovina, Georgia and the Former Yugoslav Republic of Macedonia as aspiring members.[115] In addition, NATO has established links with many other countries through various partnership programmes. The most extensive programme is the 'Euro-Atlantic Partnership', composed of the 29 NATO Member States and 21 other countries, such as Sweden and Finland – important strategic partners to NATO. The Euro-Atlantic Partnership brings together the 1994 Partnership for Peace (PfP), which focuses on practical cooperation, and the 1997 Euro-Atlantic Partnership Council (EAPC), the successor of the North Atlantic Cooperation Council (NACC). The EAPC is a multilateral forum for political discussions on security issues.[116]

[109] Judgment of 27 February 2018, *Associação Sindical dos Juízes Portugueses*, C-64/16, EU:C:2018:117, paras 30–32.

[110] S Trifunovska, *North Atlantic Treaty Organization* (Alphen aan den Rijn, Kluwer, 2010).

[111] M Williams and B Neumann, 'From Alliance to Security Community: NATO, Russia, and the Power of Identity' (2000) 29 *Millennium: Journal of International Studies* 357–62.

[112] See eg K Friis (ed), *NATO and Collective Defence in the 21st Century: An Assessment of the Warsaw Summit* (London, Routledge, 2017); M Webber and AGV Hyde-Price (eds), *Theorising NATO: New Perspectives on the Atlantic Alliance* (London, Routledge, 2016).

[113] Of which the most recent one is the Strategic Concept adopted in Lisbon (2010): NATO, *Strategic Concept* (2010), nato.int/lisbon2010/strategic-concept-2010-eng.pdf. See eg JP Shea, 'Why does NATO's New Strategic Concept Matter?' (2010) 34 *Atlantisch Perspektief* 8; D Yost, 'NATO's Evolving Purposes and the Next Strategic Concept' (2010) 86 *International Affairs* 489.

[114] Belgium, Netherlands, Luxemburg, France, Italy, Portugal, Denmark, Norway, Iceland, the UK, the US and Canada.

[115] NATO, *Encyclopedia* (2017), nato.int/nato_static_fl2014/assets/pdf/pdf_publications/20180201_2017-nato-encyclopedia-eng.pdf.

[116] S Balanzino, 'A year after Sintra: Achieving Cooperative Security through the Euro-Atlantic Partnership Council and Partnership for Peace' (1998) 46 *NATO Review* 4; I Lundestad, 'Turning Foe to Friend? US Objectives

The political dialogue within the EAPC also includes non-traditional aspects of security, such as terrorism and environmental and economic security-related issues. As indicated, PfP seeks to advance operational compatibility to enable NATO and PfP countries to act together militarily. PfP is open to all States that participate in the Organization for Security and Co-operation in Europe (OSCE) and satisfy the conditions (inter alia on democracy, human rights and respect for international law as well as OSCE commitments). Such participation takes the form of bilateral agreements (of which the content varies and is subject to the extent of cooperation the partner country wishes to establish) between NATO and each of the participating PfP States.[117]

Furthermore, NATO maintains a special relationship with Ukraine and Russia. NATO Allies meet regularly with Ukraine in the format of the 'NATO-Ukraine Commission'. In May 2002, the NATO-Russia Council was established, as a platform for undertaking joint action. Since Russia's 2014 intervention in Ukraine, NATO-Russia discussions have continued, but the relations have become more tense: NATO has suspended all practical cooperation with Russia since 2014.[118] NATO also works together with Algeria, Egypt, Israel, Jordan, Mauritania, Morocco and Tunisia in the context of the 'Mediterranean Dialogue'.[119] Lastly, in June 2004, the 'Istanbul Cooperation Initiative' was launched, which aims at strengthening ties with Bahrain, Qatar, Kuwait and the United Arab Emirates.[120]

The highest decision-making body of NATO is the North Atlantic Council (NAC).[121] The NAC is made up of the 29 Permanent Representatives of the Member States and meets at least once a week. It can also gather at a higher level without affecting the legal force of the decisions taken. The Council meets at the level of Ministers of Foreign Affairs twice a year, at the level of Defence Ministers about four times a year and occasionally at the level of heads of State and government, known as a 'NATO Summit'.[122] Decision-making within NATO is carried out by consensus, which necessitates thorough consultations.[123] While the political headquarters of NATO were originally situated in Paris, they were moved to Brussels in 1966 when France withdrew from NATO's military integrated structure, which it re-joined in 2008.[124]

Apart from the NAC, the three most important committees are the Military Committee (MC), the Defence Policy and Planning Committee (DPPC), and the Nuclear Planning Group (NPG). These bodies have the same decision-making powers within their respective domains as the NAC. In addition, there are numerous specialised committees and working

in Including Russia in Post-Cold War Euro-Atlantic Security Cooperation' (2015) 38 *The International History Review* 694, 707; S Szurek, 'L'élargissement de l'O.T.A.N. aux pays de l'Europe centrale et orientale et le Partenariat pour la paix' in P Daillier (ed), *Perspectives d'intégration des pays d'Europe centrale et orientale aux institutions de l'Europe occidentale: actes du colloque de Miskolc (Hongrie) des 4–5 octobre 1996* (Paris, Montchrestien, 1998) 85–112.

[117] C Masala, *Renewing NATO's Partnerships: Towards a Coherent and Efficient Framework 2006* (Rome, NATO Defense College Forum Paper, 2006).

[118] J Wilhelmsen and JM Godzimirski, 'NATO and Russia: Spiral of Distrust' in Friis (n 112) 63–76; and HJ Giessmann, 'Euroatlantische Partnerschaft: entbehrlich, notwendig, möglich? Die NATO und Russland – vorwärts in die Vergangenheit' (2017) 35 *S+F: Vierteljahreszeitschrift für Sicherheit und Frieden* 19.

[119] G Hauser, *The Mediterranean Dialogue: A Transatlantic Approach* (Milan, ISU Universita Cattolica, 2006); K Sipos Kecskeméthy, 'The Mediterranean' (2012) 7 *Science and Military Journal* 60, 64.

[120] Masala (n 117).

[121] See Art IX NATO Treaty.

[122] Trifunovska (n 110).

[123] DC Info Documents, *The North Atlantic Alliance: A Model for International Cooperation among Independent Sovereign States* (Brussels, North Atlantic Assembly, 1992).

[124] However, France does not take part in the Nuclear Planning Group as it stands today.

groups operating under these bodies. These civilian organs and subordinate committees are supported by the international staff.

On the military side of NATO there is the MC, which is supported by the international military staff. The MC's principal role is to provide consensus-based advice on military policy and strategy to the NAC and to the NATO Strategic Commanders. Its advice is sought prior to the authorisation by the NAC of NATO military activities or operations.[125] The military structure is comprised of two supreme commanders: SACEUR (Supreme Allied Commander Europe), head of Allied Command Operations, and SACT (Supreme Allied Commander Transformation), head of Allied Command Transformation. Both Supreme Commanders are responsible to the MC and regularly report on military issues. SACEUR's tasks are notably the overall command of NATO's military operations, military planning, and the identification of forces.[126] The Supreme Headquarters Allied Commander for Europe (SHAPE) was originally housed in Rocquencourt near Paris, but was relocated to Casteau near Mons, Belgium, when France withdrew from NATO's integrated military structure. SACT is located in Norfolk, USA. The NATO Secretary General plays one of the most important roles within the organisation. The Secretary General has three main responsibilities: he or she is the Chairman of the NAC, the principal spokesperson of NATO and the head of the international staff. One of his or her main tasks is facilitating consensus-building within NATO. The Secretary General has his or her own cabinet (Private Office), where the Deputy Secretary General is also based.[127]

Although not stipulated in the NATO Treaty, a NATO Parliamentary Assembly was established in 1955. This body sets broad strategic goals for NATO and is made up of members of parliament from the 29 Member States as well as 13 Associate Members. The NATO Parliamentary Assembly interacts directly with the parliamentary structures of the national governments of the Member States. It is, however, not an official part of NATO.[128]

NATO seeks to safeguard the freedom, common heritage and civilisation of the peoples of the Member States on the basis of the principles of democracy, individual liberty and the rule of law, as stipulated in the Preamble to the NATO Treaty. Its central task remains collective defence, as laid down in Article V NATO Treaty:

> The Parties agree that an armed attack against one or more of them in Europe or North America shall be considered an attack against them all and consequently they agree that, if such an armed attack occurs, each of them, in exercise of the right of individual or collective self-defence recognized by Article 51 of the Charter of the United Nations, will assist the Party or Parties so attacked by taking forthwith, individually and in concert with the other Parties, such action as it deems necessary, including the use of armed force, to restore and maintain the security of the North Atlantic area.

Apart from this, Article I of the NATO Treaty includes a commitment to peaceful settlement of disputes, while Article IV calls for consultation among the Allies.[129]

[125] NATO (n 115).

[126] ibid.

[127] RC Hendrickson, *Diplomacy and War at NATO: The Secretary General and Military Action after the Cold War* (Columbia, University of Missouri Press, 2006); and S Trifunovska, 'North Atlantic Treaty Organisation (NATO)' in Wouters (n 11).

[128] C Brumter, *The North Atlantic Assembly* (Dordrecht, Nijhoff, 1986); Z Sabic, 'Parliamentary Diplomacy and the US Congress: The Case of the NATO Parliamentary Assembly' (2016) 11 *The Hague Journal of Diplomacy*, 235.

[129] Art IV: 'The Parties will consult together whenever, in the opinion of any of them, the territorial integrity, political independence or security of any of the Parties is threatened'. The article has been invoked several furies, notably by Turkey.

In the 1990s and early 2000s, NATO undertook operations in Bosnia and Herzegovina and Kosovo.[130] In recent years, NATO's focus has been redirected to (military) tasks different from those originally understood under Article V, such as conflict management, peacekeeping and peace enforcement, often out of NATO territory.[131] The NAC has qualified the attacks of 11 September 2001 in the US as an armed attack within the meaning of Article V NATO Treaty, thereby invoking this article for the first – and as yet only – time in NATO's history. NATO provided military support to the US, most visibly in the form of Airborne Warning and Control System (AWACS) Radar Aircrafts that undertook policing activities in US airspace.[132] The events of 9/11 had a noticeable impact on the direction of NATO, with renewed efforts to develop the relationship with Russia (though the 2014 events in Ukraine reversed this), and focusing on the fight against terrorism and weapons of mass destruction.[133] After the fall of the Taliban, NATO also sent peacekeepers to Afghanistan, whose responsibilities have been expanded after taking over command in South Afghanistan from the US-led Coalition troops.[134]

In light of Russia's 2014 annexation of Crimea and aggression in Ukraine, the ongoing conflict in the Middle East and the instability in Northern Africa, a 'NATO Readiness Action Plan' (RAP) was announced at the Wales Summit of September 2014. The Plan foresees a constant presence and activity – albeit on a rotating basis – in the air, on the ground and in the sea at NATO's Eastern Flank, as well as a rapidly deployable respond unit, the 'Very High Readiness Joint Task Force' (VJTF).[135] Allied leaders introduced the 'Enhanced Forward Presence' (EFP) at the 2016 Warsaw Summit, as a reinforcement of the Readiness Action Plan. Four multinational battalion battle groups are currently deployed in Estonia, Latvia, Lithuania and Poland. Furthermore, as Europe faced a refugee influx, NATO has deployed a maritime force in the Aegean Sea in 2016 to conduct reconnaissance, monitoring and surveillance of illegal crossings, in support of Turkish and Greek authorities and the EU Border Agency.

Burden-sharing is an important topic within NATO. Member States have agreed to spend two per cent of their GDP on defence matters within the next decade in order to enhance NATO's capabilities.[136] Concerning cooperative security, NATO has developed institutionalised relations with the EU since 2001, as both organisations face similar challenges and share strategic interests. In 2002, the EU and NATO adopted the NATO-EU Declaration on a European Security and Defence Policy (ESDP), which outlines the principles governing their relationship.[137] Cooperation between both organisations was further developed

[130] J Deni, 'Alliance Management: NATO's Fight Against Terrorism' (2007) 60 *Studia Diplomatica* 137.

[131] See eg G Szamuely, *Bombs for Peace: NATO's Humanitarian War on Yugoslavia* (Amsterdam, Amsterdam UP, 2013); and A Buzzi, *L'intervention armée de l'OTAN en République fédérale de Yougoslavie* (Paris, Pedone, 2001).

[132] J Kriendler, 'NATO Crisis Management and Conflict Prevention' in V Kronenberger and J Wouters (eds), *The European Union and Conflict Prevention: Policy and Legal Aspects* (The Hague, TMC Asser Press, 2004) 415; D Peters, 'Conflict Prevention and Crisis Management: The Role of NATO' in E Frangou-Ikonomidou (ed), *Peace and Human Rights* (Thessaloniki, Sakkoulas, 2000) 529.

[133] See eg B Bracknell, 'NATO Approaches in Response to ISIL and International Terrorism' (2016) 49 *The International Lawyer* 417.

[134] See eg DP Auerswald and SM Saidemann, *NATO in Afghanistan: Fighting Together, Fighting Alone* (Princeton, Princeton UP, 2014); D Deschaux-Dutard, 'L'approche globale des missions de l'OTAN: le cas de l'Afghanistan' in K Bannelier and C Pison (eds), *Le recours à la force autorisé par le Conseil de sécurité: droit et responsabilité* (Paris, Pedone, 2014) 103.

[135] J Ringsmose and S Rynning, 'Can NATO's New Very High Readiness Joint Task Force Deter?' in Friis (n 112).

[136] NATO, *Wales Summit Declaration* (5 September 2014), nato.int/cps/ic/natohq/official_texts_112964.htm.

[137] NATO, 'EU-NATO Declaration on ESDP', 16 December 2002, nato.int/cps/en/natolive/official_texts_19544.htm.

in 2010, 2016 and 2017 through the implementation of various measures.[138] At the 2016 Warsaw Summit, areas for strengthened NATO-EU cooperation were identified: hybrid threats; enhancing resilience; defence capacity building; cyber defence; maritime security; exercises and more.[139] Furthermore, NATO-OSCE cooperation takes places on issues such as conflict prevention, crisis management and emerging security challenges. Concerning cooperation with the UN, it should first and foremost be noted that resolutions of the UN Security Council have served as mandate for multiple NATO operations and missions. NATO also contributes in practice to UN-sponsored operations. Regular exchanges and dialogues take place between these different institutions.[140]

D. Organization for Economic Co-operation and Development

The OECD was established by the OECD Convention, adopted on 14 December 1960 in Paris.[141] The OECD functions as the successor of the OEEC (see above, introduction to Section II).[142] The current 35 Member Countries are industrialised countries with a market economy and a system of democratic governance. The OECD is no longer a purely European organisation, as nine of its Member Countries are non-European.[143] The OECD aims to maximise the promotion of economic growth, employment and living standards in a stable financial climate, as well as further liberalisation of world trade. To achieve these aims, its activities focus on information exchange, consultations and conducting studies.[144]

The OECD bodies are the Council, the Executive Committee and the Secretariat, headed by a Secretary General. As the decision-making body of the OECD, the Council consists of one representative of each Member Country, as well as one representative of the European Commission. It frequently gathers at the level of permanent representatives, but it also meets once a year on the ministerial level to discuss important issues and determine priorities. The Council, which operates based on consensus, may make binding decisions, issue recommendations and adopt conventions.[145] Under the supervision of the Council, around 250 specialised committees, working groups and expert groups (subsidiary bodies within the meaning of Article 9 OECD Convention) operate, in which Member Countries develop ideas and evaluate progress in specific policy domains, such as trade, science, work, education, financial markets or the economy.

With regard to economic coordination, the main actors are the 'Economic Policy Committee' (EPC) and 'Economic and Development Review Committee' (EDRC). The 'Development Assistance Committee' (DAC), on the other hand, seeks to expand the volume

[138] NATO (n 115) and E Parry, 'After Prague: Relations between NATO and the EU' (2003) 148 *RUSI Journal* 46.
[139] NATO, 'Warsaw Summit Communiqué', 9 July 2016, nato.int/cps/ic/natohq/official_texts_133169.htm.
[140] D Yost, *NATO and International Organizations* (Rome, NATO Defense College Forum Paper, 2007).
[141] The original 20 Member Countries were Austria, Belgium, Canada, Denmark, France, Germany, Greece, Iceland, Ireland, Italy, Luxembourg, the Netherlands, Norway, Portugal, Spain, Sweden, Switzerland, Turkey, the UK and the US. Japan joined in 1964, Finland in 1967, Australia in 1971, New Zealand in 1973, Mexico in 1994, the Czech Republic in 1995, Hungary, Korea and Poland in 1996 and Slovakia in 2000. The newest Member Countries are Chile, Israel, Estonia and Slovenia, which acceded in 2010, and Latvia, which joined in 2016.
[142] HJ Hahn, 'La reconstitution de l'O.E.C.E. et sa continuation dans l'O.C.D.E.' (1962) 8 *Annuaire Français de Droit International* 751; and R Woodward, *The Organisation for Economic Co-operation and Development (OECD)* (London, Routledge, 2009).
[143] Australia, Canada, Chile, Israel, Japan, Korea, Mexico, New Zealand and US.
[144] See Arts 1–3 OECD Convention.
[145] See ibid, Arts 5–6.

and effectiveness of development aid and to enhance and promote a coherent approach to development policies.[146] In addition, there is the Secretariat in Paris and its Secretary General, who is elected for five years and acts as the Council's chair when it meets at the level of the permanent representatives. Furthermore, there are a number of semi-autonomous bodies, such as the International Energy Agency (IEA), the Nuclear Energy Agency (NEA), the European Conference of Ministers of Transport (ECMT), the Centre for Educational Research and Innovation (CERI), the Development Centre, and the Financial Action Task Force (FATF). The latter plays an important role in the fight against money laundering and the financing of terrorism, inter alia through the '40 recommendations against money laundering' (1996, revised in 2003–2004), the 'Nine Special Recommendations on Terrorist Financing' (2004) and a list of 'Non-Cooperative Countries and Territories' (see further below, Section VII(B)(v)).[147]

The primary function of the OECD is to assist authorities in the promotion of prosperity and in the fight against poverty through means of economic growth and financial stability. To this end, the OECD seeks to coordinate the development aid and economic and trade policies of its Member Countries, and engages in special activities for agriculture, science, technology, employment, industry, energy, nuclear energy, education and social affairs. In practice, the Secretariat collects and analyses numerous data on, inter alia, trade, education, employment, environment, health, taxation, investment, migration, public policy, science and technology (included in the OECD data network).[148] On the basis of the analyses made, the relevant specialised committees examine their area of expertise and discuss the potential policy directions. There is also a form of monitoring, called 'peer review'. This implies that the Member Countries explain their policies and provide information and answers to critical remarks. Based on this, the Board formulates decisions or recommendations, after which the government in question is encouraged to implement the decisions or recommendations. For instance, the OECD formulated recommendations in 2014 regarding international cooperation for competition procedures. In July 2014, the OECD, along with the G20 and the EU, developed the 'Global Standard for Automatic Exchange of Financial Account Information in Tax Matters' (the Standard), aiming to achieve transparency in the banking sector by means of an automatic exchange of financial account information. This Standard calls on jurisdictions to request detailed bank information of their respective national financial institutions and share the information automatically with other jurisdictions on a yearly basis (leading to the abolition of bank secrecy). The Standard also included a model convention concerning competent authorities, common reporting and due diligence standards. On the basis of this Standard, the EU and Switzerland signed a historic treaty to limit Swiss banking secrecy.[149]

[146] OECD, Development Assistance Committee, DAC Mandate 2011–2015, 18 October 2010, DCD/DAC(2010)34/FINAL.

[147] MT Nance, 'Naming and Shaming in Financial Regulation: Explaining Variation in the Financial Action Task Force on Money Laundering' in HR Friman (ed), *The Politics of Leverage in International Relations: Name, Shame, and Sanction* (Basingstoke, Palgrave MacMillan, 2015) 123; G Krämer, 'Strategien und Massnahmen der Financial Action Task Force (FATF) zur globalen Durchsetzung ihrer Regeln zur Bekämpfung der Terrorismusfinanzierung' in M Albers and L Groth (eds), *Globales Recht und Terrorismusfinanzierungsbekämpfung* (Baden-Baden, Nomos, 2015) 203; NW Turner, 'The Financial Action Task Force: International Regulatory Convergence through Soft Law' (2015) 59 *New York Law School Law Review* 547.

[148] This data is available at data.oecd.org.

[149] Amending Protocol to the Agreement between the European Community and the Swiss Confederation providing for measures equivalent to those laid down in Council Directive 2003/48/EC on taxation of savings income in the form of interest payments (adopted 27 May 2015, entered into force 1 January 2017) [2015] OJ L333/12.

Recommendations are not only directed to governments. For instance, in 1976, the OECD adopted the OECD Guidelines for Multinational Enterprises (revised in 2000 and 2011) which formulate recommendations for multinationals regarding responsible corporate behaviour (see below, Chapter 8, Section III(C)).[150]

With regard to some other issues, treaties were concluded within the OECD framework. There is, for instance, the Convention on Combating Bribery of Foreign Public Officials in International Business Transactions, adopted in Paris on 17 December 1997,[151] and the Convention on Mutual Administrative Assistance in Tax Matters, concluded in Strasbourg on 25 January 1988.[152] Within the OECD framework, a number of model treaties also came into being, such as the frequently updated OECD Model Tax Convention on Income and Capital[153] and the Model Agreements on Exchange of Information on Tax Matters (Model TIEA).[154] Moreover, the OECD publishes many comprehensive reports (eg the 'Economic Outlook', 'International Migration Outlook', and 'Employment Outlook'), magazines (eg *The OECD Observer*), statistics (eg with regard to the economic growth of some countries), work and policy documents, and books.

While not a member, the EU fully participates in the work of the OECD on the basis of the Supplementary Protocol to the OECD Convention (see also above, p 264).

E. Organization for Security and Co-operation in Europe

The OSCE is a pan-European intergovernmental organisation with a wide-ranging membership: 57 participating States from Europe, Central Asia and North America, all of which enjoy equal status. It deals with security in a broad sense, including its economic, ecological, humanitarian and politico-military aspects. This includes issues such as arms control, confidence and security-building measures, human rights, national minorities, democratisation, police strategies, counter-terrorism and economic and environmental activities. The OSCE was preceded by the 'Conference for Security and Cooperation in Europe' (CSCE), which had been established by the Helsinki Final Act of 1 August 1975 and served as a forum for dialogue between East and West (hence the membership of the United States and Canada).[155] It is generally accepted that the

[150] OECD, 'Guidelines for Multinational Enterprises' (2011) oecd.org/daf/inv/mne/48004323.pdf. See also below, p 392 and p 577.

[151] Convention on Combating Bribery of Foreign Public Officials in International Business Transactions (adopted 17 December 1997, entered into force 15 February 1999) 2802 UNTS 225. See also M Pieth, LA Low and N Bonucci (eds), *The OECD Convention on Bribery: A Commentary* (Cambridge, CUP, 2014); C Graves, 'Beyond Good Intentions: the OECD Anti-Bribery Convention's Pursuits of Prescriptive Enforcement' (2015) 38 *Suffolk Transnational Law Review* 419.

[152] Convention on Mutual Administrative Assistance in Tax Matters (adopted 25 January 1988, entered into force 1 April 1995) 1966 UNTS 215. See also AHM Daniels, 'International Cooperation between Tax Authorities: The Multilateral Convention on Mutual Administrative Assistance in Tax Matters of the Council of Europe/OECD' (1988) 1 *Legal issues of European Integration* 35.

[153] For the most recent version, see OECD, 'Model Tax Convention on Income and Capital', Condensed Version, 21 November 2017, oecd.org/ctp/treaties/model-tax-convention-on-income-and-on-capital-condensed-version-20745419.htm.

[154] OECD, 'Agreement on Exchange of Information on Tax Matters', April 2002, oecd.org/tax/exchange-of-tax-information/2082215.pdf. The Model TIEA consists of a bilateral and multilateral version. Further, see eg M Lang (ed), *The Impact of the OECD and UN Model Conventions on Bilateral Tax Treaties* (Cambridge, CUP, 2012).

[155] Final Act of the Conference for Security and Co-operation in Europe (1 August 1975) 14 ILM 1292 (Helsinki Final Act).

OSCE constitutes a regional organisation within the meaning of Chapter VIII of the UN Charter, and the OSCE has also proclaimed itself as such.

The OSCE is not based on a founding treaty, but rather on different 'acts' and 'documents', which lack treaty status (see Chapter 2, Section III(D)(i)). The aim is for the participating States to engage in political cooperation in a flexible manner. Because of this many CSCE/OSCE documents specify that they do not qualify as a treaty under Article 102 UN Charter. The main instruments that provide the foundations for the OSCE are the Helsinki Final Act (1975),[156] the Charter of Paris for a New Europe (1990),[157] the Helsinki document 'The Challenges of Change' (1992)[158] and the Budapest document 'Towards a Genuine Partnership in a New Era' (1994).[159]

The Helsinki Final Act includes a statement on the principles guiding the mutual relations of the participating States, and the implementation of these principles.[160] These principles can be grouped into three dimensions: (i) military (confidence-building measures and certain aspects of security and disarmament); (ii) economic (cooperation in the economic sphere, on science and technology and the environment); and (iii) human (cooperation on human rights and democracy).[161] The Helsinki Final Act states that the participating States are determined to continue the multilateral process initiated by the conference, through a continuous exchange of views and meetings between their representatives.

As a result of these follow-up exchanges, the CSCE gradually acquired a more permanent character. A third follow-up meeting was held in Vienna from 4 November 1986–19 January 1989. On the initiative of Soviet President M Gorbachev, a Summit meeting was held in Paris on 19–21 November 1990, during which the Charter of Paris for a new Europe was signed by the heads of State and government of the 34 participating States. Some years later, at the Budapest Summit on 6 December 1994, the CSCE was renamed, starting from 1 January 1995, the 'Organization for Security and Cooperation in Europe'. The change of name from 'Conference' to 'Organization' did not change the essentially political nature of OSCE commitments, as stated by the Budapest Document: 'The change in name from CSCE to OSCE alters neither the character of our CSCE commitments nor the status of the CSCE and its institutions' (para 29).

The main decision-making body of the OSCE is the Summit of Heads of State and Government, which meets every two years. Its action is complemented by that of the (annual) Ministerial Council, the (weekly) Permanent Council, the Economic and Environmental Forum (annual) and the Forum for Security Cooperation (weekly). There is also a Parliamentary Assembly, which meets annually and whose secretariat is in Copenhagen.

A more permanent actor is the Presidency, which rotates annually, and forms the OSCE Troika, along with the previous and the future Presidency, and the Secretary General (appointed for three years). The Secretariat Offices are located in Vienna and Prague, in addition to a liaison office in Central Asia. The Secretariat is also home to the Conflict Prevention Centre (CPC).

[156] See above (n 155).
[157] OSCE, 'Charter of Paris for a New Europe', 21 November 1990, osce.org/mc/39516.
[158] OSCE, 'The Challenges of Change', 10 July 1992, osce.org/mc/39530.
[159] OSCE, 'Towards a Genuine Partnership in a New Era', 6 December 1994, osce.org/mc/39554.
[160] A Bloed, 'OSCE Principles: Which principles?' (2014) 25 *Security and Human Rights* 210.
[161] Among these principles there are seven principles (including the VI principle of non-interference in internal affairs), which overlap with the Friendly Relations Declaration. Three other principles are more prominently highlighted than in the Friendly Relations Declaration: the inviolability of the borders (III), the territorial integrity of States (IV) and respect for human rights (VII).

There are also a number of specialised bodies: the Office for Democratic Institutions and Human Rights (ODIHR) in Warsaw, the Representative on Freedom of the Media in Vienna and the High Commissioner on National Minorities (introduced by the Helsinki Document 1992). In addition there is a Court of Conciliation and Arbitration in Geneva (on which see below, Chapter 13, Section II(C)).

Decisions are, in principle, taken by consensus. There are, however, some exceptions: where there is a 'clear, gross and uncorrected violation of [O]SCE commitments' a decision may be taken without the consent of the State concerned.[162] Certain actions qualifying as 'executive action' do not require consensus either. Some bodies, such as the Presidency, may also take 'operational initiatives' without consensus.

As briefly touched upon above, the OSCE focuses on all aspects of security and conflict prevention, but also on dispute resolution and conflict management, through field operations and CPC.[163] For example, in response to the unrest in Ukraine in 2013, the OSCE sent a special monitoring mission to the area with the aim of contributing to de-escalating tensions and promoting peace, stability and security.[164] Since the Dayton peace agreement for the former Yugoslavia,[165] the OSCE also developed expertise on post-conflict peace building (particularly the building up of democratic institutions, training and/or forming of police forces, etc).[166] Often these peace-building activities are part of a broader effort. Since 1992, the OSCE may also carry out peacekeeping missions. However, so far the OSCE has not yet conducted military peacekeeping missions. Much attention is nevertheless devoted to conflict prevention and peaceful settlement of disputes. This is, inter alia, achieved by stressing the sovereign equality and territorial integrity of the participating States, the prohibition on the use of force and other principles of international law. In terms of prevention, the CPC, the High Commissioner on National Minorities, and the Presidency and its Personal Representatives play a particularly important role. Regarding peaceful settlement of disputes various procedures are available, with the Convention on Conciliation and Arbitration,[167] which provides the basis for the Court of Conciliation and Arbitration, constituting the most prominent agreement on these matters.[168]

Another core issue, from the very start, has been disarmament. The Treaty on Conventional Armed Forces in Europe (CFE, 1990)[169] and the Treaty on Open Skies (1992),[170]

[162] OSCE, 'Prague Document on Further Development of CSCE Institutions and Structures', 31 January 1992, osce.org/mc/40270, para 16.

[163] A Bloed, 'The OSCE Main Political Bodies and Their Role in Conflict Prevention and Crisis Management' in M Bothe and N Ronzitti (eds), *The OSCE in the Maintenance of Peace and Security: Conflict Prevention, Crisis Management and Peaceful Settlement of Disputes* (The Hague, Kluwer, 1997) 35.

[164] C Neukirch, 'The Special Monitoring Mission to Ukraine in Its Second Year: Ongoing OSCE Conflict Management in Ukraine' (2015) 21 *OSCE Yearbook* 229.

[165] General Framework Agreement for Peace in Bosnia and Herzegovina (adopted 21 November 1995, entered into force 14 December 1995) 35 ILM 75 (Dayton Peace Agreement).

[166] M Ducasse-Rogier, 'The Operational Role of the OSCE in the Field of Peace-Building: The Case of Bosnia and Herzegovina' in VY Ghebali and E Rogier (eds), *The Operational Role of the OSCE in Southeastern Europe: Contributing to Regional Stability in the Balkans* (Aldershot, Ashgate, 2001) 24; and C van der Borgh, 'Post-War Peace-Building: What Role For International Organizations?' in M Kremer, P van Lieshout and R Went (eds), *Doing Good or Doing Better: Development Policies in a Globalising World* (Amsterdam, Amsterdam UP, 2009) 303.

[167] Convention on Conciliation and Arbitration within the OSCE (adopted on 15 December 1992, entered into force 5 December 1994) osce.org/cca/111409.

[168] C Tomushat, R Pisillo Mazzeschi and D Thürer (eds), *Conciliation in International Law: The OSCE Court of Conciliation and Arbitration* (Leiden, Brill Nijhoff, 2017).

[169] Treaty on Conventional Armed Forces in Europe (adopted 19 November 1990, entered into force 9 November 1992) osce.org/library/14087.

[170] Treaty on Open Skies (adopted 24 March 1992, entered into force 1 January 2002) osce.org/library/14127.

were both adopted to address this. There are also numerous agreements on 'confidence- and security building measures' (CSBMs). At the OSCE Summit in Istanbul in November 1999, the CFE Treaty was amended and the 1999 Vienna Document, dealing with CSBMs, was adopted. In 2009, at an informal meeting of the OSCE Ministers of Foreign Affairs, the 'Corfu Process' was launched. The purpose of the initiative is the advancement of existing structures, the strengthening of 'cooperative security' in the OSCE region and the full implementation of existing agreements, including those regarding conflict resolution and arms control.[171]

A third central theme is human rights and democracy (the so-called 'Human Dimension'). There have been several OSCE missions to ensure free and fair elections. Key actors here are the ODIHR and the High Commissioner for National Minorities, who often work together with other human rights monitoring and advocacy organisations, such as the Office of the United Nations High Commissioner for Human Rights (OHCHR). For instance, ODIHR and OHCHR cooperated closely on the protection of Roma and travellers, which resulted in a Contact Point for Roma and Sinti issues. Environmental, cultural and economic cooperation are also discussed within the framework of the OSCE.

Finally, the OSCE benefits from a strong relationship with the EU, and both organisations collaborate on a range of issues. In particular, at both the political and working level, the OSCE and the EU collaborate through consultations between the OSCE Troika, including the OSCE Secretary General, and the EU at both the ministerial and ambassadorial/Political Security Committee levels; cross representation at relevant meetings; and contacts between the Secretary General and the High Representative of the Union for Foreign Affairs and Security Policy and other high-level EU officials. Furthermore, annual staff-level talks on topical issues that are on the agenda of both organisations also take place.[172]

F. Sub-Regional Organisations: Benelux and Others

i. Benelux

The Benelux Union (Benelux) – not to be confused with the Belgium-Luxembourg Economic Union (BLEU) – is the current name for the former Benelux Economic Union, established by way of a Treaty of 3 February 1958.[173] The impetus for the Benelux was given on 5 September 1944, when the governments of Belgium, the Netherlands and Luxembourg (in exile) signed the London Customs Convention.[174] The Convention aspired to establish an economic union between these three countries, through gradual progressive integration. The Benelux Economic Union Treaty was initially concluded for a period of 50 years, and could thereafter be tacitly renewed every ten years. The treaty was thoroughly amended on 17 June 2008 and was renamed the Benelux Union Treaty.[175]

[171] I Cliff, 'The Corfu Process: What Was It All About?' (2011) 17 *OSCE Yearbook* 65.

[172] OSCE, 'The European Union', osce.org/partnerships/european-union.

[173] Treaty instituting the Benelux Economic Union (adopted 3 February 1958, entered into force 1 November 1960) 381 UNTS 167, amended by the Treaty revising the Treaty instituting the Benelux Economic Union signed on 3 February 1958 (adopted 17 June 2008, entered into force 1 January 2012) UNTS Registration No 5471 (Benelux Union Treaty).

[174] London Customs Convention (adopted 5 September 1944, entered into force 1 January 1948) cvce.eu/en/obj/netherlands_belgium_luxembourg_customs_convention_london_5_september_1944-en-ac12ecf6-6d89-48fc-ba05-5309aec76f78.html.

[175] See (n 173). Further, see inter alia J Wouters and M Vidal, 'The Trials and Tribulations of Benelux' in T Giegerich, DC Schmitt and S Zeitzmann (eds), *Flexibility in the EU and Beyond* (Baden-Baden, Nomos/Hart,

The Benelux Union Treaty redefined the institutional framework of the organisation. The modernisation of its functioning, inter alia by reducing the number of organs, was one of the key achievements. Moreover, the new designation indicates the broadening of the cooperation to domains beyond the purely economic sphere. The Benelux Union now has two core objectives: the pursuit of experimental cooperation initiatives that may later be implemented in the EU context (eg the Schengen system builds upon Benelux cooperation) and expansion of cross-border cooperation. Three themes are at the heart of the Benelux Union: the internal market and economic union; sustainability; and justice and home affairs. Other innovations were the recognition of the increasing role of the Belgian regions for Benelux activities, within their jurisdiction (eg recognition of diplomas for the communities or cross-mobility for the regions) and the openness towards neighbouring countries and their regions. In particular, the German region of North Rhine-Westphalia has been actively involved for several years in Benelux operations.

Formally, the Committee of Ministers, composed of the three ministers of Foreign Affairs, each with one vote (other interested ministers may attend the meetings), oversees the implementation of the Treaty and takes the necessary decisions.[176] However, in practice, the Benelux is primarily a discussion forum for civil servants and the Committee of Ministers rarely takes decisions. Following a classic intergovernmental model, the Committee takes only those decisions which bind the States and adopts the treaties which have to be ratified before their entry into force. The Interparliamentary Consultative Council is not involved in the decision-making process.[177] The Council consists of 49 members of parliament from the three countries. Its advisory role is enshrined in a separate treaty of 1955.[178] A treaty of 20 January 2015, which has not yet entered into force, renames the Council the Benelux Interparliamentary Assembly. The Secretariat-General is located in Brussels.[179] Since 1975 the Secretariat has a limited right of initiative to adopt guidelines. As the 'engine' of the Benelux, it puts forward and supervises project and policy proposals.[180] The Benelux Court of Justice was established by a treaty of 31 March 1965[181] to ensure the uniform application of common rules. It is composed of nine judges, from each country's highest national court, and three advocates-general. The Court decides by way of preliminary rulings and opinions (at the request of the Committee of Ministers).[182] In addition, since 1 September 2006, the Benelux Office for Intellectual Property (BOIP) supervises the implementation of the rules regarding trademarks, designs and models, which are commonly defined since 1960.[183] This organisation functions as an integrated administration specialised in intellectual property, which is also the main focus of the Benelux Court of Justice.

The Benelux has a special relationship with the activities and powers of its 'big sister organisation', the EU. In the pursuit of its original economic purposes (free movement

2017) 285–95; J Wouters and M Vidal: 'Towards a Rebirth of Benelux?'(2007) *Revue belge de droit international* 532–56; J Wouters et al, *De Benelux: tijd voor een wedergeboorte?* (Antwerp, Intersentia, 2006).

176 See Arts 16–22 Benelux Union Treaty (n 173).

177 ibid, Arts 15 and 16.

178 Agreement setting up a Benelux Inter-Parliamentary Advisory Council (adopted 5 November 1955, entered into force 9 September 1956) 250 UNTS 201.

179 Art 18 Benelux Union Treaty (n 173).

180 See notably ibid, Art 21(1).

181 Treaty concerning the establishment and the statute of a Benelux Court of Justice (adopted 31 March 1965, entered into force 1 January 1974) 924 UNTS 41. See also Art 17 Benelux Union Treaty (n 173).

182 A Henkes, 'La Cour de Justice Benelux, ses missions et ses compétences' (2016) 21 *Intellectuele rechten* 112; A Braun, 'The Work of the Benelux Court of Justice in the Application of the Uniform Trademark Law' (1981) 20 *Industrial Property: Monthly Review of the World Intellectual Property Organization* 70.

183 Art 31 Benelux Union Treaty (n 173).

of persons, goods, capital and services; coordination of economic, financial-monetary and social politics; common foreign trade policy), it was soon overshadowed by the European Communities, even though the Benelux was (and is) explicitly authorised to integrate further than the EU as a whole and thereby to deviate from EU provisions.[184] Often, the Benelux countries consult closely in order to determine their common position within EU discussions. The organisation also provided the basis for the well-known Schengen Agreement, which abolished internal border controls between its parties, starting from 1985.[185]

The organisation is particularly important for concrete initiatives facilitating cross-border cooperation within Benelux, on both a centralised and decentralised level. For instance, the Benelux has taken a number of initiatives to facilitate cross-border cooperation between local governments[186] and mutual assistance for emergency services (firefighting, ambulance, etc). Based on a treaty on cross-border police action of 8 June 2004,[187] agents and equipment may be exchanged between Belgium, Luxembourg and the Netherlands. Under certain conditions, they may even operate on the territory of another Benelux State. In 2014, similar arrangements were made for road inspection.[188] Furthermore, the Benelux is also active in the field of frontier workers, the environment and nature conservation, spatial planning, traffic and youth.[189]

The Benelux's international legal personality was for a long time not recognised by its Member States. However, it is now assumed that the organisation has international legal personality.[190]

ii. Other Sub-regional Organisations in Europe

Elsewhere in Europe, States have also sought to engage in closer cooperation by uniting in sub-regional organisations.[191] While it is practically impossible to give a comprehensive

[184] See Art 350 TFEU. For a commentary, see J Wouters and M Vidal, 'Article IV-441' in L Burgorgue-Larsen, A Levade and F Picod (eds), *Traité établissant une Constitution pour l'Europe. Commentaire article par article*, I (Brussels, Bruylant, 2007) 781–90.

[185] See above (n 50).

[186] See notably the Benelux Convention on Cross-Border Cooperation between Territorial Partnerships or Authorities (adopted 12 September 1986, entered into force 1 April 1991) (1986) *Dutch Treaty Series ('Tractatenblad van het Koninkrijk der Nederlanden')* No 160, 1; and the Protocol supplementing the Benelux Convention on Transfrontier Cooperation between Territorial Networks or Authorities signed in Brussels on 12 September 1986 (adopted 22 September 1998, not entered into force) (1998) *Dutch Treaty Series* No 261, 1 (this protocol extends the scope of the agreement to other bodies with legal personality governed by public and under certain conditions even private law). The most recent instrument of relevance is the Benelux Convention on Cross-Border and Interterritorial Cooperation (adopted 20 February 2014, not yet entered into force) (2014) *Dutch Treaty Series* No 62, 1, which will, according to its Article 30(1), once it enters into force between certain parties, replace the 1986 Convention in the relations between those parties; and which, according to its Article 30(2), withdraws the 1998 Protocol.

[187] Benelux Treaty concerning Cross-Border Police Intervention (adopted 8 June 2004, entered into force 13 April 2010) (2005) *Dutch Treaty Series* No 35, 1.

[188] Benelux Treaty on Cross-Border Cooperation in respect of Road Transport Inspection (adopted 3 October 2014, entered into force 1 June 2017) UNTS Registration No 54487.

[189] See eg Adviesraad Internationale Vraagstukken, *The Benelux: The Benefits and Necessity of Enhanced Cooperation* (The Hague, Advisory Council on International Affairs, 2007).

[190] See Art 28 Benelux Union Treaty (n 173).

[191] See eg AJK Bailes and KT Olafsson, 'Northern Europe and the Arctic Agenda: Roles of Nordic and other Sub-Regional Organizations' (2013) 5 *The Yearbook of Polar Law* 45; A Cottey (ed), *Subregional Cooperation in the New Europe: Building Security, Prosperity and Solidarity from the Barents to the Black Sea* (Hampshire, MacMillan, 1999); A Cottey, 'Europe's new subregionalism' (2000) 23 *Journal of Strategic Studies* 23.

overview of the various organisations that have been set up, we attempt to give at least a condensed overview of the most prominent ones in the following.

In Northern Europe, the *Council of Baltic Sea States* (CBSS) has been set up as a political forum for regional intergovernmental cooperation. Its Members are the 11 States of the Baltic region (Denmark, Estonia, Finland, Germany, Iceland, Latvia, Lithuania, Norway, Poland, Russia, Sweden) and the European Commission. The Council has three long-term priorities: building a regional identity; ensuring a safe and secure region; and promoting sustainability and prosperity.[192] In the same region, the *Barents Euro-Arctic Council* is another political forum promoting regional cooperation in the Barents area. It comprises seven members: Denmark, Finland, Iceland, Norway, Russia, Sweden and the European Commission. A number of other European countries and the United States have observer status. The main objective of the Barents cooperation is sustainable development.[193]

In Central Europe, the Visegrad Group and the Central European Initiative are the most noteworthy. The *Visegrad Group* aims at enhancing the cooperation between its four members (Czech Republic, Hungary, Poland and Slovakia), but also with other countries in the region and the EU. The objectives are to preserve and promote cultural cohesion between its members, and to contribute to European security and integration.[194] The *Central European Initiative* (CEI) is also an intergovernmental forum to support regional cooperation and integration between its 18 members (Albania, Austria, Belarus, Bosnia and Herzegovina, Bulgaria, Croatia, Czech Republic, Hungary, Italy, Macedonia, Moldova, Montenegro, Poland, Romania, Serbia, Slovakia, Slovenia and Ukraine). Its main objectives are: supporting its members in the process of European integration, promoting the alignment to EU standards, and implementing projects in various areas of cooperation.

South-Eastern Europe also has a number of sub-regional organisations aimed at enhancing regional cooperation. The *Organization of the Black Sea Economic Cooperation* (BSEC)[195] has 12 members: Albania, Armenia, Azerbaijan, Bulgaria, Georgia, Greece, Moldova, Romania, Russia, Serbia, Turkey and Ukraine. The areas of cooperation range from agriculture to tourism, banking and combating crime.[196] The *Central European Free Trade Agreement* (CEFTA)[197] has economic development as its core aim. Despite its name, this agreement now mainly concerns South East Europe, as Bulgaria, Romania and Croatia withdrew following their accession to EU. Its seven State parties (Albania, Bosnia, Macedonia, Moldova, Montenegro, Serbia and the United Nations Interim Administration Mission in Kosovo on behalf of Kosovo) have agreed to focus on four priorities: trade

[192] N Germanas, 'The Council of the Baltic Sea States (CBDD) and other Forms of Cooperation in the Baltic Sea Region' in ED Stratenschulte (ed), *Das europäische Meer: die Ostsee als Handlungsraum* (Berlin, Berliner Wissenschafts-Verlag, 2011) 21; A Krohn, 'The Council of the Baltic Sea States (CBSS): Fostering Cooperation in the Baltic Sea Region' (2000) 43 *GYIL* 65.

[193] P Aalto et al, 'The Coordination of Policy Priorities among Regional Institutions from the Baltic Sea to the Arctic: The Institutions – Coordination Dilemma' (2017) 48 *Journal of Baltic Studies* 135, 149; and P Joenniemi, 'The Barents Euro-Arctic Council' in Cottey (n 191) 23.

[194] M Dangerfield, 'The Contribution of the Visegrad Group to the European Union's 'Eastern' Policy: Rhetoric or Reality?' in J Gower and G Timmins (eds), *The European Union, Russia and the Shared Neighbourhood* (London, Routledge, 2011) 51.

[195] Charter of the Organization of the Black Sea Economic Cooperation (adopted 5 June 1998, entered into force 1 May 1999).

[196] P Naskou-Perrakis, *Black Sea Economic Cooperation: Basic Texts* (Athens, Sakkoulas, 2001); G Konidaris, 'The Black Sea Economic Cooperation Scheme' in GD Hook and I Kearns (eds), *Subregionalism and World Order* (Basingstoke, MacMillan, 1999) 41.

[197] Central European Free Trade Agreement (adopted 21 December 1992, entered into force July 1994) 34 ILM 8.

facilitation, trade in services, investment, and transparency.[198] The *Regional Cooperation Council* (RCC) is the successor of the Southeast European Cooperative Initiative (SECI) and the EU Stability Pact for South Eastern Europe, which aimed at building peace and security in the region. Its 46 participants (the EU and South-East European countries, but also the US and certain international organisations[199]) now focus more on regional integration and promoting development.[200]

G. Other Organisations in Europe

In addition to the organisations discussed above, Europe has a whole range of other – often technical – organisations. The *European Free Trade Association* (EFTA) was established in 1960 between Denmark, Norway, Portugal, the UK, Sweden and Switzerland.[201] Later, Finland, Iceland and Liechtenstein joined, but Denmark, Finland, Austria, Portugal, the UK and Sweden withdrew from EFTA when they joined the EU. Today, the organisation has four Member States: Iceland, Liechtenstein, Norway and Switzerland. On 21 June 2001, the founding treaty was revised in Vaduz. Iceland, Liechtenstein and Norway are, together with the EU Member States and the EU, also members of the *European Economic Area* (EEA).[202] In addition to a Secretariat, the EEA has a Surveillance Authority (based in Brussels) and a Court (based in Luxembourg) which monitor compliance with the EEA Agreement by Iceland, Liechtenstein and Norway. EFTA also houses the EFTA Development Fund (EFTA-DF) and the EFTA Industrial Development Fund (EFTA-IFP).[203]

The *European Bank for Reconstruction and Development* (EBRD) was founded in 1990[204] to facilitate the transition from European planned economies to market economies and has 65 Member States together with the EU and the European Investment Bank.[205] The *European Space Agency* (ESA) is discussed in Chapter 18, Section XII(D).

There are also a number of other organisations with limited membership active on the European territory, including the *Central Rhine Commission*, which focuses on the freedom of navigation, and uniform rules and equal treatment for shipping on the Rhine.

[198] M Dangerfield, *Subregional Economic Cooperation in Central and Eastern Europe: The Political Economy of CEFTA* (Cheltenham, Edward Elgar, 2000); M Petreski, 'Southeastern European Trade Analysis: A Role for Endogenous CEFTA-2006?' (2013) 49 *Emerging Markets Finance and Trade* 26.

[199] These include the EU, OSCE, EBRD, the European Investment Bank, the Council of Europe as well as its Development Bank, IOM, SECI, NATO, UN, UNDP, UN Economic Commission for Europe and the World Bank.

[200] E Busek (ed), *Ten Years Southeast European Cooperative Initiative: From Dayton to Brussels* (Wien, Springer, 2006).

[201] Convention establishing the European Free Trade Association (adopted 4 January 1960, entered into force 3 May 1960) 370 UNTS 3.

[202] See the Agreement on the European Economic Area (adopted 2 May 1992, entered into force 1 January 1994) 1801 UNTS 4.

[203] R Gschwend and P Poretti, 'The Role of the European Free Trade Association Secretariat and Select Legal Aspects of EFTA Free Trade Agreements' in AH Qureishi and X Gao (ed), *International Economic Organizations and Law: The Perspective and Role of the Legal Counsel* (Alphen aan den Rijn, Kluwer, 2012) 351.

[204] Agreement establishing the European Bank for Reconstruction and Development (adopted 29 May 1990, entered into force 28 March 1991) 1646 UNTS 97.

[205] R Kastratović, 'European Bank for Reconstruction and Development' (2015) 44(2) *Bankarstvo* 74, 77; and J Linarelli, 'The European Bank for Reconstruction and Development: legal and policy issues' (1995) 18(2) *Boston College International and Comparative Law Review* 361.

Among the rather technical organisations there are: the International Commission of Civil Status (ICCS), the European and Mediterranean Plant Protection Organization (EPPO), the North Atlantic Marine Mammal Commission (NAMCO), the North Atlantic Salmon Conservation Organization (NASCO), North-East Atlantic Fisheries Commission (NEAFC), Northwest Atlantic Fisheries Organization (NAFO), the European Organization for Nuclear Research (CERN), the European Organization of Experimental Photogrammetric Studies (OEEPE), the FAO Commission for the control of Foot-and-Mouth disease (EuFMD), the European Company for the Financing of Railroad Equipment (EUROFIMA), the European Organization for the Safety of Air Navigation (Eurocontrol), the European Organization for Astronomical Research in the Southern Hemisphere (ESO), the European Patent Office (EPO), the European Centre for Medium-Range Weather Forecasts (ECMWF), the European Organization for the Exploitation of Meteorological Satellites (EUMETSAT), the Organization for Joint Armament Cooperation (OCCAR), and the European Molecular Biology Laboratory (EMBL).

III. Regional Organisations in the Americas

A. The Organization of American States

The OAS was formed in 1948,[206] rising out of the 1910 Pan-American Union, which had in turn built on the achievements of the various inter-American Conferences that had taken place since 1890. The OAS structure is based on the 1947 Inter-American Treaty of Reciprocal Assistance (Rio Treaty),[207] which entails a collective self-defence mechanism, and the 1948 OAS Charter[208] and American Treaty on Pacific Settlement (Pact of Bogotá).[209] The OAS currently consists of 35 Member States and therefore covers virtually the entire American continent. The OAS is a typical intergovernmental organisation.[210] All its decisions are taken by consensus and do not legally bind its Member States.[211] Given its intergovernmental nature, the agenda of the OAS is determined by State and Government leaders during the Summit of the Americas. So far there have been eight of these meetings. The organs of the OAS are responsible for the implementation and the monitoring of the decisions taken at the Summit. The highest decision-making body of the OAS is the General Assembly, which consists of the foreign ministers of its Member States. The Assembly meets annually and determines the general OAS policies.

[206] Art 1 Charter of the Organization of American States (adopted 30 April 1948, entered into force 13 December 1951) 119 UNTS 3 (OAS Charter). The Charter was amended by the 1967 Buenos Aires Protocol, the 1985 Cartagena de Indias Protocol, the 1992 Washington Protocol and the 1993 Managua Protocol.

[207] Inter-American Treaty of Reciprocal Assistance and Final Act of the Inter-American Conference for the Maintenance of Continental Peace and Security (adopted 2 September 1947, entered into force 3 December 1948) 21 UNTS 147 (Rio Treaty).

[208] See above (n 206).

[209] American Treaty on Pacific Settlement (adopted 30 April 1948, entered into force 1949) 30 UNTS 55 (Pact of Bogotá).

[210] For a general overview, see eg B Horwitz, *The Transformation of the Organization of American States: A Multilateral Framework for Regional Governance* (London, Anthem Press, 2011); M Herz, *The Organization of American States (OAS): Global Governance Away from the Media* (London, Routledge, 2011); JM Arrighi (ed), *La OEA y el derecho internacional* (Mexico, Editorial Porrua, 2015).

[211] CM Shaw, *Cooperation, Conflict, and Consensus in the Organization of American States* (New York, Palgrave Macmillan, 2004).

The OAS mainly focuses on the strengthening of democracy (including through election monitoring), the protection of human rights, the promotion of peace and security, the expansion of free trade and the tackling of structural societal issues, such as poverty, drugs and corruption.[212] The 1928 Inter-American Commission of Women is part of the OAS framework. In addition, the American Declaration of Rights and Duties of Man was adopted in 1948[213] and the Inter-American Commission on Human Rights was established in 1959. In 1969, the OAS adopted the American Convention on Human Rights (Pact of San José).[214] This convention came into force in 1978, just when the Inter-American Court of Human Rights came into existence. In 1994, the Inter-American Convention on the Prevention, Punishment and Eradication of Violence against Women (Convention of Belém do Para)[215] was adopted as the first of only two legal instruments focusing on violence against women.[216] The Inter-American human rights system is discussed in more detail in Chapter 16, Section XI(A)(i).

In 2001, the OAS adopted the Inter-American Democratic Charter,[217] followed by a Social Charter in 2012.[218] Other instruments adopted within the context of the OAS are the Inter-American Convention against Corruption (1996),[219] the Inter-American Convention against Terrorism (2002),[220] the Declaration on Security in the Americas (2003),[221] the Inter-American Convention against Racism, Racial Discrimination and Related Forms of Intolerance (2013),[222] the Inter-American Convention against All Forms of Discrimination and Intolerance (2013),[223] and the Inter-American Convention on Protecting the Human Rights of Older Persons (2015).[224]

Day-to-day management is conducted by the Permanent Council, composed of one ambassador per Member State. The Council looks into matters which have been referred

[212] See eg H Caminos, 'The role of the Organization of American States in the promotion and protection of democratic governance' (1998) 273 *RdC* 103; N Ramis, 'La OEA y la promoción de la democracia en las Américas: un objetivo en construcción' (2010) ICIP working paper No 2010/07; YA Soto, 'The Role of the Organization of American States in Conflict' in A Schnabel (ed), *Conflict Prevention from Rhetoric to Reality* (Lanham, Lexington Books, 2004) 223; and E Spehar, 'Democracy in Our Hemisphere and the Role of the Organization of American States' (1998) 11 *Revue Québécoise de droit international* 35.

[213] American Declaration of Rights and Duties of Man (2 May 1948) OEA/Ser.L./V.II.23, doc 21, rev 6.

[214] American Convention on Human Rights (adopted 22 November 1969, entered into force 18 July 1978) 1144 UNTS 143 (Pact of San José). Further, see eg C Medina Quiroga, *The American Convention on Human Rights: Crucial Rights and Their Theory and Practice* (Cambridge, Intersentia, 2016).

[215] Inter-American Convention on the Prevention, Punishment and Eradication of Violence Against Women (adopted 9 June 1994, entered into force 5 March 1995) ATS No A-61 (Convention of Belém do Para).

[216] See also the Council of Europe Convention on Preventing and Combating Violence against Women and Domestic Violence (adopted 11 May 2011, entered into force 1 August 2014) CETS No 210; see above, p 312.

[217] Inter-American Democratic Charter (11 September 2001) 40 ILM 1289 (Lima Declaration). See also B Sarante, 'A System of Collective Defense of Democracy: The Case of the Inter-American Democratic Charter' (2011) 3 *Goettingen Journal of International Law* 675.

[218] Social Charter of the Americas (4 June 2012) OEA/Ser.P, AG/doc.5242/12 rev.2.

[219] Inter-American Convention against Corruption (adopted 29 March 1996, entered into force 6 March 1997) ATS No B-58.

[220] Inter-American Convention against Terrorism (adopted 3 June 2002, entered into force 10 July 2003) ATS No A-66. See also M de los Angeles Cano Linares, 'La labor de la OEA en la lucha contra el terrorismo internacional' in CM Diaz Barrado (ed), *Guía del espacio iberoamericano de paz, seguridad y defensa* (Madrid, Instituto Universitario General Gutierrez Mellado – UNED, 2010) 67.

[221] Declaration on Security in the Americas (28 October 2003) OEA/Ser.K/XXXVIII, CES/DEC.1/03 rev 1.

[222] Inter-American Convention against Racism, Racial Discrimination and Related Forms of Intolerance (adopted 5 June 2013, not entered into force) ATS No A-68.

[223] Inter-American Convention against All Forms of Discrimination and Intolerance (adopted 5 June 2013, not entered into force) ATS No A-69.

[224] Inter-American Convention on Protecting the Human Rights of Older Persons (adopted 15 June 2015, entered into force 11 January 2017) ATS No A-70.

to it by the General Assembly or the Secretary General. The Council has the competence to settle disputes peacefully. However, the unwillingness of the Member States to use the Permanent Council as a forum for discussion on domestic affairs, due to considerations of sovereignty, stands in the way of the OAS becoming a proper mechanism for the promotion of democracy through information sharing. The Secretary General acts as a catalyst and plays an important mediation role in disputes, and is thus comparable to the Secretary General of the UN.

The OAS also has a large number of bodies related to specific thematic areas, such as the Inter-American Committee against Terrorism (CICTE), the Inter-American Drug Abuse Control Commission (CICAD) and the Pan American Development Foundation (PADF).

B. Other Regional and Sub-Regional Organisations in the Americas

Apart from the OAS, the Americas count many regional organisations, such as the Southern Common Market (Mercosur), the North American Free Trade Agreement (NAFTA), the Andean Community, two Caribbean organisations (the CARICOM and the Association of Caribbean States), and other organisations like the Latin American and Caribbean Economic System (SELA), the Central American Integration System (SICA), the Latin American Integration Association (ALADI), and the Inter-American Development Bank (IADB). Each of these is discussed below.

i. Mercosur

Mercosur (*el Mercado Común del Sur* – the Southern Common Market) was founded in 1991 by Argentina, Brazil, Paraguay and Uruguay in the Treaty of Asunción.[225] Beside the four founding states, Venezuela is also full member. However, due to internal turmoil, the latter's membership was suspended in December 2016. Bolivia has been a candidate to full membership since 2015.[226] Colombia, Ecuador, Peru, Chile, Guyana and Surinam are associated members. With a GDP of US$4.6 trillion and a population of 293 million, Mercosur forms the fifth largest economic entity in the world.[227]

As stated in the Asunción Treaty, Mercosur mainly focuses on the realisation of a free trade area and customs union among its Member States.[228] By way of a system of progressive liberalisation, tariff and non-tariff barriers have for the most part been lifted. Since 2000, all products are subject to Mercosur rules. In 1995 Mercosur reached the stage of a customs union, resulting in a common trade policy in relation to third countries.

The development of Mercosur was arguably weakened with the collapse of the Argentinean economy in 2001 and internal disagreement regarding trade policies among

[225] Treaty establishing a Common Market between the Argentine Republic, the Federal Republic of Brazil, the Republic of Paraguay and the Eastern Republic of Uruguay (adopted 26 March 1991, entered into force 29 November 1991) 2140 UNTS 257 (Treaty of Asunción).

[226] Mercosur, 'Bolivia ingresa al Mercosur', July 2016, mercosur.int/innovaportal/v/6923/2/innova.front/bolivia-ingresa-al-mercosur; and ML Olivar Jimenez, 'La adhesión de nuevos miembros al Mercosur: una cuestión fundamental para la evolución de la organización' in C Flaesch-Mougin and J Lebullenger (eds), *Regards croisés sur les intégrations régionales: Europe, Amériques, Afrique* (Brussels, Bruylant, 2010) 53.

[227] These figures include Venezuela.

[228] C Edler, *Die Integration der Südamerikanischen Staaten durch den Mercosur* (München, Herbert Utz Verlag, 2013).

the four founding States. Another factor is the reliance on the existing functional domestic regulatory institutions, as opposed to introducing new supranational institutions and creating immediately enforceable rules, as the main obstacle to the harmonisation process.

The Asunción Treaty did not provide for any central institutions for Mercosur. Following the example of the EU, the institutional structure of the organisation was enshrined in the 1994 Protocol of Ouro Preto.[229] On the basis of the Protocol, Mercosur enjoys international legal personality. Although Mercosur did envisage the creation of a common market, a common policy and economic and monetary union, it functions as an intergovernmental system. Its institutions are the Council of the Common Market, in which ministers meet; the Group for the Common Market, in which ambassadors sit; and a Trade Commission.[230] Mercosur also has a large number of technical committees, working groups and ad hoc groups that specialise in areas such as industry, competition, environment, cooperation, agriculture and customs. All organs consist of representatives of the Member States, who take decisions on a consensual basis. The presidency rotates every six months among the Member States. In addition, Mercosur has several EU-inspired bodies, such as the Joint Parliamentary Committee (16 members from each national Parliament), the Economic and Social Consultative Forum (similar to the EU Economic and Social Committee) and the Administrative Secretariat of Mercosur (similar to the General Secretariat of Ministers of the EU Council).

In 2002, the Member States founded a Committee of Permanent Representatives and a dispute settlement mechanism.[231] However, as noted above, unlike the EU, Mercosur does not have strong technical bodies with the authority to adopt and implement common rules. The Permanent Representatives Committee is authorised to coordinate all Mercosur organs, to support the Mercosur Council, to develop the integration process and, in particular, to represent Mercosur in its relations with third countries and international organisations. The resolution of commercial disputes often requires the intervention of the four presidents. A permanent court now acts as the appellate court for the ad hoc arbitration mechanism established in 1991,[232] even though this court may be seised directly as well.

[229] Additional Protocol to the Treaty of Asunción on the Institutional Structure of MERCOSUR (adopted 17 December 1994, entered into force 15 December 1995) 2145 UNTS 298 (Protocol of Ouro Preto).

[230] PB Casella, 'Mercosur' in Wouters (n 11); A Dreyzin De Klor, 'The Legal-Institutional Structure of MERCOSUR' in MT Franca Filho, L Lixinski and MB Olmos Giupponi (eds), *The Law of MERCOSUR* (Oxford, Hart, 2010) 39; EI Rimoldi de Ladmann, 'La Comisión de Comercio en el Mercosur' in J Irigoin Barrenne (ed), *Chile y el Mercosur en América Latina: VI Encuentro International de Derecho en América del Sur* (Santiago, Ed Juridica de Chile, 1999) 437; and F Seatzu, 'The Southern Common Market (Mercosur)' in M Odello and F Seatzu (eds), *Latin American and Caribbean International Institutional Law* (The Hague, TMC Asser Press, 2015) 169.

[231] Olivos Protocol for the Solution of Controversies in the Mercosur (adopted 18 February 2002, entered into force 1 January 2004) 2251 UNTS 243.

[232] Brasília Protocol for the Solution of Controversies (adopted 17 December 1991, entered into force 22 April 1993) 2145 UNTS 252. See also C Castro, 'La solución de controversias entre estados miembros del Mercosur' in M Di Filippo (ed), *Organizzazioni regionali, modello sovranazionale e metodo intergovernativo: I casi dell'Unione Europea e del Mercosur* (Torino, Giappichelli, 2012) 123; EJ Rey Caro, 'La solución de controversias en el Mercosur: hacia nuevos mecanismos' in M Hinojo Rojas (ed), *Liber amicorum Profesor José Manuel Pelaez Maron: derecho internacional y derecho de la Unión Europea* (Cordoba, Universidad de Cordoba, 2012) 717; W Barral, 'Dispute Settlement and Legal Harmonization in Mercosur' in L Cata Backer (ed), *Harmonizing Law in an Era of Globalization: Convergence, Divergence, and Resistance* (Durham, Carolina Academic Press, 2007) 129; D Opertti, 'The New Mercosur Dispute Settlement Mechanism' in J Lacarte (ed), *Inter-governmental Trade Dispute Settlement: Multilateral and Regional Approaches* (London, Cameron May, 2004) 229; N Susani, *Le règlement des différends dans le Mercosur: un système de droit international pour une organisation d'intégration* (Paris, L'Harmattan, 2008).

The Ushuaia Protocol[233] has made the undisturbed functioning of democratic institutions an essential precondition for the positive evolution of the integration process. In the event of a disruption of the democratic order in any of the Member and Associated States, the other States will consult with the State in question. If the consultation proves unsuccessful, participation can be suspended, either from the decision-making organ or in terms of its rights and obligations in the framework, or in its association with Mercosur.

On 8 December 2004, at the Third South American Summit, the representatives of 12 South American countries signed the Cusco Declaration.[234] In May 2008 this led to the Union of South American States (UNASUR), which brings together Member States of the Andean Community and Mercosur.[235] The group acts as an intergovernmental forum for interaction between Member State leaders and also serves as a platform for interregional trade promotion. On 26 November 2010, during the South American Summit, an amendment was introduced to the UNASUR Treaty, specifying measures to be taken against Member States whose political choices run counter to the organisation's principles. The clause established sanctions, such as shutting down borders and trade suspension.

Mercosur has developed a strong relationship with the EU since the early 1990s. While limited cooperation agreements had already been adopted in the 1970s, the third generation cooperation agreements, signed between 1990 and 1992, paved the way for the Interinstitutional Cooperation Agreement[236] and the EU-Mercosur Interregional Framework Cooperation Agreement.[237] The first agreement aims at strengthening Mercosur by allowing it to benefit from the European experience in regional integration. The objective of the latter agreement is to allow for negotiations on an interregional association agreement between the two regional organisations.[238] Although progress has been achieved at the two negotiation rounds in 2016 and 2017, many obstacles still remain.[239]

ii. NAFTA

The North American Free Trade Agreement (NAFTA) was concluded in 1992 between Canada, the United States and Mexico and aims to ensure the free movement and liberalisation of goods and services, people and investment.[240] NAFTA is not a real international organisation, although it does have a limited institutional structure, comparable to the General Agreement on Tariffs and Trade (GATT; on which see Chapter 19, Section III(A)). In particular, the bodies of NAFTA are the Free Trade Commission and

[233] Ushuaia Protocol on Democratic Commitment in the Mercosur, the Republic of Bolivia and the Republic of Chile (adopted 24 July 1998, entered into force 17 January 2002) 2177 UNTS 373.

[234] Cusco Declaration on the South American Community of Nations, 8 December 2004, europarl.europa.eu/meetdocs/2004_2009/documents/fd/200/200412/20041216_03_d.pdf.

[235] Constitutive Treaty of the Union of South American Nations (adopted 23 May 2008, entered into force 11 March 2011) 2742 UNTS 287 (UNASUR Treaty).

[236] Interinstitutional Cooperation Agreement between the Southern Common Market Council and the Commission of the European Communities (29 May 1992).

[237] Interregional Framework Cooperation Agreement between the European Community and its Member States, of the one part, and the Southern Common Market and its Party States, of the other part (adopted 15 December 1995, entered into force 1 July 1999) [1996] OJ L69/4.

[238] GG Müller et al, *The EU-Latin American Strategic Partnership: State of Play and Ways Forward* (Brussels, European Parliament, 2017) 42–43.

[239] S Santander, 'Can Regional Blocs (Still) Talk with Each Other? The Euro-Mercosur Relationship' (2016) 2/33 *World Affairs* 83.

[240] North American Free Trade Agreement (adopted 17 December 1992, entered into force 1 January 1994) 32 ILM 289.

the NAFTA Secretariat. These institutions are responsible for the implementation of NAFTA and related agreements on labour and environmental cooperation.[241]

The Free Trade Commission is NAFTA's key institution and it brings together the Ministers of Trade of each State Party. It is not a permanent body, but gathers yearly or whenever necessary. The Commission is responsible for the implementation of NAFTA and oversees the NAFTA committees and working groups, which are in charge of the daily implementation of the Agreement. It also provides assistance to the resolution of disputes which may arise in relation to NAFTA.

The Secretariat, which consists of national sections, is responsible for providing assistance to the Commission, several dispute related panels and committees, as well as for supporting other committees and working groups. The Secretariat manages the NAFTA dispute settlement procedure under Chapters 11 (Investment Disputes), 14 (disputes concerning financial services), 19 (antidumping) and 20 (other cases), which are the principal mechanisms.[242] Each national section is responsible for the registration of proceedings taken before the panels, committees and tribunals.

iii. Andean Community

The Andean Community (*Comunidad Andina*) is a regional organisation with international legal personality, consisting of Bolivia, Colombia, Ecuador and Peru. It comprises a number of organs and institutions striving towards sub-regional integration in the Andes region.[243] The Andean Community's structure bears striking resemblance to that of the EU. Its legal system is supranational rather than merely intergovernmental. The Community rules have direct effect in the legal order of its Member States and take precedence over national legislation.

The Andean Community is rooted in the Cartagena Agreement or Andean Pact of 1969.[244] The objectives of this agreement are the liberalisation of trade in goods between the Andean countries, the introduction of a common customs tariff and the harmonisation of economic policies. In 2003, the WTO was informed that the Andean Community had become a customs union. To deepen the integration, the Trujillo Protocol[245] brought into existence an ambitious institutional structure (the Andean Integration System or AIS).

The highest body of the AIS is the Presidential Council of the Andes (similar to the European Council). The Council was established in 1979 and consists of the presidents of

[241] For a general overview, see eg RH Folsom (ed), *NAFTA and Free Trade in the Americas in a Nutshell*, 4th edn (St Paul, West, 2012); T Kay, *NAFTA and the Politics of Labor Transnationalism* (Cambridge, CUP, 2011).

[242] See eg ALC De Mestral, 'NAFTA Dispute Settlement: Creative Experiment or Confusion?' in L Bartels and F Ortino (eds), *Regional Trade Agreements and the WTO Legal System* (Oxford, OUP, 2006) 359; WA Kerr, 'Trade Dispute Settlement Mechanisms: Tthe Nafta versus the WTO' in N Perdikis and R Read (eds), *The WTO and the Regulation of International Trade: Recent Trade Disputes between the European Union and the United States* (Cheltenham, Edward Elgar, 2005) 49.

[243] For a general overview, see eg FV Garcia-Amador, *The Andean Legal Order: a New Community Law* (Dobbs Ferry, Oceana Publications, 1978); M Odello, 'The Andean Community of Nations' in Odello and Seatzu (n 230) 125; R Schembri Carrasquilla and C Nunez Rivero, 'La Comunidad Andina de Naciones (CAN)' (2015) 16 *Revista de derecho UNED* 663; A Vilela, 'Andean Common Market' in Wouters (n 11).

[244] Andean Subregional Integration Agreement (adopted 26 May 1969, entered into force 16 October 1969) (Cartagena Agreement).

[245] Protocol Modifying the Andean Subregional Integration Agreement (adopted 10 March 1996, entered into force 3 June 1997) (Trujillo Protocol). See also Vilela (n 243) 57; and JL Da Cruz Vilaça, 'Del Pacto a la Comunidad Andina: el Protocolo de Trujillo de 10 de marzo de 1996: simple reforma institucional o profundización en la integración subregional?' (1996) 26 *Gaceta jurídica de la CEE* 83.

the Member States determining the political direction of the AIS. The other political body is the Council of Ministers of Foreign Affairs of the Andes (similar to the Council of the EU). This Council is responsible for achieving the integration objectives and the foreign policy of the Andean Community. The Court of Justice oversees the implementation of the decisions taken by the latter. The Council also prepares the meetings of the Presidential Council, appoints the Secretary-General, reviews the functioning of the General Secretariat and considers the initiatives and proposals of Member States. The main policy-making body of the AIS is the Commission of the Andean Community (similar to the European Commission), which consists of a representative of each Member State. It shares the power to legislate with the Council of Ministers and takes sectoral decisions with direct effect in the Member States.

The executive agency of the AIS is the General Secretariat (also similar to the European Commission), which is supervised by the Secretary General. The General Secretariat has a right to present initiatives to the Council of Ministers and the Commission. The judicial organ of the AIS is the Court of Justice of the Andean Community, which oversees the legality of Community acts, their uniform application in the Member States and settles disputes. The Court has been in existence since 1979 and operational since 1983, and has expanded its competences particularly since 1999. The AIS also has a Parliament with a mere advisory role which currently consists of representatives of the national parliaments. Yet, the 1997 Protocol of Sucre[246] envisages directly-elected members in the future.

The Protocol on the 'Andean Community Commitment to Democracy',[247] like the Ushuaia Protocol, considers the functioning of democratic institutions in a Member State as a precondition for regional integration within the Andean Community. However, the Protocol has not yet entered into force. Under the Cusco Declaration of 8 December 2004, the Andean Community merged with Mercosur into the UNASUR (see above, Section III(B)(i)).

iv. Caribbean Organisations

Four main developments led to the establishment of the *Caribbean Community and Common Market* (CARICOM) in 1973 by way of the Treaty of Chaguaramas.[248] The rather lengthy process towards greater regional integration began with the Conference of leaders of Government in 1963, the establishment of the Caribbean Free Trade Association (CARIFTA)[249] in 1965, the establishment of a Regional Secretariat in 1968 and the Caribbean Development Bank in 1969.[250] Today, CARICOM has 15 Member States: Barbados, Jamaica, Guyana, Antigua and Barbuda, Trinidad and Tobago, Dominica, Grenada, St Kitts and Nevis, Montserrat, Belize, Bahamas, St Vincent and the Grenadines, Saint Lucia,

[246] Protocol Modifying the Andean Subregional Integration Agreement (adopted 25 June 1997, entered into force 25 June 1997) (Protocol of Sucre).

[247] Additional Protocol to the Cartagena Agreement 'Andean Community Commitment to Democracy' (adopted 27 October 1998, not entered into force) sice.oas.org/CAN/Protdemc_e.asp.

[248] Treaty establishing the Caribbean Community (adopted 4 July 1973, entered into force 1 August 1973) 946 UNTS 17 (Treaty of Chaguaramas). See also F Seatzu, 'The Caribbean Community' in Odello and Seatzu (n 230) 219; and E Vigliar, 'L'Integrazione Caribica dal CARIFTA al CARICOM' (1983) 38 *La Comunità Internazionale: rivista trimestrale delle Società Italiana per l'Organizzazione Internazionale* 513.

[249] Agreement establishing the Caribbean Free Trade Association (adopted 15 December 1965, entered into force 1 May 1968) 772 UNTS 4.

[250] Agreement establishing the Caribbean Development Bank (adopted 18 October 1969, entered into force 26 January 1970) 712 UNTS 217.

Suriname and Haiti. The organisation also has five associated members (Anguilla, Bermuda, British Virgin Islands, Cayman Islands, Turks and Caicos Islands). Since its establishment, CARICOM has focused on the integration of Caribbean economies, the coordination of the foreign policies of the Member States and functional cooperation. Since 2001, the Community has been functioning within the framework of the Revised Treaty of Chaguaramas,[251] including the establishment of the CARICOM Single Market and Economy (CSME).

CARICOM has two main bodies: the Conference of Heads of Government and the Community Council of Ministers. The Conference is its highest organ, as it determines policy direction and is responsible for the common foreign policy of the Organization. Since 1992, the Conference has had a Bureau in charge of policy preparation, building consensus between the Member States and facilitating the implementation of decisions. The Community Council of Ministers is responsible for the development of strategic planning and the coordination with regard to economic integration, functional cooperation and foreign relations. The Caribbean Development Bank and the Organization of Eastern Caribbean States (OECS)[252] are institutions associated to CARICOM. In 2001, a Caribbean Court of Justice was established,[253] which began its activities on 16 April 2005.[254]

Regional integration in the Caribbean is also pursued by the *Association of Caribbean States* (ACS),[255] established in 1994. This association has 25 Member States and 12 Associate Members, focusing on trade, transport, sustainable tourism and natural disasters. The political direction of the ACS is set at meetings between the State and government leaders. The main bodies are the Council of Ministers, which meets annually, and the Secretariat, which determines the day-to-day policy. The ACS also has a number of specialised committees and a Council of National Representatives, responsible for managing a special fund for financing project development.[256]

v. *Other Latin American Organisations*

Latin America has a number of other intergovernmental organisations, such as the Latin American Economic System, the Central American Integration System, the Latin American Integration Association and the Inter-American Development Bank.

The *Latin American and Caribbean Economic System* (SELA) was founded in 1975 by the Panama Convention[257] and brings together 28 Latin American and Caribbean

[251] Protocol on the revision of the Treaty of Chaguaramas (adopted 4 February 2002, entered into force 4 February 2002) 2260 UNTS 47.

[252] Treaty establishing the Organisation of Eastern Caribbean States (adopted 18 June 1981, entered into force 2 July 1982) 1338 UNTS 97. This organisation has four organs (the Eastern Caribbean Telecommunications Authority, the Directorate of Civil Aviation, the Eastern Caribbean Central Bank and the Eastern Caribbean Supreme Court) and 10 members (Dominica, Grenada, St Kitts and Nevis, Saint Lucia, St Vincent and the Grenadines, Martinique, Montserrat, British Virgin Islands, Anguilla, and Antigua and Barbuda).

[253] Agreement establishing the Caribbean Court of Justice (adopted 14 February 2001, entered into force 23 July 2002) 2255 UNTS 319.

[254] See eg P Thiery, 'Karibische Gemeinschaft (CARICOM)' in A Grimmel and C Jakobeit (eds), *Regionale Integration: Erklärungsansätze und Analysen zu den wichtigsten Integrationszusammenschlüssen in der Welt* (Baden-Baden, Nomos, 2015) 357; BTI Pollard, 'The Caribbean Community (CARICOM): Its Structure and Functions' (2003) 2 *Cursos de derecho internacional* 1519.

[255] Convention establishing the Association of Caribbean States (adopted 24 July 1994, entered into force 4 August 1995) 1895 UNTS 3.

[256] For a general overview, see eg AJ Payne, 'The Association of Caribbean States' in Hook and Kearns (n 196) 117. See also Seatzu (n 248) 223, fn 5.

[257] Panama Convention establishing the Latin American Economic System (SELA) (adopted 17 October 1975, entered into force 7 June 1976) 1292 UNTS 337. See eg L Marinas Otero, 'El "Sistema económico latinoamericano"

countries. The Latin American Council is its main decision-making body. Each Member State has one representative in this Council, which meets every year. It is responsible for defining the general policy direction of the organisation and takes specific decisions by consensus. The Permanent Secretariat is the technical-administrative organ of SELA. SELA also has a number of ad hoc and standing committees, which develop joint projects in specific fields of action. The organisation mainly concentrates on the integration of Latin America into the world economy.

The *Central American Integration System* (SICA) was created by the Protocol of Tegucigalpa[258] in 1991. SICA stems from the 1951 Organization of Central American States and the 1960 Central American Common Market.[259] SICA includes Guatemala, El Salvador, Honduras, Nicaragua, Costa Rica, Panama, Belize and the Dominican Republic, as well as nine regional observers and 17 extraregional observers. It aims to realise the integration of Central America by strengthening democracy and human rights protection, stimulating sustainable development and creating an economic union and common foreign policy. The Meeting of Presidents is the supreme body of SICA and it determines SICA policies on democracy, development, freedom, peace and security. The decisions of the Meeting are implemented by the Council of Ministers, the Executive Committee, the General Secretariat of SICA, the Consultative Committee, the Central American Parliament, the Central American Court of Human Rights and the Meeting of Central American Vice Presidents. A number of specialised technical secretariats work under the authority of SICA. The Secretariat for Central American Integration (SIECA) is a separate legal entity which provides technical and administrative assistance to SICA. SIECA works closely with the General Secretariat of SICA and focuses on the optimisation of the common market and the role of Central America in the global economy.[260]

The *Latin American Integration Association* (ALADI)[261] was founded by the 1980 Montevideo Convention.[262] It derives from the Latin American Free Trade Association, established in 1960. The ALADI has 12 members and pursues the establishment of a common market and policy coordination among its Member States. It considers itself an umbrella organisation aimed at supporting sub-regional integration associations. It has three political bodies: the Council of Ministers of Foreign Affairs, the Conference for Evaluation and Convergence and the Committee of Representatives. The General Secretariat is the technical body of the ALADI. The ALADI was involved in the integration of Mercosur and the Andean Community in the South American Community of Nations (now UNASUR; see above, Section III(B)(iii)).

(SELA)' (1978) 159 *Revista de política internacional* 137; and F Quispe Remón, 'The Economic System in Latin America and the Caribbean: A Commitment to the Development of the Region's Nations' in Odello and Seatzu (n 230) 1 ff.

258 Tegucigalpa Protocol to the Charter of the Organization of Central American States (OCAS) of 12 December 1962 (adopted 13 December 1991, entered into force 23 July 1992) 1695 UNTS 382.

259 Charter of the Organization of Central American States (adopted 12 December 1962, entered into force 30 March 1965) UNTS Registration No 8048.

260 For a general overview, see eg TA O'Keefe, 'The Central American Integration System (ICA) at the Dawn of a New Century: Will the Central American Isthmus Finally Be Able to Achieve Economic and Political Unity' (2001) 13 *Florida Journal of International Law* 243; RA Sánchez Sánchez, *The Politics of Central American Integration* (Abingdon, Routledge, 2009) 138 ff.

261 Treaty establishing the Latin American Integration Association (adopted 18 February 1960, entered into force 1 June 1961) UNTS Registration No 25392.

262 Treaty of Montevideo (adopted 12 August 1980, entered into force 18 March 1981) 1329 UNTS 255.

The *Inter-American Development Bank* (IADB)[263] was founded in 1959 to promote economic and social development in Latin America and the Caribbean.[264] The IADB is owned by 48 States, which are its shareholders and members. Only the 26 'borrowing' countries are able to receive loans. The other 22 States are 'non-borrowing'. The IADB Group comprises the Inter-American Investment Corporation (IIC) and the Multilateral Investment Fund (MIF), a structure similar to the World Bank Group. The IIC was founded with a view to promote economic development in the region through the financing of small- and medium-sized companies. The MIF was established in 1992 and, in particular, promotes investment reforms and encourages the development of the private sector. The highest organ of the IADB is the Board of Governors, in which each country is represented. The Board of Governors has delegated many operational responsibilities to the Board of Executive Directors.

The *Pacific Alliance*,[265] created in 2012 by Chile, Colombia, Mexico and Peru, is a trade bloc, building on already existing free trade agreements between the four countries. The aim of the Alliance is to create an area of deep integration in order to enhance the growth and development of the Member States, by moving towards free movement of goods, services, resources and people. The Alliance is strictly intergovernmental, and has no permanent secretariat or administrative body; it only consists of a Summit of heads of State, a high-level group of vice-ministers of trade and foreign affairs, technical groups and a pro-tempore presidency.

The *Bolivarian Alliance for the Peoples of our America* (ALBA)[266] was established in 2004 with an agreement between Cuba and Venezuela,[267] and expanded in 2006 with the Peoples' Trade Agreement,[268] signed together with Bolivia. ALBA now has 11 Member States throughout Latin America and the Caribbean. Its main objectives relate to poverty eradication and social inclusion. ALBA's initiatives aim to redistribute resources and regulate trade among its Member States. To do so, the Alliance sponsors a virtual currency, the SUCRE, allowing the States to conduct trade without using the US dollar.

The *Community of Latin American and Caribbean States* (CELAC)[269] is a regional bloc of 33 states, formed at the Unity Summit in February 2010. This Summit brought together the parties to the 21st Summit of the Rio Group and the 2nd Latin American and Caribbean Summit on Integration and Development (CALC) – CELAC is the successor

[263] Agreement establishing the Inter-American Development Bank (adopted 8 April 1959, entered into force 30 December 1959) 389 UNTS 69.

[264] For a general overview, see eg F Adams, 'External Financing for Development: The Role of the Inter-American Development Bank' (2005) 36 *International Studies* 301; and A Estevadeordal, 'Lessons Learned Delivering Aid for Trade in Latin America and the Caribbean: The Role of the Inter-American Development Bank' in D Njinkeu and H Cameron (eds), *Aid for Trade and Development* (New York, CUP, 2008) 234.

[265] C Daniels, 'The Pacific Alliance and Its Effect on Latin America: Must a Continental Divide Be the Cost a Pacific Alliance Success?' (2015) 37 *Loyola of Los Angeles International and Comparative Law Review* 153.

[266] W Muno, 'ALBA, UNASUR und CELAC' in Grimmel and Jakobeit (n 254) 412.

[267] Agreement between the President of the Bolivarian Republic of Venezuela and the President of the Council of State of Cuba, for the Application of the Bolivarian Alternative for the Americas (14 December 2004) cuba.cu/gobierno/discursos/2004/ing/a141204i.html.

[268] Agreement for the Application of the Bolivarian Alternative for the Peoples of Our America and the Peoples' Trade (29 April 2006) ifrc.org/docs/idrl/I542EN.pdf (Peoples' Trade Agreement).

[269] S Moran Blanco, 'La 'nueva' integración y sus reformas en America Latina y el Caribe: CELAC, UNASUR y Alianza del Pacifico' in F Aldecoa Luzarraga and M Guinea Llorente (eds), *Gobernanza y reforma internacional tras la crisis financiera y económica: el papel de la Unión Europea* (Madrid, Marcial Pons, 2014) 493; F Fernandez, 'Alba-TCP et CELAC: instruments d'une politique indépendante et souveraine' (2012) 116 *Revue générale de droit international public* 557.

of these institutions. The organisation's objective is uniting all of the Latin American and Caribbean States, in order to strengthen the political, social and cultural integration of the region, stimulate the economic growth and improve living standards. The official bodies of the organisation are the Summit of heads of State and government, the Meeting of ministers of foreign affairs, the Pro-Tempore Presidency (assisted by the States holding the Presidency before and after, together forming the Troika), and the Specialised Meetings. Moreover, the Latin American and Caribbean countries have been cooperating with the EU since 2000 and they continue to do so through the EU-CELAC partnership. In particular, the biannual EU-CELAC Summits have been the main driver of the bi-regional partnership. Moreover, according to the EU Global Strategy, the EU-CELAC partnership is the preferred region-to-region forum, even if the EU aims at maintaining good relationships with the other, smaller regional groups as well.[270]

The *Dominican Republic – Central America Free Trade Agreement* (CAFTA-DR)[271] is a free trade agreement between the United States and the Dominican Republic, Costa Rica, El Salvador, Guatemala, Nicaragua, and Honduras, signed in 2005. The CAFTA-DR aims to create economic opportunities, by opening markets, eliminating tariffs and reducing trade barriers. It is also seen as a first step towards the Free Trade Area of the Americas (FTAA).

IV. Regional Organisations in Africa

A. African Union

In 2001, the African Union (AU)[272] succeeded the Organization of African Unity (OAU).[273] The latter was the result of the merger of the Union of African States and Madagascar (formed in 1960 by 12 French-speaking African countries, called the 'Group of Brazzaville') and the Union of African States (formed by Ghana, Guinea, Mali and the North African States, the so-called 'Group of Casablanca'). The Charter of the Organization of African Unity (OAU Charter) was signed in Addis Ababa in 1963[274] and stated the main objectives of the OAU: the liberation of the African continent from the remaining vestiges of colonisation and apartheid; promoting unity and solidarity among African States; cooperation and coordination; the safeguarding of the sovereignty and territorial integrity of Member States; and fostering international cooperation in the framework of the UN. As a continental organisation, the OAU was a forum which offered Member States the possibility to

[270] Müller et al (n 238) 49–50.

[271] G Bottini, V Lavista and M Lozza, 'MERCOSUR and CAFTA' in M Bungenberg et al (eds), *International Investment Law* (Oxford, Hart, 2015) 326; and FG Sourgens, 'Free Trade à l'Américaine – NAFTA, DR-CAFTA and Beyond' in IA Laird (ed), *Investment Treaty Arbitration and International Law* (Huntington, Juris, 2013) vii.

[272] See for the Constitutive Act below n 277. For a general overview, see eg KD Magliveras and GN Naldi, 'The African Union' in Wouters (n 11); SM Makinda, W Okumu and D Mickler (eds), *The African Union: Addressing the Challenges of Peace, Security, and Governance*, 2nd edn (London, Routledge, 2016); G Mvelle and L Zang (eds), *L'Union africaine quinze ans après* (Paris, L'Harmattan, 2017); AA Yusuf and F Ouguergouz (eds), *L'Union Africaine: cadre juridique et institutionnel: manuel sur l'organisation panafricaine* (Paris, Pedone, 2013).

[273] K van Walraven, 'Heritage and Transformation: From the Organization of African Unity to the African Union' in U Engel and J Gomes Porto (eds), *Africa's New Peace and Security Architecture: Promoting Norms, Institutionalizing Solutions* (Farnham, Ashgate, 2010) 31.

[274] Charter of the Organization of African Unity (adopted 25 May 1963, entered unto force 13 September 1963) 479 UNTS 69 (OAU Charter).

adopt common positions in international forums. In July 1999, the Assembly of heads of State and government decided to establish an African Union and demand for the speedy establishment of institutions such as the Pan-African Parliament, African Central Bank, African Monetary Union and African Court of Justice. On 11 July 2000, the Constitutive Act of the African Union was signed in Lomé.[275] It entered into force on 26 May 2001, after the Lusaka Summit. On 9 July 2002, the AU replaced the OAU. The AU has 55 Member States: all UN Member States on the African continent, as well as the disputed Saharawi Arab Democratic Republic. Morocco withdrew from the OAU in 1985, following the admission of the latter as a member, represented by Polisario, a national liberation movement. Nonetheless, in January 2017, Morocco re-joined the AU after more than 30 years. The vision and objectives of the AU do not differ substantially from those of the OAU. What is innovative, however, is the extraordinary wealth of bodies within the AU.

Among the most important documents adopted by the Assembly of heads of State and government is undoubtedly the African Charter on Human and Peoples' Rights of 1981,[276] which is discussed in Chapter 16, Section XI(B)(i). In addition, in 1991 the Treaty establishing the African Economic Community (AEC)[277] was adopted, which, alongside the OAU Charter, served as the main basis for the OAU's operations. The Treaty provides that an African Economic Community must be achieved in six phases, which together should not last more than 34 years. Therefore, the Community is mainly built on existing (sub-) regional cooperation associations (Regional Economic Communities (RECs)). The main policy-making body of the AEC is the Economic and Social Council, which, together with its specialised committees, implements the objectives of the AEC.

The Assembly of heads of State and government is the supreme organ of the AU. The Assembly meets annually in ordinary session, or in extraordinary session at the request of a Member State. Notably, the Assembly may adopt its decisions by two-thirds majority if a consensus cannot be achieved. The Executive Council consists of the foreign ministers or their representatives. It meets at least twice a year in ordinary session, or at the request of a Member State in exceptional session. The Executive Council implements the decisions of the Assembly. Once again, the Council may decide by a two-thirds majority if consensus proves impossible. A number of specialised technical committees operate under the authority of the Executive Council. Similarly to the EU (see above, p 317), a Permanent Representatives Committee of the Member States exists within the AU. The Committee prepares for the activities in the Executive Council and operates under its authority. Finally, it may set up subcommittees and working groups.

The Pan-African Parliament gathered for the first time on 16 September 2004 in South Africa. It is composed of representatives of the Member States. In the first five years of its workings, it only had an advisory and consultative power. On 28 October 2009, a new five-year mandate started and the Parliament assumed full legislative powers.[278]

[275] Constitutive Act of the African Union (adopted 11 July 2000, entered into force 26 May 2001) 2158 UNTS 3.

[276] African Charter on Human and Peoples' Rights (adopted 27 June 1981, entered into force 21 October 1986) 1520 UNTS 217. See also M Hansungele, 'The African Charter on Human and Peoples' Rights' in AA Yusuf and F Ouguergouz (eds), *The African Union: Legal and Institutional Framework: A Manual on the Pan-African Organization* (Leiden, Nijhoff, 2012) 415.

[277] Treaty establishing the African Economic Community (adopted 3 June 1991, entered into force 12 May 1994) 30 ILM 1241. See also MM Mbengue and O Illy, 'The African Economic Community' in Yusuf and Ouguergouz (n 275) 185.

[278] SL Mohamed, 'The Pan-African Parliament' in Yusuf and Ouguergouz (n 276) 95; B Mbete, 'The Pan-African Parliament: Progress and Prospects' in JK Akokpari, A Ndinga-Muvumba and T Murithi (eds), *The African Union and its Institutions* (Auckland Park, Fanele, 2008) 307.

The Commission is the Secretariat of the AU. It consists of a chairman, vice-chairmen and commissioners. The Commission comprises a number of entities, not unlike the Directorates-General of the EU institutions. In 2001, a Peace and Security Council was set up, which led to an additional protocol to the Constitutive Act[279] the following year. The Peace and Security Council aims to develop a common defence policy, including an African 'standby force'.[280]

In 1998, a Protocol establishing the African Court on Human and Peoples' Rights was adopted.[281] This Court complements the protection offered by the African Commission on Human Rights, on the basis of the Charter for Human and Peoples' Rights. The Court may give advisory opinions on the interpretation of the Charter or any other human rights instrument which has been ratified by the Member States. The Protocol entered into force on 25 January 2004, and the Court finally became operational in 2006. In 2003, another protocol was adopted to create the Court of Justice of the African Union.[282] In 2008, the Assembly of the AU adopted the Protocol on the Statute of the African Court of Justice and Human Rights,[283] which aims to merge the African Court on Human and Peoples' Rights and the African Court of Justice, but has not yet entered into force. Moreover, in 2014, the Malabo Protocol was adopted,[284] which gives this Court criminal jurisdiction over an elaborate list of broadly defined crimes, but has not entered into force as of yet (see also Chapter 16, Section XI(B)(ii)).

The most important initiative established within the framework of the AU to date is arguably the New Partnership for Africa's Development (NEPAD), which was introduced in October 2001 as part of a programme of the AU.[285] The objective of NEPAD is to strengthen democracy and healthy economic development in Africa. NEPAD is primarily used to establish partnerships with industrialised countries. In this respect, the G8 adopted the Africa Action Plan in 2002 and promised a comprehensive aid package to the NEPAD countries. An important means to achieve the NEPAD objective is the so-called African Peer Review Mechanism (APRM). The APRM verifies whether the policies of the participating States are in accordance with the values and standards of the 2002 Declaration. However, participation in the APRM is optional.[286]

[279] Protocol relating to the establishment of the Peace and Security Council of the African Union (adopted 9 July 2002, entered into force 26 December 2003) au.int/en/treaties/protocol-relating-establishment-peace-and-security-council-african-union.

[280] IA Badmus, *The African Union's Role in Peacekeeping: Building on Lessons Learned from Security Operations* (Basingstoke, Palgrave Macmillan, 2015).

[281] Protocol to the African Charter on Human and Peoples' Rights on the Establishment of the African Court on Human and Peoples' Rights (adopted 9 June 1988, 25 January 2004) OAU/LEG/EXP/AFCHPR/PROT (III).

[282] Protocol of the Court of Justice of the African Union (adopted 1 July 2003, entered into force 11 February 2009) au.int/en/treaties/protocol-court-justice-african-union.

[283] Protocol on the Statute of the African Court of Justice and Human Rights (adopted 1 July 2008, not entered into force) au.int/en/treaties/protocol-statute-african-court-justice-and-human-rights.

[284] Protocol on Amendments to the Protocol on the Statute of the African Court of Justice and Human Rights (adopted 27 June 2014, not yet entered into force) au.int/en/treaties/protocol-amendments-protocol-statute-african-court-justice-and-human-rights.

[285] E Kannyo, 'The New Partnership for Africa's Development (NEPAD)' in Yusuf and Ouguergouz (n 276) 203.

[286] B Manby, 'Development, Good Governance and South-South Cooperation: The African Peer Review Mechanism' in Office of the High Commissioner for Human Rights (ed), *Realizing the Right to Development: Essays in Commemoration of 25 Years of the United Nations Declaration on the Right to Development* (New York, United Nations, 2013) 217; A Adedeji, 'NEPAD's African Peer Review Mechanism: Progress and Prospects' in Akokpari, Ndinga-Muvumba and Murithi (n 278) 241.

One of latest initiatives developed within the framework of the AU is the African Continental Free Trade Area. On 21 March 2018, the first real step towards what would be a continent-wide free trade area among all AU Member States was taken in Kigali with the signing of the African Continental Free Trade Agreement (AfCFTA) by 44 of the AU's 55 Member States.[287] On 1 July 2018, South Africa signed the Agreement,[288] while at the time of writing, it appeared that also Nigeria would do so,[289] the initiative includes the two biggest African economies. Although the AfCFTA does not directly establish a continental free trade area, the agreement will serve as an umbrella to which protocols (on trade in goods, trade in services, dispute settlement as well as on intellectual property rights, investment and competition) will be added. These instruments are still in the process of being negotiated. If successful, the African Continental Free Trade Area would resemble the EU's single market.

Finally, the AU has formally been cooperating with the EU since the adoption of the 2006 Africa-EU Strategy.[290] At the fourth EU-Africa Summit in 2014 both organisations decided to deepen their relationship. For instance, the Joint Annual Forum was created to assess the implementation of the roadmap developed during the Summit. Moreover, the African Union Support Programmes and the Pan-African Programme were established, which allow the EU to provide financial support to the AU.[291] At the 5th Summit in 2017, the organisations adopted a declaration outlining common priorities.[292]

B. Other Regional and Sub-Regional Organisations in Africa

Other important African regional organisations are the Economic Community of West African States (ECOWAS), the Southern African Development Community (SADC), the Common Market for Eastern and Southern Africa (COMESA), the Arab Maghreb Union (UMA), the Economic and Monetary Union of West Africa (UEMOA), the Economic and Monetary Community of Central Africa (CEMAC), the Economic Community of Central African States (CEEAC/ECCAS), the East African Community (EAC) and the African Development Bank (AfDB).

i. Economic Community of West African States

The Treaty establishing ECOWAS was signed in 1975 by 16 West African States.[293] It now has 15 Member States, since Mauritania withdrew in 2000. ECOWAS aims at achieving

[287] See Assembly of the African Union, 'Decision on the Draft Agreement Establishing the African Continental Free Trade Area (AfCFTA)', 21 March 2018, Ext/Assembly/AU/Dec.1(X).

[288] S Kimani, 'SA signs free trade agreement', *SABC News*, 2 July 2018, sabcnews.com/sabcnews/sa-signs-free-trade-agreement.

[289] F Onuah and C Ohuocha, 'Nigeria's President Buhari says will soon sign up to African free-trade agreement', *Reuters*, 12 July 2018, af.reuters.com/article/topNews/idAFKBN1K20H9-OZATP.

[290] The Africa-EU Strategic Partnership, 'A Joint Africa-EU Strategy', 28 April 2006, africa-eu-partnership.org//sites/default/files/documents/eas2007_joint_strategy_en.pdf.

[291] Fourth EU-Africa Summit, 'Roadmap 2014–2017', 2–3 April 2014, consilium.europa.eu/media/21520/142094.pdf.

[292] Fifth EU-Africa Summit, 'Joint Declaration of the 5th African Union-European Union Summit', 30 November 2017, AU-EU/Decl.1(V).

[293] Treaty of the Economic Community of West African States (adopted 28 May 1975, entered into force 28 May 1975) 1010 UNTS 17 (ECOWAS Treaty). The treaty was revised in 1993: Revised Treaty of the Economic

collective self-sufficiency by way of the integration of West Africa in one economic bloc with a common market and an economic and monetary union.[294] ECOWAS envisages the elimination of customs, the introduction of a single tariff for third countries, the harmonisation of economic and financial policies of the Member States and the creation of a monetary zone. ECOWAS has been successful in the area of free movement of persons, the construction of interstate roads, the development of telecommunication connections between the States and the maintenance of regional peace and security. To the outside world, ECOWAS is best known for the latter function. It has led peacekeeping missions in the region, among others in Ivory Coast and Liberia in 2003, in Mali in 2013, and in Gambia in 2017.[295] Since 2004, an early-warning system and a Rapid Reaction Force exist within ECOWAS (the ECOWAS Cease-fire Monitoring Group or ECOMOG), which may be immediately deployed in the region.

The market integration in West Africa, however, is only in its infancy. The Trade Liberalization Scheme is not yet fully operational, and the economic and financial policies are not harmonised, although a framework has been established. Nonetheless, after more than a decade, the Common External Tariff finally entered into force in January 2017, following which ECOWAS rose up to the level of a customs union. Still, the poorly-managed political and economic policies of the Member States, the weak national economies, the absence of reliable infrastructure, the plurality of regional integration organisations with overlapping objectives, the irregular payment of contributions by the Member States and the lack of involvement of non-State actors, all contribute to the rather disappointing results of ECOWAS.

The Authority of Heads of State and Government is the highest organ of ECOWAS. It meets annually and is responsible for the general direction of the Community. It may, if necessary, refer a case to the Court of Justice (see below, Section IV(B)(iii)), when it confirms that a Member State is not fulfilling its obligations or a Community organ has exceeded its powers. The Authority may also request an Advisory Opinion on a legal matter of the Court of Justice.

The Council of Ministers mainly consists of Ministers responsible for ECOWAS affairs. The Council meets in ordinary session twice a year and is responsible for the functioning and development of the Community. It makes recommendations to the Authority on any action contributing to the achievement of the Community objectives and, if the Authority has delegated this power, adopts guidelines on the coordination and harmonisation of the economic integration policy. The Council may also request the Court of Justice to deliver an Advisory Opinion.

Community of West African States (adopted 24 July 1993, entered into force 23 August 1995) 2373 UNTS 233; and in 2001, by the Protocol adopted in Dakar (adopted 21 December 2001, entered into force 10 August 2004) 2375 UNTS 516.

[294] S Riley, 'West African Subregionalism: The Case of the Economic Community of West African States (ECOWAS)' in Hook and Kearns (n 196) 63; J Ukaigwe, *Ecowas Law* (Berlin, Springer, 2016) 4; and T Zogbelemou, *Droit des organisations d'intégration économique en Afrique: CEDEAO – CEMAC – UEMOA – ZMAO* (Paris, L'Harmattan, 2014).

[295] EK Aning and S Atuobi, 'The Economic Community of West African States and the Responsibility to Protect' in WA Knight and F Egerton (eds), *The Routledge Handbook of the Responsibility to Protect* (London, Routledge, 2012) 216; PA Jenkins, 'The Economic Community of West African States and the Regional Use of Force' (2007) 35 *Denver Journal of International Law and Policy* 333; KC Omeje, 'Organizaciones regionales y resolución de conflictos en África: el caso de la CEDEAO' in OM Martin and R Grasa (eds), *¿Una nueva era para África? Nuevos desafíos y perspectivas sobre paz y seguridad en África* (Madrid, Catarata, 2014) 65; A Abass, 'La CEDEAO et le maintien de la paix et de la sécurité internationales' (2003) 14 *L'observateur des Nations Unies* 3.

ECOWAS has its own Community Court of Justice.[296] When a dispute on the interpretation or the application of the ECOWAS Treaty may not be settled out of court, each Member State or the Authority may refer the case to the Court of Justice. A Member State may also refer a case on behalf of its citizens to the Court. The decision of the Court is not subject to appeal and is binding for the Member States, the organs of the Community and individuals.

Other ECOWAS institutions are the advisory Community Parliament, the Economic and Social Council, the Executive Secretariat and the ECOWAS Bank for Investment and Development (EBID).

ii. Southern African Development Community

The South African Coordination Conference (SADCC), the predecessor to the Southern African Development Community (SADC), was founded in 1980 with the Lusaka Declaration,[297] signed by nine Southern African States. The 1992 Declaration and Treaty of the Southern African Development Community[298] replaced the Lusaka Declaration and established the SADC, in which 16 States take part.[299] The main objective of SADC is building an independent region with a high degree of harmonisation and rationalisation, similar to ECOWAS.[300] Pooling resources is seen as the basis for improving living standards across the region. SADC countries have concluded cooperation protocols regarding the most diverse matters. Moreover, the SADC EPA Group (comprising Botswana, Lesotho, Mozambique, Namibia, South Africa and Swaziland), concluded an Economic Partnership Agreement (EPA) with the EU on 10 June 2016.[301] The agreement has been provisionally applied since 10 October 2016, with Mozambique joining in February 2018.

In 1996, the SADC set up the Organ on Politics, Defence and Security Co-operation. The Organ is tasked with the prevention, management and resolution of conflicts between States, with enforcement action considered a measure of last resort where peaceful means

[296] Protocol relating to the Community Court of Justice (adopted 6 July 1991, entered into force 5 November 1996). The protocol was amended in 2005 and in 2006; the 2005 supplementary protocol expanded the Court's jurisdiction to human rights claims by individuals. See also KJ Alter, LR Helfer and JR McAllister, 'A New International Human Rights Court for West Africa: the ECOWAS Community Court of Justice' (2013) 107 *AJIL* 737; ES Nwauche, 'The ECOWAS Community Court of Justice and the horizontal application of human rights' (2013) 13 *African Human Rights Law Journal* 30.

[297] Declaration by the Governments of Independent States of Southern Africa, 'Southern Africa: Toward Economic Liberation', 1 April 1980, sadc.int/files/3014/1139/9635/SADC_Declaration_Southern_Africa_Towards_Economic_Liberalisation.PDF (Lusaka Declaration).

[298] Declaration by the Heads of State or Government of Southern African States, 'Towards the Southern African Development Community', 17 August 1992, sadc.int/files/8613/5292/8378/Declaration__Treaty_of_SADC.pdf; Treaty of the Southern African Development Community (adopted 17 August 1992, entered into force 5 October 1993) UNTS Registration No 52885.

[299] For a general overview, see eg GH Oosthuizen, *The Southern African Development Community: The Organisation, its Policies and Prospects* (Midrand, Institute for Global Dialogue, 2006); A Kösler, *Die Entwicklung der Southern African Development Community (SADC) als Building Block der panafrikanischen Einheit: die Herausforderung der doppelten Integration und wichtige Einflussfaktoren* (Hamburg, Kovac, 2010); T Huaraka, 'The Southern African Development Community' in L Boisson de Chazournes and V Gowlland-Debbas (eds), *The International Legal System in Quest of Equity and Universality* (The Hague, Nijhoff, 2001) 797.

[300] C Ng'ong'ola, 'Regional integration and trade liberalization in the Southern African Development Community' (2000) 3 *JIEL* 485.

[301] Economic Partnership Agreement between the European Union and its Member States, of the one part, and the SADC EPA States, of the other part, done at Kasane on 10 June 2016 [2016] OJ L 250/3.

have failed.[302] It may, therefore, employ a number of peaceful means such as diplomacy, negotiations, mediation, arbitration and adjudication to an international tribunal. This body consists of a Ministerial Committee, an Inter-State Politics and Diplomacy Committee, and an Inter-State Defence and Security Committee. In August 2004, the SADC Member States adopted the 'Principles and Guidelines Governing Democratic Elections',[303] on the basis of which election monitoring is conducted.

The Summit of Heads of State and Government is the highest organ of SADC. It meets twice a year and is responsible for the general policy of the Community. The Council of Ministers meets four times a year and is responsible for the functioning and the development of SADC, ensuring the proper implementation of the organisation's policies. A Standing Committee assists the Council in technical matters, while a SADC Tribunal was established in 2005 to ensure adherence to the provisions of the SADC Treaty and their proper interpretation. However, after several judgments ruling against the Zimbabwean government, the Tribunal was suspended in 2010. The 2012 SADC Summit addressed this issue, and decided that a new Tribunal should be negotiated, with a mandate confined to the interpretation of the SADC Treaty and Protocols relating to disputes between Member States.

The Secretariat is the main executive organ of SADC and is responsible for the strategic planning, coordination and management of SADC programmes. A number of centralised directorates with specific powers have been created within the Secretariat.[304] Also, SADC committees were established on the national level and are made up of representatives of government, the private sector and civil society. They give input at a national level with regard to the formulation of regional policy strategies.[305]

iii. Common Market for Eastern and Southern Africa

The Common Market for Eastern and Southern Africa (COMESA)[306] comprises 19 countries, from Egypt in the north to Namibia and Swaziland in the south. COMESA replaced the 1994 Preferential Trade Area for Eastern and Southern Africa (PTA), which had existed since 1981 within the framework of an action plan of the OAU. COMESA aims at putting in place an area with free movement of goods, services, capital, people and investment, and a customs union. In 2000, a zero tariff for all traded goods between the Participating States was introduced and a Common External Tariff became operational

[302] Protocol on Politics, Defence and Security Co-operation (adopted 14 August 2001, entered into force 2 March 2004) UNTS Registration No 52885. See also J Muntschick, *The Southern African Development Community (SADC) and the European Union (EU): Regionalism and External Influence* (London, Palgrave Macmillan, 2018) 205; and N Ngoma, *Prospects for a Security Community in Southern Africa: An Analysis of Regional Security in the Southern African Development Community* (Pretoria, Institute for Security Studies, 2005).

[303] 'SADC Principles and Guidelines Governing Democratic Election', first version adopted on 17 August 2004, saiia.org.za/images/upload/SADC_%20Principles%20and%20Guidelines%20Governing%20Democratic%20 Elections.pdf; revised version adopted on 20 July 2015, eisa.org.za/pdf/sadc2015principles.pdf.

[304] See eg the organogram 'SADC Organizational Structure', 1 February 2008, sadc.int/files/2113/6792/0281/ sadc_organogram_FINAL.pdf.

[305] C Landsberg, 'The Southern African Development Community's Decision-Making Architecture' in CC Saunders (ed), *Region-building in Southern Africa: Progress, Problems and Prospects* (London, Zed Books, 2012) 63.

[306] Treaty establishing the Common Market for Eastern and Southern Africa (adopted 5 November 1993, 8 December 1994) 2314 UNTS 265.

in 2005. The establishment of a monetary union and a fully free movement of persons is scheduled for 2025.[307]

The Authority of heads of State and government is the highest organ of COMESA and is responsible for the strategic direction of the organisation. The Council of Ministers adopts the policy decisions regarding the programmes and activities of COMESA, including the monitoring of financial and administrative management. The Committee of Governors of Central Banks manages the clearinghouse of COMESA and oversees the implementation of Monetary and Financial Cooperation programmes. The Intergovernmental Committee is composed of permanent secretaries of the Participating States and is responsible for the development and management of programmes and action plans in all areas of cooperation, with the exception of the financial and monetary sector. Technical committees are responsible for different economic sectors and for administrative and budgetary matters. The Secretariat, headed by the Secretary General, provides technical support and implementation advice to the Member States. A Consultative Committee of the business community and other interest groups facilitate dialogue between the COMESA partners. Since 1998, a Court of Justice oversees the correct interpretation and application of the Treaty rules and resolves disputes between Member States.[308]

iv. Arab Maghreb Union

The Arab Maghreb Union (AMU) was founded by the Marrakech Treaty in 1989[309] with a view to a full integration and a stronger international position of the Maghreb (Morocco, Algeria, Tunisia, Libya and Mauritania). The objectives of the AMU are the liberalisation of goods, services and people, and capital movement between the Member States, the implementation of a common policy on an industrial, social, agricultural and commercial level and the implementation of joint projects and programmes.[310]

Between 1989 and 1991, the AMU established a number of institutions: the Council of Ministers of Foreign Affairs, the Follow-up Committee, the General Secretariat, the Consultative Council, a Maghreb Bank for Investment and Foreign Trade and a number of specialised Ministerial Commissions. The AMU envisages a free-trade zone in a first phase, a customs union in a second phase, and a global economic union in a third phase. However, the process of dismantling trade barriers has only recently begun, due to the absence of a stable administrative structure and political issues between the Member States. The establishment of a Euro-Mediterranean free trade area between the EU and the Maghreb countries was envisaged for 2010. Today, European Mediterranean Association

[307] K Cheluget and S Wright, 'COMESA and the Tripartite Free Trade Area: Towards an African Economic Community?' (2017) 24 *South African Journal of International Affairs* 481, 483; HK Mutai, *Compliance with International Trade Obligations: The Common Market for Eastern and Southern Africa* (Alphen aan den Rijn, Kluwer, 2007).

[308] PT Muchlinski, 'The COMESA Common Investment Area: Substantive Standards and Procedural Problems in Dispute Settlement' in C Leng Lim (ed), *Alternative Visions of the International Law on Foreign Investment: Essays in Honour of Muthucumaraswamy Sornarajah* (Cambridge, CUP, 2016) 156; TA O'Keefe, 'Los sistemas de resolución de controversias en COMESA y SADC' in A Dreyzin de Klor (ed), *Solución de controversias* (Buenos Aires, Zavalia, 2004) 176.

[309] Treaty instituting the Arab Maghreb Union (adopted 17 February 1989, entered into force 1 July 1989) 1546 UNTS 160.

[310] For a general overview, see eg J Worrall, *International Institutions of the Middle East: the GCC, Arab League, and Arab Maghreb Union* (London, Routledge, 2017); P Charbrier, *The Arab Maghreb Union* (Washington, IMF, 1994); A El Kadiri, 'L'Union du Maghreb Arabe' (1994) 2 *African Yearbook of International Law* 141.

Agreements have been concluded with most of them (with the exception of Syria and Libya).

v. *West African Economic and Monetary Union*

The West African Economic and Monetary Union (*Union Economique et Monétaire Ouest-Africaine*, UEMOA) was established in 1994 by the Treaty of Dakar,[311] amended in 2003,[312] and includes Benin, Burkina Faso, Ivory Coast, Guinea-Bissau, Mali, Niger, Senegal and Togo. Most of these countries have used a common currency since 1945 (the '*Franc CFA*') and were already united in the UMOA (*Union Monétaire Ouest-Africaine*) since 1962. The objectives of the UEMOA are: the pursuit of a common economic policy; the strengthening of the competitiveness of economic and financial activities of the Member States; the creation of a common market[313] and a customs union; and the harmonisation of national legislation. In 1996, the UEMOA introduced a preferential tariff regime. However, since 2000, it has applied a Common External Tariff of 20 per cent.[314]

The Conference of Heads of State is the highest body of the UEMOA and may take decisions on any matter with regard to which the Council could not reach a unanimous agreement. It meets at least once a year and decides by unanimity. The Council of Ministers determines the monetary and credit policy of the Union, in order to secure the common currency and to provide for the financing of economic activity and development of the Member States. It may also change the determination of the monetary unit. Each Member State is represented by two ministers. The Council of Ministers meets at least twice a year and decides by unanimity.

The Commission of the UEMOA exercises its implementing powers in light of the good functioning and the general interest of the Union. Alongside this, it presents recommendations and advice to the Conference and Council. Finally, the Commission also sets the budget and may refer a matter to the Court of Justice of the UEMOA if a Member State does not comply with its obligations under Community law. This Court ensures the uniform interpretation and application of Union law. It also resolves disputes between Member States or between the Union and its officials. The Court of Auditors verifies the accounts of the Union's bodies and the reliability of these budgetary data.

The Inter-Parliamentary Committee has a consultative role and animates the integration debates. It receives annual reports drawn up by the Commission, drafts its own reports and issues resolutions, and meets at least once a year. The Regional Consular Chamber is a forum for dialogue between the UEMOA and the main economic actors. The Chamber is a consultative body, in charge of the involvement of the private sector in the integration process of UEMOA. The UEMOA has two autonomous specialised

[311] Traite de l'Union Economique et Monetaire Ouest Africaine (UEMOA) (adopted 10 January 1994, entered into force 1 August 1994) centif.sn/TraiteUEMOA.pdf (Treaty of Dakar).

[312] Traité modifié de l'Union Economique et Monétaire Ouest Africaine (UEMOA) (29 January 2003) uemoa.int/fr/system/files/fichier_article/traitreviseuemoa.pdf.

[313] ibid, Art 4. See also A Dioukhane, 'Le marché commun de l'UEMOA' (2000) 46 *Revue internationale de droit africain* 7.

[314] For a general overview, see eg Zogbelemou (n 294); D Kohnert, 'Die UEMOA und die CFA-Zone: eine neue Kooperationskultur im frankophonen Afrika?' in D Nabers (ed), *Regionale Integration: neue Dynamiken in Afrika, Asien und Lateinamerika* (Hamburg, Deutsches Übersee-Institut, 2005) 115; J Issa-Sayegh, 'L'ordre juridique de l'UEMOA et l'intégration juridique africaine' in JC Gautron (ed), *Les dynamiques du droit européen en début de siècle: études en l'honneur de Jean-Claude Gautron* (Paris, Pedone, 2004) 663.

institutions. The Central Bank of West African States (BCEAO) regulates the common currency of the Union. The West African Development Bank (BOAD)[315] aims to promote the development of the Member States and to stimulate their integration. It employs internal and external financial resources to finance infrastructure, means of production and new activities.

vi. Economic and Monetary Community of Central African States

The Economic and Monetary Community of Central Africa (*Communauté Economique et Monétaire de l'Afrique Centrale*, CEMAC) replaced the 1964 Customs and Economic Union of Central Africa (UDEAC) in June 1999. It consists of two unions: the UEAC (*Union Economique de l'Afrique Centrale*) and the UMAC (*Union Monétaire de l'Afrique Centrale*).[316] It is composed of six States: Cameroon, the Central African Republic, Congo-Brazzaville, Gabon, Equatorial Guinea and Chad. These countries also use the common *Franc CFA*. CEMAC envisages eliminating trade barriers, to coordinate development programmes, the harmonisation of industrial projects, the development of solidarity between Member States and the establishment of a common African market.[317]

The Conference of Heads of State is the highest organ of CEMAC and determines the orientation of the Community and its institutions. The Conference takes its decisions, depending on the matter, by consensus, qualified or simple majority. The Council of Ministers consists of three ministers from each Member State and determines the direction of the UEAC and the UMAC, oversees the Bank of Central African States, approves the budget and the accounts and examines the annual report. The Inter-State Committee prepares the deliberations of the Council of Ministers. It consists of three experts from each State.

The Executive Secretariat oversees the application of Treaty provisions and secondary law by Member States and their nationals. Under the authority of the Council of Ministers, it carries out the coordination of the institutions and the organs. The Community Court of Justice and the Community Parliament have supervisory powers. The Court of Justice may also consider the appeals by the Member States, institutions and individuals, against actions and decisions of the organs of CEMAC.[318] Within the UMAC, there are two specialised institutions: the Bank of Central African States (BEAC) and the Central African Banking Commission (COBAC).

vii. Economic Community of Central African States

In 1981, the leaders of the Central African Customs and Economic Union (UDEAC) decided to form a wider economic community. In 1983, the *Economic Community of Central African*

[315] Agreement establishing a West-African Development Bank (adopted 14 November 1973, entered into force 11 October 1974) UNTS Registration No 25270. See also M Cogen, 'The West African Development Bank' (1983) 36 *Studia Diplomatica* 559.

[316] Art 2 Traité instituant la Communauté Economique et Monétaire de l'Afrique Centrale (adopted 16 March 1994, entered into force 25 June 1999; revised on 25 June 2008) cherpaa.org/wp-content/uploads/2016/03/CEMAC-Traite-revise-CEMAC-2008.pdf.

[317] Zogbelemou (n 294); L Zang, 'L'intégration en Afrique centrale de l'UDEAC à la CEMAC' (2004) 58 *Revue juridique et politique des états francophones* 410.

[318] E Gnimpieba Tonnang and O Fandjip, 'La Cour de Justice de la CEMAC et les règles du procès équitable' (2010) 120 *Penant: revue de droit des pays d'Afrique* 329.

States (ECCAS) was founded with the aim of improving living standards and maintaining economic stability through harmonious cooperation.[319] Today it comprises 11 Member States: Angola, Burundi, Cameroon, Central African Republic, Chad, Congo-Kinshasa, Congo-Brazzaville, Equatorial Guinea, Gabon, Rwanda and São Tomé and Príncipe. The Community became operational in 1985, with the ultimate goal of establishing a Central African Common Market. To this end, a number of agreements were concluded with regard to economic integration.

ECCAS has been designated as the economic pillar of the AEC. However, the ECCAS only signed the Protocol on Relations between the AEC and the RECs[320] in 1999. Its organs are the Conference of heads of State and government, the Council of Ministers, the Secretary General, the Court of Justice and the Consultative Commission. On 17 June 2002, a Protocol was adopted establishing a network among the national parliaments (REPAC).[321] The membership of ECCAS partly overlaps with CEMAC (see above, Section IV(B)(vi)). Therefore, the EU has concluded a financial agreement with ECCAS, pending their merger, as a result of which ECCAS would take up responsibility for peace and security in the region.

ECCAS had been largely inactive since 1992 because of financial difficulties and the conflict in the Great Lakes region. In 1998, the leaders re-launched the organisation. The following year, the Council for Peace and Security in Central Africa (COPAX) was created, for the promotion, enforcement and consolidation of peace and security in Central Africa. The Protocol establishing the COPAX came into force in January 2004. This Council consists of a number of technical organs. The Central African early warning system (MARAC) collects and analyses data for the early detection and prevention of crises. In 2000, the network of Central African parliamentary members gathered for the first time. A year later, the Centre for Human Rights and Democracy was founded.

The Defence and Security Commission (CDS) is the meeting of the chiefs of staff of the national armies and commanders of the security forces of the Member States. Its role is to plan, organise and provide advice to decision-making bodies of the Community and, when necessary, to launch military operations. The Central African Multinational Force (FOMAC) is a non-permanent force consisting of military contingents of the Member States. Its task is to carry out peace and security or military missions. In 2003, a peacekeeping task force was formed to intervene in unstable areas.

The 'fresh start' of ECCAS encountered a setback with the withdrawal of Rwanda in 2007. However, various key players in international relations (such as Western powers, the EU, UN, AU and ECA) appear to have agreed that ECCAS should play a more significant role, especially with regard to issues of peace and stability in Central Africa. Nonetheless, the need to harmonise and coordinate the activities of the different Central African Communities remains a major obstacle in the workings of ECCAS.

[319] For a general overview, see eg R Adouki, 'Le Renouveau spectaculaire d'une organisation internationale sous-régionale en hibernation: la Communauté Economique des Etats de l'Afrique Centrale (CEEAC)' (2007) 72 *Revue internationale de droit africain* 57; M Kamto, 'La Communauté Economique des Etats de l'Afrique Centrale (C.E.E.A.C.): une communauté de plus?' (1987) 33 *Annuaire français de droit international* 839.

[320] Protocol on Relations between the African Economic Community and the Regional Economic Communities (25 February 1998) worldbank.org/GPTAD/PDF/annexes/AEC_protocols.pdf.

[321] Protocol establishing the Network of Parliaments of the Economic Community of Central African States (REPAC) (17 June 2002) nd.edu/~ggoertz/rei/rei220/rei220.02tt1.pdf.

viii. East African Community

The *East African Community* (EAC), created in 2000,[322] is a regional organisation of six Partner States: the Republics of Burundi, Kenya, Rwanda, South Sudan, the United Republic of Tanzania, and the Republic of Uganda, with headquarters in Arusha, Tanzania. The EAC previously functioned from 1967 to 1977 under the same name, and from 1993 to 2000 as the East African Cooperation. The EAC seeks to achieve a wider and deeper cooperation in all areas between the Partner States, through the establishment of a customs union, a common market, a monetary union and ultimately a Political Federation of East African States.[323]

The Summit of heads of State and government provides a general direction to the development and achievement of the objectives of the Community. It is held at least annually, to review the annual progress reports. The Council of Ministers is the policy-making organ of the Community. The Council promotes and supervises the implementation of Community programmes, ensures the good functioning of the organisation and meets at least twice a year. The East African Court of Justice (EACJ) has jurisdiction over the interpretation and application of the Treaty for the establishment of the EAC.[324] The EAC also has an East African Legislative Assembly with advisory powers, a Secretariat and a number of autonomous institutions such as the East African Development Bank.

ix. African Development Bank

The African Development Bank (AfDB)[325] is a multinational development bank, supported by 80 countries from Africa, America, Europe and Asia. The AfDB Group comprises the African Development Bank itself, the African Development Fund (ADF)[326] and the Nigerian Trust Fund (NTF). The AfDB was founded in 1964 and promotes economic and social development through loans, investments and technical assistance. The highest policy organ of the AfDB is the Board of Governors, in which a governor from each Member State is seated. It issues general guidelines regarding the operational policies of the AfDB and elects the AfDB President.[327] Amendments to the founding agreement of the AfDB, the admission of new members and capital increases all require the approval of the Board of Governors. However, it delegates most of its competences to the Board of Directors, which is responsible for the overall functioning of the Bank. It consists of 18 Executive Directors and it approves all loans, guarantees and investments. It also issues policy guidelines for the operations of the AfDB.

[322] Treaty for the establishment of the East African Community (adopted 30 November 1999, entered into force 7 July 2000) UNTS Registration No 37437.

[323] For a general overview, see eg P Drummond, S Kal Wajid and O Williams (eds), *The Quest for Regional Integration in the East African Community* (Washington, IMF, 2014); K Gastorn (ed), *Processes of Legal Integration in the East African Community* (Dar Es Salaam, Dar Es Salaam UP, 2011).

[324] A Possi, 'The East African Court of Justice: Towards Effective Protection of Human Rights in the African community' (2013) 17 *Max Planck Yearbook of United Nations Law* 173.

[325] Agreement establishing the African Development Bank (adopted 4 August 1963, entered into force 10 September 1964) 510 UNTS 3.

[326] Agreement establishing the African Development Fund (adopted 29 November 1972, entered into force 30 June 1973) 1197 UNTS 13.

[327] For a general overview, see eg YC Amegavie, *La Banque Africaine de Développement* (Paris, Pedone, 1977); K Gadio, 'Fostering Opportunity Through Development Finance in Africa: Legal Perspectives from the African Development Bank' (2013) 5 *The World Bank Legal Review: Law and Justice for Development* 453.

x. Community of Sahel-Saharan States

The *Community of Sahel-Saharan States* (CEN-SAD)[328] is a trade bloc aiming to create a free trade area within Africa. It was created in 1998 by six countries, but today it comprises 28 Member States. CEN-SAD has three priorities: economy, cooperation, and security. Its aim is to create an economic union, by ensuring free movement of persons, goods, services and capital, recognising the same rights to nationals of Member States, and harmonising the educational, scientific and cultural systems. The main bodies of CEN-SAD are: the Conference of Heads of State, which meets once a year; the Executive Board, responsible for the preparation of programmes and the implementation of decisions of the Conference; the General Secretariat, responsible for the daily management; the Sahel-Saharan Bank for Investment and Trade (BSIC), in charge of financing development projects; and the Economic, Social and Cultural Advisory Body.

V. Regional Organisations in Asia

Among the regional organisations in Asia, the most prominent are the Association of South East Asian Nations (ASEAN), the Asian Development Bank (ADB), the South Asian Association for Regional Cooperation (SAARC) and the Gulf Cooperation Council (GCC).[329] These will be discussed in this section.

A. Association of Southeast Asian Nations

The *Association of South East Asian Nations* (ASEAN)[330] was founded in 1967 by Indonesia, Malaysia, the Philippines, Singapore and Thailand. Later, Brunei, Vietnam, Laos, Myanmar and Cambodia joined. In 1976, the ASEAN Declaration[331] formalised the principles of peace and co-operation and is considered to be the founding document of ASEAN. It states the following objectives: the acceleration of economic growth, social progress and cultural development, in addition to promoting regional peace and stability through the respect for justice and the rule of law. In 2003, ASEAN was consolidated in a three-pillar structure, called the ASEAN Community, and consisting of an Economic Community, a Defence Community and a Socio-Cultural Community.[332]

[328] FJ Aivo, 'La Communauté des Etats Sahélo-Sahariens (CEN-SAD): acteur complémentaire ou concurrentiel de l'Union Africaine ?' (2009) 55 *Annuaire français de droit international* 469.

[329] See inter alia M Beeson (ed), *Routledge Handbook of Asian Regionalism* (London, Routledge, 2012); M Wesley (ed), *The Regional Organizations of the Asia-Pacific: Exploring Institutional Change* (Basingstoke, Palgrave Macmillan, 2003).

[330] Declaration constituting an agreement establishing the Association of South East Asian Nations (ASEAN) (adopted 8 August 1967, entered into force 8 August 1967) 1331 UNTS 235.

[331] ASEAN, 'The Declaration of ASEAN Concord', 24 February 1976, asean.org/?static_post=declaration-of-asean-concord-indonesia-24-february-1976.

[332] For a general overview, see eg S Inama and EW Sim, *The Foundation of the ASEAN Economic Community: An Institutional and Legal Profile* (Cambridge, CUP, 2015); CS Yue and MG Plummer, *ASEAN Economic Cooperation and Integration: Progress, Challenges and Future Directions* (Cambridge, CUP, 2015); CB Roberts, *ASEAN Regionalism: Cooperation, Values and Institutionalization* (London, Routledge, 2012).

The highest decision-making body of ASEAN is the Annual Meeting of State and government leaders. While foreign affairs ministers also meet annually, ministerial meetings in specific sectors are held more regularly, supported by several committees and technical groups. To promote ASEAN policies externally, it also has established committees in a number of major foreign cities. The Secretariat General of ASEAN has existed since 1979 and is tasked with initiating, advising, coordinating and implementing the organisation's activities. In addition, ASEAN has several specialised bodies promoting public cooperation in various fields, encouraging cooperation between organisations with similar objectives. ASEAN is also affiliated to a number of NGOs. All decisions within ASEAN are taken by consensus.

A number of important political agreements to avoid armed conflicts were signed among the ASEAN Member States. In 1994, the ASEAN Regional Forum (ARF) was established to focus on preventive diplomacy and conflict resolution in the region, and may issue recommendations in this regard.[333] The ARF includes the 10 ASEAN countries, 15 counterparts (including the EU, US, Japan, China and Russia)[334] and two ASEAN observers (Papua New Guinea and Timor-Leste). The Ministers of Foreign Affairs of the ARF States gather yearly under the presidency of an ASEAN Member State. Since 2002, the main focus of the ARF has been on the fight against terrorism.

Since 1993, ASEAN has been striving for the creation of a trans-ASEAN transportation network and a free trade zone (ASEAN Free Trade Area or AFTA). The backbone of the AFTA is the Common Effective Preferential Tariff (CEPT), which obliges Member States to apply a tariff rate of 0–5 per cent. Unlike the EU or the African regional organisations discussed above, the AFTA does not apply a common external tariff on imported goods.[335]

Since 1996, ASEAN has had a number of action plans for functional cooperation in domains such as social development, culture and information, science and technology, environment, drug abuse and transnational crime. In November 2007, ASEAN leaders signed the ASEAN Charter[336], which came into effect on 15 December 2008, with a view to encourage the transformation of ASEAN from a loosely-formed association to a rules-based integrated Community. However, the Charter has been marred by legitimacy concerns, more precisely due to a lack of transparency during the drafting process. In November 2012, a Declaration on Human Rights was adopted,[337] drafted by the ASEAN Intergovernmental Commission on Human Rights.[338]

ASEAN is the main interlocutor for third countries in South East Asia. For example, the political dialogue between the EU and ASEAN dates back to 1980, when the EEC signed a Cooperation Agreement with the ASEAN countries. Since then 21 ASEAN-EU Ministerial Meetings have taken place. The EU-ASEAN Joint Cooperation Committee promotes and oversees the various cooperation activities. The Committee meets every 18 months and

[333] J Haacke (ed), *Cooperative Security in the Asia-Pacific: the ASEAN Regional Forum* (London, Routledge, 2010).

[334] See eg K Weber, 'The ASEAN Regional Forum and the EU's Role in Promoting Security in the Asia-Pacific' in T Christiansen, EJ Kirchner and P Murray (eds), *The Palgrave Handbook of EU-Asia Relations* (Basingstoke, Palgrave Macmillan, 2015) 344.

[335] HE Sharmini Nesadurai, *Globalisation, Domestic Policies and Regionalism: The ASEAN Free Trade Area* (London, Routledge, 2003).

[336] Charter of the Association of Southeast Asian Nations (adopted 20 November 2007, entered into force 15 December 2008) 2624 UNTS 223.

[337] ASEAN, 'ASEAN Human Rights Declaration', 19 November 2012, asean.org/asean-human-rights-declaration.

[338] GJ Naldi and KD Magliveras, 'The ASEAN Human Rights Declaration' (2014) 3 *International Human Rights Law Review* 183.

has established a number of sub-committees. In 2007, the Nuremberg Declaration on an EU-ASEAN Enhanced Partnership was adopted,[339] which sets out a long-term vision on common goals and objectives. Following that declaration, the 'Bandar Seri Begawan Plan of Action to Strengthen the ASEAN-EU Enhanced Partnership' (2013–2017) was adopted in 2012,[340] focusing on enhancing cooperation in various areas (security, economy, trade, culture, etc).[341] The Bandar Seri Begawan Plan of Action was replaced by the 'ASEAN-EU Plan of Action (2018–2022)'.[342]

B. Other Regional and Sub-Regional Organisations in Asia

i. Asian Development Bank – Asian Infrastructure Investment Bank

The *Asian Development Bank* (ADB)[343] is a multilateral financial institution, comparable to the World Bank. It aims to reduce poverty in Asia and the Pacific. The Bank was created in 1966 and currently has 67 Members, including 19 Members located beyond the Asian-Pacific region. The two organs of the ADB are the Board of Governors, in which each country is represented, and the Board of Directors, which is composed of 12 directors. The Board of Governors has delegated many of its powers to the Board of Directors. Since 2002, the structure of the ADB has been thoroughly reformed to accommodate the needs of the developing countries. At the core of the reorganisation is the increase of the accountability duties of the Bank towards developing countries. To that end, all the developing countries are brought together into five geographical areas, each covered by a different regional department of the Bank. Finally, there is an Asian Development Bank Institute connected to the Bank, which presents studies about Asian development.

Nevertheless, the Bank's activities have been criticised from various angles. Since its early days, criticism has been directed at the significant influence over lending, policy and staffing, exerted by the two major donors of the Bank: the US and Japan.[344]

Partly for that reason, China took the initiative in 2013 to create a new multilateral development bank, the *Asian Infrastructure Investment Bank* (AIIB). The AIIB currently has 86 Member States from around the world, including a number of EU Member States. It started its operations after the agreement entered into force on 25 December 2015.[345]

[339] EU and EEAS, 'Nuremberg Declaration on an EU-ASEAN Enhanced Partnership', 15 March 2007, eeas.europa.eu/sites/eeas/files/2007_16_nuremberg_declar.pdf.

[340] 'Bandar Seri Begawan Plan of Action to Strengthen the ASEAN-EU Enhanced Partnership (2013–2017)', europarl.europa.eu/cmsdata/124481/129884.pdf.

[341] L Allison, *The EU, ASEAN and Interregionalism: Regionalism Support and Norm Diffusion between the EU and ASEAN* (Basingstoke, Palgrave Macmillan, 2015); A Berramdane and M Trochu (eds), *Le partenariat UE-ASEAN* (Brussels, Bruylant, 2013).

[342] 'ASEAN-EU Plan of Action (2018–2022)', asean.org/storage/2017/08/ASEAN-EU-POA-2018-2022-Final.pdf.

[343] Agreement establishing the Asian Development Bank (adopted 4 December 1965, entered into force 22 August 1966) 571 UNTS 123. For a general overview, see M Wesley, 'The Asian Development Bank' in Wesley (n 329) 19; and L Xing, 'The Asian Development Bank (ADB)' in Wouters (n 11).

[344] See DY Moa Lim and JR Vreeland, 'Regional organizations and International Politics: Japanese Influence over the Asian Development Bank and the UN Security council' (2013) 65 *World Politics* 34.

[345] See B Gu, 'The Chinese Multilateralism in the AIIB' (2017) 20 *Journal of International Economic Law* 1464; NG Lichtenstein, *A Comparative Guide to the Asian Infrastructure Investment Bank* (Oxford, OUP, 2018); X Wu, 'Friendly Competition for Co-Progressive Development: The Asian Infrastructure Investment Bank vs. the Bretton Woods Institutions' (2017) 16 *Chinese Journal of International Law* 41. The AIIB's Articles of Agreement can be found here: https://www.aiib.org/en/about-aiib/basic-documents/_download/articles-of-agreement/basic_document_english-bank_articles_of_agreement.pdf.

ii. South Asian Association for Regional Cooperation

The *South Asian Association for Regional Cooperation* (SAARC)[346] was established in 1985 by Bangladesh, Bhutan, India, Maldives, Nepal, Pakistan and Sri Lanka. Afghanistan joined SAARC as its eighth member in April 2007. SAARC aims to promote the economic and social development of its Member States.[347] The meeting of the heads of State or government is the highest decision-making authority. The Council of Foreign Ministers formulates the policy direction of SAARC, oversees the progress of SAARC cooperation and adopts decisions in new areas for cooperation. The Standing Committee is an executive organ which consists of representatives of the Ministers of Foreign Affairs. It is responsible for the supervision and coordination of cooperation programmes, the evaluation of projects and programmes, the determination of inter-sectoral priorities, the mobilisation of regional and external means and the identification of new areas for cooperation. Under the supervision of the Standing Committee, a number of technical committees operate. The role of the Secretariat of SAARC is to coordinate and monitor the implementation of SAARC activities and provide assistance to its meetings. The Secretariat also serves as the communication channel between SAARC and other international organisations. Decisions within SAARC are taken unanimously.

Unlike in other regional organisations, the creation of a free trade zone was not a central objective of SAARC. Nevertheless, in 1995, a preferential trade agreement (South Asian Preferential Trading Arrangement (SAPTA)) came into effect among the Member States.[348] In 2004, a framework agreement on a free trade area (South Asian Free Trade Area (SAFTA))[349] was signed, which should eventually lead to an economic union.[350] The trade flows between the SAARC States remain rather limited. The lack of progress of SAARC is mainly due to the ongoing geopolitical tensions between India and Pakistan, which have repeatedly led to the postponing of the annual Summits. A dialogue about politically sensitive issues is prohibited under the SAARC Charter, although Member States do hold informal political consultations.

iii. Cooperation Council for the Arab States of the Gulf

The Charter of the *Cooperation Council for the Arab Gulf States* (GCC)[351] was signed in 1981 between the United Arab Emirates, Bahrain, Saudi Arabia, Oman, Qatar and Kuwait. United by a common Arab heritage, the six Gulf States joined forces to strengthen

[346] Charter of the South-Asian Association for Regional Cooperation (adopted 8 December 1985, entered into force 8 December 1985) saarc-sec.org/SAARC-Charter.

[347] For a general overview, see ZS Ahmed, *Regionalism and Regional Security in South Asia: The Role of SAARC* (Farnham, Ashgate, 2013); L Saez, *The South Asian Association for Regional Cooperation (SAARC): An Emerging Collaboration Architecture* (London, Routledge, 2011); J Betz, 'Südasiatische Vereinigung für regionale Kooperation (SAARC)' in Grimmel and Jakobeit (n 254) 165.

[348] Agreement on SAARC Preferential Trading Arrangement (11 April 1993, entered into force 7 December 1995) saarc-sec.org/digital_library/detail_menu/agreement-on-saarc-preferential-trading-arrangement-sapta (SAPTA).

[349] Agreement on South Asian Free Trade Area (adopted 6 January 2004, entered into force 1 January 2006) saarc-sec.org/digital_library/detail_menu/agreement-on-south-asian-free-trade-area-safta (SAFTA).

[350] BA Iqbal, 'Is SAFTA a Myth or Reality?' (2012) 13 *Journal of World Investment and Trade* 103; S Paranjpe, 'From State-centricism to Transnationalism: SAARC, SAPTA and SAFTA' (1996) 52 *India Quarterly: A Journal of International Affairs* 95.

[351] Charter of the Co-operation Council for the Arab States of the Gulf (adopted 25 May 1981, entered into force 25 May 1981) 1288 UNTS 131.

coordination and integration among the Member States in all areas.[352] The GCC forms a customs union since January 2003. The common tariff for imported products from third countries is 5 per cent, although some products are exempted from import duties.

The Supreme Council is the highest authority and the final decision-making body of the GCC. It consists of the heads of State and government of the GCC countries, and meets annually. At the request of a Member State, supported by another Member State, special sessions may be convened. Since 1998, the Council has held a consultative meeting between the annual Summits. It also forms a Commission for Dispute Settlement, on an ad hoc basis. The Council of Ministers consists of Ministers of Foreign Affairs or their representatives. It is competent to present policy proposals and recommendations, and to encourage and coordinate the existing activities of the GCC. The Ministerial committees send their resolutions to the Council of Ministers which, in turn, refers relevant issues to the Supreme Council. The Council of Ministers decides unanimously. The Secretariat General of the GCC is responsible for preparing policy studies, drafting periodic reports on the work of the GCC, the monitoring of the implementation of the resolutions and the preparation of draft resolutions for the Council of Ministers.

In 1988, the EEC and the GCC signed a Cooperation Agreement.[353] Since then, the GCC has a Permanent Mission to the European Commission and the Ministers of Foreign Affairs of the EU and the GCC meet on an annual basis. The objective of this agreement is the simplification of trade relations and strengthening stability in the Gulf region. Negotiations regarding the conclusion of a Free Trade Agreement have been ongoing since 1990. However, they have faced several challenges and were effectively suspended in 2008, when the GCC countries withdrew from all negotiations. While, since then, periodic informal contacts have taken place to test whether a basis can nonetheless be found to resume and conclude negotiations, these have not been successful. However, in May 2017, a more structured informal EU-GCC dialogue on trade and investment was launched, in order to enhance cooperation on matters of common interest, such as market access irritants, regulatory requirements, or ways to encourage greater two-way trade and investment flow.

In 2011, Saudi Arabia presented a proposal to transform the GCC into a 'Gulf Union' with closer economic, political and military cooperation, in order to counterbalance the Iranian influence in the region. It met with a mixed response.

iv. Other Regional and Sub-Regional Organisations in Asia

The *Asia Cooperation Dialogue* (ACD) is an intergovernmental organisation aiming to build an Asian community, by bringing together separate international organisations, such as ASEAN, SAARC and the GCC. It was established in 2002, and now comprises 34 Member States. The main objectives of the ACD are: promoting the cooperation between Asian countries in various areas; expanding the trade and financial market within Asia; and,

[352] For a general overview, see eg Worrall (n 310); AD Marar, 'The Cooperation Council for the Arab States of the Gulf' (2004) 10 *Law and Business Review of the Americas* 475; S Boutros Farajallah, 'Le Conseil de Coopération des Etats Arabes du Golfe' (1991) 228 *RdC* 9.

[353] Cooperation Agreement between the European Economic Community, of the one part, and the countries parties to the Charter of the Cooperation Council for the Arab States of the Gulf (the State of the United Arab Emirates, the State of Bahrain, the Kingdom of Saudi Arabia, the Sultanate of Oman, the State of Qatar and the State of Kuwait) of the other part (adopted 15 June 1988, entered into force 1 January 1990) [1989] OJ L54/3 (EU-GCC Cooperation Agreement).

ultimately, creating an Asian community, capable of interacting with the rest of the world. The main bodies of ACD are the yearly Ministerial Meeting, which is the executive organ, and the Secretariat, with an administrative role.

The *Bay of Bengal Initiative for Multi-Sectoral Technical and Economic Cooperation* (BIMSTEC)[354] is an organisation gathering the countries dependent on the Bay of Bengal, from India to Myanmar. It was established in 1997, and now includes seven Member States. The main objective is to enhance the economic growth and development of the region, focusing on cooperation in 15 sectors, including trade, technology, transport, energy, tourism, fisheries, agriculture, public health, poverty alleviation, counter-terrorism, environment, culture, people to people contact, and climate change. Its main bodies are: the Annual Ministerial Meeting; the Senior Officials Committee, meeting on a regular basis and when required; the BIMSTEC Working Group, comprising representatives of Member States to carry on with work in between Annual Ministerial Meetings; and the Secretariat.

The *Trilateral Cooperation Secretariat* (TCS) is an organisation established in 2011, in order to promote peace and prosperity in China, Japan and South Korea. It provides support for trilateral consultative mechanisms, facilitates cooperative projects, promotes understanding of trilateral cooperation, expands the networking and cooperation with other international organisations, and compiles databases. The TCS consists of a Consultative Board with a Secretary General and two Deputy Secretary Generals, and of four Departments: Political Affairs, Economic Affairs, Socio-Cultural Affairs, and Management and Coordination.

VI. Transcontinental Regional Organisations

Among the transcontinental regional organisations, the following should be mentioned: the Arab League, the Asian-Pacific Economic Cooperation (APEC), the Secretariat of the Pacific Community (SPC), the Organization of Petroleum Exporting Countries (OPEC), the Organization of Arab Petroleum Exporting Countries (OAPEC), the Organization for Economic Cooperation of the Black Sea (BSEC), the Commonwealth of Independent States (CIS), the Organization of the Islamic Conference (OIC), the Islamic Development Bank (IDB) and the Conference of Energy Charter (ECC).

A. Arab League

The League of Arab States (LAS), or *Arab League*,[355] is an association of 22 States from Africa and the Middle East whose citizens are mainly Arabic speaking or where Arabic is an official language. The Arab League was founded in Cairo in 1945 on Egypt's initiative, with the aim of creating a full Arab Union. Its initial objectives were achieving the independence

[354] A Batra, 'Asian Economic Integration and Sub-Regionalism: A Case Study of the BIMSTEC' (2010) 47 *International Studies: Journal of the School of International Studies, Jawaharlal Nehru University* 1.

[355] Pact of the League of Arab States (adopted 22 March 1945, entered into force 10 May 1945) 70 UNTS 237. For a general overview, see eg Worrall (n 310); A Zorob, 'Arabische Liga' in Grimmel and Jakobeit (n 254) 209.

of the Arab States, putting an end to Jewish immigration to Palestine and preventing the establishment of a Jewish State. Ever since the establishment of the latter in 1948 and the Arab-Israeli war that followed, the Arab League has boycotted Israel.[356] On a more general level, it strives to strengthen the ties between Arab States, to coordinate their policies and to advance common interests.

Within the fold of the Arab League, a number of political, economic, cultural and social programmes were designed to promote the interests of the Member States. The Arab League is also a forum through which Member States coordinate their policy positions and settle disputes. However, the instruments to achieve this are lacking. The Member States of the Arab League may submit their disputes to the Council. Its majority decisions are binding. When a Member State is attacked or threatened, it may request an immediate meeting of the Council. The Council may unanimously adopt the necessary measures to repel the attack. However, in practice settlement attempts primarily take the form of informal conciliation efforts. For instance, on two occasions, the Arab League attempted to mediate between the parties to the war in Syria, without success.

The Arab League also serves as a platform for drafting instruments on economic integration, such as the Joint Arab Economic Charter of 1957. In 1953 an Arab Telecommunications Union was founded, followed by an Arab Postal Union a year later and the Arab Development Bank in 1959. The Arab Common Market was founded in 1965 and is open to all Member States of the League.[357] Yet, greater political unity among the Member States has proven difficult to attain, due to initial tensions between pro-Western countries and neutral or pro-Soviet countries and the subsequent contrast between moderates and fundamentalists.

The Council of the Arab League is composed of representatives of the Member States. It gathers twice a year in ordinary session. The Council is tasked with achieving the objectives of the League and oversees the implementation of the agreements among the Member States, regarding the matters included in the Charter. The Council's decisions, which are adopted unanimously, are binding on all Member States; other decisions are binding only for the States which accept them. However, the Member States of the Arab League do not always comply with these unanimous decisions. The Arab League has a permanent General Secretariat, which prepares the draft budget of the League and submits it for approval to the Council.

Dialogues and cooperation between the EU and the Arab league were given a boost by the Arab Spring revolts and the Libya crisis in 2011. Various high-level dialogues have since been held. Cooperation focuses on conflict prevention, early warning and crisis response.

B. Asian-Pacific Economic Cooperation

The *Asian-Pacific Economic Cooperation* (APEC)[358] consists of 21 Asian countries and countries bordering the Pacific. APEC was formed in 1989 and focuses on economic issues,

[356] MA Weiss, 'Arab League Boycott of Israel' in LH Girard (ed), *Israeli-Arab Negotiations and Issues* (New York, Nova Science, 2011).

[357] Economic and Social Commission for Western Asia, *Assessing Arab Economic Integration: Towards the Arab Customs Union* (Beirut, UNESCWA, 2015); AG Musrey, *An Arab Common Market: A Study in Inter-Arab Trade Relations, 1920–67* (New York, Praeger, 1969) 137.

[358] For a general overview, see eg J Ruland, E Manske and W Draguhn (eds), *Asia-Pacific Economic Cooperation (APEC): The First Decade* (London, Routledge, 2002).

particularly the reduction of tariffs and other trade barriers, the creation of efficient economies and the increase of exports (the so-called 'Bogor targets'). Within the context of APEC, the term 'Member Economies' is used instead of Member States. The annual rotating chairmanship of APEC is responsible for the annual Ministerial Meeting between the Ministers of Foreign Affairs and Finance. Every two years this Meeting is held in an ASEAN country. In 1995, a Business Advisory Council was also set up. This permanent council consists of more than three businessmen from all Member States and provides advice on the implementation of the APEC action plans and other specific priorities, in relation to the private sector. APEC further consists of a secretariat, committees (trade and investment, economy and technology, budget and management), working groups and some other APEC forums. All decisions are taken by consensus.

C. South Pacific Community

In 1947, Australia, France, New Zealand, the Netherlands, the UK and the US founded the *South Pacific Community* via the Canberra Agreement.[359] After all island States and territories in the Pacific became members, and the Netherlands and the UK left, in 1962 and 1994 respectively, the name of the organisation was changed to the *Secretariat of the Pacific Community* (SPC). The Secretariat is based in Noumea (New Caledonia). SPC is responsible for the social and economic development in 26 countries and territories in the Pacific. It is a non-political organisation that provides technical assistance, advice and training. Within SPC all decisions are taken by consensus. SPC has been particularly active in the fields of fisheries, health, agriculture, education and socio-economic and statistical services.

D. Organization of Petroleum Exporting Countries

The *Organization of Petroleum Exporting Countries* (OPEC)[360] is an international organisation founded by five States in Baghdad in 1960. It has been headquartered in Vienna since 1965, and consists of 15 Member Countries which are heavily dependent on oil revenues as their main source of income. The OPEC Member Countries coordinate their oil production policies in view of the stabilisation of the oil market, a reasonable return on investment for producers and a stable oil supply for consumers. OPEC membership is open to any country that is a net exporter of oil and shares the goals of the organisation. OPEC Member Countries produce 40 per cent of the world's oil and own more than three quarters of proven reserves of crude oil.[361]

The Ministers of Petroleum and Energy of the OPEC countries meet twice a year, or more often if required, in the context of a Conference to adapt the output level in light of previous and anticipated developments in the oil market. The Conference is the supreme

[359] Agreement establishing the South Pacific Commission (adopted 6 February 1947, entered into force 29 July 1948) 97 UNTS 227.

[360] Agreement concerning the creation of the Organization of Petroleum Exporting Countries (OPEC) (adopted 14 September 1960, entered into force 1 October 1960) 443 UNTS 247.

[361] See eg JM Witte and A Goldthau, *Die OPEC: Macht und Ohnmacht des Öl-Kartells* (München, Hanser, 2009); L Mihailovitch and JJ Pluchart, *L'OPEP: organisation des pays exportateurs de pétrole*, 2nd edn (Paris, Presses Universitaires de France, 1985).

organ of OPEC. It decides unanimously and its decisions are published in the form of press releases. The OPEC management is in the hands of the Board of Governors, each appointed by an OPEC Member. The Board of Governors implements the resolutions of the Conference, drafts the annual budget, looks into the reports by the Secretary General and puts forward its own reports and recommendations to the Conference. The OPEC Secretariat is a permanent intergovernmental body, which offers analytical and administrative support to the Ministerial Conference and distributes news and information on OPEC. The Secretary General is the executive head of the OPEC Secretariat and the representative of OPEC. He is assisted by his own cabinet, a research section and several other departments. The Economic Commission, a specialised body that functions under the auspices of the Secretariat, backs the OPEC in promoting the stability of the international oil prices.

The effectiveness of OPEC is undermined by a number of important oil-exporting countries which are not members of OPEC and by the recurring temptation for individual OPEC Member Countries to exceed production ceilings and pursue conflicting self-interests.

E. Organization of Arab Petroleum Exporting Countries

The *Organization of Arab Petroleum Exporting Countries* (OAPEC)[362] was founded in 1968 and should be distinguished from OPEC.[363] OAPEC's membership is limited to Arab countries with significant oil revenues (Kuwait, Libya, Saudi Arabia, Algeria, Bahrain, Egypt, Iraq, Qatar, Syria, Tunisia and the United Arab Emirates). The Tunisian membership was suspended upon their request. OAPEC is a tool for Arab cooperation and integration, with the aim of providing support to the Arab oil industry, including by sponsoring joint ventures. The determination of oil prices is not part of its mandate, as this is in the remit of OPEC. OAPEC also deals with energy issues that concern all Member States of the Arab League and gathers every four years to that end. The Ministerial Council of OAPEC is the highest body of the organisation. It is responsible for the overall policy, the strategic direction of its activities and the promulgating of rules. It meets at least twice a year. The Ministerial Council is assisted by the Executive Office. The General Secretariat is responsible for the planning, management and implementation of the activities of the organisation, in accordance with the objectives of the OAPEC Agreement and the resolutions and guidelines of the Ministerial Council.

OAPEC established a Judicial Tribunal in 1978 through a special protocol and it has been operational since 1981.[364] The Tribunal has jurisdiction over disputes with respect to the interpretation and application of the OAPEC Agreement, disputes between two or more Member States relating to oil operations, as far as they do not infringe upon the

[362] Agreement for the establishment of an Arab Organization for the Petroleum Exporting Countries (adopted 9 January 1968, entered into force 1 September 1968) 681 UNTS 247. For a general overview, see eg A Maachou, *OAPEC: An International Organization for Economic Cooperation and an Instrument for Regional Integration* (Paris, Berger-Levrault, 1982); S El-Gebali, *Die OAPEC als Organisation zur Interessenvertretung der Arabischen Öllländer in den internationalen wirtschaftlichen Beziehungen* (Frankfurt am Main, Lang, 1981).

[363] AA Khaki, 'OPEC and OAPEC: A Comparative Study in International Organizations' (1980) 36 *Revue égyptienne de droit international* 197.

[364] Protocol of the Judicial Tribunal (adopted 9 May 1978, entered into force 20 April 1980).

sovereignty of the countries, and disputes with regard to which the Ministerial Council decides on the referral to the Tribunal. With the consent of the parties, the Tribunal may decide over disputes between a Member State and an oil company operating on its territory, a dispute between a Member State and a national oil company of another Member State, and disputes between two Member States. The Tribunal also has advisory jurisdiction on matters referred to it by the Ministerial Council. The decisions of the Tribunal are not subject to appeal and are binding on the parties.

F. Organization of the Black Sea Economic Cooperation

In 1992, 11 'Black Sea countries' (Albania, Armenia, Azerbaijan, Bulgaria, Georgia, Greece, Moldova, Romania, Russia, Turkey and Ukraine) adopted the Bosporus Statement in Istanbul and established the Economic Cooperation of the Black Sea. In 2004, the State Union of Serbia and Montenegro became the twelfth member. In 1994, a Permanent International Secretariat was established within the framework of this cooperation. A few years later, in 1998, the political Bosporus Declaration was upgraded to a legal Charter at the Yalta Conference.[365] After having obtained the necessary ratifications, the *Organization of the Black Sea Economic Cooperation* (BSEC; see also above, Section II(F)(ii)) was established in 1999. According to the Yalta Charter, the BSEC concentrates primarily on trade and economic development, banking and finance, communications, energy, transportation, agriculture, healthcare, environmental protection, tourism, science and technology, the exchange of statistical economic data, the collaboration between border authorities, the fight against organised crime and illegal drug trafficking, weapons and radioactive materials, terrorism and illegal migration.

G. Commonwealth of Independent States

The *Commonwealth of Independent States* (CIS)[366] came into existence immediately after the dissolution of the Soviet Union in December 1991, and currently has nine full Member States: Armenia, Azerbaijan, Belarus, Kazakhstan, the Kyrgyz Republic, Moldova, the Russian Federation, Tajikistan, and Uzbekistan.[367] Since 1991, the CIS has served as a platform from which several initiatives for closer economic cooperation between the former Soviet States have been launched. Such attempts at economic reconnection have, inter alia, included the 1993 Treaty on the Creation of an Economic Union,[368] the 2000 Treaty on the establishment of the Eurasian Economic Community,[369] which was followed in 2007

[365] Charter of the Organization of the Black Sea Economic Cooperation (adopted 5 June 1998, entered into force 1 May 1999) internationaldemocracywatch.org/attachments/379_Charter%20of%20the%20Organization%20of%20the%20Black%20Sea%20Economic%20Cooperation.pdf (Yalta Charter).

[366] Z Kembayev, *Legal Aspects of the Regional Integration Processes in the Post-Soviet Area* (Berlin, Springer, 2009); E Engle (ed), *Russia, the European Union and the CIS* (The Hague, Eleven International Publishing, 2012).

[367] Although both Turkmenistan and Ukraine were founding States, their status is now that of 'associated' States.

[368] Treaty on creation of Economic Union (adopted 24 September 1993, entered into force provisionally 24 December 1993) 34 ILM 1303.

[369] Treaty on the establishment of the Eurasian Economic Community (adopted 10 October 2000, entered into force 30 May 2001) 2212 UNTS 257.

by a treaty setting up a customs union,[370] and the initiative to launch a single economic space in 2009.[371] These initiatives were eventually overtaken by a more far-reaching attempt at economic integration that was driven in particular by Russia, namely the Eurasian Economic Union, which was established in 2014 (see below, Section VI(H)).

However, the CIS remains operational today. The Council of heads of State is the supreme organ of the CIS and it discusses and resolves questions which concern the common interests of the Member States. The Economic Court is entrusted with ensuring the compliance with the economic commitments undertaken within the framework of the CIS. The Court settles economic disputes between States and examines them in light of the agreements and decisions of the Council of heads of State of the CIS. Its rulings, however, have the status of recommendations. The Council of Foreign Ministers is the main executive body and secures cooperation in the field of foreign policy of the Member States, while the Council of Defence Ministers is a body of the Council of Heads of State. In addition, the Executive Committee is the permanent executive, administrative and coordinating body of the CIS. It organises the activities of the councils and other bodies, prepares proposals to deepen cooperation in the framework of the CIS, particularly as far as the economy is concerned. Furthermore, an Inter-State Bank, an Inter-State Statistical Committee and a number of technical bodies were added to the CIS structure. Within the framework of the CIS, Russia, Ukraine, Belarus, Kazakhstan, Kyrgyzstan, Tajikistan, Moldova and Armenia[372] have entered into a free trade agreement, the Commonwealth of Independent States Free Trade Area Agreement, which was signed in 2011 and entered into force in 2012.[373]

H. Eurasian Economic Union

The *Eurasian Economic Union* (EAEU) was founded in 2014.[374] It is an international economic organisation, consisting of five former Soviet Republics: the Russian Federation, Belarus, Kazakhstan, the Kyrgyz Republic and Armenia.[375] Its aim is to foster closer economic cooperation, and to establish an internal single market that includes the free movement of goods, services, persons and capital. Its institutional structure mirrors to a certain extent that of the EU, and is comprised of the Supreme Eurasian Economic Council, Eurasian Intergovernmental Council, Eurasian Economic Commission, and Court of the Eurasian Economic Union.

[370] Treaty on the establishment of a Common Customs Territory and the Formation of the Customs Union (adopted 6 October 2007, fully functional as of 1 July 2011) evrazes.com/docs/view/163.

[371] R Dragneva and K Wolczuk, 'Russia, the Eurasian Customs Union and the EU: Cooperation, Stagnation or Rivalry?' (2012) Chatham House Briefing Paper 5. For more detail, see R Dragneva and K Wolczuk (eds), *Eurasian Economic Integration: Law, Policy and Politics* (Cheltenham, Edward Elgar, 2013).

[372] Later joined by Uzbekistan.

[373] Treaty on a Free Trade Area (adopted 18 October 2011, entered into force 20 September 2012) eurasiancommission.org/ru/act/trade/dotp/sogl_torg/Documents/FTA%20CIS_Text_with_protocols_ENG.pdf.

[374] Treaty on the Eurasian Economic Union (adopted 29 May 2014, entered into force 1 January 2015) UNTS Registration No 52764.

[375] For more detail, see A Di Gregorio and A Angeli, *The Eurasian Economic Union and the European Union: Moving towards a Greater Understanding* (The Hague, Eleven Law, 2017); and AA Kashirinka and AN Morozov, *Россия, Евразийский экономический союз и Всемирная торговая организация (Russia, the Eurasian Economic Union and the World Trade Organization)* (Moscow, InfraM, 2014).

I. Organization of Islamic Cooperation

The *Organization of Islamic Cooperation* (OIC)[376] is an intergovernmental organisation which consists of 57 Member States. It was founded as the Organization of the Islamic Conference in 1969 in Rabat, at a meeting of leaders of the Islamic world after an attack on the Al-Aqsa Mosque in Jerusalem. In 1970 the First Islamic Conference of Foreign Ministers took place in Jeddah and created the Permanent Secretariat, which is located there. In 1972, the Third Islamic Conference adopted the OIC Charter.[377] According to the Charter, the objective of the OIC lies in strengthening Islamic solidarity and cooperation on the political, economic, social, cultural and scientific level, safeguarding the Holy Places, supporting the struggle of the Palestinian people and the elimination of all forms of racial discrimination and colonialism. The Islamic Summit, attended by Kings, Heads of State and Government of the Member States is the highest organ of the OIC. It comes together every three years to determine the policies of the organisation.

The Islamic Conference of Foreign Ministers meets annually and examines progress reports on the implementation of the decisions taken at the Islamic Summits. The Permanent Secretariat is the executive organ of the OIC and is responsible for implementing the decisions of the Summits and Conferences. To coordinate the activities of Member States, and to streamline their views, the OIC has set up a number of specialised committees at the ministerial level, as well as several subsidiary bodies. Since 1988, the OIC has built Islamic Colleges and cultural institutes and centres to disseminate Islamic culture and the Arabic language. It was also one of the first organisations to adopt a regional instrument condemning terrorism.[378]

In 2008, the OIC amended its founding Convention. The revised text insists on the promotion of human rights, fundamental freedoms and good governance in all Member States. In 2011, the Conference of Foreign Ministers decided to change the name to Organization of Islamic Cooperation. In 2016, the OIC adopted a programme for the 2016–2025 period, focusing on 18 issues, such as peace and security, counter-terrorism, climate change or women's empowerment.[379]

J. Islamic Development Bank

The *Islamic Development Bank* (IDB)[380] is a multilateral financial institution similar to the World Bank, the AfDB (see above, Section IV(B)(ix)) or the ADB (see above,

[376] Charter of the Islamic Conference (adopted 4 March 1972, entered into force 28 February 1973) 914 UNTS 110. See also VL Gutierrez Castillo and J Cruz Angeles, 'Islam and International Organizations: the Organization of Islamic Cooperation' in R Virzo and I Ingravallo (eds), *Evolutions in the Law of International Organizations* (Leiden, Nijhoff, 2015) 171; G Bacik, 'The Genesis, History, and Functioning of the Organization of Islamic Cooperation (OIC): A Formal-Institutional Analysis' (2011) 31 *Journal of Muslim Minority Affairs* 594.

[377] See above (n 376).

[378] Convention of the Organization of the Islamic Conference on Combating International Terrorism (adopted 1 July 1999, entered into force 7 November 2002), reprinted in UN, *International Instruments related to the Prevention and Suppression of International Terrorism* (New York, UN, 2008) 204. See also KLH Samuel, 'The Legal Response to Terrorism of the Organization of Islamic Cooperation' in B Saul (ed), *Research Handbook on International Law and Terrorism* (Cheltenham, Edward Elgar, 2014) 717.

[379] OIC, 'The OIC-2025 Programme of Action', 14–15 April 2016, OIC/SUM-13/2016/POA-Final.

[380] SA Meenai, *The Islamic Development Bank: A Case-study of Islamic Co-operation* (London, Kegan Paul International, 1989); and B Turner, 'Islamic Development Bank' in B Turner (ed), *The Statesman's Yearbook* (London, Palgrave Macmillan, 2014) 51.

Section V(B)(i)). Its objective is to promote economic development and social progress in the participating countries and in Muslim communities abroad, in accordance with the principles of Islamic law (Sharia). The IDB comprises 57 Member States, all of which must also be members of the OIC. The IDB was established in 1975 pursuant to a memorandum of the Conference of Finance Ministers of Muslim Countries adopted in Jeddah in 1973.

The IDB provides loans for promising projects and enterprises and offers financial assistance to the Member States under various forms for economic and social development. In addition, it provides support to promote foreign trade between its Member States, as well as technical assistance and training opportunities. The IDB mobilises financial resources through methods compatible with Sharia. Each Member State of the IDB is represented in the Board of Governors, which meets annually to oversee the activities of the IDB during the previous year and to decide on future policies. Decisions of the Board of Governors are taken by a majority vote. As the highest decision-making body, it has exclusive responsibility regarding membership, capital change and cooperation agreements with international and regional organisations. Most other powers are delegated to the Board of Directors, in which 14 directors are seated.

K. Energy Charter Conference

The *Energy Charter Conference* (ECC)[381] is a Brussels-based intergovernmental organisation which constitutes the decision-making body of the Energy Charter process. The ECC was founded in 1994 by the Energy Charter Treaty,[382] providing a multilateral framework for energy cooperation. All States which have signed the Treaty are members of the ECC. There are 54 signatories, mainly European States and the EU. However, not all of them have ratified it. The ECC usually gathers twice a year, in the context of a conference to discuss policy issues with regard to energy cooperation between the Parties to the Treaty, to ensure the implementation of the provisions of the Treaty and the Protocol on Energy Efficiency and Related Environmental Aspects,[383] and to consider possible new tools and initiatives in the field of energy.

VII. Informal Cooperation Structures between States

A. Group of Twenty (G20)

The *Group of Twenty* (G20) is an informal forum that brings together the 20 systemically most important economies worldwide.[384] The G20 was first conceived in reaction to the G7's (see below, Section VII(B)(i)) perceived failing to adequately respond to the financial crisis that hit East Asia in the late 1990s. It was officially established on 26 September 1999,

[381] TW Wälde and A Konoplyanik, 'Energy Charter Conference' in C Tietje and A Brouder (eds), *Handbook of Transnational Economic Governance Regimes* (Leiden, Nijhoff, 2009) 827.

[382] The Energy Charter Treaty (adopted 17 December 1994, entered into force 16 April 1998) 2080 UNTS 95.

[383] Energy Charter Protocol on energy efficiency and related environmental aspects (adopted 17 December 1994, entered into force 16 April 1998) 2081 UNTS 3.

[384] S Lee, 'The Group of 20', *Council on Foreign Relations*, 30 March 2009, cfr.org/backgrounder/group-20.

at the G7's meeting of finance ministers and central bank governors.[385] First conceived as a forum for finance ministers and central bank governors, G20 meetings have been lifted to the level of Heads of State and Government with the Washington Summit in 2008, as a response to the financial crisis. Since then, a G20 Leaders' Summit is held annually (initially, during the crisis, twice a year), whereas the G20 finance ministers and central bank governors meet twice a year.

Although the G20 does not formally apply any membership criteria, its membership has remained stable, and comprises 19 States[386] and the EU. Depending on the topics under debate, the G20 Chair may also invite other States to attend the G20 Leaders' Summits.[387] In addition, international financial institutions are usually also represented at G20 Summits. Indeed, the Managing Director of the IMF, the President of the World Bank and the chairs of the International Monetary and Financial Committee and of the Development Committee of the IMF and World Bank take part in G20 meetings.[388] Since the Pittsburgh Summit, the heads of the WTO, OECD and ILO have also been invited to G20 meetings. In economic terms, the G20 membership represents five continents, 66 per cent of the world's population, approximately 85 per cent of global GDP and approximately 75 per cent of international trade.[389]

The G20's activities are not governed by an underlying founding document or charter. The G20 does not impose any formal membership conditions, nor does it employ any formal rules or mechanisms with respect to voting, decision-making or dispute resolution.[390] It also lacks a permanent secretariat and official headquarters. At its core, the G20 is designed as an international forum for debate and consensus-seeking on all matters related to global economic governance. As such, it is an inherently informal network without permanent representatives of its members.[391] The informality that characterises the G20 also applies to its decision-making, as the outcome does not amount to a legally binding commitment for its members.[392] The only exceptions to this are decisions of an entirely operational nature, such as selection of the chair and agreeing on the annual agenda.[393] The G20 has taken great care to avoid any institutionalisation of its structure. The final declaration of the 2011 G20 Summit in Cannes, for example, states that the G20 'is a leader-led and informal group and it should remain so'.[394]

The presidency of the G20 is held by the members on a rotating basis, and the chair is selected annually from a different regional group (of which there are five).[395] In order to

[385] J Lockhurst, *G20 Since the Global Crisis* (London, Palgrave Macmillan, 2016) 1.

[386] Argentina, Australia, Brazil, Canada, China, France, Germany, India, Indonesia, Italy, Japan, Mexico, the Republic of Korea, the Russian Federation, Saudi Arabia, South Africa, Turkey, the UK and the US.

[387] Spain for example is a permanent invitee, as well as the Chair of ASEAN and two African countries (the chair of the African Union and a representative of NEPAD). In addition, the presidency usually invites one or more States to participate.

[388] J Wouters and T Ramopoulos, 'The G20 and Global Economic Governance: Lessons from Multi-level European Governance' (2012) 15 *JIEL* 763.

[389] G20 Argentina 2018, 'What is the G20?', g20.org/en/g20/what-is-the-g20.

[390] Wouters and Ramopoulos (n 388).

[391] J Jokela, 'The G-20: A Pathway to Effective Multilateralism?' (2011) European Union Institute for Security Studies (ISS) Chaillot Paper No 125, 20.

[392] V Rubio-Marquez, 'The G20: A Practitioner's Perspective' in N Woods and L Martinez-Diaz (eds), *Networks of Influence? Developing Countries in a Networked Global Order* (Oxford, OUP, 2009) 22.

[393] ibid.

[394] G20 Cannes 2011, 'Cannes Summit Final Declaration: Building our Common Future: The Renewed Collective Action for the Benefit of All', 4 November 2011, g20.utoronto.ca/2011/2011-cannes-declaration-111104-en.html, para 91.

[395] In recent years, the presidency was successively assumed by Turkey (2015), China (2016), Germany (2017) and Argentina (2018).

ensure continuity, management of the G20 is structured in a so-called 'Troika', which is composed of the preceding, current and subsequent chairs.

There is a strong cooperation between the G20 and other – formal – international organisations, such as the IMF, WTO[396] and OECD. The G20 also works in cooperation with the Financial Stability Board (which it created at its London Summit in April 2009) and the Basel Committee on Banking Supervision. The EU is also very active in the G20.[397]

B. Other Informal Cooperation Fora

i. Group of Seven (G7)

The *Group of Seven* (G7) was founded in Rambouillet in 1975 by the major industrialised countries: the United States, the United Kingdom, France, Germany, Japan and Italy. Soon after, they were joined by Canada and the then EEC. In 1998, Russia was admitted to the G7, except for certain financial and economic affairs, forming the G8. However, Russia's membership was suspended in the Spring of 2014 following its annexation of Crimea.

Originally, the G7 was an exclusive economic club. Its genesis is specifically connected with the collapse of the Bretton Woods system of fixed exchange rates, the oil crisis and the subsequent economic recession in the 1970s. Later the G7's political mission, the spreading of the 'market democracy' model, was strongly emphasised. After the fall of the Berlin Wall, attention shifted to the post-communist transition, the reform of international institutions and global issues such as democratisation, the environment, drugs and terrorism.

The G7 operates on the basis of annual Summits of the Heads of State and Government of its members. Around these meetings a whole system of ministerial meetings has grown, to discuss and build consensus on specific challenges in various domains. Moreover, the coordination and planning among the 'Sherpas', ie the personal representatives of the Heads of State or Government, also takes place in the run-up of each Summit. In addition, there are also ad hoc meetings and ad hoc working groups.

The lack of institutionalisation of the G7/G8 has at the same time proven to be the strength of the forum. Informal meetings enable a faster reaching of consensus than via the formalised multilateral channels.[398]

ii. Group of 77 (G77)

The *Group of 77* (G77)[399] was established in 1964 by 77 developing countries after the first session of the United Nations Conference on Trade and Development (UNCTAD)

396 For a discussion of the interactions between the WTO and the G20, see J Wouters and I Willemyns, 'The Interplay between the G20 and the World Trade Organization: Informal Law-making in Action' in J Chaisse and T-Y Lin (eds), *International Economic Law and Governance: Essays in Honour of Mitsoa Mitsushita* (Oxford, OUP, 2016) 183.

397 See J Wouters, S Van Kerckhoven and J Odermatt, 'The EU and the G20 and the G20's Impact on the EU' in B Van Vooren, S Blockmans and J Wouters (eds), *The EU's Role in Global Governance: The Legal Dimension* (Oxford, OUP, 2013) 259.

398 See inter alia, including on the role of the EU in the G7, C Oldani and J Wouters (eds), *The G7, Anti-Globalism and the Governance of Globalisation* (London, Routledge, 2018).

399 JW Müller (ed), *Chronology, Bibliography and Index for the Group of 77 and the Non-Aligned Movement* (New York, Oceana, 1993); JFJ Toye, 'Assessing the G77: 50 Years after UNCTAD and 40 years after the NIEO' in TG Weiss and A Erthal Abdenur (eds), *Emerging Powers and the UN: What Kind of Development Partnership?* (London, Routledge, 2016).

in Geneva. In the meantime, 133 countries have become members of the G77, although the name was kept unaltered as a reminder of its origins. China participates in the G77 but does not consider itself a member: official statements are issued in the name of 'The Group of 77 and China'. The G77 held its first Ministerial Meeting in 1967, when the group adopted the Algiers Charter.[400] From then on, an institutional structure gradually developed. The G77 is a means for developing countries to promote their collective economic interests, to enhance their joint negotiating capacity on all major economic issues within the UN system, and to encourage economic and technical cooperation between these States. The G77 has representations (so-called 'Chapters') in the FAO, UNIDO, UNESCO, UNEP, the World Bank and IMF. The Chapters of the G77 have a number of minimum features in common, such as membership, the decision-making process and working methods. The activities of the G77 in the Chapters are coordinated by a president who serves as a spokesman. The Ministerial Meeting is the highest decision-making body of the G77. It is convened every year at the beginning of the UN General Assembly sessions in New York. The meetings take place periodically in preparation of the UNCTAD sessions and the General Conferences of UNIDO and UNESCO.

iii. Non-Aligned Movement

The Movement of Non-Aligned States or *Non-Aligned Movement* (NAM)[401] was initiated by Yugoslavia at a Summit in Belgrade in September 1961, in which 25 countries were represented. NAM advocates solutions to global economic problems and has deliberately avoided adopting a charter or establishing a secretariat, out of fear that formal structures would weaken the operations of the NAM, as it consists of States with very different ideologies and objectives. A Summit of the NAM countries usually takes place every three years. The Presidency of this Summit has rotated among these countries since 1997, according to a troika system in which the previous and the next president assist the incumbent one. Given the absence of a secretariat, the burden of the administrative structure falls on the NAM president. The ambassador at the UN of the country presiding over the NAM fulfils the role of the Minister of Non-Aligned Affairs for the duration of its presidency. The Coordinating Bureau of the NAM is in charge of ensuring cooperation between the NAM countries, including a united position within the UN. It monitors the NAM Working Groups, Contact Groups, Task Forces and Committees created within the fold of the NAM. The chairman of the NAM is responsible for the Coordination Office. The NAM countries which are elected in the UN Security Council constitute the Non-Aligned Security Council Caucus. This group strives to ensure that the decisions and positions of the NAM adopted at Summits, Conferences and within the Coordination Bureau are reflected in the Security Council. Regular consultations within the NAM should contribute to this.

With the end of the Cold War, the NAM had to find a new role. The Movement today focuses on contributing to the acceleration and enhancement of national development, by strengthening South-South cooperation.

[400] First Ministerial Meeting of the Group of 77, 'Charter of Algiers', 10-25 October 1967, g77.org/doc/algier~1.htm.

[401] JA Braveboy-Wagner, 'The Non-aligned Movement: Collective Diplomacy of the Global South' in BJC MacKercher (ed), *Routledge Handbook of Diplomacy and Statecraft* (London, Routledge, 2012) 274; J Singh, *Emerging International Order and Non-aligned Movement* (New Delhi, Kanishka, 1996).

iv. Paris Club

The *Paris Club*[402] is an informal group of official creditors dating back to 1956. Its role consists in devising coordinated and sustainable solutions to the difficulties that debtor States encounter in fulfilling their obligations. The creditors of the Paris Club have generally attempted to rearrange their debts by way of rescheduling or reducing payments. Since 1956, the Paris Club and its ad hoc groups have concluded 433 agreements with 90 different countries covering over US$583 billion in debt.

The Paris Club remains a strictly informal group. It gathers creditor States who want to coordinate their claims vis-à-vis developing countries, on a voluntary basis. It has neither a legal basis nor an institutional structure. Nevertheless, creditor States have reached several agreements, establishing a number of rules and principles. An important principle of the Paris Club is that of solidarity: all members of the Paris Club agree to act as a group in their dealings with a given debtor country. Another principle is that the Paris Club always decides – by consensus – on a case-by-case basis, in order to adapt to the peculiarities of each debtor State. Debt treatments are only applied with regard to countries in need of redeployment, willing to implement reforms to address their financial difficulties, usually on the basis of an adapted programme which is supported by the IMF. The creditors, on the other hand, accept implementation of the terms agreed in the framework of the Paris Club. The creditor States meet 10 to 11 times a year in Paris for negotiating sessions or to informally discuss the situation of the external debt of the State debtors. The chairman of these meetings is a high official of the French Treasury. Fifteen civil servants of the French Treasury work part-time for the permanent Secretariat of the Paris Club.

v. Financial Action Task Force on Money Laundering

The *Financial Action Task Force on Money Laundering* (FATF)[403] is an intergovernmental body which develops and promotes policies to combat the laundering of money and the financing of terrorist activities, both at national and international level. The Task Force was established at the 1989 G7 Summit in Paris, in response to the growing concern about laundering practices. The FATF currently consists of 35 member jurisdictions, and two regional entities: the European Commission and the Gulf Co-operation Council. Its mission is revised every five years. Its Secretariat is located at the OECD Headquarters in Paris.

The FATF monitors the progress of its Members in the implementation of necessary measures, keeps track of the techniques used for money laundering and terrorist financing and promotes the adoption and implementation of appropriate global counter-measures. In conducting these activities, the FATF is guided by its 40 Recommendations on Money Laundering (most recently revised in 2012) and eight Special Recommendations on Terrorist Financing. The FATF also collaborates with other international bodies, such as the IMF and the World Bank.

[402] TM Callaghy, 'The Paris Club, Debt, and Poverty Reduction: Evolving Patterns of Governance' in JA Clapp and R Wilkinson (eds), *Global Governance, Poverty and Inequality* (London, Routledge, 2010) 162; C Holmgren, *La renégociation multilatérale des dettes: le club de Paris au regard du droit international* (Brussels, Bruylant, 1998).

[403] A Damais, 'The Financial Action Task Force' in WH Muller (ed), *Anti-money Laundering: International Law and Practice* (Chichester, Wiley, 2007) 69; NW Turner, 'The Financial Action Task Force: International Regulatory Convergence through Soft Law' (2014–2015) 59 *New York Law School Law Review* 547; G Krämer, 'Strategien und Massnahmen der Financial Action Task Force (FATF) zur globalen Durchsetzung ihrer Regeln zur Bekämpfung der Terrorismusfinanzierung' in M Albers and L Groth (eds), *Globales Recht und Terrorismusfinanzierungsbekämpfung* (Baden-Baden, Nomos, 2015) 203.

vi. Commonwealth

The *Commonwealth*[404] is an association of 53 sovereign States that are mostly former territories of the British Empire. Relying on its common language and legal system, the Commonwealth focuses on the advancement of democracy, human rights and sustainable economic and social development in its Member Countries and beyond. The Commonwealth has no formal founding treaty but is based on a number of declarations, of which the main ones are the declarations of Singapore (1971)[405] and Harare (1991).[406] The Heads of State of the Commonwealth members established a Secretariat in London in 1965. The Secretariat is the main intergovernmental agency of the Commonwealth. It simplifies consultation and cooperation between the Member Countries, is headed by a Secretary General and is connected to the Commonwealth Foundation and the Commonwealth of Learning. The Commonwealth Fund for Technical Cooperation is the principal tool with which the Commonwealth advances economic and social development and encourages the reduction of poverty in its Member States. The Fund was established in 1971 and is managed by the Secretariat. It operates on the basis of the principle of mutual assistance, following which the Member States contribute financially on a voluntary basis and may obtain technical assistance.

vii. International Organization of La Francophonie

The *International Organization of La Francophonie* or Francophonie[407] (*Organisation Internationale de la Francophonie*) is the counterpart of the Commonwealth and primarily stems from a cultural impetus. The organisation brings together 84 States, many of which are former French colonies, and all have the French language in common. Summits of the Francophonie started taking place from 1986, but a proper organisation was only created in 1998. The seat of the General Secretariat of the Francophonie is in Paris.

The Heads of State and Government come together every two years. At this Summit the main political strategy is decided. The Ministerial Conference of the Francophonie meets between the Summits to ensure political continuity. The governments of the Member States are represented by their foreign minister or a minister competent for the Francophonie. The Permanent Council of the Francophonie (CPF) is responsible for the preparation and the follow-up of the Summit. The Francophonie also relies on the work and recommendations of two permanent Ministerial Conferences: the Conference of Francophone Ministers of Education (CONFEMEN) and the Conference of Francophone Ministers of Youth and Sports (CONFEJES), and a number of ministerial conferences.

[404] A Leca, 'Le Commonwealth of Nations: un produit de l'histoire, à mi-chemin entre l'organisation internationale et la confédération d'états' in JY Faberon (ed), *Destins des collectivités politiques d'Océanie: peuples, populations, nations, états, territoires, pays, patries, communautés, frontières* (Aix en Provence, Presses Universitaires d'Aix-Marseille, 2011); A Banerji, 'The Commonwealth of Nations: A Force for Democracy in the 21st Century?' (2008) 97 *The Round Table: The Commonwealth Journal of International Affairs* 813.

[405] Commonwealth, 'Singapore Declaration of Commonwealth Principles 1971', 22 January 1971, thecommonwealth.org/sites/default/files/history-items/documents/Singapore%20Declaration.pdf.

[406] Commonwealth, 'The Harare Commonwealth Declaration, 1991', 20 October 1991, thecommonwealth.org/sites/default/files/history-items/documents/Harare%20Commonwealth%20Declaration%201991.pdf.

[407] C Desouches (ed), *De Dakar à Dakar: 25 ans d'engagement de la Francophonie au service des droits de l'homme, de la démocratie et de la paix; repères* (Brussels, Bruylant, 2015); F Ramel, 'Task Sharing and Peace Operations: The Role of the Organisation Internationale de la Francophonie' in B Charbonneau and T Chafer (eds), *Peace Operations in the Francophone World: Global Governance Meets Post-colonialism* (London, Routledge, 2014) 38.

The Parliamentary Assembly of the Francophonie is the consultative body of the forum. It mainly adopts texts relating to the strengthening of democratic institutions in the Member States, and organises 'good office' missions and electoral observation missions. Besides the Parliament, the Francophonie structure has a Consultative Council which mainly acts as a study service. The main operator of the Francophonie, the Intergovernmental Agency of the Francophonie, was founded in 1970 on the initiative of three African Heads of State.[408] This Agency conducts programmes in all areas of cooperation. It has two specialized institutes and three regional offices. Within the Francophonie there are four 'direct operators': the Universitary Agency of the Francophonie, TV5, the Senghor-University of Alexandria and the International Association of Francophone Mayors.

viii. *Alliance of Small Island States*

The *Alliance of Small Island States* (AOSIS)[409] was founded in the context of the Second World Climate Conference in Geneva in November 1990. AOSIS is a coalition of small island States and low-lying coastal countries, which share similar developmental and environmental concerns. AOSIS serves as a mouthpiece for these countries in the UN. It has 39 Member States and five observers from Africa, the Caribbean, the Indian Ocean, the Mediterranean, the South Pacific and the South China Sea. AOSIS has no formal charter, no regular budget and no secretariat. The AOSIS Member States mainly cooperate through their diplomatic missions at the UN in New York, led by the mission of the President. The major policy decisions are taken in plenary sessions at the ambassadorial level.

In its negotiations, AOSIS is guided by the following principles: the principle of preventive action, the precautionary principle, the 'polluter pays' principle, the duty to cooperate, justice, the principle of common but differentiated responsibility and the development of renewable energy. On the basis of these principles, AOSIS developed a number of objectives which guide its work on the implementation of the UNFCCC, the Kyoto Protocol and the Paris Agreement: the strengthening of the commitments of the industrialised countries to reduce their emissions; the reduction of scientific and methodological uncertainty associated with the commitments and mechanisms of the Kyoto Protocol; the development of strong monitoring, verification and compliance regimes; and the development of mechanisms bearing the costs for the adaptation to the effects of climate change.

Agenda 21, adopted at the Earth Summit in Rio de Janeiro in 1992 (see below, Chapter 20 I(B)), recognises the Member States as a special case for both environmental and development efforts, because of their ecological vulnerability. A direct result of the Rio process was the convening of a Global Conference on the Sustainable Development of Small Island States in Barbados in 1994. The main AOSIS activities relate to the implementation of the Barbados Programme of Action. The AOSIS countries were among the first to ratify the Paris Agreement and are putting a lot of effort into convincing other States to ratify it and to accelerate action to reduce greenhouse gas emissions.

[408] Convention on the Agency for Cultural and Technical Cooperation (adopted 20 March 1970, entered into force 31 August 1970) 1095 UNTS 291.

[409] PS Chasek, 'Margins of Power: Coalition Building and Coalition Maintenance of the South Pacific Island States and the Alliance of Small Island States' (2005) 14 *Review of European Community and International Environmental Law* 125.

ix. BRICS

The *BRICS* grouping of Brazil, Russia, India, China and South Africa came about in 2009, when the leaders of the first four countries gathered together in Yekaterinburg and held the first BRIC summit. The goal was to discuss proposals to improve the state of the global economy, reform of financial institutions and foster cooperation and coordination between emerging economies in the future. In 2010, after the entry of South Africa, the grouping was renamed for the third summit to BRICS. The BRICS work together on an ever growing variety of topics. Its summit declarations demonstrate that the agenda has continuously grown with new issues included every year. The most remarkable achievement so far is the creation of the New Development Bank (NDB), which can be considered a partial alternative to the World Bank and the IMF.[410]

x. Nordic Council

The Nordic countries have a long history of cooperation. From 1397 to 1521 Denmark, Norway and Sweden formed a union, called the Kalmar Union. From 1815 to 1905 Sweden and Norway renewed their union, and from 1873 to 1914 Denmark, Norway and Sweden established a currency union.

In 1952, Denmark, Norway and Sweden created the *Nordic Council*. Later Finland and Iceland also joined. The Nordic Council is an inter-parliamentary forum of 87 representatives, elected from the national parliaments of these five countries. It focuses on the cooperation between these countries and three Northern autonomous territories (the Faroe Islands, Greenland and Åland). The main session of the Nordic Council is held in the autumn, while a so-called 'theme session' takes place during spring.

The Nordic Council has a Secretariat, which is divided into three committees: the Committee for Nordic Affairs, the Committee on European Affairs and the Committee on the Adjacent Areas and the Nordic Region. Each of the national delegations and the delegations of the autonomous regions has its own secretariat in the national parliament.

In 1971 the Nordic Council of Ministers was established in Helsinki, as the official cooperation body of the Nordic governments, which decides by consensus. It differs in composition, depending on the nature of the matters dealt with, and gathers a few times a year. The Council has Executive Committees, consisting of senior officials, set up to deal with specific policy areas. One of these committees is the Nordic Cooperation Committee, which is responsible for managing the Secretariat of the Council of Ministers. The Nordic prime ministers meet regularly on an informal basis, with a view to coordinating their position within the European Council.

xi. San José Dialogue

The *San José Dialogue* is a forum for dialogue between Central America and the EU founded in 1984. It consists of the Central American countries of Costa Rica,

[410] See inter alia S Kingah and C Quiliconi (eds), *Global and Regional Leadership of BRICS Countries* (Cham, Springer, 2016); RJ Neuwirth, A Svetlicinii and D De Castro Halis (eds), *The BRICS-Lawyers' Guide to Global Cooperation* (Cambridge, CUP, 2017); J Wouters and S Van Kerckhoven, 'A European Perspective on the G20 and the BRICS' (2018) 13 *International Organisations Research Journal* 60; id, 'The G20 and the BRICS on Trade and Investment: Trends and Policies' (2017) 12 *International Organisations Research Journal* 7. The NDB was created based on the Agreement on the New Development Bank, Fortaleza (adopted 15 July 2014, entered into force July 2015): https://www.ndb.int/wp-content/themes/ndb/pdf/Agreement-on-the-New-Development-Bank.pdf.

El Salvador, Guatemala, Honduras, Nicaragua and Panama. Initially, the main objective of the San José Group was to look for a solution to the armed conflicts in Central America through dialogue and negotiation. The EU set up a cooperation programme with the San José group to address the socio-economic causes of the crisis. In 2003, a Political Dialogue and Cooperation Agreement was signed, introducing new areas of cooperation. In 2012, a region-to-region Association Agreement was concluded between the EU and the six Central American states, based on three pillars: political dialogue; cooperation; and trade.[411]

xii. Asia-Europe Meeting

The *Asia-Europe Meeting* (ASEM)[412] is an informal dialogue and cooperation process between the EU Member States, the EU, the ASEAN Secretariat, 19 Asian countries and, since 1996, five additional countries. ASEM is engaged in political, economic and cultural issues. The ASEM process consists of two-yearly Summits of the Heads of State and Government, annual ministerial meetings and frequent meetings at the technical level.

xiii. Shanghai Cooperation Organization

The *Shanghai Cooperation Organization* (SCO)[413] is the continuation of 'the Shanghai Five', an informal alliance that existed since 1996 between China, Kazakhstan, Kyrgyzstan, Russia and Tajikistan. Together they founded the SCO in Uzbekistan in 2001. The Shanghai Five were principally engaged in confidence building in the military field and the reduction of border troops. According to the Shanghai Declaration of 2001, the cooperation between the eight Member States (the 'Shanghai five', India, Pakistan and Uzbekistan) aims at covering also other areas. However, the SCO currently focuses on fighting terrorism and maintaining regional stability. In order to achieve these goals, the organisation has two permanent bodies: the SCO Secretariat and the Executive Committee of the Regional Anti-Terrorist Structure (RATS).

xiv. East Asia Summit

The *East Asia Summit* (EAS) is a forum held annually by leaders of the ten ASEAN countries plus Australia, China, India, Japan, New Zealand, South Korea, the United States and Russia. The first Summit was held in December 2005 and it aims to advance closer regional integration and cooperation in the East-Asian region. The Summit takes place once a year, usually after the annual ASEAN leaders' meeting. In addition, ministerial

[411] Agreement establishing an Association between the European Union and its Member States, on the one hand, and Central America on the other (29 June 2012) [2012] OJ L346/3. See also above, p 122.

[412] YL Hwee, 'The Asia-Europe Meeting' in Christiansen, Kirchner and Murray (n 334) 330; C Mattison Dent, 'The Asia-Europe Meeting (ASEM) Process: Beyond the Triadic Political Economy?' in H Hänggi (ed), *Interregionalism and International Relations* (London, Routledge, 2006) 113.

[413] M Al-Qahtani, 'The Shanghai Cooperation Organization and the Law of International Organizations' (2006) 5 *CJIL* 129; T Tumurkhuleg, 'Does the Shanghai Cooperation Organization represent an Example of a Military Alliance?' in RE Bedeski (ed), *Eurasia's Ascent in Energy and Geopolitics: Rivalry or Partnership for China, Russia, and Central Asia?* (London, Routledge, 2012) 179; G Fei, *The Shanghai Cooperation Organization and China's New Diplomacy* (The Hague, Netherlans Institute of International Relations 'Clingendael', 2010).

and senior officials' meetings are held throughout the year in order to build consensus on proposed initiatives.

VIII. Concluding Remarks

Regional and sub-regional organisations come in a staggering variety of different shapes and sizes. They not only vary in terms of types and categories, but also fields of expertise, membership rules, financing, decision-making processes, and so on. The purpose of this chapter was not to give a comprehensive overview, but rather to highlight this diversity and to give a preliminary insight into the workings and aims of the most noteworthy regional organisations. Nevertheless, what brings these organisations together is that they all represent a recasting of the spirit of cooperation that emerged in war-torn Europe, with some even mirroring elements of the EU's institutional structure. Even if all regional and subregional organisation reflect the specific needs of the context in which they have been created, the language of (regional) cooperation appears to have become very widely shared.

After having dealt with international (Chapter 6) and regional organisations (Chapter 7), the next chapter will focus on non-State actors, in particular individuals, corporations, non-governmental organisations, armed groups, and the Holy See. Aspects of their international legal status will also be addressed in subsequent, more specific chapters, notably on the peaceful settlement of disputes (Chapter 13), armed conflicts (Chapter 15), human rights (Chapter 16), and international criminal law (Chapter 17).

Bibliography

A. Regional Organisations in Europe

Adam, R and Tizzano, A, *Lineamenti di diritto dell'Unione europea*, 4th edn (Turin, Giappichelli, 2016).
Auerswald, DP and Saidemann, SM, *NATO in Afghanistan: Fighting Together, Fighting Alone* (Princeton, Princeton UP, 2014).
Bannelier, K and Pison, C (eds), *Le recours à la force autorisé par le Conseil de sécurité: droit et responsabilité* (Paris, Pedone, 2014).
Barnard, C and Peers, S (eds), *European Union Law*, 2nd edn (Oxford, OUP, 2017).
Bieber, R, Epiney, A, Haag, M and Kotzur, M, *Die Europäische Union: Europarecht und Politik*, 12th edn (Baden-Baden, Nomos and Helbing Lichtenhahn Verlag, 2016).
Bond, M, *The Council of Europe: Structure, History and Issues in European Politics* (London, Routledge, 2012).
Bothe, M and Ronzitti, N (eds), *The OSCE in the Maintenance of Peace and Security: Conflict Prevention, Crisis Management and Peaceful Settlement of Disputes* (The Hague, Kluwer, 1997).
Brumter, C, *The North Atlantic Assembly* (Dordrecht, Nijhoff, 1986).
Busek, E (ed), *Ten Years Southeast European Cooperative Initiative: From Dayton to Brussels* (Wien, Springer, 2006).

Buzzi, A, *L'intervention armée de l'OTAN en République fédérale de Yougoslavie* (Paris, Pedone, 2001).
Cannizzaro, E, *Il diritto dell'integrazione europea: L'ordinamento dell'Unione*, 2nd edn (Turin, Giappichelli, 2017).
Cottey, A (ed), *Subregional Cooperation in the New Europe: Building, Security, Prosperity and Solidarity from the Barents to the Black Sea* (Hampshire, MacMillan, 1999).
Craig, P and de Búrca, G, *EU Law: Text, Cases and Materials*, 6th edn (Oxford, OUP, 2015).
Daillier, P (ed), *Perspectives d'intégration des pays d'Europe centrale et orientale aux institutions de l'Europe occidentale: actes du colloque de Miskolc (Hongrie) des 4–5 octobre 1996* (Paris, Montchrestien, 1998).
Dangerfield, D, *Subregional Economic Cooperation in Central and Eastern Europe: The Political Economy of CEFTA* (Cheltenham, Edward Elgar, 2000).
Dinan, D, *Europe Recast: A History of European Union*, 2nd edn (Basingstoke, Palgrave Macmillan, 2014).
Engle, E (ed), *Russia, the European Union and the CIS* (The Hague, Eleven International Publishing, 2012).
Føllesdal, A (ed), *Constituting Europe: The European Court of Human Rights in a National, European and Global Context* (Cambridge, CUP, 2013).
Friis, K (ed), *NATO and Collective Defence in the 21st Century: An Assessment of the Warsaw Summit* (London, Routledge, 2017).
Ghebali, VY and Rogier, E (eds), *The Operational Role of the OSCE in Southeastern Europe: Contributing to Regional Stability in the Balkans* (Aldershot, Ashgate, 2001).
Gower, J and Timmins, G (eds), *The European Union, Russia and the Shared Neighbourhood* (London, Routledge, 2011).
Hauser, G, *The Mediterranean Dialogue: A Transatlantic Approach* (Milan, ISU Universita Cattolica, 2006).
Hendrickson, RC, *Diplomacy and War at NATO: The Secretary General and Military Action after the Cold War* (Columbia, University of Missouri Press, 2006).
Jacqué, J-P, *Droit institutionnel de l'Union européenne*, 8th edn (Paris, Dalloz, 2015).
Lang, M (ed), *The Impact of the OECD and UN Model Conventions on Bilateral Tax Treaties* (Cambridge, CUP, 2012).
Lenaerts, K and Van Nuffel, P, *European Union Law*, 3rd edn (London, Sweet & Maxwell, 2011).
Lenaerts, K, Maselis, I and Gutman, K, *EU Procedural Law* (Oxford, OUP, 2014).
Masson, A and Nihoul, P, *Droit de l'Union européenne: droit institutionnel et droit matériel: théorie, exercices et éléments de méthodologie*, 3rd edn (Brussels, Larcier, 2011).
Naskou-Perrakis, P, *Black Sea Economic Cooperation: Basic Texts* (Athens, Sakkoulas, 2001).
Peers, S, Hervey, T, Kenner, J and Ward, A, *The EU Charter of Fundamental Rights: A Commentary* (Oxford, Hart, 2014).
Pieth, M, Low, LA and Bonucci, N (eds), *The OECD Convention on Bribery: A Commentary* (Cambridge, CUP, 2014).
Qureishi, AH and Gao, X (eds), *International Economic Organizations and Law: The Perspective and Role of the Legal Counsel* (Alphen aan den Rijn, Kluwer, 2012).
Rosas, A and Armati, L, *EU Constitutional Law: An Introduction*, 2nd edn (Oxford, Hart, 2012).

Sarmiento Ramírez-Escudero, D, *El derecho de la Unión Europea* (Madrid, Marcial Pons, 2016).
Schmahl, S and Breuer, M (eds), *The Council of Europe: Its Laws and Policies* (Oxford, OUP, 2017).
Schütze, R, *European Constitutional Law*, 2nd edn (Cambridge, CUP, 2016).
Stratenschulte, ED (ed), *Das europäische Meer: die Ostsee als Handlungsraum* (Berlin, Berliner Wissenschafts-Verlag, 2011).
Szamuely, G, *Bombs for Peace: NATO's Humanitarian War on Yugoslavia* (Amsterdam, Amsterdam UP, 2013).
Trifunovska, S, 'North Atlantic Treaty Organisation (NATO)' in Wouters, J (ed), *International Encyclopedia for Intergovernmental Organisations* (Alphen aan den Rijn, Kluwer, 2012).
Van Raepenbusch, S, *Droit institutionnel de l'Union européenne*, 2nd edn (Brussels, Larcier, 2016).
Wathelet, M, *Contentieux européen*, 2nd edn (Brussels, Larcier, 2014).
Woodward, R, *The Organisation for Economic Co-operation and Development (OECD)* (London, Routledge, 2009).
Wouters, J (ed), *International Encyclopedia of Intergovernmental Organisations* (Alphen aan den Rijn, Kluwer).
X, *The Council of Europe: Achievements and Activities* (Strasbourg, Council of Europe, 1996).

B. Regional Organisations in America

Aldecoa Luzarraga, F and Guinea Llorente, M (eds), *Gobernanza y reforma internacional tras la crisis financiera y económica: el papel de la Unión Europea* (Madrid, Marcial Pons, 2014).
Arrighi, JM (ed), *La OEA y el derecho internacional* (Mexico, Editorial Porrua, 2015).
Bungenberg, M et al (eds), *International Investment Law* (Oxford, Hart, 2015).
Casella, PB, 'Mercosur' in Wouters, J (ed), *International Encyclopedia for Intergovernmental Organisations* (Alphen aan den Rijn, Kluwer, 2007).
Cata Backer, L (ed), *Harmonizing Law in an Era of Globalization: Convergence, Divergence, and Rsesistance* (Durham, Carolina Academic Press, 2007).
Diaz Barrado, CM (ed), *Guía del espacio iberoamericano de paz, seguridad y defensa* (Madrid, Instituto Universitario General Gutierrez Mellado – UNED, 2010).
Di Filippo, M (ed), *Organizzazioni regionali, modello sovranazionale e metodo intergovernativo: I casi dell' Unione europea e del Mercosur* (Torino, Giappichelli, 2012).
Dreyzin De Klor, A, 'The Legal-Institutional Structure of MERCOSUR' in Franca Filho, MT, Lixinski, L and Olmos Giupponi, MB (eds), *The Law of MERCOSUR* (London, Hart, 2010) 29–56.
Edler, C, *Die Integration der Südamerikanischen Staaten durch den Mercosur* (München, Herbert Utz Verlag, 2013).
Flaesch-Mougin, C (ed), *Regards croisés sur les intégrations régionales: Europe, Amériques, Afrique* (Brussels, Bruylant, 2010).
Folsom, RH (ed), *NAFTA and Free Trade in the Americas in a Nutshell*, 4th edn (St Paul, West, 2012).

Garcia-Amador, FV, *The Andean Legal Order: A New Community Law* (Dobbs Ferry, Oceana Publications, 1978).
Herz, M, *The Organization of American States (OAS): Global Governance Away from the Media* (London, Routledge, 2011).
Hinojo Rojas, M (ed), *Liber amicorum Profesor José Manuel Pelaez Maron: derecho internacional y derecho de la Unión Europea* (Cordoba, Universidad de Cordoba, 2012).
Horwitz, B, *The Transformation of the Organization of American States: A Multilateral Framework for Regional Governance* (London, Anthem Press, 2011).
Irigoin Barrenne, J (ed), *Chile y el Mercosur en América Latina: VI Encuentro International de Derecho en América del Sur* (Santiago, Ed Juridica de Chile, 1999).
Kay, T, *NAFTA and the Politics of Labor Transnationalism* (Cambridge, CUP, 2011).
Medina Quiroga, C, *The American Convention on Human Rights: Crucial Rights and Their Theory and Practice* (Cambridge, Intersentia, 2016).
Njinkeu, D and Cameron, H (eds), *Aid for Trade and Development* (New York, CUP, 2008).
Odello, M and Seatzu, F (eds), *Latin American and Caribbean International Institutional Law* (The Hague, TMC Asser Press, 2015).
Perdikis, N and Read, R (eds), *The WTO and the Regulation of International Trade: Recent Trade Disputes between the European Union and the United States* (Cheltenham, Edward Elgar, 2005).
Rimoldi de Ladmann, EI, 'La Comisión de Comercio en el Mercosur' in Irigoin Barrenne, J (ed), *Chile y el Mercosur en América Latina: VI Encuentro International de Derecho en América del Sur* (Santiago, Ed. Juridica de Chile, 1999) 437–49.
Sánchez Sánchez, RA, *The Politics of Central American Integration* (Abingdon, Routledge, 2009).
Shaw, CM, *Cooperation, Conflict, and Consensus in the Organization of American States* (New York, Palgrave Macmillan, 2004).
Soto, YA, 'The Role of the Organization of American States in Conflict' in Schnabel, A (ed), *Conflict Prevention from Rhetoric to Reality* (Lanham, Lexington Books, 2004) 223–61.
Susani, N, *Le règlement des différends dans le Mercosur: un système de droit international pour une organisation d'intégration* (Paris, L'Harmattan, 2008).
Vilela, A, 'Andean Common Market' in Wouters, J (ed), *International Encyclopedia for Intergovernmental Organisations* (Alphen aan den Rijn, Kluwer, 2017).

C. Regional Organisations in Africa

Akokpari, JK, Ndinga-Muvumba, A and Murithi, T (eds), *The African Union and its Institutions* (Auckland Park, Fanele, 2008).
Amegavie, YC, *La Banque Africaine de Développement* (Paris, Pedone, 1977).
Badmus, IA, *The African Union's Role in Peacekeeping: Building on Lessons Learned from Security Operations* (Basingstoke, Palgrave Macmillan, 2015).
Boisson de Chazournes, L and Gowlland-Debbas, V (eds), *The International Legal System in Quest of Equity and Universality* (The Hague, Nijhoff, 2001).
Charbrier, P, *The Arab Maghreb Union* (Washington, IMF, 1994).
Dreyzin de Klor, A (ed), *Solución de controversias* (Buenos Aires, Zavalia, 2004).
Drummond, P, Kal Wajid, S and Williams, O (eds), *The Quest for Regional Integration in the East African Community* (Washington, IMF, 2014).
Engel, U and Gomes Porto, J (eds), *Africa's New Peace and Security Architecture: Promoting Norms, Institutionalizing Solutions* (Farnham, Ashgate, 2010).

Fau-Nougaret, M (ed), *La concurrence des organisations régionales en Afrique* (Paris, L'Harmattan, 2012).
Gastorn, K (ed), *Processes of Legal Integration in the East African Community* (Dar Es Salaam, Dar Es Salaam UP, 2011).
Gautron, JC (ed), *Les dynamiques du droit européen en début de siècle: études en l'honneur de Jean-Claude Gautron* (Paris, Pedone, 2004).
Knight, WA and Egerton, F (eds), *The Routledge Handbook of the Responsibility to Protect* (London, Routledge, 2012).
Kösler, A, *Die Entwicklung der Southern African Development Community (SADC) als Building Block der panafrikanischen Einheit: die Herausforderung der doppelten Integration und wichtige Einflussfaktoren* (Hamburg, Kovac, 2010).
Leng Lim, C (ed), *Alternative Visions of the International Law on Foreign Investment: Essays in Honour of Muthucumaraswamy Sornarajah* (Cambridge, CUP, 2016).
Magliveras, KD and Naldi, GN, 'The African Union' in Wouters, J (ed), *International Encyclopedia for Intergovernmental Organisations* (Alphen aan den Rijn, Kluwer, 2014).
Makinda, SM, Okumu, W and Mickler, D (eds), *The African Union: Addressing the Challenges of Peace, Security, and Governance*, 2nd edn (London, Routledge, 2016).
Martin, OM and Grasa, R (eds), *¿Una nueva era para África? Nuevos desafíos y perspectivas sobre paz y seguridad en África* (Madrid, Catarata, 2014).
Muntschick, J, *The Southern African Development Community (SADC) and the European Union (EU): Regionalism and External Influence* (London, Palgrave Macmillan, 2018).
Mutai, HK, *Compliance with International Trade Obligations: The Common Market for Eastern and Southern Africa* (Alphen aan den Rijn, Kluwer, 2007).
Nabers, D (ed), *Regionale Integration: neue Dynamiken in Afrika, Asien und Lateinamerika* (Hamburg, Deutsches Übersee-Institut, 2005).
Ngoma, N, *Prospects for a Security Community in Southern Africa: An Analysis of Regional Security in the Southern African Development Community* (Pretoria, Institute for Security Studies, 2005).
Oosthuizen, GH, *The Southern African Development Community: The Organisation, Its Policies and Prospects* (Midrand, Institute for Global Dialogue, 2006).
Saunders, CC (ed), *Region-building in Southern Africa: Progress, Problems and Prospects* (London, Zed Books, 2012).
Ukaigwe, J, *Ecowas Law* (Berlin, Springer, 2016).
Worrall, J, *International Institutions of the Middle East: The GCC, Arab League, and Arab Maghreb Union* (London, Routledge, 2017).
Yusuf, AA and Ouguergouz, F (eds), *L'Union Africaine: cadre juridique et institutionnel: manuel sur l'organisation panafricaine* (Paris, Pedone, 2013).
Zogbelemou, T, *Droit des organisations d'intégration économique en Afrique: CEDEAO – CEMAC – UEMOA – ZMAO* (Paris, L'Harmattan, 2014).

D. Regional Organisations in Asia

Ahmed, ZS, *Regionalism and Regional Security in South Asia: The Role of SAARC* (Farnham, Ashgate, 2013).
Allison, L, *The EU, ASEAN and Interregionalism: Regionalism Support and Norm Diffusion between the EU and ASEAN* (Basingstoke, Palgrave Macmillan, 2015).

Beeson, M (ed), *Routledge Handbook of Asian Regionalism* (London, Routledge, 2012).
Berramdane, A and Trochu, M (eds), *Le partenariat UE-ASEAN* (Brussels, Bruylant, 2013).
Christiansen, T, Kirchner, EJ and Murray, P (eds), *The Palgrave Handbook of EU-Asia Relations* (Basingstoke, Palgrave Macmillan, 2015).
Haacke, J (ed), *Cooperative Security in the Asia-Pacific: The ASEAN Regional Forum* (London, Routledge, 2010).
Inama, S and Sim, EW, *The Foundation of the ASEAN Economic Community: An Institutional and Legal Profile* (Cambridge, CUP, 2015).
Roberts, CB, *ASEAN Regionalism: Cooperation, Values and Institutionalization* (London, Routledge, 2012).
Saez, L, *The South Asian Association for Regional Cooperation (SAARC): An Emerging Collaboration Architecture* (London, Routledge, 2011).
Sharmini Nesadurai, HE, *Globalisation, Domestic Policies and Regionalism: The ASEAN Free Trade Area* (London, Routledge, 2003).
Wesley, M, *The Regional Organizations of the Asia-Pacific: Exploring Institutional Change* (Basingstoke, Palgrave Macmillan, 2003).
Worrall, J, *International Institutions of the Middle East: the GCC, Arab League and Arab Maghreb Union* (London, Routledge, 2017).
Xing, L, 'The Asian Development Bank (ADB)' in Wouters, J (ed), *International Encyclopedia for Intergovernmental Organisations* (Alphen aan den Rijn, Kluwer, 2018).
Yue, CS and Plummer, MG, *ASEAN Economic Cooperation and Integration: Progress, Challenges and Future Directions* (Cambridge, CUP, 2015).

E. Transcontinental Regional Organisations

Di Gregorio, A and Angeli, A, *The Eurasian Economic Union and the European Union: Moving towards a Greater Understanding* (The Hague, Eleven Law, 2017).
Economic and Social Commission for Western Asia, *Assessing Arab Economic Integration: towards the Arab Customs Union* (Beirut, UNESCWA, 2015).
El-Gebali, S, *Die OAPEC als Organisation zur Interessenvertretung der Arabischen Öllander in den internationalen wirtschaftlichen Beziehungen* (Frankfurt am Main, Lang, 1981).
Kashirinka, AA and Morozov, AN, *Россия, Евразийский экономический союз и Всемирная торговая организация* (*Russia, the Eurasian Economic Union and the World Trade Organization*) (Moscow, Infra-M, 2014).
Kembayev, Z, *Legal Aspects of the Regional Integration Processes in the Post-Soviet Area* (Berlin, Springer, 2009).
Maachou, A, *OAPEC: An International Organization for Economic Cooperation and an Instrument for Regional Integration* (Paris, Berger-Levrault, 1982).
Meenai, SA, *The Islamic Development Bank: A Case-study of Islamic Co-operation* (London, Kegan Paul International, 1989).
Mihailovitch, L and Pluchart, JJ, *L'OPEP: organisation des pays exportateurs de pétrole*, 2nd edn (Paris, Presses Universitaires de France, 1985).
Musrey, AG, *An Arab Common Market: A Study in Inter-Arab Trade Relations, 1920–67* (New York, Praeger, 1969).
Ruland, C, Manske, E and Draguhn, W (eds), *Asia-Pacific Economic Cooperation (APEC): The First Decade* (London, Routlegde, 2002).

Tietje, C and Brouder, A (eds), *Handbook of Transnational Economic Governance Regimes* (Leiden, Nijhoff, 2009).

Virzo, R and Ingravallo, I (eds), *Evolutions in the Law of International Organizations* (Leiden, Nijhoff, 2015).

Witte, JM and Goldthau, A, *Die OPEC: Macht und Ohnmacht des Öl-Kartells* (München, Hanser, 2009).

Worrall, J, *International Institutions of the Middle East: the GCC, Arab League, and Arab Maghreb Union* (London, Routledge, 2017).

F. Informal Cooperation Structures between States

Bedeski, RE (ed), *Eurasia's Ascent in Energy and Geopolitics: Rivalry or Partnership for China, Russia, and Central Asia?* (London, Routledge, 2012).

Faberon JY (ed), *Destins des collectivités politiques d'Océanie: peuples, populations, nations, états, territoires, pays, patries, communautés, frontières* (Aix en Provence, Presses Universitaires d'Aix-Marseille, 2011).

Fei, G, *The Shanghai Cooperation Organization and China's New Diplomacy* (The Hague, Netherlands Institute of International Relations 'Clingendael', 2010).

Hänggi, H (ed), *Interregionalism and International Relations* (London, Routledge, 2006).

Holmgren, C, *La renégociation multilatérale des dettes: le club de Paris au regard du droit international* (Brussels, Bruylant, 1998).

Larionova, M (ed), *The European Union in the G8: Promoting Consensus and Concerted Actions for Global Public Goods* (Farnham, Ashgate, 2012).

MacKercher, BJC (ed), *Routledge Handbook of Diplomacy and Statecraft* (London, Routledge, 2012).

Müller, JW (ed), *Chronology, Bibliography and Index for the Group of 77 and the Non-Aligned Movement* (New York, Oceana, 1993).

Muller, WH, Kälin, CH and Goldsworth, JG (eds), *Anti-money Laundering: International Law and Practice* (Chichester, Wiley, 2007).

Murray, P (ed), *The Palgrave Handbook of EU-Asia Relations* (Basingstoke, Palgrave Macmillan, 2015).

Singh, J, *Emerging International Order and Non-aligned Movement* (New Delhi, Kanishka, 1996).

Weiss, TG and Erthal Abdenur, A (eds), *Emerging Powers and the UN: What Kind of Development Partnership?* (London, Routledge, 2016).

Wouters, J, Van Kerckhoven, S and Odermatt, J, 'The EU and the G20 and the G20's Impact on the EU' in Van Vooren, B, Blockmans, S and Wouters, J (eds), *The EU's Role in Global Governance: The Legal Dimension* (Oxford, OUP, 2013) 259–71.

G. General

Bartels, L and Ortino, F (eds), *Regional Trade Agreements and the WTO Legal System* (Oxford, OUP, 2006).

Grimmel, A and Jakobeit, C (eds), *Regionale Integration: Erklärungsansätze und Analysen zu den wichtigsten Integrationszusammenschlüssen in der Welt* (Baden-Baden, Nomos, 2015).

Hook, GD and Kearns, I (eds), *Subregionalism and World Order* (Basingstoke, MacMillan, 1999).
Lacarte, J (ed), *Inter-governmental Trade Dispute Settlement: Multilateral and Regional Approaches* (London, Cameron May, 2004).

Further Reading

Aldecoa Luzárraga, F and Cornago Prieto, N, 'El nuevo regionalismo y reestructuratión del sistema mundial' (1998) 50 *Revista Española de Derecho Internacional* 59.
Barnard, C, *The Substantive Law of the EU: The Four Freedoms*, 5th edn (Oxford, OUP, 2016).
Boisson de Chazournes, L (ed), *Interactions between Regional and Universal Organizations: A Legal Perspective* (Leiden, Brill, 2017).
Börzel, T (ed), *Roads to Regionalism: Genesis, Design, and Effects of Regional Organizations* (Farnham, Ashgate, 2012).
Burgorgue-Larsen, L, 'Le fait régional dans la juridictionnalisation du droit international' in Société Française pour le Droit International (ed), *La Juridictionnalisation du Droit International: Colloque de Lille* (Paris, Pedone, 2003) 203–66.
Chalmers, D, Davies, G and Monti, G, *European Union Law: Text and Materials*, 3rd edn (Cambridge, CUP, 2014).
Craig, P and de Búrca, G, *The Evolution of EU Law*, 2nd edn (Oxford, OUP, 2011).
Crawford, J, 'Universalism and Regionalism from the Perspective of the Work of the ILC' in International Law Commission (ed) *International Law on the Eve of the Twenty-First Century: Views from the International Law Commission* (New York, United Nations, 1997) 99–121.
De Melo, J and Panagariya, A (eds), *New Dimensions in Regional Integration* (Cambridge, CUP, 1993).
Dwan, R, 'Divisions of Labour between International, Regional and Subregional Organizations' in SIPRI, *Preventing Violent Conflict: The Search for Political Will, Strategies and Effective Tools (Report of the Krusenberg Seminar)* (Stockholm, SIPRI, 2000) 37–44.
Grabendorff, W and Seidelmann, R (eds), *Relations between the European Union and Latin America: Biregionalism in a Changing Global System* (Baden-Baden, Nomos, 2005).
Šabič, Z (ed), *Global Impact of Regional International Organizations: Issues of Regionalism and Regional Integration* (Torun, Marszalek, 2009).
Schreuer, G, 'Regionalism v Universalism' (1995) 6 *EJIL* 477.
Société Française pour le Droit International (ed), *Actes du colloque de la Société Française pour le Droit International* Vol. 10 *Colloque de Bordeaux: Régionalisme et universalisme dans le droit international contemporain* (Paris, Pedone, 1977).
Van Vooren, B, Blockmans, S and Wouters, J (eds), *The EU's Role in Global Governance: the Legal Dimension* (Oxford, OUP, 2012).
Wallensteen, P and Bjurner, A (eds), *Regional Organizations and Peacemaking: Challengers to the UN?* (London, Routledge, 2015).
Wolfrum, R (ed), *Strengthening the World Order: Universalism v. Regionalism: Risks and Opportunities of Regionalization* (Berlin, Duncker & Humblot, 1990).

World Trade Organization (ed), *Regionalism and the World Trading System* (Geneva, WTO, 1995).

Wouters, J, Verhey, L and Kiiver, P (eds), *European Constitutionalism Beyond Lisbon* (Antwerp, Intersentia 2009).

Wouters, J, Nowak, M, Chané, A and Hachez, N (eds), *The European Union and Human Rights: Law and Policy* (Oxford, OUP, 2019).

Wyatt, D and Dashwood, A, *Wyatt and Dashwood's European Union Law*, 6th edn (Oxford, Hart, 2011).

8

Non-State Actors

I. Introduction

The international legal system considers States as the primary subjects of international law. States are seen as enjoying an international legal personality that comes with full legal capacities (international rights, obligations, privileges, etc). However, they are not the only actors in international law and governance. As gatekeepers of the system, States have allowed a number of non-State actors to participate in the shaping of world public order: they have transferred competences to intergovernmental organisations, enabled corporate actors to extend their global business activities,[1] or accredited non-governmental organisations to provide policy input or advisory services. Even where States have not formally allowed non-State actors to play a role, these actors have nevertheless carved out more or less autonomous spaces for themselves, by challenging governments, sometimes militarily, or filling governance lacunae created by failed or retreating States. The increasing relevance of non-State actors led the ICJ to observe as early as 1949, in the *Reparation for Injuries* advisory opinion, that '[t]he subjects of law in any legal system are not necessarily identical in their nature or in the extent of their rights, and their nature depends upon the needs of the community'.[2] This view has opened the door for the recognition of a 'partial' international legal personality of non-State actors, with the subsequent discussion focusing on the exact rights and duties being imposed on non-State actors as subjects of international law.

It bears emphasis that the category of non-State actors is a heterogeneous one. In essence, it encompasses all international actors that are not States. This characterisation – which Philip Alston usefully denoted as the 'not-a-cat syndrome'[3] – masks sufficient factual and legal differences between discrete categories of non-State actors. Depending on their usefulness for the system of States, some non-State actors, such as intergovernmental organisations, have been given far-reaching rights and duties, whereas others, such as

[1] For an excellent sociological account of State facilitation of global financial capitalism, see S Sassen, *Territory, Authority, Rights* (Princeton, Princeton UP, 2006).

[2] *Reparation for Injuries Suffered in the Service of the United Nations* (Advisory Opinion) [1949] ICJ Rep 174, 178.

[3] P Alston, 'The "Not-a-Cat" Syndrome: Can the International Human Rights Regime Accommodate Non-State Actors?' in P Alston (ed), *Non-State Actors in Human Rights* (Oxford, OUP, 2005).

transnational terrorist groups, have no international legal personality to speak of, except of being addressees of international criminal proscription. In view of the significant differences between various categories of non-State actors, it is advisable to discuss their legal personality – their rights and obligations – per category.

The following categories of non-State actors are typically discerned: international organisations, peoples, individuals, religious organisations, corporations, armed groups, and non-governmental organisations.[4] As the previous chapter focused on (global and regional) international organisations, the present chapter provides an overview of the position under international law of individuals, corporations, non-governmental organisations, armed groups, and the Holy See (a spiritual organisation with a historically special legal status). Aspects of their personality will also be addressed in subsequent, more specific chapters.[5] Indeed, non-State actors' exact rights and duties not only differ per category, but also per functional domain. Some areas of international law – notably human rights and international criminal law – have even placed non-State actors (individuals) at their centre of attention.

II. Individuals

International law as classically conceived is a system made by and for States. Therefore, the ultimate unit of international law's concern is the State rather than the individual, even if the State, as an abstract entity, is composed of individuals, and uses individuals as its agents.[6] According to this approach, the State is seen as mediating the interests of the individuals, who themselves remain largely invisible to international law.

A. Diplomatic Protection

The State-centeredness of the international legal system does not mean that it turns a blind eye to the legal interests of individuals.[7] Even prior to the Second World War, it was accepted that international agreements concluded by States, or customary international law for that matter, could, in principle, create individual rights and obligations enforceable by national courts,[8] even if individuals as such could not assert their rights at the international level. This did not leave individual rights unprotected, however. States, using the mechanism of diplomatic protection, had (and still have) the right – but not the duty[9] – to bring a claim

[4] Peoples, who enjoy the right to self-determination and may sometimes aspire to statehood, are addressed in Chapter 5 on States, Section II(B).

[5] Notably on the peaceful settlement of disputes (Chapter 13), the law of armed conflict (Chapter 15), human rights law (Chapter 16) and international criminal law (Chapter 17).

[6] Compare with cosmopolitan theories in international ethics, for whom the individual, rather than the State, is the ultimate unit of moral concern and worth. See K Tan, *Justice without Borders: Cosmopolitanism, Nationalism, and Patriotism* (Cambridge, CUP, 2004) 35.

[7] *Amin v Brown* [2005] EWHC 1670 (Ch) (access to an English court for an Iraqi citizen during the war).

[8] *Jurisdiction of the Courts of Danzig (Pecuniary Claims of Danzig Railway Officials who have passed into the Polish Service, Against the Polish Railways Administration)* PCIJ Series B, No 15, 17–18.

[9] See eg District Court of The Hague, (NL), *Anonymous v Netherlands (Ministry for Foreign Affairs)*, 18 March 2003, Case No KG 03/137.

against a foreign State which has violated the international rights of the former's nationals.[10] This mechanism of diplomatic protection transforms an individual-to-State claim into a State-to-State claim, and thus fits well within the State-centred system of international law.

States exercise diplomatic protection over their own nationals whose treatment by a foreign State does not meet the 'international minimum standard'. This minimum standard of treatment for aliens could even go beyond the standard of treatment which a State has reserved for its own nationals.[11] In the interwar years, the doctrine was applied and developed in a large number of cases regarding aliens suffering injuries as a result of the revolution in Mexico, cases that were heard by mixed claims commissions set up by Mexico on the one hand, and the United States and some European States on the other.[12] In *USA (LF Neer) v United Mexican States*, the Mexican-US Claims Commission defined an international delinquent treatment of an alien as 'an outrage, to bad faith, to wilful neglect of duty, or to an insufficiency of governmental action so far short of international standards that every reasonable and impartial man would readily recognize its insufficiency'.[13]

Application of the international minimum standard of treatment of aliens later largely shifted to the more specific field of international investment law, with so-called 'Friendship, Commerce, and Navigation' treaties (FCN treaties) and bilateral investment treaties further defining the standard.[14] In the currently applicable bilateral investment treaties, the international minimum standard has largely taken the shape of the fair and equitable standard of treatment, which means, according to the OECD, that 'protection afforded under the Convention shall be that generally accorded by the Party concerned to its own nationals, but, being set by international law, the standard may be more exacting where rules of national law or national administrative practices fall short of the requirements of international law'.[15]

That the international minimum standard for treatment of aliens has lost relevance, except in the field of investment law, is largely attributable to the rise of international human rights after the horrors of the Second World War. 'International human rights' are inherent entitlements of *all* individuals – irrespective of whether they are citizens or aliens – who can invoke them vis-à-vis every State on whose territory or within whose jurisdiction they find themselves.[16] The mechanism of diplomatic protection is further elaborated on in Chapter 12, Section V.

[10] See eg District Court of The Hague, (NL), *A v Minister of Immigration and Integration*, 23 August 2005, Case No AWB 05/34215; District Court of The Hague, (NL), *A v Secretary of State for Justice*, 26 September 2000, Case No AWB 99/6851.

[11] C Rousseau, *Droit International Public* Vol I (Paris, Sirey, 1970) 46.

[12] See, for an overview of the procedures before these commissions, AH Feller, *The Mexican Claims Commissions, 1923–34: A Study in the Law and Procedure of International Tribunals* (New York, MacMillan, 1935).

[13] *USA (LF Neer) v United Mexican States* (1926) 4 RIAA 60, para 4.

[14] In 1989, in the *ELSI* case, the ICJ applied the FCN treaty between Italy and the United States, holding that relevant treaty clauses which prohibited 'arbitrary and discriminatory measures' and required 'constant protection and security' to the person and property of nationals of the other party, must conform to the international minimum standard: *Elettronica Sicula SpA (ELSI) (United States of America v Italy)* [1989] ICJ Rep 15, para 108.

[15] OECD Draft Convention on the Protection of Foreign Property (adopted 12 October 1967) (1968) 7 ILM 117, Notes and Comments to Article 1, No 4(a). For an example of a treaty clause, see Art 1105 (1) of NAFTA Chapter XI: 'Each Party shall accord to investments of investors of another Party treatment in accordance with international law, including fair and equitable treatment and full protection and security'. See further Chapter 19, Section IV on International Investment Law.

[16] See eg Higher Administrative Court, (AT), *A A and Ai A v Federal Office for Migration and Asylum (Bundesamt für Fremdenwesen und Asyl)*, 15 December 2015, Ra 2015/18/0100 to 0101-12 (on the refugee law obligation of

B. International Human Rights Law

Since 1945 a large number of international human rights instruments have come into existence. In 1948, the UN General Assembly adopted the Universal Declaration of Human Rights, pursuant to which '[a]ll human beings are born free and equal in dignity and rights' and that '[e]veryone is entitled to all the rights and freedoms […] without distinction of any kind'.[17] On that same day, the General Assembly adopted the Convention on the Prevention and the Punishment of the Crime of Genocide, the first binding international human rights instrument. Other international human rights conventions followed, such as the International Convention on the Elimination of Racial Discrimination, the International Covenant on Civil and Political Rights (1966), the International Covenant on Economic and Social Rights (1966), the Convention against Torture (1984). Human rights instruments were also adopted at the regional level, eg under the auspices of the Council of Europe, such instruments as the European Convention for the Protection of Human Rights and Fundamental Freedoms and the European Social Charter were adopted. These instruments typically come with elaborate supervisory mechanisms, such as reporting obligations, and rights of individual petition to a Committee or even a Court, the European Court of Human Rights being the most notable example. The content, mechanisms, and procedures of international human rights law are dealt with in Chapter 16.

C. International Criminal Law

After the Second World War, international law not only drastically expanded the *rights* of individuals but also their *duties*, notably under international criminal law. In a famous *dictum* in 1946, the Nuremberg Tribunal, which brought to trial some of the major Nazi war criminals, abandoned the principle that only States could commit violations of international law.[18] It famously held that 'international law imposes duties and liabilities upon individuals as well as upon States' and that '[c]rimes against international law are committed by men, not by abstract entities, and only by punishing individuals who commit such crimes can the provisions of international law be enforced'.[19] Out of this Nuremberg Principle, an entirely new field of international law grew: international criminal law, by virtue of which individuals rather than States could be punished for transgressions of the basic norms of humanity (war crimes, genocide, crimes against humanity). These individual duties under international law long remained a paper tiger, mostly due to the lack of enforcement mechanisms post-Nuremberg. Since the 1990s, however, newly-established international criminal

States not to transfer personal details from the asylum-seeker to his home country in order to ensure the safety of the asylum-seeker); Higher Administrative Court of North Rhine-Westphalia, (DE), *Anonymous v Federal Government*, Judgment of 18 December 2014, Case No 4 A 2948/11 (test is respect for human rights in their entirety, not international minimum standard); Federal Supreme Court, (CH), *A v GastroSocial Compensation Office*, 18 December 2008, Case No 8C-449/2008 (on entitlement of refugees to child benefits).

[17] Arts 1 and 2 UDHR.

[18] In fact, Art 227 of the Versailles Treaty had already done so in respect of German Emperor Wilhelm II: 'The Allied and Associated Powers publicly arraign William II of Hohenzollern, formerly German Emperor, for a supreme offence against international morality and the sanctity of treaties', but this article was never acted upon.

[19] International Military Tribunal (Nuremberg), *US et al v Göring et al*, 1 October 1946, [1946] 22 IMT 203, (1947) 41 *AJIL* 172, 220–21.

tribunals, as well as national courts actively enforcing international law,[20] routinely hold individuals accountable for violations of international criminal law. The substantive principles and institutional mechanisms of international criminal law are set out in greater detail in Chapter 17 on international criminal law.

As far as the international legal personality of the individual is concerned, one can conclude that in discrete fields, international law has conferred rights and obligations directly on individuals. Accordingly, the individual has become a true addressee of international law and not just of national law. Individuals enjoy international human rights vis-à-vis the State, and possess duties under international criminal law vis-à-vis other individuals. These rights and duties can be, and have been, enforced by national and international supervisory mechanisms. The existence of far-reaching substantive rules and mechanisms of protection and accountability could not, however, prevent individual rights from continuing to be violated, and individuals from continuing to commit international crimes on a rather staggering scale.

III. Corporations

It is trite to say that transnational corporations (TNCs) occupy an increasingly prominent place in today's world. The contemporary deep economic integration, dynamic growth of international production, and 'globalisation' more generally are not so much the work of States, but have been driven by a burgeoning number of 'multinational' corporations.[21] Thousands of TNCs operate around the world today.[22] In fact, research indicates that, in 2015,[23] 69 of the world's top 100 economies[24] were corporations, with only 31 States making the list.[25]

Given their weight in the current international economic order, it is important when discussing non-State actors to also make a short stop at the role of TNCs in international law, the extent to which they have been endowed with legal personality, and are consequently bestowed rights and obligations under international law.

In principle, corporations are profit-driven entities that are incorporated in a State, and are, accordingly, subjects of domestic law. However, as corporations increasingly engage in activities outside the country of incorporation, often via subsidiaries and branches, they

[20] See eg Council of State, (NL), *A v Minister of Immigration and Integration*, 18 April 2005, Case No 200408765/1 (holding an individual responsible for war crimes under Art 1(F)(a) of the Refugee Convention).

[21] PT Muchlinski, *Multinational Enterprises and the Law*, 2nd edn (Oxford, OUP, 2007) 3; CD Wallace, *The Multinational Enterprise and Legal Control: Host State Sovereignty in an Era of Economic Globalization*, 2nd edn (London, Martinus Nijhoff, 2002) 9.

[22] J Mikler, 'Global Companies as Actors in Global Policy and Governance' in J Mikler (ed), *The Handbook of Global Companies* (New York, John Wiley and Sons Ltd, 2013) 4.

[23] Compare this to 2001, when the relation was approximately 50:50 between corporations and States. See J Bhagwati, *In Defense of Globalization* (New York, OUP, 2004) 166 and A Hennings, *Über das Verhältnis von multinationalen Unternehmen zu Menschenrechten: Eine Bestandsaufnahme aus juristischer Perspektive* (Göttingen, Universitätsverlag Göttingen, 2009) 9.

[24] The research in question used government revenues (based on the CIA World Factbook) and corporate turnover (based on Fortune Global 500) to draw up the ranking.

[25] Global Justice Now, '10 biggest corporations make more money than most countries in the world combined' (September 2016) www.globaljustice.org.uk/news/2016/sep/12/10-biggest-corporations-make-more-money-most-countries-world-combined.

have become 'transnational' or 'multinational' enterprises which have an international 'actorness' in their own right. States have conferred some international rights and obligations on TNCs.

A. Definitions

Before delving into some of the different features of TNCs' position under international law, it should be noted that the terminology that is employed with respect to TNCs is inconsistently varied and imprecise.[26] Terminological confusion persists as international instruments and literature use a variety of different terms to address essentially the same entities, and sometimes use similar terms to address functionally different entities.[27]

While in reality covering very different concepts, terms such as 'multinational enterprise', 'transnational corporation' and 'multinational corporation' are often used interchangeably.[28] The international legal instruments that attempt to delineate the abovementioned concepts are not exactly a shining example of consistency, and are of little help in elucidating the terminology. The UN, OECD and ILO, for example, each employ different concepts. Although a distinction was initially made between transnational corporations and multinational corporations, over time UN parlance has crystallised around the notion of 'transnational corporation', which is now used to cover all types of cross-border business associations that engage in direct investment.[29] The 2003 UN Draft Norms on the Responsibilities of Transnational Corporations and Other Business Enterprises with Regard to Human Rights provides that the term 'transnational corporation' refers to:

> an economic entity operating in more than one country or a cluster of economic entities operating in two or more countries – whatever their legal form, whether in their home country or country of activity, and whether taken individually or collectively.[30]

On the other hand, OECD and ILO instruments employ the term 'multinational enterprises'.[31] The OECD Guidelines for Multinational Enterprises – rejecting the need for a precise definition – describe them as follows:

> These enterprises operate in all sectors of the economy. They usually comprise companies or other entities established in more than one country and so linked that they may co-ordinate their operations in various ways. While one or more of these entities may be able to exercise a significant influence over the activities of others, their degree of autonomy within the enterprise may vary widely from one multinational enterprise to another. Ownership may be private, State or mixed.[32]

[26] C Brüls, 'Les sociétés multinationales: généralités' in C Brüls (ed), *Les Multinationales: Statut et réglementations* (Brussels, Larcier, 2013) 15.

[27] A Gatto, *Multinational Enterprises and Human Rights: Obligations under EU Law and International Law* (Cheltenham, Edward Elgar, 2011) 38; Muchlinski (n 21) 5.

[28] Gatto (n 27) 38.

[29] Muchlinski (n 21) 6.

[30] UN Commission on Human Rights, Sub-Commission on the Promotion and Protection of Human Rights, 'Norms on the Responsibilities of Transnational Corporations and Other Business Enterprises with Regard to Human Rights', 26 August 2003, UN Doc E/CN.4/Sub.2/2003/12/Rev.2, para 20.

[31] See OECD, 'Guidelines for Multinational Enterprises' (2011) oecd.org/daf/inv/mne/48004323.pdf; ILO, 'Tripartite Declaration of Principles Concerning Multinational Enterprises and Social Policy', 5th ed (2017), https://www.ilo.org/empent/areas/mne-declaration/lang--en/index.htm.

[32] OECD 'Guidelines for Multinational Enterprises' (n 31) part I, ch I, 4.

In a similar vein, the ILO also argues against the need for a precise definition, stating that multinational enterprises include:

> enterprises which own or control production, distribution, services or other facilities outside the country in which they are based. They may be large or small; and can have their headquarters in any part of the world. [...] Unless otherwise specified, the term 'multinational enterprise' is used in this Declaration to designate the various entities (parent companies or local entities or both or the organization as a whole) according to the distribution of responsibilities among them, in the expectation that they will cooperate and provide assistance to one another as necessary to facilitate observance of the principles laid down in this Declaration.[33]

The *Institut de droit international*, in a 1977 resolution, also employed the notion of multinational enterprises, and defined them as:

> Enterprises which consist of a decision-making centre located in one country and of operating centres, with or without legal personality, situated in one or more other countries.[34]

International legal scholarship has not exhibited greater consistency in its terminology relating to TNCs. Going beyond the broad underlying debate concerning the appropriate nomenclature for TNCs,[35] we follow Muchlinski's line of thinking: instead of making yet another attempt at hammering out an accurate definition of 'transnational corporations', we focus on the characteristics that distinguish TNCs from what Muchlinski refers to as 'uninational' enterprises (ie domestic corporations).[36] Grossly simplifying the various divergences, TNCs differ from domestic businesses in the sense that they: (i) operate their assets and control the use of such assets across national borders; (ii) utilise a managerial structure that allows managerial control to reach across national borders; and (iii) are able to trade across borders not only in respect of finished products but also in factor inputs, such as technical know-how and managerial skills, between affiliates and third parties.[37]

B. Rights under International Law

As far as rights are concerned, States have most conspicuously granted various procedural and substantive rights to investors (including legal persons such as TNCs) on the basis of international investment treaties. Among these rights is the right for an investor to initiate legal proceedings directly against States before international investment tribunals on the basis of a treaty violation. It bears noting, however, that corporations need not be afforded direct rights under international law for their international interests to be furthered. In fact, corporations derive considerable economic benefits from the current system of international law, such as from the law of the World Trade Organization (see Chapter 19), which has significantly reduced barriers to international trade, or from the law of the sea (see Chapter 18), which has facilitated international maritime transport. Below, we succinctly

[33] ILO 'Tripartite Declaration of Principles Concerning Multinational Enterprises and Social Policy' (n 31) 6.
[34] Institut de Droit International, *Annuaire*, Vol 57, Tome II (Session d'Oslo 1977) (München, S Karper, 1978) 194, cited by Wallace (n 21) 117.
[35] For a comprehensive and insightful overview of which we refer to Wallace (n 21).
[36] See in more detail Muchlinski (n 21) 7.
[37] Muchlinski (n 21) 7; JH Dunning, *International Production and the Multinational Enterprise* (London, Allen & Unwin, 1981) 7; OO Amao, 'The foundation for a global company law for multinational corporations' (2010) 21 *International Company and Commercial Law Review* 276.

discuss a selection of the rights granted to multinational corporations under international law, more specifically in the field of international human rights law. For the rights and protection granted to TNCs under international investment law, we refer to Chapter 19, Section IV.

Corporations, like individuals, are bearers of some fundamental rights,[38] and the area of international human rights law is becoming increasingly relevant for corporations. A first forum that might be important in this respect is the UN Human Rights Committee, which oversees the implementation of the International Covenant on Civil and Political Rights (ICCPR). Although the UN Human Rights Committee has acknowledged that legal entities do enjoy certain rights under the ICCPR, such as for example the freedom to manifest one's religion or belief and the freedom of association,[39] it is in reality impossible for corporations to bring a claim before the UN Human Rights Committee. According to Article 1 of the Optional Protocol to the ICCPR, only individuals can claim the violation of their rights before the Human Rights Committee. In consequence, corporations must rely entirely on domestic legal fora for the enforcement of their rights under the ICCPR.[40]

This differs significantly from the approach of the ECtHR, which has showed itself to be quite flexible in reviewing claims from corporate applicants, and in granting them protection under several of the ECHR rights – at times even going above and beyond the wording of the ECHR.[41] Indeed, corporations enjoy a uniquely high level of protection under the jurisdiction of the ECtHR, which has spearheaded the application of human rights to corporate applicants. Thus, it is well-accepted that corporations can petition the ECtHR, as this right is open to both natural and legal persons. According to Article 34 of the ECHR, the ECtHR may 'receive applications from any person, nongovernmental organisation or group of individuals claiming to be the victim of a violation by one of the High Contracting Parties of the rights set forth in the Convention or the Protocols thereto'. Corporations are included within the scope of the term 'nongovernmental organisation', and have made ample use of this right to bring claims before the ECtHR.[42]

The majority of the claims brought before the ECtHR by corporations relate to Articles 6(1) (right to a fair trial) and 13(1) (right to an effective remedy) of the ECHR respectively, and thus predominantly concern procedural rights.[43] The ECHR has, on multiple occasions, confirmed the right of corporations to various due process guarantees, for example, a fair and public hearing by an independent and impartial tribunal,[44] access to a court,[45] the equality of arms,[46] and the reasonable length of the proceedings.[47]

[38] P-F Docquir and L Hennebel, 'L'entreprise, titulaire et garante des droits de l'homme' in T Berns et al, *Responsabilité des entreprises et corégulation* (Brussels, Bruylant, 2007) 81.

[39] UN Human Rights Committee, General Comment No 31, 'The Nature of the General Legal Obligation Imposed on States Parties to the Covenant' (2004) UN Doc CCPR/C/21/Rev.1/Add.13 para 9.

[40] Brüls (n 26) 25.

[41] Eg in *Société Colas Est and others v France* App No 37971/97 (ECtHR, 16 April 2002) and *Comingersoll SA v Portugal* App No 35382/97 (ECtHR, 6 April 2000).

[42] M Emberland, 'Protection against Unwarranted Searches and Seizures of Corporate Premises under Article 8 of the European Convention on Human Rights: The Colas Est SA v. France Approach' (2003) 25 *MJIL* 82; LJ Dhooge, 'Human Rights for Transnational Corporations' (2007) 16 *Journal of Transnational Law & Policy* 215.

[43] Docquir and Hennebel (n 38) 87.

[44] *Sovtransavto Holding v Ukraine* App no 48553/99 (ECtHR, 25 July 2002).

[45] *Silvester's Horeca Service v Belgium* App no 47650/99 (ECtHR, 4 March 2004).

[46] *Dombo Beheer BV v the Netherlands* App No 14448/88 (ECtHR, 27 October 1993); Stran Greek Refineries and Stratis Andreadis v Greece App no 13427/87 (ECtHR, 9 December 1994).

[47] *Unión Alimentaria Sanders SA v Spain* App No 11681/85 (ECtHR, 7 July 1989).

Another ECHR right that is frequently invoked by corporations is the right to freedom of expression. Enshrined in Article 10(1) ECHR, the right to freedom of expression guarantees not only the right to hold any opinion, but also to 'receive and impart information and ideas without interference by public authority and regardless of frontiers'.[48] The right to freedom of expression has – rather unsurprisingly – most frequently been invoked by press and publishing companies.[49] The ECtHR has stated that the protection offered by Article 10 ECHR does not depend on the form or medium of the communication. For instance, it applies equally to films[50] or works of art.[51] The ECtHR has further confirmed that Article 10 ECHR also applies to corporations when the expression of opinion contains a political element,[52] or reflects 'controversial opinions pertaining to modern society in general'.[53]

In *Autronic AG v Switzerland* (1990), the ECtHR extended the protection offered by Article 10 ECHR to speech that is purely commercial. It held that corporate speech – ie communication in order to 'incite the public to purchase a particular product' – falls within the scope of Article 10 ECHR, and that it is not necessary to 'ascertain the reason and purpose for which the right is to be exercised'.[54]

Another claim that is often brought by corporations relates to the right to peaceful enjoyment of possessions.[55] Article 1 of the First Protocol to the ECHR expressly refers to both natural persons and legal persons, and protects against the deprivation of possessions.[56] In addition to possessions, the ECtHR has also extended a layer of protection over business premises (for example the corporation's registered office).[57] It did so by extending the protection offered by Article 8 ECHR, which enshrines the right to respect for private and family life, and provides that everyone has 'the right to respect for his private and family life, his home and his correspondence'. In *Société Colas Est SA and others v France* (2002) the ECtHR held that, in certain circumstances, the rights guaranteed by Article 8(1) ECHR may be construed as including the right to respect for a company's registered office, branches or other business premises.[58] In a fit of dynamic interpretation, the ECtHR thus expanded the notion of 'home' to corporate offices and facilities.

Perhaps the most innovative application of the ECHR to corporations is the ECtHR's interpretation of Article 41 ECHR with respect to 'just satisfaction'. Article 41 ECHR provides injured parties the possibility of obtaining damages in case of a violation of the ECHR or the Protocols thereto. As a consequence of *Comingersoll SA v Portugal* (2001), corporations are also entitled to monetary compensation for non-pecuniary damages in accordance with Article 41 ECHR. These non-pecuniary damages may include subjective and objective elements, such as for example the company's reputation, as well as 'uncertainty

[48] Art 10(1) ECHR.
[49] Docquir and Hennebel (n 38) 92.
[50] *Wingrove v United Kingdom* App No 17419/90 (ECtHR 25 November 1996).
[51] *Müller and others v Switzerland* App No 10737/84 (ECtHR, 24 May 1988).
[52] *Sunday Times v UK* App No 6538/74 (ECtHR, 26 April 1979).
[53] *VGT Verein gegen Tierfabriken v Switzerland* App No 24699/94 (ECtHR, 28 June 2001); see also *Sunday Times v UK* (n 52).
[54] *Autronic AG v Switzerland* App No 12726/87 (ECtHR, 22 May 1990) para 47.
[55] Docquir and Hennebel (n 38) 90.
[56] Art 1 Protocol to the Convention for the Protection of Human Rights and Fundamental Freedoms (adopted 20 March 1952, entered into force 18 May 1954) CETS No 9.
[57] Brüls (n 26) 28.
[58] *Société Colas Est SA and others v France* (n 41) para 41.

in decision-planning, disruption in the management of the company […] and […] the anxiety and inconvenience caused to the members of the management team'.[59]

C. Obligations under International Law

Because the international legal system appears to be skewed towards the interests of transnational corporations, some have argued that their powers should be constrained. In particular, it has been argued that there should be mechanisms to hold them accountable for the negative externalities caused by their activities on global values and common interests, such as human rights and the environment.

Starting in the 1970s, a number of international organisations sought to limit the adverse impact of corporations on the enjoyment of social rights and the environment. In 1977, the International Labour Organization adopted a Tripartite Declaration of Principles Concerning Multinational Enterprises and Social Policy,[60] which was revised several times, and aims at countering the negative social impact of transnational corporations' activities.[61] In parallel, the OECD has adopted (non-binding) Guidelines for Multinational Enterprises, which set out a number of recommendations regarding responsible business conduct, aiming at minimising the adverse impacts of their operations, inter alia on sustainable development and human rights.[62] These Guidelines, which have also been revised a number of times, are supported by National Contact Points, which are set up by adhering countries 'to further the effectiveness of the Guidelines by undertaking promotional activities, handling enquiries and contributing to the resolution of issues that arise relating to the implementation of the Guidelines'.[63] These National Contact Points, typically located within government ministries, may investigate complaints filed against multinational corporations, and recommend solutions, while involving the relevant stakeholders.

The EU has also taken action with respect to corporate social responsibility. The European Parliament, for instance, adopted resolutions on corporate social responsibility in international trade agreements,[64] and on accountable, transparent and responsible business behaviour and sustainable growth.[65] In addition, the EU has published a number of non-binding guidelines[66] and encouraged its Member States to adopt national action plans on

[59] *Comingersoll SA v Portugal* (n 41) para 35; Brüls (n 26) 30.

[60] See for its most recent edition: ILO, 'Tripartite Declaration of Principles Concerning Multinational enterprises and Social Policy', 5th edn (March 2017) www.ilo.org/empent/Publications/WCMS_094386/lang--en/index.htm.

[61] See on ILO standards, eg R Zandvliet and P van der Heijden, 'The Rapprochement of ILO Standards and CSR Mechanisms: towards a Positive Understanding of the 'Privatization' of International Labour Standards' in A Marx, J Wouters, G Rayp and L Beke (eds), Global Governance of Labour Rights: Assessing the Effectiveness of Public and Private Policy Initiatives (Cheltenham, Edward Elgar, 2015), 170–89.

[62] OECD Guidelines for Multinational Enterprises (n 31).

[63] ibid.

[64] European Parliament, Resolution of 25 November 2010 on corporate social responsibility in international trade agreements, 2009/2201(INI).

[65] European Parliament, Resolution of 28 January 2013 on corporate social responsibility: accountable, transparent and responsible business behaviour and sustainable growth, 2012/2098(INI).

[66] See, for example, the three EU Sector Guides on Implementing the UN Guiding Principles on Business and Human Rights: (i) for employment and recruitment agencies: publications.europa.eu/en/publication-detail/-/publication/7fa3f4c2-9f0f-46df-b698-cdd627cabe31; (ii) for the oil and gas sector: publications.europa.eu/en/publication-detail/-/publication/e05fc065-f35c-4c0d-91e9-7e500374ee0f; and (iii) for the ICT sector: publications.europa.eu/en/publication-detail/-/publication/ab151420-d60a-40a7-b264-adce304e138b.

business and human rights,[67] and has even passed binding legislation in the field. These will be discussed in more detail below.

The aforementioned initiatives are essentially *government* initiatives. In order to involve corporations more directly in the development of responsible business practices, the United Nations launched the Global Compact in 2000, an innovative learning platform in which businesses can participate to advance their operations' social and environmental sustainability.[68] Since 2000, more than 9,000 corporate participants have committed themselves to upholding ten universally accepted principles in the areas of human rights, labour, environment, and anti-corruption, and to share best practices. The mechanism has some teeth, as participating corporations' failure to annually post a Communication on Progress can result in a change in participant status and possible expulsion. On the other hand, since the annual reports are not subject to review, they have been criticised as a mere 'public relations exercise'.[69]

Participation in the Global Compact, or a host of other corporate responsibility schemes,[70] remains entirely voluntary. A failure to participate, or a failure to live up to commitments made, does not amount to an internationally wrongful act. At most, corporate misconduct can engage corporations' responsibility under domestic law. But as Host States may be more concerned with attracting inward investment, and home States may want to maximise their corporations' profits, it is doubtful whether effective domestic regulation of corporate activities, and adequate enforcement of existing domestic law, are realistic. This apparent regulatory failure explains calls by some campaigners for more far-reaching corporate obligations *under international law*.

Under international law as it currently stands, however, it is heavily disputed whether corporations have direct obligations. As far as obligations under international criminal law are concerned, for instance, the personal jurisdiction of international criminal tribunals, including of the International Criminal Court (Article 25 of the Rome Statute) is limited to natural persons. This may be explained by the fact that criminal liability of corporations and other legal persons is unknown in the domestic legal systems of a large number of States, which then opposed enshrining such liability in the Rome Statute. The jurisdictional limitations of these international tribunals need not imply, however, that there cannot be a substantive rule on criminal liability of (non-State) entities under general international law that could be applied by domestic courts. That said, there is no strong evidence of courts applying such a rule.[71] International humanitarian law, for its part, undeniably imposes

[67] So far, the UK (2013, updated in 2016), the Netherlands (2013), Denmark (2014), Finland (2014), Lithuania (2015), Sweden (2015), Italy (2016), Germany (2016), France (2017), Poland (2017), Spain (2017), Belgium (2017), and Chile (2017) have launched national action plans. The Czech Republic, Greece, Ireland, Luxembourg, Portugal and Slovenia are in the process of doing so.

[68] See United Nations Global Compact Leaders Summit 2017, unglobalcompact.org.

[69] NZ Tévar, 'Shortcomings and Disadvantages of Existing Legal Mechanisms to Hold Multinational Corporations Accountable for Human Rights Violations' (2012) 4 *Cuadernos de Derecho Transnacional* 398, 405; Administrative Court of Appeal of Île-de-France, Versailles (FR), *Association France-Palestine Solidarité (AFPS) and Palestine Liberation Organization (PLO) v Société Alstom transport SA and others*, 22 March 2013, Case No 11/05331 (UN Global Compact does not hold an obligation for corporation to abstain from enterprise in violation as it is non-binding and international human rights law is directed at States).

[70] See eg the Extractive Industries Transparency Initiative (EITI), eiti.org; the International Code of Conduct Association (ICoCA) and the International Code of Conduct for Private Security Service Providers, icoca.ch; the Voluntary Principles on Security and Human Rights, voluntaryprinciples.org; and the Responsible Jewellery Council, responsiblejewellery.com.

[71] Note that the mode of liability which prosecutors may use to indict corporations will normally be accomplice (aiding and abetting) liability rather than (in-)direct perpetration, since corporations are unlikely to be the

obligations on non-State entities provided that they are parties to an armed conflict (see also below, Section IV, on non-State armed groups). But as corporations normally do not directly participate in hostilities, they remain civilians and are not bound by norms of international humanitarian law in a combatant capacity.[72] An exception might be private military and security companies, although even these entities typically take on a support rather than a direct combat role, and thus may not be characterised as parties to a conflict.[73]

i. Human Rights Law

There is a great debate on the question whether corporations have obligations under international human rights law. This debate has culminated in the United Nations giving a mandate to a UN Special Representative on Human Rights and Transnational Corporations and other Business Enterprises, John Ruggie, to study the issue. The Special Representative's final Guiding Principles on Business and Human Rights (UNGPS) of 2011 are cautious. While enunciating as a foundational principle that '[b]usiness enterprises should respect human rights', meaning that 'they should avoid infringing on the human rights of others and should address adverse human rights impacts with which they are involved' (Principle 11), Ruggie refrains from recognising the binding character of international human rights obligations for corporations, leaving liability issues instead to national law.[74] According to this approach, direct human rights obligations are only incumbent on States, which under international law have the duty to 'protect against human rights abuse within their territory and/or jurisdiction by third parties, including business enterprises', which 'requires taking appropriate steps to prevent, investigate, punish and redress such abuse through effective policies, legislation, regulations and adjudication' (Principle 1). John Knox has similarly explained in his seminal article on horizontal human rights law that 'human rights law does not impose many correlative duties directly' – correlative duties being understood as private duties to respect the human rights of others – and 'merely contemplates that governments should protect many human rights from violation by private actors'.[75] Knox defended this

perpetrators of international crimes. Criminal cases involving businesses have been brought against individual businessmen rather than against corporations. See eg Court of Appeal of 's-Hertogenbosch (NL), 21 April 2017, *K*, Case No 20-001906-10: the District Court of The Hague convicted a businessman for supplying weapons to the regime of Charles Taylor in violation of weapon embargoes imposed by the UN Security Council; and Court of Appeal of The Hague, *Van Anraat*, 9 May 2007, Case No 2200050906-2: the same Court found a businessman guilty of complicity to war crimes committed in Iraq and Iran for selling various chemicals to the regime of Saddam Hussein. On transnational corporations' responsibility as a 'general practice': *AFPS and PLO v Société Alstom transport SA and others* (n 70). The sole finding of several soft law instruments was not sufficient to characterise States' consent to the general responsibility of transnational corporations in the event of infringements of human rights law.

[72] E Mongerald, 'Corporate Civil Liability for Violations of International Humanitarian Law' (2006) 88 *IRRC* 665.

[73] Even if they take on combat roles, they may have been incorporated into the armed forces of a State Party.

[74] ibid, Commentary to Principle 12 (submitting that 'responsibility of business enterprises to respect human rights is distinct from issues of legal liability and enforcement, which remain defined largely by national law provisions in relevant jurisdictions'). For an illustration in domestic case law, see *AFPS and PLO v Société Alstom transport SA and others* (n 70). In an earlier Report (OHCHR, 'Protect, Respect, and Remedy: A Framework for Business and Human Rights', 7 April 2008, UN Doc A/HRC/8/5, paras 54–55), the Special Representative of the Secretary General on the issue of human rights and transnational corporations and other business enterprises, John Ruggie, wrote: 'Whereas governments define the scope of legal compliance, the broader scope of the responsibility to respect is defined by social expectations – as part of what is sometimes called a company's social licence to operate. The corporate responsibility to respect exists independently of States' duties. Therefore, there is no need for the slippery distinction between "primary" State and "secondary" corporate obligations'.

[75] J Knox, 'Horizontal Human Rights Law' (2008) 102 *AJIL* 1, 2.

approach on the ground that new horizontal duties might 'open the door to converse vertical duties that would restrict human rights', and inadvertently weaken the existing system of human rights law.[76] This concern is echoed in the Special Representative's warning that the (non-legal) corporate responsibility to respect 'exists independently of States' abilities and/or willingness to fulfil their own human rights obligations, and does not diminish those obligations'.[77] For litigation purposes, in any event, the relevance of identifying direct human rights obligations incumbent on corporations appears overstated. Especially after the jurisdictional limitation of the idiosyncratic Alien Tort Statute by the US Supreme Court in the *Kiobel*[78] case, it is likely that claims with respect to human rights abuses by corporations will be reframed as simple tort claims brought before domestic courts in transnational civil litigation governed by conflict of laws rules rather than public international law.[79] However, this remains an evolving area in domestic case law.[80]

The 'Ruggie approach', according to which corporations have no direct obligations under international human rights law, but are nevertheless socially expected not to infringe on human rights, has been endorsed by the EU and the Council of Europe. The EU has committed itself to implementing the UNGPs in its 2011 CSR strategy,[81] and encourages the implementation of the UNGPs at the international level.[82] Since 2011 it has published a number of non-binding guidelines[83] and encouraged its Member States to adopt national action plans on business and human rights.[84] While EU efforts have mostly focused on non-binding instruments, the EU has also passed binding legislation in the field, including notably the 2014 Non-Financial Reporting Directive, which obliges large companies to disclose in their management report, information on policies, risks and outcomes as regards environmental matters, social and employee aspects, respect for human rights, anti-corruption and bribery issues, and diversity in their board of directors, as well as eg their environmental impact or respect for human rights,[85] and the 2017 Conflict Minerals Regulation, which sets in place a system for supply chain due diligence for importers of minerals or metals containing or consisting of tin, tantalum, tungsten or gold.[86] The Committee of

[76] ibid, 47.

[77] UNGPs, Commentary to Principle 11.

[78] United States Supreme Court, *Kiobel v Royal Dutch Petroleum Co*, 17 April 2013, 133 S Ct 1659.

[79] Corporate human rights abuses may thus be reframed as assault and battery, wrongful death and false imprisonment. See for such litigation in US State courts: symposium issue of the UC Irvine Law Review on Human Rights Litigation in State Courts and Under State Law (2013), and for such litigation in a Dutch Court: Court of Appeal The Hague (Rechtbank's Gravenhage) (NL), *Akpan and others v Royal Dutch Shell and Shell Petroleum Development Company of Nigeria, Ltd*, 18 December 2015, Case No 200.126.849-01 200.127.813-01 (holding Shell's Nigerian subsidiary responsible for violating its duty of care to prevent oil spills vis-à-vis a Nigerian farmer).

[80] See eg the active case of *Al Shimari v CACI Premier Technology, Inc* in which the Fourth Circuit held that a lawsuit by four Iraqi nationals who were imprisoned at Abu Ghraib, and who were allegedly tortured by US military contractors there, satisfied the *Kiobel* 'touch and concern' test; District Court Virginia (US), *Al Shimari v CACI*, 21 February 2018, Case No 1:08-cv-00827-LMB-JFA (denying CACI's motion to dismiss).

[81] EC, Communication, 'A Renewed EU Strategy 2011–14 for Corporate Social Responsibility', 25 October 2011, COM/2011/0681.

[82] See eg EU, Oral Statement, Open-ended intergovernmental working group on transnational corporations and other business enterprises with respect to human rights, 2nd session, Geneva, 24–28 October 2016, 161025_11.

[83] See n 67.

[84] See n 68.

[85] Directive 2014/95/EU of 22 October 2014 amending Directive 2013/34/EU as regards disclosure of non-financial and diversity information by certain large undertakings and groups Text with EEA relevance [2014] OJ L330/1.

[86] Regulation (EU) 2017/821 of 17 May 2017 laying down supply chain due diligence obligations for Union importers of tin, tantalum and tungsten, their ores, and gold originating from conflict-affected and high-risk areas [2017] OJ L130.

Ministers of the Council of Europe in turn has adopted recommendations on human rights and business, containing a guide of good practice addressing gaps in the implementation of the UNGPs at the European level.[87] At the UN level, however, efforts are underway to prepare a binding treaty on business and human rights. A working group was set up by the UN Human Rights Council in June 2014,[88] and produced a draft in July 2018.[89]

ii. Direct Legal Obligations

In contrast, in the law of the sea and environmental law, a number of conventions impose apparently direct obligations on non-State (corporate) actors. Article 137 UNCLOS prohibits natural or juridical persons (aside from States) from acquiring or exercising rights with respect to 'the Area' (ie the seabed and ocean floor and subsoil thereof, beyond the limits of national jurisdiction),[90] or from appropriating any part thereof. That said, natural and legal persons are eligible to carry out activities in the Area, in accordance with Article 153(2) UNCLOS, provided that they be either nationals of a State party or effectively controlled by its nationals, and are sponsored by such State.[91] When damage arises out of a wrongful act in the conduct of the operations of such a contractor, as a result of its activity, its responsibility or liability will be engaged in accordance with Article 22 of UNCLOS Annex III.

In an important 2011 advisory opinion, the Seabed Disputes Chamber of the International Tribunal for the Law of the Sea (ITLOS) clarified the obligations of certain non-State actors.[92] The ITLOS held, in particular, that contractors are under an obligation to cooperate with the International Seabed Authority (the Authority) – which administers the Area – in the establishment of monitoring programmes to evaluate the impact of deep seabed mining on the marine environment.[93] In addition, the ITLOS ruled that the main liability for a wrongful act committed in the conduct of the contractor's operations or in the exercise of the Authority's powers and functions rests with the contractor and the Authority, respectively, rather than with the sponsoring State.[94] This is a clear confirmation of the autonomy of the obligations of non-State actors vis-à-vis those of States (on the Area, see further Chapter 18, Section VI).

Rules on international obligations and liability of non-State economic operators can also be found in the field of civil liability for oil pollution (on which see also Chapter 20, Section IV(A)(i)). In fact, in this field, primary obligations to pay compensation rest on

[87] CoE Committee of Ministers, Recommendation CM/Rec(2016)3 on human rights and business, 2 March 2016.

[88] HRC, Resolution 26/9, Elaboration of an international legally binding instrument on transnational corporations and other business enterprises with respect to human rights, 26 June 2014. The first session of the open-ended intergovernmental working group (IGWG) took place on 6–10 July 2015 in Geneva. In these negotiations the European institutions have not been speaking with one voice so far.

[89] Legally Binding Instrument to Regulate, in International Human Rights Law, the Activities of Transnational Corporations and Other Business Enterprises, Zero Draft, 16 July 2018, https://www.ohchr.org/Documents/HRBodies/HRCouncil/WGTransCorp/Session3/DraftLBI.pdf.

[90] The definition of the 'Area' in Art 1.1(1) UNCLOS.

[91] Note that the legal status of the entities is thus effectively a function of their status under the domestic law of a State Party to UNCLOS.

[92] *Responsibilities and obligations of States with respect to activities in the Area* (Advisory Opinion) [2011] ITLOS Rep 10, 74–78.

[93] ibid, 44, para 143 (particularly through the creation of 'impact reference zones' and 'preservation reference zones').

[94] ibid, 63, para 200.

(non-State) ship-owners rather than States. Article VII of the 1992 Civil Liability Convention,[95] for instance, provides compulsory liability insurance for ship-owners registered in a Contracting State and carrying more than 2,000 tons of oil in bulk as cargo. Similar rules can be found in the 1996 International Convention on Liability and Compensation for Damage in Connection with the Carriage of Hazardous and Noxious Substances by State (the HNS Convention) and the 2001 International Convention on Civil Liability for Bunker Oil Pollution Damage.[96] The latter Convention makes it clear that it imposes obligations on *any person*, such person being defined as 'any individual or partnership or any public or private body, whether corporate or not'.[97] It is of note that under these Conventions, where the insurance does not cover an incident, or is insufficient to satisfy the claim, oil pollution funds will pay compensation.[98] A similar system has been proposed for damage done by a contractor to the Area.[99]

Direct responsibility for private operators can also be found in the field of nuclear energy. Article 3 of the OECD Paris Convention on Third Party Liability in the Field of Nuclear Energy (1960)[100] provides that the operator of a nuclear installation shall be (objectively) liable for the damage to or loss of life of any person, and damage to or loss of any property upon proof that such damage or loss was caused by a nuclear incident in such installation.[101] Similarly, the Vienna Convention on Civil Liability for Nuclear Damage (1963)[102] provides that the operator of a nuclear installation is to be liable for nuclear damage upon proof that such damage has been caused by a nuclear incident.

Ultimately, however, civil liability questions in the environmental field are governed by domestic law rather than international law. The relevant conventions only lay down minimum standards which States subsequently have to implement and enforce in their domestic legal order. As operators mainly fall under domestic law, they are subjects of domestic rather than international law, even if international law impacted on the content of domestic law.[103]

It is well-known that corporations and other non-State actors incur direct obligations under EU law, such as under rules of EU competition law (Articles 101–102 TFEU).[104]

[95] International Convention on Civil Liability for Oil Pollution Damage (adopted 29 November 1969, entered into force 19 June 1975) 973 UNTS 3 (1992 Liability Convention).

[96] International Convention on Civil Liability for Bunker Oil Pollution Damage (adopted 23 March 2001, entered into force 21 November 2008) (2002) OJ L256/9 (BUNKER Convention). For the liability rules under this Convention, see Arts 3–7.

[97] See Arts 1–2 of the BUNKER Convention.

[98] Art 4 of the 1992 Liability Convention.

[99] Y Tanaka, 'Responsibilities and Obligations of Sponsoring States Concerning Activities in the Area: Reflections on the ITLOS Advisory Opinion of 1 February 2011' (2013) 60 *NILR* 205.

[100] Convention on Third Party Liability in the Field of Nuclear Energy (adopted 29 July 1960, entered into force 1 April 1968) and Additional Protocol to the Said Convention (adopted 28 January 1964, entered into force 1 April 1968) 956 UNTS 251.

[101] For the maximum liability of the operator, see Art 7 of the Convention on Third Party Liability in the Field of Nuclear Energy.

[102] Art II Vienna Convention on Civil Liability for Nuclear Damage (adopted 21 May 1963, entered into force 12 November 1977) 1063 UNTS 265, as amended by the 1997 Protocol to Amend the 1963 Vienna Convention on Civil Liability for Nuclear Damage (adopted 12 September 1997, entered into force 4 October 2003) 2241 UNTS 270.

[103] Tomuschat has observed in this respect that the conventional regimes 'reflect a method well known to private international law, which often seeks to harmonize or make uniform the rules of internal laws by drafting an international treaty whose content will then be translated in the internal legal orders of the States parties'. See C Tomuschat, 'Private Individuals' in J Crawford, A Pellet and S Olleson (eds), *The Law of International Responsibility* (Oxford, OUP, 2010) 324.

[104] Arts 101–102 TFEU.

iii. Aid and Assistance

Where corporations and other non-State actors may not incur direct obligations under (the norms pertaining to various branches of) international law, they may well aid and assist, or be complicit in international law violations committed by subjects which do incur such obligations, notably States. Interestingly, Clapham has submitted that the rules on State responsibility for aiding and assisting may apply by analogy to corporations involved in conduct that does not rise to the level of an international crime but constitutes 'international torts'.[105] This would require a further development of Article 16 of the ILC Articles on State Responsibility in order to include aiding and assisting/complicity by non-State actors.[106]

iv. Voluntary Codes of Conduct

Corporations may subscribe to codes of conduct in which they commit themselves to respecting human rights, labour laws, and environmental law.[107] Such codes have a voluntary character, however, and can be categorised as 'soft law' rather than genuine 'law' (on soft law, see Chapter 3, Section VII). Such codes could gain teeth, however, if the norms they contain are reproduced in contracts which corporations enter into with States or international organisations – eg a contract for services between a State and a private military company, or a loan contract between a company active in the extractive sector, and an international financial institution or multilateral development). Although these norms have an international law origin – and are typically drawn from human rights and environmental law conventions – they are contractual rather than international in nature. Corporations are bound by them on the basis of (domestic/transnational) contractual law rather than directly on the basis of international law.

IV. Non-State Armed Groups

We live in an era where most armed conflicts are of a non-international character ('civil wars'), in which government forces fight against non-State armed groups (NSAGs), or NSAGs fight against others NSAGs. The law of non-international armed conflict, which is dealt with in Chapter 15, has regulated such conflicts, and in order to ensure reciprocity between States and non-State actors, has imposed a number of international humanitarian law obligations on both States and NSAGs. Common Article 3 of the Geneva Conventions 1949 can be considered seminal in this respect: it provides that '[i]n the case of armed

[105] A Clapham, *The Human Rights Obligations of Non-State Actors* (Oxford, OUP, 2006) 261–63.

[106] A non-State actor could then incur liability for aiding and assisting provided that he or she: (a) is aware of the circumstances making the activity of the assisted State a violation of international human rights law; (b) gives assistance with a view to facilitating the commission of such a violation and actually contributes significantly to the violation; and (c) the act would be internationally wrongful if the complicit entity committed the act itself (ibid, 266). For an application to corruption, see C Rose, 'The Application of Human Rights Law to Private Sector Complicity in Governmental Corruption' (2011) 24 *LJIL* 715.

[107] Apart from that, international guidelines regarding the activities of multinational corporations have been adopted by international organisations and governments, eg, the ILO Tripartite Declaration of Principles Concerning Multinational Enterprises and Social Policy (n 61) and the OECD Guidelines for Multinational Enterprises (n 31). As such, these guidelines do not have legal value.

conflict not of an international character occurring in the territory of one of the High Contracting Parties, each Party to the conflict [ie either a State or a NSAG] shall be bound to apply, as a minimum' a number of basic humanitarian provisions on the treatment of those who do not take active part in hostilities. The protection provided by this provision is less far-reaching than the protection offered by Geneva Conventions to persons caught up in international armed conflicts. But then, the article goes on to provide that '[t]he Parties to the conflict should further endeavour to bring into force, by means of special agreements, all or part of the other provisions' of the Conventions. A disclaimer has been added, however, to the effect that the application of these provisions 'shall not affect the legal status of the Parties to the conflict'. This reflects States' concern over the recognition, and thus increased legitimacy of NSAGs which may follow from their carrying international obligations, and thus possessing a measure of international legal personality.

The protections offered in non-international armed conflict, and the list of attendant obligations imposed on NSAGs, have been expanded through Additional Protocol II to the Geneva Conventions (1977), which develops and supplements Common Article 3. The material scope of the Protocol, however, is more limited than the scope of Common Article 3; as far as NSAGs in particular are concerned, the Protocol only contains obligations for NSAGs to the extent that they are involved in an armed conflict with government armed forces (so not with other NSAGs), and that they are under responsible command and exercise such control over a part of its territory as to enable them to carry out sustained and concerted military operations and to implement the Protocol.[108] Apart from these conventional obligations, it is assumed that NSAGs also possess IHL obligations under customary international law,[109] in the words of the International Criminal Tribunal for the former Yugoslavia 'whenever there is [...] protracted armed violence between governmental authorities and organised armed groups or between such groups within a State'.[110] The UN Security Council, for its part, has demanded that NSAGs 'fulfil their international obligations and their commitments under relevant agreements [and] relevant Council resolutions'.[111]

The theoretical justification of why precisely NSAGs are bound by IHL remains elusive. After all, States, through conventions and customary law, appear to have just *imposed* such obligations on NSAGs. This process is in tension with the consent-based structure of international law, but is testimony of the treatment of non-State actors as *objects*, rather than as veritable *subjects* of international law. States, as the original subjects of international law, are considered to have the power to bind non-State actors under international law, without necessarily securing their consent. Arguably, insofar as NSAGs are active in the territory of a Contracting State, such a State is allowed to regulate the former's activities, also on the basis of international law (ie the theory of legislative jurisdiction).[112]

[108] As of 27 February 2018, the Protocol had been ratified by 168 States.

[109] See Rule 139 in J-M Henckaerts and L Doswald-Beck, Customary International Humanitarian Law: Volume I: Rules (Cambridge, CUP, 2005); SCSL, Appeals Chamber, Prosecutor v Sam Hinga Norman, Decision on Preliminary Motion Based on Lack of Jurisdiction (Child Recruitment), 31 May 2004, Case No SCSL-2004-14-AR72(E), para 22: 'it is well settled that all parties to an armed conflict, whether States or non-State actors, are bound by international humanitarian law, even though only States may become parties to international treaties'.

[110] ICTY, Appeals Chamber, *Prosecutor v Tadić*, Decision on the Defence Motion for Interlocutory Appeal on Jurisdiction, 2 October 1995, Case No IT-94-1, para 70.

[111] UNSC Res 1769, 31 July 2007, UN Doc S/RES/1769, para 22; UNSC Res 1828, 31 July 2008, UN Doc S/RES/1828, para 26 (regarding the conflict in Darfur).

[112] See eg M Sassòli, A Bouvier and A Quintin (eds), How Does Law Protect in War, 3rd edn (Geneva, ICRC, 2011) 26.

Alternatively, NSAGs could be bound by IHL on the ground that their individual members are already bound by norms of international criminal law – which punish violations of IHL, on the basis of customary international law, or on the ground that treaties can create duties for third parties (NSAGs). An alternative approach finds NSAGs to be bound by international humanitarian law rules via their individual members who are individually bound to respect these rules.[113]

Whereas the theoretical basis for the binding character of IHL for NSAGs is disputed, it is a matter of near consensus that NSAGs are indeed bound by IHL norms. In contrast, there is more contestation as to whether armed groups are bound by norms of *international human rights law*. Such groups are not bound on the basis of human rights treaties, not only because they cannot become parties to these treaties, but also because such treaties do not contain provisions to the effect of binding non-State actors to the treaty norms.[114] Still, it is argued that armed groups *may* have human rights obligations under customary international law, at least if they have control over territory and thus exercise de facto governmental functions.[115] This rule has no strong grounding in State practice, however, and has mainly been based on the practice and views of UN bodies and experts.

It is of note that all these theories, while being based on legitimate considerations of humanitarian necessity, bypass NSAGs' consent to be bound. This is not only problematic from a theoretical perspective, but also from a practical one. NSAGs may reject the legitimacy of international norms which they have not agreed to – if they are aware of them in the first place – and accordingly refuse to apply them in practice. This effectiveness problem has partly been addressed with respect to peoples fighting against colonial domination and alien occupation and against racist regimes in the exercise of their right to self-determination. Conflicts pitting such national liberation movements against States have been equated with *international* armed conflict, even if in fact such conflicts are merely internal to one State, for the purpose of the application of international humanitarian law, at least by Additional Protocol I (Article 1(4)).[116] Article 96(3) of the Protocol secures such movements' consent to be bound, by stipulating that

> the authority representing a people engaged against a High Contracting Party in an armed conflict of the type referred to in Article 1, paragraph 4, may undertake to apply the Conventions and this Protocol in relation to that conflict by means of a unilateral declaration addressed to the depositary.

This provision was inserted as a result of the participation of a number of national liberation movements in the negotiations leading up to the adoption of the Protocol. The 'ownership' hopes it raised, however, have not been realised in practice. Not all States have ratified

[113] S Sivakumaran, 'Binding Armed Opposition Groups' (2006) 55 ICLQ 369; A Cassese, 'The Status of Rebels under the 1977 Geneva Protocol on Non-International Armed Conflicts' (1981) 30 ICLQ 416.

[114] See ECOSOC, Report of the Sub-Commission on Prevention of Discrimination and Protection of Minorities, Minimum Humanitarian Standards, Analytical report of the Secretary-General submitted pursuant to Commission on Human Rights Resolution 1997/21, 5 January 1998, UN Doc E/CN.4/1998/87.

[115] K Fortin, *The Accountability of Armed Groups under International Human Rights Law* (OUP, 2017); J-M Henckaerts and C Wiesener, 'Human Rights Obligations of Non-Armed Groups: A Possible Contribution from Customary International Law?' in R Kolb and G Gaggioli (eds), Research Handbook on Human Rights and Humanitarian Law (Cheltenham, Edward Elgar, 2013) 146–69; A Constantinides, 'Human Rights Obligations and Accountability of Armed Opposition Groups: The Practice of the UN Security Council' (2010) 4 Human Rights and International Legal Discourse 89; J Moore, 'From Nation State to Failed State: International Protection from Human Rights Abuses by Non-State Actors' (1999) 31 Columbia Human Rights Law Review 81; M Schoiswohl, 'De Facto Regimes and Human Rights Obligations: The Twilight Zone of Public International Law' (2003) 6 Austrian Review of International and European Law 45.

[116] Art 1(4) AP I.

the Protocol, and no declarations under Article 96(3) have so far been filed. Moreover, the special regime for national liberation movements was designed for a specific period in history (decolonisation and its aftermath); as of today, few NSAGs currently qualify as national liberation movements.[117]

A. Unilateral Declarations and Agreements

For NSAGs not falling within the scope of the aforementioned regime – in practice nearly all NSAGs – international efforts have been undertaken to secure their consent to be bound by IHL (as well as human rights) obligations through unilateral declarations and agreements. The work of Geneva Call deserves particular mention in this respect. This Geneva-based non-governmental organisation has pioneered the use of a Deed of Commitment, which allows NSAGs to pledge to respect specific humanitarian norms and be held accountable for norm violations. On the basis of this Deed of Commitment, NSAGs can formally express their agreement to be bound by IHL and related human rights norms. Three such deeds are currently in existence: the Deed of Commitment for Adherence to a Total Ban on Anti-Personnel Mines and for Cooperation in Mine Action (2000), the Deed of Commitment for the Protection of Children from the Effects of Armed Conflict (2010), and the Deed of Commitment for the Prohibition of Sexual Violence in Situations of Armed Conflict and towards the Elimination of Gender Discrimination (2012).[118] Compliance with NSAGs' pledges is monitored and assessed by Geneva Call. NSAGs not only lay down their obligations in unilateral pledges, but also in (peace) agreements signed with the governments against whom they have been fighting. Such agreements may be brokered – and later monitored – by international organisations (such as the UN and the African Union) and interested third States, a process which confers on them an international character. It is uncertain, however, whether on that basis they qualify as treaties providing for obligations under international law. Nevertheless, there is some institutional practice that considers such agreements as binding.[119]

B. International Responsibility

While a regime of NSAG *primary obligations*, especially under IHL, has been put in place, a (secondary) *responsibility* regime, governing matters such as attribution and reparations,

[117] See in particular the Palestine Liberation Organization (PLO), which holds observer status at the UN (since 1974, see UNGA Res 3237 (XXIX), 'Observer status for the Palestine Liberation Organization', 22 November 1974, UN Doc A/RES/3237), the African Union, and the Polisario Front, which represents the Sahrawi people of the Western Sahara, occupied by Morocco, and has been recognised by the UN (see Point 7, UNGA Res 34/37, 'Question of Western Sahara', 21 November 1979, UN Doc A/RES/34/37, Point 7).

[118] For more information, see Geneva Call, 'Deed of Commitment', genevacall.org/how-we-work/deed-of-commitment. As of 29 May 2018, 52 NSAGs had signed the Deed of Commitment banning AP mines, 26 had signed the Deed of Commitment protecting children in armed conflict, and 24 had signed the Deed of Commitment prohibiting sexual violence and gender discrimination.

[119] ICTY, Appeals Chamber, *Prosecutor v Galić*, 30 November 2006, Case No IT-98-29-A, para 119; ICTY, Trial Chamber, *Prosecutor v Blaškić*, 3 March 2000, Case No IT-95-14-T, para 172; UNSC, Report of the International Commission of Inquiry on Darfur to the Secretary General pursuant to Security Council Resolution 1564 (2004) of 18 September 2004, 1 February 2005, UN Doc S/2005/60, para 174, stating that 'the [NSAGs] SLM/A and the JEM possess under customary international law the power to enter into binding international agreements with the Government of Sudan'.

along the lines of the International Law Commission's Articles on the Responsibility of States for Internationally Wrongful Acts has not yet been fully developed (on the ASR, see Chapter 12). So far, when it comes to accountability, international law has mainly concerned itself with *criminalising* acts of NSAG members, or with attributing such acts to States under the principles of State responsibility. However, because the responsibility of States for the acts of a NSAG will be engaged only in limited circumstances,[120] and such responsibility will often only exist in the abstract (for lack of effective enforcement), a direct responsibility regime for NSAGs may be desirable. In the *Nicaragua* case, the International Court of Justice did not seem to exclude such responsibility, where it held that the acts committed by the paramilitary *contras* 'could easily have been committed by the *contra* force outside the control of the United States'.[121] Later, the UN Security Council condemned the activities of certain armed groups, citing their criminal acts and human rights abuses.[122] In doing so, the Security Council may have implied that such groups could incur responsibility for violations of international criminal law and human rights law. Developing a responsibility regime of armed groups is, however, politically sensitive, as such a regime could confer legitimacy on armed groups undermining the authority of the State or the international legal system (see also above on IHL obligations of NSAGs).

If a responsibility regime for NSAGs were to be developed, the rules of attribution could provide that violations committed by NSAG members are attributed to NSAGs on the basis of the organ/agency doctrine, since armed opposition groups must in any case operate under a responsible command, for a conflict to rise to the level of an armed conflict, therefore triggering the application of IHL. What the consequences of such responsibility for NSAGs are, or should be, remains somewhat unclear. Victims may bring lawsuits in tort against presumed offenders, but such suits are generally governed by domestic law rather than international law. Still, some practices appear to support the existence of a duty incumbent on NSAGs to provide reparation for damage resulting from violations of IHL,[123] and in the literature it has been argued that 'there is no justification for subjecting non-State groups to rules which are substantially different from those applicable to States'.[124] Whether such a reparation regime should mirror the regime for States and international organisations is doubtful. Tomuschat has warned that 'the consequences that the ILC articles establish for internationally wrongful acts are not generally appropriate to be applied to individuals' and that 'apologies presented by an individual are no more than a gesture of courtesy and do not have the same weight as official apologies offered by a State'.[125] Reparation could in any event appropriately consist of compensation, and to that effect an international indemnity fund that could be composed of blocked assets has been contemplated.[126]

[120] Arts 8–10 ASR.

[121] *Military and Paramilitary Activities In and Against Nicaragua* (Nicaragua v United States of America) [1986] ICJ Rep 14, paras 115–16.

[122] UNSC Res 1378, 14 November 2001, UN Doc S/RES/1378 (crimes of Al Qaeda); UNSC Res 1296, 19 April 2000, UN Doc S/RES/1296 (UNSC calling on non-State armed groups 'to comply with the provisions of the Charter of the United Nations and with rules and principles of international law, in particular international humanitarian, human rights and refugee law, and to implement fully the relevant decisions').

[123] Henckaerts and Doswald-Beck (n 109) 549–50, Rule 150.

[124] G Cahin, 'Armed Bands and Criminal Groups' in Crawford, Pellet and Olleson (n 103) 340.

[125] Tomuschat (n 103) 320.

[126] Cahin (n 124) 340.

C. Penal or Quasi-Penal Sanctions

In addition to international responsibility, specific sanctions of a penal or quasi-penal nature may have to be developed, which reflect the vertical relationship between States and international organisations on the one hand, and NSAGs on the other (as opposed to the horizontal relationship between States, as evidenced by the reparations regime in the ILC Articles on State Responsibility). A good example of such a sanctions regime is offered by the UN Security Council's practice of imposing sanctions on persons who are presumed to support terrorists,[127] on armed groups active in the DRC, Liberia and Darfur,[128] and on persons who violate the rights of the child in armed conflicts.[129] On closer inspection, however, these resolutions, rather than directly sanctioning armed groups, oblige *States* to enforce these sanctions.[130] From the perspective of the targeted person, these sanctions are domestic rather than international, and their legality may be challenged on the basis of domestic law. The *Kadi* judgment of the CJEU (2008) is a case in point: the Court did not review the *UN* resolutions and decisions concerning the sanctions taken against Mr Kadi, but instead reviewed the *European* implementing measures – which, however, had the same content and scope – in light of the fundamental rights as guaranteed in the European constitutional system.[131] Several judicial decisions show that such a review could invalidate a terrorist listing.[132] This was not only the case in *Kadi*, but also in a case involving the Tamil Tigers.[133]

Armed groups, and not only their individual members, may also be bound by international rules governing terrorism. This was the finding of the Appeals Chamber of the Special Tribunal for Lebanon, in its Interlocutory Decision on Applicable Law which held that a customary rule on terrorism imposed on rebel groups 'the obligation to refrain from engaging through their officials and agents in acts of terrorism'.[134] The Appeal Chamber's identification of a customary norm on terrorism is open to criticism, however; State practice in particular may not be as uniform as the Chamber may lead us to believe.[135] It is unclear, therefore, whether the various dimensions of the content of this norm, as they apply to non-State armed groups, represent good law.

[127] Notably the Al Qaeda and Taliban sanctions on the basis of UNSC Res 1267, 15 October 1999, UN Doc S/RES/1267.

[128] UNSC Res 1493, 28 July 2003, UN Doc S/RES/1493; UNSC Res 1521, 22 December 2003, UN Doc S/RES/1521; UNSC Res 1552, 27 July 2004, UN Doc S/RES/1552; UNSC Res 1556, 30 July 2004, UN Doc S/RES/1556; UNSC Res 1596, 18 April 2005, UN Doc S/RES/1596.

[129] See the Monitoring and Reporting Mechanism established by UNSC Res 1612, 26 July 2005, UN Doc S/RES/1612.

[130] See eg UNSC Res 1373, 28 September 2001, UN Doc S/RES/1373; UNSC Res 1540, 28 April 2004, UN Doc S/RES/1540.

[131] See Judgment of 3 September 2008, *Kadi and Al Barakaat International Foundation v Council and Commission*, C-402/05 P and C-415/05 P, EU:C:2008:461, paras 285 and 299. On the 'Kadi saga', see Chapter 4, Section V(A)(iii)(b).

[132] *Ahmed and others v Her Majesty's Treasury, Appeal decision* [2010] UKSC 2; Council of State (FR), *World Help Association of France v France*, 3 November 2004, Case No 262626.

[133] Judgment of 17 December 2014, *Hamas v Council*, T400/10, EU:C:2014:1095; and judgment of 16 October 2014, *Liberation Tigers of Tamil Eelam (LTTE) v Council*, T208/11 and T508/11, EU:C:2014:885. In the *Hamas* case, the EU General Court had earlier invalidated the listing, but its decision was overruled by the ECJ.

[134] STL, *Interlocutory Decision on the Applicable Law: Terrorism, Conspiracy, Homicide, Perpetration, Cumulative Charging*, 16 February 2011, Case No STL-11-01/I/AC/R176bis, para 102.

[135] See eg B Saul, 'Legislating from a Radical Hague: The United Nations Special Tribunal for Lebanon Invents an International Crime of Transnational Terrorism' (2011) 24 *LJIL* 677.

D. Use of Force

It is not fully clear whether NSAGs are bound by the international law norms on the use of force (on which see Chapter 14). Such rules have traditionally been viewed as regulating the use of force *between States*.[136] The question has arisen, especially since 2001, whether States may exercise their right of self-defence against non-State actors. This question is logically accompanied, or rather preceded, by the question whether non-State actors can commit an 'armed attack', in the sense of Article 51 of the UN Charter or customary international law, in the first place. In its *Wall* opinion, the ICJ ruled that Article 51 only recognises the existence of an inherent right of self-defence in the case of armed attack by, or imputable to, one State against another State.[137] However, some practice and doctrine supports the principle that non-State armed groups can indeed commit such attacks, and are thus bound by international law norms prohibiting the (transnational) use of force.[138] This in turn allows States to exercise their right to self-defence against them, even if they are found on the territory of another State.[139] Other doctrine is more cautious and supports the exercise of self-defence against these actors only if evidence is adduced that they are harboured by a State.[140] Still others outright reject the exercise of self-defence against non-State actors or States harbouring them.[141] On this issue, see further Chapter 14, Section III(B).

E. Principle of Territorial Integrity

It is similarly unclear whether NSAGs, and in fact any non-State actors, are bound by the principle of territorial integrity. In its *Kosovo* advisory opinion (2010),[142] the Court considered that the scope of the principle of territorial integrity is restricted to the sphere of inter-state relations,[143] which implies that sub-states or non-State actors are not bound by it. Accordingly, the principle was held to be irrelevant to the analysis of the legality of the unilateral declaration of independence of the Kosovo parliamentary assembly

[136] See Art 2(4) UN Charter.

[137] *Legal Consequences of the Construction of a Wall in the Occupied Palestinian Territory* (Advisory Opinion) [2004] ICJ Rep 194, para 139.

[138] eg, France invoked Art 42(7) TEU ('If a Member State is the victim of armed aggression on its territory, the other Member States shall have towards it an obligation of aid and assistance by all the means in their power, in accordance with Article 51 of the United Nations Charter. This shall not prejudice the specific character of the security and defence policy of certain Member States') after the IS-sponsored Paris attacks of November 2015: I Traynor, 'France invokes EU's article 42.7, but what does it mean?' *The Guardian*, 17 November 2015, theguardian.com/world/2015/nov/17/france-invokes-eu-article-427-what-does-it-mean.

[139] See notably the writings of Jordan Paust; eg, JJ Paust, 'Use of Armed Force against Terrorists in Afghanistan, Iraq, and beyond' (2002) 35 *Cornell International Law Journal* 533; JJ Paust, 'Self-Defense Targetings of Non-State Actors and Permissibility of U.S. Use of Drones in Pakistan' (2010) 19 *Journal of Transnational Law and Policy* 237; JJ Paust, 'Operationalizing Use of Drones Against Non-State Terrorists Under the International Law of Self-Defense' (2015) 8 *Albany Government Law Review* 166.

[140] See eg D Bethlehem, 'Self-Defense Against an Imminent or Actual Armed Attack by Nonstate Actors' (2012) 106 *AJIL* 769; KN Trapp, 'Back to Basics: Necessity, Proportionality, and the Right of Self-Defence Against Non-State Terrorist Actors' (2007) 56 *ICLQ* 141; E Wilmshurst, 'The Chatham House Principles of International Law on the Use of Force in Self-Defence' (2006) 55 *ICLQ* 963.

[141] See eg KJ Heller, 'Do Attacks on ISIS in Syria Justify the "Unwilling or Unable" Test?', *Opinio Juris*, 13 December 2014, opiniojuris.org/2014/12/13/attacks-isis-syria-justify-unwilling-unable-test.

[142] *Accordance with International Law of the Unilateral Declaration of Independence in Respect of Kosovo* (Advisory Opinion) [2010] ICJ Rep 403.

[143] ibid, para 80.

(a non-State actor).[144] One can also derive from this that the principle of territoriality similarly does not constitute an obstacle to non-State actors seceding from States. It is noted, however, that the General Assembly's Friendly Relations Declaration (1970), which was also cited by the Court in the *Kosovo* opinion, explicitly links a people's right to self-determination to the principle of territorial integrity, where it provides that the right to self-determination shall not be interpreted as 'authorizing or encouraging any action which would dismember or impair, totally or in part, the territorial integrity or political unity of sovereign and independent States'. Arguably, this Declaration also concerns itself with the *intra-State* dimension of the principle of territorial integrity, by imposing an obligation on peoples not to violate the territorial integrity of States on whose territory they find themselves, for example by seceding.[145] Accepting the existence of such an obligation for NSAGs, with respect to a State's territorial integrity, may appear to undermine the State-centred nature of international law, but in fact strengthens the State by protecting it from unilateral acts of secession carried out by NSAGs.

The EU itself has not pronounced directly on the rights or obligations of NSAGs under international law. However, it is sometimes involved as a mediator in non-international armed conflicts.[146] The EU's engagement with NSAGs may, however, be hindered where such groups are proscribed by anti-terrorism legislation, including by the EU's own legislation.[147]

V. Non-Governmental Organisations

International non-governmental organisations (NGOs) differ from international or intergovernmental organisations in that they are not normally established by States, but rather by individuals. They differ from corporations in that they are not profit-driven, but pursue idealistic aims. Non-governmental organisations are of relevance to international law as their activities may not be restricted to the territory of just one State, and contribute to the formation of a value-based international community. Their influence on the formation of international law is unmistakable. Their lobbying campaigns have led States to outlaw slavery, the use of landmines and cluster munitions, to establish the International Criminal Court, and to adopt more stringent environmental regulation. However, their international legal status is still unclear, and consists mainly of various participation rights in the deliberations of intergovernmental organisations, treaty bodies, and institutional regimes.[148]

[144] See also Chapter 5 on States, Section III(D).

[145] The binding character of the principle of territorial integrity for non-State actors has also been confirmed by Simone van den Driest in her recent study of the right to secession in international law. See SF van den Driest, *Remedial Secession: A Right to External Self-Determination as a Remedy to Serious Injustices?* (Cambridge, Intersentia, 2013).

[146] Council of the European Union, Concept on Strengthening EU Mediation and Dialogue Capacities, 10 November 2009, 15779/09.

[147] cp judgment of 18 January 2007, *PKK and KNK v Council*, C-229/05 P, EU:C:2007:32, and to the Opinions of AG Sharpston of 22 September 2016, *Council v Hamas*, C-79/15 P, EU:C:2016:722 and *Council v LTTE*, C-599/14 P, EU:C:2016:723.

[148] cp S Ripinsky and P van den Bossche, *NGO Involvement in International Organizations: A Legal Analysis* (London, British Institute of International and Comparative Law, 2007).

A. NGO Participation in International Organisations

Internationally active NGOs were first *legally* recognised in 1986 by the Council of Europe, in the framework of which a European Convention on the Recognition of the Legal Personality of International Non-Governmental Organizations was adopted.[149] This convention usefully defines NGOs as 'associations, foundations and other private institutions', which 'have a non-profit-making aim of international utility', 'have been established by an instrument governed by the internal law of a Party', 'carry on their activities with effect in at least two States'; and 'have their statutory office in the territory of a Party and the central management and control in the territory of that Party or of another Party'.[150]

The recognition which this European convention confers on NGOs cannot be separated from NGOs' important participatory status within the Council of Europe itself.[151] These NGOs form a 'Conference' which exists alongside the Committee of Ministers, the Parliamentary Assembly and the Congress of Local and Regional Authorities, as the fourth institution of the Council of Europe. While this Conference does not have formal law-making capacity – a characteristic which it shares with the other institutions of the Council for that matter – it can decide on policy lines and define or adopt action programmes.[152] More than 400 NGOs currently enjoy participatory status within the Council of Europe.

NGOs play a similarly active role in the EU. Since the Lisbon Treaty, Article 11(2) of the Treaty on European Union sets out that '[t]he EU institutions shall maintain an open, transparent and regular dialogue with representative associations and civil society'.[153] As far as the EU's external action is concerned, for instance, the EU consults regularly with NGO networks throughout the year, or on an ad hoc basis prior to Human Rights Dialogues and Consultations with non-EU countries, both on thematic issues and country situations.[154] Annually, the EU, human rights NGOs, experts, and international organisations gather for an EU NGO Human Rights Forum.[155] Quite a number of NGOs receive funding from the EU,[156] which may cast some doubt on their independence from the EU.

NGOs have acquired similar participatory rights in other international organisations and institutional arrangements, most prominently within the UN. Article 71 of the UN Charter provides that the UN Economic and Social Council 'may make suitable arrangements for consultation with non-governmental organizations which are concerned with

[149] European Convention on the Recognition of the Legal Personality of International Non-Governmental Organisations (adopted 24 April 1986, entered into force on 1 January 1991) CETS No 124. As of 1 July 2018, it had been ratified by 12 States.

[150] ibid, Art 1.

[151] See on NGO participatory rights: CoE, Committee of Ministers, Resolution 2003/8, Participatory status for international non-governmental organisations with the Council of Europe, 19 November 2003.

[152] Rules of Procedure of the Conference of International Non-Governmental Organisations (INGOs) of the Council of Europe, 24 June 2016, coe.int/en/web/ingo/rules-of-procedure.

[153] See EC, White Paper of European Governance, 25 July 2001, COM(2001) 428. See also Art 24(1) TFEU and Regulation (EU) No 211/2011 of 16 February 2011 on the citizen's initiative [2011] OJ C65/1.

[154] EEAS, 'Human Rights and Democracy', eeas.europa.eu/topics/human-rights-and-democracy_en.

[155] For the 18th session held on 1–2 December 2016, see 18th EU – NGO Forum on Human Rights, eeas.europa.eu/headquarters/headquarters-homepage_en/16240/EU-NGO%20Forum%20on%20Human%20Rights.

[156] For the legal framework of EU funding for environmental NGOs, see eg Regulation (EU) No 1293/2013 of 11 December 2013 on the establishment of a Programme for the Environment and Climate Action (LIFE) and repealing Regulation (EC) No 614/2007 [2013] OJ L347/185.

matters within its competence'. This provision has most recently been implemented by an ECOSOC Resolution of 1996, pursuant to which

> [c]onsultative arrangements are to be made, on the one hand, for the purpose of enabling the Council or one of its bodies to secure expert information or advice from organizations having special competence in the subjects for which consultative arrangements are made, and, on the other hand, to enable international, regional, sub-regional and national organizations that represent important elements of public opinion to express their views.[157]

On that basis, a large number of NGOs – currently almost 4,000 – have been accredited with ECOSOC's functional commissions, regional commissions, standing committees and other bodies. Depending on their participatory status,[158] NGOs can attend international conferences and events, make written and oral statements at these events, organise side events, enter United Nations premises, and have opportunities to network and lobby.[159]

Many others organisations and regimes similarly allow and encourage NGO participation in their activities, including the WTO[160] and the UN Framework Convention on Climate Change.[161] Many of them also share relevant information with NGOs.[162] Some institutional regimes, in particular in the field of the environment, require States to provide the public, including NGOs, with access to information.[163]

B. International Dispute Settlement

NGO participation in the international legal and governance system is not limited to rights of participation in the activities of various international organisations and regimes, but extends also to a large number of international dispute settlement mechanisms (on which see Chapter 13). While, historically, international dispute settlement mechanisms were only accessible to States as the primary subjects of international law, in more recent times, NGOs have been granted access as plaintiffs as well as *amici curiae*. As far as NGOs' *jus standi* is concerned, NGOs have notably been given the right to initiate cases before regional human rights courts, such as the European Court of Human Rights[164] and before EU courts.[165] NGOs also have access to the complaints mechanisms under the European

[157] ECOSOC Res 1996/31, 'Consultative relationship between the United Nations and non-governmental organizations', 25 July 1996, UN Doc E/RES/1996/31, part II, para 20.

[158] There are three categories of participatory statutes in the UN: Roster, General, and Special. Most new applications concern the Special category.

[159] UN, 'Working with ECOSOC: A NGOs Guide to Consultative Status' (2011) csonet.org/content/documents/Brochure.pdf, 7.

[160] Art V(2) WTO Agreement; WTO, General Council Decision, Guidelines for Arrangements on Relations with Non-Governmental Organizations, 18 July 1996, WT/L/162.

[161] Art 4(1)(i) UNFCCC (encouraging 'the widest participation in this process including that of [NGOs]').

[162] See also the UN Non-Governmental Liaison Service (NGLS), which is mandated to promote and develop constructive relations between the United Nations and civil society organisations. See un-ngls.org.

[163] Art 9 Convention for the Protection of the Marine Environment of the North-East Atlantic (adopted 22 September 1992, entered into force 25 March 1998) 2354 UNTS 67 (OSPAR Convention); Art 15 Convention on Civil Liability for Damage Resulting from Activities Dangerous to the Environment (adopted 21 June 1993, not yet entered into force) CETS No 150; Art 1 Convention on Access to Information, Public Participation in Decision-Making and Access to Justice in Environmental Matters (adopted 25 June 1998, entered into force 30 October 2001) 2161 UNTS 447 (Aarhus Convention).

[164] Art 34 ECHR.

[165] Art 263(4) TFEU; *AFPS and PLO v Société Alstom transport SA and others* (n 69).

Social Charter.[166] It is more common, however, that NGOs are granted less far-reaching participatory rights in international dispute settlement, not as full parties to the case, but rather as expert witnesses or *amici curiae*.[167]

NGO participation in proceedings of the world's principal judicial institution, the International Court of Justice, has been rather limited, which probably reflects its traditional inter-State focus.[168] The Court has never designated NGO representatives as experts, even though Article 50 of the ICJ Statute allows it to do so.[169] Neither has the Court accepted the intervention of an NGO as an *amicus curiae* in contentious proceedings.[170] In advisory proceedings, where the procedural rules are somewhat less strict,[171] the Court has accepted a written NGO statement only once, in 1950.[172] That being said, under the Court's Practice Direction XII, NGOs are allowed to submit written briefs, which, while not being part of the official case file, are made available to, and may be referred to by States and international organisations 'presenting written and oral statements in [proceedings] in the same manner as publications in the public domain'.[173] Furthermore, NGOs can use their political influence to try to convince States or international organisations to initiate proceedings before the ICJ without formally participating in ICJ proceedings. For instance, NGOs, assembled in the 'World Court Project', successfully lobbied the UN General Assembly to submit a question regarding the legality of the use or threat of nuclear weapons to the ICJ, resulting in the famous *Nuclear Weapons* advisory opinion.[174] Pressure brought to bear by civil society groups may also have influenced Australia's decision to bring an ICJ case against Japan with respect to the latter's whaling programme.[175]

In the dispute settlement mechanism of the WTO, NGOs have acquired rather more participatory rights. In the seminal *Shrimp/Turtle* case, the WTO Appellate Body held

[166] The Additional Protocol to the European Social Charter Providing for a System of Collective Complaints (adopted 9 November 1995, entered into force 9 November 1995) sets out a new supervision procedure, the collective complaints procedure, whereby allegations of breaches of the Charter or the revised Charter may be submitted to the European Committee of Social Rights.

[167] Supreme Court (NL), *Association of Lawyers for Peace (Vereniging van Juristen voor de Vrede) and others v Netherlands*, 6 February 2004, Case No C02/217HR.

[168] For an overview, see E Valencia-Ospina, 'Non-Governmental Organizations and the International Court of Justice' in T Treves et al (eds), *Civil Society, International Courts and Compliance Bodies* (The Hague, TMC Asser Press, 2005) 227–32; and Y Ronen, 'Participation of Non-State Actors in ICJ Proceedings' (2011) 11 *The Law and Practice of International Courts and Tribunals* 77.

[169] Art 50 ICJ Statute; ICJ, Rules of the Court (adopted 14 April 1978, entered into force 1 July 1978), as amended, icj-cij.org/en/rules, Arts 57 and 63.

[170] Pursuant to Art 34(2) ICJ Statute, the Court 'subject to and in conformity with its Rules, may request of public international organizations information relevant to cases before it, and shall receive such information presented by such organizations on their own initiative'.

[171] Art 66(2) ICJ Statute.

[172] Correspondence from Mr Robert Delson to the Registrar, *Re request for advisory opinion concerning the international status of South-West Africa*, 7 March 1950, Corresp pt III, 324, doc 10.

[173] ICJ Practice Directions, October 2001, as amended on 20 January 2009 and 21 March 2013, Practice Direction XII, paras 1 and 2.

[174] This 'World Court Project' campaign was launched in Geneva in 1992, originally by the International Peace Bureau (IPB), International Physicians for the Prevention of Nuclear War and the International Association of Lawyers Against Nuclear Arms. Other NGOs such as Greenpeace, joined later. The question put by the UN General Assembly to the ICJ resulted in *Legality of the Threat or Use of Nuclear Weapons* (Advisory Opinion) [1996] ICJ Rep 226.

[175] See P Dorling, '"Doomed" whaling fight aimed at saving Labor vote', *Sydney Morning Herald*, 5 January 2011, smh.com.au/environment/conservation/doomed-whaling-fight-aimed-at-saving-labor-vote-20110104-19f52.html. The article cites Wikileaks cables which report that domestic Australian politics informed the bringing of the case. The Australian Labor Party, which is notoriously more amenable to environmental pressure groups than the Liberal/National Coalition, had just been elected at that time.

that WTO Panels could consider *amicus curiae* briefs, either when they are attached to a State's own submissions, or when they are submitted by the NGO *proprio motu*. In the former case, WTO Panels are under an obligation to consider such briefs; in the latter case they can accept them at their own discretion.[176] The Appellate Body later ruled that it could also accept *amicus* briefs.[177] In international investment arbitration proceedings, NGOs have also been permitted to file *amicus briefs*, notably by tribunals established under NAFTA Chapter 11,[178] and by ICSID tribunals.[179] Such briefs are not accepted, however, in investment arbitration proceedings under the popular UNCITRAL Arbitration Rules. Furthermore, NGO *amicus* interventions are allowed in proceedings before the European Court of Human Rights, where NGOs have direct standing.[180]

The participatory status of NGOs typically comes with a number of entry and post-entry conditions,[181] which could be considered as specific obligations under international institutional law. ECOSOC Resolution 1996/31, for instance, provides that NGOs which have consultative status at the UN 'shall conform at all times to the principles governing the establishment and nature of their consultative relations with the Council',[182] and are to submit to the Council Committee on Non-Governmental Organizations a quadrennial report of activities.[183] Similar rules could be found in the context of the Ramsar Convention on Wetlands, where NGO partners who have a formal status within the regime incur certain obligations, mainly with respect to assisting governments,[184] and the Council of Europe, where NGOs which participate in the organisation's work are obliged to work constructively with the organisation.[185] Furthermore, NGOs acting as *amicus curiae* in international dispute settlement proceedings may be bound by rules of confidentiality,[186] and NGOs receiving funds from international organisations may be bound by codes of conduct, violation of which may amount to a breach of contract.[187]

NGOs can easily evade the abovementioned obligations insofar as they decide *not* to participate in the regime or arrangement which sets out the obligations. Accordingly,

[176] WTO, US: Import Prohibition of Certain Shrimp and Shrimp Products, Report of the Appellate Body, 12 October 1998, WT/DS58/AB/R, Part III – A, paras 1–13.

[177] WTO, US: Imposition of Countervailing Duties on Certain Hot-Rolled Lead and Bismuth Carbon Steel Products Originating in the UK, Report of the Appellate Body, 10 May 2000, WT/DS138/AB/R, para 42; WTO, European Communities: Measures Affecting Asbestos and Asbestos-Containing Products, Report of the Appellate Body, 12 March 2001, WT/DS135/AB/R, para 52.

[178] In the Matter of an International Arbitration under Chapter 11 of the NAFTA and the UNCITRAL Arbitration Rules, *Methanex Corporation v US*, Decision of the Tribunal on Petitions form Third Persons to Intervene as 'Amici Curiae', 15 January 2001.

[179] ICSID, *Suez, Sociedad General de Aguas de Barcelona S.A. and Vivendi Universal SA v Argentine Republic*, Order in Response to a Petition for Participation as Amicus Curiae, Case No ARB/03/19, 19 May 2005.

[180] Art 36 ECHR.

[181] eg Art 4 of the European Convention on the Recognition of the Legal Personality of International Non-Governmental Organizations (n 149). For a fine overview, see A-K Lindblom, 'Non-Governmental Organizations' in Crawford, Pellet and Olleson (n 103) 348–51.

[182] See ECOSOC Res 1996/31, 25 July 1996, UN Doc E/1996/31, para 55.

[183] ibid, para 61(c).

[184] Convention on Wetlands of International Importance Especially as Waterfowl Habitat (adopted 2 February 1971, entered into force 21 December 1975) 996 UNTS 245 (Ramsar Convention); The Conference of the Contracting Parties, Resolution VII.3, 'Partnership with International Organizations', 10–18 May 1999, para 4.7.

[185] Council of Europe, Committee of Ministers, Resolution 2003/8, 'Participatory status for international non-governmental organisations with the Council of Europe', 19 November 2003, para 9.

[186] See eg WTO, European Communities: Export Subsidies on Sugar, Complaint by Brazil, Report of the Panel WT/DS266/4, 15 October 2004, paras 7.82–7.85.

[187] See eg Food and Agricultural Organization of the United Nations, Standard Letter of Agreement, clause 3(f).

Lindblom has usefully categorised such obligations (and responsibilities) as a 'bilateral matter, in contrast to the rules on State responsibility, which define the responsibility of States generally, with no possibility for them to "opt out" of the system'.[188]

C. Other Roles of NGOs in International Law

Under international law as it currently stands, it is difficult to discern direct, non-bilateral obligations of a general character, that is, those outside the context of NGOs participating in international organisations. Most obligations are found in the domain of humanitarian law, which can obviously be explained by the nature of the activities of many NGOs. Article 10 of the First Geneva Convention (1949), for instance, provides that the High Contracting Parties may at any time agree to entrust to an organisation, which offers all guarantees of impartiality and efficacy, the duties incumbent on the Protecting Powers by virtue of the Convention. In practice, these duties have been entrusted to the International Committee of the Red Cross. Article 44 of the Convention further provides that the emblem of the Red Cross should not be employed, either in time of peace or in time of war, except to indicate or to protect the medical units and establishments, the personnel and material protected by the present Convention and other Conventions dealing with similar matters, which is a prohibition directed at all actors, including non-State actors. Of note also are NGO obligations regarding the protection of persons in the event of disasters, as currently in the process of codification by the International Law Commission.[189] Any humanitarian actor, whether State or non-State, is under the obligation to respond to disasters 'in accordance with the principles of humanity, neutrality and impartiality, and on the basis of non-discrimination, while taking into account the needs of the particularly vulnerable'[190] and to 'respect and protect the inherent dignity of the human person'.[191] When terminating their external assistance, such humanitarian actors 'shall consult with respect to the termination of external assistance and the modalities of termination' and 'provide appropriate notification'.[192]

Outside the humanitarian field, NGO obligations could be found in the field of international labour law, with, for instance, Article 8(1) of the Convention on the Freedom of Association and Protection of the Right to Organize, adopted in the framework of the International Labour Organization (ILO Convention No 87, 1948), providing that workers' and employers' organisations – which qualify as NGOs – shall, like other persons or organised collectivities, respect the law of the land in exercising the rights provided for in the Convention.[193]

Like corporations, NGOs may also adopt codes of conduct in which they commit themselves to living up to specific standards.[194] As such, these codes are deprived of legally binding

[188] Lindblom (n 181) 352.

[189] See ILC, 'Protection of persons in the event of disasters: Texts and titles of the draft articles adopted by the Drafting Committee on first reading', 15 May 2014, UN Doc A/CN.4/L.831.

[190] ibid, Art 6.

[191] ibid, Art 7, which refers specifically to 'States, competent intergovernmental organizations and *relevant non-governmental organizations*' (emphasis added).

[192] ibid, Art 15, which refers specifically to 'the affected State and assisting State, and *as appropriate other assisting actors*' (emphasis added).

[193] Lindblom has noted in respect of this provision, however, that 'the obligation is formulated in such a way that it has more the consequence of limiting convention rights than of creating actual obligations': Lindblom (n 181) 347.

[194] See eg The Code of Conduct for the International Red Cross and Red Crescent Movement and NGOs in Disaster Relief (1996) 310 *IRRC* 55, annex VI.

force, although the standards they contain can be integrated into contractual arrangements. Some have called for upgraded obligations and a more advanced responsibility regime for NGOs,[195] yet it is doubtful whether such rules are desirable. After all, they may serve only to constrain legitimate, counter-hegemonic activities of NGOs, and encourage States to eventually silence them.[196]

VI. The Holy See

A rather unique non-State actor is the Holy See. Headed by the Pope (the Supreme Pontiff), the Holy See is the seat of a non-State religious organisation – the Catholic Church – with a global ambition and following, but also a territorial base in the Vatican City. It has been recognised by a large number of States, has acceded to various conventions, and has joined several intergovernmental organisations. Accordingly, the Holy See enjoys a measure of international legal personality that includes capacities that go far beyond those other non-State actors possess, and that even rivals the status of States in international law.[197] As the authority of the Holy See is not based on territorial sovereignty over the Vatican City premises, but rather on its spiritual sovereignty over the 1.2 billion adherents to the Catholic faith,[198] the Holy See could best be characterised as a *sui generis* entity rather than as a State.

Arguably, only one other spiritual entity enjoys the same status in international law: the Sovereign Military Order of St John of Jerusalem, of Rhodes, and of Malta (the Order of Malta). Like the Holy See, this Catholic body also has the right of legation and has observer status at the UN General Assembly.[199] Unlike the Holy See, however, the Order of Malta no longer has a territorial base.

The Holy See acquired its legal status in the Middle Ages, when the Pope was not just the head of a spiritual organisation, but also the temporal ruler of the Papal States. Afterwards, as a result of the Italian reunification, the Holy See lost its territories in 1870 and its legal status remained in doubt for more than half a century. In 1929, however, it signed the Lateran Treaties with Italy, which recognised the Holy See as a separate entity and granted it the Vatican City, an enclave of 110 acres in Rome. The legal relationship between the Vatican and the Holy See is somewhat unclear.[200] Sometimes both entities are equated, for example, for the purposes of immunities.[201] Many authors take the view

[195] E Roucounas, 'Non-State Actors: Areas of International Responsibility in Need of Further Exploration' in M Ragazzi (ed), *International Responsibility Today: Essays in Memory of Oscar Schachter* (Leiden, Martinus Nijhoff Publishers, 2005) 404.

[196] Such rules may indeed embolden States that already have draconian laws in places that limit NGOs' sphere of action, eg, Russia. See International Centre for Not-for-Profit Law, 'NCO Law Monitor: Russia', 8 May 2013.

[197] Insights of this section are drawn from C Ryngaert, 'The Legal Status of the Holy See' (2011) 3 *Goettingen Journal of International Law* 829.

[198] See also AD Hertzke, 'The Catholic Church and Catholicism in Global Politics' in J Haynes (ed), *Routledge Handbook of Religion and Politics* (London, Routledge, 2009) 48.

[199] cp F Gazzoni, 'Malta, Order of' in MPEPIL.

[200] J Crawford, *The Creation of States in International Law* (Oxford, OUP, 2006) 223.

[201] See eg District Court Ghent (BE), *V and others v Holy See and others*, 1 October 2013, (2013–2014) *Rechtskundig Weekblad* 507; Court of Appeals, (US), *Dale and others v Colagiovanni and others*, 16 March 2006, 443 F3d 425

that the Vatican City is subordinated to the Holy See.[202] The latter view does not exclude considering the former as a State in its own right, with a fixed territory, population, and a government,[203] which is also constitutionally empowered to conduct international relations.[204] The Vatican has used its status as a State, or resemblance to a State, to join various international organisations of a technical nature.[205] But when it comes to projecting the core activities of the Catholic Church, pertaining to its spiritual and value-driven mission, the Church has used the Holy See as its international legal embodiment. The Holy See rather than the Vatican has thus joined the OSCE, the United Nations Conference on Trade and Development (UNCTAD), the International Atomic Energy Agency (IAEA), the Comprehensive Nuclear Test Ban Treaty Organization, the Preparatory Commission for the Comprehensive Test Ban Treaty, and the Organization for the Prohibition of Chemical Weapons. However, the Holy See is not a member of the United Nations, although it has been accredited as a permanent observer with the UN since 1964,[206] as well as with some other intergovernmental organisations.[207] As far as treaties are concerned, it has ratified the Geneva Conventions on the Law of War (1949), the Convention relating to the Status of Refugees (1951), the Vienna Convention on Diplomatic Relations (1961), the Vienna Convention on Consular Relations (1963), the International Convention on the Elimination of All Forms of Racial Discrimination (1966), the Convention against Torture and Other Cruel, Inhuman or Degrading Treatment or Punishment (1984), the Convention on the Rights of the Child (1989) and its Optional Protocols, and the Convention on Cluster Munitions. To give effect to its spiritual mission, the Holy See has not only joined some classic international organisations and multilateral treaties, but it has also negotiated a special kind of treaties with a limited number of third States, the so-called 'concordats', bilateral treaties which govern the religious affairs and activities of the Catholic Church in third States.[208] Such treaties are governed by the customary law of treaties.[209]

The pre-eminence of the Holy See in diplomatic relations, as compared to the Vatican, was in fact already borne out by the Lateran 1929 Conciliation Treaty, in which 'Italy recognizes the right of the *Holy See* to passive and active Legation, according to the general rules of *International Law*' (emphasis added).[210] Diplomatic relations are thus normally

(5th Cir 2006); Court of Appeals, (US), *O'Bryan v Holy See*, 24 November 2008, 556 F3d 361 (6th Cir 2009) (upholding the immunity of the Holy See by equating it with a foreign sovereign).

[202] J Duursma, *Fragmentation and the International Relations of Micro-States* (Cambridge, CUP, 1996); G Arangio-Ruiz, 'On the Nature of the International Personality of the Holy See' (1996) 29 *Revue belge de droit international* 354, 354.

[203] DJ Harris, *Cases and Materials on International Law*, 7th edn (London, Sweet & Maxwell, 2010) 129.

[204] Art 2 of the Fundamental Law of the Vatican City State (adopted 26 November 2000, entered into force 22 February 2001) http://www.vatican.va/news_services/press/documentazione/documents/sp_ss_scv/informazione_generale/legge-fondamentale_it.html.

[205] The Vatican has notably jointed the International Telecommunications Union (ITU), the Universal Postal Union (UPU), the International Telecommunications Satellite Organization (INTELSAT), European Telecommunications Satellite Organization (EUTELSAT), the International Institute for the Unification of Private Law (UNIDROIT), the World Intellectual Property Organization (WIPO), and the International Grain Council.

[206] See for its current status: UNGA Res 58/314, 'Participation of the Holy See in the work of the United Nations', 16 July 2004, UN Doc A/RES/58/314.

[207] For an overview, see ibid, fourth preambular paragraph.

[208] S Ferrari, 'Concordats' in MPEPIL. See eg Court of Appeal of Coimbra (PT), *Brothers of the Santa Casa da Misericórdia of Fundão v Brotherhood of the Santa Casa da Misericórdia of Fundão*, 17 May 2011, Case No 646/09.1TBFND.C1.

[209] RR Haule, *Der Heilige Stuhl/Vatikanstaat im Völkerrecht* (Lohmar, Eul Verlag, 2006) 196.

[210] Art 12 Lateran Conciliation Treaty (11 February 1929) www.vaticanstate.va/content/dam/vaticanstate/documenti/leggi-e-decreti/Normative-Penali-e-Amministrative/LateranTreaty.pdf.

conducted on behalf of the Holy See, whose particular status has led to the inclusion of its legation practice in the Vienna Convention on Diplomatic Relations.[211] When conducting diplomacy, Holy See representatives do not just further the interests of the Catholic Church proper, but may be involved in mediation efforts with respect to disputes between States, on the basis of the Lateran Conciliation Treaty.[212] Holy See mediation goes back many centuries. As early as 1500 the Pope was involved in resolving the dispute between Spain and Portugal over the division of the newly discovered Americas.[213] In more recent times, the Holy See mediated successfully in the *Beagle Channel* dispute between Chile and Argentina (1980),[214] and was instrumental in the thaw in relations between the United States and Cuba (2014).[215]

The Holy See has also established relations with the EU, and since 1970 the EU has had a delegation to the Holy See. They maintain a dialogue on a number of issues, in particular on culture and religion, poverty and development, environmental sustainability, conflict prevention and resolution, and human rights.[216] In 2014, for the first time in 26 years, the Pope addressed the European Parliament on some of these issues.[217] The EU and the Vatican have concluded a Monetary Agreement on the use of the euro as the Vatican's official currency.[218]

VII. Concluding Observations

In 1949, in its *Reparation for Injuries* advisory opinion, the ICJ held that '[t]he subjects of law in any legal system are not necessarily identical in their nature or in the extent of their rights, and their nature depends on the needs of the international community'.[219] The Court then proceeded to recognise the international legal personality of a first category of non-State actors: intergovernmental organisations with a general scope. The ICJ's dictum could also be applied to other non-State actors: apart from international organisations with a more specific scope, also individuals, corporations, NGOs, armed groups, or religious movements may enjoy international legal personality. The overview provided in this chapter shows that these categories of non-State actors have indeed acquired a measure of legal international

[211] Art 14(1) VCDR equates apostolic nuncios (the Holy See's diplomatic representatives) with ambassadors, ie, the first class of heads of mission. Art 16, which deals with the precedence of diplomatic representatives, provides in para 3 that it 'is without prejudice to any practice accepted by the receiving State regarding the precedence of the representative of the Holy See'.

[212] Art 23 Lateran Conciliation Treaty.

[213] Treaty of Tordesillas (7 June 1494), as sanctioned by the papal bull *Ea quae* in 1506. See F Gardiner Davenport and CO Paullin (eds), *European Treaties Bearing on the History of the United States and Its Dependencies to 1648* (Washington DC, Carnegie Institution of Washington, 1917) 107–11; H Harrisse, *The Diplomatic History of America: Its First Chapter 1452–1493–1494* (London, BF Stevens, 1897).

[214] *Case concerning a dispute between the Republic of Argentina and the Republic of Chile concerning the Beagle Channel* (Argentina v Chile), Report and Decision of the Court of Arbitration, 18 February 1977, 21 RIAA 53.

[215] J Hooper, 'US-Cuba deal offers reminder of Vatican's diplomatic influence' *The Guardian*, 20 December 2014, theguardian.com/world/2014/dec/20/us-cuba-vatican-diplomatic-influence-pope.

[216] See EEAS, 'The Holy See and the EU', eeas.europa.eu/delegations/un-rome/2355/holy-see-and-eu_en.

[217] EP, Press Release: 'Pope Francis delivers a message "to all the citizens of Europe" at the European Parliament', 26 November 2014, europarl.europa.eu/news/en/news-room/content/20141121IPR79832/html/Pope-Francis-delivers-a-message-in-Parliament-to-all-the-citizens-of-Europe.

[218] See Monetary Agreement Between the European Union and the Vatican City State [2010] OJ C28/13.

[219] *Reparation for Injuries* (n 2) 178.

personality. The rights and obligations that go with such personality are nevertheless rather limited, and crucially depend on the willingness of States to actually grant them.

Accordingly, States, discussed in Chapter 5, remain the primary subjects of international law. Statehood is characterised by sovereignty, which means that States are entitled to exercise legal authority within their territory, normally to the exclusion of other States. In a more technical sense, the exercise of such legal authority is denoted as the exercise of *jurisdiction*. The next chapter will give an overview of the different principles of jurisdiction in public international law.

Bibliography

Alston, P (ed), *Non-State Actors in Human Rights* (Oxford, OUP, 2005).

d'Aspremont, J (ed), *Participants in the International Legal System: Multiple Perspectives on Non-State Actors in International Law* (London, Routledge, 2011).

Bettati, M and Dupuy, PM, *Les ONG et le droit international* (Paris, Economica, 1986).

Clapham, A, *The Human Rights Obligations of Non-State Actors* (Oxford, OUP, 2006).

Daboné, Z, *Le droit international public relatif aux groupes armés non étatiques* (Zürich, Schulthess Verlag, 2012).

Dahm, G, *Die Stellung des Menschen im Völkerrecht unserer Zeit* (Tübingen, Mohr, 1961).

De LaPradelle, A, 'La place de l'homme dans la construction du droit international' (1958) 1 *Current Legal Problems* 140.

Dumberry, P, 'L'Entreprise, sujet du droit international? Retour sur la question à la lumière des développements récents du droit international es investissements' (2004) 108 *Revue générale de droit internationale public* 103.

Dupuy, PM, 'L'individu et le droit international' (1987) 32 *Archives de philosophie de droit* 119.

Fröhlich, FW, *Multinationale Unternehmen* (Baden-Baden, Nomos, 1974).

Furtak, FT, *Nichtstaatliche Akteure in den internationaler Beziehungen – NGOs in der Weltpolitik* (München, Tuduv Verlag, 1997).

Gal-Or, N, Ryngaert, C and Noortmann, M (eds), *Responsibilities of the Non-State actor in Armed Conflict and the Market Place* (The Hague, Brill, 2015).

Geldermann, H, *Völkerrechtliche Pflichten multinationaler Unternehmen* (Baden-Baden, Nomos, 2009).

Germelmann, F, 'Heiliger Stuhl und Vatikanstadt in der internationalen Gemeinschaft' (2009) 47 *Archiv des Völkerrechts* 147.

Grassi, M, *Die Rechtsstellung des Individuums im Völkerrecht* (Winterthur, Keller, 1955).

Haule, RR, *Der Heilige Stuhl Der Vatikanstaat im Völkerrech*t (Cologne, Lohmar, 2006).

Hempel, M, *Die Völkerrechtssubjektivität internationaler nichtstaatlicher Organisationen* (Berlin, Duncker & Humblot, 1999).

Hobe, S, 'Der Rechtsstatus der Nichtregierungsorganisationen nach geltendem Völkerrecht' (1999) 37 *Archiv des Völkerrechts* 152.

Köck, HF, *Die völkerrechtliche Stellung des Heiligen Stuhls: Dargestellt an seinen Beziehungen zu Staaten und internationalen Organisationen* (Berlin, Duncker & Humblot, 1975).

Kopelmanas, L, 'L'application du droit international aux sociétés multinationales' (1976) 150 *RdC* 295.

Lindblom, A-K, *Non-Governmental Organizations* (Cambridge, CUP, 2005).
Miaja de la Muele, A, 'El Derecho internacional ante las sociedades multinacionales' (1975) 2 *Anuario de Derecho Internacional* 169.
Miele, M, *La condizione giuridica internazionale della Santa Sede e della Città del Vaticano* (Milano, Giuffrè, 1937).
Muchlinski, PT, *Multinational Enterprises and the Law*, 2nd edn (Oxford, OUP, 2007).
Noortmann, M and Ryngaert, C (eds), *Non-State Actor Dynamics in International Law: from Law-Takers to Law-Makers* (Aldershot, Ashgate, 2010).
Noortmann, M, Reinisch, A and Ryngaert, C (eds), *Non-State Actors in International Law* (Oxford, Hart, 2015).
Peters, A, Koechlin, L, Förster, T and Fenner Zinkernagel, G (eds), *Non-State Actors as Standard-Setters* (Cambridge, CUP, 2010).
Peters, A and Marxen, C (eds), *Self-Defense against Non-State Actors*, special issue (2017) 3 *Heidelberg Journal of International Law (ZaöRV)* 1–94.
Ryngaert, C and Noortmann, M (eds), *Human Security and International Law: The Challenge of Non-State Actors* (Antwerp, Intersentia, 2014).
Satchivi, FAA, *Les sujets de droit: Contribution à l'Etude de la reconnaissance de l'individu comme sujet direct du droit international* (Paris, L'Harmattan, 1999).
Soumy, I, *L'accès des organisations non gouvernementales aux juridictions internationales* (Brussels, Bruylant, 2008).
Spiropoulos, J, 'L'individu et le droit international' (1929) 30 *RdC* 191.
Teijo García, C, *Organizaciones Internacionales no gubernamentales y Derecho Internacional* (Madrid, Dilex, 2005).

Further Reading

Angelo, G, 'Les sociétés multinationales' (1968) 125 *RdC* 447.
Arangio-Ruiz, G, 'L'individuo e il diritto internazionale' (1971) *Rivista di diritto internazionale* 561.
Arangio-Ruiz, G, 'On the Nature of the International Personality of the Holy See' (1996) 29 *Revue belge de droit international* 354.
Araujo, RJ, 'The International Personality and Sovereignty of the Holy See' (2001) 50 *Catholic University Law Review* 291.
Blet, P, *Histoire de la représentation diplomatique du Saint Siège des origines à l'aube du XIXe Siècle* (Città del Vaticano, Archivio Vaticano, 1982).
Lindblom, A-K, 'Non-Governmental Organizations' in Crawford, J, Pellet, A and Olleson, S (eds), *The Law of International Responsibility* (Oxford, OUP, 2010) 348–351.
Moore, J, 'From Nation State to Failed State: International Protection from Human Rights Abuses by Non-State Actors' (1999) 31 *Columbia Human Rights Law Review* 81.
Pérez-León, JP, 'El individuo como sujeto de derecho internacional: Análisis de la dimensión activa de la subjetividad jurídica internacional del individuo' (2008) 8 *Anuario Mexicano de Derecho Internacional* 599.
Puente Egido, J, *Personalidad internacional de la Ciudad del Vaticano* (Madrid, Instituto Francisco de Vitoria, 1965).

Rauch, AM, *Der Heilige Stuhl und die Europäische Union* (Baden-Baden, Nomos, 1995).
Ronen, Y, 'Participation of Non-State Actors in ICJ Proceedings' (2011) 11 *The Law and Practice of International Courts and Tribunals* 77.
Roucounas, E, 'Non-State Actors: Areas of International Responsibility in Need of Further Exploration' in Ragazzi, M (ed), *International Responsibility Today: Essays in Memory of Oscar Schachter* (Leiden, Martinus Nijhoff Publishers, 2005) 391–404.
Ryngaert, C, 'The Legal Status of the Holy See' (2011) 3 *Goettingen Journal of International Law* 829.
Schoiswohl, M, 'De Facto Regimes and Human Rights Obligations: The Twilight Zone of Public International Law' (2003) 6 *Austrian Review of International and European Law* 45.
Sivakumaran, S, 'Binding Armed Opposition Groups' (2006) 55 *ICLQ* 369.
Tomuschat, C, 'Private Individuals' in Crawford, J, Pellet, A and Olleson, S (eds), *The Law of International Responsibility* (Oxford, OUP, 2010) 317–330.
Valencia-Ospina, E, 'Non-Governmental Organizations and the International Court of Justice' in Treves, T et al (eds), *Civil Society, International Courts and Compliance Bodies* (The Hague, TMC Asser Press, 2005) 227–242.
Zambrana Tévar, N, 'Shortcomings and Disadvantages of Existing Legal Mechanisms to Hold Multinational Corporations Accountable for Human Rights Violations' (2012) 4 *Cuadernos de Derecho Transnacional* 398.
Zandvliet, R and van der Heijden, P, 'The Rapprochement of ILO Standards and CSR Mechanisms: towards a Positive Understanding of the 'Privatization' of International Labour Standards' in Marx, A, Wouters, J, Rayp, G, and Beke L (eds), *Global Governance of Labour Rights: Assessing the Effectiveness of Public and Private Policy Initiatives* (Cheltenham, Edward Elgar, 2015), 170–89.

9

Jurisdiction

I. Introduction

Jurisdiction can mean many things in international law, and even more in domestic law. In general international law, jurisdiction is commonly understood to refer to the legal authority of States to make determinations as to the legal treatment to be given to certain situations. As such, it is an aspect of the sovereignty of the State. International rules governing jurisdiction aim to delimit spheres of competence between States and thus to limit jurisdictional overlap and prevent interference in other States' affairs.

State jurisdiction has been perceived as a 'unitary phenomenon categorized by different stages of [an] exercise of authoritative power'.[1] Nevertheless, legal doctrine typically distinguishes between three modalities of the exercise of State authority: prescriptive or legislative; enforcement; and adjudicatory jurisdiction. While these modalities are subject to different international rules, they are interrelated and even sequential, as ultimately one can expect that a State wishes for the rules it prescribes to also be enforced and adjudicated. Exceptionally, States may satisfy themselves with mere symbolic prescription.[2]

The international rules on *prescriptive* jurisdiction are concerned with the permissible reach of a State's laws. In pre-modern times, jurisdiction was often considered as a function of tribal or ethnic allegiance, with tribal or ethnic law and dispute-settlement following

[1] H Maier, 'Jurisdictional Rules in Customary International Law' in KM Meessen (ed), *Extraterritorial Jurisdiction in Theory and Practice* (London, Kluwer, 1996) 78.

[2] Eg where they enact laws under the universality principle without much hope of actually bringing alleged perpetrators to justice. Such prescription without enforcement has been criticised as ineffective and even illegitimate. See A Chehtman, *The Philosophical Foundations of Extraterritorial Punishment* (Oxford, OUP, 2010) 45, declaring extraterritorial proscription and punishment to be presumptively illegitimate when they cannot actually be enforced, while nevertheless supporting universal jurisdiction to punish international crimes. See also G Binder, 'Authority to Proscribe and Punish International Crimes' (2013) 63 *University of Toronto Law Journal* 278, 308, arguing, in respect of universal jurisdiction, that '[r]ealizing human rights worldwide requires much more than denouncing a few exemplary perpetrators', and that '[t]heatrical criminal trials blame perpetrators for human rights violations, but they also absolve the international community that proscribes, prosecutes, judges, and punishes', drawing on Fuller's requirement that the law must also actually be applied to be 'moral' (ie there must be 'congruence' between what the law declares and how it is enforced); LL Fuller, *The Morality of Law*, rev edn (New Haven, Yale UP, 1969) 33–94 superfluous.

the person wherever he may go.[3] From the late Middle Ages onwards, jurisdiction became grounded in territoriality. As early as the fourteenth century, Baldus, the famous post-glossator of Roman law, wrote that 'territory and jurisdiction go together as mist to a swamp'.[4] In the Modern Age, which saw the refinement of cartographic techniques allowing for the drawing of more certain State boundaries and the attendant consolidation of State power, territoriality became the political and jurisdictional norm.[5] Thus, in his 1758 *Le droit des gens*, Vattel declared that '[t]out l'espace dans lequel une Nation étend son empire, forme le ressort de sa Jurisdiction, [et] s'appelle son *Territoire*'.[6] Territoriality also assumes a prominent place in the two defining treaties of the Modern Age, the Treaty of Westphalia (1648)[7] and the Final Act of the Congress of Vienna (1815).[8]

The crystallisation of the contemporary law of jurisdiction starts in 1927, when the Permanent Court of International Justice, in the *Lotus* case, famously ruled that a State's exercise of prescriptive jurisdiction is presumptively lawful, absent a prohibitive rule to the contrary.[9] Nevertheless, it is widely acknowledged that in principle, a jurisdictional assertion should rest on a permissive principle of international law, territoriality being the most prominent one. The principles of prescriptive jurisdiction are set out in more detail in Section IV.

The international rules on *enforcement* jurisdiction are concerned with the extent of the State's enforcement power (eg the power to arrest a fugitive), notably in another State's territory. The relevant rules can equally be found in *Lotus*, where the Court upheld a ban on the exercise of such jurisdiction absent the consent of the territorial State.[10] This ban obviously does not mean that the prohibition on extraterritorial enforcement jurisdiction is always rigorously complied with.[11]

This leaves us with the category of adjudicatory jurisdiction, which refers to the exercise of jurisdiction by courts. As courts, when establishing their jurisdiction, actualise a State's assertion of the applicability of its laws – prescriptive jurisdiction – to given conduct, one may consider enforcement jurisdiction to subsume adjudicatory jurisdiction.[12] Nevertheless,

[3] S Kassan, 'Extraterritorial Jurisdiction in the Ancient World' (1935) 29 *AJIL* 237.

[4] S Elden, *The Birth of Territory* (Princeton, Princeton UP, 2013) 36.

[5] J Branch, *The Cartographic State: Maps, Territory, and the Origins of Sovereignty* (Cambridge, CUP, 2013).

[6] Which translates into '[t]he whole space over which a nation extends its government, becomes the seat of its jurisdiction, and is called its *territory*'; see respectively E de Vattel, *Le droit des gens*, Vol I, Livre I: 'De la Nation considérée en elle-même' (London, 1758) and its 1797 translation as republished: E de Vattel, *The Law of Nations*, Book I: 'Of Nations Considered in Themselves' (Indianapolis, Liberty Fund, 2008), para 205.

[7] See Art LXXVI of the Treaty between the Holy Roman Emperor and the King of France and their respective Allies (signed 24 October 1648) 1 CTS 319, which incorporates within the Kingdom of France, 'with all manner of Jurisdiction and Sovereignty' 'all the Rights, Regales and Appurtenances, without any reserve'.

[8] See Art XIX of the Final Act of the Congress of Vienna (signed 9 June 1815) 64 CTS 453, providing that: 'His Majesty the King of Prussia and his Majesty the King of Saxony, wishing particularly to remove every object of future contest or dispute, renounce, each on his own part, and reciprocally in favour of one another, all feudal rights or pretensions, which they might exercise or might have exercised, beyond the frontiers fixed by the present Treaty'.

[9] *SS Lotus* [1927] PCIJ Series A, No 10, 18–19.

[10] ibid; 'the first and foremost restriction imposed by international law upon a State is that – failing the existence of a permissive rule to the contrary – it may not exercise its power in any form in the territory of another State. In this sense jurisdiction is certainly territorial; it cannot be exercised by a State outside its territory except by virtue of a permissive rule derived from international custom or from a convention'.

[11] See notably the kidnapping of Adolf Eichmann in Argentina by Israeli secret agents (Supreme Court (IL), *Attorney-General of the Government of Israel v Eichmann* (1968) 36 ILR 277) and the abduction of the plaintiff in Mexico by the US authorities (Supreme Court (US), *Alvarez-Machain v United States*, 504 US 655 (1992)).

[12] R O'Keefe, 'Universal Jurisdiction Clarifying the Basic Concept' (2004) 2 *JICJ* 735, 741. O'Keefe's definition of enforcement jurisdiction appears to cover action by the executive (eg the imposition of a fine on a foreign

it is analytically useful to restrict enforcement jurisdiction to executive action, and not to extend it to court litigation. Unlike executive action, court litigation does not, and cannot, take place extraterritorially, for the simple reason that States do not operate courts abroad.[13] The fact that courts are based inside the forum State's territory does not mean that the jurisdiction which they exercise is by definition lawful. In criminal and administrative (regulatory) cases, the legality of the exercise of adjudicatory jurisdiction is a function of the lawful exercise of prescriptive jurisdiction. Civil and commercial cases concern (transnational) private disputes that may not raise sovereignty concerns to the same extent that public law cases do. In such cases, the exercise of adjudicatory jurisdiction is normally governed by domestic law rather than international law and may even be entirely unrelated to the exercise of a State's prescriptive jurisdiction, as the court may well go on to apply foreign rather than domestic law.[14]

In many States, international law principles of jurisdiction can be invoked directly before the courts. However, in light of the domestic principle of legality, courts will normally not set aside domestic laws, especially not criminal laws, claimed to be in violation of the international law of jurisdiction. In some States, courts are reluctant to rely on international law altogether when it comes to determining the geographical reach of domestic law. Citing separation of powers concerns, they may leave international jurisdictional choices to the legislature and limit themselves to ascertaining the latter's legislative intent. The United States is a case in point. Since 1991, the US Supreme Court has routinely applied the presumption against extraterritoriality, pursuant to which the legislature is presumed not to have intended to give extraterritorial application to a statute.[15] This (rebuttable) presumption serves, at least in part 'to avoid the international discord that can result when U.S. law is applied to conduct in foreign countries', much like the international law principles of jurisdiction.[16] It applies even when there is no risk of conflict between a US statute and a foreign law, as the US Congress is presumed to generally legislate with domestic concerns in mind.[17] Thus, in a rather peculiar case brought by the EU and its Member States, the US Supreme Court refused to give extraterritorial effect to a provision allowing for private enforcement of a racketeering statute, even though there was no evidence that international discord would ensue in case of rebuttal of the presumption.[18] In any case, discord will not

corporation or the arrest of a fugitive), but also action by the judiciary (eg the criminal trial of the fugitive or a domestic court's hearing of a civil or commercial case).

[13] However, on the basis of 'unequal' treaties in the nineteenth century, Western courts could sit in judgment of disputes involving their own nationals in portions of foreign States' territories such as that of China and the Ottoman Empire. In respect of China, see D Wang, *China's Unequal Treaties: Narrating National History* (Lanham, Lexington Books, 2005).

[14] See eg M Akehurst, 'Jurisdiction in International Law' (1972) 46 *BYIL* 145, 170. Recently, however, transnational tort cases have raised sovereignty concerns (see Section III(D)). Adjudicatory jurisdiction in civil and commercial cases is in principle based on the legitimate expectations of the defendant to be brought before the forum State's courts, and of the plaintiff to sue in these courts. For the main instrument on adjudicatory jurisdiction within the EU, see Regulation (EU) No 1215/2012 of 12 December 2012 on jurisdiction and the recognition and enforcement of judgments in civil and commercial matters (recast) [2012] OJ L351/1 (Brussels I Regulation). Examples of how that regulation is interpreted by the Court of Justice of the EU include the judgments of 17 October 2017, *Bolagsupplysningen and Ilsjan*, C-194/16, EU:C:2017:766, and of 7 March 2018, *flightright and Others*, C-274/16, C-447/16 and C-448/16, EU:C:2018:160. See further G Van Calster, *European Private International Law*, 2nd edn (Oxford, Hart, 2016) 21–201.

[15] Supreme Court (US), *EEOC v Arabian American Oil Co ('Aramco')*, 499 US 244 (1991).

[16] Supreme Court (US), *RJR Nabisco, Inc v European Community*, 20 June 2016, Case No 15-138, 7–8.

[17] Supreme Court (US), *Morrison v National Australia Bank Ltd*, 561 US 247, 255 (2010).

[18] *Nabisco* (n 16). Private enforcement was considered to include enforcement by the EU and its Member States, which had brought this case under the *US Racketeer Influenced and Corrupt Organizations Act* (RICO) in 2000.

be avoided when it was the intention of the US Congress to apply the statute extraterritorially. US courts will normally defer to this intention, even if the extraterritorial application violates principles of international law and thus engages US responsibility.

Note that, in international law, jurisdiction can also refer to notions other than the sovereignty-based jurisdiction of the State. For example, it can refer to the power (*ratione materiae*, *ratione personae*, *ratione loci* and *ratione temporis*) of international courts and tribunals to hear cases, or concern the geographical scope of application of treaties; human rights treaties in particular. The jurisdiction of international courts is covered in Chapter 13 (Peaceful Settlement of Disputes). The notion of jurisdiction in international human rights will be addressed in this chapter, as human rights jurisdiction relates to the scope of State authority.[19]

The chapter proceeds as follows. Section II deals with territorial jurisdiction. Section III discusses nationality in international law. Section IV gives an overview of the principles of prescriptive jurisdiction as they have been developed in criminal law. Section V then examines the relevance of these principles outside the context of criminal law. In this respect, a number of assertions of regulatory jurisdiction by the EU receive particular attention. Section VI studies the concept of jurisdiction in international human rights law, focusing on relevant case law of the European Court of Human Rights. Section VII concludes.

II. Territorial Jurisdiction

In his arbitral award of 4 April 1928 in the case on the island of Palmas, arbitrator Max Huber held:

> Sovereignty in the relations between States signifies independence. Independence in regard to a portion of the globe is the right to exercise therein, to the exclusion of any other State, the functions of a State.[20]

The territorial jurisdiction of a State is characterised by the plenitude of powers and by its exclusive character (see also Chapter 5). A *plenitude of powers* refers to how the territorial jurisdiction comprises both constitutional, legislative, administrative and judicial powers.[21] These powers in principle apply to all persons situated on the territory of the State concerned, both its own nationals and aliens. The State can also grant asylum to aliens which are persecuted within the meaning of the Refugee Convention (see Chapter 16). The *exclusive character* of a State's power to exercise its authority on its territory is also an attribute of such State's sovereignty. Other States or subjects of international law – eg international organisations – can only act on the State's territory with the latter's consent (see above).

The aim was to obtain treble damages from a US cigarette producer that had colluded with drug traffickers, and in so doing destabilised the EU market. The case was brought before US courts as, in 2000, EU law was insufficiently developed to allow the case to be successful before European courts. The risk of conflict between US and foreign law was absent, as, in their capacity as plaintiffs, the EU and its Member States had themselves invoked US law.

[19] See also *Banković and others v Belgium and others* App No 52207/99 (ECtHR, 12 December 2001) paras 59–61 (referring to the notion of jurisdiction in general international law).

[20] *Island of Palmas* (Netherlands v United States of America), Award of 4 April 1928, II RIAA 829, 839.

[21] BH Oxman, 'Jurisdiction of States' in MPEPIL.

There are a number of exceptions to the plenitude and exclusive character of a State's power to exercise authority over its own territory which flow from customary international law or from treaty obligations.[22] Thus, it is a general rule of customary international law that a State may not knowingly let its territory be used in violation of the rights of other States. In its judgment in the *Corfu Channel* case the ICJ referred to 'every State's obligation not to allow knowingly its territory to be used for acts contrary to the rights of other States'.[23] It held Albania responsible for the presence of mines in its territorial seas and for the explosions and damage and loss of human life when two British warships ran into the mines, because it appeared from the circumstances that Albania knew, or should have known, about the mines. In its judgment in the *Pulp Mills* case, the Court confirmed the principle it had put forward in *Corfu Channel*.[24] In the arbitral award in the *Trail Smelter Arbitration* this principle was applied to the situation of cross-border environmental pollution: 'no State has the right to permit the use of its territory in such a manner as to cause injury by fumes in or to the territory of another State or the properties or persons therein'.[25] The arbitral college held Canada internationally responsible for the damage caused in the American State of Washington by the emission of sulphur dioxide gases by a factory located in British Columbia. Acts by individuals can therefore engage the international responsibility of a State, if the latter has not taken appropriate steps to prevent the damage (see also Chapter 12). In addition, a State cannot allow its territory to be used for disturbing order in, or for causing the demise of the political regime, in another State. The Friendly Relations Declaration stipulates in this respect:

> Every State has the duty to refrain from organizing, instigating, assisting or participating in acts of civil strife or terrorist acts in another State or acquiescing in organized activities within its territory directed towards the commission of such acts, when the acts referred to in the present paragraph involve a threat or use of force.

And:

> No State may use or encourage the use of economic political or any other type of measures to coerce another State in order to obtain from it the subordination of the exercise of its sovereign rights and to secure from it advantages of any kind. Also, no State shall organize, assist, foment, finance, incite or tolerate subversive, terrorist or armed activities directed towards the violent overthrow of the regime of another State, or interfere in civil strife in another State.[26]

In its judgment in the *Nicaragua Case* the ICJ concluded from these passages that 'these forms of action are therefore wrongful in light of both the principle of non-use of force, and that of non-intervention'.[27]

Limitations to the exercise of authority on a State's own territory may also flow from the latter's international obligations with regard to State immunity, diplomatic and consular immunities and immunities of international organisations based on the State's territory or of personnel or agents of international organisations that are active therein. Also, the

[22] See Oxman (n 21) for an overview of possible limitations.

[23] *Corfu Channel* (United Kingdom of Great Britain and Northern Ireland v Albania) [1949] ICJ Rep 4, 22.

[24] *Pulp Mills on the River Uruguay* (Argentina v Uruguay) [2010] ICJ Rep 14, para 101.

[25] *Trail Smelter Case* (United States v Canada), Award of 16 April 1938 and 11 March 1941, III RIAA 1905, 1965.

[26] Friendly Relations Declaration, principle I(9) and IIII(2).

[27] *Military and Paramilitary Activity in and against Nicaragua* (Nicaragua v United States of America) [1986] ICJ Rep 14, para 205.

international rules regarding the treatment due to foreigners can result in limitations. Last but not least, a State can voluntarily confer jurisdiction to other entities for exercising jurisdiction on its territory. Thus, the European Commission has the authority, pursuant to the Treaty on the Functioning of the European Union (TFEU), to detect and punish violations of the EU competition rules, in particular of Articles 101 and 102 TFEU.

A. Territory

A State's territory comprises both the land part and the internal waters. International watercourses often enjoy a special status under international law.

i. Land Part

A State's borders are the imaginary lines on the Earth's surface that separate the territory of one State from the territory of another State, from non-appropriated territory, or from the high seas. It is common practice that these borders are determined in boundary treaties between neighbouring States. Boundary treaties can establish borders either by specifying precise coordinates (eg the 38th parallel north between North and South Korea) or by establishing a general principle for their precise determination. In the latter case, a mixed boundary commission usually carries out the exact demarcation 'in the field' and utilises border markers if necessary. In case of a dispute regarding the exact path of the frontier, the treaty usually determines how the dispute is to be settled.[28] Boundary treaties enjoy a special status under international law. In Chapter 5 it was noted that Article 11 of the Vienna Convention on Succession of States in respect of Treaties stipulates that State succession does not as such affect a boundary established by a treaty, or the obligations and rights established by a treaty and relating to the regime of a boundary. In Chapter 2 reference was made to Article 62(2)(a) of the VCLT, pursuant to which *rebus sic stantibus* cannot be invoked as a ground for the termination of a treaty or for the withdrawal from it if the treaty establishes a boundary.[29]

International law employs a number of different general principles for the demarcation of *natural boundaries*. For *mountain ranges* that are situated on the boundary between two or more States, no single criterion applies. Given their often complex structure, it is advisable that boundary treaties accurately indicate whether the boundary line follows the crest line (ie the line which traces the highest peaks in the range), the mountain ridge, or the (continental or local) watershed line (ie the ridge or crest line that divides two separate drainage areas). This last criterion is often used in order to preserve sovereignty over natural resources.

With respect to *rivers*, a distinction is made between navigable and non-navigable rivers. In the absence of a special agreement, the demarcation line for non-navigable rivers that form the boundary between two States follows the median line of the river, or of its main

[28] See *Land and Maritime Boundary between Cameroon and Nigeria* (Cameroon v Nigeria: Equatorial Guinea intervening) [2002] ICJ Rep 303; *Kasikili/Sedudu Island* (Botswana v Namibia) [1999] ICJ Rep 1045 and *Case concerning the temple of Preah Vihear – Merits* (Cambodia v Thailand) [1962] ICJ Rep 6.

[29] Art 62(2) of the Vienna Convention on the Law of Treaties between States and International Organizations or between International Organizations contains an analogous provision.

arm if it has more than one.[30] When a navigable river forms the boundary between two States, and in the absence of an agreement to the contrary, the boundary line follows the median line of the so-called *thalweg*, ie the middle of the main navigation channel of the river in the downstream direction.[31] If the riverbed slowly shifts as a result of *accretion* (ie the addition of soil by gradual deposit) from one bank, the boundary is adjusted accordingly, unless otherwise agreed by treaty.[32] If, on the other hand, the riverbed suddenly and significantly changes (*avulsion*), the boundary remains in its original position.[33] As for *bridges* that are built over a river that forms an international boundary, the boundary line runs through the middle of the bridge unless the bridge was fully placed under the sovereignty of one State by way of treaty.[34] For *lakes* and *internal seas* situated on the boundary between two or more States, the boundary line generally follows the median line of such lake or internal sea. Often, however, such boundaries are expressly determined in boundary treaties between the riparian States.

ii. Internal Waters

Under customary international law, State sovereignty also extends to the *internal waters* of a State.[35] These are the waters located on the land side of the baseline, ie the line separating the land area from the sea.[36] A State's internal waters with a maritime character include bays, estuaries, seaports and the waters situated behind the straight baselines.[37]

The United Nations Convention on the Law of the Sea (UNCLOS), adopted in Montego Bay, Jamaica, on 10 December 1982,[38] makes a distinction between the 'normal baseline' and other baselines. By virtue of Article 5 UNCLOS, the *normal baseline* is 'the low-water line along the coast as marked on large-scale charts officially recognized by the coastal State'. However there are some cases in which the low-water line does not serve as the baseline. In places where the coastline is deeply indented and cut into, or if there is a fringe of islands along the coast in its immediate vicinity, according to Article 7(1) UNCLOS, the method of the straight baselines joining appropriate points for this purpose is used to determine the baseline. For example, the Wadden Sea and the *Zeeuwse wateren* are internal waters for the Netherlands.

[30] *Kasikili/Sedudu Island* (Botswana v Namibia) [1999] ICJ Rep 1045, 1062 and RP Anand, 'Accretion' in MPEPIL. See the Israel-Jordan Treaty of Peace (adopted and entered into force in 1994) for an example of a boundary treaty dealing with such a river.

[31] *Frontier Dispute* (Benin v Niger) [2005] ICJ Rep 90, 126 and 149; *Kasikili/Sedudu Island* (Botswana v Namibia) [1999] ICJ Rep 1045, 1062; Anand (n 30) and MH Mendelson and SG Hutson 'Iraq-Kuwait Boundary: Legal Aspects' (1990) *Revue Belge de Droit International* 293.

[32] *Land, Island and Maritime Frontier Dispute* (El Salvador v Honduras) [1992] ICJ Rep 351, 546 and Anand (n 30).

[33] ibid, 546; Supreme Court, US, *Georgia v South Carolina* [1990] 91 ILR 439; Anand (n 30) and R Jennings and A Watts, *Oppenheim's International Law*, 9th edn (London, Longman, 1992) 696.

[34] M Herdegen, 'River Bridges' in MPEPIL.

[35] Art 2(1) UNCLOS; *Case concerning Military and Paramilitary Activities in and against Nicaragua – Merits* (Nicaragua v United States), [1986] ICJ Rep 14, para 212. See Chapter 18(2)(A).

[36] Art 5(1) Convention on the Territorial Sea and Contiguous Zone (adopted 29 April 1958, entered into force 10 September 1964) 516 UNTS 205 and ILC, 'Articles concerning the Law of the Sea', *Yearbook of the International Law Commission* (1956) II, 277 and K Bangert, 'Internal Waters' in MPEPIL.

[37] See DR Rothwell and T Stephens, *The International Law of the Sea* (Oxford, Hart, 2010) 54 for more examples of internal waters.

[38] United Nations Convention on the Law of the Sea (adopted 10 December 1982, entered into force 16 November 1994) 1833 UNTS 3, 1834 UNTS 3, 1835 UNTS 3.

For a *river* that flows directly into the sea, the baseline is a straight line across the mouth of the river between points on the low-water line of its banks (Article 9 UNCLOS). In the case of *bays*[39] of which the distance between the natural access points at low water does not exceed 24 nautical miles (one nautical mile has the length of one minute of latitude, ie approximately 1,852 m), a closing line may be drawn between these two points, whereby the waters thus enclosed are considered part of the internal waters (Article 10, § 4 UNCLOS).

Finally, there is a specific arrangement for the delimitation of *ports*: pursuant to Article 11 UNCLOS, the outermost permanent harbour works that form an integral part of the harbour system (mostly harbour dams and breakwaters) are considered to form part of the coast.[40]

Seaports, whether they are located on the coast or on a natural or artificial internal watercourse, are part of the internal waters of the coastal State, which means that they fall entirely under the sovereignty of this State and are therefore in principle also subject to its legislation.[41] While there is treaty law and case law in support of the principle that a State does not have the absolute power to prohibit access to its ports,[42] State practice evidences that it is not universally accepted that a right of access to the ports or internal waters of a State exists.[43]

In the *Nicaragua* case, the ICJ confirmed that 'by virtue of its sovereignty […] the coastal State may regulate access to its ports'.[44] However, the Court specified that customary international law does recognise a right of access for foreign vessels insofar that these ships enjoy a right of innocent passage through the territorial sea of the coastal State in order to sail inland or out of internal waters: 'in order to enjoy access to ports, foreign vessels possess a customary right of innocent passage in territorial waters for the purposes of entering or leaving internal waters'.[45] It is moreover generally accepted that foreign vessels in distress have a right of access to the ports and internal waters of the coastal State, at least to the extent that such access is necessary to save lives.[46]

[39] The term 'bay' is defined in Art 10(2) UNCLOS: 'a well-marked indentation whose penetration is in such proportion to the width of its mouth as to contain land-locked waters and constitute more than a mere curvature of the coast. An indentation shall not, however, be regarded as a bay unless its area is as large as, or larger than, that of the semi-circle whose diameter is a line drawn across the mouth of that indentation'.

[40] To which Art 11 UNCLOS adds that offshore installations and artificial islands shall not be considered as permanent harbour works.

[41] See inter alia M Hayashi, 'Jurisdiction over foreign commercial ships in ports: a gap in the law of the sea codification' (2004) *Ocean Yearbook* 488–511, GC Kasoulides, *Port State Control and Jurisdiction: Evolution of the Port State Regime* (Dordrecht, Nijhoff, 1993); G Kiene, 'Investigation, detention and release of ships under the Paris MOU on port State control: a view from practice' (1996) *International Journal of Marine & Coastal Law* 217–24.

[42] Rothwell and Stephens (n 37) 55. See, for instance, Convention and Statute on the International Regime of Maritime Ports (adopted 9 December 1923, entered into force 26 July 1926) 58 LNTS 287. For general overviews of treaties and judgments, see LB Sohn et al, *Law of the Sea in a Nutshell* (St Paul, West, 2010) 172–89; DP O'Connell, *The International Law of the Sea* (Oxford, Clarendon Press, 1982) 848 and CJ Colombos, *The International Law of the Sea*, 6th edn (London, Longmans, 1967) 176–77.

[43] See inter alia Bangert (n 36); L de la Fayette, 'Access to ports in international law' (1996) *International Journal of Marine & Coastal Law* 1–22; I Laun, 'Le régime international des ports' (1926) 15 *RdC* 1–143.

[44] *Nicaragua* (n 35) para 213 *in fine*.

[45] *Nicaragua* (n 35) para 214.

[46] Bangert (n 36); RR Churchill and AV Lowe, *The Law of the Sea*, 3rd edn (Manchester, Manchester UP, 1999) 63, who remark that it is not clear as yet whether a foreign vessel also enjoys a right of access to save its cargo. See also Sohn et al (n 42) 186–89; AE Chircop, 'The Customary Law of Refuge for Ships in Distress' in AE Chircop and O Linden (eds), *Places of Refuge for Ships: Emerging Environmental Concerns of a Maritime Custom* (Leiden, Brill, 2006) 163, 185–89 and E Van Hooydonk, 'The obligation to offer a place of refuge to a ship in distress' (2004) *Lloyd's Maritime and Commercial Law Quarterly* 347–74.

The foregoing does not detract from the fact that many multilateral and bilateral treaties (often the so-called 'treaties of friendship, commerce and navigation') grant access rights to foreign vessels. Within the EU, ships flying the flag of an EU Member State have a right to access the ports of the other Member States on the basis of the free movement of goods and the freedom to provide services. Article V GATT includes a provision on the freedom of transit for vessels through the territory of the GATT Contracting Parties (now WTO Members). Broader access rights apply for the use of international watercourses (see below).

With regard to the jurisdiction which a State can exercise vis-à-vis foreign vessels located in its internal waters, it should be noted that, even though a vessel may enjoy a right of access to a port on the basis of a treaty, and even though this logically also implies a right of free passage from this port, the State in question may nonetheless impose significant restrictions in this respect.[47] The right of free passage may be restricted, for example, by a court order to protect the security or public order of the State in question, because this State has adopted international reprisals against the flag State, or because the vessel is seized following a violation of customs regulations or as collateral in a civil dispute concerning a maritime claim. The State can refuse free passage to a vessel that is not seaworthy.

Recent treaties have significantly expanded the jurisdiction of the port State with respect to the protection of the environment.[48] By virtue of Article 219 UNCLOS States which have ascertained that a vessel within one of their ports is in violation of applicable international rules and standards relating to seaworthiness of vessels and thereby threatens damage to the marine environment shall, as far as practicable, take administrative measures to prevent the vessel from sailing. They can permit the vessel to proceed only to the nearest appropriate repair yard and, upon removal of the causes of the violation, shall permit the vessel to continue immediately. The port State may institute legal proceedings in respect of such violations. Under the International Convention for the Safety of Life at Sea[49] (SOLAS), the port State can prevent the ship from sailing if its condition or equipment does not correspond substantially with the prescribed safety certificate.[50]

[47] Bangert (n 36); Rothwell and Stephens (n 37) 56; Sohn et al (n 42) 190 and PC Jessup, *The Law of Territorial Waters and Maritime Jurisdiction* (New York, GA Jennings, 1927) xxxvii. See Ch 18 section (V)(d) on port state jurisdiction.

[48] See inter alia D Anderson, 'Port States and environmental protection' in A Boyle and D Freestone (eds), *International Law and Sustainable Development: Past Achievements and Future Challenges* (Oxford, OUP, 2003) 325; Bangert (n 36); M Cuttler, 'Incentives for Reducing Oil Pollution from Ships: the Case for Enhanced Port State Control' (1995) *Georgetown International Environmental Law Review* 175; L Schiano di Pepe, 'Port State Control as an Instrument to Ensure Compliance with International Marine Environmental Obligations' in A Kirchner (ed), *International Marine Environmental Law* (The Hague, KLI, 2003) 137. EU rules have also introduced obligations for the Member States to exercise their jurisdiction to combat violations of EU environmental law. See, for example, Directive 2005/35/EC of the European Parliament and of the Council of 7 September 2005 on ship-source pollution and on the introduction of penalties for infringements [2005] OJ L255/11, the validity of which was assessed by the ECJ in the judgment of 3 June 2008, *The International Association of Independent Tanker Owners and others*, C-308/06, EU:C:2008:312. There, the Court was asked whether the strict liability regime for environmental damage occurring on the high seas under the directive was compatible with UNCLOS and with the International Convention for the Prevention of Pollution from Ships, signed in London on 2 November 1973, as supplemented by the Protocol of 17 February 1978 (MARPOL 73/78). The Court held that the validity of the directive could not be assessed on the basis of either convention. See further Chapter 20.

[49] International Convention for the Safety of Life at Sea (adopted 1 November 1974, entered into force 25 May 1980) UNTS No 18961.

[50] Regulation 6, International Convention for the Safety of Life at Sea. Note that the EU is not a party to the SOLAS Convention, but that the CJEU has held that the division of competences between the Union and its Member States must nevertheless be respected when making proposals within the framework of that Convention. In particular, the Court concluded that by submitting to the International Maritime Organisation (IMO) Maritime

In addition, since the foreign vessels involved are within its territorial jurisdiction, the coastal or riparian State can in principle also enforce its national laws and regulations vis-à-vis the vessel and those on board, except where international immunities apply. However, foreign vessels are more or less independent entities to which the law of the flag State remains applicable when they are in the internal waters of another State and in respect of which the captain and the local consul of the flag State have enforcement jurisdiction. For that reason, the coastal and riparian States, in practice, leave matters concerning the 'internal affairs' of the vessel to the authorities of the flag State and exercise their jurisdiction only in respect of certain matters that affect their interests.[51]

In practice, when it comes to exercising *criminal jurisdiction*, the authorities of the coastal and riparian State usually waive the prosecution of crimes committed on board a vessel, unless: (i) they disturb the order in the port or on internal watercourses; (ii) the captain himself requests the intervention of local authorities; or (iii) it is a serious crime that no country can leave unpunished.[52] Consular treaties and shipping agreements often include criteria in this respect.

The *civil jurisdiction* of the coastal or riparian State with respect to foreign vessels is also, in principle, unlimited, albeit once again subject to the applicable international immunities. In a number of cases, States have regulated this competence in a treaty.[53] Thus, according to the 1952 International Convention relating to the Arrest of Sea-Going Ships,[54] it is only possible to arrest a foreign sea-going ship for a maritime claim, ie a claim arising out of damage caused by a ship (due to collision or otherwise), loss of life or personal injury caused by a ship, salvage, transport agreements, loss of or damage to goods carried by a ship, general average, bottomry, towage, pilotage, disputes about ship ownership, ship mortgages, etc.[55] The 1952 International Convention on Certain Rules concerning Civil Jurisdiction in Matters of Collision[56] provides that an action for collision between seagoing vessels or between seagoing and inland navigation craft can only be introduced: (i) before the court where the defendant has his habitual residence or a place of business; (ii) before the court of the area where arrest has been effected of the defendant ship or of any other ship

Safety Committee a proposal to examine the creation of checklists or other appropriate tools for assisting the Contracting States of the SOLAS Convention in monitoring whether ships and port facilities complied with certain requirements, Greece had not respected the exclusive competence of the Union: judgment of 12 February 2009, *Commission v Greece*, C-45/07, EU:C:2009:81. See further PJ Kuijper et al, *The Law of EU External Relations: Cases, Materials, and Commentary on the EU as an International Legal Actor*, 2nd edn (Oxford, OUP, 2015) 183–86; and G De Baere, 'EU Status in Other International Organizations' in R Schütze and T Tridimas (eds), *Oxford Principles of European Union Law*, Vol 1: The European Union Legal Order (Oxford, OUP, 2018) 1266–67.

[51] See also C Gloria, 'Internationales öffentliches Seerecht' in K Ipsen, *Völkerrecht*, 5th edn (Munich, Beck, 2004) 826 and D König, 'Flag of Ships' in MPEPIL.

[52] Art 27(1) UNCLOS. As regards the Belgian-French position, reference is usually made to the advice (with force of law) of the French *Conseil d'Etat* of 20 November 1806; R Koering-Joulin and A Huet, 'Compétence des tribunaux répressifs français et de la loi pénale française' in *Juris-Classeur de droit international* (Paris, Editions du Juris-Classeur, 1995) 9, para 20, who are critical of the traditional position and are of the opinion that the current French criminal law provisions apply. More than once, the non-exercise of jurisdiction is based on reasons of courtesy: see inter alia Gloria (n 51) 830, König (n 51); Sohn et al (n 42) 190; and 'Eaux' in *Répertoire Pratique du Droit Belge* (Brussels, Bruylant, 1942) 361, no 141. Compare finally with MN Shaw, *International Law*, 8th edn (Cambridge, CUP, 2017) 413, according to whom, regardless of the theoretical divergences between the French and common law approaches, the practical reality is the same.

[53] See n 47.

[54] International Convention Relating to the Arrest of Sea-Going Ships (adopted 10 May 1952) UNTS No 6330.

[55] Arts 1 and 2 of the International Convention Relating to the Arrest of Sea-Going Ships.

[56] International Convention on Certain Rules concerning Civil Jurisdiction in Matters of Collision (adopted 10 May 1952) UNTS No 6331.

belonging to the defendant which can be lawfully arrested, or where arrest could have been effected and bail or other security has been furnished; or (iii) before the court of the place of collision when the collision has occurred within the limits of a part or in internal waters (Article 1).

iii. International Watercourses

National watercourses are waterways that are entirely (ie from source to mouth) located in the territory of a single State. The water and mouth (Article 9 UNCLOS) of such rivers form an exclusive part of the internal waters of the State in question. Also *international boundary rivers* (waterways that form the separation between several States) are part of the territory of the States which they separate, whereby, as indicated above, the boundary line usually runs through the middle of the (*thalweg* of the) river (see above).

International watercourses, which flow through different States, have a special status when they are the subject of a treaty-based arrangement concerning free navigation. Apart from shipping use, international law has seen an increasing number of treaties in recent years which also regulate other aspects of the use of transboundary waterways.[57] This also applies to some channels that are international maritime links and which are the subject of special treaty regimes.

The nineteenth century saw the emergence of a principle of free navigation on several European transboundary watercourses. The Final Act of the Congress of Vienna of 9 June 1815[58] stipulated that navigation along the entire course of the rivers flowing through the signatory States, 'from the point where each of them becomes navigable, to its mouth, shall be entirely free, and shall not, in respect to commerce, be prohibited to any one'.[59] The Final Act also stipulated that the duties on navigation would be regulated in a uniform and settled manner.[60] Special arrangements for free navigation on the Scheldt (also for non-riparian States), on the Meuse and on the Rhine were attached to the Final Act of the Congress of Vienna. In order to monitor the regime of free navigation, an international commission, which included representatives of the riparian countries, was set up for each internationalised watercourse. Still, it would take more than 50 years before free navigation on the Rhine became a reality. This was achieved with the 1868 Mannheim Act[61] and the Rhine navigation regime was further elaborated in the Treaty of Versailles.[62] As a result of the latter, Belgium and the UK have been parties to the Rhine navigation treaties since 1919, and have thus been equated with the riparian States of the Rhine. After the Second World War, the rules for free navigation on the Rhine were reconfirmed in several amendments to

[57] Art 42(1) UNCLOS stipulates which matters the strait States may regulate; SC McCaffrey, 'International Watercourses' in MPEPIL.

[58] Final Act of the Congress of Vienna (adopted 9 June 1815), in GF De Martens, *Nouveau Recueil de Traités* 1814–1845, 433 (Final Act).

[59] Art 109 Final Act.

[60] Art 111 Final Act.

[61] Convention for Rhine Navigation between France, Grand Duchy of Baden, Bavaria, Grand Duchy of Hessen, Netherlands and Prussia (adopted 17 October 1868, revised 20 November 1963) 138 CTS 167; see amongst others, CA Ferrier, *La liberté de navigation sur le Rhin de Bâle à la mer* (Winterthur, Keller, 1955); Stichting Nederlands Vervoerswetenschappelijk Instituut, *Honderd jaren Akte van Mannheim* (1969) 126.

[62] Treaty of Peace with Germany (adopted 28 June 1919, entered into force 10 January 1920) 225 CTS 188 (Treaty of Versailles).

the Mannheim Act.[63] The general principle in this respect is that vessels from all contracting States are allowed to navigate the entire Rhine freely. Disputes about shipping on the Rhine must be brought before a Rhine watercourse court, ie a court that was designated by each of the riparian States for this purpose; these courts are competent both in criminal and civil cases.[64] The management of the Rhine is carried out by the Central Commission for Navigation on the Rhine (CCR), a commission of the contracting States which has its seat in Strasbourg and has the authority to make binding decisions. It is charged with drafting treaties with respect to the Rhine navigation regime and the joint management of this regime. It is also a court of appeal that decides on certain appeals against judgments of the Rhine watercourse courts of first instance.[65]

International watercourses are also important for *non-shipping purposes*, eg for environmental protection, drinking water and energy supply. Whereas, initially, theories were put forward proclaiming the absolute sovereignty of the riparian State (the so-called 'Harmon doctrine', formulated at the time by the American minister of Justice Harmon in a dispute with Mexico),[66] international law, both with regard to shipping and other uses of international watercourses, has evolved considerably over the twentieth century, and has developed into a concept of a 'community of interest' between equal riparian States.

In a judgment of 1929 in the case concerning the River Oder, the Permanent Court of International Justice stated:

> [The] community of interest in a navigable river becomes the basis of a common legal right, the essential features of which are the perfect equality of all riparian States in the use of the whole course of the river and the exclusion of any preferential privilege of any one riparian State in relation to the others.[67]

In its 1997 judgment on the *Gabčikovo-Nagymaros Project*, the ICJ confirmed this case law and extended it to the use of international watercourses for purposes other than shipping:

> Modern development of international law has strengthened this principle for non-navigational uses of international watercourses as well, as evidenced by the adoption of the Convention of

[63] The need to amend the Mannheim Act was at issue in Opinion 1/76 (Agreement on the establishment of a European Laying-up Fund for Inland Waterway Vessels) of 26 April 1977, EU:C:1977:63. There, the ECJ held that the participation of six Member States in the draft agreement on the establishment of a European Laying-up Fund for Inland Waterway Vessels at issue was explained and justified by the fact that they had undertaken, pursuant to Art 3 of that draft agreement, to make the amendments to the Mannheim Act (as well as to Convention of Luxembourg of 27 October 1956 on the Canalization of the Moselle) necessitated by the implementation of the draft agreement. See further G De Baere, *Constitutional Principles of EU External Relations* (Oxford, OUP, 2008) 52–58.

[64] See Arts 33–40 of Mannheim Act.

[65] See Arts 43, 45 and 46 of the Mannheim Act. See inter alia A Bos, 'Reflections on the Provision of the Act of Mannheim Enshrining the Right of Complaint to the Central Commission for the Navigation of the Rhine' in N Blokker and S Muller (eds), *Towards more Effective Supervision by International Organizations. Essays in Honour of Henry G Schermers* (Dordrecht, Nijhoff, 1994) 205–15; WE Haak, 'Experience in the Netherlands Regarding the Case-law of the Chamber of Appeal of the Central Commission for Navigation on the Rhine' (1988) *NYIL* 3–51. On the relationship between the CCR and the EU, see A Bour, 'Les relations entre la Communauté Economique européenne et la Commission Centrale pour la navigation du Rhin' in A von Ziegler and T Burckhardt (eds), *Internationales Recht auf See und Binnengewässern: Festschrift für Walter Müller* (Zürich, Schulthess, 1993) 61–74; DS Collinson, 'The Rhine regime in transition: relations between the European Communities and the Central Commission for Rhine navigation' (1972) *Columbia Law Review* 485–516; F Meiβner, *Das Recht der Europäischen Wirtschaftsgemeinschaft im Verhältnis zur Rheinschiffahrtsakte von Mannheim: ein Beitrag zur völkerrechtlichen Bedeutung des Artikels 234 EWGV* (Berlin, Duncker & Humblot, 1973).

[66] See McCaffrey (n 57) and SC McCaffrey, 'The Harmon Doctrine one hundred years later: buried, not praised' (1996) *Natural Resources Journal* 725–67.

[67] *Case relating to the Territorial Jurisdiction of the International Commission of the River Oder* (United Kingdom, Czechoslovakia, Denmark, France, Germany and Sweden v Poland) [1929] PCIJ Rep A, n 23, 27.

21 May 1997 on the Law of the Non-Navigational Uses of International Watercourses by the United Nations General Assembly.[68]

An important multilateral treaty for the protection of the environment of international waterways and lakes is the 1992 *Helsinki Convention on the Protection and Use of Transboundary Watercourses and International Lakes*, also known as the UNECE Water Convention.[69] This is a framework treaty covering transboundary or border-forming waters, both groundwater and surface water,[70] with the aim of preventing, controlling and reducing the adverse transboundary effects on the environment caused by human activities. The UNECE Water Convention was drafted by the United Nations Economic Commission for Europe (UNECE) at the request of the CSCE. It has a clear structure. Part I applies to all contracting parties. They commit themselves to take all appropriate measures to prevent, control and reduce transboundary effects. To this end, the following principles are set as a basis for the water policy: (i) the precautionary principle; (ii) the polluter pays principle; and (iii) water management aimed at sustainability. The riparian States must cooperate on the basis of equality and reciprocity by means of bilateral and multilateral agreements, in order to develop policies, programmes and strategies for all parties concerned in order to protect the environment of the transboundary waters or the environment on which they have an impact (Article 2). Part II contains specific provisions for the riparian States bordering the same transboundary waters. They have to conclude bilateral or multilateral agreements on the basis of equality and reciprocity if these do not yet exist, or adapt them if necessary, in order to avoid contradictions with the fundamental principles of the UNECE Water Convention (Article 9). Consultations between the riparian States must take place on the basis of reciprocity, good faith and good-neighbourliness, and must be aimed at cooperation (Article 10). They must develop joint measurement and monitoring programmes (Article 11), carry out common research and development activities (Article 12) and exchange information (Article 13). There is also a duty to notify in alarm situations (Article 14), as well as a mutual assistance obligation in emergency situations (Article 15). Information about water quality must be made public (Article 16). Finally, Part III contains a number of institutional arrangements. There is also a Protocol on Water and Health to the UNECE Water Convention which dates from 17 June 1999 and aims to prevent, control and reduce water-related diseases.[71] Moreover, in 2003, the Protocol on Civil Liability and Compensation for Damage Caused by the Transboundary Effects of Industrial Accidents

[68] *Case concerning the Gabčikovo-Nagymaros Project* (Hungary v Slovakia) [1997] ICJ Rep 1, para 85.

[69] Convention on the Protection and Use of Transboundary Watercourses and International Lakes (adopted 17 March 1992, entered into force 6 October 1996) 1936 UNTS 269. See in this respect inter alia B Bosnjakovic, 'UN/ECE strategies for protecting the environment with respect to international watercourses: the Helsinki and Espoo conventions' in SMA Salman and L Boisson de Chazournes (eds), *International Watercourses: Enhancing Co-operation and Managing Conflict* (Washington, The World Bank, 1998) 47; A Tanzi, 'Regional Integration and the Protection of the Environment: the UN/ECE Process on Water Law' (2000) *Italian YIL* 71; M Papaconstantinou, 'The ECE Convention on the Protection and the Use of Transboundary Watercourses and International Lakes and the UN Convention on International Watercourses' (1999) *Revue hellénique de droit internationale* 263; P Wouters and S Vinogradov, 'Analysing the ECE Water Convention: What Lessons for the Regional Management of Transboundary Water Resources?' (2003–2004) *Yearbook of International Co-operation on Environment and Development* 55.

[70] See the definition of 'transboundary waters' in Art 1(1) of the Convention.

[71] Protocol on Water and Health to the Convention on the Protection and Use of Transboundary Watercourses and International Lakes (adopted 17 June 1999, entered into force 17 June 1999) 2331 UNTS 202.

on Transboundary Waters was adopted.[72] Under the UNECE Water Convention, specific treaties for the Meuse,[73] Danube[74] and Rhine[75] have been concluded.[76]

The 1997 *Convention on the Law of the Non-navigational Uses of International Watercourses* is a framework treaty drawn up within the framework of the UN – on the basis of a draft provided by the International Law Commission (above, Chapter 3) – which aims at both codification and further development of the international rules on the use of watercourses other than for shipping.[77] The Convention obliges the watercourse States to utilise an international watercourse (as defined in Article 2(b)) in a reasonable and equitable manner, with a view to attaining optimal and sustainable utilisation thereof and benefits therefrom, taking into account the interests of the other watercourse States, consistent with adequate protection of the watercourse (Article 5(1)). In its 1997 judgment on the *Gabčikovo-Nagymaros Project*, the ICJ also referred repeatedly to the right of a riparian State to a fair and reasonable part of the use of the natural resources of an international watercourse.[78] The Convention contains a general obligation for watercourse States to take all appropriate measures to prevent the causing of significant harm to other watercourse States (Article 7(1), ie the so-called '*no-harm*' principle[79]) and to cooperate (Article 8(1)), which includes a duty to exchange on a regular basis readily available data and information (Article 9). In the case of planned measures which may have a significant adverse effect upon other watercourse States, there is a duty to timely notify these States (Article 12). This should be carried out in a manner that allows the notified States a period of six months to respond to the notification (Articles 13–16). If the other watercourse State(s) is (are) of the opinion that implementation of the planned measures is inconsistent with the Convention, the notifying State and the notified State shall enter into consultations and, if necessary, negotiations (Article 17). In addition, there are specific rules applicable for the protection, conservation and management of the ecosystems of international waterways (Articles 20–26), the prevention and mitigation of harmful conditions (Article 27), emergency situations (Articles 28), and the settlement of disputes (Article 33).

iv. Canals

When canals are restricted to the territory of a single State, they fall in principle exclusively under the sovereign jurisdiction of that State. However, when they form an international

[72] Protocol on Civil Liability and Compensation for Damage Caused by the Transboundary Effects of Industrial Accidents on Transboundary Waters (adopted 21 May 2003, not yet entered into force).

[73] International Agreement on the (River) Meuse (adopted 3 December 2002, entered into force 1 December 2006) (https://iea.uoregon.edu/treaty-text/2002-protectionmeusefrtxt) (Treaty of Ghent).

[74] Convention on Cooperation for the Protection and Sustainable Use of the Danube River (adopted 29 June 1994, entered into force 22 October 1998) OJ L342/19 (1997) (Danube River Protection Convention).

[75] Convention on the Protection of the Rhine (adopted 12 April 1999, entered into force 1 January 2003) OJ L289/31 (2000) (Rhine River Protection Convention).

[76] See also, although it does not refer to the UNECE Water Convention, the Convention on the International Commission for the Protection of the River Oder against Pollution (adopted 11 April 1996, entered into force 14 January 2011) OJ L100/21 (1999).

[77] Convention on the Law of the Non-Navigational Uses of International Watercourse (adopted 21 May 1997, entered into force 17 August 2014) UNTS No 52106 (UN Watercourse Convention).

[78] *The Gabčikovo-Nagymaros Project* (Hungary v Slovakia) [1997] ICJ Rep 7, paras 78 and 85.

[79] On the status of this principle under current international law, see SC McCaffrey, 'The Contribution of the UN Convention on the Law of the Non-Navigational Uses of International Watercourses' (2001) *International Journal of Global Environmental Issues* 260; see also AE Utton, 'Which Rule Should Prevail in International Water Disputes: that of Reasonableness or that of No Harm?' (1996) *Natural Resources Journal* 635.

maritime route, special treaty regimes often apply.[80] For example, the 1888 Constantinople Convention was drawn up for the Suez Canal,[81] dug in the second half of the nineteenth century.[82] This treaty established an international and neutral status for the Suez Canal: it declared the canal open, both in time of peace as in time of war, for merchant ships and for ships of war without flag discrimination.[83] To safeguard this free passage, the canal was neutralised and demilitarised: no right of war, no act of hostility nor any act aiming at obstructing the free navigation of the canal that can prevent free shipping, may be committed in the canal, its ports and within a radius of three nautical miles from these ports.[84] Military fortifications may not be erected along the canal.[85]

The regime of the *Panama Canal*,[86] constructed between 1904 and 1914, was initially based on the so-called Hay-Bunau-Varilla Treaty[87] of 1903 between the US and Panama, which granted the US perpetual sovereign rights over the ten-mile ship canal across the isthmus of Panama. After gaining extensive experience and after many years of negotiation, on 7 September 1977 the US and Panama adopted two new treaties. The Panama Canal Treaty[88] replaced the earlier agreements and provided for a gradual takeover by Panama of the management and protection of the canal. The American rights in this area expired on 31 December 1999. The other treaty, the Treaty concerning the Permanent Neutrality and Operation of the Panama Canal,[89] placed the canal under a permanent neutrality regime, so that the canal remains open to the peaceful passage of ships, both in peace and in wartime – both merchant ships and ships of war – from all countries, without discrimination.[90]

The *Canal of Kiel*,[91] constructed at the end of the nineteenth century, connects the Baltic Sea with the North Sea over a distance of almost 99 km. Until 1919 its use was regulated solely by German legislation. The Treaty of Versailles[92] gave the canal an international status: although Germany retained sovereignty, the canal and its access roads were declared free and open to both merchant ships and ships of war, and Germany had to demilitarise the canal. In the *The SS 'Wimbledon'* case the PCIJ examined the scope of the relevant provisions of the Treaty of Versailles. It ruled that Germany had violated the Treaty by refusing passage to the British ship SS Wimbledon, on its way to Poland loaded with ammunition, in the framework of the Polish-Russian war of 1921 (in which Germany itself was neutral).[93] On 14 November 1936, Germany declared – without protests from most contracting parties – that it no longer recognised the relevant provisions of the treaty

[80] M Arcari, 'Canals' in MPEPIL.
[81] M Arcari, 'Suez Canal' in MPEPIL.
[82] Convention Respecting the Free Navigation of the Suez Maritime Canal (adopted 29 October 1888, entered into force 22 December 1888) (https://www.cvce.eu/en/obj/convention_respecting_the_free_navigation_of_the_suez_maritime_canal_constantinople_october_29_1888-en-35fba5fa-113a-4468-a6c9-efc467f13563.html) (1888 Constantinople Convention).
[83] Art I 1888 Constantinople Convention.
[84] Art IV 1888 Constantinople Convention.
[85] Art XI 1888 Constantinople Convention.
[86] M Arcari, 'Panama Canal' in MPEPIL.
[87] Convention for the Construction of a Ship Canal (adopted 18 November 1903, entered into force 26 February 1904) (http://avalon.law.yale.edu/20th_century/pan001.asp) (Hay-Bunau-Varilla Treaty).
[88] Panama Canal Treaty (adopted on 7 September 1977, entered into force 1 October 1979) UNTS No 21086.
[89] Treaty concerning the Permanent Neutrality and Operation of the Panama Canal (adopted on 7 September 1977, entered into force 1 October 1979) 1161 UNTS 177.
[90] Arts I and II Treaty concerning the Permanent Neutrality and Operation of the Panama Canal.
[91] R Lagoni, 'Kiel Canal' in MPEPIL.
[92] Above n 62.
[93] *The SS 'Wimbledon'* (United Kingdom, France, Italy, Japan v Germany) [1923] PCIJ Rep, Series A, No 1.

as binding. Today, the Canal of Kiel is under the authority and management of the Federal Republic of Germany.

B. Air Space

International air law, ie the set of international rules relating to the use of air by aviation, is a young branch of international law. With the first flight of Blériot on 25 July 1909 across the Channel from Calais to Dover, international aviation became a reality and the legal implications started to gain importance. Initially, most States were in favour of a liberal status of airspace, with the underlying State taking protective measures only to a limited extent. This liberal vision disappeared with the First World War, which for the first time involved air warfare.[94] Where the warring factions had only a very limited number of planes at the start of the war, which were used for reconnaissance, this number increased to tens of thousands of military aircrafts in 1918, often equipped with machine guns. In addition, the commercial possibilities of aviation emerged more and more clearly. In the 1919 Treaty of Paris European States determined that the airspace above a State falls within the latter's complete and exclusive sovereignty.[95] In 1928, American States concluded a similar agreement in Havana.[96] The separate development of international agreements for Europe and America proved to be outdated rather quickly. In 1927, Lindberg crossed the Atlantic: the intercontinental character of aviation was a reality.

With 192 State Parties, the 1944 Convention on International Civil Aviation or Chicago Convention,[97] which also established the Organization for International Civil Aviation (ICAO), has a quasi-universal status. In addition, the State Parties undertake to accept that the Convention will prevail over all existing obligations and agreements that are incompatible with its provisions, as well as not to enter into such obligations or agreements.[98] This feature and the universal character of the Convention mean that it can be seen as the cornerstone of international aviation law. A core provision of the Convention is Article 1: 'The contracting States recognize that every State has complete and exclusive sovereignty over the airspace above its territory'.

This principle deserves some clarification. The recognition of complete and exclusive sovereignty is not tautological, but indicates the exclusion of free passage through national airspace. Unlike the law of the sea (see Chapter 18), air law has no 'right of innocent overflight'. The absolute authority of the underlying State over its airspace implies that any unauthorised passage constitutes a violation of the sovereignty of this State and may give rise to interception.[99] The term 'recognise' indicates that the States already had sovereign rights before the entry into force of the Convention. In its *Nicaragua* judgment, the ICJ

[94] S Hobe, 'Airspace' in MPEPIL.

[95] Convention Relating to the Regulation of Aerial Navigation (with additional Protocol) (adopted 13 October 1919, entered into force 12 October 1919) 11 UNTS 173 (Treaty of Paris). In this respect reference is sometimes made to the Roman law maxim *'cuius est solum, eius est usque ad coelom et ad inferos'*: IHPh Diedericks-Verschoor and MA Butler, *An Introduction to Air Law*, 8th edn (Alphen aan den Rijn, Kluwer, 2006) 5.

[96] Pan-American Convention on Commercial Aviation (adopted 20 February 1928, entered into force 13 June 1929) 47 Stat 1901, Treaty Series 840 (Havana Convention).

[97] Convention on international civil aviation (adopted in Chicago on 7 December 1944, entered into force 30 April 1947, 'Chicago Convention') UNTS No 102.

[98] Art 82 Chicago Convention.

[99] L Tomas, 'Air Law' in MPEPIL and Shaw (n 52) 404.

confirmed that this provision, as well as Article 2 of the Chicago Convention, pursuant to which the territory also includes the territorial waters adjacent to it, 'merely respond to firmly established and longstanding tenets of customary international law'.[100] This explains why the sovereignty of '*any State*' is recognised, even of those – very few ones – which are not a party to the Convention.

As far as the geographical delineation of the airspace is concerned, a distinction can be made between horizontal and vertical delineation.[101] As regards the *horizontal* delimitation of the airspace, Article 1 of the Chicago Convention determines that sovereignty concerns airspace 'above its territory'. In conjunction with Article 2 this means that in addition to the terrestrial part, sovereignty also relates to the airspace above the territorial sea (which can be no more than 12 nautical miles wide: see Chapter 18). In the national airspace, the underlying State is free to arrange air traffic at its own discretion, with due observance of the international obligations it has entered into. Sovereignty, however, does not extend to other 'functional' maritime areas such as the contiguous zone and the exclusive economic zone.[102] By virtue of Article 58 of UNCLOS, States enjoy the same freedom to fly over the exclusive economic zone as over the high seas. Above the high seas, the provisions set by the ICAO under the Convention (Article 12) apply, while an aircraft above the territory and the territorial sea of an underlying State must comply with the regulations of the latter, which may differ from ICAO rules (Article 38). As far as the *vertical* delineation of the airspace is concerned, it should be noted that the highest rate for a conventional flight is around 40 km, while the lowest satellite rate is around 160 km. However, the Chicago Convention does not make any reference to the vertical demarcation of national airspace. Nevertheless, its importance is not to be underestimated. Whereas the passage of the national airspace is subject to the permission of the underlying State, the use of space is free and falls outside any sovereignty (see Chapter 18). Yet there is also a boundary here, albeit a functional one. International air law ceases to apply where aviation turns into space travel. In other words, only an aircraft that keeps itself in the air by using air resistance is covered by air law. Spacecraft are therefore not subject to the Chicago Convention.[103] Generally, the demarcation between airspace and outer space is currently put at 100 km above sea level.[104] It goes without saying that such a functional analysis is not easy to apply to less conventional devices. What to do with the so-called stratospheric platforms, ie structures that are placed 30 km above a fixed location on the surface of the earth and work on solar energy? According to the US Government, these platforms fall under the jurisdiction of the State above whose territory they are installed, and not under the Space Treaty.[105] It becomes even more complex with the space shuttle, which can best be described as a cross between an aircraft and a spacecraft. In a sense, a practice has emerged that allows the free overflight for spacecraft after its launch.[106]

[100] *Military and Paramilitary Activities in and against Nicaragua* (Nicaragua v United States of America) [1986] ICJ Rep 14, para 212.

[101] Hobe (n 94).

[102] ibid.

[103] See for further references, D Goedhuis, 'The problems of the frontiers of outer space and air space' (1982) 174 *Rec Cours* I 367.

[104] See further Chapter 18 section XII.

[105] See inter alia Hobe (n 94); R Ramírez de Arellano Gurría y Ramírez de Arellano, 'Stratospheric stations: do their operation cause sovereignty problems?' in *Proceedings of the 42th colloquium on the law of outer space* (1999) 118; M Rothblatt, 'Are stratospheric platforms in airspace or outer space?' (1996) *Journal of Space Law* 107.

[106] S Hobe, 'Preamble' in S Hobe, B Schmitt-Tedd and K-U Schrogl (eds), *Cologne Commentary on Space Law* (Cologne, Carl Heymans Verlag, 2009) 28 and S Hobe, 'Spacecraft, Satellites and Space Objects' in MPEPIL.

The fact that a State possesses full sovereignty over the airspace over its territory does not mean that it can act without any restriction against aircrafts entering its airspace without its consent. In most cases, airspace violations are merely reported, with or without diplomatic follow-up. In exceptional cases the interception of the aircraft is carried out, whereby there is a choice between enforcing a landing at a designated airport, imposing a flight path or returning it to the point of entry into the national airspace.[107] Yet sometimes weapons are also used when it comes to enforcing sovereignty in the own airspace. A distinction must be made here between State aircraft and civil aircraft.

There is no explicit prohibition on bringing down *State planes*, such as the shooting of a Russian warplane by Turkey in 2015. However, the State which is violated in its sovereignty may only intervene in proportion to the harmful nature of the infringement. Customary international law prohibits the aircraft from being exposed to unnecessary or unnecessarily great danger; this is the so-called 'flexible approach' of Lissitzyn.[108] Such actions are ultimately governed by the rules on the use of force.[109]

With regard to the shooting of *civil aircrafts* there is an explicit prohibition: Article 3*bis* of the Chicago Convention.[110] This article was inserted following the destruction of a South Korean Boeing 747 (flight KAL 007) by the Soviet air force on 31 August 1983.[111] All 269 occupants were killed. In Article 3*bis*, the contracting States recognise that each State must refrain from using arms against civil aircrafts in flight and that, in case of interception, the lives of persons on board and the safety of the aircraft must not be jeopardised. Although this provision entered into force only on 1 October 1998, the rule was already part of customary international law. This conclusion can at least be drawn from the condemnation by the UN Security Council of the shooting of two American Cessna planes above Cuban territory in 1996.[112] In the aftermath of the downing of Malaysia Arlines Flight MH17 in 2014, ICAO's Council reaffirmed Article 3*bis* and urged 'States to take all necessary measures to safeguard the safety of air navigation'.[113]

[107] Hobe (n 94) and AJ Williams, 'A crisis in aerial sovereignty? Considering the implications of recent military violations ofnational airspace' (2010) 42(1) *Area* 51. See T Ruys, *'Armed Attack' and Article 51 of the UN Charter* (Cambridge, CUP, 2010) 349 for examples of non-forcible measures a State is allowed to take under international law.

[108] See OJ Lissitzyn, 'The Treatment of Aerial Intruders in Recent Practice and International Law' (1953) 47 *AJIL* 559. See also J Sundberg, 'Legitimate Responses to Aerial Intruders: the View from a Neutral State' (1985) 10 *Annals of Air and Space Law* 251.

[109] See Chapter 14.

[110] Lissitzyn (n 108).

[111] See inter alia IHP Diederiks-Verschoor, *An Introduction to Air Law* (Alphen aan den Rijn, Kluwer, 2012) 28; GF FitzGerald, 'The Use of Force against Civil Aircraft: The Aftermath of the KAL Flight 007 Incident' (1984) 22 *Canadian YIL* 291; IL Jahn, 'Applying International Law to the Downing of Korean Air Lines Flight 007 on September 1, 1983' (1984) *GYIL* 444; M Kido, 'The Korean Airlines Incident on September 1, 1983 and Some Measures Following It' (1997) 62 *Journal of Air Law and Commerce* 1049; J-C Piris, 'De quelques controverses juridiques consécutives à la destruction du Boeing 747 de la KAL le 1er septembre 1983' (1986) 90 *RGDIP* 815; 'Legal Argumentation in International Crises: The Downing of Korean Air Lines Flight 007' (1984) 97 *Harv LR* 1198.

[112] Declaration by the President of the UN Security Council (27 February 1996) UN Doc S/PRST/1996/9: 'The Security Council recalls that according to international law, as reflected in Article 3bis [...] States must refrain from the use of weapons against civil aircraft in flight and must not endanger the lives of persons on board and the safety of aircraft. States are obliged to respect international law and human rights norms in all circumstances'.

[113] ICAO Council, 'Council Resolution on Malaysia Airlines Flight MH17, destroyed over Eastern Ukraine on 17 July 2014' (2014) https://www.icao.int/Newsroom/NewsDoc2014/COUNCIL%20RESOLUTION%20ON%20MALAYSIA%20AIRLINES%20FLIGHT%20MH17.pdf.

III. Nationality

Nationality is the legal relationship between an individual[114] and a State. This relationship is of fundamental importance to the status of the individual in international law: through his nationality, an individual enjoys the rights and protection granted to him by international law.[115] The relationship of nationality forms the basis of the right of entry and residence of the individual in his homeland and offers the latter the possibility to grant diplomatic protection to its subjects (see Chapter 12). The ICJ described nationality in the *Nottebohm* case (1955) as

> a legal bond having as its basis a social fact of attachment, a genuine connection of existence and sentiments, together with the existence of reciprocal rights and duties. It may be said to constitute a juridical expression of the fact that the individual upon whom it is conferred, either directly by the law or as a result of an act of the authorities, is in fact more closely connected with the population of the State conferring nationality than with that of any other State.[116]

Whereas individuals with one or more nationalities stand at one end of the spectrum, stateless persons stand at the other end. The latter are individuals who are not considered citizens or nations under the operation of the laws of any State.[117] Statelessness implies that no State protects them against unlawful treatment by another State. They also do not enjoy entry or residence rights in any country.[118] The international community has made various efforts to remedy statelessness, either by attempting to prevent it or by mitigating its effects. In the first category of efforts one can place the *European Convention on Nationality*,[119] which was adopted in 1997 within the Council of Europe.[120] This Convention entered into force on

[114] Also in relation to legal persons (eg companies, associations, etc), a 'nationality' is often referred to, whereby the criterion of the statutory or the real corporate seat is generally used. See inter alia O Beygo, 'Nationality of Corporations in International Claims Arising Out of Foreign Investment Disputes' (1993) 46 *Revue hellenique de droits internationales* 33; M Rahman, 'Determination of Nationality of Transnational Corporations (TNCs): a Functional Approach' (1988) 28 *Ind J Int L* 222; M Travers, 'La nationalité des sociétés commerciales' (1930) 33 *Rec Cours* III 1.

[115] H Arendt, *The Origins of Totalitarianism* (New York, Harcourt, Brace & Jovanovich, 1979) 298–99; O Dörr, 'Nationality' in MPEPIL and Oxman (n 21).

[116] *Nottebohm Case* (Liechtenstein v Guatemala) [1955] ICJ Rep 4, 23.

[117] Art 1(1) Convention relating to the Status of Stateless Persons (adopted 28 September 1954, entered into force 6 June 1960) 360 UNTS 117. For an elaborate explanation of the term 'stateless person', see UNHCR, 'Guidelines on Statelessness No 1: The definition of "Stateless Person" in Article 1(1) of the 1954 Convention relating to the Status of Stateless Persons', UN Doc No HCR/GS/12/01, 20 February 2012, paras 10–11.

[118] Dörr (n 113) and K Göcke, 'Stateless Persons' in MPEPIL.

[119] European Convention on Nationality (done in Strasbourg on 6 November 1997) ETS No 166. See inter alia GR de Groot, 'The European Convention on Nationality: a Step Towards a Ius Commune in the Field of Nationality Law' (2000) 7 *Maastricht Journal of European and Comparative Law* 117; S Hall, 'The European Convention on Nationality and the Right to Have Rights' (1999) 24 *European Law Review* 586; B Knocke, *Das europäische Übereinkommen über die Staatsangehörigkeit als Schranke für die Regelung des nationalen Staatsangehörigkeitsrechts: Stand der Vereinbarkeit des Staatsangehörigkeitsrechts der Schweiz, der Bundesrepublik Deutschland, des Vereinigten Königreichs und Frankreichs mit den Vorgaben des Übereinkommens* (Herdecke, GCA-Verlag, 2005); R Schärer, 'The European Convention on Nationality' (1998) 40 *German Yearbook of International Law* 438.

[120] See also Convention on the Reduction of Cases of Multiple Nationality and on Military Obligations in Cases of Multiple Nationality (adopted 6 May 1963, entered into force 28 March 1968) ETS No 43; Protocol amending the Convention on the Reduction of Cases of Multiple Nationality and Military Obligations in Cases of Multiple Nationality (adopted 24 November 1977, entered into force 8 September 1978) ETS No 95; and Additional Protocol to the Convention on the Reduction of Cases of Multiple Nationality and Military Obligations in Cases

1 March 2000 and is currently ratified or acceded to by 21 States. The Convention stipulates that a State may not deprive a national of its nationality if this would lead to statelessness, with a few minor exceptions.[121] Various legislators have also taken action at national level to prevent statelessness.

The Convention on the Status of Stateless Persons, done in New York on 28 September 1954, belongs to the category of treaties that grant a number of minimum rights to stateless persons.[122] However, the number of rights granted to such persons is limited and only 90 States are party to the Convention. It was supplemented by the 1961 Convention on the Reduction of Statelessness. 71 States are party to this Convention.[123]

The granting of nationality falls within the exclusive competence of the States, each of which may determine the criteria for granting their nationality.[124] Since the nineteenth century there are *grosso modo* two criteria that have been used to grant nationality: *jus sanguinis* and *jus soli*.[125] The *jus sanguinis* relies on kinship or parentage as the main criterion for the granting of nationality. It can be found in the legislation of most continental European States (eg Belgium, France and Germany). Yet, the same principle also is applied by many African and South-East Asian States. Under the *jus soli* principle, the birthplace of the child is decisive for determining the nationality. This tradition mainly occurs in the common law countries (US, UK) but equally in the majority of South American States.

Although each State may determine the conditions under which an individual obtains his or her nationality, there are limits to the international law of opposability of nationality allocation by States. In the *Nottebohm* case (1955), the ICJ ruled that, in order to be enforceable against third States, there must at least be an effective link between the State and its national.[126] This 'genuine link' (*lien effectif*) can be derived from factors such as the normal place of residence, the centre of interests, family ties or participation in public life.[127] In the *Nottebohm* case, the absence of such a tie led to the conclusion of the ICJ that Liechtenstein was not entitled to exercise diplomatic protection for Mr Nottebohm against Guatemala. It is unclear, however, whether the existence of a 'genuine link' with the State of nationality is indispensable to make the conferral of nationality opposable to third States.[128]

Finally, while under international law it is in principle for each State to lay down the conditions for the acquisition and loss of nationality, it is settled case law of the CJEU that, with respect to EU Member States, this competence must be exercised having due regard to EU law.[129] *Rottmann* concerned a decision by German authorities to withdraw from an Austrian citizen by birth the naturalisation into German nationality, which would

of Multiple Nationality (adopted 24 November 1977, entered into force 17 October 1983) ETS No 96. For the sake of completeness, it should be noted that there is another amendment protocol to this Convention, Second Protocol amending the Convention on the Reduction of Cases of Multiple Nationality and Military Obligations in Cases of Multiple Nationality (adopted 2 February 1977, entered into force 24 March 1995) ETS No 149, with only two State parties (Italy and the Netherlands – France withdrew in 2009).

[121] Art 7(3) European Convention on Nationality.

[122] Above n 117.

[123] Convention on the Reduction of Statelessness (adopted 30 August 1961, entered into force 13 December 1975) 989 UNTS 175.

[124] *Nationality Decrees in Tunis and Morocco* [1923] PCIJ, Series B, Advisory Opinion No 4; Dörr (n 115) and Shaw (n 52) 494.

[125] Dörr (n 115); Shaw (n 52) 495.

[126] Above n 116.

[127] ibid and Dörr (n 115).

[128] See Chapter 12 section V.B.

[129] See the judgments of 7 July 1992, *Micheletti and others*, C-369/90, EU:C:1992:295, para 10; of 11 November 1999, *Mesbah*, C-179/98, EU:C:1999:549, para 29; of 20 February 2001, *Kaur*, C-192/99, EU:C:2001:106, para 19; of 19 October 2004, *Zhu and Chen*, C-200/02, EU:C:2004:639, para 37, and of 2 March 2010, *Rottmann*, C-135/08,

have had as a likely consequence that Mr Rottmann would have lost both nationalities (the initial German naturalisation having caused him to lose his Austrian nationality) and become a stateless person. Notably, the Court held that when a Member State's competence with respect to nationality is exercised in respect of a Union citizen and affects the rights conferred and protected by the legal order of the Union, it is subject to judicial review carried out in the light of EU law. Nevertheless, in the case at issue, the Court concluded that it is not contrary to EU law for a Member State to withdraw from a citizen of the Union the nationality of that State acquired by naturalisation when that nationality has been obtained by deception, on condition that the decision to withdraw observes the principle of proportionality.[130]

IV. Principles of Prescriptive Criminal Jurisdiction

The international law of jurisdiction has developed largely with respect to assertions of criminal jurisdiction. Such assertions bring the State's authority most starkly into relief, and entail the biggest potential for interference in other States' sovereignty and, hence, international tensions. In *Lotus*, the PCIJ rather categorically ruled that States are not allowed to exercise their criminal enforcement jurisdiction abroad.[131] Few would indeed doubt that extraterritorial law enforcement violates the territorial State's sovereignty, as it entails the forces of one State physically entering the territory of another State without the latter's consent.

From a sovereignty perspective, extraterritorial *prescriptive* jurisdiction appears less problematic: when a State simply enacts laws that apply to foreign activity, it does not physically enforce its laws on foreign territory. Such laws only provide that, under certain circumstances, persons who have committed crimes abroad can be prosecuted before the domestic courts of the State concerned. Nevertheless, by regulating activities that take place on another State's territory, a State may displace local regulatory choices and thus meddle in the latter's domestic affairs. Fear of foreign prosecution or lawsuits may impel individuals and corporations to conduct themselves in a manner that is not required, and sometimes even not allowed under domestic law. Extraterritorial prescriptive jurisdiction can also give rise to fierce international conflict, notably where one State subjects foreign officials to its laws in respect of foreign activity, as the backlash against assertions of universal jurisdiction has shown (see below, Section IV(B)(v)(b)). The controversial character of extraterritorial jurisdiction explains why States ordinarily apply their laws only to criminal acts that occurred within their own territory, and only rarely to acts that occurred outside of it.

Most domestic criminal codes, including those of many European States, thus affirm territorial jurisdiction as the norm, and extraterritorial jurisdiction as the exception.[132] The principles of extraterritorial jurisdiction are, like territoriality, based on a nexus with the

EU:C:2010:104, para 45. See also the Opinion of AG Szpunar in *Rendón Marín and CS*, C-165/14 and C-304/14, EU:C:2016:75, point 113, and the Opinion of AG Bot in *Lounes*, C-165/16, EU:C:2017:407, point 40.

[130] Rottmann (n 129), paras 39–59.

[131] *Lotus* (n 9) 18–19.

[132] See eg in Europe: Art 113-2 of the French Code Penal; Art 2 of the Dutch Penal Code; para 3 of the German Strafgesetzbuch (StGB); Arts 3–4 of the Belgian Penal Code.

State, such as the nationality of the perpetrator (active personality principle) or the victim (passive personality principle), or the State's political independence (protective or security principle). Only exceptionally, with respect to particularly grave crimes, does international law allow or even oblige States to establish jurisdiction absent any particular nexus (universal jurisdiction).

A. The *Lotus* Case

The PCIJ and ICJ have only on rare occasions addressed questions of prescriptive jurisdiction. The leading case remains the PCIJ's 1927 *Lotus* judgment. The question at issue in *Lotus* was whether the flag State of a vessel colliding with another vessel on the high seas had exclusive criminal jurisdiction over the case. At that time, the rule of exclusive flag State jurisdiction had not yet fully crystallised.[133] Accordingly, the Court refrained from affirming it. But as the case concerned jurisdiction on the high seas, the PCIJ could have limited itself to addressing this specific issue. Nevertheless, in a famous dictum, it laid down a general rule pursuant to which a State's exercise of jurisdiction is presumptively lawful, absent proof that such exercise is prohibited by a norm of international law:

> It does not, however, follow that international law prohibits a State from exercising jurisdiction in its own territory, in respect of any case which relates to acts which have taken place abroad, and in which it cannot rely on some permissive rule of international law. Such a view would only be tenable if international law contained a general prohibition to States to extend the application of their laws and the jurisdiction of their courts to persons, property and acts outside their territory, and if, as an exception to this general prohibition, it allowed States to do so in certain specific cases. But this is certainly not the case under international law as it stands at present. Far from laying down a general prohibition to the effect that States may not extend the application of their laws and the jurisdiction of their courts to persons, property and acts outside their territory, it leaves them in this respect a wide measure of discretion which is only limited in certain cases by prohibitive rules; as regards other cases, every State remains free to adopt the principles which it regards as best and most suitable.[134]

The Court's dictum that what is not prohibited is allowed has also echoed beyond the law of jurisdiction. For instance, the ICJ's view that Kosovo's unilateral declaration of independence was lawful, as there was no rule of international law prohibiting it,[135] is informed by the same idea.

B. The Permissive Principles of Jurisdiction

In the years since *Lotus*, the liberal rule of jurisdiction gradually lost its force. It was perceived that *Lotus* may not have reflected existing law, and drew upon a discredited

[133] Since 1958, when the first law of the sea conventions were adopted, the rule of exclusive flag State jurisdiction has clearly been established. See Art 11 UNCLOS: 'In the event of a collision or any other incident of navigation concerning a ship on the high seas, involving the penal or disciplinary responsibility of the master or of any other person in the service of the ship, no penal or disciplinary proceedings may be instituted against such person except before the judicial or administrative authorities either of the flag State or of the State of which such person is a national'.

[134] *Lotus* (n 9) 18–19.

[135] *Accordance with International Law of the Unilateral Declaration of Independence in Respect of Kosovo* [2010] ICJ Rep 403, Declaration of Judge Simma, para 2.

positivist international law paradigm that considered State sovereignty as superior to the law, rather than based on, or restricted by the law.[136] In 1935, scholars at Harvard University drew up a Draft Convention on Jurisdiction with Respect to Crime, which abandoned the jurisdictional freedom of *Lotus*, set forth territoriality as the basic principle of jurisdiction, and elaborated a limited number of principles of extraterritorial jurisdiction as the exception.[137] In this conception of jurisdiction, the lawfulness of a jurisdictional assertion depends on the existence of a permissive principle that allows the State to exercise jurisdiction, being the principle of territoriality, nationality, security or universality.

By and large, States have followed the permissive principles approach when justifying a jurisdictional assertion. However, the jurisdictional principles, and that of territoriality in particular, have been construed broadly. It suffices that one constituent element of a crime has materialised on a State's territory for territorial jurisdiction to be legitimately established.[138] Where this constituent element relates to the initiation of the crime (eg the firing of a gun), a State can exercise subjective territorial jurisdiction. Where it relates to the completion of the crime (eg the bullet striking the victim), a State can exercise objective territorial jurisdiction. In economic law, a variation of the objective territoriality principle considers that even the mere adverse *effects* that materialise on a State's territory but originate from extraterritorial conduct are sufficient to ground territorial jurisdiction.[139] In the contemporary, densely interconnected world, a wholesale application of the effects doctrine that, for example, extends to harmful cyber-activity, risks allowing almost every State to exercise jurisdiction. The upshot of a broad interpretation of the permissive principles is that States enjoy considerable latitude to exercise jurisdiction as they please, as long as they can identify some nexus under one of the principles. Accordingly, in terms of their practical consequences, somewhat ironically perhaps, the permissive principles may yield results that are not very different from those of the *Lotus* approach.

Most States recognise the following grounds of extraterritorial jurisdiction, subject to a number of restrictive conditions: active personality or nationality; passive personality or nationality; protection or security; representation and universality.

i. The Active Personality Principle

The active personality or nationality principle allows States to exercise jurisdiction over crimes committed by their nationals abroad.[140] This ground serves as the natural counterpart of States' reluctance to extradite their own nationals.[141] In order to see justice done

[136] A Mills, 'Rethinking Jurisdiction in International Law' (2014) 84 *BYIL* 187, 190–91.

[137] Harvard Research on International Law, 'Draft Convention on Jurisdiction with Respect to Crime' (1935) 29 *AJIL* 439.

[138] For an analysis of how some European States have applied the principle of territoriality based on the constituent elements approach or 'ubiquity theory', see C Ryngaert, 'Territorial Jurisdiction over Cross-Frontier Offences: Revisiting a Classic Problem of International Criminal Law' (2009) 9 *International Criminal Law Review* 187.

[139] For the US, see Court of Appeals for the Second Circuit (US), *United States v Aluminium Corp of America*, 148 F2d 416 (1945). Europe is somewhat more reluctant to recognise this effects doctrine. In cartel matters, the CJEU has required that the foreign cartel be *implemented* on the territory of the EU (judgment of 31 March 1993, *Ahlström Osakeyhtiö and others v Commission ('Wood Pulp')*, C-89/85, C-104/85, C-114/85, C-116/85, C-117/85 and C-125/85 to C-129/85, EU:C:1993:120). With respect to merger control, the Court has satisfied itself with territorial *effects* being established (judgment of 25 March 1999, *Gencor v Commission*, T-102/96, EU:T:1999:65).

[140] See eg Art 5 Dutch Penal Code; Art 113-6 French Criminal Code; Section 7(2)1 German Criminal Code; Art 9(1) and (2) Romanian Criminal Code.

[141] See eg Arts 1 and 3 of the Treaty between the United Kingdom of Great Britain and Ireland and the Argentine Republic for the Mutual Extradition of Fugitive Criminals (adopted and entered into force 22 May 1889);

and to prevent these persons from wreaking havoc outside their State's territory, jurisdiction based on nationality had to be established. The exercise of active personality-based jurisdiction may be circumscribed by the requirement that the crime be serious, or that the crime be criminalised in both the territorial and the forum State (ie the principle of 'double criminality'), but it is doubtful whether this is required by international law.

ii. The Passive Personality Principle

The passive personality principle, which allows States to exercise jurisdiction over crimes committed *against* their nationals abroad is more controversial than the active personality principle. It subjects persons to foreign criminal law without having known this before committing the act.[142] It is typically used for serious crimes. Various anti-terrorism conventions and the UN Torture Convention list it as an acceptable ground of jurisdiction.[143] Also domestic penal codes may contain a general grant of passive personality-based jurisdiction over all serious crimes.[144] The active or passive personality principle is sometimes extended to include permanent residents.[145]

iii. The Protective Principle

The protective principle allows States to exercise jurisdiction over crimes committed against the security of the State or its political independence. Examples of crimes giving rise to such jurisdiction are plots to overthrow the State's government or counterfeiting the State's currency.[146] Although not widely used, the protective principle is an uncontroversial ground of jurisdiction that is codified in most penal codes.[147]

iv. The Representation Principle

A few European States allow for the exercise of representational or vicarious jurisdiction, that is extraterritorial jurisdiction over offences committed abroad where extradition is impossible for reasons not related to the nature of the crime. When States exercise such jurisdiction, they can be considered to 'represent' the territorial State, although they will apply their own criminal laws.[148]

Art 6(1)(a) of the European Convention on Extradition (adopted 13 December 1957, entered into force 18 April 1960) CETS No 24.

[142] See eg GR Watson, 'Offenders Abroad: A Case for Nationality-Based Criminal Jurisdiction' (1992) 17 *Yale Journal of International Law* 41, 79.

[143] Art 5(1)(c) of the UN Convention against Torture. See also Art 4(b) of the Convention of Offences and Certain Other Acts Committed on Board Aircraft (adopted 14 September 1963, entered into force 4 December 1969) 704 UNTS 219; Art 6(2)(b) of the Convention for the Suppression of Unlawful Acts Against the Safety of Maritime Navigation (adopted 10 March 1988, entered into force 1 March 1992) 1678 UNTS 221.

[144] See eg Art 10(5) Preliminary Title Belgian Code of Criminal Procedure; Art 113-7 French Criminal Code; Section 7(1) German Criminal Code; Article 10(1) Romanian Criminal Code.

[145] For an example with respect to the active personality principle, see eg Arts 6–7 Preliminary Title Belgian Code of Criminal Procedure.

[146] For the latter, see eg Art 10(2) and (3) Preliminary Title Belgian Code of Criminal Procedure.

[147] For a classic continental European perspective, see HFA Donnedieu de Vabres, *Les principes modernes du droit pénal international* (Paris, Recueil Sirey, 1928) 87. See currently Section 5 of the German Criminal Code; Art 10(2) and (3) Preliminary Title Belgian Code of Criminal Procedure.

[148] See eg Art 113-8-1 French Criminal Code; Section 7(2)2° German Criminal Code. The principle requires that the foreign criminal norm be 'identical' to the domestic criminal norm for the latter to be legitimately applied.

v. The Universality Principle

The most controversial ground of jurisdiction is the universality principle. Unlike the other grounds of jurisdiction, universal jurisdiction is exercised without the asserting State having a nexus with the crime;[149] such jurisdiction is based on the *gravity* of the crime alone. The exercise of such jurisdiction may run counter to the principle of non-intervention, as it allows any State to exercise jurisdiction over crimes committed on the territory of another State. However, where States have signed and ratified treaties that provide for some form of universal jurisdiction over certain crimes, the principle loses its force, as the ratifying States may be considered to have consented a priori to the exercise of universal jurisdiction.[150]

a. Crimes Amenable to Universal Jurisdiction

A considerable number of other crimes are amenable to universal jurisdiction, on the basis of either treaty law or customary international law. Treaty-based universal jurisdiction often flows from an *aut dedere aut judicare* clause, which requires that States Parties either extradite the offender, or prosecute him or her on the basis of universal jurisdiction. Usually, the *aut dedere aut judicare* clause is made conditional upon the requirement that the State concerned is the *forum deprehensionis*, ie provided that the suspect can be found on its territory. Examples of such clauses can be found in the 1949 Geneva Conventions,[151] the UN Convention against Torture,[152] the Enforced Disappearance Convention[153] and a number of counter-terrorism conventions, including the Council of Europe Convention on the Prevention of Terrorism.[154] Crimes that are amenable to universal jurisdiction under customary international law include the crime of genocide,[155] crimes against humanity,[156] war crimes[157] and sexual offences committed against minors.[158]

The identity requirement also extends to the amenability to prosecution, which implies for instance that a person who has been amnestied abroad is not subject to prosecution in Germany under the representation principle. See A Eser, 'Grundlagen und Grenzen "stellvertretender Strafrechtspflege": (para 7 Abs 2 Nr 2 StGB)' (1993) 48 *JuristenZeitung* 875 (with case examples).

[149] See eg Federal Criminal Court (CH), *A v Ministère Public de la Confédération, B and C*, 25 July 2012, Case No BB.2011.140, para 3.3 (holding that 'l'argument du recourant quant à l'exigence de prendre en considération l'existence d'un lien étroit en vertu du droit coutumier [concerning the exercise of jurisdiction over war crimes] tombe à faux').

[150] ibid, para. 3.5.

[151] Arts 49 GC I; Art 50 GC II; Art 129 GC III; Art 146 GC IV.

[152] Art 5(2) Convention against Torture.

[153] Art 9(2) Enforced Disappearance Convention.

[154] Art 14(3) Council of Europe Convention on the Prevention of Terrorism (adopted 16 May 2005, entered into force 1 June 2007) CETS No 196.

[155] Federal Constitutional Court (DE), *Jorgić*, 12 December 2000, 2 BvR 1290/99 ('Genocide is, as the most severe violation of human rights, […] the classic case for application of universal jurisdiction, the purpose of which is to make possible the most thorough prosecution of crimes perpetrated against the especially important legal interests of the international community of states'). The Genocide Convention itself does not provide for universal jurisdiction.

[156] Eg *Eichmann* (n 11) 304; High Court (AU), *Polyukhovich v The Commonwealth* [1991] HCA 32, Judge Toohey J, para 35; Tribunal of First Instance Brussels (BE), *Aguilar Diaz et al v Pinochet*, 6 November 1998, *Journal des Tribunaux* No 5924 – 1999/16, 308.

[157] J-M Henckaerts and L Doswald-Beck, *Customary International Humanitarian Law* (Cambridge, ICRC/CUP, 2005) 604, Rule 157: 'States have the right to vest universal jurisdiction in their national courts over war crimes'.

[158] UNGA, Sixth Committee, 'The Scope and Application of the Principle of Universal Jurisdiction (Agenda Item 86)', 65th session, 2010, Observations by Belgium on the scope and application of the principle of universal jurisdiction, para 16.

b. The Exercise of Universal Jurisdiction

Universal jurisdiction has been exercised most actively by European courts, particularly in Belgium, Spain,[159] the Netherlands,[160] and Germany.[161] This activism has been spurred by a combination of different factors, such as the availability of civil party petition, the presence of large communities of victims in Europe, and the zeal of prosecutors and investigating judges. One European State, Belgium, has even taken another State, Senegal, to the ICJ on the grounds that Senegal failed to either extradite (to Belgium, where he would be tried under the universality principle) or prosecute Hissène Habré, the former Head of State of Chad, for crimes of torture, in violation of its obligations under the UN Convention against Torture.[162] After the ICJ held that Senegal had indeed violated the Convention, Senegal set up Extraordinary Chambers in its domestic courts, which tried and convicted Habré on the basis of the universality principle.[163] Outside Europe, prosecutions on the basis of universality have also been reported in South Africa[164] and Argentina.[165] In the United States, federal courts have exercised universal jurisdiction in *civil* (tort) cases under the Alien Tort Claims Act (ATCA),[166] as well as the Torture Victim Protection Act.[167] In such cases, victims attempt to obtain damages from the perpetrator rather than a criminal conviction. In this regard, the ECtHR ruled that Article 3 of the ECHR does not oblige States to exercise – or establish, for that matter – universal civil jurisdiction over torture.[168] However, 'given the dynamic nature of this area, the Court [did] not rule out the possibility of developments in the future'.[169]

[159] See below (n 170) for the relevant statutes and evolutions in Belgium and Spain.

[160] Act of 19 June 2003 containing rules concerning serious violations of international humanitarian law (International Crimes Act), *Dutch Official Gazette ('Staatsblad')* No 270 of 3 July 2003.

[161] Act to Introduce the Code of Crimes against International Law of 26 June 2002 (Code of Crimes against International Law), *Federal Gazette ('Bundesgesetzblatt')* 2002, Part I, No 42, 29 June 2002, 2254–60. As of 2016 only two persons had been convicted on the basis of this Code. For a discussion of the Code's potential to bring justice for the atrocities committed in Syria, see P Kroker and AL Kather, 'Justice for Syria? Opportunities and Limitations of Universal Jurisdiction Trials in Germany', *EJIL: Talk!*, 12 August 2016, ejiltalk.org/justice-for-syria-opportunities-and-limitations-of-universal-jurisdiction-trials-in-germany/, calling on German prosecutors to charge individuals involved in the Syrian civil war not only with terrorism, but also with war crimes.

[162] *Questions relating to the Obligation to Prosecute or Extradite* (Belgium v Senegal) [2012] ICJ Rep 422. For the Senegalese Supreme Court's decision on the absence of jurisdiction for Senegalese courts, see Court of Cassation (SN), *Habré (Hissène) v Guengueng (Souleymane) and others*, 20 March 2001, Cassation No 14, (2002) AHRLR 183 (SeCC 2001).

[163] Extraordinary African Chambers (SN), *Ministère Public v Hissein Habré*, 30 May 2016.

[164] Constitutional Court South Africa (ZA), *National Commissioner of The South African Police Service v Southern African Human Rights Litigation Centre and Another*, 30 October 2014, Case No CCT 02/14 [2014] ZACC 30, para 40, ruling that South Africa is required 'to exercise universal jurisdiction in relation to [international] crimes as they offend against the human conscience and our international and domestic law obligations'.

[165] 'Argentina judge asks Spain to extradite 20 Franco-era officials', *Jurist*, 3 November 2014, jurist.org/paperchase/2014/11/argentina-judge-asks-spain-to-extradite-20-franco-era-spanish-officials.php. Argentina is particularly interested in the prosecution of crimes committed during the Franco dictatorship in Spain; under a Spanish amnesty law, such crimes cannot be prosecuted in Spain.

[166] See US Alien Tort Statute (28 USC § 1350), also known as the Alien Tort Claims Act (ATCA): 'The district courts shall have original jurisdiction of any civil action by an alien for a tort only, committed in violation of the law of nations or a treaty of the United States'. For an application, see eg Supreme Court (US), *Sosa v Alvarez-Machain*, 542 US 692 (2004). However, options under the Act have been seriously circumscribed since the Supreme Court's judgment in *Kiobel v Royal Dutch Petroleum Co*, 133 S Ct 1659 (2013). See further below, Section V(F).

[167] Public Law No 102-256, 12 March 1992, 106 Stat 73; providing for civil remedies over torture and extrajudicial killing. Unlike the ATCA, the Torture Victim Protection Act, at Section 2(b), requires exhaustion of internal remedies in the territorial State. In Supreme Court (US), *Mohamad v Palestinian Authority*, 132 S Ct 1702, 1705 (2012) the Court held that the Act only applied to natural persons (individuals).

[168] *Naït-Liman v Switzerland* App no 51357/07 (ECtHR, 15 March 2018) paras 187–88 and 198.

[169] ibid, para 220.

European activism regarding universal criminal jurisdiction has led to a diplomatic backlash. As prosecutors started to exercise jurisdiction over (current or former) high-ranking State officials, even in their absence (universal jurisdiction *in absentia*), and private plaintiffs, encouraged by NGOs, had the right to initiate proceedings, this resulted in a push against universal jurisdiction. Sustained foreign pressure led Belgium (2003) and Spain (2009, 2014) to restrict the scope of their universality laws and require a nexus.[170] Even after these restrictions, the exercise of universal jurisdiction, or rather the modalities of its application, have remained controversial, with notably the African Union (AU) leading the charge.[171]

In spite of these evolutions, research has shown that, in the wake of the implementation of the Statute of the ICC, more States have incorporated the universality principle in their legislation as far as core crimes are concerned. Moreover, the number of prosecutions based on the universality principle has not decreased.[172] However, most prosecutions are brought against lower-ranking perpetrators who have voluntarily fled their own State, amongst whom former Nazis and those who committed crimes in the former Yugoslavia or Rwanda. States subject these persons to universal jurisdiction to deny them a safe haven. There has been very little protest against such prosecutions. But overall, States remain rather reluctant to act as 'global enforcers' of international law, as they fear to upset foreign nations and waste scarce resources.[173]

c. The Modalities of the Exercise of Universal Jurisdiction

As a result of controversies over the scope of universal jurisdiction, the exact modalities and limitations of the exercise of the universality principle remain somewhat unclear. It is not fully settled yet whether States should exercise universal jurisdiction only on a subsidiary basis; that is, only provided that the territorial or national State is unable or unwilling to prosecute the suspect. Nor is it clear whether universal jurisdiction can be exercised *in absentia*; that is, in the absence of the suspect on the territory. In her dissenting opinion in the *Arrest Warrant* case, Judge Van den Wyngaert defended the lawfulness of the exercise of such jurisdiction.[174] Still, most domestic statutes and courts in Europe do require the presence of the offender.[175] In principle, transitory presence may suffice. This may also

[170] For Belgium: Grave Breaches of International Humanitarian Law Act of 5 August 2003, *Belgian Official Gazette ('Belgisch Staatsblad')* of 7 August 2003, requiring Belgian nationality or residence of the perpetrator or the victim; for Spain: Ley Orgánica 1/2009, de 3 de noviembre complementaria de la Ley de reforma de la legislación procesal para la implantación de la nueva Oficina judicial, por la que se modifica la Ley Orgánica 6/1985, de 1 de julio, del Poder Judicial, *Spanish Official Gazette ('Boletín Oficial Del Estado')* No 266 of 4 November 2009, 92089, requiring Spanish nationality of the victim, amended by Ley Orgánica 1/2014, de 13 marzo, de modificación de la Ley Orgánica 6/1985, de 1 de julio, del Poder Judicial, relativa a la justicia universal, *Spanish Official Gazette* No 63 of 14 March 2014, 23026, also requiring Spanish nationality of the perpetrator.

[171] For the African Union, see Assembly of the African Union, 'Decision on the Report of the Commission on the Abuse of the Principle of Universal Jurisdiction', Decision No Assembly/AU/Dec.199 (XI), AU Doc Assembly/AU/14 (XI), 30 June–1 July 2008, para 5 and paras ii and iii.

[172] M Langer, 'The Diplomacy of Universal Jurisdiction: The Political Branches and the Transnational Prosecution of International Crimes' (2011) 105 *AJIL* 1.

[173] On the distinction between the 'no safe haven' and the 'global enforcer' model of universal jurisdiction, see M Langer, 'Universal Jurisdiction is Not Disappearing: The Shift from "Global Enforcer" to "No Safe Haven" Universal Jurisdiction' (2015) 13 *JICJ* 245.

[174] *Arrest Warrant of 11 April 2000* (Democratic Republic of Congo *v* Belgium) [2002] ICJ Rep 3, Dissenting Opinion of Judge ad hoc Van den Wyngaert, paras 58 and 62.

[175] See eg Section 2(1)(a) Dutch International Crimes Act (n 160); Art 264(m) Swiss Criminal Code.

imply that a suspect can be brought to justice even if he or she could no longer be found on the territory, provided that he or she was present at the moment the proceedings were initiated.[176] But then, during the person's stay in the territory, the authorities may not have been able to identify the person as a suspect, which is precisely the trigger for the exercise of universal jurisdiction.[177] Neither is it clear whether prosecutors should refrain from exercising universal jurisdiction in the face of local political or transitional justice processes that may defer or exclude criminal prosecution (eg amnesties).

d. Universal Jurisdiction over Piracy

Universal jurisdiction does not only apply to violations of the interests of humanity: it also extends to crimes that threaten the joint interests of States, such as terrorist acts or acts of piracy. In fact, piracy is the oldest crime over which States are allowed to exercise universal jurisdiction. Currently, UNCLOS provides for universal jurisdiction over piracy:

> On the high seas, or in any place outside the jurisdiction of any State, every State may seize a pirate ship or aircraft, or a ship or aircraft taken by piracy and under the control of pirates, and arrest the persons and seize the property on board. The courts of the State which carried out the seizure may decide upon the penalties to be imposed, and may also determine the action to be taken with regard to the ships, aircraft or property, subject to the rights of third parties acting in good faith.[178]

This article has taken on increased significance since Somali pirates became active off the Horn of Africa in the 2000s, in the context of the Somali government's continued failure to establish control over its territory. In the face of these piracy activities, which threatened to disrupt international maritime traffic, the UN Security Council adopted various resolutions, which, among other things, allowed anti-piracy operations in Somalia's territorial sea and even allowed the taking of measures on Somali territory for the purpose of suppressing acts of piracy and armed robbery at sea.[179]

A number of States and international organisations heeded the UNSC's call for a coordinated response to the piracy threat, including the EU, which established military operation 'Atalanta' pursuant to EU Joint Action 2008/851/CSFP.[180] The competent authorities of an EU ship that takes pirates captive could bring these pirates to justice under the universality principle. However, mindful of the political realities – prosecutors are often not particularly interested in initiating criminal proceedings against foreign pirates in light of limited resources and uncertainties regarding *refoulement* of the pirate after serving the sentence – the EU Joint Action contemplates the transfer by flag State authorities who cannot or do not wish to exercise their jurisdiction of arrested persons to 'a Member

[176] Court of Cassation (BE), *FE alias NY v DS*, 18 September 2007, Case No P.07.0571.N; *A v Ministère Public de la Confédération, B and C* (n 149) para 3.1.

[177] See Hague Court of Appeal (NL), *Al Shami v Ayalon*, 26 October 2009, ECLI:NL:GHSGR:2009:BK1478, paras 12(b)–16.

[178] Art 105 UNCLOS.

[179] See in particular UNSC Res 1815, 2 June 2008, UN Doc S/RES/1815. For a broader discussion of the international community's anti-piracy measures, see T Treves, 'Piracy, Law of the Sea, and Use of Force: Developments off the Coast of Somalia' (2009) 20 *EJIL* 399.

[180] Council Joint Action 2008/851/CFSP of 10 November 2008 on a European Union military operation to contribute to the deterrence, prevention and repression of acts of piracy and armed robbery off the Somali coast [2008] OJ L301/33. See also Chapter 14, Section VI(C).

State or any third State which wishes to exercise its jurisdiction over the aforementioned persons'.[181] In 2009 the EU entered into an Exchange of Letters with Kenya concerning the transfer of suspected persons to Kenyan authorities, and provided for *non-refoulement* in case of inadequate human rights protection of the captured pirates.[182] The Exchange of Letters guarantees human rights and due process, including a provision that no such transferred person will be subjected to the death penalty. The agreement gives rise to a number of questions under international law regarding the legality of third party prosecution of piracy, since Article 105 UNCLOS authorises the prosecution of piracy by a capturing State.[183]

V. The Exercise of Jurisdiction Outside the Criminal Law Context

The law of jurisdiction has developed for the most part with respect to assertions of criminal law by States. States, as well as organisations on which States have conferred legislative competences – notably the EU – could, however, also resort to non-penal measures to regulate foreign activities which they consider to be harmful. Such assertions of jurisdiction are likewise subject to the international rules of jurisdiction. In this Section, extraterritorial action with respect to competition law, environmental law, fisheries law/the law of the sea, data protection, economic sanctions, and civil/tort matters will be discussed.

A. Competition Law[184]

The United States was the first State to apply its antitrust (competition) laws to foreign conspiracies adversely affecting its markets. In the *Alcoa* case (1945), the US Court of Appeal for the Second Circuit famously held that 'it is settled law [...] that any state may impose liabilities, even upon persons not within its allegiance, for conduct outside its borders that has consequences within its borders which the state reprehends; and these liabilities other states will ordinarily recognize'.[185] In Europe, the validity of this 'effects doctrine'

[181] ibid, Art 12(1).

[182] Council Decision 2009/293/CFSP of 26 February 2009 concerning the Exchange of Letters between the European Union and the Government of Kenya on the conditions and modalities for the transfer of persons suspected of having committed acts of piracy and detained by the European Union-led naval force (EUNAVFOR), and seized property in the possession of EUNAVFOR, from EUNAVFOR to Kenya and for their treatment after such transfer [2009] OJ L79/49.

[183] See E Kontorovich, 'Introductory Note to Exchange of Letters between the European Union and the Government of Kenya on the Conditions and Modalities for the Transfer of Persons Suspected of Having Committed Acts of Piracy' (2009) 48 *ILM* 747. See also Chapter 18, Section V(E)(i)(a) on jurisdiction over piracy on the high seas.

[184] For an extensive discussion, see C Ryngaert, *Jurisdiction over Antitrust Violations in International Law* (Antwerp, Intersentia, 2008).

[185] *United States v Aluminium Corp of America* (n 139). For later landmark international antitrust cases, see Court of Appeals for the Ninth Circuit (US), *Timberlane Lumber Co v Bank of America ('Timberlane')*, 27 December 1976, 549 F2d 597, introducing an interest-balancing test to mitigate the impact of the effects doctrine; Supreme Court (US), *Hartford Fire Insurance v California*, 509 US 764 (1993), limiting the *Timberlane* interest-balancing

in competition law, which may be considered as a modality of the territoriality principle (see above, Section IV(B)), was confirmed by the German Federal Court of Justice (*Bundesgerichtshof*) in the 1973 *Ölfeldrohre* case.[186] The CJEU did not recognise the effects doctrine in the 1988 *Wood Pulp* case, only holding an 'implementation doctrine' to be lawful under public international law:

> If the applicability of prohibitions laid down under competition law were made to depend on the place where the agreement, decision or concerted practice was formed, the result would obviously be to give undertakings an easy means of evading those prohibitions. The decisive factor is therefore the place where it is implemented.
>
> The producers in this case implemented their pricing agreement within the common market. It is immaterial in that respect whether or not they had recourse to subsidiaries, agents, sub-agents, or branches within the Community in order to make their contacts with purchasers within the Community.
>
> Accordingly the Community's jurisdiction to apply its competition rules to such conduct is covered by the territoriality principle as universally recognized in public international law.[187]

It is not fully clear how the implementation doctrine differs from the effects doctrine in practical terms. Possibly, producers' decisions *not* to sell products in the EU may fail to be 'implemented' in the EU, while still causing effects there. That being said, the Commission has endorsed the effects doctrine in cartel matters. In its 2004 Guidelines on the effect on trade concept, it stipulated that

> Articles 81 and 82 [the provisions of the former EC Treaty that prohibited cartels] apply irrespective of where the undertakings are located or where the agreement has been concluded, provided that the agreement or practice is either implemented inside the Community, or produce effects inside the Community.[188]

The effects doctrine has less ambiguously been confirmed with respect to European merger control. In the *Gencor* case (1999), the Court of First Instance (now General Court), held that '[a]pplication of the [EC Merger Control] Regulation is justified under public international law when it is foreseeable that a proposed concentration will have an immediate and substantial effect in the Community'.[189] It went on to find that, in that case, a concentration between two South African platinum mining companies caused immediate, substantial and foreseeable effects within the then European Community, and that, accordingly, the Commission was entitled to block it. An Austrian court has also applied the effects doctrine to a proposed merger, coming to a negative conclusion. It decided that the application of domestic merger control legislation to the purchase by one company of two other companies was precluded by the general rule of international law limiting jurisdiction to cases where a purchase had a direct or immediate effect on the domestic market, while the acquisitions at hand could only have an indirect effect.[190]

test to 'true conflicts' between US law and foreign law; Supreme Court (US), *F Hoffman-La Roche Ltd et al v Empagran SA et al*, 124 S Ct 2359 (2004), deciding that foreign-based plaintiffs would have standing in US courts for foreign harm caused by a global cartel, but only if that harm was dependent upon US harm.

[186] Federal Court of Justice (GE), *Ölfeldrohre*, 12 July 1973, WuW/E BGH 1276.

[187] *Wood Pulp* (n 139) paras 16–18.

[188] European Commission, Guidelines on the effect on trade concept contained in Articles 81 and 82 of the Treaty (2004/C 101/07) [2004] OJ C101/81, para 100.

[189] *Gencor* (n 139), para 90.

[190] Supreme Court of Justice (AT), *E v Bundeskartellanwalt and Bundeswettbewerbsbehörde*, 27 February 2006, 16 Ok 49/05, paras 27–28.

However, in *Intel*,[191] the General Court unequivocally recognised the so-called 'qualified effects doctrine' as a lawful basis for the extraterritorial application of EU competition law. In an action for annulment of the decision[192] in which the Commission found that Intel had infringed what is now Article 102 TFEU[193] (or, alternatively, annulment or reduction of the fine imposed on Intel), the General Court pointed out that in order to justify the Commission's jurisdiction under public international law, it is sufficient to establish either the qualified effects of the practice in the EU or that it was implemented in the EU.[194] The Court held that the conduct of Intel was capable of having immediate, substantial and foreseeable effects within the EEA, while taking the view that the Commission's jurisdiction was based not only on the qualified effects doctrine but also on the implementation doctrine.[195] On appeal, the CJEU recalled that the fact that an undertaking participating in an agreement is situated in a third country does not prevent the application of that provision if that agreement is operative on the territory of the internal market, and that the application of the implementation test is justified by the fact that if the applicability of prohibitions laid down under competition law were made to depend on the place where the agreement, decision or concerted practice was formed, the result would obviously be to give undertakings an easy means of evading those prohibitions.[196] According to the Court, the qualified effects test pursues the same objective, namely preventing conduct which, while not adopted within the EU, has anticompetitive effects liable to have an impact on the EU market. The Court therefore dismissed as incorrect Intel's argument that the qualified effects test cannot serve as a basis for the Commission's jurisdiction.[197]

B. Environmental Law

In the field of environmental law, the EU controversially extended the territorial scope of its Aviation Directive to fight climate change.[198] The Directive required airlines to surrender emissions allowances with respect to flights that arrived at or departed from an aerodrome situated in the territory of a Member State, including to flights by aircraft registered in third States and flights that took place significantly over the territory of non-EU States or over the high seas. This led to protests from foreign States and airlines alike, and resulted in a lawsuit being launched in the UK by a number of air transport associations, which ended up before the CJEU. In its preliminary ruling, the CJEU held that the geographical scope of the Aviation Directive did not violate the territoriality principle or the sovereignty of other

[191] Judgment of 12 June 2014, *Intel v Commission*, T-286/09, EU:T:2014:547.
[192] Commission Decision C(2009) 3726 final of 13 May 2009 relating to a proceeding under Article 82 [EC] and Article 54 of the EEA Agreement (Case COMP/C-3/37.990 – Intel).
[193] As well as the corresponding provision of the Agreement on the European Economic Area (EEA): Art 54.
[194] *Intel I* (n 191), para 244.
[195] ibid, paras 221–321.
[196] Judgment of 6 September 2017, *Intel v Commission*, C-413/14 P, EU:C:2017:632, paras 43–44.
[197] ibid, paras 45–46. Note that the Court of Justice set aside the judgment under appeal on other grounds, and referred the case back to General Court: *Intel v Commission*, T-286/09 RENV, pending.
[198] Directive 2008/101/EC of 19 November 2008 amending Directive 2003/87/EC so as to include aviation activities in the scheme for greenhouse gas emission allowance trading within the Community [2009] OJ L8/3.

nations, in light of the strong links of the regulated activity with the EU. In *Air Transport Association of America* the Court held:[199]

> In laying down a criterion for Directive 2008/101 to be applicable to operators of aircraft registered in a Member State or in a third State that is founded on the fact that those aircraft perform a flight which departs from or arrives at an aerodrome situated in the territory of one of the Member States, Directive 2008/101, inasmuch as it extends application of the scheme laid down by Directive 2003/87 to aviation, does not infringe the principle of territoriality or the sovereignty which the third States from or to which such flights are performed have over the airspace above their territory, since those aircraft are physically in the territory of one of the Member States of the European Union and are thus subject on that basis to the unlimited jurisdiction of the European Union.
>
> […]
>
> It is only if the operator of such an aircraft has chosen to operate a commercial air route arriving at or departing from an aerodrome situated in the territory of a Member State that the operator, because its aircraft is in the territory of that Member State, will be subject to the allowance trading scheme.

The Directive did not proclaim 'universal' jurisdiction, by applying as such to aircraft registered in third States that flew over third States or the high seas.[200] Yet it remains no less true that the Directive did have extraterritorial effects, in that it subjected aircraft to the Directive provided that they arrived or departed from an aerodrome situated in the territory of a Member State. The CJEU countered this argument by pointing out that the territoriality principle does not require that the event that is the subject of regulation occurs *entirely* on EU territory. In the Court's view, it would suffice that such an event occurred at least *in part* on EU territory:

> the fact that, in the context of applying European Union environmental legislation, certain matters contributing to the pollution of the air, sea or land territory of the Member States originate in an event which occurs partly outside that territory is not such as to call into question, in the light of the principles of customary international law capable of being relied upon in the main proceedings, the full applicability of European Union law in that territory.[201]

It seems hard to contest that aircraft arriving or departing from EU territory do emit greenhouse gases *in the EU*, and that the EU can set environmental standards for such activities, all the more so if international agreements oblige the EU to take environmental action:

> the European Union legislature may in principle choose to permit a commercial activity, in this instance air transport, to be carried out in the territory of the European Union only on condition that operators comply with the criteria that have been established by the European Union and are designed to fulfil the environmental protection objectives which it has set for itself, in particular where those objectives follow on from an international agreement to which the European Union is a signatory, such as the Framework Convention and the Kyoto Protocol.[202]

[199] Judgment of 21 December 2011, *Air Transport Association of America and others ('ATAA')*, C-366/10, EU:C:2011:864, paras 125 and 127. See G De Baere and C Ryngaert, 'The ECJ's Judgment in Air Transport Association of America and the International Legal Context of the EU's Climate Change Policy' (2013) 18 *European Foreign Affairs Review* 389.

[200] ibid, para 122.

[201] ibid, para 129.

[202] ibid, para 128.

In spite of the Directive's link to the EU's territory, its geographic scope was so severely contested internationally that the EU temporarily limited its reach to intra-EEA flights,[203] until a satisfactory multilateral solution within the International Civil Aviation Organization (ICAO) could be found. In late 2016, the ICAO adopted a Carbon Offsetting and Reduction Scheme for International Aviation (CORSIA), which was supported by the EU in March 2018.[204]

Ultimately, unilateral assertions of jurisdiction are difficult to defend when it comes to protecting global public goods, such as the atmosphere, or even global cartels threatening worldwide consumer welfare. Such public goods ought to be protected by international solutions. But when international agreements are not forthcoming because some nations drag their feet (eg with respect to curbing greenhouse gas emissions),[205] individual States or regional groupings such as the EU may arguably do it alone and extend their territorial jurisdiction,[206] provided that the global public goods which they protect are laid down in international instruments with a global reach, whether they are binding or not (such as the Kyoto Protocol and the Paris Agreement).[207]

C. Fisheries Regulation

Assertions of extraterritorial jurisdiction may also occur in the area of the law of the sea. As far as the EU is concerned, this particularly concerns fisheries, given the EU's Common Fisheries Policy. For instance, Article 6(1) of a 1986 Regulation provided, with regard to salmon and sea trout, that, where those fish have been caught outside waters under the sovereignty or jurisdiction of the Member States in certain regions, they may not be retained on board, transshipped, landed, transported, stored, sold, displayed or offered for sale, but must be returned immediately to the sea.[208] This provision had an extraterritorial aspect in that it regulated fishing on the high seas, outside Member States' functional jurisdiction over their maritime zones. As in *Air Transport Association of America* discussed above, the object of the regulation was a global public good, that is, conservation of threatened fish stocks. This found its legal basis in an international convention to which the Community

[203] Council and Parliament Decision (EU) 377/2013/EU of 24 April 2013 derogating temporarily from Directive 2003/87/EC establishing a scheme for greenhouse gas emission allowance trading within the Community [2013] OJ L113/1.

[204] ICAO Resolution A39-3 (2016): Consolidated statement of continuing ICAO policies and practices related to environmental protection – Global Market-based Measure (MBM) scheme; EU reply to CORSIA state letter, 6 March 2018, available at https://ec.europa.eu/transport/sites/transport/files/2018-03-01-eu-reply-to-corsia-state-letter.pdf.

[205] For example, on 1 June 2017, President Donald Trump announced the US' withdrawal from the Paris Agreement (adopted 12 December 2015, entered into force 4 November 2016) as annexed to UN Doc FCCC/CP/2015/L.9/Rev.1: see White House, 'Statement by President Trump on the Paris Climate Accord', 1 June 2017, whitehouse.gov/briefings-statements/statement-president-trump-paris-climate-accord/.

[206] See J Scott, 'Extraterritoriality and Territorial Extension in EU Law' (2014) 62 *American Journal of Comparative Law* 87.

[207] That is, provided that they respect international agreements and norms of customary international law. Such agreements and norms may remain silent on their enforcement, however, which creates opportunities for unilateral action.

[208] Council Regulation (EEC) No 3094/86 of 7 October 1986 laying down certain technical measures for the conservation of fishery resources OJ L288/1.

was a party, namely the Convention for the Conservation of Salmon in the North Atlantic Ocean.[209]

In its judgment on a reference for a preliminary ruling, the CJEU, in *Poulsen and Diva Navigation*, interpreted the Regulation as follows:[210]

> Community legislation may be applied to [a vessel registered in a non-member country] when it sails in the inland waters or, more especially, is in a port of a Member State, where it is generally subject to the unlimited jurisdiction of that State.
>
> [...]
>
> [T]echnical measures for the conservation of fishery resources may in principle be applied to a vessel registered in a non-member country [...] when that vessel is in the inland waters or in the port of a Member State.
>
> [...]
>
> [T]he national court may in principle order the confiscation of a cargo of salmon caught in the areas referred to in Article 6(l)(b) of Council Regulation (EEC) No 3094/86 of 7 October 1986 laying down certain technical measures for the conservation of fishery resources, which is in transit in waters under Community jurisdiction and is kept aboard a vessel registered in a non-member country and belonging to a company established in that State, [...] when that vessel is in the inland waters or in the port of a Member State.

In so doing, the CJEU drew attention to the EU's territorial *enforcement* jurisdiction, which is indeed hardly contested. But the fact remains that the Union's *legislative* jurisdiction over the relevant events (the catching of the fish) extended to areas beyond national or EU jurisdiction: parts of the high seas. The CJEU judgment does not justify this exercise of extraterritorial jurisdiction, but arguably – as in *Air Transport Association of America* – it may be based on the international convention that protected threatened fish stocks on the high seas.

Similar assertions of extraterritorial jurisdiction can be exercised by port States, with respect to marine conservation, pollution or employment conditions. Such port States can deny entry to, or even impose administrative or penal sanctions on foreign vessels that are not in compliance with international or even national standards with respect to activities in areas beyond national jurisdiction.[211]

D. Data Protection Law

The EU has lately cast itself as an international champion of data protection. In our current data-driven economy, in which data controllers amass large amounts of personal information for commercial and surveillance purposes, such protection is obviously relevant. As data easily cross territorial boundaries, the question whether the EU has jurisdiction over non-EU corporations controlling and processing EU persons' data has particular salience.

[209] Convention for the Conservation of Salmon in the North Atlantic Ocean (adopted 2 March 1982, entered into force 1 October 1983) 1338 UNTS 33 (NASCO).

[210] Judgment of 24 November 1992, *Poulsen and Diva Navigation*, C-286/90, EU:C:1992:453, paras 28–29 and 34.

[211] On port State jurisdiction, see further Chapter 18, Section V(C).

As early as 1995, when internet-based communication was still in its infancy, the EU adopted a Data Protection Directive (DPD),[212] which applies as soon as data processing occurs 'in the context of the activities of an establishment of the controller on the territory of the Member State', and when a controller not on EU territory nevertheless 'makes use of equipment [...] situated on the territory of the said Member State', except when the equipment is used for data in transit through EU territory.[213] This jurisdictional clause may appear to be firmly based on the territoriality principle. Still, if the broad interpretation of the notion of 'equipment' by the Article 29 working group (that is the EU advisory body set up under the DPD) is followed, EU data protection law may in fact apply 'where the processing in question has no real connection with the EU'.[214] The Commission even raised the spectre that this wide reach of EU law could lead to international legal conflict.[215] The cases discussed below show that regulators and courts do at times construe their jurisdiction broadly, resulting in international – notably transatlantic – tension.

From 25 May 2018 onwards, the General Data Protection Regulation (GDPR) has replaced the DPD.[216] Arguably, the GDPR better responds to the data protection challenges brought about by rapid technological development. Jurisdiction under the GDPR appears to be even broader than under the DPD. As to its territorial scope, Article 3 provides as follows:

> 1 This Regulation applies to the processing of personal data in the context of the activities of an establishment of a controller or a processor in the Union, regardless of whether the processing takes place in the Union or not.
>
> 2 This Regulation applies to the processing of personal data of data subjects who are in the Union by a controller or processor not established in the Union, where the processing activities are related to:
>
> (a) the offering of goods or services, irrespective of whether a payment of the data subject is required, to such data subjects in the Union; or
>
> (b) the monitoring of their behaviour as far as their behaviour takes place within the Union.

Thus, a foreign corporation that offers goods and services to, or 'targets' persons in, the EU will be subject to the GDPR, without any additional territorial connection being required.[217] The broad jurisdictional reach of the GDPR may again give rise to additional international tension. Such tension is not just theoretical. Since 2000, the EU, which construes its jurisdiction under the DPD broadly, has clashed several times with the US and US corporations offering services in the EU. This clash also relates to different views on substantive law. In the US, the level of data protection is generally lower than in the EU, as law-enforcement agencies have more powers and the freedom of speech has fewer restrictions, arguably to the detriment of individuals' data privacy.

[212] Directive 95/46/EC of 24 October 1995 on the protection of individuals with regard to the processing of personal data and on the free movement of such data [1995] OJ L281/31 (DPD).

[213] ibid, Art 4(1)(a) and (c).

[214] European Commission, Article 29 Data Protection Working Party, 'Opinion 8/2010 on applicable law', 16 December 2010, 0836-02/10/EN, WP 179, 29.

[215] Commission of the European Communities, 'First report on the implementation of the Data Protection Directive (95/46/EC)', 15 May 2003, COM(2003) 265 final, 17.

[216] Regulation (EU) 2016/679 of 27 April 2016 on the protection of natural persons with regard to the processing of personal data and on the free movement of such data, and repealing Directive 95/46/EC [2016] OJ L119/1.

[217] For a critique, see D Svantesson, 'Extraterritoriality and Targeting in EU Data Privacy Law: The Weak Spot Undermining the Regulation' (2015) 5 *International Data Privacy Law Journal* 226.

The first legal-cultural collision between Europe and the US in this field arguably occurred in 2000, when French courts ordered US Internet provider Yahoo! to prevent, through geo-location technology, the online sale of Nazi memorabilia – which is illegal in France – to French residents.[218] The courts' decisions could jurisdictionally be justified by reference to the territorial effects doctrine (the effects of the online sale could clearly be felt in France), but also raised the more fundamental question whether France could impose 'European' restrictions on a US corporation's freedom of speech.[219] While the *Yahoo!* case did not pertain to data protection as such, it served as a harbinger of – as of yet not fully resolved – tensions between the EU and the US over the regulation of cyberspace. Many of the current tensions relate to the exact balance to be struck between data protection and other rights (eg freedom of speech and freedom of information) or interests (commercial and governmental). Two examples are discussed below: the vicissitudes of the Passenger Name Records agreements between the EU and the US, and the conflict over US-based corporations' implementation of the data protection-based EU right to erasure.

Starting in the early 2000s, in the context of the post-9/11 fight against terrorism, the EU and the US have been at loggerheads over the US' desire to record and store personal data of all passengers boarding EU-US flights. Such recording and storing by the US authorities would require a transfer of data from the EU to the US. The EU was initially of the view that the US did not ensure an adequate level of data protection, and as a consequence data transfers from the EU to the US had to be prohibited pursuant to the DPD.[220] This stance led to EU-US negotiations over permissible data transfers, which resulted in various Passenger Name Records (PNR) agreements. In 2004, the Commission and the US Government concluded a first PNR agreement. However, this agreement was annulled by the CJEU for lack of EU legal basis.[221] The Commission subsequently concluded a PNR agreement with the US in 2007, which was only applied provisionally because the European Parliament voiced its concerns over the compatibility of the agreement with EU data protection law.[222] After laborious EU-US negotiations, a more permanent PNR was adopted in 2011 and approved by the European Parliament in 2012.[223] The end result is a 'territorial extension' of some aspects of EU data protection legislation to the activities of US law-enforcement authorities. Whether an adequate balance has been struck between the imperative to prevent

[218] Tribunal de Grande Instance de Paris (FR), *Union des Etudiant Juifs de France and Ligue contre le Racisme et l'Antisemitisme v Yahoo! and Yahoo France*, 22 May 2000, Case No RG: 00/05308.

[219] See further H Muir Watt, '*Yahoo!* Cyber Collision Of Cultures: Who Regulates?' (2003) 24 *MJIL* 673, 674.

[220] Art 25 DPD (n 212); European Commission, 'Report from the Commission to the European Parliament and the Council on the joint review of the implementation of the Agreement between the European Union and the United States of America on the processing and transfer of passenger name records in the United States Department of Homeland Security', 27 November 2013, COM(2013) 844 final.

[221] Judgment of 30 May 2006, *Parliament v Council and Commission*, C-317/04 and C-318/04, EU:C:2006:346, para 50.

[222] Council Decision 2007/551/CFSP/JHA of 23 July 2007 on the signing, on behalf of the European Union, of an Agreement between the European Union and the United States of America on the processing and transfer of Passenger Name Record (PNR) data by air carriers to the United States Department of Homeland Security (DHS) [2007] OJ L204/16 (2007 PNR Agreement).

[223] Council Decision of 26 April 2012 on the conclusion of the Agreement between the United States of America and the European Union on the use and transfer of passenger name records to the United States Department of Homeland Security (2012/472/EU) [2012] OJ L215/4, preamble; Agreement between the United States of America and the European Union on the use and transfer of passenger name records to the United States Department of Homeland Security (adopted 14 December 2011, entered into force 1 July 2012) [2012] OJ L215/5 (2011 PNR Agreement).

and combat terrorism and the protection of personal data (while satisfying the requirements of EU data protection law) remains to be seen.[224]

A second major clash resulting from the EU's desire to give its data protection legislation a wide geographic scope was one between the EU and a US-based corporation, occurring in respect of the individual right to erasure or right to be forgotten, an aspect of the right to data privacy. In the 2014 *Google Spain* case[225] before the CJEU, the question arose as to whether US-based internet corporation Google was under an obligation to remove search results featuring a newspaper article discussing a Spanish national's personal debts. The CJEU admitted that the actual processing of this person's data via Google search did not as such take place in the EU, but nevertheless held that Google fell within the reach of the DPD. This was because the selling of advertising space by Google's Spanish subsidiary constituted data processing 'in the context of the activities of an establishment of the controller on the territory of a member state'.[226] In the CJEU's view, 'territorial' jurisdiction was based on the inextricable link between the activities of the controller (Google Inc) and of its Spanish establishment (Google Spain).[227]

In the aftermath of this decision, a tug-of-war ensued between Google and EU and EU Member State data protection agencies over the precise implementation of the decision. Google argued that the EU right to erasure was limited to search results obtained on EU Google search domains.[228] This stance allowed users – or at least users from a State other than the State from which the delisting request came – to obtain non-redacted results by simply using google.com. EU and EU Member State data protection regulators considered this to be insufficient to protect EU persons' right to data protection, and instead advanced a model of universal implementation. The Article 29 Working Party advised delisting on 'all relevant domains, including .com'.[229] In 2016, the French Data Protection Agency even fined Google €100,000 for its failure to give universal implementation to delisting

[224] For instance, in an intra-EU context, the CJEU annulled the Data Retention Directive, which requires that Member States retain EU citizens' telecommunications data for between six months and two years to help in the fight serious crime and terrorism. According to the Court, the Directive violated the principles of proportionality and necessity and seriously interfered with fundamental rights; judgment of 8 April 2014, *Digital Rights Ireland and others*, C-293/12 and C-594/12, EU:C:2014:238, para 73. It is possible that the 2011 PNR agreement (n 219) does not withstand this test. Note that the CJEU held the draft Agreement between Canada and the European Union on the transfer and processing of Passenger Name Record data to be incompatible with Arts 7, 8 and 21 and Art 52(1) of the Charter of Fundamental Rights of the European Union in so far as it did not preclude the transfer of sensitive data from the European Union to Canada and the use and retention of that data: Opinion 1/15 (EU-Canada PNR Agreement) of 26 July 2017, EU:C:2017:592.

[225] Judgment of 13 May 2014, *Google Spain and Google*, C-131/12, EU:C:2014:317.

[226] *Google Spain* (n 225) para 60.

[227] ibid, para 56. With respect to EU jurisdiction regarding data protection, see eg also the judgment of 6 October 2015, *Schrems*, C-362/14, EU:C:2015:650. On that case and its implications, see eg L Azoulai and M van der Sluis, 'Institutionalizing personal data protection in times of global institutional distrust: *Schrems*' (2016) *Common Market Law Review* 1343; T Ojanen, 'Making the Essence of Fundamental Rights Real: The Court of Justice of the European Union Clarifies the Structure of Fundamental Rights under the Charter' (2016) 12 *European Constitutional Law Review* 318; RA Epstein, 'The ECJ's Fatal Imbalance: Its cavalier treatment of national security issues poses serious risk to public safety and sound commercial practices' (2016) 12 *European Constitutional Law Review* 330; M Scheinin, 'Towards evidence-based discussion on surveillance: A Rejoinder to Richard A Epstein' (2016) 12 *European Constitutional Law Review* 341.

[228] For Google's position, see P Fleischer, 'Adapting our approach to the European right to be forgotten', *Google*, 4 March 2016, blog.google/topics/google-europe/adapting-our-approach-to-european-rig/.

[229] European Commission, Article 29 Data Protection Working Party, 'Guidelines on the implementation of the Court of Justice of the European Union judgment on "Google Spain and inc v Agencia Española de Protección de Datos (AEPD) and Mario Costeja González" C-131/12', 26 November 2014, 14/EN WP 225, 9.

decisions.[230] It is uncertain whether the universal implementation model is compatible with the law of jurisdiction, as it forces a data controller to comply with EU law abroad, even if the goal is to protect the data privacy rights of EU residents. On the other hand, the territorial model favoured by Google, while prima facie more in keeping with traditional principles of jurisdiction, may do insufficient justice to EU residents' fundamental rights. These rights may be compromised if users outside the State where the delisting request originated can see non-redacted results by using google.com rather than an EU top level domain name.[231]

E. Economic Sanctions[232]

States sometimes resort to economic sanctions against other States on the grounds that the latter pose a security threat or engage in gross human rights violations. When sanctions imply an outright ban on trading, one speaks of an embargo or boycott. Sanctions are administrative measures of a non-criminal nature,[233] even if they are perceived as punitive by foreign States and businesses.[234]

Sanctions are relatively uncontroversial under the law of jurisdiction insofar as they are 'primary'; that is, only directed against economic transactions originating from the sanctioning State's territory (territoriality principle), or involving that State's nationals (personality principle). This is obviously not to say that they may not be opposed by the target State: as the aim of the sanctions is precisely to put pressure on the target to change its behaviour, or to bring about a change in its political regime, such sanctions are likely to engender protest on grounds of undue interference in the target's internal affairs.[235] Under the law of jurisdiction, the international legality of sanctions is most fiercely contested when they are 'secondary'; that is, when they apply to the dealings of foreign persons with sanctioned States.[236] Such measures could be considered as extraterritorial in that they operate on the basis of only a tenuous connection between the sanctioning State and the foreign national. They reduce the foreign policy discretion that third States can exercise vis-à-vis the sanctioned State,[237] and may thus give rise to international tension.

[230] Commission Nationale de l'Informatique et des Libertés, 'Decision no. 2016-054 of March 10, 2016 of the Restricted Committee issuing Google Inc. with a financial penalty', sites.les.univr.it/cybercrime/wp-content/uploads/2017/08/2016-google.pdf.

[231] For an insightful reasonableness application of the law of jurisdiction to the implementation of the *Google Spain* judgment, informed by the jurisdictional principle of reasonableness, see B van Alsenoy and M Koekkoek, 'Internet and Jurisdiction after *Google Spain*: The Extraterritorial Reach of the "Right to be Delisted"' (2015) 5 *International Data Privacy Law* 105.

[232] This discussion is partly based on ALM Schaap and C Ryngaert, 'De internationale onrechtmatigheid van Amerikaanse secundaire sanctiewetgeving' (2015) *Tijdschrift voor Sanctierecht en Onderneming* 9.

[233] See in that sense eg the Opinion of AG Bot in Joined Cases *Commission and others v Kadi*, C-584/10 P, C-593/10 P and C-595/10 P, EU:C:2013:176, point 68.

[234] See eg judgment of 30 September 2010, *Kadi v Commission*, T-85/09, EU:T:2010:418, paras 150–51, questioning the classification of long-term santions as preventative rather than punitive.

[235] See eg the Declaration of the Russian Federation and the People's Republic of China on the Promotion of International Law, 25 June 2016, mid.ru/en/foreign_policy/news/-/asset_publisher/cKNonkJE02Bw/content/id/2331698, para 4: 'The Russian Federation and the People's Republic of China fully support the principle of non-intervention in the internal or external affairs of States, and condemn as a violation of this principle any interference by States in the internal affairs of other States with the aim of forging change of legitimate governments'.

[236] For a more extensive discussion, see: C Ryngaert, 'Extraterritorial Export Controls (Secondary Boycotts)' (2008) 7 *CJIL* 625, 629–30.

[237] See eg European Communities, 'Comments on the US Regulations Concerning Trade With the USSR Presented to the United States Department of State on 12 August 1982' (1982) 21 ILM 891, 895 (EEC Memorandum): 'The

The United States in particular has imposed secondary sanctions on foreign persons,[238] often to the consternation of the EU, European States, and affected European corporations. Arguably, the first extraterritorial application of US sanctions legislation occurred when, in the 1960s, the US Ministry of the Treasury, acting on the basis of the 1917 Trading with the Enemy Act, ordered the French corporation Fruehauf to denounce a contractual agreement with China.[239] The US reasoned that it had jurisdiction because a US corporation held the majority of stock in, and thus controlled Fruehauf.[240]

In the 1980s, the 'Soviet Pipeline Regulations', a secondary boycott aimed at weakening the Soviet Union's economy,[241] led to considerable controversy. These Regulations prohibited the export to the Soviet Union of products by subsidiaries of US concerns and of goods produced in the US or used with US technology.[242] The Regulations were again based on the control theory, but unlike in *Fruehauf*, actual international protest, especially from Europe, was strong. The European Commission accused the US of violating international law,[243] and the District Court of The Hague declared the 'extraterritorial application' of the Regulations to be incompatible with international law.[244] The US eventually withdrew the Regulations after sustained diplomatic protest.[245] Clearly, it was the international community's view that the extraterritorial 'control-based' application of the US Regulations could not be based on the established principles of jurisdiction. The control theory appears to be an overly extensive interpretation of the nationality principle,[246] and is in tension with the ICJ's decision in the *Barcelona Traction* case that a corporation's nationality depends on the place of incorporation or statutory seat.[247]

After the debacle of the Soviet Pipeline Regulations, the US did not relent in its quest to give extraterritorial application to sanctions legislation. In 1996, it adopted the Cuban Liberty and Democratic Solidarity Act, also called the Helms-Burton Act after its promoters,[248] as well as the Iran Libya Sanctions Act (ILSA).[249] The Helms-Burton Act prohibited any person, whatever his or her nationality, from 'trafficking' in confiscated property belonging to Americans or Cubans who later acquired American citizenship, and also applied to foreign persons. ILSA applied to every natural or legal person investing more

practical impact of the Amendments to the Export Administration Regulations is that E.C. companies are pressed into service to carry out US trade policy towards the USSR, even though these companies are incorporated and have their registered office within the Community which has its own trade policy towards the USSR. The public policy ("ordre public") of the European Community and of its Member States is thus purportedly replaced by US public policy which European companies are forced to carry out within the EC, if they are not to lose export privileges in the US or to face other sanctions. This is an unacceptable interference in the affairs of the European Community'.

[238] It should be emphasised that not all US sanctions laws have an extraterritorial dimension.

[239] Trading With the Enemy Act of 1917, 50 App USCA § 10; Fed Reg 2503-04 (1942).

[240] Executive Order No 9193, 3 CFR 1174 (938-43 Comp); Executive Order No 9989, 3 CFR 748 (1943–48 Comp); Ryngaert (n 233) 629–30. WF Craig, 'Applications of the Trading with the Enemy Act to Foreign Corporations Owned by Americans: Reflections on Fruehauf v. Massardy' (1970) 83 *Harvard Law Review* 579.

[241] Export Administration Amendment Act of 1981 (1982) 21 ILM 164.

[242] C Staker, 'Jurisdiction' in MD Evans (ed), *International Law*, 4th edn (Oxford, OUP, 2014) 309.

[243] European Community, 'Note and Comments on the Amendments of 22 June 1982 to the Export Administration Act, Presented to the United States Department of State on 12 August 1982' (1982) 21 ILM 891.

[244] District Court The Hague (NL), *Compagnie européenne des Pétroles SA v Sensor Nederland BV*, 17 September 1982, (1983) 22 ILM 66.

[245] 47 Fed Reg 51,858 (18 Nov 1982), amending 15 CFR pts 379, 385, 390, 399.

[246] Court of Appeal Paris (FR), *Société Fruehauf Corp v Massardy*, 22 May 1965, (1966) 5 ILM 476.

[247] *Barcelona Traction Power & Light Company, Limited* (Belgium v Spain) [1970] ICJ Rep 3.

[248] Cuban Liberty and Democratic Solidarity (Libertad) Act of 1996, Public Law 104-114, 110 Stat 785, 22 USC 6021.

[249] Iran and Libya Sanctions Act of 1996, Public Law 104-172, 110 Stat 1541, 50 USC 1701.

than US$20 million in the development of the petroleum industry in Iran or Libya. Again, these acts were widely condemned. Canada and Mexico considered the Helms-Burton Act to be in violation of US obligations under the North American Free Trade Agreement (NAFTA),[250] and the (then) European Community challenged both acts before the World Trade Organization.[251] The EU also adopted Regulation 2271/96, prohibiting natural and legal persons within the Community from giving effect to the relevant US sanctions.[252] Canada, Mexico and the UK enacted similar blocking legislation.[253] Blocking legislation also applied to subsidiaries of US parent corporations, which previously complied with US law on the basis of the control theory. The 'blocking statutes' were not always consistently applied, however. In addition, the WTO procedure was aborted after the US suspended the extraterritorial application of the acts.[254] At any rate, the overwhelmingly negative legal reactions demonstrate the controversial character, if not unlawfulness of US secondary sanctions of the type of Helms-Burton and ILSA, the scope of which goes even beyond the already disputed control theory.

More recently, the US has started targeting foreign providers of financial services doing business with 'rogue States',[255] insofar as these providers use the US financial system via US correspondent or payable-through accounts. As most international banks carry out transactions in US dollars, for which they have to hold US bank accounts, they are subject to US sanctions law. In case of violations, they can expect large fines and may lose access to the US financial market. New US sanctions are vigorously enforced: the Office of Foreign Assets Control (OFAC) recently imposed rather hefty fines on foreign corporations (banks).[256]

However, European protest against recent US assertions has remained muted. If protest arises, it focuses on the disproportionality of the fine rather than on the authority of the US to enact the sanctions in the first place.[257] Some States even take the view that it falls to targeted corporations rather than States to challenge foreign States' extraterritorial

[250] North American Free Trade Agreement (adopted 17 December 1992, entered into force 1 January 1994) 32 ILM 289.

[251] The case was later settled; see 'Current Developments: The EU-U.S. Compromise on the Helms-Burton and D'Amato Acts' (1999) 93 *AJIL* 227.

[252] Council Regulation (EC) No 2271/96 of 22 November 1996 protecting against the effects of the extra-territorial application of legislation adopted by a third country, and actions based thereon or resulting therefrom [1996] OJ L309/1.

[253] UK: Protection of Trading Interest Act (1980), 1980 Chapter 11; Canada: Foreign Extraterritorial Measures Act (1985) RSC, 1985, Chapter F-29, as amended by Act to Amend the Foreign Extraterritorial Measures Act (1996) RSC, 1996, Chapter 28, as reprinted in (1997) 36 ILM 117 (FEMA); Mexico: Ley de Protección al Comercio y la Inversión de Normas Extranjeras que Contravenganel Derecho Internacional (1996), *Official Gazette of the Federation* ('*Diario Oficial de la Federación*') of 23 October 1996; for the English version, see 'Act to Protect Trade and Investment from Foreign Norms that Contravene International Law' (1997) 36 ILM 145.

[254] Memorandum of Understanding between the United States and the European Union concerning the US Helms-Burton Act and the US Iran and Libya Sanctions Act, 11 April 1997, (1997) 36 ILM 530.

[255] Comprehensive Iran Sanctions, Accountability, and Divestment Act of 2010, Public Law 111-195, 124 Stat 1312, 22 USC 8501 (CISADA); Iran Freedom and Counter Proliferation Act (2012), as part of Public Law 112-239, 22 USC Chapter 95, 8801; National Defense Authorization Act for Fiscal Year 2012 (2011), HR 1540, Public Law 112-81, 125 Stat 1298.

[256] For recent information on enforcement, see US Department of the Treasury, Resource Center, 'Civil Penalties and Enforcement Information', treasury.gov/resource-center/sanctions/CivPen/Pages/civpen-index2.aspx.

[257] See eg French President Hollande's reaction to the US$9 billion fine imposed by US regulators on French bank BNP Paribas: A de Guigné and P-Y Dugua, 'BNP Paribas: Obama refuse de se mêler de l'affaire judiciare', *Le Figaro*, 5 June 2014, lefigaro.fr/societes/2014/06/05/20005-20140605ARTFIG00009-l-affaire-bnp-paribas-s-invite-au-diner-entre-hollande-et-obama.php.

sanctions.[258] It seems that, more than before, the international community substantively agrees on the taking of sanctions against specific regimes, which obviates the need for protest.[259] For instance, the EU simply followed suit, at least with primary sanctions, after the US strengthened its sanctions against Iran.[260] The sanctions imposed on the Russian Federation by the US and the EU in 2014 are largely similar.[261] However, things changed after US President Trump announced the US withdrawal from the 2015 Joint Comprehensive Plan of Action, *i.e.*, the Iran nuclear deal, in 2018, and reimposed sanctions with extraterritorial effects.[262] The EU reacted by adopting the aforementioned blocking legislation. This legislation allows EU operators to recover damages arising from the extraterritorial sanctions within its scope from the persons causing them and nullifies the effect in the EU of any foreign court rulings based on them. It also forbids EU persons from complying with those sanctions, unless exceptionally authorised to do so by the Commission in case non-compliance seriously damages their interests or the interests of the Union.[263]

The EU's reaction to the reimposition of extraterritorial US sanctions against Iran shows that it considers extraterritorial legislation to be contrary to international law.[264] The EU's own sanctions legislation is always based on an unambiguous territorial or personal link with the EU, and is clearly of a primary nature.[265] Still, from a substantive perspective,

[258] See eg for the Netherlands: Rijksoverheid, Internationale Sancties, Sancties tegen Iran, 'Doorwerking Amerikaanse sancties Iran', rijksoverheid.nl/onderwerpen/internationale-sancties/sancties-tegen-iran/doorwerking-amerikaanse-sancties-iran.

[259] 'Developments in the Law: Extraterritoriality' (2011) 124 *Harvard Law Review* 1227, 1250–55.

[260] Council Decision 2010/413/CFSP of 26 July 2010 concerning restrictive measures against Iran and repealing Common Position [2010] OJ L195/39; Council Regulation (EU) No 267/2012 of 23 March 2012 concerning restrictive measures against Iran and repealing Regulation (EU) No 961/2010 [2012] OJ L88/1. For relevant case law, see eg judgments of 5 March 2015, *Europäisch-Iranische Handelsbank v Council*, C-585/13 P, EU:C:2015:145, and of 1 March 2016, *National Iranian Oil Company v Council*, C-440/14 P, EU:C:2016:128. However, diplomatic talks between Iran and the 'E3/EU+3' (France, UK, Germany, and the EU+ the USA, Russia, and China) on nuclear-proliferation led to an agreement on a Joint Comprehensive Plan of Action (JCPOA) on 14 July 2015. On 16 January 2016 (Implementation Day), the UN lifted certain of its nuclear-related restrictive measures, as set by UN Security Council Resolution 2231 (2015). On the same day, the Council lifted all nuclear-related economic and financial EU sanctions against Iran, while some restrictions remain in force. However, the current US administration decided to abandon the nuclear deal and to reinstate sanctions: see eg M Landler, 'Trump Abandons Iran Nuclear Deal He Long Scorned', *The New York Times*, 8 May 2018, https://www.nytimes.com/2018/05/08/world/middleeast/trump-iran-nuclear-deal.html; P Wintour, 'US faces European backlash against Iran sanctions: Senior politician says Europe will consider countermeasures to keep trading with Iran', *The Guardian*, 11 May 2018.

[261] Compare 31 CFR Part 589 – Ukraine-Related Sanctions Regulations and the Executive Orders 13660, 13661, 13662, 13685, with Council Regulation (EU) No 1290/2014 of 4 December 2014 amending Regulation (EU) No 833/2014 concerning restrictive measures in view of Russia's actions destabilising the situation in Ukraine, and amending Regulation (EU) No 960/2014 amending Regulation (EU) No 833/2014 [2014] OJ L349/20.

[262] US President Executive Order 13846 of August 6, 2018. Reimposing Certain Sanctions With Respect to Iran.

[263] Commission Implementing Regulation (EU) 2018/1101 of 3 August 2018 laying down the criteria for the application of the second paragraph of Article 5 of Council Regulation (EC) No 2271/96 protecting against the effects of the extra-territorial application of legislation adopted by a third country, and actions based thereon or resulting therefrom [2018] OJ L 199I/7; Commission Delegated Regulation (EU) 2018/1100 of 6 June 2018 amending the Annex to Council Regulation (EC) No 2271/96 protecting against the effects of extra-territorial application of legislation adopted by a third country, and actions based thereon or resulting therefrom [2018] OJ L 199I/1.

[264] Commission Delegated Regulation (EU) 2018/1100 of 6 June 2018, preambular paragraph 2. See also Council of the EU (Press Office), Factsheet: 'EU restrictive measures', 29 April 2014, consilium.europa.eu/uedocs/cms_Data/docs/pressdata/EN/foraff/135804.pdf, 3.

[265] See eg Art 49 of Council Regulation (EU) No 267/2012 of 23 March 2012 concerning restrictive measures against Iran [2012] OJ L88/1: 'This Regulation shall apply: (a) within the territory of the Union, including its airspace; (b) on board any aircraft or any vessel under the jurisdiction of a Member State; (c) to any person inside or outside the territory of the Union who is a national of a Member State; (d) to any legal person, entity or body, inside or outside the territory of the Union, which is incorporated or constituted under the law of a Member State; (e) to any legal person, entity or body in respect of any business done in whole or in part within the Union'.

EU sanctions, even if not jurisdictionally 'extraterritorial', can be very drastic and, while using EU territorial and personal links, are unambiguously aimed at effecting extraterritorial change, as for instance EU sanctions against Russia and Iran show. Other States, such as China, India and South Africa, have also continued to condemn sanctions imposed without a territorial or personal link.[266] In light of these positions, it is unlikely that the customary international law bases regarding the legitimation of sanctions have shifted.

F. Civil Jurisdiction

The concept of jurisdiction is not only a fundamental notion in public international law, but also in private international law, where it pertains to the competence of a court to adjudicate a claim in civil or commercial matters. The jurisdictional rules of private international law often have a national or regional character, but nevertheless operate against the background of, and should comply with, rules of public international law. As far as the EU is concerned, the rules of adjudicatory jurisdiction are laid down in the 'Brussels Regulation' on jurisdiction, recognition and enforcement of judgments in civil and commercial matters (recast 2012).[267] The basic jurisdictional principle of the Regulation is that a plaintiff can sue a defendant in the State where the latter is domiciled, even if he or she has another nationality.[268] The Regulation defines the domicile of a company or other legal person as the place where it has its statutory seat, its central administration, or its principal place of business.[269] This implies that a corporation can be sued in its home State, even where it has committed tortious acts on another State's territory, for example, where a Western-based multinational corporation is alleged to be complicit in human rights violations committed in a developing State. The Regulation also provides for a large number of special rules of jurisdiction;[270] these rules include the classic territoriality principle, pursuant to which, in matters relating to tort, delict or quasi-delict, a person may be sued in the courts of the place where the harmful event occurred or may occur.[271] Some of these jurisdictional rules also depend on the subject-matter of the dispute, and can for example differ depending on whether it concerns an insurance, employment or consumer contract.[272]

The Brussels Regulation does not provide for 'universal tort jurisdiction'; that is jurisdiction absent any nexus with the forum, based on the gravity of the crime (as opposed to universal criminal jurisdiction). This need not mean that, from a European perspective, such jurisdiction would be considered illegal. In fact, in its *amicus curiae* brief in the US *Kiobel* litigation (2013) – which concerned the reach of the US ATCA (see above, Section IV(B)(v)(a)) – the European Commission supported the exercise of universal tort jurisdiction, subject to certain limitations, such as the duty to exhaust internal remedies.[273]

[266] See eg The State Council of the People's Republic of China, 'China rejects U.S. unilateral sanctions on third country', 12 June 2012, gov.cn/misc/2012-06/12/content_2159186.htm; Asian-African Legal Consultative Organization (AALCO), 'Extraterritorial Application of National Legislation: Sanctions Imposed against Third Parties', AALCO/53/TEHRAN/2014/SD/S6, 11.
[267] The Brussels I Regulation (n 14).
[268] ibid, Art 4(1).
[269] ibid, Art 63.
[270] ibid, Section 2.
[271] ibid, Art 7(2).
[272] ibid, Sections 3–5.
[273] *Kiobel* (n 166) 33, Supplemental Brief of the European Commission on Behalf of the European Union as *Amicus Curiae* in Support of Neither Party.

The UK and the Netherlands are far less enthusiastic about such jurisdiction: in their brief in *Kiobel*, they expressed concern that the exercise of universal civil jurisdiction could impede a foreign nation's prerogative to 'regulate its own commercial affairs', and could adversely affect 'much needed direct foreign investment' in host countries.[274] In *Kiobel*, the US Supreme Court, relying on the congressional presumption against extraterritoriality, eventually limited the scope of the ATCA to claims that 'touch and concern' the US, thus rejecting the universal reach of the Act.[275]

In spite of the reservations that some States may harbour regarding universal tort jurisdiction, quite a number of European States, as well as Canada, provide for necessity-based jurisdiction, pursuant to which their courts may exercise exceptional jurisdiction so as to avert a denial of justice.[276] Such jurisdiction comes close to universal tort jurisdiction, although States often require at least some connection of the claim with the forum for necessity-based jurisdiction to be exercised. The Swiss Code of Private International Law, for instance, provides that

> [i]f this Code does not provide for jurisdiction in Switzerland and if proceedings abroad are impossible or cannot reasonably be required to be brought, the Swiss judicial or administrative authorities at the place with which the facts of the case are sufficiently connected shall have jurisdiction.[277]

Forum of necessity clauses have particular relevance for public international law claims, as adequate dispute-settlement mechanisms for such claims may be lacking, for instance because Host States may be unable or unwilling to provide a forum to a tort victim. Dutch courts, for instance, established necessity-based jurisdiction over a tort claim filed by a foreign victim of torture committed abroad, on the grounds that the victim did not have access to any alternative forum.[278] Forum of necessity may also hold some potential for human rights claims against multinational corporations in respect of the adverse impact of their overseas activities on human rights or the environment.[279]

EU Member States may not only exercise exceptional civil jurisdiction to prevent a denial of justice, but also for reasons of procedural economy. For instance, this is the case where they exercise jurisdiction over a claim brought against one person that is connected to a claim brought against another person over whom jurisdiction could duly be established on the basis of an accepted jurisdictional principle, such as domicile or territory. In an extraterritorial environmental tort case, for example, the District Court of The Hague established jurisdiction over the victims' claim filed against Shell's Nigerian subsidiary on the ground that it had jurisdiction over the subsidiary's parent company on the basis of the domicile principle.[280]

[274] ibid, 26 and 31.
[275] ibid.
[276] See A Nuyts, 'Study on Residual Jurisdiction: 'Review of the Member States' Rules concerning the "Residual Jurisdiction" of their courts in Civil and Commercial Matters pursuant to the Brussels I and II Regulations', 3 September 2007, ec.europa.eu/civiljustice/news/docs/study_residual_jurisdiction_en.pdf.
[277] Code of Private International Law (*Bundesgesetz über das International Privatrecht*) of 8 December 1987, Systematic Collection of Federal Law (*Systematische Sammlung des Bundesrechts*) (SR) 291, Art 3.
[278] See District Court The Hague (NL), *El-Hojouj*, 21 March 2012, NL:RBSGR:2012:BV9748.
[279] C Nwapi, 'Jurisdiction by Necessity and the Regulation of the Transnational Corporate Actor' (2014) 20 *Utrecht Journal of International and European Law* 24, 33.
[280] District Court The Hague (NL), *Oruma v Royal Dutch Shell*, 30 December 2009, ECLI:NL:RBSGR:2009:BK8616, paras 3.4–3.6 (applying Art 7 of the Dutch Code of Civil Procedure).

VI. Jurisdiction in International Human Rights Treaties: The Role of the European Court of Human Rights[281]

The concept of jurisdiction not only figures in general public international law and private international law, but also in international human rights treaties. In human rights law, jurisdiction is not so much aimed at delimiting competences and preventing sovereignties from clashing. Rather, it aims at defining the group of persons whose rights the State has to respect and protect. It is concerned with the geographic scope of application of a State's primary human rights obligations.

In human rights law, unlike general international law, jurisdiction takes on an *obligatory* rather than a permissive or prohibitive character. Indeed, human rights treaties typically *oblige* a contracting State to guarantee the rights provided for in the treaty to all persons 'within its jurisdiction'. If a contracting State fails to guarantee such rights to persons within its jurisdiction, it may ultimately incur State responsibility, provided that the violation of a substantive treaty provision has been established. Accordingly, in the context of human rights treaties, the concept of jurisdiction should be understood against the backdrop of the law on State responsibility,[282] while nevertheless being analytically distinct from it.[283] Notably the ECtHR has contributed significantly to the development of the concept of jurisdiction in human rights law. Accordingly, the emphasis of the discussion in this section will be on the ECtHR's relevant case law. The Court has mainly addressed the issue of jurisdiction in the context of contracting States' overseas military operations. However, the issue is also relevant in non-military contexts; for instance, does the right to privacy have extraterritorial application in the face of cross-border State surveillance?[284]

A. The Geographic Scope of Human Rights Treaties

The geographic scope of human rights treaties crucially depends on the interpretation of the notion of 'jurisdiction', which is often used in human rights treaties. Thus, Article 1 ECHR provides that 'The High Contracting Parties shall secure to everyone *within their jurisdiction* the rights and freedoms defined in Section I of this Convention' (emphasis added). Similarly, Article 2(1) ICCPR provides that 'each State Party [...] undertakes to respect and ensure to all individuals within its territory and *subject to its jurisdiction* the rights recognized in the present Covenant' (emphasis added), and Article 2(1) of the Convention on the Rights of the Child requires that States Parties 'respect and ensure the rights set forth in the present Convention to each child *within their jurisdiction*' (emphasis added). International supervisory bodies have interpreted these jurisdictional clauses as giving rise to some extraterritorial obligations, notably with respect to persons finding themselves outside of the

[281] This discussion draws on Section 1.5 of C Ryngaert, *Jurisdiction in International Law*, 2nd edn (Oxford, OUP, 2015).

[282] See Chapter 12.

[283] Compare in this respect *Ilascu and others v Moldova and Russia* App no 48787/99 (ECtHR, 8 July 2004) para 311 with *Jaloud v The Netherlands* App no 47708/08 (ECtHR, 20 November 2014) para 154.

[284] See further M Milanovic, 'Human Rights Treaties and Foreign Surveillance: Privacy in the Digital Age' (2015) 56 *Harvard International Law Journal* 81.

territory of the State Party but nevertheless within its jurisdictional control.[285] Thus, both the ICJ and the Human Rights Committee held that the ICCPR is applicable in occupied territories.[286] However, some States, notably the US and Israel, have rejected the extraterritorial application of the ICCPR.[287]

Not all human rights treaties feature a jurisdictional clause. The ICESCR, for instance, does not.[288] As the ICJ ruled, '[t]his may be explicable by the fact that this Covenant guarantees rights which are essentially territorial'.[289] At the same time, the absence of a jurisdictional clause may lead one to believe that such treaties give rise to unlimited 'global duties'.[290] Still, State obligations such as those under the ICESCR cannot be considered as entirely borderless either. This is all the more so in respect of positive obligations: one cannot expect a State to respect, protect and promote the full panoply of economic, social, and cultural rights of individuals outside its borders and territorial control. Thus, the Committee on Economic, Social and Cultural Rights (CESCR) held that economic, social and cultural rights apply when States exercise 'effective control' on the territory of another State, such as in case of occupation.[291] Nevertheless, according to the Committee, States also have 'extraterritorial' positive obligations absent such extraterritorial 'effective control'. This includes, for example, the obligation to protect individuals abroad from the adverse consequences on the right to health and the right to water flowing from conduct of corporations over which those States can exercise influence.[292]

B. The Territorial Model of Jurisdiction

The jurisdictional reach of the ECHR came to the fore in the *Banković* case (2001),[293] in which the jurisdictional question at the admissibility stage was whether the victims of a bombing raid by NATO fighter jets on Belgrade were 'within the jurisdiction' of the Member States of NATO that were also Contracting Parties to the ECHR.[294] In this case,

[285] Eg HRCttee, *Lopez Burgos v Uruguay*, 29 July 1981, Communication No 52/1979, UN Doc CCPR/C/13/D/52/1979; Inter-American Commission on Human Rights (IACHR), *Coard et al v United States*, 29 September 1999, Report No 109/99, Case No 10.951, para 37. See the subsections below for a discussion of the ECtHR's case law.

[286] *Legal Consequences of the Construction of a Wall in Occupied Palestinian Territory* (Advisory Opinion) [2004] ICJ Rep 136, paras 108–11; HRCttee, Consideration of Reports Submitted by States Parties under Article 40 of the Covenant, Concluding observations, Israel, 21 August 2003, UN Doc CCPR/CO/78/ISR, para 11.

[287] HRCttee, Statement of US State Department Legal Adviser, Conrad Harper, 24 April 1995, UN Doc CCPR/C/SR.1405, para 20; HRCttee, Replies of the Government of Israel to the List of Issues (CCPR/C/ISR/Q/3), to be taken up in connection with the consideration of the third periodic report of Israel (CCPRICI/SR/3), 12 July 2010, UN Doc CCPR/C/ISR/Q/3/Add.1, 3.

[288] Art 2(1) ICESCR only declares that 'Each State Party to the present Covenant undertakes to take steps, individually and through international assistance and co-operation, especially economic and technical, to the maximum of its available resources, with a view to achieving progressively the full realization of the rights recognized in the present Covenant by all appropriate means, including particularly the adoption of legislative measures'.

[289] *Wall* Opinion (n 286) para 112.

[290] For a discussion of the geographic scope of economic, social, cultural rights, see M Langford et al (eds), *Global Justice, Global Duties* (Cambridge, CUP, 2014).

[291] See CESCR, Consideration of Reports Submitted by States Parties under Articles 16 and 17 of the Covenant, Concluding observations, Israel, 4 December 1998, UN Doc E/C.12/1/Add.27, para 8.

[292] CESCR, General Comment No 14: 'The right to the highest attainable standard of health (article 12 of the International Covenant on Economic, Social and Cultural Rights)', 11 August 2000, UN Doc E/C12/2000/4, para 39; General Comment No 15, 'The Right to Water', 20 January 2003, UN Doc E/C.12/2002/11, para 33.

[293] *Banković* (n 19).

[294] As NATO itself is not a Party to the ECHR, the case could not be brought against the organisation, but only against the Member States that were Parties. Along the same lines, Serbia and Montenegro could not bring a case

the ECtHR controversially attempted to derive the meaning of the Convention's concept of jurisdiction as set out in Article 1 ECHR from general international law:

> As to the 'ordinary meaning' of the relevant term in Article 1 of the Convention, the Court is satisfied that, from the standpoint of public international law, the jurisdictional competence of a State is primarily territorial. While international law does not exclude a State's exercise of jurisdiction extra-territorially, the suggested bases of such jurisdiction (including nationality, flag, diplomatic and consular relations, effect, protection, passive personality and universality) are, as a general rule, defined and limited by the sovereign territorial rights of the other relevant States. [...] The Court is of the view, therefore, that Article 1 of the Convention must be considered to reflect this ordinary and essentially territorial notion of jurisdiction, other bases of jurisdiction being exceptional and requiring special justification in the particular circumstances of each case.[295]

As noted above, basing the meaning of jurisdiction in human rights law on general international law is problematic in that the two concepts of jurisdiction serve different purposes. Whereas the former essentially aims to *limit* expansive assertions of State jurisdiction, the latter aims at widening the net of State human rights obligations. It is recalled in that regard that the Committee of Experts drafting the ECHR jettisoned the concepts of 'residing' or 'living' within the territories of the Contracting Parties in favour of the presumably wider concept of 'within the jurisdiction' with a view to 'widen[ing] as far as possible the categories of persons who are to benefit by the guarantees contained in the Convention'.[296] Using principles of general international law to construe the jurisdictional clause in human rights treaties is bound to limit the categories of persons protected by the treaties. The rigidity flowing from the Court's statement in *Banković*, which unsurprisingly led the Court to declare the case inadmissible, has been considerably softened in later cases.

Even before *Banković*, the Court did not restrict a State's human rights obligations to persons finding themselves within the State's territory. In *Loizidou v Turkey*, the Court held that,

> in conformity with the relevant principles of international law governing State responsibility, [...] the responsibility of a Contracting Party could also arise when as a consequence of military action it exercises effective control – whether lawful or unlawful – of an area outside its national territory.[297]

Thus, ECHR Contracting Parties occupying foreign territory, which ordinarily also implies exercising effective control over it, are required to ensure the Convention rights of individuals in the controlled area.[298]

The 'effective control' standard in the law of human rights jurisdiction is not necessarily coterminous with the 'effective control' standard as espoused by the ICJ in the *Nicaragua* case,[299] nor with the 'overall control' standard as put forward by the ICTY in the

before the ICJ concerning the legality of the use of force by NATO in 1999 against NATO itself, but only against NATO Member States. The ICJ eventually declared that since Serbia was not a UN Member State in 1999, the Court had no jurisdiction to entertain the claims made. See *Case concerning the Legality of the Use of Force* (Serbia and Montenegro v Belgium) [2004] ICJ Rep 279, para 79.

[295] *Banković* (n 19) paras 59–61.

[296] *Collected Edition of the 'Travaux préparatoires' of the European Convention on Human Rights, Volume II: Consultative Assembly, Second Session of the Committee of Ministers, Standing Committee of the Assembly (10 August–19 November 1949)* (The Hague, Nijhoff, 1975) 200.

[297] *Loizidou v Turkey* App no 15318/89 (ECtHR, 23 March 1995) para 62.

[298] See also *Wall* Opinion (n 286) para 109.

[299] *Case Concerning the Military and Paramilitary Activity in and against Nicaragua* (Nicaragua v United States of America) [1986] ICJ Rep 14.

Tadić case.[300] After all, those standards serve different purposes. While the ECtHR standard governs the jurisdictional reach of human rights treaties, the *Nicaragua* test indicates the level of State control required for conduct of non-State actors to be attributable to the State.[301] The *Tadić* test, on the other hand, deals with the point at which a non-international armed conflict becomes an international armed conflict as a result of the control exercised by a State over a non-State actor involved in the conflict, and serves to determine the applicable branch of the law of armed conflict.[302]

Even putting aside the different purposes of the various tests, when comparing the operation of the ECtHR's control test with the operation of the ICJ's, it becomes clear that, while the ICJ requires that the State has 'directed or enforced the perpetration of the acts contrary to human rights',[303] the ECtHR merely requires that the State exercise factual or legal authority over a certain territory, irrespective of whether it holds a valid legal title with respect to that territory. At times the exercise of authority is even decoupled from the exercise of territorial control. In *Ilascu and others v Moldova and Russia*, for instance, the applicant was held to have fallen within the jurisdiction of both Moldova and Russia, although Moldova could not enforce its laws in the separatist region where the rights violations took place (Transnistria),[304] while Russia possibly only had a 'decisive influence' over the separatist regime and only provided 'military, economic and political support',[305] a yardstick which would fall well short of the one used by the ICJ for the purposes of attributing responsibility.[306] Possibly, it is 'overall control', as was required by the ICTY in *Tadić*, that the ECtHR demands after all. In that respect, it was in the seminal *Loizidou* case that the Court somewhat confusingly held that the Turkish army exercises 'effective overall control' over the northern part of Cyprus, and that it was 'not necessary to determine whether […] Turkey actually exercises detailed control over the policies and actions of the [Turkish Republic of Northern Cyprus]'.[307] In other cases, the requirement of territorial control has been even more relaxed. The Court has indeed found that individuals on a vessel on the high seas were considered to be within the jurisdiction of the State intercepting it or colliding with it (through a State vessel),[308] and that a person arrested abroad by security forces of a contracting State was within the jurisdiction of that State.[309]

C. From Territorial to State Agent Control

The ECtHR is still struggling to devise a bright-line rule as to the precise circumstances under which individuals outside the territory of a contracting State fall within the latter's jurisdiction.[310] The difficulties appear to stem primarily from the Court's strenuous efforts to square the emphasis that the general law of jurisdiction puts on territoriality with the human rights principle that a State, whether acting intra- or extraterritorially, should be

[300] ICTY, Appeals Chamber, *Prosecutor v Tadić*, 15 July 1999, Case No IT-94-1-A.
[301] *Nicaragua* (n 299) para 115.
[302] *Tadić* (n 300) paras 115–45. On this, see further Chapter 13, Section II(B).
[303] *Nicaragua* (n 299) para 115.
[304] *Assanidze v Georgia* App no 71503/01 (ECtHR, 8 April 2004) paras 139–47.
[305] *Ilascu* (n 283) paras 392–94.
[306] *Nicaragua* (n 299) para 115.
[307] *Loizidou* (n 297) para 56.
[308] *Xhavara v Italy and Albania* App no 39473/98 (ECtHR,11 January 2001); *Medvedyev v France* App no 3394/03 (ECtHR, 10 July 2008) para 50 and the Grand Chamber judgment (ECtHR, 29 March 2010) paras 62–67.
[309] *Öcalan v Turkey* App no 46221/99 (ECtHR, 12 May 2005) para 91.
[310] See also at length M Milanovic, *Extraterritorial Application of Human Rights Treaties: Law, Principles and Policy* (Oxford, OUP, 2011).

held accountable for its acts vis-à-vis persons over whom it exercises control. It was anticipated that the ECtHR would clarify matters in its judgment in *Al-Skeini* (2011), which concerned the question whether Iraqi citizens killed in combat by UK troops in Iraq fell within the UK's human rights jurisdiction. In *Al-Skeini*, the Court reaffirmed both the effective control standard and the State agent control standard which it had previously applied, and, on the facts of the case, considered that

> following the removal from power of the Ba'ath regime and until the accession of the Interim Government, the United Kingdom (together with the United States) assumed in Iraq the exercise of some of the public powers normally to be exercised by a sovereign government. In particular, the United Kingdom assumed authority and responsibility for the maintenance of security in South East Iraq. In these exceptional circumstances, the Court considers that the United Kingdom, through its soldiers engaged in security operations in Basrah during the period in question, exercised authority and control over individuals killed in the course of such security operations, so as to establish a jurisdictional link between the deceased and the United Kingdom for the purposes of Article 1 of the Convention.[311]

This dictum falls short of a wholesale endorsement of the State agent control standard, however. It indicates the importance which the Court continues to attach to the exercise of some measure of territorial control by an ECHR State Party for individuals to fall within the latter's jurisdiction.[312] The hybrid approach to jurisdiction – combining elements of territorial and personal control – can also be gleaned from later cases, such as *Hassan v UK*,[313] or *Jaloud v the Netherlands*,[314] although these cases give more prominence to the State agent control model. In *Jaloud*, for instance, the Court was satisfied that the Netherlands exercised its jurisdiction for the purpose of asserting authority and control over persons passing through a checkpoint in Iraq (a person was killed by shots fired from soldiers at the checkpoint).[315] In the future, perhaps, the Court may hold that persons injured or killed by patrols may also fall within the jurisdiction of the State. It is unclear, however, whether victims of extraterritorial bombing raids or drone attacks, assuming that the acting State has no territorial control, fall within the State's jurisdiction.

VII. Concluding Remarks

Jurisdiction is a multifaceted concept. Still, the various instantiations of jurisdiction have one thing in common: they imply the exercise of State authority. The rules of international law on jurisdiction provide that the exercise of jurisdiction is not just discretionary, but is either restricted or, rather exceptionally, required by international law. The PCIJ's *Lotus* judgment having lost much of its authority, the exercise of jurisdiction is not just a projection of factual power, but rather rests on an authorisation under international law.

[311] *Al-Skeini and others v The United Kingdom* App no 55721/07 (ECtHR, 7 July 2011) para 149.

[312] The UK may not have effectively controlled the Basrah territory through military occupation, but its strong territorial presence in the area was crucial for the Court's determination that the deceased individuals fell within the UK's jurisdiction. Moreover, the Court noted that these were 'exceptional circumstances', in the absence of which the individuals would arguably not have fallen within the UK's jurisdiction, even if the UK exercised control over their lives under the personal model of jurisdiction.

[313] *Hassan v The United Kingdom* App no 29750/09 (ECtHR, 16 September 2014) para 76: 'Following his capture by British troops […] Tarek Hassan was within the physical power and control of the United Kingdom soldiers and therefore fell within United Kingdom jurisdiction under the principles outlined in […] Al-Skeini'.

[314] *Jaloud v the Netherlands* App no 47708/08 (ECtHR, 20 November 2014).

[315] ibid, para 152.

In international law, jurisdiction is largely based on the principle of territoriality, which reflects the territorial structure of the system of States. Still, principles of extraterritorial jurisdiction, often based on a nexus with the State, have developed alongside that of territoriality, and have been codified in the criminal codes of European States. A similar evolution can be witnessed in human rights law, where the ECtHR has held that individuals not only fall within the jurisdiction of a State on the basis of the latter's territorial control, but also on the basis of State agent or 'personal' control.

The general international law of jurisdiction mainly applies to the exercise of criminal jurisdiction. However, its principles could equally apply to assertions of civil or regulatory jurisdiction, as such assertions, when having extraterritorial effects, could in equal measure interfere with other States' sovereignty. Thus, the law of jurisdiction also applies to the external regulatory action of the EU, as evidenced by the CJEU's judgments regarding the purported extraterritorial reach of the EU Aviation Directive and Data Protection Directive.

Even if the permissive principles of jurisdiction are by now rather clear, the law of jurisdiction remains in flux, largely because the exact scope of the principles is undetermined, and because of technological, social and moral evolutions. Due to the increased interconnectedness of the world, just one action, such as an act of cybercrime, could produce ripple effects everywhere, thus possibly allowing any State to exercise territorial jurisdiction. This would largely negate the ordering potential of territoriality – indeed, territoriality originally had an exclusive character – and call for the further development of second-order principles of jurisdiction. At the same time, increased global interconnectedness also translates into greater solidarity among States and among individuals, thus grounding a mandate for States to exercise jurisdiction in the interest of the international community, even absent a strong nexus of the asserting State. For instance, on the basis of treaty and customary law, any State can, or even must, exercise jurisdiction over grave crimes, such as torture or war crimes. Given the overlapping jurisdiction and international strife that such universality inevitably causes, the exact modalities and scope of universal jurisdiction, also outside the realm of criminal law, remain controversial.

In actual practice, head-on jurisdictional collisions between States nonetheless remain rather limited, possibly reflecting the fact that (transnational) crime and harmful activity is under- rather than over-enforced. The (non-)exercise of jurisdiction over foreign corrupt practices and cybercrime is a case in point. Where important political or economic interests are at stake, however, vigorous jurisdictional assertions remain likely to engender foreign opposition, and may lead to jurisdictional backpedalling by the asserting States. The fate of Belgium's and Spain's universality laws can serve as a cautionary tale in this respect.

We must also keep in mind that even when jurisdiction is claimed in legal proceedings, immunities of States, State officials, or international organisations and their officials may stand in the way of courts actually exercising their jurisdiction. This is further discussed in Chapter 11 on Immunities.

Bibliography

Akehurst, M, 'Jurisdiction in International Law' (1972) 46 *BYIL* 145.
Chehtman, A, *The Philosophical Foundations of Extraterritorial Punishment* (Oxford, OUP, 2010).

Lowe, V, *Extraterritorial Jurisdiction* (Cambridge, Grotius, 1983).
Staker, C, 'Jurisdiction' in MD Evans (ed), *International Law*, 4th edn (Oxford, OUP, 2014) 309–335.
Mann, F, 'The Doctrine of Jurisdiction in International Law' (1964) 111 *Recueil des Cours* 39.
Meessen, KM (ed), *Extraterritorial Jurisdiction in Theory and Practice* (London, Kluwer, 1996).
Reydams, L, *Universal Jurisdiction: International and Municipal Legal Perspectives* (Oxford, OUP, 2003).
Rothwell, DR and Stephens, T, *The International Law of the Sea* (Oxford, Hart, 2010).
Ryngaert, C, *Jurisdiction in International Law*, 2nd edn (Oxford, OUP, 2015).
Ryngaert, C, *Unilateral Jurisdiction and Global Values* (Utrecht, Eleven Publishing, 2015).
Sohn, LB, Gustafson Juras, K, Noyes, JE and Franckx, E, *Law of the Seas in a Nutshell* (St Paul, West Publishing, 2010).
Société française pour le droit international (ed), *Les compétences de l'Etat en droit international: colloque de Rennes* (Paris, Pedone, 2005).

Further Reading

Arnell, P, 'The Case for Nationality-Based Jurisdiction' (2001) 50 *ICLQ* 955.
Buxbaum, HL, 'Territory, Territoriality, and the Resolution of Jurisdictional Conflict' (2009) 57 *American Journal of Comparative Law* 631.
Colangelo, AJ, 'Universal Jurisdiction as an International "False Conflict" of Laws' (2008) 30 *MJIL* 881.
de La Pradelle, G, 'La compétence universelle' in Ascencio, H, Decaux, E and Pellet, A, *Droit international pénal*, 2nd edn (Paris, Pedone, 2012) 1007–1026.
Knox, JH, 'A Presumption Against Extrajurisdictionality' (2010) 104 *AJIL* 351.
Langer, M, 'The Diplomacy of Universal Jurisdiction: The Political Branches and the Transnational Prosecution of International Crimes' (2011) 105 *AJIL* 1.
Mills, A, 'Rethinking Jurisdiction in International Law' (2014) 84 *BYIL* 187.
O'Keefe, R, 'Universal Jurisdiction Clarifying the Basic Concept' (2004) 2 *JICJ* 735.
Scott, J, 'Extraterritoriality and Territorial Extension in EU law' (2014) 62 *American Journal of Comparative Law* 87.
Slot, PJ and Bulterman, M (eds), *Globalisation & Jurisdiction* (Alphen aan den Rijn, Kluwer, 2004).
Spiro, PJ, 'A new international law of citizenship' (2011) 105 *American Journal of International Law* 694.
Vallejo Peña, C, *El Estado de la jurisdicción universal en el Derecho Internacional y en el derecho interno español* (Valencia, Tirant lo Blanch, 2016).
Van Calster, G, *European Private International Law*, 2nd edn (Oxford, Hart, 2016).

10

Diplomatic and Consular Relations

CO-AUTHORED WITH SANDERIJN DUQUET

I. Introduction

Diplomatic and consular intercourse is at the heart of international relations. It enables States to maintain mutual relations and to communicate with nationals living or travelling abroad, as well as with foreign audiences. Virtually every State conducts permanent diplomatic relations with other States. It therefore maintains an embassy in the capital city of a foreign country, led by an ambassador whose main task consists of representing the sending State in the receiving State. The ambassador interacts with the official counterparts at the highest political level. In addition, a State may open one or more consulates per country, either in the capital or elsewhere. Although a consul also functions as the official representative of one State in the territory of another, his or her tasks are of a more administrative and economic nature compared to those of an ambassador. A consulate maintains regular contacts with local authorities, businesses, and its nationals; it also facilitates trade and friendship between two countries in a geographically limited area, called the consular district.

The formal and permanent conduct of diplomatic and consular relations is associated with the birth of the modern nation State in the sixteenth and seventeenth centuries. Most early writings on the law of nations included a section on the right of legation, which consists of the (active) right to send and the (passive) right to receive diplomatic and consular representatives.[1] Customary international law was, and continues to be, the basis for the system of diplomatic and consular exchanges. The first attempts at codification were made in 1815 (in the form of a regulation adopted by the Congress of Vienna on the classes of heads of diplomatic missions) and in 1818 (a protocol adopted by the Congress of Aix-la-Chapelle on diplomatic precedence and etiquette). In the early 1950s, the law of diplomatic and consular intercourse was one of the first to be selected by the UN General Assembly for further study by the International Law Commission (ILC), with the adoption of treaties

[1] See eg A Gentili, *De Legationibus, Libri Tres* (Excudebat Thomas Vautrollerius, 1585) 40 ff; H Grotius, *De Iure Belli Ac Pacis, Libri Tres* (Apud Nicolavm Bvon, 1625) vol 2, Ch XVIII, 366, I; E de Vattel, *Le Droit Des Gens, Ou Principes de La Loi Naturelle, Appliqués À La Conduite et Aux Affaires Des Nations et Des Souverains, Livre IV, Chapitre V* (1758) para 57 ff.

on both subjects as a consequence. The 1961 Vienna Convention on Diplomatic Relations (VCDR)[2] and the 1963 Vienna Convention on Consular Relations (VCCR)[3] are the starting point of our analysis. Measuring by the high degree of observance and their influence on international and national legal orders, the VCDR and VCCR are among the most successful international instruments ever to be drawn up under the auspices of the UN. To a large extent, the VCDR codified customary rules on bilateral diplomatic relations between States.[4] Meanwhile, its provisions have largely become part of general international law itself.[5] With 191 State Parties, its application is truly global.[6] The VCCR is not considered to be a simple codification of customary international law, although its main provisions have acquired customary status over time and 179 States have ratified it.[7]

The European continent – birthplace of the sovereign State – has been fertile soil for the growth and development of diplomatic and consular interactions. European States traditionally maintain large and influential networks of permanent missions. It is no surprise that Europe, too, has set afoot a new non-sovereign actor in diplomacy. Over five decades ago, the EU first claimed that it possessed a right of legation under public international law.[8]

This chapter discusses the legal framework on diplomatic and consular relations. It examines the diplomatic and consular functions (Section II), the establishment and termination of diplomatic and consular relations (Section III), the rights and obligations of diplomats and consuls (Section IV), and the application of diplomatic law by the EU and the joint efforts of its Member States in consular affairs (Section V).

II. Diplomatic and Consular Functions

A. Diplomatic Functions

Article 3(1) of the Convention on Diplomatic Relations enumerates the functions of a diplomatic mission, without being exhaustive:

(a) representing the sending State in the receiving State;

[2] VCDR (191 State Parties). Two optional protocols were added to the Convention: the Optional Protocol to the Vienna Convention on Diplomatic Relations concerning Acquisition of Nationality (adopted 18 April 1961, entered into force 24 April 1964) 500 UNTS 223 (51 State parties) and the Optional Protocol to the Vienna Convention on Diplomatic Relations concerning Compulsory Settlement of Disputes (adopted 18 April 1961, entered into force 24 April 1964) 500 UNTS 241 (71 State Parties).

[3] VCCR (179 State Parties). Two optional protocols were added to the Convention: the Optional Protocol to the Vienna Convention on Consular Relations concerning Acquisition of Nationality (adopted 24 April 1963, entered into force 19 March 1967) 596 UNTS 469 (41 State Parties) and the Optional Protocol to the Vienna Convention on Consular Relations concerning the Compulsory Settlement of Disputes (adopted 24 April 1963, entered into force 19 March 1967) 596 UNTS 487 (51 State Parties).

[4] G Berridge, *Diplomacy: Theory and Practice*, 4th edn (Basingstoke, Palgrave Macmillan, 2010) 109–10; E Denza, *Diplomatic Law: Commentary on the Vienna Convention on Diplomatic Relations*, 4th edn (Oxford, OUP, 2016) 2–5; J Verhoeven, *Droit International Public* (Brussels, Éditions Larcier, 2000) 106.

[5] See *Case concerning United States Diplomatic and Consular Staff in Tehran* (United States of America v Iran) [1980] ICJ Rep 3, paras 45 and 62; *Case concerning the Arrest Warrant of 11 April 2000* (Democratic Republic of the Congo v Belgium) [2002] ICJ Rep 3, para 52.

[6] Denza (n 4) 1.

[7] *Tehran Hostage Case* (n 5) para 62; LT Lee and JB Quigley, *Consular Law and Practice*, 3rd edn (Oxford, OUP, 2008) 21–23.

[8] Résolution adoptée par l'Assemblée Parlementaire Européenne relative aux problèmes que posent les relations des Communautés européennes avec l'extérieur, en particulier le droit de légation et de pavillon, 29 November 1960, OJ 1496/60.

(b) protecting in the receiving State the interests of the sending State and of its nationals, within the limits permitted by international law;
(c) negotiating with the Government of the receiving State;
(d) ascertaining by all lawful means conditions and developments in the receiving State, and reporting thereon to the Government of the sending State;
(e) promoting friendly relations between the sending State and the receiving State, and developing their economic, cultural and scientific relations.

The first function of representation is often overlooked or naively minimised, according to Berridge,[9] although it embraces all functions subsequently listed in Article 3 VCDR.[10] Three subsidiary functions can be distinguished as being part of the representational function: protection, negotiation and observation.[11] Of these functions, the ICJ has stressed diplomacy's role in the peaceful settlement of disputes,[12] while the ILC has emphasised the importance of the communication function.[13]

Article 3(2) VCDR stipulates that the performance of consular functions by a diplomatic mission should not be prevented. The legal framework for the performance of all consular functions by diplomats is the VCCR rather than the VCDR.[14] A diplomat performing consular tasks is granted diplomatic immunity according to the provisions of the latter Convention, since he or she is acting within his or her official functions.[15] The names of members of a diplomatic mission assigned to the consular section are submitted to the Ministry of Foreign Affairs (MFA) of the receiving State.[16]

The basic functions of diplomats have changed surprisingly little over time.[17] The context of diplomatic practice, on the contrary, has changed significantly. Since the introduction of the VCDR, a major shift has been brought about by globalisation processes.[18] Complex global problems have transformed a 'strict foreign policy', traditionally including matters of trade and security, into a 'broad foreign policy', which includes environmental, social, and human rights concerns. This evolution has been matched by a change in the methods used and a broadening of the membership of the diplomatic community. A wide range of less traditional actors, including governmental and non-governmental organisations, sub-State governments, parliaments, technical experts, and business representatives have become involved in diplomacy in the broader sense of the word.[19] Under the influence of these new circumstances, the focus and procedures of diplomatic practice have also

[9] Berridge (n 4) 114.
[10] I Roberts (ed), *Satow's Diplomatic Practice*, 6th edn (Oxford, OUP, 2011) 77.
[11] Denza (n 4) 35.
[12] In the words of the Court: '[t]he institution of diplomacy [...] proved to be an instrument essential for effective co-operation in the international community, and for enabling States, irrespective of their differing constitutional and social systems, to achieve mutual understanding and to resolve their differences by peaceful means': *Tehran Hostage Case* (n 5) para 39.
[13] In the 'Draft Articles on the Responsibility of States for Internationally Wrongful Acts with commentaries' *YBILC* vol II, Part Two, 131 and 133, the ILC recalls that 'the maintenance of channels of communication between the two States concerned' and 'the resolution of the dispute between the parties' are essential functions of the diplomatic system'.
[14] Arts 3 and 70(1) VCCR (n 3).
[15] ibid, Art 70(4) VCCR (n 3).
[16] ibid, Art 70(2) VCCR (n 3); Art 11 VCCR stipulates that they do not have to request a consular *exequatur*. See Lee and Quigley (n 7) 551; J Salmon, *Manuel de Droit Diplomatique* (Brussels, Bruylant, 1994) 526.
[17] Denza (n 4) 35; Roberts (n 10) 77; RP Barston, *Modern Diplomacy*, 4th edn (Harlow, Pearson, 2013) 4; S Sofer, 'Old and New Diplomacy: A Debate Revisited' in C Jönsson and R Langhorne (eds), *Diplomacy*, 2nd edn (London, Sage, 2004) 395.
[18] AF Cooper, 'The Changing Nature of Diplomacy' in AF Cooper, J Heine and R Thakur (eds), *The Oxford Handbook of Modern Diplomacy* (Oxford, OUP, 2013) 49.
[19] Barston (n 17) 6; K Mahbubani, 'Multilateral Diplomacy' in AF Cooper, Jorge Heine and Ramesh Thakur (eds), *The Oxford Handbook of Modern Diplomacy* (Oxford, OUP, 2013).

changed. Diplomatic and consular relations traditionally have been defined as being at the most formal end of the spectrum of international communication.[20] This function has not disappeared, but significantly more attention is now paid by diplomats to the informing and mobilising of citizens. Such public outreach ('public diplomacy') is seen as an essential element of the traditional function to promote friendly relations among States.[21] The age of digitalisation has reinforced this trend: many diplomatic missions have set up a website and manage social media accounts, which allow for a more direct communication with audiences in the Host State.[22] Furthermore, there is the growing influence of multilateralism as well as specialisation on diplomacy: international topics such as climate change, energy policy, and HIV/AIDS are tackled at international conferences dedicated to these topics. Although the public is most accustomed to Heads of State/Government and ministers representing countries in such settings, diplomatic missions play an important role in respect of the preparation, negotiation, and follow-up of these summits. The exercise of diplomatic functions has become more demanding in a world characterised by technological developments, the altered expectations of citizens, and increased global interactions. Yet the Vienna Convention's description of diplomatic functions proves to be flexible enough to be interpreted to include these trends and developments. It is well accepted that the interests of a State may nowadays include transnational and global themes. Nothing in Article 3 VCDR's language, moreover, suggests that those interests may not be represented via electronic means. The outreach to foreign audiences, it can be argued, has become a standard diplomatic function: learning the views of academia, civil society, and opposition parties in the receiving State will contribute not only to the 'promotion of friendly relations' between the sending State and the receiving State (and not just their governments), but also to the development of their economic, cultural and scientific relations (Article 3(1)(e) VCDR) and to ascertaining 'conditions and developments' in the receiving State (Article 3(1)(d) VCDR). Many States have seized the potential for creativity in the VCDR's application, although occasionally accusations of meddling in the receiving State's internal affairs (Article 41(1) VCDR) have also been voiced.

B. Consular Functions

One of the major challenges during the 1963 Vienna negotiations was to define a consular agent's functions. Article 5 VCCR therefore enumerates a broad range of tasks.[23]

> According to the 1963 Vienna Convention consular tasks include: (a) protecting the interests of the sending State and of its nationals; (b) furthering the development of commercial, economic, cultural, and scientific relations between the sending and the receiving State; (c) ascertaining conditions and developments in the commercial, economic, cultural, and scientific life of the receiving State; (d) issuing passports and travel documents; (e) helping and assisting nationals; (f) and (g) performing notarial and administrative functions; (h) and (i) safeguarding the interests

[20] J Crawford, *Brownlie's Principles of Public International Law* (Oxford, OUP, 2012) 395.

[21] J Melissen (ed), *The New Public Diplomacy: Soft Power in International Relations* (Basingstoke, Palgrave Macmillan, 2005).

[22] J Heine, 'On the Manner of Practising the New Diplomacy' (2006) *CIGI* 15; Michael Koch, 'Wozu noch Diplomaten?' in E Brandt and C Buck (eds), *Auswärtiges Amt: Diplomatie als Beruf* (Wiesbaden, Verlag für Sozialwissenschaften, 2005) 346, 358.

[23] VM Uribe, 'Consuls at Work: Universal Instruments of Human Rights and Consular Protection in the Context of Criminal Justice' (1997) 2 *Houston Journal of International Law* 375, 386; Lee and Quigley (n 7) 107; Crawford (n 20) 411.

of minors and other persons lacking full capacity who are nationals of the sending State; (j) transmitting and executing judicial and extrajudicial documents; (k) and (l) exercising rights of supervision and inspection in respect of vessels and aircrafts having the nationality of or which are registered in the sending State and extending assistance to these vessels and aircraft and to their crews.

As the final paragraph (m) of Article 5 VCCR spells out, consular agents are also permitted to perform any other function entrusted by the sending State which is not prohibited by the laws of the receiving State. In special circumstances and with the consent of the receiving State, consular functions can be exercised outside the consular district (Article 6 VCCR), in another State (upon notification to the receiving State; Article 7 VCCR), or in the receiving State on behalf of a third State (Article 8 VCCR). In certain prescribed circumstances, consular officers can even perform diplomatic acts. Their exercise, however, is of an extraordinary character and does not confer upon a consular agent any right to claim diplomatic privileges and immunities.[24]

Another legal instrument – adopted in the framework of the Council of Europe – that defines consular functions is the 1967 European Convention on Consular Functions.[25] Articles 2–16 of this Paris Convention extend the scope of such functions, adapt them to the European consular context, and grant new functions to consular officers in those fields where their role was considered most useful,[26] leading to a more tailored codification of consular functions compared to Article 5 VCCR.

The consular agent performs administrative, legal, and notarial functions in the receiving State,[27] all of which demand a basic knowledge of the local laws and regulations.[28] These tasks include the issuance of passports, visas, and other travel documents recognised by a sending State;[29] notarial and registration services such as declarations of adoption or parenthood, the administration of estates, marriage and divorce; depositions, service of process, and the transmittance of judicial and extrajudicial documents. The consul renders services in the clear interest of the sending State and under its instruction. Yet, when exercising public authority, consular agents are under a general duty to respect the laws and regulations of the receiving State (Article 55 VCCR), which distinguishes their position from that of government officials performing similar functions at home.

Consular functions that are particularly relevant for individuals include the different forms of consular assistance and protection offered abroad.[30] After a consular officer has established that an individual is a national of the sending State, the agent may coordinate his or her repatriation, mediate in disputes with local authorities or private actors, and assist in emergency situations. As a result of growing global mobility, the number of foreigners being charged with criminal offences, and thus in need of consular access, has also increased.[31] Article 36(1)(b) VCCR acknowledges that free communication between a consular agent and a national faced with criminal charges is a prerequisite for consular

[24] Art 17(1) VCCR (n 3); Salmon (n 16) 524.

[25] European Convention on Consular Functions (adopted 11 December 1967, entered into force 9 June 2011) CETS No 061 (five ratifications).

[26] General Consideration No 6, European Convention on Consular Functions – Explanatory Report, 11 December 1967, [1967] COETSER 4 conventions.coe.int/Treaty/en/Reports/Html/061.htm.

[27] See Arts 5(d), (f), (g), (i), (j) and (k) VCCR (n 3).

[28] Roberts (n 10) 261.

[29] French consular agents are granted the authority to effect final decisions on requests to issue visa to enter France; see Conseil d'Etat (FR), statuant au contentieux, 27 May 1998, Case No 181092.

[30] Art 5(a), (e), (i) VCCR (n 3).

[31] Lee and Quigley (n 7) 139.

assistance.[32] The VCCR further provides a sending State tools to watch over the (fair) treatment of its nationals by a local police corps and the judicial system.[33] However, neither Article 5 nor Article 36 VCCR imposes an obligation on the part of the sending State to exercise consular protection.[34]

Article 36 has provoked a considerable number of judicial decisions. Case law typically tackles questions with regard to the existence of a duty of the receiving State's officials to inform foreigners of their rights to consular access and, if they fail to do so, on the appropriate judicial remedy.[35]

In 1999, the Inter-American Court on Human Rights was the first international adjudication body to issue an advisory opinion that recognised that Article 36 VCCR creates individual rights.[36] Soon thereafter, the ICJ addressed the topic on the merits both in the 2001 *LaGrand*[37] and the 2004 *Avena and Other Mexican Nationals* judgments.[38] The first case concerned two German brothers sentenced to death in the United States. The ICJ noted that the language of Article 36(1)(b) VCCR does not leave room for misinterpretation where it stipulates that 'the said authorities shall inform the person concerned *without delay*[39] of his or her rights under this subparagraph'.[40] It continued by stating that Article 36 provides a rare instance in which a treaty obligation – the right to consular assistance of nationals of the sending State in a receiving State – was recognised to affect both the rights of the sending State (the so-called 'right to consul') and the individual rights of the national concerned. Moreover, it was decided that both are subject to international adjudication.[41] The *Avena* case concerned 52 Mexican nationals facing the death penalty in the US who were unable to, or not told that they could, communicate with the Mexican consulate.[42] The US was found to be in violation of the VCCR's information duty with respect

[32] Art 36 includes three distinctive rights: (1) a freedom of communication; (2) an obligation to forward any communication addressed to the consular post by the person in detention without delay; (3) the right to visit a national in prison, custody, or detention, to converse and correspond with him and to arrange for his legal representation: MJ Kadish, 'Article 36 of the Vienna Convention on Consular Relations: A Search for the Right to Consul' (1996) 18 *MJIL* 565, 569.

[33] Uribe (n 23) 390; Lee and Quigley (n 7) 140; Canadian Alberta Court of Appeal (CA), *R v Van Bergen*, 26 July 2000, [2000] AJ No 882 (QL), 225 WAC 386.

[34] In the past, European citizens have challenged their State, without success, for a perceived lack of assistance. See for instance: Court of Appeal of The Hague (NL) *Van Dam v The Netherlands*, 25 November 2004, LJN: AR7484; Conseil d'Etat (FR), 29 January 1993, Case No 11946, 111949.

[35] Certain national courts consider a non-notification of rights under Art 36 VCCR a violation of an individual right; see Bundesverfassungsgericht (DE), *German Consular Notification Case*, 19 September 2006, 2 BvR 2115/01; Court of First Instance's-Gravenhage (NL), 25 April 2007, [2006] AWB 08/34834.

[36] Advisory Opinion OC-16/99, 1 October 1999, IACtHR Series A No 16 (1999), para 87.

[37] *LaGrand* (Germany v United States of America) [2001] ICJ Rep 466.

[38] *Avena and Other Mexican Nationals* (Mexico v United States of America) [2004] ICJ Rep 12. In 1998, the ICJ had already issued provisional measures calling upon the United States not to execute a Paraguayan national, Angel Breard, who had not been made aware of rights to consular access. Although the US Supreme Court declined the ruling, Paraguay decided to dismiss the case after Breard was executed: *Case Concerning the Vienna Convention on Consular Relations* (Paraguay v United States of America) [1998] ICJ Rep 426.

[39] *Avena* (n 38) para 63. A delay of ten days to notify consular authorities of an alien's detention constitutes a breach of Art 36(1)(b) VCCR (n 3): District Court The Hague (NL), *A v Minister of Immigration and Integration*, 23 August 2005, AWB 05/34215 VRWET [2005].

[40] J Fitzpatrick, 'The Unreality of International Law in the United States and the LaGrand Case' (2002) 27 *Yale Journal of International Law* 427, 428.

[41] See paras 77 and 125, *LaGrand Case* (n 37). For a more detailed assessment, see JB Quigley, 'LaGrand: A Challenge to the US Judiciary' (2002) 27 *Yale Journal of International Law* 435; Fitzpatrick (n 40).

[42] *Avena* (n 38) para 40 and Request for Interpretation of the Judgment of 31 March 2004, 9 January 2009, in the same case.

to 51 of those cases;[43] in 49 cases, the US had deprived the individuals of the right to communicate, in a timely fashion, with the consulate. The influence of the *Avena* decision was soon measured in the United States' domestic legal order, when one of the nationals involved in the case, Mr Medellin, was denied relief by a federal appellate court following the ICJ's ruling. The holding of the *Avena* case was not considered to be binding on US federal courts[44] as was later confirmed by the US Supreme Court.[45] In the direct aftermath, the US also withdrew from the Optional Protocol to the VCCR concerning the compulsory settlement of disputes, which had formed the basis for ICJ jurisdiction in the discussed *LaGrand* and *Avena* cases.[46]

C. Diplomatic and Consular Functions Compared

The functions of a diplomatic and a consular agent are to be distinguished. Generally speaking, consular functions do not have a representative or political character but are instead of a more commercial, practical, and administrative nature.[47] The absence of the representational function prevents a consular agent from being authorised to bring or defend legal proceedings on behalf of his or her State in the receiving country, except when expressly mandated to do so.[48] The diplomatic functions are mostly carried out by interacting with the central government of the receiving State, as opposed to consular functions, which are performed through contacts with local actors such as businesses, police or prison officers, the cultural sector, and so on.

Granted that there are important differences between the descriptions of functions in the two Vienna Conventions, clear intersections are also to be observed.[49] Firstly, because of the growing interconnectedness of politics and commercial affairs, in many instances a complete distinction of diplomatic and consular functions is considered unfeasible.[50] Article 5(a) VCCR, for example, tasks the consul to protect *all* interests of the sending State and of its nationals, both individuals and enterprises, in the receiving State, without further specification. Article 3(1)(b) VCDR similarly defines the protection of interests in a manner that includes both commercial and political interests. Secondly, as already explained, the

[43] N Klein, 'Avena and Other Mexican Nationals (Mexico v United States of America)' (2004) 11 *Australian Journal of International Law* 143, 151.

[44] Supreme Court (US), *Medellin v Dretke*, 10 December 2004, 371 F3d 270 (5th Cir 2004). See also, Supreme Court (US) *Sánchez-Llamas v Oregon*, 28 June 2006, 548 US 331 (2006) para 43; MJ Kadish, 'Article 36 of the Vienna Convention on Consular Relations : The International Court of Justice in Mexico v. United States (Avena) Speaks Emphatically to the Supreme Court of the United States about Fundamental Nature of the Right to Consul' (2004) 36 *GJIL* 1, 9–17.

[45] See Supreme Court (US) *Medellín v Texas*, 25 March 2008 552 US 491; S Charnovitz, 'Correcting America's Continuing Failure to Comply with the Avena Judgment' (2012) 106 *AJIL* 572.

[46] On 7 March 2005, the UN Secretary General received a communication from the US Government notifying its withdrawal from the Optional Protocol, the exact consequences of which are debated in lack of a denunciation clause in the Protocol; JB Quigley, 'The United States' Withdrawal From International Court of Justice Jurisdiction in Consular Cases: Reasons and Consequences' (2008) 19 *Duke Journal of Comparative and International Law* 263. See for a discussion of the effect of these judgments in domestic courts, Chapter 4 on the relationship and interactions between international law, EU law and national law.

[47] Roberts (n 10) 249 and 260.

[48] Salmon (n 16) 461 and 522.

[49] Denza (n 4) 32; M Okano-Heijmans, 'Consular Affairs' in AF Cooper, J Heine and R Thakur (eds), *The Oxford Handbook of Modern Diplomacy* (Oxford, OUP, 2013) 473, 482.

[50] Lee and Quigley (n 7) 541. In the same sense: Roberts (n 10) 260.

Conventions foresee the possibility of consular functions being performed by diplomatic agents and diplomatic functions being performed by consular mission respectively. Thirdly, although the functions listed in Article 5 VCCR are intended to be more detailed and specific in comparison to the broadly formulated functions in Article 3 VCDR, neither article is exhaustive. In a modern context, diplomatic and consular functions may therefore best be distinguished based on how they are carried out and by methods used rather than by a mere textual reading of Articles 3 VCDR and 5 VCCR.[51]

III. The Establishment of Diplomatic and Consular Relations

The recognition of a State (see Chapter 5 on States), the establishment of diplomatic and/or consular relations, and the establishment of a permanent mission are separate international legal acts.[52] As a result, the establishment of diplomatic and/or consular relations can precede the opening of a representation office.[53] The establishment of such relations and missions is carried out by mutual consent (Article 2 VCDR and Article 2(1) VCCR); most commonly a formal request is made by the MFA of the sending State to the receiving State's authorities. The actual decision on whether to open a mission is taken by the Head of State or Government.[54] States deciding to establish diplomatic relations concurrently imply the establishment of consular relations, unless stated otherwise (Article 2(2) VCCR). Consular relations can also be established regardless of the existence of diplomatic relations;[55] the termination of diplomatic relations does not therefore *ipso facto* involve the severance or termination of consular relations.[56]

International diplomatic law governs the accreditation process of diplomatic agents.[57] When the Head of the sending State appoints a diplomatic representative,[58] this is announced in a 'Letter of Credence' addressed to the Head of the receiving State, in order to receive *agrément*.[59] Since the essence of the *agrément* procedure is its informality, the VCDR does not prescribe a form or method to be used.[60] The MFA of the receiving State is notified of

[51] Denza (n 4) 32. For example, both Art 3 VCDR (n 2) and Art 5 VCCR (n 3) list the protection of nationals as a core function; however, while a diplomat will protect in a more collective, general sense, the consular agent will protect the national in individual cases upon concrete needs; see Roberts (n 10) 249 and 260.

[52] Roberts (n 10) 71. Although different legal acts, the distinct steps can take place at the same time.

[53] M Zieck, 'Diplomatiek En Consulair Recht' in N Horbach, R Lefeber and O Ribbelink (eds), *Handboek Internationaal Recht* (The Hague, TMC Asser Press, 2007) 275, 278.

[54] B Sen, *A Diplomat's Handbook of International Law and Practice*, 3rd edn (Dordrecht, Martinus Nijhoff Publishers, 1988) 22.

[55] Roberts (n 10) 227.

[56] Art 2(3) VCCR (n 3). Following the invasion of the Falkland Islands (1982), all diplomatic and consular relations between the United Kingdom and Argentina were severed. In a joint statement of 19 October 1989 the re-establishment of consular relations was announced (Art 4), a full year before the re-establishment of diplomatic relations; MD Evans, 'The Restoration of Diplomatic Relations Between Argentina and the United Kingdom' (1991) 40 *ICLQ* 473.

[57] Denza (n 4) 40.

[58] Sen (n 54) 34; Roberts (n 10) 84; MN Shaw, *International Law*, 6th edn (Cambridge, Cambridge University Press, 2014) 547.

[59] Sen (n 54) 50; Zieck (n 53) 281; Crawford (n 20) 400.

[60] Denza (n 4) 40. Members of a diplomatic mission other than the head of the mission are not subject to the previous *agrément* of the receiving State (Art 7 VCDR (n 2)).

the details of the appointment of other members of the mission.[61] The head of a diplomatic mission is considered as having taken up his or her functions in the receiving State either following the presentation of his or her credentials or following a notification of his or her arrival and the presentation of a true copy of the credentials to the MFA of the receiving State.[62] Similarly, the sending State will request the receiving State to grant an *exequatur* to admit a commissioned head of a consular post to the exercise of his or her functions.[63] The VCCR does not spell out any formal requirements for the consular exequatur, but does require the receiving State to immediately notify the competent authorities of the consular district of its admittance of a head of a consular post to enable the (provisional) exercise of consular functions.[64] The Conventions do not compel a receiving State to give reasons for a decision not to grant the necessary authorisation to a foreign diplomat or consul.[65]

IV. Diplomatic and Consular Rights and Obligations

The Vienna Conventions cover a wide variety of topics that relate to the sending and receiving of diplomats and consuls. The majority of these provisions concern the rights of the missions and their staff, conceptualised as immunities, inviolabilities, privileges, and entitlements. As a result of these, the State Parties accept restrictions on the exclusive jurisdiction over their own territory:[66] certain laws and regulations either do not apply (privileges) or cannot be enforced (immunities and inviolabilities). The far-reaching restrictions on the sovereignty of States would not have withstood the test of time if there had not been certain strings attached. The quasi-unchallengeable rights of diplomats and (to a lesser extent) of consuls bring about obligations to be observed when stationed abroad. Therefore, the literature often notes that most, if not all, duties of diplomats serve as the corollary of the immunities. In other words, diplomatic and consular rights and duties are seen as corresponding notions.[67] This is correct, in the sense that the Vienna Conventions adhere to a certain balance between rights and duties of receiving and sending States, which enables the diplomatic and consular systems – historically grounded in the principle of reciprocity – to function. Yet, the system is not in every aspect based on mutual obligations. Strict adherence to the reciprocity principle might hinder equal treatment of missions, as it would enable States to discriminate according to immunities and privileges received by their own missions abroad. Such acts would be irreconcilable with the text of Articles 47 VCDR and 72 VCCR,

[61] Art 10 VCDR (n 2).
[62] Art 13(1) VCDR (n 2).
[63] Art 12 VCCR (n 3); Shaw (n 58) 561. In order receive exequatur, the sending State will provide the head of a consular post with a document called 'a commission', certifying its capacity and consular rank and class; Art 11(1) VCCR (n 3). Some governments require by law or regulations that consular officers, other than the head of mission, also receive exequatur, see Art 19(3)–(4) VCCR (n 3); Roberts (n 10) 214; Lee and Quigley (n 7) 83.
[64] Arts 12(1) and 14 VCCR (n 3).
[65] Art 4(2) VCDR (n 2) and Art 12(2) VCCR (n 3). The decision of the French government not to grant approval for the opening of a consular post of the Republic of Albania in Caen, and subsequently, its refusal of the necessary exequatur for the Albanian honorary consul, cannot be appealed before the French administrative court system; Administrative Court of Appeal (*Cour administrative d'appel*) (FR), 23 June 2005, [2005] *Jurisprudence Jus Luminum* n° J185700.
[66] Crawford (n 20) 204.
[67] Roberts (n 10) 150; S Lechner, 'What Difference Does Ius Inter Gentes Make? Changing Diplomatic Rights and Duties and the Modern European States-System' (2006) 1 *The Hague Journal of Diplomacy* 235, 240–241.

which contains a straightforward prohibition of parties discriminating between States. As a result, receiving States are under a duty to treat all diplomats and consuls within their territory according to a general standard of treatment, both in law and in practice. They do not, however, prohibit a receiving State, under the specific circumstances spelled out in Articles 47(2) and 72(2) VCDR, from granting treatment more favourable than the general standard to particular sending States, nor from applying diplomatic and consular privileges restrictively because of a restrictive application of that provision to its own missions in the sending State.[68] However, the ILC ruled out the idea that a State only has to grant immunities if an envoy fulfils his or her duties in the receiving State. In its 1958 Commentary to the Draft Articles on Diplomatic Intercourse and Immunities, the ILC submitted that '[f]ailure by a diplomatic agent to fulfil his obligations does not absolve the receiving State from its duty to respect the agent's immunity'.[69] This section studies the diplomatic and consular rights and obligations and their interactions in more detail and also comments on the interface between these concepts and human rights law.

A. Privileges, Immunities, and Inviolability[70]

Both the VCDR and the VCCR include provisions on privileges, immunities, and inviolability. However, neither Convention defines these terms. In general, a distinction between the different concepts has been made as follows:[71] 'immunity' encompasses the immunity from jurisdiction (Article 31(1) VCDR; Article 43 VCCR) and the immunity from execution (Article 31(3) VCDR; Article 45(4) VCCR). 'Inviolability' entails on the one hand a special positive duty of protection for the receiving State, and on the other hand a negative duty for the latter to abstain from exercising any sovereign right, in particular enforcement rights.[72] 'Privileges', in turn, can be best understood as 'other advantages than immunities and inviolability'.[73] Contrary to immunities, which are procedural in nature, privileges are substantive rights. A privilege denotes an exemption from laws or regulations, while immunity does not imply any exemption from substantive law, but confers procedural protection from the enforcement processes in the receiving State.[74] The rules laid down in the VCDR regarding diplomatic privileges, immunities, and inviolability are mainly based

[68] Art 47 VCDR (n 2) and Art 72 VCCR (n 3) allow less and more favourable treatment. First, a receiving State may apply a VCDR/VCCR provision 'restrictively because of a restrictive application of that provision to its mission in the sending State' (Art 47(2)(a) VCDR and Art 72(2)(a) VCCR). Consequently, States can opt for a restrictive reading of the Conventions when another State does so, on the basis of reciprocity in a specific bilateral relationship, under the condition that no breach occurs. Second, no discrimination takes place when 'States extend to each other more favourable treatment' than is required by the Vienna Conventions (Art 47(2)(b) VCDR and Art 72(2)(b) VCCR). The legal basis for such favourable treatment may either be a rule of custom or an agreement between states, for which no reciprocity is required. Nonetheless, in practice, the main reason why States grant additional privileges will be because their missions abroad are receiving additional rights and privileges. In practice, these rules result in the fact that quota for products that can be imported duty free or the number of diplomatic licence plates (ie, topics not regulated by the Vienna Conventions) differs from one country to another, and within one country, from one mission to another.

[69] ILC, 'Draft Articles on Diplomatic Intercourse and Immunities with commentaries' (1958) II *YILC* 104.

[70] See also Chapter 11 on immunities.

[71] The distinction between a 'privilege' and an 'immunity' is not easy to make, and the terms are sometimes used interchangeably; Roberts (n 10) 121–22; Lee and Quigley (n 7) 341.

[72] Denza (n 4) 105–106; Zieck (n 53) 284.

[73] Zieck (n 53) 284; Lee and Quigley (n 7) 341.

[74] Roberts (n 10) 121–22.

on customary international law and have become international custom themselves.[75] This is different for the VCCR, which came into being when only some consular immunities and inviolabilities, and virtually no privileges, had the status of general international law.[76] Today, however, most rules laid down in the VCCR regarding consular privileges, immunities, and inviolability are also recognised as customary international law.[77]

The preambles of both Vienna Conventions state that the 'purpose of such privileges and immunities is not to benefit individuals but to ensure the efficient performance of the functions' of 'diplomatic missions as representing States' (VCDR) and by 'consular posts on behalf of their respective States' (VCCR).[78] This formulation reflects that in the 1960s a compromise needed to be found between two theoretical bases that historically have been used to justify diplomatic and consular benefits: the functional necessity theory (diplomatic and consular advantages serve a functional need) and the representative character principle (diplomats – and to a lesser extent consuls – are the direct representatives of the sending State).[79] The functional necessity theory has clearly prevailed. The rationale for diplomatic and consular immunities may thus be similar; the scope of diplomatic/consular immunity varies according to the content of diplomatic and consular functions performed. The more sensitive work carried out by diplomats requires a more extensive protection and a guaranteed confidentiality.[80] Consequently, the protection of diplomats has a broader scope than that of consuls.

Since States have a reciprocal interest in upholding diplomatic and consular law (being both sending and receiving State), immunities, inviolabilities, and privileges are in general well respected. Certain bilateral agreements also accord consular agents rights beyond what is essential for their official functions on a mutual basis. In this regard, one should note that the VCCR expressly allows for the conclusion of agreements supplementing, extending, or amplifying its provisions (Article 73).[81] Conversely, privileges and immunities accorded to honorary consuls are more limited than those enjoyed by career consuls, whose status, competences, functions, and wages differ substantially. An honorary consul is not a professional consul and is often appointed from among the nationals of the receiving State because he or she is well integrated in the area and speaks a local language. The honorary functions vary from State to State but generally include activities that are politically less sensitive and can be combined with another daytime job (eg, as a lawyer or business representative). Consequently, honorary consuls are called upon to provide administrative and consular assistance to citizens, serve as liaison with local authorities, and to build commercial, economic, cultural, and touristic contacts in the area – duties for which they may be paid a small honorarium. The legal distinction between consuls and honorary consuls is

[75] *Tehran Hostage Case* (n 5) para 62; *Arrest Warrant Case* (n 5) para 52. See also Verhoeven (n 4) 106.

[76] Before the VCCR came into force, only the inviolability of consular archives and the immunity of consuls with regard to their official acts were recognised as customary international law. See WE Beckett, 'Consular Immunities' (1944) 21 *BYIL* 34; Lee and Quigley (n 7) 341; Roberts (n 10) 265–66.

[77] *Tehran Hostage Case* (n 5) para 62; *Arrest Warrant Case* (n 5) para 52. See also CJ Milhaupt, 'The Scope of Consular Immunity under the Vienna Convention on Consular Relations: Towards a Principled Interpretation' (1988) 88 *CLR* 845, 841; Lee and Quigley (n 7) 341.

[78] See Art 25 VCDR (n 2) and Art 28 VCCR (n 3).

[79] K Bruns, *A Cornerstone of Modern Diplomacy: Britain and the Negotiation of the 1961 Vienna Convention on Diplomatic Relations* (New York, Bloomsbury Academic, 2014) 133.

[80] Salmon (n 16) 521–22.

[81] See, for further reading, S Kho, 'Article 73 of the Vienna Convention on Consular Relations: The Relationship between the Vienna Consular Convention and Other International Consular Agreements' (1994) 13 *Chinese (Taiwan) Yearbook of International Law and Affairs* 235.

reflected in the VCCR. Chapter II applies to consular posts headed by career consuls, while the provisions of Chapter III VCCR govern consular posts headed by honorary consular officers (Article 1(2) VCCR). This chapter focuses on the status of career consuls, although reference will be made to the applicable rules for honorary consuls.

B. Inviolability of Diplomatic and Consular Premises

The inviolability of diplomatic (Article 22 VCDR) and consular premises (Article 31 VCCR) is underpinned by the same principles as discussed above. A receiving State must take all appropriate steps to protect such premises (positive duty), while its agents are prohibited from entering them without due consent of the head of the mission (negative duty). Notable differences nevertheless exist with regard to the definition of the premises of the mission. Under Article 1(i) VCDR, the premises of the diplomatic mission are 'the buildings or parts of buildings and the land ancillary thereto, irrespective of ownership, used for the purposes of the mission including the residence of the head of the mission'.[82] Diplomatic premises are thus broadly defined to also include the private residence of a diplomatic agent, which enjoys the same inviolability and protection as the premises of the mission (Article 30(1) VCDR). The private residence of a consul, in contrast, is not considered as being part of the 'consular premises' and does not enjoy inviolability (Article 31(1) VCCR).[83]

With regard to the negative obligation, the receiving State is under different obligations when dealing with diplomatic and consular premises. Firstly, the inviolability of diplomatic missions is strictly interpreted. The receiving State's agents may not enter it without the express consent of the head of the mission (Article 22(1) VCDR). The consent of the head of mission, unless agreed to the contrary, is not presumed, not even in emergency or exceptional situations (a fire, etc). The inviolability goes together with a prohibition on all coercive measures (search, requisition, attachment or execution, see Article 22(3) VCDR)[84] and applies to members of the armed forces, the police, officials of the tax, employment or customs administrations, as well as to bailiffs in the context of the service of documents on the premises of the mission.[85] Even when the receiving State believes that the inviolability is being abused and the premises are used in a manner 'incompatible with the functions of the mission' (prohibited under Article 41 VCDR), the receiving State does not have a right

[82] The qualification as 'premises of the mission' does not depend on a title to property but relates to the Art 3 VCDR (n 2) activities performed on those premises: Salmon (n 16) 90. According to the ECtHR '[i]t is sufficient for the property to be "used for the purposes of the mission" of the foreign State'. See *Manoilescu and Dobrescu v Romania and Russia* App no 60861/00 (ECtHR, 3 March 2005) para 77.

[83] Consequently, even when located in the same premises, the residence of a consul and the area used for consular activities have a separate status. A consular post headed by an honorary consul is not inviolable, but must be protected by the receiving State against intrusion, damage, and impairment of dignity (Art 59 VCCR (n 3)).

[84] In 2011 and 2012 French authorities conducted searches in the Parisian mansion of the Vice-President of Equatorial Guinea, in the context of a money laundering investigation. Because the property had been recently sold by the Vice-President to the State of Equatorial Guinea, the country asserted that it formed part of its embassy. France claimed it had never recognised the diplomatic status of the premises and was not under an obligation to grant them inviolability under Art 22 VCDR. By an Order of 7 December 2016 the ICJ indicated that, pending a final decision in the case, France was to ensure the inviolability of the premises presented by Equatorial Guinea as housing their diplomatic mission. By its Judgment of 6 June 2018, the Court declared that it had jurisdiction to hear Equatorial Guinea's claims under the VCDR (*Immunities and Criminal Proceedings (Equatorial Guinea v France)*, preliminary objections [2018] ICJ Rep 163).

[85] F Dopagne, S Duquet and B Theeuwes, *Diplomatiek recht toegepast in België* (Antwerp, Maklu, 2014) 51.

of entry.[86] If illegal activities take place in a diplomatic mission, a solution should be found through diplomatic negotiation.[87]

One infamous case concerns an 1984 incident that took place in London. At a peaceful protest outside the Libyan embassy, a young police officer, Yvonne Fletcher, was fatally shot and 11 people were hurt after gunfire was discharged at the protesters from within the embassy.[88] Even in this event the inviolability of the diplomatic mission was strictly interpreted by the UK government. Instead of entering the mission, local authorities laid siege to the embassy for the next 11 days. All diplomatic relations with Libya were severed and the staff was requested to leave the country, but no official charges were filed against them.

The protection provided by the VCCR is more limited in three ways. Under Article 1(1)(j) VCCR, firstly, consular premises are the buildings exclusively used for the purpose of consular work. Consequently, other parts (eg, a kitchen) can be entered in accordance with local rules. Secondly, consent for an entry may not be given only by the head of the consular post, but also by a designee or by the head of the diplomatic mission of the sending State. Thirdly, the consent of the head of the consular post may be assumed in case of fire or of other disaster requiring prompt action. The more limited protection of consular posts finds its origins in the idea that, traditionally (ie, before the VCCR), inviolability of consular posts was not recognised as a rule of customary international law.[89]

A final element of inviolability is that the premises of a diplomatic mission, their furnishings (and other property thereon), and the means of transport of the mission are immune from search, requisition, attachment, or execution (Article 22(3) VCDR). The VCCR's immunity from execution, in contrast, is limited to a protection against any form of requisition for the purposes of national defence or public utility (Article 31(4) VCCR). Since the coming into force of the 1961 Vienna Convention, discussion has emerged in the literature as well as in many national courts regarding the question whether a mission's bank accounts are covered by Article 22 VCDR.[90] One of the main problems is that such accounts are not held on the mission's premises as required by the wording of the article. State practice by and large accepts a functional interpretation: since bank accounts serve the functioning of an embassy, they cannot be made subject to measures of attachment or execution.[91]

[86] Salmon (n 16) 198–99; Roberts (n 10) 102.

[87] *Tehran Hostage Case* (n 5) paras 83–87. The Eritrea-Ethiopia Claims Commission concluded that Ethiopia had breached Art 22 VCDR by sealing off the Eritrean embassy without its consent on the basis of suspicion of criminal activity taking place in the embassy. See Eritrea-Ethiopia Claims Commission, Partial Award: *Diplomatic Claim – Eritrea's Claim 20* (Eritrea v Ethiopia), 19 December 2005, 381 RIAA, paras 46–47.

[88] S Tendler, 'Fletcher, Yvonne Joyce (1958–1984)' in *Oxford Dictionary of National Biography* (Oxford, OUP, 2010); Denza (n 4) 147; C Chatterjee, *International Law and Diplomacy* (London, Routledge, 2007) 232.

[89] Art 31(2) VCCR (n 3) should therefore be seen as the result of a compromise between States that favoured absolute immunity of consular posts (such as the former Communist States), and States that favoured conditional immunity of consular posts (such as Nigeria, Greece, Japan, and the UK). See United Nations, 'Official Records of the United Nations Conference on Consular Relations, Vienna, 4 March–22 April 1963' (1963) *Volume I: Summary records of plenary meetings and of the meetings of the First and Second Committees* A/CONF 25/16 22.

[90] See, for instance, Bundesverfassungsgericht (DE), 13 December 1977, 2 BvM 1/76, ILR, vol 65 and 6 December 2006, 2 BvM 9/03; House of Lords (UK), *Alcom Ltd/Republic*, 12 April 1984, ILR, vol 74, 170; Oberster Gerichtshof (AU), *Republic of «A» Embassy Bank Account Case*, 30 April 1986, 77 ILR 488; Cass. (IT), *Capizzi/Embassy of Algeria*, 4 May 1989, 87 ILR 56.

[91] The Court of Cassation (BE), 22 November 2012, C.11.0688.F and 11 December 2014, C.13.0537.F/1, which adheres to the French Court of Cassation on the issue (Cass (FR), *NML Capital Ltd/République Argentine*, 28 September 2011, no 09-72.057; *NML Capital Ltd./Argentine*, 28 March 2013, no 11-10.450; *Commisimpex/République du Congo* (DRC), 13 May 2015, no 13-17751, explicitly relies on this functional theory, while finding

The other side of the inviolability coin concerns a positive duty for the receiving State to take all appropriate steps to protect diplomatic and consular premises against any intrusion or damage and to prevent the disturbance of the peace of the premises or impairment of their dignity (Article 22(2) VCDR; Article 31(3) VCCR). According to the ICJ this includes an obligation to take measures to repel any armed attack on the premises by private actors, such as armed militia groups.[92]

The legal rules on the protection of an embassy were tested during the infamous 1979 Iran hostage crisis, and later gave rise to one of the most cited ICJ cases on diplomatic relations. On 4 November 1979, a militant group of Iranian students entered the US Embassy in Tehran and overtook it, taking its 52 occupants hostage. In the 1980 *Tehran Hostages* judgment, the Court found the receiving State, Iran, in violation of the VCDR.[93] Despite the fact that the hostage takers were not agents of the State, the Court concluded that Iran, which had proved itself unwilling to prevent the takeover or to end it, was responsible for its inactions.[94] The moment Iranian authorities had become aware of appeals for help from the US government, an obligation to comply with obligations under the VCDR had arisen which required the receiving State to take action to protect the embassy with the means at its disposal.[95]

Compliance with the provision on the inviolability of diplomatic premises may thus in certain circumstances require the taking of preventive measures by the receiving State. Article 22(3) refers to 'appropriate steps'; these are measures which are proportionate in light of the security risk at hand.[96] Appropriate steps can be enshrined in domestic laws (eg, on the instalment of a secure perimeter around an embassy or consulate) or may be left to the discretion of the police in the circumstances of each case. No permanent surveillance can be expected, but when authorities are aware of specific threats, they are obliged to provide an appropriate level of protection.[97] Where the receiving State does not provide the appropriate protection against intrusion of diplomatic or consular premises or the occurrence of damage, this can trigger its international responsibility.[98] The 1980 Tehran Hostage Case confirmed these principles when it decided that Iran had incurred responsibility

support in Art 25 VCDR, and even more prominently, in the customary principle 'ne impediatur legatio'. The ILC confirms the presumption that such accounts serve sovereign purposes ('Report of the International Law Commission on the Work of Its Forty-Third Session, Forty-Sixth Session, 29 April–19 July 1991, Supplement No. 10, UN Doc A/46/10). See for further reading on the issue: Verhoeven (n 4) 115; Jean-Paul Pancracio, *Droit et Institutions Diplomatiques* (Paris, Pédone, 2007) 233–34; Salmon (n 16) 202–206; Pierre d'Argent, 'Case Note: Cass. (1re Ch.), 22 Novembre 2012' (2013) 113 *Journal des tribunaux* 290; S Duquet and J Wouters, 'De (On)beslagbaarheid van Bankrekeningen van Buitenlandse Ambassades' (2016) 79 *Rechtskundig Weekblad* 1483. See for critical reflections and an analysis from the point of view of the legitimate interests of creditors: C Ryngaert, 'Embassy Bank Accounts and State Immunity from Execution: Doing Justice to the Financial Interests of Creditors' (2013) 26 *LJIL* 73.

[92] *Armed Activities on the Territory of the Congo* (Democratic Republic of the Congo v Uganda) [2005] ICJ Rep 168, paras 337–40.

[93] *Tehran Hostage Case* (n 5) para 61: '[b]y a number of provisions of the Vienna Conventions of 1961 and 1963, Iran was placed under the most categorical obligations, as a receiving State, to take appropriate steps to ensure the protection of the United States Embassy and Consulates, their staffs, their archives, their means of communication and the freedom of movement of the members of their staffs'.

[94] ibid, para 67.

[95] ibid, para 68.

[96] *Tehran Hostage Case* (n 5) para 63; Constitutional Court Latvia (LV) *Agesins v Parliament of Latvia (Saeima) (Assemblies Case)*, 23 November 2006, Case No 2006-03-0106.

[97] The UN Security Council regularly recalls the applicable rules concerning the inviolability of premises. See, for example, UNSC Res 2216, 14 April 2015, S/RES/2216 (2015), para 11 (on Yemen, referring both to the VCDR and the VCCR).

[98] *Tehran Hostage Case* (n 5) para 95; Shaw (n 58) 549.

towards the US by committing breaches of the obligations laid upon it by the VCDR, and that this entailed an obligation to make reparation for the injury thereby caused.[99]

C. Privileges and Immunities of Diplomatic and Consular Agents

The VCDR accords more immunities to diplomats than the VCCR accords to consuls. Diplomats enjoy personal immunity (Article 31 VCDR), whereas consuls only enjoy a functional immunity in relation to official consular acts (Article 43(1) VCCR) and a limited personal inviolability.[100] Diplomatic immunity encompasses criminal as well as civil and administrative immunity from jurisdiction. The diplomatic immunity from criminal jurisdiction is absolute, while the VCDR formulates three exceptions with regard to civil and administrative jurisdiction concerning: (a) real actions relating to private immovable property; (b) actions relating to private succession matters; and (c) actions relating to professional or commercial activities exercised by the diplomatic agent.[101]

The immunity from jurisdiction is broad and applies to legal proceedings based upon official acts, but also in the private sphere (for example, an application for a divorce or a dispute stemming from the rental of personal accommodation). In addition to immunity from jurisdiction, diplomats enjoy immunity from execution (Article 31(3) VCDR) to which the three exceptions referred to in the field of civil and administrative immunity also apply. Diplomatic immunity continues to exist after the termination of the diplomatic function (Article 39(2) VCDR) with the caveat that for acts not performed by the diplomat in the exercise of official functions, the immunity only continues until the agent leaves the country or until a 'reasonable period' to do so has expired (Article 39(2) VCDR).[102] A functional approach to immunity is adopted regarding a diplomatic agent who is a national or permanent resident of the receiving State (Article 38(1) VCDR). Likewise, the immunity from jurisdiction of consular officers and consular employees is limited to acts performed in the exercise of their function (Article 43(1) VCCR).[103] However, since the list of consular functions provided by the Article 5 VCCR is not exhaustive, the scope of the consular immunity also depends on the interpretation of courts and may therefore differ in individual cases and from one country to another.[104] There are two exceptions to the principle of functional

[99] *Tehran Hostage Case* (n 5) para 90.

[100] Honorary consular officers enjoy an 'official acts' immunity and do not enjoy personal inviolability (Art 58(2) VCCR (n 3)). See Court of Cassation (BE), 10 September 2002, AR P.01.0531.N, 9 *Arr Cass* 2002, 1774: the commute by an honorary consul to the consulate was not accepted as 'an act performed in the exercise of his consular functions'.

[101] Art 31(1) VCDR (n 2); see US District Court of Columbia (US), *Sabbithi v Al Saleh*, 20 March 2009, 605 F Supp 2d 122: 'When examined in context, the term "commercial activity" [as used in the VCDR] does not have so broad a meaning as to include occasional service contracts as [plaintiff] contends, but rather relates only to trade or business activity engaged in for personal profit'. For a more detailed analysis of these exceptions, see Pancracio (n 91) 217–18; Salmon (n 16) 309–16; Roberts (n 10) 130–32. In the 2017 *Reyes v. Al-Malki* case, a majority in the UK Supreme Court indicated that human trafficking can be considered a commercial activity, albeit an illicit one, for the purposes of the exception to immunity from civil and administrative jurisdiction as listed in Art. 31(1)(c) VCDR (UKSC, Reyes v Al-Malki [2017] UKSC 61).

[102] M Richtsteig, *Wiener Übereinkommen über diplomatische und konsularische Beziehungen: Entstehungsgeschichte, Kommentierung, Praxis*, 2nd edn (Baden-Baden, Nomos, 2010) 96–99.

[103] In Belgium, there is no presumption that acts were performed in the exercise of the consular function; see for an application Court of Cassation (BE), 30 October 2001, AR P.00.0401.N, *Arr Cass* 2001, vol 9, 1811.

[104] Milhaupt (n 77); Lee and Quigley (n 7) 448–51. See for an application, Court of Appeal (Oberlandesgericht Düsseldorf) (DE), 3 May 1996 juris.de: the VCDR does not prevent the prosecution of a consular agent for an offence committed during a private holiday with a motor vehicle carrying an official consular badge.

immunity. A consul never enjoys personal immunity in respect of a civil action arising out of a contract, unless her or she expressly or impliedly contracted as an agent of the sending State (Article 43(2)(a)), in which case the rules of State immunity apply. Moreover, regardless of whether it was in the exercise of their function, a consular officer or employee does not enjoy immunity regarding damage arising from an accident in the receiving State caused by a vehicle, vessel, or aircraft (Article 43(2)(b)). In line with the rules laid down in the VCDR, the immunity for consuls continues to exist after the termination of the consular function (Article 53(4) VCCR), but for acts not performed by the consul in the exercise of official functions, the immunity ends when the consular agent leaves the country or after a 'reasonable period of time' to do so (Article 53(3) VCCR).

Diplomats enjoy a personal inviolability, and are not liable to any form of arrest or detention (Article 29 VCDR). The receiving State is under the positive obligation to treat the diplomat with due respect and has to take all appropriate steps to prevent any attack on his or her person, freedom, or dignity (Article 29 VCDR), by its authorities as well as by individuals.[105] The last sentence of Article 29 VCDR is replicated in Article 40 of the VCCR. However, the inviolability of consular officers is more limited than that of diplomats.[106] In case of a 'grave crime'[107] and pursuant to a decision by the competent judicial authority, consular agents can be arrested or detained (Article 41(1) VCCR). If so, the head of post must be notified (Article 42 VCCR), and proceedings against the consular officer must be instituted with the minimum of delay (Article 41(3) VCCR). Both diplomats and consuls enjoy exemptions from social security (Article 33 VCDR; Article 48 VCCR), taxation (albeit with some exceptions; Article 34 VCDR; Article 49 VCCR), and custom duties (Article 36 VCDR; Article 50 VCCR).[108]

The rules on immunities, privileges, and inviolabilities of diplomatic and consular agents are among the oldest in international law and indispensable for the functioning of international intercourse. It has frequently been observed that there is generally good compliance with the law of diplomatic and consular immunity by receiving States. This is remarkable, considering the distress an abuse of immunities can cause to citizens and/or society – think of a diplomat that does not pay rent or commits traffic offences.[109] Occasional abuses of immunity traditionally receive ample attention by media, sometimes feeding prejudices of the public without correctly stating the purpose, scope, and consequences of the protection granted to diplomats and consuls. At the same time, one cannot turn a blind eye to certain persisting issues, which mostly arise with regard to diplomats, who are granted quasi-absolute immunity in a receiving State, and sending States that do not sanction irresponsible

[105] The Convention on the Prevention and Punishment of Crimes against Internationally Protected Persons, including Diplomatic Agents (adopted 14 December 1973, entered into force 20 February 1977) 1035 UNTS 167, may be mentioned in this regard. Committing a murder, a kidnapping or another attack against the person or liberty of a diplomatic agent, as well as the threat, attempt, or participation in such an attack (Art 2(1)(a) and (c)–(e) of that Convention), are subject to punishment in States party to the Convention.

[106] Honorary consuls do not enjoy inviolability, but the receiving State is under a duty to accord such protection as may be required by reason of his official position (Art 64 VCCR (n 3)).

[107] The term 'grave crime' is not defined in the VCCR. Definitions can be found in national laws, including in the UK's Consular Relations Act 1968 (c 18), s 1(2), which construes it as meaning 'any offence punishable (on a first conviction) with imprisonment for a term that may extend to five years or with a more severe sentence'; Roberts (n 10) 271.

[108] For privileges of honorary consuls, see Art 62 VCCR (exemption from customs duties); Art 66 VCCR (exemption from taxation); Art 67 VCCR (exemption from personal services and contributions) (n 3).

[109] In 2016, the Belgium Court of Cassation annulled the judgment of a lower court that had ordered a diplomatic agent to pay rent arrears and damages; see Court of Cassation (BE), 28 October 2016, Case No C.16.0039.N.

behaviour of their agents abroad. Sub-section F below deals with the particular tension that exists between human rights law, on the one hand, and diplomatic and consular law, on the other.

D. Inviolability of Diplomatic and Consular Communication and Documents

One of the aims of the Vienna Conventions is to facilitate and protect inter-State communication, including its secret character.[110] For reasons related to the effective functioning of embassies and consular posts, the provisions on the inviolability of correspondence, archives and documents of diplomatic missions are among the most relevant. The inviolability of archives and documents, even the consular ones, has long been accepted as a rule of customary international law.[111] The Vienna Conventions codified those rules, and combined them with a protection of free communication.

Both the VCDR and the VCCR state that documents and archives of the mission 'shall be inviolable at all times and wherever they may be' (Article 24 VCDR; Article 33 VCCR).[112] While the term archives is not further defined in the VCDR nor in the commentaries to the ILC's 1958 Draft Articles, it is defined in the VCCR. The latter Convention refers to 'all the papers, documents, correspondence, books, films, tapes and registers of the consular post, together with the ciphers and codes, the card-indexes and any article of furniture intended for their protection or safe keeping' (Article 1(1) *k* VCCR). Scholars have argued that the broad definition applies by analogy to diplomatic archives but does not exclude other forms of information[113] and modern forms of storage, such as computer files and USB keys.[114] This view in the literature was recently confirmed by the UN General Assembly in Resolution 69/121,[115] which featured the first express confirmation of a broad understanding of diplomatic documents and archives, where it notes:

> [...] that diplomatic and consular missions may maintain archives and documents in various forms, that official correspondence may take a variety of forms and that diplomatic and consular missions may use a variety of means of communication.

The inviolability of diplomatic/consular archives and documents entails that they cannot be opened, searched, or requisitioned without consent and cannot be used as evidence in a court of law.

The Vienna Conventions permit diplomatic missions and consular posts to communicate freely with their government and the other missions of the sending State by 'all appropriate means' (Article 27(1) VCDR; Article 35(1) VCCR). In interacting with its sending State, the mission may employ traditional means such as a diplomatic or consular bag and messages in code or cipher, as well as more modern communication means such as mobile telecommunication, fax, and email.[116] The receiving State has to permit and protect such

[110] Berridge (n 4) 109–10.
[111] Beckett (n 76); Lee and Quigley (n 7) 389.
[112] The consular archives and documents of an honorary consular officer are inviolable, provided that they are kept separate from other papers and documents (Art 61 VCCR (n 3)).
[113] Salmon (n 16) 209; Denza (n 4) 160–61.
[114] Roberts (n 10) 113; W-M Choi, 'Diplomatic and Consular Law in the Internet Age' (2006) 10 *SYBIL* 117.
[115] UNGA Res 69/121 on the consideration of effective measures to enhance the protection, security and safety of diplomatic and consular missions and representatives, 10 December 2014, A/RES/69/121.
[116] Choi (n 114) 125.

communication to the extent that it is used for 'official purposes', although the consent of the receiving State is imperative for the installation and use of wireless transmitters (Article 27(1) VCDR; Article 35(1) VCCR). The interception of, or any attempt to become acquainted with, the content of diplomatic or consular communication is prohibited. Yet observers of international relations provide ample examples of receiving States that have installed listening devices or bugged telephones of diplomatic missions on their territory.[117] The Vienna Conventions do not expressly deal with the reverse situation, namely secret intelligence gathering by diplomats and consuls in the receiving State. Espionage as such is not prohibited under public international law and State-led surveillance operations seem to be ever-present.[118] With more States possessing the technical capability for interception, it has been suggested that such practices are even on the rise.[119] However, the ICJ has considered acts of espionage by diplomatic agents to be an 'abuse of [diplomatic] functions', making their performance by diplomatic agents unlawful.[120]

Diplomatic and consular bags are protected by the Vienna Conventions if they bear visible external marks of their character and if they contain documents or articles intended for official use (Article 27(4) VCDR; Article 35(4) VCCR).[121] To add to its protection, States can opt to have the bag carried by a diplomatic or consular courier (Article 27(5) VCDR; Article 35(5) VCCR). The VCCR permits competent authorities of the receiving State suspecting misuse of the consular bag to request an authorised representative of the sending State to open it in their presence or to return the bag to its place of origin (Article 35(3) VCCR). The VCDR is stricter where it states that the diplomatic bag cannot be opened or detained (Article 27(3) VCDR).[122] The prohibition on opening the diplomatic bag is and has been subject to controversy, as it allows for abuses such as drug or weapon trafficking.[123] Several States entered into reservations seeking to limit the diplomatic bag's inviolability while reserving the right to open or return it in specific circumstances.[124] Other States objected to these reservations,[125] arguing inter alia that these go against the object and purpose of the VCDR[126] and, for that reason, are invalid.[127] In practice, we observe that the relevance of this legal-technical discussion has waned: States use alternative means to protect their communication and have a common interest in preventing misuse of the

[117] Richtsteig (n 102) 61.
[118] A Colson, 'The Ambassador Between Light and Shade: The Emergence of Secrecy as the Norm for International Negotiation' (2008) 13 *International Negotiation* 179.
[119] Barston (n 17) 11. Edward Snowden's 2013 leak of classified NSA documents revealed the conduct of acts of espionage from the rooftop of the US Embassy in Berlin by a special unit of the CIA and NSA, which allegedly monitored telephone communication in Germany's government quarter.
[120] *Tehran Hostage Case* (n 5) para 84.
[121] See Court of First Instance (Rechtbank) Haarlem (NL), 23 June 2006, no 15/500349-06. This case concerned the transport of cocaine in a 'diplomatic' bag, which although sealed, did not bear visible external marks of its character and did not meet its requirements.
[122] The VCDR (n 2) is also stricter than customary international law that applied prior to its entry into force. The customary rule allowed – as the VCCR does – requests to open the diplomatic bag if there was suspicion of abuse; JF Addicott, 'The Status of the Diplomatic Bag: A Proposed United States Position' (1991) 13 *Houston Journal of International Law* 221, 224–25.
[123] Salmon (n 16) 247–49; A Zeidman, 'The Abuse of the Diplomatic Bag: A Proposed Solution' (1989) 11 *Cardozo Law Review* 427.
[124] See the reservations of Bahrain, Qatar, Kuwait, Libya, and Saudi Arabia: UN Treaty Collection, treaties.un.org/Pages/ViewDetails.aspx?src=TREATY&mtdsg_no=III-3&chapter=3&lang=en.
[125] ibid. See in particular the objections of Australia, France, the UK, Ireland, and the US.
[126] See in this regard the objections of Mongolia, Poland, and the Soviet Union.
[127] See Art 19(c) VCLT.

diplomatic and consular bag. Most countries now accept the use of techniques that allow for the screening of a diplomatic bag for the presence of explosives, metal, drugs, or nuclear substances without opening it. Scholarship agrees that sniffer dogs and scanning methods are not prohibited by the text of the Vienna Convention: Article 27(3) VCDR is silent on external controls of bags; Article 27(4) VCDR spells out that these may only contain articles intended for official use.[128]

Increased air traffic is another factor in the emergence of a more uniform practice. It is now generally accepted that airline authorities can scan diplomatic bags and even refuse their transport where a threat to aircraft safety is presumed; most diplomats adopt a cooperative attitude in this regard.[129] In the context of the EU, however, Member States are still entitled to policy space. Harmonised legislation on aviation security standards states that the appropriate authority 'may allow a diplomatic bag to be exempted from screening or to be subjected to special security procedures provided that the requirements of the Vienna Convention on Diplomatic Relations are met'.[130] Overall, the increased controls on diplomatic bags and baggage have resulted in the more extensive diplomatic protection being replaced by the practices that are in force with regard to consular protection. As a result, the textual difference between the two Conventions concerning the treatment of diplomatic bags and consular bags has become blurred in practice.[131]

E. The Obligations of Diplomats and Consuls

In contrast to the comprehensive obligations to be observed by receiving States in respecting the rights of envoys and missions, the Vienna Conventions offer less detailed guidance with regard to the duties of sending States and the diplomats and consuls that are granted privileges and immunities.[132] The individual obligations of diplomats and consuls can be summarised as follows: (i) an obligation to respect the laws and regulations of the receiving State;[133] (ii) an obligation to not interfere in the internal affairs of the receiving State;[134] and (iii) an obligation to abstain from professional and commercial activities.[135] The mission as a whole is obliged to not use its premises in any manner incompatible with its official functions.[136] Moreover, diplomatic representations, unlike consular ones, are also obliged to conduct official business with or through the receiving State's MFA 'or such other ministry as may be agreed'.[137] While the Vienna Conventions are thus relatively brief on this topic, there exist uniform practices in the interpretation of the duties of diplomats and consuls. The duty for diplomats and consuls to adhere to the rules of the receiving State, for

[128] Denza (n 4) 202; Roberts (n 10) 117.

[129] Addicott (n 122) 236–37. Sending States are still allowed to refuse the scan of a diplomatic bag by airline authorities, but will have to search for other means of transportation as a consequence of that decision.

[130] Commission Regulation (EU) No 185/2010 of 4 March 2010 laying down detailed measures for the implementation of the common basic standards on aviation security [2010] OJ L 55/1, Annex 4.1.2.11.

[131] In 1989, the ILC still proposed to prohibit examination 'through electronic or other technical devices'; see Art 28(1) of its 'Draft Articles on the Status of the Diplomatic Courier and the Diplomatic Bag Not Accompanied by Diplomatic Courier and Draft Optional Protocols' (1989) II *YILC*.

[132] See for a detailed discussion: S Duquet and J Wouters, 'What Diplomats Must Do: The Continuing Relevance of the Vienna Convention' in P Behrens (ed), *Diplomatic Law in a New Millennium* (Oxford, OUP, 2017).

[133] Art 41(1) VCDR (n 2); Art 55(1) VCCR (n 3).

[134] Art 41(1) VCDR (n 2); Art 55(1) VCCR (n 3).

[135] Art 42 VCDR (n 2); Art 57 VCCR (n 3).

[136] Art 41(3) VCDR (n 2); Art 55(2) VCCR (n 3).

[137] Art 41(2) VCDR (n 2).

instance, applies to their official as well as private activities.[138] Obligations can stem from contract law (eg, the payment of rent or debts owed to providers of services), public law (eg, marriages cannot be performed in the consulate's or embassy's premises unless it is permitted under local law), labour law (eg, the duties of a diplomat as a responsible employer), penal law (eg, the duty to respect the physical integrity of others), human rights law, or – an area of great concern worldwide – traffic laws and regulations: most receiving States explicitly request diplomats to abide by traffic regulations upon arrival and remind them of this regularly.[139] It is thus necessary for agents to be knowledgeable about local laws and regulations. Generally, legal scholars note the existence of a strong responsibility of diplomats to respect obligations in the receiving State.[140]

F. Reconciling Human Rights Law with Diplomatic and Consular Law

A certain tension exists between a number of the typical features of diplomatic and consular law, on the one hand, and human rights law, on the other.[141] Problems arise, firstly, with regard to the interpretation of diplomatic functions and obligations. For instance, there is some debate whether diplomats can publicly condemn a grave human rights violation that occurred in a receiving State. Quite a number of States consider it an improper interference in domestic affairs when diplomats actively get involved in human rights-related issues in the receiving State.[142] The taking part in anti-government protests or commenting on a pending outcome in court case are likely to be perceived as such interference. In other instances, diplomatic actions may be justified. International human rights law requires diplomats, as agents of their government, to respect, protect and promote human rights obligations entered into by the sending State.[143] This would entail that diplomats, in the appropriate fora, have a right and even a duty to speak up. Sending states' responsibility can be engaged by acts or omissions in the human rights sphere by their diplomatic or consular agents, when these constitute an extra-territorial exercise of jurisdiction.[144] Some of the discussion is based on the misconception that diplomatic law does not allow

[138] Roberts (n 10) 151.

[139] See, for example, the French directives www.diplomatie.gouv.fr/en/the-ministry-of-foreign-affairs-158/protocol/immunities/article/respect-for-local-laws-and, and the Belgian Circular Note of 18 March 2014 ('Respect for traffic rules and regulations').

[140] Denza (n 4) 374 and references therein.

[141] V Orrego, 'Diplomatic and Consular Immunities and Human Rights' (1991) 40 *ICLQ* 34; A Plantey, *Principes de Diplomatie*, 2nd edn (Paris, Pedone, 2000) 24.

[142] Salmon (n 16) 129; Richtsteig (n 102) 103.

[143] Behrens (n 132).

[144] The European Commission of Human Rights addressed the issue on two occasions, finding both times that acts of diplomatic and consular agents were conducted within the jurisdiction of the sending State's authorities, engaging the latter's responsibility. See *X v Federal Republic of Germany*, App no 1611/62 (ECtHR, 25 September 1965); *WM v Denmark*, App no 17392/90 (ECtHR, 14 October 1993). The ECtHR has recognised that activities of diplomatic or consular agents abroad can be considered an extraterritorial exercise of jurisdiction in *Banković and others v Belgium and others* App no 52207/99 (ECtHR, 19 December 2001) para 73; and, more recently, in *Hirsi Jamaa and others v Italy* App no 27765/09 (ECtHR, 23 February 2012) para 75. For a more elaborate discussion of extraterritoriality, see Chapter 10 on jurisdiction.

for interaction with the human rights regime.[145] Yet the Vienna Conventions do not rule out this possibility. In their preambles it is affirmed that matters not expressly regulated their provisions continue to be governed continue to be governed by the rules of customary international law. The difficulty lies in reconciling the two coexisting regimes in practice. This requires a reading of diplomatic functions and obligations in light of obligations stemming from human rights law. The receiving State will be the final arbiter of this exercise because it has the tools to sanction the individual diplomat or the sending State (see sub-section G).

Secondly, persons enjoying immunities have occasionally engaged in human rights violations themselves. In various countries where cases of child or partner abuse and inhuman treatment of domestic workers have been reported, immunities impeded victims from exercising their right to access to court or governments to take protective measures. What commonly happens in such cases, is that a sending State will request to waive an agent's immunity, if the receiving State has not already voluntarily recalled its agent. When the receiving State proves unwilling to do so, national courts have in rare instances of grave violations stepped in and not granted immunities.[146] The international community also expressed its interest in finding a more durable solution by suggesting the limiting of immunities in cases of abuse.[147] Reference can be made to the recommendation of the Parliamentary Assembly of the Council of Europe on 'domestic slavery', in which it recommends Member States to 'amend the Vienna Convention in order to waive diplomatic immunity for all offences committed in private life'.[148] To date, however, no such amendment has been accepted. The matter is somewhat less pressing in the case of consular law, since consular officers and employees are granted immunity only in respect of acts performed in the exercise of consular functions.

A third discussion that has emerged concerns the freedom of the press to report on diplomacy and whether that includes a right to publish secret information.[149] In recent years, the

[145] Much of this confusion has its origins in the ICJ's *Tehran Hostage Case* (n 5). At para 86, the ICJ referred to the diplomatic system as a 'self-contained system', the rules of which must be understood in line with the specific rationale of diplomatic law. In its aftermath, scholarly discussions centred around the question whether diplomatic law is to be treated as some sort of closed or autonomous sub-system within international law, and, if so, the legal effects this brings about. The ICJ judgment provoked considerable criticism (B Simma and D Pulkowski, 'Of Planets and the Universe: Self-Contained Regimes in International Law' (2006) 17 *EJIL* 483) and some even argued that it might add to the fragmentation of public international law (ILC, Report of the study group on Fragmentation of International Law: Difficulties Arising from the Diversification and Expansion of International Law, 3 May to 4 June and 5 July to 6 August 2004, 58th session, UN Doc A/CN 4/L 682, paras 192–193). To understand the self-contained regime reference, it is crucial to recall the particular issue addressed by the ICJ. The dictum in *Tehran Hostages* merely relates to the conditions for and limitations on the taking of countermeasures by an injured State in a diplomatic context (para 83). When wrongdoing occurs in that specific context – in this case the alleged illicit activities carried out by members of a diplomatic mission – a receiving State has to resort to means of defence and sanctions provided for in diplomatic law itself (para 87).

[146] One example from the Belgian practice concerns a minor who was abused by its parent, who enjoyed diplomatic status in the country. The Court had to define whether and how Belgium, signatory party to the Convention on the Rights of the Child (CRC), had to comply with its duty to take preventive protection measures (Art 3(2) CRC) with both the child and its abusive parent enjoying diplomatic immunity. The solution put forward by a Belgian Court to give priority to the CRC on the basis of the *lex posterior derogat legi priori* adagio was legally flawed, but deemed necessary for humanitarian reasons. See Court of Appeal Brussels (BE), 1 March 2002, 66 *Rechtskundig Weekblad*, 301 and annotation.

[147] R Higgins, 'The Abuse of Diplomatic Privileges and Immunities: Recent United Kingdom Experience' (1985) 79 *AJIL* 641; WG Morris, 'Constitutional Solutions to the Problem of Diplomatic Crime and Immunity' (2007) 36 *Hofstra Law Review* 601.

[148] PACE, Recommendation 1523 (2001) on Domestic Slavery, 26 June 2001, Art 10 (iv).

[149] See, for an analysis, S Duquet and J Wouters, 'Diplomacy, Secrecy and the Law' in C Bjola and S Murray (eds), *Secret Diplomacy: Concepts, Contexts and Cases* (Abingdon, Routledge, 2016) 85–107.

content of diplomatic documents via the secret-sharing website WikiLeaks, as reprinted and commented upon in newspapers all over the world, has entered the public domain. When reporting on matters of diplomacy, however, both traditional and non-traditional press have to take into account limits imposed upon the right of the public to be informed so as to allow for secrecy and confidentiality in diplomatic relations.

In 2007, a case was brought before the ECtHR on the protection of diplomatic cables at the expense of the freedom of the press.[150] The applicant, Mr. Stoll, was a journalist who had been convicted for reporting on a confidential briefing document prepared by the Swiss ambassador in Washington DC, leaked to him by a Swiss government official. The disclosure of diplomatic documents is a crime under Swiss law and the journalist had been sentenced to pay a fine of 800 Swiss Francs. The ECtHR's case law on freedom of speech consistently takes the view that the media has an important role in informing the public on matters of public interest, including in circumstances where State actions are not automatically subject to democratic control or judicial review due to their confidential nature.[151] These principles were confirmed in *Stoll v Switzerland*. However, since Mr Stoll had only been sentenced to pay a small fine, which had not prevented him from expressing his views, the ECtHR decided that the conviction had not amounted to censorship and, consequently, that Article 10 ECHR had not been violated.[152]

WikiLeaks' 2010 'Cablegate' has put on the agenda questions related to whether there should be a public debate on the content of diplomatic affairs. While WikiLeaks has provided scholars and journalists alike with abundant material for thought and study, its legality is disputed.[153] However, in the controversial Bancoult No 3 judgement ([2018] UKSC 3), the UK Supreme Court allowed a diplomatic communication cable between the US Embassy in London to the US Embassy in Mauritius as evidence in court, after it had been published by WikiLeaks and several newspapers. Regrettably, the Court ignored the possibility that the cable was inviolable as an archive of a foreign sovereign State. At the same time, the consequences of WikiLeaks for the conduct of diplomacy should not be exaggerated. In practice, the absolute protection of free and safe diplomatic communication can never be guaranteed, and it does not seem to have caused fundamental changes to the way diplomacy is conducted.[154]

G. Sanctions in the Diplomatic and Consular Regimes

Immunity is only procedural in nature, and should not be confused with impunity.[155] The Vienna Conventions contain certain safety brakes and even allow for a number of

[150] *Stoll v Switzerland* App no 69698/01 (ECtHR, 10 December 2007).

[151] *Eerikäinen v Finland* App no 3514/02 (ECtHR, 10 February 2009); *Times Newspapers Ltd v United Kingdom* App nos 3002/03 and 23676/03 (ECtHR, 10 March 2009), *Times Newspapers Ltd v United Kingdom*; *Sanoma Uitgevers v Nederland* App no 38224/03 (ECtHR, 14 September 2010).

[152] *Stoll v Switzerland* (n 150) para 162.

[153] In the US, the taking of diplomatic information is an offence under the national Espionage Act. A former US Army Intelligence Analyst, Bradley (now, Chelsea) Manning, was convicted to 35 years in prison for copying classified reports and transferring them to WikiLeaks founder Julian Assange.

[154] Pancracio (n 91) 248; Plantey (n 141) 293; Salmon (n 16) 250.

[155] In the words of the ICJ: '[i]mmunity from criminal jurisdiction and individual criminal responsibility are quite separate concepts. While jurisdictional immunity is procedural in nature, criminal responsibility is a question of substantive law. Jurisdictional immunity may well bar prosecution for a certain period or for certain offences; it cannot exonerate the person whom it applies from all criminal responsibility': *Arrest Warrant Case* (n 5) para 60. See MA Summers, 'Diplomatic Immunity Ratione Personae: Did the International Court of Justice Create a New Customary Law Rule in Congo v Belgium?' (2007) 16 *MJIL* 459.

sanctions to be taken. First, minor offences may be drawn to the attention of the head of mission or the foreign government. A receiving State may also ask the agent to voluntarily remedy any damage caused or, where appropriate, to voluntarily pay a fine, without the immunity being lifted. The receiving State can also request the sending State to waive its agent's immunity (Article 32 VCDR; Article 45 VCCR).[156] In a second step, grave breaches of diplomatic obligations or the recurrent occurrence of minor offences may give rise to more resolute measures. The receiving State can withhold certain privileges enjoyed by the mission. There have been numerous applications in practice: a request to downsize the mission (Article 11 VCDR), a prohibition to use radio communication equipment (Article 27(1) VCDR), and the adoption of quotas on the import of certain products by the mission (Article 36(1) VCDR). Ultimately, it is possible for the receiving State to have the diplomat in question removed from the territory. Although both concepts are often confused, a request to the sending State to recall the agent usually will precede a *persona non grata* declaration. The consequences are alike: the diplomat will return to the sending State, or, at least, terminate his or her functions with the mission (Article 9 VCDR; Article 23 VCCR).[157] This decision is a political one for which no reasons have to be given and against which no judicial appeal lies.[158] As an ultimate sanction, when the general relations have deteriorated and diplomatic relations between sending and receiving States are in a difficult condition, the severance or termination of diplomatic (and sometimes also consular) relations is possible.

V. The EU as a Diplomatic and Consular Actor

States have historically enjoyed a monopoly in diplomatic and consular affairs, and they remain particularly protective of these rights. This leaves hardly any room for non-State entities to participate. The Vienna Conventions reflect this, since they reserve their scope of application to States.[159] Yet, two UN observers that do not (straightforwardly) classify as a State are signatory parties: the Holy See has been fully involved since the Vienna Conventions' codification process and the State of Palestine acceded the VCDR/VCCR tandem in 2014. In the past, city-states and provinces sometimes also exercised a right of legation and, in more modern times, we have seen claims made – with varying degrees of success and enthusiasm – by sub-state entities (eg, German *Länder*, Belgian federated entities, Spanish *autonomías*, and French regions) and the Sovereign Military Order of Saint John of Jerusalem (Order of Malta).[160]

[156] Shaw nevertheless observes that waivers are unusual in diplomatic practice: Shaw (n 58) 560.

[157] Salmon (n 16) 348; Roberts (n 10) 206–15. During the time period communicated by the receiving State for the diplomat or consul to leave its territory (commonly between 48 hours and two weeks), the agent still enjoys all privileges and immunities. A *persona non grata* declaration is often followed by a reciprocal sanction in the sending State. When the UK expelled 23 Russian diplomats as a reaction to the 2018 poisoning of Sergei and Yulia Skripal in Salisbury, Moscow retaliated by sending the same number of UK diplomats back home. The Russian Federation equally announced the expulsion of agents of over 20 EU and NATO member States that had taken similar measures.

[158] See, for the Belgian practice, Conseil d'État (BE), 9 April 1998, n° 73.027.

[159] Arts 48 and 50 VCDR (n 2); Art 74 VCCR (n 3).

[160] See for further reading Chapter 8 on Non-State Actors.

One non-traditional diplomatic and (to some extent) consular actor – the EU – stands out for applying creative legal techniques to engage in formal international intercourse. Unlike other international organisations – most of which exercise a passive right of legation[161] – the broad array of competences allocated to the Union by the Member States has resulted in a need to also actively pursue common interests via diplomatic tools. Over the past five decades, the Union increasingly has become a global player. Via a worldwide bilateral and multilateral diplomatic network consisting of 'Union Delegations' that represent the EU in third States and at international organisations, it exercises an active right of legation.[162] Recent debates also focused on the further integration of European consular services. This section discusses how public international law and EU institutional law developed in relation to the Union's diplomatic and consular aspirations.[163]

A. The EU and International Diplomatic Law

The Union's active right of legation is largely managed by the European External Action Service (EEAS). The Service's external arm consists of 133 bilateral Delegations accredited to 163 countries, which are placed under the authority of the High Representative of the Union for Foreign Affairs and Security Policy. To become a diplomatic actor, however, the EU needed to do more than update its internal system: it required the recognition by third States of a capacity to enter into diplomatic relations. Since diplomatic relations exist by virtue of mutual consent (Article 2 VCDR), there is neither a right nor an entitlement to them under international law.[164] In other words, international law does not oblige States to grant a special status to other missions unless they have entered into a specific agreement.[165] To enable its Delegations to take part in the diplomatic system on the same basis as States, the European Commission and – since the Lisbon Treaty – the High Representative thus had to find an agreement with third States. Overall, this has been a success story. The Union, on an ad hoc basis, entered into bilateral agreements that establish diplomatic relations between the parties and spell out the legal framework under which these will be maintained (Article 5(6) EEAS Decision).[166] In these so-called 'establishment agreements', third States allow the Union to establish a diplomatic mission and to perform diplomatic functions, and grant those EU Delegations and their staff full diplomatic privileges and immunities. The agreements also contain a clause that makes the VCDR applicable to the EU's diplomatic

[161] Quite a number of international organisations exercise a passive legation right, some of them (for example, the League of Arab States and the African Union) also send ambassadors to other international organisations. See: HG Schermers and NM Blokker, *International Institutional Law: Unity Within Diversity*, 5th edn (Leiden, Martinus Nijhoff Publishers, 2011) 1159. However, the EU remains unrivalled with regard to the size of its diplomatic network.

[162] Art 221(1) TFEU and Arts 1(4) and 5 of the Council Decision 2010/427/EU of 26 July 2010 Establishing the Organization and Functioning of the European External Action Service [2010] OJ L 201/30 (EEAS Decision).

[163] See, on this topic, J Wouters and S Duquet, 'The EU and International Diplomatic Law: New Horizons?' (2012) 7 *The Hague Journal of Diplomacy* 31; J Wouters and S Duquet, 'Unus Inter Plures? The EEAS, the Vienna Convention and International Diplomatic Practice' in D Spence and J Bátora (eds), *The European External Action Service: European Diplomacy Post-Westphalia* (Basingstoke, Palgrave Macmillan, 2015) 159–74.

[164] Shaw (n 58) 546–47.

[165] YL Ling, 'A Comparative Study of the Privileges and Immunities of United Nations Member Representatives and Officials with the Traditional Privileges and Immunities of Diplomatic Agents' (1976) 33 *Washington and Lee Law Review* 127.

[166] E Baroncini, 'Le Delegazioni dell'Unione Europea Dopo Il Trattato Di Lisbona. Struttura, Status E Funzioni' (2014) 6 *Cuadernos de Derecho Transnacional* 68, 99.

activities. As a result, although the Union cannot ratify the 1961 Vienna Convention, its rules and obligations will apply in parallel on the basis of a bilateral agreement.

Delegations' activities do not differ substantially from the functions executed by other diplomatic representatives as described in Article 3 VCDR. In a Host State, EU diplomats represent and protect the Union's interests as well as those of its citizens, promote friendly relations, observe local developments and report them to EU Institutions and Bodies. One crucial difference has to be emphasised: a Union Delegation's mandate is more restricted than that of national diplomatic missions since their competences are limited to EU powers – that is, the competences conferred upon the EU by its Member States.[167] While the Delegation has *carte blanche* to inform foreign governments and citizens about what the EU is and does and to represent the Union in legal proceedings, its representational functions are more limited when it comes to presenting, explaining, and implementing concrete policies. When exercising diplomatic functions, there is a thematic predominance with regard to matters in which the EU enjoys exclusive, shared, and parallel competencies, such as trade and aid (Articles 3–4 TFEU).[168] The range of tasks performed by Delegations may also be broader than that of States. Comparatively speaking, the EU spends more resources on coordination activities and on information sharing. These activities are intended to benefit other diplomatic missions, which makes them atypical in the diplomatic sphere characterised by the pursuit of individual interests and secrecy. Moreover, Delegations have important administrative roles now that they execute a large number of European Commission policies on the international stage, ranging from development aid to human rights protection programmes.

The EU also exercises a passive right of legation. Through the years, the scope and number of diplomatic missions accredited to the EU in Brussels have significantly expanded. Three types can be discerned: the permanent representations of EU Member States; diplomatic missions of third States; and diplomatic missions of international organisations and other non-State entities, such as the International Committee of the Red Cross. In line with Article 5 VCDR, missions may be simultaneously accredited to Belgium and/or other international organisations headquartered in Belgium. Article 16 of Protocol No 7 on the privileges and immunities of the EU tasks the Member State in whose territory the Union has its seat – in other words, Belgium – 'to accord the customary diplomatic immunities and privileges to missions of third countries accredited to the Union'.[169] As a result, the EU is able to reciprocate the diplomatic status granted to its diplomatic agents in third countries. Diplomats accredited to the EU are entitled to exercise all normal diplomatic functions.[170] The Union, at this point, does not accredit diplomatic missions of States that are not formally recognised by all 28 Member States. The pragmatic solution has been to accredit such missions as a liaison or a representative office. These will lack formal diplomatic status, but are commonly given facilities that resemble those granted to

[167] On the principle of conferral, see Arts 4(1) and 5(1)–(2) TEU; specifically as to the action of EU institutions, see Art 13(2) TEU.

[168] Notwithstanding, Delegations have been involved in the execution of environmental programmes and mobility partnerships in which they often assume the first point of entry for local authorities and partners. By way of example, see the Delegation's role in the execution of the EU-Cape Verde mobility partnership, as explained by Ane Kristine Djupedal, 'Recent Developments in the EU Migration Management Policy EU-Cape Verde Mobility Partnership, Frontex and the Management of the European Borders', 26 November2011, ARENA Report No 7/11.

[169] Protocol No 7 on the Privileges and Immunities of the European Union attached to the EU Treaties [2012] OJ C326.

[170] Roberts (n 10) 408.

diplomats.[171] Yet the question remains whether the Union could accredit a representative, or declare him or her persona non grata, against the will of the Member States, and in particular Host State Belgium.

B. The EU and International Consular Law

Since the 1992 Treaty of Maastricht, any person who holds the nationality of an EU country is automatically also granted EU citizenship. As an EU citizen, a person is entitled to a number of rights spelled out in the EU Treaties, such as the right to move and reside freely within the Union. One of these entitlements listed in the EU Treaties has a purely external dimension: it grants citizens traveling or working abroad the right to be protected by the diplomatic and consular authorities of any other EU Member State. In this respect, Article 23 TFEU reads:

> Every citizen of the Union shall, in the territory of a third country in which the Member State of which he is a national is not represented, be entitled to protection by the diplomatic or consular authorities of any Member State, on the same conditions as the nationals of that State. Member States shall adopt the necessary provisions and start the international negotiations required to secure this protection.

While the wording of the article refers to 'protection by diplomatic and consular authorities', the intention of the drafters was solely to regulate consular protection, which can be delivered by both diplomatic and consular authorities of the Member States through cooperation schemes.[172] The Lisbon Treaty further strengthened the consular protection of non-represented Union citizens abroad and clarified that the role for the Union Delegations is to 'contribute' to the implementation of the right in cooperation with the Member States (Article 35 TEU).[173] In the same vein, the Council Decision establishing the EEAS gives the Delegations a supportive role when it specifies that the Union Delegations can, upon request by a Member State, support that country to provide consular protection to citizens of the Union in third countries.

Since 1992, the EU has been working on practical guidelines for the Member States whose missions abroad had to put the right to consular protection into practice.[174] Due to the changing social and economic patterns – making it for citizens easier and cheaper to travel the world and more attractive to work or study abroad – mobility has only increased. At the same time, there is a trend for Member States, related to the general tendency seen all over Europe to cut government spending, to close missions in third States. Moreover, the number of third States where all Member States are represented is three: the US, the Russian Federation, and the People's Republic of China. In practical terms, this can lead to a situation where an EU citizen requiring (medical, legal, administrative) assistance in

[171] See, for instance, the General Delegation of Palestine, a liaison office that is listed as an 'other representation' in the Union's protocol list. The Union also entertains non-diplomatic relations with Taiwan, Kosovo, Hong Kong, and Macao; the last two each manage an Economic and Trade Office in Brussels at the non-ambassadorial level.

[172] J Weyland, 'La Protection Diplomatique et Consulaire des Citoyens de l'Union Européenne' in EA Marias (ed), *European Citizenship* (Maastricht, EIPA, 1994) 64.

[173] See E Tichy-Fisslberger, 'Der Schutz Der EU-Bürger Durch Die Diplomatischen Und Konsularischen Vertretungsbehörden' (2012) 13 *Europarecht* 217.

[174] See, for a more detailed discussion, J Wouters, S Duquet and K Meuwissen, 'Caring for Citizens Abroad: The European Union and Consular Tasks' (2014) 19 *European Foreign Affairs Review* 563.

a foreign country following a personal (eg, an accident or a detention) or general crisis (eg, a war, tsunami, or earthquake) may not be able to call on consular representation by his or her own Member State. Finally, in 2015, the Council adopted a Directive on consular protection for EU citizens in third countries to remedy this situation.[175] The Directive lays down when and how unrepresented EU citizens can receive consular assistance from other EU countries' embassies or consulates.[176] In line with the Lisbon Treaty, the Union Delegations were not assigned a particular role in this; the Directive focuses on the cooperation between the consular authorities of the Member States. Consequently, the role the EU plays in consular affairs – beyond allowing for the coordination and cooperation between Member States – is minimal when compared to its diplomatic practices.[177]

The relationship between consular protection as conceptualised within the EU legal framework and international consular law has received scant attention thus far. Article 8 VCCR allows for the exercise of consular functions by third States but also makes explicit that the receiving State can object to this. For that reason, Article 23 TFEU tasks the Member States to 'adopt the necessary provisions and start the international negotiations required to secure [consular] protection'. Negotiations can result in: (i) a bilateral agreement between an EU Member State and a third State for the protection of non-nationals; (ii) a multilateral agreement between EU Member States and a (number of) third State(s); or (iii) a mixed agreement between (a number of) third States, the EU and its Member States. Currently, few agreements exist with third States that implement Article 23 TFEU.[178] In practice, however, third States have not invoked their right under Article 8 VCCR to oppose European practices in their territory. Without an explicit confirmation, in an international agreement, however, receiving States – for example in a general crisis situation or when diplomatic or consular relations deteriorate – revise the previously tolerated situation. So far, no bilateral agreements have been concluded on the application of consular law by the EU. This is due to the more limited role played by those Delegations in consular affairs, now that their main task in this field is to support the Member States in their roles as consular actors.

VI. Concluding Remarks

The rules laid down in the VCDR and VCCR continue to show their durability, as evidenced by their customary law status, broad application in the diplomatic and consular corps

[175] Council Directive (EU) 2015/637 of 20 April 2015 on the coordination and cooperation measures to facilitate consular protection for unrepresented citizens of the Union in third countries and repealing Decision 95/553/EC [2015] OJ L106/1; see also Art 23 (para 2) TEU.

[176] Art 6 Council Directive 2015/637 defines the absence of representation as the situation in which 'a Member State is not represented in a third country if it has no embassy or consulate established there on a permanent basis, or if it has no embassy, consulate or honorary consul there which is effectively in a position to provide consular protection in a given case'.

[177] When Member States decide to set up a joint evacuation of citizens in a crisis situation, Union Delegations seem to automatically assume a more active role. We have seen this, for instance, when in 2011 a nuclear disaster hit Japan and revolutionary protests broke out in Libya.

[178] Care Project (Citizens Consular Assistance Regulation in Europe), 'Consular and Diplomatic Protection Legal Framework in the EU Member States', December 2010, 36–38 and 592–603, www.careproject.eu/images/stories/ConsularAndDiplomaticProtection.pdf; A Vermeer-Künzli, 'Where the Law Becomes Irrelevant: Consular Assistance and the European Union' (2011) 60 *ICLQ* 965, 970–71.

around the world, and in the general interaction between States. At the same time, international diplomatic and consular law has substantially evolved in practice. A number of these developments have been discussed in this chapter. Due to globalisation and technological developments, the functions of diplomats and consuls have been subject to change. Furthermore, individual rights and entitlements have been put to the forefront. This is reflected in a growing body of case law interpreting Article 36 VCCR on individual consular protection as well as in the collective efforts of EU Member States to develop a common protection system to assist Union citizens abroad. At the same time, States face the challenge of complying with obligations to respect and protect individual human rights, both as sending and receiving States, while also conferring diplomatic and consular immunities, privileges and inviolabilities, and respecting diplomatic and consular duties. This tension, however, seems to be inherent to the way both systems – each with their own rationale and priorities – were set up. From a legal perspective, general principles of harmonisation may offer a way out of conflicts between diplomatic/consular and human rights law.

Against the backdrop of global changes and related diplomatic and consular challenges, the Vienna Conventions provide a remarkably stable and flexible legal framework for the conduct of diplomatic and consular activities. While frictions do occur, only rarely has it been suggested that the Conventions should be amended in order to respond to these evolutions. At the same time, it may be observed that the interpretation of VCDR/VCCR rules by government bodies (in diplomatic and consular codes), the UN General Assembly (in its Resolution on diplomatic documents and archives) and in case law, contributes to the constant refinement of the existing legal regimes. The Conventions are living instruments that allow interpretation with a view to their creative application to new situations (eg, external checks of the diplomatic bag to respond to a need for security in airspace), actors (eg, the EU), and tools (eg, digital communication).

Bibliography

Abrisqueta, J, *El Derecho consular internacional* (Madrid, Reus, 1974).

Ballesteros, A, *Diplomacia y Relaciones Internacionales*, 3rd edn (Madrid, Ministerio de Asuntos Exteriores y de Cooperación, 1995).

Baroncini, E, 'Le Delegazioni dell'Unione Europea Dopo Il Trattato Di Lisbona. Struttura, Status E Funzioni' (2014) 6 *Cuadernos de Derecho Transnacional* 68.

Barston, RP, *Modern Diplomacy*, 4th edn (Harlow, Pearson, 2013).

Berridge, G, *Diplomacy: Theory and Practice*, 4th edn (Basingstoke, Palgrave Macmillan, 2010) 109–10.

Chatterjee, C, *International Law and Diplomacy* (London, Routledge, 2007).

Cooper, AF, Heine, J and Thakur, R (eds), *The Oxford Handbook of Modern Diplomacy* (Oxford, OUP, 2013).

Denza, E, *Diplomatic Law: Commentary on the Vienna Convention on Diplomatic Relations*, 4th edn (Oxford, OUP, 2016).

Lee, LT and Quigley, JB, *Consular Law and Practice*, 3rd edn (Oxford, OUP, 2008).

Pancracio, JP, *Droit et institutions diplomatiques* (Paris, Pedone, 2007).

Plantey, A, *Principes de Diplomatie*, 2nd edn (Paris, Pedone, 2000).

Richtsteig, M, *Wiener Übereinkommen über diplomatische und konsularische Beziehungen: Entstehungsgeschichte, Kommentierung, Praxis*, 2nd edn (Baden-Baden, Nomos, 2010).
Salmon, J, *Manuel de Droit Diplomatique* (Brussels, Bruylant, 1994).
Roberts, I (ed), *Satow's Diplomatic Practice*, 6th edn (Oxford, OUP, 2011).
Vilariño Pintos, E, *Curso de derecho diplomático y consular*, 3rd edn (Madrid, Tecnos, 2007).
Wouters, J and Duquet, S, 'The EU and International Diplomatic Law: New Horizons?' (2012) 7 *The Hague Journal of Diplomacy* 31.
Wouters, J, Duquet, S and Meuwissen, K, 'Caring for Citizens Abroad: The European Union and Consular Tasks' (2014) 19 *European Foreign Affairs Review* 563.

Further Reading

Bolewski, W, 'Les privilèges diplomatiques dans la pratique' (2005) *Revue de Droit international et de Droit comparé* 95.
Bruns, K, *A Cornerstone of Modern Diplomacy: Britain and the Negotiation of the 1961 Vienna Convention on Diplomatic Relations* (New York, Bloomsbury Academic, 2014).
Charnovitz, S, 'Correcting America's Continuing Failure to Comply with the Avena Judgment' (2012) 106 AJIL 572.
Choi, W-M, 'Diplomatic and Consular Law in the Internet Age' (2006) 10 *Singapore Yearbook of International Law* 117.
Duquet, S and Wouters, J, 'Diplomatic and Consular Relations', in Malone, D, Chesterman, S and Villalpando, S (eds), *Oxford Handbook on UN Treaties* (Oxford, OUP, 2018).
Higgins, R, 'The Abuse of Diplomatic Privileges and Immunities: Recent United Kingdom Experience' (1985) 79 *AJIL* 641.
Koch, M, 'Wozu noch Diplomaten?' in Brandt, E and Buck, C (eds), *Auswärtiges Amt: Diplomatie als Beruf* (Wiesbaden, Verlag für Sozialwissenschaften, 2005).
Lechner, S, 'What Difference Does Ius Inter Gentes Make? Changing Diplomatic Rights and Duties and the Modern European States-System' (2006) 1 *The Hague Journal of Diplomacy* 235.
Orrego, V, 'Diplomatic and Consular Immunities and Human Rights' (1991) 40 *ICLQ* 34.
Milhaupt, CJ, 'The Scope of Consular Immunity under the Vienna Convention on Consular Relations: Towards a Principled Interpretation' (1988) 88 *CLR* 845.
Quel López, FJ, *Los privilegios e inmunidades de los agentes diplomáticos en el Derecho Internacional y en la práctica española* (Madrid, Civitas, 1993).
Quigley, JB, 'The United States' Withdrawal From International Court of Justice Jurisdiction in Consular Cases: Reasons and Consequences' (2008) 19 *Duke Journal of Comparative and International Law* 263.
Tichy-Fisslberger, E, 'Der Schutz Der EU-Bürger Durch Die Diplomatischen Und Konsularischen Vertretungsbehörden' (2012) 13 *Europarecht* 217.
Virally, M, Gerbet, P and Salmon, J, *Les missions permanentes auprès des organisations internationales* (Brussels, Bruylant, 1971).

11

Immunities

I. Introduction

Even when States can establish jurisdiction on lawful grounds, the exercise of that jurisdiction may be impeded by an immunity. In international law, immunities accrue to States and international organisations, as well as their officials, because of their special status as subjects of international law.

Immunity is a procedural impediment to the exercise of jurisdiction. It does not imply that its beneficiary is exempt from the law, but merely that legal proceedings are barred or suspended. This feature distinguishes immunities from privileges, which are substantive exemptions from local law, typically tax and social security legislation. Immunity should also be distinguished, at least partly, from inviolability, which refers to the prohibition to trespass on, or interfere with, property, assets, or personal liberty (by means of arrest, detention or compulsion).[1] A distinction is also made between immunity from jurisdiction, which bars a court before which a protected person is sued from establishing its adjudicatory jurisdiction, and immunity from execution or enforcement, which bars the taking of measures of constraint, such as attachment or arrest, against property of a protected person, whether pre- or post-judgment. The extent of immunity varies depending on the nature of the protected person. Thus, it is important to ascertain the distinct regimes applying to States, international organisations, diplomats, State officials, officials of international organisations, etc. The sources of these regimes are varied. While multilateral or bilateral treaties have increasingly codified immunity regimes, some regimes, such as the law of State immunity, remain governed by customary international law.

Immunities are not necessarily absolute. They can be waived by the State or the international organisation which is entitled to them. Also, treaty-based immunity regimes may allow for limited, and at times far-reaching exceptions to the principle of immunity.

[1] To the extent that such interference may result from judicial action, eg court-ordered enforcement action, inviolability may overlap with immunity (from execution).

Furthermore, human rights and accountability considerations have led to a reinterpretation and relaxation of immunities conferred by treaty or customary law.[2]

Note that States may also confer immunities on their own officials, such as ministers or members of parliament, under national law. As such immunities are governed by national constitutional or administrative law, they are not addressed here. That said, national law remains important to the law of international immunities, as international law only provides a framework that is, or at least can be, further refined by national legislation and case law.[3] Accordingly, a State's application of international immunities can take on a peculiarly domestic flavour. This chapter discusses respectively the immunity of States (Section II), State officials (Section III) and international organisations (Section IV).

II. State Immunity

The rule that States enjoy immunity from the jurisdiction of other States' courts finds its roots in the principle of sovereign equality, which harks back to the 1648 Peace of Westphalia. Pursuant to this principle, States are not allowed to exercise jurisdiction over their peers, captured in the Latin adage *par in parem non habet imperium*. Deciding otherwise would arguably lead to international tension and disorder. Historically speaking, legal practice and doctrine has paid more attention to the immunity of *State representatives*, in particular of the Head of State, as the distinction between the State as an abstract concept and its personification in the form of the prince, ruler or monarch had not yet been made. This changed in the early nineteenth century, as epitomised by the US Supreme Court decision in the 1812 case of *The Schooner Exchange v McFaddon*, in which Chief Justice Marshall upheld a foreign State's immunity in respect of the latter's captured warships on grounds of comity and the 'equal rights and independence' of sovereigns.[4]

The international law of the immunity of States before the courts of other States is mainly customary in nature. Two conventions regarding immunities of States have been concluded, but these have not been particularly successful. The European Convention on State Immunity (1972)[5] counts only eight States Parties,[6] whereas the UN Convention on the Jurisdictional Immunities of States and their Property (2004) has not yet entered into force.[7]

[2] See notably the case law of the ECtHR with respect to the immunity of international organisations (Section IV) and the – only partly successful – efforts of anti-impunity campaigners to carve out an exception to the immunity of States and their officials in respect of international crimes (Section II(C)).

[3] Notably in common law countries international immunities are typically laid down in separate legislative acts. See, eg, the UK State Immunity Act 1978 (1978 c 33) and the US Foreign Sovereign Immunities Act of 1976, Public Law 94-583, 90 Stat 2891.

[4] Supreme Court (US), *The Schooner Exchange v McFaddon and others*, 24 February 1812, 11 US 116.

[5] European Convention on State Immunity (adopted 16 May 1972, entered into force 11 June 1976) CETS No 74 (European Convention).

[6] Austria, Belgium, Cyprus, Germany, Luxembourg, the Netherlands, Switzerland and UK.

[7] United Nations Convention on Jurisdictional Immunities of States and Their Property (adopted 2 December 2004, not yet entered into force), UN Doc A/59/508, 3 (UN Convention). On 27 December 2009, this Convention had been signed by 7 States and obtained 8 instruments of ratification, acceptance, approval or accession. Today it has 21 States Parties and 28 Signatories. Art 30 of the Convention provides that it will enter into force on the thirtieth day following the date of deposit of the thirtieth such instrument.

Still, provisions of these treaties are regularly referenced by domestic courts, to the extent that they are codifications of customary international law.[8]

States enjoy both immunity from *jurisdiction* and *execution* (enforcement) in the courts of other States. The regimes of immunity from jurisdiction and execution are governed by different legal rules. This has as a consequence that a State's waiver of immunity from jurisdiction does not imply that the State also waives its immunity from execution. Also, foreign domestic courts may well uphold a State's immunity from execution after having rejected its immunity from jurisdiction at an earlier stage.

A. State Immunity from Jurisdiction

In the past, State immunity from jurisdiction was held to be absolute. The basic premise of the modern law of State immunity is that States do not enjoy such absolute immunity,[9] although some States may espouse a more conservative approach.[10] Nevertheless, there is relative agreement that immunity from jurisdiction only attaches to *acta jure imperii* (sovereign acts of the State),[11] and not to *acta jure gestionis* (managerial or commercial acts),[12] a distinction originally introduced by Italian and Belgian courts in the late nineteenth century.[13] As States carry out the latter activities as if they were private persons, it is not considered fair to award States preferential treatment as grantees of immunity. Denial of immunity for non-sovereign activities is also in the interest of States, as private parties may be reluctant to contract with States that can invoke their immunity in legal proceedings.

It is now widely accepted that, in a considerable number of disputes concerning States' non-sovereign activities, immunity cannot be invoked, and the forum State can exercise its jurisdiction. Most notably, where a State engages in a commercial transaction with a foreign natural or juridical person, the State cannot invoke immunity from jurisdiction before the courts of another State which has jurisdiction by virtue of the applicable rules of private international law.[14] By the same token, a State is not normally allowed to invoke immunity from jurisdiction before a court of another State in a proceeding which relates to a contract of employment between that first State and an individual for work performed or

[8] Domestic courts, especially in continental Europe, tend to apply international law norms on State immunity directly. In common law countries, however, immunities are typically governed by statute; see above (n 3).

[9] This process unfolded throughout the early twentieth century, with, by the mid-twentieth century, absolutists and restrictionists being equally divided. cp S Sucharitkul, *State Immunities and Trading Activities in International Law* (London, Stevens & Sons, 1959) (defending restrictive immunity). Common law countries, however, clung for a relatively long time to an absolute approach to immunity. In the UK, this approach was only abandoned by the Court of Appeal (UK) in *Trendtex Trading Corpn v Central Bank of Nigeria* [1977] QB 529, and by the State Immunity Act 1978 (n 3).

[10] eg The Declaration of the Russian Federation and the People's Republic of China on the Promotion of International Law, 25 June 2016, mid.ru/en/foreign_policy/news/-/asset_publisher/cKNonkJE02Bw/content/id/2331698, para 8: 'The Russian Federation and the People's Republic of China assert that international obligations regarding immunity of States, their property and officials must be honored by States at all times. Violations of these obligations are not in conformity with the principle of sovereign equality of States and may contribute to the escalation of tensions'. This paragraph does not state, however, that immunities are necessarily absolute.

[11] Art 5 UN Convention (n 7).

[12] ibid, Art 10 ff.

[13] For relevant case law, see ILC, 'Draft Articles on Jurisdictional Immunities of States and Their Property, with commentaries' (1991) *YILC*, Vol II, Part Two, 36.

[14] Art 10 UN Convention (n 7).

to be performed, in whole or in part, in the territory of that other State.[15] The latter rule is typically applied in disputes between embassy staff and the foreign State. It is subject to exceptions, however. These include instances where the employee has been recruited to perform particular functions in the exercise of governmental authority, where the employee is a diplomatic agent or consular officer, where the security interests of the State are at stake, or where the employee is a national of the employer State.[16]

States can also not invoke immunity in a proceeding

> which relates to pecuniary compensation for death or injury to the person, or damage to or loss of tangible property, caused by an act or omission which is alleged to be attributable to the State, if the act or omission occurred in whole or in part in the territory of that other State and if the author of the act or omission was present in that territory at the time of the act or omission.[17]

This territorial tort principle mainly applies to traffic accidents caused by vehicles belonging to a State.[18] In its 2012 judgment in the case of *Jurisdictional Immunities of the State* (Germany v Italy), the ICJ held that this does not extend to civil proceedings for acts occasioning death, personal injury or damage to property committed by the armed forces and other organs of a State in the conduct of armed conflict.[19] Thus, according to the Court, the decision of the Italian courts to deny immunity to Germany in respect of injury caused by German troops on Italian soil during the Second World War could not be justified on the basis of this principle.[20]

Other exceptions to immunity from jurisdiction apply to proceedings relating to State ownership, possession and use of property, intellectual and industrial property, participation in companies or other collective bodies, and ships owned or operated by a State.[21] Also, a State cannot invoke immunity if it has entered into an agreement with a foreign person to submit to arbitration differences relating to a commercial transaction.[22] There is a substantial amount of practice in domestic courts in Europe which confirms the absence of immunity with respect to *acta jure gestionis*, especially in employment matters.[23]

This practice may not have been very uniform in the past, but convergence is expected in the wake of a number of judgments at the European level. For example, there have been a number of ECtHR judgments which have held that granting State immunity beyond what the UN Convention allows[24] unreasonably and disproportionally restricts the claimant's right of access to a court under Article 6 ECHR.[25] Further convergence in the application of State immunity in employment matters may come about as a result of the CJEU's decision in *Mahamdia* (2012).[26] This case did not concern the compatibility of immunity with

[15] ibid, Art 11(1).
[16] ibid, Art 11(2).
[17] ibid, Art 12.
[18] ILC Draft Articles (n 13), Commentary (4) to Art 12, 45 ('the article covers most areas of accidents involved in the transport of goods and passengers by rail, road, air or waterways').
[19] *Jurisdictional Immunities of the State* (Germany v Italy: Greece Intervening) [2012] ICJ Rep 99, para 77.
[20] ibid, para 79.
[21] Arts 13–16 UN Convention (n 7).
[22] ibid, Art 17.
[23] For cases, see H Fox and P Webb, *The Law of State Immunity*, 3rd edn (Oxford, OUP, 2013) 437 ff.
[24] Art 11 UN Convention (n 7).
[25] *Sabeh El Leil v France* App no 34869/05 (ECtHR, 29 June 2011), paras 66–68; *Cudak v Lithuania* App no 15869/02 (ECtHR, 23 March 2010); *Guadagnino v Italy and France* App no 2555/03 (ECtHR, 18 January 2011).
[26] Judgment of 19 July 2012, *Ahmed Mahamdia v People's Democratic Republic of Algeria*, C-154/11, EU:C:2012:491.

human rights, but rather with the claimants' access to EU-based courts under the Brussels Regulation on jurisdiction and the recognition and enforcement of judgments in civil and commercial matters.[27] Article 18(2) of this Regulation provides that

> [w]here an employee enters into an individual contract of employment with an employer who is not domiciled in a Member State but has a branch, agency or other establishment in one of the Member States, the employer shall, in disputes arising out of the operations of the branch, agency or establishment, be deemed to be domiciled in that Member State.

On its face, this provision allows employees of foreign embassies based in an EU Member State to sue the foreign State operating the embassy. Quite obviously, this would enable these employees to circumvent public international law rules on State immunity by relying on EU law. The CJEU has found a way out of this conundrum, however, by relying on the distinction between *acta jure gestionis* and *acta jure imperii*, with immunity only attaching to the latter, and with Article 18(2) of the Brussels Regulation thus granting a right of access to an EU Member State court with respect to non-sovereign acts of foreign States.[28] This could be seen as an example of the CJEU interpreting EU law in harmony with rules of public international law.

B. State Immunity from Enforcement

The immunity of States does not only apply to the establishment of jurisdiction, but also to the taking of enforcement or execution measures against foreign States. This immunity from enforcement is equally governed by the European and UN Conventions mentioned above. Like jurisdictional immunity, State immunity from enforcement is not absolute. The European Convention provides that

> [n]o measures of execution or preventative measures against the property of a Contracting State may be taken in the territory of another Contracting State except where and to the extent that the State has expressly consented thereto in writing in any particular case.[29]

The more recent UN Convention, however, *allows* execution if

> it has been established that the property is specifically in use or intended for use by the State for other than government non-commercial purposes and is in the territory of the State of the forum, provided that post-judgment measures of constraint may only be taken against property that has a connection with the entity against which the proceeding was directed.[30]

In the case of *Jurisdictional Immunities of the State* (Germany v Italy), the ICJ held that the latter principle represents customary international law.[31] According to the ICJ, measures

[27] Council Regulation No 44/2001 of 22 December 2000 on jurisdiction and the recognition of enforcement of judgements in civil and commercial matters [2001] OJ L12/1; Council Regulation No 1215/2012 of 20 December 2012 on jurisdiction and the recognition and enforcement of judgements in civil and commercial matters (recast) [2012] OJ L351/1.

[28] *Ahmed Mahamdia* (n 26) para 57.

[29] Art 23 European Convention (n 5).

[30] Art 19(c) UN Convention (n 7). Art 21(1) of the UN Convention, however, excludes a number of categories of property of State from being considered as property specifically in use or intended for use by the State for other than government non-commercial purposes under Art 19(c).

[31] *Jurisdictional Immunities* (n 19) para 117 (doubting, however, 'whether all aspects of Art 19 reflect current customary international law').

of constraint may be taken against property belonging to a foreign State, but only where the property in question is in use for an activity not pursuing government non-commercial purposes, the State which owns the property has expressly consented to the taking of a measure of constraint, or that State has allocated the property in question for the satisfaction of a judicial claim.[32] Some categories of State property are clearly not subject to enforcement, such as property of a military character, property of the central bank or other monetary authority of the State, property forming part of the cultural heritage of the State or part of its archives and not placed or intended to be placed on sale, or property forming part of an exhibition of objects of scientific, cultural or historical interest and not placed or intended to be placed on sale.[33]

There is again a sizeable amount of case law, also from domestic courts in Europe, which supports the principle that execution measures can, under certain circumstances, be taken against State property.[34] In respect of bank accounts, however, most courts are reluctant to lift the State's immunity, even if such accounts may well be used for commercial purposes. This is evidenced by the following leading decision of the German Federal Constitutional Court (1982):

> There exists the following general rule of international law: Forced execution of judgment by the State of the forum under a writ of execution against a foreign State which has been issued in respect of non-sovereign acts (acta iure gestionis) of that State, on property of that State which is present or situated in the territory of the State of the forum is inadmissible without the consent of the foreign State if, at the time of the initiation of the measure of execution, such property serves sovereign purposes of the foreign State. Claims against a general current bank account of the embassy of a foreign State which exists in the State of the forum and the purpose of which is to cover the embassy's costs and expenses are not subject to forced execution by the State of the forum. This rule forms part of federal law.[35]

This principle has found its way into the UN Convention, which provides that

> any bank account, which is used or intended for use in the performance of the functions of the diplomatic mission of the State or its consular posts, special missions, missions to international organisations or delegations to organs of international organisations or to international conferences […] shall not be considered as property specifically in use or intended for use by the State for other than government non-commercial purposes.[36]

Based on the limited exception for enforcement measures against foreign States, execution proceedings against Argentinian State property were initiated in France and Belgium by investment funds which had purchased debt from the defaulting Argentinian government. These procedures were largely unsuccessful: the French and Belgian Supreme Courts upheld Argentina's immunity from execution with respect to various diplomatic and non-diplomatic properties.[37] In 2015, shareholders seeking to enforce the largest arbitral award

[32] ibid, para 118.

[33] Art 21(b)–(e) UN Convention (n 7).

[34] Constitutional Court (DE), *Philippine Embassy*, 13 December 1977, 2 BvM 1/76, 46 BVerfGE 342, 65 ILR 146; Federal Tribunal (CH), *Kingdom of Spain v Société X*, 30 April 1986, (1986) 43 *Annuaire suisse de droit international* 158, 82 ILR 44; House of Lords (UK), *Alcom Ltd v Republic of Colombia* [1984] 1 AC 580 (HL), 74 ILR 170 and Constitutional Court (ES), *Abbott v Republic of South Africa*, 1 July 1992, (1992) 44 *Revista española de derecho international* 565, 113 ILR 414.

[35] *Philippine Embassy* (n 34) 150.

[36] Art 21 UN Convention (n 7).

[37] Court of Cassation (FR), *Argentina v NML Capital*, 28 September 2011, Arrêt n° 867 (09-72.057); 28 March 2013, Arrêt n° 394 (10-25.938); Arrêt n° 395 (11-10.450); Arrêt n° 396 (11-13.323); Court of Cassation (BE); *Argentina, v NML Capital*, 11 December 2014, C.13.0537.F.

ever rendered (US$50 billion), against Russia in the *Yukos* litigation in 2014 (an award that was later annulled by the Hague District Court),[38] initiated execution proceedings in the same countries (France, Belgium, the US and the UK). The shareholders moved to attach embassy bank accounts and announced that they might target other State assets too, including assets of State-owned energy corporations.[39] These execution proceedings were again unsuccessful, with Belgium for instance unblocking attached Russian bank accounts after Russian protest.[40] The chances of success were further diminished after the Russian Federation adopted a 'claw-back law' that allowed Russia to seize assets of foreign States which wrongfully seized Russian property.[41] It is expected that such a law may have a major deterrent effect on foreign States' willingness to take enforcement measures. Belgium and France later tightened, or envisaged tightening their laws to make execution procedures against State property more difficult.[42] These vicissitudes show that obtaining a favourable judgment against a foreign State may be one thing, but having the judgment enforced is quite another.

C. State Immunity and International Crimes

The question has arisen whether there is an additional exception to State immunity from jurisdiction in relation to allegations of gross human rights violations or international crimes, even if such acts could not qualify as *acta jure gestionis*.[43] One of the leading cases in this respect is *Jurisdictional Immunities of the State* (Germany v Italy) before the ICJ, which reviewed the legality of tort proceedings before Italian courts against Germany in respect of international crimes committed by the Nazi regime in Italy during the Second World War. Related or similar cases were heard by various national courts in Europe (in Italy, Greece and Germany), by the ECtHR,[44] and by the CJEU.[45] The cases mainly revolved around the question whether Germany could avail itself of its immunity in proceedings brought before Italian courts in respect of international crimes. Some Italian and Greek courts had taken the view that it could not, and then proceeded to hold that victims of Nazi atrocities and their relatives could sue Germany before foreign courts.[46] After the Italian Court of

[38] *Yukos Universal Limited (Isle of Man) v The Russian Federation*, 28 July 2014, PCA Case No AA 227; District Court The Hague (NL), *Russian Federation v Yukos et al*, 20 April 2016, ECLI:NL:RBDHA:2016:4229.

[39] 'Russia and Yukos: Bound Over', *The Economist*, 25 June 2015, economist.com/news/leaders/21656186-kremlin-cares-little-rule-law-home-western-courts-are-less-malleable-bound.

[40] M Hanrahan, 'Belgium Unfreezes Russian Assets Seized In Yukos Legal Fight', *International Business Times*, 21 June 2015, ibtimes.com/belgium-unfreezes-russian-assets-seized-yukos-legal-fight-1976386.

[41] 'Putin signs law allowing retaliatory sequestration of foreign property in Russia', *Russia Today*, 4 November 2015, rt.com/politics/320741-putin-property-sequestration-abroad/.

[42] For Belgium: Art 1412*quinquies* Code of Civil Procedure; added by the Law introducing an Article 1412quinquies in the Code of Civil Procedure, concerning the seizure of property of a foreign power or of a public law supranational or international organisation, 23 August 2015, *Belgian Official Gazette* of 3 September 2015. For France: Art L111-1-3 Code of Civil Enforcement Procedures (as lastly amended 1 January 2018); added by Loi n° 2016-1691 du 9 décembre 2016 relative à la transparence, à la lutte contre la corruption et à la modernisation de la vie économique (Loi Sapin 2), ECFM1605542L, *Journal officiel de la république française* No 0287 of 10 December 2016, Text No 2.

[43] For a study, see R van Alebeek, *The Immunity of States and their Officials in International Criminal Law and International Human Rights Law* (Oxford, OUP, 2008).

[44] *Kalogeropoulou and others v Greece and Germany* App no 59021/00 (ECtHR, 12 December 2002).

[45] Judgment of 15 February 2007, *Lechouritou and others v Dimosio tis Omospondiakis Dimokratias tis Germanias*, C-292/05, EU:C:2007:102.

[46] Court of Cassation (IT), *Ferrini v Germany*, 11 March 2004, Case No 5044/4; Supreme Court (GR), *Germany v Prefecture of Voiotia*, 4 May 2000, Case No 11/2000.

Cassation upheld this approach[47] and Greek victims sought to execute Greek judgments against German property in Italy, Germany filed an application with the ICJ against Italy (Greece intervening), arguing that it enjoyed immunity before Italian courts and that no exception applied. The ICJ followed this argument and held that there is no territorial tort exception to immunity in relation to acts committed by military forces,[48] and that immunity continues to apply in the face of international crimes or violations of *jus cogens*. According to the Court, the argument centred on a perceived hierarchy of norms – in the case the posited prevalence of *jus cogens* over the rules of immunity – is beside the point in that there is no conflict between a rule of *jus cogens* and the customary rule of State immunity that necessitate recourse to higher norms as a conflict-resolution mechanism.[49] In the Court's view, immunity is only of a procedural character, and does not bear on the substantive (un-)lawfulness of the impugned conduct.[50] It is recalled indeed that a State's entitlement to immunity in relation to international crimes does not mean that it is not responsible for the crimes it may have committed;[51] in fact, Germany had assumed responsibility for crimes committed by the Nazi regime in the Second World War. Moreover, the ICJ discerned a logical problem in lifting State immunity with respect to international crimes: the mere allegation of an international crime by victims might suffice for a State to forfeit its immunity without the Court having been able to enquire into the merits of the case to determine whether such a crime had actually occurred.[52] This speaks to a legitimate concern over frivolous, but long drawn-out lawsuits being filed against States that ultimately may turn out to be baseless, while tarnishing the States' reputations.

While the ICJ opposed the lifting of State immunity in view of the importance of the stability of inter-State relations, it is not blind to the need for accountability in respect of these crimes. It suggested in particular that the victims' State of nationality may want to pursue diplomatic negotiations with the allegedly responsible State.[53] One could also think of the victims initiating proceedings against the responsible State before its own courts. For instance, relatives of victims of the Srebrenica massacre sued the Dutch government before Dutch courts.[54] Prior settlement agreements and domestic doctrines restricting litigation against the government may nevertheless limit the success of these avenues.[55] According to the ICJ, the fact that the chances of success are slight is not an argument to lift the allegedly responsible State's immunity.[56] Reflecting on this, one wonders whether the ICJ is taking the

[47] *Ferrini v Germany* (n 46).

[48] *Jurisdictional Immunities* (n 19) para 77: citing *Grosz v France* App no 14717/06 (ECtHR, 16 June 2009); *Kalogeropoulou and others v Greece and Germany* (n 44).

[49] *Jurisdictional Immunities* (n 19) para 93.

[50] ibid.

[51] ibid, para 108.

[52] ibid, para 106.

[53] See eg ibid, para 104.

[54] See eg *Stichting Mothers of Srebrenica and others v the Netherlands and the United Nations*: Supreme Court (NL), 13 April 2012, ECLI:NL:HR:2012:BW1999; Court of Appeal The Hague (NL), 30 March 2010, ECLI:NL:GHSGR:2010:BL8979; Court of First Instance The Hague (NL), 10 July 2008, ECLI:NL:RBSGR:2008:BD6796.

[55] For a prior settlement agreement, see eg Art 77(4) of the Peace Treaty of the Allied Powers with Italy (adopted 10 February 1947, entered into force 15 September 1947) 49 UNTS 3. For domestic doctrines excluding claims for compensation for damage resulting from foreign combat operations, see eg Foreign Claims Act, 10 USC § 2734 (2006); Federal Court of Justice (DE), 2 November 2006, Case No III ZR 190/05, BGHZ 169, 348. For a discussion, see H Krieger, 'Addressing the Accountability Gap in Peacekeeping: Law-Making by Domestic Courts As a Way to Avoid UN Reform?' (2015) 62 *NILR* 259.

[56] *Jurisdictional Immunities* (n 19) para 101.

individual's fundamental human right to a remedy sufficiently seriously.[57] Of note in this respect is that in *Simoncioni*, the Italian Constitutional Court disallowed the application of the international law of State immunity in case of conflict with the fundamental (constitutional) principle of access to justice,[58] and for that reason annulled a law seeking to give effect to the ICJ's judgment in the *Jurisdictional Immunities of the State* case.[59] It is not excluded, insofar as other domestic courts are following this reasoning, that a new customary exception to the principle of State immunity for international crimes may emerge in due course. As we write, however, there is no evidence of such a tendency, rather on the contrary: in *Jones v UK*, the ECtHR, citing the ICJ's judgment, considered the conferral of immunity on a foreign State accused of crimes of torture to be compatible with Article 6 ECHR.[60] In so doing, with an even larger majority of judges, it reaffirmed its decision in *Al Adsani v UK*, in which it had held that

> [n]otwithstanding the special character of the prohibition of torture in international law, the Court is unable to discern in the international instruments, judicial authorities or other materials before it any firm basis for concluding that, as a matter of international law, a State no longer enjoys immunity from civil suit in the courts of another State where acts of torture are alleged.[61]

The United States and Canada make an additional (and controversial) exception to State immunity for acts of terrorism. Thus, the US Foreign Sovereign Immunities Act, amended for that purpose in 1996, provides that

> [a] foreign state shall not be immune from the jurisdiction of courts of the United States or of the States in any case […] in which money damages are sought against a foreign state for personal injury or death that was caused by an act of torture, extrajudicial killing, aircraft sabotage, hostage taking, or the provision of material support or resources for such an act if such act or provision of material support or resources is engaged in by an official, employee, or agent of such foreign state while acting within the scope of his or her office, employment, or agency.[62]

In practice, States' immunity from execution proved a potent obstacle to the effective application of the exception. This changed after US law-makers moved to allow such execution measures, the constitutionality of which was upheld by the US Supreme Court in 2016, in a case against Iran.[63] Members of the Non-Aligned Movement denounced this 'unilateral action' as a violation of the international law of State immunity in a letter addressed to the UN Secretary General.[64] Iran itself initiated proceedings against the United States before

[57] R van Alebeek, 'Domestic Courts as Agents of Development of International Immunity Rules' (2013) 26 *LJIL* 559, 578: 'It is to be hoped that domestic courts will not be blinded by the undisputed authority of these venerable international institutions, but undertake an independent assessment of the relationship between immunity rules and fundamental rights under international law'.

[58] Constitutional Court (IT), *Simoncioni and others v Germany and President of the Council of Ministers of the Italian Republic (intervening)*, 22 October 2014, Decision No 238/2014. It is noted that the Italian Court of Cassation had earlier held that Italian courts were obliged to apply an Italian statute requiring them to give effect to ICJ decisions (Art 3 of Law 5/2013 on the accession of Italy to the United Nations Convention on Jurisdictional Immunities of States and their Property, 14 January 2013): Court of Cassation (IT), *Federal Republic of Germany v Ferrini and Ferrini*, 21 January 2014, Case No 1136.

[59] *Jurisdictional Immunities* (n 19).

[60] *Jones and others v UK* App nos 34356/06 and 40528/06 (ECtHR, 14 January 2014). See also *Jurisdictional Immunities* (n 19) para 85.

[61] *Al-Adsani v UK* App no 35763/97 (ECtHR, 21 November 2001), para 61.

[62] US Foreign Sovereign Immunities Act of 1976 (n 3) § 1605A(a).

[63] Supreme Court (US), *Bank Markazi, aka Central Bank of Iran v Deborah Peterson et al*, 20 April 2016, Case No 14–770.

[64] Letter dated 5 May 2016 from the Permanent Representative of the Islamic Republic of Iran to the United Nations addressed to the Secretary General, Annex: 'Communiqué by the Coordinating Bureau of the

the ICJ under a Treaty of Amity, which both States had concluded in 1955.[65] In Canada, similar evolutions have taken place. In 2012, the Justice for Victims of Terrorism Act (JVTA) was enacted to create an exception to State immunity for terrorist offences, including those committed by States.[66] In 2016, the Ontario Superior Court of Justice held that US judgments based on the aforementioned US legislation and the JVTA are enforceable in Canada, in the case against Iran.[67]

III. Immunity of Foreign State Officials

The immunity of the State ordinarily trickles down to the person performing State acts in an official capacity. This immunity *ratione materiae* or functional/conduct-based immunity can be relied on by any person acting on behalf of the State, in particular State officials, including former State officials.[68] The rationale for this immunity is that allowing a State official to be sued before a foreign State's court in respect of its official acts could amount to allowing the *State* to be *indirectly* sued, and thus to circumvent the principle of State immunity. After all, States, being abstract entities, necessarily rely on natural persons – State officials – to carry out the official activities of the State. Thus, the UN Convention provides that 'State' not only means 'the State and its various organs of government', but also 'agencies or instrumentalities of the State or other entities, to the extent that they are entitled to perform and are actually performing acts in the exercise of sovereign authority of the State', and 'representatives of the State acting in that capacity'.[69] Relying on this rule, in *Jones v UK*, the ECtHR confirmed that the definition of 'State' includes its representatives.[70]

Again, the question has arisen whether State officials could avail themselves of immunity in respect of international crimes. Two categories of State officials should be distinguished in this respect: on the one hand all State officials, who are normally entitled to immunity *ratione materiae*, *i.e.*, limited to their official acts and on the other hand, a limited number of high-ranking State officials, who are normally entitled to immunity *ratione personae* which also extends to non-official acts.

A. Immunity Ratione Materiae

After the ICJ's judgment in *Germany v Italy* it has become clear that there is no exception to State immunity for grave crimes. This decision is not necessarily dispositive of the immunity

Non-Aligned Movement in Rejection of Unilateral Actions by the United States in Contravention of International Law, in Particular the Principle of State Immunity', 6 May 2016, UN Doc A/70/861-S/2016/420, 2.

[65] Certain Iranian Assets (Islamic Republic of Iran v United States of America), Application of 14 June 2016 before the ICJ.

[66] Justice for Victims of Terrorism Act, SC 2012, Chapter 1, Section 2.

[67] Ontario Superior Court of Justice (CA), *Tracy v The Iranian Ministry of Information and Security*, 2016 ONSC 3759.

[68] D Akande and S Shah, 'Immunities of State Officials, International Crimes, and Foreign Domestic Courts' (2010) 21 *EJIL* 815, 825.

[69] Art 2(1)(b) UN Convention (n 7).

[70] *Jones v UK* (n 60) para 202. For the UK House of Lords' decisions in the case, see House of Lords (UK), *Jones v Saudi Arabia* [2006] UKHL 26, [2007] 1 AC 270, para 10. See also the Supreme Court of Canada's

ratione materiae of State *officials*, however. In fact, there is a tendency to *deny* immunity to State officials in case of grave crimes, at least in criminal proceedings. In its seminal *Pinochet* judgment, the UK House of Lords held that a former Head of State could not avail himself of his immunity as a State official in respect of alleged crimes of torture, as deciding otherwise would frustrate the object and purpose of the UN Convention against Torture:[71]

> The alleged acts of torture by Senator Pinochet were carried out under colour of his position as head of state, but they cannot be regarded as functions of a head of state under international law when international law expressly prohibits torture as a measure which a state can employ in any circumstances whatsoever and has made it an international crime.[72]
>
> So far as the states that are parties to the convention are concerned, I cannot see how, so far as torture is concerned, this immunity can exist consistently with the terms of that Convention. Each State Party has agreed that the other State Parties can exercise jurisdiction over alleged official torturers found within their territories [...] and thus, to my mind, can hardly simultaneously claim an immunity from extradition or prosecution that is necessarily based on the official nature of the alleged torture.[73]

Also in respect of crimes of torture, the Court of Appeal of Amsterdam held that 'the commission of very grave criminal offences of this kind cannot be regarded as part of the official duties of a Head of State'.[74] The Swiss Federal Criminal Court similarly held that a former major-general of the Algerian army was not entitled to immunity *ratione materiae* for war crimes, because it would be contradictory for, on the one hand, the legislative branch of the Swiss Government to commit to combating impunity by implementing the Rome Statute establishing the ICC, and on the other, the courts to espouse a wide interpretation of functional immunity.[75] In 2017, the International Law Commission provisionally adopted draft Article 7 on immunity of State officials from foreign criminal jurisdiction, which provides that '[i]mmunity ratione materiae from the exercise of foreign criminal jurisdiction shall not apply in respect of the following crimes under international law:

(a) crime of genocide;
(b) crimes against humanity;
(c) war crimes;
(d) crime of apartheid;
(e) torture;
(f) enforced disappearance.[76]

ruling in *Kazemi Estate v Islamic Republic of Iran* [2014] SCC 62 (ruling that the Canadian State Immunity Act does not provide for an exception to foreign State immunity from civil suits alleging acts of torture occurring outside Canada, and that public officials must be included in the meaning of 'government' as it is used in the Act); but see Supreme Court (US), *Samantar v Yousuf et al*, 8 US 1555 (2010) (holding that State officials do not fall within the statutory definition of 'State' in the Foreign Sovereign Immunities Act of 1976 (n 3)).

[71] House of Lords (UK), *R v Bartle and the Commissioner of Police for the Metropolis and others, ex parte Pinochet (No 3)* (*Pinochet No 3*) [1999] UKHL 17, [2000] 1 AC 147, (1999) 38 ILM 581.

[72] *Pinochet No 3* (n 71) (per Lord Hutton) (1999) 38 ILM 638.

[73] *Pinochet No 3* (n 71) (per Lord Saville of Newdigate) (1999) 38 ILM 642–43.

[74] Court of Appeal Amsterdam (NL), *Re Bouterse*, 20 November 2000, ECLI:NL:GHAMS:2000:AA8395, para 4.2. For a comment, see L Zegveld, 'The Bouterse case' (2001) 32 *NYIL* 97.

[75] Federal Criminal Court (CH), *A and Ministère Public de la Confédération v B and C*, 25 July 2012, Case No BB.2011.140, para 5.4.4.

[76] ILC, Report on the work of the sixty-ninth session (2017), UN Doc. A/72/10, 176.

It bears notice that in civil (tort) cases – filed by victims claiming compensation – State officials' immunity *ratione materiae* may still stand, even in the face of torture allegations. At least, such immunity has been upheld by the ECtHR in *Jones v UK*, although the Court recognised that State practice in this field was in a 'state of flux'.[77] It is not fully clear on what grounds State officials could continue to avail themselves of their immunity *ratione materiae* in civil cases, while such immunity would no longer hold in criminal cases. After all, the underlying violation is the same, and the impact on inter-State relations is comparable. Future State practice will be instructive in this regard, although the ECtHR has obviously not encouraged more progressively-inclined courts to reject immunity in civil cases.

B. Immunity Ratione Personae

While all State officials enjoy immunity *ratione materiae* (whether or not subject to an exception for international crimes), some State officials also enjoy immunity *ratione personae*, that is, a (quasi-)absolute immunity during their time in office, including in relation to private acts, even if committed before taking office. Officials who can avail themselves of immunity *ratione personae* include diplomatic agents and a few high-ranking government members, in particular Heads of State, Heads of Government, and Ministers for Foreign Affairs.[78] Such immunity is accorded not for their personal benefit, 'but to ensure the effective performance of their functions on behalf of their respective States'.[79] In the absence of immunity, States may well hinder this performance, as the relevant State representatives may have to defend themselves in court to the detriment of the effective discharge of their State duties. Accordingly, the rationale of immunity *ratione personae* lies in the principles of comity and non-intervention, and the international community's desire to facilitate the smooth conduct of international relations in the interest of international peace.

Diplomatic agents enjoy absolute immunity *ratione personae* in criminal matters, and quasi-absolute immunity in civil and administrative matters pursuant to Article 31 of the 1961 Vienna Convention on Diplomatic Relations (VCDR).[80] High-ranking government members enjoy absolute immunity in criminal matters under customary international law, although it is not fully clear whether they also enjoy absolute immunity in other matters.[81]

The immunity of high-ranking office-holders also extends to international crimes. In the *Arrest Warrant* case before the ICJ, the Democratic Republic of Congo (DRC) was of the view that a Belgian investigating judge's issuance of an arrest warrant against the incumbent Minister for Foreign Affairs of the DRC for incitement to genocide was a violation of the law of immunity. The ICJ agreed with this position and clarified that there is no customary

[77] See *Jones v UK* (n 60) para 213.

[78] See for the latter *Arrest Warrant of 11 April 2000* (Democratic Republic of the Congo v Belgium) [2002] ICJ Rep 3, para 53.

[79] ibid.

[80] Pursuant to Art 31 VCDR, the diplomatic agent does not enjoy immunity in the case of '(a) A real action relating to private immovable property situated in the territory of the receiving State, unless he holds it on behalf of the sending State for the purposes of the mission; (b) An action relating to succession in which the diplomatic agent is involved as executor, administrator, heir or legatee as a private person and not on behalf of the sending State; (c) An action relating to any professional or commercial activity exercised by the diplomatic agent in the receiving State outside his official functions'.

[81] See, in respect of Heads of State: Institut de Droit International, 'Immunities from Jurisdiction and Execution of Heads of State and of Government in International Law', 26 August 2001, idi-iil.org/app/uploads/2017/06/2001_van_02_en.pdf, Art 3.

law-based exception to senior State officials' immunity in criminal matters, not even for international crimes:

> The Court has carefully examined State practice, including national legislation and those few decisions of national higher courts, such as the House of Lords or the French Court of Cassation. It has been unable to deduce from this practice that there exists under customary international law any form of exception to the rule according immunity from criminal jurisdiction and inviolability to incumbent Ministers for Foreign Affairs, where they are suspected of having committed war crimes or crimes against humanity.[82]

The Court added, however, that immunity does not mean impunity: '[j]urisdictional immunity may well bar prosecution for a certain period or for certain offences; it cannot exonerate the person to whom it applies from all criminal responsibility'.[83] According to the Court, the immunities enjoyed under international law by an incumbent or former Minister for Foreign Affairs do not necessarily represent a bar to criminal prosecution. Such persons can be prosecuted in their own country, the State which they represent can waive their immunity, they can be tried in other States after ceasing to hold office, and they could be subject to criminal proceedings before certain international courts and tribunals such as the ICC[84] (according to Article 27 of the ICC Statute, immunities related to a person's official capacity do not constitute a bar to the Court's jurisdiction, on which see Chapter 17, Section V(C)(ii)). In practice, however, these avenues may not be available for political, practical or legal reasons. States are unlikely to prosecute their own high-office holders, or waive their immunity, unless they have fallen out of favour. Incumbents may be reluctant to give up their office for fear of prosecution when they step down. Even if they do so, few States may be willing to exercise universal jurisdiction over high-ranking foreign officials. Finally, and as discussed in Chapter 17, Section V(B), the ICC has a limited remit: it only has jurisdiction over acts committed after 1 July 2002, and it can only exercise jurisdiction over individuals who committed a crime on the territory of a State Party, who are nationals of a State Party, or who committed a crime referred to it by the UN Security Council. Therefore, the principle of immunity *ratione personae* may well leave the victim without a remedy.

Domestic courts in Europe have complied with the rule that at least high-ranking office holders such as Heads of State, Heads of Government, Ministers of Foreign Affairs and diplomats enjoy immunity *ratione personae*, also in relation to international crimes.[85] In one case, a UK court even extended this immunity to foreign Ministers of Defence.[86] This may expand the narrow circle of senior office-holders traditionally considered to enjoy immunity *ratione personae*, but it seems to be in keeping with the functional rationale for such immunity identified by the ICJ in *Arrest Warrant*, namely that such immunity ensures the effective performance of their functions on behalf of their State. It is arguable that, just like a Minister of Foreign Affairs, a Minister of Defence also often represents the State in international negotiations and intergovernmental meetings, is frequently required to travel internationally, must be in a position to do so freely whenever the need should arise, and

[82] *Arrest Warrant* (n 78) para 58. See, however, the dissenting opinion of Judge van den Wyngaert, criticising the Court for not giving more thought and consideration to the balancing of the relative normative status of international *jus cogens* crimes and immunities.

[83] ibid, para 60.

[84] ibid, para 61.

[85] Court of Cassation (FR), *Re Qadhafi*, 13 March 2001, Appeal No 00-87215; Court of Cassation (BE), *Re Sharon and Yaron*, 12 February 2003, Case No P.02.1139.F/2.

[86] Bow Street Magistrates' Court (UK), *Re Mofaz*, 12 February 2004, as reproduced in (2004) 53 *ICLQ* 771.

must be in constant communication with the Government.[87] However, a slippery slope is discernable here, as these days many ministers and other senior officials are required to represent the State abroad. Further expansions of immunity *ratione personae* risk running afoul of individual claimants' right of access to a court, as laid down in Article 6 ECHR, and may have to be opposed. Thus, the French Court of Cassation rejected the immunity of a vice-president of Equatorial Guinea (2015).[88] The French position led to an application to the ICJ by Equatorial Guinea (2016), which was of the view that vice-presidents are also entitled to immunity *ratione personae*.[89] In its judgment on preliminary objections (2018), however, the ICJ held that it does not have jurisdiction to address this aspect of the case.[90]

Foreign State officials may also enjoy immunity *ratione personae* on the basis of the UN Convention on Special Missions.[91] The Convention defines a special mission as

> a temporary mission, representing the State, which is sent by one State to another State with the consent of the latter for the purpose of dealing with it on specific questions or of performing in relation to it a specific task.[92]

It confers quasi-absolute immunity, including absolute immunity in criminal matters, on the representatives of the sending State in the special mission on a par with diplomatic representatives.[93] However, the Convention has attracted a relatively low number of ratifications (39), and few European States are parties to it. Still, in particular on the grounds that the Convention was adopted by a UN General Assembly resolution with 98 states in favour, none against and only one abstention, in 2018, the Court of Appeal for England and Wales considered the Convention to represent customary international law.[94]

IV. Immunities of International Organisations and Their Officials

Apart from States and their officials, international organisations and their officials also generally enjoy immunity. This immunity is usually laid down in specific agreements with host States that provide for the privileges and immunities of the organisation and its staff from the jurisdiction of the host State, or in the constituent instruments of the international organisation. These privileges and immunities aim to safeguard the autonomy of the organisation – which is vested with separate international legal personality – from judicial and political interference by (Member) States.

[87] *Arrest Warrant* (n 78) para 53.

[88] Court of Cassation (FR), *Re Teodoro Nguema Obiang Mangue*, 15 December 2015, Appeal No 15-83156.

[89] Immunities and Criminal Proceedings (Equatorial Guinea v France), Application of 13 June 2016 before the ICJ.

[90] ICJ, *Immunities and Criminal Proceedings* (*Equatorial Guinea v France*), Preliminary Objections, Judgment of 6 June 2018, para. 118 (ruling that it lacks jurisdiction pursuant to the Palermo Convention to entertain Equatorial Guinea's Application regarding its vice-president's immunity).

[91] Convention on Special Missions (adopted 8 December 1969, entered into force 21 June 1985) 1400 UNTS 231.

[92] ibid, Art 1(a).

[93] ibid, Art 31. For a discussion: A Sanger and M Wood, 'The Immunities of Members of Special Missions', forthcoming in T Ruys, N Angelet, L Ferro (eds), *The Cambridge Handbook of Immunities and International Law*.

[94] [2018] EWCA Civ 1719.

It is not fully clear whether in the absence of a treaty, an international organisation could avail itself of immunity under customary international law or general principles of law. The case law is somewhat contradictory in this respect: in 1986, the Dutch Supreme Court held that the Iran-US Claims Tribunal enjoys immunity under customary international law,[95] whereas in 2001, the Belgian Supreme Court ruled that there is no general principle of international law pursuant to which the League of Arab States enjoys immunity.[96] Also, in 2012, the Supreme Court of New York held that the IMF Managing Director Dominique Strauss-Kahn did not enjoy absolute immunity under customary international law in the absence of the US ratification of the UN Convention on the Immunities and Privileges of the Specialized Agencies[97] (which does provide for such immunity).[98] It appears that, unlike with respect to the immunity of States, there is insufficient State practice and *opinio juris* to the effect of conferring immunity on international organisations and their officials under customary international law. The relevance of the issue should not be exaggerated, however, as international organisations typically enter into rather detailed headquarters or other agreements with the host States, providing for immunities and privileges of the organisation and its staff.

These agreements usually provide for the *functional* immunity from jurisdiction of the organisation (as well as its representatives), meaning that the organisation enjoys immunity insofar as it acts for the fulfilment of the organisation's purposes, that is insofar as the organisation is exercising the powers which its Member States have attributed to it. This immunity cannot readily be compared with the immunity accorded to States, which is based on the principle of sovereignty. While States exercise sovereignty, international organisations only exercise delegated powers. Still, an argument can be made that, when exercising functional authority, international organisations should only enjoy immunity in respect of acts that form the core of their activity – comparable to the *acta jure imperii* in the law of State immunity – and not for acts that are ancillary to its main goals – comparable to the *acta jure gestionis* in the law of State immunity. Thus, the Court of Appeal of Amsterdam, in a criminal case against Euratom, dismissed the organisation's immunity on the grounds that violating Dutch environmental regulations did not form part of the organisation's functions.[99] The Court of Appeal of The Hague, for its part, in a procurement case against the European Patent Organisation, dismissed the organisation's claim to immunity on the grounds that offering catering facilities was unrelated to the organisation's role of issuing patents.[100] By and large, however, domestic courts are reluctant to inquire into whether a particular activity is essential for, or just ancillary to,

[95] Supreme Court (NL), *Spaans v Iran-United States Claims Tribunal*, 18 April 1986, Case No 12627.

[96] Court of Cassation (BE), *Re League of Arab States v TM*, 12 March 2001, Case No S.99.0103.F. For voices in the literature, see CH Brower, 'International Immunities: Some Dissident Views on the Role of Municipal Courts' (2000) 41 *Virginia Journal of International Law* 1, 22–23; M Singer, 'Jurisdictional Immunity of International Organizations: Human Rights and Functional Necessity Concerns' (1995) 36 *Virginia Journal of International Law* 53, 98; K Tesfagabir, 'The State of Functional Immunity of International Organizations and Their Officials and Why It Should be Streamlined' (2011) 10 *CJIL* 97, 107–108.

[97] Convention on the Privileges and Immunities of the Specialized Agencies (adopted 21 November 1947, entered into force 2 December 1948) 33 UNTS 261.

[98] Supreme Court New York (US), *Nafissatou Diallo v Dominique Strauss-Kahn*, 11 June 2012, Case No 307065/11.

[99] The Court of Appeal was overruled by the Supreme Court, however, which did grant the organisation functional immunity. See Supreme Court Amsterdam (NL), *Re Euratom*, 13 November 2007, Case No LJN: BA9173, and the summary of the Court of Appeal's judgment contained therein.

[100] Court of Appeal The Hague (NL), *European Patent Organisation v Stichting Restaurant de la Tour*, 21 June 2011, LJN: BR0188.

an organisation's exercise of its competences, for fear of interfering into matters internal to the international organisation.

This Section gives an overview of the regime of functional immunity as it applies, in accordance with relevant treaties, to the UN (Section A), the EU (Section B), and to a certain extent also to Status of Forces Agreements governing the legal position of international military missions stationed in the host State concerned (Section C). Acknowledging that international organisations do not usually act ultra vires and thus that application of the 'functional necessity' doctrine will ordinarily lead to the conferral of immunity on the international organisation, Section D examines the human rights-based exceptions that have been carved out with respect to the organisation's immunity, to prevent third parties from having no remedy against the organisation.

A. Immunities of the UN

To determine whether a given international organisation and its officials enjoy immunity in a specific situation, the terms of the agreement between the organisation and its host State(s) have to be examined. This section covers the immunity regime with respect to the UN, as it has provided a model for other international organisations.

The principle of 'functional' immunity of the UN is laid down in Article 105 of the UN Charter, which provides that the UN:

> shall enjoy in the territory of each of its Members such privileges and immunities as are necessary for the fulfillment of its purposes and that representatives of the Members of the United Nations and officials of the Organization shall similarly enjoy such privileges and immunities as are necessary for the independent exercise of their functions in connection with the Organization.

Section 2 of the General Convention on the Privileges and Immunities of the United Nations (1946) elaborates on Article 105 of the Charter by setting out that '[t]he United Nations, its property and assets wherever located and by whomsoever held, shall enjoy immunity from every form of legal process except insofar as in any particular case it has expressly waived its immunity'.[101] UN officials, for their part, are 'immune from legal process in respect of words spoken or written and all acts performed by them in an official capacity',[102] and enjoy a number of privileges in relation to taxation and national services obligations.[103] The UN Secretary General and the Assistant Secretaries General enjoy more far-reaching privileges, immunities, exemptions and facilities, equivalent to those accorded to diplomatic envoys.[104] The '[p]rivileges and immunities are granted to officials in the interest of the United Nations', however, 'and not for the personal benefit of the individuals themselves'.[105] This explains why

> the Secretary General shall have the right and the duty to waive the immunity of any official in any case where, in his opinion, the immunity would impede the course of justice and can be waived without prejudice to the interests of the United Nations.[106]

[101] Convention on the Privileges and Immunities of the United Nations (adopted 13 February 1946, entered into force 14 December 1946) 1 UNTS 15 (General Convention).

[102] ibid, Section 18(a).

[103] ibid, Section 18(b)–(c) and (g).

[104] ibid, Section 19.

[105] ibid, Section 20.

[106] ibid.

Nonetheless, victims do not have a subjective right to have a UN official's immunity waived.

Apart from UN officials, pursuant to Section 22 of the General Convention, experts

> performing missions for the United Nations are also accorded certain privileges and immunities, to the extent necessary for the independent exercise of their functions during the period of their missions, including the time spent on journeys in connection with their missions.

The ICJ has twice been called on to clarify the scope of this provision. In 1989, it held that the special rapporteur of the Sub-Commission on Prevention of Discrimination and Protection of Minorities, Mr Mazilu, whom the Romanian authorities had refused a travel permit, was entitled to the immunities accruing to an expert on mission as defined in Section 22.[107] In 1999, after Malaysia had prosecuted the UN Special Rapporteur of the Commission on Human Rights on the independence of judges and lawyers, Mr Cumaraswamy, for a critical interview he gave, the ICJ clarified who could make the determination whether the words spoken or written and acts done by experts on mission were really in the course of the performance of their mission, in which case they would be entitled to immunity pursuant to Section 22(b). In its advisory opinion (which was in fact binding on the parties pursuant to Section 30 of the General Convention),[108] the ICJ averred that it is up to the UN Secretary General as the chief administrative officer of the Organization, 'to assess whether its agents acted within the scope of their functions and, where he so concludes, to protect these agents, including experts on mission, by asserting their immunity', which means that he

> has the authority and responsibility to inform the Government of a Member State of his finding and, where appropriate, to request it to act accordingly and, in particular, to request it to bring his finding to the knowledge of the local courts if acts of an agent have given or may give rise to court proceedings.[109]

According to the Court, while such a determination is not, as such, binding on the Member State, it nevertheless 'creates a presumption which can only be set aside for the most compelling reasons and is thus to be given the greatest weight by national courts'.[110]

B. Immunities of the EU

The regime of the UN General Convention is largely replicated for other international organisations, such as the Council of Europe and the EU. The General Agreement on Privileges and Immunities of the Council of Europe (1949), for instance, provides that State representatives and officials of the Council of Europe enjoy immunity from legal process in respect of words spoken or written and acts done by them in their official capacity and, as far as the Council's officials are concerned, within the limit of their authority.[111] Also, the

[107] *Applicability of Article VI, Section 22, of the Convention on the Privileges and Immunities of the United Nations* (Advisory Opinion) [1989] ICJ Rep 177.

[108] Section 30 UN Convention (n 7) provides that '[a]ll differences arising out of the interpretation or application of the present convention shall be referred to the International Court of Justice, unless in any case it is agreed by the parties to have recourse to another mode of settlement' and that '[t]he opinion given by the Court shall be accepted as decisive by the parties'.

[109] *Difference Relating to Immunity from Legal Process of a Special Rapporteur of the Commission on Human Rights* (Advisory Opinion) [1999] ICJ Rep 62, para 60.

[110] ibid, para 61.

[111] General Agreement on Privileges and Immunities of the Council of Europe (adopted 2 September 1949, entered into force 10 September 1949) CETS No 2, Arts 9(a) and 18(a).

Agreement provides that such immunity could be waived in any case where the immunity would impede the course of justice, and where it can be waived without prejudice to the purpose for which the immunity is accorded, ie to protect the interests of the Council of Europe.[112]

As far as the EU is concerned, the Protocol on Privileges and Immunities of the European Union[113] provides that members of the European Parliament can only claim inviolability and immunity in respect of opinions expressed or votes cast by them in the performance of their duties,[114] while excluding immunity when a member 'is found in the act of committing an offence'.[115] Along the same lines, officials and other servants of the EU, in the territory of each Member State, only enjoy immunity from legal proceedings in respect of acts performed by them in their official capacity,[116] and each institution of the Union is required to waive the immunity accorded to an official or other servant wherever that institution considers that the waiver of such immunity is not contrary to the interests of the Union.[117] To (members of) missions of third States accredited to the Union, the customary diplomatic privileges and immunities are awarded.[118]

The EU considers itself, and its staff, immune from the jurisdiction of foreign courts, all the more so since the Lisbon Treaty explicitly recognised the EU's legal personality.[119] The Commission has observed that lawsuits have been brought against the EU, an EU institution, an EU delegation, or even named EU staff working in a delegation, in non-EU States (often in relation to claims of private parties concerning the execution of programmes of financial and technical assistance which the EU provides to non-EU countries), but that 'there is no indication that there is a single instance in which a non-EU court has denied the jurisdictional immunity of the European Union'.[120] The EU can often rely on express provisions regarding jurisdictional immunity laid down in agreements with the host State regarding the establishment of the EU delegation and in the relevant framework agreement concluded by the EU with the beneficiary non-EU State regarding the provision of financial and technical assistance. EU missions deployed in third countries are typically covered by Status of Forces or Status of Mission Agreements. But even in the absence of such agreements, the EU and its staff enjoy functional immunity, that is the immunity that is necessary for the EU and its staff to fulfil the tasks that are entrusted to it by the Member States.[121]

It is not fully clear whether diplomatic representatives of the EU enjoy the same privileges and immunities as State diplomats under the Vienna Convention on Diplomatic Relations. As far as the EU is concerned, it appears that it uses its bilateral bargaining power to ensure that third States do indeed grant EU diplomats such privileges and immunities. In practice, the EU invokes its immunity as follows:

> In cases where such jurisdictional immunity will need to be invoked in foreign local courts or administrative tribunals, the European Commission will via the EU delegation respond by way

[112] ibid, Arts 11 and 19.
[113] Protocol on Privileges and Immunities of the European Union [2004] OJ C310/261.
[114] ibid, Art 8.
[115] ibid, Art 9.
[116] ibid, Art 11a.
[117] ibid, Art 17.
[118] ibid, Art 16.
[119] Art 47 TEU. See EC, 'A Contribution on its Practice Regarding Lawsuits in Third Countries', March 2010, coe.int/t/dlapil/cahdi/Source/state_immunities/EU%20Immunities.pdf.
[120] EC, 'A Contribution on its Practice Regarding Lawsuits in Third Countries' (n 119).
[121] ibid.

of Note Verbale, informing the Ministry of Foreign Affairs of the non-EU country concerned that it invokes immunity from jurisdiction. In such a Note Verbale the delegation will also usually ask the Department of Foreign Affairs to take the appropriate steps to confirm with local courts that immunity is invoked. Where considered necessary or useful local counsel will be appointed to follow the proceedings and/or for to invoke jurisdictional immunity on behalf of the EU and/ or its staff.[122]

i. Immunities in Status of Forces Agreements

In the context of multinational military operations with the consent of the host State, the international organisation commanding the troops and the host State ordinarily conclude international agreements which confer on the organisation's mission and members privileges and immunities from the jurisdiction of the host State. These 'Status of Forces Agreements' (SOFAs) are often based on model agreements. Examples include the UN Model SOFA for peacekeeping operations (1990),[123] the NATO SOFA (1951)[124] and the EU SOFA (2003).[125] In this section, the main aspects of the UN Model SOFA will be highlighted. Other SOFAs, such as the NATO and EU SOFAs, contain similar provisions. The EU SOFA is largely inspired by the NATO SOFA.

The UN Model SOFA provides for specific privileges for forces contributed to UN peacekeeping operations and provides for immunity from prosecution in the host State. Contributing forces are considered members of the UN peacekeeping mission via a 'Transfer of Authority' (TOA) agreement made between the UN and the troop-contributing States. The peacekeeping operation enjoys such privileges as the right to communication,[126] freedom of movement,[127] the importation of all goods free of duty which are for the use of the operation,[128] and the use of premises required for the operational and administrative activities of the operation.[129] Members of the peacekeeping operation are exempt from taxation,[130] have the right to import their personal effects free of duty,[131] and have the right to enter into, reside in, and depart from the territory of the host State.[132]

The military police of the peacekeeping operation have the power of arrest over the military members of the operation. UN personnel could also take into custody any other person on the premises of the operation, although such person must be delivered

[122] ibid.

[123] UNGA Res 45/594, 9 October 1990, UN Doc A/45/594, Annex: 'Draft Model Status-of-Forces Agreement between the United Nations and Host Countries'.

[124] Agreement between the Parties to the North Atlantic Treaty regarding the Status of their Forces (adopted 19 June 1951, entered into force 23 August 1953) 199 UNTS 67.

[125] Agreement between the Member States of the European Union concerning the status of military and civilian staff seconded to the institutions of the European Union, of the headquarters and forces which may be made available to the European Union in the context of the preparation and execution of the tasks referred to in Art 17(2) of the Treaty on European Union, including exercises, and of the military and civilian staff of the Member States put at the disposal of the European Union to act in this context (EU SOFA) [2003] OJ C321/6. For a discussion, see A Sari, 'The European Union Status of Forces Agreement (EU SOFA)' (2008) 13 *Journal of Conflict and Security Law* 353; A Sari, 'Status of Forces and Status of Mission Agreements under the ESDP: The EU's Evolving Practice' (2008) 19 *EJIL* 67.

[126] UN Model SOFA (n 123) paras 10–11.

[127] ibid, paras 12–14.

[128] ibid, para 15.

[129] ibid, paras 16–19.

[130] ibid, paras 20–21.

[131] ibid, para 30.

[132] ibid, paras 32–34.

immediately to the host State authorities.[133] Host State authorities can only take into custody a member of the peacekeeping operation when so requested by the operation's commander or Special Representative, or when apprehended in the (attempted) commission of a criminal offence, although in the latter situation this person has to be delivered immediately to a representative of the peacekeeping operation.[134] The host State is under an obligation to prosecute persons accused of acts in relation to the operation or its members.[135] These provisions suffer from some deficits both with regard to what constitutes a criminal offence which would require detention and the limitations on the exercise of powers of detention. UN peacekeepers have the right to use force in self-defence and in carrying out their UN mandate which will often be included in the Rules of Engagement (ROE) and would normally contravene national law, but rules on use of force are not dealt with expressly in the SOFA. Also, applicable bodies of international law, such as international humanitarian law[136] or international human rights law,[137] are not expressly referenced in the SOFA. Neither is there any express mention of the role of the ICC in carrying out prosecutions.

Importantly, all members of the peacekeeping mission enjoy *immunity from legal process* in respect of words spoken or written and all acts performed by them in an official capacity, even after they cease to be members.[138] This is in fact the immunity *ratione materiae* which any State official enjoys abroad. In addition, members of the military component of the mission enjoy absolute immunity from the host State's criminal jurisdiction; they are subject to the exclusive jurisdiction of their troop-contributing State.[139] Civilian members of the mission, in contrast, may under some circumstances be prosecuted by local authorities.[140] Local authorities also have jurisdiction in civil proceedings against members of the operation insofar as they are unrelated to their official duties and subject to certification by the commander or Special Representative.[141]

To prevent immunity from becoming impunity, the UN Model SOFA provides that the UN Secretary General will obtain assurances from governments of participating States that they will be prepared to exercise jurisdiction with respect to crimes or offences which may be committed by members of their national contingents.[142] However, under the SOFA these States do not have a concrete legal duty to exercise their jurisdiction, so that impunity may well ensue in any case.

International reports and media disclosure of offences committed by peacekeepers – notably the revelations in 2004 of sexual exploitation and abuse by a significant number of UN peacekeeping personnel in the DRC under peacekeeping mission MONUC – may keep up the pressure on troop-contributing States to tackle such impunity.[143] There is no

[133] ibid, para 41.
[134] ibid, para 42.
[135] ibid, para 45.
[136] See Chapter 15.
[137] See Chapter 16.
[138] UN Model SOFA (n 123) para 46.
[139] ibid, para 47(b).
[140] ibid, para 47(a).
[141] ibid, para 49.
[142] ibid, para 48.
[143] EF Defeis, 'UN Peacekeepers and Sexual Abuse and Exploitation: An End to Impunity' (2008) 7 *Washington University Global Law Review* 185. France, for instance, ordered a criminal investigation into allegations that French peacekeeping soldiers raped children and demanded sex for food in the Central African Republic following revelations in *The Guardian* that a senior UN official had been suspended for leaking details

reliable data, however, on the number of completed prosecutions brought by States contributing troops to UN peacekeeping missions.[144] Since 2006, the UN General Assembly Sixth Committee has been carrying out work to eliminate potential jurisdictional gaps and enhance international cooperation among States to ensure the criminal accountability of UN officials and experts on mission.[145]

C. Immunities of International Organisations and Human Rights

In practice, the functional immunity enjoyed by international organisations on the basis of various agreements amounts to a quasi-absolute immunity, as organisations do not normally act outside the powers conferred upon them. This may obviously be to the detriment of the legitimate interests of claimants who have a grievance against the organisation. Within the context of the Council of Europe, claimants – often in employment disputes – have framed these interests as rights of access to a court under Article 6 ECHR. They have argued that domestic courts, when upholding an organisation's functional immunity, may unjustifiably give precedence to the treaty obligation providing for immunity over the State's ECHR obligations to offer an effective remedy.[146] In the cases of *Waite and Kennedy* and *Beer and Regan v Germany* (1999), the ECtHR solved this dilemma by accepting domestic courts' recognition of an organisation's immunity insofar as the organisation offered to the claimant reasonably available alternative mechanisms of dispute settlement:

> The Court is of the opinion that where States establish international organisations in order to pursue or strengthen their cooperation in certain fields of activities, and where they attribute to these organisations certain competences and accord them immunities, there may be implications as to the protection of fundamental rights. It would be incompatible with the purpose and object of the Convention, however, if the Contracting States were thereby absolved from their responsibility under the Convention in relation to the field of activity covered by such attribution. It should be recalled that the Convention is intended to guarantee not theoretical or illusory rights, but rights that are practical and effective. This is particularly true for the right of access to the

of the alleged abuse to the French government: 'France launches criminal inquiry into alleged sex abuse by peacekeepers', *The Guardian*, 7 May 2015, theguardian.com/world/2015/may/07/france-criminal-inquiry-alleged-sex-abuse-french-soldiers-un-central-african-republic.

[144] The UN Department of Field Support's Conduct and Discipline Unit publishes only generalised statistics. See C Ferstman, 'Criminalizing Sexual Exploitation and Abuse by Peacekeepers', US Institute of Peace, Special Report 335, September 2013, usip.org/sites/default/files/SR335-Criminalizing%20Sexual%20Exploitation%20and%20Abuse%20by%20Peacekeepers.pdf, 4.

[145] In 2005, the UNGA adopted the recommendations of the report of the Adviser to the Secretary General, 'A comprehensive strategy to eliminate future sexual exploitation and abuse in United Nations peacekeeping operations' (Zeid Report), as annexed to UNGA Res 59/710, 24 March 2005, UN Doc A/RES/59/170, which pertained to standards of conduct, the investigative process, organisational, managerial and command responsibility, and individual disciplinary, financial and criminal accountability (UNGA Res 59/300, 30 June 2005, UN Doc A/RES/59/300). In 2006, the UNGA established an Ad Hoc Committee for the purpose of considering the 'Report of the Group of Legal Experts on ensuring the accountability of United Nations staff and experts on mission with respect to criminal acts committed in peacekeeping operations', as contained in UNGA Res 60/980, 16 August 2006, UN Doc A/RES/60/980. The Ad Hoc Committee was established by UNGA Res 61/29, 18 December 2006, UN Doc A/RES/61/29. After 2008, the work of the Committee has continued in the framework of a working group of the Sixth Committee; see UN, Office of Legal Affairs, Codification Division, 'Ad Hoc Committee on the criminal accountability of United Nations officials and experts on mission', legal.un.org/committees/criminal_accountability.

[146] See eg C Ryngaert, 'The Immunity of International Organizations Before Domestic Courts: Recent Trends' (2010) 7 *International Organizations Law Review* 121.

> courts in view of the prominent place held in a democratic society by the right to a fair trial [...]. For the Court, a material factor in determining whether granting ESA immunity from German jurisdiction is permissible under the Convention is whether the applicants had available to them reasonable alternative means to protect effectively their rights under the Convention.[147]

Most cases decided on the basis of *Waite and Kennedy* relate to individual employment disputes, although collective employment and commercial contract cases have been reported as well.[148] In practice, most courts tend to apply the *Waite and Kennedy* test with a rather light touch and defer to the international organisation.[149] However, there are examples of domestic courts in Europe rejecting an organisation's immunity on the ground that a dispute-settlement mechanism, which the organisation made available to a claimant, did not offer adequate procedural safeguards in light of Article 6 ECHR[150] or simply on the ground that the organisation violated the fundamental rights of the claimants.[151]

Where a domestic court refuses to grant immunity on the ground of incompatibility with Article 6 ECHR and renders a judgment on the merits against the organisation, it is hardly certain that such a judgment will also be enforced. After all, the organisation, or the executive of the host State for that matter, may still avail itself of the organisation's treaty-based immunity from execution to block enforcement. Thus, after a Dutch court rejected the European Patent Organisation's immunity from jurisdiction on human rights grounds,[152] the Dutch Minister of Justice enjoined law-enforcement authorities not to enforce the judgment on the ground that the organisation enjoys immunity from execution on the basis of a relevant treaty.[153] The ECtHR has not yet ruled on the compatibility of the organisation's treaty-based immunity from execution with Article 6 ECHR, although at least one domestic court in Europe has applied the above-mentioned *Waite and Kennedy* principle to execution procedures.[154]

The *Waite and Kennedy* principle does not seem to extend to claims brought against the UN, at least not with respect to acts or omissions in the fulfilment of its collective security mandate. In a tort case brought against the UN with respect to peace operations in the former Yugoslavia (the *Mothers of Srebrenica* case), the Dutch Supreme Court decided that the *Waite and Kennedy* criteria did not apply to the immunity of the UN, given the UN's special place in international law.[155] According to the Court, the immunity of the UN was absolute, at least in the context of the maintenance of international peace and security.

[147] *Beer and Regan v Germany* App no 28934/95 (ECtHR,18 February 1999) paras 58–59; *Waite and Kennedy v Germany* App no 26083/94 (ECtHR, 18 February 1999) paras 67–68.

[148] Court of Appeal The Hague (NL), *VEOB and SUEPO v European Patent Organisation*, 17 February 2015, ECLI:NL:GHDHA:2015:255 (collective employment conditions); Court of Appeal Brussels (BE), *SA Energies Nouvelles et Environnement v Agence Spatiale Européenne*, 23 March 2011, Case No 2011/2013 (commercial contract).

[149] See eg High Court of Justice, Queen's Bench Division, Commercial Court (UK), *Entico Corporation Ltd v UNESCO* [2008] EWHC 531 (Comm).

[150] See eg the progressive case law of the Belgian Court of Cassation: *Western European Union v Siedler M*, 21 December 2009, Case No S.04.0129.F; *General Secretariat of the ACP Group v Lutchmaya M*, 21 December 2009, Case No C.03.0328.F; *General Secretariat of the ACP Group v BD*, 21 December 2009, Case No C.07.0407.F.

[151] *European Patent Organisation* (n 148).

[152] ibid.

[153] The Netherlands, Ministerie van Veiligheid en Justitie, Directoraat-Generaal Rechtspleging en Rechtshandhaving, Directie Juridische en Operationele Aangelegenheden, 'Aanzegging ex artikel 3a, tweede lid, van de Gerechtsdeurwaarderswet', 23 February 2015.

[154] Court of Cassation (BE), *Lutchmaya v General Secretariat of the ACP*, 4 March 2003, Case No C07.0407F.

[155] Supreme Court (NL), *Stichting Mothers of Srebrenica and others v the Netherlands and the United Nations* (n 54) paras 4.3.3–4.3.4.

Moreover, States would be under an obligation, pursuant to Article 103 of the UN Charter, to give priority to their UN obligations over obligations flowing from any other international agreements (such as the ECHR).[156] This approach has been upheld by the ECtHR, which ruled in 2013 that it does not follow from *Waite and Kennedy* that in 'the absence of an alternative remedy the recognition of immunity is ipso facto constitutive of a violation of the right of access to a court'.[157] The Court considered that such a rule may perhaps be applicable to employment disputes, but that the *Srebrenica* case was 'fundamentally different from [these] earlier cases'[158] given the 'special nature' of the UN as a collective security organisation:

> The Court finds that since operations established by United Nations Security Council Resolutions under Chapter VII of the United Nations Charter are fundamental to the mission of the United Nations to secure international peace and security, the Convention cannot be interpreted in a manner which would subject the acts and omissions of the Security Council to domestic jurisdiction without the accord of the United Nations.[159]

This argument may open up an accountability gap for victims of UN action: while Section 29 of the General Convention on the Privileges and Immunities of the United Nations provides that the UN shall make provisions for appropriate modes of settlement of disputes arising out of contracts or other disputes of a private law character to which the UN is a party, such modes have never been established. In practice, the UN settles disputes arising out of peacekeeping operations administratively, via *ex gratia* payments or lump sum agreements with host States, without offering judicial guarantees.[160] Courts, however, have ruled that the UN's failure to give effect to Section 29 has no bearing on its immunity. In its 1969 decision in *Manderlier*, the Court of Appeal of Brussels held that

> the immunity from every form of legal process granted to the United Nations under the Convention on the Privileges and Immunities of the United Nations is unconditional and is not limited by article VIII, Section 29 of the Convention in question, or by article 10 of the Universal Declaration on Human Rights, or by Art 105 of the United Nations Charter'.[161]

Similarly, US courts have held that 'construing the UN's failure to provide "appropriate modes of settlement" for Plaintiffs' claims as subjecting the UN to Plaintiffs' suit would read

[156] ibid, paras 4.3.5–4.3.6.

[157] *Stichting Mothers of Srebrenica and others v the Netherlands* App no 65542/12 (ECtHR, 27 June 2013) para 164. The Court drew attention to *Waite and Kennedy*'s enunciation that the absence of an alternative dispute-settlement mechanism was only a '"material factor" in determining whether granting an international organization immunity from domestic jurisdiction was permissible' (ibid, para 163).

[158] ibid, para 165 *juncto* para 149.

[159] ibid, para 154, citing its decision in *Behrami*, in which it refused to hold UN Member States responsible for violations committed in the context of UN peace operations: *Behrami and Behrami v France and Saramati v France, Germany and Norway* App nos 71412/01 and 78166/01 (ECtHR, 2 May 2007).

[160] See K Schmalenbach, 'Third Party Liability of International Organizations: A Study on Claim Settlement in the Course of Military Operations and International Administrations' (2006) 10 *International Peacekeeping* 33. Note that for the UN Interim Administration Mission in Kosovo (UNMIK), which was a territorial administration rather than a peacekeeping operation, a Human Rights Advisory Panel had jurisdiction over complaints relating to alleged violations of human rights attributable to UNMIK; UNMIK Regulation No 2006/12, 23 March 2006, UN Doc UNMIK/REG/2006/12. See eg the lead poisoning case: Human Rights Advisory Panel, *NM and others v UNMIK*, Case No 26/08, Opinion of 26 February 2016. The Panel's opinions may recommend the paying of compensation, but UNMIK may not act on them; see eg K Boon, 'New Decision Finds UN Responsible in Kosovo Lead Poisoning Case', *Opinio Juris*, 14 April 2016, opiniojuris.org/2016/04/14/32510.

[161] Court of Appeal Brussels (BE), *Manderlier v United Nations and Belgian State*, 15 September 1969, as summarised in (1969) *United Nations Juridical Yearbook* 236.

the strict express waiver requirement out of the [UN Convention]'.[162] This occurred most recently in a case brought against the UN in relation to the outbreak of a cholera epidemic in Haiti allegedly caused by untreated sewage from a UN peacekeeping compound.[163] In spite of the immunity obstacles, there is a silver lining for the plaintiffs in that the very initiation of proceedings against the UN before domestic courts, even if these are not successful, may raise awareness and put political pressure on the UN to change its ways.

V. Concluding Remarks

In order to properly carry out their international activities, States, international organisations and their officials have been granted functional immunities. These immunities have been justified on the grounds that they protect States from policy interference by foreign States and safeguard the autonomy of international organisations from their Member States.

In a time when international actors are expected to account for their acts, especially those that affect individuals, the importance of immunities may be waning. This explains why exceptions to immunities have gradually been carved out. States no longer enjoy immunity from jurisdiction in disputes over non-sovereign matters, nor do they enjoy immunity from enforcement with respect to property that is used for commercial purposes. State officials may no longer enjoy immunity *ratione materiae* in criminal proceedings with respect to international crimes. International organisations may only invoke their immunity in cases where they have reasonably available alternative mechanisms for dispute resolution at their disposal.

In recent years, however, this accountability-inspired evolution appears to have ground to a halt. No exception to the quasi-absolute immunity *ratione personae* of high-ranking State officials, including diplomats, has been accepted. State immunity has been upheld even in the case of international crimes. And with respect to the immunity of international organisations, courts have not applied the 'alternative means' test very strictly, and have sometimes abandoned it altogether.

Ultimately, the law on immunities is a legal grey area that is in a constant state of flux.[164] Its pendulum swings back and forth between the protection of State sovereignty or the autonomy of the international organisation on the one hand, and aggrieved third parties' right to a remedy on the other. The former imperative militates in favour of a broad grant of immunity; the latter in favour of a more restrictive one. Every equilibrium between these counteracting considerations is necessarily a precarious one. As the *Pinochet* case demonstrates, it can easily be upset by new dynamics in State and institutional practice that suggest novel interpretations of treaty and customary international law.

[162] District Court, Southern District of New York (US), *Delama Georges et al v United Nations*, 9 January 2015, 13-CV-7146 (JPO), 5, as confirmed by Court of Appeals for the Second Circuit (US), *Delama Georges et al v United Nations*, 18 August 2016, No 15-455-cv. See also already Court of Appeals for the Second Circuit (US), *Brzak v United Nations*, 2 March 2010, 597 F3d 107, 112.

[163] *Delama Georges et al v United Nations* (n 160).

[164] We borrow from *Jones v UK* (n 60) para 213.

An immunity is a procedural impediment to the exercise of jurisdiction, which bars (domestic) courts from addressing the merits of the claim against the holder of immunity, and thus from potentially finding this actor responsible for wrongful conduct in a court of law. For a court to grant immunity to an actor does not mean, however, that it considers this actor not to be responsible, be it under domestic or international law. Such responsibility may exist regardless of the availability of an immunity. The next chapter addresses the elements of international responsibility.

Bibliography

Dickinson, A, Lindsay, R and Loonam, JP, *State Immunity: Selected Materials and Commentary* (Oxford, OUP, 2004).

Fox, H and Webb, P, *The Law of State Immunity*, 3rd edn (Oxford, OUP, 2013).

Hafner, G, Kohen, M and Breau, S (eds), *State Practice regarding State Immunities: La pratique des Etats concernant les immunités des Etats, in English and French* (Strasbourg, Council of Europe, 2006).

Jenks, CW, *International Immunities* (London, Stevens, 1961).

O'Keefe, R and Tams, CJ (eds), *The UN Convention on Jurisdictional Immunities of States and Their Property: A Commentary* (Oxford, OUP, 2013).

Peters, A, Lagrange, E, Oeter, S and Tomuschat, C (eds), *Immunities in the Age of Global Constitutionalism* (Leiden, Brill Nijhoff, 2015).

Reinisch, A, *International Organizations before National Courts* (Cambridge, CUP, 2000).

Reinisch, A (ed), *The Privileges and Immunities of International Organizations in Domestic Courts* (Oxford, OUP, 2013).

Talmon, S, *Immunität von Staatsbediensteten* (Heidelberg, CF Müller, 2014).

van Alebeek, R, *The Immunities of States and Their Officials in International Criminal Law and International Human Rights Law* (Oxford, OUP, 2008).

Yang, X, *State Immunity in International Law* (Cambridge, CUP, 2012).

Further Reading

Akande, D and Shah, S, 'Immunities of State Officials, International Crimes, and Foreign Domestic Courts' (2010) 21 *EJIL* 815.

Dominicé, C, 'Quelques observations sur l'immunité de juridiction pénale de l'ancien chef d'Etat' (1999) *Revue générale de droit international public* 297.

Dupuy, P-M, 'Crimes et immunités' (1999) 103 *Revue générale de droit international public* 289.

Falk Lengelsen, R, *Aktuelle Probleme der Staatenimmunität im Verfahren vor den Zivil- und Verwaltungsgerichten* (Frankfurt am Main, Peter Lang, 2011).

Gaillard, E and Pingel-Lenuzza, I, 'International Organizations and Immunity from Jurisdiction: To Restrict or to Bypass' (2002) 51 *ICLQ* 1.

Lauterpacht, H, 'The Problem of Jurisdictional Immunities of Foreign States' (1951) 28 *BYIL* 220.

Reinisch, A, 'Recent Practice of European Courts with Regard to State Immunity from Enforcement Measures' (2006) 17 *EJIL* 4.
Ryngaert, C, 'The Immunity of International Organizations Before Domestic Courts: Recent Trends' (2010) 7 *International Organizations Law Review* 121.
Sanger, A, 'Immunity of State Officials from the Criminal Jurisdiction of a Foreign State' (2013) 62 *ICLQ* 193.
Sari, A, 'Status of Forces and Status of Mission Agreements under the ESDP: The EU's Evolving Practice' (2008) 19 *EJIL* 67.
Schmitt, P, *Access to Justice and International Organizations: The Case of Individual Victims of Human Rights Violations* (Cheltenham, Edward Elgar, 2017).
Wood, M, 'The Immunity of Official Visitors' (2012) 16 *Max Planck Yearbook of United Nations Law* 35.
Wood, M, 'Do International Organizations Enjoy Immunity under Customary International Law' (2014) 10 *International Organizations Law Review* 287.
Wuerth, I, 'Foreign Official Immunity: Invocation, Purpose and Exceptions' (2013) 23 *Swiss Review of International and European Law* 207.

12

International Responsibility

I. Introduction

It is a well-established principle of international law that whenever a State breaches an international obligation, it is liable to make reparation in an adequate form.[1] This concept of State responsibility[2] for breaches of international law is a fundamental pillar of the international legal order and flows from the sovereignty and equality of States. International responsibility is not limited exclusively to States, but also applies to international organisations that have been granted international legal personality by their founding Member States.[3] No equivalent general international responsibility exists, however, on the part of private persons and companies.

The law of international responsibility encompasses the secondary rules determining inter alia when States and international organisations incur responsibility under international law, what consequences flow from this, and who can invoke such responsibility. They have been shaped and clarified primarily through the case law of arbitral tribunals, the PCIJ and the ICJ. In the 1950s, the International Law Commission embarked on an ambitious project to codify the customary rules concerned. It took several decades and the cumulative efforts of multiple special rapporteurs (including Roberto Ago and, as final rapporteur, James Crawford), for the ILC to finally adopt its Draft Articles on State Responsibility in 2001 (ASR). Another ten years later, the ILC adopted a second text, containing a set of 'Draft Articles on the Responsibility of International Organizations' (ARIO). Although neither text constitutes a legally binding instrument – the UN General Assembly has welcomed the efforts of the ILC, but has so far not proceeded to convert either into a multilateral treaty – the authority of the two sets of Articles, and their respective Commentaries,

[1] *The Factory at Chorzów* (Germany v Poland) (Jurisdiction) [1927] PCIJ Series A, No 9, 21.

[2] Useful works on the law of State responsibility include J Crawford, *State Responsibility: The General Part* (Cambridge, CUP, 2013); J Crawford, A Pellet and S Olleson (eds), *The Law of International Responsibility* (Oxford, OUP, 2010); R Provost (ed), *State Responsibility in International Law* (Dartmouth, Ashgate, 2002); M Ragazzi (ed), *International Responsibility Today: Essays in Memory of Oscar Schachter* (Leiden, Brill, 2005).

[3] Useful works on the responsibility of international organisations include M Ragazzi, *Responsibility of International Organizations: Essays in Memory of Sir Ian Brownlie* (Leiden, Nijhoff, 2013); D Sarooshi, *Remedies and Responsibility for the Actions of International Organizations* (Leiden, Nijhoff, 2014).

can hardly be overestimated. Both instruments qualify in large part as a restatement of the pre-existing customary law on international responsibility. Even if the ILC's Articles are not entirely free from criticism and leave a number of questions unanswered,[4] they undeniably constitute the main point of departure to examine the law of international responsibility and have been relied upon by the ICJ,[5] as well as by other international and national[6] judicial bodies, including the CJEU[7] and the ECHR.[8] Importantly, whereas the Articles can be said to spell out the *general* law on international responsibility, this does not, however, exclude that there may be situations where the conditions for the existence of an internationally wrongful act or the content or implementation of the responsibility of a State or IO is governed by more specific (*lex specialis*) rules of international law.[9] The WTO system of remedies, for instance, constitutes a conspicuous example of *lex specialis*.[10]

The present chapter is, however, concerned first and foremost with the *lex generalis* of State responsibility. In particular, the present chapter first addresses the twin constituents of State responsibility: the requirement of an internationally wrongful act and the requirement of State imputability of the act concerned. Next, the chapter examines the consequences of international responsibility and the question who can invoke this responsibility. Special attention is reserved for the question of countermeasures. While the focus of the chapter rests with the international responsibility of *States*, the final section addresses some specific issues related to the responsibility of international organisations.

II. Internationally Wrongful Conduct

A. General Characteristics

Established case law confirms that State responsibility presupposes two cumulative elements, notably internationally wrongful conduct and State imputability. In relation to the hostage-taking at the US embassy in Tehran in 1979, for instance, the ICJ held as follows:

> First, [the Court] must determine how far, legally, the acts in question may be regarded as imputable to the Iranian State. Secondly, it must consider their compatibility or incompatibility with the obligations of Iran under treaties in force or under any other rules of international law that may be applicable.[11]

[4] See eg below, Section VI(B), on the permissibility of third-State countermeasures.

[5] See eg *Application of the Convention on the Prevention and Punishment of the Crime of Genocide* (Bosnia and Herzegovina v Serbia and Montenegro) [2007] ICJ Rep 43, paras 385, 398, 401, 407, 414, 420, 431 and 460.

[6] eg Supreme Court (NL), *Nuhanovic*, 6 September 2013, LJN BZ9225, para 3.10.1 (referring to Arts 6–7 ARIO).

[7] Judgment of 6 May 2010, *Walz v Clickair SA*, C-63/09, EU:2010:251, para 27 (referring to the definition of 'damage' in Art 31(2) ASR).

[8] eg *Jaloud v the Netherlands* App no 47708/08 (ECtHR, 20 November 2014) paras 98 and 151.

[9] Art 55 ASR; Art 64 ARIO. See also *Bosnian Genocide* (n 5) para 401 (finding that, absent *lex specialis*, the general rules apply for purposes of determining whether genocide is attributable to a State).

[10] See J Gomula, 'Responsibility and the World Trade Organization' in Crawford, Pellet and Olleson (n 2) 797 ff (thus, while WTO law is part of general public international law, the WTO system of remedies focuses on cessation instead of reparation; it does not rely on the traditional concept of 'injury', and has its own system of unilateral measures).

[11] *United States Diplomatic and Consular Staff in Tehran* (United States of America v Iran) [1980] ICJ Rep 3, para 56.

Internationally wrongful conduct presupposes a breach by a State of an international legal obligation incumbent upon it. The nature of the obligation concerned (whether, for instance, it is a treaty or a customary rule) is irrelevant.[12] At the same time, it is clear that the obligation must have been binding upon the State at the time of the contested act(s).[13] As explained by Max Huber in the *Island of Palmas* case: 'a juridical fact must be appreciated in light of the law contemporary with it, and not of the law in force at the time when the dispute in regard to it arises or fails to be settled'.[14] For instance, a State cannot retroactively be held accountable for involvement in the slave trade at a time when the prohibition of slavery was not yet part and parcel of customary international law or of treaty law binding upon it. Furthermore, breaches can be 'instantaneous' or 'continuing'. In the former case, the act and its consequences are fixed at a particular point in time.[15] By contrast, in the latter case, the wrongful act is characterised by a course of conduct which extends over a period of time. Thus, a breach of the prohibition of torture constitutes an example of an instantaneous breach, whereas unlawful occupation qualifies as a continuing breach.[16]

Internationally wrongful conduct may consist of one or more acts, as well as of a failure to act (an omission). This may be the case where a State is under an obligation to take action (eg, to prevent an event from occurring[17]), but fails to take proper action. Thus, in the *Corfu Channel* case, the ICJ held Albania responsible for the explosions damaging two British ships and resulting in several casualties on account of its failure to notify shipping of the existence of mines in her waters.[18] In the *Bosnian Genocide* case,[19] the ICJ found that, even if Serbia was not complicit in genocide, it had breached its *obligation to prevent* genocide in respect of the events in Srebrenica in 1995.

Wrongful conduct may consist of a single act or omission, yet it may also be of a 'composite' nature in that the wrongful character may result from the aggregate of a series of actions or omissions. A classic example of a composite breach concerns the prohibition of genocide. Indeed, in accordance with Article II(a) of the Genocide Convention, genocide presupposes an accumulation of acts of murder, causing serious bodily or mental harm, etc, committed with the intent to destroy, in whole or in part, a national, ethnical, racial or religious group. Yet, once the required threshold is exceeded, the wrongful character will extend over the entire period starting with the first acts of the series and will last for as long as these acts are repeated.[20]

In accordance with the theory of 'objective responsibility', international responsibility in principle flows from the act or omission itself, without there being need for some form of *culpa* or (malicious) intent on the part of the State. This approach finds support in

[12] *Gabčíkovo-Nagymaros Project* (Hungary v Slovakia) [1997] ICJ Rep 7, para 47.

[13] Art 13 ASR; Art 11 ARIO.

[14] *Island of Palmas* (Netherlands v United States), Award of 4 April 1928, 2 RIAA 829, 845.

[15] Art 14(1) ASR; Art 12 (1) ARIO; Crawford (n 2) 254. See further J Salmon, 'Duration of the Breach' in Crawford, Pellet and Olleson (n 2) 383–96.

[16] Art 14(2) ASR; Art 12(2) ARIO. Crawford (n 2) 259. The continuous character of the breach may have repercussions for the jurisdiction of international courts or tribunals to consider questions of responsibility. Thus, in *Loizidou*, the ECtHR confirmed that it had jurisdiction over allegations of a violation of the applicant's property rights which originated prior to Turkey's accession of the ECHR, but which continued thereafter. Conversely, the Court did not have jurisdiction over instantaneous breaches preceding Turkey's accession: *Loizidou v Turkey* App no 15318/89 (ECtHR, 23 February 1995) paras 99–105.

[17] On the temporal aspect of such scenario, see Art 14(3) ASR; Art 12(3) ARIO.

[18] *Corfu Channel* (United Kingdom of Great Britain and Northern Ireland v Albania) [1949] ICJ Rep 4, 22–23.

[19] *Bosnian Genocide* (n 5).

[20] Art 15(2) ASR; Art 13(2) ARIO. The provisions apply equally to acts and omissions.

State practice and in the jurisprudence of both arbitral tribunals[21] and the ICJ[22] – although there are exceptions which seemingly render support to the *culpa* doctrine[23] – and arguably constitutes the majority view in legal doctrine.[24] It follows that a plea before an international court or tribunal that acts resulted from a mistake, or were conducted in good faith, will generally fall on deaf ears. At the same time, it is worth recalling that international law consists of a diverse range of both 'obligations of result' as well as 'obligations of means'.[25] In the former case, the factual outcome itself determines whether internationally wrongful conduct exists. In the latter case, however, the intent or prior knowledge of the State may well be relevant factors. Thus, to revisit the example mentioned above, no genocide can take place without proof of a genocidal intent. In a similar vein, a State's authorisation of arms transfers to another State that uses these arms in the commission of crimes against humanity or war crimes, will only give rise to a breach of Article 6(3) of the Arms Trade Treaty if the former State had 'knowledge at the time of the authorisation that the arms or items would be used' in such manner. Furthermore, where international rules require a State to take action to prevent certain acts (eg, trans-boundary environmental harm) from occurring, considerations of good faith and 'due diligence' standards inevitably arise. This is not as a matter of 'secondary' law, but as part of the assessment of the scope of the primary rule at hand. Thus, while 'objective responsibility' is sometimes put forward as the default modus, the reality is more complex.

Exceptionally, the primary rules may (as a matter of *lex specialis*) provide that a State will be liable to repair the consequences of acts which do not as such amount to a breach of international law. Article 110 UNCLOS, for instance, holds that States may board vessels sailing the flag of a third State on the high seas when there is reasonable ground for suspecting piracy or certain other activities, but must in principle compensate for any loss or damage that may have been sustained at boarding if the suspicions subsequently prove unfounded. Such 'liability without fault' is often called for in relation to (lawful) activities that engender a high risk of trans-boundary harm, in particular environmental pollution.[26] In its 2006 'Draft Principles on the Allocation of Loss in the Case of Transboundary Harm Arising out of Hazardous Activities', the ILC proclaims that '[e]ach State should take all necessary measures to ensure that prompt and adequate compensation is available for victims of transboundary damage caused by hazardous activities located within its territory or otherwise under its jurisdiction or control', and make available additional financial resources if need be.[27] At the same time, the Commentary acknowledges that the Draft Principles leave unaffected the rules on State responsibility, and that the State itself is not legally obliged to pay compensation, and will only be internationally responsible if it actually breaches an obligation of prevention under international law.[28] In the end, examples of truly faultless

[21] eg *Caire* (France v Mexico), Award of 7 June 1929, 5 RIAA 516, 529.

[22] eg *Bosnian Genocide* (n 5) para 385.

[23] eg *Corfu Channel* (n 18) 18.

[24] See Crawford (n 2) 556–59.

[25] CP Economides, 'Content of the Obligation: Obligations of Means and Obligations of Result' in Crawford, Pellet and Olleson (n 2) 371–81.

[26] See in this context the famous *Trail Smelter* case between Canada and the United States: *Trail Smelter Case* (United States v Canada), Award of 11 March 1941, 3 RIAA 1905.

[27] ILC, 'Draft Principles on the Allocation of Loss in the Case of Transboundary Harm arising out of Hazardous Activities, with Commentaries' (2006) *YILC*, Vol II, Part Two, Principles 4(1) and 4(5). See further RM Bratspies and RA Miller (eds), *Transboundary Harm in International Law: Lessons from the 'Trail Smelter' Arbitration* (New York, CUP, 2006).

[28] ILC (n 27) 152. See also preamble, para 8.

liability (not contingent upon a State failing to act with proper diligence) remain rare. A conspicuous example is the absolute liability of States to pay compensation for damage caused by space objects.[29]

Finally, there is no general requirement of harm or damage for a State to incur international responsibility for internationally wrongful conduct. In certain situations, the mere occurrence of the wrongful conduct may suffice, and may prompt an international court or tribunal to adopt a declaratory relief, finding that a breach has occurred. In other situations, however, the need for some form of identifiable damage is intrinsic in the primary norm itself (eg, in case of a claim that a State has breached its duty to prevent transboundary environmental pollution).

B. Circumstances Precluding Wrongfulness

States can never invoke their municipal law as a justification for a refusal or failure to comply with their international obligations. This is so even if their national law would *oblige* them to act in a way that is contrary to their international obligations. This fundamental principle, expressed in Article 3 ASR and Article 27 Vienna Convention on the Law of Treaties (VCLT), reflects the autonomy of international law as a distinct system of law (see Chapter 4).

Articles 20–25 ASR nonetheless set forth a series of 'circumstances precluding wrongfulness' which States can invoke as 'excuses', 'defences' or 'exceptions' to exclude responsibility for conduct that would otherwise be wrongful under international law.[30] These are: consent (Article 20); self-defence (Article 21); countermeasures (discussed in Section VI below) (Article 22); *force majeure* (Article 23); distress (Article 24) and necessity (Article 25). The classification of these five circumstances is not entirely logical, especially inasmuch as some of the grounds, in particular consent and self-defence, may rather be construed as an aspect of the scope of the 'primary' rules, rather than as 'secondary' norms. Article 26 ASR confirms that no grounds precluding wrongfulness can justify a breach of *jus cogens*. It follows that distress or necessity cannot be invoked to justify recourse to torture as an interrogation method. Nor can self-defence, for instance, justify acts of genocide. Furthermore, a party invoking one of the listed grounds bears the burden of proof to demonstrate that the requirements are met.

First, consent by a State can preclude the wrongfulness of another State's conduct in relation to the former State. This presupposes: (i) that the consent is valid, that is, that it is given prior to the act concerned;[31] (ii) that it emanates from a person that has the authority to express the will of the State in the matter; and (iii) that it remains within the limits of that consent.[32] Consent can be invoked in a variety of scenarios, for example, to justify the boarding of a vessel flying the flag of a third-State on the high seas or the arrest of a suspect

[29] Art II Convention on International Liability for Damage Caused by Space Objects (adopted 29 March 1972, entered into force 1 September 1972) 961 UNTS 187.

[30] Note that the primary rules themselves may also allow for specific justifications for certain conduct. For example, Art 23(g) of the Hague Rules annexed to the Fourth Hague Convention prohibits the destruction or seizure of enemy property 'unless such destruction or seizure be imperatively demanded by the necessities of war' (Convention with Respect to the Laws and Customs of War by Land and its Annex: Regulations Respecting the Laws and Customs of War on Land (adopted 18 October 1907, entered into force 26 January 1910) 205 CTS 277)).

[31] Note that approbation expressed after the fact may nonetheless qualify as a waiver of claim.

[32] ILC ASR, 73.

in foreign territory, or to justify the entering by police personnel of a foreign embassy. Consent can also justify the presence of military troops on the territory of another State, for instance, pursuant to a troop-stationing agreement or a 'hot pursuit' agreement, or pursuant to ad hoc consent to establish a peacekeeping operation.[33]

Second, when the conduct of a State constitutes a lawful measure of self-defence taken in conformity with the UN Charter, the wrongfulness of that conduct is precluded vis-à-vis the State whose armed attack triggered the right of self-defence. It follows that self-defence may justify the non-performance of certain obligations other than the prohibition on the use of force, provided that such non-performance is related to the breach of that prohibition. Breaches of the law of armed conflict or non-derogable human rights provisions cannot, however, be justified on this basis.[34]

In certain circumstances, the commission by one State of an internationally wrongful act may justify another State injured by that act in taking non-forcible countermeasures as a means of 'self-help'. Recourse to countermeasures is, however, circumscribed by the conditions spelled out in Articles 49–54 ASR. The legality of countermeasures is further examined below.

This leaves three further circumstances precluding wrongfulness: *force majeure*, distress and necessity. Force majeure presupposes that the wrongful conduct is due to the occurrence of an irresistible force or of an unforeseen event beyond the control of the State, making it materially impossible in the circumstances to perform the obligation.[35] The key element, and which distinguishes *force majeure* from distress and necessity, is that the conduct of the State which would otherwise be internationally wrongful, is involuntary or at least involves no element of free choice. The irresistible force or unforeseen event may consist either of a natural or physical event, such as a flood or earthquake, or a human intervention, such as a military intervention by a third State. An example of *force majeure* would be a situation where a State aircraft is forced, due to loss of control of the aircraft owing to weather, into the airspace of another State without the latter's authorisation.[36] If compliance with one's obligations is not made 'materially impossible', but simply more difficult, *force majeure* cannot successfully be relied upon. Nor can it be invoked where a State has itself contributed to the situation giving rise to *force majeure*, or has assumed the risk of the situation occurring.

Distress operates to excuse conduct where the author of the act had no other way of 'saving the author's life or the lives of other persons entrusted to the author's care'.[37] Typical examples are situations involving aircraft or ships entering State territory to avoid bad weather.[38] Another illustration can be found in the 1990 *Rainbow Warrior* arbitration between New Zealand and France. In this case, the arbitral tribunal accepted that the evacuation of Major Mafart – whom France had agreed to transfer to the island of Hao for a period of three years in light of his involvement in the sinking of the *Rainbow Warrior* – was

[33] Note that, having regard to the *jus cogens* character of the prohibition on the use of force, the possibility to rely on consent to justify military intervention abroad is not unfettered. Clearly, consent expressed through a pre-existing bilateral treaty cannot be invoked to justify the invasion and occupation of another State. On the doctrine of 'intervention by invitation', see Chapter 14.

[34] ILC ASR, 74.

[35] Art 23 ASR.

[36] ILC ASR, 77.

[37] Art 24(1) ASR.

[38] Note that the distinction between distress and *force majeure* may not always be clear-cut in such settings.

justified in light of his medical condition.[39] Reliance on distress is excluded if the State has itself contributed to the situation giving rise to distress, or if the act in question is likely to create a comparable or greater peril.

The final ground precluding wrongfulness is necessity. This concept, which finds substantial support in nineteenth century practice, is rather controversial in light of the fact that it is quite vague and accordingly prone to abuse.[40] On balance, State practice and judicial decisions support the view that necessity may constitute a circumstance precluding wrongfulness under certain very limited conditions.[41] In particular, necessity may not be invoked unless the conduct at stake is 'the only way for the State to safeguard an essential interest against a grave and imminent peril', and it does not seriously impair an essential interest of the State or States towards which the underlying obligation exists, or the international community as a whole.[42] Additionally, necessity may not be invoked in respect of international obligations which themselves exclude this possibility, or if the State has contributed to the situation of necessity.[43] An interesting illustration of (the limited scope of) the concept of necessity can be found in the *Gabcikovo-Nagymaros* case. In this case, the ICJ was asked to consider whether there was a state of necessity which would have permitted Hungary to suspend and abandon works on a dam over the Danube River that it was committed to perform pursuant to a treaty concluded with Czechoslovakia. The Court recognised that the environmental concerns raised by Hungary could theoretically qualify as affecting an 'essential interest' of the State, but ultimately found that the peril was insufficiently grave and imminent, and that Hungary had itself contributed to the situation of necessity.[44] In general, States' occasional attempts to play the 'necessity' card have by and large not been successful.[45]

Two final observations are due. First, reliance on a ground precluding wrongfulness is permitted only for as long as the circumstance exists. Thus, if the original conduct giving rise to recourse to countermeasures ceases, the latter must be withdrawn.[46] By way of illustration, in the *Rainbow Warrior* arbitration discussed above, the arbitral tribunal agreed that the evacuation for medical reasons of Major Mafart was justified due to distress, but found that France should have returned Mafart to the island of Hao after his medical condition had improved.[47] Second, a State (successfully) relying on a ground precluding wrongfulness

[39] *Case concerning the difference between New Zealand and France concerning the interpretation or application of two agreements, concluded on 9 July 1986 between the two States and which related to the problems arising from the Rainbow Warrior Affair*, Award of 30 April 1990, 20 RIAA 215, paras 80–88.

[40] This is illustrated by the fact that some authors (unconvincingly) construe necessity as a possible justification for certain military interventions. See eg J Raby, 'The State of Necessity and the Use of Force to Protect Nationals' (1988) 26 *Canadian Yearbook of International Law* 253; A Laursen, 'The Use of Force and (the State of) Necessity' (2004) 37 *Vanderbilt Journal of Transnational Law* 485. For a powerful rebuttal, see O Corten, 'L'état de nécessité peut-il justifier un recours à la force non constitutif d'agression?' (2004) 1 *Global Community* 11.

[41] ILC ASR, 83.

[42] Art 25(1) ASR.

[43] ibid.

[44] *Gabčíkovo-Nagymaros* (n 12) paras 49–58.

[45] In recent years, for instance, Argentina has sought to rely on a state of necessity as justifying the measures it adopted to deal with its financial crisis in 1999–2002 and which resulted in a large number of claims under bilateral investment treaties. These pleas have generally been dismissed. See J Crawford and S Olleson, 'The Character and Forms of International Responsibility' in MD Evans (ed), *International Law*, 4th edn (Oxford, OUP, 2014) 466 (with references). For an illustration in national case law, see Constitutional Court (DE), *K and others v Argentina (represented by President Néstor Kirchner)*, 8 May 2007, 2 BvM 1-5/03, 1, 2/06, Vol 118, 124, in which Argentina's attempt to rely on necessity for its failure to fulfil contractual obligations in relation to private individuals was unsuccessful, as there was no State practice nor *opinio juris* to substantiate the extension of the concept beyond interstate relations.

[46] Art 27(1) ASR.

[47] *Rainbow Warrior* (n 39) para 88.

may under certain circumstances still be expected to make good any material loss suffered by the State affected by its conduct.[48] Thus, in the *Gabcikovo-Nagymaros* case, Hungary expressly acknowledged that, in any event, the alleged state of necessity 'would not exempt it from its duty to compensate its partner'.[49]

III. State Imputability

A. De Jure Organs and Other Persons and Entities Authorised to Exercise Elements of Governmental Authority

For a State to incur international responsibility there must not only be an internationally wrongful act, but that act must also be attributable to the State. This imputability or attributability requirement reflects the reality that States are legal abstractions that can only act through the conduct of individuals or groups of individuals.[50] The general point of departure is that States are only responsible for the conduct of their organs, provided the latter are acting in their capacity of State organs. By contrast, the conduct of private individuals cannot normally be imputed to the State, except in exceptional circumstances.

First, the conduct of a State organ shall be considered an act of that State under international law.[51] This rule is not limited to senior State officials, or even to individuals that are competent to enter into obligations on behalf of the State on the international plane, but equally covers other State officials. It extends first and foremost to members of the executive branch, obvious examples being military or police personnel. It is irrelevant whether a person is an organ of the central government or of a territorial unit of the State. States cannot hide behind the domestic distribution of functions to circumvent responsibility. Furthermore, a State can also incur responsibility for the activities of its legislature(s) and judicial organs.

The decisive criterion for characterising a person or entity as a State organ is their formal status under the State's domestic law[52] (hence the label of 'de jure organs'). At the same time, States cannot avoid responsibility for particular conduct by delegating governmental functions to private entities, such as by employing private firms to guard prison facilities or to perform immigration duties at a national airport. Pursuant to Article 5 ASR, conduct of persons or entities empowered to exercise elements of governmental authority will effectively be considered an act of the State provided the person or entity is acting in that capacity in a particular instance.[53] Furthermore, a State will be responsible for the conduct of organs placed at the disposal of a State by another State 'if the organ is acting

[48] Art 27(2) ASR; Crawford (n 2) 318–320.

[49] *Gabčíkovo-Nagymaros* (n 12) para 48. The ASR does not lay down specific rules. The Commentary simply observes that '[i]t will be for the State invoking a circumstance precluding wrongfulness to agree with any affected States on the possibility and extent of compensation payable in a given case' (ILC ASR, 86).

[50] Note, the same acts may of course simultaneously give rise to State responsibility and international criminal responsibility of individuals. This will be the case, for example, where State armed forces involved in an international armed conflict commit war crimes. On international criminal responsibility, see Chapter 17.

[51] Art 4 ASR.

[52] Art 4(2) ASR.

[53] Note that corporate entities with ties to the government (eg shareholdings) are not automatically considered agents of the State pursuant to Art 5 ASR. See Crawford (n 2) 128–29.

in the exercise of elements of the governmental authority of the State at whose disposal it is placed'.[54] Such a scenario may arise, for instance, where military troops are placed at the disposal of another State.

In each of the cases mentioned above, the acts of the individuals or entities concerned will be attributable to the State, even if they have been acting ultra vires or in contravention of instructions.[55] For instance, in the *Caire* case, Mexico was held responsible for the conduct of members of its armed forces who had shot a French national after the latter refused to pay a bribe.[56] In the *Youmans* case, Mexico was found liable for the killing of a number of US citizens by Mexican soldiers opening fire on a house contrary to orders.[57] This is not to say, of course, that conduct of military or police personnel acting in a purely private capacity gives rise to State responsibility. Rather, for ultra vires acts to be imputable to the State, the persons concerned 'must have acted at least to all appearances as competent officials or organs, or they must have used powers or methods appropriate to their official capacity'.[58]

B. Conduct of Private Persons

Whereas the imputability to the State of the conduct of organs and other persons and entities authorised to exercise elements of governmental authority is construed broadly, the conduct of private persons will not normally be imputed to the State. Thus, in the *Tehran* case, the ICJ found that the *initial* attack by militants on the US embassy in Tehran on 4 November 1979 was not in itself imputable to Iran.[59] Exceptional circumstances may nonetheless warrant attributing the conduct of private individuals to the State.

Apart from the aforementioned situation spelled out in Article 5 ASR, a first exception concerns the scenario where persons, groups or entities act 'in complete dependence' on the State. This situation is not expressly envisaged in the ASR, but was entertained by the ICJ in the *Nicaragua* and *Bosnian Genocide* cases. In *Nicaragua*, the ICJ examined whether the right-wing *contras*, battling the Sandinista government in Nicaragua, could be regarded as being completely dependent on the United States, so as to make the acts committed by them imputable to the United States.[60] In *Bosnian Genocide*, the Court similarly examined whether the (non-State) Bosnian Serb Army, which carried out the genocide at Srebrenica, was 'completely dependent' on Serbia.[61] The two cases affirm that, once the 'complete dependency' threshold is achieved, the individuals or groups concerned are effectively regarded as 'de facto organs' of the State, whose conduct can be imputed to the State without requiring further proof of instructions, etc, in respect of *specific* acts or operations. It is clear, however, that a very high threshold applies. In both cases, the Court found

[54] Art 6 ASR. The ILC Commentary does not attempt to identify precisely the scope of 'governmental authority' for the purpose of attribution of the conduct of an entity to the State, but recognises that what is regarded as 'governmental' depends in part on the particular society, its history and traditions: ILC ASR, 43.

[55] Art 7 ASR.

[56] *Caire* (n 21).

[57] *Thomas H Youmans (USA) v United Mexican States*, Award of 23 November 1926, 4 RIAA 110.

[58] *Caire* (n 21) 531.

[59] *Tehran* (n 11) paras 56–61.

[60] *Military and Paramilitary Activity in and against Nicaragua* (Nicaragua v United States of America) [1986] ICJ Rep 14, paras 109–12.

[61] *Bosnian Genocide* (n 5) paras 390–95. See further M Milanovic, 'State Responsibility for Genocide' (2006) 17 *EJIL* 553.

that, in spite of their close ties to the United States and Serbia respectively (eg, in the form of weapons supplies, strategic advice, financial support, etc), the *contras* and the Bosnian Serb Army could not be regarded as mere instruments of the States concerned, but instead enjoyed a certain margin of independence. In light of this, the Court ultimately concluded that neither of the armed groups could be regarded as 'completely dependent' on the State.

Even absent 'complete dependence', conduct will still be considered an act of a State under international law 'if the person or group of persons is in fact acting on the instructions of, or under the direction or control of, that State in carrying out the conduct'.[62] The idea that conduct pursuant to 'instructions' of a State is imputable to the latter is fairly straightforward. The concept of 'direction or control' is more complex. In the *Nicaragua* case, the ICJ asserted that 'United States participation, even if preponderant or decisive, in the financing, organising, training, supplying and equipping of the *contras*, the selection of its [...] targets and the planning of the whole of its operation' was still insufficient, for the purpose of attributing to the US the breaches of the law of armed conflict committed by the *contras*.[63] According to the Court, for this to be the case, it would have to be demonstrated that the US had 'effective control' of the operations in the course of which the alleged violations were committed.[64] In its 1999 Judgment in the *Tadić* case, however, the Appeals Chamber of the ICTY harshly criticised the high threshold imposed by the *Nicaragua* case.[65] According to the ICTY, the *Nicaragua* test was not consonant with the logic of the law of State responsibility in that it would seem to permit States to escape international responsibility by having private individuals carry out certain tasks. Nor was the test deemed compatible with prior judicial and State practice. Instead, the ICTY set forth an alternative 'overall control' threshold in respect of organised armed groups, which was said to be met when State involvement went 'beyond the mere financing and equipping of such forces and involving also participation in the planning and supervision of military operations'.[66] In *Bosnian Genocide*, however, the ICJ expressly reaffirmed the need for 'effective control'. According to the Court, 'overall control' might well be a proper test to determine the 'internationalisation' of a non-international armed conflict, but had no place in the law of international responsibility, as it disregarded the fundamental principle that 'a State is responsibly only for its own conduct, that is to say the conduct of persons acting, on whatever basis, on its behalf'.[67] The ILC Commentary similarly seems to stick to the 'effective control' test.[68]

There are several other exceptions to the rule that the conduct of private persons cannot be imputed to the State. Thus, conduct by private persons is imputed to the State 'if and to the extent that the State acknowledges and adopts the conduct in question as its own'.[69] Such a situation presented itself in the *Tehran* case. As mentioned above, the ICJ

[62] Art 8 ASR.
[63] *Nicaragua* (n 60) para 115.
[64] ibid (demanding evidence that the US 'directed or enforced the perpetration of the acts contrary to human rights and humanitarian law alleged by the applicant State').
[65] ICTY, Appeals Chamber, *Prosecutor v Tadić*, 15 July 1999, Case No IT-94-1-A, paras 99–145 (while accepting such threshold for the conduct of single individuals, it regarded it as ill-suited in relation to the conduct of organised non-State armed groups).
[66] ibid, para 145.
[67] *Bosnian Genocide* (n 5) para 406 (noting that the overall control test 'stretches too far, almost to breaking point, the connection which must exist between the conduct of a State's organs and its international responsibility').
[68] ILC ASR, 48. See also the reference to 'effective control' in Art 7 ARIO.
[69] Art 11 ASR.

held that the *initial* attack on, and occupation of, the US embassy in Tehran was not as such attributable to Iran. Yet, the Court found that, as time went on, the Iranian authorities began using the occupation of the embassy as leverage in diplomatic negotiations with the United States, asserting inter alia that the hostages would not be released until certain demands were met.[70] The Court found that the authorities' collusion with the militants fundamentally transformed the legal nature of the situation, turning the continued occupation of the embassy and the detention of the hostages into acts of the State.[71] At the same time, this basis for imputing private conduct to a State must be interpreted narrowly. 'Mere support or endorsement' of certain acts is insufficient.[72] By way of illustration, the mere fact that a State expresses sympathy, or even outright support, for the acts of a non-State armed group abroad obviously does not convert the latter's conduct into acts of the former State.

Another, somewhat mysterious, exception is found in Article 9 ASR. This provision deals with the exceptional case of conduct in the exercise of elements of the governmental authority by a person or group of persons acting in the absence of the official authorities and without any actual authority to do so.[73] Such cases may, for instance, occur during a revolution, armed conflict or foreign occupation. The provision sets forth three cumulative conditions: (i) the conduct must effectively relate to the exercise of elements of the governmental authority; (ii) it must have been carried out in the absence or default of the official authorities; and (iii) the circumstances must have been such as to call for the exercise of those elements of authority.[74] A rare example is found in the *Yeager* case of the Iran-US Claims Tribunal,[75] concerning the activities of the Revolutionary Guards or 'Komitehs' in the immediate aftermath of the Islamic revolution of 1979. The Tribunal held that the Guards' activities of performing immigration, customs and similar functions at Tehran airport, even if not actually authorised by the Government, should nonetheless be regarded as acts of the State under international law, as the Government had to be aware of these activities and did not object.[76]

The conduct of insurrectional movements is only imputable to the territorial State if either of the abovementioned hypotheses is applicable – which will not normally be the case if the insurgents are engaged in hostilities with the government. An insurgency or major upheaval creates a situation of (man-made) *force majeure* on the part of the territorial State, whereby the latter will only incur responsibility for negligent failure to suppress the insurgents.[77] The situation is different, however, if the insurrectional movement is successful and becomes the new government of the State. In such case, its acts will *ab initio* be regarded as acts of the State.[78]

[70] *Tehran* (n 11) paras 69–75.
[71] ibid, para 74.
[72] ILC ASR, 53.
[73] ibid, 49. According to the ILC Commentary, this rule owes something to the old idea of the *levée en masse*.
[74] ibid.
[75] Iran-United States Claims Tribunal, *Kenneth P Yeager v The Islamic Republic of Iran*, 2 November 1987, Partial Award No 324-10199, reprinted in 17 Iran-United States Claims Tribunal Reports 92, 101–102.
[76] ibid, para 43.
[77] Crawford (n 2) 552. As Crawford observes: 'In fact there is no modern example of a state being held responsible for negligent failure to suppress insurgents'. See also A McNair, *International Law Opinions, Vol II: Peace* (Cambridge, CUP, 1956) 245.
[78] Art 10 ASR. See eg Mixed Claims Commission Great Britain-Venezuela, *Bolivar Railway*, 9 RIAA 445, 453. Note, pursuant to Art 10(2) ASR the same is true, mutatis mutandis, where an insurrectional or other movement succeeds in establishing a new State.

C. Acts Which Are Not as Such Imputable to the State

Even if certain acts cannot be attributed to a State along the lines described above, this does not necessarily prevent the State from incurring State responsibility *in connection with* that act, notably when a related, but distinct, primary rule has been breached. Again, while the initial attack on the US embassy premises was not imputable to Iran, the latter State was nonetheless found to have breached its obligation under the Vienna Convention on Diplomatic Relations to take appropriate steps to protect foreign embassies on its soil.[79] In a similar vein, while Serbia was not itself responsible for the genocide at Srebrenica, the ICJ concluded that Serbia had nonetheless breached its obligation under the Genocide Convention to take proper steps *to prevent* genocide from taking place. In sum, even if acts by private individuals or groups cannot be equated to acts of the State, they may trigger the State's liability for failure to prevent those acts, or, for instance, for failure to prosecute or extradite a person suspected of an international crime. The plurality of primary rules should not be ignored.

Furthermore, leaving aside the situation where multiple States are jointly responsible for wrongful acts, Articles 16–18 ASR identify a number of scenarios where a State may incur responsibility in connection with the act of another State. The provisions refer to the situation where a State 'directs and controls' another State in the commission of an internationally wrongful act,[80] or 'coerces' another State into committing such act, in full knowledge of the circumstances thereof.[81] In addition, Article 16 ASR refers to the responsibility of a State for 'aid or assistance in the commission of an internationally wrongful act' by another State.[82] This last provision has a 'vast field of potential application'[83] and can theoretically be used to hold third States liable for complicity in wrongful conduct of others (eg, where a State furnishes logistical or other support to a State that is involved in widespread human rights violations and/or war crimes).[84] So far, however, practice remains scarce. In two recent cases, the ECtHR held Poland responsible for its involvement in the CIA's programme of secret detention and extraordinary renditions of suspected terrorists.[85] Both judgments effectively cite Article 16 ASR, but ultimately find Poland responsible for an (autonomous) breach of Article 3 ECHR.[86] In *Bosnian Genocide*, the ICJ confirmed the customary status of Article 16 ASR,[87] but found that the conditions were not fulfilled, since it was not established beyond doubt that Serbia, which furnished aid and assistance to the Bosnian Serb Army, was aware that genocide was about to take place.[88] Article 16(a) ASR indeed clarifies that ancillary responsibility only arises where the State providing aid or assistance did so 'with knowledge of the circumstances of the internationally wrongful act'.

[79] *Tehran* (n 11) paras 60–67.
[80] Art 17 ASR.
[81] ibid, Art 18.
[82] See further HP Aust, *Complicity and the Law of State Responsibility* (Cambridge, CUP, 2011); M Jackson, *Complicity in International Law* (Oxford, OUP, 2015).
[83] Aust (n 82) 239.
[84] See eg Federal Administrative Court (DE), *Attorney of the Federal Armed Forces v Anonymous (a Major of the Armed Forces)*, 21 June 2005, BverwG 2 WD 12.04 (German participation in attacks against Iraq March 2003).
[85] *Al Nashiri v Poland* App no 28761/11 (ECtHR, 24 July 2014); *Husayn (Abu Zubaydah) v Poland* App no 7511/13 (ECtHR, 24 July 2014).
[86] See para 5 of the dispositive of both judgments.
[87] *Bosnian Genocide* (n 5) para 420.
[88] ibid, para 422.

The potential scope of Article 16 ASR is moreover circumscribed by the ILC Commentary, which states that 'the aid or assistance must be given *with a view to facilitating* the commission of [the wrongful] act, and must actually do so'.[89] At the same time, there is no requirement that the aid or assistance should have been essential to the performance of the wrongful act; it is sufficient if it contributed significantly.[90]

IV. Consequences of State Responsibility

A. Cessation and Reparation

The general consequences of a finding that a State is responsible for a breach of international law are essentially twofold and encompass both a prospective and a retrospective component. First, to remedy the situation for the future, States are required to cease the internationally wrongful conduct (if it is continuing) and/or to offer appropriate assurances and guarantees of non-repetition, if circumstances so require.[91] Thus, in the *Whaling in the Antarctic* case (Australia v Japan), the ICJ, having found Japan's 'scientific' whaling program to be unlawful, ordered Japan to revoke any extant whaling permits and to refrain from granting any further permits.[92] In the *LaGrand* and *Avena* cases, the Court simply observed that the commitments expressed by the United States to ensure compliance with its obligations under Article 36 of the Vienna Convention on Consular Relations had to be regarded as 'meeting the request by [Mexico] for guarantees and assurances of non-repetition'.[93]

Second, the responsible State is under an obligation to make full reparation for the injury caused by the internationally wrongful act. Such reparation does not absolve the State from its continued duty to perform the obligation breached,[94] but operates separately therefrom. The injury for which the responsible State must make reparation includes 'any damage, whether material or moral, caused by the internationally wrongful act'.[95] As the text suggests, there must be a causal link between the wrongful conduct and the injury suffered.[96] In *Bosnian Genocide*, the ICJ found that even if Serbia had breached its obligation to take proper measures to prevent the genocide at Srebrenica, it was not liable to pay compensation for the material or moral damage caused by the genocide.[97] Having regard to the fact that the genocide was not as such imputable to Serbia (see above), the Court found the requisite causal nexus between the wrongful conduct and the injury suffered lacking. According to the Court, such nexus could only be established if the Court were able to

[89] ILC ASR, 66 (emphasis added). Further 'A State is not responsible for aid or assistance under Article 16 unless the relevant State organ intended, by the aid or assistance given, to facilitate the occurrence of the wrongful conduct'.

[90] ibid. See also at 67.

[91] Art 30 ASR.

[92] *Whaling in the Antarctic* (Australia v Japan: New Zealand intervening) [2014] ICJ Rep 226.

[93] *LaGrand* (Germany v United States of America) [2001] ICJ Rep 466, para 124; *Avena and Other Mexican Nationals* (Mexico v United States of America) [2004] ICJ Rep 12, para 150.

[94] Art 29 ASR.

[95] Art 31(2) ASR.

[96] ILC ASR, 92–93.

[97] *Bosnian Genocide* (n 5) paras 459–62.

conclude with a sufficient degree of certainty that the genocide at Srebrenica would not have taken place if Serbia had complied with its legal obligations – *quod non*. The challenges of causation are amply illustrated by the findings of the Eritrea-Ethiopia Claims Commission in relation to Eritrea's unlawful recourse to force against Ethiopia in 1998.[98] In its Final Award of 2009 on Ethiopia's Damages Claims, the Commission emphasised that '[a] breach of the *jus ad bellum* by a State does not create liability for all that comes after. Instead, there must be a sufficient causal connection'.[99] To establish this causal connection, the Commission relied on the concept of 'proximate cause', which was influenced inter alia by the extent to which certain consequences could reasonably be foreseen by the party breaching the prohibition on the use of force.[100] In cases involving a breach of obligations protecting collective/community interests (such as *Whaling in the Antarctic* case), however, (causally related) damage may be difficult to identify and define, and international courts and tribunals may limit themselves to a declaratory judgment, possibly combined with requiring guarantees of non-repetition.[101]

Articles 35–37 ASR spell out three possible forms of reparation, listed in order of preference, which may moreover be combined. The first is restitution (or *restitutio ad integrum*), which involves the re-establishment of the situation which existed before the wrongful act was committed. Obvious examples consist in the return of stolen cultural artefacts or the release of persons wrongly detained. An example of a form of 'juridical restitution',[102] can be found in the *Avena* case, where the ICJ ordered the United States to 'provide, by means of its own choosing, review and reconsideration of the convictions and sentences' of a number of Mexican nationals on death row who had been denied their right to consular assistance under Article 36 of the Vienna Convention on Consular Relations.[103] In many cases, however, restitution will simply be excluded because it is impossible to turn back the clock and undo the wrongful act, for instance, where a person has been tortured, genocide has been committed, or property has been destroyed. In addition, restitution is excluded, not only when it is materially impossible, but also when the resulting burden would be disproportionate to the benefit deriving therefrom.[104] In the end, while restitution is in a sense the most 'pure', and accordingly preferred, form of reparation,[105] it remains rather exceptional, and is limited mostly to situations in which it is expressly provided for.[106]

Insofar as damage is not (fully) covered by restitution, Article 36 ASR provides for compensation on a subsidiary basis. Compensation shall cover 'any financially assessable damage', including loss of profits 'insofar as established',[107] and can be increased

[98] See, Ethiopia-Eritrea Claims Commission, Partial Award *Jus ad Bellum*, Ethiopia Claims 1–8, 19 December 2005; Eritrea-Ethiopia Claims Commission, Guidance regarding *Jus ad Bellum* Liability, Decision Number 7, 27 July 2007; Eritrea Ethiopia Claims Commission, Final Award Ethiopia's Damages Claims, 17 August 2009, 26 RIAA 631.

[99] ibid, para 289.

[100] ibid. See further SD Murphy, W Kidane and TR Snider, *Litigating War: Arbitration of Civil Injury by the Eritrea-Ethiopia Claims Commission* (New York, OUP, 2013).

[101] See also below on the limitations posed by Art 48 ASR.

[102] Juridical restitution is a form of restitution involving the modification of a legal situation either within the legal system of the responsible State or in its legal relations with the injured State. See ILC ASR, 97.

[103] *Avena* (n 93).

[104] Art 35 ASR.

[105] See the essential aim of reparation is that it 'must, as far as possible, wipe out all the consequences of the illegal act and re-establish the situation which would, in all probability, have exited if that act had not been committed'; *The Factory at Chorzów* [1928] PCIJ Series A, No 17, 47.

[106] Crawford (n 2) 570.

[107] Art 36(2) ASR.

with interest.[108] Financially assessable damage encompasses damage suffered by the State itself, such as damage to its property or personnel, or in respect of expenditures incurred to remedy or mitigate damage flowing from an internationally wrongful act. It also covers damage suffered by nationals, whether persons or companies, on whose behalf the State is claiming within the framework of diplomatic protection.[109] As for the latter category, compensable injury encompasses not only material losses, including loss of earnings, medical expenses, etc, which can be fairly straightforward to identify and quantify. It also includes non-material or 'moral' damage, which, even if difficult to measure or estimate by monetary standards, is nonetheless deemed financially assessable. 'Moral' damage includes such items as individual pain and suffering (eg, pursuant to a person's arbitrary deprivation of liberty for a prolonged period of time), loss of loved ones, personal affront associated with an intrusion on one's home or private life, etc.[110] Compensation is arguably the most commonly sought form of reparation in international practice. Ample case law exists, for instance, awarding pecuniary compensation in investment arbitration.[111]

Insofar as injury cannot (or not entirely) be made good by restitution or compensation, Article 37 ASR provides for a third form of reparation, notably satisfaction. Satisfaction can be useful where a wrongful act causes non-material injury to a State, which is not 'financially assessable' in the sense of Article 36 ASR, but may rather be symbolic in nature. Examples include unlawful acts affecting the honour, dignity or prestige of a State, such as a result of a violation of a State's territorial integrity or violations of the premises of embassies. Satisfaction can take multiple forms, including, for instance, a formal (written or verbal) apology,[112] an acknowledgment of the breach, or an expression of regret. The modalities listed in Article 37(2) ASR are not exhaustive, but merely illustrative. Thus, satisfaction may equally consist of a pecuniary 'indemnity' for injury that is not financially assessable (and accordingly does not qualify for compensation properly speaking). It may also take other forms. In the initial 1986 *Rainbow Warrior* arbitration,[113] the UN Secretary General, apart from awarding US$7 million in compensation for damages, ordered France to apologise to New Zealand for the sinking of the Greenpeace vessel in the port of Auckland by French agents, and to transfer two French agents involved in the operation to the French military facility on the isolated island of Hao for a period of three years. Satisfaction may also take the form of a purely declaratory relief. Thus, in the *Corfu Channel* case, the ICJ '[gave] judgment that by reason of [the mine-sweeping operation] of the British Navy in Albanian waters [...], the United Kingdom violated the sovereignty of [Albania]', adding that 'this declaration by the Court constitutes in itself appropriate satisfaction'.[114]

[108] Art 38 ASR. The case law on the award of interest is, however, not very consistent (Crawford (n 24) 577). Pursuant to Art 38(2) ASR interest 'runs from the date when the principal sum should have been paid until the date the obligation to pay is fulfilled.'

[109] ILC ASR, 99–102.

[110] ibid 92.

[111] Further, see eg B Sabahi, *Compensation and Restitution in Investor-State Arbitration: Principles and Practice* (Oxford, OUP, 2011) 189 (affirming that reparation in international investment law mainly takes the form of compensation).

[112] eg *I'm Alone* (Canada v United States), Award of 30 June 1933 and 5 January 1935, 3 RIAA 1609. But see *LaGrand* (n 93) para 123 (where the Court found the willingness of the United States to present an apology to Germany to be insufficient in a case 'where foreign nationals have not been advised without delay of their rights [to consular assistance] and have been subject to prolonged detention or sentenced to severe penalties').

[113] Case concerning the Differences between New Zealand and France Arising from the Rainbow Warrior Affair, Ruling of 6 July 1986 by the Secretary General of the United Nations, 19 RIAA 199.

[114] *Corfu Chanel* (n 18) 35.

In accordance with Article 37(3) ASR, satisfaction shall not be out of proportion to the injury and may not take a form humiliating to the responsible State.

It will not always be easy to distinguish between cessation/non-repetition, on the one hand, and reparation, on the other hand.[115] In a similar vein, it may be hard to distinguish between compensation for moral damage and pecuniary satisfaction. In all, the outcome of inter-State litigation may vary considerably, depending on the international court or tribunal concerned, on the nature of the primary rules, on the precise demands of the applicant State, etc. Pursuant to Article 39 ASR, account shall be taken of the contribution to the injury by wilful or negligent action or omission of the injured State or any person or entity in relation to whom reparation is sought.[116] In its Final Award on Ethiopia's Damages Claims, the Eritrea-Ethiopia Claims Commission moreover recognised that the parties' 'economic capacity' had to be taken into account for purposes of determining compensation.[117]

Article 33 ASR asserts that the rules on cessation and reparation are 'without prejudice to any right, arising from the international responsibility of a State, which may accrue directly to any person or entity other than a State'. This provision thus refers, for instance, to the access to international investment arbitration of multinational undertakings under bilateral investment treaties, or to the access of affected individuals to regional human rights courts. Overall, the rules and principles developed by these tribunals and courts with regard to reparation can be seen as manifestations of the general principles laid down in the ASR.[118] At the same time, each of these organs has its own particularities, and occasionally *lex specialis* rules may apply. One such *lex specialis* rule identified in the ASR Commentary[119] concerns Article 41 ECHR, which provides for 'just satisfaction', rather than full reparation, 'if the national law of the High Contracting Party concerned allows only partial reparation to be made'.[120] Interestingly, in its judgment of 12 May 2014 in *Cyprus v Turkey*, the ECtHR for the first time applied the just satisfaction rule in the context of an inter-State case.[121] The Court stressed that the logic of Article 41 ECHR is 'directly derived from the principles of public international law relating to State liability, and has to be construed in this context'.[122] Bearing in mind the *lex specialis* nature of the provision, the Court found that it should not be interpreted in such a narrow way as to exclude inter-State applications from its scope.[123] At the same time, the judgment suggests that just satisfaction claims in inter-State cases before the Strasbourg Court will only be successful if they concern damage suffered by individual nationals of the State ('in the context of diplomatic protection').[124]

B. Punitive Damages and the Special Consequences of Breaches of *Jus Cogens*

While both issues gave rise to discussion throughout the preparatory works of the ASR, the Articles ultimately recognise neither the concept of 'punitive damages', nor that of

[115] ILC ASR, 89–90.

[116] In the *LaGrand* case, the ICJ was critical of Germany's delay in instituting proceedings and stated that it would have taken this factor into account had Germany sought a claim for indemnification: *LaGrand* (n 93) paras 57 and 116.

[117] See Final Award Ethiopia's Damages Claims (n 98) paras 18, 26 and 61.

[118] ILC ASR, 100 and 102.

[119] ibid, 94.

[120] Further O Ichim, *Just Satisfaction under the European Convention on Human Rights* (Cambridge, CUP, 2014).

[121] *Cyprus v Turkey* App no 25781/94 (ECtHR, 12 May 2014) para 39 ff.

[122] ibid, paras 40–41.

[123] ibid, para 42.

[124] ibid, para 43–47.

'State crimes'. Instead, the ILC Commentary rightly observes that the award of punitive damages is not recognised in international law and that the function of damages is essentially compensatory.[125] Elsewhere, it is stressed that 'satisfaction is not intended to be punitive in character, nor does it include punitive damages'.[126] This approach appears to be generally consistent with the contemporary practice of international courts and tribunals.[127] Thus, the Eritrea-Ethiopia Commission has previously stressed that compensation has a remedial, rather than a punitive function.[128] In a similar vein, the ECtHR has consistently rejected claims for punitive damages.[129] On a related note, the ILC Commentary observes that there has been 'no development of penal consequences for States of breaches of [...] fundamental norms' of international law,[130] stressing that it remains the case, as the Nuremberg Tribunal asserted in 1946, that '[c]rimes against international law are committed by men, not by abstract entities, and only by punishing individuals who commit such crimes can the provisions of international law be enforced'.[131]

The ASR nonetheless attach particular consequences to certain breaches that affect the international community as a whole and/or that are deemed particularly reprehensible. First, when the breach is one pertaining to an *erga omnes* norm, this affects the possibility for others to invoke State responsibility (see below). Second, certain additional consequences apply in relation to 'serious'[132] breaches of obligations under peremptory norms of general international law, such as the prohibition of genocide or the prohibition against torture.[133] The consequences in such scenarios are essentially threefold.

First, third States are under a duty 'to refrain from acts and actions, or from taking attitudes, that imply the recognition of the acts offending against peremptory norms in a variety of international legal relations'.[134] The archetypical example of the general duty of non-recognition enshrined in Article 41(2) ASR, is the non-recognition of territorial acquisition through conquest.[135] This principle, which is tackled in greater detail in Chapter 5 on States,[136] has been affirmed in the UN General Assembly's Friendly Relations Declaration,[137] and in the Definition of Aggression,[138] and has been applied on several

[125] ILC ASR, 111.

[126] ibid,107.

[127] See Crawford (n 2) 523–25; S Wittich, 'Punitive Damages' in Crawford, Pellet and Olleson (n 2) 671.

[128] Final Award Ethiopia's Damages Claims (n 98) 26: 'Compensation has a limited function. Its role is to restore an injured party, in so far as possible, to the position it would have occupied but for the injury. This function is remedial, not punitive'.

[129] Varnava and others v Turkey App nos 16064/90, 16065/90, 16066/90, 16068/90, 16069/90, 16070/90, 16071/90, 16072/90 and 16073/90 (ECtHR, 18 September 2009) para 223.

[130] ILC ASR, 111.

[131] International Military Tribunal (Nuremberg), *US et al v Göring et al*, 1 October 1946, 22 IMT 203, reprinted in (1947) 41 *AJIL* 172, 221. See also *Bosnian Genocide* (n 5) para 170.

[132] A serious breach is defined as one which involves 'a gross or systematic failure by the responsible State to fulfil the obligation': Art 40(2) ASR. The ILC Commentary provides further guidance on establishing the 'seriousness' of the breach, while stressing that 'some of the peremptory norms in question, most notably the prohibitions of aggression and genocide, by their very nature require an intentional violation on a large scale': ILC ASR, 113.

[133] Art 40 ASR.

[134] A Orakhelashvili, *Peremptory Norms in International Law* (Oxford, OUP, 2006) 282.

[135] But see Y Dinstein, *War, Aggression and Self-defence*, 6th edn (Cambridge, CUP, 2017) 193–94 (pragmatically observing that if the de facto control of territory annexed by an aggressor State continues uninterrupted for generations, international law may ultimately have no choice but to 'capitulate to the facts').

[136] See Chapter 5, Section IV.

[137] Friendly Relations Declaration: 'No territorial acquisition resulting from the threat or use of force shall be recognised as legal'.

[138] UNGA, 'Definition of Aggression', 14 December 1974, Annex to UNGA Res 3314 (XXIX), Art 5(3).

occasions by the UN Security Council.[139] The duty of non-recognition is not, however, unqualified. Thus, in the *Namibia* Advisory Opinion, the ICJ stressed that one should not treat as illegal and invalid acts (such as registrations of births, and marriages) that can only be ignored 'to the detriment of the inhabitants' of the territory under the jurisdiction of the offending State.[140] This '*Namibia* principle', which accepts the recognition of certain everyday transactions that are unavoidable in the daily relations of individuals,[141] was also applied by the ECtHR in a number of cases concerning the so-called Turkish Republic of Northern Cyprus.[142]

In the *Anastasiou I* case, the European Court of Justice nonetheless took the view that certificates of origin produced by the authorities of the so-called Turkish Republic of Northern Cyprus held no validity under the Association Agreement between the European Communities and the Republic of Cyprus of 1972 and the 1977 Protocol.[143] The Court found in this case that the practice of the parties, in particular the de facto acceptance of certificates issued by the Turkish Republic of Northern Cyprus did not 'warrant a departure from the clear, precise and unconditional provisions'[144] of the 1977 Protocol.

Second, States are prohibited from rendering 'aid or assistance' in maintaining the situation created by a breach of *jus cogens*. This rule is reflected in a variety of Security Council resolutions prohibiting aid or assistance to apartheid regimes or colonial oppressors.[145] In the *Ferrini* case, the Italian Court of Cassation explicitly referred to Articles 40–41 ASR to support the conclusion that Germany's State immunity could be set aside in respect of violations of *jus cogens* (committed in the course of the Second World War).[146] The ICJ nonetheless rejected this argument and condemned Italy for flouting Germany's immunity. According to the Court

> recognizing the immunity of a foreign State in accordance with customary international law does not amount to recognizing as lawful a situation created by the breach of a *jus cogens* rule, or rendering aid and assistance in maintaining that situation, and so cannot contravene the principle in Article 41 [ASR].[147]

[139] eg UNSC Res 662, 9 August 1990, UN Doc S/RES/662.

[140] *Legal Consequences for States of the Continued Presence of South Africa in Namibia (South West Africa) notwithstanding Security Council Resolution 276* [1971] ICJ Rep 16, para 125.

[141] LG Loucaides, 'Is the European Court of Human Rights Still a Principled Court of Human Rights After the *Demopoulos* Case?' (2011) 24 *LJIL* 435, 446 (but criticising the ECtHR's application of the principle).

[142] *Loizidou v Turkey* App no 15318/89 (ECtHR, 18 December 1996); *Demopoulos v Turkey* App no 46113/99 (ECtHR, 3 January 2010) 68–129.

[143] Judgment of 5 July 1994, *Anastasiou*, C-432/92, EU:C:1994:277.

[144] ibid, para 37.

[145] eg UNSC Res 218, 23 November 1965, UN Doc S/RES/218; UNSC Res 418, 4 November 1977, UN Doc S/RES/418; UNSC Res 569, 26 July 1985, UN Doc S/RES/569. Note: inasmuch as the ILC Commentary stresses that the concepts of 'aid or assistance' must be read in connection with Art 16 ASR the question arises to what extent this rule imposes more far-reaching restraints on third States than Art 16 ASR. See T Ruys, 'Of Arms, Funding and "Non-Lethal Assistance" – Issues Surrounding Third-State Intervention in the Syrian Civil War' (2014) 13 *CJIL* 13, 19.

[146] Supreme Court of Cassation (IT), *Germany v Mantelli and others*, 29 May 2008, Case No 14201/2008, (2008) *Rivista di diritto internazionale* 896 (where immunity conflicts with fundamental rights, the conflict must be solved in favour of the latter). A similar argument was amade in Supreme Court (GR), *Germany v Prefecture of Voiotia (Representing 118 persons from Distomo village)*, 4 May 2000, Case No 11/2000, (2000) 49 *Nomiko Vima* 212 but was overturned in Special Supreme Court (GR), *Germany v Margellos and 18 other natural and legal persons (intervening)*, 17 September 2002, Case No 6/2002.

[147] *Jurisdictional Immunities of the State* (Germany v Italy: Greece Intervening) [2012] ICJ Rep 99, para 93. Italy's response to this judgment can be found in Constitutional Court (IT), *Simoncioni and others v Germany and President of the Council of Ministers of the Italian Republic (intervening)*, 22 October 2014, Case No 238/2014 (the maintenance of peaceful interstate relations does not justify limiting access to justice in cases of grave human rights abuses) and Supreme Court of Cassation (IT), *'Podrute Massacre case', Opačić*, 29 October 2015,

Finally, States are under a positive duty to cooperate to bring the breach to an end 'through lawful means'.[148] The provision does not clarify what is meant by 'lawful means', nor does it otherwise prescribe what measures States ought to take. State practice is extremely sparse and the ILC Commentary itself admits that '[i]t may be open to question whether general international law at present prescribes a positive duty of cooperation'.[149] In the end, cooperative measures to enforce international law are essentially a question of political will.[150]

V. The Invocation of State Responsibility

A. General

For States to have the *locus standi* to invoke the international responsibility of another State, they must possess the requisite legal interest. Absent such legal interest, their claims will be held inadmissible. This was the case, for instance, with the claims of Ethiopia and Liberia in respect of South Africa's policy of racial discrimination in the *South West Africa* cases.[151] The traditional view has long been that only the State that is injured pursuant to the alleged wrongful act can invoke the offender's responsibility. More recently, the concept of legal interest has come to be understood in a more flexible manner, at least in respect of breaches of norms that are deemed to protect collective interests or that are owed to the international community as a whole. This bifurcated approach is reflected in the ASR, which distinguish between the invocation of State responsibility by the 'injured State',[152] on the one hand, and, the invocation of responsibility by a State 'other than an injured State',[153] on the other hand.

Invocation by the 'injured State' remains the default option. A State may sustain (material or non-material) injury triggering its *locus standi* in two ways, either directly or indirectly. Injury to the State's *direct* interests can take various forms, such as material damage to a State's warships, diplomatic missions, its armed forces, the executive and damage to State property,[154] but also non-material injury resulting from a breach of the State's territorial integrity or the inviolability of its diplomatic premises.

A State may also suffer injury to its *indirect* interests, notably when an internationally wrongful act causes injury to a natural or legal person that is a national of the State

Case No 43696/2015 (exhaustion of judicial remedies not a requirement for State immunity to be set aside in case of a *jus cogens* violation).

[148] Art 41(1) ASR.

[149] ILC ASR, 114. The uncertain status and impact of the provision is reflected in the ICJ's *Wall* Opinion. In this case the Court called upon States 'not to recognise' the situation resulting from the unlawful construction of a wall in the Occupied Palestinian Territory and 'not to render aid or assistance' in maintaining it. By contrast, the Court refrained from affirming a positive duty to cooperate to end the breach. Instead, it recalled the (more specific) duty on the part of States to 'respect and ensure respect' with international humanitarian law in accordance with Common Article 1 of the Geneva Conventions. In addition, it stressed – without further explanation – that '[t]he United Nations […] should consider what further action is required to bring to an end the illegal situation'. *Legal Consequences of the Construction of a Wall in the Occupied Palestinian Territories* [2004] ICJ Rep 136, paras 159–60 and dispositive.

[150] Crawford (n 2) 388.

[151] *South West Africa* (Ethiopia v South Africa; Liberia v South Africa) [1966] ICJ Rep 6, para 99.

[152] Art 42 ASR.

[153] ibid, Art 48.

[154] P Okowa, 'Issues of Admissibility and the Law on International Responsibility' in Evans (n 45) 480.

concerned. Possible scenarios include, for instance, the mistreatment of a national abroad or the unlawful expropriation of a multinational company. Pursuant to the long-established doctrine of 'diplomatic protection', the State concerned can in such scenarios invoke the responsibility of the offending State, so as to seek reparation for the injury indirectly suffered. The limits to the exercise of diplomatic protection are further examined in the subsequent section. It must be stressed, however, that the dividing line between (direct) injury to a State and (indirect) injury to a national of the State may not always be easy to determine, and that some claims may contain elements of both. For instance, when a State raises a claim in relation to injury caused by the unlawful pursuit and arrest of a commercial vessel flying its flag, it is first and foremost challenging direct violations of the rights owed to it under the law of the sea.[155] Yet, when it raises a claim in respect of mistreatment of persons on board the ship, this will come under the rubric of diplomatic protection.

'Injury' can result first and foremost from a breach of an obligation owed to the State 'individually'.[156] This will be fairly straightforward in case of a breach of a bilateral treaty, stipulating reciprocal commitments between two States. Yet, Article 42(a) ASR also covers multilateral treaties that create bundles of bilateral relations.[157] By way of illustration, under the Vienna Convention on Diplomatic Relations, two States, A and B, owe each other obligations to respect the inviolability of diplomatic premises and the immunities of diplomatic personnel. While these obligations are not 'exclusive' to the relationship between A and B (the same obligations will apply between A and C, or C and D), they are nonetheless owed on an 'individual' basis in the sense of Article 42 ASR. The situation is quite different, however, if the breach relates to an obligation owed to 'a group of States including that State, or the international community as a whole'.[158] In such scenario, it may nonetheless be possible to identify an 'injured State' in one of two ways. First, a State may be 'specially affected' by the breach.[159] For instance, while the prohibition on the use of force enshrined in Article 2(4) UN Charter applies to the international community as a whole, breaches thereof will 'specially affect' the State on whose territory aggression is committed.[160] This State should accordingly be competent, not only to invoke the responsibility of the aggressor, but also to seek redress using the full set of tools under the law of international responsibility.

Second, the breach of an obligation owed to multiple States may be 'of such character as radically to change the position of all the other States to which the obligation is owed with respect to the further performance of the obligation'.[161] This scenario refers to 'interdependent' obligations that operate on an all-or-nothing basis, and where the breach by one State threatens the structure of the entire regime. This may be the case in the context of a disarmament treaty or a nuclear-free zone treaty.[162]

Invocation of State responsibility is not – or, rather, is no longer – the exclusive prerogative of the 'injured State'. Indeed, in its judgment in the *Barcelona Traction* case (1970), the ICJ – seemingly retreating from its more conservative (and criticised) stance in the *South West Africa* cases[163] – drew a distinction between obligations vis-à-vis another State in the

[155] *M/V 'SAIGA' (No 2)* (Saint Vincent and the Grenadines v Guinea) (Prompt Release) [1997] ITLOS Rep 16, paras 95–102.
[156] Art 42(a) ASR.
[157] Crawford (n 2) 546.
[158] Art 42(b) ASR.
[159] ibid, Art 42(b)(i).
[160] Crawford (n 2) 546.
[161] Art 42(b)(ii) ASR.
[162] ILC ASR, 119.
[163] See *South West Africa* (n 151).

field of diplomatic protection, and 'obligations of a State towards the international community as a whole', and which 'by their very nature [...] are the concern of all States'.[164] The Court's recognition of so-called '*erga omnes*' norms – which have since become an accepted feature of international law – paved the way for the adoption, by way of progressive development of the law, of Article 48 ASR. This provision effectively proclaims that States other than the injured State are entitled to invoke the responsibility of another State if: (a) the obligation breached is owed to a group of States including that State, and is established for the protection of a collective interest of the group (*erga omnes partes*);[165] or (b) the obligation breached is owed to the international community as a whole (*erga omnes*). States other than the 'injured' State have no right to claim reparation for themselves, or to claim 'punitive' damages. Pursuant to Article 48(2) ASR, their entitlement to claim is limited to seeking cessation and guarantees of non-repetition, as well as seeking reparation in the interest of the injured State.[166] The concept of community interest or collective interest claims has been recognised only gradually in international law and is unlikely to be put into practice on a frequent basis.[167]

Nonetheless, Article 48 ASR marks an important step forward in the promotion of the international rule of law. The provision was explicitly invoked by the International Tribunal for the Law of the Sea (ITLOS) Seabed Disputes Chamber to support the argument that third States may be entitled to claim compensation for damage caused to the marine environment of the high seas and the deep seabed in light of the *erga omnes* character of the obligations concerned.[168] In addition, the *Whaling in the Antarctic* case,[169] where Australia and New Zealand challenged the legality of Japan's allegedly 'scientific' whaling programme, is a successful invocation of State responsibility by a State that is neither 'injured' nor 'specially affected'.

The ASR provides further guidance on the claims process. Thus, Article 43 ASR stipulates that States invoking the responsibility of another State shall give notice thereof. Article 45 ASR acknowledges that States lose the right to invoke State responsibility when they have validly waived a claim (or part thereof), or, by reason of their conduct, have validly acquiesced in the lapse thereof. The ICJ judgments in the *Certain Phosphate Lands* and *LaGrand* cases, for instance, confirm that loss of the right to invoke responsibility may occur where a State has long remained idle and where, having regard to the circumstances, the respondent State could reasonably expect that the claim would no longer be pursued.[170] Articles 46–47 ASR deal with claims where there is a plurality of injured States or a plurality of responsible States.[171]

The mere fact that a State has the required legal interest to invoke another State's international responsibility does not automatically imply that it will be able to initiate a case before an international or national judicial body. In order to bring a case before an international

[164] *Barcelona Traction, Light and Power Co Limited* (Belgium v Spain) [1970] ICJ Rep 3, para 33.

[165] Note that there is no need for the States concerned to cooperate in making a claim.

[166] It has been very rare for States other than injured States to claim reparation: G Gaja, 'State Having an Interest in Compliance with the Obligation Breached' in Crawford, Pellet and Olleson (n 2) 962.

[167] Crawford (n 2) 531–32.

[168] *Responsibilities and Obligations of States Sponsoring Persons and Entities with Respect to Activities in the Area* (Advisory Opinion) [2011] ITLOS Rep 10, 180.

[169] See *Whaling in the Antarctic* (n 92).

[170] *Certain Phosphate Lands in Nauru* (Nauru v Australia) [1992] ICJ Rep 240, 253–54; *LaGrand* (n 93) 508; Crawford (n 2) 560–63.

[171] In the latter scenario, an injured State may not recover, by way of compensation, more than the damage it has suffered.

court or tribunal, the respondent State must have recognised the jurisdiction of the body in one way or another (see Chapter 13 on Peaceful Dispute Settlement).[172] In cases before the national courts of a third State, the respondent State may of course be able to rely on its jurisdictional immunity (see Chapter 11 on Immunities).

B. Limitations to the Exercise of Diplomatic Protection

Traditionally, international law conceived of natural and legal persons as (passive) 'objects', rather than as 'subjects', of international law. Thus, it was accepted that natural and legal persons could benefit from a certain degree of international protection vis-à-vis third States pursuant to the international minimum standards for the treatment of aliens. The underlying obligations were not, however, 'owed' to these persons as individuals, but rather to their State of nationality. Procedurally, this meant that, while affected individuals could of course initiate procedures before the national courts of the Host State under the latter State's domestic law, only the State of nationality could invoke the *international* responsibility of the offending State. Each State indeed has the right to exercise 'diplomatic protection'[173] – by invoking the responsibility of another State through diplomatic action or other means of peaceful settlement – in respect of its 'nationals' that are injured by internationally wrongful conduct. As the PCIJ put it in the *Mavrommatis Palestine Concessions* case:

> It is an elementary principle of international law that a State is entitled to protect its subject, when injured by acts contrary to international law committed by another State, from whom they have been unable to obtain satisfaction through the ordinary channels. [...] [B]y taking up the case of one of its subjects and by resorting to diplomatic protection or international judicial proceedings on his behalf, a State is in reality asserting its own rights [...].[174]

While diminished in relevance (see below), the exercise of diplomatic protection remains an accepted feature of international law. The underlying principles, elaborated by the ILC in its 2006 Articles on Diplomatic Protection (ADP), have largely remained unaltered. A recent application can be found in the *Diallo* case, where the Democratic Republic of Congo was held responsible for having breached various international obligations by detaining a businessman of Guinean nationality, by expelling him from Congolese territory, and by failing to inform him of his right to consular assistance.[175] As this case illustrates, the exercise of diplomatic protection is not limited to the traditional customary rules on the treatment of aliens, but equally extends to other international obligations whose breach may cause injury to natural or legal persons, chiefly international human rights law.[176]

It is important to emphasise that the State of nationality in principle decides on a discretionary basis whether or not to exercise diplomatic protection on behalf of one of its nationals abroad (possibly even against the wishes of the latter): 'The State must be viewed as the sole judge to decide whether its protection will be granted, to what extent it is granted, and when it will cease'.[177] The proposal to provide for a *duty* to exercise diplomatic

[172] Of course, the respondent State may also raise other challenges to the admissibility of a case, pertaining, for instance, to the absence of a 'dispute' between the parties concerned. See further Chapter 13 on Immunities.

[173] Not to be confused with consular assistance.

[174] *The Mavrommatis Palestine Concessions* (Greece v UK) [1924] PCIJ Series A, No 2. On a related note, individuals cannot validly waive any entitlement to diplomatic protection by their national State.

[175] *Ahmadou Sadio Diallo* (Republic of Guinea v Democratic Republic of the Congo) [2010] ICJ Rep 639.

[176] *Ahmadou Sadio Diallo* (Republic of Guinea v Democratic Republic of the Congo) [2007] ICJ Rep 582, para 39.

[177] *Barcelona Traction* (n 164) para 79.

protection in certain cases ultimately did not find its way to the ADP. Instead, Article 19(a) ADP merely 'recommends' that States give 'due consideration to the possibility of exercising diplomatic protection'. The case law of national courts generally affirms the wide discretion of States in this matter. For instance, in *Abbasi v Secretary of State*, concerning a British national detained at the US military base at Guantanamo Bay, the English Court of Appeal agreed that the UK Foreign Office had a 'very wide' discretion whether 'to exercise this right [...] to protect British citizens', while nonetheless noting that 'there is no reason why its decision or inaction should not be reviewable if it can be shown that the same were irrational or contrary to legitimate expectation'.[178] Several national constitutions provide for a right of protection enforceable against the State of which the person is a national, but in practice these provisions are still interpreted as granting the executive a wide discretion.[179]

On a related note, the State exercising diplomatic protection is traditionally not *legally obliged* to transfer to the injured person or entity the compensation obtained for the injury from the responsible State, although it will often do so voluntarily. Article 19 ADP 'recommends' that States do so. Furthermore, in international case law, there has been increased pressure for States to transfer compensation obtained to the injured person or entity. Thus, in *Diallo*, the Court '[recalled] that the sum awarded to Guinea in the exercise of diplomatic protection of Mr Diallo is intended to provide reparation for the latter's injury'.[180] In *Cyprus v Turkey*, the ECtHR stressed that 'if just satisfaction is afforded [pursuant to Article 41 ECHR] in an inter-State case, it should always be done for the benefit of individual victims'.[181]

Recourse to diplomatic protection is only possible for the State of nationality of the injured person(s) concerned. This nationality requirement must in principle be fulfilled continuously from the date of injury to the date of the official presentation of the claim – although exceptions to this principle exist.[182] Nationality issues are governed first and foremost by municipal law, and international law poses only few limits to the discretion of States to confer nationality. Some restrictions may flow, for example, from the non-intervention principle or from international human rights law.[183] Nationality presupposes some form of factual connection with the State, whether through birth, descent, naturalisation, or as a result of State succession.[184] In the *Nottebohm* case, the ICJ nonetheless found that Liechtenstein could not extend diplomatic protection to a person who originally held German nationality (through birth) and subsequently obtained the nationality of Liechtenstein (through naturalisation), who had been detained and expelled by Guatemala, and whose property

[178] Court of Appeal (UK), *R v Secretary of State for Foreign and Commonwealth Affairs and Secretary of State for the Home Department* [2002] EWCA Civ 1598, 106 (emphasising that 'the court cannot enter the forbidden areas, including decisions affecting foreign policy').

[179] See eg Federal Supreme Court (CH), *Consortium X v Switzerland*, 2 July 2004, BGE 130 I 312 (Switzerland was free to decide whether it made such protection available to a national or not; there existed no right to diplomatic protection as long as the decision did not seem arbitrary); Okowa (n 154) 482–83.

[180] *Ahmadou Sadio Diallo* (Republic of Guinea v Democratic Republic of the Congo) [2012] ICJ Rep 324, para 57.

[181] See eg *Cyprus v Turkey* (n 121) paras 46, 59 (the Court left it to the Cypriot government to set up an effective mechanism to distribute the awarded sums to the individual victims).

[182] Art 5 ADP.

[183] See eg Art 1 of the 1930 Hague Convention on Certain Questions relating to the Conflict of Nationality Laws (adopted 12 April 1930, entered into force 1 July 1937) 179 LNTS 90: 'It is for each State to determine under its own law who are its nationals. This law shall be recognised by other States in so far as it is consistent with international conventions, international custom, and the principles of law generally recognised with regard to nationality'.

[184] Art 4 ADP. On the impact of State succession on questions of nationality, see ILC Articles on Nationality.

had been seized by the latter State without compensation. The reason for this was that Mr Nottebohm, who had been living in Guatemala for over 34 years, was found not to have a 'genuine connection' with Liechtenstein.[185] It has been questioned whether this case should be read as implying that the existence of some form of 'genuine link' with the State of nationality is indispensable to make the conferral of nationality opposable to third States. Such requirement is said to unduly curtail the conferring State's sovereign right to confer nationality and to create an element of uncertainty. In addition, it has been argued that it is not supported by State practice or other case law, such as the more recent *Diallo* case.[186] Still, there may be exceptional cases where a conferral of nationality is not opposable to third States and cannot serve as a basis to exercise diplomatic protection. This would be the case, for example, where it has been extended in bad faith or in a manner incompatible with fundamental principles, such as those prohibiting racial discrimination.[187] By way of illustration, in its Report of 2009, the EU-established Independent International Fact-Finding Mission on the Conflict in Georgia found Russia's collective naturalisation ('passportisation') of Georgian nationals residing in Georgia to be contrary to international law, and held that Russia could not exercise diplomatic protection for the persons concerned.[188]

In addition, it is accepted that, in cases where a person has multiple nationalities, both (or all) of the States of nationality may in principle exercise diplomatic protection in his/her respect against third States.[189] In the relations between the different States of nationality, however, only the State whose nationality is in fact 'predominant' will be able to bring a claim against the other(s).[190] The nationality requirement may of course be waived, either on an ad hoc basis, or pursuant to a pre-existing treaty. Article 23 TFEU, for instance, could be read as creating a treaty-based right of consular protection for all EU nationals in a third State (see Chapter 10 on Diplomatic and Consular Relations).[191]

In the *Barcelona Traction* case, the ICJ stressed that the right of diplomatic protection of a corporate entity belongs 'to the State under the laws of which it is incorporated and in whose territory it has its registered office'.[192] Accordingly, the Court denied that Belgium could exercise diplomatic protection in respect of a company incorporated in Canada, even if 88 per cent of the shareholders were Belgian. At the same time, the Court recognised that the State of nationality of the shareholders is entitled to bring a claim where the direct rights of shareholders (as distinct from the rights of the company) are infringed.[193] This twofold approach is repeated in Articles 9 and 12 ADP. At the same time, the ADP contain

[185] *Nottebohm Case* (Liechtenstein v Guatemala) [1955] ICJ Rep 4, 23.

[186] Further, see ILC ADP 33; Okowa (n 154) 486–87; Crawford (n 2) 574–75.

[187] Okowa (n 154) 487; Crawford (n 2) 706.

[188] Report of the Independent international Fact-Finding Mission on the Conflict in Georgia, September 2009, Vol II www.mpil.de/en/pub/publications/archive/independent_international_fact.cfm 155–83.

[189] Art 6 ADP.

[190] ibid, Art 7.

[191] Okowa (n 154) 493; J Dugard, 'Fifth Report on Diplomatic Protection', 4 March 2004, UN Doc A/CN.4/538, 8. According to Art 23 TFEU, '[e]very citizen of the Union shall, in the territory of a third country in which the Member State of which he is a national is not represented, be entitled to protection by the diplomatic or consular authorities of any Member State, on the same conditions as the nationals of that State. Member States shall adopt the necessary provisions and start the international negotiations required to secure this protection'. As Dugard observes, 'it is difficult to suggest that a third State which has not consented to the exercise of diplomatic protection by a European State of which the injured person is not a national could be bound in law to recognize the right of such a State to protect a non-national' (ibid, 8).

[192] *Barcelona Traction* (n 164) para 70.

[193] ibid, para 47. Examples listed by the Court include, eg, the right of shareholders to dividends or the right to attend and vote at general meetings.

several other exceptions to the general rule laid down in *Barcelona Traction*. Thus, pursuant to Article 11(a) ADP diplomatic protection may be exercised by the State of nationality of the shareholders when the company has ceased to exist for a reason unrelated to the injury. More controversial are the exceptions enshrined in Articles 9 and 11(b) ADP.[194] First, whereas Article 9 affirms the basic premise of the *Barcelona Traction* case that it is incorporation that confers nationality on a corporation for the purpose of diplomatic protection, it subsequently makes exception, in a manner reminiscent of the treatment of the concept of 'genuine connection' in the *Nottebohm* case, for situations where there is no significant link or connection between the corporation and the State of incorporation. In particular, the provision refers to situations where the corporation has no substantial business activities in the State of incorporation, is controlled by nationals of another State and where both the seat of management and the financial control of the corporation are located in another State.

Where these conditions are (cumulatively) met, Article 9 stipulates that it is the State in which the corporation has its seat of management and in which it is financially controlled that shall be regarded as the State of nationality. Article 11(b) ADP in turn suggests that the State of nationality of the shareholders may step in where the injury to the corporation was caused by the State of nationality of the corporation, and incorporation in the State was required by the latter as a precondition for doing business there. In *Diallo*, the ICJ nonetheless rejected the idea that there exists a general entitlement under customary international law to diplomatic protection for shareholders whenever a company has the nationality of the wrong-doing State.[195]

The exercise of diplomatic protection also presupposes that the injured person or entity has exhausted all local remedies available in the Host State.[196] The underlying idea is that, out of respect for State sovereignty and as a matter of practical convenience (since local tribunals will normally be best placed to offer swift and appropriate redress), the State where the violation occurred should have an opportunity to redress it by its own means, within the framework of its own domestic legal system.[197] It follows that the claim must have been brought before the competent tribunals and pursued as far as permitted by local law, without success.[198] While Article 14(2) ADP spells out a broad definition of 'local remedies',[199] case law demonstrates that the 'local remedies' rule is applied with a degree of flexibility, and that remedies that are discretionary or available as a matter of grace need not be exhausted.[200] Thus, the fact that Diallo could have submitted a request to the Congolese Prime Minister to reconsider his expulsion from the DRC was not seen by the ICJ as a hurdle preventing Guinea from exercising diplomatic protection.[201] This flexible approach is reflected in Article 15 ADP, which spells out five exceptions to the local remedies rule. The main exception pertains to situations where 'there are no reasonably available

[194] See Crawford (n 2) 578–80.
[195] *Diallo* (n 180) paras 88–93.
[196] *Mavrommatis Palestine Concessions* (n 174) 12. See further, CF Amerasinghe, *Local Remedies in International Law*, 2nd edn (Cambridge, CUP, 2004); AA Cançado Trindade, *The Application of the Rule of Exhaustion of Local Remedies in International Law* (Cambridge, CUP, 1983).
[197] *Interhandel* (Switzerland v United States) [1959] ICJ Rep 6, 27. Note: there is discussion as to whether the local remedies rule is a procedural rule or a rule of substance. See Okowa (n 154) 503–504.
[198] *Elettronica Sicula SpA (ELSI)* (United States of America v Italy) [1989] ICJ Rep 15, 46.
[199] Local remedies are defined as 'legal remedies which are open to an injured person before the judicial or administrative courts or bodies, whether ordinary or special, of the State alleged to be responsible for causing the injury'.
[200] Okowa (n 154) 501.
[201] See eg *Diallo* (n 176) para 47.

local remedies to provide effective redress, or the local remedies provide no reasonable possibility of such redress'.[202]

Furthermore, the rule does not apply in cases where: (i) there is undue delay in the remedial process which is attributable to the Host State;[203] (ii) there was no relevant connection between the injured person and the wrong-doing State;[204] (iii) the injured person is manifestly precluded from pursuing local remedies;[205] or (iv) the wrong-doing State has waived the local remedies rule, such as in the context of a bilateral investment treaty. When a State brings a 'mixed' claim against another State on the basis of *both* an injury to a natural or legal person that is a national of the claimant State *and* an injury to its direct interests, the local remedies rule will only apply where the former aspect is 'preponderant'.[206] This rule would apply, for instance, where a State brings a claim pursuant to injury to crew members of a commercial vessel as well as a parallel claim in respect of a breach of its direct rights under the law of the sea. As far as the burden of proof is concerned, when the responsibility of the wrong-doing State is raised at the international level, it is 'incumbent upon the applicant to prove that local remedies were indeed exhausted or to establish that exceptional circumstances relieved the allegedly injured person [...] of the obligation to exhaust available local remedies'.[207] Conversely, it is for the respondent State 'to convince the Court that there were effective remedies in its domestic legal system that were not exhausted'.[208]

On a final note, it is worth recalling that the customary rules pertaining to the exercise of diplomatic protection were developed at a time when natural or legal persons had no standing whatsoever to invoke the international responsibility of the State. Clearly, the situation is fundamentally different today. A variety of regional human rights regimes now empower individuals to bring claims at the international level. Thus, individuals that come within the jurisdiction of one of the 47 Member States of the ECHR, may (after having exhausted available local remedies) themselves seek redress before the Strasbourg Court for alleged violations of the Convention. Furthermore, there are now numerous investment treaties that empower multinational companies to bring claims against a Host State and to trigger direct investor-State arbitration. Many Bilateral Investment Treaties (BITs) moreover expressly dispense with the requirement that companies first exhaust local remedies. At times, treaties will explicitly stipulate that recourse to direct investor-State arbitration precludes the exercise of diplomatic protection by the State of nationality.[209]

Yet, even where recourse to diplomatic protection is not so excluded, direct claims brought by natural or legal persons under human rights or investment treaties carry undeniable advantages. For instance, these procedures involve less uncertainty and delays compared to the exercise of diplomatic protection.[210] Another advantage relates to the

[202] Art 15(a) ADP. For a recent illustration, see *Chiragov and others v Armenia* App no 13216/05 (ECtHR, 16 June 2015) para 119.

[203] Art 15(b) ADP.

[204] ibid, Art 15(c) ADP. See eg *M/V 'SAIGA' (No 2)* (n 155) paras 99–100.

[205] ibid, 15(d) ADP.

[206] ibid, 14(3) ADP. See also eg *M/V 'Virginia G' Case* (Panama v Guinea-Bissau) [2014] ITLOS Rep 4, paras 152–60.

[207] *Diallo* (n 176) para 44.

[208] ibid.

[209] See eg Art 27(1) ICSID: 'No Contracting State shall give diplomatic protection, or bring an international claim, in respect of a dispute which one of its nationals and another Contracting State shall have consented to submit or shall have submitted to arbitration under this Convention, unless such other Contracting State shall have failed to abide by and comply with the award rendered in such dispute'.

[210] The litigation in the *Barcelona Traction* case lasted almost two decades. The *Diallo* case took more than ten years to reach final judgment; Okowa (n 154) 491.

direct enforceability of investment awards. The implication is that the exercise of diplomatic protection has 'faded'[211] somewhat, and that the relevance of this tool is limited mainly to situations where no direct avenues are provided for.[212] At the same time, it would be premature to conclude that the rules are no longer valid or have somehow become obsolete.

VI. Countermeasures

A. General

A State's breach of an international obligation incumbent upon it may cause repercussions beyond the possibility for injured (and possibly non-injured) States invoking its international responsibility and seeking reparation. Pursuant to the law of treaties, for instance, a 'material' breach of a treaty enables other State Parties to terminate or suspend its operation (see Chapter 2 on Treaty Law).[213] Whether there is an independent exception of non-performance (*exceptio non-adimpleti contractus*) justifying the non-performance of an obligation in situations not covered by Article 60 VCLT, remains uncertain.[214] In any case, under the law of international responsibility, internationally wrongful conduct by one State may lead other, injured, States to adopt 'countermeasures', that is, to engage in an act of non-compliance with an international obligation owed to the State that committed the initial breach. Countermeasures thus constitute both a 'consequence' of international responsibility, as well as a 'ground precluding wrongfulness' on the part of the State taking them.

Countermeasures are in essence a form of 'self-help' and constitute a remnant of the nineteenth century doctrine of (peacetime) 'reprisals'.[215] Reprisals were defined in the *Naulilaa* case as 'acts of self-help by the injured State, acts in retaliation for acts contrary to international law on the part of the offending State, which have remained unredressed after a demand for amends.'[216]

The permissibility of reprisals was seen as an inevitable corollary of the imperfect state of international law and the absence of a 'Court [or] central authority above the Sovereign States which could compel a delinquent State to give reparation'.[217] Reprisals could take many forms, including the refusal to pay a debt or the detention of foreign ships in a State's ports, but also recourse to armed force. With the introduction of the prohibition on the use of force in the twentieth century and the creation of a global collective security architecture (Chapter 14 on the Use of Force and Collective Security), however, the vocabulary of

[211] *Diallo* (n 176) para 88.

[212] For an exceptional case where a State exercised its right of diplomatic protection in spite of the possibility for the legal person concerned to initiate direct investor-State arbitration, see *Italy v Cuba*, Interim Award of 15 March 2005, (2011) *Oxford Reports on International Investment Claims* 518.

[213] Art 60 VCLT.

[214] See Crawford (n 2) 678–82. See also D Azaria, 'Exception of Non-performance' in MPEPIL.

[215] See further OY Elaraby, *The Legality of Non-Forcible Countermeasures* (Oxford, Clarendon Press, 1988); LA Sicilianos, *Les reactions décentralisées à l'illicite: des contre-mesures à la légitime défense* (Paris, LGDJ, 1990). Peacetime reprisals should not be confused with 'belligerent reprisals' undertaken in the context of an armed conflict.

[216] *Naulilaa* (Portugal v Germany), Award of 31 July 1928, 2 RIAA 1012.

[217] L Oppenheim, *International Law: A Treatise, Vol 2: War and Neutrality*, 2nd edn (London, Longmans, 1912) para 43.

'reprisals', comprising of both measures using force and other non-forcible measures, was replaced with new concepts: (i) self-defence, temporarily sanctioning the use of force, but contingent on the occurrence of an 'armed attack'; and (ii) countermeasures, which may be triggered by any internationally wrongful conduct, but can only be non-forcible in nature.[218]

Countermeasures are fundamentally different from 'retorsion' in that the latter concept refers to measures of discourtesy or unfriendliness towards another State,[219] but which do not of themselves give rise to a breach of an international obligation, and which are therefore essentially unregulated by international law. Examples are the severing of diplomatic relations or the withdrawal of voluntary aid programmes. By contrast, when the measure taken would normally qualify as a breach of an international obligation, it no longer qualifies as a 'retorsion' but as a 'countermeasure'. Determining whether a unilateral measure falls in one category or the other can be a complex endeavour and may require a careful scrutiny of the measure under relevant customary international law (such as the principle of non-intervention, which prohibits 'coercive' interference in a State's internal affairs[220]), bilateral treaty law (eg, in the form of bilateral treaties of friendship and commerce or BITs) or multilateral treaty law (eg, the GATT prohibits a variety of unilateral trade restrictions, but nonetheless contains a 'national security' exception).[221]

Countermeasures remain controversial as ever. This is due to a variety of factors, including the fact that they generally favour the stronger party over the weaker, as well as the risk that they result in the escalation of inter-State disputes. This is especially the case since the States concerned often hold genuinely different views on whether the initial conduct was unlawful or not. In light of this, building on existing case law, the ASR imposes a variety of restrictions on the use of countermeasures.

The core limitations can be summarised as follows. First, an injured State may only take countermeasures against a State which is responsible for an internationally wrongful act.[222] Clearly, where the existence of an internationally wrongful act is disputed, the State resorting to countermeasures does so at its own risk, and may incur responsibility if its assessment is held to be unfounded by an international judicial body.[223] Second, the countermeasures must be directed against the wrong-doing State (to the exclusion of third States), and must aim at inducing the State to comply with the obligation(s) concerned. In other words, they must be done with the purpose of changing the behaviour constituting the breach, and should not be punitive in nature. In *Interim Accord*, for instance, the ICJ found that Greece's objections to the Former Yugoslav Republic of Macedonia's (FYROM) admission to NATO could not be justified as proportionate countermeasures since the objection was not aimed at achieving the cessation of a wrongful act by the latter State.[224] Third, countermeasures must be halted when the wrong-doing State resumes the performance of its obligations, and must therefore normally be reversible in nature.[225] Fourth, to avoid escalation and abuse, an essential requirement is that countermeasures be *proportional* to the initial wrongful act. Thus, in *Gabcikovo-Nagymaros*, the ICJ found that Czechoslovakia's unilaterally assuming

[218] Crawford (n 2) 586.
[219] Note that retorsions can also be a response to conduct of another State that is not as such unlawful.
[220] See, M Jamnejad and M Wood, 'The Principle of Non-intervention' (2009) 22 *LJIL* 345.
[221] Art XXI GATT.
[222] Art 49(1) ASR.
[223] Crawford (n 2) 686.
[224] *Application of the Interim Accord of 13 September 1995* (the Former Yugoslav Republic of Macedonia v Greece) [2011] ICJ Rep 644, para 164.
[225] Arts 49(2)–(3) ASR. The duty to choose measures that are reversible is not absolute. See ILC ASR, 131.

control over a large percentage of the waters of the Danube was not commensurate with Hungary's suspension and abandonment of the construction works it was held to.[226] By contrast, in the *US-France Air Services Agreement* arbitration, the arbitral tribunal found that US measures prohibiting certain flights to the US were not disproportionate to France's preventing PanAm passengers from disembarking in Paris.[227] Often, evaluating proportionality 'can at best be accomplished by approximation'.[228] Although countermeasures need not necessarily be related to the same (type of) obligation as the one originally breached, those that do are more likely to satisfy the proportionality requirement.

Certain countermeasures are prohibited having regard to 'the experiences of humanity and the rules of good faith'.[229] In particular, as mentioned before, countermeasures may not affect the obligation to refrain from the threat or use of force.[230] 'Armed reprisals' are no longer permitted in the UN Charter era.[231] In addition, countermeasures may not affect fundamental human rights norms, the obligations under international humanitarian law prohibiting reprisals, or other *jus cogens* norms.[232]

Article 50(2)(a) ASR moreover affirms that a State taking countermeasures is not relieved from fulfilling its obligations under any dispute settlement procedure applicable between it and the responsible State. Finally, countermeasures may not affect the inviolability of diplomatic or consular agents, premises, archives and documents.[233] Indeed, as the ILC Commentary explains, if diplomatic or consular personnel could be targeted by way of countermeasures, they would in effect constitute resident hostages against perceived wrongs of the sending State, undermining the institution of diplomatic and consular relations.[234] Countermeasures are also subject to a number of procedural conditions. Thus, a State should first call upon the responsible State to fulfil its obligations,[235] and should moreover notify the target State of its intentions and offer to negotiate, save inasmuch as urgent countermeasures would be necessary to preserve its rights.[236] Finally, countermeasures are excluded while the underlying dispute is pending before an international judicial body.[237]

Like States, international organisations can resort to countermeasures when they suffer injury as a result of the internationally wrongful conduct of a State or international organisation. Mutatis mutandis, the possibility for injured international organisations to apply countermeasures is affirmed and defined in Articles 22 and 51–56 ARIO in much the same way as in the corresponding provisions of the ARS. Special restrictions nonetheless apply with regard to the recourse to countermeasures by an international organisation against its Member States and vice versa (see below, Section VII).[238]

[226] *Gabčíkovo-Nagymaros* (n 12) paras 83–87.

[227] Air Services Agreement of 27 March 1946 between the United States of America and France, Award of 9 December 1978, 28 RIAA 417.

[228] ibid, para 83.

[229] *Naulilaa* (n 216) 1026.

[230] Art 50(1)(a) ASR.

[231] *Guyana and Suriname*, Award of 17 September 2007, 139 ILR 566, 702; UNGA Res 2625 (XXV), 24 October 1970, UN Doc A/RES/25/2625, Principle 1, para 6.

[232] Art 50(1)(a)–(c) ASR. See eg Ethiopia-Eritrea Claims Commission, Prisoners of War – Eritrea's Claim 17, 1 July 2003, 135 ILR 199, 247: 'Ethiopia's suspension of prisoner of war exchanges cannot be justified as a non-forcible countermeasure [...] because, as Article 50 [ASR] emphasises, such measures may not affect "obligations for the protection of fundamental human rights", or "obligations of a humanitarian character prohibiting reprisals"'.

[233] Art 50(2)(b) ASR. Consider also *Tehran* (n 11) para 86.

[234] ILC ASR, 134.

[235] See eg *Gabčíkovo-Nagymaros* (n 12) para 84.

[236] Art 52 ASR.

[237] ibid, Art 52(3)(b); *Air Services Agreement* (n 227) 96.

[238] See Arts 22(2)–(3) and 52(1)–(2) ARIO.

The general law of international responsibility cannot be transplanted to the responsibility of EU Member States and EU institutions in the context of the EU legal order.[239] The CJEU has made it clear that EU Member States may not resort, for instance, to traditional countermeasures against other Member States for breaches of EU law. In *Commission v Luxembourg & Belgium* the Court held that

> the Treaty is not limited to creating reciprocal obligations between the different natural and legal persons to whom it is applicable, but establishes a new legal order which governs the powers, rights and obligations of the said persons, as well as the necessary procedures for taking cognizance of and penalizing any breach of it. Therefore, except where otherwise expressly provided, the basic concept of the Treaty requires that the Member States shall not take the law into their own hands.[240]

Since the general law of international responsibility does not apply within the EU legal order, which contains a complete system of rights and remedies, there has been discussion as to whether the EU might constitute a 'self-contained regime' in international law.[241] It should be pointed out that this applies to the internal legal order of the EU, and the responsibility of Member States within that system. The EU, like other international organisations, is still bound by general rules of international law.

B. Third-party Countermeasures

So far, we have dealt with the possible recourse to countermeasures by a State that is itself injured by the internationally wrongful conduct of another State. Even more controversial, however, is the permissibility of countermeasures by non-injured States (or non-injured international organisations) (so called 'third-party' countermeasures).[242] The importance of the discussion can hardly be overestimated. On the one hand, it is argued that to allow such countermeasures would contribute to strengthening the international rule of law, inasmuch as it would increase the cost of non-compliance with international law. This is the case especially where there is no directly injured State, such as when a regime commits widespread human rights violations against its own population, or where the State injured by the breach is not in a position to engage in countermeasures against a more powerful offending State.

On the other hand, some caution that to leave the enforcement of collective/community interests at the mercy of individual States, acting based on their own understanding of international legality, is a recipe for chaos and subjectivism.[243] Previously, it was noted that States can invoke an offending State's international responsibility even if they are not injured by internationally wrongful conduct, at least with regard to breaches of obligations

[239] See, J-M Thouvenin, 'Responsibility in the Context of the European Union Legal Order' in Crawford, Pellet and Olleson (n 2) 861–75 (the author notes, for instance, that not all wrongful acts entail Community responsibility (see 868)).

[240] Judgment of 13 November 1964, *Commission v Luxembourg & Belgium*, Joined Cases 90/63 and 91/63, EU:C:1964:80, 631.

[241] B Simma and D Pulkowski, 'Of Planets and the Universe: Self-contained Regimes in International Law' (2006) 17 *EJIL* 483, 518.

[242] Further, see eg C Tams, *Enforcing Obligations Erga Omnes in International Law* (Cambridge, CUP, 2005); EK Proukaki, *The Problem of Enforcement in International Law: Countermeasures, the Non-Injured State and the Idea of International Community* (London, Routledge, 2010), M Dawidowicz, Third-Party Countermeasures in International Law (Cambridge, CUP, 2017).

[243] eg B Simma, 'From Bilateralism to Community Interest in International Law' (1994) 250 *RdC* 217, 331.

'*erga omnes partes*' and obligations '*erga omnes*'.[244] Whether in such scenarios third States can moreover engage in countermeasures remains as yet unsettled.

Ever since the 1990s, there has been increasing recourse to 'sanctions' – both of a general nature (eg, trade embargos) and more 'targeted' sanctions (eg, asset freezes and travel bans against individual persons). Such sanctions have been adopted not only by the UN Security Council,[245] but also by individual States (eg, the United States) and regional organisations.

The European Union, for example, has in place a wide range of 'restrictive measures' against third countries, individuals and entities.[246] Some of the underlying Council Decisions and Council (Implementing) Regulations merely seek to implement mandatory Security Council sanctions at the EU level. Others, however, are imposed 'autonomously' by the EU as such. Thus, Council Regulation (EU) No 359/2011 and Council Decision 2010/413/CFSP and related EU instruments contained a variety of import and export restrictions (including an arms embargo and an import ban on crude oil and petroleum products) targeting Iran as well as asset freezes targeting specific Iranian individuals and entities.[247] In a similar vein, pursuant to the Russian intervention in Ukraine, the EU 'blacklisted' a variety of Russian individuals and entities, while also imposing measures of a more general nature, such as an arms embargo, or controls on the export of certain equipment for the oil industry.[248]

While the States and regional organisations adopting such 'sanctions' generally remain silent on their qualification under international law, and some of these may be more akin to retorsions than countermeasures, many sanctions regimes, including many EU restrictive measures, are ostensibly inspired by breaches of international law (eg, breaches of international human rights law, of the law of armed conflict, of the prohibition on the use of force).

In 2001, the ILC nonetheless concluded that

> the current state of international law on countermeasures taken in the general or collective interest is uncertain. State practice is sparse and involves a limited number of States. At present, there appears to be no clearly recognized entitlement of States referred to in Article 48 to take countermeasures in the collective interest.[249]

[244] Art 48 ASR.

[245] For an overview of the UNSC's Sanctions Committees, see UNSC, 'Subsidiary Organs', 'Sanctions', un.org/sc/suborg/en.

[246] For a regularly updated list of restrictive measures, see EU, 'Restrictive measures (sanctions) in force', eeas.europa.eu/cfsp/sanctions/docs/measures_en.pdf. See also EEAS, 'Consolidated list of persons, groups and entities subject to EU financial sanctions', eeas.europa.eu/topics/sanctions-policy/8442/consolidated-list-of-sanctions_en. At the EU level, these measures find their legal basis first and foremost in Art 215 TFEU, which refers to decisions providing 'for the interruption or reduction, in part or completely, of the Union's economic and financial relations with one or more third countries, where such restrictive measures are necessary to achieve the objectives of the [CFSP]'.

[247] These measures have, however, been suspended or abolished in large part in the wake of the so-called Joint Comprehensive Plan of Action of 2015. See eg Council Regulation (EU) 2015/1861 of 18 October 2015 amending Regulation (EU) No 267/2012 concerning restrictive measures against Iran [2015] OJ L274/1; Council Implementing Regulation (EU) 2015/1862 of 18 October 2015 implementing Regulation (EU) No 267/2012 concerning restrictive measures against Iran [2015] OJ L274/161; Council Decision (CFSP) 2015/1863 of 18 October 2015 amending Decision 2010/413/CFSP concerning restrictive measures against Iran [2015] OJ L274/174; Council Decision (CFSP) 2016/37 of 16 January 2016 concerning the date of application of Decision (CFSP) 2015/1863 amending Decision 2010/413/CFSP concerning restrictive measures against Iran [2016] OJ L11 I/1.

[248] See eg Council Decision 2014/512/CFSP of 31 July 2014 concerning restrictive measures in view of Russia's actions destabilising the situation in Ukraine [2014] OJ L229/13 and Council Regulation (EU) No 833/2014 of 31 July 2014 concerning restrictive measures in view of Russia's actions destabilising the situation in Ukraine [2014] OJ L229/1.

[249] ILC ASR, 139.

In light thereof, it decided to leave the matter open, to be determined by the further development of international law. The 'savings clause' of Article 54 ASR thus provides, in a circular manner, that the ASR '[do] not prejudice the right of any State [other than an injured State], entitled [...] to invoke the responsibility of another State, to take *lawful* measures against that State to ensure the cessation of the breach'.[250]

VII. International Organisations and the Law of International Responsibility

The ascendancy of international organisations, as well as their potential to commit internationally wrongful acts, spurred the ILC to include the topic of 'responsibility of international organisations' in its program of work. The ILC's study of the topic resulted in the adoption of the Articles on the Responsibility of International Organizations by the UN General Assembly in 2011. The provisions of the ARIO are largely modelled on those of the ASR, although the ARIO contain a number of innovative clauses regarding the attribution of responsibility in the relations between international organisations and their Member States. The ILC used the ASR by analogy, for conceptual and pragmatic reasons. As international organisations are international legal subjects, just like States, use of state responsibility analogies was arguably warranted. Moreover, practice regarding the responsibility of international organisations was scarce, so that analogies were most welcome to fill gaps in the responsibility system. Still, the ILC could have given sounder underpinnings to its use of analogies.[251]

It is observed in passing that recourse to analogies is not exceptional in international law. Private law has informed the formation of general principles of international law,[252] and the 1986 Vienna Convention on the Law of Treaties between States and International Organizations and between International Organizations[253] was modelled on the 1969 Vienna Convention on the Law of Treaties between States. Nonetheless, there are important differences between States and international organisations, and specific rules needed to be developed to take them into account. For instance, since international organisations are composite legal actors, made up of Member States who themselves possess international legal personality, the ILC had to take into account these issues in the ARIO.

One of the many issues faced by the ILC was how to deal with regional economic integration organisations, and more specifically, the European Union. The EU argued that since it was a rather unique type of international organisation, specific rules should be developed to take this into account. The nature of competences within the EU legal order, the relationship between the EU and the Member States (specifically the model of 'executive

[250] Emphasis added.

[251] ILA, Report of the Study Group on the Responsibility of International Organizations, Sofia Conference (2012) 10–11; J Wouters and J Odermatt, 'Are All International Organizations Created Equal?' (2012) 9 *International Organizations Law Review* 7.

[252] H Lauterpacht, 'The Doctrine of Non-Justifiable Disputes in International Law' (1928) 24 *Economica* 277.

[253] Vienna Convention on the Law of Treaties between States and International Organizations or between International Organizations (adopted 20 March 1986, not yet entered into force) 25 ILM 543.

federalism'[254]) and the fact that the EU acts in a 'state-like' manner on the international plane, were put forward as reasons for the creation of a specific set of rules.[255] One question that arose in this regard was whether a special rule of attribution had developed in the EU context whereby the actions of the organs of the EU Member States would be attributed to the EU (to the extent of its competence).[256] The ILC and the Special Rapporteur rejected such an approach, however, deciding instead to develop rules of general application, which would be capable of applying to the EU as well as any other international organisation.

The responsibility regime for international organisations operates in very much the same manner as the State responsibility regime. International responsibility occurs when conduct consisting of an action or omission: (i) is attributable to that organisation under international law; and (ii) constitutes a breach of an international obligation of that organisation.[257] That international organisations can possess international obligations is no longer contested. In fact, it is a logical corollary of their possessing international legal personality, confirmed by the ICJ in the 1949 *Reparation* case.[258] In *Interpretation of the Agreement of 25 March 1951 between the WHO and Egypt* (1980), the ICJ unambiguously ruled that '[i]nternational organizations are subjects of international law and, as such, are bound by any obligations incumbent upon them under general rules of international law, under their constitutions or under international agreements to which they are parties'.[259] To the extent that international organisations are bound by international legal norms, they can be held internationally responsible for violating them, at least provided that the impugned acts are attributable to them.

Where the responsibility of an international organisation is engaged, the organisation may still invoke circumstances precluding wrongfulness well-known also to the law of State responsibility.[260] The legal consequences of a finding of responsibility, as well as the rules regarding the invocation of responsibility and countermeasures,[261] also echo the relevant State responsibility rules. They will not be discussed in detail here.

A major limitation of the rules laid down in the ARIO, unlike the ASR, is that their application in actual disputes will be rather limited, as international and national courts and tribunals do not normally have jurisdiction over disputes involving international organisations. International organisations for the most part cannot be sued before international tribunals, and may enjoy immunity before domestic courts. That being said, the ARIO may well be invoked in judicial proceedings filed against States in connection with acts of international organisations, such as proceedings against States contributing troops to UN military operations, as well as by domestic courts not accepting the immunity of the organisation. The ARIO could obviously also play its part outside the judicial context, in diplomatic and institutional practice, as do the ASR.

[254] See R Schütze, 'From Rome to Lisbon: "Executive Federalism" in the (New) European Union' (2010) 47 *CMLR* 1385.

[255] See P-J Kuijper and E Paasivirta, 'EU International Responsibility and its Attribution: From the Inside Looking Out' in M Evans and P Koutrakos (eds), *The International Responsibility of the European Union: European and International Perspectives* (Oxford, Hart, 2013) 35–71. E Paasivirta and P-J Kuijper, 'Does One Size Fit All? The European Community and the Responsibility of International Organizations' (2005) 36 *NILR* 169.

[256] Observations of Mr Kuijper, Observer for the European Commission, UNGA Sixth Committee, Summary Record of its 21st Meeting, 18 November 2004, UN Doc A/C.6/59/SR.21, para 18.

[257] Art 4 ARIO.

[258] *Reparation for Injuries Suffered in the Service of the United Nations* [1949] ICJ Rep 174, 185.

[259] *Interpretation of the Agreement of 25 March 1951 between the WHO and Egypt* [1980] ICJ Rep 73, para 37.

[260] Arts 20–27 ARIO.

[261] ibid, Arts 43–57.

A. Attribution of Conduct to International Organisations

The ARIO rules on attribution of conduct resemble those of the ASR but are not co-extensive. Like the ASR, the ARIO feature a provision on organic or agency attribution: they consider the conduct of organs or agents of an international organisation in the performance of functions of that organ or agent an act of that organisation under international law, whatever position the organ or agent holds in respect of the organisation.[262] Who is an organ or agent may seem straightforward enough: an organ or an agent is any official of the organisation and any other person acting for the organisation on the basis of functions conferred by an organ of the organisation.[263] In some circumstances, however, the characterisation of an actor as an agent, or not, of an organisation has been the subject of controversy. This is because it is often Member States who are implementing or exercising the powers of the international organisation, rather than the 'organs' of the organisation itself. In particular, the United Nations considers Member State troop contingents involved in UN peacekeeping operations as subsidiary organs of the United Nations in the sense of Article 6 ARIO.[264] Any wrongful acts committed by such contingents would then automatically be attributable to the UN. This view was apparently confirmed by the ECtHR, which ruled in the *Behrami* case that the decisive factor for attribution purposes was whether 'the United Nations Security Council retained ultimate authority and control so that operational command only was delegated'.[265] As a result, the conduct of member State forces placed at the disposal of the United Nations Interim Administration Mission in Kosovo or authorised by the United Nations was held to be attributable to the UN rather than to the Member States, even though the UN had no effective operational control over this conduct. Under another view, however, such troop contingents are considered as organs of the State providing them. They are never fully seconded to the UN but remain under the command of a national commander, and the State retains penal and disciplinary powers in respect of misconduct by its soldiers. Conduct of such troops, it is argued, should thus be attributed to the State under the rules of State responsibility. For these military operations, the ILC opted for a middle way in the ARIO, which provide that

> [t]he conduct of an organ of a State or an organ or agent of an international organization that is placed at the disposal of another international organization shall be considered under international law an act of the latter organization if the organization exercises effective control over that conduct.[266]

In so doing, they repudiate the UN's view on attribution in peacekeeping operations, while nevertheless providing for attribution of acts to the international organisation in international peacekeeping or military operations insofar as the organisation exercises 'effective control'.

[262] Art 6 ARIO.

[263] ILC, Commentary (3) to ARIO.

[264] Letter of 3 February 2004 by the United Nations Legal Counsel to the Director of the Codification Division, A/CN.4/545, Sect II.G.

[265] *Behrami and Behrami v France and Saramati v France, Germany and Norway* App nos 71412/01 and 78166/01 (ECtHR, 2 May 2007) para 133.

[266] Art 7 ARIO; applied in House of Lords (UK), *R (on the application of Al-Jedda) v Secretary of State for Defence* [2007] UKHL 58 (no effective control); and Higher Administrative Court of North Rhine-Westphalia (DE), *Anonymous v Federal Government*, 18 September 2014, Case No 4 A 2948/11, (2015) *Deutsches Verwaltungsblatt* 375 (no effective control). In Court of First Instance Brussels (BE), *Mukeshimana-Ngulinzira and others v Belgium and others*, 8 December 2010, RG No 04/4807/A and 07/15547/A, the Belgian court did not cite the ARIO but sought to determine factual operational control.

'Effective control' may be said to denote factual, operational control on the ground. This is at least the interpretation of courts in the Netherlands, hearing a number of cases that arose as a result of a Dutch UN peacekeeping contingent's failure to prevent acts of genocide in the vicinity of the Bosnian town of Srebrenica in 1995. So far, Dutch courts are the only courts that have engaged in-depth with the effective control standard as laid down in Article 7 ARIO. Accordingly, they can be seen as trailblazers to which other courts may turn for guidance. The *Srebrenica* litigation in the Netherlands consists of two sets of cases, one set known as *Mustafic* and *Nuhanovic*, and the other as *Mothers of Srebrenica*.[267]

Mustafic and *Nuhanovic* is a set of cases heard on final appeal by the Dutch Supreme Court in 2013. The case concerned the damage suffered by the relatives of a Bosnian electrician (*Mustafic*) who worked as a local employee for the Dutch peacekeeping force known as 'Dutchbat' and who was killed by the Bosnian Serbs, and for damages suffered by an interpreter who worked as a UN employee for Dutchbat and whose father and brother (*Nuhanovic*) also after eviction from the Dutchbat compound, suffered violent deaths at the hands of the troops of the Bosnian Serbs.[268]

Mothers of Srebrenica, for its part, was heard at first instance by the District Court of The Hague, and concerns the damages incurred by relatives of approximately 320 victims of the Srebrenica massacre,[269] resulting from the cooperation between Dutchbat and the Bosnian Serbs in the deportation of male Muslim refugees from Dutchbat's compound on 13 July 1995, refugees who were subsequently killed by Bosnian Serb militia.[270] *Mothers of Srebrenica* had initially also been brought against the United Nations, but the Dutch courts, up to the Supreme Court, as well as the European Court of Human Rights, had upheld the immunity of the UN.[271]

What is important for our purposes is that the various courts attributed a number of acts carried out within the framework of a UN peacekeeping operation to the Netherlands as a troop-contributing state on the basis of the 'effective control' standard, understood as operating on the basis of 'actual say or factual control'.[272] On the basis of this standard, the District Court in *Mothers of Srebrenica* attributed to the Netherlands, among other acts, separating the Bosnian Muslim men from the other refugees during the evacuation and cooperating in evacuating refugees who had sought refuge in the compound.[273]

However, this attribution of wrongful acts to the State does not exclude simultaneous attribution to the international organisation. It is certainly possible that in the *Srebrenica*

[267] The effective control standard espoused in the appeals judgments in the former set of cases was cited approvingly by the ILC in its 2011 ARIO Commentary to Art 7 ARIO, 90–91, comment no 15. Neither the Supreme Court decision in these cases, nor the first instance decision in *Mothers of Srebrenica* (see below, respectively (n 268) and (n 270)) had yet been rendered at the time of drafting the commentary. As these decisions also applied the effective control standard, one can safely assume that the ILC would have approved of them as well.

[268] Supreme Court (NL), *State of the Netherlands v Mustafic et al*, 6 September 2013, NL:HR:2013:BZ9228 (AG's advisory opinion: conclusion NL:PHR:2013:BZ9228); *State of the Netherlands et al v Nuhanovic*, 6 September 2013, NL:HR:2013:BZ9225 (AG's advisory opinion: NL:PHR:2013:BZ9225).

[269] The case was brought by ten individual claimants and by the foundation *Mothers of Srebrenica*, a legal person which promotes the interests of approximately 6,000 surviving relatives of the Srebrenica victims.

[270] District Court of The Hague (NL), *Mothers of Srebrenica v State of the Netherlands*, 16 July 2014, NL:RBDHA:2014:8562. The ECLI number of the unofficial English translation is NL:RBDHA:2014:8748.

[271] Supreme Court (NL), 13 April 2012, NJ 2014/262, NL:HR:BW1999, with annotation by NJ Schrijver; *Stichting Mothers of Srebrenica and others v the Netherlands* App no 65542/12 (ECtHR, 27 June 2013). See also annotation ThM de Boer 'Netherlands Judicial Decisions Involving Questions of Private International Law: Can the United Nations be Sued for its Role in the Srebrenica Massacre?' (2013) *NILR* 121.

[272] *Mothers of Srebrenica* (n 270) para 4.34.

[273] ibid, para 4.144.

cases, both the Netherlands and the UN exercised effective command and control over the events at the time, and that Dutchbat's failure to act could have been attributable to both.

In *Mustafic and Nuhanovic*, the Supreme Court drew attention to Article 48 ARIO in this respect, which provides that '[w]here an international organization and one or more States or other international organizations are responsible for the same internationally wrongful act, the responsibility of each State or organization may be invoked in relation to that act'. According to the Court this provision 'expressly leaves open the possibility [...] of dual attribution to the international organization and the State concerned' and thus to 'more than one State or organization being held responsible for the consequences of an internationally wrongful act'.[274] It is observed, however, that Article 48 ARIO does not necessarily acknowledge a principle of dual *attribution*, but rather of dual *responsibility*. The responsibility of a State and an international organisation may be engaged not on the basis of the single wrongful act being attributed to both of them, but rather on the basis of *parallel* attribution based on *independent acts*.[275]

What can ultimately be gathered from the *Srebrenica* cases in terms of attribution, is that the effective control standard is a *factual* one which does not concern itself with *formal* authority structures. Where such formal structures do not correspond to reality, the actual control structure will prevail. As national contingents always remain to a certain extent under the command and control of States, even when placed at the disposal of an international organisation, it would seem that their acts are attributable to troop-contributing States in the first place, and only secondarily to the organisation, to the extent that proof is offered of effective control also being exercised by the latter. Sole attribution to the organisation on the basis of Article 7 ARIO would then be rather exceptional. This may in fact also be the inference to be drawn from the *Jaloud* judgment (2014) of the ECtHR, which attributed a wrongful act committed by Dutch troops deployed in Iraq in the framework of a multinational operation to the Netherlands, even though Dutch troops were under the command of an officer from the United Kingdom.[276] The Court reasoned that the Netherlands assumed responsibility for providing security in south-eastern Iraq 'to the exclusion of other participating States, and retained full command over its contingent there'.[277] In so doing, the Court seemed to equate 'full command' with 'effective control' for attribution purposes. As States always retain the power to take disciplinary action and impose criminal sanctions, they can be said to necessarily retain 'full command', and accordingly, all acts of national troop contingents are per se attributable to the State. Such an interpretation may be undesirable, however, as it would allow international organisations to escape all responsibility. The better view arguably is that, while States may retain command over their forces, an international organisation could well have effective control over these forces' acts.[278]

The practice cited by the ILC in its Commentary to Article 7 ARIO almost exclusively concerns military action, as it is mostly in such an operational context that organs (troops) of a State or international organisation are placed at the disposal of an(other) international organisation. Still, in its Commentary the ILC also refers to an agreement between the

[274] *Mustafic* (n 268) para 3.9.4.

[275] A Nollkaemper and D Jacobs, 'Shared Responsibility in International Law: A Conceptual Framework' (2013) 34 *MJIL* 359.

[276] *Jaloud* (n 8).

[277] ibid, para 149.

[278] A Sari, 'Untangling Extra-territorial Jurisdiction from International Responsibility in *Jaloud v Netherlands*: Old Problem, New Solutions?' (2015) 54 *Military Law and Law of War Review* 12.

WHO and the PAHO, pursuant to which the latter is to serve as the Regional Committee and the Regional Office of the WHO, engaging the WHO's responsibility.[279]

Apart from provisions on organic attribution and 'effective control'-based attribution to international organisations, the ARIO also contain two other provisions on attribution of conduct copied straight from the ASR. The first is a provision on ultra vires that stipulates that the conduct of an organ or agent is attributable to the organisation if (s)he acts in an official capacity and within the overall functions of that organisation, even if the conduct exceeds the authority of that organ or agent or contravenes instructions.[280] The second is a provision which sets out that conduct is attributable to an organisation when it is acknowledged and adopted by an international organisation as its own.[281] This second provision is based on Article 11 ASR, which involves States acknowledging the acts of private entities as their own. There is little – if any – practice of an international organisation doing so.

As far as attribution with respect to the EU is concerned, it bears noting that the ILC has referred to the on-going debate concerning a purported *lex specialis* character of rules of attribution of Member State conduct to the EU. It could be argued that conduct of EU Member States implementing binding acts of the EU could be attributed to the EU,[282] because the Member States were acting as organs or agents of the EU in the sense of Article 6 ARIO. A WTO panel has indeed held so much in 2005, accepting

> the European Communities' explanation of what amounts to its *sui generis* domestic constitutional arrangements that Community laws are generally not executed through authorities at Community level but rather through recourse to the authorities of its Member States which, in such a situation, "act de facto as organs of the Community, for which the Community would be responsible under WTO law and international law in general".[283]

The European Court of Human Rights, in the *Bosphorus* case, however, has attributed Member State action giving effect to binding EU legislation regarding the imposition of sanctions on economic operators, to the Member States themselves rather than to the EU.[284]

B. Attribution of Responsibility to International Organisations

The ARIO feature a number of provisions on attribution of responsibility, short of conduct, to international organisations. Some of these are directly borrowed from the ASR. An international organisation is internationally responsible, for instance, where it aids or assists, directs or controls, or coerces a State or another international organisation in the commission of an internationally wrongful act by the State or the latter organisation.[285] Another

[279] ARIO, Commentary (16) to Art 7.

[280] Art 8 ARIO.

[281] Art 9 ARIO.

[282] Commentary (2) to Article 64 ARIO, 166.

[283] WTO Panel Report, European Communities – Protection of Trademarks and Geographical Indications for Agricultural Products and Foodstuffs – Complaint by the United States (EC – Trademarks and Geographical Indications (US)), 20 April 2005, WT/DS174/R, para 7.725.

[284] *Bosphorus Hava Yollari Turizm ve Ticaret AS v Ireland* App no 45036/98 (ECtHR, 30 June 2005) para 137. However, EU Member States were eventually allowed to rely on the EU system in this case, as the latter provided 'equivalent' human rights protection, which was not manifestly deficient in individual cases.

[285] Arts 14–16 ARIO, based on Art 16–18 ASR.

provision on attribution of responsibility is unique to the ARIO, namely Article 17, which provides that an international organisation incurs international responsibility if it circumvents one of its international obligations by adopting a decision binding Member States to commit an act, or authorising Member States to commit an act that would be internationally wrongful if committed by the former organisation.[286] The ILC has justified the inclusion of this article on the ground that

> the relations between an international organization and its Member States … may allow the former organization to influence the conduct of members also in cases that are not envisaged in Articles 16 to 18 on the responsibility of States for internationally wrongful acts.[287]

It is not fully clear in what circumstances Article 17 ARIO could exactly be applied. The commentary only cites some hypothetical and rather unspecific cases. Note that the scenario enshrined in Article 17 ARIO constitutes the reverse scenario of the one contemplated in Article 61 ARIO (see below).

C. Countermeasures

The ARIO, just like the ASR, allow for the taking of countermeasures, in this case by an injured State or international organisation against an international organisation, which is responsible for an internationally wrongful act.[288] It remains that practice regarding countermeasures taken against international organisations is extremely rare, and is largely limited to the rather special regime of the WTO, which allows for the taking of institutionally supervised countermeasures by or against the EU (a member of the WTO) in case of non-compliance. Still, as a matter of principle, the taking of countermeasures against international organisations should not be excluded. Therefore, the ARIO provide for a rather elaborate regime governing such measures. This regime is largely a copy of the relevant ASR regime, but with some special rules for international organisations.

Thus, the ARIO, cognisant of the tasks entrusted to the international organisation by the Member States, specify, that 'countermeasures shall, as far as possible, be taken in such a way as to limit their effects on the exercise by the responsible international organisation of its functions'.[289] Also, members of an international organisation may only in exceptional circumstances resort to countermeasures against the organisation, namely when the general conditions for countermeasures are met, when the countermeasures are not inconsistent with the rules of the organisation; and no appropriate means are available for otherwise inducing compliance with the obligations of the responsible international organisation concerning cessation of the breach and reparation.[290] They cannot be taken in response to a breach of an international obligation under the rules of the organisation unless such countermeasures are provided for by those rules.[291]

[286] Art 17 ARIO.
[287] ILC, Commentary (3) to Chapter 4 ARIO.
[288] Arts 51–57 ARIO. These provisions develop Art 22 ARIO, which characterises countermeasures as circumstances precluding wrongfulness, just like the ILC did in the ASR. See also F Dopagne, *Les contre-mesures des organisations internationales* (Paris, LGDJ, 2010).
[289] Art 51(4) ARIO.
[290] ibid, Art 52(1).
[291] ibid, Art 52(2).

VIII. Responsibility of States in Connection with the Conduct of International Organisations

The special relationship between international organisations and States, in particular their Member States, has warranted the inclusion of a separate Part V in the ARIO, which addresses the responsibility of States in connection with the conduct of international organisations. It should be clear up front, however, that as international organisations are separate legal persons their liabilities can ordinarily *not* be attributed to the Member States that established them. In this respect, organisations somewhat resemble limited liability corporations, whose shareholders are not liable for the liabilities of the corporations whose stock they hold. Still, there may be circumstances of a (member) State influencing the commission of a wrongful act by an international organisation. These circumstances may engage the responsibility of the Member State, possibly alongside the responsibility of the organisation. To a large extent they mirror the circumstances concerning the attribution of responsibility to international organisations discussed above.[292]

Articles 58–60 ARIO provide for the responsibility of a State aiding or assisting, directing or controlling, or coercing an international organisation to commit an internationally wrongful act. Again, the practice cited by the ILC in its Commentaries is scarce, so that it remains elusive when exactly these articles could be applied, all the more so because it is indicated that acts taken by a Member State in accordance with the rules of the organisation cannot qualify as unlawful aid, assistance, direction, control or coercion.[293] The latter disclaimer might imply that, for instance, the use of a veto by a Member State in the context of institutional decision-making, resulting in a wrongful failure to act by the organisation, would not engage the Member State's responsibility.

Article 61 ARIO, as discussed above, is the reverse scenario of Article 17 ARIO, and provides that a State member of an international organisation incurs international responsibility if, by taking advantage of the fact that the organisation has competence in relation to the subject-matter of one of the State's international obligations, it circumvents that obligation by causing the organisation to commit an act that, if committed by the State, would have constituted a breach of the obligation. In essence, this rather laboriously formulated provision aims to ensure that Member States, by transferring competences to an international organisation, do not also transfer their responsibility for wrongful acts. This principle was most famously laid down by the European Court of Human Rights in the *Bosphorus* case, where the Court held that Member States might retain responsibility under the ECHR when transferring functions to international organisations, on the ground that

> absolving Contracting States completely from their Convention responsibility in the areas covered by such a transfer would be incompatible with the purpose and object of the Convention; the guarantees of the Convention could be limited or excluded at will, thereby depriving it of its peremptory character and undermining the practical and effective nature of its safeguards [...]. The State is considered to retain Convention liability in respect of treaty commitments subsequent to the entry into force of the Convention [...].[294]

[292] Arts 14–17 ARIO.
[293] Commentary (4) to Art 58 ARIO, Commentary (4) to Art 59 ARIO, and Commentary (3) to Art 60 ARIO.
[294] *Bosphorus* (n 284) para 154.

An absolute interpretation of this principle may, however, result in the responsibility of Member States by virtue of their mere membership. This would fly in the face of the separate legal personality of organisations and their Member States. To prevent this outcome, the ARIO require that there be a significant link between the conduct of the circumventing Member State and that of the international organisation, in the sense that the act of the international organisation be caused by the Member State.[295] There is a rather rich case law of the European Court of Human Rights, which ascertains intervening Member State action in the context of activity of an international organisation – the EU in particular – for purposes of attributing responsibility to the Member State under the ECHR.[296]

In the relevant cases, a finding of Member State responsibility is, however, not just dependent on an intervening act of the Member State, but also on the absence of equivalent protection of rights offered by the organisation, and the absence of manifest deficiencies in the system of rights protection.[297] Because of this rather high threshold, the Court has so far not actually held a Member State responsible for violations committed by an international organisation.[298]

Article 62 ARIO, finally, provides that a State member of an international organisation is responsible for an internationally wrongful act of that organisation if: (i) it has accepted responsibility for that act towards the injured party; or (ii) it has led the injured party to rely on its responsibility. Acceptance could for instance result from a constituent instrument of the international organisation, which provides for Member State responsibility vis-à-vis third parties. As far as reliance is concerned, there is no presumption that a third party should be able to rely on the responsibility of Member States, although reliance can be inferred from the circumstances. There is some judicial practice applying the principle: an arbitral tribunal hearing a case brought by a creditor against Member States of the liquidated Arab Organization for Industrialization cited 'the trust of third parties contracting with the organization as to its ability to cope with its commitments because of the constant support of the Member States' in support of an argument in favour of Member State liability in the case.[299]

Note that Part V ARIO is not normally applicable to the scenario of States exercising their *discretion* in the context of international institutional decision-making. Such States will be held responsible *for their own acts*, and there is no need to inquire whether the requirements for attribution of responsibility under Articles 58–61 ARIO are satisfied. Thus, in the *Matthews* case (1999), the ECtHR held the United Kingdom responsible for its own conduct when freely entering into an international agreement under EU auspices – primary EU law that is only binding upon acceptance by the Member States – that deprived residents of Gibraltar of the right to vote in European elections.[300]

[295] See also Commentary (7) to Art 61 ARIO.

[296] eg *Boivin v 34 Member States of the Council of Europe* App no 73250/01 (ECtHR, 9 September 2008); *Kokkelvisserij v the Netherlands* App no 13645/05 (ECtHR, 20 January 2009); *Gasparini v Italy and Belgium* App no 10750/03 (ECtHR, 12 May 2009); *Ullens de Schooten et Rezabek contre Belgique* App nos 3989/07 and 38353/07 (ECtHR, 20 September 2011); *Ferreira Santos Pardal contre Portugal* App no 30123/10 (ECtHR, 4 September 2012) (only in French); *Djokaba Lambi Longa v the Netherlands* App no 33917/12 (ECtHR, 9 October 2012); *Michaud v France* App no 12323/11 (ECtHR, 6 December 2012) (only in French).

[297] eg *Bosphorus* (n 284); *Gasparini* (n 296).

[298] For a discussion, see C Ryngaert, 'Oscillating Between Embracing and Avoiding Bosphorus: The European Court of Human Rights on Member State Responsibility for Acts of International Organisations and the Case of the European Union' (2014) 2 *ELR* 176.

[299] *Westland Helicopters Ltd v Arab Organization for Industrialization and Others*, Second Arbitral Award, 21 July 1991, 429–30, para 56.

[300] *Matthews v United Kingdom* App no 24833/94 (ECtHR, 18 February 1999) para 33.

Somewhat similarly, the ICJ held in the *Application of the Interim Accord* Case (2011) that Greece was responsible for its own acts preventing the FYROM from acceding to NATO, in violation of the provisions of an Interim Accord of 1995, even if such acts had consequences on the actual final decision of an international organisation – NATO – regarding whether or not to invite FYROM for membership. The Court held in this respect that

> [t]he issue before the Court is thus not whether NATO's decision may be attributed to the Respondent, but rather whether the Respondent violated the Interim Accord as a result of its own conduct. Nothing in the Application before the Court can be interpreted as requesting the Court to pronounce on whether NATO acted legally in deferring the Applicant's invitation for membership in NATO. Therefore, the dispute does not concern, as contended by the Respondent, the conduct of NATO or the Member States of NATO, but rather solely the conduct of the Respondent.[301]

Bibliography

Ago, R, 'Le délit international' (1939) 68 *RdC* 419.

Amerasinghe, CF, *Local Remedies in International Law*, 2nd edn (Cambridge, CUP, 2004).

Anzilotti, D, *Teoria generale della responsabilità dello stato nel diritto internazionale* (Florence, Lumachi, 1902).

Boisson de Chazournes, L, *Les contre-mesures dans les relations internationales économiques* (Paris, Pedone, 1992).

Cohn, G, 'La théorie de la responsabilité internationale' (1939) 68 *RdC* 207.

Crawford, J and Olleson, S, 'The Character and Forms of International Responsibility' in MD Evans (ed), *International Law*, 4th edn (Oxford, OUP, 2014) 443–76.

Crawford, J, Pellet, A and Olleson, S (eds), *The Law of International Responsibility* (Oxford, OUP, 2010).

Crawford, J, *State Responsibility: The General Part* (Cambridge, CUP, 2013).

De Visscher, C, 'La responsabilité des États' (1923) 2 *RdC* 89.

Dopagne, F, *Les contre-mesures des organisations internationales* (Paris, LGDJ, 2010).

Dupuy, PM, 'Le fait générateur de la responsabilité internationale des Etats' (1984) 188 *RdC* 9.

Epiney, A, *Die völkerrechtliche Verantwortlichkeit von Staaten für rechtswidriges Verhalten im Zusammenhang mit Aktionen Privater* (Berlin, Nomos, 1992).

Eustathiades, CT, 'Les sujets de Droit International et la responsabilité internationale : nouvelles tendances' (1953) 84 *RdC* 397.

Focarelli, C, *Le contromisure nel diritto internazionale* (Milan, Giuffrè, 1994).

Giegerich, T, 'Verantwortlichkeit und Haftung für Akte internationaler und supranationaler Organisationen' (2005) 104 *Zeitschrift für vergleichende Rechtswissenschaft* 163.

Gutiérrez Espada, C, *El hecho ilícito internacional* (Madrid, Dickinson, 2005).

Hartwig, M, *Die Haftung der Mitgliedstaaten für Internationale Organisationen* (Heidelberg, Springer, 1993).

Milanovic, M, 'State Responsibility for Genocide' (2006) 17 *EJIL* 553.

Paasivirta, E and Kuijper, P-J, 'Does One Size Fit All? The European Community and the Responsibility of International Organizations' (2005) 36 *NYIL* 169.

[301] *Application of the Interim Accord* (n 224) para 42.

Pernice, I, 'Die Haftung internationaler Organisationen und ihrer Mitarbeiter' (1988) 26 *Archiv des Völkerrechts* 406.

Provost, R (ed), *State Responsibility in International Law* (Dartmouth, Ashgate, 2002).

Ragazzi, M (ed), *International Responsibility Today: Essays in Memory of Oscar Schachter* (Leiden, Brill, 2005).

Ragazzi, M, *Responsibility of International Organizations: Essays in Memory of Sir Ian Brownlie* (Leiden, Nijhoff, 2013).

Ruiloba Santana, E, 'Consideraciones sobre el concepto y elementos del acto ilícito en Derecho internacional' in *Symbolae García Arias (Estudios de derecho internacional)* (Zaragoza, Temis, 1974) 381–405.

Ruiloba Alvariño, J, *Las contramedidas: Análisis de la práctica española* (Paracuellos de Jarama, Dilex, 2012).

Sarooshi, D, *Remedies and Responsibility for the Actions of International Organizations* (Leiden, Nijhoff, 2014).

Sicilianos, LA, *Les reactions décentralisées à l'illicite : des contre-mesures à la légitime défense* (Paris, LGDJ, 1990).

Further Reading

Bratspies, RM and Miller, RA (eds), *Transboundary Harm in International Law: Lessons from the 'Trail Smelter' Arbitration* (New York, CUP, 2006).

Corten, O, 'L'état de nécessité peut-il justifier un recours à la force non constitutif d'agression?' (2004) 1 *The Global Community Yearbook of International Law and Jurisprudence* 11.

Dawidowicz, M, Third-Party Countermeasures in International Law (Cambridge, CUP, 2017).

Dublin, L, 'Les garanties de non-répétition à l'aune des affaires LaGrand et Avena: la révolution n'aura pas lieu' (2005) *Revue Generale de Droit International Public* 859.

Garibian, S, 'Vers l'émergence d'un droit individuel à la protection diplomatique?' (2008) 54 *Annuaire français de droit international* 119.

Ichim, O, *Just Satisfaction under the European Convention on Human Rights* (Cambridge, CUP, 2014).

Laursen, A, 'The Use of Force and (the State of) Necessity' (2004) 37 *Vanderbilt Journal of Transnational Law* 485.

Nollkaemper, A and Jacobs, D, 'Shared Responsibility in International Law: A Conceptual Framework' (2013) 34 *MJIL* 359.

Meng, W, 'Internationale Organisationen im völkerrechtlichen Deliktsrecht' (1985) 45 *ZaöRV* 324.

Reuter, P, 'Le dommage comme condition de la responsabilité internationale' in *Estudios de derecho internacional: homenaje al profesor Miaja de la Muela* (Madrid, Éditorial Tecnos, 1979) 837–46.

Ruys, T, 'Of Arms, Funding and "Non-Lethal Assistance" – Issues Surrounding Third-State Intervention in the Syrian Civil War' (2014) 13 *CJIL* 13.

Ryngaert, C, 'Oscillating Between Embracing and Avoiding Bosphorus: The European Court of Human Rights on Member State Responsibility for Acts of International Organisations and the Case of the European Union' (2014) 2 *ELR* 176.

Sabahi, B, *Compensation and Restitution in Investor-State Arbitration: Principles and Practice* (Oxford, OUP, 2011).

Schmalenbach, K, *Die Haftung Internationaler Organisationen im Rahmen von Militäreinsätzen und Territorialverwaltungen* (Frankfurt, Lang, 2004).

Touzé, S, *La protection des droits des nationaux à l'etranger: recherches sur la protection diplomatique* (Paris, Pedone, 2007).

Villalpando, S, *L'émergence de la communauté internationale dans la responsabilité des États* (Geneva, Presses Universitaires de France, 2005).

Wouters, J and Odermatt, J, 'Are All International Organizations Created Equal?' (2012) 9 *International Organizations Law Review* 7.

13

Peaceful Settlement of Disputes

I. Introduction

Having international law is one thing; ensuring that international law is complied with, and that disputes are settled, is quite another. Procedures and institutions that ensure compliance and settle disputes are crucial to promote the rule of law at the international level. (The threat of) decisions, awards, judgments and enforcement help to stimulate compliance with international legal rules.

While the institutionalisation of compliance-monitoring and dispute settlement mechanisms at the international level lags far behind institutionalisation at the domestic level, it is nevertheless remarkable how many international supervisory bodies,[1] fact-finding commissions, compliance committees, courts, tribunals, etc have been established over the years.[2] James Crawford has observed in this respect: 'It is more common for practitioners these days to have the choice between methods of dispute settlement than to have none, whereas not so long ago it was more common not to have any forum to appeal to'.[3]

This chapter provides an overview of the varied mechanisms of peaceful dispute settlement in international law. It first briefly introduces the different non-binding, diplomatic and non-judicial methods of dispute settlement (Section II), before discussing the binding judicial methods of dispute settlement (Section III). Particular prominence is reserved for the jurisdiction and procedure of the ICJ, the main judicial organ of the UN, in both

[1] Notably in environmental law and human rights law, where the risk of violations is sizable, a host of compliance-monitoring bodies has been established. Regarding the environment, see eg the Conference of the Parties under the United Nations Convention to Combat Desertification in Countries Experiencing Serious Drought and/or Desertification, Particularly in Africa (adopted 17 May 1994, entered into force 26 December 1996) 1954 UNTS 3; and the Conference of the Parties under the United Nations Framework Convention on Climate Change (adopted 9 May 1992, entered into force 21 March 1994) 1771 UNTS 107. Regarding human rights law, see notably the different treaty bodies that monitor the implementation of their respective human rights treaties, as discussed in Chapter 16, Section VI(A).

[2] This has led to the establishment of a new *Journal of International Dispute Settlement* (Oxford, 2010). As the editorial to the first issue notes: 'The causes of this surge in interest are multiple, and lie both in the quantitative importance of international dispute resolution and in the qualitative significance of the legal, economic and sociological issues raised': T Schultz, 'Editorial' (2010) 1 *JIDS* 1.

[3] J Crawford, 'Continuity and Discontinuity in International Dispute Settlement: An Inaugural Lecture' (2010) 1 *JIDS* 3, 14.

contentious (between States) and advisory cases. Some brief reflections on the relationship between the ICJ and the UNSC,[4] on dispute settlement within Europe, and on the proliferation of international courts and tribunals,[5] follow. In Section IV, concluding observations consider the question of compliance with international decisions purporting to settle disputes.

II. Diplomatic and Non-Judicial Methods

A. Diplomatic Versus Judicial Methods

A cardinal principle laid down in Article 2(3) UN Charter, is that disputes are to be settled peacefully.[6] This principle also features in a number of other international and regional treaties, such as the European Convention for the Peaceful Settlement of Disputes (ECPSD) of 1957 adopted within the framework of the Council of Europe,[7] and is further developed in the 'Manila Declaration on the Peaceful Settlement of International Disputes', adopted by the UN General Assembly in 1982. The principle that disputes are to be settled peacefully does not mean that States are obliged to settle every dispute they are involved in. It merely implies that, for the purposes of settling their disputes, States may not engage in the threat or use of force.[8] An exception to the freedom of States to settle their disputes are disputes 'the continuance of which is likely to endanger the maintenance of international peace and security'.[9] According to Article 33 UN Charter, the parties to such disputes 'shall' seek a solution. Nonetheless, even in the context of such disputes, States retain a 'right of free choice of means', ie the right to choose between the means listed in Article 33.[10] The UN

[4] On the UN and its principal organs, see Chapter 6, Section VIII.

[5] For a comprehensive overview of regional organisations and their courts and tribunals which have mushroomed across the globe in recent years, see Chapter 7.

[6] Art 2(3) UN Charter: 'All Members shall settle their international disputes by peaceful means in such a manner that international peace and security, and justice, are not endangered'. See also Art 33(1) UN Charter, which contains an explicit obligation to settle disputes that are likely to endanger international peace and security.

[7] European Convention for the Peaceful Settlement of Disputes (adopted on 29 April 1957, entered into force on 30 April 1958) CETS No 23. As of 12 May 2018, the ECPSD has been ratified by 14 States, out of which 11 are Member States of the EU. See further eg H Wehberg, 'La Convention européenne pour le règlement pacifique des différends' in *Varia Juris Gentium* (Leiden, Sijthoff, 1959) 391–99; H Miehsler, 'The European Convention for the Peaceful Settlement of Disputes' in H Kipp, F Meyer and A Steinkamm (eds), *Um Recht und Freiheit Festschrift für Friedrich August Freiherr von der Heydte* (Berlin, Duncker & Humblot, 1977) 355–61; and S Torres Bernárdez, 'L'arbitrage interétatique avec des références particulières à la Convention européenne pour le règlement des différends du 29 avril 1957' in D Bardonnet (ed), *The Peaceful Settlement of International Disputes in Europe* (Dordrecht, Nijhoff, 1991) 205–67. For other examples of legal instruments confirming the principle, see eg Preamble, para 11 Friendly Relations Declaration; Art 279 UNCLOS; Art 1 NATO Treaty; Art X Treaty for Collaboration in Economic, Social, and Cultural Matters, and for Collective Self-Defence (adopted 17 March 1948, entered into force 25 August 1948) 19 UNTS 51, ie the 'Brussels Treaty' which constituted the preconfiguration of the later Western European Union, as amended by the Protocol Modifying and Completing the Brussels Treaty (adopted 23 October 1954, entered into force 6 May 1955); and Arts 1–2 American Treaty on Pacific Settlement (adopted 30 April 1948, entered into force 6 May 1949) 30 UNTS 50 (Pact of Bogotá). Also the OSCE framework encompasses a number of mechanisms for peaceful dispute settlement, on which see Section II(C).

[8] Art 2(4) UN Charter.

[9] Art 33 UN Charter.

[10] Part I, paras 3 and 10 Manila Declaration. This right of free choice was reaffirmed by UNGA Res 53/101, 'Principles and Guidelines for International Negotiations', 20 January 1999, UN Doc A/RES/53/101. See also *Legality of Use of Force* (Yugoslavia v Belgium) (Order) [1999] ICJ Rep 124, para 48.

General Assembly has 'invite[d] all Member States to resort more often to the peaceful settlement of disputes and conflicts by the means provided for in the Charter'.[11]

Apart from the possibility to resort to regional agencies or arrangements,[12] Article 33 envisages dispute settlement through either diplomatic or judicial means. The settlement of a dispute through diplomatic means, including negotiation, good offices, mediation, fact-finding and conciliation, is not binding. The settlement of disputes through judicial means, including arbitration and judicial settlement, is binding. Non-judicial or informal mechanisms are particularly attractive in cases where the stakes are high, or where truly *legal* questions may be too narrowly framed and neglect political, social and economic dimensions which may be germane to eventually solve the conflict.[13]

Still, international law may play its role in the context of diplomatic methods. It may, for instance, facilitate negotiations. After all, international law is supposed to constitute common ground for all parties (although their respective interpretations may of course differ considerably). At the same time, international law may serve to strengthen the position of weaker parties in international negotiations, as it protects them from unfair terms imposed by stronger parties. Conversely, diplomatic methods may continue to play a role where a dispute has been submitted to judicial or quasi-judicial dispute settlement. For example, negotiations between the parties to a WTO dispute are incorporated in the first stage of dispute settlement under the WTO Dispute Settlement Understanding (the 60 days consultation stage), during which time the WTO Director-General may also act as a mediator.[14] Along the same lines, the ICJ held that 'the fact that negotiations are being actively pursued during the proceedings is not, legally, any obstacle to the exercise by the Court of its judicial function'.[15]

B. The Different Diplomatic or Non-Judicial Methods

i. Negotiation

The most common method by which States settle their disputes is negotiation.[16] Negotiations consist of discussions between the parties to a dispute with a view to reconciling, or at least coming to an understanding of, their diverging opinions.[17] Thus, 'the concept of

[11] UNGA Res 2627 (XXV), 'Declaration on the Occasion of the Twenty-fifth Anniversary of the United Nations', UN Doc A/RES/26/27, 24 October 1970, para 4.

[12] On which see Chapter 7.

[13] cp the US amendment of its Declaration in the *Nicaragua* case, just before Nicaragua filed its application: 'Notwithstanding the terms of the aforesaid declaration, this proviso shall take effect immediately and shall remain in force for two years, so as to foster the continuing regional dispute settlement process which seeks a negotiated solution to the interrelated political, economic and security problems of Central America': *Military and Paramilitary Activities in and against Nicaragua* (Nicaragua v United States of America) [1984] ICJ Rep 392, para 13.

[14] WTO Agreement, Annex 2: 'Understanding On Rules And Procedures Governing The Settlement Of Disputes' in *The Legal Texts: The Results Of The Uruguay Round Of Multilateral Trade Negotiations* (Cambridge, CUP, 1994), Art 4(3). On WTO dispute settlement, see further Chapter 19, Section III(A).

[15] *Aegean Sea Continental Shelf* (Greece v Turkey) [1978] ICJ Rep 1, para 29.

[16] cp JG Merrills, *International Dispute Settlement*, 6th edn (Cambridge, CUP, 2017) 2: 'negotiation is employed more frequently than all the other methods put together'.

[17] MN Shaw, *International Law*, 8th edn (Cambridge, CUP, 2017) 767; J Wouters, 'Government by Negotiation' in S Cassese (ed), *Research Handbook on Global Administrative Law* (Cheltenham, Edward Elgar, 2016) 196–211.

"negotiations" differs from the concept of "dispute", and requires – at the very least – a genuine attempt by one of the disputing parties to engage in discussions with the other disputing party with a view to resolving the dispute'.[18] What differentiates negotiations from other means of dispute settlement is that they do not involve a third party.[19] Moreover, a negotiated settlement is not binding, unless the negotiating States agree it is so, in which case the negotiations result in a treaty.[20] Even when negotiations do not by themselves lead to a settlement, they may constitute a useful precursor to other settlement procedures and facilitate the latter by clearly defining the subject matter of the dispute and what is at stake.[21]

The 'Principles and Guidelines for International Negotiation' adopted by the UN General Assembly in 1999 stress 'the important role that constructive and effective negotiations can play in attaining the purposes of the Charter by contributing to [inter alia] the peaceful settlement of disputes'.[22] According to the Manila Declaration, 'States should, without prejudice to the right of free choice of means, bear in mind that direct negotiations are a flexible and effective means of peaceful settlement of their disputes'.[23]

There is no general obligation under customary international law for States to settle their dispute by means of negotiation.[24] Nevertheless, in particular situations, the ICJ has recognised that the State Parties to a dispute are under a customary international law duty to enter into negotiations.[25] Also, some treaties explicitly provide for a duty to negotiate before recourse is had to other methods of dispute settlement.[26] While there may not be a general obligation to settle disputes by means of negotiation, the Manila Declaration provides that when States resort to negotiation, they should negotiate 'meaningfully, in order to arrive at an early settlement acceptable to the parties'.[27] According to the Negotiation Principles, '[n]egotiations should be conducted in good faith'.[28] Thus, States are required 'to act honestly and reasonably and to make a genuine attempt to reach a settlement' once they have voluntarily entered into negotiations'.[29]

[18] *Application of the International Convention on the Elimination of All Forms of Racial Discrimination* (Georgia v Russian Federation) [2011] ICJ Rep 70, para 157.

[19] Shaw (n 17) 767.

[20] M Dixon, *Textbook on International Law*, 7th edn (Oxford, OUP, 2013) 287. cp Chapter 2 on Sources: Treaty Law, Section V(A)(i): 'As a general rule, treaties are the result of a negotiation process'.

[21] cp *The Mavrommatis Palestine Concessions* (Greece v Britain) [1924] PCIJ Series A, No 2, 15: 'before a dispute can be made the subject of an action at law, its subject matter should have been clearly defined by means of diplomatic negotiations'.

[22] UNGA Res 53/101 (n 10) preamble, para 7.

[23] Part I, para 10 Manila Declaration. See also UNGA Res 53/101 (n 10) preamble, para 4.

[24] Dixon (n 20) 288.

[25] *North Sea Continental Shelf* [1969] ICJ Rep 3, para 85: 'in accordance with the ideas which have always underlain the development of the legal régime of the continental shelf in this field, namely: (a) the parties are under an obligation to enter into negotiations with a view to arriving at an agreement […]'. For a more general statement, see eg *Fisheries Jurisdiction* (United Kingdom of Great Britain and Northern Ireland v Iceland) [1973] ICJ Rep 3, Dissenting Opinion of Judge Nervo, 45: 'The obligation to negotiate is a principle of general international law'.

[26] eg Art 283(1) UNCLOS.

[27] Part I, para 10 Manila Declaration.

[28] UNGA Res 53/101 (n 10) operative clause 2(a). What this entails is further specified in clauses 2(b)–(g).

[29] Dixon (n 20) 288; still, Dixon considers such an obligation to be 'too vague to be of any practical value'. On negotiation as a means of dispute settlement, see further Merrills (n 16) 1–25 and RP Jr Barnidge, 'The International Law of Negotiation as a Means of Dispute Settlement' (2013) 36 *Fordham International Law Journal* 545.

ii. Good Offices and Mediation

When negotiations between the parties to a dispute are stalled, the parties may employ other diplomatic methods of dispute settlement, such as good offices, mediation, inquiry/fact-finding and conciliation. In the case of good offices, a third party, normally a 'neutral trusted by both sides',[30] offers its services and acts as a facilitating go-between, providing the parties to the dispute with an additional channel of communication.[31] This third party can be one or several individuals, a State or group of States, an international organisation or a non-governmental organisation.[32] As the party offering its good offices will attempt to persuade the parties to the dispute to negotiate and to reach a satisfactory settlement by themselves, good offices and negotiation are normally part of the same process.[33]

If the third party takes on a more active role, it will be termed a 'mediator'. The line between good offices and mediation is often a fine one. Still, indications of mediation are that the parties to the dispute were brought together by the third party, that the latter interprets their proposals, and that it is authorised and expected to actively take part in the negotiations, notably by advancing fresh proposals and suggesting terms of settlement.[34] Good offices or mediation cannot be forced on the parties to the dispute, but can only take place with their consent. Relatedly, a mediator's proposals are not binding.[35] The prospects of success essentially hinge on the willingness of the parties to the dispute to make concessions, which can be encouraged by the skilfulness of the mediator.[36]

An important third party which often offers its good offices in disputes between States and which may take on the role of a mediator once the parties have come together is the UN Secretary General, be it in person or through senior representatives.[37] For example, on 10 July 2014, then UN Secretary General Ban Ki-moon appointed the Italian-Swedish diplomat Staffan de Mistura as his Special Envoy for Syria to 'provide good offices aimed at bringing an end to all violence and human rights violations, and promoting a peaceful solution to the Syrian crisis'.[38] The UN General Assembly has made persistent efforts to strengthen 'the role of mediation in the peaceful settlement of disputes, conflict prevention and resolution'.[39] Upon the request of the UNGA, the UN Secretary General prepared a report for that purpose, including the 'UN Guidance for Effective Mediation'.[40] Also the

[30] Dixon (n 20) 288.
[31] Merrills (n 16) 26 and 34.
[32] ibid, 27; Shaw (n 17) 770.
[33] Shaw (n 17) 770.
[34] Dixon (n 20) 288; Merrills (n 16) 26; Shaw (n 17) 770.
[35] Merrills (n 16) 29–30.
[36] ibid, 39.
[37] According to the Report of the Secretary General, 'In Larger Freedom: Towards Development, Security and Human Rights for All', 21 March 2005, UN Doc A/59/2005, para 108, 'the United Nations has almost certainly prevented many wars by using the Secretary General's "good offices" to help resolve conflicts peacefully'. cp UNGA Res 60/1, '2005 World Summit Outcome', 16 September 2005, UN Doc A/RES/60/1, para 76: 'Recognizing the important role of the good offices of the Secretary General, including in the mediation of disputes, we support the Secretary General's efforts to strengthen his capacity in this area'.
[38] UN, Press Release: 'Secretary General Appoints Staffan de Mistura Special Envoy for Syria, Ramzy Ezzeldin Ramzy Deputy Special Envoy for Syria', 10 July 2014, SG/A/1480, un.org/press/en/2014/sga1480.doc.htm.
[39] See notably UNGA Res 65/283, 22 June 2011, UN Doc A/RES/65/283; UNGA Res 66/291, 13 September 2012, UN Doc A/RES/66/291; UNGA Res 68/303, 31 July 2014, UN Doc A/RES/68/303; and UNGA Res 70/304, 26 September 2016, UN Doc A/RES/70/304, all entitled 'Strengthening the role of mediation in the peaceful settlement of disputes, conflict prevention and resolution'.
[40] UNSG, 'Strengthening the role of mediation in the peaceful settlement of disputes, conflict prevention and resolution', 25 June 2012, UN Doc A/66/811, including Annex I: 'Guidance for Effective Mediation'.

UN Security Council has repeatedly underlined the importance of mediation and encouraged its use for the peaceful settlement of disputes.[41]

From a European perspective, it can be noted that the European Community offered its good offices to resolve the crisis in the Balkans in the 1990s, albeit largely in vain. Norway has brought Israelis and Palestinians somewhat closer to one another[42] and has offered its good offices to settle the dispute between the government of Sri Lanka and the Tamil Tiger rebels.[43] Lastly, it is a little-known fact that the ECtHR can act as a mediator to settle disputes in a friendly manner, a role which is in principle not limited to disputes between individuals and States, but can extend to inter-State disputes.[44]

iii. Inquiry

Disputes between parties often revolve around different ideas about, or different interpretations of certain facts (eg, the occurrence/scale of certain atrocities), possibly connected to legal issues (eg, whether or not these atrocities took place in the context of an armed conflict and constituted war crimes). To the extent that such ideas or interpretations are difficult or impossible to reconcile, negotiation, even when backed by good offices or mediation, does not constitute an adequate means of dispute settlement.[45] If a dispute is largely one of fact rather than law or policy and if no other procedure is being employed, an independent commission of inquiry or fact-finding mission can help to resolve the dispute, provided of course that the parties are willing to accept its findings, also when these differ from their version of the events.[46]

Such commissions of inquiry can be traced back to the 1899/1907 Hague Conventions. After the US battleship *Maine* exploded in the harbour of Havana on 15 February 1898, a Spanish commission of inquiry found the explosion to have had an internal cause, while the rival American commission concluded that it was destroyed by a submarine mine, leaving unresolved the dispute between the US and Spain as regards the explosion. This episode caused the Hague Peace Conference of 1899 to regulate the conditions under which international commissions of inquiry should be established.[47] The 1907 Hague Convention further developed the rather rudimentary provisions contained in the 1899 Convention devoted to organisation and procedure.[48] While there were a number of early successful examples, only few commissions of inquiry have been established in accordance with the Hague Conventions.[49] More often, States rely on an inquiry within specified institutional

[41] See most explicitly UNSC, Statement by the President of the Security Council, 23 September 2008, UN Doc S/PRST/2008/36.

[42] eg Declaration of Principles on Interim Self-Government Arrangements (13 September 1993) (Oslo I Accord).

[43] Consider also The Elders, founded by Nelson Mandela and chaired by Kofi Annan, which is an independent group of public figures 'who offer their collective influence and experience to support peace building, help address major causes of human suffering and promote the shared interests of humanity' and have mediated in various notorious disputes and other global dilemmas; see theelders.org.

[44] Art 39 ECHR (on friendly settlements). For an overview of friendly settlements, see H Keller, M Forowicz and L Engi, *Friendly Settlements before the European Court of Human Rights: Theory and Practice* (Oxford, OUP, 2010).

[45] Merrills (n 16) 43.

[46] ibid, 61.

[47] ibid, 43–44. See Hague Convention I – Pacific Settlement of International Disputes (adopted 29 July 1899, entered into force 4 September 1900) 187 CTS 410, Arts 9–14.

[48] Merrills (n 16) 46. See Hague Convention I – Pacific Settlement of International Disputes (adopted 18 October 1907, entered into force 26 January 1910) 205 CTS 233, Arts 9–36.

[49] Shaw (n 17) 772.

frameworks and/or alternatives to the traditional inquiry commission as proposed by the Conventions.[50]

For example, a fact-finding commission established by the EU inquired into the violations carried out during, and the causes of, the brief Russio-Georgian armed conflict of August 2008.[51] Similarly, a UN commission inquired into the violations of the laws of war allegedly perpetrated by Israel and Hamas between December 2008 and January 2009 during the Gaza conflict.[52] Following persistent indications that chemical weapons were being used in the conflict in Syria, in 2014, the Organisation for the Prohibition on Chemical Weapons (OPCW) Fact Finding Mission (FFM) was created 'to establish facts surrounding allegations of the use of toxic chemicals, reportedly chlorine, for hostile purposes in the Syrian Arab Republic', and has deployed several missions since.[53] An example of a permanent inquiry body is the International Humanitarian Fact-Finding Commission (IHFFC), established pursuant to Article 90 of the First Additional Protocol of 1977 to the Geneva Conventions of 1949, which can investigate allegations of serious violations of international humanitarian law when the parties to an international armed conflict have submitted a declaration accepting the IHFFC's competence, or when they request the Commission's involvement (on the IHFFC, see Chapter 15, Section VI(C)).[54]

iv. Conciliation

The process of conciliation involves an impartial third party, usually a conciliation commission, set up by the parties to the dispute, which investigates the dispute and attempts to define the terms of a settlement that would be acceptable to the parties, generally by submitting a report, or which actively helps the parties to reach such settlement on the basis of its investigation.[55] Conciliation involves elements of inquiry as well as mediation, although, as opposed to what is the case for inquiry, the fact-finding exercise is not essential.[56] In terms of composition and working methods, conciliation commissions often resemble arbitral tribunals. However, unlike decisions of arbitral tribunals, the reports or proposals of conciliation commissions are not legally binding.[57]

For a limited number of mainly European States, conciliation procedures are regulated by the General Act on the Pacific Settlement of Disputes of 1928,[58] as revised in 1949,[59] Article 1 of which provides that 'disputes of every kind' between the parties thereto which

[50] ibid, 772–73; Merrills (n 16) 61.

[51] This 'Independent International Fact-Finding Commission' was established by Council Decision 2008/901/CFSP of 2 December 2008 concerning an independent international fact-finding mission on the conflict in Georgia [2008] OJ L323/66. The Commission delivered its report in September 2009.

[52] HRC, 'Report of the United Nations Fact-Finding Mission on the Gaza Conflict', 25 September 2009, UN Doc A/HRC/12/48.

[53] For more information on and the reports of the FFM, see OPCW, 'The Fact-Finding Mission (FFM)', opcw.org/special-sections/syria/the-fact-finding-mission.

[54] On inquiry, see further Merrills (n 16) 43–61.

[55] Institut de Droit International, 'Regulations on the Procedure of International Conciliation', 11 September 1961, idi-iil.org/app/uploads/2017/06/1961_salz_02_en.pdf, Art 1; Shaw (n 17) 773.

[56] Merrills (n 20) 62; Shaw (n 17) 773.

[57] eg Shaw (n 17) 773.

[58] General Act for the Pacific Settlement of International Disputes (adopted 26 September 1928, entered into force 16 August 1929) 93 LNTS 343.

[59] Revised General Act for the Pacific Settlement of International Disputes (adopted 28 April 1949, entered into force 20 September 1950) 71 UNTS 101. The State Parties are: Belgium, Burkina Faso, Denmark, Estonia, Luxembourg, the Netherlands, Norway and Sweden.

could not be settled by diplomacy shall be submitted to conciliation. The parties to the General Act agreed to submit their disputes to permanent bilateral conciliation commissions or, failing the establishment of the relevant permanent commission, to an ad hoc conciliation commission.[60] Under the General Act, conciliation is compulsory, except for 'disputes with regard to which the parties are in conflict as to their respective rights', which shall, on the condition that the parties to the dispute recognise the jurisdiction of the ICJ,[61] be submitted to the ICJ, unless the parties agree to have resort to arbitration.[62] Also for such disputes, the parties remain free to opt for conciliation.[63] If the conciliation proceedings fail, the dispute shall be brought before an arbitral tribunal.[64]

The General Act served as the basis for the European Convention on the Pacific Settlement of Disputes (ECPSD), which essentially contains the same provisions, but slightly tipped the balance towards judicial settlement by swapping the rule and the exception. Article 1 of the ECPSD provides that the parties shall submit all their 'international legal disputes' to the ICJ, in particular including the disputes referred to in Article 36(2) of the ICJ Statute, the list of which is copied into Article 1 (see below, Section III(B)(ii)(b)).[65] The States that do not recognise the jurisdiction of the ICJ 'shall carry out the measures necessary to enable them to have access thereto'.[66] Article 4(1) ECPSD then provides that the parties 'shall submit to conciliation all disputes which may arise between them, other than disputes falling within the scope of Article 1', unless they agree to resort to arbitration.[67] If conciliation proceedings fail, the parties are also to have recourse to arbitration.[68]

An historical example is the conciliation between Iceland and Norway concerning the delimitation of the continental shelf between Iceland and the Jan Mayen island.[69] In this dispute, the parties agreed to establish a conciliation commission composed of two members appointed by the respective countries, and a chairman appointed by both parties jointly.[70] The Commission was to submit recommendations with regard to the delimitation, for which purpose it had to 'take into account Iceland's strong economic interests in these sea areas, the existing geographical and geological factors and other special circumstances'.[71] Also, it was specified that the recommendations would not be binding, but that 'during their further negotiations the Parties [would] pay reasonable regard to them'.[72] The solution with which the Commission eventually came up, ie a joint development zone, would not have been reached through judicial settlement, which focuses on the rights the parties are entitled to, and thus illustrates the flexibility and added value of the conciliation process.[73]

[60] ibid, Art 2. cp Art 5 ECPSD (n 7).
[61] ibid, Art 20(2).
[62] ibid, Art 17.
[63] ibid, Art 20(1).
[64] ibid, Art 21.
[65] cp Art 17 of the Revised General Act: 'It is understood that the disputes referred to above include in particular those mentioned in Article 36 of the Statute of the International Court of Justice'.
[66] Art 3 ECPSD (n 7).
[67] ibid, Art 4(2).
[68] ibid, Art 19.
[69] Conciliation Commission on the Continental Shelf area between Iceland and Jan Mayen, 'Report and Recommendations to the Governments of Iceland and Norway', Decision of June 1981, 27 RIAA 1.
[70] Art 9 Agreement between Norway and Iceland on Fishery and Continental Shelf Questions (adopted 28 May 1980, entered into force 13 June 1980) 2124 UNTS 226.
[71] ibid.
[72] ibid.
[73] Shaw (n 17) 774. On conciliation, see further Merrills (n 16) 62–87.

C. Regional Non-Judicial Dispute Settlement Mechanisms in Europe

In the Manila Declaration, the UN General Assembly stressed the role of regional arrangements in the process of the peaceful settlement of disputes.[74] Given the high degree of regional integration within Europe, a substantial number of regional non-judicial dispute settlement mechanisms are available.[75] It is noted that the regional international organisations of (chiefly) European membership are particularly well-suited for the amicable settlement of disputes between the members, even if such disputes relate to matters that do not fall within the competency of the organisation. Of note in this respect is the role of NATO – whose membership is mainly European – as a means of settling the dispute between the United Kingdom and Iceland over the so-called 'cod wars' in the 1960s and 1970s, relating to Iceland's extension of its fishing zone to first 12 miles and later 200 miles, to the detriment of UK fishermen. The NATO membership of both the United Kingdom and Iceland, coupled with substantial pressure by NATO's most powerful member, the United States, diffused tensions and eventually led to an agreement acceptable to both parties.[76]

Some European international organisations provide for formal or informal mechanisms that allow for the non-binding settlement of disputes between Member States, institutional organs, or third parties, drawing rights from the organisation's rule-making procedures. The National Contact Points of the OECD, an organisation that mainly counts European States among its Members, provide a good example of an informal non-judicial mechanism set up to settle disputes relating to multinational enterprises' allegedly harmful business conduct in violation of the OECD Guidelines for Multinational Enterprises. Those OECD National Contact Points, which are typically established within a government ministry, are open to interested parties (in practice normally employee organisations or other non-governmental organisations) that are affected by the violation, and facilitate – but do not impose – a settlement of the dispute between the parties.[77] Another example of an informal dispute settlement mechanism in the economic sphere is the European Bank for Reconstruction and Development's (EBRD) Independent Recourse Mechanism.[78]

A somewhat more formal dispute settlement mechanism is the Court of Conciliation and Arbitration of the OSCE, which forms part of a wider OSCE system of settling disputes between States that affect peace and security in Europe.[79] This little-known and little-used Court, based in Geneva, was established in 1995 on the basis of an OSCE Convention on

[74] Part I, para 6 Manila Declaration.

[75] Although the dispute settlement provisions of the UN Charter have a universal scope, Art 52(2) of the UN Charter provides for the settlement of local/regional disputes by regional agencies or arrangements. See also the Manila Declaration and further Chapter 7 on Regional Organisations.

[76] Also in J Merrills, 'The Means of Dispute Settlement' in MD Evans, *International Law*, 4th edn (Oxford, OUP, 2014) 563–88.

[77] The National Contact Points were established by the 2000 review of the OECD Guidelines for Multinational Enterprises, the latest (2011) edition of which is available at oecd.org/corporate/mne/48004323.pdf. Part II, 'Implementation Procedures of the OECD Guidelines for Multinational Enterprises', principle I.1, provides: 'Adhering countries shall set up National Contact Points for undertaking promotional activities, handling inquiries and for discussions with the parties concerned on all matters covered by the Guidelines so that they can contribute to the solution of problems which may arise in this connection, taking due account of the attached procedural guidance'.

[78] For more information, see EBRD, 'Independent Recourse Mechanism: The Guide to Making a Complaint about an EBRD-financed Project', July 2004, ebrd.com/downloads/research/policies/irm.pdf.

[79] cp M Bothe, N Ronzitti and A Rosas (eds), *The OSCE in the Maintenance of Peace and Security: Conflict Prevention, Crisis Management and Peaceful Settlement of Disputes* (The Hague, Kluwer, 1997).

Conciliation and Arbitration (1992), to which 33 States are parties.[80] Its position resembles the position of the Permanent Court of Arbitration (PCA) in The Hague, as neither is a 'permanent court' in the strict sense of the word. Rather, both are conduits through which arbitral tribunals are set up. In spite of its very elaborate provisions, States seem to have neglected the possibilities of conciliation and arbitration offered by the OSCE Convention.[81] No arbitral awards have indeed been rendered so far,[82] and it is unclear whether, and if so, how often, the conciliation procedure is used, as the entire proceedings are confidential.[83]

III. Judicial Methods

Negotiations, good office, mediation, fact-finding, and conciliation are diplomatic, non-judicial mechanisms of dispute settlement. This entails that the substantive outcomes of recourse to those mechanisms, such as reports or recommendations, are not binding on the parties to the dispute. Only if the parties submit their dispute to an arbitral tribunal or a court, will the outcome be binding on them. Given that there is no generalised system of compulsory jurisdiction in international law, since States wish to retain control over disputes,[84] submission to binding dispute settlement will necessarily be ad hoc or partial. Still, some instances of compulsory jurisdiction of permanent institutions are discernible in international law. For one thing, when taking part in a certain regime, States may be required to accept binding dispute settlement in respect of the regime's obligations. This is the case with the World Trade Organization. WTO Member States *ipso facto* accept the compulsory jurisdiction of the WTO Dispute Settlement Mechanism over disputes arising under WTO law. States may also voluntarily submit to the compulsory jurisdiction of an arbitral tribunal or a court by unilaterally accepting the jurisdiction of the tribunal or court for an unlimited number of future cases. This is the case with the ICJ, the compulsory jurisdiction of which States can accept by declaration under the 'optional clause' of the ICJ Statute.[85]

A. Arbitration

From a historical perspective, binding dispute settlement by permanent (quasi-)judicial institutions, such as the ICJ, the WTO Dispute Settlement Mechanism, the ICC, the ECtHR,

[80] Convention on Conciliation and Arbitration within the OSCE (adopted on 15 December 1992, entered into force 5 December 1994).

[81] Therefore, the New York University Project on International Court and Tribunals, 'The International Judiciary in Context', pict-pcti.org/publications/synoptic_chart/synop_c4.pdf, has categorised the OSCE Court of Conciliation and Arbitration as 'dormant'. However, States still appoint members and alternate members to the Court; see OSCE, 'List of appointed members and alternate members of the Court', 16 October 2017, osce.org/cca/25460.

[82] OSCE, Court of Conciliation and Arbitration, *Periodic Report 2013–2016 to the States Parties to the Convention on Conciliation and Arbitration within the OSCE*, 12 January 2017, osce.org/cca/293571.

[83] Art 23(1) OSCE Convention.

[84] See A Guzman, *How International Law Works* (Oxford, OUP, 2008) 136.

[85] Art 36(2) ICJ Statute.

or arbitral panels established through the Permanent Court of Arbitration (PCA) or International Centre for Settlement of Investment Disputes (ICSID), has been the exception rather than the rule.[86] If binding dispute settlement was opted for at all, it was ad hoc, by an arbitral tribunal established for the purpose of settling one dispute, or a string of disputes relating to the same situation.[87] Early in the twentieth century, a PCA came into being.[88] Still, the institutionalisation of binding dispute settlement through the establishment of the PCA should not be overstated. After all, the PCA is not a court in itself but a mechanism facilitating the constitution of arbitral panels dealing ad hoc with certain disputes. This lack of institutionalisation and uniformity has its advantages, of course, otherwise ad hoc-ism would not persist. It allows the parties to a dispute to select the arbiters (the parties are ordinarily not allowed to choose the judges of a permanent court),[89] to select the applicable law and procedure,[90] and to oppose publication of the award.

The importance of arbitral tribunals for the further development of international law should not be underestimated, however. States have submitted a large number of cases to arbitral tribunals due to their continued reliance on such tribunals for the settlement of their disputes.[91] In light of the role of international arbitration in settling international investment disputes, their importance is set to grow even further. Currently, a major part of international arbitration cases are 'hybrid' investment arbitrations between States on the one hand, and natural or corporate persons (investors) on the other hand (on which see Chapter 19, Section IV(E)).

The jurisdictional bases for these arbitrations are found in numerous bilateral investment treaties (BITs) between Host States (receiving the investment) and Home States (the States where the investors are incorporated). This so-called 'BIT revolution' has yielded a string of dispute settlement mechanisms for investment-related disputes, such as ICSID,[92]

[86] Crawford (n 3) 13: 'In clear contrast with Grotius' view of international law as institution-less, the 20th century saw the development of a large number of institutions and the struggle against the "ad hoc": not a struggle against the existing conception of arbitration, but rather a struggle against ad hoc arrangements for dispute settlement'.

[87] eg the Jay Treaties between the UK and the US, ushering in the new era of binding dispute settlement through international arbitration: Treaty of Amity, Commerce and Navigation between His Britannic Majesty and the United States of America (adopted on 19 November 1794, entered into force 29 February 1796) (Jay Treaty).

[88] The Permanent Court of Arbitration was established in 1899 to facilitate arbitration and other forms of dispute resolution between States, by way of the Hague Convention for the Pacific Settlement of International Disputes (adopted 29 July 1899, entered into force 4 September 1900) 187 CTS 410, replaced by the Hague Convention for the Pacific Settlement of International Disputes (adopted 18 October 1907, entered into force 26 January 1910) 205 CTS 233.

[89] See however Art 26 of the ICJ Statute, pursuant to which Chambers of the Court can be constituted at the request of the parties. The Chamber structure leaves more choice for the parties and may resemble arbitration. It may also limit the overload of the Court; see further H Thirlway, 'The International Court of Justice' in Evans (n 76) 589–618. However, as Dixon observed, 'if states believe they can eliminate those judges thought to be too "political" or "unsympathetic"', this 'would nullify the advantages of a broadly based judicial body capable of developing international law beyond the narrower perspectives of a few like-minded judges': M Dixon, *Textbook on International* Law, 6th edn (Oxford, OUP, 2007) 284 (this statement was omitted from the 7th edn (2013)).

[90] For instance, for environmental disputes, the PCA proposes three sets of rules: (1) using procedural rules based on arbitration rules of the UN Commission on International Trade Law (UNCITRAL); (2) using Optional Rules for Arbitration of Disputes Relating to Natural Resources and/or the Environment (2001); (3) using Optional Rules for Conciliation of Disputes Relating to Natural Resources and/or the Environment (2002). Procedural rules may also cut back on the length of proceedings before arbitral tribunals. Thirlway has observed that the current length of proceedings before the ICJ may well put off States: Thirlway (n 89) 586–87.

[91] Arbitration also plays an increasingly important role in maritime delimitation. See Chapter 18, Section VII.

[92] The relevant provisions of the Convention on the Settlement of Investment Disputes between States and Nationals of Other States (adopted 18 March 1965, entered into force 14 October 1966) 575 UNTS 159 (ICSID Convention) read as follows: Art 1(2): 'The purpose of the Centre shall be to provide facilities for conciliation and arbitration of investment disputes between Contracting States and nationals of other Contracting States in

the PCA, the International Chamber of Commerce, the London Court of International Arbitration, the Stockholm Chamber of Commerce, tribunals established in accordance with UNCITRAL rules, and ad hoc tribunals.[93] Different rules of substantive law may apply before these tribunals.

The most conspicuous feature of investment arbitration and investment-related arbitral tribunals is that they blur the dividing line between public and private law. Institutionally, investment arbitration allows private persons (non-State actors) to have access to international tribunals, which were traditionally only accessible to *States*. This right of access and the substantive rights that investors can invoke before the tribunals may imply that investors are endowed with international legal personality (at least insofar as such rights have been granted to them by an investment treaty). This is revolutionary in light of the historical State-centered focus of international law and international dispute settlement.[94] An 'international' dispute may arise as soon as an investment deal involving a corporation from one State investing in another State turns sour. The BIT revolution has, however, not only blurred the line between the public and the private, but also between monism and dualism, the two systems of giving effect to international law in domestic law. For example, the UK Court of Appeal ruled in 2005 that BIT awards are directly enforceable in English courts,[95] although the English legal system has traditionally been a dualist one. This BIT revolution is not uncontroversial, especially because the granting of rights to investors may limit States' legitimate policy freedom. States and civil society groups have notably criticised the investor-state dispute settlement mechanism envisaged in the EU-US Transatlantic Trade and Investment Partnership.[96]

B. The International Court of Justice

The binding settlement of disputes by standing courts and tribunals, as opposed to ad hoc arbitration panels, is the last method of international dispute settlement. There are various such courts and tribunals dealing with disputes relating to a specific subject-matter,[97] or to a specific region.[98] Only the ICJ, one of the principal organs of the UN,[99] is, like its predecessor the PCIJ, a court of general jurisdiction open to all States. The Court differs from

accordance with the provisions of this Convention'; Art 25(1): 'The jurisdiction of the Centre shall extend to any legal dispute arising directly out of an investment, between a Contracting State (or any constituent subdivision or agency of a Contracting State designated to the Centre by that State) and a national of another Contracting State, which the parties to the dispute consent in writing to submit to the Centre. When the parties have given their consent, no party may withdraw its consent unilaterally'.

[93] Thanks to Tarcisio Gazzini for pointing this out to the authors.

[94] cp *Plama Consortium Limited v Bulgaria*, Award of 8 February 2005, ICSID ARB/03/24, para 141 (holding that Art 26 of the Energy Charter Treaty (adopted 17 December 1994, entered into force 16 April 1998) 2080 UNTS 95 'is a very important feature of the ECT which is itself a very significant treaty for investors, marking another step in their transition from objects to subjects of international law').

[95] cp Crawford (n 3).

[96] See eg the action group's website: stop-ttip.org. The compatibility with EU law of the mechanism for the resolution of investment disputes between investors and States as contained in the Comprehensive Economic and Trade Agreement between Canada, of the one part, and the European Union and its Member States, of the other part, signed in Brussels on 30 October 2016 (CETA) is currently before the CJEU: see request for an Opinion 1/17, pending (see further Chapter 4, Section V(B)(i)).

[97] eg, the international criminal tribunals with jurisdiction over a number of international crimes, or ITLOS.

[98] eg, the regional human rights courts, or the courts established by a number of regional organisations settling disputes between the member States and the institutions, or between the institutions *inter se*.

[99] On the UN and its principal organs, see Chapter 6, Section VIII.

an arbitral tribunal in that it is a permanent institution with appointed judges, having its own Statute, and applying only international law.[100] It has the jurisdiction to settle concrete disputes between States (contentious proceedings) and to render advisory opinions at the request of UN organs or UN specialised agencies.

i. Access to the ICJ

Pursuant to Article 34 of the ICJ Statute, the Court is only open to States for contentious proceedings. Non-State actors, such as individuals or international organisations, do not have access to the Court. UN organs and UN specialised agencies, however, can request an advisory opinion from the Court (see below Section III(B)(ii)(d)(3)).

The rule that only States have access to the Court may seem straightforward enough. The rule has only led to some problems of application when doubt was cast over the statehood of the applicant. This occurred notably in two 'European' disputes involving Serbia and Montenegro in the aftermath of the break-up of the Federal Republic of Yugoslavia (FRY), where the Court reached apparently different conclusions as to Serbia and Montenegro's right to access the Court. In the *Legality of the Use of Force* decision (2004), the Court inferred from the suspension of the applicant's UN membership that it was no longer a member of the United Nations. Thus, it was no longer a party to the ICJ Statute, at least not in that capacity, and therefore the Court was not open to it under Article 35(1) of the Statute.[101] Nor was the Court open to it, in the Court's view, under Article 35(2) of the Statute, which provides that States may have access to the Court on the basis of 'special provisions contained in treaties in force', on the ground that the reference to such treaties 'applies only to treaties in force at the date of the entry into force of the Statute, and not to any treaties concluded since that date'.[102] The entry into force of the ICJ Statute predated the entry into force of the treaty invoked by Serbia and Montenegro – the Genocide Convention, which featured a 'compromissory clause' conferring compulsory jurisdiction on the ICJ regarding the interpretation and application of the treaty. However, in *Bosnia Genocide*, a case also involving Serbia and Montenegro as a party (respondent), the Court ruled in 1996 that the very same compromissory clause sufficed for access to the court. The Court saw no problem in Serbia's suspension from UN membership between 1992 and 2000.[103] This position was confirmed as *res judicata* in 2007.[104] Dixon observed that these inconsistent findings damaged the integrity of the Court,[105] although Klabbers called for sympathy with the Court in view of the muddled approach of the UN's political organs vis-à-vis Serbia.[106] At any rate, the judgment did not particularly promote the trust of Serbia's citizens in international justice, which was already at low ebb due to the perceived anti-Serb bias of the ICTY.

[100] It is noted, however, that States often have the choice, even under particular treaties, to submit one and the same dispute either to the ICJ or an arbitral panel, or even another international court; see eg the UNCLOS dispute settlement regime, as discussed in Chapter 18, Section IX.
[101] *Legality of Use of Force* (Serbia and Montenegro v UK) [2004] ICJ Rep 1307, para 89.
[102] ibid, para 94.
[103] *Application of the Convention on the Prevention and Punishment of the Crime of Genocide* (Bosnia and Herzegovina v Yugoslavia) [1996] ICJ Rep 595.
[104] *Application of the Convention on the Prevention and Punishment of the Crime of Genocide* (Bosnia and Herzegovina v Serbia and Montenegro) [2007] ICJ Rep 43, para 139.
[105] Dixon (n 20) 297.
[106] J Klabbers, *Introduction to International Institutional Law* (Cambridge, CUP, 2009) 106.

ii. Jurisdiction

As has been noted, the ICJ does not have compulsory jurisdiction over inter-State disputes. Its jurisdiction needs to be accepted by States, either ad hoc (through special agreement/compromise, or on the basis of *forum prorogatum*) or beforehand (pursuant to a compromissory clause in a treaty or a declaration filed unilaterally in accordance with the optional clause of the ICJ Statute). If the Court's jurisdiction is disputed in a given case – for instance, if the respondent argues that it has not accepted the Court's jurisdiction – it is for the Court to determine its jurisdiction, not for a party or the parties.[107] This also means that none of the parties is expected to discharge a burden of proof in the matter of jurisdiction.[108]

Objections to the jurisdiction of the Court are normally addressed by the Court in a judgment on preliminary objections. The Court will only consider such objections provided that they have an exclusively preliminary character.[109] If that is not the case, they are dealt with in the merits phase.[110] This may obviously lead to rather long procedural delays. Changes to the Court's procedures are not self-evident, however, as they would need the support of the States appearing before them. Quite a number of States appreciate the opportunity to explain their case at length before the Court; moreover, the long proceedings before the ICJ allow States to 'cool off' difficult political problems.[111]

a. Optional Clause

Acceptance of the ICJ's jurisdiction can take place on the basis of the so-called 'optional clause' under Article 36(2) of the ICJ Statute, pursuant to which States can file a declaration accepting the jurisdiction of the Court for an unlimited number of future cases.[112] Such acceptances of the Court's jurisdiction are not absolute, however. For one thing, a State can withdraw its declaration. Many declarations provide for withdrawal, sometimes at a few months' notice. A State may not withdraw its declaration, however, when another State, relying on the former State's declaration, has filed suit against it.

States can also append reservations to their declaration, thus limiting the Court's jurisdiction. As the acceptance of the Court's jurisdiction is optional under Article 36(2) of the ICJ Statute, States' power to append reservations is hardly circumscribed. Some problems have, however, arisen in relation to automatic or self-judging reservations, according to which the declaring/reserving State is the sole judge of whether the ICJ has jurisdiction pursuant to the State's declaration. In the *Norwegians Loans* case, the Court accepted France's reservation pertaining to 'differences relating to matters which are essentially within the national jurisdiction' on the basis that it represented the 'common will' of the parties. The validity of the reservation had not been questioned by either party as France fully

[107] cp Art 36(6) ICJ Statute. This is known as the principle of *compétence de la compétence*.

[108] *Fisheries Jurisdiction* (Spain v Canada) [2007] ICJ Rep 43, paras 36–38.

[109] cp Rules of the ICJ (adopted 14 April 1978, entered into force 1 July 1978), Art 79(7).

[110] eg *Questions of Interpretation and Application of the 1971 Montreal Convention arising from the Aerial Incident at Lockerbie* (Libyan Arab Jamahiriya v United States of America) [1998] ICJ Rep 115.

[111] S Talmon, 'Article 43' in A Zimmermann, K Oellers-Frahm, C Tomuschat and CJ Tams (eds), *The Statute of the International Court of Justice: A Commentary*, 2nd edn (Oxford, OUP, 2012) 1088–1171.

[112] Art 36(2) ICJ Statute: 'The States Parties to the present Statute may at any time declare that they recognise as compulsory *ipso facto* and without special agreement, in relation to any other State accepting the same obligation, the jurisdiction of the Court in all legal disputes concerning: (a) the interpretation of a treaty; (b) any question of international law; (c) the existence of any fact which, if established, would constitute a breach of an international obligation; (d) the nature or extent of the reparation to be made for the breach of an international obligation'.

maintained its reservation and Norway sought to rely on it in the dispute.[113] Some authors and judges believe such reservations to be unlawful, however, and have urged the Court to sever the automatic reservation from the State's otherwise valid declaration.[114]

The Court is often called upon to interpret declarations under the optional clause in the preliminary objections phase of contentious proceedings. In the *Fisheries* case it usefully set out the principles guiding this interpretative exercise.[115] The ICJ bases its interpretation by analogy on the reservation regime set out in Article 19 and following of the VCLT. It warned, however, that the regimes are not identical. Interpretation should instead be carried out in a natural and reasonable way, having due regard to the intention of the State concerned at the time when it accepted the compulsory jurisdiction of the Court (text, context, and circumstances could be relevant here), and the effect sought by the State. The Court added that there is no rule that in case of doubt, jurisdiction would obtain (no *contra preferentem* rule). In the Court's view, when making a reservation to the jurisdiction of the Court, a State does not necessarily derogate from a wider acceptance of jurisdiction already given. All of this means that reservations to declarations need not be interpreted restrictively, and that the State's 'subjective' intent remains a decisive factor. The regime of reservations to treaties under the VCLT, by contrast, appears to opt for a more objective and restrictive approach: reservations are invalid if they are incompatible with the object and purpose of the treaty.[116]

A leading principle governing the system of optional declarations is 'reciprocity'. Reciprocity implies that the Court can only have jurisdiction if both States Parties to a dispute have made a declaration of which the scope coincides. In practice, this typically means that the respondent can rely on reservations made by the applicant, even if the respondent has not made such reservations for itself, and that the narrowest acceptance of the Court's jurisdiction will govern the case. In the *Norwegians Loans* case, for instance, Norway successfully relied on France's reservation as to domestic competence, although it had not made such a reservation for itself.[117] The principle of reciprocity only governs substantive matters, as opposed to procedural matters, however. In the *Nicaragua* case, the United States was not allowed to rely on Nicaragua's declaration that the declaration was terminable without notice. Accordingly, the Court did not recognise the US termination of its own declaration without notice. Instead, it held that the US was required to comply with its own declaration pursuant to which it would give six months' notice when terminating its declaration.[118] The US challenge to the Court's jurisdiction on this ground thus failed.

Pursuant to Article 36(5) of the ICJ Statute, declarations of acceptance of the jurisdiction of the PCIJ are transferable to the ICJ. Such an automatic transfer of jurisdiction will, however, only take place if the relevant State has been a party to the ICJ Statute since 1945. Therefore, in the *Aerial Incident Case*, the Court declined jurisdiction because Bulgaria only became party to the ICJ Statute in 1955.[119]

[113] *Norwegian Loans* (France v Norway) [1957] ICJ Rep 9, 21–22.
[114] eg Lauterpacht in *Norwegians Loans* (n 113) and *Interhandel* (Switzerland v United States) [1959] ICJ Rep 6; Dixon (n 20) 308.
[115] *Fisheries* (n 108) paras 39–56.
[116] Art 19(c) VCLT.
[117] *Norwegian Loans* (n 113).
[118] *Nicaragua* (n 13) para 65. For criticism of the distinction between 'substantive' and 'procedural' reservations for the purpose of the application of the principle of reciprocity, see Dixon (n 20) 311.
[119] *Aerial Incident of July 27th, 1955* (Israel v Bulgaria) [1959] ICJ Rep 127.

A substantial number of States, including 23 EU Member States and four non-EU European States, have filed a declaration accepting the Court's jurisdiction under Article 36(2) of the ICJ Statute.[120] However, many States have appended reservations to their declarations with a view to limiting the Court's jurisdiction over disputes to which they are parties.

Declarations by European States often state that they 'do not apply to any dispute in respect of which the parties thereto have agreed or shall agree to have recourse to other means of peaceful settlement for its final and binding decision'.[121] This is really an innocuous statement as it guarantees that disputes are somehow subjected to binding dispute settlement resembling ICJ dispute settlement. Equally innocuous is the 'reservation' pursuant to which the Court does not have jurisdiction over 'disputes relating to questions which fall within the domestic jurisdiction' of the reserving State.[122] To the extent that reservations of this type are not 'automatic' or 'self-judging', in that they preclude the assessment of whether a particular question falls within the domestic jurisdiction of the State by the Court, as opposed to merely the State, such reservations are in fact redundant, as the Court can ordinarily not address questions that fall within the domestic jurisdiction of a State and do not raise international law issues.

Quite a number of declarations by European States exclude disputes with States that have accepted the compulsory jurisdiction of the ICJ pursuant to Article 36(2) 'less than twelve months prior to filing an application bringing the dispute before the Court or where such acceptance has been made only for the purpose of a particular dispute'.[123] This is a logical limitation of the Court's jurisdiction, aiming to preclude essentially ad hoc acceptances of jurisdiction from producing legal effects against the respondent State.[124]

Some States have made more far-reaching declarations that exclude politically sensitive disputes from the jurisdiction of the Court, such as disputes with military aspects,[125] or disputes relating to the law of the sea.[126] Malta and Poland seem to have gone the furthest

[120] In total, 73 States have filed a Declaration: see ICJ, 'Declarations recognizing the jurisdiction of the Court as compulsory', icj-cij.org/en/declarations.

[121] See the declarations of Austria, Belgium, Estonia, Germany, Hungary, Luxembourg, Malta, the Netherlands, Poland, Portugal, Spain and the UK.

[122] See the declarations of Cyprus, Hungary, Malta, Poland and Slovakia.

[123] See the declarations of Bulgaria, Cyprus, Germany, Hungary, Malta, Poland, Portugal, Slovakia, Spain and the UK.

[124] The Court has not ruled out that ad hoc acceptance of jurisdiction could produce legal effects. The Court has held it was not necessary that the respondent State was informed of the applicant's (possibly ad hoc) acceptance of the Court's jurisdiction: *Right of Passage over Indian Territory* (Portugal v Italy) [1960] ICJ Rep 6.

[125] eg, Germany's exclusion of 'any dispute which (a) relates to, arises from or is connected with the deployment of armed forces abroad, involvement in such deployments or decisions thereon, or (b) relates to, arises from or is connected with the use for military purposes of the territory of the Federal Republic of Germany, including its airspace, as well as maritime areas subject to German sovereign rights and jurisdiction'; Greece's exclusion of 'any dispute relating to defensive military action taken by the Hellenic Republic for reasons of national defense'; Hungary's exclusion of 'disputes relating to, or connected with, facts or situations of hostilities, war, armed conflicts, individual or collective actions taken in self-defense or the discharge of any functions pursuant to any resolution or recommendation of the United Nations, and other similar or related acts, measures or situations in which the Republic of Hungary is, has been or may in the future be involved'; Malta's exclusion of 'disputes concerning any question relating to or arising out of belligerent or military occupation or the discharge of any functions pursuant to any recommendation or decision of an organ of the United Nations, in accordance with which the Government of Malta have accepted obligations'.

[126] Norway, for instance, added to its Declaration that 'the limitations and exceptions relating to the settlement of disputes pursuant to the provisions of, and the Norwegian declarations applicable at any given time to UNCLOS and the Agreement for the Implementation of the Provisions of the United Nations Convention on the Law of the Sea of 10 December 1982 relating to the Conservation and Management of Straddling Fish Stocks and Highly Migratory Fish Stocks, shall apply to all disputes concerning the law of the sea'.

in their reservations. Malta, for instance, in addition to excluding the type of disputes mentioned above, also excluded disputes with other members of the (British) Commonwealth (as did the United Kingdom); disputes arising under a multilateral treaty if not all parties to the treaty affected by the decision are also parties to the case before the Court;[127] disputes relating to matters excluded from adjudication or arbitration under a treaty; and disputes in respect of which 'arbitral or judicial proceedings are taking, or have taken place with any State which, at the date of the commencement of the proceedings, had not itself accepted the compulsory jurisdiction of the International Court of Justice'. Poland, for its part, aside from the usual exclusions, also excluded territorial disputes, disputes with regard to environmental protection,[128] and disputes with regard to foreign liabilities or debts. It may be said that, by and large, European States' declarations and reservations with respect to the jurisdiction of the Court do not qualitatively differ from such declarations and reservations by other States.

b. Other Methods of Accepting the Jurisdiction of the ICJ: Compromissory Clause, Compromise and Forum Prorogatum

The first 'jurisdictional' provision of the ICJ Statute refers to the 'compromise' or 'special agreement' as a mechanism triggering the jurisdiction of the Court. Pursuant to a compromise, States can accept the jurisdiction of the Court ad hoc, for one dispute only by means of an agreement (treaty) between them (Article 36(1) ICJ Statute). This is a remnant of the classic system of international arbitration. In the compromise, the parties frame the questions to be put to the Court.

Acceptance of the ICJ's jurisdiction can also take place on the basis of a 'compromissory clause'. This is a clause in a bilateral or multilateral treaty conferring compulsory jurisdiction on the ICJ as to disputes relating to the interpretation and application of the treaty's provisions.[129] Such a clause can be 'optional' in that it may feature in an optional protocol to the treaty containing the substantive provisions,[130] or in that States can make reservations to the clause. In the latter case, the question may arise whether such a reservation is valid at all under Article 19 of the VCLT, notably whether it is compatible with the object and purpose of the treaty at issue.[131] It is noted that, pursuant to Article 37 of the ICJ Statute, ICJ jurisdiction also obtains on the basis of compromissory treaty clauses providing for PCIJ jurisdiction. Unlike with respect to transferability of declarations under the optional clause, States Parties to the dispute need not have been party to the ICJ Statute since 1945, although quite obviously they should still be parties to the relevant treaty. In a number of

[127] See also the US reservation in *Nicaragua* (n 13) para 13.

[128] See also Slovakia's declaration.

[129] Thirlway has noted that few new treaties in fact provide for such a compromissory clause: Thirlway (n 89) 587.

[130] See Optional Protocol to the Vienna Convention on Diplomatic Relations, concerning the Compulsory Settlement of Disputes (adopted 18 April 1961, entered into force 24 April 1964) 500 UNTS 241; and Optional Protocol to the Vienna Convention on Consular Relations concerning the Compulsory Settlement of Disputes (adopted 24 April 1963, entered into force 19 March 1967) 596 UNTS 487. See also *United States Diplomatic and Consular Staff in Tehran* (USA v Iran) [1980] ICJ Rep 3; and *Avena and Other Mexican Nationals* (Mexico v USA) [2004] ICJ Rep 12.

[131] The US Reservation to the Genocide Convention Art IX(1), which reads: 'That with reference to article IX of the Convention, before any dispute to which the United States is a party may be submitted to the jurisdiction of the International Court of Justice under this article, the specific consent of the United States is required in each case', was objected to by Greece, Mexico, the Netherlands and the UK on the basis that it was incompatible with the object and purpose of the Convention.

recent ICJ disputes between European States, jurisdiction was claimed on the basis of a compromissory clause. In the *Genocide Case* (*Bosnia v Serbia*) (2007)[132] jurisdiction was accepted on the basis of Article IX of the Genocide Convention,[133] and in *Application of the International Convention on the Elimination of All Forms of Racial Discrimination*,[134] jurisdiction was claimed on the basis of Article 22 of the said convention, but was not accepted.

A variation on a compromissory clause is the compromissory treaty, which does not deal with any substantive matter, but only confers compulsory jurisdiction on the ICJ in respect of disputes between States Parties to the treaty, generally States belonging to the same region. The two best known such treaties are the American Treaty on Pacific Settlement (Pact of Bogota) of 1948,[135] and the ECPSD.[136] As alluded to above (in Section II(B)(4)), the latter stipulates in its first article:

> The High Contracting Parties shall submit to the judgement of the International Court of Justice all international legal disputes which may arise between them including, in particular, those concerning:
>
> (a) the interpretation of a treaty;
> (b) any question of international law;
> (c) the existence of any fact which, if established, would constitute a breach of an international obligation;
> (d) the nature or extent of the reparation to be made for the breach of an international obligation.[137]

The ICJ has accepted jurisdiction on the basis of this Convention in the recent cases of *Greece v Macedonia*,[138] and *Jurisdictional Immunities of the State* (Germany v Italy).[139]

A final method of accepting the jurisdiction of the ICJ is by *forum prorogatum*. This will typically occur when a party informally consents to the jurisdiction of the Court, for example, when a State that has not otherwise accepted the jurisdiction of the Court responds to a unilateral application and accepts the jurisdiction of the Court ad hoc. In the *Corfu Channel* case,[140] for instance, Albania consented by letter to the jurisdiction of the Court. It is noted that the mere appearance of a State should not be equated with the acceptance of jurisdiction, as that State may precisely have made its appearance to contest the jurisdiction of the Court.

c. Other Issues of Jurisdiction and Admissibility in ICJ Cases

Even where the ICJ has jurisdiction on the basis of one of the aforementioned consent-based means of accepting its jurisdiction, it remains to be established that there is an actual

[132] See above (n 104).
[133] 'Disputes between the Contracting Parties relating to the interpretation, application or fulfillment of the present Convention, including those relating to the responsibility of a State for genocide or for any of the other acts enumerated in article III, shall be submitted to the International Court of Justice at the request of any of the parties to the dispute'.
[134] *Application of the International Convention on the Elimination of All Forms of Racial Discrimination* (n 18).
[135] See above (n 7).
[136] ibid.
[137] Art 1 Pact of Bogotá (n 7).
[138] *Application of the Interim Accord of 13 September 1995* (the Former Yugoslav Republic of Macedonia v Greece) [2011] ICJ Rep 644.
[139] *Jurisdictional Immunities of the State* (Germany v Italy: Greece intervening) [2012] ICJ Rep 99.
[140] *Corfu Channel* (United Kingdom of Great Britain and Northern Ireland v Albania) [1949] ICJ Rep 4.

dispute between the parties. The existence of a legal dispute is a precondition for its jurisdiction, as obviously in contentious proceedings, in the absence of a dispute, there is not much to decide for the Court. The ICJ has defined a dispute as 'a disagreement on a point of law or fact, a conflict of legal views or of interests between parties',[141] and required that for a dispute to exist, '[i]t must be shown that the claim of one party is positively opposed by the other'.[142] Until recently, this test was an informal one, as a result of which a dispute was always found to exist. In its 2016 judgments in the *Marshall Islands* cases,[143] however, the ICJ formalised the test by requiring that the respondent was aware, or could not have been unaware that the applicant was making an allegation that the respondent was in breach of its obligations,[144] without nevertheless requiring notification. Applying the test to the cases before it, the ICJ concluded for the first time in its history that it lacked jurisdiction based on the absence of a dispute between the parties.[145]

Apart from contesting that there is a dispute, respondent States may also contest the 'admissibility' of the case. Objections to admissibility are all preliminary objections that do not relate to the jurisdiction of the Court.[146] Such objections often fall flat, however. The *Nicaragua* case provides a good illustration of this. In this case, the US advanced five grounds of inadmissibility, all of them rejected by the Court. No 'indispensable parties rule', by virtue of which the respondent should have brought before the Court parties whose presence and participation is necessary for the rights of those parties to be protected and for the adjudication of the issues raised in the application, was found to exist.[147] Nor did the Court discern a rule pursuant to which a case is admissible on the grounds that its subject-matter falls within the competence of the UNSC,[148] or that the judicial function is unable to deal with situations involving ongoing armed conflict.[149] The Court also refused to accept a requirement of prior exhaustion of regional negotiating processes as a precondition to seising the Court.[150]

In other cases, the 'political question' objection, which has quite some force in US law, has been given short shrift by the Court, which consistently held that the political (or more generally non-legal) overtones of a legal question do not suffice for the Court to declare a case inadmissible.[151] The most potent objection to admissibility may be one State's objection that the person over whom another State exercises diplomatic protection vis-à-vis the

[141] *Mavrommatis Palestine Concessions* [1924] PCIJ Series A, No 2, 11.
[142] *South West Africa* (Ethiopia v South Africa; Liberia v South Africa) [1962] ICJ Rep 319, 328; *Alleged Violations of Sovereign Rights and Maritime Spaces in the Caribbean Sea* (Nicaragua v Colombia) [2016] ICJ Rep 3, para 50.
[143] The Marshall Islands cases consisted of three separate but largely similar cases, brought against India, Pakistan and the United Kingdom, the only nuclear weapons States over which the ICJ could exercise consent-based jurisdiction.
[144] *Obligations Concerning Negotiations Relating to Cessation of the Nuclear Arms Race and to Nuclear Disarmament* (Marshall Islands v India) [2016] ICJ Rep 255, para 48.
[145] This decision was severely criticised by the minority judges. In the case involving the UK, the casting vote of the ICJ President had to decide. In an earlier case, *Questions relating to the Obligation to Prosecute or Extradite* (Belgium v Senegal) [2012] ICJ Rep 422, paras 50–55, the ICJ had concluded to the absence of a dispute based on violations of customary international law, but the consequences of this decision were negligible as the Court had already established that there was a dispute between the parties regarding obligations under treaty law.
[146] Thirlway (n 89) 574.
[147] *Nicaragua* (n 13) paras 85–88.
[148] ibid, paras 89–98.
[149] ibid, paras 99–101.
[150] ibid, paras 102–108.
[151] *South West Africa* (n 142); *Legal Consequences of the Construction of a Wall in the Occupied Palestinian Territory* [2004] ICJ Rep 136; *Tehran* (n 130) para 36.

former State is not its national or that such person has failed to exhaust domestic remedies in the former State.

d. Some Procedural Issues before the ICJ

Although the limited scope of this chapter does not permit us to discuss the procedure applicable before the ICJ in great detail, two procedural issues will be briefly highlighted: interim or provisional measures, and the intervention of third parties in proceedings before the Court.

1. Interim or Provisional Measures

Like many courts, the ICJ has the power to order interim or provisional measures in urgent cases in order to protect the rights of either party against irreparable injury.[152] In recent years, there has been a significant increase in the use of the Court's incidental jurisdiction.[153] Two legal issues arise in this respect: (i) whether such orders are binding on the parties; and (ii) what the incidence of objections to the jurisdiction of the Court on its power to order provisional measures is. As the Statute uses the word 'indicate' instead of the more compelling 'order', it was long unclear whether provisional measures were actually binding on the parties. Since the Court's affirmation of the binding nature of those measures in the *LaGrand* case, the controversy seems to have settled.[154] As to the second issue, it is noted that the Court has to rule on the urgent request for provisional measures *before* it addresses the preliminary objections, which typically relate to the Court's jurisdiction (if such objections are made of course). It may be the case that the Court is asked to order provisional measures when its very jurisdiction over the dispute is in doubt. The Court has solved this conundrum by considering that objections to jurisdiction do not necessarily preclude it from ordering provisional measures, but that a manifest lack of jurisdiction does.[155] It is noted that the ICJ does not, as a matter of course, accede to requests for the indication/order of provisional measures.[156] Even if it accedes to such requests and orders provisional measures – which are now considered as binding – it is unfortunately not a given that States will comply.[157]

2. Third Parties

As far as the role of third parties is concerned, the ICJ Statute provides that a State may submit a request to the Court to be permitted to intervene if it considers 'that it has an interest of a legal nature which may be affected by the decision in the case'.[158] Such a State may intervene even if it has not accepted the jurisdiction of the Court. After all, by intervening it does not necessarily become a party to the dispute. Another consequence of the State

[152] Art 41 ICJ Statute, providing that the Court can 'indicate, if it considers that circumstances so require, any provisional measures which ought to be taken to preserve the respective rights of either party'.

[153] See further, D Akande, 'Selection of the International Court of Justice as a Forum for Contentious and Advisory Proceedings (Including Jurisdiction)' (2016) 7 *JIDS* 320.

[154] *LaGrand* (Germany v United States) [2001] ICJ Rep 501, para 98 ff (confirming the binding character of its order for provisional measures made in that case).

[155] cp *Legality of Use of Force* (Yugoslavia v United States of America) [1999] ICJ Rep 916, para 29; see also *Bosnian Genocide* [1996] (n 103).

[156] For a rejection, see eg *Passage through the Great Belt* (Finland v Denmark) [1991] ICJ Rep 218.

[157] For lack of compliance on the part of European States, see eg *Fisheries* (n 108) and *Bosnian Genocide* [2007] (n 104).

[158] Art 62 ICJ Statute.

not being a party to the dispute is also that it is not bound by the Court's decision.[159] The ICJ is not required to invite third parties to intervene if their interests may be affected by a decision in a given case, let alone decline jurisdiction over the case. Things might be different, however, if a decision does not simply 'affect' a State's interests, but if the rights and obligations of a third party are at the heart of the dispute. Thus, in the *Monetary Gold Case*, in which the Court was called on to pronounce itself on the international responsibility of Albania – which was not a party to the proceedings and had not accepted the jurisdiction of the Court – the Court declined to exercise jurisdiction, given the lack of consent by Albania.[160]

It is finally pointed out that the Court is not bound by precedent, although obviously it attaches great authority to its prior statements of the law.[161] The judgment is only binding upon the parties to the case, who are required to comply with the Court's ruling.[162] As is usual in international dispute settlement, the ICJ's judgment cannot be appealed.[163] Still, '[i]n the event of dispute as to the meaning or scope of the judgment', any party can submit a request for interpretation to the Court,[164] and 'upon the discovery of some fact of such a nature as to be a decisive factor', an application for revision of a judgment may be made.[165] In the history of the ICJ, States have filed a number of applications requesting the Court to revise an earlier judgment. The best 'European' example is the former FRY 2001 application for revision of the 1996 judgment in the Case concerning Application of the Convention on the Prevention and Punishment of the Crime of Genocide. In this application, the FRY argued that its admission to the UN in 2000 constituted a new fact. The ICJ, however, held that a fact which occurs several years after a judgment has been given is not a 'new' fact, irrespective of the legal consequences that such a fact may have, and thus found the application inadmissible.[166]

3. Advisory Opinions

A number of international courts not only have the power to settle disputes between parties, but also to give advisory opinions at the request of an entity to which they are institutionally linked. Typically this involves a request by another organ of the international organisation to which the Court is linked. The ICJ is the best-known example of an international court invested with this advisory jurisdiction, although it is not the only one. In fact, the ICJ's predecessor, the PCIJ, gave in its relatively short lifespan more advisory opinions than

[159] Art 63 ICJ Statute also grants third States a right to intervene in the proceedings '[w]henever the construction of a convention to which states other than those concerned in the case are parties is in question'. Art 63 clarifies that, unlike the situation with respect to Art 62, if the State uses this right of intervention, 'the construction given by the judgment will be equally binding upon it'. Still, even if the State does not intervene, it will be hard-pressed to cast aside an authoritative interpretation of the convention by the ICJ. cp Thirlway (n 89) 578.

[160] *Monetary Gold Removed from Rome in 1943* [1954] ICJ Rep 19, 32–33. *East Timor (Portugal v. Australia), Judgment*, [1995] ICJ Rep 90, 105 (Court ruling that it cannot exercise its jurisdiction because 'in order to decide the claims of Portugal, it would have to rule, as a prerequisite, on the lawfulness of Indonesia's conduct in the absence of that State's consent').

[161] Art 59 ICJ Statute.

[162] Art 94(1) of the UN Charter. Instances of non-compliance can be brought before the UN Security Council by virtue of Art 94(2) of the UN Charter.

[163] Decisions of WTO panels, as well as decisions of international criminal tribunals, can be appealed, however.

[164] Art 60 ICJ Statute.

[165] Art 61 ICJ Statute.

[166] *Application for Revision of the Judgment of 11 July 1996 in the Case concerning Application of the Convention on the Prevention and Punishment of the Crime of Genocide* (Yugoslavia v Bosnia and Herzegovina) [2003] ICJ Rep 7.

the ICJ: 27 opinions to the ICJ's 24.[167] This may be explained by the fact that the Council of the League of Nations – a political body that could request an advisory opinion from the Court – often referred a legal dispute to the Court for an advisory opinion so as to avoid making a (politically sensitive) decision.[168] The PCIJ's advisory opinions in fact settled contentious disputes (albeit in a non-binding manner), rather than 'giving advice' in the current sense of the term.

Other international and regional tribunals also have the power to issue advisory opinions, such as ITLOS, the ECtHR, or binding opinions outside the context of a dispute, in particular the CJEU. The Seabed Disputes Chamber of ITLOS has advisory jurisdiction with respect to the exploration and exploitation of the deep seabed directly on the basis of UNCLOS.[169] The ITLOS has advisory jurisdiction over any law of the sea question on the basis of its own procedural rules, provided that an international agreement related to the purposes of UNCLOS specifically provides for the submission to the Tribunal of a request for such an opinion.[170] Both the Seabed Disputes Chamber and ITLOS itself have each issued one opinion so far.[171] The ECHR for its part provides in Articles 47–49 that the ECtHR may give an advisory opinion on a legal question put to it by the Committee of Ministers concerning the interpretation of the ECHR and its Protocols.[172] Only very rarely has the Committee made a request for an advisory opinion. In 2002, a request was made concerning the co-existence of the ECHR and the Commonwealth of Independent States Convention of 1995. It was rejected by the Court in 2004 as being beyond its competence.[173] A second request concerned Ukraine's withdrawal of Court candidates, in which the Court upheld the position, taken by the Parliamentary Assembly, that withdrawal of candidates could only take place before the deadline as set.[174] Finally, the CJEU has jurisdiction to deliver an Opinion on the compatibility of an agreement concluded between the EU and one or more third countries or international organisations.[175] For example, in Opinion 2/13 of 2014, the CJEU famously held that the agreement on the accession of the European Union to the European Convention on Human Rights was 'not compatible with Article 6(2) TEU or with Protocol (No 8) relating to Article 6(2) of the Treaty on European Union on the accession of the Union to the European Convention

[167] Art 14 of the Covenant of the League of Nations provided that the PCIJ 'may also give an Advisory Opinion upon any dispute or question referred to it by the Council or the Assembly [of the League]'. The power to give an advisory opinion did not figure in the PCIJ Statute, however. It does in the ICJ Statute, Chapter IV.

[168] A Aust, 'Advisory Opinions' (2010) 1 *JIDS* 123, 129. The UN Security Council, the main political organ of the UN, in contrast, requested only one advisory opinion: *Legal Consequences for States of the Continued Presence of South Africa in Namibia (South West Africa) notwithstanding Security Council Resolution 276 (1970)* [1971] ICJ Rep 16. Political organs' decisions to refer nettlesome legal questions to courts elicit the question as to whether a court receiving an advisory question should not sometimes refuse to render an opinion. See below, this section.

[169] Art 191 UNCLOS. On the Seabed Disputes Chamber, see also Chapter 18, Section IX(B).

[170] ITLOS, *Rules of the Tribunal*, 17 March 2009, ITLOS/8, Art 138.

[171] *Responsibilities and obligations of States with respect to activities in the Area* (Advisory Opinion) [2011] ITLOS Rep 10; *Request submitted by the Sub-Regional Fisheries Commission* (Advisory Opinion) [2015] ITLOS Rep 4.

[172] Art 47(1) ECHR: 'The Court may, at the request of the Committee of Ministers, give advisory opinions on legal questions concerning the interpretation of the Convention and the Protocols thereto'. The use of the word 'may' suggests that the ECtHR, like the ICJ, is not *required* to give an advisory opinion.

[173] *Decision on the Competence of the Court to Give an Advisory Opinion* (ECtHR, 2 June 2004).

[174] *Advisory opinion on certain legal questions concerning the lists of candidates submitted with a view to the election of judges to the European Court of Human Rights (No 2)* (ECtHR, 22 January 2010).

[175] Art 218 (11) TFEU: 'A Member State, the European Parliament, the Council or the Commission may obtain the opinion of the Court of Justice as to whether an agreement envisaged is compatible with the Treaties. Where the opinion of the Court is adverse, the agreement envisaged may not enter into force unless it is amended or the Treaties are revised'.

on the Protection of Human Rights and Fundamental Freedoms'.[176] The CJEU also has the jurisdiction to decide on Member States' courts' references for a preliminary ruling on the interpretation or validity of EU law.[177] However, neither Opinions pursuant to Article 218(11) TFEU nor preliminary rulings are advisory opinions, as both are binding.

Only the ICJ can give advisory opinions on questions of general international law. The UN Charter provides for ICJ advisory jurisdiction in Article 96, whereas the ICJ Statute sets out the principles governing advisory opinions in Articles 65–68. Article 65(1) of the Statute provides that the ICJ 'may give an Advisory Opinion on any legal question', that may have to be construed as any *international* legal question. Not all international legal persons can request an advisory opinion. Only the main organs of the UN as well as a number of specialised international agencies (in case their constituent instruments give them this power) can do so. The UN General Assembly and Security Council can request an opinion on any legal question. The other UN bodies and agencies must ask a question that falls within the scope of their activities. So far, most requests have emanated from the UN General Assembly. ECOSOC has requested two opinions,[178] and the UNSC only one.[179] The specialised agencies have similarly requested only a few opinions (UNESCO, IMCO, WHO).[180]

By their very nature, ICJ advisory opinions are merely advisory in nature, and not binding. States and organisations are of course free to nevertheless accept the Court's advisory opinions as binding. For example, Section 30 of the General Convention on the Privileges and Immunities of the Specialized Agencies of the UN of 1946 provides that an advisory opinion of the ICJ 'shall be accepted as decisive' by the parties. The Court has so far rendered two such 'binding' opinions on the privileges and immunities of UN special rapporteurs.[181] It is noted that the generally non-binding character of ICJ advisory opinions does not exercise a particularly strong pull towards compliance. It is, for instance, well-known that Israel did not act upon the findings of the Court in the *Wall* case, where

[176] Opinion of 18 December 2014, Accession of the EU to the ECHR, 2/13, EU:C:2014:2454 (Opinion 2/13). See further eg P Eeckhout, 'Opinion 2/13 on EU Accession to the ECHR and Judicial Dialogue: Autonomy or Autarky' (2015) 38 *Fordham International Law Journal* 955–92; J Odermatt, 'A Giant Step Backwards? Opinion 2/13 on the EU's Accession to the European Convention on Human Rights' (2015) 47 *NYU Journal of International Law and Politics* 783.

[177] Art 267 TFEU, on which see K Lenaerts, I Maselis and K Gutman (JT Nowak ed), *EU Procedural Law* (Oxford, OUP, 2014) chapters 6, 10, and 24.

[178] See *Applicability of Article VI, Section 22, of the Convention on the Privileges and Immunities of the United Nations ('Mazilu')* (Advisory Opinion) [1989] ICJ Rep 177; and *Difference Relating to Immunity from Legal Process of a Special Rapporteur of the Commission on Human Rights ('Cumaraswamy')* (Advisory Opinion) [1999] ICJ Rep 62.

[179] See *Legal Consequences for States of the Continued Presence of South Africa in Namibia (South West Africa) notwithstanding Security Council Resolution 276 (1970)* (n 168). The circumstances that allowed this question to be put to the Court were probably unique: no great power felt the need to 'protect' an outcast such as South Africa from the advisory jurisdiction of the Court.

[180] See *Judgments of the Administrative Tribunal of the ILO upon Complaints made against UNESCO* (Advisory Opinion) [1956] ICJ Rep 77; *Constitution of the Maritime Safety Committee of IMCO* (Advisory Opinion) [1960] ICJ Rep 150; and *Interpretation of the Agreement of 25 March 1951 between the WHO and Egypt* (Advisory Opinion) [1980] ICJ Rep 73. A second Advisory Opinion requested by the WHO, on the Legality of the Threat or Use by a State of Nuclear Weapons in Armed Conflict, was rejected by the ICJ because the question of the legality of such action did not arise within the scope of the activities of' the WHO; *Legality of the Threat or Use by a State of Nuclear Weapons in Armed Conflict* [1996] ICJ Rep 66.

[181] See *Mazilu* and *Cumaraswamy* (n 178).

the Court found Israel's building of a security fence separating the occupied Palestinian Territories from Israel to be in breach of international human rights and humanitarian law.

The aforementioned *Wall* case raises the question whether the Court should refrain from laying down the rights and duties of a State in an advisory opinion, especially if that State is embroiled in a legal dispute with another State or entity, and has not given its consent, as was the case with Israel. This argument has informed the PCIJ's refusal to render an advisory opinion in the *Eastern Carelia* case, on the ground that the case in question really concerned a dispute between two States (Finland and the USSR), one of which had not consented to the Court's jurisdiction and was not even a member of the League of Nations in the first place.[182] It was affirmed by the ICJ in the *Western Sahara* case, where the Court recognised 'that lack of consent might constitute a ground for declining to give the Opinion requested if, in the circumstances of a given case, considerations of judicial propriety should oblige the Court to refuse an Opinion', for example 'when the circumstances disclose that to give a reply would have the effect of circumventing the principle that a State is not obliged to allow its disputes to be submitted to judicial settlement without its consent'.[183] Still, the ICJ has never found such circumstances to be present. It has never held cases to be inadmissible on the ground that the case was of a contentious nature,[184] although at times the Court's opinions may govern the legal responsibilities of States, as in the *Wall* opinion. This has led Dixon to argue that such advisory opinions 'may effectively crystallize those responsibilities at the date of judgment'.[185]

States whose responsibilities may thus be determined, obviously have a strong interest in having their views heard by the Court. In fact, *all* States, while not being entitled to put requests for an advisory opinion to the ICJ, are allowed to make representations (written or oral statements). As far as the ICJ's three opinions that are most well-known in the political arena are concerned, it is noted that in the *Nuclear Weapons* opinion of 1996, written statements were filed by eight EU Member States and three other European States, in the *Wall* opinion of 2004, by 13 EU Member States, three other European States and by the EU itself (through the Irish presidency), and in the *Kosovo* opinion,[186] by 18 EU Member States and five other European States. These data suggest more European interest in the advisory jurisdiction of the ICJ, although one should not overlook that there was a worldwide increase in the number of States filing written statements in advisory proceedings before the ICJ,[187] and that European States had an obvious interest in the *Kosovo* opinion. It can be argued that the EU as such may also be entitled to give its opinion where it is a party to a treaty that is being interpreted, since the ICJ Statute allows not only States but also international organisations to file a written statement.[188] Exceptionally, also other non-State actors – or at least territorial actors whose statehood may be in doubt – may file

[182] *Eastern Carelia* [1923] PCIJ Series B, No 5.
[183] *Western Sahara* [1975] ICJ Rep 12, paras 32–33.
[184] It is noted, in passing, that in advisory proceedings, unlike in contentious proceedings, the Court does not render a separate opinion addressing preliminary observations concerning jurisdiction, admissibility, or the exercise of discretion for that matter. The Court tackles such preliminary matters and the merits in one and the same opinion.
[185] Dixon (n 20) 318.
[186] *Accordance with International Law of the Unilateral Declaration of Independence in Respect of Kosovo* (Advisory Opinion) [2010] ICJ Rep 403.
[187] Akande (n 153).
[188] Art 66(2) ICJ Statute.

such a statement. In the *Kosovo* opinion, the Court allowed the authors of the unilateral declaration of independence (the Kosovo provisional institutions for self-government) to file a written contribution.[189]

As only international organisations and their organs have the power to put questions to the Court, the Court has been mainly confronted with internal institutional 'housekeeping' questions on which the Court is then supposed to give guidance to the requesting institutions.[190] Such questions are often not particularly controversial, and therefore, it is not surprising that the Court has so far not yet used its discretion *not* to give an opinion.[191] It has held consistently that only 'for compelling reasons' would it refuse to give an opinion (without such compelling reasons ever been considered present by the Court).[192] This stance is justified by the institutional role of the Court within the UN and the wider UN system. The Court has held in this respect that an advisory opinion represents the Court's 'participation in the activities of the Organization, and [therefore], in principle, should not be refused'.[193] Occasionally, however, advisory opinions involve serious political questions, eg, the *Wall*, *Kosovo* and *Nuclear Weapons* opinions. Other advisory opinions may seem to be technical but have behind them a greater political conflict, eg, *Certain Expenses*, which concerned the legality of UN peacekeeping operations. It is expected that in such cases the ICJ may use its power not to give an opinion. In the *Nuclear Weapons* case, the Court came quite close to refusal. Eventually, the opinion was given, because of the casting vote of the President. It was also in this case that the ICJ for the first and only time ruled that it could not entertain a legal question put to it on the ground that it did not fall within the scope of the activities of the requesting organisation/agency. The WHO was considered not to have the power to ask a question concerning the legality of nuclear weapons, since 'none of the functions of the WHO [which relate to health] is dependent upon the legality of the situations upon which it must act'.[194] In contrast, the Court did entertain the same question as put to it by the UN General Assembly. Replying to the objection that the UNGA did not need such an opinion, the Court forcefully stated that

> it is not for the ICJ itself to purport to decide whether or not an Advisory Opinion is needed by the Assembly for the performance of its functions. The General Assembly has the right to decide for itself on the usefulness of an Opinion in the light of its own needs.[195]

In so doing, the Court showed its reluctance to pass judgment on how the other organs of the UN perceive their powers and jurisdiction, thereby in fact reiterating a stance already

[189] *Accordance with International Law of the Unilateral Declaration of Independence in Respect of Kosovo*, Written Contribution of the Authors of the Unilateral Ceclaration of Independence, 17 April 2009, icj-cij.org/files/case-related/141/15678.pdf. This written contribution was formally filed by the Republic of Kosovo.

[190] cp *Reservations to the Convention on the Prevention and Punishment of the Crime of Genocide* [1951] ICJ Rep 15, 19: 'The object of this request for an Opinion is to guide the United Nations in respect of its own action'. See also *Legal Consequences for States of the Continued Presence of South Africa in Namibia (South West Africa) notwithstanding Security Council Resolution 276 (1970)* (n 168) para 32: 'The request is put forward by a United Nations organ with reference to its own decisions and it seeks legal advice from the Court on the consequences and implications of these decisions'.

[191] Art 65(1) ICJ Statute provides that the ICJ '*may* give an Advisory Opinion on any legal question' (emphasis added).

[192] *Certain Expenses of the United Nations* [1962] ICJ Rep 151, 155; *Cumaraswamy* (n 178); *Wall* (n 151) para 65.

[193] *Interpretation of Peace Treaties* [1950] ICJ Rep 65, 71.

[194] *Legality of Nuclear Weapons* (n 180).

[195] ibid, para 16.

enunciated in the *Certain Expenses* case: 'each [UN] organ must, in the first place at least, determine its own jurisdiction'.[196]

Still, the fact that the ICJ in the *Nuclear Weapons* case nearly declined to render an opinion, points to the politically controversial nature of the question asked. While the UNGA undeniably has the power to ask a question concerning the legality of the use of nuclear weapons, and while the question may truly be a *legal* question,[197] the Court may possibly have been well-advised to use its discretionary power *not* to answer the question on the grounds that the question was politically motivated, and that rendering an opinion would complicate negotiations and fail to address the broader political issue. The same observations may be made regarding those two other politically sensitive requests: the *Wall* and *Kosovo*.[198] The ICJ may especially want to abstain from interposing itself where both the UNGA and the UNSC are dealing with the same issues.[199]

iii. The ICJ versus the UN Security Council

In light of the pre-eminence of the UNSC in matters of peace and security, in particular its powers to take binding measures under Chapter VII of the UN Charter in response to a threat to the peace, a breach of the peace, or an act of aggression, it could be argued that the ICJ should defer to the Council where the latter is addressing a case that is put before the Court. This would be true regardless of whether the case was put before the Court on the basis of an application for the opening of contentious proceedings or on the basis of a request for an advisory opinion. Such a stance would, however, negate the judicial role of the ICJ, a main organ of the UN. Moreover, the ICJ seems to have guarded its judicial prerogatives. In circumstances where a matter was also before the Security Council, the Court has, only in the *Lockerbie* case and only with respect to Libya's request for provisional measures, deferred to the Council. In that case, it refused to order provisional measures on the ground that the UNSC had made a determination under Chapter VII of the Charter. It noted, in particular, that the rights which the US and the UK (against which the case was brought and which are permanent members of the Security Council) enjoyed pursuant to the relevant resolution would be prejudiced if the Court were to accede to the request.[200]

[196] *Certain Expenses* (n 192) 168; adding that '[p]roposals made during the drafting of the Charter to place the ultimate authority to interpret the Charter in the International Court of Justice were not accepted; the opinion which the Court is in course of rendering is an *advisory* opinion'.

[197] Quite obviously, the Court will declare inadmissible purely political, moral or factual questions that have no legal dimension. With respect to moral questions, see eg *International Status of South-West Africa* (Advisory Opinion) [1950] ICJ Rep 128. The Court has noted, however, that 'a mixed question of law and fact is nonetheless a legal question within the meaning of art 96(1)' of the UN Charter; cp *Western Sahara* (n 183) paras 32–33.

[198] Aust (n 168) 149–51; highlighting the relevance of the voting pattern of UN General Assembly resolutions requesting an advisory opinion (eg, the *Kosovo* request which was made by 77 States with 6 objecting and 74 abstentions); and pointing out that the 'ICJ professes to ignore [...] the politically controversial nature of the two latest requests [*Wall* (n 151) and *Kosovo* (n 186)]' and that the *Wall* and *Nuclear Weapons* advisory opinions 'were on politically controversial matters that will never be solved by an Advisory Opinion'.

[199] Note that where a particular subject-matter is before both the UNSC and the UNGA, both organs may nevertheless address discrete issues, thus not necessarily barring the ICJ's exercise of advisory jurisdiction. See *Wall* (n 151) para 27: 'It is often the case that, while the Security Council has tended to focus on the aspects of such matters related to international peace and security, the General Assembly has taken a broader view'.

[200] *Questions of Interpretation and Application of the 1971 Montreal Convention arising from the Aerial Incident at Lockerbie* (Libyan Arab Jamahiriya v United States of America) [1992] ICJ Rep 114, para 42. The Resolution's obligations prima facie overrode any rights claimed by Libya under the Convention for the Suppression of Unlawful Acts Against the Safety of Civil Aviation (adopted 23 September 1971, entered into force 26 January 1973) 974 UNTS 177, by virtue of Arts 25 and 103 of the UN Charter.

Still, in the same case, in the later preliminary objections phase, the ICJ refused to declare the application inadmissible, pointing out that Libya had filed its application with the Court when the Council had only adopted a resolution that 'was a mere recommendation without binding effect'.[201] By the same token, in the *Congo v Uganda* case, the ICJ granted interim measures because the Council had not taken a binding decision, but only 'demanded' the cessation of hostilities between the parties.[202] In general, the Court has not viewed the fact that the UNSC was considering a specific matter, or certain aspects of a dispute, as a bar to its jurisdiction. In the *Nicaragua* case, the Court stated in this respect:

> The Court is of the opinion that the fact that a matter is before the Security Council should not prevent it from being dealt with by the Court and that both proceedings could be pursued pari passu. The Council has functions of a political nature assigned to it, whereas the Court exercises purely judicial functions. Both organs can therefore perform their separate but complementary functions with respect to the same events.[203]

A somewhat related matter is whether the ICJ could review resolutions of the Security Council in light of higher norms of international law, for example, norms of *jus cogens*. An affirmative answer to this question would cast doubt on the traditional interpretation of Article 103 of the UN Charter, which is seen as protecting the hierarchically higher status of Security Council resolutions (those instruments contain the main obligations which UN member States can have under the Charter). In any event, as the ICJ is not – unlike the CJEU – a constitutional court, neither States nor other organs of the UN can directly apply for the annulment of a Security Council resolution considered as ultra vires. There is, however, still the option of incidental review of a resolution in contentious proceedings, where one party invokes the invalidity of a resolution advanced by the other. No such review has so far occurred.[204]

C. Binding Dispute Settlement Mechanisms in Europe

European States often make use of universal dispute settlement mechanisms such as the ICJ, the PCA, or the WTO. Still, quite a number of regional dispute settlement mechanisms have been established within Europe. Reference has already been made to the seldom-used OSCE Court of Conciliation and Arbitration. Of much greater importance, however, is the CJEU. A detailed discussion of the powers of review of those courts is beyond the scope of this book but it should be noted that they provide a high level of judicial protection: they provide access to justice for individuals (notably the ECtHR, but also the CJEU). The CJEU even serves as a full-fledged constitutional court hearing disputes between organs

[201] *Lockerbie* [1998] (n 110) para 44.

[202] *Armed Activities on the Territory of the Congo* (Democratic Republic of the Congo v Uganda) [2000] ICJ Rep 111, para 36.

[203] *Nicaragua* (n 13) paras 89–98. See also *Tehran* (n 130) and *Wall* (n 151).

[204] *Jus cogens* incompatibility of a UN Security Council resolution was however raised in a 'European' dispute before the ICJ. In *Bosnian Genocide Case*, Bosnia raised the argument that UNSC Res 713 (1991), 25 September 1991, UN Doc S/RES/713, which imposed an arms embargo on Yugoslavia, violated *jus cogens*, since an all-out embargo – relating to the entire territory of Yugoslavia, including Bosnia – facilitated the genocide of Bosnian Muslims by the already more heavily armed Serbs. The argument was not addressed by the Court, but it was touched upon ad hoc by judge Lauterpacht in his separate opinion; cp *Application of the Convention on the Prevention and Punishment of the Crime of Genocide* (Bosnia and Herzegovina v Serbia and Montenegro) (Order) [1993] ICJ Rep 325, Separate Opinion of Judge Lauterpacht, para 104. See further Klabbers (n 106) 225.

and Member States of the organisation.[205] One should not fail to note that the CJEU has a sister court sitting opposite its own premises in Luxembourg, the EFTA Court, which serves the parties to the EFTA/EEA.[206] The Benelux for its part has had its Court of Justice since 1974 and may resort to a (so far dormant) Arbitral College. Most European organisations also provide for internal administrative tribunals that can hear staff disputes; appeals boards have been established at the OECD, the CoE, NATO, and the European Space Agency. Finally, of note are the claims and compensation bodies that dealt rather belatedly with individuals' loss of assets during the Second World War: the Claims Resolution Tribunal for Dormant Accounts in Switzerland (1997) and the German Forced Labour Compensation Programme (2000).

D. Proliferation of International Courts and Problems of Coordination

As may be clear from the discussion in this chapter, many international dispute settlement mechanisms have been established. This proliferation of international courts, tribunals,[207] and other mechanisms can lead to forum-shopping by parties and to coordination problems. It is indeed not excluded that several mechanisms can have jurisdiction over a dispute that raises issues straddling different fields of the law. Institutional turf wars may ensue when those mechanisms actually exercise their jurisdiction. Even worse, when reaching a decision, they may apply and interpret the law differently or come to contradictory conclusions. While some judicial pluralism may seem desirable, in that competition may tend to raise standards, ultimately, incoherence in the law and uncertainty as to the competent dispute settlement mechanism does not particularly further trust in international law and institutions.[208]

From a European perspective, the judicial vagaries of the MOX Plant litigation deserve some attention here. When in 2001, the United Kingdom started operating a Mixed Oxide (MOX) plant in Sellafield, on the Irish Sea, Ireland initiated legal proceedings against the UK, claiming that the UK had violated rules of international environmental law, with an UNCLOS arbitral tribunal, the ITLOS (provisional measures jurisdiction), and with a tribunal established under the 1992 Convention for the Protection of the Marine Environment of the North East Atlantic (OSPAR Convention). Subsequently, the European Commission initiated proceedings against Ireland before the ECJ on the grounds that Ireland had had recourse to another dispute settlement mechanism in violation of the duty of loyal cooperation as laid down in Article 10 TEC (now Article 4(3) TEU) and

[205] See further eg E Sharpston and G De Baere, 'The Court of Justice as a Constitutional Adjudicator' in A Arnull, C Barnard, M Dougan, E Spaventa (eds), *A Constitutional Order of States? Essays in EU Law in Honour of Alan Dashwood* (Oxford, Hart, 2011) 123–50. On the CJEU, see also Chapter 7 on Regional Organisations, Section II(B)(ii).

[206] Only Norway, Iceland, and Liechtenstein. It is mainly competent to deal with disputes between the parties (Art 32), infringement actions brought by the EFTA Surveillance Authority against the EFTA State (Arts 31 and 35), appeals brought against the EFTA Surveillance Authority (Art 35) and advisory opinions on the interpretation of EEA rules (Art 36): Agreement between the EFTA States on the Establishment of a Surveillance Authority and a Court of Justice (adopted 2 May 1992, entered into force 1 January 1994) OJ L344/1.

[207] T Buergenthal, 'Proliferation of International Courts and Tribunals: Is It Good or Bad?' (2001) 14 *LJIL* 267.

[208] ILC, Report of the Study Group of the International Law Commission Fragmentation of International Law: 'Difficulties Arising from the Diversification and Expansion of International Law', finalised by Martti Koskenniemi, 13 April 2006, UN Doc A/CN.4/L.682.

Article 192 Euratom Treaty, and of Article 292 TEC (now Article 344 TFEU) pursuant to which 'Member States undertake not to submit a dispute concerning the interpretation or application of this Treaty to any method of settlement other than those provided for therein'.

Of the four mechanisms that dealt with the dispute, only one – the UNCLOS arbitral tribunal – appeared to realise and acknowledge that the dispute was heard by several courts and tribunals, and that perhaps some institutional coordination or deference was called for. Pending the outcome of the case brought before the ECJ, it suspended its own proceedings on grounds of mutual respect and comity.[209] Such jurisdictional reluctance was almost entirely absent at the OSPAR arbitration tribunal, ITLOS, and the ECJ. The OSPAR tribunal refused to pay heed to relevant EU law, ruling that the OSPAR Convention and EU law were distinct legal regimes.[210] Similarly, ITLOS held that the rights and obligations under the OSPAR Convention, the EC Treaty and the Euratom Treaty have a separate existence from those under UNCLOS, and took the reaching of different results by various dispute settlement mechanisms for granted.[211]

The ECJ for its part held that, although 'environment' is a competence shared between the Community and the Member States, the EC was a party to UNCLOS (which thus qualified as a 'mixed' agreement) and had 'very largely regulated' the areas submitted by Ireland to the UNCLOS arbitral tribunal.[212] Therefore, according to the Court, the provisions of UNCLOS came within the scope of EU law, which then triggered the exclusive jurisdiction of the ECJ.[213] The Court added that Ireland had violated its duty of loyalty by failing to consult with the Commission before starting proceedings under UNCLOS.[214] While, under EU law, this conclusion may well be warranted, it may fail to catch the bigger picture: the need to limit competition and to further cooperation between different dispute settlement mechanisms. While the ECJ may now have brought some welcome clarity with respect to matters that are governed by mixed agreements, one may wonder whether it has not unduly outmanoeuvered other relevant dispute settlement mechanisms. In particular, it is important to bear in mind that Article 282 of UNCLOS specifically regulates the relationship between obligations under that treaty and obligations under general, regional, or bilateral agreements, and contains a 'friendly' conflict rule with respect to other dispute

[209] *MOX Plant* (Ireland v United Kingdom), Award of 24 June 2003, PCA Order No 3, para 28: 'In the circumstances, and bearing in mind considerations of mutual respect and comity which should prevail between judicial institutions both of which may be called upon to determine rights and obligations as between two States, the Tribunal considers that it would be inappropriate for it to proceed further with hearing the Parties on the merits of the dispute in the absence of a resolution of the problems referred to. Moreover, a procedure that might result in two conflicting decisions on the same issue would not be helpful to the resolution of the dispute between the Parties'. In 2000, an UNCLOS arbitral panel had espoused a similar approach in the *Southern Bluefin Tuna* case, in relation to fishing programs implemented by Japan, when it incorporated non-UNCLOS law in its decision: *Southern Bluefin Tuna* (Australia and New Zealand v Japan), Award of 4 August 2000, 39 ILM 1359, para 54: 'The Parties to this dispute – the real terms of which have been defined above – are the same Parties grappling not with two separate disputes but with what in fact is a single dispute arising under both Conventions. To find that, in this case, there is a dispute actually arising under UNCLOS which is distinct from the dispute that arose under the CCSBT (Convention for the Conservation of Southern Bluefin Tuna) would be artificial'.

[210] *MOX Plant* (n 209) para 142. For a critical commentary, see Y Shany, 'The first MOX Plant Award: The Need to Harmonize Competing Environmental Regimes and Dispute Settlement Procedures' (2004) 17 *LJIL* 815.

[211] *MOX Plant* (Ireland v United Kingdom) (Order) [2001] ITLOS Rep 95, paras 49–51.

[212] Judgment of 30 May 2006 *European Commission v Ireland*, C-459/03, EU:C:2006:345, para 110.

[213] ibid, paras 127–28.

[214] ibid, paras 179–81.

settlement mechanisms.[215] This raises the question of what would happen if an international agreement in question does not contain such a rule.[216] The absence of a similar provision in the ECHR was one of the elements that led the CJEU in Opinion 2/13 to the conclusion that the Draft agreement on the accession of the EU to the ECHR was liable to affect Article 344 TFEU. The Court explicitly contrasted the set-up in the ECHR with that at issue in *MOX Plant*.[217] Opinion 2/13 appears to imply that provisions in an international agreement much like Article 344 TFEU, which prevent parties from bringing disputes pertaining to the agreement in question before other dispute settlement mechanisms, are inherently problematic.[218] An example is Article 23(1) of the WTO Dispute Settlement Understanding (DSU),[219] which appears to imply that two EU Member States bringing a case against each other on matters of WTO law before the ECJ would violate Article 23(1) DSU. Conversely, if two EU Member States brought a dispute between them on WTO law before the DSB, they would violate Article 344 TFEU. Neither the judgment in *MOX Plant* nor Opinion 2/13 appear to be helpful in indicating how such conflicts could be resolved,[220] except of course by persuading the other parties to the 'non-compliant' international agreement to amend the agreement by inserting a 'friendly' conflict rule akin to Article 282 UNCLOS. That said, at least with respect to the WTO, problems in that regard are in practice unlikely to occur, as cases brought against EU Member States under the DSU are as a rule taken up by the Union, represented by the Commission.[221]

Possibly, giving direct effect to the treaties that constitute the applicable law before those mechanisms may go some way to close the legitimacy gap opened by the ECJ claiming exclusive jurisdiction over mixed agreements.[222]

[215] 'If the States Parties which are parties to a dispute concerning the interpretation or application of this Convention have agreed, through a general, regional or bilateral agreement or otherwise, that such dispute shall, at the request of any party to the dispute, be submitted to a procedure that entails a binding decision, that procedure shall apply in lieu of the procedures provided for in this Part, unless the parties to the dispute otherwise agree'.

[216] G De Baere, 'EU Status in Other International Organizations' in R Schütze and T Tridimas (eds), *Oxford Principles of European Union Law*, Vol 1: The European Union Legal Order (Oxford, OUP, 2018) 1249–50.

[217] Opinion 2/13 (n 176), para 205: 'Unlike the international convention at issue in the case giving rise to the judgment in *Commission v Ireland* (EU:C:2006:345, paras 124 and 125), which expressly provided that the system for the resolution of disputes set out in EU law must in principle take precedence over that established by that convention, the procedure for the resolution of disputes provided for in Article 33 of the ECHR could apply to any Contracting Party and, therefore, also to disputes between the Member States, or between those Member States and the EU, even though it is EU law that is in issue'.

[218] De Baere (n 216) 1250–52.

[219] 'When Members seek the redress of a violation of obligations or other nullification or impairment of benefits under the covered agreements or an impediment to the attainment of any objective of the covered agreements, they shall have recourse to, and abide by, the rules and procedures of this Understanding'.

[220] With respect to *Mox Plant*, see P Eeckhout, *EU External Relations Law* (2nd edn, OUP, 2011) 240.

[221] F Hoffmeister, 'Outsider or Frontrunner? Recent Developments under International and European Law on the Status of the European Union in International Organizations and Treaty Bodies' (2007) 44 *Common Market Law Review* 41, 43; De Baere (n 216) 1252.

[222] cp PJ Caldwell and D French, 'Who Decides? The ECJ's Judgment on Jurisdiction in the *MOX Plant* Dispute' (2007) 19 *JEL* 121. Conferring the power to apply and interpret a convention of universal scope on as active a regional international court as the ECJ may, in light of the relative inactivity of the ITLOS, UNCLOS arbitral panels, and the ICJ in relation to law of the sea and environmental matters, create its own legitimacy problems, however. On the CJEU as an enforcement mechanism of international environmental treaties, as illustrated notably by the example of the Convention on Access to Information, Public Participation in Decision-Making and Access to Justice in Environmental Matters (the Aarhus Convention, on which see Chapter 20, Section II(A)(iv)), see G De Baere and JT Nowak, 'The Right to "Not Prohibitively Expensive" Judicial Proceedings under the Aarhus Convention and the ECJ as an International (Environmental) Law Court: *Edwards and Pallikaropoulos*' (2016) 53 *CMLR* 1727–52 (in particular from 1742 onward).

Interestingly, the ECJ's jealous guarding of its own jurisdiction vis-à-vis other courts and tribunals may have received a setback by the decision of the arbitral tribunal in the Arbitration regarding the Iron Rhine Railway.[223] In this decision, also concerning the application of international environmental law, the arbitral tribunal considered itself entitled to consider EU law as long as such would not require an 'interpretation' of EU law in the sense of conclusiveness or relevance.[224] The tribunal subsequently found that EU law was not applicable. It has been suggested that 'the very attempt by the tribunal to delimit jurisdiction in this way – through an "interpretation" of when EC treaty articles become operational – is itself an infringement of the jurisdiction of the ECJ',[225] and that the Commission could have brought proceedings against either Belgium or the Netherlands, like it had against Ireland in the *MOX Plant* case.[226]

IV. Concluding Remarks

The above overview goes to show that there exist a large number of international dispute settlement mechanisms, to the extent that States may even go forum-shopping for the most amenable mechanism. In spite of international courts' and tribunals' prevalence, however, few of them have busy dockets. It appears that only where individuals or other private persons have the right to sue (States) before dispute settlement mechanisms – notably in the human rights and investment context – will such mechanisms have more than a handful of cases to deal with.[227] A further reason for pause is that, even where dispute settlement mechanisms have jurisdiction, hear cases and issue rulings, these mechanisms will not necessarily be effective.[228] Indeed, as international courts and tribunals lack enforcement powers – unlike their domestic counterparts – it is uncertain whether they can command sufficient respect and compliance from States. This question of compliance obviously goes to the heart of international law as a legal system and has informed claims that international law is, given the lack of enforcement, not really law.[229]

As far as dispute settlement is concerned, it may, however, be noted that decisions of the various mechanisms are generally complied with. This compliance may perhaps not be so much a function of an internal 'pull for compliance', exerted by the authority of the decision itself, but rather by reputational and retaliatory consequences that could follow in case of non-compliance. From a law and economics perspective, apart from clarifying facts and the law, and thus reducing uncertainty, decisions by dispute settlement mechanisms generate important changes to the payoffs for States. Non-compliance by the losing

[223] *Arbitration Regarding the Iron Rhine ('IJzeren Rijn') Railway* (Belgium v Netherlands), Award of 24 May 2005, 27 RIAA 35.

[224] ibid, para 106.

[225] Caldwell (n 222).

[226] Crawford (n 3) note 85.

[227] The State-to-State dispute settlement mechanism of the WTO may be an exception.

[228] 'It is not enough to have courts and tribunals capable of handing down legal decisions. [States should be persuaded] to use them and mak[e] their decisions effective'; Merrills (n 76) 549.

[229] See further Chapter 1, Section V on Theory of International Law.

State will cause other States to update beliefs about the losing State's willingness to comply, and thereby possibly exclude the latter from benefits flowing from future cooperation (in economic terms, the non-complying State will have a higher discount rate).[230] Guzman has observed that compliance will generally be higher in case of tribunals that are (in terms of composition, funding, etc) largely dependent on the parties (eg investment tribunals). Rulings of such tribunals may indeed resemble settlements 'owned' by the parties, and accordingly be more effective than truly independent tribunals (eg, the ICJ, although this court also, to a limited extent, allows the parties to appoint their own ad hoc judges).[231] If that is true, judicial dependence may have to be relaxed. However, this may well go to the detriment of the fairness and integrity of the proceedings, especially where the parties to the litigation are not just States, but also individuals, such as in international human rights or international criminal law cases. Moreover, 'ownership' or 'privatisation' of dispute settlement – in essence a return to arbitration – may have an exclusionary effect on non-Western or weaker States, and raise questions of equity. Compliance expectations should thus only be one parameter in the design of dispute settlement mechanisms.

Under international law, States should settle their disputes peacefully. However, where a peaceful solution to a dispute cannot be obtained, a party may well contemplate resorting to armed force. The next chapter discusses the legal rules governing the use of force in international relations.

Bibliography

Aust, A, 'Advisory Opinions' (2010) 1 *JIDS* 123.

Akande, D, 'Selection of the International Court of Justice as a Forum for Contentious and Advisory Proceedings (Including Jurisdiction)' (2016) 7 *JIDS* 320.

Buergenthal, T, 'Proliferation of International Courts and Tribunals: Is It Good or Bad?' (2001) 14 *LJIL* 267.

Crawford, J, 'Continuity and Discontinuity in International Dispute Settlement: An Inaugural Lecture' (2010) 1 *JIDS* 3.

De Baere, G and Wouters, J (eds), *The Contribution of International and Supranational Courts to the Rule of Law* (Cheltenham, Edward Elgar, 2015).

Guzman, A, *How International Law Works* (Oxford, OUP, 2008).

Merrills, J, 'The Means of Dispute Settlement' in Evans, MD, *International Law*, 4th edn (Oxford, OUP, 2014) 563–88.

Merrills, J, *International Dispute Settlement*, 6th edn (Cambridge, CUP, 2017).

Thirlway, H, 'The International Court of Justice' in Evans, MD, *International Law*, 4th edn (Oxford, OUP, 2014) 589–617.

Zimmermann, A, Oellers-Frahm, K, Tomuschat, C, and Tams, CJ (eds), *The Statute of the International Court of Justice: A Commentary* (Oxford, OUP, 2007).

[230] Guzman (n 84) 51–52.
[231] ibid, 53.

Further Reading

Amr, MSM, *The Role of the International Court of Justice as the Principal Judicial Organ of the United Nations* (The Hague, Kluwer, 2003).

Bercovitch, J (ed), *Resolving International Conflicts: The Theory and Practice of Mediation* (London, Lynne Rienner, 1996).

Collier, J and Lowe, A, *The Settlement of Disputes in International Law* (Oxford, OUP, 1999).

Crawford, J and Nevill, P, 'Relations between International Courts and Tribunals: The "Regime Problem' in Young, MA (ed), *Regime Interaction in International Law* (Cambridge, CUP, 2012) 235–60.

De Baere, G, Chané, AL and Wouters, J, 'International Courts as Keepers of the Rule of Law: Achievements, Challenges, and Opportunities' (2016) 48 *New York University Journal of International Law & Politics* 715.

French, D, Saul, M and White, ND (eds), *International Law and Dispute Settlement* (Oxford, Hart, 2010).

Gray, C and Kingsbury, B, 'Developments in Dispute Settlement: Inter-State Arbitration since 1945' (1992) 63 *BYIL* 97.

Greenberg, MC, Barton, JH, and McGuinness, ME (eds), *Words over War: Mediation and Arbitration to Prevent Deadly Conflict* (Lanham, Rowman and Littlefield, 2000).

Kolb, R, *The International Court of Justice* (Oxford, Hart, 2013).

Lowe, V, 'The Function of Litigation in International Society' (2012) 61 *ICLQ* 209.

Rosenne, S, *The Law and Practice of the International Court, 1920–1996* (The Hague, Nijhoff, 1997).

Schneider, P, *Internationale Gerichtsbarkeit als Instrument friedlicher Streitbeilegung: von einer empirisch fundierten Theorie zu einem innovativen Konzept* (Baden-Baden, Nomos, 2003).

Shany, Y, *The Competing Jurisdictions of International Courts and Tribunals* (Oxford, OUP, 2003).

14

Use of Force and Collective Security[1]

I. Introduction

The present chapter examines the law regarding the use of force and collective security in international law. The laws of war, that is, the law governing the conduct of hostilities and the protection of persons *hors de combat* during armed conflict, is dealt with in Chapter 15.

The first part of this chapter deals with the prohibition on the use of force (Section II) and the exceptions to this rule under international law, addressing the right of self-defence (Section III) and other possibilities for unilateral recourse to force (Section IV). The second half turns towards collective security, examining action by the UN Security Council under Chapter VII of the UN Charter (Section V) and peacekeeping (Section VI). Lastly, this chapter turns to Chapter VIII of the UN Charter by addressing peacekeeping and enforcement action by regional organisations (Section VII).

II. The Prohibition on the Use of Force

A. From Jus ad Bellum to Jus Contra Bellum

For countless ages, States have invoked the rhetoric of justice when resorting to war. From the Roman era onwards, philosophers, theologians and natural law jurists have distinguished between just and unjust wars. Numerous authors, from St Augustine to Grotius, have drafted catalogues of criteria to determine when war was considered permissible. The main common denominator was the need for a 'just cause', by which it was understood that resort to war ought to occur only when provoked by another State's behaviour, and ought to constitute a reaction against a prior violation.[2]

[1] This chapter is a revised version of T Ruys, 'International Law on the Use of Force' in J Wouters, P De Man and N Verlinden (eds), *Armed Conflicts and the Law* (Antwerp, Intersentia, 2016) 107–40.

[2] The 'just war' doctrine nonetheless suffered from several fundamental weaknesses, chiefly the lack of an agreed set of 'just causes' and the absence of an impartial authority to assess the justness of war. The extent to

With the advance of positivist legal thinking in post-Westphalian Europe, the *bellum justum* doctrine was eventually abandoned. By the nineteenth century, it was generally accepted that, whereas international law imposed limitations on certain so-called 'measures short of war' (chiefly retorsions and reprisals)[3] and restricted the situations in which States could intervene in another State's domestic affairs, it did not forbid actual resort to war.[4] In short, war was regarded as a permissible (if perhaps 'last resort') means of settling inter-State disputes.[5] War was, as von Clausewitz famously put it, 'the continuation of politics by other means'.[6]

Eventually, the birth of total warfare, with its *levée en masse* and modern weaponry, compelled States to adopt legal restrictions on the recourse to war. The first modest initiatives were undertaken during the Hague Peace Conferences of 1899 and 1907, which led to the adoption of the Hague Convention (I) for the Pacific Settlement of International Disputes and the Hague Convention (II) Respecting the Limitation of the Employment of Force for the Recovery of Contract Debts.[7] Next, the Covenant of the League of Nations,[8] established in the aftermath of the First World War, required Member States to submit their disputes to arbitration, judicial settlement or inquiry by the League's Council.[9] Members were bound not to resort to war until three months after the award or decision, and consented not to go to war when the other State complied with the outcome of the settlement. Nevertheless, the Covenant's procedure contained so many gaps that Member States felt it necessary to develop further constraints to strengthen the Covenant framework.[10]

With the adoption of the General Treaty for the Renunciation of War on 28 April 1919,[11] a comprehensive prohibition on the recourse to war first came into being. The Treaty, better known as the Kellogg-Briand Pact or the Pact of Paris, obliged contracting parties to settle their disputes by pacific means only. It 'condemned' recourse to war for the solving of international disputes and renounced such measures as an instrument of national policy. Although the Pact did not provide for any exceptions to the outlawing of war itself, many States issued reservations, confirming the generally accepted view that it did not exclude the right of legitimate self-defence.[12]

which it constituted a form of 'law', rather than a matter of morality, concerned with the individual conscience of the sovereign princes of the day, remains contested. For a critical review, see A Nussbaum, 'Just War – a Legal Concept?' (1943) 42 *Michigan Law Review* 453.

[3] See Chapter 12 on International Responsibility, Section VI(A).

[4] See further J von Elbe, 'The Evolution of the Concept of the Just War in International Law' (1939) 33 *AJIL* 665; JL Kunz, 'Bellum Justum and Bellum Legale' (1951) 45 *AJIL* 528.

[5] For a critique of the theory of 'indifference', see A Verdebout, 'The Contemporary Discourse on the Use of Force in the Nineteenth Century: A Diachronic and Critical Analysis' (2014) 1 *Journal on Use Force and International Law* 223.

[6] C von Clausewitz, *Vom Kriege* (Berlin, Dümmler, 1832) Book 1, Section 24.

[7] Hague Convention (I) for the Pacific Settlement of International Disputes (adopted 29 July 1899, entered into force 4 September 1900) 187 CTS 410, revised by the Hague Convention for the Pacific Settlement of International Disputes (adopted 18 October 1907, entered into force 26 January 1910) 205 CTS 233; Hague Convention (II) Respecting the Limitation of the Employment of Force for the Recovery of Contract Debts (adopted 18 October 1907, entered into force 26 January 1910) (1908) 2 *AJIL* 81. The First Convention obliged States to have recourse to the good offices or mediation 'as far as circumstances allowed' before going to war (Art 2). The Second Convention prohibited the 'recourse to armed force' for the recovery of contract debts due to a State's nationals (but not in absolute terms) (Art 1).

[8] Covenant of the League of Nations (adopted 28 April 1919, entered into force 10 January 1920) 225 CTS 195.

[9] ibid, Arts 11–17.

[10] Consider eg the Protocol for the Pacific Settlement of International Disputes, adopted by League of Nations Assembly Resolution of 2 October 1924, which, however, never entered into force due to a lack of ratifications.

[11] General Treaty for the Renunciation of War as an Instrument of National Policy (adopted 27 August 1928, entered into force 24 July 1929) 94 LNTS 57.

[12] Q Wright, 'The Meaning of the Pact of Paris' (1933) 27 *AJIL* 39, 42–43.

The Kellogg-Briand Pact signalled the transition of the *jus ad bellum* – the law governing the recourse to force – to the *jus contra bellum*, a transition that was later completed with the acceptance of the UN Charter. The Pact had a significant influence on the practice of States during the interwar period and provided a legal basis for the charges of crimes against the peace at the Nuremberg and Tokyo Military Tribunals.[13] Nevertheless, the Pact also suffered from a number of crucial shortcomings. For instance, by condemning only the recourse to 'war', it left an opening for States to argue that it did not ban uses of force 'short of war' (especially armed reprisals) or that it only applied to war in the formal sense, requiring an intention to fight (*animus belligerendi*) on the part of either party to the conflict.[14]

The weakness of the League of Nations framework and the Kellogg-Briand Pact was amply exposed when the world was drawn into the Second World War. For this reason, States decided to establish the United Nations, whose aim is, first and foremost, to maintain international peace and security.[15] The UN Charter succeeded in tackling many shortcomings of preceding international instruments. It provided for a comprehensive collective security system, revolving around the primary role of the UN Security Council. Contrary to the Pact of Paris, it also incorporated an express provision regarding self-defence, defining the modalities of this right. Finally, it extended the condemnation of war to a general prohibition on the threat or use of force, enshrined in Article 2(4) of the Charter.

B. Scope of Article 2(4) of the UN Charter

Article 2(4), which is considered the cornerstone of the Charter system, proclaims that '[a]ll Members shall refrain in their international relations from the threat or use of force against the territorial integrity or political independence of any State, or in any other manner inconsistent with the Purposes of the United Nations'. This prohibition is recognised as a norm of customary international law, and even as a norm of *jus cogens*.[16] An important corollary of the prohibition is the doctrine of non-recognition of territorial acquisition through conquest (see Chapter 5 on States, Section IV (on the role of recognition) and Section V (on the acquisition of territory)).[17]

[13] I Brownlie, *International Law and the Use of Force by States* (Oxford, OUP, 1963) 75–80. For an argument that the Kellogg-Briand Pact has contributed to an evolution towards peace that lasts up until today, see OA Hathaway and SJ Shapiro, *The Internationalists: How a Radical Plan to Outlaw War Remade the World* (New York, Simon & Schuster, 2017).

[14] On the contested concept of 'war', see further Q Wright, 'When Does War Exist?' (1932) 26 *AJIL* 362; H Lauterpacht, '"Resort to War" and the Interpretation of the Covenant during the Manchurian Dispute' (1934) 28 *AJIL* 43.

[15] Art 1(1) UN Charter.

[16] *Military and Paramilitary Activity in and against Nicaragua* (Nicaragua v United States of America) [1986] ICJ Rep 14, para 190 (favourably quoting a statement made by the ILC to this end). See also D Schindler and K Hailbronner, *Die Grenzen des völkerrechtlichen Gewaltverbots* (Heidelberg, Müller Juristischer Verlag, 1986) 14; O Corten, *Le droit contre la guerre: L'interdiction du recours à la force en droit international contemporain*, 2nd edn (Paris, Pédone, 2014) 341–59. But see J Green, 'Questioning the Peremptory Status of the Prohibition on the Use of Force' (2011) 32 *MJIL* 215. Some authors limit the peremptory character to an allegedly narrower core of '(acts of) aggression'. See eg the position of Roberto Ago in ILC, 'Addendum to the Eight Report on State responsibility' (1980) *YILC*, Vol II, Part 1, 44; and L Hannikainen, *Peremptory Norms (Jus cogens) in International Law* (Helsinki, Lakimiesliiton Kustannus, 1988) 356.

[17] See eg League of Nations Assembly Resolution of 11 March 1932, (1932) *League of Nations Official Journal*, Special Supplement No 101, 87–88 (in the context of the Manchurian conflict). The doctrine is better known as the Stimson doctrine, after a similar declaration by US Secretary of State Henry L Stimson: see 'Identic Notes from the US Secretary of State to the Chinese and Japanese governments', 8 January 1932, reprinted in (1932) *Documents on International Affairs* 262.

Breaches of the prohibition on the use of force in the first place give rise to *State* responsibility. However, they may also give rise to *individual* criminal responsibility on the part of those 'in a position effectively to exercise control over or to direct the political or military action of a State'.[18] Thus, by sanctioning the 'crime of aggression', Article 8*bis* of the amended ICC Statute added a criminal layer to the public international law prohibition on the use of force.[19] However, the scope of the 'crime of aggression' as understood under this provision is narrower than that of the prohibition on the use of force. In particular, the former concept is limited to acts of aggression 'which by [their] character, gravity and scale, constitut[e] manifest violation[s]' of the UN Charter.[20]

There is broad agreement today, confirmed by general practice, that the term 'force' only covers armed force and not, for example, economic or psychological pressure.[21] On the other hand, the concept of 'armed force' is construed broadly and entails both direct and indirect force.[22] Thus, in the 1986 *Nicaragua* case, the ICJ held that the US had violated Article 2(4) by 'arming and training' rebels.[23] The same could not be said for the 'mere supply of funds', which nonetheless infringed the broader prohibition on the non-intervention in another State's internal affairs.[24] Small-scale cross-border strikes against individual targets are not as such outside the scope of Article 2(4),[25] nor are 'cyber attacks'.[26] Apart from the actual use of force, Article 2(4) also forbids States to threaten with force that would itself be unlawful,[27] as was the case when France and the UK issued an ultimatum to Egypt and Israel in 1956, demanding a ceasefire within 12 hours.[28] Complaints that cite threats of the use force are nonetheless relatively uncommon in State practice.

[18] Art 8*bis*(1) ICC Statute.

[19] The ICC Statute was amended to include the crime of aggression during the Review Conference of the Rome Statute of 2010, which took place at Kampala (Uganda); see Res RC/Res.6, 11 June 2010, RC/11.

[20] Art 8*bis*(1) ICC Statute. On 14 December 2017, the ICC Assembly of State Parties adopted draft resolution ICC-ASP/16/L.10 and 'decide[d] to activate the Court's jurisdiction over the crime of aggression as of 17 July 2018', thus meeting the condition set out in Art 15*bis*(3) ICC Statute that '[t]he Court shall exercise jurisdiction over the crime of aggression [...] subject to a decision to be taken after 1 January 2017 by the same majority of States Parties as is required for the adoption of an amendment to the Statute', after the amendments to the ICC Statute concerning the crime of aggression had been ratified or accepted by (at least) 30 State Parties (as required by Art 15*bis*(2) ICC Statute). See further C Kress and S Barriga (eds), *The Crime of Aggression: A Commentary* (Cambridge, CUP, 2016). On the possible impact of the ICC's jurisdiction over the crime of aggression on the *jus ad bellum*, see T Ruys, 'Criminalizing Aggression: How the Future of the Law on the Use of Force Rests in the Hands of the ICC' *EJIL* (forthcoming).

[21] A Randelzhofer, 'Article 2(4)' in B Simma et al (eds), *The Charter of the United Nations: A Commentary*, 3rd edn (Oxford, OUP, 2012) 209. See also Y Dinstein, *War, Aggression and Self-Defence*, 6th edn (Cambridge, CUP, 2017) 90. More nuanced is TJ Farer, 'Political and Economic Coercion in Contemporary International Law' (1985) 79 *AJIL* 413. During the Charter negotiations, a Brazilian proposal to insert a reference to 'armed and economic force' was dismissed.

[22] See eg H Wehberg, 'L'interdiction du recours à la force: le principe et les problèmes qui se posent' (1951) 78 *RdC* 68–69; P Cahier, 'Changements et continuité du droit international' (1985) 195 *RdC* 68–69; R Higgins, *Problems and Process: International Law and How We Use It* (Oxford, Clarendon, 1994) 249.

[23] *Nicaragua* (n 16) para 228.

[24] See UNGA Res 2131 (XX), 'Declaration on the Inadmissibility of Intervention in the Domestic Affairs of States and the Protection of their Independence and Sovereignty', 21 September 1965, UN Doc A/RES/2131 and the Friendly Relations Declaration.

[25] See T Ruys, 'The Meaning of "Force" and the Boundaries of the Jus ad Bellum: Are "Minimal" Uses of Force Excluded from UN Charter Article 2(4)?' (2014) 108 *AJIL* 159. It is worth noting, for instance, that the UK regarded the use of a nerve agent on British soil against Sergei Skripal in March 2018 as 'an unlawful use of force' by Russia: UNSC Official Records, Seventy-third year, 8203rd meeting, 14 March 2018, UN Doc S/PV.8203, 2.

[26] The (non-binding) Tallinn Manual finds that a cyber-operation constitutes a use of force 'when its scale and effects are comparable to non-cyber operations rising to the level of a use of force': M Schmitt, *Tallinn Manual on the International Law Applicable to Cyber Warfare* (Cambridge, CUP, 2013) Rule 11.

[27] *Legality of the Threat or Use of Nuclear Weapons* (Advisory Opinion) [1996] ICJ Rep 226, para 47. On 'threats of force', see N Stürchler, *The Threat of Force in International Law* (Cambridge, CUP, 2007).

[28] See 'The Suez Canal question (July–October 1956)' (1956) *Yearbook of the United Nations* 19 ff.

The main source of controversy regarding the scope of the prohibition on the threat or use of force lies in the second part of Article 2(4), which refers to the 'territorial integrity or political independence' of States. Should this phrase be regarded as a limitation on the prohibition or merely as an emphasis on the importance of these two principles? The first option was followed by the UK in the *Corfu Channel* case.[29] The UK argued that British minesweeping operations in Albanian waters, following damage to British ships, did not fall within the ambit of Article 2(4), since they did not affect Albania's independence or territorial integrity. However, the ICJ did not accept that argument. Other instances where States have relied on a narrow reading of Article 2(4) have been both rare and disputed.[30] In the end, the reference to 'other purposes of the United Nations', the *travaux préparatoires* of the Charter and general practice all make clear that the prohibition on the threat or use of force is to be understood broadly and extends to rather small-scale operations that do not necessarily impinge on a State's borders or political establishment.[31]

Still, some authors argue that certain interventions involving the use of force fall beyond the scope of Article 2(4) on the ground that they are consistent with the purposes of the UN Charter. Such controversial claims advocate the legality of humanitarian or ideological interventions, as well as interventions to assist peoples fighting a 'war of national liberation'. The validity of these claims will be addressed below (Section IV).

For now, it suffices to point out that only one form of intervention is universally accepted not to infringe Article 2(4), namely intervention at the request of the government of a State.[32] Such a request has to be issued prior to intervention and must emanate from the de jure government, which will normally be the regime holding de facto control over the State's territory, and which is generally recognised as the legitimate government of the State.[33] Intervention by invitation can be invoked, for example, to restore order in the face of local disorders or riots. However, the majority view holds that, in conformity with the non-intervention principle[34] and the right of self-determination, it cannot be invoked to justify intervention in a civil war, except when there has been prior foreign intervention against the government requesting assistance.[35] The intervention should, moreover, cease as soon as the territorial State's consent is withdrawn.[36]

Even if the basic principles underlying 'intervention by invitation' are relatively straightforward, the problem lies in their practical application. Practice is indeed replete with

[29] *Corfu Channel* case (United Kingdom of Great Britain and Northern Ireland v Albania) [1949] ICJ Rep 4.

[30] See C Gray, *International Law and the Use of Force*, 4th edn (Oxford, OUP, 2018) 32–40. But see, for instance, A D'Amato, 'Israel's Air Strike upon the Iraqi Nuclear Reactor' (1983) 77 *AJIL* 584.

[31] See also Gray (n 30) 37–40; Dinstein (n 21) 93–94.

[32] *Nicaragua* (n 16) para 246. See also, a contrario, UNGA Res 3314 (XXIX), Annex: 'Definition of Aggression', 14 December 1974, UN Doc A/RES/3314.

[33] See L Doswald-Beck, 'The Legal Validity of Military Intervention by Invitation of the Government' (1985) 56 *BYIL* 189; Institut de Droit International, 10th Commission, 'Present Problems of the Use of Force in International Law: Intervention by Invitation', Preliminary Draft of Rapporteur Gerhard Hafner and Comments (2011) 74 *Yearbook of the Institute for International Law* 227; Corten (n 16) 409–512. General practice suggests that a high degree of international recognition may occasionally compensate for a lesser degree of control over territory. However, a request by the political opposition will not justify an intervention: *Nicaragua* (n 16) para 246.

[34] See above (n 24).

[35] See Doswald-Beck (n 33) 213 and 251; Gray (n 30) 84–85 and 95 ff. This was also the position of the Institut de Droit International, see Institut de Droit International, 'The Principle of Non-intervention in Civil Wars', 14 August 1975, idi-iil.org/app/uploads/2017/06/1975_wies_03_en.pdf, Art 2(1). But see eg Dinstein (n 21) 125–27. Some authors have argued that consensual operations against terrorist groups do not amount to intervention in civil war and accordingly remain permissible: eg K Bannelier-Christakis, 'Military Interventions against ISIL in Iraq, Syria and Libya, and the Legal Basis of Consent' (2016) 29 *LJIL* 743.

[36] See *Armed Activities on the Territory of the Congo* (Democratic Republic of the Congo v Uganda) [2005] ICJ Rep 116, paras 39–71.

highly controversial and sometimes manifestly abusive claims of intervention by invitation. Historical examples include, for example, the US interventions in the Dominican Republic (1965) and Grenada (1983), as well as the Soviet intervention in Hungary (1956).[37] More recently, the doctrine was invoked (in part) by France in relation to *Opération Serval* in Mali (2013).[38] Also Russia relied (in part) on a request by the ousted Ukrainian President Yanukovych and by the regional authorities of Crimea to justify its intervention on the Crimean peninsula in March 2014, albeit that this argument was dismissed by numerous States.[39] Another example is the Saudi-led military intervention in Yemen in 2015, upon request of the internationally recognised, but domestically opposed, President Hadi.[40]

III. Right of Self-Defence

A. An Inherent Right Subject to Limitations

The UN Charter allows for only one explicit exception to the prohibition on the use of force whereby States can lawfully claim unilateral recourse to force. This possibility is laid down in Article 51, which proclaims that '[n]othing in the present Charter shall impair the inherent right of individual or collective self-defence if an armed attack occurs [...]'. In the *Nicaragua* case, the ICJ acknowledged that this 'inherent' right forms part of customary international law.[41] The Court, moreover, made clear that two further criteria, those of 'necessity' and 'proportionality', should be added to the requirements listed in Article 51.[42] Both criteria are generally traced back to the diplomatic exchange of letters following the British attack in 1837 on the *Caroline*, a ship used by US citizens to assist Canadian rebels.[43] The attack led an angry US Secretary of State Webster to request his British counterpart to 'show a necessity of self-defence, instant, overwhelming, leaving no choice of means, and no moment for deliberation',[44] a formula that subsequently became known as the *Caroline* doctrine. Thus, as it stands, the right of self-defence is governed by two formal and three substantive limitations.

The first formal requirement is the obligation of States to immediately report measures undertaken in self-defence to the UNSC. According to the ICJ, this requirement does not reflect customary international law.[45] Nevertheless, the absence of a report can weaken a State's claim of self-defence, as it constitutes one of the factors indicating whether the

[37] See Gray (n 30) 92 ff.

[38] See eg R Van Steenberghe, 'Les interventions française et africaines au Mali au nom de la lutte armée contre le terrorisme' (2014) 118 *Revue générale de droit international public* 273.

[39] See eg T Ruys and N Verlinden, 'Digest of State Practice 1 January–30 June 2014' (2014) 1 *Journal on the Use of Force and International Law* 324.

[40] T Ruys and L Ferro, 'Weathering the Storm: Legality and Legal Implications of the Saudi-led Military Intervention in Yemen' (2016) 65 *ICLQ* 61.

[41] *Nicaragua* (n 16) para 193.

[42] Ibid, paras 183, 193, 195 and 211.

[43] See R Jennings, 'The Caroline and MacLeod Cases' (1938) 32 *AJIL* 82.

[44] 'Correspondence between Great Britain and The United States, respecting the Arrest and Imprisonment of Mr McLeod, for the Destruction of the Steamboat Caroline' (1840–1841) 29 *British and Foreign State Papers* 1126, 1138; 'Correspondence between Great Britain and The United States, respecting the Destruction of the Steamboat Caroline' (1841–1842) 30 *British and Foreign State Papers* 193, 196.

[45] *Nicaragua* (n 16) para 200.

State in question was itself convinced that it was acting in self-defence.[46] The second formal requirement is the time limit imposed on the exercise of self-defence. Article 51 indeed prescribes that States can exercise their right of self-defence *until* the UNSC has taken the measures necessary to maintain international peace and security.[47]

B. The 'Armed Attack' Requirement

The first substantive limitation concerns the requirement of an 'armed attack'. This concept was not defined in the Charter, but was partially clarified by the ICJ in *Nicaragua*.[48] The Court made clear that armed attacks need to attain a minimal threshold of severity, by distinguishing the 'most grave' forms of use of force, those constituting an armed attack, from forms of use of force of a lesser severity. At the same time, this *de minimis* threshold should not be set too high. In the *Oil Platforms* case, for instance, the Court did not exclude that the mining of a single military vessel could amount to an armed attack.[49] According to Dinstein, an armed attack presupposes at least 'a use of force producing (or liable to produce) some painful consequences'.[50] When different minor incidents are interlinked, they may be taken cumulatively in order to assess whether the armed attack requirement is met (in line with the 'accumulation of events' theory).[51] Furthermore, in *Nicaragua*, the ICJ distinguished armed attacks from 'mere frontier incidents'.[52] This distinction seems to be inspired by the desire to prevent smaller incidents from escalating. It does not exclude a priori that armed confrontations near a border, or isolated encounters between military units, may – singularly or cumulatively – reach the *de minimis* threshold and warrant on-the-spot action in self-defence.[53] Uses of force that do not reach the *de minimis* threshold may give rise to non-forcible countermeasures (see Chapter 12, Section VI), yet do not warrant a forcible response in self-defence.

Several aspects of the armed attack requirement remain highly contentious. The first concerns the long-standing debate as to whether an attack must already have occurred in order to trigger the right of self-defence or whether it may be anticipated. A first group of

[46] Ibid. On the reporting obligation, see eg JA Green, 'The Article 51 Reporting Requirement for Self-Defense Actions' (2015) 55 *Virginia Journal of International Law* 563.

[47] What measures are envisaged is not entirely clear. Merely holding UNSC debates on a conflict certainly does not abrogate the right of self-defence. Conversely, there can be little doubt that military actions must come to an end when the UNSC explicitly calls for a ceasefire or orders one or more States to withdraw their troops. In similar vein, military enforcement action by the UNSC will 'de-activate' Art 51 UN Charter. Whether economic sanctions have a similar effect is less clear. Further, see EV Rostow, 'Until What? Enforcement Action or Collective Self-Defense?' (1991) 85 *AJIL* 506; M Halberstam, 'The Right to Self-Defense Once the Security Council Takes Action' (1996) 17 *MJIL* 229.

[48] *Nicaragua* (n 16) paras 191 and 195.

[49] *Oil Platforms* (Islamic Republic of Iran v United States of America) [2003] ICJ Rep 161, paras 64 and 72.

[50] Dinstein (n 21) 206; cp Y Dinstein, *War, Aggression and Self-Defence*, 5th edn (Cambridge, CUP, 2011) 208: 'an armed attack presupposes a use of force producing (or liable to produce) serious consequences, epitomized by territorial intrusions, human casualties or considerable destruction of property'.

[51] *Nicaragua* (n 16) para 231; *Oil Platforms* case (n 49) paras 64 and 72.

[52] *Nicaragua* (n 16) para 195. For a critique, see eg JL Hargrove, 'The *Nicaragua* Judgment and the Future of the Law of Force and Self-Defense' (1987) 81 *AJIL* 135, 139–40; Dinstein (n 21) 209–11.

[53] See T Ruys, *'Armed attack' and Article 51 of the UN Charter* (Cambridge, CUP, 2010) 139–249. Going against the ICJ's case law, the US rejects the idea that there is a 'gap' between the 'use of force' and any 'armed attack' and that the latter concept is subject to a further gravity threshold; eg US Department of Defense, 'Law of War Manual', June 2015, archive.defense.gov/pubs/law-of-war-manual-june-2015.pdf, 47, para 1.11.5.2: 'The United States has long taken the position that the inherent right of self-defense potentially applies against any illegal use of force'.

scholars has traditionally rejected 'anticipatory self-defence' by virtue of a literal interpretation of the phrase 'if an armed attack occurs' and the argument that, as an exception to the general prohibition to use force, Article 51 should be construed narrowly.[54] The opposing side argues that the reference to the 'inherent' right of self-defence preserves earlier customary law, which allowed for anticipatory action.[55] Proponents of a broad reading of self-defence invoke the *Caroline* incident as a precedent to their claims, suggesting that in the nuclear era States cannot be expected to await a 'first strike'. The former group conversely rejects the precedent value of the *Caroline* incident based on the fact that it precedes the outlawing of the use of force,[56] and warns of the risk of escalation if anticipatory action is permitted.

Throughout the Cold War era, general practice and *opinio juris* rendered little support to the legality of anticipatory self-defence. On many occasions where it would have been open for States to invoke this doctrine, they chose instead to rely on other arguments, such as the presence of a prior armed attack (eg the Six Day War in 1967)[57] or regional peacekeeping (eg the Cuban missile crisis in 1962).[58] By contrast, when in 1981 Israel relied on anticipatory self-defence to justify its raid on an Iraqi nuclear reactor, its claim was defeated by a majority of States, several of whom expressly stressed the illegality of anticipatory action.[59]

This situation has changed dramatically since the events of 11 September 2001, and more specifically since the promulgation of the 2002 American National Security Strategy by the Bush administration.[60] The latter document not only claimed the right to take pre-emptive measures of self-defence in response to *imminent* threats, as was traditionally argued by proponents of a broad interpretation of Article 51, but extended anticipatory self-defence to include preventive action in response to *non-imminent* threats.[61] Since then, States and scholars have increasingly come to endorse the view that self-defence against imminent threats of armed attacks should be considered lawful,[62] with some States effectively invoking such right in the context of military operations against non-State actors abroad (see also below, this section).[63] At the same time, the attempt to broaden the scope

[54] eg H Kelsen, *The Law of the United Nations: A Critical Analysis of Its Fundamental Problems* (London, Stevens & Sons, 1950) 913–14; E Jiménez De Arechaga, 'International Law in the Past Third of a Century' (1978) 159 *RdC* 9; L Henkin, *How Nations Behave*, 2nd edn (New York, Columbia University Press, 1979) 141–42.

[55] eg DW Bowett, *Self-Defence in International Law* (Manchester, Manchester University Press, 1958) 188–92; MS McDougal and FP Feliciano, *Law and Minimum World Public Order* (New Haven, Yale University Press, 1961) 237.

[56] J Crawford, *Brownlie's Principles of Public International Law*, 8th edn (Oxford, OUP, 2012) 751.

[57] See Report of the 1348th Meeting of the UNSC, 6 June 1967, UN Doc S/PV.1348.

[58] See eg A Chayes, 'Law and the Quarantaine of Cuba' (1962–1963) 41 *Foreign Affairs* 550.

[59] See UNSC Res 487, 19 June 1981, UN Doc S/RES/487. See further Report of the 2283rd Meeting of the UNSC, 15 June 1981, UN Doc S/PV.2283.

[60] The White House, 'The National Security Strategy of the United States of America', September 2002, state.gov/documents/organization/63562.pdf.

[61] ibid, 15.

[62] eg A Randelzhofer and G Nolte, 'Article 51' in Simma (n 21) 1423–24 (referring to the 'prevailing opinion among commentators today') and references in fn 183; WM Reisman and A Armstrong, 'The Past and Future of the Claim of Preemptive Self-defense' (2006) 100 *AJIL* 525; Report of the Special Rapporteur on Extrajudicial, Summary or Arbitrary executions (Philip Alston), Addendum: Study on Targeted Killings, 28 May 2010, UN Doc A/HRC/14/24/Add.6, para 45; Advisory Committee on Issues of Public International Law (Netherlands), 'Advisory Report on Armed Drones', July 2013, cms.webbeat.net/ContentSuite/upload/cav/doc/CAVV_advisory_report_on_armed_drones_(English_translation_-_final)_(2).pdf, 13; ILA Committee on the Use of Force, 'Final Report on Aggression and the Use of Force', Sydney, 2018, http://www.ila-hq.org/index.php/committees, 14–19, Statement of UK Attorney-General Lord Goldsmith before the House of Lords, 21 April 2004, 660 *House of Lords Hansard* 370–71, publications.parliament.uk/pa/ld200304/ldhansrd/vo040421/text/40421-07.htm.

[63] See eg the following letters to the UN Security Council: S/2014/695 (US), S/2015/688 (UK). On the concept of self-defence against 'imminent' attacks by non-State actors, see D Bethlehem, 'Self-Defense against an Imminent

of self-defence to include preventive action against non-imminent threats has been widely criticised by legal scholars and officials alike, and was implicitly denounced by the ICJ in the *Armed Activities* case.[64]

Even if pre-emptive self-defence is not without problems – there indeed exists little clarity on what qualifies as an imminent threat or on the burden of proof to be applied[65] – it appears that the tide in legal doctrine has slowly turned in favour of those acknowledging the recourse to self-defence against 'imminent threats of armed attack'.[66] A number of authorities nonetheless continue to plead for a more cautious approach, insisting that self-defence only be exercised to 'intercept' an armed attack that is irrevocably being mounted.[67]

The second contentious aspect of the armed attack requirement has to do with the nature of the entity committing the armed attack (the *ratione personae* question).[68] While the text of Article 51 does not in any way define or restrict the scope of armed attacks, legal literature and general practice have traditionally linked the concept to acts of *States*.[69] On the other hand, it was argued that this should be given a broad interpretation, including not only attacks actually carried out by a State, but also attacks by private actors for which States shared a certain degree of responsibility.[70] The latter type was sometimes described as 'indirect', as opposed to 'direct' military aggression, carried out by State agents.[71]

The distinction between these two main types of armed attacks was confirmed by the ICJ in the *Nicaragua* case. The Court first affirmed that armed action undertaken by regular armed forces across an international border constitutes an armed attack.[72] Relying on Article 3(g) of the UNGA Definition of Aggression,[73] it subsequently asserted that the notion of armed attack equally covers

> the sending by or on behalf of a State of armed bands, irregulars or mercenaries carrying out acts of armed force as well as a State's substantial involvement therein, provided the scale and effects of the attacks exceeded those of mere frontier incidents.[74]

or Actual Armed Attack by Nonstate Actors' (2012) 106 *AJIL* 774. In the course of 2016–2017, the 'Bethlehem principles' were explicitly endorsed by the US, the UK and Australia.

[64] *Armed Activities* (n 36) paras 119, 143 and 148.

[65] For a rare attempt at elucidation, see N Lubell, 'The Problem of Imminence in an Uncertain World' in M Weller (ed), *The Oxford Handbook of the Use of Force in International Law* (Oxford, OUP, 2015) 697–719. According to Lubell, there must be 'an impending attack over which there is a reasonable level of certainty that it will occur in the foreseeable future; and it must be a specific and identifiable attack' (ibid, 718).

[66] This evolution is reflected in the Report of the High-level Panel on Threats, Challenges and Change, 'A more Secure World: Our Shared Responsibility', 2 December 2004, UN Doc A/59/565, paras 188–92. Former UNSG Kofi Annan similarly accepted the legality of pre-emptive self-defence: Report of the Secretary General, 'In Larger Freedom: Towards Development, Security and Human Rights for All', 21 March 2005, UN Doc A/59/2005, para 124.

[67] ie so-called 'interceptory' self-defence. See eg Brownlie (n 13) 276; L-A Sicilianos, *Les réactions décentralisées à l'illicité: des contre-mesures à la légitime defense* (Paris, LGDJ, 1990) 403–405; T Christakis, 'Vers une connaissance de la notion de guerre preventive?' in K Bannelier (ed), *L'intervention en Irak et le droit international* (Paris, Pédone, 2004) 9–45; Dinstein (n 21) 231–33. Further: Corten (n 16) 662 ff (rejecting pre-emptive self-defence).

[68] See eg N Lubell, *Extraterritorial Use of Force against Non-State Actors* (Oxford, OUP, 2010); C Kress, *Gewaltverbod und Selbstverteidigungsrecht nach der Satzung der Vereinten Nationen bei staatlicher Verwicklung in Gewaltakte Privater* (Berlin, Duncker & Humblot, 1995).

[69] eg JL Kunz, 'Individual and Collective Self-Defence in Article 51 of the Charter of the United Nations' (1947) 41 *AJIL* 872, 878; A Cassese, 'The International Community's "Legal" Response to Terrorism' (1989) 38 *ICLQ* 589, 596 ff.

[70] I Brownlie, 'The Use of Force in Self-Defence' (1961) 37 *BYIL* 193, 245; US Senate, 'Report of the Committee on Foreign Relations on the North Atlantic Treaty', Executive Report No 8, 6 June 1949, 13.

[71] eg PL Zanardi, 'Indirect Military Aggression' in A Cassese (ed), *The Current Legal Regulation on the Use of Force* (Dordrecht, Nijhoff, 1986) 111–19.

[72] *Nicaragua* (n 16) para 195.

[73] See above (n 32).

[74] *Nicaragua* (n 16) para 195.

The Court rejected the idea that the assistance to rebels in the form of the provision of weapons or 'logistical or other support' falls within the ambit of 'substantial involvement'.[75] This interpretation was heavily criticised by a number of scholars as well as some ICJ judges for being overly restrictive.[76] Others have pointed out that the ICJ's approach accurately reflects general practice in preceding decades.[77]

In any event, the Court's view has increasingly come under pressure as a result of recent practice whereby States have justified the recourse to self-defence against other States by virtue of their active support to non-State actors carrying out cross-border attacks, or by reference to their unwillingness or inability to prevent cross-border attacks from their territory.[78] US operations against Sudan and Afghanistan in the wake of the 1998 embassy bombings were, for example, justified on self-defence grounds.[79] In particular, the controversy regarding self-defence against attacks by non-State actors acquired a new dimension after 9/11. On 12 September 2001, the UNSC adopted Resolution 1368.[80] In its preamble, the resolution, which unequivocally condemned the 9/11 attacks, recognised 'the inherent right of individual or collective self-defence in accordance with the Charter', without making any reference to State involvement in the attacks. Moreover, NATO for the first time in its history invoked collective self-defence, stating that the attack 'was directed from abroad and shall therefore be regarded as an action covered by Article 5 of the Washington Treaty'.[81]

Be it in an ambiguous manner, the ICJ has ostensibly refused to open the door for a broader right of self-defence against non-State attacks in its *Wall* Opinion (2004)[82] and its *Armed Activities* judgment (2005),[83] to the discontent of some of its judges.[84] Yet, developments in general practice after 9/11 confirm that the scope of self-defence vis-à-vis non-State attacks is undergoing a transformation. For instance, in its 2002 National Security Strategy, the US declared that it would make no distinction 'between terrorists and those who knowingly harbour or provide aid to them'.[85] Furthermore, even if the response of the

[75] ibid.

[76] eg *Nicaragua* (n 16), Dissenting Opinion of Judge Jennings, 543; Dissenting Opinion of Judge Schwebel, para 171; JN Moore, 'The *Nicaragua* Case and the Deterioration of World Order' (1987) 81 *AJIL* 151, 152 and 154–55; Higgins (n 22) 250–51.

[77] eg Zanardi (n 71) 113–15; Sicilianos (n 67) 325; A Constantinou, *The Right of Self-Defence Under Customary International Law and Article 51 of the UN Charter* (Brussel, Bruylant, 2000) 94 and 103–10; Gray (n 30) 136–39 and 183.

[78] See T Ruys and S Verhoeven, 'Attacks by Private Actors and the Right of Self-Defence' (2005) 10 *Journal of Conflict and Security Law* 289, 294–96.

[79] (1998) 52 *Yearbook of the United Nations* 185–86 and 1219–20; Letter from the Permanent Representative of the United States of America addressed to the President of the Security Council, 20 August 1998, UN Doc S/1998/780.

[80] UNSC Res 1368, 12 September 2001, UN Doc S/RES/1369, preamble para 3. See also UNSC Res 1373, 28 September 2001, UN Doc S/RES/1373, preamble para 4.

[81] Statement by NATO Secretary General, Lord Robertson, 2 October 2001, reprinted in (2001) 40 *ILM* 1267. The Organization of American States (OAS) made an analogous statement: OAS, 'Terrorist Threat to the Americas', Resolution adopted at the First Plenary Session of the Twenty-Fourth Meeting of Consultation of Ministers of Foreign Affairs, 21 September 2001, OAS Doc OEA/Ser.F/II.24/RC.24/RES.1/01, reprinted in (2001) 40 *ILM* 1270.

[82] *Legal Consequences of the Construction of a Wall in the Occupied Palestinian Territories* (Advisory Opinion) [2004] ICJ Rep 163, para 139. See further CJ Tams, 'Light Treatment of a Complex Problem: The Law of Self-Defence in the Wall Case' (2006) 16 *EJIL* 963.

[83] *Armed Activities* (n 36) paras 146–47. See further J Kammerhofer, 'The *Armed Activities* Case and Non-state Actors in Self-Defence Law' (2007) 20 *LJIL* 89.

[84] *Wall* Opinion (n 82), Separate Opinion Judge Kooijmans, para 35, Declaration of Judge Buergenthal, para 6 and Separate Opinion of Judge Higgins, para 33; *Armed Activities* (n 36), Separate Opinion Judge Kooijmans, para 25 and Separate Opinion Judge Simma, para 8.

[85] 'The National Security Strategy of the United States of America' (n 60) 5 and 19.

international community has at times been inconsistent, actual practice in recent years abounds with cross-border interventions that are difficult to reconcile with Article 3(g) of the UNGA Definition of Aggression or the ICJ's interpretation thereof, such as the Israeli intervention in Lebanon in 2006 or the Turkish intervention in northern Iraq in 2007–2008.[86] The right of self-defence has in particular been invoked as a justification for strikes against Islamic State (IS) targets in Syria in the context of the US-led military coalition against IS, including by several European States.[87]

Both among States and scholars, there is growing support for the view that attacks by non-State actors may qualify as armed attacks, at least if they are of considerable gravity or form part of a sustained campaign of cross-border attacks, and that they can trigger the right of self-defence, even if they are not as such attributable to a State.[88] Even so, self-defence will only be permissible if it is reasonably clear that the territorial State is 'unwilling or unable' to take appropriate action within its borders.[89] Unless the non-State attacks can be imputed to the territorial State in accordance with the secondary rules on State responsibility, defensive measures should strictly target the non-State presence abroad.[90] Still, if credible evidence points at a more flexible interpretation of the right of self-defence in relation to cross-border attacks by non-State armed groups, it remains to a certain extent unclear how the 'unable or unwilling' threshold is to be operationalised. In any case, several scholars continue to insist on a more restrictive reading of Article 51 UN Charter when it comes to non-State attacks.[91]

The third and last controversy relating to the armed attack criterion concerns the question whether armed attacks may include attacks against a State's nationals abroad, or, in other words, whether States can resort to the use of force in order to protect their nationals in another State without the host State's consent.[92] Proponents fall back on the idea that

[86] See further Ruys (n 53) 447–72.

[87] See eg the following letters to the UNSC: 23 September 2014, UN Doc S/2014/695 (US); 25 November 2014, S/2014/851 (UK); 24 July 2015, S/2015/563 (Turkey); 7 September 2015, S/2015/688 (UK); 8 September 2015, S/2015/745 (France); 9 September 2015, S/2015/693 (Australia); 3 December 2015, S/2015/928 (UK); 10 December 2015, UN Doc S/2015/946 (Germany); 13 January 2016, UN Doc S/2016/34 (Denmark); 10 February 2016, UN Doc S/2016/132 (Netherlands); 3 June 2016, UN Doc S/2016/513 (Norway); 9 June 2016, UN Doc S/2016/523 (Belgium). But see the letter from the Syrian representative to the UNSC of 21 September 2015 (UN Doc S/2015/719), speaking of a 'distorted reading of the intention of Article 51 of the Charter'.

[88] See eg Chatham House, 'Principles of International Law on the Use of Force by States in Self-Defence', October 2005, chathamhouse.org/publications/papers/view/108106, 13; 'Leiden Policy Recommendations on Counter-terrorism and International Law', Annexed to L van den Herik and N Schrijver (eds), *Counter-Terrorism Strategies in a Fragmented International Legal Order: Meeting the Challenges* (Cambridge, CUP, 2013) 706–26, paras 38–39; Bethlehem (n 63); Advisory Committee on Issues of Public International Law (Netherlands) (n 62).

[89] On the 'unable or unwilling' standard, see eg AS Deeks, '"Unwilling or Unable": Toward a Normative Framework for Extraterritorial Self-Defense' (2012) 52 *Virginia Journal of International Law* 483. The unable or unwilling criterion can be regarded as an application of the necessity and proportionality standards (see below, Section III(C)) and has been confirmed (explicitly or implicitly) by a number of States. See eg the following letters to the UNSC: 23 September 2014, UN Doc S/2014/695 (US); 31 March 2015, UN Doc S/2015/221 (Canada); 24 July 2015, UN Doc S/2015/563 (Turkey); 9 September 2015, UN Doc S/2015/693 (Australia).

[90] eg 'Leiden Policy Recommendations on Counter-terrorism and International Law' (n 88) para 43.

[91] eg Corten (n 16) 717–58; C Gray, 'Targeted Killings: Recent US Attempts to Create a Legal Framework' (2013) 66 *Current Legal Problems* 75. Consider also the following open letter signed by more than 200 scholars worldwide: 'A plea against the abusive invocation of self-defence as a response to terrorism', July 2016, cdi.ulb.ac.be/contre-invocation-abusive-de-legitime-defense-faire-face-defi-terrorisme.

[92] This form of intervention – not to be confused with 'humanitarian intervention' (see below, Section IV(B)) – is often seen as an application of the right of self-defence, although some see it as a separate customary exception to the prohibition on the use of force, or even as a type of intervention that is somehow not covered by Art 2(4). While 'protection of nationals' was widely accepted in earlier times, it has become controversial since the adoption of the UN Charter. See further N Ronzitti, *Rescuing Nationals abroad through Military Coercion and Intervention on Grounds of Humanity* (Dordrecht, Nijhoff, 1985).

Article 51 preserves earlier customary law and argue that it should be subject to a number of strict conditions. There should be: (i) an imminent threat of injury to nationals; (ii) a failure or inability on the part of the territorial sovereign to protect them; and (iii) measures of protection should be strictly confined to the object of protecting them against injury.[93] The right to protect one's nationals has been invoked by a minority of States, eg the US, the UK, France, Israel and Belgium.[94] Interventions on this basis were condemned by a majority of UN Members, although it may be argued that this had more to do with the interventions' alleged failure to meet the requirements of necessity and proportionality (see below, Section III(C)) rather than with the validity of the claimed right to protect one's nationals.[95] Recent practice indicates a tendency to at least condone interventions aimed at the evacuation of nationals abroad threatened by civil war or internal unrest.[96] Several States have, moreover, adopted military doctrines on so-called 'non-combatant evacuation operations', asserting that such operations do not necessarily require Host State consent.[97] On the other hand, many developing countries continue to regard the 'protection of nationals' doctrine as a pretext for other states intervening in their domestic affairs.[98] Recent invocations of the doctrine by Russia in relation to its interventions in Georgia and Ukraine illustrate the potential for abuse.[99]

C. Necessity and Proportionality

Apart from the need for an 'armed attack', the two final substantive constraints on the right of self-defence are the criteria of necessity and proportionality.[100] These criteria were not incorporated in Article 51, yet their applicability as rules of customary law has been consistently affirmed by the ICJ.[101] These two standards both stress that self-defence is restricted to the repulsion of an armed attack and may never involve retaliatory or punitive actions, thus distinguishing lawful recourse to self-defence from unlawful armed reprisals.[102]

'Necessity' entails that no alternative means of redress may be available and that force should in principle be directed against the source(s) of the armed attack(s). Moreover, necessity requires the time lapse between the armed attack and the recourse to self-defence to be reasonably short, taking account of the need to carry out investigations and/or negotiations or to take military preparations. 'Proportionality' presupposes that the exercise of

[93] eg CHM Waldock, 'The Regulation of the Use of Force by Individual States in International Law' (1952) 81 *RdC* 451, 467.

[94] See TC Wingfield and JE Meyen (eds), *Lillich on the Forcible Protection of Nationals Abroad* (Newport, Naval War College, 2002) 41 ff.

[95] Gray (n 30) 166–67.

[96] eg F Grimal and G Melling, 'The Protection of Nationals Abroad: Lawfulness or Toleration? A Commentary' (2011) 16 *Journal Conflict and Security Law* 541.

[97] See T Ruys, 'The "Protection of Nationals" Doctrine Revisited' (2008) 13 *Journal Conflict and Security Law* 233.

[98] Corten (n 16) 836–39.

[99] See eg JA Green, 'The Annexation of Crimea: Russia, Passportization and the Protection of Nationals Revisited' (2014) 1 *Journal on Use of Force and International Law* 3; Report of the Independent International Fact-Finding Mission on the Conflict in Georgia, September 2009, Vol II, mpil.de//files/pdf4/IIFFMCG_Volume_II1.pdf, 227 ff.

[100] eg J Gardam, *Necessity, Proportionality and the Use of Force by States* (Cambridge, CUP, 2004) xxiv.

[101] *Nicaragua* (n 16) para 176; *Legality of the Threat or Use of Nuclear Weapons* (n 27) para 41; *Oil Platforms* (n 49) paras 43 and 73–77.

[102] See further D Kretzmer, 'The Inherent Right of Self-Defence and Proportionality in Jus ad Bellum' (2013) 24 *EJIL* 235.

self-defence is proportionate to the initial armed attack(s), not only in terms of gravity or intensity, but also in terms of duration, location and the range of targets selected.[103]

Both criteria should be interpreted in a flexible manner, having regard to the factual circumstances of the case and the aims of the defensive response. Thus, the weapons or the amount of force used in self-defence need not be exactly the same as in the initial attack. Nor should there be a strict quantitative symmetry in terms of casualties or damage caused. The need to limit self-defence to the repelling of an armed attack does not prohibit a State from pursuing troops across the border into their own territory. Still, even on a flexible reading, it is clear that a number of recent interventions are hard to reconcile with the aforementioned principles.[104]

D. Collective Self-Defence

The various conditions set out above all apply to both individual and collective self-defence.[105] As regards the latter, the ICJ has spelled out two additional requirements.[106] It found that States can only provide military support in the exercise of the right of collective self-defence where the State concerned has declared itself to be the victim of an armed attack and has issued a formal request for assistance.[107]

Collective self-defence can be based on a pre-existing mutual defence agreement or a collective self-defence clause in a (sub-)regional treaty. Examples are Article V of the NATO Treaty, first triggered after the 9/11 attacks, Article 3 of the Inter-American Treaty of Reciprocal Assistance[108] or Article 2 of the Arab League's Treaty of Joint Defense.[109] Another example can be found in Article 42(7) TEU, which states that

> [i]f a Member State is the victim of armed aggression on its territory, the other Member States shall have towards it an obligation of aid and assistance by all the means in their power, in accordance with Article 51 of the United Nations Charter.

[103] R Ago, 'Addendum to the eighth Report on State Responsibility' (1980) *YILC*, Vol II, Part One, 69; O Schachter, 'The Right of States to Use Armed Force' (1984) 82 *Michigan Law Review* 1620, 1637.

[104] In 2006, for instance, Israel responded to a Hezbollah attack on a border patrol by means of a large-scale military operation, which inter alia resulted in the destruction of approximately 15,000 Lebanese houses and apartments, as well as 680 km of roads; 'Middle East Crisis: Facts and Figures', *BBC News*, 31 August 2006, news.bbc.co.uk/2/hi/middle_east/5257128.stm.

[105] *Nicaragua* (n 16) paras 105, 110 and 121–23.

[106] ibid, para 232.

[107] ibid, paras 194–98. For an illustration of such request, see eg the following letters from the Permanent Representative of Iraq to the United Nations: 25 June 2014, UN Doc S/2014/440; 22 September 2014, UN Doc S/2014/691. The requirement of a formal request, which aims at preventing possible abuses, was criticised by a number of ICJ judges and scholars for being excessively formalistic (*Nicaragua* (n 16), Dissenting Opinion Judge Schwebel, paras 191 and 221–27; Dissenting Opinion Judge Jennings, paras 544–45). The Court's phrasing that a victim State should 'normally' make an explicit request for support indicates that it should not be interpreted as an absolute condition, and that it may be set aside for example when a State is overrun by and invading army, thus rendering it impossible to issue a formal request. cp Gray (n 30) 185–88; see further J Green, 'The "Additional" Criteria for Collective Self-Defence: Request but Not Declaration' (2017) 4 *Journal on the Use of Force and International Law* 4.

[108] Inter-American Treaty of Reciprocal Assistance (adopted 2 September 1947, entered into force 3 December 1948) 21 UNTS 77.

[109] Treaty of Joint Defence and Economic Co-operation of the League of Arab States (adopted 18 June 1950, entered into force 22 August 1952), avalon.law.yale.edu/20th_century/arabjoin.asp. A 'softer' version of a collective defence clause can be found in Art V of the Security Treaty Between the United States, Australia, and New Zealand (adopted 1 September 1951, entered into force 29 April 1952) 131 UNTS 83.

In particular to accommodate the concerns of permanently neutral States, the provision adds that this obligation 'shall not prejudice the specific character of the security and defence policy of certain Member States'. Furthermore, the provision stresses the primacy of the NATO collective defence arrangement.[110] Article 42(7) TEU was first invoked by France following the Paris attacks by terrorists affiliated to Islamic State on 13 November 2015.[111]

The existence of a prior collective defence agreement does not preclude the need for the ad hoc consent of the victim State. Conversely, action in collective self-defence can also be undertaken on an ad hoc basis in the absence of a formal mutual defence agreement. This is illustrated by the reliance by several States on the right of collective self-defence (in support of Iraq) as a justification for military operations against Islamic State in 2014 and beyond.[112]

IV. Other Possibilities for Unilateral Recourse to Force

A. Wars of National Liberation

Since 1945, a number of claims have been made (at times reflecting a partial return to natural law) alleging that self-defence is not the only option for States in resorting to unilateral force.[113] A first example concerns the idea that in situations of colonial domination or foreign occupation it is lawful for States to give armed support to 'national liberation movements' in their struggle for self-determination (see Chapter V on States, Section III(B)).[114] Newly independent and socialist States supported this right as a legitimate struggle to end the yoke of colonialism. Western States opposed it on the basis that it eroded the prohibition on the use of force and was dangerously open to abuse. The main UNGA resolutions touching upon the question were deliberately drafted in ambiguous and circular terms so as to secure consensus among both blocs rather than to resolve the disagreement.[115]

[110] Art 42(7) TEU, para 2: 'Commitments and cooperation in this area shall be consistent with commitments under the North Atlantic Treaty Organisation, which, for those States which are members of it, remains the foundation of their collective defence and the forum for its implementation'.

[111] Elysée, 'Discours du président de la République devant le Parlement réuni en congrès', 16 November 2015, elysee.fr/declarations/article/discours-du-president-de-la-republique-devant-le-parlement-reuni-en-congres. The provision was subsequently invoked by the German Bundestag in its resolution authorising German troop deployment abroad: Deutscher Bundestag, Antrag der Bundesregierung: 'Einsatz bewaffneter deutscher Streitkräfte zur Verhütung und Unterbindung terroristischer Handlungen durch die Terrororganisation IS auf Grundlage von Artikel 51 der Satzung der Vereinten Nationen in Verbindung mit Artikel 42 Absatz 7 des Vertrages über die Europäische Union sowie den Resolutionen 2170 (2014), 2199 (2015), 2249 (2015) des Sicherheitsrates der Vereinten Nationen', 1 December 2015, Drucksache 18/6866; as approved by the Bundestag on 4 December 2015; The Federal Government (GE), 'Bundestag Approves Mandate for Syria Mission', 4 December 2015, bundesregierung.de/Content/EN/Artikel/2015/12_en/2015-12-01-syrien-mandat-bundeswehr.html.

[112] See the references above (n 87).

[113] One such example pertains to the idea of a so-called 'pro-democratic' intervention. This notion is not explored in greater detail here, as there is virtually no support in general practice for the legality of unilateral pro-democratic intervention and the concept also enjoys very little support in legal doctrine. Further, see eg O Corten, 'La résolution 940 du Conseil de Sécurité autorisant une intervention militaire en Haïti: L'émergence d'un principe de légitimité démocratique en droit international?' (1995) 6 *EJIL* 116; GH Fox and BR Roth (eds), *Democratic Governance and International Law* (Cambridge, CUP, 2000).

[114] eg HA Wilson, *International Law and the Use of Force by National Liberation Movements* (Oxford, Clarendon Press, 1988).

[115] See Arts 1 and 7 of the Friendly Relations Declaration; Art 7 Annex UNGA Res 3314 (n 32); R Rosenstock, 'The Declaration on Principles of International Law Concerning Friendly Relations: A Survey' (1971) 65 *AJIL*

In the end, the practical importance of the debate has decreased significantly since the end of the colonial era.

B. Humanitarian Intervention

Today, the controversy regarding wars of national liberation has largely been replaced by the doctrinal divide on the legality of unilateral 'humanitarian interventions', that is, the use of force (that is not authorised by the UNSC; see below, Section V) to protect individuals or groups of individuals against massive human rights violations in their own State.[116] The debate on humanitarian intervention has deep historic roots. Nevertheless, in the Cold War era, general practice showed little support for the doctrine. Several actions that could have fallen under the heading of humanitarian interventions, including the Indian intervention in Bangladesh (1971),[117] the Vietnamese intervention in Cambodia (1978)[118] and the Tanzanian intervention in Uganda (1979),[119] were justified on the basis of self-defence. Furthermore, in *Nicaragua*, the ICJ seemed to reject unilateral humanitarian intervention, stating that, 'while the United States might form its own appraisal of the situation as to respect for human rights in Nicaragua, the use of force could not be the appropriate method to monitor or ensure such respect'.[120]

This situation has changed since the end of the Cold War. When the UK, the US and France created no-fly zones in Iraq to protect the Kurds and Shiites from persecution by the Hussein regime in 1991, the UK became the first country to openly argue that intervention without invitation can be justified 'in cases of extreme humanitarian need'. The Foreign and Commonwealth Office spelled out four limitations: (i) there should be a compelling and urgent situation of extreme humanitarian distress; (ii) the territorial State must be unable or unwilling to act; (iii) there may be no practical alternative; and (iv) the intervention should be limited in time and scope.[121]

Moreover, the legality of humanitarian intervention became the centre of attention in 1999, when, following a diplomatic deadlock in the UNSC, NATO forces launched a bombing campaign against the Federal Republic of Yugoslavia in order to call an end to the massive human rights violations against the Kosovar Albanese minority. Whereas NATO claimed to be acting 'to avert a humanitarian catastrophe',[122] Member States seemed to disagree considerably as to the concrete legal basis of the operation, and several States took care to stress that the operation should not be seen as a precedent for future interventions.[123]

713, 732–33; BB Ferencz, *Defining International Aggression, the Search for World Peace: A Documentary History and Analysis*, Vol II (New York, Oceana, 1975) 49.

[116] See generally S Chesterman, *Just War or Just Peace? Humanitarian Intervention and International Law* (Oxford, OUP, 2001); JL Holzgrefe and RO Keohane (eds), *Humanitarian Intervention: Ethical, Legal and Political Dilemmas* (Cambridge, CUP, 2003); A Orford, *Reading Humanitarian Intervention: Human Rights and the Use of Force in International Law* (Cambridge, CUP, 2003).

[117] (1971) 25 *Yearbook of the United Nations* 144.

[118] (1978) 32 *Yearbook of the United Nations* 281.

[119] (1979) 33 *Yearbook of the United Nations* 262.

[120] *Nicaragua* (n 16) para 268.

[121] G Marston, 'United Kingdom Materials on International Law' (1992) 63 *BYIL* 615, 824–27.

[122] Dr Javier Solana, Secretary General of NATO, Press Statement, 23 March 1999, nato.int/DOCU/pr/1999/p99-040e.htm.

[123] (1999) 53 *Yearbook of the United Nations* 342; Report of the 3988th Meeting of the UNSC, 24 March 1999, UN Doc S/PV.3988; Gray (n 30) 50–51; M Byers and S Chesterman, 'Changing the Rules about Rules? Unilateral Humanitarian Intervention and the Future of International Law' in Holzgrefe and Keohane (n 116) 199.

The bombing campaign, moreover, provoked strong criticism from several other countries, such as Russia and China.[124] Significantly, the G-77 adopted a Declaration, rejecting 'the so-called right of humanitarian intervention, which has no basis in [...] international law'.[125]

In its submission to the High-Level Panel on Threats, Challenges and Change, the General Affairs and External Relations Council of the EU in 2004 stressed that 'there is a need to clarify the international principles that would authorise, in exceptional circumstances, outside intervention in the territory of a sovereign country to prevent a humanitarian catastrophe'.[126] It is also interesting to note that Article 4(h) of the African Union's Constitutive Act (2000)[127] provides for 'the right of the Union to intervene in a Member State pursuant to a decision of the Assembly in respect of grave circumstances, namely: war crimes, genocide and crimes against humanity' (see below (Section VI)). In practice, however, the AU has not proved enthusiastic about forcible unilateral intervention on these grounds.[128] Debates pertaining to the permissibility of unilateral humanitarian intervention have resurfaced with renewed vigour in the context of threats of military strikes (in 2013) and actual military strikes (in 2017 and again in 2018) against the Syrian regime in reaction to the latter's use of chemical weapons.[129]

In the end, (unilateral) humanitarian intervention continues to be extremely controversial. Proponents point to the growing importance of human rights and to the fact that in accordance with Article 1 of the 1948 Genocide Convention, States have agreed that genocide is a crime which they undertake to prevent and punish. The opposing side points to the risk that States will invoke the prevention of human rights violations as a pretext to further their own political agendas. The conclusion seems to be that, although humanitarian interventions cannot be said to be 'unambiguously illegal',[130] the concept lacks the necessary support to have become part of customary international law. Consequently, interventions for humanitarian motives should be left to the discretion of the UNSC.[131]

C. Responsibility to Protect

This arguably remains the majority position in spite of the advance of the Responsibility to Protect (R2P) principle. This principle was endorsed in the final declaration of the Heads

[124] See Report of the 3988th Meeting of the UNSC (n 123).

[125] G-77 Ministerial Declaration, 24 September 1999, g77.org/doc/Decl1999.html, para 69.

[126] General Affairs and External Relations Council, 'Draft Paper for the submission to the High-Level Panel on Threats, Challenges and Change', 11 May 2004, Doc 9165/04, 12.

[127] Constitutive Act of the African Union (adopted 11 July 2000, entered into force 26 May 2001) 2158 UNTS 3.

[128] C Gray, 'The Use of Force for Humanitarian Purposes' in ND White and C Henderson (eds), *Research Handbook on International Conflict and Security Law* (Cheltenham, Edward Elgar, 2013) 237.

[129] In 2013, the UK relied on the humanitarian intervention doctrine to justify possible air strikes against the Assad regime: UK Prime Minister's Office, 'Guidance – Chemical Weapon Use by Syrian Regime: UK Government Legal Position', 29 August 2013, gov.uk/government/publications/chemical-weapon-use-by-syrian-regime-uk-government-legal-position/chemical-weapon-use-by-syrian-regime-uk-government-legal-position-html-version. At the same time, the US refrained from invoking the doctrine to justify missile strikes against Syrian military installations in 2017 and 2018. More generally, the 2015 US Law of War Manual (n 53) observes that the US 'has not adopted this legal rationale' (para 1.11.4.4).

[130] G Marston, 'United Kingdom Materials on International Law' (1986) 57 *BYIL* 614. It has also been argued that a 'genuine' humanitarian intervention cannot amount to a 'crime of aggression' in the sense of the Rome Statute: J Trahan, 'Defining the "Grey Area" Where Humanitarian Intervention May Not Be Fully Legal, but Is Not the Crime of Aggression' (2015) 2 *Journal on the Use of Force and International Law* 42.

[131] This was also the view shared by the High-Level Panel on Threats, Challenges and Change in 2004 (n 66), at paras 199–203.

of State and Government at the UN World Summit in September 2005,[132] and features inter alia in the 2008 Report on the Implementation of the European Security Strategy.[133] R2P implies that States have a responsibility to protect the welfare of their own people. When States fail to abide by this responsibility, the wider international community must step in, if necessary through the use of force. Opinions are divided on whether the R2P principle merely belongs to the realm of political rhetoric or whether it also has legal implications.[134] Several States have expressly stressed that it should not be regarded as a licence for unilateral action.[135]

Generally, the R2P principle can be said to differ from the doctrine of humanitarian intervention in that it is both broader and narrower than the latter. First, it is broader, because it comprises three responsibilities: the responsibility to prevent, to react and to rebuild. Humanitarian intervention, then, is merely one way to fulfil the responsibility to react. On the other hand, the R2P principle is narrower than the doctrine of humanitarian intervention, as – at least according to its version adopted at the 2005 UN World Summit – it only allows for collective action taken through the UNSC.[136] In this light, the R2P principle has found its way into several UNSC resolutions,[137] including the resolution authorising the use of force for purposes of protecting the civilian population in the context of the Libyan civil war in 2011.[138]

V. Chapter VII Action by the UN Security Council

A. Primary Responsibility for International Peace and Security

The collective security system that saw the light of day at the 1945 San Francisco Conference essentially revolves around the central role of the UNSC as the primary body responsible for the maintenance of international peace and security.[139] The UNSC's competence is divided

[132] UNGA Res 60/1, '2005 World Summit Outcome', 16 September 2005, UN Doc A/RES/60/1, paras 138–39. The concept finds its origins in the report of the International Commission on Intervention and State Sovereignty, 'The Responsibility to Protect', December 2001, responsibilitytoprotect.org/ICISS%20Report.pdf.

[133] Report on the Implementation of the European Security Strategy; 'Providing Security in a Changing World', approved by the European Council held in Brussels on 11 and 12 December 2008, Doc S407/08, at 2. Consider also G De Baere, 'The EU and the Responsibility to Protect' in B Van Vooren, S Blockmans and J Wouters (eds), *The EU's Role in Global Governance: The Legal Dimension* (Oxford, OUP, 2013) 95–109.

[134] eg C Stahn, 'Responsibility to Protect: Political Rhetoric or Emerging Legal Norm?' (2007) 101 *AJIL* 99–120. Further M Vashakmadze, 'Responsibility to Protect' in Simma (n 21) 1201–36.

[135] Gray (n 128) 253 (noting that no State took the opposite position at 244). If R2P was initially seen as a more attractive alternative to humanitarian intervention, some of the suspicion that had been attached to that doctrine has now transferred to R2P (ibid, 254–55). This is at least partly a consequence of the NATO operation in Libya in 2011, which was undertaken under the R2P flag, but which several States perceived as exceeding the authorisation granted by the UNSC. See further G Beestermöller, *Libyen: Missbrauch der Responsibility to Protect?* (Baden-Baden, Nomos, 2014).

[136] J Pattison, *Humanitarian Intervention and the Responsibility to Protect: Who Should Intervene?* (Oxford, OUP, 2010) 12–15.

[137] eg UNSC Res 1674, 28 April 2006, UN Doc S/RES/1674 (on protection of civilians in armed conflict); UNSC Res 1970, 26 February 2011, UN Doc S/RES/1970 (imposing an arms embargo, a travel ban and an assets freeze in connection with the situation in the Libyan Arab Jamahiriya); UNSC Res 1975, 30 March 2011, UN Doc S/RES/1975 (imposing sanctions on Laurent Gbagbo – the then President of Côte d'Ivoire – and his circle).

[138] UNSC Res 1973, 17 March 2011, UN Doc S/RES/1973; but see above (n 135).

[139] Art 24(1) UN Charter. See further C Henderson, 'The Centrality of the United Nations Security Council in the Legal Regime Governing the Use of Force' in White and Henderson (n 128) 120–69.

among Chapters VI and VII of the UN Charter. The first addresses the peaceful settlement of disputes (see Chapter 13) and empowers the UNSC to investigate disputes or situations which might lead to a dispute, as well as to recommend appropriate methods or procedures of adjustment. The UNSC should thereby take into consideration dispute settlement procedures already adopted by the parties, as well the fact that legal disputes should generally be referred by the parties to the ICJ. Recommendations of this kind are not binding on UN Members, although non-compliance may prompt the UNSC to act under Chapter VII.

Chapter VII allows the UNSC to issue not only recommendations, but also decisions, aimed at the maintenance or restoration of international peace and security. Although such recommendations are again non-binding, decisions made under Chapter VII are binding on UN Member States, who agree to accept and carry out the decisions of the UNSC in accordance with the UN Charter.[140]

B. Chapter VII Jurisdiction

In order to act under Chapter VII, the UN Security Council must first determine that there exists a 'threat to the peace', a 'breach of the peace' or 'an act of aggression'.[141] While none of these concepts are defined in the UN Charter, 'threats to the peace' clearly constitutes the broadest of the three notions.[142] Although it was initially understood to imply a threat to *international* peace, UNSC practice illustrates that determinations of this kind may also be made in essentially internal situations.[143] It should be stressed that this practice does not infringe upon the prohibition placed on the UN when intervening in 'matters which are essentially within the domestic jurisdiction' of a State,[144] as Article 2(7) UN Charter provides for an explicit exception with regard to enforcement measures under Chapter VII. UNSC practice, moreover, indicates that threats to the peace are not limited to 'threats of force'. Thus, violations of human rights and humanitarian law have been labelled as threats to the peace, as well as terrorist activities or violations of democratic principles.[145] In the *Tadić* case, the ICTY argued that the Council's discretion to determine a threat to the peace was not 'totally unfettered', and should remain at least within the limits of the purposes and principles of the Charter.[146] Yet, it is difficult to envisage situations where a determination under Article 39 would as such violate the purposes and principles of the UN Charter.

[140] Art 25 UN Charter. See also *Legal Consequences for States of the Continued Presence of South Africa in Namibia (South West Africa) notwithstanding Security Council resolution 276 (1970)* (Advisory Opinion) [1971] ICJ Rep 16, 52–53.

[141] Art 39 UN Charter.

[142] See further I Osterdahl, *Threat to the Peace: The Interpretation by the Security Council of Article 39 of the UN Charter* (Uppsala, Iustus Förlag, 1998); N Krisch, 'Article 39' in Simma (n 21) 1278–79.

[143] eg on Southern Rodesia: UNSC Res 216, 12 November 1965, UN Doc S/RES/216; UNSC Res 217, 20 November 1965, UN Doc S/RES/217; UNSC Res 221, 9 April 1966, UN Doc S/RES/221; and UNSC Res 232, 16 December 1966, UN Doc S/RES/232.

[144] Art 2(7) UN Charter.

[145] Examples include the overthrowing of the democratically elected president of Haiti (UNSC Res 875, 16 October 1993, UN Doc S/RES/875; UNSC Res 940, 31 July 1994, UN Doc S/RES/940); the Libyan refusal to extradite the Lockerbie suspects (UNSC Res 748, 31 March 1992, UN Doc S/RES/748); the Ebola outbreak in West Africa (UNSC Res 2177, 18 September 2014, UN Doc S/RES/2177). See also UNSC Res 2134 of 28 January 2014, UN Doc S/RES/2134 and UNSC Res 2136, 30 January 2014, UN Doc S/RES/2136 on wildlife poaching.

[146] ICTY, *Prosecutor v Tadić*, IT-94-1-AR72, Appeals Chamber, Decision of the Defence Motion for Interlocutory Appeal on Jurisdiction, 2 October 1995, para 29.

Ultimately, what constitutes threats to the peace seems to depend on whatever the Council decides as constituting a threat.[147]

'Breaches of the peace' and 'acts of aggression' should be construed more narrowly and presume that armed force has already been used. As the UN Security Council has only referred to these concepts on rare occasions,[148] its resolutions on these two notions offer little guidance in distinguishing them. The main difference arguably lies in the fact that aggression places the liability with one or more of the parties to a dispute, whereas a breach of peace is considered a more neutral term. The term aggression is furthermore elaborated by the UNGA in its resolution on the definition of aggression,[149] which, although not binding upon the UNSC, seems to have influenced its practice to some extent.

C. Chapter VII Powers

i. Article 40: Provisional Measures

Chapter VII provides for three types of Council 'decisions', all of which are binding upon UN Member States.[150] In accordance with Article 40 UN Charter, the UNSC can adopt provisional measures in order to prevent a situation from deteriorating, such as through the imposition of a ceasefire or the deployment of UN observers. These measures may not prejudice the rights or position of the parties concerned.

ii. Article 41: Sanctions

Article 41 UN Charter empowers the UN Security Council to adopt (non-provisional) measures not involving the use of armed force. A non-exhaustive list is added, including the interruption of economic relations, means of communication or transportation, and the severance of diplomatic relations. Mandatory sanctions of this kind were rare during the Cold War.[151] Since the 1991 Gulf War they have become much more common, being imposed on States as well as on non-State actors.[152]

The increased recourse to mandatory sanctions has not gone unchallenged. They may produce unwanted results, such as economic losses for trading partners of the targeted State, unintentional favouring of one party to a dispute[153] or extensive suffering on behalf of the civilian population resulting from a lack of food and/or medical supplies. Only the

[147] Dinstein (n 21) 335. See also A Orakhelashvili, 'The Power of the UN Security Council to Determine the Existence of a "Threat to the Peace"' (2006) 1 *Irish Yearbook International Law* 61.

[148] eg UNSC Res 82, 25 June 1950, UN Doc S/RES/82 (Korean War); UNSC Res 502, 3 April 1982, UN Doc S/RES/502 (Falkland War); UNSC Res 598, 20 July 1987, UN Doc S/RES/598 (Iran-Iraq War).

[149] Annex UNGA Res 3314 (n 32), especially Art 4.

[150] See generally E De Wet, *The Chapter VII Powers of the United Nations Security Council* (Oxford, Hart, 2004).

[151] For rare exceptions, see UNSC Res 232, 16 December 1966, UN Doc S/RES/232 (Southern Rhodesia); UNSC Res 460, 21 December 1966, UN Doc S/RES/460 (Southern Rhodesia); UNSC Res 418, 4 November 1977, UN Doc S/RES/418 (South Africa); UNSC Res 919, 26 May 1994, UN Doc S/RES/919 (South Africa); UNSC Res 930, 27 June 1994, UN Doc S/RES/930 (South Africa).

[152] During the 1990s, sometimes dubbed the 'sanctions decade', the UNSC utilised Art 41 on numerous occasions. See Dinstein (n 21) 351–52; and further D Cortright and GA Lopez, *The Sanctions Decade: Assessing UN Strategies in the 1990s* (Boulder, Rienner, 2000); L Van den Herik, *Research Handbook on UN Sanctions* (Cheltenham, Edward Elgar, 2017).

[153] eg, the arms embargo during the Balkan War in the early 1990s clearly favoured the Serb side, as it already possessed a far larger quantity of heavy weaponry.

first by-product is addressed in the UN Charter, namely in Article 50, which provides for a right to consult the UNSC for those States experiencing 'special economic problems' arising from the carrying out of the sanctions regime.[154] Yet, it was primarily the suffering of the civilian population, evidenced by the strong increase in malnutrition and infant mortality in Iraq, which provoked the most criticism. This situation led to a growing consensus among legal scholars that the authority of the UNSC to impose sanctions is limited by certain standards of international human rights and international humanitarian law as well as *jus cogens* norms and the principle of proportionality.[155] Unfortunately, the complete failure of the notorious oil-for-food programme,[156] set up in 1995 in order to allow Iraq to sell oil to finance the purchase of humanitarian goods, demonstrates that the proper implementation of humanitarian exemptions remains a challenge. After the 1990s, the UN Security Council has increasingly shifted its attention to the imposition of so-called 'smart' or 'targeted sanctions', such as travel bans or the freezing of funds vis-à-vis individual government officials, rebel leaders or presumed terrorists. This new policy has met with some success.[157] Yet, the Council's 'listing' and 'de-listing' procedures have also been criticised for being incompatible with international human rights standards, in particular with fair trial standards.[158]

The EU implements all sanctions imposed by the UN Security Council. In addition, the EU adopts so-called 'autonomous' sanctions of its own initiative, and increasingly so (eg when the veto of a permanent member of the UNSC prevents the adoption of sanctions at the UN level).[159] These sanctions are mostly adopted pursuant to Article 215 TFEU,[160] which states that

> Where a decision, adopted in accordance with Chapter 2 of Title V of the Treaty on European Union [governing the Common Foreign and Security Policy (CFSP)], provides for the interruption or reduction, in part or completely, of economic and financial relations with one or more third countries, the Council [...] shall adopt the necessary measures.[161]

[154] For an overview of practice, see A Reinisch and M Nowak, 'Article 50' in Simma (n 21) 1391–96 (the authors conclude that the UN has yet to develop a functioning institutional response to assist third States affected by sanctions, while observing that the problem has become less acute as a result of the shift towards more targeted sanctions).

[155] See eg M Craven, 'Humanitarianism and the Quest for Smarter Sanctions' (2002) 13 *EJIL* 43; ME O'Connell, 'Debating the Law of Sanctions' (2002) 13 *EJIL* 63; and further A Peters, 'Article 25' in Simma (n 21) 789–854.

[156] UNSC Res 986, 14 April 1995, UN Doc S/RES/986. Further, see L Oette, 'Die Entwicklung des Oil for Food-Programms und die gegenwärtige humanitäre Lage im Irak' (1999) 59 *ZaöRV* 839.

[157] For an assessment of the effectiveness of such sanctions, see Targeted Sanctions Consortium, 'The Effectiveness of United Nations Targeted Sanctions', November 2013, repository.graduateinstitute.ch/record/287976/files/effectiveness_TCS_nov_2013.pdf. In 2015, the so-called 'High-Level Review of United Nations Sanctions' produced a compendium listing 150 recommendations for reforming and strengthening the UN sanctions framework, as annexed to UN Doc A/69/941–S/2015/432 of 12 June 2015.

[158] See Federal Supreme Court (CH), *Youssef Nada v State Secretariat for Economic Affairs and Federal Department of Economic Affairs*, 14 November 2007, Case No 1A 45/2007, BGE 133 II 450, para 8.3; *Nada v Switzerland* App no 10593/08 (ECHR, 12 September 2012); judgment of 3 September 2008, *Kadi and Al Barakaat International Foundation v Council and Commission ('Kadi 2008')*, C-402/05 P and C-415/05 P, EU:C:2008:461; *Al-Dulimi v Switzerland* App no 5809/08 (ECHR, 21 June 2016) as discussed in Chapter 4, Sections IV(D) and V(B)(iii)(b). See further D Hovell, *The Power of Process: The Value of Due Process in Security Council Sanctions Decision-Making* (Oxford, OUP, 2016).

[159] For an overview, see EC (Service for Foreign Policy Instruments), 'European Union Restrictive Measures (Sanctions) in Force', last updated 7 July 2016, eeas.europa.eu/cfsp/sanctions/docs/measures_en.pdf.

[160] Another legal basis is found in Art 75 TFEU. On the relationship between the two provisions, see the judgment of 19 July 2012, *European Parliament v Council*, C-130/10, ECLI:EU:C:2012:472.

[161] Of course Art 215 TFEU constitutes a *res inter alios acta* for non-EU Member States, and cannot therefore, from an international law perspective, provide a legal basis for sanctions against third States that would otherwise be contrary to international law (eg because they fail to comply with the rules on the adoption of countermeasures (see Chapter 12, Section VI)).

The sanctions take the form of 'restrictive measures' that are imposed through a CFSP Council Decision adopted by unanimity. Inasmuch as they entail economic measures such as asset freezes and export bans that fall under the competence of the EU, separate implementing legislation is required in the form of a Council Regulation, which is directly binding on EU citizens and businesses. The increased recourse to autonomous sanctions by the EU as well as by individual States has fuelled a debate over the permissibility of so-called third-party countermeasures (see Chapter 12, Section VI(B)).

iii. Article 42: Use of Force and the 'Authorisation Model'

When mandatory sanctions are insufficient, the UNSC can resort to the third type of Chapter VII decisions, spelled out in Article 42 UN Charter: action involving the use of force by air, sea or land forces. Originally, the Charter envisaged the conclusion of bilateral agreements between the UN and the Member States whereby the latter would make available to the UNSC 'armed forces, assistance, and facilities [...] necessary for the purpose of maintaining international peace and security'.[162] These troops would operate under UN command, directed by the Military Staff Committee.[163] Nevertheless, these plans have never materialised as Member States have failed to agree on their relative contributions and the location of the forces.

Although no single agreement under Article 43 UN Charter has ever been concluded, the UN Security Council has not remained idle, but has instead developed two alternative mechanisms. On the one hand, it has started to organise so-called peacekeeping operations, which are discussed below (Section V). On the other hand, instead of ordering States to use armed force, it has chosen to 'authorise' Member States or regional organisations to undertake military action, leaving it to the latter to decide whether, to what degree and for how long to take part in collective security measures, within the parameters defined by the UNSC.[164] As far as regional organisations are concerned, the 'subcontracting' option is expressly foreseen in Chapter VIII of the UN Charter, which is discussed below (Section VI). By contrast, the UN Charter does not provide an express legal basis for authorising individual Member States to use force on behalf of the UNSC. This option has simply grown from UN practice and has today become a generally accepted feature of the UN collective security mechanism.

Notwithstanding some early precursors,[165] the breakthrough of the 'authorisation model' coincided with the end of the Cold War. When Iraqi forces occupied Kuwait in 1990, the UNSC reacted with unprecedented vigour, 'authori[zing] Member States cooperating with the Government of Kuwait [...] to use all necessary means [...] to restore international peace and security in the area'.[166] Since then, the UNSC has authorised military

[162] Art 43(1) UN Charter.

[163] Art 47(3) UN Charter.

[164] See L-A Sicilianos, 'L'autorisation par le Conseil de Sécurité de recourir à la force: une tentative d'évaluation' (2002) 106 *Revue générale de droit international public* 5.

[165] See notably the resolutions adopted at the time of the Korea War: UNSC Res 82, 25 June 1950, UN Doc S/RES/82; UNSC Res 83, 27 June 1950, UN Doc S/RES/83; UNSC Res 84, 7 July 1950, UN Doc S/RES/84. Note: these resolutions are sometimes seen as merely affirming the right of collective self-defence; eg Gray (n 30) 266–67. See also UNSC Res 221, 9 April 1966, UN Doc S/RES/221, operative clause 5, 'calling upon' the UK to prevent 'by the use of force if necessary' the arrival of oil shipments destined for Rhodesia.

[166] UNSC Res 678, 29 November 1990, UN Doc S/RES/678, operative clause 2.

interventions inter alia in Somalia, Bosnia, Haiti, Rwanda and the Democratic Republic of the Congo (DRC).[167]

This is not to say that the 'authorisation' model is completely free from criticism. Several authors have challenged the legality of the lack of overall control by the UNSC over subcontracting operations.[168] Furthermore, States have occasionally attempted to justify unilateral recourse to force on the grounds that they were enforcing UNSC resolutions, thereby claiming 'implied authorisation' to use force.[169] This was part of the justification given for the NATO intervention in the Federal Republic of Yugoslavia in 1999 (see further below (Section VI)). The United States, the United Kingdom and Australia used a similar argument in relation to Operation 'Iraqi Freedom' in 2003.[170] The latter intervention was, however, contested by a majority of UN Members. Several States, including a number of NATO Members, expressly renounced the possibility of implied authorisation.[171] Another controversial precedent concerns the NATO operation in Libya in 2011, which gave rise to deep divisions between States as to whether the operation had remained within the confines of the mandate granted by the UNSC[172] to use all necessary measures 'to protect civilians and civilian populated areas under threat of attack'.[173] In light of these precedents, certain Security Council members have come to insist that Chapter VII resolutions refer to specific Charter articles, in order to prevent any invocation of those resolutions to justify the use of force.[174] This has not prevented the Council from continuing to adopt resolutions whose language is rather ambiguous.[175] Still, the proper view is that UNSC authorisation must – as one State put it – be 'express, affirmative and prior'.[176]

D. Expanding Mandate

The end of the Cold War marked a radical revitalisation of the UN Security Council. The Council took a broad approach to 'threats to peace', expanding its jurisdiction to situations essentially within the domestic sphere. This evolution was underscored in 2004 in the

[167] For a (somewhat dated) list, see Y Dinstein, *War, Aggression and Self-Defence*, 4th edn (Cambridge, CUP, 2005) 303–304.

[168] See eg J Quigley, 'The "Privatization" of Security Council Enforcement Action: A Threat to Multilateralism' (1996) 17 *MJIL* 249; N Blokker, 'Is the Authorization Authorized? Powers and Practice of the UN Security Council to Authorize the Use of Force by "Coalitions of the Able and Willing"' (2000) 11 *EJIL* 541. But see C Gray, 'The Use of Force and the International Legal Order' in MD Evans (ed), *International Law*, 4th edn (Oxford, OUP, 2014) 638 (observing that the situation has improved since the early 1990s).

[169] See eg J Lobel and M Ratner, 'Bypassing the Security Council: Ambiguous Authorizations to Use Force, Cease-fires and the Iraqi Inspection Regime' (1999) 93 *AJIL* 124; O Corten and F Dubuisson, 'L'hypothèse d'une règle émergente fondant une intervention militaire sur une "autorisation implicite" du Conseil de Sécurité' (2000) 104 *Revue générale de droit international public* 873.

[170] See further O Corten, 'Opération Iraqi Freedom: Peut-on admettre l'argument de l'autorisation implicite du Conseil de Sécurité?' (2003) 36 *Revue Belge du Droit International* 205.

[171] See the various statements in UNSC Verbatim Record, 26 March 2003, UN Doc S/PV.4726. Consider also the Statement by the Troika of the Non-Aligned Movement (South Africa, Malaysia and Cuba), 19 March 2003, Annex to UN Doc S/2003/357.

[172] UNSC Res 1973 (n 138).

[173] See eg G Ulfstein and HF Christiansen, 'The legality of the NATO bombing in Libya' (2013) 62 *ICLQ* 159.

[174] Gray (n 168) 636.

[175] See eg UNSC Res 2249 (2015), 20 November 2015, UN Doc S/RES/249 ('calling upon' States 'to take all necessary measures, in compliance with international law, in particular with the United Nations Charter' against ISIL/Da'esh in Syria and Iraq). See also UNSC Res 2337, 19 January 2017, UN Doc S/RES/2337 (concerning the Gambia).

[176] UNSC Verbatim Record, 19 January 2017, UN Doc S/PV.7866, 3 (Uruguay).

UN High-Level Panel's designation of the UNSC as the proper authority to step in when States fail to live up to their responsibility to protect the wellbeing of their inhabitants.[177] The UNSC has also taken a liberal view as regards the instruments at its disposal. Not only has it made frequent use of the possibilities expressly foreseen in the UN Charter, interpreting Chapter VII as implicitly allowing the delegation of military enforcement, it has also utilised a wide array of measures not listed in the UN Charter. For example, it has adopted resolutions on the creation of international protectorates, has demanded the extradition of individuals, has awarded compensation, and has established international criminal tribunals.[178]

This evolution was generally welcomed by States and scholars, who applauded the UNSC for finally living up to the aspirations of a truly collective security system. However, many have expressed concern about the expanding reach of the UNSC, warning that the body has rapidly outgrown the constitutional role originally envisaged by the drafters of the UN Charter.[179] These authors argue that although the UNSC was initially established to act as an executive organ, it is increasingly assuming quasi-judicial and quasi-legislative functions. Controversial examples are Resolution 687 (1991), which demarcated the Iraq-Kuwait boundary,[180] Resolution 1373 (2001), which laid down a series of general rules with regard to counter-terrorism,[181] and Resolution 1540 (2004), dealing with the non-proliferation of weapons of mass destruction.[182] Another example concerns Resolution 2178 (2014), which imposed several obligations on UN Member States to prevent the travel of, and support for, 'foreign terrorist fighters'.[183]

In the *Tadić* case, the ICTY held that, however broad its powers may be, the Security Council remains subject to certain constitutional limitations.[184] Therefore, it seems fair to state that the UNSC is not only bound by *jus cogens* and basic legal standards of human rights and international humanitarian law, but also by a certain division of powers. Quasi-judicial and quasi-legislative decisions should be confined to cases where they are indispensable for the exercise of the police function of the Council; effects of such decisions should in principle be limited to a particular situation. On the other hand, as long as States do not object, decisions such as Resolution 1373 may well serve as a precedent, leading in time to a shift in the original UN Charter paradigm.

[177] Report of the High-level Panel on Threats, Challenges and Change (n 66) paras 202–203.

[178] eg UNSC Res 748, 31 March 1992, UN Doc S/RES/748 (imposing an arms embargo and selective travel ban on Libya, and establishing a sanctions committee); UNSC Res 827, 25 May 1993, UN Doc S/RES/827 (establishing the International Criminal Tribunal for the former Yugoslavia); UNSC Res 955, 8 November 1994, UN Doc S/RES/955 (establishing the International Criminal Tribunal for Rwanda); UNSC Res 1244, 10 June 1999, UN Doc S/RES/1244 (authorising NATO to secure and enforce the withdrawal of Federal Republic of Yugoslavia forces from Kosovo and establishing UNMIK).

[179] See eg K Harper, 'Does the United Nations Security Council Have the Competence to Act as a Court and Legislature?' (1994) 27 *New York University Journal of International Law and Politics* 103; M Koskenniemi, 'The Police in the Temple – Order, Justice and the UN: A Dialectical View' (1995) 6 *EJIL* 325; P Szasz, 'The Security Council Starts Legislating' (2002) 96 *AJIL* 901; MCE Happold, 'Security Council Resolution 1373 and the Constitution of the United Nations' (2003) 16 *LJIL* 593; J Wouters and J Odermatt, 'Quis Custodiet Consilium Securitatis?: Reflections on the Law-making Powers of the Security Council' in V Popovski and T Fraser (eds), *The Security Council as a Global Legislator* (London, Routledge, 2014) 71–96.

[180] UNSC Res 687, 3 April 1991, UN Doc S/RES/687, paras 2–4.

[181] UNSC Res 1373, 28 September 2001, UN Doc S/RES/1373. See also E Rosand, 'Security Council Resolution 1373, the Counter-Terrorism Committee, and the Fight against Terrorism' (2003) 97 *AJIL* 333.

[182] UNSC Res 1540, 28 April 2004, UN Doc S/RES/1540. See R Lavalle, 'A Novel, if Awkward, Exercise in International Law-making: Security Council Resolution 1540 (2004)' (2004) 51 *NILR* 411.

[183] UNSC Res 2178, 24 September 2014, UN Doc S/RES/2178.

[184] ICTY, *Prosecutor v Tadić* (n 146) para 28.

The expanding mandate of the Security Council has also given rise to growing calls for judicial review of its resolutions by the ICJ, which in turn does not appear to exclude the possibility of such review per se. Thus, in the *Lockerbie* case,[185] the Court initially denied Libya's request for provisional measures by deferring to the UNSC, but eventually declared the case admissible, accepting the argument that Libya had filed its application at a time the UNSC had only adopted a resolution that was a recommendation without binding effect (see Chapter 13, Section III(B)(iii)). As the UNSC grows ever more active, the prospect of legal clashes with regional or national judicial authorities has increasingly begun to materialise.[186] Some have even argued that States can rely on the concept of 'countermeasures' to justify a refusal to implement unlawful sanctions imposed by the UN Security Council.[187] Finally, it should be stressed that the controversy concerning the authority of the Security Council cannot be disconnected from the long-standing debate over UNSC reform (see Chapter 6, Section VIII(C)(ii)(c)).

VI. Peacekeeping

A. Background

As discussed above (Section V(C)), due to the absence of Article 43 agreements, the UN Security Council has had to find alternatives for military action, one of which concerns the authorisation of UN Member States to resort to force. The second option concerns the creation of peacekeeping operations.[188] The origins of peacekeeping operations are to be traced back to the beginning of the Charter era, when UNSC action was brought to a standstill as a result of the Cold War divide. In light of this situation, the UNGA sought to assume a greater role with regard to international peace and security, arguing that the UNSC was merely the 'primary' and not the 'exclusive' actor in this field. Article 11(2) UN Charter indeed empowers the UNGA to discuss questions relating to international

[185] *Questions of interpretation and application of the 1971 Montreal Convention arising from the aerial incident at Lockerbie* (Libyan Arab Jamahiriya v United Kingdom) [1992] ICJ Rep 3, [1998] ICJ Rep 9. On this case, see further V Gowland-Debbas, 'The Relationship between the International Court of Justice and the Security Council in the light of the Lockerbie Case' (1994) 88 *AJIL* 643; B Martenczuk, 'The Security Council, the International Court and Judicial Review: What Lessons from Lockerbie? (1999) 10 *EJIL* 514; ND White, 'To Review or not to Review? The Lockerbie Cases before the World Court' (1999) 12 *LJIL* 401.

[186] See the references to the case law of the Swiss Federal Supreme Court, the ECtHR and the CJEU above (n 158) and the discussion in Chapter 4, Sections IV(D) and V(B)(iii)(b)). See further E De Wet and A Nollkaemper (eds), *Review of the Security Council by Member States* (Antwerp, Intersentia, 2003); A Tzanakopoulos, 'Domestic Court Reactions to UN Security Council Sanctions' in A Reinisch (ed), *Challenging Acts of International Organizations before National Courts* (Oxford, OUP, 2010) 54–76. For a comparison of the approach of the ECtHR and the CJEU, see E De Wet, 'From *Kadi* to *Nada*: Judicial Techniques Favouring Human Rights over United Nations Security Council Sanctions' (2013) 12 *CJIL* 787.

[187] See A Tzanakopoulos, *Disobeying the Security Council: Countermeasures against Wrongful Sanctions* (Oxford, OUP, 2011). See also Peters (n 155) 846–48.

[188] See generally ND White, *Keeping the Peace: The United Nations and the Maintenance of International Peace and Security*, 2nd edn (Manchester, Manchester UP, 1997); R Murphy, *UN Peacekeeping in Lebanon, Somalia and Kosovo: Operational and Legal Issues in Practice* (Cambridge, CUP, 2007); AJ Bellamy and PD Williams, *Understanding Peacekeeping*, 2nd edn (Cambridge, Polity, 2010); M Bothe, 'Peacekeeping' in Simma (n 21) 1171–99; J Koopes, N MacQueen, T Tardy and PD Williams (eds), *The Oxford Handbook of United Nations Peacekeeping Operations* (Oxford, OUP, 2015).

peace and security and make recommendations. This competence is limited by the fact that any question for which action is necessary must be referred to the UNSC,[189] and by the rule that the UNGA may not issue recommendations on a dispute or situation under consideration in the UNSC, unless the latter body so requests.[190] Nevertheless, the UNGA chose to interpret these limitations narrowly. This is evident from the adoption of the 'Uniting for Peace' Resolution in 1950.[191] This resolution allows the UNGA to call emergency meetings in the event of UNSC failure due to a lack of unanimity between permanent members in any case in which there appears to be a threat to the peace, breach of the peace or act of aggression.[192] The UNGA may then recommend collective measures, including the use of force if necessary. The latter option was implemented during the Korean crisis, where the UNGA called upon States to place their troops under UN command and recommended the imposition of a weapons embargo.[193] After 1951, the UNGA has frequently relied on the Uniting for Peace Resolution to convoke emergency sessions, where it has called for ceasefires or condemned certain behaviour.[194] Nevertheless, since the Korean crisis, the UNGA has never invoked the resolution to recommend the use of force.[195] It did, however, use the procedure in 1956 to set up the First United Nations Emergency Force (UNEF I),[196] which was charged with the supervision of the cessation of hostilities following the Suez crisis and was established with the consent of the parties concerned. Although UNEF I was, strictly speaking, not the first peacekeeping operation (the UNSC established some limited observation forces in the late 1940s),[197] it proved to be the breakthrough and blueprint for this emerging model.

Beyond the creation of UNEF,[198] the UNGA has only rarely initiated peacekeeping. In 1960 it renewed the mandate of the UN Operation in Congo (ONUC).[199] In 1962, it approved the creation of the UN Security Force in West New Guinea pursuant to an Agreement between the Netherlands and Indonesia.[200] In general, however, the establishment of peacekeeping forces was gradually taken over by the UNSC, which followed the consensual model developed by the UNGA, while asserting its supremacy in peacekeeping. Over time, the number and scope of UN peacekeeping operations has increased significantly.[201]

[189] Art 11(2) UN Charter.

[190] Art 12 UN Charter.

[191] UNGA Res 377 (V), 'Uniting for Peace', 3 November 1950, UN Doc A/RES/377. See J Andrassy, 'Uniting for Peace' (1956) 50 *AJIL* 563; H Reicher, 'The Uniting for Peace Resolution on the Thirtieth Anniversary of its Passage' (1982) 20 *Columbia Journal of Transnational Law* 25; D Zaum, 'The Security Council, the General Assembly, and War: The Uniting for Peace Resolution' in V Lowe (ed), *The United Nations Security Council and War: The Evolution of Thought and Practice since 1945* (Oxford, OUP, 2008) 154–74.

[192] The validity of this procedure was endorsed by the ICJ in *Oil Platforms* (n 49) paras 24–35.

[193] See respectively UNGA Res 498 (V), 1 February 1951, UN Doc A/RES/498; and UNGA Res 500 (V), 18 May 1951, UN Doc A/RES/500.

[194] See UNGA, 'Emergency Special Sessions', un.org/ga/sessions/emergency.shtml.

[195] Note that a mere recommendation by the UNGA, acting under the 'Uniting for Peace' procedure, to use force, does not constitute an autonomous legal basis for recourse to force separate from self-defence or UNSC authorisation: Dinstein (n 21) 365–68.

[196] See UNGA Res 998 (ES-1), 4 November 1956, UN Doc A/RES/998; UNGA Res 1000 (ES-1), 5 November 1956, UN Doc A/RES/1000.

[197] See the overview of operations (with relevant legal basis) in Bothe (n 188) 1194.

[198] ie 'UNEF I'. The Second United Nations Emergency Force (UNEF II) was established by the UN Security Council (to supervise the ceasefire between Egyptian and Israeli forces after the Arab-Israeli War (Yom Kippur War) of 1973); see UNSC Res 340, 25 October 1973, UN Doc S/RES/340, operative clause 3.

[199] UNGA Res 1474 (ES-IV), 20 September 1960, UN Doc A/RES/1474.

[200] UNGA Res 1752 (XVII), 21 September 1962, UN Doc A/RES/1752.

[201] United Nations Peacekeeping, 'Data', peacekeeping.un.org/en/data.

From 1948 to June 2018, 71 operations were set up. In June 2018, 104,680 UN 'blue helmets' were deployed in 14 operations all over the world.[202]

Peacekeeping has thus become one of the UN's main enterprises, covering a wide array of activities, ranging from the operation of more traditional observation or ceasefire supervision forces to multi-dimensional operations, engaging in electoral assistance, human rights promotion, civilian policing, humanitarian assistance and even temporary governmental administration (as in Kosovo and East Timor). Although peacekeeping has no express basis in the UN Charter, the competence of the UNSC to set up peacekeeping operations is not contested. Peacekeeping operations are considered to fall somewhere between Chapter VI and Chapter VII of the UN Charter, and are hence often labelled 'Chapter VI½ operations'.[203] The competence of the UNGA to set up peacekeeping operations was affirmed by the ICJ in the *Certain Expenses* case.[204] It should finally be pointed out that as long as they refrain from actually engaging in military enforcement and are conducted with the consent of the territorial State, individual States, groups of States and regional organisations can also mount peacekeeping operations without the express approval from the UNSC (see also below, Section VII(B)). Such operations could be regarded as a form of 'intervention by invitation' (see above, Section II(B)) and normally fall beyond the scope of Article 2(4) UN Charter.

B. Characteristics

UN peacekeeping operations are conducted under the direction of the UNSG. They receive their planning, management, direction and support from the UN Department of Peacekeeping Operations and the Department of Field Support. Peacekeeping operations are founded on three basic characteristics that are interrelated and mutually reinforcing.[205] First of all, in order to enjoy the necessary freedom of action to carry out their mandated tasks, they require the consent of the parties involved.[206] This principle is evident in inter-State disputes. Thus, when Egypt withdrew its support for UNEF in 1967, UN forces were pulled out instantly. Similarly, in 1996 the UN Assistance Mission for Rwanda (UNAMIR) was terminated at Rwanda's request. Moreover, following the problems encountered by UN Interim Force in Lebanon (UNIFIL) in southern Lebanon,[207] the UN has also admitted that it is best to secure the consent of all factions involved in intra-State conflicts as well, so as to guarantee the effectiveness of the operation and the safety of the personnel.

[202] ibid, referring to 76,453 contingent troops, 1,273 experts on mission, 10,705 police, 2,023 staff officers, 12,932 civilian personnel and 1,294 UN volunteers.

[203] On this issue, see ND White, 'The UN Charter and Peacekeeping Forces: Constitutional Issues' (1996) 3 *International Peacekeeping* 43.

[204] *Certain Expenses of the United Nations* (Advisory Opinion) [1962] ICJ Rep 151, 162 ff.

[205] See UN Department of Peacekeeping Operations and Department of Field Support, 'United Nations Peacekeeping Operations: Principles and Guidelines', January 2008, un.org/en/peacekeeping/documents/capstone_eng.pdf, 31–35; and further N Tsagourias, 'Consent, Neutrality/Impartiality and the Use of Force in Peacekeeping: Their Constitutional Dimension' (2006) 11 *Journal Conflict and Security Law* 465.

[206] See further C Gray, 'Host-state Consent and United Nations Peacekeeping in Yugoslavia' (1996) 7 *Duke Journal of Comparative and International Law* 241; D Roberts, 'More Honoured in the Breach: Consent and Impartiality in the Cambodian Peacekeeping Operation' (1997) 4 *International Law Peacekeeping* 1; I Johnstone, 'Managing Consent in Contemporary Peacekeeping Operations' (2011) 18 *International Law Peacekeeping* 168.

[207] This operation was established at the request of the government, yet without the support of the various warring factions. Since its creation in 1978, UNIFIL has lost more than 100 soldiers following hostile acts.

The UN has indeed gone to great lengths to acquire the cooperation of warring parties in situations such as those in Yugoslavia and Angola. A second prerequisite for peacekeeping concerns the impartiality of the operation (not to be confused with neutrality or inactivity).[208] Contrary to enforcement actions, which generally provide a military advantage to one side, peacekeeping missions must at all times remain impartial regardless of the actual mandate of the operation. Thirdly, peacekeeping forces may only use force in self-defence, ie when UN personnel become the object of an attack, and in defence of their mandate.[209] This rule was initially spelled out by the UNSG and was later made explicit in the mandates of various operations. A corollary of this feature is that peacekeeping forces are generally only lightly armed, as they are not designed for genuine combat situations.

Throughout most of the UN Charter era, these preconditions were observed fairly well. The only notable exception relates to ONUC, established in 1960 to provide assistance in maintaining law and order following the decolonisation of the Congo.[210] Whereas ONUC came into being as a consensual, non-offensive operation, it was gradually given a broader mandate and granted permission to use force beyond the purview of self-defence. Resolution 161 (1961) urged ONUC 'to take all appropriate measures to prevent the occurrence of civil war [...] including the use of force, if necessary, in the last resort'.[211] Resolution 169 (1961) widened this mandate even further and authorised the use of force 'to expel foreign troops and mercenaries if necessary'.[212]

C. Robust Peacekeeping

For a long time, the near disaster of ONUC, which had become involved in fighting with secessionist groups, led to a return to traditional peacekeeping operations in accordance with the aforementioned principles. However, with the end of the Cold War, calls for a larger role for peacekeeping operations swelled. In 1992, the UNSG took heed of these pleas, advocating a new concept of 'robust peacekeeping' or 'peacemaking', based on Article 40 UN Charter, whereby UN forces would enforce rather than merely monitor ceasefires.[213] This eventually led to the blurring of the traditional distinction between enforcement action and peacekeeping, illustrated by the events in Somalia and the former Yugoslavia.[214]

In both countries, peacekeeping operations were set up in extremely volatile circumstances, with no real ceasefire in place. Moreover, on both occasions peacekeeping went far beyond traditional boundaries and overlapped partly with Chapter VII enforcement

[208] See further S Vohra, 'Impartiality in United Nations Peace-keeping' (1996) 9 *LJIL* 63; D Donald, 'Neutrality, Impartiality and UN Peacekeeping at the Beginning of the 21st century' (2002) 9 *International Peacekeeping* 21; A Hughes, 'Impartiality and the UN Observation Group in Lebanon' (2002) 9 *International Peacekeeping* 1.

[209] See further KE Cox, 'Beyond Self-Defense: United Nations Peacekeeping Operations & the Use of Force' (1999) 27 *Denver Journal of International Law and Policy* 239; M Berdal, 'Lessons not Learned: The Use of Force in "Peace Operations" in the 1990s' (2001) 7 *Internationoal Peacekeeping* 55; R Murphy, 'United Nations Peacekeeping in Lebanon and Somalia, and the Use of Force' (2003) 8 *Journal of Conflict and Security Law* 71; R Zacklin, 'The Use of Force in Peacekeeping Operations' in N Blokker and N Schrijver (eds), *The Security Council and the Use of Force: Theory and Reality – A Need for Change?* (Dordrecht, Nijhoff, 2005) 91–106.

[210] See Gray (n 30) 271–72.

[211] UNSC Res 161, 21 February 1961, UN Doc S/RES/161.

[212] UNSC Res 169, 24 November 1961, UN Doc S/RES/169.

[213] UNSG, 'An Agenda for Peace: Preventive Diplomacy, Peacemaking and Peace-Keeping', 17 June 1992, UN Doc A/47/277-S/24111, paras 34–45.

[214] See Gray (n 30) 289–95.

operations. In Yugoslavia, the UN Protection Force (UNPROFOR) was authorised to use force to secure the delivery of humanitarian aid and to protect the 'safe havens'.[215] Although coercive action was in fact left to NATO forces authorised to use force under Chapter VII, the UN set aside the impartiality of UNPROFOR, exposing it to attacks. This was illustrated in 1995, when 300 UN personnel were taken hostage. In Somalia, the initial peacekeeping operation, the UN Operation in Somalia (UNOSOM I), was supplemented with parallel Chapter VII enforcement action in the form of the Unified Task Force (UNITAF). Both operations were subsequently transformed into the broadly mandated peacekeeping operation UNISOM II, which was drawn into the civil war and suffered heavy casualties.

The harsh experiences of the early 1990s led the UNSG to announce a return to traditional peacekeeping operations in his 'Supplement to an Agenda for Peace'.[216] This document recognised the enormous danger for a peacekeeping operation when asked to use force while being denied the necessary capabilities. It stressed that peacekeeping and enforcement action should be seen as separate techniques rather than as adjacent points on a continuum. The UNSG's report paved the way for a partial reversion of the traditional features of peacekeeping. The Brahimi Report[217] launched a set of reform proposals which were endorsed by the UNSC in 2000[218] and addressed, amongst other things, the need for adequate financial support for UN peacekeeping, the need for clear and credible mandates, the relationship between the UNSC, the Secretariat and the Troop-Contributing Countries (TCCs), and the importance of rapid deployment. Many of these recommendations have been implemented over the years.[219] Efforts to review and reform UN peacekeeping have continued ever since.[220]

D. Pragmatic Practice

In spite of a professed return to the traditional parameters of peacekeeping, the distinction between Chapter VI½ operations and Chapter VII enforcement action continues to be blurred, with more robust peacekeeping operations at times being deployed to volatile areas.[221] In eastern Congo, for instance, UN peacekeepers, fighting alongside Congolese armed forces, have engaged in offensive military operations against various armed rebel groups. To this end, an 'Intervention Brigade' was set up within the UN Organization Stabilization Mission in the DRC, 'with the responsibility of neutralizing armed groups [...] and the objective of contributing to reducing the threat posed by armed groups to state authority and civilian security in eastern DRC and to make space for stabilization

[215] UNSC Res 776, 14 September 1992, UN Doc S/RES/776; UNSC Res 836, 4 June 1993, UN Doc S/RES/836.
[216] UNSG, 'Supplement to An Agenda for Peace', 3 January 1995, UN Doc A/50/60-S/1995/1, paras 33–46.
[217] 'Report of the Panel on United Nations Peace Operations', UN Doc A/55/305-S/2000/809, 21 August 2000, v-58 (Brahimi Report).
[218] UNSC Res 1318, 7 September 2000, UN Doc S/RES/1318.
[219] See eg UNSC Res 1327, 13 November 2000, UN Doc S/RES/1327 (agreeing to strengthening the system of consultations with TCCs through the holding of private meetings with them and stating a possibility to consider using the Military Staff Committee as one of the means of enhancing UN peacekeeping capacity); UNSC Res 1353, 13 June 2001, UN Doc S/RES/1353 (adopting a statement of principles on cooperation with TCCs).
[220] See eg 'Report of the High-level Independent Panel on Peace Operations on uniting our strengths for peace: politics, partnership and people', 17 June 2015, UN Doc A/70/95–S/2015/446, 7-104.
[221] UN Department of Peacekeeping Operations and Department of Field Support (n 205) 19. Consider eg UNSC Res 2364, 29 June 2017, UN Doc S/RES/2364 (in relation to the UN Multidimensional Integrated Stabilization Mission in Mali).

activities'.[222] The relevant UNSC resolutions emphasise that this approach should not be seen as a 'precedent' and is not intended to cause 'any prejudice to the agreed principles of peacekeeping'.[223] Nevertheless, not much later the UNSC later also established the United Nations Multidimensional Integrated Stabilization Mission in Mali (MINUSMA), which was authorised 'to use all necessary means [...] to carry out its mandate'[224] and had to operate alongside a French military force that was fighting terrorist groups.[225] Upon the request of the government of Mali, the UNSC even requested MINUSMA 'to move to a more proactive and robust posture to carry out its mandate'.[226]

While these two operations have caused much discussion, it is hard to tell whether they mark a real change in the practice of the UNSC and the UN Secretariat.[227] What is evident from practice over the past decades is that the implementation of the UN's collective security mechanism is steered by a pragmatic case-by-case analysis of the exigencies and complexities of the situations under consideration, rather than by a formalistic adherence to legal constructs.

The main problem confronting UN peacekeeping today concerns the fact that the UN's resources and capacities are over-stretched, in combination with the reluctance, especially on behalf of developed countries, to duly provide the UN with (rapidly deployable) military and civilian personnel and corresponding resources.[228] Closely related to this is the notable trend towards the outsourcing by the UN of its collective security role to regional and sub-regional organisations, both in terms of peacekeeping and peace enforcement.

VII. Chapter VIII: Peacekeeping and Enforcement Action by Regional Organisations

A. Role of Regional Organisations

Chapter VIII of the UN Charter opens with Article 52, which stresses the primary role of regional organisations vis-à-vis the peaceful settlement of disputes within their region. This follows logically from the fact that the UNSC has the *primary* but not *exclusive* responsibility for maintaining international peace and security; it only has a monopoly on (the authorisation of) the use of force. As mentioned above (Section V(C)(iii)), the UNSC has the option to subcontract peacekeeping and enforcement action to regional organisations. Thus, Article 53(1) of the UN Charter provides that:

> The Security Council shall, where appropriate, utilize such regional arrangements or agencies for enforcement action under its authority. But no enforcement action shall be taken under regional arrangements or by regional agencies without the authorization of the Security Council [...].

[222] See UNSC Res 2098, 28 March 2013, UN Doc S/RES/2098, operative clause 9.
[223] ibid; UNSC Res 2147, 28 March 2014, UN Doc S/RES/2147, operative clause 1; UNSC Res 2211, 26 March 2015, UN Doc S/RES/2211, operative clause 1; UNSC Res 2277, 30 March 2016, UN Doc S/RES/2277, operative clause 27; UNSC Res 2348, 31 March 2017, UN Doc S/RES/2348, operative clause 26.
[224] UNSC Res 2100, 25 April 2013, UN Doc S/RES/2100, operative clauses 7 and 17.
[225] Gray (n 30) 336.
[226] UNSC Res 2295, 29 June 2016, UN Doc S/RES/2295, operative clause 18.
[227] Gray (n 30) 338.
[228] See further AJ Bellamy and PD Williams (eds), *Providing Peacekeepers: The Politics, Challenges and Future of United Nations Peacekeeping Contributions* (Oxford, OUP, 2013).

The UN Charter does not contain a definition of 'regional arrangements or agencies', a concept that was deliberately left vague by its drafters.[229] Accordingly, the UN(SC) has taken a very flexible and non-formal approach regarding the notion.[230] Even an ad hoc group of States merely coordinating national action through common organs suffices for the purpose of Chapter VIII, provided that it has 'as its purpose the settlement at a regional level of matters relating to the maintenance of international peace and security'.[231] Article 54 adds that the UNSC must at all times be kept fully informed of the activities undertaken by these entities for the maintenance of international peace and security.[232]

Not surprisingly, the breakthrough of the authorisation model at the end of the Cold War not only led to calls for a larger role for UN peacekeeping operations, but simultaneously gave rise to increased expectations of partnerships with regional organisations.[233] In his Agenda for Peace (1992), the UNSG stressed that the UNSC keeps the 'primary responsibility for maintaining international peace and security', but expressed his hope that 'regional action as a matter of decentralization, delegation and cooperation with United Nations efforts could not only lighten the burden of the Council but also contribute to a deeper sense of participation, consensus and democratization in international affairs'.[234] Since then, there has been a steady increase in regional peacekeeping and enforcement action. In particular, African and European (sub)regional organisations have taken on an important role in this regard, with the African Union (AU) and the EU becoming the most important actors.[235] In this context, Article 42(1) TEU provides that '[t]he common security and defence policy [...] shall provide the Union with an operational capacity drawing on civilian and military assets', which the EU may use 'on missions outside the Union for peace-keeping, conflict prevention and strengthening international security in accordance with the principles of the United Nations Charter'.

Regional peacekeeping and enforcement action raises delicate questions concerning the legitimacy and accountability of these operations, as well as the relationship between the organisations concerned and the UNSC.[236] Although the UN remains the world's most important provider of peacekeeping operations, the increase in regional action has at least partly affected the organisation's role in this regard.[237] As more and more UN peacekeeping missions are deployed concurrent with or following regional operations,[238] the UN often has to focus on coordination. It is in this light that it has attempted to set up institutional

[229] T Gazzini, *The Changing Rules on the Use of Force in International Law* (Manchester, Manchester UP, 2005) 106.

[230] Gray (n 30) 411–16.

[231] *Land and Maritime Boundary between Cameroon and Nigeria* (Cameroon v Nigeria) (Preliminary Objections) [1998] ICJ Rep 275, para 67. But note that since it is undisputed that the UNSC is entitled to authorise individual Member States to use force, the issue of whether a regional organisation is qualified for the purpose of Art 53 appears to have lost its practical relevance; see Gazzini (n 229) 106–108.

[232] An obligation 'reiterated' in UNSC Res 1631, 17 October 2005, UN Doc S/RES/1631, operative clause 9.

[233] Gray (n 30) 387–88.

[234] An Agenda for Peace (n 213) para 64.

[235] H Yamashita, 'Peacekeeping Cooperation between the United Nations and Regional Organisations' (2012) 38 *Review of International Studies* 165, 165; S Angerbauer, 'Die Beiträge der Europäischen Union zum Krisenmanagement der Vereinten Nationen' (2014) 1 *Strategie und Sicherheit* 305, 306 and 311.

[236] See eg M Griffin, 'Blue Helmet Blues: Assessing the Trend towards "Subcontracting" UN Peace Operations' (1999) 30 *Security Dialogue* 43; I Martin, 'Is the Regionalization of Peace Operations Desirable?' in M Pugh and WPS Sidhu (eds), *The United Nations and Regional Security* (Boulder, Rienner, 2003) 47–54; J Delbrück, 'The Role of Regional Organizations in Maintaining Peace and Security' in M Bothe et al (eds), *Redefining Sovereignty: The Use of Force after the Cold War* (Ardsley, Transnational Publishers, 2005) 145–60.

[237] Yamashita (n 235) 166 and 183.

[238] ibid, 166.

partnerships – as opposed to mere operational collaboration relationships – with the two main actors, the AU[239] and the EU.[240] It appears that the increase in regional action has not necessarily eased the burden on the UN's shoulders, as it has become engaged with the development of African peacekeeping capacity, and the need to organise follow-on missions to regional operations has remained.[241]

B. Regional Peacekeeping

Regional action short of enforcement action, such as a regional peacekeeping operation, does not require UNSC authorisation (see above, Section VI(A)). There have been several instances of regional peacekeeping operations with which the UNSC was involved only limitedly and/or which it did not authorise. For example, when in 1993 after a failed coup the Organisation of African Unity (OAU) – now the AU – sent military observers to Burundi, the UNSC simply welcomed this operation[242] and expressed its appreciation for the work done by the OAU[243] – an approval it repeated after the military coup in 1996.[244] In 2003, the AU then established the African Union Mission in Burundi (AMIB), after which the UNSC welcomed its efforts and those of 'the contingents from South Africa, Ethiopia and Mozambique which make it up', to eventually establish the UN operation in Burundi, which took over from AMIB.[245] A similar situation presented itself in Darfur (Sudan), after conflict broke out in 2003. With the consent of the government of Sudan and various rebel groups, the AU deployed the AU Mission in Sudan (AMIS), a monitoring mission that developed into a peacekeeping force. AMIS was endorsed by the UNSC,[246] to eventually be replaced by the now UN-'authorised' AU/UN Hybrid Operation in Darfur (UNAMID) after the conclusion of the Comprehensive Peace Agreement in 2006.[247]

Another example is the EU's first military European Security and Defence Policy (ESDP) operation.[248] In 2003, CONCORDIA took over from NATO's peacekeeping mission in the Former Yugoslav Republic of Macedonia (FYROM) 'to further contribute to a stable, secure environment, [and] to allow the FYROM Government to implement the Ohrid Framework Agreement'.[249] The mission was established following a request by the President of FYROM, and welcomed by the UNSC, which expressed its strong support.[250]

[239] See eg the joint declaration 'Enhancing UN-AU Cooperation: Framework for the Ten-year Capacity Building Programme for the African Union', 16 November 2006, UN Doc A/61/630, Annex.

[240] See eg 'Joint Declaration on UN-EU Co-operation in Crisis Management', 24 September 2003, consilium.europa.eu/uedocs/cms_data/docs/pressdata/en/misc/77348.pdf; 'Joint Statement on UN-EU Cooperation in Crisis Management', 7 June 2007, consilium.europa.eu/uedocs/cmsUpload/EU-UNstatmntoncrsmngmnt.pdf; EEAS (Crisis Management and Planning Department), 'Strengthening the UN-EU Strategic Partnership on Peacekeeping and Crisis Management: Priorities 2015–2018', EEAS 458/15, 23 March 2015, data.consilium.europa.eu/doc/document/ST-7632-2015-INIT/en/pdf. See Yamashita (n 235) 177–180 (AU) and 181–182 (EU).

[241] Yamashita (n 235) 183.

[242] Statement by the President of the UNSC 1994/60, 21 October 1994, UN Doc S/PRST/1994/60.

[243] Statement by the President of the UNSC 1994/82, 22 December 1994, UN Doc S/PRST/1994/82.

[244] UNSC Res 1072, 30 August 1996, UN Doc S/RES/1072.

[245] UNSC Res 1545, 21 May 2004, UN Doc S/RES/1545. See Gray (n 30) 392–93.

[246] UNSC Res 1556, 30 July 2004, UN Doc S/RES/1556.

[247] UNSC Res 1769, 31 July 2007, UN Doc S/RES/1769. See Gray (n 30) 401–404.

[248] F Naert, *International Law Aspects of the EU's Security and Defence Policy, with a Particular Focus on the Law of Armed Conflict and Human Rights* (Antwerp, Intersentia, 2010) 106–107.

[249] Council Joint Action 2003/92/CFSP of 27 January 2003 on the European Union military operation in the Former Yugoslav Republic of Macedonia, OJ L34/26, recital (1).

[250] UNSC Res 1371, 26 September 2001, UN Doc S/RES/1371.

C. Regional Enforcement Action within the Authorisation Model

Further, the UNSC has authorised enforcement action by regional organisations in several situations and for varied purposes.[251] It did so for the first time in relation to a trade embargo against Serbia and Montenegro in the context of the conflict in Yugoslavia in 1992. 'Acting under Chapters VII and VIII', the UNSC called upon States, 'acting nationally or through regional agencies or arrangements', to take the necessary measures to enforce the embargo[252] (implicitly addressing NATO and the Western European Union).[253] Subsequent resolutions regarding Yugoslavia have authorised the facilitation of access for humanitarian assistance,[254] the enforcement of a flight ban[255] and the protection of safe areas.[256]

Similar authorisations to enforce trade embargos followed regarding Haiti[257] and Sierra Leone.[258] It was only in the context of the situation in Sierra Leone that the UNSC for the first time explicitly referred to a regional organisation – the Economic Community of West-African States (ECOWAS) – by name.[259] Later, ECOWAS was also authorised to use force in Côte d'Ivoire, 'to guarantee the security and freedom of movement of their personnel and to ensure [...] the protection of civilians immediately threatened with physical violence'.[260] With regard to the situation in Liberia, the UNSC explicitly recognised the central role of ECOWAS when it gave a mandate 'to establish a Multinational Force in Liberia to support the implementation of the 17 June 2003 ceasefire agreement', authorising the participating UN Member States 'to take all necessary measures to fulfil its mandate'.[261] Somalia can serve as an example involving the AU. There, the UNSC authorised 'Member States of the African Union to establish [...] a mission in Somalia [AMISOM], which shall be authorised to take all necessary measures as appropriate to carry out [its] mandate'.[262]

There are also several examples of EU regional action within the authorisation model. In 2003, the UNSC authorised the EU-led Interim Emergency Multinational Force – named operation ARTEMIS – 'to contribute to the stabilization of the security conditions and the improvement of the humanitarian situation in Bunia' and 'to take all necessary measures to fulfil its mandate' in support of the UN Mission in the DRC (MONUC).[263] In 2004, the UNSC authorised the ESDP operation ALTHEA to take over the military presence of the NATO-led Stabilisation Force (SFOR) in Bosnia and Herzegovina (BiH) to ensure

[251] Note that the fact that the UNSC has authorised regional action does not make it enforcement action, as regional organisations generally defer to the UNSC to authorise or at least endorse eg peacekeeping operations also when this is strictly speaking not required under international law (see above, Section VI(A)).

[252] UNSC Res 787, 16 November 1992, UN Doc S/RES/787.

[253] Gray (n 30) 413–14; cp C Gray, *International Law and the Use of Force*, 3rd edn (Oxford, OUP, 2008) 385 and 423.

[254] UNSC Res 770, 13 August 1992, UN Doc S/RES/770.

[255] UNSC Res 816, 31 March 1993, UN Doc S/RES/816.

[256] UNSC Res 836, 4 June 1993, UN Doc S/RES/836.

[257] UNSC Res 875, 16 October 1993, UN Doc S/RES/875.

[258] UNSC Res 1132, 8 October 1997, UN Doc S/RES/1132.

[259] Gray (2008) (n 253) 423–24.

[260] UNSC Res 1464, 4 February 2003, UN Doc S/RES/1464. Mainly due to ECOWAS' limited resources, its mission in Côte d'Ivoire (ECOMICI) was first complemented by a small UN mission and later replaced by a multi-dimensional operation (UNOCI); Gray (n 30) 446–48.

[261] UNSC Res 1497, 1 August 2003, UN Doc S/RES/1497.

[262] UNSC Res 1744, 21 February 2007, UN Doc S/RES/1744. As AMISON faced difficulties in securing troops and was subjected to repeated attacks, it was not able to effectively carry out its mission; Gray (n 30) 397–400.

[263] UNSC Resolution 1484, 30 May 2003, UN Doc S/RES/1484 (not explicitly referring to the EU); Naert (n 248) 111–14.

compliance with the Dayton Peace Agreement and to contribute to a safe and secure environment in BiH.[264] In 2006, the UNSC authorised the deployment of EUFOR RD Congo, an autonomous EU operation to support MONUC during the 2006 elections.[265] In 2007, the UNSC authorised the EU to deploy an operation (EUFOR Tchad/RCA) in Chad and the CAR that could take all necessary measures to protect civilians in danger, to facilitate the delivery of humanitarian aid and to protect UN personnel and facilities.[266] A last example is the EU's involvement in counter-piracy operations in Somalia, discussed further in Chapter 18, Section V(E)(i)(a) on piracy. In all resolutions concerning the EU, the UNSC referred only to Chapter VII, omitting any reference to Chapter VIII. This lack of reference could be explained by the fact that these were not the type of Chapter VIII operations originally envisaged by the drafters of the UN Charter, as these operations were not carried out *within* the EU.[267]

D. Regional Action Challenging the Authorisation Model

As mentioned above (Section VII(A)), Article 53(1) of the UN Charter provides that no enforcement action can be taken by regional organisations without the authorisation of the UNSC. Nevertheless, regional practice has at times challenged the authorisation model. For example, several ECOWAS operations used force before the UNSC gave its authorisation, or went beyond the limits of such authorisation.[268] In 1990, before the UNSC got involved, the ECOWAS Standing Mediation Committee established a multilateral armed force in the form of a 'Monitoring Group' (ECOMOG) in Liberia. ECOMOG secured territory against the National Patriotic Front of Liberia of Charles Taylor and in 1992 even recaptured territory occupied by the latter, going beyond peacekeeping.[269] The first UNSC resolution on the situation was adopted only at the end of the same year, commending ECOWAS 'for its efforts to restore peace, security and stability in Liberia'.[270] All of this occurred despite considerable uncertainty as to whether Liberia consented to ECOMOG's presence, at least at the time it was established and entered the country.[271] Still, as stated above (Section V(C)(iii)), some have argued, unconvincingly, that the UNSC may authorise enforcement action implicitly. As the UNSC had been informed by ECOWAS' activities in Liberia and later approved its actions, this may have been an example of an 'implicit but certain authorization'.[272] To the extent that this approach relies on authorisation *subsequent to* regional action, it should be rejected. On the other hand, the situation in Liberia leaves

[264] UNSC Res 1575, 22 November 2004, UN Doc S/RES/1575; Council Joint Action 2004/570/CFSP of 12 July 2004 on the European Union military operation in Bosnia and Herzegovina, OJ L252/10; Naert (n 248) 124–27.
[265] UNSC Res 1671, 25 April 2006, UN Doc S/RES/1671; Naert (n 248) 150–52.
[266] UNSC Res 1778, 25 September 2007, UN Doc S/RES/1778; Naert (n 248) 159–62.
[267] Gray (2008) (n 253) 385–86. In any case, whether or not the UNSC explicitly refers to Chapter VIII is a matter of 'no obvious legal or practical significance'; Gray (n 30) 415.
[268] Gazzini (n 229) 112.
[269] Gray (n 30) 428.
[270] UNSC Res 788, 19 November 1992, UN Doc S/RES/788.
[271] While President Doe, who was in power until Charles Taylor challenged him, and Prince Johnson (who broke away from Charles Taylor) consented to this presence, Charles Taylor, who controlled 90% of Liberia's territory, did not. Later, ECOWAS claimed that there was consent on the part of President Sawyer, who was in charge of the interim government set up under the auspices of ECOWAS by the end of 1990; Gray (n 30) 429–31.
[272] U Villani, 'The Security Council's Authorization of Enforcement Action by Regional Organizations' (2002) 6 *Max Planck Yearbook of United Nations Law Online* 535, 542–43.

open the possibility of authorisation after the *beginning* of the action, following which the UNSC can still control the operation, which it did in the case at hand by establishing the UN Observer Mission in Liberia.[273]

Another case of regional enforcement action at odds with the authorisation model is the NATO intervention in Kosovo. While NATO had always based coercive action on relevant UNSC authorisations (although sometimes substantial or procedural limits were disregarded), the 1999 operation was perceived as a challenge to the UNSC monopoly on the use of force.[274] It has again been attempted to argue that NATO's actions were 'consistent with the orientation' of the UNSC and to infer an implicit authorisation from several UNSC resolutions that condemned the violence,[275] determined that the situation constituted a threat to peace and security in the region, reserved the possibility for further enforcement action[276] and welcomed the conditions for the cessation of hostilities.[277] The observation that two permanent members of the UNSC – China and Russia – unequivocally condemned NATO's intervention appears to preclude such a conclusion.[278] Similarly, it is contested whether the NATO operation in Libya in 2011 remained within the confines of what the UNSC authorised (see above, Section V(C)(iii)).

Lastly, Article 4(h) of the Constitutive Act of the AU appears to contravene the authorisation model. As mentioned above regarding the doctrine of humanitarian intervention (Section IV(B)), it provides for 'the right of the Union to intervene in a Member State pursuant to a decision of the Assembly in respect of grave circumstances, namely: war crimes, genocide and crimes against humanity'.[279] However, as the doctrine of humanitarian intervention is not part of customary international law, interventions for humanitarian motives should be left to the discretion of the UNSC. It has been argued that 'through binding themselves to the Act, AU Member States have consented to making themselves subject to intervention'.[280] Still, as stated above with regard to the existence of a prior collective defence agreement (Section III(D)), this does not preclude the need for the ad hoc consent of the State concerned. Accordingly, Article 4(h) cannot provide an exception to the prohibition of the use of force. If applied without Host State consent, the AU would act in contravention of Article 2(4) of the UN Charter more generally, and Article 53(1) in particular.[281]

[273] ibid, 550–51. cp UNSC Res 1132, 8 October 1997, UN Doc S/RES/1132, authorising ECOWAS to undertake certain enforcement actions in Sierra Leone after ECOWAS had already initiated them, following which the UN Observer Mission in Sierra Leone (UNOMSIL) and later the UN Mission in Sierra Leone (UNAMSIL) progressively took over; ibid, 553–54.

[274] Gazzini (n 229) 111.

[275] eg UNSC Res 1160, 31 March 1998, UN Doc S/RES/1160.

[276] UNSC Res 1199, 23 September 1998, UN Doc S/RES/1199.

[277] UNSC Res 1244, 19 June 1999, UN Doc S/RES/1244; see Villani (n 272) 544.

[278] Villani (n 272) 546.

[279] See above (n 127). The Protocol on Amendments to the Constitutive Act of the African Union (adopted 11 July 2003, not yet entered into force) adds to Art 4(h) 'as well as a serious threat to legitimate order to restore peace and stability to the Member State of the Union upon the recommendation of the [AU] Peace and Security Council', challenging the monopoly of the UNSC on (the authorisation of) the use of force. As to date, it only obtained 28 of the required 37 ratifications (ie a 2/3rd majority of 55 Member States; see AU, 'List of countries which have signed, ratified/acceded to the Protocol on the Amendments to the Constitutive Act of the African Union', last updated 15 June 2017, au.int/sites/default/files/treaties/7785-sl-protocol_on_the_amendments_to_the_constitutive_act_of_the_african_union_.pdf), the Protocol has not (yet) entered into force.

[280] D Kuwali, *The Responsibility to Protect: Implementation of Article 4(h) Intervention* (Leiden, Nijhoff, 2011) 140.

[281] Gazzini (n 229) 113–14. For a comprehensive discussion of the provision and the amendment thereto and a position that does not outright reject their illegality, see B Kioko, 'The Right of Intervention under the African Unions Constitutive Act: From Non-interference to Non-Intervention' (2003) 85 *IRRC* 807.

In this regard, a more recent initiative by the League of Arab States (LAS) appears less problematic. At the closing of its March 2015 Summit, the LAS laid the ground for the creation of the so-called Joint Defence Arab Forces 'to face the challenges threatening the security and safety of any of the member states, its national sovereignty and that represent a direct threat to the "Arab National Security", including the threats of terrorist organisations'.[282] However, as any intervention by the Forces would require the consent of the State concerned, the idea does not immediately challenge the authorisation model.[283]

VIII. Concluding Remarks

The twentieth century saw the transition from a *jus ad bellum* to a *jus contra bellum*, culminating in the adoption of the UN Charter. The Charter provides for a comprehensive collective security system that revolves around the primary role of the UN Security Council and is built on Article 2(4), containing the prohibition on the threat or use of force. The only uncontested form of intervention considered to fall beyond the scope of Article 2(4) is intervention at the request of the de jure government of a State. However, history is replete with highly controversial claims of intervention by invitation. The only exception to Article 2(4), allowing States to claim unilateral recourse to force, is the right of self-defence enshrined in Article 51 of the UN Charter.

The exercise of the right of self-defence requires the existence of an armed attack. Traditionally, there was agreement that such an attack had to have taken place before States could use force in self-defence. Since the events of 11 September 2001, it is increasingly recognised that pre-emptive measures against an imminent attack are also allowed. The possibility of preventive measures against a non-imminent attack is generally rejected. Furthermore, in the post-9/11 word, the ICJ's *Nicaragua* approach, according to which an 'armed attack' presupposes State imputability or substantial State involvement, has increasingly come under pressure, as exemplified by State action in Afghanistan and, most recently, Syria/Iraq. Lastly, it is contested whether States can resort to force to protect their nationals abroad without the host State's consent. While this ground for the use of force is open for abuse, there is a tendency in recent general practice to at least condone interventions aimed at the evacuation of nationals abroad threatened by civil war or internal unrest.

Although the UN Charter contains only one exception to the prohibition on the unilateral recourse to force, additional exceptions have at times been claimed to exist. While there has been considerable debate about the use of force in support of national liberation wars, today, the debate centres around the permissibility of unilateral humanitarian interventions. Yet, as notably illustrated by the controversy surrounding NATO's intervention in Kosovo, the concept lacks the necessary support to have become part of customary international law. Humanitarian interventions may not be 'unambiguously illegal', but should, even in spite of the advance of the R2P principle, be left to the discretion of the UNSC.

Indeed, the collective security system as established by the UN Charter revolves around the UNSC. Carrying the primary responsibility for the maintenance of international peace

[282] NI Diab, 'Enforcement Action by Regional Organisations Revisited: The Prospective Joint Arab Forces' (2017) 4 *Journal on the Use of Force and International Law* 86, 86.
[283] ibid, 87 and 100–103.

and security, the UNSC can adopt non-binding recommendations regarding methods or procedures for the peaceful settlement of disputes between States (Chapter VI), but also binding decisions aimed at maintaining or restoring international peace and security (Chapter VII). While to act under Chapter VII, the UNSC must first establish the existence of a 'threat to the peace', it has interpreted this concept flexibly as to include a broad array of 'threats'. Moreover, the UNSC has at times assumed the role of a quasi-judicial or quasi-legislative body. It is submitted that such a role should be confined to cases where it is indispensable for the exercise of the UNSC's police function, and that effects of such decisions should in principle be limited to a particular situation. However, as long as States do not object, the original UN Charter paradigm may well shift in time. In the latter case, reforms to make the UNSC a more legitimate body and strengthen its authority are even more necessary.

Under Chapter VII, the UNSC can also adopt measures that involve the use of force. As UN Member States have never agreed to structurally make available troops to the UN, the UNSC has resorted to two alternative mechanisms: it has started to organise peacekeeping operations and authorise individual Member States and/or regional organisations to use force. While UN peacekeeping operations must be impartial and may only use force in self-defence, calls for a larger role for peacekeeping led to the idea of 'robust peacekeeping', blurring the traditional lines between peacekeeping and enforcement action. As the UN's peacekeeping practice largely depends on the exigencies of the situations concerned, the professed return to the traditional parameters of peacekeeping has not remedied this blurring of the distinction between Chapter VI½ operations and Chapter VII enforcement action.

Further, there is a notable trend towards outsourcing peacekeeping and enforcement action to regional and sub-regional organisations. With several organisations, such as the AU and the EU, increasingly profiling themselves as regional security providers, this trend is bound to persist in the future. However, regional organisations at times challenge the primary role of the UNSC as regards the maintenance of international peace and security by acting outside of the authorisation model. Delicate questions arise concerning the legitimacy and accountability of such regional operations, as well as the relationship between these organisations and the UN(SC). A lasting equilibrium has yet to be found, and may eventually require a fundamental revision of the Charter framework.

Bibliography

Bellamy, AJ and Williams, PD, *Understanding Peacekeeping*, 2nd edn (Cambridge, Polity, 2010).

Blokker, N and Schrijver, N (eds), *The Security Council and the Use of Force: Theory and Reality – A Need for Change?* (Dordrecht, Nijhoff, 2005).

Bothe, M et al (eds), *Redefining Sovereignty: The Use of Force after the Cold War* (Ardsley, Transnational Publishers, 2005).

Brownlie, I, *International Law and the Use of Force by States* (Oxford, OUP, 1963).

Brownlie, I, 'The Use of Force in Self-Defence' (1961) 37 *BYIL* 193.

Cassese, A (ed), *The Current Legal Regulation on the Use of Force* (Dordrecht, Nijhoff, 1986).

Chesterman, S, *Just War or Just Peace? Humanitarian Intervention and International Law* (Oxford, OUP, 2001).

Corten, O, *Le droit contre la guerre: L'interdiction du recours à la force en droit international contemporain*, 2nd edn (Paris, Pédone, 2014).

De Wet, E, *The Chapter VII Powers of the United Nations Security Council* (Oxford, Hart, 2004).

Dinstein, Y, *War, Aggression and Self-Defence*, 6th edn (Cambridge, CUP, 2017).

Doswald-Beck, L, 'The Legal Validity of Military Intervention by Invitation of the Government' (1985) 56 *BYIL* 189.

Gardam, J, *Necessity, Proportionality and the Use of Force by States* (Cambridge, CUP, 2004).

Gazzini, T, *The Changing Rules on the Use of Force in International Law* (Manchester, Manchester UP, 2005).

Gray, C, *International Law and the Use of Force*, 4th edn (Oxford, OUP, 2018).

Holzgrefe, JL and Keohane, RO (eds), *Humanitarian Intervention: Ethical, Legal and Political Dilemmas* (Cambridge, CUP, 2003).

Kress, C, *Gewaltverbod und Selbstverteidigungsrecht nach der Satzung der Vereinten Nationen bei staatlicher Verwicklung in Gewaltakte Privater* (Berlin, Duncker & Humblot, 1995).

Lubell, N, *Extraterritorial Use of Force against Non-State Actors* (Oxford, OUP, 2010).

Naert, F, *International Law Aspects of the EU's Security and Defence Policy, with a Particular Focus on the Law of Armed Conflict and Human Rights* (Antwerp, Intersentia, 2010).

Orford, A, *Reading Humanitarian Intervention: Human Rights and the Use of Force in International Law* (Cambridge, CUP, 2003).

Osterdahl, I, *Threat to the Peace: The Interpretation by the Security Council of Article 39 of the UN Charter* (Uppsala, Iustus Förlag, 1998).

Quigley, J, 'The "Privatization" of Security Council Enforcement Action: A Threat to Multilateralism' (1996) 17 *MJIL* 249.

Ruys, T, *'Armed Attack' and Article 51 of the UN Charter* (Cambridge, CUP, 2010).

Ruys, T and Corten, O (eds), *The Use of Force in International Law: A Case-Based Approach* (Oxford, OUP, 2018).

Schachter, O, 'The Right of States to Use Armed Force' (1984) 82 *Michigan Law Review* 1620.

Sicilianos, L-A, 'L'autorisation par le Conseil de Sécurité de recourir à la force: Une tentative d'évaluation' (2002) 106 *Revue générale de droit international public* 5.

Sicilianos, L-A, *Les réactions décentralisées à l'illicité: Des contre-mesures à la légitime defense* (Paris, Librairie Générale de Droit et de Jurisprudence, 1990).

Simma, B et al (eds), *The Charter of the United Nations: A Commentary*, 3rd edn (Oxford, OUP, 2012).

Waldock, CHM, 'The Regulation of the Use of Force by Individual States in International Law' (1952) 81 *RdC* 451.

Weller, M (ed), *The Oxford Handbook of the Use of Force in International Law* (Oxford, OUP, 2015).

White, ND, *Keeping the Peace: The United Nations and the Maintenance of International Peace and Security*, 2nd edn (Manchester, Manchester UP, 1997).

White, ND and Henderson, C (eds), *Research Handbook on International Conflict and Security Law* (Cheltenham, Edward Elgar, 2013).

Wilson, HA, *International Law and the Use of Force by National Liberation Movements* (Oxford, Clarendon Press, 1988).

Further Reading

Blokker, N, 'Is the Authorization Authorized? Powers and Practice of the UN Security Council to Authorize the Use of Force by "Coalitions of the Able and Willing"' (2000) 11 *EJIL* 541.

Cox, KE, 'Beyond Self-defense: United Nations Peacekeeping Operations & the Use of Force' (1999) 27 *Denver Journal of International Law and Policy* 239.

Dubuisson, F, 'L'hypothèse d'une règle émergente fondant une intervention militaire sur une "autorisation implicite" du Conseil de Sécurité' (2000) 104 *Revue générale de droit international public* 873.

Griffin, M, 'Blue Helmet Blues: Assessing the Trend towards "Subcontracting" UN Peace Operations' (1999) 30 *Security Dialogue* 43.

Grimal, F and Melling, G, 'The Protection of Nationals Abroad: Lawfulness or Toleration? A Commentary' (2011) 16 *Journal Conflict and Security Law* 541.

Harper, K, 'Does the United Nations Security Council Have the Competence to Act as a Court and Legislature?' (1994) 27 *New York University Journal of International Law and Politics* 103.

Hovell, D, *The Power of Process: The Value of Due Process in Security Council Sanctions Decision-Making* (Oxford, OUP, 2016).

Johnstone, I, 'Managing Consent in Contemporary Peacekeeping Operations' (2011) 18 *International Law Peacekeeping* 168.

Koskenniemi, M, 'The Police in the Temple – Order, Justice and the UN: A Dialectical View' (1995) 6 *EJIL* 325.

Kretzmer, D, 'The Inherent Right of Self-defence and Proportionality in Jus ad Bellum' (2013) 24 *EJIL* 235.

Lubell, N, 'The Problem of Imminence in an Uncertain World' in Weller, M (ed), *The Oxford Handbook of the Use of Force in International Law* (Oxford, OUP, 2015) 697–719.

Martin, I, 'Is the Regionalization of Peace Operations Desirable?' in Pugh, M and Sidhu, WPS (eds), *The United Nations and Regional Security* (Boulder, Rienner, 2003) 47–54.

Orakhelashvili, A, 'The Power of the UN Security Council to Determine the Existence of a "Threat to the Peace"' (2006) 1 *Irish Yearbook International Law* 61.

Ruys, T and Verhoeven, S, 'Attacks by Private Actors and the Right of Self-defence' (2005) 10 *Journal of Conflict and Security Law* 289.

Stahn, C, 'Responsibility to Protect: Political Rhetoric or Emerging Legal Norm?' (2007) 101 *AJIL* 99.

Tsagourias, N, 'Consent, Neutrality/Impartiality and the Use of Force in Peacekeeping: Their Constitutional Dimension' (2006) 11 *Journal Conflict and Security Law* 465.

Villani, U, 'The Security Council's Authorization of Enforcement Action by Regional Organizations' (2002) 6 *Max Planck Yearbook of United Nations Law Online* 535.

White, ND, 'The UN Charter and Peacekeeping Forces: Constitutional Issues' (1996) 3 *International Peacekeeping* 43.

Yamashita, H, 'Peacekeeping Cooperation between the United Nations and Regional Organisations' (2012) 38 *Review of International Studies* 165.

15

The Law of Armed Conflict

I. Introduction

The law of armed conflict (LOAC), also known as the 'law of war', 'international humanitarian law' (IHL) or the '*jus in bello*',[1] is the branch of international law that governs the conduct of hostilities and the protection of victims in armed conflict. LOAC does not seek to render it impossible to wage war, nor does it distinguish between the 'aggressor' and the 'victim' in an international armed conflict; it necessarily applies in equal fashion to both.[2] Furthermore, non-compliance by one party does not release the other party from its obligations.[3] Principally, LOAC accepts that armed conflicts occur, but holds that the conduct of hostilities is subject to certain rules that balance the exigencies of military necessity and considerations of humanity and that seek to protect those who do not, or no longer, participate in hostilities.

The birth of the modern-day law of armed conflict is commonly traced back to the 1860s, when three key instruments were adopted. The first was the Lieber Code of 1863, a manual drafted for the purposes of guiding the conduct of the Union army in the American Civil War.[4] Second, the 1864 Geneva Convention for the Amelioration of the Condition of the Wounded in Armies in the Field[5] was the first of many 'Geneva' Conventions dealing with the protection of persons *hors de combat* (out of combat). The third major instrument was the Saint Petersburg Declaration of 1868,[6] which constituted the first international

[1] As opposed to the *jus ad bellum*, on which see Chapter 14 on the Use of Force.

[2] However, the position of the parties under the law of neutrality may be different. See A Orakhelashvili, 'Overlap and Convergence: The Interaction between Jus ad Bellum and Jus in Bello' (2007) 12 *Journal of Conflict and Security Law* 157, 185–93.

[3] Although LOAC provides for some, very limited, leeway in such context for the latter party to have recourse to belligerent reprisals. See further F Kalshoven, *Belligerent Reprisals*, 2nd edn (Leiden, Nijhoff, 2005).

[4] Instructions for the Government of Armies of the United States in the Field (Lieber Code), 24 April 1863, ihl-databases.icrc.org/ihl/INTRO/110.

[5] Its adoption resulted from the lobbying efforts of Henry Dunant, who had founded the International Committee of the Red Cross (ICRC) one year earlier, after witnessing the battle of Solferino in 1859 (on which see Henry Dunant, *Un souvenir de Solférino* (Geneva, ICRC, 1862)).

[6] Declaration Renouncing the Use, in Time of War, of Explosive Projectiles Under 400 Grammes Weight (Saint Petersburg Declaration), 29 November/11 December 1868, ihl-databases.icrc.org/ihl/INTRO/130?OpenDocument.

agreement outlawing the use of a specific weapon/projectile. It was also the first instrument to set forth the fundamental principle that parties to a conflict should not use arms that cause 'unnecessary suffering', a principle that has inspired the adoption of several other instruments restricting or prohibiting the use of specific weapons.

Numerous other treaties saw the light after the 1860s.[7] Major codification efforts took place in The Hague in 1899 and 1907. While most of the resulting 'Hague' Conventions (HC) have long become obsolete, the Fourth Hague Convention Respecting the Laws and Customs of War on Land (HC IV) and the Regulations annexed thereto (the Hague Regulations)[8] remain valid and relevant today. Another major codification effort took place in 1949, when States, influenced by the atrocities of the Second World War, adopted the four Geneva Conventions (GCs), each of which deals with a separate category of persons *hors de combat*: (i) the wounded and sick in armed forces in the field (GC I); (ii) the wounded, sick and shipwrecked at sea (GC II); (iii) prisoners of war (GC III); and (iv) civilians (GC IV).[9] It is often suggested that the Hague Conventions were written primarily from the perspective of the combatant taking part in hostilities, whereas the Geneva Conventions are primarily conceived from the point of view of the victim of the armed conflict. Accordingly, a distinction is sometimes made between so-called 'Hague law' and 'Geneva law'. In 1977, two other key instruments were adopted, namely the two Additional Protocols to the Geneva Conventions (APs). These treaties deal respectively with international armed conflicts (AP I) and non-international armed conflicts (AP II). Both additional protocols contain a mixture of both Hague law and Geneva law.[10]

Together, the Hague Conventions, the four Geneva Conventions and the two Additional Protocols form the core of the modern law of armed conflict. They are supplemented by numerous other treaties, including a substantial number of treaties governing the use of specific weapons (see below, Section V), but also, for instance, instruments dealing with the protection of cultural property in armed conflict (see below, Section III(C)).

Whereas these treaties constitute the main sources of LOAC, customary international law remains of crucial importance in subdomains such as the law of naval warfare or the law of non-international armed conflict, that have not, or have only partially, been codified in written texts. Furthermore, in relation to those rules that have been enshrined in treaty law but are not universally ratified (as opposed to the four Geneva Conventions, which enjoy universal ratification), customary international law broadens the legally binding character of those rules to non-State Parties. On the basis of an in-depth analysis of all available practice, the International Committee of the Red Cross (ICRC) in 2005 published its Customary International Humanitarian Law Study, which identified 161 rules having

[7] See the ICRC Treaty Database at icrc.org/ihl.

[8] Hague Convention (IV) of 1907 Respecting the Laws and Customs of War on Land and its annex: Regulations Concerning the Laws and Customs of War on Land (adopted 18 October 1907, entered into force 26 January 2010) 205 CTS 277.

[9] Geneva Convention (I) for the Amelioration of the Condition of the Wounded and Sick in Armed Forces in the Field (adopted 12 August 1949, entered into force 21 October 1950) 75 UNTS 31; Geneva Convention (II) for the Amelioration of the Condition of Wounded, Sick and Shipwrecked Members of Armed Forces at Sea (adopted 12 August 1949, entered into force 21 October 1950) 75 UNTS 85; Geneva Convention (III) Relative to the Treatment of Prisoners of War (adopted 12 August 1949, entered into force 21 October 1950) 75 UNTS 135; Geneva Convention (IV) Relative to the Protection of Civilian Persons in Time of War (adopted 12 August 1949, entered into force 21 October 1950) 755 UNTS 287.

[10] It follows that no strict distinction can be maintained in modern-day LOAC between so-called Hague law and Geneva law, although the distinction may still be useful for didactical purposes.

the status of customary law.[11] Some of the findings of this study have nonetheless sparked debate, as has the underlying methodology the ICRC used to come to these findings.[12]

Lastly, useful subsidiary guidance on the content of LOAC can be found in a variety of non-binding manuals, such as the 1994 San Remo Manual (on warfare at sea),[13] the 2009 HPCR Manual (on air and missile warfare),[14] and the 2013 Tallinn Manual (on cyber warfare),[15] as well as in the commentaries to the Geneva Conventions and the Additional Protocols that were prepared under the auspices of the ICRC.[16]

LOAC is a broad field, which is often confronted with, and at times forced to adapt to, new evolutions in the nature of warfare. In recent years, this has included the advance of cyber warfare and drone warfare. At the same time, LOAC ultimately rests on a few fundamental principles, chiefly the principle of distinction and the principle of unnecessary suffering.[17] The former requires combatants to distinguish themselves from civilians, and to distinguish between civilians and civilian objects on the one hand and military objectives on the other in their targeting decisions and in their choice of means and methods of warfare.[18] Unnecessary suffering or superfluous injury is caused by the use of means and methods of warfare whose foreseeable harm is excessive in relation to the lawful military advantage intended.[19] Reference can also be made to the principle of humanity, which acts as an important limiting factor in LOAC and resists the idea that belligerents have the right to do whatever is required to prevail in armed conflict.[20]

[11] J-M Henckaerts and L Doswald-Beck (eds), *Customary International Humanitarian Law – Volume I: Rules* (Cambridge, CUP, 2005); J-M Henckaerts and L Doswald-Beck (eds), *Customary International Humanitarian Law – Volume II: Practice* (Cambridge, CUP, 2005). The 'Rules' and the 'Practice' section (updated on a regular basis) can also be consulted online via icrc.org/customary-ihl/eng/docs/home.

[12] See in particular JB Bellinger III and WJ Haynes II, 'A US Government Response to the International Committee of the Red Cross Study Customary International Humanitarian Law' (2007) 89 *IRRC* 443.

[13] L Doswald-Beck (ed), *San Remo Manual on International Law applicable to Armed Conflicts at Sea* (Cambridge, CUP, 1995).

[14] Program on Humanitarian Policy and Conflict Research at Harvard University (HPCR), *HPCR Manual on International Law applicable to Air and Missile Warfare* (New York, CUP, 2013).

[15] MN Schmitt, *Tallinn Manual on the International Law applicable to Cyber Warfare* (Cambridge, CUP, 2013).

[16] The original commentaries to the GCs were prepared under the general editorship of Jean Pictet and were published between 1952 and 1960: JS Pictet (ed), *Commentary I: Geneva Convention for the Amelioration of the Condition of the Wounded and Sick in Armed Forces in the Field* (Geneva, ICRC, 1952), mutatis mutandis for GC II (1960), GC III (1960) and GC IV (1958). Commentaries to the APs were published in 1987: Y Sandoz, C Swinarski and B Zimmerman (eds), *Commentary on the Additional Protocols of 8 June 1977 to the Geneva Conventions of 12 August 1949* (Geneva, ICRC, 1987)). More recently, the ICRC has embarked upon the preparation of new commentaries to each of the GCs. New commentaries to GC I and GC II were published in 2016 and 2017 respectively: ICRC, *Commentary on the First Geneva Convention* (Cambridge, CUP, 2016), mutatis mutandis for GC II (2017). All ICRC Commentaries are available via the ICRC Treaty Database (n7).

[17] Legality of the Threat or Use of Nuclear Weapons (Advisory Opinion) [1996] ICJ Rep, paras 78–79.

[18] See further N Melzer, 'The Principle of Distinction between Civilians and Combatants' in A Clapham and P Gaeta (eds), *The Oxford Handbook of International Law in Armed Conflict* (Oxford, OUP, 2014) 296–31.

[19] S Oeter, 'Methods and Means of Combat' in D Fleck, *The Handbook of International Humanitarian Law*, 3rd edn (Oxford, OUP, 2013) 115–230, 125. See further H Meyrowitz, 'The Principle of Superfluous Injury or Unnecessary Suffering' (1994) 34 *IRRC* 98.

[20] The principle of humanity is included in the so-called 'Martens clause', which can be found in several LOAC instruments. Pursuant to the 'Martens clause', in cases not covered by treaty law, civilians and combatants remain under the protection of the principles of international law derived not only from custom, but also from 'the principles of humanity' and 'the dictates of public conscience'. See the preamble of Hague Convention (II) with Respect to the Laws and Customs of War on Land (adopted 29 July 1899, entered into force 4 September 1900) 187 CTS 429 and Hague Convention (IV) (n8), as well as Art 1(2) AP I. See further M Salter, 'Reinterpreting Competing Interpretations of the Scope and Potential of the Martens Clause' (2012) 17 *Journal of Conflict and Security Law* 403; A Cassese, 'The Martens Clause: Half a Loaf or Simply Pie in the Sky?' (2000) 11 *EJIL* 187.

The present chapter deals with only the tip of the LOAC iceberg. Various sub-fields and sub-topics, such as the law of belligerent occupation,[21] the law of neutrality,[22] the law of naval warfare[23] and the rules governing the protection of the environment[24] are left aside.

II. Scope of Application of the Law of Armed Conflict

A. Relevance

The application of LOAC depends on two fundamental classification questions. The first relates to the classification of the conflict; the second to the classification of the affected individual (either as a combatant or as a civilian). The first question pertains to the scope of application of LOAC, which is limited to situations of 'armed conflict'.[25] In the past, its application was often considered dependent upon the existence of a '(state of) war', a concept that was sometimes linked to the issuing of a declaration of war. However, the 1949 Geneva Conventions have replaced the concept of 'war' as a trigger for the application of LOAC by the more objective, factual concept of armed conflict. Thus, Common Article[26] 2 of the Geneva Conventions asserts that the Conventions shall apply 'to all cases of declared war or of any other armed conflict between two or more of the High Contracting Parties, even if the state of war is not recognized by them'.[27] It follows that a declaration of war is sufficient to trigger the application of the Conventions, but is not necessary to this end. More generally, to determine whether LOAC applies, it is necessary to look at the situation on the ground. The label used to describe a conflict (eg a 'war on drugs' or a 'war on terror') bears no autonomous relevance.

[21] Further, see eg E Benvenisti, *The International Law of Occupation*, 2nd edn (Oxford, OUP, 2012); V Koutroulis, *Le début et la fin de l'application du droit de l'occupation* (Paris, Pedone, 2010); R Kolb and S Vité, *Le droit de l'occupation militaire: perspectives historiques et enjeux juridiques actuels* (Brussels, Bruylant, 2009); Y Dinstein, *The International Law of Belligerent Occupation* (Cambridge, CUP, 2009).

[22] Further, see eg M Bothe, 'The Law of Neutrality' in Fleck (n 19) 549–80; W Heintschel von Heinegg, '"Benevolent" Third States in International Armed Conflicts: The Myth of the Irrelevance of the Law of Neutrality' in MN Schmitt and J Peijic (eds), *International Law and Armed Conflict: Exploring the Faultlines: Essays in Honour of Yoram Dinstein* (Leiden, Nijhoff, 2007) 543–68; P Seger, 'The law of Neutrality' in Clapham and Gaeta (n 18) 248–70; N Verlinden, 'The Law of Neutrality' in J Wouters, P De Man and N Verlinden, *Armed Conflicts and the Law* (Antwerp, Intersentia, 2016) 75–106.

[23] Further, see eg W Heintschel von Heinegg, 'The Law of Armed Conflict at Sea' in Fleck (n 19) 463–48; N Ronzitti, *The Law of Naval Warfare: A Collection of Agreements and Documents with Commentaries* (Dordrecht, Nijhoff, 1988).

[24] Further, see eg R Rayfuse (ed), *War and the Environment: New Approaches to Protecting the Environment in relation to Armed Conflict* (Leiden, Nijhoff, 2014); J-M Henckaerts and D Constantin, 'Protection of the Natural Environment' in Clapham and Gaeta (n 18) 469–91; RJ Grunawalt et al (eds), *Protection of the Environment During Armed Conflict*, International Law Studies – Vol 69 (Newport, Naval War College, 1996).

[25] Further, see eg ES Wilmshurst (ed), *International Law and the Classification of Conflicts* (Oxford, OUP, 2012); ILA Committee on the Use of Force, 'Final Report on the Meaning of Armed Conflict in International Law', 2010, ila-hq.org/index.php/committees; ME O'Connell (ed), *What is War? An Investigation in the Wake of 9/11* (Leiden, Nijhoff, 2012); M Milanovic and V Hadzi-Vidanovic, 'A Taxonomy of Armed Conflict' in ND White and C Henderson (eds), *Research Handbook on International Conflict and Security Law* (Cheltenham, Edward Elgar, 2013) 256–13; Y Dinstein, *Non-International Armed Conflicts in International Law* (Cambridge, CUP, 2014) 20–57; S Vité, 'Typology of Armed Conflicts in International Humanitarian Law: Legal Concept and Actual Situations' (2009) 91 *IRRC* 69.

[26] The term 'Common Article' refers to those provisions that are common to each of the four GCs.

[27] Consider also Art 1(3) AP I and Art 1(1) AP II.

An armed conflict may be classified as an international armed conflict (IAC) or a non-international armed conflict (NIAC). The distinction between the two categories is of considerable importance, as the rights and obligations applicable in the scenarios are not identical. For instance, the degree of protection granted to persons *hors de combat* is higher in an IAC (see below, Section IV). This discrepancy is due to the fact that States originally regarded NIACs as a purely internal matter subject to national law only, and with which the international community should not interfere save in the exceptional (and now historical) case of a 'recognition of belligerency'.[28] It was only gradually that States came to accept that LOAC can, and should, also regulate the conduct of parties embroiled in a NIAC. Except for Common Article 3, which spells out the minimum fundamental guarantees applicable in every NIAC (such as the prohibition of torture), the manifold provisions of the four Geneva Conventions apply exclusively to IACs. It was not until the adoption of the 1977 Second Additional Protocol that States first introduced a treaty devoted to the regulation of NIACs.[29] In the meantime, the gap in protection between IACs and NIACs has been reduced considerably, by developments in customary international law and by the advance of international criminal law.[30] For instance, numerous grave breaches are now regarded as international crimes *both* in IACs and in NIACs regardless of the classification of the conflict.[31] The gap in protection has also been addressed, more indirectly, by the injection of human rights law into the realm of armed conflict (see below, Section II(E)). In spite of these developments, important differences remain. Crucially, in a NIAC, rebels fighting the de jure government will enjoy no combatant privilege and can, upon capture, be prosecuted under domestic law (eg for murder) even if they comply with the prescripts of LOAC.[32]

B. International and Non-International Armed Conflicts

i. Distinction between IAC and NIAC

An authoritative definition of the twin concepts of IAC and NIAC, repeatedly confirmed in the case law of international courts and tribunals,[33] can be found in the *Tadić* judgment of the ICTY. In this case, the ICTY held that an armed conflict exists 'whenever there is a resort to armed force between States or protracted armed violence between governmental authorities and organised groups or between such groups within a State'.[34]

[28] See further S Sivakumaran, *The Law of Non-International Armed Conflict* (Oxford, OUP, 2012) 9–20. See also Chapter V, Section IV(B) on the recognition of governments.

[29] Note moreover that AP II contains only 28 articles, whereas AP I (devoted to IACs) counts over a hundred articles. With 168 State Parties (as of April 2018), AP II is also less widely ratified than AP I (174), and certainly less widely ratified than the GCs (196).

[30] On customary international law, see Chapter 3, Section II; on international criminal law, see Chapter 17.

[31] Note, however, that under Art 8(2) of the ICC Statute certain acts qualify as war crimes when committed in an IAC, but not when committed in a NIAC.

[32] For a critique, see T Ruys, 'The Syrian Civil War and the Achilles' Heel of the Law of Non-International Armed Conflict' (2013) 50 *Stanford Journal of International Law* 247. However, the de jure government may unilaterally agree to borrow from the law on IACs (eg by treating captured rebels in a similar fashion as prisoners of war (POWs), on which see Section IV(A)). Alternatively, the warring parties may conclude special agreements to apply (part of) the law relating to IACs to a NIAC scenario (Common Article 3 GCs in fact encourages the conclusion of such agreements). See Sivakumaran (n 28) 113 ff.

[33] eg ICC, Trial Chamber I, *Prosecutor v Thomas Lubanga Dyilo*, 14 March 2012, Case No ICC-01/04-01/06, para 533.

[34] ICTY, Appeals Chamber, *Prosecutor v Duško Tadić*, Decision of the Defence Motion for Interlocutory Appeal on Jurisdiction, 2 October 1995, Case No IT-94-1-A, para 70.

It follows that, for an IAC to arise, any 'resort to armed force' between States is sufficient. Opinions are divided on whether this implies that even a single and short-lived confrontation can trigger the application of LOAC, or whether some minimum level of violence is required.[35] What is clear is that IACs require a resort to force between *States*.[36] Recognition of the other State or government is irrelevant. Violence by private individuals is not covered. Furthermore, as indicated in Common Article 2(2) GCs, LOAC applies to all cases of partial or total occupation of the territory of one State by another, 'even if the said occupation meets with no armed resistance'.

It is uncontested that for NIACs, a higher threshold applies. Thus, even if this is not made explicit in Common Article 3 GCs, the above quote from the *Tadić* judgment illustrates that there must be 'protracted armed violence' between governmental authorities and organised armed groups or between such groups within a State. Situations of internal disturbances and tensions, such as riots, isolated and sporadic acts of violence, are not regarded as NIACs.[37] More specifically, the case law of the ICTY makes clear that there must be a minimum degree of 'intensity' for a NIAC to exist, as well as a minimum degree of 'organisation' on the part of the non-State armed group(s) involved.[38] The former criterion relates to the number of combatants involved, the frequency of attacks, the type of weapons deployed, etc. The latter criterion chiefly implies that the non-State groups should be capable of sustaining military operations over a longer span of time, and that they possess a hierarchical structure making it possible to implement LOAC and impose disciplinary measures. Furthermore, the scope of application of the Second Additional Protocol is more limited than that of Common Article 3 GCs. First, AP II applies exclusively to armed conflicts between a de jure government on the one hand, and one or more non-State armed groups on the other, whereas Common Article 3 GCs also applies to fighting between different non-State groups. Second, the conflict must take place on the territory of the State involved in the armed conflict.[39] Third, the insurgents must have some degree of control over territory.[40]

The CJEU has made clear that the concept of 'internal armed conflict' as used in the Qualification Directive,[41] which forms one of the pillars of the Common European Asylum System,[42] has a different meaning to the concept of NIAC under LOAC. This is so because of the different aim pursued by the Directive, which seeks to establish whether individuals

[35] See Milanovic and Hadzi-Vidanovic (n 25) 274 (with references). The need for a minimum level of violence is rejected by the ICRC in its 2016 Commentary to GC I (n 16) at paras 236–44.

[36] But see below, Section II(B)(ii) on the internationalisation of NIACs.

[37] This is explicitly affirmed in Art 1(2) AP II.

[38] See in particular ICTY, Trial Chamber, *Prosecutor v Boškoski and Tarčulovski*, 10 July 2008, Case No IT-04-82-T, paras 175 ff; ICTY, Trial Chamber, *Prosecutor v Haradinaj*, 29 November 2012, Case No IT-04-84bid-T, para 392 ff. But see, for a rather flexible application of the NIAC concept: Inter-American Commission on Human Rights (IACHR), *Juan Carlos Abella v Argentina* (*Tablada* case), 18 November 1997, Case No 11.137, Report No 55/97, OEA/Ser.L/V/II.98, Doc 6 rev (13 April 1998) paras 146–56. According to the ICRC, 'duration', while relevant, should not be construed as an independent criterion: ICRC (2016) (n 16) paras 438–44.

[39] Art 1(1) AP II provides that the Protocol applies to armed conflicts 'which take place in the territory of a High Contracting Party between its armed forces and dissident armed forces or other organized armed groups [...]'.

[40] ibid: '[...] which, under responsible command, exercise such control over a part of its territory as to enable them to carry out sustained and concerted military operations and to implement this Protocol'.

[41] Directive 2011/95/EU of the European Parliament and of the Council of 13 December 2011 on standards for the qualification of third-country nationals or stateless persons as beneficiaries of international protection, for a uniform status for refugees or for persons eligible for subsidiary protection, and for the content of the protection granted (recast) [2011] OJ L337/9.

[42] On which see Chapter 16, Section V.

entering the EU qualify for 'subsidiary protection'. Thus, for purposes of the Directive, an 'internal armed conflict' was stated to exist 'if a State's armed forces confront one or more armed groups or if two or more armed groups confront each other'.[43] The Court adds that

> [i]t is not necessary for that conflict to be categorised as 'armed conflict not of an international character' under international humanitarian law; nor is it necessary to carry out, in addition to an appraisal of the level of violence present in the territory concerned, a separate assessment of the intensity of the armed confrontations, the level of organisation of the armed forces involved or the duration of the conflict.[44]

ii. Special Cases

Having summarily sketched the main requirements for the existence of an IAC or a NIAC, it is important to emphasise that many borderline and special cases exist. This makes the identification of an armed conflict and its classification a complex, and often sensitive, exercise. First, a NIAC may gradually turn into an IAC, as the State in which an internal conflict takes place breaks up into newly-independent entities (as happened with the disintegration of the SFRY). Second, a NIAC may be 'internationalised' when a third State engages in 'proxy warfare', eg by providing arms, training and intelligence support to a non-State armed group, and that State exercises 'overall control' over the latter group.[45] Alternatively, an IAC may exist alongside a NIAC,[46] resulting in a fragmentary application of LOAC.[47]

When a third State intervenes in support of a de jure government that is involved in a NIAC with a non-State armed group on its soil, such intervention is generally deemed not to internationalise the conflict. The relations between the third State and the non-State group will be regarded as a NIAC.[48] What if a State intervenes on the territory of another State to undertake military action against a non-State actor, yet without the consent of the territorial State? This scenario took place in 2006, when Israel launched a military operation against Hezbollah in Lebanon. According to the ICRC, absent consent of the territorial State, the situation will automatically qualify as an IAC, possibly existing in parallel to a NIAC between the intervening State and the non-State armed group.[49] Other approaches could be envisaged, however, depending on a number of factors, such as the link between the non-State group and the territorial government and the targets of the operation.[50]

[43] Judgment of 30 January 2014, *Aboubacar Diakité v Commissaire général aux réfugiés et aux apatrides*, C-285/12, ECLI:EU:2014:39, para 19 ff.

[44] ibid.

[45] According to the ICTY, such 'overall control' exists when a State 'has a role in organizing, coordinating or planning the military actions of the military group, in addition to financing, training and equipping or providing operational support to that group'. ICTY, Appeals Chamber, *Prosecutor v Duško Tadić*, 15 July 1999, Case No IT-94-1-A, paras 137 and 145. For the ICRC's approach (which is not without controversy), see ICRC (2016) (n 16) paras 265–73.

[46] This fragmentary application is illustrated by the *Nicaragua* case, where the ICJ held that the relations between the contras and the government of Nicaragua were governed by the law applicable to NIAC, whereas the relation between Nicaragua and the US fell under the legal rules relating to IAC (*Military and Paramilitary Activities in and against Nicaragua* (Nicaragua v United States of America) [1986] ICJ Rep 14, para 219).

[47] The implication is eg that a captured person's status may be different depending on the identity of his/her capturer.

[48] See, in this sense, ICRC (2016) (n 16) para 259; Milanovic and Hadzi-Vidanovic (n 25) 295. On the legality of such intervention under the *jus ad bellum*, see Chapter 14, Section II(B).

[49] ICRC (2016) (n 16) paras 261–63 and 477.

[50] See Milanovic and Hadzi-Vidanovic (n 25) 295–97.

Pursuant to Article 1(4) AP I, 'armed conflicts in which peoples are fighting against colonial domination and alien occupation and against racist regimes in the exercise of their right of self-determination' are equated to IACs.[51] The rationale is that peoples fighting for national liberation should be treated as a State for LOAC purposes, even if they have yet to achieve external self-determination.[52] However, at the time of its adoption, the provision proved highly controversial; for instance, it was one of the main reasons why Israel refused to ratify AP I. Accordingly, it cannot be said to have achieved customary status.

As acknowledged in the 1999 UN Secretary General's 'Bulletin on the Observance by United Nations Forces of International Humanitarian Law', UN peacekeepers are not as such excluded from the scope of application of LOAC.[53] If UN peacekeepers are actively engaged in hostilities (which involves more than isolated cases of limited use of force in self-defence or for mission accomplishment),[54] they may themselves become a party to the conflict (whether an IAC or a NIAC, depending on the identity of the adverse party) and thus lose their protection from attack.[55] The same applies in respect of operations under NATO auspices[56] and military operations conducted under the EU's Common Security and Defence Policy.[57]

C. Geographical Application

The application of LOAC is geographically limited in scope. Thus, as indicated in the *Tadić* case, in the event of an IAC, LOAC applies in 'the whole territory of the warring parties'.[58] The application of LOAC in NIACs is similarly geographically limited to the 'territory under the control of a party, whether or not actual combat takes place there'.[59] Clearly, the geographical scope of a conflict can widen when it spills over into the territory of another State and gives rise to intense and protracted hostilities in the new location. However, the idea of a 'global' NIAC against a transnational terrorist group such as Al-Qaeda[60] must

[51] According to Art 96(3) AP I, this presupposes that the authority representing the people concerned makes a declaration undertaking to apply the GCs and AP I. This possibility has been used only once, namely by the Polisario Front (in 2015).

[52] On which see Chapter 5, Section III(B) and (D).

[53] Secretary General's Bulletin, 'Observance by United Nations Forces of International Humanitarian Law', 6 August 1999, UN Doc ST/SGB/1999/13. The application of the normal rules of LOAC to UN peacekeepers and troops engaged in UN-authorised military operations may, however, be somewhat modified by binding Chapter VII resolutions of the UNSC pursuant to Arts 25 and 103 UN Charter.

[54] F Naert, *International Law Aspects of the EU's Security and Defence Policy* (Antwerp, Intersentia, 2010) 537.

[55] By contrast, attacks against personnel of a peacekeeping mission that is not actively engaged in hostilities amounts to a war crime under Arts 8(2)(b)(iii) and 8(2)(e)(iii) of the Rome Statute.

[56] See further M Zwanenburg, *Accountability under International Humanitarian Law for United Nations and North Atlantic Treaty Organization Peace Support Operations* (Leiden, EM Meijers Instituut, 2004).

[57] See further Naert (n 54) 463–40.

[58] ICTY, Appeals Chamber, *Tadić* (Jurisdiction) (n 34) para 70. Beyond this, the 'area of war' also extends to the high seas and exclusive economic zones: J Kleffner, 'Scope of Application of International Humanitarian Law' in Fleck (n 19) 43–78 and 56–57. Furthermore, certain specific areas can exceptionally be excluded from the conflict zone or be placed under special protection. See eg Art 23 GC I (on the mutual recognition of hospital zones and localities), Art 6 AP I (on demilitarised zones) and Art 59 AP I (on non-defended localities).

[59] ICTY, Appeals Chamber, *Tadić* (Jurisdiction) (n 34) para 70. However, the applicability of humanitarian law in the whole of the territory of a State Party to the conflict does not mean that all acts within that territory necessarily fall under the LOAC regime. See further ICRC (2016) (n 16) para 460 ff. Consider also ICTR, Trial Chamber, *Prosecutor v Rutaganda*, 6 December 1999, Case No ICTR-96-3-T, para 102, according to which LOAC 'extends throughout the territory of the State where the hostilities are occurring'.

[60] See eg US Department of Justice, White Paper: 'Lawfulness of a Lethal Operation Directed against a US Citizen Who Is a Senior Operational Leader of Al-Qa'ida or an Associated Force', msnbcmedia.msn.com/i/msnbc/sections/news/020413_DOJ_White_Paper.pdf, 4.

be dismissed.[61] As Dinstein explains, military operations directed against a transnational terrorist group can 'blend into both an IAC and a NIAC waged in [the] country [concerned]', but they do not create a separate global 'war' on terrorism.[62] More generally, the concept of a third category of so-called 'transnational' armed conflicts, in addition to the traditional binary distinction between IACs and NIACs, is not supported by general practice, and does not seem desirable from a policy perspective.[63]

D. Temporal Application

Just as the beginning of the applicability of LOAC is a matter of fact, so too is the end of that applicability.[64] In IACs, LOAC ceases to apply on the generalised close of military operations.[65] This may take the form of a formal peace agreement, or it may simply be inferred from the termination of hostilities. Special rules apply to the conclusion of ceasefires, which are generally of a temporary nature, and armistices, which are intended to pave the way for a permanent termination of hostilities.[66] However, even upon a general close of military operations persons deprived of their liberty or whose liberty has been restricted for reasons related to an armed conflict (eg prisoners of war) will continue to benefit from the protections of LOAC until the end of such deprivation or restriction of liberty (eg repatriation in case of POWs).[67] Also NIACs continue to be governed by LOAC until 'a peaceful settlement is reached'.[68] The law of belligerent occupation continues to apply until the occupation is terminated.[69]

E. The Law of Armed Conflict and Human Rights Law

Although international human rights law (IHRL) was primarily designed to apply in times of peace, the application of LOAC to an armed conflict does not as such exclude the application of IHRL.[70] Quite the contrary, IHRL in principle continues to apply – at least to *States*[71] – in situations of armed conflict. Various human rights instruments admittedly provide that States may derogate from certain human rights obligations in times of war or

[61] See, in this sense, eg Milanovic and Hadzi-Vidanovic (n 25) 307; Dinstein (n 25) 27.
[62] Dinstein (n 25) 27.
[63] ibid, 24; Milanovic and Hadzi-Vidanovic (n 25) 304–12. The ICRC has also observed that State practice in support of a global or transnational NIAC 'remains isolated'; ICRC (2016) (n 16) para 482.
[64] See further Kleffner (n 58) 60–70.
[65] See Arts 6(2) GC IV and 3(b) AP I.
[66] See eg Arts 36–41 Hague Regulations, 15 GC I, 18 GC II and 17 GC IV. An indefinite ceasefire or prolonged cessation of hostilities would appear to reactivate the rules of the *jus ad bellum*, implying that hostilities can only lawfully be resumed in accordance with the right of self-defence (on which see Chapter 14, Section III); Kleffner (n 58) 66–67.
[67] Kleffner (n 58) 60. See eg Art 3(b) AP I.
[68] ICTY, Appeals Chamber, *Tadić* (Jurisdiction) (n 34) para 70.
[69] Art 3(b) AP I. But see Art 6(3) GC IV, according to which part of the law of belligerent occupation ceases to apply 'one year after the general close of military operations', as applied by the ICJ in *Legal Consequences of the Construction of a Wall in Occupied Palestinian Territory* (Advisory Opinion) [2004] ICJ Rep 136, para 125.
[70] See further G Oberleitner, *Human Rights in Armed Conflict: Law, Practice, Policy* (Cambridge, CUP, 2015); D Jinks, 'International Human Rights Law in Time of Armed Conflict' in Clapham and Gaeta (n 18) 656–74.
[71] The extent to which non-State armed groups may be subject to obligations under IHRL is contested. See Chapter 8, Section IV and further eg D Murray, *Human Rights Obligations of Non-State Armed Groups* (Oxford, Hart, 2016); K Fortin, *The Accountability of Armed Groups under Human Rights Law* (Oxford, OUP, 2017).

other 'public emergency which threatens the life of the nation', when this is 'strictly required by the exigencies of the situation'.[72] However, absent an officially proclaimed derogation, the obligations concerned will continue to apply.[73] In addition, certain fundamental rights, such as the prohibition of torture, are in any case 'non-derogable'.[74]

As the ICJ held in its *Wall* Advisory Opinion, three scenarios are possible in a situation of armed conflict: 'some rights may be exclusively matters of international humanitarian law; others may be exclusively matters of international human rights law; yet others may be matters of both these branches of international law'.[75] In the last scenario (which arises in particular in situations of deprivation of liberty or deliberate use of lethal force), the ICJ has made it clear that interpretive problems should be solved by reference to the *lex specialis* principle, according to which precedence should be given to the more detailed and specific legal norm.[76] This principle should not be understood as automatically resulting in the total displacement of IHRL in favour of LOAC.[77] Rather, a rule-specific approach is needed, whereby the rule of LOAC will not necessarily be the more 'specific' rule, and the interpretation of a norm of IHRL may be informed by a related norm of LOAC, and vice versa.[78]

The continued relevance of IHRL is not limited to the scenario where a State is engaged in a NIAC within its own territory. It has become increasingly accepted that the human rights obligations enshrined in the various treaties – including the ECHR – also apply extraterritorially, in particular in respect of individuals that come within the jurisdiction of the State with whose armed forces they come into contact.[79] This potentially brings a broad array of conduct of military personnel abroad (eg shooting incidents at a checkpoint manned by troops participating in a multinational operation)[80] under the purview of the ECtHR. The increased judicial scrutiny of military operations abroad on the basis of IHRL indirectly contributes to a better enforcement of LOAC. Conversely, this trend has also given rise to criticism by some who claim that the 'judicialisation of war' is harming military efforts abroad and/or provides Member States of the Council of Europe with a competitive disadvantage.[81] Either way, the trend is unlikely to reverse.[82]

[72] See eg Arts 4 ICCPR (on which see Chapter 16, Section II(A)(i)), 15 ECHR (on which see Chapter 16, Section IX(A)(i)) and 27(1) ACHR.

[73] But see *Hassan v UK* App no 29750/09 (ECtHR, 16 September 2014), as discussed in Chapter 2, Section VII(B)(iii).

[74] See again Chapter 16, Section II(A)(i) and Section IX(A)(i).

[75] *Wall* Opinion (n69) para 106.

[76] *Nuclear Weapons* (n 17) para 25.

[77] Consider eg *Hassan v UK* (n 73) paras 96–107; High Court of Justice (UK), *Serdar Mohammed v Ministry of Defence* [2014] EWHC 1369 (QB), paras 273–94. See also M Milanovic, 'The Lost Origins of Lex Specialis: Rethinking the Relationship between Human Rights and International Humanitarian Law' in JD Ohlin (ed), *Theoretical Boundaries of Armed Conflict and Human Rights* (Cambridge, CUP, 2016) 78–117; T Ruys and C De Koker, 'Foregoing Lex Specialis? Exclusivist v Symbiotic Approaches to the Concurrent Application of International Humanitarian Law and Human Rights Law' (2016) *Revue belge de droit international* 244.

[78] See eg *Varnava and others v Turkey* App nos 16064/90, 16065/90, 16066/90, 16068/90, 16069/90, 16070/90, 16071/90, 16072/90 and 16073/90 (ECtHR, 18 September 2009) para 185.

[79] See Chapter 9, Section IV on jurisdiction in international human rights treaties. See further M Milanovic, *Extraterritorial Application of Human Rights Treaties: Law, Principles and Policy* (Oxford, OUP, 2011). Note that the precise definition of the scope of application of the different human rights treaties is not always identical, adding to the complexity of the issue; Kleffner (n 58) 75.

[80] For this scenario, see *Jaloud v the Netherlands* App no 47708/08 (ECHR, 20 November 2014) paras 139–53.

[81] For a (rather unconvincing) critique, see eg R Elkins, J Morgan and T Tugendhat, 'Clearing the Fog of Law: Saving our Armed Forces from Defeat by Judicial Diktat', *Policy Exchange*, 2015, policyexchange.org.uk/wp-content/uploads/2016/09/clearing-the-fog-of-law.pdf. See also below (n 190).

[82] In a leaked memo on the extraterritorial application of the Convention against Torture, US Legal Adviser Harold Koh noted that '[t]he international trend toward recognizing some form of extraterritorial application of

If the application of LOAC does not as such displace the application of IHRL, more generally, the existence of an armed conflict does not *ipso facto* terminate or suspend the operation of other rules of treaty or customary international law. In its 'Draft Articles on the Effects of Armed Conflicts on Treaties' of 2011, the ILC identifies a list of treaties 'the subject-matter of which involves an implication that they continue in operation, in whole or in part, during armed conflict', including not only human rights treaties, but also treaties on international criminal justice or treaties relating to the protection of the environment.[83] In a similar vein, in a judgment of 2014 relating to an EU asset freeze targeting the Liberation Tigers of Tamil Eelam (LTTE) in Sri Lanka, the General Court insisted that 'the existence of an armed conflict [...] does not exclude the application of provisions of EU law concerning terrorism to any acts of terrorism committed in that context'.[84] Accordingly, the fact that the LTTE was an organised group engaged in a NIAC did not bar the EU from imposing restrictive measures on the group pursuant to Regulation No 2580/2001.[85]

Unlike IHRL, LOAC does not leave any room for derogation, based, for instance, on considerations of military necessity. It follows that one can only deviate from a rule of LOAC inasmuch as the rule itself foresees this possibility.[86]

III. The Principle of Distinction and Targeting Rules

A. The Distinction between Civilians/Civilian Objects and Combatants/Military Objectives

The distinction between civilians and combatants is a cardinal aspect of LOAC. It determines whether or not a person may lawfully be the target of an attack in armed conflict.[87] It also carries repercussions for the extent to which a person *hors de combat* is entitled to the protection offered by the various protective regimes installed by LOAC (see below, Section IV).

In an IAC, the notion of 'combatants' refers to the members of the (organised) regular or irregular armed forces belonging to a party to the conflict (but excluding medical and religious personnel). It also applies to participants in a so-called *levée en masse*; that is,

human rights treaty obligations [...] has left the United States increasingly isolated in its legal positions in relation to the allies with which it collaborates'. According to Koh, it was 'not legally available to policymakers to claim [...] a categorical bar' against the Convention against Torture's extraterritorial scope or its application in armed conflict. See US Department of State, Office of the Legal Adviser, 'Memorandum Opinion on the Geographic Scope of the Convention against Torture and its Application in Situations of Armed Conflict', 21 January 2013, nytimes.com/interactive/2014/03/07/world/state-department-koh.html, 3 and 6.

[83] ILC, 'Draft Articles on the Effects of Armed Conflicts on Treaties' (2011) *YILC*, Vol II, Part Two, Art 7 and Annex. See also Chapter 2, Section XI(I) on outbreak of armed conflict as a ground for the termination of treaties.

[84] Judgment of 16 October 2014, *Liberation Tigers of Tamil Eelam (LTTE) v Council of the European Union*, T-208/11 and T-508/11, ECLI:EU:T:2014:885, para 56 ff.

[85] Council Regulation (EC) No 2580/2001 of 27 December 2001 on specific restrictive measures directed against certain persons and entities with a view to combating terrorism, OJ L344/70.

[86] See eg Art 23(g) Hague Regulations, which prohibits the destruction or seizure of enemy property 'unless such destruction or seizure be imperatively demanded by the necessities of war'.

[87] On the law of targeting, see further WH Boothby, *The Law of Targeting* (Oxford, OUP, 2012); IS Henderson, *The Contemporary Law of Targeting* (Leiden, Nijhoff, 2009); A Jachec-Neale, *The Concept of Military Objectives in International Law and Practice* (London, Routledge, 2015); Y Dinstein, *The Conduct of Hostilities under the Law of International Armed Conflict*, 2nd edn (Cambridge, CUP, 2010) at 89–196; D Turns, 'Targets' in White and Henderson (n 25) 342–74.

a spontaneous uprising by the population against an invading army.[88] In a NIAC, combatants include the armed forces of the State concerned as well as the members of the organised armed forces of a non-State Party to the conflict that have a 'continuous combat function'.[89] The notion of 'civilians' is defined in the negative. In other words, civilians are all those who do not qualify as combatants.[90] In case of doubt, a person must be regarded as a civilian.[91]

Combatants, as defined above, may always be lawfully attacked, irrespective of time and place and regardless of their specific tasks within the armed forces; that is, even when they are not taking direct part in hostilities at the time of attack or if they have no fighting role.[92] LOAC does not prohibit the singling out of a combatant in an attack, unless the attack is perfidious[93] or otherwise contrary to the rules of LOAC. The exposure of combatants to (lawful) attack continues until they withdraw from hostilities by retiring or demobilising, or when they become *hors de combat*, either on a voluntary basis (eg by surrendering) or by force.[94] Unlike combatants, civilians may not be directly targeted,[95] and to do so amounts to a war crime. However, the immunity of civilians from attack is not absolute, and will be lost if and for such time as they take a 'direct part in hostilities' (see below, Section III(B)(iii)).[96]

For targeting purposes, a distinction must be made between civilian objects and military objectives, analogous to the distinction between combatants and civilians. Only military objectives may be the lawful target of an attack.[97] In accordance with Article 52 AP I, military objectives are limited

> to those objects which by their nature, location, purpose or use make an effective contribution to military action and whose total or partial destruction, capture or neutralisation, in the circumstances ruling at the time, offers a definite military advantage.

Again, in cases of doubt, objects shall be treated as civilian.[98] It follows that, rather than setting forth a limitative list of possible military objectives, LOAC adopts a generic approach based on two cumulative criteria. Something is a military objective if: (i) it makes an effective contribution to military action; and (ii) targeting it offers a definite military advantage. Whether an object makes an effective contribution to military action must be determined by reference to one or more out of four factors: the object's nature, location,

[88] ICRC, 'Interpretive Guidance on the Notion of Direct Participation in Hostilities under International Humanitarian Law', adopted by the ICRC Assembly on 26 February 2009, (2008) 90 *IRRC* 991, at 998 ff; T Ruys and C De Cock, 'Protected Persons in International Armed Conflicts' in White and Henderson (n 25) 378–79.

[89] ICRC, Interpretive Guidance (n88) 1002 ff.

[90] eg Art 50(1) AP I.

[91] ibid.

[92] When civilians are in the line of fire, the proportionality principle and the duty to take reasonable precautions must nonetheless be observed. See further below, Section III(B)(ii).

[93] Art 37 AP I; Art 23(b) Hague Regulations. The essence of perfidy is the intentional misuse of a protected or particular status to invite or encourage an adversary to believe that the person acting perfidiously is immune from attack (E Crawford and A Pert, *International Humanitarian Law* (Cambridge, CUP, 2015) 212). Examples include the feigning of surrender or the feigning of civilian status. Perfidy must be distinguished from (lawful) ruses of war. On the prohibition of perfidy, see eg M Madden, 'Of Wolves and Sheep: A Purposive Analysis of Perfidy Prohibitions in International Humanitarian Law' (2012) 17 *Journal of Conflict and Security Law* 439.

[94] T Ruys and De Cock (n88) 382. Note that whether there are situations where warring parties may be under an obligation to 'capture' rather than 'kill' an opponent is subject to debate. For a position in favour of such an obligation, see eg R Goodman, 'The Power to Kill or Capture Enemy Combatants' (2013) 24 *EJIL* 819.

[95] See, however, below (Section III(B)(ii)) on the legality under LOAC of attacks causing proportionate 'collateral' damage among civilians.

[96] See further E Crawford, *Identifying the Enemy: Civilian Participation in Armed Conflict* (Oxford, OUP, 2015).

[97] Art 48 AP I.

[98] Article 52(3) AP I.

purpose and/or use.[99] For some objects, such as military depots or warships, their military 'nature' is beyond question.[100] Yet, the reference to 'use' and 'purpose' (or intended future use) makes clear that even objects such as schools, churches or hospitals may exceptionally turn into a lawful military target (eg when a church tower is used as a firing position for snipers).

B. The Immunity from Attack of Civilians and Civilian Objects

i. Indiscriminate Attacks

As mentioned above, civilians and civilian objects enjoy immunity from attack and can never be *deliberately* targeted.[101] In addition, LOAC outlaws so-called 'indiscriminate' attacks.[102] Indiscriminate attacks take place when an attacker is not actually trying to harm civilians, but acts in a reckless manner, without making any effort to keep civilians out of harm's way. For instance, an attacker may use a weapon that cannot be targeted against a specific military objective (eg an imprecise missile) or simply fire artillery 'blindly' into territory controlled by the enemy. Thus, in 2007, the ICTY found the firing of non-guided rockets with cluster munitions at the city of Zagreb from a distance of around 50 kilometres to constitute an indiscriminate attack.[103]

ii. The Principle of Proportionality

Even if an attack is properly directed against a military target and is not indiscriminate in nature, the attacker must ascertain that it will not cause loss of civilian life or damage to civilian objects that would be '*excessive* in relation to the concrete and direct military advantage anticipated'.[104] In other words, the attacker must conduct a proportionality analysis, weighing the envisaged military advantage against the expected 'collateral damage'. Whether collateral damage is 'excessive' must be determined on a case-by-case basis from the perspective of the person instructing the attack and the information available to him/her at that time, and not after the fact on the basis of the consequences of the attack. Proportionality cannot be decided by reference to some quantitative formula, but inherently entails a value judgment. In reality, exposure to incidental injury is strongly influenced by the 'proximity' of civilians to military objectives. Thus, civilian contractors accompanying regular armed forces are more likely to get caught in the crossfire.[105] Lastly, the foregoing should be read in conjunction with the obligation to 'take all feasible precautions' with a view to avoiding and minimising collateral damage.[106] Precautionary measures may, for

[99] For an example, see ICTY, 'Final Report to the Prosecutor by the Committee Established to Review the NATO Bombing Campaign against the Federal Republic of Yugoslavia', June 2000, icty.org/x/file/Press/nato061300.pdf, paras 71–79. Controversially, the US extends the notion of military target to include a variety of economic targets that may indirectly support the enemy's war-fighting capability. See further Dinstein (n87) 95–96.
[100] For a non-exhaustive enumeration of military objectives 'by nature', see ibid, 96–97.
[101] Arts 51(2) and 52(1) AP I; Art 13(2) AP II. See also the criminalisation of such behaviour in both IACs and NIACs under Arts 8(2)(b)(i)–(ii) and 8(2)(e)(i)–(ii) ICC Statute.
[102] Art 51(4) AP I.
[103] ICTY, Trial Chamber, *Prosecutor v Milan Martić*, 12 June 2007, Case No IT-95-11-T, para 463.
[104] Art 51(5)(b) AP I (emphasis added).
[105] Ruys and De Cock (n88) 382.
[106] Art 57(2)(a)(ii) AP I.

example, relate to the choice of ammunition or the timing[107] of an attack. They also involve the obligation to give an advance warning of an impending attack (for instance, by using flyers or radio messages) if circumstances so permit.[108]

iii. Direct Participation in Hostilities

As alluded to above, in accordance with Article 51(3) AP I, civilians lose their immunity from attack if 'and for such time as they take a direct part in hostilities'. This rule also applies to personnel of private military or security companies not integrated into the armed forces.[109] Determining the nature of the acts that amount to, and establishing the duration of, 'direct participation in hostilities' (DPH) has proven to be one of the most controversial questions of LOAC, particularly since 9/11. Following a series of expert meetings, the ICRC in 2009 published a detailed 'Interpretive Guidance on the Notion of Direct Participation in Hostilities'.[110] The Guidance distinguishes between members of organised groups belonging to a non-State Party to an armed conflict, who lose protection against direct attack for the duration of their 'continuous combat function', on the one hand, and civilians taking direct part in hostilities, who only lose protection from attack 'for the duration of each specific act amounting to direct participation in hostilities', on the other.[111] Although the ICRC's approach is not without controversy,[112] the Guidance authoritatively interprets the concept of DPH. Acts are deemed to give rise to DPH when they meet the following cumulative requirements:[113]

(1) the act must be likely to adversely affect the military operations or military capacity of a party to an armed conflict or, alternatively, to inflict death, injury, or destruction on persons or objects protected against direct attack (threshold of harm);
(2) there must be a direct causal link between the act and the harm likely to result either from that act, or from a coordinated military operation of which that act constitutes an integral part (direct causation);
(3) the act must be specifically designed to directly cause the required threshold of harm in support of a party to the conflict and to the detriment of another (belligerent nexus).[114]

Involuntary 'human shields', who are compelled to accompany combatants in the course of military operations, cannot be regarded as directly participating in hostilities, but qualify

[107] For instance, an attacker may choose to attack a munitions factory at night, rather than during the day, if it knows or can assume that there will be fewer civilian workers present.
[108] Art 57(2)(c) AP I.
[109] On the position and legal obligations of private military and security companies during armed conflict, see eg 'The Montreux Document: On Pertinent Legal Obligations and Good Practice for States related to Operations of Private Military and Security Companies during Armed Conflict', August 2009, icrc.org/eng/assets/files/other/icrc_002_0996.pdf; C Seiberth, *Private Military and Security Companies in International Law: A Challenge for Non-binding Norms* (Antwerp, Intersentia, 2014); L Cameron and V Chetail, *Privatizing War: Private Military and Security Companies under Public International Law* (Cambridge, CUP, 2013).
[110] ICRC Interpretive Guidance (n88).
[111] ibid, Recommendation VII.
[112] See in particular the contributions of B Boothby, W Hays Parks, MN Schmitt and K Watkin, as well as the defence of N Melzer in (2010) 42 *New York University Journal of International Law and Politics*. See also D Akande, 'Clearing the Fog of War?: The ICRC's Interpretive Guidance on Direct Participation in Hostilities' (2010) 59 *ICLQ* 180; WJ Fenrick, 'ICRC Guidance on Direct Participation in Hostilities' (2009) 12 *Yearbook of International Humanitarian Law* 287; APV Rogers, 'Direct Participation in Hostilities: Some Personal Reflections' (2009) 48 *Military Law and the Law of War Review* 143.
[113] ICRC Interpretive Guidance (n88) Recommendation V.
[114] This includes the preparatory stage of the attack, as well as the return from the location where the attack is executed; ibid, Recommendations VI and VII.

as ordinary civilians for the purpose of the principle of distinction and the proportionality assessment.[115] In any case, the use of involuntary human shields is in clear breach of LOAC[116] and amounts to a war crime under Article 8(2)(b)(xxiii) of the ICC Statute. Some have argued that civilians *voluntarily* attempting to shield a military objective by their presence against an attack (voluntary human shields) ought to be excluded in the estimation of incidental injury when assessing proportionality. To the extent that they do not physically inhibit the execution of an attack, this position is rejected by the ICRC.[117] Overall, whether voluntary human shields may or may not be considered to engage in DPH remains disputed.[118]

C. Specific Targeting Rules

In addition to the general targeting principles discussed above, there exists a wide array of rules providing for specific protection from attack for certain categories of persons or certain categories of goods. Persons entitled to special protection include inter alia combatants *hors de combat* (eg those expressing an intention to surrender),[119] medical and religious personnel, civil defence personnel, and relief personnel.[120] However, this special protection from attack is conditional, as those concerned lose it if they engage respectively in 'hostile acts' or 'acts harmful to the enemy outside their humanitarian duties'.[121]

Certain objects also enjoy special protection. In particular, LOAC provides for special protection for medical units (eg hospitals) and medical transports (eg ambulances). To facilitate their identification, it prescribes the use of special 'distinctive emblems' to mark medical units, notably the Red Cross, the Red Crescent and the Red Crystal.[122] Intentional attacks against medical units, regardless of whether they use a distinctive emblem, constitute a war crime under the ICC Statute.[123] Like medical personnel, medical units lose their protection from attack 'if they are used to commit, outside their humanitarian duties, acts harmful to the enemy'.[124] Even so, no attack can take place until 'due warning' is given and that warning has remained unheeded.[125]

In light of their irreplaceable nature and their symbolic importance for mankind, LOAC has long sought to protect cultural property from damage and destruction.[126] The 1899

[115] This follows from Art 51(n 8) AP I. But see Dinstein (n87) 155.
[116] Art 51(n 7) AP I.
[117] See Dinstein (n87) 153–54.
[118] During the ICRC meetings, the experts were largely unable to agree on the circumstances in which acting as a voluntary human shield would, or would not, amount to DPH. ICRC Interpretive Guidance (n88) 57, note 141. See also HPCR (n 14) commentary to Rule 45, para 7.
[119] See eg Arts 12 GC I, 12 GC II, 41(1)–(2) AP I and 23(c) Hague Regulations. According to Art 23(d) Hague Regulations and Art 40 AP I it is forbidden to issue a declaration that no quarter shall be given.
[120] For a detailed overview, see Dinstein (n87) 156–70.
[121] See respectively Art 41(2)(c) AP I for combatants *hors de combat* and Arts 19/21 GC I and 19 GC IV on hospitals/medical units, by analogy applicable to medical/religious personnel.
[122] See Art 42 GC I, 43 GC II, 18 and 21–22 GC IV, 18 AP I and 12 AP II.
[123] See Art 8(2)(b)(ix), (xxiv) and 8(2)(e)(iv) of the Rome Statute.
[124] Art 21 GC I and Art 13(1) AP I.
[125] The aim of this warning is to enable the adverse party to end the abuse or to evacuate the wounded and sick; Dinstein (n87) 191.
[126] On the protection of cultural property in armed conflict, see eg R O'Keefe, *The Protection of Cultural Property in Armed Conflict* (Cambridge, CUP, 2006); R O'Keefe, 'Protection of Cultural Property' in Clapham and Gaeta (n 18) 492–520; JD Kila and JA Zeidler, *Cultural Heritage in the Crosshairs: Protecting Cultural Property During Conflict* (Leiden, Brill, 2013); Dinstein (n87) 170–85.

Hague Rules stipulated that warring parties should take all necessary steps in sieges and bombardments to spare 'as far as possible' buildings dedicated to religion, art, science, or historic monuments, 'provided they are not being used at the time for military purposes'.[127] LOAC has since strengthened the protection for cultural property, primarily as a result of the adoption of the 1954 Hague Convention for the Protection of Cultural Property in the Event of Armed Conflict,[128] the First Additional Protocol of 1977,[129] and the Second Protocol to the 1954 Hague Convention of 1999.[130] The result of these different instruments is a rather complex web of overlapping provisions, providing for different degrees of immunity from attack for different types of cultural property. The 1954 Hague Convention has also introduced a distinctive emblem to facilitate the identification of cultural property, namely the blue-white shield.

In spite of the criminalisation of intentional attacks against medical units and cultural property in IACs and NIACs under the Rome Statute,[131] such attacks are regrettably becoming a common occurrence in various armed conflicts.[132] This is particularly evident from several attacks against medical units by different parties in the conflict in Syria and Iraq and the systematic destruction of religious and other monuments by Islamic State (IS).

IV. Protection of Persons *hors de combat*[133]

A. Prisoners of War

The 1949 Geneva Conventions have established four categories of 'protected persons' in IACs. These are: (i) the sick and wounded on land (GC I); (ii) the shipwrecked at sea (GC II); (iii) POWs (GC III); and (iv) civilians (GC IV). Of the three regimes dealing with

[127] Art 27 Hague Regulations.

[128] Convention for the Protection of Cultural Property in the Event of Armed Conflict (adopted 14 May 1954, entered into force 7 August 1956) 249 UNTS 215.

[129] Art 53 AP I.

[130] Second Protocol to The Hague Convention of 1954 for the Protection of Cultural Property in the Event of Armed Conflict (adopted 26 March 1999, entered into force 9 March 2004) 2253 UNTS 172.

[131] For medical units, see above (n 123); for cultural property, see respectively Art 8(2)(b)(ix) and 8(2)(e)(iv) of the ICC Statute. For a (first) conviction on the latter basis, see ICC, Trial Chamber VIII, *Prosecutor v Ahmad Al Faqi Al Mahdi*, 27 September 2016, Case No ICC-01/12-01/15 (concerning a jihadi leader responsible for demolishing ancient mausoleums in Timbuktu, Mali).

[132] Experience regrettably shows that medical personnel are often prevented from carrying out their tasks or are themselves the object of attack. This has inspired the ICRC to set up the 'health care in danger' project, which aims at the adoption of specific measures designed to help ensure that the sick and wounded have safe access to effective and impartial health care in situations of armed conflict. See ICRC, 'Health Care in Danger: Making the Case. A Sixteen-Country Study', July 2011, icrc.org/eng/assets/files/reports/4073-002-16-country-study.pdf; and, in this context, ICRC, 'Domestic Normative Frameworks for the Protection of Health Care', January 2015, icrc.org/eng/resources/documents/publication/p4215.htm. In October 2015, the US Air Force attacked a hospital in Kunduz, Afghanistan, operated by Médecins Sans Frontières (MSF), resulting in 42 casualties and over 30 injured. A controversial CIA Report nonetheless concluded that the personnel involved had not committed a war crime, since the investigation had shown that the personnel did not know that they were striking a medical facility. See US Forces-Afghanistan (USFOR-A), 'Investigation Report of the Airstrike on Médecins Sans Frontières / Doctors Without Borders Trauma Center in Kunduz, Afghanistan on 3 October 2015', 11 November 2015, fpp.cc/wp-content/uploads/01.-AR-15-6-Inv-Rpt-Doctors-Without-Borders-3-Oct-15_CLEAR.pdf.

[133] This section is based in part on Ruys and De Cock (n88). Certain sections of the latter chapter are reproduced here with the approval of the two authors as well as that of the publisher.

combatants *hors de combat*, the POW regime is undoubtedly the most detailed.[134] The linchpin provision establishing the personal scope of application of the POW regime is found in Article 4(A) GC III (identical provisions can be found in Articles 13 GC I and 13 GC II). This provision refers first and foremost to the three categories of so-called 'lawful combatants'. Lawful combatants are those that enjoy the 'combatant privilege' and are therefore entitled under LOAC to take a direct part in hostilities, subject to certain requirements. Upon capture, they become POWs. Crucially, POWs cannot be punished for their mere participation in hostilities, but only for specific breaches of LOAC. Importantly, lawful combatants exist only in IACs. By contrast, rebels engaged in a NIAC do not have an equivalent right to participate in hostilities, and can be prosecuted under domestic law for any criminal offences they may have committed, irrespective of compliance with LOAC.

The three categories of lawful combatants are:

(1) members of the regular armed forces of a Party to the conflict, as well as members of militias or volunteer corps forming part of such armed forces;[135]
(2) members of other (ie irregular) militias and other volunteer corps, including those of organised resistance movements, which are being commanded by a person responsible for his subordinates, and belonging to a Party to the conflict;[136]
(3) participants in a *levée en masse* in non-occupied territory.[137]

In addition, for combatants to lawfully take part in hostilities, they must in principle fulfil three cumulative conditions: (i) they must carry their arms openly; (ii) they must conduct their operations in accordance with the laws and customs of war; and (iii) save for participants in a *levée en masse*, they must have a fixed distinctive sign recognisable at a distance (eg a uniform, armband or particular headgear).[138]

The extent to which non-compliance with the criteria mentioned above results in the loss of POW status upon capture is subject to debate. The Third Geneva Convention does not offer a general answer, but merely observes that POWs that are prosecuted, or even convicted, for acts committed prior to capture, shall retain the benefits of the Convention, thus indicating that breaches of LOAC do not normally result in loss of POW status if the other requirements are met.[139] Controversially, however, Article 44(3) AP I further restricts possible loss of POW status by asserting that there are 'situations in armed conflicts where, owing to the nature of the hostilities an armed combatant cannot so distinguish himself', and where combatants need only comply with the obligation to carry their arms openly upon capture to qualify as POWs. Even if the latter obligation is ignored, Article 44(4) AP I states that captured combatants, while no longer qualifying as POWs, should be given 'protections equivalent' to those enshrined in GC III and AP I. The inclusion of the latter provisions was inspired by the concern for better protection for certain guerrilla liberation

[134] The regime governing the wounded, sick and shipwrecked combatants will not be discussed separately in the present chapter. Suffice it to note that the personal scope of application is mutatis mutandis the same as that of GC III. As soon as the sick, wounded and shipwrecked of a belligerent fall into enemy hands, their situation is no longer governed by GC I or II, but by the POW regime of GC III. See further Ruys and De Cock (n88) 388–89 and 395–98.

[135] Art 4(A)(1) GC III.

[136] Art 4(A)(2) GC III.

[137] Art 4(A)(n 6) GC III.

[138] See further Ruys and De Cock (n88) 377–81 and 385–86. Note that Art 4(A) GC III only lists these requirements in relation to irregular armed forces. This should not be read as implying that they do not apply to regular armed forces, but merely reflects the (logical) assumption that the latter normally comply with these requirements.

[139] Art 85 GC III. In a similar vein, see Art 44(2)–(3) AP I. But see Dinstein (n87) 50.

movements in the decolonisation period. Yet, Articles 44(3)–(4) AP I have been criticised for reducing the incentive for combatants to properly distinguish themselves from the civilian population and thus leading to greater exposure of civilians to the harmful effects of hostilities.[140]

Apart from the categories of combatants discussed above, Article 4(A) GC III also extends POW status to certain categories of non-combatants, provided they take no direct part in hostilities. One such category consists of 'persons who accompany the armed forces without actually being members thereof', such as certain civilian contractors or embedded journalists, provided that they have received authorisation from the armed forces whom they accompany. On the other hand, pursuant to Article 47 AP I (which has a very restricted scope), mercenaries who participate in armed conflict for financial gain do not have the right to POW status and are explicitly denied combatant privilege. Spies caught in the act and not wearing their uniform cannot claim POW status either, but may be punished by the capturing State under its domestic law.[141] Medical and religious personnel cannot be held as POWs upon capture, but can under certain conditions be held as 'retainees' with a view to assisting POWs.[142]

According to Article 5 GC III, should 'any doubt arise' as to whether persons having fallen into the hands of the enemy qualify as POWs, such persons shall enjoy the protection of GC III until their status has been determined 'by a competent tribunal'.[143] In the wake of the 9/11 attacks, the Bush administration initially refused to organise Article 5 hearings to determine the status of captured Al Qaeda or Taliban members because, according to the administration, there could be no doubt that they did not deserve such status. This decision resulted in the detention of some apparently uninvolved civilians for years longer than necessary. Eventually, following the US Supreme Court decisions in *Rasul v Bush*[144] and *Hamdi v Rumsfeld*,[145] the US set up Combatant Status Review Tribunals to comply with its obligations under Article 5 GC III.

As a rule, belligerent Parties have the right to intern POWs for the duration of the conflict to prevent their continued participation in hostilities, save for certain categories of wounded and sick persons who qualify for direct repatriation.[146] An in-depth analysis of the substantive POW regime is beyond the purview of this chapter. Following the structure of the Convention, the main rights and obligations can broadly be divided into four groups:

— general protection: POWs must always be treated humanely and cannot, for instance, be subjected to physical mutilation, medical experiments or reprisals. They may not be put on display for propaganda purposes, but must be protected against 'acts of violence or intimidation and against insults and public curiosity';[147]

[140] Ruys and De Cock (n88) 386. It has been argued that Art 44(3)–(4) AP I does not form part of customary law, implying that there are two different standards of lawful combatancy, depending on whether the States party to an IAC have ratified AP I; C Greenwood, 'The Law of War (International Humanitarian Law)' in MD Evans (ed), *International Law*, 2nd edn (Oxford, OUP, 2006) 790.

[141] Art 46 AP I and Arts 29–31 Hague Regulations. However, a spy that is caught only after having re-joined his armed forces is entitled to POW status and can no longer be prosecuted for prior acts of espionage.

[142] Art 4(c) and 33 GC III.

[143] Discriminatory treatment is in principle prohibited, although exception is made for specific provisions relating to rank and sex (eg separate dormitories for men and women). See Art 5 GC III and Art 45(1)–(2) AP I.

[144] Supreme Court (US), *Rasul v Bush*, 542 US 466 (2004).

[145] Supreme Court (US), *Hamdi v Rumsfeld*, 542 US 507 (2004).

[146] Art 110 GC III.

[147] Art 13 GC III.

— the beginning of captivity: GC III regulates interrogation of POWs upon capture (no coercion whatsoever is permitted), and determines the extent to which certain items can be confiscated. POWs must be evacuated to internment camps removed from the combat zone as soon as possible;[148]

— the conditions of internment: States are obliged to provide POWs with adequate food, clothing and medical attention.[149] Other provisions relate to the right of POWs to practise their religion;[150] the extent to which the Detaining Power may utilise the labour of POWs and the conditions applicable thereto;[151] the possibility for POWs to communicate with the outside world;[152] and the possibility to impose penal and disciplinary sanctions on POWs.[153] While the relevant provisions of GC III often go into considerable detail, it has been observed that they must be interpreted having regard to the situation on the ground and the capacities of the warring Parties;[154]

— termination of captivity: captivity may end as a result of a prisoner's successful escape,[155] or as a result of his death in captivity (which triggers specific obligations under Articles 120–121 GC III). Otherwise, all POWs must be repatriated without delay after the cessation of active hostilities.[156]

B. The Protection of Civilians in International Armed Conflicts

The Fourth Geneva Convention contains a series of protective provisions that are of general application and cover the 'whole of the populations of the countries' in an IAC.[157] The thrust of the Convention is found in Part III (Articles 27–141), which deals with the 'status and treatment of protected persons'. Just as the concept of 'civilian' is defined negatively for the purposes of determining one's individual battlefield status,[158] the notion of 'protected person' is partly defined in a negative manner. Article 4(4) GC IV indeed holds that POWs protected by GC III, as well as sick, wounded or shipwrecked combatants protected by GC I or II are excluded from its scope of application. Otherwise, to qualify as a 'protected person' under GC IV, a person: (i) should be in the hands of a Party to the conflict or Occupying Power;[159] and (ii) not have the nationality of that Party or Occupying Power.[160]

[148] Arts 17, 18 and 19 GC III.
[149] Arts 25–32 GC III.
[150] Art 34 GC III.
[151] Arts 49–57 GC III.
[152] Arts 70–71 GC III.
[153] Art 82 ff GC III.
[154] See eg Eritrea Ethiopia Claims Commission, Partial Award: Prisoners of War, Ethiopia's Claim 4, 1 July 2003, (2003) 42 ILM 1056, paras 70, 73–74 and 142–43.
[155] Art 91 GC III.
[156] Art 118 GC III. Repatriation may be postponed if a POW is awaiting trial or serving a sentence following trial (Art 119 GC III).
[157] Part II (Arts 13–26) GC IV.
[158] Art 50(1) AP I.
[159] There is some discussion as to whether Part III GC IV also applies to the so-called invasion phase preceding actual occupation; see eg K Dörmann, 'The Legal Situation of Unlawful/Unprivileged Combatants' (2003) 85 *IRRC* 45, 61–64.
[160] But see ICTY, Appeals Chamber, *Tadić* (Merits) (n 45) para 166. Furthermore, pursuant to Art 4(2) GC IV, nationals of a State that is not bound by the Convention, nationals of a neutral State and nationals of a co-belligerent State cannot qualify as 'protected persons'.

Article 5(1) GC IV goes on to stipulate that persons who are 'definitely suspected of or engaged in activities hostile to the security of the State' shall not be entitled to claim such rights and privileges as would be 'prejudicial to the security of such State'. The implication is that, while such persons in principle remain 'protected persons', the State may curtail their rights under GC IV when it has determined, on an individualised basis,[161] that the person concerned poses a risk to its security. At the same time, these persons must still be treated with humanity and shall not be deprived of their rights of fair trial.[162] Restrictions imposed on the basis of Article 5 GC IV must be lifted as soon as they are no longer justified by security reasons.

Another question arises regarding those persons who participate directly in hostilities, yet who do not meet the requirements for POW status, such as members of organised irregular forces who fail to distinguish themselves from the civilian population (as many non-State armed groups do). In the wake of the 9/11-attacks, the Bush administration took the view that such persons could not be regarded as 'protected persons'. Rather, they were regarded as 'unlawful' or 'unprivileged' combatants, entitled only to the minimum fundamental guarantees set forth in Article 75 AP I (eg minimum fair trial guarantees).[163] However, this goes against the traditional view, adhered to by the ICRC as well as numerous scholars, that there exists no third category of 'unlawful combatants' that falls between the cracks of GC III (POWs) and GC IV (protected civilians).[164] Thus, according to the Commentary to GC IV:

> If members of a resistance movement who have fallen in to enemy hands do not fulfill [the] conditions [for POW status], they must be considered to be protected persons within the meaning of [GC IV]. That does not mean that they cannot be punished for their acts, but the trial and sentence must take place in accordance with the provisions of Article 64 and the Articles which follow it.[165]

As indicated above, it must be kept in mind that Article 5 GC IV can be invoked to limit the claims and privileges to which 'unlawful combatants' are entitled.[166]

Following the structure of the Convention, the main rights and obligations can (non-exhaustively) be summed up as follows:

— general protection: protected persons must, like POWs, at all times be humanely treated, and be protected especially against all acts of violence or threats thereof and against insults and public curiosity.[167] LOAC prohibits the use of protected persons as human shields,[168] as well as pillage, collective penalties and reprisals against them.[169] The taking of hostages is similarly prohibited.[170] Parties must also allow for the free passage of

[161] In this sense, see ICTY, Appeals Chamber, *Prosecutor v Zejnil Delalić et al*, 20 February 2001, Case No IT-96-21-A, para 327.

[162] Art 5(3) GC IV.

[163] Article 75 API identifies the fundamental guarantees owed to persons in the power of a Party to the conflict and who do not benefit from more favourable treatment under the GCs or AP I.

[164] See the list of authors cited by Dörmann (n 159) 59, note 36. Consider also: Supreme Court (IL), *Public Committee against Torture in Israel v Government of Israel*, 13 December 2006, Case No HCJ 769/02, para 28; ICTY, Trial Chamber, *Prosecutor v Zejnil Delalić et al*, 16 November 1998, Case No IT-96-21-T, para 271. See further K Dörmann, 'Unlawful Combatants' in Clapham and Gaeta (n 18) 605–23.

[165] Pictet, *Commentary IV* (n 16) 51.

[166] Dörmann (n 159) 50.

[167] Art 27 GC IV.

[168] Art 28 GC IV.

[169] Art 33 GC IV.

[170] Art 34 GC IV.

certain goods essential for the civilian population and should not arbitrarily withhold their consent to relief actions;[171]

— aliens in the own territory of a Party to the conflict: civilians are entitled to leave the territory at the outset of, or during the armed conflict, unless their departure is contrary to the national interests of the State, in which case they will be informed of the reasons for refusal;[172]
— occupation: situations of belligerent occupation are subject to a specific corpus of rules, an overview of which is beyond the scope of this chapter.[173] Occupying Powers have more far-reaching *positive* obligations. For instance, an Occupying Power has the duty of ensuring, to the fullest extent of the means available to it, the food and medical supplies of the population, and 'should, in particular, bring in the necessary foodstuffs, medical stores and other articles if the resources of the occupied territory are inadequate'.[174] If the population is inadequately supplied, it is obliged to accept offers of relief actions.[175] GC IV also prohibits mass forcible transfers and deportations of protected persons from occupied territory to other States, regardless of the underlying motive;[176]
— internment: civilians may be interned or placed in assigned residence only for imperative security reasons.[177] For civilians interned for reasons relating to the armed conflict, GC IV contains detailed provisions on the conditions the detention regime needs to fulfil.[178] Internees shall be accommodated and administered separately from POWs and persons deprived of their liberty for any other reason. The State concerned must take the necessary measures regarding health and hygiene, and provide proper food rations. Interned persons must be released as soon as the reasons which necessitated their internment no longer exist.[179]

In addition, special protection exists for certain groups that are deemed particularly vulnerable in situations of armed conflict, especially women[180] and children.[181]

[171] Art 23 GC IV and Art 70 AP I. See further Y Dinstein, 'Siege Warfare and the Starvation of Civilians' in AJM Delissen and GJ Tanja (eds), *Humanitarian Law of Armed Conflict: Challenges Ahead – Essays in Honour of Frits Kalshoven* (Dordrecht, Nijhoff, 1991) 145–52; D Akande and E Gillard, 'Oxford Guidance on Humanitarian Relief Operations', Commissioned by the United Nations Office for the Coordination of Humanitarian Affairs, October 2016, unocha.org/sites/dms/Documents/Oxford%20Guidance%20pdf.pdf.

[172] Art 35 GC IV.

[173] See the references above (n 21).

[174] Art 55 GC IV.

[175] Art 59 GC IV and Art 69 AP I.

[176] See in particular Art 49 GC IV and Art 78 AP I.

[177] Art 42 GC IV (for the own territory of a Party to the conflict) and Art 78 (for occupied territory).

[178] Arts 79–141 GC IV.

[179] Art 132 GC IV.

[180] See in particular Art 27(2) GC IV and Arts 75(5) and 76 AP I. Consider also UNSC Res 1325, 31 October 2000, UN Doc S/RES/1325 (the first UNSC Res on Women, Peace and Security). Further, see eg A Barrow, 'UN Security Council Resolutions 1325 and 1820: Constructing Gender in Armed Conflict and International Humanitarian Law' (2010) 92 *IRRC* 221; H Durham, 'Women, Armed Conflict and International Law' (2002) 84 *IRRC* 655.

[181] See eg Arts 24 and 50 GC IV; Art 77(1) AP I; Art 38 Convention on the Rights of the Child; Arts 1–3 Optional Protocol to the CRC on the Involvement of Children in Armed Conflict (adopted 25 May 2000, entered into force 12 February 2002) 2173 UNTS 222; Art 8(2)(b)(xxvi) and 8(2)(e)(vii) ICC Statute; UNSC Res 1612, 26 July 2005, UN Doc S/RES/1612 (setting up the UNC's Working Group on Children and Armed Conflict (WGCAAC). See also the webpage of the WGCAAC: un.org/sc/suborg/en/subsidiary/wgcaac. See further S Vité, 'Protecting Children During Armed Conflict: International Humanitarian Law' (2011) 5 *Human Rights and International Legal Discourse* 40; G Waschefort, *International Law and Child Soldiers* (Oxford, Hart, 2015).

C. Protection of Persons *hors de combat* in Non-International Armed Conflicts

So far, we have looked primarily at the treatment of persons *hors de combat* – chiefly POWs and civilians – in situations of IAC. In NIACs, the four Geneva Conventions and AP I do not apply, except for the minimum guarantees contained in Common Article 3. Indeed, the concepts of POW status/treatment for combatants and 'protected person' status/treatment for civilians are in principle unknown to the law of NIAC.[182]

However, as far as the general protection of persons *hors de combat* is concerned, many of the rights and obligations discussed above apply not only to IACs, but also to NIACs. Several of these rules are equally enshrined in AP II. For example, Article 4(3)(c) AP II states that children under 15 'shall neither be recruited in the armed forces or groups nor allowed to take part in hostilities'. Article 17 AP II prohibits the forced movement of civilians, and Article 18 AP II provides for relief operations when the civilian population is suffering undue hardship, albeit subject to the consent of the State concerned. However, AP II only applies to certain NIACs (see above, Section II(B)(i)) and only when the State where the NIAC takes place has ratified it. Still, many of the rules pertaining to the protection of persons *hors de combat* in IACs apply by analogy to NIACs because they form part of the customary international law of NIAC.[183] It is also worth recalling that certain conduct is considered to be a war crime (in particular under the ICC Statute) in both types of armed conflict.[184]

A crucial gap nonetheless remains when it comes to the deprivation of liberty in NIACs.[185] Whereas GC III and GC IV together contain more than 175 rules on the detention of POWs and the internment of protected persons, there is simply no comparable regime for NIACs. Thus, while Article 5 AP II contains a handful of requirements concerning the conditions of internment or detention and Article 6 AP II deals with penal prosecutions of criminal offences related to the armed conflict, AP II and Common Article 3 GCs are completely silent when it comes to the grounds for internment for security reasons in NIACs and the relevant procedural safeguards (eg review of internment decisions and right to information). Moreover, uncertainty exists as to the existence and content of customary rules on detention in NIACs. Against this background, several initiatives have been set up to remedy this conundrum. The Danish government launched an international consultation process, which in 2012 resulted in the adoption of the 'Copenhagen Process Principles and Guidelines', a set of non-binding principles and guidelines on the detention of persons in the context of an international military operation.[186] The ICRC, for its part, considers that also in NIACs, there is an 'inherent power to detain', while additional authority related to

[182] As mentioned above (Section II(A)), rebels taking part in a NIAC in principle do not enjoy any right to participate in hostilities, but can be prosecuted under domestic law for any criminal offences they may have committed. At the same time, the warring parties may nonetheless agree to grant protection equivalent to that existing in NIACs, or a party may decide to do so unilaterally; see above (n 32).

[183] See the ICRC Customary Study (n 11).

[184] See Art 8 ICC Statute.

[185] Further, see eg L Hill-Cawthorne, *Detention in Non-International Armed Conflict* (Oxford, OUP, 2016); E Debuf, *Captured in War: Lawful Internment in Armed Conflict* (Oxford, Hart, 2013) 449 ff; R Goodman, 'The Detention of Civilians in Armed Conflict' (2009) 103 *AJIL* 48; J Pejic, 'Procedural Principles and Safeguards for Internment/Administrative Detention in Armed Conflict and Other Situations of Violence' (2005) 87 *IRRC* 375.

[186] The Copenhagen Process on the Handling of Detainees in International Military Operations, 'The Copenhagen Process: Principles and Guidelines', um.dk/en/~/media/UM/English-site/Documents/Politics-and-diplomacy/Copenhagen%20Process%20Principles%20and%20Guidelines.pdf. Principle 16 nonetheless asserts that the Copenhagen Principles and Guidelines are not intended as a restatement of customary international law.

the grounds and procedure for deprivation of liberty in non-international armed conflict must in all cases be provided'.[187] In light of these considerations, it set up a consultation process on how to strengthen the legal protection of persons deprived of their liberty in relation to NIACs.[188]

In the meantime, legal questions surrounding the detention of persons in armed conflict have been raised before domestic courts and the ECtHR. In the *Serdar Mohammed* case, English courts by and large rejected the idea of an inherent right to detain in NIAC.[189] In the *Hassan* case, the ECtHR held that the grounds of permitted deprivation of liberty under Article 5 ECHR should be 'accommodated' to allow for a right to detain without a trial under LOAC, but explicitly limited this recognition to situations of IAC.[190] The resulting (and still evolving) case law attests to the valuable contribution of IHRL with regard to the protection of persons deprived of their liberty in NIACs. At the same time, an additional challenge stems from the fact that, contrary to LOAC, IHRL does not as such bind non-State armed groups engaged in a NIAC, but is addressed to States only.[191]

V. Means of Warfare[192]

Article 35 AP I articulates the basic rule that '[i]n any armed conflict, the right of the Parties to the conflict to choose methods or means of warfare is not unlimited'. The choice of

[187] ICRC (2016) (n 16) para 728.

[188] See ICRC, 'Detention in non-international armed conflict: The ICRC's work on strengthening legal protection', 21 April 2015, icrc.org/eng/what-we-do/other-activities/development-ihl/strengthening-legal-protection-ihl-detention.htm.

[189] High Court of Justice (UK), *Serdar Mohammed* (n77) paras 228–94. Justice Legatt held that (1) LOAC (whether treaty law or customary law) does not provide a legal basis for detention by UK armed forces operating in the NIAC in Afghanistan; and (2) there was no scope for contending that LOAC operates during a NIAC to displace or qualify Art 5 ECHR. Upheld on appeal, see Court of Appeal (UK), *Serdar Mohammed and others v Secretary of State for Defence* [2015] EWCA Civ 843 (QB). Somewhat more cautious: Supreme Court (UK), *Abd Ali Hameed Al-Waheed v Ministry of Defence, Serdar Mohammed v Ministry of Defence* [2017] UKSC 2, Lord Sumption, para 14. Unlike the lower courts, the justices of the Supreme Court mostly refrained from explicitly pronouncing on whether customary international law provided an inherent basis to detain in NIACs, probably because they saw the matter as evolving, and because they could resolve the case on other grounds (ie the existence of an authority to detain pursuant to applicable UNSC resolutions).

[190] *Hassan v UK* App no 29750/09 (ECtHR, 16 September 2014) para 104: 'It can only be in cases of international armed conflict, where the taking of prisoners of war and the detention of civilians who pose a threat to the security are accepted features of international humanitarian law, that Article 5 could be interpreted as permitting the exercise of such broad powers', being the deprivation of liberty for security reasons. This *dictum* could be read as implying *a contrario* that Art 5 ECHR prohibits the detention/internment of persons for safety reasons in NIACs, save pursuant to a formal derogation by the State Party under Art 15 ECHR. This may help to explain why in late 2016, the UK government announced an intention to derogate from the ECHR in future military operations abroad: UK Minister of Defence, 'Government to protect Armed Forces from persistent legal claims in future overseas operations', 4 October 2016, gov.uk/government/news/government-to-protect-armed-forces-from-persistent-legal-claims-in-future-overseas-operations. In the *Serdar Mohammed* judgment of the UK Supreme Court (n 189), Lord Sumption expanded the application of the ECtHR's *Hassan* reasoning to detention in NIAC, at least where such detention would be authorised by some norm of international law, such as a UNSC resolution.

[191] ICRC, 'Strengthening Legal Protection for Persons Deprived of their Liberty in relation to Non-International Armed Conflict', Regional Consultations 2012–2013, Background Paper, icrc.org/eng/assets/files/2013/strengthening-legal-protection-detention-consultations-2012-2013-icrc.pdf, 5, 10 ('detention by non-state armed groups is usually prohibited as a matter of domestic law. The application of IHL does not provide legitimacy to such detention') and 12–13. But see above (n71).

[192] This section is based on B Demeyere and T Ruys, 'Means and Methods of Warfare' in Wouters, De Man and Verlinden (n 22) (some sections are reproduced here with the permission of the authors). See also S Oeter (n 19);

'means' of warfare is restricted, for example, by the prohibition to inflict superfluous injury and the prohibition of indiscriminate attacks. In addition, a wide range of treaties restricts, or bans altogether, the use of specific weapons in situations of international and/or non-international armed conflict.[193]

Among the oldest examples in this area are the 1868 Saint Petersburg Declaration prohibiting the use of explosive projectiles below 400 grams of weight[194] and the prohibition of 'expanding bullets' in Hague Declaration IV of 1899.[195] As for non-conventional weapons, the majority of the rules relating to biological weapons are found in the 1972 Biological Weapons Convention.[196] This Convention builds on the 1925 Gas Protocol,[197] whose scope already extended to 'bacteriological methods of warfare'. Whereas the 1925 prohibition only related to the use of these agents, the 1972 Convention equally bans their development and production, ordering the destruction of existing stockpiles.[198]

In a similar vein, the 1993 Chemical Weapons Convention (CWC)[199] prohibits the use of chemical weapons and includes an elaborate and detailed regime geared towards their destruction, under the international oversight of the Organisation for the Prohibition of Chemical Weapons. Article 1(5) CWC also prohibits the use of 'riot control agents', such as tear gas, as a method of warfare once the threshold for the law of armed conflict to apply has been crossed. Below that threshold, their use may be lawful, eg as a matter of law enforcement to disperse a rioting crowd. Although the prohibition on the use of chemical weapons now forms part of customary international law,[200] chemical agents have occasionally been used in armed conflict both before and after 1993, including eg the Iran-Iraq war in the 1980s, as well as, more recently, the Syrian civil war.[201]

As far as conventional weapons are concerned, the 1980 Convention on Conventional Weapons (CCW)[202] serves as a framework agreement, to which substantive obligations have been added in the form of separate protocols. Five Protocols have been adopted over time, dealing respectively with non-detectable fragments;[203] the use of mines, booby-traps and

W Hays Parks, 'Means and Methods of Warfare' (2006) 38 *George Washington International Law Review* 511. The present section is limited to restrictions on the 'means' of warfare, this term being understood as referring to weapons, as well as weapons launch and delivery systems.

193 Further, see eg WH Boothby, *Weapons and the Law of Armed Conflict*, 2nd edn (Oxford, OUP, 2016).

194 Saint Petersburg Declaration Renouncing the Use, in Time of War, of Explosive Projectiles under 400 Grammes Weight, 29 November / 11 December 1868, ihl-databases.icrc.org/ihl/INTRO/130?OpenDocument.

195 Commonly known as 'dum dum' bullets. Further, see eg A Vanheusden, W Hays Parks and WH Boothby, 'The Use of Expanding Bullets in Military Operations: Examining the Kampala Consensus' (2011) 50 *Military Law and the Law of War Review* 535. See also Art 23(a) Hague Regulations on the use of poisonous weapons.

196 Biological Weapons Convention (adopted 10 April 1972, entered into force 26 March 1975) 1015 UNTS 163. Further, see eg J Goldblat, 'The Biological Weapons Convention: An Overview' (1997) 37 *IRRC* 251.

197 Protocol for the Prohibition of the Use of Asphyxiating, Poisonous or Other Gases, and of Bacteriological Methods of Warfare (adopted 17 June 1925, entered into force 8 February 1928) 94 LNTS 65. Further, see eg JN Moore, 'Ratification of the Geneva Protocol on Gas and Bacteriological Warfare: A Legal and Political Analysis' (1972) 58 *Virginia Law Review* 419.

198 Art 1 Biological Weapons Convention.

199 Further, see eg W Krutsch, EPJ Myjer and R Trapp (eds), *The Chemical Weapons Convention: A Commentary* (Oxford, OUP, 2014).

200 See the ICRC Customary Study (n 11) 259.

201 Further, see eg R Trapp, 'Elimination of the Chemical Weapons Stockpile of Syria' (2014) 19 *Journal of Conflict and Security Law* 7.

202 Convention on Prohibitions or Restrictions on the Use of Certain Conventional Weapons which may be deemed to be Excessively Injurious or to have Indiscriminate Effects (adopted 10 October 1980, entered into force 2 December 1983) 1342 UNTS 137.

203 Protocol on Non-Detectable Fragments (Protocol I) (adopted 10 October 1980, entered into force 2 December 1983) 1342 UNTS 168: 'It is prohibited to use any weapon the primary effect of which is to injure by fragments which in the human body escape detection by X-rays'.

other devices;[204] the use of incendiary weapons;[205] blinding laser weapons;[206] and explosive remnants of war.[207] For several years, negotiations have also been ongoing within the CCW framework on the possible conclusion of further instruments dealing specifically with 'mines other than anti-personnel mines' and lethal autonomous weapon systems.[208] On occasion, States have adopted instruments outside the CCW framework, often due to a lack of agreement among the CCW States Parties. First, the 1997 Ottawa Convention on Anti-Personnel Mines[209] goes beyond the (amended) Protocol II to the CCW by banning (rather than merely restricting) the use of anti-personnel mines.[210] It also contains sweeping obligations on the destruction of existing stockpiles of anti-personnel mines and on the destruction of such mines in mined areas.[211] Although 164 States were party to the Convention by April 2018, several important players, including China, Russia and the United States, have so far refused to join.[212] Second, pursuant to an international advocacy campaign, the international community in 2008 concluded a treaty on the prohibition of cluster munitions.[213] While the treaty entered into force in 2010 and has attracted a total of 103 States Parties by April 2018, it has met with strong opposition from a number of (militarily important) States, some of which continue to use cluster munitions in military operations.

In addition to the foregoing instruments, reference must be made to a number of treaties that exclusively address the possession, production or transfer of certain weapons, without specifically tackling their *use* in armed conflict. An example is the Non-Proliferation Treaty (NPT),[214] which stipulates that non-nuclear States Parties undertake not to acquire nuclear

[204] Protocol on Prohibitions or Restrictions on the Use of Mines, Booby-Traps and Other Devices (Protocol II) (adopted 10 October 1980, entered into force 2 December 1983) 1342 UNTS 168, as amended in 1996. Further, see eg MJ Matheson, 'The Revision of the Mines Protocol' (1997) 91 *AJIL* 158.

[205] Protocol on Prohibitions or Restrictions on the Use of Incendiary Weapons (adopted 10 October 1980, entered into force 2 December 1983) 1342 UNTS 171. Further, see eg W Hays Parks, 'The Protocol on Incendiary Weapons' (1990) 30 *IRRC* 535.

[206] Protocol on Blinding Laser Weapons (Protocol IV) (13 October 1995, 30 July 1998) 1380 UNTS 370. Further, see eg L Doswald-Beck, 'New Protocol on Blinding Laser Weapons' (1996) 36 *IRRC* 272.

[207] Protocol on Explosive Remnants of War (Protocol V) (adopted 28 November 2003, entered into force 12 November 2006) 2399 UNTS 100. Further, see eg L Maresca, 'A New Protocol on Explosive Remnants of War: The History and Negotiation of Protocol V to the 1980 Convention on Certain Conventional Weapons' (2004) 86 *IRRC* 815.

[208] For the latest information on these negotiations, see the CCW webpage: unog.ch/80256EE600585943/(httpPages)/4F0DEF093B4860B4C1257180004B1B30?OpenDocument. Further, see eg N Davison, 'A Legal Perspective: Autonomous Weapon Systems under International Humanitarian Law' in *UNODA Occasional Papers: Perspectives on Lethal Autonomous Weapon Systems* (New York, UN, 2017) 5–18.

[209] Convention on the Prohibition of the Use, Stockpiling, Production and Transfer of Anti-Personnel Mines and on their Destruction (adopted 18 September 1997, entered into force 1 March 1999) 2056 UNTS 211. See further eg S Maslen, *Commentaries on Arms Control Treaties – Volume 1: The Convention on the Prohibition of the Use, Stockpiling, Production, and Transfer of Anti-Personnel Mines and on Their Destruction*, 2nd edn (Oxford, OUP, 2005).

[210] However, as with other instruments, it is crucial to properly construe the type of weapons covered. Art 2(1) defines an 'anti-personnel mine' as a 'mine *designed to* be exploded by the presence, proximity or contact of a person and that will incapacitate, injure or kill one or more persons' (emphasis added).

[211] Arts 4–5 of the Ottawa Convention. The implementation of these obligations is monitored through periodic reports to be submitted by the States Parties; Art 7 Ottawa Convention.

[212] In 2014, the US nonetheless decided to 'align' its policy to the key requirements under the Ottawa Convention, inter alia by announcing that it would no longer use anti-personnel mines outside the Korean Peninsula; White House, Office of the Press Secretary, 'Fact Sheet: Changes to U.S. Anti-Personnel Landmine Policy', 23 September 2014, obamawhitehouse.archives.gov/the-press-office/2014/09/23/fact-sheet-changes-us-anti-personnel-landmine-policy.

[213] Convention on Cluster Munitions (adopted 30 May 2008, entered into force 1 August 2010) 2688 UNTS 39. Further, see eg G Nystuen and S Casey-Maslen (eds), *The Convention on Cluster Munitions: A Commentary* (Oxford, OUP, 2010).

[214] Treaty on the Non-Proliferation of Nuclear Weapons (adopted 1 July 1968, entered into force 5 March 1970) 729 UNTS 169.

weapons,[215] whereas nuclear States Parties undertake to pursue good faith negotiations to achieve nuclear disarmament.[216] The use of nuclear weapons in armed conflict is not addressed.[217] In its 1996 *Nuclear Weapons* Advisory Opinion, the ICJ affirmed that such use is subject to inter alia the principles of distinction and proportionality. However, the Court did not affirm or reject the existence of an absolute ban against their use under international law.[218] The recently adopted Treaty on the Prohibition of Nuclear Weapons of 2017 expressly sets forth a blanket prohibition on the use of nuclear weapons and prohibits State Parties, for instance, to allow nuclear weapons to be stationed on their territory.[219] However, the vast majority of European States have refrained from signing the treaty, as have the (other) nuclear-weapon States.[220]

Finally, reference must be made to the Arms Trade Treaty, Article 6(3) of which prohibits State Parties from authorising any transfer of conventional arms covered by the treaty if they have

> knowledge at the time of authorization that the arms or items would be used in the commission of [...] grave breaches of the Geneva Conventions of 1949, attacks directed against civilian objects or civilians protected as such, or other war crimes as defined by international agreements to which it is a party.[221]

In 2016, the Campaign against Arms Trade (CAAT), a UK-based NGO, challenged the legality of the UK government's decision to continue to licence the export of military equipment to Saudi Arabia, in light of reports of grave breaches of LOAC in the context of the Saudi military intervention in Yemen. The High Court of Justice dismissed the CAAT's claim for judicial review as it found the UK Secretary of State was 'rationally entitled to conclude [...] that there was no "clear risk" that there might be "serious violations" of [LOAC]' in the sense of the Consolidated EU and National Arms Exporting Licensing Criteria.[222] The CAAT has been granted permission to appeal the judgment.[223]

[215] Art II NPT.

[216] ibid, Art IV. In April 2014, the Marshall Islands instituted proceedings before the ICJ against a number of nuclear States accusing them of having breached this obligation (and its supposed customary equivalent). However, the ICJ upheld the objections made by the nuclear States that there was no actual dispute, following which it ruled that it did not have jurisdiction: *Obligations Concerning Negotiations Relating to Cessation of the Nuclear Arms Race and to Nuclear Disarmament* (Marshall Islands v India/Pakistan/United Kingdom) (Preliminary Objections) [2016] ICJ Rep 833.

[217] Note that upon ratifying AP I, a number of States emphasised that it only addressed conventional weapons: F Kalshoven, 'Arms, Armaments and International Law' (1985) II 191 *RdC* 183, 287.

[218] *Nuclear weapons* (n 17) 256.

[219] Treaty on the Prohibition of Nuclear Weapons (adopted 7 July 2017, not yet in force (April 2018)), UN Doc A/CONF.229/2017/8.

[220] The European signatories are: Austria, the Holy See, Liechtenstein and San Marino.

[221] Arms Trade Treaty (adopted 2 April 2013, entered into force 24 December 2014), UN Doc A/CONF.217/2013/L.3. Further, see eg NHB Jorgensen, 'State Responsibility for Aiding or Assisting International Crimes in the context of the Arms Trade Treaty' (2014) 108 *AJIL* 722.

[222] High Court of Justice (UK), *Campaign against Arms Trade*, [2017] EWHC 1726 (QB). According to the Court, the UK Secretary of State 'was rationally entitled to conclude as follows: (i) the [Saudi-led] Coalition were not deliberately targeting civilians; (ii) Saudi processes and procedures have been put in place to secure respect for the principles of [LAOC]; (iii) the Coalition was investigating incidents of controversy, including those involving civilian casualties; (iv) the Saudi authorities have throughout engaged in constructive dialogue with the UK about both its processes and incidents of concern; (v) Saudi Arabia has been and remains genuinely committed to compliance with [LOAC]; and (vi) that there was no "clear risk" that there might be "serious violations" of [LOAC] (in its various manifestations)'.

[223] Court of Appeal (UK), *Campaign against Arms Trade* [2018] EWCA Civ 1010.

VI. The Enforcement of the Law of Armed Conflict

A. The Achilles' Heel of the Law of Armed Conflict

Lingering controversies exist in relation to a number of important issues of LOAC, including the precise scope of 'direct participation in hostilities', the position of 'unlawful combatants' and the legal framework governing detention in NIACs. Yet, it is clear that LOAC has developed enormously since the 1860s. The problem then is not so much a lack of regulation, but one of enforcement, as daily reports of widespread LOAC violations in various corners of the world remind us.

Upon capture, persons taking a direct part in hostilities are regularly treated in manners that are incompatible with LOAC standards, as was illustrated in recent years by the maltreatment of detainees at the Abu Ghraib facility in Iraq,[224] by the US' 'extraordinary rendition' programme (concerning the extrajudicial transfer of detainees to third countries) or the harsh 'enhanced' interrogation methods used by the CIA under the Bush administration.[225] In a similar vein, the death toll among civilians is often high, raising serious questions over the compatibility of eg US drone strikes (in Pakistan, Yemen and elsewhere) or Israeli military operations in Gaza[226] with LOAC targeting principles. Violations of LOAC are particularly widespread in NIACs. A gruesome illustration is offered by the armed conflict in Syria and Iraq, where practices including torture, summary execution, rape and sexual slavery and deliberate attacks on residential areas, hospitals and cultural property are rife, in particular (but certainly not exclusively) on the part of the so-called Islamic State.[227] In light of this, the enforcement of LOAC merits further attention.

B. Compliance-inducing Factors

The various factors inducing compliance with LOAC are well documented in existing literature.[228] Such factors include considerations of reciprocity and fears of reprisals. According to this logic, a party that complies with LOAC (eg by treating captured enemies in a humane manner) knows that its adversary will be more inclined to reciprocate, and vice

[224] See the (normally confidential, but leaked) 'Report of the International Committee of the Red Cross (ICRC) on the Treatment by the Coalition Forces of Prisoners of War and Other Protected Persons by the Geneva Conventions in Iraq During Arrest, Internment and Interrogation', February 2004, washingtonmonthly.com/2004/05/10/red-cross-report-on-abu-ghraib/.

[225] See Open Society Justice Initiative, 'Globalizing Torture: CIA Secret Detention and Extraordinary Rendition', February 2013, opensocietyfoundations.org/sites/default/files/globalizing-torture-20120205.pdf.

[226] Consider eg the following statement by the UN Special Coordinator for the Middle East Peace Process on Operation 'Protective Edge': 'A total of almost 2,000 Palestinians have been killed […]. Civilians represent more than two thirds of that total': UNSC Verbatim Record, 18 August 2014, UN Doc S/PV.7243, 2–4.

[227] See eg the many reports of the Independent International Commission of Inquiry on the Syrian Arab Republic (established by the Human Rights Council): ohchr.org/EN/HRBodies/HRC/IICISyria/Pages/Documentation.aspx.

[228] See eg S Vöneky, 'Implementation and Enforcement of International Humanitarian Law' in Fleck (n 19) 647–700; MN Schmitt and W Heintschel von Heinegg, *The Implementation and Enforcement of International Humanitarian Law* (Farnham, Ashgate, 2012); O Bangerter, 'Les raisons pour les groupes armés de choisir de respecter le droit international humanitaire, ou pas' (2011) 93 *IRRC* 51.

versa. Another factor is the intrinsic value and moral appeal of the rules vis-à-vis individual combatants. LOAC also has the utility of helping to maintain discipline among a party's armed forces.[229] Lastly, compliance with LOAC plays an important role as part of the effort to win the 'hearts and minds', both at the national and the international level. A marked disregard of LOAC often results in diplomatic reactions and a loss of political support at the international level, and may inspire sanctions by third States and/or international organisations.[230]

C. Institutional Oversight

The ICRC occupies a special place as the guardian of LOAC.[231] The ICRC, which professes a strict neutrality and impartiality, is endowed with the task of ensuring observation of the rights of protected persons.[232] In IACs, the Geneva Conventions provide the ICRC with a legal right to access places of detention where protected persons are held.[233] It may also offer, and does offer, its services to the Parties engaged in a NIAC as part of its right of humanitarian initiative.[234]

The International Humanitarian Fact-Finding Commission (IHFFC) can investigate allegations of serious violations of LOAC when the parties to an IAC have submitted a declaration accepting the IHFFC's competence, or when they request the Commission's involvement.[235] However, so far, no State has requested the services of the IHFFC.[236] The only crack in the IHFFC's status of inactivity resulted from the request in 2017 by the OSCE to the IHFFC to lead an independent forensic investigation into an incident in Eastern Ukraine that caused the death of a paramedic and the injury of two monitors of the OSCE's Special Monitoring Mission to Ukraine (SMM). Even if the OSCE is not a State and can strictly speaking not trigger the competence of the IHFFC, the latter heeded the request, resulting in its first ever investigation.[237]

[229] For a useful overview, see Vöneky (n 228) 652.

[230] The UNSC, for instance, has repeatedly qualified gross human rights violations and war crimes as 'threats to the peace', triggering enforcement action under Chapter VII of the UN Charter. Further, see eg M Roscini, 'The United Nations Security Council and the Enforcement of International Humanitarian Law' (2010) 43 *Israel Law Review* 330–59.

[231] Further, see eg J Kellenberger, 'The Role of the International Committee of the Red Cross' in Clapham and Gaeta (n 18) 20–34; DP Forsythe and BAJ Rieffer-Flanagan, *The International Committee of the Red Cross: A Neutral Humanitarian Actor*, 2nd edn (London, Routledge, 2016).

[232] Note that the ICRC may also assume the role of a substitute of a 'Protecting Power' (see eg Art 10 GC I), but instead prefers to act on the basis of the right of humanitarian initiative conferred on it. See ICRC (2016) (n 16) para 1258.

[233] Art 126 GC III and Art 143 GC IV.

[234] Common Art 3 GCs.

[235] Art 90 AP I.

[236] Following a US attack against a hospital run by MSF in Kunduz (see above (n 132)), MSF requested that the incident be investigated by the IHFFC. However, the offer by the IHFFC to launch an investigation was not approved by the US. See eg C Harwood, 'Will the 'Sleeping Beauty' Awaken? The Kunduz Hospital Attack and the International Humanitarian Fact-Finding Commission', 15 October 2015, *EJIL: Talk!*, ejiltalk.org/will-the-sleeping-beauty-awaken-the-kunduz-hospital-attack-and-the-international-humanitarian-fact-finding-commission.

[237] IHFFC, 'International Humanitarian Fact-Finding Commission to lead an independent forensic investigation in Eastern Ukraine (Luhansk province)', 19 May 2017, ihffc.org/index.asp?page=news&mode=newsarchive. The Independent Forensic Investigation (IFI) team assembled and deployed by IHFFC concluded that the OSCE SMM was not targeted: IHFFC, 'OSCE Special Monitoring Mission was not targeted, concludes Independent Forensic Investigation into tragic incident of 23 April 2017', 7 September 2017, ibid.

NGOs also play an important role, not only in directly assisting the victims of armed conflict and lobbying for the further development of LOAC, but also in flagging abuses and raising awareness with the public at large.[238] In the same vein, the impact of mass media is not to be underestimated.

D. Peacetime Obligations

LOAC also imposes a variety of obligations that must be implemented in peacetime, and which aim at securing better protection in case an armed conflict actually breaks out. Numerous treaties not only restrict or outlaw the use of specific weapons in armed conflict, but also prohibit their production or order the destruction of existing stockpiles. In addition, with regard to the development of new weapons, Article 36 AP I obliges States to conduct a review to determine whether their employment would, in some or all circumstances, breach LOAC.[239] LOAC instruments contain several other obligations that apply (also) in time of peace but that intend to facilitate war-time compliance, such as the duty to take proper precautions by avoiding locating military objectives within or near densely populated areas, or by using a distinctive emblem.[240] Of paramount importance is the obligation to ensure the widest possible dissemination of LOAC and to provide for proper LOAC training of armed forces,[241] as well as the obligation to make available legal advisers to military commanders.[242] Clearly, a first step towards compliance with LOAC is to ensure that those taking part in hostilities are familiar with the core rules and principles.

E. State Responsibility

When violations take place, this raises the prospect of judicial enforcement.[243] First, States may be held accountable at the international level pursuant to the normal rules on State responsibility.[244] For example, in several cases, including the *Nicaragua* case[245] and the *Armed Activities* case,[246] the ICJ has found States internationally responsible for breaches of LOAC and ordered that reparation be provided.[247] Of course, such inter-State judicial enforcement is possible only when the parties to the dispute have accepted the jurisdiction of the judicial body concerned.

[238] Consider in this regard in particular the role of Amnesty International and Human Rights Watch, whose reports on LOAC violations are usually very well-researched and widely distributed and relied upon.

[239] See further ICRC, 'A Guide to the Legal Review of New Weapons, Means and Methods of Warfare: Measures to Implement Article 36 of Additional Protocol I of 1977' (2006) 88 *IRRC* 931.

[240] Art 58 AP I. See Dinstein (n87) 145.

[241] See in particular Arts 47 GC I, 48 GC II, 127 GC III, 144 GC IV, 83 AP I, Art 25 Hague Cultural Property Convention (n 128) and Art 6 CCW (n 202).

[242] Art 82 AP I.

[243] See further C Tomuschat, 'State Responsibility and the Individual Right to Compensation before National Courts' in Clapham and Gaeta (n 18) 811–39.

[244] See Chapter 12 on International Responsibility.

[245] *Nicaragua* (n 47).

[246] *Armed Activities on the Territory of the Congo* (Democratic Republic of the Congo v Uganda) [2005] ICJ Rep 116.

[247] Consider also the awards of the Eritrea Ethiopia Claims Commission (n 154). See further SD Murphy, W Kidane and TR Snider, *Litigating War: Arbitration of Civil Injury by the Eritrea-Ethiopia Commission* (Oxford, OUP, 2013).

Another question arises regarding individual victims and their families. Pursuant to Article 3 HC IV, affirmed in Article 91 AP I, a belligerent Party that violates LOAC is 'liable to pay compensation'. However, save for some exceptions, this obligation has traditionally been implemented at the inter-State level, with States being allowed to discretionarily decide on how to distribute reparation on behalf of their citizens.[248] In spite of a notable trend towards recognising an individual right to reparation,[249] and notwithstanding the occasional payment of *ex gratia* compensation, a directly enforceable right for victims of breaches of LOAC to obtain reparation has yet to emerge.[250] At the same time, it is not excluded that individual victims can rely on alternative legal bases under domestic law for damage resulting from breaches of LOAC.[251]

In Germany, for instance, there has been a string of cases on whether State conduct during armed conflicts can form the basis of claims for governmental liability under domestic law. A first series of cases revolved around Germany's involvement in NATO's decision to bomb the bridge of Varvarin in Serbia in 1999. The German Constitutional Court denied the existence of a customary right to reparation for individuals for breaches of LOAC, but left open the question of a right to reparation pursuant to German domestic law.[252] Another notable claim was brought by victims of a controversial German airstrike against two fuel trucks near the NATO camp in Kunduz, Afghanistan, in 2009, which left 142 individuals dead. In this case, the Court of First Instance in Bonn confirmed government liability on the basis of domestic law, but found that the colonel ordering the air strike had committed no breach of LOAC.[253] While the decision was upheld on appeal by the Appeals Court of Cologne,[254] the Federal Court of Justice in 2016 ruled that the domestic State liability regime does not apply to actions of the German army in the context of armed conflicts.[255]

IHRL may provide an alternative legal basis to obtain compensation. Thus, in the *Serdar Mohammed* case mentioned above (Section IV(C)), the UK Courts have held that

[248] A Muleefu, *Reparation for Victims of Collateral Damage: A Normative and Theoretical Inquiry* (Oisterwijk, Wolff Legal Publishers, 2014) 53.

[249] See further UNGA Res 60/147, 'Basic Principles and Guidelines on the Right to a Remedy and Reparation for Victims of Gross Violations of International Human Rights Law and Serious Violations of International Humanitarian Law', 16 December 2005, UN Doc A/RES/60/147, Annex, in particular paras 15–23; ILA, 'Declaration of International Law Principles on Reparation for Victims of Armed Conflict', Resolution No 2/2010, August 2010, ila-hq.org/index.php/committees; C Evans, *The Right to Reparation in International Law for Victims of Armed Conflict* (Cambridge, CUP, 2012).

[250] Consider eg *Jurisdictional Immunities of the State* (Germany v Italy; Greece intervening) [2012] ICJ Rep 99, para 108; Federal Constitutional Court (GE), *Bridge of Varvarin*, 13 August 2013, Case Nos 2 BvR 2660/06 and 2 BvR 487/07, in particular paras 45–47. See further Tomuschat (n 243). Adopting a pragmatic approach, Tomuschat suggests that the best approach would be to strive for the establishment of procedures for collective reparation under international supervision (similar to the UN Compensation Commission, established by the UNSC in the wake of Iraq's invasion of Kuwait).

[251] Note that victims may also be able to obtain some form of (limited) reparation from the ICC's Trust Fund pursuant to criminal proceedings before the ICC (see Art 75 Rome Statute). See further C McCarthy, *Reparations and Victim Support in the International Criminal Court* (Cambridge, CUP, 2012).

[252] Federal Constitutional Court (GE), *Bridge of Varvarin* (n 250).

[253] Regional Court Bonn (GE), *In re Kunduz*, 11 December 2013, Case No 1 O 460/11. See EV Henn, 'The Development of German Jurisprudence on Individual Compensation for Victims of Armed Conflicts: The *Kunduz* Case' (2014) 12 *JICJ* 615.

[254] Higher Regional Court Cologne (GE), *In re Kunduz*, 30 April 2015, Case No 7 U 4/14.

[255] Federal Court of Justice (GE), *In re Kunduz*, 6 October 2016, Case No III ZR 140/15. The judgment also confirms that international law does not confer upon individuals the right to claim compensation for breaches of LOAC and treats questions of compensation as purely interstate matters pursuant to Art 91 AP I. A complaint against the Court's judgment was lodged before the German Constitutional Court (pending at the time of writing).

the claimant – an individual detained in contravention of LOAC by British armed forces operating in Afghanistan – had an 'enforceable right to compensation' under Article 5(5) ECHR.[256]

In the end, the prospect of obtaining individual reparation before a national court may vary depending on the domestic legal bases, the integration of international law in the domestic legal system concerned, and the propensity of national judges to scrutinise the conduct of the armed forces.[257] It must, moreover, be recalled that it would be highly difficult for such claims to be heard before the national courts of third States, especially since the ICJ has confirmed that the doctrine of State immunity also applies to war crimes and crimes against humanity (see Chapter 11, Section II(C)). Of course, the doctrine of State immunity does not apply before regional human rights courts. Where a regional human rights court has competence, victims of breaches of LOAC may try to seek redress before that court, where appropriate invoking the extraterritorial application of the human rights instrument concerned. The ECtHR in particular has repeatedly condemned States for breaches of human rights committed as part of military operations abroad. In *Jaloud v the Netherlands*, for instance, the Court held that the Netherlands breached the procedural obligation of Article 2 ECHR by failing properly to investigate a shooting incident at an Iraqi military checkpoint, and ordered it to pay damages to the father of the Iraqi national killed in the incident.[258]

Furthermore, a State may incur liability not only for direct breaches of LOAC, but also for its involvement in breaches committed by other States. First, the former State's involvement may qualify as an autonomous breach of its human rights obligations.[259] Second, also as a matter of primary law, the acts concerned may qualify as a breach of the duty to 'respect and ensure respect' with LOAC.[260] Third, as a matter of secondary law, third States can in principle incur State responsibility for aiding or assisting in the commission of breaches of LOAC in the sense of Article 16 of the Draft Articles on State Responsibility (see Chapter 12, Section III(C)).

F. Individual Criminal Responsibility

Holding States accountable for breaches of LOAC is one thing; holding individual perpetrators criminally responsible is quite another. The development of international criminal

[256] High Court of Justice (UK), *Serdar Mohammed* (n77) para 357; Supreme Court (UK), *Serdar Mohammed* (n 189) para 111.

[257] Note that in many national jurisdictions there are possible 'escape routes' that national courts may (or must) use to refrain from scrutinising combat operations of the armed forces. In the UK, for instance, the principle of 'combat immunity' prevents courts from adjudicating disputes on occurrences during actual fighting. See eg Supreme Court (UK), *Smith v Ministry of Defence* [2013] UKSC 41, [2013] WLR 239.

[258] *Jaloud v the Netherlands* (n80). For other examples, see the periodically updated factsheet of the ECtHR Press Unit on 'Armed Conflicts': echr.coe.int/Documents/FS_Armed_conflicts_ENG.pdf.

[259] In two rulings of 2014 the ECtHR found Poland guilty of breaching a number of ECHR provisions by hosting a CIA black site and by otherwise participating in the US programme of secret detention and extraordinary renditions: see *Al Nashiri v Poland* App no 28761/11 (ECtHR, 24 July 2014); *Husayn (Abu Zubaydah) v Poland* App no 7511/13 (ECtHR, 24 July 2014).

[260] Common Art 1 GCs and Art 1(1) AP I. Further, see eg F Kalshoven, 'The Undertaking to Respect and Ensure Respect in All Circumstances: From Tiny Seed to Ripening Fruit' (1999) 2 *Yearbook of International Humanitarian Law* 3. In the *Nicaragua* case, the ICJ found that the US had breached the duty to 'ensure respect' with LOAC by producing and disseminating to the contras a manual on psychological operations encouraging the 'neutralisation' of certain targets, such as judges and police officers, in breach of LOAC; *Nicaragua* (n 47) para 219.

law is indeed also of key importance, not only for the development of LOAC,[261] but also for its enforcement.[262]

According to the Geneva Conventions and AP I, States are under an obligation to criminalise the so-called 'grave breaches' enumerated in the aforementioned instruments, and to prosecute and punish offenders.[263] The prosecution of war crimes is first and foremost a task for the Host State of the offender. At the same time, States often lack the capability or the political will to prosecute suspected war criminals. They may also lack the will to comply with their subsidiary duty to extradite suspects whom they do not themselves wish to prosecute. In such scenarios, as long as a suspect is not an acting Head of State, Head of Government or Minister of Foreign Affairs (see Chapter 11, Section III on the immunity of foreign State officials), third States may initiate criminal prosecution, mainly on the basis of the passive personality principle or – most likely – on the basis of domestic legislation enabling the exercise of universal jurisdiction in respect of certain crimes (see Chapter 9, Section II on the principles of prescriptive criminal jurisdiction).

For instance, in the wake of the conflict in Syria and Iraq, domestic courts in some European States have initiated prosecutions for war crimes against so-called 'foreign fighters' with their respective nationality on the one hand, and refugees with Syrian/Iraqi nationality on the other. In Germany, courts have exercised jurisdiction based on the principle of active personality to convict German foreign fighters of the war crime of committing outrages upon personal dignity.[264] Following an exercise of universal jurisdiction, a member of the Iraqi armed forces was convicted of the same charge.[265] Also in Finland, Iraqi refugees have been convicted of the war crime of committing outrages upon personal dignity.[266] Alleged members of Islamic State were prosecuted for, but acquitted, of having wilfully killed persons *hors de combat*.[267] In Sweden, lastly, Syrian refugees have been convicted of 'crimes under international law' because they participated in the torture and extrajudicial killing of persons *hors de combat*.[268]

Furthermore, over the past 25 years, a variety of international criminal tribunals have been set up, as well as a number of mixed or 'hybrid' criminal courts. Since the entry into force of the Rome Statute in 2002, the permanent International Criminal Court (ICC)

[261] As mentioned above (Section II(A)), the development of international criminal law has contributed indirectly to narrowing the gap in protection between IACs and NIACs by identifying a variety of acts that qualify as international crimes in both types of armed conflict. More generally, the case law of the ad hoc criminal tribunals and of the ICC has an important impact on the development and interpretation of LOAC. Consider eg N Ousman, *The Contribution of the Special Court for Sierra Leone to the Development of International Humanitarian Law* (Berlin, Duncker & Humblot, 2013).

[262] See eg N Grono and A de Courcy Wheeler, 'The Deterrent Effect of the ICC on the Commission of International Crimes by Government Leaders' in C Stahn (ed), *The Law and Practice of the International Criminal Court* (Oxford, OUP, 2015) 1225–44.

[263] On the special responsibility of commanders, see eg G Mettraux, *The Law of Command Responsibility* (Oxford, OUP, 2009).

[264] eg Higher Regional Court Frankfurt am Mein (GE), *Prosecutor v Aria L*, 12 July 2016, Case No 5-3 StE 2/16 – 4 – 1/16; Higher Regional Court Frankfurt am Mein (GE), *Prosecutor v Abdelkarim El B*, 8 November 2016, Case No 5-3 StE 4/16 – 4 – 3/16.

[265] Court of Appeal Berlin (GE), *Prosecutor v Rami K*, 1 March 2017, Case No (2A) 172 OJs 26/16 (3/16).

[266] District Court Pirkanmaa (FI), *Prosecutor v Jebbar Salman Amar*, 18 March 2016, Case No R 16/1304; District Court Kanta-Hame (FI), *Prosecutor v Hadi Habeeb Hilal*, 22 March 2016, Case No R 16/214.

[267] District Court Pirkanmaa (FI), *Prosecutor v Ahmad Shhab Hamad and Daham Shhab Hamad*, 24 May 2017, Case No R 16/6930 (at the time of writing, the case is still under appeal).

[268] Court of Appeal Svea (SE), *Public Prosecutor v Mouhannad Droubi*, 5 August 2016, Case No B 4770-16 (torture); District Court Stockholm (SE), *Public Prosecutor v Haisam Omar Sakhanh*, 16 February 2017, Case No B 3787-16 (extrajudicial killing).

has become operational. The material jurisdiction of the ICC extends inter alia to a variety of war crimes listed in Article 8 of the Rome Statute. These crimes relate to IACs (Article 8(2)(a)–(b)) as well as NIACs (Article 8(2)(c)–(f)), albeit that the lists applicable to the respective types of conflict are not identical.[269] The development of international criminal law is addressed in greater detail in Chapter 17.

G. Further Initiatives

In spite of the welcome advance in international criminal law in recent years, and in spite of the increased human rights scrutiny of military conduct, in particular by the ECtHR, there is much room for improving the implementation and enforcement of LOAC. Several initiatives have been taken to remedy this situation. The EU, for instance, has adopted a set of 'Guidelines on Promoting Compliance with International Humanitarian Law', which lists various possible means of promoting LOAC compliance, such as recourse to restrictive measures (sanctions) or LOAC training in third countries.[270]

The ICRC has published a manual on 'domestic implementation of international humanitarian law'[271] together with a database of national implementation measures,[272] in order to assist policy-makers, legislators and other stakeholders in adhering to LOAC. Together with the Swiss government, the ICRC organised a major consultation process between 2012 and 2015 to address the institutional vacuum in the area of LOAC implementation, in particular through the possible establishment of a regular conference of State Parties to the Geneva Conventions or a similar type of institutional forum in which States can discuss the application of LOAC and the related challenges.[273] Nonetheless, a joint Swiss-ICRC draft resolution to this end failed to attract sufficient State support at the 32nd International Conference of the Red Cross and Red Crescent.[274]

VII. Concluding Remarks

LOAC is a relatively old branch of law – older than IHRL, notably – that has grown throughout the adoption of numerous conventions. Nonetheless, it is clear that the core of modern LOAC is formed by the four 1949 Geneva Conventions and their two 1977 Additional Protocols. While the latter are supplemented by several more 'sectoral' conventions

[269] Note that while the case law of the ad hoc criminal tribunals and the ICC as well as the ICC Statute have indirectly contributed to the development of the law of NIAC (see above (n 261)), inasmuch as an amendment of the ICC Statute with a view to expanding the list of war crimes in NIACs is unlikely, to some extent, the ICC Statute also freezes the law of NIAC.

[270] Council of the EU, 'Updated European Union Guidelines on promoting compliance with international humanitarian law', 2009/C 303/06, OJ C303/12.

[271] ICRC, 'The Domestic Implementation of International Humanitarian Law: A Manual', April 2013, icrc.org/eng/assets/files/publications/icrc-002-4028.pdf.

[272] The National Implementation Database is available at icrc.org/ihl-nat.

[273] See ICRC, 'Strengthening compliance with international humanitarian law (IHL): The work of the ICRC and the Swiss government', 21 April 2015, icrc.org/eng/what-we-do/other-activities/development-ihl/strengthening-legal-protection-compliance.htm.

[274] ICRC, 'No agreement by States on mechanism to strengthen compliance with rules of war', 10 December 2015, icrc.org/en/document/no-agreement-states-mechanism-strengthen-compliance-rules-war.

dealing with issues such as the use of a certain kind of weapons, customary international law is also an important source of obligations, in particular in NIACs. Lastly, LOAC rests upon a few cardinal principles, especially the principle of distinction and the principle of unnecessary suffering.

The very idea of LOAC is intertwined with its scope of application: it aims to protect certain persons in a certain situation, ie one of armed conflict. Whether an armed conflict exists is a matter of fact. An IAC exists whenever there is any resort to armed force between States; NIACs require a certain degree of intensity, while the non-State armed group(s) involved must show a sufficient level of organisation. In addition, for there to be a NIAC under AP II, the non-State armed group must have a certain degree of control over the territory of the State it is fighting. The geographical application of LOAC is limited to the territory of the State(s) on which the armed conflict is occurring, while temporally, it applies until the general close of military operations (IAC) or until a peaceful settlement is reached (NIAC). Also IHRL continues to apply during situations of armed conflict. In situations where both branches of law govern a certain matter, the applicable rule must be determined and/or interpreted by reference to the *lex specialis* principle.

Pursuant to the principle of distinction, warring parties must differentiate between combatants and civilians. In an IAC, combatants are members of the armed forces belonging to a party to the conflict, additionally including those members of a non-State armed group with a continuous combat function in a NIAC. They may be the target of an attack. Civilians, on the other hand, may not be targeted, except if and for such time as they take a direct part in hostilities. A similar distinction is made between civilian objects and military objectives. Indiscriminate attacks are prohibited, while every attack must comply with the principle of proportionality. Lastly, some categories of persons and objects, notably including combatants *hors de combat* and medical personnel and units, enjoy special protection and may not be attacked, unless more stringent conditions are satisfied.

The distinction between combatants and civilians not only has consequences during the conduct of hostilities, but also when persons are *hors de combat*. Provided that they meet the relevant requirements, in an IAC, lawful combatants in the hands of the enemy enjoy POW status: they cannot be punished for their mere participation in hostilities, but can be detained until the cessation of hostilities. Still in an IAC, civilians in the hands of the enemy are 'protected persons' in the sense of GC IV and benefit from its protection. They may only be detained for imperative reasons of security. A third category of 'unlawful combatants' falling in between the cracks of GC III (POWs) and GC IV (civilians) is generally rejected. Many of the same rules apply also in a NIAC, be it through the application of AP II or customary international law. However, there is a notable gap as regards the issue of detention. While the ICRC considers that in NIACs, there is also an inherent right to detain, this position has been rejected by UK courts. It appears that, at least for now, IHRL is the *lex specialis* governing this issue.

As to the means and methods of warfare, the options for parties to a conflict are not unlimited. In particular, the principle of avoiding unnecessary suffering and the prohibition of indiscriminate attacks must be complied with. Even then, the possession, production and transfer of several kinds of weapons is restricted by specific weapon conventions, which sometimes also restrict and/or prohibit the use of these weapons.

Eventually, the problem of LOAC is not so much the lack of appropriate rules, but the lack of enforcement of the existing rules. Due to certain compliance-inducing factors, parties to an armed conflict do have an incentive to comply with LOAC. There is oversight notably by (other) States, the ICRC, NGOs and the public at large. Moreover, peacetime obligations resting upon States, such as the obligation to disseminate knowledge about LOAC as widely as possible, must facilitate compliance with LOAC in war time. Lastly, both States and individuals can legally be held responsible for LOAC violations. Still, LOAC's enforcement remains its 'Achilles' heel'. As evidenced by contemporary armed conflicts, there is much to be done about LOAC's implementation. However, the rejection of the recent initiative of the ICRC and the Swiss government to establish a regular conference of States Parties to the Geneva Conventions illustrates that States are very reluctant to take on more obligations in this regard. As a result, LOAC is increasingly enforced through IHRL and human rights bodies, notably including the ECtHR, to be discussed in the following chapter.

Bibliography

Clapham, A and Gaeta, P (eds), *The Oxford Handbook of International Law in Armed Conflict* (Oxford, OUP, 2014).
Clapham, A, Gaeta P and Sassòli, M (eds), *The 1949 Geneva Conventions: A Commentary* (Oxford, OUP, 2015).
Crawford, E and Pert, A, *International Humanitarian Law* (Cambridge, CUP, 2015).
Cullen, A, *The Concept of Non-International Armed Conflict in International Humanitarian Law* (Cambridge, CUP, 2010).
David, E, *Principes de droit des conflits armés*, 5th edn (Brussels, Bruylant, 2012).
Dinstein, Y, *Non-International Armed Conflicts in International Law* (Cambridge, CUP, 2014).
Dinstein, Y, *The Conduct of Hostilities under the Law of International Armed Conflict*, 2nd edn (Cambridge, CUP, 2010).
Fleck, D, *The Handbook of International Humanitarian Law*, 3rd edn (Oxford, OUP, 2013).
Gill, T and Fleck, D (eds), *Handbook of the International Law of Military Operations*, 2nd edn (Oxford, OUP, 2015).
Sassòli, M, Bouvier, AA and Quintin, A, *How Does Law Protect in War? Cases, Documents and Teaching Materials on Contemporary Practice in International Humanitarian Law*, 3rd edn (Geneva, ICRC, 2011).
Sivakumaran, S, *The Law of Non-International Armed Conflict* (Oxford, OUP, 2012).
Solis, GD, *The Law of Armed Conflict* (Cambridge, CUP, 2010).
White, ND and Henderson, C (eds), *Research Handbook on International Conflict and Security Law* (Cheltenham, Edward Elgar, 2013).
Wouters, J, De Man, P and Verlinden, N, *Armed Conflicts and the Law* (Antwerp, Intersentia, 2016).

Further Reading

Benvenisti, E, *The International Law of Occupation*, 2nd edn (Oxford, OUP, 2012).
Boothby, WH, *The Law of Targeting* (Oxford, OUP, 2012).
Boothby, WH, *Weapons and the Law of Armed Conflict*, 2nd edn (Oxford, OUP, 2016).

Crawford, E, *Identifying the Enemy: Civilian Participation in Armed Conflict* (Oxford, OUP, 2015).

Debuf, E, *Captured in War: Lawful Internment in Armed Conflict* (Oxford, Hart, 2013).

Dinstein, Y, *The International Law of Belligerent Occupation* (Cambridge, CUP, 2009).

Dörmann, K, 'The Legal Situation of Unlawful/Unprivileged Combatants' (2003) 85 *IRRC* 45.

Evans, C, *The Right to Reparation in International Law for Victims of Armed Conflict* (Cambridge, CUP, 2012).

Forsythe, DP and Rieffer-Flanagan, BAJ, *The International Committee of the Red Cross: A Neutral Humanitarian Actor*, 2nd edn (London, Routledge, 2016).

Goodman, R, 'The Detention of Civilians in Armed Conflict' (2009) 103 *AJIL* 48.

Goodman, R, 'The Power to Kill or Capture Enemy Combatants' (2013) 24 *EJIL* 819.

Heintschel von Heinegg, W, *The Implementation and Enforcement of International Humanitarian Law* (Farnham, Ashgate, 2012).

Hill-Cawthorne, L, *Detention in Non-International Armed Conflict* (Oxford, OUP, 2016).

Jachec-Neale, A, *The Concept of Military Objectives in International Law and Practice* (London, Routledge, 2015).

Kalshoven, F, *Belligerent Reprisals*, 2nd edn (Leiden, Nijhoff, 2005).

Kalshoven, F, 'The Undertaking to Respect and Ensure Respect in All Circumstances: From Tiny Seed to Ripening Fruit' (1999) 2 *Yearbook of International Humanitarian Law* 3.

Kila, JD and Zeidler, JA, *Cultural Heritage in the Crosshairs: Protecting Cultural Property During Conflict* (Leiden, Brill, 2013).

Kolb, R and Vité, S, *Le droit de l'occupation militaire : perspectives historiques et enjeux juridiques actuels* (Brussels, Bruylant, 2009).

Koutroulis, V, *Le début et la fin de l'application du droit de l'occupation* (Paris, Pedone, 2010).

Oberleitner, G, *Human Rights in Armed Conflict: Law, Practice, Policy* (Cambridge, CUP, 2015).

O'Connell, ME (ed), *What is War? An Investigation in the Wake of 9/11* (Leiden, Nijhoff, 2012).

O'Keefe, R, *The Protection of Cultural Property in Armed Conflict* (Cambridge, CUP, 2006).

Rayfuse, R, *War and the Environment: New Approaches to Protecting the Environment in Relation to Armed Conflict* (Leiden, Nijhoff, 2014).

Ronzitti, N, *The Law of Naval Warfare: A Collection of Agreements and Documents with Commentaries* (Dordrecht, Nijhoff, 1988).

Waschefort, G, *International Law and Child Soldiers* (Oxford, Hart, 2015).

Wilmshurst, ES (ed), *International Law and the Classification of Conflicts* (Oxford, OUP, 2012).

16

Human Rights Law

I. Introduction

Human rights are fundamental rights that are inherent to every human being and attach to the human person's very dignity.[1] As they are universal, human rights intrinsically relate to international law. They are a matter for the international community, laid down in numerous international and regional treaties and soft law instruments, the implementation of which is monitored by the respective international and regional organisations or bodies to which they relate. In addition, human rights are part of customary international law, while some human rights have reached the status of *jus cogens* norms.

This chapter aims at introducing the main international human rights regimes that operate at global and regional levels today. The first section provides a brief historical overview of the emergence of international human rights law. Sections II–V provide an overview of the *global* human rights instruments adopted under the auspices of the UN, while Section VI elaborates on their monitoring mechanisms. Section VII discusses the main UN intergovernmental body that deals with human rights, ie, the Human Rights Council (HRC). Section VIII briefly touches upon the Office of the UN High Commissioner for Human Rights (OHCHR). Together, Sections II–VIII give a comprehensive overview of what is usually called the 'UN human rights system'. The last sections discuss the most important *regional* human rights mechanisms, with a special focus on Europe. They respectively discuss the Council of Europe (Section IX), the EU (Section X) and the American and African (Section XI) human rights system. To highlight the important position of the ECHR and the pioneering role of the ECtHR and its case law, a more substantive discussion of the most important human rights is reserved for Section IX.

A. Historical Overview

Before the twentieth century, the theme of human rights was a matter that fell almost exclusively within the sovereign jurisdiction of States. Some of the nineteenth century

[1] On the universality of human rights, see Subsection (B).

forerunners to the international system of human rights protection were the minimum standard of treatment for foreigners, the movement towards the abolition of the slave trade and the emergence of certain norms of international humanitarian law. After the First World War, the situation gradually started to change with the protection of national minorities in the League of Nations and the work of the International Labour Organization (ILO) on social rights and standards. However, the major breakthrough of international human rights law only occurred after the Second World War with the adoption and implementation of the UN Charter.[2]

Partially as a reaction to the atrocities committed by the Nazi regime, which had demonstrated that human rights could not be left exclusively to nation States, it was made one of the purposes of the UN '[t]o achieve international co-operation [...] in promoting and encouraging respect for human rights and for fundamental freedoms for all without distinction as to race, sex, language or religion'.[3] Article 55(c) of the UN Charter tasks the UN with 'promot[ing] universal respect for, and observance of, human rights and fundamental freedoms for all without distinction as to race, sex, language or religion'. Moreover, pursuant to Article 56 of the UN Charter, '[a]ll Members pledge themselves to take joint and separate action in co-operation with the Organization for the achievement of the purposes set forth in Article 55'. These provisions ultimately instigated the adoption of a large number of global human rights treaties and their monitoring mechanisms within the framework of the UN.[4]

In its efforts within the area of human rights, the UN has often encountered strong resistance by States insisting on their sovereignty. These States typically rely on Article 2(7) of the UN Charter, according to which the UN does not have the competence 'to intervene in matters which are essentially within the domestic jurisdiction of any State'. Over time, it has however come to be accepted that Article 2(7) does not mean that the UN should remain indifferent in situations where grave and widespread violations of human rights occur (see also above, pp. 194 and 257).[5]

B. Universal Declaration of Human Rights

The UN Charter fell short of providing a definition or catalogue of human rights. It therefore did not come as a surprise that the UN's first initiative within the field of human rights was to establish the Universal Declaration of Human Rights (UDHR). The UDHR was drafted by the UN Commission on Human Rights and adopted on 10 December 1948 by the UN General Assembly with merely eight abstentions and no dissenting votes.[6]

[2] For an overview of the history of human rights law, see eg E Bates 'History' in D Moeckli et al (eds), *International Human Rights Law* (Oxford, OUP, 2014) 15–32; W Osiatyński, 'The Historical Development of Human Rights' in S Sheeran and N Rodley, *Routledge Handbook of International Human Rights Law* (London, Routledge, 2013) 9–24; MH Randall, 'The History of International Human Rights Law' in R Kolb and G Gaggioli (eds), *Research Handbook on Human Rights and Humanitarian Law* (Cheltenham, Edward Elgar, 2013) 3–34; and further, CNJ Roberts, *The Contentious History of the International Bill of Human Rights* (Cambridge, CUP, 2014).

[3] Art 1(3) UN Charter.

[4] These treaties and their monitoring mechanisms are discussed below. For more information, see the webpage of the OHCHR: www.ohchr.org/EN/HRBodies/Pages/TreatyBodies.aspx.

[5] See further, J Donnelly, 'State Sovereignty and International Human Rights' (2014) 28 *Ethics and International Affairs* 225; J Shen, 'National Sovereignty and Human Rights in a Positive Law Context' (2000) 26 *Brooklyn Journal of International Law* 417.

[6] UNGA Res 3/217, 10 December 1948, UN Doc A/RES/3/217A. On the genesis of the UDHR see MA Glendon, *A World Made New: Eleanor Roosevelt and the Universal Declaration of Human Rights* (New York,

The UDHR is based on the fundamental premise that '[a]ll human beings are born free and equal in dignity and rights' (Article 1). The Declaration contains 30 rights and freedoms, ranging from classic rights, such as the right to life and the prohibition of torture and slavery, to socio-economic rights, such as the right to education and the protection of intellectual property. The different rights and freedoms contained in the Declaration can be more or less classified into five categories. The first category comprises the inherently personal freedoms: these are the rights and freedoms that are inseparably connected to every person. They concern, amongst others, the right to life (Article 3), the right not to be held in slavery (Article 4), the right not to be subjected to torture (Article 5), and the right to equal protection before the law (Article 7). A second category consists of the rights and freedoms that guarantee personal safety. Some examples of these rights are the right not to be subjected to arbitrary arrest (Article 9), the right to be presumed innocent until proven guilty (Article 11), and the right to seek asylum in another country (Article 14). The rights concerning the political life of the individual, such as the right to freedom of opinion (Article 19), the right to take part in the government of one's country (Article 21(1)) and the right to participate in elections to choose said government (Article 21(3)) constitute the third category of rights and freedoms. The fourth category concerns economic and social rights, such as the right to own property (Article 17), the right to an adequate standard of living (Article 25(1)) and the right to participate freely in cultural life (Article 27). The final category includes the rights concerned with the social and legal life of the individual, such as the right to leave any country (Article 13), the right to a nationality (Article 15) and the right to marry and found a family (Article 16).

Notwithstanding its significant moral and political value, it is important to point out that the UDHR is only a recommendation of the UN General Assembly. From a formal point of view, it is therefore not legally binding: as its preamble makes clear, it constitutes a 'common standard of achievement' (Preamble). Nevertheless, many of its provisions nowadays reflect customary international law.[7] Moreover, certain provisions, such as the prohibition of torture and of slavery, have reached *jus cogens* status.[8] At the very least, the UDHR gives a particularly authoritative interpretation of the human rights obligations of UN Member States (see also above, p 165).

Although the universality of human rights is emphasised by the UDHR, some States have asserted that the concept of human rights in the Declaration is a primarily Western concept and argue in favour of cultural relativism about human rights.[9] Nevertheless, the World Conference on Human Rights of 1993 in Vienna agreed that:

> All human rights are universal, indivisible and interdependent and interrelated. The international community must treat human rights globally in a fair and equal manner, on the same footing, and with the same emphasis. While the significance of national and regional particularities and various

Random House, 2001); J Morsink, *The Universal Declaration of Human Rights: Origins, Drafting and Intent* (Philadelphia, University of Philadelphia Press, 1999); WA Schabas, *The Universal Declaration of Human Rights: The 'Travaux Préparatoires'* (Cambridge, CUP, 2013).

[7] O De Schutter, *International Human Rights Law: Cases, Materials, Commentary*, 2nd edn (Cambridge, CUP, 2015) 63.

[8] For the prohibition of torture, see *Questions relating to the Obligation to Prosecute or Extradite* (Belgium v Senegal) [2012] ICJ Rep 422, para 99.

[9] See further O Bring, 'The Notion of Human Rights and the Issue of Cultural Relativism' in J Crawford et al (eds), *The International Legal Order: Current Needs and Possible Responses Essays in Honour of Djamchid Momtaz* (Leiden, Brill Nijhoff, 2017) 544–58; J Donnelly, 'Cultural Relativism and Universal Human Rights' (1984) 6 *Human Rights Quarterly* 400; M Freeman, 'Universalism of Human Rights and Cultural Relativism' in Sheeran and Rodley (n 2) 49–62.

> historical, cultural and religious backgrounds must be borne in mind, it is the duty of States, regardless of their political, economic and cultural systems, to promote and protect all human rights and fundamental freedoms.[10]

This language resonates with Article 21(1) TEU, pursuant to which

> The Union's action on the international scene shall be guided by the principles which have inspired its own creation, development and enlargement, and which it seeks to advance in the wider world: democracy, the rule of law, the universality and indivisibility of human rights and fundamental freedoms, respect for human dignity, the principles of equality and solidarity, and respect for the principles of the United Nations Charter and international law.[11]

II. Three Generations of Human Rights

A. The First and Second Generation

Because of the formally non-binding character of the UDHR and the absence of any monitoring mechanism, the UN Commission on Human Rights has continued its work by further developing draft versions of international human rights treaties. However, after the Second World War, the ideological differences between the 'capitalist world' on the one hand and the 'socialist bloc' on the other hand continued to grow. Whereas the former emphasised the importance of civil and political rights or 'first generation' rights, the latter focused on the importance of economic and social rights or 'second generation' rights. Eventually, the decision was made to draft two treaties, both of which would take into account the different characteristics of the two categories of rights. On the one hand, a covenant on civil and political rights would mainly concern rights that, in essence, impose upon a government the *immediate* obligation to *refrain* from committing certain acts (negative obligations). These rights and freedoms contrast with economic, social and cultural rights, which in the first place require an active *intervention* on the part of the government in view of their *progressive* realisation (positive obligations). However, this distinction is far from absolute. Governments also need to intervene actively to ensure the (progressive) realisation of civil and political rights, for instance by ensuring an effective court system. On the other hand, they should (immediately) refrain from intervening with economic, social and cultural rights where such an intervention would amount to a violation thereof (eg, with respect to the right to form a trade union).[12]

Eventually, both treaties were adopted by the Commission on 16 April 1954 and subsequently sent to the Third Committee of the UN General Assembly. Nonetheless, it took 12 years before the International Covenant on Civil and Political Rights (ICCPR) and the International Covenant on Economic, Social and Cultural Rights (ICESCR) were adopted

[10] The World Conference on Human Rights, 'Vienna Declaration and Programme of Action', 12 July 1993, UN Doc A/CONF.157/23, Section I, para 5.

[11] See J Wouters 'The EU's Post-Lisbon legal and Institutional Architecture on Human Rights and Democracy' in F Gómez, C Churucca and J Wouters (eds) *EU Human Rights and Democratization Policies: Achievements and Challenges* (London, Routledge, 2018) 27.

[12] See T van Boven, 'Categories of Rights' in Moeckli et al (n 2) 143–56; see also D Shelton and A Gould, 'Positive and Negative Obligations' in D Shelton (ed), *The Oxford Handbook of International Human Rights Law* (Oxford, OUP, 2013) 562–84.

on 16 December 1966, and an additional ten years before they both entered into force internationally in 1976. Today, they have 172 and 169 States Parties respectively, including all EU Member States.

i. The International Covenant on Civil and Political Rights

The ICCPR's main purpose is to further specify the rights and freedoms contained in the UDHR and to incorporate them into an instrument with legally binding force. The Covenant predominantly recognises classic civil and political rights, including the most fundamental ones such as the right to life (Article 6) and the prohibition of torture (Article 7). Other prominent rights include the right to liberty (Article 9) and the right to a fair trial (Article 14). As the ICCPR was adopted in times of decolonisation, there is also a strong emphasis on the right to self-determination, as well as the right to freely dispose of natural wealth and resources.[13]

Not all rights contained in the ICCPR are absolute. Indeed, some civil and political rights allow for *restrictions* or *limitations*. For example, the right to freedom of movement 'shall not be subject to any restrictions except those which are provided by law, are necessary to protect national security, public order (*ordre public*), public health or morals or the rights and freedoms of others'.[14] However, this does not give States Parties a 'carte blanche'. Generally, any measures affecting a right that can be limited must pursue one of the enumerated – but admittedly broadly formulated – legitimate aims, and be necessary for and proportionate to the achievement of that aim. Apart from restrictions or limitations, Article 4 provides for the possibility to *derogate* from certain rights contained in the ICCPR 'in time of public emergency which threatens the life of the nation', 'to the extent strictly required by the exigencies of the situation'. This implies that measures derogating from the provisions of the ICCPR must be exceptional, temporary and proportionate to the achievement of their aim. In addition, a state of public emergency must be officially proclaimed. Even then, there are certain rights that cannot be derogated from under any circumstances (eg the right to life).[15] These rights can be considered to be a set of 'core' or 'non-derogable' human rights.[16]

On 15 December 1989, a (Second[17]) Optional Protocol[18] to the ICCPR was adopted by the UN General Assembly. This Protocol aims to abolish the death penalty. It entered into force on 11 July 1991, and it currently has 85 State Parties, including all EU Member States.

ii. International Covenant on Economic, Social and Cultural Rights

In contrast to the UDHR, which contained only six provisions dealing with social rights, the ICESCR is much more elaborate on that matter. Amongst other rights, it recognises

[13] Art 1 ICCPR.

[14] ibid, Art 12(3).

[15] ibid, Art 4(2).

[16] van Boven (n 12) 150. See further Human Rights Committee (HRCttee), 'General Comment No 29: Derogations During a State of Emergency', 31 August 2001, UN Doc CCPR/C/21/Rev1/Add11. On derogations more generally, see further, EM Hafner-Burton, LR Helfer and CJ Fariss, 'Emergency and Escape: Explaining Derogations from Human Rights Treaties' in EJ Criddle (ed), *Human Rights in Emergencies* (New York, CUP, 2016) 83–123.

[17] Second Optional Protocol to the International Covenant on Civil and Political Rights, aiming at the abolition of the death penalty (adopted 15 December 1989, entered into force 11 July 1991) 1642 UNTS 414.

[18] The First Optional Protocol to the International Covenant on Civil and Political Rights (adopted 16 December 1966, 23 March 1976) 999 UNTS 171, concerned the individual complaints procedure before the HRCttee (on the individual complaints mechanism, see below, Section VI(D)).

the right to work (Article 6), the right to enjoy just and favourable working conditions (Article 7), the right to social security (Article 9), the right to an adequate standard of living (Article 11), the right to enjoy the highest standard of physical and mental health (Article 12), the right to education (Article 13) and the right to take part in cultural life (Article 15). Unlike the obligation to (immediately) respect the rights and freedoms in the ICCPR,[19] the ICESCR requires active intervention of a government 'to the maximum of its available resources, with a view to achieving progressively the full realisation of the rights recognised in the present Covenant'.[20] Consequently, the provisions of the ICESCR do not easily lend themselves to immediate judicial application.[21]

Also unlike the ICCPR, the ICESCR does not contain absolute rights. Accordingly, it contains a general permission to *limit* the rights contained therein in Article 4, which provides that 'the State may subject such rights only to such limitations as are determined by law only in so far as this may be compatible with the nature of these rights and solely for the purpose of promoting the general welfare in a democratic society'. In a similar vein, and again unlike the ICCPR, the ICESCR does not contain a derogation clause.[22]

B. A Third Generation

i. Collective or Peoples' Rights

In the second half of the twentieth century, so-called 'collective rights', 'people's rights' or 'third generation rights' were added to the spectrum of individual rights. Initially, States only recognised individual rights, such as the right to life, the right to physical integrity and the right to freedom of opinion. It is only recently that States have come to recognise rights that are not granted to individuals separately, but rather to a group of persons, such as environmental and developmental rights, the right to self-determination and the rights of minorities and indigenous peoples. As noted in Chapter 5, Section III(D), regarding the right to self-determination, the concept of a 'people' is not authoritatively defined, but is generally considered to refer to a group of persons characterised by a degree of homogeneity in terms of their language, culture, religion, ethnicity and/or history. Accordingly, 'peoples tend to be seen as large, anonymous human groups possessing certain national characteristics', while what those national characteristics exactly are is left open.[23] The process of the recognition of collective rights is not self-evident, as is illustrated in particular by the right to self-determination.[24] In a similar vein, to make sure that any separatist ambitions that minorities may pursue are not legitimised, minorities, as collectives, are often not referred to as beneficiaries of rights. Instead, human rights instruments usually refer to the 'persons

[19] Art 2 ICCPR.

[20] Art 2(1) ICESCR.

[21] See further Committee on Economic, Social and Cultural Rights (CESCR), 'General Comment No 3: The Nature of States Parties' Obligations', 1 January 1991, UN Doc E/1991/23; 'General Comment No 9: The Domestic Application of the Covenant', 3 December 1998, UN Doc E/C12/1998/24; F Coomans, *Justiciability of Economic and Social Rights: Experiences from Domestic Systems* (Antwerp, Intersentia, 2006); MJ Dennis and DP Stewart, 'Justiciability of Economic, Social, and Cultural Rights: Should There Be an International Complaints Mechanism to Adjudicate the Rights to Food, Water, Housing, and Health?' (2004) 98 *AJIL* 462.

[22] See further A Müller, 'Limitations to and Derogations from Economic, Social and Cultural Rights' (2009) 9 *Human Rights Law Review* 557.

[23] J Summers, *Peoples and International Law*, 2nd edn (Leiden, Martinus Nijhoff, 2014) 7.

[24] For a detailed discussion of the right to self-determination, see Chapter 5 on States, Section III(B).

belonging to such minorities'.[25] From a human rights perspective, the rights of minorities and indigenous people deserve further attention.[26]

ii. The Rights of Minorities

There is no universally agreed definition of a minority. The most widely accepted definition is the one prepared by Francesco Capotorti, then Special Rapporteur on Prevention of Discrimination and Protection of Minorities. He defined a minority as follows:

> A group numerically inferior to the rest of the population of a State, in a non-dominant position, whose members – being nationals of the State – possess ethnic, religious or linguistic characteristics differing from those of the rest of the population and show, if only implicitly, a sense of solidarity, directed towards preserving their culture, traditions, religion or language.[27]

Even if applying such an abstract definition may in practice be difficult, it is possible to deduce certain objective and subjective criteria therefrom. A first objective criterion is whether the part of the population concerned of a particular State forms a numerical minority in that State.[28] Second, to be considered a minority, that part of the population should be in a 'non-dominant position' on a political, economic, social and/or cultural level. Subjective criteria then include a mutual sense of solidarity and the shared aim of preserving the group's own cultural, religious and/or linguistic identity.

Historically, minority rights find their roots in the framework for the protection of national minorities of the League of Nations (see above, Section I(A)). Article 27 ICCPR then became the first provision to consider the issue from a human rights perspective, and the first provision to do so in a binding manner. It provides that '[i]n those States in which ethnic, religious or linguistic minorities exist, persons belonging to such minorities shall not be denied the right, in community with the other members of their group, to enjoy their own culture, to profess and practise their own religion, or to use their own language'.[29] Article 27 ICCPR is complemented by the UN General Assembly's 1992 Declaration on the Rights of Persons Belonging to National or Ethnic, Religious and Linguistic Minorities (Minorities Declaration).[30] The central idea of the Minorities Declaration is captured in Article 1 thereof, stating that 'States shall protect the existence and the national or ethnic, cultural, religious and linguistic identity of minorities within their respective territories and shall encourage conditions for the promotion of that identity'. Further, the

[25] See eg Art 27 ICCPR.

[26] On peoples' rights more generally, see further P Alston, *Peoples' Rights* (Oxford, OUP, 2001) and J Crawford, *The Rights of Peoples* (Oxford, Clarendon Press, 1988). See also B Algan, 'Rethinking "Third Generation" Human Rights' (2004) 1 *Ankara Law Review* 121.

[27] F Capotorti, 'Study on the Rights of Persons Belonging to Ethnic, Religious and Linguistic Minorities' (1979), UN Doc E/CN4/Sub2/384/Rev1, para 568. In 1985, the Sub-Commission on the Prevention of Discrimination and the Protection of Minorities submitted to the Commission on Human Rights an updated definition of a minority, prepared by Jules Deschênes (J Deschênes, 'Proposal Concerning a Definition of the Term Minority' (14 May 1985), UN Doc E/CN4/Sub2/1985/31/Corr1, para 181), which was however not accepted by the Commission. See B Uddin Khan and M Mahbubur Rahman, *Protection of Minorities: Regimes, Norms and Issues in South Asia* (Newcastle upon Tyne, Cambridge Scholars Publishing, 2012) 2.

[28] Thus, the HRCttee considered that 'English speaking citizens of Canada cannot be considered a linguistic minority' (HRCttee, *Ballantyne et al v Canada*, Communications Nos 359/1989 and 385/1989, 5 May 1993, UN Doc CCPR/C/47/D/359/1989 and 385/1989/Rev.1, para 11.2).

[29] See further HRCttee, 'General Comment No 23: Article 27 (Rights of Minorities)', 8 April 1994, UN Doc CCPR/C/21/Rev1/Add5.

[30] UNGA Res 47/135, 18 December 1992, UN Doc A/RES/47/135.

Declaration contains more specific rights of persons belonging to minorities and measures States should take to ensure the enjoyment thereof. While it is not a legally binding instrument and has no monitoring body,[31] the UN Forum on Minority Issues, whose work is guided by the UN Special Rapporteur on Minority Issues,[32] analyses best practices, challenges, opportunities and initiatives for the further implementation of the Minorities Declaration.[33] In addition, and to enhance dialogue and cooperation between relevant UN Departments, Agencies, Programmes and Funds, the UN Secretariat has established the UN Network on Racial Discrimination and Protection of Minorities.[34]

In addition to Article 27 ICCPR and the Minorities Declaration, other international human rights instruments are relevant. First, the principle of non-discrimination and equality, upon which all human rights treaties rely, form the fundamental pillar of the minority rights regime. Second, in practice, the Committee on the Elimination of Racial Discrimination (CERD) supervises the implementation of certain minority rights.[35]

iii. The Rights of Indigenous Peoples

A category of peoples with specific needs is that of *indigenous peoples*. Again, there is no universally agreed definition, but indigenous peoples are usually defined according to the definition of José Martínez Cobo, then Special Rapporteur of the Human Rights Commission's Sub-Commission on Prevention of Discrimination and Protection of Minorities:

> Indigenous communities, peoples and nations are those which, having a historical continuity with pre-invasion and pre-colonial societies that developed on their territories, consider themselves distinct from other sectors of the societies now prevailing in those territories, or parts of them. They form at present non-dominant sectors of society and are determined to preserve, develop and transmit to future generations their ancestral territories, and their ethnic identity, as the basis of their continued existence as peoples, in accordance with their own cultural patterns, social institutions and legal systems.[36]

The rights of indigenous peoples are laid down in the 2007 UN General Assembly Declaration on the Rights of Indigenous Peoples.[37] This Declaration contains rights that especially affect the situation of indigenous people, and is particular in its 'collectivist' or 'peoples-oriented' approach.[38] Thus, Article 1 of the Declaration provides that '[i]ndigenous peoples have the right to the full enjoyment, *as a collective or as individuals*, of all human rights and fundamental freedoms as recognized in the UN Charter, the UDHR, and international human rights law' (emphasis added). Also there is a Permanent Forum on Indigenous Issues, which is a high-level advisory body to the UN Economic and Social Council (ECOSOC), with the mandate to deal with indigenous issues related to economic

[31] See below, Section VI for a discussion of the treaty monitoring bodies.

[32] Whose mandate was established by Commission on Human Rights Resolution 2005/79 of 21 April 2005, and most recently extended by HRC Res 34/6, 23 March 2017, UN Doc A/HRC/RES/34/6.

[33] HRC Res 6/15, 28 September 2007, UN Doc A/HRC/RES/6/15 (as renewed by Res 19/23, 23 March 2012, UN Doc A/HRC/RES/19/23), operative clause 1.

[34] UNSG, Decision of the Policy Committee, 6 March 2012, No 2012/4.

[35] On the CERD, see further Section VI.

[36] JR Martínez Cobo, 'Study of the Problem of Discrimination Against Indigenous Populations', 11 March 1986, UN Doc E/CN4/Sub2/1986/7/Add2.

[37] UNGA Res 61/295, 13 September 2007, UN Doc A/RES/61/295.

[38] van Boven (n 12) 145–47.

and social development, culture, the environment, education, health and human rights.[39] In addition, the HRC established an Expert Mechanism on the Rights of Indigenous Peoples,[40] which has the mandate to assist the Council with expertise and advice on the rights of indigenous peoples as set out in the Declaration on the Rights of Indigenous Peoples, and assist Member States in achieving the ends of the Declaration through the promotion, protection and fulfilment of the rights of indigenous peoples.[41] Lastly, there is a Special Rapporteur on the Rights of Indigenous Peoples.[42] All three mechanisms are to coordinate their work.[43] Lastly, in 2014 the first – and so far only – World Conference on Indigenous Peoples was held, providing an opportunity to share perspectives and best practices on the realisation of the rights of indigenous peoples, as especially laid down in the Declaration on the Rights of Indigenous Peoples.[44]

III. The Human Rights Obligation to Criminalise

A second category of global international human rights instruments concerns those that primarily oblige States to criminalise, investigate, prosecute and/or punish specific behaviour that would strongly affect the human rights of any victim of such behaviour. This is not to say that these Conventions cannot be relied upon for other than criminal purposes, for example to hold a State liable for an internationally wrongful act or for tort litigation before national courts. This category includes the Genocide Convention, the Convention against Torture and the Enforced Disappearance Convention.

A. Genocide Convention

The Convention on the Prevention and Punishment of the Genocide Convention was adopted by the UN General Assembly in Paris on 9 December 1948 and entered into force on 12 January 1951. There are currently 149 States Parties to the Convention, including all EU Member States.

According to Article I of the Genocide Convention, 'The Contracting Parties confirm that genocide […] is a crime under international law which they undertake to prevent and to punish'. Article II defines genocide as

> any of the following acts committed with intent to destroy, in whole or in part, a national, ethnical, racial or religious group, as such:
>
> (a) Killing members of the group;
> (b) Causing serious bodily or mental harm to members of the group;

[39] ECOSOC Res 2000/22, 28 July 2000, UN Doc ECOSOC/RES/2000/22, operative clause 2.
[40] HRC Res 6/36, 14 December 2007, UN Doc A/HRC/RES/6/36.
[41] HRC Res 33/25, 5 October 2016, UN Doc A/HRC/RES/33/25, operative clause 1.
[42] Whose mandate was established by Commission on Human Rights (CHR) Res 2001/57, 24 April 2001, and most recently extended by HRC Res 33/12, 6 October 2016, UN Doc A/HRC/RES/33/12.
[43] See eg HRC Res 33/25 (n 41) operative clause 10.
[44] For the outcome document of the World Conference, see UNGA Res 69/2, 25 September 2014, UN Doc A/RES/69/2.

(c) Deliberately inflicting on the group conditions of life calculated to bring about its physical destruction in whole or in part;
(d) Imposing measures intended to prevent births within the group;
(e) Forcibly transferring children of the group to another group.[45]

This definition explicitly states that the concerned acts must have been committed 'with intent' to exterminate certain population groups. This intentional element on the part of the perpetrator (often referred to as a '*dolus specialis*') is a decisive element in the determination of the crime.[46]

The Genocide Convention undoubtedly constitutes an important step forward in the fight against the crime of genocide. However, it needs to be noted that only those population groups that are distinguishable on the basis of their nationality, ethnicity, religion or race (and not on the basis of culture, language or political conviction) fall within the scope of protection of the Convention.[47] Moreover, the Convention does not provide for a particular monitoring mechanism. It refers to the States Parties, which have the obligation 'to enact [...] the necessary legislation to give effect to the provisions of the [...] Convention'.[48] Article VI further states that '[p]ersons charged with genocide [...] *shall* be tried by a competent tribunal of the State *in the territory of which the act was committed*' (emphasis added). Thus, only the territorial State has an obligation to prosecute and punish the crime of genocide. This is problematic, as it is precisely that State that may not be willing and/or able to prosecute alleged perpetrators.[49]

This territorial jurisdiction is complemented by the possibility of jurisdiction by 'such international penal tribunal as may have jurisdiction with respect to those Contracting Parties which shall have accepted its jurisdiction'.[50] It is therefore possible to establish an ad hoc tribunal with jurisdiction over violations of the Convention. Both the ICTY and ICTR were given the necessary jurisdiction to prosecute the crime of genocide.[51] However, the Genocide Convention neither created an international body that could prosecute all violations of its provisions on a permanent basis, nor did it establish an organisation that could assure the prevention of genocide. In the meantime, the ICC has permanent jurisdiction to prosecute crimes of genocide.[52] Even though the Rome Statute does not explicitly refer to the Genocide Convention, it has adopted the same definition.[53]

The principles contained in the Genocide Convention have been recognised as reflecting customary international law by the ICJ in its 1951 Advisory Opinion on *Reservations to the Convention on the Prevention and Punishment of the Crime of Genocide*:[54] 'the principles underlying the Convention are principles which are recognised by civilised nations as binding on States, even without any conventional obligation'.[55] More recently, the ICJ ruled on

[45] On the physical element or *actus reus* of genocide, see further, WA Schabas, *Genocide in International Law: The Crime of Crimes*, 2nd edn (Cambridge, CUP, 2009) 172–240.
[46] See further, ibid, 241–306.
[47] See further, ibid, 117–71. See also F Martin, 'The Notion of "Protected Groups" in the Genocide Convention and Its Application' in P Gaeta (ed), *The UN Genocide Convention: A Commentary* (Oxford, OUP, 2009) 112–27.
[48] Art V Genocide Convention.
[49] See further V Thalmann, 'National Criminal Jurisdiction over Genocide' in Gaeta (n 47) 231–58.
[50] Art VI Genocide Convention.
[51] Art 4 ICTY Statute; Art 2 ICTR Statute.
[52] Art 5(1) Rome Statute.
[53] ibid, Art. See further, S Zappalà, 'International Criminal Jurisdiction over Genocide' in Gaeta (n 47) 259–77.
[54] *Reservations to the Convention on the Prevention and Punishment of the Crime of Genocide* [1951] ICJ Rep 15, 23.
[55] ibid, 23; See also, *Case Concerning Armed Activities on the Territory of the Congo (New Application: 2002)* (Democratic Republic of the Congo v Rwanda) [2006] ICJ Rep 6, 32, where the ICJ declared that the prohibition of genocide 'assuredly' is a *jus cogens* norm.

the genocide allegedly committed in 1995 against Bosnian Muslims in Srebrenica.[56] It held that Article I of the Convention also imposes upon *States* the obligation not to *commit* genocide.[57] The Court then found that the acts of genocide concerned could not be attributed to organs of the Serbian State or persons wholly dependent upon it;[58] nor did that State direct or control the relevant operations.[59] Subsequently, however, the ICJ ruled that although the Serbian State had the means to prevent the genocide, it refrained from using them and it failed in its duty to cooperate fully with the ICTY. As such, its responsibility under international law was engaged following respectively the violation of its obligation to *prevent* and to *punish* genocide.[60]

B. Convention against Torture

A second global human rights instrument that obliges States to criminalise certain behaviour is the Convention against Torture. The Convention was adopted by the UN General Assembly on 10 December 1984 and entered into force on 26 June 1987. It currently has 163 States Parties, including all EU Member States. The Convention begins by defining torture in Article 1. For the purposes of the Convention, 'torture' means

> any act by which severe pain or suffering, whether physical or mental, is intentionally inflicted on a person for such purposes as obtaining from him or a third person information or a confession, punishing him for an act he or a third person has committed or is suspected of having committed, or intimidating or coercing him or a third person, or for any reason based on discrimination of any kind, when such pain or suffering is inflicted by or at the instigation of or with the consent or acquiescence of a public official or other person acting in an official capacity. It does not include pain or suffering arising only from, inherent in or incidental to lawful sanctions.[61]

Further, the Convention contains the obligation of States to take effective measures in order to prevent torture (Article 2), other acts of cruel, inhuman or degrading treatment or punishment which do not amount to torture as defined in Article I (Article 16),[62] and to ensure that all acts of torture are made offences under their respective criminal legislation (Article 4). One of the most important contributions of the Convention lies in the principle of *non-refoulement*, according to which 'no State shall expel, return (*refouler*) or extradite a person to another State where there are substantial grounds for believing that he would be in danger of being subjected to torture'.[63]

[56] *Application of the Convention on the Prevention and Punishment of the Crime of Genocide* (Bosnia and Herzegovina v Serbia and Montenegro) [2007] ICJ Rep 43.

[57] Notwithstanding the Article's literal provision that '[t]he Contracting Parties confirm that genocide, whether committed in time of peace or in time of war, is a crime under international law which they undertake to *prevent* and to *punish*' (emphasis added); ibid, paras 155–79.

[58] ibid, para 395.

[59] ibid, para 412.

[60] As provided for in Art I Genocide Convention; ibid, paras 438, and 449–50. See further, OB Naftali, 'The Obligation to Prevent and to Punish Genocide' in Gaeta (n 47) 27–57.

[61] Art 1(2) Convention against Torture adds that this article is without prejudice to any international instrument or national legislation which does or may contain provisions of wider application.

[62] See further Committee against Torture (CAT), 'General Comment No 2: Implementation of Article 2 by States Parties', 24 January 2008, UN Doc CAT/C/GC/2. At para 3, the Committee held that '[t]he obligations to prevent torture and other cruel, inhuman or degrading treatment or punishment […] are indivisible, interdependent and interrelated'.

[63] Art 3(1) Convention against Torture. See further, E Hamdan, *The Principle of Non-Refoulement under the ECHR and the UN Convention against Torture and Other Cruel, Inhuman or Degrading Treatment or Punishment* (Leiden, Brill, 2016).

Regarding the exercise of criminal jurisdiction, Article 5(1) obliges States Parties to take all necessary measures to establish jurisdiction over all acts of torture. There are three situations in which a State needs to assert this jurisdiction: when the offences are committed in any territory under its jurisdiction (territoriality principle); when the alleged offender is a national of that State (active personality principle); and when the victim is a national of that State, if that State considers it appropriate (passive personality principle).[64] Article 5(2) also provides for the obligation to establish universal jurisdiction in cases where the alleged offender is present in any territory under a State's jurisdiction (conditional universal jurisdiction, subject to the principle of *forum deprehensionis*) and that State does not extradite him (*aut dedere, aut judicare*). Article 5(3) further states that the Convention 'does not exclude any criminal jurisdiction in accordance with internal law', and thus allows – but does not oblige – States to establish unconditional universal jurisdiction (not subject to the principle of *forum deprehensionis*).[65]

The Convention against Torture (as implemented in the United Kingdom's national law) was famously applied by the House of Lords in the *Pinochet* case. The issue was whether the former Chilean dictator General Augusto Pinochet could be extradited to Spain based on allegations of (amongst others) torture during his period of office (1973–1990). The judges first considered that to qualify as an extraditable crime, the crime must have been a crime under UK law *at the time it was committed*. However, as 'extraterritorial torture did not become a crime in the United Kingdom until section 134 of the Criminal Justice Act 1988 came into effect on 29 September 1988 [...] all the alleged offences of torture [...] before that date [...] which did not occur in Spain were crimes for which the applicant could not be extradited'.[66] Second, the House of Lord famously held that 'there had been a universal jurisdiction in all the Convention state parties to either extradite or punish a public official who committed torture', and that 'since Chile, Spain and the United Kingdom had all ratified the Convention by 8 December 1988 the applicant could have no immunity for crimes of torture [...] after that date [...] and the extradition could proceed on those charges'.[67] A second notable application of the Convention against Torture is that by the ICJ in *Belgium v Senegal*.[68] Belgium had exercised unconditional universal jurisdiction and asked for the extradition of Mr Hissène Habré, the former President of the Republic Chad, amongst others based on the Convention against Torture. In line with Article 5(2) of the Convention, the ICJ found Senegal to be in breach of Articles 6(2) and 7(1) of the Convention against Torture, and ruled that 'Senegal must therefore take without further delay the necessary measures to submit the case to its competent authorities for the purpose of prosecution, if it does not extradite Mr Habré'.[69]

[64] Art 5(1) Convention against Torture.

[65] On the principles of prescriptive criminal jurisdiction in general, see Chapter 9, Section IV; see further A Boulesbaa, *The UN Convention on Torture and the Prospects for Enforcement* (The Hague, Martinus Nijhoff, 1999); C Ryngaert, 'Universal Criminal Jurisdiction over Torture: A State of Affairs after 20 Years UN Torture Convention' (2005) 23 *Netherlands Quarterly of Human Rights* 571.

[66] *R v Bow Street Metropolitan Stipendiary Magistrate and others, ex parte Pinochet Ugarte (No 3)* [2000] 1 AC 147 (HL).

[67] ibid; see further, R Brody and M Ratner, *The Pinochet Papers: The Case of Augusto Pinochet in Spain and Britain* (The Hague, Kluwer, 2000); D Woodhouse, *The Pinochet Case: A Legal and Constitutional Analysis* (Oxford, Hart, 2000).

[68] *Belgium v Senegal* (n 8).

[69] ibid, para 121; see further, M Andenas and T Weatherall, 'International Court of Justice: Questions Relating to the Obligation to Extradite or Prosecute (Belgium v Senegal) Judgment of 20 July 2012' (2013) 62 *ICLQ* 753; S Shah, 'Questions Relating to the Obligation to Prosecute or Extradite (*Belgium v Senegal*)' (2013) 2 *Human Rights Law Review* 351.

C. Enforced Disappearance Convention

A last example of a global human rights instrument that obliges States to criminalise certain behaviour is the more recent International Convention for the Protection of All Persons from Enforced Disappearance. The Enforced Disappearance Convention was adopted by the UN General Assembly on 20 December 2006. It entered into force on 23 December 2010. To date, it has been ratified by 58 States. The Convention states that 'no one shall be subjected to enforced disappearance'.[70] Enforced disappearance is defined in Article 2 as

> the arrest, detention, abduction or any other form of deprivation of liberty by agents of the State or by persons or groups of persons acting with the authorization, support or acquiescence of the State, followed by a refusal to acknowledge the deprivation of liberty or by concealment of the fate or whereabouts of the disappeared person, which place such a person outside the protection of the law.

The particularity of the crime of enforced disappearance is that it is a phenomenon that encapsulates a severe violation of several (other) human rights, while it does not concern one human right or a violation thereof as such. As argued by the UN General Assembly Declaration on the Protection of all Persons from Enforced Disappearance, which paved the way for the Enforced Disappearance Convention, an act of enforced disappearance

> constitutes a violation of the rules of international law guaranteeing, inter alia, the right to recognition as a person before the law, the right to liberty and security of the person and the right not to be subjected to torture and other cruel, inhuman or degrading treatment or punishment. It also violates or constitutes a grave threat to the right to life.[71]

IV. The Protection of Vulnerable Groups

A third category of global international human rights instruments to be discerned is one that concerns vulnerable groups. Specific conventions protect groups that have historically been shown to be particularly vulnerable to discrimination and other human rights violations, and thus deserve special attention. It concerns people with a particular race, colour, descent, or national or ethnic origin that usually are minorities (Racial Discrimination Convention), women (Convention on Discrimination against Women), children (Convention on the Rights of the Child), migrant workers (Migrants' Rights Convention) and persons with disabilities (Disability Rights Convention).[72]

[70] Art 1 Enforced Disappearance Convention.

[71] See further, N Kyriakou, 'The International Convention for the Protection of All Persons from Enforced Disappearance and Its Contributions to International Human Rights Law, with Specific Reference to Extraordinary Rendition' (2012) 13 *Melbourne Journal of International Law* 424; L Ott, *Enforced Disappearance in International Law* (Antwerp, Intersentia, 2011); T Scovazzi and G Citroni, *The Struggle against Enforced Disappearance and the 2007 United Nations Convention* (Leiden, Martinus Nijhoff, 2007).

[72] See further, I Nifosi-Sutton, *The Protection of Vulnerable Groups under International Human Rights Law* (Abingdon, Routledge, 2017).

A. Racial Discrimination Convention

After having adopted a UN Declaration on the matter, the UN General Assembly adopted the International Convention on the Elimination of All Forms of Racial Discrimination on 21 December 1965, which entered into force on 4 January 1969. There are currently 179 States Parties to this Convention, including all EU Member States. 'Racial discrimination' is defined in Article 1(1) of the Convention as

> any distinction, exclusion, restriction or preference based on race, colour, descent, or national or ethnic origin which has the purpose or effect of nullifying or impairing the recognition, enjoyment or exercise, on an equal footing, of human rights and fundamental freedoms in the political, economic, social, cultural or any other field of public life.

States Parties to the Racial Discrimination Convention undertake to refrain from engaging in and supporting racial discrimination, and are obliged to prohibit and bring to an end racial discrimination by private persons.[73] To this end, they must criminalise 'all dissemination of ideas based on racial superiority or hatred, incitement to racial discrimination, as well as all acts of violence or incitement to such acts against any race'.[74] Lastly, States Parties also have to take positive measures. In particular, they must 'guarantee the right of everyone, without distinction as to race, colour, or national or ethnic origin, to equality before the law', notably in the enjoyment of a number of rights that are prone to discrimination.[75]

B. Convention on the Elimination of All Forms of Discrimination against Women

After having adopted a 'Declaration on the Elimination of Discrimination against Women' in 1967,[76] the UN General Assembly adopted the CEDAW on 18 December 1979. The Convention entered into force on 3 September 1981. It presently has 189 States Parties, including all EU Member States. 'Discrimination against women' is defined in Article 1 of the Convention as:

> any distinction, exclusion or restriction made on the basis of sex which has the effect or purpose of impairing or nullifying the recognition, enjoyment or exercise by women, irrespective of their marital status, on a basis of equality of men and women, of human rights and fundamental freedoms in the political, economic, social, cultural, civil or any other field.

States Parties to the Convention on Discrimination against Women undertake to refrain from engaging in discrimination against women, to prohibit and bring to an end discrimi-

[73] Art 2 Racial Discrimination Convention.

[74] ibid, Art 4(a); P Thornberry, 'International Convention on the Elimination of All Forms of Racial Discrimination: The Prohibition of "Racist Hate Speech"' in T McGonagle and Y Donders (eds), *The United Nations and Freedom of Expression and Information: Critical Perspectives* (Cambridge, CUP, 2015) 121–44.

[75] Art 5 Racial Discrimination Convention; see further, D Keane and J Castellino, 'Is the International Convention on the Elimination of All Forms of Racial Discrimination the *De Facto* Minority Rights Treaty?' in CM Buckley, A Donald and P Leach (eds), *Towards Convergence in International Human Rights Law: Approaches of Regional and International Systems* (Leiden, Brill, 2016) 275–95; N Lerner, *The UN Convention on the Elimination of All Forms of Racial Discrimination* (Leiden, Brill, 2014); P Thornberry, *The International Convention on the Elimination of All Forms of Racial Discrimination: A Commentary* (Oxford, OUP, 2016).

[76] UNGA Res 2263 (XXII), 'Declaration on the Elimination of Discrimination Against Women', 7 November 1967, UN Doc A/RES/2263(XXII).

nation against women by private persons, and to realise the equality of men and women.[77] Further, the Convention primarily imposes positive obligations upon States Parties in view of the empowerment of women that require the active involvement of their respective governments. For this purpose, the Convention allows for affirmative action (positive discrimination).[78] Also, the Convention obliges States Parties to ensure a number of rights that particularly affect women and/or must be geared to their situation (eg, the right to equal remuneration[79]). However, the nature of the rights contained in the Convention does not immediately lend them to judicial application.[80]

C. Convention on the Rights of the Child

The CRC was adopted by the UN General Assembly on 20 November 1989 and entered into force on 2 September 1990. With 196 States Parties (including all EU Member States), it is the human rights treaty with the most ratifications. According to Article 1, 'a child means every human being below the age of eighteen years unless under the law applicable to the child, majority is attained earlier'. The CRC affirms the right of children not to be discriminated against,[81] and requires that '[i]n all actions concerning children, […] the best interests of the child shall be a primary consideration'.[82] States Parties to the CRC recognise the inherent right to life of every child, and are required to 'ensure to the maximum extent possible the survival and development of the child'.[83] In addition, the Convention provides all children with a number of rights that are largely already contained in general human rights instruments, but that may particularly affect children and/or must be geared to their situation (eg, the right to education[84]). The Convention calls upon the States Parties to 'undertake all appropriate legislative, administrative, and other measures for the implementation of the rights recognized [by it]'.[85]

On 25 May 2000, the UN General Assembly adopted two Optional Protocols to the Convention on the Rights of the Child. The First Optional Protocol prohibits the use of child soldiers in armed conflicts.[86] 167 States are a party to this Protocol. The Protocol does not prohibit children under the age of 18 from being part of States Parties' regular armed forces. It does however prohibit their direct participation in hostilities, their submission to compulsory recruitment and their enlistment with rebel groups.[87] The Second

[77] Art 2 CEDAW.
[78] ibid, Art 4.
[79] ibid, Art 11(1)(d).
[80] See further, MA Freeman, C Chinkin and B Rudolf, *The UN Convention on the Elimination of All Forms of Discrimination Against Women: A Commentary* (Oxford, OUP, 2012).
[81] Art 2 CRC.
[82] ibid, Art 3.
[83] ibid, Art 6.
[84] ibid, Art 28.
[85] ibid, Art 4. See further A Alen et al (eds), *A Commentary on the United Nations Convention on the Rights of the Child* (Leiden, Brill, 2005–2015); O Cvejić Jančić, *The Rights of the Child in a Changing World: 25 Years after The UN Convention on the Rights of the Child* (Cham, Springer, 2016); T Liefaard and J Sloth-Nielsen, *The United Nations Convention on the Rights of the Child: Taking Stock after 25 Years and Looking Ahead* (Leiden, Brill Nijhoff, 2017).
[86] Optional Protocol to the Convention on the Rights of the Child on the Involvement of Children in Armed Conflict (adopted 25 May 2000, entered into force 12 February 2002) 2173 UNTS 222.
[87] See ibid, respectively Arts 1, 2 and 4. See further, C Poulatova, *Children and Armed Conflict* (Newcastle upon Tyne, Cambridge Scholars Publishing, 2013).

Optional Protocol prohibits the sale of children, child prostitution and child pornography.[88] It currently has 174 States Parties. The Protocol contains provisions concerning the criminalisation of certain acts such as offering children for sexual exploitation or forced labour.[89]

D. The Migrants' Rights Convention

The International Convention on the Protection of the Rights of All Migrant Workers and Members of their Families was adopted by the UN General Assembly on 18 December 1990. Even though the resolution was adopted by consensus, the Migrants' Rights Convention only entered into force on 1 July 2003.[90] Amongst the 51 States that are a party to the Convention, there is not one EU Member State, nor any other western country.

Again, the majority of rights and freedoms guaranteed in the Convention to migrants and their family members, such as the right to life, the right to freedom of expression and the right to protection against torture, are already guaranteed vis-à-vis all human beings in other human rights treaties. In addition, the Migrants' Rights Convention contains provisions with a particular focus on the protection of migrants. An example can be found in Article 22, which stipulates that '[m]igrant workers and members of their families shall not be subject to measures of collective expulsion' and that '[e]ach case of expulsion shall be examined and decided individually'.[91]

E. Convention on the Rights of Persons with Disabilities

The most recent example of an international human rights instrument that aims to protect a vulnerable group is the Convention on the Rights of Persons with Disabilities (CRPD). The CRPD was adopted by the UN General Assembly on 13 December 2006 and entered into force on 3 May 2008.[92] At the moment, it has 177 States Parties, including all EU Member States and the EU itself. The EU ratified the Convention on 23 December 2010, and it entered into force for the EU on 22 January 2011.

The purpose of the CRPD 'is to promote, protect and ensure the full and equal enjoyment of all human rights and fundamental freedoms by all persons with disabilities, and to promote respect for their inherent dignity'.[93] For the purpose of the Convention, Article 1 defines persons with disabilities as including 'those who have long-term physical, mental, intellectual or sensory impairments which in interaction with various barriers may hinder

[88] Optional Protocol to the Convention on the Rights of the Child on the Sale of Children, Child Prostitution and Child Pornography (adopted 25 May 2000, entered into force 18 January 2002) 2171 UNTS 227.

[89] ibid, Art 3. See further, M Santos Pais, 'The Protection of Children from Sexual Exploitation Optional Protocol to the Convention on the Rights of the Child on the Sale of Children, Child Prostitution and Child Pornography' (2010) 18 *The International Journal of Children's Rights* 551.

[90] Convention on the Protection of the Rights of All Migrant Workers and Members of their Families (adopted 18 December 1990, entered into force 1 July 2003) 2220 UNTS 3.

[91] See further, P de Guchteneire, A Pécoud and R Cholewinski (eds), *Migration and Human Rights: The United Nations Convention on Migrant Workers' Rights* (Cambridge, CUP, 2009).

[92] Convention on the Rights of Persons with Disabilities (adopted 13 December 2006, entered into force 3 May 2008) 2515 UNTS 3.

[93] Art 1 CRPD.

their full and effective participation in society on an equal basis with others'. In addition to general principles and obligations and specific obligations with regard to women and children with disabilities, the Convention reaffirms certain rights already contained in general human rights instruments and obliges States Parties to take positive measures in view of issues that particularly affect persons with disabilities (eg, access to transport and inclusion and participation in the community).[94]

The CRPD is the first universal human rights treaty the EU has become a party to.[95] Article 19(1) TFEU provides that

> without prejudice to the other provisions of the Treaties and within the limits of the powers conferred by them upon the Union, the Council [...] may take appropriate action to combat discrimination based on sex, racial or ethnic origin, religion or belief, *disability*, age or sexual orientation. (emphasis added)

On this basis,[96] on 26 November 2009, the Council decided to conclude the Convention.[97] In addition, the Treaty of Lisbon, which entered into force on 1 December 2009, introduced the 'policy mainstreaming' Article 10 TFEU, providing that in the development of its policies and activities, the EU shall aim to combat discrimination, inter alia based on disability. The Treaty of Lisbon also gave binding treaty force to the EU Charter. The EU Charter provides that discrimination based on disability shall be prohibited,[98] adding that the EU 'recognises and respects the right of persons with disabilities to benefit from measures designed to ensure their independence, social and occupational integration and participation in the life of the community'.[99]

Both the EU and its Member States have competence in the fields covered by the CRPD, which is why they can both become Parties to it.[100] This entails different possible scenarios as regards the respective competence of the EU and its Member States with regard to individual provisions. In particular, the EU or the Member States can have the exclusive competence *or* the EU and the Member States can share the competence to act.[101] This complexity required the adoption of a 'Declaration of Competence', identifying the areas of exclusive and shared competences,[102] and a 'Code of Conduct', setting out the internal arrangements for the implementation of the Convention.[103] For example, both the EU and

[94] See ibid, respectively Arts 9 and 19. See further, OM Arnardóttir and G Quinn (eds), *The UN Convention on the Rights of Persons with Disabilities: European and Scandinavian Perspectives* (Leiden, Brill, 2009).

[95] P Craig and G de Búrca, *EU Law: Text, Cases and Materials* (Oxford, OUP, 2015) 392.

[96] In combination with Art 114 TFEU, providing the EU's competence for the adoption of measures for the approximation of provisions which have as their object the establishment and functioning of the internal market (note that, technically, the Council acted on the corresponding pre-Lisbon bases).

[97] Council Decision 2010/48/EC of 26 November 2009 concerning the conclusion, by the European Community, of the United Nations Convention on the Rights of Persons with Disabilities [2010] OJ L303/16.

[98] Art 21 EU Charter.

[99] ibid, Art 26.

[100] Council Decision 2010/48/EC (n 97) Recital 7. So far the EU and 27 EU Member States have ratified the Convention. Ireland signed the Convention on 30 May 2007 but has not yet ratified it.

[101] L Waddington, 'The European Union and the United Nations Convention on the Rights of Persons with Disabilities: A Story of Exclusive and Shared Competences' (2011) 18 *Maastricht Journal of European and Comparative Law* 431, 438.

[102] Declaration concerning the competence of the European Community with regard to matters governed by the United Nations Convention on the Rights of Persons with Disabilities, as annexed (Annex II) to Council Decision 2010/48/EC (n 97).

[103] Code of Conduct 2010/C 340/08 between the Council, the Member States and the Commission setting out internal arrangements for the implementation by and representation of the European Union relating to the United Nations Convention on the Rights of Persons with Disabilities [2010] OJ C340/11.

its Member States report to the Committee on the Rights of Persons with Disabilities on issues which fall under their respective competences.

In the policy fields in which competences are shared and as long as the EU has not acted, it is in principle the Member States that have the obligation to comply with the Convention. However, while in this regard the EU does not have an obligation under international law to act, any action taken by the EU must be in compliance with the Convention. For example, when adopting instruments in the realm of transport, a policy field of shared competence,[104] the EU has repeatedly included provisions addressing disability accessibility to ensure the rights of disabled persons. Nevertheless, also in policy fields with shared competences, action on the part of the EU can be highly desirable, for example when differing national measures hamper the free movement of (disabled) persons.[105]

Following the case law of the CJEU, the CRPD does not have direct effect in the EU's legal order. However, EU law 'must, as far as possible, be interpreted in a manner that is consistent with that convention'.[106]

V. Refugee Convention

The last Convention to be discussed is the 1951 Refugee Convention. Although opinions differ on whether it is or is not a human rights instrument,[107] the Refugee Convention addresses the issue of refugees by guaranteeing (potential) refugees particular rights, following which the Convention interacts with (other) human rights treaties and must (also) be considered from a human rights perspective.[108]

The Refugee Convention was adopted on 28 July 1951, and complemented by the Protocol of New York, adopted on 31 January 1967. According to Article 1 of the Convention, a refugee is a person who,

> owing to well-founded fear of being persecuted for reasons of race, religion, nationality, membership of a particular social group or political opinion, is outside the country of his nationality and is unable or, owing to such fear, is unwilling to avail himself of the protection of that country.

[104] Art 4(2) TFEU.

[105] When taking action in policy realms with shared competences, the EU has to act in conformity with the principle of subsidiarity. More generally, for the exercise of any (including exclusive) competences, the EU has to respect the proportionality principle: see Art 5(3) and (4) TEU 13; Waddington (n 101) 448–51.

[106] See eg Judgment of 1 December 2016, *Daouidi*, C-395/15, EU:C:2016:917, para 41; and, more recently, Judgment of 9 March 2017, *Milkova*, C 406/15, EU:C:2017:198, para 48.

[107] As part of the ongoing debate on the lack of a strong, encompassing international refugee law framework, scholars have been interpreting provisions of the international refugee framework in the light of international human rights law; see eg DE Anker, 'Refugee Law, Gender, and the Human Rights Paradigm' (2002) 15 *Harvard Human Rights Journal* 133; C Harvey, 'Time for Reform? Refugees, Asylum-seekers, and Protection Under International Human Rights Law' (2015) 34 *Refugee Survey Quarterly* 43. Others have gone a step further and support the view that refugee law is fundamentally a mechanism of human rights protection; see eg JC Hathaway, 'Why Refugee Law Still Matters' (2007) 8 *MJIL* 88; Chétail V, 'Are Refugee Rights Human Rights? Some Unorthodox Questioning on the Relations between International Refugee Law and International Human Rights Law' in R Rubio Marin (ed), *Human Rights and Immigration, Collected Courses of the Academy of European Law* (Oxford, OUP, 2014) 19–72. Interestingly, in practice, this technique has rarely been extended to other areas than the refugee definition; see eg DJ Cantor, 'The End of Refugee Law' (2017) 9 *Journal of Human Rights Practice* 203.

[108] See further, T Clark and F Crépeau, 'Mainstreaming Refugee Rights: The 1951 Refugee Convention and International Human Rights Law' (1999) 17 *Netherlands Quarterly of Human Rights* 389.

The words 'well-founded fear' contain a subjective element (fear), referring to the refugee's state of mind, that must be supported by an objective situation (well-founded).[109] Another important principle of the Refugee Convention is the principle of *non-refoulement*. Article 33(1) defines this principle in the following way:

> No Contracting State shall expel or return ('refouler') a refugee in any manner whatsoever to the frontiers of territories where his life or freedom would be threatened on account of his race, religion, nationality, membership of a particular social group or political opinion.

Article 33(2) establishes an exception with regard to refugees for whom there are reasonable grounds to consider them a danger to the security of the country in which they reside or who, having been convicted by a final judgment of a particularly serious crime, constitute a danger to the community of that country. The principle of *non-refoulement* contained in the Refugee Convention intersects with human rights law. Explicit recognitions of the principle can be found in the Convention against Torture,[110] the Enforced Disappearance Convention[111] and the EU Charter.[112] As for the ECHR and the ICCPR, the principle of *non-refoulement* has been recognised in connection to the prohibition of torture respectively by the ECtHR[113] and the HRCttee.[114] As opposed to what is the case under the Refugee Convention, the principle of *non-refoulement* under human rights law knows no exceptions, and is thus absolute.[115]

From 1999 onwards, the EU has built its own asylum framework CEAS, 'based on the full and inclusive application of the Geneva Convention'.[116] Article 78(1) TFEU indeed proclaims that '[t]he Union shall develop a common policy on asylum, subsidiary protection and temporary protection with a view to offering appropriate status to any third-country national requiring international protection and ensuring compliance with the principle of *non-refoulement*. This policy must be in accordance with the Geneva Convention of 28 July 1951 and the Protocol of 31 January 1967 relating to the status of refugees, and other relevant treaties'.

The CEAS has been given shape by several legal instruments. First, the EU has implemented the Refugee Convention primarily through the Qualification Directive,[117] which

[109] UNHCR, Handbook and Guidelines on Procedures and Criteria for Determining Refugee Status under the 1951 Convention and the 1967 Protocol relating to the Status of Refugees (reissued), December 2011, UN Doc HCR/1P/4/ENG/REV3, 11–13, www.unhcr.org/3d58e13b4.pdf.

[110] Art 3 Convention against Torture.

[111] Art 16 Enforced Disappearance Convention.

[112] Art 19(2) EU Charter.

[113] *Soering v UK* App no 14038/88 (ECtHR, 7 July 1989) paras 88–91.

[114] HRC, 'General Comment No 20: Article 7 (Prohibition of Torture, or Other Cruel, Inhuman or Degrading Treatment or Punishment', 10 March 1992, para 9.

[115] See eg *Chahal v UK* App no 22414/93 (ECHR, 15 November 1996) paras 72–82. At para 80, the ECtHR held: 'The prohibition provided by Article 3 (art. 3) against ill-treatment is equally absolute in expulsion cases. […], the activities of the individual in question, however undesirable or dangerous, cannot be a material consideration. The protection afforded by Article 3 […] is thus wider than that provided by Articles 32 and 33 of the United Nations 1951 Convention on the Status of Refugees […]'. See further O Delas, *Principe de non-refoulement dans la jurisprudence internationale des droits de l'homme* (Brussels, Bruylant, 2011); E Hamdan, *The Principle of Non-Refoulement under the ECHR and the UN Convention against Torture and Other Cruel, Inhuman or Degrading Treatment or Punishment* (Leiden, Brill Nijhoff, 2016); O Thurin, *Der Schutz des Fremden vor rechtswidriger Abschiebung: das Prinzip des Non-Refoulement nach Artikel 3 EMRK* (Vienna, Springer, 2009); RMM Wallace, 'The Principle of "Non-Refoulement" in International Refugee Law' in V Chetail and C Bauloz, *Research Handbook on International Law and Migration* (Cheltenham, Edward Elgar, 2014) 417–38.

[116] European Council, 'Tampere Presidency Conclusions', 15–16 October 1999, para 13.

[117] Directive 2011/95/EU of 13 December 2011 on standards for the qualification of third-country nationals or stateless persons as beneficiaries of international protection, for a uniform status for refugees or for persons eligible

clarifies the grounds for granting international protection (which can consist either of a *refugee* status, or of *subsidiary protection*). Thus, the Qualification Directive implements Article 1 (refugee definition) of the Refugee Convention in EU law by setting out the elements essential for the recognition of refugee status: acts of persecution (Article 9), reasons for persecution (Article 10), actors of persecution (Article 6), (the absence of) actors of protection (Article 7) and (the absence of) an internal flight alternative (Article 8). In addition, the Directive provides for the regime of 'subsidiary protection', which is peculiar to the EU. Applicants that do not qualify for refugee status (eg, because they are not persecuted for one of the recognised reasons) can still qualify for subsidiary protection if there is a real risk of suffering 'serious harm', defined as: (i) the death penalty or execution; (ii) torture or inhuman or degrading treatment; or (iii) 'serious and individual threat to a civilian's life or person by reason of indiscriminate violence in situations of international or internal armed conflict'.[118] Lastly, the Qualification Directive specifies the rights of recognised refugees or those enjoying subsidiary protection by setting out the 'content of international protection', including protection from *refoulement*.[119]

Second, the EU has built its CEAS on the 'Dublin Regime',[120] delineating responsibility among EU Member States for the examination of asylum applications

> to prevent multiple claims and 'forum shopping' by asylum seekers and also to prevent the situation of refugees 'in orbit' passing between States with no one State having responsibility for examining the asylum application, by guaranteeing a determination of the asylum claim in one country.[121]

While there are several possible criteria based upon which a Member State can be responsible to examine an asylum application, the criterion almost exclusively applied in practice is that the applicant has 'irregularly crossed the border into [that] Member State'.[122] As painfully exposed by the migration crisis of 2015–2017, the Dublin regime puts disproportionate pressure on EU border States like Italy and Greece.[123] The European Commission

for subsidiary protection, and for the content of the protection granted (recast) [2011] OJ L337/9. However, this implementation was rather imperfect. For example, according to a literal reading of Art 10(1)(d) of the Directive, in order to enjoy protection as part of 'a social group', the individual should not only objectively be part of a persecuted group, but should also be perceived to be so by his or her environment. In that way, it goes beyond what is required under the 1951 Refugee Convention. Nevertheless, various EU Member State courts do not adopt this strict approach within their case law.

[118] ibid, Art 15.

[119] ibid, Chapter VII (Arts 20–35).

[120] For the 'Dublin instrument' currently in force, see Regulation (EU) 604/2013 of 26 June 2013 establishing the criteria and mechanisms for determining the Member State responsible for examining an application for international protection lodged in one of the Member States by a third-country national or a stateless person (recast) [2013] OJ L180/31 (Dublin Regulation).

[121] *Zhanje, Re Judicial Review* [2007] NIQB 14 para 3. See also Opinion of 12 January 2012, *Kastrati*, C-620/10, EU:C:2012:10, para 25.

[122] Art 13(1) Dublin Regulation.

[123] Moreover, the Dublin regime was de facto suspended with regard to Greece by the ECtHR after Belgium was convicted for having violated Art 3 ECHR by sending an asylum seeker back to Greece even if 'substantial grounds [had] been shown for believing that the person concerned face[d] a real risk of being subjected to torture or inhuman or degrading treatment' due to the detention conditions in Greece: *MSS v Belgium* App no 30696/09 (ECtHR, 21 January 2011) para 365. The CJEU, in turn, stressed the principle of mutual trust among EU Member States, and that 'it must be assumed that the treatment of asylum seekers in all Member States complies with the requirements of the Charter, the Geneva Convention and the ECHR'. Increasing the threshold set by the ECtHR, it held that only 'if there are substantial grounds for believing that there are *systemic flaws* in the asylum procedure and reception conditions for asylum applicants in the Member State responsible, resulting in inhuman or degrading treatment, within the meaning of Article 4 of the Charter, of asylum seekers transferred to the territory of that Member State, the transfer would be incompatible with that provision' (emphasis added); Judgment

has submitted a proposal to remedy the Dublin system,[124] but has been criticised for not being willing to 'fundamentally overhaul' it.[125]

Third, the Asylum Procedures Directive (APD) lays down minimum standards regarding the *procedure* for granting or withdrawing international protection, aiming at fair and quick asylum decisions of good quality.[126] Important is that the APD allows EU Member States to provide that nationals or habitual residents from listed 'safe countries of origin' must go through an accelerated procedure that consists in a de facto rebuttable presumption that they do not require international protection.[127] Moreover, applications from persons who can apply for refugee status in a 'safe third country' are inadmissible.[128] It was according to this rule that the EU argued it could conclude the infamous 'EU-Turkey deal' that allowed it to return all new asylum seekers crossing from Turkey back to Greece, resettling one Syrian to the EU from Turkey directly for every Syrian returned to Turkey.[129] Lastly, the Reception Conditions Directive aims at humane *material* reception conditions for asylum seekers across the EU by laying down minimum standards, for example regarding detention.[130]

With regard to the protection of refugees in the framework of the UN, reference needs to be made to two important UN agencies. Firstly, there is the UNRWA established by the UN General Assembly following the 1948 Arab-Israeli conflict, in order to carry out direct relief and works programmes for Palestinian refugees.[131] The UNRWA provides assistance (mainly education and health care) and protection for some five million Palestinian refugees in Jordan, Syria, Lebanon, the West Bank and the Gaza Strip.[132] The second UN agency is UNHCR, directed by the UN High Commissioner for Refugees and established by the UN General Assembly in 1949.[133] The agency is mandated to lead and co-ordinate

of 21 December 2011, *NS and others*, C-411/10 and C-493/10, EU:C:2011:865, paras 78–86. The ECtHR took note of the CJEU's judgment, but reaffirmed its case law in *Tarakhel v Switzerland* App no 29216/12 (ECtHR, 4 November 2014), at para 105 in a case that concerned the particular situation of detention conditions for a family with young children in Italy. On 8 December 2016, the European Commission announced that from 15 March onwards, asylum seekers could again be sent back to Greece; Commission Recommendation of 8 December 2016 addressed to the Member States on the resumption of transfers to Greece under Regulation (EU) No 604/2013, C(2016) 8525 final.

[124] EC, Proposal for a Regulation of the European Parliament and of the Council establishing the criteria and mechanisms for determining the Member State responsible for examining an application for international protection lodged in one of the Member States by a third-country national or a stateless person (recast), 4 May 2016, COM(2016) 270 final, 2016/0133 (COD).

[125] See eg D Ivanov (European Parliamentary Research Service), 'Reform of the Dublin System', 10 March 2017, www.europarl.europa.eu/RegData/etudes/BRIE/2016/586639/EPRS_BRI(2016)586639_EN.pdf.

[126] Directive 2013/32/EU of 26 June 2013 on common procedures for granting and withdrawing international protection (recast) [2013] OJ L180/60.

[127] See Arts 31(8)(b), 36, 37 and Annex I APD.

[128] See Arts 33(2)(c) and 38 APD. This requires 'a connection between the applicant and the third country concerned on the basis of which it would be reasonable for that person to go to that country' (Art 38(2)(a) APD). See UNCHR, 'Improving Asylum Procedures: Comparative Analysis and Recommendations for Law and Practice', March 2010, www.unhcr.it/wp-content/uploads/2016/01/5improving_asylum_procedures.pdf, 63.

[129] European Council, 'EU-Turkey Statement', 18 March 2016, consilium.europa.eu/en/press/press-releases/2016/03/18/eu-turkey-statement. See also the orders of the General Court of the EU of 28 February 2017, *NF v European Council*, T-192/16, EU:T:2017:128; NG v European Council, T-193/16, EU:T:2017:129; and *NM v European Council*, T-257/16, EU:T:2017:130; and the order of the Court of Justice of the EU of 12 September 2018, *NF and Others v European Council*, C-208/17 P to C-210/17 P, not published, EU:C:2018:705.

[130] Directive 2013/33/EU of the European Parliament and of the Council of 26 June 2013 laying down standards for the reception of applicants for international protection (recast) [2013] OJ L180/96.

[131] UNGA Res 302 (IV), 8 December 1949 UN Doc A/RES/320 (IV).

[132] For more information, see unrwa.org.

[133] UNGA Res 319 (IV), 3 December 1949, UN Doc A/RES/319 (IV).

international action to protect refugees and resolve refugee problems worldwide.[134] In practice, the UNHCR has received more and more humanitarian tasks and provides assistance and protection to 'people of concern', meaning not only to refugees in the sense of the Convention but also to internally displaced persons, asylum seekers, returnees, stateless people, etc.[135] Even if the UNHCR has the mandate to supervise the application of the Refugee Convention,[136] it has never established a true monitoring mechanism involving a reporting obligation for States Parties to the Refugee Convention and/or the possibility for individuals to submit complaints, as is the case for nearly all human rights instruments.[137]

VI. Monitoring Mechanisms

This section first discusses the treaty bodies connected to the respective UN human rights instruments discussed above. Second, it discusses the different monitoring mechanisms that exist thereunder; ie, respectively, the duty to report, the inter-State complaints mechanisms, the individual complaints mechanism, the inquiry procedure and urgent action mechanisms. Lastly, it briefly discusses the issues the treaty bodies are faced with, and the more recent proposals to reform the monitoring system. It concludes with a summary table of all treaties and related data.

A. UN Treaty Bodies

With the exception of the Genocide Convention and the Refugee Convention, the (human rights) instruments discussed above have their own treaty bodies that monitor the implementation of the respective convention. These are: for the ICCPR, the HRCttee;[138] for the ICESCR, the Committee on Economic, Social and Cultural Rights (CESCR);[139] for the Convention against Torture, the CAT;[140] for the Enforced Disappearance Convention, the Committee on Enforced Disappearances (CED);[141] for the Convention on the Elimination of Racial Discrimination the Committee on the Elimination of Racial Discrimination (CERD);[142] for the Convention on the Elimination of All Forms of Discrimination

[134] UNGA Res 428 (V), 'Statute of the Office of the United Nations High Commissioner for Refugees', 14 December 1950, UN Doc A/RES/319 (IV) (Annex), para 1.

[135] For more information, see www.unhcr.org.

[136] Art 35 Refugee Convention.

[137] See further, A Blackham, 'A Proposal for Enhanced Supervision of the Refugee Convention' (2013) 26 *Journal of Refugee Studies* 392; S Takahashi, 'Recourse to Human Rights Treaty Bodies for Monitoring of the Refugee Convention' (2002) 20 *Netherlands Quarterly of Human Rights* 53.

[138] Art 28 ICCPR.

[139] Technically, the CESCR is not a UN treaty body, as it is established by ECOSOC Res 1985/17, 28 May 1985, UN Doc E/RES/1985/17 (and not the ICESCR). The Covenant initially only foresaw an obligation for States to report to ECOSOC, which had established a working group to fulfil this obligation. In 1985, ECOSOC decided to change this working group into the CESCR. Apart from this technicality, the CESCR is nevertheless considered to be part of the 'UN treaty body family'.

[140] Art 17 Convention against Torture.

[141] Art 26 Enforced Disappearance Convention.

[142] Art 8(1) CERD.

against Women the Committee on the Elimination of Discrimination against Women (CEDAW);[143] for the CRC, the Committee on the Rights of the Child;[144] for the Migrants' Rights Convention, the Committee on the Protection of the Rights of All Migrant Workers and Members of their Families;[145] and for the CRPD, the Committee on the Rights of Persons with Disabilities (CRPD).[146]

A last and special treaty body within the UN human rights system is the Subcommittee on Prevention of Torture and Other Cruel, Inhuman or Degrading Treatment or Punishment (SPT). The SPT has a preventive mandate and was created on 18 December 2002, when the UN General Assembly adopted an Optional Protocol to the Convention against Torture,[147] the aim of which is to 'establish a system of regular visits undertaken by independent international and national bodies to places where people are deprived of their liberty, in order to prevent torture and other cruel, inhuman and degrading treatment or punishment'.[148] All States that are a party to the Optional Protocol are required to allow this Subcommittee to undertake visits to those locations on their territory 'where persons are or may be deprived of their liberty'.[149] In addition, they are required to 'set up, designate or maintain at the domestic level one or several visiting bodies' (a national preventive mechanism).[150] At the moment, 84 States have become a party to this Optional Protocol.[151]

UN treaty bodies are composed of a number of experts (ranging from 10 to 23, but most commonly 18) that are proposed by the States Parties of which they are nationals, and that are normally elected for a term of four years.[152] They are not representatives of their respective governments, but independent experts who serve in their personal capacity.[153] As any recommendations or decisions by UN treaty bodies are not binding, they are usually considered to be 'quasi-judicial' bodies (especially when acting in response to complaints). However, these recommendations and decisions are publicly available and are widely resorted to by practitioners seeking authoritative interpretations of the respective conventions. With slight variations depending on the committee concerned, UN treaty bodies' main tasks consist of reviewing reports of States Parties and adopting recommendations in view thereof, adopting decisions following inter-State or individual complaints and launching inquiries when considered necessary.[154] These respective monitoring mechanisms will be discussed subsequently. Lastly, two 'oddities' amongst the monitoring mechanisms are discussed: the urgent action mechanisms under the Racial Discrimination Convention and the Enforced Disappearance Convention, and the Subcommittee on Prevention of Torture and Other Cruel, Inhuman or Degrading Treatment or Punishment.

[143] Art 17 CEDAW.
[144] Art 43 CRC.
[145] Art 72 Migrants' Rights Convention.
[146] Art 34 CRPD.
[147] Optional Protocol to the Convention against Torture and other Cruel, Inhuman or Degrading Treatment or Punishment (adopted 18 December 2002, entered into force 22 June 2006) 2375 UNTS 237.
[148] Art 1 Optional Protocol to the Convention against Torture.
[149] ibid, Art 4.
[150] ibid, Art 3.
[151] See further R Murray et al, *The Optional Protocol to the UN Convention Against Torture* (Oxford, OUP, 2011).
[152] See eg Art 32 ICCPR for the HRC.
[153] See eg Arts 28 and 29 ICCPR for the HRC.
[154] See further H Keller and G Ulfstein (eds), *UN Human Rights Treaty Bodies: Law and Legitimacy* (Cambridge, CUP, 2012).

B. Duty to Report

All UN human rights treaties to which a treaty body is connected provide for a reporting obligation for the States Parties to their respective committee.[155] Usually, States Parties are required to report on the legislative, judicial, administrative or other measures they have taken to implement the provisions of the relevant convention within one or two years after it entered into force for them,[156] following which the reporting obligation becomes periodic (ie, every four or five years, and whenever the committee so requests).[157] Following the report, the UN treaty body concerned issues recommendations for improvement by adopting concluding observations.

For a range of reasons, this mechanism is fairly weak. First, the States concerned draw up their own reports. If they fail to do so or are late, or if their reports are inadequate, there are no sanctions available.[158] Moreover, the number of reports States must submit causes a certain 'reporting fatigue' that affects the quality of the reports. Second, reporting only works *a posteriori*: these are not prevention mechanisms that could altogether preclude violations from happening. Third, the Committees that are in charge of assessing the reports often have only limited resources and suffer from backlogs. Finally, and as alluded to above, the conclusions that are adopted by the Committees are not legally binding. Notwithstanding its flaws, the value of the reporting system should not be underestimated, since its goal is to establish and maintain a constructive dialogue between the monitoring organ and the States Parties of the respective human rights treaty.[159]

C. Inter-State Complaints Mechanism

With the exception of the Convention on Discrimination against Women and the CRPD, all UN human rights conventions to which a treaty body is connected provide for an inter-State complaints mechanism.[160] In general, the mechanism is optional, which means that the complaint can only be dealt with by the relevant committee if both the complaining State and the respondent State have accepted the competence of the committee. There are two exceptions to this: both the Racial Discrimination Convention[161] and the ECHR provide for a compulsory inter-State complaints mechanism. In practice, States have never

[155] See respectively Art 40 ICCPR; Art 9 Racial Discrimination Convention; Art 19 Convention against Torture; Art 18 Convention on the Elimination of All Forms of Discrimination against Women; Art 35 CRPD; Art 29 Enforced Disappearance Convention; Art 16 ICESCR; Art 44 CRC; Art 73 Migrant Rights' Convention.

[156] See eg Art 40(1)(a) ICCPR, which provides for an initial term of one year.

[157] See eg Art 19(1) Convention against Torture, which provides for a periodic term of four years. Even if Art 40(1)(b) ICCPR provides for an obligation to submit a report whenever the HRCttee so requests after the initial term of one year, the Committee usually does so every four years.

[158] See further LJ LeBlanc, A Huibregtse, and T Meister, 'Compliance with the Reporting Requirements of Human Rights Conventions' (2010) 14 *The International Journal of Human Rights* 789.

[159] See further W Kälin, 'Examination of State Reports' in Keller and Ulfstein (n 154) 16–72; J Krommendijk, *The Domestic Impact and Effectiveness of the Process of State Reporting under UN Human Rights Treaties in the Netherlands, New Zealand and Finland: Paper-pushing or Policy Prompting?* (Cambridge, Intersentia, 2014).

[160] See respectively Arts 41–43 ICCPR; Arts 11–13 Racial Discrimination Convention; Art 21 Convention Against Torture; Art 32 Enforced Disappearance Convention; Art 10 Optional Protocol to the International Covenant on Economic, Social and Cultural Rights, 10 December 2008, UN Doc A/RES/63/435; Art 12 Optional Protocol to the Convention on the Rights of the Child on a Communications Procedure (adopted 19 December 2011, entered into force 14 April 2014) UN Doc A/RES/66/138; Art 74 Migrant Rights Convention.

[161] Arts 11–13 CERD.

made use of this mechanism. They do not have any direct interest in doing so, and/or are concerned that they might themselves become the subject of such a complaint.[162]

The Racial Discrimination Convention, Convention on Discrimination against Women, Convention against Torture, Migrants' Rights Convention and Enforced Disappearance Convention (also) provide for alternative mechanisms to resolve inter-State disputes concerning the interpretation or application of the respective Conventions.[163] States Parties should resolve these disputes in the first instance by negotiation or, failing that, and as provided for in some of the conventions, arbitration.[164] In last instance, they can refer their case to the ICJ.[165] More recently, the ICJ has been seised of a matter relating to the application of the Racial Discrimination Convention,[166] based on Article 22 thereof.[167] In 2008, Georgia had filed an application accusing the Russian Federation of having engaged in ethnic cleansing of Georgians in South Ossetia and Abkhazia. However, deciding on the preliminary objections raised by the Russian Federation, the ICJ ruled that Georgia had not first used or attempted to use the procedures provided for in the Convention (namely the inter-State complaint mechanism before the CERD), nor did it try to negotiate with the Russian Federation. Thus, the Court concluded that it did not have jurisdiction on the matter.[168]

D. Individual Complaints Mechanism

Currently, eight of the human rights treaty bodies (CCPR, CERD, CAT, CEDAW, CRPD, CED, CESCR and CRC) may, under certain conditions, receive and consider individual complaints or communications from individuals (or, for the CERD, CEDAW, CRPD, CESCR and CRC, groups of individuals).[169] For the Committee on Migrant Workers, the individual complaints mechanism has not yet entered into force. The individual complaints mechanism is always optional. Globally, the only exceptions to this are the American Declaration on Human Rights and the ECHR, as modified by the Eleventh Additional Protocol.[170]

The exercise of the right of individual complaint is subject to a number of conditions. First of all, the State concerned needs to have accepted the competence of the committee

[162] See further S Leckie, 'The Inter-State Complaint Procedure in International Human Rights Law: Hopeful Prospects or Wishful Thinking?' (1988) 10 *Human Rights Quarterly* 249.

[163] See respectively, Art 22 CERD; Art 29 CEDAW; Art 30 Convention against Torture; Art 92 Migrant Rights' Convention; and Art 32 Enforced Disappearance Convention.

[164] See eg Art 29 Convention on Discrimination against Women.

[165] On the peaceful settlement of disputes, see Chapter 13.

[166] *Application of the International Convention on the Elimination of All Forms of Racial Discrimination* (Georgia v Russian Federation) [2011] ICJ Rep 70.

[167] Which provides that '[a]ny dispute between two or more States Parties with respect to the interpretation or application of this Convention, which is not settled by negotiation or by the procedures expressly provided for in this Convention, shall, at the request of any of the parties to the dispute, be referred to the [ICJ] for decision, unless the disputants agree to another mode of settlement'.

[168] *Georgia v Russian Federation* (n 166), respectively paras 149, 182 and 187. For a succinct discussion of the judgement, see K Parlett, 'The International Court of Justice's Decision on Preliminary Objections in Georgia v. Russia: Towards Formalism?' (2012) 71 *The Cambridge Law Journal* 56.

[169] See respectively, Art 1 First Optional Protocol to the ICCPR; Art 14 Racial Discrimination Convention; Art 22 Convention against Torture; Art 2 Optional Protocol to the CEDAW (adopted 6 October 1999, entered into force 22 December 2000) 2131 UNTS 83; Art 1 Optional Protocol to the CRPD (adopted 13 December 2006, entered into force 3 May 2008) 2518 UNTS 283; Art 31 Enforced Disappearance Convention; Art 2 Optional Protocol to the ICESCR; Art 5 Optional Protocol on Communications Procedure to the CRC.

[170] Protocol No 11 to the Convention for the Protection of Human Rights and Fundamental Freedoms, restructuring the control machinery established thereby (adopted 11 May 1994, entered into force 1 November 1998) ETS 155.

concerned. In addition, the 'local remedies rule' offers States the possibility to first settle disputes within the domestic legal order. This rule prevents international monitoring mechanisms from becoming overburdened with complaints. It has been made more flexible throughout the years. When internal remedies are not actual, relevant and accessible, when the receipt of a judicial remedy is highly unlikely, or when a decision has been absent for an unreasonable period of time, the rule will not hinder the involvement of an international organ. Anonymous complaints and complaints that are manifestly unfounded or abusive are inadmissible. The complaint often has to be filed within a certain period of time. Whenever a committee decides that the complaint before it is admissible, it will ask the State concerned for a reaction. If the committee finds the complaint to be well-founded and consequently establishes a violation of the treaty on the part of the State, it shall communicate its findings to the State concerned. However, as mentioned above, the State is not legally bound by these findings.[171]

i. Inquiry Procedure

Upon receipt of reliable information on serious, grave or systematic violations by a State Party, a number of the UN human rights treaty bodies (CAT, CEDAW, CRPD, CED, CESCR and CRC) may, on their own initiative, initiate inquiries.[172] They may only conduct such inquiries with respect to States Parties that have recognised their competence to that effect. States may opt out from the inquiry procedure when they sign, ratify or accede to the convention in question, or anytime later.[173] An exception is the CED, as its competence to conduct inquiries is not subject to the acceptance by States Parties.[174]

E. Urgent Action Mechanisms

The CERD has created an additional mechanism for 'early warning and urgent action procedures'. This mechanism allows the CERD to take certain measures to avoid the escalation of a conflict and to prevent or limit imminent and grave breaches of the Convention.[175] Under these procedures, the CERD has issued a number of decisions and statements, and sent a number of letters to States Parties.[176]

Second, under Article 30 of the Enforced Disappearance Convention, it is possible to submit a request to the CED that a disappeared person is to be sought and found. In the

[171] See further OHCHR, Individual Complaint Procedures under the United Nations Human Rights Treaties, New York, 2013, Fact Sheet No 7/Rev 2, www.ohchr.org/Documents/Publications/FactSheet7Rev.2.pdf; G Ulfstein, 'Individual Complaints' in Keller and Ulfstein (n 154) 73–115; N Weiß, 'Überblick über die Erfahrungen mit Individualbeschwerden unter verschiedenen Menschenrechtsabkommen' (2004) 42 *Archiv des Völkerrechts* 142.

[172] See respectively, Art 20 Convention against Torture; Art 8 Optional Protocol to the CEDAW; Art 6 Optional Protocol to the CRPD; Art 33 Enforced Disappearance Convention; Art 11 Optional Protocol to the ICESCR; Art 13 Optional Protocol on communications procedure to CRC.

[173] See respectively Art 28 Convention against Torture; Art 10 Optional Protocol to the CEDAW; Art 8 Optional Protocol to the CRPD; Art 11(8) Optional Protocol to the ICESCR; Art 13(7) Optional Protocol on communications procedure to CRC.

[174] Art 33 Enforced Disappearance Convention.

[175] CERD, Prevention of Racial Discrimination, Including Early Warning and Urgent Procedures: Working Paper Adopted by the Committee on the Elimination of Racial Discrimination, 1993, UN Doc A/48/18 (Annex III); CERD, Guidelines for the Early Warning and Urgent Action Procedures, 2007, UN Doc A/62/18 (Annexes, Chapter III).

[176] See www.ohchr.org/EN/HRBodies/CERD/Pages/EarlyWarningProcedure.aspx.

most urgent cases, it is possible for the CED to adopt interim measures by asking the State Party concerned 'to adopt measures to avoid irreparable damage to the persons concerned or […] relevant to locating the disappeared person'.[177]

F. Proposals for Reform

Even though the UN treaty bodies are of fundamental importance to the international human rights system, they face significant obstacles to their effectiveness. Together with issues related to compliance and implementation, the increase in human rights instruments, their respective committees and ratifications over the last decades and a chronic lack of resources have caused significant backlogs. In 2009, the then UN High Commissioner for Human Rights, Navi Pillay, initiated the 'Dublin Process' that involved a range of stakeholders. When the process was nearing its conclusion in 2011, a group of States opposed the outcome as it did not sufficiently reflect their interests. Eventually, the UN General Assembly formally adopted a compromise in 2014 by means of Resolution 69/268.[178]

The Resolution increases the UN treaty bodies' meeting time, but does not substantially increase their resources. It also allocates a budget to the creation of a capacity-building program within the OHCHR to provide assistance to States that require aid in the preparation of their reports. Even if one of the High Commissioner's and States' desires was the harmonisation of treaty body procedures, as exemplified by an initial proposal on the part of High Commissioner Louise Arbour for a 'Unified Standing Treaty Body',[179] the Resolution merely '[e]ncourages the human rights treaty bodies to continue to enhance their efforts towards achieving greater […] harmonization through their working methods'. Lastly, and although high-quality reporting and an increased implementation of treaty recommendations by States was a concern, the Resolution merely '[r]ecognizes that some States parties consider that they would benefit from improved coordination of reporting at the national level'.

Accordingly, and even if the UN General Assembly 'addressed some of the system's most pressing resource concerns, much remains to be done to strengthen the treaty bodies'.[180] In this light, it was even proposed that a 'World Court of Human Rights' 'would take over from the treaty bodies the jurisdiction to decide on individual and inter-State complaints as well as to initiate inquire procedures', while they would remain competent for the examination of State reports.[181]

[177] CED, 'Guidance for the Submission of a Request for Urgent Action to the Committee', 29 April 2004, UN Doc CED/C/4. See further CED, 'Report on Requests for Urgent Action Submitted under Article 30 of the Convention', 14 November 2016, UN Doc CED/C/11/3.

[178] UNGA Res 69/268, 21 April 2014, UN Doc A/RES/68/268.

[179] UN High Commissioner for Human Rights, 'Concept Paper on the High Commissioner's Proposal for a Unified Standing Treaty Body', 14 March 2006, UN Doc HRI/MC/2006/CRP1 (Annexes I–III); M Bowman, 'Towards a Unified Treaty Body for Monitoring Compliance with UN Human Rights Conventions? Legal Mechanisms for Treaty Reform' (2007) 7 *Human Rights Law Review* 225; M O'Flaherty and C O'Brien, 'Reform of UN Human Rights Treaty Monitoring Bodies: A Critique of the Concept Paper on the High Commissioner's Proposal for a Unified Standing Treaty Body' (2007) 7 *Human Rights Law Review* 141.

[180] C Broecker, 'The Reform of the United Nations' Human Rights Treaty Bodies', *American Society of International Law*, 8 August 2014, www.asil.org/insights/volume/18/issue/16/reform-united-nations%E2%80%99-human-rights-treaty-bodies. See further, S Egan, 'Strengthening the United Nations Human Rights Treaty Body System' (2013) 13 *Human Rights Law Review* 209; J Pedone and AR Kloster, 'New Proposals for Human Rights Treaty Body Reform' (2012) 22 *Journal of Transnational Law and Policy* 29.

[181] M Nowak, 'The Need for a World Court of Human Rights' (2007) 7 *Human Rights Law Review* 251, 256.

Table 6 UN Human Rights Treaties

Treaty	**Genocide**	**ICERD**	**ICESCR**	**ICCPR**	**CEDAW**	**CAT**	**CRC**	**ICRMW**	**CRPD**	**ICCPED**
Opened for signature	1948	1965	19/12/1966	19/12/1966	1/3/1980	1984	1989	1990	2006	2006
Entry into force	12/1/1951	12/3/1969	3/1/1976 (Opt. Prot. 2013)	23/3/1976 (1st Opt. Prot. 1976, 2nd Opt. Prot. 1991)	3/9/1981 (Opt. Prot. 2000)	1987 (Opt. Prot. 2002)	1990 (1st/2nd Opt. Prot. 2002, 3rd Opt. Prot. 2014)	2003	2008 (Opt. Prot. 2008)	2010
Signatories	41	88	71	74	99	83	140	38	161	97
States Parties (October 2017)	149 (incl. 28 EUMS	179 (incl. 28 EUMS)	169 (incl. 28 EUMS) Opt. Prot. 22 (incl. 8 EUMS)	172 (incl. 28 EUMS) 1st Opt. Prot. 116 (incl. 26 EUMS) 2nd Opt. Prot. 85 (incl. 28 EUMS)	189 (incl. 28 EUMS) Opt. Prot. 109 (incl. 25 EUMS)	163 (incl. 28 EUMS) Opt. Prot. 84 (incl. 24 EUMS)	196 (incl. 28 EUMS) 1st Opt. Prot. 167 (incl. 28 EUMS), 2nd Opt. Prot. 174 (incl. 27 EUMS), 3rd Opt. Prot. 39 (incl. 15 EUMS)	51 (no EUMS)	177 (incl. 28 EUMS + EU) Opt. Prot. 92 (incl. 21 EUMS)	58 (incl. 13 EUMS)

(*continued*)

Table 6 ***(Continued)***

Treaty	**Genocide**	**ICERD**	**ICESCR**	**ICCPR**	**CEDAW**	**CAT**	**CRC**	**ICRMW**	**CRPD**	**ICCPED**
Monitoring Committee	None	CERD	CESCR	HRCttee	CEDAW	CAT	CRC	CMW	CRPD	CED
Reporting + period	No	Yes 2 years	Yes 5 years	Yes 5 years	Yes 4 years	Yes 4 years	Yes 5 years	Yes 5 years	Yes 4 years	Yes 2 years after entry into force
State-to-State Right of Complaint	No	Yes	Opt., Opt. Prot.	Opt.	No	Opt.	Opt, 3rd Opt. Prot.	Yes	No	Opt.
Individual rights of complaint	No	Opt.	Opt., Opt. Prot.	Opt., 1st Opt. Prot.	Opt., Opt. Prot.	Opt.	Opt., 3rd Opt. Prot.	No	Opt., Opt. Prot.	Opt.
Inquiry	No	No	Opt., Opt. Prot.	No	Opt., Opt. Prot.	Yes, but opt-out possible	Opt., 3rd Opt. Prot.	No	Opt., Opt. Prot.	Yes

Notes:

A number of additional treaties are mentioned among 'human rights treaties' on the UN Treaty Collection website. These include:

1) The 1968 Convention on the Non-Applicability of Statutory Limitations to War Crimes and Crimes against Humanity;[182]
2) The 1973 International Convention on the Suppression and Punishment of the Crime of Apartheid;[183]
3) The 1985 International Convention against Apartheid in Sports.[184]

[182] (adopted 26 November 1968, entered into force 11 November 1970) 754 UNTS 73, 55 Parties, including 11 EU MS.
[183] (adopted 30 November 1973, entered into force 18 July 1976) 1015 UNTS 243, 109 Parties, including 10 EU MS.
[184] (adopted 10 December 1985, entered into force 3 April 1988) 1500 UNTS 161, 62 Parties, including 6 EUMS.

VII. The UN Human Rights Council

A. General Overview

In March 2006, the UN Human Rights Council replaced the UN Commission on Human Rights. There were several reasons for this change. One of the major points of critique was the lack of credibility and professionalism of the Commission, as well as its politicised nature.[185] As then UN Secretary General Kofi Annan pointed out, 'States ha[d] sought membership of the Commission not to strengthen human rights but to protect themselves against criticism or to criticize others'.[186] The absence of membership criteria eventually led to known human rights abusers being admitted into the Commission, as well as one of them becoming its chair.[187] The EU had also been critical of the work of the Commission and played a constructive role in the negotiations for a new HRC.[188]

Resolution 60/251 established the United Nations HRC as a subsidiary organ of the UN General Assembly. The Council is composed by 47 Member States of the UN. Based on an equitable geographic distribution, members are 'directly and individually' elected by secret ballot by the UN General Assembly for a period of three years (with a maximum of two consecutive terms).[189] The Council's main tasks are to promote the full implementation of human rights obligations, to make recommendations to address situations of violations of human rights, and to promote the effective coordination and the mainstreaming of human rights within the UN system. The Council must schedule no fewer than three sessions per year, for a total duration of no less than ten weeks.[190]

Resolution 60/251 recognises the work undertaken by the Commission on Human Rights and acknowledges the need to preserve and build on what it had achieved. Moreover, the Council has been tasked with 'assum[ing], review[ing] and, where necessary, improv[ing] and rationaliz[ing] all mandates, mechanisms, functions and responsibilities of the Commission'.[191] Accordingly, the Council has taken over the complaint procedure and

[185] See further eg M Kothari, 'From Commission to the Council: Evolution of UN Charter Bodies' in Shelton (n 12) 587–620.

[186] UNSG, 'In Larger Freedom: Towards Development, Security and Human Rights for All', 21 March 2005, UN Doc A/59/2005, para 182; see also UNSG, 'High-Level Panel on Threats, Challenges and Change, "A More Secure World: Our Shared Responsibility"', 1 December 2004, UN Doc A/59/565, para 283.

[187] Namely Libya, the African Union candidate elected to be the chair of the Commission in 2003. After an objection by the United States, Libya became the first chair of the Commission to be elected by secret ballot instead of acclamation; UN, Press Release: 'Commission on Human Rights Elects Chairperson and Bureau for Fifty-ninth Session', 20 January 2003, HR/CN/991, www.un.org/press/en/2003/hrcn991.doc.htm; R Freedman, *The United Nations Human Rights Council, A Critique and Early Assessment* (Oxon, Routledge 2013) 19–26.

[188] The EU's vision on the matter was reflected in the following statement made by the Representative of Luxembourg to the United Nations on 21 June 2005 (UN Doc PRES05-079EN) paras 25–26: 'A Human Rights Council, whose membership is elected at a two thirds majority of the General Assembly on the basis of equitable geographic representation, will gain in status and legitimacy. An equitable peer review mechanism could be established. The Human Rights Council should address urgent human rights violations in an effective manner and promote the mainstreaming of human rights, while maintaining the main tasks of the CHR. [...] We do not need to reinvent the wheel. Central features of the CHR, such as the special procedures and the very positive participation of NGOs as well as national human rights institutions in the proceedings of the CHR, are to be maintained and further strengthened'.

[189] UNGA Res 60/251, 3 April 2006, UN Doc A/RES/60/251, para 7.

[190] ibid, para 10.

[191] ibid, para 6.

special procedures,[192] albeit with slight modifications.[193] The Council also has a number of new characteristics as compared to its predecessor. Whereas the Commission did not have any membership criteria, when electing members to the HRC UN Member States 'shall take into account the contribution of candidates to the promotion and protection of human rights and their voluntary pledges and commitments made thereto'.[194] The UN General Assembly may suspend the rights of membership in the Council of a member of the Council that commits gross and systematic violations of human rights by a two-thirds majority of the members present and voting.[195] An important novelty of the HRC is the Universal Periodic Review (UPR) mechanism.[196]

Even though the politicised nature of the Commission was one of the main driving factors behind the reform, the HRC itself has also been criticised for being 'politicised and selective'.[197] The membership criteria are not strict, it has failed to take effective action regarding country-specific situations (such as Myanmar, Somalia and Zimbabwe), and certain States have sought to change the interpretation or application of human rights in order to advance cultural or political aims.[198]

Resolution 60/251, which laid the foundation for the establishment of the HRC, also provided for a review process 'within five years'.[199] This process would entail a review of the status of the Council by the UN General Assembly,[200] as well as a review by the Council of its own work and functioning.[201] In March and June 2011, the HRC and the UN General Assembly respectively adopted their outcome resolutions.[202] The review led to a few procedural and technical changes, but it is generally seen to have produced only minimal results, and it has consequently been criticised.[203]

The EU has a role to play in the HRC, both directly and indirectly. On a direct level, it has observer status in the Council, so it is able to make statements, to have EU Member States table draft resolutions on behalf of the EU, and to engage in negotiations. It is, however, excluded from the right to vote. Indirectly, EU Member States which are elected to the Council as full members are endowed with voting rights. Article 34(1) of the TEU requires these EU Member States to coordinate whatever action they might take within the HRC and to uphold the position of the EU. While formally, this provision only applies to

[192] See below, Subsection (B).

[193] See further, LS Sunga, 'What Effect if Any Will the UN Human Rights Council Have on Special Procedures?' in G Alfredsson et al (eds), *International Human Rights Monitoring Mechanisms: Essays in Honour of Jakob Th. Möller*, 2nd edn (Leiden, Martinus Nijhoff, 2009) 169–84.

[194] UNGA Res 60/251 (n 189) para 8.

[195] ibid.

[196] See below, Subsection (C).

[197] HRC, Report of the Human Rights Council on its Thirteenth Session, 7 April 2010, UN Doc A/HRC/13/56, para 311: 'Turkey considered that the integrity of the UPR must be upheld, the rules must be fully respected, and its politicisation must be avoided'.

[198] Freedman (n 187) 145; J Wouters and K Meuwissen, 'The European Union at the UN Human Rights Council: Multilateral Human Rights Protection Coming of Age?' (2014) *European Journal of Human Rights* 135, 140–41.

[199] UNGA Res 60/251 (n 189) para 1.

[200] ibid.

[201] ibid, para 16.

[202] HRC Res 16/21, 12 April 2011, UN Doc A/HRC/RES/16/21; UNGA Res 65/281, 20 July 2011, UN Doc A/RES/65/281.

[203] UNGA, Report of the Open-ended Intergovernmental Working Group on the Review of the Work and Functioning of the Human Rights Council, 22 March 2011, UN Doc A/HRC/WG.8/2/1, under IIE, para 17(a), where the USA particularly referred to the review process as a 'race to the bottom'; for the EU, see ibid, para 17(i). On the HRC more generally, see eg M Zani, 'Le Conseil des droits de l'homme des Nations Unies' (2008) 39 *Études internationales* 433.

the EU's CFSP,[204] EU Member States tend to apply at least its spirit also in other contexts, including the HRC.[205] In Brussels, it is the Council Working Group on Human Rights (COHOM) which develops the EU's human rights policy and coordinates its position on human rights issues in the HRC. On the ground in Geneva, the EU delegation leads the coordination process between the 28 EU Member States and ensures the external representation of the Union. In order to efficiently manage the high workload, the delegations resort to 'burden sharing', dividing the follow-up of ongoing negotiations among each other.

The EU underlined its commitment for the HRC in the 2012 Strategic Framework on Human Rights and Democracy.[206] Every year, it develops a list of thematic and country-specific priorities that it intends to support at the Council. Traditionally, EU Member States jointly table resolutions on freedom of religion or belief, children's rights and the human rights situations in North Korea, Myanmar and Belarus. For example, the Union successfully sought the appointment of a Special Rapporteur on the situation of human rights in Belarus,[207] the establishment of a Commission of Inquiry on North Korea,[208] and, more recently, the sending of an independent international fact-finding mission to Myanmar.[209] In addition, EU Member States sponsor a variety of resolutions covering a broad range of human rights issues, with an increasing tendency towards national instead of joint EU initiatives. Overall, the Union tends to support resolutions on civil and political, economic, social and cultural rights, as well as country-specific resolutions, but is more lukewarm with regard to so-called 'third generation rights',[210] or proposals for new binding human rights instruments, eg on business and human rights, the right to development or the rights of older persons.

B. Special Procedures

Special procedures involve independent human rights experts with mandates to report and advise on human rights. The special procedures consist of thematic procedures (procedures concerning a particular type of human rights violation, such as disappearances, summary executions, torture, arbitrary arrest, or a particular motive for human rights violations, such as religious intolerance) and country-specific procedures (procedures concerning human rights violations in specific countries). As of 1 August 2017, there are 44 thematic and 12 country mandates. After the completion of the review, according to paragraph six of Resolution 60/251, many thematic and country mandates were extended. With regard to the former, recent mandates include those on cultural rights,[211] transnational corporations

[204] See the fact that it is located under Title V (General Provisions on the Union's External Action and Specific Provisions on the Common Foreign and Security Policy), Chapter II (Specific Provisions on the Common Foreign and Security Policy) TEU.

[205] See eg KE Smith, 'The European Union at the Human Rights Council: Speaking with One Voice but Having Little Influence' (2010) 17 *Journal of European Public Policy* 224.

[206] Council of the EU, 'EU Strategic Framework and Action Plan on Human Rights and Democracy', 25 June 2012, Doc No 11855/12.

[207] HRC Res 20/13, 'Situation of human rights in Belarus', 5 July 2012, UN Doc A/HRC/RES/20/13.

[208] HRC Res 22/13, 'The situation of human rights in the Democratic People's Republic of Korea', 21 March 2013, UN Doc A/HRC/RES/22/13.

[209] HRC Res 34/22, 'Situation of human rights in Myanmar', 24 March 2017, UN Doc A/HRC/RES/34/22.

[210] A Chané and A Sharma, 'Universal Human Rights? Exploring Contestation and Consensus in the UN Human Rights Council' (2016) 10 *Human Rights & International Legal Discourse* 219.

[211] HRC Res 10/23, 26 March 2009, UN Doc A/HRC/RES/10/23; extended by HRC Res 28/9, 10 April 2015, UN Doc A/HRC/RES/28/9.

and business[212] and the right to privacy.[213] Regarding the latter, recent country mandates include those on Iran,[214] Eritrea[215] and the Central African Republic.[216] The individuals involved are usually called 'Special Rapporteur', 'Special Representative of the Secretary General' or 'Independent Expert'. It is also possible that a group of individuals is involved as a working group. Mandate-holders conduct a (wide) range of activities. Amongst others, they undertake fact-finding missions to countries, they issue communications and urgent appeals to governments and they contribute to the elaboration of human rights standards falling within their mandate.[217]

Special procedures, and especially country-specific mandates, have been unpopular with a number of States.[218] Partly for that reason the special procedures have been codified further.[219] Resolution 5/2 adopted by the HRC is an example this process.[220] It is a Code of Conduct which is meant to 'enhance the effectiveness of the system of special procedures by defining the standards of ethical behaviour and professional conduct that special procedures mandate-holders of the Human Rights Council [...] shall observe whilst discharging their mandates'.[221]

The special procedures have been shown to work complementarily with the UN treaty bodies in a wide range of ways. For example, where treaty bodies will operate on a bilateral level, special procedures work on a multilateral level. Also, many of the UN human rights treaties, complemented by the work of their respective treaty bodies, help to legitimise the activities of the special procedures mandate-holders. The other way around, special procedures promote the ratification of UN human rights treaties and, in doing so, they promote the work of the treaty bodies. Finally, treaty bodies may inform mandate-holders of special procedures of their work and vice versa.[222]

C. Universal Periodic Review

The UPR entails a peer review procedure of the human rights situation in each country every four years, and was introduced to overcome certain issues of selectivity by which the Commission was plagued. Resolution 60/251 left the precise content of the UPR to be determined by the HRC. In June 2007, the HRC adopted Resolution 5/1, which outlines the structure of the entire review procedure. Reviews are undertaken by the UPR Working Group, which is composed of all UN Member States that are members of the HRC,

[212] HRC Res 17/4, 6 July 2011, UN Doc A/HRC/RES/17/4, extended by HRC Res 26/22, 15 July 2014, UN Doc A/HRC/RES/26/22.
[213] HRC Res 28/16, 1 April 2015, UN Doc A/HRC/RES/28/16.
[214] HRC Res 16/9, 8 April 2011, UN Doc A/HRC/RES/16/9, extended by HRC Res 28/21, 27 March 2015, UN Doc A/HRC/RES/28/21.
[215] HRC Res 20/20, 17 July 2012, UN Doc A/HRC/RES/20/20, extended by HRC Res 26/24, 27 June 2014, UN Doc A/HRC/RES/26/24.
[216] HRC Res 24/34, 9 October 2013, UN Doc A/HRC/RES/24/34, extended by HRC Res S-20/1, 21 January 2014, UN Doc A/HRC/RES/S-20/1.
[217] See further H Cantú Rivera (ed), *The Special Procedures of the Human Rights Council: A Brief Look from the Inside and Perspectives from Outside* (Cambridge, Intersentia, 2015).
[218] De Schutter (n 7) 967–68.
[219] ibid, 968.
[220] HRC Res 5/2, 18 June 2007, UN Doc A/HRC/RES/5/2.
[221] ibid, Art 1.
[222] N Rodley, 'United Nations Human Rights Treaty Bodies and Special Procedures of the Commission on Human Rights – Complementarity or Competition?' (2003) 25 *Human Rights Quarterly* 882.

and which is chaired by the President of the HRC. Other stakeholders include NGOs, but these are not allowed to take the floor. To facilitate the review process, for each State, a so-called 'troika' is established. The troika is composed of three members of the HRC, who are required to be from a different regional grouping/group. It receives written questions and/or issues raised by States and submits them to the Secretariat, which eventually transmits them to the State under review no later than ten days before the review in the Working Group. The troika also prepares the outcome report of the Working Group.

The proceedings usually take around three-and-a-half hours. The process can be divided into different phases. The first phase involves the presentation of the State under review, as well as responses to written questions. The second phase entails an interactive dialogue between the State under review and the other members of the HRC. Phase three allows the State under review to make its Concluding Remarks. The human rights obligations that are addressed are those that stem from the standards found in the UDHR, the UN Charter, the UN human rights treaties to which the relevant State is a party and all the voluntary pledges that have been made by that State. The review itself is based on a range of documents. First, there is the information prepared by the State that is under review. Second, there is a compilation that has been prepared by the Office of the High Commissioner for Human Rights. This compilation consists of, among other documents, reports of treaty bodies and information contained in special procedures. Finally, there is the 'credible and reliable information' prepared by relevant stakeholders, including NGOs.[223] The outcome of the UPR consists of a report summarising the proceedings of the review process and containing the different conclusions and/or recommendations, as well as the voluntary commitments of the States that have been reviewed. Future review cycles will then focus on the implementation of the outcome by the State concerned. The first review cycle was finalised in October 2011. The second cycle was started in June 2012 and completed in November 2016. The third cycle started in May 2017, and will finish in November 2021. While the UPR is seen as one of the major innovations of the HRC, it also has to deal with some flaws and problems, some of which derive from its politicised nature.[224]

D. Complaints Mechanism

The HRC largely reproduced the complaints procedure which already existed for the Commission on Human Rights, and is shown in Table 7.[225] The mechanism is aimed at 'address[ing] consistent patterns of gross and reliably attested violations of all human rights and all fundamental freedoms occurring in any part of the world and under any circumstances'.[226] The procedure is principally confidential,[227] so as to enhance cooperation

[223] UNHRC Res 5/1, 18 June 2007, UN Doc A/HRC/RES/5/1, para 15(c).

[224] Freedman (n 187) 278: 'Various tactics were used to deflect attention from sensitive issues or to protect states from particular scrutiny [...] regionalism was used in the UPR process in much the same way as it has throughout Council sessions and proceedings'. See further, H Charlesworth and E Larking (eds), *Human Rights and the Universal Periodic Review: Rituals and Ritualism* (Cambridge, CUP 2015); I Fassasi, 'L'examen périodique universel devant le Conseil des droits de l'homme des Nations Unies' (2009) 20 *Revue trimestrielle des droits de l'homme* 739; A-M Thévenot-Werner, 'L'examen périodique universel du Conseil des droits de l'homme des Nations Unies au regard du droit international' (2012) 139 *Journal du droit international*.

[225] See ECOSOC Res 1235 (XLII), 6 June 1967, UN Doc E/4393, and ECOSOC Res 1503 (XLVIII), 27 May 1970, UN Doc E/4832/Add1.

[226] UNHRC Res 5/1 (n 223) para 85.

[227] ibid, paras 100, 102 and 104.

with States. Communications are submitted either by individuals, by groups of individuals or by NGOs. The self-proclaimed improvements of the current complaints mechanism to the system that existed for the Commission are that it is 'impartial, objective, efficient, victims-oriented and conducted in a timely manner'.[228]

Table 7 HRC Complaints Mechanism

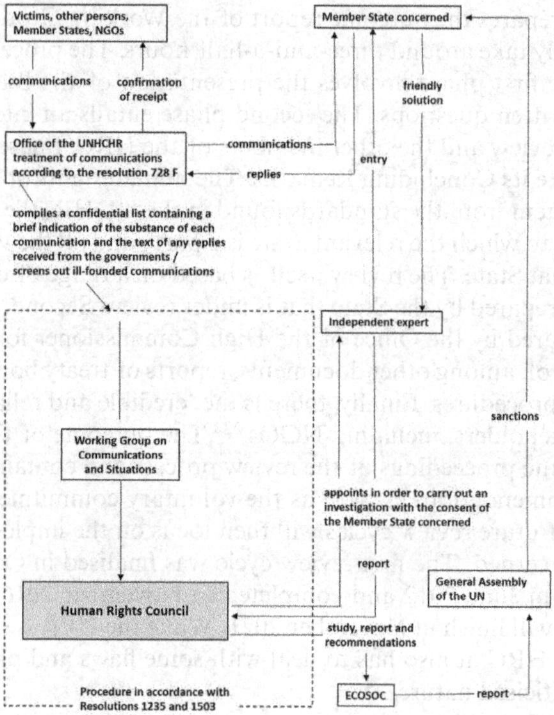

VIII. Office of the UN High Commissioner for Human Rights

On 20 December 1993, the UN General Assembly created the OHCHR.[229] The OHCHR is headed by the UN High Commissioner for Human Rights, who has the general mandate to 'promote and protect the effective enjoyment by all of all civil, cultural, economic, political and social rights'.[230] The High Commissioner reports annually about his work and that of the OHCHR to the HRC, ECOSOC and the UN General Assembly.[231] The creation of the

[228] ibid, para 86.
[229] UNGA Res 48/141, 20 December 1993, UN Doc A/RES/48/141.
[230] ibid, operative clause 4(a).
[231] ibid, operative clause 5; BG Ramcharan, 'The Office of UN High Commissioner for Human Rights' in Alfredsson et al (n 193) 199, 200.

mandate of the High Commissioner was an important part of the effort to 'mainstream' human rights throughout all political, developmental and other initiatives by the UN during the 1990s.[232] Thus, his initial mandate and activity focused on the streamlining, rationalisation and coordination of the UN human rights machinery and the improvement of its efficiency and effectiveness.[233]

Over the years, the scope of the activities and services performed by the OHCHR, the mandates it supports, and the human and financial resources made available to it have grown exponentially.[234] Today, its work mainly focuses on human rights standard-setting, human rights monitoring and supporting human rights implementation at the country level.[235] In these areas, the OHCHR provides substantive and technical support to the HRC as well as the UN treaty bodies. In addition, it contributes to the implementation of human rights and the monitoring thereof at the national level, in particular through country-specific or regional teams that provide expert advice and assistance requested by governments.[236] In this sense, there has been a shift of emphasis away from the OHCHR headquarters, which have taken on a more supportive role, to the field.[237] This is the case especially for the OHCHR's activity in connection with violent contexts, regarding which its approach can be conceptualised in three phases: (i) the prevention of human rights violations; (ii) rapid deployment in case of human rights emergencies and the constant monitoring thereof; and (iii) addressing post-conflict situations.[238] Thus, the OHCHR can be a part of peacekeeping or peacebuilding missions.[239] Lastly, it is to be noted that the OHCHR also cooperates with regional organisations[240] as well as the international criminal tribunals, including the ICC.[241]

IX. Council of Europe

A. European Convention on Human Rights

After the atrocities of the Second World War, many sought to pursue international protection of the individual against arbitrary power and oppression. The previous section already discussed the instruments adopted at the global level in the wake of these developments, such as the UDHR. Also on the European continent, a multitude of 'European Movements' started to arise as a response to the threats against human rights and political freedom. In 1948, the Committee of Movements for European Unity organised a Congress

[232] H Hannum, 'Human Rights in Conflict Resolution: The Role of the Office of the High Commissioner for Human Rights in UN Peacemaking and Peacebuilding' (2006) 28 *Human Rights Quarterly* 1, 4.
[233] UNGA Res 48/141 (n 229) perambulatory clauses.
[234] J Connors and M Schmidt, 'United Nations' in Moeckli et al (n 2) 359, 388.
[235] ibid, 389.
[236] ibid; Ramcharan (n 231) 200.
[237] Connors and Schmidt (n 234) 389.
[238] A Bellal, 'Building Respect for the Rule of Law in Violent Contexts: The Office of the High Commissioner for Human Rights' Experience and Approach' (2014) 96 *International Review of the Red Cross* 881, 884.
[239] See further, Hannum (n 232).
[240] For example, the Regional Office for Europe of OHCHR (ROE-OHCHR) plays a leading role in human rights standard-setting and monitoring within Europe, and therefore works in close dialogue with the EU and Council of Europe institutions. See www.europe.ohchr.org for a regular update on its workings.
[241] Ramcharan (n 231) 200.

of Europe in The Hague. This congress resulted in the establishment of the Council of Europe (CoE), and in the drafting of the ECHR.[242] Even though the ECHR is the centre-piece of the CoE, several other important human rights treaties have originated from the Council. Amongst them are the ESC (see below, Subsection (B)) and the European Convention for the Prevention of Torture and Inhuman or Degrading Treatment or Punishment (see below, Subsection (C)).[243]

The ECHR was signed on 4 November 1950 and entered into force on 3 September 1953. The provisions of the ECHR concern the classical rights and freedoms already contained in the UDHR. Those were the rights which the 12 European States signing the ECHR in 1950 could agree upon. The more controversial rights, such as the right to asylum, were left outside the scope of the Convention. However, the ECHR describes these rights in a much more detailed manner than the UDHR does. Moreover, the circumstances in which a State might derogate from the exercise of certain rights are more specifically set out in the ECHR.[244] Also, some of the disputed rights were added later, either through an additional protocol to the ECHR (eg, the right to property[245]) or in the ESC (eg, the right to work[246]).

Within the ECHR, it is necessary to distinguish between normative provisions, which secure rights and freedoms, and institutional provisions, which establish a monitoring mechanism. The Protocols to the ECHR do not alter its normative provisions. They merely add additional rights to the existing catalogue of rights (the actual additional protocols) or they modify the monitoring mechanisms (procedural protocols). The actual additional protocols only need to be ratified by a limited number of States (Contracting Parties) in order to enter into force (eg, the entry into force of the First Protocol only required ten ratifications).[247] Procedural protocols need to be ratified by all Contracting Parties given that they contain rules of procedure and hence modify the (procedural) provisions of the ECHR as such. Examples of these procedural protocols are the Eleventh Protocol[248] and the Fourteenth Protocol.[249]

i. Normative Provisions

The original text of the ECHR essentially deals with the right to live a free life, and all of the different modalities that this freedom can assume. Article 2 concerns the right to *life*. First, the article makes an exception for the death penalty. However, this exception has over time become redundant. The Sixth Protocol, adopted in 1983, prohibits the death penalty in peace time.[250] In 2002, the Thirteenth Protocol abolished the death

[242] See further, V Butkevych, 'The European Convention on Human Rights in the Context of the History of International Law' in L Caflisch, and L Wildhaber (eds), *Liber Amicorum Luzius Wildhaber: Human Rights – Strasbourg Views* (Kehl, Engel, 2007) 41–64.

[243] European Convention for the Prevention of Torture and Inhuman or Degrading Treatment or Punishment (adopted 26 November 1987, entered into force 1 February 1989) ETS 126 (Convention on the Prevention of Torture).

[244] See Art 15 ECHR.

[245] See Art 1 Protocol to the Convention for the Protection of Human Rights and Fundamental Freedoms (adopted 20 March 1952, entered into force 18 May 1954) ETS 9 (First Protocol).

[246] See Art 1 ESC.

[247] Art 6 First Protocol.

[248] See above (n 170).

[249] Protocol No 14 to the Convention for the Protection of Human Rights and Fundamental Freedoms, amending the control system of the Convention (adopted 13 May 2004, entered into force 1 June 2010) ETS 194.

[250] Protocol No 6 to the Convention for the Protection of Human Rights and Fundamental Freedoms concerning the Abolition of the Death Penalty (adopted 28 April 1983, entered into force 1 March 1985) ETS 114.

penalty in all circumstances.[251] In 2010 the ECtHR found that the ratification rate of the Thirteenth Protocol and 'consistent State practice in observing the moratorium on capital punishment, are strongly indicative that Article 2 has been amended so as to prohibit the death penalty in all circumstances'.[252]

Article 2 also makes an exception for the use of force which is absolutely necessary[253] for an exhaustive list of three enumerated purposes, namely: (i) self-defence and the defence of others; (ii) the execution of a lawful arrest or the prevention of the escape of a person lawfully detained; and (iii) quelling a riot or insurrection. The ECtHR has made clear that the requirement that the force used must be absolutely necessary also entails that it must be strictly proportionate to any of the three aims pursued.[254] Lastly, the right to life can be derogated from 'in respect of deaths resulting from lawful acts of war'.[255]

Article 3 contains the prohibition of *torture*, inhuman or degrading treatment or punishment. As opposed to the right to life, the prohibition of torture is an absolute right that does not allow for limitations or derogations.[256] The ECtHR has ruled that the distinction between torture and inhuman or degrading treatment 'derives principally from a difference in the intensity of the suffering inflicted'.[257] Even though a separate European Torture Prevention Convention was adopted in the framework of the Council of Europe,[258] the provision nonetheless does not lose its importance, given that that Convention – as opposed to the ECHR – does not foresee a possible review before the ECtHR where there is a violation thereof.[259]

Article 4 offers protection against *slavery*, servitude and forced or compulsory labour. Again, there is a difference in degree between the three prohibitions.[260] The ECtHR has ruled that also trafficking in human beings, even if not expressly mentioned in the Convention, falls within the scope of Article 4 ECHR.[261] The term forced or compulsory labour does

[251] Protocol No 13 to the Convention for the Protection of Human Rights and Fundamental Freedoms, concerning the abolition of the death penalty in all circumstances (adopted 3 May 2002, entered into force 1 July 2003) ETS 187. See further J Yorke, 'The Right to Life and Abolition of the Death Penalty in the Council of Europe' (2009) 34 *European Law Review* 205.

[252] *Al-Saadoon and Mufdhi v UK* App no 61498/08 (ECtHR, 2 March 2010) para 120.

[253] As regards the condition that any use of force affecting the right to life must be 'absolutely necessary', see the seminal judgment of the ECHR: *McCann and others v UK* App no 18984/91 (ECtHR, 27 September 1995), in particular paras 146–50.

[254] ibid, para 149.

[255] Art 15(2) ECHR. On the right to life, see further, L Early et al (eds), *The Right to Life under Article 2 of the European Convention on Human Rights: Twenty Years of Legal Developments since McCann v. the United Kingdom* (Oisterwijk, Wolf Legal Publishers, 2016); and WA Schabas, 'Article 2. Right to Life' in WA Schabas, *The European Convention on Human Rights: A Commentary* (Oxford, OUP, 2015) 117–63.

[256] ibid; *Soering v UK* (n 113) para 88.

[257] *Torture* concerns 'deliberate inhuman treatment causing very serious and cruel suffering', and thus 'constitutes an aggravated and deliberate form of cruel, inhuman or degrading treatment or punishment', to which a special stigma is to be attached. *Inhuman treatment* causes, 'if not actual bodily injury, at least intense physical and mental suffering to the persons subjected thereto'. Acts of *degrading treatment* are 'such as to arouse in their victims feelings of fear, anguish and inferiority capable of humiliating and debasing them and possibly breaking their physical or moral resistance': *Ireland v UK* App no 5310/71 (ECtHR, 18 January 1978) para 167.

[258] See below, Subsection (C).

[259] See further WA Schabas, 'Article 3. Prohibition of Torture' in Schabas (n 255) 164–200.

[260] *Siliadin v France* App no 73316/01 (ECtHR, 26 July 2005). Referring to the 1927 Slavery Convention, the ECtHR considered that *slavery* 'is the status or condition of a person over whom any or all of the powers attaching to the right of ownership are exercised' (para 122). *Servitude* 'means an obligation to provide one's services that is imposed by the use of coercion, and is to be linked with the concept of "slavery"' (para 124). *Forced or compulsory labour*, lastly, 'brings to mind the idea of physical or mental constraint'. 'What there has to be is work "exacted … under the menace of any penalty" and also performed against the will of the person concerned, that is work for which he "has not offered himself voluntarily"' (para 117).

[261] *Rantsev v Cyprus and Russia* App no 25965/04 (ECtHR, 7 January 2010) paras 277–82.

not include work required to be done in the ordinary course of detention[262] and military service.[263] Also the obligation to provide free lawyer services to indigent defendants as a pupil lawyer was found not to be in breach of the ECHR.[264]

Article 5 guarantees the right to *liberty* and security. Only in six exhaustively enumerated and strictly circumscribed cases can persons be deprived of their liberty.[265] Even then, there are a number of procedural safeguards and judicial guarantees to be complied with. First, everyone who is arrested has to be informed promptly of the reasons of his or her arrest, and of any charges against him or her.[266] Second, anyone facing criminal charges must be brought promptly before a judge.[267] Third, everyone deprived of his or her liberty has the right to have the legality of his or her detention reviewed by a judge (*habeas corpus*).[268] Lastly, everyone who has been the victim of an arrest or detention in contravention of Article 5 has an enforceable right to compensation.[269]

Article 6(1) lays down the right to a *fair trial*. Its scope of application is limited to civil and criminal cases. These are however 'autonomous' notions, interpreted flexibly by the ECtHR.[270] Article 6(1) guarantees that everyone is entitled to a fair and public hearing within a reasonable time and by an independent and impartial tribunal established by law.[271] Judgments are, apart from enumerated grounds that can justify an exception, to be pronounced publicly. Article 6(2) only applies to criminal cases, and contains the presumption of innocence.[272] Article 6(3), too, only applies to criminal cases, and contains particular rights, such as the right to be informed promptly of the nature and cause of any accusation, the right to have adequate time and facilities for the preparation of one's defence and the

[262] Recently, see eg *Meier v Switzerland* App no 10109/14 (ECtHR, 9 February 2016), in which the Court found that Switzerland did not violate Art 4 because it had obliged a prisoner to work beyond retirement age.

[263] Art 4(3) ECHR.

[264] *Van der Mussele v Belgium* App no 8919/80 (ECtHR, 23 November 1983). See further WA Schabas, 'Article 4. Prohibition of Slavery and Forced Labour' in Schabas (n 255) 201–18.

[265] See Art 5(1) ECHR.

[266] ibid, Art 5(2).

[267] ibid, Art 5(3).

[268] ibid, Art 5(4).

[269] ibid, Art 5(5). See further, WA Schabas 'Article 5. Right to Liberty and Security' in Schabas (n 255) 219–63.

[270] eg, in *Le Compte, Van Leuven and De Meyere v Belgium* App nos 6878/75 and 7238/75 (ECtHR, 23 June 1981) paras 46–48, the ECtHR found that a decision from an administrative body that prevented the applicants from exercising the medical profession concerned their civil rights and obligations. In *Engel and others v the Netherlands* App nos 5100/71, 5101/71, 5102/71, 5354/72 and 5370/72 (ECtHR, 8 June 1976) para 82, the ECtHR ruled that the criminal nature of cases is to be determined on the basis of: (i) 'whether the provision(s) defining the offence charged belong, according to the legal system of the respondent State, to criminal law' (a criterion that 'provides no more than a starting point'); (ii) 'the very nature of the offence'; and (iii) 'the degree of severity of the penalty that the person concerned risks incurring'.

[271] 'The reasonableness of the length of proceedings is to be determined in the light of […] the complexity of the case, the conduct of the applicant and of the relevant authorities, and what was at stake for the applicant in the dispute'; eg, *Comingersoll SA v Portugal* App no 35382/97 (ECtHR, 6 April 2000) para 19. On the requirement of independence and impartiality, see *Findlay v UK* App no 22107/93 (ECtHR, 25 February 1997) para 73: for the independence of a tribunal 'regard must be had, inter alia, to the manner of appointment of its members and their term of office, the existence of guarantees against outside pressures and the question whether the body presents an appearance of independence'. For its impartiality: 'First, the tribunal must be subjectively free of personal prejudice or bias. Secondly, it must also be impartial from an objective viewpoint, that is, it must offer sufficient guarantees to exclude any legitimate doubt in this respect'. However, '[t]he concepts of independence and objective impartiality are closely linked'.

[272] For example, in *Allenet de Ribemont v France* App no 15175/89 (ECtHR, 10 February 1995) para 41, the ECtHR found that the fact that during a judicial investigation 'some of the highest-ranking officers in the French police referred to Mr Allenet de Ribemont, without any qualification or reservation, as one of the instigators of a murder' violated Art 6(2) ECHR.

right to defend oneself or to legal assistance.[273] Article 7 contains the related *principle of legality*, and more particularly protects against retroactive criminal offences (*nullum crimen sine lege*) and penalties (*nulla poena sine lege*) to the detriment of the accused. However, with the Nuremberg trials and judgment in mind, the drafters provided that this 'shall not prejudice the trial and punishment of any person for any act or omission which, at the time when it was committed, was criminal according to the general principles of law recognised by civilised nations'.[274]

Article 8 refers to the right to respect for *private and family life*. Traditionally, it covers a person's home and correspondence. However, over time, the ECtHR has broadened the scope of Article 8, which has come to encompass the privacy of decisions, including issues relating to one's sexual[275] and reproductive life[276] and the right to health. It also protects a person's personal data. In this light, the phenomenon of 'mass surveillance' has become a particular issue.[277] The right to the respect for private and family life is not absolute; hence, Article 8(2) ECHR provides a number of grounds in the pursuit of which necessary and proportionate measures can lawfully limit it.[278] Related is Article 12, which ensures the right to *marry* for men and women of marriageable age as well as the right to found a family in accordance with the national laws governing the exercise of this right. The ECtHR has so far not recognised the right to marry for same-sex couples.[279]

Article 9 guarantees the right to freedom of *thought, conscience and religion*, and includes the freedom to manifest one's religion or belief, be it alone or in community with others and in private or in public. As exemplified in the case *SAS v France*,[280] in which the ECtHR upheld the French law prohibiting the wearing of the full-face veil in public, this right also can be subject to limitations.[281] Article 10 protects the related right to freedom of *expression*. This includes 'not only "information" or "ideas" that are favourably received or regarded as inoffensive or as a matter of indifference, but also those that offend, shock or disturb the State or any sector of the population'.[282] Some forms of expression, like political expression, require a high level of protection.[283] On the other hand, the freedom

[273] See further WA Schabas 'Article 6. Right to a Fair Trial' in Schabas (n 255) 264–327.

[274] Art 7(2) ECHR. See further, WA Schabas, 'Article 7. No Punishment without Law' in Schabas (n 255) 328–57.

[275] See in particular *Dudgeon v UK* App no 7525/76 (ECtHR, 22 October 1981), where the Court held that in so far as the English Criminal Law Amendment Act 1885 criminalised homosexual acts between consenting adult males, it violated Art 8 ECHR.

[276] See in particular *Dickson v UK* App no 44362/04 (ECtHR, 4 December 2007), where the Court found the UK to be in violation of Art 8 ECHR because it refused access to artificial insemination facilities to a prisoner (serving a life sentence) and his wife; and *P and S v Poland* App no 57375/08 (ECtHR, 30 October 2012), where the Court found Poland to be in breach of Art 8 (and 3) ECHR because of the numerous humiliating obstacles a 14-year-old teenager encountered in her search for abortion after she had been raped.

[277] See in particular *Roman Zakharov v Russia* App no 47143/06 (ECtHR, 4 December 2015), where Russia was found to be in violation of Art 8 because its provisions governing the interception of mobile telephone communications did not provide sufficient guarantees against arbitrariness and the risk of abuse.

[278] See further WA Schabas, 'Article 8. Right to Respect for Private and Family Life' in Schabas (n 255) 358–411.

[279] *Schalk and Kopf v Austria* App no 30141/04 (ECtHR, 24 June 2010). However, it did recognise their right to a private and family life (para 94). See further, WA Schabas, 'Article 12. Right to Marry' in Schabas (n 255) 528–45. The ECtHR did rule that, where a CoE Member State extends a right to adopt to unmarried different-sex couples, it should to same-sex couples as well (*X and others v Austria* App no 19010/07 (ECtHR, 19 February 2013)). The CJEU has itself pronounced on the free movement/residence rights of same-sex couples in its judgment of 5 June 2018, *Coman and others*, C-673/16, ECLI:EU:C:2018:385.

[280] *SAS v France* App no 43835/11 (ECtHR, 1 July 2014).

[281] See Art 9(2) ECHR. See further, WA Schabas, 'Article 9. Freedom of Thought, Conscience and Religion' in Schabas (n 255) 412–43.

[282] *Handyside v UK* App no 5493/72 (ECtHR, 7 December 1976) para 49.

[283] *Steel and Morris v UK* App no 68416/01 (ECtHR, 15 February 2005) para 88.

of expression is not absolute.[284] Moreover, there are forms of expression that are not protected, in particular hate speech. Hate speech is normally considered to be an abuse of rights, which is prohibited under Article 17 ECHR, and thus removed from the protection of Article 10.[285] Article 11 guarantees the rights to freedom of *peaceful assembly and association* with others. In addition to the traditional limitations to this right on the basis for example of public safety, limitations can also be brought upon the exercise of this right by members of the armed forces, of the police or the administration of the State.[286]

Article 13 foresees the right to an *effective remedy* before a national authority for everyone whose rights and freedoms as set forth in the Convention have been violated. This provision is at the same time accessory and autonomous: accessory because its violation has to relate to another Convention right, but autonomous because that other right does not have to be *violated*: it is sufficient that the applicant presents an *arguable claim* that his or her rights under the Convention have been violated.[287]

Article 14, lastly, does not refer to a specific right but prohibits *discrimination* with regard to the enjoyment of the rights and freedoms set forth in the ECHR. The provision mentions certain grounds based upon which one cannot be discriminated (eg, sex), but the 'such as' makes this list open-ended. Article 14 is accessory, and must relate to rights safeguarded by other provisions of the ECHR or additional protocols. However, Article 14 'does not necessarily presuppose a breach of those provisions – and to this extent it is autonomous'; nevertheless, 'there can be no room for its application unless the facts in issue fall within the ambit of one of the latter provisions'.[288] A general prohibition of discrimination, meaning one that also covers discrimination not related to a Convention right (eg, rights merely laid down in national legislation), is foreseen in the Twelfth Protocol.[289] Discrimination can exist not only when States treat persons in analogous situations differently, but also when they fail to treat differently persons whose situations are significantly different.[290] Even if Article 14 ECHR and Article 1 of the Twelfth Protocol are drafted in absolute terms, discrimination can be allowed if it has an objective and reasonable justification, pursues a legitimate aim, and if there is 'a reasonable relationship of proportionality between the means employed and the aim sought to be realised':[291] 'there must be no other means of achieving the same end that would interfere less seriously with the fundamental right concerned'.[292] However, there are grounds of discrimination for which the ECtHR will apply a stricter test, and thus limit the margin of appreciation of States (eg, race, colour or ethnic origin[293] and disability[294]).

[284] See Art 10(2) ECHR.

[285] *Seurot v France* App no 57383/00 (ECtHR, 18 May 2004). See further, WA Schabas, 'Article 10. Freedom of Expression' in Schabas (n 255) 444–82.

[286] Art 11(2) ECHR. See further WA Schabas, 'Article 11. Freedom of Assembly and Association' in Schabas (n 255) 483–527.

[287] *Klass and others v Germany* App no 5029/71 (ECtHR, 6 September 1978) para 64; *Boyle and Rice v UK* App nos 9659/82 and 9658/82 (ECtHR, 27 April 1988). See further, WA Schabas, 'Article 13. Right to an Effective Remedy' in Schabas (n 255) 546–54.

[288] *Glor v Switzerland* App no 13444/04 (ECtHR, 30 April 2009), para 45. See further, WA Schabas, 'Article 14. Prohibition of Discrimination' in Schabas (n 255) 555–86.

[289] Protocol No 12 to the Convention for the Protection of Human Rights and Fundamental Freedoms (adopted 4 November 2000, entered into force 1 April 2005) ETS 177.

[290] *Thlimmenos v Greece* App no 34369/97 (ECtHR, 6 April 2000), para 44.

[291] *Case 'Relating to Certain Aspects of the Laws on the Use of Languages in Education in Belgium' v Belgium*, App nos 1474/62; 1677/62; 1691/62; 1769/63; 1994/63 and 2126/64 (ECtHR, 23 July 1968) para 10.

[292] *Glor v Switzerland*, above (n 288) para 94.

[293] *DH v Czech Republic* App no 57325/00 (ECtHR, 13 November 2007) para 196.

[294] *Glor v Switzerland*, above (n 288) para 84.

Other Protocols than the ones already discussed that added rights to the ECHR are the First (the right to property, education and free and secret elections),[295] the Fourth (the prohibition of imprisonment for debt or inability to fulfil a contractual obligation, the right to liberty of movement and freedom to choose one's residence, the prohibition of expulsion of nationals and the collective expulsion of aliens)[296] and the Seventh Additional Protocol (procedural safeguards relating to the expulsion of aliens, the right of appeal in criminal matters, compensation for wrongful conviction, the right not to be tried or punished twice (*non bis in idem*) and equality between spouses).[297]

As alluded to on several occasions, the ECHR provides its Contracting Parties with the possibility to limit the exercise of or derogate from certain rights and freedoms guaranteed by the Convention under certain circumstances. First, some provisions foresee the possibility to *limit* or *restrict* the exercise of the right guaranteed. Similarly as for the ICCPR, these limitations must be foreseen by law, pursue a legitimate purpose, be necessary in a democratic society for the pursuance of that aim, and be proportionate thereto. They may also not discriminate.[298] For example, Article 8(2), concerning the right to respect for private and family life, states that:

> [t]here shall be no interference by a public authority with the exercise of this right except such as is in accordance with the law and is necessary on a democratic society, in the interests of national security, public safety or the economic well-being of the country, for the prevention of disorder or crime, for the protection of health and morals, or for the protection of the rights and freedoms of others.

A similar possibility is foreseen in Articles 9(2), 10(2), and 11(2).

Second, Article 15 stipulates that

> [i]n time of war or other public emergency threatening the life of the nation[299] any High Contracting Party [may] take measures *derogating* from [their] obligations under this Convention to the extent strictly required by the exigencies of the situation, provided that such measures are not inconsistent with its other obligations under international law.

Such derogations cannot, however, be established with regard to the right to life foreseen in Article 2, except in cases of death as a consequence of lawful acts of war, and Articles 3, 4(1) and 7. Moreover, the derogating State has to keep the Secretary General of the Council of Europe fully informed of the measures which it has taken and the reasons therefore.[300] Nevertheless, the ECtHR has recognised that 'the national authorities are in principle in

[295] See above (n 245).

[296] Protocol No 4 to the Convention for the Protection of Human Rights and Fundamental Freedoms, securing certain rights and freedoms other than those already included in the Convention and in the first Protocol thereto (adopted 16 September 1963, entered into force 2 May 1968) ETS 46.

[297] Protocol No 7 to the Convention for the Protection of Human Rights and Fundamental Freedoms (adopted 22 November 1984, entered into force 1 November 1988) ETS 117.

[298] See Art 14 ECHR.

[299] In *Lawless v Ireland (No 3)* App no 332/57 (ECtHR, 1 July 1961) para 28, the Court clarified that 'the words "other public emergency threatening the life of the nation" [...] refer to an exceptional situation of crisis or emergency which affects the whole population and constitutes a threat to the organized life of the community of which the State is composed'.

[300] Art 15(3) ECHR. But see *Hassan v UK* App no 29750/09 (ECtHR, 16 September 2014) paras 101–107, where the Court dispensed with the requirement to formally lodge a derogation in view of the possibility for the UK to (administratively) detain persons in a situation of international armed conflict on grounds not provided for in Art 5 ECHR, based on the argument that 'no State has ever made a derogation pursuant to Article 15 of the Convention in respect of these activities'.

a better position than the international judge to decide both on the presence of such an emergency and on the nature and scope of derogations necessary to avert it', leaving them 'a wide margin of appreciation […] accompanied by a European supervision'.[301]

Article 17 further specifies that

> [n]othing in this Convention may be interpreted as implying for any State, group or person any right to engage in any activity or perform any act aimed at the destruction of any of the rights and freedoms set forth herein or at their limitation to a greater extent than is provided for in the Convention.

It thus contains a general prohibition of *abuse of the rights* guaranteed in the Convention. This provision is used for example to remove hate speech from the protection of Article 10 ECHR.[302] Article 18, lastly, clearly establishes that the restrictions permitted under the Convention shall not be applied for any purpose other than those for which they have been prescribed.[303]

ii. Interpretation

As already alluded to with regard to certain specific rights, over the years, the ECtHR has adopted a particular evolutive-teleological approach in applying the ECHR, emphasising that the Convention is a living instrument to be interpreted in the light of present-day conditions, and that the object and purpose of the Convention require that its provisions should be implemented so as to make its safeguards effective.[304] Furthermore, the Court has broadly interpreted the notion of jurisdiction, as referred to in Article 1 ECHR.[305] On occasion, the approach of the ECtHR has led CoE Member States to accuse the Court of judicial activism, and to refuse to implement its rulings. For example, even if the ECtHR repeatedly ruled that the United Kingdom violated Article 3 of the First Protocol with its blanket ban on prisoner voting,[306] the country has consistently refused to adapt its legislation. On the other hand, when it is faced with what it feels is more an issue of policy than law, the ECtHR generally tries to exercise restraint and to take into account Member States' interests through its doctrine of the margin of appreciation (see eg, above on derogations). This way, the Court can also factor in the diversity in relevant approaches taken by the different CoE Member States.[307] However, overall, it is rather unclear when exactly the doctrine of the margin of appreciation should be used, what its precise limits and contours are, and which exact consequences flow from invoking it.[308]

[301] *Ireland v UK* (n 257) para 207. See further, WA Schabas, 'Article 15. Derogation in Time of Emergency' in Schabas (n 255) 587–605.

[302] See further, WA Schabas, 'Article 17. Prohibition of Abuse of Rights' in Schabas (n 255) 611–22.

[303] See further WA Schabas, 'Article 18. Limitation on Use of Restrictions on Rights' in Schabas (n 255) 623–30.

[304] See eg *Soering v UK* (n 113) paras 87, 90 and 102. See also Chapter 2 on Treaty Law, Section VII(A)(i).

[305] See further Chapter 9 on Jurisdiction, Section VI.

[306] See *Hirst v UK (No 2)* App no 74025/01 (ECtHR, 6 October 2005); and, most importantly, *McHugh and others v UK* App no 51987/08 and 1,014 others (ECtHR, 10 February 2015).

[307] E Brems, 'The Margin of Appreciation Doctrine of the European Court of Human Rights: Accommodating Diversity within Europe' in DP Forsythe and PC McMahon (eds), *Human Rights and Diversity: Area Studies Revisited* (Lincoln, University of Nebraska Press, 2003) 81–110.

[308] J Kratochvíl, 'The Inflation of the Margin of Appreciation by the European Court of Human Rights' (2011) 29 *Netherlands Quarterly of Human Rights* 324, 325.

iii. Institutional Provisions

The ECHR provides a high and effective level of protection. First, it has a compulsory inter-State complaint mechanism that is only rarely used.[309] Second, and more importantly, it provides for a right for individuals to directly introduce complaints before the ECtHR.[310] Filing a complaint to the Registry of the ECtHR is not very formalistic. However, there are a number of criteria for a complaint to be admissible. First, the Court may only deal with applications that have exhausted all domestic remedies and that are filed within a period of six months from the date on which the final decision was taken.[311] In addition, the Court shall not deal with any individual application: (i) that is anonymous;[312] (ii) that is substantially the same as a matter that has already been examined by the Court or that has already been submitted to another procedure of international investigation or settlement;[313] (iii) that is manifestly ill-founded or an abuse of the right of individual application;[314] or (iv) where the applicant has not suffered a significant disadvantage, unless respect for human rights requires an examination of the application and provided that no case may be rejected on this ground which has not been duly considered by a domestic tribunal.[315]

At any stage of the proceedings, the Court may place itself at the disposal of the parties concerned with a view to securing a friendly settlement of the matter in confidential proceedings.[316] If no such settlement is reached, contentious proceedings follow. Hearings are public, unless the Court decides otherwise in exceptional circumstances.[317] The parties appear before the Court, where each Contracting Party has one judge.[318] The judges are independent, sit in their personal capacity and do not represent their State.[319] They can sit in different formations: the Court sits in a single-judge formation, committees of three judges, Chambers of seven judges (including the 'national' judge) or in a Grand Chamber of 17 judges (including the President of the Court, the Vice-Presidents, the Presidents of the Chambers and the 'national' judge).[320]

[309] Art 33 ECHR. See eg *Ireland v UK* (n 257); *Cyprus v Turkey* App no 25781/94 (ECtHR, 10 May 2001). Following the violence in Eastern Ukraine and Crimea, several *Ukraine v Russia* cases are pending before the ECtHR. See further, SC Prebensen 'Inter-State Complaints Under Treaty Provisions – The Experience of the European Convention on Human Rights' in Alfredsson et al (n 193) 441–64.

[310] Before the entry into force of (Art 34 of) the Eleventh Protocol (n 170), this was only an optional possibility. Moreover, originally, individuals did not have direct access to the ECtHR: they had to apply to the European Commission on Human Rights, which would decide whether their case was well-founded and, if so, bring it before the ECtHR on their behalf. See further M Pellonpää, 'From the European Commission of Human Rights to the European Court of Human Rights' (2014) 35 *Human Rights Law Journal* 256.

[311] Art 35(1) ECHR. From the moment Protocol No 15 enters into force, the time limit is shortened from six to four months. See Protocol No 15 amending the Convention for the Protection of Human Rights and Fundamental Freedoms (adopted 24 June 2013, not yet entered into force) CETS 213.

[312] Art 35(2)(a) ECHR.

[313] ibid, Art 35(2)(b).

[314] ibid, Art 35(3)(a).

[315] ibid, Art 35(3)(b). From the moment Protocol No 15 enters into force, the words 'and provided that no case may be rejected on this ground which has not been duly considered by a domestic tribunal' shall be deleted.

[316] Art 39(1) and (2) ECHR. See further, I Cabral Barreto, 'Le règlement amiable devant la Cour Européenne des droits de l'homme' (2002) 10 *Bulletin des droits de l'homme* 27; H Keller, M Forowicz, and L Engi, *Friendly Settlements before the European Court of Human Rights: Theory and Practice* (Oxford, OUP, 2010).

[317] Arts 39(2) and 40(1) ECHR.

[318] Art 20 ECHR. Being a judge at the ECtHR is a full-time job. The judges are elected for a period of nine years, and they may not be re-elected (Art 23(1) ECHR). The term of office of judges expires when they reach the age of 70 (Art 23(2) ECHR). From the moment Protocol No 15 enters into force, this changes into the requirement that '[c]andidates shall be less than 65 years of age at the date by which the list of three candidates has been requested by the Parliamentary Assembly' (future Art 21(2) ECHR).

[319] ibid, Art 21(2).

[320] ibid, Art 26(1), (4) and (5).

A single judge may declare inadmissible or strike out of the Court's list of cases an application where such a decision can be taken without further examination.[321] No appeal against such a decision is possible.[322] If the single judge does not declare an application inadmissible or strike it out, he or she forwards it to a committee or Chamber.[323] A committee of three judges may then, by unanimous vote: (i) declare the application inadmissible or strike it out of its list of cases (a 'decision'); or (ii) declare it admissible and at the same time render a judgment on the merits, if the underlying question in the case is already the subject of well-established case law of the Court (a 'judgment').[324] Such decisions and judgments are final as well.[325] If there is no unanimity on the matter, or the single judge referred the case to a Chamber of seven judges immediately, the latter will treat the case. The Chamber then decides both on the admissibility and the merits.[326] However, where the case raises a serious question affecting the interpretation of the ECHR, or where it may lead to a result inconsistent with a previous judgment of the Court, the Chamber may relinquish jurisdiction in favour of the Grand Chamber, unless one of the parties to the case objects.[327] A party to the case can, in exceptional cases, request that the case be referred to the Grand Chamber within a period of three months from the date of the judgment of the Chamber.[328] Judgments of the Grand Chamber are always final.[329] The final judgment must be published,[330] and reasons must be given for all decisions and judgments.[331]

Before coming to a final judgment, the ECtHR can in certain circumstances adopt provisional measures.[332] If the Court finds that there has been a violation, and if the internal law of the High Contracting Party concerned allows only partial reparation to be made, the Court may afford just satisfaction to the injured party.[333] The Court can also decide that the judgment recognising the violation in itself constitutes just satisfaction. The High Contracting Parties undertake to abide by the final judgment of the Court in any case to which they are parties.[334] The Committee of Ministers, an intergovernmental body – theoretically – composed of the Ministers of Foreign Affairs of the 47 CoE Member States or – in practice – their Permanent Representatives in Strasbourg, supervises the execution of the Court's judgments.[335]

[321] ibid, Art 27(1).
[322] ibid, Art 27(2).
[323] ibid, Art 27(3).
[324] ibid, Art 28, respectively (a) and (b).
[325] ibid, Art 28(1).
[326] ibid, Art 29(1).
[327] ibid, Art 30. From the moment Protocol No 15 enters into force, the right of the parties to a case to object to relinquishment of jurisdiction over it by a Chamber in favour of the Grand Chamber is removed.
[328] ibid, Art 43(1). In such cases, a panel of five judges of the Grand Chamber will first assess if the exceptional circumstances needed for such a referral are met. Concretely, this means that the case needs to raise a serious question affecting the interpretation or application of the Convention or Protocols thereto or raise a serious issue of general importance (ibid, Art 43(2)).
[329] ibid, Art 44(1).
[330] ibid, Art 44(3).
[331] ibid, Art 45(1).
[332] See Rule 39 of the Rules of Court (adopted and entered into force 14 November 2016). See further O De Schutter, 'The Binding Character of the Provisional Measures adopted by the European Court of Human Rights' (2005) 7 *International Law FORUM du droit international* 16; S Watthée, *Les mesures provisoires devant la Cour européenne des droits de l'homme : la protection préventive des droits conventionnels en puissance ?* (Limal, Anthemis, 2014).
[333] Art 41 ECHR.
[334] ibid, Art 46(1).
[335] ibid, Art 46(2). More specifically, it is usually legal experts located in ministries of justice or foreign affairs or the permanent missions that attend the (quarterly) human rights meetings of the Committee. As soon as a

iv. Reform of the Court

Over time, the ECtHR has become the victim of its own success. As the Court kept receiving more and more individual applications (considering also the exponential increase in CoE Member States from the 1990s onwards), the Eleventh (1994) and Fourteenth (2004) Protocol[336] have institutionally reformed the 'control machinery' established by the ECHR to make it more efficient.[337] Nevertheless, the ECtHR remains flooded with complaints. For that reason, and as already alluded to, a Fifteenth Protocol (which has not yet entered into force) was adopted in June 2013 to maintain the effectiveness of the Court.[338] This Protocol shortens the time limit within which an application must be made from six to four months; amends the 'significant disadvantage' admissibility criterion by removing the second safeguard preventing rejection of an application that has not been duly considered by a domestic tribunal; removes the right of the parties to a case to object to relinquishment of jurisdiction over it by a Chamber in favour of the Grand Chamber; and replaces the upper age limit of 70 years for judges by a requirement that candidates for the post of judge be less than 65 years of age at the date by which the list of candidates has been requested by the Parliamentary Assembly. Lastly, the Sixteenth Protocol now allows the highest courts and tribunals of States that have ratified it, as specified by the latter, to request the ECtHR to give advisory opinions on questions of principle relating to the interpretation or application of the rights and freedoms defined in the ECHR or the protocols thereto.[339] Before, the Court could give such advisory opinions only at the request of the Committee of Ministers.[340]

B. The European Social Charter

The ESC guarantees fundamental social and economic rights. It is the counterpart of the ECHR, which contains civil and political rights. The ESC opened for signature on 18 October 1961 in Turin. It entered into force in February 1965 and has been ratified by 27 States. Over the years, three protocols were added to the ESC. While the First added substantive rights to the ESC,[341] the Second and Third Additional Protocol concerned its monitoring mechanism.[342]

violation is found, the matter is placed on the agenda of the Committee and remains there until the government in question has implemented the necessary measures (see Rules 3 and 4 of the Rules of Procedure of the Committee of Ministers). See further B Çali and A Koch, 'Foxes Guarding the Foxes? The Peer Review of Human Rights Judgments by the Committee of Ministers of the Council of Europe' (2014) 14 *Human Rights Law Review* 301.

[336] See above, respectively (n 170) and (n 249).

[337] See further C Hioureas, 'Behind the Scenes of Protocol No 14: Politics in Reforming the European Court of Human Rights' (2006) 24 *Berkeley Journal of International Law* 718; P Lemmens and W Vandenhole (eds), *Protocol No 14 and the Reform of the European Court of Human Rights* (Antwerp, Intersentia, 2005); C Paraskeva, 'Reforming the European Court of Human Rights: An Ongoing Challenge' (2007) 76 *Nordic Journal of International Law* 185.

[338] See above (n 311).

[339] Protocol No 16 to the Convention for the Protection of Human Rights and Fundamental Freedoms (adopted 2 October 2013, entered into force 1 August 2018) CETS 214.

[340] Art 47 ECHR.

[341] Additional Protocol to the European Social Charter (adopted 5 May 1988, entered into force 4 September 1992) ETS 128.

[342] Protocol amending the European Social Charter (adopted 21 October 1991, not yet entered into force) ETS 142; Additional Protocol to the European Social Charter Providing for a System of Collective Complaints (adopted 9 November 1995, entered into force 1 July 1998) ETS 158.

On 1 July 1999 the Revised European Social Charter (Revised Charter), adopted on 3 May 1996, entered into force.[343] This Revised Charter contains different provisions of the original ESC combined with some slightly modified provisions of the First Protocol and complemented with some rights that where neither contained in the original ESC nor in the Protocol. Enforcement of the Revised Charter is submitted to the same monitoring mechanism as the original ESC.[344] There are 34 States Parties to the Revised Charter. As such, 43 out of 47 Member States are a party to either the ESC or the Revised Charter.[345]

The original ESC of 1961 mainly contains standards with regard to social rights and social security rights. These rights can be classified in different subcategories: (i) labour rights, such as the right to work, the right to just conditions of work, the right to safe and healthy working conditions and the right to a fair remuneration (Articles 1–4); (ii) union rights, including the right to freedom of association and the right to bargain collectively (Articles 5–6); (iii) the protection of labouring children, young persons and women (Articles 7–8); (iv) the right to vocational guidance and training (Articles 9–10); (v) the right to social security and social and medical assistance (Articles 11–17); and (vi) the right to engage in a gainful occupation in the territory of any other Party, with special attention for the rights of migrant workers (Articles 18–19). The First Protocol contains provisions guaranteeing equal opportunities and equal treatment in matters of employment and occupation without discrimination on the grounds of sex.[346]

The ESC is a so-called *à la carte* treaty. States are not obliged to accept all of its provisions. They can choose by which provisions of the Charter they want to be bound. This choice is, however, not completely free: Article 20(1) of the Charter establishes certain limitations in this regard. According to Article 20(1)(a), States must consider themselves bound by at least five out of seven ESC core articles (the right to work, the right to organise, the right to bargain collectively, the right to social security, the right to social and medical assistance, the right of the family to social, legal and economic protection and the right of migrant workers and their families to protection and assistance). Article 20(1)(b) adds to this that the total number of (substantive) articles or paragraphs by which a State considers itself bound should not be less than 10 articles or 45 paragraphs. Most of the contracting parties have accepted more provisions than minimally required.

As opposed to what is the case for the ECHR, the ESC does not have a court, but committees to supervise its implementation. While those cannot take binding decisions and thus hardly be as effective as the ECtHR, the Second and Third Additional Protocols improve the supervisory machinery of the ESC. The Second Protocol mainly clarifies and strengthens the role of the European Committee of Social Rights and the Governmental Committee,[347] and reinforces the participation of social partners and NGOs.[348] Given that it modifies the content of the ESC it will only enter into force when all the States Parties to the ESC have ratified it, which is not yet the case. Nevertheless, following a decision of the Committee of Ministers of 11 December 1991, the reporting system has 'taken account' of all but one of its provisions, which are in practice applied.[349]

[343] European Social Charter (revised) (adopted 3 May 1996, entered into force 1 July 1999) ETS 163 (Revised Charter).

[344] See below, this subsection.

[345] Only Liechtenstein, Monaco, San Marino and Switzerland ratified neither of the two.

[346] See above (n 341).

[347] See below, this subsection.

[348] See above (n 342).

[349] The only article of the Protocol which is still not (fully) being applied is Art 3, and more particularly its provision modifying Art 25(1) ESC, concerning the election of members of the European Committee of Social Rights by the Parliamentary Assembly instead of the Committee of Ministers.

The ESC's supervisory mechanism is comparable to the one of the ILO. The contracting parties are obliged to send a report to the Secretary General of the Council of Europe at two-yearly intervals concerning the application of the provisions that they have accepted.[350] These reports are examined by a Committee of Independent Experts, which has taken the operational shape of the European Committee of Social Rights (ECSR).[351] On completion of its examination, the ECSR draws up a report containing its conclusions, which is made public.[352] The reports of the Contracting Parties and the conclusions of the ECSR are then submitted for examination to the Governmental Committee of the European Social Charter and European Code of Social Security (Governmental Committee).[353] The Governmental Committee is composed of one representative of each of the Contracting Parties as well as observers of (no more than) two international organisations of employers and two international trade union organisations.[354] In a report that is made public, the Governmental Committee prepares the decisions of the Committee of Ministers, in particular by selecting the situations which should, in its view, be the subject of recommendations by the latter.[355] The Committee of Ministers then, by a majority of two-thirds of its members, adopts a resolution covering the entire supervision cycle and containing individual recommendations to the Contracting Parties concerned.[356]

The Third Protocol, lastly, establishes a collective complaints procedure.[357] The Contracting Parties recognise the right to submit complaints to the ECSR alleging unsatisfactory application of the ESC of (i) international organisations of employers and trade unions; (ii) other non-governmental organisations which have consultative status with the Council of Europe; and (iii) representative national organisations of employers and trade unions.[358] Subsequently, the ECSR takes a decision on the merits of the complaint,[359] which it transmits to the Committee of Ministers in a report, which is then made public within four months.[360] On the basis of the report of the ECSR, the Committee of Ministers adopts a resolution by a simple majority. If it finds that the ESC is not applied in a satisfactory manner, the Committee can, by a two third majority, adopt a recommendation specifying the measures to be taken by the State concerned to bring the situation into line with the Charter.[361]

[350] Art 21 ESC.

[351] See, for example, European Committee of Social Rights, Rules (as amended on 6 July 2016), rm.coe.int/168069fae6, preamble.

[352] Art 24 ESC, as informally amended by Art 2 of the Second Protocol.

[353] ibid, Art 27(1), as informally amended by Art 4 the Second Protocol. See also Governmental Committee of the European Social Charter and European Code of Social Security, Rules of Procedure (adopted and entered into force 25 November 2016), GC(2016)16, rm.coe.int/16806c0f41.

[354] Art 27(2) ESC, as informally amended by Art 4 of the Second Protocol.

[355] ibid, Art 27(3), as informally amended by Art 4 of the Second Protocol.

[356] ibid, Art 29, as informally amended by Art 5 of the Second Protocol. On the ECSR, see further, O De Schutter and M Sant'Ana, 'The European Committee of Social Rights (The ECSR)' in G de Beco (ed), *Human Rights Monitoring Mechanisms of the Council of Europe* (London, Routledge, 2012) 71–99.

[357] See above (n 342).

[358] Art 1 Third Protocol.

[359] ibid, Art 8(1).

[360] ibid, Art 8(2).

[361] ibid, Art 9(1). On the collective complaint procedure, see R Churchill and U Khaliq, 'The Collective Complaints System of the European Social Charter: An Effective Mechanism for Ensuring Compliance with Economic and Social Rights?' (2004) 15 *EJIL* 417. On the European Social Charter in general, see O De Schutter (ed), *The European Social Charter: A social constitution for Europe – La charte sociale européenne: une constitution sociale pour l'Europe* (Brussels, Bruylant, 2010); O Dörr, 'European Social Charter' in S Schmahl and M Breuer (eds), *The Council of Europe: Its Law and Policies* (Oxford, OUP, 2017) 507–41; and M D'Amico and G Guiglia (eds), *European Social Charter and the Challenges of the XXI Century* (Napoli, Edizioni Scientifiche Italiane, 2014).

C. European Prevention of Torture Convention

On 26 November 1987, the Council of Europe adopted the European Convention for the Prevention of Torture and Inhuman and Degrading Treatment or Punishment (European Prevention of Torture Convention). Its ratification is a precondition for joining the Council of Europe.[362] The European Prevention of Torture Convention is rather unique given that it does not contain any provision determining its scope of application *ratione materiae*. Contrary to the UN Convention against Torture, it does not even contain a definition of 'torture'. However, in its preamble, it does refer to Article 3 ECHR stating that 'no one shall be subjected to torture or to inhuman or degrading treatment or punishment'. In the same vein, the European Committee for the Prevention of Torture uses the case law of the ECtHR as interpretative guidance.

The merit of this Convention lies in the fact that it enhances the protection of persons against torture and inhuman and degrading treatment through the introduction of 'non-judicial means of a preventive character'.[363] For this purpose, the Convention established a European Committee for the Prevention of Torture and Inhuman and Degrading Treatment or Punishment (CPT).[364] The CPT has a wide range of competences in order to, by means of visits, examine the treatment of persons deprived of their liberty.[365] Each Contracting Party has the obligation to allow these visits to any place within its jurisdiction where persons are deprived of their liberty by a public authority.[366] Only in exceptional circumstances, exhaustively written down in the Convention, may a Contracting Party oppose to a visit at the time or the particular place proposed by the Committee.[367] In principle, the Committee organises periodic visits. However, when required by the circumstances at hand, it can also organise ad hoc visits to the above-mentioned places.[368] Following the visit, the CPT drafts a report that is transmitted to the State Party concerned and that remains confidential until that State decides to make it public.[369] However, when a State refuses to cooperate, the Committee may decide to issue a public statement by a 2/3 majority.[370]

D. Framework Convention for the Protection of National Minorities

The Framework Convention for the Protection of National Minorities (Framework Convention) was opened for signature by Council of Europe Member States on 1 February 1995

[362] European Convention for the Prevention of Torture and Inhuman or Degrading Treatment or Punishment (adopted 26 November 1987, entered into force 1 February 1989) ETS 126.

[363] Preamble, fifth indent, European Prevention of Torture Convention.

[364] Each State Party has one expert in the CPT (Art 1). These experts are elected by an absolute majority of votes by the Committee of Ministers, from a list presented by the Parliamentary Assembly of the Council of Europe (Art 5(1)) for a period of four years (Art 5(3) European Prevention of Torture Convention).

[365] ibid, Art 1.

[366] ibid, Art 2.

[367] These exceptional circumstances can only concern 'grounds of national defence, public safety, serious disorder in places where persons are deprived of their liberty, the medical condition of a person or that an urgent interrogation relating to a serious crime is in progress'; ibid, Art 9(1).

[368] ibid, Art 7(1).

[369] ibid, Art 11 and Rule 39 of the CPT's Rules of Procedure (as amended on 7 March 2008) CPT/Inf/C (2008) 1, rm.coe.int/16806db824.

[370] Art 12 European Prevention of Torture Convention. On the European Prevention of Torture Convention more generally, see further, E Svanidze, 'The European Convention for the Prevention of Torture' in Alfredsson et al (n 193) 493–502. On the CPT, see further R Kicker, 'The European Committee for the Prevention of Torture and Inhuman or Degrading Treatment or Punishment (The CPT)' in de Beco (ed) (n 356) 43–70.

and has been ratified by 39 of them.[371] The Convention sets out the legal principles which States must respect in order to ensure the protection of national minorities and to enable them to preserve and develop their culture and retain their identity. Article 3(2) specifies that '[p]ersons belonging to national minorities may exercise the rights and enjoy the freedoms flowing from the principles enshrined in the present framework Convention individually as well as in community with others'.

Amongst others, the Framework Convention obliges the States Parties 'to guarantee to persons belonging to national minorities the right of equality before the law and of equal protection of the law'.[372] They are also bound 'to promote the conditions necessary for persons belonging to national minorities to maintain and develop their culture, and to preserve the essential elements of their identity, namely their religion, language, traditions and cultural heritage',[373] and 'to refrain from policies or practices aimed at assimilation of persons belonging to national minorities against their will and shall protect these persons from any action aimed at such assimilation'.[374] They shall further 'ensure respect for the right of every person belonging to a national minority to freedom of peaceful assembly, freedom of association, freedom of expression, and freedom of thought, conscience and religion'.[375]

The States Parties also strive to ensure, as far as possible, the conditions which would make it possible to use the minority language in relations with administrative authorities 'in areas inhabited by persons belonging to national minorities traditionally or in substantial numbers' and 'if those persons so request and where such a request corresponds to a real need'.[376] They also strive to ensure in the said areas 'that persons belonging to those minorities have adequate opportunities for being taught the minority language or for receiving instruction in this language'.[377] Relatedly, according to Article 13(1), States Parties recognise that persons belonging to a national minority have the right to set up and to manage their own private educational and training establishments.

The implementation of the Framework Convention is monitored by the Committee of Ministers of the Council of Europe,[378] for which it is assisted by an Advisory Committee on the Framework Convention for the Protection of National Minorities.[379] The Advisory Committee considers periodic State reports and transmits its opinions thereon to the Committee of Ministers.[380] For this purpose, it can organise meetings with government as well as minority representatives.[381]

Even though the Convention ensures an important number of minority rights, its range is limited. This is due to the fact that the provisions require the intervention of the national legislator in order to be invoked in front of a national judge, which is evident from

[371] Framework Convention for the Protection of National Minorities (adopted 1 February 1995, entered into force 1 February 1995) ETS 157.

[372] ibid, Art 4(1).

[373] ibid, Art 5(1).

[374] ibid, Art 5(2).

[375] ibid, Art 7.

[376] ibid, Art 10(2).

[377] ibid, Art 14(2).

[378] ibid, Art 24(1).

[379] ibid, Art 26(1).

[380] Advisory Committee on the Framework Convention for the Protection of National Minorities, Rules of Procedure (adopted and entered into force 29 October 1998) ACFC/INF (98) 2, www.coe.int/en/web/minorities/rules-of-procedure, Rule 34.

[381] ibid, Rule 37, as applied in practice.

the formulation 'the Parties undertake to' that commences every provision containing a commitment on the part of the States Parties. Moreover, the Convention does not contain a definition of 'national minority'.[382]

X. The EU and Human Rights

A. Constitutional Scheme

Article 2 of the TEU proclaims that the EU is 'founded on the values of respect for human dignity, freedom, democracy, equality, the rule of law and respect for human rights, including the rights of persons belonging to minorities'. Nevertheless, as regards the EU's *internal* policies, there is no Treaty provision that confers upon the EU any general power to enact rules on human rights. However, this does not mean that the EU lacks any competence in this regard. Rather, every policy field the EU is competent for, comes with the responsibility to promote and protect human rights within that field.[383] For example, although there is no explicit reference to the rights of disabled people in the TFEU Chapter relating to transport, the EU has long included references to the needs of passengers with a disability in legislation adopted under this Chapter.[384] In addition, there are two specific legal bases which allow the EU to enact legislation concerning data protection (Article 16 TFEU) and non-discrimination (Article 19 TFEU).

Moreover, although the EU did not have a human rights instrument until the proclamation of the EU Charter in 2000, fundamental rights have long been a part of EU law as general principles of Community law viz. Union law. As early as 1969, the CJEU ruled that fundamental rights were enshrined in the general principles of Community law and protected by the Court.[385] For the recognition of these principles, 'the Court is bound to draw inspiration from constitutional traditions common to the Member States' and 'international treaties for the protection of human rights' to which Member States are signatories. The CJEU made clear that it would declare invalid measures incompatible with fundamental rights.[386]

As regards the EU's *external* policies, Article 3(5) TEU provides that in its relations with the wider world, the EU shall contribute to the protection of human rights. Article 21(1) TEU specifies that the EU's action on the international scene is to be guided by the principles of 'democracy, the rule of law, the universality and indivisibility of human rights and fundamental freedoms, respect for human dignity, the principles of equality and solidarity'. These provisions have given the EU an extensive mandate to integrate human

[382] See further G de Beco and E Lantschner, 'The Advisory Committee on the Framework Convention for the Protection of National Minorities (the ACFC)' in de Beco (ed) (n 356) 100–26; and A Philips, 'The Council of Europe Framework Convention for the Protection of National Minorities: Minority Rights, Diversity and Participation' in D Thürer (ed), *International Protection of Minorities: Challenges in Practice and Doctrine* (Zurich, Schulthess, 2014) 95–105.

[383] Craig and de Búrca, above (n 96) 392–94.

[384] Waddington (n 101) 434.

[385] Judgment 12 November 1969, *Stauder*, 29/69, EU:C:1969:57, para 7.

[386] Judgment of 14 May 1974, *Nold*, 4/73, EU:C:1974:51, para 13. See further B de Witte, 'The Past and Future Role of the European Court of Justice in the Protection of Human Rights' in P Alston (ed), *The EU and Human Rights* (Oxford, OUP, 1999) 859–98.

rights protection into its external relations policies.[387] For example, the EU consistently includes human rights clauses in bilateral cooperation and trade agreements.[388] However, as generally the EU's competences regarding its external policies do not concern human rights *law* in the strict sense, this section focuses on human rights in the EU's internal legal framework.

B. Charter of Fundamental Rights of the European Union

An EU system of fundamental rights protection was present, but was – and largely still is – grounded in a plurality of sources.[389] To clarify the position of human rights in the EU's legal framework and reinforce its internal commitment to human rights, the EU, in 2000, 'solemnly proclaimed' the EU Charter, which, after being slightly amended and again proclaimed in 2007, has the same legal value as the EU's founding Treaties since the entry into force of the Treaty of Lisbon on 1 December 2009.[390]

The Charter groups its substantive provisions under six titles: dignity, freedoms, equality, solidarity, citizen's rights and justice. Apart from some rights connected with citizenship of the EU, the rights contained in the Charter may be invoked in the context of EU law by anyone, including persons who are not nationals of Member States.[391] It is a relatively recent catalogue of human rights that in some ways goes beyond the traditional dichotomy of civil and political and economic, social and cultural rights. It contains rights whose meaning and/or scope is wider than that of similar rights in existing human rights instruments such as the ECHR, or even rights that these instruments do not contain.[392] Not all rights in the Charter are enforceable as such. In this regard, Article 52(5) Charter distinguishes 'principles' from 'rights'. Unlike the latter, principles do not give rise to direct claims for positive action, but are only 'judicially cognisable' when EU law or acts implementing it are interpreted or reviewed.[393]

It is important to note that the scope of application of the Charter is limited. According to Article 51(1) Charter, it applies to the institutions, bodies, offices and agencies of the EU and to Member States, but to the latter *only* 'when they are implementing EU law'. While this requirement has at times been interpreted broadly by the CJEU,[394] it now has taken a more restrictive approach on the matter.[395]

[387] Craig and de Búrca (n 95) 392–94. Further, see eg A Clapham, 'Where is the EU's Human Rights Common Foreign Policy, and How is it Manifested in Multilateral Fora?' in Alston (ed) (n 386), 627–87.

[388] On this, see Chapter 2, Section XI(E).

[389] K Lenaerts and JA Gutiérrez, 'The Place of the Charter in the EU Constitutional Edifice' in S Peers et al (eds), *The EU Charter of Fundamental Rights: A Commentary* (Oxford, Hart, 2014) 1559–61, and 1592–93.

[390] That is the TEU and the TFEU; Art 6(1) TEU.

[391] K Lenaerts and P Van Nuffel, *European Union Law* (London, Sweet & Maxwell, 2011) 831.

[392] Lenaerts and Gutiérrez (n 389) 1576, 1582 and 1584.

[393] However, the distinction between rights and principles is unclear, which leaves it up to the CJEU to clarify the matter; ibid, 1576–78.

[394] See for example in the Judgment of 26 February 2013, *Åkerberg Fransson*, C-617/10, EU:C:2013:105, in particular at para 28, where a remote connection between the national legislation concerned and EU rules on Value Added Tax (VAT) collection was considered sufficient; ibid, 1561–1571 and E Spaventa, 'A Very Fearful Court? The Protection of Fundamental Rights in the European Union after Opinion 2/13' (2015) 22 *Maastricht Journal of European and Comparative Law* 1, 39. On the Charter, see further, DF Giacomo, *The EU Charter of Fundamental Rights: From Declaration to Binding Instrument* (Dordrecht, Springer 2011); Peers et al (n 389).

[395] The Court has clarified that the concept of 'implementing Union law', as referred to in Art 51 of the Charter, presupposes a degree of connection between the measure of EU law and the national measure at issue which goes beyond the matters covered being closely related or one of those matters having an indirect impact on the other.

C. Judicial Protection

Institutionally, the EU's judicial order in the first place relies on the national courts of the Member States to apply EU law, including its general principles and the Charter. Nevertheless, the ultimate interpretation thereof lies with the CJEU, and more particularly the Court of Justice, the CJEU's highest Court. Thus, the main bulk of judicial proceedings conducted before the Court of Justice concerns references for a preliminary ruling coming from Member State courts.[396] National courts can either ask the Court to interpret primary (ie, the TEU, TFEU and the Charter) or secondary (ie, acts of the institutions, bodies, offices or agencies of the Union) EU law, following which it is up to the national court to decide whether the *national* measure at issue is compatible with EU law as interpreted by the Court, or contest the validity of secondary *EU law* in light of primary EU law (including the Charter).[397] Article 53 of the Charter provides that nothing in the Charter shall be interpreted as restricting human rights as recognised by EU law, international law (including the ECHR) and by the Member States' constitutions. Although this means that, regarding the implementation of EU law, national courts remain free to apply (higher) national standards of protection, the CJEU has ruled that they can only do so provided that 'the primacy, unity and effectiveness of EU law are not thereby compromised'.[398]

To challenge acts of *EU law* in light of the Charter, other procedures can be relied upon. In this regard, the CJEU has ruled that the EU's legal system, which is based upon the rule of law, provides for a 'complete system of legal remedies and procedures' to review the legality of measures adopted by the EU institutions.[399] Thus, before the General Court, individuals can initiate an action for annulment of a measure of EU law[400] and proceedings for a failure to act on the part of an EU institution, body, office or agency.[401] However, they can do so only in limited circumstances: for *legislative* acts when they are 'directly' concerned (that is 'directly affected'[402] by a measure leaving 'no discretion' in view of its implementation[403]) and 'individually' concerned (that is if the applicant is the addressee of the measure or in a situation that distinguishes him or her individually just as in the case of

In particular, the Court has found that fundamental EU rights could not be applied in relation to national legislation because the provisions of EU law in the area concerned did not impose any specific obligation on Member States with regard to the situation at issue in the main proceedings. Consequently, the mere fact that a national measure comes within an area in which the Union has powers cannot bring it within the scope of EU law, and, therefore, cannot render the Charter applicable. In order to determine whether a national measure involves the implementation of EU law for the purposes of Art 51(1) of the Charter, it is necessary to determine, inter alia, whether that national legislation is intended to implement a provision of EU law; the nature of the legislation at issue and whether it pursues objectives other than those covered by EU law, even if it is capable of indirectly affecting EU law; and also whether there are specific rules of EU law on the matter or rules which are capable of affecting it: *Julián Hernández and others*, C-198/13, EU:C:2014:2055, paras 34–37. For a recent example, see Judgment of 9 March 2017, *Milkova*, C-406/15, EU:C:2017:198, paras 50–54.

[396] For the period 2012–2016, 67.92% of the proceedings conducted before the Court of Justice concerned references for a preliminary ruling: CJEU, 'Annual Report 2016: Judicial Activity', 2017, curia.europa.eu/jcms/upload/docs/application/pdf/2017-03/ra_jur_2016_en_web.pdf.

[397] Art 267 TFEU.

[398] Judgment of 26 February 2013, *Melloni*, C-399/11, EU:C:2013:107, para 60. Thus, Spain could not refuse to execute a European Arrest Warrant for the reason that a conviction *in absentia* would not be open to review in Italy, although in this case, the (interpretation of) the Spanish constitution provides for a right to retrial.

[399] As complemented by Art 267 TFEU; Judgment of 23 April 1986, *Les Verts*, 294/83, EU:C:1986:166, para 23. See more recently, Judgment of 28 March 2017, *Rosneft*, C-72/15, EU:C:2017:236, paras 66–67.

[400] Art 263 TFEU.

[401] ibid, Art 265.

[402] Judgment of 29 June 2004, *Front National v Parliament*, C-486/01 P, EU:C:2004:394, para 24.

[403] Judgment of 2 May 2006, *Regione Siciliana v Commission*, C-417/04 P, EU:C:2006:282, paras 28 and 57.

the addressee).[404] For *regulatory* acts that do not entail implementing measures, applicants only have to be directly concerned.[405] Next, during proceedings before the CJEU, it is possible to object to the application of an act of general application based on its illegality when the latter is relied upon for implementing measures concerning the applicant.[406] Albeit only under certain conditions, it is possible to claim damages from both Member States and the EU when the applicant has suffered harm following a violation of the Charter in the exercise of their respective competences.[407] The CJEU has explicitly recognised this as a possibility – however theoretical in view of the difficulty of fulfilling the conditions for liability – in the context of the Commission's role in the imposition of austerity measures which led to the restrictions of the right to property, protected by Article 17(1) of the Charter, of some Cypriot citizens during the Eurozone crisis.[408] Although the restrictions were found not to be unjustified, the Court acknowledged the Commission's responsibility to ensure that the memorandum of understanding implementing the austerity measures was consistent with rights guaranteed by the Charter.[409]

In addition, the European Commission can initiate infringement proceedings before the CJEU following an alleged failure of an EU Member State to fulfil its obligations under the Charter.[410] Before the Court is seised of such a matter, the Commission issues a reasoned opinion and the State concerned has the opportunity to submit observations and rectify the situation.[411] Lastly, a serious and persistent breach of fundamental rights by a Member State may result in the suspension of certain membership rights (including voting rights).[412] This latter mechanism enshrined in Article 7 TEU is unique, as well as politically difficult to activate, in that its application is in principle not limited to Member State actions which come within the ambit of EU law, as is normally required for EU rules, including those concerning EU fundamental rights protection, to be applicable in the case at hand.

D. The EU and the ECHR

i. Relation between the EU and the ECHR

The EU itself is not a party to the ECHR, and the ECtHR cannot hold the EU accountable for violations of the Convention. Nevertheless, all EU Member States are Contracting

[404] Judgment of 15 July 1963, *Plaumann v Commission*, 25/62, EU:C:1963:17, 107.
[405] Art 263 TFEU.
[406] ibid, Art 277.
[407] Judgment of 19 November 1991, *Francovich and others*, C-6/90 and C-9/90, EU:C:1991:428, para 37; see respectively Arts 268 and 340 TFEU (the action for damages can be brought in combination with the actions discussed above).
[408] Judgment of 20 September 2016, *Ledra Advertising and others*, C-8/15 P to C-10/15 P, EU:C:2016:701.
[409] ibid, paras 74 and 67.
[410] For example, in 2015, the Commission initiated infringement proceedings against Hungary inter alia for concerns in view of Art 47 of the Charter (right to an effective remedy and to a fair trial) regarding asylum applicants. More recently, the Commission decided to follow up on these proceedings, as 'Hungarian law does not allow for applications to be submitted outside of special transit zones at the borders, and restricts access to these zones, thus failing to provide an effective access to asylum procedures' and 'the systematic and indefinite confinement of asylum seekers, including minors over 14, in closed facilities in the transit zone without respecting required procedural safeguards, such as the right to appeal, leads to systematic detentions, which are in breach of the EU law on reception conditions and the Charter of Fundamental Rights of the EU'; EC, 'Commission Follows Up On Infringement Procedure against Hungary Concerning Its Asylum Law' (Press release, 17 May 2017) europa.eu/rapid/press-release_IP-17-1285_en.htm.
[411] Art 258, respectively Arts 259 and 260 TFEU.
[412] Art 7 TEU; Lenaerts and Van Nuffel (n 391) 826.

Parties thereto. Consequently, the ECtHR considers EU Member States to be fully responsible under the Convention for all acts falling outside their strict obligations under EU law.[413] However, the ECtHR did not rule out that it can hold EU Member States responsible for violations of the ECHR also when they are implementing EU law. This can lead to a (rare) situation in which an EU Member State finds itself confronted with conflicting obligations under EU law on the one hand, and the ECHR on the other.[414]

To avoid such a situation as much as possible, the ECtHR has tried to come to a middle ground when it has to judge the compliance with the ECHR of measures of EU Member States that implement EU obligations, and has developed the so called 'Bosphorus doctrine'. This doctrine entails that Member State action taken in compliance with EU obligations is justified as long as the EU is considered to protect human rights, both substantively as well as regards the controlling mechanisms, in a manner at least equivalent to that provided for by the ECHR.[415] Thus, considering especially the proactive role the CJEU has taken on in this regard, the ECtHR considered the level of human rights protection provided for by EU law to be equivalent to that of the Convention system. Only when the protection of the applicant's rights under the ECHR is 'manifestly deficient' can this 'presumption of Convention compliance' be rebutted.[416]

Conversely, Article 6(3) TEU provides that fundamental rights, as guaranteed by the ECHR, constitute general principles of EU law. Moreover, when the Charter contains rights which correspond to rights guaranteed by the ECHR, the meaning and scope of those rights shall be the same as those laid down by the said Convention.[417] However, this does not prevent EU law from providing more extensive protection.[418] Thus, when the ECtHR raises the level of protection of a right also contained in the Charter or expands its scope, the CJEU is obliged to adapt its interpretation of the respective right. On the other hand, when the protection provided by the ECtHR is lower, the CJEU should adhere to the higher standards laid down in the Charter (as interpreted by the Court).[419]

However, issues as regards the relationship between the EU and the ECHR remain. Although the Bosphorus doctrine is in place, in exceptional circumstances, EU Member States can still be squeezed between their obligations (or rights) under EU law and the ECHR.[420] Moreover, when the ECtHR holds an EU Member State responsible for a violation of the ECHR when it is implementing EU law, that Member State alone might not be in a position to unilaterally remedy that breach of the Convention. Lastly, the EU's legal system, both institutionally and substantively, might benefit from independent, 'external'

[413] *Bosphorus Hava Yollari Turizm Ve Ticaret Anonim Şirketi v Ireland* App no 45036/98 (ECtHR, 30 June 2005) para 157.

[414] Lenaerts and Van Nuffel (n 391) 842.

[415] ibid, 841.

[416] *Bosphorus* (n 413) paras 155–66. On the Bosphorus doctrine, see further C Costello, 'The Bosphorus Ruling of the European Court of Human Rights: Fundamental Rights and Blurred Boundaries in Europe' (2006) 6 *Human Rights Law Review* 87; O De Schutter, '"Bosphorus" Post-Accession: Redefining the Relationships between the European Court of Human Rights and the Parties to the Convention' in V Kosta, N Skoutaris and VP Tzevelekos (eds), *The EU Accession to the ECHR* (Oxford, Hart, 2014) 177–89.

[417] Art 52(3) EU Charter.

[418] ibid.

[419] Lenaerts and Gutiérrez (n 389) 1580–82.

[420] Lenaerts and Van Nuffel (n 391) 842. An example of a situation where an EU Member State violated the ECHR by implementing EU law can be found in the *MMS v Belgium* case discussed above (n 123), where Belgium implemented the Dublin Regulation by sending an asylum seeker back to Greece, but violated Art 3 ECHR by doing so.

scrutiny by the ECtHR, which would enhance its credibility, both in relation to its Member States and on the international plane.[421]

ii. Accession of the EU to the ECHR

Consequently, 'to enhance coherence in human rights protection in Europe',[422] it was considered necessary for the EU to be bound by human rights in the same manner as its Member States. Therefore, the Treaty of Lisbon not only equipped the EU with its own catalogue of human rights (the EU Charter), but also provided that the EU shall accede to the ECHR.[423] Protocol No 8 to the Lisbon Treaty set out the conditions for accession, stressing that the eventual accession could not affect the competences of the EU, nor affect the situation of EU Member States in relation to the ECHR.[424]

In 2013, then, the Draft Agreement on the Accession of the EU to the ECHR was adopted.[425] In particular, the Draft Agreement provided for a 'co-respondent mechanism'. The EU could become co-respondent to a case against an EU Member State when the alleged violation of the ECHR called into question the compatibility of a measure of EU law with the Convention. Conversely, EU Member States could become co-respondents to a case against the EU when the alleged violation of the ECHR called into question the compatibility of a measure of EU primary law with the Convention.[426] Becoming a co-respondent would only be possible following the acceptance of an invitation of the ECtHR or by a decision of the latter following a request of the EU, respectively an EU Member State. However, the ECtHR would only assess whether it was 'plausible' that the conditions to become co-respondent were met.[427] If a case to which the EU was a co-respondent concerned an issue of compatibility of EU law with the ECHR the CJEU had not yet assessed, the latter was allowed sufficient time to do so.[428] Lastly, if a violation was established in a case with a co-respondent, the respondent and the co-respondent were to be held jointly liable, unless the ECtHR decided otherwise.[429]

The Draft Agreement was referred to the CJEU with a view to its opinion on the compatibility thereof with EU law.[430] Although the observations submitted by the Commission, the Parliament, the Council of the EU and the 24 governments of EU Member States concluded that the Draft Agreement was compatible with the EU's founding Treaties, in December 2014, the CJEU ruled differently and rendered a negative opinion.[431]

[421] Spaventa (n 394) 38–44.

[422] Draft revised agreement on the accession of the [EU] to the [ECHR] (10 June 2013), as annexed to the 'Final report to the CDDH' of the 'Fifth negotiation meeting between the CDDH ad hoc Negotiation Group and the European Commission on the Accession of the [EU] to the [ECHR]', 47+1(2013)008rev2, Preamble, fourth indent.

[423] Art 6(2) TEU; Spaventa (n 394) 36.

[424] Art 2 of the Protocol (No 8) relating to Article 6(2) of the Treaty on European Union on the accession of the Union to the European Convention on the Protection of Human Rights and Fundamental Freedoms, as attached to the Treaty of Lisbon [2012] OJ C326/1, 273.

[425] See above (n 422).

[426] Art 3(2), respectively (3) Draft Agreement.

[427] ibid, Art 3(5).

[428] ibid, Art 3(6).

[429] ibid, Art 3(7). On the Draft Agreement, see further, P Gragl, 'A Giant Leap for European Human Rights? The Final Agreement on the European Union's Accession to the European Convention on Human Rights' (2014) 51 *Common Market Law Review* 13; and, on an earlier version of the Draft Agreement, T Lock, 'End of an Epic? The Draft Agreement on the EU's Accession to the ECHR' (2012) 31 *Yearbook of European Law* 162.

[430] Final report to the CDDH (n 422) point 8; as well as Art 218(11) TFEU.

[431] Opinion of 18 December 2014, *Accession of the EU to the ECHR*, 2/13, EU:C:2014:2454, paras 108–109 and 258.

First, the CJEU stressed that the EU is not a State, but a new kind of legal order. In this regard, the Court argued that it should be ensured that Article 53 ECHR, which provides that nothing in the Convention shall be construed as limiting or derogating from any of the rights which are ensured under the laws of any State Party, does not compromise the 'primacy, unity and effectiveness' of EU law.[432] Moreover, upon accession, EU States could be required by the ECHR to check whether another EU State has observed fundamental rights in spite of the principle of mutual trust governing their mutual relations, which is problematic especially as regards EU measures in relation to the Area of Freedom, Security and Justice.[433] Also, Protocol No 16 to the ECHR, which will allow the highest courts of EU Member States to request advisory opinions of the ECtHR, would be liable to affect the effectiveness of the preliminary ruling procedure provided for in Article 267 TFEU.[434] For these reasons, accession would adversely affect the specific characteristics of EU law and its autonomy.[435] Similarly, accession would make it possible that disputes between EU Member States or between Member States and the EU in relation to the application of the ECHR, but within the scope of EU law, would be referred to the ECtHR. The CJEU found this to be at variance with Article 344 TFEU, which provides that disputes concerning the interpretation or application of the Treaties cannot be submitted to any method of settlement other than those provided for therein.[436]

Subsequently, the Court analysed the co-respondent mechanism. In this regard, it held that it is problematic that in reviewing a request to become co-respondent and in deciding on the apportionment of liability, the ECtHR would be required to assess the rules of EU law governing the division of powers between the EU and its Member States.[437] As regards the prior involvement procedure, the CJEU argued that it should be ensured that it is the CJEU and not the ECtHR that assesses whether or not the former has already given a ruling on the underlying issue of compatibility of EU law with the ECHR.[438] Lastly, the CJEU found it problematic that given its limited jurisdiction in the realm of the EU's CFSP,[439] the ECtHR would obtain a general competence to carry out a judicial review of acts of EU institutions in this regard.[440]

While many of the CJEU's objections are of an institutional or procedural nature (for example regarding the co-respondent mechanism) and can relatively easily be remedied in a possible future accession agreement, that is less so for arguments pertaining to the exceptional nature of the EU's legal order (for example regarding the principle of mutual trust). Accordingly, the Court blocked the accession of the EU to the ECHR at least for a number of years by setting out conditions of which it is not clear whether they will be negotiable to non-EU Member States such as Russia or Turkey, in particular in the current political climate.[441] In any case, most of these objections relate to jurisdiction of the ECtHR

[432] ibid, paras 186–90. Here, the ECJ defends its decision in *Melloni* (n 398).
[433] ibid, paras 155, 164 and 193–194. On this issue, see Judgment of 21 December 2011, *NS and others*, C-411/10 and C-493/10, EU:C:2011:865, especially paras 75–86.
[434] ibid, paras 196–99.
[435] ibid, para 200.
[436] ibid, paras 201–14.
[437] ibid, paras 222–25 and 229–34.
[438] ibid, paras 236–41. Moreover, it was problematic that the scope of the prior involvement procedure, in the case of secondary law, was limited solely to questions of validity and not interpretation; paras 242–47.
[439] See Art 275 TFEU.
[440] ibid, paras 249–57.
[441] A Lazowski and R Wessel, 'When Caveats Turn into Locks: Opinion 2/13 on Accession of the European Union to the ECHR' (2015) 16 *German Law Journal* 179, 210.

that the latter already has (with the formal difference that without accession, the EU as such is not bound by any decision of the ECtHR). Moreover, the ECtHR has shown to be committed to 'ensure that there is no legal vacuum in human rights protection on the Convention's territory, whether the violation can be imputed to a State or to a supranational institution'.[442]

XI. Other Regional Protection Mechanisms

The previous sections gave an overview of the systems for human rights protection in Europe. This section briefly turns towards regions outside Europe. In doing so, it focuses on two regions that are considered to have developed a proper system of human rights protection – albeit certainly to a different degree: the Americas and Africa. It does not discuss two geographical areas that are generally considered not to have developed a proper system of human rights protection (yet): the Arab world[443] and Asia.[444]

A. American Continent

i. Inter-American Human Rights System

The inter-American Human Rights system was born with the adoption of the American Declaration of the Rights and Duties of Man in 1948.[445] This was the first international human rights instrument of a general nature to be adopted. As it concerns a declaration, its text is not legally binding. Nevertheless, the IACtHR and the IACHR consider the Declaration to be a source of binding obligations for the Member States of the Organization of American States (OAS).[446]

[442] D Spielmann, President of the ECtHR, Opening Speech: 'Solemn Hearing for the Opening of the Judicial Year of the European Court of Human Rights', 30 January 2015) www.echr.coe.int/Documents/Speech_20150130_Solemn_Hearing_2015_ENG.pdf, 5; Spaventa (n 394) 53–56. See further, V Kosta, N Skoutaris and VP Tzevelekos (eds), *The EU Accession to the ECHR* (Oxford, Hart, 2014); S Morano-Foadi and L Vickers (eds), *Fundamental Rights in the EU: A Matter for Two Courts* (Oxford, Hart, 2015).

[443] But see further eg, W Allam, 'The Arab Charter on Human Rights: Main Features' (2014) 28 *Arab Law Quarterly* 40; S Alshehri, 'An Arab Court of Human Rights: The Dream Desired' (2016) 30 *Arab Law Quarterly* 34; KD Magliveras, 'Completing the Institutional Mechanism of the Arab Human Rights System' (2017) 6 *International Human Rights Law Review* 30.

[444] But see further eg, JD Ciorciari, 'Institutionalizing Human Rights in Southeast Asia' (2012) 34 *Human Rights Quarterly* 695; T Hsien-Li, *The ASEAN Intergovernmental Commission on Human Rights: Institutionalising Human Rights in Southeast Asia* (Cambridge, CUP, 2011); B Saul and C Renshaw (eds), *Human Rights in Asia and the Pacific* (New York, Routledge, 2014).

[445] Ninth International Conference of American States, 'American Declaration of the Rights and Duties of Man', 2 May 1948, OAS/Ser.L/V/I.4 rev 13 (2010).

[446] The OAS, which had 21 founding Member States attending the Ninth International Conference of American States, today has 35 Member States and geographically covers almost the entirety of the Americas. For more information, see www.oas.org. Functionally, the Declaration is largely replaced by the ACHR. However, the Declaration is still enforced with respect to those States that have not ratified the ACHR (including the United States and Canada). See in particular IACtHR, *Interpretation of the American Declaration of the Rights and Duties of Man Within the Framework of Article 64 of the American Convention on Human Rights*, 14 July 1989, Advisory Opinion OC-10/89, IACtHR Ser A, No 10, paras 45–46.

Articles I–XXVIII of the Declaration set forth a catalogue of civil and political rights (such as the right to life, liberty, and personal security; the right to equality; the right to a fair trial, the right to freedom of investigation, opinion, expression and dissemination; and the right of assembly), as well as economic, social, and cultural rights (such as the right to education, the right to the preservation of health and to well-being, the right to work and to fair remuneration, and the right to social security). Interestingly, Articles XXIX–XXXVIII set forth a list of duties owed by individuals (such as the duty to vote, to obey the law, to pay taxes, to work, to receive instruction).

During the conference another significant international instrument was adopted, namely the Charter of the OAS.[447] The Charter not only created the OAS but also proclaimed the fundamental rights of the individual without distinction as to race, nationality, creed, or sex. Furthermore, and of paramount importance, it also formally established the IACHR as one of the principal organs of the OAS. The IACHR's function is to promote the observance and protection of human rights and to serve as a consultative organ of the OAS in these matters. However, the Charter did not regulate the structure and competence of, nor the procedure to be followed by or before the IACHR, but instead left this to be determined by an inter-American convention on human rights.[448] It was not until 1959 that the IACHR was actually created. The Council of the OAS approved the Commission's Statute on 25 May 1960, and elected its first members on 29 June 1960. That same year it held its first session, and by 1961 it began to make on-site visits to observe the general human rights situation in States or to investigate specific situations. A major step in the development of the system was taken in 1965, when the Commission was expressly authorised to examine specific cases of human rights violations on its own initiative.[449]

ii. American Convention on Human Rights

The American Convention on Human Rights (ACHR) of 1969 (also known as the 'Pact of San José, Costa Rica') largely superseded the American Declaration of the Rights and Duties of Man.[450] Today, the Convention has been ratified by 25 American States. However, two of them have subsequently denounced it, namely Trinidad and Tobago in 1998 and Venezuela in 2012, thus bringing the number of States Parties to 23.[451]

Part I of the ACHR begins with Chapter I, which establishes the general obligations of the Member States to 'undertake to respect the rights and freedoms recognized [t]herein and to ensure to all persons subject to their jurisdiction the free and full exercise of those rights and freedoms, without any discrimination'.[452] Chapter II establishes a detailed list

[447] Charter of the Organization of American States (adopted 30 April 1948, entered into force 13 December 1951) 119 UNTS 3 (Charter of the OAS) (as amended).

[448] Art 106 Charter of the OAS.

[449] See Second Special Inter-American Conference, Res XXII: 'Expanded Functions of the Inter-American Commission on Human Rights', November 1965; IACHR, Annual Report 1976, 10 March 1977, OEA/Ser.L/VII.40, Doc 5 corr 1, first section.

[450] American Convention on Human Rights 'Pact of San José, Costa Rica' (adopted 22 November 1969, entered into force 18 July 1978) 1144 UNTS 123 (ACHR).

[451] See www.oas.org/dil/treaties_B-32_American_Convention_on_Human_Rights_sign.htm.

[452] Art 1 ACHR. The IACtHR interpreted these undertakings in the *Velasquez* case. It considered that they imply that 'the exercise of public authority has certain limits which derive from the fact that human rights are inherent attributes of human dignity and are, therefore, superior to the power of the State' and that the latter 'must prevent, investigate and punish any violation of the rights recognized by the Convention and, moreover, if possible attempt

of civil and political rights. In contrast, Chapter III, titled 'Economic, Social and Cultural Rights', only contains Article 26, which deals with the progressive realisation of these rights in a cursory way.[453] Chapter IV deals with suspensions of guarantees. In the same vein as the ECHR, Article 27 limits the possibility of suspension by listing a number of articles that cannot be derogated from and provides for the obligation to inform the other States Parties of the provisions subject to suspension, the reasons thereto, and the date set for the termination thereof. Chapter V, 'Personal Responsibilities', concludes Part I by pointing out that 'the rights of each person are limited by the rights of others, by the security of all, and by the just demands of the general welfare, in a democratic society'.[454] Part II follows with provisions for the creation and operation of the two 'organs that shall have competence with respect to matters relating to the fulfilment of the commitments made by the States Parties', those being the IACHR and the IACtHR.[455]

In 1988, the General Assembly of the OAS adopted the Additional Protocol to the American Convention on Human Rights in the Area of Economic, Social and Cultural Rights, also called the 'Protocol of San Salvador',[456] to fill the gap left by Chapter III of the ACHR. The Protocol contains a detailed list of economic, social and cultural rights. Lastly, in 1990, the General Assembly also adopted the Protocol to the American Convention on Human Rights to Abolish the Death Penalty.[457] This Protocol does not allow reservations, except for 'the death penalty in wartime in accordance with international law, for extremely serious crimes of a military nature'.[458]

iii. Inter-American Commission and Court of Human Rights

The IACHR's Statute clearly distinguishes the Commission's powers with respect to the States Party to the ACHR from those with regard to the Member States of the OAS not party to the ACHR. With regard to the latter, the Commission can make recommendations on the adoption of progressive measures in favour of human rights. For this purpose, it can request reports on measures Member States adopt and, with the consent or at the invitation of the respective government, conduct on-site observations. It also has the power to examine specific cases of human rights violations. Lastly, it can respond to inquiries made by any Member State and provide it with advisory services, and prepare any studies or reports it considers feasible to perform its duties.[459] With respect to States Party to the ACHR, the Commission has additional competences. It can act on petitions and other communications, appear before the IACtHR in cases provided for in the Convention, request the Court to

to restore the right violated and provide compensation as warranted for damages resulting from the violation': IACtHR, *Velasquez Rodriguez Case*, 29 July 1988, InterAmCtHR Ser C No 4 (1988), paras 165–66.

[453] These rights have been given a more detailed legal definition in the Protocol of San Salvador (see below (n 456)).

[454] Art 32 ACHR.

[455] ibid, Art 33. See further, TM Antkowiak and A Gonza, *The American Convention on Human Rights: Essential Rights* (Oxford, OUP, 2017).

[456] Additional Protocol to the American Convention on Human Rights in the Area of Economic, Social, and Cultural Rights 'Protocol of San Salvador' (adopted 17 November 1988, entered into force 16 November 1999) OAS TS 69. The Protocol currently has 16 States Parties; www.oas.org/juridico/english/sigs/a-52.html.

[457] Protocol to the American Convention on Human Rights to Abolish the Death Penalty (adopted 8 June 1990, entered into force 28 August 1991) OAS TS 73. The Protocol currently has 13 States Parties; www.oas.org/juridico/english/sigs/a-53.html.

[458] Art 2(1) Protocol to the American Convention on Human Rights to Abolish the Death Penalty.

[459] OAS General Assembly Res 447, 'Statute of the Inter-American Commission on Human Rights', 1 October 1979, OAS Off Rec OEA/Ser.P/IX.0.2/80, Vol 1 at 88 (as amended) (IACHR Statute), Arts 18 and 20.

take such provisional measures as it considers appropriate in serious and urgent cases which have not yet been submitted to it for consideration, consult it on the interpretation of the ACHR or other treaties and submit additional draft protocols or proposed amendments to the ACHR to the General Assembly.[460]

Furthermore, two important competences of the Commission are established in Articles 44 and 45 of the ACHR. The first provides for the right of individual petition to the Commission for a person, group of persons or recognised NGO. Second, Article 45 provides for an inter-State complaints procedure, which requires a specific declaration whereby the State concerned recognises the competence of the Commission to examine communications brought against another State Party having made the same declaration.[461]

The other treaty-based organ that has the competence to deal with matters relating to the fulfilment of the commitments made by the States Parties is the IACtHR.[462] The Court has two functions: a judicial one and an advisory one. With regard to its first function, the jurisdiction of the Court comprises all cases concerning the interpretation and application of the provisions of the Convention that are submitted to it.[463] However, for a case to be brought before the Court against a State Party, the latter must make a special declaration in which it recognises the jurisdiction of the Court to interpret and apply the ACHR.[464] Currently, 22 States have done so.[465] Unlike the situation with the ECtHR, individuals are not granted the right to submit a case before the Court; only the States Parties and the IACHR are authorised to do so.[466] As regards the advisory function of the Court, the ACHR provides that any Member State of the OAS may consult the Court regarding the interpretation of the Convention or other treaties concerning the protection of human rights in the American States.[467]

B. African Continent

i. *African Charter on Human and Peoples' Rights*

The African Charter on Human and Peoples' Rights, also known as the 'Banjul Charter',[468] is intended to promote and protect human rights and basic freedoms on the

[460] Art 19 IACHR Statute.

[461] To date, only 10 States have accepted the competence of the Commission under Art 45 of the ACHR; www.cidh.oas.org/basicos/english/Basic4.Amer.Conv.Ratif.htm. See further, RK Goldman, 'History and Action: The Inter-American Human Rights System and the Role of the Inter-American Commission on Human Rights' (2009) 31 *Human Rights Quarterly* 856; F González Morales, 'La Comisión Interamericana de Derechos Humanos: antecedentes, funciones y otros aspectos' (2009) 5 *Anuario de Derechos Humanos* 35.

[462] The Court consists of seven judges, who all have to be from different States (Art 52 ACHR). They are elected in their individual capacity, for a term of six years and may be re-elected only once (ibid, Art 54).

[463] ibid, Art 62(3).

[464] ibid, Art 62(1).

[465] See link above (n 461).

[466] Art 61 ACHR.

[467] ibid, Art 64. On the IACtHR, see further, CM Cerna, 'The Inter-American Commission on Human Rights and the Inter-American Court of Human Rights' in C Giorgetti (ed), *The Rules, Practice, and Jurisprudence of International Courts and Tribunals* (Leiden, Martinus Nijhoff, 2012) 365–92; JM Pasqualucci, *The Practice and Procedure of the Inter-American Court of Human Rights*, 2nd edn (Cambridge, CUP, 2013).

[468] African Charter on Human and Peoples' Rights 'Banjul Charter' (adopted 27 June 1981, entered into force 21 October 1986) 1520 UNTS 217. In honour thereof, 21 October was declared 'African Human Rights Day'.

African continent. It was adopted by the Assembly of Heads of State and Government (the Assembly) of the OAU, later replaced by the AU in 1981. To date, there are 53 States that have ratified the Charter.[469]

Part I begins with Chapter I, 'Human and Peoples' Rights', providing that States Parties 'shall recognise the rights, duties and freedoms enshrined in the Charter and shall undertake to adopt legislative or other measures to give effect to them'.[470] Subsequently, Articles 2–18, in a rather succinct manner, recognise a range of mainly civil and political, but also economic, social and cultural *individual* rights.[471] Next, the Charter recognises a number of rights of *peoples*, stressing that 'all peoples shall be equal'.[472] The first Chapter concludes with the State's duty to promote education and to guarantee the independence of the courts.[473] Unlike the American and European Conventions on Human Rights, the Banjul Charter does not provide for any right of derogation for the States Parties in case of public emergency. However, the absence of a derogation clause needs to be nuanced in light of the many so-called 'claw-back' clauses included in the Charter, which limit the exercise of the rights concerned *ab initio* (see for example Article 9, which provides that '[e]very individual shall have the right to express and disseminate his opinions *within the law*' (emphasis added)) and the general limitations clause contained in Article 27(2), pursuant to which '[t]he rights and freedoms of each individual shall be exercised with due regard to the rights of others, collective security, morality and common interest'.[474]

Chapter II, titled 'Duties', is particular to the Banjul Charter and establishes that '[e]very individual shall have duties towards his family and society, the State and other legally recognised communities and the international community'.[475] Amongst others, the individual has the duty to preserve the harmonious development of the family, to serve his national community by placing his physical and intellectual abilities at its service, and to preserve and strengthen positive African cultural values.[476]

ii. *African Commission and Court on Human and Peoples' Rights*

Part II of the Banjul Charter is dedicated to the African Commission on Human and Peoples' Rights (the Commission), whose function is twofold: the promotion and protection of these rights.[477] In particular, the Commission has the competence to undertake research

[469] For more information, including on the number of States Parties to the Charter and 1998 Protocol, see www.achpr.org.

[470] Art 1 Banjul Charter.

[471] See further, respectively, O Amao, 'Civil and Political Rights in the African Charter' (29–54) and M Ssenyonjo, 'Economic, Social and Cultural Rights in the African Charter' (55–100) in M Ssenyonjo (ed), *The African Regional Human Rights System: 30 Years after the African Charter on Human and Peoples' Rights* (Leiden, Martinus Nijhoff, 2012).

[472] Art 19 Banjul Charter, which is the counterpart of Art 2 that tackles the traditional non-discrimination principle (with regard to individuals). On group rights, see further, B Ugochukwu, O Badaru and O Okafor, 'Group Rights under the African Charter on Human and Peoples' Rights: Concept, Praxis and Prospects' in Ssenyonjo (n 471) 101–18.

[473] See Art 25 and 26 Banjul Charter, respectively.

[474] See further L Sermet, 'The Absence of a Derogation Clause from the African Charter on Human and Peoples' Rights: A Critical Discussion' (2007) 7 *African Human Rights Law Journal* 142.

[475] Art 27 Banjul Charter.

[476] ibid, Art 29. See further EK Quashigah, 'Scope of Individual Duties in the African Charter' in Ssenyonjo (n 471) 119–33.

[477] Art 30 Banjul Charter.

on and raise awareness of African problems in the field of human and peoples' rights. If necessary, it can give its views or make recommendations to governments.[478] It can also lay down principles and rules aimed at solving relevant legal problems upon which these governments may base their legislation.[479] It has the competence to interpret all the provisions of the Charter at the request of a State Party, an institution of the AU or an African organisation recognised thereby.[480]

Another main function of the Commission is to receive and assess inter-State communications. If a State Party has good reasons to believe that another State Party violates the provisions of the Charter, it may draw the latter's attention to the matter,[481] giving that State three months to submit an explanation. If, afterwards, the respective States cannot settle the matter bilaterally, either one of them can bring the matter to the attention of the Commission.[482] Notwithstanding these provisions, a State may also refer such a matter to the Commission directly.[483] After having tried to reach an amicable solution, the Commission then prepares a report,[484] following which it may make recommendations to the Assembly.[485]

The Charter does not specifically provide for the possibility of individual complaints, but Article 55 states that, before each session of the Commission, its Secretary 'shall make a list of the communications other than those of States Parties [...] and transmit them to Members of the Commission, who shall indicate which communications should be considered' by it.[486] When communications relate to special cases that reveal 'the existence of a series of serious or massive violations of human and peoples' rights', the Commission informs the Assembly.[487] The latter may then request the Commission 'to undertake an in-depth study' of these cases.[488] In the same vein, the Charter provides for a procedure for emergency cases to be submitted by the Commission to the Chairman of the Assembly.[489]

In 1998, a Protocol on the Establishment of the African Court on Human and Peoples' Rights was adopted.[490] This Court, which was finally established in 2006, has to supplement and reinforce the work of the Commission.[491] To date, 24 States have ratified the Protocol.[492] In the same vein as the IACtHR, the Court has both a judicial and an advisory

[478] ibid, Art 45(1)(a).
[479] ibid, Art 45(2)(b).
[480] ibid, Art 45(3).
[481] ibid, Art 47.
[482] ibid, Art 48.
[483] ibid, Art 49.
[484] ibid, Art 52.
[485] ibid, Art 53.
[486] Before a substantive consideration is made of a communication, that communication must be brought to the attention of the State concerned (ibid, Art 57).
[487] ibid, Art 58(1).
[488] ibid, Art 58(2).
[489] ibid, Art 58(3). On the Commission, see further, M Killander, 'The African Commission on Human and Peoples' Rights' in Ssenyonjo (n 471) 235–48; RI Maikassoua, *La Commission africaine des droits de l'homme et des peuples : un organe de contrôle au service de la Charte africaine* (Paris, Karthala, 2013).
[490] Protocol to the African Charter on Human and Peoples' Rights on the Establishment of the African Court on Human and Peoples' Rights (adopted 9 June 1988, 25 January 2004) OAU/LEG/EXP/AFCHPR/PROT (III). The Court is composed of 11 judges, who are to be nationals of Member States of the African Union (Art 11 Protocol), and are elected for a six-year term that can be renewed once (Art 15 Protocol).
[491] Art 2 1998 Protocol.
[492] See above (n 469).

function. As regards the judicial function, the Court has jurisdiction over all cases and disputes submitted to it concerning the interpretation and application of the Charter, the Protocol and any other relevant human rights instrument ratified by the States concerned.[493] The interrelation between the Commission and the Court is evidenced by the list of those that can submit a case to the latter: (i) the Commission; (ii) a State Party that lodged a complaint to the Commission; (iii) a State Party against which a complaint has been lodged;(iv) the State Party whose citizen is a victim of a human rights violation; and (v) African intergovernmental organisations.[494] In addition, the Court may entitle NGOs with observer status before the Commission and individuals to do so.[495] However, the last of these is only possible when the State Party concerned has made a declaration accepting the competence of the Court in such a situation.[496] As regards its advisory function, the Court may, at the request of an African Union (AU) Member State, the AU, any of its organs, or any African organisation recognised by the AU, provide an opinion on any legal matter relating to the Charter or any other relevant human rights instruments, provided that the subject matter of the opinion is not related to a matter being examined by the Commission.[497]

In 2008, the Assembly of the AU adopted the Protocol on the Statute of the African Court of Justice and Human Rights.[498] As its name suggests, the Protocol merges the African Court on Human and Peoples' Rights and the African Court of Justice – which is modelled on the International Court of Justice – putting in place a new, pan-African judicial entity: the African Court of Justice and Human and Peoples' Rights.[499] As, so far, the Protocol has been ratified by only six out of the 15 required Member States of the AU, it has not yet entered into force.[500] First, the Court would be unique because it combines the jurisdiction of the judicial organ of an intergovernmental organisation and that of a regional human rights court.[501] Second, in 2014 the AU Member States adopted the 'Malabo Protocol',[502] which gives the (future) Court criminal jurisdiction over an elaborate list of broadly defined (international) crimes. This would make the Court the first 'regional criminal court'. This development must be seen in light of the deteriorated relationship between the International Criminal Court and (many) African States. The Malabo Protocol has not yet been ratified by any State.[503] As both Protocols contain significant flaws, many

[493] Art 3 1998 Protocol.
[494] ibid, Art 5(1).
[495] ibid, Art 5(3).
[496] ibid, Art 34(6). To date, there are only eight States that have done so; see www.acthprmonitor.org/country-tracker/.
[497] Art 4 1998 Protocol.
[498] Protocol on the Statute of the African Court of Justice and Human Rights (adopted 1 July 2008, not yet entered into force).
[499] Art 2 2008 Protocol.
[500] Art 9(1) 2008 Protocol; see the Status List, au.int/en/treaties/protocol-statute-african-court-justice-and-human-rights.
[501] GJ Naldi and KD Magliveras, 'The African Court of Justice and Human Rights: A Judicial Curate's Egg' (2012) 9 *International Organizations Law Review* 383, 383.
[502] Protocol on Amendments to the Protocol on the Statute of the African Court of Justice and Human Rights (adopted 27 June 2014, not yet entered into force); see the Status List, au.int/sites/default/files/treaties/7804-sl-protocol_on_amendments_to_the_protocol_on_the_statute_of_the_african_court_of_justice_and_human_rights_5.pdf
[503] See further, G Werle and M Vormbaum (eds), *The African Criminal Court: A Commentary on the Malabo Protocol* (The Hague, TMC Asser Press, 2017).

observers have called the merger of both courts and/or the expansion of its jurisdiction to criminal matters ill-advised.[504]

XII. Concluding Remarks

Since the Second World War and the establishment of the UN, a significant number of global treaties have been adopted that incorporate a wide range of human rights, from civil, political, economic, social and cultural rights to the obligation to criminalise and the protection of vulnerable groups. Together with the UDHR, these ever more widely ratified treaties constitute the backbone of the international human rights protection system. International human rights law has therefore become an essential and dynamic branch of international law. Nevertheless, some treaties have limited ratification records and some regions have particularly low ratification rates. In addition, the effective implementation of treaties is hampered by reservations made by States and a limited acceptance of the possibility of individual complaints and inquiry procedures.

To monitor and ensure compliance with the respective treaties, the UN human rights system relies on two main pillars: the treaty bodies on the one hand, and the Charter-based bodies (the HRC and the OHCHR) on the other. The treaty bodies play a primordial role, primarily by examining the reports submitted by States Parties and individual complaints. However, as their recommendations and decisions are not legally binding and as they face severe resource constraints, their impact is – at least for now – limited. Also, the HRC forms a cornerstone of the UN human rights system, providing for an intergovernmental forum where States address human rights concerns, in particular through the UPR mechanism. Nevertheless, and even if this was one of the reasons why the HRC replaced the UN Commission on Human Rights, the agenda and work of the HRC is often tainted by political considerations and block dynamics.

Human rights treaties and protection mechanisms have proliferated not only at the international, but also at the regional level. In Europe, the most important organisation in this regard is the Council of Europe, in the framework of which the ECHR was adopted. Not least because it is enforced in a binding manner by the ECtHR, to which individuals have direct access, the ECHR has grown to become the most effective human rights convention in the world. The EU has seen its own interesting human rights dynamics in recent years, with the changes laid down in the Treaty of Lisbon as a culmination point. The promotion of the 'universality and indivisibility of human rights' is one of the key foreign relations objectives of the EU. However, it should be noted that the EU Charter only applies in relation to EU law, and the EU has not, as yet, acceded to the ECHR.

Two other regional organisations with important human rights instruments and monitoring mechanisms are the OAS and the AU. While in the Americas, the duo of the IACHR and the IACtHR has markedly contributed to the protection of human rights, and made the American human rights system one of the two strongest in the world, the African human

[504] Naldi and Magliveras (n 501) 383–87. On the African human rights system more generally, see H Kembo Takam Gatsing, *Le système africain de protection des droits de l'homme : un système en quête de cohérence* (Paris, l'Harmattan, 2014).

rights system struggles to become more effective. In particular, the (potential) establishment of the African Court of Justice and Human and Peoples' Rights, which would also have criminal jurisdiction, leaves the system in an uncertain state of flux.

Bibliography

Alston, P and Goodman, R, *International Human Rights* (Oxford, OUP, 2012).

Benedek, W, *Menschenrechte verstehen: Handbuch zur Menschenrechtsbildung*, 3rd edn (Berlin, Berliner Wissenschaftsverlag, 2017).

De Schutter, O, *International Human Rights Law: Cases, Materials, Commentary*, 2nd edn (Cambridge, CUP, 2015).

Hannum, H, Anaya, SJ, and Shelton, DL, *International Human Rights: Problems of Law, Policy, and Practice*, 5th edn (New York, Aspen, 2011).

Hennebel, L and Tigroudja, H, *Traité de droit international des droits de l'homme* (Paris, Pedone, 2016).

Moeckli, D, Shah, S, Sivakumaran, S (eds) and Harris, D (consultant ed), *International Human Rights Law*, 3rd edn (Oxford, OUP, 2018).

Peers, S, Hervey, T, Kenner, J, Ward, A (eds), *The EU Charter of Fundamental Rights: A Commentary* (Oxford, Hart, 2014).

Pollmann, A and Lohmann, G (eds), *Menschenrechte: ein interdisziplinäres Handbuch* (Stuttgart, Metzler, 2012).

Rodley, N, 'International Human Rights Law' in Evans, MD (ed), *International Law*, 4th edn (Oxford, OUP, 2014) 783–820.

Schabas, WA, *The European Convention on Human Rights: A Commentary* (Oxford, OUP, 2015).

Sheeran, S and Rodley, N, *Routledge Handbook of International Human Rights Law* (London, Routledge, 2013).

Shelton, D (ed), *The Oxford Handbook of International Human Rights Law* (Oxford, OUP, 2013).

Sudre, F, *Droit européen et international des droits de l'homme*, 13th edn (Paris, PUF, 2016).

Further Reading

Alston, P (ed), *The EU and Human Rights* (Oxford, OUP, 1999).

Antkowiak, TM and Gonza, A, *The American Convention on Human Rights: Essential Rights* (Oxford, OUP, 2017).

Charlesworth, H and Larking, E (eds), *Human Rights and the Universal Periodic Review: Rituals and Ritualism* (Cambridge, CUP, 2015).

Criddle, EJ (ed), *Human Rights in Emergencies* (New York, CUP, 2016).

Freedman, R, *The United Nations Human Rights Council, A Critique and Early Assessment* (Oxon, Routledge, 2013).

Giacomo, DF, *The EU Charter of Fundamental Rights: From Declaration to Binding Instrument* (Dordrecht, Springer, 2011).

Keller, H and Ulfstein, G (eds), *UN Human Rights Treaty Bodies: Law and Legitimacy* (Cambridge, CUP, 2012).

Kembo Takam Gatsing, H, *Le système africain de protection des droits de l'homme : un système en quête de cohérence* (Paris, l'Harmattan, 2014).

Kosta, V, Skoutaris, N and Tzevelekos, VP (eds), *The EU Accession to the ECHR* (Oxford, Hart, 2014).

Morano-Foadi, S and Vickers, L (eds), *Fundamental Rights in the EU: A Matter for Two Courts* (Oxford, Hart, 2015).

Nifosi-Sutton, I, *The Protection of Vulnerable Groups under International Human Rights Law* (Abingdon, Routledge, 2017).

Pasqualucci, JM, *The Practice and Procedure of the Inter-American Court of Human Rights*, 2nd edn (Cambridge, CUP, 2013).

Wouters, J and Meuwissen, K, 'The European Union at the UN Human Rights Council: Multilateral Human Rights Protection Coming of Age?' (2014) *European Journal of Human Rights* 135.

Wouters, J, Nowak, M, Chané, AL and Hachez, N (eds), *The European Union and Human Rights: Law and Policy* (Oxford, OUP, 2019).

Wouters, J and Ovadek, M, *The European Union and Human Rights: Analysis, Cases and Materials* (Oxford, OUP, 2019).

17

International Criminal Law

CO-AUTHORED WITH THOMAS VAN POECKE

I. Introduction

International criminal law (ICL) was originally concerned with horizontal judicial cooperation between States in the fight against crime. In the nineteenth century, States embarked on the creation of a vast web of multilateral and in particular bilateral extradition treaties enabling the transfer of sought individuals from one State to another. In the twentieth century, States started to tackle transnational crime phenomena by means of international conventions, giving a more uniform definition to crimes and facilitating international cooperation. Before the Second World War, international conventions on crimes as counterfeiting, slavery and the trafficking of women and children were concluded.[1] From the 1970s onwards, they were complemented by conventions on terrorism, corruption and money-laundering.[2] These conventions form the backbone of the field of *transnational* criminal law, a body of rules and procedures created by States to smoothen international cooperation in respect of forms of criminality threatening State interests.[3]

International criminal law in the strict sense, by contrast, represses attacks against the basic values of the international community, as epitomised by systematic or large-scale violence,[4] rather than attacks against the joint interests of States. To address these crimes, supranational prosecutorial and judicial mechanisms, rather than mere enhanced inter-State

[1] eg International Convention for the Suppression of Counterfeiting Currency (adopted 20 April 1929, entered into force 22 February 1931) 112 LNTS 371; Convention to Suppress the Slave Trade and Slavery (adopted 25 September 1926, entered into force) 212 UNTS 17; Supplementary Convention on the Abolition of Slavery, the Slave Trade, and Institutions and Practices Similar to Slavery (adopted 7 September 1956, entered into force 30 April 1957) 266 UNTS 3.

[2] eg Convention on Offences and Certain Other Acts Committed on Board Aircraft (adopted 14 September 1963, entered into force 4 December 1969) 704 UNTS 219; United Nations Convention against Corruption (adopted 31 October 2003, entered into force 14 December 2005) 2349 UNTS 41 (UN Convention against Corruption); United Nations Convention against Transnational Organized Crime (adopted 15 November 2000, entered into force 29 September 2003) 2225 UNTS 209.

[3] N Boister, *An Introduction to Transnational Criminal Law* (Oxford, OUP, 2012) 3.

[4] G Werle, 'General Principles of International Criminal Law' in A Cassese (ed), *The Oxford Companion to International Criminal Justice* (Oxford, OUP, 2009) 55.

cooperation procedures, have been put in place. That is the case because these crimes are often committed by States themselves, following which they may have little incentive to investigate and prosecute them.

ICL has been developed through case law,[5] a limited number of subject-matter-specific treaties,[6] and the codification of customary international law.[7] It encompasses not only the law concerned with such crimes as war crimes, crimes against humanity and genocide, but also the principles and procedures governing the international investigation and prosecution of these crimes. These are crimes over which: (i) international criminal tribunals established ad hoc by the UN Security Council, ie the International Criminal Tribunal for the former Yugoslavia (ICTY) and the International Criminal Tribunal for Rwanda (ICTR); (ii) 'mixed', 'hybrid' or 'internationalised' courts, tribunals or chambers, such as the Special Court for Sierra Leone (SCSL), the Special Tribunal for Lebanon (STL) or the Extraordinary Chambers in the Courts of Cambodia (ECCC); and (iii) the International Criminal Court (ICC) have jurisdiction.[8] ICL may also be concerned with aggression, torture and terrorism, but most international tribunals do not have jurisdiction over these crimes as such.[9]

This chapter does not discuss questions of transnational criminal law, including questions of mutual legal assistance, as such questions are of a criminal rather than public international law nature. An exception is made for: (i) the crimes of terrorism and torture, which, strictly speaking, are transnational 'treaty crimes', but may have entered the realm of ICL; and (ii) the law of extradition, as public international law sources, such as international human rights norms, have had a considerable impact on it. In this context, attention will also be devoted to the surrender procedures which apply within the EU on the basis of the 2002 Framework Decision on the European Arrest Warrant.[10] When discussing such issues as definitions of crimes, individual responsibility, jurisdiction and criminal procedure, this chapter does not limit itself to the ICC Statute, but refers to all the main sources of ICL.

II. Elements of the Crimes

All crimes consist of a material (*actus reus*) and a mental (*mens rea*) element. Pertinent to the material element are the perpetrator's conduct (eg using prohibited weapons, even absent harmful effects), consequences (eg killing civilians), and/or circumstances (eg recruiting child soldiers, 'age' being the relevant circumstance). The material element is normally established in the definition of the crime.

[5] eg Internatinal Military Tribunal (Nuremberg), *US et al v Göring et al*, 1 October 1946, 22 IMT 203.
[6] eg the Genocide Convention and the four 1949 Geneva Conventions.
[7] eg J-M Henckaerts and L Doswald-Beck (eds), *Customary International Humanitarian Law – Volume I: Rules and Volume II: Practice* (Cambridge, CUP, 2005). For general principles of ICL, see F Raimondo, *General Principles of Law in the Decisions of the International Criminal Courts and Tribunals* (Leiden, Nijhoff, 2008).
[8] See below, Section V(A) on the establishment and design of international criminal tribunals.
[9] The ICC has jurisdiction over aggression; see below, Section III(D). Via the Lebanese Criminal Code, the STL had jurisdiction over terrorism and torture; see Art 2 Statute of the Special Tribunal for Lebanon (UNSC Res 1757, 30 May 2007, UN Doc S/RES/1757). See also STL, *Interlocutory Decision on the Applicable Law: Terrorism, Conspiracy, Homicide, Perpetration, Cumulative Charging*, 16 February 2011, Case No STL-11-01/I/AC/R176bis, para 62, holding that the STL may refer to international sources of law, including on terrorism, to assist it in interpreting and applying Lebanese law.
[10] Council Framework Decision of 13 June 2002 on the European Arrest Warrant and the surrender procedures between Member States (2002/584/JHA) [2012] OJ L190/1 (EAW Framework Decision).

The mental element, referring to the perpetrator's state of mind when committing the crime, is often not established in the definition of the crime, which explains why a specific provision in the ICC Statute is devoted to it. Under Article 30(1) of the Statute, a person shall be criminally responsible and liable for punishment for a crime within the jurisdiction of the Court only if the material elements are committed with intent and knowledge.[11] Definitions of crimes may provide for a different *mens rea*. For instance, and as will be discussed below (Section III(A)), genocide requires a 'special intent'.

Pursuant to Article 9 of the ICC Statute, 'Elements of Crimes', which assist the Court in the interpretation and application of the substantive crimes by further specifying their respective elements, have been adopted by the Assembly of States Parties to the ICC Statute.[12]

III. Definitions of International Crimes

All modern-day international criminal tribunals – ie the ICTY, ICTR and ICC – have (or, for the ICTY and ICTR, 'had'; see below, Section V(A)) jurisdiction over three categories of crimes: genocide, crimes against humanity and war crimes. These crimes are characterised as 'core crimes' against international law. Only the ICC has jurisdiction over the crime of aggression. The essentials of the four crimes are discussed respectively, following which the 'treaty crimes' terrorism and torture are also considered.

A. Crime of Genocide[13]

The crime of genocide refers to a number of acts committed with the intent to destroy, in whole or in part, a national, ethnical, racial or religious group, as such.[14] The seriousness of the crime is underlined by the fact that – immediately after World War II – it was codified by means of the 1948 Genocide Convention, and that its prohibition has since been recognised to have attained the status of a *jus cogens* norm[15] and to impose an *erga omnes* obligation on States.[16]

[11] Art 30(2) ICC Statute goes on to state that 'a person has intent where (a) [i]n relation to conduct, that person means to engage in the conduct; (b) [i]n relation to a consequence, that person means to cause that consequence or is aware that it will occur in the ordinary course of events'. Art 30(3) provides that '"knowledge" means awareness that a circumstance exists or a consequence will occur in the ordinary course of events'.

[12] ICC 'Elements of Crimes', 9 September 2002, ICC-ASP/1/3, Part II.B, as amended by Res RC/Res.6 of 11 June 2010, RC/11.

[13] See also Chapter 16, Section III(A), which deals with genocide from a human rights law perspective.

[14] Art 6 ICC Statute; Art 4 Statute of the International Criminal Tribunal for the Former Yugoslavia, adopted by UNSC Res 827, 25 May 1993, UN Doc S/RES/827, as amended, consolidated version as of September 2009: icty.org/x/file/Legal%20Library/Statute/statute_sept09_en.pdf (ICTY Statute); Art 2 Statute of the International Criminal Tribunal for Rwanda, adopted by and annexed to UNSC Res 955, 8 November 1994, UN Doc S/RES/995, as amended, consolidated version as of 31 January 2010: unictr.unmict.org/sites/unictr.org/files/legal-library/100131_Statute_en_fr_0.pdf (ICTR Statute). These articles all copy the definition of genocide contained in Art II of the Genocide Convention.

[15] *Armed Activities on the Territory of the Congo* (Democratic Republic of the Congo v Rwanda) [2006] ICJ Rep 6, para 64.

[16] *Reservations to the Convention on the Prevention and Punishment of the Crime of Genocide* (Advisory Opinion) [1951] ICJ Rep 15, 23.

The specific forms of genocide, which form part of the objective elements of the crime, concern:

(a) Killing members of the group;
(b) Causing serious bodily or mental harm to members of the group;
(c) Deliberately inflicting on the group conditions of life calculated to bring about its physical destruction in whole or in part;
(d) Imposing measures intended to prevent births within the group;
(e) Forcibly transferring children of the group to another group.[17]

While these forms of genocide are relatively clear, it is noteworthy that in its quintessential *Akayesu* judgment, the ICTR established that rape and sexual violence may also amount to genocide (if committed with genocidal intent, on which see immediately below).[18]

Judicial authorities faced more ambiguities in establishing the fulfilment of the notion 'group'. In *Akayesu*, the ICTR first put forward an objective approach, requiring 'stable' rather than 'mobile' groups; referring to groups 'constituted in a permanent fashion and membership of which is determined by birth' rather than 'voluntary commitment'.[19] Eventually – still in *Akayesu* – the ICTR inserted a subjective element in its test, noting 'that all the Rwandan witnesses who appeared before it invariably answered spontaneously and without hesitation the questions [...] regarding their ethnic identity'.[20] A subjective approach was confirmed in later ICTY cases, considering that 'it is more appropriate to evaluate the status of a national, ethnical or racial group from the point of view of those persons who wish to single that group out from the rest of the community' and that it is 'the stigmatisation of a group [...] which allows it to be determined whether a targeted population constitutes a national, ethnical or racial group in the eyes of the alleged perpetrators'.[21]

This approach is in line with the requirement of a special, genocidal intent (*dolus specialis*), which sets genocide apart from the other international crimes. The gravity of genocide is marked by its subjective element or *mens rea*, namely the intent to destroy one of the protected groups.[22] That is so because perpetrators of genocide 'do not see the victim as a human being, but only as a member of the persecuted group' and do not target the victim in his or her capacity as an individual.[23] Accordingly, Article II of the Genocide Convention requires intent to destroy the group 'as such'. In *Mpambara*, the ICTR held that 'the commission of even a single instance of one of the prohibited acts is sufficient, provided that the accused genuinely intends by that act to destroy at least a substantial part of the group'.[24] Thus, what is required is 'genuine intent'.[25]

[17] Art II Genocide Convention.

[18] ICTR, Trial Chamber, *Prosecutor v Akayesu*, 2 September 1998, Case No ICTR-96-4-T, para 731; as 'rape and sexual violence certainly constitute infliction of serious bodily and mental harm on the victims and are even, according to the Chamber, one of the worst ways of [*sic*] inflict harm on the victim as he or she suffers both bodily and mental harm' (ibid). This has been confirmed by Art 6(b)(1), fn 3 of the ICC Elements of Crimes (n 12).

[19] *Akayesu* (n 18) para 511.

[20] ibid, para 702.

[21] ICTY, Trial Chamber, *Prosecutor v Jelisić*, 14 December 1999, Case No IT-95-10-T, para 70. See also ICTY, Trial Chamber, *Prosecutor v Krstić*, 2 August 2001, Case No IT-98-33-T, paras 559–60; A Cassese, *International Criminal Law*, 3rd edn (Oxford, OUP, 2013) 120–21.

[22] R Cryer et al, *An Introduction to International Criminal Law and Procedure*, 2nd edn (Cambridge, CUP, 2010) 206. See also *Jelisić* (n 21) para 66 and Court of Bosnia and Herzegovina, the Panel of the Appellate Division, the Section I for War Crimes, *Prosecutor's Office of Bosnia and Herzegovina v Stevanović Miladin*, 9 November 2009, Case No X-KRŽ-05/24-2, paras 55–58.

[23] Federal Court of Justice (GE), *Prosecutor v Jorgić*, 30 April 1999, Case No 3 StR 215/98, para 37.

[24] ICTR, Trial Chamber, *Prosecutor v Mpambara*, 11 September 2006, Case No ICTR-01-65-T, para 8.

[25] Cassese (n 21) 118–19.

The ICTY has clarified that the term 'destroy' should be interpreted as referring to the physical or biological destruction of the group and not, for example, to attacking 'the cultural or sociological characteristics of a group in order to remove its separate identity'[26] (a so-called 'cultural genocide'). In the same vein, genocide should not be confused with 'ethnic cleansing', which 'has no legal significance of its own',[27] but can be defined as 'rendering an area ethnically homogeneous by using force or intimidation to remove persons of given groups from the area'.[28] According to the ICJ, the 'deportation or displacement of the members of a group, even if effected by force, is not necessarily equivalent to destruction of that group, nor is such destruction an automatic consequence of the displacement'.[29]

B. Crimes against Humanity

Crimes against humanity concern a number of acts committed as part of a widespread or systematic attack directed against any civilian population, with knowledge of the attack.[30] As of yet, and as opposed to what is the case for genocide, there is no separate convention on crimes against humanity. Since 2014, the ILC has been in the process of drafting such a global convention.[31]

Traditionally, the specific forms of crimes against humanity concern acts such as murder, extermination, enslavement, deportation, imprisonment, torture, rape and persecution.[32] Article 7 of the ICC Statute, which constitutes a codification as well as a progressive development of customary international law,[33] specified that also other forms of sexual violence are included, and added enforced disappearance and the crime of apartheid to the list. Noteworthy is that the list of acts that can constitute crimes against humanity includes a catch-all clause, referring to 'other inhumane acts of a similar character intentionally causing great suffering, or serious injury to body or to mental or physical health'.[34]

[26] ICTY, Appeals Chamber, *Prosecutor v Krstić*, 19 April 2004, Case No IT-98-33-A, para 25. Although, while not sufficient in and of themselves, simultaneous attacks on cultural and religious property and symbols are often connected to the crime of genocide.

[27] *Application of the Convention on the Prevention and Punishment of the Crime of Genocide* (Bosnia and Herzegovina v Serbia and Montenegro) [2007] ICJ Rep 43, para 190.

[28] Final Report of the Commission of Experts Established Pursuant to Security Council Resolution 780 (1992), 27 May 1994, UN Doc S/1994/674, Annex, para 129.

[29] 'This is not to say that acts described as "ethnic cleansing" may never constitute genocide': they do if they can be characterised as one of the specific forms of genocide and are 'carried out with the necessary specific intent *(dolus specialis)*, that is to say with a view to the destruction of the group, as distinct from its removal from the region'. Still, 'it is clear that acts of "ethnic cleansing" may occur in parallel to acts [of genocide], and may be significant as indicative of the presence of a specific intent *(dolus specialis)* inspiring those acts'; *Application of the Convention on the Prevention and Punishment of the Crime of Genocide* (n 27) para 190.

[30] Art 5 ICTY Statute; Art 3 ICTR Statute; Art 7 ICC Statute. Art 5 ICTY Statute requires a nexus with an armed conflict (see below) and does not refer to the prerequisite of a widespread or systematic attack. However, the latter requirement was included in the jurisprudence of the ICTY: see ICTY, Trial Chamber, *Prosecutor v Tadić*, 7 May 1997, Case No IT-94-1-T, para 644 ff. Art 3 ICTR Statute adds the requirement that the attack be committed 'on national, political, ethnic, racial or religious grounds'.

[31] For more information, see ILC, 'Analytical Guide to the Work of the International Law Commission: Crimes Against Humanity', legal.un.org/ilc/guide/7_7.shtml.

[32] Art 5 ICTY Statute; Art 3 ICTR Statute; Art 7(1) ICC Statute.

[33] K Ambos, *Treatise on International Criminal Law – Volume II: The Crimes and Sentencing* (Oxford, OUP, 2014) 49.

[34] Art 7(1)(k) ICC Statute. Art 5(i) ICTY Statute and Art 3(1) ICTR Statute simply refer to 'other inhumane acts'.

This catch-all clause illustrates that the characteristic element of crimes against humanity does not so much concern the specific acts through which they can materialise. Rather, it is the required contextual element that sets crimes against humanity apart from the other international crimes. The 1945 Nuremberg Charter was the first legal instrument to criminalise crimes against humanity, but required a link with an armed conflict.[35] However, when France, the UK, the US and the USSR later that year adopted Control Council Law No 10,[36] which served as a basis to prosecute perpetrators of international crimes committed during World War II who would not be prosecuted by the International Military Tribunal (IMT or Nuremberg Tribunal), they dropped the link between crimes against humanity and armed conflict.[37] After the ICTY Statute had again stipulated the requirement of a connection with an armed conflict,[38] the ICTR Statute contributed to the evolution of crimes against humanity towards a truly self-standing international crime, instead requiring the contextual element of a 'widespread or systematic attack' against any civilian population.[39] The ICC Statute has consolidated this evolution.[40] Thus, what distinguishes crimes against humanity from war crimes is that the former do not need to be committed during an armed conflict.[41]

The widespread or systematic test is disjunctive, meaning that only one of its two elements needs to be satisfied. The term 'widespread' generally connotes the large-scale nature of the attack and the number of victims, while the term 'systematic' refers to the high degree of organisation of the attack.[42] The ICC Statute establishes that the requirement of an attack includes a policy element, meaning that a plan or policy to commit the crimes by a government or an organisation must exist;[43] an element the statutes and case law of the ad hoc tribunals did not require.[44] The requirement that the attack be directed against any civilian population entails: (i) that attacks by a State or organisation against its own population or that of its allies are also covered;[45] but (ii) that attacks against combatants are not covered.[46] As to the subjective element, it is required that the perpetrator is aware of the existence of a widespread or systematic attack, and the link between his or her crime and that attack.[47]

[35] Agreement for the Prosecution and Punishment of the Major War Criminals of the European Axis, Annex: Charter of the International Military Tribunal (8 August 1945) 82 UNTS (Nuremberg Charter) 279, Art 6(c).

[36] Control Council Law No 10 on the Punishment of Persons Guilty of War Crimes, Crimes Against Peace and Against Humanity, 20 December 1945, (1946) 3 *Official Gazette Control Council for Germany* 50.

[37] ibid, Art II(1)(c); Cassese (n 21) 90.

[38] Art 5 ICTY Statute.

[39] Art 3 ICTR Statute.

[40] Art 7(1) ICC Statute.

[41] Although, when the underlying crimes are committed during an armed conflict, it is not excluded that they qualify as crimes against humanity. For an application before a national court, see eg Regional Court of Ljubljana (SI), *Supreme State Prosecutor v Ribičič (Mitja)*, 27 June 2006, Case No Ks 962/2006, para 14, relying on the provisions of several international instruments to come to the conclusion that crimes against humanity can be committed in time of peace.

[42] *Akayesu* (n 18) para 580.

[43] According to Art 7(2)(a) ICC Statute, the attack requirement refers to 'a course of conduct involving the multiple commission of acts [...] pursuant to or in furtherance of a State or organizational policy'. The ICC Elements of Crimes (n 12) add that the policy element 'requires that the State or organization actively promote or encourage' the attack.

[44] eg ICTY, Appeals Chamber, *Prosecutor v Kunarac*, 12 June 2002, IT-96-23 & 23/1-A, para 98.

[45] Cassese (n 21) 101–102.

[46] Even if combatants can still be the individual victims of the underlying crimes part of an attack against a civilian population; ibid, 102.

[47] ibid, 98–100.

C. War Crimes

War crimes are grave breaches of the 1949 Geneva Conventions,[48] or other serious violations of the laws and customs applicable in international or non-international armed conflict.[49] Thus, according to the ICTY, for there to be a war crime, (i) there must be a violation constituting 'an infringement of a rule of international humanitarian law' (IHL);[50] (ii) the rule violated must either be part of customary international law or of an applicable treaty; (iii) the violation must be 'serious', meaning that it 'must constitute a breach of a rule protecting important values, and the breach must involve grave consequences for the victim'; and (iv) 'the violation of the rule must entail, under customary or conventional law, the individual criminal responsibility of the person breaching the rule'.[51]

As war crimes concern violations of IHL, they must be committed in the context of an armed conflict, be it an international (IAC) or non-international armed conflict (NIAC). Accordingly, what distinguishes war crimes from the other international crimes is the required contextual element: unlike genocide or crimes against humanity,[52] war crimes must have a 'nexus' with an armed conflict. The nexus requirement entails that the criminal conduct must be 'closely related to the hostilities'.[53] It follows that while crimes against humanity require the contextual element of a widespread or systematic attack against a civilian population, war crimes do not; a single crime – with a nexus to an armed conflict – can constitute a war crime. Article 8(1) of the ICC Statute nuances this by providing a 'practical guideline' as to the war crimes the ICC, and especially its prosecutor, should focus on,[54] specifying that '[t]he Court shall have jurisdiction in respect of war crimes *in particular* when committed as part of a plan or policy or as part of a large-scale commission of such crimes'.[55]

According to Cassese, six types of war crimes can be distinguished: (i) crimes against persons not, or no longer, taking part in hostilities (eg rape); (ii) crimes involving prohibited methods of warfare (eg intentionally directing an attack against the civilian population); (iii) crimes involving prohibited means of warfare (eg employing weapons that are of a nature to cause superfluous injury or unnecessary suffering); (iv) crimes against specially protected persons or objects (eg intentionally directing an attack against medical personnel); (v) crimes involving the improper use of protected signs or emblems (eg the improper use of a flag of truce resulting in death or serious personal injury); and (vi) 'conscripting or enlisting children under the age of 15 years or using them to participate actively in hostilities'.[56]

D. Crime of Aggression

Crimes of aggression are the modern-day versions of crimes against the peace, with which the Treaty of Versailles (1919)[57] charged the German Emperor and which were made

[48] Art 8(2)(a) ICC Statute; Art 2 ICTY Statute.
[49] Art 8(2)(b)–(e) ICC Statute; Art 3 ICTY Statute; Art 4 ICTR Statute.
[50] Or the law of armed conflict (LOAC), on which see Chapter 15.
[51] ICTY, Appeals Chamber, *Prosecutor v Tadić*, Decision on the Defence Motion for Interlocutory Appeal on Jurisdiction, 2 October 1995, Case No IT-94-1, para 94; see also Cassese (n 21) 65.
[52] See, however, above (Subsection (B)) on the Nuremberg Charter and the ICTY Statute.
[53] Cassese (n 21) 77.
[54] M Cottier, 'Article 8: War Crimes' in O Triffterer and K Ambos, *The Rome Statute of the International Criminal Court: A Commentary*, 3rd edn (München, Beck, 2016) 321–22.
[55] Emphasis added.
[56] Cassese (n 21) 71–75.
[57] Art 227 Treaty of Peace with Germany (adopted 28 June 1919, entered into force 10 January 1920) 225 CTS 188 (Treaty of Versailles).

punishable by the Nuremberg Charter.[58] In 1974, UN General Assembly Resolution 3314 (XXIX) defined aggression as 'the use of armed force by a State against the sovereignty, territorial integrity or political independence of another State, or in any other manner inconsistent with the Charter of the United Nations'.[59]

Today, the ICC Statute is the sole legal instrument containing the crime of aggression. Initially, Article 5(1) of the ICC Statute simply mentioned that the crime of aggression was a crime within the jurisdiction of the Court, while Article 5(2) of the Statute provided that '[t]he Court shall exercise jurisdiction over the crime of aggression once a provision is adopted [...] defining the crime and setting out the conditions under which the Court shall exercise jurisdiction with respect to this crime.' At the Kampala Conference in 2010, an amendment to the ICC Statute was adopted, defining the crime of aggression.[60] Still, according to the new Article 15*bis*(3) of the ICC Statute, the Court could only exercise jurisdiction over the crime of aggression: (i) 'subject to a decision to be taken after 1 January 2017 by the same majority of States Parties as is required for the adoption of an amendment to the Statute'; and (ii) after the amendments to the ICC Statute concerning the crime of aggression had been ratified or accepted by (at least) 30 States Parties.[61] At the end of 2017, the Assembly of States Parties was finally able 'to activate the Court's jurisdiction over the crime of aggression as of 17 July 2018'.[62]

Article 8*bis* of the ICC Statute heavily borrows from UN General Assembly Resolution 3314.[63] However, as the UNGA dealt with aggression as a matter of public international law and the ICC Statute does so as a matter of international criminal law, differences exist. Thus, Article 8*bis*(1) separately defines the *crime* of aggression, specifying two additional elements. First, the crime of aggression can only be committed 'by a person in a position effectively to exercise control over or to direct the political or military action of a State'.[64] Thus, it excludes: (i) leaders of non-State armed groups; and (ii) State agents that are not in a leadership position. Second, the Statute inserts a qualified threshold by requiring an act of aggression that 'by its *character, gravity and scale*, constitutes a *manifest* violation of the Charter of the United Nations'.[65] Article 8*bis*(2) then defines what constitutes an 'act of aggression' under the Statute by copying the list contained in Article 3 of UNGA Resolution 3314. It should be noted, however, that while Article 4 of the UNGA Resolution provides that the list of acts enumerated in Article 3 thereof is not exhaustive, the ICC Statute does not contain such a provision, following which the list of Article 8*bis*(2) must be considered to be exhaustive.

E. International Treaty Crimes

International 'treaty crimes' are those crimes that are the subject of multilateral treaties because the international community has an interest in suppressing them, but the status

[58] Art 6(a) Nuremberg Charter (n 35).

[59] UNGA, 'Definition of Aggression', Annex to UNGA Res 3314 (XXIX), 14 December 1974, UN Doc A/RES/3314 (XXIX), Art 1. Art 3 then contains a (non-exhaustive (see Art 4)) list of specific acts that qualify as acts of aggression.

[60] See Assembly of States Parties, Res RC/Res.6, 11 June 2010, RC/11.

[61] Art 15*bis*(2) ICC Statute. See further C Kreß and L von Holtzendorff, 'The Kampala Compromise on the Crime of Aggression' (2010) 8 *JICJ* 1179.

[62] Assembly of States Parties, 'Draft resolution proposed by the Vice-Presidents of the Assembly Activation of the jurisdiction of the Court over the crime of aggression', 14 December 2017, ICC-ASP/16/L.10, operative clause 1.

[63] See above (n 59).

[64] Art 8*bis*(1) ICC Statute.

[65] ibid (emphasis added).

of which as a distinct crime under customary international law is uncertain and/or over which no supranational criminal jurisdiction can be exercised. They belong to the realm of 'transnational criminal law' (see above, Section I). Terrorism and torture are transnational crimes that may nevertheless have entered the realm of international criminal law, and will be discussed respectively. Treaty crimes that will not be discussed notably include piracy,[66] drug trafficking,[67] trafficking in persons[68] and the crime of enforced disappearance.[69]

i. Crime of Terrorism

Various manifestations of terrorism have been criminalised by sectoral international conventions on terrorism.[70] Yet, it is unclear whether terrorism constitutes a crime under customary international law in and of itself. The STL has held that 'a customary rule of international law regarding the crime of terrorism, at least *in time of peace*, has indeed emerged'.[71] In the STL's view, this crime of terrorism consists of:

> (i) the perpetration of a criminal act (such as murder, kidnapping, hostage-taking, arson, and so on), or threatening such an act; (ii) the intent to spread fear among the population (which would generally entail the creation of public danger) or directly or indirectly coerce a national or international authority to take some action, or to refrain from taking it; (iii) when the act involves a transnational element.[72]

However, this finding of the STL has been heavily criticised.[73] Mainly because on the international level, there is no generally accepted definition of terrorism, most agree that 'there is currently no solid consensus in international practice as to the existence of the international crime of terrorism in customary international law'.[74]

The disagreement on the international level as regards the definition of terrorism is best illustrated by the failure to reach consensus on a (Draft) Comprehensive Convention on International Terrorism (CCIT).[75] In 1996, the UN General Assembly established an

[66] cp Ambos (n 33) 241: 'piracy comes very close to an international crime *stricto sensu*'. For the definition of piracy, see Art 101 UNCLOS. From the perspective of the law of the sea, see Chapter 18, Section V(E)(i)(a).

[67] See the United Nations Convention against the Illicit Traffic in Narcotic Drugs and Psychotropic Substances (adopted 20 December 1988, entered into force 11 November 1990) 1582 UNTS 95.

[68] See the Protocol to Prevent, Suppress and Punish Trafficking in Persons, Especially Women and Children (adopted 15 November 2000, entered into force 25 December 2003) 2237 UNTS 319, supplementing the United Nations Convention against Transnational Organized Crime (n 2), with a definition of 'trafficking in persons' in Art 3(a).

[69] Enforced disappearance can constitute a crime against humanity (eg Art 7(1)(i) ICC Statute). For a definition, see Art 2 Enforced Disappearance Convention. From a human rights law perspective, see Chapter 16, Section III(C). Further, see eg B Finucane, 'Enforced Disappearance as a Crime under International Law: A Neglected Origin in the Laws of War' (2010) 35 *Yale Journal of International Law* 171.

[70] See eg above (n 2). For the full list of the 12 sectoral international conventions dealing with terrorism, see UN Office of Counter-Terrorism, 'International Legal Instruments', un.org/en/counterterrorism/legal-instruments.shtml.

[71] STL, *Interlocutory Decision* (n 9) para 85. Note that terrorism in time of armed conflict is – at least according to most – a different matter, and one that goes beyond the scope of this chapter. See further A Bianchi and Y Naqvi, *International Humanitarian Law and Terrorism* (Oxford, Hart, 2011).

[72] STL, *Interlocutory Decision* (n 9) para 85.

[73] See eg B Saul, 'Legislating from a Radical Hague: The United Nations Special Tribunal for Lebanon Invents an International Crime of Transnational Terrorism' (2011) 24 *LJIL* 677.

[74] Bianchi and Naqvi (n 71) 285. Further, see notably B Saul, *Defining Terrorism in International Law* (Oxford, OUP, 2006) 191–270, concluding that 'arguments that terrorism is a customary international crime are premature' (ibid, 270). But see Cassese (n 21) 148–49, arguing that such a crime exists.

[75] See the Annexes to the Report of the Ad Hoc Committee established by General Assembly resolution 51/210 of 17 December 1996, Sixth session (28 January–1 February 2002), GAOR Fifty-seventh Session, Supplement No 37, 11 February 2002, UN Doc A/57/37.

Ad Hoc Committee, inter alia to develop 'a comprehensive legal framework of conventions dealing with international terrorism'.[76] While the debate on the CCIT has been going on since 2000,[77] there is persistent disagreement among States mainly as to whether armed struggles for self-determination, or, more generally, the activities of non-State parties to an armed conflict, should be excluded from the scope of the Convention, as well as to whether 'State terrorism' should fall within the CCIT's scope of application.[78] While, in December 2016, the UNGA revived the process by recommending its Sixth Committee to 'establish a working group with a view to finalizing the process on the draft comprehensive convention on international terrorism',[79] it remains to be seen whether States will reach an agreement on the CCIT any time soon.

ii. Crime of Torture[80]

Unlike what is the case for terrorism, most agree that torture is an international crime.[81] The crime of torture is outlawed by the 1984 UN Convention against Torture, as well as the 1985 Inter-American Convention to Prevent and Punish Torture.[82] In *Questions relating to the Obligation to Prosecute or Extradite*, the ICJ noted that 'the Parties agree that acts of torture are regarded by customary international law as international crimes, independently of the [UN Convention] against torture',[83] and held that 'the prohibition of torture is part of customary international law and it has become a peremptory norm (*jus cogens*)'.[84] The international community accepts the main elements of the definition of torture as contained in Article 1(1) of the UN Convention against Torture,[85] providing that

> the term 'torture' means any act by which severe pain or suffering, whether physical or mental, is intentionally inflicted on a person for such purposes as obtaining from him or a third person information or a confession, punishing him for an act he or a third person has committed or is suspected of having committed, or intimidating or coercing him or a third person, or for any reason based on discrimination of any kind, when such pain or suffering is inflicted by or at the instigation of or with the consent or acquiescence of a public official or other person acting in an

[76] UNGA Res 51/210, 17 December 1996, UN Doc A/RES/51/210, operative clause 9.

[77] See the initial 'Draft Comprehensive Convention on International Terrorism', Working document submitted by India, 28 August 2000, UN Doc A/C.6/55/1.

[78] M Hmoud, 'Negotiating the Draft Comprehensive Convention on International Terrorism Major Bones of Contention' (2006) 4 *Journal of International Criminal Justice* 1031, 1031–43.

[79] UNGA Res 71/151, 20 December 2016, UN Doc A/RES/71/151.

[80] See also Chapter 16, Section III(B), which deals with torture from a human rights law perspective.

[81] eg Cassese (n 21) 134. See, however, Ambos (n 33) 245, holding that 'it is doubtful whether the fact that torture constitutes a dignity violation suffices to make it a true international crime' and that 'isolated incidents of torture do not amount to true international crimes'.

[82] Inter-American Convention to Prevent and Punish Torture (adopted 9 December 1985, entered into force 28 February 1987) OAS Treaty Series No 67. See also the European Convention for the Prevention of Torture and Inhuman or Degrading Treatment or Punishment (adopted 26 November 1987, entered into force 1 February 1989) CETS No 126, which does not serve to outlaw the crime of torture, but relies on the prohibition of torture contained in Art 3 ECHR to establish 'a European Committee for the Prevention of Torture and Inhuman or Degrading Treatment or Punishment' (CPT), on which see Chapter 16, Section IX(C).

[83] *Questions relating to the Obligation to Prosecute or Extradite* (Belgium v Senegal) [2012] ICJ Rep 422, para 97.

[84] ibid, para 99.

[85] ICTY, Trial Chamber, *Prosecutor v Delalić et al*, 16 November 1998, Case No IT-96-21-T, paras 455–74; ICTY, Trial Chamber, *Prosecutor v Furundzija*, 10 December 1998, IT-95-17/1-T, para 257; *Kunarac* (n 44) paras 483–97; see Cassese (n 21) 132.

official capacity. It does not include pain or suffering arising only from, inherent in or incidental to lawful sanctions.

The different elements of the crime of torture deserve to be highlighted. First, it must concern 'severe' pain or suffering.[86] Second, the infliction of the suffering must be intentional. Third, the UN Convention against Torture introduces a purpose requirement. Even if torture can be committed not only for the purpose of obtaining information or a confession, punishment, intimidation or coercion, but also 'for any other purpose based on discrimination of any kind' – a fairly open-ended formula – an instrumental purpose remains required, distinguishing 'the phenomenon of torture from isolated sadism more properly the concern of domestic law'.[87] Lastly, the 'participation of a de jure or de facto state official' is required.[88] Note that while torture can constitute a crime of genocide, crime against humanity or war crime,[89] the distinct international crime of torture does not require the specific elements that attach to the respective core crimes of international law.[90]

IV. Individual Criminal Responsibility

A. Modes of Liability

International crimes, apart from war crimes perhaps, are, unlike regular crimes, not normally committed by just one person. They are collective crimes, in which often a large number of individuals at multiple levels of responsibility are involved. In ICL, 'the paradigmatic offender is often the person who orders, masterminds, or takes part in a plan at a high level'.[91] The collective nature of international criminality does not do away with the need to establish individualised guilt and responsibility. This explains why ICL has developed rather intricate 'modes of liability'. In the ICC Statute, for example, these modes of liability are laid down in Article 25.

The basic premise of responsibility in ICL is that an individual's criminal responsibility can only be engaged if he or she is personally culpable of a crime; collective punishment is not allowed.[92] Obviously, those who commit a crime as a principal perpetrator or co-perpetrator can be punished.[93] But a host of other forms of participation can also engage an individual's criminal responsibility, such as planning (at the ad hoc tribunals, not the ICC);[94] ordering,[95] instigating (at the ad hoc tribunals)[96] or soliciting/inducing

[86] See Chapter 16, Section IX(A)(i), n 257 on the ECtHR's jurisprudence on the required degree of intensity. See, however, Art 2 of the Inter-American Convention to Prevent and Punish Torture (n 82), which does not require that the suffering be 'severe'.
[87] Cassese (n 21) 133.
[88] ibid, 133. See also Art 3 of the Inter-American Convention to Prevent and Punish Torture (n 82).
[89] Ambos (n 33) 245.
[90] eg, the crime of torture may be committed in time of peace or in time of war; *Kunarac* (n 44) paras 488–97.
[91] Cryer et al (n 22) 361.
[92] Art 25(2) ICC Statute; Art 7 ICTY Statute; Art 6 ICTR Statute. See also ICTY, Appeals Chamber, *Prosecutor v Tadić*, 15 July 1999, Case No IT-94-1-A, para 186.
[93] Art 25(3)(a) ICC Statute; Art 7 ICTY Statute; Art 6 ICTR Statute.
[94] Art 7 ICTY Statute; Art 6 ICTR Statute.
[95] Art 25(3)(b) ICC Statute; Art 7 ICTY Statute; Art 6 ICTR Statute.
[96] Art 7 ICTY Statute; Art 6 ICTR Statute.

(at the ICC);[97] aiding and abetting;[98] and in any other way contributing to a crime by a group acting with a common purpose (at the ICC, not the ad hoc tribunals).[99] While, before the ad hoc tribunals, the relevant modes of liability required that the crime was eventually perpetrated, at the ICC it suffices that the crime was attempted.[100] This is linked with the fact that, as opposed to the statutes of the ad hoc tribunals, Article 25 of the ICC Statute also criminalises the attempt to commit a crime, provided that the perpetrator takes action that commences the execution of a crime by means of a substantial step, but the crime does not occur because of circumstances independent of his or her intentions.[101]

ICL does not criminalise conspiracy, ie an agreement to commit a crime regardless of whether that crime materialises, with the exception of conspiracy to commit genocide (at the ad hoc tribunals, not the ICC),[102] which is a distinct, inchoate offence rather than a mode of liability.[103] The same goes for direct and public incitement to commit genocide,[104] which is criminalised by the statutes of the ad hoc tribunals as well as the ICC.[105]

B. Joint Criminal Enterprise

The ICTY did not consider the modes of liability contained in its Statute to be sufficient to capture the responsibility of notably those who planned or designed international crimes at hierarchically higher levels. In 1999, in the *Tadić* case, the ICTY Appeals Chamber derived the concept of 'joint criminal enterprise' (JCE) from the object and purpose of the ICTY Statute and the Nuremberg case law, in order to be able to punish criminal leaders who did not physically commit any crimes.[106]

The *actus reus* of a JCE consists of: (i) 'a plurality of persons', who 'need not be organised in a military, political or administrative structure'; and who have (ii) 'a common plan, design or purpose which amounts to or involves the commission of a crime provided for in the [ICTY] Statute'.[107] It is not required that this plan, design or purpose has been 'previously arranged or formulated'.[108] Moreover, '[t]he common plan or purpose may materialize extemporaneously and be inferred from the fact that a plurality of persons acts in unison to put into effect a [JCE]'.[109] Third, (iii) the accused must have participated in the common plan or purpose. 'This participation need not involve the commission of a specific crime [...], but may take the form of assistance in, or contribution to, the execution of the common plan or

[97] Art 25(3)(b) ICC Statute.

[98] Art 25(3)(c) ICC Statute; Art 7 ICTY Statute; Art 6 ICTR Statute. 'Aiding' refers to practical assistance, whereas 'abetting' refers to moral assistance. A suspect must knowingly provide a substantial contribution to the commission of the crime before he or she can be held accountable as an aider or abettor.

[99] Art 25(3)(d) ICC Statute.

[100] Art 25(3)(b)–(d) ICC Statute.

[101] Art 25(3)(f) ICC Statute.

[102] Art 3(b) Genocide Convention; Art 4(3)(b) ICTY Statute; Art 2(3)(b) ICTR Statute. But see also *US et al v Göring et al* (n 5) 447, finding conspiracy to commit aggression to be criminal.

[103] See eg ICTY, Appeals Chamber, *Prosecutor v Tolimir*, 8 April 2015, Case No IT-05-88/2-A, para 582.

[104] See eg ICTR, Appeals Chamber, *Nahimana, Barayagwiza and Ngeze v Prosecutor*, 28 November 2007, Case No ICTR-99-52-A, para 678.

[105] Art 25(3)(e) ICC Statute; Art 4 ICTY Statute; Art 2 ICTR Statute.

[106] *Tadić* (n 92) paras 185–229.

[107] ibid, para 227.

[108] ibid.

[109] ibid.

purpose'.[110] The participation need not constitute a *conditio sine qua non* for the execution of the plan or purpose. But, as the ICTY Appeals Chamber held in *Brđanin*: 'although the contribution need not be necessary or substantial, it should at least be a *significant* contribution to the crimes for which the accused is to be found responsible' (emphasis added).[111]

JCE may come in three categories: a basic (JCE I), systematic (JCE II) and extended (JCE III) version. The basic category concerns a form of co-perpetration, where all co-defendants, acting pursuant to a common design, possess the same criminal intention, and one or more of them actually perpetrates the crime.[112] The systematic category, which is a variant of the basic version, punishes participation in the design of an organised system to ill-treat detainees and commit various crimes (the concentration camp scenario).[113] The extended category pertains to 'a common design to pursue one course of conduct where one of the perpetrators commits an act which, while outside the common design, was nevertheless a natural and foreseeable consequence of the effecting of that common purpose'.[114]

While the *actus reus* is the same for all JCE categories, the *mens rea* differs according to the category of JCE under consideration.[115] Still in *Tadić*, the ICTY Appeals Chamber held that:

> With regard to the first category, what is required is the intent to perpetrate a certain crime (this being the shared intent on the part of all co-perpetrators). With regard to the second category [...], personal knowledge of the system of ill-treatment is required [...], as well as the intent to further this common concerted system of ill-treatment. With regard to the third category, what is required is the intention to participate in and further the criminal activity or the criminal purpose of a group and to contribute to the joint criminal enterprise or in any event to the commission of a crime by the group. In addition, responsibility for a crime other than the one agreed upon in the common plan arises only if, under the circumstances of the case, (i) it was foreseeable that such a crime might be perpetrated by one or other members of the group and (ii) the accused willingly took that risk.[116]

Every person who participates in a JCE is considered to be a *principal* perpetrator. Thus, the JCE doctrine follows a subjective approach, which

> moves the focus from the level of contribution to the commission of the offence as the distinguishing criterion between principals and accessories, and places it instead on the state of mind in which the contribution to the crime was made. As a result, only those who make their contribution with the shared intent to commit the offence can be principals to the crime, regardless of the level of their contribution to its commission.[117]

Perhaps not surprisingly, 'the vague "elastic" nature of the doctrine has led to claims that it is overbroad, thus reliant on prosecutorial discretion rather than law to keep it in check'.[118]

[110] ibid; eg *Stevanović* (n 22) para 57: the accused needs to assist or contribute. Mere presence does not suffice in and of itself for the accused to be considered part of a JCE.
[111] ICTY, Appeals Chamber, *Prosecutor v Brđanin*, 3 April 2007, Case No IT-99-36-A, para 430.
[112] *Tadić* (n 92) para 196.
[113] ibid, para 202.
[114] ibid, para 204.
[115] ibid, para 228.
[116] ibid, para 228.
[117] ICC, Pre-Trial Chamber I, *Prosecutor v Lubanga*, Decision on the Confirmation of Charges, 29 January 2007, Case No ICC-01/04-01/06, para 329.
[118] Cryer et al (n 22) 373.

According to some, the doctrine, and especially its extended version (JCE III), constitutes 'a violation of the basic principle that individuals should only be criminally liable to the extent of their own culpability' (see above, Section IV(A)).[119] Again others argue that the doctrine, including JCE III, 'is firmly established in customary international law'.[120]

C. Co-Perpetration by Control over the Crime

When faced with situations similar to the ones outlined as regards JCE, the ICC relies on a different mode of liability. Article 25(3)(a) of the ICC Statute provides that a person is criminally responsible if he or she '[c]ommits [...] a crime, whether as an individual, jointly with another or through another person, regardless of whether that other person is criminally responsible'. Based on a reading of that provision in conjunction with Article 25(3)(d) of the ICC Statute,[121] the Statute is considered to exclude the (subjective) JCE doctrine developed by the ICTY.[122] Neither does the ICC accept an objective approach, according to which 'only those who physically carry out one or more of the objective elements of the offence can be considered principals to the crime'.[123] The ICC follows a third approach, namely 'co-perpetration by control over the crime', which was originally developed by the German scholar Claus Roxin.[124] According to ICC Trial Chamber I:

> The notion underpinning this third approach is that principals to a crime are not limited to those who physically carry out the objective elements of the offence, but also include those who, in spite of being removed from the scene of the crime, control or mastermind its commission because they decide whether and how the offence will be committed.[125]

As is the case for JCE, co-perpetration by control over the crime requires the objective element of an agreement or common plan.[126] This agreement or common plan must include an 'element of criminality', but must not be specifically directed at the commission of a crime.[127] It need not be previously arranged, but can arise contemporaneously,[128]

[119] JD Ohlin, 'Three Conceptual Problems with the Doctrine of Joint Criminal Enterprise' (2007) 5 *JICJ* 69, 71 and 76.
[120] Cassese (n 21) 170.
[121] Art 25(3)(d) ICC Statute holds criminally responsible the person who: 'In any other way contributes to the commission or attempted commission of such a crime by a group of persons acting with a common purpose. Such contribution shall be intentional and shall either: (i) Be made with the aim of furthering the criminal activity or criminal purpose of the group, where such activity or purpose involves the commission of a crime within the jurisdiction of the Court; or (ii) Be made in the knowledge of the intention of the group to commit the crime'; see also above, Section IV(A), n 99.
[122] *Lubanga*, Confirmation of Charges (n 117) paras 322–41; cp G Bitti, 'Article 21 and the Hierarchy of Sources of Law before the ICC' in C Stahn, *The Law and Practice of the International Criminal Court* (Oxford, OUP, 2015) 431.
[123] *Lubanga*, Confirmation of Charges (n 117) para 328.
[124] See notably C Roxin, 'Crimes as Part of Organized Power Structures' (2011) 9 *JICJ* 193.
[125] *Lubanga*, Confirmation of Charges (n 117) para 330.
[126] ibid, para 343. ICC, Pre-Trial Chamber II, *Prosecutor v Bemba*, Decision Pursuant to Article 61(7)(a) and (b) of the Rome Statute on the Charges of the Prosecutor Against Jean-Pierre Bemba Gombo, 15 June 2009, Case No ICC-01/05-01/08, para 350.
[127] *Lubanga*, Confirmation of Charges (n 117) para 344.
[128] ICC, Appeals Chamber, *Prosecutor v Lubanga*, Judgment on the Appeal of Mr Thomas Lubanga Dyilo against His Conviction, 1 December 2014, Case No ICC-01/04-01/06 A 5, para 445.

and must not be explicit, but 'can be inferred from the subsequent concerted action of the co-perpetrators'.[129] In addition, each co-perpetrator must make an '*essential* contribution [...] resulting in the realisation of the objective elements of the crime' (emphasis added).[130] In this respect, co-perpetration differs from JCE, which only requires a 'significant' contribution (see above, Section IV(B)). Indeed, while for a JCE, it is not required that the contribution of the accused constitutes a *conditio sine qua non*, for co-perpetration, 'only those to whom essential tasks have been assigned – and who, consequently, have the power to frustrate the commission of the crime by not performing their tasks – can be said to have joint control over the crime'.[131]

With respect to the *mens rea*, the co-perpetrator must first fulfil the subjective elements of the crime in question.[132] Second, co-perpetrators: (i) must be mutually aware that 'implementing the common plan will result in the fulfilment of the material elements of the crimes'; and (ii) nevertheless purposefully 'bring about the material elements of the crimes', *or* be 'aware that in the ordinary course of events, the fulfilment of the material elements will be a virtually certain consequence of their actions'.[133] Third, the co-perpetrator must be aware of 'the factual circumstances enabling him or her to jointly control the crime'.[134]

D. Command Responsibility

A last mode of liability that is characteristic for ICL and largely unknown to domestic law[135] concerns command or superior responsibility.[136] Again, because the commission of international crimes almost always involves the machinery of the State or at least an organised entity, the need was felt to hold military commanders as well as civilian superiors responsible even if they did not directly commit any crimes. What characterises command responsibility is that it concerns a form of *omission* liability attached to a failure to comply with particular *duties* that rest upon commanders or superiors.

Commanders and superiors are criminally responsible for crimes committed by forces under their command, respectively authority, if they fail to prevent or punish these crimes. Accordingly, a first requirement is that there is a 'relationship of subordination' between the

[129] ibid; *Lubanga*, Confirmation of Charges (n 117) para 345.
[130] *Lubanga*, Confirmation of Charges (n 117) para 346; *Bemba* (n 126) para 350.
[131] *Lubanga*, Confirmation of Charges (n 117) para 347; *Lubanga*, Appeal (n 128) para 469.
[132] *Lubanga*, Confirmation of Charges (n 117) para 349.
[133] *Bemba* (n 126) para 370; *Lubanga*, Appeal (n 128) paras 447–51.
[134] *Lubanga*, Confirmation of Charges (n 117) para 366; *Bemba* (n 126) para 371.
[135] However, it is included in Section 4 of the German Code of Crimes against International Law, (2002) 42 *Bundesgesetzblatt*, Part I, 2254 and Art 9(1) of the Dutch Act of 19 June 2003 containing rules concerning serious violations of international humanitarian law (International Crimes Act), (2003) *Staasblad* 270. For an application, see respectively Federal Court of Justice (DE), *IM*, Decision on Pretrial Detention, 17 June 2010, Case No AK 3/10; District Court of The Hague (NL), *Public Prosecutor v F*, 25 June 2007, NL:GHSGR:2009:BK8758.
[136] See Art 28 ICC Statute; Art 7(3) ICTY Statute; Art 6(3) ICTR Statute. It is contested wheter command responsibility constitutes a mode of liability or a crime per se; cp Cassese (n 21) 191–92. Arguably, it has a '*sui generis*, uniqe nature'; ibid, 191. It is a 'hybrid form of liability, combining aspects of a mode of liability and a separate offence liability'; E van Sliedregt, *Individual Criminal Responsibility in International Law* (Oxford, OUP, 2012) 196. See further C Meloni, 'Command Responsibility: Mode of Liability for the Crimes of Subordinates or Separate Offence of the Superior? (2007) 5 *JICJ* 619.

commander or superior and the subordinate(s) concerned – be it de jure or de facto – in the context of which the former exercises 'effective control' over the latter.[137]

Second, commanders or superiors can only be held criminally responsible if they had 'actual or contructive knowledge' – ie if they knew or should have known – that their forces were committing or were about to commit such crimes.[138] For the ICTY, constructive knowledge means 'reason to know', meaning that a commander or superior would be criminally responsible 'only if information was available to him which would have put him on notice of offences committed by subordinates'.[139] The ICC Statute requires that the military commander 'should have known, owing to the circumstances at the time'.[140] This is interpreted as a 'form of negligence',[141] requiring 'more of an active duty on the part of the superior to take the necessary measures to secure knowledge of the conduct of his troops and to inquire, regardless of the availability of information at the time on [*sic*] the commission of the crime'.[142] In the case of civilian superiors, on the other hand, the Statute requires that they 'either knew, or consciously disregarded information which clearly indicated, that the subordinates were committing or about to commit such crimes'.[143]

Third and lastly, to be liable for the crimes concerned, the commander or superior must have 'failed to take all necessary and reasonable measures within his or her power to prevent or repress their commission'.[144] The duties to prevent and repress or punish are distinct; a failure to prevent certain crimes cannot be cured by the subsequent punishment of these crimes.[145] What is expected from the commander or superior is 'inextricably linked to the facts of each particular situation'[146] and depends on 'the degree of effective control he wielded over his subordinates'.[147]

E. Defences: Justifications and Excuses

In a limited number of situations, individuals can escape criminal responsibility by invoking a defence, be it a justification or excuse. Criminal conduct may be 'justified' because it was preferable to even worse alternatives, or it can be 'excused' when 'it was produced by an impairment of a person's autonomy to such a degree as to negate [its] blameworthiness'.[148]

[137] ICTY, Appeals Chamber, *Prosecutor v Delalić et al*, 20 February 2001, Case No IT-96-21-A, paras 197–98; *Bemba* (n 126) paras 411–15. For factors that are indicative of effective control, see *Bemba* (n 126) para 417. See further Cassese (n 21) 187–89.
[138] Cassese (n 21) 189.
[139] *Delalić* (n 137) para 241.
[140] Art 28(2) ICC Statute.
[141] *Bemba* (n 126) para 429.
[142] ibid, para 433. See Cassese (n 21) 190.
[143] Art 28(b)(i) ICC Statute.
[144] ibid, Art 28(a)(ii) and (b)(iii), which add '[…] or to submit the matter to the competent authorities for investigation and prosecution'. Art 7 ICTY Statute and Art 6 ICTR Statute contain a nearly identical provision, but do not explicitly include the latter option, which would nevertheless normally also under the ICTY and ICTR Statute discharge the commander or superior of his or her duties.
[145] ICTY, Trial Chamber, *Prosecutor v Blaškić*, 3 March 2000, Case No IT-95-14-T, para 336.
[146] *Delalić* (n 137) para 394.
[147] ICTY, Appeals Chamber, *Prosecutor v Blaškić*, 29 July 2004, Case No IT-95-14-A, para 72.
[148] Cassese (n 21) 210.

Article 31(1) of the ICC Statute lists one justification: self-defence.[149] An action taken in self-defence which is normally criminal is not unlawful if: (i) it responds to an imminent or actual unlawful use of force against the person acting in self-defence or another person; (ii) there is no alternative way to stop or prevent that use of force; (iii) the person acting in self-defence has not caused the use of force; and (iv) the action taken in self-defence is proportionate to the use of force to which it reacts.[150] The ICC Statute controversially adds the possibility to act in self-defence in response to war crimes against 'property which is essential for the survival of the person or another person or property which is essential for accomplishing a military mission'.[151]

Article 31(1) also lists three excuses: a mental disease or defect,[152] a state of intoxication[153] and duress.[154] As to the last excuse, it must concern duress

> resulting from a threat of imminent death or of continuing or imminent serious bodily harm against that person or another person, and the person [must act] necessarily and reasonably to avoid this threat, provided that the person does not intend to cause a greater harm than the one sought to be avoided. Such a threat may either be:
>
> (i) Made by other persons; or
> (ii) Constituted by other circumstances beyond that person's control.

As illustrated by the *Erdemović* case at the ICTY, duress is not easily accepted. Erdemović was a member of the Bosnian Serb Army who, as a member of an execution squad, participated in the shooting of unarmed Bosnian Muslims. He argued that when he had refused to shoot the civilians, his commander had threatened to kill him as well. Nevertheless, the ICTY Appeals Chamber found 'that duress does not afford a complete defence to a soldier charged with a crime against humanity and/or a war crime involving the killing of innocent human beings'.[155]

Further, criminal responsibility is excused before the ICC in the exceptional case that a mistake of fact (eg executing a person assuming that he or she had been duly convicted)[156] or mistake of law negates the mental element required by the crime concerned.[157] 'Obedience to superior orders' can be considered to constitute a particular type of mistake of law which may excuse criminal responsibility in exceptional circumstances.[158] Article 33 of the ICC Statute provides that the fact that a crime has been committed pursuant to an order by a superior 'shall not relieve that person of criminal responsibility unless: (a) [t]he person was under a legal obligation to obey orders'; (b) 'did not know that the

[149] Art 31(1)(c).
[150] Cassese (n 21) 211.
[151] See ibid, 212–13, arguing that the extension to acts of self-defence against property is problematic and that it broadens the customary international law definition of self-defence.
[152] Art 31(1)(a) ICC Statute.
[153] ibid, Art 31(1)(b). This ground cannot be invoked where 'the person has become voluntarily intoxicated under such circumstances that the person knew, or disregarded the risk, that, as a result of the intoxication, he or she was likely to engage in conduct constituting a crime within the jurisdiction of the Court'.
[154] ibid, Art 31(1)(d).
[155] ICTY, Appeals Chamber, *Prosecutor v Erdemović*, 7 October 1997, Case No IT-96-22-A, para 19. Note that two of the five judges on the bench dissented. See Cassese (n 21) 218.
[156] Art 32(1) ICC Statute.
[157] ibid, Art 32(2).
[158] cp Cassese (n 21) 231.

order was unlawful; and (c) [t]he order was not manifestly unlawful'. However, 'orders to commit genocide or crimes against humanity are manifestly unlawful'.[159] Thus, the defence of superior orders can never relieve the subordinate of responsibility for such crimes, but can exceptionally do so for war crimes. This defence prevents insubordination and avoids soldiers having to decide on controversial legal questions. Nevertheless, it is excluded by the statutes of the ICTY and ICTR,[160] appears to be at odds with customary international law and has rarely been accepted in case law.[161]

V. International Criminal Tribunals

A. Establishment and Design

International criminal tribunals were only established after the end of the Second World War. Typically, they were established ad hoc, ie in relation to specific events that are circumscribed in time and place. However, the ICC has been established as a permanent international tribunal with a quasi-universal remit.

The first international criminal tribunals were the International Military Tribunal (IMT) at Nuremberg,[162] and the International Military Tribunal for the Far East (IMTFE) at Tokyo,[163] which were established in the immediate aftermath of World War II. The IMT brought to justice the major war criminals belonging to Nazi Germany,[164] 12 of whom were eventually executed. The IMTFE prosecuted the major Japanese war criminals,[165] seven of whom were executed. There is no doubt that these prosecutions represented victor's justice, as the tribunals did not have jurisdiction over crimes committed by the Allied Powers and were composed of representatives of the war's victorious nations. Nevertheless, they represented a watershed: the international community had finally signalled that atrocities would no longer go unpunished. The most famous holding of the IMT, which has become a 'foundational statement' in ICL,[166] was probably the following:

> Crimes against international law are committed by men, not abstract entities, and only by punishing individuals who commit such crimes can the provisions of international law be enforced. [...] [I]ndividuals have international duties which transcend the national obligations of obedience imposed by the individual state.[167]

In 1950, the legal legacy of the tribunals was laid down in the ILC's 'Principles of International Law Recognized in the Charter of the Nuremberg Tribunal and in the Judgment of the Tribunal'.[168]

[159] Art 33(2) ICC Statute.
[160] Art 7(4) ICTY Statute; Art 6(4) ICTR Statute.
[161] See Cassese (n 21) 231–37.
[162] See above (n 35).
[163] See the Charter of the International Military Tribunal for the Far East (19 January 1946) 82 UNTS 284 (IMTFE Charter).
[164] See Arts 1 and 6 Nuremberg Charter (n 35), referring to 'the major war criminals of the European Axis'. However, no war criminals belonging to the Italian Fascist regime appeared before the IMT.
[165] See Arts 1 and 5 IMTFE Charter (n 163), respectively referring to 'the major war criminals in the Far East' and 'Far Eastern war criminals'.
[166] Cryer et al (n 22) 113.
[167] *US et al v Göring et al* (n 5) 447.
[168] ILC, 'Principles of International Law Recognized in the Charter of the Nuremberg Tribunal and in the Judgment of the Tribunal' (1950) *YILC*, Vol II, 374–78.

While East-West tensions precluded the establishment of international criminal tribunals during the Cold War, the Nuremberg paradigm paved the way for the establishment, in the 1990s, of two ad hoc tribunals to prosecute the perpetrators of international crimes committed in Yugoslavia (ICTY) and Rwanda (ICTR), as well as the ICC. The ICTY and ICTR were established on the basis of resolutions of the UN Security Council,[169] a process the legality of which was confirmed by the ICTY in the *Tadić* case.[170] After more than 20 years since their establishment, the ICTR closed on 31 December 2015 and the ICTY on 31 December 2017. In 2010, 'in view of the substantially reduced nature of the residual functions' of both tribunals, the UN Security Council established the United Nations Mechanism for International Criminal Tribunals (MICT), 'a small, temporary and efficient structure', which continues 'the jurisdiction, rights and obligations and essential functions of the ICTY and the ICTR' and will finish their work.[171] As opposed to the ICTY and ICTR, the ICC came into being on the basis of a multilateral treaty, the Rome Statute of the International Criminal Court (ICC Statute),[172] which, in October 2018, counts 123 State Parties.[173]

The EU and its Member States were particularly instrumental in the establishment of the ICC Statute,[174] and all EU Member States have ratified it. Since its establishment, the EU and its Member States have been the staunchest supporters of the Court.[175] In 2011, the Council adopted a decision on the ICC.[176] This decision aims to: (i) advance universal support for the ICC by promoting the widest possible participation in its Statute; (ii) preserve the integrity of the Court; (iii) support its independence and its effective and efficient functioning; (iv) enhance cooperation with the Court; and (v) support the implementation of the principle of complementarity (on which see below, Section V(C)(i)).[177] The implementation of the decision is furthered by the Council's Action Plan of 2011.[178] In particular, the EU aims to encourage States which have not yet ratified the ICC Statute to do so, and to provide technical and/or financial assistance to those States that may

[169] See respectively UNSC Res 827 (n 14) and UNSC Res 955 (n 14).

[170] *Tadić*, Decision on the Defence Motion for Interlocutory Appeal on Jurisdiction (n 51) paras 28–48.

[171] UNSC Res 1966, 22 December 2010, UN Doc S/RES/1966, preambular para 7 and operative clauses 1 and 4.

[172] Rome Statute of the International Criminal Court (adopted 17 July 1998, entered into force on 1 July 2002) 2187 UNTS 90.

[173] Note that the last change in the number of State Parties to the ICC Statute was caused by the withdrawal of Burundi (notified 27 October 2016, effective as of 27 October 2017) in a context of troubled relations between the ICC and many African countries. While South Africa and Gambia had also formally notified the UN Secretary General that they would withdraw from the ICC Statute on respectively 19 October 2016 and 10 November 2016, they withdrew these notifications on 7 March 2017 and 10 February 2017 respectively. The Philippines has notified the UNSG that it will withdraw from the ICC Statute on 17 March 2018 – a notification which, when it becomes effective on 17 March 2019, will reduce the number of State Parties to the ICC Statute to 122. See UN Treaty Collection, 'Rome Statute of the International Criminal Court', status as at 1 October 2018, treaties.un.org/Pages/ShowMTDSGDetails.aspx?src=UNTSONLINE&tabid=2&mtdsg_no=XVIII-10&chapter=18&lang=en.

[174] See further J Wouters and S Basu, 'The Creation of a Global Criminal Justice System: The European Union and the International Criminal Court' in C Ryngaert (ed), *The Effectiveness of International Criminal Justice* (Antwerp, Intersentia, 2009) 117–42.

[175] O Bekou, 'Mainstreaming Support for the ICC in the EU's Policies', Study for the Directorate-General for External Policies of the Union of the European Parliament, March 2014, EXPO/B/DROI/2013/28, 8. Further, see eg M Groenleer, 'The United States, the European Union, and the International Criminal Court: Similar Values, Different Interests?' (2015) 13 *I•CON* 923.

[176] Council Decision 2011/168/CFSP of 21 March 2011 on the International Criminal Court and repealing Common Position 2003/444/CFSP [2011] OJ L76/56.

[177] ibid, Art 1(2).

[178] Council of the EU, 'Action Plan to follow-up on the Decision on the International Criminal Court', 12 July 2011, 12080/11, Annex.

be willing but are unable to do so.[179] Through their 2006 Agreement on Cooperation and Assistance, the EU and the ICC have mutually committed themselves to cooperate closely and consult each other on matters of mutual interest.[180] To further the implementation of the principle of complementarity, the European Commission and the High Representative have jointly adopted a 'Complementarity Toolkit', the aim of which is to provide practical guidance to EU officials, Union Delegations and Member States on how to support and reinforce justice systems in third countries so that they can fully exercise their jurisdiction over crimes that fall within the purview of the ICC Statute.[181]

The ICC, ICTY and ICTR are all truly international tribunals, which apply international (criminal) law and are composed of international judges and prosecutors. In the early 2000s, however, to create more local ownership of accountability efforts, as well as to cut costs, the international community pressed for the establishment of 'mixed', 'hybrid' or 'internationalised' tribunals. These would apply a mixture of international and domestic criminal law, be based in the country were the crimes were committed,[182] would be composed of international and domestic prosecutors and judges, and could entrench the rule of law locally. Thus, on the basis of cooperation between the UN and the State concerned, the STL,[183] the SCSL,[184] the ECCC[185] and the Special Panels for East Timor[186] were established.

Sometimes, regional organisations play a primary role in the establishment of hybrid tribunals. Thus, on the basis of an agreement concluded between the African Union and Senegal,[187] Extraordinary African Chambers were established to try the former Chadian dictator Hissène Habré, after the ICJ ruled that Senegal had violated the UN Convention

[179] ibid, 7–8.

[180] Agreement between the International Criminal Court and the European Union on Cooperation and Assistance (adopted 10 April 2006, entered into force 1 May 2006) [2006] OJ L115/50, Art 4. See further G Hafner, 'Selected Legal and Policy Implications Arising from the EU–ICC Agreement of 2006' in FANJ Goudappel and EMH Hirsch Ballin (eds), *Democracy and Rule of Law in the European Union* (The Hague, TMC Asser, 2016) 203–24.

[181] EC and High Representative of the Union for Foreign Affairs and Security Policy, 'Joint Staff Working Document on Advancing the Principle of Complementarity: Toolkit for Briding the Gap between International and National Justice', 31 January 2013, SWD(2013) 26 final, 2. Further, see eg A Antoniadis and O Bekou, 'The European Union and the International Criminal Court: An Awkward Symbiosis in Interesting Times' (2007) 7 *International Criminal Law Review* 621.

[182] The ICTY was and the ICC is based in The Hague (the Netherlands); the ICTR in Arusha (Tanzania).

[183] See the Agreement between the United Nations and the Lebanese Republic on the Establishment of a Special Tribunal for Lebanon (adopted 22 January 2007 (Beirut) – 6 February 2007 (New York), entered into force 10 June 2007) 2461 UNTS 257. As eventually the Lebanese parliament did not convene to vote on the ratification of the Agreement, it was UNSC Res 1757, 30 May 2007, UN Doc S/RES/1757, which formally made the Agreement enter into force and established the STL, rather than the Agreement itself.

[184] See the Agreement between the United Nations and the Government of Sierra Leone on the Establishment of a Special Court for Sierra Leone (adopted 16 January 2002, entered into force 12 April 2002) 2178 UNTS 137.

[185] See the Law on the Establishment of Extraordinary Chambers in the Courts of Cambodia for the Prosecution of Crimes Committed during the Period of Democratic Kampuchea, 10 August 2001, Preah Reach Kram No NS/RKM/0801/12, as amended on 27 October 2004, Preah Reach Kram No NS/RKM/1004/006. The law was endorsed by the Agreement between the United Nations and the Royal Government of Cambodia concerning the Prosecution under Cambodian Law of Crimes Committed during the Period of Democratic Kampuchea (adopted 6 June 2003, entered into force 29 April 2005) 2329 UNTS 117.

[186] In full the District Court of Dili Special Panels of Serious Crimes (SPSC). The SPSC were established by the UN Transitional Administration in East Timor (UNTAET) by Regulation No 2000/15 on the Establishment of Panels with Exclusive Jurisdiction over Serious Criminal Offences, 6 June 2000, UNTAET/REG/2000/15; the UNTAET was in turn mandated by UNSC Res 1272, 25 October 1999, UN Doc S/RES/1272.

[187] Agreement between the Government of the Republic of Senegal and the African Union on the Establishment of Extraordinary African Chambers within the Senegalese Judicial System (adopted 22 August 2012, entered into force 30 January 2013) 52 ILM 1024.

against Torture by failing to prosecute Habré, who had found refuge in Senegal.[188] Pursuant to an agreement between the EU and the Kosovo authorities,[189] the Kosovo Specialist Chambers and Specialist Prosecutor's Office have been established.[190] The Chambers and Prosecutor have jurisdiction over crimes against humanity, war crimes, and a number of other crimes under Kosovo law committed in Kosovo from 1 January 1998 to 31 December 2000, ie during the Kosovo war.[191]

All these tribunals receive substantial financial backing from the EU and its Member States, either via contributions to the UN budget in the case of the ad hoc tribunals, via assessed contributions to the ICC, or through voluntary contributions to the hybrid tribunals.[192] In spite of European generosity, the funding of international tribunals remains a continuing challenge.

B. Jurisdiction

The statutes of the tribunals normally begin by delimiting the tribunals' jurisdiction, which is closely related to their mandate. For instance, the ICTY has 'the power to prosecute persons responsible for serious violations of international humanitarian law committed in the territory of the former Yugoslavia since 1991'.[193] The ICTR, in turn, has the power to prosecute IHL violations committed in the territory of Rwanda and by Rwandan citizens in the territory of neighbouring States between 1 January 1994 and 31 December 1994.[194]

The ICC's jurisdiction has been defined somewhat more carefully. In principle, temporally, the ICC only has prospective jurisdiction, ie jurisdiction over crimes committed after the entry into force of the Statute for the State Party in question;[195] the earliest from 1 July 2002 onwards.[196] As to the geographical and personal scope of its jurisdiction, it should be recalled that the ICC was established by a treaty. Thus, it may only exercise jurisdiction over crimes committed on the territory of a State Party and/or by a national of a State Party, unless the UN Security Council has referred a situation to the Court.[197] States may also accept the jurisdiction of the Court on an ad hoc basis for a period that they were not yet a

[188] See *Questions relating to the Obligation to Prosecute or Extradite* (n 83); see also Chapter 9, Section IV(B)(v)(b), on the exercise of universal jurisdiction and Chapter 16, Section III(B), on the UN Convention against Torture.

[189] See Assembly of Republic of Kosovo, Law No 04/L-274 on Ratification of the International Agreement between the Republic of Kosovo and the European Union on the European Union Rule of Law Mission in Kosovo, 23 April 2014, kuvendikosoves.org/common/docs/ligjet/04-L-274%20a.pdf.

[190] See Assembly of Republic of Kosovo, Law No 05/L-053 on Specialist Chambers and Specialist Prosecutor's Office, 3 August 2015, kuvendikosoves.org/common/docs/ligjet/05-L-053%20a.pdf.

[191] ibid, Arts 6–8 and 13–15.

[192] The EU Member States fund approximately 38% of the UN's regular budget; Permanent Delegation of the European Union to the UN Office and other International Organizations in Geneva, 'The EU and the UN', eeas.europa.eu/delegations/un_geneva/eu_un_geneva/index_en.htm. The EU also provides for over 60% of the ICC's funding, see African Business Magazine, 'Who Pays for the ICC?', 1 October 2011, africanbusinessmagazine.com/special-reports/who-pays-for-the-icc. By way of example, the EU has since 2007 contributed more than US$15 million to the ECCC, complemented by bilateral contributions from EU Member States totalling more than €36 million; Delegation of the European Union to Cambodia, 'Cambodia and the EU', 11 May 2016, eeas.europa.eu/delegations/cambodia_en/1006/Cambodia%20and%20the%20EU.

[193] Art 1 ICTY Statute.

[194] Art 1 ICTR Statute.

[195] Art 11(2) ICC Statute.

[196] ie the date the ICC Statute (internationally) entered into force (see above (n 172)); ibid, Art 11(1).

[197] ibid, Art 12(2).

party to the Statute, or without becoming a party to the Statute at all.[198] In the case of an ad hoc declaration, the State concerned may thus grant the ICC retroactive jurisdiction (ie over crimes committed before it became a Party to the Statute),[199] be it that it may not go back further than 1 July 2002.[200] The international crimes that fall within the material jurisdiction of the ICC (and that of the ICTY and ICTR) have been discussed above (Section III).

There are three ways of bringing a 'situation' before the ICC: its jurisdiction can be triggered through (i) a State Party referral, (ii) a *proprio motu* investigation by the Prosecutor, or (iii) a referral by the UN Security Council.[201] In October 2018, eleven situations were officially under investigation by the Office of the Prosecutor (OTP),[202] for which purposes all three trigger mechanisms had been used.[203] It concerns situations 'in which one or more crimes within the jurisdiction of the Court appear to have been committed'.[204] The notion 'situation' is not defined in the ICC Statute, but refers to 'a description of facts, defined by space and time, which circumscribe the prevailing circumstances at the time' (ie the conflict scenario), establishing the broader context in which the crimes have been committed[205] and from which one or more cases may spring.[206] Prosecutions thus proceed in stages that 'begin with a "situation" and end with a concrete "case", where one or more suspects have been identified for the purpose of prosecution'.[207] In the framework of the situations currently under investigation before the ICC, 26 cases have been brought before the Court.[208]

C. Bars to the Exercise of Jurisdiction

i. Admissibility

Even where the jurisdiction of the ICC over a situation has been triggered, a specific case will only be held admissible when there have not been or are no relevant national investigations or prosecutions, and where the State which has jurisdiction over it 'is unwilling or unable genuinely to carry out the investigation or prosecution'.[209] This rule is known as the 'complementarity principle', which aims to respect national sovereignty and ensures that international criminal justice only becomes operational as a stopgap measure in case of

[198] ibid, Art 12(3).
[199] WA Schabas and G Pecorella, 'Article 12: Preconditions to the Exercise of Jurisdiction' in Triffterer and Ambos (n 54) 686–87.
[200] Art 11(1) ICC Statute.
[201] ibid, Art 13.
[202] Burundi, Central African Republic (I and II), Côte d'Ivoire, Darfur (Sudan), Democratic Republic of the Congo, Georgia, Kenya, Libya, Mali and Uganda. See ICC, 'Situations under Invstigation', icc-cpi.int/Pages/Situations.aspx.
[203] Four State Parties to the ICC Statute – Uganda, the Democratic Republic of the Congo, the Central African Republic (twice) and Mali – have referred situations occurring on their territory to the Court. The situations in Darfur (Sudan) and Libya, both concerning non-States Parties, have been referred to the Prosecutor by the UNSC. The Prosecutor has been granted authorisation to open an investigation *proprio motu* into the situation in Kenya, Côte d'Ivoire and South Ossetia (Georgia); ICC, 'Situations under Investigation', icc-cpi.int/pages/situation.aspx.
[204] See Arts 13–14 ICC Statute.
[205] A Marchesi and E Chaitidou, 'Article 14: Referral of a Situation by a State Party' in Triffterer and Ambos (n 54) 716–17.
[206] WA Schabas, 'Selecting Situations and Cases' in Stahn (n 122) 367.
[207] ibid, citing ICC, Pre-Trial Chamber II, Decision Pursuant to Article 15 of the Rome Statute on the Authorization of an Investigation into the Situation in the Republic of Kenya, Situation in the Republic of Kenya, Case No ICC-01/09-19-Corr, 31 March 2010, para 41.
[208] ICC, 'Cases', icc-cpi.int/Pages/cases.aspx.
[209] Art 17(1)(a)–(b) ICC Statute.

investigative and/or prosecutorial failures by States. This represents a departure from the model of the ad hoc tribunals, which was based on the primacy of the tribunals vis-à-vis national courts.[210] Still, also in the waning days of those tribunals, complementarity has played its role: in order to complete their work on time, a number of cases pending before the ICTY and ICTR were referred back to the national level for prosecution and trial.[211]

The first isssue of admissibility is an 'empirical' one, and involves a determination of whether relevant investigations or prosecutions have been or are being conducted.[212] If there are no national proceedings, this domestic inactivity renders the case admissible and no question of unwillingness or inability arises.[213] This assessment must be based on the facts as they exist at the time of the examination and not on hypothetical proceedings.[214] While, 'the taking of steps directed at ascertaining whether [the suspect is] responsible for that conduct' is sufficient, 'the mere preparedness to take such steps or the investigation of other suspects is not sufficient'.[215] Thus, the proceedings must concern the same person and substantially the same conduct, meaning that 'the case that the State is investigating sufficiently mirrors the one that the Prosecutor is investigating'.[216]

Only if there are relevant proceedings, it must be assessed whether 'the State is unwilling or unable genuinely to carry out the investigation or prosecution'.[217] Article 17(2) of the ICC Statute establishes how to determine *unwillingness* according to three criteria:

(a) The proceedings were or are being undertaken or the national decision was made for the purpose of shielding the person concerned from criminal responsibility [...];
(b) There has been an unjustified delay in the proceedings which in the circumstances is inconsistent with an intent to bring the person concerned to justice; [or]
(c) The proceedings were not or are not being conducted independently or impartially, and they were or are being conducted in a manner which, in the circumstances, is inconsistent with an intent to bring the person concerned to justice.

According to the ICC Appeals Chamber, the primary purpose of the unwillingness test is to avoid sham trials that allow the accused to evade justice.[218] Considering that 'the Court

[210] Art 9(2) ICTY Statute; Art 8(2) ICTR Statute.

[211] The legal basis for these referrals is Rule 11*bis* of respectively ICTY, 'Rules of Procedure and Evidence', 11 February 1994, last amended 8 July 2015, IT/32/Rev.50; and ICTR, 'Rules of Procedure and Evidence', 29 June 1995, last amended 13 May 2015, unictr.unmict.org/sites/unictr.org/files/legal-library/150513-rpe-en-fr.pdf. For the first referral, see ICTR, *Prosecutor v Uwinkindi*, Decision on Prosecutor's Request for Referral to the Republic of Rwanda, 28 June 2011, Case No ICTR-2001-75-R11bis.

[212] ICC, Appeals Chamber, *Prosecutor v Katanga and Ngudjolo Chui*, Judgment on the Appeal of Mr Germain Katanga against the Oral Decision of Trial Chamber II of 12 June 2009 on the Admissibility of the Case, 25 September 2009, Case No ICC-01/04-01/07 OA 8, para 78; ICC, OTP, 'Policy Paper on Preliminary Examinations', November 2013, legal-tools.org/doc/acb906/pdf, para 47. Note that Art 17(c) of the ICC Statute provides that if the person has already been tried for the conduct which is the subject of the complaint, a trial by the ICC is normally not permitted due to the *ne bis in idem* principle and will make the case inadmissible, except for the limited exceptions set out in Art 20 ICC Statute.

[213] *Katanga and Ngudjolo Chui* (n 212) para 78; OTP (n 212) para 47.

[214] OTP (n 212) para 47.

[215] ICC, Appeals Chamber, *Prosecutor v Muthaura, Kenyatta and Ali*, Judgment on the Appeal of the Republic of Kenya against the Decision of Pre-Trial Chamber II of 30 May 2011 entitled 'Decision on the Application by the Government of Kenya Challenging the Admissibility of the Case Pursuant to Article 19(2)(b) of the Statute', 30 August 2011, Case No ICC-01/09-02/11-274, paras 1 and 40.

[216] ICC, Appeals Chamber, *Prosecutor v Saif Gaddafu and Al-Senussi*, Judgment on the Appeal of Libya against the Decision of Pre-Trial Chamber I of 31 May 2013 Entitled 'Decision on the Admissibility of the Case against Saif Al-Islam Gaddafi', 21 May 2014, Case No ICC-01/11-01/11 OA 4, para 73.

[217] Art 17(a) ICC Statute.

[218] ICC, Appeals Chamber, *Prosecutor v Gaddafi and Al-Senussi*, Judgment on the Appeal of Mr Abdullah Al-Senussi against the Decision of Pre-Trial Chamber I of 11 October 2013 Entitled 'Decision on the Admissibility

was not established to be an international court of human rights, sitting in judgment over domestic legal systems to ensure that they are compliant with international standards of human rights',[219] this test 'is not one that involves an assessment of whether the due process rights of a suspect have been breached per se'.[220] Still, there may be situations where 'violations of the rights of the suspect are so egregious that the proceedings can no longer be regarded as being capable of providing any genuine form of justice'.[221]

Article 17(3) provides that, to determine *inability*,

> the Court shall consider whether, due to a total or substantial collapse or unavailability of its national judicial system, the State is unable to obtain the accused or the necessary evidence and testimony or otherwise unable to carry out its proceedings.

Thus, in the *Gaddafi* case, Pre-Trial Chamber I found that Libya faced 'substantial difficulties in exercising its judicial powers fully across the entire territory' and that 'its national system [could not] yet be applied in full in areas or aspects relevant to the case', thus being 'unavailable'.[222] The Chamber set forth how Libya was unable to find Mr Gaddafi and obtain the necessary testimony, as well as how it was otherwise unable to carry out the proceedings against him, referring to the failing attempts to secure legal representation for Mr Gaddafi.[223]

Lastly, to be admissible before the ICC, a case must be of sufficient 'gravity'.[224] Accordingly, 'the fact that a case addresses one of the most serious crimes for the international community as a whole is not sufficient for it to be admissible before the Court'.[225] The gravity of a case should not only be assessed from a quantitative, but also from a qualitative perspective.[226] Relevant factors include 'the scale, nature and manner of commission of the alleged crimes, their impact on victims, and the existence of any aggravating circumstances'.[227]

ii. Immunities

The international criminal tribunals that have so far been established only have jurisdiction over natural persons,[228] and not over entities such as armed groups, corporations[229]

of the Case against Abdullah Al-Senussi', 24 July 2014, Case No ICC-01/11-01/11 OA 6, paras 2, 218, 222 and 224.

[219] ibid, para 219.

[220] ibid, para 2. See also paras 219–28.

[221] ibid, para 3. See also para 230.

[222] ICC, Pre-Trial Chamber I, *Prosecutor v Gaddafi and Al-Senussi*, Decision on the Admissibility of the Case against Saif Al-Islam Gaddafi, 31 May 2013, Case No ICC-01/11-01/11, para 205.

[223] ibid, paras 206–14.

[224] Art 17(1)(d) ICC Statute.

[225] ICC, Pre-Trial Chamber I, Situation in the Democratic Republic of Congo, Decision on the Prosecutor's Application for Warrants of Arrests, Article 58, 10 February 2016, Case No ICC-01/04-01/07, para 42.

[226] ICC, Pre-Trial Chamber I, *Prosecutor v Abu Garda*, Decision on the Confirmation of Charges, 8 February 2010, Case No ICC-02/05-02/09, para 31.

[227] ICC, Pre-Trial Chamber II, *Muthaura, Kenyatta and Ali*, Decision on the Confinnation of Charges Pursuant to Article 61(7)(a) and (b) of the Rome Statute, 23 January 2012, Case No ICC-01/09-02/11, para 50.

[228] Art 25 ICC Statute.

[229] Note, however, that according to Art 46C, entitled 'Corporate Criminal Liability', of the Protocol on Amendments to the Protocol on the Statute of the African Court of Justice and Human Rights (adopted

or States.[230] However, the absence of international jurisdiction over such entities need not mean that no criminal responsibility can be engaged. The natural persons who are responsible for the crimes committed by armed groups or corporations over whom the tribunals have jurisdiction can be prosecuted. Also, State officials are not allowed to hide behind their official capacity: unlike domestic courts, the tribunals do not recognise immunities.

Thus, Article 27 of the ICC Statute provides that (1) the 'Statute shall apply equally to all persons without any distinction based on official capacity' (referring to immunities *ratione materiae*); and that (2) '[i]mmunities or special procedural rules which may attach to the official capacity of a person [...] shall not bar the Court from exercising its jurisdiction over such a person' (referring to immunities *ratione personae*).[231] However, the irrelevance of official capacity only pertains to the ICC's adjudicatory jurisdiction (ie where an individual is before the ICC), not its executive jurisdiction (eg where the ICC issues an arrest warrant in view of bringing the individual before the Court). As regards its executive jurisdiction, reference needs to be made to Article 98(1) of the ICC Statute, which provides that the ICC

> may not proceed with a request for surrender or assistance which would require the requested State to act inconsistently with its obligations under international law with respect to the State or diplomatic immunity of a person or property of a third State, unless the Court can first obtain the cooperation of that third State for the waiver of the immunity.[232]

This provision concerns a 'triangular relation': on the one hand, it concerns the vertical relation between the ICC and the requested State Party; on the other, it relates to the horizontal relation between the requested State Party and a 'third State'.[233] Irrespective of whether the notion 'third State' refers to 'a State other than the requested State' (including State Parties to the ICC Statute) or only to 'a non-State Party',[234] in as much as it concerns a State that is party to the ICC Statute, that State is considered to have waived the immunity of its officials by accepting Article 27 of the Statute and is under an obligation to cooperate with the Court.[235] Accordingly, and irrespective of whether the request concerning one of its officials is addressed to that State itself or – as in the scenario of Article 98 – a different State, that State must comply with any request for surrender or assistance.[236]

If the request concerns an official of a third State that is not a party to the ICC Statute, that State has not accepted Article 27 of the ICC Statute, neither is it under an obligation

27 June 2014, not yet entered into force), the future African Court of Justice and Human and Peoples' Rights 'shall have jurisdiction over legal persons, with the exception of States'. On this Court, see Chapter 16, Section XI(B)(ii).

230 In an earlier draft of its ASR, the ILC had included the notion 'State crime' in Art 19; see ILC, Report of the Commission to the General Assembly on the work of its forty-eighth session (6 May–26 July 1996), UN Doc A/51/10, (1996) *YILC*, Vol II, Part Two, 60.

231 See also Art 7(2) ICTY Statute; Art 6(2) ICTR Statute. On immunities more generally, see Chapter 11. On this interpretation of Art 27 ICC Statute, see eg O Triffterer and C Burchard, 'Article 27: Irrelevance of Official Capacity' in Triffterer and Ambos (n 54) 1040.

232 See also the similar provision contained in Art 98(2) ICC Statute, pertaining to relevant international agreements between the requested State Party and the 'sending State'.

233 Triffterer and Burchard (n 231) 1040.

234 Which is the subject of discussion; cp C Kreß and K Prost, 'Article 98: Cooperation with respect to Waiver of Immunity and Consent' in Triffterer and Ambos (n 54) 2123.

235 ibid, 2125. For the general obligation of State Parties to cooperate with the Court, see Art 86 ICC Statute.

236 P Gaeta, 'Does President Al Bashir Enjoy Immunity from Arrest?' (2009) 7 *JICJ* 315, 328; Kreß and Prost (n 234) 2125.

to cooperate with the Court.[237] Article 98(1) should then ensure that State Parties do not have to act in contravention of their obligation to respect the immunity of a foreign State official. According to some, State Parties would nevertheless be obliged to comply with any request for surrender or assistance concerning such an official, because also under customary international law, there is an exception to the immunity of State officials before international courts (ie on the vertical level), which 'encompasses State measures of arrest and surrender of a person sought by the Court'.[238] This was the position taken by ICC Pre-Trial Chamber I in 2011, finding that Malawi and Chad (State Parties to the ICC Statue) had failed to comply with the Court's requests to arrest and surrender the Sudanese President Omar Al Bashir (Sudan not being a State Party to the ICC Statute).[239] However, at least for immunities *ratione personae*, this position can be questioned. While for international crimes, there is an exception to the immunity *ratione materiae* of State officials before foreign domestic courts (ie on the horizontal level), such is not the case for immunities *ratione personae* (see Chapter 11, Section III). Principally, Al Bashir still enjoys personal immunity vis-à-vis other States, including State Parties to the ICC Statute. Unless the Court would first have obtained Sudan's cooperation for the waiver of Al Bashir's immunity (which was not the case), these States are thus 'not obliged to execute the ICC request for surrender of President Al Bashir, and can lawfully decide not to comply with it'.[240]

The matter becomes even more complicated if it concerns a situation that was referred to the ICC by the UN Security Council, as was the case for the situation in Darfur (Sudan).[241] In 2014, Pre-Trial Chamber II found that the Democratic Republic of the Congo (DRC) – a State Party to the ICC Statute – failed to comply with the requests to arrest and surrender Al Bashir, but changed the reasoning adopted by Pre-Trial Chamber I. It found that, as the UNSC had decided that Sudan 'shall cooperate fully' with the ICC,[242] this implied that the UNSC had implicitly waived the immunity of Al Bashir and thus lifted any impediment at the horizontal level between the DRC and Sudan as to the extradition of Al Bashir.[243] Consequently, the DRC should have complied with the requests to arrest and surrender him. This reasoning has been criticised, primarily because it can hardly be argued that the UNSC has the power to affect the rights and powers of an international organisation – the ICC – by modifying its constituent treaty, ie by dispensing with the requirement of Article 98(1) to obtain the cooperation of Sudan for the waiver of the immunity of Al Bashir.[244]

[237] Except where that third State accepts the exercise of jurisdiction by the Court on an ad hoc basis (see Art 12(3) ICC Statute, and the discussion thereof above, Section V(B)); Triffterer and Burchard (n 231) 1042.

[238] Kreß and Prost (n 234) 2127 (as regards immunity *ratione materiae*).

[239] ICC, Pre-Trial Chamber I, *Prosecutor v Al Bashir*, Decision Pursuant to Article 87(7) of the Rome Statute on the Failure by the Republic of Malawi [Chad] to Comply with the Cooperation Requests Issued by the Court with Respect to the Arrest and Surrender of Omar Hassan Ahmad Al Bashir, 12 [13] December 2011, Case No ICC-02/05-01/09, paras 22–47 [para 13, citing the *Malawi* decision].

[240] Gaeta (n 236) 329; cp ICC, Pre-Trial Chamber II, *Prosecutor v Al Bashir*, Decision under Article 87(7) of the Rome Statute on the Non-compliance by South Africa with the Request by the Court for the Arrest and Surrender of Omar Al-Bashir, Case No ICC-02/05-01/09, 6 July 2017, para 68: 'The Chamber is unable to identify a rule in customary international law that would exclude immunity for Heads of State when their arrest is sought for international crimes by another State, even when the arrest is sought on behalf of an international court, including, specifically, this Court.'

[241] See UNSC Res 1593, 31 March 2005, UN Doc S/RES/1593.

[242] ibid, operative clause 2.

[243] ICC, Pre-Trial Chamber II, *Prosecutor v Al Bashir*, Decision on the Cooperation of the Democratic Republic of the Congo Regarding Omar Al Bashir's Arrest and Surrender to the Court, 9 April 2014, Case No ICC-02/05-01/09, para 29.

[244] P Gaeta, 'Guest Post: The ICC Changes Its Mind on the Immunity from Arrest of President Al Bashir, But It Is Wrong Again', *Opinio Juris*, 23 April 2014, opiniojuris.org/2014/04/23/guest-post-icc-changes-mind-immunity-arrest-president-al-bashir-wrong.

In the latest episode of the 'Al Bashir saga', Pre-Trial Chamber II found that South Africa failed to comply with its obligations under the Statute to arrest Al Bashir and surrender him to the Court, again adopting a different reasoning.[245] It now argued that

> the necessary effect of the Security Council resolution triggering the Court's jurisdiction […] and imposing on Sudan the obligation to cooperate fully with the Court, is that, for the limited purpose of the situation in Darfur, Sudan has rights and duties analogous to those of States Parties to the Statute.[246]

Accordingly, Sudan would, like State Parties to the ICC Statute, be bound by Article 27 and the obligation to cooperate with the Court, following which South Africa was under an obligation to arrest Al Bashir when it had the chance to do so. As the Chamber acknowledged, 'this is an expansion of the applicability of an international treaty to a State which has not voluntarily accepted it as such'.[247] Nevertheless, the Chamber considered that the UN Charter permits the UNSC to impose such obligations on States.[248] Again, others have contested this, arguing that the UNSC has the power to refer situations to the ICC based on the ICC Statute as a treaty, rather than that it has the power to create a distinct source of jurisdiction for the ICC based upon which the Court can treat States that have not consented to the ICC Statute as 'quasi-State parties'.[249]

iii. Minors

Lastly, it is to be noted that persons under 18 years old at the time of the alleged commission of a crime are excluded from the personal jurisdiction of the ICC.[250] Crimes committed against minors are obviously subject to the jurisdiction of the Court, notably including the crime of '[c]onscripting or enlisting children under the age of fifteen years into [armed forces] or using them to participate actively in hostilities'.[251]

D. Procedure

It would lead us too far to discuss the procedures before the various international criminal tribunals. It suffices here to give a general overview of the functioning of the ICC, as laid down in the ICC Statute and its Rules of Procedure and Evidence.[252]

i. Preliminary Investigation

After a situation has been referred to the Court by a State Party or the UN Security Council, or before the Prosecutor decides to request the authorisation to open an official

[245] cp *Al Bashir* (2017) (n 240) para 134: 'It is also acknowledged that previous decisions by the Court, while invariably concluding that States Parties to the Statute have a duty to arrest Omar Al-Bashir and surrender him to the Court, have not employed exactly the same legal argumentation on the matter.'

[246] *Al Bashir* (2017) (n 240) para 88. This approach was proposed by D Akande, 'The Legal Nature of Security Council Referrals to the ICC and its Impact on Al Bashir's Immunities' (2009) 7 *JICJ* 333.

[247] *Al-Bashir* (2017) (n 240) para 89.

[248] ibid.

[249] Gaeta (n 244).

[250] Art 26 ICC Statute.

[251] Art 8(2)(b)(xxvi) and 8(2)(e)(vii) ICC Statute.

[252] ICC, 'Rules of Procedure and Evidence', 9 September 2002, ICC-ASP/1/3, Part II-A, as amended by ICC-ASP/10/Res.1 of 20 December 2011, ICC-ASP/11/Res.2 of 21 November 2012 and ICC-ASP/12/Res.7 of 12 November 2013.

investigation into a certain situation following a *proprio motu* initiative, the OTP first conducts a preliminary investigation into that situation. In October 2018, a preliminary investigation was ongoing for nine situations, while it had been closed with a decision not to proceed for five situations.[253] During such an investigation, the Prosecutor must determine whether there is a 'reasonable basis to proceed' with the initiation of an 'official' investigation.[254] More specifically: (i) the information available to the Prosecutor must provide 'a reasonable basis to believe' that a crime within the temporal, material and geopgraphical or personal jurisdiction of the Court 'has been or is being committed' (on jurisdiction, see above, Section V(B)); (ii) the case should be admissible (on admissibility, see above, Section V(C)(i)); and (iii) 'taking into account the gravity of the crime and the interests of the victims', there must be no 'substantial reasons to believe that an investigation would not serve the interests of justice'.[255]

As alluded to above (Section V(B)), at the preliminary stage of the proceedings, this assessment is to be made at the 'situation' rather than 'case' level, as concrete cases only spring from the official investigation of a situation. The jurisdictional scope of the Court serves to determine the situation within which the OTP conducts its investigative activities by means of objective parameters.[256] The consideration of admissibility, which includes complementarity and gravity, takes into account 'potential cases' that would probably arise from an official investigation into the situation.[257] For example, when the OTP received information on alleged war crimes committed by officials of the UK in the context of the armed conflict in Iraq and its subsequent occupation (2003–2008), the Prosecutor found that '[t]he number of potential victims of crimes within the jurisdiction of the Court in this situation – 4 to 12 victims of wilful killing and a limited number of victims of inhuman treatment – was of a different order than the number of victims found in other situations under investigation or analysis by the Office', concluding that the OTP would not seek authorisation to initiate an official investigation.[258] However, when the OTP declined to initiate an official investigation into the 'Flotilla incident',[259] which concerned the attack by Israeli forces of an activist humanitarian aid convoy that intended to break the naval blockade of Gaza in 2010 and was referred to the ICC by the Union of the Comoros, Pre-Trial Chamber I considered that 'ten killings, 50–55 injuries, and possibly hundreds of instances of outrages upon personal dignity, or torture or inhuman treatment, [...] are a compelling indicator of sufficient, and not of insufficient gravity'.[260]

[253] Afghanistan, Colombia, Gabon (closed), Guinea, Honduras (closed), Iraq/UK, Nigeria, Palestine, the Philippines, Registered Vessels of Comoros, Greece and Cambodia (closed), Republic of Korea (closed), Ukraine, Venezuela I (closed) and II. See ICC, 'Preliminary Investigations', icc-cpi.int/pages/pe.aspx. Of course, the situations currently under official investigation as enumerated above (n 202) also went through the preliminary investigation phase.

[254] Art 53(1) ICC Statute.

[255] ibid.

[256] OTP (n 212) para 41.

[257] ibid, para 43.

[258] ICC, OTP, Louis-Moreno-Ocampo, Chief Prosecutor of the International Criminal Court, 'OTP response to communications received concerning Iraq', 9 February 2006, icc-cpi.int/NR/rdonlyres/04D143C8-19FB-466C-AB77-4CDB2FDEBEF7/143682/OTP_letter_to_senders_re_Iraq_9_February_2006.pdf, 9. See, however, ICC, 'Prosecutor of the International Criminal Court, Fatou Bensouda, re-opens the preliminary examination of the situation in Iraq', 13 May 2014, icc-cpi.int//Pages/item.aspx?name=otp-statement-iraq-13-05-2014.

[259] See ICC, OTP, 'Situation on Registered Vessels of Comoros, Greece and Cambodia: Article 53(1) Report', 6 November 2014, icc-cpi.int/iccdocs/otp/OTP-COM-Article_53(1)-Report-06Nov2014Eng.pdf.

[260] ICC, Pre-Trial Chamber I, Decision on the Request of the Union of the Comoros to Review the Prosecutor's Decision Not to Initiate an Investigation, 16 July 2016, Case No ICC-01/13-34, para 26. Nevertheless, on 29 November 2017, the Prosecutor took the 'final decision' not to proceed with the investigation; ICC, OTP, Situation on the Registered Vessels of the Union of the Comoros, The Hellenic Republic and the Kingdom of Cambodia, 'Notice of Prosecutor's Final Decision under Rule 108(3)', 29 November 2017, Case No ICC-01/13.

The interests of justice, lastly, only need to be considered where jurisdiction and admissibility have been established.[261] These interests should be determined in dialogue with the victims and respected intermediaries or representatives (eg local leaders, other States, international organisations, and/or NGOs).[262] They should not be conflated with the interests of peace, which fall within the mandate of other institutions.[263] The OTP has stressed that there is a presumption in favour of investigation, and that it will exercise its discretion not to initiate an investigation based on considerations of the interests of justice only exceptionally and as a 'last resort'.[264]

ii. Official Investigation

If the Prosecutor initiates an investigation *proprio motu*, it can only open an official investigation after the Pre-Trial Chamber authorises him or her to do so.[265] This requirement was introduced into the ICC Statute as some States feared 'politically motivated or frivolous *proprio motu* proceedings'.[266] If it concerns a situation that was referred to the Prosecutor by a State Party or the UN Security Council, no such authorisation is required, and the Prosecutor can decide to proceed from a preliminary to an official investigation independently. Once an official investigation is opened, the Pre-Trial Chamber may issue arrest warrants or summonses to appear (see eg above, Section V(C)(ii), on the arrest warrants issued against Al Bashir).[267] The Pre-Trial Chamber may, upon the request of the Prosecutor, take such measures as may be necessary to ensure the efficiency and integrity of the proceedings and, in particular, to protect the rights of the defence.[268] The Pre-Trial Chamber subsequently holds a hearing to confirm the charges against the person charged, normally in the latter's presence.[269] The indictment must include the 'material facts' underpinning the charges, which must be given with enough detail to inform the defendant clearly of the charges and allow him or her to prepare a defence.[270]

iii. Trial

When the charges are confirmed, a trial is conducted, always in the presence of the accused.[271] The trial itself follows a straightforward scheme: opening statements, presentation of evidence, closing arguments, deliberations and judgment.[272] Victims may, under certain conditions, participate in the trial.[273] In the event of a conviction, a sentence will be imposed;[274] the maximum sentence is life imprisonment.[275] The Trial Chamber can

261 ICC, OTP, 'Policy Paper on the Interests of Justice', September 2007, icc-cpi.int/NR/rdonlyres/772C95C9-F54D-4321-BF09-73422BB23528/143640/ICCOTPInterestsOfJustice.pdf, 2.
262 ibid, 6.
263 ibid, 1.
264 ibid, 1 and 9.
265 Arts 13(c) and 15(3)–(4) ICC Statute.
266 M Bergsmo, J Pejic and D Zhu, 'Article 15: Prosecutor' in Triffterer and Ambos (n 54) 727.
267 Art 58 ICC Statute.
268 ibid, Art 56.
269 ibid, Art 61. This is a feature that is known within the frameworks of the ICC and the ECCC only.
270 Cryer et al (n 22) 456.
271 Part VI ICC Statute.
272 Cryer et al (n 22) 469.
273 Art 68(3) ICC Statute.
274 ibid, Art 76.
275 ibid, Art 77(1)(b).

also order reparations to be made to the victims.[276] The Trial Chamber's decisions can be appealed or revised.[277] The ICC Statute lists the grounds of appeal as procedural error, error of fact, and error of law, and as an additional ground in case of conviction '[a]ny other ground that affects the fairness or reliability of the proceedings or decision'.[278] In the event of a sentence of imprisonment, the sentence is not served at the ICC's premises, but in a State designated by the Court from a list of States which have indicated to the Court their willingness to accept sentenced persons.[279]

International criminal tribunals have given rather strong protection to the rights of the accused, even if the latter have been accused of the most horrific crimes.[280] The case law of the ECtHR has partly influenced the protective scope of these rights, in particular with respect to the right to a fair trial, the length of the proceedings, the scope of appeals, the equality of arms, the adversarial nature of the hearing, and judicial independence and impartiality.[281]

VI. Limitations of International Criminal Justice

International criminal justice's aspirations to bring about a more just world through the meting out of accountability for the gravest crimes should be nuanced. First, international criminal tribunals, given logistical and financial constraints, can only try a handful of criminals.[282] This means that most international criminals must be tried by domestic courts, which may lack the resources, legislation, jurisdiction and/or willingness to do so.[283]

Second, international criminal tribunals are crucially dependent on the cooperation of States for the arrest of suspects and the gathering of evidence.[284] Practice has demonstrated that such cooperation is not self-evident, especially not if the investigation and prosecution concern senior leaders or commanders. ICTY fugitives such as Karadžić and Mladić could remain on the run for many years, apparently protected by segments of the Serbian security services. The ICC as well has had its fair share of cooperation problems, as particularly illustrated by the Al Bashir saga (see above, Section V(C)(ii)). Due to such problems, a number of prosecutions were suspended or even discontinued, notably including the

[276] ibid, Art 75. For this purpose, a Trust Fund has been established in accordance with Art 79.

[277] Part VIII ICC Statute.

[278] ibid, Art 81(1).

[279] ibid, Art 103. The States which have indicated this are Austria, Belgium, Colombia, Denmark, Finland, Mali, Serbia and the UK.

[280] Note that Art 21(3) ICC Statute provides that the application of the law of the ICC should be consistent with internationally recognised human rights.

[281] See WA Schabas, 'Synergy or Fragmentation? International Criminal Caw and the European Convention on Human Rights' (2011) 9 *JICJ* 609.

[282] This explains why the statutes of a number of tribunals stipulate that they focus only on the most responsible persons; see eg Art 1 ECCC Statute and Art 1(1) SCSL Statute. See also ICC, OTP, 'Strategic Plan, 2016–2018', 16 November 2015, icc-cpi.int/iccdocs/otp/EN-OTP_Strategic_Plan_2016-2018.pdf, 16.

[283] International crimes can also be prosecuted by third States on the basis of the universality principle, on which see Chapter 9, Section IV(B)(v).

[284] The entire Part IX of the ICC Statute is devoted to issues of international cooperation and judicial assistance.

case against Uhuru Kenyatta, the president of Kenya.[285] Such problems may seriously dent the legitimacy of the ICC, which may be perceived as not being able to deliver on its promises.

Third, the retributive criminal justice paradigm may not always be appropriate to provide accountability or to offer affected societies a sense of closure. Instead, non-criminal 'transitional justice' solutions have been suggested that would be more attuned to local cultural sensitivities and could further peace and reconciliation in ways that criminal law cannot. Two such mechanisms stand out: amnesties and truth and reconciliation commissions. Thoughtfully drafted amnesty laws, which protect their beneficiaries from prosecution, can bring an end to vicious conflicts and smooth democratic transition processes.[286] A truth and reconciliation commission, such as the one established in post-apartheid South Africa,[287] may promise non-prosecution in return for truth-telling, can allow victims to reconcile with perpetrators,[288] and establish a historical record. It is unclear whether such mechanisms, insofar as they shield perpetrators of international crimes from justice, are compatible with the duty to prosecute underlying the ICC's principle of complementarity.[289]

The EU chooses to promote national criminal investigations and prosecutions. The EU Day Against Impunity for genocide, crimes against humanity and war crimes, is a special annual event at the EU level (organised by the Presidency of the Council of the EU, the European Commission, the Network for investigation and prosecution of genocide, crimes against humanity and war crimes and Eurojust) to commemorate the victims of core international crimes and to raise awareness and promote the fight against impunity. In addition to the promotion of criminal investigations and prosecutions, the event is intended to appropriately recognise the common efforts of the EU Member States and the EU in enforcing ICL, to address the position and participation of victims in criminal proceedings, and to reinvigorate Europe-wide commitment to the continuing fight against impunity.[290]

[285] See ICC, Trial Chamber V(B), *Prosecutor v Uhuru Muigai Kenyatta*, Notice of Withdrawal of the Charges against Uhuru Muigai Kenyatta, 5 December 2014, Case No ICC-01/09-02/11.

[286] Amnesty laws should carefully balance the interests of peace and justice. Thus, 'self-amnesty laws' (adopted by authoritarian regimes to bar the prosecution of their crimes) or 'blanket amnesty laws' (exempting entire groups from prosecution without making a distinction based on the role of individuals or the gravity of their crimes) are problematic from a human rights law perspective. Eg, in 1995, Peruvian President Alberto Fijumori enacted Amnesty Law 26479 (confirmed and extended by Amnesty Law 26492 later that year), granting a general amnesty to all military, police and civilian personnel involved in human rights violations in relation to the fight against terrorism (ie against the guerilla groups the Shining Path and the Túpac Amaru Revolutionary Movement (MRTA)). However, when called upon to adjugde the compatibility of the Amnesty Laws with the IACHR, the IACtHR ruled that 'all amnesty provisions [...] are inadmissible, because they are intended to prevent the investigation and punishment of those responsible for serious human rights violations'; IACtHR, *Barrios Altos v Peru*, 14 March 2001, IACtHR Ser C No 83, para 41. On the situation in Peru, see C Sandoval, 'The Challenge of Impunity in Peru: The Significance of the Inter-American Court of Human Rights' (2008) 5 *Essex Human Rights Review* 1. On the issue more generally, see L Mallinder, 'Can Amnesties and International Justice Be Reconciled?' (2007) 1 *International Journal of Transitional Justice* 208.

[287] See South African Truth and Reconciliation Commission, 'Final Report', 29 October 1998, justice.gov.za/trc/report.

[288] However, it is not fully clear whether truth-telling does lead to reconciliation. Moreover, victims are often not satisfied with truth *an sich*. See further OHCHR, 'Rule-of-Law Tools for Post-Conflict States: Truth Commissions', 2006, HR/PUB/06/1.

[289] See notably Art 17(2)(a) ICC Statute, as discussed above, Section V(C)(i).

[290] See Eurojust, 'Strategy of the EU Genocide Network to combat impunity for the crime of genocide, crimes against humanity and war crimes within the European Union and its Member States', November 2014, eurojust.europa.eu/Practitioners/Genocide-Network/Pages/strategy.aspx, measure 7c.

VII. Extradition

A. General System

So far, this chapter has been concerned with substantive ICL and the supranational mechanisms enforcing it. As pointed out, ICL and its machinery are of rather recent vintage, starting with the 1946 Nuremberg trials. Horizontal State cooperation in criminal matters is much older: the first extradition treaty was arguably signed as early as the thirteenth century BC, between the Egyptian Pharaoh Ramesses II and the Hittite King Hattusili III.[291] Given the abiding practical relevance of extradition for common crimes (and to a lesser extent international crimes), as well as public international law's imprint on current extradition practices, the basic features of the law of extradition will be outlined here.

The law of extradition is related to the law of jurisdiction in criminal matters (on which see Chapter 9, Section IV). A State may have jurisdiction under international law over a crime, eg, on the basis of the territoriality or nationality principle, but it may not have custody of the presumed offender. The latter may well have fled to another State, and in order to gain custody and bring him or her to justice before its own courts, the forum State will have to file an extradition request with the custodial State. Indeed, in light of the prohibition of extraterritorial enforcement jurisdiction,[292] international law does not allow the forum State to enforce its arrest warrants abroad. That being said, a person who has been arrested in violation of this prohibitive rule may not be allowed to invoke irregularities in his or her arrest or detention procedure when brought to justice in the forum State (principle of *male captus bene detentus*),[293] although in some common law countries, judges can resort to the abuse of process doctrine to avert a miscarriage of justice.[294]

Extradition is governed partly by international and partly by national (criminal/administrative) law, which explains the wide variety in extradition practices. However, such practices evince a number of commonalities. Most European States have entered into a considerable number of bilateral and multilateral extradition treaties with other States, as without a treaty, extradition will not normally be possible. There is obviously no duty to conclude extradition treaties. As a result, a patchwork of treaties, especially bilateral ones, has seen the light. In practice, no State has extradition agreements with all other States, especially not with States whose legal or political system is not deemed trustworthy.

The precise extradition rules and procedures are laid down in domestic legislation, especially of the requested State. Such legislation typically provides for a diplomatic or political rather than a judicial decision-making process, which explains why the processing of an

[291] See Treaty Between Hattusili and Ramesses II, paras 11–14, as translated in S Langdon and AH Gardiner, 'The Treaty of Alliance Between Hattusili, King of the Hittites, and the Pharaoh Ramesses II of Egypt' (1920) 6 *Journal of Egyptian Archaeology* 179, 192–94.

[292] *SS Lotus* [1927] PCIJ Series A, No 10, 18–19. See also Chapter 9, Section I.

[293] See eg *Stocké v Germany* App no 11755/85 (ECtHR, 13 December 1989); *Öcalan v Turkey* App no 46221/99 (ECtHR, 12 March 2003).

[294] The principle of *male captus bene detentus* was applied in the UK. See eg King's Bench (UK), *Ex parte Susanna Scott* [1829] 109 Eng Rep 166; King's Bench Divisional Court (UK), *Ex parte Elliot* [1949] 1 All ER 373; until the House of Lords reversed its case law in *R v Horseferry Road Magistrates' Court, ex parte Bennett* [1993] 3 WLR 90.

extradition request may take a rather long time.[295] Still, as decisions on extradition are administrative acts, they may be subject to judicial review.[296]

Extradition is not normally possible for all crimes: treaties or domestic laws either enumerate the crimes eligible for extradition, or lay down a severity threshold (eg, all crimes punishable by at least one year's imprisonment).[297] Also, they normally require double criminality: the act for which extradition is sought should be a crime in both the requesting and the requested State.[298] Specific categories of crimes may be excluded from extradition; eg, political[299] or fiscal offences.[300] States may also refuse to extradite their own nationals.[301] Once a person has been extradited, States can only try that person for the offences for which he or she has been extradited (a rule referred to as the 'principle of specialty').[302]

While extradition law is to an important extent governed by domestic law, international law has had a sizable impact on extradition practices. Some international treaties on specific crimes provide for a State's duty to either prosecute or extradite the person who has presumably committed the crime and who is present on its territory (*aut dedere aut judicare*). However, *aut dedere aut judicare* is no general principle of international law, and is limited to more serious crimes, often violations of international law, such as war crimes,[303] torture,[304] terrorism,[305] apartheid[306] or corruption.[307] In respect of these crimes, State Parties to the relevant conventions are under an obligation to extradite the alleged perpetrator if they do not prosecute him or her. In *Questions relating to the Obligation to Prosecute or Extradite* (Belgium v Senegal), the ICJ has held, at least as far as the *aut dedere aut judicare* clause of the UN Convention against Torture is concerned,[308] that 'the choice between extradition or submission for prosecution, pursuant to the Convention, does not mean that the

[295] This explains in turn the adoption of the EAW Framework Decision (n 10), the execution of which has been entrusted to judicial authorities who can process surrender requests more speedily.

[296] See eg the UK House of Lords' review of the decision to extradite General Pinochet to Spain: *R v Bow Street Metropolitan Stipendiary Magistrate, ex parte Pinochet Ugarte (No 1)* [1998] 3 WLR 1456.

[297] For an example of the former, see eg Art II Convention on Extradition Between the United States of America and Sweden (adopted 24 October 1961, entered into force 3 December 1963) 494 UNTS 141. For examples of the latter, see eg Art 2(1) European Convention on Extradition (adopted 13 December 1957, entered into force 18 April 1960) CETS No 24.

[298] Requiring double criminality, see eg Art 2(1) European Convention on Extradition (n 297); Art 2(1) Extradition Treaty between the United States of America and the United Kingdom of Great Britain and Northern Ireland (adopted 31 March 2003, entered into force 26 April 2007) 2490 UNTS 249: 'An offense shall be an extraditable offense if the conduct on which the offense is based is *punishable under the laws in both States* by deprivation of liberty for a period of one year or more or by a more severe penalty' (emphasis added).

[299] See eg C van Den Wyngaert, 'The Political Offence Exception to Extradition: Defining the Issues and Searching a Feasible Alternative' (1983) 20 *Revue belge de droit international* 741.

[300] Art 5 European Convention on Extradition (n 297).

[301] eg Austria (see Section 12 of the Austrian Extradition and Legal Assistance Act (4 December 1979)), the Czech Republic (see Art 14(4) of the Charter of Fundamental Rights and Freedoms (1 January 1991)), France (see Arts 696-1 to 696-7 of the Code of Criminal Procedure (25 January 1974)), Germany (except to a Member State of the EU or to an international court, see Art 16(2) Basic Law for the Federal Republic of Germany (8 May 1949)).

[302] See eg Art 14(1) European Convention on Extradition (n 297); Court of Appeal Antwerp (BE), *NV ICLBLTR and NV S v JS*, 25 October 2006, (2008–2009) *Rechtskundig Weekblad* 460.

[303] See respectively Arts 49, 50, 129 and 146 of GC I, II, III and IV.

[304] See Arts 5(2) and 7(1) UN Convention against Torture.

[305] See Art 7 Convention for the Suppression of Unlawful Seizure of Aircraft (16 December 1970, entered into force 14 October 1971) 860 UNTS 105.

[306] See Art XI(2) International Convention on the Suppression and Punishment of the Crime of Apartheid (adopted 30 November 1973, entered into force 18 July 1976) 1015 UNTS 243.

[307] See Art 44(11) UN Convention against Corruption (n 2).

[308] Art 7(1) UN Convention against Torture.

two alternatives are to be given the same weight'; according to the Court, '[e]xtradition is an option offered to the State by the Convention, whereas prosecution is an international obligation under the Convention, the violation of which is a wrongful act engaging the responsibility of the State'.[309]

Also international human rights treaties have influenced, or rather limited, States' extradition practices. This applies in particular to Europe, where the ECtHR is the final arbitrator of the compatibility of judicial and administrative decisions taken by ECHR Contracting Parties.[310] The ECtHR case law has a broad application: it applies to decisions regarding extradition, deportation, expulsion, or any other form of removal from the territory. In the seminal *Soering* case of 1989, the ECtHR held that the United Kingdom violated Article 3 ECHR, which prohibits inhuman and degrading treatment, by extraditing an individual to the United States, where he would possibly be exposed to the death row phenomenon.[311] In later cases, the risk of being sentenced to death,[312] or even to life imprisonment without parole in the third State,[313] have been considered to fall within the scope of Article 3 ECHR.[314] The Court has confirmed that this provision is absolute, which means that it is not possible to weigh the risk of ill-treatment against the reasons for extraditing or deporting the person.[315] The ECtHR not only reviews extradition or deportation decisions in light of Article 3 ECHR, but also in light of Article 13 ECHR (right to an effective remedy, ie judicial review),[316] Article 5 ECHR (right to liberty) and Article 6 ECHR (right to a fair trial) provided that the breaches are flagrant.[317] In *Abu Qatada*, the ECtHR for the first time held there to be a real risk that an individual's retrial in a third State after deportation would amount to a flagrant denial of justice.[318] However, under certain conditions, the ECtHR is willing to accept diplomatic assurances from the receiving State that the extradited or deported individual's rights, especially his or her right not to be ill-treated, will not be violated.[319]

In the fight against terrorism, regular extradition procedures have at times been circumvented through extraordinary renditions – secret transfers from one State to another, often combined with secret detention where torture is employed during interrogation sessions. European States have cooperated with the United States in extraordinary rendition programs; the Council of Europe and the ECtHR have condemned such practices as violations of the ECHR.[320]

[309] *Questions relating to the Obligation to Prosecute or Extradite* (n 83) para 95.
[310] On the ECHR and the ECtHR, see Chapter 16, Section IX.
[311] *Soering v UK* App no 14038/88 (ECtHR, 7 July 1989).
[312] ibid.
[313] *Trabelsi v Belgium* App no 140/10 (ECtHR, 4 September 2014).
[314] See also Chapter 16, Section IX(A)(i) on the normative provisions of the ECHR.
[315] *Saadi v Italy* App no 37201/06 (ECtHR, 28 February 2008) paras 125 and 138.
[316] *A v the Netherlands* App no 4900/06 (ECtHR, 20 July 2010).
[317] *Soering v UK* (n 311) para 113; *Mamatkulov and Askarov v Turkey* App nos 46827/99 and 46951/99 (ECtHR, 4 February 2005) paras 90 and 91; *Al-Saadoon and Mufdhi v UK* App no 61498/08 (ECtHR, 2 March 2010) para 149; *Othman (Abu Qatada) v UK* App no 8139/09 (ECtHR, 17 January 2012) paras 233 and 258.
[318] *Abu Qatada v UK* (n 317) para 288.
[319] The Court assesses the quality of assurances given and whether, in light of the receiving State's practices, they can be relied upon. For 11 factors taken into account by the Court in this assessment, see *Abu Qatada v UK* (n 317) para 189. In that case, the Court accepted the receiving State's diplomatic assurances that on the individual's return he would not be exposed to a real risk of ill-treatment (paras 186–207).
[320] Parliamentary Assembly of the Council of Europe, Committee on Legal Affairs and Human Rights, 'Alleged secret detentions and unlawful inter-state transfers involving Council of Europe member states', Draft report – Part II (Explanatory memorandum), 7 June 2006, AS/Jur (2006) 16 Part II; Parliamentary Assembly of the Council of Europe, Committee on Legal Affairs and Human Rights, 'Secret detentions and illegal transfers of

B. Extradition Procedures in Europe

Specifically for European States, one has seen the coming about of a multiplicity of multilateral instruments on extradition at the regional and subregional level over the past six decades, including: (i) the 1957 European Convention on Extradition, negotiated within the framework of the Council of Europe;[321] (ii) the 1962 Benelux Extradition Treaty (between Belgium, the Netherlands and Luxembourg);[322] (iii) the 1990 Convention implementing the Schengen Agreement (making the European Extradition Convention applicable amongst the Schengen States);[323] and (iv) the 1995 and 1996 EU Extradition Conventions.[324]

The main extradition instrument has for a long time been the European Extradition Convention. This Convention is a classic extradition treaty, which provides for traditional extradition exceptions,[325] and does not do away with the rather cumbersome diplomatic extradition procedures.[326] However, in the relations between EU Member States and for the offences that fall within its scope,[327] all instruments concerning extradition have been replaced by the 2002 EU Framework Decision on the European Arrest Warrant (EAW).[328] The EAW is based on the principle of mutual trust and smooths the extradition process. Departing from the ordinary international extradition practice, 'surrender' – so no longer 'extradition' – procedures on the basis of the EAW Framework Decision are depoliticised and only involve judicial authorities, require Member States to surrender their own nationals, and abandon the requirement of double criminality for 32 (serious) crimes (eg terrorism and trafficking in human beings).[329] However, the issuing Member State cannot issue an arrest warrant for *any* act: acts should be punishable by the law of the issuing Member State

detainees involving Council of Europe member states: second report', 11 June 2007, Doc 11302 rev; *Babar Ahmad and others v UK* App nos 24027/07, 11949/08, 36742/08, 66911/09 and 67354/09 (ECtHR, 10 April 2012); *Husayn (Abu Zubaydah) v Poland* App no 7511/13 (ECtHR, 24 July 2014); *Al Nashiri v Poland* App no 28761/11 (ECtHR, 24 July 2014); finding violations of Arts 3, 5, 6(1), 8 and 13 ECHR.

321 See above (n 297).

322 Treaty Concerning Extradition and Mutual Assistance in Criminal Matters between the Kingdom of Belgium, the Grand Duchy of Luxembourg and the Kingdom of the Netherlands (adopted 27 June 1962, entered into force 11 December 1967) UNTS No 8893. Nothwithstanding the European Convention on Extradition, the Benelux Extradition Treaty governed the relevant relations between Belgium, the Netherlands and Luxembourg, as those countries made reservations to the European Convention for that purpose.

323 Convention implementing the Schengen Agreement of 14 June 1985 between the Governments of the States of the Benelux Economic Union, the Federal Republic of Germany and the French Republic on the Gradual Abolition of Checks at Their Common Borders (adopted 19 June 1990, entered into force 1 September 1993) [2000] OJ L239/19, Art 60.

324 Convention Drawn up on the Basis of Article K.3 of the Treaty on European Union, on Simplified Extradition Procedure between the Member States of the European Union (adopted 10 March 1995, not entered into force) [1995] OJ C78/2; Convention drawn up on the basis of Article K.3 of the Treaty on European Union relating to Extradition between the Member States of the European Union (adopted 27 September 1996, not entered into force) [1996] OJ C313/11. Even if these EU Extradition Conventions have never entered into force because they were not ratified by all then EU Member States, they applied between those Member States that made declarations in that respect; see eg Art 16 of the 1995 Convention.

325 See Arts 3–6 of the European Convention on Extradition (n 297).

326 ibid, Art 21.

327 See Recital 11 EAW Framework Decision (n 10), making this replacement explicit; and ibid, Art 2, enumerating the offences that fall within the EAW Framework Decision's scope.

328 See above (n 10).

329 Art 2(2) EAW Framework Decision.

by a custodial sentence or a detention order for a maximum period of at least 12 months or, where a sentence has been passed or a detention order has been made, for sentences of at least four months.[330]

Judicial authorities of the Member State of execution (ie, the State which receives the surrender request) are normally required to execute the EAW. However, the EAW Framework Decision lists a number of grounds for mandatory and optional non-execution of the EAW. Mandatory grounds include amnesty, double jeopardy and age,[331] whereas optional grounds include absence of double criminality, prosecution in the executing State, applicability of a statute of limitations, final judgment in a third State, execution of a sentence in the executing State, and extraterritorial offences.[332] In a number of scenarios, the executing State can also subject the execution of the EAW to certain guarantees, namely where the EAW has been issued for the purposes of executing a sentence or a detention order imposed by a decision rendered *in absentia*, where the offence is punishable by a custodial life sentence or life-time detention order, and where a person who is the subject of a EAW for the purposes of prosecution is a national or resident of the executing State.[333] In the latter scenario, the executing State may subject surrender to the condition that the person, after being heard, is returned to the executing Member State in order to serve the custodial sentence or detention order passed against him or her in the issuing Member State.[334]

The EAW Framework Decision provides for strict time limits for the execution of the EAW. In cases where the requested person consents to his or her surrender, the final decision on the execution of the EAW should be taken within a period of 10 days after consent has been given.[335] In other cases, the final decision on the execution of the EAW should be taken within a period of 60 days after the arrest of the requested person.[336] The time limits can exceptionally be extended for a further 30 days.[337] The person must be surrendered no later than 10 days after the final decision on the execution of the EAW.[338]

The specialty principle, as it applies under ordinary extradition law, continues to apply under the EAW regime, subject to limited exceptions. Thus, a person surrendered may not normally be prosecuted, sentenced or otherwise deprived of his or her liberty for an offence committed prior to his or her surrender other than that for which he or she was surrendered.[339]

The EAW has been criticised by human rights advocates and defence lawyers, who feared that the smoother surrender procedures under the EAW could go to the detriment of individual rights guarantees,[340] even if the preamble of the Framework Decision confirms the applicability of human rights in EAW surrender proceedings.[341] Various aspects of the EAW, and its interpretation and application, have been challenged before the CJEU, but the

[330] ibid, Art 2(1).
[331] ibid, Art 3.
[332] ibid, Art 4.
[333] Judgment of 17 July 2008, *Kozłowski*, C-66/08 EU:C:2008:437.
[334] Art 5 EAW Framework Decision.
[335] ibid, Art 17(2). Consent can be given on the basis of Art 13.
[336] ibid, Art 17(3).
[337] ibid, Art 17(4).
[338] ibid, Art 23(2).
[339] ibid, Art 27(2). The exceptions are listed in Art 27(1) and (3).
[340] See eg L Marin, 'The European Arrest Warrant and Domestic Legal Orders: Tensions between Mutual Recognition and Fundamental Rights: The Italian Case' (2008) 15 *Maastricht Journal of European and Comparative Law* 473; JAE Vervaele, 'The Transnational *ne bis in idem* Principle in the EU Mutual Recognition and Equivalent Protection of Human Rights' (2005) 1 *Utrecht Law Review* 100.
[341] EAW Framework Decision, recitals (12) and (13).

Court has not proved willing to subject the operation of the EAW to stringent human rights requirements. In *Advocaten voor de Wereld* (2007),[342] it rejected claims that the EAW should have been regulated by a treaty rather than a Framework Decision,[343] or that the abandonment of the condition of double criminality in Article 2(2) of the Framework Decision violated the principle of legality of criminal offences and penalties.[344] In *Radu* (2013), it held that 'the executing judicial authorities cannot refuse to execute a European arrest warrant issued for the purposes of conducting a criminal prosecution on the ground that the requested person was not heard in the issuing Member State before that arrest warrant was issued'.[345] In *Melloni* (2013), it ruled that Article 53 of the EU Charter does not allow an executing Member State to apply its own constitutional standards on the right to a fair trial and the rights of the defence, rather than the issuing Member State's standards, when making the surrender of a person convicted *in absentia* conditional upon the conviction being open to review in the issuing Member State.[346] In the Court's view, a contrary interpretation of Article 53 of the Charter 'would undermine the principle of the primacy of EU law inasmuch as it would allow a Member State to disapply EU legal rules which are fully in compliance with the Charter where they infringe the fundamental rights guaranteed by that State's constitution'.[347] All these decisions confirm the principle of mutual trust between Member States underpinning the EAW, a principle that should not be undermined by spurious human rights arguments.

One should realise that the EAW only applies to the relations *between* EU Member States. In the relations between the EU and its Member States on the one hand, and third States on the other, the classic extradition rules continue to apply. Extradition treaties have also been concluded by the EU itself, most notably with the United States.[348] These agreements affect but do not invalidate bilateral extradition treaties existing in the relations between a Member State and the third State, nor do they preclude the conclusion of bilateral extradition treaties after the entry into force of the EU agreement.[349] Such bilateral treaties should, however, comply with the framework rules set out in the EU agreement. Under the EU-US Agreement, for instance, Member States are precluded from extraditing a person to the US if the offence is not punishable under the laws of the requesting and requested State by deprivation of liberty for a maximum period of more than one year or by a more severe penalty,[350] or where the offence for which extradition is sought is punishable by death in the United States, if assurances are not provided that the death penalty shall not be imposed or carried out.[351]

[342] Judgment of 3 May 2007, *Advocaten voor de Wereld VZW v Leden van de Ministerraad*, C-303/05, EU:C:2007:261.

[343] The Court found that Art 34 TEU did not establish any order of priority between the different instruments listed in that provision, and thus that the Council legitimately opted for a Framework Decision, even in a field that was previously regulated by conventions; ibid, paras 41–42.

[344] ibid, para 57.

[345] Judgment of 29 January 2013, *Ciprian Vasile Radu*, C-396/11, EU:C:2013:39, para 43.

[346] Judgment of 26 February 2013, *Stefano Melloni v Ministerio Fiscal*, C-399/11, EU:C:2013:107, para 64.

[347] ibid, para 58.

[348] Agreement on Extradition between the European Union and the United States of America (adopted 25 June 2003, entered into force 1 February 2010) [2003] OJ L181/27.

[349] By virtue of Art 3 of the EU-US Agreement, the EU ensures 'that the provisions of this Agreement are applied in relation to bilateral extradition treaties between its Member States and the [US], in force at the time of the entry into force of this Agreement'. Nevertheless, as specified in Art 18, the Agreement does 'not preclude the conclusion, after its entry into force, of bilateral Agreements between a Member State and the [US] consistent with this Agreement'.

[350] Art 4(1) EU-US Agreement.

[351] ibid, Art 13.

VIII. Concluding Observations

ICL started its ascendancy only after the Second World War and is a rather new functional domain of public international law. It is an important field, however, not only because, in a departure from the State-centric perspective of international law, it provides for the responsibility of individuals, but also because the establishment of international criminal tribunals, and especially the ICC, has raised the prospect that those who commit unspeakable atrocities, wherever on earth, will no longer escape accountability.

While the vertical cooperation between international criminal tribunals and States has not gone smoothly, horizontal cooperation in criminal matters in contrast, given its long pedigree, is likely to stay with us. Mechanisms of extradition and surrender of (mostly common) criminals between States are firmly in place, and are expected to gain in prominence as transnational criminality spreads with increased opportunities of international exchange and commerce. It remains a challenge, however, to ensure that States' desire to facilitate extradition and surrender procedures does not undermine the individual rights of presumed offenders. Courts, including the ECtHR and the CJEU, play a key role in this respect.

Bibliography

Ambos, K, *Internationales Strafrecht: Strafanwendungsrecht, Völkerstrafrecht, Europäisches Strafrecht, Rechtshilfe*, 5th edn (München, Beck, 2018).

Ambos, K, *Treatise on International Criminal Law*, 2 Vols (Oxford, OUP, 2013–2014).

Ascensio, H, Decaux, E and Pellet, A (eds), *Droit international pénal*, 2nd edn (Paris, Pedone, 2012).

Bantekas, I, *International Criminal Law*, 4th edn (Oxford, Hart, 2010).

Bassiouni, MC (ed), *International Criminal Law*, 3rd edn, 3 Vols (Leiden, Nijhoff, 2008).

Bassiouni, MC, *Introduction au droit pénal international* (Brussels, Bruylant, 2002).

Bassiouni, MC, *Introduction to International Criminal Law*, 2nd edn (Dordrecht, Nijhoff, 2012).

Bueno Arús, F and de Miguel Zaragoza, J, *Manual de derecho penal internacional* (Madrid, Universidad Pontificia de Comillas, 2003).

Cassese, A, *International Criminal Law*, 3rd edn (Oxford, OUP, 2013).

Cassese, A (ed), *The Oxford Companion to International Criminal Justice* (Oxford, OUP, 2009).

Cassese, A, Gaeta, P and Jones, JRWD (eds), *The Rome Statute of the International Criminal Court: A Commentary*, 2 Vols (Oxford, OUP, 2002).

Cryer, R, 'International Criminal Law' in Evans, MD, *International Law*, 4th edn (Oxford, OUP, 2014) 752–82.

Cryer, R, Friman, H, Robinson, D and Wilmshurst, E, *An Introduction to International Criminal Law and Procedure*, 3rd edn (Cambridge, CUP, 2014).

Donnedieu de Vabres, H, *Les principes modernes du droit pénal international* (Paris, Editions Panthéon-Assas, 2004).

Huet, A and Koering-Joulin, R, *Droit pénal international*, 3rd edn (Paris, PUF, 2005).
Jones, JRWD and Powles, S, *International Criminal Practice*, 3rd edn (Ardsley, Transnational, 2003).
Kolb, R and Scalia, D (eds), *Droit international pénal: prècis*, 2nd edn (Basel, Helbing & Lichtenhahn, 2012).
L Reydams, J Wouters and C Ryngaert (eds), *International Prosecutors* (Oxford, OUP, 2012).
Schabas, WA, *An Introduction to the International Criminal Court*, 5th edn (Cambridge, CUP, 2017).
Schabas, WA, *The International Criminal Court: A Commentary on the Rome Statute*, 2nd edn (Oxford, OUP, 2016).
Stahn, C (ed), *The Law and Practice of the International Criminal Court* (Oxford, OUP, 2015).
Triffterer, O and Ambos, K (eds), *Rome Statute of the International Criminal Court: A Commentary*, 3rd edn (München, Beck, 2016).
Werle, G and Jeßberger, F, *Völkerstrafrecht*, 4th edn (Tübingen, Mohr Siebeck, 2016).
Werle, G and Jeßberger, F, *Principles of International Criminal Law*, 3rd edn (Oxford, OUP, 2014).

Further Reading

Bohlander, M (ed), *International Criminal Justice: A Critical Analysis of Procedures and Institutions* (London, Cameron May, 2007).
Boister, H, *An Introduction to Transnational Criminal Law* (Oxford, OUP, 2012).
Ferdinandusse, W, *Direct Application of International Criminal Law in National Courts* (Den Haag, TMC Asser Press, 2006).
Lawther, C, Moffett, L and Jacobs, D, *Research Handbook on Transitional Justice* (Cheltenham, Edward Elgar, 2017).
Mettraux, G, *International Crimes and the ad hoc Tribunals* (Oxford, OUP, 2005).
Politi, P and Gioia, F (eds), *The International Criminal Court and National Jurisdictions* (Aldershot, Ashgate, 2008).
Ratner, SR, Abrams, JS and Bischoff, JL, *Accountability for Human Rights Atrocities in International Law: Beyond the Nuremberg Legacy*, 3rd edn (Oxford, OUP, 2009).
Schabas, WA, McDermott, Y and Hayes, N (eds), *The Ashgate Research Companion to International Criminal Law: Critical Perspectives* (Farnham, Ashgate, 2013).
Schiff, BN, *Building the International Criminal Court* (Cambridge, CUP, 2008).
Simbeye, Y, *Immunity and International Criminal Law* (Aldershot, Ashgate, 2004).
Stigen, J, *The Relationship between the International Criminal Court and National Jurisdictions: The Principle of Complementarity* (Leiden, Nijhoff, 2008).
J Wouters, S Verhoeven and B Demeyere, 'The International Criminal Court's Office of the Prosecutor: Navigating between Independence and Accountability?' (2008) 8 *International Criminal Law Review* 273.
Yokaris, A, *La répression pénale en droit international public* (Brussels, Bruylant, 2007).

18

Law of the Sea and Global Commons

I. Introduction: Codification of the Law of the Sea

A. Historical Background

Oceans cover no less than 70 per cent of our planet's surface. They are of crucial importance for mankind for trade, transportation and communication. They contain vast reserves of natural resources, be it in terms of fishing stocks in the water columns, oil and gas reserves in the subsoil or minerals dispersed over the deep seabed. Moreover, they have been, and continue to be, of great military and geo-strategic importance. It is no wonder that the international law of the sea constitutes one of the oldest branches of international law.

The law of the sea has always been characterised by an inherent tension between the attempts of individual States to lay claim to certain parts, or usages, of the sea, and the need to safeguard the use of the sea for the international community as a whole.[1] This persistent tension between competing claims is well illustrated by the publication of two very different works in the first half of the seventeenth century. The first, *Mare Liberum* (1609) by the famous Dutch scholar Hugo Grotius, staunchly advocated the freedom of the high seas. The second, *Mare Clausum* (1635) by the British scholar Selden, by contrast, claimed that it was possible for States to lay sovereign claim over parts of the seas. Competing claims relating to the use of the oceans still surface on a recurring basis. It is no coincidence, for instance, that a considerable share of the cases brought before the ICJ concern disputes over maritime delimitation and jurisdiction.[2] Maritime disputes have also given rise to a substantial number of arbitral cases. Examples of important maritime disputes which remain to be conclusively settled include the Chinese claims over large swathes of the South China Sea on the basis of historic entitlements (demarcated by the notorious

[1] Consider eg L Oppenheim, *International Law, A Treatise – Volume 1: Peace*, 2nd edn (New York, Longmans, 1912) para 248; observing that '[t]hese claims have been more or less successfully asserted for several hundreds of years'.

[2] In 2014 Boyle identified 43 cases since 1996 dealing with the law of the sea, making it 'the second largest category of inter-state cases outside the WTO': A Boyle, 'UNCLOS Dispute Settlement: Uses and Abuses of Part XV' (2014) 47 *Revue Belge de Droit International* 182, 185.

'nine-dash line')[3] and the competing claims of several States vis-à-vis the continental shelf underlying the Arctic ocean.[4]

For centuries, the law of the sea was governed essentially by general and regional custom, as well as by bilateral treaties. The basic division dominating the law of the sea was that between the 'territorial sea', on the one hand, and the 'high seas' on the other. Put simply: the former zone fell within the jurisdiction of the coastal State; the latter was deemed open to all. Throughout the twentieth century, however, the need for codification and further 'progressive development' of the law of the sea became clear. Various factors account for this, including economic and technological developments, which made it possible to exploit natural resources hitherto inaccessible or to do so at faraway locations, growing awareness of environmental issues, such as overfishing, shifting strategic interests and the strong increase in maritime trade. A first attempt to arrive at codification at the 1930 Hague Conference failed. A second attempt, culminating in the First UN Conference on the Law of the Sea in Geneva in 1958, proved more successful. Four separate 'Geneva Conventions' were adopted, dealing respectively with: (i) the territorial sea and the contiguous zone;[5] (ii) the high seas;[6] (iii) the continental shelf;[7] and (iv) fisheries and the conservation of the living resources of the high seas.[8]

While the 1958 Geneva Conventions constituted an important step forward, it soon became clear that they fell short of what was actually needed. They had left several important issues, such as the breadth of the territorial sea, open. In addition, many newly-independent countries felt that the Conventions did not properly reflect their interests, in particular as regards fishing rights. As early as 1960, a second UN Conference on the Law of the Sea was convened to address some of these issues, albeit in vain. A third UN Conference on the Law of the Sea was convened at the instigation of the UN General Assembly in 1973, and continued to meet until the adoption of a broad package deal in Montego Bay (Jamaica) in 1982.

B. UNCLOS

With its 320 articles and nine annexes spanning all aspects of ocean governance, such as delimitation, environmental control, marine scientific research, economic and commercial activities, transfer of technology and the settlement of disputes relating to ocean

[3] See eg F Dupuy and P-M Dupuy, 'A Legal Analysis of China's Historic Rights Claim in the South China Sea' (2013) 107 *AJIL* 124; R Beckman, 'The UN Convention on the Law of the Sea and the Maritime Disputes in the South China Sea' (2013) 107 *AJIL* 142; S Talmon and BB Jia (eds), *The South China Sea Arbitration: A Chinese Perspective* (Oxford, Hart, 2014). On 12 July 2016 there was a first and (so far) only decision in the South China Sea dispute by the PCA in a case between the Philippines and China: *South China Sea Arbitration* (Philippines v China), Award of 12 July 2016, PCA Case No 2013-19. See further below, Section VII(B).

[4] See eg M Byers and JE Baker, *International Law and the Arctic* (Cambridge, CUP, 2013); S Holmes, 'Breaking The Ice: Emerging Legal Issues in Arctic Sovereignty' (2008) 9 *Chicago Journal of International Law* 323.

[5] Convention on the Territorial Sea and the Contiguous Zone (adopted 29 April 1958, entered into force 10 September 1964) 516 UNTS 205 (1958 Territorial Sea Convention).

[6] Convention on the High Seas (adopted 29 April 1958, entered into force 30 September 1962) 450 UNTS 11 (1958 High Seas Convention).

[7] Convention on the Continental Shelf (adopted 29 April 1958, entered into force 10 June 1964) 499 UNTS 311 (1958 Continental Shelf Convention).

[8] Convention on Fishing and Conservation of the Living Resources of the High Seas (adopted 29 April 1958, entered into force 20 March 1966) 559 UNTS 285 (1958 Fisheries Convention).

matters, the 1982 UN Convention on the Law of the Sea (UNCLOS) or 'Montego Bay Convention'[9] constitutes a unique document, which truly forms the 'constitution for the oceans'.[10]

At the outset, the future success of the Convention was anything but certain. Even though in 1994 the Convention succeeded in obtaining the required number of ratifications needed to enter into force, 59 out of 60 ratifications emanated from developing countries. In contrast, the lion's share of developed countries refused to ratify, in particular due to their discontent with Part XI of the Convention, dealing with the 'Area' or deep seabed. From the 1950s–1960s onwards, there was a widespread (yet somewhat premature) conviction that it would soon become technologically and commercially possible to explore and exploit the vast natural resources of the deep seabed. In 1967, the Maltese UN ambassador Arvid Pardo warned that if it were accepted that individual States would be free to exploit these resources, this would result in a scramble for resources at the expense of the developing world, and possibly in (yet another) 'tragedy of the commons'. Instead, Pardo argued that the deep seabed should be considered a 'common heritage of mankind', only to be exploited for the benefit of the international community as a whole. UNCLOS effectively integrated Pardo's proposal. What is more, the Convention also introduced a far-reaching institutional regime, including a supranational 'Enterprise' that would itself undertake mining activity and distribute the revenues among the State Parties. The Convention's deep seabed regime proved completely unacceptable to most developed countries. Eventually, a separate treaty was adopted in July 1994 in order to accommodate the latter's objections by (instantly) amending the original 'Part XI'.[11] The rather euphemistically entitled 'Implementation Agreement' substantially waters down the original regime, which is replaced by a more market-oriented approach (see further below, Section VI).

Following the adoption of the Implementation Agreement, the number of ratifications steadily increased. As of June 2017, 168 Parties (including the EU)[12] had ratified or acceded to UNCLOS. The United States is one of a handful of coastal States that has not ratified the Convention. This is so in spite of the fact that, ever since 1994, successive US administrations have consistently pressed for ratification of the Convention at the domestic level.[13] In any case, it is generally accepted – including by the US – that most provisions of UNCLOS reflect customary international law and are accordingly binding on all States.

[9] United Nations Convention on the Law of the Sea (adopted 10 December 1982, entered into force 16 November 1994) 1833 UNTS 397 (UNCLOS).

[10] 'A Constitution for the Oceans', Remarks by Tommy TB Koh, of Singapore, President of the Third United Nations Conference on the Law of the Sea, un.org/depts/los/convention_agreements/texts/koh_english.pdf.

[11] Agreement relating to the Implementation of Part XI of the United Nations Convention on the Law of the Sea of 10 December 1982 (adopted 28 July 1994, entered into force 28 July 1996) 1836 UNTS 3. Note: Art 2 of the Agreement provides: 'The provision of this Agreement and Part XI shall be interpreted and applied together as a single instrument. In the event of any inconsistency between this Agreement and Part XI, the provisions of this Agreement shall prevail'. Art 7 of the Agreement provides for the provisional application of the Agreement once UNCLOS enters into force, so as to avoid that States would ever be bound by the original 'Part XI' as set out in the Convention. Art 4 provides that, after the adoption of the 1994 Agreement, any instrument of ratification or accession to UNCLOS will also represent consent to be bound by the 1994 Agreement.

[12] Still, it is to be noted that the CJEU has held that UNCLOS lacks direct effect and accordingly cannot be invoked before the CJEU to challenge the vailidy of EU law; judgment of 3 June 2008, *International Association of Independent Tanker Owners (Intertanko) and others v Secretary of State for Transport*, C-308/06, ECLI:EU:C:2008:312, concluding at paras 64–65.

[13] See JE Noyes, 'The Law of the Sea Convention and the United States of America' (2014) 47 *Revue Belge de Droit International* 15.

Pursuant to Article 309 UNCLOS, States are not permitted to make reservations or exceptions to the Convention save insofar as this is (exceptionally) permitted by specific provisions thereof. An important novelty of UNCLOS, as compared to the four 1958 Geneva Conventions, is moreover that it contains a compulsory dispute settlement mechanism. States acceding to the Convention thus accept that, save for a number of exceptions, disputes with other States Parties concerning the application and interpretation of the Convention can in principle be submitted to a judicial body (see below, Section IX).

C. Other Instruments

While UNCLOS constitutes one of the most ambitious and extensive multilateral agreements ever to be drafted, it is not the only treaty instrument to address the use of the world's oceans. Numerous bilateral, regional and multilateral treaties implement and/or supplement the 1982 Convention. Such agreements include bilateral delimitation agreements, multilateral and regional agreements on fisheries or on the protection of the marine environment from pollution, and agreements criminalising certain conduct and/or providing for mutual legal assistance. They include a variety of treaties, such as the 1992 UN Biodiversity Convention,[14] that cannot be regarded as belonging to the realm of the law of the sea as such, but nonetheless impact upon the use of the oceans. As an exhaustive overview of these instruments is beyond the scope of the present chapter, it will focus on the core rules of the law of the sea, as laid down first and foremost in UNCLOS.

The chapter first examines the legal regimes applicable to the different maritime zones identified in the 1982 Convention. As a general rule, coastal States have the largest degree of jurisdictional competence over those zones that are closest to their coast.

Table 8 Maritime Zones

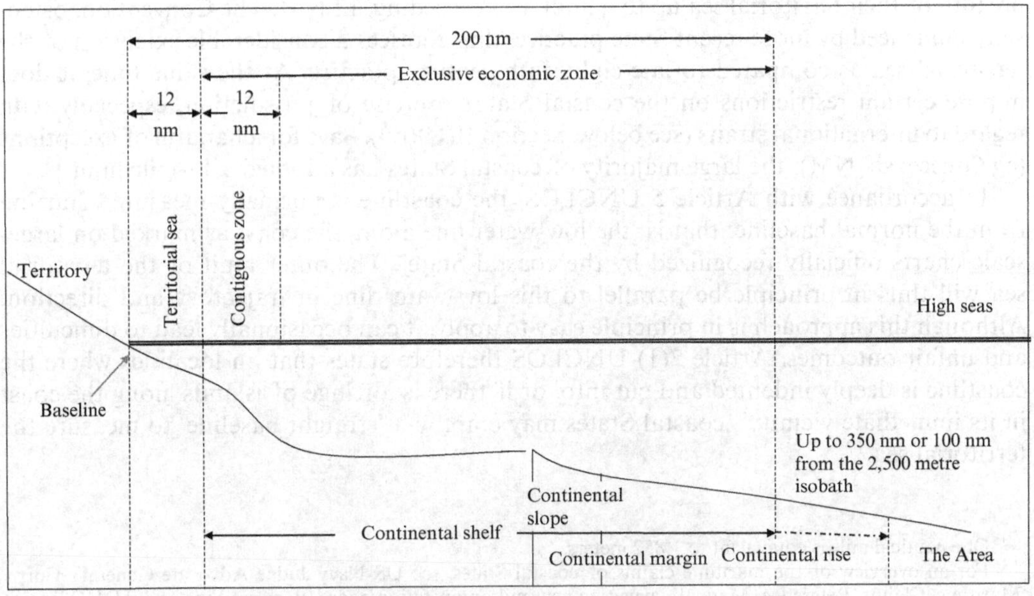

[14] Convention on Biological Diversity (adopted 5 June 1992, entered into force 29 December 1993) 1760 UNTS 79.

II. The Territorial Sea and the Contiguous Zone

A. The Territorial Sea and Internal Waters

Article 2(1) UNCLOS confirms the long-established rule that the sovereignty of the coastal State extends beyond its territory and internal waters, to a belt of sea adjacent to its coastline, described as the territorial sea. Article 2(2) adds that this sovereignty extends to the air space over the territorial sea as well as to its bed and subsoil. It follows that the coastal State can exercise prescriptive and enforcement jurisdiction in respect of its territorial sea. It has, for instance, exclusive control over the natural resources (living and non-living) within the territorial sea. It can also decree laws and regulations concerning issues such as immigration and customs in respect of this zone. On the other hand, the sovereign control over the territorial sea is not unfettered. Article 2(3) makes clear that it must be exercised in conformity with the rules of UNCLOS and with other rules of international law. The Convention itself contains several important restrictions on the coastal State's jurisdiction (see below, Section II(C)).

In the eighteenth and nineteenth centuries, several States took the view that the territorial sea could extend up to three nautical miles (NM) from the coastline.[15] This three-mile limit corresponded to the shooting range of coastal artillery at the time. State practice throughout the nineteenth and twentieth centuries was far from uniform. Some coastal States adopted a four- or six-mile limit, or claimed broader zones in which they could undertake enforcement action and which extended beyond the three-mile limit. During the 1958 and 1960 UN Law of the Sea Conferences, finding a consensus on the issue proved impossible.

The 1982 Convention cut the Gordian knot by stipulating that States can establish the breadth of their territorial sea up to a limit 'not exceeding' 12 NM. The Convention, ostensibly influenced by more recent State practice, thus foresees a considerable extension of the territorial sea as compared to late-eighteenth century practice. At the same time, it does impose certain restrictions on the coastal State's exercise of jurisdiction, especially with regard to international straits (see below, Section II(C)(iv)). Save for a handful of exceptions (eg Greece: six NM), the large majority of coastal States has adopted a 12-mile limit.[16]

In accordance with Article 5 UNCLOS, the coastline is normally measured starting from the normal baseline; that is 'the low-water line along the coast as marked on large-scale charts officially recognized by the coastal State'. The outer limit of the territorial sea will thus in principle be parallel to this low-water line in trajectory and direction. Although this approach is in principle easy to apply, it can occasionally lead to difficulties and unfair outcomes. Article 7(1) UNCLOS therefore states that 'in localities where the coastline is deeply indented and cut into, or if there is a fringe of islands along the coast in its immediate vicinity', coastal States may employ a 'straight baseline' to measure the territorial sea.[17]

[15] One nautical mile is equivalent to 1,852 meters.

[16] For an overview of the maritime claims of coastal States, see US Navy Judge Advocate General's Corps, 'Maritime Claims Reference Manual', www.jag.navy.mil/organization/code_10_mcrm.htm and UN Office of Legal Affairs, Division for Ocean Affairs and the Law of the Sea, 'Table of Claims to Maritime Jurisdiction (as at 15 July 2011)', un.org/Depts/los/LEGISLATIONANDTREATIES/PDFFILES/table_summary_of_claims.pdf.

[17] A identical provision was already contained in Art 4(1) of the 1958 Territorial Sea Convention (n 5).

Article 7(1) UNCLOS mirrors the position of the ICJ in its 1951 judgment in the *Anglo-Norwegian Fisheries* case.[18] This case was initiated by the UK pursuant to a series of incidents involving British fishing vessels. According to the UK, Norway had unlawfully interfered with the activities of vessels which were outside the permissible limits of Norway's territorial sea, and was therefore liable to pay compensation. The Court nonetheless agreed with Norway that it was not legally obliged to use the low water line along its coast for purposes of drawing its territorial sea. Rather, it emphasised the broken and indented character of the Norwegian coastline, with its multitudes of fjords, and found that a baseline along the outer limit of the *skjaergaard* (ie the rampart of rocks and islands off the Norwegian coast) was a solution 'dictated by geographical realities'.[19] Echoing the ICJ's approach, Article 7(3) UNCLOS cautions that straight baselines should not depart to any appreciable extent from the general direction of the coast, and that the sea areas lying within the lines must show a sufficiently close nexus to the coast.[20]

In *Commission v United Kingdom*,[21] the CJEU was asked to assess whether British legislation fixing new baselines, which were shifted further out to sea than those previously in force (thus impacting fishing activities off the coast of the UK), were compatible with EU law. While there was no suggestion that the new legislation was at variance with the rules of international law relating to the demarcation of the territorial sea and the drawing of baselines (para 18), the Court held that it contravened the UK's obligations under EU law for various reasons. The case illustrates that, while international law may authorise certain behaviour, this cannot be used as a defence against violations of EU law.

Waters located on the seaward side of the baseline fall within the territorial sea (up to a maximum breadth of 12 NM). Waters located on the landward side of the baseline qualify as 'internal waters'. Use of those waters is not governed by the law of the sea and is fully subject to domestic legislation. The internal waters include the coastal State's lakes, rivers and ports. Bays also qualify as internal waters, rather than as part of the territorial sea, when they present a closer nexus to the land than to the sea. To determine whether this is the case, Article 10 UNCLOS foresees a complex mechanism[22] whereby one must: (i) identify the 'natural entrance points' of the bay; (ii) examine whether the area of water within the bay is larger or smaller than a semi-circle whose diameter is drawn between these points,[23] and; (iii) calculate the distance between the points.[24] Article 10 UNCLOS does not apply to 'historic bays'; that is, bays that are claimed to form part of a State's internal

[18] *Fisheries case* (United Kingdom v Norway) [1951] ICJ Rep 1951, para 116.

[19] ibid, para 128.

[20] Art 7(4) adds that '[s]traight baselines shall not be drawn to and from low-tide elevations, unless lighthouses or similar installations which are permanently above sea level have been built on them or except in instances where the drawing of baselines to and from such elevations has received general international recognition'. Art 7(5) accepts that 'economic interests peculiar to the region concerned' can be taken into account for purposes of employing straight baselines.

[21] Judgment of 9 July 1991, *Commission v United Kingdom*, C-146/89, ECLI:EU:C:1991:294.

[22] Note: this provision only applies to bays the coasts of which belong to a single State. On 'pluri-State' bays, see Art 15 UNCLOS and *Land, Island and Maritime Frontier Dispute* (El Salvador/Honduras v Nicaragua) [1992] ICJ Rep 351, para 395.

[23] Art 10(2) UNCLOS: 'An indentation shall not [...] be regarded as a bay unless its area is as large as, or larger than, that of the semi-circle whose diameter is a line drawn across the mouth of that indentation'.

[24] Art 10(4) UNCLOS: 'If the distance between the low-water marks of the natural entrance points of a bay does not exceed 24 NM, a closing line may be drawn between the two points, and the waters enclosed thereby shall be considered as internal waters'. In the alternative scenario, Art 10(5) UNCLOS provides that 'a straight baseline of 24 NM shall be drawn within the bay in such a manner as to enclose the maximum area of water that is possible with a line of that length'.

waters on the basis of long-standing claims and acquiescence by third States.[25] Waters enclosed by the archipelagic baselines of so-called 'archipelagic States'[26] are not regarded as internal waters, but as 'archipelagic waters' subject to the specific regime of Articles 49–54 UNCLOS (see also below, Section II(C)(v)).

B. Islands

The regime for islands deserves specific mention. Every 'island' is entitled to its own territorial sea, contiguous zone, exclusive economic zone and continental shelf, irrespective of its size, but '[r]ocks which cannot sustain human habitation or economic life of their own shall have no exclusive economic zone or continental shelf'.[27] Pursuant to Article 121(1) UNCLOS, an island is 'a naturally formed area of land, surrounded by water, which is above water at high tide'. An island's natural formation opposes it to artificial islands, eg resulting from land-reclamation activities around reefs that are submerged at least part of the time. The elevation above water at high tide distinguishes islands from low-tide elevations.[28]

C. Jurisdiction of the Coastal State

As mentioned above, the territorial sea falls under the sovereignty of the coastal State. It follows that the coastal State has exclusive control over the natural resources within the territorial sea, and that in principle the entire body of State law applies.

i. Right of Innocent Passage

The law of the sea nonetheless imposes important restrictions on the coastal State's powers in respect of its territorial sea. The fundamental point of departure is that vessels of all

[25] The concept of 'historic bays' has nonetheless given rise to controversy in the past, as in the case of the Libyan claim to the 'Gulf of Sirte'. For an overview of bays that are regarded as historic bays or are claimed to be so by the State concerned, see Secretariat of the UN, 'Historic Bays' (Memorandum), *Official Records of the United Nations Conference on the Law of the Sea, Volume I: Preparatory Documents*, UN Doc A/CONF.13/1, 3.

[26] Art 46(1) UNCLOS defines an archipelagic State as 'a State constituted wholly by one or more archipelagos[, which] may include other islands'. Art 46(2) specifies that an archipelago is 'a group of islands, including parts of islands, interconnecting waters and other natural features which are so closely interrelated that they form an intrinsic geographical, economic and political entity, or which have historically been regarded as such'. Art 47 UNCLOS nonetheless imposes certain restrictions on the drawing of 'archipelagic baselines' joining the outermost points of the outermost islands and drying reefs of the archipelago. The result is that archipelagic States that primarily consist of a few large islands (eg the UK) or that are composed of small and widely dispersed islands (eg Kiribati) cannot draw archipelagic baselines; MD Evans, 'The Law of the Sea' in MD Evans (ed), *International Law*, 4th edn (Oxford, OUP, 2014) 651, 656.

[27] Art 121(3) UNCLOS.

[28] One of the key questions the Philippines put before the Tribunal in the *South China Sea Arbitration* (n 3) was whether certain formations should be regarded as 'islands' or rather as rocks that cannot sustain human habitation or economic life. In its Award, the Tribunal elaborated at length on the interpretation of Art 121 UNCLOS (see in particular paras 475–553). With regard to China's land reclamation campaign, the Tribunal asserted that 'human modification cannot change the seabed into a low-tide elevation or a low-tide elevation into an island' (para 305), and 'that the status of a feature must be ascertained on the basis of its earlier, natural condition, prior to the onset of significant human modification' (para 306) (see again para 508).

States enjoy the long-established 'right of innocent passage'. This means that they are free to navigate through the territorial sea in a 'continuous and expeditious'[29] manner for the purpose of traversing that sea without entering the internal waters, or for the purpose of travelling to or from the internal waters (and/or calling a port).[30] Passage is deemed 'innocent' as long as it is 'not prejudicial to the peace, good order or security of the coastal State'.[31] Article 19(2) UNCLOS gives an exhaustive overview of activities that are not considered to be 'innocent'. Examples include, for instance, weapons exercises, espionage, propaganda activities, wilful and serious pollution, fishing activities and research or survey activities. Article 19(2)(l) contains a catch-all provision, referring to 'any other activity not having a direct bearing on passage'.

Vessels exercising their right of innocent passage are not exempt from the coastal State's legislation. At the same time, Article 21 UNCLOS makes clear that the coastal State may only legislate on certain issues, including inter alia: the safety of navigation and the regulation of maritime traffic, the protection of cables and pipelines, fisheries, pollution control, marine scientific research and customs, fiscal, immigration or sanitary matters. Legislation concerning the design, construction, manning or equipment of foreign ships is only permissible insofar as it gives effect to 'generally accepted international rules or standards',[32] that is, standards adopted under the auspices of the International Maritime Organization (IMO). The laws and regulations imposed by the coastal State may not be overly burdensome and must not erode the right of innocent passage.[33] Nor may they be discriminatory in nature.[34] The coastal State may take steps to prevent passage which is not innocent.[35] It may also temporarily suspend the innocent passage of foreign ships if such suspension is essential for the protection of its security and has been duly published.[36] Foreign vessels may not be levied charges merely for passing through the territorial sea, but only for specific services rendered to the ship.[37] UNCLOS contains indications that the right of innocent passage also extends to foreign warships, although State practice is not uniform on this subject and a number of coastal States (such as China)[38] require prior notification or even prior authorisation for such passage.[39] In any case, submarines travelling through the territorial sea must navigate on the surface and show their flag.[40] Warships and other government ships operated for non-commercial purposes enjoy immunity[41] and thus

[29] Still, Art 18(2) UNCLOS provides that ships may stop and anchor for purposes of ordinary navigation or when rendered necessary by force majeure or distress.

[30] Art 18 UNCLOS. Note: there exists no corresponding right of 'innocent overflight'. Aircraft can only traverse the airspace over the territorial sea if the coastal State has consented to that traverse.

[31] Art 19(1) UNCLOS.

[32] ibid, Art 21(2).

[33] ibid, Art 24(1)(a).

[34] ibid, Art 24(1)(b).

[35] ibid, Art 25(1).

[36] ibid, Art 25(3).

[37] ibid, Art 26.

[38] Art 6(2) of the People's Republic of China's Law on the Territorial Sea and the Contiguous Zone of 25 February 1992, promulgated by Order No 55 of the President of the People's Republic of China on 25 February 1992 and effective on the date of promulgation, provides that the entry of a foreign military ship into the territorial sea of China is subject to approval by the Chinese government.

[39] See eg WK Agyebeng, 'Theory in Search of Practice: The Right of Innocent Passage in the Territorial Sea' (2006) 39 *Cornell International Law Journal* 371.

[40] Art 20 UNCLOS.

[41] ibid, Art 32.

cannot be arrested when they are found breaching the laws and regulations of the coastal State.[42] The coastal State may nonetheless request such vessels to leave the territorial sea immediately.

ii. Enforcement Action against Foreign Ships

Articles 27 and 28 UNCLOS moreover impose important restrictions on the possibility for the coastal State to take enforcement action against foreign ships passing through its territorial sea. First, the coastal State should not exercise criminal jurisdiction vis-à-vis a foreign ship passing through the territorial sea in connection with any crime committed on board the ship during its passage, save in certain exceptional circumstances. In accordance with Article 27(1) UNCLOS, exercising criminal jurisdiction is permissible only: (i) when the consequences of the crime extend to the coastal State; (ii) when the crime was of a kind to disturb the peace of the country or the good order of the territorial sea; (iii) when assistance was requested by the master of the ship or by the flag State; or (iv) in respect of illicit traffic in drugs. These restrictions do not apply in relation to a vessel that has just left the State's internal waters. Conversely, the coastal State in principle cannot exercise criminal jurisdiction in respect of crimes committed before a ship entered its territorial sea.[43]

Article 28 UNCLOS deals with the exercise of civil jurisdiction. The thrust of the provision is that the coastal State should not stop or divert a vessel to exercise civil jurisdiction in relation to a person on board the ship, but only in respect of the activities of the vessel itself. However, if the ship is passing through the territorial sea after leaving internal waters, civil jurisdiction may be exercised under Article 28(3) UNCLOS.

iii. Jurisdiction over Internal Waters

The aforementioned restrictions do not apply in respect of the coastal State's internal waters (as defined above), including its ports. Coastal States are indeed free to regulate, restrict and even exclude entry of their internal waters. States are not legally obliged to grant vessels a right of entry into their ports,[44] albeit that: (i) such a right is sometimes enshrined in bilateral or multilateral treaties;[45] and (ii) it can be presumed that the ports of the coastal State are normally open to merchant vessels unless otherwise provided.[46] Once a foreign vessel is within the coastal State's internal waters it is as such subject to that State's domestic legislation, which can moreover be enforced against it. Considering foreign vessels' temporary presence and the legal competences of the flag State,[47] coastal States generally exercise restraint in respect of acts on board foreign vessels within their ports. At the same time, States will sometimes prevent vessels from entering or leaving their ports due to non-compliance with minimum safety, health or environmental standards. Such exercise of 'port state control' has grown out of dissatisfaction with some flag States' failure

[42] In accordance with general international law, a warship also enjoys immunity within the internal waters of another State. See eg *"Ara Libertad"* (Argentina v Ghana) [2012] ITLOS Rep 332, para 95.
[43] Art 27(5) UNCLOS.
[44] eg MD Fink, 'Naval Blockade and the Humanitarian Crisis in Yemen' (2017) 64 *NILR* 291, 301.
[45] See eg Art XIX(2) of the Treaty of Friendship, Commerce and Navigation concluded between the Netherlands and the United States (adopted 27 March 1956, entered into force 5 December 1957) 285 UNTS 232.
[46] Y Tanaka, *The International Law of the Sea*, 2nd edn (Cambridge, CUP, 2012) 80–81.
[47] On the competences of the flag State, see below, throughout the different sections.

to properly ensure that vessels carrying their flag meet minimum international standards (see below, Section V(C)).

iv. *Transit Passage*

One of the consequences of the extension of the territorial sea from the traditional three-mile-limit to 12 NM has been that many major international waterways, such as the Strait of Dover, where the freedom of navigation traditionally applied, were swallowed up by the territorial seas of the respective coastal State(s). Given their importance for trade, but also for military purposes, it was agreed to further curtail the ability of the coastal State(s) to restrict passage in these straits. Articles 37–44 UNCLOS effectively introduce a more flexible regime of 'transit passage' (exclusively) in respect of 'straits which are used for international navigation between one part of the high seas or an exclusive economic zone and another part of the high seas or an exclusive economic zone'. The regime of transit passage is different from the ordinary regime of innocent passage in that: (i) it applies to vessels as well as to aircraft; (ii) submarines are not required to navigate on the surface; (iii) it cannot be temporarily suspended; and (iv) coastal States have less leeway to regulate activities within these straits.[48] It does not apply: (1) if there is a convenient route through the strait itself, which is not covered by territorial sea;[49] (2) if there exists another convenient alternative route through the high seas or through an exclusive economic zone;[50] or (3) if the strait is governed by a particular treaty regime (as is the case, for instance, for the Dardanelles and the Bosphorus).[51]

Straits used for international navigation that do not fall within the scope of the transit passage regime, are covered by the normal rules on innocent passage as discussed above (Section II(C)(i)). The sole difference with the normal regime is that the coastal State cannot suspend innocent passage through such straits.[52]

v. *Archipelagic Waters*

Finally, the rules on innocent passage also apply *mutatis mutandis* to 'archipelagic waters'.[53] Nonetheless, Article 53(1) UNCLOS provides that 'an archipelagic State may designate sea lanes and air routes thereabove, suitable for the continuous and expeditious passage of foreign ships and aircraft through or over its archipelagic waters and the adjacent territorial sea' in which 'all ships and aircraft enjoy the right of archipelagic sea lane passage'.[54] This type of passage is comparable to transit passage (it also applies to aircraft, for instance). If the coastal State does not designate sea lanes or air routes in which this type of passage applies, archipelagic sea lane passage may be exercised throughout 'the routes normally used for international navigation'.[55]

[48] Compare the list in Art 42 (transit passage) to the list in Art 21 UNCLOS (innocent passage).
[49] Art 36 UNCLOS.
[50] ibid, Art 38(1).
[51] ibid, Art 35(c).
[52] ibid, Art 45. This prohibition was affirmed in *Corfu Channel* (Albania v United Kingdom) [1949] ICJ Rep 4, 28.
[53] As defined above (n 26); Art 52 UNCLOS. Note: Art 52(2) UNCLOS similarly acknowledges the possibility to temporarily suspend innocent passage if essential for the protection of the coastal State's security and after due publication.
[54] Art 53(2) UNCLOS.
[55] ibid, Art 53(12).

D. The Contiguous Zone

In order to facilitate the enforcement by the coastal State of the laws and regulations applicable in its territorial sea, Article 33 UNCLOS – like Article 24 of the 1958 Territorial Sea Convention[56] – provides for a separate zone where the coastal State has a limited degree of functional jurisdiction. Mainly to prevent vessels that commit offences in the territorial sea from escaping arrest simply by moving (just) outside this zone, the provision foresees that coastal States can establish a so-called 'contiguous zone'. This zone is adjacent to the territorial sea and can stretch up to 24 NM from the baselines (irrespective of the breadth of the territorial sea).[57]

Within this zone, the coastal State can take action to 'prevent' and 'punish' infringements of the laws and regulations applicable in its territorial sea.[58] The implication is that the coastal State can prevent a vessel from entering its territorial sea when it has (credible) reasons to believe that a breach will be committed. Conversely, when a breach has been committed within the territorial sea, the vessel may be arrested within the contiguous zone.

Still, a number of restrictions apply. First, enforcement action is limited to actual or impending breaches of the coastal State's customs, fiscal, immigration or sanitary laws and regulations.[59] Second, enforcement action is excluded vis-à-vis vessels that merely traverse the contiguous zone, without entering, or having entered, the territorial sea. Third, the contiguous zone must be 'declared' by the coastal State. Considering the usefulness of this regime, numerous coastal States – including several European States – have done so.[60]

III. The Continental Shelf

A. Geographical and Legal Concept

As mentioned at the outset, the law of the sea traditionally distinguished between two zones only: the territorial sea and the high seas. This simple dichotomy has long been changed by the creation of new zones, chiefly the continental shelf and the exclusive economic zone, in respect of which States enjoy a certain circumscribed 'functional jurisdiction'. It must be kept in mind that the legal regime applicable to these zones differs substantially from

[56] See above (n 5).

[57] This was only 12 NM under Art 24 of the 1958 Territorial Sea Convention (n 5). Note: the contiguous zone does not extend to the airspace over these waters.

[58] See respectively Art 33(1)(a) and 33(1)(b) UNCLOS.

[59] ibid.

[60] Contiguous zones have been declared (in various terms, eg sometimes limited to customs matters only) by Belgium, Bulgaria, Cyprus, Denmark, Finland (but only 14 NM), France, Ireland, Italy, Malta, Netherlands, Norway, Portugal, Romania, the Russian Federation, Spain and Lithuania. By contrast, no such declaration has been issued by Albania, Bosnia-Herzegovina, Croatia, Estonia, Germany, Greece, Iceland, Latvia, Monaco, Montenegro, Poland, Slovenia, Sweden, Ukraine or the UK. See the US Navy Judge Advocate General's Corps' 'Maritime Claims Reference Manual' and UN Office of Legal Affairs' 'Table of Claims to Maritime Jurisdiction' (n 16).

that of the territorial sea. Indeed, the territorial sea is subject to the full sovereign prerogatives of the coastal State, save insofar as the law of the sea restricts these. In respect of the different zones where coastal States enjoy a more limited functional jurisdiction, the point of departure is exactly the opposite. These zones are in principle governed by the different freedoms of the high seas (see below, Section V), or by the common heritage of mankind regime applicable to the deep seabed (see below, Section VI), save insofar as the law of the sea grants the coastal State specific and exclusive rights.

The continental shelf is first and foremost a geological concept. It refers to the 'natural prolongation'[61] of the gently sloping seabed off a coast (the continental margin), where the waters are relatively shallow, until there is a steep incline (the continental slope) and the seabed plunges to great depths (the 'abyssal plain'). The continental shelf is in other words considered to be geographically part of the continent, as opposed to the deep seabed. The depth of the continental shelf ranges from 50 to 550 metres (compared to a maximum-known depth of the deep seabed of 10.9 km below sea level). The width of the continental shelf varies remarkably. In some parts of the world, the geological continental shelf has a width of only a few miles off the coast. In other parts of the world it extends up to several hundreds of miles. The North Sea mainly consists of continental shelf, while the same is not true for the Mediterranean Sea.

The concept of the continental shelf acquired a second, somewhat distinct, legal connotation as of the 1940s, as improvements in technology made it possible and economically viable to exploit the vast oil and gas reserves in the (geological) continental shelf. The main catalyst in this context was the promulgation in 1945 of the 'Truman Proclamation', in which the United States declared that it regarded 'the natural resources of the subsoil and seabed of the continental shelf [...] contiguous to the coasts of the US as appertaining to the US, subject to its jurisdiction and control'.[62] The Truman Proclamation proved to establish an attractive precedent and generated a snowball effect. Numerous States (Arab, Latin-American and other) quickly followed, similarly asserting claims over the resources of the seabed and subsoil of the continental shelf, without necessarily calling into question the freedom of fishing in the water columns above. The idea of a legal 'continental shelf' over which the coastal State retained resource jurisdiction was born. It was formally adopted in the 1958 Continental Shelf Convention,[63] and subsequently included in UNCLOS.

B. Entitlement to a Continental Shelf

Article 76 UNCLOS now provides that coastal States are automatically entitled to a 'legal' continental shelf of 200 NM from the baseline, even if the 'geological' continental shelf is (far) less wide. If the geological continental shelf extends beyond 200 NM, States can lay claim to this continental shelf up to the outer edge of the continental margin. In the latter case, States must choose to apply one of the limits provided for in Article 76(5) UNCLOS: (i) either the continental shelf cannot extend beyond 350 NM from the baseline; (ii) or it cannot extend more than 100 NM from the point at which the depth of the water reaches

[61] *North Sea Continental Shelf cases* (Germany v Denmark and the Netherlands) [1969] ICJ Rep 3, para 19.

[62] US President Harry Truman, Proclamation 2667: 'Policy of the United States with respect to the Natural Resources of the Subsoil and Sea Bed of the Continental Shelf', 28 September 1945.

[63] See above (n 7).

2,500 metres. Furthermore, where States wish to claim a continental shelf of more than 200 NM, they must provide detailed information to the Commission on the Limits of the Continental Shelf (CLCS) in accordance with Article 76(8) UNCLOS. The Commission will then make recommendations on the basis of which the coastal State shall establish the final boundary.[64] As already mentioned above (Section II(B)), naturally formed islands are also entitled to a continental shelf.

C. Legal Regime

Articles 77–81 UNCLOS sum up the rights of the coastal State with regard to the continental shelf. First and foremost, the coastal State exercises sovereign rights for the purposes of exploring it and exploiting its natural resources. This rule extends to the non-living resources of the seabed and subsoil as well as sedentary species living on the seabed. The coastal State also has the exclusive right to authorise and regulate artificial islands, installations and other structures on the continental shelf[65] and drilling.[66] Even where the coastal State does not make use of these rights, other States are prevented from undertaking these activities without the consent of the coastal State.[67] Pursuant to Article 82 UNCLOS, exploitation beyond the fixed 200 NM limit is nonetheless subject to the coastal State making 'payments or contributions in kind' to the International Seabed Authority (on this institution, see below, Section VI(B)).[68] Moreover, all States remain entitled to lay submarine cables and pipelines on the continental shelf, subject to certain conditions.[69]

The CJEU has on repeated occasions affirmed that work carried out on fixed or floating installations (such as gas-drilling platforms) positioned on the continental shelf in the context of the prospection and/or exploitation of natural resources is to be regarded as work carried out in the territory of that State for the purposes of applying EU law.[70] Notably, this implies that the EU law provisions on free movement apply in respect thereof.[71]

The regime concerning the continental shelf does not affect the legal status of the superjacent (overlying) waters. These waters will normally form part of the high seas or of the

[64] Art 4 Annex II UNCLOS originally decreed that States should submit their detailed claims to the CLCS within a period of 10 years following the entry into force of the Convention (in respect of the State concerned). This deadline has been postponed to the fixed date of 13 May 2009 for those States for whom the ten-year limit would previously have expired; UNCLOS Meeting of States Parties, 'Decision regarding the date of commencement of the ten-year period for making submissions to the Commission on the Limits of the Continental Shelf set out in article 4 of Annex II to the United Nations Convention on the Law of the Sea', 29 May 2001, UN Doc SPLOS/72. As of 26 October 2017, the Commission had received 78 submissions and had issued 29 recommendations (the full content of which is not made public); UN Division for Ocean Affairs and the Law of the Sea, 'Submissions, through the Secretary-General of the United Nations, to the Commission on the Limits of the Continental Shelf, pursuant to article 76, paragraph 8, of the United Nations Convention on the Law of the Sea of 10 December 1982', un.org/depts/los/clcs_new/commission_submissions.htm.

[65] Art 80 UNCLOS, referring to the rules applicable in the exclusive economic zone (on which see below, Section IV).

[66] ibid, Art 81. This does not, however, prejudice the right of coastal States to exploit the subsoil by means of tunnelling (ibid, Art 85).

[67] ibid, Art 77(2).

[68] See International Seabed Authority, 'Implementation of Article 82 of the United Nations Convention on the Law of the Sea', ISA Technical Study No 12, 2013, isa.org.jm/files/documents/EN/Pubs/TS12-web.pdf.

[69] ibid, Art 79.

[70] Judgment of 27 February 2002, *Weber*, C-37/00, ECLI:EU:C:2002:122, para 36; judgment of 17 January 2012, *Salemink*, C-347/10, ECLI:EU:C:2012:17, para 35.

[71] *Salemink* (n 70), para 36.

exclusive economic zone, depending on whether or not the coastal State has declared such a zone (see below, Section IV).

IV. The Exclusive Economic Zone

A. Origins

While the emergence of the continental shelf doctrine in the 1940s helped coastal States secure their claims to the resources of the seabed and subsoil off their coast, several States soon started pressing for similar recognition of preferential access to the fish stocks lying beyond their territorial sea. An important factor was the desire of developing countries to control and preserve their fish stocks in the face of growing operations by extra-regional fishing fleets (often from developed countries). Against this background, States not only claimed control over the resources of the seabed and subsoil (see above, Section III(A)), but also began establishing so-called 'exclusive fishing zones', in which they claimed exclusive jurisdiction over fisheries. The permissibility of such exclusive fishing zones gradually received broad recognition, and was recognised as a customary rule by the ICJ.[72]

In the 1960s and 1970s several States eventually began to advance claims asserting resource jurisdiction encompassing both the natural resources of the seabed and subsoil, as well as the superjacent waters in a zone of 200 NM in breadth. This idea received widespread support in the course of the Third UN Law of the Sea Conference, where it was decided that coastal States could establish a so-called exclusive economic zone (EEZ) of up to a distance of 200 NM from their baseline. Again, naturally formed islands are also entitled to their own EEZ (see above, Section II(B)). This explains why France and the United Kingdom – both of which control several overseas territories (*territoires outre mer*) – rank among the States with the largest EEZ, and why a small island State like Kiribati controls the twelfth largest EEZ in the world.

It needs to be observed that even if UNCLOS contains no reference to it, States are still permitted under customary international law to establish 'Exclusive Fishing Zones' up to 200 NM (covering only the water columns). A number of States still apply exclusive fishing zones, although these zones mostly overlap in their entirety with a co-existing EEZ. One of the few exceptions is Malta, which has established a 25 NM exclusive fishing zone, without having declared a (broader) EEZ.[73]

B. Relation with the Continental Shelf

The EEZ regime is different from that governing the continental shelf in the sense that coastal States can only benefit from it if they effectively claim an EEZ (and only for the distance claimed). Should all coastal States claim a 200 NM EEZ – as most have indeed

[72] *Fisheries Jurisdiction* (United Kingdom v Iceland) [1974] ICJ Rep 3, 23–31; *Maritime Delimitation in the Area between Greenland and Jan Mayen* (Denmark v Norway) [1993] ICJ Rep 38, throughout the judgment (paras 41–94).

[73] See the US Navy Judge Advocate General's Corps' 'Maritime Claims Reference Manual' (n 16) concerning Malta, as of May 2014: jag.navy.mil/organization/documents/mcrm/Malta2014.pdf.

done – these zones would cover approximately a third of all sea surface, and cover the lion's share of all commercially exploitable fish stocks.

Another obvious difference between the EEZ and the continental shelf is that the latter grants the coastal State jurisdiction over the natural resources of the seabed and subsoil only, whereas the former also covers the superjacent water columns. Article 56(1)(a) UNCLOS grants the coastal State 'sovereign rights for the purpose of exploring and exploiting, conserving and managing the natural resources, whether living or non-living', of the waters, the seabed and the subsoil of the EEZ. The coastal State can determine, for instance, who is allowed to fish in its EEZ and subject to what conditions (in terms of licence fees, species, quotas, fishing seasons and areas). This is indeed the core feature of EEZ jurisdiction. It follows that there is an important overlap between the jurisdictional regimes governing the EEZ and the continental shelf. For a coastal State that has declared a 200 NM EEZ, the continental shelf regime becomes redundant. For such a State, the rules concerning the continental shelf will be of added value only inasmuch as the State claims (and can validly claim) a continental shelf beyond the 200 NM width (see above, Section III(B)).

C. Further Legal Regime

The EEZ regime moreover provides for a number of additional rights on the part of the coastal State. Article 56(1) UNCLOS, for instance, refers to 'other activities for the economic exploitation and exploration of the zone, such as the production of energy from the water, currents and winds'.[74] The provision also grants the coastal State jurisdiction 'with regard to (i) the establishment and use of artificial islands, installations and structures; (ii) marine scientific research; [and] (iii) the protection and preservation of the marine environment'.[75] As far as artificial islands and related installations are concerned, Article 60 UNCLOS sets out that such installations must not be established where they would interfere with the navigation in recognised sea lanes.[76] The coastal State must give due notice of the construction of these installations and can establish safety zones not exceeding 500 metres around them.[77]

Except insofar as UNCLOS grants specific rights to the coastal State, the freedoms of the high seas (see below, Section V(A)) apply *mutatis mutandis* to the EEZ. Thus, Article 58 UNCLOS affirms that all States enjoy freedom of navigation and freedom of overflight in the EEZ. Third States moreover enjoy the right to install submarine cables and pipelines and engage in related activities in accordance with the general framework for the high seas. Article 58(3) UNCLOS does recall in general terms that third States shall have due regard to the rights and duties of the coastal State and comply with the provision of the Convention and other relevant rules of international law.

[74] Art 56(1)(a) UNCLOS.

[75] ibid, Art 56(1)(b).

[76] This provision also applies where a coastal State has not declared an EEZ but wishes to construe artificial islands or related installations on its continental shelf (ibid, Art 80).

[77] In the *Arctic Sunrise* case, the Arbitral Tribunal rejected the Dutch claim that Russia had breached Art 60 UNCLOS by establishing a three-nautical mile safety zone around the *Prirazlomnaya* offshore oil platform in Russia's EEZ. According to the Tribunal, the contested Russian notice to mariners merely served as an encouragement to ships to communicate with the platform in an effort to reduce the risk of collision or any other accident. The notice could not by contrast in and of itself create a safety zone in the sense of Art 60 UNCLOS; *Arctic Sunrise Arbitration* (Netherlands v Russia), Award of 14 August 2015, PCA Case No 2014-02, paras 202–20.

Coastal States can engage in enforcement action (including by boarding, inspecting and arresting vessels in their EEZ), but only in relation to activities for which the Convention grants them jurisdiction. Article 73 UNCLOS makes clear that penalties for violations of fishery laws and regulations in the EEZ may normally not include imprisonment or any other form of corporal punishment. It moreover states that arrested vessels and their crews shall be 'promptly released' upon the posting of a reasonable bond or security, and that the vessels' flag State be notified of any action taken.

Occasionally, discussion arises as to what activities not explicitly addressed by UNCLOS are permitted or forbidden in the EEZ, and whether or not coastal States – which sometimes seem to flirt with the outer limits of coastal State jurisdiction[78] – can take enforcement action. Article 59 UNCLOS merely provides that in cases where the Convention does not attribute rights or jurisdiction to the coastal State or to other States in the EEZ, conflicts should be resolved 'on the basis of equity and in the light of all the relevant circumstances, taking into account the respective importance of the interests involved to the parties as well as to the international community as a whole'.

Clearly, this provision does not offer much guidance. A number of issues have in the meantime been clarified in case law. Thus, in the 1986 *Franco-Canadian Fisheries Arbitration*, the Tribunal took the view that a vessel engaged in processing fish at sea fell outside the range of activities over which the coastal State could exercise (and enforce) jurisdiction.[79] Conversely, in the *Virginia G* case, the International Tribunal for the Law of the Sea (ITLOS) held that the bunkering of foreign vessels engaged in fishing in the EEZ is an activity that coastal States may regulate,[80] an issue that was previously left unanswered in the *M/V SAIGA* case.[81] Furthermore, in the *Arctic Sunrise* Award, concerning Russia's arrest of a *Greenpeace* vessel staging protests at an offshore oil platform in Russia's EEZ, the Arbitral Tribunal found that a coastal State should tolerate some level of nuisance through civilian protest as long as it does not amount to an 'interference with the exercise of its sovereign rights'.[82]

At the same time, there still exists controversy on the extent to which freedom of navigation in the EEZ extends to certain military activities, such as military exercises or surveillance activities.[83] A considerable group of (developed) States, most notably including

[78] See B Oxman, 'The Territorial Temptation: A Siren Song at Sea' (2006) 100 *AJIL* 830.

[79] *Franco-Canadian Fisheries Arbitration*, Award of 17 July 1986, as reprinted in (1986) 90 *Revue générale de droit international public* 713.

[80] *M/V 'Virginia G'* (Panama v Guinea-Bissau) [2014] ITLOS Rep 4, paras 223–24. ITLOS nonetheless held that '[t]he coastal State, however, does not have such competence with regard to other bunkering activities, unless otherwise determined in accordance with the Convention' (para 223).

[81] *M/V 'SAIGA' (No 2)* (Saint Vincent and the Grenadines v Guinea) [1999] ITLOS Rep 10. ITLOS found that Guinea could not rely on grounds of 'public interest' or 'necessity' to justify the creation of a customs radius including parts of its EEZ and, more specifically, to justify enforcement action against a foreign bunkering vessel supplying gas oil to fishing vessels in its EEZ (paras 116–38). The Tribunal nonetheless refrained from determining whether bunkering in the EEZ constituted a lawful application of the freedom of navigation in the EEZ, or rather an unlawful activity harming the (fiscal) interests of the coastal State.

[82] *Arctic Sunrise Arbitration* (n 77) paras 328–30. Note: the Tribunal did acknowledge that the Greenpeace protesters may have breached the coastal State laws applicable to the artificial island concerned, but found that the arrest of the vessel was carried out in disregard of the hot pursuit requirements of Art 111 UNCLOS (ibid, paras 242–75).

[83] See eg R Pedrozo, 'Preserving Navigational Rights and Freedoms: The Right to Conduct Military Activities in China's Exclusive Economic Zone' (2010) 9 *CJIL* 9; Z Haiwen, 'Is It Safeguarding the Freedom of Navigation or Maritime Hegemony of the United States? – Comments on R Pedrozo's Article on Military Activities in the EEZ' (2010) 9 *CJIL* 31; E Franckx, 'American and Chinese Views on Navigational Rights of Warships' (2011) 10 *CJIL* 187; H Heintschel von Heinegg, 'Military Activities in the Exclusive Economic Zone' (2014) 47 *Revue belge de droit international* 45.

the United States, relies inter alia on the preparatory works of UNCLOS to claim that the aforementioned acts are normally lawful (ie as long as they do not give rise, eg, to a threat or use of force or a breach of the non-intervention principle).[84] This position is challenged by a number of other (developing) States, including China.

V. The High Seas

A. Freedoms of the High Seas

The 'high seas' are negatively defined as covering all parts of the sea that are not included in the EEZ, in the territorial sea or in the internal waters of a State, or in the archipelagic waters of an archipelagic State.[85] In accordance with long-established customary international law, UNCLOS affirms that the high seas are a *res communis* 'open to all States, whether coastal or land-locked'.[86] No State may validly purport to subject any part of the high seas to its sovereignty.[87] Accordingly, Article 87(1) UNCLOS articulates six freedoms of the high seas: (a) freedom of navigation; (b) freedom of overflight; (c) freedom to lay submarine cables and pipelines; (d) freedom to construct artificial islands and other installations permitted under international law; (e) freedom of fishing; and (f) freedom of scientific research.

The Convention imposes several general as well as specific limitations on the exercise of the aforementioned freedoms. In general terms, the six freedoms must be exercised in a peaceful manner,[88] and 'with due regard for the interests of other States'[89] (this excludes, for instance, the use of long fishing nets over busy shipping routes). Further, all freedoms are subject to specific limitations. While UNCLOS does not impose particular restrictions on the freedom of navigation of the high seas, subsequent practice has developed certain limitations on that freedom. Thus, to promote the safety of shipping and the cleanliness of oceans, the IMO adopts 'routeing measures' that control the navigation of vessels and monitor their progress.[90]

The freedom of overflight, in turn, does not prevent coastal States from establishing additional zones of aerial control beyond their territorial airspace in which approaching aircraft are required to identify themselves and provide certain information.[91] Such 'air defence identification zones' (ADIZ), inspired by national security concerns, have indeed been established by several States (most overlap with (part of) the coastal State's EEZ). The establishment in late 2013 of a Chinese ADIZ in the East China Sea nonetheless gave rise

[84] The US regularly asserts its position by engaging in so-called 'freedom of navigation' (FON) operations, including in the South China Sea. The US Department of Defense keeps annual records of naval operations that are aimed at challenging what the US regards as excessive maritime claims. See US Department of Defense, 'DoD Annual Freedom of Navigation (FON) Reports', policy.defense.gov/OUSDP-Offices/FON/.

[85] Art 86 UNCLOS.

[86] ibid, Art 87(1).

[87] ibid, Art 89.

[88] ibid, Art 88.

[89] ibid, Art 87(2).

[90] See further IMO, *Ship's Routeing, 2017 Edition* (London, IMO Publishing, 2017).

[91] See in particular PA Dutton, 'Caelum Liberam: Air Defense Identification Zones Outside Sovereign Airspace' (2009) 103 *AJIL* 1; J Odom, 'A "Rules-based Approach" to Airspace Defense: A U.S. Perspective on

to considerable controversy, with several States asserting that ADIZ requirements can only be imposed on aircraft flying to or from the coastal State, and that forcible interception of non-compliant aircraft is only permitted in accordance with the right of self-defence.[92]

The freedom to construct artificial islands and to lay submarine cables and pipelines is limited by the relevant articles of Part VI, governing (activities on) the continental shelf. The freedom of fishing is subject to the provisions of Part VII, Section 2 UNCLOS, which provides that States must cooperate for the conservation and management of the living resources of the high seas (see below, Section VIII(A)). Moreover, on the high seas, there is no corollary to the freedom of fishing allowing for the free exploration and exploitation of the seabed. Such activities are governed by the separate regime concerning 'the Area', laid down in Part XI of the Convention (see below, Section VI). The freedom of scientific research, lastly, is subjected to further limitations in Part XIII UNCLOS on 'marine scientific research'.

B. Exclusive Jurisdiction of the Flag State

The key to regulating activities in the high seas is the concept of flag State jurisdiction.[93] Article 90 UNCLOS confirms that every State, whether coastal or land-locked,[94] has the right to sail ships flying its flag on the high seas. Ships must sail under the flag of one State only and are, save for exceptional cases (see below, Subsection (E)), subject to that State's exclusive jurisdiction on the high seas,[95] as was confirmed by the PCIJ in the *Lotus* case.[96] To this end, each State shall fix the conditions for the grant of 'nationality' to ships and for the right to fly its flag.[97] Vessels are subject to the exclusive legislative and enforcement jurisdiction of their flag State, at least while within its territorial sea or EEZ, or while on the high seas (ie when not in the territorial sea or EEZ of another State, in which case they also fall within the jurisdiction of the coastal State). Thus, in matters of collision or any other incident of navigation on the high seas, only the flag State can order the arrest or detention of a ship.[98] When a ship flies multiple flags, or flies no flag at all, all States can take enforcement action against it while on the high seas.[99] Yet, judicial practice makes clear that the alleged

the International Law of the Sea and Airspace, Air Defence Measures, and the Freedom of Navigation' (2014) 47 *Revue belge de droit international* 65.

[92] See eg T Ruys, 'Digest of State Practice – 1 July – 31 December 2013' (2014) 1 *Journal on the Use of Force and International Law* 149, 162–66.

[93] Evans (n 26) 665.

[94] Land-locked States also have a right of access to and from the sea for purposes of exercising the freedom of the high seas. To this end, Art 125(1) UNCLOS provides that they shall enjoy freedom of transit through the territory of transit States by all means of transport. Pursuant to Art 125(2) UNCLOS, the terms and modalities for exercising freedom of transit shall be agreed between the land-locked States and transit States concerned through bilateral, subregional or regional agreements. Transit States cannot, however, arbitrarily deny the freedom of transit of land-locked States. See further L Caflisch, 'Land-locked States and Their Access to and From the Sea' (1978) 49 *BYIL* 71.

[95] Art 92(1) UNCLOS.

[96] *SS Lotus* (France v Turkey) [1927] PCIJ Series A, No 10, 25.

[97] Art 91 UNCLOS.

[98] ibid, Art 97. The provision does acknowledge that penal or disciplinary proceedings may be instituted against individual persons not only by the vessel's flag State, but also by the State of which the person concerned is a national. This (restrictive) position considerably differs from the flexible position set forth by the PCIJ in the *Lotus* case (n 96).

[99] Art 92(2) UNCLOS.

(or actual) absence of a 'genuine link' between the ship and its flag State cannot be invoked to qualify the vessel as being 'stateless' and subject to the jurisdiction of all States.[100]

Even so, a flag State not only holds certain (exclusive) prerogatives in respect of vessels flying its flag but also a number of concomitant responsibilities. Article 94 UNCLOS enumerates several duties of the flag State. Flag States must maintain shipping registers and assume jurisdiction over vessels carrying their flag 'in respect of administrative, technical and social matters'.[101] They must take measures to ensure the seaworthiness of ships and to ensure that the master and officers of the ship possess appropriate qualifications, and they must do so in conformity with generally accepted regulations, procedures and practices.[102] Flag States must conduct investigations with respect to a specific vessel whenever a third State signals an issue. They must also hold an inquiry in cases of marine casualties or navigation incidents. Finally, they must require the masters of ships flying their flag to render assistance to persons or vessels in distress (eg when a collision has taken place).

C. Flags of Convenience

The problem is that many States simply do not have the capacity (if only because the vessels never enter their ports) or the will to properly impose and enforce their laws and/or generally accepted minimum standards in respect of vessels flying their flag. In particular, it is well-known that several States apply more 'attractive' requirements regarding fiscal matters or minimum labour standards, regarding the construction, equipment or seaworthiness of vessels, or regarding environmental standards. Such 'flags of convenience' (also called 'open registries') are attractive for ship-owners because they allow them to reduce operations costs and avoid more stringent regulations. The State, for its part, benefits from receiving registry fees and annual fees.

It is accordingly no coincidence that over half of the world's fleet flies the flag of only a handful of smaller States, such as Panama, Liberia, the Marshall Islands, the Bahamas, Malta and Cyprus. Neither is it a coincidence that many naval incidents concern vessels flying flags of convenience (consider eg the massive oil spill caused by the Liberian-flagged tanker *Amoco Cadiz* which ran aground off the coast of France in 1978), or that vessels engaged in 'illegal, unreported and unregulated' (IUU) fishing often fly such flags. In 1986, the UN Registration Convention on Conditions for Registrations of Ships[103] was adopted to tighten the requirement of a genuine link between a flag State and 'its' vessels by elaborating a number of obligations for flag States. The Convention has, however, been ratified by only a small number of States and has not yet entered into force. 'Flag of convenience' States may moreover have little incentive to accede to the Convention.

In the *Poulsen* case,[104] the CJEU affirmed the legality of such 'flags of convenience', entailing that a vessel can be registered in a State and have the nationality of that State, even though the owners of the ship have no genuine link with that State. Mr Poulsen, master

[100] See eg *M/V 'SAIGA' (No 2)* (n 81) paras 102–18; *M/V 'Virginia G'* (n 80) paras 110 and 113.
[101] Art 94(2) UNCLOS.
[102] See in this context IMO Assembly, 'Code for the Implementation of Mandatory IMO Instruments, 2011', 20 December 2011, A 27/Res.1054(27). On the meaning of the phrase 'generally accepted', see GK Walker (ed), *Definitions for the Law of the Sea – Terms Not Defined by the 1982 Convention* (Leiden, Nijhoff, 2012) 92–97.
[103] UN Registration Convention on Conditions for Registrations of Ships (adopted 7 February 1986, not yet entered into force) 26 ILM 1229.
[104] Judgment of 24 November 1992, *Poulsen*, C-286/90, ECLI:EU:C:1992:453.

of the *Onkel Sam*, was being prosecuted in Denmark on charges that the vessel had transported and stored on board salmon caught in the North Atlantic in contravention of an EU Regulation laying down technical measures for the conservation of fishery resources. The company that owned the vessel was registered in Panama, and the vessel was registered in Panama and flew the Panamanian flag. The master and crew were Danish, and the vessel was normally berthed in Denmark between voyages. The Court confirmed that, pursuant to the relevant law of the sea conventions, a vessel in principle has only one nationality, which must be respected by third States even if the sole link between a vessel and the State of which it holds the nationality is the administrative formality of registration, and the vessel allegedly has a genuine link with an(other) EU Member State.[105]

In a similar vein, the CJEU confirmed that the law governing the crew's activities depends on the State in which a vessel is registered, rather than the nationality of the crew members.[106] The Court held that EU legislation could not be applied against a vessel exercising its freedom of navigation in the EEZ of a Member State, nor in respect of a vessel exercising its right of innocent passage in the territorial waters of a Member State. Only when the vessel sails in the inland waters or, more particularly, is in a port of a Member State, does it become 'generally subject to the unlimited jurisdiction of that State'.[107]

If the CJEU in *Poulsen* accepted that international law essentially grants absolute discretion to States to determine the conditions on which they would grant nationality to vessels,[108] it follows from the *Factortame* case[109] that, as far as EU Member States are concerned, this discretion is nonetheless curtailed by relevant EU law. *In casu*, the UK had altered the conditions for registration of vessels through the Merchant Shipping Act 1988 in order to prevent its fishing quotas from being 'plundered' by vessels flying the British flag but lacking any genuine link with the United Kingdom.[110] The UK defended its action, arguing that under customary international law there had to be a 'genuine link' between a State and a vessel flying its flag.[111] The Court responded that, while the UK was entitled to require a 'genuine link' between the registering State and the vessel, in accordance with international law, this did not absolve the UK from its obligations under EU law, including freedom of establishment.[112] A requirement that the owners of the vessel should have the nationality of the Member State was deemed contrary to the freedom of establishment.[113] The requirement according to which the vessel ought to be managed and its operations directed and controlled from within the Member State concerned was not.[114]

In reaction to the failure of flag States to properly exercise jurisdiction over vessels flying their flag, (other) States have developed alternative mechanisms, involving the exercise of 'port State jurisdiction' and 'port State control'. In addition, UNCLOS contains several exceptions to the principle that only the flag State can take enforcement action in respect of a vessel on the high seas. Several other treaties have moreover contributed to the

[105] ibid, paras 13–16.
[106] ibid, paras 18–20.
[107] ibid, para 28.
[108] ibid, para 15.
[109] Judgment of 25 July 1991, *Factortame and others ('Factortame II')*, C-221/89, ECLI:EU:C:1991:320.
[110] ibid, para 4.
[111] ibid, para 15.
[112] ibid, para 23.
[113] ibid, para 30.
[114] ibid, para 36.

gradual erosion of the exclusive jurisdiction of the flag State. Subsection (D) first looks at the concepts of port State jurisdiction and port State control, after which Subsection (E) examines the exceptions to the exclusive jurisdiction of the flag State on the high seas.

D. Port State Jurisdiction and Port State Control

States can exceptionally exercise jurisdiction in respect of past activities by foreign vessels on the high seas, insofar as such vessels voluntarily find themselves within their ports. Although port State jurisdiction and control have grown in importance for the enforcement of various international rules and standards (from fisheries to ship safety standards), UNCLOS makes reference to port States only once. Article 218(1) UNCLOS provides that when a vessel voluntarily finds itself in a port, the relevant port State can undertake investigations and institute proceedings 'in respect of any discharge from [the vessel concerned]' on the high seas in violation of applicable international rules and standards.[115] Such exercise of port State jurisdiction may contribute to protecting the marine environment against vessel-source pollution. At the same time, it is subject to substantial restrictions.[116] Moreover, the exercise of such jurisdiction is not free from difficulty in practice, as port States may have little incentive to exercise such jurisdiction or because evidence of violations may be difficult to detect.[117]

'Port State control' is different from port State jurisdiction in that it does not confer on States a right to prosecute breaches of international rules and standards on the high seas, but rather permits – or even obliges them – to undertake administrative measures of verification, including possibly the temporary detention of a vessel. Many treaties involving the regulation of marine pollution, marine safety or seafarers' working conditions have indeed introduced some form of port State control.

By way of illustration, Regulation 11 of MARPOL Annex I provides that when there are clear grounds for believing that the master or crew of a vessel are not familiar with essential shipboard procedures relating to the prevention of pollution by oil, the vessel is subject to inspection by the State in whose port the vessel is located. In addition, that State must ensure that the ship does not set sail until the situation is remedied. In a similar vein, several treaties require States to prevent substandard vessels from entering their ports.[118]

[115] ie the standards imposed by the International Convention for the Prevention of Pollution from Ships (adopted 2 November 1973, entered into force 2 October 1983) 1340 UNTS 61 as modified by the Protocol of 1978 relating to the International Convention for the prevention of pollution from ships, 1973 (adopted 17 February 1978, entered into force 2 October 1983) 1340 UNTS 61 (MARPOL 73/78). In the *Intertanko* case, several members of the European oil tanker industry, including Intertanko, argued that Directive 2005/35/EC on ship-source pollution and on the introduction of penalties for infringements violated international law of the sea. This argument was mainly based on a perceived higher level of stringency of the then EC's directive vis-à-vis the relevant international standards (namely Annex I and II to MARPOL 73/78), violating Art 211(5) UNCLOS which provides that coastal State may 'adopt laws and regulations [regarding pollution from vessels] conforming to and giving effect to generally accepted international rules and standards. The CJEU did not render a judgment on the merits of the case, as it considered that UNCLOS lacked direct effect, and could thus not be invoked by Intertanko to challenge the validity of EU law, or domestic laws for that matter; judgment of 3 June 2008, *Intertanko* (n 12) para 64. See also the discussion of the *Intertanko* case in Chapter 4, n 70 and Section V(B).

[116] eg, Art 226(1)(a) states that physical inspection of a foreign vessel shall in principle be limited to documentary examination. In accordance with Art 226(1)(b) UNCLOS, vessels must be promptly released upon the posting of a reasonable bond or other financial security.

[117] Tanaka (n 46) 296–97.

[118] Consider eg the provisions on port State control in the following instruments: the International Convention for the Safety of Life at Sea (adopted 1 November 1974, entered into force 25 May 1980) 1184 UNTS 278 (SOLAS),

In order to enhance the efficiency of port State control (eg by sharing information and avoiding duplication of efforts), and to limit the risk of 'port shopping', several memoranda of understanding on regional port State control have been established. The oldest example is the 'Paris MoU on Port State control', which establishes a regional institution consisting of 27 participating States (as of March 2018) and covers the waters of the European coastal States and the North Atlantic basin from North America to Europe.[119] Each year, over 18,000 inspections take place on board foreign ships in the Paris MoU ports (brought together in a central inspection database). Ships that are found to be deficient can be detained and, in case of repeat offenders, be refused access to any port in the region. Other relevant mechanisms include the 'Mediterranean MoU',[120] bringing together several southern and eastern Mediterranean countries, and the 'Black Sea MoU',[121] which brings together the six States bordering the Black Sea. At the EU level, there exists specific maritime legislation, notably in the form of Directive 2009/16/EC on port State control and its three implementing regulations.[122] Technical responsibility for monitoring port State control rests with the European Maritime Safety Agency (EMSA),[123] which also participates in the meetings of the Paris MoU on behalf of the European Commission. The activity (eg inspection rate) and efficiency of the different regional MoUs varies strongly. Port State control not only plays an important role in the fight against substandard shipping, but also in the context of the fight against IUU fishing (on which see below, Section VIII).

E. Exceptions to Exclusive Flag State Jurisdiction

It is long accepted under customary international law that all States can board and arrest vessels engaged in piracy on the high seas. Over time, several further exceptions have developed, eroding the rule that vessels sailing the high seas can never be subject to enforcement action except by their own flag State or without their flag State's consent.[124] UNCLOS essentially provides for two important exceptions to the principle of exclusive flag State

ILO Convention No 147 concerning Minimum Standards in Merchant Ships (adopted 29 October 1976, entered into force 28 Nov 1981) 1259 UNTS 336, MARPOL 73/78 and its annexes (n 115), or the Maritime Labour Convention (adopted 23 February 2006, entered into force 20 August 2013) 2952 UNTS 1 (MLC).

[119] Paris Memorandum of Understanding on Port State Control (adopted 26 January 1982, entered into force 1 July 1982), including 40th Amendment (adopted 26 May 2017, entered into force 1 July 2017), parismou.org/inspections-risk/library-faq/memorandum. Save for Canada, the Paris MoU members are all European States.

[120] Memorandum of Understanding on Port State Control in the Mediterranean Region (adopted 11 July 1997, entered into force for each Authority on the date duly notified to the Secretariat), 2017 Revision, 197.230.62.214/Publications/Med%20MoU%202017%20Revision.pdf.

[121] Black Sea Memorandum of Understanding on Port State Control (adopted 7 April 2000, entered into force 19 December 2000), including 11th amendment (adopted 14 April 2016, entered into force 1 January 2017), bsmou.org/downloads/reference/bsmou_text_2017.pdf.

[122] Directive 2009/16/EC of the European Parliament and of the Council of 23 April 2009 on port State control (Recast) [2009] OJ L131/57, as amended by Directive 2013/38/EU of the European Parliament and of the Council of 12 August 2013 amending Directive 2009/16/EC on port State control [2013] OJ L218/1; Commission Regulation EU 801/2010 of 13 September 2010 implementing Article 10(3) of Directive 2009/16/EC of the European Parliament and of the Council as regards the flag State criteria [2010] OJ L241/1; Commission Regulation EU 802/2010 of 13 September 2010 implementing Article 10(3) and Article 27 of Directive 2009/16/EC of the European Parliament and of the Council as regards company performance [2010] OJ L241/4; Commission Regulation EU 428/2010 of 20 May 2010 implementing Article 14 of Directive 2009/16/EC of the European Parliament and of the Council as regards expanded inspections of ships [2010] OJ L125/2.

[123] See EMSA, Implementation Tasks, 'Port State Control', emsa.europa.eu/implementation-tasks/port-state-control.html.

[124] See further D Guilfoyle, *Shipping Interdiction and the Law of the Sea* (Cambridge, CUP, 2009).

jurisdiction: a right to visit foreign ships on the high seas under certain conditions, and the right to hot pursuit.

i. Right to Visit

First, Article 110 UNCLOS decrees that there is a 'right of visit' of foreign ships on the high seas when there is 'reasonable ground for suspecting' that:

> (a) the ship is engaged in piracy; (b) the ship is engaged in slave trade; (c) the ship is engaged in unauthorized broadcasting [...]; (d) the ship is without nationality; (e) though flying a foreign flag or refusing to show its flag, the ship is, in reality of the same nationality as the warship [exercising the right to visit].

If the suspicions ultimately prove to be unfounded, and provided that the ship boarded has not committed any act justifying them, it shall be compensated for any loss or damage that may have been sustained.

The situations referred to in Article 110(d)–(e) UNCLOS are fairly straightforward. They reflect the customary rule that a ship without nationality is without protection. Application of these provisions may, for instance, be triggered where a flag State has revoked the registration of the vessel because of non-compliance with its laws and regulations. By way of illustration, in 2014, North Korea revoked the registration of a tanker illegally loading crude oil from a rebel-controlled port in Libya.[125] The tanker was subsequently boarded by US Special Forces.[126] The situations referred to in Article 110(a)–(c) are respectively discussed below.

a. Piracy

The possibility to take enforcement action against pirate ships (or aircraft) is further clarified in Articles 100–107 UNCLOS. Piracy is defined (rather narrowly) as referring to 'illegal acts of violence or detention, or any act of depredation, committed for private ends'. Key is the phrase 'committed for private ends', which excludes, for instance, the hijacking of vessels for political purposes. States have a duty to cooperate in the repression of piracy on the high seas. Any State may arrest a pirate ship, and arrest the persons and seize the property on board. States may moreover try the persons concerned in accordance with their national criminal legislation.

In past years, the surge in acts of piracy, especially off the coast of the Horn of Africa led to renewed attention for piracy as a threat to maritime trade and navigation.[127] The UN Security Council has adopted a number of resolutions temporarily and conditionally authorising States to take enforcement action against suspected pirates in the territorial waters of Somalia.[128] In the framework of this authorisation, NATO conducted several naval operations around the Horn of Africa and in the Indian Ocean between 2008 and

[125] 'North Korea denies role in tanker loaded with crude at rebel-held Libya port', *Reuters*, 13 March 2014, reuters.com/article/us-korea-north-libya/north-korea-denies-role-in-tanker-loaded-with-crude-at-rebel-held-libya-port-idUSBREA2C15120140313.

[126] 'US Navy SEALs board rogue Libya oil tanker', *Al Jazeera*, 17 March 2014, aljazeera.com/news/africa/2014/03/us-navy-seals-board-rouge-libya-oil-tanker-201431710529805169.html.

[127] See eg P Koutrakos and A Skordas (eds), *The Law and Practice of Piracy at Sea: European and International Perspectives* (Oxford, Hart, 2014); D Guilfoyle (ed), *Modern Piracy: Legal Challenges and Responses* (Cheltenham, Elgar, 2013).

[128] UNSC Res 1816, 2 June 2008, UN Doc S/RES/1816; and even in Somalia itself: UNSC Res 1851, 16 December 2008, UN Doc S/RES/1851.

2016. The EU for its part established the 'European Naval Force Somalia' or 'Operation Atalanta' under the Common Security and Defence Policy in December 2008.[129] Well over 1,000 suspects have been, or are being, prosecuted in different countries, including in several EU Member States. Calls to create a special international tribunal to prosecute suspected pirates have gone unheeded.[130] To facilitate swift prosecution, the EU nonetheless signed several transfer agreements with countries in the region (eg the Seychelles and Mauritius), enabling for arrested suspects to be prosecuted in countries bordering the Indian Ocean.[131] The concerted efforts to tackle the piracy problem off the coast of Somalia has resulted in a substantial decrease in attacks in the region. At the same time, pirate attacks continue to plague shipping in other regions, chiefly the Gulf of Guinea, the Singapore Strait and the Strait of Malacca.

b. Slave Trade

Ships engaged in slave trade can be boarded under Article 110(b) UNCLOS. Contrary to what is the case for piracy, UNCLOS does not provide for universal jurisdiction enabling States to arrest and prosecute the persons involved in slave trade. Instead, Article 99 UNCLOS merely provides that every State shall take effective measures to prevent and punish the transport of slaves 'in ships authorised to fly its flag'. The provision does add that '[a]ny slave taking refuge on board any ship, whatever its flag, shall *ipso facto* be free'. The right to visit can thus be exercised by any State in such a way as to organise the escape and 'liberation' of the slaves being transported.[132]

c. Unauthorised Broadcasting

The inclusion of 'unauthorised broadcasting' among the different activities that trigger the right to visit under Article 110 UNCLOS seems somewhat out of place. Obviously, unauthorised broadcasting poses less of a threat to international security or community interests than piracy or slave trade. Its inclusion stems from the rise of commercial broadcasting from foreign vessels on the high seas in the 1960s, enabling broadcasters to evade administrative control and taxation by the States where the transmissions were received. This new phenomenon led to cooperation between States bordering the North Sea and eventually found its way into the list of activities giving rise to a right to visit under Article 110 UNCLOS. The right to visit is, however, somewhat more circumscribed than it is in relation to piracy or slave trade. It can only be exercised by States that have jurisdiction to prosecute the persons engaged in unauthorised broadcasting and to seize the broadcasting apparatus. In accordance with Article 109 UNCLOS, such jurisdiction is granted only to:

> (a) the flag State of the ship; (b) the State of registry of the installation; (c) the State of which the person is a national; (d) any State where the transmission can be received; or (e) any State where authorized radio communication is suffering interference.

[129] The EU has also adopted a 'Strategic Framework on the Horn of Africa' in 2011 and appointed a 'Special Representative to the Horn of Africa' early 2012. See EEAS, 'Fight Against Piracy', 3 May 2016, eeas.europa.eu/headquarters/headquarters-homepage/428/fight-against-piracy_en/. The EU has moreover been active in the broader 'Contact Group on Piracy off the Coast of Somalia' (CGPCS), created pursuant to UNSC Res 1851 (128).

[130] Consider eg UNSC Res 1918, 27 April 2010, UN Doc S/RES/1918.

[131] See also Chapter 9, Section IV(B)(v)(d) on universal jurisdiction over piracy and Chapter 14, Section VII(C) on regional enforcement action.

[132] Evans (n 26) 668.

The definition of unauthorised broadcasting is wide, so that it could cover vessels engaged in the spreading of political messages (eg in the context of pro-democratic protest).[133] As with slave trade, Article 109(1) UNCLOS provides that all States shall cooperate in the suppression of unauthorised broadcasting from the high seas.

ii. Right to Hot Pursuit

In addition to the right to visit under Article 110 UNCLOS, UNCLOS affirms a second general exception to the exclusive jurisdiction of the flag State vis-à-vis vessels on the high seas: the right of 'hot pursuit'. Hot pursuit can be defined as the 'legitimate chase of a foreign vessel on the high seas following a violation of the law of the pursuing State committed by the vessel within the marine spaces under the pursuing State's jurisdiction'.[134] The right of hot pursuit serves a similar purpose as the contiguous zone (see above, Section II(D)), in that it provides a means to prevent vessels from evading arrest simply by sailing away from the zone in which the breach has been committed.

The exercise of the right is subject to the cumulative preconditions of Article 111 UNCLOS. First, it may only be undertaken by 'warships or military aircraft, or other ships or aircraft clearly marked and identifiable as being on government service'.[135] Second, hot pursuit is only triggered where the coastal State has good reason to believe that the ship has violated the laws and regulations of that State within a zone over which the State exercises jurisdiction.[136] The breach concerned may be a violation of the customs, fiscal, immigration or sanitary laws that apply within the territorial sea. Yet, the right of hot pursuit also applies *mutatis mutandis* to violations in the EEZ or on the continental shelf,[137] such as illegal fishing within the EEZ or unauthorised drilling on the coastal State's continental shelf. Third, hot pursuit must commence when the foreign ship is still within the maritime zone where the violation has taken place.[138] Fourth, it may only be commenced after a visual or auditory signal to stop has been given 'at a distance which enables it to be seen or heard by the foreign ship',[139] although the transmission of radio signals can be sufficient to this end. Fifth, the pursuit must be continuous,[140] implying, for instance, that an aircraft giving an order to stop must itself actively pursue the ship until a ship or another aircraft of the coastal State arrives to take over the pursuit, unless the aircraft is itself able to arrest the ship.[141] States may nonetheless work together without this necessarily undermining the continuity of the pursuit.[142] Sixth, the right of hot pursuit ceases as soon as the

[133] Art 109(2) UNCLOS defines unauthorised broadcasting as 'the transmission of sound radio or television broadcasts from a ship or installation on the high seas intended for reception by the general public contrary to international regulations, but excluding the transmission of distress calls'.

[134] Tanaka (n 46) 168–69.

[135] Art 111(5) UNCLOS.

[136] ibid, Art 111(1).

[137] ibid, Art 111(2).

[138] ibid, Art 111(1).

[139] ibid, Art 111(4).

[140] ibid, Art 111(1).

[141] Tanaka (n 46) 164. For an illustration of a pursuit that was found to be interrupted, see *Arctic Sunrise Arbitration* (n 77) paras 269–75.

[142] Consider eg the Treaty between the Government of Australia and the Government of the French Republic on Cooperation in the Maritime Areas Adjacent to the French Southern and Antarctic Territories (TAAF), Heard Island and the McDonald Islands (adopted 24 November 2003, entered into force 1 February 2005), as reprinted in (2004) 19 *International Journal of Marine and Coastal Law* 545.

ship enters the territorial sea of its own State or of a third State[143] (by contrast, hot pursuit can continue within the EEZ of a third State). Seventh, where a ship is stopped 'outside the territorial sea in circumstances that do not justify the exercise of the right of hot pursuit, it shall be compensated for any loss or damage' caused.[144] Lastly, the exercise of the right of hot pursuit is subject to the rule that force can only be used as a last resort.[145] That being said, this principle applies to any form of law enforcement against vessels more generally.

When breaches are committed by smaller boats dispatched from a 'mother' ship which remains itself beyond the zone where the breach (eg illegal fishing) is committed, the right of hot pursuit can also be exercised against the latter vessel; this is the doctrine of 'constructive presence'.[146] It is unclear how broadly this doctrine must be interpreted, or, conversely, how loose the nexus between the colluding ships can be without removing the right of hot pursuit.

iii. Other Exceptions

Apart from the two general exceptions to flag State jurisdiction spelled out above, several others exist. Some exceptions flow from customary international law or UNCLOS. Others are established by separate bilateral or multilateral treaties. On a related note, in several domains, States have created cooperative regimes to facilitate the boarding of vessels suspected of engaging in unlawful activities without however removing the need for prior consent by the flag State. Without claiming to be exhaustive, what follows gives an overview of the most important scenarios concerning further exceptions to exclusive flag State jurisdiction.

a. Jus ad bellum and jus in bello

There are two exceptions possible under the *jus ad bellum*, that coincide with the two broadly accepted exceptions to the prohibition on the use of force.[147] First, States may engage in forcible acts against vessels on the basis of the right of individual or collective self-defence, subject of course to the requirements of Article 51 of the UN Charter, in particular the occurrence of an 'armed attack'.[148]

Second, the UN Security Council can set aside the principle of exclusive flag State jurisdiction by taking enforcement action under Chapter VII of the UN Charter. Thus, in Resolution 221 (1966), the UNSC called upon the UK to prevent, by the use of force if necessary, the arrival of oil shipments in southern Rhodesia, and empowered the UK to arrest and detain the *Joanna V*.[149] In Resolution 1874 (2009), the UNSC called upon States

[143] Art 111(3) UNCLOS.
[144] ibid, Art 111(8).
[145] *M/V 'SAIGA' (No 2)* (n 81) para 156: 'The normal practice used to stop a ship at sea is first to give an auditory or visual signal to stop, using internationally recognised signals. Where this does not succeed, a variety of actions may be taken, including the firing of shots across the bows of the ship. It is only after the appropriate actions fail that the pursuing vessel may, as a last resort, use force'. Here, Guinea was found to have breached this rule by indiscriminately firing on a much slower bunkering vessel filled with gas oil.
[146] See eg *Arctic Sunrise Arbitration* (n 77) paras 247–53, finding that incursions by rigid-hulled inflatable boats (RHIBs) into the safety zone surrounding a Russian drilling platform justified engaging in a hot pursuit against the mother vessel (Greenpeace's *Arctic Sunrise*).
[147] On the *jus ad bellum* and the use of force, see Chapter 14.
[148] See Chapter 14, Section III on the right of self-defence.
[149] UNSC Res 221, 9 April 1966, UN Doc S/RES/221, operative clause 5.

to inspect vessels on the high seas if they had reasons to believe that a vessel was carrying nuclear material to the Democratic People's Republic of Korea (DPRK).[150] As mentioned above (Section V(E)(i)(a)), the UNSC has also authorised States to enter Somali territorial waters for the purpose of repressing piracy 'in a manner consistent with such action permitted on the high seas'.[151] Against the background of the refugee crisis, and at the request of the EU, in 2015 the UNSC also authorised States to inspect and seize vessels engaged in human trafficking and migrant smuggling on the high seas off the coast of Libya,[152] thus giving greater leeway to the EU's 'EUNVAFOR Med Operation' (Operation SOPHIA).[153] In 2016, in an effort to implement the arms embargo imposed on Libya, the UNSC also authorised UN Member States, acting nationally or through regional organisations, to inspect vessels on the high seas off the coast of Libya believed to be in violation of the embargo.[154]

Lastly, also under the *jus in bello*,[155] the proper enforcement of a naval blockade pursuant to the law of armed conflict constitutes an exception to the exclusive jurisdiction of the flag State.[156]

b. Criminal Activities

Further, there are some exceptions that mainly relate to the fight against criminal activities on the high seas. As mentioned above, the definition of piracy is limited to acts conducted for private ends, which excludes, for instance, terrorist acts such as the hijacking of a vessel for political purposes. In the wake of the *Achille Lauro* incident involving an Italian cruise liner hijacked by members of the Palestine Liberation Front, the view emerged that this left a legal vacuum that needed to be addressed. A few years later, the 1988 Convention for the Suppression of Unlawful Acts against the Safety of Maritime Navigation (SUA Convention)[157] was adopted under the auspices of the IMO. The SUA Convention applies to a variety of acts of violence against ships or persons on board a ship, or otherwise endangering maritime navigation. The Convention sets out an extensive range of offences which States Parties are required to criminalise under their domestic law and sets forth an

[150] UNSC Res 1874, 12 June 2009, UN Doc S/RES/1874, operative clauses 12–13. The inspection is subjected to the prior consent of the flag State. Absent consent of the flag State, operative clause 13 calls upon States to direct the vessel 'to proceed to an appropriate and convenient port for the required inspection by the local authorities'. For nearly identical provisions concerning the DPRK, see UNSC Res 2375, 11 September 2017, UN Doc S/RES/2375, operative clauses 7–8.

[151] UNSC Res 1816 (n 128), operative clause 7(b).

[152] UNSC Res 2240, 9 October 2015, UN Doc S/RES/2240, operative clauses 7–8 and 10. The Resolution nonetheless requires States to undertake good faith efforts to obtain the consent of the vessel's flag State prior to using the authority granted by the Resolution.

[153] EU Council Decision (CFSP) 2015/778 of 18 May 2015 on a European military operation in the Southern Central Mediterranean (EUNAVFOR MED) [2015] OJ L122/31.

[154] UNSC Res 2292, 14 June 2016, UN DOC S/RES/2292.

[155] On the law of armed conflict or *jus in bello*, see Chapter 15.

[156] See eg in relation to the 2010 'Gaza flotilla raid': UN, Report of the Secretary-General's Panel of Inquiry on the 31 May 2010 Flotilla Incident, September 2011, un.org/News/dh/infocus/middle_east/Gaza_Flotilla_Panel_Report.pdf, paras 82, 104 and 117; at para 104: 'We have made it clear that we consider that Israel was entitled to impose the naval blockade. It follows that Israel was also entitled to enforce it. The manner of its enforcement, however, raises serious issues of concern'. See also ICC, Office of the Prosecutor, Situation on Registered Vessels of Comoros, Greece and Cambodia, Article 53(1) Report, 6 November 2014, icc-cpi.int/iccdocs/otp/otp-com-article_53(1)-report-06nov2014eng.pdf, paras 30–35, leaving open whether the blockade was lawful or not.

[157] Convention for the Suppression of Unlawful Acts against the Safety of Maritime Navigation (adopted 10 March 1988, entered into force 1 March 1992) 1678 UNTS 201.

obligation to 'prosecute or extradite' suspected individuals within their jurisdiction. It also creates a framework to facilitate cooperation between States, including by providing procedures for flag States to authorise the boarding and searching of vessels. No right to visit exists, however, absent consent of the flag State.[158]

In 2005, the IMO adopted a Protocol modifying the SUA,[159] chiefly requiring States to criminalise the intentional transport of any material, equipment, or software that is intended to be used to produce a biological, chemical, or nuclear weapon.[160] The 2005 Protocol was inspired by the broad concern within the international community over the proliferation of weapons of mass destruction following the 9/11 attacks. It followed a prior US initiative, the 'Proliferation Security Initiative' (PSI),[161] which was created in 2003 to facilitate cooperation between States. On the basis of the PSI, which was endorsed by more than 100 States, the United States has entered into a number of bilateral ship boarding agreements, which inter alia provide that if the other State does not respond to a request to authorise the boarding and searching of a vessel carrying its flag within a specified period of time, it is presumed to have given its consent. The same mechanism has also been integrated in the 2005 Protocol to the SUA Convention: once alerted of the intention to board a ship, the flag State has four hours to either deny or approve the boarding. If no response is received within four hours, the requesting State is allowed to board and inspect the vessel.[162]

Also the use of private vessels for illicit traffic in narcotic drugs has long posed a serious challenge to the international community. In spite of the magnitude of the problem, UNCLOS does not offer much assistance. Article 108 UNCLOS merely states that all States 'shall cooperate' to suppress drug trafficking on the high seas. Article 108(2) indicates that only the flag State can visit and arrest a vessel engaged in drug trafficking on the high seas, or request the cooperation of other States to this end. States have sought to remedy the shortcomings of Article 108 UNCLOS by developing separate instruments to tackle the problem, in particular the 1988 Vienna Convention against Illicit Traffic in Narcotic Drugs and Psychotropic Substances,[163] which was regionally supplemented by the 1995 Agreement on Illicit Traffic by Sea, adopted under the auspices of the Council of Europe.[164] While both instruments promote cooperation between States to suppress illicit traffic by sea, the boarding and arrest of vessels on the high seas ultimately remains subject to the consent of the flag State. In this sense, neither instrument undermines the principle of

[158] See Art 9 SUA Convention: 'Nothing in this Convention shall affect in any way the rules of international law pertaining to the competence of States to exercise investigative or enforcement jurisdiction on board ships not flying their flag'.

[159] Protocol of 2005 to the Convention for the Suppression of Unlawful Acts Against the Safety of Maritime Navigation (adopted 14 October 2005, entered into force 28 July 2010) IMO Doc LEG/CONF.15/21.

[160] ibid, Art 4(5). See further N Klein, 'The Right of Visit and the 2005 Protocol on the Suppression of Unlawful Acts against the Safety of Maritime Navigation' (2007) 35 *Denver Journal of International Law and Policy* 287. Note: the 2005 Protocol is not the only Protocol to the SUA Convention. In 1988, States adopted the Protocol for the Suppression of Unlawful Acts against the Safety of Fixed Platforms Located on the Continental Shelf (adopted 10 March 1988, entered into force 1 March 1992) 1678 UNTS 304.

[161] See US Department of State, Under Secretary for Arms Control and International Security, Bureau of International Security and Nonproliferation (ISN), 'Proliferation Security Initiative', state.gov/t/isn/c10390.htm.

[162] Art 8(2)(5)(d) SUA Convention, as amended by the 2005 Protocol (n 159).

[163] United Nations Convention against Illicit Traffic in Narcotic Drugs and Psychotropic Substances (adopted 20 December 1988, entered into force 11 November 1990) 1582 UNTS 95.

[164] Agreement on Illicit Traffic by Sea, implementing Article 17 of the United Nations Convention against Illicit Traffic in Narcotic Drugs and Psychotropic Substances (adopted 31 January 1995, entered into force 1 May 2000) CETS No 156.

exclusive jurisdiction of the flag State. Several treaties in which States dispense with the need for prior consent on a bilateral basis have nonetheless been adopted over the years. For example, in 1990, Spain and Italy concluded a treaty recognising the mutual right to board and search commercial ships displaying the flag of the other State.[165] Similar treaties have been concluded by other States.

Another relevant instrument is the 'Migrant Smuggling Protocol' to the UN Convention against Transnational Organized Crime.[166] Articles 7–9 of the Protocol deal with the smuggling of migrants by sea and again provide for a framework for cooperation to this end. Vessels can, however, only be boarded subject to the prior (and possibly conditional) consent of the flag State (unless of course, the UNSC authorises third States to inspect suspected vessels, as it did in respect of human traffickers operating from Libya (see above, Section V(E)(iii)(a)).

c. Environmental Protection

In the wake of the 1967 *Torrey Canyon* incident, during which the British air force bombed a stranded oil tanker in an effort to reduce the oil spill off its coast, the question arose to what extent States can take enforcement jurisdiction on the high seas to prevent and control marine pollution. In 1969, the IMO adopted the International Convention relating to Intervention on the High Seas in cases of Oil Pollution Casualties.[167] The Convention explicitly allows States parties – subject to certain conditions (eg consultation with the flag State) – to 'take such measures as may be necessary to prevent, mitigate or eliminate grave and imminent danger to their coastline or related interests from pollution or threat of pollution of the sea by oil', resulting from a maritime casualty.[168] The 1973 Protocol to the Convention broadens its scope as to include other forms of pollution (caused by substances other than oil).[169] The right to take action to prevent pollution has also been acknowledged by Article 221 UNCLOS.[170] At-sea inspection of vessels suspected of being engaged in IUU fishing is discussed further below (Section VIII(B)(ii)).

d. Additional Comments

With regard to jurisdiction on the high seas, two final comments can be made. First, whenever there is a legal basis permitting a State to visit, and possibly arrest, a foreign vessel on

[165] Treaty between the Kingdom of Spain and the Republic of Italy to Combat Illicit Drug Trafficking at Sea (adopted 23 March 1990, entered into force on 7 May 1994) 1776 UNTS 230 (Spanish), reprinted in (1995) 29 *Law of the Sea Bulletin* 77 (English).

[166] Protocol against the Smuggling of Migrants by Land, Sea and Air, supplementing the United Nations Convention against Transnational Organized Crime (adopted 15 November 2000, entered into force 28 January 2004) 2241 UNTS 507.

[167] International Convention relating to Intervention on the High Seas in cases of Oil Pollution Casualties (adopted 29 November 1969, entered into force 6 May 1975) 970 UNTS 211.

[168] ibid, Art 1(1).

[169] Protocol Relating to Intervention on the High Seas in Cases of Pollution by Substances other than Oil (adopted 2 November 1973, entered into force 30 March 1983) 1313 UNTS 4.

[170] Providing: 'Nothing in this Part shall prejudice the right of States, pursuant to international law, both customary and conventional, to take and enforce measures beyond the territorial sea proportionate to the actual or threatened damage to protect their coastline or related interests, including fishing, from pollution or threat of pollution following upon a maritime casualty or acts relating to such a casualty, which may reasonably be expected to result in major harmful consequences'.

the high seas, the coastal State can a fortiori visit/arrest said foreign vessel within its EEZ. Second, it must be kept in mind that these restrictions to the principle of flag State jurisdiction relate to the activities of commercial vessels. By contrast, as Articles 95–96 UNCLOS affirm, respectively warships and ships used only on government non-commercial service shall, on the high seas, enjoy complete immunity from the jurisdiction of any State other than the flag State.[171]

F. Biodiversity beyond National Jurisdiction

At the end of this section on the high seas, reference should be made to the ongoing development of a new legal instrument relating to biodiversity in areas beyond national jurisdiction. After lengthy discussion in the Ad Hoc Open-ended Informal Working Group to study issues relating to the conservation and sustainable use of marine biological diversity beyond areas of national jurisdiction (BBNJ Working Group) between 2006 and 2015, the UN General Assembly decided in 2015 to establish a Preparatory Committee for the purpose of developing an international legally binding instrument under UNCLOS (ie a new implementing agreement).[172] This Preparatory Committee held two sessions in 2016 and in 2017 and delivered its final report to the UN General Assembly on 31 July 2017.[173] Despite the connection to UNCLOS of the instrument under development, both the Preparatory Committee and the BBNJ Working Group were open to all States Members of the UN.

Throughout the process, disagreement persisted regarding which topics should form part of the negotiations. Nevertheless, the UN General Assembly confirmed that the Preparatory Committee and any further negotiations should

> address the topics identified in the package agreed in 2011, namely the conservation and sustainable use of marine biological diversity of areas beyond national jurisdiction, in particular, together and as a whole, marine genetic resources, including questions on the sharing of benefits, measures such as area-based management tools, including marine protected areas, environmental impact assessments and capacity-building and the transfer of marine technology.[174]

Given the high levels of dissension concerning several of these topics, the report of the Preparatory Committee remained relatively vague and many issues remain unresolved, such as which benefits are to be shared and how and what kind of institutional structure would be set up. With regard to the decision-making body, for example, it is stated that '[t]he text would set out an institutional framework for decision-making, as well as the functions that could be performed', before enumerating several possible functions such a body could perform.[175] These issues will thus require resolution during the intergovernmental conference to be convened.[176]

[171] This immunity can only be curtailed when the right of self-defence applies or when the UNSC has taken enforcement action under Chapter VII (see above, Subsection (E)(ii)(a)), or, exceptionally, when waived by the flag State itself. On the immunity of these vessels in the territorial sea, see above, Section II(C)(i).

[172] UNGA Res 69/292, 6 July 2015, UN Doc A/RES/69/292, operative clause 1.

[173] Report of the Preparatory Committee established by General Assembly resolution 69/292: Development of an international legally binding instrument under the United Nations Convention on the Law of the Sea on the conservation and sustainable use of marine biological diversity of areas beyond national jurisdiction, 31 July 2017, UN Doc A/AC.287/2017/PC.4/2.

[174] UNGA Res 69/292 (n 172), operative clause 2.

[175] Report of the Preparatory Committee (n 173), Section A(VI)(1).

[176] In UNGA Res 72/249 the General Assembly decided to convene this intergovernmental conference under the auspices of the UN, in order to consider the recommendations of the Preparatory Committee and to elaborate the

VI. The Deep Seabed

A. Common Heritage of Mankind

As mentioned at the outset (Section I(B)), UNCLOS dedicates a separate chapter to another maritime zone, namely the 'Area' or 'deep seabed'. The term refers to all parts of the seabed beyond States' territorial seas and beyond States' continental shelves (in the legal sense). The deep seabed attracted considerable attention in the 1950s and 1960s, as many believed that it would soon become commercially viable to explore and exploit nodules scattered over the deep seabed surface and containing valuable minerals, such as nickel, copper and cobalt. Against this background, it was agreed that the deep seabed should not be regarded as a *res communis* (free to exploit for all), nor as a *res nullius* (free to occupy and appropriate by interested States). Such an approach, it was felt, would only benefit technologically developed States at the expense of developing countries, and potentially sow the seeds for another tragedy of the commons. At the initiative of the Maltese Ambassador Arvid Pardo, the UN General Assembly in 1970 passed a resolution declaring that: 'The seabed and ocean floor, and the subsoil thereof, beyond the limits of national jurisdiction […], as well as the resources of the area, are the common heritage of mankind'.[177]

Whether the principle of common heritage of mankind relates solely to mineral resources, or whether it also applies to other activities on the deep seabed beyond States' continental shelves, remains hotly debated. This discussion proved especially relevant in the BBNJ negotiations (see also section V(F) above). At the 2010 meeting of the BBNJ Working Group, participants discussed the legal status of marine genetic resources found on the deep seabed, and whether these fell under the regime of the common heritage of mankind, or under the high seas regime. Whereas some States argued that the principle of the common heritage of mankind applied to all activities in the Area, others held that this principle's scope of application was limited to mineral resources.[178]

The qualification of the Area as 'common heritage of mankind' is reiterated in Article 136 UNCLOS. The Convention clarifies that no State shall claim or exercise sovereignty or sovereign rights over any part of the Area or its resources,[179] and that activities in the Area shall be carried out for the benefit of mankind as a whole,[180] with special attention

text of an international legally binding instrument under UNCLOS on the conservation and sustainable use of marine biological diversity of areas beyond national jurisdiction. The conference will meet in New York for four substantive sessions (4–17 September 2018; the second and third sessions will take place in 2019; the fourth session in the first half of 2020).

[177] UNGA Res 2749 (XXV), 17 December 1970, UN Doc A/RES/2749 (XXV) (adopted with 108 votes in favour, 0 against and 14 abstentions).

[178] See BBNJ Working Group 2010 Meeting Report, 17 March 2010, UN Doc A/65/68, paras 71–72: '71. […] Several delegations […] emphasized that the common heritage of mankind, including the fair and equitable sharing of benefits, applied to the biological resources of the area. […] Some delegations also stressed that, under the Convention, the legal regime applicable to marine resources was defined by the maritime zone in which they were found, not by their nature as mineral or biological resources. 72. Other delegations stressed that Part XI only addressed mineral resources, and expressed the view that marine genetic resources beyond areas of national jurisdiction were regulated by the high seas regime in Part VII of the Convention'.

[179] Art 137(1) UNCLOS.

[180] ibid, Art 140.

for the interests and needs of developing countries. The Area shall be used exclusively for peaceful purposes.[181]

B. International Seabed Authority

UNCLOS moreover puts in place a detailed regime governing activities within the Area. Key is the creation of an 'International Seabed Authority',[182] based in Jamaica[183] and consisting of a plenary Assembly, a Council (ie the executive body) and a Secretariat.[184] The Authority is granted exclusive legislative and enforcement jurisdiction with respect to activities in the Area.[185] It is a supranational institution empowered to take regulatory action concerning matters such as the exploration and exploitation of the Area, the distribution of profits derived therefrom and the protection of the marine environment. Its enforcement powers include the right to inspect installations and to sanction non-compliance (eg by revoking rights to explore or exploit the area or by imposing monetary fines).[186] With regard to the actual exploration and exploitation of the resources of the Area, UNCLOS foresees that the Authority can itself conduct such activities through its operational organ, the so-called 'Enterprise', charged with transporting, processing and marketing the minerals recovered from the Area.[187] In addition, commercial operators, including States Parties, States enterprises and national or legal persons possessing the nationality of States Parties, can submit a request to the Authority with a view to obtaining a concession to explore or exploit a specific area of the deep seabed. In so doing, they must normally propose two separate (exploration/mining) zones. The Authority can subsequently reserve one of the two zones for its own activities. The other zone will be reserved to the applicant.[188]

C. Implementation Agreement

In spite of some early concessions made in the margin of the Third UN Conference on the Law of Sea (in particular with a view to protecting prior investments by so-called 'pioneer investors'), the deep seabed regime set out in Part XI UNCLOS proved to be a bridge too far for most industrialised countries. Faced with fierce opposition of several States, some of whom proceeded to adopt domestic legislation in relation to deep seabed mining, new consultations were started so as to soften some of the sharper edges of the original regime. Eventually, in 1994, States adopted the so-called 'Implementation Agreement',[189] which instantly amends Part XI UNCLOS and opened the door to broad participation of developed countries in the Convention (see above, Section I(B)).

[181] ibid, Art 141.
[182] ibid, Art 156(1).
[183] ibid, Art 156(4).
[184] ibid, Art 158(1).
[185] ibid, Art 157(1).
[186] ibid, Art 153(5).
[187] ibid, Art 170(1).
[188] Art 8 Annex III UNCLOS.
[189] Agreement relating to the Implementation Part XI of the United Nations Convention on the Law of the Sea of 10 December 1982 (adopted 28 July 1994, entered into force 11 December 2001) 1836 UNTS 3 (Implementation Agreement).

The Implementation Agreement contains several important modifications watering down the original deep seabed regime. Thus, the creation of the so-called 'Enterprise' is postponed, and its functions are performed by the Authority Secretariat for the time being.[190] Operating costs are minimised in order to reduce the budgetary burden on developed countries.[191] The Implementation Agreement also calls for a more 'market-oriented' approach to the exploration and exploitation of the area.[192] This is illustrated by the removal of production limitations originally foreseen in Article 151 UNCLOS[193] and in the removal of the duty on the part of developed countries to transfer technology to the Enterprise.[194] Application fees to obtain a concession were lowered substantially.[195] Finally, the decision-making procedure was modified, introducing a consensus procedure and a collective veto system, thus enabling States to block decisions deemed contrary to their interests.[196] At the same time, the original premise that the Area qualifies as 'common heritage of mankind' has remained intact.[197]

D. Deep Seabed Mining

Contrary to what was thought in the 1950s and 1960s, commercially viable deep seabed mining has long remained a remote prospect. The International Seabed Authority has nonetheless concluded several 15-year contracts for the exploration of certain mineral resources in the meantime.[198] By October 2017, the Authority had 27 exploration contracts, mostly with government entities, but also with some private companies (pursuant to a State-sponsored application).[199] The Authority has also developed an elaborate 'Mining Code', a comprehensive set of rules and procedures to regulate the prospection, exploration and exploitation of various minerals in the seabed and subsoil of the Area.[200]

In an advisory opinion of 2011, ITLOS's Deep Seabed Chamber made clear that sponsoring States are bound by an obligation of 'due diligence' to secure compliance with the applicable laws and regulations by the sponsored contractors, and can be held liable in case of failure to comply with that obligation.[201]

190 Annex to the Implementation Agreement, Section 2 on 'The Enterprise' and Section 2(1) more specifically.
191 ibid, Section 1 on 'Costs to States Parties and Institutional Arrangements'.
192 ibid, Section 6 on 'Production Policy'.
193 This measure was intended to prevent deep seabed mining from having negative effects on the economies of developing countries with land-based mining operations. However, Section 6(1) of the Annex to the Implementation Agreement provides that '[d]evelopment of the resources of the Area shall take place in accordance with sound commercial principles'.
194 ibid, Section 5 on 'Transfer of Technology'.
195 ibid, Section 8 on 'Financial Terms of Contracts'.
196 ibid, Section 3 on 'Decision-Making'.
197 Preamble, para 2 Implementation Agreement.
198 Most of these contracts are for the exploration of polymetallic nodules in the Clarion-Clipperton Fracture Zone and the Central Indian Ocean Basin. Some relate to activities in the South West Indian Ridge, the Central Indian Ridge, the Mid-Atlantic Ridge and the Western Pacific Ocean.
199 For an overview, see International Seabed Authority, 'Deep Seabed Minerals Contractors', isa.org.jm/deep-seabed-minerals-contractors. Examples of government entities having entered into a contract with the Authority are the Federal Institute for Geosciences and Natural Resources of Germany and the *Institut français de recherché pour l'exploitation de la mer*. An example of a private contractor is Global Sea Mineral Resources NV, a Belgian-based private undertaking which signed a contract with the Authority in 2013 (with Belgium acting as the sponsoring State).
200 See further International Seabed Authority, 'The Mining Code', isa.org.jm/mining-code.
201 *Responsibilities and obligations of States with respect to activities in the Area* (Advisory Opinion) [2011] ITLOS Rep 10, 74–78.

VII. Maritime Delimitation

It will often be impossible for coastal States to extend their jurisdiction as far seawards as international law permits, due to overlapping claims of other opposite or adjacent coastal States. In such scenarios, the need for 'maritime delimitation' arises, in order to define the spatial ambit of each coastal State's jurisdiction. Questions of maritime delimitation have given rise to a large number of ICJ and arbitral cases. This case law is highly technical and to a large extent case-specific. Some cases concern the delimitation of the territorial seas of adjacent or opposite coastal States. Others concern the delimitation of their EEZ or continental shelf, or aim at drawing a single maritime boundary covering multiple maritime zones. An in-depth analysis of the case law is beyond the scope of the present chapter.[202] A number of general observations can nonetheless be made.

A. UNCLOS Regime

As far as the delimitation of the territorial sea is concerned, Article 15 UNCLOS spells out a triple rule (copying Article 12 of the 1958 Territorial Sea Convention[203]). The first step is to verify whether the parties concerned have concluded an agreement amongst themselves. If such an agreement exists,[204] this normally closes the matter. Absent such an agreement, it is necessary to apply the equidistance principle, or, put differently, to draw a line every point of which is equidistant from the coasts of the States concerned. The maritime delimitation thus obtained may, however, be adjusted and deviated from where this is 'necessary by reason of historical title or other special circumstances'.[205] Hence, even if the equidistance principle provides a practical and objective mechanism to settle conflicting maritime claims, its applicability is not absolute.

With regard to the delimitation of the continental shelves of adjacent or opposite States, UNCLOS adopted the same triple rule, emphasising the role of the equidistance method as the residuary mechanism. However, in the *North Sea Continental Shelf* case,[206] the ICJ determined that the provision concerned (Article 6 of the 1958 Continental Shelf Convention[207]) did not form part of customary international law and was accordingly not binding on Germany (which had not ratified the Convention).[208] In the case concerned, the ICJ moreover held that the application of the equidistance principle would lead to an inequitable outcome in light of the concave shape of the German coast.[209] In the context of

[202] See further eg Y Tanaka, *Predictability and Flexibility in the Law of Maritime Delimitation* (Oxford, Hart, 2006); S Fietta and R Cleverly, *A Practitioner's Guide to Maritime Boundary Delimitation* (Oxford, OUP, 2016) 52–95.

[203] See above (n 5).

[204] See eg the Agreement between the Government of the French Republic and the Government of the Kingdom of Belgium on the Delimitation of the Territorial Sea (adopted 8 October 1990, entered into force 7 April 1993), as reprinted in (1991) 19 *Law of the Sea Bulletin* 27.

[205] Art 15 UNCLOS.

[206] *North Sea Continental Shelf* (n 61).

[207] See above (n 7).

[208] *North Sea Continental Shelf* (n 61), paras 60–82.

[209] ibid, paras 89–91.

the Third UN Conference on the Law of the Sea, intense discussions arose between those favouring reliance on the equidistance method (holding the benefit of predictability, but the disadvantage of inflexibility), and those preferring delimitation on the basis of 'equitable principles' (leaving more room for flexibility, but generating a greater degree of legal uncertainty). A compromise between these approaches is reflected in the identical rules that were adopted for the delimitation of the continental shelf[210] and for the EEZ.[211] No reference is made to the equidistance rule. Instead, both provisions decree that delimitation must be effected 'by agreement on the basis of international law [...] in order to achieve an equitable solution'. In light of the vagueness of the provisions, it comes as no surprise that the law of maritime delimitation has primarily developed through the case law of international courts and tribunals.[212]

B. Approach in Case Law

The case law can be divided broadly into two phases.[213] First, between 1969 and 1992, international courts and tribunals basically adopted a 'result-oriented equity approach', focusing on the 'equitable result' to be achieved and dismissing mandatory reliance on the equidistance principle as the proper point of departure.[214] After 1992, however, it appears that case law has abandoned this flexible, yet highly unpredictable, 'result-oriented' approach and instead embraced a 'corrective-equity approach' as properly reflecting customary international law.[215] According to this approach, it is necessary to first establish the equidistance line as a provisional line and subsequently ask whether 'special circumstances' require any adjustment or shifting of that line. A new, three-staged variant of the 'corrective-equity' approach was first applied in the ICJ's 2009 *Black Sea* judgment,[216] and has since been confirmed in subsequent case law of the ICJ and ITLOS.[217] This method introduces a third stage – after the identification of the provisional equidistance line (the first phase) and the possible adjustment of that line in light of 'relevant circumstances' (the second phase) – consisting of an *ex post facto* check of non-disproportionality of the result reached at the second stage. This is slightly different from the ordinary 'corrective-equity' approach which construes 'proportionality' as one of several 'special circumstances' that may justify an adjustment of the provisional equidistance line (in the second phase). In any case, it is clear

[210] Art 83(1) UNCLOS.

[211] ibid, Art 74(1).

[212] In this sense, see eg *Delimitation of the maritime boundary in the Bay of Bengal* (Bangladesh v Myanmar) [2012] ITLOS Reports 4, para 226.

[213] See Tanaka (n 46) 202–208.

[214] See eg *North Sea Continental Shelf* (n 61) paras 83–85; *Continental Shelf* (Tunisia v Libyan Arab Jamahiriya) [1982] ICJ Rep 1982, paras 70–71.

[215] See in particular: *Jan Mayen* (n 72); *Land and Maritime Boundary between Cameroon and Nigeria* (Cameroon v Nigeria; Equatorial Guinea intervening) [2002] ICJ Rep 303; *Maritime Delimitation and Territorial Questions between Qatar and Bahrain* (Qatar v Bahrain) [2001] ICJ Rep 40; *Eritrea v Yemen*, Award of 17 December 1999, 22 RIAA 335; *Guyana v Suriname*, Award of 17 September 2007, 30 RIAA 1. But see *Territorial and Maritime Dispute between Nicaragua and Honduras in the Caribbean Sea* (Nicaragua v Honduras) [2007] ICJ Rep 659, partially departing from the aforementioned jurisprudence.

[216] *Maritime delimitation in the Black Sea* (Romania v Ukraine) [2009] ICJ Rep 61.

[217] *Territorial and Maritime Dispute* (Nicaragua v Colombia) [2012] ICJ Rep 695, paras 190–93; *Maritime Dispute* (Peru v Chile) [2014] ICJ Rep 3, para 180; *Bay of Bengal Maritime Boundary Arbitration* (Bangladesh v India), Award of 7 July 2014, PCA Case No 2010-16, para 341; *Dispute Concerning Delimitation of the Maritime Boundary Delimitation between Ghana and Côte d'Ivoire in the Atlantic Ocean* (Ghana v Côte D'Ivoire), Judgment of 23 September 2017, ITLOS Case No 23, paras 533–37.

that the equidistance rule still constitutes the proper point of departure for the delimitation of the territorial sea, the EEZ and the continental shelf.

The question next arises what 'relevant circumstances' may necessitate an adjustment of the provisional equidistance line. Again, case law is highly specific and rather unpredictable.[218] Overall, however, geographical factors are of more importance than non-geographical factors. In particular, the configuration of the coast – eg the concavity or convexity of the coastline and the general direction of the coast – plays an essential role in the delimitation process.[219] Furthermore, proportionality plays a role in most cases, whether as a 'relevant circumstance' or in the context of an *ex post facto* equity check. A recurring question in this context is whether the respective maritime spaces attributed to each Party are proportionate to the relative length of their respective coastlines. The presence of islands within the delimitation zone also plays a role, although the legal effect of the presence of islands varies from case to case.[220] Geological and geomorphological factors seem less relevant.

Overall, non-geographical factors play but a modest role in the delimitation process. Economic factors, such as the existence of natural resource exploitation or fishing interests, have often been invoked, yet mostly without success.[221] The relative economic fortune of the littoral States has been found equally irrelevant in delimiting maritime boundaries.[222]

Likewise, 'historic rights' based on alleged continuous and public usage from time immemorial and acquiesced by other States, have rarely been taken into account by international courts and tribunals,[223] even though the notion of 'historic title' surfaces in Article 15 UNCLOS concerning the delimitation of the territorial sea. It may be noted that China's extensive maritime claims in the South China Sea – which are dismissed by the other coastal States concerned – essentially rest on such 'historic rights'.[224] The 2016 arbitral award in the case brought against China by the Philippines, while excluding from its scope the question of maritime delimitation, nonetheless appears to have greatly diminished the future possibility of relying on 'historic rights' by ruling that UNCLOS 'supersede[s] any historic rights or other sovereign rights or jurisdiction in excess of the limits imposed therein'.[225] Other non-geographical factors, such as security interests and environmental factors, have never been taken into account, although this does not automatically imply they are intrinsically incapable of qualifying as 'relevant circumstances'.[226]

[218] Evans (n 26) 679.
[219] See eg *North Sea Continental Shelf* (n 61); *Bay of Bengal Maritime Boundary Arbitration* (n 217).
[220] Consider eg *Maritime delimitation in the Black Sea* (n 216) paras 185–88.
[221] In the *Jan Mayen* case, the ICJ accepted that it was necessary to ensure that the delimitation should not entail catastrophic repercussions for the livelihood and economic well-being of the population of the countries concerned and adjusted the provisional equidistance line in order to give Denmark equitable access to the fish stocks concerned (*Jan Mayen* (n 72)). However, reliance on fishing interests proved unsuccessful in *Barbados v Trinidad and Tobago*, Award of 11 April 2006, 27 RIAA 147 and in the *Bay of Bengal Maritime Boundary Arbitration* (n 217) (para 424).
[222] *Continental Shelf* (Libyan Arab Jamahiriya v Malta) [1985] ICJ Rep 13, para 50; *Continental Shelf* (Tunisia v Libyan Arab Jamahiriya) (n 214) paras 106–107.
[223] Tanaka (n 46) 225. See also *Maritime Delimitation and Territorial Questions between Qatar and Bahrain* (n 215) para 236, relating to historic pearl-fishing activity.
[224] See further eg Dupuy and Dupuy (n 3).
[225] *South China Sea Arbitration* (n 3) para 278.
[226] For instance, *In the Matter of an Arbitration under the Arbitration Agreement between the Government of the Republic of Croatia and the Government of the Republic of Slovenia* (Croatia v Slovenia), Final Award of 29 June 2017, PCA Case No 2012-04, the tribunal adjusted the provisional equidistant line to remedy a 'boxed-in' effect that would have otherwise resulted from a sharp turn in Croatia's coastline near its territorial border (paras 1011–14).

As a final point, recent cases confirm that in situations where States claim a continental shelf beyond 200 NM, maritime delimitation can lead to a situation of 'bifurcation' whereby one State holds (functional) jurisdiction over the water columns in a certain area of the seas, with another State having (functional) jurisdiction over the seabed and subsoil of the same area. The EEZ and the continental shelf are indeed seen as severable layers of jurisdiction.[227] Situations where two States share the same maritime space may of course create practical difficulties, requiring States to work out arrangements for the exercise of their respective rights.

VIII. Fisheries Regulation

A. UNCLOS Regime

One of the great challenges for modern-day international law of the sea concerns the conservation of marine living resources. Indeed, while marine living resources are of vital importance for mankind due to their nutritional value and the economic interests involved, existing fish stocks are at serious risk due to overfishing, illegal,[228] unregulated[229] and unreported[230] (IUU) fishing[231] and marine pollution.[232]

At the same time, this is an area where UNCLOS provides few workable answers. Under the UNCLOS regime, States are under no explicit obligation to conserve marine living resources in the marine spaces that are under their territorial sovereignty, being their

While Slovenia had argued that this effect greatly affected its navigational and security interests, the tribunal qualified this relevant circumstance as geographical in nature (paras 984–88).

[227] See *Bay of Bengal Maritime Boundary Arbitration* (n 217); *Delimitation of the maritime boundary in the Bay of Bengal* (Bangladesh v Myanmar) [2012] ITLOS Rep 4.

[228] Food and Agriculture Organization of the United Nations (FAO), 'International Plan of Action to Prevent, Deter and Eliminate Illegal, Unreported and Unregulated Fishing' (2001), fao.org/3/a-y1224e.pdf, 2: 'Illegal fishing refers to activities: [i] conducted by national or foreign vessels in waters under the jurisdiction of a State, without the permission of that State, or in contravention of its laws and regulations; [ii] conducted by vessels flying the flag of States that are parties to a relevant regional fisheries management organization but operate in contravention of the conservation and management measures adopted by that organization and by which the States are bound, or relevant provisions of the applicable international law; or [iii] in violation of national laws or international obligations, including those undertaken by cooperating States to a relevant regional fisheries management organization'.

[229] ibid: 'Unreported fishing refers to fishing activities: [i] which have not been reported, or have been misreported, to the relevant national authority, in contravention of national laws and regulations; or [ii] undertaken in the area of competence of a relevant regional fisheries management organization which have not been reported or have been misreported, in contravention of the reporting procedures of that organization'.

[230] ibid: 'Unregulated fishing refers to fishing activities: [i] in the area of application of a relevant regional fisheries management organization that are conducted by vessels without nationality, or by those flying the flag of a State not party to that organization, or by a fishing entity, in a manner that is not consistent with or contravenes the conservation and management measures of that organization; or [ii] in areas or for fish stocks in relation to which there are no applicable conservation or management measures and where such fishing activities are conducted in a manner inconsistent with State responsibilities for the conservation of living marine resources under international law'.

[231] It is believed that IUU fishing has escalated over the past 20 years, especially in the high seas. An estimated 11–26 million tonnes of fish is thought to be harvested illicitly each year, equivalent to a worth between US$10–23 billion. See FAO, Fisheries and Aquaculture Department, 'Voluntary Guidelines on Flag State Performance', fao.org/fishery/topic/16159/en.

[232] See Tanaka (n 46) 219–20.

internal waters, territorial seas and archipelagic waters. The situation is different in the EEZ. In the EEZ – which is estimated to encompass around 90 per cent of all commercially exploitable fish stocks[233] – coastal States in principle have exclusive jurisdiction over all fishing activities. Nonetheless, Articles 61–62 UNCLOS oblige coastal States to ensure that the maintenance of the living resources in their EEZ is not endangered by over-exploitation. To this end, coastal States must determine the total allowable catch (TAC) of the living resources in their EEZ, in a manner designed to maintain or restore populations of harvested species at levels which can produce the maximum sustainable yield.[234] Coastal States must moreover determine their capacity to harvest the entire allowable catch. If the State's harvest capacity falls short of the allowable catch, it must give other States access to the surplus, having particular regard to the interests of developing States and those of land-locked and geographically disadvantaged States.[235] Clearly, coastal States can easily avoid the duty to allocate surpluses to other States by setting the allowable catch at such a level as to establish a zero surplus.

Articles 64–67 UNCLOS contain specific provisions dealing with the conservation of particular categories of species such as highly migratory species, marine mammals, anadromous stock and catadromous species. In essence, the various provisions call upon States to cooperate, either directly or through appropriate international, regional or subregional organisations, to ensure the conservation and development of the species concerned. The success of this system stands or falls with the will and capacity of the coastal State to implement it in good faith. Some States indeed choose short-term economic (fishing) interests over the long-term interests in the conservation of marine living resources and refuse to take appropriate measures within their own EEZ and/or to enter into cooperative arrangements with other States. Other States simply lack the means to tackle illegal fishing off their coast.

Similar concerns arise over fishing on the high seas. As mentioned above, one of the fundamental freedoms of the high seas is the freedom of fishing. Article 116 UNCLOS confirms that 'all States have the right for their nationals to engage in fishing on the high seas'. Still, this right is subject to: (i) restrictions flowing from their treaty obligations; (ii) the rights and duties as well as the interests of coastal States provided for, inter alia, in Articles 63(2)–67 UNCLOS (dealing with specific types of species); and (iii) the provisions of Part VII, Section 2 UNCLOS dealing with 'conservation and management of the living resources on the high seas'. The latter section sets out two main obligations. First, '[a]ll States have the duty to take, or to cooperate with other States in taking, such measures for their respective nationals as may be necessary for the conservation of the living resources of the high seas'.[236] This is not merely an obligation to regulate the conduct of flag vessels; it arguably extends to all nationals of the State irrespective of the flag they sail under.[237] Inasmuch as the implementation of this provision rests

[233] ibid, 223.
[234] Art 61 UNCLOS.
[235] ibid, Art 62(1). The situation is somewhat different for *developing* land-locked and geographically disadvantaged States, because the surplus rule does not seem to apply to them (Arts 69(3) and 70(4) UNCLOS). The fact remains that the exercise of their right to participate in the fishing in the EEZ of coastal States in the same subregion or region depends inter alia on the 'terms and modalities' of special agreements to be concluded with these coastal States; Tanaka (n 46) 410–13. Further, see eg AM Punal, 'Right of Land-Locked and Geographically Disadvantaged States in Exclusive Economic Zones' (1992) 23 *Journal Of Maritime Law And Commerce* 429.
[236] Art 117 UNCLOS.
[237] Guilfoyle (n 124) 101.

on unilateral determinations and self-imposed restrictions, it is little short of wishful thinking.[238] Second, Article 118 UNCLOS provides that States shall cooperate with each other in the conservation and management of living resources in the high seas and shall, as appropriate, cooperate to establish regional or subregional fisheries organisations to this end. However, no specific guidance is given as to evaluate whether or not this obligation has been breached. Nor is there any sanction to punish States unwilling to enter into cooperative arrangements.

B. Specific Instruments and Regional Fishing Management Organisations

i. General Framework

When it comes to the protection of marine living resources, UNCLOS merely provides a framework for further bilateral and multilateral cooperation and leaves much to be desired. Numerous bilateral, multilateral and regional instruments have been adopted over the past years and decades to partially address this legal vacuum. Many of these instruments concern the conservation of specific species and/or establish so-called marine protected areas, such as the 1946 International Convention on the Regulation of Whaling[239] or the 1990 Agreement on the Conservation of Seals in the Wadden Sea.[240]

Of particular importance in the present context are the various regional fisheries management organisations (RFMOs) and other regional fishing bodies (RFBs) established to manage high seas fisheries for certain stocks within certain areas.[241] While the competences may vary, the aim of these bodies is to keep track of statistics and to monitor the evolution of fish stocks, to determine the total allowable catch, regulate the equipment and maintain oversight of scientific research.[242] Many RFMO agreements contain dispute settlement provisions and/or provide for other compliance tools.[243] There are over 50 regional fishing bodies.[244]

[238] Evans (n 26) 682.

[239] International Convention for the Regulation of Whaling (adopted 2 December 1946, entered into force 10 November 1948) 161 UNTS 72.

[240] Agreement on the Conservation of Seals in the Wadden Sea (adopted 16 October 1990, entered into force 1 October 1991), (1990) *Dutch Treaty Series ('Tractatenblad van het Koninkrijk der Nederlanden')* No 174, 1; concluded between Denmark, Germany and the Netherlands. Other examples include the Agreement on the Conservation of Small Cetaceans of the Baltic, North East Atlantic, Irish and North Seas (adopted 17 March 1992, entered into force 29 March 1994) 1772 UNTS 217; the Convention for the Protection of the Marine Environment of the North-East Atlantic (adopted 22 September 1992, entered into force 25 March 1998) 2354 UNTS 67; the Protocol concerning Specially Protected Areas and Biological Diversity in the Mediterranean (adopted 10 June 1995, entered into force 12 December 1999) [1999] OJ L322/3; and the Agreement concerning the Creation of a Marine Mammal Sanctuary in the Mediterranean (adopted 25 November 1999, entered into force 21 February 2002) 2176 UNTS 247.

[241] RFMOs are RFBs that have a management mandate and that can adopt fisheries conservation and management measures that are binding on their members. See further eg T Henriksen, G Honneland and A Sydnes, *Law and Politics in Ocean Governance: The UN Fish Stocks Agreement and Regional Fisheries Management Regimes* (Leiden, Nijhoff, 2006).

[242] J Crawford, *Brownlie's Principles of Public International Law*, 8th edn (Oxford, OUP, 2012) 323.

[243] For an overview of these dispute settlement provisions, see J Peel, 'A Paper Umbrella which Dissolves in the Rain? The Future for Resolving Fisheries Disputes under UNCLOS in the aftermath of the Southern Bluefin Tuna Arbitration' (2002) 3 *Melbourne Journal of International Law* 53, Appendix A: Dispute Settlement Provisions in Regional Fisheries Agreements.

[244] See http://www.fao.org/fishery/rfb/en.

The creation and success of RFMOs is heavily indebted to the adoption of the 1995 UN Agreement on Straddling Stocks and Highly Migratory Species, ratified by more than eighty States, including the US.[245] The Straddling Stocks Agreement implements the relevant provisions of UNCLOS by further clarifying the framework for establishing subregional or regional fisheries management organisations and arrangements, as well as the functioning and the competences of these organisations. Crucially, Articles 8(4) and 17 of the Agreement provide that, whenever an RFMO has been established for a specific region or species, States parties to the Agreement can only fish in that region or fish those species within the framework established by this organisation. The implication is that fishing can only be undertaken by those States (parties to the Agreement) that play by the rules.

ii. Enforcement

Enforcement of the various instruments dealing with the conservation of marine living resources takes three different forms: (i) flag State responsibility; (ii) at-sea inspection by non-flag States; and (iii) port State control.

First, as mentioned above (Section VIII(A)), States are under an obligation to take such measures regarding vessels flying their flag as may be necessary for the conservation of the living resources of the high seas. Still, the obligation enshrined in UNCLOS remains very vague. Moreover, flag States, especially those of 'flags of convenience', may lack the will or capacity to regulate and monitor the fishing activities of vessels flying their flag. Additional difficulties stem from the practice of 're-flagging' vessels in order to avoid flag State regulation, as well as from the practice of illegal fishing. A number of binding and non-binding instruments have nonetheless been adopted, especially in the context of the UN Food and Agriculture Organization (FAO), to clarify and strengthen the flag State's responsibility. For example, the 1993 Agreement to Promote Compliance with International Conservation and Management Measures[246] inter alia prohibits States Parties from authorising any fishing vessel entitled to fly its flag to be used for fishing on the high seas unless the State is satisfied that it is able to exercise effectively its responsibilities of control.[247] The same rule is found in Article 18(2) of the Straddling Stocks Agreement,[248] which lays down obligations for States to maintain a national record of fishing vessels authorised to fish on the high seas, together with information on their authorisation to fish, such as the species they may fish for and the type of gear they may use. Under the Agreement, States must moreover take such measures as necessary to ensure that vessels flying their flag comply with subregional and regional conservation and management measures and that they do not engage in any activity which undermines the effectiveness of such measures. Similar measures, including measures against 'flag hopping' to dodge detection, can be found in the 1995 FAO Code of Conduct for Responsible Fisheries,[249] the 2001 FAO International Plan of Action to Prevent Deter and Eliminate IUU Fishing,[250] and, more recently, the 2014 FAO Voluntary

[245] Agreement for the Implementation of the Provisions of the United Nations Convention on the Law of the Sea of 10 December 1982 relating to the Conservation and Management of Straddling Stocks and Highly Migratory Fish Stocks (adopted 4 December 1995, entered into force 11 December 2001) 2167 UNTS 3.

[246] Agreement to Promote Compliance with International Conservation and Management Measures (adopted 24 November 1993, entered into force 24 April 2003) 2221 UNTS 91.

[247] ibid, Art III(3).

[248] See above (n 245).

[249] FAO, 'Code of Conduct for Responsible Fisheries', 1995, fao.org/3/a-v9878e.pdf.

[250] See above (n 228).

Guidelines for flag State performance.[251] However, flag State jurisdiction alone is plainly inadequate to ensure the conservation of marine living resources, if only because 'flag of convenience' States can simply choose not to be bound by any of the aforementioned instruments.

A second mechanism to tackle illegal fishing concerns the at-sea inspection of vessels by non-flag States. Key in this context is the Straddling Stocks Agreement,[252] which lays down a general boarding, inspection and enforcement regime, to be operationalised through subregional or regional fisheries management organisations or arrangements.

The thrust of the regime is that members of RFMOs are instructed to establish schemes whereby one member of the RFMO can board and inspect vessels of any other State Party to the Agreement (irrespective of whether it is actually a member of the RFMO). According to Article 22, flag States must 'ensure that [...] vessel masters accept and facilitate prompt and safe boarding by the inspectors'.[253] In the event that the master of a vessel refuses to accept boarding and inspection, the flag State must direct the master of the vessel to submit immediately to boarding and inspection and, if the master does not comply, suspend the vessel's authorisation to fish and order it to return immediately to port.[254] Where inspection reveals incriminating evidence, the flag State is either bound to take enforcement action itself, or to authorise the inspecting State to do so.[255] The flag State can at any time require that the vessel be released to it.[256] Several RFMOs effectively engage in at-sea inspections of vessels of contracting States. A number of RFMOs moreover undertake at-sea inspections of vessels of non-contracting States.[257] While at-sea inspection provides a useful tool, it must be emphasised that the ultimate discretion with regard to prosecution and sanction is always left to the flag State.[258] In addition, at-sea inspection is a very costly mechanism.[259]

Finally, several coastal States engage in port State control of fishing vessels. Article 23 of the Straddling Stocks Agreement, for instance, declares that port States have the right and duty to take non-discriminatory measures to promote the effectiveness of subregional, regional and global conservation and management measures.[260] They may inter alia inspect documents, fishing gear and catch on board fishing vessels when such vessels are voluntarily in their ports or offshore terminals.[261] They may moreover prohibit landing and transhipments where illegal fishing is detected.[262] Several RFMOs indeed apply port-State

[251] FAO, 'Voluntary Guidelines for Flag State Performance', 2015, fao.org/3/a-i4577t.pdf.
[252] See above (n 245).
[253] Art 22(3)(a) Straddling Stocks Agreement.
[254] ibid, Art 22(4).
[255] ibid, Art 21(6).
[256] ibid, Art 21(12).
[257] By way of illustration, Art 38 of the North East Atlantic Fisheries Commission (NEAFC) Scheme of Control and Enforcement provides that NEAFC inspectors can request the master of the vessel permission to board and inspect non-Contracting Party vessels. If such request is denied, the vessel will be presumed to have engaged in illegal fishing; North East Atlantic Fisheries Commission Scheme of Control and Enforcement (adopted 15 November 2006, entered into force 1 May 2007), including changes in force as of 13 February 2018, neafc.org/scheme; as implemented into the EU legal order through Regulation (EU) No 1236/2010 of the European Parliament and of the Council of 15 December 2010 laying down a scheme of control and enforcement applicable in the area covered by the Convention on future multilateral cooperation in the North-East Atlantic fisheries and repealing Council Regulation (EC) No 2791/1999 [2010] OJ L348/17.
[258] Tanaka (n 46) 259.
[259] ibid.
[260] Art 23(1) Straddling Stocks Agreement.
[261] ibid, Art 23(2).
[262] ibid, Art 23(3).

inspection regimes. Often, vessels intending to call into a port will be required to give prior notice to the port State authorities and will be subject to prior inspection of their documents, log books, fishing gear, catch, etc. No vessel will be allowed to land or tranship until inspection has taken place. Several RFMOs moreover provide for port State inspection of contracting States' vessels and non-contracting States' vessels alike.[263] The problem with port-State control is that this mechanism suffers from certain inefficiencies, due to insufficient vessel information and lack of compliance among port States, enabling vessels to seek out 'ports of convenience'.[264] In order to address some of these deficiencies and to establish a more robust and comprehensive regime for port State control, the FAO Conference in 2009 adopted the Agreement on Port State Measures to Prevent, Deter and Eliminate Illegal, Unreported and Unregulated Fishing.[265] The Agreement aims at harmonising port State measures, enhancing regional and international cooperation and blocking the flow of illegally caught fish into national and international markets. However, the Agreement only entered into force in 2016 and it remains to be seen whether it will be a success.[266]

The adoption and enforcement of measures for the protection of marine living resources is sometimes claimed to contravene States' obligations under the WTO Agreements. For example, GATT panels previously held a US embargo on tuna caught using fishing methods resulting in a high level of dolphin mortality to be unjustified under the provisions of the GATT.[267] Reference can also be made to the dispute over swordfish in the South Pacific between Chile and the EU. In this case, the EU instituted WTO proceedings against Chile, claiming that the denial of port access violated Article V of the GATT.[268] Chile in turn lodged a claim before ITLOS accusing the EU of having failed to cooperate to ensure the conservation of highly migratory swordfish stocks. The case was eventually removed from the ITLOS docket in 2009 after the two parties reached a compromise agreement.[269]

C. EU Common Fisheries Policy

Article 3(d) TFEU provides the EU with exclusive competence in respect of 'the conservation of marine biological resources under the common fisheries policy'. Pursuant to this competence, the EU has developed a set of rules for managing European fishing fleets and for the conservation of fish stocks. The EU, as represented by the Commission, also

[263] As mentioned above (Section II(A)), a State's ports form part of its internal waters. States are in principle free to regulate, restrict and even exclude entry of their internal waters.

[264] Tanaka (n 46) 263–64.

[265] Agreement on Port State Measures to Prevent, Deter and Eliminate Illegal, Unreported and Unregulated Fishing (adopted 22 November 2009, entered into force 5 June 2016), fao.org/3/a-i5469t.pdf.

[266] See eg D Desierto, 'First Global Treaty Against Illegal, Unreported, and Unregulated (IUU) Fishing Entry into Force', *EJIL: Talk!*, 9 June 2017, ejiltalk.org/first-global-treaty-against-illegal-unreported-and-unregulated-iuu-fishing-enters-into-force/, stressing several promising aspects of the new treaty.

[267] See *United States – Restrictions on Imports of Tuna*, 3 September 1991, GATT Doc DS21/R, (1991) 30 ILM 1594; *United States – Restrictions on Imports of Tuna*, 16 June 1994, GATT Doc DS29/R, (1994) 33 ILM 839.

[268] See *Chile – Measures Affecting the Transit and Importation of Swordfish, request for consultation by the European Communities*, 26 April 2000, WTO Doc WT/DS193/1; *Chile – Measures Affecting the Transit and Importation of Swordfish, Request for the Establishment of a Panel by the European* Communities, 7 November 2000, WTO Doc WT/DS193/2.

[269] *Conservation and Sustainable Exploitation of Swordfish Stocks in the South-Eastern Pacific Ocean* (Chile v European Union) (Order of 16 December 2009) [2008–2010] ITLOS Rep 13.

participates in six RFMOs managing highly-migratory species (mainly tuna),[270] and in 11 RFMOs covering a certain geographical area.[271] By contrast, in spite of the fact that it plays an active role in other maritime domains[272] such as maritime safety,[273] maritime transport[274] and maritime pollution,[275] the EU is not a member of the IMO, nor is it a party to most conventions adopted under the auspices of the IMO.[276]

As part of the 'Common Fisheries Policy' (CFP), overall TACs are set for most commercial fish stocks. These TACs are shared between EU countries in the form of national quotas. Member States can exchange quotas with other Member States.[277] To ensure that the CFP rules are complied with, an elaborate control system has been introduced,[278] with checks being conducted at sea, in ports, but also during transport in processing facilities and at markets where fish is sold. Infringements are sanctioned in a harmonised manner inter alia by means of a point system which may result in a vessel's licence temporarily being suspended. Fisheries controls are conducted through the national authorities and their inspectors, while the European Fisheries Control Agency (EFCA) has been created to encourage closer collaboration and exchange best practices. The Commission has its own inspectors, whose task is to verify that the national authorities implement the EU rules correctly (in case of breach, funds can temporarily be withheld or national quotas can be reduced). For certain species and certain fishing zones, the CFP works with a system of designated ports. The aim of this mechanism is to make it easier to control sensitive catches by making it compulsory for the vessels concerned to land at specific ports. In 2008, the EU adopted a Regulation establishing a system to prevent, deter and eliminate illegal, unreported and unregulated fishing (the 'IUU Regulation'), which entered into force in 2010.[279] Under this system, only marine fisheries products validated as legal by the competent flag

[270] The six RFMOs concerned are: the International Commission for the Conservation of Atlantic Tunas (ICCAT), the Indian Ocean Tuna Commission (IOTC), the Western and Central Pacific Fisheries Commission (WCPFC), the Inter-American Tropical Tuna Commission (IATTC), the Agreement on the International Dolphin Conservation Programme (AIDC) and the Commission for the Conservation of Southern Bluefin Tuna (CCSBT); EC, 'Regional Fisheries Management Organisations (RFMOs)', ec.europa.eu/fisheries/cfp/international/rfmo/index_en.htm.

[271] ibid. The 11 RFMOs concerned are: NEAFC (see also above (n 257)), the Northwest Atlantic Fisheries Organization (NAFO), the North Atlantic Salmon Conservation Organisation (NASCO), the South-East Atlantic Fisheries Organisation (SEAFO), the South Indian Ocean Fisheries Agreement (SIOFA), the South Pacific Regional Fisheries Management Organisation (SPRFMO), the Convention on Conservation of Antarctic Marine Living Resources (CCAMLR), the General Fisheries Commission for the Mediterranean (GFCM), the Convention on the Conservation and Management of Pollock Resources in the Central Bering Sea (CCBSP), the Western Central Atlantic Fisheries Commission (WECAFC) and the Fisheries Committee for the Eastern Central Atlantic (CECAF). The last two bodies only have an advisory status.

[272] See eg Art 4(2)(d) TFEU, designating 'fisheries' as a shared competence. See further EC, 'Maritime Affairs', ec.europa.eu/maritimeaffairs/index_en.htm.

[273] See above (nn 122–123).

[274] See eg EC, 'Strategic Goals and Recommendations for the EU's Maritime Transport Policy Until 2018', 21 January 2009, COM(2009) 8 final.

[275] See eg EC, European Civil Protection and Humanitarian Aid Operations, 'Response to Maritime Pollution', ec.europa.eu/echo/what/civil-protection/response-to-marine-pollution_en.

[276] The EC does, however, hold observer status in the IMO. See further L Nengye and F Maes, 'Legal Constraints to the European Union's Accession to the International Maritime Organization' (2012) 43 *Journal of Maritime Law and Commerce* 279; C Gulbrandsen, 'Navigating from Conflict to Working Arrangement: EU Coordination in the International Maritime Organization' (2013) 35 *Journal of European Integration* 749.

[277] EC, 'Fishing Quotas', ec.europa.eu/fisheries/cfp/fishing_rules/tacs/index_en.htm.

[278] Council Regulation (EC) No 1224/2009 of 20 November 2009 establishing a Community control system for ensuring compliance with the rules of the common fisheries policy [2009] OJ L343/1.

[279] Council Regulation (EC) No 1005/2008 of 29 September 2008 establishing a Community system to prevent, deter and eliminate illegal, unreported and unregulated fishing [2008] OJ L286/1 (as amended).

State or exporting State can be imported to, or exported from, the EU.[280] An IUU vessel list is issued on a regular basis, in order to keep track of non-compliant vessels identified by RFMOs. The Regulation also offers the possibility to blacklist States that turn a blind eye to illegal fishing activities. EU operators who fish illegally, under any flag, face substantial penalties proportionate to the economic value of their catch.

It is estimated that more than a quarter of the fish caught by European fishing boats are taken outside EU waters.[281] Around eight per cent of EU catches (2004–2006) are made under bilateral fishing agreements with countries outside the EU,[282] while another 20 per cent are taken on the high seas, mainly in regions under the care of RFMOs.

IX. The UNCLOS Dispute Settlement Regime

A. General Regime

When States adopted the four Geneva Conventions on the law of the sea in 1958 (see above, Section I(A)), they also adopted an Optional Protocol concerning the Compulsory Settlement of Disputes.[283] As the title indicates, the Protocol provides for a mechanism for the compulsory settlement of disputes arising under the 1958 law of the sea Conventions, albeit only in relation to disputes between the States that have ratified the Protocol. However, in the course of the third UN Convention on the Law of the Sea States opted for a radically different approach, deciding that States signing up to the Convention should *ipso facto* accept compulsory dispute settlement.[284]

As a result, Article 279 UNCLOS provides that all States Parties are under an obligation to settle disputes between them by peaceful means. When a dispute arises, parties should exchange views expeditiously.[285] They can invite one another to submit the dispute to a five-member conciliation commission established in accordance with Annex V to the 1982 Convention[286] or agree at any time to settle the dispute between them by any peaceful means of their own choice.[287] If no agreement can be reached on the mode of dispute settlement, and insofar as no existing agreement between the parties applies[288] (such as a regional fisheries agreement providing for consultations only),[289] any party to the

[280] EC, 'Illegal Fishing (IUU)', ec.europa.eu/fisheries/cfp/illegal_fishing/index_en.htm.

[281] EC, 'Fishing Outside the EU', ec.europa.eu/fisheries/cfp/international/index_en.htm.

[282] For an overview, see EC, 'Bilateral Agreements with Countries outside the EU', ec.europa.eu/fisheries/cfp/international/agreements/index_en.htm. On the controversial Fisheries Partnership Agreement with Morocco and its application to the non-self-governing Western Sahara, see Chapter 5 on States, n 82.

[283] Optional Protocol concerning the Compulsory Settlement of Disputes (adopted 19 April 1958, entered into force 30 September 1962) 450 UNTS 169.

[284] For an excellent overview of the use of the UNCLOS dispute settlement mechanism, see Boyle (n 2).

[285] Art 283 UNCLOS.

[286] ibid, Art 284.

[287] ibid, Art 280.

[288] Art 282 UNCLOS refers to the scenario whereby the States parties to a dispute have agreed, 'through a general, regional or bilateral agreement or otherwise', to a binding dispute settlement procedure.

[289] For example, in *Southern Bluefin Tuna* (New Zealand v Japan/Australia v Japan), Award on Jurisdiction and Admissibility of 4 August 2000, 23 RIAA 1, at para 44, the arbitral tribunal held it had no jurisdiction to rule on the claims by Australia and New Zealand against Japan because Art 16 of the Convention for the Conservation of Southern Bluefin Tuna (adopted 10 May 1993, entered into force 20 May 1194) 1819 UNTS 306 provided for dispute settlement by means of peaceful means by the parties' own choice, accordingly trumping binding dispute settlement through arbitration pursuant to the UNCLOS provisions. For a critique, see Peel (n 243).

dispute can activate the residuary compulsory dispute settlement mechanism of Part XV, Section 2 UNCLOS.[290]

At the time of the negotiation of UNCLOS, States failed to agree on a single specific method of dispute settlement. Some States expressed a preference for dispute settlement by the ICJ, while others favoured the creation of ad hoc arbitral panels. Eventually, as no consensus could be found, it was decided not to impose a single procedure, but to allow States Parties to make a written declaration establishing their preferred dispute settlement method. In so doing, States can choose one or more of the four following options.[291] First, States can opt to settle their dispute through the ICJ.[292] The second possibility is to have recourse to ITLOS, a standing Tribunal established in accordance with Article 1 of Annex VI to the Convention, containing the ITLOS Statute.[293] Third, States can opt to have their dispute settled by an arbitral tribunal constituted in accordance with Annex VII to the Convention.[294] Lastly, a special arbitral tribunal can be constituted in accordance with Annex VIII to deal with disputes 'relating to (1) fisheries; (2) protection and preservation of the marine environment; (3) marine scientific research, or (4) navigation, including pollution from vessels and dumping'.[295]

As a general rule then, when a dispute arises, it is necessary to compare the choices made by the parties to the dispute. If the parties have accepted the same procedure for the settlement of the dispute, it may be submitted only to that procedure, unless the parties otherwise agree.[296] In the alternative scenario, if the parties have opted for different dispute settlement procedures, the dispute may be submitted only to (Annex VII) arbitration – which thus constitutes the residuary option – unless, again, the parties otherwise agree.[297]

B. Exceptions

A few exceptions exist to the general regime just described. First, pursuant to Article 186 UNCLOS, the ITLOS Seabed Disputes Chamber automatically has exclusive jurisdiction over all disputes with respect to activities in the Area. The Seabed Disputes Chamber has a broad personal jurisdiction and can hear disputes involving not only States, but also the International Seabed Authority, the (as yet non-existent) 'Enterprise', State enterprises and

[290] See further N Klein, *Dispute Settlement in the UN Convention on the Law of the Sea* (Cambridge, CUP, 2005).
[291] Art 287(1) UNCLOS.
[292] See Chapter 13 on Peaceful Dispute Settlement, Section III(B) on the ICJ.
[293] ITLOS is based in Hamburg (Art 1(2) ITLOS Statute), composed of 21 judges with recognised competence in the field of the law of the sea (ibid, Art 2(1)) who are elected for a (renewable) period of nine years (ibid, Art 5(1)). ITLOS has several standing Chambers, in particular (1) a Seabed Disputes Chamber (Art 14), composed of 11 judges (ibid, Art 35(1)) elected for a three-year period (ibid, Art 35(3)), which has specific jurisdiction in respect of disputes regarding activities in the Area (Art 187 UNCLOS); (2) a Chamber of Summary Procedure (Art 15(3) ITLOS Statute); (3) a Chamber for Fisheries Disputes (established under Art 15(1) ITLOS Statute); and (4) a Chamber for Maritime Delimitation Disputes (ibid). Separate ad hoc Chambers may moreover be established to deal with a particular dispute if the parties so request (ibid, Art 15(2)).
[294] Arbitral tribunals normally consist of five members (Art 3(a) Annex VII UNCLOS), chosen from a list of possible arbitrators drawn up and maintained by the UNSG (ibid, Art 2(1)).
[295] Art 1 Annex VIII UNCLOS. Special arbitral tribunals normally consist of five members (ibid, Art 3(a)), chosen from lists of arbitrators drawn up and maintained by the FAO, the UN Environment Programme, the Intergovernmental Oceanographic Commission or the IMO, depending on which of the four aforementioned topics the dispute relates to (ibid, Art 2(1)).
[296] Art 287(4) UNCLOS.
[297] ibid, Art 287(5).

natural or juridical persons engaged in activities in the Area.[298] Second, ITLOS has residual compulsory jurisdiction with respect to provisional measures, notably in situations where the constitution of an arbitral tribunal is pending.[299] Third, a special procedure also applies where the authorities of a State party have detained a foreign vessel 'and it is alleged that the detaining State has not complied with the provisions of [UNCLOS] for the prompt release of the vessel or its crew upon the posting of a reasonable bond or other financial security'.[300] Such prompt release provisions apply first and foremost in relation to the detention of vessels for illegal fishing in the State's EEZ.[301] In such a scenario, an application for the vessel's release may be introduced by its flag State to: (i) any court or tribunal agreed upon by the parties, or, failing such an agreement; (ii) to a court or tribunal selected by the detaining State under Article 287 UNCLOS (see above, Subsection (A)); or (iii) to ITLOS, again granting ITLOS residual compulsory jurisdiction.[302]

Finally, there are some types of disputes that do not fall under the compulsory dispute settlement regime at all. First, States are not obliged to accept the submission to such settlement of any dispute relating to the exercise of discretionary powers by the coastal State over fishing or marine scientific research in the EEZ.[303] This reflects the sensitivities of coastal States on these issues.[304] Second, States can opt out of the compulsory dispute settlement mechanism by means of a written declaration for three types of disputes: (i) disputes relating to sea boundary delimitations, or those involving historic bays or titles; (ii) disputes concerning military activities and disputes concerning law enforcement activities in relation to fishing and marine scientific research in the EEZ; and (iii) disputes in respect of which the UN Security Council is exercising its functions under the UN Charter.[305] Opt-out declarations always operate in a reciprocal manner. Thus, a State Party which has made such a declaration is not entitled to submit a dispute falling within the excepted category of disputes for compulsory settlement against another State Party, unless the latter so accepts.[306] This opt-out regime partly explains why many sensitive disputes involving competing maritime claims – whether in the South China Sea or in the Arctic – cannot simply be brought before an arbitral body, ITLOS or the ICJ.[307] On the other hand, irrespective of the exceptions to compulsory jurisdiction,

[298] ibid, Art 187. Note that ITLOS itself is also open to entities other than States Parties, ie States or intergovernmental organisations that are not a party to the Convention, and to State enterprises and private entities 'in any case expressly provided for in Part XI or in any case submitted pursuant to any other agreement conferring jurisdiction on the Tribunal which is accepted by all the parties to that case' (Art 20 ITLOS Statute).

[299] Art 290 UNCLOS. For example, ITLOS exercised this jurisdiction in the *Arctic Sunrise Arbitration* (n 77), where the Netherlands sought and obtained the imposition of provisional measures against Russia pending the constitution of an arbitral tribunal; *The 'Arctic Sunrise' Case* (Kingdom of the Netherlands v Russian Federation) – Provisional Measures, Order of 22 November 2013, ITLOS Case No 22. For a critical analysis of the Order, see D Guilfoyle, 'Provisional Measures and the MV Arctic Sunrise' (2014) 108 *AJIL* 271. In the subsequent Award on the merits, the Arbitral Tribunal condemned Russia for failing to comply with the ITLOS Order. See *Arctic Sunrise Arbitration* (n 77) para 334.

[300] Art 292(1) UNCLOS.

[301] Which is possible under Art 73 UNCLOS (see above, Section IV(C)).

[302] Art 292(1) UNCLOS.

[303] ibid, Art 297(2)(a)(i).

[304] Tanaka (n 46) 428.

[305] Art 298(1), respectively (a), (b) and (c) UNCLOS.

[306] ibid, Art 298(3).

[307] eg, China made the following declaration under Art 298 UNCLOS: 'The Government of the People's Republic of China does not accept any of the procedures provided for in Section 2 of Part XV of the Convention with respect to all the categories of disputes referred to in paragraph 1(a) (b) and (c) of Article 298 of the Convention'. In the *South China Sea Arbitration* (n 3), the tribunal nonetheless concluded that the Chinese reservation did not

States can of course always decide to proceed to judicial settlement by mutual agreement. Furthermore, even where compulsory jurisdiction of a dispute is excluded, States may nonetheless be obliged to accept that the dispute be submitted to conciliation under Annex V to the Convention, albeit that the outcome of such conciliation procedure is of course not legally binding.[308]

C. Practice

The UNCLOS dispute settlement regime has produced a fair amount of litigation, including the aforementioned *Swordfish* case between Chile and the EU (see above, Section VIII(B)(ii)). As far as ITLOS is concerned, the lion's share of procedures have been 'prompt release' proceedings and requests for provisional measures. At the same time, the Tribunal has also dealt with several more substantive disputes in recent years, including some maritime delimitation cases.[309]

In 2015, ITLOS also rendered its first advisory opinion acting as the full Tribunal in accordance with Article 138 of its Rules of Procedure,[310] pursuant to a request from the west-African Sub-Regional Fisheries Commission (SRFC) concerning the liability of States for illegal fishing by vessels flying their flag.[311] In the context of the SRFC procedure, the European Commission submitted observations on behalf of the EU pursuant to its exclusive competence under Article 3(d) TFEU. The Council of the EU nonetheless lodged a procedure before the CJEU, insisting that the Commission should have sought the Council's approval prior to doing so. The Court in turn found that the Commission had committed no breach of Articles 218(9) or 335 TFEU, and had not committed a breach of the principle of sincere cooperation.[312] Accordingly, the action was dismissed.

Since the entry into force of UNCLOS in 1994, there have moreover been over a dozen Annex VII arbitral cases. Especially in recent years, there has been an upsurge of high-profile arbitral cases, including the arbitration instituted by the Philippines against China (relating to maritime jurisdiction in the South China Sea),[313] and the proceedings instituted by Mauritius against the UK (concerning the UK's declaration of a marine protected area in the British Indian Ocean Territory (BIOT)).[314] Several of the cases initiated have nonetheless raised intricate questions regarding the scope of jurisdiction and the impact of the

prevent it inter alia from qualifying certain contested formations as rocks or 'islands', or from ruling on the (in) compatibility of China's claim to historic rights over the South China Sea with the UNCLOS regimes.

[308] In 2016, Timor-Leste commenced the first ever compulsory conciliation procedure under the UNCLOS regime. See *The Democratic Republic of Timor-Leste and the Commonwealth of Australia*, Decision on Australia's Objections to Competence, 19 September 2016, PCA Case No 2016-1, with the Conciliation Commission declaring itself competent at para 111.A.

[309] *Delimitation of the maritime boundary in the Bay of Bengal* (n 227); *Dispute Concerning Delimitation of the Maritime Boundary Delimitation between Ghana and Côte d'Ivoire in the Atlantic Ocean* (n 217).

[310] ITLOS, 'Rules of the Tribunal', 17 March 2009, ITLOS/8.

[311] *Request for an Advisory Opinion submitted by the Sub-Regional Fisheries Commission* (Advisory Opinion) [2015] ITLOS Rep 4. For a critical appraisal of the Tribunal's (assertion of its) advisory competence, see T Ruys and A Soete, '"Creeping" Advisory Jurisdiction of International Courts and Tribunals? The Case of the International Tribunal for the Law of the Sea' (2016) 29 *LJIL* 155.

[312] Judgment of 6 October 2015, *Council v Commission*, C-73/14, ECLI:EU:C:2015:663.

[313] See above (n 3), as also discussed in Section VII(B).

[314] *In the matter of the Chagos Marine Protected Area Arbitration* (Mauritius v United Kingdom), Award of 18 March 2015, PCA Case No 2011-03.

exceptions to compulsory jurisdiction of Articles 297–298 UNCLOS.[315] However, refusals on the part of China and Russia to participate in specific Annex VII proceedings have not prevented the tribunals concerned from confirming their jurisdiction and from rendering an award on the merits.

X. The Arctic

A. The Arctic and Law of the Sea

The Arctic is often included in the list of the Earth's global commons. From a legal perspective, this qualification can be misleading if global commons are defined as 'areas over which no State can exercise or claim sovereignty'. Only certain parts of the Arctic region can be considered as completely 'beyond national jurisdiction'. The Arctic consists of an ice-covered ocean surrounded by continents. Accordingly, only those parts of the Arctic that constitute high seas or form part of the Area are truly 'beyond national jurisdiction'. The Arctic is, however, generally considered to cover a larger area. Some define the region as everything North of 66°32' Northern Latitude, whereas others use more elaborate definitions based on different elements, such as political, jurisdictional or administrative borders, vegetation boundaries, permafrost limits, major oceanographic features and cultural and social factors. Even within the Arctic Council, different working groups employ different definitions of the Arctic region, depending on the subject matter at hand. In other words, there is no fixed (legal) definition of the Arctic.

Thus, in 1998, the Arctic Monitoring and Assessment Program (AMAP), one of the Arctic Council's Working Groups, defined the Arctic as

> essentially the terrestrial and marine areas north of the Arctic Circle (66°32'N), and north of 62°N in Asia and 60°N in North America, modified to include the marine areas north of the Aleutian chain, Hudson Bay, and parts of the North Atlantic Ocean including the Labrador Sea.[316]

The 2004 and 2014 Arctic Human Development Reports (AHDRs), which were commissioned by the Arctic Council, took the AMAP definition as a basis but adapted the definition 'for reasons having to do mainly with the location of jurisdictional or administrative boundaries and the availability of data'.[317] The 2004 AHDR then defines the Arctic as 'all of Alaska, Canada North of 60°N together with northern Quebec and Labrador, all of Greenland, the Faroe Islands, and Iceland, and the northernmost counties of Norway, Sweden and Finland' together with the following Russian territories: 'the Murmansk Oblast, the Nenets, Yamalo-Nenets, Taimyr, and Chukotka autonomusokrugs, Vorkuta City in the Komi Republic, Norilsk and Igsrka in Krasnoyarsky Kray, and those parts of the Sakha

[315] See eg ibid, para 160 and *In the matter of an Arbitration before an Arbitral Tribunal Constituted under Annex VII to the 1982 UN Convention on the Law of the Sea* (Philippines v China), Award on Jurisdiction and Admissibility of 29 October 2015, PCA Case No 2013-19.

[316] AMAP, 'Assessment Report: Arctic Pollution Issues', 1998, amap.no/documents/doc/amap-assessment-report-arctic-pollution-issues/68, 10.

[317] N Einarsson et al, 'Arctic Human Development Report' (Stefansson Arctic Institute, 2004), oaarchive.arctic-council.org/handle/11374/51, 18.

Republic whose boundaries lie closest to the Arctic Circle'.[318] The Conservation of Arctic Flora and Fauna (CAFF), another Arctic Council working group, defines the Arctic yet differently, basing the boundary mainly on the treeline.

As the Arctic largely constitutes frozen ocean surrounded by continents, the law of the sea plays a prominent role in Arctic governance. This was explicitly recognised by the five Arctic coastal States (Denmark, Russia, the US, Canada and Norway – also referred to as 'the Arctic Five') in their 2008 Ilulissat Declaration:

> we recall that an extensive international legal framework applies to the Arctic Ocean […]. Notably, the law of the sea provides for important rights and obligations concerning the delineation of the outer limits of the continental shelf, the protection of the marine environment, including ice-covered areas, freedom of navigation, marine scientific research, and other uses of the sea. We remain committed to this legal framework.[319]

As this declaration was mainly a response to claims for the negotiation of a comprehensive multilateral convention dealing with all Arctic matters, the Arctic Five added that they saw 'no need to develop a new comprehensive international legal regime to govern the Arctic Ocean'.[320]

Still, UNCLOS contains no specific provisions relating to the Arctic (nor to the Antarctic), even though some States argued in favour of such provisions during the Third UN Conference on the Law of the Sea. However, Article 234 of the Convention does provide for stronger coastal State jurisdiction 'for the prevention, reduction and control of marine pollution from vessels' for ice-covered areas within coastal States' EEZs. This rule was proposed and lobbied for by Canada with its Arctic waters in mind, and although the Arctic region is not explicitly mentioned in the article, it is widely acknowledged that it was designed specifically for this region.

B. Sovereignty and Jurisdictional Claims

In the past decades, the Arctic has drawn increased attention as extensive claims of coastal State jurisdiction were made by the Arctic coastal States. Already at several points in the course of the twentieth century, officials from both Canada[321] and Russia have argued for the existence of a 'sector theory' on the basis of geographical proximity.[322] According to this theory, all lands and islands within a pie-slice-shaped area defined by the northern coastline of the continent and meridians of longitude extending from the North Pole to the most western and eastern points of this coastline are part of the sovereign territory of the relevant coastal State. Canadian and Russian positions on this theory have varied considerably from government to government, while the US and Norway have consistently rejected this theory.

More recently, extended continental shelf claims (beyond the 200NM limit) put forward by several Arctic states through the submission of information to the CLCS between 2001

[318] ibid, 18–19. J Nymand Larsen and G Fondahl (eds), 'Arctic Human Development Report: Regional Processes and Global Linkages' (Norden, 2014), norden.diva-portal.org/smash/get/diva2:788965/FULLTEXT03.pdf, works with the same definition.

[319] The Ilulissat Declaration, Arctic Ocean Conference (Ilulissat, Greenland), 29 May 2008, (2009) 48 ILM 382.

[320] ibid.

[321] See IL Head, 'Canadian Claims to Territorial Sovereignty in the Arctic Regions' (1960) 9 *McGill Law Journal* 200.

[322] This theory was first put forward by Pascal Poirier, a Canadian senator, in 1907, but was initially greeted with a lack of support within the Canadian government.

and 2015 have shaken up the region.[323] Several of these claims overlap and stretch up to and beyond the North Pole. On 20 December 2001, the Russian government was first to submit information to the CLCS regarding the outer limits of its continental shelf.[324] Subsequently, Norway made a partial submission for its Arctic claims on 27 November 2006. Denmark submitted information regarding the northern extended continental shelf of the Faroe Islands (which stretches into the Arctic circle) on 29 April 2009, and made a partial submission relating to the outer limits of Greenland's continental shelf on 14 June 2012 (southern continental shelf), 26 November 2013 (north-eastern continental shelf) and 15 December 2014 (northern continental shelf). Canada submitted information on 6 December 2013 regarding the outer limit of its continental shelves, with the exception of the Arctic Ocean.[325] The US is not in a position to submit information to the CLCS, as it has not ratified UNCLOS.

The growing economic and strategic importance of the Arctic region, in particular in the light of the rapidly melting sea ice, ensures that debates over sovereignty and jurisdiction are likely to continue for the foreseeable future. Such debates will concern the resources of the Arctic, both living (see below, Subsection (C)(iii) on the fisheries agreement for the Central Arctic Ocean) and non-living (most notably gas and oil), as well as control over (the potential revenues generated by) the Arctic sea routes, both in the Western and in the Eastern hemisphere, and growing environmental challenges, including the linkages between the Arctic and the global climate.[326]

C. International Cooperation

Although important geostrategic interests are involved and the Arctic Five have opposed the negotiation of a comprehensive multilateral treaty or international organisation governing the Arctic, bilateral and multilateral cooperation have nevertheless featured prominently in Arctic governance.

i. Bilateral Cooperation

Bilateral cooperation is evident, for example, on the matter of maritime delimitation, as demonstrated by the Barents Sea Treaty concluded between Russia and Norway in 2010 after almost 40 years of negotiation.[327] Canada and the US have also closely cooperated in developing Arctic policies. Despite disagreement regarding the legal status of passage through the Northwest passage (the shipping lane running along the northern coast of

[323] For an overview of the claims, see the link above (n 64).

[324] At the request of the CLCS, Russia provided more detailed and substantiated information on 3 August 2015.

[325] Canada informed the CLCS of its intention to provide information regarding the outer limits of its Arctic continental shelf at a later date, but has not done so as of March 2018. For more information, see the link above (n 64).

[326] The Russian flag planting at the North Pole in 2007 symbolises the importance Arctic States attach to their Arctic territories and maritime zones, even though the Russian government has consistently argued that the flag planting held no legal value.

[327] Treaty between the Kingdom of Norway and the Russian Federation concerning Maritime Delimitation and Cooperation in the Barents Sea and the Arctic Ocean (adopted on 15 September 2010, entered into force 7 July 2011). See O Jensen, 'Treaty Between Norway and the Russian Federation Concerning Maritime Delimitation and Cooperation in the Barents Sea and the Arctic Ocean' (2011) 26 *International Journal of Marine and Coastal Law* 151, to which the Treaty is attached (at 159) and T Henriksen and G Ulfstein, 'Maritime Delimitation in the Arctic: The Barents Sea Treaty' (2011) 42 *Ocean Development and International Law* 1.

both States), they concluded a bilateral agreement in 1988 allowing for practical cooperation on this issue.[328] Furthermore, on 10 March 2016, Canadian Prime Minister Trudeau and former US President Obama issued a joint statement on 'climate, energy, and Arctic leadership'.[329] This statement sets out four joint objectives for both States with regard to Arctic governance: 'conserving Arctic biodiversity through science-based decision making', 'incorporating indigenous science and traditional knowledge into decision-making', 'building a sustainable Arctic economy', and 'supporting strong Arctic communities'.[330]

ii. Multilateral Cooperation: The Arctic Council

On the multilateral level, the most important institution is the Arctic Council, which was established by the 1996 Ottawa Declaration.[331] The membership of the Arctic Council consists of those (eight) States that have territories within the Arctic circle (the Arctic Five plus Iceland, Finland and Sweden). Furthermore, the special status of indigenous peoples in the Arctic is recognised, as six organisations representing Arctic indigenous peoples are entitled to 'active participation and full consultation' as Permanent Participants.[332] Finally, observer status is open to 'non-Arctic states; inter-governmental and inter-parliamentary organizations, global and regional; and non-governmental organizations that the Council determines can contribute to its work'.[333]

In 2011, the Arctic Council adopted a set of criteria for the accreditation of observers (the 'Nuuk criteria'). These criteria were added to the Council's Rules of Procedure as Annex 2, and stipulate that the suitability of applicants will inter alia be assessed on the acceptance of the premises of the Ilulissat Declaration, respect for and willingness to support indigenous peoples' rights, demonstration of the applicant's Arctic interest and expertise and on the concrete added value to the work of the Arctic Council, 'including through partnerships with member states and Permanent Participants bringing Arctic concerns to global decision-making bodies'.[334] Nevertheless, as the final decision regarding accreditation is taken by the Arctic Council and decisions within the Council are taken by consensus, every Member State of the Arctic Council can veto the admission of a certain State or organisation as observer. Allegedly, this is what happened when the EU received permanent observer status in 2013, but had the implementation of this status put on hold. This situation has been attributed to Canadian resistance, triggered by EU secondary legislation relating to the trade of seal products,[335] and later to Russian resistance, linked to the EU's condemnation of the Crimean annexation.

[328] Agreement between the Government of Canada and the Government of the United States of America on Arctic Cooperation (adopted and entered into force 11 January 1988) 1852 UNTS 60.

[329] 'US-Canada Joint Statement on Climate, Energy, and Arctic Leadership' (Washington DC, United States), 10 March 2016, pm.gc.ca/eng/news/2016/03/10/us-canada-joint-statement-climate-energy-and-arctic-leadership.

[330] ibid.

[331] Declaration on the Establishment of the Arctic Council (Ottawa, Canada), 19 September 1996, oaarchive.arctic-council.org/handle/11374/85.

[332] ibid, Art 2.

[333] ibid, Art 3.

[334] Arctic Council, Rules of Procedure (adopted at the First Arctic Council Ministerial Meeting on 17–18 September 1998, as revised at the Eight Arctic Council Ministerial Meeting on 15 May 2013), oaarchive.arctic-council.org/handle/11374/940, Annex 2, provision 6.

[335] This same legislation gave rise to a dispute before the WTO Dispute Settlement Bodies. See *European Communities – Measures Prohibiting the Importation and Marketing of Seal Products*, 22 May 2014, WTO Docs WT/DS400/AB/R and WT/DS401/AB/R.

The Arctic Council constitutes a high-level forum established to facilitate international cooperation, coordination and interaction in particular on issues of sustainable development and protection of the environment.[336] 'Matters related to military security' are explicitly excluded from the deliberations of the Council,[337] and fisheries-related matters have de facto also been excluded. The Arctic Council has purposely been designed as an informal institution without the mandate to develop legally binding instruments, mainly because the Arctic States considered that a more formal form of cooperation might undermine their sovereign rights and jurisdiction in the region. Therefore, the Council does not constitute a fully-fledged intergovernmental organisation, even though it established a secretariat in Trømso in 2013.

The supreme organ of the Arctic Council is the Ministerial Meeting which meets biennially, with chairmanship rotating among the Arctic States. These meetings are followed-up and supported by meetings of Senior Arctic Officials (SAOs), whom each Arctic State has to designate and who meet twice a year. However, most of the work is done in the Council's six Working Groups: the Arctic Contaminants Action Program (ACAP), the Arctic Monitoring and Assessment Program (AMAP), the Conservation of Arctic Flora and Fauna (CAFF), the Emergency Prevention, Preparedness and Response (EPPR), the Protection of the Arctic Marine Environment (PAME), and the Sustainable Development Working Group (SDWG). Four of these Working Groups (AMAP, CAFF, PAME and EPPR) were taken over from the Arctic Council's predecessor, the Arctic Environmental Protection Strategy (AEPS) established in 1991,[338] as was the Indigenous Peoples' Secretariat. Finally, the Arctic Council has established several Task Forces over recent decades. Currently, two Task Forces, the Task Force on Arctic Marine Cooperation and the Task Force on Improved Connectivity in the Arctic, are in operation.

Despite the general reluctance to enter into binding agreements pertaining to Arctic matters, three legally binding agreements have been negotiated under the auspices of the Arctic Council: the 2011 Agreement on Cooperation on Aeronautical and Maritime Search and Rescue in the Arctic,[339] the 2013 Agreement on Cooperation on Marine Oil Pollution Preparedness and Response in the Arctic,[340] and the 2017 Agreement on Enhancing International Arctic Scientific Cooperation.[341] However, despite their negotiation under the auspices of the Arctic Council, these agreements have not been adopted by or in the Arctic Council as this would surpass its mandate.

iii. Other Multilateral Cooperation

Besides the Arctic Council, other multilateral institutions also deal with Arctic issues, such as the Barents Euro-Arctic Council (BEAC), the Barents Regional Council (BRC) and the Nordic Council of Ministers. The first two of these organisations were set up in 1993 in

[336] Art 1 Ottawa Declaration (n 331).
[337] ibid, fn 1.
[338] The AEPS fully transitioned into the Arctic Council in 1997.
[339] Agreement on Cooperation on Aeronautical and Maritime Search and Rescue in the Arctic (adopted on 12 May 2011, entered into force 19 January 2013) 50 ILM 1119.
[340] Agreement on Cooperation on Marine Oil Pollution Preparedness and Response in the Arctic (adopted on 15 May 2013, entered into force 25 March 2016), oaarchive.arctic-council.org/handle/11374/529.
[341] Agreement on Enhancing International Arctic Scientific Cooperation (adopted on 11 May 2017, not yet entered into force), oaarchive.arctic-council.org/handle/11374/1916.

order to promote sustainable development in the Barents region.[342] Whereas the BEAC was designed as a more traditional intergovernmental forum (with Denmark, Finland, Iceland, Norway, Russia, Sweden and the European Commission as members), the BRC constitutes an interregional forum, bringing together 14 subnational entities. The special status of indigenous peoples in the Arctic is also recognised in these organisations as representatives of the three indigenous peoples living in the Barents region cooperate in the Working Group of Indigenous Peoples (WGIP), through which indigenous peoples can participate in all bodies (primary and subsidiary) established by both organisations. In 2008, the International Barents Secretariat was established in Kirkenes in order to provide administrative support to both the BEAC and the BRC.

Interparliamentary cooperation also features prominently within the Arctic region. In the Joint Communiqué adjoined to the Ottawa Declaration, the contribution of the Standing Committee of the Parliamentarians of the Arctic Region was explicitly recognised and its future participation was welcomed. As such, the Standing Committee was one of the first organisations to be granted observer status in the Arctic Council. In addition, the Nordic Council of Ministers is supported by the Nordic Council, which was established in 1952 and groups 87 members from Denmark, Finland, Iceland, Norway, Sweden, the Faroe Islands, Greenland and Åland.

A final instance of multilateralism as a characteristic of Arctic governance relates to the management of fisheries in the Central Arctic Ocean (CAO). While other RFMOs (in particular the North Atlantic Fisheries Organization (NAFO) and the North East Atlantic Fisheries Commission (NEAFC)) are already active in parts of the Arctic, the American Senate urged its government in 2007 to commence negotiations on an international fisheries agreement for the CAO. Consultation with Canada and Russia pointed out that these States were unwilling to involve the UN General Assembly, the FAO or even the Arctic Council in these matters. Negotiations were therefore started within the framework of the Arctic Five, holding separate policy and science meetings. Eventually, the Arctic Five adopted a 'Declaration concerning the Prevention of Unregulated High Seas Fishing in the Central Arctic Ocean' at the end of their 2015 policy meeting in Oslo.[343] This Oslo Declaration established a (non-binding) moratorium on commercial fisheries in the CAO until such time as a RFMO or similar arrangement was established. In addition, the declaration explicitly acknowledged the interests of States other than the Arctic Five in regulating high seas fisheries in the CAO and envisioned a broader process to develop relevant measures. Consequently, four other States (Iceland, Japan, South Korea and China) and one international organisation (the EU) were included in this broader process (known since as the 'Five-plus-Five').

At the last meeting of the Arctic Five-plus-Five in November 2017, a draft 'Agreement to Prevent Unregulated High Seas Fisheries in the Central Arctic Ocean' was concluded. The Agreement 'will prevent unregulated commercial fishing in the high seas portion of

[342] See Declaration on Cooperation in the Barents Euro-Arctic Region, Conference of Foreign Ministers (Kirkenes, Norway), 11 January 1993, barentsinfo.fi/beac/docs/459_doc_KirkenesDeclaration.pdf (Kirkenes Declaration). The Members' commitment was reaffirmed in 2013; see Declaration on the 20th Anniversary of the Barents Euro-Arctic Cooperation, Barents Summit (Kirkenes, Norway), 4 June 2013, regjeringen.no/globalassets/upload/ud/vedlegg/nordomrc3a5dene/barentssamarbeidet/barentssummitdeclaration2013.pdf (Kirkenes II Declaration).

[343] See Declaration concerning the Prevention of Unregulated High Seas Fishing in the Central Arctic Ocean (Oslo, Norway), 16 July 2015, regjeringen.no/globalassets/departementene/ud/vedlegg/folkerett/declaration-on-arctic-fisheries-16-july-2015.pdf.

the central Arctic Ocean', 'establish and operate a Joint Program of Scientific Research and Monitoring with the aim of improving the understanding of the ecosystem(s) of this area' and 'envisions the possibility that one or more additional regional fisheries management organisations or arrangements may be established for this area in the future'. The Agreement is expected to be formally adopted in the second half of 2018.[344]

D. The EU in the Arctic

The EU is closely connected with the Arctic region, not only for reasons of proximity, but also because several of its Member States (Denmark, Finland and Sweden) exercise sovereignty over parts of this region. The close connection between the Arctic and global climate change further solidifies the EU's interest in this region. The origins of the EU's involvement in the Arctic actually stretch back to the establishment of the Northern Dimension in the 1990s. The Northern Dimension mainly focused on relations between Russia and members and candidate members in the Baltic Sea area. An Arctic Window was developed in 2002 in the framework of this policy, although the Northern Dimension in general and the Arctic Window in particular remained relatively low-key policies throughout most of the 2000s.

The EU has only really engaged in the region since 2008, when the European Parliament adopted a resolution in which it urged the Commission to take a proactive role in the Arctic – inter alia by attaining observer status in the Arctic Council – and suggested that the Commission prepare for the negotiation of a treaty for the protection of the Arctic, inspired by the Antarctic treaty.[345] Furthermore, the Parliament identified four issues that should be dealt with in the EU's Arctic policy, which the Commission had begun to develop since the publication of its 2007 Integrated Maritime Policy[346] and a 2008 joint policy paper by the Commission and the High Representative relating to climate change and international security.[347]

The basis for the EU's Arctic policy was then laid by the European Commission in a 2008 Communication on the European Union and the Arctic region.[348] The Communication laid out the groundwork for the EU's involvement in the Arctic by focusing on three main policy objectives: protecting and preserving the Arctic in unison with its population; promoting the sustainable use of resources; and contributing to enhanced Arctic multilateral governance. The progress in the wake of this Communication was assessed in a 2012 Joint Communication from the Commission and the High Representative, which also set the EU on the path towards the elaboration of a fully-fledged Arctic policy.[349] The need

[344] EC, Proposal for a Council Decision on the signing, on behalf of the European Union, of the Agreement to prevent unregulated high seas fisheries in the Central Arctic Ocean, 12 June 2018 (COM/2018/454final).

[345] European Parliament, Resolution on Arctic governance, 9 October 2008, P6_TA(2008)0474.

[346] Communication from the Commission to the European Parliament, the Council, the European Economic and Social Committee and the Committee of the Regions, 'An Integrated Maritime Policy for the European Union', 10 October 2007, COM(2007) 574 final.

[347] Joint Policy Paper from the High Representative and the European Commission to the European Council, 'Climate Change and International Security', 14 March 2008, S113/08.

[348] Communication from the Commission to the European Parliament and the Council, 'The European Union and the Arctic Region', 20 November 2008, COM(2008) 763 final.

[349] Joint Communication from the Commission and the High Representative to the European Parliament and the Council, 'Developing a European Union Policy towards the Arctic Region: progress since 2008 and next steps', 26 June 2012, JOIN(2012) 19 final.

to develop a coherent and integrated Arctic policy was further stressed by the European Parliament[350] and the Council[351] in 2014. In 2015, stakeholder consultations were organised and in April 2016 an integrated EU policy for the Arctic was presented by the Commission and the High Representative.[352] This Arctic policy focuses on three priority areas: climate change and safeguarding the Arctic environment; sustainable development in and around the Arctic; and international cooperation on Arctic issues. Furthermore, a prominent role for 'research, science and innovation' is envisaged[353] and the policy is framed particularly in terms of the UN's Sustainable Development Goals.

Even before the adoption of the EU's integrated Arctic policy in 2016, the EU has actively participated in a plethora of multilateral fora engaged with Arctic matters, such as the Arctic Council, the Barents Euro-Arctic Council, the Northern Dimension policy, and the Nordic Council. Where the EU applied for permanent observer status at the 2013 Ministerial Meeting of the Arctic Council, a final decision was deferred (see above, Subsection (C)(ii)). Nevertheless, some EU Member States have already been approved as observers, namely France, Germany, Italy, the Netherlands, Poland, Spain and the UK.

XI. Antarctica

In contrast with the Arctic region, which is in essence an ice-covered ocean surrounded by land, Antarctica consists of a landmass covered by an ice sheet, surrounded by ice-covered seas. Antarctica is the highest, driest, windiest, and coldest continent on earth. Historically uninhabited, it was the last continent to be discovered and explored. Both scientifically and resource-wise, Antarctica is of global importance. It is central to scientific research on climate change and global warming, and contains the world's greatest reserve of fresh water (albeit in frozen form). Moreover, it contains considerable amounts of both mineral and living resources, including some bio-organisms with great potential for bioprospecting.

A. Origins of the Antarctic Treaty System

Between 1907 and 1942, seven States (Argentina, Australia, Chile, France, New Zealand, Norway and the UK) made (mostly sectoral) claims to the Antarctic continent on several grounds, including discovery (and subsequent occupation), exploration, geographical proximity and geological affinity. Only a small part of the Antarctic, known as Marie Byrd Land, remains unclaimed; according to some, this piece of land constitutes the last *terra nullius* on earth. Three of the existing claims overlap (the Argentinian, the Chilean and the British), and none of the seven claims are recognised by non-claimant

[350] European Parliament, Resolution on the EU strategy for the Arctic, 12 March 2014, 2013/2595(RSP), P7_TA(2014)0236.

[351] Council conclusions on developing a European Union Policy towards the Arctic Region, 12 May 2014.

[352] Joint Communication from the Commission and the High Representative to the European Parliament and the Council, 'An integrated European Union policy for the Arctic', 27 April 2016, JOIN(2016) 21 final.

[353] ibid, 4.

States. As this situation gave rise to increasing tensions shortly after the Second World War, the States involved looked to defuse this situation. The success of the International Geophysical Year (1957–1958) (IGY), during which national expeditions from different States managed to cooperate peacefully to further scientific knowledge of the Antarctic continent, gave the much needed impetus to settle these issues. Shortly afterwards, in 1959, the Antarctic Treaty[354] was adopted by the 12 States[355] engaged in the IGY. In the course of the next 60 years, this treaty was complemented by several other treaties and instruments. The collection of these instruments is known as the Antarctic Treaty System (ATS), which still governs the Antarctic region.

B. The Antarctic Treaty

i. Claims Regime

The Antarctic Treaty did not resolve the sovereignty issues surrounding the Antarctic continent. Rather, the original signatories agreed to disagree on these matters in order to promote peaceful international cooperation and scientific research on the continent. Thus, the claims dispute was 'frozen' in accordance with a formula laid down in Article IV of the Antarctic Treaty.

Article IV(1)(a) protects the position of the claimant States; it stipulates that nothing in the Antarctic Treaty should be read as a renunciation of the existing claims. Article IV(1)(c) protects the position of the non-claimant States, confirming that ratification of the agreement is not to be interpreted as either recognition or non-recognition of any of the claims. Article IV(1)(b) protects the interests of two specific States, namely Russia and the US. Although neither have yet made a claim to the Antarctic continent, both retain the right to make claims at a later date (read: if the Antarctic Treaty should fall apart). Therefore, this Article protects their right to maintain this 'claim to make a claim'.

Article IV(2) contains two main elements: (i) no acts or activities undertaken while the Treaty is in force will constitute a 'basis for asserting, supporting or denying a claim to sovereignty in Antarctica'; and (ii) the assertion of new claims or the enlargement of existing claims is prohibited while the Treaty is in force. On the basis of the latter element, the ability of claimant States to claim maritime zones, such an EEZ and an extended continental shelf, has been challenged. Therefore, most claimant States adopted a diplomatic approach in submitting their information to the CLCS in accordance with Article 76(8) UNCLOS.[356]

One common misconception with regard to Article IV is that it results in a 'freezing of the claims', rather than a 'freezing of the claims *dispute*'. There is an important difference between both formulations. While freezing the claims would result in the claimant States not being able to exercise their claimed sovereignty, the freezing of the claims dispute does not have this effect. Claimant States remain free to perform acts of sovereignty, while

[354] Antarctic Treaty (adopted 1 December 1959, entered into force 23 June 1961) 402 UNTS 71.

[355] These 12 states include the seven claimant states mentioned earlier and Belgium, Japan, South Africa, the Soviet Union and the US.

[356] See above, Section III(B). See further R Baird, 'Can Australia Assert an Extended Continental Shelf off the Australian Antarctic Territory Consistent with the Law of the Sea and within the Constraints of the Antarctic Treaty?' (2004) *Maritime Studies* 1; J Jabour, 'High Latitude Diplomacy: Australia's Antarctic Extended Continental Shelf' (2006) 30 *Marine Policy* 197.

other States remain free to stress their non-recognition of the claims. Although claimant States, due to the sensitive political situation, have limited themselves to more symbolic acts of sovereignty, they have by no means stopped performing sovereign acts.[357] Thus, these claims still play an important role in the functioning of the Antarctic Treaty System: it has been forced to adopt a 'bifocal approach' in its further development to accommodate the views of both claimant and non-claimant States.[358] Consequently, provisions often require a vague formulation which is acceptable to both claimant and non-claimant States, and explicit rules on jurisdiction are largely absent from the ATS (see however below, Subsection (ii), on Article VIII).

ii. Three Main Principles

The freezing of the claims dispute allowed for peaceful coexistence and even cooperation on the Antarctic continent. Indeed, the Antarctic Treaty rests on three main principles. First, Article I of the Antarctic Treaty provides that the Antarctic should be used 'for peaceful purposes only'.[359] Any measures of a military nature, 'such as the establishment of military bases and fortifications, the carrying out of military maneuvers, as well as the testing of any type of weapons' are prohibited.[360] Nevertheless, military personnel and equipment can be used for scientific purposes 'or for any other peaceful purpose'.[361] Indeed, scientific research in Antarctica would prove practically impossible without these means. To ensure compliance with this provision, Article VII has established a system of observers. Consultative Parties can designate observers among their own nationals, who 'shall have complete freedom of access at any time to any or all areas of Antarctica'.[362] This includes 'all stations, installations and equipment within those areas, and all ships and aircraft at points of discharging or embarking cargoes or personnel in Antarctica'.[363] These observers are subject only to the jurisdiction of their own State.[364]

Second, Article II of the Antarctic Treaty proclaims 'the freedom of scientific investigation in Antarctica and cooperation toward that end'. Article III clarifies that the promotion of international cooperation requires the Contracting Parties to, 'to the greatest extent feasible and practicable': (i) exchange information regarding plans for scientific research; (ii) exchange personnel between expeditions and stations; and (iii) make freely available scientific observations and results. This last provision raises questions with regard to the patentability of inventions stemming from Antarctic research, especially in light of the possible commercial applications of research with regard to bio-organisms in Antarctica (in the process of bioprospecting). Despite these encouragements, international cooperation in view of scientific research remains limited. There is, for example,

[357] See further KJ Dodds and AD Hemmings, 'Frontier Vigilantism? Australia and Contemporary Representations of Australian Antarctic Territory' (2009) 55 *Australian Journal of Politics and History* 513; KJ Dodds, 'Sovereignty Watch: Claimant States, Resources, and Territory in Contemporary Antarctica' (2011) 47 *Polar Record* 231.

[358] See ML Lee, 'The 1959 Antarctic Treaty: The Freezing and Bifocalism Formula' (2000) *Australian International Law Journal* 200.

[359] Art I(1) Antarctic Treaty (n 354).

[360] ibid.

[361] ibid, Art I(2).

[362] ibid, Art VII(2).

[363] ibid, Art VII(3).

[364] ibid, Art VIII(1).

still no international research station in Antarctica equivalent to the International Space Station.[365]

The third principle is that of protection of the Antarctic environment. Although this principle plays only a limited role in the Antarctic Treaty itself, it has become one of the main pillars of the ATS as a whole. The Antarctic Treaty contains a ban on nuclear tests and the disposal of radioactive waste in Antarctica,[366] as well as a provision putting 'the preservation and conservation of living resources in Antarctica' on the agenda of the Antarctic Treaty Consultative Meetings (ATCMs, on which see below, Subsection (iv)).[367] These provisions have not only been complemented by two treaties and a protocol with an environmental focus (see below, Subsection C), but also by recommendations, resolutions, and measures relating to environmental protection. For example, through these instruments, guidelines for tourists and visitors have been adopted.[368]

iii. Scope

The Antarctic Treaty applies to the Antarctic treaty area, which is the area south of 60° South Latitude, 'including all ice shelves'.[369] However, it is expressly stated that this leaves the rights of any State with regard to the high seas unaffected.[370] Given the subsequent evolutions in the law of the sea, the exact meaning of this provision has become contested, and has given rise to serious questions about the relationship between the ATS and the law of the sea.

The Treaty has been adopted for an unlimited duration, although Article XII(2) did provide for the possibility of convening a Conference of the Parties to review the treaty after 30 years, if one of the Consultative Parties so requested. Formally, no use was made of this provision. However, the Madrid Protocol was adopted around this time (in 1991).[371]

There exists some debate on whether the Antarctic Treaty binds third States. Those answering in the affirmative have largely relied on the theory of objective regimes. Others have referred to the principle of *res inter alios acta*, according to which a treaty does not create obligations or rights for a third State without its consent.[372] This latter view seems to be most in line with positive law, especially as the objective regime theory was rejected during the negotiations of the VCLT. In any case, Article X of the Antarctic Treaty requires Contracting Parties 'to exert appropriate efforts […] to the end that no one engages in any activity in Antarctica contrary to the principles or purposes' of the Antarctic Treaty.

[365] AD Hemmings, 'Why Did We Get an International Space Station before an International Antarctic Station?' (2011) 1 *The Polar Journal* 5.

[366] Art V Antarctic Treaty (n 354).

[367] ibid, Art IX(1)(f).

[368] See eg Annex to Recommendation XVIII-1, adopted at the XVIIIth ATCM (Kyoto, Japan), 11–22 April 1994, effective as of 11 May 2016 (guidelines for tourism); Annex to Resolution 3, adopted at the XXXIVth ATCM – XIVth Committee for Environmental Protection Meeting (CEP), adopted 1 July 2011, not yet effective (General Guidelines for Visitors to the Antarctic); Annex to Resolution 6, adopted at the XLth ATCM – XXth CEP (Beijing, China), adopted 1 June 2017, not yet effective (Guidelines on Contingency Planning, Insurance and Other Matters for Tourist and Other Non-Governmental Activities in the Antarctic Treaty Area).

[369] Art VI Antarctic Treaty (n 354).

[370] ibid.

[371] Protocol on Environmental Protection to the Antarctic Treaty (adopted 4 October 1991, entered into force 14 January 1998) 30 ILM 1455 (Madrid Protocol).

[372] See Chapter 3, Section VIII on consequences of treaties for third parties.

In other words, Contracting Parties are expected to exert political pressure on States wanting to engage in Antarctic activities to comply with the rules of the ATS.

iv. Institutional Framework

Currently, the Antarctic Treaty counts 53 States Parties, of which only 29 have consultative status. Consultative status is awarded to the 12 original signatories and to all other States Parties that demonstrate their interest in Antarctica 'by conducting substantial scientific research there'.[373] The Antarctic Treaty Consultative Parties (ATCPs) have the right to vote during the annual ATCMs,[374] whereas the non-Consultative Parties can participate but cannot vote. During the ATCM, the Consultative Parties adopt decisions, resolutions and measures. Decisions (which only concern internal organisational matters for the ATCM) and resolutions are hortatory texts, whereas measures become binding on the Consultative Parties once they have been approved by them.[375]

The Antarctic Treaty did not establish an international organisation to monitor the implementation of and compliance with the Treaty. Some claimant States vehemently opposed any proposals to this end, as they considered that this could weaken their sovereignty claims in the long term. Instead, the ATCPs jointly manage this task, generally through their annual ATCMs. Despite continuing resistance from some claimant States, the Antarctic Treaty finally established a Secretariat on 1 September 2004 to support the annual ATCMs.[376]

Several other organisations play an important role in Antarctica, namely the Council of Managers of National Antarctic Programs (COMNAP), the Scientific Committee on Antarctic Research (SCAR), and the International Association of Antarctic Tour Operators (IAATO). These organisations support the work of the ATCMs and facilitate cooperation between the different Contracting Parties.

C. Additional Treaties

The ATS consists not only of the Antarctic Treaty, but includes also 'the measures in effect under that Treaty, its associated separate international instruments in force and the measures in effect under those instruments'.[377] In addition to instruments adopted in the ATCMs, over time, the Antarctic Treaty has been supplemented by other international agreements, such as the 1972 Convention for the Conservation of Antarctic Seals.[378]

Another example of such an agreement is the 1980 Convention for the Conservation of Antarctic Marine Living Resources (CCAMLR).[379] In line with the ecosystem approach adopted in this Convention, its territorial scope of application is broader than that of the

[373] Art XI.2 Antarctic Treaty (n 354).
[374] These ATCMs are organised each year on the territory of a different State Party.
[375] See Secretariat of the Antarctic Treaty, 'The Antarctic Treaty Consultative Meeting (ATCM)', ats.aq/e/ats_meetings_atcm.htm.
[376] K Scott, 'Institutional Developments within the Antarctic Treaty System' (2003) 52 *ICLQ* 473.
[377] Art 1 Madrid Protocol (n 371).
[378] Convention on the Conservation of Antarctic Seals (adopted 1 June 1972, entered into force 11 March 1978) 1080 UNTS 175 (Seals Convention).
[379] Convention on the Conservation of Antarctic Marine Living Resources (adopted 20 May 1980, entered into force 7 April 1982) 1329 UNTS 48 (CCAMLR).

Antarctic Treaty. More specifically, it reaches up to the Antarctic Convergence as defined in Article I(4) CCAMLR. Thus, it includes some recognised maritime zones stretching into the Antarctic Convergence from sub-Antarctic islands. CCAMLR counts only 25 Members, including the EU. These Members are bound to respect the 'principles and purposes' of the Antarctic Treaty, including the compromise of Article IV of the Antarctic Treaty.[380] CCAMLR has also established a separate but connected institutional framework, with a Commission consisting of delegates from the member States but with separate legal personality,[381] a Scientific Committee[382] and a Secretariat.[383] The connection between both institutional frameworks is exemplified by the permanent observer status of the CCAMLR Commission at the ATCMs.

Lastly, there is the 1991 Protocol on Environmental Protection to the Antarctic Treaty (Madrid Protocol).[384] Between 1982 and 1988, the ATCPs had been negotiating an agreement to allow for mineral exploitation in the Antarctic, despite great protest coming from the Group of 77 in the UN General Assembly. However, shortly after the conclusion of the so-called Convention on the Regulation of Antarctic Mineral Resource Activities (CRAMRA),[385] France and Australia, pressured by environmental NGOs and out of fear that this agreement might weaken their territorial claims, started a campaign against this Convention. Instead, the Madrid Protocol was negotiated, which designated Antarctica as a 'Special Conservation Area' and stipulated the 'protection of the Antarctic environment and dependent and associated ecosystems and the intrinsic value of Antarctica'.[386] In addition to requiring an environmental impact assessment to be undertaken for every activity taking place in Antarctica,[387] the Protocol banned all mineral activities other than scientific research from the Antarctic Treaty area for at least a period of 50 years.[388] Moreover, the Madrid Protocol established a Committee on Environmental Protection (CEP), which gathers annually at the same time and in the same place as the ATCM. The CEP consists of delegates from the Member States and provides advice to the ATCM for the adoption of environmental protection measures. The Madrid Protocol has been further elaborated through the adoption of annexes.

D. The EU in the Antarctic

Despite its (growing) interest in Arctic governance (see above, Section X(D)), Antarctica has never been high on the EU's policy agenda. A notable exception is the EU's engagement in the CCAMLR. The EU is one of the founding members of CCAMLR, and remains an active participant in the CCAMLR Commission. In 2013, for example, it tabled a proposal to establish an East Antarctic Representative System of Marine Protected Areas (EARMSPA), together with Australia and France. This proposal is currently still under

380 ibid, Art III; see also Art IV.
381 ibid, Arts VII–VIII.
382 ibid, Art XIV.
383 ibid, Art XVII.
384 See above (n 371).
385 Convention on the Regulation of Antarctic Mineral Resource Activities (adopted 2 June 1988, not entered into force) 27 ILM 868.
386 Art 3 Madrid Protocol (n 371).
387 ibid, Art 8.
388 ibid, Art 7 *juncto* Art 25.

debate, and has not yet been implemented. Nevertheless, it illustrates the leading role adopted by the EU in CCAMLR.

Besides its engagement in CCAMLR, the EU has only participated four times in ATS proceedings, ie during the negotiation of the Madrid Protocol. Ever since, it has shown very little interest in further involvement. In 2015, this lack of interest was acknowledged by European Commissioner Karmenu Vella in response to a parliamentary question in the European Parliament. He stated that, besides its engagement in CCAMLR, 'other avenues for participating in the Antarctic Treaty System, including a possible accession by the EU to the Antarctic Treaty, have not yet been explored'.[389]

XII. Outer Space

The launch of Sputnik I on 4 October 1957 marked the first successful activity to be undertaken by a State in outer space. To regulate the activities of exploration and use in this new realm, States were quick to develop the basics of an international legal regime in the form of a limited set of resolutions and treaties negotiated between 1963 and 1979 in the UN Committee on the Peaceful Uses of Outer Space. Though modern spacefaring differs drastically from the activities undertaken and envisaged at the time of negotiation of the UN framework, these instruments remain the basis for international space law to this day.

A. Sources

From the outset it became clear that rules related to territorial sovereignty and jurisdiction could not apply to outer space. As a rule, it is accepted that State sovereignty ends where outer space begins, though States have yet to agree on a lower limit of outer space (or an upper limit of airspace). A physical distinction between the two generally puts the demarcation line between airspace and outer space at 100 km above sea level. Some national space laws, like the Australian Space Activities Act of 21 December 1998,[390] apply this limit to determine whether operators should apply for a space licence. An alternative approach is to operate a functional criterion, distinguishing between airspace and outer space on the basis of the highest possible altitude that can be reached by an aeroplane, and contrasting this with the lowest possible orbit of a space object. This criterion would put the demarcation line anywhere between 80 and 110 km.

Although the lower limit of outer space determines the limit of State sovereignty, its meaning is largely theoretical. The UN space resolutions and treaties regulate the exploration

[389] 'Answer given by Mr Vella on behalf of the Commission', 24 September 2015, europarl.europa.eu/sides/getAllAnswers.do?reference=E-2015-010071&language=EN. See further N Vanstappen and J Wouters, 'The EU and the Antarctic: Strange Bedfellows?' in AD Hemmings, K Dodds and P Roberts (eds), *Handbook on the Politics of Antarctica* (Cheltenham, Edward Elgar, 2017) 269–83; N Vanstappen and J Wouters, 'Quel rôle pour l'Union européenne dans l'Arctique et dans l'Antarctique?' in J Auvret-Finck (ed), *La dimension environnementale de l'action extérieure de l'Union européenne* (Paris, Pedone, 2018).

[390] Space Activities Act 1998, No 123, Compilation No 7, as of 10 March 2016, legislation.gov.au/Details/C2016C00627.

and use of outer space rather than the status of the physical environment of outer space as such. The key international legal text on space law in this respect is the Treaty on Principles Governing the Activities of States in Outer Space, including the Moon and Other Celestial Bodies (Outer Space Treaty or OST) of 1967.[391] The treaty is a codification of the principles contained in UNGA Resolution 1962 of 13 December 1963.[392] The OST principles have in turn been further developed in a series of four UN treaties adopted between 1967 and 1979.[393] These treaties are chronologically characterised by a dwindling number of ratifications, however, and little legal progress has been made in international space law after the adoption of the last treaty in 1979.

Despite the lack of new international space law treaties, the legal regulation of activities in outer space has not come to a halt. First, issues not explicitly covered by the UN treaties on space law remain governed by general international law. In particular, Article III of the Outer Space Treaty requires that States carry on their activities in outer space 'in accordance with international law, including the Charter of the United Nations, in the interest of maintaining international peace and security'. Second, the general principles of the UN space regime are increasingly being complemented by legal developments at the national level. The most expansive national space law regime has been developed by the US.[394] In addition, national space laws have been adopted by more than 20 States, including European space players such as France, the UK and Belgium.[395] Finally, specific aspects related to the placement and operation of satellites in orbit around the Earth are governed by the law of the International Telecommunication Union (ITU), which is regularly updated and revised to keep up with the latest technological advances.[396]

B. Space Activities

The fundamental principles of international space law are enshrined in the Outer Space Treaty of 1967. Although this treaty applies to outer space, including the Moon and other celestial bodies, the Agreement Governing the Activities of States on the Moon and Other Celestial Bodies of 1979 (Moon Agreement)[397] repeats most of these principles and clarifies their application to celestial bodies in the solar system. Despite their similarity in content,

[391] Treaty on Principles Governing the Activities of States in the Exploration and Use of Outer Space, including the Moon and Other Celestial Bodies (adopted 27 January 1967, entered into force 10 October 1967) 610 UNTS 205.

[392] UNGA Res 1962 (XVIII), 'Declaration of Legal Principles Governing the Activities of States in the Exploration and Use of Outer Space', 13 December 1963, UN Doc A/RES/1962 (XVIII).

[393] Agreement on the Rescue of Astronauts, the Return of Astronauts and the Return of Objects Launched into Outer Space (adopted 19 December 1967, entered into force on 3 December 1968) 672 UNTS 119 (Rescue Agreement or ARRA); Convention on International Liability for Damage Caused by Space Objects (adopted 29 November 1971, entered into force 1 September 1972) 961 UNTS 187 (Liability Convention or LIAB); Convention on Registration of Objects Launched into Outer Space (adopted 12 November 1974, entered into force 15 September 1976) 1023 UNTS 15 (Registration Convention or REG); Agreement Governing the Activities of States on the Moon and Other Celestial Bodies (adopted 5 December 1979, entered into force 11 July 1984) 1363 UNTS 3 (Moon Agreement).

[394] See eg JI Gabrynowicz, 'One Half Century and Counting: The Evolution of U.S. National Space Laws' (2010) 4 *Harvard Law and Policy Review* 405.

[395] For updates, see UN Office for Outer Space Affairs, 'National Space Law Collection', unoosa.org/oosa/en/ourwork/spacelaw/nationalspacelaw/index.html.

[396] See ITU, 'Collection of the Basic Texts Adopted by the Plenipotentiary Conference', Edition 2015, search.itu.int/history/HistoryDigitalCollectionDocLibrary/5.21.61.en.100.pdf.

[397] See above (n 393).

the two treaties have very different ratification records: the Outer Space Treaty has been ratified by over 100 States, including almost all of the major spacefaring nations, and many of its principles are considered customary international law. The Moon Agreement, on the other hand, has only been ratified by 16 States, including a number of European countries, though none of the major spacefaring nations. Belgium and the Netherlands have ratified the agreement; France has only signed it. Most of the controversy surrounding the Moon Agreement concerns the regulation of the exploitation of natural resources of celestial bodies.

The following principles apply to all activities of States in outer space:

— the exploration and use of outer space, including celestial bodies, shall be carried out for the benefit and in the interests of all countries;[398]

— outer space, including celestial bodies, is free for exploration and use by all States, on a basis of equality and in accordance with international law;[399]

— outer space, including celestial bodies, is not subject to national appropriation by claim of sovereignty, by means of use or occupation, or by any other means;[400]

— the Moon and other celestial bodies must be used exclusively for peaceful purposes; States may not place weapons of mass destruction in other parts of outer space;[401]

— States bear international responsibility for the activities of their nationals in outer space, including celestial bodies, must authorise these activities and exercise continuing supervision over them; responsibility for the activities of international organisations in space rests with the international organisation and its Member States;[402]

— control and jurisdiction over space objects and the personnel thereof, even when they are in outer space or on a celestial body, rest with the State of registry of those objects;[403]

— in exploring and using outer space, including celestial bodies, States shall be guided by the principle of cooperation and mutual assistance; States must have due regard for the activities of others in outer space and may request to undertake appropriate international consultations with those States whose activities may harmfully interfere with their own;[404]

— States shall avoid harmful contamination of outer space, including celestial bodies.[405]

These principles apply to all activities undertaken by governmental and non-governmental actors in space and on celestial bodies, including private nationals and international organisations.[406]

Though national appropriation of outer space, including celestial bodies, is not allowed, it is unclear whether this prohibition extends to the natural resources of asteroids and other celestial bodies. In this respect, the Moon Agreement adds that natural resources 'in place' on celestial bodies remain covered by the non-appropriation principle,[407] leaving

[398] See notably Art I Outer Space Treaty (n 391).
[399] ibid.
[400] ibid, Art II.
[401] ibid, Art IV.
[402] ibid, Art VI.
[403] ibid, Art VIII.
[404] ibid, Art IX.
[405] ibid.
[406] See eg ibid, Art VI.
[407] Art 11(3) Moon Agreement (n 393).

unresolved whether these resources can become property when no longer in place. In any case, the uncertainty at the international level has not stopped countries from adopting national space legislation on asteroid mining. The US Commercial Space Launch Competitiveness Act of 2015[408] is the first to grant property rights to private companies that exploit asteroids in outer space. European countries are now starting to follow suit. In 2017, Luxembourg became the first country to model its legislation after the American example.[409]

C. Astronauts and Space Objects

In addition to the abovementioned fundamental principles that characterise all activities in outer space, the OST contains a number of key provisions on the rescue and return of astronauts, the return and registration of space objects and the liability for damage caused by these objects. Unlike the principles on space activities, the provisions on astronauts and space objects have also been elaborated in separate UN treaties. As a result, their interpretation is less problematic, though issues related to the application of these treaties to modern spacefaring activities remain.

Article V OST declares that government astronauts should be considered envoys of mankind. States should therefore render all possible assistance to them in the event of accident, distress or an emergency landing both on Earth and in outer space. The Agreement on the Rescue of Astronauts, the Return of Astronauts and the Return of Objects Launched into Outer Space of 1968 (Rescue Agreement or ARRA) expands upon this principle.[410] Astronauts who or space objects that have landed on the territory of another State should be rescued and/or returned to the launching State.[411] In case of an emergency landing on the high seas or in other territory on Earth not covered by national jurisdiction, this obligation extends only to those States that are in a position to render assistance.[412]

Article VII OST determines that each launching State is internationally liable for damages to other States or their natural or juridical persons caused by its space objects. Every State that launched or procures the launching of a space object, and from whose territory or facility such an object is launched, is considered a launching State. The Convention on International Liability for Damage Caused by Space Objects of 1972 (Liability Convention or LIAB)[413] distinguishes between damage caused on Earth or to aircraft in flight, on the one hand, and damage done in outer space. In the former case, liability is absolute;[414] in the latter, it is fault-based.[415] In the event of multiple launching States, all

[408] US Commercial Space Launch Competitiveness Act, 25 November 2015, Public Law 114-90, 129 Stat 704.
[409] The Government of the Grand Duchy of Luxembourg, 'A legal framework for space exploration', 13 July 2017, luxembourg.public.lu/en/actualites/2017/07/21-spaceresources/index.html. The law, as contained in the *Projet de loi sur l'exploration et l'utilisation des ressources de l'espace*, is available via the same link. It was adopted on 13 July 2017 and entered into force on 1 August 2017. See further J Wouters, P De Man, and R Hansen (eds), *Commercial Uses of Space and Space Tourism. Legal and Policy Aspects* (Cheltenham, Edward Elgar, 2017).
[410] See above (n 393).
[411] Art 2 ARRA.
[412] ibid, Art 3.
[413] See above (n 393).
[414] Art II LIAB.
[415] ibid, Art III.

shall be held jointly and severally liable for any damage caused.[416] Such joint liability also extends to damages caused by a space object launched by an international organisation, in which case liability is incurred by the international organisation and those of its Member States that have ratified the Liability Convention.[417]

Article VIII OST provides that ownership of space objects when in space or on a celestial body shall remain with the State of registry. The Convention on Registration of Objects Launched into Outer Space of 1975 (REG)[418] contains specific details on the nature and content of such space registries. States have to register objects that are launched in orbit around the Earth both at the national level and the international level. The content of national registries is generally left to the decision of individual States, which are only required to maintain an 'appropriate' national registry.[419] Most national space laws require operators to at least list the information that States have to convey to the UN Secretary General for inclusion in the international registry.[420] This includes such information on the space object as the date and location of launch, its orbital parameters and the general function of the space object, though not necessarily its functionality.[421]

D. The EU and the European Space Agency

The EU has recently acquired competences with respect to outer space. Since the entry into force of the Lisbon Treaty, Article 4(3) TFEU lists research, technological development and space amongst the competences that are shared between the Union and its Member States. However, unlike the situation most other shared competences, exercise of its 'space competence' by the EU does not result in Member States being prevented from exercising theirs.[422] The EU cannot harmonise national approaches to space undertaken by its Member States. This has led some to qualify space as a parallel rather than shared EU competence. The space competence of the EU largely consists of defining and implementing space programmes, such as the European flagship programmes Galileo[423] and Copernicus.[424] More recently, the EU has developed regulatory frameworks on other issues, such as space surveillance and tracking (SST).[425] The EU is also tasked with developing a space policy and fleshing out the relations with the European Space Agency (ESA).[426]

[416] ibid, Art V.
[417] ibid, Art XXII.
[418] See above (n 393).
[419] Art II REG.
[420] See ibid, Art III.
[421] ibid, Art IV.
[422] Art 4(3) TFEU. See J Wouters, 'The EU and Space Policy: Constitutional and Institutional Aspects' in S Hobe, B Schmidt-Tedd and KU Schrogl (eds), *Legal Aspects of the Future Institutional Relationship between the European Union and the European Space Agency* (Cologne, Institute of Air and Space Law, 2003) 17.
[423] For more information, see galileognss.eu.
[424] For more information, see copernicus.eu.
[425] See notably Decision No 541/2014/EU of the European Parliament and of the Council of 16 April 2014 establishing a Framework for Space Surveillance and Tracking Support [2014] OJ L158/227 and Commission Implementing Decision of 12.9.2014 on the procedure for participation of the Member States in the Space Surveillance and Tracking Support Framework, C(2014) 6342 final.
[426] Art 189 TFEU. On 6 June 2018 the Commission issued a proposal for a Regulation of the European Parliament and of the Council establishing the space programme of the Union and the European Union Agency for the Space Programme and repealing Regulations (EU) No 912/2010, (EU) No 1285/2013, (EU) No 377/2014 and Decision 541/2014/EU.

The ESA is governed by its constitutive Convention of 1975.[427] Its current membership of 22 States largely overlaps with that of the EU, although not entirely. Obviously, the goals of the Agency are much more limited than those of the EU. Whereas space is but one of the competences for the EU to realise its myriad of goals, including military objectives, ESA solely aims to provide for and to promote cooperation among European States in space research and technology, for exclusively peaceful purposes.[428] The parallel existence of 'two Europes in space' with differing membership, financing rules and decision-making procedures has strained relations between the EU and ESA. A 2004 EU-ESA Framework Agreement[429] has set up minimal forms of cooperation and a basic division of tasks, underpinned by a skeleton institutional framework headed by the so-called Space Council, which brings together Ministers of the Council of the EU and the ESA Council at ministerial level.[430] Despite the recently acquired space competence of the EU, European participation in global spacefaring affairs is still mainly realised through ESA.

The Member States of ESA, as well as any other European State that would like to accede to the agreement, together constitute the European Partner to the International Space Station.[431] However, in practice, most of the rights and responsibilities of the European Partner are delegated to ESA. This is due to the fact that the Agency, unlike the EU, is bound by the international rules on spacefaring developed by the UN. It has declared its acceptance of the rights and obligations laid down in the Rescue Agreement, the Liability Convention and the Registration Convention. The European Organization for the Exploitation of Meteorological Satellites (EUMETSAT) is bound by the same treaties. In addition, the rules of the Liability and Registration Conventions apply to the European Telecommunications Satellite Organization (EUTELSAT). Indeed, any intergovernmental international organisation can make such a declaration if the majority of its Member States are parties to the Outer Space Treaty and to the treaty by which the international organisation wishes to be bound.[432] The limited space competences of the EU and its difficult relationship with ESA have so far prevented the Union from doing so.

XIII. Concluding Remarks

If global commons are defined as those areas over which no State can exercise or claim sovereignty, four such areas can be identified: the high seas, the deep seabed, outer space and Antarctica (although controversy persists regarding the legal status of the latter). Despite some common characteristics, the legal regimes governing them differ considerably.

[427] Convention for the Establishment of a European Space Agency (adopted 30 May 1975, entered into force 30 October 1980), as published in the ESA Annual Report 1975, Annex X.

[428] ibid, Art II.

[429] Framework Agreement between the European Community and the European Space Agency (adopted 25 November 2003, entered into force 28 May 2004) [2004] OJ L261/64.

[430] ibid, Art 8.

[431] Art 3(b) of the Agreement among the Government of Canada, Governments of Member States of the European Space Agency, the Government of Japan, the Government of the Russian Federation, and the Government of the United States of America concerning Cooperation on the Civil International Space Station (adopted 29 January 1998, entered into force 27 March 2001), as published in K-H Böckstiegel, M Benkö and S Hobe (eds), *Space Law: Basic Legal Documents* (Dordrecht, Nijhoff, 1990) and on state.gov/documents/organization/107683.pdf.

[432] See Arts 6 ARRA, XXII LIAB and VII REG.

Global commons have been a perennial feature of (modern) international law. In his seminal work *Mare Liberum*, Grotius argued that the sea is 'common to all because it is so limitless that it cannot become a possession of any one, and because it is adapted for the use of all, whether we consider it from the point of view of navigation or of fisheries'.[433] Despite some early resistance, Grotius' theory became widely accepted and the oceans (high seas) were considered the first global commons in modern international law. Moreover, Grotius also set out the two basic principles governing these areas, namely the non-appropriability thereof on the one hand and the freedom to use them on the other. These principles would also serve as a basis for the rules regarding outer space. Antarctica is, however, a different matter, as seven States still hold sovereignty claims over part of the continent and the freedom to use the seventh continent has been substantively curtailed (eg through the moratorium on commercial mining).

These basic ordering principles have come under increasing pressure in subsequent centuries, especially the law of the sea. An exception was created in the course of the seventeenth century for territorial seas, to ensure the security of the coastal State. More importantly, however, although Grotius argued that the seas were 'adapted for the use of all', it has increasingly become clear that the oceans' resources are not inexhaustible. Instead, there existed – and continues to exist – a serious risk of a 'tragedy of the commons'. In addition, the basic principle of freedom of use was deemed to favour major developed States who could make full use of this freedom. Accordingly, the oceans were ordered into different zones over the course of the twentieth century, with varying degrees of jurisdiction for coastal States. Moreover, the deep seabed was set aside as the common heritage of mankind to be exploited for the benefit of mankind as a whole and the developing States in particular. At the same time, the function of the global commons as means of communication, trade and navigation between States was maintained through the principle of freedom of navigation. These evolutions and compromises were codified in UNCLOS. Whereas outer space was not divided up into zones of jurisdiction, other means were found to ensure equitable sharing of limited resources, such as satellite lanes, through international institutions, such as the ITU.

Over recent decades these compromises have been criticised, in particular because they splintered the exercise of jurisdiction where more holistic and integrated approaches were needed. Neither fish stocks nor pollution stop at borders. Accordingly, it has been argued that governance arrangements should adopt more integrated approaches, spanning across borders, but also across functional domains. Outer space activities could, for example, serve to monitor ocean acidification or the movement of fish stocks. These issues could then be regulated through an ecosystem-based approach spanning across EEZs and the high seas. Within the EU's domain, for example, this search for a more holistic approach formed the basis for the development of an Integrated Maritime Policy and the concomitant adoption of the Maritime Spatial Planning Directive (2014).[434]

In all, through the governance of the global commons, States have increasingly become aware of the interconnectedness of our Earth's different parts and phenomena and of how much they depend on each other to find adequate solutions. This increasing consciousness

[433] H Grotius, *Mare Liberum* (1609), as translated: R Van Deman Magoffin, *The Freedom of the Seas* (New York, OUP, 1916) 28.

[434] Directive 2014/89/EU of the European Parliament and of the Council of 23 July 2014 establishing a framework for maritime spatial planning [2014] OJ L257/135.

of all States' interdependence has also greatly affected international environmental law and international economic law, matters which the following chapters discuss in greater detail.

Bibliography

Baslar, K, *The Concept of the Common Heritage of Mankind in International Law* (The Hague, Nijhoff, 1998).
Byers, M, *International Law and the Arctic* (Cambridge, CUP, 2013).
Churchill, RR and Lowe, AV, *The Law of the Sea*, 3rd edn (Manchester, Manchester UP, 1999).
Evans, MD, 'The Law of the Sea' in Evans, MD (ed), *International Law*, 4th edn (Oxford, OUP, 2014) 651–687.
Forteau, M and Thouvenin, JM (eds), *Traité de droit international de la mer* (Paris, Pedone, 2017).
Institut du droit économique de la mer (ed), *Droit international de la mer et droit de l'Union européenne: cohabitation, confrontation, coopération?* (Paris, Pedone, 2014).
Molenaar, EJ, Oude Elferink, AG, Rothwell, DR, *The Law of the Sea and the Polar Regions: Interactions between Global and Regional Regimes* (Leiden, Nijhoff, 2013).
Pancracio, J-P, *Droit de la mer* (Paris, Dalloz, 2010).
Proelß, A (ed), *The United Nations Convention on the Law of the Sea: A Commentary* (Munich, Beck, 2017).
Ranganathan, S, 'Global Commons' (2016) 27 *EJIL* 693.
Rothwell, DR, Oude Elferink, AG, Scott, KN and Stephens, T (eds), *The Oxford Handbook of the Law of the Sea* (Oxford, OUP, 2015).
Smolinska AM, *Le droit de la mer entre universalisme et régionalisme* (Brussels, Bruylant, 2014).
Tanaka, Y, *The International Law of the Sea*, 2nd edn (Cambridge, CUP, 2015).
Treves, T and Pineschi, L (eds), *The Law of the Sea: the European Union and its Member States* (The Hague, Martinus Nijhoff Publishers, 1997).
Vanstappen, N and Wouters, J, 'The EU and the Antarctic: Strange Bedfellows?' in Hemmings, AD, Dodds, K and Roberts, P (eds), *Handbook on the Politics of Antarctica* (Cheltenham, Edward Elgar, 2017) 269–283.
von der Dunk, FG, *Handbook of Space Law* (Cheltenham, Edward Elgar, 2015).

Further Reading

Allott, P, 'Mare Nostrum: A New International Law of the Sea' (1992) 86 *AJIL* 764.
Brunnée J, 'Common Areas, Common Heritage, and Common Concern' in Bodansky, D, Brunnée, J and Hey, E (eds), *Oxford Handbook of International Environmental Law* (Oxford, OUP, 2007) 550–573.
Churchill, R and Owen, D, *The EC Common Fisheries Policy* (Oxford, OUP, 2010).

Franckx, E, 'The International Seabed Authority and the Common Heritage of Mankind: The Need for States to Establish the Outer Limits of their Continental Shelf' (2010) 25 *International Journal of Marine and Coastal Law* 543.

Freestone, D, 'International Governance, Responsibility and Management of Areas beyond National Jurisdiction' (2012) 27 *International Journal of Marine and Coastal Law* 191.

Hoefsmit, CA, 'Southern Ocean Shakeup: Establishing Sovereignty in Antarctica and the Consequences for Fishery Management' (2010) 15 *Roger Williams University Law Review* 547.

Jakhu, R, 'Legal Issues Relating to the Global Public Interest in Outer Space' (2006) 32 *Journal of Space Law* 31.

Joyner, CJ, *Antarctica and the Law of the Sea* (Dordrecht, Nijhoff, 1992).

Koivurova, T, 'The Arctic Council: A Testing Ground for New International Environmental Governance' (2012) 19 *The Brown Journal of World Affairs* 131.

Lefeber, R, 'The Exercise of Jurisdiction in the Antarctic Region and the Changing Structure of International Law: The International Community and Common Interests' (1990) 21 *NYIL* 81.

JG Mahinga, *Le tribunal international du droit de la mer: organisation, compétence et procédure* (Brussels, Larcier, 2013).

Molenaar, EJ, 'Current and Prospective Roles of the Arctic Council System within the Context of the Law of the Sea' (2012) 27 *International Journal of Marine and Coastal Law* 553.

Oxman, BH, 'The Territorial Temptation: A Siren Song at Sea' (2006) 100 *AJIL* 830.

Rayfuse, R and Warner, R, 'Securing a Sustainable Future for the Oceans beyond National Jurisdiction: The Legal Basis for an Integrated Cross-Sectoral Regime for High Seas Governance for the 21st Century' (2008) 23 *International Journal of Marine and Coastal Law* 399.

Schrijver, N and Prislan, V, 'From Mare Liberum to the Global Commons: Building on the Grotian Heritage' (2009) 30 *Grotiana* 168.

Serdy, A, 'Postmodern International Fisheries Law, or We Are All Coastal States Now' (2011) 60 *ICLQ* 387.

Vanstappen, N and Wouters, J, 'Quel rôle pour l'Union européenne dans l'Arctique et dans l'Antarctique?' in Auvret-Finck, J (ed), *La dimension environnementale de l'action extérieure de l'Union européenne* (Paris, Pedone, 2018).

Wolfrum, R, *Die Internationalisierung staatsfreier Räume* (Vienna, Springer, 1984).

Wolfrum, R, 'Common Heritage of Mankind' (2009) in Wolfrum, R (ed), *Max Planck Encyclopedia of Public International Law* (Oxford, OUP).

19

International Economic Law

I. Introduction

International economic law is composed of a number of areas that contain specific sets of norms of public international law governing the economic relations between States and between States and other subjects of international law, including international organisations and private actors. It encompasses international trade law, economic integration law, investment law, antitrust (or competition) law, intellectual property law and monetary law.[1] This chapter will start with a short overview of the history and the institutions of international economic law. Hereafter, specific attention will be devoted to international trade law, especially the functioning of the World Trade Organization (WTO), regional economic integration (through regional trade agreements), and the protection of foreign investments in international investment law.

II. History and Institutions

International norms concerning economic relations between States are of relatively recent origin. During the nineteenth century most States adopted a laissez-faire policy with respect to international economic relations; apart from customs regulations and import restrictions there were hardly any controls and restrictions on trade and financial transactions with foreigners. Towards the end of the nineteenth century the international trading system was mainly based on liberal national legislation (including those on the gold standard and convertibility of national currencies), and bilateral trade and investment agreements. With the commencement of the First World War, this system collapsed. The period between the two World Wars was characterised by monetary instability, in the aftermath of the crash of Wall Street in 1929, as the post-war restored gold standard was based on unrealistic exchange rates, especially for the British Pound. When the Pound was disconnected from the

[1] M Herdegen, *Principles of International Economic Law*, 2nd edn (Oxford, OUP, 2016) 8–11.

gold standard in 1931, this gave rise to a series of competitive devaluations between countries and a spiral of protectionist measures, whereby States adopted trade barriers to protect their economies, with similar countermeasures in other States.[2] As a result thereof, between 1929 and 1932, the value of world trade fell by as much as 60 per cent. The collapse of the world economy and the ensuing Great Depression of the 1930s led to political instability and helped lay the foundation for the rise of fascism in Europe, which ultimately culminated in the outbreak of World War II.

During the Second World War, plans were made for a new international economic order. In the early 1940s the British economist John Maynard Keynes and American economist Harry Dexter White almost simultaneously developed plans for a new international monetary system in order to stabilise exchange rates and promote free trade. In order to achieve these objectives a permanent institution would be required, rather than the conferences of the major countries which were hitherto held at irregular intervals (and failed because of deep disagreements). In July 1944, negotiations took place in Bretton Woods, New Hampshire, where an agreement was reached on the statutes of the to-be established 'Bretton Woods institutions', in particular the IMF[3] (on which see Chapter 6, Section IX(E)) and the International Bank for Reconstruction and Development (IBRD)[4] (part of the World Bank Group) (on which see Chapter 6, Section IX(F)). In addition to these two financial institutions, plans were made to also establish an International Trade Organization (ITO). All three of these institutions were meant to be specialised agencies of the UN.[5] In anticipation of the adoption and entry into force of the ITO Charter,[6] some of the participating States started negotiations on the General Agreement on Tariffs and Trade 1947 (GATT 1947), which became provisionally applicable in January 1948.[7] Even though the ITO Charter had been adopted in Havana in 1948, it never entered into force due to the unwillingness of the United States to submit the Charter to the Senate for its advice and consent.[8] The 'provisionally applied' GATT evolved into a de facto organisation, with a secretariat in Geneva.[9]

The liberal character of this post-war international financial and economic order is striking: it is based on the theory of comparative advantage in international economic relations, as developed by the British economists David Ricardo and John Stuart Mill.[10] This theory

[2] J Wouters and B De Meester, *The World Trade Organization: A Legal and Institutional Analysis* (Oxford, Intersentia, 2007) 8.

[3] Articles of Agreement of the International Monetary Fund (adopted 22 July 1944, entered into force 27 December 1945) 2 UNTS 39.

[4] Articles of Agreement for the International Bank for Reconstruction and Development (adopted 22 July 1944, entered into force 27 December 1945) 2 UNTS 134.

[5] T Flory, *L'organisation mondiale de commerce : droit institutionnel et substantiel* (Brussels, Bruylant, 1999) 3.

[6] Havana Charter for an International Trade Organisation (adopted 24 March 1948, never entered into force).

[7] Protocol on the Provisional Application of the GATT of 30 October 1947, 61 Stat A2051; 55 UNTS 308; JH Jackson, *The Jurisprudence of GATT and the WTO. Insights on Treaty Law and Economic Relations* (Cambridge, CUP, 2000) 24–27.

[8] For more information on the 'failure' of the ITO, see eg W Diebold, *The End of ITO. Essays in International Finance no 16* (Princeton, Princeton UP, 1952); JH Jackson, *World Trade Law and the Law of GATT: A Legal Analysis of the General Agreement on Tariffs and Trade* (Michigan, Bobbs-Merrill Company, 1969); JH Jackson, *The World Trading System. Law and Policy of International Economic Relations* (Cambridge, MIT Press, 1997); J-C Graz, *Aux sources de l'OMC: la Charte de la Havane 1941–1950 / Precursor of the WTO: the stillborn Havana Charter 1941–1950* (Geneva, Droz, 1999); AF Lowenfeld, *International Economic Law*, 2nd edn (Oxford, OUP, 2008).

[9] For more information on the provisional application of the GATT, see Wouters and De Meester (n 2) 10.

[10] D Ricardo, *The Principles of Political Economy and Taxation* (London, John Murray, 1817). See also A Smith, *An Inquiry into the Nature and Causes of the Wealth of Nations* (London, Methuen & Co Ltd, 1776).

assumes that liberalised international trade and the accompanying international division of labour yields benefits to all participating national economies.[11] The consequent phasing out of restrictions on access to international markets and on financial transactions, along with the stabilisation of the international monetary relations, was seen as a prerequisite for a high level of employment, increasing prosperity and optimising the use of production factors. This liberal character helps explain why the Soviet Union (which initially sat at the table at Bretton Woods) dropped out, with the Eastern Bloc countries following in its wake during the Cold War.

In addition to the IMF, the World Bank and the – later established – WTO,[12] the OECD (on which see Chapter 7, Section II(D))[13] plays an important role in the framework of global economic governance. The OECD brings together the major industrialised countries, in order to promote policies that improve the economic and social well-being of people around the world.[14] Moreover, within the framework of the UN system, several programs and specialised agencies are concerned with economics and development. These include the United Nations Conference on Trade and Development (UNCTAD) and the United Nations Development Programme (UNDP), both working under the auspices of the UN General Assembly and the UN Economic and Social Council (ECOSOC).[15] In addition, several UN specialised agencies are concerned with raising the standard of living and the economic development of developing countries: the Food and Agriculture Organization (FAO) (on which see Chapter 6, Section IX(D)), the United Nations Industrial Development Organization (UNIDO) and the International Fund for Agricultural Development (IFAD). Even though the WTO itself is not a specialised agency of the UN, it does interact with it in several instances, including through the International Trade Centre (ITC) (as a 'joint subsidiary organ'), on technical assistance to developing countries (via UNCTAD) and on issues such as food security (through FAO) and sustainable development (through UNDP). The relationship between the GATT and the UN was set out in a 1973 UN General Assembly document.[16]

From a European perspective, special mention should be made of the UN Economic Commission for Europe (UNECE), one of the five regional economic commissions which saw the light of day under ECOSOC.[17] UNECE was founded in 1947 to strengthen the economic reconstruction of Europe and the economic relations between European countries and the rest of the world. UNECE has 56 members in Europe (including Israel) and North America.[18] The principal activities of UNECE are in the fields of environment,

[11] See AO Sykes, 'Comparative Advantage and the Normative Economics of International Trade Policy' (1998) 1 *JIEL* 49.

[12] See the WTO Agreement, also referred to as the Marrakesh Agreement.

[13] OECD Convention.

[14] OECD, 'About', oecd.org/about.

[15] United Nations System Organization Chart, July 2015, un.org/en/aboutun/structure/pdfs/UN_System_Chart_30June2015.pdf.

[16] UN General Assembly, *Relations of the General Agreement on Tariffs and Trade with the United Nations*, 9 March 1973, UN Doc A/AC.179/5.

[17] The others being the: Economic Commission for Africa (ECA), Economic and Social Commission for Asia and the Pacific (ESCAP), Economic Commission for Latin America and the Caribbean (ECLAC) and Economic and Social Commission for Western Asia (ESCWA).

[18] Albania, Andorra, Armenia, Austria, Azerbaijan, Belarus, Belgium, Bosnia and Herzegovina, Bulgaria, Canada, Croatia, Cyprus, Czech Republic, Denmark, Estonia, Finland, France, Georgia, Germany, Greece, Hungary, Iceland, Ireland, Israel, Italy, Kazakhstan, Kyrgyzstan, Latvia, Liechtenstein, Lithuania, Luxembourg,

transport, statistics, trade facilitation, industry, agriculture and forestry, housing, building, and planning. UNECE also assists countries in Central and Eastern Europe in their transition to a market economy. It has been instrumental in developing various standards and international conventions (on this, see also Chapter 20).

Reference should also be made to the following types of international agreements that relate to international economic law. Firstly, *International Commodity Agreements* between importing and exporting countries: for a number of goods, international agreements are concluded between the major exporting and importing countries with a view to achieving greater price stability in the interest of developing countries that depend heavily on these products. For example, there are the international coffee,[19] rubber,[20] tea,[21] wood,[22] cocoa,[23] olive oil,[24] wheat,[25] copper[26] and jute[27] agreements. Some of these agreements provide only for the elimination of trade barriers; others provide a direct intervention on supply and demand. A specific agreement is the 1994 Energy Charter Treaty, a multilateral investment and trade agreement which has been signed or acceded to by 52 States (including all EU Member States, Central and Eastern European countries, all former Soviet countries, Japan and Australia), the EU and Euratom.[28]

Secondly, reference should be made to *International Agreements between Exporting Countries:* the best known example is the Organization for Petroleum Exporting Countries (OPEC), founded in 1960 in Baghdad. Since the first oil crisis in 1973, OPEC sees to the unilateral pricing of oil. OPEC Members agree on quotas among themselves, but these are not always observed due a lack of mutual solidarity. Thirdly, *Regional Trade Agreements* are agreements that reciprocally lower barriers to trade between two or more countries. During recent decades the establishment of such agreements has mushroomed (see below, Section III(B)).

Malta, Monaco, Montenegro, the Netherlands, Norway, Poland, Portugal, Republic of Moldova, Romania, the Russian Federation, San Marino, Serbia, Slovak Republic, Slovenia, Spain, Sweden, Switzerland, Tajikistan, the Former Yugoslav Republic of Macedonia, Turkey, Turkmenistan, Ukraine, United Kingdom of Great Britain and Northern Ireland, United States of America, Uzbekistan.

[19] International Coffee Agreement (adopted 28 September 2000, entered into force 17 May 2005) 2161 UNTS 308.

[20] International Natural Rubber Agreement (adopted 17 February 1995, entered into force 14 February 1997, ended 13 October 1999) 1964 UNTS 3.

[21] Agreement Establishing the International Tea Promotion Association (adopted 31 March 1977, entered into force 23 February 1979) 1128 UNTS 367.

[22] International Tropical Timber Agreement (adopted 1 February 2006, entered into force 7 December 2011) 2791 UNTS 75.

[23] International Cocoa Agreement (adopted 2 March 2001, entered into force 2 November 2005) 2229 UNTS 2; International Cocoa Agreement (adopted 25 July 2010, entered into force provisionally 1 October 2012) 2871 UNTS 3.

[24] International Agreement on Olive Oil and Table Olives (adopted 1 July 1986, entered into force 25 March 1994) 1772 UNTS 342. It was amended and extended by protocol of 10 March 1993, and then ended 1 January 2006).

[25] International Wheat Agreement (adopted 14 March 1986, entered into force 1 July 1986) 1429 UNTS 71. It ended 30 June 1995.

[26] Terms of Reference of the International Copper Study Group (adopted 24 February 1989, entered into force 23 January 1992) 1662 UNTS 229.

[27] International Agreement on Jute and Jute Products (adopted 3 November 1989, entered into force provisionally 12 April 1991) 1605 UNTS 211. It ended 11 April 2000.

[28] Energy Charter Treaty (ECT) (adopted 17 December 1994, entered into force 16 April 1998) 2080 UNTS 95; 34 ILM 360 (1995).

III. International Trade Law

International trade law regulates the exchange of goods and services across borders. In the first section we will discuss the WTO, an international organisation which deals with the global rules of trade between nations and whose main purpose is to promote and manage international trade. Subsequently, we will discuss initiatives for regional economic integration, while in a third section we will discuss the relationship between EU law and WTO law.

A. The World Trade Organization

i. Genesis

In contrast to the establishment of the IMF and the World Bank, after Bretton Woods a further three years of negotiations were spent on creating the multilateral trading system. In 1948, the Havana Charter was established, which provided for the establishment of an ITO which, however, never became a reality (see above, Section II). The GATT 1947, which incorporated elements of the Charter, did take 'provisional' effect on 1 January 1948 because the Contracting Parties were able to agree on a protocol of provisional application.[29] The GATT 1947 evolved slowly and in a very pragmatic way during 47 years as one of a multilateral trade agreement to a de facto international trade organisation.[30] Its success, however, has never managed to conceal major shortcomings, such as the absence of a genuine institutional framework (there was only a small secretariat in Geneva) and a lack of competences with respect to regulation and dispute resolution. These shortcomings were largely ended by the establishment of the WTO, on 1 January 1995, an intergovernmental organisation with legal personality.[31] The GATT 1947 is still a core part of the WTO system. The agreement is understood to be an integral part of the WTO Covered Agreements that were agreed upon in the framework of the Uruguay Round (1986–1994).[32]

ii. Membership

Any State or customs union that is capable of autonomously conducting its trade policies may join the WTO.[33] All WTO Members must approve the terms of accession. A working

[29] See JH Jackson, *The World Trade Organization: Constitution and Jurisprudence* (London, Royal Institute of International Affairs, 1998) 15–18.

[30] P Van den Bossche and W Zdouc, *The Law and Policy of the World Trade Organization*, 4th edn (Cambridge, CUP, 2017) 84.

[31] Art VIII WTO Agreement. For more information on the process of the establishment of the WTO, especially the Uruguay Round of Multilateral Trade Negotiations, see E-U Petersmann and M Hilf (eds), *The New GATT Round of Multilateral Trade Negotiations: Legal and Economic Problems* (Alphen aan den Rijn, Kluwer, 1991); T Stewart (ed), *The GATT Uruguay Round* (Alphen aan den Rijn, Kluwer, 1993); Jackson (n 29).

[32] As stated in the first paragraph of the GATT 1994: 'The General Agreement on Tariffs and Trade 1994 ("GATT 1994") shall consist of: [...] the provisions in the General Agreement on Tariffs and Trade, dated 30 October 1947; [and] the provisions of the legal instruments set forth below that have entered into force under the GATT 1947 before the date of entry into force of the WTO Agreement'.

[33] See Art XII WTO Agreement.

party in which all Members can participate, investigates the circumstances under which the accession candidate wishes to join. Hereafter, the various Members negotiate separately with the accession candidate as each Member has a specific number of trade interests it wants to further. Given the principle of most favoured nation (MFN) (on which see below, Subsection (A)(v)(b)), concessions are also immediately applicable to all other Members. Once the working party has completed its analysis and bilateral negotiations have been concluded, a Protocol of Accession (a draft membership agreement) is drafted. Eventually, at least two-thirds of the membership must approve the accession. In practice, however, decision-making takes place by means of consensus among all WTO Members.[34] The Protocol of Accession becomes an integral part of the Marrakesh Agreement and becomes enforceable in dispute settlement.[35] Special effort is taken to promote the successful accession of least developed countries (LDCs).[36]

As of August 2018, there are 164 Members (including the EU and its Member States as separate Members) to the WTO. Within the WTO, Members whose interests are related to one another form alliances or (in)formal groups. Even though the EU is not an official 'negotiation group', the European Commission represents the EU and its Member States (after prior coordination with the latter) at almost all WTO meetings. This leads to a completely integrated approach by the EU and its Member States. Various regional 'negotiation groups' exist which are much less integrated but regularly hold joint positions, including the ASEAN. A well-known alliance of a different kind is the 'Cairns Group'. It concerns a group of 19 countries from four continents, which have in common that they wish to liberalise international trade in agricultural products.[37] There are also groups such as the ACP,[38] the Common Market of the South (Mercosur),[39] the LDCs[40] and

[34] Van den Bossche and Zdouc (n 30) 120.

[35] See Panel Report, *China – Raw Materials* (2012).

[36] As mandated by the Preamble to the WTO Agreement: 'Recognizing further that there is need for positive efforts designed to ensure that developing countries, and especially the least developed among them, secure a share in the growth in international trade commensurate with the needs of their economic development'. A detailed list of all 'special and differential treatment' provisions in the WTO covered agreements, benefiting developing and least-developed countries, can be found in the 2001 WTO Secretariat Note on 'Implementation of Special and Differential Treatment Provisions in WTO Agreements and Decisions'.

[37] Its membership consisting of: Argentina, Australia, Brazil, Canada, Chile, Colombia, Costa Rica, Guatemala, Indonesia, Malaysia, New Zealand, Pakistan, Paraguay, Peru, Philippines, South Africa, Thailand, Uruguay, Vietnam.

[38] Representing both Members (Angola, Antigua and Barbuda, Barbados, Belize, Benin, Botswana, Burkina Faso, Burundi, Cameroon, Cabo Verde, Central African Republic, Chad, Congo, Côte d'Ivoire, Cuba, Democratic Republic of the Congo, Djibouti, Dominica, Dominican Republic, Fiji, Gabon, Gambia, Ghana, Grenada, Guinea, Guinea-Bissau, Guyana, Haiti, Jamaica, Kenya, Lesotho, Liberia, Madagascar, Malawi, Mali, Mauritania, Mauritius, Mozambique, Namibia, Niger, Nigeria, Papua New Guinea, Rwanda, Saint Kitts and Nevis, Saint Lucia, Saint Vincent and the Grenadines, Samoa, Senegal, Sierra Leone, Seychelles, Solomon Islands, South Africa, Suriname, Swaziland, Tanzania, Togo, Tonga, Trinidad and Tobago, Uganda, Vanuatu, Zambia, Zimbabwe), and Observers (Bahamas, Comoros, Equatorial Guinea, Ethiopia, Sao Tomé and Principe, Somalia, Sudan, Timor-Leste), and non-Members/Observers (Cook Islands, Eritrea, Federated States of Micronesia, Kiribati, Marshall Islands, Nauru, Niue, Palau, Tuvalu).

[39] Which currently has four members: Argentina, Brazil, Paraguay, and Uruguay.

[40] Also representing both WTO Members (Afghanistan, Angola, Bangladesh, Benin, Burkina Faso, Burundi, Cambodia, Central African Republic, Chad, Democratic Republic of the Congo, Djibouti, Gambia, Guinea, Guinea-Bissau, Haiti, Lao People's Democratic Republic, Lesotho, Liberia, Madagascar, Malawi, Mali, Mauritania, Mozambique, Myanmar, Nepal, Niger, Rwanda, Senegal, Sierra Leone, Solomon Islands, Tanzania, Togo, Uganda, Vanuatu, Yemen, Zambia), Observers (Bhutan, Comoros, Equatorial Guinea, Ethiopia, Sao Tomé and Principe, Somalia, Sudan, Timor-Leste), and non-Members/Observers (Eritrea, Kiribati, South Sudan, Tuvalu).

the Small and Vulnerable economies (SVEs).[41] At the Ministerial Conference in Cancun in September 2003 a new coalition of developing countries (the G20) arose, which, led by China, India, Brazil and South Africa, formed a front against the (richer) industrialised countries. The group's membership appears to fluctuate greatly, but interaction between this new coalition and the WTO has been frequent.[42]

The peculiar membership situation of the EU and its Member States deserves special mention. Both the EU as well as all of its Member States are *full* WTO Members, with all rights and obligations applying equally to all of them. The European Communities were not a member to the GATT 1947, but their acceptance of certain GATT-related agreements was explicitly recorded.[43] Moreover, most agreements negotiated in the GATT framework after 1970 were accepted only by the European Communities, without separate acceptance by Member States (thereby arguably indicating a de facto membership).[44] In the *Italian Finance Administration v SPI and SAMI* case, the CJEU clarified that the GATT only became an act of the Community institutions in 1968, the moment at which the EC Member States agreed upon the common external tariff.[45] Contrary to the GATT 1947, the Marrakesh Agreement did foresee EU membership. The accession of the European Union (then 'European Communities') as an original Member of the WTO was explicitly recognised in Article XI of the WTO Agreement.[46] It should be highlighted that, in the context of WTO meetings and negotiations, the European Commission acts and speaks for both the European Union and its Member States. The sole exception to this rule of representation is matters relating to the WTO budget.[47]

iii. Organs and Decision-Making

The WTO Members in principle meet at least once every two years in a Ministerial Conference. The Ministerial Conference is the top of the institutional structure of the WTO and consists of representatives of all Members, in principle, ministers of foreign trade.[48]

[41] Consisting of 26 WTO Members (Antigua and Barbuda, Barbados, Belize, Bolivia, Cuba, Dominica, Dominican Republic, El Salvador, Ecuador, Fiji, Grenada, Guatemala, Honduras, Jamaica, Mauritania, Nicaragua, Panama, Papua New Guinea, Saint Kitts and Nevis, Saint Lucia, Saint Vincent and the Grenadines, Samoa, Seychelles, Sri Lanka, Tonga, Trinidad and Tobago), and one Observer (Bahamas).

[42] For more information see, J Wouters and I Willemyns, 'The Interplay between the G20 and the World Trade Organization' in J Chaisse and T Lin (eds), *International Economic Law and Governance. Essays in Honour of Mitsuo Matsushita* (Oxford, OUP, 2016) 183–200.

[43] Importantly, in the landmark *International Fruit Company Case*, the CJEU accepted that certain provisions of the GATT 1947 were binding on the EEC, even though it was not originally a Contracting Party. It thereby recognised that the EEC had succeeded to the obligations of its Member States. See Judgment of 12 December 1972, *International Fruit Company NV v Productschap voor Groenten en Fruit*, Joined Cases 21 to 24/72, EU:C:1972:115, paras 17–18.

[44] J Brsakoska Bazerkoska, 'The European Union and the World Trade Organization: Problems and Challenges' (2011) 7 *Croatian Yearbook of European Law and Policy* 277, 279.

[45] The Court of Justice of the European Union presented a detailed analysis on the relationship of the (then) European Communities and the GATT 1947 in the Judgment of 16 March 1983, *Amministrazione delle Finanze dello Stato v. Società Petrolifera Italiana SpA (SPI) and SpA Michelin Italiana (SAMI) (Italian Finance Administration v SPI and SAMI)*, Joined Cases 267 to 269/81, EU:C:1983:78, 824.

[46] Art XI, para 1, WTO Agreement.

[47] Van den Bossche and Zdouc (n 30) 116.

[48] The creation of the Ministerial Conference is mandated by Art IV(1) WTO Agreement. The specific powers granted to it (on top of its broad decision-making power) can be found in Arts VI (appointing Director-General and setting out his powers, duties, conditions of service and terms of office), IX (exclusive authority to adopt interpretations of the covered agreements and authority to, in exceptional circumstances, waive obligations imposed on a Member by the covered agreements), X (adopt proposed amendments) and XII (decide upon accession of new Members) of the WTO Agreement.

Immediately below that is the General Council, which is the real engine of the WTO.[49] This body also consists of representatives of all Members, usually Ambassadors and Heads of Delegation in Geneva. In addition to fulfilling the functions of the Ministerial Conference when it is not in session, the General Council also acts in two other capacities: (i) as the Dispute Settlement Body;[50] and (ii) as the Trade Policy Review Body.[51] Under the supervision of the General Council there are three specific councils: the Council for Trade in Goods, the Council for Trade in Services and the Council for Trade-Related Aspects of Intellectual Property Rights (TRIPS Council).[52] Respectively, these councils oversee the operation of the agreements on the liberalisation of goods (such as GATT), the General Agreement on Trade in Services (GATS) and the Agreement on Trade-Related Aspects of Intellectual Property Rights (TRIPS). Additionally, the WTO includes a large number of specialised committees, working groups and working parties which focus on specific agreements and other areas such as environment,[53] development[54] and regional trade agreements.[55] Additionally the Trade Negotiations Committee (TNC) supervises the conduct of the negotiations in the ongoing Doha Negotiation Round that are conducted in the TNC itself as well as in its subsidiary negotiation bodies.[56] Unlike the World Bank or the IMF, the WTO does not have an executive organ with a limited number of Members who represent specific countries or groups of countries: in principle, all Members are represented in all of the above bodies and committees. The Secretariat of the WTO is based in Geneva[57] and headed by a Director-General (since 1 September 2013, the Brazilian Roberto Azevêdo), appointed by the Ministerial Conference.[58] The Secretariat and the Director-General have very limited powers. For example, the Secretariat itself may not start a dispute settlement procedure. It should also not interpret multilateral agreements nor judge whether the policy of a Member is in accordance with the WTO rules. Still, the Secretariat plays an important role, including through the provision of technical assistance to developing countries, studies, informing the public and the media about the WTO and its role as registrar

[49] As set out by Art IV(2) of the WTO Agreement: 'There shall be a General Council composed of representatives of all the Members, which shall meet as appropriate. In the intervals between meetings of the Ministerial Conference, its functions shall be conducted by the General Council'.

[50] See Art IV(3) WTO Agreement: 'The General Council shall convene as appropriate to discharge the responsibilities of the Dispute Settlement Body provided for in the Dispute Settlement Understanding'.

[51] See Art IV(4) WTO Agreement: 'The General Council shall convene as appropriate to discharge the responsibilities of the Trade Policy Review Body provided for in the TPRM'.

[52] As provided for in Art IV(5) WTO Agreement. The rules of conduct of these councils can be found respectively in: WTO, 'Rules of Procedure for Meetings of the Council for Trade in Goods', 7 August 1995, WT/L/79; WTO, 'Rules of Procedure for Meetings of the Council for Trade in Services', 19 October 1995, S/L/15; WTO, 'Rules of Procedure for Meetings of the Council for TRIPS', 28 September 1995, IP/C/1.

[53] The Committee on Trade and Environment, established on 14 April 1994 (1994 Ministerial Decision on Trade and Environment, MTN.TNC/45(Min)).

[54] The Committee on Trade and Development, established by the General Council on 31 January 1995 (28 February 1995, WT/GC/M/1).

[55] The Committee on Regional Trade Agreements, established by the General Council on 6 February 1996 (6 March 1996, WT/GC/M/10).

[56] The TNC was established on 14 November 2001 at the Doha Ministerial Conference, WT/MIN(01)/DEC/1, dated 20 November 2001.

[57] The duties of the WTO Secretariat are described in Van den Bossche and Zdouc (n 30) 142–43: (i) providing technical, secretarial and professional support to other WTO bodies; (ii) providing technical assistance to developing-country Members; (iii) monitoring and analysing developments in world trade; (iv) advising governments of countries wishing to accede; (v) providing information to the public and the media; and (vi) providing administrative support and legal assistance to WTO dispute settlement panels.

[58] See Art VI(1) and (2) of the WTO Agreement. Impartiality of both the Secretariat as well as the Director-General are mandated by Art VI(4) of the WTO Agreement.

(and secretary) of the panels and the Appellate Body in the framework of the dispute settlement mechanism.

Decision-making in the WTO takes place, in principle, by consensus. In a number of cases, however, decisions can be taken by special majority. If consensus appears impossible, in accordance with the WTO Agreement – aside from a few important exceptions – decisions are taken through ballot, where a majority of votes cast (each Member, independent of its economic importance, has one formal vote) is sufficient.[59] In practice, however, this has never occurred. The WTO is fundamentally a 'Member-driven organisation'.[60] It is the membership, not the WTO Secretariat or the Director-General, which determines the agenda of the WTO and makes decisions. The WTO dispute settlement mechanism (on which see below, Subsection (vii)) is entitled to impose obligations on Members.

Table 9 WTO Structure

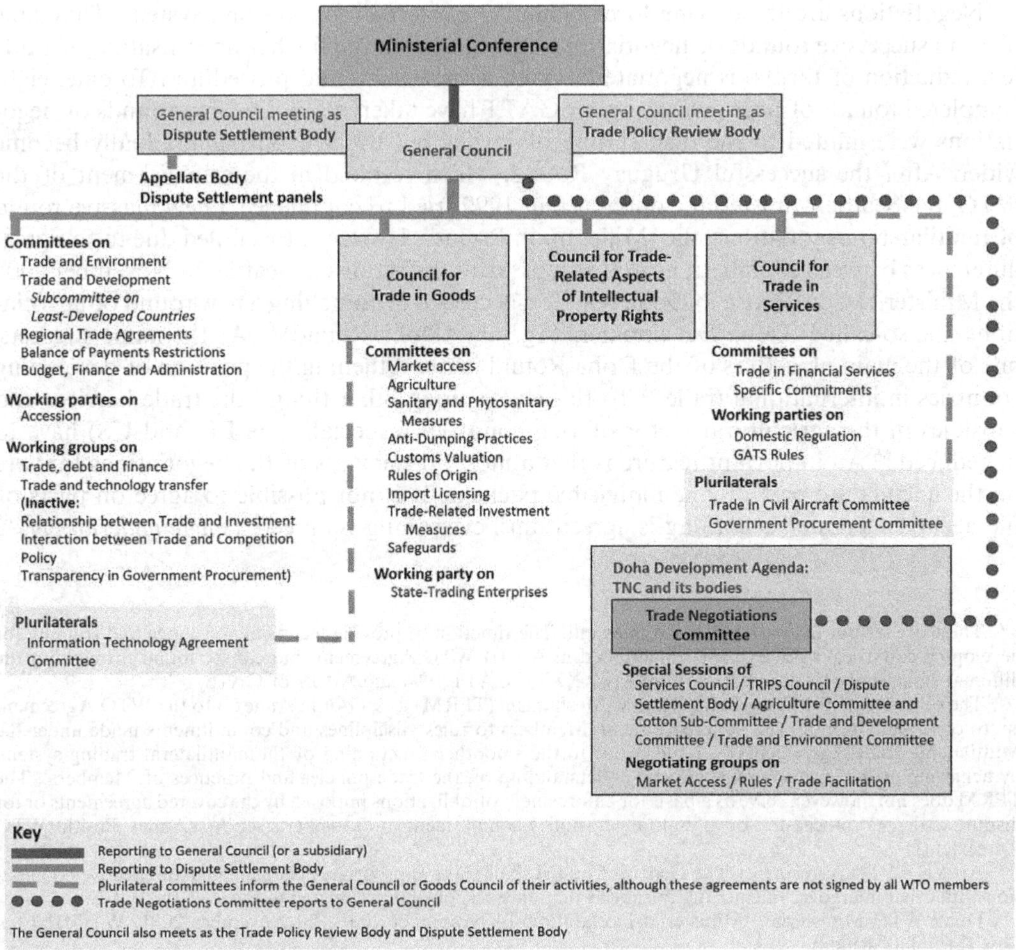

Source: WTO.org.

[59] See Art IX(1) of the WTO Agreement.
[60] For more on this, see, Jackson (n 29) 45; and, Van den Bossche and Zdouc (n 30) 151–52.

iv. Tasks

The WTO has six major functions.[61] Firstly, its primary task is to manage and implement the multilateral and plurilateral trade agreements which together make up the WTO agreements. Secondly, the WTO provides a forum for continuing multilateral negotiations among its Members to further reduce trade barriers. The third task of the WTO consists of resolving disputes among its Members concerning existing obligations under the agreements (see below, Subsection (vii)). Fourthly, the WTO assesses the national trade policies of its Members periodically (the frequency depends on the importance of each Member in world trade during a reference period) to the agreements.[62] Fifthly, the WTO also cooperates with other international institutions engaged in formulating global economic policy. Thus, the WTO has concluded a cooperation agreement with the IMF and the World Bank and coordinates its action with these institutions.[63] Finally, the WTO focuses on providing technical assistance and training for developing countries.

Negotiations are the driving force behind the international trading system. They take place in successive rounds of negotiations, in which both the further liberalisation of trade (eg, reduction of tariffs) is negotiated as well as new rules and procedures. To date, eight completed rounds of negotiations under GATT have taken place. The first rounds of negotiations were limited to the dismantling of tariffs, but the agenda has gradually become wider. After the successful Uruguay Round, which resulted in the establishment of the WTO, the Seattle Ministerial Conference in 1999 tried to commence a new massive round of multilateral negotiations, the 'Millennium Round'. However, this failed due to too great differences between Members, as well as mass demonstrations in Seattle. In November 2001 the Ministerial Conference in Doha (Qatar) succeeded in launching a new round of negotiations, the so-called 'Doha Development Agenda' (Doha Round).[64] As the name suggests, one of the main objectives of the Doha Round is strengthening the position of developing countries in international trade.[65] To this end, among other things, the trade barriers and subsidies in the agricultural sector of rich countries (especially the EU and US) have to be reduced.[66] An important feature is that almost all elements of the negotiations that are on the agenda are part of one indivisible package. It is not possible to agree on parts of the agenda separately: 'nothing is agreed until everything is agreed' (*single undertaking*).[67]

[61] These are set out in Art III WTO Agreement. The function to provide technical assistance and training for developing countries is not explicitly mentioned in Art III WTO Agreement, but can be found throughout the different agreements. Examples hereof are Art XXXVII GATT 1994 and Art IV of GATS.

[62] The objective of the Trade Policy Review Mechanism (TPRM) as set out in Annex 3 to the WTO Agreement is: 'to contribute to improved adherence by all Members to rules, disciplines and commitments made under the Multilateral Trade Agreements [...] and hence to the smoother functioning of the multilateral trading system, by achieving greater transparency in, and understanding of, the trade policies and practices of Members'. The TPRM does not, however, serve as a basis for enforcement of obligations imposed by the covered agreements or for dispute settlement procedures or to impose new policy commitments on Members (see A(i) Annex 3 to the WTO Agreement).

[63] Art V(1) WTO Agreement: 'The General Council shall make appropriate arrangements for effective cooperation with other intergovernmental organizations that have responsibilities related to those of the WTO'.

[64] Doha WTO Ministerial, 'Ministerial Declaration 14 November 2001', 20 November 2001, WT/MIN(01)/DEC/1 (Doha Agenda).

[65] This is exemplified by various paragraphs in the Doha Agenda: paras 2 (promotion of economic development and the alleviation of poverty), 3 (particular vulnerability of the least-developed countries), 35 (small economies), 38–41 (technical cooperation and capacity building), 42–43 (least-developed countries), and 44 (special and differential treatment).

[66] Doha Agenda, paras 13 and 14 (Commitments on negotiations on agriculture).

[67] Doha Agenda, para 47.

Given the impasse in the negotiations on, among others, the liberalisation of agriculture, the Doha Round does not yet provide for further liberalisation of trade in non-primary goods and services, or new rules and procedures.

Table 10 Rounds of Negotiations in the Framework of GATT and WTO

Period	**Place/name**	**Subjects**	**Number of countries**
1947	Geneva	Tariffs	23
1949	Annecy	Tariffs	13
1951	Torquay	Tariffs	38
1956	Geneva	Tariffs	26
1960–61	Geneva (Dillon Round)	Tariffs	26
1964–67	Geneva (Kennedy Round)	Tariffs and anti-dumping measures	62
1973–79	Geneva (Tokyo Round)	Tariffs, Non-tariff barriers, framework agreements	102
1986–1994	Geneva (Uruguay Round)	Tariffs, Non-tariff barriers, services, intellectual property protection, dispute settlement, textile, agriculture, establishment WTO	123
2001–?	Doha (Doha Development Round)	Further liberalisation in agriculture, services and non-essential products; intellectual property; transparency; 'Trade facilitation'; new rules in several areas, including subsidies and dispute resolution.	153 (164 from 2016)

v. Fundamental Principles and Exceptions

The States that drafted the GATT 1947 had envisioned an open and unobstructed trading system in which – through increasing trade – more investment, production, employment and ultimately development of all States would be realised.[68] The underlying economic theory is that by eliminating all trade barriers, optimal global efficiency will be reached: each country will produce that at which it is (relatively) the best, resulting in the lowest possible production costs (*comparative advantage*) (see above, Section II). In order to promote freedom and transparency of trade as much as possible, quantitative restrictions were prohibited[69] and Members were stimulated to use tariffs as the preferred instrument to influence trade. Tariffs are preferable to quantitative restrictions (quotas) because a

[68] This aim is set out in the Preamble to the GATT 1947, stating: '[Contracting parties are] desirous of contributing to [the objectives of raising standards of living, ensuring full employment and a large and steadily growing volume of real income and effective demand, developing the full use of the resources of the world and expanding the production and exchange of goods] by entering into reciprocal and mutually advantageous arrangements directed to the substantial reduction of tariffs and other barriers to trade and to the elimination of discriminatory treatment in international commerce'. Very similar wording can be found in the preamble to the WTO Agreement.

[69] See Art XI GATT 1994.

quantitative restriction defines the trading volume at a specific level; tariffs, by contrast, are taxes on goods crossing the border (and passing through customs) and in principle allow for an undistorted volume of import. Moreover, tariffs provide for more transparency than quantitative restrictions. Once WTO Members only use tariffs to protect their production, it is the intention to reduce these rates systematically and eventually to make them disappear altogether. To this end, Members negotiate in the context of successive rounds of negotiations and commit themselves to lower 'bound tariffs' (per product).[70]

Two basic principles permeate the entire body of WTO law: market access and non-discrimination. Various exceptions apply to these obligations.

a. Market Access Principle

The market access principle is, as far as goods are concerned, not an operational norm as such, but is developed in several WTO rules, each of which is based on concessions over which agreement was reached 'on the basis of reciprocity and mutual benefit'.[71] Economic operators from the various WTO Members must in principle have unrestricted access to the market of another Member. Although customs duties undoubtedly impede access, they are not prohibited as such under WTO law.[72] This is a clear indication that the WTO's main objective is not the liberalisation of trade per se, but rather ensuring a predictable and stable environment for international trade. Customs duties were the subject of repeated rounds of negotiations under GATT (see above, Subsection (iv)) and as a result thereof, the import duties on industrial products gradually decreased from 40 per cent in the 1940s to between 3 and 5 per cent today. Charges other than customs duties on the import of products are allowed only in as far as they are contained in a list (schedule) which is specific for each Member.[73] Non-tariff restrictions on the quantity of imported products, ie quantitative restrictions, are prohibited in principle: except for duties, taxes or other charges, a WTO Member may not impose quotas, import and export licences or other measures with equivalent effect (measures that do not take the form of quotas but do have a similar effect) on imports of products originating in any other Member or on the exportation of any product destined for the territory of another Member.[74] Moreover, the use of non-tariff barriers is restrained (see below). With respect to trade in services, Article XVI of GATS is the operational standard for market access in trade in services (see below).

b. Non-Discrimination Principle

It is not sufficient that access to the markets of other WTO Members is available: such access should also take place on a non-discriminatory basis. The principle of non-discrimination is the leitmotif of WTO law and there are two manifestations hereof in

[70] Art II GATT 1994 read in conjunction with Art XXVIII*bis*(1) GATT 1994. The so-called 'bound tariff' is the maximum rate at which a certain Member can impose a tariff on a certain product. These bound tariffs are not necessarily a reflection of the tariff that is actually applied. Generally, WTO Members apply tariffs (far) below their bound rate ('*applied tariff*').

[71] Art XXVIII *bis* GATT 1994.

[72] Art II.1 (a) and (b), first sentence GATT 1994.

[73] Art II.1 (b) second sentence, and II.2 GATT 1994. Such other charges include financial charges in various forms (that are not customs duties), like: import surcharges, security deposits, statistical taxes, customs fees, transitional surcharges and foreign exchange fees. See Van den Bossche and Zdouc (n 30) 464.

[74] Art XI GATT 1994.

the relevant WTO rules on goods, services and intellectual property. On the one hand, a Member shall not discriminate among various WTO trading partners. This is the principle referred to as the principle of the most favoured nation. On the other hand, once foreign products and services have crossed the border they may be given no less favourable treatment than the domestic products or services. Imported products or services must, in other words, be granted national treatment.

The most favoured nation principle, included in Article I GATT 1994, Article II GATS and Article 4 TRIPS, is a cornerstone of international trade law: when a WTO Member grants an advantage to any country, whether or not a WTO Member, this right should also apply to all other Members. As far as goods are concerned, the MFN principle comes down to the obligation for a Member to extend any advantage, favour, privilege or immunity (eg, from customs duties, so-called tariff concession, or other charges) which it grants to any product originating in any other country, unconditionally to all relevant products from all other WTO Members.[75]

The MFN principle implicitly or explicitly also features in a number of other GATT 1994 provisions: among others, in Article XIII (accepted quantitative restrictions should be applied to all trading partners) and Article XIX (emergency measures in case of unforeseen massive imports of a product which threatens serious damage to domestic producers). However, various instances exist in which preferential treatment is granted to specific trading partners such as customs unions (like the EU),[76] free trade areas (like NAFTA),[77] and developing countries. How can these be reconciled with the MFN principle? Because they lead to regional economic integration, regional trade agreements can play an important role in the liberalisation and expansion of world trade that cannot be reached at the multilateral level.[78] Article XXIV GATT 1994, Article V GATS, Article V *bis* GATS, and Article 2(c) of the 'Decision on Differential and More Favourable Treatment' (the so-called 'Enabling Clause') of 28 November 1979 therefore allow for the establishment of such regional trade agreements, albeit under strict conditions (see below).

The Enabling Clause has both a vertical and a horizontal dimension. Its horizontal dimension includes regional or global trade arrangements *among developing countries*.[79] The horizontal dimension will be discussed in more detail below (see Subsection (B)(ii)(c)). The vertical dimension allows for differential and more favourable treatment *by developed countries in favour of developing and least developed countries*, in particular: (i) preferential tariff treatment accorded by developed countries to products originating in developing countries in accordance with the Generalized System of Preferences (GSP);[80]

[75] Art I GATT 1994.

[76] A union of States in which barriers to trade between the members are mutually eliminated and a common customs tariff applies to goods from third countries. The requirements for a WTO-consistent customs union can be found in Art XXIV (para 8(a)) GATT 1994.

[77] An area in which the participating parties only remove obstacles to trade inter se but each of the parties maintains its own trade barriers against third countries. The requirements for a WTO-consistent free trade area can be found in Art XXIV (para 8(b)) GATT 1994.

[78] As stated in the Preamble to the Understanding on the Interpretation of Article XXIV of the GATT 1994 (Understanding on Article XXIV): 'Recognizing the contribution to the expansion of world trade that may be made by closer integration between the economies of the parties to such agreements'. This Understanding is part of the Annex 1A to the WTO Agreement.

[79] Para 2(c) Enabling Clause.

[80] ibid, para 2(a). The EU has several of these types of preferential arrangements in place under its GSP. See, for a discussion of the legality of these conditional preferences, L Bartels, 'The WTO Enabling Clause and Positive Conditionality in the European Community's GSP Program' (2003) 6(2) *JIEL* 507.

(ii) differential and more favourable treatment concerning non-tariff measures negotiated under the GATT auspices;[81] and (iii) special treatment of the 'least developed among the developing countries' in the context of any general or specific measures in favour of developing countries.[82] These commitments are *not reciprocal* and must be non-discriminatory.[83] The EU has several of these types of preferential agreements in place, among others, under its 'Generalized Scheme of Preferences'.

Finally, the General Council may also confer an exemption (*waiver*) under Article XXV (para 5) GATT 1994 to certain WTO rules under the procedure of Article IX WTO Agreement. Such an exemption was given to, among others, the least developed countries in order to extend the transition period for the implementation of TRIPS obligations in respect of patents for pharmaceutical products until early 2033.[84]

The second form of non-discrimination, the principle of national treatment, is laid down in Article III GATT 1994 and Article XVII GATS. Once a product is allowed on the market, national regulations and internal taxes or other internal charges may not be applied to imported products in a way which would provide protection to domestic production. Despite its complex terms, Article III GATT 1994 has a logical structure. It involves on the one hand, internal charges (eg, VAT taxes or sales taxes such as excise duties: Article III(2) GATT) and on the other hand, regulations (Article III(4) GATT 1994). With regard to internal charges the first sentence of Article III(2) stipulates that imported products must not be taxed higher than 'directly or indirectly corresponding' products of domestic origin. In this context, the slightest difference in the rate of charge is sufficient for a violation of Article III(2).[85] This is different with respect to the second sentence of Article III(2). This sentence concerns products that are not similar to such an extent that one can speak of 'similar products', but are still in a 'competitive relationship'.[86] To speak of a violation in this case, in addition to a difference in charge (not similarly taxed), evidence is needed that this difference is applied in such a manner that the domestic product is protected.[87]

With regard to regulation, Article III(4) GATT 1994 endorses the application of regulation with regard to the sale, supply, purchase, transportation, distribution or use. When imported products enjoy a less favourable treatment which is aimed to provide protection to corresponding domestic products, this provision is violated. This general provision was seen as a threat to national sovereignty. Virtually any legislation can have an effect on trade and would therefore fall within the scope of Article III(4). Taking into account the need

[81] Para 2(b) Enabling Clause.

[82] ibid, para 2(d).

[83] WTO, *Report of the Appellate Body*, 'European Communities: Conditions for the Granting of Tariff Preferences to Developing Countries', 7 April 2004, WT/DS246/AB/R, para 165.

[84] Council for Trade-Related Aspects of Intellectual Property Rights, Extension of the Transition Period Under Art 66.1 of the TRIPS Agreement for Least Developed Country Members for Certain Obligations with Respect to Pharmaceutical Products, 6 November 2015, IP/C/73.

[85] Relevant case law includes: WTO Dispute Settlement, *Japan – Alcoholic Beverages II*, Appellate Body Report, 4 October 1996, WT/DS8/AB/R; WT/DS10/AB/R; WT/DS11/AB/R; *Dominican Republic – Import and Sale of Cigarettes*, Panel Report, 26 November 2004, WT/DS302/R; *Mexico – Taxes on Soft Drinks*, Panel Report, 7 October 2005, WT/DS308/R; *Thailand – Cigarettes (Philippines)*, Appellate Body Report, 17 June 2011, WT/DS371/AB/R; and, *Philippines – Taxes on Distilled Spirits*, Panel Report, 15 August 2011, WT/DS396/R; WT/DS403/R.

[86] Relevant case law includes: WTO Dispute Settlement, *Japan – Alcoholic Beverages II* (n 85); and, *Korea – Alcoholic Beverages*, Appellate Body Report, 18 January 1999, WT/DS75/AB/R; WT/DS84/AB/R.

[87] Relevant case law includes: WTO Dispute Settlement, *Japan – Alcoholic Beverages II* (n 85); *Chile – Alcoholic Beverages*, Appellate Body Report, 13 December 1999, WT/DS87/AB/R; WT/DS110/AB/R; and, *Philippines – Distilled Spirits*, Appellate Body Report, 21 December 2011, WT/DS396/AB/R; WT/DS403/AB/R.

for some degree of regulatory autonomy, the widespread use of certain "technical barriers to trade" and "sanitary and phytosanitary measures" and the possibility of a legitimate regulatory distinction, there was a need for clarification. The Agreement on Technical Barriers to Trade (TBT) and the Agreement on Sanitary and Phytosanitary Measures (SPS) provide basic rules for such measures in accordance with the fundamental principles of the GATT 1994.

c. Exceptions

The WTO Covered Agreements provide for exceptions to the aforementioned basic principles. This involves an often delicate balance between free trade and other important societal objectives.[88] The exceptions allow WTO Members to make sovereign policy choices without, however, creating disproportionate barriers to trade. Experience shows that in cases of dispute, the panels and the Appellate Body are entitled to make this assessment, partly on the basis of the principle of proportionality: the question is whether alternative measures are available, which are less trade restrictive than the current measure, but can also achieve the policy objective pursued (environmental protection, protection of health or public morals, etc).[89]

In the first place, apart from the aforementioned exceptions to MFN, the general exceptions for trade in goods are exhaustively contained in Article XX (a)–(j) of the GATT 1994. These are inter alia measures for the protection of (a) public morals, (b) life or health of humans, animals or plants, and (g) conservation of exhaustible natural resources. In its *chapeau*, Article XX determines that the exceptions cannot be applied in a way that either forms a means of arbitrary or unjustifiable discrimination between countries where the same conditions prevail, or a disguised restriction on international trade. These strict requirements were added with the aim of avoiding abuse of these general exceptions.[90] In considering these general exceptions, it should be noted that Article XX is first and foremost a balancing measure, trying to find an equilibrium between the restriction to international trade and other societal values.[91] Very similar general exceptions applying to trade in services can be found in Article XIV GATS.[92]

Secondly, Article XXI GATT 1994 and Article XIV*bis* GATS provide exceptions relating to national security. Thirdly, safeguard measures constitute a specific exemption.[93] A WTO Member may temporarily restrict imports of a product by taking safeguard

[88] These objectives can be either non-economic or economic. Examples of the former can be found in Art XX GATT 1994 and Art XIV GATS: public morals, human health, protection of the environment, etc. Examples of the latter can be found in inter alia Arts XII, XIX and XXIV GATT 1994 and Arts V, X and XII GATS: safeguarding the external financial position (balance of payments), emergency action to protect markets from being flooded with foreign products and pursuing regional economic integration.

[89] For more information on the proportionality principle in WTO law: A Desmedt, 'Proportionality in WTO Law' (2001) 4(3) *JIEL* 441.

[90] WTO Dispute Settlement, *US – Standards for Reformulated and Conventional Gasoline*, Appellate Body Report, 29 April 1996, WT/DS2/AB/R, para 22.

[91] *Thailand – Cigarettes* (n 85) para 173.

[92] Even though Art XX GATT 1994 and Art XIV GATS are very similar, some differences can be spotted, the main one being that the listed justifications in both articles are not identical and each contains justifications that cannot be found in the other. Jurisprudence on Art XX GATT 1994 has explicitly been recognised by the Appellate Body as guidance on the interpretation of Art XIV GATS. See WTO Dispute Settlement, *US – Measures Affecting the Cross-Border Supply of Gambling and Betting Services*, Appellate Body Report, 7 April 2005, WT/DS285/AB/R, para 291.

[93] Art XIX GATT 1994.

measures, if the domestic industry experiences serious injury or threat thereof caused by a sudden increase in imports of the product concerned. This sudden increase in imports must be due to unforeseeable circumstances, combined with tariff concessions which were made by the relevant WTO Member. The safeguard measure consists of an increase in the tariff or the imposition of a quantitative restriction for the relevant product. The safeguard measures under GATT 1947 were based solely on Article XIX GATT. This possibility was rarely used. Governments opted for other measures to protect their domestic industry, the GATT conformity of which, however, was debatable. For example, use was made of 'voluntary export restraints' which involved exporting countries 'voluntarily' accepting to limit their exports to a certain level.[94] The *Agreement on Safeguards* elaborates Article XIX GATT.[95] It prohibits 'voluntary export restraints' and places time constraints on the use of safeguard measures.[96] Except in exceptional circumstances, the protective measures cannot be directed against imports from one country (ie, they should be applied on an MFN basis).[97]

Finally, the GATT 1994 provides for an exception for Members with balance of payments problems.[98]

vi. Other Substantive WTO Norms

a. Trade in Goods

With respect to trade in goods, 11 agreements are annexed to the GATT 1994 (Annex 1A). Some of these agreements are new, others resume – with some modifications – agreements that were concluded in the context of previous GATT rounds, with the important difference that, whereas GATT Contracting Parties could decide autonomously which agreement they wanted to join, this is no longer possible under the WTO. A Member must accept the entire package of multilateral agreements (see below on 'plurilateral agreements'). These agreements include: the Agreement on Agriculture;[99] the Agreement on Sanitary and Phytosanitary Measures (SPS Agreement);[100] Technical Barriers to Trade (TBT Agreement);[101] the Agreement on Trade-Related Investment Measures (TRIMS);[102] the Anti-dumping Agreement;[103] the Customs Valuation Agreement;[104] Agreement on Pre-Shipment Inspection;[105] Agreement on Rules of Origin;[106] Agreement on Import Licensing;[107] the Agreement on Subsidies and Countervailing Measures;[108] the Agreement on Safeguards.[109]

[94] For more information on these 'voluntary export restraints', see Van den Bossche and Zdouc (n 30) 632.
[95] Agreement on Safeguards, 1869 UNTS 154.
[96] Arts 11(b) and 7 Agreement on Safeguards.
[97] ibid, Art 2.
[98] Arts XII and XVIII(B) GATT 1994.
[99] Agreement on Agriculture, 1867 UNTS 410.
[100] Agreement on the Application of Sanitary and Phytosanitary Measures, 1867 UNTS 493.
[101] Agreement on Technical Barriers to Trade, 1868 UNTS 120.
[102] Agreement on Trade Related Investment Measures, 1868 UNTS 186.
[103] Agreement on Implementation of Article VI of the General Agreement on Tariffs and Trade 1994 (Anti-Dumping Agreement) 1868 UNTS 201.
[104] Agreement on Implementation of Article VII of the General Agreement on Tariffs and Trade 1994 (Customs Valuation Agreement) 1868 UNTS 279.
[105] Agreement on Pre-Shipment Inspection, 1868 UNTS 368.
[106] Agreement on Rules of Origin, 1868 UNTS 397.
[107] Agreement on Import Licensing Procedures, 1868 UNTS 436.
[108] Agreement on Subsidies and Countervailing Measures (SCM) 1869 UNTS 14.
[109] Agreement on Safeguards, 1869 UNTS 154.

The TBT Agreement applies to *technical regulations and standards* which determine specific characteristics of a product (eg, the size, shape, features, functionality, packaging, labeling and permitted production methods).[110] These measures may aim at protecting legitimate policy objectives, including the protection of human health, safety or the environment.[111] At the same time these measures may not discriminate against like foreign products. Given the prohibition of quantitative restrictions and reduced tariffs, States also protect domestic production at times simply through such measures. One way to ensure that technical regulations are not an obstacle to trade is the requirement that these technical regulations are based on international standards.[112] If there is a relevant international standard and that standard is used by the WTO Member that has taken the measure, there is a rebuttable presumption that the measure does not raise an unnecessary barrier to trade.[113] However, when a Member enters a regime which is more stringent (more protective, and therefore often more obstructive), it must prove that the international standard was not effective or was inappropriate to achieve the legitimate objectives pursued by it.[114] If no relevant international standard exists, the Member must notify other Members of the proposed technical regulation, if that measure could have a significant effect on the trade of other Members.[115] Nevertheless, it must ensure that the scheme is not more trade restrictive than necessary to pursue the legitimate objective.

WTO Members may not only demand that products meet technical requirements, but may also impose sanitary and phytosanitary regulations. These are rules to protect human and animal life against additives, pollution, poisons or disease-causing organisms in food. Furthermore, these rules are intended to protect human life against diseases of plants or animals within them. Animal and plant life can also be protected from pests, diseases or disease-causing organisms. Finally, such rules can attempt to shield a country from the entering, establishment or spreading of pests.[116] The SPS Agreement provides rules to be observed by WTO Members if they wish to take sanitary or phytosanitary measures. The difference with technical arrangements lies in the objective of the measures.[117] The objectives of sanitary and phytosanitary measures are clearly specified, while technical arrangements may have diverse goals. The SPS Agreement aims to prevent measures being used as an excuse to protect domestic producers. Here, too, WTO Members have to base their regulatory measures on international standards, guidelines or recommendations, drawn up by international bodies in which they must try to participate as much as possible.[118] If, however, a Member wishes to impose a higher standard, it must justify this as much as possible on the basis of scientific data.[119] A Member should therefore carefully consider the risks and the appropriate level of protection.

[110] Art 1.2 TBT Agreement read in conjunction with Annex 1.
[111] ibid, Art 2.2.
[112] ibid, Art 2.4.
[113] ibid, Art 2.5.
[114] ibid, Art 2.4.
[115] ibid, Art 2.9.
[116] More information on the scope of the SPS Agreement can be found in Art 1.1 and Annex A of this Agreement. The latter contains the definition of 'sanitary or phytosanitary measure'.
[117] As stated by the Appellate Body in *Australia – Apples* (2010), the appropriate level of protection, determined by a Member when implementing an SPS measure, is the *objective* of this measure and the SPS measure is an instrument chosen to attain or implement that objective (WTO Dispute Settlement, *Australia – Measures Affecting the Importation of Apples from New Zealand*, Appellate Body Report, 29 November 2010, WT/DS367/AB/R, para 172).
[118] Arts 3.1 and 3.2 SPS Agreement.
[119] Art 3.3 read in conjunction with Art 5 SPS Agreement.

b. Trade in Services

International trade in services is becoming increasingly important and the GATS provides the multilateral legal framework for this expanding part of global trade. The GATS constitutes a framework agreement that assumes to a great extent the GATT principles, but for its implementation mainly depends on further negotiations. The agreement has a broad scope, including 'any service in any sector except services supplied in the exercise of governmental authority'.[120] The GATS applies to four different modes of supply: (i) cross-border services, where the service crosses the border without the service provider or the receiver having to move; (ii) consumption abroad, whereby the consumer moves abroad to consume the service; (iii) commercial presence, where the provider moves abroad under any form of trade or business establishment; and (iv) the temporary presence of natural persons abroad to provide services there.[121]

Article II and Article XVII GATS express the general principle of non-discrimination. The MFN principle, as stated in Article II, however, differs from Article I GATT in that it is possible for WTO Members to negotiate one-off exceptions to its application. These may in principle have a duration of no longer than 10 years.[122] The stipulated exceptions are listed in the Annex to Article II GATS; they do not end automatically and are therefore still in effect. Article V GATS foresees, as indicated above, in regional trade with a similar exception as Article XXIV GATT 1994. As far as the principles of market access (Article XVI GATS) and national treatment (Article XVII GATS) of foreign services and service suppliers are concerned, WTO Members are only bound by the specific commitments they have entered into.[123] Unlike trade in goods, trade in services is not protected by tariffs, but rather by regulatory measures. Each WTO Member commits to gradually eliminate (or adapt) regulations that would impede trade in services. For the obligation to provide market access, this happens through the registration of specific commitments (indicated for specific service sectors and modes of supply) to not maintain or create measures which impede the market and which are of the type listed in Article XVI(2) GATS (measures of a quantitative nature). In a similar fashion, every WTO Member individually agrees to grant national treatment as provided for in Article XVII GATS for certain service sectors (ie, with specific commitments for specific service sector and modes of supply). The extent to which this occurs depends on the progress in the negotiations.

In those sectors for which a Member has agreed to specific commitments, WTO law has an impact on domestic laws and regulations. For these types of legislation, Article VI(1) GATS determines that 'all measures of general application affecting trade in services [must be applied] in a reasonable, objective and impartial manner'. The Council for Trade in Services has the authority to draft so-called 'disciplines', which should ensure that qualifications and procedures, technical standards and permits do not form unnecessary obstacles to trade in services.[124] Just as Members want to maintain some form of control on the sale of goods to protect consumers (see above on TBT and SPS), such control may equally be

[120] Art I(3)(b) GATS.
[121] Art I(2) GATS.
[122] Paragraph 6 of the Annex on Art II Exemptions, see Art II(2) GATS.
[123] These specific commitments can be found in each Member's Schedule of Specific Commitments (Services Schedule). Specific guidelines have been issued in order to assist in the drafting and reading of these Services Schedules: WTO Council for Trade in Services, 'Guidelines for the Scheduling of Specific Commitments under the General Agreement on Trade in Services', 28 March 2001, WTO Doc SL/92.
[124] Art VI(4) GATS.

necessary to ensure the quality of services. For example, certain diplomas, certificates or permits may be required. Lack of knowledge of the obscure and complex internal legislation of another Member to service providers who are from another State often forms a major obstacle. Mutual recognition of required qualifications, permits or certificates can help prevent these schemes constituting an obstacle to trade.[125] To ensure the quality of services in sensitive sectors, States also often provide for arrangements that grant exclusive rights to certain service providers. WTO Members have the obligation to ensure that in such cases, the exclusive service suppliers do not abuse their monopoly or exclusive rights.[126] The GATS also has general exceptions to its basic principles (see above).[127]

The EU (at the time still the European Economic Community) played a signification role in the drafting of the GATS, as it had already gained important experience on harmonisation and regulation of trade in services.[128] A draft agreement proposed by the EU helped to ensure that the third mode of supply of services (commercial presence in a Host State) was made subject to the disciplines of the GATS.[129] The text of other provisions in the GATS, like Article VI and Article XIV, also indicates some EU influence.[130]

c. Intellectual Property Rights

The regulation of intellectual property today is significantly influenced by WTO law. The TRIPS aims to strengthen and harmonise the level of protection of intellectual property and provides for more effective enforcement at both national and international level.[131]

Intellectual property rights allow owners to enjoy the fruits of their intellectual and creative work and also stimulate further innovation through the granting of *copyrights*,[132] *patents*[133] and *industrial design*.[134] Some intellectual property rights are not granted so much to encourage innovation but to avoid abuse by third parties of a labouriously constructed product image through trademarks, as well as to ensure the quality and product properties of specific regional products (through appellations of origin, geographical indications).[135] It goes without saying that these intellectual property rights may signify a serious disruption of free trade. The holder of an intellectual property right may prevent products being produced in a particular country or prevent products being sold and executed under a particular name. TRIPS seeks a balance between, on the one hand, the importance of protecting intellectual property and, on the other hand, to avoid national regulations concerning

[125] Art VII GATS.
[126] Art VIII GATS.
[127] Art XIV GATS.
[128] Whereas up until the negotiations at the Uruguay round, there had been a significant lack of research and analysis of international trade in services.
[129] W Kennet, 'The European Community and the General Agreement on Trade in Services' in N Emiliou and D O'Keeffe, *The European Union and World Trade Law. After the GATT Uruguay Round* (Chichester, John Wiley & Sons, 1996) 137.
[130] ibid; eg, the uncanny resemblance between a footnote to Art XIV(a) and the language of the Judgment of 27 October 1977, *R v Bouchereau*, Case 30-77, EU:C:1977:172.
[131] The Preamble to the TRIPS Agreement identifies the objective as follows: 'Desiring to reduce distortions and impediments to international trade, and taking into account the need to promote effective and adequate protection of intellectual property rights, and to ensure that measures and procedures to enforce intellectual property rights do not themselves become barriers to legitimate trade'.
[132] Covered by Arts 9–14 (Part II, Section 1) TRIPS Agreement.
[133] ibid, Arts 27–34 (Part II, Section 5).
[134] ibid, Arts 25–26 (Part II, Section 4).
[135] Trademarks are covered by ibid, Arts 15–21 (Part II, Section 2).

intellectual property disrupting or hindering international trade.[136] It is important to note that the TRIPS Agreement does not affect existing conventions on intellectual property. Moreover, it explicitly refers to the various WIPO Conventions.[137] TRIPS first establishes a number of basic principles.[138] For example, Article 3 TRIPS provides for the principle of *national treatment*. WTO Members may not offer nationals of other Members less favourable protection of intellectual property than their own nationals. Moreover, TRIPS also includes the *most favoured nation principle*.[139] When a Member, for example, grants a more advantageous procedure for the enforcement of copyright to nationals of a particular Member, this advantage should be granted to all Members. Furthermore, TRIPS prescribes standards concerning the availability, scope and use of various intellectual property rights (eg, the length of protection). It is important to note here as well that TRIPS merely sets a minimum level of protection and Members are free to determine a higher level of protection in their own legal systems.[140]

d. Multilateral vs Plurilateral Agreements

The aforementioned agreements on trade in goods, services and commercial aspects of intellectual property are multilateral agreements. This means that all WTO Members must be a party to them. In addition, there are two plurilateral trade agreements on, respectively, trade in civil aircraft and government procurement.[141] Although they are concluded between a limited number of WTO Members (including the EU), other Members are free to accede to these agreements. Plurilateral agreements form an integral part of the WTO system: the mechanisms for dispute settlement and review of trade policy are applicable. As plurilateral agreements allow for cooperation between a smaller subset of WTO Members, they have been suggested as a good alternative negotiating forum in light of the stalled multilateral negotiations.[142]

vii. Dispute Settlement Mechanism

One of the major innovations of the Uruguay Round agreements is the *Understanding on Rules and Procedures concerning the Settlement of Disputes* (the DSU), which is attached

[136] See T Cottier, 'The Agreement on Trade-Related Aspects of Intellectual Property Rights' in PFJ Macrory, AE Appleton and MG Plummer (eds), *The World Trade Organization: Legal, Economic and Political Analysis* (New York, Springer, 2005) 1054.

[137] Specifically, the Paris Convention for the Protection of Industrial Property of 1883, as revised in the Stockholm Act of 1967, 21 UST 1583, 828 UNTS 305; the Berne Convention for the Protection of Literary and Artistic Works of 1886, as revised in the Paris Act of 1971, S Treaty Doc No 99-27 (1986); the International Convention for the Protection of Performers, Producers of Phonograms and Broadcasting Organizations of 1961, 496 UNTS 43; and the Treaty on Intellectual Property in Respect of Integrated Circuits of 1989, 28 ILM 1477.

[138] Part I TRIPS Agreement.

[139] Art 4 TRIPS Agreement.

[140] WTO Dispute Settlement, *India – Patent Protection for Pharmaceutical and Agricultural Chemical Products*, Appellate Body Report, 19 December 1997, WT/DS50/AB/R, para 59; *European Communities – Protection of Trademarks and Geographical Indications for Agricultural Products and Foodstuffs*, Panel Report, 15 March 2005, WT/DS290/R, paras 7.762–7.766.

[141] The Agreement on Government Procurement (GPA 1996) (adopted 15 April 1994, entered into force on 1 January 1996); and the Agreement on Civil Aircraft (adopted 12 April 1979, entered into force 1 January 1980).

[142] For a discussion on the advantages and disadvantages of plurilateral agreements, see BM Hoekman and PC Mavroidis, 'WTO "à la carte" or "menu du jour"? Assessing the Case for More Plurilateral Agreements' (2015) 26(2) *EJIL* 319.

to the WTO Agreement.[143] The dispute settlement mechanism can rightly be called the crown jewel of WTO law. The proper functioning of this mechanism explains a large part of the WTO's success. During the GATT era (1947–1994) there were no fixed time limits for settling disputes and decisions could easily be blocked. This was changed and the dispute settlement procedure in the WTO is tightly regulated in terms of both the time frame and the procedure.[144] At the time of the GATT, dispute settlement was characterised by its eminently diplomatic character. In the WTO, it is a quasi-judicial system, which still has some diplomatic characteristics: the emphasis remains on mutual solution and discussion of the dispute between the Members concerned. This explains why the first stage of the procedure consists of consultations between the governments concerned, and even when the case is in a different phase, consultation and mediation continue to be available at any time.[145] The WTO dispute settlement system distinguishes itself from other international courts through its jurisdiction, which is compulsory,[146] exclusive,[147] and contentious.[148]

Settling disputes is the responsibility of the Dispute Settlement Body (DSB), ie, the General Council wearing a different hat. The DSB has the exclusive power to appoint panels of experts and to accept or reject the findings of these panels (or the results of an appeal).[149] The DSB oversees the implementation of the rulings and recommendations, and has the authority to give permission to retaliate if a Member fails to comply with a decision.[150]

The phases of the dispute settlement mechanism can be summarised as follows. Prior to any other action, the Members involved in the conflict have to consult with each other to determine whether they can settle the conflict among themselves. This first phase is called the consultations, and may take up to 60 days. If that fails, they can also ask the WTO Director-General to mediate or help in any other way.[151] The panel stage, which is the second stage, may take up to seven and a half months (45 days to appoint a panel, plus six months for the panel to reach its decision). If the consultations fail, the complaining party may request that a panel be appointed.[152] The defending Member may block an appointed panel once, but when the DSB meets for a second time, the appointment can no longer be prevented, unless there is a consensus against the appointment (the rule of reverse consensus).[153] Panels meet behind closed doors and must decide in principle within six months (in case of emergency within three months). The final panel report is adopted by the DSB within 60 days unless

[143] Understanding on Rules and Procedures Governing the Settlement of Disputes (DSU) 1869 UNTS 401; 33 ILM 1226 (1994).

[144] For more information on the GATT dispute settlement system see EU Petersmann, *The GATT/WTO Dispute Settlement System: International Law, International Organizations and Dispute Settlement* (London, Kluwer, 1997) 66–91.

[145] Art 11 DSU: panels are required to give the parties to the dispute adequate opportunity to develop a mutually satisfactory solution.

[146] ibid, Art 6.1.

[147] ibid, Art 23.1. The Panel in *US – Section 301 Trade Act* (2000) clarified that this provision imposes an obligation on all Members to have recourse to the multilateral process when they seek the redress of WTO inconsistency (WTO Dispute Settlement, *US – Sections 301–310 of the Trade Act 1974*, Panel Report, 22 December 1999, WT/DS152/R, para 7.43).

[148] *US – Measures Affecting Imports of Woven Wool Shirts and Blouses from India*, Appellate Body Report, 25 April 1997, WT/DS33/AB/R, para 340.

[149] Art 2.1 DSU.

[150] ibid, Art 21.

[151] ibid, Art 4.

[152] ibid, Art 6.

[153] ibid, Arts 6.1, 16.4, 17.14, and 22.6.

there is a consensus to reject it (reverse consensus) or unless one of the parties to the dispute (not third parties) appeals the report.

In a third phase, an appeal may be filed with the Appellate Body (60–90 days).[154] An appeal against the panel report must be based on points of law.[155] As part of the appeal existing evidence cannot be re-examined, let alone that new evidence can be adduced. The Appellate Body is composed of seven members, appointed for a term of four years. Members of the Appellate Body must be people with proven experience in the field of law and international trade. They should not be affiliated with any government and should not participate in the consideration of any disputes that may directly or indirectly lead to a conflict of interest.[156] The Appellate Body may uphold, modify or annul the legal findings and conclusions of the panel, and shall do so in principle within 60 days.[157] The report of the Appellate Body is adopted by the DSB and accepted unconditionally by the parties to the dispute, unless the DSB within 30 days after sending the report to the WTO Members, decides by consensus not to adopt the report (reverse consensus).[158]

Decisions holding that a Member's measure breaches WTO provisions would have little effect if no sanctions can be imposed to enforce them. However, even after a dispute is settled, *trade sanctions* cannot simply be imposed on a losing party. At that stage, it is up to that party to bring its policy in line with the ruling or recommendations.[159] At a meeting of the DSB, which should be held within 30 days of the adoption of the report by a panel or the Appellate Body, the Member concerned must inform the DSB of its intentions in respect of implementation of the recommendations and rulings of the DSB.[160] If unable to comply immediately, the Member concerned shall have a reasonable period in which it may take the necessary measures. If the Member fails to act within this period, it must enter into negotiations with the complainant(s) to agree upon a mutually acceptable compensation (for example lowering of tariffs in areas of particular interest to the complainant(s)).[161] If after 20 days no satisfactory compensation has been established, the complainant may request the DSB to give permission to impose limited trade sanctions (suspension of concessions or obligations) onto the losing party. The DSB must authorise this agreement within 30 days after a reasonable period has lapsed, unless there is a consensus against this request (reverse consensus).[162] In principle, sanctions, which must be equivalent to the damage suffered by non-implementation, must be imposed in the same sector as those in which the dispute is concerned.[163] If this is not practical or would not be effective, the sanctions can be imposed in a different sector of the same agreement.[164] If this in turn is not practical or effective, action can be taken under another WTO agreement (so-called '*cross-retaliation*').[165] Trade sanctions should be used only as a last resort. Such sanctions indeed oppose the

[154] ibid, Art 17.
[155] ibid, Art 17.6.
[156] ibid, Art 17.3.
[157] ibid, Art 17.5.
[158] ibid, Art 17.14.
[159] ibid, Art 21.
[160] ibid, Art 21.3.
[161] ibid, Art 22.2.
[162] ibid, Art 22.6.
[163] ibid, Art 22.3(a).
[164] ibid, Art 22.3(b).
[165] ibid, Art 22.3(c).

'raison d'être' of the WTO (trade liberalisation). In any event, the DSB will supervise how decisions are implemented. Each pending case remains on its agenda until the issue has been resolved.

B. Regional Economic Integration

i. Regional Trade Agreements: An Introduction

As seen in Chapter 7, regional economic integration whereby States seek to strengthen their economies by entering into regional arrangements – as opposed to a global trading regime, such as created by the WTO – has become a major trend. Regional economic integration is realised by the negotiation and conclusion of regional trade agreements[166] and other forms of regional cooperation. The term 'regional trade agreement' (RTA) refers to: (i) agreements establishing free trade areas (whereby the participating parties mutually remove obstacles to trade between them but each of the parties maintains its own trade barriers against third countries)[167] or customs unions (whereby barriers to trade between the parties are mutually eliminated and a common customs tariff applies to goods from third countries);[168] (ii) economic integration agreements liberalising trade in services and labour market integration arrangements; and (iii) preferential trade agreements between developing countries.[169]

Although the majority of RTAs are bilateral, there are also a number of regional agreements that include more than two parties, often located within the same geographical region, such as NAFTA, the EU, the Eurasian Economic Union, the African Continental Free Trade Area, ASEAN, and Mercosur. Moreover, many RTAs not only set out substantive rules on competition and investment, but also incorporate certain human rights, labour, and environmental standards.[170]

ii. Legal Framework

The conditions under which WTO Members may enter into RTAs are set out in the following three sets of rules.

a. RTAs Covering Trade in Goods

Article XXIV GATT 1994 permits the establishment of customs unions, free trade areas, and interim agreements necessary for the formation of a customs union or a free trade area, provided that: (i) these agreements cover 'substantially all trade' between the parties;[171] (ii) the import duties and other trade rules, on the whole, are not higher or more restrictive to

[166] The importance of RTAs has increased substantially over the years. See, for a more detailed analysis of different RTAs, L Bartels and F Ortino (eds), *Regional Trade Agreements and the WTO Legal System* (Oxford, OUP, 2006); Herdegen (n 1) 319–47; S Lester and B Mercurio, *Bilateral and Regional Trade Agreements: Case Studies* (Cambridge, CUP, 2009); JH Mathis and JN Bhagwati, *Regional Trade Agreements in the GATT/WTO: Article XXIV and the Internal Trade Requirement* (The Hague, TMC Asser Press, 2002).

[167] The requirements for a WTO-consistent free trade area can be found in Art XXIV:8(b) GATT 1994.

[168] The requirements for a WTO-consistent customs union can be found in Art XXIV:8(a) GATT 1994.

[169] L Bartels, 'Regional Trade Agreements' in *Max Planck Institute of Public International Law* (Oxford Public International law, last updated in March 2013), para 1.

[170] ibid.

[171] ibid, Art XXIV (para 8) GATT 1994.

trade with other WTO Members than before the creation of the free trade area or customs union;[172] (iii) if, by setting up the customs union or free trade area, a Member deviates from the tariffs to which he had previously committed himself towards another Member, these rates should be renegotiated to restore the former balance;[173] and (iv) an interim agreement that puts a timetable to establish a customs union or free trade is conducted within a reasonable period.[174] Together with Article XXIV GATT 1994, the Understanding on the Interpretation of Article XXIV of the General Agreement on Tariffs and Trade 1994 provides for the legal framework for RTAs covering the formation and operation of customs unions and free trade areas covering trade in goods. There remains, however, plenty of disagreement among WTO Members regarding the interpretation of Article XXIV GATT 1994.[175]

b. RTAs Covering Trade in Services and Labour Market Integrations Arrangements

In the field of services, similar conditions are imposed by Article V GATS, which provides for 'economic integration' agreements, and Article V*bis* GATS, which provides for Labour Market Integration Agreements. The underlying rationale in the cases of services is the same: the regional trade agreement has to cover sufficient trade and may not create new obstacles for WTO Members who are not party to the agreement.

c. RTAs Covering Trade in Goods between Developing Countries

To regulate RTAs among developing countries, the signatories of the GATT issued the above mentioned 'Enabling Clause' of 28 November 1979, allowing for a derogation to the MFN treatment in favour of developing countries. Article 2(c) of the Enabling Clause permits 'horizontal' reciprocal preferential (tariff and non-tariff) trade agreements covering trade in goods among developing countries. In accordance with Article 3 of the Enabling Clause, any differential and more favourable treatment is allowed provided that it: (i) facilitates and promotes trade of developing countries and does not raise barriers to or create undue difficulties for the trade of any other Contracting Parties; and (ii) does not constitute an impediment to the reduction or elimination of tariffs and other restrictions to trade on a most favoured nation basis.

iii. The EU and Regional Economic Integration

The EU is one of the trading blocs with the largest amount of regional trade agreements. The proliferation of (regional) free trade initiatives that involve the EU can be divided into three categories of agreements: (i) customs unions;[176] (ii) (Stabilisation and) Association

[172] ibid, Art XXIV (para 5).
[173] ibid, Art XXIV (para 6).
[174] The reasonable period of time shall not exceed ten years, except in exceptional circumstances. See the Understanding on Article XXIV, para 3.
[175] N Lockhart and AD Mitchell, 'Regional Trade Agreements Under GATT 1994: An Exception and Its Limits' in AD Mitchell (ed), *Challenges and Prospects for the WTO* (London, Cameron May, 2005).
[176] Examples include: the Agreement of 28 June 1990 between the Principality of Andorra and the European Economic Community [1990] OJ L374/14; and, Decision No 1/95 of the EC-Turkey Association Council of 22 December 1995 on implementing the final phase of the Customs Union [1996] OJ L 035.

Agreements,[177] Economic Partnership Agreements[178] and (Deep and Comprehensive) Free Trade Agreements ((DC)FTAs);[179] and (iii) Partnership and Cooperation Agreements.[180] Its common commercial policy being one of its strongest, and exclusive, competences, the unity of the EU in international trade negotiations is both its strength as well as a potential weakness: in those cases where the EU was unable to unify its voice and unite its Member States, little leverage in the negotiations could be used.[181] Recent changes in public opinion have had a significant impact on the ongoing trade negotiations conducted by the European Commission, with increased calls for transparency and preservation of national sovereignty.[182]

So far, the EU has notified 37 RTAs which are still in force and has made an early announcement for 15 others.[183] Notably, the EU is at the time of writing negotiating FTAs with, among others, India, China, Tunisia, and Indonesia.[184] In September 2014, the EU concluded negotiations with Canada on a free trade and investment agreement between the EU and Canada (Comprehensive Economic and Trade Agreement (CETA)) and on 15 February 2017, the European Parliament voted in favour of CETA.[185] In order to enter into force, the EU national parliaments must approve CETA. The EU completed negotiations for a comprehensive free trade agreement with Singapore in October 2014 (ESFTA)[186]

[177] Used in the commercial policy with neighbouring countries. Recent examples include: Association Agreement of 21 March 2014 between the European Union and its Member States, of the one part, and Ukraine, of the other part (Ukraine Association Agreement) [2014] OJ L161/3; Association Agreement of 27 June 2014 between the European Union and the European Atomic Energy Community and their Member States, of the one part, and the Republic of Moldova, of the other part (Moldova Association Agreement) [2014] OJ L260/4; Association Agreement of 27 June 2014 between the European Union and the European Atomic Energy Community and their Member States, of the one part, and Georgia, of the other part (Georgia Association Agreement) [2014] OJ L261/4; and, Stabilization and Association Agreement of 18 July 2016 between the European Union and the European Atomic Energy Community, of the one part, and Kosovo, of the other part (Kosovo Stabilization and Association Agreement) [2016] OJ L71/3.

[178] These are trade and development agreements negotiated between the EU and ACP partners engaged in regional economic integration processes (EC, DG Trade, 'Economic Partnerships', 19 October 2017, ec.europa.eu/trade/policy/countries-and-regions/development/economic-partnerships).

[179] eg, Free Trade Agreement between the European Union and its Member States, of the one part, and the Republic of Korea, of the other part (EU-Korea FTA) [2011] OJ L127/1.

[180] These Agreements are concluded with various trading partners all over the world. Recent examples include: Partnership and Cooperation Agreement of 17 January 2013 between the European Union and its Member States, of the one part, and the Republic of Iraq, of the other part [2012] OJ L204/20; Enhanced Partnership and Cooperation Agreement of 21 December 2015 between the European Union and its Member States, of the one part, and the Republic of Kazakhstan, of the other part [2016] OJ L29/3.

[181] S Meunier, *Trading Voices: the European Union in International Commercial Negotiations* (Princeton, Princeton UP, 2005) 2.

[182] In his 2017 State of the Union, President Jean-Claude Juncker stated that the Commission would from then on publish any new proposal for negotiating mandates. See EC, Press release: 'State of the Union 2017 – Trade Package: Commission unveils initiatives for a balanced and progressive trade policy', 14 September 2017, europa.eu/rapid/press-release_IP-17-3182_en.htm; 'If the EU cannot do trade, what can it do? The CETA debacle heralds the age of "vetocracy"', *The Economist*, 29 October 2016, economist.com/news/europe/21709330-ceta-debacle-heralds-age-vetocracy-if-eu-cannot-do-trade-what-can-it-do; H Von Der Burchard, 'EU-New Zealand Trade Deal in 'Deep Trouble', *Politico*, 9 January 2017, politico.eu/article/eu-new-zealand-trade-deal-in-deep-trouble.

[183] To illustrate these numbers: runners-up are Iceland (29), Switzerland (29), Norway (28), Chile (27) and Liechtenstein (27). The United States has 'only' 14 RTAs notified to the WTO and currently in force (WTO, RTA Database, 'Regional trade agreements notified to the GATT/WTO and in force. By country/territory', 9 January 2017, rtais.wto.org/ui/publicPreDefRepByCountry.aspx).

[184] EC, 'Investment', ec.europa.eu/trade/policy/accessing-markets/investment/.

[185] Comprehensive Economic and Trade Agreement between the European Union and the Government of Canada (CETA) (adopted 26 September 2014, provisionally applied since 21 September 2017); ec.europa.eu/trade/policy/in-focus/ceta/ceta-chapter-by-chapter/.

[186] Free Trade Agreement between the European Union and Singapore (ESFTA) (adopted May 2015, not yet entered into force) trade.ec.europa.eu/doclib/press/index.cfm?id=96.

and with Vietnam in December 2015 (EVFTA).[187] The EU finalised negotiations for a trade agreement with Japan on 8 December 2017. The negotiations for a Trans-Atlantic Partnership Agreement (TTIP) between the EU and the United States were paused in 2016.

Importantly, there has been discussion on whether or not the EU has the exclusive competence to sign and conclude ESFTA by itself or whether this is a shared competence with the EU Member States. ESFTA is an example of a so-called '*new generation*' bilateral free trade agreement[188] which not only includes the traditional barriers to trade in goods and services, but also provisions on a number of other matters related to trade, including for example direct and indirect foreign investment, competition, sustainable development, intellectual property protection, and dispute settlement between States and investors. On 16 May 2017, the Court of Justice of the European Union issued an opinion on these questions.[189] The CJEU held that the EU cannot conclude ESFTA alone, since some of the provisions fall within the competences shared between the EU and the EU Member States.[190] In particular with respect to portfolio investments and the regime governing dispute settlement between investors and States (ISDS), the EU has a shared competence with the EU Member States.[191] Accordingly, it follows from this opinion that ESFTA can only be concluded by the EU and the EU Member States jointly, requiring an institutional involvement by the Member States' national parliaments in the ratification procedure of this FTA. This opinion will have far-reaching consequences for the EU investment program and the ongoing negotiation procedures between the EU and third countries, as it has now been confirmed that some of the elements contained in FTAs qualify as shared competences.[192]

C. The Relationship between WTO Law and EU Law

The above discussion on the WTO makes clear that the impact of WTO trade rules on the EU can be significant. The EU is in a unique position in that respect, as it is the only regional organisation that provides for in-depth market integration. The question then arises what the influence is of WTO law in the EU. As the WTO covered agreements are international agreements, the question has arisen whether at least some of their provisions might have direct effect.[193] However, according to well-established CJEU case law, the provisions of the

[187] Free Trade Agreement between the European Union and Socialist Republic of Vietnam (EVFTA) (adopted January 2016, entered into force October 2016) trade.ec.europa.eu/doclib/press/index.cfm?id=1437.

[188] Opinion of the Court of 16 May 2017, *Opinion delivered pursuant to Art 218(11) TFEU – Free Trade Agreement between the European Union and the Republic of Singapore*, 2/15, EU:C:2017:376, para 17 (Opinion 2/15).

[189] ibid.

[190] The CJEU did confirm that the EU is indeed endowed with exclusive competence over the reduction of custom duties and of non-tariff barriers in the fields of trade in goods and services, intellectual property protection, direct foreign investment protection, public procurement, competition, sustainable development and the rules on transparency unless those rules relate to the field of non-direct foreign investment (the so-called portfolio investments, which should be understood as investments made without the intention to influence the management and control of an undertaking). See ibid, paras 41, 43, 45, 48, 74, 77, 82, 102, 130, 138, 167, 172, 193, 202, 217, 224, 225, 243, 252, 277, 283, and 305.

[191] ibid, para 305.

[192] This increased involvement of EU Member States opens the door for increased blockage by national (or even regional) parliaments.

[193] See on earlier agreements Judgment of 26 October 1982, *Kupferberg*, C-104/81, EU:C:1982:362, paras 20–22, 26–27. See also Judgment of 10 January 2006, *R (on the application of International Air Transport Association) v European Low Fares Airline Association v Department for Transport*, C-344/04, EU:C:2006:10, para 39.

WTO agreements as well as the outcomes of WTO dispute settlement proceedings, do not enjoy direct effect in the EU, meaning that individuals cannot invoke WTO law to challenge EU measures.[194] This does not mean that the CJEU ignores WTO law completely when reviewing EU measures. Only when an EU act explicitly refers to specific provisions of WTO law[195] or when the EU intends to implement a particular WTO obligation,[196] can the CJEU review the legality of the EU measure against WTO agreements.[197] There is a limited possibility for direct effect of those measures for which it is clear that the EU legislator has intended to implement WTO law.[198] Although in principle such intention can be found in any area of EU law, so far the 'intention argument' has only been accepted in the case of anti-dumping legislation[199] and in the case of the EC Trade Barriers Regulation.[200] That being said, the CJEU goes to great lengths to avoid finding conflict between WTO law and EU law. Although it is not willing to test the legality of an EU measure on the basis of WTO law, it engages in consistent interpretation.[201] Since both the EU and its Member States are full WTO Members, bound by all of its obligations, the EU is responsible for ensuring that its Member States respect WTO law.[202]

Interestingly, the CJEU seems to purposefully hold any potential interaction with WTO panels and/or the WTO Appellate Body at bay. A famous example is a 2001 case in which the Appellate Body first held that an EC anti-dumping duty was in breach of WTO law as it was an application of the practice of zeroing.[203] When the same measure was challenged in front of the CJEU, the latter refused to rely on the reasoning of the Appellate Body and instead applied its own reasoning.[204] However, even though the CJEU relied on its own assessment of the measure, it did not contradict the Appellate Body. It can arguably be concluded that there is in fact an indirect dialogue between EU law and

[194] The Court first decided on this matter in Judgment of 23 November 1999, *Portugal v Council*, C-149/9, EU:C:1999:574. More recent judgments are Judgment of 3 September 2008, *Kadi and Al Barakaat International Foundation*, C-402/05 P and C-415/05, EU:C:2008:461, paras 307–308; Judgment of 30 September 2003, *Biret*, C-93 and 94/02, EU:C:2003:518, paras 65–67; Judgment of 9 September 2008, *FIAMM and Fedion*, C-120/06 P and C-121/06 P, EU:C:2008:476, para 176. See also M Bronckers, 'From "Direct Effect" to "Muted Dialogue"'(2008) 11(4) *JIEL* 885; M Dani, 'Remedying European Legal Pluralism: The FIAMM and Fedion Litigation and the Judicial Protection of International Trade Bystanders' (2010) 21(2) *EJIL* 303; J Wouters, D Coppens and D Geraets, 'The influence of general principles of law' in S Gaines, E Olsen and K Engsig Sørensen (eds), *Liberalising Trade in the EU and the WTO: A Legal Comparison* (Cambridge, CUP, 2012). See also Chapter 4, Section V(B).

[195] eg, Council Regulation No 2641/84 of 17 September 1984 on the strengthening of the common commercial policy with regard in particular to protection against illicit commercial practices [1984] OJ L252/1.

[196] eg, in the case of EU anti-dumping regulations, including Council Regulation (EEC) No 2423/88 of 11 July 1988 on protection against dumped or subsidised imports from countries not members of the European Economic Community [1988] OJ L209/1.

[197] See Judgment of 7 May 1991, *Nakajima All Precision Co Ltd v Council of the European Communities*, C-69/89, EU:C:1991:186 (*Nakajima v Council*); and, Judgment of the Court of 22 June 1989, *Fediol v Commission*, 70/87, EU:C:1989:254 (*Fediol*).

[198] *Nakajima v Council* (n 197). Note that the Court required the intention to be explicitly included in the relevant legislation.

[199] Judgment of 3 February 2005, *Chiquita v Commission*, T-19/01, EU:T:2005:31, para 124.

[200] *Fediol* (n 197).

[201] This is limited to secondary EU legislation, see Judgment of 17 September 2007, *Microsoft v Commission*, T-201/04, EU:T:2007:289, para 798.

[202] This includes, if necessary, bringing an action against that Member State under Arts 258 and 259 TFEU; B Egelund Olsen, M Steinicke and K Engsig Sørensen, 'The WTO and the EU' in B Egelund Olsen, M Steinicke and K Engsig Sørensen (eds), *WTO Law. From a European Perspective* (Alphen aan den Rijn, Wolters Kluwer, 2012) 109.

[203] WTO Dispute Settlement, European Communities – Anti-Dumping Duties on Imports of Cotton-Type Bed Linen from India (EC-Bed Linen), Appellate Body Report, 1 March 2001, WT/DS141/AB/R.

[204] Judgment of 27 September 2007, *IKEA v Commissioners of Customs & Excise*, C-351/04, EU:C:2007:547, paras 26–35.

WTO law, despite the absence of direct effect, albeit a 'muted dialogue'.[205] Interestingly, the CJEU appears to take a different approach when it comes to the possible direct effect of other international agreements. It has been noted that when interpreting international agreements, the Court usually looks at the wording of provisions, in contrast to the analysis of structure and purpose it applies to WTO law.[206] Still, this observation has been found to not always be correct.[207] It has been said by some commentators that the CJEU's caution to allow direct effect to the WTO may be understandable, as the alternative would potentially overly restrain legitimate political choices made by EU legislators.[208] Direct effect could also overly empower individuals that could overtake the interest of the EU as a whole. Denying direct effect, thus, would be a way to ensure that EU trade policy decisions are kept with the legitimate authority.[209] Another reason lies in the fact that the EU and the WTO are different organisations that influence the municipal laws of their Member States or Members in different ways.[210]

The EU is recognised as a strong actor within the WTO framework, with a leading role in both the Uruguay Negotiation Round that conceived the WTO as well as in the ongoing Doha Development Round.[211] The EU's strong position within the WTO has sometimes led it to, in rather exceptional circumstances, trying to 'abuse' its dominant position. An example of this can be found in the European Parliament's official call to ignore the Panel Report in the *EC – Hormones* dispute, which ruled against the EU, and continue to apply bans on beef containing hormones.[212] It should be noted that similar 'flexing of muscles' at the WTO has been done by many Members, both big and small.[213] The EU has equally used its strong position to advocate further liberalisation of international trade, with remarkable leadership in the ongoing negotiations on the Trade in Services Agreements (TiSA).[214] The EU's 'deep trade agenda' includes furthering environmental protection, labour standards, protection of intellectual property rights, competition policy, etc, both at the multilateral as well as the plurilateral level.[215]

[205] Bronckers (n 194) 890.
[206] ibid, 894.
[207] Judgment of 3 June 2008, *Intertanko v Secretary of State for Transport*, C-308/06, EU:C:2008:312, paras 54 and 64–65.
[208] J Jackson, 'Direct Effect of Treaties in the US and EU, the Case of the WTO: Some Perceptions and Proposals' in A Arnull, P Eeckhout and T Tridimas (eds), *Continuity and Change in EU Law: Essays in Honour of Sir Francis Jacobs* (Oxford, OUP, 2007) 361–82.
[209] PJ Kuijper and M Bronckers, 'WTO Law in the European Court of Justice' (2005) 42(5) *CMLR* 1313, 1341.
[210] A Sennekamp and I Van Damme, 'A Practical Perspective on Treaty Interpretation: The Court of Justice of the European Union and the WTO Dispute Settlement System' (2014) 4(2) *CJICL* 489, 494.
[211] T Gehring, S Oberthür and M Mühleck, 'European Union Actorness in International Institutions: Why the EU is Recognized as an Actor in Some International Institutions, but Not in Others' (2013) 51(5) *Journal of Common Market Studies* 849, 855.
[212] EP Resolution of 5 May 1999 on the Transatlantic Economic Partnership and EU/US – trade disputes, especially hormones, bananas and hushkits of 4 May 1999 [1999] OJ C279/215, para 16.
[213] See R Senti, 'The Role of the EU as an Economic Actor Within the WTO' (2002) 7(1) *European Foreign Affairs Review* 111, 112.
[214] TiSA is a trade agreement currently being negotiated between 23 WTO Members (Australia, Canada, Chile, Chinese Taipei, Colombia, Costa Rica, the EU, Hong Kong China, Iceland, Israel, Japan, Korea, Liechtenstein, Mauritius, Mexico, New Zealand, Norway, Pakistan, Panama, Peru, Switzerland, Turkey and the United States). The aim of this agreement is to provide a framework for the further liberalisation of trade in services, building on existing obligations as set out in the GATS. More specifically, 'TiSA aims at opening up markets and improving rules in areas such as licensing, financial services, telecoms, e-commerce, maritime transport, and professionals moving abroad temporarily to provide services' (EC, DG Trade, 'Trade in Services Agreement (TiSA)', 14 July 2017, ec.europa.eu/trade/policy/in-focus/tisa/).
[215] For more information on this 'deep trade agenda', see AR Young and J Peterson, 'The EU and the new trade politics' (2006) 13(6) *Journal of European Public Policy* 803; and BAM Araujo, *The EU Deep Trade Agenda. Law and Policy* (Oxford, OUP, 2016).

IV. International Investment Law

International investment law encompasses a legal framework for the promotion of foreign investment and the protection of private foreign investors against interferences by Host States, including legal safeguards for the stability of legal conditions, predictability of State action, and due process.[216]

A. Definitions of Foreign Direct Investment, Investor and Investments

According to the OECD, foreign direct investment (FDI) 'reflects the objective of establishing a lasting interest by a resident enterprise in one economy (direct investor) in an enterprise (direct investment enterprise) that is resident in an economy other than that of the direct investor'.[217] The lasting interest assumes the existence of a long-term relationship between the direct investor and the direct investment enterprise as well as a significant degree of influence on the management of the latter.[218]

While the definition of foreign direct investment is rather straightforward, general consensus has not yet been reached on the definitions of 'investment' and 'investor'. Determining the scope of these concepts is, however, important for ensuring investment protection under customary international law and provisions under international investment agreements (IIAs). In practice, arbitral tribunals ruling over investor-state disputes are left with the difficult task of determining on a case-by-case basis whether the definitions are satisfied in order to have jurisdiction over a certain claim and apply the substantive standards guaranteed in the IIAs.[219]

The definition of investment involves questions concerning the nature of the commercial venture undertaken by the private person in the Host State.[220] Drafters of IIAs often leave the concept of investment undefined, or they deliberately adopt an open-ended approach which favours a broad definition of investment. For example, CETA defines investments as

> every kind of asset that an investor owns or controls, directly or indirectly, that has the characteristics of an investment, which includes a certain duration and other characteristics such as the commitment of capital or other resources, the expectation of gain or profit, or the assumption of risk.

This is followed by a non-exhaustive list of examples, including but not limited to, enterprises, shares, stocks or other forms of equity participation in enterprises, bonds debentures and other debt instruments of an enterprise, and intellectual property rights.[221]

[216] M Herdegen, 'International Economic Law' in MPEPIL.

[217] OECD, 'OECD Benchmark Definition of Foreign Direct Investment', 4th edn, 2008, oecd.org/daf/inv/investmentstatisticsandanalysis/40193734.pdf, 48.

[218] A long-term relationship is considered to exist if the investor is the direct or indirect owner of 10% or more of the voting power of an enterprise resident in an economy other than that of the investor. See OECD (n 217) 48–49.

[219] D Collins, *An Introduction to International Investment Law* (Cambridge, CUP, 2017) 3–4.

[220] ibid, 75 and 81.

[221] Art 8(1) CETA.

The Convention on the Settlement of disputes relating to investments between States and Nationals of other States (ICSID Convention), contrarily, does not contain a definition of investment, but simply requires that the dispute should arise directly out of an investment.[222]

The definition of investor involves questions of nationality and the relationship of the private person with his home State. Generally, an investor is a foreign person who made an investment in a Host State and is either an individual (a natural person) or a company (a legal person) of a specific nationality.[223] Some IIAs give a detailed description of the concept of investor to clearly delineate the scope of the treaty's intended beneficiaries. For example, the Energy Charter Treaty (ECT) defines 'investor of a Contracting Party' as 'a natural person having the citizenship or nationality of or who is permanently residing in that Contracting Party in accordance with its applicable law or a company or other organisation organised in accordance with the law applicable in that Contracting Party'.[224] The ICSID Convention, on the other hand, does not use the term 'investor' and instead refers to persons who are 'nationals' of the home State.[225] An investor will only have standing to bring a claim under the ECT or the ICSID Convention when it can prove it is foreign and has the nationality of one of the State Parties to the respective treaties. An individual investor's nationality is determined by the relevant national laws.[226] Determining the nationality of legal persons is generally more difficult given that there are more grounds upon which the nationality can be based.[227] IIAs most commonly invoked include the place of incorporation or legal establishment, or the place of the principal seat of business as the bases for nationality claims. Alternatively, the place of the central administration or effective seat is included.

[222] See Art 25(1) ICSID Convention: 'The jurisdiction of the Centre shall extend to any legal dispute arising directly out of an investment, between a Contracting State (or any constituent subdivision or agency of a Contracting State designated to the Centre by that State) and a national of another Contracting State, which the parties to the dispute consent in writing to submit to the Centre. When the parties have given their consent, no party may withdraw its consent unilaterally' (Convention on the Settlement of disputes relating to investments between States and Nationals of other States (adopted 18 March 1965, entered into force 14 October 1966) 17 UST 1270, TIAS 6090, 575 UNTS 159 (ICSID Convention)).

[223] R Dolzer and C Schreuer, *Principles of International Investment Law* (Oxford, OUP, 2012) 44; K Nadakavukaren Schefer, *International Investment Law. Text, Cases and Materials*, 2nd edn (Cheltenham, Edward Elgar, 2016) 135; R Wisner and N Gallus, 'Nationality Requirements in Investor-State Arbitration' (2004) 5 *Journal of World Investment & Trade* 927.

[224] Art 1(7) ECT.

[225] See Art 25(2) ICSID Convention: '"National of another Contracting State" means:(a) any natural person who had the nationality of a Contracting State other than the State party to the dispute on the date on which the parties consented to submit such dispute to conciliation or arbitration as well as on the date on which the request was registered pursuant to paragraph (3) of Article 28 or paragraph (3) of Article 36, but does not include any person who on either date also had the nationality of the Contracting State party to the dispute; and, (b) any juridical person which had the nationality of a Contracting State other than the State party to the dispute on the date on which the parties consented to submit such dispute to conciliation or arbitration and any juridical person which had the nationality of the Contracting State party to the dispute on that date and which, because of foreign control, the parties have agreed should be treated as a national of another Contracting State for the purposes of this Convention'.

[226] *Champion Trading Company, Ameritrade International, Inc v Arab Republic of Egypt*, 21 October 2003, ICSID Case No ARB/02/9; *Victor Pey Casado and President Allende Foundation v Republic of Chile*, 8 May 2008, ICSID ARB Case No ARB/98/2; *Soufraki v United Arab Emirates*, 7 July 2007, ICSID Case No ARB/02/07; Wisner and Gallus (n 223) 928.

[227] M Sornarajah, *The International Law on Foreign Investment*, 3rd edn (Cambridge, CUP, 2010) 8; Nadakavukaren Schefer (n 223) 147.

B. Protection of Investments under the Sources of International Investment Law

Today foreign investors use international investment agreements as the primary means to protect their investments from undue interferences by Host States. IIAs include: (i) bilateral investment treaties (BITs) (eg the BIT between the United Kingdom and Colombia[228]); (ii) regional investment treaties (eg the ASEAN Comprehensive Investment Agreement); and (iii) agreements with investment protection provisions, including trade agreements between States from certain regions (eg NAFTA) and agreements for specific sectors (eg ECT). In addition to seeking protection for their investments under IIAs, foreign investors may also invoke customary international law and investment contracts concluded with the Host State or a State-owned enterprise. On a final note, some Host States have adopted investment codes which are designed to both attract foreign investment and maintain control over it; these will not be further discussed here.

i. Protection of Investments under Customary International Law

The existence of a number of customary rules regarding the protection of FDI was not controversial until the First World War.[229] While a State could treat its own nationals in any way it deemed fit, an international minimum standard existed for the treatment of foreigners in general and foreign investors in particular. The major European States were among the first to conclude treaties containing reciprocal obligations to protect foreigners and their property.[230]

The Russian Revolution and the widespread nationalisations that followed, on the one hand, and the desire for economic independence of Latin American countries, on the other hand, put an end to this consensus.[231] In the Soviet Union, this was legitimised on ideological grounds, while in Latin America this was grounded in the teachings of the Argentine jurist Carlos Calvo. Under the so-called *Calvo-doctrine*, the existence of an international minimum standard was denied and the doctrine of national treatment was honoured.[232] Under the Calvo-doctrine, a foreign investor would only receive compensation when being expropriated by the Host State if a domestic investor would receive compensation in the same situation.[233]

[228] Bilateral Agreement for the Promotion and Protection of Investments between the Government of the United Kingdom of Great-Britain and Northern Ireland and Republic of Colombia (adopted 17 March 2010, entered into force 10 October 2014) TS No 24, Cm 8973.

[229] These customary rules include the rules on state responsibility (on which see Chapter 12). See Nadakavukaren Schefer (n 223) 44–57; KJ Vandevelde, 'A Brief History of International Investment Agreement' in KP Sauvant and LE Sachs (eds), *The Effect of Treaties on Foreign Direct Investment: Bilateral Investment Treaties, Double Taxation Treaties, and Investment Flows* (Oxford, OUP, 2009) 4–5.

[230] Nadakavukaren Schefer (n 223) 6.

[231] Opposition had always been voiced by socialist states, contesting the notion of private property, but became louder after these developments. See P Muchlinski, 'Policy Issues' in P Muchlinski, F Ortino and C Schreuer (eds), *The Oxford Handbook of International Investment Law* (Oxford, OUP, 2008) 4.

[232] Calvo argued that the treatment that foreign investors should receive should be strictly limited to what is received by the like domestic investors. This included foreign investors searching for remedies, being limited to the jurisdiction of national courts: 'International law, in short, would be substantially removed from investment law': Nadakavukaren Schefer (n 223) 7.

[233] Some States took this Calvo-doctrine further and included in agreements with foreigners a so-called Calvo-clause, causing investments to be placed under the exclusive jurisdiction of the national courts and waived the diplomatic protection of the foreign investor from his State. This clause, however, was not considered valid because diplomatic protection is a right that belongs to the State and not the individual. Indeed, a State has an interest in ensuring compliance with international law.

Contrarily, developed States continued to defend the existence of an international minimum standard, requiring States to uphold a certain common standard of treatment to aliens (including foreign investors) in their territory. In case of expropriation, the developed nations considered the *Hull-formula*, requiring prompt, adequate, and effective compensation, as the international minimum standard (see below) – even if a domestic investor would not receive compensation in the same situation.

This discord in doctrine between the international minimum standard and national treatment would continue to influence the debate and was enhanced because of the decolonisation process after 1960.[234] This had an impact in practice, which was not unequivocal: both Mexico[235] and the USSR[236] went ahead despite their principled position on national treatment on the payment of compensation, with respect to which they denied any value of precedence. On the other hand, the Supreme Court of the United States stated in 1964 that '[t]here are few issues in international law today on which opinion seems to be so divided as the limitations on a state's power to expropriate the property of aliens'[237] and refused to grant the claims against the nationalised Bank of Cuba.

The efforts of the United Nations in the 1960s and 1970s to codify customary international law in this field by means of declarations, contributed to the confusion due to the divided international community. In retrospect, however, it can be maintained that the resolutions of the General Assembly on the New International Economic Order[238] cannot be considered to be an accurate reflection of customary international law. Still, these resolutions were a clear reflection of the demise of the *Hull-formula*.[239] Among the other General Assembly resolutions mentioned above,[240] neither the Resolution on the permanent sovereignty over natural resources[241] from 1962 nor the Charter of Economic Rights and Duties[242] from 1974, required a compensation to be calculated on the basis of the *Hull-formula*. The former Resolution, however, does show a consensus within the various schools in the international community on a number of principles: (i) appropriate compensation must be payed after expropriation of foreign property; (ii) this compensation should be paid in accordance with rules of international law; (iii) investment contracts between States and foreign investors are binding; and (iv) arbitration agreements between States and foreign investors prevail.

Various factors have contributed to the widespread acceptance of *international standards of treatment*: (i) the demise of the Socialist Bloc; (ii) the effects of the 1980s debt crisis on loan capital with FDI becoming a major source of capital in developing countries; and (iii) the increased acceptance by international governments of market-based approaches

[234] For more information on the developments of international economic policies between the 1940s and the 1970s see C Lipson, *Standing Guard: Protecting Foreign Capital in the Nineteenth and Twentieth Centuries* (Berkeley, University of California Press, 1985).
[235] *US Dept of State Bull* [22 November 1941] 399–403.
[236] Representation of the agreement in *United States v Pink* [1942] 315 US 203.
[237] Supreme Court (US), *Banco Nacional de Cuba v Sabbatino*, 23 March 1964, 376 US 398.
[238] These resolutions emphasised the sovereign rights to regulate and control foreign investors and investments, as well as the recognition of permanent national sovereignty over natural wealth and resources; UNGA Res 2158(XXI), 25 November 1966, UN Doc A/RES/2158(XXI); UNGA Res 3171(XXVIII), 17 December 1973, UN Doc A/RES/3171(XXVIII); and, UNGA Res 3281(XXIX), 'Charter on the Economic Rights and Duties of States', 12 December 1974, UN Doc A/RES/3281(XXIX).
[239] AT Guzman, 'Explaining the Popularity of Bilateral Investment Treaties' in Sauvant and Sachs (n 229) 77.
[240] UNGA Res 2158(XXI) (n 238); UNGA Res 3171(XXVIII) (n 238); and UNGA Res 3281(XXIX) (n 238).
[241] UNGA Res 1803(XVII), 14 December 1962, UN Doc A/RES/1803(XVII).
[242] UNGA Res 3281(XXIX) (n 238).

to economic development.[243] As to the substance of the international rules on damages there was – and still is – no consensus. An attempt to find these is often based on legal doctrine, the extensive body of international dispute settlement by a large number of arbitral tribunals,[244] and the case law of the ICJ[245] and its predecessor the PCIJ.[246]

The above discussion about the applicability of the international minimum standard of treatment or national treatment has, however, become less relevant with the arrival of international investment agreements. IIAs now include their own standards of protection against interferences by Host States in investors' property rights. The international minimum standard for the treatment of aliens, however, remains relevant in a number of contexts, including cases of denial of justice.[247] Moreover, customary international law still remains relevant for other aspects of the investment arbitration practice, including but not limited to the rules on nationality of the investor and expropriation.[248] Interestingly, although the *Hull-formula* did not become customary international law, many BITs include a similar standard.[249]

ii. Bilateral Protection of Investments

Nowadays, bilateral investment agreements are the most important source of international investment law.[250] A quick search on UNCTAD's Investment Policy Hub results in a list of almost 3,000 bilateral investment agreements at the time of writing.[251] A bilateral investment agreement may be understood as a reciprocal legal agreement between two sovereign States regulating the promotion and protection of investments made by their nationals in each other's territory. They generally include the following elements: (i) the title and preamble indicating the intentions of the State Parties; (ii) definitions, especially of the concepts 'investment' and 'investor' (see also above, Subsection (A)); (iii) substantive provisions on the protection of investors and investments, including but not limited to provisions

[243] Muchlinski (n 231) 4.
[244] Norwegian Shipowners Claims *(Norway v United States)*, Award of 13 October 1922, RIAA 307; De Sabla Claim *(United States v Panama)*, Award of 29 June 1933, 28 AJIL 602; BP v Libya, Award of 10 October 1973, 53 ILR 297; Texaco & Calasiatic v Libya, Award of 19 January 1977, 17 ILM 1; Liamco v Libya, Award of 12 April 1977, 20 ILM 1; Aminoil v Kuwait, Award of 24 March 1982, 21 ILM 976; Phillips Petroleum v Iran, 30 December 1982, 1 Iran-US CTR 487; ITT Industries v. Iran, 26 May 1983, 2 Iran-US CTR Reports 348; Tippett, Abbett, McCarthy, Stratton v TAMS-AFFA Consulting Engineers of Iran, Award of 29 June 1984, 6 Iran-US CTR 219; INA Corporation v Iran, Award of 13 August 1985, 8 Iran-US CTR 373; Phelps Dodge v Iran, Award of 19 March 1986, 10 Iran-US CTR 121.
[245] Anglo-Iranian Oil Company (*United Kingdom v Iran*) [1952] ICJ Rep 1952, 20; Barcelona Traction, Light & Power Co (*Belgium v Spain*) [1970] ICJ Rep 1970, 3 CASES, IB14; Elettronica Sicula SpA (ELSI) (*United States v Italy*) [1989] ICJ Rep 1989, 15.
[246] Certain German interests in Polish Upper Silesia and the Factory at Chorzow (*Germany v Poland*) [1928] PCIJ Ser A No 17; German Interests in Upper Silesia (*Germany v Poland*) [1925] PCIJ Ser A No 6.
[247] C Schreuer, 'Investments, International Protection' in MPEPIL, para 22.
[248] Dolzer and Schreuer (n 223) 17.
[249] H Dickerson, 'Minimum Standards' in MPEPIL, para 16.
[250] Bilateral investment agreements between States themselves should still be distinguished from '*internationalised*' investment agreements or investment contracts between States and investors. These instruments also intend to protect investments by withdrawing them from the national law of the Host State. However, contrary to BITs which are concluded between States, investment contracts are directly concluded between a Host State and a foreign investor.
[251] UNCTAD's Investment Policy Hub is available at investmentpolicyhub.unctad.org. The countries with the most BITs are: Germany (135), China (129), Switzerland (114), the United Kingdom (106), and France (104).

on the prohibition of expropriation, discrimination, and unfair and inequitable treatment; (iv) provisions on the settlement of disputes between States Parties and disputes between investors and Host States;[252] and (v) final provisions determining territorial and temporal application, as well as the possibilities for terminating or amending the BIT.[253]

The predecessors of the BITs were the so-called Friendship, Commerce and Navigation Agreements, bilateral treaties which envisaged facilitating commerce, investment, and navigation between State Parties. However, they did not offer a conclusive answer to the increased uncertainty about the international law of foreign investment. In 1959, West Germany was the first State to sign a bilateral investment agreement with Pakistan.[254] Other Western European States, notably France, Belgium and Switzerland, and the United States, soon followed.[255]

At first these BITs were concluded between traditional capital exporting countries from Western Europe and North America on the one hand, and developing countries and transition countries of Central and Eastern Europe on the other hand.[256] This led to the developed countries drafting these treaties and offering them for signature to the developing or transition country, the latter accepting in order to attract foreign investment.[257] The motivation for the developed country to go through the trouble of drafting and concluding these bilateral agreements, was to obtain clear and straightforward protection of its foreign investments.[258] In recent years, however, agreements are increasingly being concluded between developing countries and transition countries *inter se*.[259]

The conclusion of a bilateral investment treaty has two main merits: the avoidance of disputes (a State wants to avoid the reputation that it is on record as a State that does not respect its international commitments) and the creation of a framework for dispute resolution. A bilateral investment agreement thus contributes to creating a climate of trust. However, the relation between the existence of an investment agreement and an increase in investment is disputed.[260] Businesses, when choosing a suitable location for their investment, are guided, after all, not only by legal considerations, but more so by economic factors.

[252] Until the mid-twentieth century, foreign investors seeking damages for injury caused by a Host State were dependent on the discretionary decision of their State of nationality to exercise diplomatic protection on their behalf or the establishment of specialised claims commissions. Moreover, customary international law requires foreign investors to exhaust local remedies to obtain satisfaction before a Host State can effectuate an investor's claim through diplomatic protection (on which see Chapter 12, Section V). Investment dispute settlement provisions under BITs now grant foreign investors direct access to international arbitration.

[253] M Jacobs, 'Investments, Bilateral Treaties' in *Max Planck Institute of Public International Law* (Oxford Public International law, last updated in June 2014).

[254] Treaty for the Promotion and Protection of Investments (with Protocol and exchange of notes) (adopted 25 November 1959, entered into force 28 April 1962) 457 UNTS 23.

[255] More information on the development of these early BITs can be found in R Dolzer and M Stevens, *Bilateral Investment Treaties* (The Hague, Kluwer, 1995); MI Khalil, 'Treatment of Foreign Investment in Bilateral Investment Treaties' (1992) 7 *ICSID Review* 399; T Modibo Ocran, 'Bilateral Investment Protection Treaties: A Comparative Study' (1987) 8 *New York Law School Journal of International and Comparative Law* 401; JW Salacuse, 'BIT by BIT: The Growth of Bilateral Investment Treaties and Their Impact on Foreign Investment in Developing Countries' (1990) 24 *International Law* 655; M Sornarajah, 'State Responsibility and Bilateral Investment Treaties' (1986) 20 *Journal of World Trade Law* 79.

[256] UNCTAD, *Bilateral Investment Treaties in the Mid-1990s* (New York, UN Publications, 1998) 8–19.

[257] Vandevelde (n 229) 15.

[258] UNCTAD (n 256) 2–6.

[259] UNCTAD, World Investment Report 2006: FDI from Developing and Transition Economies: Implications for Development, (New York, United Nations, 2007) 119.

[260] Found positive impact: E Neumayer and L Spess, 'Do Bilateral Investment Treaties Increase Foreign Direct Investment to Developing Countries' in Sauvant and Sachs (n 229) 225–52; found no impact: M Hallward-Dreimeier,

The existence of such a network of bilateral investment agreements, in which, nowadays, almost all States are involved, has led some authors to conclude that the international community has reached consensus again on the customary status of the protection of foreign investments,[261] while others point to the differences in power between the parties to such agreements and the fact that a bilateral investment agreement is often part of a package of agreements in which concessions are exchanged for each other, so that no rules of customary law can be deduced.[262]

iii. Multilateral Protection of Investments

If a bilateral investment agreement had been concluded between every State or customs territory, so that in every situation it would be possible to fall back on treaty for protection, a network of more than 20,000 agreements would exist. It is therefore not surprising that initiatives at the multilateral level were undertaken to achieve a multilateral investment agreement. However, so far all attempts to arrive at a comprehensive multilateral investment agreement have failed, and there are only multilateral agreements on (procedural) aspects of international investment law and general agreements on specific investments or between a limited number of States. In addition to these limited multilateral agreements on *protection* of foreign investments, a number of investment banks may be mentioned that were established by multilateral agreements with a view to *promoting* investment in developing countries or countries in transition.[263] Finally, the treaties establishing regional economic integration organisations[264] include provisions on effective investment protection measures. Also, Article 1 of the First Protocol to the ECHR can be seen as providing protection against property depriving measures with respect to investments in a Member State of the Council of Europe.

a. Initiatives of the World Bank

The most successful multilateral agreements on foreign investments were drafted in the context of the World Bank (on which see also Chapter 6, Section IX(F)). The secret of their success may lie in the fact that they do not as such deal with substantive investment law, but, on the one hand, provide a procedural framework for disputes between investors and Host States and on the other hand, create an international system of investment guarantees.

'Do bilateral investment treaties attract FDI? Only a bit … and it might bite' *World Bank Policy Research Working Paper* No 3121 (Washington DC, World Bank, 2003); JW Salacuse and NP Sullivan, 'Do BITs really work? An evaluation of bilateral investment treaties and their grand bargain' (2005) 46 *Harvard International Law Journal* 161; J Tobin and S Rose-Acherman, 'Foreign direct investment and the business environment in developing countries: the impact of bilateral investment treaties' *Economics and Public Policy Research Paper* No 293 (New Haven, Yale Law School Center for Law, 2005).

[261] PE Comeaux and NS Kinsella, *Protecting Foreign Investment under International Law* (New York, Oceana, 1997) 74–76.

[262] M Sornarajah, *The International Law on Foreign Investment*, 3rd edn (Cambridge, CUP, 2010) 225–29. On this discussion see also JP Sasse, *An Economic Analysis of Bilateral Investment Treaties* (The Netherlands, Gabler, 2011) 64–65.

[263] eg, the International Investment Bank (IIB), founded in 1970 on the basis of an intergovernmental agreement, the European Investment Bank (EIB), founded in 1958 under the Treaty of Rome, and the much more recent Asian Infrastructure Investment Bank (AAIB), its Memorandum of Understanding signed by 21 member states in Beijing on 24 October 2015 and the Bank being 'open for business' as from 16 January 2016. As of 12 July 2018, the AAIB has 42 regional and 17 non-regional members. More information can be obtained at aiib.org.

[264] Such as the AU, the CARICOM, the EFTA, etc.

A familiar example is the International Centre for Settlement of Investment Disputes established by the Convention on the Settlement of disputes relating to investments between States and Nationals of other States, with 153 State Parties so far.[265] ICSID is an autonomous international organisation with close ties to the World Bank, which offers parties to the Convention the possibility of mediation and arbitration on investment disputes between States and nationals – mostly enterprises – of other States. Furthermore, the Centre is engaged in providing advice and research. The ICSID has an Administrative Council and a Secretariat. The Administrative Council is chaired by the President of the World Bank and is further comprised of one representative of each State Party to the ICSID Convention.[266]

The role of this Centre is similar to that of the Permanent Court of Arbitration.[267] However, important differences exist. For example, ICSID itself is not involved in mediation or arbitration: mediators and arbitrators are appointed by the parties in accordance with the ICSID Convention. A State may, once it has accepted the arbitration agreement, no longer withdraw its consent. Many governments have committed themselves to refer disputes to ICSID through multilateral treaties, eg, NAFTA,[268] the ECT,[269] and bilateral agreements.[270] Also in treaties between States to which not all parties are a party to the ICSID Convention, it is likely that ICSID plays a role, through the so-called '*Additional Facility*', provided that either the home State of the investor or the Host State is a party to the Convention.[271] All States party to the ICSID Convention, regardless of whether they are parties to the conflict, are obliged to recognise and execute the decisions of the arbitration tribunal. The ICSID awards are, in other words, enforceable.[272]

[265] See Art 1 ICSID Convention: (1) There is hereby established the International Centre for Settlement of Investment Disputes (hereinafter called the Centre); and, (2) The purpose of the Centre shall be to provide facilities for conciliation and arbitration of investment disputes between Contracting States and nationals of other Contracting States in accordance with the provisions of this Convention.

[266] See Arts 4–8 ICSID Convention.

[267] The Permanent Court of Arbitration (PCA) was established in 1899 to facilitate arbitration and other forms of dispute resolution between States, by way of the Hague Convention for the Pacific Settlement of International Disputes, replaced by the Hague Convention for the Pacific Settlement of International Disputes. On the PCA, see Chapter 13, Section III(A).

[268] Art 1120 NAFTA on 'Submission of a Claim to Arbitration'.

[269] Art 26 ECT on 'Settlement of Disputes between an Investor and a Contracting Party'. For more information on investment arbitration in the Energy Charter see T Wälde, 'Investment Arbitration under the Energy Charter Treaty – From Dispute Settlement to Treaty Implementation' (1996) 12(4) *Arbitration International* 429; and K Hober, 'Investment Arbitration and the Energy Charter Treaty' (2010) 1(1) *JIDS* 153.

[270] Various degrees of reference to BITs exist: (1) 'binding offer of consent by the host state': jurisdiction of ICSID is mandatory. Examples include: the Sri Lanka – United Kingdom BIT (1980); Democratic Republic of Congo – US BIT (1984); The Netherlands – Venezuela BIT (1991) (terminated); and the model BITs of China (2003), Germany (2008), the UK (2005) and the US (2012). These model BITs can be found in Dolzer and Schreuer (n 223) 358–405; (2) 'prospect of future consent': an undertaking by the host state to consent to ICSID jurisdiction in the future. Examples include: the France – Malaysia BIT (1975); Japan – Egypt BIT (1977); UK – Philippines BIT (1980); Netherlands – Pakistan BIT (1988); Australia – Czech Republic BIT (1993); Japan – Pakistan BIT (1998); (3) 'consent to different forms of arbitration': parties are given several possibilities, including ICSID. Examples include: the Argentina – US BIT (1991); Switzerland – Paraguay BIT (1992); Lithuania – Poland BIT (1992); Ukraine – US BIT (1994); (4) 'acceptance by the investor': the States offers recourse to ICSID, but the investor has to accept. Examples include: the France – Nigeria BIT (1990), Austria – Morocco BIT (1992); UK model BIT (2005). See C Schreuer et al, *The ICSID Convention: A Commentary*, 2nd edn (Cambridge, CUP, 2009) 205–14.

[271] Adopted by the ICSID in 1978. These Rules offer arbitration, conciliation, and fact-finding services for certain disputes that fall outside the scope of the ICSID Convention. For example, in the case of NAFTA, only the United States is a party to ICSID, so that US investors may still invoke the procedure, while Mexican or Canadian investors can only do this in disputes with the US authorities.

[272] See the text of Arts 53 and 54 of the ICSID Convention: Art 53 '(1) The award shall be binding on the parties and shall not be subject to any appeal or to any other remedy except those provided for in this Convention. Each

The Multilateral Investment Guarantee Agency (MIGA) also plays a role in connection with investments, as the largest and most important of the public investment insurance providers.[273] As a Member of the World Bank, one of MIGA's main aims is to promote foreign direct investment in developing countries.[274] MIGA is based on the Agreement Establishing the Multilateral Investment Guarantee Agency (MIGA Convention), which was adopted in Seoul on 11 October 1985, and ensures investment activities from MIGA countries against political risks.[275] In addition to the role of ensuring guarantees, MIGA in accordance with Article 23 of its founding convention, is also committed to promoting investments, through encouraging bilateral investment agreements and membership in ICSID or by ensuring the peaceful settlement of disputes.

On a final note, in 1992, the World Bank developed Guidelines on the Treatment of Foreign Direct Investment. The Guidelines provide for a general framework for the treatment of foreign investors by Host States.[276] In particular, with a view to encouraging and protecting foreign investment, the Guidelines establish 'standards' promoting fair and equitable treatment of investments, most-favoured nation treatment, and national treatment, and by imposing strict limits on nationalisation.

b. Initiatives of the OECD

From 1995 to 1998, negotiations on a Multilateral Agreement on Investment (MAI) took place within the framework of the OECD.[277] The Member States of this organisation wanted to draft an agreement on mutual investment protection, after which other States

party shall abide by and comply with the terms of the award except to the extent that enforcement shall have been stayed pursuant to the relevant provisions of this Convention; and (2) For the purposes of this Section, "award" shall include any decision interpreting, revising or annulling such award pursuant to Articles 50, 51 or 52'; Art 54 '(1) Each Contracting State shall recognize an award rendered pursuant to this Convention as binding and enforce the pecuniary obligations imposed by that award within its territories as if it were a final judgment of a court in that State. A Contracting State with a federal constitution may enforce such an award in or through its federal courts and may provide that such courts shall treat the award as if it were a final judgment of the courts of a constituent state; (2) A party seeking recognition or enforcement in the territories of a Contracting State shall furnish to a competent court or other authority which such State shall have designated for this purpose a copy of the award certified by the Secretary-General. Each Contracting State shall notify the Secretary-General of the designation of the competent court or other authority for this purpose and of any subsequent change in such designation; and (3) Execution of the award shall be governed by the laws concerning the execution of judgments in force in the State in whose territories such execution is sought'.

[273] Nadakavukaren Schefer (n 223) 608.

[274] See Art 2 MIGA Convention: 'The objectives of the Agency shall be to encourage the flow of investments for productive purposes among member countries, and in particular to developing member countries, thus supplementing the activities of the International Bank for Reconstruction and Development (hereinafter referred to as the Bank), the International Finance Corporation and other international development finance institutions' (Convention establishing the Multilateral Investment Guarantee Agency (MIGA Convention) (adopted 11 October 1985, entered into force 12 April 1988) 1508 UNTS 99 (I-26012)).

[275] See Arts 11–18 MIGA Convention.

[276] The drafters did not intend to establish new norms, but rather extract standards from various preceding multilateral instruments as well as the practice of Western countries and bilateral investment treaties they have concluded.

[277] The mandate for the negotiations stating: '[the agreement is to] provide for a broad multilateral agreement for international investment with high standards for the liberalization of investment regimes and investment protection with effective dispute settlement procedures; [and] be a free-standing international treaty open to all OECD Members and the European Communities and to accession by non-OECD Member countries, which will be consulted as negotiations progress'. Source: *Report by the Committee on International Investment and Multinational Enterprises (CIME) and the Committee on Capital Movements and Invisible Transactions (CMIT)*, 5 May 1995, DAFFE/CMIT/CIME(95)13/FINAL, para 3.

would be invited to accede to this agreement. However, the choice for the OECD as a forum for negotiations was one of the reasons for the failure of this initiative. The OECD Member States at that time, with the exception of Mexico, Turkey, and South Korea, all belonged to the group of capital-exporting countries. But they wanted the membership of the agreement to reach further, including as many developing and transition countries to this agreement as possible, without them being involved in the negotiations.[278] Due to the financial potential of the OECD countries, the developing countries could thus willy-nilly be forced into such an agreement. This method caused many protests in development circles, and was also evidenced by the fact that the text referred only to obligations of the host country and was silent on social obligations of multinational companies. In that respect, there was only a brief reference to the OECD Guidelines for Multinational Enterprises.

A second problem was the broad scope of the agreement: as mentioned before, international law not only imposes restrictions on nationalisation *sensu stricto*, but also on other ownership restrictive measures. The MAI, however, contained such a broad provision in this regard that the tightening of labour, social protection, and environmental regulation could be considered as custodial measures.[279]

Eventually, several domestic motives in the OECD Member States ensured that the negotiations in 1998 were postponed *sine die*: whereas the US feared that its unilateral extra-territorial measures would be difficult to realise in the future, France felt that its cultural identity was threatened since due to the absolute obligation of national treatment the French cultural industry could no longer be subsidised.[280]

c. Initiatives of the WTO

With the failure of the ITO, rules on foreign investments were not part of the multilateral trade law framework until 1994.[281] Foreign investments do play a role at the WTO, but so far this has been limited to trade-related aspects of international investment law.[282] In the context of investment regulations, trade restrictive conditions indeed can be imposed, such as the obligation to purchase raw materials locally. Even before the establishment of the WTO, Canada had been condemned under the GATT for imposing such an obligation.[283]

[278] J Kurtz, 'A General Investment Agreement in the WTO – Lessons from Chapter 11 NAFTA and the OECD Multilateral Agreement on Investment' (2002) 23 *University of Pennsylvania Journal of International Economic Law* 713, 714.

[279] The leaking of a negotiation draft of the MAI to Public Citizen, a US NGO, in February 1997 triggered a vigorous debate on the balance between investment liberalisation and regulatory autonomy of the member states. See Kurtz (n 278) 768 ff.

[280] PT Muchlinski, 'The Rise and Fall of the Multilateral Agreement on Investment: Lessons for the Regulation of International Business' in IF Fletcher, LA Mistelis and M Cremona (eds), *Foundations and Perspectives of International Trade Law* (London, Sweet & Maxwell, 2001) 114, 129 ff.

[281] For more information on the institutional divide between trade and investment since the conclusion of the GATT 1947, see Kurtz (n 278) 718–19.

[282] A first attempt by the United States to include investment in the Tokyo Round Declarations failed due to opposition by developing countries. A second attempt was undertaken by the US during the Punta del Este GATT Ministerial Meeting in 1986. Again, developing countries resisted the proposal of a comprehensive investment agreement, but a compromise was reached to cover only trade-related investment issues. See TL Brewer and S Young, *The Multilateral Investment System and Multinational Enterprises* (Oxford, OUP, 1998) 122 ff; TP Stewart (ed), *The GATT Uruguay Negotiation Round: A Negotiation History (1986–1992)* (The Hague, Kluwer, 1993) 2069 ff; Kurtz (n 278) 722.

[283] *Canada – Administration of the Foreign Investment Review Act*, Panel Report, 7 February 1984, L/5504 – 30S/140.

In the Uruguay Round, three instruments were developed which directly affect investments and through which the WTO assumed new competences over foreign investment: (i) TRIPS; (ii) GATS; and (iii) the Agreement on Trade-Related Investment Measures (TRIMS). TRIPS aims to strengthen and harmonise the level of protection of intellectual property – an asset which is generally recognised as falling under the definition of investment – and provides for more effective enforcement at both national and international level. GATS deals with services and explicitly includes services supplied by foreign investors within another State (mode 3). Foreign direct investment is thereby recognised as one of the covered modes to supply services. It also provides for a general application of the most-favoured nation standard whereas the national treatment and market access obligations only apply in so far as specific commitments have been undertaken in the third mode of supply.[284] The TRIMS does not contain rules on international investment law that are not related to trade (such as unlawful expropriation): it is limited to a ban on investment measures contrary to Article III GATT (national treatment) and Article XI (prohibition of quantitative restrictions – market access).

On a final note, investment is one of the so-called 'Singapore issues' on which future negotiations can take place within the framework of the WTO.[285] This organisation is, partly due to its almost universal membership, regarded as the most likely forum for a possible future multilateral investment treaty.[286] Since 1995 little progress has been made on the multilateral rules on foreign investment, but the need for a multilateral initiative has not yet subsided.[287]

d. Initiatives of the UN

A number of other multilateral initiatives were undertaken by the UN which are relevant to foreign investors. Firstly, the Convention on the Recognition and Enforcement of Foreign Arbitral Awards (the New York Convention),[288] a multilateral instrument which requires the signatory States to: (i) recognise and enforce foreign arbitral awards;[289] and (ii) give effect to an arbitral clause in a contract or an arbitration agreement by referring the parties to the conflict, at the request of one of the parties, to arbitration.[290] Secondly, the UNCITRAL Arbitration Rules (with new Article 1, paragraph 4, as adopted in 2013) (UNCITRAL Arbitration Rules 2013),[291] a set of procedural rules upon which

[284] The inclusion of a 'third mode' of supply of services that can be found in Art I.2(c) leads to the GATS also applying to foreign direct investment: 'For the purposes of this Agreement, trade in services is defined as the supply of a service: [...] by a service supplier of one Member, through commercial presence in the territory of any other Member'.

[285] Together with competition policy, government procurement and trade facilitation. See WTO, *World Trade Organization: Singapore Ministerial Declaration*, 13 December 1996, WT/MIN(96)/DEC, (1997) 36 ILM 218, paras 20–23.

[286] For a comprehensive analysis of the contents of such prospective multilateral investment agreement in the framework of the WTO, see, Kurtz (n 278) 773–88.

[287] A Åslund, 'The World Needs a Multilateral Investment Agreement', *Peterson Institute for International Economics*, Policy Brief 13-01, January 2013, piie.com/publications/pb/pb13-1.pdf.

[288] Convention on the Recognition and Enforcement of Foreign Arbitral Awards (the New York Convention) (adopted 10 June 1985, entered into force 7 June 1959) 330 UNTS 38.

[289] Art I of the New York Convention.

[290] ibid, Art II(3).

[291] UNCITRAL Arbitration Rules (adopted in 1976, entered into force on 15 August 2010) uncitral.org/pdf/english/texts/arbitration/arb-rules-2013/UNCITRAL-Arbitration-Rules-2013-e.pdf.

disputing parties can agree for the conduct of arbitral proceedings arising out of inter alia investor-State disputes or State-to-State disputes. Contrary to the ICSID Convention, UNCITRAL does not provide for an institutional setting for an arbitration; it solely offers a model system of procedural rules for international arbitration.[292] Thirdly, the UNCITRAL Rules on Transparency in Treaty-based Investor-State Arbitration (UNCITRAL Transparency Rules),[293] a set of procedural rules which provide for transparency and accessibility to the public of treaty-based investor-State arbitration. The UNCITRAL Transparency Rules apply to all treaty-based investor-State arbitration proceedings taking place under the UNCITRAL Arbitration Rules, unless the disputing parties agree otherwise. The Rules consist of the United Nations Convention on Transparency in Treaty-based Investor-State Arbitration (the Mauritius Convention on Transparency),[294] an instrument by which parties to existing international investment agreements concluded before 1 April 2014 express their consent to apply the UNCITRAL Transparency Rules; and, the United Nations Draft Code of Conduct on Transnational Corporations,[295] a code which was meant to establish a multilateral framework to control the conduct of transnational corporations. In line with MAI, the UN Draft Code of Conduct never received acceptance.[296]

e. Sectoral and Regional Economic Integration Initiatives

There are also a number of regional and sectoral initiatives which seek to protect foreign investors and their investments (see also Chapter 7 on Regional Organisations), such as the Regional investment agreements (RIAs), which may be understood as reciprocal legal agreements between sovereign States from a given region regulating the promotion and protection of investments made by their nationals in each other's territory. Examples of RIAs include the China–Japan–South Korea Trilateral Investment Agreement (CJKTIA),[297] ASEAN Comprehensive Investment Agreement (ACIA),[298] and the Organization of the Islamic Conference Investment Agreement (OICIA).[299] In 2007, the Common Market for Eastern and Southern Africa (COMESA) signed the Investment Agreement for the COMESA Common Investment Area (CCIA).[300] Another form of such regional and sectoral initiatives are the Agreements with investment provisions, including regional trade agreements

[292] Collins (n 219) 242.

[293] UNGA Res 68/109, UNCITRAL Rules on Transparency in Treaty-based Investor-State Arbitration, 16 December 2013, UN Doc A/RES/68/109.

[294] UNGA Res 69/116, the United Nations Convention on Transparency in Treaty-based Investor-State Arbitration (the Mauritius Convention on Transparency), 18 December 2014, UN Doc A/RES/69/116.

[295] UNGA Res 45/186, United Nations Code of Conduct for Transnational Corporations, 21 December 1990, UN Doc A/RES/45/186.

[296] For a comprehensive overview of the issues surrounding the negotiations of the UN Code of Conduct, see, K Sauvant, 'The Negotiations of the United Nations Code of Conduct on Transnational Corporations: Experience and Lessons Learned' (2015) 16 *The Journal of World Investment & Trade* 11.

[297] China-Japan-Korea Trilateral Investment Agreement (CJKTIA) (adopted on 13 May 2012, entered into force 20 December 2015), investmentpolicyhub.unctad.org/Download/TreatyFile/2633.

[298] ASEAN Comprehensive Investment Agreement (ACIA) (adopted 26 February 2009, 24 February 2012) asean.org/storage/images/2013/economic/aia/ACIA_Final_Text_26%20Feb%202009.pdf.

[299] Organisation of the Islamic Conference Investment Agreement (OICIA) (adopted 5 June 1981, entered into force 23 September 1986) investmentpolicyhub.unctad.org/Download/TreatyFile/2399.

[300] Investment Agreement for the COMESA Common Investment Area (CCIA) (adopted 23 February 2007), investmentpolicyhub.unctad.org/IIA/treaty/3225. As of 12 July 2018, this agreement was not yet in force.

(eg, NAFTA,[301] EFTA,[302] CAFTA-DR,[303] the Cotonou Agreement,[304] or the SADC Protocol on Finance and Investment[305]), or sectoral trade agreements (eg, the ECT[306]).

f. The EU's New Competence over Foreign Direct Investment

Under the Treaty of Lisbon,[307] the EU has assumed a new exclusive competence over the conclusion of treaties covering foreign direct investment.[308] Article 206 TFEU provides for the EU to contribute to the progressive abolition of restrictions on foreign direct investment. Article 207 TFEU adds foreign direct investment to the EU's treaty-making power by including it as an aspect of the EU's common commercial policy. In accordance with Article 3(e) TFEU, the EU has an exclusive competence in the area of common commercial policy. Since the entry into force of the Treaty of Lisbon, the European Commission has sought to develop a comprehensive EU common investment policy and replace old BITs concluded by EU Member States with third countries by new ones.

In a communication of July 2010, the European Commission set out its approach for the EU's future common investment policy,[309] accompanied by a legislative proposal aiming to introduce a comprehensive policy and establishing transitional arrangements for BITs between the EU Member States and third countries.[310] After negotiations between the Council, the EU Member States, and third countries on the Commission's legislative proposal, the European Parliament and the Council adopted Regulation No 1219/2012

[301] Chapter 11 of the NAFTA was remarkable for its far-reaching commitments in this regard: it set very high standards regarding investment liberalisation, investment protection and dispute settlement. For more on this chapter, see Kurtz (n 278) 732–56.

[302] Arts 23–28 EFTA.

[303] Dominican Republic-Central America Free Trade Agreement (CAFTA-DR) (adopted 5 August 2004, entered into force for the United States, El Salvador, Guatemala, Honduras, and Nicaragua in 2006, for the Dominican Republic in 2007, and for Costa Rica in 2009) ustr.gov/trade-agreements/free-trade-agreements/cafta-dr-dominican-republic-central-america-fta/final-text, Arts 10.1–10.28.

[304] Partnership Agreement between the members of the African, Caribbean and Pacific Group of States of the one part, and the European Community and its Member States, of the other part, signed in Cotonou (Cotonou Agreement) (adopted 23 June 2000, entered into force 15 December 2000) OJ L317/3, Art 21 and Arts 74–78.

[305] South African Development Community Protocol on Finance and Investment (adopted 18 August 2006, entered into force 16 April 2010) investmentpolicyhub.unctad.org/Download/TreatyFile/2730, Art 3 and Annex 1.

[306] Arts 10–17 and 26 ECT. It is important to note that the Energy Charter Treaty only covers investments in the energy sector

[307] Treaty of Lisbon amending the Treaty on European Union and the Treaty establishing the European Community (adopted 13 December 2007, entered into force 1 December 2009) 2007/C 306/01.

[308] For a comprehensive overview of the evolution of the legal competences of the European Union in international investment regulation, see R Basedow, 'A Legal History of the EU's International Investment Policy' (2016) 17 *The Journal of World Investment & Trade* 743.

[309] EC, 'Communication from the Commission to the European Parliament, The Council, the European Economic and Social Committee and the Committee of the Regions, Towards a comprehensive European international investment policy', 7 July 2010, COM(2010) 343 final 4, trade.ec.europa.eu/doclib/docs/2011/may/tradoc_147884.pdf.

[310] The European Commission indicated that the EU common investment policy seeks to integrate investment liberalisation by providing EU investors with market access as well as substantive protection of their investments by providing a stable, predictable, fair, and properly regulated environment in which to conduct their business. It was intended that this investment policy would also contribute to the objectives set out in the Europe 2020 Strategy, a strategy for smart, sustainable, and inclusive growth. See EC, 'Proposal for a regulation of the European Parliament and of the Council establishing transitional arrangements for bilateral investment agreements between the Member States and third countries', 7 July 2010, COM(2010) 344 final, europarl.europa.eu/registre/docs_autres_institutions/commission_europeenne/com/2010/0344/COM_COM(2010)0344_EN.pdf; EC, 'Europe 2020: A strategy for smart, sustainable and inclusive growth', 3 March 3010, COM (2010) 2020.

on 20 December 2012.[311] This represented a first effort to establish a legal framework to regulate BITs between EU Member States and third countries. It also marked an important step toward the adoption of a common EU investment policy on FDI. On 14 October 2015, the European Commission issued a communication setting out an updated EU trade and investment policy, *'Trade for all: Towards a more responsible trade and investment policy'*.[312] In its policy, the Commission made clear that it sought to integrate investment and investment protection provisions in its broader trade agreements instead of negotiating these provisions separately.[313]

The exact scope of the new investment competence, however, remains unclear and disagreement persists between the EU Member States and the Commission about the joint reading of Articles 206 and 207 FTEU.[314] Article 207 TFEU, for example, does not include a definition of the term *'foreign direct investment'*, making it unclear whether the EU competence only covers market access, or also post-admission treatment and operation of foreign investment; whether the scope of application is extended to portfolio investments, concession contracts and state contract; or whether the EU has the competence to regulate protection of foreign investment against expropriation and other political risks.[315] One of these latter questions has been clarified by the Court in its Opinion 2/15 on the EU's competences in negotiating the EU-Singapore FTA. The Court held that portfolio investments did not fall within EU exclusive competence (and therefore not fully within the scope of Article 207 TFEU) and that inclusion of provisions dealing with this kind of investment in FTAs required ratification by Member States.[316]

Moreover, the transfer of competence to conclude BITs from the EU Member States to the EU has affected BITs between EU Member States and third countries, as well as intra-EU BITs concluded between EU Member States. As noted above, EU Regulation No 1219/2012 now governs BITs concluded between EU Member States and third countries, providing that those BITs will remain in force until being replaced by a BIT between the EU and the other BIT party on the same subject matter.[317] However, the Commission can, under certain circumstances, still authorise EU Member States to amend or conclude BITs with third countries with which the EU does not plan to negotiate in the near future.[318]

With regard to intra-EU BITs, Regulation 1219/2012 remains silent, yet the Commission has requested EU Member States to terminate their intra-EU BITs, arguing that they are incompatible with the provisions of the EU Treaties and should therefore be considered invalid.[319] The Commission also argued that intra-EU BITs provide for parallel case law

[311] Regulation No 1219/2012 of 12 December 2012 establishing transitional arrangements for bilateral investment treaties between Member States and third countries [2012] OJ L351/40.

[312] EC, 'Trade for all: Towards a more responsible trade and investment policy', 14 October 2015, trade.ec.europa.eu/doclib/docs/2015/october/tradoc_153846.pdf.

[313] ibid.

[314] Basedow (n 308) 770. See also M Bungenberg, 'The Divison of Competences Between the EU and Its Member States in the Area of Investment Disputes' in M Bungenberg, J Griebel and S Hindelang (eds), *International Investment Law and EU Law* (Berlin, Springer Berlin Heidelberg, 2011) 29, 40–42; A Reinisch, 'The Divison of Powers Between the EU and Its Member States "After Lisbon"' in ibid, 99–111.

[315] For a comprehensive discussion of the scope of the EU investment competence, see A Dimopoulos, *EU Foreign Investment Law* (Oxford, OUP, 2011) 65–124.

[316] Opinion 2/15 (n 188) para 305.

[317] See Regulation No 1219/2012 of 12 December 2012 establishing transitional arrangements for bilateral investment treaties between Member States and third countries [2012] OJ L351/40, Chapter II; European Commission, 'Investment', ec.europa.eu/trade/policy/accessing-markets/investment/.

[318] Regulation No 1219/2012, Chapter III.

[319] Decision No 2015/1470 of 30 March 2015 on State aid, SA 38517 (2014/C) (ex 2014/NN) implemented by Romania – Arbitral award Micula v Romania [2013] OJ L232/43, para 128. For a comprehensive analysis of

through arbitration.[320] In reality, however, foreign investors have continued to seek protection under intra-EU BITs before investment tribunals. The Commission has intervened in a number of cases (eg by submitting amicus curiae briefs or other written communications) to convince investment tribunals not to assume jurisdiction, yet without much success.[321] In June 2015, the Commission initiated infringement proceedings against five Member States (the Netherlands, Slovakia, Sweden, Austria, and Romania) with a view to compelling these Member States to terminate their intra-EU BITs.[322] In addition, the Commission initiated an administrative dialogue with 21 other Member States who declined to terminate their intra-EU BITs.[323] On 3 March 2016, the German Federal Court of Justice referred the *Achmea (Eureko) v Slovakia* case to the CJEU to request for a preliminary ruling on the compatibility with EU law of provisions in BITs allowing foreign investors to bring proceedings against Host States before an arbitral tribunal.[324] On 6 March 2018, the CJEU ruled that the BIT between the Netherlands and Slovakia established a mechanism for the settlement of disputes that is incapable of ensuring that those disputes will be decided by a court within the EU's judicial system.[325] It therefore found that the arbitration clause in that BIT had an adverse effect on the autonomy of EU law, since only courts within the judicial system of the EU can ensure the full effectiveness of EU law. The arbitration clause was found incompatible with EU law.

iv. Investment Contracts

Although there is no generally accepted definition of investment contracts, the term generally refers to an agreement negotiated directly between a foreign investor and a Host State

aspects of intra-EU BITs, see C Binder, 'A Treaty Law Perspective on Intra-EU BITs' (2016) 17 *The Journal of World Investment & Trade* 964; M Bungenberg and A Reinisch, 'Special Issue: Legal Problems of Intra-EU BITs: An Introduction' (2016) 17 *The Journal of World Investment & Trade* 871; M Burgstaller, 'The Future of Bilateral Investment Treaties of EU Member States' in Bungenberg, Griebel and Hindelang (n 314) 55–77; M Wierzbowski and A Gubrynowicz, 'Conflict of Norms Stemming From Intra-EU BITs and EU Legal Obligations: Some Remarks on Possible Solutions' in C Binder et al (eds), *International Investment Law for the 21st Century: Essays in Honour of Christoph Schreuer* (Oxford, OUP, 2009) 544–60.

320 eg, in *Achmea (Eureko) v Slovakia*, the Commission took the view that: 'There are some provisions of the Dutch-Slovak BIT 'that raise fundamental questions regarding compatibility with EU law. Most prominent among these are the provisions of the BIT providing for an investor-State arbitral mechanism (set out in Art 8), and the provisions of the BIT providing for an inter-State arbitral mechanism (set out in Art 10). These provisions conflict with EU law on the exclusive competence of EU courts for claims which involve EU law, even for claims where EU law would only partially be affected. The European Commission must therefore [...] express its reservation with respect to the Arbitral Tribunal's competence to arbitrate the claim brought before it by Eureko B.V'. See *Achmea BV v The Slovak Republic (formerly Eureko BV v The Slovak Republic)*, Award of 26 October 2010, PCA Case No 2008-13, para 193.

321 *Eastern Sugar BV (Netherlands) v The Czech Republic*, Partial Award of 27 March 2007, SCC Case No 088/2004; *AES Summit Generation Limited and AES-Tisza Erömü Kft v The Republic of Hungary*, Award of 23 September 2010, ICSID Case No ARB/07/22; *Electrabel SA v Republic of Hungary*, Decision of 30 November 2012, ICSID Case No ARB/07/19; *Achmea BV v The Slovak Republic* (n 320); *European American Investment Bank AG v The Slovak Republic*, Award of 22 October 2002, PCA Case No 2010-17.

322 EC, Press release: 'Commission asks Member States to terminate their intra-EU bilateral investment treaties', 18 June 2015, europa.eu/rapid/press-release_IP-15-5198_en.htm.

323 On 8 March 2017, the Romanian Parliament approved legislation for terminating 22 intra-EU BITs between Romania and other EU Member States. Following the example set by Ireland and Italy in 2012 and 2013 respectively, Romania is the third EU Member State to do so. See EC Press release, 'Commission asks Member States to terminate their intra-EU bilateral investment treaties', 18 June 2015, europa.eu/rapid/press-release_IP-15-5198_en.htm; V Fietta, 'Romania Set to Terminate Its Intra-EU BITs Lexology', *Lexology*, 28 March 2017, lexology.com/library/detail.aspx?g=89abdc5f-4749-4f27-9edb-a4714c09dfc4.

324 Judgment of 6 March 2018, *Achmea*, C-284/16, EU:C:2018:158.

325 ibid.

(or government agency), which often concerns large-scale investments and creates mutual obligations between the State (or government agency) and the foreign investor.[326] Examples include concessions, licences, joint-venture agreements, build and operate agreements, profit sharing agreements, management and service agreements, and production-sharing agreements.

Investment contracts generally lay down the rights, responsibilities, and risks of both the foreign investor and the Host State (or government agency). Many investment contracts also include a choice of law clause to determine the applicable law. The underlying reason is that the Host State will typically prefer to apply its own legal framework, whereas the foreign investor seeks a system that provides a stable and secure legal environment.[327] In order to strike the right balance between these competing interests, investment contracts provide for a choice of law clause which, for example, refers to international law and/or the general principles of law as the applicable law or invokes a combination of different legal systems or principles, such as the common legal principles of the contracting State and the home State of the foreign investor. Sometimes, investment contracts also insert a so-called stabilisation clause which refers to the legal regime of the contracting State at the time of the conclusion of the contract. Moreover, since a Host State prefers to bring disputes before its local courts while a foreign investor seeks an independent and impartial forum for dispute resolution, investment contracts tend to include a dispute resolution clause. These dispute resolution clauses generally provide for the settlement of disputes through international arbitration (eg, in the framework of ICSID) or arbitration under domestic law.[328]

C. Expropriation and Nationalisation

International law does not know an absolute right to the protection of property. Territorial sovereignty implies the right to take property owned by nationals or aliens within the State's territory through nationalisation or expropriation.[329] This sovereign right is as such not subject to much controversy, yet the exact meaning of the conditions and limitations placed on expropriation remains controversial.[330] International law, moreover, not only establishes restrictions on expropriation *sensu stricto*, but also to other measures that amount to a taking of property,[331] though there is no consensus on the practical implications of these restrictions.

The terms 'expropriation' and 'nationalisation' cover a similar, yet not identical meaning. Expropriation may be understood as the taking of property in the form of (i) the deprivation

[326] I Marboe and A Reinisch, 'Contracts between States and Foreign Private Law Persons' in MPEPIL, para 9; Nadakavukaren Schefer (n 223).

[327] Dolzer and Schreuer (n 223) 81.

[328] Marboe and Reinisch (n 326) para 31.

[329] UNCTAD, 'Expropriation: the Sequel' in *Series on Issues in International Investment Agreements II* (New York, UN, 2012) 1.

[330] Even in the context of the North-South ideological divide on the right to compensation for expropriations, the industrialised countries supported the right to expropriate. This, however, was only under the condition that such expropriation was done 'for a public purpose, non-discriminatory, and compensated fully'; see Nadakavukaren Schefer (n 223) 9.

[331] Tippetts, Abbett, McCarthy, Stratton v TAMS-AFFA Consulting Engineers of Iran, Award of 29 June 1984, 6 Iran-US CTR 219; INA Corporation v Iran, Award of 13 August 1985, 8 Iran-US CTR 373; Phelps Dodge v Iran, Award of 19 March 1986, 10 Iran-US CTR 121.

of the owner of its legal title to its property or its outright physical seizure for the benefit of the State or a third party mandated by the State (so-called direct expropriation), or (ii) the taking of measures which deprive the foreign investor of the substantial benefit of ownership, yet without a formal taking of property rights or outright physical seizure (so-called indirect or de facto expropriation).[332] Nationalisation is generally understood as the massive or large-scale takings of private property as part of a governmental economic or social program. It may concern large takings of property in all economic sectors or an entire industry.[333] Both direct expropriation and nationalisation involve the transfer of the investor's legal title and/or outright physical seizure. Conversely, indirect expropriation involves an interference with a property resulting in a total or near-total deprivation of the possibility of utilising the investment in a meaningful way, yet without a formal transfer of legal title or outright seizure. In the context of foreign direct investment, 'property' refers to 'investment'. Only when the owner of property is foreign can it seek protection under international investment law.

It is commonly accepted that, in order to be lawful, the expropriation must meet four conditions. These conditions are incorporated in most IIAs and are generally perceived to be part of customary international law.[334] First of all, the property must be taken for a public purpose. International law has, because of the differences in development and the diversity of socio-economic systems, no definition of this term. Only flagrant violations of this requirement, such as expropriation for the personal enrichment of a head of State, could be qualified as an unlawful deprivation of property. Consistent with this prerequisite is the second condition of the non-discriminatory nature of the expropriation. These may not be specific to a particular person or a particular group of people, for example, a group of a particular nationality. A measure, however, is not *ipso facto* discriminatory merely because of the fact that a particular economic activity is only practiced by a particular group. A third condition is that due process should be followed. The measures should be taken on the basis of a certain (constitutional) legal norm and should be challengeable in court. Finally, the expropriating State is obligated to pay damages to the dispossessed foreigner.[335] The international minimum standard for such damages was based on the *Hull-formula*.[336] The compensation must be immediate ('prompt', this means from the moment of deprivation of ownership), complete ('adequate') and actual ('effective', this means in convertible currency and without the hindrance of transfer of the capital).[337] Here, the second criterion especially is often a source of controversy. First, there is disagreement about the value of investments; this can be done on the basis of various criteria (eg, book value, market value or replacement value) and at different times (after all, the market value of an investment declines upon the announcement of a possible expropriation). Conversely, it is also argued that the socio-economic reforms that give rise to an expropriation are precisely what stand

[332] UNCTAD (n 329) 6–7.

[333] ibid, 5.

[334] Dolzer and Schreuer (n 223) 99–100.

[335] Brownlie qualifies the compensation principle as 'yet another aspect of the international minimum standard governing the treatment of aliens'. See I Brownlie, *Principles of Public International Law* (Oxford, OUP, 2008) 534; dissenting opinion of Judge Carneiro in *Anglo-Iranian Oil Company* [1952] ICJ Rep 93; dissenting opinion of Judge Gros in *Barcelona Traction, Light & Power Co* [1970] ICJ Rep 1.

[336] Named after US Secretary of State which explicated these requirements in a correspondence with the Mexican authorities from 1938 to 1941.

[337] More on the *Hull-formula*: see KJ Vandevelde, *United States Investment Treaties: Policy and Practice* (The Hague, Kluwer, 1992) 21.

in the way of full compensation.[338] Finally, clauses in concession agreements between the Host State and a foreign investor can give rise to a higher standard of compensation.

If in case of an expropriation the aforementioned conditions were not met, higher compensation is required.[339] In that case: 'Reparation must, as far as possible, wipe out all the consequences of the illegal act and re-establish the situation which would have existed if that act had not been committed'.[340] Moreover, an unlawful expropriation is a violation of international law because of which the home State of an aggrieved investor would be entitled to additional compensation.

D. Standards of Protection

IIAs typically provide for a number of obligations a Host State has toward foreign investors. These protection standards can either be an aspect of customary international law, or they can be treaty-based. The most common protection standards are the following. Firstly, the standard of national treatment, which provides that the Host State shall permit and treat the foreign investor and its investment on a basis no less favourable than the Host State treats its own investors in like situations.[341] The underlying purpose is to protect foreign investors from internal regulation affording more favourable treatment to national investors.[342] National treatment is not a feature of customary international law, yet most IIAs have incorporated this standard of protection.[343] Secondly, the MFN obligation which is one of the most important standards of protection and is included in almost all BITs and multilateral treaties.[344] Yet, as with national treatment, it is not required under customary international law, allowing foreign investors to only invoke the standard if it has been included in the relevant treaty upon which it bases its claims.[345] The purpose of MFN clauses in IIAs is to ensure that the States concerned treat each other's investors at least as favourably as they treat third parties.[346] Accordingly, as soon as a Host State grants benefits to investors from another country, this benefit is automatically extended to the beneficiaries of the MFN clause.

Thirdly, the fair and equitable treatment (FET) standard protects foreign investors against 'serious instances of arbitrary, discriminatory or abusive conduct by Host States'.[347]

[338] Individual opinion of Judge Lagergren in INA Corporation v Iran (n 331); Phelps Dodge v Iran (n 331).

[339] *Texaco/Calasiatic v Libya*, Award of 19 January 1977, ILM 1978, 1–37, CASES, IH4, para 112.

[340] *Germany v Poland* (n 246).

[341] This concept should not be confused with the notion of national treatment under the *Calvo-doctrine* (see above). Under this doctrine, the concept of national treatment was formulated as to limit as much as possible the protection of foreign investors under international law by entitling foreign investors only to the same treatment accorded to national investors of the Host State under its national laws. Conversely, the standard of national treatment as included in IIAs recognises the possibility of a more favourable treatment for foreign investors by including the wording '*no less favorable*'. A better treatment will even be required if the international standards are higher than the ones applying to national investors. See Dolzer and Schreuer (n 223) 198; UNCTAD, 'National Treatment' in *Series on Issues in International Investment Agreements* (New York, UN, 1999) 6.

[342] Although the standard of national treatment under international trade law is prompted by the same economic objective, it does differ in scope and purpose: ibid, 8–10.

[343] For example, CETA in Art 8(6), ECT in Art 10(3) and (7), ACIA in Art 5, and NAFTA in Art 1102.

[344] For example, CETA in Art 8(7), ECT in Art 10(3) and (7), ACIA in Art 6, and NAFTA in Art 1103. See further, P Acconci, 'Most-Favoured-Nation Treatment' in Muchlinski, Ortino, and Schreuer (n 231) 374.

[345] ILC, 'Report of the International Law Commission to the General Assembly on the work of its Thirtieth session, 8 May–28 July 1978', UN Doc A/33/10, 25.

[346] Collins (n 219) 109.

[347] UNCTAD, Fair and Equitable Treatment in *Series on Issues in International Investment Agreements II* (New York, UN, 2012).

Unlike the standards of national treatment and MFN, the FET standard is a generally applicable minimum standard which is exclusively governed by international law and is independent from the treatment the State accords to its domestic investors and investors of third States.[348] A general definition is lacking, yet arbitral tribunals have attempted to determine the substantive content of the FET standard on a case-by-case basis.[349] This has resulted in a number of concepts which have been identified as relevant in the context of fair and equitable treatment, including but not limited to: (i) defeating the investor's legitimate expectations;[350] (ii) manifest arbitrariness in decision-making;[351] (iii) denial of justice and due process;[352] (iv) discrimination;[353] and (v) outright abusive treatment of investors.[354] Fourthly, in first instance, the full protection and security (FPS) standard requires Host States to grant physical protection and security to foreign investment to protect them from adverse effects.[355] More precisely, it imposes on the Host State both a negative and a positive obligation: first, the Host State is under the negative obligation not to harm the foreign investments by actions of the Host State's police or military personnel.[356] Second, the Host State has the positive obligation to protect foreign investments against interferences by third parties, including insurgents or rioting groups, by actively deploying police or military personnel.[357]

In more recent cases, foreign investors have also invoked the FPS standard in cases where the Host State allegedly failed to ensure legal security, as opposed to physical security.[358] In these cases it was argued that the FPS standard also requires Host States to ensure a stable legal regime and provide for timely access to court proceedings for the foreign

[348] *Alex Genin, Eastern Credit Limited, Inc, and AS Baltoil v The Republic of Estonia*, Award of 24 Feburary 2014, ICSID Case No ARB/99/2, (2002) 17 *ICSID Review – Foreign Investment Law Journal* 395, para 367; *SD Myers, Inc v Government of Canada*, Award of 13 November 2000, para 259; *CME Czech Republic BV v The Czech Republic*, Award of 13 September 2001, para 611; *United Parcel Service of America Inc v Government of Canada*, Award of 22 November 2002, para 80; *El Paso Energy International Company v The Argentine Republic*, Award of 31 October 2011, ICSID Case No ARB/03/15, paras 228–31; S Vasciannie, 'The Fair and Equitable Treatment Standard in International Investment Law and Practice' (1999) 70(1) *BYIL* 99, 105–107.

[349] UNCTAD (n 347) 1.

[350] *Técnicas Medioambientales Tecmed, SA v The United Mexican States*, Award of 29 May2003, ICSID Case No ARB (AF)/00/2, para 154; *CMS Gas Transmission Company v The Republic of Argentina*, Award of 12 May 2005, ICSID Case No ARB/01/8, para 274; and *Enron Corporation and Ponderosa Assets, LP v Argentine Republic*, Award of 22 May 2007, ICSID Case No ARB/01/3, para 260.

[351] *Enron Corporation and Ponderosa Assets, LP v Argentine Republic* (n 350) para 281; *LG&E Energy Corp, LG&E Capital Corp, and LG&E International, Inc v Argentine Republic*, Decision of 3 October 2006, ICSID Case No ARB/02/1, para 162.

[352] *Petrobart Limited v The Kyrgyz Republic*, Award of 29 March 2005, SCC Case No 126/2003, 28; *Loewen Group, Inc and Raymond L Loewen v United States of America*, Award of 26 June2003, ICSID Case No ARB(AF)/98/3, para 135.

[353] *Saluka Investments BV v The Czech Republic*, Award of 7 March 2006, para 461; *Loewen Group, Inc and Raymond L Loewen v United States of America*, Award of 26 June 2003, ICSID Case No ARB(AF)/98/3, para 123; *Waste Management, Inc v United Mexican States ('Number 2')*, Award of 30 April2004, ICSID Case No ARB(AF)/00/3, para 98; and *CMS Gas Transmission Company v The Republic of Argentina*, Award of 12 May 2005, ICSID Case No ARB/01/8, para 287.

[354] *Saluka Investments BV v The Czech Republic* (n 353) para 308; *Desert Line Projects LLC v Yemen*, Award of 6 February 2008), ICSID Case No ARB/05/17, paras 179, 185–187, 190 and 193. CETA includes a similar standard in Art 8(10).

[355] *American Manufacturing & Trading, Inc v Republic of Zaire* (Award), [1997] ICSID Case No ARB/93/1, (1997) 36 ILM 1534, paras 6.02–6.11; *Asian Agricultural Products Ltd v Republic of Sri Lanka* (Final Award), [1990] ICSID Case No ARB/87/3, para 45 ff, 78 ff; *Wena Hotels Ltd v Arab Republic of Egypt* (Award), [2000] ICSID Case No ARB/98/4, (2002) 41 ILM 896, para 84.

[356] Collins (n 219) 138.

[357] ibid.

[358] Nadakavukaren Schefer (n 223) 366.

investor.[359] Fifthly, an umbrella clause is a provision in an IIA which elevates a breach of an investment contract between a Host State and a foreign investor or a failure to comply with unilateral representations made by a Host State to the international level. A breach of contract or other commitments becomes a treaty violation and imposes Host State liability. The wording of umbrella clauses in IIAs varies widely and has raised substantial debate as to their interpretation.[360] Most IIAs provide for protection against arbitrary or discriminatory treatment, yet the precise wording varies. Whereas some IIAs use the term 'arbitrary or discriminatory', others use 'unjustified or discriminatory' or 'unreasonable or discriminatory'.[361]

According to Dolzer and Schreuer, the following measures may be identified as arbitrary:

> (a) a measure that inflicts damage on the investor without serving any apparent legitimate purpose; (b) a measure that is not based on legal standards but on discretion, prejudice, or personal preference; (c) a measure taken for reasons that are different from those put forward by the decision maker; (d) a measure taken in willful disregard of due process and proper procedure.[362]

The principle of *non-discrimination* is fundamental to international investment law and is accordingly included in both the national treatment and MFN standard, and in a general obligation of non-discrimination.[363] The general obligation of non-discrimination prohibits the unjustified unequal treatment of a foreign investor and may be based on race, sex, gender, nationality, religion, political affiliation or a number of other aspects.

E. Dispute Resolution

Several dispute settlement mechanisms allow for remedying investments 'gone wrong' and therefore, in practice, deserve some specific attention. Such dispute resolution can involve either both the Host State and the home State of the investor or the investor and the Host State.

i. State-to-State Dispute Resolution

Under State-to-state investment dispute resolution, the home State of the investor can bring a claim against the Host State in order to protect its foreign investments. Clauses stipulating the possibility of State-to-State dispute resolution can be found in BITs, often providing

[359] *Azurix Corp v The Argentine Republic*, Award of 14 July 2006, ICSID Case No ARB/01/12, paras 406–408; *Biwater Gauff (Tanzania) Ltd v United Republic of Tanzania*, Award of 24 July 2008, ICSID Case No ARB/05/22, paras 725–30; *CME Czech Republic BV v The Czech Republic* (n 348), para 613; *Total SA v The Argentine Republic*, Decision of 27 December 2010, ICSID Case No ARB/04/01, para 343; Nadakavukaren Schefer (n 223) 361; Dolzer and Schreuer (n 223) 163–65.

[360] Art 10(1) ECT provides for an umbrella clause. ACIA, NAFTA, and CETA do not appear to contain an explicit umbrella clause. See further, Dolzer and Schreuer (n 223) 166–78; C Schreuer, 'Travelling the BIT Route: Of Waiting Periods, Umbrella Clauses and Forks in the Road' (2004) 5 *The Journal of World Investment & Trade* 231; AC Sinclair, 'The Origins of the Umbrella Clause in the International Law of Investment Protection' (2004) 20 *Arbitration International* 411; TW Wälde, 'The "Umbrella" Clause in Investment Arbitration: A Comment on Original Intentions and Recent Cases' (2005) 6 *The Journal of World Investment & Trade* 183.

[361] As defined in the often-quoted *Elettronica Sicula Case*, 'arbitrariness is not so much something opposed to a rule of law, as something opposed to the rule of law'. See ELSI case (n 245) para 128; Schreuer (n 247) para 58.

[362] Dolzer and Schreuer (n 223) 193.

[363] Art 10(1) ECT includes such a general protection standard, whereas CETA, ACIA, and NAFTA, although having incorporated the national treatment and the MFN standard, do not provide for an explicit general provision.

the choice between recourse to the ICJ or to arbitration.[364] In the context of modern BIT dispute resolution procedures, sovereign arbitration on investment claims has become less common.[365]

ii. Investor-to-State Dispute Settlement

Investor-State dispute settlement (ISDS) allows investors to bring claims against the Host State directly. The main advantage of this type of dispute resolution is that it allows the investor to make its own claims and collect damages directly.[366] Additionally, it allows Host States to market themselves as having an investment-friendly climate.[367] The disadvantage to ISDS is that it affects the sovereignty of the home State, which will have agreed to being sued for governmental action within its own sovereign territory.[368] It has been argued that sovereign States' right to regulate can be infringed by claims by foreign investors.[369]

Various fora exist for the resolution of investor-State disputes. An important forum is the ICSID, which is part of the World Bank. The ICSID Convention stipulates that its purpose is 'to provide facilities for conciliation and arbitration of investment disputes between Contracting States and nationals of other Contracting States in accordance with the provisions of this Convention'.[370] The Convention provides for standard clauses the parties can use, rules of procedure and institutional support.[371] Other investor-State arbitration institutions include the International Chamber of Commerce (ICC), the London Court of International Arbitration (LCIA), the PCA and the Stockholm Chamber of Commerce's Institute of Arbitration. In addition, almost all international investment agreements allow for ad hoc arbitration, giving the parties to the dispute the freedom to follow either the UNCITRAL rules on arbitration or to use their own agreed-upon rules.[372]

However, several concerns have been raised in the context of ISDS, including concerns relating to the lack of transparency in these arbitration proceedings, the lack of independence of arbitrators, the lack of access to appeal proceedings and lack of coherent case law.[373] These widely acknowledged concerns have prompted the EU to look for a solution.[374] On 23 July 2014, the European Parliament and the Council adopted Regulation

[364] An example can be found in the Investment Promotion and Protection Agreement (United Republic of Tanzania) Regulations 2009, [Mauritius] Government Notice No 131 of 2009, Art 9. Only a very limited number of investment cases have been brought before the ICJ, of which the most important ones are: Case Concerning Barcelona Traction, Light & Power Co (*Belgium v Spain*) [1970] ICJ Rep 1970, 3 CASES, IB14; ELSI case (n 245).

[365] Nadakavukaren Schefer (n 223) 432.

[366] ibid, 433.

[367] Dolzer and Schreuer (n 223) 236.

[368] A De Nanteuil, *Droit international de l'investissement*, 2nd edn (Paris, Pedone, 2017) 229; Nadakavukaren Schefer (n 223) 434.

[369] And rather lead to a 'fright to regulate'. See eg V Korzun, 'The Right to Regulate in Investor-State Arbitration: Slicing and Dicing Regulatory Carve-Outs' (2016) 50 *Vanderbilt Journal of Transnational Law* 355.

[370] Art 1(2) ICSID Convention.

[371] Dolzer and Schreuer (n 223) 238.

[372] Nadakavukaren Schefer (n 223) 448.

[373] De Nanteuil (n 368) 229; Dolzer and Schreuer (n 223) 286–87; K Yannaca-Small, 'Improving the System of Investor-State Dispute Settlement', *OECD Working Papers on International Investment*, Working Paper No 2006/01, February 2006, oecd.org/china/WP-2006_1.pdf, 8–14.

[374] EC, Press release: 'Commission proposes new Investment Court System for TTIP and other EU trade and investment negotiations', 16 September 2015, trade.ec.europa.eu/doclib/press/index.cfm?id=1364.

No 912/2014 to establish an internal legal and financial framework for investor-to-State dispute settlement between the EU and its trading partners.[375] In November 2015, the EU agreed on a reformed investment dispute settlement policy which envisages the establishment of a permanent Investment Court System and a set of rules on investment protection.[376] The EU's unilateral reform through the Investment Court System has been included in CETA and EVFTA, but has not yet been put into practice. It has also been proposed in the negotiations with the US on TTIP. In March 2018, the EU Council gave directives to the Commission to negotiate, under the auspices of UNCITRAL, a Convention Establishing a Multilateral Court for the Settlement of Investment Disputes.[377]

V. Concluding Remarks

The World Trade Organization has undergone a significant transformation in the last century, evolving from a de facto organisation in 1947 to a full-fledged international organisation in 1995. As a member-driven organisation with a strong enforcement mechanism (its dispute settlement mechanism), the WTO has successfully provided a forum for multilateral negotiations on the international legal framework applicable to international trade. In the area of investment law, we have seen a significant growth in global foreign investment and the growing realisation that general principles of public international law could not adequately regulate these foreign investments. Consequently, states had recourse to BITs and IIAs to provide a better legal framework for foreign investments. This framework has, however, been challenged from various angles, mainly due to the inconsistency in the application and interpretation of key principles of international investment law.[378]

Similarly, the WTO's position has not remained unchallenged in recent years. We have witnessed a large-scale shift from multilateralism to plurilateralism, with a steep proliferation of bilateral, regional and preferential trade agreements. An excellent example of this shift is reflected in the trade policy of the European Union, which has concluded a significant number of bilateral/regional trade agreements in recent decades. Many reasons have been proffered to account for this shift, from the increased number of developing countries participating in the negotiations, to the demise of the Quad as a strong negotiation group and the consideration that liberalisation remains to be negotiated on the most contentious issues.[379] All of these reasons are, however, linked to the deadlock in the Doha Development Round. Even though this latest round was launched in November 2001, it has not yet been concluded.

[375] Regulation No 912/2014 of 23 July 2014 establishing a framework for managing financial responsibility linked to investor-to-state dispute settlement tribunals established by international agreements to which the European Union is party [2014] OJ L257/121.

[376] EC Press release, 'EU finalizes proposal for investment protection and Court System for TTIP', 12 November 2015, europa.eu/rapid/press-release_IP-15-6059_en.htm.

[377] Council Doc. 12981/17, ADD 1 DCL 1 (20 March 2018), http://data.consilium.europa.eu/doc/document/ST-12981-2017-ADD-1-DCL-1/en/pdf.

[378] N Butler and S Subedi, 'The Future of International Investment Regulation: Toward a World Investment Organisation?' (2017) 64 *NILR* 43.

[379] Including agriculture, subsidies and services.

In addition to the arduous multilateral negotiations, the WTO has been confronted with other challenges in recent years. How can it best address the rise of protectionism and the increased threat of trade wars? How should the membership remedy the US' blocking of the (re-)appointment of Appellate Body Members? Are the existing rules still adequate in the face of technological advancement? The WTO will have to effectively address these challenges in order to ensure its continued relevance as the multilateral forum for trade matters.

Lastly, we also see an increased awareness of environmental protection and sustainable development as global goals. So far, the WTO has been accused of struggling to find a balance between further international trade and respecting environmental laws and concerns. A similar observation can be made for the relationship between international investment law and the environment, with little language referring to environmental concerns included in IIAs. In an ever globalising world, the importance of environmental law and its relationship to international economic law cannot be stressed enough.

Bibliography

Carreau, D and Juillard, P, *Droit international économique*, 5th edn (Paris, Dalloz, 2013).

Collins, D, *An Introduction to International Investment Law* (Cambridge, CUP, 2017).

Dolzer, R, and Schreuer, C, *Principles of International Investment Law* (Oxford, OUP, 2012).

Herdegen, M, *Principles of International Economic Law*, 2nd edn (Oxford, OUP, 2016).

Herdegen, M, *Internationales Wirtschaftsrecht*,10th edn (Munich, Beck, 2014).

Hilf, M and Oeter, S, *WTO-Recht. Rechtsordnung des Welthandels*, 2nd edn (Baden-Baden, Nomos, 2010).

Hoekman, BM and Mavroidis, P, *The World Trade Organization. Law, Economics and Politics*, 2nd edn (London, Routledge, 2016).

Jackson, J, *The World Trade Organization: Constitution and Jurisprudence* (London, Royal Institute of International Affairs, 1998).

Jackson, J, *The Jurisprudence of GATT and the WTO. Insights on Treaty Law and Economic Relations* (Cambridge, CUP, 2000).

Kronke, H, Melis, W and Kuhn, H (eds), *Handbuch internationales Wirtschaftsrecht*, 2nd edn (Cologne, Otto Schmidt, 2017).

Lowenfeld, AF, *International Economic Law*, 2nd edn (Oxford, OUP, 2008).

Luff, D, *Le droit de l'Organisation mondiale du commerce: analyse critique* (Brussels, Bruylant, 2004).

Matsushita, M, Schoenbaum, TJ, Mavroidis, PC and Hahn, M, *The World Trade Organization. Law, Practice and Policy*, 3rd edn (Oxford, OUP, 2015).

Muchlinski, P, Ortino, F and Schreuer, C (eds), *The Oxford Handbook of International Investment Law* (Oxford, OUP, 2008).

Nadakavukaren Schefer, K, *International Investment Law. Text, Cases and Materials*, 2nd edn (Cheltenham, Edward Elgar, 2016).

Subedi, PS, 'International Investment Law' in Evans, MD (ed), *International Law*, 4th edn (Oxford, OUP, 2014) 727.

Tietje, C (ed), *Internationales Wirtschaftsrecht*, 2nd edn (Berlin, De Gruyter, 2015).

Trebilcock, M, Howse, R and Eliason, A, *The Regulation of International Trade*, 4th edn (London, Routledge, 2013).

Van den Bossche, P and Zdouc, W, *The Law and Policy of the World Trade Organization* 4th edn (Cambridge, CUP, 2017).
Venturini, G, *L'Organizzazione Mondiale del Commercio*, 3rd edn (Milan, Giuffrè, 2015).
Vincent, P, *Institutions économiques internationales: éléments de droit international économique*, 2nd edn (Brussels, Larcier, 2013).
Weiß, W, Hermann, C and Ohler, C, *Welthandelsrecht*, 2nd edn (Munich, Beck, 2007).
Wouters, J and De Meester, B, *The World Trade Organization. A Legal and Institutional Analysis* (Oxford, Intersentia, 2007).

Further Reading

Adlung, R and Carzaniga, A, 'MFN Exemptions under the General Agreements on Trade in Services: Grandfathers Striving for Immortality?' (2009) 12 *JIEL* 357.
Altemöller, F, 'A Future for Multilateralism? New Regionalism, Counter-Multilateralism and Perspectives for the World Trade System after the Bali Ministerial Conference' (2015) 10 *Global Trade and Customs Journal* 42.
Baldwin, R, 'The World Trade Organization and the Future of Multilateralism' (2016) 30 *Journal of Economic Perspectives* 95.
Bartels, L, 'The Chapeau of the General Exceptions in the WTO GATT and GATS Agreements: A Reconstruction' (2015) 109 *AJIL* 95.
Bourgeois, J, Bronckers, M and Quick, R, *WTO Dispute Settlement: A Check-up* (Brussels, Peter Lang, 2017).
Cottier, T, 'International Economic Law in Transition from Trade Liberalization to Trade Regulation' (2014) 17 *JIEL* 671.
Davey, W, 'The WTO and Rules-Based Dispute Settlement: Historical Evolution, Operational Success, and Future Challenges' (2014) 17 *JIEL* 679.
De Bièvre, D, Poletti, A, Hanegraaff, M and Beyers, J, 'International Institutions and Interest Mobilization: the WTO and Lobbying in EU and US Trade Policy' (2016) 50 *Journal of World Trade* 289.
Du, M, '"Treatment No Less Favourable" and the Future of National Treatment Obligation in GATT Article III:4 after EC-Seal Products' (2015) *World Trade Review* 1.
Ehring, L, 'De Facto Discrimination in WTO Law: National and Most-Favoured-Nation Treatment – or Equal Treatment' (2002) 36 *Journal of World Trade* 921.
Flett, J, 'WTO Space for National Regulation: Requiem for a Diagonal Vector Test' (2013) 16 *JIEL* 37.
Howse, R, 'The World Trade Organization 20 Years On: Global Governance by Judiciary' (2016) 27 *EJIL* 1.
Marceau, G and Wyatt, J, 'The WTO's Efforts to Balance Economic Development and Environmental Protection: A Short Review of Appellate Body Jurisprudence' (2013) 1 *Latin American Journal of International Trade Law* 291.
McRae, D, 'MFN in the GATT and the WTO' (2012) 7 *Asian Journal of WTO and International Health Law and Policy* 1.
Meagher, N, 'Regulatory Convergence and Dispute Settlement in the WTO' (2015) 14 *Journal of International Trade Law and Policy* 157.

Pauwelyn, J, '*Rien ne va plus?* Distinguishing Domestic Regulation from Market Access in GATT and GATS' (2005) 4 *World Trade Review* 131.

Peng, S, 'Renegotiate the WTO "Schedules of Commitments"?: Technological Development and Industrial Tariff Liberalization' (2012) 45 *Cornell International Law Journal* 403.

Wouters, J and Coppens, D, 'GATS and Domestic Regulation: The Right to Regulate and Trade Liberalization' in Alexander, K and Andenas, M (eds), *The World Trade Organization and Trade in Services* (Leiden, Martinus Nijhoff Publishers, 2008) 207.

Wouters, J and Coppens, D, 'International Economic Policy-Making: Exploring the Legal Linkages between the World Trade Organization and the Bretton Woods Institutions' (2005) 3 *International Organizations Law Review* 267.

Wouters, J and De Meester, B, 'Safeguarding coherence in global policy-making on trade and health: the EU-WHO-WTO triangle' (2005) 2 *International Organizations Law Review* 395.

Yoo, J and Ahn, D, 'Security Exceptions in the WTO System: Bridge or Bottle Neck for Trade and Security' (2016) 19 *JIEL* 417.

20

International Environmental Law

I. Genesis and Development

The past decades have witnessed a remarkable development and expansion of international environmental law, one of the youngest branches of international law. The worsening condition of the environment has been amply scientifically documented, and includes phenomena such as atmospheric and marine pollution, deforestation, an increasing amount of nuclear and other hazardous wastes, the greenhouse effect, global warming, and the endangerment of wild flora and fauna. Adding to the intractability of these issues is the fact that they all have an inherently transnational character: they usually cause cross-border problems that cannot be tackled adequately by actions of States individually. Reaching consensus in negotiations on global environmental and climate change-related problems is at the same time highly arduous and absolutely essential. Amongst the reasons that reaching political consensus is especially difficult in this area is its interconnectivity to economic wellbeing and security and the increasing divisions between rich and poor,[1] all of which seem unlikely to disappear in the foreseeable future. International environmental law also suffers from a paradox, in that while it deals with matters of eminently global importance, such as climate change, it is characterised by the presence of a significant amount of 'soft law', general principles, and often aspirational treaties with exhortatory compliance mechanisms.[2] Furthermore, the implementation of international environmental law is characterised by a number of specific features giving rise to implementation challenges, such as resistance from economic interest groups, political and strategic considerations, and the need to adapt to constantly evolving scientific and technological insights and innovations.[3] As a consequence, compliance with international environmental obligations remains a significant challenge. In response, existing compliance mechanisms have been further developed, and new approaches have been explored.[4]

[1] CP Carlarne, *Climate Change Law and Policy: EU and US Approaches* (Oxford, OUP, 2010) 348–49.
[2] S Humphreys and Y Otomo, 'Theorizing International Environmental Law' in A Orford and F Hoffmann (eds), *The Oxford Handbook of the Theory of International Law* (Oxford, OUP, 2016) 798.
[3] PM Dupuy and JE Viñuales, *International Environmental Law* (Cambridge, CUP, 2015) 37.
[4] P Sands and J Peel, *Principles of International Environmental Law*, 3rd edn (Cambridge, CUP, 2012) 135–38.

The starting point for intensive international action and collaboration in the field of international environmental law was the United Nations Conference on the Human Environment, held in Stockholm in June 1972. On the basis of the acknowledgement of 'the need for a common outlook and for common principles to inspire and guide the peoples of the world in the preservation and enhancement of the human environment',[5] the Conference adopted the Stockholm Declaration.[6] Attached to the Declaration was a list containing 26 Principles, of which Principles 21 and 22 in particular can be considered as the cornerstones of current international environmental law.[7]

> Principle 21
>
> States have, in accordance with the Charter of the United Nations and the principles of international law, the sovereign right to exploit their own resources pursuant to their own environmental policies, and the responsibility to ensure that activities within their jurisdiction or control do not cause damage to the environment of other States or of areas beyond the limits of national jurisdiction.
>
> Principle 22
>
> States shall cooperate to develop further the international law regarding liability and compensation for the victims of pollution and other environmental damage caused by activities within the jurisdiction or control of such States to areas beyond their jurisdiction.

The responsibility in Principle 21 to ensure that activities within their jurisdiction or control do not cause damage to the environment of other States or of areas beyond the limits of national jurisdiction can be traced back to the *Trail Smelter* arbitration, which provided compensation to the United States for damage to land and property caused by sulphur dioxide emissions from a smelter across the border in Trail, British Columbia, Canada.[8] The obligation to prevent transboundary environmental damage was restated in the second Principle of the Rio Declaration.

The development of international environmental law after the Stockholm Conference can be largely divided into two stages. During the first stage from the 1970s until the mid-1980s, the United Nations Environmental Programme (UNEP) was established, and the development of legal instruments for the prevention and reparation of and liability for the pollution of water, air and soil by industrial activities was emphasised. During the second stage, from the mid-1980s onwards, the focus shifted somewhat to new global environmental problems, such as the depletion of the ozone layer, climate change caused by the greenhouse effect, declining biodiversity, and escalating deforestation and desertification.

A. The Brundtland Report

The second stage is also characterised by an increasingly unified approach of environmental and economic development. The Brundtland Report[9] was highly influential in that regard, by emphasising the necessity of international cooperation and responsibility to fight the

[5] Preamble to the Stockholm Declaration.

[6] Declaration of the United Nations Conference on the Human Environment, 16 June 1972, A/CONF.48/14/Rev.1.

[7] These principles were also included in Art 30 of the Charter of Economic Rights and Duties of States, contained in the UNGA Res 3281 (XXIX), 12 December 1974, A/RES/29/3281.

[8] *Trail Smelter Arbitration* (United States v Canada), Award of 11 March 1941, 3 RIAA 1905, 1965.

[9] *Report of the World Commission on Environment and Development: Our Common Future*, Transmitted to the UNGA as an Annex to UN Secretary General, *Development and International Co-operation: Environment, Report*

increasing exhaustion of resources and environmental pollution. The Report, formally called 'Our Common Future', was written by the World Commission on Environment and Development and published in 1987 with the aim of discussing environmental and development matters as a single issue and raising political awareness of the topic. The Report introduced the concept of 'sustainable development', thereby establishing the link between the environment and development. In the Report, the notion of sustainable development is defined as 'development that meets the needs of the present without compromising the ability of future generations to meet their own needs'.[10] More specifically, sustainable development consists of two key concepts. The first is 'the concept of "needs", in particular the essential needs of the world's poor, to which overriding priority should be given'. The second is 'the idea of limitations imposed by the state of technology and social organization on the environment's ability to meet present and future needs'. The latter component is also separately mentioned as the principle of inter-generational equity,[11] which provides that 'States shall conserve and use the environment and natural resources for the benefit of present and future generations'.

B. Rio Earth Summit

Subsequent to the Brundtland Report, the UN Conference on Environment and Development, also referred to as the 'Earth Summit', was held in Rio de Janeiro in 1992. At this Conference, a number of important texts were adopted. First, Agenda 21[12] is a non-binding, voluntarily implemented comprehensive plan of action, aimed at realising different developmental and environmental objectives in the twenty-first century. In addition to national governments and the UN system itself, other international, regional and sub-regional organisations as well as NGOs are encouraged to cooperate. The document identifies different programme areas related to environmental problems. Second, the United Nations Framework Convention on Climate Change (UNFCCC),[13] and third, the Convention on Biological Diversity[14] were adopted, which will both be discussed in more detail later in this chapter. Fourth, the Statement of Forest Principles[15] is a 'non-legally binding authoritative statement of principles for a global consensus on the management, conservation and sustainable development of all types of forests', and contains guidelines for sustainable forest management. It advocates providing financial resources to developing countries with significant forest areas, in order to create alternative economic and social programmes to conserve forests. Lastly, all participating States unanimously adopted the Rio Declaration on Environment and Development. This Declaration reaffirms the Stockholm Declaration and is based upon the basic principles identified therein. It contains

of the World Commission on Environment and Development, Note by the Secretary-General, UN Doc A/42/427 and endorsed in UNGA, *Report of the World Commission on Environment and Development*, UN Doc A/RES/42/187.

[10] ibid, 40.

[11] Annex I to the Brundtland Report contains a summary of proposed legal principles for environmental protection and sustainable development, which was adopted by the WCED Experts Group on Environmental Law.

[12] See www.sustainabledevelopment.un.org/content/documents/Agenda21.pdf.

[13] UN Framework Convention on Climate Change (adopted 9 May 1992, entered into force 21 March 1994) 1771 UNTS 107; S. Treaty Doc No. 102–38; UN Doc A/AC.237/18 (Part II)/Add.1; 31 ILM 849 (1992) (UNFCCC).

[14] Convention on Biological Diversity (adopted 5 June 1992, entered into force 29 December 1993) 1760 UNTS 79.

[15] This document is attached to the UNGA, Report of the Conference on Environment and Development, 12 August 1992, UN Doc A/CONF151/26 (Vol III).

various principles referring to, inter alia, the right to development and environment related information, States' common though differentiated responsibilities with regard to their respective contributions to global environment deterioration and the need for reducing and eliminating unsustainable production and consumption patterns. The precautionary principle is expressly emphasised.[16] Following the Earth Summit, the Commission on Sustainable Development was created as a mechanism to follow-up its implementation. As a consequence of these evolutions, the principle of sustainable development[17] emerged as a principle of international cooperation in the domain of environmental protection.[18]

C. Kyoto Protocol

After the Earth Summit, the development of international environmental law accelerated. However, tensions between industrial and developmental countries often obstructed a consensus. That is illustrated by the adoption in 1997 of the Kyoto Protocol,[19] pursuant to which industrial countries need to reduce greenhouse gas emissions. The Protocol only entered into force on 16 February 2005 after a long and difficult process, following ratification by Russia and Canada,[20] in accordance with Article 25 of the Protocol.[21] Furthermore, the World Summit on Sustainable Development held in Johannesburg in 2002, often referred to as the Earth Summit + 10, did not succeed in reaching a breakthrough with regard to institutional reform or new multilateral conventions. Likewise, the 2009 Copenhagen Summit[22] did not meet expectations and was not considered a great success. However, the 2015 UN Climate Change Conference held in Paris did manage to adopt a binding agreement, and generally received more positive reviews.[23]

II. Sources

This section considers the sources of international environmental law. After an overview of the applicable general principles of law, the central position of treaties as a source of law – characteristic of international environmental law – is briefly considered. That is followed by a concise look at other sources of law, in particular non-legally binding though politically influential soft law instruments, which play a significant role in international environmental law, and customary international law.

[16] This principle will be discussed more fully in Section II(B)(ii)(c).

[17] See below Subsection (B)(ii)(a), and the discussion on the *Gabcikovo-Nagymaros Project* case and the *Pulp Mills* case.

[18] MN Shaw, *International Law*, 8th edn (Cambridge, CUP, 2017) 658–59.

[19] Kyoto Protocol to the UN Framework Convention on Climate Change (adopted 11 December 1997, entered into force 16 February 2005) 2303 UNTS 148.

[20] Russia and Canada ratified the Protocol in 2002.

[21] With Russia's ratification, the threshold contained in Art 25 of the Protocol was met, since '55 Parties to the Convention, incorporating Parties included in Annex I which accounted in total for at least 55 per cent of the total carbon dioxide emissions for 1990 of the Parties included in Annex I, have deposited their instruments of ratification, acceptance, approval or accession'.

[22] See below Section IV(B)(ii).

[23] The Copenhagen Summit and the Paris Conference are further explained when discussing the issue of climate change.

A. General Principles of International Environmental Law

A number of general principles of law are regularly applied to environmental issues, such as the principles of *sic utere tuo ut alienum non laedas* (one should use one's own property in such a way as not to injure others), abuse of law, territorial integrity and good neighbourliness. However, complex issues and disputes concerning environmental law are often difficult to resolve on the basis of such principles alone. In addition to general principles of law, international environmental law therefore increasingly makes use of what could be termed 'general principles of international environmental law', which are discussed more in detail in this section. While specific to environmental law, the following principles are still quite general in nature, and their scope is often subject to controversy.[24]

i. The Principle of Sustainable Development

The concept of sustainable development or the sustainable use of natural resources emerged in the context of the Rio Conference, was further developed in the Brundtland Report[25] and subsequently refined. It has been included in the texts of various treaties[26] and other instruments and has been increasingly applied, directly or indirectly, in case law. Notably, the ICJ referred to the concept of sustainable development in *Gabcikovo-Nagymaros*:[27]

> In order to evaluate the environmental risks, current standards must be taken into account. […] New norms and standards have been developed, set forth in a great number of instruments during the last two decades. Such new norms have to be taken into consideration, and such new standards given proper weight, not only when States contemplate new activities but also when continuing with activities begun in the past. This need to reconcile economic development with protection of the environment is aptly expressed in the concept of sustainable development.

The Court referred to it again in the *Pulp Mills* case,[28] by emphasising

> the need to strike a balance between the use of the waters and the protection of the river consistent with the objective of sustainable development. […] Consequently, it is the opinion of the Court that [the provision at issue] embodies this interconnectedness between equitable and reasonable utilization of a shared resource and the balance between economic development and environmental protection that is the essence of sustainable development.

Although the exact content and meaning of the concept of sustainable development remain uncertain, it seems to consist of four recurring elements that define its scope. First, it entails the need to conserve the environment and natural resources for the benefit of future generations. Second, the 'sustainable exploitation' of natural resources refers to the cautious, rational, wise or appropriate manner in which this should be done. Third, States should use natural resources equitably, thereby taking into account the needs and interests of other States. Lastly, environmental concerns should be integrated in broader economic and other developmental programmes and projects, and the need for development should be taken into account in the application of ecological objectives. These elements are highly interlinked and often used in combination and will be further developed and refined over time.

[24] On general principles of law as sources of international law, see Chapter 3, Section III.
[25] See n 9 ff.
[26] eg WTO agreement, preamble; Art 11 TEU.
[27] *Gabcikovo-Nagymaros Project* (Hungary v Slovakia) [1997] ICJ Rep 7, 140.
[28] *Pulp Mills* (Argentina v Uruguay) [2010] ICJ Rep 14, 177.

Nevertheless, since it remains disputed whether the principle of sustainable development may evolve into a legally binding norm or whether it is merely a policy goal, its normative status is contested.[29] Be that as it may, the principle of sustainable development is recognised as a general principle of EU law, both as an environmental principle and as an 'overarching long-term goal of the EU'.[30] It is included in Article 11 TFEU, which provides for environmental protection requirements to be 'integrated into the definition and implementation of the Union's policies and activities, in particular with a view to promoting sustainable development'.[31]

ii. The Preventive Principle

The preventive principle, also referred to as the 'no harm' principle,[32] implies the obligation to prevent environmental harm and to reduce, limit and control activities possibly causing such harm. It requires action to be taken at an early stage and, if possible, before the damage actually occurs. The preventive principle finds support in a substantial amount of national legislation, international environmental standards, access to information concerning the environment and the need for assessing certain activities' environmental impact. Consequently, it can take many forms, including sanctions and the determination of liability. This is illustrated clearly in the 2001 ILC Draft Articles on the Prevention of Transboundary Harm from Hazardous Activities, which provide that prevention in the sense of these Draft Articles 'deals with the phase prior to the situation where significant harm or damage might actually occur, requiring States concerned to invoke remedial or compensatory measures, which often involve issues concerning liability'.[33]

The preventive approach in international environmental law was further developed by the Stockholm Declaration, the operation of UNEP and the World Charter for Nature.[34] As will be discussed in the section on Treaty Law below, the principle finds expression in a number of international conventions. It is recognised in Principles 11 and 14 of the Rio Declaration, obliging States to enact effective legislation and to prevent the transfer of hazardous substances and activities. Further, it is mentioned in conventions concerning the environment in general as well as conventions dealing with specific environmental issues.[35] This indicates that the preventive principle is broadly accepted in international environmental law.

[29] U Beyerlin and T Marauhn, *International Environmental Law* (Oxford, Hart, 2011) 79–82; PP Rogers, KF Jalal and JA Boyd, *An Introduction to Sustainable Development* (London, Earthscan, 2008) 193–200.

[30] European Commission, *Mainstreaming Sustainable Development into EU Policies: 2009 Review of the European Union Strategy for Sustainable Development*, COM (2009) 400. See also European Commission, Communication from the Commission to the European Parliament, the Council, the European Economic and Social Committee and the Committee of the Regions, *Next steps for a sustainable European future: European action for sustainability*, COM(2016) 739 final. See further G Van Calster and L Reins, *EU Environmental Law* (Cheltenham, Edward Elgar, 2017) 9–10 and 24–27.

[31] See further below Section IV(b).

[32] See for example Beyerlin and Marauhn (n 29) 39 ff.

[33] Draft articles on Prevention of Transboundary Harm from Hazardous Activities, with commentaries (2010) *YILC*, II, General Commentary, para (1).

[34] UNGA, World Charter for Nature, 28 October 1982, UN Doc A/RES/37/7.

[35] See, for example, Art 1 Convention on the Prevention of Marine Pollution by Dumping of Wastes and Other Matter (adopted 29 December 1972, entered into force 30 August 1975) 1046 UNTS 120 (London Dumping Convention), Art 194(1) United Nations Convention on the Law of the Sea (adopted 10 December 1982, entered into force 16 November 1994) 1833 UNTS 3, 1834 UNTS 3, 1835 UNTS 3 (UNCLOS), Art II(4)(b) Convention on the Conservation of Migratory Species of Wild Animals (adopted 23 June 1973, entered into force 1 November 1983) 1651 UNTS 333 (Bonn Convention), Art 2 UNFCCC, Preamble, and Art I Convention on Biological Diversity (n 14).

iii. The Precautionary Principle

Although the precautionary principle was already part of certain national environmental legislation, and is currently mentioned in various international conventions,[36] it only emerged as a principle of international environmental law in the 1980s. In particular, Principle 15 of the Rio Declaration states that

> in order to protect the environment, the precautionary approach shall be widely applied by States according to their capabilities. Where there are threats of serious or irreversible damage, lack of full scientific certainty shall not be used as a reason for postponing cost-effective measures to prevent environmental degradation.

The exact meaning of the precautionary principle remains subject to debate.[37] Whereas some consider it to be the ground for early action concerning gravely threatening environmental problems, others fear for overregulation and limitation of human activities. Nevertheless, what seems to be clear is that the precautionary principle responds to the limitations of science in assessing global ecological risks that typically raise serious difficulties as to understanding the chain of causation and predicting outcomes.[38]

In the EU, the principle is often applied as a risk management principle in the areas of health protection and food safety, for example regarding nanotechnology and the use of genetically modified organisms (GMO). The principle was first mentioned by the European Court of Justice[39] in the 1998 *Bergaderm*[40] case. A year later, in *Pfizer*[41] the European General Court clarified its application and introduced some limitations to the applications of the principle. It held: 'a preventive measure cannot properly be based on a purely hypothetical approach to the risk, founded on mere conjecture which has not been scientifically verified'. Rather, according to the General Court, it follows from the Union Courts' interpretation of the precautionary principle

> that a preventive measure may be taken only if the risk, although the reality and extent thereof have not been 'fully' demonstrated by conclusive scientific evidence, appears nevertheless to be adequately backed up by the scientific data available at the time when the measure was taken.[42]

[36] See, for example, Art 3 UNFCCC, the Preamble to the Vienna Convention for the Protection of the Ozone Layer (adopted 22 March 1985, entered into force 22 September 1988) 1513 UNTS 323, the Preamble to the Montreal Protocol on Substances that Deplete the Ozone Layer (adopted 16 September 1987, entered into force 1 January 1989) 1522 UNTS 3, Art VI Convention on Biological Diversity (n 14).

[37] See eg C Sunstein, *The Laws of Fear. Beyond the Precautionary Principle* (Cambridge, CUP, 2005).

[38] Beyerlin and Marauhn (n 29) 52–53.

[39] Under Art 19(1), first subpara TEU, the institution of the CJEU encompasses the Court of Justice, the General Court and specialised courts. This chapter refers to the Court of Justice as the European Court of Justice (ECJ) in the sense of the highest court of this institution, and to the General Court as the European General Court (EGC) in the sense of the first instance court of that same institution.

[40] Judgment of 4 July 2000, *Bergaderm and Goupil v Commission*, C-352/98 P, EU:C:2000:361.

[41] Judgment of 11 September 2002, *Pfizer Animal Health v Council*, T-13/99, EU:T:2002:209. For a detailed discussion of the case see G Van Calster, 'Note under case T-70/99, Alpharma Inc v Council of the European Union (Alpharma), 11 September 2002 and case T-13/99, Pfizer animal health SA v Council of the European Union (Pfizer)' (2003) 12(1) *Review of European Community & International Environmental Law* 109.

[42] *Pfizer* (n 41) paras 143–44. See more recently ECJ, judgment of 9 June 2016, *Pesce and Others*, C-78/16 and C-79/16, EU:C:2016:428, para 47, holding that 'the EU legislature must take account of the precautionary principle, according to which, where there is uncertainty as to the existence or extent of risks to human health, protective measures may be taken without having to wait until the reality and seriousness of those risks become fully apparent. Where it proves to be impossible to determine with certainty the existence or extent of the alleged risk because of the insufficiency, inconclusiveness or imprecision of the results of studies conducted, but the likelihood of real harm to public health persists should the risk materialise, the precautionary principle justifies the adoption of restrictive measures'. See also EGC, judgment of 17 May 2018, *Bayer CropScience and Others v Commission*, T-429/13 and T-451/13, EU:T:2018:280, paras 109–111.

The 2000 Commission Communication on the precautionary principle established 6 criteria for measures based on the principle. They need to be inter alia: '*proportional* to the chosen level of protection, *non-discriminatory* in their application, *consistent* with similar measures already taken, *based on an examination of the potential benefits and costs* of action or lack of action (including, where appropriate and feasible, an economic cost/benefit analysis), *subject to review,* in the light of new scientific data, and *capable of assigning responsibility for producing the scientific evidence* necessary for a more comprehensive risk assessment'.[43]

The European Court of Human Rights has also relied on the precautionary principle in its case law, doing so for the first time in *Tătar v Romania*. There, after a brief overview of the precautionary principle in EU law and the relevant case law of the ECJ, the Court recalled that the precautionary principle recommends that States not delay taking preventive action simply because of scientific uncertainty, holding that Romania should have addressed in advance the potential risk of the mine at issue on the environment and the health of the population.[44]

Generally, the precautionary principle brings about an obligation for States to act cautiously and foresightedly when taking decisions that might affect the environment. More concrete definitions of the principle, such as the obligation to restrict or prohibit possibly hazardous activities and substances despite the absence of conclusive evidence, remain controversial.

Controversy also exists regarding the question as to who carries the burden of proof concerning the possible harm an activity or substance might cause in cases of insufficient scientific data. Traditionally, it is the opponent of an activity or product who carries this burden of proof and consequently has to prove the high probability that environmental harm will be caused. However, some commentators argue that the precautionary principle shifts this burden of proof to the proponents of an activity or product, who thereby have to prove that no such harm will be caused.[45]

iv. The Polluter Pays Principle

The polluter pays principle mainly obliges the polluter to bear the costs of the environmental harm that they have caused. Its exact scope and application to concrete cases remains subject to interpretation, especially with regard to the nature and extent of the costs and the situations in which the principle does not apply. The polluter pays principle is expressed in Principle 16 of the Rio Declaration, which provides that

> national authorities should endeavour to promote the internalization of environmental costs and the use of economic instruments, taking into account the approach that the polluter should, in principle, bear the cost of pollution, with due regard to the public interest and without distorting international trade and investment.

This wording also shows the compromise that often has to be made regarding this principle, which still faces resistance both from certain developing and industrialised countries, who

[43] Communication from the Commission on the precautionary principle, COM(2000) 1.

[44] *Tătar v Romania* App No 67021/01 (ECtHR, 27 January 2009) paras 109 and 120. See further, A Gouritin, 'Sustainable Development Principles in the European Court of Human Rights' in M-C Cordonnier Segger and CG Weeramantry (eds), *Sustainable Development Principles in the Decisions of International Courts and Tribunals 1992–2012* (London, Routledge, 2017) 529–30.

[45] See further, A Trouwborst, *Evolution and Status of the Precautionary Principle in International Law* (Deventer, Kluwer, 2002) 193–227.

argue that it should be applied on the national level only and does not govern relationships and liability amongst States internationally.

Despite its broad acceptance, the polluter pays principle has less support than the preventive principle and has gained less attention than the precautionary principle. Nevertheless, apart from frequently serving as the source of inspiration for domestic regulatory or legislative initiatives, for example within the area of taxation, it is contained in various conventions[46] and has gained particular significance in the context of the EU, the Organisation for Economic Co-operation and Development (OECD) and the United Nations Economic Commission for Europe (UNECE), a regional commission set up in 1947 by the Economic and Social Council of the UN (ECOSOC).

In EU law, waste legislation (for instance, the Packaging and Packaging Waste Directive or the Landfill Directive[47]) in particular is a practical application of the polluter pays principle. A common tool to implement the principle in practice is the establishment of standards, such as environmental quality standards, product and process standards or operational standards. In addition to standards, or in combination therewith, charges likewise serve as an incentive for pollution reduction, ensuring that the polluter pays.

v. *The Principle of Participation*

Principle 10 of the Rio Declaration provides for public participation in environmental decision-making and judicial and administrative proceedings:

> Principle 10
>
> Environmental issues are best handled with participation of all concerned citizens, at the relevant level. At the national level, each individual shall have appropriate access to information concerning the environment that is held by public authorities, including information on hazardous materials and activities in their communities, and the opportunity to participate in decision-making processes. States shall facilitate and encourage public awareness and participation by making information widely available. Effective access to judicial and administrative proceedings, including redress and remedy, shall be provided.

That suggests that public participation is not just important in terms of democratic accountability and public deliberation, but also as a means to operationalise the preventive principle.[48] Arguably the most important international instrument in that regard is the Convention on Access to Information, Public Participation in Decision-Making and Access to Justice in Environmental Matters (the Aarhus Convention), which provides for citizens to have a right to access to information, to be entitled to participate in decision-making and to have access to justice in environmental matters. It was adopted by the then European Community, its Member States and 19 other States on 25 June 1998 in Aarhus, Denmark,

[46] The International Convention on the Establishment of an International Fund for Compensation for Oil Pollution Damage (adopted 18 December 1971, entered into force 16 October 1978) 1110 UNTS 57; Convention on the Protection and Use of Transboundary Watercourses and International Lakes (adopted 17 March 1992, entered into force 6 October 1996) 1936 UNTS 269 (Water Convention); Vienna Convention on Civil Liability for Nuclear Damage (adopted 21 May 1963, entered into force 12 November 1977) 1063 UNTS 265; Protocol to the Convention on the Prevention of Marine Pollution by Dumping of Wastes and Other Matter (adopted 7 November 1996, entered into force 24 March 2006) 36 ILM 1.

[47] Directive 94/62 of 20 December 1994 on packaging and packaging waste [1994] OJ L365/10; and Directive 1999/31 of 26 April 1999 on the landfill of waste [1999] OJ L182/1. See further in general: G Van Calster, *EU Waste Law*, 2nd edn (Oxford, OUP 2015).

[48] Dupuy and Viñuales (n 3) 76.

within the framework of UNECE. It entered into force definitively on 30 October 2001. Former UN Secretary General Kofi Annan has emphasised that while it is 'regional in scope, the significance of the Aarhus Convention is global', calling it 'by far the most impressive elaboration of Principle 10 of the Rio Declaration'.[49]

The Aarhus Convention was approved on behalf of the then European Community by Council Decision 2005/370/EC of 17 February 2005.[50] The EU adopted two Directives concerning the first and second 'pillars' of the Aarhus Convention in 2003 on public access to environmental information[51] and on public participation in respect of the drawing up of certain plans and programmes relating to the environment, respectively.[52] The Aarhus Convention was further implemented in EU law by the 'Aarhus Regulation',[53] which applies the provisions of the Convention to EU institutions and bodies. Furthermore, the Court of Justice of the EU has been interpreting and applying the Convention either directly or through the EU implementing legislation in a growing number of cases,[54] thereby acting as an additional (and more powerful) enforcement mechanism of the Aarhus Convention.[55]

The Aarhus Convention is based on the premise that every person has the right to live in an environment adequate to his or her health and well-being, and even the duty, both individually and in association with others, to protect and improve the environment for the benefit of present and future generations. To be able to assert this right and observe this duty, the Aarhus Convention rests on three 'pillars': citizens must have access to information; be entitled to participate in decision-making; and have access to justice in environmental matters. These pillars depend on each other for the full implementation of the Convention's objectives.[56] The Convention acknowledges that citizens may need assistance in order to exercise their rights. Furthermore, effective judicial mechanisms should be accessible to the public, including organisations, so that its legitimate interests are protected and the law is enforced.[57]

The Aarhus Convention has also been relied on in the case law of the European Court of Human Rights. Notably, in *Tătar v Romania*, the Court found a violation of Article 8 ECHR on the right to private life inter alia on the basis that the national authorities had

[49] K Annan, Foreword to UNECE: The Aarhus Convention: an implementation guide, UN Doc ECE/CEP/72, v.

[50] Council Decision 2005/370/EC on the conclusion, on behalf of the European Community, of the Convention on access to information, public participation in decision-making and access to justice in environmental matters [2005] OJ L124/1.

[51] Directive 2003/4/EC on public access to environmental information and repealing Council Directive 90/313/EEC [2003] OJ L41/26.

[52] Directive 2003/35/EC providing for public participation in respect of the drawing up of certain plans and programmes relating to the environment and amending with regard to public participation and access to justice Council Directives 85/337/EEC and 96/61/EC [2003] OJ L156/17.

[53] Regulation (EC) No 1367/2006 on the application of the provisions of the Aarhus Convention on Access to Information, Public Participation in Decision-making and Access to Justice in Environmental Matters to Community institutions and bodies [2006] OJ L264/13. Further on the implementation of the Aarhus Convention in the EU Member States and its application to the EU institutions and bodies, see Van Calster and Reins (n 30) 81–107.

[54] See most recently judgment of 15 March 2018, *North East Pylon Pressure Campaign and Sheehy*, C-470/16, EU:C:2018:185, and the Opinion of Advocate General Bobek, EU:C:2017:781, as well as judgment of 4 September 2018, *ClientEarth v Commission*, C-57/16 P, EU:C:2018:660, and the Opinion of Advocate General Bot, EU:C:2017:909.

[55] See further G De Baere and JT Nowak, 'The right to access to 'not prohibitively expensive' judicial proceedings under the Aarhus Convention and the Court of Justice as an international (environmental) law court' (2016) 53(6) *CMLR* 1727.

[56] UNECE, *The Aarhus Convention: An Implementation Guide, Second edition, 2014*, UN Doc ECE/CEP/72/Rev1, 19.

[57] See the 7th, 8th, and 18th recital in the preamble and Art 1 Aarhus Convention.

failed to ensure public access to the conclusions of investigations and studies, reiterating that the State had a duty to guarantee the right of members of the public to participate in the decision-making process concerning environmental issues.[58]

B. Treaty Law

Apart from the abovementioned Aarhus Convention, a significant number of other bilateral, regional, and multilateral treaties in the field of international environmental law have been concluded in recent decades. However, an integrated approach, whereby treaties with respect to specific sectors and regional treaties would be complemented by cross-sectorial treaties and treaties with a global focus, is lacking. Consequently, instead of a coherent system – let alone a hierarchy of norms of some description – international environmental treaties form a fairly complex web of diverse subject areas.

A common problem in this regard is that most of these treaties lack a clear implementation, enforcement or compliance mechanism. More broadly, classic enforcement avenues at the international level are less common in international environmental law than more 'soft' mechanisms such as 'naming and shaming' or monitoring, or than enforcement at the domestic level, even if through domestic (civil) principles.[59]

Furthermore, besides the fact that it has been increasingly difficult to conclude international environmental treaties, their entry into force is often a long drawn-out and tortuous process. Given that many environmental issues require a rapid response, delayed entry into force may diminish or even nullify the relevance of the treaty in question.

The most significant relevant treaties will be discussed thematically below as part of the overview of the main themes in international environmental law.

C. Other Sources

As already mentioned, even though treaties play the most significant role in the field of international environmental law, other sources too are relevant. Soft law instruments in particular play an important role.

[58] *Tătar v Romania* (n 44) paras 115–25.

[59] See, for example, The Hague District Court (Netherlands), *Urgenda Foundation v Netherlands*, 24 June 2015, C/09/456689 / HA ZA 13-1396. The court held it to be 'established that any anthropogenic greenhouse gas emission, no matter how minor, contributes to an increase in CO_2 levels in the atmosphere and therefore to hazardous climate change. Emission reduction therefore concerns both a joint and individual responsibility of the signatories to the UN Climate Change Convention' (para 4.79). In addition, the Court found that a sufficient causal link could be assumed to exist between the Dutch greenhouse gas emissions, global climate change and the effects on the Dutch living climate. The Court ordered the Dutch State to limit the joint volume of Dutch annual greenhouse gas emissions, or have them limited, so that this volume will have reduced by at least 25% at the end of 2020 compared to the level of the year 1990. See also Court of First Instance of Brussels, *VZW Klimaatzaak v Kingdom of Belgium and others*. Similar to the *Urgenda* case, *Klimaatzaak* was brought by an organization of concerned citizens arguing that Belgian law requires the Belgian government's approach to reducing greenhouse gas emissions to be more ambitious. To date, the court has issued a ruling on procedural matters raised by the Flemish government. On 20 April 2018, the Court of Cassation rejected the appeal against that ruling. Any decision on the merits is still pending. And see *Lungowe and others v Vedanta Resources Plc and another* [2017] EWCA Civ 1528, [2017] WLR (D) 741, which found that Vendata, a UK company, could be held responsible under UK law for the actions of its Zambian subsidiary, Konkola Copper Mines, which was accused of causing significant harm to local waterways through water discharged from one of its copper mines.

i. Soft Law

In international environmental law, instruments are frequently adopted that are not conventions or treaties as such, but political declarations of intent, resolutions, recommendations or guidelines. The Stockholm Declaration, the Rio Declaration, Agenda 21 and the Forest Principles are but a few examples in this respect. Although these documents are not legally binding, they often have significant political and legal relevance. In this regard, they may confirm already existing customary law[60] or serve as the benchmark for the further development of rules and principles of environmental law, by either subsequently becoming part of a treaty or by gaining the status of customary law.

ii. Customary Law

When compared with other domains of international law, specific norms of international customary law are rather scarce in the area of environmental law, given its recent emergence. The most well-known example in this respect is the obligation to prevent transboundary environmental damage established in the *Trail Smelter* Arbitration, as confirmed in the second Principle of the Rio Declaration and Principle 21 of the Stockholm Declaration. The ICJ acknowledged that this principle 'is now part of the corpus of international law relating to the environment' in its advisory opinion concerning the legality of the threat or use of nuclear weapons.[61]

In *Pulp Mills*, the ICJ based some of its findings on customary international law.[62] Notably, the Court recalled 'the general obligation of States to ensure that activities within their jurisdiction and control respect the environment of other States or of areas beyond national control is now part of the corpus of international law relating to the environment',[63] concluding that

> it may now be considered a requirement under general international law to undertake an environmental impact assessment where there is a risk that the proposed industrial activity may have a significant adverse impact in a transboundary context, in particular, on a shared resource. Moreover, due diligence, and the duty of vigilance and prevention which it implies, would not be considered to have been exercised, if a party planning works liable to affect the régime of the river or the quality of its waters did not undertake an environmental impact assessment on the potential effects of such works.[64]

More generally, given the rapid developments within this field, other principles and rules may gain the status of customary international law in the future.

III. Institutions

International environmental law lacks a leading global institution enforcing and controlling compliance. Nevertheless, there are quite a few institutions actively involved in that domain, both at the global and the regional (here European Union) level.

[60] See, for example, Principle 21 of the Stockholm Declaration.
[61] *Legality of the Threat or Use of Nuclear Weapons* [1996] ICJ Rep 66, para 29.
[62] *Pulp Mills* (n 28). See the discussion below.
[63] ibid, para 193, citing *Legality of the Threat or Use of Nuclear Weapons* (n 61) para 29.
[64] ibid, para 204.

A. Institutions on the Global Level

On the global level, there is first UNEP, which was mentioned at the very beginning of this chapter.[65] Further, various specialised organisations and agencies were established in the context of the UN, which focus on specific environmental issues. In this regard, the International Maritime Organization (IMO) should be mentioned, which is responsible for the safety and security of shipping and the prevention of marine pollution by ships.[66] The IMO has produced various broadly ratified conventions[67] and its Legal Committee and Marine Environment Protection Committee issue recommendations and non-binding guidelines. The WHO established the WHO Commission on Health and Environment, which was influential with respect to the inclusion of health considerations in Agenda 21. The WHO further sets out quality requirements concerning drinking water in the context of international health regulations, which has had an important impact on environmental measures.

Furthermore, the World Meteorological Organisation (WMO) provides and facilitates the exchange of data and information about the impact of environmental pollution on the climate and weather conditions.[68] Through various Programmes, notably the World Weather Watch, the World Climate Programme and the Atmospheric Research and Environmental Programme, the WMO contributes to the monitoring and protection of the environment. Together with UNEP, it established the Intergovernmental Panel on Climate Change, which issues scientific, technical and socio-economic recommendations regarding climate change, and has contributed to the creation of regulations concerning the ozone layer, climate change and transboundary air pollution. Finally, global institutions not specifically in the area of environmental policy have also addressed environmental issues. For example, the UN Security Council has discussed climate change as a security threat on a number of occasions since it first considered the issue in 2007,[69] and has adopted resolutions condemning wildlife poaching and trafficking in connection to conflicts.[70]

B. Institutions on the European Level

At the European level, various organisations and institutions play an important role in the field of environmental law. First, the UNECE has adopted a significant number of treaties

[65] The EU has a preference for upgrading UNEP to a UN specialised agency under Art 57 UN Charter: see further T Delreux, 'The EU and multilateralism in the environmental field. UNEP reform and external representation in environmental negotiations' in E Drieskens and L van Schaik (eds), *The EU and Effective Multilateralism. Internal and External Reform Practices* (Abingdon, Routledge, 2014) 68–74.

[66] See www.imo.org. However, the task of preventing marine pollution was not mentioned in its founding Treaty.

[67] For example the International Convention for the Prevention of the Pollution of the Sea by Oil (adopted 12 May 1954, entered into force 26 July 1958) 327 UNTS 3, and the International Convention for the Prevention of Pollution from Ships, 1973, as modified by the Protocol of 1978 relating thereto (adopted 2 November 1973, entered into force 2 October 1983) 1340 UNTS 184; 12 ILM 1319 (1973) (MARPOL 73/78).

[68] See www.wmo.int.

[69] See UN Doc S/PV.6587. See further eg, SV Scott, 'Implications of climate change for the UN Security Council: mapping the range of potential policy responses' (2015) 91(6) *International Affairs* 1317.

[70] See eg UN Doc S/RES/2389 (2017) on the situation in the Great Lakes region, which recalls 'the linkage between the illegal exploitation and trade of natural resources, including poaching and illegal trafficking of wildlife, and the proliferation and trafficking of arms as one of the major factors fuelling and exacerbating conflicts in the Great Lakes region' (9th recital in the preamble), and stresses the need 'to undertake further efforts to cut off financing for armed groups involved in destabilizing activities through the illicit trade of natural resources, including gold or wildlife products' (para 17).

in the environmental field, including the Convention on Environmental Impact Assessment in a Transboundary Context[71] and the Water Convention.[72] The OECD too is concerned with environmental issues. Under its auspices, conventions[73] as well as legally non-binding instruments[74] have been established and its Recommendations on specific environmental problems have further developed environmental protection.[75] Second, the Council of Europe has produced a number of environmental instruments, such as the Convention on the Conservation of European Wildlife and Natural Habitats,[76] the Convention on Civil Liability for Damage resulting from Activities Dangerous to the Environment,[77] and the Convention on the Protection of Environment through Criminal Law.[78] Furthermore, the case law of the European Court of Human Rights contains quite a number of examples in which adverse environmental factors were the cause of breaches of one of the human rights protected by the ECHR.[79]

Third, environmental protection features prominently among the EU's aims and objectives.[80] It is first mentioned in the ninth recital in the preamble to the EU Treaty, intended to reassure EU citizens that economic integration within the Union must not come at the cost of other societal goals, notably those of social progress, sustainable development, and environmental protection. That commitment is confirmed in Article 3(3) TEU, which lists the establishment of an internal market as one of the aims of the Union, but adds that the Union is to 'work for the sustainable development of Europe', aiming inter alia at 'a high level of protection and improvement of the quality of the environment'. In addition, Article 37 of the Charter of Fundamental Rights of the EU provides that a 'high level of environmental protection and the improvement of the quality of the environment must be integrated into the policies of the Union and ensured in accordance with the principle of sustainable development'.[81] With respect to EU external action, Article 3(5) TEU provides that the Union is to contribute to 'the sustainable development of the Earth'. Furthermore, the protection of the environment is twice mentioned among the basic objectives of the Union's external action listed in Article 21(2) TEU. Pursuant to that provision, the Union is to define and pursue common policies and actions, and is to work for a high degree of cooperation in all fields of international relations, inter alia in order to 'foster the sustainable economic, social and environmental development of developing countries, with the primary aim of eradicating poverty' and to 'help develop international measures to preserve and improve the quality of the environment and the sustainable management of global natural resources, in order to ensure sustainable development'.[82]

[71] Convention on Environmental Impact Assessment in a Transboundary Context (adopted 25 February 1991, entered into force 10 September 1997) 1989 UNTS 309.

[72] See n 46.

[73] For example the Convention on Third Party Liability in the Field of Nuclear Energy (adopted 29 July 1960, entered into force 1 April 1968) 956 UNTS 251.

[74] Various OECD Recommendations were influential for the development of the polluter pays principle; Beyerlin and Marauhn (n 29) 57.

[75] Beyerlin and Marauhn (n 29) 12.

[76] (adopted 19 September 1979, entered into force 1 June 1982) ETS No 104.

[77] (adopted 21 June 1993, not yet entered into force) ETS No 150.

[78] (adopted 4 November 1998, not yet entered into force) ETS No 172.

[79] See eg *Tătar v Romania* (n 44) above.

[80] See further Van Calster and Reins (n 30) 8–14.

[81] See further E Morgera and G Marín Durán, 'Environmental Protection', in S Peers, T Hervey, J Kenner and A Ward (eds), *The EU Charter of Fundamental Rights: A Commentary* (London, Hart Publishing, 2014) 983–1004.

[82] Art 21(2)(d) and (f) TEU.

The Union's action on the international scene is to be guided by those principles and objectives.[83] Furthermore, Article 11 TFEU provides that environmental protection requirements 'must be integrated into the definition and implementation of the Union's policies and activities, in particular with a view to promoting sustainable development'. That implies an obligation for the Union not only to mainstream environmental protection and sustainable development into its policies, but also to ensure consistency between environmental policy and its other policies.[84] Furthermore, 'to improve environmental integration and policy coherence' is one of the priority objectives of the 7th Environment Action Programme, and so is 'to increase the Union's effectiveness in addressing international environmental and climate-related challenges'.[85] 'Environment' is listed as a shared competence under Article 4(2)(e) TFEU, which implies, pursuant to Article 2(2) TFEU, that the Union and the Member States may legislate and adopt legally binding acts in that area. The Member States are to exercise their competence to the extent that the Union has not exercised its competence, and are again to exercise their competence to the extent that the Union has decided to cease exercising its competence. Nevertheless, as now explicitly confirmed in Article 3(1)(d) TFEU, the conservation of marine biological resources under the common fisheries policy[86] belongs to the a priori exclusive competences of the Union. While not strictly speaking part of EU environmental policy within the meaning of Article 4(2)(e) TFEU, it clearly belongs to environmental policy in a broader functional sense.[87] The legal bases for EU external environmental law are to be found in Articles 191 and 192 in Title XX of Part Three of the TFEU.[88] Article 193 TFEU[89] further clarifies that measures taken on the basis of Article 192 TFEU are to be minimum requirements. Concern for the environment outside the Union forms part of the core objectives of EU environmental policy, as Article 191(1), fourth dash, provides for Union policy on the environment to contribute to the pursuit of a list of objectives that include 'promoting measures at international level to deal with regional or worldwide environmental problems, and in particular combating climate change'.

As a rule, all Free Trade Agreements (FTAs) that the Union has recently concluded contain provisions aiming at the protection of the environment or, more broadly, sustainable development.[90] Taking the Free Trade Agreement between the European Union and the Republic of Singapore ('the EUSFTA')[91] as an example, according to its preamble, the Parties are 'determined to strengthen their economic, trade, and investment relations in accordance with the objective of sustainable development, in its economic, social and environmental dimensions'. Articles 13.1 and 13.2 then state that sustainable development,

[83] Art 205 TFEU. That commitment is also specifically confirmed in Arts 207(1) (common commercial policy), 208(1) (development cooperation), 212(1) (economic, financial and technical cooperation with third countries), and 214(1) TEU (humanitarian aid).

[84] M Cremona, 'Coherence and EU external environmental policy' in E Morgera (ed), *The External Environmental Policy of the European Union: EU and International Law Perspectives* (Cambridge, CUP, 2012) 33, 36.

[85] Art 2(1)(g) and (i) of Decision No 1386/2013/EU of the European Parliament and of the Council on a General Union Environment Action Programme to 2020 'Living well, within the limits of our planet' [2013] OJ L354/171.

[86] On which see Chapter 18, Section VII.

[87] In that sense, see H Vedder, 'The formalities and substance of EU external environmental competence: stuck between climate change and competitiveness' in Morgera (n 84) 11 and 15.

[88] Ex Arts 174 and 175 TEC.

[89] Ex Art 176 TEC.

[90] See further G De Baere, *EU External Environmental Policy After Lisbon: The Legal Framework and Its Context* (Stockholm, Swedish Institute for European Policy Studies, forthcoming 2018).

[91] See further E Roussou, *Free Trade Agreement between the EU and the Republic of Singapore – Analysis* (European Parliament, Directorate-General for External Policies, Policy Department, 2018).

of which the social protection of workers and environmental protection are mutually reinforcing components, forms part of the objectives of trade relations between the EU and Singapore. More specifically with respect to environmental protection, Articles 13.6 to 13.10 include, in addition to various commitments of the Parties to cooperate, exchange information, and take account of scientific information, the obligation to implement effectively the multilateral environmental agreements to which they are party,[92] to address trade in illegally harvested timber and timber products,[93] to comply with sustainable exploitation of fish stocks as defined in the international instruments ratified by the Parties,[94] to combat illegal, unreported and unregulated fishing,[95] and to adopt effective monitoring and control measures to ensure compliance with conservation measures.[96] Article 13.6.4 adds the important proviso that the Parties are prohibited from applying measures adopted or maintained to implement a multilateral environmental agreement in a manner that would constitute a means of arbitrary or unjustifiable discrimination between the Parties or a disguised restriction on trade. As summed up by the CJEU in Opinion 2/15 on the competence of the EU to conclude the EUSFTA, by the provisions of Chapter 13, the EU and Singapore 'undertake, essentially, to ensure that trade between them takes place in compliance with the obligations that stem from the international agreements concerning social protection of workers and environmental protection to which they are party'.[97] It seems clear that Opinion 2/15 has significantly reinforced the nexus between trade and sustainable development under EU law, in particular by confirming that the objective of sustainable development henceforth forms an integral part of the common commercial policy (ie the EU's external trade policy).[98]

IV. Main Themes

A. The Protection of the Marine Environment and Freshwater Resources

i. The Protection of the Marine Environment

Concerns about marine pollution started taking a central position in international rulemaking processes in the 1970s. In particular, the protection of the marine environment was one of the main themes during the Stockholm Conference, and various relevant bilateral and multilateral treaties were concluded, such as the (global) London Dumping Convention,[99] the (regional) Oslo Dumping Convention[100] and MARPOL 73/78.[101] The coinciding

[92] Article 13.6.2 EUSFTA.
[93] Article 13.7(b) EUSFTA.
[94] Article 13.8(a) EUSFTA.
[95] Article 13.8(b) EUSFTA.
[96] Article 13.8(c) EUSFTA.
[97] Opinion 2/15 (EU-Singapore Free Trade Agreement) of 16 May 2017, EU:C:2017:376, para 152.
[98] Ibid, para 147. See further on trade and the environment in EU law: Van Calster and Reins (n 30) 308–329.
[99] n 35.
[100] Convention for the Prevention of Marine Pollution by Dumping from Ships and Aircraft, Oslo (adopted 15 February 1972, 7 April 1974) 932 UNTS 3. The Convention for the Protection of The Mediterranean Sea against Pollution (adopted 16 February 1976, entered into force 12 February 1978) 1102 UNTS 27 (Barcelona Convention) is another well-known and influential regional Convention in this domain.
[101] n 67.

negotiations on the UNCLOS had both a remarkable impact on and were influenced by these developments, and the resulting UNCLOS implicitly recognised the existing treaties on marine pollution.

With regard to dumping, a licensing system was initially used, on the basis of which dumping as such was not in principle prohibited, with the exception of the dumping of substances that were explicitly categorised as dangerous. This policy was reversed with the OSPAR Convention[102] and the 1996 Protocol to the London Dumping Convention,[103] which prohibited dumping at sea in principle, but explicitly identified certain exceptions to this general ban. In addition to this shift from permissiveness to restrictiveness,[104] the London Protocol stresses the importance of the principle of precautionary action[105] and takes the approach that, in principle, the polluter carries the burden of proof that dumping causes no serious damage to the marine environment and should bear the cost of pollution.[106]

Due to widely publicised oil spills, the issue of marine pollution from ships gained much attention and became subject to a number of international treaties. An infamous example that sparked much debate is the March 1967 incident involving 'The Torrey Canyon', a US-owned oil tanker registered in Liberia, which ran aground on submerged rocks off the coast of Cornwall outside British territorial waters, spilling large amounts of oil that threatened the English coastline.[107] After various remedial attempts had failed, the British Government decided to bomb the ship to burn the remaining oil, emphasising the existence of a situation of extreme danger and claiming that the decision to bomb the ship had been taken only after all other means had failed.[108] The oil spill caused exceptional marine pollution and showed the insufficiency of the applicable international regulatory framework. After the event, the International Convention relating to Intervention on the High Seas in Cases of Oil Pollution Casualties[109] was concluded to cover future cases where intervention might prove necessary to avert serious oil pollution.

MARPOL 73/78 in turn aims to achieve the 'complete elimination of intentional pollution of the marine environment by oil and other harmful substances and the minimisation of accidental discharge of such substances'.[110] The Convention includes six technical Annexes[111] and was modified by several Protocols and other amendments. Annexes I and

[102] Convention for the Protection of the Marine Environment of the North-East Atlantic (adopted 22 September 1992, entered into force 25 March 1998) 2354 UNTS 67.

[103] 1996 Protocol to the Convention on the Prevention of Marine Pollution by Dumping of Wastes and Other Matter (adopted 7 November 1996, entered into force 24 March 2006) 36 ILM 1 (1997) (London Protocol).

[104] B Sage-Fuller, *The Precautionary Principle in Marine Environmental Law: With Special Reference to High Risk Vessels* (Abingdon, Routledge, 2013) 71.

[105] Art 3 of the Protocol states that 'in implementing this Protocol, Contracting Parties shall apply a precautionary approach to environmental protection from dumping of wastes or other matter whereby appropriate preventative measures are taken when there is reason to believe that wastes or other matter introduced into the marine environment are likely to cause harm even when there is no conclusive evidence to prove a causal relation between inputs and their effects'.

[106] See above on the polluter pays principle and the burden of proof in this regard.

[107] Command Paper 3246, *The 'Torrey Canyon'* (London, HM Stationery Office, 1967). See also Chapter 18.

[108] The incident can arguably be regarded as an example of 'necessity' as a circumstance precluding wrongfulness in the sense of Art 25 of the Articles on State Responsibility. See the International Law Commission's Articles on the Responsibility of States for Internationally Wrongful Acts (2001) *YILC* II, and Annex to UNGA Res 56/83, 12 December 2001, corrected by UN Doc A/56/49(Vol I)/Corr4. See further Chapter 10.

[109] Adopted 29 November 1969, entered into force 6 May 1975, 970 UNTS 211.

[110] Fourth recital in the preamble to MARPOL 73/78.

[111] These Annexes deal with regulations for the prevention of pollution by oil and for the control of pollution by noxious liquid substances in bulk, prevention of pollution by harmful substances carried by sea in packaged form and of pollution by sewage and garbage from ships and, lastly, prevention of air pollution from ships.

II are binding upon all State Parties, whereas the other Annexes are optional. Especially Annex I is relevant here, since it focuses on oil pollution by ships. In particular, it prohibits the operational discharge of oil and oily mixtures from ships into the sea when various conditions are not satisfied, and requires the State Parties to provide for adequate facilities for the reception of oil residues. Furthermore, several areas are identified as Special Areas in which strictly no oil pollution is allowed.[112]

The liability for marine pollution was regulated through the conclusion of a number of treaties, such as the International Convention on Civil Liability for Oil Pollution Damage[113] and the International Convention on the Establishment of an International Fund for Compensation for Oil Pollution Damage,[114] both modified by Protocols. According to these treaties, the ship-owner is strictly liable[115] for the damage caused. The latter treaty provides for compensation to the extent that the protection offered by the first is not sufficient and the Fund it established is financed by those States importing oil by sea. This system enables victims of oil pollution to receive compensation reasonably expeditiously.

The EU is a party to UNCLOS, but not to MARPOL 73/78. In *Intertanko*,[116] the ECJ was asked whether the strict liability regime for environmental damage occurring on the high seas under Directive 2005/35/EC[117] was compatible with both conventions. As the EU is a party to UNCLOS,[118] its provisions are binding upon EU institutions and Member States[119] and prevail over EU acts.[120] However, the ECJ held that UNCLOS 'does not establish rules intended to apply directly and immediately to individuals and to confer upon them rights or freedoms capable of being relied upon against States', and that it 'follows that the nature and the broad logic of UNCLOS' prevent the ECJ from being able to assess the validity of an EU measure in the light of it.[121] That position is undoubtedly problematic from an international law point of view.[122] Nevertheless, whether or not UNCLOS as such or customary law of the sea can be invoked before EU courts, the EU *is* required to abide by the Convention both under international law and EU law.

The ECJ also held that, given that the EU is not a party to MARPOL 73/78, the validity of Directive 2005/35/EC could not be assessed in the light of that convention. Nevertheless, the Court also noted that the fact that all Member States are parties to MARPOL 73/78 was liable to have consequences for the interpretation of UNCLOS and the provisions of

[112] These areas are inter alia the Mediterranean Sea area, the Baltic Sea area, the Red Sea area and the 'Gulfs area', which are further defined in Regulation 10 of Annex I.

[113] International Convention on Civil Liability for Oil Pollution Damage (adopted 29 November 1969, entered into force 19 June 1975) 973 UNTS 3.

[114] International Convention on the Establishment of an International Fund for Compensation for Oil Pollution Damage (adopted 18 December 1971, entered into force 16 October 1978) 1110 UNTS 57.

[115] Nevertheless, this strict liability is limited, unless there is a fault on the side of the shipowner. In order to cover his liability, the shipowner should hold insurance.

[116] Judgment of 3 June 2008, *Intertanko and others*, C-308/06, EU:C:2008:312.

[117] Directive 2005/35/EC of the European Parliament and of the Council of 7 September 2005 on ship-source pollution and on the introduction of penalties for infringements [2005] OJ L255/11.

[118] Council Decision 98/392/EC concerning the conclusion by the European Community of the United Nations Convention of 10 December 1982 on the Law of the Sea and the Agreement of 28 July 1994 relating to the implementation of Part XI thereof [1998] OJ L179/1.

[119] Art 216(2) TFEU.

[120] Judgment of 21 December 2011, *Air Transport Association of America and others*, C-366/10, EU:C:2011:864, para 50.

[121] *Intertanko* (n 116) paras 64–65.

[122] See eg P Eeckhout, 'Case C-308/06, The Queen on the application of Intertanko and Others v Secretary of State for Transport, judgment of the Court of Justice (Grand Chamber) of 3 June 2008' (2009) 46 *CMLR* 2041 at 2055.

EU secondary law that fall within the field of application of MARPOL 73/78, concluding that in view 'of the customary principle of good faith, which forms part of general international law, and of Article [4(3) TEU], it is incumbent upon the Court to interpret those provisions taking account of Marpol 73/78'.[123] Nevertheless, the Court did not explain how precisely it had taken account of MARPOL 73/78 in its interpretation of Directive 2005/35/EC.

ii. The Protection of Freshwater Resources

A sufficient supply of fresh water, which can be mainly found in rivers, lakes, ground waters and basins, is essential for human, animal and plant life. However, a NASA-led study has found that current unsustainable groundwater use threatens the resilience of aquifer systems and their ability to provide a long-term water source, and that an important number of the world's freshwater sources are being drained faster than they are being replenished.[124] Serious water shortages cause a lack of access to clean water and basic sanitation, and create fundamental environmental problems. Even though initially international environmental law did not focus on these issues as such, they are increasingly part of the debate.[125] While treaties arguably form the most important source for this evolution, general international law and judicial decisions have played a significant role as well. Indeed, as mentioned above, in *Pulp Mills*, the ICJ based some of its findings on customary international law instead of on treaty law.[126]

One of the main general instruments dealing with this topic is the UN Convention on the Law of the Non-Navigational Uses of International Watercourses,[127] which was based on a draft of the ILC and entered into force on 17 August 2014. It is a global framework instrument governing the non-navigational use of international watercourses,[128] and partly codifies relevant customary international law. The Convention does not affect existing watercourse agreements, but allows parties to harmonise such agreements with the principles of the Convention, and to enter into watercourse agreements that apply and adjust the provisions of the Convention to the characteristics and uses of a particular international watercourse.[129] The Convention contains several general principles, such as the principle of equitable and reasonable utilisation. The principle states that international watercourses and the arising benefits thereof are to be used and developed in an optimal and sustainable manner, consistent with adequate protection of the watercourse.[130] Other general principles include the obligation not to cause significant harm, the obligation to cooperate and the regular exchange of data and information.[131] In addition to these principles, the Convention

[123] *Intertanko* (n 116) para 52.

[124] See AS Richey et al, 'Uncertainty in global groundwater storage estimates in a Total Groundwater Stress framework' (2015) 51 *Water Resources Research* 5198; and AS Richey et al, 'Quantifying renewable groundwater stress with GRACE'(2015) 51 *Water Resources Research* 5217.

[125] P Birnie, B Alan and C Redgwell, *International Law and the Environment* (Oxford, OUP, 2009) 535–36. Nevertheless, the subject of freshwater is mainly discussed within the broader framework of other subjects, such as international watercourses or marine pollution.

[126] *Pulp Mills* (n 28).

[127] UN Convention on the Law of the Non-Navigational Uses of International Watercourses (adopted 21 May 1997, entered into force 17 August 2014) 36 ILM 700, adopted as an annex to UNGA Res 51/229, 8 July 1997, A/RES/51/229 (UN Watercourses Convention).

[128] For an elaborate discussion of the content and implications of this Convention, including case studies and commentary, see A Rieu-Clarke, R Moynihan and BO Magsig, *UN Watercourses Convention User's Guide* discovery.dundee.ac.uk/ws/files/1477328/UN_Watercourses_Convention_User_s_Guide.pdf.

[129] Art 3(1)–(3) UN Watercourses Convention.

[130] Art 5 UN Watercourses Convention. In the *Gabčíkovo-Nagymaros Project* case, the ICJ referred explicitly to this provision: *Gabčíkovo-Nagymaros Project* (n 27) 150.

[131] Arts 6–9 UN Watercourses Convention.

contains procedural requirements for cooperation and obligations concerning the protection, conservation and management of the ecosystems of international watercourses for riparian States. Lastly, the Convention regulates measures to prevent or mitigate harmful conditions and emergency situations.

The Water Convention[132] has significant importance in Europe. The Parties to this Convention are to take all appropriate measures to prevent, control and reduce pollution of waters causing or likely to cause transboundary harm. They are to ensure that transboundary waters are used with the aim of ecologically sound and rational water management and the conservation of water resources and environmental protection, and that they are used in a reasonable and equitable way. They are further to ensure conservation and restoration of ecosystems. These measures are, if possible, to be taken at source and not to result in a transfer of pollution to other parts of the environment. Moreover, the Convention provides that the Parties are to be guided by the precautionary principle, the polluter pays principle and the principle of intergenerational equity.[133] The Convention contains specific obligations for riparian Parties.[134] In 2003, the Convention was amended, allowing all UN Member States to accede to it. The amendment entered into force on 6 February 2013, turning the initially regional Convention into a universal legal framework for transboundary water cooperation.[135]

The Draft Articles on the Law of Transboundary Aquifers, adopted by the ILC in 2008, developed the international law on transboundary groundwater resources.[136] The Draft Articles contain several general principles similar to those of the UN Watercourses Convention such as equitable and reasonable utilisation, the obligation not to cause significant harm, the obligation to cooperate and the regular exchange of data and information. They also refer to the precautionary principle. Whether the Draft Articles will lead to a binding Convention remains unclear. The ILC itself proposed a two-step approach, by which the UN General Assembly should, firstly, take note of the articles and, secondly, consider whether they should form the basis for concluding a convention.[137] If such a Convention were to be negotiated on the basis of these Draft Articles, it would be necessary to abolish the overlapping scope with regard to aquifers of the Articles and the UN Watercourses Convention in order to avoid confusion.[138]

B. The Protection of the Atmosphere

The atmosphere is protected by three different layers of international environmental law, viz regimes concerning transboundary air pollution, depletion of the ozone layer and climate change, respectively. Given the global dimension of these problems, these regimes are global in nature.

[132] n 46.
[133] Art 2 of the Water Convention.
[134] These provisions are concerned with cooperation and consultation, joint monitoring and assessment, exchange of information, common research and development, the installation of warning and alarm systems, mutual assistance and public information.
[135] www.unece.org/env/water/.
[136] Beyerlin and Marauhn (n 29) 98.
[137] The UNGA did so in GA Res 63/124. SC McCaffrey, 'The International Law Commission Adopts Draft Articles on Transboundary Aquifers' (2009) 103 *AJIL* 272, at 292–93.
[138] K Mechlem, 'Moving Ahead in Protecting Freshwater Resources: The International Law Commission's Draft Articles on Transboundary Aquifers' (2009) 22 *LJIL* 801, at 821.

i. Transboundary Air Pollution

Transboundary air pollution is one of the oldest cross-border environmental problems.[139] Its causes and harmful consequences are increasingly complex and wide-ranging. That is one of the reasons why the process to conclude the Convention on Long-range Transboundary Air Pollution[140] was so lengthy and tortuous. In the context of this Convention, which is the main regional multilateral treaty in this area, long-range transboundary air pollution is defined as

> air pollution whose physical origin is situated wholly or in part within the area under the national jurisdiction of one State and which has adverse effects in the area under the jurisdiction of another State at such a distance that it is not generally possible to distinguish the contribution of individual emission sources or groups of sources.[141]

The Contracting Parties aimed to limit and gradually reduce and prevent air pollution including long-range transboundary air pollution, both from new and existing sources. The Convention itself does not contain specific targets concerning reduction, but rather serves as a framework within which the Contracting Parties should, by way of exchanges of information, consultation, research and monitoring, develop policies and strategies to combat the discharge of air pollutants. Currently, there exist eight Protocols to the Convention,[142] which taken together considerably expand the initial obligations of the Contracting Parties.

ii. The Depletion of the Ozone Layer

Ozone (O_3) is a gas occurring naturally in small amounts in the upper atmosphere (the stratosphere). It absorbs most of the ultraviolet (UV) radiation from the Sun, thereby protecting life on Earth. However, human activities have had a significant effect on the global concentration and distribution of stratospheric ozone since before the second half of the twentieth century, and large annual decreases in average ozone concentrations began to occur by at least 1980. In particular, increased levels of human-produced gases such as CFCs (chlorofluorocarbons) led to increased rates of ozone destruction.[143]

The Vienna Convention for the Protection of the Ozone Layer[144] contained few concrete obligations, and stressed the need to assess the causes and consequences of ozone depletion and cooperation to exchange information and technology. The lack of strong provisions is the result of an awkward compromise and, as a result, the Convention is often considered a largely empty framework.[145] However, the Montreal Protocol to this Convention[146]

[139] This issue gave rise to a dispute already in the *Trail Smelter Arbitration* (n 8).

[140] Convention on Long-range Transboundary Air Pollution (adopted 13 November 1979, entered into force 16 March 1983) 1302 UNTS 217.

[141] Art 1 of the Convention.

[142] The 1984 Protocol on Long-term Financing of the Cooperative Programme for Monitoring and Evaluation of the Long-range Transmission of Air Pollutants in Europe (EMEP); The 1985 Protocol on the Reduction of Sulphur Emissions or their Transboundary Fluxes by at least 30 per cent; The 1988 Protocol concerning the Control of Nitrogen Oxides or their Transboundary Fluxes; The 1991 Protocol concerning the Control of Emissions of Volatile Organic Compounds or their Transboundary Fluxes; The 1994 Protocol on Further Reduction of Sulphur Emissions; The 1998 Protocol on Heavy Metals and its 2012 amended version; The 1998 Protocol on Persistent Organic Pollutants (POPs) and its 2009 amended version; The 1999 Protocol to Abate Acidification, Eutrophication and Ground-level Ozone and its 2012 amended version.

[143] See ozonewatch.gsfc.nasa.gov/facts/SH.html.

[144] n 36.

[145] Birnie, Alan and Redgwell (n 125) 350.

[146] n 36.

significantly changed the situation by setting concrete targets for the reduction and elimination of ozone-depleting substances. Moreover, the Protocol contains special provisions to meet the specific needs of developing countries and to encourage their participation and compliance, by creating financial and technical incentives, such as the establishment of a multilateral fund. Importantly, the Protocol provides for a formal procedure of non-compliance, which is a system of 'soft enforcement', enabling Sates to fulfil their obligations and providing for possible sanctions. Subsequent amendments have further refined these targets and provisions.

The Montreal Protocol is widely considered to be one of the most important and successful international environmental agreements. Recent studies have found that it has slowed the rate of stratospheric ozone depletion, and there are now signs that the ozone abundance over Antarctica has begun to increase.[147]

iii. Climate Change

As the Intergovernmental Panel on Climate Change (IPCC) has noted in its Fifth Assessment Report, each of the last three decades has been successively warmer at the Earth's surface than any preceding decade since 1850.[148] The period from 1983 to 2012 was probably the warmest 30-year period of the last 1,400 years in the Northern Hemisphere. In short, warming of the climate system is unequivocal, and since the 1950s, many of the observed changes are unprecedented over decades to millennia. The atmosphere and ocean have warmed, the amounts of snow and ice have diminished, and sea level has risen. At the same time, anthropogenic greenhouse gas emissions have increased since the pre-industrial era, driven largely by economic and population growth, and are now higher than ever. This has led to atmospheric concentrations of carbon dioxide, methane and nitrous oxide that are unprecedented in at least the last 800,000 years. Their effects, together with those of other anthropogenic drivers, have been detected throughout the climate system and are extremely likely to have been the dominant cause of the observed warming since the mid-twentieth century.[149]

The UNFCCC forms the cornerstone of the international law regime to combat climate change. Its main objective is 'to achieve, in accordance with the relevant provisions of the Convention, stabilization of greenhouse gas concentrations in the atmosphere at a level that would prevent dangerous anthropogenic interference with the climate system'.[150] In their actions to achieve that objective, the Parties are to be guided by a number of principles, which include equity and common but differentiated responsibilities,[151] sustainable development,[152] and the precautionary principle.[153] Despite being mainly a framework, the UNFCCC contains concrete commitments in Article 4. Some of these obligations are addressed to all Parties, for example those on the creation of inventories of anthropogenic emissions and programmes to mitigate climate change and on cooperation on the

[147] See S Solomon et al, 'Emergence of healing in the Antarctic ozone layer' (2016) 353 *Science* 269; and SE Strahan and AR Douglass, 'Decline in Antarctic ozone depletion and lower stratospheric chlorine determined from Aura Microwave Limb Sounder observations' (2017) *Geophysical Research Letters* 44.

[148] Intergovernmental Panel on Climate Change (IPCC), Fifth Assessment Report – Synthesis Report, 2014, 2.

[149] ibid, 4.

[150] Art 2 UNFCCC.

[151] ibid, Art 3(1). See also Art 4.

[152] ibid, Art 3(3).

[153] ibid, Art 3(4).

adaptation to the impacts of climate change, whereas other obligations focus on developed countries, who are expected to take the lead in achieving these goals.

The UNFCCC provides for the Parties to be able to adopt protocols to the Convention,[154] and on 11 December 1997, the Conference of the Parties (COP) adopted the Kyoto Protocol. The Protocol contains binding quantified emission limitation and reduction commitments,[155] in order to promote sustainable development, and contains a fairly strong compliance regime. Article 18 of the Kyoto Protocol provides for the Conference of the Parties serving as the meeting of the Parties (CMP) at its first session to approve

> appropriate and effective procedures and mechanisms to determine and to address cases of non-compliance with the provisions of this Protocol, including through the development of an indicative list of consequences, taking into account the cause, type, degree and frequency of non-compliance.

At its first session, held in Montreal from 28 November to 10 December 2005, the CMP adopted Decision 27/CMP.1, which provides inter alia for a Compliance Committee.[156] The fact that the compliance mechanism was adopted by the CMP rather than through an amendment to the Kyoto Protocol was the price to pay for convincing the Russian Federation and Japan to join the Kyoto process.[157] At any rate, only with the Kyoto Protocol did industrial countries become subject to concrete and clear objectives and timetables to reduce their emission of greenhouse gases and to create mechanisms to ensure its enforcement. Their main obligation was to reduce greenhouse gas emissions 'by at least 5 per cent below 1990 levels in the commitment period 2008 to 2012'.[158]

A system of emission trading allows a State Party to exceed its emissions by buying credits from another State Party.[159] Furthermore, the system of Joint Implementation, whereby a State Party can earn credits by supporting emission reduction projects in another country, helps the Parties to reach the targets.[160] The first commitment period of the Kyoto Protocol expired in 2012. In 2007, the Bali Road Map was adopted,[161] which aimed to agree upon a post-2012 governance framework and contained the Bali Action Plan, indicating the way forward for future negotiation processes. On that basis, a new Protocol was meant to be adopted at the Copenhagen Summit in 2009, one of the largest environmental conferences in history. That Summit aimed at enhancing the Kyoto Protocol by clarifying legal uncertainty over its future and by encouraging developed States to upgrade their participation and to take on more responsibility. Nevertheless, the Summit was widely considered as having failed to deliver on its numerous and ambitious expectations and as indicating the lack of consensus of the participating States. The most important outcome was the adoption of the Copenhagen Accord. In the Accord, the parties put forward that they stress

[154] ibid, Art 17.
[155] Art 3 Kyoto Protocol.
[156] Decision 27/CMP.1, 'Procedures and mechanisms relating to compliance under the Kyoto Protocol', UN Doc FCCC/KP/CMP/2005/8/Add.3. See eg Conference of the Parties serving as the meeting of the Parties to the Kyoto Protocol, 'Annual report of the Compliance Committee to the Conference of the Parties serving as the meeting of the Parties to the Kyoto Protocol', Tenth session 1–12 December 2014, UN Doc FCCC/KP/CMP/2014/2.
[157] L Massai, 'Is there anybody out there? EU climate diplomacy before and after Copenhagen' in WT Douma and S Van der Velde (eds), *EU Environmental Norms and Third Countries: the EU as a Global Role Model?* (2013) CLEER Working Paper 2013/5, 65.
[158] Art 3(1) Kyoto Protocol.
[159] ibid, Art 17.
[160] ibid, Art 6.
[161] The Bali Road Map was adopted in 2007 at the Bali Climate Change Conference.

the challenge that climate change poses to the world and the political will to mitigate the phenomenon in accordance with the principle of common but differentiated responsibilities and respective capabilities.

Nevertheless, the Copenhagen Conference did not live up to the lofty declarations and great expectations that preceded it. Suffice it to say that the Copenhagen Accord was hashed out in the final hours of COP15 by a high-level group of heads of state and government led inter alia by the USA, and that the COP limited itself to the following laconic statement: '*The Conference of the Parties, Takes note* of the Copenhagen Accord of 18 December 2009'.[162] In other words, the Accord, essentially a register for voluntary commitments, is neither a treaty nor any other type of legally binding instrument, and has been referred to as nothing more than a 'poor political compromise'.[163] On 8 December 2012, the Parties to the Kyoto Protocol adopted the Doha Amendment to the Kyoto Protocol,[164] providing for new commitments setting goals to be achieved in a second commitment period.[165] With this amendment, developed countries committed to reducing their emissions significantly further than the percentage agreed upon in the first commitment period.[166] However, the Doha amendment has not yet entered into force.[167] Nevertheless, Parties may provisionally apply the amendment pending its entry into force in accordance with Articles 20 and 21 of the Kyoto Protocol, and even Parties that do not provisionally apply the amendment will implement their commitments and other responsibilities in relation to the second commitment period, in a manner consistent with their national legislation or domestic processes, as of 1 January 2013 and pending the entry into force of the amendment.[168] This essentially means that the amendment can be de facto applied, even if it never enters into force.[169]

In December 2015, the 21st UN Climate Change Conference was held in Paris. The conference followed on from the Durban Platform, established in 2011 and adopted an agreement with legal force, binding on all UNFCCC Parties. The Paris Agreement includes the target of keeping global warming below 2°C, at best below 1.5°C. States submitted Nationally Determined Contributions (NDCs), including the national climate change commitments. New, more ambitious NDCs are to be submitted every five years. The Agreement entered into force on 4 November 2016 and, in 2018, the Parties will evaluate the collective efforts in relation to progress towards the goal set and to inform the preparation of NDCs. The EU and its Member States committed to at least a 40 per cent domestic reduction in greenhouse gas emissions by 2030 compared to 1990. The EU NDC covers the following sectors: Energy; Industrial processes and product use; Agriculture; Waste; Land Use; Land-Use Change; and Forestry. Whereas the Agreement as

[162] Decision 2/CP.15, 'Copenhagen Accord', UN Doc FCCC/CP/2009/11/Add1.
[163] Beyerlin and Marauhn (n 29) 169–70.
[164] Decision 1/CMP.8 'Amendment to the Kyoto Protocol pursuant to its Article 3, paragraph 9 (the Doha Amendment)', UN Doc FCCC/KP/CMP/2012/13/Add.1.This amendment was adopted at the eighth session of the Conference of the Parties serving as the meeting of the Parties to the Kyoto Protocol held in Doha, in accordance with Arts 20 and 21 of the Kyoto Protocol.
[165] This second commitment period started on 1 January 2013 and expires on 31 December 2020.
[166] Whereas the reduction of emissions was set at 5 per cent in the first commitment period, this level has now been raised to no less than 18 per cent below 1990 levels. However, the parties of the second commitment period are not entirely the same as those of the first.
[167] As of August 2018, 114 countries have ratified the Doha Amendment. In accordance with Art 20, para 4, the amendment will enter into force for those Parties having accepted it on the ninetieth day after the date of receipt by the Depositary of an instrument of acceptance by at least three quarters of the Parties to the Kyoto Protocol.
[168] Decision 1/CMP.8 (n 164) paras 5 and 6.
[169] D Bodansky, J Brunnée, and L Rajamani, *International Climate Change Law* (Oxford, OUP, 2017) 204.

such is binding, it often includes soft language, such as the use of 'should' instead of 'shall' and the enforcement measures are rather lax. Sanctions are not included in the Agreement.

The EU has set itself a goal to lead the way with respect to measures to address climate change. Since the Treaty of Lisbon, that goal has been reflected in the fourth indent of Article 191(1) TFEU, which provides for Union policy on the environment to contribute to promoting measures at international level to deal with 'regional or worldwide environmental problems, and in particular combating climate change'. With this strong mandate, the Union seeks to establish itself as the world leader in climate change abatement technology.[170] The EU is a party to both the UNFCCC and the Kyoto Protocol. In 2003, the EU decided to set up a scheme for greenhouse gas emission allowance trading as a central element of European policy to combat climate change.[171] This was intended as a model for non-EU countries to follow.[172] Indeed, while the Union's attempts to strengthen the multilateral framework to combat climate change through the UNFCCC has had only modest results, its efforts to lead by example have arguably been more successful.[173] Initially, the EU emissions trading scheme (ETS) did not cover greenhouse gas emissions from air transport. The ETS was amended to include aviation, in the face of strong international opposition.[174] From 1 January 2012 all airlines – including those of third countries – had to acquire and surrender emission allowances for their flights that depart from and arrive at European airports.[175]

Airlines and groups representing the airline industry,[176] all of whose headquarters are in the USA, contested the measures transposing Directive 2008/101 in the UK, the administering Member State responsible for them for the purposes of the ETS. They contended

[170] H Vedder, 'Diplomacy by Directive? An Analysis of the International Context of the Emissions Trading Scheme Directive' in M Evans and P Koutrakos (eds), *Beyond the Established Legal Orders: Policy Interconnections between the EU and the Rest of the World* (Oxford, Hart, 2011) 105–106. See further J Scott, 'The Multi-Level Governance of Climate Change' in P Craig and G de Búrca (eds), *The Evolution of EU Law*, 2nd edn (Oxford, OUP, 2011) 805–35, as well as K Kulovesi, 'Climate change in EU external relations: please follow my example (or I might force you)' in Morgera (n 84) 116, and Van Calster and Reins (n 30) 253–263.

[171] Directive 2003/87/EC establishing a scheme for greenhouse gas emission allowance trading within the Community and amending Council Directive 96/61/EC [2003] OJ L275/32.

[172] See recital 17 in the preamble to Directive 2008/101/EC amending Directive 2003/87/EC so as to include aviation activities in the scheme for greenhouse gas emission allowance trading within the Community [2009] OJ L8/3. cf K Inglis, 'EU environmental law and its green footprints in the world' in A Dashwood and M Maresceau (eds), *Law and Practice of EU External Relations. Salient Features of a Changing Landscape* (Cambridge, CUP, 2008) 453–54.

[173] Kulovesi (n 170) 115.

[174] See Council of the International Civil Aviation Organization (ICAO), Declaration, Second Meeting of the 194th Session, 2 November 2011, C-DEC 194/2, which opposes 'the EU's plan to include all flights by non-EU carriers to/from an airport in the territory of an EU Member State in its emissions trading system (EU Directive 2008/101/EC), which is inconsistent with applicable international law'(para 5) and urges the EU and its Member States 'to refrain from including flights by non-EU carriers to/from an airport in the territory of an EU Member State in its emissions trading system' and 'to work collaboratively with the rest of the international community to address aviation emissions' (paras 6–7).

[175] See for the list of operators (including foreign operators) covered by the Directive: Commission Regulation (EU) No 100/2012 amending Regulation (EC) No 748/2009 on the list of aircraft operators that performed an aviation activity listed in Annex I to Directive 2003/87/EC of the European Parliament and of the Council on or after 1 January 2006 specifying the administering Member State for each aircraft operator also taking into consideration the expansion of the Union emission trading scheme to EEA-EFTA countries [2010] OJ L39/1.

[176] Air Transport Association of America (ATA), which has been renamed 'Airlines for America (A4A)', is a non-profit trade and service association of airlines in the USA. AA, Continental and UAL are airlines whose headquarters are in the USA and which operate worldwide, also serving destinations within the EU.

that, in adopting the directive, the EU infringed a number of principles of customary international law and various international agreements: the Chicago Convention,[177] the Kyoto Protocol,[178] and the Open Skies Agreement.[179] They argued that the ETS imposed a form of tax on fuel consumption. Second, they argued that it breached certain principles of customary international law in that it sought to apply the allowance trading scheme beyond the EU's territorial jurisdiction. The High Court of Justice of England and Wales, Queen's Bench Division (Administrative Court) asked the ECJ whether the directive was valid in the light of those rules of international law. That gave the Court the opportunity to deliver a densely reasoned judgment that is, while upholding the validity of Directive 2008/101, of crucial importance for the EU's climate change policy and its relationship to international law.[180]

The EU's decision to 'go it alone' in this regard must be understood against the background of its frustration with the lethargic pace at which international negotiations on the reduction of emissions from international aviation proceed. It inevitably raises questions on the effect of the applicable international norms in the EU legal order and on the international legality of the EU's action.[181] On 12 November 2012, the EU announced that it would not require allowances to be surrendered for emissions from international flights during 2012 in order to create space for political negotiations within the International Civil Aviation Organization (ICAO) regarding a global solution to address emissions from aviation.[182] That 'stopping of the clocks' was further extended for the period 2013–2016, so that only emissions from flights within the EEA fall under the EU ETS.[183] In light of a resolution agreed by the ICAO in October 2016, the European Commission proposed to continue this approach beyond 2016. Indeed, the ICAO decided on a Global Marked-based Measure (MBM) scheme, in order to reduce CO_2 emissions on a global scale.[184] 72 States, representing 87.7 per cent of international aviation activity, intend to voluntarily participate in this global scheme. All EU Member States will participate from the start.[185]

[177] Convention on International Civil Aviation (adopted 7 December 1944, entered into force 4 April 1947) 61 Stat 1180; 15 UNTS 295.

[178] See n 19.

[179] Air Transport Agreement between the United States of America, of the one part, and the European Community and its Member States, of the other part (adopted 25 and 30 April 2007, provisionally applied from 21 June 2011) [2007] OJ L134/4.

[180] *Air Transport Association of America and Others* (n 120). See further, G De Baere and C Ryngaert, 'The ECJ's Judgment in Air Transport Association of America and the International Legal Context of the EU's Climate Change Policy' (2013) 18(3) *European Foreign Affairs Review* 389. On the relationship between EU law and general international law, see Chapter 4.

[181] Kulovesi (n 170) 144.

[182] EC, MEMO/12/854, 12 November 2012 ('Stopping the clock of ETS and aviation emissions following last week's International Civil Aviation Organisation (ICAO) Council'); see also ICAO, COM 20/12, 15 November 2012. The 'stopping of the clocks' was confirmed by Decision No 377/2013/EU derogating temporarily from Directive 2003/87/EC establishing a scheme for greenhouse gas emission allowance trading within the Community Text with EEA relevance [2013] OJ L113/1.

[183] Regulation (EU) No 421/2014 of the European Parliament and of the Council of 16 April 2014 amending Directive 2003/87/EC establishing a scheme for greenhouse gas emission allowance trading within the Community, in view of the implementation by 2020 of an international agreement applying a single global market-based measure to international aviation emissions Text with EEA relevance [2014] OJ L129/1.

[184] International Civil Aviation Organization, Resolution A39-3: Consolidated statement of continuing ICAO policies and practices related to environmental protection – Global Market-based Measure (MBM) scheme, 6 October 2016.

[185] see also Chapter 9.V.B.

C. Hazardous Substances and Activities

i. Nuclear Energy

Given the immense risks associated with nuclear energy and its clear transboundary dimension, it should not come as a surprise that this issue is well regulated internationally. Initially, international regulation was mainly concerned with liability and compensation in case of nuclear disasters, and safeguarding the commercial exploitation of nuclear energy was the main concern. In this regard, the Paris Convention on Third Party Liability in the Field of Nuclear Energy[186] aims to harmonise legislation to ensure both the goals of compensation for victims and the exploitation of nuclear energy. It does so through a system whereby liability is tiered and financially limited on each level: the operator of the nuclear installation is held liable first, followed by the State in which the installation is located and, in the final instance, all State Parties. By adding a Protocol in 1988, the Convention was connected to the global Vienna Convention on Civil Liability for Nuclear Damage.[187]

Since the former Soviet Union was not a Contracting Party, the Paris Convention did not apply to the Chernobyl disaster. Nevertheless, the incident showed the enormous risks nuclear power creates for all States, including radioactive contamination and the spread of hazardous substances. In addition to bringing these dangers and their transboundary dimension to the fore, the incident exposed important gaps in international regulation, which led to the adoption (under the auspices of the IAEA) of new Conventions intensifying nuclear safety.[188] The Fukushima Daiichi accident, although leading to the release of fewer radioactive substances, was a multi-unit accident and showed the need for the international community, acting within the existing regulatory framework, to enhance diligence and commitment to the existing principles on this issue.[189]

ii. Chemicals

In 1998 the Rotterdam Convention was adopted,[190] which concerns the issue of toxic chemicals. The Convention's objectives are, amongst others, the promotion of shared responsibility and cooperation among the Parties in the area of international trade of

[186] The Convention was amended by the Additional Protocol to the Convention to the Convention on Third Party Liability in the Field of Nuclear Energy (adopted 28 January 1964, entered into force 1 April 1968) 956 UNTS 335.

[187] Vienna Convention on Civil Liability for Nuclear Damage (adopted 21 May 1963, entered into force 12 November 1977) 1063 UNTS 265, adopted under the auspices of IAEA. See further also the Convention relating to Civil Liability in the Field of Maritime Carriage of Nuclear Material (adopted 17 December 1971, entered into force 15 July 1975) 974 UNTS 255.

[188] The Convention on Early Notification of a Nuclear Accident (adopted 26 September 1986, entered into force 27 October 1986) 1439 UNTS 275 and the Convention on Assistance in the Case of a Nuclear Accident or Radiological Emergency (adopted 26 September 1986, entered into force 26 February 1987) 1457 UNTS 133. See also the Convention on Nuclear Safety (adopted 20 September 1964, entered into force 24 October 1966) 1963 UNTS 293, concerned with the safety of nuclear power plants.

[189] SG Burns, 'The Fukushima Daiichi Accident: The International Community Responds' (2012) *Washington University Global Studies Law Review* 739.

[190] Rotterdam Convention on the Prior Informed Consent Procedure for Certain Hazardous Chemicals and Pesticides in International Trade (adopted 10 September 1998, entered into force 24 February 2004) 2244 UNTS 337. The Rotterdam Convention was signed by the then European Community on 11 September 1998 and approved by Council Decision 2003/106/EC [2003] OJ L63/27. The further implementation of the Convention in EU law gave rise to litigation before the ECJ with respect to the appropriate legal basis: see Judgments of 10 January 2006, *Commission v Council*, C-94/03, EU:C:2006:2; and *Commission v Parliament and Council*, C-178/03, EU:C:2006:4.

certain hazardous chemicals in order to protect human health and the environment. Parties are obliged to contribute to the environmentally sound use of these chemicals through an exchange of information on the characteristics of the chemicals, as well as by establishing a national decision-making process on their import and export.[191]

To achieve these objectives, the Convention contains two essential mechanisms. First, the Prior Informed Consent (PIC) Procedure requires all Parties to decide whether they allow the import of the chemicals enlisted in Annex III of the Convention, which should be respected by exporting Parties. Second, the Information Exchange mechanism provides for information exchange between the Parties for numerous potentially toxic chemicals. When banning or severely restricting a certain chemical, the Parties are to notify the Secretariat.

In addition, the Stockholm Convention[192] is a multilateral agreement the objective of which is, in accordance with its Article 1, to protect human health and the environment from Persistent Organic Pollutants (POPs), '[m]indful of the precautionary approach as set forth in Principle 15 of the Rio Declaration on Environment and Development'. The first recital in the preamble to the Convention specifies that POPs, for example DDT (Dichloro-diphenyl-trichloroethane), which was used as an agricultural and household pesticide, possess toxic properties, resist degradation, bioaccumulate[193] and are transported, through air, water and migratory species, across international boundaries and deposited far from their place of release, where they accumulate in terrestrial and aquatic ecosystems. Both the Union[194] and all EU Member States[195] are parties to the Convention.[196] It requires

[191] Art 1 Rotterdam Convention.

[192] Stockholm Convention on Persistent Organic Pollutants (adopted 22 May 2001, entered into force 17 May 2004) 2256 UNTS 119; 40 ILM 532 (2001). The Stockholm Convention entered into force, in accordance with its Art 26(1), on 17 May 2004. See, in general, JA Mintz, 'Two Cheers For Global POPs: A Summary and Assessment of the Stockholm Convention on Persistent Organic Pollutants' (2001) 14 *Georgetown International Environmental Law Review* 319; AJ Yoder, 'Lessons from Stockholm: Evaluating the Global Convention on Persistent Organic Pollutants' (2003) 10 *Indiana Journal of Global Legal Studies* 113.

[193] A pollutant bioaccumulates when it reaches a concentration within an organism that is higher than found in the environment: MK Hill, *Understanding Environmental Pollution*, 3rd edn (Cambridge, CUP, 2010) 67.

[194] Council Decision 2006/507/EC concerning the conclusion, on behalf of the European Community, of the Stockholm Convention on Persistent Organic Pollutants [2006] OJ L209/1. Art 2(a) of the Convention defines a 'party' as 'a State or regional economic integration organization that has consented to be bound by this Convention and for which the Convention is in force'. Art 2(b) defines a 'Regional economic integration organization' as 'an organization constituted by sovereign States of a given region to which its member States have transferred competence in respect of matters governed by this Convention and which has been duly authorized, in accordance with its internal procedures, to sign, ratify, accept, approve or accede to this Convention'. See B de Witte, 'The Emergence of a European System of Public International Law: the EU and its Member States as Strange Subjects' in J Wouters, A Nollkaemper, E de Wet (eds), *The Europeanisation of International Law. The Status of International Law in the EU and its Member States* (The Hague, TMC Asser Press, 2008) 39, 40, noting that many multilateral treaty provisions 'use the terms "international organisation" or "regional international economic organisation" where it is clear from the context that the (only) organisation that is intended by that term is the European Community'. Further on 'regional economic integration organization' (REIO) and 'regional integration organization' (RIO) clauses: G De Baere, 'EU Status in Other International Organizations' in R Schütze and T Tridimas (eds), *Oxford Principles of European Union Law*, Vol 1: The European Union Legal Order (Oxford, OUP, 2018) 1241.

[195] See judgment of 20 April 2010, *Commission v Sweden ('PFOS')*, C-246/07, EU:C:2010:203, para 19.

[196] Under EU law, this means the Convention is a so-called 'mixed agreement'. See further: J Heliskoski, *Mixed Agreements as a Technique for Organizing the International Relations of the European Community and Its Member States* (The Hague/London/New York: Kluwer, 2001); C Hillion and P Koutrakos, *Mixed Agreements Revisited: The EU and Its Member States in the World* (Oxford, Hart, 2010); G De Baere, 'EU External Action' in C Barnard and S Peers (eds), *European Union Law*, 2nd edn (Oxford, Oxford University Press, 2017) 746–748. In Opinion 2/15 (n 97) para 29, the CJEU defined a mixed agreement simply as an agreement that has to be 'signed and concluded both by the European Union and by each of its Member States'.

parties to eliminate or restrict the production, use, import and export of POPs listed in its annexes.[197] Any Party to the Convention may submit a proposal to the Secretariat that a substance be considered a POP and added to the annexes to the Convention.[198]

POPs are also regulated by the Protocol to the 1979 UNECE Convention on Long-range Transboundary Air Pollution on Persistent Organic Pollutants (the Aarhus Protocol or the Protocol),[199] which seeks to control, reduce or eliminate discharges, emissions and losses of POPs.[200] The Aarhus Protocol was to be open for signature by States that are members of the UNECE, States having consultative status with that Commission and regional economic integration organisations constituted by sovereign States members of that Commission.[201] As with the Stockholm Convention, any Party may propose amendments to the Annexes of the protocol.[202] The Union[203] is a party to the Protocol, though not all EU Member States are.[204]

The cross-border negative effects of POPs have also led to their regulation at the Union level, most notably by Regulation No 850/2004 (the POPs regulation).[205] The Stockholm Convention gave rise to litigation within the EU, when the European Commission brought infringement proceedings against Sweden for having unilaterally proposed that perfluorooctane sulfonate (PFOS) be added to Annex A to the Stockholm Convention.[206] Under Article 193 TFEU, a Member State is free to adopt measures providing for a higher level of protection within its own jurisdiction. However, proposing such measures within the framework of an international agreement to which the Union is a party, which would imply that the Union may be bound by a more stringent measure with which it did not express its agreement, does not fall within the scope of Article 193 TFEU.[207] In exercising its own competence, the principle of sincere cooperation (now Article 4(3) TEU) required Sweden to take into account the fact that the Union too is competent in the matter and that a strategy had been agreed within the Council.

Furthermore, the potentially adverse environmental effects of the presence of mercury, a shiny, silver-white metal that is a liquid at room temperature and is or was traditionally used in thermometers, have been well documented.[208] In 2010 the UNEP Governing Council set up an intergovernmental negotiating committee with the plan to establish a binding instrument on mercury by 2013.[209] By Decision 25/5 III, the UNEP Governing Council requested the Executive Director to convene an intergovernmental negotiating committee (INC) with the mandate to prepare a global legally binding instrument on mercury, with

[197] Art 3 of the Convention.
[198] Art 8(1) of the Convention.
[199] Protocol to the 1979 United Nations' Convention on Long-range Transboundary Air Pollution (adopted 24 June 1998, entered into force 23 October 2003) TIAS 10541; 1302 UNTS 217; 18 ILM 1442 (1979).
[200] Art 2 of the Aarhus Protocol.
[201] Art 15(1) of the Aarhus Protocol.
[202] Art 14(1)–(3) of the Aarhus Protocol.
[203] Council Decision 2004/259/EC concerning the conclusion, on behalf of the Community, of the Protocol to the 1979 Convention on Long Range Transboundary Air Pollution on Persistent Organic Pollutants [2004] OJ L81/35.
[204] *PFOS* (n 195).
[205] Regulation (EC) No 850/2004 on persistent organic pollutants and amending Directive 79/117/EEC [2004] OJ L158/7, and corrigendum [2004] OJ L229/5.
[206] *PFOS* (n 195). See further, G De Baere, '"O, Where is Faith? O, Where is Loyalty?" Some Thoughts on the Duty of Loyal Co-operation and the Union's External Environmental Competences in the Light of the PFOS Case' (2011) 36 *ELR* 405.
[207] *PFOS* (n 195) para 102.
[208] UNEP, Global Mercury Assessment, December 2002, 40.
[209] Decision 25/5: Chemicals management, including mercury, UN Doc UNEP/GC25/17, 26.

the goal of completing its work by 2013.[210] Further to Decision 25/5, the Commission on 15 July 2009 submitted a recommendation to the Council of the EU on the participation of the then European Community in the negotiations.[211] After a very public falling out between the European Commission and the Council of the EU on how the negotiations were to be conducted,[212] a compromise was finally reached in late 2010.[213] Despite that, all Member States in substance agree that mercury should be phased out. The mercury negotiations should therefore have been relatively easy from a technical point of view.

The international mercury negotiations culminated in January 2013 in the adoption of the text of a global legally binding instrument on mercury called the 'Minamata Convention on Mercury'.[214] The Convention, which entered into force on 16 August 2017,[215] arguably constitutes an important step in the search for an integrated approach to the regulation of chemicals in general, and mercury in particular. The Convention has a global scope, and aims to encompass the entire life cycle of mercury, from mining, use and release, trade and storage, to disposal. It relies on successful techniques developed in other conventions, and notably includes an important institutional and compliance component.[216]

D. Environmental Governance and Protection of Animal Species

The first international environmental treaties mainly dealt with the issue of environmental governance and the protection of animal species. These issues are the focus of numerous bilateral, regional and multilateral treaties. In what follows, the most important treaties in this regard will be discussed, which are referred to as 'the big five conventions', as well as one example of a convention with respect to the protection of a specific species.

i. The Ramsar Convention

The mission of the Convention on Wetlands of International Importance, especially as Waterfowl Habitat (Ramsar Convention)[217] is:

> the conservation and wise use of all wetlands through local and national actions and international cooperation, as a contribution towards achieving sustainable development throughout the world.[218]

The objectives and concepts of the Convention were further refined and broadened over time. In particular, 'wise use' is considered to mean 'sustainable use' and the concept of

[210] ibid.

[211] Recommendation from the Commission to the Council on the participation of the European Community in negotiations on a legally binding instrument on mercury further to Decision 25/5 of the Governing Council of the UNEP, SEC(2009) 983 final.

[212] Further G De Baere, '*Mercury Rising*: The European Union and the International Negotiations for a Globally Binding Instrument on Mercury' (2012) 37 *ELR* 640.

[213] Art 1 Council Decision on the participation of the Union in negotiations on a legally binding instrument on mercury further to Decision 25/5 of the Governing Council of the UNEP, Council Doc 16632/10.

[214] See Annex to the report of the intergovernmental negotiating committee to prepare a global legally binding instrument on mercury on the work of its fifth session, UN Doc UNEP(DTIE)/Hg/INC.5/7 (Draft Minamata Convention on Mercury).

[215] As of August 2018, there were 128 signatories and 95 parties to the Convention.

[216] Dupuy and Viñuales (n 3) 229–32.

[217] Convention on Wetlands of International Importance especially as Waterfowl Habitat (adopted 2 February 1971, entered into force 21 December 1975) 996 UNTS 245, which currently has 170 Contracting Parties.

[218] www.ramsar.org/about/the-ramsar-convention-and-its-mission.

'wetland' also includes fish and birds species and their habitat. The limited provisions were further supplemented by decisions of the Conference of the Contracting Parties (COP), which meets every three years, most recently in Punta del Este, Uruguay, on 1–9 June 2015 (COP12).[219] The Convention protects wetland sites by putting them onto a list. These sites should be protected by national policies and can be added to the Wetlands of International Importance List.[220] To ensure that a lack of financial means would not cause insufficient protection of wetlands, the Small Grants Fund for Wetland Conservation and Wise Use was established. The Ramsar Advisory Mission provides technical support to the Contracting Parties.

ii. The World Heritage Convention

The World Heritage Convention,[221] adopted under the auspices of UNESCO, aims at 'ensuring the identification, protection, conservation, presentation and transmission to future generations of the cultural and natural heritage'.[222] Cultural and natural heritage is protected by putting properties considered as having outstanding universal value in terms of certain criteria on a World Heritage List.[223] It is, therefore, a hybrid convention, in the sense that it protects both cultural monuments and elements of the natural environment.[224] This happens on the basis of inventories drafted by the Contracting Parties, which have the exclusive competence to identify these properties in their territory.[225] In doing so, the Convention embodies the inherent tension between the interest of the international community in seeing certain sites protected as 'world heritage' on the one hand, and the fact that such sites are located with the territory of one or more States.[226] Two Advisory Bodies[227] guarantee the evaluation of the identified properties in the light of the criteria. These Criteria for Selection are explained in the Operational Guidelines for the Implementation of the World Heritage Convention, which are regularly revised by the World Heritage Committee to reflect evolutions in the concept of World Heritage itself. Currently, the World Heritage List consists of no less than 1092 properties, of which 845 are cultural, 209 natural and 38 mixed.[228] The Convention also provides for the first treaty-specific environmental fund, the World Heritage Fund, created under Article 15 of the Convention, and compulsory

[219] COP13 will be held in October 2018 in Dubai, United Arab Emirates.

[220] As of August 2018, the so-called Ramsar List counts 2323 sites.

[221] Convention Concerning the Protection of the World Cultural and Natural Heritage (adopted 16 November 1972, entered into force 17 December 1975) 1037 UNTS 151, which currently has 193 Contracting Parties. Participation of developing States is supported by the World Heritage Fund, financed by compulsory and voluntary contributions of the Contracting Parties.

[222] ibid, Art 4.

[223] ibid, Art 11.

[224] Dupuy and Viñuales (n 3) 178.

[225] ibid, Arts 2 and 11. Consequently, UNESCO itself has no competence to identify such properties of its own motion.

[226] Dupuy and Viñuales (n 3) 178. See, for example, the Preah Vihear temple, which gave rise to litigation before the ICJ between Cambodia and Thailand: *Case concerning the Temple of Preah Vihear (Cambodia v Thailand)* [1962] 6; and *Request for Interpretation of the Judgment of 15 June 1962 in the Case concerning the Temple of Preah Vihear* (Cambodia v Thailand) [2013] ICJ Rep 281.

[227] The International Council on Monuments and Sites for cultural heritage and the World Conservation Union (IUCN) for natural heritage, respectively.

[228] Further on the World Heritage Convention's strengths in nature conservation: EJ Goodwin, 'The World Heritage Convention, the environment, and compliance' (2009) 20(2) *Colorado Journal of International Environmental Law and Policy* 157.

and voluntary contributions by States, as well as donations from other entities. The funds are allocated primarily to activities involving capacity-building of States Parties and other forms of technical assistance.[229]

iii. CITES

The Convention on International Trade in Endangered Species of Wild Fauna and Flora (CITES)[230] restricts or prohibits international trade in specimens of wild animals and plants so that their survival is not threatened. Currently, 35,000 species of animals and plants fall under its protection. The import and export of endangered species is internationally controlled by way of a permit system, managed by national authorities.

Appendix I includes all species threatened with extinction which are or may be affected by trade. Trade in such specimens is subject to particularly strict regulation and only authorised in exceptional circumstances.[231] Appendix II includes species that, although not necessarily now threatened with extinction, may become so unless trade in specimens of such species is subject to strict regulation in order to avoid utilisation incompatible with their survival; and other species which must be subject to regulation in order that trade in specimens of certain species just referred to may be brought under effective control. This category is governed by a system of export permits and re-export certificates.[232] Appendix III includes all species that any Party identifies as being subject to regulation within its jurisdiction for the purpose of preventing or restricting exploitation, and as needing the co-operation of other Parties in the control of trade. For this last category, an export permit is required.[233] A list modification system allows for the list to be updated to reflect an evolved understanding or evolving circumstances.[234]

The State Parties are to appoint at least one management authority, responsible for granting permits and certificates, and one scientific authority.[235] The Secretariat examines the implementation of the Convention and exchanges information.[236] Implementation is reviewed by the Conference of the Parties to which the Secretariat sends reports. Where a violation occurs, trade with the violating Party is suspended.[237] While CITES is not designed to address important threats to the preservation of species posed by factors such as the destruction or deterioration of habitats, it counts as an effective multilateral instrument for the protection of species, as is illustrated for example by the improved circumstances of the African elephant and the sturgeon.[238]

On 30 April 1983, at the second extraordinary meeting of the Conference of the Parties (Gaborone, Botswana), Article XXI of CITES was amended to make the Convention open to accession by organisations of regional economic integration composed of sovereign States, such as the then European Community. In accordance with Article XVII, paragraph 3, of CITES, the Gaborone amendment entered into force on 29 November 2013, 60 days

[229] See Dupuy and Viñuales (n 3) 274–75.

[230] Convention on International Trade in Endangered Species of Wild Fauna and Flora (adopted 3 March 1973, entered into force 1 July 1975) 993 UNTS 243 (CITES Convention). It currently has 183 Parties.

[231] ibid, Arts II and III.

[232] ibid, Arts II and IV.

[233] ibid, Arts II and V.

[234] ibid, Arts XV and XVI. See Dupuy and Viñuales (n 3) 167–68.

[235] ibid, Art IX.

[236] ibid, Art XII.

[237] ibid, Art VIII.

[238] See Dupuy and Viñuales (n 3) 171–72.

after 54 (two-thirds) of the 80 States that were party to CITES on 30 April 1983 deposited their instrument of acceptance of the amendment. At that time, it entered into force only for those States that had accepted the amendment. The amended text of the Convention will apply automatically to any State that becomes a Party after 29 November 2013. For States that became party to the Convention before that date and have not accepted the amendment, it will enter into force 60 days after they accept it.[239] The Commission submitted a proposal for a Council decision on the accession to CITES in December 2013.[240] The European Parliament consented to the accession on 16 December 2014,[241] and on 6 March 2015, the Council approved the Union's accession to CITES.[242] On 9 April 2015, the European Union acceded to CITES, which entered into force for the Union on 8 July 2015.

iv. The Bonn Convention

The Bonn Convention[243] aims at the conservation of migratory species and their habitat. To reach this objective, the Convention mainly provides for two mechanisms. First, with regard to endangered migratory species, which are listed in Appendix I, the Contracting Parties are obliged to conserve and restore their habitat and remove obstacles impeding or preventing their migration. The taking of animals belonging to such species is to be prohibited by national legislation.[244] Second, Appendix II lists

> migratory species which have an unfavourable conservation status and which require international agreements for their conservation and management, as well as those which have a conservation status which would significantly benefit from the international cooperation that could be achieved by an international agreement.[245]

With regard to these species, Contracting Parties should conclude agreements for their benefit and prioritisation. Species may be included in more than one list.

v. The Convention on Biological Diversity

To fill the remaining gaps in international environmental law caused by the lack of an overarching instrument linking species and their habitat to ecosystems, the Convention on Biological Diversity[246] was adopted at the Rio Conference on 5 June 1992 at the initiative of UNEP. The objectives of this Convention are to conserve biological diversity, to use its components in a sustainable manner, and the fair and equitable sharing of the benefits arising out of the utilisation of genetic resources. This includes appropriate access to genetic

[239] See www.cites.org/eng/disc/gaborone.php.

[240] Proposal for a Council Decision on the Accession of the European Union to the Convention on International Trade in Endangered Species of Wild Fauna and Flora (CITES), COM(2013) 867 final. The proposal is based on Arts 192, 207, and 218(6)(a) TFEU.

[241] EP, 'Legislative resolution on the draft Council decision concerning the accession of the European Union to the Convention on International Trade in Endangered Species of Wild Fauna and Flora (CITES)', 16 December 2014, P8_TA-PROV(2014)0075.

[242] Council Decision (EU) 2015/451 concerning the accession of the European Union to the Convention on International Trade in Endangered Species of Wild Fauna and Flora (CITES) [2015] OJL75/1.

[243] n 35. There are currently 126 Contracting Parties.

[244] ibid, Art III.

[245] ibid, Art IV.

[246] See n 14. It currently has 196 Contracting Parties, which gives the Convention a quasi-universal reach.

resources and technology transfer.[247] The main responsibility for implementation lies with the Contracting Parties, which should develop national strategies, whereby their particular conditions and capabilities are taken into account. Implementation is further controlled by the Conference of the Parties. Given that already existing treaties contained concrete obligations regarding specific species and their habitat, this Convention does not identify specific goals or lists of species and habitats falling under its protection. Nevertheless, additional obligations aim to enhance cooperation.

Amongst the Contracting Parties are a remarkable number of developing States. Their participation was essential for the effectiveness of the Convention, since the most biologically rich areas of the planet are mainly situated in these countries. Their participation was made possible by providing funds and differentiating between Parties' obligations depending on their respective capacities. The Convention further creates a framework for the adoption of national legislation facilitating the access to genetic resources and the sharing of benefits arising from their commercial utilisation.

The Cartagena Protocol on Biosafety,[248] which supplements the Convention on Biological Diversity, was adopted in 2000. The Protocol explicitly mentions the precautionary principle and refers to Principle 15 of the Rio Declaration. It seeks to protect biological diversity from the risks associated with modern biotechnology, taking into account risks to human health, focusing particularly on transboundary movements.[249] An essential aspect is the advance informed agreement procedure, which ensures that Contracting Parties receive necessary information to make an informed decision before consenting to the import of living modified organisms (LMOs).

The Nagoya Protocol,[250] another supplement to the Convention on Biodiversity, was adopted in 2010. The Protocol aims to contribute to the conservation of biological diversity and to sharing the benefits arising from the utilisation of genetic resources in a fair and equitable manner.[251] Contracting Parties should develop national policies to achieve the Protocol's objectives, and are further encouraged to consider the need for a global multilateral benefit-sharing mechanism and to strive for transboundary cooperation. In the context of this Protocol, the Access and Benefit-sharing Clearing-House (ABS-CH) was established, which is a platform for exchanging information on access and benefit-sharing and a key tool for facilitating the Protocol's implementation.[252]

vi. Protection of a Specific Species: The Example of the Whaling Convention

In addition to these general legal regimes, there are also treaty regimes aimed at protecting and preserving particular species. An example of this is the International Convention for

[247] ibid, Art 1.

[248] Cartagena Protocol on Biosafety to the Convention on Biological Diversity (adopted 29 January 2000, entered into force 11 September 2003) 2226 UNTS 208. At the level of the EU, the Cartagena Protocol was the subject of Opinion 2/00 (Cartagena Protocol on Biosafety) of 6 December 2001, EU:C:2001:664, in which the CJEU determined that substantive international environmental agreements concluded by the Union had to be based on what was then Article 175 TEC and now Article 192 TFEU.

[249] ibid, Art 1.

[250] Nagoya Protocol on Access to Genetic Resources and the Fair and Equitable Sharing of Benefits Arising from their Utilization to the Convention on Biological Diversity (adopted 29 October 2010, entered into force 12 October 2014).

[251] ibid, Art 1.

[252] absch.cbd.int/.

the Regulation of Whaling (the Whaling Convention or the ICRW),[253] which was adopted in 1946.[254] The ICRW does not contain substantive provisions regulating the conservation of whale stocks or the management of the whaling industry. Instead, these are contained in the Schedule, which 'forms an integral part' of the Convention,[255] which explains which species may or may not be hunted, establishes sanctuaries, and sets forth periods during which whaling is in principle prohibited. The Schedule is subject to amendments, to be adopted by the International Whaling Commission (IWC). Established under Article III, paragraph 1 ICRW, the IWC has a significant role in the regulation of whaling through its competence for the conservation and management of whale stocks. It is composed of one member from each Contracting Government.

Membership of the IWC is only open to governments that adhere to the Whaling Convention. In other words, an amendment to the Whaling Convention allowing the EU to become a member would require the ratification of a protocol by all IWC members. The European Commission adopted a proposal in 1992 to negotiate the accession of the then Community to the Whaling Convention,[256] but the Council of the EU has not followed up on this proposal.[257] The EU is therefore not a party, but merely an observer to the Whaling Convention.[258]

The adoption by the IWC of amendments to the Schedule requires a three-fourths majority of votes cast.[259] An amendment becomes binding on a State Party unless it presents an

[253] International Convention for the Regulation of Whaling (adopted 2 December 1946, entered into force 10 November 1948) 62 Stat 1716; 161 UNTS 72.

[254] See also the earlier Geneva Convention for Regulation of Whaling (adopted 24 September 1931, entered into force 16 January 1935) 155 LNTS 349; and, the Agreement for the Regulation of Whaling (adopted 8 June 1937, entered into force 7 May 1938) 190 LNTS 79.

[255] Art I, para 1 ICRW.

[256] Draft Council Decision authorizing the Commission to negotiate, on behalf of the Community, a protocol amending the international Convention on the regulation of whaling, 2 December 1946, COM(92) 316.

[257] See Proposal for a Council decision establishing the position to be adopted on behalf of the European Community with regard to proposals for amendments to the International Convention on the Regulation of Whaling and its Schedule, 6 November 2008, COM(2008) 711 final, Point 6 of the Explanatory Memorandum.

[258] However, in the context of the current talks about the reform of the IWC the Commission proposes to support proposals for revision of the Convention, including the possibility for the EU to become a party to the IWC: Proposal for a Council Decision establishing the position to be adopted on behalf of the European Union at the next five meetings of the International Whaling Commission including the related inter-sessional meetings with regard to proposals for amendments to the International Convention on the Regulation of Whaling and its Schedule, 25 August 2011, COM(2011) 495 final. In a more recent proposal, the Commission noted that although 'it seems unlikely that the efforts by the current Japanese Chair of the IWC to initiate discussions on "The IWC in the Future" will lead to calls for treaty amendments, the EU and its Member States should take advantage of any opportunities that arise which would advance the cause of EU membership', and that in the absence of EU membership 'it becomes even more important that Member States use their collective weight to the full to defend EU positions in the IWC, in accordance with the principle of sincere cooperation reflected in Article 4(3) [TEU] and the principle of the unity in the external representation of the EU', adding that a united EU position is also essential as it is a prerequisite for achieving consensus or unanimity within the IWC, which is especially important in light of the finding of the ICJ in *Whaling in the Antarctic (Australia v. Japan: New Zealand Intervening)* (Judgment) [2014] ICJ Rep 226, para 46 that IWC Resolutions may be relevant for the interpretation of the Convention or its Schedule if they are adopted by consensus or unanimous vote: Proposal for a Council Decision on the position to be adopted, on behalf of the European Union, at the next three meetings of the International Whaling Commission including related inter-sessional meetings and actions (COM(2017) 463 final) 8 para 3.3. EU regulatory activity as regards matters pertaining to whaling does not come under the exclusive common fisheries policy (Art 3(1)(d) TFEU), but under the shared competence on the environment (Art 4(2)(e) TFEU). Annex I to the TFEU lists the products coming under Art. 38 TFEU on the common agriculture and fisheries policy. Chapter 3 mentions 'Fish, crustaceans and molluscs', but not marine mammals. The latter are only mentioned in Chapter 15.04: 'Fats and oil, of fish and marine mammals, whether or not refined'. At any rate, EU action on whaling has, as a rule, been taken under environmental competence.

[259] Art III, para 2 ICRW.

objection, in which case the amendment does not become effective in respect of that State until the objection is withdrawn. The IWC has amended the Schedule many times. As the ICJ noted in *Whaling in the Antarctic*, the functions conferred on the IWC 'have made the Convention an evolving instrument'.[260]

While the Convention originally established a framework for the exploitation of whales as a resource, an amendment to paragraph 10(e) of the Schedule[261] has established a moratorium on commercial whaling in place since 1982.[262] That amendment turned the ICRW into a proper instrument for the conservation of whales[263] Nevertheless, Article VIII of the Convention allows a Contracting Government to grant authorisations for its nations to participate in whaling for 'purposes of scientific research'.[264] On that basis, Japan has launched whaling programmes in the Antarctic (JARPA I and II). Australia (New Zealand intervening) challenged the compatibility of JARPA II before the ICJ, which held that Japan had violated: (i) the moratorium on commercial whaling in each of the years during which it had set catch limits above zero for minke whales, fin whales and humpback whales under JARPA II; (ii) the factory ship moratorium[265] in each of the seasons during which fin whales were taken, killed and treated under JARPA II; and (iii) the prohibition of commercial whaling in the Southern Ocean Sanctuary in each of the seasons during which fin whales have been taken under JARPA II.[266] The interpretation and application of Article VIII of the Convention was central to the case. The ICJ took the view that while this article gives discretion to a State Party to the Convention to reject the request for a special permit or to specify the conditions under which a permit will be granted, the question of whether the killing, taking and treating of whales pursuant to a requested special permit is for purposes of scientific research cannot depend simply on that State's perception. In particular, in order to ascertain whether a programme's use of lethal methods is 'for purposes of' scientific research, the Court considered whether the elements of such a programme's design and implementation are reasonable in relation to its stated research objectives. The judgment *Whaling in the Antarctic* is not only of interest because of the ICJ's handling of the concept of 'scientific', but also as an illustration of the challenge international courts and tribunals face when the treaty underlying a dispute was agreed in a distant past. In its judgment in *Whaling in the Antarctic* the ICJ focused particularly on procedural arrangements overseen by the IWC, and put forward a 'duty to cooperate'.[267]

260 *Whaling in the Antarctic* (n 258) para 45.
261 'Notwithstanding the other provisions of paragraph 10, catch limits for the killing for commercial purposes of whales from all stocks for the 1986 coastal and the 1985/86 pelagic seasons and thereafter shall be zero. This provision will be kept under review, based upon the best scientific advice, and by 1990 at the latest the Commission will undertake a comprehensive assessment of the effects of this decision on whale stocks and consider modification of this provision and the establishment of other catch limits'.
262 Norway and Iceland hunt whales commercially at present, either under objection to the moratorium decision, or under reservation to it.
263 Dupuy and Viñuales (n 3) 166–67.
264 Art VIII(1) ICRW.
265 The factory ship moratorium in para 10(d) of the ICRW Schedule provides: 'Notwithstanding the other provisions of paragraph 10, there shall be a moratorium on the taking, killing or treating of whales, except minke whales, by factory ships or whale catchers attached to factory ships. This moratorium applies to sperm whales, killer whales and baleen whales, except minke whales'.
266 *Whaling in the Antarctic* (n 258) para 247.
267 See MA Young and SR Sullivan, 'Evolution through the Duty to Cooperate: Implications of the Whaling Case at the International Court of Justice' (2015) 16 *Melbourne Journal of International Law* 311.

At the level of the EU, the two main instruments for nature and biodiversity protection are the Birds[268] and Habitats[269] Directives.[270] The Birds Directive, which was originally adopted in 1979,[271] aims to protect all naturally occurring wild birds and their eggs, nests, and habitats across the EU.[272] It was adopted in response to public concern with customary hunting of migratory birds, and constituted the first piece of environmental legislation enacted at EU level.[273] Member States are to take the requisite measures to ensure that the population of bird species is maintained at or adapted to a level that corresponds to ecological, scientific, and cultural requirements, while taking account of economic and recreational requirements.[274] To that end, Member States must, on the one hand, take the necessary measures to 'preserve, maintain or re-establish' a sufficient diversity and area of habitats for all the species of birds to which the directive applies, and on the other hand, classify the most suitable territories as special protection areas (SPAs) for the conservation of the species listed in Annex I to the Birds Directive in the geographical sea and land area where the directive applies, while taking similar measures for regularly occurring migratory species not listed in Annex I.[275] Within these protection areas, Member States are to take appropriate steps to avoid significant pollution or deterioration of habitats or any significant disturbances affecting the birds. Outside these protection areas, Member States must also strive to avoid pollution or deterioration of habitats.[276] The Birds Directive also prohibits certain practices harmful to birds, such as deliberate killing or capture or deliberate destruction of, or damage to, their nests and eggs or removal of their nests,[277] the sale, transport for sale, keeping for sale and the offering for sale of live or dead birds,[278] severely restricts any hunting of birds,[279] and bans the use of all means, arrangements or methods used for the large-scale or non-selective capture or killing of birds or capable of causing the local disappearance of a species.[280] Derogations are only permissible for reasons of public health and safety, air safety, and specific reasons of nature conservation and prevention of damage to agriculture.[281] Economic development as such does not constitute a sufficient reason for derogating from the obligations under the Birds Directive.[282]

The Habitats Directive, adopted in 1992, provides for similar measures but has a much broader scope, covering around 230 rare habitat types[283] and more than 1000 rare, threatened

[268] Directive 2009/147/EC of the European Parliament and of the Council of 30 November 2009 on the conservation of wild birds [2010] OJ L20/7.
[269] Council Directive 92/43/EEC on the conservation of natural habitats and of wild fauna and flora [1992] OJ L206/7.
[270] See further Van Calster and Reins (n 30) 181–206.
[271] Council Directive 79/409/EEC on the conservation of wild birds [1979] OJ L103/1.
[272] Art 1 Birds Directive.
[273] S Kingston, V Heyvaert and A Čavoški, *European Environmental Law* (Cambridge, CUP, 2017) 416.
[274] Art 2 Birds Directive.
[275] ibid, Arts 3 and 4(1) and (2).
[276] ibid, Art 4(4). See eg Judgment of 24 November 2016, *Commission v Spain*, C-461/14, EU:C:2016:895; and Opinion of AG Wahl of 23 February 2016, *Commission v Spain*, C-461/14, EU:C:2016:110. With respect to the corresponding provision in the 1979 Birds Directive, see eg Judgment of 20 September 2007, *Commission v Italy*, C-388/05, EU:C:2007:533; and Opinion of AG Sharpston of 3 May 2007, *Commission v Italy*, C-388/05, EU:C:2007:263.
[277] Art 5(a) and (b) Birds Directive.
[278] ibid, Art 6(1).
[279] ibid, Art 7.
[280] ibid, Art 8.
[281] ibid, Art 9.
[282] Kingston, Heyvaert and Čavoški (n 273) 417.
[283] Annex I Habitats Directive.

or endemic species of wild animals and plants.[284] The directive also provides for a coherent European ecological network of special areas of conservation (SACs) to be set up under the title Natura 2000, composed of sites hosting the natural habitat types and habitats of the species covered by the directive. The Natura 2000 network, which also includes the SPAs classified by the Member States pursuant to the Birds Directive, is to enable the natural habitat types and the species' habitats concerned to be maintained or, where appropriate, restored at a favourable conservation status. Each Member State is to contribute to the creation of Natura 2000 in proportion to the representation within its territory of the natural habitat types and the habitats of species covered by the Habitats Directive, and must designate sites as SACs to that effect.[285] Article 4 of the Habitats Directive sets out the procedure for classifying natural sites as SACs, divided into several stages with corresponding legal effects.[286] The ECJ has clarified that the designation of SACs must only happen on the basis of ecological criteria,[287] and that the Habitats Directive does not allow a Member State to refuse to agree to the Commission's draft list of sites of Community importance (SCIs) on grounds other than nature conservation grounds.[288]

More generally, EU action in the area of biodiversity lies not only at the intersection of environmental law and trade law, but equally cuts across development cooperation and human rights law, as actors need to embed action in the area of biodiversity in what is sometimes referred to as a 'holistic' approach to nature conservation, which takes into account the role of, and impact on, local and indigenous communities.[289] That much is clear, for example, from the controversy and litigation surrounding the seal products regulation.

In 2009, the European Parliament and the Council adopted legislation banning within the European Union both the trade in seal products produced in the EU and in imported seal products,[290] which was further implemented by the Commission.[291] The legislation

[284] ibid, Annexes II, IV, and V.

[285] ibid, Art 3.

[286] See the summary in Opinion of AG Sharpston of 9 July 2009, *Stadt Papenburg*, C-226/08, EU:C:2009:440, point 24: Under Stage 1, on the basis of the applicable criteria set out in Annex III to the Habitats Directive together with relevant scientific information, each Member State is to propose and transmit to the Commission a list of sites, indicating which natural habitat types in Annex I and native species in Annex II are to be found there (Art 4(1)). Under Stage 2, the Commission is to establish, on the basis of the applicable criteria set out in Annex III and in agreement with each Member State, a draft list of sites of Community importance (SCIs) drawn from the Member States' lists. The list of sites selected as SCIs, identifying those which host one or more priority natural habitat types or priority species, is adopted by the Commission (Art 4(2)). Once a SCI has been so adopted, the Member State concerned must designate that site as a SAC (Art 4(4)). As soon as a site is placed on the list adopted by the Commission in accordance with the third subparagraph of Art 4(2), it is subject to Art 6(2), (3) and (4) (Art 4(5)).

[287] Judgment of 7 November 2000, *First Corporate Shipping*, C-371/98, EU:C:2000:600.

[288] Judgment of 14 January 2010, *Stadt Papenburg*, C-226/08, EU:C:2010:10; and Opinion of AG Sharpston (n 286). As Van Calster and Reins observe, the appropriate post-Lisbon jargon would appear to have to be 'site of Union importance (SUI)', yet the terminology has not yet been formally updated in that regard: Van Calster and Reins (n 30) 186.

[289] E Morgera, 'The trajectory of EU biodiversity cooperation: supporting environmental multilateralism through EU external action' in Morgera (n 84) 237–38. See further E Desmet, *Indigenous Rights Entwined with Nature Conservation* (Antwerp, Intersentia, 2011).

[290] Regulation (EC) No 1007/2009 of the European Parliament and of the Council of 16 September 2009 on trade in seal products (Text with EEA relevance) [2009] OJ L286/36.

[291] Commission Regulation (EU) No 737/2010 laying down detailed rules for the implementation of Regulation (EC) No 1007/2009 of the European Parliament and of the Council on trade in seal products (Text with EEA relevance) [2010] OJ L216/1 (Seals Products Regulation). See also the actions for annulment of the Seals Products Regulation brought by an association representing the interests of Canadian Inuit: Order of 6 September 2011, *Inuit Tapiriit Kanatami and others v Parliament and Council*, T-18/10, EU:T:2011:419; Judgment of 3 October 2013, *Inuit*

provides for a so-called 'Inuit exception', which allows seal products that result from hunts traditionally conducted by Inuit and other indigenous communities to be placed on the Union market if the applicable conditions have been met.[292]

Canada and Norway launched WTO dispute settlement proceedings against the EU's Seal regime in 2009. The Panel and Appellate Body rejected the claims of Canada and Norway against the ban itself, accepting that the ban pursues a legitimate objective (public moral concerns on seal welfare) and is not more trade restrictive than necessary.[293] However, the Appellate Body found that there was a de facto violation of the most-favoured nation treatment obligation,[294] because seal products from Greenland were treated more favourably than seal products from Canada through the exception for products derived from Inuit hunts. It found that this difference in treatment could in principle be justified under the exception of GATT for public morals,[295] but found that the EU had failed to design the legislation to prevent arbitrary discrimination and should have made more efforts to encourage Canadian Inuit to use the exception. The ban was amended in 2015 in order to reflect that outcome.[296]

V. Concluding Remarks

The above has provided a concise overview of the development of international environmental law, as well as of its main sources, institutions, and themes. It has illustrated that international environmental law is a fast developing field, characterised by the tension between the drive for stricter standards through treaties on the one hand, and the reluctance of States to be bound, on the other hand, resulting in often weak enforcement mechanisms and a proliferation of soft law. At the same time, it is perhaps the paradigmatic example of a field of international law in which the need for regulation and governance at the global level is generally recognised. Notwithstanding that, the most recent developments regarding the

Tapiriit Kanatami and others v Parliament and Council, C-583/11 P, EU:C:2013:625; Judgment of 25 April 2013, *Inuit Tapiriit Kanatami and others v Commission*, T-526/10, EU:T:2013:215; and Judgment of 3 September 2015, *Inuit Tapiriit Kanatami and others v Commission*, C-398/13 P, EU:C:2015:535. For a commentary, see eg T Perišin, 'Is the EU Seal Products Regulation a Sealed Deal? EU and WTO Challenges' (2013) 62 *ICLQ* 373; A Kornezov, 'Shaping the New Architecture of the EU System of Judicial Remedies: Comment on Inuit' (2014) *ELR* 251; T Bombois and D Waelbroeck, 'Des requérants "privilégiés" et des autres …' (2014) *Cahiers de droit européen* 22; P-A Van Malleghem, N Baeten, 'Before the law stands a gatekeeper – Or, what is a "regulatory act" in Article 263(4) TFEU?' (2014) *CMLR* 1187.

[292] Art 3(1) Seals Products Regulation.

[293] Panel Reports, *European Communities – Measures Prohibiting the Importation and Marketing of Seal Products*, 18 June 2014, WT/DS400/R and Add.1 / WT/DS401/R and Add.1, as modified by Appellate Body Reports WT/DS400/AB/R / WT/DS401/AB/R, DSR 2014:II, 365; Appellate Body Reports, *European Communities – Measures Prohibiting the Importation and Marketing of Seal Products*, adopted 18 June 2014, WT/DS400/AB/R / WT/DS401/AB/R, DSR 2014:I, 7.

[294] Art I GATT.

[295] ibid, Art XX.

[296] Regulation (EU) 2015/1775 amending Regulation (EC) No 1007/2009 on trade in seal products and repealing Commission Regulation (EU) No 737/2010 (Text with EEA relevance) [2015] OJ L262/1–6; Commission Implementing Regulation (EU) 2015/1850 laying down detailed rules for the implementation of Regulation (EC) No 1007/2009 of the European Parliament and of the Council on trade in seal products (Text with EEA relevance) [2015] OJ L271/1–11.

engagement and disengagement of global players with respect to environmental obligations, in particular regarding climate change, demonstrates that the existing tensions are unlikely to diminish in the foreseeable future.

Bibliography

Beurier, J-P, *Droit international de l'environnement*, 5th edn (Paris, Pedone, 2017).

Beyerlin, U, and Marauhn, T, *International Environmental Law* (Oxford, Hart, 2011).

Birnie, P, Alan, B, and Redgwell, C, *International Law and the Environment* (Oxford, OUP, 2009).

Bodansky, D, Brunnée, J, and Rajamani, L, *International Climate Change Law* (Oxford, OUP, 2017).

Carlarne, CP, *Climate Change Law and Policy: EU and US Approaches* (Oxford, OUP, 2010).

Dupuy, P-M and Viñuales, JE, *Introduction au droit international de l'environnement* (Brussels, Bruylant, 2015).

Dupuy, P-M and Viñuales, JE, *International Environmental Law* (Cambridge, CUP, 2015).

Lavielle, J-M, Delzangles, H and Le Bris, C, *Droit international de l'environnement*, 4th edn (Paris, Ellipses, 2018).

Morgera, E (ed), *The External Environmental Policy of the European Union: EU and International Law Perspectives* (Cambridge, CUP, 2012).

Postiglione, A, *Diritto internazionale dell'ambiente* (Roma, Aracne, 2013).

Proelß, A (ed), *Internationales Umweltrecht* (Berlin, De Gruyter, 2017).

Redgwell, C, 'International Environmental Law' in Evans, MD (ed), *International Law*, 4th edn (Oxford, OUP, 2012) 688–726.

Rogers, PP, Jalal, KF and Boyd, JA, *An Introduction to Sustainable Development* (London, Earthscan, 2008).

Sands, P, and Peel, J, *Principles of International Environmental Law*, 3rd edn (Cambridge, CUP, 2012).

Trouwborst, A, *Evolution and Status of the Precautionary Principle in International Law* (Deventer, Kluwer, 2002).

Further Reading

Beyerlin, U, Stoll, PT, and Wolfrum, R (eds), *Ensuring Compliance with Multilateral Environmental Agreements: A Dialogue between Practitioners and Academia* (Leiden, Nijhoff, 2006).

Bowman, M, 'The Ramsar Convention on Wetlands: Has it Made a Difference?' (2002) 10 *Yearbook of International Co-operation on Environment and Development* 61.

Diaz Barrado, CM, 'Los objetivos de desarollo sostenible: un principio de naturaleza incierta y varias dimensiones fragmentadas' (2016) 32 *Anuario español de derecho internacional* 9.

Dominicé, C, 'Le principe de prévention en droit international de l'environnement' (1998) 1 *Zeitschrift für europarechtliche Studien* 329.

Fitzmaurice-Lachs, M, 'The International Convention for the Regulation of Whaling and International Whaling Commission: Conservation or Preservation: can the Gordian Knot be cut (or untangled)?' (2013) 5 *The Yearbook of Polar Law* 451.

Harrad, S (ed), *Persistent Organic Pollutants* (West Sussex, Blackwell Publishing Ltd, 2010).

Harrison, J, *Saving the Oceans through Law: The International Legal Framework for the Protection of the Marine Environment* (Oxford, OUP, 2017).

Hildering, A, *International Law, Sustainable Development and Water Management* (Delft, Eburon, 2004).

Hinteregger, M (ed), *Environmental Liability and Ecological Damage in European Law* (Cambridge, CUP, 2008).

Humphreys, S and Otomo, Y, 'Theorizing International Environmental Law' in Orford, A and Hoffmann, F (eds), *The Oxford Handbook of the Theory of International Law* (Oxford, OUP, 2016) 797–819.

Kingston, S, Heyvaert, V and Čavoški, A, *European Environmental Law* (Cambridge, CUP, 2017).

Klein, D, Pia Carazo, M, Doelle, M, Bulmer, J and Higham, A (eds), *The Paris Agreement on Climate Change: Analysis and Commentary* (Oxford, OUP, 2017).

Koester, V, 'The Nature of the Convention on Biological Diversity and its Application of Components of the Concept of Sustainable Development' (2006) 16 *Italian Yearbook of International Law* 57.

Matz, N, 'Chaos or Coherence? Implementing and Enforcing the Conservation of Migratory Species through Various Legal Instruments' (2005) 65 *Zeitschrift für ausländisches öffentliches Recht und Völkerrecht* 197.

Maurmann, D, *Rechtsgrundsätze im Völkerrecht am Beispiel des Vorsorgeprinzips* (Baden-Baden, Nomos, 2008).

McIntyre, O, 'The Protection of Freshwater Ecosystems Revisited: towards a Common Understanding of the "Ecosystems Approach" to the Protection of Transboundary Water Resources' (2014) 23 *Review of European Community and International Environmental Law* 88.

McPherson, AM, 'Let Them Eat Carbon: the End of the Kyoto Protocol' (2012) 41 *Georgia Journal of International and Comparative Law* 219.

Michallet, I, *La protection des espèces migratrices en droit international et en droit communautaire* (Lyon, Université Jean Moulin, 2000).

Morgera, E, 'The Ecosystem Approach and the Precautionary Principle' in Morgera, E and Razzaque, J (eds), *Elgar Encyclopedia of Environmental Law*, Vol III (Cheltenham, Edward Elgar, 2017).

Romanin Jacur, F, 'The Kyoto Protocol's Compliance Mechanism' in Farber, DA and Peeters, M (eds), *Elgar Encyclopedia of Environmental Law*, Vol I (Cheltenham, Edward Elgar, 2016).

de Sadeleer, N, *Environmental Principles: From Political Slogans to Legal Rules* (Oxford, OUP, 2002).

de Sadeleer, N, 'The Precautionary Principle as a Device for Greater Environmental Protection: Lessons from EC Courts' (2009) 18 *Review of European, Comparative and International Environmental Law* 3.

Sand, PH, 'Transboundary Air Pollution' in Nollkaemper, A and Plakokefalos, I (eds), *The Practice of Shared Responsibility in International Law* (Cambridge, CUP, 2017).

Selin, H, 'Global Environmental Law and Treaty-Making on Hazardous Substances: The Minamata Convention and Mercury Abatement' (2014) 14 *Global Environmental Politics* 1.

Székely, A, 'The Promise of the Brundtland Report: Honored or Betrayed?' (2008) 21 *Pacific McGeorge Global Business and Development Law Journal* 159.

Tabau, AS, *La mise en oeuvre du Protocole de Kyoto en Europe: interactions des contrôles international et communautaire* (Brussels, Bruylant, 2011).

Van Calster, G and Reins, L, *EU Environmental Law* (Cheltenham, Edward Elgar, 2017).

Verschuuren, JM, 'The Growing Significance of the Principle of Sustainable Development as a Legal Norm' in Fisher, D (ed), *Research Handbook on Fundamental Concepts of Environmental Law* (Cheltenham, Edward Elgar, 2016).

Wiersema, A, 'The New International Law-Makers? Conferences of the Parties to Multilateral Environmental Agreements' (2009) 31 *MJIL* 231.

Wiersema, A, 'The Precautionary Principle in Environmental Governance' in Fisher, D (ed), *Research Handbook on Fundamental Concepts of Environmental Law* (Cheltenham, Edward Elgar, 2016).

Wolff, N and Köck, W (eds), *10 Jahre Übereinkommen über die biologische Vielfalt* (Baden-Baden, Nomos, 2004).

Wolfrum, R, and Matz, N, *Conflicts in International Environmental Law* (Berlin, Springer, 2003).

Wolfrum, R, Langenfeld, C and Minnerop, P (eds), *Environmental Liability in International Law: Towards a Coherent Conception* (Berlin, Erich Schmidt, 2005).

Young, M, *Trading Fish, Saving Fish: The Interaction between Regimes in International Law* (Cambridge, CUP, 2013).

Appendix I

Overview of Treaty Ratification

R: Ratification ♦ AA: Approval/Acceptance ♦ A: Accession ♦ S: Signature ♦ (S): Succession

* Not yet in effect as of 18 June 2018.

Treaty	Austria	Belgium	Bulgaria	Croatia	Cyprus	Czech Republic	Denmark	Estonia	European Union	Finland	France	Germany	Greece	Hungary	Iceland	Ireland	Italy
Treaty Law																	
Vienna Convention on the Law of Treaties (1969)	A	A	A	R(S)	A	A(S)	R	A		R		R	A	A		A	R
Vienna Convention on the Law of Treaties between States and International Organizations or between International Organizations (1986)*	R	R	A	A	R	A(S)	R	A				R	R	A			R
States																	
Vienna Convention on Succession of States in Respect of Treaties (1978)				R(S)	A	R		A									
Vienna Convention on Succession of States in Respect of State Property, Archives and Debts (1983)*				A				A									

International Organizations																	
Charter of the United Nations (1945)	A	R	A	A	A	A	R	A		A	R	A	R	A	A	A	A
Agreement Establishing the World Trade Organization (WTO) (1994)	R	R	A	A	R	AA	R	A	AA	R	R	R	AA	R	R	R	R
Regional Organizations																	
North-Atlantic Treaty (NATO Agreement) (1949)		R	A	A		A	R	A			R	R	A	A	R		R
Non-State Actors																	
European Convention on the Recognition of the Legal Personality of International Non-Governmental Organisations (1986)	R	R			R						R		R				
Jurisdiction																	
Chicago Convention on International Civil Aviation (1944)	A	R	A	R	A	R	R	A		A	R	A	R	A	R	R	R
Convention relating to the Status of Stateless Persons (1954)	A	R	A	A(S)		A	R			A	R	R	A	A		A	R
Convention on the Reduction of Statelessness (1961)	A	A	A	A		A	A			A	S	A		A		A	A
European Convention on Nationality (1997)	R		R	S		R	R			R	S	R	S	R	R		S
Diplomatic and Consular Relations																	
Vienna Convention on Diplomatic Relations (1961)	R	R	R(S)	R	A	R(S)	R	A		R	R	R	R	R	A	R	R
Optional Protocol to the Vienna Convention on Diplomatic Relations, concerning the Compulsory Settlement of Disputes (1961)	R	R	A				R	A		R	R	R		A	A	S	R
Vienna Convention on Consular Relations (1963)	R	R	A	R(S)	A	R(S)	R	A		R	R	R	A	A	A	R	R

(continued)

Treaty	Austria	Belgium	Bulgaria	Croatia	Cyprus	Czech Republic	Denmark	Estonia	European Union	Finland	France	Germany	Greece	Hungary	Iceland	Ireland	Italy
Optional Protocol to the Vienna Convention on Consular Relations concerning the Compulsory Settlement of Disputes (1963)	R	R	A				R	A		R	R	R		A	A	S	R
Convention on the Prevention and Punishment of Crimes against Internationally Protected Persons, including Diplomatic Agents (1973)	A	A	R	R(S)	A	R(S)	R	A		R	A	R	A	R	R	A	R
Immunities																	
Convention on the Privileges and Immunities of the United Nations (1946)	A	A	A	A(S)	R(S)	A(S)	A	A		A	A	A	A	A	A	A	A
Convention on the Privileges and Immunities of the Specialized Agencies (1947)	A	A	A	A(S)	A(S)	A(S)	A	A		A	A	A	A	A	A	A	A
Convention on Special Missions (1969)	A		A	R(S)	R	A(S)		A		S							
European Convention on State Immunity (1972)	R	R			R							R					
Vienna Convention on the Representation of States in their Relations with International Organisations of Universal Character (1975)*			R	R(S)	A	R(S)		A						R			
United Nations Convention on Jurisdictional Immunities of States and Their Property (2004)*	R	S				R	S	S		R	R				S		A
Peaceful Settlement of Disputes																	
Statute of the International Court of Justice (1945)	A	R	A	A	A	A	R	A		A	R	A	R	A	A	A	A
European Convention for the Peaceful Settlement of Disputes (1957)	R	R					R				S	R	S		S	S	R
Convention on the Recognition and Enforcement of Foreign Arbitral Awards (1958)	A	R	R	A(S)	A	R(S)	A	A		R	R	R	A	A	A	A	A

Convention on the Settlement of Investment Disputes Between States and Nationals of Other States (ICSID Convention) (1965)	R	R	R		R	R	R	R		R	R	R	R	R	R	R	R
Law of Armed Conflict																	
First Geneva Convention (1949)	R	R	R	R(S)	A	R(S)	R	A		R	R	A	R	R	A	R	R
Second Geneva Convention (1949)	R	R	R	R(S)	A	R(S)	R	A		R	R	A	R	R	A	R	R
Third Geneva Convention (1949)	R	R	R	R(S)	A	R(S)	R	A		R	R	A	R	R	A	R	R
Fourth Geneva Convention (1949)	R	R	R	R(S)	A	R(S)	R	A		R	R	A	R	R	A	R	R
Treaty on the Non-Proliferation of Nuclear Weapons (1968)	R	R	R		R	R(S)	R	R		R	A	R	R	R	R	R	R
Protocol Additional to the Geneva Conventions of 12 August 1949, and relating to the Protection of Victims of International Armed Conflicts (Protocol I) (1977)	R	R	R	R(S)	A	R(S)	R	A		R	A	R	A	R	R	R	R
Protocol Additional to the Geneva Conventions of 12 August 1949, and relating to the Protection of Victims of Non-International Armed Conflicts (Protocol II) (1977)	R	R	R	R(S)	A	R(S)	R	A		R	A	R	A	R	R	R	R
Convention on Prohibitions or Restrictions on the Use of Certain Conventional Weapons which may be Deemed to be Excessively Injurious or to Have Indiscriminate Effects (1980)	R	R	R	R(S)	A	R(S)	R	A		R	R	R	R	R	R	R	R
Chemical Weapons Convention (1992)	R	R	R	R	R	R	R	R		R	R	R	R	R	R	R	R
Arms Trade Treaty (2014)	R	R	R	R	R	R	AA	AA		R	R	R	R	R	R	R	R
Treaty on the Prohibition of Nuclear Weapons (2017)*	R															S	

(continued)

Treaty	Austria	Belgium	Bulgaria	Croatia	Cyprus	Czech Republic	Denmark	Estonia	European Union	Finland	France	Germany	Greece	Hungary	Iceland	Ireland	Italy
Human Rights																	
Convention on the Prevention and Punishment of the Crime of Genocide (1948)	A	R	A	R(S)	A	R(S)	R	A		A	R	A	R	A	R	A	A
European Convention for the Protection of Human Rights and Fundamental Freedoms (1950)	R	R	R	R		R	R	R		R	R	R	R	R	R	R	R
Convention Relating to the Status of Refugees (1951)	R	R	A	R(S)	R(S)	A(S)	R	A		A	R	R	R	A	A	A	R
International Convention on the Elimination of All Forms of Racial Discrimination (1966)	R	R	R	R(S)	R	R(S)	R	A		R	A	R	R	R	R	R	R
International Covenant on Civil and Political Rights (1966)	R	R	R	R(S)	R	R(S)	R	A		R	A	R	A	R	R	R	R
International Covenant on Economic, Social and Cultural Rights (1966)	R	R	R	R(S)	R	R(S)	R	A		R	A	R	A	R	R	R	R
Protocol Relating to the Status of Refugees (1967)	A	A	A	A(S)	A	A(S)	A	A		A	A	A	A	A	A	A	A
International Convention on the Suppression and Punishment of the Crime of Apartheid (ICSPCA) (1973)			R	R(S)		R(S)		A						R			
Convention on the Elimination of All Forms of Discrimination Against Women (1979)	R	R	R	R(S)	A	R(S)	R	A		R	R	R	R	R	R	A	R
Convention Against Torture and Other Cruel, Inhuman or Degrading Treatment or Punishment (1984)	R	R	R	R(S)	R	R(S)	R	A		R	R	R	R	R	R	R	R

European Convention for the Prevention of Torture and Inhuman or Degrading Treatment or Punishment (1987)	R	R	R	R	R	R	R	R		AA	AA	R	R	R	R	R	R
Convention on the Rights of the Child (1989)	R	R	R	R(S)	R	R(S)	R	A		R	R	R	R	R	R	R	R
Council of Europe Framework Convention on National Minorities (1995)	R	S	R	R	R	R	R	R		R		R	S	R	S	R	R
Optional Protocol to the Convention on the Rights of the Child on the Sale of Children, Child Prostitution and Child Pornography (2000)	R	R	R	R	R	R	R	R		R	R	R	R	R	R	S	R
Optional Protocol to the Convention on the Rights of the Child on the Involvement of Children in Armed Conflicts (2000)	R	R	R	R	R	R	R	R		R	R	R	R	R	R	R	R
Convention on the Rights of Persons with Disabilities (2006)	R	R	R	R	R	R	R	R	AA	R	R	R	R	R	R	R	R
International Convention for the Protection of All Persons from Enforced Disappearance (2006)	R	R	S	S	S	R	S			S	R	R	R		S	S	R
Council of Europe Convention on Preventing and Combating Violence against Women and Domestic Violence (2011)	R	R	S	R	R	S	R	R	S	R	R	R	R	S	R	R	R
International Criminal Law																	
Rome Statute of the International Criminal Court (1998)	R	R	R	R	R	R	R	R		R	R	R	R	R	R	R	R
Convention on the Non-applicability of Statutory Limitations to War Crimes and Crimes against Humanity (1968)			R	R(S)		R(S)		A						R			
United Nations Convention Against Illicit Traffic in Narcotic Drugs and Psychotropic Substances (1988)	R	R	R	R(S)	R	R(S)	R	A	AA	AA	AA	R	R	R	A	R	AA

(continued)

Treaty	Austria	Belgium	Bulgaria	Croatia	Cyprus	Czech Republic	Denmark	Estonia	European Union	Finland	France	Germany	Greece	Hungary	Iceland	Ireland	Italy
Convention on Combating Bribery of Foreign Public Officials in International Business Transactions (OECD Anti-Bribery Convention) (1997)	R	R	R			R	R	R		R	R	R	R	R	R	R	R
United Nations Convention Against Transnational Organized Crime (TOC) (2000)	R	R	R	R	R	R	R	R	AA	R	R	R	R	R	R	R	R
United Nations Convention against Corruption (2003)	R	R	R	R	R	R	R	A	AA	AA	R	R	R	R	A	R	R
Council of Europe Convention on Laundering, Search, Seizure and Confiscation of the Proceeds from Crime and on the Financing of Terrorism (2005)		R	R	R	R		R					R	R	R			R
Amendments on the Crime of Aggression to the Rome Statute of the International Criminal Court (2010)	R	R		R	R	AA		R		R		AA			R		
Law of the Sea and Global Commons																	
Antarctic Treaty (1959)		R				A(S)	A				R	R					
Treaty on Principles Governing the Activities of States in the Exploration and Use of Outer Space, Including the Moon and Other Celestial Bodies (1967)	R	R	R		R	R(S)	R			R	R	R	R	R	R	R	R
Convention concerning the Protection of the World Cultural and Natural Heritage (1972)	R	R	AA	R(S)	AA	AA(S)	R	R		R	AA	R	R	AA	R	R	R
Agreement Governing the Activities of States on the Moon and Other Celestial Bodies (Moon Agreement) (1979)	R	A									S						

Convention on the Conservation of Antarctic Marine Living Resources (1980)		R	A						A	A	R	R	A				A
United Nations Convention on the Law of the Sea (1982) (Montego Bay Convention)	R	R	R	R(S)	R	R	R	A	S	R	R	A	R	R	R	R	R
Protocol on Environmental Protection to the Antarctic Treaty (1991)		R	A			R				AA	AA	R	R				R
Agreement Relating to the Implementation of Part XI of the United Nations Convention on the Law of the Sea (1994)	R	AA	A	R	R	R	R	A	AA	R	R	R	R	A	R	R	R
Convention for the Safeguarding of the Intangible Cultural Heritage (2003)	R	R	A	R(S)	A	R(S)	R	A		A	R	R	R	R			R
Agreement on Port State Measures to Prevent, Deter, and Eliminate Illegal, Unreported and Unregulated Fishing (2009)*									AA		AA				R		
International Economic Law																	
Energy Charter Treaty (ECT) (1994)	R	R	R	R	R	R	R	R	AA	R		R	R	R			R
Comprehensive Economic and Trade Agreement (CETA) (2016)*	S	S	S	R	S	R	R	R	S	S	S	S	S	S		S	S
International Environmental Law																	
International Convention for the Regulation of Whaling (1946)							R				R				A		
RAMSAR Convention (1971)	A	R	S	A(S)	A	A(S)	A	R		R	R	R	A	A	A	R	R
Convention on International Trade in Endangered Species of Wild Fauna and Flora (CITES) (1973)	R	R	A	A	R	A(S)	R	A	A	A	AA	R	A	A	A	R	R
Vienna Convention for the Protection of the Ozone Layer (1985)	R	R	A	A(S)	A	A(S)	R	A	AA	R	AA	R	R	A	A	A	R

(continued)

Treaty	Austria	Belgium	Bulgaria	Croatia	Cyprus	Czech Republic	Denmark	Estonia	European Union	Finland	France	Germany	Greece	Hungary	Iceland	Ireland	Italy
Basel Convention on the Control of Transboundary Movements of Hazardous Wastes and their Disposal (Basel Convention) (1989)	R	R	A	A	R	A(S)	AA	A	AA	AA	AA	R	R	AA	A	R	R
Convention on Environmental Impact Assessment in a Transboundary Context (Espoo Convention) (1991)	R	R	R	A	A	R	AA	A	AA	AA	AA	R	R	R	S	R	R
Convention on the Protection and Use of Transboundary Watercourses and International Lakes (UNECE Water Convention) (1992)	R	R	R	A		A	AA	R	AA	AA	AA	R	R	AA			R
United Nations Framework Convention on Climate Change (1992)	R	R	R	AA	R	AA	R	R	AA	AA	R	R	R	R	R	R	R
Convention on Biological Diversity (1992)	R	R	R	R	R	AA	R	R	AA	AA	R	R	R	R	R	R	R
United Nations Convention to Combat Desertification (1994)	A	A	A	AA	A	A	R	A	R	AA	R	R	R	A	A	R	R
Agreement for the Implementation of the Provisions of the United Nations Convention on the Law of the Sea relating to the Conservation and Management of Straddling Fish Stocks and Highly Migratory Fish Stocks (1995)	R	R	A	A	A	A	R	A	R	R	R	R	R	A	R	R	R
Convention on the Law of Non-Navigational Uses of International Watercourses (1997)							A			AA	A	R	A	AA		A	A
Kyoto Protocol to the United Nations Framework Convention on Climate Change (1997)	R	R	R	R	A	AA	R	R	AA	R	AA	R	R	A	A	R	R

Convention on Access to Information, Public Participation in Decision-making and Access to Justice in Environmental Matters (Aarhus Convention) (1998)	R	R	R	R	R	R	AA	R	AA	AA	AA	R	R	R	R	R	R
Protocol on Water and Health to the 1992 Convention on the Protection and Use of Transboundary Watercourses and International Lakes (1999)		R	S	R	S	R	S	R		AA	AA	R	S	AA	S		S
Cartagena Protocol on Biosafety to the Convention on Biological Diversity (Cartagena Protocol) (2000)	R	R	R	R	A	R	R	R	AA	R	AA	R	R	R	S	R	R
Nagoya Protocol on Access to Genetic Resources and the Fair and Equitable Sharing of Benefits Arising from their Utilization to the Convention on Biological Diversity (2010)	S	R	R	A	S	R	AA		AA	AA	R	R	S	R		S	S
Paris Agreement on Climate Change (2015)	R	R	R	R	R	R	AA	R	R	R	R	R	R	R	A	R	R

Treaty	Latvia	Lithuania	Luxembourg	Malta	Netherlands	Norway	Poland	Portugal	Romania	Russian Federation	Serbia	Slovak Republic	Slovenia	Spain	Sweden	Switzerland	Turkey	United Kingdom
Treaty Law																		
Vienna Convention on the Law of Treaties (1969)	A	A	R	A	A		A	A		A	R(S)	A(S)	R(S)	A	R	A		R
Vienna Convention on the Law of Treaties between States and International Organizations or between International Organizations (1986)*				A	R						S	A(S)		A	R	A		R
States																		
Vienna Convention on Succession of States in Respect of Treaties (1978)							S				R(S)	R	R(S)					
Vienna Convention on Succession of States in Respect of State Property, Archives and Debts (1983)*											S(S)		A					
International Organizations																		
Charter of the United Nations (1945)	A	A	R	A	R	R	R	A	A	R	A	A	A	A	A	A	R	R
Agreement Establishing the World Trade Organization (WTO) (1994)	A	A	R	R	AA	R	R	R	R	A		AA	R	R	R	R	R	R
Regional Organizations																		
North-Atlantic Treaty (NATO Agreement) (1949)	A	A	R		R	R	A	R	A			A	A	A			A	R

Non-State Actors																		
European Convention on the Recognition of the Legal Personality of International Non-Governmental Organisations (1986)					AA			R					S			R		R
Jurisdiction																		
Chicago Convention on International Civil Aviation (1944)	A	A	R	A	R	R	R	R	A	A	R	R	R	R	R	R	R	R
Convention relating to the Status of Stateless Persons (1954)	A	A	R		R	R		A	A		A(S)	A	A(S)	A	R	R	A	R
Convention on the Reduction of Statelessness (1961)	A	A	A		R	A		A	A		A	A			A			R
European Convention on Nationality (1997)	S		R	S	R	R	S	R	R	S		R			R			
Diplomatic and Consular Relations																		
Vienna Convention on Diplomatic Relations (1961)	A	A	R	R(S)	A	R	R	A	R	R	R(S)	R(S)	R(S)	A	R	R	A	R
Optional Protocol to the Vienna Convention on Diplomatic Relations, concerning the Compulsory Settlement of Disputes (1961)		A	R	R(S)	A	R			A		R(S)	A	R(S)	A	R	R		R
Vienna Convention on Consular Relations (1963)	A	A	R	A	A	R	R	A	A	A	R(S)	R(S)	R(S)	A	R	R	A	R
Optional Protocol to the Vienna Convention on Consular Relations concerning the Compulsory Settlement of Disputes (1963)		A	R		A	R			A		S(S)	A		A	R	R		R

(continued)

Treaty	Latvia	Lithuania	Luxembourg	Malta	Netherlands	Norway	Poland	Portugal	Romania	Russian Federation	Serbia	Slovak Republic	Slovenia	Spain	Sweden	Switzerland	Turkey	United Kingdom
Convention on the Prevention and Punishment of Crimes against Internationally Protected Persons, including Diplomatic Agents (1973)	A	A	A	A	A	R	R	A	R	R	R(S)	R(S)	R(S)	A	R	A	A	R
Immunities																		
Convention on the Privileges and Immunities of the United Nations (1946)	A	A	A	R(S)	A	A	A	A	A	A	A(S)	A(S)	A(S)	A	A	A	A	A
Convention on the Privileges and Immunities of the Specialized Agencies (1947)	A	A	A	A(S)	A	A	A	A	A	A	A(S)	A(S)	A(S)	A	A	A		A
Convention on Special Missions (1969)		A					A				R(S)	A(S)	R(S)	A		R		S
European Convention on State Immunity (1972)			R		R											R		R
Convention on the Representation of States in their Relations with International Organisations of Universal Character (1975)*							R			R	R(S)	R(S)	R(S)				S	
United Nations Convention on Jurisdictional Immunities of States and Their Property (2004)*	A					R		R	R	S		R		A	R	R		S

Peaceful Settlement of Disputes																		
Statute of the International Court of Justice (1945)	A	A	R	A	R	R	R	A	A	R	A	A	A	A	A	A	R	R
European Convention for the Peaceful Settlement of Disputes (1957)			R	R	R	R						R			R	R	S	R
Convention on the Recognition and Enforcement of Foreign Arbitral Awards (1958)	A	A	R	A	R	A	R	A	A	R	A(S)	R(S)	A(S)	A	R	R	A	A
Convention on the Settlement of Investment Disputes Between States and Nationals of Other States (ICSID Convention) (1965)	R	R	S	R	R	R		R			R	R	R	R	R	R	R	R
Law of Armed Conflict																		
First Geneva Convention (1949)	A	A	R	S(S)	R	R	R	R	R	R(S)	R(S)	R(S)	R(S)	R	R	R	R	R
Second Geneva Convention (1949)	A	A	R	S(S)	R	R	R	R	R	R(S)	R(S)	R(S)	R(S)	R	R	R	R	R
Third Geneva Convention (1949)	A	A	R	S(S)	R	R	R	R	R	R(S)	R(S)	R(S)	R(S)	R	R	R	R	R
Fourth Geneva Convention (1949)	A	A	R	S(S)	R	R	R	R	R	R(S)	R(S)	R(S)	R(S)	R	R	R	R	R
Treaty on the Non-Proliferation of Nuclear Weapons (1968)	A	A	R	R	R	R	R	A	R	R(S)	R(S)	R(S)	R(S)	A	R	R	R	R
Protocol Additional to the Geneva Conventions of 12 August 1949, and relating to the Protection of Victims of International Armed Conflicts (Protocol I) (1977)	A	A	R	A	R	R	R	R	R	R(S)	R(S)	R(S)	R(S)	R	R	R		R

(continued)

Treaty	Latvia	Lithuania	Luxembourg	Malta	Netherlands	Norway	Poland	Portugal	Romania	Russian Federation	Serbia	Slovak Republic	Slovenia	Spain	Sweden	Switzerland	Turkey	United Kingdom
Protocol Additional to the Geneva Conventions of 12 August 1949, and relating to the Protection of Victims of Non-International Armed Conflicts (Protocol II) (1977)	A	A	R	A	R	R	R	R	R	R(S)	R(S)	R(S)	R(S)	R	R	R		R
Convention on Prohibitions or Restrictions on the Use of Certain Conventional Weapons which may be Deemed to be Excessively Injurious or to Have Indiscriminate Effects (1980)	A	A	R	A	A	R	R	R	R	R	R(S)	R(S)	R(S)	R	R	R	R	R
Chemical Weapons Convention (1992)	R	R	R	R	R	R	R	R	R	R	A	R	R	R	R	R	R	R
Arms Trade Treaty (2014)	R	R	R	R	AA	R	R	R	R		R	R	R	R	R	R	S	R
Treaty on the Prohibition of Nuclear Weapons (2017)*																		
Human Rights																		
Convention on the Prevention and Punishment of the Crime of Genocide (1948)	A	A	A	A	A	R	A	A	A	R	A	R(S)	R(S)	A	R	A	A	A
European Convention for the Protection of Human Rights and Fundamental Freedoms (1950)	R	R	R	R	R	R	R	R	R		R	R	R	R	R	R	R	R

Convention Relating to the Status of Refugees (1951)	A	A	R	A	R	R	A	A	A	A	R(S)	A(S)	R(S)	A	R	R	R	R
International Convention on the Elimination of All Forms of Racial Discrimination (1966)	A	R	R	R	R	R	R	A	A	R	R(S)	R(S)	R(S)	A	R	A	R	R
International Covenant on Civil and Political Rights (1966)	A	A	R	A	R	R	R	R	R	R	R(S)	R(S)	R(S)	R	R	A	R	R
International Covenant on Economic, Social and Cultural Rights (1966)	A	A	R	R	R	R	R	R	R	R	R(S)	R(S)	R(S)	R	R	A	R	R
Protocol Relating to the Status of Refugees (1967)	A	A	A	A	A	A	A	A	A	A	A(S)	A(S)	A(S)	A	A	A	A	A
International Convention on the Suppression and Punishment of the Crime of Apartheid (ICSPCA) (1973)	A						R		R	R	R(S)	R(S)	R(S)					
Convention on the Elimination of All Forms of Discrimination Against Women (1979)	A	A	R	A	R	R	R	R	R	R	R(S)	R(S)	R(S)	R	R	R	A	R
Convention Against Torture and Other Cruel, Inhuman or Degrading Treatment or Punishment (1984)	A	A	R	A	R	R	R	R	A	R	R(S)	R(S)	R(S)	R	R	R	R	R
European Convention for the Prevention of Torture and Inhuman or Degrading Treatment or Punishment (1987)	R	R	R	R	AA	R	R	R	R	R	R	R	R	R	R	R	R	R
Convention on the Rights of the Child (1989)	A	A	R	R	AA	R	R	R	R	R	R(S)	R(S)	R(S)	R	R	R	R	R

(continued)

Treaty	Latvia	Lithuania	Luxembourg	Malta	Netherlands	Norway	Poland	Portugal	Romania	Russian Federation	Serbia	Slovak Republic	Slovenia	Spain	Sweden	Switzerland	Turkey	United Kingdom
Council of Europe Framework Convention on National Minorities (1995)	R	R	S	R	R	R	R	R	R	R	R	R	R	R	R	R		R
Optional Protocol to the Convention on the Rights of the Child on the Sale of Children, Child Prostitution and Child Pornography (2000)	R	A	R	A	R	R	R	R	R	R	R	R	R	R	R	R	R	R
Optional Protocol to the Convention on the Rights of the Child on the Involvement of Children in Armed Conflicts (2000)	R	R	R	R	R	R	R	R	R	R	R	R	R	R	R	R	R	R
Convention on the Rights of Persons with Disabilities (2006)	R	R	R	R	R	R	R	R	R	R	R	R	R	R	R	A	R	R
International Convention for the Protection of All Persons from Enforced Disappearance (2006)		R	S	R	R	S	S	R	S		R	R	S	R	S	R		
Council of Europe Convention on Preventing and Combating Violence against Women and Domestic Violence (2011)	S	S	S	R	R	R	R	R	R		R	S	R	R	R	R	R	S

International Criminal Law																		
Rome Statute of the International Criminal Court (1998)	R	R	R	R	AA	R	R	R	R	S	R	R	R	R	R	R		R
Convention on the Non-applicability of Statutory Limitations to War Crimes and Crimes against Humanity (1968)	A	A					R		R	R	R(S)	R(S)	R(S)					
United Nations Convention Against Illicit Traffic in Narcotic Drugs and Psychotropic Substances (1988)	A	A	R	A	AA	R	R	R	A	R	R(S)	R(S)	R(S)	R	R	R	R	R
Convention on Combating Bribery of Foreign Public Officials in International Business Transactions (OECD Anti-Bribery Convention) (1997)	R	R	R		R	R	R	R		R		R	R	R	R	R	R	R
United Nations Convention Against Transnational Organized Crime (TOC) (2000)	R	R	R	R	R	R	R	R	R	R	R	R	R	R	R	R	R	R
United Nations Convention against Corruption (2003)	R	R	R	R	AA	R	R	R	R	R	R	R	A	R	R	R	R	R
Council of Europe Convention on Laundering, Search, Seizure and Confiscation of the Proceeds from Crime and on the Financing of Terrorism (2005)	R			R	R		R	R	R		R	R	R	R	R			
Amendments on the Crime of Aggression to the Rome Statute of the International Criminal Court (2010)	R	R	R	R	AA		R	R		R		AA	R	R		R		

(continued)

Treaty	Latvia	Lithuania	Luxembourg	Malta	Netherlands	Norway	Poland	Portugal	Romania	Russian Federation	Serbia	Slovak Republic	Slovenia	Spain	Sweden	Switzerland	Turkey	United Kingdom
Law of the Sea and Global Commons																		
Antarctic Treaty (1959)					A	R	A		A	R(S)								R
Treaty on Principles Governing the Activities of States in the Exploration and Use of Outer Space, Including the Moon and Other Celestial Bodies (1967)			R		R	R	R	A	R	R(S)	S(S)	R(S)		A	R	R	R	R
Convention concerning the Protection of the World Cultural and Natural Heritage (1972)	AA	AA	R	AA	AA	R	R	R	AA	R(S)	R(S)	AA(S)	R(S)	AA	R	R	R	R
Agreement Governing the Activities of States on the Moon and Other Celestial Bodies (Moon Agreement) (1979)					R				S								A	
Convention on the Conservation of Antarctic Marine Living Resources (1980)					A	R	R			AA(S)				A	A			R
United Nations Convention on the Law of the Sea (1982) (Montego Bay Convention)	A	A	R	R	R	R	R	R	R	R	R(S)	R	R(S)	R	R	R		A
Protocol on Environmental Protection to the Antarctic Treaty (1991)					AA	R	R		R	R				R	R			R

Agreement Relating to the Implementation of Part XI of the United Nations Convention on the Law of the Sea (1994)	A	A	R	R	R	A	R	R	A	A	R	R	R	R	R	R		R
Convention for the Safeguarding of the Intangible Cultural Heritage (2003)	A	A	R	R	R	R	R	R	R	R	R(S)	R(S)	R(S)	R	A	A	A	R
Agreement on Port State Measures to Prevent, Deter, and Eliminate Illegal, Unreported and Unregulated Fishing (2009)*						R				S							S	
International Economic Law																		
Energy Charter Treaty (ECT) (1994)	R	R	R		AA			R	R			R	R	R	R	R		R
Comprehensive Economic and Trade Agreement (CETA) (2016)*	R	R	S	R	S		S	R	S			S	S	R	S			S
International Environmental Law																		
International Convention for the Regulation of Whaling (1946)					R	R				R(S)				A	A			R
RAMSAR Convention (1971)	A	A	R	A	A	S	A	R	A	R(S)	A(S)	A(S)	A(S)	A	S	R	A	R
Convention on International Trade in Endangered Species of Wild Fauna and Flora (CITES) (1973)	A	A	R	A	R	R	R	R	A	R(S)	A	R(S)	A	A	R	R	A	R
Vienna Convention for the Protection of the Ozone Layer (1985)	A	A	R	A	AA	R	A	A	A	AA	A(S)	A(S)	A(S)	A	R	R	A	R

(continued)

Treaty	Latvia	Lithuania	Luxembourg	Malta	Netherlands	Norway	Poland	Portugal	Romania	Russian Federation	Serbia	Slovak Republic	Slovenia	Spain	Sweden	Switzerland	Turkey	United Kingdom
Basel Convention on the Control of Transboundary Movements of Hazardous Wastes and their Disposal (Basel Convention) (1989)	A	A	R	A	AA	R	R	R	A	R	A	A(S)	A	R	R	R	R	R
Convention on Environmental Impact Assessment in a Transboundary Context (Espoo Convention) (1991)	A	A	R	A	AA	R	R	R	R	S	A	R	A	R	R	A		R
Convention on the Protection and Use of Transboundary Watercourses and International Lakes (UNECE Water Convention) (1992)	R	R	R		AA	AA	R	R	R	AA	A	A	A	R	R	R		S
United Nations Framework Convention on Climate Change (1992)	R	R	R	R	AA	R	R	R	R	R	A	AA	R	R	R	R	A	R
Convention on Biological Diversity (1992)	R	R	R	R	AA	R	R	R	R	R	R	AA	R	R	R	R	R	R
United Nations Convention to Combat Desertification (1994)	A	A	R	R	AA	R	A	R	A	A	A	A	A	R	R	R	R	R

Agreement for the Implementation of the Provisions of the United Nations Convention on the Law of the Sea relating to the Conservation and Management of Straddling Fish Stocks and Highly Migratory Fish Stocks (1995)	A	A	R	A	R	R	A	R	A	R		A	A	R	R			R
Convention on the Law of Non-Navigational Uses of International Watercourses (1997)			R		AA	R		R						A	A			A
Kyoto Protocol to the United Nations Framework Convention on Climate Change (1997)	R	R	R	R	AA	R	R	AA	R	R	A	R	R	R	R	R	A	R
Convention on Access to Information, Public Participation in Decision-making and Access to Justice in Environmental Matters (Aarhus Convention) (1998)	R	R	R	R	AA	R	R	R	R		A	A	R	R	R	R		R
Protocol on Water and Health to the 1992 Convention on the Protection and Use of Transboundary Watercourses and International Lakes (1999)	R	R	R	S	AA	R	S	AA	R	AA	A	R	S	R	S	R		S
Cartagena Protocol on Biosafety to the Convention on Biological Diversity (Cartagena Protocol) (2000)	A	R	R	A	AA	R	R	AA	R		A	R	R	R	R	R	R	R

(continued)

Treaty	Latvia	Lithuania	Luxembourg	Malta	Netherlands	Norway	Poland	Portugal	Romania	Russian Federation	Serbia	Slovak Republic	Slovenia	Spain	Sweden	Switzerland	Turkey	United Kingdom
Nagoya Protocol on Access to Genetic Resources and the Fair and Equitable Sharing of Benefits Arising from their Utilization to the Convention on Biological Diversity (2010)		S	R	A	AA	R	S	AA	S		S	A	S	R	R	R		R
Paris Agreement on Climate Change (2015)	R	R	R	R	A	R	R	R	R	S	R	R	R	R	R	R	S	R

Appendix II

Basic Bibliography and Websites on International Law

I. Basic Works

A. General International Law

i. Textbooks

Aledo, L-A, *Le droit international public*, 3rd edn (Paris, Dalloz, 2014).
Alland, D, *Manuel de droit international public*, 3rd edn (Paris, Presses universitaires de France, 2016).
Armstrong, D (ed), *Routledge Handbook of International Law* (London, Routledge, 2009).
Bederman, DJ and Keitner, CI, *International Law Frameworks (Concepts and Insights)*, 4th edn (New York, Foundation Press, 2016).
Besson, S and Tasioulas, J (eds), *The Philosophy of International Law* (Oxford, OUP, 2010).
Blay, S, Piotrowicz, R and Tsamenyi, M (eds), *Public International Law. An Australian Perspective*, 2nd edn (Melbourne, OUP, 2005).
Bossuyt, M and Wouters, J, *Grondlijnen van internationaal recht* (Antwerp, Intersentia, 2005).
Buergenthal, T and Murphy, SD, *Public International Law in a Nutshell*, 5th edn (St Paul, West, 2013).
Canal-Forgues, E and Rambaud, P, *Droit international public*, 3rd edn (Paris, Flammarion, 2016).
Carreau, D and Marrella, F, *Droit international*, 11th edn (Paris, Pedone, 2012).

Carter, BE and Weiner, AS, *International Law*, 6th edn (New York, Aspen, 2011).
Cassese, A, *International Law in a Divided World* (Oxford, Clarendon, 1986).
Cassese, A, *International Law*, 2nd edn (Oxford, OUP, 2004).
Chen, L-C, *An Introduction to Contemporary International Law. A Policy-Oriented Perspective*, 3rd edn (Oxford, OUP, 2015).
Clapham, A, *Brierly's Law of Nations: An Introduction to the Role of International Law in International Relations*, 7th edn (Oxford, OUP, 2012).
Cogen, M, *The Comprehensive Guide to International Law* (Bruges, Die Keure, 2008).
Combacau, J and Sur, S, *Droit international public*, 12th edn (Paris, Montchrestien, 2016).
Conforti, B, *Diritto internazionale*, 11th edn (Napels, Editoriale Scientifica, 2018).
Crawford, J, *The Creation of States in International Law*, 2nd edn (Oxford, OUP, 2007).
Crawford, J, *Brownlie's Principles of Public International Law*, 8th edn (Oxford, OUP, 2012).
Crawford, J and Koskenniemi, M (eds), *The Cambridge Companion to International Law* (Cambridge, CUP, 2012).
Daillier, P, Forteau, M, Quoc Dinh, N and Pellet, A, *Droit international public*, 8th edn (Paris, LGDJ, 2009).
Decaux, E and de Frouville, O, *Droit international public*, 10th edn (Paris, Dalloz, 2016).
Deyra, M, *Droit international public*, 6th edn (Issy-les-Moulineaux, Gualino, 2018).
Diez de Velasco Vallejo, M, *Instituciones de derecho internacional público*, 18th edn (Madrid, Tecnos, 2013).
Dixon, M, *Textbook on International Law*, 7th edn (Oxford, OUP, 2013).
Doehring, K, *Völkerrecht. Ein Lehrbuch*, 2nd edn (Heidelberg, Müller, 2004).
Dreyfus, S, *Droit des relations internationales. Eléments de droit international public*, 4th edn (Paris, Cujas, 1997).
Dugard, J, *International Law. A South African Perspective*, 4th edn (Cape Town, Juta & Co, 2011).
Dupuy, P-M and Kerbrat, Y, *Droit international public*, 13th edn (Paris, Dalloz, 2016).
Dupuy, R-J, *Le droit international*, 12th edn (Paris, Presses universitaires de France, 2001).
Emanuelli, C, *Droit international public. Contribution à l'étude du droit international selon une perspective canadienne*, 3rd edn (Montreal, Wilson & Lafleur, 2010).
Evans, MD (ed), *International Law*, 4th edn (Oxford, OUP, 2014).
Fassbender, B and Peters, A (eds), *The Oxford Handbook of the History of International Law* (Oxford, OUP, 2012).
Fischer, P and Köck, HF, *Völkerrecht: das Recht der universellen Staatengemeinschaft* (Vienna, Linde, 2004).
Herdegen, M, *Völkerrecht*, 15th edn (Munich, Beck, 2016).
Higgins, R, *Problems and Process. International Law and How We Use It* (Oxford, Clarendon, 1995).
Hillier, T, *Principles of Public International Law*, 2nd edn (London, Cavendish, 1999).
Hobe, S, *Einführung in das Völkerrecht*, 10th edn (Tübingen, A Francke, 2014).
Horbach, N, Lefeber, R and Ribbelink, O, *Handboek internationaal recht* (The Hague, TMC Asser Press, 2007).
Ipsen, K (ed), *Völkerrecht. Ein Studienbuch*, 6th edn (Munich, Beck, 2014).
Jennings, R and Watts, A (eds), *Oppenheim's International Law*, 9th edn (Oxford, OUP, 2008).
Joyner, CC, *International Law in the 21st Century. Rules for Global Governance* (Lanham, Rowman & Littlefield, 2005).
Kaczorowska-Ireland, A, *Public International Law*, 5th edn (London, Routledge, 2015).
Kälin, W, Epiney, A, Caroni, M and Künzli, J, *Völkerrecht: eine Einführung*, 3rd edn (Bern, Stämpfli, 2010).
Kempen, B and Hillgruber, C, *Völkerrecht*, 2nd edn (Munich, Beck, 2012).
Klabbers, J, *International Law*, 2nd edn (Cambridge, CUP, 2017).
Kokott, J, Doehring, K and Buergenthal, T, *Grundzüge des Völkerrechts*, 3rd edn (Heidelberg, Müller, 2003).

Kooijmans, PH, *Internationaal publiekrecht in vogelvlucht*, 10 edn (Deventer, Kluwer, 2008).
Ku, C and Diehl, PF (eds), *International Law. Classic and Contemporary Readings*, 3rd edn (Boulder, Lynne Rienner, 2008).
Lascombe, M, *Le droit international public* (Paris, Dalloz, 1996).
Malanczuk, P, *Akehurst's Modern Introduction to International Law*, 7th edn (London, Routledge, 1997).
Müller, JP and Wildhaber, L (eds), *Praxis des Völkerrechts*, 3rd edn (Bern, Stämpfli, 2000).
Murphy, SD, *Principles of International Law*, 2nd edn (St Paul, West, 2012).
Nollkaemper, A, *Kern van het internationaal publiekrecht*, 7th edn (The Hague, Boom Juridische Uitgevers, 2016).
O'Brien, J, *International Law* (London, Cavendish, 2001).
Orakhelashvili, A (ed), *Research Handbook on the Theory and History of International Law* (Cheltenham, Edward Elgar, 2011).
Orford, A and Hoffmann, F (eds), *The Oxford Handbook of the Theory of International Law* (Oxford, OUP, 2016).
Perrin, GJ, *Droit international public. Sources, sujets, caractéristiques* (Zürich, Schulthess, 1999).
Perrin de Brichambaut, M and Dobelle, J-F, *Leçons de droit international public*, 2nd edn (Paris, Dalloz/Presses de Sciences Po, 2011).
Reinisch, A, *Österreichisches Handbuch des Völkerrechts*, 5th edn (Vienna, Manz, 2013).
Reisman, WM, Arsanjani, MH, Westerman, GS and Wiessner, S, *International Law in Contemporary Perspective*, 2nd edn (New York, Foundation Press, 2004).
Roche, C, *L'essentiel du droit international public* (Issy-les-Moulineaux, Gualino, 2016).
Rosenne, S, *The Perplexities of Modern International Law* (Leiden, Nijhoff, 2003).
Rosenne, S, *Essays on International Law and Practice* (Leiden, Nijhoff, 2007).
Ruzié, D and Teboul, G, *Droit international public*, 23rd edn (Paris, Dalloz, 2015).
Schachter, O, *International Law in Theory and Practice* (Dordrecht, Nijhoff, 1991).
Schwarzenberger, G, *International Law as Applied by International Courts and Tribunals*, 3rd edn (London, Stevens, 1986).
Shaw, MN, *International Law*, 8th edn (Cambridge, CUP, 2017).
Shearer, IA, *Starke's International Law*, 11th edn (London, Butterworths, 1994).
Slomanson, WR, *Fundamental Perspectives on International Law*, 6th edn (Boston, Thomson-Wadsworth, 2011).
Tomuschat, C and Walter, C, *Völkerrecht*, 7th edn (Baden-Baden, Nomos, 2016).
Torsten, S and von Buttlar, C, *Völkerrecht*, 13th edn (Munich, Franz Vahlen, 2012).
Tourme-Jouannet, E, *Le droit international* (Paris, Presses universitaires de France, 2013).
Touscoz, J, *Droit international*, (Paris, Presses universitaires de France, 1993).
Van Dervort, TR, *International Law and Organization: An Introduction* (Thousand Oaks, Sage, 1997).
Verhoeven, J, *Droit international public* (Brussels, Larcier, 2000).
Vitzthum, WG and Proelß, A (eds), *Völkerrecht*, 7th edn (Berlin, De Gruyter, 2016).
von Arnauld, A, *Völkerrecht*, 2nd edn (Heidelberg, Müller, 2012).
Wallace, RMM and Holliday, A, *International Law*, 2nd edn (London, Sweet & Maxwell, 2010).
Wallace, RMM and Martin-Ortega, O, *International Law*, 8th edn (London, Sweet & Maxwell, 2016).
Zarka, J-C, *Droit international public*, 2nd edn (Paris, Ellipses, 2011).
Ziegler, AR, *Einführung in das Völkerrecht*, 3rd edn (Bern, Stämpfli, 2015).

ii. Casebooks and Exercises

Blumenwitz, D, *Fälle und Lösungen zum Völkerrecht: Übungsklausuren mit gutachterlichen Lösungen und Erläuterungen*, 2nd edn (Stuttgart, Boorberg 2005).
Bretton, P, *Travaux dirigés de droit international public et de relations internationales: commentaire de textes, note de synthèse, cas pratique, dissertation* (Paris, Litec, 1991).

Casanovas, O and Rodrigo, AJ, *Casos y textos de derecho internacional público*, 6th edn (Madrid, Tecnos, 2010).
Damrosch, L, Henkin, L, Murphy, S and Smit, H, *International Law: Cases and Materials*, 5th edn (St Paul, West, 2009).
Distefano, G and Buzzini, GP, *Bréviaire de jurisprudence internationale: les fondamentaux du droit international public* (Brussels, Bruylant, 2010).
Dixon, M, McCorquodale, R and Williams, S, *Cases & Materials on International Law*, 6th edn (Oxford, OUP, 2016).
Fernández Tomás, A, *Derecho internacional público: casos y materiales*, 5th edn (Valencia, Tirant lo Blanch, 2001).
Harris, DJ and Sivakumaran, S, *Cases and Materials on International Law*, 8th edn (London, Sweet & Maxwell, 2015).
Heintschel von Heinegg, W, *Casebook Völkerrecht* (Munich, Beck, 2005).
Janis, MW and Noyes, JE, *International Law: Cases and Commentary*, 5th edn (St Paul, West, 2014).
Kempen, B and Hillgruber, C, *Fälle zum Völkerrecht*, 2nd edn (Munich, Beck, 2012).
Kunig, P and Uerpmann-Wittzack, R, *Übungen im Völkerrecht*, 2nd edn (Berlin, De Gruyter, 2006).
Menzel, J, Pierlings, T and Hoffman, J, *Völkerrechtsprechung: ausgewählte Entscheidungen zum Völkerrecht in Retrospektive* (Tübingen, Mohr Siebeck, 2005).
Milhat, C, *Les indispensables du droit international public* (Paris, Ellipses, 2016).
O'Connell, ME, Scott, RF, Roht-Arriaza, N and Bradlow, DD, *The International Legal System: Cases and Materials*, 7th edn (New York, Foundation Press, 2015).
Odendahl, K and Odendahl, G, *Völkerrecht – Sammlung höchstrichterlicher Rechtsprechung: Entscheidungsauszüge, Kommentierungen, Kontrollfragen* (Neuwied, Luchterhand, 1999).
Partan, DG, *The International Law Process: Cases and Materials* (Durham, Carolina Academic Press, 1992).
Reimann, MW, Hathaway, JC, Dickinson, TL and Samuels, JH, *Transnational Law: Cases and Materials* (St Paul, West, 2013).
Ruzié, D and Teboul, G, *Droit international public*, 23rd edn (Paris, Dalloz, 2015).
Sapienza, R, *Diritto internazionale: casi e materiali*, 4th edn (Turin, Giappichelli, 2014).
Scovazzi, T, *Esercitazioni di diritto internazionale* (Milan, Giuffrè, 1994).
Shaw, MN, *Rosenne's Law and Practice of the International Court: 1920–2015*, 5th edn (Leiden, Brill Nijhoff 2016).
Steiner, HJ and Vagts, DF, *Transnational Legal Problems: Materials and Text*, 4th edn (Mineola, Foundation Press, 1994).
Von Arnauld, A, *Klausenkurs im Völkerrecht*, 2nd edn (Heidelberg, Müller, 2012).
Weber, A, *Fälle zum Völker- und Europarecht* (Munich, Beck, 1992).
Weston, BH, Falk, RA, Charlesworth, H and Strauss, AL, *International Law and World Order. A Problem-Oriented Coursebook*, 4th edn (St Paul, West, 2006).
Wouters, J, *Cases van internationaal recht* (Antwerp, Intersentia, 2005).

iii. Encyclopedias – Legal Dictionaries

Bernhardt, R (ed), *Encyclopedia of Public International Law* (Amsterdam, North-Holland, 1992).
Bledsoe, RL and Boczek, BA, *The International Law Dictionary* (Oxford, Clio, 1987).
Boczek, BA, *International Law: A Dictionary* (Lanham, Scarecrow Press, 2005).
Grant, JP and Barker, JC, *Encyclopaedic Dictionary of International Law*, 3rd edn (Oxford, OUP, 2009).
Kdhir, M, *Dictionnaire juridique de la Cour internationale de justice*, 2nd edn (Brussels, Bruylant, 2000).
Salmon, J (ed), *Dictionnaire de droit international public* (Brussels, Bruylant, 2001).

Schiavone, G, *International Organizations: A Dictionary and Directory*, 7th edn (New York, Palgrave, 2008).
Seidl-Hohenveldern, I, *Lexikon des Rechts. Völkerrecht* (Darmstadt, Luchterhand, 2001).
Volger, H (ed), *A Concise Encyclopedia of the United Nations*, 2nd edn (The Hague, Nijhoff, 2009).
Wolfrum, R (ed), *The Max Planck Encyclopedia of Public International Law*, 2nd edn (Oxford, OUP, 2013).

iv. Sourcebooks

Brownlie, I, *Basic Documents in International Law*, 6th edn (Oxford, OUP, 2008).
Dupuy, P-M and Kerbrat, Y, *Les grands textes de droit international public*, 8th edn (Paris, Dalloz, 2012).
Evans, MD, *Blackstone's International Law Documents*, 12th edn (Oxford, OUP, 2015).
Guerrero Mayorga, O, *Recopilación de textos básicos de derecho internacional público* (Managua, Somarriba, 1999).
Neuhold, H, Hummer, W and Schreuer, C, *Österreichisches Handbuch des Völkerrechts. Band II Materialienteil*, 5th edn (Vienna, Manz, 2013).
Randelzhofer, A, *Völkerrechtliche Verträge*, 13th edn (Munich, Deutscher Taschenbuch Verlag, 2013).
Suy, E, *Corpus Iuris Gentium*, 2nd edn (Leuven, Acco, 1996).
Van Alebeek, R, Brölmann, C, den Heijer, M and Nollkaemper, A, *Jurisprudentie en documentatie internationaal publiekrecht*, 7th edn (The Hague, Boom Juridische Uitgevers, 2016).
World Trade Organization, *The Legal Texts. The Results of the Uruguay Round of Multilateral Trade Negotiations* (Cambridge, CUP, 1999).
Wouters, J, *Bronnen van Internationaal Recht* (Antwerp, Intersentia, 2004).

B. Specific Fields of International Law

i. International Organisations

Alvarez, JA, *International Organizations as Law-Makers* (Oxford, OUP, 2006).
Amerasinghe, CF, *Principles of the Institutional Law of International Organizations*, 2nd edn (Cambridge, CUP, 2005).
Archer, C, *International Organizations*, 4th edn (London, Routledge, 2015).
Boisson de Chazournes, C, Romano, CPR and Mackenzie, R (eds), *International Organizations and International Dispute Settlement: Trends and Prospects* (Ardsley, Transnational, 2002).
Charpentier, J and Sierpinski, B, *Institutions Internationales*, 18th edn (Paris, Dalloz, 2012).
Cogan, JK, Hurd, I and Johnstone, I (eds), *The Oxford Handbook of International Organizations* (Oxford, OUP, 2017).
Coicauld, J-M and Heiskanen, V (eds), *The Legitimacy of International Organizations* (Tokyo, United Nations UP, 2001).
Colliard, C-A, *Institutions internationales*, 10th edn (Paris, Dalloz, 1995).
David, E, *Droit des organisations internationales* (Bruxelles, Bruylant, 2016).
Diez de Velasco, M, *Las Organisaciones Internacionales*, 16th edn (Madrid, Tecnos, 2010).
Dupuy, R (ed), *Manuel sur les organisations internationales/A Handbook on International Organizations*, 2nd edn (Dordrecht, Nijhoff, 1998).
Feld, WJ, Jordan, RS and Hurwitz, L, *International Organizations. A Comparative Approach*, 3rd edn (Westport – London, Praeger, 1994).
Karns, MP, Mingst, KA and Stiles, KW, *International Organizations: The Politics and Processes of Global Governance* (Boulder, Lynne Rienner, 2015).
Kirgis, FL, *International Organizations in their Legal Setting*, 2nd edn (St Paul, West, 1993).
Klabbers, J (ed), *International Organizations* (Aldershot, Ashgate, 2005).

Klabbers, J, *An Introduction to International Organizations Law*, 3rd edn (Cambridge, CUP, 2015).
Klabbers, J, *Advanced Introduction to the Law of International Organizations* (Cheltenham, Edward Elgar, 2015).
Klabbers, J and Wallendahl, A (eds), *Research Handbook on the Law of International Organizations* (Cheltenham, Edward Elgar, 2011).
Lagrange, E, *La représentation institutionnelle dans l'ordre international: une contribution à la théorie de la personnalité morale des organisations internationales* (The Hague, KLI, 2002).
LeRoy Bennett, A, *International Organizations. Principles and Issues*, 7th edn (New York, Pearson, 2001).
Reinalda, B, *Decision-Making within International Organisations* (London, Routledge, 2004).
Ruffert, M and Walter, C, *Institutionalisiertes Völkerrecht*, 2nd edn (Munich, Beck, 2015).
Sands, P and Klein, P, *Bowett's Law of International Institutions*, 6th edn (London, Sweet & Maxwell, 2009).
Schermers, H and Blokker, NM, *International Institutional Law: Unity within Diversity*, 5th edn (Leiden, Nijhoff, 2011).
Schiavone, G, *International Organizations: A Dictionary and Directory*, 7th edn (New York, Palgrave, 2008).
Seidl-Hohenveldern, I and Loibl, G, *Das Recht der Internationalen Organisationen einschließlich der Supranationalen Gemeinschaften*, 7th edn (Cologne, Heymann, 2000).
White, ND, *The Law of International Organisations*, 2nd edn (Manchester, Manchester UP, 2005).

ii. United Nations

Alger, CF, *The United Nations System: A Reference Handbook* (Santa Barbara, ABC-CLIO, 2006).
Baehr, P and Gordenker, L, *De Verenigde Naties. Ideaal en werkelijkheid*, 4th edn (Amsterdam, Boom, 2006).
Cede, F and Sucharipa-Behrmann, L (eds), *The United Nations: Law and Practice* (The Hague, KLI, 2001).
Conforti, B and Focarelli, C, *The Law and Practice of the United Nations*, 4th edn (Leiden, Nijhoff, 2010).
Conforti, B and Focarelli, C, *Le Nazioni Unite*, 12th edn (Milan, Kluwer, 2015).
Cot, JP, Pellet, A and Forteau, M (eds), *La Charte des Nations Unies: commentaire article par article*, 3rd edn (Paris, Economica 2005).
Denis, C, *Le pouvoir normatif du Conseil de securité des Nations Unies: portées et limites* (Brussels, Bruylant, 2004).
Diallo, A, *Les Nations Unies face aux nouveaux enjeux de la paix et de la sécurité internationales* (Paris, L'Harmattan, 2005).
Dienst Informatie van de Verenigde Naties, *ABC van de Verenigde Naties* (2006) https://www.unric.org/html/nederlands/un/abc.html.
Gareis, SB, *United Nations: An Introduction*, 2nd edn (Basingstoke, Palgrave, Macmillan 2012).
Gareis, SB and Varwick, J, *Die Vereinten Nationen. Aufgaben, Instrumenten und Reformen*, 5th edn (Stuttgart, UTB, 2014).
Kennedy, P, *The Parliament of Man. The United Nations and the Quest for World Government* (London, Allen Lane, 2006).
Knipping, F, von Mangoldt, H and Rittberger, V (eds), *The United Nations System and its Predecessors* (Oxford, OUP, 1997).
Lee, RS (ed), *Swords into Plowshares: Building Peace through the United Nations* (Leiden, Nijhoff, 2005).
Meyer, V, *Die internationale Verwaltung durch die Vereinten Nationen: Die Aufrechterhaltung von Sicherheit und Ordnung* (Hamburg, Kovac, 2006).
Moore, JA and Pubantz, J, *The New United Nations: International Organization in the Twenty-first Century* (Upper Saddle River, Pearson Education, 2006).

Ozmanczyk, EJ and Mango, A (eds), *Encyclopedia of the United Nations and International Agreements*, 3rd edn (New York, Routledge, 2003).
Ryngaert, C, *De gespecialiseerde organisaties van de Verenigde Naties* (Leuven, Acco, 2011).
Schlesinger, SC, *Act of Creation. The Founding of the United Nations. A Story of Superpowers, Secret Agents, Wartime Allies and Enemies, and their Quest for a Peaceful World* (Cambridge, Westview Press, 2004).
Simma, B, Khan, D-E, Nolte, G and Paulus, A (eds), *The Charter of the United Nations: A Commentary*, 3rd edn (Oxford, OUP, 2012).
Singh, MK and Kumar, A, *United Nations Organisation* (New Delhi, KK Publications, 2001).
Taylor, P and Groom, AJR (eds), *The United Nations at the Millennium. The Principal Organs* (London, Continuum, 2000).
Tehindrazanarivelo, DL, *Les sanctions des Nations Unies et leurs effets secondaires : assistance aux victimes et voies juridiques de prévention* (Paris, Presses universitaires de France, 2005).
Thakur, R, *The United Nations, Peace and Security: From Collective Security to the Responsibility to Protect* (Cambridge, CUP, 2006).
Thomé, N, *Les pouvoirs du Conseil de sécurité au regard de la pratique récente du chapitre VII de la Charte des Nations Unies* (Aix-Marseille, Presses Universitaires d'Aix-Marseilles, 2006).
Varwick, J and Zimmerman, A (eds), *Die Reform der Vereinten Nationen: Bilanz und Perspektiven* (Berlin, Duncker & Humblot, 2006).
Volger, H (ed), *A Concise Encyclopedia of the United Nations*, 2nd edn (The Hague, Nijhoff, 2009).
Weiss, TG and Daws, S (eds), *The Oxford Handbook on the United Nations* (Oxford, OUP, 2008).
White, ND, *The United Nations System: Toward International Justice* (Boulder, Rienner, 2002).
Wouters, J and Ryngaert, C (eds), *De Verenigde Naties: een wereld van verschil?* (Leuven, Acco, 2005).
Ziring, L, Riggs, R and Plano, J, *The United Nations: International Organization and World Politics*, 4th edn (Belmont, Thomson Wadsworth, 2005).

iii. Law of the Sea

Beckert, E and Breuer, G, *Öffentliches Seerecht* (Berlin, De Gruyter, 1991).
Caminos, H (ed), *Law of the Sea* (Aldershot, Ashgate, 2001).
Churchill, RR and Lowe, AV, *The Law of the Sea*, 3rd edn (Manchester, Manchester UP, 1999).
Combacau, J, *Le droit international de la mer* (Paris, Presses universitaires de France, 1985).
Forteau, M and Thouvenin, JM (eds), *Traité de droit international de la mer* (Paris, Pedone, 2017).
Freestone, D, Barnes, R and Ong, DM (eds), *The Law of the Sea: Progress and Prospects* (Oxford, OUP, 2006).
Gupta, UN (ed), *The Law of the Sea* (New Delhi, Atlantic, 2005).
Klein, N, *Dispute Settlement in the UN Convention on Law of the Sea* (Cambridge, CUP, 2005).
Lowe, V and Talmon, S (eds), *The Legal Order of the Oceans: Basic Documents on Law of the Sea* (Oxford, Hart, 2009).
Lucchini, L and Voelckel, M, *Droit de la mer* (Paris, Pedone, 1990–1996).
Nordquist, MH, Sadan, SN and Rosenne, S (eds), *United Nations Convention on the Law of the Sea, 1982: A Commentary* (Dordrecht, Martinus Nijhoff, 1985–2011).
Oda, S, *Fifty Years of the Law of the Sea: With a Special Section on the International Court of Justice: Selected Writings of Shigeru Oda, Judge of the International Court of Justice* (The Hague, KLI, 2003).
Oude Elferink, AG (ed), *Stability and Change in the Law of the Sea: The Role of the LOS Convention* (Leiden, Martinus Nijhoff, 2005).
Pancracio, J-P, *Droit de la mer* (Paris, Dalloz, 2010).
Proelß, A (ed), *The United Nations Convention on the Law of the Sea: A Commentary* (Munich, Beck, 2017).
Rothwell, DR, Oude Elferink, AG, Scott, KN and Stephens, T (eds), *The Oxford Handbook of the Law of the Sea* (Oxford, OUP, 2015).

Rothwell, DR and Stephens, T, *The International Law of the Sea*, 2nd edn (Oxford, Hart, 2016).
Smolinska AM, *Le droit de la mer entre universalisme et régionalisme* (Brussels, Bruylant, 2014).
Somers, E, *Inleiding tot het internationaal zeerecht*, 5th edn (Mechelen, Wolters Kluwer, 2010).
Tanaka, Y, *The International Law of the Sea* (Cambridge, CUP, 2012).
Treves, T and Pineschi, L (eds), *The Law of the Sea: the European Union and its Member States* (The Hague, Martinus Nijhoff Publishers, 1997).
Vukas, B, *The Law of the Sea: Selected Writings* (Leiden, Nijhoff, 2004).

iv. Treaty Law

Aryal, RS, *Interpretation of Treaties: Law and Practice* (New Delhi, Deep & Deep, 2003).
Aust, A, *Modern Treaty Law and Practice*, 3rd edn (Cambridge, CUP, 2013).
Bastid, S, *Les traités dans la vie internationale: conclusion et effets* (Paris, Economica, 1985).
Combacau, J, *Le droit des traités* (Paris, Presses universitaires de France, 1991).
Corten, O and Klein, P (eds), *Les Conventions de Vienne sur le droit des traités : commentaire article par article* (Brussels, Bruylant, 2006).
Corten, O and Klein, P (eds), *The Vienna Conventions on the Law of Treaties: A Commentary*, Vol 2 (Oxford, OUP, 2011).
Davidson, S (ed), *The Law of Treaties* (Aldershot, Ashgate, 2004).
Dörr, O and Schmalenbach, K (eds), *Vienna Convention on the Law of Treaties: A Commentary*, 2nd edn (Heidelberg, Springer, 2018).
Elias, TO, *The Modern Law of Treaties* (Dobbs Ferry, Oceana Publications, 1974).
Ferrari, F, Kieninger, E-M, Mankowski, P, Otte, K, Saenger, I, Schulze, G and Staudinger, A, *Internationales Vertragsrecht* 3rd edn (Munich, Beck, 2018).
Fitzmaurice, M and Elias, OA, *Contemporary Issues in the Law of Treaties* (Utrecht, Eleven International Publishing, 2005).
Gardiner, R, *Treaty Interpretation*, 2nd edn (Oxford, OUP, 2015).
Gautier, P, *Essai sur la définition des traités entre Etats. La pratique de la Belgique aux confins du droit des traités* (Brussels, Bruylant, 1993).
Gowlland-Debbas, V, *Multilateral Treaty-Making: The Current Status of Challenges to and Reforms Needed in the International Legislative Process* (The Hague, Nijhoff, 2000).
Haraszti, G, *Some Fundamental Problems of the Law of Treaties* (Budapest, Akadémiai Kiadó, 1973).
Hingst, U, *Auswirkungen der Globalisierung auf das Recht der völkerrechtlichen Verträge* (Berlin, Duncker & Humblot, 2001).
Hollis, DB (ed), *The Oxford Guide to Treaties* (Oxford, OUP, 2012).
Holloway, K, *Modern Trends in Treaty Law: Constitutional Law, Reservations and the Three Modes of Legislation* (London, Stevens, 1967).
Klabbers, J, *The Concept of Treaty in International Law* (The Hague, Kluwer, 1996).
Klabbers, J and Lefeber, R (eds), *Essays on the Law of Treaties. A Collection of Essays in Honour of Bert Vierdag* (The Hague, Nijhoff, 1998).
Kolb, R, *The Law of Treaties: An Introduction* (Cheltenham, Edward Elgar, 2016).
McNair, AD, *The Law of Treaties*, 2nd edn (Oxford, OUP, 1986).
Masquelin, J, *Le droit des traités dans l'ordre juridique et dans la pratique diplomatique belges* (Brussels, Bruylant, 1980).
Nolte, G (ed), *Treaties and Subsequent Practice* (Oxford, OUP, 2013).
Poirat, F, *Le traité, acte juridique international: recherches sur le traité international comme mode de production et comme produit* (Leiden, Nijhoff, 2004).
Reuter, P, *La Convention de Vienne du 29 mai 1969 sur le droit des traités* (Paris, Colin, 1970).
Reuter, P, *Introduction au droit des traités*, 3rd edn (Paris, Presses universitaires de France, 1995).
Rosenne, S, *The Law of Treaties. A Guide to the Legislative History of the Vienna Convention* (Leiden, Sijthof, 1970).
Rosenne, S, *Developments in the Law of Treaties 1945–1986* (Cambridge, CUP, 1989).

Sinclair, I, *The Vienna Convention on the Law of Treaties*, 2nd edn (Manchester, Manchester UP, 1984).
Strozzi, G, *Il diritto dei trattati* (Turin, Giappichelli, 1999).
Tams, CJ, Tzanakopoulos, A and Zimmermann, A (eds), *Research Handbook on the Law of Treaties* (Chelthenham, Edward Elgar, 2014).
Verwey, D, *The European Community, the European Union and the International Law of Treaties* (The Hague, TMC Asser Press, 2004).
Villiger, ME, *Commentary on the 1969 Vienna Convention on the Law of Treaties* (Leiden, Nijhoff, 2009).
Vischer, F, Huber, L and Oser, D, *Internationales Vertragsrecht*, 2nd edn (Bern, Stämpfli, 2000).
Wetzel, RG and Rauschning, D, *The Vienna Convention on the Law of Treaties: Travaux préparatoires* (Frankfurt am Main, Metzner, 1978).
Wolfrum, R and Röben, V (eds), *Developments of International Law in Treaty Making* (Berlin, Springer, 2005).

v. International Court of Justice

Amr, MSM, *The Role of the International Court of Justice as the Principal Judicial Organ of the United Nations* (The Hague, KLI, 2003).
Bekker, PHF, *World Court Decisions at the Turn of the Millenium (1997–2001)* (The Hague, Nijhoff, 2002).
Fitzmaurice, G, *The Law and Procedure of the International Court of Justice* (Cambridge, Grotius Publications, 1986).
Gill, TD (ed), *Rosenne's The World Court: What It Is and How It Works*, 6th edn (Leiden, Nijhoff, 2003).
Guillaume, G, *La Cour internationale de Justice à l'aube du XXIème siècle: le regard d'un juge* (Paris, Pedone, 2003).
Meyer, HN, *The World Court in Action: Judging among the Nations* (Lanham, Rowman & Littlefield, 2002).
Patel, BN, *The World Court Reference Guide. Judgments, Advisory Opinions and Orders of the Permanent Court of International Justice and the International Court of Justice (1922–2000)* (The Hague, KLI, 2002).
Schulte, C, *Compliance with Decisions of the International Court of Justice* (Oxford, OUP, 2004).
Shaw, MN, *Rosenne's Law and Practice of the International Court: 1920–2015*, 5th edn (Leiden, Brill Nijhoff, 2016).
Zimmerman, A, Oellers-Frahm, K, Tomuschat, C and Tams, CJ, *The Statute of the International Court of Justice: A Commentary*, 2nd edn (Oxford, OUP, 2012).
Zyberi, G, *The Humanitarian Face of the International Court of Justice: Its Contribution to Interpreting and Developing International Human Rights and Humanitarian Law Rules and Principles* (Antwerp, Intersentia, 2008).

vi. Human Rights

Addo, MK, *International Law of Human Rights* (Aldershot, Ashgate, 2006).
Addo, MK, *The Legal Nature of International Human Rights* (Leiden, Nijhoff, 2010).
Alston, P (ed), *Non-State Actors in Human Rights* (Oxford, OUP, 2005).
Alston, P and Goodman, R, *International Human Rights: The Successor to International Human Rights in Context* (Oxford, OUP, 2012).
Barkhuysen, T, van Emmerik, ML and Rieter, ER, *Procederen over mensenrechten onder het EVRM, het IVBPR en andere VN-verdragen* (Nijmegen, Ars Aequi Libri, 2002).

Benedek, W, *Menschenrechte verstehen: Handbuch zur Menschenrechtsbildung*, 3rd edn (Berlin, Berliner Wissenschaftsverlag, 2017).

Ben-Naftali, O (ed), *International Humanitarian Law and International Human Rights Law: Pas de deux* (Oxford, OUP, 2011).

Bossuyt, MJ, *Guide to the 'Travaux Préparatoires' of the International Covenant on Civil and Political Rights* (Dordrecht, Nijhoff, 1987).

Bouziri, N, *La protection des droits civils et politiques par l'O. N. U.: l'œuvre du Comité des Droits de l'Homme* (Paris, L'Harmattan, 2003).

Buergenthal, T, Shelton, D and Stewart, DP, *International Human Rights in a Nutshell*, 4th edn (St Paul, West, 2009).

Carlson, S and Gisvold, G, *Practical Guide to the International* Covenant on Civil *and Political Rights* (Ardsley, Transnational, 2003).

Clapham, A, *The Human Rights Obligations of Non-State Actors* (Oxford, OUP, 2006).

Cohen-Jonathan, G and Flauss, JF (eds), *International Human Rights Law and Non-Governmental Organizations* (Brussels, Bruylant, 2005).

Conforti, B and Francioni, F (eds), *Enforcing International Human Rights in Domestic Courts* (The Hague, Nijhoff, 1997).

Courtis, C, *Courts and the Legal Enforcement of Economic, Social and Cultural Rights: Comparative Experiences of Justiciability* (Geneva, International Commission of Jurists, 2008).

Craven, MCR, *The International Covenant on Economic, Social and Cultural Rights. A Perspective on its Development* (Oxford, Clarendon, 1998).

De Frouville, O, *L'intangibilité des droits de l'Homme and droit international: régime conventionnel des droits de l'Homme et droit des traités* (Paris, Pedone, 2004).

De Schutter, O, *International Human Rights Law: Cases, Materials, Commentary*, 2nd edn (Cambridge, CUP, 2014).

Doebler, CFJ, *International Human Rights Law: Cases and Materials* (Washington, CD Publishing, 2004).

Donnelly, J, *International Human Rights*, 4th edn (Boulder, Westview, 2012).

Doswald-Beck, L and Kolb, R, *Judicial Process and Human Rights: United Nations, European, American and African Systems: Texts and Summaries of International Case-Law* (Kehl, Engel, 2004).

Evans, M and Murray, R, *The African Charter on Human and Peoples' Rights: The System in Practice 1986–2006*, 2nd edn (Cambridge, CUP, 2008).

Evans, T (ed), *Human Rights Fifty Years On. A Reappraisal* (Manchester, Manchester UP, 1998).

Hannum, H (ed), *Guide to International Human Rights Practice*, 4th edn (Ardsley, Transnational, 2004).

Hannum, H, Anaya, SJ and Shelton, DL, *International Human Rights: Problems of Law, Policy and Practice*, 5th edn (New York, Aspen, 2011).

Hanski, R and Suksi, M (eds), *An Introduction to the International Protection of Human Rights. A Textbook*, 2nd edn (Turku, Abo, 1999).

Hennebel, L and Tigroudja, H, *Traité de droit international des droits de l'homme* (Paris, Pedone, 2016).

Henrard, K, *Mensenrechten vanuit internationaal and nationaal perspectief*, 2nd edn (The Hague, Boom Juridische Uitgevers, 2008).

Joseph, S and Castan, M, *The International Covenant on Civil and Political Rights: Cases, Materials and Commentary*, 3rd edn (Oxford, OUP, 2013).

Lawson, E (ed), *Encyclopedia of Human Rights*, 2nd edn (Washington, Taylor & Francis, 1996).

Manisuli, S, *Economic, Social and Cultural Rights in International Law* (Oxford, Hart, 2009).

Marauhn, T (ed), *Die Rechtsstellung des Menschen im Völkerrecht: Entwicklungen und Perspektiven* (Tübingen, Mohr Siebeck, 2003).

Martin, FF, Schnably, SJ, Wilson, RJ, Simon, JS and Tushnet, MV, *International Human Rights and Humanitarian Law: Treaties, Cases and Analysis* (Cambridge, CUP, 2006).

Meyer-Ladewig, J, *Konvention zum Schutz der Menschenrechte und Grundfreiheiten: Handkommentar* (Baden-Baden, Nomos, 2003).
Moeckli, D, Shah, S, Sivakumaran, S (eds) and Harris, D (consultant ed), *International Human Rights Law*, 3rd edn (Oxford, OUP, 2018).
Moriarty, B and Massa, E (eds), *Human Rights Law*, 4th edn (Oxford, OUP, 2012).
Nowak, M, *UN Covenant on Civil and Political Rights. CCPR Commentary*, 2nd edn (Kehl, Engel, 2005).
Peces-Barba Martinez, G, *Théorie générale de droits fondamentaux* (Paris, LGDJ, 2004).
Peers, S, Hervey, T, Kenner, J and Ward, A (eds), *The EU Charter of Fundamental Rights: A Commentary* (Oxford, Hart, 2014).
Pentassuglia, G, *Les minorités and droit international: une étude introductive* (Strasbourg, Council of Europe, 2004).
Pollmann, A and Lohmann, G (eds), *Menschenrechte: ein interdisziplinäres Handbuch* (Stuttgart, Metzler, 2012).
Rainey, B, Wicks, E and Ovey, C, *Jacobs, White & Ovey: The European Convention on Human Rights*, 6th edn (Oxford, OUP, 2014).
Ramcharan, BG (ed), *Human Rights Protection in the Field* (Leiden, Nijhoff, 2005).
Risse, T, Ropp, SC and Sikkink, K (eds), *The Persistent Power of Human Rights: From Commitment to Compliance* (Cambridge, CUP, 2013).
Robertson, AH and Merrills, JG, *Human Rights in the World: An Introduction to the Study of the International Protection of Human Rights*, 4th edn (Manchester, Manchester UP, 1996).
Robinson, M and Boyle, K (ed), *A Voice for Human Rights* (Philadelphia, University of Pennsylvania Press, 2006).
Sachleben, M, *Human Rights Treaties: Considering Patterns of Participation, 1948–2000* (New York, Routledge, 2006).
Schabas, WA, *The European Convention on Human Rights: A Commentary* (Oxford, OUP, 2015).
Sciotti-Lam, C, *L'applicabilité des traités internationaux relatifs aux droits de l'homme and droit interne* (Brussels, Bruylant, 2004).
Sheeran, S and Rodley, N, *Routledge Handbook of International Human Rights Law* (London, Routledge, 2013).
Shelton, D, *Remedies in International Human Rights Law*, 2nd edn (Oxford, OUP, 2005).
Shelton, D, *The Oxford Handbook of International Human Rights Law* (Oxford, OUP, 2013).
Smis, S, Janssens, C, Mirgaux, S and Van Laethem, K, *Handboek mensenrechten: de internationale bescherming van de rechten van de mens* (Antwerp, Intersentia, 2011).
Smith, RKM, *Textbook on International Human Rights*, 7th edn (Oxford, OUP, 2016).
Sudre, F, *La Convention européenne des droits de l'homme*, 10th edn (Paris, Presses universitaires de France, 2015).
Sudre, F, *Droit européen et international des droits de l'homme*, 12th edn (Paris, Presses universitaires de France, 2015).
Wachsmann, P, *Les droits de l'homme*, 5th edn (Paris, Dalloz, 2008).
Wallace, R, *International Human Rights. Text & Materials*, 2nd edn (London, Sweet & Maxwell, 2001).
Weber, A, *Menschenrechte: Texte und Fallpraxis* (Munich, Sellier, 2004).

vii. International Criminal Law

Ahlbrecht, H, Böhm, K-M, Esser, R, Hugger, H, Kirsch, S and Rosenthal, M, *Internationales Strafrecht in der Praxis* (Heidelberg, Müller, 2008).
Ambos, K, *Treatise on International Criminal Law*, 2 Vols (Oxford, OUP, 2013–2014).
Ambos, K, *Internationales Strafrecht: Strafanwendungsrecht, Völkerstrafrecht, Europäisches Strafrecht, Rechtshilfe*, 5th edn (Munich, Beck, 2018).
Ascensio, H, Decaux, E and Pellet, A (eds), *Droit international pénal*, 2nd edn (Paris, Pedone, 2012).

Bantekas, I, *International Criminal Law*, 4th edn (Oxford, Hart, 2010).
Bassiouni, MC, *Introduction au droit pénal international* (Brussels, Bruylant, 2002).
Bassiouni, MC (ed), *International Criminal Law*, 3rd edn (Leiden, Nijhoff, 2008).
Bassiouni, MC, *Introduction to International Criminal Law*, 2nd edn (Dordrecht, Nijhoff, 2012).
Bohlander, M (ed), *International Criminal Justice: A Critical Analysis of Procedures and Institutions* (London, Cameron May, 2007).
Bueno Arús, F and de Miguel Zaragoza, J, *Manual de derecho penal internacional* (Madrid, Universidad Pontificia Comillas, 2003).
Cassese, A (ed), *The Oxford Companion to International Criminal Justice* (Oxford, OUP, 2009).
Cassese, A, Gaeta, P, Baig, L, Fan, M, Gosnell, C and Whiting, A, *Cassese's International Criminal Law*, 3rd edn (Oxford, OUP, 2013).
Cassese, A, Gaeta, P and Jones, JRWD (eds), *The Rome Statute of the International Criminal Court: A Commentary* (Oxford, OUP, 2002).
Cryer, R, Friman, H, Robinson, D and Wilmshurst, E, *An Introduction to International Criminal Law and Procedure*, 3rd edn (Cambridge, CUP, 2014).
De Hert, P, Flamme, J, Holvoet, M and Struyven, O, *Code of International Criminal Law and Procedure, Annotated* (Brussels, Larcier, 2013).
Delmas-Marty, M (ed), *Les sources du droit international pénal: l'expérience des tribunaux pénaux internationaux et le statut de la Cour Pénale Internationale* (Paris, Societé de Législation Comparée, 2005).
Donnedieu de Vabres, H, *Les principes modernes du droit pénal international* (Paris, Editions Panthéon-Assas, 2004).
Dugard, J and Van den Wyngaert, C (eds), *International Criminal Law and Procedure* (Dartmouth, Aldershot, 1996).
Ferdinandusse, W, *Direct Application of International Criminal Law in National Courts* (The Hague, TMC Asser Press, 2006).
Findlay, M, *Governing through Globalised Crime: Futures for International Criminal Justice* (Uffculme, Willan, 2008).
Glaser, S, *Droit international pénal conventionnel* (Brussels, Bruylant, 1970–1978).
Grant, JP, and Barker, JC, *International Criminal Law Deskbook* (London, Cavendish, 2006).
Huet, A and Koering-Joullin, R, *Droit pénal international*, 3rd edn (Paris, Presses universitaires de France, 2005).
Jones, JRWD and Powles, S, *International Criminal Practice*, 3rd edn (Ardsley, Transnational, 2003).
Kittichaisaree, K, *International Criminal Law* (Oxford, OUP, 2001).
Kolb, R and Scalia, D, *Droit international pénal: prècis*, 2nd edn (Basel, Helbing Lichtenhahn, 2012).
Mettraux, G, *International Crimes and the Ad Hoc Tribunals* (Oxford, OUP, 2005).
Politi, M and Gioia, F (eds), *The International Criminal Court and National Jurisdictions* (Aldershot, Ashgate, 2008).
Ratner, SR, Abrams, JS and Bischoff, JL, *Accountability for Human Rights Atrocities in International Law: Beyond the Nuremberg Legacy*, 3rd edn (Oxford, OUP, 2009).
Reydams, L, Wouters, J and Ryngaert, C (eds), *International Prosecutors* (Oxford, OUP, 2012).
Schabas, WA, *An Introduction to the International Criminal Court*, 5th edn (Cambridge, CUP, 2017).
Schabas, WA and Bernaz, N (eds), *Routledge Handbook of International Criminal Law* (London, Routledge, 2013).
Schabas, WA, McDermott, Y and Hayes, N (eds), *The Ashgate Research Companion to International Criminal Law. Critical Perspectives* (Farnham, Ashgate, 2013).
Schiff, BN, *Building the International Criminal Court* (Cambridge, CUP, 2008).
Simbeye, Y, *Immunity and International Criminal Law* (Aldershot, Ashgate, 2004).
Sjöcrona, JM and Orie, AMM, *Internationaal strafrecht vanuit Nederlands perspectief*, 3rd edn (Deventer, Kluwer, 2003).
Stahn, C (ed), *The Law and Practice of the International Criminal Court* (Oxford, OUP, 2015).

Stigen, J, *The Relationship between the International Criminal Court and National Jurisdictions: The Principle of Complementarity* (Leiden, Nijhoff, 2008).

Triffterer, O and Ambos, K (eds), *Rome Statute of the International Criminal Court: A commentary*, 3rd edn (Oxford, Hart, 2016).

Van den Wyngaert, C, *Kennismaking met het Internationaal and Europees Strafrecht* (Antwerp, Maklu, 2003).

Van den Wyngaert, C, Stessens, G and Janssens, L (eds), *International Criminal Law: A Collection of International and European Instruments*, 3rd edn (Leiden, Nijhoff, 2005).

Van Elst, R and Van Sliedregt, E, *Handboek internationaal strafrecht: internationaal and Europees strafrecht vanuit Nederlands perspectief* (Deventer, Kluwer, 2015).

Van Sliedregt, E, Orie, AMM and Sjöcrana, JM (eds), *Handboek internationaal strafrecht: schets van het Europese and internationale strafrecht* (Deventer, Kluwer, 2008).

Werle, G, *Völkerstrafrecht*, 3rd edn (Tübingen, Mohr Siebeck, 2012).

Werle, G and Jeßberger, F, *Principles of International Criminal Law* (Oxford, OUP, 2014).

Wouters, J and Panken, H (eds), *De Genocidewet in internationaal perspectief* (Gent, Larcier, 2002).

Wouters, J and Pattyn, B (eds), *Misdaden tegen de mensheid. De internationale strijd tegen straffeloosheid* (Leuven, Acco, 2006).

Yokaris, A, *La répression pénale en droit international public* (Brussels, Bruylant, 2005).

Zahar, A and Sluiter, GK, *International Criminal Law: A Critical Introduction* (Oxford, OUP, 2007).

viii. International Economic Law

Barton, JH, Goldstein, JL, Josling, TE and Steinberg, RH, *The Evolution of the Trade Regime: Politics, Law, and Economics of the GATT and the WTO* (Princeton, Princeton UP, 2006).

Belanger, M, *Institutions économiques internationales: la mondialisation économique et ses limites*, 6th edn (Paris, Economica, 1997).

Bhala, R, *International Trade Law: Interdisciplinary Theory and Practice*, 3rd edn (London, Lexis Nexis, 2008).

Braune, B, *Rechtsfragen der nachhaltigen Entwicklung im Völkerrecht: eine Untersuchung unter besonderer Berücksichtigung des Handels- und Investitionsrechts* (Frankfurt am Main, Peter Lang, 2005).

Bronckers, MCEJ, *A Cross-Section of WTO Law* (London, Cameron May, 2000).

Carreau, D and Juillard, P, *Droit international économique*, 5th edn (Paris, Dalloz, 2013).

Cass, D, *The Constitutionalization of the World Trade Organization. Legitimacy, Democracy and Community in the International Trading System* (Oxford, OUP, 2005).

Collins, D, *An Introduction to International Investment Law* (Cambridge, CUP, 2017).

Cuyvers, L and Kerremans, B, *Internationale economische organisaties*, 2nd edn (Leuven, Garant, 2005).

Dolzer, R and Schreuer, C, *Principles of International Investment Law* (Oxford, OUP, 2012).

Fletcher, IF, Cremona, M and Mistelis, L (eds), *Foundations and Perspectives of International Trade Law* (London, Sweet & Maxwell, 2001).

Flory, T, *L'Organisation mondiale du commerce. Droit institutionnel et substantiel* (Brussels, Bruylant, 1999).

Footer, M, *An Institutional and Normative Analysis of the World Trade Organization* (Rotterdam, Erasmus Universiteit, 2006).

Herdegen, M, *Internationales Wirtschaftsrecht*,10th edn (Munich, Beck, 2014).

Herdegen, M, *Principles of International Economic Law*, 2nd edn (Oxford, OUP, 2016).

Hilf, M and Oeter, S, *WTO-Recht. Rechtsordnung des Welthandels*, 2nd edn (Baden-Baden, Nomos, 2010).

Hoekman, BM and Mavroidis, P, *The World Trade Organization. Law, Economics and Politics*, 2nd edn (London, Routledge, 2016).

Irwin, D, Mavroidis, P and Sykes, A, *The Genesis of the GATT* (Cambridge, CUP, 2008).

Jackson, JH, *The World Trading System. Law and Policy of International Economic Relations*, 2nd edn (Cambridge, MIT Press, 1997).
Jackson, JH, *The World Trade Organization. Constitution and Jurisprudence* (London, Royal Institute of International Affairs, 1998).
Jackson, JH, *The Jurisprudence of GATT and the WTO. Insights on treaty law and Economic Relations* (Cambridge, CUP, 2000).
Jackson, JH, *Sovereignty, the WTO and Changing Fundamentals of International Law* (Cambridge, CUP, 2006).
Jackson, JH, Davey, WJ and Sykes, AO, *Legal Problems of International Economic Relations. Cases, Materials and Text*, 5th edn (St Paul, West, 2008).
Kieffer, B, *L'Organisation Mondiale du Commerce et l'évolution du droit international public* (Brussels, Larcier, 2008).
Kohona, PTB, *The Regulation of International Economic Relations Through Law* (Dordrecht, Nijhoff, 1985).
Kronke, H, Melis, W and Kuhn, H (eds), *Handbuch internationales Wirtschaftsrecht*, 2nd edn (Cologne, Otto Schmidt, 2017).
Krueger, AO (ed), *The WTO as an International Organization* (Chicago, University of Chicago Press, 1998).
Lester, S, Mercurio, B and Davies, A, *World Trade Law: Text, Materials and Commentary*, 2nd edn (Oxford, Hart, 2012).
Lowenfeld, A, *International Economic Law*, 2nd edn (Oxford, OUP, 2008).
Luff, D, *Le droit de l'Organisation mondiale du commerce: analyse critique* (Brussels, Bruylant, 2004).
Macrory, P, Appleton, A and Plummer, M (eds), *The World Trade Organization. Legal, Economic and Political Analysis* (New York, Springer, 2005).
Matsushita, M, Schoenbaum, TJ, Mavroidis, PC and Hahn, M, *The World Trade Organization. Law, Practice and Policy*, 3rd edn (Oxford, OUP, 2015).
Mavroidis, PC, *The General Agreement on Tariffs and Trade. A Commentary* (Oxford, OUP, 2005).
Mavroidis, PC, *Trade in Goods: The GATT and the Other Agreements Regulating Trade in Goods*, 2nd edn (Oxford, OUP, 2012).
Mavroidis, PC and Sykes, AO (eds), *The WTO and International Trade Law: Dispute Settlement* (Aldershot, Elgar, 2005).
Muchlinski, P, Ortino, F and Schreuer, C (eds), *The Oxford Handbook of International Investment Law* (Oxford, OUP, 2008).
Nadakavukaren Schefer, K, *International Investment Law. Text, Cases and Materials*, 2nd edn (Cheltenham, Edward Elgar, 2016).
Narlikar, A, *The World Trade Organization. A Very Short Introduction* (Oxford, OUP, 2005).
Organization for Economic Co-operation and Development, *Droit international de l'investissement: un domaine and mouvement: complément aux perspectives de l'investissement international* (Paris, OECD, 2005).
Pissoort, W and Saerens, P, *Initiation au droit commercial international* (Brussels, De Boeck, 2004).
Pryles, M, Waincymer, J and Davies, M, *International Trade Law: Commentary and Materials*, 2nd edn (Pyrmont, Lawbook, 2004).
Rey, J-J and Dutry, J, *Institutions économiques internationales*, 3rd edn (Brussels, Bruylant, 2001).
Schnitzer, S, *Understanding International Trade Law* (Exeter, Law Matters, 2006).
Seidl-Hohenveldern, I, *International Economic Law*, 3rd edn (Dordrecht, Nijhoff, 1999).
Senti, R, *WTO. System und Funktionsweise der Welthandelsordnung* (Zürich, Schulthess, 2000).
Stoll, P-T and Schorkopf, F, *WTO. Welthandelsordnung und Welthandelsrecht* (Cologne, Heymann, 2002).
Stoll, P-T and Schorkopf, F, *WTO. World Economic Order, World Trade Law* (Leiden, Nijhoff, 2006).
Tietje, C (ed), *Internationales Wirtschaftsrecht*, 2d edn (Berlin, De Gruyter, 2015).
Trebilcock, M, Howse, R and Eliason, A, *The Regulation of International Trade*, 4th edn (London, Routledge, 2013).

Van den Bossche, P and Zdouc, W, *The Law and Policy of the World Trade Organization. Text, Cases and Materials*, 4th edn (Cambridge, CUP, 2017).
Van Houtte, H, *The Law of International Trade*, 2nd edn (London, Sweet & Maxwell, 2001).
Venturini, G, *L'Organizzazione Mondiale del Commercio*, 3rd edn (Milan, Giuffrè, 2015).
Vincent, P, *Institutions économiques internationales*, 2nd edn (Brussels, Larcier, 2013).
Wallach, L and Woodall, P, *Whose Trade Organization: A Comprehensive Guide to the WTO*, 2nd edn (New York, New Press, 2004).
Weiler, JHH (ed), *The EU, the WTO and the NAFTA: Towards a Common Law of International Trade?* (Oxford, OUP, 2000).
Weiß, W, Hermann, C and Ohler, C, *Welthandelsrecht*, 2nd edn (Munich, Beck, 2007).
Wouters, J and De Meester, B, *The World Trade Organization. A Legal and Institutional Analysis* (Antwerp, Intersentia, 2007).

ix. International Environmental Law

Barnes, R, *Property Rights and Natural Resources* (Oxford, Hart, 2009).
Beurier, J-P, *Droit international de l'environnement*, 4th edn (Paris, Pedone, 2010).
Beyerlin, U and Marauhn, T, *International Environmental Law* (Oxford, Hart, 2011).
Birnie, P, Boyle, A and Redgwell, C, *International Law and the Environment* (Oxford, OUP, 2009).
Bodansky, D, Brunnée, J and Rajamani, L, *International Climate Change Law* (Oxford, OUP, 2017).
Boisson de Chazournes, L, Desgagne, R and Mbengue, MM, *Protection internationale de l'environnement* (Paris, Pedone, 2005).
Boisson de Chazournes, L and Salman, SMA (eds), *Les ressources en eau et le droit international* (The Hague, Nijhoff, 2005).
Brunnée, J, Bodansky, D and Hey, E (eds), *The Oxford Handbook of International Environmental Law* (Oxford, OUP, 2007).
Carlarne, CP, *Climate Change Law and Policy: EU and US Approaches* (Oxford, OUP, 2010).
Cullet, P and Gowlland-Gualtieri, A (eds), *Key Materials in International Environmental Law* (Aldershot, Ashgate, 2004).
Desai, BH, *Institutionalizing International Environmental Law* (Ardsley, Transnational, 2004).
Dupuy, P-M and Viñuales, JE, *Introduction au droit international de l'environnement* (Brussels, Bruylant, 2015).
Dupuy, P-M and Viñuales, JE, *International Environmental Law* (Cambridge, CUP, 2015).
Fisher, E, Lange, B and Scotford, E, *Environmental Law: Text, Cases and Materials* (Oxford, OUP, 2013).
Gillespie, A, *International Environmental Law, Policy and Ethics*, 2nd edn (Oxford, OUP, 2014).
Guruswamy, LD, *International Environmental Law in a Nutshell*, 4th edn (St Paul, West, 2011).
Kiss, A and Shelton, D, *International Environmental Law*, 3rd edn (Ardsley, Transnational, 2004).
Lavieille, J-M, *Droit international de l'environnement*, 3rd edn (Paris, Ellipses, 2010).
Morgera, E (ed), *The External Environmental Policy of the European Union: EU and International Law Perspectives* (Cambridge, CUP, 2012).
Postiglione, A, *Diritto internazionale dell'ambiente* (Roma, Aracne, 2013).
Proelß, A (ed), *Internationales Umweltrecht* (Berlin, De Gruyter, 2017).
Rajamani, L, *Differential Treatment in International Environmental Law* (Oxford, OUP, 2006).
Rogers, PP, Jalal KF and Boyd, JA, *An Introduction to Sustainable Development* (London, Earthscan, 2008).
Romi, R, *Droit international et européen de l'environnement*, 2nd edn (Paris, Montchrestien, 2013).
Sands, P and Galizzi, P (eds), *Documents in International Environmental Law*, 2nd edn (Cambridge, CUP, 2004).
Sands, P and Peel, J, *Principles of International Environmental Law*, 4th edn (Cambridge, CUP, 2018).

x. International Humanitarian Law and Law on the Use of Force

Arai-Takahashi, Y, *The Law of Occupation: Continuity and Change of International Humanitarian Law, and Its Interaction With International Human Rights Law* (Leiden, Nijhoff, 2009).
Belanger, M, *Droit international humanitaire général*, 2nd edn (Paris, Gualino, 2007).
Bellamy, AJ and Williams, PD, *Understanding Peacekeeping*, 2nd edn (Cambridge, Polity, 2010).
Benvenisti, E, *The International Law of Occupation*, 2nd edn (Oxford, OUP, 2012).
Bettati, M, *Droit humanitaire* (Paris, Dalloz, 2012).
Biad, A and Tavernier, P (eds), *Le droit international humanitaire face aux défis du XXIe siècle* (Brussels, Bruylant, 2012).
Blokker, N and Schrijver, N (eds), *The Security Council and the Use of Force: Theory and Reality – A Need for Change?* (Dordrecht, Nijhoff, 2005).
Boothby, WH, *Weapons and the Law of Armed Conflict*, 2nd edn (Oxford, OUP, 2016).
Bothe, M et al (eds), *Redefining Sovereignty: The Use of Force after the Cold War* (Ardsley, Transnational Publishers, 2005).
Bothe, M, Partsch, KJ and Solf, WA, *New Rules for Victims of Armed Conflicts: Commentary on the Two 1977 Protocols Additional to the Geneva Conventions of 1949*, 2nd edn (Leiden, Nijhoff, 2013).
Bouchet-Saulnier, F, *Dictionnaire pratique de droit humanitaire*, 4th edn (Paris, La Découverte, 2013).
Bowden, B, Charlesworth, H and Farall, J, *The Role of International Law in Rebuilding Societies after Conflict* (Cambridge, CUP, 2009).
Bowett, D, *Self-Defence in International Law* (New York, Lawbook Exchange, 1958).
Brownlie, I, *International Law and the Use of Force by States* (Oxford, OUP, 1963).
Bugnion, F, *The International Committee of the Red Cross and the Protection of War Victims* (Geneva, International Committee of the Red Cross, 2003).
Carey J, Dunlap, W and Pritchard, J (eds), *International Humanitarian Law* (Ardsley, Transnational, 2004).
Cassese, A (ed), *The Current Legal Regulation on the Use of Force* (Dordrecht, Nijhoff, 1986).
Chesterman, S, *Just War or Just Peace? Humanitarian Intervention and International Law* (Oxford, OUP, 2001).
Clapham, A and Gaeta, P (eds), *The Oxford Handbook of International Law in Armed Conflict* (Oxford, OUP, 2014).
Clapham, A, Gaeta P and Sassòli, M (eds), *The 1949 Geneva Conventions: A Commentary* (Oxford, OUP, 2015).
Coolen, G, *Humanitair oorlogsrecht* (Deventer, Tjeenk Willink, 1998).
Corn, G, Hansen, V, Jackson, R, Jenks, C, Jensen, E and Schoettler, J, *The Law of Armed Conflict: An Operational Approach* (New York, Wolters Kluwer, 2012).
Corten, O, *The Law Against War: The Prohibition on the Use of Force in Contemporary International Law* (Oxford, Hart, 2010).
Corten, O, *Le droit contre la guerre: l'interdiction du recours à la force en droit international contemporain*, 2nd edn (Paris, Pedone, 2014).
Crawford, E and Pert, A, *International Humanitarian Law* (Cambridge, CUP, 2015).
Cullen, A, *The Concept of Non-International Armed Conflict in International Humanitarian Law* (Cambridge, CUP, 2010).
Daboné, Z, *Le droit international public relatif aux groupes armés non étatiques* (Zürich, Schulthess Verlag, 2012).
David, E, *Principes de droit des conflits armés*, 5th edn (Brussels, Bruylant, 2012).
David, E, Tulkens, F and Vandermeersch, D, *Code de droit international humanitaire*, 7th edn (Brussels, Bruylant, 2016).
De Wet, E, *The Chapter VII Powers of the United Nations Security Council* (Oxford, Hart, 2004).
Dinstein, Y, *The International Law of Belligerent Occupation* (Cambridge, CUP, 2009).
Dinstein, Y, *The Conduct of Hostilities under the Law of International Armed Conflict*, 2nd edn (Cambridge, CUP, 2010).
Dinstein, Y, *War, Aggression and Self-Defence*, 5th edn (Cambridge, CUP, 2011).

Dinstein, Y, *Non-International Armed Conflicts in International Law* (Cambridge, CUP, 2014).
Fleck, D, *The Handbook of International Humanitarian Law*, 3rd edn (Oxford, OUP, 2013).
Gardam, J, *Necessity, Proportionality and the Use of Force by States* (Cambridge, CUP, 2004).
Gazzini, T, *The Changing Rules on the Use of Force in International Law* (Manchester, Manchester UP, 2005).
Gill, TD and Fleck, D, *The Handbook of the International Law of Military Operations*, 2nd edn (Oxford, OUP, 2015).
Gray, C, *International Law and the Use of Force*, 4th edn (Oxford, OUP, 2018).
Harouel-Bureloup, V, *Traité de droit humanitaire* (Paris, Presses universitaires de France, 2005).
Hasse, J, Müller, E and Scheider, P (eds), *Humanitäres Völkerrecht: politische, rechtliche und strafgerichtliche Dimensionen* (Baden-Baden, Nomos, 2001).
Henckaerts, J-M and Doswald-Beck, L (eds), *Customary International Humanitarian Law* (Cambridge, CUP, 2005).
International Institute of Humanitarian Law, *San Remo Manual on International Law Applicable to Armed Conflicts at Sea* (Cambridge, CUP, 1995).
Kalshoven, F, *Zwijgt het recht als de wapens spreken?*, 2nd edn (The Hague, Staatsuitgeverij, 1985).
Kalshoven, F and Zegveld, L, *Constraints on the Waging of War. An Introduction to International Humanitarian Law*, 4th edn (Cambridge, CUP, 2011).
Kolb, R, *Droit humanitaire et opérations de paix internationales: les modalités d'application du droit international humanitaire dans les opérations de maintien ou de rétablissement de la paix auxquelles concourt une organisation internationale (en particulier les Nations Unies)*, 2nd edn (Basel, Helbing & Lichtenhahn, 2006).
Kolb, R and Gaggioli, C (eds), *Research Handbook on Human Rights and Humanitarian Law* (Cheltenham, Edward Elgar, 2013).
Kolb, R and Hyde, R, *An Introduction to the International Law of Armed Conflicts* (Oxford, Hart, 2008).
Kolb, R, Poretto, G and Vité, S, *L'application du droit international humanitaire et des droits de l'homme aux organisations internationales: forces de paix et administrations civiles transitoires* (Brussels, Bruylant, 2005).
Kress, C, *Gewaltverbod und Selbstverteidigungsrecht nach der Satzung der Vereinten Nationen bei staatlicher Verwicklung in Gewaltakte Privater* (Berlin, Duncker & Humblot, 1995).
McCoubrey, H, *International Humanitarian Law: The Regulation of Armed Conflicts* (Aldershot, Dartmouth, 1990).
Martin, FF, Schnabli, SJ, Wilson, RJ, Simon, JS and Tushnet, MV, *International Human Rights and Humanitarian Law: Treaties, Cases and Analysis* (Cambridge, CUP, 2006).
Moir, L, *The Law of Internal Armed Conflict* (Cambridge, CUP, 2002).
Naert, F, *International Law Aspects of the EU's Security and Defence Policy, with a Particular Focus on the Law of Armed Conflict and Human Rights* (Antwerp, Intersentia, 2010).
Program on Humanitarian Policy and Conflict Research at Harvard University, *HPCR Manual on International Law Applicable to Air and Missile Warfare* (Cambridge, CUP, 2013).
Rogers, APV, *Law on the Battlefield* (Manchester, Manchester UP, 2004).
Rogers, APV, Malherbe, P and Doppler, B, *Fight it Right: Model Manual on the Law of Armed Conflict for Armed Forces* (Geneva, International Committee of the Red Cross, 1999).
Ronzitti, N and Venturini, G (eds), *The Law of Air Warfare: Contemporary Issues* (Utrecht, Eleven International Publishing, 2006).
Rowe, P, *The Impact of Human Rights Law on Armed Forces* (Cambridge, CUP, 2006).
Ruys, T, *'Armed Attack' and Article 51 of the UN Charter* (Cambridge, CUP, 2010).
Ruys, T and Corten, O (eds), *The Use of Force in International Law: A Case-Based Approach* (Oxford, OUP, 2018).
Sassòli, M, Bouvier, AA and Quintin, A, *How Does Law Protect in War? Cases, Documents and Teaching Materials on Contemporary Practice in International Humanitarian Law*, 3rd edn (Geneva, International Committee of the Red Cross, 2006).

Sassòli, M, Bouvier, AA, Quintin, A and Garcia, J, *Un droit dans la guerre? Cas, documents et supports d'enseignement relatifs à la pratique du droit international humanitaire*, 2nd edn (Geneva, Comité International de la Croix-Rouge, 2012).
Schmitt, M (ed), *Tallinn Manual on International Law Applicable to Cyber Warfare* (Cambridge, CUP, 2013).
Sicilianos, L-A, *Les réactions décentralisées à l'illicité: des contre-mesures à la légitime défense* (Paris, Librairie Générale de Droit et de Jurisprudence, 1990).
Sivakumaran, S, *The Law of Non-International Armed Conflict* (Oxford, OUP, 2012).
Solis, GD, *The Law of Armed Conflict: International Humanitarian Law in War*, 2nd edn (Cambridge, CUP, 2016).
Stürchler, N, *Threat of Force in International Law* (Cambridge, CUP, 2009).
Thomas, F and Cuvelier, B, *Inleiding tot het humanitair recht* (Antwerp, Kluwer, 1990).
Torrelli, M, *Le droit international humanitaire*, 2nd edn (Paris, Presses universitaires de France, 1989).
Volk, D, *Die Begrenzung kriegerischer Konflikte durch das moderne Völkerrecht* (Frankfurt am Main, Peter Lang, 2005).
Weller, M (ed), *The Oxford Handbook of the Use of Force in International Law* (Oxford, OUP, 2015).
White, ND, *Keeping the Peace: The United Nations and the Maintenance of International Peace and Security*, 2nd edn (Manchester, Manchester UP, 1997).
White, N, *Advanced Introduction to International Conflict and Security Law* (Cheltenham, Edward Elgar, 2014).
White, ND and Henderson, C (eds), *Research Handbook on International Conflict and Security Law* (Cheltenham, Edward Elgar, 2013).
Wieczorek, J, *Unrechtmäßige Kombattanten und humanitäres Völkerrecht* (Berlin, Duncker & Humblot, 2005).
Wouters, J, De Man, P and Verlinden, N (eds), *Armed Conflicts and the Law* (Antwerp, Intersentia, 2016).

xi. Air and Space Law

Benkö, M and Kroll, W (eds), *Air and Space Law in the 21st Century: Liber Amicorum Professor Karl-Heinz Böckstiegel* (Cologne, Heymann, 2001).
Benkö, M and Schrogl, K-U (eds), *Space Law: Current Problems and Perspectives for Future Regulation* (Utrecht, Eleven International Publishing, 2005).
Cheng, B, *Studies in International Space Law* (Oxford, Clarendon, 1997).
Christol, CQ, *The Modern International Law of Outer Space* (New York, Pergamon, 1982).
Christol, CQ, *Space Law: Past, Present, and Future* (Deventer, Kluwer, 1991).
Diederiks-Verschoor, IHP and Kopal, V, *An Introduction to Space Law*, 3rd edn (Alphen aan de Rijn, KLI, 2008).
Diederiks-Verschoor, IHP and Mendes de Leon, P, *An Introduction to Air Law*, 9th edn (Alphen aan de Rijn, KLI, 2012).
Du Pontavice, E, Dutheil de la Rochère, J, Miller, GM and de Juglart, M, *Traité de droit aérien*, 2nd edn (Paris, Librairie Générale de Droit et de Jurisprudence, 1989–1992).
European Space Agency, *International Organisations and Space Law: Their Role and Contributions* (Noordwijk, European Space Agency, 1999).
Gal, G, *Space Law* (Leiden, Sijthoff, 1969).
Gangale, T, *The Development of Outer Space: Sovereignty and Property Rights in International Space Law* (Santa Barbara, ABC-CLIO, 2009).
Goh, GM, *Dispute Settlement in International Space Law: A Multi-door Courthouse for Outer Space* (Leiden, Nijhoff, 2007).
Grard, L, *Le droit aérien* (Paris, Presses universitaires de France, 1995).
Hobe, S, Schmidt-Tedd, B and Schrogl, K-U, *Cologne Commentary on Space Law* (Cologne, Heymanns, 2009–2013).

Jasentuliyana, N, *Space Law: Development and Scope* (Westport, Praeger, 1992).
Jasentuliyana, N and Lee, RSK (eds), *Manual on Space Law* (Dobbs Ferry, Oceana Publications, 1979–1981).
Jenks, CW, *Space Law* (London, Stevens, 1965).
Kean, A (ed), *Essays in Air Law* (The Hague, Nijhoff, 1982).
Litvine, M and Moury, A, *Droit aérien. Notions de droit belge et de droit international* (Brussels, Bruylant, 1970).
Lyall, F and Larsen, PB, *Space Law: A Treatise* (Aldershot, Ashgate, 2009).
Marchán, J, *Derecho internacional del espacio. Teoria y politica*, 2nd edn (Madrid, Civitas, 1990).
Matte, NM, *Treatise on Air-Aeronautical Law* (Toronto, Carswell, 1981).
McClean, JD et al (eds), *Shawcross and Beaumont: Air Law* (London, Butterworths, 2018).
McNair, A, *The Law of the Air*, 3rd edn (London, Stevens, 1964).
Naveau, J, *Droit du transport aérien international* (Brussels, Bruylant, 1980).
Naveau, J, Godfroid, M and Frühling, P, *Précis de droit aérien*, 2nd edn (Brussels, Bruylant, 2006).
Ogunbanwo, OO, *International Law and Outer Space Activities* (The Hague, Nijhoff, 1975).
Peyrefitte, L, *Droit de l'espace* (Paris, Dalloz, 1993).
Tronchetti, F, *The Exploitation of Natual Resources of the Moon and Other Celestial Bodies: A Proposal for a Legal Regime* (Leiden, Nijhoff, 2008).
Van Bogaert, ERC, *Eléments de droit aérien* (Brussels, Story-Scientia, 1987).
Videla Escalada, FN, *Aeronautical Law* (Alphen aan den Rijn, Sijthoff & Noordhoff, 1979).
Von der Dunk, F and Tronchetti, F (eds), *Handbook of Space Law* (Cheltenham, Elgar, 2015).

C. EU Law

Adam, R and Tizzano, A, *Manuale di diritto dell'Unione Europea*, 2nd edn (Turin, G Giappichelli Editore, 2017).
Arnull, A and Chalmers, D (eds), *The Oxford Handbook of European Union Law* (Oxford, OUP, 2015).
Barents, R, *Remedies and Procedures before the EU Courts* (Antwerp, Kluwer, 2016).
Barents, R and Brinkhorst, LJ, *Grondlijnen van Europees Recht*, 13th edn (Antwerp, Kluwer, 2012).
Barnard, C, *The Substantive Law of the EU: The Four Freedoms*, 5th edn (Oxford, OUP, 2016).
Barnard, C and Peers, S (eds), *European Union Law*, 2nd edn (Oxford, OUP, 2017).
Barnard, C and Scott, J, *The Law of the Single European Market* (Oxford, Hart, 2002).
Bieber, R, Epiney, A, Haag, M and Kotzur, M, *Die Europäische Union: Europarecht und Politik*, 12th edn (Baden, Nomos, 2016).
Chalmers, D, Davies, G and Monti, G, *European Union Law: Text and Materials*, 3rd edn (Cambridge, CUP, 2014).
Cloots, E, De Baere, G and Sottiaux, S (eds), *Federalism in the European Union* (Oxford, Hart, 2012).
Craig, P, *The Lisbon Treaty, Law, Politics and Treaty Reform* (Oxford, OUP, 2010).
Craig, P, *EU Administrative Law*, 2nd edn (Oxford, OUP, 2012).
Craig, P and De Burca, G, *EU Law: Texts, Cases and Materials*, 6th edn (Oxford, OUP, 2015).
Craig, P and De Burca, G (eds), *The Evolution of EU Law*, 2nd edn (Oxford, OUP, 2011).
Griller, S and Ziller, J, *The Lisbon Treaty, EU Constitutionalism Without a Constitutional Treaty* (New York, Springer, 2008).
Hartley, TC, *The Foundations of European Union Law: An Introduction to the Constitutional and Administrative Law of the European Union*, 8th edn (Oxford, OUP, 2014).
Jacqué, JP, *Droit institutionnel de l'Union européenne*, 9th edn (Paris, Dalloz, 2018).
Kuijper, PJ, Wouters, J, Hoffmeister, F, De Baere, G and Ramopoulos, T, *The Law of EU External Relations: Cases, Materials, and Commentary on the EU as an International Legal Actor*, 2nd edn (New York, OUP, 2015).

Lenaerts, K, Maselis, I and Gutman, K, *EU Procedural Law* (Oxford, OUP, 2014).
Lenaerts, K and Van Nuffel, P, *European Union Law* (London, Sweet & Maxwell, 2011).
Masson, A and Nihoul, PL, *Droit de l'Union européenne: droit institutionnel et droit matériel: théorie, exercices et éléments de méthodologie*, 3rd edn (Brussels, Larcier, 2011).
Piris, JC, *The Lisbon Treaty, A Legal and Political Analysis* (Cambridge, CUP, 2010).
Rosas, A and Armati, L, *EU Constitutional Law: An Introduction*, 2nd edn (Oxford, Hart, 2012).
Sarmiento Ramírez-Escudero, D, *El Derecho de la Unión Europea* (Madrid, Marcial Pons Ediciones Jurídicas y Sociales, 2016).
Schütze, R and Tridimas, T (eds), *Oxford Principles of European Union Law, Volume 1: The European Union Legal Order* (New York, OUP, 2018).
Schütze, R, *European Union Law* (Cambridge, CUP, 2015).
Schwarze, J (ed), *EU-Kommentar*, 3rd edn (Munich, Beck, 2012).
Tridimas, T, *The General Principles of EU Law*, 2nd edn (New York, OUP, 2007).
Van Gerven, W, *The European Union: A Polity of States and Peoples*, (Oxford, Hart, 2005).
Van Raepenbusch, S, *Droit institutionnel de l'Union européenne*, 2nd edn (Brussels, Larcier, 2016).
Vedder, C and Heintschel Von Heinegg, W (eds), *Europäisches Unionsrecht: EUV, AEUV, Grundrechte-Charta: Handkommentar*, 2nd edn (Baden, Nomos, 2012).
Wallace, H, Pollack, M and Young, A, *Policy-Making in the European Union*, 7th edn (New York, OUP, 2014).
Wathelet, M, *Contentieux européen*, 2nd edn (Brussels, Larcier, 2014).
Weiler, JHH, *The Constitution of Europe: 'Do the New Clothes Have an Emperor?' and Other Essays on European Integration* (Cambridge, CUP, 1999).
Wyatt, D and Dashwood, A, *Wyatt and Dashwood's European Union Law*, 6th edn (Oxford, Hart, 2011).

II. Periodicals

A. General Periodicals

American Journal of International Law
American Society of International Law. Proceedings of the Annual Meeting
Asian Journal of International Law
Australian International Law Journal
Austrian Journal of Public and International Law
Austrian Review of International and European Law
Belgisch Tijdschrift voor Internationaal Recht
Brooklyn Journal of International Law
Cambridge Journal of International and Comparative Law
Chinese Journal of International Law
Columbia Journal of Transnational Law
Connecticut Journal of International Law
Cornell International Law Journal
Denver Journal of International Law and Policy
Duke Journal of Comparative and International Law
Emory International Law Review
European Journal of International Law
Fordham International Law Journal
Foreign Affairs
Georgia Journal of International and Comparative Law

Georgetown Journal of International Law
Harvard International Law Journal
Indiana International and Comparative Law Review
Indiana Journal of Global Legal Studies
International Affairs
International and Comparative Law Quarterly
International Community Law Review
Internationale Spectator
International Law Forum du droit international
(The) International Lawyer
Journal du droit international
Journal of Transnational Law and Policy
Leiden Journal of International Law
Melbourne Journal of International Law
Michigan Journal of International Law
Netherlands International Law Review
New York University Journal of International Law and Politics
Nordic Journal of International Law
Pace International Law Review
Recueil des Cours de l'Académie de droit international de la Haye
Revue belge de droit international / Belgisch Tijdschrift voor Internationaal Recht
Revue de droit international, de sciences diplomatiques et politiques
Revue de droit international et de droit comparé
Revue générale de droit international public
Stanford Journal of International Law
Studia Diplomatica
Texas International Law Journal
Tilburg Law Review: Journal of International and European Law
Transaktie
Tulane Journal of International and Comparative Law
Vanderbilt Journal of Transnational Law
Yale Journal of International Law
Zeitschrift für ausländisches öffentliches Recht und Völkerrecht

B. Specialised Periodicals

i. International Economic Law

George Washington Journal of International Law and Economics
ICSID Review: Foreign Investment Law Journal
International Financial Law Review
International Trade Law and Regulation
Journal de droit des affaires internationales
Journal of International Economic Law
Journal of International Law and Economics
Journal of World Investment & Trade: Law, Economics, Politics
Journal of World Trade
Law and Policy in International Business
Northwestern Journal of International Law and Business
Revue internationale de droit économique
Revue internationale de la propriété industrielle et artistique

Shipping and Trade Law
World Trade Review

ii. International Humanitarian and Criminal Law

Criminal Law Forum
Global Justice Monitor (before November 2010 *International Criminal Court Monitor*)
Helsinki Monitor: quarterly on security and cooperation in Europe
Internationaal Humanitair Recht in de Kijker
International Criminal Law Review
International Journal of Transitional Justice
International Review of the Red Cross
Journal of Conflict and Security Law
Journal of International Criminal Justice
Tijdschrift voor Militair Strafrecht en Oorlogsrecht
United States Naval War College – International Law Studies
Zoeklicht: viermaandelijks tijdschrift voor internationaal humanitair recht

iii. Law of the Sea, Air and Space Law

Air and Space Law (before 1992 *Air Law*)
(The) Air and Space Lawyer
Annals of Air and Space Law
International Journal of Marine and Coastal Law
Journal of Air Law and Commerce
Journal of Space Law
Ocean Development and International Law
Proceedings IISL Colloquia
Revue française de droit aérien et spatial
Zeitschrift für Luft- und Weltraumrecht

iv. Human Rights

Asia-Pacific Journal on Human Rights and the Law
Business and Human Rights Journal
Columbia Human Rights Law Review
Europäische Grundrechte-Zeitschrift
European Human Rights Law Review
European Human Rights Reports
European Journal of Human Rights/Journal européen des droits de l'homme
Harvard Human Rights Journal
Human Rights & International Legal Discourse
Human Rights Internet Reporter
Human Rights Journal/Journal des droits de l'homme
Human Rights Law Journal
Human Rights Quarterly
International Journal of Children's Rights
International Journal of Discrimination and the Law
International Journal of Group Rights
International Journal of Human Rights
International Journal on Minority and Group Rights

International Journal of Refugee Law
Netherlands Quarterly of Human Rights
NJCM-Bulletin. Nederlands Tijdschrift voor de Mensenrechten
Revue trimestrielle des droits de l'homme
Revue universelle des droits de l'homme
Security and Human Rights

v. *International Environmental Law*

Carbon & Climate Law Review
Colorado Journal of International Environmental Law and Policy
Columbia Journal of Environmental Law
Environmental Policy and Law
European Energy and Environmental Law Review (before 2008 *European Environmental Law Review*)
Georgetown International Environmental Law Review
International Environmental Agreements: Politics, Law and Econcomics
Journal of Energy and Natural Resources Law

vi. *United Nations, International Organisations and International Tribunals*

Helsinki Monitor (about the OSCE)
International Organization
International Organizations Law Review
Law and Practice of International Courts and Tribunals
L'Observateur des Nations Unies
Vereinte Nationen
Wereldbeeld. Tijdschrift voor de Verenigde Naties (before 2004 *VVN-Berichten*)

vii. *Other Specialised Periodicals*

Arbitration International
Chinese (Taiwan) Yearbook of International Law and Affairs
East Asia Law Review
Global Responsibility to Protect
ICC International Court of Arbitration Bulletin
International Arbitration Law Review
International Negotiation
International Peacekeeping
Journal of the History of International Law / Revue d'histoire du droit international
Journal of the Use of Force and International Law
Non-State Actors and International Law

viii. *Periodicals with Official Documents*

Archiv des Völkerrechts
Documents d'actualité internationale
European Commission of Human Rights: Decisions and reports – Commission européenne des droits de l'homme: décisions et rapports
Human Rights Case Digest
Human Rights – Information Bulletin
International Court of Justice. Reports of judgments, advisory opinions and orders

International Law in Brief (only electronic version)
International Legal Materials
Nations Unies. PIDCP. Comité des droits de l'homme. Comptes rendus
Publications of the European Court of Human Rights – Publications de la Cour européenne des droits de l'homme
Series A – Série A (Judgements and Decisions – arrêts et décisions)
Series B – Série B (Pleadings, Oral Arguments and Documents – mémoires, plaidoiries et documents)
Reports of International Arbitral Awards
United Nations Juridical Yearbook
World Trade and Arbitration Materials

ix. EU Law

Cahiers de Droit Européen
Cambridge Yearbook of European Legal Studies
Columbia Journal of European Law
Common Market Law Review
Europarecht
Europe and the World: A Law Review
European Constitutional Law Review
European Foreign Affairs Review
European Law Journal
European Law Review
European Public Law
Maastricht Journal of European and Comparative Law
Nederlands Tijdschrift voor Europees Recht
Revue du Droit de l'Union Européenne
Revue du Marché Commun
Revue du Marché Commun et de l'Union Européenne
SEW: Tijdschrift voor Europees en Economisch Recht

III. Yearbooks

Amnesty International Jaarboek
Annuaire de droit maritime et océanique
Annuaire de l'Institut de droit international
Annuaire français de droit international
Australian Yearbook of International Law
British Yearbook of International Law
Canadian Yearbook of International Law
Czech Yearbook of Public and Private International Law
Finnish Yearbook of International Law
German Yearbook of International Law
Inter-American Yearbook on Human Rights
International Court of Justice. Yearbook
Italian Yearbook of International Law
Jaarboek van het Interuniversitair Centrum voor Mensenrechten
Jahrbuch für internationales Recht
Japanese Yearbook of International Law (before 2008 *Japanese Annual of International Law*)

Max Planck Yearbook of United Nations Law
Netherlands Yearbook of International Law
South African Yearbook of International Law
UNCITRAL Yearbook
United Nations Yearbook of the Human Rights Committee
Yearbook of European Law
Yearbook of International Environmental Law
Yearbook of International Humanitarian Law
Yearbook of International Organizations
Yearbook of the European Convention on Human Rights – Annuaire de la Convention européenne des droits de l'homme
Yearbook of the International Law Commission

IV. Websites

This is a selective bibliography of websites on international law and international organisations and a number of other pertinent websites.

A. International Organisations

i. Collections of Links to International Organisations

International Law Institute	www.ili.org
Northwestern University Library	libguides.northwestern.edu/IGO
Project on International Courts and Tribunals (links to pages with links to dispute settlement organs)	www.pict-pcti.org/site_map.html
UN Organizational Chart	www.unsceb.org/organizationchart

ii. Global International Organisations

BIS	www.bis.org
BITD	www.bitd.org
CAT	www.ohchr.org/en/hrbodies/cat/pages/catindex.aspx
CEDAW	www.un.org/womenwatch/daw/cedaw
CERD	www.ohchr.org/EN/HRBodies/CERD/Pages/CERDIndex.aspx
CESCR	www.ohchr.org/en/hrbodies/cescr/pages/cescrindex.aspx
CIEC (ICCS)	www.ciec1.org
CLCS	www.un.org/Depts/los/clcs_new/clcs_home.htm
CRC	www.ohchr.org/EN/HRBodies/CRC/Pages/CRCIndex.aspx
CTBTO (PrepCom)	www.ctbto.org
FAO	www.fao.org

Hague Conference IPL	www.hcch.net
Human Rights Committee	www.ohchr.org/EN/HRBodies/CCPR/Pages/CCPRIndex.aspx
Human Rights Council	www.ohchr.org/EN/HRBodies/HRC/Pages/HRCIndex.aspx
IAEA	www.iaea.org
IBRD	www.worldbank.org/ibrd
ICAO	www.icao.org
ICC	www.icc-cpi.int
ICES	www.ices.dk
ICSID	www.worldbank.org/icsid
ICTR (lifted)	unictr.unmict.org
ICTY	www.un.org/icty
IDA	www.worldbank.org/ida
IFAD	www.ifad.org
IFC	www.ifc.org
IGH	See UN, ICJ
IHO	www.iho.int/srv1/index.php?lang=en
ILC	See UN, ILC
ILO	www.ilo.org
ILO Admin Tribunal	www.ilo.org/tribunal/lang--en/index.htm
IMF	www.imf.org
IMO	www.imo.org
Interpol	www.interpol.int
IOC (within UNESCO)	www.unesco.org/new/en/natural-sciences/ioc-oceans
IOM	www.iom.int
IPU	www.ipu.org
ISA	www.isa.org.jm
ISH	See ICC
ISO	www.iso.org
ITC	www.intracen.org
ITLOS	www.itlos.org
ITSO	www.itso.int
ITU	www.itu.int
IUCN	www.iucn.org (partly NGO)
IWC	www.iwc.int/home
MIGA	www.miga.org
OHCHR / UNHCHR	www.ohchr.org
OOSA	www.unoosa.org
OPCW	www.opcw.org
PCA (CPA)	www.pca-cpa.org
UN	www.un.org

– Administrative Tribunal	untreaty.un.org/UNAT
– Documentation Centre (per category and year, i.a. all resolutions General Assembly and Security Council)	www.un.org/en/documents/index.html
– Official Document System of the United Nations (ODS) (search function)	documents.un.org
– ICJ (CIJ)	www.icj-cij.org
– ILC	legal.un.org/ilc
– Human Rights Council	www.ohchr.org
– News Centre	www.un.org/News
– Organizational chart	www.unsceb.org/organizationchart
– UNBISnet	unbisnet.un.org (search in UN-publications and documents)
– UNECA	www.uneca.org
– UNECE	www.unece.org
– UNECLAC	www.cepal.org
– UNESCAP	www.unescap.org
– UNESCWA	www.unescwa.org
UNCC	www.uncc.ch
UNCITRAL	www.uncitral.org
UNCTAD	www.unctad.org
UNDP	www.undp.org
UNEP	www.unep.org
UNESCO	www.unesco.org
UNHCHR/OHCHR	www.ohchr.org
UNHCR	www.unhcr.org
UNICEF	www.unicef.org
UNIDIR	www.unidir.org
UNIDO	www.unido.org
UNIDROIT	www.unidroit.org
UPU	www.upu.int
WCO	www.wcoomd.org
WFP	www1.wfp.org
WHO	www.who.int
WIPO	www.wipo.org
– mediation and arbitration centre	www.wipo.int/amc
WMO	www.wmo.int
World Bank Group	www.worldbank.org (IBRD, IFA, ICSID, MIGA, …)
WTO	www.wto.org

– documents	docsonline.wto.org
– documents concerning dispute settlement	www.wto.org/english/tratop_e/dispu_e/dispu_e.htm
WT(ourism)O	www2.unwto.org

iii. Regional Organisations in Europe

Baltic Assembly	www.baltasam.org
Benelux	www.benelux.int
– Court	www.courbeneluxhof.be
– Parliament	www.beneluxparl.eu
Intellectual property	www.boip.int
CERN	www.cern.ch
CCNR	www.ccr-zkr.org
Commission Internationale de la Meuse	www.meuse-maas.be
Commission Internationale de l'Escaut	www.isc-cie.com
Council of Europe	www.coe.int
– ECtHR	www.echr.coe.int
– Committee of Ministers	www.coe.int/t/cm
– Parliamentary Assembly	assembly.coe.int
– Database complaints ESC	hudoc.esc.coe.int
– Documents Committee Prevention Torture	www.cpt.coe.int
– State Reports Minorities Treaty	www.coe.int/en/web/minorities/home
Dutch Language Union	www.taalunie.org
EBRD	www.ebrd.com
EC	See EU
EFTA	www.efta.int
– EFTA Court	www.eftacourt.int
ECtHR	See Council of Europe
EIB	www.eib.org
EIF	www.eif.org
ESA	www.esa.int
ESO	www.eso.org
EU	www.europa.eu
– documents	europa.eu/european-union/documents-publications/official-documents_en
– ECB	www.ecb.eu
– EU Bulletin	ec.europa.eu/archives/bulletin/en/bullset.htm
– EurLex	eur-lex.europa.eu
– consolidated legislation	eur-lex.europa.eu/collection/eu-law/consleg.html?locale=nl

– ECJ	curia.europa.eu
– Newsroom	europa.eu/newsroom
– Official Journal	eur-lex.europa.eu/oj/direct-access.html?locale=nl
– index council documents	register.consilium.europa.eu
– legislative observatory	www.europarl.europa.eu/oeil
EUMETSAT	www.eumetsat.int
Euratom	See EU
Eurocontrol	www.eurocontrol.int
Eurojust	www.eurojust.eu
European Patent Office and EPO	www.epo.org
Europol	www.europol.europa.eu
NATO	www.nato.int
Nordic Council	www.norden.org
OCCAR	www.occar.int
OECD (OESO)	www.oecd.org
OSCE	www.osce.org
– Office for Democratic Institutions and Human Rights (ODIHR)	www.osce.org/odihr
– Court of Conciliation and Arbitration	www.osce.org/cca
– High Commissioner on National Minorities (HCNM)	www.osce.org/hcnm
Western European Union (lifted)	www.weu.int

iv. Regional Organisations in America

ACS	www.acs-aec.org
ALADI	www.aladi.org
Andean Community	www.comunidadandina.org
– Court of Justice	www.tribunalandino.org.ec
CARICOM	www.caricom.org
CDB	www.caribank.org
FTAA	www.ftaa-alca.org
IAComHR	www.oas.org/en/iachr
IACtHR	www.corteidh.or.cr
IADB	www.iadb.org
IAIC	www.iic.org
Mercosur	www.mercosur.int
NAFTA	www.nafta-sec-alena.org
OAS	www.oas.org

OECS	www.oecs.org
SELA	www.sela.org
SICA	www.sica.int
SIECA	www.sieca.int

v. Regional Organisations in Africa

AfDB	www.afdb.org
AU	www.au.int
– NEPAD	www.nepad.org
CEEAC (ECCAS)	www.ceeac-eccas.org
CEMAC	www.ccmac.int
COMESA	www.comesa.int
EAC	www.eac.int
ECOWAS	www.ecowas.int
SADC	www.sadc.int
UEMOA	www.uemoa.int
– BCEAO	www.bceao.int
– BOAD	www.boad.org
AMU	www.maghrebarabe.org

vi. Regional Organizations in Asia

AsDB	www.adb.org
ASEAN	www.asean.org
GCC	www.gcc-sg.org
SAARC	www.saarc-sec.org

vii. Transcontinental Regional Organisations

Arab League	www.arableagueonline.org
APEC	www.apecsec.org.sg
CIS	www.cisstat.com (via CIS Interstate Statistical Committee)
– Executive Committee	www.cis.minsk.by
EAEU	www.eaeunion.org
ECC	www.encharter.org
IDB	www.isdb-pilot.org
NATO	www.nato.int (see also regional organisations in Europe)
OAPEC	www.oapecorg.org
OBSEC	www.bsec-organization.org
OECD (OESO)	www.oecd.org (see also regional organisations in Europe)

– IEA	www.iea.org
– NEA	www.oecd-nea.org
OESO	See OECD
OIC	www.oic-oci.org
OPEC	www.opec.org
OSCE	www.osce.org (see also regional organisations in Europe)
Pacific Community	www.spc.int

viii. Informal Groupings

ACP	www.acp.int
AOSIS	www.aosis.org
Australia Group (AG)	www.australiagroup.net
CBSS	www.cbss.org
Commonwealth	www.thecommonwealth.org
FATF	www.fatf-gafi.org
G-8	www.g8.utoronto.ca (unofficial)
G-20	www.g20.org
G-24	g24.org
G-77	www.g77.org
MTCR	www.mtcr.info
NAM	www.nam.gov.za
NSG	www.nuclearsuppliersgroup.org
OIF	www.francophonie.org
Paris Club	www.clubdeparis.org
SCO	www.infoshos.ru
Wassenaar Arrangement	www.wassenaar.org
Zangger Committee	www.foi.se/en/Customer--Partners/Projects/zc/zangger

B. Treaties

i. General Sites on Treaty Law and Treaty Search Engines

Fundamentals of Treaty Research (Electronic Resources) (L Louis-Jacques, University of Chicago Library)	www.lib.uchicago.edu/~llou/treaties.html
International Legal Research Tutorial – Treaties and Agreements (Duke University and Berkeley School of Law)	www.law.duke.edu/ilrt/treaties_1.htm
Researching Non-US Treaties (S Weigmann, LLRX)	www.llrx.com/2001/05/features-researching-non-u-s-treaties-and-agreements/

Researching US Treaties and Agreements (M Hoffman, LLRX)	www.llrx.com/2001/05/features-researching-u-s-treaties-and-agreements/
UN Treaty Handbook	treaties.un.org/Pages/Resource.aspx?path=Publication/TH/Page1_en.xml

ii. General Collections

ASIL Electronic Information System for International Law (EISIL) (very well-structured, extensive, with links to text and background information)	www.eisil.org
Avalon Project (Yale, also older treaties and documents)	avalon.law.yale.edu
UN Treaty Collection (most recent information on all UN Treaties)	treaties.un.org
UN Treaty Series Online	https://treaties.un.org/Pages/AdvanceSearch.aspx?tab=UNTS&clang=_en
Viadrina International Law Project (VILP) (well-structured and multilingual (EN, FR, DE, PL and SP))	www.vilp.de
WorldLII (extensive, with links to text and at times status)	www.worldlii.org/catalog/2266.html

iii. Treaties within International Organisations

Andean Community (ES)	www.comunidadandina.org/tratados.aspx
COE, (C)ETS (status, five languages)	https://www.coe.int/en/web/conventions/
EU	
– EU and EC Treaties	eur-lex.europa.eu/collection/eu-law/treaties.html
– international agreements	eur-lex.europa.eu/collection/eu-law/inter-agree.html
FAO (status)	www.fao.org/legal/treaties/treaties-under-article-xiv
ICAO (status)	www.icao.int/secretariat/legal/Pages/TreatyCollection.aspx
ILO (status)	www.ilo.org/dyn/normlex/en/f?p=1000:12000:0
IMO (status)	www.imo.org/en/About/Conventions/ListOfConventions
OAS	
– bilateral agreements	www.oas.org/en/sla/dil/bilateral_agreements.asp
– inter-American treaties (status)	www.oas.org/en/sla/dil/inter_american_treaties.asp
OECD Decisions and Legal Instruments	webnet.oecd.org/oecdacts
UNCITRAL (status)	www.uncitral.org/uncitral/en/uncitral_texts.html
UNIDROIT (status)	www.unidroit.org/news (select instruments)
UNTS	treaties.un.org/pages/untsonline.aspx?id=1
WIPO (status)	www.wipo.int/treaties
WTO	www.wto.org/english/docs_e/legal_e/legal_e.htm

iv. Antarctica

Antarctic Treaty Database	www.ats.aq/devAS/info_measures_list.aspx

v. Economic Law

Bilateral investment treaties 1959–2014 (ICSID)	https://icsid.worldbank.org/en/Pages/resources/Bilateral-Investment-Treaties-Database.aspx
Bilateral investment treaties (UNCTAD)	
– 1959–1999	www.unctad.org/en/docs/poiteiiad2.en.pdf
– 1995–2006	www.unctad.org/en/Docs/iteiia20065_en.pdf
International Investment Agreements Navigator (UNCTAD)	investmentpolicyhub.unctad.org/IIA
International Investment Instruments: A Compendium (UNCTAD)	http://unctad.org/en/Pages/DIAE/DIAE%20Publications%20-%20Bibliographic%20Index/International-Investment-Instruments-A-Compendium.aspx
International Trade Instruments (Lex Mercatoria)	www.jus.uio.no/lm/treaties.and.organisations/doc.html

See also the UNCITRAL-, UNIDROIT-, WIPO-,WTO-collections (above) and treaties for the creation of regional economic organisations (above).

vi. Humanitarian and Criminal Law

ICRC (very accurate and extensive)	ihl-databases.icrc.org/ihl
University of Minnesota	hrlibrary.umn.edu/instree/auoy.htm (armed conflict)
	hrlibrary.umn.edu/instree/auox.htm (international crimes)
ICC's Legal Tools Database	www.legal-tools.org

vii. Human Rights

English text of human rights instruments (University of Minnesota, very extensive)	hrlibrary.umn.edu
UN Treaty Bodies Jurisprudence Database (OHCHR)	juris.ohchr.org

viii. Environmental Law

ECOLEX (treaties and other instruments)	www.ecolex.org
ENTRI (very extensive)	sedac.ciesin.columbia.edu/entri/index.jsp
TMC Asser Institute – European Environmental Law (treaties and other instruments)	www.asser.nl/eel/legal-texts
UNEP – Links to secretariats of environmental law treaties (mostly with text and status)	www.unep.org/Documents/Default.asp?DocumentID=43&ArticleID=234

ix. Disarmament

Federation of American Scientists	fas.org
UN Office for Disarmament Affairs (UNODA)	www.un.org/disarmament
– Disarmament Treaties	disarmament.un.org/treaties
– UNODA Documents Library	disarmament-library.un.org
US Bureau of Arms Control, Verification and Compliance	www.state.gov/t/avc
– Treaties and Agreements	www.state.gov/t/avc/trty/index.htm

x. Space Law

OOSA space law page	www.unoosa.org/oosa/en/SpaceLaw/index.html
– Documents and resolutions database	www.unoosa.org/oosa/documents-and-resolutions/search.jspx?&view=resolutions

xi. Terrorism

UN Security Council Counter-Terrorism Committee:	www.un.org/sc/ctc
– Conventions (with summary and status)	https://www.un.org/sc/ctc/resources/international-legal-instruments/

xii. Peace Agreements

UN Peacemaker (database)	www.peacemaker.un.org
US Institute of Peace	www.usip.org/library/pa.html
Incore	www.incore.ulst.ac.uk/services/cds/agreements

xiii. Law of the Sea

Committe Maritime International (status)	www.comitemaritime.org/publication-documents/ratifications/
UN Division for Ocean Affairs and the Law of the Sea	www.un.org/Depts/los

C. Academic Sites on International Law

i. General International Law

American Bar Association, Section of International Law	www.americanbar.org/groups/international_law.html
American Society of International Law (ASIL)	www.asil.org
– Electronic Resource Guide	www.asil.org/resources/electronic-resource-guide-erg
Amsterdam Center for International Law	www.acil.uva.nl

Library Peace Palace (ICJ, with i.a. catalogue and topic search)	www.peacepalacelibrary.nl
British Institute of International and Comparative Law	www.biicl.org
Cambridge University Lauterpacht Research Centre for International Law	www.lcil.law.cam.ac.uk
Canadian Council on International Law	www.ccil-ccdi.ca
Cornell University Library Foreign and International Law Guide	guides.library.cornell.edu/Foreign_and_International_Law_Guide
EJIL: Talk! – Blog of the European Journal of International Law	www.ejiltalk.org
Electronic Information System for International Law	www.eisil.org
European Society of International Law (ESIL)	www.esil-sedi.eu
Globelaw	www.globelaw.com
Georgetown Law Library Foreign and Comparative Law Research Guide	guides.ll.georgetown.edu/ForeignandComparativeLaw
(The) Hague Academy of International Law	www.hagueacademy.nl
Institut de Droit International	www.justitiaetpace.org
Institut de Recherche and Droit International et Européen de la Sorbonne (IREDIES)	www.univ-paris1.fr/unites-de-recherche/iredies
Instituut voor Internationaal Recht (KU Leuven)	www.law.kuleuven.be/iir
International Commission of Jurists	www.icj.org
International Law Association (ILA)	www.ila-hq.org
Koninklijke Nederlandse Vereniging voor Internationaal Recht	www.knvir.org
Nederlandse Vereniging voor de VN	www.nvvn.nl
Max Planck Institute for International Law (with extensive online catalogue)	www.mpil.de
Opinio Juris (international law forum)	www.opiniojuris.org
Project on International Courts and Tribunals	www.pict-pcti.org
Répertoire Paix et Sécurité Internationales (French, a lot of links)	www.toile.org/psi/dip.html
Société Française pour le Droit International	www.sfdi.org
TMC Asser Instituut	www.asser.nl
(Vlaamse) Vereniging voor de VN	www.vvn.be
UN page international law (including ILC)	www.un.org/en/globalissues/internationallaw
Washburn University Foreign and International Law Resources (links)	www.washlaw.edu/forint
World Courts	www.worldcourts.com
World Federation of United Nations Associations (WFUNA) (with links to national UN associations)	www.wfuna.org

ii. Economic Law and Arbitration

CISG-online.ch	www.cisg-online.ch
Institute of International Commercial Law (Pace Univ., incl. database Vienna Convention Sale of Goods (CISG))	www.iicl.law.pace.edu/cisg/cisg
Institute of International Economic Law (Georgetown)	www.law.georgetown.edu/iiel
Internationaal Juridisch Instituut (NL)	www.iji.nl
International Chamber of Commerce	www.iccwbo.org
Lex Mercatoria	www.jus.uio.no/lm
NAFTA claims	www.naftaclaims.com
World Trade Institute	www.wti.org
WorldTradeLaw.net	www.worldtradelaw.net

See also Hague Conference on Private International Law, ICSID, PCA, OECD, UNCITRAL, UNCTAD, UNIDROIT, WIPO, WTO and regional economic organisations (above).

iii. International Humanitarian and Criminal Law

AI Vlaanderen	www.aivl.be
Amnesty International	www.amnesty.org
Geneva Academy of International Humanitarian Law and Human Rights Law	www.geneva-academy.ch
Harvard Law School Library, Nuremberg Trials Project (Digital Document Collection)	nuremberg.law.harvard.edu
Human Rights First (previously LCHR)	www.humanrightsfirst.org
Human Rights Watch	www.hrw.org
Institute for International Law of Peace and Armed Conflict (Bochum)	www.ifhv.de
– BOFAXE: short comments on current events (EN / DE)	www.ifhv.de/index.php/publications/bofaxe
International Committee of the Red Cross	www.icrc.org
– international humanitarian law	www.icrc.org/en/war-and-law
International Criminal Law Network	www.icln.net
International Criminal Law Society	www.icls.de
International Humanitarian Law Research Initiative	https://worldwide.harvard.edu/international-humanitarian-law-research-initiative
International Law of War Association	www.lawofwar.org (not updated since 2010)
International Society for Military Law and the Law of War	www.ismllw.org
Max Planck Institute for Foreign and International Criminal Law	www.mpicc.de/en/home.cfm

Prevent Genocide International	www.preventgenocide.org
San Remo Institute for International Humanitarian Law	www.iihl.org

See also ICC, ICTY, ICTR, SCSL, Lebanon Tribunal, etc.

iv. Human Rights, Minorities and Refugees

African Commission on Human and Peoples' Rights	www.achpr.org
Center for World Indigenous Studies	www.cwis.org
Council of Europe – Human Rights and Rule of Law	www.coe.int/en/web/human-rights-rule-of-law
European Centre for Minority Issues	www.ecmi.de
Equipo Nizkor – Derechos Human Rights	www.derechos.org/nizkor/eng.html
Fédération Internationale des Ligues des Droits de l'Homme	www.fidh.org
Human Rights Internet (impressive – probably the home page for human rights research)	www.hri.ca
– Human Rights Database	www.hri.ca/database
Human Rights Library (University of Minnesota, very extensive)	hrlibrary.umn.edu/
Human Rights First	www.humanrightsfirst.org
Human Rights Watch	www.hrw.org
Internal Displacement Monitoring Centre (Norwegian Refugee Council)	www.internal-displacement.org
International Association of Refugee Law Judges	www.iarlj.nl
International Commission of Jurists (very useful)	www.icj.org
Liga voor Mensenrechten	www.mensenrechten.be
Minority Rights Group International	www.minorityrights.org
Minority Rights Information System (MIRIS)	www.eurac.edu/MIRIS
NativeWeb (indigenous peoples)	www.nativeweb.org
Nederlands Juristen Comité voor de Mensenrechten (NCJM)	www.njcm.nl
Project Diana (Yale University)	avalon.law.yale.edu/subject_menus/diana.asp (limited)
Reflaw	www.reflaw.org
Studie- en Informatiecentrum Mensenrechten (University of Utrecht)	sim.rebo.uu.nl
StateWatch	www.statewatch.org
UN Treaty Bodies Jurisprudence Database (OHCHR)	juris.ohchr.org
UN Division for Social Policy and Development – Indigenous Peoples	www.un.org/development/desa/indigenouspeoples
UN human rights page	www.un.org/en/sections/what-we-do/protect-human-rights/index.html

See also Council of Europe (including ECtHR), UN Commission on Human Rights, UNHCHR, UNHCR, UN Human Rights Committee, and other human rights organs (above).

v. Environmental Law

Center for International Environmental Law (CIEL)	www.ciel.org
Environmental Law Network International (ELNI)	www.elni.org
TMC Asser Institute – European Environmental Law	www.asser.nl/eel
Greenpeace	www.greenpeace.org
Institute for Environmental and Energy Law, KU Leuven	www.law.kuleuven.be/imer
International Environmental Law Research Centre	www.ielrc.org

See also UNEP and IUCN (above).

vi. Disarmament

Arms Control Association	www.armscontrol.org
Acronym Institute	www.acronym.org.uk
Federation of American Scientists (very extensive)	www.fas.org
International Campaign to Ban Landmines	www.icbl.org
NGO Committee on Disarmament, Peace and Security (limited, last updated 2013)	www.ngocdps.wordpress.com
UN Office for Disarmament Affairs (UNODA)	www.un.org/disarmament
– UN Conference on Disarmament	www.un.org/disarmament/geneva/cd
US Under Secretary for Arms Control and International Security (incl. different Bureaux)	www.state.gov/t

See also IAEA, PrepCom. CTBT, OPCW, MTCR, NSG, Zangger Committee, Australia Group and Wassenaar Arrangement (above).

vii. Air and Space Law

Archimedes Institute	www.permanent.com/archimedes
CataLaw – Aviation and Space Law (links)	www.catalaw.com/cattopics/Aviation.shtml
European Centre for Space Law	www.esa.int/SPECIALS/ECSL
Institute of Air and Space Law (Cologne)	www.ilwr.de
Institute of Air and Space Law (McGill)	www.iasl.mcgill.ca
International Institute of Air and Space Law (Leiden)	www.universiteitleiden.nl/en/law/institute-of-public-law/institute-for-air-space-law
International Institute of Space Law (International Astronautical Federation)	www.iislweb.org

National Center for Remote Sensing, Air and Space Law (University of Mississippi School of Law)	www.spacelaw.olemiss.edu
OOSA space law page	www.unoosa.org/oosa/en/SpaceLaw/index.html

See also ESA, OOSA and ICAO (above).

viii. Terrorism

Center for Terrorism Law (St Mary's University School of Law)	law.stmarytx.edu/academics/center-for-terrorism-law

ix. Law of the Sea and Waterways

Admiralty and Maritime Law Guide	www.admiraltylawguide.com
Baltic and International Maritime Council (BIMCO)	www.bimco.org
Centre de Droit Maritime et Océanique (Nantes)	www.cdmo.univ-nantes.fr
Center for International Ocean Law	www.oceanandlaw.org
Center for Oceans Law and Policy (University of Virginia School of Law)	www.virginia.edu/colp
Comité Maritime International (CMI)	www.comitemaritime.org
FAO Fisheries Department	www.fao.org/fishery
International Law of the Sea (Gallagher Law Library, University of Washington)	lib.law.washington.edu/ref/LOS1.html
Netherlands Institute for the Law of the Sea	https://www.uu.nl/en/netherlands-institute-for-the-law-of-the-sea-nilos
Paris Memorandum of Understanding on Port State Control	www.parismou.org
UN sea law page	www.un.org/Depts/los

See also IMO, ISA, ITLOS, CLCS, IOC, ICES and IWC (above).

Index

Please note that page references in **bold** refer to information in tables and those in *italics* refer to information in figures.